D0941461

GREAT BOOKS
OF THE WESTERN WORLD

ROBERT MAYNARD HUTCHINS, *EDITOR IN CHIEF*

20.

THOMAS AQUINAS: II

THE
SUMMA THEOLOGICA

OF SAINT THOMAS AQUINAS

Translated by Fathers of the English Dominican Province

Revised by Daniel J. Sullivan

VOLUME II

WILLIAM BENTON, *Publisher*

ENCYCLOPÆDIA BRITANNICA, INC.

CHICAGO · LONDON · TORONTO · GENEVA

The text of this edition is derived from the translation of *The Summa Theologica* by Fathers of the English Dominican Province by arrangement with Burns, Oates & Washbourne Ltd., London, and Benziger Brothers, Inc., New York.

The bibliographical footnotes and bibliography in this edition are derived from the Piana Edition of the *Summa Theologiae* published by the Dominican Fathers in Ottawa by arrangement with the Institute of Medieval Studies Albert le Grand of the University of Montreal. Copyright, 1941, by College Dominicain d'Ottawa.

THE UNIVERSITY OF CHICAGO

The Great Books
is published with the editorial advice of the faculties
of The University of Chicago

GENERAL CONTENTS, VOL. II

CONTENTS, VOLUME II

vii

Treatise on Active and Contemplative Life

Treatise on the States of Life

THIRD PART (QQ. 1–26; 60–65)

Treatise on the Incarnation

Treatise on the Sacraments

BIBLIOGRAPHY OF FOOTNOTE REFERENCES

ABBREVIATIONS

DZ—DENZINGER, H., and BANNWART, C., *Enchiridion Symbolorum Definitionum et Declarationum de Rebus Fidei et Morum*, 16th–17th edition by J. P. Umberg, Freiburg, 1928.

MA—MANSI, J D., *Sacrorum Conciliorum Nova et Amplissima Collectio*, 54 vols., Paris and Leipsig, 1901–1927.

PG—MIGNE, J. P., *Patrologiae Cursus Completus, Series Graeca*, 166 vols., Paris, 1857–1866.

PL—MIGNE, J. P., *Patrologiae Cursus Completus, Series Latina*, 217 vols. text, 4 vols. indices, Paris, 1844–1855.

SOURCES

ABELARD, *Opera*, PL 178.

Acta Sanctorum, ed. I. Bollandus, and others [BL], 60 vols., Paris, 1863–1870 and 6 vols., Brussels, 1883–1925.

AGATHO, Epistola I, *Ad Augustos Imperatores*, PL 87, 1161–1214.

———, Epistola III, *Epistola Agathonis et Romanae Synodi*, PL 87, 1215–1248.

ALAN OF LILLE, *Theologicae Regulae*, PL 210, 621–684.

ALBERT THE GREAT, *Opera*, ed. A. Borgnet [BO], 38 vols., Paris, 1890–1899.

———, *De quindecim Problematibus*, ed. P. Mandonett [MD] in *Siger de Brabant et l'Averroisme Latin*, Louvain, 1908.

ALCHER OF CLAIRVAUX (PSEUDO-AUGUSTINE), *De Spiritu et Anima*, PL 40, 779–832.

ALCUIN, *Opera*, PL 100–101.

ALEXANDER, *Epistola Alexandri de Ariana Haeresi*, PG 18, 547–582.

ALEXANDER III, Epistola DCCXLIV, *Ad Willelmum Archiepiscopum Senonensem*, PL 200, 685.

ALEXANDER OF APHRODISIAS, *De Intellectu et Intellecto* in G. Théry [TH], *Alexandre d'Aphrodise* (Bibliothèque Thomiste, VII), Kain, 1926.

———, *Praeter Commentaria Scripta Minora: De Anima Liber cum Mantissa*, ed. I. Bruns (Supplementum Aristotle [SA], Vol. II. P. 1), Berlin, 1887.

ALEXANDER OF HALES, *Summa Theologica*, 3 vols., Quarrachi [QR], Florence, 1924–1930.

———, *Summa Theologica*, 4 vols., Lyons, A. Koburger, 1515–1516.

ALFARABI, *Al Farabi's philosophische Abhandlungen*, aus dem Arabischen übersetzt von F. Dieterici [DI], Leinden, 1892.

———, *De Intellectu*, in Avicenna, *Opera*, Venice, 1508.

———, *De Intellectu et Intellecto*, ed. E. Gilson [GI], in Archives d'histoire doctrinale et littéraire du moyen-âge, IV, 1929.

ALGAZEL, *Metaphysica*, ed. J. T. Muckle [MK], Toronto, 1933.

AMBROSE, *Opera*, PL 14–17.

PSEUDO-AMBROSE, Epistola I, *Ad Virgines Sacras*, PL 17, 813–821.

AMBROSIASTER, *Commentaria in Duodecim Epistolas Beati Pauli*, PL 17, 45–536.

———, *Quaestiones Veteris et Novi Testamenti*, PL 35, 2213–2416.

ANONYMOUS, *Presbyterum et Diaconorum Achaiae Epistola de Martyrio Sancti Andreae Apostoli*, PG, 2, 1217–1248.

ANONYMOUS (PSEUDO-HUGH OF ST. VICTOR), *Summa Sententiarum septem Tractatibus Distincta*, PL 176, 41–174.

ANSELM, *Opera*, PL 158–159.

APULEIUS, *De Deo Socratis Liber*, Firmin-Didot [DD], Paris, 1842.

ARISTOTLE, *Aristotelis Opera*, ex recensione I. Bekkeri, edidit Academia Regia Borussica, 5 vols., Berlin, 1831.

———, *The Works of Aristotle*, ed. W. D. Ross, 11 vols., Oxford, 1928–1931.

———, For *The Works of Aristotle,* see volumes 8 and 9 of this set.

[ARNIM, H. VON] *Stoicorum Veterum Fragmenta*, 4 vols., Leipsig, 1921–1924.

ATHANASIUS, *Opera*, PG 25–28.

PSEUDO-ATHANASIUS, *Symbolum*, MA II, 1353–1356; DZ no. 39–40.

AUGUSTINE, *Opera*, PL 32–46.

———, For *The Confessions, The City of God,* and *On Christian Doctrine,* see volume 18 of this set.

PSEUDO-AUGUSTINE, *Hypomnesticon contra Pelagianos et Caelestianos vulgo Libri Hypognosticon*, PL 45, 1611–1664.

AVERROES, *Commentaria in Opera Aristotelis*, 12 vols., Venice, 1562–1576.

AVICEBRON, *Fons Vitae*, ed. C. BAEUMKER [BK], (Beiträge zur Geschichte der Philos. und Theol. des Mittelalters, I, 2–4), Münster, 1892–1895.

AVICENNA, *Opera*, trans. by Dominic Gundissalinus, Venice, 1508.

BARONIUS, C., and others, *Annales Ecclesiastici*, ed. A. Theiner, 37 vols., Paris and Freiburg, Surtz., 1864–1883.

BASIL, *Opera*, PG 29–32.

BEDE, *Opera*, PL 90–95.

BEDE (?), *Sententiae sive Axiomata Philosophica ex Aristotele et alia Praestantibus Collecta*, PL 90, 965–1090.

BENEDICT, *Regula, cum Commentariis*, PL 66, 215–932.

BERNARD, *Opera*, PL 182–185.

BOËTHIUS, *Opera*, PL 63–64.

BONAVENTURE, *Opera*, 10 vols., Quarrachi [QR], 1882–1902.

[BREMOND, A.] *Bullarium Ordinis FF, Praedicatorum*, 8 vols., Rome, 1729–1740.

CAESAR, *Commentarii de Bello Gallico*, Firmin-Didot [DD], Paris, 1879.

CAIUS ROMANUS, *Fragmenta ex Dialogo sive Disputatione adversus Proclum*, PG 10, 25–26.

CANDIDUS ARIANUS, *Liber de Generatione Divina*, PL 8, 1013–1020.

CASSIANUS, *Collationum XXIV Collectio in tres Partes Divisa*, PL 49, 477–1328.

——, *De Coenobiorum Institutis Libri duodecim*, PL 49, 53–476.

CASSIODORUS, *De Anima*, PL 70, 1279–1308.

——, *In Psalterium Expositio*, PL 70, 25–1056.

CASSIODORUS (?), *Expositio in Cantica Canticorum*, PL 70, 1055–1106.

CHALCIDIUS, *Timaeus ex Platonis Dialogo translatus et in eundem Commentarius (Fragmenta Philosophorum Graecorum*, Firmin-Didot [DD] Vol. II), Paris, 1862.

CICERO, *Oeuvres Complètes*, Firmin-Didot [DD], Paris, 1881.

PSEUDO-CLEMENT OF ROME, *De Actibus, Peregrinationibus et Praedicationibus S. Petri*, PG 2, 469–604.

CORNELIUS (CYPRIANUS?), *Epistola X, Ad Antonianum*, PL 3, 787–820.

[CORSSEN, P.] *Monarchianische Prologe zu den vier Evangelien*, Leipsig, 1896.

COSTA-BEN-LUCA, *De Differentia Animae et Spiritus*, ed. C. S. Barach [BH], Innsbruck, 1878.

CYPRIAN, *De Oratione Dominica Liber*, PL 4, 535–562.

——, *Epistola LXX, Ad Januarium*, PL 3, 1073–1082; cf. PL 4, 421.

——, *Liber de Habitu Virginum*, PL 4, 451–478.

CYPRIAN (CORNELIUS?), *Epistola LII, Ad Antonianum, De Cornelio et Novatiano*, PL 4, 355; cf. PL 3, 787–820.

CYRIL OF ALEXANDRIA, *Opera*, PG 68–77.

DECIUS AUSONIUS, *Epigrammata, Idyllia, Epistolae, etc.*, PL 19, 817–958.

Decretales Gregorii in *Corpus Iuris Canonici*, ed. Richter and Friedberg [RF], Leipsig, 1922.

[DENIFLE, H. and CHATELAIN, E.] *Chartularium Universitatis Parisiensis*, 4 vols, Paris, 1889–1897.

DIDYMUS OF ALEXANDRIA, *Liber de Spiritu Sancto*, trans. Jerome, PG 39, 1029–1110.

[DIELS, H.] *Die Fragmente der Vorsokratiker*, 3 vols., Berlin, 1910–1912.

——, *Doxographia Graeci*, Berlin and Leipsig, 1929.

Digesta, ed. T. Mommsen, rev. P. Krueger [KR]

in *Corpus Iuris Civilis*, 15th edition, Vol. I, Berlin, 1928.

DIOGENES LAËRTIUS, *De Clarorum Philosophorum Vitis*, Firmin-Didot [DD], Paris, 1878.

DIONYSIUS OF ALEXANDRIA, *Interpretatio in S. Evangelii secundum Lucam* PG 10, 1589–1596.

DIONYSIUS THE PSEUDO-AREOPAGITE, *Opera*, PG 3–4.

EADMER, *Liber de Sancti Anselmi Similitudinibus*, PL 159, 605–708.

EPIPHANIUS, *Adversus Octoginta Haereses Panarium*, PG 41, 173–42, 774.

——, *Epistola ad Ioannem*, PG 43, 379–392.

EUCLID, *Geometria*, tr. Boëthius, PL 63, 1307–1364.

——, **For *The Thirteen Books of Euclid's Elements,* see volume 11 of this set.**

EUSEBIUS, *Historia Ecclesiastica*, PG 20, 9–906.

EUSTRATIUS, *In Ethica Nicomachea Commentaria*, ed. G. Heylbut (*Commentaria in Aristotelem Graeca* (CG), XX), Berlin, 1892.

FRONTINUS, *Strategematicon Libri quatuor*, Firmin-Didot [DD], Paris, 1878.

FULGENTIUS (PSEUDO-AUGUSTINE), *De Fide ad Petrum*, PL 65, 671–708.

—— *Liber de duplici Praedestinatione Dei*, PL 65, 153–178.

GALEN, *Opera Omnia*, ed. D. C. Gottlob Kühn [KU], 20 vols., Leipsig, 1821–1833.

GENNADIUS (PSEUDO-AUGUSTINE), *Liber de Ecclesiasticis Dogmatibus*, PL 58, 979–1000.

GERHOHUS, *Epistola VII, Ad Adamum Abbatem Eberacensem*, PL 193, 496–500.

——, *Epistola VIII, Ad Eberhardum Archiepiscopum Salzburgensem*, PL 193, 500–514.

GILBERT DE LA PORRÉE, *Commentaria in Librum De Trinitate* (Boëthius), PL 64, 1255–1300.

——, *Commentaria in Librum de Praedicatione trium Personarum*, (Boëthius), PL 64, 1302–1310.

——, *Liber de Sex Principiis*, PL 188, 1257–1270.

Glossa in Decretum Gratiani (*Decretum Gratiani Emendatum et Notationibus Illustratum una cum Glossis*), 2 vols., Venice, 1595.

Glossa (*Glossa ordin. and Glossa interl.*) *cum expositione Lyre Litterali et morali, necnon additionibus et relicis*, 6 v., Basel, 1506–1508.

GRATIAN, *Decretum Magistri Gratiani in Corpus Iuris Canonici*, ed. Richter and Friedberg [RF], Leipsig, 1922.

GREGORY NAZIANZEN, *Opera*, PG 35–38.

GREGORY OF NYSSA, *Opera*, PG 44–46.

GREGORY OF TOURS, *Historiae Ecclesiasticae Francorum Libri Decem*, PL 71, 161–572.

GREGORY THE GREAT, *Opera*, PL 75–79.

GUNDISSALINUS, *De Anima*, ed. J. T. Muckle [MK] (Medieval Studies, II), New York–London, 1940.

HAYMO, *Opera*, PL 116–117.

PSEUDO-HERMES TRISMEGISTUS, *Liber XXIV Philosophorum*, ed. Baeumker [BK], in Abhandlungen aus dem Gebiete der Philosophie und ihrer Geschichte, Freiburg, 1913.

HESYCHIUS, *Commentarius in Leviticum*, PG 93, 787–1180.

HILARY, *Opera*, PL 9–10.

HILDEBERT, *Versus de Excidio Troiae*, PL 171, 1447–1453.

HUGH OF ST. CHER, *Opera Omnia in Universum Vetus, et Novum Testamentum*, 8 vols., Venice, 1754.

HUGH OF ST. VICTOR, *Opera*, PL 175–177.

PSEUDO-HUGH OF ST. VICTOR, *Summa Sententiarum septem Tractatibus Distincta*, PL 176, 41–174.

INNOCENT I, Epistola II, *Ad Victricium Episcopum Rotomagensem*, PL 20, 469–481.

———, Epistola XVII, *Ad Rufinum, Eusebium, etc.*, PL 20, 526–537.

IRENAEUS, *Contra Haereses Libri Quinque*, PG 7, 433–1224.

ISAAC ISRAELI, *Liber de Definicionibus* ed. Muckle in Archives d'histoire doctrinale et littéraire du moyen-âge [AHDLM], XII-XIII, 1937–1938.

ISIDORE, *Opera*, PL 81–84.

JEROME, *Opera*, PL 22–30.

JOHN CHRYSOSTOM, *Opera*, PG 47–64.

PSEUDO-JOHN CHRYSOSTOM, *Opus, Imperfectum in Matthaeum*, PG 56, 611–946.

JOHN DAMASCENE, *Opera*, PG 94–96.

JOHN OF SALISBURY, *Vita Sancti Thomae Cantuariensis*, PL 190, 195–208.

JOSEPHUS, *Works*, trans. by H. Thackeray and R. Marcus, Loeb Classical Library, Cambridge, Mass., 1926.

JULIAN OF TOLEDO, *Prognosticon Futuri Saeculi Libri tres*, PL 96, 453–524.

JULIANUS POMERIUS, *De Vita Contemplativa Libri tres*, PL 59, 415–520.

JUSTINIAN, *Codex Justinianus*, ed. Paul Krueger [KR], in *Corpus Iuris Civilis*, 9th edition, Vol. II, Berlin, 1915.

———, *Digesta*, ed. T. Mommsen, rev. P. Krueger [KR] in *Corpus Iuris Civilis*, 15th edition, Vol. I, Berlin, 1928.

Koran, trans. by G. Sale [SL], London, 1863.

LANFRANC, *De Corpore et Sanguine Domini adversus Berengarium Turonensem*, PL 150, 407–442.

———, *In Omnes Pauli Epistolas Commentarii cum Glossula Interiecta*, PL 150, 101–406.

LEO THE GREAT, *Epistles and Sermons*, PL 54.

Liber de Causis, ed. O Bardenhewer [BA], Freiburg i. B., 1882.

MACROBIUS, *Commentarius ex Cicerone in Somnum Scipionis*, Firmin-Didot [DD], Paris, 1875

MAIMONIDES, *Guide for the Perplexed*, trans. by M. Friedlander [FR], London, 1928.

MAXIMUS, *Commentaria in S. Dionysii Areopagitae Librum de Caelesti Hierarchia*, PG 4, 29–114.

——— *Commentaria in Librum de Ecclesiastica Hierarchia*, PG 4, 115–184.

MAXIMUS OF TURIN, *Sermones in tres Classes Distributi*, PL 57, 529–760.

MOMBRITIUS, B., *Sanctuarium seu Vitae Sanctorum*, 2 vols., Paris, 1910.

NEMESIUS EMESENUS (PSEUDO-GREGORY OF NYSSA), *De Natura Hominis*, PG 40, 503–818.

NESTOR, *Blasphemarium Capitula XII*, trans. by M. Mercator, PL 48, 907–923.

NESTOR, Epistola II, *Ad Cyrillum*, PG 77, 49–58; Cf. Mercator's translation, PL 48, 818–827.

ORIGEN, *Opera*, PG 11–17.

OVID, *Oeuvres complètes*, Firmin-Didot [DD], Paris, 1881.

PASCHASIUS DIACONUS, *De Spiritu Sancto Libri Duo*, PL 62, 9–40.

PAUL THE DEACON, *Liber Exhortationis, Vulgo De Salutaribus Documentis ad Hencricum Comitem*, PL 99, 197–282; item, PL 40, 1047–1078.

PELAGIUS, *Commentarius in Evangelium secundum Marcum*, PL 30, 609–668.

———, Epistola I, *Ad Demetriadem*, PL 30, 16–47.

———, *Libellus Fidei Pelagii ad Innocentium*, PL 45, 1716–1718.

PETER DAMIAN, *De Novissimis et Antichristo*, PL 145, 837–842.

PETER THE EATER, *Historia Scholastica*, PL 198, 1053–1722.

PETER LOMBARD, *Glosses*, PL 191, 55–192, 520.

——— *Liber IV Sententiarum*, 2 vols., Quaracchi [QR], 1916.

PETER OF POITIERS, *Sententiarum Libri Quinque*, PL 211, 783–1280.

PHILIP THE CHANCELLOR, *Summa Quaestionum Theologicarum (Summa de Bono)*, MS. Tolosae 192, 171 ff.

PLATO, *The Dialogues of Plato*, 5 vols., trans. by B. Jowett, Oxford, 1871.

———, for *The Dialogues of Plato*, see volume 7 of this set.

PLOTINUS, *Ennéades*, ed. and trans. by E. Bréhier, 6 vols. (édition Budé [BU]), Paris, 1924–1938.

———, for the *Ennéads*, see volume 17 of this set.

PORPHYRY, *Isagoge*, ed. A. Busse (Commentaria in Aristotelem Graeca [CG], vol. IV, part 1), Berlin, 1887.

PRAEPOSITINUS, *Summa*, MS. Turone, 142 ff. 53–127.

PROCLUS, *Institutio Theologica*, ed. F. Dubner, Firmin-Didot [DD], Paris, 1855.

PROSPER OF AQUITAINE, *Sententiarum ex Operibus S. Aug. Delibatarum Liber Unus*, PL 51, 427–496.

PTOLEMY, *Liber Ptholemei quattuor tractatuum (Quadripartitum) cum Centiloquio*, Venice, 1484.

———, *Syntaxis Mathematica (Almagest)*, 2 vols., ed. J. L. Heiberg [HB], Leipsig, 1898–1903.

———, for *The Almagest*, see volume 16 of this set.

RAYMOND OF PENNAFORT, *Summa*, Verona, 1744.

RHABANUS MAURUS, *Opera*, PL 107–112.

RICHARD OF ST. VICTOR, *Opera*, PL 196.

ROBERT GROSSETESTE, *An unedited text by Robert Grosseteste on the subject-matter of theology (Hexaëmeron)*, ed. G. B. Phelan in Revue néo-scholastique de philosophie [RNP], XXXVI (Mélanges de Wulf), 1934.

———, *Die philosophischen Werke des Robert Grosseteste*, ed. L. Baur [BR], in Beiträge zur Geschichte der Philosophie des Mittelalters, Band IX, Münster, 1912.

ROBERT KILWARDBY, *De Natura Theologiae*, ed. F. Stegmüller, Münster, 1935.

RUFINUS, *Orationum Gregorii Naziazeni novem in-*

terpretatio, ed. A. Engelbrecht (Corpus script. eccles. lat. [CV] t. 46), Vindob., 1910.

RUPERT, *De Gloria et Honore Filii Hominis super Matthaeum*, PL 168, 1307–1634.

———, *De Trinitate*, PL 167, 199–1828.

SALLUST, *Conjuration de Catilina—Guerre de Jugurtha*, ed. and trans. by J. Roman (éditions Budé [BU]), Paris, 1924.

SEDULIUS SCOTUS, *Collectanea in Omnes B. Pauli Epistolas*, PL 103, 9–270.

SENECA, *Works*, Firmin-Didot [DD], Paris, 1887.

SIMPLICIUS, *In Aristotelis Categorias Commentarium*, ed. C. Kalbfleisch (Commentaria in Aristotelem Graeca [CG], VIII), Berlin, 1907.

SIRICIUS, Epistola VII, *Ad Diversos Episcopos Missa adversus Iovinianum Haereticum*, PL 13, 1168–1172.

SOCRATES SCHOLASTICUS, *Historia Ecclesiastica*, PG 67, 29–842.

STOBAEUS, *Eglogarum Physicarum et Ethicarum Libri Duo*, ed. T. Gaisford, Oxford, 1850.

TERTULLIAN, *Adversus Valentinianos Liber*, PL 2, 557–632.

THEMISTIUS, *In Libros Aristotelis de Anima Paraphrasis*, ed. R. Heinze (Commentaria in Aristotelem Graeca [CG] V, 3), Berlin, 1899.

THEODORE OF MOPSUESTIA, *Ex Epistola ad Domnum Fragmenta*, PG 66, 1011–1014.

———, *Fragmenta ex Libris de Incarnatione Filii Dei*, PG 66, 969–994.

THEODORE THE NESTORIAN, *Epistolae ad Ioannem, Antiochenum Episcopum*, PG 83, 1483–1486.

———, *Haereticarum Fabularum Compendium*, PG 83, 335–556.

THEODOTUS OF ANCYRA, *Homiliae*, PG 77, 1349–1432.

THEOPHANES, *Chronographia Annorum DXXVIII*, PG 108, 55–1164.

THEOPHILUS OF ALEXANDRIA, *Epistola Altera Paschalis Anni 402 Ad Totius Aegypti Episcopos*, trans. by Jerome, PL 22, 792–812.

[THIEL, A.] *Epistolae Romanorum Pontificum Genuinae et Quae ad Eos Scriptae Sunt a S. Hilaro usque ad Pelagium II*, Brunsbergae, 1868.

THOMAS AQUINAS, *Opera Omnia*, ed. E. Fretté and P. Maré, 34 vols., Paris, 1872–1880.

———, *Summa Theologiae*, cura et studio Instituti Studiorum Medievalium Ottaviensis, 5 vols., Ottawa, 1941–1945.

———, *Opuscula Omnia*, ed. P. Mandonnet, 5 vols., Paris, 1927.

TICHONIUS AFER, *Liber de Septem Regulis*, PL 18, 15–66.

VALERIUS MAXIMUS, *Factorum et Dictorum Memorabilium Libri novem*, Firmin-Didot [DD], Paris, 1841.

VARRO, *De Lingua Latina ad Ciceronem*, Firmin-Didot [DD], Paris, 1875.

VEGETIUS RENATUS, *Institutorum Rei Militaris*, Firmin-Didot [DD], Paris, 1878.

VIGILIUS TAPSENSIS, *Contra Arianos etc. Dialogus*, PL 62, 179–238.

VIGILIUS TAPSENSIS (PS.-AUGUSTINE), *Contra Felicianum et Arianum De Unitate Trinitatis ad Optatum Liber*, PL 62, 333–352; Cf. PL 42, 1157–1172.

Vitae Patrum sive Historiae Eremetricae Libri Decem, PL 73, 89–74, 240.

VOLUSIANUS, Inter Epistolas Augustini Epistola CXXXV, *Ad Augustinum Episcopum*, PL 33, 512–514.

WILLIAM OF AUXERRE, *Summa Aurea*, MS. Paris, Bibl. Nat., lat. 15.746, 330 ff.

WILLIAM OF PARIS (WILLIAM OF AUVERGNE), *Works*, 2 vols., Venice, 1591; 2 vols., Paris, 1674.

WILLIAM OF ST. THIERRY, *Tractatus de Natura et Dignitate Amoris*, PL 184, 379–408.

WILLIAM OF SHYRESWOOD, *Introductiones in Logicam*, ed. Grabmann, Munich, 1937.

SECONDARY WORKS

BAEUMKER, C. *Witelo, ein Philosoph und Naturforscher des XII. Jahrhunderts* (Beiträge zur Geschichte der Philosophie und Theologie des Mittelalters, III, 2), Münster, 1908.

BERGERON, M., *La Structure du concept latin de Personne*, in Etudes d'histoire littéraire et doctrinale du XIII siècle [EHLD], II, Ottawa, 1932.

BRUNET, P. and MIELI, A., *Histoire des Sciences-Antiquité*, Paris, 1935.

CAPELLE, G. C., *Amaury de Bène (Autour du décret de 1210*, III [Bibliothèque Thomiste, vol. XVI]), Paris, 1932.

CHENU, M. D., *Grammaire et théologie au XIIe et XIIIe siècles*, Archives d'histoire doctrinale et littéraire du moyen-âge [AHDLM], X-XI, 1935–1936.

———, *La psychologie de la foi dans la théologie du XIIIe siècle*, Etudes d'histoire littéraire et doctrinale du XIIIe siècle [EHLD], deuxième série, Paris and Ottawa, 1932.

CHENU, M.D., *Les réponses de S. Thomas et de Kilwardby à la consultation de Jean de Verceil (1271)*, Mélanges Mandonnet, I, (Bibliothèque Thomiste, XIII) Paris, 1930.

———, *Notes de Lexicographie philosophique médiévale—Antiqui, Moderni*, Revue des sciences philosophiques et théologiques [RSPT], XVII, 1928.

DESTREZ, J., *La lettre de Saint Thomas d'Aquin dite lettre au Lecieur de Venise*, Mél. Mandonnet, I (Bibliothèque Thomiste, XIII), Paris, 1930.

DEVAUX, R., *Note conjointe sur un texte retrouvé de David de Dinant*, Revue des sciences philosophiques et théologiques [RSPT], XXII, 1933.

[DTC] *Dictionnaire de théologie catholique*, ed. A. Vacant, and others, Paris, 1923–1939.

DuCANGE D., DuFRESNE, C., *Glossarium ad Scriptores Mediae et Infimae Latinatis*, Venice, 1736–1740.

DUHEM, P., *Le Système du Monde,* 5 vols., Paris, 1913–1917.

GEYER, B., *Die Übersetzunges der Aristotelischen Metaphysik bei Albertus Magnus und Thomas von Aquin,* Philosophisches Jahrb. [PJ], XXX, 1917.

GILSON, E., *La Philosophie de saint Bonaventure,* Paris, 1924.

———, *L'Esprit de la philosophie médiévale,* 2 vols., Paris, 1932.

———, *Les sources gréco-arabes de l'augustinisme avicennisant,* Archives d'histoire doctrinale et littéraire de moyen-âge [AHDLM], IV, 1929.

———, *Pourquoi saint Thomas a critiqué saint Augustin,* Archives d'histoire doctrinale et littéraire de moyen-âge [AHDLM], I, 1926.

GLORIEUX, P., *"Contra Geraldinos." L'enchaînement des polémiques.* Recherches de théologie ancienne et médiévale [RTAM], VII, 1935.

———, *Le "Contra Impugnantes" de s. Thomas. Ses sources—son plan.* Mélanges Mandonnet, I, (Bibliothèque Thomiste, XIII), Paris, 1930.

———, *Les polémiques "contra Geraldinos." Les pièces du dossier,* Recherches de théologie ancienne et médiévale [RTAM], VI, 1934.

GRABMANN, M., *Forschungen über die Lateinischen Aristotelesübersetzungen des XIII. Jahrhunderts* (Beiträge zur Geschichte der Philosophie des Mittelalters, XVII, 5–6), Münster, 1916.

GRUNDMANN, H., *Studien über Joachim von Floris* (Beiträge zur Kulturgeschichte des Mittelalters und der Renaissance), Leipsig and Berlin, 1927.

KLEINEIDAM, E., *Das Problem der hylemorphen Zusammensetzung der geistigen Substanzen im 13. Jahrhundert, behandelt bis Thomas von Aquin,* Breslau, 1930.

KORS, J. B., *La Justice primitive et le Péché originel d'après S. Thomas,* (Bibliothéque Thomiste, II), Le Saulchoir, 1922.

LAGRANGE, M. J., *Evangile selon saint Marc,* Paris, 1929.

LEBON, J., *Le Monophysisme sévérien,* Louvain, 1909.

LOTTIN, O., *La composition hylémorphique des substances spirituelles,* Revue néo-scolastique de philosophie [RNP], XXXIV, 1932, pp. 21–41.

———, *La nature du péché d'ignorance,* Revue thomiste [RT], XXXVII, 1932.

———, *La pluralité des formes substantielles avant s. Thomas d'Aquin,* Revue néo-scolastique de philosophie [RNP] XXXIV, 1932, pp. 449–467.

———, *La syndérèse chez les premiers maîtres franciscains de Paris,* Revue néo-scolastique de philosophie [RNP], XXIV, 1927.

———, *La théorie des vertus cardinales de 1230 à 1250,* Mélanges Mandonnet, II (Bibliothéque Thomiste, XIV), Paris, 1930.

———, *La théorie du libre-arbitre depuis saint Anselme jusqu'à saint Thomas d'Aquin,* Saint Maximin, 1929.

———, *Le droit naturel chez s. Thomas d'Aquin et ses prédécesseurs,* Zème édition, Bruges, 1931.

———, *Les dons du Saint-Esprit chez les théologiens depuis P. Lombard jusqu'à S. Thomas d'Aquin,* Recherches de théologie ancienne et médiévale [RTAM], 1929, I.

LOTTIN, O., *Les premiers définitions et classifications des vertus au moyen-âge,* Revue des sciences philosoph. et théologiques [RSPT], XVIII, 1929.

———, *Les premiers linéaments du traité de la syndérèse au moyen-âge,* Revue néo-scolastique de philosophie [RNP], XXVIII, 1926.

———, *L'identité de l'âme et des facultés pendant la première moitié de XIIIe siècle,* Revue néo-scolastique de philosophie, XXXIV (Mélanges de Wulf, février 1934).

LUYCKX, B., *Die Erkenntnislehre Bonaventuras* (Beiträge zur Geschichte der Philosophie und Theologie des Mittelalters, XXIII, 3–4) Münster, 1923.

MANSER, G. M., *Johann von Rupella,* Jahrbuch für Philosophie und speculative Theologie [JPST], XXVI, 1912.

MARTIN, J., *Priscillianus oder Justantius?* Historisches Jahrbuch, XLVII, 1927.

MOTTE, A. M., *Une fausse accusation contre Abélard et Arnaud de Brescia,* Revue des sciences philosophiques et théologiques [RSPT], XXII, 1933.

MUCKLE, J. T. *Isaac Israeli's Definition of Truth,* Archives d'histoire doctrinale et littéraire du moyen-âge [AHDLM], VIII, 1933.

PARENT, J. M. *La Notion de Dogma au XIIIe siècle,* in Etudes d'histoire littéraire et doctrinale du XIIIe siècle [EHLD], première série, Paris and Ottawa, 1932.

PEGIS, A. C., *St. Thomas and the Greeks,* Milwaukee, 1939.

———, *St. Thomas and the Problem of the Soul in the Thirteenth Century,* Toronto, 1934.

PERGAMO, B., *La Dottrina della "Gratia Unionis" in Allexandro d'Hales,* Studi Francescani, XXIV, 1932.

PRANTL, C., *Geschichte der Logik im Abendlande,* 4 vols., Leipsig, 1855.

ROUSSELOT, P., *Pour l'histoire du problème de l'amour au moyen-âge* (Beiträge zur Geschichte der Philosophie und Theologie des Mittelalters, VI, 6), Münster, 1908.

SARTON, G., *Introduction to the History of Science,* 2 vols., Baltimore, 1927–1931.

SCHMAUS, M., *Die Texte der Trinitatslehre in den Sententiae des Simon von Tournai,* Rech. de théologie ancienne et médiévale [RTAM] IV, 1932.

SIMONIN, H. D. and MEERSSEMAN, S., *De Sacramentorum Efficentia apud Theologos Ord. Praed.,* Rome, 1936.

THORNDIKE, L., *A History of Magic and Experimental Science during the First Thirteen Centuries of our Era,* 2 vols., New York, 1929.

[TJE] *The Jewish Encyclopaedia,* 12 vols., ed. I. Singer, New York, 1901–1906.

[UJE] *The Universal Jewish Encyclopaedia,* 10 vols., ed. I. Landmann, L. RITTENBERG, and others, New York, 1939–1943.

VON LIESHOUT, H., *La théorie plotinienne de la vertu,* Fribourg, Switz., 1926.

TREATISE ON HABITS

1. IN GENERAL

QUESTION XLIX

OF HABITS IN GENERAL, AS TO THEIR
SUBSTANCE

(*In Four Articles*)

AFTER treating of human acts and passions, we now pass on to the consideration of the principles of human acts, and first, of intrinsic principles, second, of extrinsic principles, (Q. XC). The intrinsic principle is power and habit; but as we have treated of powers in the First Part (Q. LXXVII. *sqq.*), it remains for us to consider habits. And first we shall consider them in general; second, we shall consider virtues and vices and other like habits, which are the principles of human acts (Q. LV).

Concerning habits in general there are four points to be considered: First, the substance of habits; second, their subject (Q. L); third, the cause of their generation, increase, and corruption (Q. LI); fourth, how they are distinguished from one another (Q. LIV).

Under the first head, there are four points of inquiry: (1) Whether habit is a quality? (2) Whether it is a distinct species of quality? (3) Whether habit implies an order to an act? (4) Of the necessity of habit.

ARTICLE 1. *Whether Habit Is a Quality?*

We proceed thus to the First Article: It would seem that habit is not a quality.

Objection 1. For Augustine says (QQ. LXXXIII, qu. 73):[1] "This word 'habit' is derived from the verb 'To have.'" But "To have" pertains not only to quality, but also to the other categories, for we speak of ourselves as having quantity and money and other like things. Therefore habit is not a quality.

Obj. 2. Further, habit is considered as one of the predicaments, as may be clearly seen in the *Book on the Predicaments*.[2] But one predicament is not contained under another. Therefore habit is not a quality.

Obj. 3. Further, "every habit is a disposi-

tion," as is stated in the *Book on the Predicaments*.[3] Now disposition is "the order of that which has parts," as stated in the *Metaphysics*.[4] But this belongs to the predicament Position. Therefore habit is not a quality.

On the contrary, The Philosopher says, in the *Book on the Predicaments*,[5] that "habit is a quality which it is difficult to change."

I answer that, This word *habitus* (habit) is derived from *habere* (to have). Now habit is taken from this word in two ways; in one way, according as man, or any other thing, is said to have something; in another way, according as a particular thing is ordered (*se habet*) in a certain way either in regard to itself, or in regard to something else.

Concerning the first, we must observe that "to have," as said in regard to anything that is had, is common to different genera. And so the Philosopher puts "to have" among the post-predicaments,[6] so called because they result from the different genera of things; as, for instance, opposition, priority, posterity, and the like. Now among things which are had, there seems to be this distinction, that there are some in which there is no medium between the haver and that which is had; as, for instance, there is no medium between the subject and quality or quantity. Then there are some in which there is a medium, but only a relation; as for instance a man is said to have a companion or a friend. And, further, there are some in which there is a medium, not indeed an action or a passion, but something after the manner of action or passion; thus, for instance, something adorns or covers, and something else is adorned or covered. Therefore the Philosopher says[7] that "a habit is said to be, as it were, an action or a passion of the haver and that which is had," as is the case in those things which we have about ourselves. And therefore these constitute a special genus of things, which is called the predicament of Habit, of which the Philosopher says[8] that

[1] PL 40, 84.
[2] Aristotle, *Categories*, 8 (8b26).
[3] *Ibid.* (9a10).   [4] Aristotle, v, 19 (1022b1).
[5] *Categories*, 8 (9a3).   [6] *Ibid.*, 15 (15b17).
[7] *Metaphysics*, v, 20 (1022b4).   [8] *Ibid.*

"there is a habit between clothing and the man who is clothed."

But if "to have" be taken according as a thing is ordered in regard to itself or to something else, in that case habit is a quality, since this mode of having is in respect of some quality; and of this the Philosopher says[1] that "habit is a disposition whereby that which is disposed is disposed well or ill, and this, either in regard to itself or in regard to another; thus health is a habit." And in this sense we speak of habit now. Therefore we must say that habit is a quality.

Reply Ob. 1. This argument takes "to have" in the general sense, for in this sense it is common to many predicaments, as we have said.

Reply Obj. 2. This argument takes habit in the sense in which we understand it to be a medium between the haver and that which is had, and in this sense it is a predicament, as we have said.

Reply Obj. 3. Disposition does always, indeed, imply an order of that which has parts. But this happens in three ways, as the Philosopher goes on at once to say: namely, "either as to place, or as to power, or as to species." "In saying this," as Simplicius observes in his *Commentary on the Predicaments,*[2] "he includes all dispositions:—bodily dispositions, when he says 'as to place,'" and this belongs to the predicament Position, which is the order of parts in a place. "When he says 'as to power,' he includes all those dispositions which are in course of formation and not yet arrived at perfect usefulness," such as undeveloped science and virtue. "And when he says, 'as to species,' he includes perfect dispositions, which are called habits," such as perfected science and virtue.

ARTICLE 2. *Whether Habit Is a Distinct Species of Quality?*

We thus proceed to the Second Article: It would seem that habit is not a distinct species of quality.

Objection 1. Because, as we have said (A. 1), habit, in so far as it is a quality, is a disposition whereby that which is disposed is disposed well or ill. But this happens in regard to any quality, for a thing happens to be well or ill disposed in regard also to shape, and in like manner in regard to heat and cold, and in regard to all such things. Therefore habit is not a distinct species of quality.

Obj. 2. Further, the Philosopher says in the *Book on the Predicaments*[3] that "heat and cold are said to be dispositions or habits, just as sickness and health." But heat and cold are in the third species of quality. Therefore habit or disposition is not distinct from the other species of quality.

Obj. 3. Further, "difficult to change" is not a difference belonging to the predicament of quality, but rather to movement or passion. Now no genus is determined to a species by a difference of another genus, but differences should be proper to a genus, as the Philosopher says in the *Metaphysics.*[4] Therefore, since habit is said to be a quality difficult to change,[5] it does not seem to be a distinct species of quality.

On the contrary, The Philosopher says in the *Book on the Predicaments*[6] that "one species of quality is habit and disposition."

I answer that, The Philosopher in the *Book on the Predicaments*[7] considers disposition and habit as the first among the four species of quality. Now Simplicius, in his *Commentary on the Predicaments,* explains the difference of these species as follows.[8] He says that "some qualities are natural, and are in their subject in virtue of its nature, and are always there; but some are adventitious, being caused from without, and these can be lost. Now the latter, that is, those which are adventitious are habits and dispositions, differing in the point of being easily or difficultly lost. As to natural qualities, some regard a thing in the point of its being in a state of potency, and thus we have the second species of quality; while others regard a thing which is in act, and this either deeply rooted in it or only on its surface. If deeply rooted, we have the third species of quality; if on the surface, we have the fourth species of quality, as shape, and form which is the shape of an animated being." But this distinction of the species of quality seems unsuitable. For there are many shapes, and qualities pertaining to passion which are not natural but adventitious; and there are also many dispositions which are not adventitious but natural, as health, beauty and the like. Moreover, it does not suit the order of the species, since that which is the more natural is always first.

Therefore we must explain otherwise the distinction of dispositions and habits from other qualities. For quality, properly speaking, implies a certain mode of substance. Now mode, as Augustine says (*Gen. ad. lit.* iv, 3),[9] "is that which

---

[1] *Metaphysics,* V, 20 (1022[b]10).
[2] *In Cat.,* VIII (CG VIII, 240.30).　[3] *Categories,* 8 (8[b]36).
[4] VII, 12 (1038[a]9).　　[5] Aristotle, *Categories,* 8 (9[a]3).
[6] *Ibid.* (8[b]26).　　　　[7] *Ibid.*
[8] *In Cat.,* VIII (CG VIII, 228.19).
[9] PL 34, 299.

a measure determines"; hence it implies a certain determination according to a certain measure. Therefore, just as that in accordance with which the potency of matter is determined to its substantial being, is called quality, which is a difference affecting substance, so that in accordance with which the potency of the subject is determined to its accidental being is called an accidental quality, which is also a kind of difference, as is clear from the Philosopher.[1]

Now the mode or determination of the subject according to accidental being may be taken either in relation to the very nature of the subject, or according to the action and passion resulting from its natural principles, which are matter and form; or again according to quantity. If we take the mode or determination of the subject in regard to quantity, we shall then have the fourth species of quality. And because quantity, considered in itself, is devoid of movement, and does not imply the notion of good or evil, so it does not concern the fourth species of quality whether a thing be well or ill disposed, nor quickly or slowly moving.

But the mode or determination of the subject according to action or passion is considered in the second and third species of quality. And therefore in both, we take into account whether a thing be done with ease or difficulty; whether it be transitory or lasting. But in them, we do not consider anything pertaining to the notion of good or evil, because movements and passions have not the aspect of an end, while good and evil are said in respect of an end.

On the other hand, the mode or determination of the subject in regard to the nature of the thing belongs to the first species of quality, which is habit and disposition; for the Philosopher says,[2] when speaking of habits of the soul and of the body, that they are "dispositions of the perfect to the best; and by perfect I mean that which is disposed in accordance with its nature." And since "the form itself and the nature of a thing is the end and the cause why a thing is made,"[3] therefore in the first species we consider both evil and good, and also changeableness, whether easy or difficult according, as a certain nature is the end of generation and movement. And so the Philosopher[4] defines habit, "a disposition whereby someone is disposed, well or ill"; and in the *Ethics*[5] he says that "by habits we are directed well or ill in

reference to the passions." For when the mode is suitable to the thing's nature, it has the aspect of good, and when it is unsuitable, it has the aspect of evil. And since nature is the first object of consideration in anything, for this reason habit is counted as the first species of quality.

Reply Obj. 1. Disposition implies a certain order, as stated above (A. 1, Reply 3). Hence a man is not said to be disposed by some quality except in relation to something else. And if we add "well or ill," which belongs to the notion of habit, we must consider the quality's relation to the nature, which is the end. So in regard to shape, or heat, or cold, a man is not said to be well or ill disposed except by reason of a relation to the nature of a thing, with regard to its suitability or unsuitability. Consequently even shapes and qualities pertaining to passion, in so far as they are considered to be suitable or unsuitable to the nature of a thing, belong to habits or dispositions; for shape and colour, according to their suitability to the nature of a thing, concern beauty; while heat and cold, according to their suitability to the nature of a thing, concern health. And in this way heat and cold are put, by the Philosopher, in the first species of quality. Therefore the answer to the second objection, though some give another solution, as Simplicius says in his *Commentary on the Predicaments*.[6]

Reply Obj. 3. This difference, "difficult to change," does not distinguish habit from the other species of quality, but from disposition. Now disposition may be taken in two ways: in one way, as the genus of habit, for disposition is included in the definition of habit;[7] in another way, according as it is divided against habit. Again, disposition, properly so called, can be divided against habit in two ways. First, as perfect and imperfect within the same species, and thus we call it a disposition, retaining the name of the genus, when it is had imperfectly, so as to be easily lost; but we call it a habit when it is had perfectly, so as not to be lost easily. And thus a disposition becomes a habit, just as a boy becomes a man. Secondly, they may be distinguished as different species of the one subaltern genus, so that we call dispositions those qualities of the first species which by reason of their very nature are easily lost, because they have changeable causes; for example, sickness and health. But we call habits those qualities which, by reason of their very nature, are not

[1] *Metaphysics*, V, 14 (1020ᵃ33).
[2] *Physics*, VII, 3 (246ᵃ13).
[3] *Ibid.*, II, 7 (198ᵇ3).
[4] *Metaphysics*, V, 20 (1022ᵇ10).   [5] II, 5 (1105ᵇ25).

[6] *In Cat.*, VIII (CG VIII, 233.10; 256.16).
[7] Aristotle, *Metaphysics*, V, 20 (1022ᵇ4).

easily changed, because they have unchangeable causes, for example, sciences and virtues. And in this sense, disposition does not become habit. The latter explanation seems more in keeping with the intention of Aristotle; for in order to confirm this distinction he invokes the common mode of speaking, according to which when a quality is by reason of its nature easily changeable, and, through some accident, becomes changeable with difficulty, then it is called a habit, while the contrary happens in regard to qualities by reason of their nature changeable with difficulty; for supposing a man to have a science imperfectly, so as to be liable to lose it easily, we say that he is disposed to that science, rather than that he has the science. From this it is clear that the word habit implies a certain lastingness: while the word disposition does not.

Nor does it matter that "to be easy and difficult to change" are specific differences (of a quality), although they belong to passion and movement, and not to the genus of quality. For these differences, though apparently accidental to quality, nevertheless designate differences which are proper and essential to quality. In the same way, in the genus of substance we often take accidental instead of substantial differences, in so far as by the former essential principles are designated.

ARTICLE 3. *Whether Habit Implies Order to an Act?*

We proceed thus to the Third Article: It would seem that habit does not imply order to an act.

Objection 1. For everything acts according as it is in act. But the Philosopher says[1] that "when one is become knowing by habit, one is still in a state of potency, but otherwise than before learning." Therefore habit does not imply the relation of a principle to an act.

Obj. 2. Further, that which is put in the definition of a thing, belongs to it essentially. But to be a principle of action, is put in the definition of power, as we read in the *Metaphysics*.[2] Therefore to be the principle of an act belongs to power essentially. Now that which is essential is first in every genus. If therefore, habit also is a principle of act, it follows that it is posterior to power. And so habit and disposition will not be the first species of quality.

Obj. 3. Further, health is sometimes a habit, and so are leanness and beauty. But these do not indicate relation to an act. Therefore it is not essential to habit to be a principle of act.

On the contrary, Augustine says (*De Bono Conjug.* xxi)[3] that "habit is that by which something is done when necessary." And the Commentator says (*De Anima,* iii)[4] that "habit is that by which we act when we will."

I answer that, To have relation to an act may belong to habit both according to the notion of habit, and according to the subject in which the habit is. According to the notion of habit, it belongs to every habit to have relation to an act. For it is of the very notion of habit to imply some relation to a thing's nature, in so far as it is suitable or unsuitable thereto. But a thing's nature, which is the end of generation, is further ordered to another end, which is either an operation, or the product of an operation, to which one attains by means of operation. Therefore habit implies relation not only to the very nature of a thing, but also, consequently, to operation, in so far as this is the end of nature, or conducive to the end. Hence also it is stated[5] in the definition of habit that it is "a disposition whereby that which is disposed, is well or ill disposed either in regard to itself," that is, to its nature, "or in regard to something else," that is, to the end.

But there are some habits, which even on the part of the subject in which they are, imply primarily and principally relation to an act. For, as we have said (A. 2), habit primarily and of itself implies a relation to the thing's nature. If therefore the nature of the thing in which the habit is consists in this very relation to an act, it follows that the habit principally implies relation to an act. Now it is clear that the nature and the notion of power is that it should be a principle of act. Therefore every habit which is in a power, as in its subject, implies principally relation to an act.

Reply Obj. 1. Habit is an act, in so far as it is a quality, and in this respect it can be a principle of operation. It is, however, in a state of potency in respect to operation. Therefore habit is called first act, and operation second act, as is explained in the book on the *Soul*.[6]

Reply Obj. 2. It is not of the essence of habit to be related to power, but to be related to nature. And as nature precedes action, to which power is related, therefore habit is put before power as a species of quality.

Reply Obj. 3. Health is said to be a habit, or a habitual disposition, in relation to nature, as

[1] *Soul,* III, 4 (429[b]6).   [2] Aristotle, v, 12 (1019[a]15).

[3] PL 40, 390.
[4] Comm. 18 (VI, 2, 161B).
[5] Aristotle, *Metaphysics*, v, 20 (1022[b]10).
[6] Aristotle, II, 1 (412[a]22).

stated above (A. 2, Reply 1). But in so far as nature is a principle of act, it consequently implies a relation to act. Therefore the Philosopher says[1] that man, or one of his members, is called healthy, when he can perform the operation of a healthy man. And the same applies to other habits.

ARTICLE 4. *Whether Habits Are Necessary?*

We proceed thus to the Fourth Article: It would seem that habits are not necessary.

Objection 1. For by habits we are well or ill disposed in respect of something, as stated above (A. 2). But a thing is well or ill disposed by its form, for in respect of its form a thing is good, even as it is a being. Therefore there is no necessity for habits.

Obj. 2. Further, habit implies relation to an act. But power implies sufficiently a principle of act; for even the natural powers, without any habits, are principles of acts. Therefore there was no necessity for habits.

Obj. 3. Further, as power is related to good and evil, so also is habit; and as power does not always act, so neither does habit. Given, therefore, the powers, habits become superfluous.

On the contrary, "Habits are perfections."[2] But perfection is of the greatest necessity to a thing, since it has the character of an end. Therefore it was necessary that there should be habits.

I answer that, As we have said above (AA. 2, 3), habit implies a disposition in relation to a thing's nature, and to its operation or end, by reason of which disposition a thing is well or ill disposed to this. Now for a thing to need to be disposed to something else, three conditions are necessary. The first condition is that that which is disposed should be distinct from that to which it is disposed; and so, that it should be related to it as potency is to act. Hence, if there is a being whose nature is not composed of potency and act, and whose substance is its own operation, which itself exists for itself, there can be there no room for habit and disposition, as is clearly the case in God.

The second condition is, that that which is in a state of potency in regard to something else be capable of determination in several ways and to various things. Hence if something be in a state of potency in regard to something else, but in regard to that only, there can be there no room for disposition and habit, for such a sub-

ject from its own nature has the due relation to such an act. Therefore if a heavenly body be composed of matter and form, since that matter is not in a state of potency to another form, as we said in the First Part (Q. LXVI, A. 2), there is no need for disposition or habit in respect of the form, or even in respect of operation, since the nature of the heavenly body is not in a state of potency to more than one fixed movement.

The third condition is that in disposing the subject to one of those things to which it is in potency several things should come together, capable of being adjusted in various ways, so as to dispose the subject well or ill to its form or to its operation. Hence the simple qualities of the elements which suit the natures of the elements in one single fixed way are not called dispositions or habits, but simple qualities; but such things as health, beauty, and so forth, which imply the adjustment of several things which may vary in their relative adjustability we call dispositions or habits. For this reason the Philosopher says[3] that "habit is a disposition"; and "disposition is the order of that which has parts either as to place, or as to potency, or as to species, as we have said above (A. 1, Reply 3). Therefore, since there are many beings for whose natures and operations several things which may vary in their relative adjustability must concur, it follows that habit is necessary.

Reply Obj. 1. By the form the nature of a thing is perfected; yet the subject needs to be disposed in regard to the form by some disposition. But the form itself is further ordered to operation, which is either the end, or the means to the end. And if the form is limited to one fixed operation, no further disposition, besides the form itself, is needed for the operation. But if the form be such that it can operate in different ways, as the soul, it needs to be disposed to its operations by means of habits.

Reply Obj. 2. Power sometimes has a relation to many things, and then it needs to be determined by something else. But if a power does not have a relation to many things, it does not need a habit to determine it, as we have said. For this reason the natural forces do not perform their operations by means of habits, because they are of themselves determined to one mode of operation.

Reply Obj. 3. The same habit does not have a relation to good and evil, as will be made clear further on (Q. LIV, A. 3), but the same power has a relation to good and evil. And, therefore,

---

[1] *History of Animals*, X, 1 (633[b]23).
[2] Aristotle, *Physics*, VII, 3 (246[a]11).

[3] *Metaphysics*, V, 19, 20 (1022[b]1; [b]10).

habits are necessary that powers be determined to good.

QUESTION L
OF THE SUBJECT OF HABITS
(*In Six Articles*)

WE consider next the subject of habits: and under this head there are six points of inquiry: (1) Whether there is a habit in the body? (2) Whether the soul is a subject of habit according to its essence or according to its power? (3) Whether in the powers of the sensitive part there can be a habit? (4) Whether there is a habit in the intellect? (5) Whether there is a habit in the will? (6) Whether there is a habit in separate substances?

ARTICLE 1. *Whether There Is a Habit in the Body?*

We proceed thus to the First Article: It would seem that there is not a habit in the body.

Objection 1. For, as the Commentator says (*De Anima*, iii),[1] a habit is that by which we act when we will. But bodily actions are not subject to the will, since they are natural. Therefore there can be no habit in the body.

Obj. 2. Further, all bodily dispositions are easy to change. But habit is a quality difficult to change. Therefore no bodily disposition can be a habit.

Obj. 3. Further, all bodily dispositions are subject to change. But change can only be in the third species of quality, which is divided against habit. Therefore there is no habit in the body.

On the contrary, The Philosopher says in the *Book of Predicaments*[2] that health of the body and incurable disease are called habits.

I answer that, As we have said above (Q. XLIX, AA. 2, 3, 4,) habit is a disposition of a subject which is in a state of potency either to form or to operation. Therefore in so far as habit implies disposition to operation, no habit is principally in the body as its subject. For every operation of the body proceeds either from a natural quality of the body or from the soul moving the body. Consequently, as to those operations which proceed from its nature, the body is not disposed by a habit, because the natural powers are determined to one mode of operation, and we have already said (Q. XLIX, A. 4) that it is when the subject is in potency to many things that a habitual disposition is required. As to the operations which proceed from

the soul through the body, they belong principally to the soul, and secondarily to the body. Now habits are proportioned to their operations; hence "by like acts like habits are formed."[3] And therefore the dispositions to such operations are principally in the soul. But they can be secondarily in the body, in so far, that is, as the body is disposed and enabled with promptitude to help in the operations of the soul.

If, however, we speak of the disposition of the subject to form, in this way a habitual disposition can be in the body, which is related to the soul as a subject is to its form. And in this way health and beauty and the like are called habitual dispositions. Yet they do not have the nature of habit perfectly, because their causes of their very nature are easily changeable.

On the other hand, as Simplicius reports in his *Commentary on the Predicaments*,[4] Alexander denied absolutely that habits or dispositions of the first species are in the body, and held that the first species of quality belonged to the soul alone. And he held that Aristotle mentions health and sickness in the book on the *Predicaments*[5] not as though they belonged to the first species of quality, but by way of example, so that he would mean that just as health and sickness may be easy or difficult to change, so also are all the qualities of the first species, which are called habits and dispositions. But this is clearly contrary to the intention of Aristotle, both because he speaks in the same way of health and sickness as examples, as of virtue and science; and because in the *Physics*[6] he expressly mentions beauty and health among habits.

Reply Obj. 1. This objection runs in the sense of habit as a disposition to operation, and of those actions of the body which are from nature, but not in the sense of those actions which proceed from the soul, and the principle of which is the will.

Reply Obj. 2. Bodily dispositions are not difficult, absolutely, to change, on account of the changeableness of their bodily causes. But they may be difficult to change by comparison to such a subject, because, namely, as long as such a subject endures, they cannot be removed; or because they are difficult to change by comparison to other dispositions. But qualities of the soul are difficult, absolutely, to change, on account of the unchangeableness of the subject.

---

[1] Comm. 18 (VI, 2, 161B).
[2] *Categories*, 8 (9ᵃ1).
[3] Aristotle, *Ethics*, II, 1 (1103ᵇ21).
[4] *In Cat.*, VIII (CG VIII, 233.16; 241.27).
[5] *Categories*, 8 (8ᵇ36).
[6] VII, 3 (246ᵇ4).

And therefore he does not say that health which is difficult to change is a habit absolutely, but that it is "as a habit," as we read in the Greek.[1] On the other hand, the qualities of the soul are called habits absolutely.

Reply Obj. 3. Bodily dispositions which are in the first species of quality, as some maintained[2] differ from qualities of the third species in this, that the qualities of the third species consist in becoming and movement, as it were, and so they are called passions or passible qualities . But when they have attained to perfection (specific perfection, so to speak), they have then passed into the first species of quality. But Simplicius in his *Commentary*[3] disapproves of this, for in this way, heating would be in the third species, and heat in the first species of quality; Aristotle, however, puts heat in the third.

Therefore Porphyrius, as Simplicius reports,[4] says that passion or passible quality, disposition and habit, differ in bodies by way of intensity and abatement. For when a thing receives heat in this only that it is being heated, and not so as to be able to give heat, then we have passion, if it goes quickly, or passible quality if it is permanent. But when it has been brought to the point that it is able to heat something else, then it is a disposition; and if it goes so far as to be firmly fixed and to become difficult to change, then it will be a habit, so that disposition would be a certain intensity or perfection of passion or passible quality, and habit an intensity or perfection of disposition. But Simplicius disapproves of this,[5] for such intensity and abatement do not imply diversity on the part of the form itself, but on the part of the diverse participation in it by the subject, so that there would be no diversity among the species of quality.

And therefore we must say otherwise that, as was explained above (Q. XLIX, A. 2, Reply 1), the adjustment of the passible qualities themselves, according to their suitability to nature, implies the notion of disposition; and so, when a change takes place in these same passible qualities, which are heat and cold, moisture and dryness, there results a change as to sickness and health. But change does not occur primarily and of themselves in regard to habits and dispositions of this kind.

[1] *Categories*, 8 (9ᵃ3).
[2] Unnamed, in Simplicius, *In Cat.*, VIII (CG VIII, 233.22; 234.11).
[3] *In Cat.*, VIII (CG VIII, 234.23).
[4] *Ibid.* (234.30).
[5] *In Cat.*, VIII (CG VIII, 234.6).

ARTICLE 2. *Whether the Soul Is the Subject of Habit According to Its Essence or According to its Power?*

We proceed thus to the Second Article: It would seem that habit is in the soul according to its essence rather than according to its powers.

Objection 1. For we speak of dispositions and habits in relation to nature, as stated above (Q. XLIX, A. 2). But nature regards the essence of the soul rather than the powers, because it is in respect of its essence that the soul is the nature of such a body and its form. Therefore habits are in the soul in respect of its essence and not in respect of its powers.

Obj. 2. Further, accident is not the subject of accident. Now habit is an accident. But the powers of the soul are in the genus of accident, as we have said in the First Part (Q. LXXVII, A. 1, Reply 5). Therefore habit is not in the soul in respect of its powers.

Obj. 3. Further, the subject is prior to that which is in the subject. But since habit belongs to the first species of quality, it is prior to power, which belongs to the second species. Therefore habit is not in a power of the soul as its subject.

On the contrary, The Philosopher puts various habits in the various powers of the soul.[6]

I answer that, As we have said above (Q. XLIX, AA. 2, 3), habit implies a certain disposition in relation to nature or to operation. If therefore we take habit as having a relation to nature, it cannot be in the soul—that is, if we speak of human nature, for the soul itself is the form completing the human nature; so that, regarded in this way, habit or disposition is rather to be found in the body by reason of its relation to the soul, that in the soul by reason of its relation to the body.—But if we speak of a higher nature, of which man may become a partaker, according to II Peter 1, *that we may be partakers of the Divine Nature,* then nothing hinders some habit, namely, grace, from being in the soul according to its essence, as we shall state later on (Q. CX, A. 4).

On the other hand, if we take habit in its relation to operation, it is in this way chiefly that habits are found in the soul, in so far as the soul is not determined to one operation but is indifferent to many, which is a condition for a habit, as we have said above (Q. XLIX, A. 4). And since the soul is the principle of operation through its powers, therefore, regarded in this sense, habits are in the soul in respect of its powers.

[6] *Ethics,* I, 13 (1103ᵃ3).

Reply Obj. 1. The essence of the soul pertains to human nature not as a subject requiring to be disposed to something further, but as a form and nature to which someone is disposed.

Reply Obj. 2. Accident is not of itself the subject of accident. But since among accidents themselves there is a certain order, the subject, according as it is under one accident, is conceived as the subject of a further accident. In this way we say that one accident is the subject of another; as for instance, a surface is the subject of colour, in which sense power can be the subject of habit.

Reply Obj. 3. Habit takes precedence of power according as it implies a disposition to nature, as but power always implies a relation to operation, which is posterior, since nature is the principle of operation. But the habit whose subject is a power does not imply relation to nature, but to operation. Therefore it is posterior to power. Or, we may say that habit takes precedence of power as the complete takes precedence of the incomplete, and as act takes precedence of potency. For act is naturally prior to potency, though potency is prior in the order of generation and time, as stated in the *Metaphysics*.[1]

ARTICLE 3. *Whether There Can Be Any Habits in the Powers of the Sensitive Part?*

We proceed thus to the Third Article: It would seem that there cannot be any habits in the powers of the sensitive part.

Objection 1. For as the nutritive power is an irrational part, so is the sensitive power. But there can be no habits in the powers of the nutritive part. Therefore we ought not to put any habit in the powers of the sensitive part.

Obj. 2. Further, the sensitive parts are common to us and the brutes. But there are not any habits in brutes, for in them there is no will, which is put in the definition of habit, as we have said above (Q. XLIX, A. 3). Therefore there are no habits in the sensitive powers.

Obj. 3. Further, the habits of the soul are sciences and virtues, and just as science is related to the apprehensive power, so is virtue related to the appetitive power. But in the sensitive powers there are no sciences, since science is of universals, which the sensitive powers cannot apprehend. Therefore, neither can there be habits of virtue in the sensitive part.

On the contrary, The Philosopher says[2] that "some virtues, namely, temperance and fortitude, belong to the irrational part."

I answer that, The sensitive powers can be considered in two ways: first, according as they act from natural instinct; secondly, according as they act at the command of reason. According as they act from natural instinct, they are ordered to one thing, just as nature is; but according as they act at the command of reason, they can be ordered to various things. And thus there can be habits in them, by which they are well or ill disposed in regard to something.

Reply Obj. 1. The powers of the nutritive part do not have an inborn aptitude to obey the command of reason, and therefore there are no habits in them. But the sensitive powers have an inborn aptitude to obey the command of reason, and therefore habits can be in them; for in so far as they obey reason, in a certain sense they are said to be rational, as stated in the *Ethics*.[3]

Reply Obj. 2. The sensitive powers of dumb animals do not act at the command of reason, but if they are left to themselves, such animals act from natural instinct, and so there are no habits in them ordered to operations. There are in them, however, certain dispositions in relation to nature, such as health and beauty. But because by man's reason brutes are disposed by a sort of custom to do things in this or that way, in this sense, after a fashion, we can admit the existence of habits in dumb animals; hence Augustine says (QQ. LXXXIII, *qu.* 36):[4] "We find the most untamed beasts deterred by fear of pain from that wherein they took the keenest pleasure; and when this has become a custom in them, we say that they are tame and gentle." But the habit is incomplete as to the use of the will, for they do not have that power of using or of refraining which seems to belong to the notion of habit, and therefore, properly speaking, there can be no habits in them.

Reply Obj. 3. The sensitive appetite has an inborn aptitude to be moved by the rational appetite, as stated in the book on the *Soul*;[5] but the rational powers of apprehension have an inborn aptitude to receive from the sensitive powers. And therefore it is more suitable that habits should be in the powers of sensitive appetite than in the powers of sensitive apprehension, since in the powers of sensitive appetite habits do not exist except according as they act at the command of the reason. And yet even

---

[1] Aristotle, VII, 3 (1029ᵃ5); IX, 8 (1049ᵇ4). Cf. St. Thomas, *In Meta.*, VIII, 2.
[2] *Ethics*, III, 10 (1117ᵇ23).

[3] Aristotle, I, 13 (1102ᵇ25).
[4] PL 40, 25.
[5] Aristotle, III, 11 (434ᵃ12).

in the interior powers of sensitive apprehension we may admit of certain habits whereby man has a facility of memory, thought or imagination; hence also the Philosopher says[1] that custom conduces much to a good memory. The reason for this is that these powers also are moved to act at the command of the reason.

On the other hand the exterior apprehensive powers, as sight, hearing and the like, are not susceptive of habits, but are ordered to their fixed acts according to the disposition of their nature, just as the members of the body, for there are no habits in them, but rather in the powers which command their movements.

ARTICLE 4. *Whether There Is Any Habit in the Intellect?*

We *proceed thus to the Fourth Article:* It would seem that there are no habits in the intellect.

Objection 1. For habits are in conformity with operations, as stated above (A. 1). But the operations of man are common to soul and body, as stated in the treatise on the *Soul.*[2] Therefore also are habits. But the intellect is not an act of the body.[3] Therefore the intellect is not the subject of a habit.

Obj. 2. Further, whatever is in a thing is there according to the mode of that in which it is. But that which is form without matter, is act only while what is composed of form and matter has potency and act at the same time. Therefore nothing at the same time potential and actual can be in that which is form only, but only in that which is composed of matter and form. Now the intellect is form without matter. Therefore habit, which has potency at the same time as act, being a sort of medium between the two, cannot be in the intellect but only in the composite being, which is composed of soul and body.

Obj. 3. Further, "habit is a disposition whereby we are well or ill disposed in regard to something," as is said.[4] But that anyone should be well or ill disposed to an act of the intellect is due to some disposition of the body; hence also it is stated[5] that "we observe men with soft flesh to be quick witted." Therefore the habits of knowledge are not in the intellect, which is separate, but in some power which is the act of some part of the body.

On the contrary, The Philosopher[6] puts science, wisdom and understanding, which is the habit of first principles, in the intellectual part of the soul.

I answer that, Concerning habits of knowing there have been various opinions. Some, supposing that there was only one possible intellect for all men, were bound to hold that habits of knowledge are not in the intellect itself, but in the interior sensitive powers.[7] For it is manifest that men differ in habits, and so it was impossible to put the habits of knowledge directly in that, which, being numerically one, would be common to all men. Therefore if there were but one single possible intellect of all men, the habits of science, in which men differ from one another, could not be in the possible intellect as their subject, but would be in the interior sensitive powers, which differ in various men.

Now this supposition in the first place is contrary to the mind of Aristotle. For it is manifest that the sensitive powers are rational not by their essence, but only by participation.[8] Now the Philosopher puts the intellectual virtues, which are wisdom, science and understanding, in that which is rational by its essence.[9] Therefore they are not in the sensitive powers, but in the intellect itself. Moreover he says expressly[10] that when the possible intellect "thus becomes each thing, that is, when it is reduced to act in respect of singulars by the intelligible species, then it is said to be in act, as the knower is said to be in act; and this happens when the intellect can act of itself," that is, by considering; "and even then it is in potency in a sense; but not however absolutely, as before learning and discovering." Therefore the possible intellect itself is the subject of the habit of science, by which the intellect, even though it be not actually considering, is able to consider. In the second place, this supposition is contrary to the truth. For just as to whom belongs the operation belongs also the power to operate, so to whom belongs the operation belongs also the habit. But to understand and to consider is the proper act of the intellect. Therefore also the habit by which one considers is properly in the intellect itself.

Reply Obj. 1. Some said, as Simplicius reports in his *Commentary on the Predicaments,*[11] that, since every operation of man is to a certain extent an operation of the composite, as the Philosopher says,[12] therefore no habit is in the soul only, but in the composite. And from this it

---

[1] *Memory and Reminiscence,* 2 (452ᵃ28).
[2] Aristotle, I, 1 (403ᵃ8); cf. also I, 4 (408ᵇ8).
[3] *Ibid.*, III, 4 (429ᵃ24).
[4] Aristotle, *Metaphysics,* V, 20 (1022ᵇ10).
[5] Aristotle, *Soul,* II, 9 (421ᵃ26).   [6] *Ethics,* VI, 3 (1139ᵇ16).
[7] Averroes, *In De An.,* III, 5, dig., T. V (VI, 2, 148D).
[8] *Ethics,* I, 13 (1102ᵇ13).   [9] *Ethics,* VI, 3 (1139ᵇ16).
[10] *Soul,* III, 4 (429ᵇ6).   [11] *In Cat.,* VIII (CG VIII, 233.22).
[12] *Soul,* I, 1, 4 (403ᵃ8; 408ᵇ8).

follows[1] that no habit is in the intellect, for the intellect is separate, as ran the argument given above. But the argument is not cogent. For habit is not a disposition of the object to the power, but rather a disposition of the power to the object. Therefore the habit must be in that power which is principle of the act, and not in that which is related to the power as its object.

Now the act of understanding is not said to be common to soul and body, except in respect of the phantasm, as is stated in the book on the *Soul*.[2] But it is clear that the phantasm is related as object to the possible intellect.[3] Hence it follows that the intellectual habit is chiefly on the part of the intellect itself, and not on the part of the phantasm, which is common to soul and body. And therefore we must say that the possible intellect is the subject of habit; for that is able to be a subject of habit which is in potency to many, and this belongs, above all, to the possible intellect. Therefore the possible intellect is the subject of intellectual habits.

Reply Obj. 2. As potency to sensible being belongs to corporeal matter, so potency to intellectual being belongs to the possible intellect. Therefore nothing prevents habit from being in the possible intellect, for it is midway between pure potency and perfect act.

Reply Obj. 3. Because the apprehensive powers inwardly prepare their proper objects for the possible intellect, therefore it is by the good disposition of these powers, to which the good disposition of the body co-operates, that man is rendered apt to understand. And so in a secondary way the intellectual habit can be in these powers. But principally it is in the possible intellect.

ARTICLE 5. *Whether Any Habit Is in the Will?*

We proceed thus to the Fifth Article: It would seem that there is not a habit in the will.

Objection 1. For the habit which is in the intellect is made up of the intelligible species, by means of which the intellect actually understands. But the will does not act by means of species. Therefore the will is not the subject of habit.

Obj. 2. Further, no habit is allotted to the agent intellect, as there is to the possible intellect, because the former is an active power. But the will is above all an active power, because it moves all the powers to their acts, as

stated above (Q. IX, A. 1). Therefore there is no habit in the will.

Obj. 3. Further, in the natural powers there is no habit, because, by reason of their nature, they are determined to one thing. But the will, by reason of its nature, is ordained to tend to the good which reason directs. Therefore there is no habit in the will.

On the contrary, Justice is a habit. But justice is in the will, for it is "a habit whereby men will and do that which is just."[4] Therefore the will is the subject of a habit.

I answer that, Every power which may be variously directed to act needs a habit whereby it is well disposed to its act. Now since the will is a rational power, it may be variously directed to act. And therefore in the will we must admit the presence of a habit by which it is well disposed to its act. Moreover, from the very notion of habit, it is clear that it is principally related to the will, since habit is that which one uses when one wills, as stated above (A. 1; Q. XLIX, A. 3).

Reply Obj. 1. Even as in the intellect there is a species which is the likeness of the object, so in the will, and in every appetitive power, there must be something by which the power is inclined to its object; for the act of the appetitive power is nothing but a certain inclination, as we have said above (Q. VI, A. 4). And therefore in respect of those things to which it is inclined sufficiently by the nature of the power itself, the power needs no quality to incline it. But since it is necessary for the end of human life that the appetitive power be inclined to something fixed, to which it is not inclined by the nature of the power, which has a relation to many and various things, therefore it is necessary that in the will and in the other appetitive powers there be certain qualities to incline them, and these are called habits.

Reply Obj. 2. The agent intellect is active only, and in no way passive. But the will, and every appetitive power, is both "mover and moved."[5] And therefore the comparison between them does not hold; for to be susceptible of habit belongs to that which is somehow in potency.

Reply Obj. 3. The will from the very nature of the power is inclined to the good of the reason. But because this good is varied in many ways, the will needs to be inclined, by means of a habit, to some fixed good of the reason, in order that action may follow more promptly.

---

[1] Cf. Simplicius, *In Cat.*, VIII (CG VIII, 241.23); Plotinus, VI, *Ennead*, I, 12 (BU VI, 76).

[2] Aristotle, I, 1 (403ª5).

[3] Aristotle, *Soul*, III, 7 (431ª14); cf. I, 1 (403ª8).

[4] Aristotle, *Ethics*, V, 1 (1129ª7).

[5] *Soul*, III, 10 (433ᵇ16).

ARTICLE 6. *Whether There Are Habits in the Angels?*

We proceed thus to the Sixth Article: It would seem that there are no habits in the angels.

Objection 1. For Maximus, commentator of Dionysius (*Cæl. Hier.* vii),[1] says: "It is not proper to suppose that there are intellectual (i.e., spiritual) powers in the divine intelligences (i.e., in the angels) after the manner of accidents, as in us, as though one were in the other as in a subject; for accident of any kind is foreign to them." But every habit is an accident. Therefore there are no habits in the angels.

Obj. 2. Further, as Dionysius says (*Cæl. Hier.* iv) :[2] "The holy dispositions of the heavenly essences participate, above all other things, in God's goodness." But that which is of itself *(per se)* is always prior to and more powerful than that which is by another *(per aliud).* Therefore the angelic essences are perfected of themselves to conformity with God, and therefore not by means of habits. And this seems to have been the reasoning of Maximus, who in the same passage adds:[3] "For if this were the case, surely their essence would not remain in itself, nor could it have been as far as possible deified of itself."

Obj. 3. Further, "habit is a disposition."[4] But disposition, as is said in the same book, is "the order of that which has parts." Since, therefore, angels are simple substances, it seems that there are no dispositions and habits in them.

On the contrary, Dionysius says (*Cæl. Hier.* vii)[5] that the angels of the first hierarchy are called: "Fire-bearers and Thrones and Out-pouring of Wisdom, by which is indicated the godlike nature of their habits."

I answer that, Some have thought that there are no habits in the angels, and that whatever is said of them is said essentially. Hence Maximus, after the words which we have quoted, says: "Their dispositions, and the powers which are in them, are essential, through the absence of matter in them." And Simplicius says the same in his *Commentary on the Predicaments:*[6] "Wisdom which is in the Soul is its habit, but that which is in the intellect, is its substance. For everything divine is sufficient of itself, and exists in itself."

[1] Sect. 1 (PG 4, 65).
[2] Sect. 2 (PG 3, 180).
[3] *In De Cæl. Hier.,* VII, 1 (PG 4, 65).
[4] Aristotle, *Metaphysics,* V, 20 (1022[b]10.)
[5] Sect. 1 (PG 3, 205).
[6] *In. Cat.,* VIII (CG VIII, 241.30).

Now this opinion contains some truth, and some error. For it is manifest from what we have said (Q. XLIX, A. 4) that only a being in potency is the subject of habit. So the above-mentioned commentators considered that angels are immaterial substances, and that there is no material potency in them, and on that account, excluded from them habit and any kind of accident. Yet since though there is no material potency in angels, there is still some potency in them (for to be pure act belongs to God alone), and therefore, as far as potency is found to be in them, so far may habits be found in them. But because the potency of matter and the potency of intellectual substance are not of the same kind, so neither are the respective habits of the same kind. And so, Simplicius says in his *Commentary on the Predicaments*[7] that "The habits of the intellectual substance are not like the habits here below, but rather are they like simple and immaterial species which it contains in itself."

However, the angelic intellect and the human intellect differ with regard to this habit. For the human intellect, being the lowest in the intellectual order, is in potency as regards all intelligible things, just as prime matter is in respect of all sensible forms; and therefore for the understanding of all things, it needs some habit. But the angelic intellect is not as a pure potency in the genus of intelligible things, but as an act; not indeed as pure act (for this belongs to God alone), but with an admixture of some potency; and the higher it is, the less potency it has. And therefore, as we said in the First Part (Q. LV, A. 1), so far as it is in potency, so far is it in need of habitual perfection by means of intelligible species in regard to its proper operation; but so far as it is in act, through its own essence it can understand some things, at least itself, and other things according to the mode of its substance, as stated in *De Causis;*[8] and the more perfect it is, the more perfectly will it understand.

But since no angel attains to the perfection of God, but all are infinitely distant from Him, for this reason, in order to attain to God Himself through intellect and will, the angels need some habits, being as it were in potency in regard to that Pure Act. And so Dionysius says (*Cæl. Hier.* vii)[9] that "their habits are godlike," that is to say, that by them they are made like to God.

[7] *In Cat.,* VIII (VIII, 241.28).
[8] Sect. 7 (BA 170.25; 171.2).
[9] Sect. 1 (PG 3, 205).

But those habits that are dispositions to natural being are not in angels, since they are immaterial.

Reply Obj. 1. This saying of Maximus must be understood of material habits and accidents.

Reply Obj. 2. As to that which belongs to angels by their essence, they do not need a habit. But as they are not so far beings of themselves as not to partake of Divine wisdom and goodness, therefore, so far as they need to partake of something from without, so far do they need to have habits.

Reply Obj. 3. In angels there are no essential parts. But there are potential parts, in so far as their intellect is perfected by several species, and in so far as their will has a relation to several things.

QUESTION LI
OF THE CAUSE OF HABITS, AS TO THEIR
FORMATION
(*In Four Articles*)

WE must next consider the cause of habits, and first, as to their formation; secondly, as to their increase (Q. LII); thirdly, as to their diminution and corruption (Q. LIII). Under the first head there are four points of inquiry: (1) Whether any habit is from nature? (2) Whether any habit is caused by acts? (3) Whether a habit can be caused by one act? (4) Whether any habits are infused in man by God?

ARTICLE 1. *Whether Any Habit Is from Nature?*

We proceed thus to the First Article: It would seem that no habit is from nature.

Objection 1. For the use of those things which are from nature does not depend on the will. But habit is that which we use when we will, as the Commentator says on *De Anima*, iii[1] Therefore habit is not from nature.

Obj. 2. Further, nature does not employ two where one is sufficient. But the powers of the soul are from nature. If therefore the habits of the powers were from nature, habit and power would be one.

Obj. 3. Further, nature does not fail in necessaries. But habits are necessary in order to act well, as we have stated above (Q. XLIX, A. 4). If therefore any habits were from nature, it seems that nature would not fail to cause all necessary habits. But this is clearly false. Therefore habits are not from nature.

On the contrary, In the *Ethics*,[2] among other

habits, place is given to understanding of first principles, which habit is from nature; hence also first principles are said to be known naturally.[3]

I answer that, One thing can be natural to another in two ways. First in respect of the specific nature, as to be able to laugh is natural to man, and it is natural to fire to have an upward tendency. Secondly, in respect of the individual nature, as it is natural to Socrates or Plato to be prone to sickness or inclined to health, in accordance with their respective temperaments. Again, in respect of both natures, something may be called natural in two ways: first, because it entirely is from the nature; secondly, because it is partly from nature, and partly from an extrinsic principle. For instance, when a man is healed by himself, his health is entirely from nature; but when a man is healed by means of medicine, health is partly from nature, partly from an extrinsic principle.

Thus then, if we speak of habit as a disposition of the subject in relation to form or nature, it may be natural in either of the foregoing ways. For there is a certain natural disposition demanded by the human species, so that no man can be without it. And this disposition is natural in respect of the specific nature. But since such a disposition has a certain latitude, it happens that different grades of this disposition are suitable to different men in respect of the individual nature. And this disposition may be either entirely from nature, or partly from nature and partly from an extrinsic principle, as we have said of those who are healed by means of art.

But the habit which is a disposition to operation, and whose subject is a power of the soul, as stated above (Q. L, A. 2), may be natural whether in respect of the specific nature or in respect of the individual nature:—in respect of the specific nature, on the part of the soul itself, which, since it is the form of the body, is the specific principle; but in respect of the individual nature, on the part of the body, which is the material principle. Yet in neither way does it happen that there are natural habits in man, so that they are entirely from nature. In the angels, indeed, this does happen, since they have intelligible species naturally infused in them, which cannot be said of the human nature, as we said in the First Part (Q. LV, A. 2; Q. LXXXIV, A. 3).

---

[1] Comm. 18 (VI, 2, 161B).
[2] Aristotle, VI, 6 (1141ᵃ5).

[3] See especially ALBERT, *Summa de Bono*, in Lottin, *Le Droit Naturel*, p. 117. Cf. also William of Auxerre, *Summa Aurea* II, tr. 12, Q. 1 (fol. 66 ra).

There are, therefore, in man certain natural habits, owing their existence partly to nature and partly to some extrinsic principle: in one way, indeed, in the apprehensive powers; in another way, in the appetitive powers. For in the apprehensive powers there may be a natural habit by way of a beginning, both in respect of the specific nature, and in respect of the individual nature. This happens with regard to the specific nature, on the part of the soul itself; thus the understanding of first principles is called a natural habit.[1] For it is owing to the very nature of the intellectual soul that man, having once grasped what is a whole and what is a part, should at once perceive that every whole is larger than its part; and in like manner with regard to other such principles. Yet what is a whole, and what is a part—this he cannot know except through the intelligible species which he has received from phantasms. And for this reason, the Philosopher at the end of the *Posterior Analytics*[2] shows that knowledge of principles comes to us from the senses.

But in respect of the individual nature, a habit of knowledge is natural as to its beginning in so far as one man, from the disposition of his organs of sense, is more apt than another to understand well, since we need the sensitive powers for the operation of the intellect.

In the appetitive powers, however, no habit is natural in its beginning on the part of the soul itself, as to the substance of the habit; but only as to certain of its principles, as, for instance, the principles of common law are said to be the *seeds of the virtues*.[3] The reason of this is because the inclination to its proper objects, which seems to be the beginning of a habit, does not belong to the habit, but rather to the very nature of the powers.

But on the part of the body, in respect of the individual nature, there are some appetitive habits by way of natural beginnings. For some are disposed from their own bodily temperament to chastity or meekness or the like.

Reply Obj. 1. This objection takes nature as divided against reason and will; but reason itself and will belong to the nature of man.

Reply Obj. 2. Something may be added even naturally to the nature of a power, which however cannot pertain to the power itself. For instance, with regard to the angels, it cannot pertain to the intellectual power itself to be of itself capable of knowing all things, for thus it would have to be the act of all things, which belongs to God alone. Because that by which something is known, must be the actual likeness of the thing known. Hence it would follow, if the power of the angel knew all things by itself, that it was the likeness and act of all things. Therefore there must be added to the angels' intellectual power some intelligible species, which are likenesses of things understood; for it is by participation of the Divine wisdom and not by their own essense that their intellect can be actually those things which they understand. And so it is clear that not everything pertaining to a natural habit can belong to the power.

Reply Obj. 3. Nature is not equally inclined to cause all the various kinds of habits, since some can be caused by nature, and some not, as we have said above. And so it does not follow that because some habits are natural that therefore all are natural.

ARTICLE 2. *Whether Any Habit Is Caused by Acts?*

We proceed thus to the Second Article: It would seem that no habit can be caused by acts.

Objection 1. For habit is a quality, as we have said above (Q. XLIX, A. 1). Now every quality is caused in a subject, according as the latter is able to receive something. Since then the agent, from the fact that it acts, does not receive but rather gives, it seems impossible for a habit to be caused in an agent by its own acts.

Obj. 2. Further, the thing in which a quality is caused is moved to that quality, as may be clearly seen in that which is heated or cooled; but that which produces the act that causes the quality, moves, as may be seen in that which heats or cools. If therefore habits were caused in anything by its own act, it would follow that the same would be mover and moved, active and passive, which is impossible, as stated in the *Physics*.[4]

Obj. 3. Further, the effect cannot be more excellent than its cause. But habit is more excellent than the act which precedes the habit, as is clear from the fact that the latter produces more excellent acts. Therefore habit cannot be caused by an act which precedes the habit.

On the contrary, The Philosopher teaches[5] that habits of virtue and vice are caused by acts.

I answer that, In the agent there is sometimes only the active principle of its act; for instance

---

[1] On this point cf. Alexander of Hales, John of Rochelle, Odo Rigaldus, in Lottin (RNP-1927, p. 269, 273, 277).

[2] II, 19 (100ª3).

[3] Cf. especially Albert, *Summa de Bono*, in Lottin, *Le Droit Naturel*, p. 117.

[4] Aristotle, VII, 1 (241ᵇ24).

[5] *Ethics*, II, 1 (1103ª31).

in fire there is only the active principle of heat-ing. And in such an agent a habit cannot be caused by its own act, for which reason natural things cannot become accustomed or unaccus-tomed, as is stated in the *Ethics*.[1] But a certain agent is to be found in which there is both the active and the passive principle of its act, as we see in human acts. For the acts of the appeti-tive power proceed from that same power ac-cording as it is moved by the apprehensive pow-er presenting the object; and further, the intel-lectual power, according as it reasons about conclusions, has, as it were, an active principle in a self-evident proposition. Therefore by such acts habits can be caused in their agents; not in-deed with regard to the first active principle, but with regard to that principle of the act which is a mover moved. For everything that is passive and moved by another is disposed by the action of the agent; therefore if the acts be multiplied a certain quality is formed in the power which is passive and moved, which qual-ity is called a habit; just as the habits of moral virtue are caused in the appetitive powers ac-cording as they are moved by the reason, and as the habits of science are caused in the intellect according as it is moved by first propositions.

Reply Obj. 1. The agent, as agent, does not receive anything. But in so far as it moves through being moved by another, it receives something from that which moves it; and thus is a habit caused.

Reply Obj. 2. The same thing, and in the same respect, cannot be mover and moved; but noth-ing prevents a thing from being moved by itself as to different respects, as is proved in the *Physics*.[2]

Reply Obj. 3. The act which precedes the hab-it, in so far as it comes from an active prin-ciple, proceeds from a more excellent principle than is the habit caused by it; just as the reason is a more excellent principle than the habit of moral virtue produced in the appetitive power by repeated acts, and as the understanding of first principles is a more excellent principle than the science of conclusions.

ARTICLE 3. *Whether a Habit Can Be Caused by One Act?*

We proceed thus to the Third Article: It would seem that a habit can be caused by one act.

Objection 1. For demonstration is an act of reason. But science, which is the habit of one

conclusion, is caused by one demonstration. Therefore habit can be caused by one act.

Obj. 2. Further, as acts may increase by multiplication, so may they increase by inten-sity. But a habit is caused by multiplication of acts. Therefore also if an act be very intense, it can be the generating cause of a habit.

Obj. 3. Further, health and sickness are hab-its. But it happens that a man is healed or becomes ill, by one act. Therefore one act can cause a habit.

On the contrary, The Philosopher says:[3] "As neither does one swallow nor one day make spring, so neither does one day nor a short time make a man blessed and happy." But "happiness is an operation in respect of a habit of perfect virtue."[4] Therefore a habit of virtue, and for the same reason, other habits, are not caused by one act.

I answer that, As we have said already (A. 2), habit is caused by act, in so far as a passive pow-er is moved by an active principle. But in order that some quality be caused in that which is passive, the active principle must entirely overcome the passive. Hence we see that be-cause fire cannot at once overcome the com-bustible, it does not enkindle at once; but it gradually expels contrary dispositions, so that by overcoming it entirely, it may impress its likeness on it. Now it is clear that the active principle which is reason cannot entirely over-come the appetitive power in one act, because the appetitive power is inclined variously and to many things, while the reason judges in a single act, what should be willed in regard to various aspects and circumstances. Therefore the appetitive power is not entirely overcome by it, so as to be inclined as though naturally to the same thing in the majority of cases; which inclination belongs to the habit of virtue. There-fore a habit of virtue cannot be caused by one act, but only by many.

But in the apprehensive powers, we must ob-serve that there are two passive principals: one is the possible intellect itself; the other is the intellect which Aristotle[5] calls "passive," and is the particular reason, that is the cogitative power,[6] with memory and imagination. With regard then to the former passive principle, it is possible for a certain active principle to en-tirely overcome, by one act, the power of its passive principle; thus one self-evident proposi-

---

[1] Aristotle, II, 1 (1103ᵃ19).
[2] Aristotle, VIII, 5 (257ᵃ31).

[3] *Ethics*, I, 7 (1098ᵃ18).
[4] Aristotle, *Ethics*, I, 7, 13 (1098ᵃ16; 1102ᵃ5).
[5] *Soul*, III, 5 (430ᵃ24).
[6] Cf. Part I, Q. LXXVIII, A. 4.

tion convinces the intellect, so that it gives a firm assent to the conclusion, but a probable proposition cannot do this. Therefore a habit of opinion needs to be caused by many acts of the reason, even on the part of the possible intellect; but a habit of science can be caused by a single act of the reason, so far as the possible intellect is concerned. But with regard to the lower apprehensive powers, the same acts need to be repeated many times for anything to be firmly impressed on the memory. And so the Philosopher says that "meditation strengthens memory."[1] Bodily habits, however, can be caused by one act if the active principle is of great power; sometimes, for instance, a strong dose of medicine restores health at once. Hence the *solutions to the objections* are clear.

ARTICLE 4. *Whether Any Habits Are Infused in Man by God?*

We proceed thus to the Fourth Article: It would seem that no habit is infused in man by God.

Objection 1. For God treats all equally. If therefore He infuses habits into some, He would infuse them into all which is clearly untrue.

Obj. 2. Further, God works in all things according to the mode which is suitable to their nature for "it belongs to Divine providence to preserve nature," as Dionysius says *(Div. Nom.* iv).[2] But habits are naturally caused in man by acts, as we have said above (A. 2). Therefore God does not cause habits to be in man except by acts.

Obj. 3. Further, if any habit be infused into man by God, man can by that habit perform many acts. But "from those acts a like habit is caused."[3] Consequently there will be two habits of the same species in the same man, one acquired, the other infused. Now this seems impossible, for two forms of the same species cannot be in the same subject. Therefore a habit is not infused into man by God.

On the contrary, It is written (Ecclus. 15. 5): *God filled him with the spirit of wisdom and understanding.* Now wisdom and understanding are habits. Therefore some habits are infused into man by God.

I answer that, Some habits are infused by God into man, for two reasons. The first reason is because there are some habits by which man is well disposed to an end which exceeds the power of human nature, namely, the ultimate and perfect happiness of man, as stated above (Q. V, A. 5). And since habits must be in proportion with that to which man is disposed by them, therefore it is necessary that those habits, which dispose to this end, exceed the power of human nature. Hence such habits can never be in man except by Divine infusion, as is the case with all gratuitous virtues.

The other reason is, because God can produce the effects of second causes without these second causes, as we have said in the First Part (Q. CV, A. 6). Just as, therefore, sometimes, in order to show His power, He causes health without its natural cause, but which nature could have caused, so also, at times, for the manifestation of His power, He infuses into man even those habits which can be caused by a natural power. Thus He gave to the Apostles the science of the Scriptures and of all tongues, which men can acquire by study or by custom, though not so perfectly.

Reply Obj. 1. God, in respect of His Nature, is the same to all, but, in respect of the order of His Wisdom, for some unerring reason, gives certain things to some which He does not give to others.

Reply Obj. 2. That God works in all according to their mode does not prevent God from doing what nature cannot do; but it follows from this that He does nothing contrary to that which is suitable to nature.

Reply Obj. 3. Acts produced by an infused habit do not cause a habit, but strengthen the already existing habit, just as the remedies of medicine given to a man who is naturally healthy do not cause a kind of health, but give new strength to the health he had before.

QUESTION LII

OF THE INCREASE OF HABITS

(In Three Articles)

WE have now to consider the increase of habits; under which head there are three points of inquiry: (1) Whether habits increase? (2) Whether they increase by addition? (3) Whether each act increases the habit?

ARTICLE 1. *Whether Habits Increase?*

We proceed thus to the First Article: It would seem that habits cannot increase.

Objection 1. For increase concerns quantity.[4] But habits are not in the genus quantity, but

---

[1] *Memory and Reminiscence,* 1 (451ᵃ12).
[2] Sect. 33 (PG 3, 733).
[3] Aristotle, *Ethics,* II, 1 (1103ᵇ21).
[4] Aristotle, *Physics,* V, 2 (226ᵃ30).

in that of quality. Therefore there can be no increase of habits.

Obj. 2. Further, "habit is a perfection."[1] But since perfection conveys a notion of end and term, it seems that it cannot be more or less. Therefore a habit cannot increase.

Obj. 3. Further, those things which can be more or less are subject to alteration, for that which from being less hot becomes more hot, is said to be altered. But in habits there is no alteration, as is proved in the *Physics*.[2] Therefore habits cannot increase.

On the contrary, Faith is a habit, and yet it increases; hence "the Disciples said to our Lord (Luke 17. 5): *Lord, increase our faith.* Therefore habits increase.

I answer that, Increase, like other things pertaining to quantity, is transferred from bodily quantities to intellectual and spiritual things, on account of the natural connection of the intellect with corporeal things, which come under the imagination. Now in corporeal quantities, a thing is said to be great according as it reaches the perfection of quantity due to it; hence a certain quantity is considered great in man which is not considered great in an elephant. And so also in forms, we say a thing is great because it is perfect. And since good has the character of perfection, therefore "in things which are great, but not in quantity, to be greater is the same as to be better," as Augustine says (*De Trin.* vi. 8).[3]

Now the perfection of a form may be considered in two ways: first, in respect of the form itself; secondly, in respect of the participation of the form by its subject. In so far as we consider the perfections of a form in respect of the form itself, in this way the form is said to be little or great; for instance great or little health or science. But in so far as we consider the perfection of a form in respect of the participation of it by the subject, it is said to be more or less; for instance more or less white or healthy. Now this distinction is not to be understood as implying that the form has a being outside its matter or subject, but that it is one thing to consider the form according to its specific nature and another to consider it in respect of its participation by a subject.

In this way, then, there were four opinions among philosophers concerning intensity and abatement of habits and forms, as Simplicius relates in his *Commentary on the Predicaments*.[4]

For Plotinus[5] and the other Platonists[6] held that qualities and habits themselves were susceptible of more or less, for the reason that they were material, and so had a certain indetermination on account of the infinity of matter. Others,[7] on the contrary, held that qualities and habits of themselves were not susceptible of more or less, but that the things affected by them *(qualia)* are said to be more or less according to diversity in participation; that, for instance, justice is not more or less, but the just thing. Aristotle alludes to this opinion in the *Predicaments*.[8] The third opinion was that of the Stoics,[9] and lies between the two preceding opinions. For they held that some habits are of themselves susceptible of more and less, for instance, the arts; and that some are not, such as the virtues. The fourth opinion was held by some who said that qualities and immaterial forms are not susceptible of more or less, but that material forms are.[10]

In order that the truth in this matter be made clear, we must observe that that in respect of which a thing receives its species must be something fixed and stationary, and as it were indivisible; for whatever attains to that thing is contained under the species, and whatever recedes from it more or less, belongs to another species, more or less perfect. Hence the Philosopher says[11] that "species of things are like numbers," in which addition or subtraction changes the species. If, therefore, a form, or anything at all, receives its specific nature in respect of itself, or in respect of something belonging to it, it is necessary that, considered in itself, it be something of a definite nature, which can be neither more nor less. Such are heat, whiteness and other like qualities which are not denominated from a relation to something else, and much more so substance, which is *per se* being. But those things which receive their species from something to which they are related can be diversified, in respect of themselves, according to more or less; and none the less they remain in the same species, on account of the one-ness of that to which they are related, and from which they receive their species. For example, movement is in itself more intense or more diminished, and yet it remains in the same

---

[1] Aristotle, *Physics*, VII, 3 (246ᵃ13).
[2] *Ibid.* (246ᵇ10).   [3] PL 42, 929.
[4] *In Cat.*, VIII (CG VIII, 284.12).

[5] Cf. Simplicius, *In Cat.*, VIII (CG VIII, 284.14); Plotinus, VI *Ennead*, TR. III, 20 (BU VI, 149).
[6] Cf. Simplicius, *In Cat.*, VIII.   [7] *Ibid.* (CG VIII, 233.10).
[8] *Categories*, 8 (10ᵃ30); cf. Simplicius, *In Cat.*, VIII (CG VIII, 284.25).
[9] Cf. Simplicius, *In Cat.*, VIII (CG VIII, 284.32).
[10] Cf. Simplicius, *Ibid.* (285.1).
[11] *Metaphysics*, VIII, 3 (1043ᵇ33).

species, on account of the one-ness of the term by which it is specifiied. We may observe the same thing in health; for a body attains to the nature of health, according as it has a disposition suitable to an animal's nature, to which various dispositions may be suitable. This disposition is therefore variable as regards more or less, and nevertheless the nature of health remains. Hence the Philosopher says:[1] "Health itself may be more or less; for the measure is not the same in all, nor is it always the same in one individual; but down to a certain point it may decrease and still remain health."

Now these various dispositions and measures of health are by way of excess and defect. And so if the name of health were given to the most perfect measure, then we should not speak of health as greater or less. Thus therefore it is clear how a quality or form may increase or decrease in itself, and how it cannot.

But if we consider a quality or form in respect of its participation by the subject, thus again we find that some qualities and forms are susceptive of more or less, and some not. Now Simplicius[2] assigns the cause of this diversity to the fact that substance in itself cannot be susceptible of more or less, because it is *per se* being. And therefore every form which is participated substantially by its subject, cannot vary in intensity and lessening; therefore in the genus of substance nothing is said to be more or less. And because quantity is near to substance, and because shape follows on quantity, therefore is it that neither in these can there be such a thing as more or less. And so the Philosopher says[3] that when a thing receives form and shape, it is not said to be altered, but to be made. But other qualities which are further removed from substance, and are connected with passions and actions, are susceptible of more or less in respect of their participation by the subject.

Now it is possible to explain yet further the reason of this diversity. For, as we have said, that from which a thing receives its species must remain fixed and constant in something indivisible. Therefore in two ways it may happen that a form cannot be participated according to more or less. First because the participator has its species in respect of that form. And for this reason no substantial form is participated according to more or less. And therefore the Philosopher says[4] that, "as a number cannot

be more or less, so neither can that which is in the species of substance," that is, in respect of its participation of the specific form; "but in so far as substance may be with matter," that is, in respect of material dispositions, more and less are found in substance.

Secondly this may happen from the fact that the form is essentially indivisible; and so if anything participate that form, it must participate it in respect of its character of indivisibility. For this reason we do not speak of the species of number as varying in respect of more and less, because each species of number is constituted by an indivisible unity. The same is to be said of the species of continuous quantity, which are denominated from numbers, such as two-cubits-long, three-cubits-long, and of relations of quantity, such as double and treble, and of figures of quantity, such as triangle and tetragon.

This same explanation is given by Aristotle in the *Predicaments*,[5] where, in explaining why figures are not susceptible of more or less, he says: "Things which are given the nature of a triangle or a circle, are likewise triangles and circles," because indivisibility is essential to the very notion of such, and so whatever participates their nature must participate it in its indivisibility.

It is clear, therefore, since we speak of habits and dispositions in respect of a relation to something,[6] that in two ways intensity and lessening may be observed in habits and dispositions. First, in respect of the habit itself: thus, for instance, we speak of greater or less health; or greater or less science, which extends to more or fewer things. Secondly, in respect of participation by the subject; in so far namely, as equal science or health is participated more in one than in another, according to a difference in aptitude arising either from nature, or from custom. For habit and disposition do not give species to the subject: nor again do they include indivisibility in their very notion.

We shall say further on (Q. LXVI, A. 1) how it is with the virtues.

Reply Obj. 1. As the word "great" is taken from corporeal quantities and applied to the intelligible perfections of forms, so also is the word "growth," the term of which is something great.

Reply Obj. 2. Habit is indeed a perfection, but not a perfection which is the term of its subject; for instance, a term giving the subject

---

[1] *Ethics*, x, 3 (1173ª24).
[2] *In Cat.*, VIII (CG VIII, 285.27).
[3] *Physics*, VII, 3 (246ª1).
[4] *Metaphysics*, VIII, 3 (1044ª9).

[5] *Categories*, 8 (11ª7).
[6] *Physics*, VII, 3 (246ᵇ3; 247ª1).

its specific being. Nor again does the notion of a habit include the notion of term, as do the species of numbers. Therefore there is nothing to hinder it from being susceptive of more or less.

Reply Obj. 3. Alteration is primarily indeed in the qualities of the third species; but secondarily it may be in the qualities of the first species. For, supposing an alteration as to hot and cold, there follows in an animal an alteration as to health and sickness. In like manner, if an alteration take place in the passions of the sensitive appetite, or the sensitive powers of apprehension, an alteration follows as to science and virtue.[1]

ARTICLE 2. *Whether Habit Increases by Addition?*

We proceed thus to the Second Article: It would seem that the increase of habits is by way of addition.

Objection 1. For the word "increase," as we have said (A. 2), is transferred to forms from corporeal quantities. But in corporeal quantities there is no increase without addition; hence it is said[2] that "increase is an addition to a magnitude already existing." Therefore in habits also there is no increase without addition.

Obj. 2. Further, habit is not increased except by means of some agent. But every agent does something in the passive subject; for instance, that which heats causes heat in that which is heated. Therefore there is no increase without addition.

Obj. 3. Further, as that which is not white, is in potency to be white, so that which is less white is in potency to be more white. But that which is not white is not made white except by the addition of whiteness. Therefore that which is less white is not made more white except by an added whiteness.

On the contrary, The Philosopher says:[3] "That which is hot is made hotter without making something hot in the matter that was not hot when the thing was less hot." Therefore, in like manner, neither is any addition made in other forms when they increase.

I answer that, The solution of this question depends on what we have said above (A. 1). For we said that increase and decrease in forms which are capable of intensity and abatement happen in one way not on the part of the very form considered in itself, but through a differ-

ence in participation in it by the subject. And therefore such increase of habits and other forms is not caused by an addition of form to form, but by the subject participating more or less perfectly one and the same form. And just as by an agent which is in act something is made actually hot, beginning, as it were, to participate a form, not as though the form itself were made, as is proved in the *Metaphysics*,[4] so, by an intense action of the agent itself, something is made more hot, as it were participating the form more perfectly, not as though something were added to the form.

For if this increase in forms were understood to be by way of addition, this could only be either in the form itself or in the subject. If it be understood of the form itself, it has already been stated (A. 1) that such an addition or subtraction would change the species, even as the species of colour is changed when a thing from being pale becomes white.—If, on the other hand, this addition be understood as applying to the subject, this could only be either because one part of the subject receives a form which it had not previously (thus we may say that cold increases in a man who, after being cold in one part of his body, is cold in several parts), or because some other subject is added, sharing in the same form (as when a hot thing is added to another, or one white thing to another). But in either of these two ways we have not a more white or a more hot thing, but a greater white or hot thing.

Since, however, as stated above (A. 1), certain accidents are of themselves susceptible of more or less, in some of these we may find increase by addition. For movement increases by an addition either to the time it lasts, or to the course it follows; and yet the species remains the same on account of the one-ness of the term. Nevertheless movement increases in intensity as to participation in its subject; that is, in so far as the same movement can be executed more or less speedily or readily. In like manner, science can increase in itself by addition; thus when anyone learns several conclusions of geometry, the same specific habit of science increases in that man. Yet a man's science increases, as to the subject's participation in it, in intensity, in so far as one man is quicker and readier than another in considering the same conclusions.

As to bodily habits, it does not seem very probable that they receive increase by way of addition. For an animal is not said absolutely to

---

[1] Aristotle, *Physics*, VII, 3 (247ª6; 248ª6).
[2] Aristotle, *Generation and Corruption*, I, 5 (320ᵇ30).
[3] *Physics*, IV, 9 (217ª34).
[4] Aristotle, VII, 8, 9 (1033ᵇ5; 1034ᵇ7).

be healthy or beautiful unless it be such in all its parts. And if it be brought to a more perfect measure, this is the result of a change in the simple qualities, which are not susceptible of increase save in intensity on the part of the subject partaking of them.

How this question affects virtues we shall state further on (Q. LXVI, A. 1).

Reply Obj. 1. Even in bodily bulk increase is twofold. First, by addition of one subject to another; such is the increase of living things. Secondly, by mere intensity, without any addition at all; such is the case with things subject to rarefaction, as is stated in the *Physics.*[1]

Reply Obj. 2. The cause that increases a habit, always effects something in the subject, not however a new form. But it causes the subject to partake more perfectly of a pre-existing form, or it makes the form to extend further.

Reply Obj. 3. What is not already white is in potency to that form, as not yet possessing the form of whiteness; hence the agent causes a new form in the subject. But that which is less hot or white, is not in potency to those forms, since it has them already actually; but it is in potency to a perfect mode of participation, and this it receives through the agent's action.

ARTICLE 3. *Whether Every Act Increases Its Habit?*

We proceed thus to the Third Article: It would seem that every act increases its habit.

Objection 1. For when the cause is increased the effect is increased. Now acts are causes of habits, as stated above (Q. LI, A. 2). Therefore a habit increases when its acts are multiplied.

Obj. 2. Further, of like things a like judgment should be formed. But all the acts proceeding from one and the same habit are alike.[2] Therefore if some acts increase a habit, every act should increase it.

Obj. 3. Further, like is increased by like. But any act is like the habit from which it proceeds. Therefore every act increases its habit.

On the contrary, Opposite effects do not result from the same cause. But according to the *Ethics,*[3] some acts lessen the habit from which they proceed, for instance if they be done carelessly. Therefore not every act increases its habit.

I answer that, "Like acts cause like habits."[4] Now things are like or unlike not only in respect

of their qualities being the same or different, but also in respect of the same or a different mode of participation. For not only is black unlike white, but also less white is unlike more white, since there is movement from less white to more white, even as from one opposite to another, as is stated in the *Physics.*[5]

But since use of habits depends on the will, as was shown above (Q. L, A. 5), just as one who has a habit may fail to use it or may act contrary to it, so also he may happen to use the habit in performing an act that is not in proportion to the intensity of the habit. Accordingly, if the intensity of the act correspond in proportion to the intensity of the habit, or even surpass it, every such act either increases the habit or disposes to an increase of it, if we may speak of the increase of habits as we do of the increase of an animal. For not every morsel of food actually increases the animal's size, as neither does every drop of water hollow out the stone: but the multiplication of food results at last in an increase of the body. So, too, repeated acts cause a habit to grow. If, however, the intensity of the act falls short proportionately of the intensity of the habit, such an act does not dispose to an increase of that habit, but rather to a lessening of it.

From this it is clear how to solve *the objections.*

QUESTION LIII

HOW HABITS ARE CORRUPTED OR DIMINISHED

(In Three Articles)

WE must now consider how habits are lost and weakened; and under this head there are three points of inquiry: (1) Whether a habit can be corrupted? (2) Whether it can be diminished? (3) How are habits corrupted or diminished?

ARTICLE 1. *Whether a Habit Can Be Corrupted?*

We proceed thus to the First Article: It would seem that a habit cannot be corrupted.

Objection 1. For habit is within its subject like a second nature; (hence it is pleasant to act from habit.) Now so long as a thing is, its nature is not corrupted. Therefore neither can a habit be corrupted so long as its subject remains.

Obj. 2. Further, whenever a form is corrupted, this is due either to corruption of its subject, or to its contrary; thus sickness ceases through corruption of the animal, or through the advent of health. Now science, which is a habit, can-

---

[1] Aristotle, IV, 7 (214b2).
[2] Aristotle, *Ethics,* II, 2 (1104a29).
[3] Aristotle, *Ibid.* (1104a18).
[4] *Ibid.,* II, 1 (1103b21).

[5] Aristotle, V, 5 (229b14).

not be lost through corruption of its subject, since the intellect, which is its subject, "is a substance and is incorruptible."[1] In like manner, neither can it be lost through the action of its contrary, for intelligible species are not contrary to one another.[2] Therefore the habit of science can in no way be lost.

Obj. 3. Further, all corruption results from some movement. But the habit of science, which is in the soul, cannot be corrupted by a direct movement of the soul itself, since the soul is not moved directly. It is, however, moved indirectly through the movement of the body. And yet no bodily change seems capable of corrupting the intelligible species residing in the intellect, since the intellect independently of the body is the proper abode of the species; for which reason it is held that habits are not lost either through old age or through death. Therefore science cannot be corrupted. For the same reason neither can habits or virtue be corrupted since they also are in the rational soul, and, as the Philosopher declares,[3] "virtue is more lasting than learning."

On the contrary, The Philosopher says[4] that "forgetfulness and deception are the corruption of science." Moreover, by sinning a man loses a habit of virtue; and again, virtues are engendered and corrupted by contrary acts.[5]

I answer that, A form is said to be corrupted in itself by its contrary; accidentally, through its subject being corrupted. When therefore a habit has a corruptible subject, and a cause that has a contrary, it can be corrupted both ways. This is clearly the case with bodily habits—for instance, health and sickness. But those habits that have an incorruptible subject cannot be corrupted indirectly. There are, however, some habits which, while residing chiefly in an incorruptible subject, reside nevertheless secondarily in a corruptible subject; such is the habit of science which is chiefly indeed in the possible intellect, but secondarily in the sensitive powers of apprehension, as stated above (Q. L, A. 3, REPLY 3). Consequently the habit of science cannot be corrupted accidentally, on the part of the possible intellect, but only on the part of the lower sensitive powers.

We must therefore inquire whether habits of this kind can be corrupted in themselves. If then there be a habit having a contrary, either on the part of itself or on the part of its

cause, it can be corrupted in itself; but if it has no contrary, it cannot be corrupted in itself. Now it is evident that an intelligible species residing in the possible intellect, has no contrary; nor can the agent intellect, which is the cause of that species, have a contrary. Therefore if in the possible intellect there be a habit caused immediately by the agent intellect, such a habit is incorruptible both in itself and accidentally. Such are the habits of the first principles, both speculative and practical, which cannot be corrupted by any forgetfulness or deception whatever, even as the Philosopher says about prudence,[6] that it cannot be lost by being forgotten.—There is, however, in the possible intellect a habit caused by the reason, namely, the habit of conclusions, which is called science, to the cause of which something may be contrary in two ways. First, on the part of those very propositions which are the starting-point of the reason; for the assertion "Good is not good" is contrary to the assertion "Good is good."[7] Secondly, on the part of the process of reasoning, according as a sophistical syllogism is contrary to a dialectic or demonstrative syllogism. Hence it is clear that a false reason can corrupt the habit of a true opinion or even of science. And so the Philosopher, as stated above, says that "deception is the corruption of science."

As to virtues, some of them are intellectual, residing in reason itself, as stated in the *Ethics*,[8] and to these applies what we have said of science and opinion.—Some, however, namely the moral virtues, are in the appetitive part of the soul, and the same may be said of the contrary vices. Now these habits of the appetitive part are caused because it is natural to it to be moved by the reason. Therefore a habit either of virtue or of vice may be corrupted by a judgment of reason, whenever its motion is contrary to such vice or virtue, whether through ignorance, passion or deliberate choice.

Reply Obj. 1. As stated in the *Ethics*,[9] a habit is like a second nature, and yet it falls short of it. And so it is that while the nature of a thing cannot in any way be taken away from a thing, a habit is removed, though with difficulty.

Reply Obj. 2. Although there is no contrary to intelligible species, yet there can be a contrary to assertions and to the process of reason, as stated above.

[1] Aristotle, *Soul*, I, 4 (408[b]18).
[2] Aristotle, *Metaphysics*, VII, 7 (1032[b]2).
[3] *Ethics*, I, 10 (1100[b]14).
[4] *Longevity*, 2 (465[a]23).
[5] *Ethics*, II, 1, 3 (1103[b]7; 1105[a]15).
[6] *Ibid.*, VI, 5 (1140[b]29).
[7] *Interpretation*, 14 (24[a]2).
[8] Aristotle, VI, 1, 2 (1139[a]1; [b]12).
[9] Aristotle, VII, 10 (1152[a]31).

Reply Obj. 3. Science is not taken away by movement of the body, if we consider the root itself of the habit, but only as it may prove an obstacle to the act of science, in so far as the intellect, in its act, has need of the sensitive powers, which are impeded by corporal change. But the intelligible movement of the reason can corrupt the habit of science, even as regards the very root of the habit. In like manner a habit of virtue can be corrupted.—Nevertheless when it is said that "virtue is more lasting than learning," this must be understood in respect, not of the subject or cause, but of the act; for the use of virtue continues through the whole of life, but the use of learning does not.

ARTICLE 2. *Whether a Habit Can Diminish?*

We proceed thus to the Second Article: It would seem that a habit cannot diminish.

Objection 1. Because a habit is a simple quality and form. Now a simple thing is possessed either wholly or not at all. Therefore although a habit can be lost it cannot diminish.

Obj. 2. Further, if a thing is befitting an accident, this is by reason either of the accident or of its subject. Now a habit does not become more or less intense by reason of itself; otherwise it would follow that a species might be predicated of its individuals according to more or less. And if it can become less intense according to its participation by its subject, it would follow that the habit has something proper to it which is not common to the habit and its subject. Now whenever a form has something proper to it besides its subject, that form can be separate, as stated in the book on the *Soul*.[1] Hence it follows that a habit is a separable form, which is impossible.

Obj. 3. Further, the very notion and nature of a habit as of any accident, is inherence in a subject, and therefore any accident is defined with reference to its subject. Therefore if a habit does not become more or less intense in itself, neither can it be diminished in its inherence in its subject, and consequently it will be in no way less intense.

On the contrary, It is natural for contraries to be applicable to the same thing. Now increase and decrease are contraries. Since therefore a habit can increase, it seems that it can also diminish.

I answer that, Habits diminish, just as they increase, in two ways, as we have already explained (Q. LII, A. I). And since they increase through the same cause as that which engenders

[1] Aristotle, I, I (403ª10).

them, so too they diminish by the same cause as that which corrupts them; for the diminishing of a habit is the road which leads to its corruption, even as, on the other hand, the engendering of a habit is a foundation of its increase.

Reply Obj. 1. A habit, considered in itself, is a simple form. It is not thus that it is subject to decrease, but according to the different ways in which its subject participates in it. This is due to the fact that the subject's potency is indeterminate, through its being able namely, to participate a form in various ways, or to extend to a greater or a smaller number of things.

Reply Obj. 2. This argument would hold, if the essence itself of a habit were in no way subject to decrease. This we do not say, but rather that a certain decrease in the essence of a habit has its origin, not in the habit, but in its subject.

Reply Obj. 3. No matter how we take an accident, its very notion implies dependence on a subject, but in different ways. For if we take an accident in the abstract, it implies relation to a subject, which relation begins in the accident and terminates in the subject; for whiteness is called "that by which a thing is white." Accordingly in defining an accident in the abstract, we do not put the subject as though it were the first part of the definition, namely the genus, but we give it the second place, which is that of the difference; thus we say that *simitas* is "a curvature of the nose." But if we take accidents in the concrete, the relation begins in the subject and terminates at the accident, for a white thing is called "something that has whiteness." Accordingly in defining this kind of accident, we place the subject as the genus, which is the first part of a definition; for we say that a *simum* is "a snub-nose." Accordingly whatever is befitting an accident on the part of the subject, but is not of the very notion of the accident is ascribed to that accident not in the abstract, but in the concrete. Such are increase and decrease in certain accidents; and therefore to be more or less white is not ascribed to whiteness but to a white thing. The same applies to habits and other qualities, save that certain habits increase or diminish by a kind of addition, as appears from what we have already said (Q. LII, A. 2).

ARTICLE 3. *Whether a Habit Is Corrupted or Diminished Through Mere Cessation from Act?*

We proceed thus to the Third Article: It would seem that a habit is not corrupted or diminished through mere cessation from act.

Objection 1. For habits are more lasting than

passible qualities, as we have explained above (Q. XLIX, A. 2, Reply 3; Q. L, A. 1). But passible qualities are neither corrupted nor diminished by cessation from act; for whiteness is not lessened through not changing the sight, nor heat through ceasing to make something hot. Therefore neither are habits diminished or corrupted through cessation from act.

Obj. 2. Further, corruption and diminution are changes. Now nothing is changed without a moving cause. Since therefore cessation from act does not imply a moving cause, it does not appear how a habit can be diminished or corrupted through cessation from act.

Obj. 3. Further, the habits of science and virtue are in the intellectual soul which is above time. Now those things that are above time are neither destroyed nor diminished by length of time. Neither, therefore, are such habits destroyed or diminished through length of time, if one fails for long to exercise them.

On the contrary, The Philosopher says[1] that "not only deception but also forgetfulness is the corruption of science." Moreover he says[2] that "want of intercourse has dissolved many a friendship." In like manner other habits of virtue are diminished or destroyed through cessation from act.

I answer that, As stated in the *Physics*[3] a thing is a cause of movement in two ways. First, of itself, and such a thing causes movement by reason of its own form; thus fire causes heat. Secondly, accidentally; for instance, that which removes an obstacle. It is in this latter way that the destruction or diminution of a habit results through cessation from act, in so far, that is, as we cease from exercising an act which overcame the causes that destroyed or weakened that habit. For it has been stated (A. 1) that habits are destroyed or diminished directly through some contrary agency. Consequently all habits that are gradually undermined by contrary agencies which need to be counteracted by acts proceeding from those habits are diminished or even destroyed altogether by long cessation from act, as is clearly seen in the case both of science and of virtue. For it is evident that a habit of moral virtue makes a man ready to choose the mean in deeds and passions. And when a man fails to make use of his virtuous habit in order to moderate his own passions or deeds, the necessary result is that many passions and deeds occur outside the mode of virtue, by reason

of the inclination of the sensitive appetite and of other external agencies. Therefore virtue is destroyed or lessened through cessation from act.—The same applies to the intellectual habits, which render man ready to judge rightly of those things that are pictured by his imagination. Hence when man ceases to make use of his intellectual habits, strange fancies, sometimes in opposition to them, arise in his imagination, so that unless those fancies be, as it were, cut off or kept back by frequent use of his intellectual habits, man becomes less fit to judge rightly and sometimes is even wholly disposed to the contrary; and thus the intellectual habit is diminished or even wholly destroyed by cessation from act.

Reply Obj. 1. Even heat would be destroyed through ceasing to give heat, if, for this same reason, cold which is destructive of heat were to increase.

Reply Obj. 2. Cessation from act is a moving cause conducive to corruption or diminution by removing the obstacles to them, as explained above.

Reply Obj. 3. The intellectual part of the soul, considered in itself, is above time, but the sensitive part is subject to time, and therefore in course of time it undergoes change as to the passions of the appetitive part, and also as to the powers of apprehension. Hence the Philosopher says[4] that time makes us forget.

QUESTION LIV

OF THE DISTINCTION OF HABITS

(In Four Articles)

WE have now to consider the distinction of habits; and under this head there are four points of inquiry (1) Whether many habits can be in one power? (2) Whether habits are distinguished by their objects? (3) Whether habits are divided into good and bad? (4) Whether one habit may be made up of many habits?

ARTICLE 1. *Whether Many Habits Can Be in One Power?*

We proceed thus to the First Article: It would seem that there cannot be many habits in one power.

Objection 1. For when several things are distinguished in respect of the same thing, if one of them be multiplied the others are too. Now habits and powers are distinguished in respect of the same thing, namely their acts and objects. Therefore they are multiplied in like

---

[1] *Longevity*, 2 (465ᵃ23).
[2] *Ethics*, VIII, 5 (1157ᵇ13).
[3] Aristotle, *Physics*, VIII, 4 (254ᵇ7).

[4] *Ibid.*, IV, 12, 13 (221ᵃ32; 222ᵇ16).

manner. Therefore there cannot be many habits in one power.

Obj. 2. Further, a power is a simple force. Now in one simple subject there cannot be diversity of accidents, for the subject is the cause of its accidents; and it does not appear how diverse effects can proceed from one simple cause. Therefore there cannot be many habits in one power.

Obj. 3. Further, just as the body is informed by its shape, so is a power informed by a habit. But one body cannot be informed at the same time by various shapes. Therefore neither can a power be informed at the same time by many habits. Therefore several habits cannot be at the same time in one power.

On the contrary, The intellect is one power, in which nevertheless, are the habits of various sciences.

I answer that, As stated above (Q. XLIX, A. 4), habits are dispositions of a thing that is in potency to something, either to nature, or to operation, which is the end of nature. As to those habits which are dispositions to nature, it is clear that several can be in one subject, since in one subject we may consider parts in various ways, according to the various dispositions of which parts there are various habits. Thus, if we take the humours as being parts of the human body, according to their disposition in respect of human nature we have the habit or disposition of health; while, if we take like parts, such as nerves, bones, and flesh, the disposition of these in respect of nature is strength or leanness; and if we take the limbs, that is, the hands, feet, and so on, the disposition of these in harmony with nature is beauty; and thus there are several habits or dispositions in the same subject.

If, however, we speak of those habits that are dispositions to operation, and belong properly to the powers, thus, again, there may be several habits in one power. The reason for this is that the subject of a habit is a passive power, as stated above (Q. LI, A. 2); for it is only an active power that cannot be the subject of a habit, as was shown above (*ibid.*). Now a passive power is compared to the determinate act of any species as matter to form, because, just as matter is determined to one form by one agent, so, too, is a passive power determined by the nature of one active object to an act specifically one. Therefore, just as several objects can move one passive power, so can one passive power be the subject of several acts or perfections specifically diverse. Now habits are qualities or forms inher-

ing in a power, and inclining that power to acts of a determinate species. Consequently several habits, even as several specifically different acts, can belong to one power.

Reply Obj. 1. Just as in natural things diversity of species is according to the form, and diversity of genus according to matter, as stated in the *Metaphysics*[1] (since things that differ in matter belong to different genera), so, too, generic diversity of objects entails a difference of powers (therefore the Philosopher says in the *Ethics*[2] that "those objects that differ generically belong to different parts of the soul"). But specific difference of objects entails a specific difference of acts, and consequently of habits also. Now things that differ in genus differ in species, but not vice versa. Therefore the acts and habits of different powers differ in species, but it does not follow that different habits are in different powers, for several can be in one power. And even as several genera may be included in one genus, and several species be contained in one species, so does it happen that there are several species of habits and powers.

Reply Obj. 2. Although a power is simple as to its essence, it is multiple virtually, according as it extends to many specifically different acts. Consequently there is nothing to prevent many specifically different habits from being in one power.

Reply Obj. 3. A body is informed by its shape as by its own terminal boundaries; a habit however is not the terminal boundary of a power, but the disposition of a power to an act as to its ultimate term. Consequently one power cannot have several acts at the same time, except in so far as it might occur that one act is comprised in another; just as neither can a body have several shapes, except in so far as one shape enters into another, as a three-sided in a four-sided figure. For the intellect cannot understand several things at the same time actually; and yet it can know several things at the same time habitually.

ARTICLE 2. *Whether Habits Are Distinguished by Their Objects?*

We proceed thus to the Second Article: It would seem that habits are not distinguished by their objects.

Objection 1. For contraries differ in species. Now the same habit of science regards contraries; thus medicine regards the healthy and the unhealthy. Therefore habits are not distinguished by objects specifically distinct.

[1] Aristotle, v, 28 (1024^b9); cf. x, 3 (1054^b26).
[2] VI, I (1139^a8).

Obj. 2. Further, different sciences are different habits. But the same scientific truth belongs to different sciences; thus both the natural philosopher and the astronomer prove the earth to be round, as stated in the *Physics*.[1] Therefore habits are not distinguished by their objects.

Obj. 3. Further, wherever the act is the same, the object is the same. But the same act can belong to different habits of virtue, if it be directed to different ends; thus to give money to anyone, if it be done for God's sake, is an act of charity, while if it be done in order to pay a debt it is an act of justice. Therefore the same object can also belong to different habits. Therefore diversity of habits does not follow diversity of objects.

On the contrary, Acts differ in species according to the diversity of their objects, as stated above (Q. XVIII, A. 5). But habits are dispositions to acts. Therefore habits also are distinguished according to the diversity of objects.

I answer that, A habit is both a form and a habit. Hence the specific distinction of habits may be taken in the ordinary way in which forms differ specifically, or according to that mode of distinction which is proper to habits. Accordingly forms are distinguished from one another in reference to the diversity of their active principles, since every agent produces its like in species. Habits, however, imply order to something, and all things that imply order to something, are distinguished according to the distinction of the things to which they are ordered. Now a habit is a disposition implying a twofold order, namely, to nature, and to an operation consequent to nature. Accordingly habits are specifically distinct in respect of three things. First, in respect of the active principles of such dispositions; secondly, in respect of nature; thirdly, in respect of specifically different objects, as will appear from what follows. (Reply 1, 2, 3; A. 3).

Reply Obj. 1. In distinguishing powers, or also habits, we must consider the object not in its material but in its formal aspect, which may differ in species or even in genus. And though the distinction between specific contraries is a real distinction, yet they are both known under one aspect, since one is known through the other. And consequently in so far as they agree in the one aspect of knowability, they belong to one cognitive habit.

Reply Obj. 2. The natural philosopher proves the earth to be round by one means, the astronomer by another; for the latter proves this by means of mathematics, for example, by the shapes of eclipses, or something of the sort,

while the former proves it by means of natural processes, for example, by the movement of heavy bodies towards the centre, and so forth. Now the whole force of a demonstration, which is "a syllogism producing science," as stated in the *Posterior Analytics*,[2] depends on the mean. And consequently various means are as so many active principles, in respect of which the habits of science are distinguished.

Reply Obj. 3. As the Philosopher says,[3] "the end is, in practical matters, what the principle is in speculative matters." Consequently diversity of ends demands a diversity of virtues, even as diversity of active principles does. Moreover the ends are objects of the internal acts, with which, above all, the virtues are concerned, as is evident from what has been said (Q. XVIII, A. 6; Q. XIX, A. 2, Reply 1; Q. XXXIV, A. 4).

ARTICLE 3. *Whether Habits Are Divided into Good and Bad?*

We proceed thus to the Third Article: It would seem that habits are not divided into good and bad.

Objection 1. For good and bad are contraries. Now the same habit regards contraries, as was stated above (A. 2, obj. 1). Therefore habits are not divided into good and bad.

Obj. 2. Further, good is convertible with being; so that, since it is common to all, it cannot be accounted a specific difference, as the Philosopher declares.[4] Again, evil, since it is a privation and a non-being, cannot differentiate any being. Therefore habits cannot be specifically divided into good and evil.

Obj. 3. Further, there can be different evil habits about one same object, for instance, intemperance and insensibility about matters of concupiscence; and in like manner there can be several good habits, for instance, human virtue and heroic or godlike virtue, as the Philosopher clearly states.[5] Therefore, habits are not divided into good and bad.

On the contrary, A good habit is contrary to a bad habit, as virtue to vice. Now contraries are distinct specifically. Therefore habits are divided specifically into good and bad habits.

I answer that, As stated above (A. 2), habits are specifically distinct not only in respect of their objects and active principles, but also in their relation to nature. Now, this happens in two ways. First, by reason of their suitableness or unsuitableness to nature. In this way a good habit is specifically distinct from a bad habit,

[1] Aristotle, II, 2 (193[b]25).

[2] Aristotle, I, 2 (71[b]18).
[3] *Physics*, II, 9 (200[a]15); *Ethics*, VII, 8 (1151[a]16).
[4] *Topics*, IV, 6 (127[a]26).   [5] *Ethics*, VII, 1 (1145[a]15).

since a good habit is one which disposes to an act suitable to the agent's nature, while an evil habit is one which disposes to an act unsuitable to nature. Thus, acts of virtue are suitable to human nature, since they are according to reason, while acts of vice are discordant with human nature since they are against reason. Hence it is clear that habits are distinguished specifically by the difference of good and bad.

Secondly, habits are distinguished in relation to nature, from the fact that one habit disposes to an act that is suitable to a lower nature, while another habit disposes to an act befitting a higher nature. And thus human virtue, which disposes to an act befitting human nature, is distinct from godlike or heroic virtue, which disposes to an act befitting some higher nature.

Reply Obj. 1. The same habit may be about contraries, in so far as contraries agree in one common aspect. Never, however, does it happen that contrary habits are in one species, since contrariety of habits follows contrariety of aspect. Accordingly habits are divided into good and bad, namely, according as one habit is good, and another bad; but not by reason of one habit being about something good, and another about something bad.

Reply Obj. 2. The good which is common to every being, is not the difference constituting the species of a habit, but some determinate good by reason of suitability to some determinate, namely, the human, nature. In like manner the evil that constitutes a difference of habits is not a pure privation, but something determinate contrary to a determinate nature.

Reply Obj. 3. Several good habits about one same specific thing are distinct in reference to their suitability to various natures, as stated above. But several bad habits in respect of one action are distinct in reference to their diverse incompatibility to that which is in keeping with nature; thus, various vices about one same matter are contrary to one virtue.

ARTICLE 4. *Whether One Habit Is Made up of Many Habits?*

We proceed thus to the Fourth Article: It would seem that one habit is made up of many habits.

Objection 1. For whatever is engendered, not at once, but little by little, seems to be made up of several parts. But a habit is engendered, not at once, but little by little, out of several acts, as stated above (Q. LI, A. 3). Therefore one habit is made up of several.

Obj. 2. Further, a whole is made up of its parts. Now many parts are assigned to one hab-

it; thus Tully assigns many parts of fortitude, temperance, and other virtues.[1] Therefore one habit is made up of many.

Obj. 3. Further, one conclusion suffices both for an act and for a habit of scientific knowledge. But many conclusions belong to but one science, to geometry, for instance, or to arithmetic. Therefore one habit is made up of many.

On the contrary, A habit, since it is a quality, is a simple form. But nothing simple is made up of many. Therefore one habit is not made up of many.

I answer that, A habit directed to operation, such as we are chiefly concerned with at present, is a perfection of a power. Now every perfection is proportioned to that which it perfects. Hence, just as a power, though it is one, extends to many things in so far as they have something in common, that is, some general aspect of the object, so also a habit extends to many things in so far as they are related to one, for instance, to some specific aspect of the object, or to one nature, or to one principle, as was clearly stated above (AA. 2, 3).

If then we consider a habit as to the things to which it extends, we shall find in it a certain multiplicity. But since this multiplicity is directed to one thing, to which the habit looks to chiefly, hence it is that a habit is a simple quality, not composed of several habits, even though it extend to many things. For a habit does not extend to many things save in relation to something, from which it derives its unity.

Reply Obj. 1. That a habit is engendered little by little is due not to one part being engendered after another, but to the fact that the subject does not acquire all at once a firm and difficultly changeable disposition, and also to the fact that it begins by being imperfectly in the subject, and is gradually perfected. The same applies to other qualities.

Reply Obj. 2. The parts which are assigned to each cardinal virtue, are not integral parts that combine to form a whole, but subjective or potential parts, as we shall explain further on (Q. LVII, A. 6, Ans. 4; Part II-II, Q. XLVIII).

Reply Obj. 3. In any science, he who acquires by demonstration scientific knowledge of one conclusion, has the habit indeed, yet imperfectly. And when he obtains by demonstration the scientific knowledge of another conclusion, no additional habit is engendered in him; but the habit which was in him previously is perfected, since it extends to more things, because the conclusions and demonstrations of one science are co-ordinate, and one flows from another.

---

[1] *Rhetor.,* II, 54 (DD I, 165).

2. In Particular
(a) Good Habits—that is, Virtues

QUESTION LV
Of the Virtues, as to their Essence
(In Four Articles)

WE come now to the consideration of habits individually. And since habits, as we have said (Q. LIV, A. 3), are divided into good and bad, we must speak in the first place of good habits, which are virtues, and of other matters connected with them, namely the Gifts, Beatitudes and Fruits (Q. LXVIII); in the second place, of bad habits, namely of vices and sins (Q. LXXI). Now five things must be considered about virtues: (1) the essence of virtue; (2) its subject (Q. LVI); (3) the division of virtue (Q. LVII); (4) the cause of virtue (Q. LXIII); (5) certain properties of virtue (Q. LXIV).

Under the first head, there are four points of inquiry: (1) Whether human virtue is a habit? (2) Whether it is an operative habit? (3) Whether it is a good habit? (4) Of the definition of virtue.

ARTICLE 1. *Whether Human Virtue Is a Habit?*

We proceed thus to the First Article: It would seem that human virtue is not a habit.

Objection 1. For virtue is "the ultimate degree of power."[1] But the ultimate degree of anything is reducible to the genus of that of which it is the ultimate degree, as a point is reducible to the genus of line. Therefore virtue is reducible to the genus of power, and not to the genus of habit.

Obj. 2. Further, Augustine says (*De Lib. Arb.* ii, 19)[2] that "virtue is good use of free choice." But use of free choice is an act. Therefore virtue is not a habit, but an act.

Obj. 3. Further, we do not merit by our habits, but by our actions; otherwise a man would merit continually, even while asleep. But we do merit by our virtues. Therefore virtues are not habits, but acts.

Obj. 4. Further, Augustine says, (*De Moribus Eccl.* xv)[3] that "virtue is the order of love," and (QQ. LXXXIII, *qu.* 30)[4] that "the ordering which is called virtue consists in enjoying what we ought to enjoy, and using what we ought to use." Now order, or ordering, denominates either an action or a relation. Therefore virtue is not a habit, but an action or a relation.

Obj. 5. Further, just as there are human virtues, so are there natural virtues. But natural virtues are not habits, but powers. Neither therefore are human virtues habits.

On the contrary, The Philosopher says[5] that "science and virtue are habits."

I answer that, Virtue denotes a certain perfection of a power. Now a thing's perfection is considered chiefly in relation to its end. But the end of power is act. Therefore power is said to be perfect according as it is determined to its act.

Now there are some powers which of themselves are determinate to their acts; for instance, the active natural powers. And therefore these natural powers are in themselves called virtues. But the rational powers, which are proper to man, are not determined to one particular action, but are inclined indifferently to many, and they are determined to acts by means of habits, as is clear from what we have said above (Q. XLIX, A. 4). Therefore human virtues are habits.

Reply Obj. 1. Sometimes we give the name of a virtue to that to which the virtue is directed, namely, either to its object, or to its act; for instance, we give the name Faith, to that which we believe, or to the act of believing, as also to the habit by which we believe. When therefore we say that "virtue is the highest degree of power," virtue is taken for the object of virtue. For the furthest point to which a power can reach is said to be its virtue; for instance, if a man can carry a hundredweight and not more, his virtue[6] is put at a hundredweight, and not at sixty. But the objection takes virtue as being essentially the highest degree of power.

Reply Obj. 2. Good use of free choice is said to be a virtue, in the same sense as above (Reply 1); that is to say, because it is that to which virtue is directed as to its proper act. For the act of virtue is nothing else than the good use of free choice.

Reply Obj. 3. We are said to merit by something in two ways. First, as by merit itself, just as we are said to run by running; and thus we merit by acts. Secondly, we are said to merit by something as by the principle by which we

---

[1] Aristotle, *Heavens,* I, 11 (281ᵃ14; ᵃ18); cf. St. Thomas, *In De Cælo,* I, 25.
[2] PL 32, 1268; *Retract.,* I, 9 (PL 32, 598).
[3] PL 32, 1322; *City of God,* XV, 22 (PL 41, 467).
[4] PL 40, 19.
[5] *Categories,* 8 (8ᵇ29).
[6] In English we should say "strength," which is the original meaning of the Latin *virtus*; thus we speak of an engine being so many horse-power, to indicate its strength.

merit, as we are said to run by the power of movement; and thus are we said to merit by virtues and habits.

Reply Obj. 4. When we say that virtue is the order or ordering of love, we refer to the end to which virtue is ordered, because in us love is set in order by virtue.

Reply Obj. 5. Natural powers are of themselves determined to one act, but not the rational powers. And so there is no comparison, as we have said.

ARTICLE 2. *Whether Human Virtue Is an Operative Habit?*

We proceed thus to the Second Article: It would seem that it is not essential to human virtue to be an operative habit.

Objection 1. For Tully says (*Tuscul.* iv, 13)[1] that as health and beauty belong to the body, so virtue belongs to the soul. But health and beauty are not operative habits. Therefore neither is virtue.

Obj. 2. Further, in natural things we find virtue not only in reference to act, but also in reference to being, as is clear from the Philosopher,[2] since some have a virtue to be always, while some have a virtue to be not always, but at some definite time. Now as natural virtue is in natural things, so is human virtue in rational beings. Therefore also human virtue is referred not only to act, but also to being.

Obj. 3. Further, the Philosopher says[3] that virtue "is the disposition of a perfect thing to that which is best." Now the best thing to which man needs to be disposed by virtue is God Himself, as Augustine proves (*De Moribus Eccl.* II, 3),[4] to Whom the soul is disposed by being made like to Him. Therefore it seems that virtue is called a quality of the soul in reference to God (likening it, as it were, to Him), but not in reference to operation. It is not, therefore, an operative habit.

On the contrary, The Philosopher says[5] that "the virtue of a thing is that which makes its work good."

I answer that, Virtue, from the very nature of the word, implies some perfection of power, as we have said above (A. 1). Therefore, since power is of two kinds, namely power in reference to being, and power in reference to act; the perfection of each of these is called virtue. But power in reference to being is on the part

[1] DD iv, 30.
[2] *Heavens,* I, 12 (281ª28).
[3] *Physics,* VII, 3 (246ª13).
[4] PL 32, 1347.
[5] *Ethics,* II, 6 (1106ª15).

of matter, which is potential being, but power in reference to act, is on the part of the form, which is the principle of action, since everything acts in so far as it is in act.

Now man is so constituted that the body holds the place of matter, the soul that of form. The body, indeed, man has in common with other animals, and the same is to be said of the powers which are common to the soul and body. Only those powers which are proper to the soul, namely, the rational forces, belong to man alone. And therefore, human virtue, of which we are speaking now, cannot belong to the body, but belongs only to that which is proper to the soul. Therefore human virtue does not imply reference to being, but rather to act. Consequently it is essential to human virtue to be an operative habit.

Reply Obj. 1. Mode of action follows on the disposition of the agent; for such as a thing is, such is its act. And therefore, since virtue is the principle of some kind of operation, there must pre-exist in the operator in respect of virtue some corresponding disposition. Now virtue causes an ordered operation. Therefore virtue itself is an ordered disposition of the soul, in so far as, namely, the powers of the soul are in some way ordered to one another, and to that which is outside. Hence virtue, in so far as it is a suitable disposition of the soul, is like health and beauty, which are suitable dispositions of the body. But this does not hinder virtue from being a principle of operation.

Reply Obj. 2. Virtue which is referred to being is not proper to man, but only that virtue which is referred to works of reason, which are proper to man.

Reply Obj. 3. As God's substance is His act, the highest likeness of man to God is in respect of some operation. Therefore, as we have said above (Q. III, A. 2), happiness or beatitude by which man is made most perfectly conformed to God, and which is the end of human life, consists in an operation.

ARTICLE 3. *Whether Human Virtue Is a Good Habit?*

We proceed thus to the Third Article: It would seem that it is not essential to virtue that it should be a good habit.

Objection 1. For sin is always taken in a bad sense. But there is a virtue even of sin; according to I Cor. 15. 56: *The virtue* (Douay,—strength) *of sin is the Law.* Therefore virtue is not always a good habit.

Obj. 2. Further, virtue corresponds to power.

But power is not only referred to good, but also to evil, according to Isa. 5. 22: *Woe to you that are mighty to drink wine, and stout men at drunkenness.* Therefore virtue also is referred to good and evil.

Obj. 3. Further, according to the Apostle (II Cor. 12. 9): *Virtue* (Douay,—*Power*) *is made perfect in infirmity.* But infirmity is an evil. Therefore virtue is referred not only to good, but also to evil.

On the contrary, Augustine says (*De Moribus Eccl.* VI):[1] "No one can doubt that virtue makes the soul exceeding good"; and the Philosopher says:[2] "Virtue is that which makes its possessor good, and his work good likewise."

I answer that, As we have said above (A. 1), virtue implies a perfection of power; hence "the virtue of a thing is fixed by the highest degree of its power."[3] Now the highest degree of any power must be good, for all evil implies defect; therefore Dionysius says (*Div. Nom.* II)[4] that "every evil is a weakness." And for this reason the virtue of a thing must be regarded in reference to good. Therefore human virtue which is an operative habit, is a good habit, productive of good works.

Reply Obj. 1. Just as bad things are said metaphorically to be perfect, so are they said to be good; for we speak of a perfect thief or robber, and of a good thief or robber, as the Philosopher explains.[5] In this way therefore virtue is applied metaphorically to evil things, so that the *virtue of sin* is said to be the law in so far as occasionally sin is aggravated through the law, so as to attain to the limit of its possibility.

Reply Obj. 2. The evil of drunkenness and excessive drink consists in a falling away from the order of reason. Now it happens that, together with this falling away from reason, some lower power is perfect in reference to that which belongs to its own kind, even in direct opposition to reason, or with some falling away from it. But the perfection of that power, since it is accompanied by a falling away from reason, cannot be called a human virtue.

Reply Obj. 3. Reason is shown to be so much the more perfect according as it is able to overcome or endure more easily the weakness of the body and of the lower powers. And therefore human virtue, which is attributed to reason, is said to be *made perfect in infirmity,* not of the

reason indeed, but of the body and of the lower powers.

ARTICLE 4. *Whether Virtue Is Suitably Defined?*

We proceed thus to the Fourth Article: It would seem that the definition, usually given, of virtue, is not suitable, namely: Virtue is a good quality of the mind, by which we live rightly, of which no one can make bad use, which God works in us, without us.[6]

Objection 1. For virtue is man's goodness, since it is virtue that makes its subject good. But goodness does not seem to be good, as neither is whiteness white. It is therefore unsuitable to describe virtue as a "good quality."

Obj. 2. Further, no difference is more common than its genus, since it is that which divides the genus. But good is more common than quality, for it is convertible with being. Therefore "good" should not be put in the definition of virtue, as a difference of quality.

Obj. 3. Further, as Augustine says (*De Trin.* XII, 8):[7] "When we come across anything that is not common to us and the beasts of the field, it is something appertaining to the mind." But there are virtues even of the irrational parts, as the Philosopher says.[8] Every virtue, therefore, is not a good quality "of the mind."

Obj. 4. Further, righteousness seems to belong to justice; hence the righteous are called just. But justice is a species of virtue. It is therefore unsuitable to put righteous in the definition of virtue, when we say that virtue is that "by which we live rightly."

Obj. 5. Further, whoever is proud of a thing, makes bad use of it. But many are proud of virtue for Augustine says in his Rule,[9] that "pride lies in wait for good works in order to slay them." It is untrue, therefore, that "no one can make bad use of virtue."

Obj. 6. Further, man is justified by virtue. But Augustine commenting on John 15. 11: *He shall do greater things than these,* says:[10] "He who created thee without thee, will not justify thee without thee." It is therefore unsuitable to say that "God works virtue in us, without us."

On the contrary, We have the authority of

---

[1] PL 32, 1314.
[2] *Ethics,* II, 6 (1106[a]15).
[3] Aristotle, *Heavens,* I, II (281[a]14; [a]18).
[4] Sect. 32 (PG 3, 732).
[5] *Metaphysics,* V, 16 (1021[b]17).

[6] Cf. Peter Lombard, *Sent.,* II, d. 27, chap. 5 (QR 1, 446); the form of this definition seems rather to come from Peter of Poitiers, *Sent.,* III, chap. 1 (PL 211, 1041). Cf. Lottin, RSPT (1929), p. 371.
[7] PL 42, 1005.
[8] *Ethics,* III, 10 (1117[b]23).
[9] *Epist.,* CCXI (PL 33, 960).
[10] *Serm.,* CLXIX, 11 (PL 38, 923); Tract. LXXII *in Joann.* (PL 35, 1823).

Augustine, from whose words this definition is gathered, and principally in *De Libero Arbitrio*.[1]

I answer that, This definition comprises perfectly the whole notion of virtue. For the perfect notion of anything is gathered from all its causes. Now the above definition comprises all the causes of virtue. For the formal cause of virtue, as of everything, is gathered from its genus and difference, when it is defined as a good quality; for quality is the genus of virtue, and the difference, good. But the definition would be more suitable if for quality we substitute habit, which is the proximate genus.

Now virtue has no matter "out of which" it is formed, as neither has any other accident; but it has matter "about which" it is concerned, and matter "in which" it exists, namely, the subject. The matter about which virtue is concerned is its object, and this could not be included in the above definition, because the object determines the virtue to a certain species, and here we are giving the definition of virtue in general. And in place of the material cause we put the subject, which is mentioned when we say that virtue is a good quality "of the mind."

The end of virtue, since it is an operative habit, is operation itself. But it must be observed, that some operative habits are always referred to evil, such as vicious habits; others are sometimes referred to good, sometimes to evil, for instance, opinion is referred both to the true and to the untrue. But virtue is a habit which is always referred to good, and so the distinction of virtue from those habits which are always referred to evil is expressed in the words "by which we live rightly"; and its distinction from those habits which are sometimes directed to good, sometimes to evil, in the words, "of which no one makes bad use."

Lastly, God is the efficient cause of infused virtue, to which this definition applies; and this is expressed in the words "which God works in us without us." If we omit this phrase, the remainder of the definition will apply to all virtues in general, whether acquired or infused.

Reply Obj. 1. That which first falls under the intellect is being, and so everything that we apprehend we consider as being, and consequently as one, and as good, which are convertible with being. Therefore we say that essence is being and is one and is good; and that one-ness is being and one and good; and in like manner goodness. But this is not the case with specific forms, such as whiteness and health; for everything that we apprehend is not apprehended

under the aspect of white and healthy. We must, however, observe that as accidents and non-subsistent forms are called beings, not as if they themselves had being, but because things are by them, so also are they called good or one, not by some distinct goodness or one-ness, but because by them something is good or one. So also virtue is called good, because by it something is good.

Reply Obj. 2. Good, which is put in the definition of virtue, is not good in general which is convertible with being, and which extends further than quality, but the good of the reason, with regard to which Dionysius says (*Div. Nom.* iv)[2] that the good of the soul is to be in accord with reason.

Reply Obj. 3. Virtue cannot be in the irrational part of the soul except in so far as this participates in the reason.[3] And therefore reason, or the mind, is the proper subject of human virtue.

Reply Obj. 4. Justice has a righteousness of its own by which it puts those outward things right which come into human use, and are the proper matter of justice, as we shall show further on (Q. LX, A. 2; Part II-II, Q. LVIII, A, 8). But the righteousness which denotes order to a due end and to the Divine law, which is the rule of the human will, as stated above (Q. XIX, A. 4), is common to all virtues.

Reply Obj. 5. One can make bad use of a virtue taken as an object, for instance, by having evil thoughts about a virtue, that is, by hating it, or by being proud of it; but one cannot make bad use of virtue as principle of action, so that an act of virtue be evil.

Reply Obj. 6. Infused virtue is caused in us by God without any action on our part, but not without our consent. This is the sense of the words, "which God works in us without us." As to those things which are done by us, God causes them in us, yet not without action on our part, for He works in every will and in every nature.

QUESTION LVI
OF THE SUBJECT OF VIRTUE
(*In Six Articles*)

WE now have to consider the subject of virtue, about which there are six points of inquiry: (1) Whether the subject of virtue is in a power of the soul as in a subject? (2) Whether one virtue can be in several powers? (3) Whether the intellect can be the subject of virtue? (4) Wheth-

---

[1] II, 19 (PL 32, 1268).

[2] Sect. 32 (PG 3, 733).
[3] Aristotle, *Ethics*, I, 13 (1102^{b}13).

er the irascible and concupiscible powers can be the subject of virtue? (5) Whether the sensitive powers of apprehension can be the subject of virtue? (6) Whether the will can be the subject of virtue?

ARTICLE 1. *Whether the Subject of Virtue Is in a Power of the Soul as in a Subject?*

We proceed thus to the First Article: It would seem that virtue is not in a power of the soul as in a subject.

Objection 1. For Augustine says (*De Lib. Arb.* II, 19)[1] that "virtue is that by which we live rightly." But we live by the essence of the soul, and not by a power of the soul. Therefore virtue is not in a power, but in the essence of the soul.

Obj. 2. Further, the Philosopher says[2] that "virtue is that which makes its possessor good, and his work good likewise." But as work is set up by power, so he that has a virtue is set up by the essence of the soul. Therefore virtue does not belong more to the power than to the essence of the soul.

Obj. 3. Further, power is in the second species of quality. But virtue is a quality, as we have said above (Q. LV, A. 4), and quality is not the subject of quality. Therefore human virtue is in a power of the soul as in a subject.

On the contrary, "Virtue is the highest degree of power."[3] But the limit is in that of which it is the limit. Therefore virtue is in a power of the soul.

I answer that, It can be proved in three ways that virtue belongs to a power of the soul. First, from the very notion of virtue, which implies perfection of a power; for perfection is in that which it perfects. Secondly, from the fact that virtue is an operative habit, as we have said above (Q. LV, A. 2); for all operation proceeds from the soul through a power. Thirdly, from the fact that virtue disposes to that which is best; for the best is the end, which is either a thing's operation, or something acquired by an operation proceeding from the thing's power. Therefore a power of the soul is the subject of virtue.

Reply Obj. 1. "To live" may be taken in two ways. Sometimes it is taken for the very being of the living thing; in this way it belongs to the essence of the soul, which is the principle of being in the living thing. But sometimes "to live" is taken for the operation of the living thing; in

this sense, by virtue we live rightly, in so far as by virtue we act rightly.

Reply Obj. 2. Good is either the end or something related to the end. And therefore, since the good of the worker consists in the work, this fact also, that virtue makes the worker good, is referred to the work, and consequently to the power.

Reply Obj. 3. One accident is said to be in another as in a subject not as though one accident could uphold another, but because one accident inheres to substance by means of another, as colour to the body by means of the surface, so that surface is said to be the subject of colour. In this way a power of the soul is said to be the subject of virtue.

ARTICLE 2. *Whether One Virtue Can Be in Several Powers?*

We proceed thus to the Second Article: It would seem that one virtue can be in several powers.

Objection 1. For habits are known by their acts. But one act proceeds in various ways from several powers; thus walking proceeds from the reason as directing, from the will as moving, and from the moving power as executing. Therefore also one habit can be in several powers.

Obj. 2. Further, the Philosopher says[4] that three things are required for virtue, namely: "to know, to will, and to work steadfastly." But to know belongs to the intellect, and to will belongs to the will. Therefore virtue can be in several powers.

Obj. 3. Further, prudence is in the reason, since it is "the right reason of things to be done."[5] And it is also in the will: for it cannot exist together with a perverse will.[6] Therefore one virtue can be in two powers.

On the contrary, The subject of virtue is a power of the soul. But the same accident cannot be in several subjects. Therefore one virtue cannot be in several powers of the soul.

I answer that, One thing can be in two subjects in two ways. First, so that it is in both on an equal footing. In this way it is impossible for one virtue to be in two powers, since diversity of powers follows the general conditions of the objects, while diversity of habits follows their special conditions; and so wherever there is diversity of powers, there is diversity of habits, but not vice versa. In another way one thing can be in two or more subjects, not on an equal

---

[1] *PL* 32, 1268.
[2] *Ethics,* II, 6 (1106ª15).
[3] Aristotle, *Heavens,* I, 11 (281ª14); cf. Thomas, *In De Cælo,* I, 25.

[4] *Ethics,* II, 4 (1105ª31).
[5] *Ibid.,* VI, 5 (1140ᵇ4).
[6] *Ibid.,* VI, 12 (1144ª36).

footing, but in a certain order. And thus one virtue can belong to several powers, so that it is in one chiefly, while it extends to others by a kind of diffusion, or by way of a disposition, according as one power is moved by another, and one power receives from another.

Reply Obj. 1. One act cannot belong to several powers equally, and in the same order, but only from different points of view, and in various orders.

Reply Obj. 2. "To know" is a condition required for moral virtue, in so far as moral virtue works according to right reason. But moral virtue is essentially in the appetite.

Reply Obj. 3. Prudence is really in the reason as in a subject, but it presupposes as its principle the rectitude of the will, as we shall see further on (A. 3; Q. LVII, A. 4).

ARTICLE 3. *Whether the Intellect Can Be the Subject of Virtue?*

We proceed thus to the Third Article: It would seem that the intellect is not the subject of virtue.

Objection 1. For Augustine says (*De Moribus Eccl.* XV)[1] that all virtue is love. But the subject of love is not the intellect, but the appetitive power alone. Therefore no virtue is in the intellect.

Obj. 2. Further, virtue is ordered to good, as is clear from what has been said above (Q. LV, A. 3). Now good is not the object of the intellect, but of the appetitive power. Therefore the subject of virtue is not the intellect, but the appetitive power.

Obj. 3. Further, "virtue is that which makes its possessor good," as the Philosopher says.[2] But the habit which perfects the intellect does not make its possessor good, since a man is not said to be a good man on account of his science or his art. Therefore the intellect is not the subject of virtue.

On the contrary, The mind is chiefly called the intellect. But the subject of virtue is the mind, as is clear from the definition, above given, of virtue (Q. LV, A. 4). Therefore the intellect is the subject of virtue.

I answer that, As we have said above (Q. LV, A. 3), virtue is a habit by which we work well. Now a habit may be ordered to a good act in two ways. First, in so far as by the habit a man acquires an aptness to a good act; for instance, by the habit of grammar man has the aptness to speak correctly. But grammar does not make

a man always speak correctly, for a grammarian may be guilty of a barbarism or make a solecism, and the case is the same with other sciences and arts. Secondly, a habit may confer not only aptness to act, but also the right use of that aptness; for instance, justice not only gives man the prompt will to do just actions, but also makes him act justly.

And since good, and, in like manner, being, is said of a thing absolutely, in respect not of what it is potentially, but of what it is actually, therefore from having habits of the latter sort, man is said absolutely to do good, and to be good; for instance, because he is just, or temperate, and in like manner as regards other such virtues. And since virtue is that which makes its possessor good, and his work good likewise, these latter habits are called virtuous absolutely; because they make the work to be actually good, and the subject good absolutely. But the first kind of habits are not called virtues absolutely, because they do not make the work good except in regard to a certain aptness, nor do they make their possessor good absolutely. For through being gifted in science or art, a man is said to be good, not absolutely, but relatively; for instance, a good grammarian, or a good smith. And for this reason science and art are often divided against virtue, while at other times they are called virtues.[3]

Hence the subject of a habit which is called a virtue in a relative sense can be the intellect, and not only the practical intellect, but also the speculative, without any reference to the will; for thus the Philosopher holds that science, wisdom and understanding, and also art, are intellectual virtues.[4] But the subject of a habit which is called a virtue absolutely can only be the will, or some power in so far as it is moved by the will. And the reason of this is that the will moves to their acts all those other powers that are in some way rational, as we have said above (Q. IX, A. 1; Q. XVII, AA. 1, 5; Part I, Q. LXXXII, A. 4); and therefore if man do well actually, this is because he has a good will. Therefore the virtue which makes a man to do well actually, and not merely to have the aptness to do well, must be either in the will itself, or in some power as moved by the will.

Now it happens that the intellect is moved by the will, just as are the other powers, for a man considers something actually because he wills to do so. And therefore the intellect, in so far as it is subordinate to the will, can be the

[1] PL 32, 1322.
[2] *Ethics,* II, 6 (1106ᵃ15).

[3] Aristotle, *Ethics,* VI, 2 (1139ᵇ13).
[4] *Ibid.,* VI, 3 (1139ᵇ16).

subject of virtue absolutely so called. And in this way the speculative intellect, or the reason, is the subject of faith; for the intellect is moved by the command of the will to assent to what is of faith; for "no man believeth, unless he will."[1] But the practical intellect is the subject of prudence. For since prudence is the right reason of things to be done, it is a condition of prudence that man be rightly disposed in regard to the principles of this reason of things to be done, that is, in regard to their ends, to which man is rightly disposed by the rectitude of the will, just as to the principles of speculative truth he is rightly disposed by the natural light of the agent intellect. And therefore as the subject of science, which is the right reason of speculative truths, is the speculative intellect in its relation to the agent intellect, so the subject of prudence is the practical intellect in its relation to the right will.

Reply Obj. 1. The saying of Augustine is to be understood of virtue so called absolutely; not that every such virtue is love absolutely, but that it depends in some way on love, in so far as it depends on the will, whose first movement consists in love, as we have said above (Q. XXV, AA. 1, 2, 3; Q. XXVII, A. 4; Part I, Q. XX, A. 1).

Reply Obj. 2. The good of each thing is its end, and therefore, as truth is the end of the intellect, so to know truth is the good act of the intellect. Hence the habit which perfects the intellect in regard to the knowledge of truth, whether speculative or practical, is a virtue.

Reply Obj. 3. This objection considers virtue so called absolutely.

ARTICLE 4. *Whether the Irascible and Concupiscible Powers Are the Subject of Virtue?*

We proceed thus to the Fourth Article: It would seem that the irascible and concupiscible powers cannot be the subject of virtue.

Objection 1. For these powers are common to us and dumb animals. But we are now speaking of virtue as proper to man, since for this reason it is called human virtue. It is therefore impossible for human virtue to be in the irascible and concupiscible powers which are parts of the sensitive appetite, as we have said in the First Part (Q. LXXXI, A. 2).

Obj. 2. Further, the sensitive appetite is a power which makes use of a corporeal organ. But the good of virtue cannot be in man's body; for the Apostle says (Rom. 7.18): *I know that good does not dwell in my flesh.* Therefore the sensitive appetite cannot be the subject of virtue.

Obj. 3. Further, Augustine proves *(De Moribus Eccl.* v)[2] that virtue is not in the body but in the soul, for the reason that the body is ruled by the soul; therefore it is entirely due to his soul that a man make good use of his body: "For instance, if my coachman, through obedience to my orders, guides well the horses which he is driving, this is all due to me." But just as the soul rules the body, so also does the reason rule the sensitive appetite. Therefore that the irascible and concupiscible powers are rightly ruled is entirely due to the rational powers. Now "virtue is that by which we live rightly," as we have said above (Q. LV, A. 4). Therefore virtue is not in the irascible and concupiscible powers, but only in the rational part.

Obj. 4. Further, "the principal act of moral virtue is choice."[3] Now choice is not an act of the irascible and concupiscible powers, but of the reason, as we have said above (Q. XIII, A. 2). Therefore moral virtue is not in the irascible and concupiscible powers, but in the reason.

On the contrary, Fortitude is assigned to the irascible power, and temperance to the concupiscible power. Hence the Philosopher says[4] that "these virtues belong to the irrational part of the soul."

I answer that, The irascible and concupiscible powers can be considered in two ways. First, in themselves, in so far as they are parts of the sensitive appetite; and in this way they are not able to be the subject of virtue. Secondly, they can be considered as participating in the reason, from the fact that they have a natural aptitude to obey reason. And thus the irascible or concupiscible power can be the subject of human virtue; for, in so far as it participates in the reason, it is the principle of a human act. And to these powers we must assign virtues.

For it is clear that there are some virtues in the irascible and concupiscible powers. Because an act which proceeds from one power according as it is moved by another power, cannot be perfect, unless both powers be well disposed to the act; for instance, the act of a craftsman cannot be successful unless both the craftsman and his instrument be well disposed to act. Therefore in the matter of the operations of the irascible and concupiscible powers, according as they are moved by reason, there

---

[1] Augustine: *Tract.* XXVI. *in Joann.*, on 6.44 (PL 35; 1607).

[2] PL 32, 1314.
[3] *Ethics*, VIII, 13 (1163ª22).
[4] *Ibid.*, III, 10 (1117ᵇ23).

must be some habit perfecting (in respect of acting well) not only the reason, but also the irascible and concupiscible powers. And since the good disposition of the power which moves through being moved depends on its conformity with the power that moves it, therefore the virtue which is in the irascible and concupiscible powers is nothing else but a certain habitual conformity of these powers to reason.

Reply Obj. 1. The irascible and concupiscible powers considered in themselves, as parts of the sensitive appetite, are common to us and dumb animals. But in so far as they are rational by participation, and are obedient to the reason, they are proper to man. And in this way they can be the subject of human virtue.

Reply Obj. 2. Just as human flesh has not of itself the good of virtue, but is made the instrument of a virtuous act, in so far as, being moved by reason we *yield our members to serve justice,* so also, the irascible and concupiscible powers of themselves indeed, have not the good of virtue, but rather the infection of the "fomes"; but in so far as they are in conformity with reason, the good of reason is engendered in them.

Reply Obj. 3. The body is ruled by the soul, and the irascible and concupiscible powers by the reason, but in different ways. For the body obeys the soul blindly without any contradiction, in those things in which it is naturally moved by the soul; hence the Philosopher says[1] that "the soul rules the body with a despotic command," as the master rules his slave: hence the entire movement of the body is referred to the soul. For this reason virtue is not in the body, but only in the soul. But the irascible and concupiscible powers do not obey the reason blindly; on the contrary, they have their own proper movements, by which, at times, they go against reason, and so the Philosopher says[2] that the "reason rules the irascible and concupiscible powers by a political command," such as that by which free men are ruled, who have in some respects a will of their own. And for this reason also must there be some virtues in the irascible and concupiscible powers, by which these powers are well disposed to act.

Reply Obj. 4. In choice there are two things, namely, the intention of the end, and this belongs to the moral virtue; and the choice of means, and this belongs to prudence.[3] But that the irascible and concupiscible powers have a right intention of the end in regard to the passions of the soul is due to the good disposition of those powers. And therefore those moral virtues which are concerned with the passions are in the irascible and concupiscible powers, but prudence is in the reason.

ARTICLE 5. *Whether the Sensitive Powers of Apprehension Are the Subject of Virtue?*

We proceed thus to the Fifth Article: It would seem that it is possible for virtue to be in the interior sensitive powers of apprehension.

Objection 1. For the sensitive appetite can be the subject of virtue in so far as it obeys reason. But the interior sensitive powers of apprehension obey reason: for the powers of imagination, of cogitation, and of memory act at the command of reason. Therefore in these powers there can be virtue.

Obj. 2. Further, as the rational appetite, which is the will, can be hindered or helped in its act by the sensitive appetite, so also can the intellect or reason be hindered or helped by the powers mentioned above. As, therefore, there can be virtue in the sensitive powers of appetite, so also can there be virtue in the powers of apprehension.

Obj. 3. Further, prudence is a virtue, of which Cicero (*De Invent. Rhetor.* ii, 53)[4] says that memory is a part. Therefore also in the power of memory there can be a virtue; and in like manner, in the other interior powers of apprehension.

On the contrary, All virtues are either intellectual or moral.[5] Now all the moral virtues are in the appetite, while the intellectual virtues are in the intellect or reason, as is clear from the *Ethics.*[6] Therefore there is no virtue in the interior sensitive powers of apprehension.

I answer that, In the interior sensitive powers of apprehension there are some habits. And this is made clear principally from what the Philosopher says,[7] that "in remembering one thing after another, we become used to it; and use is a second nature." Now a habit of use is nothing else than a habit acquired by use, which is like nature. Therefore Tully says of virtue in his *Rhetoric (loc. cit.)* that "it is a habit like a second nature in accord with reason." Yet in man, that which he acquires by use, in his memory and other sensitive powers of apprehension, is not a habit properly so called, but

[1] *Politics,* I, 2 (1254[b]4).
[2] *Ibid.*
[3] *Ethics,* VI, 12 (1144[a]6).
[4] DD I, 165.
[5] Aristotle, *Ethics,* II, I (1103[a]14).
[6] *Ibid.,* VI, I (1138[b]35).
[7] *Memory and Reminiscence,* 2 (452[a]27).

something annexed to the habits of the intellective part, as we have said above (Q. L, A. 4, Reply 3).

Nevertheless even if there be habits in such powers, they cannot be called virtues. For virtue is a perfect habit, by which it never happens that anything but good is done; and so virtue must be in that power which brings the good act to completion. But the knowledge of truth is not consummated in the sensitive powers of apprehension, for such powers prepare the way to the intellectual knowledge. And therefore in these powers there are none of the virtues by which we know truth; these are rather in the intellect or reason.

Reply Obj. 1. The sensitive appetite is related to the will, which is the rational appetite, through being moved by it. And therefore the act of the appetitive power is consummated in the sensitive appetite, and for this reason the sensitive appetite is the subject of virtue. But the sensitive powers of apprehension are related to the intellect rather through moving it, for the reason that the phantasms are related to the intellectual soul as colours to sight.[1] And therefore the act of knowledge is terminated in the intellect; and for this reason the virtues of knowing are in the intellect itself, or the reason.

And thus is made clear the *reply to the second objection.*

Reply Obj. 3. Memory is not a part of prudence, as species is of a genus, as though memory were a virtue properly so called; but one of the conditions required for prudence is a good memory, so that, in a fashion, it is after the manner of an integral part.

ARTICLE 6. *Whether the Will Can Be the Subject of Virtue?*

We proceed thus to the Sixth Article: It would seem that the will is not the subject of virtue.

Objection 1. Because no habit is required for that which belongs to a power by reason of its very nature. But since the will is in the reason, it is of the very notion of the will, according to the Philosopher,[2] to tend to that which is good according to reason. And to this good every virtue is ordered, since everything naturally desires its own good; for virtue, as Tully says in his *Rhetoric*,[3] is "a habit like a second nature in accord with reason." Therefore the will is not the subject of virtue.

Obj. 2. Further, every virtue is either intel-

lectual or moral.[4] But intellectual virtue is in the intellect and reason as in a subject, and not in the will, while moral virtue has its subject in the irascible and concupiscible powers which are rational by participation. Therefore no virtue is in the will as in a subject.

Obj. 3. Further, all human acts, to which virtues are ordered, are voluntary. If therefore there be a virtue in the will in respect of some human acts, in like manner there will be a virtue in the will in respect of all human acts. Either, therefore, there will be no virtue in any other power, or there will be two virtues ordered to the same act, which seems unreasonable. Therefore the will cannot be the subject of virtue.

On the contrary, Greater perfection is required in the mover than in the moved. But the will moves the irascible and concupiscible powers. Much more therefore should there be virtue in the will than in the irascible and concupiscible powers.

I answer that, Since the habit perfects the power in reference to act, the power needs a habit perfecting it for doing well, which habit is a virtue, when the power's own proper nature does not suffice for the purpose.

Now the proper nature of a power is seen in its relation to its object. Since, therefore, as we have said above (Q. XIX, A. 3), the object of the will is the good of reason proportionate to the will, in respect of this the will does not need a virtue perfecting it. But if man's will is confronted with a good that exceeds its capacity, whether as regards the whole human species (such as Divine good, which transcends the limits of human nature), or as regards the individual, (such as the good of one's neighbour), at that point the will needs virtue. And therefore such virtues as those which direct man's affections to God or to his neighbour as charity, justice, and the like, are in the will as their subject.

Reply Obj. 1. This objection is true of those virtues which are ordered to the willer's own good, such as temperance and fortitude, which are concerned with the human passions, and the like, as is clear from what we have said (Q. XXV, A. 6, Reply 3; Part I, Q. XXI, A. 1, Reply 1; Q. LIX, A. 4, Reply 3).

Reply Obj. 2. Not only the irascible and concupiscible powers are rational by participation, but the appetitive power altogether, that is, in its entirety.[5] Now the will is included in the

---

[1] Aristotle, *Soul,* III, 7 (431ª14).
[2] *Ibid.,* III, 9 (432ᵇ5).   [3] Bk. II, chap. 53 (DD T, 165).

[4] Aristotle, *Ethics,* I, 13 (1103ª4); II, 1 (1103ª14).
[5] *Ibid.,* I, 13 (1102ᵇ30).

appetitive power. And therefore whatever virtue is in the will must be a moral virtue, unless it be theological, as we shall see later on (Q. LXII, A. 3).

Reply Obj. 3. Some virtues are directed to the good of moderated passion, which is the proper good of this or that man; and in these cases there is no need for virtue in the will, for the nature of the power suffices for the purpose, as we have said. This need exists only in the case of virtues which are directed to some extrinsic good.

QUESTION LVII
OF THE INTELLECTUAL VIRTUES
(*In Six Articles*)

WE now have to consider the various kinds of virtue: (1) the intellectual virtues; (2) the moral virtues (Q. LVIII); (3) the theological virtues (Q. LXII). Concerning the first there are six points of inquiry: (1) Whether habits of the speculative intellect are virtues? (2) Whether they are three, namely, wisdom, science, and understanding? (3) Whether the intellectual habit, which is art, is a virtue? (4) Whether prudence is a virtue distinct from art? (5) Whether prudence is a virtue necessary to man? (6) Whether *eubulia, synesis* and *gnome* are virtues joined to prudence?

ARTICLE 1. *Whether the Habits of the Speculative Intellect Are Virtues?*

We proceed thus to the First Article: It would seem that the habits of the speculative intellect are not virtues.

Objection 1. For virtue is an operative habit, as we have said above (Q. LV, A. 2). But speculative habits are not operative, for the speculative order is distinct from the practical, that is, operative order. Therefore the habits of the speculative intellect are not virtues.

Obj. 2. Further, virtue is about those things by which man is made happy or blessed; for "happiness is the reward of virtue."[1] Now intellectual habits do not consider human acts or other human goods, by which man acquires happiness, but rather things pertaining to nature or to God. Therefore habits of this kind cannot be called virtues.

Obj. 3. Further, science is a speculative habit. But science and virtue are distinguished as genera which are not subalternate, as the Philosopher proves in the *Topics*.[2] Therefore speculative habits are not virtues.

On the contrary, The speculative habits alone consider necessary things which cannot be otherwise than they are. Now the Philosopher[3] places certain intellectual virtues in that part of the soul which considers necessary things that cannot be otherwise than they are. Therefore the habits of the speculative intellect are virtues.

I answer that, Since every virtue is ordered to some good, as stated above (Q. LV, A. 3), a habit, as we have already observed (Q. LVI, A. 3), may be called a virtue for two reasons: first, because it confers aptness in doing good; secondly, because besides aptness, it confers the good use of it. The latter condition, as above stated (*ibid.*), belongs to those habits alone which affect the appetitive part of the soul, since it is the soul's appetitive power that puts all the powers and habits to their respective uses.

Since, then, the habits of the speculative intellect do not perfect the appetitive part, nor affect it in any way, but only the intellective part, they may indeed be called virtues in so far as they confer aptness for a good work, namely, the consideration of truth (since this is the good work of the intellect); yet they are not called virtues in the second way, as though they conferred the good use of a power or habit. For if a man possess a habit of speculative science, it does not follow that he is inclined to make use of it, but he is made able to consider the truth in those matters of which he has scientific knowledge:—that he make use of the knowledge which he has is due to the motion of his will. Consequently a virtue which perfects the will, such as charity or justice, confers the good use of these speculative habits. And in this way too there can be merit in the acts of these habits, if they be done out of charity; thus Gregory says (*Moral.* vi)[4] that "the contemplative life has greater merit than the active life."

Reply Obj. 1. Work is of two kinds, exterior and interior. Accordingly practical or operative which is divided against speculative, is concerned with exterior work, to which the speculative habit is not ordered. Yet it is ordered to the interior act of the intellect which is to consider the truth. And in this way it is an operative habit.

Reply Obj. 2. Virtue is about certain things in two ways. In the first place a virtue is about its object. And thus these speculative virtues are not about those things by which man is

---

[1] Aristotle, *Ethics*, I, 9 (1099^{b}16).   [2] IV, 2 (121^{b}34).

[3] *Ethics*, VI, 1 (1139^{a}7).
[4] PL 75, 764.

made happy; except perhaps in so far as "by which" indicates the efficient cause or object of complete happiness, that is, God, Who is the supreme object of contemplation. Secondly, a virtue is said to be about its acts, and in this sense the intellectual virtues are about those things by which a man is made happy; both because the acts of these virtues can be meritorious, as stated above, and because they are a kind of beginning of perfect bliss, which consists in the contemplation of truth, as we have already stated (Q. III, A. 7).

Reply Obj. 3. Science is divided against virtue taken in the second sense, where it belongs to the appetitive power.

ARTICLE 2. *Whether There Are Only Three Habits of the Speculative Intellect, Namely, Wisdom, Science and Understanding?*

We proceed thus to the Second Article: It would seem unfitting to distinguish three virtues of the speculative intellect, namely, wisdom, science and understanding.

Objection 1. Because a species should not be divided with its genus. But wisdom is a kind of science, as stated in the *Ethics.*[1] Therefore wisdom should not be divided with science among the intellectual virtues.

Obj. 2. Further, in differentiating powers, habits and acts in respect of their objects, we consider chiefly the formal aspect of these objects, as we have already explained (Q. LIV, A. 2, REPLY 1; Part I, Q. LXXVII, A. 3). Therefore the diversity of habits is taken, not from their material objects, but from the formal aspect of those objects. Now the principle of a demonstration is the formal aspect under which the conclusion is known. Therefore the understanding of principles should not be set down as a habit or virtue distinct from the knowledge of conclusions.

Obj. 3. Further, an intellectual virtue is one which resides in the essentially rational part. Now even the speculative reason employs the dialectic syllogism, just as it employs the demonstrative syllogism. Therefore as science, which is the result of a demonstrative syllogism, is set down as a virtue of the speculative intellect, so also should opinion be.

On the contrary, The Philosopher[2] sets down these three alone as being virtues of the speculative intellect, namely, wisdom, science and understanding.

I answer that, As already stated (A. 1), the virtues of the speculative intellect are those which perfect the speculative intellect for the consideration of truth, for this is its good work. Now a truth is subject to a twofold consideration,—as known in itself, and as known through another. What is known in itself is as a principle, and is at once understood by the intellect; therefore the habit that perfects the intellect for the consideration of such truth is called understanding, which is the habit of principles.

On the other hand, a truth which is known through another, is understood by the intellect not at once, but by means of the reason's inquiry, and is as a term. This may happen in two ways: first, so that it is the last in some particular genus; secondly, so that it is the ultimate term of all human knowledge. And, since "things that are knowable last from our standpoint, are knowable first and chiefly in their nature,"[3] hence that which is last with respect to all human knowledge is that which is knowable first and chiefly in its nature. And concerning these there is "wisdom, which considers the highest causes," as stated in the *Metaphysics.*[4] Therefore it rightly judges all things and sets them in order, because there can be no perfect and universal judgment that is not resolved into first causes. But in regard to that which is last in this or that genus of knowable things, it is science that perfects the intellect. Therefore according to the different genera of knowable things, there are different habits of sciences; although there is but one wisdom.

Reply Obj. 1. Wisdom is a kind of science in so far as it has that which is common to all the sciences, namely, to demonstrate conclusions from principles. But since it has something proper to itself above the other sciences, in so far, that is, as it judges of them all, not only as to their conclusions, but also as to their first principles, therefore it is a more perfect virtue than science.

Reply Obj. 2. When the formal aspect of the object is referred to a power or habit by one same act, there is no distinction of habit or power in respect of the formal aspect and of the material object; thus it pertains to the same power of sight to see both colour and light, which latter is the formal aspect under which colour is seen, and is seen at the same time as the colour. On the other hand, the principles of a demonstration can be considered apart, without the conclusion being considered at all. Again, they can be considered together with

[1] Aristotle, VI, 7 (1141ᵃ19).
[2] *Ethics,* VI, 7 (1141ᵃ19); VI, 3 (1139ᵇ16).
[3] *Physics,* I, 1 (184ᵃ18).
[4] Aristotle, I, 1, 2 (981ᵇ28; 982ᵇ9).

the conclusions, since the conclusions can be deduced from them. Accordingly, to consider the principles in this second way pertains to science, which considers the conclusions also, while to consider the principles in themselves pertains to understanding.

Consequently, if we consider the point rightly, these three virtues are distinct not as being on a par with one another, but in a certain order. The same is to be observed in potential wholes, in which one part is more perfect than another; for instance, the rational soul is more perfect than the sensitive soul, and the sensitive, than the vegetative. For it is in this way that science depends on understanding as on a virtue of higher degree; and both of these depend on wisdom, as being in the highest place, and containing beneath itself both understanding and science, by judging both of the conclusions of science, and of the principles on which they are based.

Reply Obj. 3. As stated above (Q. LV, AA. 3, 4), a virtuous habit has a fixed relation to good, and is in no way referrible to evil. Now the good of the intellect is truth, and falsehood is its evil. Therefore those habits alone are called intellectual virtues by which we always speak the truth and never a falsehood. But opinion and suspicion can be about both the true and the false; and so, as stated in the *Ethics*,[1] they are not intellectual virtues.

ARTICLE 3. *Whether the Intellectual Habit Art Is a Virtue?*

We proceed thus to the Third Article: It would seem that art is not an intellectual virtue.

Objection 1. For Augustine says (*De Lib. Arb.* ii, 18, 19)[2] that "no one makes bad use of virtue." But one may make bad use of art, for a craftsman can work badly according to the knowledge of his art. Therefore art is not a virtue.

Obj. 2. Further, there is no virtue of a virtue. But "there is a virtue of art," according to the Philosopher.[3] Therefore art is not a virtue.

Obj. 3. Further, the liberal arts excel the mechanical arts. But just as the mechanical arts are practical, so the liberal arts are speculative. Therefore, if art were an intellectual virtue, it would have to be numbered among the speculative virtues.

On the contrary, The Philosopher says[4] that

[1] Aristotle, VI, 3 (1139^{b}17).
[2] PL 32, 1267, 1268.
[3] *Ethics*, VI, 5 (1140^{b}22).
[4] *Ibid.*, VI, 3, 7 (1139^{b}16; 1141^{a}19).

art is a virtue; and yet he does not number it among the speculative virtues, which, according to him, reside in the scientific part of the soul.

I answer that, Art is nothing else but the right reason about certain works to be made. And yet the good of these things depends, not on man's appetite being affected in this or that way, but on the goodness of the work done. For a craftsman, as such, is commendable not for the will with which he does a work, but for the quality of the work. Art, therefore, properly speaking, is an operative habit. And yet it has something in common with the speculative habits, since the quality of the object considered by the latter is a matter of concern to them also, but not how the human appetite may be affected towards that object. For as long as the geometrician demonstrates the truth, it does not matter how his appetitive part may be affected, whether he be joyful or angry, even as neither does this matter in a craftsman, as we have observed. And so art has the nature of a virtue in the same way as the speculative habits, in so far, that is, as neither art nor speculative habit makes a good work as regards the use of the habit, which is proper to a virtue that perfects the appetite, but only as regards the aptness to work well.

Reply Obj. 1. When anyone endowed with an art produces bad workmanship, this is not the work of that art, but rather is contrary to the art, even as when a man lies while knowing the truth, his words are not in accord with his knowledge, but contrary to it. Therefore, just as science has always a relation to good, as stated above (A. 2, REPLY 3), so it is with art, and it is for this reason that it is called a virtue. And yet it falls short of being a perfect virtue, because it does not make its possessor use it well, for which purpose something further is requisite, although there cannot be a good use without the art.

Reply Obj. 2. In order that man may make good use of the art he has, he needs a good will, which is perfected by moral virtue; and for this reason the Philosopher says that there is a virtue of art, namely, a moral virtue, in so far as the good use of art requires a moral virtue. For it is evident that a craftsman is inclined by justice, which rectifies his will, to do his work faithfully.

Reply Obj. 3. Even in speculative matters there is something by way of work; for example, the making of a syllogism or of a fitting speech, or the work of counting or measuring. Hence whatever habits are ordered to such works of the speculative reason, are by a kind of comparison called arts indeed, but liberal arts, in order to distinguish them from those arts that are ordered to works done by the body, which arts are, in a fashion, servile, in so far as the body is in servile subjection to the soul, and man, as regards his soul, is free *(liber)*. On the other hand, those sciences which are not ordered to any work of this kind, are called sciences absolutely, and not arts. Nor, if the liberal arts be more excellent, does it follow that the notion of art is more applicable to them.

Article 4. *Whether Prudence Is a Distinct Virtue from Art?*

We proceed thus to the Fourth Article: It would seem that prudence is not a distinct virtue from art.

Objection 1. For art is the right reason about certain works. But diversity of works does not make a habit cease to be an art, since there are various arts concerned with works widely different. Since therefore prudence is also right reason about works, it seems that it too should be called an art.

Obj. 2. Further, prudence has more in common with art than the speculative habits have; for they are both "about contingent matters that may be otherwise than they are."[1] Now some speculative habits are called arts. Much more, therefore, should prudence be called an art.

Obj. 3. Further, "it pertains to prudence to be of good counsel."[2] But counselling takes place in certain arts also, as stated in *Ethics*,[3] for example, in the arts of warfare, of government, and of medicine. Therefore prudence is not distinct from art.

On the contrary, The Philosopher distinguishes prudence from art.[4]

I answer that, Where the nature of virtue differs, there is a different kind of virtue. Now it has been stated above (A. 1; Q. LVI, A. 3) that some habits have the nature of virtue through merely conferring aptness for a good work, while some habits are virtues not only through conferring aptness for a good work, but also through conferring the use. But art confers only the aptness for good work, since it does not regard the appetite; prudence however confers not only aptness for a good work, but also the use,

for it regards the appetite, since it presupposes the rectitude of the appetite.

The reason for this difference is that art is the right reason of things to be made, while prudence is the right reason of things to be done. Now making and doing differ, as stated in the *Metaphysics*,[5] in that making is an action passing into outward matter, for example, to build, to saw, and so forth; while doing is an action abiding in the agent, for example, to see, to will, and the like. Accordingly prudence stands in the same relation to this kind of human actions, consisting in the use of powers and habits, as art does to outward makings, since each is the perfect reason about the things with which it is concerned. But perfection and rectitude of reason in speculative matters depend on the principles from which reason argues, just as we have said above (A. 2, Reply 2) that science depends on and presupposes understanding, which is the habit of principles. Now "in human acts the end is what the principles are in speculative matters," as stated in the *Ethics*.[6] Consequently, it is requisite for prudence, which is right reason about things to be done, that man be well disposed with regard to the ends, and this depends on the rectitude of his appetite. Therefore, for prudence there is need of a moral virtue, which rectifies the appetite. On the other hand, the good of things made by art is not the good of man's appetite, but the good of those artificial things themselves, and therefore art does not presuppose rectitude of the appetite. The consequence is that more praise is given to a craftsman who is at fault willingly, than to one who is unwillingly; but it is more contrary to prudence to sin willingly than unwillingly, since rectitude of the will is essential to prudence, but not to art. Accordingly it is evident that prudence is a virtue distinct from art.

Reply Obj. 1. The various kinds of things made by art are all external to man, and therefore they do not cause a different kind of virtue. But prudence is right reason about human acts themselves, and so it is a distinct kind of virtue, as stated above.

Reply Obj. 2. Prudence has more in common with art than a speculative habit has if we consider their subject and matter; for they are both in the part of the soul which deals with matters of opinion, and about things that may be otherwise than they are. But if we consider them as virtues, then art has more in common

[1] Aristotle, *Ethics*, VI, 6 (1140[b]35).
[2] *Ibid.*, VI, 5 (1140[a]25).
[3] *Ibid.*, III, 3 (1112[b]3).
[4] *Ibid.*, VI, 3, 5 (1139[b]16; 1140[b]2).

[5] Aristotle, IX, 8 (1050[a]30).
[6] Aristotle, VII, 8 (1151[a]16).

with the speculative habits than with prudence, as is clear from what has been said.

Reply Obj. 3. Prudence is of good counsel about matters regarding man's entire life, and the end of human life. But in some arts there is counsel about matters concerning the ends proper to those arts. Hence some men, in so far as they are good counsellors in matters of warfare, or government, are said to be prudent officers or rulers, but not prudent absolutely; only those are prudent absolutely who give good counsel about all the concerns of life.

ARTICLE 5. *Whether Prudence Is a Virtue Necessary to Man?*

We proceed thus to the Fifth Article: It would seem that prudence is not a virtue necessary to lead a good life.

Objection 1. For as art is to things that are made, of which it is the right reason, so is prudence to things that are done, in respect of which we judge of a man's life; for prudence is the right reason about these things, as stated in the *Ethics*.[1] Now art is not necessary in things that are made, save in order that they be made, but not after they have been made. Neither therefore is prudence necessary to man in order to lead a good life, after he has become virtuous, but only perhaps in order that he may become virtuous.

Obj. 2. Further, "It is by prudence that we are of good counsel," as stated in the *Ethics*.[2] But man can act not only from his own, but also from another's good counsel. Therefore man does not need prudence in order to lead a good life, but it is enough that he follow the counsels of prudent men.

Obj. 3. Further, an intellectual virtue is one by which one always says the true, and never the false. But this does not seem to be the case with prudence; for it is not human never to err in taking counsel about what is to be done, since human actions are about things that may be otherwise than they are. Hence it is written (Wisd. 9. 14): *The thoughts of mortal men are fearful, and our counsels uncertain.* Therefore it seems that prudence should not be accounted an intellectual virtue.

On the contrary, It is numbered with other virtues necessary for human life, when it is written (Wisd. 8. 7) of Divine Wisdom: *She teacheth temperance and prudence and justice and fortitude, which are such things as men can have nothing more profitable in life.*

I answer that, Prudence is a virtue most nec-

essary for human life. For a good life consists in good deeds. Now in order to do good deeds, it matters not only what a man does but also how he does it; that is, that he do it from right choice and not merely from impulse or passion. And, since choice is about things in reference to the end, rectitude of choice requires two things; namely, the due end, and something suitably ordered to that due end. Now man is suitably directed to his due end by a virtue which perfects the soul in the appetitive part, the object of which is the good and the end. And to that which is suitably ordered to the due end man needs to be rightly disposed by a habit in his reason, because counsel and choice, which are about things ordered to the end, are acts of the reason. Consequently an intellectual virtue is needed in the reason, to perfect the reason, and make it suitably disposed towards things ordered to the end; and this virtue is prudence. Consequently prudence is a virtue necessary to lead a good life.

Reply Obj. 1. The good of an art is to be found not in the craftsman himself, but in the product of the art, since art is right reason about things to be made. For since the making of a thing passes into external matter, it is a perfection not of the maker, but of the thing made, even as movement is the act of the thing moved; art however is concerned with the making of things. On the other hand, the good of prudence is in the agent himself, whose perfection is action itself; for prudence is right reason about things to be done, as stated above (A. 4). Consequently art does not require of the craftsman that his act be a good act, but that his work be good. Rather would it be necessary for the thing made to act well (for example, that a knife should carve well, or that a saw should cut well), if it were proper to such things to act rather than to be acted on, because they do not have dominion over their actions. Therefore the craftsman needs art not that he may live well, but that he may produce a good work of art, and preserve it. But prudence is necessary to man that he may lead a good life, and not merely that he may be a good man.

Reply Obj. 2. When a man does a good deed not of his own counsel, but moved by that of another, his deed is not yet quite perfect, as regards reason directing him and appetite moving him. Therefore, if he do a good deed, he does not do well absolutely; and yet this is required in order that he may lead a good life.

Reply Obj. 3. As stated in *Ethics*,[3] truth is

[1] Aristotle, VI, 5 (1140ᵇ3).   [2] *Ibid.* (1140ᵃ25).

[3] Aristotle, VI, 2 (1139ᵃ26).

not the same for the practical as for the speculative intellect. For the truth of the speculative intellect depends on conformity between the intellect and the thing. And since the intellect cannot be infallibly in conformity with things in contingent matters, but only in necessary matters, therefore no speculative habit about contingent things is an intellectual virtue, but only such as is about necessary things. On the other hand, the truth of the practical intellect depends on conformity with a right appetite. This conformity has no place in necessary matters, which are not affected by the human will, but only in contingent matters which can be effected by us, whether they be matters of interior action, or the products of external work. Hence it is only about contingent matters that an intellectual virtue is assigned to the practical intellect, namely, art, as regards things to be made, and prudence, as regards things to be done.

ARTICLE 6. *Whether "Eubulia, Synesis and Gnome" Are Virtues Annexed to Prudence?*

We proceed thus to the Sixth Article: It would seem that εὐβουλία, σύνεσις and γνώμη are unfittingly assigned as virtues joined to prudence.

Objection 1. For εὐβουλία is a habit whereby we take good counsel.[1] Now "it belongs to prudence to take good counsel," as stated.[2] Therefore εὐβουλία is not a virtue joined to prudence, but rather is prudence itself.

Obj. 2. Further, it belongs to the higher to judge of the lower. The highest virtue would therefore seem to be the one whose act is judgment. Now σύνεσις enables us to judge well. Therefore σύνεσις is not a virtue joined to prudence, but rather is a principal virtue.

Obj. 3. Further, just as there are various matters to pass judgment on, so are there different points on which one has to take counsel. But there is one virtue referring to all matters of counsel. Therefore, in order to judge well of what has to be done, there is no need, besides σύνεσις, of the virtue of γνώμη.

Obj. 4. Further, Cicero (*De Invent. Rhet.* ii, 53)[3] mentions three other parts of prudence; namely, "memory of the past, understanding of the present, and foresight of the future." Moreover, Macrobius (*Super Somn. Scip.* i, 8)[4] mentions yet others: namely, caution, docility, and the like. Therefore it seems that the above

[1] Aristotle, *Ethics*, VI, 9 (1142^{b}16).
[2] *Ibid.*, VI, 5, 7 (1140^{a}25; 1141^{b}9).
[3] DD I, 165.   [4] DD 33.

are not the only virtues joined to prudence.

On the contrary stands the authority of the Philosopher,[5] who assigns these three virtues as being annexed to prudence.

I answer that, Wherever several powers are ordered to one another, that power is the highest which is ordered to the highest act. Now there are three acts of reason in respect of anything to be done by man; the first of these is counsel, the second, judgment, the third, command. The first two correspond to those acts of the speculative intellect which are inquiry and judgment, for counsel is a kind of inquiry, but the third is proper to the practical intellect, in so far as this is ordered to operation; for reason does not have command in things that man cannot do. Now it is evident that in things done by man the chief act is that of command, to which all the rest are subordinate. Consequently, that virtue which perfects the command, namely, prudence, as having the highest place, has other secondary virtues joined to it, namely, εὐβουλία, which perfects counsel, and σύνεσις and γνώμη, which are parts of prudence in relation to judgment, and of whose distinction we shall speak further on (REPLY 3).

Reply Obj. 1. Prudence makes us be of good counsel not as though its immediate act consisted in being of good counsel, but because it perfects the latter act by means of a subordinate virtue, namely, εὐβουλία.

Reply Obj. 2. Judgment about what is to be done is directed to something further, for it may happen in some matter of action that a man's judgment is sound, while his execution is wrong. But the matter attains its final completion when the reason has commanded rightly in the point of what has to be done.

Reply Obj. 3. Judgment of anything should be based on that thing's proper principles. But inquiry does not reach to the proper principles, because, if we were in possession of these, we should no more need to inquire, for the truth would be already discovered. Hence only one virtue is directed to being of good counsel, while there are two virtues for good judgment; for difference is based not on common but on proper principles. Consequently in speculative matters also there is one science of dialectics, which inquires about all matters; but demonstrative sciences, which pronounce judgment, differ according to their different objects. Σύνεσις and γνώμη differ in respect of the different rules on which judgment is based, for σύνεσις judges of actions according to the common law, while

[5] *Ethics*, VI, 11 (1143^{a}25).

γνώμη bases its judgment on the natural law, in those cases where the common law fails to apply, as we shall explain further on (Part II-II, Q. LI, A. 4).

Reply Obj. 4. Memory, understanding, and foresight, as also caution and docility and the like, are not virtues distinct from prudence, but are, as it were, integral parts of it, in so far as they are all requisite for perfect prudence. There are, moreover, subjective parts or species of prudence, for example, domestic and political economy, and the like. But the three first named are, in a fashion, potential parts of prudence, because they are subordinate to it, as secondary virtues to a principal virtue. We shall speak of them later (Part II-II, Q. XLVIII, *sqq.*).

QUESTION LVIII
OF THE DIFFERENCE BETWEEN MORAL AND INTELLECTUAL VIRTUES
(*In Five Articles*)

WE must now consider moral virtues. We shall speak (1) of the difference between them and intellectual virtues; (2) of their distinction, one from another, in respect of their proper matter (Q. LIX); (3) of the difference between the chief or cardinal virtues and the others (Q. LXI).

Under the first head there are five points of inquiry: (1) Whether every virtue is a moral virtue? (2) Whether moral virtue differs from intellectual virtue? (3) Whether virtue is adequately divided into moral and intellectual virtue? (4) Whether there can be moral without intellectual virtue? (5) Whether, on the other hand, there can be intellectual without moral virtue?

ARTICLE I. *Whether Every Virtue Is a Moral Virtue?*

We proceed thus to the First Article: It would seem that every virtue is a moral virtue.

Objection 1. Because moral virtue is so called from the Latin *mos*, that is, custom. Now, we can accustom ourselves to the acts of all the virtues. Therefore every virtue is a moral virtue.

Obj. 2. Further, the Philosopher says[1] that moral virtue is "a habit of choosing the rational mean." But every virtue seems to be a habit of choosing, since the acts of any virtue can be done from choice. And, moreover, every virtue consists in following the rational mean in some way, as we shall explain further on (Q. LXIV, AA. 1, 2, 3). Therefore every virtue is a moral virtue.

[1] *Ethics*, II, 6 (1106ᵇ36).

Obj. 3. Further, Cicero says (*De Invent. Rhet.* ii, 53)[2] that "virtue is a habit like a second nature, in accord with reason." But since every human virtue is directed to man's good, it must be in accord with reason, since man's good consists in that which agrees with his reason, as Dionysius states (*Div. Nom.* iv, 32).[3] Therefore every virtue is a moral virtue.

On the contrary, The Philosopher says:[4] "When we speak of a man's morals, we do not say that he is wise or intelligent, but that he is gentle or sober." Accordingly, then, wisdom and understanding are not moral virtues; and yet they are virtues, as stated above (Q. LVII, A. 2). Therefore not every virtue is a moral virtue.

I answer that, In order to answer this question clearly, we must consider the meaning of the Latin word *mos*, for thus we shall be able to discover what a "moral" virtue is. Now *mos* has a twofold meaning. For sometimes it means custom, in which sense we read (Acts 15. 1): *Except you be circumcised after the manner (morem) of Moses, you cannot be saved.* Sometimes it means a natural or quasi-natural inclination to do some particular action, in which sense the word is applied to dumb animals. Thus we read (II Macc. 1. 11) that *rushing violently upon the enemy, like lions (Leonum more), they slew them;* and the word is used in the same sense in Ps. 67. 7, where we read: *Who maketh men of one manner (moris) to dwell in a house.* For both these significations there is but one word in Latin; but in Greek there is a distinct word for each, for the word *ethos* which signifies our word *mos* sometimes has the first e long and is written η and sometimes has the first e short and is written ε.

Now moral virtue is so called from *mos* in the sense of a natural or quasi-natural inclination to do some particular action. And the other meaning of *mos*, that is, custom, is akin to this, because custom somehow becomes a second nature, and produces an inclination similar to a natural one. But it is evident that inclination to an action belongs properly to the appetitive power, whose function it is to move all the powers to their acts, as explained above (Q. IX, A. 1). Therefore not every virtue is a moral virtue, but only those that are in the appetitive power.

Reply Obj. 1. This argument takes *mos* in the sense of custom.

Reply Obj. 2. Every act of virtue can be done from choice. But no virtue makes us choose

[2] DD I, 165.   [3] PG 3, 733.
[4] *Ethics*, I, 13 (1103ᵃ7).

rightly except that which is in the appetitive part of the soul; for it has been stated above that choice is an act of the appetitive part (Q. XIII, A. 1). Therefore a habit of choosing, that is, a habit which is the principle by which we choose, is that habit alone which perfects the appetitive power; although the acts of other habits also may be a matter of choice.

Reply Obj. 3. "Nature is the principle of movement."[1] Now to move to action is the proper function of the appetitive part. Consequently to become as a second nature by consenting to the reason is proper to those virtues which are in the appetitive power.

ARTICLE 2. *Whether Moral Virtue Differs from Intellectual Virtue?*

We proceed thus to the Second Article: It would seem that moral virtue does not differ from intellectual virtue.

Objection 1. For Augustine says[2] that "virtue is the art of right conduct." But art is an intellectual virtue. Therefore moral and intellectual virtue do not differ.

Obj. 2. Further, some authors put science in the definition of virtues; thus some define perseverance as "a science or habit regarding those things to which we should hold or not hold"; and holiness as "a science which makes man to be faithful and to do his duty to God."[3] Now science is an intellectual virtue. Therefore moral virtue should not be distinguished from intellectual virtue.

Obj. 3. Further, Augustine says (*Soliloq.* i, 6)[4] that "virtue is the rectitude and perfection of reason." But this belongs to the intellectual virtues, as stated in the *Ethics*.[5] Therefore moral virtue does not differ from intellectual.

Obj. 4. Further, a thing does not differ from that which is included in its definition. But intellectual virtue is included in the definition of moral virtue, for the Philosopher says[6] that "moral virtue is a habit of choosing the mean appointed by reason as a wise man would appoint it." Now this right reason that fixes the mean of moral virtue belongs to an intellectual virtue, as stated in the *Ethics*.[7] Therefore moral virtue does not differ from intellectual.

On the contrary, It is stated in the *Ethics*[8] that "there are two kinds of virtue: some we call intellectual; some, moral."

I answer that, Reason is the first principle of all human acts, and whatever other principles of human acts may be found, they obey reason in some fashion, but in various ways. For some obey reason blindly and without any contradiction whatever; such are the limbs of the body, provided they be in a healthy condition, for as soon reason commands, the hand or the foot proceeds to action. Hence the Philosopher says[9] that "the soul rules the body like a despot," that is, as a master rules his slave, who has no right to go against him. Accordingly some held that all the active principles in man are subordinate to reason in this way. If this were true, for man to act well it would suffice that his reason be perfect. Consequently, since virtue is a habit perfecting man in view of his doing good actions, it would follow that it is only in the reason, so that there would be none but intellectual virtues. This was the opinion of Socrates, who said "every virtue is a kind of prudence," as stated in the *Ethics*.[10] Hence he maintained[11] that as long as a man is in possession of knowledge, he cannot sin, and that every one who sins does so through ignorance.

Now this is based on a false supposition. Because the appetitive part obeys the reason, not blindly, but with a certain power of opposition; hence the Philosopher says[12] that "reason commands the appetitive part by a politic power," the rule, that is, by which a man rules over subjects that are free, having a certain right of opposition. Hence Augustine says on Ps. 118 *(serm.* 8)[13] that "sometimes understanding goes before while desire is slow, or follows not at all," in so far as the habits or passions of the appetitive part cause the use of reason to be impeded in some particular action. And in this way, there is some truth in the saying of Socrates that so long as a man is in possession of knowledge he does not sin, provided, however, that this knowledge is made to include the use of reason in this individual act of choice.

Accordingly for a man to do a good deed, it is requisite not only that his reason be well disposed by means of a habit of intellectual virtue, but also that his appetite be well dis-

---

[1] Aristotle, *Physics*, II, 1 (192[b]21).

[2] *City of God*, IV, 21 (PL 41, 128); cf. XXII, 24 (PL 41, 789).

[3] Andronicus of Rhodes, Diogenes Laertius, Stobaeus, Clement of Alexandria. in Arnim, *Fragmenta*, Vol. III; cf. Thomas, *Summa*, II-II, Q. CXXXVII, A. 1, Sed contra.

[4] PL 32, 876.

[5] Aristotle, VI, 13 (1144[b]21).

[6] *Ethics*, II, 6 (1106[b]36).   [7] VI, 13 (1144[b]21).

[8] I, 13 (1103[a]3).

[9] *Politics*, I, 5 (1254[b]4).

[10] VI, 13 (1144[b]19).

[11] Cf. Aristotle, *Ethics*, VII, 2 (1145[b]23); *Protagoras*, 352; 355; 357.

[12] *Politics*, I, 5 (1254[b]5).

[13] PL 37, 1522.

posed by means of a habit of moral virtue. And so moral differs from intellectual virtue even as the appetite differs from the reason. Hence just as the appetite is the principle of human acts in so far as it partakes of reason, so are moral habits to be considered virtues in so far as they are in conformity with reason.

Reply Obj. 1. Augustine usually applies the term art to any form of right reason, in which sense art includes prudence which is the right reason about things to be done, just as art is the right reason about things to be made. Accordingly, when he says that virtue is the art of right conduct, this applies to prudence essentially, but to other virtues by participation, according as they are directed by prudence.

Reply Obj. 2. All such definitions, no matter where they are found, were based on the Socratic theory, and should be explained according to what we have said about art (REPLY 1).

The same applies to the Third Objection.

Reply Obj. 4. Right reason, which flows from prudence is included in the definition of moral virtue, not as part of its essence, but as something belonging by way of participation to all the moral virtues, in so far as they are all under the direction of prudence.

ARTICLE 3. *Whether Virtue Is Adequately Divided into Moral and Intellectual?*

We proceed thus to the Third Article: It would seem that virtue is not adequately divided into moral and intellectual.

Objection 1. For prudence seems to be a mean between moral and intellectual virtue, since it is numbered among the intellectual virtues;[1] and again is placed by all among the four cardinal virtues, which are moral virtues, as we shall show further on (Q. LXI, A. 1). Therefore virtue is not adequately divided into intellectual and moral, as though there were no mean between them.

Obj. 2. Further, continence, perseverance, and patience are not counted among the intellectual virtues. Yet neither are they moral virtues, since they do not reduce the passions to a mean, and are consistent with an abundance of passion. Therefore virtue is not adequately divided into intellectual and moral.

Obj. 3. Further, faith, hope, and charity are virtues. Yet they are not intellectual virtues, for there are only five of these, namely, science, wisdom, understanding, prudence, and art, as stated above (Q. LVII, AA. 2, 3, 5). Neither are they moral virtues, since they are not about the passions, which are the chief concern of moral virtue. Therefore virtue is not adequately divided into intellectual and moral.

On the contrary, The Philosopher says[2] that "virtue is twofold, intellectual and moral."

I answer that, Human virtue is a habit perfecting man in view of his doing good deeds. Now, in man there are but two principles of human actions, namely, the intellect or reason and the appetite; for these are the two principles of movement in man as stated in the book on the *Soul.*[3] Consequently every human virtue must be a perfection of one of these principles. Accordingly if it perfects man's speculative or practical intellect in order that his deed may be good, it will be an intellectual virtue, but if it perfects his appetite, it will be a moral virtue. It follows therefore that every human virtue is either intellectual or moral.

Reply Obj. 1. Prudence is essentially an intellectual virtue. But considered on the part of its matter, it has something in common with the moral virtues, for it is right reason about things to be done, as stated above (Q. LVII, A. 4). It is in this sense that it is numbered among the moral virtues.

Reply Obj. 2. Continence and perseverance are not perfections of the sensitive appetite. This is clear from the fact that disorderly passions abound in the continent and persevering man, which would not be the case if his sensitive appetite were perfected by a habit making it conformable to reason. Continence and perseverance are, however, perfections of the rational part, and withstand the passions lest reason be led astray. But they fall short of being virtues, since intellectual virtue, which makes reason maintain itself well in respect of moral matters, presupposes a right appetite of the end, so that it may maintain itself rightly in respect of principles, that is, the ends, from which it reasons; and this is wanting in the continent and persevering man.—Nor again can an action proceeding from two principles be perfect unless each principle be perfected by the habit corresponding to that operation; thus, however perfect be the principal agent employing an instrument, it will produce an imperfect effect if the instrument be not well disposed also. Hence if the sensitive appetite, which is moved by the rational part, is not perfect, however perfect the rational faculty may be the resulting action will be imperfect. And consequently the principle of that action will not be a virtue.

---

[1] Aristotle, *Ethics,* VI, 3, 5 (1139^{b}16; 1140^{b}28).

[2] *Ethics,* II, 1 (1103^{a}14).

[3] Aristotle, III, 10 (433^{a}9).

And for this reason, continence, refraining from pleasures, and perseverance in the midst of pains, are not virtues, but something less than a virtue, as the Philosopher maintains.[1]

Reply Obj. 3. Faith, hope, and charity are superhuman virtues, for they are virtues of man as sharing in the grace of God.

ARTICLE 4. *Whether There Can Be Moral Without Intellectual Virtue?*

We proceed thus to the Fourth Article: It would seem that moral virtue can be without intellectual virtue.

Objection 1. Because moral virtue, as Cicero says (*De Invent. Rhet.* ii, 53),[2] is "a habit like a second nature in accord with reason." Now though nature may be in accord with some superior reason that moves it, there is no need for that reason to be united to nature in the same subject, as is evident of natural things devoid of knowledge. Therefore in a man there may be a moral virtue like a second nature, inclining him to consent to his reason without his reason being perfected by an intellectual virtue.

Obj. 2. Further, by means of intellectual virtue man obtains perfect use of reason. But it happens at times that men are virtuous and acceptable to God without being vigorous in the use of reason. Therefore it seems that moral virtue can be without intellectual.

Obj. 3. Further, moral virtue makes us inclined to do good works. But some, without depending on the judgment of reason, have a natural inclination to do good works. Therefore moral virtues can be without intellectual virtues.

On the contrary, Gregory says (*Moral.* xxii, 1)[3] that "the other virtues, unless we do prudently what we desire to do, cannot be real virtues." But prudence is an intellectual virtue, as stated above (Q. LVII, A. 5). Therefore moral virtues cannot be without intellectual virtues.

I answer that, Moral virtue can be without some of the intellectual virtues, namely, wisdom, science, and art, but not without understanding and prudence. Moral virtue cannot be without prudence, because moral virtue is a habit of choosing, that is, making us choose well. Now in order that a choice be good, two things are required. First, that the intention be directed to a due end; and this is done by moral virtue, which inclines the appetitive power to the good that is in accord with reason, which is a due end. Secondly, that man take rightly those things which have reference to the end, and he cannot do this unless his reason counsel, judge and command rightly, which is the function of prudence and the virtues joined to it, as stated above (Q. LVII, AA. 5, 6). Therefore there can be no moral virtue without prudence. And consequently neither can there be without understanding. For it is by the virtue of understanding that we know naturally known principles both in speculative and in practical matters. Consequently just as right reason in speculative matters, in so far as it proceeds from naturally known principles, presupposes the understanding of those principles, so also does prudence, which is the right reason about things to be done.

Reply Obj. 1. The inclination of nature in things lacking reason is without choice, and therefore such an inclination does not of necessity require reason. But the inclination of moral virtue is with choice, and consequently in order that it may be perfect it requires that reason be perfected by intellectual virtue.

Reply Obj. 2. A man may be virtuous without having full use of reason as to everything, provided he have it with regard to those things which have to be done virtuously. In this way all virtuous men have full use of reason. Hence even those who seem to be simple, through lack of worldly cunning, can be prudent, according to Matt. 10. 16: *Be ye therefore prudent* (Douay,—*wise*) *as serpents, and simple as doves.*

Reply Obj. 3. The natural inclination to a good of virtue is a kind of beginning of virtue, but is not perfect virtue. For the stronger this inclination is, the more perilous may it prove to be, unless it be accompanied by right reason, which rectifies the choice of fitting means towards the due end. Thus if a running horse be blind, the faster it runs the more heavily will it fall, and the more grievously will it be hurt. And consequently, although moral virtue is not right reason, as Socrates held,[4] yet not only is it according to right reason, in so far as it inclines man to that which is according to right reason, as the Platonists maintained,[5] but also it needs to be joined with right reason, as Aristotle declares.[6]

ARTICLE 5. *Whether There Can Be Intellectual Without Moral Virtue?*

We proceed thus to the Fifth Article: It would seem that there can be intellectual without moral virtue.

[1] *Ethics*, VII, 1, 9 (1145^{b}1; 1151^{b}32).
[2] DD I, 165.   [3] PL 76, 212.
[4] Cf. Aristotle, *Ethics*, VI, 13 (1144^{b}19).
[5] Cf. Aristotle, *Ibid.* Cf. Thomas, *In Eth.*, VI, 11.
[6] *Ethics*, VI, 13 (1144^{b}21).

Objection 1. Because perfection of what precedes does not depend on the perfection of what follows. Now reason precedes and moves the sensitive appetite. Therefore intellectual virtue, which is a perfection of the reason, does not depend on moral virtue, which is a perfection of the appetitive part, and can be without it.

Obj. 2. Further, morals are the matter of prudence, even as things makeable are the matter of art. Now art can be without its proper matter, as a smith without iron. Therefore prudence can be without the moral virtues, although of all the intellectual virtues, it seems most akin to the moral virtues.

Obj. 3. Further, prudence is "a virtue whereby we are of good counsel."[1] Now many are of good counsel without having the moral virtues. Therefore prudence can be without a moral virtue.

On the contrary, To wish to do evil is directly opposed to moral virtue; and yet it is not opposed to anything that can be without moral virtue. Now it is contrary to prudence to sin willingly.[2] Therefore prudence cannot be without moral virtue.

I answer that, Other intellectual virtues can, but prudence cannot, be without moral virtue. The reason for this is that prudence is the right reason about things to be done, and this not merely in general, but also in the particular, with which actions are concerned. Now right reason demands principles from which reason proceeds. And when reason argues about particular cases, it needs not only universal but also particular principles. As to universal principles of action, man is rightly disposed by the natural understanding of principles, by which he knows that he should do no evil; or again by some practical science. But this is not enough in order that man may reason rightly about particular cases. For it happens sometimes that this kind of universal principle, known by means of understanding or science, is destroyed in a particular case by a passion; thus to one who is swayed by concupiscence, when he is overcome by it, the object of his desire seems good, although it is opposed to the universal judgment of his reason. Consequently, just as by the natural understanding or by the habit of science, man is made to be rightly disposed in regard to the universal principles of action, so, in order that he be rightly disposed with regard to the particular principles of action, namely, the ends, he needs to be perfected by certain habits, by

which it becomes connatural, as it were, to man to judge rightly of the end. This is done by moral virtue; for the virtuous man judges rightly of the end of virtue because "such as a man is, such does the end seem to him."[3] Consequently the right reason about things to be done, namely, prudence, requires man to have moral virtue.

Reply Obj. 1. Reason, as apprehending the end, precedes the appetite for the end; but appetite for the end as arguing about the choice of the means, which is the concern of prudence, precedes the reason. Just as also in speculative matters the understanding of principles is the foundation on which the syllogism of the reason is based.

Reply Obj. 2. It does not depend on the disposition of our appetite whether we judge well or ill of the principles of art, as it does when we judge of the end which is the principle in moral matters; in the former case our judgment depends on reason alone. Hence art does not require a virtue perfecting the appetite as prudence does.

Reply Obj. 3. Prudence not only helps us to be of good counsel, but also to judge and command well. This is not possible unless the impediment of the passions, destroying the judgment and command of prudence, be removed; and this is done by moral virtue.

QUESTION LIX

OF MORAL VIRTUE IN RELATION TO THE PASSIONS

(In Five Articles)

WE must now consider the difference of one moral virtue from another. And since those moral virtues which are about the passions differ according to the difference of passions, we must consider (1) the relation of virtue in general to passion; (2) the different kinds of moral virtue in relation to the passions (Q. LX). Under the first head there are five points of inquiry: (1) Whether moral virtue is a passion? (2) Whether there can be moral virtue with passion? (3) Whether sorrow is compatible with moral virtue? (4) Whether every moral virtue is about a passion? (5) Whether there can be moral virtue without passion?

ARTICLE 1. *Whether Moral Virtue Is a Passion?*

We proceed thus to the First Article: It would seem that moral virtue is a passion.

Objection 1. For the mean is of the same ge-

---

[1] *Ibid.,* VI, 5, 7 (1140ª25; 1141ᵇ10).
[2] *Ibid.,* VI, 5 (1140ᵇ22).
[3] Aristotle, *Ethics,* III, 5 (1114ª32).

nus as the extremes. But moral virtue is a mean between passions. Therefore moral virtue is a passion.

Obj. 2. Further, virtue and vice, being contrary to one another, are in the same genus. But some passions are said to be vices, such as envy and anger. Therefore some passions are virtues.

Obj. 3. Further, pity is a passion, since it is sorrow for another's ills, as stated above (Q. XXXV, A. 8). Now "Cicero the renowned orator did not hesitate to call pity a virtue," as Augustine states in the *City of God*.[1] Therefore a passion may be a moral virtue.

On the contrary, It is stated in the *Ethics*[2] that "passions are neither virtues nor vices."

I answer that, Moral virtue cannot be a passion. This is clear for three reasons. First, because a passion is a movement of the sensitive appetite, as stated above (Q. XXII, A. 3). But moral virtue is not a movement, but rather a principle of the movement of the appetite, being a kind of habit. Secondly, because passions are not in themselves good or evil. For man's good or evil is something in reference to reason; hence the passions, considered in themselves, are referrible both to good and to evil, according as they may be in accord or disaccord with reason. Now nothing of this sort can be a virtue, since virtue is referrible to good alone, as stated above (Q. LV, A. 3). Thirdly, because, granted that some passions are, in some way, referrible to good only or to evil only, nevertheless the movement of passion, as passion, begins in the appetite, and ends in the reason, since the appetite tends to conformity with reason. On the other hand, the movement of virtue is the reverse, for it begins in the reason and ends in the appetite, according as the latter is moved by reason. Hence the definition of moral virtue states that it is "a habit of choosing the mean appointed by reason as a wise man would appoint it."[3]

Reply Obj. 1. Virtue is a mean between passions, not by reason of its essence, but on account of its effect; because, that is, it establishes the mean between passions.

Reply Obj. 2. If by vice we understand a habit of doing evil deeds, it is evident that no passion is a vice. But if vice is taken to mean sin, which is a vicious act, nothing prevents a passion from being a vice, or, on the other hand, from concurring in an act of virtue, in so far as a passion is either opposed to reason or in accordance with reason.

Reply Obj. 3. Pity is said to be a virtue, that is, an act of virtue, in so far as "that movement of the soul is obedient to reason; namely, when pity is bestowed without violating justice, as when the poor are relieved, or the penitent forgiven," as Augustine says (*ibid.*). But if by pity we understand a habit perfecting man so that he bestows pity reasonably, nothing prevents pity, in this sense, from being a virtue. The same applies to similar passions.

ARTICLE 2. *Whether There Can Be Moral Virtue With Passion?*

We proceed thus to the Second Article: It would seem that moral virtue cannot be with passion.

Objection 1. For the Philosopher says[4] that "a gentle man is one who is not passionate; but a patient man is one who is passionate but does not give way." The same applies to all the moral virtues. Therefore all moral virtues are without passion.

Obj. 2. Further, virtue is a right disposition of the soul, as health is of the body, as stated in the *Physics*;[5] therefore "virtue seems to be a kind of health of the soul," as Cicero says (*Quæst. Tuscul.* iv, 13).[6] But the soul's passions are the soul's diseases, as he says in the same book.[7] Now health is incompatible with disease. Therefore neither is passion compatible with virtue.

Obj. 3. Further, moral virtue requires perfect use of reason even in particular matters. But the passions are an obstacle to this, for the Philosopher says[8] that pleasures destroy the judgment of prudence; and Sallust says (*Catilin.*)[9] that "when they," that is, the soul's passions, "interfere, it is not easy for the mind to grasp the truth." Therefore passion is incompatible with moral virtue.

On the contrary, Augustine says,[10] "If the will is perverse, these movements," namely, the passions, "are perverse also; but if it is upright, they are not only blameless, but even praiseworthy." But nothing praiseworthy is incompatible with moral virtue. Therefore moral virtue does not exclude the passions, but is consistent with them.

I answer that, The Stoics and Peripatetics disagreed on this point, as Augustine relates.[11]

---

[1] IX, 5 (PL 41, 261).
[2] Aristotle, II, 5 (1105^{b}28).
[3] *Ibid.*, II, 6 (1106^{b}36).
[4] *Topics*, IV, 5 (125^{b}22).
[5] Aristotle, VII, 3 (246^{b}2; 247^{a}2).
[6] DD IV, 30.
[7] Chap. 10 (DD IV, 29).
[8] *Ethics*, VI, 5 (1140^{b}12).
[9] Chap. 51 (BU 47).
[10] *City of God*, XIV, 6 (PL 41, 409).
[11] *Ibid.*, IX, 4 (PL 41, 258); cf. Q. XXIV, A. 2.

For the Stoics held that the soul's passions cannot be in a wise or virtuous man; but the Peripatetics, who were founded by Aristotle, as Augustine says,[1] maintained that the passions are compatible with moral virtue, if they be reduced to the mean.

This difference, as Augustine observes, was one of words rather than of opinions. Because the Stoics, through not discriminating between the intellectual appetite, that is, the will, and the sensitive appetite, which is divided into irascible and concupiscible, did not, as the Peripatetics did, distinguish the passions from the other affections of the human soul, in the point of their being movements of the sensitive appetite, (whereas the other emotions of the soul, which are not passions, are movements of the intellectual appetite or will), but only in the point of the passions being, as they maintained, any affections in disaccord with reason. These affections could not be in a wise or virtuous man if they arose deliberately, but it would be possible for them to be in a wise man if they arose suddenly, because, in the words of Aulus Gellius,[2] "it is not in our power to call up the visions of the soul, known as its fancies; and when they arise from awesome things, they must needs disturb the mind of a wise man, so that he is slightly startled by fear, or depressed with sorrow, as if these passions forestalled the use of reason without his approving of such things or consenting to them."

Accordingly, if the passions be taken for inordinate affections they cannot be in a virtuous man, in such a way that he consent to them deliberately, as the Stoics maintained. But if the passions be taken for any movements of the sensitive appetite, they can be in a virtuous man, in so far as they are subordinate to reason. Hence Aristotle says[3] that "some describe virtue as being a kind of freedom from passion and disturbance; this is incorrect, because the assertion should be qualified"; they should have said that virtue is freedom from those passions "that are not as they should be as to manner and time."

Reply Obj. 1. The Philosopher quotes this, as well as many other examples in his books on Logic, in order to illustrate not his own mind, but that of others. It was the opinion of the Stoics that the passions of the soul were incompatible with virtue;[4] and the Philosopher rejects this opinion,[5] when he says that "virtue is not free-

dom from passion." It may be said, however, that when he says that a gentle man is not passionate, we are to understand this of inordinate passion.

Reply Obj. 2. This and all similar arguments which Tully brings forward in *De Tuscul. Quæst.* take the passions in the sense of inordinate affections.

Reply Obj. 3. When a passion forestalls the judgment of reason so as to prevail on the mind to give its consent, it hinders counsel and the judgment of reason. But when it follows that judgment, as though commanded by reason, it helps toward the execution of reason's command.

ARTICLE 3. *Whether Sorrow Is Compatible with Moral Virtue?*

We proceed thus to the Third Article: It would seem that sorrow is incompatible with virtue.

Objection 1. Because the virtues are effects of wisdom, according to Wisd. 8. 7: *She*, that is, Divine wisdom, *teacheth temperance, and prudence, and justice, and fortitude.* Now the *conversation* of wisdom *hath no bitterness*, as we read further on (*verse* 16). Therefore sorrow is incompatible with virtue also.

Obj. 2. Further, sorrow is a hindrance to work, as the Philosopher states.[6] But a hindrance to good works is incompatible with virtue. Therefore sorrow is incompatible with virtue.

Obj. 3. Further, Tully calls sorrow "a disease of the soul" (*Tusc. Quæst.* iv, 7).[7] But disease of the soul is incompatible with virtue, which is a good condition of the soul. Therefore sorrow is opposed to virtue and is incompatible with it.

On the contrary, Christ was perfect in virtue. But there was sorrow in Him, for He said (Matt. 26. 38): *My soul is sorrowful even unto death.* Therefore sorrow is compatible with virtue.

I answer that, As Augustine says,[8] "the Stoics held that in the soul of the wise man there are three εὐπάθειαι," that is, three good passions, "in place of the three disturbances: namely, instead of covetousness, desire; instead of mirth, joy; instead of fear, caution." But they denied that anything corresponding to sorrow could be in the mind of a wise man, for two reasons. First, because sorrow is for an evil that is already present. Now they held that no evil can happen to a wise man, for they thought that, just as man's only good is virtue, and bodily goods are no good

---

[1] *Ibid.*   [2] *Ibid.*
[3] *Ethics*, II, 3 (1104b24).
[4] Cf. Cicero, *Tuscul.*, III, 4 (DD IV, 3).
[5] *Loc. cit.*

[6] *Ethics*, VII, 13 (1153b2); X, 5 (1175b17).
[7] DD IV, 5.
[8] *City of God*, XIV, 8 (PL 41, 411).

to man, so man's only evil is vice, which cannot be in a virtuous man. But this is unreasonable. For, since man is composed of soul and body, whatever conduces to preserve the life of the body is some good to man, although not his supreme good, because he can abuse it. Consequently the evil which is contrary to this good can be in a wise man, and can cause him moderate sorrow. Again, although a virtuous man can be without grave sin, yet no man is to be found to live without committing slight sins, according to I John 1. 8: *If we say that we have no sin, we deceive ourselves.* A third reason is because a virtuous man, though not actually in a state of sin, may have been so in the past. And he is to be commended if he sorrow for that sin, according to II Cor. 7. 10: *The sorrow that is according to God worketh penance steadfast unto salvation.* Fourthly, because he may praiseworthily sorrow for another's sin. Therefore sorrow is compatible with moral virtue in the same way as the other passions are when moderated by reason.

Their second reason for holding this opinion was that sorrow is about evil present, while fear is for evil to come, even as pleasure is about a present good, while desire is for a future good. Now the enjoyment of a good possessed, or the desire to have good that one does not possess or even the avoidance of future evil, may be consistent with virtue. But depression of the soul resulting from sorrow for a present evil is altogether contrary to reason, and therefore it is incompatible with virtue. But this is unreasonable. For there is an evil which can be present to the virtuous man, as we have just stated, which is rejected by reason. Therefore the sensitive appetite follows reason's rejection by sorrowing for that evil, yet moderately, according as reason dictates. Now it pertains to virtue that the sensitive appetite be conformed to reason, as stated above (A. 1, reply 2). Hence moderated sorrow for an object which ought to make us sorrowful is a mark of virtue, as the Philosopher also says.[1] Moreover, this proves useful for avoiding evil, since just as good is more readily sought for the sake of pleasure, so is evil more strongly shunned on account of sorrow.

Accordingly we must allow that sorrow for things pertaining to virtue is incompatible with virtue, since virtue rejoices in its own. On the other hand, virtue sorrows moderately for all that thwarts virtue, no matter how.

Reply Obj. 1. The passage quoted proves that the wise man is not made sorrowful by wisdom.

[1] *Ethics*, II, 6 (1106[b]20).

Yet he sorrows for anything that hinders wisdom. Consequently there is no room for sorrow in the blessed, in whom there can be no hindrance to wisdom.

Reply Obj. 2. Sorrow hinders the work that makes us sorrowful, but it helps us to do more readily whatever banishes sorrow.

Reply Obj. 3. Immoderate sorrow is a disease of the mind, but moderate sorrow is the mark of a well disposed soul according to the present state of life.

ARTICLE 4. *Whether All the Moral Virtues Are Concerned with the Passions?*

We proceed thus to the Fourth Article: It would seem that all the moral virtues are concerned with the passions.

Objection 1. For the Philosopher says[2] that "moral virtue is about objects of pleasure and sorrow." But pleasure and sorrow are passions, as stated above (Q. XXIII, A. 4; Q. XXXI, A. 1; Q. XXXV, AA. 1, 2). Therefore all the mortal virtues are about the passions.

Obj. 2. Further, the subject of the moral virtues is that which is rational by participation, as the Philosopher states.[3] But the passions are in this part of the soul, as stated above (Q. XXII, A. 3). Therefore every moral virtue is about the passions.

Obj. 3. Further, some passion is to be found in every moral virtue, and so either all are about the passions, or none are. But some are about the passions, as fortitude and temperance, as stated in the *Ethics*.[4] Therefore all the moral virtues are about the passions.

On the contrary, Justice, which is a moral virtue, is not about the passions, as stated in the *Ethics*.[5]

I answer that, Moral virtue perfects the appetitive part of the soul by ordering it to good of reason. Now the good of reason is that which is moderated or ordered by reason. Consequently there are moral virtues about all matters that are subject to reason's ordering and moderation. Now reason orders not only the passions of the sensitive appetite, but also the operations of the intellectual appetite, that is, the will, which is not the subject of a passion, as stated above (Q. XXII, A. 3). Therefore not all the moral virtues are about passions, but some are about passions, some about operations.

Reply Obj. 1. The moral virtues are not all about pleasures and sorrows as about their prop-

[2] *Ethics*, II, 3 (1104[b]8).   [3] *Ibid.*, I, 13 (1103[a]1).
[4] *Ibid.*, III, 6, 10 (1115[a]6; 1117[b]25); cf. II, 12 (1107[a]33).
[5] *Ibid.*, V, 1 (1129[a]4); cf. Thomas, *In Eth.*, V, 1.

er matter, but as about something resulting from their proper acts. For every virtuous man rejoices in acts of virtue, and sorrows for the contrary. Hence the Philosopher, after the words quoted, adds, "virtues are about actions and passions; now every action and passion is followed by pleasure or sorrow, so that in this way virtue is about pleasures and sorrows," namely, as about something that results from virtue.

Reply Obj. 2. Not only the sensitive appetite which is the subject of the passions, is rational by participation, but also the will, where there are no passions, as stated above.

Reply Obj. 3. Some virtues have passions as their proper matter, but some virtues not. Hence the comparison does not hold for all cases, as we will show below (Q. LX, A. 2).

ARTICLE 5. *Whether There Can Be Moral Virtue Without Passion?*

We proceed thus to the Fifth Article: It would seem that moral virtue can be without passion.

Objection 1. For the more perfect moral virtue is, the more does it overcome the passions. Therefore at its highest point of perfection it is altogether without passion.

Obj. 2. Further, a thing is perfect when it is removed from its contrary and from whatever inclines to its contrary. Now the passions incline us to sin which is contrary to virtue; hence (Rom. 7. 5) they are called *passions of sins.* Therefore perfect virtue is altogether without passion.

Obj. 3. Further, we are conformed to God by virtue, as Augustine declares (*De Morib. Eccl.* vi, xi, xiii).[1] But God does all things without passion. Therefore the most perfect virtue is without any passion at all.

On the contrary, "No man is just who rejoices not in just deeds," as stated in the *Ethics.*[2] But joy is a passion. Therefore justice cannot be without passion, and still less can the other virtues be.

I answer that, If we take the passions as being disordered affections, as the Stoics did,[3] it is evident that in this sense perfect virtue is without the passions. But if by passions we understand any movement of the sensitive appetite, it is plain that moral virtues, which are about the passions as about their proper matter, cannot be without passions. The reason for this is that otherwise it would follow that moral virtue makes the sensitive appetite altogether useless, and it

[1] PL 32, 1315, 1319, 1321.
[2] Aristotle, I, 8 (1099ª17).   [3] Cf. above, A. 2.

is not the function of virtue to deprive the powers subordinate to reason of their proper activities, but to make them execute the commands of reason by exercising their proper acts. Therefore just as virtue disposes the bodily limbs to their due external acts, so does it direct the sensitive appetite to its proper regulated movements.

Those moral virtues, however, which are not about the passions, but about operations, can be without passions. Such a virtue is justice, because it applies the will to its proper act, which is not a passion. Nevertheless, joy results from the act of justice, at least in the will, in which case it is not a passion. And if this joy be increased through the perfection of justice, it will overflow into the sensitive appetite, in so far as the lower powers follow the movement of the higher, as stated above (Q. XVII, A. 7; Q. XXIV, A. 3). Therefore by reason of this kind of overflow, the more perfect a virtue is, the more does it cause passion.

Reply Obj. 1. Virtue overcomes disordered passion and produces moderated passion.

Reply Obj. 2. Disordered, not moderated, passion leads to sin.

Reply Obj. 3. The good of anything depends on the condition of its nature. Now there is no sensitive appetite in God and the angels, as there is in man. Consequently good operation in God and the angels is altogether without passion, as it is without a body; but the good operation of man is with passion, even as it is produced with the body's help.

QUESTION LX

How THE MORAL VIRTUES DIFFER FROM ONE ANOTHER
(*In Five Articles*)

WE must now consider how the moral virtues differ from one another, under which head there are five points of inquiry: (1) Whether there is only one moral virtue? (2) Whether those moral virtues which are about operations are distinct from those which are about passions? (3) Whether there is but one moral virtue about operations? (4) Whether there are different moral virtues about different passions? (5) Whether the moral virtues differ in point of the various objects of the passions?

ARTICLE 1. *Whether There Is Only One Moral Virtue?*

We proceed thus to the First Article: It would seem that there is only one moral virtue.

Objection 1. Because just as the direction of

moral actions belongs to reason which is the subject of the intellectual virtues, so does their inclination belong to the appetite which is the subject of moral virtues. But there is only one intellectual virtue to direct all moral acts, namely, prudence. Therefore there is also but one moral virtue to give all moral acts their respective inclinations.

Obj. 2. Further, habits differ not in respect of their material objects, but according to the formal aspect of their objects. Now the formal aspect of the good to which moral virtue is directed, is one, namely, the measure of reason. Therefore, it seems that there is but one moral virtue.

Obj. 3. Further, things pertaining to morals are specified by their end, as stated above (Q. I, A. 3). Now there is but one common end of all moral virtues, namely happiness, while the proper and proximate ends are infinite in number. But the moral virtues themselves are not infinite in number. Therefore it seems that there is but one.

On the contrary, One habit cannot be in several powers, as stated above (Q. LVI, A. 2). But the subject of the moral virtues is the appetitive part of the soul, which is divided into several powers, as stated in the First Part (Q. LXXX, A. 2; Q. LXXXI, A. 2). Therefore there cannot be only one moral virtue.

I answer that, As stated above (Q. LVIII, AA. I, 2, 3), the moral virtues are habits of the appetitive part. Now habits differ specifically according to the special differences of their objects, as stated above (Q. LIV, A. 2). Again, the species of the object of appetite, as of any thing, depends on its specific form which it receives from the agent. But we must observe that the matter of the passive subject bears a twofold relation to the agent. For sometimes it receives the form of the agent in the same kind as the agent has that form, as happens with all univocal agents, so that if the agent be one specifically, the matter must of necessity receive a form specifically one; thus the univocal effect of fire is of necessity something in the species of fire. Sometimes, however, the matter receives the form from the agent, but not in the same kind specifically as the agent, as is the case with non-univocal causes of generation; thus an animal is generated by the sun. In this case the forms received into matter are not of one species, but vary according to the adaptability of the matter to receive the influx of the agent; for instance, we see that owing to the one action of the sun, animals of various species are produced by putrefaction according to the various adaptability of matter.

Now it is evident that in moral matters the reason holds the place of commander and mover, while the appetitive power is commanded and moved. But the appetite does not receive the impression of reason univocally, as it were, because it is rational not essentially, but by participation.[1] Consequently, objects made desirable by the direction of reason belong to various species according to their various relations to reason, so that it follows that moral virtues are of various species and are not one only.

Reply Obj. I. The object of the reason is truth. Now in all moral matters, which are contingent matters of action, there is but one kind of truth. Consequently, there is but one virtue to direct all such matters, namely prudence. On the other hand, the object of the appetitive power is the appetible good, which varies in kind according to its various relations to reason, the directing power.

Reply Obj. 2. This formal element is one generically on account of the unity of the agent; but it varies in species, on account of the various relations of the receiving matter, as explained above.

Reply Obj. 3. Moral matters do not receive their species from the last end, but from their proximate ends; and these, although they are infinite in number, are not infinite in species.

ARTICLE 2. *Whether Moral Virtues About Operations Are Different From Those That Are About Passions?*

We proceed thus to the Second Article: It would seem that moral virtues are not divided into those which are about operations and those which are about passions.

Objection I. For the Philosopher says[2] that "moral virtue is an operative habit whereby we do what is best in matters of pleasure or sorrow." Now pleasure and sorrow are passions, as stated above (Q. XXXI, A. I; Q. XXXV, A. I). Therefore the same virtue which is about passions is also about operations, since it is an operative habit.

Obj. 2. Further, the passions are principles of external action. If therefore some virtues regulate the passions, they must, as a consequence, regulate operations also. Therefore the same moral virtues are about both passions and operations.

Obj. 3. Further, the sensitive appetite is moved well or ill towards every external operation. Now movements of the sensitive appetite

---

[1] Aristotle, *Ethics*, I, 13 (1102^{b}13).

[2] *Ibid.*, II, 3 (1104^{b}27).

are passions. Therefore the same virtues that are about operations are also about passions.

On the contrary, The Philosopher reckons justice to be about operations; and temperance, fortitude, and gentleness, about passions.[1]

I answer that, Operation and passion stand in a twofold relation to virtue. First, as its effects. And in this way every moral virtue has some good operations as its product; and a certain pleasure or sorrow, which are passions, as stated above (Q. LIX, A. 4, REPLY 1). Secondly, operation may be compared to moral virtue as the matter about which virtue is concerned, and in this sense those moral virtues which are about operations must be different from those which are about passions. The reason for this is that good and evil, in certain operations, are taken from the very nature of those operations, no matter how man may be affected towards them; in so far namely as good and evil in them depend on their being commensurate with something else. In operations of this kind there needs to be some power to regulate the operations in themselves; such are buying and selling, and all such operations in which there is an element of something due or undue to another. For this reason justice and its parts are properly about operations as their proper matter. On the other hand, in some operations, good and evil depend only on commensuration with the agent. Consequently good and evil in these operations depend on the way in which man is affected to them. And for this reason in such operations virtue must be chiefly about internal affections which are called the passions of the soul, as is evidently the case with temperance, fortitude, and the like.

It happens, however, in operations which are directed to another, that the good of virtue is set aside by reason of some inordinate passion of the soul. In such cases justice is destroyed in so far as the due measure of the external act is destroyed, while some other virtue is destroyed in so far as the internal passions exceed their due measure. Thus when through anger, one man strikes another, justice is destroyed in the undue blow, while gentleness is destroyed by the immoderate anger. The same may be clearly applied to other virtues.

This suffices for the *Replies to the Objections.* For the first considers operations as the effect of virtue, while the other two consider operation and passion as concurring in the same effect. But in some cases virtue is chiefly about operations, in others, about passions, for the reason given above.

ARTICLE 3. *Whether There Is Only One Moral Virtue About Operations?*

We proceed thus to the Third Article: It would seem that there is but one moral virtue about operations.

Objection 1. Because the rectitude of all external operations seems to pertain to justice. Now justice is but one virtue. Therefore there is but one virtue about operations.

Obj. 2. Further, those operations seem to differ most which are directed on the one side to the good of the individual and on the other to the good of the many. But this diversity does not cause diversity among the moral virtues; for the Philosopher says[2] that legal justice, which directs human acts to the common good, does not differ, save logically, from the virtue which directs a man's actions to one man only. Therefore diversity of operations does not cause a diversity of moral virtues.

Obj. 3. Further, if there are various moral virtues about various operations, diversity of moral virtues would necessarily follow diversity of operations. But this is clearly untrue, for it is the function of justice to establish rectitude in various kinds of exchanges, and again in distributions, as is set down in the *Ethics.*[3] Therefore there are not different virtues about different operations.

On the contrary, Religion is a virtue distinct from piety, both of which are about operations.

I answer that, All the moral virtues that are about operations agree in the one general notion of justice, which is in respect of something due to another, but they differ in respect of various special notions. The reason for this is that in external operations the order of reason is established, as we have stated (A. 2), not according as how man is affected towards such operations, but according to the suitability of the thing itself, from which suitability we derive the notion of something due which is the formal aspect of justice; for it seems to pertain to justice that a man give another his due. Therefore all such virtues as are about operations, bear, in some way, the character of justice. But the thing due is not of the same kind in all these virtues; for something is due to an equal in one way, to a superior, in another way, to an inferior, in yet another, and the nature of a debt differs according as it arises from a contract, a promise, or a favour already conferred. And corresponding to these various kinds of things due there are various virtues: for example, Religion, by which we pay

---

[1] *Ibid.,* V, 1, 5 (1129^{a}4; 1133^{b}32).   [2] *Ethics,* V, 1 (1130^{a}12).   [3] V, 2 (1130^{b}3).

our debt to God; Piety, by which we pay our debt to our parents or to our country; Gratitude, by which we pay our debt to our benefactors, and so forth.

Reply Obj. 1. Justice properly so called is one special virtue, whose object is the perfect due, which can be paid according to an exact equivalence. But the name of justice is extended also to all cases in which something due is rendered. In this sense it is not a special virtue.

Reply Obj. 2. That justice which seeks the common good is a different virtue from that which is directed to the private good of an individual; therefore common right differs from private right, and Tully (*De Inv.* ii, 53)[1] reckons as a special virtue, piety which directs man to the good of his country. But that justice which directs man to the common good is a general virtue through its act of command, since it directs all the acts of the virtues to its own end, namely, the common good. And the virtues, in so far as they are commanded by that justice, receive the name of justice, and in this way virtue does not differ, save logically, from legal justice; just as there is only a logical difference between a virtue which acts of itself, and a virtue which acts through the command of another virtue.

Reply Obj. 3. There is the same kind of due in all the operations belonging to special justice. Consequently, there is the same virtue of justice, especially in regard to exchanges. For it may be that distributive justice is of another species from commutative justice; but about this we shall inquire later on (Part II-II, Q. LXI, A. 1).

ARTICLE 4. *Whether There Are Different Moral Virtues About Different Passions?*

We proceed thus to the Fourth Article: It would seem that there are not different moral virtues about different passions.

Objection 1. For there is but one habit about things that concur in their principle and end, as is evident especially in the case of sciences. But the passions all concur in one principle, namely, love; and they all terminate in the same end, namely, joy or sorrow, as we stated above (Q. XXV, AA. 1, 2, 4; Q. XXVII, A. 4). Therefore there is but one moral virtue about all the passions.

Obj. 2. Further, if there were different moral virtues about different passions, it would follow that there are as many moral virtues as passions. But this clearly is not the case, since there is one moral virtue about contrary passions; namely, fortitude, about fear and daring; temperance,

about pleasure and sorrow. Therefore there is no need for different moral virtues about different passions.

Obj. 3. Further, love, concupiscence, and pleasure are passions of different species, as stated above (Q. XXIII, A. 4). Now there is but one virtue about all these three, namely, temperance. Therefore there are not different moral virtues about different passions.

On the contrary, Fortitude is about fear and daring; temperance about concupiscence; meekness about anger; as stated in the *Ethics.*[2]

I answer that, It cannot be said that there is only one moral virtue about all the passions, since some passions are not in the same power as other passions; for some belong to the irascible, others to the concupiscible part, as stated above (Q. XXIII, A. 1).

On the other hand, neither does every diversity of passions necessarily suffice for a diversity of moral virtues. First, because some passions are in contrary opposition to one another, such as joy and sorrow, fear and daring, and so on. About such passions as are thus in opposition to one another there must be one and the same virtue. Because, since moral virtue consists in a kind of mean, the mean in contrary passions stands in the same ratio to both, even as in the natural order there is but one mean between contraries, for example, between black and white. Secondly, because there are different passions which oppose reason in the same manner, for example, by impelling to that which is contrary to reason, or by withdrawing from that which is in accord with reason. Therefore the different passions of the concupiscible part do not require different moral virtues, because their movements follow one another in a certain order, as being directed to the one same thing, namely, the attainment of some good or the avoidance of some evil; thus from love proceeds concupiscence, and from concupiscence we arrive at pleasure; and it is the same with the opposite passions, for hatred leads to avoidance or dislike, and this leads to sorrow. On the other hand, the irascible passions are not all of one order, but are directed to different things; for daring and fear are about some great danger, hope and despair are about some difficult good, while anger seeks to overcome something contrary which has brought harm. Consequently there are different virtues about passions of this kind: for example, temperance, about the concupiscible passions; fortitude, about fear and daring; mag-

---

[1] DD1, 165.

[2] Aristotle, III, 5 (1115^{a}6); III, 10 (1117^{b}25); IV, 5 (1125^{b}26); cf. II, 7 (1107^{a}33; 1108^{a}6).

nanimity, about hope and despair; meekness, about anger.

Reply Obj. 1. All the passions concur in one common principle and end, but not in one proper principle or end. And so this does not suffice for the unity of moral virtue.

Reply Obj. 2. Just as in natural things the same principle causes movement from one extreme and movement towards the other, and just as in the intellectual order contraries have one common notion, so too between contrary passions there is but one moral virtue, which, like a second nature, consents to reason's dictates.

Reply Obj. 3. Those three passions are directed to the same object in a certain order, as stated above. And so they belong to the same virtue.

ARTICLE 5. *Whether the Moral Virtues Differ According to the Various Objects of the Passion?*

We proceed thus to the Fifth Article: It would seem that the moral virtues do not differ according to the objects of the passions.

Objection 1. For just as there are objects of passions, so are there objects of operations. Now those moral virtues that are about operations do not differ according to the objects of those operations; for the buying and selling either of a house or of a horse belong to the one same virtue of justice. Therefore neither do those moral virtues that are about passions differ according to the objects of those passions.

Obj. 2. Further, the passions are acts or movements of the sensitive appetite. Now it needs a greater difference to differentiate habits than acts. Hence diverse objects which do not diversify the species of passions, do not diversify the species of moral virtue, so that there is but one moral virtue about all objects of pleasure. And the same applies to the other passions.

Obj. 3. Further, more or less do not change a species. Now various objects of pleasure differ only by reason of being more or less pleasurable. Therefore all objects of pleasure belong to one species of virtue. And for the same reason so do all fearful objects, and the same applies to others. Therefore moral virtue is not diversified according to the objects of the passions.

Obj. 4. Further, virtue hinders evil, even as it produces good. But there are various virtues about the desires for good things; thus temperance is about desires for the pleasure of touch, and playfulness (εὐτραπελία) about pleasures in games. Therefore there should be different virtues about fears of evils.

On the contrary, Chastity is about sexual pleasures, abstinence about pleasures of the table, and playfulness about pleasures in games.

I answer that, The perfection of a virtue depends on the reason, while the perfection of a passion depends on the sensitive appetite. Consequently virtues must be differentiated according to their relation to reason, but the passions according to their relation to the appetite. Hence the objects of the passions, according as they are variously related to the sensitive appetite, cause the different species of passions, while, according as they are related to reason, they cause the different species of virtues. Now the movement of the reason is not the same as that of the sensitive appetite. Therefore nothing hinders a difference of objects from causing diversity of passions without causing diversity of virtues, as when one virtue is about several passions, as stated above (A. 4); and again, a difference of objects from causing different virtues without causing a difference of passions, since several virtues are directed towards one passion, for example, pleasure.

And because diverse passions belonging to diverse powers always belong to diverse virtues, as stated above (A. 4), therefore a difference of objects that corresponds to a difference of powers always causes a specific difference of virtues,—for instance the difference between that which is good absolutely speaking, and that which is good and difficult to obtain.—Moreover since the reason rules man's lower powers in a certain order, and even extends to outward things, hence, one single object of the passions, according as it is apprehended by sense, imagination, or reason, and again, according as it belongs to the soul, body, or external things, has various relations to reason, and consequently is of a nature to cause a difference of virtues. Consequently man's good which is the object of love, concupiscence and pleasure, may be taken as referred either to a bodily sense, or to the inner apprehension of the soul; and this same good may be directed to man's good in himself, either in his body or in his soul, or to man's good in relation to other men. And every such difference, being differently related to reason, differentiates virtues.

Accordingly, if we take a good, and it be something discerned by the sense of touch, and something pertaining to the upkeep of human life either in the individual or in the species, such as the pleasures of the table or of sexual intercourse, it will belong to the virtue of temperance. As regards the pleasures of the other senses, they are not intense, and so do not present much difficulty to the reason. Hence there is no virtue corresponding to them; for virtue, "like art, is about difficult things."[1]

On the other hand, good discerned not by the senses, but by an inner power, and belonging to man in himself, is like money and honour; the former, by its very nature, is employable for the good of the body, while the latter is based on the apprehension of the soul. These goods again may be considered either absolutely, in which way they concern the concupiscible part, or as being difficult to obtain, in which way they belong to the irascible part. This distinction, however, has no place in pleasurable objects of touch, since such are of base condition, and belong to man in so far as he has something in common with irrational animals. Accordingly in reference to money considered as a good absolutely, as an object of concupiscence, pleasure, or love, there is liberality; but if we consider this good as difficult to get, and as being the object of our hope, there is magnificence. With regard to that good which we call honour, taken absolutely, as the object of love, we have a virtue called "philotimia," that is, love of honour;[2] while if we consider it as hard to attain, and as an object of hope, then we have magnanimity. And so liberality and love of honor seem to be in the concupiscible part, while magnificence and magnanimity are in the irascible.

As regards man's good in relation to other men, it does not seem hard to obtain, but is considered absolutely, as the object of the concupiscible passions. This good may be pleasurable to a man in his behaviour towards another either in some serious matter, in actions, namely, that are directed by reason to a due end; or in playful actions, those, that is, that are done for mere pleasure, and which do not stand in the same relation to reason as the former. Now one man behaves towards another in serious matters in two ways. First, as being pleasant in his regard, by becoming speech and deeds, and this belongs to a virtue which Aristotle calls friendship,[3] and may be rendered affability. Secondly, one man behaves towards another by being frank with him, in words and deeds: this belongs to another virtue which he calls truthfulness.[4] For frankness is more akin to the reason than pleasure, and serious matters likewise are closer to reason than play. Hence there is another virtue about the pleasures of games, which

the Philosopher calls playfulness (εὐτραπελία).[5]

It is therefore evident that, according to Aristotle[6] there are ten moral virtues about the passions, namely, fortitude, temperance, liberality, magnificence, magnanimity, love of honor, gentleness, friendship, truthfulness, and playfulness all of which differ in respect of their different matter, passions, or objects. If therefore we add justice, which is about operations, there will be eleven in all.

Reply Obj. 1. All objects of the same specific operation have the same relation to reason, but not all the objects of the same specific passion; because operations do not go against reason as the passions do.

Reply Obj. 2. Passions are not differentiated by the same rule as virtues are, as stated above.

Reply Obj. 3. More and less do not cause a difference of species, unless they bear different relations to reason.

Reply Obj. 4. Good is a more potent mover than evil, because evil does not act save in virtue of good, as Dionysius states (*Div. Nom.* iv).[7] Hence an evil does not prove an obstacle to reason so as to require virtues unless that evil be great (there being, it seems, one such evil corresponding to each kind of passion). Hence there is but one virtue, meekness, for every form of anger; and again, but one virtue, fortitude, for all forms of daring. On the other hand good involves difficulty, which requires virtue, even if it be not a great good in that particular kind of passion. Consequently there are various moral virtues about desires, as stated above.

QUESTION LXI
OF THE CARDINAL VIRTUES
(In Five Articles)

WE must now consider the cardinal virtues, under which head there are five points of inquiry: (1) Whether the moral virtues should be called cardinal or principal virtues? (2) Of their number. (3) Which are they? (4) Whether they differ from one another? (5) Whether they are fittingly divided into political, cleansing virtues, virtues of the cleansed soul, and exemplar virtues?

ARTICLE 1. *Whether the Moral Virtues Should Be Called Cardinal or Principal Virtues?*

We proceed thus to the First Article: It would seem that moral virtues should not be called cardinal or principal virtues.

Objection 1. For "the opposite members of a

---

[1] Aristotle, *Ethics*, II, 3 (1105ᵃ9).
[2] Cf. Aristotle, *Ethics*, II, 7 (1107ᵇ32).
[3] *Ibid.* (1108ᵃ28).   [4] *Ibid.* (1108ᵃ20).
[5] *Ibid.* (1108ᵃ24). [6] *Ibid.* (1107ᵃ32). [7] Sect. 31 (PG 3, 732).

division are by nature together,"[1] so that one is not principal rather than another. Now all the virtues are opposite members of the division of the genus virtue. Therefore none of them should be called principal.

Obj. 2. Further, the end is principal as compared to the means. But the theological virtues are about the end, while the moral virtues are about the means. Therefore the theological virtues, rather than the moral virtues, should be called principal or cardinal.

Obj. 3. Further, that which is essentially so is principal in comparison with that which is so by participation. But the intellectual virtues belong to that which is essentially rational, while the moral virtues belong to that which is rational by participation, as stated above (Q. LVI, A. 6, REPLY 2; Q. LVIII, A. 3). Therefore the intellectual virtues are principal, rather than the moral virtues.

On the contrary, Ambrose in explaining the words, *Blessed are the poor in spirit* (Luke 6. 20) says:[2] "We know that there are four cardinal virtues, namely, temperance, justice, prudence, and fortitude." But these are moral virtues. Therefore the moral virtues are cardinal virtues.

I answer that, When we speak of virtue absolutely, we are understood to speak of human virtue. Now human virtue, as stated above (Q. LVI, A. 3), answers to the perfect notion of virtue when it requires rectitude of the appetite; for such virtue not only confers the power of doing well, but also causes the exercise of the good deed. On the other hand, the name virtue, according to the imperfect notion of virtue, is applied to one that does not require rectitude of the appetite, because it merely confers the power of doing well without causing the use of the good deed. Now it is evident that the perfect is principal as compared to the imperfect, and so those virtues which imply rectitude of the appetite are called principal virtues. Such are the moral virtues, and prudence alone, of the intellectual virtues, for it is also something of a moral virtue, according to its matter, as was shown above (Q. LVII, A. 4). Consequently, those virtues which are called principal or cardinal are fittingly placed among the moral virtues.

Reply Obj. 1. When a univocal genus is divided into its species, the members of the division are on a par in the point of the generic idea; although considered in their nature as things, one species may surpass another in rank

and perfection, as man in respect of other animals. But when we divide an analogous term, which is applied to several things, but to one before it is applied to another, nothing hinders one from ranking before another, even in the point of the common notion, as the notion of being is applied to substance principally in relation to accident. Such is the division of virtue into the various kinds of virtue, since the good of reason is not found in the same way in all things.

Reply Obj. 2. The theological virtues are above man, as stated above (Q. LVIII, A. 3, REPLY 3). Hence they should properly be called not human, but super-human or godlike virtues.

Reply Obj. 3. Although the intellectual virtues, except in prudence, rank before the moral virtues in point of their subject, they do not rank before them as virtues; for a virtue, as such, regards good, which is the object of the appetite.

ARTICLE 2. *Whether There Are Four Cardinal Virtues?*

We proceed thus to the Second Article: It would seem that there are not four cardinal virtues.

Objection 1. For prudence is the directing principle of the other moral virtues, as is clear from what has been said above (Q. LVIII, A. 4). But that which directs other things ranks before them. Therefore prudence alone is a principal virtue.

Obj. 2. Further, the principal virtues are, in a way, moral virtues. Now we are directed to moral works both by the practical reason, and by a right appetite, as stated in the *Ethics*.[3] Therefore there are only two cardinal virtues.

Obj. 3. Further, even among the other virtues one ranks higher than another. But in order that a virtue be principal, it needs not to rank above all the others, but above some. Therefore it seems that there are many more principal virtues.

On the contrary, Gregory says (*Moral.* ii, 49):[4] "The entire structure of good works is built on four virtues."

I answer that, Things may be numbered either in respect of their formal principles, or according to their subjects, and in either way we find that there are four cardinal virtues.

For the formal principle of the virtue of which we speak now is the good of reason, which good can be considered in two ways. First, as consisting in the consideration itself of reason;

---

[1] Aristotle, *Categories*, 13 (14^b33).
[2] Bk. v (PL 15, 1738).
[3] Aristotle, VI, 2 (1139^a24).   [4] PL 76, 592.

and thus we have one principal virtue, called Prudence.—Secondly, according as the reason puts its order into something else: either into operations, and then we have Justice; or into passions, and then there must be two virtues. For the need of putting the order of reason into the passions is due to their going against reason, and this occurs in two ways. First, by the passions inciting to something against reason, and then the passions need a curb, which we call Temperance. Secondly, by the passions withdrawing us from following the dictate of reason, for instance, through .fear of danger or toil, and then man needs to be strengthened for that which reason dictates, lest he turn back; and to this end there is Fortitude.

In like manner, we find the same number if we consider the subjects of virtue. For there are four subjects of the virtue we speak of now: namely, the power which is rational in its essence, and this is perfected by Prudence; and that which is rational by participation, and is threefold, the will, subject of Justice, the concupiscible part, subject of Temperance, and the irascible part, subject of Fortitude.

Reply Obj. 1. Prudence is the principal of all the virtues absolutely. The others are principal each in its own genus.

Reply Obj. 2. That part of the soul which is rational by participation is threefold, as stated above.

Reply Obj. 3. All the other virtues among which one ranks before another are reducible to the above four, both as to the subject and as to the formal principle.

ARTICLE 3. *Whether Any Other Virtues Should Be Called Principal Rather than These?*

We proceed thus to the Third Article: It would seem that other virtues should be called principal rather than these.

Objection 1. For it seems that the greatest is the principal in any genus. Now "magnanimity has a great influence on all the virtues."[1] Therefore magnanimity should more than any be called a principal virtue.

Obj. 2. Further, that which strengthens the other virtues should above all be called a principal virtue. But such is humility, for Gregory says (*Hom.* vii *in Ev.*)[2] that "he who gathers the other virtues without humility is as one who carries straw against the wind." Therefore humility seems above all to be a principal virtue.

Obj. 3. Further, that which is most perfect seems to be principal. But this applies to pa-

[1] Aristotle, *Ethics*, IV, 3 (1123ᵇ30).　　[2] PL 76, 1103.

tience, according to James 1. 4: *Patience hath a perfect work.* Therefore patience should be reckoned a principal virtue.

On the contrary, Cicero reduces all other virtues to these four (*De Invent. Rhet.* ii, 53).[3]

I answer that, As stated above (A. 2), these four are taken as cardinal virtues in respect of the four formal principles of virtue as we understand it now. These principles are found chiefly in certain acts and passions. Thus the good which consists in the consideration of reason is found chiefly in reason's command, but not in its counsel or its judgment, as stated above (Q. LVII, A. 6). Again, good as defined by reason and put into our operations as something right and due, is found chiefly in exchanges and distributions in respect of another person, and on a basis of equality. The good of curbing the passions is found chiefly in those passions which are most difficult to curb, namely, in the pleasures of touch. The good of being firm in holding to the good of reason against the impulse of passion is found chiefly in perils of death, which are most difficult to withstand.

Accordingly the above four virtues may be considered in two ways. First, in respect of their common formal principles. In this way they are called principal, being general, as it were, in comparison with all the virtues. Thus, for instance, any virtue that causes good in reason's act of consideration may be called prudence; every virtue that causes the good of right and due in operations, called justice; every virtue that curbs and represses the passions, called temperance; and every virtue that strengthens the mind against any passions whatever, called fortitude. Many, both holy doctors[4] as well as philosophers,[5] speak about these virtues in this sense. And in this way the other virtues are contained under them. —Therefore all the objections fail.

Secondly, they may be considered in point of their being denominated from that which is foremost in the respective matter of each, and thus they are specific virtues, codivided with the others. Yet they are called principal in comparison with the other virtues on account of the importance of their matter, so that prudence is the virtue which commands; justice, the virtue which is about due actions between equals; temperance, the virtue which suppresses desires for the pleasures of touch; and fortitude, the virtue

[3] DD 1, 165.

[4] Ambrose, *De Offic. Ministr.*, I, 36 (PL 16, 82); Augustine, *De Mor. Eccl. Cathel.*, I, 15 (PL 32, 1322); Gregory, *Moral.*, XXII, 1 (PL 76, 212).

[5] Seneca, *Ad Lucilium*, Epist., LXVII (DD 651).

which strengthens against dangers of death.—
Thus again do the objections fail, because the
other virtues may be principal in some other
way, but these are called principal by reason of
their matter, as stated above.

ARTICLE 4. *Whether the Four Cardinal Virtues Differ From One Another?*

We proceed thus to the Fourth Article: It
would seem that the above four virtues are not
different and distinct from one another.

Objection 1. For Gregory says (*Moral.* xxii,
1):[1] "There is no true prudence, unless it be
just, temperate and brave; no perfect temperance, that is not brave, just and prudent; no
sound fortitude, that is not prudent, temperate
and just; no real justice, without prudence, fortitude and temperance." But this would not be
so if the above four virtues were distinct from
one another since the different species of one
genus do not qualify one another. Therefore
these virtues are not distinct from one another.

Obj. 2. Further, among things distinct from
one another what belongs to one is not attributed to another. But what belongs to temperance is attributed to fortitude, for Ambrose says
(*De Offic.* xxxvi)[2] "Rightly do we call it fortitude, when a man conquers himself, and is not
weakened and bent by any enticement." And
of temperance he says (*ibid.,* xxiv)[3] that "it
safeguards the manner and order in all things
that we decide to do and say." Therefore it
seems that these virtues are not distinct from
one another.

Obj. 3. Further, the Philosopher says[4] that the
necessary conditions of virtue are first of all
"that a man should have knowledge; secondly,
that he should exercise choice for a particular
end; thirdly, that he should possess the habit
and act with firmness and steadfastness." But
the first of these seems to belong to prudence
which is right reason in things to be done; the
second, that is, choice, belongs to temperance,
by which a man, holding his passions in check,
acts not from passion but from choice; the third,
that a man should act for the sake of a due end,
implies a certain rectitude, which seems to pertain to justice; while the last, namely, firmness
and steadfastness, belongs to fortitude. Therefore each of these virtues is general in comparison to other virtues. Therefore they are not distinct from one another.

On the contrary, Augustine says (*De Moribus
Eccl.* xv)[5] that "there are four virtues, cor-

responding to the various affections of love,"
and he applies this to the four virtues mentioned
above. Therefore these four virtues are distinct
from one another.

I answer that, As stated above (A. 3), these
four virtues are understood differently by various writers. For some[6] take them as signifying
certain general conditions of the human soul, to
be found in all the virtues, so that, namely, prudence is merely a certain rectitude of discernment in any actions or matters whatever; justice, a certain rectitude of the soul by which
man does what he ought in any matters; temperance, a disposition of the soul moderating
any passions or operations, so as to keep them
within bounds; and fortitude, a disposition by
which the soul is strengthened for that which
is in accord with reason, against any assaults
of the passions, or the toil involved by any
operations. To distinguish these four virtues in
this way does not imply that justice, temperance and fortitude are distinct virtuous habits.
For it pertains to every moral virtue, from the
fact that it is a habit, that it should be accompanied by a certain firmness so as not to be
moved by its contrary, and this, we have said,
belongs to fortitude. Moreover, since it is a
virtue, it is directed to good which involves
the notion of right and due, and this, we have
said, belongs to justice. Again, owing to the
fact that it is a moral virtue partaking of reason, it observes the mode of reason in all things,
and does not exceed its bounds, which has been
stated to belong to temperance. It is only in
the point of having discernment which we
ascribed to prudence, that there seems to be a
distinction from the other three, since discernment belongs essentially to reason; but the
other three imply a certain participation of
reason by way of a kind of application (of reason) to passions or operations. According to the
above explanation, then, prudence would be
distinct from the other three virtues but these
would not be distinct from one another; for it is
evident that one and the same virtue is both
habit, and virtue, and moral virtue.

Others,[7] however, with better reason, take
these four virtues, according as they have their
special determinate matter, each its own matter, in which special praise is given to that
general condition from which the virtue's name
is taken as stated above (A. 3). In this way it

[1] PL 76, 212.   [2] PL 16, 82.   [3] PL 16, 62.
[4] *Ethics,* ii, 4 (1105[a]31).   [5] PL 32, 1322.

[6] Cf. Lottin, *Mél. Mandonnet* (ii, 252).
[7] Aristotle, *Ethics,* ii, 7 (1107[a]33); Cicero, *De Invent.,*
ii, 53 (DD i, 165); Albert the Great, *Summa de Bono,* in
Lottin, *Mél. Mandonnet* (ii, 258).

is clear that the aforesaid virtues are distinct habits, differentiated in respect of their diverse objects.

Reply Obj. 1. Gregory is speaking of these four virtues in the first sense given above. It may also be said that these four virtues qualify one another by a kind of overflow. For the qualities of prudence overflow on to the other virtues in so far as they are directed by prudence. And each of the others overflows on to the rest, for the reason that whoever can do what is harder, can do what is less difficult. Therefore whoever can curb his desires for the pleasures of touch, so that they keep within bounds, which is a very hard thing to do, for this very reason is more able to check his daring in dangers of death, so as not to go too far, which is much easier; and in this sense fortitude is said to be temperate. Again, temperance is said to be brave, by reason of fortitude overflowing into temperance, in so far, namely, as he whose soul is strengthened by fortitude against dangers of death, which is a matter of very great difficulty, is more able to remain firm against the onslaught of pleasures; for as Cicero says (*De Offic.* i, 20),[1] it would be inconsistent for a man to be unbroken by fear, and yet vanquished by cupidity; or that he should be conquered by lust, after showing himself to be unconquered by toil."

From this the *Reply to the Second Objection* is clear. For temperance observes the mean in all things, and fortitude keeps the soul unbent by the enticements of pleasures,—either in so far as these virtues are taken to denote certain general conditions of virtue, or in the sense that they overflow on to one another, as explained above.

Reply Obj. 3. These four general conditions of virtue set down by the Philosopher, are not proper to the above mentioned virtues. They may, however, be appropriated to them, in the way above stated.

ARTICLE 5. *Whether the Cardinal Virtues Are Fittingly Divided Into Political Virtues, Cleansing Virtues, Virtues of the Cleansed Soul, and Exemplar Virtues?*

We proceed thus to the Fifth Article: It would seem that these four virtues are unfittingly divided into exemplar virtues, cleansing virtues, virtues of the cleansed soul, and political virtues.[2]

Objection 1. For as Macrobius says (*Super Somn, Scip.* 1, 8)[3] "the exemplar virtues are such as exist in the mind of God." Now the Philosopher says[4] (*Ethics*) that it is absurd to ascribe justice, fortitude, temperance, and prudence to God. Therefore these virtues cannot be exemplar.

Obj. 2. Further, the virtues of the cleansed soul are those which are without any passion; for Macrobius says (*ibid.*) that "in a soul that is cleansed it pertains to temperance not to repress worldly desires, but to forget about them completely; to fortitude to be unaware of the passions, not to conquer them." Now it was stated above (Q. LIX, A. 5) that these virtues cannot be without passions. Therefore there is no such thing as these virtues of the cleansed soul.

Obj. 3. Further, he says (Macrobius,—*ibid.*) that the cleansing virtues are those of the man "who flies from human affairs and devotes himself exclusively to the things of God." But it seems wrong to do this; for Cicero says (*De Offic.* i, 21):[5] "I deem that it is not only unworthy of praise, but wicked for a man to say that he despises what most men admire, namely, power and office." Therefore there are no cleansing virtues.

Obj. 4. Further, he says (Macrobius,—*ibid.*)[6] that the political virtues are those "whereby good men work for the good of their country and for the safety of the city." But it is only legal justice that is directed to the common good, as the Philosopher states (*Ethics*).[7] Therefore other virtues should not be called political.

On the contrary, Macrobius says (*ibid.*):[8] "Plotinus, together with Plato foremost among teachers of philosophy, says: 'The four kinds of virtue are fourfold. In the first place there are political virtues; secondly, there are cleansing virtues; thirdly, there are the virtues of the cleansed soul; and fourthly, there are exemplar virtues.'"

I answer that, As Augustine says (*De Moribus Eccl.* vi),[9] "the soul needs to follow something in order to give birth to virtue. This something is God; if we follow Him we shall live well." Consequently the exemplar of human virtue must pre-exist in God, just as in Him

---

[1] DD IV, 441.
[2] Cf. Augustine, *De Quant. An.*, 23 (PL 32, 1073); *De Musica*, VI, 13 (PL 32, 1183); for this doctrine in Manegold of Lautenbach and Peter Abelard, see Van Lieshout, *La Théorie Plotinienne* (p. 127).
[3] DD 33.
[4] X, 8 (1178^{b}10).
[5] DD IV, 441.
[6] DD 32.
[7] V, 1 (1129^{b}15).
[8] DD 32; cf. Plotinus, I, *Ennead*, II, 2–7 (BU I, 53–59).
[9] PL 32, 1314.

pre-exist the types of all things. Accordingly virtue may be considered as existing by way of origin in God, and thus we speak of exemplar virtues. Thus in God the Divine Mind itself may be called prudence, while temperance is the turning of God's gaze on Himself, even as in us it is that which conforms concupiscence to reason. God's fortitude is His unchangeableness; His justice is the observance of the Eternal Law in His works, as Plotinus states. (Cf. Macrobius,—*ibid.*).

Again, since man by his nature is a political animal, these virtues, in so far as they are in him according to the condition of his nature, are called political virtues; since it is by reason of them that man behaves himself well in the conduct of human affairs. It is in this sense that we have been speaking of these virtues until now.

But since it is given to man to do his utmost to strive onward even to Divine things, as even the Philosopher declares in the *Ethics*,[1] and as Scripture often admonishes us,—for instance: *Be ye ... perfect, as your heavenly Father is perfect* (Matt. 5. 48), we must place some virtues between the political, which are the human virtues, and the exemplar virtues which are Divine. Now these virtues differ by reason of a difference of movement and term. Some are virtues of men who are on their way and tending towards the Divine likeness; and these are called cleansing virtues. Thus prudence, by contemplating the things of God, counts as nothing all things of the world, and directs all the thoughts of the soul to God alone; temperance, so far as nature allows, neglects the needs of the body; fortitude prevents the soul from being afraid of neglecting the body and rising to heavenly things; and justice consists in the soul giving a whole-hearted consent to follow the way thus proposed. Besides these there are the virtues of those who have already attained to the Divine likeness; these are called the virtues of the soul already cleansed. Thus prudence sees nothing but the things of God; temperance knows no earthly desires; fortitude has no knowledge of passion; and justice, by imitating the Divine Mind, is united to it by an everlasting covenant. Such are the virtues attributed to the Blessed, or, in this life, to some who are at the summit of perfection.

Reply Obj. 1. The Philosopher is speaking of these virtues according as they relate to human affairs; for instance, justice about buying and selling, fortitude about fear, temperance about

desires; for in this sense it is absurd to attribute them to God.

Reply Obj. 2. Human virtues, that is to say, virtues of men living together in this world, are about the passions. But the virtues of those who have attained to full happiness are without passions. Hence Plotinus says (cf. Macrobius,—*loc. cit.*) that the political virtues check the passions, that is, they bring them to the mean; the second kind, namely, the cleansing virtues, uproot them; the third kind, namely, the virtues of the cleansed soul, forget them; while it is impious to mention them in connection with virtues of the fourth kind, namely, the exemplar virtues.—It may also be said that here he is speaking of passions as denoting inordinate movements.

Reply Obj. 3. To neglect human affairs when necessity forbids is wicked; otherwise it is virtuous. Hence Cicero says a little earlier (*ibid.*): "Perhaps one should make allowances for those who by reason of their exceptional talents have devoted themselves to learning; as also to those who have retired from public life on account of failing health, or for some other yet weightier motive; when such men yielded to others the power and renown of authority." This agrees with what Augustine says:[2] "The love of truth demands a hallowed leisure; charity necessitates good works. If no one lays this burden on us we may devote ourselves to the study and contemplation of truth; but if the burden is laid on us it is to be taken up under the pressure of charity."

Reply Obj. 4. Legal justice alone looks to the common good directly; but by commanding the other virtues it draws them all into the service of the common good, as the Philosopher declares.[3] For we must take note that it concerns the political virtues, as we understand them here, to do well not only towards the community, but also towards the parts of the community, namely, towards the household, or even towards one individual.

QUESTION LXII
OF THE THEOLOGICAL VIRTUES
(In Four Articles)

WE must now consider the Theological Virtues, under which head there are four points of inquiry: (1) Whether there are any theological virtues? (2) Whether the theological virtues are distinct from the intellectual and moral

---

[1] x, 7 (1177^b26).

[2] *City of God*, XIX, 19 (PL 41, 647).

[3] *Ethics*, v, 1 (1129^b31).

virtues? (3) How many, and which are they? (4) Of their order.

ARTICLE 1. *Whether There Are Any Theological Virtues?*

We proceed thus to the First Article: It would seem that there are not any theological virtues.

Objection 1. For according to the *Physics*,[1] "virtue is the disposition of a perfect thing to that which is best; and by perfect, I mean that which is disposed according to nature." But that which is Divine is above man's nature. Therefore the theological virtues are not virtues of a man.

Obj. 2. Further, theological virtues are quasi-Divine virtues. But the Divine virtues are exemplars, as stated above (Q. LXI, A. 5), which are not in us but in God. Therefore the theological virtues are not virtues of man.

Obj. 3. Further, the theological virtues are so called because they direct us to God, Who is the first beginning and last end. But by the very nature of his reason and will man is directed to his first beginning and last end. Therefore there is no need for any habits of theological virtue, to direct the reason and will to God.

On the contrary, The precepts of the Law are about acts of virtue. Now the Divine Law contains precepts about the acts of faith, hope, and charity, for it is written *(Ecclus.* 2. 8, *sqq.): Ye that fear the Lord believe Him,* and again, *hope in Him,* and again, *love Him.* Therefore faith, hope, and charity are virtues directing us to God. Therefore they are theological virtues.

I answer that, Man is perfected by virtue for those actions by which he is directed to happiness, as was explained above (Q. V, A. 7). Now man's happiness is twofold, as was also stated above *(ibid.,* A. 5). One is proportionate to human nature, a happiness, namely, which man can obtain by means of the principles of his nature. The other is a happiness surpassing man's nature, and which man can obtain by the power of God alone, by a kind of participation of the Godhead, about which it is written (II Pet. 1. 4) that by Christ we are made *partakers of the Divine nature.* And because such happiness surpasses the proportion of human nature, man's natural principles which enable him to act well according to his capacity do not suffice to direct man to this same happiness. Hence it is necessary for man to receive from God some addition-

al principles, by means of which he may be directed to supernatural happiness, even as he is directed to his connatural end by means of his natural principles, although not without the Divine assistance. Such principles are called theological virtues:[2] first, because their object is God, because they direct us rightly to God; secondly, because they are infused in us by God alone; thirdly, because these virtues are not made known to us except by Divine revelation, contained in Holy Writ.

Reply Obj. 1. A certain nature may be ascribed to a certain thing in two ways. First, essentially: and thus these theological virtues surpass the nature of man. Secondly, by participation, as kindled wood partakes of the nature of fire, and thus, after a fashion, man becomes a partaker of the Divine Nature, as stated above. And so these virtues belong to man in respect of the Nature of which he is made a partaker.

Reply Obj. 2. These virtues are called Divine not as though God were virtuous by reason of them, but because by them God makes us virtuous, and directs us to Himself. Hence they are not exemplar virtues but virtues resulting from the exemplar.

Reply Obj. 3. The reason and will are naturally directed to God, according as He is the beginning and end of nature, but in proportion to nature. But the reason and will, according to their nature, are not sufficiently directed to Him in so far as He is the object of supernatural happiness.

ARTICLE 2. *Whether the Theological Virtues Are Distinct from the Intellectual and Moral Virtues?*

We proceed thus to the Second Article: It would seem that the theological virtues are not distinct from the moral and intellectual virtues.

Objection 1. For the theological virtues, if they are in a human soul, must perfect it either as to the intellectual or as to the appetitive part. Now the virtues which perfect the intellectual part are called intellectual, and the virtues which perfect the appetitive, are called moral. Therefore, the theological virtues are not distinct from the moral and intellectual virtues.

Obj. 2. Further, the theological virtues are those which direct us to God. Now, among the intellectual virtues there is one which directs us to God, namely wisdom, which is about Di-

---

[1] Aristotle, VII, 3 (246ª13).

[2] Cf. Wm. of Auxerre, *Summa Aurea,* PT. III, tr. 2, chap. 2 (fol. 130 ra); cf. Lottin, RSPT (1929) p. 374 and *passim; Mél. Mandonnet* (II, 233; 253).

vine things, since it considers the highest cause. Therefore the theological virtues are not distinct from the intellectual virtues.

Obj. 3. Further, Augustine *(De Moribus Eccl.* xv)[1] shows how the four cardinal virtues are the order of love. Now love is charity, which is a theological virtue. Therefore the moral virtues are not distinct from the theological.

On the contrary, That which is above man's nature is distinct from that which is according to his nature. But the theological virtues are above man's nature, while the intellectual and moral virtues are in proportion to his nature, as shown above (Q. LVIII, A. 3). Therefore they are distinct from one another.

I answer that, As stated above (Q. LIV, A. 2, REPLY 1), habits are specifically distinct from one another in respect of the formal difference of their objects. Now the object of the theological virtues is God Himself, Who is the last end of things, as surpassing the knowledge of our reason. On the other hand, the object of the intellectual and moral virtues is something comprehensible to human reason. Therefore the theological virtues are specifically distinct from the moral and intellectual virtues.

Reply Obj. 1. The intellectual and moral virtues perfect man's intellect and appetite according to the proportion of human nature; the theological virtues, supernaturally.

Reply Obj. 2. The wisdom which the Philosopher puts as an intellectual virtue considers Divine things so far as they are open to the inquiry of human reason.[2] Theological virtue, on the other hand, is about those same things so far as they surpass human reason.

Reply Obj. 3. Though charity is love, yet not all love is charity. When, then, it is stated that every virtue is the order of love, this can be understood either of love in the general sense, or of the love of charity. If it be understood of love commonly so called, then each virtue is stated to be the order of love, in so far as each cardinal virtue requires ordered affection; and love is the root and principle of every affection, as stated above (Q. XXVII, A. 4; Q. XXVIII, A. 6, REPLY 2; Q. XLI, A. 2, REPLY 1). If, however, it be understood of the love of charity, it does not mean that every other virtue is charity essentially, but that all other virtues depend on charity in some way, as we shall show further on (Q. LXV, AA. 2, 4; Part II-II, Q. XXIII, A. 7).

[1] PL 32, 1322.
[2] *Ethics,* VI, 3 (1139ᵇ17).

ARTICLE 3. *Whether Faith, Hope, and Charity Are Fittingly Put as Theological Virtues?*

We proceed thus to the Third Article: It would seem that faith, hope, and charity are not fittingly put as three theological virtues.

Objection 1. For the theological virtues are in relation to Divine happiness, what the natural inclination is in relation to the connatural end. Now among the virtues directed to the connatural end there is but one natural virtue, namely, the understanding of principles. Therefore there should be but one theological virtue.

Obj. 2. Further, the theological virtues are more perfect than the intellectual and moral virtues. Now faith is not put among the intellectual virtues, but is something less than a virtue, since it is imperfect knowledge. Likewise hope is not put among the moral virtues, but is something less than a virtue, since it is a passion. Much less therefore should they be accounted as theological virtues.

Obj. 3. Further, the theological virtues direct man's soul to God. Now man's soul cannot be directed to God, save through the intellectual part, where the intellect and will are. Therefore there should be only two theological virtues, one perfecting the intellect, the other, the will.

On the contrary, The Apostle says (I Cor. 13. 13): *Now there remain faith, hope, charity, these three.*

I answer that, As stated above (A. 1), the theological virtues direct man to supernatural happiness in the same way as by the natural inclination man is directed to his connatural end. Now the latter happens in respect of two things. First, in respect of the reason or intellect, in so far as it contains the first universal principles which are known to us by the natural light of the intellect, and which are reason's starting-point, both in speculative and in practical matters. Secondly, through the rectitude of the will which tends naturally to the good of reason.

But these two fall short of the order of supernatural happiness, according to I Cor. 2. 9: *The eye hath not seen, nor ear heard, neither hath it entered into the heart of man, what things God hath prepared for them that love Him.* Consequently in respect of both the above things man needed to receive in addition something supernatural to direct him to a supernatural end. First, as regards the intellect, man receives certain supernatural principles, which are held by means of a Divine light: these are the articles of faith, about which is faith. Secondly, the will is directed to this end, both as to the movement of intention, which tends to that end as something attainable,—and this pertains to hope,—and as to a certain spiritual union, by which the will is, so to speak, transformed into that end,—and this belongs to charity. For the appetite of a thing is moved and tends towards its connatural end naturally, and this movement is due to a certain conformity of the thing with its end.

Reply Obj. 1. The intellect needs intelligible species by which it understands; consequently there is need of a natural habit in addition to the power. But the very nature of the will suffices for it to be directed naturally to the end, both as to the intention of the end and as to its conformity with the end. But the nature of the power is insufficient in either of these respects in relation to things that are above its nature. Consequently there was need for an additional supernatural habit in both respects.

Reply Obj. 2. Faith and hope imply a certain imperfection, since faith is of things unseen, and hope, of thing not possessed. Hence faith and hope in things that are subject to human power fall short of the notion of virtue. But faith and hope in things which are above the power of human nature surpass all virtue that is in proportion to man, according to I Cor. 1. 25: *The weakness of God is stronger than men.*

Reply Obj. 3. Two things pertain to the appetite, namely, movement to the end, and conformity with the end by means of love. Hence there must be two theological virtues in the human appetite, namely, hope and charity.

ARTICLE 4. *Whether Faith Precedes Hope, and Hope Charity?*

We proceed thus to the Fourth Article: It would seem that the order of the theological virtues is not that faith precedes hope, and hope charity.

Objection 1. For the root precedes that which grows from it. Now charity is the root of all the virtues, according to Ephes. 3. 17: *Being rooted and founded in charity.* Therefore charity precedes the others.

Obj. 2. Further, Augustine says,[1] "A man cannot love what he does not believe to exist. But if he believes and loves, by doing good works he ends in hoping." Therefore it seems that faith precedes charity, and charity hope.

Obj. 3. Further, love is the principle of all affection, as stated above (A. 2, Reply 3). Now

[1] *Christian Doctrine,* I, 37 (PL 34, 35).

hope is a kind of affection, since it is a passion, as stated above (Q. XXIII, A. 4). Therefore charity, which is love, precedes hope.

On the contrary, The Apostle enumerates them thus (I Cor. 13. 13): *Now there remain faith, hope, charity.*

I answer that, Order is twofold: order of generation, and order of perfection. By order of generation, in respect of which matter precedes form, and the imperfect precedes the perfect, in one and the same subject, faith precedes hope, and hope charity, as to their acts; for the habits are infused at the same time. For the movement of the appetite cannot tend to anything, either by hoping or loving, unless that thing be apprehended by the sense or by the intellect. Now it is by faith that the intellect apprehends the object of hope and love. Hence in the order of generation, faith must precede hope and charity. In like manner a man loves a thing because he apprehends it as his good. Now from the very fact that a man hopes to be able to obtain some good through someone, he looks on the man in whom he hopes as a good of his own. Hence from the very fact that a man hopes in someone, he proceeds to love him, so that in the order of generation, hope precedes charity as regards their respective acts.

But in the order of perfection, charity precedes faith and hope, because both faith and hope are formed by charity, and receive from charity their perfection as virtues. For thus charity is the mother and the root of all the virtues, since it is the form of them all, as we shall state further on (Part II-II, Q. XXIII, A. 8).

This suffices for the *Reply to the First Objection.*

Reply Obj. 2. Augustine is speaking of that hope by which a man hopes to obtain Happiness through the merits which he has already, and this belongs to hope formed by and following charity. But it is possible for a man before having charity to hope through merits not already possessed, but which he hopes to possess.

Reply Obj. 3. As stated above (Q. XL, A. 7), in treating of the passions, hope regards two things. One as its principal object, namely, the good hoped for. With regard to this love always precedes hope, for good is never hoped for unless it be desired and loved. Hope also regards the person from whom a man hopes to be able to obtain some good. With regard to this, hope precedes love at first, though afterwards hope is increased by love. Because from the fact that a man thinks that he can obtain a good through someone, he begins to love him and from this very fact that he loves him, he then hopes all the more in him.

QUESTION LXIII
OF THE CAUSE OF VIRTUES
(In Four Articles)

WE must now consider the cause of virtues; and under this head there are four points of inquiry: (1) Whether virtue is in us by nature? (2) Whether any virtue is caused in us by habituation? (3) Whether any moral virtues are in us by infusion? (4) Whether virtue acquired by habituation is of the same species as infused virtue?

ARTICLE 1. *Whether Virtue Is in Us by Nature?*

We proceed thus to the First Article: It would seem that virtue is in us by nature.

Objection 1. For Damascene says (*De Fide Orthod.* iii, 14):[1] "Virtues are natural to us and are equally in all of us." And Antony says in his sermon to the monks:[2] "If the will contradicts nature it is perverse, if it follow nature, it is virtuous." Moreover, a gloss on Matt. 4. 23, *Jesus went about,* etc., says:[3] "He taught them natural virtues, that is, chastity, justice, humility, which man possesses naturally."

Obj. 2. Further, the good of virtue consists in accord with reason, as was clearly shown above (Q. LV, A. 4, reply 2). But that which accords with reason is natural to man; since reason is part of man's nature. Therefore virtue is in man by nature.

Obj. 3. Further, that which is in us from birth is said to be natural to us. Now virtues are in some from birth, for it is written (Job 31. 18): *From my infancy mercy grew up with me; and it came out with me from my mother's womb.* Therefore virtue is in man by nature.

On the contrary, Whatever is in man by nature is common to all men, and is not taken away by sin, since even in the demons natural gifts remain, as Dionysius states *(Div. Nom.* iv).[4] But virtue is not in all men; and is cast out by sin. Therefore it is not in man by nature.

I answer that, With regard to corporeal forms, it has been maintained by some that they are wholly from within, by those, for instance, who upheld the theory of latent forms.[5] Others held that forms are entirely from without; those,

for instance, who thought that corporeal forms originated from some separate cause.[6] Others, however, held that they are partly from within, in so far as they pre-exist potentially in matter, and partly from without, in so far as they are brought into act by the agent.[7]

In like manner with regard to sciences and virtues, some held[8] that they are wholly from within, so that all virtues and sciences would pre-exist in the soul naturally, but that the hindrances to science and virtue, which are due to the soul being weighed down by the body, are removed by study and practice, even as iron is made bright by being polished. This was the opinion of the Platonists. Others said that they are wholly from without, being due to the inflow of the agent intellect, as Avicenna maintained.[9] Others said that sciences and virtues are in us by nature, so far as we have an aptitude for them, but not in their perfection; this is the teaching of the Philosopher[10] and is nearer the truth.

To make this clear, it must be observed that there are two ways in which something is said to be natural to a man; one is according to his specific nature, the other according to his individual nature. And, since each thing derives its species from its form, and its individuation from matter, and, again, since man's form is his rational soul, while his matter is his body, whatever belongs to him in respect of his rational soul is natural to him according to his specific nature; while whatever belongs to him in respect of the particular temperament of his body, is natural to him according to his individual nature. For whatever is natural to man in respect of his body, considered as part of his species, is to be referred, in a way, to the soul, in so far as this particular body is proportioned to this particular soul.

In both these ways virtue is natural to man according to a kind of beginning. This is so in respect of the specific nature, in so far as in man's reason are to be found instilled by nature certain naturally known principles of both knowledge and action, which are the nurseries of intellectual and moral virtues, and in so far as there is in the will a natural appetite for good in accordance with reason. Again, this is so in respect of the individual nature, in so far as by reason of a disposition in the body some are disposed either well or ill to certain virtues: be-

---

[1] PG 94, 1045.   [2] Cf. Athanasius, *Vita S. Antonii,* trans. of Evagrius (PG 26, 873).
[3] *Glossa ordin.* (V, 17E).   [4] Sect. 23 (PG 3, 725).
[5] Cf. above, Part I, Q. XLV, A. 8.

[6] *Ibid.*   [7] *Ibid.*
[8] Cf. above, Part I, Q. LXXXIV, A. 3, Arg. 3; cf. Albert, *In Eth.,* I, 7, 4 (BO VII, 112).
[9] *De An.,* V, 5 (25 rb).
[10] *Ethics,* II, 1 (1103ª25); cf. the doctrine of the Stoics, in Cicero, *De Finibus,* III, 6 (DDIII, 546).

cause, namely, certain sensitive powers are acts of certain parts of the body, according to the disposition of which these powers are helped or hindered in the exercise of their acts, and, in consequence, the rational powers also, which these sensitive powers assist. In this way one man has a natural aptitude for science, another for fortitude, another for temperance, and in these ways, both intellectual and moral virtues are in us naturally, as an undeveloped aptitude. But they are not in us perfectly, since nature is determined to one thing, while the perfection of these virtues does not depend on one particular mode of action, but on various modes, in respect of the various matters which constitute the sphere of action of the virtues, and according to various circumstances.

It is therefore evident that all virtues are in us by nature, according to aptitude and beginning, but not according to perfection, except the theological virtues, which are entirely from without.

This suffices for the *Replies to the Objections.* For the first two argue about the nurseries of virtue which are in us by nature, in so far as we are rational beings. The third objection must be taken in the sense that, owing to the natural disposition which the body has from birth, one has an aptitude for pity, another for living temperately, another for some other virtue.

ARTICLE 2. *Whether Any Virtue Is Caused in Us by Habituation?*

We proceed thus to the Second Article: It would seem that virtues cannot be caused in us by habituation.

Objection 1. Because a gloss of Augustine,[1] commenting on Rom. 14. 23, *All that is not of faith is sin,* says: "The whole life of an unbeliever is a sin; and there is no good without the Sovereign Good. Where knowledge of the truth is lacking, virtue is false even in the best behaved people." Now faith cannot be acquired by means of works, but is caused in us by God, according to Eph. 2. 8: *By grace you are saved through faith.* Therefore no acquired virtue can be in us by habituation.

Obj. 2. Further, sin and virtue are contraries, so that they are incompatible. Now man cannot avoid sin except by the grace of God, according to Wisd. 8. 21: *I knew that I could not otherwise be continent, except God gave it.* Therefore neither can any virtues be caused in us by habituation, but only by the gift of God.

[1] *Glossa ordin.* (VI, 30B); *Glossa* Lombardi (PL 191, 1520); Prosper of Aquitaine, *Sent.,* CVI (PL 51, 441).

Obj. 3. Further, actions which lead towards virtue lack the perfection of virtue. But an effect cannot be more perfect than its cause. Therefore a virtue cannot be caused by actions that precede it.

On the contrary, Dionysius says *(Div. Nom.* iv)[2] that good is more efficacious than evil. But vicious habits are caused by evil acts. Much more, therefore, can virtuous habits be caused by good acts.

I answer that, We have spoken above (Q. LI, AA. 2, 3) in a general way about the production of habits from acts; and speaking now in a special way of this matter in relation to virtue, we must take note that, as stated above (Q. LV, AA. 3, 4), man's virtue perfects him in relation to good. Now since the notion of good consists in "mode, species, and order," as Augustine states *(De Nat. Boni,* iii),[3] or in *number, weight, and measure,* as expressed in Wisd. 11, 21, man's good must be appraised with respect to some rule. Now this rule is twofold, as stated above (Q. XIX, AA. 3, 4), namely, human reason and Divine Law. And since Divine Law is the higher rule, it extends to more things, so that whatever is ruled by human reason is ruled by the Divine Law too; but the converse does not hold.

It follows that human virtue directed to the good which is defined according to the rule of human reason can be caused by human acts, in so far as such acts proceed from reason, by whose power and rule such good is established. On the other hand, virtue which directs man to good as defined by the Divine Law, and not by human reason, cannot be caused by human acts, the principle of which is reason, but is produced in us by the Divine operation alone. Hence Augustine in giving the definition of the latter virtue inserts the words, "which God works in us without us."[4] It is also of this virtue that the *First Objection* holds good.

Reply Obj. 2. Mortal sin is incompatible with divinely infused virtue, especially if this be considered in its perfect state. But actual sin, even mortal, is compatible with humanly acquired virtue, because the use of a habit in us is subject to our will, as stated above (Q. XLIX, A. 3), and one sinful act does not destroy a habit of acquired virtue, since it is not an act but a habit that is directly contrary to a habit. Therefore, though man cannot avoid mortal sin without grace, so as never to sin mortally, yet he is not hindered from acquiring a habit

[2] Sects. 20, 32 (PG 3, 717, 732).
[3] PL 42, 553.
[4] Cf. above, Q. LV, A. 4, obj. 1.

of virtue by which he may abstain from evil in the majority of cases, and chiefly in matters most opposed to reason. There are also certain mortal sins which man can in no way avoid without grace, those, namely, which are directly opposed to the theological virtues, which are in us through the gift of grace. This, however, will be more fully explained later (Q. CIX, A. 4).

Reply Obj. 3. As stated above (A. 1; Q. LI, A. 1), certain seeds or principles of acquired virtue pre-exist in us by nature. These principles are more excellent than the virtues acquired through them, just as the understanding of speculative principles is more excellent than the science of conclusions, and the natural rectitude of the reason is more excellent than the rectification of the appetite which results through the appetite partaking of reason, which rectification belongs to moral virtue. Accordingly human acts, in so far as they proceed from higher principles, can cause acquired human virtues.

ARTICLE 3. *Whether Any Moral Virtues Are in Us by Infusion?*

We proceed thus to the Third Article: It would seem that no virtues besides the theological virtues are infused in us by God.

Objection 1. Because God does not do by Himself, save perhaps sometimes miraculously, those things that can be done by second causes; for, as Dionysius says (*Cæl. Hier.* iv)[1] it is God's rule to bring about extremes through the mean. Now intellectual and moral virtues can be caused in us by our acts, as stated above (A. 2). Therefore it is not reasonable that they should be caused in us by infusion.

Obj. 2. Further, much less is there anything superfluous in God's works than in the works of nature. Now the theological virtues suffice to direct us to supernatural good. Therefore there are no other supernatural virtues which have to be caused in us by God.

Obj. 3. Further, nature does not employ two means where one suffices, and much less does God. But God sowed the seeds of virtue in our souls, according to a gloss on Heb. 1.[2] Therefore it is unfitting for him to cause in us other virtues by means of infusion.

On the contrary, It is written (Wisd. 8. 7): *She teacheth temperance and prudence and justice and fortitude.*

[1] Sect. 3 (PG 3, 181).
[2] *Glossa ordin.* (VI, 79E); cf. Jerome on Gal. 1.15 (PL 26, 351).

I answer that, Effects must be proportionate to their causes and principles. Now all virtues, intellectual and moral, that are acquired by our actions, arise from certain natural principles pre-existing in us, as above stated (A. 1; Q. LI, A. 1). Instead of these natural principles, God bestows on us the theological virtues, by which we are directed to a supernatural end, as stated (Q. LXII, A. 1). Therefore we need to receive from God other habits corresponding, in due proportion, to the theological virtues, which habits are to the theological virtues what the moral and intellectual virtues are to the natural principles of virtue.

Reply Obj. 1. Some moral and intellectual virtues can indeed be caused in us by our actions, but they are not proportioned to the theological virtues. Therefore it was necessary for us to receive immediately from God others that are proportionate to those virtues.

Reply Obj. 2. The theological virtues direct us sufficiently, according to a certain beginning, to our supernatural end, that is, to that which concerns God Himself immediately. But the soul needs further to be perfected by infused virtues in regard to other things, yet in relation to God.

Reply Obj. 3. The power of those naturally instilled principles does not extend beyond the capacity of nature. Consequently man needs in addition to be perfected by other principles in relation to his supernatural end.

ARTICLE 4. *Whether Virtue Acquired by Habituation Belongs to the Same Species as Infused Virtue?*

We proceed thus to the Fourth Article: It would seem that infused virtue does not differ in species from acquired virtue.

Objection 1. Because acquired and infused virtues, according to what has been said (A. 3), do not seem to differ save in relation to the last end. Now human habits and acts are specified not by their last, but by their proximate end. Therefore the infused moral or intellectual virtue does not differ from the acquired virtue.

Obj. 2. Further, habits are known by their acts. But the act of infused and acquired temperance is the same, namely, to moderate desires of touch. Therefore they do not differ in species.

Obj. 3. Further, acquired and infused virtue differ as that which is wrought by God immediately from that which is wrought by a creature. But the man whom God made is of the same species as a man begotten naturally;

and the eye which He gave to the man born blind as one produced by the power of generation. Therefore it seems that acquired and infused virtue belong to the same species.

On the contrary, Any change introduced into the difference expressed in a definition involves a difference of species. But the definition of infused virtue contains the words, "which God works in us without us," as stated above (A. 2; Q. LV, A. 4). Therefore acquired virtue, to which these words cannot apply, is not of the same species as infused virtue.

I answer that, There is a twofold specific difference among habits. The first, as stated above (Q. LIV, A. 2; Q. LVI, A. 2; Q. LX, A. 1), is taken from the special and formal aspects of their objects. Now the object of every virtue is a good considered as in that virtue's proper matter; thus the object of temperance is a good in respect of the pleasures connected with the concupiscence of touch. The formal aspect of this object is from reason which fixes the mean in these concupiscenses, while the material element is something on the part of the concupiscences. Now it is evident that the mean that is appointed in such concupiscences according to the rule of human reason is seen under a different aspect from the mean which is fixed according to the Divine rule. For instance, in the consumption of food, the mean fixed by human reason is that food should not harm the health of the body, nor hinder the act of reason; but according to the Divine rule, man is required to *chastise* his *body, and bring it into subjection* (I Cor. 9. 27), by abstinence in food, drink and the like. It is therefore evident that infused and acquired temperance differ in species, and the same applies to the other virtues.

The chief specific difference among habits is taken from the things to which they are directed. For a man's health and a horse's are not of the same species, on account of the difference between the natures to which their respective healths are directed. In the same sense, the Philosopher says[1] that citizens have different virtues according as they are well directed to different forms of government. In the same way, too, those infused moral virtues by which men behave well in respect of their being *fellow-citizens with the saints, and of the household* (Douay,—*domestics*) *of God* (Eph. 2. 19), differ from the acquired virtues, by which man behaves well in respect of human affairs.

Reply Obj. 1. Infused and acquired virtue differ not only in relation to the ultimate end,

[1] *Politics,* III, 2 (1276ᵇ31).

but also in relation to their proper objects, as stated.

Reply Obj. 2. Both acquired and infused temperance moderate desires for pleasures of touch, but for different reasons, as stated; therefore their respective acts are not identical.

Reply Obj. 3. God gave the man born blind an eye for the same act as the act for which other eyes are formed naturally, and consequently it was of the same species. It would be the same if God wished to give a man miraculously virtues such as those that are acquired by acts. But the case is not so in the question before us, as stated.

QUESTION LXIV

OF THE MEAN OF VIRTUE

(*In Four Articles*)

WE must now consider the properties of virtues, and (1) the mean of virtue, (2) the connection between virtues (Q. LXV), (3) equality of virtues (Q. LXVI), (4) the duration of virtues (Q. LXVII). Under the first head there are four points of inquiry: (1) Whether moral virtue observes the mean? (2) Whether the mean of moral virtue is the mean of the thing or the mean of reason? (3) Whether the intellectual virtues observe the mean? (4) Whether the theological virtues do?

ARTICLE 1. *Whether Moral Virtues Observe the Mean?*

We proceed thus to the First Article: It would seem that moral virtue does not observe the mean.

Objection 1. For the nature of a mean is incompatible with that which is extreme. Now the nature of virtue is to be something extreme, for it is stated in the *Heavens*[2] that "virtue is the limit of power." Therefore moral virtue does not observe the mean.

Obj. 2. Further, the maximum is not a mean. Now some moral virtues tend to something maximum; for instance magnanimity to very great honours, and magnificence to very large expenditure, as stated in the *Ethics*.[3] Therefore not every moral virtue observes the mean.

Obj. 3. Further, if it is of the very notion of a moral virtue to observe the mean, it follows that a moral virtue is not perfected, but on the contrary corrupted, through tending to something extreme. Now some moral virtues are perfected by tending to something extreme; thus

[2] Aristotle, I, 11 (281ᵃ11); cf. Thomas, *In De Cælo,* I, 25.
[3] Aristotle, IV, 2, 3 (1122ᵃ18; 1123ᵃ34).

virginity, which abstains from all sexual pleasure, observes the extreme, and is the most perfect chastity; and to give all to the poor is the most perfect mercy or liberality. Therefore it seems that it is not essential to moral virtue that it should observe the mean.

On the contrary, The Philosopher says[1] that "moral virtue is a habit of choosing while observing a mean."

I answer that, As already explained (Q. LV, A. 3), the nature of virtue is that it should order man to good. Now moral virtue is properly a perfection of the appetitive part of the soul in regard to some determinate matter. And the measure or rule of the appetitive movement in respect of appetible objects is the reason. But the good of that which is measured or ruled consists in its conformity with its rule; thus the good of things made by art is that they follow the rule of art. Consequently, in things of this sort evil consists in discordance from their rule or measure. Now this may happen either by their exceeding the measure or by their falling short of it, as is clearly the case in all things ruled or measured. Hence it is evident that the good of moral virtue consists in conformity with the rule of reason. Now it is clear that between excess and deficiency the mean is equality or conformity. Therefore it is evident that moral virtue observes the mean.

Reply Obj. 1. Moral virtue derives goodness from the rule of reason, while its matter consists in passions or operations. If therefore we compare moral virtue to reason, then, if we look at that which it has of reason, it holds the position of one extreme, namely conformity, while excess and defect take the position of the other extreme, namely deformity. But if we consider moral virtue in respect of its matter, then it holds the position of a mean, in so far as it makes the passion conform to the rule of reason. Hence the Philosopher says[2] that "virtue, as to its substance, is a mean state," in so far as the rule of virtue is imposed on its proper matter; "'but it is an extreme in reference to the 'best' and 'the excellent,'" namely as to its conformity with reason.

Reply Obj. 2. In actions and passions the mean and the extremes depend on various circumstances. Hence nothing hinders something from being extreme in a particular virtue as to one circumstance, while the same thing is a mean in respect of other circumstances, through being in conformity with reason. This is the case with magnanimity and magnificence. For if we

look at the absolute quantity of the respective objects of these virtues, we shall call it an extreme and a maximum; but if we consider the quantity in relation to other circumstances, then it has the character of a mean, since these virtues tend to this maximum in accordance with the rule of reason, that is where it is right, when it is right, and for an end that is right. There will be excess if one tends to this maximum when it is not right, or where it is not right, or for an undue end; and there will be deficiency if one fails to tend to it where one ought, and when one ought. This agrees with the saying of the Philosopher that "the magnanimous man observes the extreme in quantity, but the mean in the right mode of his action."[3]

Reply Obj. 3. The same is to be said of virginity and poverty as of magnanimity. For virginity abstains from all sexual matters, and poverty from all wealth, for a right end, and in a right manner, that is, according to God's word, and for the sake of eternal life. But if this be done in an undue manner, that is, out of unlawful superstition, or again for vainglory, it will be in excess. And if it be not done when it ought to be done, or as it ought to be done, it is a vice by deficiency; for instance, in those who break their vows of virginity or poverty.

ARTICLE 2. *Whether the Mean of Moral Virtue Is the Mean of the Thing or the Mean of Reason?*

We proceed thus to the Second Article: It would seem that the mean of moral virtue is not the mean of reason, but the mean of the thing.

Objection 1. For the good of moral virtue consists in its observing the mean. Now, good, as stated in the *Metaphysics*,[4] is in things themselves. Therefore the mean of moral virtue is a mean of the thing.

Obj. 2. Further, the reason is a power of apprehension. But moral virtue does not consist in a mean between apprehensions, but rather a mean between operations or passions. Therefore the mean of moral virtue is not the mean of reason, but the mean of the thing.

Obj. 3. Further, a mean that is observed according to arithmetical or geometrical proportion is a mean of the thing. Now such is the mean of justice, as stated in the *Ethics*.[5] Therefore the mean of moral virtue is not the mean of reason, but the mean of the thing.

[1] *Ethics,* II, 6 (1106^b36).   [2] *Ibid.* (1107^a7).

[3] *Ethics,* IV, 3 (1123^b13).
[4] Aristotle, VI, 4 (1027^b26).
[5] Aristotle, V, 3 (1131^b13); also V, 4 (1132^a2); II, 6 (1106^a28).

On the contrary, The Philosopher says[1] that "moral virtue observes the mean fixed, in our regard, by reason."

I answer that, The mean of reason can be understood in two ways. First, according as the mean is observed in the act itself of reason, as though the very act of reason were reduced to the mean. In this sense, since moral virtue perfects not the act of reason, but the act of the appetitive power, the mean of moral virtue is not the mean of reason. Secondly, the mean of reason may be considered as that which the reason puts into some particular matter. In this sense every mean of moral virtue is a mean of reason, since, as above stated (A. 1), moral virtue is said to observe the mean through conformity with right reason.

But it happens sometimes that the mean of reason is also the mean of the thing in which case the mean of moral virtue is the mean of the thing, for instance, in justice. On the other hand, sometimes the mean of reason is not the mean of the thing, but is a mean fixed in relation to us, and such is the mean in all the other moral virtues. The reason for this is that justice is about operations, which deal with external things, where right has to be established in itself and absolutely, as stated above (Q. LX, A. 2). Therefore the mean of reason in justice is the same as the mean of the thing, in so far, namely, as justice gives to each one his due, neither more nor less. But the other moral virtues deal with interior passions, where the right cannot be established in the same way, since men are variously situated in relation to their passions; hence when it is a question of the passions the rectitude of reason has to be established in relation to us, who are moved in respect of the passions.

This suffices for the *replies to the objections.* For the first two arguments take the mean of reason as being in the very act of reason, while the third argues from the mean of justice.

ARTICLE 3. *Whether the Intellectual Virtues Observe the Mean?*

We proceed thus to the Third Article: It would seem that the intellectual virtues do not observe the mean.

Objection 1. Because moral virtue observes the mean by conforming to the rule of reason. But the intellectual virtues are in reason itself, so that they seem to have no higher rule. Therefore the intellectual virtues do not observe the mean.

Obj. 2. Further, the mean of moral virtue is fixed by an intellectual virtue; for it is stated in the *Ethics*[2] that "virtue observes the mean appointed by reason, as a wise man would appoint it." If therefore intellectual virtues also observe the mean, this mean will have to be appointed for them by another virtue, so that there would be an infinite series of virtues.

Obj. 3. Further, "a mean is, properly speaking, between contraries," as the Philosopher explains.[3] But there seems to be no contrariety in the intellect; since contraries themselves, as they are in the intellect, are not in opposition to one another, but are understood together, as white and black, healthy and sick. Therefore there is no mean in the intellectual virtues.

On the contrary, Art is an intellectual virtue,[4] and yet there is a mean in art.[5] Therefore also intellectual virtue observes the mean.

I answer that, The good of anything consists in its observing the mean, by conforming with a rule or measure in respect of which it may happen to be excessive or deficient, as stated above (A. 1). Now intellectual virtue, like moral virtue, is ordered to the good, as stated above (Q. LVI, A. 3). Hence the good of an intellectual virtue consists in observing the mean, in so far as it is subject to a measure. Now the good of intellectual virtue is the true; in the case of contemplative virtue, it is the true taken absolutely;[6] in the case of practical virtue, it is the true in conformity with a right appetite.

Now truth apprehended by our intellect, if we consider it absolutely, is measured by things, since things are the measure of our intellect, as stated in the *Metaphysics;*[7] because there is truth in what we think or say, according as the thing is so or not. Accordingly the good of speculative intellectual virtue consists in a certain mean, by way of conformity with things themselves, in so far as the intellect says that what is, is, and what is not, is not; and it is in this that the notion of the true consists. There will be excess if something false is affirmed, as though something were which in reality is not; and there will be deficiency if something is falsely denied, and that is declared not to be which in reality is.

The truth of practical intellectual virtue, if we consider it in relation to things, has the character of that which is measured. Thus both in practical and in speculative intellectual virtues,

[1] *Ethics,* II, 6 (1106[b]36).
[2] Aristotle, II, 6 (1106[b]36).
[3] *Metaphysics,* X, 7 (1057[a]30).
[4] *Ethics,* VI, 3 (1139[b]16).
[5] *Ibid.,* II, 6 (1106[b]13).
[6] *Ethics,* VI, 2 (1139[a]29).
[7] Aristotle, X, 1 (1053[a]33).

the mean consists in conformity with things. But if we consider it in relation to the appetite, it has the character of a rule and measure. Consequently the rectitude of reason is the mean of moral virtue, and also the mean of prudence,— of prudence as ruling and measuring, of moral virtue, as ruled and measured by that mean. In like manner the difference between excess and deficiency is to be applied in both cases.

Reply Obj. 1. Intellectual virtues also have their measure, as stated, and they observe the mean according as they conform to that measure.

Reply Obj. 2. There is no need for an infinite series of virtues because the measure and rule of intellectual virtue is not another kind of virtue but things themselves.

Reply Obj. 3. The things themselves that are contrary have no contrariety in the mind, because one is the reason for knowing the other. Nevertheless there is in the intellect contrariety of affirmation and negation, which are contraries, as stated at the end of the treatise on *Interpretation.*[1] For though to be and not to be are not in contrary, but in contradictory opposition to one another, so long as we consider their signification in things themselves, for on the one hand we have being and on the other we have non-being absolutely; yet if we refer them to the act of the mind, there is something positive in both cases. Hence to be and not to be are contradictory: but the opinion stating that good is good is contrary to the opinion stating that good is not good; and between two such contraries intellectual virtue observes the mean.

ARTICLE 4. *Whether the Theological Virtues Observe the Mean?*

We proceed thus to the Fourth Article: It would seem that theological virtue observes the mean.

Objection 1. For the good of other virtues consists in their observing the mean. Now the theological virtues surpass the others in goodness. Therefore much more does theological virtue observe the mean.

Obj. 2. Further, the mean of moral virtue depends on the appetite being ruled by reason, while the mean of intellectual virtue consists in the intellect being measured by things. Now theological virtue perfects both intellect and appetite, as stated above (Q. LXII, A. 3). Therefore theological virtue also observes the mean.

Obj. 3. Further, Hope, which is a theological virtue, is a mean between despair and presump-

tion. Likewise faith holds "a middle course between contrary heresies," as Boethius states (*De Duab. Natur.* vii) ;[2] thus, by confessing one Person and two natures in Christ, we observe the mean between the heresy of Nestorius, who maintained the existence of two persons and two natures, and the heresy of Eutyches, who held to one person and one nature. Therefore theological virtue observes the mean.

On the contrary, Wherever virtue observes the mean it is possible to sin by excess as well as by deficiency. But there is no sinning by excess against God, Who is the object of theological virtue. For it is written (Ecclus. 43. 33): *Blessing the Lord, exalt Him as much as you can: for He is above all praise.* Therefore theological virtue does not observe the mean.

I answer that, As stated above (A. 1), the mean of virtue depends on conformity with virtue's rule or measure, in so far as one may exceed or fall short of that rule. Now the measure of theological virtue may be twofold. One is taken from the very notion of virtue, and thus the measure and rule of theological virtue is God Himself, because our faith is ruled according to Divine truth, charity, according to His goodness, hope, according to the immensity of His omnipotence and loving kindness. This measure surpasses all human power, so that never can we love God as much as He ought to be loved, nor believe and hope in Him as much as we should. Much less therefore can there be excess in such things. Accordingly the good of such virtues does not consist in a mean, but increases the more we approach to the summit.

The other rule or measure of theological virtue is by comparison with us. For although we cannot be borne towards God as much as we ought, yet we should approach to Him by believing, hoping and loving, according to the measure of our condition. Consequently it is possible to find a mean and extremes in theological virtue, accidentally and in reference to us.

Reply Obj. 1. The good of intellectual and moral virtues consists in a mean by reason of conformity with a measure that may be exceeded, which is not so in the case of theological virtue, considered in itself, as stated above.

Reply Obj. 2. Moral and intellectual virtues perfect our intellect and appetite in relation to a created measure and rule, while the theological virtues perfect them in relation to an uncreated rule and measure. Therefore the comparison fails.

Reply Obj. 3. Hope observes the mean be-

---

[1] Aristotle, 14 (23ª27).   [2] PL 64, 1352.

tween presumption and despair in relation to us, in so far, that is, as a man is said to be presumptuous through hoping to receive from God a good in excess of his condition, or to despair through failing to hope for that which according to his condition he might hope for. But there can be no excess of hope in comparison with God, Whose goodness is infinite. In like manner faith holds a middle course between contrary heresies, not by comparison with its object, which is God, in Whom we cannot believe too much, but in so far as human opinion itself takes a middle position between contrary opinions, as was explained above.

QUESTION LXV
OF THE CONNECTION OF VIRTUES
(In Five Articles)

WE must now consider the connection of virtues, under which head there are five points of inquiry: (1) Whether the moral virtues are connected with one another? (2) Whether the moral virtues can be without charity? (3) Whether charity can be without them? (4) Whether faith and hope can be without charity? (4) Whether charity can be without them?

ARTICLE 1. *Whether the Moral Virtues Are Connected with One Another?*

We proceed thus to the First Article: It would seem that the moral virtues are not connected with one another.

Objection 1. Because moral virtues are sometimes caused by the exercise of acts, as is proved in the *Ethics.*[1] But man can exercise himself in the acts of one virtue without exercising himself in the acts of some other virtue. Therefore it is possible to have one moral virtue without another.

Obj. 2. Further, magnificence and magnanimity are moral virtues. Now a man may have other moral virtues without having magnificence or magnanimity; for the Philosopher says[2] that "a poor man cannot be magnificent," and yet he may have other virtues; and[3] that "he who is worthy of small things, and so accounts his worth, is modest, but not magnanimous." Therefore the moral virtues are not connected with one another.

Obj. 3. Further, as the moral virtues perfect the appetitive part of the soul, so do the intellectual virtues perfect the intellectual part. But the intellectual virtues are not connected, since

we may have one science without having another. Neither, therefore, are the moral virtues connected with one another.

Obj. 4. Further, if the moral virtues are connected, this can only be because they are united together in prudence. But this does not suffice to connect the moral virtues together. For it seems that one may be prudent about things to be done in relation to one virtue without being prudent in those that concern another virtue, even as one may have the art of making certain things without the art of making certain others. Now prudence is right reason about things to be done. Therefore the moral virtues are not necessarily connected with one another.

On the contrary, Ambrose says[4] on Luke 6. 20: "The virtues are connected and linked together, so that whoever has one, is seen to have several"; and Augustine says (*De Trin.* vi, 4)[5] that "the virtues that reside in the human mind are quite inseparable from one another"; and Gregory says (*Moral.* xxii, 1)[6] that "one virtue without the other is either of no account whatever, or very imperfect"; and Cicero says (*Quæst. Tusc.* ii, 14).[7] "If you confess to not having one particular virtue, it must be that you have none at all."

I answer that, Moral virtue may be considered either as perfect or as imperfect. An imperfect moral virtue, temperance for instance, or fortitude, is nothing but an inclination in us to do some kind of good deed, whether such inclination be in us by nature or by habituation. If we take the moral virtues in this way, they are not connected, since we find men who, by natural temperament or by being so accustomed, are prompt in doing deeds of liberality, but are not prompt in doing deeds of chastity.

But the perfect moral virtue is a habit that inclines us to do a good deed well; and if we take moral virtues in this way, we must say that they are connected, as nearly all are agreed in saying. For this two reasons are given, corresponding to the different ways of assigning the distinction of the cardinal virtues. For, as we stated above (Q. LXI, AA. 3, 4), some distinguish them according to certain general properties of the virtues; for instance, by saying that discretion belongs to prudence, rectitude to justice, moderation to temperance and strength of mind to fortitude, in whatever matter we consider these properties. In this way the reason for the connection is evident, for strength of mind is not commended as

---

[1] Aristotle, II, 1 (1103ª31).
[2] *Ethics,* IV, 2 (1122ᵇ26).   [3] *Ibid.* (1123ᵇ5).

[4] Bk. v (PL 15, 1738).
[5] PL 42, 927.   [6] PL 76, 212.
[7] DD III, 661; cf. Jerome, *Epist.,* LXVI (PL 22, 640).

virtuous if it be without moderation or rectitude or discretion; and so forth. This, too, is the reason assigned for the connection by Gregory, who says (*Moral.* xxii, 1)[1] that "a virtue cannot be perfect as a virtue, if isolated from the others; for there can be no true prudence without temperance, justice and fortitude"; and he continues to speak in like manner of the other virtues. Augustine also gives the same reason (*De Trin.* vi, 4).[2]

Others, however differentiate these virtues in respect of their matters,[3] and it is in this way that Aristotle assigns the reason for their connection.[4] Because, as stated above (Q. LVIII, A. 4), no moral virtue can be without prudence, for the reason that it is proper to moral virtue to make a right choice, since it is an elective habit. Now right choice requires not only the inclination to a due end, which inclination is the direct outcome of moral virtue, but also the right choice of means, which choice is made by prudence, that counsels, judges, and commands in those things that are directed to the end. In like manner one cannot have prudence unless one has the moral virtues, since prudence is right reason about things to be done, and the starting-point of reason is the end of the thing to be done, to which end man is rightly disposed by moral virtue. Hence, just as we cannot have speculative science unless we have the understanding of the principles, so neither can we have prudence without the moral virtues. And from this it follows clearly that the moral virtues are connected with one another.

Reply Obj. 1. Some moral virtues perfect man as regards his general state, in other words, with regard to those things which have to be done in every kind of human life. Hence man needs to exercise himself at the same time in the matters of all moral virtues. And if he exercise himself by good deeds in all such matters, he will acquire the habits of all the moral virtues. But if he exercise himself by good deeds in regard to one matter but not in regard to another, for instance, by behaving well in matters of anger, but not in matters of concupiscence, he will indeed acquire a certain habit of restraining his anger; but this habit will lack the nature of virtue, through the absence of prudence, which is wanting in matters of concupiscence. In the same way, natural inclinations fail to have the complete character of virtue if prudence is lacking.

But there are some moral virtues which perfect man with regard to some eminent state, such as magnificence and magnanimity; and since it does not happen to all in common to be exercised in the matter of such virtues, it is possible for a man to have the other moral virtues without actually having the habits of these virtues, speaking in the sense of acquired virtue. Nevertheless, when once a man has acquired those other virtues he possesses these in proximate potency. Because when, by practice, a man has acquired liberality in small gifts and expenditure, if he were to come in for a large sum of money, he would acquire the habit of magnificence with but little practice; even as a geometrician, by dint of little study, acquires scientific knowledge about some conclusion which had never been presented to his mind before. Now we speak of having a thing when we can easily acquire it, according to the saying of the Philosopher:[5] "That which is scarcely lacking is as though it were not lacking at all."

This suffices for the *Reply to the Second Objection.*

Reply Obj. 3. The intellectual virtues are about different matters having no relation to one another, as is clearly the case with the various sciences and arts. Hence we do not observe in them the connection that is to be found among the moral virtues, which are about passions and operations, which are clearly related to one another. For all the passions have their rise in certain primary passions, namely, love and hatred, and terminate in certain others, namely, pleasure and sorrow. In like manner all the operations that are the matter of moral virtue are related to one another, and also to the passions. Hence the whole matter of moral virtues falls under the one rule of prudence.

Nevertheless, all intelligibles are related to first principles. And in this way, all the intellectual virtues depend on the understanding of principles; even as prudence depends on the moral virtues, as we have said. On the other hand, the universal principles which are the object of the understanding of principles do not depend on the conclusions, which are the objects of the other intellectual virtues, as the moral virtues do depend on prudence, from the fact that the appetite, in a fashion, moves the reason, and the reason the appetite, as stated above (Q. IX, A. 1; Q. LVIII, A. 5, Reply 1).

Reply Obj. 4. Those things to which the moral virtues incline are as the principles of prudence; the products of art however are not the principles, but the matter of art. Now it is evident that, though reason may be right in one

---

[1] PL 76, 212.   [2] PL 42, 927.
[3] Cf. above, Q. LXI, A. 4.   [4] *Ethics,* VI, 13 (1144^{b}36).

[5] *Physics,* II, 5 (197^{a}29).

part of the matter, and not in another, yet in no way can it be called right reason if it be deficient in any principle whatever. Thus, if a man be wrong about the principle, A whole is greater than its part, he cannot acquire the science of geometry, because he must necessarily wander far from the truth in his conclusion.—Moreover, things *done* are related to one another, but not things *made*, as stated above (Reply 3). Consequently the lack of prudence in one part of things to be done would result in a deficiency affecting other things to be done, which does not occur in things to be made.

ARTICLE 2. *Whether Moral Virtues Can Be Without Charity?*

We proceed thus to the Second Article: It would seem that moral virtue can be without charity.

Objection 1. For it is stated in the *Liber Sentent. Prosperi*, vii,[1] that "every virtue save charity may be common to the good and bad." But "charity can be in none except the good," as stated in the same book. Therefore the other virtues can be had without charity.

Obj. 2. Further, moral virtues can be acquired by means of human acts, as stated in the *Ethics*,[2] while charity cannot be had otherwise than by infusion, according to Rom. 5. 5: *The charity of God is poured forth in our hearts by the Holy Ghost Who is given to us.* Therefore it is possible to have the other virtues without charity.

Obj. 3. Further, the moral virtues are connected together, in so far as they depend on prudence. But charity does not depend on prudence; indeed, it surpasses prudence, according to Eph. 3. 19: *The charity of Christ, which surpasseth all knowledge.* Therefore the moral virtues are not connected with charity, and can be without it.

On the contrary, It is written (I John 3. 14): *He that loveth not, abideth in death.* Now the spiritual life is perfected by the virtues, since it is by them that we lead a good life, as Augustine states (*De Lib. Arb.* ii, 19).[3] Therefore they cannot be without the love of charity.

I answer that, As stated above (Q. LXIII, A. 2), it is possible by means of human works to acquire moral virtues, in so far as they produce good works that are directed to an end not surpassing the natural power of man; and when they are acquired thus, they can be without charity, even as they were in many of the Gen-

tiles.—But in so far as they produce good works in relation to a supernatural last end, thus they have the character of virtue, truly and perfectly, and cannot be acquired by human acts, but are infused by God. Such moral virtues cannot be without charity. For it has been stated above (A. 1; Q. LVIII, AA. 4, 5) that the other moral virtues cannot be without prudence, and that prudence cannot be without the moral virtues, because these latter make man well disposed to certain ends, from which the notion of prudence arises. Now for the right notion of prudence, it is much more necessary that man be well disposed towards his ultimate end, which is the effect of charity, than that he be well disposed in respect of other ends, which is the effect of moral virtue; just as in speculative matters right reason has greatest need of the first indemonstrable principle, that contradictories cannot both be true at the same time. It is therefore evident that neither can infused prudence be without charity; nor, consequently, the other moral virtues, since they cannot be without prudence.

It is therefore clear from what has been said that only the infused virtues are perfect, and deserve to be called virtues absolutely, since they direct man well to the ultimate end. But the other virtues, those, namely, that are acquired, are virtues in a restricted sense, but not absolutely; for they direct man well in respect of the last end in some particular genus of action, but not in respect of the last end absolutely. Hence a gloss of Augustine on the words, *All that is not of faith is sin* (Rom. 14. 23), says:[4] "He that fails to acknowledge the truth has no true virtue, even if his conduct be good."

Reply Obj. 1. Virtue, in the words quoted, denotes imperfect virtue. Otherwise, if we take moral virtue in its perfect state, it makes its possessor good, and consequently cannot be in the wicked.

Reply Obj. 2. This argument holds good of virtue in the sense of acquired virtue.

Reply Obj. 3. Though charity surpasses science and prudence, yet prudence depends on charity, as we have said; and consequently so do all the infused moral virtues.

ARTICLE 3. *Whether Charity Can Be Without Moral Virtue?*

We proceed thus to the Third Article: It would seem possible to have charity without the moral virtues.

---

[1] Prosper of Aquitaine (PL 51, 428).
[2] Aristotle, II, 1 (1103ª31).
[3] PL 32, 1268; cf. above, Q. LV, A. 4, obj. 1.

[4] *Glossa ordin.* (VI, 30B); *Glossa* Lombard I (PL 191, 1520); cf. Prosper of Aquitaine, *Sent.*, Sent. 106 (PL 51, 441).

Objection 1. For when one thing suffices for a certain purpose, it is superfluous to employ others. Now charity alone suffices for the fulfilment of all the works of virtue, as is clear from I Cor. 13. 4, *sqq.*: *Charity is patient, is kind*, etc. Therefore it seems that if one has charity, other virtues are superfluous.

Obj. 2. Further, he that has a habit of virtue easily performs the works of that virtue, and those works are pleasing to him for their own sake; hence "pleasure taken in a work is a sign of habit."[1] Now many have charity, being free from mortal sin, and yet they find it difficult to do works of virtue; nor are these works pleasing to them for their own sake, but only for the sake of charity. Therefore many have charity without the other virtues.

Obj. 3. Further, charity is to be found in every saint, and yet there are some saints who are without certain virtues. For Bede says[2] (on Luke 17. 10) that the saints are more humbled on account of their not having certain virtues than rejoiced at the virtues they have. Therefore, if a man has charity, it does not follow of necessity that he has all the moral virtues.

On the contrary, The whole Law is fulfilled through charity, for it is written (Rom. 8. 8): *He that loveth his neighbour, hath fulfilled the Law*. Now it is not possible to fulfil the whole Law without having all the moral virtues, since the law contains precepts about all acts of virtue, as stated in the *Ethics*.[3] Therefore he that has charity has all the moral virtues. Moreover, Augustine says in a letter (*Epist.* clxvii),[4] that charity contains all the cardinal virtues.

I answer that, All the moral virtues are infused together with charity. The reason for this is that God operates no less perfectly in works of grace than in works of nature. Now, in the works of nature, we find that whenever a thing contains a principle of certain works, it has also whatever is necessary for their execution; thus animals are provided with organs by which they are able to perform the actions that their souls enable them to do. Now it is evident that charity, since it directs man to his last end, is the principle of all the good works that are referrible to his last end. Therefore all the moral virtues must be infused together with charity, since it is through them that man performs each different kind of good work.

It is therefore clear that the infused moral virtues are joined not only through prudence,

but also on account of charity; and, again, that whoever loses charity through mortal sin, forfeits all the infused moral virtues.

Reply Obj. 1. In order that the act of a lower power be perfect, not only must there be perfection in the higher, but also in the lower power; for if the principal agent were well disposed, perfect action would not follow if the instrument also were not well disposed. Consequently, in order that man work well in things referred to the end, he needs not only a virtue disposing him well to the end, but also those virtues which dispose him well to whatever is a means to the end. For the virtue which regards the end is the chief and moving principle in respect of the means to the end. Therefore it is necessary to have the moral virtues together with charity.

Reply Obj. 2. It happens sometimes that a man who has a habit finds it difficult to act in accordance with the habit, and consequently feels no pleasure and satisfaction in the act, on account of some impediment supervening from without; thus a man who has a habit of science finds it difficult to understand through being sleepy or unwell. In like manner sometimes the habits of infused moral virtue experience difficulty in their works by reason of certain contrary dispositions remaining from previous acts. This difficulty does not occur in respect of acquired moral virtue, because the repeated acts by which they are acquired remove also the contrary dispositions.

Reply Obj. 3. Certain saints are said not to have certain virtues in so far as they experience difficulty in the acts of those virtues, for the reason already stated (Reply 2), although they have the habits of all the virtues.

ARTICLE 4. *Whether Faith and Hope Can Be Without Charity?*

We proceed thus to the Fourth Article: It would seem that faith and hope are never without charity.

Objection 1. Because, since they are theological virtues, they seem to be more excellent than even the infused moral virtues. But the infused moral virtues cannot be without charity. Neither therefore can faith and hope be without charity.

Obj. 2. Further, "no man believes unwillingly" as Augustine says (*Tract.* xxvi *in Joann.*).[5] But charity is in the will as a perfection of the will, as stated above (Q. LXII, A. 3). Therefore faith cannot be without charity.

Obj. 3. Further, Augustine says (*Enchiridion*, viii)[6] that "there can be no hope without love."

---

[1] Aristotle, *Ethics*, II, 3 (1104ᵇ3).
[2] PL 92, 541.   [3] Aristotle, V, 1 (1129ᵇ23).
[4] PL 33, 738; cf. *De Mor. Eccl.*, I, 15 (PL 32, 1322).
[5] PL 35, 1607.   [6] PL 40, 235.

But love is charity, for it is of this love that he speaks. Therefore hope cannot be without charity.

On the contrary, A gloss on Matt. I. 2 says[1] that faith begets hope, and hope, charity. Now the begetter precedes the begotten, and can be without it. Therefore faith can be without hope; and hope, without charity.

I answer that, Faith and hope, like the moral virtues, can be considered in two ways; first according to a certain beginning; secondly, as complete virtues. For since virtue is directed to the doing of good works, perfect virtue is that which gives the power of doing a perfectly good work, and this consists in not only doing what is good, but also in doing it well. Otherwise, if what is done is good, but not well done, it will not be perfectly good; therefore neither will the habit that is the principle of such an act have the perfect character of virtue. For instance, if a man do what is just, what he does is good; but it will not be the work of a perfect virtue unless he do it well, that is, by choosing rightly, which is the result of prudence; for which reason justice cannot be a perfect virtue without prudence.

Accordingly faith and hope can exist indeed in a fashion without charity; but they have not the perfect character of virtue without charity. For, since the act of faith is to believe in God, and since to believe is to assent to someone of one's own will, to will not as one ought, will not be a perfect act of faith. To will as one ought is the outcome of charity which perfects the will; for every right movement of the will proceeds from a right love, as Augustine says.[2] Hence faith may be without charity, but not as a perfect virtue; just as temperance and fortitude can be without prudence. The same applies to hope. For the act of hope consists in looking to God for future Happiness. This act is perfect if it is based on the merits which we have, and this cannot be without charity. But to expect future Happiness through merits which one has not yet, but which one proposes to acquire at some future time, will be an imperfect act; and this is possible without charity. Consequently, faith and hope can be without charity; yet, without charity, they are not virtues properly so-called, because the nature of virtue requires that by it, we should not only do what is good, but also that we should do it well.[3]

Reply Obj. I. Moral virtue depends on prudence, and not even infused prudence has the character of prudence without charity; for this involves the absence of due order to the first principle, namely, the ultimate end. On the other hand faith and hope, as such, do not depend either on prudence or charity, so that they can be without charity, although they are not virtues without charity, as stated.

Reply Obj. 2. This argument is true of faith considered as perfect virtue.

Reply Obj. 3. Augustine is speaking here of that hope by which we look to gain future Happiness through merits which we have already; and this is not without charity.

ARTICLE 5. *Whether Charity Can Be Without Faith and Hope?*

We proceed thus to the Fifth Article: It would seem that charity can be without faith and hope.

Objection I. For charity is the love of God. But it is possible for us to love God naturally, without already having faith, or the hope of future Happiness. Therefore charity can be without faith and hope.

Obj. 2. Further, charity is the root of all the virtues, according to Ephes. 3. 17: *Rooted and founded in charity.* Now the root is sometimes without branches. Therefore charity can sometimes be without faith and hope, and the other virtues.

Obj. 3. Further, there was perfect charity in Christ. And yet He had neither faith nor hope, because He was a perfect comprehensor, as we shall explain further on (Part III, Q. VII, AA. 3, 4). Therefore charity can be without faith and hope.

On the contrary, The Apostle says (Heb. 11. 6): *Without faith it is impossible to please God;* and this evidently belongs most to charity, according to Prov. 8. 17: *I love them that love me.* Again, it is by hope that we are brought to charity, as stated above (Q. LXII, A. 4). Therefore it is not possible to have charity without faith and hope.

I answer that, Charity signifies not only the love of God but also a certain friendship with Him; and this implies, besides love, a certain mutual return of love, together with mutual communion, as stated in the *Ethics.*[4] That this belongs to charity is evident from I John 4. 16: *He that abideth in charity, abideth in God, and God in him,* and from I Cor. 1. 9, where it is written: *God is faithful, by Whom you are called unto the fellowship of His Son.* Now this fellowship of man with God, which consists in

---

[1] *Glossa interl.* (v, 5r).
[2] *City of God,* XIV, 9 (PL 41, 413).
[3] Aristotle, *Ethics,* II, 6 (1106ª23).
[4] Aristotle, VIII, 2, 12 (1155ᵇ28; 1161ᵇ11).

a certain familiar intercourse with Him, is begun here, in this life, by grace, but will be perfected in the future life, by glory; each of which things we hold by faith and hope. Therefore just as friendship with a person would be impossible if one disbelieved in, or despaired of, the possibility of his fellowship or familiar intercourse, so too, friendship with God, which is charity, is impossible without faith, so as to believe in this fellowship and intercourse with God, and to hope to attain to this fellowship. Therefore charity is altogether impossible without faith and hope.

Reply Obj. 1. Charity is not any kind of love of God, but that love of God by which He is loved as the object of Happiness to which object we are directed by faith and hope.

Reply Obj. 2. Charity is the root of faith and hope in so far as it gives them the perfection of virtue. But faith and hope as such are presupposed to charity, as stated above (Q. LXII, A. 4), and so charity is impossible without them.

Reply Obj. 3. In Christ there was neither faith nor hope, on account of their implying an imperfection. But instead of faith, He had manifest vision, and instead of hope, full comprehension, so that in Him was perfect charity.

QUESTION LXVI
Of equality among the virtues
(*In Six Articles*)

We must now consider equality among the virtues, under which head there are six points of inquiry: (1) Whether one virtue can be greater or less than another? (2) Whether all the virtues existing together in one subject are equal? (3) Of moral virtue in comparison with intellectual virtue. (4) Of the moral virtues as compared with one another. (5) Of the intellectual virtues in comparison with one another. (6) Of the theological virtues in comparison with one another.

Article 1. *Whether One Virtue Can Be Greater or Less than Another?*

We proceed thus to the First Article: It would seem that one virtue cannot be greater or less than another.

Objection 1. For it is written (Apoc. 21. 16) that the sides of the city of Jerusalem are equal; and a gloss says that the sides denote the virtues.[1] Therefore all virtues are equal; and consequently one cannot be greater than another.

Obj. 2. Further, a thing that by its nature con-

[1] *Glossa ordin.* (VI, 272E).

sists in a maximum cannot be more or less. Now the nature of virtue consists in a maximum, for virtue is "the limit of power" as the Philosopher states;[2] and Augustine says (*De Lib. Arb.* ii, 18)[3] that "virtues are very great goods, and no one can use them to evil purpose." Therefore it seems that one virtue cannot be greater or less than another.

Obj. 3. Further, the quantity of an effect is measured by the power of the agent. But perfect, that is infused virtues, are from God Whose power is uniform and infinite. Therefore it seems that one virtue cannot be greater than another.

On the contrary, Wherever there can be increase and greater abundance, there can be inequality. Now virtues admit of greater abundance and increase, for it is written (Matt. 5. 20): *Unless your justice abound more than that of the Scribes and Pharisees, you shall not enter into the kingdom of heaven;* and (Prov. 15. 5): *In abundant justice there is the greatest strength* (*virtus*). Therefore it seems that a virtue can be greater or less than another.

I answer that, When it is asked whether one virtue can be greater than another, the question can be taken in two senses. First, as applying to virtues of different species. In this sense it is clear that one virtue is greater than another. For a cause is always more excellent than its effect, and among effects those nearest to the cause are the most excellent. Now it is clear from what has been said (Q. XVIII, A. 5; Q. LXI, A. 2) that the cause and root of human good is the reason. Hence prudence which perfects the reason, surpasses in goodness the other moral virtues which perfect the appetitive power, in so far as it partakes of reason. And among these, one is better than another according as it approaches nearer to the reason. Consequently justice, which is in the will, excels the remaining moral virtues; and fortitude, which is in the irascible part, stands before temperance, which is in the concupiscible, which has a smaller share of reason, as stated in the *Ethics.*[4]

The question can be taken in another way, as referring to virtues of the same species. In this way, according to what was said above (Q. LII, A. 1) when we were treating of the intensity of habits, virtue may be said to be greater or less in two ways: first, in itself; secondly with regard to the subject that participates in it. If we

[2] *Heavens,* I, 11 (281ª11); cf. Thomas, *In De Cælo,* I, 25.

[3] PL 32, 1267.

[4] Aristotle, VII, 6 (1149ᵇ1).

consider it in itself, we shall call it great or little according to the things to which it extends. Now whoever has a virtue, for example, temperance, has it in respect of all the things to which temperance extends. But this does not apply to science and art, for every grammarian does not know everything relating to grammar. And in this sense the Stoics said rightly, as Simplicius states in his *Commentary on the Predicaments*,[1] that virtue cannot be more or less, as science and art can; because the nature of virtue consists in a maximum.

If, however, we consider virtue on the part of the subject, it may then be greater or less, either in relation to different times, or in different men. Because one man is better disposed than another to attain to the mean of virtue which is conformed to right reason; and this, on account of either greater habituation, or a better natural disposition, or a more discerning judgment of reason, or again a greater gift of grace, which is given to each one *according to the measure of the giving of Christ*, as stated in Ephes. 4. 9. And here the Stoics erred,[2] for they held that no man should be called virtuous, unless he were, in the highest degree, disposed to virtue. Because the nature of virtue does not require that man should reach the mean of right reason as though it were an indivisible point, as the Stoics thought, but it is enough that he should approach the mean, as stated in the *Ethics*.[3] Moreover, one identical indivisible mark is reached more nearly and more readily by one than by another, as may be seen when several archers aim at a fixed target.

Reply Obj. 1. This equality is not one of absolute quantity, but of proportion, because all virtues grow in a man proportionately, as we shall see further on (A. 2).

Reply Obj. 2. This "limit" which belongs to virtue, can have the character of something more or less good, in the ways explained above, since, as we have said, it is not an indivisible limit.

Reply Obj. 3. God does not work by necessity of nature, but according to the order of His wisdom, by which He bestows on men various measures of virtue, according to Ephes. 4. 7: *To every one of you* (Vulg., *us*) *is given grace according to the measure of the giving of Christ.*

ARTICLE 2. *Whether All the Virtues That Are Together in One Man, Are Equal?*

We proceed thus to the Second Article: It would seem that the virtues in one and the same man are not all equally intense.

Objection 1. For the Apostle says (I Cor. 7. 7): *Everyone hath his proper gift from God; one after this manner, and another after that.* Now one gift would not be more proper than another to a man if God infused all the virtues equally into each man. Therefore it seems that the virtues are not all equal in one and the same man.

Obj. 2. Further, if all the virtues were equally intense in one and the same man, it would follow that whoever surpasses another in one virtue would surpass him in all the others. But this is clearly not the case, since various saints are specially praised for different virtues; for example, Abraham for faith (Rom. 4), Moses for his meekness (Num. 7. 3), Job for his patience (Tob. 2. 12). This is why of each Confessor the Church sings:[4] *There was not found his like in keeping the law of the most High*, since each one was remarkable for some virtue or other. Therefore the virtues are not all equal in one and the same man.

Obj. 3. Further, the more intense a habit is, the greater one's pleasure and readiness in making use of it. Now experience shows that a man is more pleased and ready to make use of one virtue than of another. Therefore the virtues are not all equal in one and the same man.

On the contrary, Augustine says (*De Trin.* vi, 4)[5] that "those who are equal in fortitude are equal in prudence and temperance," and so on. Now it would not be so, unless all the virtues in one man were equal. Therefore all virtues are equal in one man.

I answer that, As explained above (A. 1), the greatness of virtues can be understood in two ways. First, as referring to their specific nature. And in this way there is no doubt that in a man one virtue is greater than another, for example, charity, than faith and hope. Secondly, it may be taken as referring to the degree of participation by the subject, according as a virtue becomes intense or slackened in its subject. In this sense all the virtues in one man are equal with an equality of proportion, in so far as their growth in man is equal; thus the fingers are un-

[1] *In Cat.* VII (CG VIII, 284.32; 237.28).
[2] Cf. Augustine, *Epist.* CLXVII, Chap. 3 (PL 33, 738); Cicero, *De Finibus*, III, 9 (DD III, 549).
[3] Aristotle, II, 9 (1109ᵇ18).
[4] See the Epistle in the Mass *Statuit* (Dominican Missal); cf. Eccl. 44.20.
[5] PL 42, 927.

equal in size, but equal in proportion, since they grow in proportion to one another.

Now the nature of this equality is to be explained in the same way as the connection of virtues; for equality among virtues is their connection as to greatness. Now it has been stated above (Q. LXV, A. 1) that a twofold connection of virtues may be assigned. The first is according to the opinion of those who understood these four virtues to be four general properties of virtues, each of which is found together with the other in any matter.[1] In this way virtues cannot be said to be equal in any matter unless they have all these properties equal. Augustine alludes to this kind of equality (*De Trin.* vi, 4)[2] when he says: "If you say these men are equal in fortitude, but that one is more prudent than the other, it follows that the fortitude of the latter is less prudent. Consequently they are not really equal in fortitude, since the former's fortitude is more prudent. You will find that this applies to the other virtues if you run over them all in the same way."

The other kind of connection among virtues followed the opinion of those who hold these virtues to have their own proper respective matters (Q. LXV, AA. 1, 2).[3] In this way the connection among moral virtues results from prudence, and, as to the infused virtues, from charity, and not from the inclination, which is on the part of the subject, as stated above (Q. LXV, A. 1). Accordingly the nature of the equality among virtues can also be considered on the part of prudence, in regard to that which is formal in all the moral virtues; for in one and the same man, so long as his reason has the same degree of perfection, the mean must be proportionately defined according to right reason in each matter of virtue.

But in regard to that which is material in the moral virtues, namely the inclination itself to the virtuous act, one may be readier to perform the act of one virtue than the act of another virtue, and this either from nature, or from habituation, or again by the grace of God.

Reply Obj. 1. This saying of the Apostle may be taken to refer to the gifts of gratuitous grace, which are not common to all, nor are all of them equal in one and the same subject. We might also say that it refers to the measure of sanctifying grace, by reason of which one man has all the virtues in greater abundance than another man, on account of his greater abundance of prudence, or also of charity, in which all the infused virtues are connected.

Reply Obj. 2. One saint is praised chiefly for one virtue, another saint for another virtue, on account of his more excellent readiness for the act of one virtue than for the act of another virtue.

This suffices for the *Reply to the Third Objection.*

ARTICLE. 3. *Whether the Moral Virtues Are Better than the Intellectual Virtues?*

We proceed thus to the Third Article: It would seem that the moral virtues are better than the intellectual.

Objection 1. Because that which is more necessary and more lasting is better. Now the moral virtues are more lasting even than the sciences,[4] which are intellectual virtues; and, moreover, they are more necessary for human life. Therefore they are preferable to the intellectual virtues.

Obj. 2. Further, virtue is defined as that which makes its possessor good. Now man is said to be good in respect of moral virtue, and not in respect of intellectual virtue, except perhaps in respect of prudence alone. Therefore moral is better than intellectual virtue.

Obj. 3. Further, the end is more excellent than the means. But according to the *Ethics,*[5] "moral virtue gives right intention of the end; prudence however gives right choice of the means." Therefore moral virtue is more excellent than prudence, which is the intellectual virtue that regards moral matters.

On the contrary, Moral virtue is in that part of the soul which is rational by participation, while intellectual virtue is in the essentially rational part, as stated in the *Ethics.*[6] Now rational by essence is more excellent than rational by participation. Therefore intellectual virtue is better than moral virtue.

I answer that, A thing may be said to be greater or less in two ways: first, absolutely; secondly, relatively. For nothing hinders something from being better absolutely, for example to philosophize rather than to gain riches, and yet not better relatively, that is, for one who is in want.[7] Now to consider a thing absolutely is to consider it in its proper specific nature. Ac-

---

[1] Cf. above, Q. LXI, A. 4.

[2] PL 42, 927.

[3] Cf. above, Q. LXI, A. 4.

[4] Aristotle, *Ethics*, I, 10 (1100[b]14).

[5] Aristotle, VI, 12 (1144[a]8).

[6] Aristotle, I, 13 (1103[a]1).

[7] Cf. Aristotle, *Topics*, III, 2 (118[a]10).

cordingly, a virtue takes its species from its object, as explained above (Q. LIV, A. 2; Q. LX, A. 1). Hence, speaking absolutely, that virtue is more excellent which has the more excellent object. Now it is evident that the object of the reason is more excellent than the object of the appetite, since the reason apprehends things in the universal, while the appetite tends to things themselves, whose being is restricted to the particular. Consequently, speaking absolutely, the intellectual virtues, which perfect the reason, are more excellent than the moral virtues, which perfect the appetite.

But if we consider virtue in its relation to act, then moral virtue, which perfects the appetite, whose function it is to move the other powers to act, as stated above (Q. IX, A. 1), is more excellent. And since virtue is called so from its being a principle of action, for it is the perfection of a power, it follows again that the nature of virtue agrees more with moral than with intellectual virtue, though the intellectual virtues are more excellent habits, absolutely speaking.

Reply Obj. 1. The moral virtues are more lasting than the intellectual virtues because they are practised in matters pertaining to life in general. Yet it is evident that the objects of the sciences, which are necessary and invariable, are more lasting than the objects of moral virtue, which are certain particular matters of action. That the moral virtues are more necessary for human life proves that they are more excellent, not absolutely, but relatively. Indeed, the speculative intellectual virtues, from the very fact that they are not referred to something else, as a useful thing is referred to an end, are more excellent. The reason for this is that in them we have a kind of beginning of that happiness which consists in the knowledge of truth, as stated above (Q. III, A. 6).

Reply Obj. 2. The reason why man is said to be good absolutely in respect of moral virtue, but not in respect of intellectual virtue, is because the appetite moves the other powers to their acts, as stated above (Q. LVI, A. 3). Therefore this argument, too, proves merely that moral virtue is better relatively.

Reply Obj. 3. Prudence directs the moral virtues not only in the choice of the means, but also in appointing the end. Now the end of each moral virtue is to attain the mean in the matter proper to that virtue, which mean is appointed according to the right reason of prudence, as stated in the *Ethics*.[1]

[1] Aristotle, II, 6 (1107ª1); VI, 13 (1144ᵇ21).

ARTICLE 4. *Whether Justice Is the Chief of the Moral Virtues?*

We proceed thus to the Fourth Article: It would seem that justice is not the chief of the moral virtues.

Objection 1. For it is better to give of one's own than to pay what is due. Now the former belongs to liberality, the latter to justice. Therefore liberality is apparently a greater virtue than justice.

Obj. 2. Further, the chief quality in a thing is, it seems, that in which it is most perfect. Now, according to James 1. 4, *Patience hath a perfect work.* Therefore it would seem that patience is greater than justice.

Obj. 3. Further, "Magnanimity has a great influence on every virtue," as stated in the *Ethics*.[2] Therefore it magnifies even justice Therefore it is greater than justice.

On the contrary, The Philosopher says[3] that "justice is the most excellent of the virtues."

I answer that, A virtue considered in its species may be greater or less, either absolutely or relatively. That virtue is said to be greater absolutely in which a greater good of reason shines forth, as stated above (A. 1). In this way justice is the most excellent of all the moral virtues, as being most akin to reason. This is clear both from its subject and its object: its subject, because this is the will, and the will is the rational appetite, as stated above (Q. VIII, A. 1; Q. XXVI, A. 1); its object or matter, because it is about operations, by which man is set in order not only in himself but also in regard to another. Hence "justice is the most excellent of virtues." Among the other moral virtues, which are about the passions, the more excellent the matter in which the appetitive movement is subjected to reason, so much the more does the good of reason shine forth in each. Now in things touching man, the chief of all is life, on which all other things depend. Consequently fortitude which subjects the appetitive movement to reason in matters of life and death, holds the first place among those moral virtues that are about the passions, but is subordinate to justice. Hence the Philosopher says[4] that "those virtues must necessarily be greatest which receive the most praise, since virtue is a power of doing good. Hence the brave man and the just man are honoured more than others; because the former, (that is, fortitude), is useful in war, and the latter, (that is,

[2] Aristotle, IV, 3 (1123ᵇ30).
[3] *Ibid.*, V, 1 (1129ᵇ27).
[4] *Rhetoric*, I, 9 (1366ᵇ3).

justice), both in war and in peace."—After fortitude comes temperance, which subjects the appetite to reason in matters directly relating to life, either in his numerical identity or in his specific identity, namely, in matters of food and of sex.—And so these three virtues, together with prudence, are called principal virtues in excellence also.

A virtue is said to be greater relatively by reason of its helping or adorning a principal virtue, even as substance is more excellent absolutely than accident; and yet relatively some particular accident is more excellent than substance in so far as it perfects substance in some accidental mode of being.

Reply Obj. 1. The act of liberality needs to be founded on an act of justice, for "a man is not liberal in giving unless he gives of his own."[1] Hence there could be no liberality apart from justice, which discerns between what is mine and what is not mine. Justice however can be without liberality. Hence justice is greater absolutely than liberality, as being more universal, and as being its foundation while liberality is greater relatively since it is an ornament and an addition to justice.

Reply Obj. 2. Patience is said to have *a perfect work*, by enduring evils, where it excludes not only unjust revenge, which is also excluded by justice; not only hatred, which is also suppressed by charity; nor only anger, which is calmed by gentleness; but also inordinate sorrow, which is the root of all the above. Therefore it is more perfect and excellent through plucking up the root in this matter. It is not, however, more perfect than all the other virtues absolutely. Because fortitude not only endures trouble without being disturbed, but also fights against it if necessary. Hence whoever is brave is patient, but the converse does not hold; for patience is a part of fortitude.

Reply Obj. 3. There can be no magnanimity without the other virtues, as stated in the *Ethics*.[2] Hence it is compared to them as their ornament, so that relatively it is greater than all the others, but not absolutely.

ARTICLE 5. *Whether Wisdom Is the Greatest of the Intellectual Virtues?*

We proceed thus to the Fifth Article: It would seem that wisdom is not the greatest of the intellectual virtues.

Objection 1. Because the commander is greater than the one commanded. Now prudence seems to command wisdom, for it is stated in the *Ethics*[3] that political science, which belongs to prudence,[4] "orders that sciences should be cultivated in states, and to which of these each individual should devote himself, and to what extent." Since, then, wisdom is one of the sciences, it seems that prudence is greater than wisdom.

Obj. 2. Further, it belongs to the nature of virtue to direct man to happiness, because virtue is "the disposition of a perfect thing to that which is best," as stated in the *Physics*.[5] Now prudence is right reason about things to be done, by which man is brought to happiness; but wisdom does not consider human acts by which man attains happiness. Therefore prudence is a greater virtue than wisdom.

Obj. 3. Further, the more perfect knowledge is, the greater it seems to be. Now we can have more perfect knowledge of human affairs, which are the subject of science, than of Divine things, which are the object of wisdom, which is the distinction given by Augustine (*De Trin.* xii, 14),[6] because Divine things are incomprehensible, according to Job 26. 26: *Behold God is great, exceeding our knowledge.* Therefore science is a greater virtue than wisdom.

Obj. 4. Further, knowledge of principles is more excellent than knowledge of conclusions. But wisdom draws conclusions from indemonstrable principles which are the object of the virtue of understanding, even as other sciences do. Therefore understanding is a greater virtue than wisdom.

On the contrary, The Philosopher says[7] that "wisdom is the head among the intellectual virtues."

I answer that, As stated above (A. 3), the greatness of a virtue, as to its species, is taken from its object. Now the object of wisdom surpasses the objects of all the intellectual virtues because wisdom considers the Supreme Cause, which is God, as stated at the beginning of the *Metaphysics*.[8] And since it is by the cause that we judge of an effect, and by the higher cause that we judge of the lower effects, hence it is that wisdom exercises judgment over all the other intellectual virtues, orders them all, and is as it were the architect of them all.

Reply Obj. 1. Since prudence is about human affairs, and wisdom about the Supreme Cause, it is impossible for prudence to be a greater

---

[1] *Politics*, II, 5 (1263[b]13).
[2] Aristotle, IV, 3 (1124[a]2).
[3] Aristotle, I, 2 (1094[a]28).
[4] *Ibid.*, VI, 8 (1141[a]20).
[5] Aristotle, VII, 3 (246[a]13).
[6] PL 42, 1009.
[7] *Ethics*, VI, 7 (1141[a]19).
[8] Aristotle, I, 2 (982[b]9; 983[a]7).

virtue than wisdom, unless, as stated in the *Ethics*,[1] "man were the greatest thing in the world." Therefore we must say, as stated in the same book,[2] that "prudence does not command wisdom," but vice versa, because *the spiritual man judgeth all things; and he himself is judged of no man* (I Cor. 2. 15). For prudence has no business with supreme matters which are the object of wisdom, but its command covers things ordered to wisdom, namely, how men are to obtain wisdom. Therefore prudence, or political science, is, in this way, the servant of wisdom, for it leads to wisdom, preparing the way for her, as the porter for the king.

Reply Obj. 2. Prudence considers the means of acquiring happiness, but wisdom considers the very object of happiness, namely, the Supreme Intelligible. And if indeed the consideration of wisdom were perfect in respect of its object, there would be perfect happines in the act of wisdom; but as, in this life, the act of wisdom is imperfect in respect of its principal object, which is God, it follows that the act of wisdom is a kind of beginning or participation of future happiness, so that wisdom is nearer than prudence to happiness.

Reply Obj. 3. As the Philosopher says,[3] "one knowledge is preferable to another, either because it is about a higher object, or because it is more certain." Hence if the subject be equally good and sublime, that virtue will be the greater which possesses more certain knowledge. But a virtue which is less certain about a higher and better object, is preferable to that which is more certain about an object of inferior degree. Hence the Philosopher says[4] that it is a great thing to be able to know something about celestial beings, though it be based on weak and probable reasoning; and again,[5] that it is better to know a little about sublime things, than much about mean things. Accordingly wisdom, to which knowledge about God pertains, is beyond the reach of man, especially in this life, so as to be his possession, for this belongs to God alone;[6] and yet this little knowledge about God which we can have through wisdom is preferable to all other knowledge.

Reply Obj. 4. The truth and knowledge of indemonstrable principles depends on the meaning of the terms, for as soon as we know what is a whole, and what is a part, we know at once that every whole is greater than its part. Now

to know the meaning of being and non-being, of whole and part, and of other things which follow on being, which are the terms of which indemonstrable principles are constituted, is the function of wisdom, because being in general is the proper effect of the Supreme Cause, which is God. And so wisdom makes use of indemonstrable principles which are the object of understanding, not only by drawing conclusions from them, as other sciences do, but also by passing its judgment on them, and by vindicating them against those who deny them. Hence it follows that wisdom is a greater virtue than understanding.

ARTICLE 6. *Whether Charity Is the Greatest of the Theological Virtues?*

We proceed thus to the Sixth Article: It would seem that charity is not the greatest of the theological virtues.

Objection 1. Because, since faith is in the intellect, while hope and charity are in the appetitive power, as we have said above (Q. LXII, A. 3), it seems that faith is compared to hope and charity as intellectual to moral virtue. Now intellectual virtue is greater than moral virtue, as was made evident above (A. 3). Therefore faith is greater than hope and charity.

Obj. 2. Further, when two things are added together, the result is greater than either one. Now hope results from something added to charity, for it presupposes love, as Augustine says (*Enchirid.* viii),[7] and it adds a certain movement of stretching forward to the beloved. Therefore hope is greater than charity.

Obj. 3. Further, a cause is more noble than its effect. Now faith and hope are the cause of charity; for a gloss on Matt. 1. 3 says[8] that faith begets hope, and hope charity. Therefore faith and hope are greater than charity.

On the contrary, The Apostle says (I Cor. 13. 13): *Now there remain faith, hope, charity, these three; but the greatest of these is charity.*

I answer that, As stated above (A. 3), the greatness of a virtue, as to its species, is taken from its object. Now, since the three theological virtues look at God as their proper object, it cannot be said that any one of them is greater than another by reason of its having a greater object, but only from the fact that it approaches nearer than another to that object. And in this way charity is greater than the others, because the others, in their very nature, imply a certain distance from the object; for faith is of

---

[1] Aristotle, VI, 7 (1141ª21).   [2] *Ibid.*, 13 (1145ª6).
[3] *Soul*, I, 1 (402ª2).   [4] *Heavens*, II, 12 (291ᵇ27).
[5] *Parts of Animals*, I, 5 (644ᵇ31).
[6] Aristotle, *Metaphysics*, I, 2 (982ᵇ28).

[7] PL 40, 235.   [8] *Glossa interl.* (V, 51).

what is not seen, and hope is of what is not possessed. But the love of charity is of that which is already possessed, since the beloved is, in a manner, in the lover, and, again, the lover is drawn by desire to union with the beloved; hence it is written (I John 4. 16): *He that abideth in charity, abideth in God, and God in him.*

Reply Obj. 1. Faith and hope are not related to charity in the same way as prudence to moral virtue, and for two reasons. First, because the theological virtues have an object surpassing the human soul, while prudence and the moral virtues are about things beneath man. Now in things that are above man, to love them is more excellent than to know them, because knowledge is perfected by the known being in the knower, while love is perfected by the lover being drawn to the beloved. Now that which is above man is more excellent in itself than in man, since a thing is in another according to the mode of that in which it is. But it is the other way about in things beneath man. Secondly, because prudence moderates the appetitive movements pertaining to the moral virtues, while faith does not moderate the appetitive movement tending to God, which movement belongs to the theological virtues, but only shows the object. And this appetitive movement towards its object surpasses human knowledge, according to Ephes. 3. 19: *The charity of Christ which surpasseth all knowledge.*

Reply Obj. 2. Hope presupposes love of that which a man hopes to obtain; and such love is love of concupiscence, by which he who desires good loves himself rather than something else. On the other hand, charity implies love of friendship, to which we are led by hope, as stated above (Q. LXII, A. 4).

Reply Obj. 3. An efficient cause is more noble than its effect, but not a disposing cause. For otherwise the heat of fire would be more noble than the soul, to which the heat disposes the matter. It is in this way that faith begets hope, and hope charity, in the sense, that is, that one is a disposition to the other.

QUESTION LXVII

OF THE DURATION OF VIRTUES AFTER THIS LIFE

(In Six Articles)

WE must now consider the duration of virtues after this life, under which head there are six points of inquiry: (1) Whether the moral virtues remain after this life? (2) Whether the intellectual virtues remain? (3) Whether faith remains? (4) Whether hope remains? (5) Whether anything remains of faith or hope? (6) Whether charity remains.

ARTICLE 1. *Whether the Moral Virtues Remain After This Life?*

We proceed thus to the First Article: It would seem that the moral virtues do not remain after this life.

Objection 1. For in the future state of glory men will be like angels, according to Matt. 22. 30. But it is absurd to put moral virtues in the angels, as stated in the *Ethics*.[1] Therefore neither in man will there be moral virtues after this life.

Obj. 2. Further, moral virtues perfect man in the active life. But the active life does not remain after this life; for Gregory says (*Moral.* iv, 37):[2] "The works of the active life pass away with the body." Therefore moral virtues do not remain after this life.

Obj. 3. Further, temperance and fortitude, which are moral virtues, are in the irrational parts of the soul, as the Philosopher states.[3] Now the irrational parts of the soul are corrupted when the body is corrupted, since they are acts of bodily organs. Therefore it seems that the moral virtues do not remain after this life.

On the contrary, It is written (Wisd. 1. 15) that justice is perpetual and immortal.

I answer that, As Augustine says (*De Trin.* xiv, 9),[4] Cicero held[5] that the four cardinal virtues do not remain after this life, and that, as Augustine says (*ibid.*), "in the other life men are made happy by the mere knowledge of that nature than which nothing is better or more lovable, that Nature, namely, which created all others." Afterwards he concludes that these four virtues remain in the future life, but after a different manner.

In order to make this evident, we must note that in these virtues there is a formal element, and a quasi-material element. The material element in these virtues is a certain inclination of the appetitive part to the passions and operations according to a certain mode,—and since this mode is fixed by reason, the formal element is precisely this order of reason.

Accordingly we must say that these moral

---

[1] Aristotle, x, 8 (1178ᵇ8).
[2] PL 75, 764.
[3] *Ethics*, III, 10 (1117ᵇ23).
[4] PL 42, 1046.
[5] In the lost work *Hortensius*.

virtues do not remain in the future life, as regards their material element. For in the future life there will be no concupiscences and pleasures in matters of food and sex, nor fear and daring about dangers of death, nor distributions and exchanges of things employed in this present life. But, as regards the formal element, they will remain most perfect, after this life, in the Blessed, since each one's reason will have most perfect rectitude in regard to things concerning him in respect of that state of life, and his appetitive power will be moved entirely according to the order of reason in things pertaining to that same state. Hence Augustine says (ibid.) that "prudence will be there without any danger of error; fortitude, without the anxiety of bearing with evil; temperance, without the rebellion of the desires: so that prudence will neither prefer nor equal any good to God; fortitude will adhere to Him most steadfastly; and temperance will delight in Him Who knows no imperfection." As to justice, it is yet more evident what will be its act in that life, namely, to be subject to God, because even in this life subjection to a superior is part of justice.

Reply Obj. 1. The Philosopher is speaking there of these moral virtues as to their material element; thus he speaks of justice, as regards exchanging and distributions; of fortitude, as to matters of terror and danger; of temperance, in respect of lewd desires.

The same applies to the Second Objection. For those things that concern the active life belong to the material element of the virtues.

Reply Obj. 3. There is a twofold state after this life: one before the resurrection, during which the soul will be separate from the body; the other, after the resurrection, when the souls will be reunited to their bodies. In this state of resurrection, the irrational powers will be in the bodily organs, just as they now are. Hence it will be possible for fortitude to be in the irascible, and temperance in the concupiscible part, in so far as each power will be perfectly disposed to obey the reason. But in the state preceding the resurrection, the irrational parts will not be in the soul actually, but only radically in its essence, as stated in the First Part (Q. LXXVII, A. 8). Therefore neither will these virtues be actually, but only in their root, that is, in the reason and will, in which are certain nurseries of these virtues, as stated above (Q. LXIII, A. 1). Justice, however, will remain even actually because it is in the will. Hence of justice is it specially said that it is perpetual and immortal; both by reason of its subject, since

the will is incorruptible, and because its act will not change, as we have said.

ARTICLE 2. Whether the Intellectual Virtues Remain After This Life?

We proceed thus to the Second Article: It would seem that the intellectual virtues do not remain after this life.

Objection 1. For the Apostle says (I Cor. 13. 8, 9) that knowledge shall be destroyed, and he states the reason to be because we know in part. Now just as the knowledge of science is in part, that is, imperfect; so also is the knowledge of the other intellectual virtues, as long as this life lasts. Therefore all the intellectual virtues will cease after this life.

Obj. 2. Further, the Philosopher says[1] that since science is a habit, it is a quality difficult to remove; for it is not easily lost, except by reason of some great change or sickness. But no bodily change is so great as that of death. Therefore science and the other intellectual virtues do not remain after death.

Obj. 3. Further, the intellectual virtues perfect the intellect so that it may perform its proper act well. Now there seems to be no act of the intellect after this life, since "the soul understands nothing without a phantasm,"[2] and, after this life, the phantasms do not remain, since their only subject is an organ of the body. Therefore the intellectual virtues do not remain after this life.

On the contrary, The knowledge of what is universal and necessary is more stable than that of particular and contingent things. Now the knowledge of contingent particulars remains in man after this life; for instance, the knowledge of what one has done or suffered, according to Luke 16. 25: Son, remember that thou didst receive good things in thy life-time, and likewise Lazarus evil things. Much more, therefore, does the knowledge of universal and necessary things remain, which pertains to science and the other intellectual virtues.

I answer that, As stated in the First Part (Q. LXXIX, A. 6), some have held[3] that the intelligible species do not remain in the possible intellect except when it actually understands, and that so long as actual consideration ceases, the species are not preserved save in the sensitive powers which are acts of bodily organs, namely, in the powers of imagination and memory. Now these powers cease when the body is corrupted,

[1] Categories, 8 (8ᵇ29).
[2] Aristotle, Soul, III, 7 (431ᵃ16).
[3] Avicenna, De An., V, 6 (26rb).

and consequently, according to this opinion, neither science nor any other intellectual virtue will remain after this life when once the body is corrupted.

But this opinion is contrary to the mind of Aristotle, who states[1] that "the possible intellect is in act when it becomes each thing through knowing it; and yet, even then, it is in potency to considering it actually."—It is also contrary to reason, because intelligible species are contained by the possible intellect immovably, according to the mode of their receiver. Hence the possible intellect is called "the abode of the species"[2] because, as it were, it preserves the intelligible species.

And yet the phantasms, by turning to which man understands in this life, by applying the intelligible species to them as stated in the First Part (Q. LXXXIV, A. 7; Q. LXXXV, A. 1, reply 5), cease as soon as the body is corrupted. Hence, so far as the phantasms are concerned, which are the quasi-material element in the intellectual virtues, these latter cease when the body is destroyed; but as regards the intelligible species, which are in the possible intellect, the intellectual virtues remain. Now the species are as the formal element of the intellectual virtues. Therefore these remain after this life, as regards their formal element, but not as regards their material element, just as we have stated concerning the moral virtues (A. 1).

Reply Obj. 1. The saying of the Apostle is to be understood as referring to the material element in science, and to the mode of understanding; because, namely, neither do the phantasms remain when the body is destroyed, nor will there be use of science by turning to the phantasms.

Reply Obj. 2. Sickness destroys the habit of science as to its material element, namely, the phantasms, but not as to the intelligible species, which are in the possible intellect.

Reply Obj. 3. As stated in the First Part (Q. LXXXIX, A. 1), the separated soul has a mode of understanding other than by turning to the phantasms. Consequently science remains, yet not as to the same mode of operation; as we have stated concerning the moral virtues (A. 1).

ARTICLE 3. *Whether Faith Remains After This Life?*

We proceed thus to the Third Article: It would seem that faith remains after this life.

Objection 1. Because faith is more excellent than science. Now science remains after this

life, as stated above (A. 2). Therefore faith remains also.

Obj. 2. Further, it is written (I Cor. 3. 11): *Other foundation no man can lay, but that which is laid; which is Christ Jesus,* that is, faith in Jesus Christ. Now if the foundation is removed, that which is built upon it remains no more. Therefore, if faith remains not after this life, no other virtue remains.

Obj. 3. Further, the knowledge of faith and the knowledge of glory differ as perfect from imperfect. Now imperfect knowledge is compatible with perfect knowledge; thus in an angel there can be *evening* and *morning* knowledge,[3] and a man can have science through a demonstrative syllogism, together with opinion through a probable syllogism, about one same conclusion. Therefore after this life faith also is compatible with the knowledge of glory.

On the contrary, The Apostle says (II Cor. 5. 6, 7): *While we are in the body, we are absent from the Lord: for we walk by faith and not by sight.* But those who are in glory are not absent from the Lord, but present to Him. Therefore after this life faith does not remain in the life of glory.

I answer that, Opposition is of itself the proper cause of one thing being excluded from another, in so far, that is, as wherever two things are opposite to one another, we find opposition of affirmation and negation. Now in some things we find opposition in respect of contrary forms; thus in colours we find white and black. In others we find opposition in respect of perfection and imperfection; hence in alterations more and less are considered to be contraries, as when a thing from being less hot is made more hot.[4] And since perfect and imperfect are opposite to one another, it is impossible for perfection and imperfection to affect the same thing at the same time.

Now we must take note that sometimes imperfection belongs to a thing's very nature, and pertains to its species, even as lack of reason belongs to the very notion of the species of a horse and an ox. And since a thing, so long as it remains the same identically, cannot pass from one species to another, it follows that if such an imperfection be removed, the species of that thing is changed, even as it would no longer be an ox or a horse, were it to be rational. Sometimes, however, the imperfection does not belong to the notion of the species, but is accidental to the individual by reason of something

---

[1] *Soul,* III, 4 (429ᵇ6).　　[2] *Ibid.* (429ᵃ27).

[3] Cf. Part I., Q. LVIII, A. 6.

[4] Aristotle, *Physics,* V, 2 (226ᵇ2).

else, even as sometimes lack of reason is accidental to a man, because he is asleep, or because he is drunk, or for some like reason; and it is evident that if such an imperfection be removed, the substance of the thing nevertheless remains.

Now it is clear that imperfect knowledge belongs to the very notion of faith, for it is included in its definition, faith being defined as *the substance of things to be hoped for, the evidence of things that appear not* (Heb. II. I). Hence Augustine says (*Tract.* xl *in Joann.*):[1] "What is faith? Believing without seeing." But it is an imperfect knowledge that is of things unapparent or unseen. Consequently imperfect knowledge belongs to the very notion of faith. Therefore it is clear that the knowledge of faith cannot be perfect and remain identically the same.

But we must also consider whether it is compatible with perfect knowledge, for there is nothing to prevent some kind of imperfect knowledge from being sometimes with perfect knowledge. Accordingly we must observe that knowledge can be imperfect in three ways: first, on the part of the knowable object; secondly, on the part of the means; thirdly, on the part of the subject. The difference of perfect and imperfect knowledge on the part of the knowable object is seen in the "morning" and "evening" knowledge of the angels; for the "morning" knowledge is about things according to the being which they have in the Word, while the "evening" knowledge is about things according as they have being in their own natures, which being is imperfect in comparison with the First Being. On the part of the means, perfect and imperfect knowledge are exemplified in the knowledge of a conclusion through a demonstrative means, and through a probable means. On the part of the subject the difference of perfect and imperfect knowledge applies to opinion, faith, and science. For it is essential to opinion that we assent to one of two opposite assertions with fear of the other, so that our adhesion is not firm; to science it is essential to have firm adhesion with intellectual vision, for science possesses certitude which results from the understanding of principles; while faith holds a middle place, for it surpasses opinion in so far as its adhesion is firm, but falls short of science in so far as it lacks vision.

Now it is evident that a thing cannot be perfect and imperfect in the same respect; yet the things which differ as perfect and imperfect can

be together in the same respect in one and the same other thing. Accordingly, knowledge which is perfect on the part of the object is altogether incompatible with imperfect knowledge about the same object; but they are compatible with one another in respect of the same means or the same subject. For nothing hinders a man from having at one and the same time, through one and the same means, perfect and imperfect knowledge about two things, one perfect, the other imperfect, for example about health and sickness, good and evil. In like manner knowledge that is perfect on the part of the means is incompatible with imperfect knowledge through one and the same means. But nothing hinders them being about the same object or in the same subject, for one man can know the same conclusions through a probable and through a demonstrative means. Again, knowledge that is perfect on the part of the subject is incompatible with imperfect knowledge in the same subject. Now faith, of its very nature, contains an imperfection on the part of the subject, namely that the believer sees not what he believes. But Happiness, of its very nature, implies perfection on the part of the subject, namely that the Blessed see that which makes them happy, as stated above (Q. III, A. 8). Hence it is manifest that faith and Happiness are incompatible in one and the same subject.

Reply Obj. 1. Faith is more excellent than science on the part of the object, because its object is the First Truth. Yet science has a more perfect mode of knowing which is not incompatible with vision which is the perfection of Happiness, as the mode of faith is incompatible.

Reply Obj. 2. Faith is the foundation in so far as it is knowledge. Consequently when this knowledge is perfected, the foundation will be perfected also.

The *Reply to the Third Objection* is clear from what has been said.

ARTICLE 4. *Whether Hope Remains After Death, in the State of Glory?*

We proceed thus to the Fourth Article: It would seem that hope remains after death, in the state of glory.

Objection 1. Because hope perfects the human appetite in a more excellent manner than the moral virtues. But the moral virtues remain after this life, as Augustine clearly states (*De Trin.* xiv, 9).[2] Much more then does hope remain.

[1] PL 35, 1690.

[2] PL 42, 1045.

Obj. 2. Further, fear is opposed to hope. But fear remains after this life:—in the Blessed, filial fear, which abides for ever—in the lost, the fear of punishment. Therefore, in a like manner, hope can remain.

Obj. 3. Further, just as hope is of future good, so is desire. Now in the Blessed there is desire for future good, both for the glory of the body, which the souls of the Blessed desire, as Augustine declares (*Gen. ad. lit.* 12, 35),[1] and for the glory of the soul, according to Ecclus. 24. 29: *They that eat me, shall yet hunger, and they that drink me, shall yet thirst*, and I Pet. 1. 12: *On Whom the angels desire to look*. Therefore it seems that there can be hope in the Blessed after this life is past.

On the contrary, The Apostle says (Rom. 8. 24): *What a man seeth, why doth he hope for?* But the Blessed see that which is the object of hope, namely God. Therefore they do not hope.

I answer that, As stated above (A. 3), that which, in its very nature, implies imperfection of its subject is incompatible with the opposite perfection in that subject. Thus it is evident that movement of its very nature implies imperfection of its subject, since it is the act of that which is in potency in so far as it is in potency, so that as soon as this potency is reduced to act, the movement ceases; for a thing does not continue to become white when once it is made white. Now hope denotes a movement towards that which is not possessed, as is clear from what we have said above about the passion of hope (Q. XL, AA. 1, 2). Therefore when we possess that which we hope for, namely the enjoyment of God, it will no longer be possible to have hope.

Reply Obj. 1. Hope surpasses the moral virtues as to its object, which is God. But the acts of the moral virtues are not incompatible with the perfection of happiness, as the act of hope is; except perhaps, as regards their matter, in respect of which they do not remain. For moral virtue perfects the appetite not only in respect of what is not yet possessed, but also as regards something which is in our actual possession.

Reply Obj. 2. Fear is twofold, servile and filial, as we shall state further on (Part II-II, Q. XIX, A. 2). Servile fear regards punishment, and will be impossible in the life of glory, since there will no longer be possibility of being punished. Filial fear has two acts: one is an act of reverence to God, and with regard to this act, it remains; the other is an act of fear lest we be

separated from God, and as regards this act, it does not remain. For separation from God is in the nature of an evil, and no evil will be feared there, according to Prov. 1. 33: *He . . . shall enjoy abundance without fear of evils*. Now fear is opposed to hope by opposition of good and evil, as stated above (Q. XXIII, A. 2; Q. XL, A. 1), and therefore the fear which will remain in glory is not opposed to hope.

In the lost there can be fear of punishment to a greater degree than hope of glory in the Blessed. Because in the lost there will be a succession of punishments, so that the notion of something future remains there, which is the object of fear. But the glory of the saints has no succession, by reason of its being a kind of participation of eternity, in which there is neither past nor future, but only the present. And yet, properly speaking, neither in the lost is there fear. For, as stated above (Q. XLII, A. 2), fear is never without some hope of escape, and the lost will have no such hope. Consequently neither will there be fear in them, except speaking in a general way, in so far as any expectation of future evil is called fear.

Reply Obj. 3. As to the glory of the soul, there can be no desire in the Blessed, in so far as desire looks for something future, for the reason already given (Reply 2). Yet hunger and thirst are said to be in them because they never weary, and for the same reason desire is said to be in the angels. With regard to the glory of the body, there can be desire in the souls of the saints, but not hope, properly speaking; neither as a theological virtue, for thus its object is God, and not a created good; nor in its general signification. Because the object of hope is something difficult, as stated above (Q. XL, A. 1), while a good whose unerring cause we already possess is not related to us as something difficult. Hence he that has money is not, properly speaking, said to hope for what he can buy at once. In like manner those who have the glory of the soul are not, properly speaking, said to hope for the glory of the body, but only to desire it.

ARTICLE 5. *Whether Anything of Faith or Hope Remains in Glory?*

We proceed thus to the Fifth Article: It would seem that something of faith and hope remains in glory.

Objection 1. For when that which is proper to a thing is removed, there remains what is common; thus it is stated in *De Causis*[2] that

---

[1] PL 34, 183.

[2] Sect. 1 (BA 163.21).

if you take away rational, there remains living, and when you remove living, there remains being. Now in faith there is something that it has in common with Happiness, namely knowledge, and there is something proper to it, namely darkness, for faith is knowledge in a dark manner. Therefore, the darkness of faith removed, the knowledge of faith still remains.

Obj. 2. Further, faith is a spiritual light of the soul, according to Ephes. i. 17, 18: *The eyes of your heart enlightened . . . in the knowledge of* God; yet this light is imperfect in comparison with the light of glory, of which it is written (Ps. 35. 10): *In Thy light we shall see light*. Now an imperfect light remains when a perfect light supervenes, for a candle is not extinguished when the sun's rays appear. Therefore it seems that the light of faith itself remains with the light of glory.

Obj. 3. Further, the substance of a habit does not cease through the withdrawal of its matter, for a man may retain the habit of liberality though he has lost his money; yet he cannot exercise the act. Now the object of faith is the First Truth as unseen. Therefore when this ceases through the First Truth being seen, the habit of faith can still remain.

On the contrary, Faith is a simple habit. Now a simple thing is either withdrawn entirely or remains entirely. Since therefore faith does not remain entirely, but is taken away as stated above (A. 3), it seems that it is withdrawn entirely.

I answer that, Some have held[1] that hope is taken away entirely, but that faith is taken away in part, that is, as to its obscurity, and remains in part, that is, as to the substance of its knowledge. And if this be understood to mean that it remains the same not identically but generically, it is absolutely true; for faith is of the same genus, namely knowledge, as the beatific vision. On the other hand, hope is not of the same genus as Beatitude, because it is compared to the enjoyment of Happiness as movement is to rest in the term of movement.

But if it be understood to mean that in heaven the knowledge of faith remains identically the same, this is absolutely impossible. Because when you remove a specific difference, the substance of the genus does not remain identically the same: thus if you remove the difference constituting whiteness, the substance of colour

does not remain identically the same, as though the identical colour were at one time whiteness, and, at another, blackness. The reason is that genus is not related to difference as matter to form, so that the substance of the genus remains identically the same when the difference is removed, as the substance of matter remains identically the same when the form is changed. For genus and difference are not the parts of a species; otherwise they would not be predicated of the species. But even as the species denotes the whole, that is, the composite of matter and form in material things, so does the difference, and likewise the genus. The genus denotes the whole from that which plays the role of matter; the difference, from that which plays the role of form; the species, from both. Thus, in man, the sensitive nature is as matter to the intellectual nature, and animal is predicated of that which has a sensitive nature, rational of that which has an intellectual nature, and man of that which has both. So that the one same whole is denoted by these three, but not under the same aspect.

It is therefore evident that, since the signification of the difference is confined to the genus, if the difference be removed the substance of the genus cannot remain the same; for the same animal nature does not remain if another kind of soul constitute the animal. Hence it is impossible for the identical knowledge which was previously obscure to become clear vision. It is therefore evident that, in heaven, nothing remains of faith, either identically or specifically the same, but only generically.

Reply Obj. 1. If "rational" be withdrawn, the remaining "living" thing is the same, not identically, but generically, as stated.

Reply Obj. 2. The imperfection of candle-light is not opposed to the perfection of sun-light, since they do not regard the same subject. But the imperfection of faith and the perfection of glory are opposed to one another and regard the same subject. Consequently they are incompatible with one another, just as light and darkness in the air.

Reply Obj. 3. He that loses his money does not lose the possibility of having money, and therefore it is fitting for the habit of liberality to remain. But in the state of glory not only is the object of faith, which is the unseen, removed actually, but even its possibility, by reason of the unchangeableness of Happiness. And therefore such a habit would remain to no purpose.

---

[1] William of Auxerre, *Summa Aurea*, pt. iii, tr. 5, q. 5 (fol. 138va); Albert, *In Sent.*, iii, d. 31, a. 7 (BO xxviii, 586); a. 8 (BO xxviii, 587).

ARTICLE 6. *Whether Charity Remains After This Life, in Glory?*

We proceed thus to the Sixth Article: It would seem that charity does not remain after this life, in glory.

Objection 1. Because according to I Cor. 13. 10, *when that which is perfect is come, that which is in part,* that is, that which is imperfect, *shall be done away.* Now the charity of the wayfarer is imperfect. Therefore it will be done away when the perfection of glory is attained.

Obj. 2. Further, habits and acts are differentiated by their objects. But the object of love is good apprehended. Since therefore the apprehension of the present life differs from the apprehension of the life to come, it seems that charity is not the same in both cases.

Obj. 3. Further, things of the same kind can advance from imperfection to perfection by continuous increase. But the charity of the wayfarer can never attain to equality, with the charity of heaven, however much it be increased. Therefore it seems that the charity of the wayfarer does not remain in heaven.

On the contrary, The Apostle says (I Cor. 13. 8): *Charity never falleth away.*

I answer that, As stated above (A. 3), when the imperfection of a thing does not belong to its specific nature, there is nothing to hinder the same identical thing passing from imperfection to perfection, even as man is perfected by growth, and whiteness by intensity. Now charity is love, the nature of which does not include imperfection, since it may relate to an object either possessed or not possessed, either seen or not seen. Therefore charity is not done away by the perfection of glory, but remains identically the same.

Reply Obj. 1. The imperfection of charity is accidental to it, because imperfection is not included in the notion of love. Now even though that which is accidental to a thing be withdrawn, the substance remains. Hence the imperfection of charity being done away, charity itself is not done away.

Reply Obj. 2. The object of charity is not knowledge itself; if it were, the charity of the wayfarer would not be the same as the charity of heaven. Its object is the thing known, which remains the same, namely God Himself.

Reply Obj. 3. The reason why the charity of the wayfarer cannot attain to the perfection of the charity of heaven is a difference on the part of the cause; for vision is a cause of love, as stated in the *Ethics*,[1] and the more perfectly we know God, the more perfectly we love Him.

QUESTION LXVIII
OF THE GIFTS
(In Eight Articles)

WE now come to consider the Gifts, under which head there are eight points of inquiry: (1) Whether the Gifts differ from the virtues? (2) Of the necessity of the Gifts. (3) Whether the Gifts are habits? (4) Which, and how many are they? (5) Whether the Gifts are connected? (6) Whether they remain in heaven? (7) Of their comparison with one another. (8) Of their comparison with the virtues.

ARTICLE 1. *Whether the Gifts Differ From the Virtues?*

We proceed thus to the First Article: It would seem that the gifts do not differ from the virtues.[2]

Objection 1. For Gregory commenting on Job 1. 2, *There were born to him seven sons,* says (*Moral.* i, 27):[3] "Seven sons are born to us, when through the conception of good thoughts, the seven virtues of the Holy Ghost take birth in us"; and he quotes the words of Isaias (11. 2, 3): *And the Spirit . . . of understanding . . . shall rest upon him,* etc. where the seven gifts of the Holy Ghost are enumerated. Therefore the seven gifts of the Holy Ghost are virtues.

Obj. 2. Further, Augustine commenting on Matt. 12. 45, *Then he goeth and taketh with him seven other spirits,* etc., says (*De Quæst. Evang.* i, qu. 8):[4] "The seven vices are opposed to the seven virtues of the Holy Ghost," that is, to the seven gifts. Now the seven vices are opposed to the seven virtues, commonly so called. Therefore the gifts do not differ from the virtues commonly so called.

Obj. 3. Further, things whose definitions are the same are themselves the same. But the definition of virtue applies to the gifts, for each gift is a good quality of the mind, by which we lead a good life, etc.[5] Likewise the definition of a gift can apply to the infused virtues, for "a gift is an unreturnable giving," according to the Philosopher.[6] Therefore the virtues and gifts do not differ from one another.

---

[1] Aristotle, IX, 5 (1167ª4).
[2] For the history and bibliography of this problem, See Lottin, RTAM (1929), p. 42.
[3] PL 75, 544.   [4] PL 35, 1325.
[5] Cf. Q. LV, A. 4.
[6] *Topics,* IV, 4 (125ª18).

Obj. 4. Several of the things mentioned among the gifts, are virtues; for, as stated above (Q. LVII, A. 2), wisdom, understanding, and knowledge are intellectual virtues; now counsel pertains to prudence, piety is a kind of justice, and fortitude is a moral virtue. Therefore it seems that the gifts do not differ from the virtues.

On the contrary, Gregory (*Moral.* i, 27)[1] distinguishes seven gifts, which he states to be denoted by the seven sons of Job, from the three theological virtues, which, he says, are signified by Job's three daughters. He also distinguishes (*Moral.* ii, 49)[2] the same seven gifts from the four cardinal virtues, which he says were signified by the four corners of the house.

I answer that, If we speak of gift and virtue with regard to the notion conveyed by the words themselves, there is no opposition between them. Because the word virtue conveys the notion that it perfects man in relation to well-doing, as we have said above (Q. LV, AA. 3, 4), while the word gift refers to the cause from which it proceeds. Now there is no reason why that which proceeds from one as a gift should not perfect another in well-doing, especially since, as we have already stated (Q. LXIII, A. 3) that some virtues are infused into us by God. Therefore in this respect we cannot differentiate gifts from virtues. Consequently some have held that the gifts are not to be distinguished from the virtues.[3] But there remains no less a difficulty for them to solve, for they must explain why some virtues are called gifts and some not, and why among the gifts there are some, fear, for instance, that are not accounted virtues.

Hence it is that others have said that the gifts should be held as being distinct from the virtues;[4] yet they have not assigned a suitable reason for this distinction, a reason, namely, which would apply either to all the virtues, and to none of the gifts, or vice versa. For some,[5] seeing that of the seven gifts, four belong to the reason, namely wisdom, science, understanding and counsel, and three to the appetite, namely fortitude, piety and fear, held that the gifts perfect free choice according as it is a power of

the reason, while the virtues perfect it as a power of the will; for they found only two virtues in the reason or intellect, namely faith and prudence, the others being in the appetitive power or the affections. If this distinction were true, all the virtues would have to be in the appetite, and all the gifts in the reason.

Others observing that Gregory says (*Moral.* ii, 49)[6] that "the gift of the Holy Ghost, by coming into the mind endows it with prudence, temperance, justice, and fortitude, and at the same time strengthens it against every kind of temptation by His sevenfold gift," said that the virtues are given us that we may do good works, and the gifts that we may resist temptation.[7] —But neither is this distinction sufficient. Because the virtues also resist those temptations which lead to the sins that are contrary to the virtues; for everything naturally resists its contrary, which is especially clear with regard to charity, of which it is written (Cant. 8. 7): *Many waters cannot quench charity.*

Others again,[8] seeing that these gifts are set down in Holy Writ as having been in Christ, according to Isa. 11. 2, 3, said that the virtues are given simply that we may do good works, but the gifts in order to conform us to Christ, chiefly with regard to His Passion, for it was then that these gifts shone with the greatest splendour. Yet neither does this appear to be a satisfactory distinction. Because Our Lord Himself wished us to be conformed to Him chiefly in humility and meekness, according to Matt. 11. 29: *Learn of Me, because I am meek and humble of heart,* and in charity, according to John 15. 12: *Love one another, as I have loved you.* Moreover, these virtues were especially resplendent in Christ's Passion.

Accordingly, in order to differentiate the gifts from the virtues, we must be guided by the way in which Scripture expresses itself, for we find there that the term employed is spirit rather than gift. For thus it is written (Isa. 11. 2, 3): *The spirit . . . of wisdom and of understanding . . . shall rest upon him,* etc., from which words we are clearly given to understand that these seven are there set down as being in us by Divine inspiration. Now inspiration denotes motion from without. For it must be noted that in man there is a twofold principle of movement: one within him, namely the reason; the other extrinsic to him, namely God, as stated above (Q.

---

[1] PL 75, 544.

[2] PL 75, 592.

[3] This doctrine was held from the middle of the twelfth century by theologians from Peter Lombard to William of Auxerre. See Lombard, *Sent.*, III, d. 34, chap. 2 (QR II, 699); cf. Lottin, RTAM (1929), p. 41; p. 70. St. Thomas is here following the exposition of Albert the Great, *In Sent.*, III, d. 34, A. 1 (BO XXVIII, 616), and of Bonaventure, *In Sent.*, III, d. 34, A. 1, Q. 1 (QR III, 735).

[4] Philip the Chancellor; cf. Lottin, RTAM (1929) pp. 49, 79.

[5] Praepositinus. Cf. Lottin, *Ibid.*, pp. 42, 66.

[6] PL 75, 592.

[7] Philip the Chancellor; cf. Lottin, *op. cit.* pp. 35, 76. Cf. p. 48.

[8] Philip the Chancellor, cf. Lottin, *op. cit.*, p. 80.

IX, AA. 4, 6): moreover the Philosopher says this in the chapter *On Good Fortune.*[1]

Now it is evident that whatever is moved must be proportionate to its mover, and the perfection of that which is moved, as such, consists in a disposition by which it is disposed to be well moved by its mover. Hence the more exalted the mover, the more perfect must be the disposition by which that which is moved is made proportionate to its mover; thus we see that a disciple needs a more perfect disposition in order to grasp a higher teaching from his master. Now it is manifest that human virtues perfect man according as it is natural for him to be moved by his reason in his interior and exterior actions. Consequently man needs yet higher perfections by which he may be disposed to be moved by God. These perfections are called gifts, not only because they are infused by God, but also because by them man is disposed to become amenable to the Divine inspiration, according to Isa. 50. 5: *The Lord . . . hath opened my ear, and I do not resist; I have not gone back.* Even the Philosopher says in the chapter *On Good Fortune* that for those who are moved by Divine prompting there is no need to take counsel according to human reason, but only to follow their inner promptings, since they are moved by a principle higher than human reason. This then is what some say,[2] namely that the gifts perfect man for acts which are higher than acts of virtue.

Reply Obj. 1. Sometimes these gifts are called virtues in the broad sense of the word. Nevertheless, they have something over and above the virtues understood in this broad way, in so far as they are Divine virtues, perfecting man as moved by God. Hence the Philosopher above virtue commonly so called, places a kind of heroic or divine virtue, in respect of which some men are called divine.[3]

Reply Obj. 2. The vices are opposed to the virtues, in so far as they are opposed to the good of reason; but they are opposed to the gifts in so far as they are opposed to the Divine impulse. For the same thing is opposed both to God and to reason, whose light flows from God.

Reply Obj. 3. This definition applies to virtue taken in its general sense. Consequently, if we wish to restrict it to virtue as distinguished from the gifts, we must explain the words, by which we lead a good life as referring to the rectitude

of life which is measured by the rule of reason. Likewise the gifts, as distinct from infused virtue, may be defined as something given by God in relation to His motion; something, that is, that makes man to follow well the promptings of God.

Reply Obj. 4. Wisdom is called an intellectual virtue in so far as it proceeds from the judgment of reason; but it is called a gift according as its work proceeds from the Divine prompting. The same applies to the other virtues.

ARTICLE 2. *Whether the Gifts Are Necessary to Man for Salvation?*

We proceed thus to the Second Article: It would seem that the gifts are not necessary to man for salvation.

Objection 1. Because the gifts are ordered to a perfection surpassing the ordinary perfection of virtue. Now it is not necessary for man's salvation that he should attain to a perfection surpassing the ordinary standard of virtue, because such perfection falls, not under the precept, but under a counsel. Therefore the gifts are not necessary to man for salvation.

Obj. 2. Further, it is enough, for man's salvation, that he behave well in matters concerning God and matters concerning man. Now man's behaviour to God is sufficiently directed by the theological virtues, and his behaviour towards men by the moral virtues. Therefore the gifts are not necessary to man for salvation.

Obj. 3. Further, Gregory says (*Moral.* ii, 49)[4] that "the Holy Ghost gives wisdom against folly, understanding against dullness, counsel against rashness, fortitude against fears, science against ignorance, piety against hardness of our heart, and fear against pride." But a sufficient remedy for all these things is to be found in the virtues. Therefore the gifts are not necessary to man for salvation.

On the contrary, Of all the gifts, wisdom seems to be the highest, and fear the lowest. Now each of these is necessary for salvation, since of wisdom it is written (Wisd. 7. 28): *God loveth none but him that dwelleth with wisdom,* and of fear (Ecclus. 1. 28): *He that is without fear cannot be justified.* Therefore the other gifts that are placed between these are also necessary for salvation.

I answer that, As stated above (A. 1), the gifts are perfections of man, by which he is disposed so as to follow well the promptings of God. Therefore in those matters where the prompting of reason is not sufficient and there

---

[1] *Eudemian Ethics,* VII, 14 (1248ª14).
[2] Albert and Bonaventure, as referred to above.
[3] *Ethics,* VII, 1 (1145ᵇ20).
[4] PL 75, 592.

is need for the prompting of the Holy Ghost, there is, in consequence, need for a gift.

Now man's reason is perfected by God in two ways: first, with its natural perfection, that is, the natural light of reason; secondly, with a supernatural perfection, that is, the theological virtues, as stated above (Q. LXII, A. 1). And, though this latter perfection is greater than the former, yet the former is possessed by man in a more perfect manner than the latter, because man has the former in his full possession while he possesses the latter imperfectly, since we love and know God imperfectly. Now it is evident that anything that has a nature or a form or a virtue perfectly, can of itself work according to it, not, however, excluding the operation of God, Who works inwardly in every nature and in every will. On the other hand, that which has a nature, or form, or virtue imperfectly, cannot of itself work unless it be moved by another. Thus the sun which possesses light perfectly can shine by itself; but the moon which has the nature of light imperfectly, sheds only a borrowed light. Again, a physician who knows the medical art perfectly can work by himself; but his pupil, who is not yet fully instructed, cannot work by himself, but needs to receive instructions from him.

Accordingly, in matters subject to human reason, and directed to man's connatural end, man can work through the judgment of his reason. If, however, even in these things man receive help in the shape of special promptings from God, this will be out of God's superabundant goodness; hence, according to the philosophers, not every one that had the acquired moral virtues, had also the heroic or divine virtues.[1] But in matters directed to the supernatural end, to which man's reason moves him according as it is in a manner and imperfectly informed by the theological virtues, the motion of reason does not suffice, unless it receive in addition the prompting or motion of the Holy Ghost, according to Rom. 8. 14, 17: *Whosoever are led by the Spirit of God, they are the sons of God . . . and if sons, heirs also;* and Ps. 142. 10: *Thy good Spirit shall lead me into the right land,* because, that is, none can receive the inheritance of that land of the Blessed except he be moved and led to it by the Holy Ghost. Therefore, in order to accomplish this end, it is necessary for man to have the gift of the Holy Ghost.

Reply Obj. 1. The gifts surpass the ordinary perfection of the virtues not as regards the kind of works (in the way that the counsels surpass the commandments), but as regards the manner of working, in respect of man being moved by a higher principle.

Reply Obj. 2. By the theological and moral virtues, man is not so perfected in respect of his last end as not to stand in continual need of being moved by the yet higher promptings of the Holy Ghost, for the reason already given.

Reply Obj. 3. Whether we consider human reason as perfected in its natural perfection, or as perfected by the theological virtues, it does not know all things, nor are all things possible to it. Consequently it is unable to avoid folly and the other like things mentioned in the objection. God, however, to Whose knowledge and power all things are subject, by His motion safeguards us from all folly, ignorance, dullness of mind and hardness of heart, and the rest. Consequently the gifts of the Holy Ghost, which make us amenable to His promptings, are said to be given as remedies to these defects.

ARTICLE 3. *Whether the Gifts of the Holy Ghost Are Habits?*

We proceed thus to the Third Article: It would seem that the gifts of the Holy Ghost are not habits.

Objection 1. For a habit is a quality abiding in man, being defined as "a quality difficult to remove," as stated in the *Predicaments*.[2] Now it is proper to Christ that the gifts of the Holy Ghost rest in Him, as stated in Isa. 11. 2, 3. Moreover, it is written (John 1. 33): *He upon Whom thou shalt see the Spirit descending and remaining upon Him, He it is that baptizeth,* on which words Gregory comments as follows (*Moral.* ii, 56):[3] "The Holy Ghost comes upon all the faithful; but, in a singular way, He dwells always only in the Mediator." Therefore the gifts of the Holy Ghost are not habits.

Obj. 2. Further, the gifts of the Holy Ghost perfect man according as he is moved by the Spirit of God, as stated above (AA. 1, 2). But in so far as man is moved by the Spirit of God, he is somewhat like an instrument in His regard. Now to be perfected by a habit is befitting, not an instrument, but a principal agent. Therefore the gifts of the Holy Ghost are not habits.

Obj. 3. Further, as the gifts of the Holy Ghost are due to Divine inspiration, so is the gift of prophecy. Now prophecy is not a habit, for "the

[1] Aristotle, *Ethics*, VII, 1 (1145ᵃ20); Albert also names Plotinus, the Stoics, Plato and Aristotle, *in Eth.*, VII, 1, 1 (BO VII, 463).

[2] Aristotle, *Categories*, 8 (8ᵇ30).
[3] PL 75, 598.

spirit of prophecy does not always reside in the prophets," as Gregory states (*Hom.* i *in Ezechiel*).[1] Neither, therefore, are the gifts of the Holy Ghost habits.

On the contrary, Our Lord in speaking of the Holy Ghost said to His disciples (John 14. 17): *He shall abide with you, and shall be in you.* Now the Holy Ghost is not in a man without His gifts. Therefore His gifts abide in man. Therefore they are not merely acts or passions but lasting habits.

I answer that, As stated above (A. 1), the gifts are perfections of man by which he follows well the promptings of the Holy Ghost. Now it is evident from what has been already said (Q. LVIII, A. 2), that the moral virtues perfect the appetitive power according as it partakes somewhat of the reason, in so far, that is, as it has a natural aptitude to be moved by the command of reason. Accordingly the gifts of the Holy Ghost are to man in relation to the Holy Ghost even as the moral virtues are to the appetitive power in relation to reason. Now the moral virtues are habits, by which the powers of appetite are disposed to obey reason promptly. Therefore the gifts of the Holy Ghost are habits by which man is perfected to obey readily the Holy Ghost.

Reply Obj. 1. Gregory solves this objection (*ibid.*) by saying that "by those gifts without which one cannot obtain life the Holy Ghost ever abides in all the elect, but not by His other gifts." Now the seven gifts are necessary for salvation, as stated above (A. 2). Therefore, with regard to them, the Holy Ghost remains always in holy men.

Reply Obj. 2. This argument holds in the case of an instrument which has no power of action, but only of being acted upon. But man is not an instrument of that kind; for he is so acted upon by the Holy Ghost that he also acts himself, in so far as he has free choice. Therefore he needs a habit.

Reply Obj. 3. Prophecy is one of those gifts which are for the manifestation of the Spirit, not for the necessity of salvation; hence the comparison fails.

ARTICLE 4. *Whether the Seven Gifts of the Holy Ghost Are Suitably Enumerated?*

We proceed thus to the Fourth Article: It would seem that the seven gifts of the Holy Ghost are unsuitably enumerated.

Objection 1. For in that enumeration four are set down corresponding to the intellectual virtues, namely wisdom, understanding, science,

[1] PL 76, 788.

and counsel, which corresponds to prudence; but nothing is set down corresponding to art, which is the fifth intellectual virtue. Moreover, something is included corresponding to justice, namely piety, and something corresponding to fortitude, namely the gift of fortitude, while there is nothing to correspond to temperance. Therefore the gifts are enumerated insufficiently.

Obj. 2. Further, piety is a part of justice. But no part of fortitude is assigned to correspond to it, but rather fortitude itself. Therefore justice itself, and not piety, ought to have been set down.

Obj. 3. Further, the theological virtues, more than any, order us to God. Since, then, the gifts perfect man according as he is moved by God, it seems that some gifts, corresponding to the theological virtues should have been included.

Obj. 4. Further, even as God is an object of fear, so is He of love, of hope, and of joy. Now love, hope, and joy are passions divided with fear. Therefore, as fear is set down as a gift, so ought the other three.

Obj. 5. Further, wisdom is added in order to direct understanding; counsel, to direct fortitude; knowledge, to direct piety. Therefore, some gift should have been added for the purpose of directing fear. Therefore the seven gifts of the Holy Ghost are unsuitably enumerated.

On the contrary stands the authority of Holy Writ (Isa. 11. 2, 3).

I answer that, As stated above (A. 3), the gifts are habits perfecting man so that he is ready to follow the promptings of the Holy Ghost, even as the moral virtues perfect the appetitive powers so that they obey the reason. Now just as it is natural for the appetitive powers to be moved by the command of reason, so it is natural for all the forces in man to be moved by the prompting of God, as by a superior power. Therefore whatever powers in man can be the principles of human actions can also be the subjects of gifts, even as they are of virtues; and such powers are the reason and appetite.

Now the reason is speculative and practical, and in both we find the apprehension of truth, which pertains to the discovery of truth, and to the judgment of truth. Accordingly, for the apprehension of truth, the speculative reason is perfected by understanding, the practical reason, by counsel. In order to judge rightly, the speculative reason is perfected by wisdom, the practical reason by knowledge. The appetitive power, in matters touching a man's relations to another, is perfected by piety; in matters touching himself, it is perfected by fortitude against the fear of dangers; and against inordinate lust for pleasures, by fear, according to Prov. 15. 27: *By the fear of the Lord every one declineth from evil*, and Ps. 118. 120: *Pierce Thou my flesh with Thy fear: for I am afraid of Thy judgments*. Hence it is clear that these gifts extend to all those things to which the virtues, both intellectual and moral, extend.

Reply Obj. 1. The gifts of the Holy Ghost perfect man in matters concerning a good life, while art is not directed to such matters, but to external things that can be made, since art is the right reason, not about things to be done, but about things to be made.[1] However, we may say that, as regards the infusion of the gifts, there is art on the part of the Holy Ghost, Who is the principal mover, and not on the part of men, who are His organs when He moves them. The gift of fear corresponds, in a manner, to temperance; for just as it belongs to temperance, properly speaking, to restrain man from evil pleasures for the sake of the good appointed by reason, so does it belong to the gift of fear to withdraw man from evil pleasures through fear of God.

Reply Obj. 2. Justice is called so from the rectitude of the reason, and so it is more suitably called a virtue than a gift. But the name of piety denotes the reverence which we give to our father and to our country. And since God is the Father of all, the worship of God is also called piety, as Augustine states.[2] Therefore the gift by which a man, through reverence for God, works good to all, is fittingly called piety.

Reply Obj. 3. The mind of man is not moved by the Holy Ghost unless in some way it be united to Him, even as the instrument is not moved by the craftsman unless there be contact or some other kind of union between them. Now the primal union of man with God is by faith, hope, and charity, and hence these virtues are presupposed to the gifts, as being their roots. Therefore all the gifts correspond to these three virtues, as being derived therefrom.

Reply Obj. 4. Love, hope and joy have good for their object. Now God is the Sovereign Good. Therefore the names of these passions are transferred to the theological virtues which unite man to God. On the other hand the object of fear is evil, which can in no way apply to God; hence fear does not denote union with God, but rather withdrawal from certain things through reverence for God. Hence it does not give its

name to a theological virtue, but to a gift, which withdraws us from evil for higher motives than moral virtue does.

Reply Obj. 5. Wisdom directs both the intellect and the affections of man. Hence two gifts are set down as corresponding to wisdom as their directing principle; on the part of the intellect, the gift of understanding; on the part of the affections, the gift of fear. Because the principal reason for fearing God is taken from a consideration of the Divine excellence, which wisdom considers.

ARTICLE 5. *Whether the Gifts of the Holy Ghost Are Connected?*

We proceed thus to the Fifth Article: It would seem that the gifts are not connected.

Objection 1. For the Apostle says (I Cor. 12. 8): *To one . . . by the Spirit, is given the word of wisdom, and to another, the word of knowledge (scientia), according to the same Spirit.* Now wisdom and knowledge are counted among the gifts of the Holy Ghost. Therefore the gifts of the Holy Ghost are given to different men, and are not connected together in the same man.

Obj. 2. Further, Augustine says (*De Trin.* xiv, 1)[3] that "many of the faithful are not strong in science, though they are strong in faith." But some of the gifts, at least the gift of fear, accompany faith. Therefore it seems that gifts are not necessarily connected together in one and the same man.

Obj. 3. Further, Gregory says (*Moral.* i, 32)[4] that "wisdom is of small account if it lack understanding, and understanding is wholly useless if it be not based upon wisdom. . . . Counsel is worthless, when the strength of fortitude is lacking thereto, . . . and fortitude is very weak if it be not supported by counsel. . . . Science is nought if it hath not the use of piety, . . . and piety is very useless if it lack the discernment of science, . . . and assuredly, unless it has these virtues with it, fear itself rises up to the doing of no good action," from which it seems that it is possible to have one gift without another. Therefore the gifts of the Holy Ghost are not connected.

On the contrary, Gregory prefaces the passage quoted above with the following remark: "It is worthy of note in this feast of Job's sons that by turns they feed one another. Now the sons of Job, of whom he is speaking, denote the gifts of the Holy Ghost. Therefore the gifts of the Holy Ghost are connected together by strengthening one another.

---

[1] Aristotle, *Ethics*, VI, 4 (1140ª10).
[2] *City of God*, X, 1 (PL 41, 279).

[3] PL 42, 1037.   [4] PL 75, 547.

I answer that, The true answer to this question is easily gathered from what has been already set down. For it has been stated (A. 3) that as the powers of appetite are disposed by the moral virtues in relation to the rule of reason, so all the powers of the soul are disposed by the gifts in relation to the motion of Holy Ghost. Now the Holy Ghost dwells in us by charity, according to Rom. 5. 5: *The charity of God is poured forth in our hearts by the Holy Ghost, Who is given to us,* even as our reason is perfected by prudence. Therefore, just as the moral virtues are united together in prudence, so the gifts of the Holy Ghost are connected together in charity, so that whoever has charity has all the gifts of the Holy Ghost, none of which can one possess without charity.

Reply Obj. 1. Wisdom and science can be considered in one way as gratuitous graces, in so far, that is, as man so far abounds in the knowledge of things Divine and human that he is able both to instruct the believer and confound the unbeliever. It is in this sense that the Apostle speaks, in this passage, about wisdom and science; hence he mentions pointedly the *word* of wisdom and the *word* of science. They may be taken in another way for the gifts of the Holy Ghost, and thus wisdom and science are nothing else but perfections of the human mind, rendering it amenable to the promptings of the Holy Ghost in the knowledge of things Divine and human. Consequently it is clear that these gifts are in all who are possessed of charity.

Reply Obj. 2. Augustine is speaking there of science while expounding the passage of the Apostle quoted above (obj. 1); hence he is referring to science in the sense already explained, as a gratuitous grace. This is clear from the context which follows: "For it is one thing to know only what a man must believe in order to gain the Happy life, which is no other than eternal life; and another, to know how to impart this to godly souls, and to defend it against the ungodly, which latter the Apostle seems to have styled by the proper name of knowledge (*scientia*)."

Reply Obj. 3. Just as the connection of the cardinal virtues is proved in one way from the fact that one is, in a manner, perfected by another, as stated above (Q. LXV, A. 1), so Gregory wishes to prove the connection of the gifts in the same way, from the fact that one cannot be perfect without the other. Hence he had already observed that "each particular virtue is to the last degree destitute, unless one virtue lend its support to another." We are therefore not to understand that one gift can be without another, but that if understanding were without wisdom it would not be a gift; even as temperance, without justice, would not be a virtue.

ARTICLE 6. *Whether the Gifts of the Holy Ghost Remain in Heaven?*

We proceed thus to the Sixth Article: It would seem that the gifts of the Holy Ghost do not remain in heaven.

Objection 1. For Gregory says (*Moral.* ii, 49)[1] that "by means of His sevenfold gift the Holy Ghost instructs the mind against all temptations." Now there will be no temptations in heaven, according to Isa. 11. 9: *They shall not hurt, nor shall they kill in all My holy mountain.* Therefore there will be no gifts of the Holy Ghost in heaven.

Obj. 2. Further, the gifts of the Holy Ghost are habits, as stated above (A. 3). But habits are of no use where their acts are impossible. Now the acts of some gifts are not possible in heaven; for Gregory says (*Moral.* i, 32)[2] that "understanding . . . penetrates the truths heard, . . . counsel . . . stays us from acting rashly, . . . fortitude . . . has no fear of adversity, . . . piety satisfies the inmost heart with deeds of mercy," all of which are incompatible with the heavenly state. Therefore these gifts will not remain in the state of glory.

Obj. 3. Further, some of the gifts perfect man in the contemplative life, for example, wisdom and understanding, and some in the active life, for example, piety and fortitude. Now "the active life ends with this life," as Gregory states (*Moral.* vi, 37).[3] Therefore not all the gifts of the Holy Ghost will be in the state of glory.

On the contrary, Ambrose says (*De Spiritu Sancto*):[4] "The city of God, the heavenly Jerusalem is not washed with the waters of an earthly river; it is the Holy Ghost, of Whose outpouring we but taste, Who, proceeding from the Fount of life, seems to flow more abundantly in those celestial spirits, a seething torrent of sevenfold heavenly virtue."

I answer that, We may speak of the gifts in two ways. First, as to their essence, and thus they will be most perfectly in heaven, as may be gathered from the passage of Ambrose, just quoted. The reason for this is that the gifts of the Holy Ghost perfect the human mind for following the motion of the Holy Ghost, which will be especially realized in heaven, where God will be *all in all* (I Cor. 15. 28), and man entirely

[1] PL 75, 592.   [2] PL 75, 547.
[3] PL 75, 764.
[4] Chap. 16 (PL 16, 770).

subject unto Him. Secondly, they may be considered as regards the matter about which their operations are, and thus, in the present life they have an operation about a matter in respect of which they will have no operation in the state of glory. Considered in this way, they will not remain in the state of glory, just as we have stated to be the case with regard to the cardinal virtues (Q. LXVII, A. 1).

Reply Obj. 1. Gregory is speaking there of the gifts according as they are compatible with the present state, for it is thus that they afford us protection against evil temptations. But in the state of glory, where all evil will have ceased, we shall be perfected in good by the gifts of the Holy Ghost.

Reply Obj. 2. Gregory, in almost every gift, includes something that passes away with the present state, and something that remains in the future state. For he says[1] that "wisdom strengthens the mind with the hope and certainty of eternal things," of which two, hope passes and certainty remains. Of understanding, he says that "it penetrates the truths heard, refreshing the heart and enlightening its darkness," of which hearing passes away, since *they shall teach no more every man . . . his brother* (Jerem. 31. 3, 4); but the enlightening of the mind remains. Of counsel he says that it "prevents us from being impetuous," which is necessary in the present life; and also that "it makes the mind full of reason," which is necessary even in the future state. Of fortitude he says that it "fears not adversity," which is necessary in the present life; and further, that "it sets before us the viands of confidence," which remains also in the future life. With regard to science he mentions only one thing, namely that "she overcomes the void of ignorance," which refers to the present state. When, however, he adds "in the womb of the mind," this may refer figuratively to the fullness of knowledge, which belongs to the future state. Of piety he says that "it satisfies the inmost heart with deeds of mercy." These words taken literally refer only to the present state; yet the inward regard for our neighbour, signified by "the inmost heart," belongs also to the future state, when piety will achieve, not works of mercy, but fellowship of joy. Of fear he says that "it oppresses the mind, lest it pride itself in present things," which refers to the present state, and that "it strengthens it with the meat of hope for the future," which also belongs to the present state, as regards hope, but may also refer to the future

state, as regards being strengthened for things we hope for here and obtain there.

Reply Obj. 3. This argument considers the gifts as to their matter. For the matter of the gifts will not be works of the active life, but all the gifts will have their respective acts about things pertaining to the contemplative life, which is the life of Happiness.

ARTICLE 7. *Whether the Gifts Are Set Down by Isaias in Their Order of Dignity?*

We proceed thus to the Seventh Article: It would seem that the gifts are not set down by Isaias in their order of dignity.

Objection 1. For it seems that the principal gift is that which, more than the others, God requires of man. Now God requires of man fear, more than the other gifts; for it is written (Deut. 10. 12): *And now, Israel, what doth the Lord thy God require of thee, but that thou fear the Lord thy God?* and (Malach. 1. 6): *If . . . I be a master, where is My fear?* Therefore it seems that fear, which is mentioned last, is not the lowest but the greatest of the gifts.

Obj. 2. Further, piety seems to be a kind of universal good, since the Apostle says (I Tim. 4. 8): *Piety* (Douay,—*Godliness*) *is profitable to all things.* Now a universal good is preferable to particular goods. Therefore piety, which is given the last place but one, seems to be the most excellent gift.

Obj. 3. Further, science perfects man's judgment, while counsel pertains to inquiry. But judgment is more excellent than inquiry. Therefore science is a more excellent gift than counsel, and yet it is set down as being below it.

Obj. 4. Further, fortitude pertains to the appetitive power, while science belongs to reason. But reason is a more excellent power than the appetite. Therefore science is a more excellent gift than fortitude, and yet the latter is given the precedence. Therefore the gifts are not set down in their order of dignity.

On the contrary, Augustine says (*De Serm. Dom. in Monte*, i, 4):[2] "It seems to me that the sevenfold operation of the Holy Ghost, of which Isaias speaks, agrees in degrees and expression with these" (of which we read in Matt. 5. 3); "but there is a difference of order, for there (namely in Isaias) the enumeration begins with the more excellent gifts, here, with the lower gifts."

I answer that, The excellence of the gifts can be measured in two ways: first, absolutely, that is, in relation to their proper acts as proceeding

---

[1] *Moral.,* I, 32 (PL 75, 547).　　　　[2] PL 34, 1234.

from their principles; secondly, relatively, that is, in relation to their matter. If we consider the excellence of the gifts absolutely, they follow the same rule as the virtues, as to their relation one with another, because the gifts perfect man for all the acts of the soul's powers, even as the virtues do, as stated above (A. 4). Hence, as the intellectual virtues have the precedence of the moral virtues, and among the intellectual virtues the contemplative are preferable to the active, namely wisdom, understanding and science to prudence and art (yet so that wisdom stands before understanding, and understanding before science, and prudence and synesis before eubulia), so also among the gifts, wisdom, understanding, science, and counsel are more excellent than piety, fortitude, and fear; and among the latter, piety excels fortitude, and fortitude fear, even as justice surpasses fortitude, and fortitude temperance. But in regard to their matter, fortitude and counsel precede science and piety because fortitude and counsel are concerned with difficult matters, while piety and knowledge regard ordinary matters. Consequently the excellence of the gifts corresponds with the order in which they are enumerated; but so far as wisdom and understanding are given the preference to the others, their excellence is considered absolutely, while so far as counsel and fortitude are preferred to science and piety their excellence is considered with regard to their matter.

Reply Obj. 1. Fear is chiefly required as being the foundation, so to speak, of the perfection of the other gifts, for *the fear of the Lord is the beginning of wisdom* (Ps 110. 10; Ecclus. 1. 16), and not as though it were more excellent than the others. Because, in order of generation, man departs from evil on account of fear (Prov. 16. 16) before doing good works, which result from the other gifts.

Reply Obj. 2. In the words quoted from the Apostle, piety is not compared with all God's gifts, but only with *bodily exercise,* of which he had said that it *is profitable to little.*

Reply Obj. 3. Although science stands before counsel by reason of its judgment, yet counsel is more excellent by reason of its matter, for counsel is only concerned with matters of difficulty[1] while the judgment of science embraces all matters.

Reply Obj. 4. The directive gifts which pertain to the reason are more excellent than the executive gifts if we consider them in relation to their acts as proceeding from their powers, because reason transcends the appetite as a rule

transcends the thing ruled. But on the part of the matter, counsel is united to fortitude as the directive power to the executive, and so also is science united to piety; for counsel and fortitude are concerned with matters of difficulty, while science and piety are concerned with ordinary matters. Hence counsel together with fortitude, by reason of their matter, are numbered ahead of science and piety.

ARTICLE 8. *Whether the Virtues Are More Excellent Than the Gifts?*

We proceed thus to the Eighth Article: It would seem that the virtues are more excellent than the gifts.

Objection 1. For Augustine says (*De Trin.* xv, 18)[2] while speaking of charity: "No gift of God is more excellent than this. It is this alone which divides the children of the eternal kingdom from the children of eternal damnation. Other gifts are bestowed by the Holy Ghost, but, without charity, they avail nothing." But charity is a virtue. Therefore a virtue is more excellent than the gifts of the Holy Ghost.

Obj. 2. Further, that which is first naturally, seems to be more excellent. Now the virtues precede the gifts of the Holy Ghost; for Gregory says (*Moral.* ii, 49)[3] that "the gift of the Holy Ghost in the mind it works on forms first of all justice, prudence, fortitude, temperance . . . and afterwards tempers the mind in the seven virtues (namely, the gifts), so as against folly to bestow wisdom; against dullness, understanding; against rashness, counsel; against fear, fortitude; against ignorance, science; against hardness of heart, piety; against pride, fear." Therefore the virtues are more excellent than the gifts.

Obj. 3. Further, Augustine says (*De Lib. Arb.* ii, 18, 19)[4] that "the virtues cannot be used to evil purpose." But it is possible to make evil use of the gifts, for Gregory says (*Moral.* i, 35):[5] "We offer up the sacrifice of prayer . . . lest wisdom may uplift; or understanding, while it runs nimbly, deviate from the right path; or counsel, while it multiplies itself, grow into confusion; that fortitude, while it gives confidence, may not make us rash; lest science, while it knows and yet loves not, may swell the mind; lest piety, while it swerves from the right line, may become distorted; and lest fear, while it is unduly alarmed, may plunge us into the pit of despair." Therefore the virtues are more excellent than the gifts of the Holy Ghost.

---

[1] Aristotle, *Ethics,* III, 3 (1112^{b}9).

[2] PL 42, 1082.   [3] PL 75, 592.
[4] PL 32, 1267, 1268.   [5] PL 75, 549.

On the contrary, The gifts are bestowed to assist the virtues and to remedy certain defects, as is shown in the passage quoted (Obj. 2), so that it seems that they accomplish what the virtues cannot. Therefore the gifts are more excellent than the virtues.

I answer that, As was shown above (Q. LVIII, A. 3; Q. LXII, A. 1), there are three kinds of virtues; for some are theological, some intellectual, and some moral. The theological virtues are those by which man's mind is united to God; the intellectual virtues are those by which reason itself is perfected; and the moral virtues are those which perfect the powers of appetite in obedience to the reason. On the other hand the gifts of the Holy Ghost dispose all the powers of the soul to be subject to the Divine motion.

Accordingly the gifts seem to be compared to the theological virtues, by which man is united to the Holy Ghost his Mover, in the same way as the moral virtues are compared to the intellectual virtues, which perfect the reason, the moving principle of the moral virtues. Therefore as the intellectual virtues are more excellent than the moral virtues and control them, so the theological virtues are more excellent than the gifts of the Holy Ghost and regulate them. Hence Gregory says (*Moral.* i, 27)[1] that "the seven sons, (that is, the seven gifts), never attain the perfection of the number ten, unless all that they do be done in faith, hope, and charity."

But if we compare the gifts to the other virtues, intellectual and moral, then the gifts have the precedence of the virtues. Because the gifts perfect the soul's powers in relation to the Holy Ghost their Mover; but the virtues perfect either the reason itself or the other powers in relation to reason; and it is evident that the more exalted the mover, the more excellent the disposition by which the thing moved requires to be disposed. Therefore the gifts are more perfect than the virtues.

Reply Obj. 1. Charity is a theological virtue; and such we grant to be more perfect than the gifts.

Reply Obj. 2. There are two ways in which one thing precedes another. One is in order of perfection and dignity, as love of God precedes love of our neighbor, and in this way the gifts precede the intellectual and moral virtues, but follow the theological virtues. The other is the order of generation or disposition; thus love of one's neighbour precedes love of God, as regards

[1] PL 75, 544.

the act. And in this way moral and intellectual virtues precede the gifts, since man, through being well subordinate to his own reason, is disposed to be rightly subordinate to God.

Reply Obj. 3. Wisdom and understanding and the like are gifts of the Holy Ghost, according as they are informed by charity, which *dealeth not perversely* (I Cor. 13. 4). Consequently wisdom and understanding and the like cannot be used to evil purpose, in so far as they are gifts of the Holy Ghost. But, lest they depart from the perfection of charity, they assist one another. This is what Gregory means to say.

QUESTION LXIX
OF THE BEATITUDES
(*In Four Articles*)

WE must now consider the beatitudes, under which head there are four points of inquiry: (1) Whether the beatitudes differ from the gifts and virtues? (2) Of the rewards of the beatitudes, and whether they refer to this life? (3) Of the number of the beatitudes. (4) Of the fittingness of the rewards ascribed to the beatitudes.

ARTICLE 1. *Whether the Beatitudes Differ From the Virtues and Gifts?*

We thus proceed to the First Article: It would seem that the beatitudes do not differ from the virtues and gifts.

Objection 1. For Augustine (*De Serm. Dom. in Monte,* i, 4)[2] assigns the beatitudes recited by Matthew (5. 3, *sqq.*) to the gifts of the Holy Ghost; and Ambrose in his commentary on Luke 6. 20, *sqq.,*[3] ascribes the beatitudes mentioned there, to the four cardinal virtues. Therefore the beatitudes do not differ from the virtues and gifts.

Obj. 2. Further, there are but two rules of the human will,—the reason and the eternal law, as stated above (Q. XIX, AA. 3, 4; Q. XXI, A. 1). Now the virtues perfect man in relation to reason, while the gifts perfect him in relation to the eternal law of the Holy Ghost, as is clear from what has been said (Q. LXVIII, AA. 1, 3). Therefore there cannot be anything else pertaining to the rectitude of the human will other than the virtues and gifts. Therefore the beatitudes do not differ from them.

Obj. 3. Further, among the beatitudes are included meekness, justice, and mercy, which are said to be virtues. Therefore the beatitudes do not differ from the virtues and gifts.

[2] PL 34, 1234.　　　　[3] PL 15, 1734.

On the contrary, Certain things are included among the beatitudes that are neither virtues nor gifts, for example poverty, mourning, and peace. Therefore the beatitudes differ from the virtues and gifts.

I answer that, As stated above (Q. II, A. 7; Q. III, A. 1), happiness is the last end of human life. Now one is said to possess the end already, when one hopes to possess it; hence the Philosopher says[1] that "children are said to be happy because they are full of hope"; and the Apostle says (Rom. 8. 24): *We are saved by hope.* Again, we hope to obtain an end because we are suitably moved towards that end, and approach it, and this is done through some action. And a man is moved towards and approaches the happy end by works of virtue, and above all by the works of the gifts, if we speak of eternal happiness, for which our reason is not sufficient, since we need to be moved by the Holy Ghost, and to be perfected with His gifts that we may obey and follow Him. Consequently the beatitudes differ from the virtues and gifts, not as habit from habit, but as act from habit.

Reply Obj. 1. Augustine and Ambrose assign the beatitudes to the gifts and virtues as acts are ascribed to habits. But the gifts are more excellent than the cardinal virtues, as stated above (Q. LXVIII, A. 8). Therefore Ambrose, in explaining the beatitudes propounded to the throng, assigns them to the cardinal virtues, but Augustine, who is explaining the beatitudes delivered to the disciples on the mountain, and so to those who were more perfect, ascribes them to the gifts of the Holy Ghost.

Reply Obj. 2. This argument proves that no other habits, besides the virtues and gifts, rectify human conduct.

Reply Obj. 3. Meekness is to be taken as denoting the act of meekness, and the same applies to justice and mercy. And though these might seem to be virtues, they are nevertheless ascribed to gifts, because the gifts perfect man in all matters wherein the virtues perfect him, as stated above (Q. LXVIII, A. 2).

ARTICLE 2. *Whether the Rewards Assigned to the Beatitudes Refer to This Life?*

We proceed thus to the Second Article: It would seem that the rewards assigned to the beatitudes do not refer to this life.

Objection 1. Because some are said to be happy because they hope for a reward, as stated above (A. 1). Now the object of hope is future

happiness. Therefore these rewards refer to the life to come.

Obj. 2. Further, certain punishments are set down in opposition to the beatitudes in Luke 6. 25, where we read: *Woe to you that are filled; for you shall hunger. Woe to you that now laugh, for you shall mourn and weep.* Now these punishments do not refer to this life, because frequently men are not punished in this life, according to Job 21. 13: *They spend their days in wealth.* Therefore neither do the rewards of the beatitudes refer to this life.

Obj. 3. Further, the kingdom of heaven which is set down as the reward of poverty is the happiness of heaven, as Augustine says.[2] Again, abundant fullness is not to be had save in the life to come, according to Ps. 16. 15: *I shall be filled* (Douay,—*satisfied*) *when Thy glory shall appear.* Again, it is only in the future life that we shall see God, and that our Divine sonship will be made manifest, according to I John 3. 2: *We are now the sons of God; and it hath not yet appeared what we shall be. We know that, when He shall appear, we shall be like to Him, because we shall see Him as He is.* Therefore these rewards refer to the future life.

On the contrary, Augustine says (*De Serm. Dom. in Monte,* i, 4):[3] "These promises can be fulfilled in this life, as we believe them to have been fulfilled in the apostles. For no words can express that complete change into the likeness even of an angel, which is promised to us after this life."

I answer that, Expounders of Holy Writ are not agreed in speaking of these rewards. For some, with Ambrose (*Super Luc.* 5),[4] hold that all these rewards refer to the life to come; while Augustine (*loc. cit.*) holds them to refer to the present life; and Chrysostom in his homilies (In Matt. 15)[5] says that some refer to the future life, and some to the present life.

In order to make the matter clear we must take note that hope of future happiness may be in us for two reasons. First, by reason of our having a preparation for, or a disposition to, future happiness, and this is by way of merit; secondly, by a kind of imperfect beginning of future happiness in holy men, even in this life. For it is one thing to hope that the tree will bear fruit when the leaves begin to appear, and another when we see the first signs of the fruit.

Accordingly, those things which are set down as merits in the beatitudes are a kind of prep-

[1] *Ethics,* I, 9 (1100ª3).

[2] *City of God,* XVII, 7 (PL 41, 539); cf. *De Serm. Dom.* I, I (PL 34, 1231).   [3] PL 34, 1235.
[4] PL 15, 1738.   [5] PG 57, 223.

aration for, or disposition to happiness, either perfect or in its beginning; while those that are assigned as rewards may be either perfect happiness, so as to refer to the future life, or some beginning of happiness, such as is found in those who have attained perfection, in which case they refer to the present life. Because when a man begins to make progress in the acts of the virtues and gifts it is to be hoped that he will arrive at perfection, both as a wayfarer and as a citizen of the heavenly kingdom.

Reply Obj. 1. Hope regards future happiness as the last end; but it may also be of the assistance of grace as that which leads to that end, according to Ps. 27. 7: *In Him hath my heart hoped, and I have been helped.*

Reply Obj. 2. Although sometimes the wicked do not undergo temporal punishment in this life, yet they suffer spiritual punishment. Hence Augustine says,[1] "Thou has decreed, and it is so, Lord, that the disordered mind should be its own punishment." The Philosopher, too, says of the wicked[2] that "their soul is divided against itself, . . . one part pulls this way, another that;" and afterwards he concludes, saying: "If wickedness makes a man so miserable, he should strain every nerve to avoid vice." In like manner, although, on the other hand, the good sometimes do not receive material rewards in this life, yet they never lack spiritual rewards, even in this life, according to Matt. 19. 29, and Mark 10. 30: *Ye shall receive a hundred times as much* even *in this time.*

Reply Obj. 3. All these rewards will be fully consummated in the life to come; but meanwhile they are, in a manner, begun, even in this life. Because the kingdom of heaven, as Augustine says,[3] can denote the beginning of perfect wisdom, in so far as the spirit begins to reign in men.—The possession of the land denotes the well-ordered affections of the soul that rests, by its desire, on the solid foundation of the eternal inheritance, signified by the land.—They are comforted in this life, by receiving the Holy Ghost, Who is called the Paraclete, that is, the Comforter.—They have their fill, even in this life, of that food of which Our Lord said (John 4. 34): *My meat is to do the will of Him that sent Me.*—Again, in this life, men obtain God's mercy.—Again, the eye being cleansed by the gift of understanding, we can, so to speak, see God.—Likewise, in this life, those who pacify their own movements approach

to likeness to God, and are called the children of God.—Nevertheless these things will be more perfectly fulfilled in heaven.

ARTICLE 3. *Whether the Beatitudes Are Suitably Enumerated?*

We proceed thus to the Third Article: It would seem that the beatitudes are unsuitably enumerated.

Objection 1. For the beatitudes are assigned to the gifts, as stated above (A. 1, REPLY 1). Now some of the gifts, namely, wisdom and understanding, belong to the contemplative life; yet no beatitude is assigned to the act of contemplation, for all are assigned to matters connected with the active life. Therefore the beatitudes are insufficiently enumerated.

Obj. 2. Further, not only do the executive gifts belong to the active life, but also some of the directive gifts, for instance science and counsel; yet none of the beatitudes seem to be directly connected with the acts of science or counsel. Therefore the beatitudes are insufficiently indicated.

Obj. 3. Further, among the executive gifts connected with the active life fear is said to be connected with poverty, while piety seems to correspond to the beatitude of mercy; yet nothing is included directly connected with justice. Therefore the beatitudes are insufficiently enumerated.

Obj. 4. Further, many other beatitudes are mentioned in Holy Writ. Thus, it is written (Job. 5. 17): *Blessed is the man whom God correcteth;* and (Ps. 1. 1.): *Blessed is the man who hath not walked in the counsel of the ungodly;* and (Prov. 3. 13): *Blessed is the man that findeth wisdom.* Therefore the beatitudes are insufficiently enumerated.

Obj. 5. On the other hand, it seems that too many are mentioned. For there are seven gifts of the Holy Ghost, but eight beatitudes are indicated.

Obj. 6. Further, only four beatitudes are indicated in the sixth chapter of Luke. Therefore the seven or eight mentioned in Matt. 5. are too many.

I answer that, These beatitudes are most suitably enumerated. To make this evident it must be observed that happiness has been held[4] to consist in one of three things: for some have ascribed it to a sensual life, some to an active life, and some to a contemplative life. Now these three kinds of happiness stand in differ-

[1] *Confessions,* I, 19 (PL 32, 670).
[2] *Ethics,* IX, 4 (1166[b]19).
[3] *De Serm. Dom.,* I, 4 (PL 34, 1235).

[4] Cf. Aristotle, *Ethics,* I, 5 (1095[b]16); Thomas, *In Eth.,* I, 5.

ent relations to future Happiness, by hoping for which we are said to be happy. Because sensual happiness, being false and contrary to reason, is an obstacle to future Happiness, while happiness of the active life is a disposition to future Happiness, and contemplative happiness, if perfect, is the very essence of future Happiness, and, if imperfect, is a beginning of it.

And so Our Lord, in the first place, indicated certain beatitudes as removing the obstacle of sensual happiness. For a life of pleasure consists of two things. First, in the affluence of external goods, whether riches or honours. Man is withdrawn from these by a virtue, so that he uses them in moderation; and by a gift, in a more excellent way, so that he despises them altogether. Hence the first beatitude is: *Blessed are the poor in spirit*, which may refer either to the contempt of riches, or to the contempt of honours, which results from humility. Secondly, the sensual life consists in following the bent of one's passions, whether irascible or concupiscible. Man is withdrawn from following the irascible passions by a virtue, so that they are kept within the bounds appointed by the ruling of reason; and by a gift, in a more excellent manner, so that man, according to God's will, is altogether undisturbed by them. Hence the second beatitude is: *Blessed are the meek*. Man is withdrawn from following the concupiscible passions by a virtue so that man uses these passions in moderation; and by a gift, so that, if necessary, he casts them aside altogether; nay more, so that if need be, he makes a deliberate choice of sorrow. Hence the third beatitude is: *Blessed are they that mourn*.

Active life consists chiefly in man's relations with his neighbour, either by way of duty or by way of spontaneous benefit. To the former we are disposed by a virtue, so that we do not refuse to do our duty to our neighbour, which pertains to justice; and by a gift, so that we do the same much more heartily, by accomplishing works of justice with an ardent desire, even as a hungry and thirsty man eats and drinks with eager appetite. Hence the fourth beatitude is: *Blessed are they that hunger and thirst after justice*. With regard to spontaneous favours we are perfected by a virtue, so that we give where reason dictates we should give, for example to our friends or others united to us, which pertains to the virtue of liberality; and by a gift, so that, through reverence for God, we consider only the needs of those on whom we bestow our gratuitous bounty. Hence it is writ-

ten (Luke 14. 12, 13): *When thou makest a dinner or supper, call not thy friends, nor thy brethren*, etc. . . . *but . . . call the poor, the maimed*, etc.; which, properly is to have mercy. Hence the fifth beatitude is: *Blessed are the merciful*.

Those things which concern the contemplative life are either final Happiness itself, or some beginning of it, and so they are included in the beatitudes not as merits, but as rewards. Yet the effects of the active life, which dispose man for the contemplative life, are included in the beatitudes as merits. Now the effect of the active life as regards those virtues and gifts by which man is perfected in himself by the cleansing of man's heart, so that it is not defiled by the passions. Hence the sixth beatitude is: *Blessed are the clean of heart*. But as regards the virtues and gifts by which man is perfected in relation to his neighbour, the effect of the active life is peace, according to Isaias 32. 17: *The work of justice shall be peace*. Hence the seventh beatitude is: *Blessed are the peacemakers*.

Reply Obj. 1. The acts of the gifts which belong to the active life are indicated in the merits, but the acts of gifts pertaining to the contemplative life are indicated in the rewards, for the reason given above. Because to *see God* corresponds to the gift of understanding, and to be like God by being adopted *children of God*, corresponds to the gift of wisdom.

Reply Obj. 2. In things pertaining to the active life, knowledge is not sought for its own sake, but for the sake of operation, as even the Philosopher states.[1] And therefore, since Happiness implies something ultimate, the beatitudes do not include the acts of those gifts which direct man in the active life (such acts, that is, as are elicited by those gifts, as, for example to counsel is the act of counsel, and to judge, the act of knowledge); but, on the other hand, they include those operative acts of which the gifts have the direction, as, for example mourning in respect of science and mercy in respect of counsel.

Reply Obj. 3. In applying the beatitudes to the gifts we may consider two things. One is likeness of matter. In this way all the first five beatitudes may be assigned to science and counsel as to their directing principles. But they must be distributed among the executive gifts, so that, namely, hunger and thirst for justice, and mercy too, correspond to piety, which perfects man in his relations to others; meekness to

[1] *Ethics*, II, 2 (1103[b]27).

fortitude, for Ambrose says on Luke 6. 22:[1] "It is the business of fortitude to conquer anger, and to curb indignation," fortitude being about the irascible passions; poverty and mourning to the gift of fear, by which man withdraws from the lusts and pleasures of the world.

Secondly, we may consider the motives of the beatitudes, and, in this way, some of them will have to be assigned differently. Because the principal motive for meekness is reverence for God which belongs to piety. The chief motive for mourning is science, by which man knows his failings and those of worldly things, according to Eccles. 1. 18: *He that addeth knowledge, addeth also sorrow* (Vulg.,—*labour*). The principal motive for hungering after the works of justice, is fortitude of the soul. And the chief motive for being merciful is God's counsel, according to Dan 4. 24: *Let my counsel be acceptable to the king* (Vulg.,—*to thee, O king*): *and redeem thou thy sins with alms, and thy iniquities with works of mercy to the poor.* It is thus that Augustine assigns them (*De Serm. Dom. in Monte*, i, 4).[2]

Reply Obj. 4. All the beatitudes mentioned in Holy Writ must be reduced to these, either as to the merits or as to the rewards, because they must all belong either to the active or to the contemplative life. Accordingly, when we read, *Blessed is the man whom the Lord correcteth*, we must refer this to the beatitude of mourning. When we read, *Blessed is the man that hath not walked in the counsel of the ungodly*, we must refer it to cleanness of heart. And when we read, *Blessed is the man that findeth wisdom*, this must be referred to the reward of the seventh beatitude. The same applies to all others that can be brought forward.

Reply Obj. 5. The eighth beatitude is a confirmation and declaration of all those that precede. Because from the very fact that a man is confirmed in poverty of spirit, meekness, and the rest, it follows that no persecution will induce him to renounce them. Hence the eighth beatitude corresponds, in a way, to all preceding seven.

Reply Obj. 6. Luke relates Our Lord's sermon as addressed to the multitude (6. 17). Hence he sets down the beatitudes according to the capacity of the multitude, who know no other happiness than pleasure, temporal and earthly. Therefore by these four beatitudes Our Lord excludes four things which seem to belong to such happiness. The first of these is abundance of external goods, which he sets aside

by saying: *Blessed are ye poor.* The second is that man be well off as to his body, in food and drink and so forth; this he excludes by saying in the second place: *Blessed are ye that hunger.* The third is that it should be well with man as to joyfulness of heart, and this he puts aside by saying: *Blessed are ye that weep now.* The fourth is the outward favour of man, and this he excludes, saying fourthly: *Blessed shall you be, when men shall hate you.* And as Ambrose says on Luke 6. 20,[3] "poverty pertains to temperance, which is unmoved by delights; hunger, to justice, since who hungers is compassionate and, through compassion gives; mourning, to prudence, which deplores perishable things; endurance of men's hatred belongs to fortitude."

ARTICLE 4. *Whether the Rewards of the Beatitudes Are Suitably Enumerated?*

We proceed thus to the Fourth Article: It would seem that the rewards of the beatitudes are unsuitably enumerated.

Objection 1. Because the kingdom of heaven, which is eternal life, contains all good things. Therefore, once given the kingdom of heaven, no other rewards should be mentioned.

Obj. 2. Further, the kingdom of heaven is assigned as the reward both of the first and of the eighth beatitude. Therefore, on the same ground, it should have been assigned to all.

Obj. 3. Further, the beatitudes are arranged in the ascending order, as Augustine remarks (*De Serm. Dom. in Monte*, i, 4).[4] But the rewards seem to be placed in the descending order, since to *possess the land* is less than to possess *the kingdom of heaven*. Therefore these rewards are unsuitably enumerated.

On the contrary stands the authority of Our Lord Who propounded these rewards.

I answer that, These rewards are most suitably assigned, considering the nature of the beatitudes in relation to the three kinds of happiness indicated above (A. 3). For the first three beatitudes concerned the withdrawal of man from those things in which sensual happiness consists, which happiness man desires by seeking the object of his natural desire, not where he should seek it, namely in God, but in temporal and perishable things. Therefore the rewards of the first three beatitudes correspond to these things which some men seek to find in earthly happiness. For men seek in external things, that is, riches and honours, a certain excellence and abundance, both of which are implied in the kingdom of heaven, by which man attains to excellence and abundance of good things in God. Hence Our Lord promised the kingdom of heaven to the poor in spirit. Again, cruel and pitiless men seek by wrangling and fighting to destroy their enemies so as to gain security for themselves. Hence Our Lord promised the meek a secure and peaceful possession of the land of the living, by which the solid reality of eternal goods is denoted. Again, men seek consolation for the toils of the present life, in the lusts and pleasures of the world. Hence our Lord promises comfort to those that mourn.

Two other beatitudes pertain to the works of active happiness, which are the works of virtues directing man in his relations to his neighbour, from which operations some men withdraw through inordinate love of their own good. Hence Our Lord assigns to these beatitudes rewards in correspondence with the motives for which men recede from them. For there are some who recede from acts of justice, and instead of rendering what is due, lay hands on what is not theirs, that they may abound in temporal goods. Therefore Our Lord promised those who hunger after justice that they shall have their fill. Some, again, recede from works of mercy lest they be busied with other people's misery. Hence Our Lord promised the merciful that they should obtain mercy, and be delivered from all misery.

The last two beatitudes belong to contemplative happiness or beatitude, and therefore the rewards are assigned in correspondence with the dispositions included in the merit. For cleanness of the eye disposes one to see clearly; hence the clean of heart are promised that they shall see God.—Again, to make peace either in oneself or among others shows a man to be a follower of God, Who is the God of unity and peace. Hence, as a reward he is promised the glory of the Divine sonship, consisting in perfect union with God through consummate wisdom.

Reply Obj. 1. As Chrysostom says *(Hom. xv in Matt.)*,[1] all these rewards are one in reality, namely eternal happiness, which the human intellect cannot grasp. Hence it was necessary to describe it by means of various goods known to us, while observing due proportion to the merits to which those rewards are assigned.

Reply Obj. 2. Just as the eighth beatitude is a confirmation of all the beatitudes, so it deserves all the rewards of the beatitudes. Hence it returns to the first, that we may understand that all the other rewards that follow are to be attributed to it. Or else, according to Ambrose

[1] PG 57, 228.

(Super Luc. 5),[2] the kingdom of heaven is promised to the poor in spirit as regards the glory of the soul; but to those who suffer persecution in their bodies, it is promised as regards the glory of the body.

Reply Obj. 3. The rewards are also arranged in ascending order. For it is more to possess the land of the heavenly kingdom than simply to have it, since we have many things without possessing them firmly and peacefully. Again, it is more to be comforted in the kingdom than to have and possess it, for there are many things the possession of which is accompanied by sorrow. Again, it is more to have one's fill than simply to be comforted, because fullness implies abundance of comfort. And mercy surpasses satiety, for thus man receives more than he merited or was able to desire. And yet more is it to see God, even as he is a greater man who not only dines at court, but also sees the king's countenance. Lastly, the highest place in the royal palace belongs to the king's son.

QUESTION LXX
OF THE FRUITS OF THE HOLY GHOST
(In Four Articles)

WE must now consider the Fruits of the Holy Ghost, under which head there are four points of inquiry: (1) Whether the fruits of the Holy Ghosts are acts? (2) Whether they differ from the beatitudes? (3) Of their number? (4) Of their opposition to the works of the flesh.

ARTICLE 1. *Whether the Fruits of the Holy Ghost Which the Apostle Enumerates* (Gal. 5) *Are Acts?*

We proceed thus to the First Article: It would seem that the fruits of the Holy Ghost, enumerated by the Apostle (Gal. 5. 22, 23), are not acts.

Objection 1. For that which bears fruit should not itself be called a fruit; otherwise we should go on indefinitely. But our actions bear fruit, for it is written (Wisd. 3. 15): *The fruit of good labour is glorious,* and (John 4. 36): *He that reapeth receiveth wages, and gathereth fruit unto life everlasting.* Therefore our actions are not to be called fruits.

Obj. 2. Further, as Augustine says *(De Trin.* x, 10),[3] "we enjoy[4] the things we know, when the will rests by rejoicing in them." But our

[2] PL 15, 1737.
[3] PL 42, 981.
[4] *Fruimur,* from which verb we have the Latin *fructus* and the English *fruit.*

will should not rest in our actions for their own sake. Therefore our actions should not be called fruits.

Obj. 3. Further, among the fruits of the Holy Ghost, the Apostle numbers certain virtues, namely charity, meekness, faith, and chastity. Now virtues are not actions but habits, as stated above (Q. LV, A. 1). Therefore the fruits are not actions.

On the contrary, It is written (Matt. 12. 33): *By the fruit the tree is known;* that is to say, man is known by his works, as holy men explain the passage.[1] Therefore human actions themselves are called fruits.

I answer that, The word fruit has been transferred from the material to the spiritual world. Now fruit, among material things, is the product of a plant when it comes to perfection, and has a certain sweetness. This fruit has a twofold relation—to the tree that produces it, and to the man who gathers the fruit from the tree. Accordingly, in spiritual matters, we may take the word fruit in two ways: first, so that the fruit of man, who is likened to the tree, is that which he produces; secondly, so that man's fruit is what he gathers.

Yet not all that man gathers is fruit, but only that which is last and gives pleasure. For a man has both a field and a tree, and yet these are not called fruits, but that only which is last, namely, that which man intends to gather from the field and from the tree. In this sense man's fruit is his last end which is intended for his enjoyment.

If, however, by man's fruit we understand a product of man, then human actions are called fruits, because operation is the second act of the operator, and gives pleasure if it is suitable to him. If then man's operation proceeds from man in virtue of his reason, it is said to be the fruit of his reason. But if it proceeds from him in respect of a higher power, which is the power of the Holy Ghost, then man's operation is said to be the fruit of the Holy Ghost, as of a Divine seed, for it is written (I John 3. 9): *Whosoever is born of God, committeth no sin, for His seed abideth in him.*

Reply Obj. 1. Since fruit is something last and final, nothing hinders one fruit bearing another fruit, even as one end is subordinate to another. And so our works, in so far as they are produced by the Holy Ghost working in us, are fruits. But, in so far as they are referred to the end which is eternal life, they should rather be called flowers; hence it is written (Ecclus.

24. 23): *My flowers are the fruits of honour and riches.*

Reply Obj. 2. When the will is said to delight in a thing for its own sake, this may be understood in two ways. First, so that the expression "for the sake of" be taken to designate the final cause; and in this way, man delights in nothing for its own sake, except the last end. Secondly, so that it express the formal cause; and in this way a man may delight in anything that is delightful by reason of its form. Thus it is clear that a sick man delights in health, for its own sake, as in an end; in an agreeable medicine, not as in an end, but as in something tasty; and in a harsh medicine, not in any way for its own sake, but only for the sake of something else. Accordingly we must say that man must delight in God for His own sake, as being his last end, and in virtuous deeds, not as being his end, but for the sake of their inherent goodness which is delightful to the virtuous. Hence Ambrose says (*De Parad.* xiii)[2] that virtuous deeds are called fruits because they refresh those that have them, with a holy and genuine delight.

Reply Obj. 3. Sometimes the names of the virtues are applied to their actions; thus Augustine writes (*Tract.* xl *in Joann.*):[3] "Faith is to believe what thou seest not": and:[4] Charity is the movement of the soul "in loving God and our neighbour." It is thus that the names of the virtues are used in numbering the fruits.

ARTICLE 2. *Whether the Fruits Differ From the Beatitudes?*

We proceed thus to the Second Article: It would seem that the fruits do not differ from the beatitudes.

Objection 1. For the beatitudes are assigned to the gifts, as stated above (Q. LXIX, A. 1, Reply 1). But the gifts perfect man in so far as he is moved by the Holy Ghost. Therefore the beatitudes themselves are fruits of the Holy Ghost.

Obj. 2. Further, as the fruit of eternal life is to future beatitude which is that of actual possession, so are the fruits of the present life to the beatitudes of the present life, which are based on hope. Now the fruit of eternal life is identified with future beatitude. Therefore the fruits of the present life are the beatitudes.

Obj. 3. Further, fruit is essentially something ultimate and delightful. Now this is the very nature of beatitude, as stated above (Q. III,

---

[1] *Glossa ordin.* (v, 29B); see below, Q. LXXIII, A. 6.

[2] PL 14, 325.
[3] PL 35, 1690.
[4] *Christian Doctrine,* III, 10 (PL 34, 71).

A. 1; Q. IV, A. 1). Therefore fruit and beatitude have the same nature, and consequently should not be distinguished from one another.

On the contrary, Things divided into different species, differ from one another. But fruits and beatitudes are divided into different parts, as is clear from the way in which they are enumerated. Therefore the fruits differ from the beatitudes.

I answer that, More is required for a beatitude than for a fruit. Because it is sufficient for a fruit to be something ultimate and delightful, while for a beatitude it must be something perfect and excellent. Hence all the beatitudes may be called fruits, but not vice versa. For the fruits are any virtuous deeds in which one delights, but the beatitudes are none but perfect works, and which, by reason of their perfection, are assigned to the gifts rather than to the virtues, as already stated (Q. LXIX, A. 1, Reply 1).

Reply Obj. 1. This argument proves the beatitudes to be fruits, but not that all the fruits are beatitudes.

Reply Obj. 2. The fruit of eternal life is ultimate and perfect absolutely; hence it in no way differs from future beatitude. On the other hand the fruits of the present life are not ultimate and perfect absolutely. Therefore not all the fruits are beatitudes.

Reply Obj. 3. More is required for a beatitude than for a fruit, as we have said.

ARTICLE 3. *Whether the Fruits Are Suitably Enumerated by the Apostle?*

We proceed thus to the Third Article: It would seem that the fruits are unsuitably enumerated by the Apostle (Gal. 5. 22, 23).

Objection 1. For, elsewhere he says that there is only one fruit of the present life, according to Rom. 6. 22: *You have your fruit unto sanctification.* Moreover it is written (Isa. 27. 9): *This is all the fruit . . . that the sin . . . be taken away.* Therefore we should not number twelve fruits.

Obj. 2. Further, fruit is the product of spiritual seed, as stated (A. 1). But Our Lord mentions (Matt. 13. 23) a threefold fruit as growing from a spiritual seed in a good ground, namely *hundredfold, sixtyfold* and *thirtyfold.* Therefore one should not put down twelve fruits.

Obj. 3. Further, the very nature of fruit is to be something ultimate and delightful. But this does not apply to all the fruits mentioned by the Apostle; for patience and long-suffering seem to be in painful things, while faith is not something ultimate, but rather something pri-

mary and fundamental. Therefore too many fruits are enumerated.

Obj. 4. *On the other hand,* It seems that they are enumerated insufficiently and incompletely. For it has been stated (A. 2) that all the beatitudes may be called fruits, yet not all are mentioned here. Nor is there anything corresponding to the acts of wisdom, and of many other virtues. Therefore it seems that the fruits are insufficiently enumerated.

I answer that, The number of the twelve fruits enumerated by the Apostle is suitable, and that there may also be a reference to them in the twelve fruits of which it is written (Apoc. 22. 2): *On both sides of the river was the tree of life bearing twelve fruits.* Since, however, a fruit is something that proceeds from a source as from a seed or root, the difference between these fruits must be gathered from the various ways in which the Holy Ghost proceeds in us. The process of the Holy Ghost consists in this, that the mind of man is set in order, first of all in regard to itself; secondly, in regard to things that are near it; thirdly, in regard to things that are below it.

Accordingly man's mind is well disposed in regard to itself when it has a good disposition towards good things and towards evil things. Now the first disposition of the human mind towards the good is effected by love, which is the first of our affections and the root of them all, as stated above (Q. XXVII, A. 4). Therefore among the fruits of the Holy Ghost, we place "charity," in which the Holy Ghost is given in a special manner, as in His own likeness, since He Himself is love. Hence it is written (Rom. 5. 5): *The Charity of God is poured forth in our hearts by the Holy Ghost, Who is given to us.*

The necessary result of the love of charity is joy. For every lover rejoices at being united to the beloved. Now charity has always actual presence of God Whom it loves, according to 1 John 4. 16: *He that abideth in charity, abideth in God, and God in Him,* and therefore the sequel of charity is "joy." Now the perfection of joy is peace, in two respects. First, as regards freedom from outward disturbance; for it is impossible to rejoice perfectly in the beloved good, if one is disturbed in its enjoyment; and again, if a man's heart is perfectly set at peace on one object, he cannot be disquieted by any other, since he accounts all others as nothing; hence it is written (Ps. 118. 165): *Much peace have they that love Thy Law, and to them there is no stumbling-block,* because, namely, external things do not disturb them in their enjoyment of God. Secondly, as regards the calming of the restless desire; for he does not perfectly rejoice who is not satisfied with the object of his joy. Now peace implies these two things, namely, that we be not disturbed by external things, and that our desires rest altogether in one object. Therefore after charity and joy, "peace" is given the third place.

In evil things the mind has a good disposition, in respect of two things. First, by not being disturbed whenever evil threatens, which pertains to "patience"; secondly, by not being disturbed whenever good things are delayed; which belongs to "long-suffering," since to lack good is a kind of evil.[1]

Man's mind is well disposed as regards what is near him, namely his neighbour, first, as to the will to do good; and to this belongs "goodness." Secondly, as to the execution of welldoing; and to this belongs "benignity," for the benign are those in whom the salutary flame (bonus ignis) of love has enkindled the desire to be kind to their neighbour. Thirdly, as to his suffering with equanimity the evils his neighbour inflicts on him. To this belongs "meekness," which curbs anger. Fourthly, in the point of our refraining from doing harm to our neighbour not only through anger, but also through fraud or deceit. To this pertains "faith," if we take it as denoting fidelity. But if we take it for the faith by which we believe in God, then man is directed by it to that which is above him, so that he subject his intellect and, consequently, all that is his, to God.

Man is well disposed in respect of that which is below him, as regards external action, by "modesty," by which we observe the "mode" in all our words and deeds; as regards internal desires, by "continency" and "chastity": whether these two differ because chastity withdraws man from unlawful desires, continency also from lawful desires; or because the continent man is subject to concupiscence, but is not led away, while the chaste man is neither subject to nor led away by them.

Reply Obj. 1. Sanctification is effected by all the virtues, by which also sins are taken away. Consequently fruit is mentioned there in the singular on account of its being generically one, though divided into many species which are spoken of as so many fruits.

Reply Obj. 2. The hundredfold, sixtyfold, and thirtyfold fruits do not differ as various

species of virtuous acts, but as various degrees of perfection, even in the same virtue. Thus continency of the married state is said to be signified by the thirtyfold fruit; the continency of widowhood, by the sixtyfold; and virginal continency, by the hundredfold fruit.[2] There are, moreover, other ways in which holy men distinguish three evangelical fruits according to the three degrees of virtue.[3] And they speak of three degrees, because the perfection of anything is considered with respect to its beginning, its middle, and its end.

Reply Obj. 3. The fact of not being disturbed by painful things is something to delight in. And as to faith, if we consider it as the foundation, it has the aspect of being ultimate and delightful according as it contains certainty; hence a gloss expounds thus: "Faith, which is certainty about the unseen."[4]

Reply Obj. 4. As Augustine says on Gal. 5. 22, 23,[5] "the Apostle had no intention of teaching us how many either works of the flesh, or fruits of the Spirit there are, but to show how the former should be avoided, and the latter sought after." Hence either more or fewer fruits might have been mentioned. Nevertheless, all the acts of the gifts and virtues can be reduced to these by a certain kind of fittingness, in so far as all the virtues and gifts must direct the mind in one of the above-mentioned ways. Therefore the acts of wisdom and of any gifts directing to good, are reduced to charity, joy, and peace. The reason why he mentions these rather than others is that these imply either enjoyment of good things, or relief from evils, which things seem to belong to the notion of fruit.

ARTICLE 4. Whether the Fruits of the Holy Ghost Are Contrary to the Works of the Flesh?

We proceed thus to the Fourth Article: It would seem that the fruits of the Holy Ghost are not contrary to the works of the flesh which the Apostle enumerates (Gal. 5. 19, sqq.).

Objection 1. Because contraries are in the same genus. But the works of the flesh are not called fruits. Therefore the fruits of the Spirit are not contrary to them.

Obj. 2. Further, one thing has one contrary. Now the Apostle mentions more works of the flesh than fruits of the Spirit. Therefore the

[1] Aristotle, Ethics, v, 3 (1131ᵇ21); cf. Cicero, Tuscul., I, 36 (DD III, 644).

[2] Jerome, Adv. Iovin., I, 3 (PL 23, 223).
[3] See Augustine, Quaest. Evang., I, 9, on Matt. 13.13 (PL 35, 1325); Thomas, Cat. Aurea, In Matt. 13, on verse 13.
[4] Glossa Interl., on Gal. 5.23 (VI, 87V); Glossa Lombardi, on Gal. 5.23 (PL 192, 160).
[5] PL 35, 2141.

fruits of the Spirit and the works of the flesh are not contrary to one another.

Obj. 3. Further, among the fruits of the Spirit, the first place is given to charity, joy, and peace; to which, fornication, uncleanness, and immodesty, which are the first of the works of the flesh, are not opposed. Therefore the fruits of the Spirit are not contrary to the works of the flesh.

On the contrary, The Apostle says *(ibid.* 17) that *the flesh lusteth against the spirit, and the spirit against the flesh.*

I answer that, The works of the flesh and the fruits of the Spirit may be taken in two ways. First, in general. And in this way the fruits of the Holy Ghost considered in general are contrary to the works of the flesh. Because the Holy Ghost moves the human mind to that which is in accord with reason, or rather to that which is above reason; but the fleshly, that is, the sensitive appetite draws man to sensible goods which are beneath him. Therefore, since upward and downward are contrary movements in the physical order, so in human actions the works of the flesh are contrary to the fruits of the Spirit.

Secondly, both fruits and fleshly works as enumerated may be considered singly, each according to its specific nature. And in this way they are not of necessity contrary each to each, because, as stated above (A. 3, ʀᴇᴘʟʏ 4), the Apostle did not intend to enumerate all the works, whether spiritual or carnal.—However, by a kind of adaptation, Augustine, commenting on Gal. 5. 22, 23,[1] contrasts the fruits with the carnal works, each to each. Thus "to fornication, which is the love of satisfying lust outside lawful wedlock, we may contrast charity, whereby the soul is wedded to God, wherein also is true chastity. By uncleanness we must understand whatever disturbances arise from fornication, and to these the joy of tranquillity is opposed. Idolatry, by reason of which war was waged against the Gospel of God, is opposed to peace. Against witchcrafts, enmities, contentions, emulations, wraths and quarrels, there is long-suffering, which helps us to bear the evils inflicted on us by those among whom we dwell; while kindness helps us to cure those evils; and goodness, to forgive them. In contrast to heresy there is faith; to envy, mildness; to drunkenness and revellings, continency."

Reply Obj. 1. That which proceeds from a tree against the tree's nature, is not called its fruit, but rather its corruption. And since works of

[1] PL 35, 2141.

virtue are connatural to reason, while works of vice are contrary to reason, therefore it is that works of virtue are called fruits, but not so works of vice.

Reply Obj. 2. Good happens in one way, evil in all manner of ways, as Dionysius says *(Div. Nom.* iv),[2] so that to one virtue many vices are contrary. Consequently we must not be surprised if the works of the flesh are more numerous than the fruits of the spirit.

The Reply to the Third Objection is clear from what has been said.

(b) Evil Habits—that is, Vices
QUESTION LXXI
Oꜰ Vɪᴄᴇ ᴀɴᴅ Sɪɴ Cᴏɴsɪᴅᴇʀᴇᴅ ɪɴ Tʜᴇᴍsᴇʟᴠᴇs
(In Six Articles)

Wᴇ have in the next place to consider vice and sin, about which six points have to be considered: (1) Vice and sin considered in themselves; (2) their distinction (Q. ʟxxɪɪ); (3) their comparison with one another (Q. ʟxxɪɪɪ); (4) the subject of sin (Q. ʟxxɪᴠ); (5) the cause of sin (Q. ʟxxᴠ); (6) the effect of sin (Q. ʟxxxᴠ).

Under the first head there are six points of inquiry: (1) Whether vice is contrary to virtue? (2) Whether vice is contrary to nature? (3) Which is worse, a vice or a vicious act? (4) Whether a vicious act is compatible with virtue? (5) Whether every sin includes action? (6) Of the definition of sin proposed by Augustine *(Contra Faust.* xxii, 27):[3] "Sin is a word, deed, or desire against the eternal law."

Aʀᴛɪᴄʟᴇ 1. *Whether Vice Is Contrary to Virtue?*

We proceed thus to the First Article: It would seem that vice is not contrary to virtue.

Objection 1. For "one thing has one contrary," as proved in the *Metaphysics.*[4] Now sin and malice are contrary to virtue. Therefore vice is not contrary to it, since vice applies also to undue disposition of bodily members or of any things whatever.

Obj. 2. Further, virtue denotes a certain perfection of power. But vice does not denote anything pertaining to power. Therefore vice is not contrary to virtue.

Obj. 3. Further, Cicero says *(De Quæst. Tusc.* iv, 13)[5] that virtue is the soul's health. Now sickness or disease, rather than vice, is opposed to health. Therefore vice is not contrary to virtue.

On the contrary, Augustine says *(De Perfect.*

[2] Sect. 31 (PG 3, 732).   [3] PL 42, 418.
[4] Aristotle, X, 4 (1055ᵃ19).   [5] DD ɪᴠ, 30.

Justit. ii)[1] that "vice is a quality in respect of which the soul is evil." But virtue is a quality which makes its subject good, as was shown above (Q. LV, AA. 3, 4). Therefore vice is contrary to virtue.

I answer that, Two things may be considered in virtue,—the essence of virtue, and that to which virtue is ordered. In the essence of virtue we may consider something directly, and we may consider something which is a consequence. Virtue implies *directly* a disposition by which the subject is well disposed according to the mode of its nature; hence the Philosopher says[2] that "virtue is a disposition of a perfect thing to that which is best; and by perfect I mean that which is disposed according to its nature." That which virtue implies *as a consequence* is that it is a kind of goodness, because the goodness of a thing consists in its being well disposed according to the mode of its nature. But that to which virtue is directed is a good act, as was shown above (Q. LVI, A. 3).

Accordingly three things are found to be contrary to virtue. One of these is sin, which is opposed to virtue in respect of that to which virtue is ordered; for, properly speaking, sin denotes a disordered act, just as an act of virtue is an ordered and due act. In respect of that which virtue implies as a consequence, namely that it is a kind of goodness, the contrary of virtue is malice; while in respect of that which belongs to the essence of virtue directly, its contrary is vice; for the vice of a thing seems to consist in its not being disposed in a way befitting its nature. Hence Augustine says (*De Lib. Arb.* iii, 14):[3] "Whatever is lacking for a thing's natural perfection may be called a vice."

Reply Obj. 1. These three things are contrary to virtue, but not in the same respect. For sin is opposed to virtue, according as the latter is productive of a good work, malice according as virtue is a kind of goodness, while vice is opposed to virtue properly as such.

Reply Obj. 2. Virtue implies not only perfection of power, which is the principle of action, but also the due disposition of its subject. The reason for this is because a thing operates according as it is in act, so that a thing needs to be well disposed if it has to produce a good work. It is in this respect that vice is contrary to virtue.

Reply Obj. 3. As Cicero says (*De Quæst. Tusc.* iv, 13),[4] "disease and sickness are vicious

qualities," for in speaking of the body he calls it disease "when the whole body is infected," for instance, with fever or the like; he calls it sickness "when the disease is attended with weakness"; and vice "when the parts of the body are not well compacted together." And although at times there may be disease in the body without sickness, for instance, when a man has a hidden complaint without being hindered outwardly from his accustomed occupations yet, in the soul, as he says, these two things are indistinguishable, except in thought. For whenever a man is ill-disposed inwardly, through some disordered affection, he is thus rendered unfit for fulfilling his duties, since *a tree is known by its fruit,* that is, man by his works, according to Matt. 12. 33. But "vice of the soul," as Cicero says (*ibid.*), "is a habit or affection of the soul discordant and inconsistent with itself through life"; and this is to be found even without disease and sickness, for example when a man sins from weakness or passion. Consequently vice is of wider extent than sickness or disease, even as virtue extends to more things than health; for health itself is reckoned a kind of virtue.[5] Consequently vice is more fittingly opposed to virtue than sickness or disease.

ARTICLE 2. *Whether Vice Is Contrary to Nature?*

We proceed thus to the Second Article: It would seem that vice is not contrary to nature.

Objection 1. Because vice is contrary to virtue, as stated above (A. 1). Now virtue is in us not by nature but by infusion or habituation, as stated above (Q. LXIII, AA. 1, 2, 3). Therefore vice is not contrary to nature.

Obj. 2. Further, it is impossible to become habituated to that which is contrary to nature; thus "a stone never becomes habituated to upward movement."[6] But some men become habituated to vice. Therefore vice is not contrary to nature.

Obj. 3. Further, anything contrary to a nature is not found in the greater number of individuals possessed of that nature. Now vice is found in the greater number of men; for it is written (Matt. 7, 13): *Broad is the way that leadeth to destruction, and many there are who go in thereat.* Therefore vice is not contrary to nature.

Obj. 4. Further, sin is compared to vice as act to habit, as stated above (A. 1). Now sin is defined as "a word, deed, or desire, contrary to the Law of God," as Augustine shows (*Contra Faust.* xxii, 27).[7] But the Law of God is above

---

[1] PL 44, 294.   [2] *Physics,* VII, 3 (246ª13).
[3] PL 32, 1291.   [4] DD IV, 30.

[5] Aristotle, *Physics,* VII, 3 (246ᵇ4).
[6] Aristotle, *Ethics,* II, 1 (1103ª20).   [7] PL 42, 418.

nature. Therefore we should say that vice is contrary to the Law, rather than to nature.

On the contrary, Augustine says (*De Lib. Arb.* iii, 13):[1] "Every vice, simply because it is a vice, is contrary to nature."

I answer that, As stated above (A. 1), vice is contrary to virtue. Now the virtue of a thing consists in its being well disposed in a manner befitting its nature, as stated above (A. 1). Hence the vice of any thing consists in its being disposed in a manner not befitting its nature, and for this reason is that thing "vituperated," which word is derived from vice according to Augustine (*De Lib. Arb.* iii, 14).[2]

But it must be observed that the nature of a thing is chiefly the form from which that thing derives its species. Now man derives his species from his rational soul, and consequently whatever is contrary to the order of reason is, properly speaking, contrary to the nature of man, as man; while whatever is in accord with reason, is in accord with the nature of man, as man. Now man's good is to be in accord with reason, and "his evil is to be against reason," as Dionysius states (*Div. Nom.* iv).[3] Therefore human virtue, which makes a man good, and his work good, is in accord with man's nature to the extent that it accords with his reason; while vice is contrary to man's nature to the extent that it is contrary to the order of reason.

Reply Obj. 1. Although the virtues are not caused by nature as regards their perfection of being, yet they incline us to that which accords with nature, that is, with the order of reason. For Cicero says (*De Inv. Rhet.* ii, 53)[4] that "virtue is a habit in accord with reason, like a second nature"; and it is in this sense that virtue is said to be in accord with nature, and on the other hand that vice is contrary to nature.

Reply Obj. 2. The Philosopher is speaking there of a thing being against nature in so far as being against nature is contrary to being from nature, and not in so far as being against nature is contrary to being in accord with nature, in which latter sense virtues are said to be in accord with nature, in so far as they incline us to that which is suitable to nature.

Reply Obj. 3. There is a twofold nature in man, rational nature, and the sensitive nature. And since it is through the operation of his senses that man accomplishes acts of reason, hence there are more who follow the inclinations of the sensitive nature than who follow the order of reason; for more reach the begin-

ning of a thing than achieve its completion. Now the presence of vices and sins in man is owing to the fact that he follows the inclination of his sensitive nature against the order of his reason.

Reply Obj. 4. Whatever is contrary to the nature of a work of art is contrary to the nature of the art which produced that work. Now the eternal law is compared to the order of human reason as art to a work of art. Therefore it amounts to the same that vice and sin are against the order of human reason, and that they are contrary to the eternal law. Hence Augustine says (*De Lib. Arb.* iii, 15)[5] that "every nature, as such, is from God; and is a vicious nature, in so far as it fails from the Divine art whereby it was made."

ARTICLE 3. *Whether Vice Is Worse Than a Vicious Act?*

We proceed thus to the Third Article: It would seem that vice, that is, a bad habit, is worse than a sin, that is, a bad act.

Objection 1. For, as the more lasting a good is the better it is, so the longer an evil lasts the worse it is. Now a vicious habit is more lasting than vicious acts, that pass away at once. Therefore a vicious habit is worse than a vicious act.

Obj. 2. Further, several evils are more to be shunned than one. But a bad habit is virtually the cause of many bad acts. Therefore a vicious habit is worse than a vicious act.

Obj. 3. Further, a cause is more potent than its effect. But a habit perfects its actions both as to their goodness and as to their badness. Therefore a habit is more potent than its act, both in goodness and in badness.

On the contrary, A man is justly punished for a vicious act, but not for a vicious habit, so long as no act ensues. Therefore a vicious action is worse than a vicious habit.

I answer that, A habit stands midway between power and act. Now it is evident that both in good and in evil act precedes power, as stated in the *Metaphysics.*[6] For it is better to do well than to be able to do well, and in like manner it is more blameworthy to do evil than to be able to do evil. Hence it also follows that both in goodness and in badness habit stands midway between power and act, so that, namely, even as a good or evil habit stands above the corresponding power in goodness or in badness, so does it stand below the corresponding act. This also appears from the fact that a habit is not called good or bad save in so far as it induces

[1] PL 32, 1290.   [2] PL 32, 1291.
[3] Sect. 32 (PG 3, 733).   [4] DD 1, 165.
[5] PL 32, 1291.   [6] Aristotle, IX, 9 (1051ᵃ4).

to a good or bad act; and therefore a habit is called good or bad by reason of the goodness or badness of its act; and so an act surpasses its habit in goodness or badness, since the cause of a thing being such is itself yet more so.

Reply Obj. 1. Nothing hinders one thing from standing above another absolutely, and below it in some respect. Now a thing is judged to be above another absolutely if it surpasses it in a point which is proper to both; while it is deemed above it in a certain respect if it surpasses it in something which is accidental to both. Now it has been shown from the very nature of act and habit, that act surpasses habit both in goodness and in badness. But the fact that habit is more lasting than act is accidental to them, and is due to the fact that they are both found in a nature such that it cannot always be in action, and whose action consists in a transient movement. Consequently act excels absolutely in goodness and badness, but habit excels in a certain respect.

Reply Obj. 2. A habit is several acts not absolutely, but in a certain respect, that is, virtually. Hence this does not prove that habit precedes act absolutely both in goodness and in badness.

Reply Obj. 3. Habit causes act by way of efficient causality; but act causes habit by way of final causality, in respect of which we consider the nature of good and evil. Consequently act surpasses habit both in goodness and in badness.

ARTICLE 4. *Whether Sin Is Compatible with Virtue?*

We proceed thus to the Fourth Article: It would seem that a vicious act, that is, sin, is incompatible with virtue.

Objection 1. For contraries cannot be together in the same subject. Now sin is, in some way, contrary to virtue, as stated above (A. 1). Therefore sin is incompatible with virtue.

Obj. 2. Further, sin is worse than vice, that is, an evil act is worse than an evil habit. But vice cannot be in the same subject with virtue; neither, therefore, can sin.

Obj. 3. Further, sin occurs in natural things, even as in voluntary things.[1] Now sin never happens in natural things except through some corruption of the natural power; thus monsters are due to corruption of some elemental force in the seed, as stated in the *Physics*.[2] Therefore no sin occurs in voluntary matters except through the corruption of some virtue in the

soul, so that sin and virtue cannot be together in the same subject.

On the contrary, The Philosopher says[3] that virtue is engendered and corrupted by contrary causes. Now one virtuous act does not cause a virtue, as stated above (Q. LI, A. 3), and, consequently, one sinful act does not corrupt virtue. Therefore they can be together in the same subject.

I answer that, Sin is compared to virtue as evil act to good habit. Now the way a habit is in the soul is not the same as that of a form in a natural thing. For the form of a natural thing produces of necessity an operation befitting itself, and therefore a natural form is incompatible with the act of a contrary form; thus heat is incompatible with the act of cooling, and lightness with downward movement (unless perhaps violence is used by some extrinsic mover). But the habit that resides in the soul does not of necessity produce its operation, but is used by man when he wills. Consequently man, while possessing a habit, may either fail to use the habit, or produce a contrary act; and so a man having a virtue may produce an act of sin. And this sinful act, so long as there is but one, cannot corrupt virtue, if we compare the act to the virtue itself as a habit; for, just as habit is not engendered by one act, so neither is it destroyed by one act, as stated above (Q. LXIII, A. 2, Reply 2). But if we compare the sinful act to the cause of the virtues, then it is possible for some virtues to be destroyed by one sinful act. For every mortal sin is contrary to charity, which is the root of all the infused virtues, as virtues; and consequently, charity being banished by one act of mortal sin, it follows that all the infused virtues are expelled in so far as they are virtues. And I say this on account of faith and hope, whose habits remain unformed after mortal sin, so that they are no longer virtues. On the other hand, since venial sin is neither contrary to charity nor banishes it, as a consequence neither does it expel the other virtues. As to the acquired virtues, they are not destroyed by one act of any kind of sin.

Accordingly, mortal sin is incompatible with the infused virtues, but is consistent with acquired virtue, while venial sin is compatible with virtues, whether infused or acquired.

Reply Obj. 1. Sin is contrary to virtue not by reason of itself, but by reason of its act. Hence sin is incompatible with the act, but not with the habit, of virtue.

[1] Aristotle, *Physics*, II, 8 (199ª33).
[2] *Ibid.* (199ᵇ4).

[3] *Ethics*, II, 3 (1105ª14).

Reply Obj. 2. Vice is directly contrary to virtue, even as sin to virtuous act, and so vice excludes virtue, just as sin excludes acts of virtue.

Reply Obj. 3. The natural powers act of necessity, and hence so long as the power is unimpaired, no sin can be found in the act. On the other hand, the virtues of the soul do not produce their acts of necessity; hence the comparison fails.

ARTICLE 5. *Whether Every Sin Includes an Action?*

We proceed thus to the Fifth Article: It would seem that every sin includes an action.

Objection 1. For as merit is compared with virtue, even so is sin compared with vice. Now there can be no merit without an action. Neither, therefore, can there be sin without action.

Obj. 2. Further, Augustine says (*De Lib. Arb.* iii, 18):[1] "So true is it that every sin is voluntary, that, unless it be voluntary, it is no sin at all." Now nothing can be voluntary save through an act of the will. Therefore every sin implies an act.

Obj. 3. Further, if sin could be without act, it would follow that a man sins as soon as he ceases doing what he ought. Now he who never does something that he ought to do ceases continually doing what he ought. Therefore it would follow that he sins continually; and this is untrue. Therefore there is no sin without an act.

On the contrary, It is written (James 4. 17): *To him . . . who knoweth to do good, and doth it not, to him it is a sin.* Now "not to do" does not imply an act. Therefore sin can be without act.

I answer that, The reason for urging this question has reference to the sin of omission, about which there have been various opinions. For some say[2] that in every sin of omission there is some act, either interior or exterior: interior, as when a man wills not to go to church when he is bound to go; exterior, as when a man at the very hour that he is bound to go to church (or even before), occupies himself in such a way that he is hindered from going. This seems, in a way, to amount to the same as the first, for whoever wills one thing that is incompatible with this other, wills, consequently, to go without this other; unless, perhaps, it does not occur to him that what he wishes to do will hinder him from that which he is bound to do, in which case he might be deemed guilty of negligence. On the other hand, others say,[3] that a sin of omission does not necessarily suppose an act; for the mere fact of not doing what one is bound to do is a sin.

Now each of these opinions has some truth in it. For if in the sin of omission we look merely at that in which the essence of the sin consists, the sin of omission will be sometimes with an interior act, as when a man wills not to go to church, while sometimes it will be without any act at all, whether interior or exterior, as when a man at the time that he is bound to go to church does not think of going or not going to church.

If, however, in the sin of omission, we consider also the causes, or occasions of the omission, then the sin of omission must of necessity include some act. For there is no sin of omission, unless we omit what we can do or not do; and that we turn aside so as not to do what we can do or not do, must be due to some cause or occasion, either united with the omission or preceding it. Now if this cause be not in man's power, the omission will not be sinful, as when anyone omits going to church on account of sickness. But if the cause or occasion be subject to the will, the omission is sinful; and such a cause, in so far as it is voluntary, must always include some act, at least the interior act of the will.

This act sometimes bears directly on the omission, as when a man wills not to go to church because it is too much trouble; and in this case this act, of its very nature, belongs to the omission, because the willing of any sin whatever pertains of itself to that sin, since voluntariness is essential to sin. Sometimes, however, the act of the will bears directly on something else, which hinders man from doing what he ought, whether this something else be united with the omission, as when a man wills to play at the time he ought to go to church, or whether it precedes the omission, as when a man wills to sit up late at night, the result being that he does not go to church in the morning. In this case the act, interior or exterior, is accidental to the omission, since the omission follows outside the intention, and that which is outside the intention is said to be accidental.[4] Therefore it is evident that then the sin of omission has indeed an act united

---

[1] PL 32, 1295; cf. *De Vera Relig.*, XIV. (PL 34, 133).

[2] Referred to anonymously by Peter Lombard, *Sent.*, II, d. 35, chap. 3 (QR 1, 495); cf. also Albert, *In Sent.*, II, d. 22, A. 7; d. 35, A. 3 (BO XXVII, 381, 565); also Bonaventure, *In Sent.*, II, d. 35, dub. 1 (QR. II, 836).

[3] Cf. Albert, *In Sent.*, II, d. 35, A. 3 (BO XXVII, 565).

[4] Aristotle, *Physics*, II, 5 (196^{b}23).

with, or preceding the omission, but that this act is accidental to the sin of omission.

Now in judging about things, we must be guided by that which is proper to them, and not by that which is accidental; and consequently it is truer to say that a sin can be without any act; otherwise circumstantial acts and occasions would be essential to other actual sins.

Reply Obj. 1. More things are required for good than for evil, since "good results from a whole and entire cause, while evil results from each single defect," as Dionysius states (*Div. Nom.* iv),[1] so that sin may arise from a man doing what he ought not, or by his not doing what he ought, while there can be no merit unless a man do willingly what he ought to do. Therefore there can be no merit without act, but there can be sin without act.

Reply Obj. 2. The term voluntary is applied not only to that on which the act of the will is brought to bear, but also to that which we have the power to do or not to do, as stated in the *Ethics.*[2] Hence even "not to will" may be called voluntary, in so far as man has it in his power to will and not to will.

Reply Obj. 3. The sin of omission is contrary to an affirmative precept which binds always, but not for always. Hence by omitting to act a man sins only for the time at which the affirmative precept binds him to act.

ARTICLE 6. *Whether Sin Is Fittingly Defined As a Word, Deed, or Desire Contrary to the Eternal Law?*

We proceed thus to the Sixth Article: It would seem that sin is unfittingly defined by saying: "Sin is a word, deed, or desire, contrary to the eternal law."[3]

Objection 1. Because word, deed, and desire imply an act; but not every sin implies an act, as stated above (A. 5). Therefore this definition does not include every sin.

Obj. 2. Further, Augustine says (*De duab. anim.* xi):[4] "Sin is the will to retain or obtain what justice forbids." Now will is comprised under desire, in so far as desire denotes any act of the appetite. Therefore it was enough to say: "Sin is a desire contrary to the eternal law," nor was there need to add "word" or "deed."

Obj. 3. Further, sin seems to consist properly

[1] Sect. 30 (PG 3, 729).
[2] Aristotle, III, 5 (1113^{b}20).
[3] In Peter Lombard, *Sent.*, II, d. 35, chap. 1 (QR 1, 491), taken from Augustine, *Contra Faust.*, XXII, 27 (PL 42, 418).
[4] PL 42, 105.

in turning away from the end, because good and evil are measured chiefly with regard to the end, as explained above (Q. XVIII, A. 6); therefore Augustine (*De Lib. Arb.* i, 11)[5] defines sin in reference to the end, by saying that "sin is nothing else than to neglect eternal things, and seek after temporal things"; and again he says (QQ. lxxxiii, qu. 30)[6] that "all human wickedness consists in using what we should enjoy, and in enjoying what we should use." Now the definition in question contains no mention of turning away from our due end. Therefore it is an insufficient definition of sin.

Obj. 4. Further, a thing is said to be forbidden, because it is contrary to the law. Now not all sins are evil through being forbidden, but some are forbidden because they are evil. Therefore sin in general should not be defined as being against the law of God.

Obj. 5. Further, a sin denotes an evil human act, as was explained above (A. 1; Q. XXI, A. 1). Now "man's evil is to be against reason," as Dionysius states (*Div. Nom.* iv).[7] Therefore it would have been better to say that sin is against reason than to say that it is contrary to the eternal law.

On the contrary, the authority of Augustine suffices (*Contra Faust.* xxii, 27).[8]

I answer that, As was shown above (A. 1), sin is nothing else than a bad human act. Now that an act is a human act is due to its being voluntary, as stated above (Q. 1, A. 1), whether it be voluntary as being elicited by the will, for example to will or to choose, or as being commanded by the will, for example the exterior actions of speech or operation. Again, a human act is evil through lacking conformity with its due measure, and conformity of measure in a thing depends on a rule, and if that thing depart from it, it is incommensurate. Now there are two rules of the human will: one is proximate and homogeneous, namely the human reason; the other is the first rule, namely the eternal law, which is God's reason, so to speak. Accordingly Augustine (*loc. cit.*) includes two things in the definition of sin: one, pertaining to the substance of a human act, and which is the matter, so to speak, of sin, when he says, "word, deed, or desire"; the other pertaining to the nature of evil, and which is the form, as it were, of sin, when he says, "contrary to the eternal law."

Reply Obj. 1. Affirmation and negation are reduced to the same genus; for example in Di-

[5] PL 32, 1233.   [6] PL 40, 19.
[7] Sect. 32 (PG 3, 733).   [8] PL 42, 418.

vine things, begotten and unbegotten are reduced to the genus relation, as Augustine states
(*De Trin.* v, 6, 7);[1] and so "word" and "deed"
denote equally what is said and what is not said,
what is done and what is not done.

Reply Obj. 2. The first cause of sin is in the
will, which commands all voluntary acts, in
which alone is sin to be found; and hence Augustine sometimes defines sin in reference to the
will alone. But since external acts also pertain
to the substance of sin, through being evil of
themselves, as stated (Q. XX, AA. 1, 2, 3), it was
necessary in defining sin to include something
referring to external action.

Reply Obj. 3. The eternal law first and foremost directs man to his end, and in consequence,
makes man to be well disposed in regard to
things which are directed to the end; hence
when he says, "contrary to the eternal law,"
he includes turning away from the end and all
other kinds of disorder.

Reply Obj. 4. When it is said that not every
sin is evil through being forbidden, this must
be understood of prohibition by positive law.
If, however, the prohibition be referred to the
natural law, which is contained primarily in the
eternal law, but secondarily in the natural power of judging of the human reason, then every
sin is evil through being prohibited; for it is
contrary to natural law, precisely because it is
disordered.

Reply Obj. 5. The theologian considers sin
chiefly as an offence against God, and the moral
philosopher as something contrary to reason.
Hence Augustine defines sin with reference to
its being "contrary to the eternal law" more
fittingly than with reference to its being contrary to reason; the more so, as the eternal
law directs us in many things that surpass human reason, for example in matters of faith.

QUESTION LXXII
OF THE DISTINCTION OF SINS
(*In Nine Articles*)

WE must now consider the distinction of sins
or vices, under which head there are nine points
of inquiry: (1) Whether sins are distinguished
specifically by their objects? (2) Of the distinction between spiritual and carnal sins. (3)
Whether sins differ in reference to their causes?
(4) Whether they differ with respect to those
who are sinned against? (5) Whether sins differ
in relation to the debt of punishment? (6)
Whether they differ in regard to omission and
commission? (7) Whether they differ according to their various stages? (8) Whether they
differ in respect of excess and deficiency? (9)
Whether they differ according to their various
circumstances?

ARTICLE 1. *Whether Sins Differ in Species
According to Their Objects?*

We proceed thus to the First Article: It
would seem that sins do not differ in species,
according to their objects.

Objection 1. For acts are said to be good
or evil in relation, chiefly, to their end, as shown
above (Q. XVIII, A. 6). Since then sin is nothing
else than an evil human act, as stated above
(Q. LXXI, A. 1), it seems that sins should differ
specifically according to their ends rather than
according to their objects.

Obj. 2. Further, evil, being a privation, differs specifically according to the different species of its opposites. Now sin is an evil in the
genus of human acts. Therefore sins differ specifically according to their opposites rather than
according to their objects.

Obj. 3. Further, if sins differed specifically
according to their objects, it would be impossible to find the same specific sin with different
objects, and yet such sins are to be found. For
pride is about things spiritual and material, as
Gregory says (*Moral.* xxxiv, 23),[2] and avarice
is about different kinds of things. Therefore
sins do not differ in species according to their
objects.

On the contrary, "Sin is a word, deed, or desire against God's law."[3] Now words, deeds,
and desires differ in species according to their
various objects, since acts differ by their objects,
as stated above (Q. XVIII, A. 5). Therefore sins
also differ in species according to their objects.

I answer that, As stated above (Q. LXXI, A. 6),
two things concur in the nature of sin, namely
the voluntary act, and its lack of order, which
consists in departing from God's law. Of these
two, one is referred essentially to the sinner,
who intends such and such an act in such and
such matter; while the other, namely the lack
of order in the act, is referred accidentally to
the intention of the sinner, for "no one acts
intending evil," as Dionysius declares (*Div.
Nom.* iv).[4] Now it is evident that a thing derives its species from that which is essential
and not from that which is accidental, because
what is accidental is outside the notion of the

[1] PL 42, 914, 915.

[2] PL 76, 744.
[3] Augustine, *Contra Faust.*, XXII, 27 (PL 42, 418).
[4] Sects. 19, 31 (PG 3, 716, 732).

species. Consequently sins differ specifically on the part of the voluntary acts rather than of the lack of order inherent to sin. Now voluntary acts differ in species according to their objects, as was proved above (Q. XVIII, A. 5). Therefore it follows that sins are properly distinguished in species by their objects.

Reply Obj. 1. The aspect of good is found chiefly in the end, and therefore the end stands in the relation of object to the act of the will which is at the root of every sin. Consequently it amounts to the same whether sins differ by their objects or by their ends.

Reply Obj. 2. Sin is not a pure privation but an act deprived of its due order; hence sins differ specifically according to the objects of their acts rather than according to their opposites, although, even if they were distinguished in reference to their opposite virtues it would come to the same, since virtues differ specifically according to their objects, as stated above (Q. LX, A. 5).

Reply Obj. 3. In various things, differing in species or genus nothing hinders our finding one formal aspect of the object, from which aspect sin receives its species. It is thus that pride seeks excellence in reference to various things, and avarice seeks abundance of things adapted to human use.

ARTICLE 2. *Whether Spiritual Sins Are Fittingly Distinguished from Carnal Sins?*

We proceed thus to the Second Article: It would seem that spiritual sins are unfittingly distinguished from carnal sins.

Objection 1. For the Apostle says (Gal. 5. 19): *The works of the flesh are manifest, which are fornication, uncleanness, immodesty, luxury, idolatry, witchcrafts,* etc., from which it seems that all kinds of sins are works of the flesh. Now carnal sins are called works of the flesh. Therefore carnal sins should not be distinguished from spiritual sins.

Obj. 2. Further, whosoever sins, walks according to the flesh, as stated in Rom. 8. 13: *If you live according to the flesh, you shall die. But if by the spirit you mortify the deeds of the flesh, you shall live.* Now to live or walk according to the flesh seems to pertain to the nature of carnal sin. Therefore carnal sins should not be distinguished from spiritual sins.

Obj. 3. Further, the higher part of the soul, which is the mind or reason, is called the spirit, according to Eph. 4. 23: *Be renewed in the spirit of your mind,* where spirit stands for reason, according to a gloss.[1] Now every sin, which is committed in accordance with the flesh, flows from the reason by its consent, since consent in a sinful act belongs to the higher reason, as we shall state further on (Q. LXXIV, A. 7). Therefore the same sins are both carnal and spiritual, and consequently they should not be distinguished from one another.

Obj. 4. Further, if some sins are carnal specifically, this, it seems, should apply chiefly to those sins by which man sins against his own body. But, according to the Apostle (I Cor. 6. 18), *every sin that a man doth, is without the body: but he that committeth fornication, sinneth against his own body.* Therefore fornication would be the only carnal sin, although nevertheless the Apostle (Eph. 5. 3) numbers covetousness with the carnal sins.

On the contrary, Gregory (*Moral.* xxxi, 45)[2] says that "of the seven capital sins five are spiritual, and two carnal."

I answer that, As stated above (A. 1), sins take their species from their objects. Now every sin consists in the desire for some changeable good for which man has an inordinate desire, and the possession of which gives him inordinate pleasure. Now, as explained above (Q. XXXI, A. 3), pleasure is twofold. One belongs to the soul, and is consummated in the mere apprehension of a thing possessed in accordance with desire; this can also be called spiritual pleasure, for example when one takes pleasure in human praise or the like. The other pleasure is bodily or natural, and is realized in bodily touch, and this can also be called carnal pleasure.

Accordingly, those sins which consist in spiritual pleasure are called spiritual sins, while those which consist in carnal pleasure, are called carnal sins, for example gluttony, which consists in the pleasures of the table, and lust, which consists in sexual pleasures. Hence the Apostle says (II Cor. 7. 1): *Let us cleanse ourselves from all defilement of the flesh and of the spirit.*

Reply Obj. 1. As a gloss says on the same passage,[3] these vices are not called works of the flesh, because they consisted in carnal pleasure; but flesh here denotes man, who is said to live according to the flesh when he lives according to himself, as Augustine says.[4] The rea-

---

[1] *Glossa ordin.* (VI, 94F); *Glossa interl.* (VI, 94v), *Glossa* Lombardi (PL 192, 205); cf. Augustine, *De Trin.*, XIV, 16 (PL 42, 1053); *De Gen. ad Litt.*, III, 20 (PL 34, 292).   [2] PL 76, 621.
[3] *Glossa ordin.* (VI, 87E); *Glossa* Lombardi (PL 191, 159). Cf. Augustine, *City of God,* XIV, 2 (PL 41, 404).
[4] *City of God,* XIV, 2, 3 (PL 41, 404; 406).

son of this is because every failing in the human reason is due in some way to the carnal sense.

This suffices for the *Reply to the Second Objection.*

Reply Obj. 3. Even in the carnal sins there is a spiritual act, namely the act of reason; but the end of these sins, from which they are named, is carnal pleasure.

Reply Obj. 4. As the gloss says on the same passage,[1] "in the sin of fornication the soul is the body's slave in a special sense, because at the moment of sinning it can think of nothing else"; but the pleasure of gluttony, although carnal, does not so utterly absorb the reason. It may also be said that in this sin an injury is done to the body also, for it is defiled inordinately; therefore by this sin alone is man said specially to sin against his body. But covetousness, which is numbered among the carnal sins, stands here for adultery, which is the unjust appropriation of another's wife. Again, it may be said that the thing in which the covetous man takes pleasure is something bodily, and in this respect covetousness is numbered with the carnal sins. But the pleasure itself does not belong to the body, but to the spirit, and therefore Gregory says *(loc. cit.)* that it is a spiritual sin.

ARTICLE 3. *Whether Sins Differ Specifically in Reference to Their Causes?*

We proceed thus to the Third Article: It would seem that sins differ specifically in reference to their causes.

Objection 1. For a thing takes its species from that from which it derives its being. Now sins derive their being from their causes. Therefore they take their species from them also. Therefore they differ specifically in reference to their causes.

Obj. 2. Further, of all the causes the material cause seems to have least reference to the species. Now the object in a sin is like its material cause. Since, therefore, sins differ specifically according to their objects, it seems that they differ much more in reference to their other causes.

Obj. 3. Further, Augustine, commenting on Ps. 79. 17, *Things set on fire and dug down,* says that "every sin is due either to fear inducing false humility, or to love enkindling us to undue ardour."[2] For it is written (I John 2. 16) that *all that is in the world, is the concupis-*

cence of the flesh, or (Vulg.,—and) the concupiscence of the eyes, or (Vulg.,—and) the pride of life. Now a thing is said to be in the world on account of sin, since "the world denotes lovers of the world," as Augustine observes (*Tract* ii *in Joann.*).[3] Gregory, too (*Moral.* xxxi, 45);[4] distinguishes all sins according to the seven capital vices. Now all these divisions refer to the causes of sins. Therefore it seems that sins differ specifically according to the difference of their causes.

On the contrary, If this were the case all sins would belong to one species, since they are due to one cause. For it is written (Ecclus. 10. 15) that *pride is the beginning of all sin* and (I Tim. 6. 10) that *the desire of money is the root of all evils.* Now it is evident that there are various species of sins. Therefore sins do not differ specifically according to their different causes.

I answer that, Since there are four kinds of causes, they are attributed to various things in various ways. Because the formal and the material cause regard properly the substance of a thing, and consequently substances differ in respect of their matter and form, both in species and in genus.—The agent and the end regard directly movement and operation, and therefore movements and operations differ specifically in respect of these causes; in different ways, however, because the natural active principles are always determined to the same acts, so that the different species of natural acts are taken not only from the objects, which are the ends or terms of those acts, but also from their active principles; thus heating and cooling are specifically distinct with reference to hot and cold. On the other hand, the active principles in voluntary acts, such as the acts of sins, are not determined of necessity to one act, and consequently from one active or moving principle, different species of sins can proceed; thus from fear engendering false humility man may proceed to theft, or murder, or to neglect the flock committed to his care; and these same things may proceed from love enkindling to undue ardour. Hence it is evident that sins do not differ specifically according to their various active or moving causes, but only in respect of difference in the final cause, which is the end and object of the will. For it has been shown above (Q. I, A. 3; Q. XVIII, A. 6) that human acts take their species from the end.

Reply Obj. 1. The active principles in voluntary acts, not being determined to one act, do

---

[1] *Glossa* Lombardi (PL 191, 1584); cf. *Glossa ordin.* (VI, 41F).
[2] *Ennar. in Ps.* (PL 36, 1027).

[3] PL 35, 1393.
[4] PL 76, 621.

not suffice for the production of human acts, unless the will be determined to one by the intention of the end, as the Philosopher proves,[1] and consequently sin derives both its being and its species from the end.

Reply Obj. 2. Objects, in relation to external acts, have the character of matter "about which"; but, in relation to the interior act of the will, they have the character of end, and it is owing to this that they give the act its species. Nevertheless, even considered as the matter "about which," they have the character of term, from which movement takes its species;[2] yet even terms of movement specify movements, in so far as term has the character of end.

Reply Obj. 3. These distinctions of sins are given not as distinct species of sins, but to show their various causes.

ARTICLE 4. *Whether Sin Is Fittingly Divided into Sin against God, against Oneself, and against One's Neighbour?*

We proceed thus to the Fourth Article: It would seem that sin is unfittingly divided into sin against God, against one's neighbour, and against oneself.

Objection 1. For that which is common to all sins should not be put as a part in the division of sin. But it is common to all sins to be against God, for it is stated in the definition of sin that it is "against God's law," as stated above (Q. LXXI, A. 6). Therefore sin against God should not be put as a part of the division of sin.

Obj. 2. Further, every division should consist of things in opposition to one another. But these three kinds of sin are not opposed to one another; for whoever sins against his neighbour, sins against himself and against God. Therefore sin is not fittingly divided into these three.

Obj. 3. Further, specification is not taken from things external. But God and our neighbour are external to us. Therefore sins are not distinguished specifically with regard to them. Consequently sin is unfittingly divided according to these three.

On the contrary, Isidore (*De Summo Bono*),[3] in giving the division of sins, says that man is said to sin against himself against God, and against his neighbour.

I answer that, As stated above (Q. LXXI, A. 1), sin is a disordered act. Now there should be a threefold order in man. One is in relation to the rule of reason, in so far as all our actions and passions should be commensurate with the rule of reason. Another order is in relation to the rule of the Divine law, by which man should be directed in all things. If man were by nature a solitary animal, this twofold order would suffice; but since "man is naturally a political and social animal," as is proved in the *Politics*,[4] hence a third order is necessary, by which man is directed in relation to other men among whom he has to dwell. Of these orders the first contains the second and surpasses it.[5] For whatever things are comprised under the order of reason, are comprised under the order of God Himself. Yet some things are comprised under the order of God which surpass the human reason, such as matters of faith, and things due to God alone. Hence he that sins in such matters, for instance, by heresy, sacrilege, or blasphemy, is said to sin against God. In like manner, the second order includes the third and surpasses it, because in all things in which we are directed in reference to our neighbour, we need to be directed according to the order of reason. Yet in some things we are directed according to reason in relation to ourselves only, and not in reference to our neighbour; and when man sins in these matters, he is said to sin against himself, as is seen in the glutton, the lustful, and the prodigal. But when man sins in matters concerning his neighbour, he said to sin against his neighbour, as appears in the thief and the murderer. Now the things by which man is ordered to God, his neighbour, and himself are different. Therefore this distinction of sins is in respect of their objects, according to which the species of sins are diversified. Consequently this distinction of sins is properly one of different species of sins; for the virtues also, to which sins are opposed, differ specifically in respect of these three. For it is evident from what has been said (Q. LXII, A. 1; Q. LXVI, AA. 4, 6) that by the theological virtues man is directed to God; by temperance and fortitude, to himself; and by justice to his neighbour.

Reply Obj. 1. To sin against God is common to all sins, in so far as the order to God includes every human order; but in so far as order to God surpasses the other two orders, sin against God is a special kind of sin.

Reply Obj. 2. When several things, of which

---

[1] *Metaphysics*, IX, 5 (1048a10).
[2] Aristotle, *Physics*, V, 1 (224b7); *Ethics*, X, 4 (1174b4).
[3] This distinction comes from the unknown author of the *Summa Sent.*, III, 16 (PL 176, 113).

[4] Aristotle, I, 2 (1253a2).
[5] The "first order" refers to the order of God, the "second order," the order of reason, and the "third order," the order of man in relation to his neighbor.

one includes another, are distinct from one another, this distinction is understood to refer, not to the part contained in another, but to that in which one goes beyond another. This may be seen in the division of numbers and figures: for a triangle is distinguished from a four-sided figure not in respect of its being contained in it, but in respect of that in which it is surpassed by it; and the same applies to the numbers three and four.

Reply Obj. 3. Although God and our neighbour are external to the sinner himself, they are not external to the act of sin, but are related to it as its proper object.

ARTICLE 5. *Whether the Division of Sins According to Their Debt of Punishment Diversifies Their Species?*

We proceed thus to the Fifth Article: It would seem that the division of sins according to their debt of punishment diversifies their species; for instance, when sin is divided into mortal and venial.

Objection 1. For things which are infinitely apart cannot belong to the same species, nor even to the same genus. But venial and mortal sin are infinitely apart, since temporal punishment is due to venial sin, and eternal punishment to mortal sin; and the measure of the punishment corresponds to the gravity of the fault, according to Deut. 25. 2: *According to the measure of the sin shall the measure also of the stripes be.* Therefore venial and mortal sin are not of the same genus, nor can they be said to belong to the same species.

Obj. 2. Further, some sins are mortal in virtue of their kind, such as murder and adultery; and some are venial in virtue of their kind, such as an idle word, and excessive laughter. Therefore venial and mortal sin differ specifically.

Obj. 3. Further, just as a virtuous act stands in relation to its reward, so does sin stand in relation to punishment. But the reward is the end of the virtuous act. Therefore punishment is the end of sin. Now sins differ specifically in relation to their ends, as stated above (A. 3). Therefore they are also specifically distinct according to the debt of punishment.

On the contrary, Those things that constitute a species are prior to the species, for example specific differences. But punishment follows sin as its effect. Therefore sins do not differ specifically according to the debt of punishment.

I answer that, In things that differ specifically we find a twofold difference. The first causes the diversity of species, and is never found in the same species, for example rational and irrational, animate, and inanimate. The other difference is consequent to specific diversity, and though, in some cases, it may be a consequence of specific diversity, yet in others it may be found within the same species; thus white and black are consequent upon the specific diversity of crow and swan, and yet this difference is found within the one species of man.

We must therefore say that the difference between venial and mortal sin, or any other difference in respect of the debt of punishment, cannot be a difference constituting specific diversity. For what is accidental never constitutes a species, and what is outside the agent's intention is accidental.[1] Now it is evident that punishment is outside the intention of the sinner. Therefore it is accidentally related to sin on the part of the sinner. Nevertheless it is related to sin by an extrinsic principle, namely the justice of the judge, who imposes various punishments according to the various manners of sin. Therefore the difference derived from the debt of punishment, may be consequent to the specific diversity of sins, but cannot constitute it.

Now the difference between venial and mortal sin is consequent upon the diversity of that lack of order which constitutes the notion of sin. For lack of order is twofold, one that destroys the principle of order, and another that, without destroying the principle of order, implies lack of order in the things which follow the principle; thus, the disposition of an animal's body may be so out of order that the vital principle is destroyed, and this is death; while, on the other hand, though the vital principle is sound, there may be disorder in the bodily humours; and then there is sickness. Now the principle of the entire moral order is the last end, "which stands in the same relation to matters of action as the indemonstrable principle does to matters of speculation."[2] Therefore when the soul is so disordered by sin as to turn away from its last end, namely God, to Whom it is united by charity, there is mortal sin; but when it is disordered without turning away from God, there is venial sin. For even as in the body, the disorder of death which results from the destruction of the principle of life is irreparable according to nature, while the disorder of sickness can be repaired by reason of the vital principle being preserved, so it is in matters concerning the soul. Because, in speculative matters, it is impossible to persuade one who

[1] Aristotle, *Physics*, II, 5 (196^{b}23).
[2] Aristotle, *Ethics*, VII, 8 (1151^{a}16).

errs in the principles; while one who errs but retains the principles can be brought back to the truth by means of the principles. Likewise in practical matters, he who, by sinning, turns away from his last end, if we consider the nature of his sin, falls irreparably, and therefore is said to sin mortally and to deserve eternal punishment; but when a man sins without turning away from God, by the very nature of his sin his disorder can be repaired, because the principle of the order is not destroyed. Therefore he is said to sin venially, because, that is, he does not sin so as to deserve to be punished endlessly.

Reply Obj. 1. Mortal and venial sin are infinitely apart as regards what they turn away from, not as regards what they turn to, namely, the object which specifies them. Hence nothing hinders the same species from including mortal and venial sins; for instance, in the species adultery the first movement is a venial sin, while an idle word, which is, generally speaking, venial, may even be a mortal sin.

Reply Obj. 2. From the fact that one sin is mortal by reason of its kind, and another venial by reason of its kind, it follows that this difference is consequent upon the specific difference of sins, not that it is their cause. And this difference may be found even in things of the same species, as stated above.

Reply Obj. 3. The reward is intended by him that merits or acts virtuously; but the punishment is not intended by the sinner, but, on the contrary, is against his will. Hence the comparison fails.

ARTICLE 6. *Whether Sins of Commission and Omission Differ Specifically?*

We *proceed thus to the Sixth Article:* It would seem that sins of commission and omission differ specifically.

Objection 1. For "offence" and "sin" are divided against one another (Eph. 2. 1), where it is written: *When you were dead in your offences and sins,* which words a gloss explains,[1] saying: " 'Offences,' by omitting to do what was commanded, and 'sins,' by doing what was forbidden." From this it is evident that offence here denotes sins of omission, while sin denotes sins of commission. Therefore they differ specifically, since they are contrasted with one another as different species.

Obj. 2. Further, It is essential to sin to be against God's law, for this is part of its defini-

[1] *Glossa interl.* (VI, 911); *Glossa* Lombardi (PL 192, 179).

tion, as is clear from what has been said (Q. LXXI, A. 6). Now in God's law, the affirmative precepts, against which is the sin of omission, are different from the negative precepts, against which is the sin of commission. Therefore sins of omission and commission differ specifically.

Obj. 3. Further, omission and commission differ as affirmation and negation. Now affirmation and negation cannot be in the same species, since negation has no species; for "there is neither species nor difference of non-being," as the Philosopher states.[2] Therefore omission and commission cannot belong to the same species.

On the contrary, Omission and commission are found in the same species of sin. For the covetous man both takes what belongs to others, which is a sin of commission, and gives not of his own to whom he should give, which is a sin of omission. Therefore omission and commission do not differ specifically.

I answer that, There is a twofold difference in sins: a material difference and a formal difference. The material difference is to be observed in the natural species of sinful acts; while the formal difference is gathered from their relation to one proper end, which is also their proper object. Hence we find certain acts differing materially from one another in species which are nevertheless formally in the same species of sin, because they are directed to the one same end; thus strangling, stoning, and stabbing come under the one species of murder, although the actions themselves differ specifically according to the natural species.—Accordingly, if we refer to the species in sins of omission and commission, they differ materially, using species in a broad sense, in so far as negation and privation may have a species.— But if we refer to the species in sins of omission and commission formally, they do not differ in species, because they are directed to the same end, and proceed from the same motive. For the covetous man, in order to hoard money, both robs, and omits to give what he ought, and in like manner, the glutton, to satiate his appetite, both eats too much and omits the prescribed fasts. The same applies to other sins; for in things, negation is always founded on affirmation, which in a manner, is its cause. Hence in the physical order it comes under the same head that fire gives forth heat and that it does not give forth cold.

Reply Obj. 1. This division in respect of commission and omission is not according to species different formally, but only according to species different materially, as stated.

[2] *Physics,* IV, 8 (215ª10).

Reply Obj. 2. In God's law, various affirmative and negative precepts were necessary so that men might be gradually led to virtue, first by abstaining from evil, being induced to this by the negative precepts, and afterwards by doing good, to which we are induced by the affirmative precepts. Therefore the affirmative and negative precepts do not belong to different virtues, but to different degrees of virtue, and consequently they are not, of necessity, opposed to sins of different species. Moreover sin is not specified by that from which it turns away, because in this respect it is a negation or privation, but by that to which it turns, in so far as sin is an act. Consequently sins do not differ specifically according to the various precepts of the Law.

Reply Obj. 3. This objection considers the material diversity of sins. It must be observed, however, that although, properly speaking, negation is not in a species, yet it is allotted to a species by reduction to the affirmation on which it is based.

ARTICLE 7. *Whether Sins Are Fittingly Divided into Sins of Thought, Word, and Deed?*

We proceed thus to the Seventh Article: It would seem that sins are unfittingly divided into sins of thought, word, and deed.

Objection 1. For Augustine (*De Trin.* xii, 12)[1] describes three stages of sin, of which the first is "when the carnal sense offers a bait," which is the sin of thought; the second stage is reached "when one is satisfied with the mere pleasure of thought"; and the third stage, "when consent is given to the deed." Now these three belong to the sin of thought. Therefore it is unfitting to put sin of thought as one kind of sin.

Obj. 2. Further, Gregory (*Moral.* iv, 27)[2] reckons "four degrees of sin: the first of which is a fault hidden in the heart; the second, when it is done openly; the third, when it is formed into a habit; and the fourth, when man goes so far as to presume on God's mercy or to give himself up to dsepair." No distinction is made between sins of deed and sins of word, and two other degrees of sin are added. Therefore the first division was unfitting.

Obj. 3. Further, there can be no sin of word or deed unless there precede sin of thought. Therefore these sins do not differ specifically. Therefore they should not be divided against one another.

On the contrary, Jerome in commenting on

Ezech. 43. 23, says:[3] "The human race is subject to three kinds of sin, for when we sin, it is either by thought, or word, or deed."

I answer that, Things differ specifically in two ways. First, when each has its complete species; thus a horse and an ox differ specifically. Secondly, when the diversity of species is derived from diversity of degree in generation or movement; thus the building is the complete generation of a house, while the laying of the foundations, and the setting up of the walls are incomplete species, as the Philosopher declares;[4] and the same can apply to the generation of animals.—Accordingly sins are divided into these three, namely, sins of thought, word, and deed, not as into various complete species, for the consummation of sin is in the deed, and so sins of deed have the complete species; but the first beginning of sin is its foundation, as it were, in the sin of thought; the second degree is the sin of word, in so far as man is ready to break out into a declaration of his thought; while the third degree consists in the consummation of sin. Consequently these three differ in respect of the various degrees of sin. Nevertheless it is evident that these three belong to the one complete species of sin, since they proceed from the same motive. For the angry man, through desire of vengeance, is at first disturbed in thought, then he breaks out into words of abuse, and lastly he goes on to wrongful deeds. And the same applies to lust and to any other sin.

Reply Obj. 1. All sins of thought have the common note of secrecy, in respect of which they form one degree, which is, however, divided into three stages, namely of cogitation, pleasure, and consent.

Reply Obj. 2. Sins of word and deed are both done openly, and for this reason Gregory (*loc. cit.*) reckons them under one head; but Jerome (*loc. cit.*) distinguishes between them, because in sins of word there is nothing but manifestation which is intended principally; in sins of deed, however, it is the consummation of the inward thought which is principally intended, and the outward manifestation is by way of sequel. Habit and despair are stages following the complete species of sin, even as boyhood and youth follow the complete generation of a man.

Reply Obj. 3. Sin of thought and sin of word are not distinct from the sin of deed when they are united together with it, but when each is found by itself; even as one part of a move-

---

[1] PL 42, 1008.
[2] PL 75, 661.

[3] Bk XIII (PL 25, 446).
[4] *Ethics*, x, 4 (1174ᵃ19).

ment is not distinct from the whole movement, when the movement is continuous, but only when there is a break in the movement.

ARTICLE 8. *Whether Excess and Deficiency Diversify the Species of Sins.*

We proceed thus to the Eighth Article: It would seem that excess and deficiency do not diversify the species of sins.

Objection 1. For excess and deficiency differ in respect of more and less. Now more and less do not diversify a species. Therefore excess and deficiency do not diversify the species of sins.

Obj. 2. Further, just as sin, in matters of action, is due to straying from the rectitude of reason, so falsehood, in speculative matters, is due to straying from the truth of the thing. Now the species of falsehood is not diversified by saying more or less than is in the thing. Therefore neither is the species of sin diversified by straying more or less from the rectitude of reason.

Obj. 3. Further, "one species cannot be made out of two," as Porphyry declares.[1] Now excess and deficiency are united in one sin; for some are at once illiberal and wasteful—illiberality being a sin by deficiency, and prodigality, by excess. Therefore excess and deficiency do not diversify the species of sins.

On the contrary, Contraries differ specifically, for contrariety is a difference of form, as stated in the *Metaphysics*.[2] Now vices that differ according to excess and deficiency are contrary to one another, as illiberality to wastefulness. Therefore they differ specifically.

I answer that, Although there are two things in sin, namely the act itself and its lack of order, in so far as sin is a departure from the order of reason and the Divine law, the species of sin is gathered, not from its lack of order, which is outside the sinner's intention, as stated above (A. 1), but rather from the act itself as terminating in the object to which the sinner's intention is directed. Consequently wherever we find a different motive inclining the intention to sin there will be a different species of sin. Now it is evident that the motive for sinning in sins by excess is not the same as the motive for sinning in sins by deficiency; in fact, they are contrary to one another, just as the motive in the sin of intemperance is love for bodily pleasures, while the motive in the sin of insensibility is hatred of the same. Therefore these sins not only differ specifically, but are contrary to one another.

Reply Obj. 1. Although more and less do not cause diversity of species, yet they are sometimes consequent to specific difference, in so far as they are the result of diversity of form; thus we may say that fire is lighter than air. Hence the Philosopher says[3] that those who held that there are no different species of friendship "by reason of its admitting of degree, were led by insufficient proof." In this way to exceed reason or to fall short of it belongs to sins specifically different, in so far as they result from different motives.

Reply Obj. 2. It is not the sinner's intention to depart from reason; and so sins of excess and deficiency do not become of one kind through departing from the one rectitude of reason. On the other hand, sometimes he who utters a falsehood intends to hide the truth, and therefore in this respect, it does not matter whether he tells more or less. If, however, departure from the truth is not outside the intention, it is evident that then one is moved by different causes to tell more or less; and in this respect there are different kinds of falsehood, as is evident of the boaster, who exceeds in telling untruths for the sake of glory, and the cheat, who tells less than the truth in order to escape from paying his debts. This also explains how some false opinions are contrary to one another.

Reply Obj. 3. One may be prodigal and illiberal with regard to different objects; for instance one may be illiberal in taking what one ought not, and prodigal in giving what one ought not. But nothing hinders contraries from being in the same subject, in different respects.

ARTICLE 9. *Whether Sins Differ Specifically in Respect of Different Circumstances?*

We proceed thus to the Ninth Article: It would seem that vices and sins differ specifically in respect of different circumstances.

Objection 1. For, as Dionysius says (*Div. Nom.* iv),[4] "evil results from each single defect." Now individual defects are corruptions of individual circumstances. Therefore from the corruption of each circumstance there results a corresponding species of sin.

Obj. 2. Further, sins are human acts. But human acts sometimes take their species from circumstances, as stated above (Q. XVIII, A. 10). Therefore sins differ specifically according as different circumstances are corrupted.

---

[1] *Isagoge,* Trans. of Boëthius (PL 64, 150).
[2] Aristotle, X, 4 (1055ª3).

[3] *Ethics,* VIII, 1 (1155ᵇ13).
[4] Sect. 30 (PG3, 729).

Obj. 3. Further, diverse species are assigned to gluttony, according to the words contained in the following verse:

Hastily, sumptuously, too much, greedily, daintily.

Now these pertain to various circumstances, for hastily means sooner than is right; too much, more than is right, and so on with the others. Therefore the species of sin is diversified according to the various circumstances.

On the contrary, The Philosopher says[1] that every vice sins by doing more than one ought, and when one ought not; and in like manner as to the other circumstances. Therefore the species of sins are not diversified in this respect.

I answer that, As stated above (A. 8), wherever there is a special motive for sinning, there is a different species of sin, because the motive for sinning is the end and object of sin. Now it happens sometimes that although different circumstances are corrupted, there is but one motive; thus the illiberal man, for the same motive, takes when he ought not, where he ought not, and more than he ought, and so on with the other circumstances, since he does this through an inordinate desire of hoarding money. And in such cases the corruption of different circumstances does not diversify the species of sins, but belongs to one and the same species.

Sometimes, however, the corruption of different circumstances arises from different motives; for instance that a man eat hastily may be due to the fact that he cannot brook the delay in taking food, on account of a rapid exhaustion of the digestive humours; and that he desire too much food may be due to a naturally strong digestion; that he desire choice meats is due to his desire for pleasure in taking food. Hence in such matters, the corruption of different circumstances entails different species of sins.

Reply Obj. 1. Evil, as such, is a privation, and so it has different species in respect of the things of which the subject is deprived, even as other privations. But sin does not take its species from the privation or aversion, as stated above (A. 1), but from turning to the object of the act.

Reply Obj. 2. A circumstance never transfers an act from one species to another, save when there is another motive.

Reply Obj. 3. In the various species of gluttony there are various motives, as stated.

[1] *Ethics*, III, 7 (1115^{b}15); IV, I (1119^{b}22).

QUESTION LXXIII

OF THE COMPARISON OF ONE SIN WITH ANOTHER

(*In Ten Articles*)

WE must now consider the comparison of one sin with another, under which head there are ten points of inquiry: (1) Whether all sins and vices are connected with one another? (2) Whether all are equal? (3) Whether the gravity of sin depends on its object? (4) Whether it depends on the excellence of the virtue to which it is opposed? (5) Whether carnal sins are more grievous than spiritual sins? (6) Whether the gravity of sins depends on their causes? (7) Whether it depends on their circumstances? (8) Whether it depends on how much harm ensues? (9) Whether on the condition of the person sinned against? (10) Whether sin is aggravated by reason of the excellence of the person sinning?

ARTICLE 1. *Whether All Sins Are Connected with One Another?*

We proceed thus to the First Article: It would seem that all sins are connected.

Objection 1. For it is written (James 2. 10): *Whosoever shall keep the whole Law, but offend in one point, is become guilty of all.* Now to be guilty of transgressing all the precepts of Law, is the same as to commit all sins, because as Ambrose says (*De Parad.* viii),[2] "sin is a transgression of the Divine law, and disobedience of the heavenly commandments." Therefore whoever commits one sin is guilty of all.

Obj. 2. Further, each sin excludes its opposite virtue. Now whoever lacks one virtue lacks them all, as was shown above (Q. LXV, A. 1). Therefore whoever commits one sin, is deprived of all the virtues. But whoever lacks a virtue, has its opposite vice. Therefore whoever commits one sin is guilty of all sins.

Obj. 3. Further, all virtues which have a principle in common are connected, as stated above (Q. LXV, AA. 1, 2). Now as the virtues have a common principle, so have sins, because, as the love of God, which builds the City of God, is the beginning and root of all the virtues, so self-love, which builds the City of Babylon, is the root of all sins, as Augustine declares.[3] Therefore all vices and sins are also connected so that whoever has one has them all.

[2] PL 14, 309.
[3] *City of God*, XIV, 28 (PL 41, 436); *Ennar. in Ps.* 64.1 (PL 36, 775).

On the contrary, Some vices are contrary to one another, as the Philosopher states.[1] But contraries cannot be together in the same subject. Therefore it is impossible for all sins and vices to be connected with one another.

I answer that, The intention of the man who acts according to virtue in pursuance of his reason is different from the intention of the sinner in straying from the path of reason. For the intention of every man acting according to virtue is to follow the rule of reason, and so the intention of all the virtues, is directed to the same end, so that all the virtues are connected together in the right reason of things to be done, namely prudence, as stated above (Q. LXV, A. 1). But the intention of the sinner is not directed to the point of straying from the path of reason; rather is it directed to tend to some desirable good from which it derives its species. Now these goods, to which the sinner's intention is directed when departing from reason, are of various kinds, having no mutual connection; in fact they are sometimes contrary to one another. Since, therefore, vices and sins take their species from that to which they turn, it is evident that, in respect of that which completes a sin's species, sins are not connected with one another. For sin does not consist in passing from the many to the one, as is the case with virtues, which are connected, but rather in forsaking the one for the many.

Reply Obj. 1. James is speaking of sin not as regards the thing to which it turns, and which causes the distinction of sins, as stated above (Q. LXXII, A. 1), but as regards that from which sin turns away, in so far as man, by sinning, departs from a commandment of the law. Now all the commandments of the law are from one and the same, as he also says in the same passage, so that the same God is despised in every sin. And in this sense he says that whoever *offends in one point, is become guilty of all,* since by committing one sin, he incurs the debt of punishment through his contempt of God, which is the origin of all sins.

Reply Obj. 2. As stated above (Q. LXXI, A. 4), the opposite virtue is not banished by every act of sin; because venial sin does not destroy virtue, while mortal sin destroys infused virtue, by turning man away from God. Yet one act, even of mortal sin, does not destroy the habit of acquired virtue; though if such acts be repeated so as to engender a contrary habit, the habit of acquired virtue is destroyed, the destruction of which entails the loss of prudence,

since when man acts against any virtue whatever, he acts against prudence, without which no moral virtue is possible, as stated above (Q. LVIII, A. 4; Q. LXV, A. 1). Consequently all the moral virtues are destroyed as to the perfect and formal being of virtue, which they have in so far as they partake of prudence; nevertheless there remain the inclinations to virtuous acts, which inclinations, however, are not virtues. Nevertheless it does not follow that for this reason man contracts all vices or sins. First, because several vices are opposed to one virtue, so that a virtue can be destroyed by one of them without the others being present. Secondly, because sin is directly opposed to virtue, as regards the virtue's inclination to act, as stated above (Q. LXXI, A. 1). Therefore, as long as any virtuous inclinations remain, it cannot be said that man has the opposite vices or sins.

Reply Obj. 3. The love of God is unitive, in so far as it draws man's affections from the many to the one, so that the virtues, which flow from the love of God, are connected together. But self-love disperses man's affections among different things, in so far as man loves himself by desiring for himself temporal goods, which are various and of many kinds. Hence vices and sins, which arise from self-love, are not connected together.

ARTICLE 2. *Whether All Sins Are Equal?*

We proceed thus to the Second Article: It would seem that all sins are equal.

Objection 1. Because sin is to do what is unlawful. Now to do what is unlawful is reproved in one and the same way in all things. Therefore sin is reproved in one and the same way. Therefore one sin is not graver than another.

Obj. 2. Further, every sin is a transgression of the rule of reason, which is to human acts what a linear rule is in corporeal things. Therefore to sin is the same as to pass over a line. But passing over a line occurs equally and in the same way even if one go a long way from it or stay near it, since privations do not admit of more or less. Therefore all sins are equal.

Obj. 3. Further, sins are opposed to virtues. But all virtues are equal, as Cicero states (*Paradox,* iii).[2] Therefore all sins are equal.

On the contrary, Our Lord said to Pilate (John 19. 11): *He that hath delivered me to thee, hath the greater sin,* and yet it is evident that Pilate was guilty of some sin. Therefore one sin is greater than another.

I answer that, The opinion of the Stoics,

---

[1] *Ethics,* II, 8 (1108ᵇ27).

[2] DD 1, 545.

which Cicero adopts in the book on *Paradoxes* (*loc. cit.*), was that all sins are equal.[1] From this opinion arose the error of certain heretics, who not only hold all sins to be equal, but also maintain that all the pains of hell are equal.[2] So far as can be gathered from the words of Cicero the Stoics arrived at their conclusion through looking at sin on the side of the privation only, in so far, that is, as it is a departure from reason; therefore considering absolutely that no privation admits of more or less, they held that all sins are equal.

Yet, if we consider the matter carefully, we shall see that there are two kinds of privation. For there is an absolute and pure privation, which consists, so to speak, in being corrupted; thus death is privation of life, and darkness is privation of light. Such privations do not admit of more or less, because nothing remains of the opposite habit. Hence a man is not less dead on the first day after his death, or on the third or fourth days, than after a year, when his corpse is already dissolved; and, in like manner, a house is no darker if the light be covered with several shades than if it were covered by a single shade shutting out all the light.—There is, however, another privation which is not absolute, but retains something of the opposite habit. It consists in becoming corrupted rather than in being corrupted, like sickness which is a privation of the due proportion of the humours, yet so that something remains of that proportion, for otherwise the animal would cease to live; and the same applies to deformity and the like. Such privations admit of more or less on the part of what remains or the contrary habit. For it matters much in sickness or deformity, whether one departs more or less from the due proportion of humours or members. The same applies to vices and sins, because in them the privation of the due proportion of reason is such as not to destroy the order of reason altogether; otherwise "evil, if total, destroys itself," as stated in the *Ethics*.[3] For the substance of the act or the affection of the agent could not remain unless something remained of the order of reason. Therefore it matters much to the gravity of a sin whether one departs more or less from the rectitude of reason. And accordingly we must say that sins are not all equal.

Reply Obj. 1. To commit sin is unlawful on account of some lack of order therein; therefore those which contain a greater lack of order are more unlawful, and consequently graver sins.

Reply Obj. 2. This argument looks upon sin as though it were a pure privation.

Reply Obj. 3. Virtues are proportionately equal in one and the same subject; yet one virtue surpasses another in excellence according to its species. And again, one man is more virtuous than another, in the same species of virtue, as stated above (Q. LXVI, AA. 1, 2). Moreover, even if virtues were equal, it would not follow that vices are equal, since virtues are connected, and vices or sins are not.

ARTICLE 3. *Whether the Gravity of Sins Varies According to Their Objects?*

We proceed thus to the Third Article: It would seem that the gravity of sins does not vary according to their objects.

Objection 1. For the gravity of a sin pertains to its mode or quality but the object is the matter of the sin. Therefore the gravity of sins does not vary according to their various objects.

Obj. 2. Further, the gravity of a sin is the intensity of its malice. Now sin does not derive its malice from its proper object to which it turns, and which is some desirable good, but rather from that which it turns away from. Therefore the gravity of sins does not vary according to their various objects.

Obj. 3. Further, sins that have different objects are of different kinds. But things of different kinds cannot be compared with one another, as is proved in the *Physics*.[4] Therefore one sin is not graver than another by reason of the difference of objects.

On the contrary, Sins take their species from their objects, as was shown above (Q. LXXII, A. 1). But some sins are graver than others in respect of their species, as murder is graver than theft. Therefore the gravity of sins varies according to their objects.

I answer that, As is clear from what has been said (A. 2), the gravity of sins varies in the same way as one sickness is graver than another. For just as the good of health consists in a certain balance of the humours in keeping with an animal's nature, so the good of virtue consists in a certain proportion of the human act in accord with the rule of reason. Now it is evident that the higher the principle whose disorder causes the disorder in the humours, the graver is the sickness; thus a sickness which comes on the hu-

[1] Cf. Jerome, *Adv. Iovin.*, II, 21 (PL 23, 329); also Augustine, *Epist.*, CLXVII, 2 (PL 33, 735); *Contra Mendac.*, XV (PL 40, 539).

[2] Cf. Jerome, *Ibid.*, II, 18, 31 (PL 23, 326); also Augustine, *De Hæres*, 82 (PL 42, 45).

[3] Aristotle, IV, 5 (1126ᵃ12).

[4] Aristotle, VII, 4 (248ᵇ6).

man body from the heart, which is the principle of life, or from some neighbouring part, is more dangerous. Therefore it must be that a sin is so much the graver according as the disorder occurs in a principle which is higher in the order of reason. Now in matters of action the reason directs all things in view of the end; hence the higher the end which attaches to sins in human acts, the graver the sin. Now the object of an act is its end, as stated above (Q. LXXII, A. 3, REPLY 2); and consequently the difference of gravity in sins depends on their objects. Thus it is clear that external things are directed to man as their end, while man is further directed to God as his end. Therefore a sin which is about the very substance of man, for example murder, is graver than a sin which is about external things, for instance theft; and graver still is a sin committed directly against God, for example unbelief, blasphemy, and the like; and in each of these grades of sin, one sin will be graver than another according as it is about a higher or a lower principle. And because sins take their species from their objects, the difference of gravity which is derived from the objects is first and foremost, resulting as it were from their species.

Reply Obj. 1. Although the object is the matter about which an act is concerned, yet it has the character of an end, in so far as the intention of the agent is fixed on it, as stated above (Q. LXXII, A. 3, REPLY 2). Now the form of a moral act depends on the end, as was shown above (Q. XVIII, A. 6; Q. LXXII, A. 6).

Reply Obj. 2. From the very fact that man turns unduly to some changeable good, it follows that he turns away from the unchangeable Good, which aversion completes the character of evil. Hence the various degrees of malice in sins must follow the diversity of those things to which man turns.

Reply Obj. 3. All the objects of human acts are related to one another, and therefore all human acts are in a way of one kind, in so far as they are directed to the last end. Therefore nothing prevents all sins from being compared with one another.

ARTICLE 4. *Whether the Gravity of Sins Depends on the Excellence of the Virtues to Which They Are Opposed?*

We proceed thus to the Fourth Article: It would seem that the gravity of sins does not vary according to the excellence of the virtues to which they are opposed, so that, namely, the graver sin is opposed to the greater virtue.

Objection 1. For, according to Prov. 15. 5, *In abundant justice there is the greatest strength.* Now, as Our Lord says (Matt. 5. 20, *sqq.*), abundant justice restrains anger, which is a less grievous sin than murder, which less abundant justice restrains. Therefore the least grievous sin is opposed to the greatest virtue.

Obj. 2. Further, it is stated in the *Ethics*,[1] that "virtue is about the difficult and the good." Hence it seems to follow that the greater virtue is about what is more difficult. But it is a less grievous sin to fail in what is more difficult than in what is less difficult. Therefore the less grievous sin is opposed to the greater virtue.

Obj. 3. Further, charity is a greater virtue than faith or hope (I Cor. 13. 13). Now hatred, which is opposed to charity, is a less grievous sin than unbelief or despair, which are opposed to faith and hope. Therefore the less grievous sin is opposed to the greater virtue.

On the contrary, The Philosopher says[2] that "the worst is opposed to the best." Now in morals the best is the greatest virtue, and the worst is the most grievous sin. Therefore the most grievous sin is opposed to the greatest virtue.

I answer that, A sin is opposed to a virtue in two ways. First, principally and directly—that sin, namely, which is about the same object as the virtue, because contraries are about the same thing. In this way, it must be that the more grievous sin is opposed to the greater virtue. Because, just as the degrees of gravity in a sin depend on the object, so also does the greatness of a virtue, since both sin and virtue take their species from the object, as shown above (Q. LX, A. 5; Q. LXXII, A. 1). Therefore the greatest sin must be directly opposed to the greatest virtue, as being farthest removed from it in the same genus. Secondly, the opposition of virtue to sin may be considered in respect of a certain extension of the virtue in checking sin. For the greater a virtue is, the farther it removes man from the contrary sin, so that it withdraws man not only from that sin, but also from whatever leads to it. And thus it is evident that the greater a virtue is, the more it withdraws man also from less grievous sins; even as the more perfect health is, the more does it ward off even minor ailments. And in this way the less grievous sin is opposed to the greater virtue, on the part of the latter's effect.

Reply Obj. 1. This argument considers the opposition which consists in restraining from sin; for thus abundant justice checks even minor sins.

[1] Aristotle, II, 3 (1105ᵃ9).   [2] *Ethics*, VIII, 10 (1160ᵇ9).

Reply Obj. 2. The greater virtue which is about a more difficult good, is opposed directly to the sin which is about a more difficult evil. For in each case there is a certain superiority, in that the will is shown to be more intent on good or evil through not being overcome by the difficulty.

Reply Obj. 3. Charity is not any kind of love, but the love of God. Hence not any kind of hatred is opposed to it directly, but the hatred of God, which is the most grievous of all sins.

ARTICLE 5. *Whether Carnal Sins Are of Less Guilt than Spiritual Sins?*

We proceed thus to the Fifth Article: It would seem that carnal sins are not of less guilt than spiritual sins.

Objection 1. Because adultery is a more grievous sin than theft; for it is written (Prov. 6. 30, 32): *The fault is not so great when a man has stolen, . . . but he that is an adulterer, for the folly of his heart shall destroy his own soul.* Now theft belongs to covetousness, which is a spiritual sin, while adultery pertains to lust, which is a carnal sin. Therefore carnal sins are of greater guilt than spiritual sins.

Obj. 2. Further, Augustine says in his commentary on Leviticus[1] that the devil rejoices chiefly in lust and idolatry. But he rejoices more in the greater sin. Therefore, since lust is a carnal sin, it seems that the carnal sins are of most guilt.

Obj. 3. Further, the Philosopher proves[2] that "it is more shameful to be incontinent in lust than in anger." But anger is a spiritual sin, according to Gregory (*Moral.* xxxi, 45),[3] while lust pertains to carnal sins. Therefore carnal sin is more grievous than spiritual sin.

On the contrary, Gregory says (*Moral.* xxxiii, 12)[4] that carnal sins are of less guilt, but of more shame than spiritual sins.

I answer that, Spiritual sins are of greater guilt than carnal sins. This, however, does not mean that each spiritual sin is of greater guilt than each carnal sin, but that, considering the sole difference between spiritual and carnal, spiritual sins are more grievous than carnal sins, other things being equal. Three reasons may be assigned for this. The first is on the part of the subject. For spiritual sins belong to the spirit, to which it is proper to turn to God, and to turn away from Him; carnal sins, however, are consummated in the carnal pleasure of the appe-tite, to which it chiefly belongs to turn to goods of the body. And therefore carnal sin, as such, denotes more a turning to something, and for that reason, implies a closer cleaving; but spiritual sin denotes more a turning from something, from which the notion of guilt arises. And for this reason it involves greater guilt.

A second reason may be taken on the part of the person against whom sin is committed. For carnal sin, as such, is against the sinner's own body, which he ought to love less, in the order of charity, than God and his neighbour, against whom he commits spiritual sins, and consequently spiritual sins, as such, are of greater guilt.

A third reason may be taken from the motive, since the stronger the impulse to sin, the less grievous the sin, as we shall state further on (A. 6). Now carnal sins have a stronger impulse, namely our innate concupiscence of the flesh. Therefore spiritual sins, as such, are of greater guilt.

Reply Obj. 1. Adultery belongs not only to the sin of lust, but also to the sin of injustice, and in this respect may be brought under the head of covetousness, as a gloss observes[5] on Eph. 5. 5, *No fornicator, or unclean, or covetous person,* etc.; so that adultery is so much the more grievous than theft as a man loves his wife more than his chattels.

Reply Obj. 2. The devil is said to rejoice chiefly in the sin of lust because it is of the greatest adhesion, and man can only with difficulty be withdrawn from it. "For the desire of pleasure is insatiable," as the Philosopher states.[6]

Reply Obj. 3. As the Philosopher himself says,[7] the reason why "it is more shameful to be incontinent in lust than in anger" is that lust partakes less of reason. And in the same sense he says[8] that "sins of intemperance are most worthy of reproach, because they are about those pleasures which are common to us and irrational animals"; hence, by these sins man is, so to speak, brutalized. For which same reason Gregory says (*loc. cit.*) that they are more shameful.

ARTICLE 6. *Whether the Gravity of a Sin Depends on Its Cause?*

We proceed thus to the Sixth Article: It would seem that the gravity of a sin does not depend on its cause.

[1] Cf. *City of God,* II, 4, 26 (PL 41, 50; 74).
[2] *Ethics,* VII, 6 (1149^{b}2).
[3] PL 76, 62.   [4] PL 76, 688.

[5] *Glossa ordin.* (VI, 95E); *Glossa* Lombardi (PL 192, 209); cf. Jerome, *In Eph.* III, on 5.5 (PL 26, 554).
[6] *Ethics,* III, 12 (1119^{b}8).
[7] *Ibid.,* VII, 6 (1149^{b}2).
[8] *Ibid.,* III, 10 (1118^{b}2).

Objection 1. Because the greater a sin's cause, the more forcibly it moves to sin, and so the more difficult is it to resist. But sin is lessened by the fact that it is difficult to resist, for it denotes weakness in the sinner, if he cannot easily resist sin, and a sin that is due to weakness is deemed less grievous. Therefore sin does not derive its gravity from its cause.

Obj. 2. Further, concupiscence is a general cause of sin. Hence a gloss on Rom. 7. 7, *For I had not known concupiscence*, says:[1] "The law is good, since by forbidding concupiscence it forbids all evils." Now the greater the concupiscence by which man is overcome, the less grievous his sin. Therefore the gravity of a sin is diminished by the greatness of its cause.

Obj. 3. Further, as rectitude of the reason is the cause of a virtuous act, so defect in the reason seems to be the cause of sin. Now the greater the defect in the reason, the less grievous the sin; so much so that he who lacks the use of reason is altogether excused from sin, and he who sins through ignorance, sins less grievously. Therefore the gravity of a sin is not increased by the greatness of its cause.

On the contrary, If the cause be increased, the effect is increased. Therefore the greater the cause of sin, the more grievous the sin.

I answer that, In the genus of sin, as in every other genus, two causes may be observed. The first is the direct and proper cause of sin, and is the will to sin; for it is compared to the sinful act as a tree to its fruit, as a gloss observes[2] on Matt. 7. 18, *A good tree cannot bring forth evil fruit.* And the greater this cause is, the more grievous will the sin be, since the greater the will to sin, the more grievously does man sin.

The other causes of sin are extrinsic and remote, as it were, being those by which the will is inclined to sin. Among these causes we must make a distinction. For some of them induce the will to sin in accord with the very nature of the will; such is the end, which is the proper object of the will. And by such a cause sin is made more grievous, because a man sins more grievously if his will is induced to sin by the intention of a more evil end. Other causes incline the will to sin against the nature and order of the will, whose natural inclination is to be moved freely of itself in accord with the judgment of reason. Therefore those causes which weaken the judgment of reason (for example ignorance), or which weaken the free movement of the will (for example weakness, violence, fear, or the like), diminish the gravity of sin, even as they diminish its voluntariness; and so much so that if the act be altogether involuntary it is no longer sinful.

Reply Obj. 1. This argument considers the extrinsic moving cause, which diminishes voluntariness. The increase of such a cause diminishes the sin, as stated.

Reply Obj. 2. If concupiscence be understood to include the movement of the will, then, where there is greater concupiscence, there is a greater sin. But if by concupiscence we understand a passion, which is a movement of the concupiscible power, then a greater concupiscence, forestalling the judgment of reason and the movement of the will, diminishes the sin. Because the man who sins because he is stimulated by a greater concupiscence falls through a more grievous temptation, and therefore he is less to be blamed. On the other hand, if concupiscence taken in this sense follows the judgment of reason and the movement of the will, then the greater the concupiscence the graver the sin. For sometimes the movement of concupiscence is redoubled by the will tending unrestrainedly to its object.

Reply Obj. 3. This argument considers the cause which renders the act involuntary, and such a cause diminishes the gravity of sin, as stated.

Article 7. *Whether a Circumstance Aggravates a Sin?*

We proceed thus to the Seventh Article: It would seem that a circumstance does not aggravate a sin.

Objection 1. Because sin takes its gravity from its species. Now a circumstance does not specify a sin, for it is an accident of sin. Therefore the gravity of a sin is not taken from a circumstance.

Obj. 2. Further, a circumstance is either evil or not. If it is evil, it causes, of itself, a species of evil; and if it is not evil, it cannot make a thing worse. Therefore a circumstance in no way aggravates a sin.

Obj. 3. Further, the malice of a sin is derived from its turning away (from God). But circumstances affect sin on the part of the object to which it turns. Therefore they do not add to the sin's malice.

On the contrary, Ignorance of a circumstance diminishes sin. For he who sins through ignorance of a circumstance, deserves to be forgiven.[3]

---

[1] *Glossa ordin.* (VI, 16E); *Glossa interl.* (VI, 16v); *Glossa Lombardi* (PL 191, 1416). Cf. Augustine, *De Spir. et Litt.*, IV (PL 44, 204).　　[2] *Glossa ordin.* (V, 29B).

[3] Aristotle, *Ethics*, III, 1 (1111ᵃ1).

Now this would not be the case unless a circumstance aggravated a sin. Therefore a circumstance makes a sin more grievous.

I answer that, As the Philosopher says in speaking of habits of virtue,[1] it is natural for a thing to be increased by that which causes it. Now it is evident that a sin is caused by a defect in some circumstance; for the fact that a man departs from the order of reason is due to his not observing the due circumstances in his action. Therefore it is evident that it is natural for a sin to be aggravated by reason of its circumstances.

This happens in three ways. First, in so far as a circumstance draws a sin from one genus to another. Thus fornication is the intercourse of a man with one who is not his wife; but if to this be added the circumstance that the latter is the wife of another, the sin is drawn to another kind of sin, namely injustice, in so far as he usurps another's property; and in this respect adultery is a more grievous sin than fornication.

Secondly, a circumstance aggravates a sin, not by drawing it into another genus, but only by multiplying the character of sin. Thus if a wasteful man gives both when he ought not, and to whom he ought not to give, he commits the same kind of sin in more ways than if he were merely to give to whom he ought not, and for that very reason his sin is more grievous, even as that sickness is the graver which affects more parts of the body. Hence Cicero says (*Paradox.* iii)[2] that "in taking his father's life a man commits many sins; for he outrages one who begot him, who fed him, who educated him, to whom he owes his lands, his house, his position in the republic."

Thirdly, a circumstance aggravates a sin by adding to the deformity which the sin derives from another circumstance. Thus, taking another's property constitutes the sin of theft; but if to this be added the circumstance that much is taken of another's property, the sin will be more grievous, although in itself, to take more or less has not the character of a good or of an evil act.

Reply Obj. 1. Some circumstances do specify a moral act, as stated above (Q. XVIII, A. 10). Nevertheless a circumstance which does not give the species may aggravate a sin. Because, even as the goodness of a thing is weighed not only in reference to its species, but also in reference to an accident, so the malice of an act is measured

not only according to the species of that act, but also according to a circumstance.

Reply Obj. 2. A circumstance may aggravate a sin either way. For if it is evil, it does not follow that it constitutes the sin's species; for it may multiply the ratio of evil within the same species, as stated above. And if it be not evil, it may aggravate a sin in relation to the malice of another circumstance.

Reply Obj. 3. Reason should direct the action not only as regards the object, but also as regards every circumstance. Therefore one may turn aside from the rule of reason through corruption of any single circumstance; for instance, by doing something when one ought not or where one ought not. And to depart thus from the rule of reason suffices to make the act evil. This turning aside from the rule of reason results from man's turning away from God, to Whom man ought to be united by right reason.

ARTICLE 8. *Whether Sin Is Aggravated by Reason of Its Causing More Harm?*

We proceed thus to the Eighth Article: It would seem that a sin is not aggravated by reason of its causing more harm.

Objection 1. Because the harm done is an issue consequent to the sinful act. But the issue of an act does not add to its goodness or malice, as stated above (Q. XX, A. 5). Therefore a sin is not aggravated on account of its causing more harm.

Obj. 2. Further, harm is inflicted chiefly by sins against our neighbour, because no one wishes to harm himself, and no one can harm God, according to Job 35. 6, 8: *If thy iniquities be multiplied, what shalt thou do against Him?* ... *Thy wickedness may hurt a man that is like thee.* If, therefore, sins were aggravated through causing more harm, it would follow that sins against our neighbour are more grievous than sins against God or oneself.

Obj. 3. Further, greater harm is inflicted on a man by depriving him of the life of grace than by taking away his natural life, because the life of grace is better than the life of nature, so far that man ought to despise his natural life lest he lose the life of grace. Now, speaking absolutely, a man who leads a woman to commit fornication deprives her of the life of grace by leading her into mortal sin. If therefore a sin were more grievous on account of its causing a greater harm, it would follow that fornication, absolutely speaking, is a more grievous sin than murder, which is evidently untrue. Therefore a sin

---

[1] *Ibid.*, II, 2 (1104ª27).
[2] DD I, 546.

is not more grievous on account of its causing a greater harm.

On the contrary, Augustine says (*De Lib. Arb.* iii, 14):[1] "Since vice is contrary to nature, a vice is the more grievous according as it diminishes the integrity of nature." Now the lessening of the integrity of nature is a harm. Therefore a sin is graver according as it does more harm.

I answer that, Harm may bear a threefold relation to sin. Because sometimes the harm resulting from a sin is foreseen and intended, as when a man does something with a mind to harm another, for example a murderer or a thief. In this case the quantity of harm aggravates the sin directly, because then the harm is the direct object of the sin.

Sometimes the harm is foreseen, but not intended, for instance, when a man takes a short cut through a field, the result being that he knowingly injures the growing crops, although his intention is not to do this harm, but to commit fornication. In this case again the quantity of the harm done aggravates the sin; indirectly, however, in so far, that is, as it is owing to his will being strongly inclined to sin that a man does not forbear from doing, to himself or to another, a harm which he would not wish absolutely. Sometimes, however, the harm is neither foreseen nor intended. And then if this harm is connected with the sin accidentally, it does not aggravate the sin directly. But, on account of his neglecting to consider the harm that might ensue, a man is deemed punishable for the evil results of his action if it be unlawful. If, on the other hand, the harm follows directly from the sinful act, although it be neither foreseen nor intended, it aggravates the sin directly, because whatever is directly consequent to a sin belongs, in a manner, to the very species of that sin; for instance, if a man is a notorious fornicator, the result is that many are scandalized, and although such was not his intention, nor was it perhaps foreseen by him, yet it aggravates his sin directly.

But this does not seem to apply to penal harm, which the sinner himself incurs. Such harm, if accidentally connected with the sinful act, and if neither foreseen nor intended, does not aggravate a sin, nor does it correspond with the gravity of the sin; for instance, if a man in running to slay, slips and hurts his foot. If, on the other hand, this harm is directly consequent to the sinful act, although perhaps it be neither foreseen nor intended, then greater harm does not make

[1] PL 32, 1291.

greater sin, but, on the contrary, a graver sin calls for the infliction of a greater harm. Thus, an unbeliever who has heard nothing about the pains of hell would suffer greater pain in hell for a sin of murder than for a sin of theft. But his sin is not aggravated on account of his neither intending nor foreseeing this, as it would be in the case of a believer, who, it seems sins more grievously in the very fact that he despises a greater punishment, that he may satisfy his desire to sin. But the gravity of this harm is caused solely by the gravity of sin.

Reply Obj. 1. As we have already stated (Q. XX, A. 5) in treating of the goodness and malice of external actions, the result of an action if foreseen and intended adds to the goodness and malice of an act.

Reply Obj. 2. Although the harm done aggravates a sin, it does not follow that this alone renders a sin more grievous; in fact, it is lack of order which of itself aggravates a sin. Therefore the harm itself that ensues aggravates a sin in so far only as it renders the act more disordered. Hence it does not follow, supposing harm to be inflicted chiefly by sins against our neighbour, that such sins are the most grievous, since a much greater lack of order is to be found in sins which man commits against God, and in some which he commits against himself. Moreover we might say that although no man can do God any harm in His substance, yet he can endeavour to do so in things concerning Him, for example by destroying faith, or by outraging holy things, which are most grievous sins. Again, a man sometimes knowingly and freely inflicts harm on himself, as in the case of suicide, though this may be referred finally to some apparent good, for example, delivery from some anxiety.

Reply Obj. 3. This argument does not prove, for two reasons. First, because the murderer intends directly to do harm to his neighbours, while the fornicator who solicits the woman intends not harm but pleasure. Secondly, because murder is the direct and sufficient cause of bodily death, while no man can of himself be the sufficient cause of another's spiritual death, because no man dies spiritually except by sinning of his own will.

ARTICLE 9. *Whether a Sin Is Aggravated by Reason of the Condition of the Person against Whom It Is Committed?*

We proceed thus to the Ninth Article: It would seem that sin is not aggravated by reason of the condition of the person against whom it is committed.

Objection 1. For if this were the case a sin would be aggravated chiefly by being committed against a just and holy man. But this does not aggravate a sin, because a virtuous man who bears a wrong with equanimity is less harmed by the wrong done him, than others, who, through being scandalized, are also hurt inwardly. Therefore the condition of the person against whom a sin is committed does not aggravate the sin.

Obj. 2. Further, if the condition of the person aggravated the sin, this would be still more the case if the person be near of kin, because, as Cicero says (*Paradox.* iii)[1] "The man who kills his slave sins once; he that takes his father's life sins many times." But the kinship of a person sinned against does not apparently aggravate a sin, because every man is most near to himself, and yet it is less grievous to harm oneself than another, for example to kill one's own, than another's horse, as the Philosopher declares.[2] Therefore kinship of the person sinned against does not aggravate the sin.

Obj. 3. Further, the condition of the person who sins aggravates a sin chiefly on account of his dignity or knowledge, according to Wis. 6. 7: *The mighty shall be mightily tormented,* and Luke 12. 47: *The servant who knew the will of his lord . . . and did it not . . . shall be beaten with many stripes.* Therefore, in like manner, on the part of the person sinned against, the sin is made more grievous by reason of his dignity and knowledge. But, apparently, it is not a more grievous sin to inflict an injury on a rich and powerful person than on a poor man, since *there is no respect of persons with God* (Col. 3. 25), according to Whose judgment the gravity of a sin is measured. Therefore the condition of the person sinned against does not aggravate the sin.

On the contrary, Holy Writ censures especially those sins that are committed against the servants of God. Thus it is written (III Kings 19. 14): *They have destroyed Thy altars, they have slain Thy prophets with the sword.* Moreover much blame is attached to the sin committed by a man against those who are akin to him, according to Mich. 7. 6: *The son dishonoureth the father, and the daughter riseth up against her mother.* Furthermore, sins committed against persons of rank are expressly condemned; thus it is written (Job 34. 18): *Who saith to the king: "Thou art an apostate"; who calleth rulers ungodly.* Therefore the condition of the person sinned against aggravates the sin.

[1] DD 1, 546.
[2] *Ethics,* v, 11 (1138ª28).

I answer that, The person sinned against is, in a manner, the object of the sin. Now it has been stated above (A. 3) that the primary gravity of a sin is derived from its object, so that a sin is deemed to be so much the more grave as its object is a more principal end. But the principal ends of human acts are God, man himself, and his neighbour, for whatever we do, it is on account of one of these that we do it, although there is a subordination of one to the other. Therefore the greater or lesser gravity of a sin, in respect of the person sinned against, may be considered on the part of these three.

First, on the part of God, to Whom man is the more closely united according as he is the more virtuous or more sacred to God, so that an injury inflicted on such a person comes back upon God, according to Zach. 2. 8: *He that toucheth you, toucheth the apple of My eye.* Therefore a sin is the more grievous according as it is committed against a person more closely united to God by reason of personal sanctity, or official station. On the part of man himself, it is evident that he sins all the more grievously according as the person against whom he sins is more united to him, either through natural affinity or kindness received or any other bond; because he seems to sin against himself rather than the other, and, for this very reason sins all the more grievously, according to Ecclus. 14. 5: *He that is evil to himself, to whom will he be good?* On the part of his neighbour, a man sins the more grievously according as his sin affects more persons, so that a sin committed against a public personage, for example a king or a prince who stands in the place of the whole people, is more grievous than a sin committed against a private person; hence it is expressly prohibited (Exod. 22. 28): *The prince of thy people thou shalt not curse.* In like manner it would seem that an injury done to a person of prominence is all the more grave on account of the scandal and the disturbance it would cause among many people.

Reply Obj. 1. He who inflicts an injury on a virtuous person, so far as the former is concerned, disturbs him internally and externally; but that the latter is not disturbed internally is due to his goodness, which does not extenuate the sin of the injurer.

Reply Obj. 2. The injury which a man inflicts on himself in those things which are subject to the dominion of his own will, for instance his possessions, is less sinful than if it were inflicted on another, because he does it of his own will. But in those things that are not subject to the dominion of his will, such as natural and spiritual goods, it is a graver sin to inflict an injury on oneself; for it is a more grievous sin for a man to kill himself than another. Since, however, things belonging to our neighbour are not subject to the dominion of our will, the argument fails to prove, in respect of injuries done to such things, that it is less grievous to sin in their regard, unless indeed our neighbour be willing, or give his approval.

Reply Obj. 3. There is no respect for persons if God punishes more severely those who sin against a person of higher rank; for this is done because such an injury redounds to the harm of many.

ARTICLE 10. *Whether the Excellence of the Person Sinning Aggravates the Sin?*

We proceed thus to the Tenth Article: It would seem that the excellence of the person sinning does not aggravate the sin.

Objection 1. For man becomes great chiefly by cleaving to God, according to Ecclus. 25. 13: *How great is he that findeth wisdom and knowledge! but there is none above him that feareth the Lord.* Now the more a man cleaves to God, the less is a sin imputed to him; for it is written (II Paral. 30. 18, 19): *The Lord Who is good will show mercy to all them, who with their whole heart seek the Lord the God of their fathers; and will not impute it to them that they are not sanctified.* Therefore a sin is not aggravated by the excellence of the person sinning.

Obj. 2. Further, *there is no respect of persons with God* (Rom. 2. 11). Therefore He does not punish one man more than another for one and the same sin. Therefore a sin is not aggravated by the excellence of the person sinning.

Obj. 3. Further, no one should reap disadvantage from good. But he would if his action were the more blameworthy on account of his goodness. Therefore a sin is not aggravated by reason of the excellence of the person sinning.

On the contrary, Isidore says (*De Summo Bono,* ii, 18).[1] "A sin is deemed so much the more grievous as the sinner is held to be a more excellent person."

I answer that, Sin is twofold. There is a sin which takes us unawares on account of the weakness of human nature, and such sins are less imputable to one who is more virtuous, because he is less negligent in checking those sins, which nevertheless human weakness does not allow us to escape altogether. But there are other sins which proceed from deliberation. And these sins are all the more imputed to a man according as

[1] PL 83, 621.

he is more excellent. Four reasons may be assigned for this. First, because a more excellent person, for instance one who excels in knowledge and virtue, can more easily resist sin; hence Our Lord said (Luke 12. 47) that the *servant who knew the will of his lord, . . . and did it not . . . shall be beaten with many stripes.* Secondly, on account of ingratitude, because every good in which a man excels is a gift of God, to Whom man is ungrateful when he sins; and in this respect any excellence, even in temporal goods, aggravates a sin, according to Wis. 6. 7: *The mighty shall be mightily tormented.* Thirdly, on account of the sinful act being specially inconsistent with the excellence of the person sinning; for instance, if a prince, who is set up as the guardian of justice, were to violate justice, or if a priest, who has taken the vow of chastity, were to be a fornicator. Fourthly, on account of the example or scandal; because, as Gregory says (*Pastor.* i, 2):[2] "Sin becomes much more scandalous when the sinner is honoured for his position"; and the sins of the great are much more notorious and men bear them with more indignation.

Reply Obj. 1. The passage quoted alludes to those things which are done negligently when we are taken unawares through human weakness.

Reply Obj. 2. God does not respect persons in punishing the great more severely, because their excellence conduces to the gravity of their sin, as stated.

Reply Obj. 3. The man who excels in anything reaps disadvantage not from the good which he has, but from his abuse of it.

QUESTION LXXIV
OF THE SUBJECT OF SIN
(*In Ten Articles*)

WE must now consider the subject of vice or sin, under which head there are ten points of inquiry: (1) Whether the will can be the subject of sin? (2) Whether the will alone is the subject of sin? (3) Whether the sensuality can be the subject of sin? (4) Whether it can be the subject of mortal sin? (5) Whether the reason can be the subject of sin? (6) Whether lingering pleasure or non-lingering pleasure are in the higher reason as in a subject? (7) Whether the sin of consent in the act of sin is as in a subject in the higher reason? (8) Whether the lower reason can be the subject of mortal sin? (9) Whether the higher reason can be the subject of venial sin? (10) Whether there can be in the

[2] PL 77, 16.

higher reason a venial sin directed to its proper object?

ARTICLE 1. *Whether the Will Is a Subject of Sin?*

We proceed thus to the First Article: It would seem that the will cannot be a subject of sin.

Objection 1. For Dionysius says (*Div. Nom.* iv)[1] that "evil is outside the will and the intention." But sin has the character of evil. Therefore sin cannot be in the will.

Obj. 2. Further, the will is directed either to the good or to what seems good. Now from the fact that the will wishes the good, it does not sin; and that it wishes what seems good but is not truly good points to a defect in the apprehensive power rather than in the will. Therefore sin is in no way in the will.

Obj. 3. Further, the same thing cannot be both subject and efficient cause of sin, because the efficient and the material cause do not coincide.[2] Now the will is the efficient cause of sin, because the first cause of sinning is the will, as Augustine states (*De Duabus Anim.* x, 10, 11).[3] Therefore it is not the subject of sin.

On the contrary, Augustine says (*Retract.* i, 9)[4] that "it is by the will that we sin, and live righteously."

I answer that, Sin is an act, as stated above (Q. XXI, A. 1; Q. LXXI, AA. 1, 6). Now some acts pass into external matter, for example to cut and to burn; and such acts have for their matter and subject the thing into which the action passes. Thus the Philosopher states[5] that "movement is the act of the thing moved, caused by a mover." On the other hand, there are acts which do not pass into external matter, but remain in the agent, for example to desire and to know; and such are all moral acts, whether virtuous or sinful. Consequently the proper subject of sin has to be the power which is the principle of the act. Now since it is proper to moral acts that they are voluntary, as stated above (Q. I, A. 1; Q. XVIII, A. 6), it follows that the will, which is the principle of voluntary acts, both of good acts and of evil acts or sins, is the principle of sins. Therefore it follows that sin is in the will as its subject.

Reply Obj. 1. Evil is said to be outside the will because the will does not tend to it under the aspect of evil. But since some evil is an ap-

parent good, the will sometimes desires an evil, and in this sense sin is in the will.

Reply Obj. 2. If the defect in the apprehensive power were in no way subject to the will, there would be no sin, either in the will, or in the apprehensive power, as in the case of those whose ignorance is invincible. It remains therefore that when there is in the apprehensive power a defect that is subject to the will, this defect also is deemed a sin.

Reply Obj. 3. This argument applies to those efficient causes whose actions pass into external matter, and which do not move themselves, but move other things. The contrary of this is to be observed in the will; hence the argument does not prove.

ARTICLE 2. *Whether the Will Alone Is the Subject of Sin?*

We proceed thus to the Second Article: It would seem that the will alone is the subject of sin.

Objection 1. For Augustine says (*De Duabus Anim.* x, 10)[6] that "no one sins except by the will." Now the subject of sin is the power by which we sin. Therefore the will alone is the subject of sin.

Obj. 2. Further, sin is an evil contrary to reason. Now good and evil pertaining to reason are the object of the will alone. Therefore the will alone is the subject of sin.

Obj. 3. Further, every sin is a voluntary act, because, as Augustine states (*De Lib. Arb.* iii, 18),[7] "so true is it that every sin is voluntary, that unless it be voluntary it is no sin at all." Now the acts of the other powers are not voluntary, except in so far as those powers are moved by the will; nor does this suffice for them to be the subject of sin, because then even the external members of the body, which are moved by the will, would be a subject of sin, which is clearly untrue. Therefore the will alone is the subject of sin.

On the contrary, Sin is contrary to virtue, and contraries are about one same thing. But the other powers of the soul besides the will are the subject of virtues, as stated above (Q. LVI, AA. 3, 6). Therefore the will is not the only subject of sin.

I answer that, As was shown above (A. 1), whatever is a principle of a voluntary act is a subject of sin. Now voluntary acts are not only those which are elicited by the will, but also those which are commanded by the will, as we

[1] Sect. 32 (PG 3, 732).
[2] Aristotle, *Physics*, II, 7 (198ª24).
[3] PL 42, 104, 105; cf. *De Lib. Arb.*, III, 7 (PL 32, 1295).
[4] PL 32, 596.
[5] *Physics*, III, 3 (202ª13).
[6] PL 42, 104.
[7] PL 32, 1295; *De Vera Relig.*, XIV (PL 34, 133).

stated above (Q. VI, A. 4) in treating of voluntariness. Therefore not only the will can be a subject of sin, but also all those powers which can be moved to their acts, or restrained from their acts, by the will. And these same powers are the subjects of good and evil moral habits, because act and habit belong to the same subject.

Reply Obj. 1. We do not sin except by the will as first mover; but we sin by the other powers as moved by the will.

Reply Obj. 2. Good and evil pertain to the will as its proper objects. But the other powers have certain determinate goods and evils, by reason of which they can be the subject of virtue, vice, and sin, in so far as they partake of will and reason.

Reply Obj. 3. The members of the body are not principles but merely organs of action. Therefore they are compared to the soul which moves them as a slave who is moved but moves no other. On the other hand, the internal appetitive powers are compared to reason as free agents, because they both act and are acted upon, as is made clear in the *Politics*.[1] Moreover, the acts of the external members are actions that pass into external matter, as may be seen in the blow that is inflicted in the sin of murder. Consequently there is no comparison.

ARTICLE 3. *Whether There Can Be Sin in the Sensuality?*

We proceed thus to the Third Article: It would seem that there cannot be sin in the sensuality.

Objection 1. For sin is proper to man who is praised or blamed for his actions. Now the sensuality is common to us and irrational animals. Therefore sin cannot be in the sensuality.

Obj. 2. Further, "no man sins in what he cannot avoid," as Augustine states (*De Lib. Arb.* iii, 18).[2] But man cannot prevent the movement of the sensuality from being inordinate, since the sensuality ever remains corrupt, so long as we abide in this mortal life; hence it is signified by the serpent, as Augustine declares (*De Trin.* xii, 12, 13).[3] Therefore the inordinate movement of the sensuality is not a sin.

Obj. 3. Further, that which man himself does not do is not imputed to him as a sin. Now, that alone do we seem to do ourselves, which we do

with the deliberation of reason, as the Philosopher says.[4] Therefore the movement of the sensuality, which is without the deliberation of reason, is not imputed to a man as a sin.

On the contrary, It is written (Rom. 7. 19): *The good which I will I do not; but the evil which I will not, that I do*, which words Augustine explains (*Contra Julian.* iii, 26),[5] as referring to the evil of concupiscence, which is clearly a movement of the sensuality. Therefore there can be sin in the sensuality.

I answer that, As stated above (A. 2), sin may be found in any power whose act can be voluntary and disordered, in which consists the nature of sin. Now it is evident that the act of the sensuality can be voluntary, in so far as the sensuality, or sensitive appetite, is naturally inclined to be moved by the will. Therefore it follows that sin can be in the sensuality.

Reply Obj. 1. Although some of the powers of the sensitive part are common to us and irrational animals, nevertheless in us they have a certain excellence through being united to the reason; thus we surpass other animals in the sensitive part because we have the powers of cogitation and reminiscence, as stated in the First Part (Q. LXXVIII, A. 4). In the same way our sensitive appetite surpasses that of other animals by reason of a certain excellence consisting in its natural aptitude to obey the reason. And in this respect it can be the principle of a voluntary action, and, consequently, the subject of sin.

Reply Obj. 2. The continual corruption of the sensuality is to be understood as referring to the "fomes," which is never completely destroyed in this life, since, though the stain of original sin passes, its effect remains. However, this corruption of the "fomes" does not hinder man from using his rational will to check individual inordinate movements, if he be presentient of them, for instance by turning his thoughts to other things. Yet while he is turning his thoughts to something else, an inordinate movement may arise about this also; thus when a man, in order to avoid the movements of concupiscence, turns his thoughts away from carnal pleasures to the considerations of science, sometimes an unpremeditated movement of vainglory will arise. Consequently a man cannot avoid all such movements, on account of the corruption we have just spoken about. But it is enough, for the conditions of a volun-

---

[1] Aristotle, I, 5 (1254^b4).

[2] PL 32, 1295.

[3] PL 42, 1007, 1009; cf. Peter Lombard, *Sent.*, II, d. 24, chap. 6 (QR 1, 423).

[4] *Ethics*, IX, 8 (1168^b35).

[5] PL 44, 733; *Serm. ad Pop.*, serm. XXX, 2, 3 (PL 38, 188, 189).

tary sin that he be able to avoid each single one.

Reply Obj. 3. Man does not do perfectly himself what he does without the deliberation of reason, since the principal part of man does nothing there. Hence such an act is not perfectly a human act, and consequently it cannot be a perfect act of virtue or of sin, but is something imperfect of that kind. Therefore such movement of the sensuality as forestalls the reason is a venial sin, which is something imperfect in the genus of sin.

ARTICLE 4. *Whether Mortal Sin Can Be in the Sensuality?*

We proceed thus to the Fourth Article: It would seem that mortal sin can be in the sensuality.

Objection 1. Because an act is known by its object. Now it is possible to commit a mortal sin about the objects of the sensuality, for example about carnal pleasures. Therefore the act of the sensuality can be a mortal sin, so that mortal sin can be found in the sensuality.

Obj. 2. Further, mortal sin is opposed to virtue. But virtue can be in the sensuality, for temperance and fortitude are virtues of the irrational parts, as the Philosopher states.[1] Therefore, since it is natural to contraries to be about the same subject, sensuality can be the subject of mortal sin.

Obj. 3. Further, venial sin is a disposition to mortal sin. Now disposition and habit are in the same subject. Since therefore venial sin may be in the sensuality, as stated above (A. 3, Reply 3), mortal sin can be there also.

On the contrary, Augustine says (*Retract.* i, 23),[2] and a gloss on Rom. 7. 14 also says[3] that the inordinate movement of concupiscence, which is the sin of the sensuality, can even be in those who are in a state of grace, in whom, however, mortal sin is not to be found. Therefore the inordinate movement of the sensuality is not a mortal sin.

I answer that, Just as a disorder which destroys the principle of the body's life causes the body's death, so too a disorder which destroys the principle of spiritual life, which is the last end, causes spiritual death, which is mortal sin, as stated above (Q. LXXII, A. 5). Now it belongs to the reason alone, and not to the sensuality, to order anything to the end, and

[1] *Ethics*, III, 10 (1117ᵇ23).
[2] PL 32, 621.
[3] *Glossa ordin.* (VI, 17E); *Glossa* Lombardi (PL 191, 1421).

disorder in respect of the end can only belong to the power whose function it is to order others to the end. Therefore mortal sin cannot be in the sensuality, but only in the reason.

Reply Obj. 1. The act of the sensuality can concur towards a mortal sin. Yet the fact of its being a mortal sin is due not to its being an act of the sensuality, but to its being an act of reason, to whom the ordering to the end belongs. Consequently mortal sin is imputed, not to the sensuality, but to reason.

Reply Obj. 2. An act of virtue is perfected not only in that it is an act of the sensuality, but still more in the fact of its being an act of reason and will, whose function it is to choose; for the act of moral virtue is not without the exercise of choice. Therefore the act of moral virtue, which perfects the appetitive power, is always accompanied by an act of prudence, which perfects the rational power; and the same applies to mortal sin, as just stated (Reply 1).

Reply Obj. 3. A disposition may be related in three ways to that to which it disposes. For sometimes it is the same thing and is in the same subject; thus undeveloped science is a disposition to perfect science. Sometimes it is in the same subject, but is not the same thing; thus heat is a disposition to the form of fire. Sometimes it is neither the same thing, nor in the same subject, as in those things which are ordered to one another in such a way that we can arrive at one through the other; for example goodness of the imagination is a disposition to science, which is in the intellect. In this way the venial sin that is in the sensuality may be a disposition to mortal sin, which is in the reason.

ARTICLE 5. *Whether Sin Can Be in the Reason?*

We proceed thus to the Fifth Article: It would seem that sin cannot be in the reason.

Objection 1. For the sin of any power is a defect in it. But the fault of the reason is not a sin; on the contrary, it excuses sin. For a man is excused from sin on account of ignorance. Therefore sin cannot be in the reason.

Obj. 2. Further, the primary subject of sin is the will, as stated above (A. 1). Now reason precedes the will, since it directs it. Therefore sin cannot be in the reason.

Obj. 3. Further, there can be no sin except about things which are under our control. Now perfection and defect of reason are not among those things which are under our control, since by nature some are mentally deficient, and some sagacious. Therefore no sin is in the reason.

On the contrary, Augustine says (*De Trin.* xii, 12)[1] that sin is in the lower and in the higher reason.

I answer that, The sin of any power is an act of that power, as we have clearly shown (AA. 1, 2, 3). Now reason has a twofold act: one is its proper act in respect of its proper object, and this is the act of knowing a truth; the other is the act of the reason as directing the other powers. Now in both of these ways there may be sin in the reason. First, in so far as it errs in the knowledge of truth, which error is imputed to the reason as a sin when it is in ignorance or error about what it is able and ought to know. Secondly, when it either commands the disordered movements of the lower powers, or deliberately fails to check them.

Reply Obj. 1. This argument considers the defect in the proper act of the reason in respect of its proper object, and with regard to the case when it is a defect of knowledge about something which one is unable to know; for then this defect of reason is not a sin, and excuses from sin, as is evident with regard to the actions of madmen. If, however, the defect of reason be about something which a man is able and ought to know, he is not altogether excused from sin, and the defect is imputed to him as a sin. The defect which belongs only to the act of directing the other powers is always imputed to reason as a sin, because it can always obviate this defect by means of its proper act.

Reply Obj. 2. As stated above (Q. XVII, A. 1), when we were treating of the acts of the will and reason, the will moves and precedes the reason in one way, and the reason moves and precedes the will in another, so that both the movement of the will can be called rational, and the act of the reason, voluntary. Accordingly sin is found in the reason either through being a voluntary defect of the reason, or through the reason being the principle of the will's act.

The Reply to the Third Objection is evident from what has been said (REPLY 1).

ARTICLE 6. *Whether the Sin of Lingering Pleasure Is in the Reason?*

We proceed thus to the Sixth Article: It would seem that the sin of lingering pleasure (*morosa delectatio*) is not in the reason.[2]

Objection 1. For pleasure denotes a movement of the appetitive power, as stated above (Q. XXXI, A. 1). But the appetitive power is distinct from the reason, which is an apprehensive power. Therefore lingering pleasure is not in the reason.

Obj. 2. Further, the object shows to which power an act belongs, since it is through the act that the power is directed to its object. Now a lingering pleasure is sometimes about sensible goods, and not about the goods of the reason. Therefore the sin of lingering pleasure is not in the reason.

Obj. 3. Further, a thing is said to be lingering (*morosus*)[3] through taking a length of time. But length of time is no reason why an act should belong to a particular power. Therefore lingering pleasure does not belong to the reason.

On the contrary, Augustine says (*De Trin.* xii, 12)[4] that if the consent to a sensual pleasure "goes no further than the mere thought of the pleasure, I deem this to be like as though the woman alone had partaken of the forbidden fruit." Now "the woman" denotes the lower reason, as he himself explains (*ibid.*). Therefore the sin of lingering pleasure is in the reason.

I answer that, As already stated (A. 5), sin may sometimes be in the reason in so far as it directs human actions. Now it is evident that reason directs not only external acts, but also internal passions. Consequently when the reason fails in directing the internal passions, sin is said to be in the reason, just as when it fails in directing external actions. Now it fails, in two ways, in directing internal passions. First, when it commands unlawful passions; for instance when a man deliberately provokes himself to a movement of anger, or of concupiscence. Secondly, when it fails to check the unlawful movement of a passion; for instance, when a man, having deliberately considered that a rising movement of passion is inordinate, continues, notwithstanding, to dwell (*immoratur*) upon it, and fails to drive it away. And in this sense the sin of lingering pleasure is said to be in the reason.

Reply Obj. 1. Pleasure is indeed in the appetitive power as its proximate principle; but it is in the reason as its first mover, in accordance with what has been stated above (A. 1),

---

[1] PL 42, 1008.

[2] On this problem and those which follow to the end of the question cf. Peter Lombard, *Sent.,* II, d. 24, chaps.

5–13 (QR 1, 422, 428); Albert the Great, *Summa de Creatur.,* pt. I, tr. 4, Q. 69, A. 3 (BO XXXIV, 700).

[3] From the Latin, *mora*—delay.

[4] PL 42, 1007.

namely that actions which do not pass into external matter are in their principles as in their subjects.

Reply Obj. 2. Reason has its proper elicited act about its proper object, but it exercises the direction of all the objects of those lower powers that can be directed by the reason. And accordingly pleasure about sensible objects comes also under the direction of reason.

Reply Obj. 3. Pleasure is said to be lingering not from a delay of time, but because the reason in deliberating dwells (*immoratur*) upon it, and fails to drive it away, "deliberately holding and turning over what should have been cast aside as soon as it touched the mind," as Augustine says (*De Trin.* xii, 12).[1]

ARTICLE 7. *Whether the Sin of Consent to the Act Is in the Higher Reason?*

We proceed thus to the Seventh Article: It would seem that the sin of consent to the act is not in the higher reason.

Objection 1. For consent is an act of the appetitive power, as stated above (Q. XV, A. 1). But the reason is an apprehensive power. Therefore the sin of consent to the act is not in the higher reason.

Obj. 2. Further, "the higher reason is intent on contemplating and consulting the eternal types," as Augustine states (*De Trin.* xii, 7).[2] But sometimes consent is given to an act, without consulting the eternal types, since man does not always think about Divine things whenever he consents to an act. Therefore the sin of consent to the act is not always in the higher reason.

Obj. 3. Further, just as man can regulate his external actions according to the eternal law, so can he regulate his internal pleasures or other passions. But consent to a pleasure without deciding to fulfil it by deed, belongs to the lower reason, as Augustine states (*De Trin.* xii, 12).[3] Therefore the consent to a sinful act should also be sometimes ascribed to the lower reason.

Obj. 4. Further, just as the higher reason excels the lower, so does the reason excel the imagination. Now sometimes man proceeds to act through the apprehension of the power of imagination, without any deliberation of his reason, as when, without premeditation, he moves his hand or foot. Therefore sometimes also the lower reason may consent to a sinful act, independently of the higher reason.

On the contrary, Augustine says (*De Trin.*

xii, 12):[4] "If the consent to the evil use of things that can be perceived by the bodily senses so far approves of any sin, as to point, if possible, to its consummation by deed, we are to understand that the woman has offered the forbidden fruit to her husband."

I answer that, Consent implies a judgment about the thing to which consent is given. For just as the speculative reason judges and delivers its sentence about intelligible matters, so the practical reason judges and pronounces sentence on matters of action. Now we must observe that in every case brought up for judgment the final sentence belongs to the supreme court, even as we see that in speculative matters the final sentence touching any proposition is delivered by resolving it into the first principles, since, so long as there remains a yet higher principle, the question can yet be submitted to it, and therefore the judgment is still in suspense, the final sentence not being as yet pronounced. But it is evident that human acts can be regulated by the rule of human reason, which rule is derived from the created things that man knows naturally; and further still, from the rule of the Divine law, as stated above (Q. XIX, A. 4; Q. LXXI, A. 6). Consequently, since the rule of the Divine law is the higher rule, it follows that the ultimate sentence, by which judgment is finally pronounced, belongs to the higher reason which is intent on the eternal types. Now when judgment has to be pronounced on several points, the final judgment deals with that which comes last; and, in human acts, the act itself comes last, and the pleasure which is the inducement to the act is a preamble to the act. Therefore the consent to an act belongs properly to the higher reason, while the preliminary judgment which is about the pleasure belongs to the lower reason, which delivers judgment in a lower court; although the higher reason can also judge of the pleasure, since whatever is subject to the judgment of the lower court, is subject also to the judgment of the higher court, but not conversely.

Reply Obj. 1. Consent is an act of the appetitive power, not absolutely, but in consequence of an act of reason deliberating and judging, as stated above (Q. XV, A. 3). Because the fact that the consent is finally given to a thing is due to the fact that the will tends to that upon which the reason has already passed its judgment. Hence consent may be ascribed both to the will and to the reason.

[1] PL 42, 1008.   [2] PL 42, 1005.   [3] PL 42, 1008.   [4] PL 42, 1008.

Reply Obj. 2. The higher reason is said to consent from the very fact that it fails to direct the human act according to the Divine law in hindering the act of sin, whether or not it advert to the eternal law. For if it thinks of God's law, it holds it in actual contempt; and if not, it neglects it by a kind of omission. Therefore the consent to a sinful act always proceeds from the higher reason. Because, as Augustine says (*De Trin.* xii, 12),[1] "the mind cannot effectively decide on the commission of a sin, unless by its consent, whereby it wields its sovereign power of moving the members to action, or of restraining them from action, it become the servant or slave of the evil deed."

Reply Obj. 3. The higher reason, by considering the eternal law, can direct or restrain the internal pleasure, just as it can direct or restrain the external action. Nevertheless, before the judgment of the higher reason is pronounced, the lower reason, while deliberating the matter in reference to temporal principles, sometimes approves of this pleasure as soon as it is proposed by the sensuality, and then the consent to the pleasure belongs to the lower reason. If, however, after considering the eternal law, man persists in giving the same consent, such consent will then belong to the higher reason.

Reply Obj. 4. The apprehension of the power of imagination is sudden and without deliberation, and so it can cause an act before the higher or lower reason has time to deliberate. But the judgment of the lower reason is deliberate, and so requires time, during which the higher reason can also deliberate. Consequently, if by its deliberation it does not check the sinful act, this will be imputed to it.

ARTICLE 8. *Whether Consent to Pleasure Is a Mortal Sin?*

We proceed thus to the Eighth Article: It would seem that consent to pleasure is not a mortal sin.

Objection 1. For consent to pleasure belongs to the lower reason, which does not consider the eternal types, that is, the eternal law, and consequently does not turn away from them. Now every mortal sin consists in turning away from the Divine law, as is evident from Augustine's definition of mortal sin, which was quoted above (Q. LXXI, A. 6). Therefore consent to pleasure is not a mortal sin.

Obj. 2. Further consent to a thing is not evil

unless the thing to which consent is given be evil. Now the cause of anything being such is yet more so, or at any rate not less. Consequently the thing to which a man consents cannot be a lesser evil than his consent. But pleasure without deed is not a mortal sin but only a venial sin. Therefore neither is the consent to the pleasure a mortal sin.

Obj. 3. Further, pleasures differ in goodness and malice, according to the difference of the deeds, as the Philosopher states.[2] Now the inward thought is one thing, and the outward deed, for example fornication, is another. Therefore the pleasure consequent to the act of inward thought differs in goodness and malice from the pleasure of fornication, as much as the inward thought differs from the outward deed; and consequently there is a like difference of consent on either hand. But the inward thought is not a mortal sin, nor is the consent to that thought; and therefore neither is the consent to the pleasure.

Obj. 4. Further, the external act of fornication or adultery is a mortal sin, not by reason of the pleasure, since this is found also in the marriage act, but by reason of a lack of order in the act itself. Now he that consents to the pleasure does not, for this reason, consent to the lack of order of the act. Therefore he seems not to sin mortally.

Obj. 5. Further, the sin of murder is more grievous than simple fornication. Now it is not a mortal sin to consent to the pleasure resulting from the thought of murder. Much less therefore is it a mortal sin to consent to the pleasure resulting from the thought of fornication.

Obj. 6. Further the Lord's Prayer is recited every day for the remission of venial sins, as Augustine asserts (*Enchirid.* LXXI).[3] Now Augustine teaches that consent to pleasure may be driven away by means of the Lord's Prayer, for he says (*De Trin.* xii, 12)[4] that "this sin is much less grievous than if it be decided to fulfil it by deed; therefore we ought to ask pardon for such thoughts also, and we should strike our breasts and say: 'Forgive us our trespasses.'" Therefore consent to pleasure is a venial sin.

On the contrary, Augustine adds after a few words: "Man will be altogether lost unless, through the grace of the Mediator, he be forgiven those things which are deemed mere sins of thought, since without the will to do them,

---

[1] PL 42, 1008.

[2] *Ethics*, X, 5 (1175^{b}26).

[3] PL 40, 265; *De Fide et Oper.*, XXVI (PL 40, 228).

[4] PL 42, 1008.

he desires nevertheless to enjoy them." But no man is lost except through mortal sin. Therefore consent to pleasure is a mortal sin.

I answer that, There have been various opinions on this point, for some have held that consent to pleasure is not a mortal sin, but only a venial sin,[1] while others have held it to be a mortal sin, and this opinion is more common and more probable.[2] For we must take note that since every pleasure results from some action, as stated in the *Ethics,*[3] and again, that since every pleasure has an object, it follows that every pleasure may be compared to two things, namely to the operation from which it results, and to the object in which a person takes delight. Now it happens that an action, just as a thing, is an object of pleasure, because the action itself can be considered as a good and an end, in which the person who delights in it, rests. Sometimes the action itself which results in pleasure is the object of pleasure, in so far as the appetitive power, to which it belongs to take delight in anything, is brought to bear on the action itself as a good; for instance, when a man thinks and delights in his thought in so far as his thought pleases him. At other times the pleasure consequent to an action, for example a thought, has for its object another action, as being the object of his thought; and then pleasure of this kind proceeds from the inclination of the appetite, not indeed to the thought, but to the action thought of.

Accordingly a man who is thinking of fornication may delight in either of two things: first, in the thought itself, secondly, in the fornication thought of. Now the pleasure in the thought itself results from the inclination of the affection to the thought itself; and the thought itself is not in itself a mortal sin; sometimes indeed it is only a venial sin, as when a man thinks of such a thing for no purpose, and sometimes it is no sin at all, as when a man has a purpose in thinking of it, for instance, he may wish to preach or dispute about it. Consequently such affection or pleasure in respect of the thought of fornication is not a mortal sin in virtue of its genus, but is sometimes a venial sin and sometimes no sin at all; and hence neither is it a mortal sin to consent to such a thought. In this sense the first opinion is true.

But that a man in thinking of fornication takes pleasure in the act thought of is due to his affection being inclined to this act. Therefore the fact that a man consents to such a pleasure amounts to nothing less than a consent to the inclination of his affection to fornication; for no man takes pleasure except in that which is in conformity with his appetite. Now it is a mortal sin if a man deliberately chooses that his affection be conformed to what is in itself a mortal sin. Therefore such a consent to pleasure in a mortal sin is itself a mortal sin, as the second opinion maintains.

Reply Obj. 1. Consent to pleasure may be not only in the lower reason, but also in the higher reason, as stated above (A. 7). Nevertheless the lower reason may turn away from the eternal types, for, though it is not intent on them, as regulating according to them, which is proper to the higher reason, yet, it is intent on them as being regulated according to them. And by turning from them in this sense, it may sin mortally, since even the acts of the lower powers and of the external members may be mortal sins in so far as the direction of the higher reason fails in directing them according to the eternal types.

Reply Obj. 2. Consent to a sin that is venial in its genus, is itself a venial sin, and accordingly one may conclude that the consent to take pleasure in a useless thought about fornication is a venial sin. But pleasure in the act itself of fornication is, in its genus, a mortal sin, and that it be a venial sin before the consent is given, is accidental, namely on account of the incompleteness of the act, which incompleteness ceases when the deliberate consent has been given, so that therefore it has its complete nature and is a mortal sin.

Reply Obj. 3. This argument considers the pleasure which has the thought for its object.

Reply Obj. 4. The pleasure which has an external act for its object cannot be without pleasure in the external act as such, even though there be no decision to fulfil it, on account of the prohibition of some higher authority. Therefore the act is without order, and consequently the pleasure will be lacking in order also.

Reply Obj. 5. The consent to pleasure resulting from pleasure in an act of murder thought of, is a mortal sin also; but not the consent to pleasure resulting from pleasure in the thought of murder.

Reply Obj. 6. The Lord's Prayer is to be said

[1] Cf. Albert, *Summa de Creat.,* Pt. I, tr. 4, Q. 69, A. 3 (BO xxxiv, 713b); also Sed contra 2 (709). See also *Summa Theol.,* Pt. II, tr. 15, Q. 94, m. 6 (BO xxxiii, 208, 209).

[2] Cf. Bonaventure, *In Sent.,* II, d. 24, Pt. 2, A. 2, Q. 2 (QR II, 582).

[3] Aristotle, X, 4 (1175ª5).

in order that we may be preserved not only from venial sin, but also from mortal sin.

ARTICLE 9. *Whether There Can Be Venial Sin in the Higher Reason as Directing the Lower Powers?*

We proceed thus to the Ninth Article: It would seem that there cannot be venial sin in the higher reason as directing the lower powers, that is, as consenting to a sinful act.

Objection 1. For Augustine says (*De Trin.* xii, 7)[1] that the higher reason "cleaves to the eternal types." But mortal sin consists in turning away from the eternal law. Therefore it seems that there can be no other mortal sin in the higher reason.

Obj. 2. Further, the higher reason is the principle of the spiritual life, as the heart is of the body's life. But the diseases of the heart are deadly. Therefore the sins of the higher reason are mortal.

Obj. 3. Further, a venial sin becomes a mortal sin if it be done out of contempt. But it would seem impossible to commit even a venial sin, deliberately, without contempt. Since then the consent of the higher reason is always accompanied by deliberate consideration of the Divine law, it seems that it cannot be without mortal sin, on account of the contempt of the Divine law.

On the contrary, Consent to a sinful act belongs to the higher reason, as stated above (A. 8). But consent to an act of venial sin is itself a venial sin. Therefore a venial sin can be in the higher reason.

I answer that, As Augustine says (*De Trin.* xii, 7),[1] the higher reason "is intent on contemplating or consulting the eternal types." It contemplates them by considering their truth; it consults them by judging and directing other things according to them—and to this pertains the fact that by deliberating through the eternal types it consents to an act or dissents from it. Now it may happen that the lack of order of the act to which it consents is not contrary to the eternal types in the same way as mortal sin is, because it does not imply turning away from the last end, but is outside that law, as an act of venial sin is. Therefore when the higher reason consents to the act of a venial sin, it does not turn away from the eternal types. Therefore it sins, not mortally, but venially.

This suffices for the *Reply to the First Objection.*

[1] PL 42, 1005.

Reply Obj. 2. Disease of the heart is twofold. One is in the very substance of the heart, and affects its natural temperament, and such a disease is always mortal. The other is a disease of the heart consisting in some disorder either of the movement or of the parts surrounding the heart, and such a disease is not always mortal. In like manner there is mortal sin in the higher reason whenever the order itself of the higher reason to its proper object, which is the eternal types, is destroyed. But when the disorder leaves this untouched, the sin is not mortal but venial.

Reply Obj. 3. Deliberate consent to a sin does not always amount to contempt of the Divine law, but only when the sin is contrary to the Divine law.

ARTICLE 10. *Whether Venial Sin Can Be in the Higher Reason As Such?*

We proceed thus to the Tenth Article: It would seem that venial sin cannot be in the higher reason as such, that is, as considering the eternal types.

Objection 1. For the act of a power is not found to fail except that power be inordinately disposed with regard to its object. Now the object of the higher reason is the eternal types, in respect of which there can be no disorder without mortal sin. Therefore there can be no venial sin in the higher reason as such.

Obj. 2. Further, since the reason is a deliberative power, there can be no act of reason without deliberation. Now every inordinate movement in things concerning God, if it be deliberate, is a mortal sin. Therefore venial sin is never in the higher reason as such.

Obj. 3. Further, it happens sometimes that a sin which takes us unawares is a venial sin. Now a deliberate sin is a mortal sin, through the reason, in deliberating, having recourse to some higher good, by acting against which higher good man sins more grievously; just as when the reason in deliberating about an inordinate pleasurable act considers that it is contrary to the law of God, it sins more grievously in consenting, than if it only considered that it is contrary to moral virtue. But the higher reason cannot have recourse to any higher tribunal than its own object. Therefore if a movement that takes us unawares is not a mortal sin, neither will the subsequent deliberation make it a mortal sin; which is clearly false. Therefore there can be no venial sin in the higher reason as such.

On the contrary, A sudden movement of unbelief is a venial sin. But it pertains to the higher reason as such. Therefore there can be a venial sin in the higher reason as such.

I answer that, The higher reason regards its own object otherwise than the objects of the lower powers that are directed by the higher reason. For it does not regard the objects of the lower powers except in so far as it consults the eternal types about them, and so it does not regard them save by way of deliberation. Now deliberate consent to what is a mortal sin in its genus is itself a mortal sin; and consequently the higher reason always sins mortally if the acts of the lower powers to which it consents are mortal sins.

With regard to its own object it has a twofold act, namely simple intuition, and deliberation, in respect of which it again consults the eternal types about its own object. But in respect of simple intuition, it can have an inordinate movement about Divine things, as for instance when a man suffers a sudden movement of unbelief. And although unbelief, in its genus, is a mortal sin, yet a sudden movement of unbelief is a venial sin, because there is no mortal sin unless it be contrary to the law of God. Now it is possible for one of the articles of faith to present itself to the reason suddenly under some other aspect, before the eternal type, that is, the law of God, is consulted, or can be consulted, on the matter; as, for instance, when a man suddenly apprehends the resurrection of the dead as impossible naturally, and rejects it, as soon as he has thus apprehended it, before he has had time to deliberate and consider that this is proposed to our belief in accordance with the Divine law. If, however, the movement of unbelief remains after this deliberation, it is a mortal sin. Therefore, in sudden movements, the higher reason may sin venially in respect of its proper object, even if it be a mortal sin in its genus; or it may sin mortally by giving a deliberate consent. But in things pertaining to the lower powers, it always sins mortally in things which are mortal sins in their genus, but not in those which are venial sins in their genus.

Reply Obj. 1. A sin which is against the eternal types, though it be mortal in its genus, may nevertheless be venial on account of the incompleteness of a sudden action, as stated.

Reply Obj. 2. In matters of action, the simple intuition of the principles from which deliberation proceeds belongs to the reason, as does the act of deliberation; even as in speculative matters it belongs to the reason both to syllogize and to form propositions. Consequently the reason also can have a sudden movement.

Reply Obj. 3. One and the same thing may be the subject of different considerations, of which one is higher than the other; thus the existence of God may be considered either as possible to be known by the human reason, or as delivered to us by Divine revelation, which is a higher consideration. And therefore, although the object of the higher reason is, in its nature, something sublime, yet it is reducible to some yet higher consideration. And in this way, that which in the sudden movement was not a mortal sin, becomes a mortal sin in virtue of the deliberation which brought it into the light of a higher consideration, as was explained above.

QUESTION LXXV
OF THE CAUSES OF SIN, IN GENERAL
(*In Four Articles*)

WE must now consider the causes of sin: (1) in general; (2) in particular. (Q. LXXVI) Under the first head there are four points of inquiry: (1) Whether sin has a cause? (2) Whether it has an internal cause? (3) Whether it has an external cause? (4) Whether one sin is the cause of another?

ARTICLE 1. *Whether Sin Has a Cause?*

We proceed thus to the First Article: It would seem that sin has no cause.

Objection 1. For sin has the nature of evil, as stated above (Q. LXXI, A. 6). But "evil has no cause," as Dionysius says (*Div. Nom.* iv).[1] Therefore sin has no cause.

Obj. 2. Further, a cause is that from which something follows of necessity. Now that which is of necessity seems to be no sin, for every sin is voluntary. Therefore sin has no cause.

Obj. 3. Further, if sin has a cause, this cause is either good or evil. It is not a good, because good produces nothing but good, for *a good tree cannot bring forth evil fruit* (Matt. 7. 18). Likewise neither can evil be the cause of sin, because the evil of punishment is a sequel to sin, and the evil of guilt is the same as sin. Therefore sin has no cause.

On the contrary, Whatever is done has a cause, for, according to Job 5. 6, *nothing upon earth is done without a cause.* But sin is something done, since it is "a word, deed, or desire contrary to the law of God."[2] Therefore sin has a cause.

---

[1] Sect. 30 (PG 3, 732).
[2] Augustine, *Contra Faust.,* XXII, 27 (PL 42, 418).

I answer that, A sin is a disordered act. Accordingly, so far as it is an act, it can have a direct cause, even as any other act; but so far as it is inordinate, it has a cause in the same way as a negation or privation can have a cause. Now two causes may be assigned to a negation. In the first place, absence of the cause of affirmation; that is, the negation of the cause itself, is the cause of the negation in itself, since the result of removing the cause is the removal of the effect; thus the absence of the sun is the cause of darkness. In the second place, the cause of an affirmation of which a negation is a sequel is the accidental cause of the resulting negation; thus fire by causing heat in virtue of its principal tendency, consequently causes a privation of cold. The first of these suffices to cause a simple negation. But, since the lack of order of sin and of every evil is not a simple negation, but the privation of that which something ought naturally to have, such lack of order needs to have an accidental efficient cause. For that which naturally is and ought to be in a thing is never lacking except on account of some impeding cause. And accordingly we are accustomed to say that evil, which consists in a certain privation, has a deficient cause, or an accidental efficient cause. Now every accidental cause is reducible to the direct cause. Since then sin, on the part of its lack of order, has an accidental efficient cause, and on the part of the act, a direct efficient cause, it follows that the lack of order of sin is a result of the cause of the act. Accordingly then, the will lacking the direction of the rule of reason and of the Divine law, and intent on some changeable good, causes the act of sin directly, and the lack of order of the act indirectly, and beside the intention; for the lack of order in the act results from the lack of direction in the will.

Reply Obj. 1. Sin signifies not only the privation of good, which privation is its lack of order, but also the act which is the subject of that privation, which has the nature of evil; and how this evil has a cause, has been explained.

Reply Obj. 2. If this definition of cause is to be verified in all cases, it must be understood as applying to a cause which is sufficient and not impeded. For it happens that a thing is the sufficient cause of something else, and that the effect does not follow of necessity, on account of some supervening impediment; otherwise it would follow that all things happen of necessity, as is proved in the *Metaphysics*.[1] Accord-

ingly, though sin has a cause, it does not follow that this is a necessary cause, since its effect can be impeded.

Reply Obj. 3. As stated above, the will in failing to apply the rule of reason or of the Divine law is the cause of sin. Now the fact of not applying the rule of reason or of the Divine law has not in itself the nature of evil, whether of punishment or of guilt, before it is applied to the act. And so accordingly, evil is not the cause of the first sin, but some good lacking some other good.

Article 2. *Whether Sin Has an Internal Cause?*

We proceed thus to the Second Article: It would seem that sin has no internal cause.

Objection 1. For that which is within a thing is always in it. If therefore sin had an internal cause, man would always be sinning, since given the cause, the effect follows.

Obj. 2. Further, a thing is not its own cause. But the internal movements of a man are sins. Therefore they are not the cause of sin.

Obj. 3. Further, whatever is within man is either natural or voluntary. Now that which is natural cannot be the cause of sin, for sin is contrary to nature, as Damascene states (*De Fide Orthod.* ii, 4, 30; iv, 20);[2] while that which is voluntary, if it be inordinate, is already a sin. Therefore nothing intrinsic can be the cause of the first sin.

On the contrary, Augustine says (*De Duabus Anim.* x, 11)[3] that "the will is the cause of sin."

I answer that, As stated above (A. 1), the direct cause of sin must be considered on the part of the act. Now we may distinguish a twofold internal cause of human acts, one mediate, the other immediate. The immediate internal cause of the human act is the reason and will, in respect of which man has free choice, while the mediate cause is the apprehension of the sensitive part, and also the sensitive appetite. For just as it is due to the judgment of reason that the will is moved to something in accord with reason, so it is due to an apprehension of the senses that the sensitive appetite is inclined to something, which inclination sometimes influences the will and reason, as we shall explain further on (Q. LXXVII, A. 1). Accordingly a double interior cause of sin may be assigned: one proximate, on the part of the reason and will; the other remote, on the part of the imagination or sensitive appetite.

[1] Aristotle, VI, 3 (1027ª29).

[2] PG 94, 876; 976; 1196.

[3] PL 42, 104, 105; *De Lib. Arb.*, III, 17 (PL 32, 1294).

But since we have said above (A. 1, Reply 3) that the cause of sin is some apparent good as motive, yet lacking the due motive, namely the rule of reason or the Divine law, this motive which is an apparent good pertains to the apprehension of the senses and to the appetite. But the absence of the due rule pertains to the reason, whose nature it is to consider this rule; and the completeness of the voluntary sinful act pertains to the will, so that the act of the will, given the conditions we have just mentioned, is already a sin.

Reply Obj. 1. That which is within a thing as its natural power, is always in it. But that which is within it as the internal act of the appetitive or apprehensive power, is not always in it. Now the power of the will is the potential cause of sin, but is made actual by the preceeding movements, both of the sensitive part, in the first place, and afterwards, of the reason. For it is because a thing is proposed as desirable to the senses, and because the appetite is inclined, that the reason sometimes fails to consider the due rule, so that the will produces the act of sin. Since therefore the movements that precede it are not always actual, neither is man always actually sinning.

Reply Obj. 2. It is not true that all the internal acts belong to the substance of sin, for this consists principally in the act of the will; but some precede and some follow the sin itself.

Reply Obj. 3. That which causes sin, just as a power producing its act, is natural; and again, the movement of the sensitive part, from which sin follows, is natural sometimes, as, for instance, when anyone sins through appetite for food. Yet sin results in being unnatural from the very fact that the natural rule fails, which man, in accord with his nature, ought to observe.

ARTICLE 3. *Whether Sin Has an External Cause?*

We proceed thus to the Third Article: It would seem that sin has no external cause.

Objection 1. For sin is a voluntary act. Now voluntary acts belong to principles that are within us, so that they have no external cause. Therefore sin has no external cause.

Obj. 2. Further, just as nature is an internal principle, so is the will. Now in natural things sin can be due to no other than an internal cause; for instance, the birth of a monster is due to the corruption of some internal principle. Therefore in the moral order, sin can arise from

no other than an internal cause. Therefore it has no external cause.

Obj. 3. Further, if the cause is multiplied, the effect is multiplied. Now the more numerous and weighty the external inducements to sin are, the less is a man's inordinate act imputed to him as a sin. Therefore nothing external is a cause of sin.

On the contrary, It is written (Num. 21. 16): *Are not these they, that deceived the children of Israel by the counsel of Balaam, and made you transgress against the Lord by the sin of Phogor?* Therefore something external can be a cause of sin.

I answer that, As stated above (A. 2), the internal cause of sin is both the will, as completing the sinful act; and the reason, as lacking the due rule, and the sensitive appetite, as inclining to sin. Accordingly something external might be a cause of sin in three ways, either by moving the will itself immediately, or by moving the reason, or by moving the sensitive appetite. Now, as stated above (Q. IX, A. 6), none can move the will inwardly save God alone, Who cannot be a cause of sin, as we shall prove further on (Q. LXXIX, A. 1). Hence it follows that nothing external can be a cause of sin, except by moving the reason, as a man or devil by enticing to sin; or by moving the sensitive appetite, as certain external sensibles move it. Yet neither does external enticement move the reason of necessity in matters of action, nor do things proposed externally of necessity move the sensitive appetite, except perhaps it be disposed thereto in a certain way; and even the sensitive appetite does not, of necessity, move the reason and will. Therefore something external can be a cause moving to sin, but not so as to be a sufficient cause. The will alone is the sufficient cause of sin being accomplished.

Reply Obj. 1. From the very fact that the external moving causes of sin do not lead to sin sufficiently and necessarily, it follows that it remains in our power to sin or not to sin.

Reply Obj. 2. The fact that sin has an internal cause does not prevent its having an external cause; for nothing external is a cause of sin, except through the medium of the internal cause, as stated.

Reply Obj. 3. If the external causes inclining to sin be multiplied, the sinful acts are multiplied, because they incline to the sinful act in both greater numbers and greater frequency. Nevertheless the character of guilt is lessened, since this depends on the act being voluntary and in our power.

ARTICLE 4. *Whether One Sin Is a Cause of Another?*

We proceed thus to the Fourth Article: It would seem that one sin cannot be the cause of another.

Objection 1. For there are four kinds of cause, none of which will fit in with one sin causing another. Because the end has the character of good, which is inconsistent with sin, which has the character of evil. In like manner neither can a sin be an efficient cause, since "evil is not an efficient cause, but is weak and powerless," as Dionysius declares (*Div. Nom.* iv).[1] The material and formal cause seems to have no place except in natural bodies, which are composed of matter and form. Therefore sin cannot have either a material or a formal cause.

Obj. 2. Further, "to produce its like belongs to a perfect thing," as stated in the *Meteorology.*[2] But sin is of its very notion something imperfect. Therefore one sin cannot be a cause of another.

Obj. 3. Further, if one sin is the cause of a second sin, in the same way, yet another sin will be the cause of the first, and thus we go on indefinitely, which is absurd. Therefore one sin is not the cause of another.

On the contrary, Gregory says on Ezechiel (*Hom.* xi).[3] "A sin that is not quickly blotted out by repentance is both a sin and a cause of sin."

I answer that, Since a sin has a cause on the part of the act of sin, it is possible for one sin to be the cause of another in the same way as one human act is the cause of another. Hence it happens that one sin may be the cause of another in respect of the four kinds of causes. First, after the manner of an efficient or moving cause, both directly and accidentally. Accidentally, in the same way as that which removes an impediment is called an accidental cause of movement; for when man, by one sinful act, loses grace, or charity, or shame, or anything else that withdraws him from sin, he thereby falls into another sin, so that the first sin is the accidental cause of the second. Directly, as when, by one sinful act, man is disposed to commit more readily another like act; because acts cause dispositions and habits inclining to like acts. Secondly, after the manner of a material cause, one sin is the cause of another by preparing its matter; thus covetousness prepares the matter for strife,

[1] Sect. 31 (PG 3, 732).
[2] Aristotle, IV, 3 (380ᵃ14).
[3] PL 76, 915.

which is often about the wealth a man has amassed together. Thirdly, after the manner of a final cause, one sin causes another, in so far as a man commits one sin for the sake of another which is his end; as when a man is guilty of simony for the end of ambition, or fornication for the purpose of theft. And since the end gives the form in moral matters, as stated above (Q. I, A. 3; Q. XVIII, A. 6), it follows that one sin is also the formal cause of another; for in the act of fornication committed for the purpose of theft, the former is material while the latter is formal.

Reply Obj. 1. Sin, in so far as it is disordered, has the character of evil; but, in so far as it is an act, it has some good, at least apparent, for its end. And thus, as an act (but not as being inordinate), it can be the cause, both final and efficient, of another sin. A sin has matter, not "of which" but "about which" it is; and it has its form from its end. Consequently one sin can be the cause of another in respect of the four kinds of cause, as stated above.

Reply Obj. 2. Sin is something imperfect on account of the moral imperfection on the part of lack of order. Nevertheless, as an act it can have natural perfection, and thus it can be the cause of another sin.

Reply Obj. 3. Not every cause of one sin is another sin. Hence there is no need to go on to infinity, for one may come to one sin which is not caused by another sin.

QUESTION LXXVI

OF THE CAUSES OF SIN, IN PARTICULAR

(In Four Articles)

WE must now consider the causes of sin, in particular, and (1) The internal causes of sin; (2) its external causes (Q. LXXIX); and (3) sins which are the causes of other sins (Q. LXXXIV). In view of what has been said above, the first consideration will be threefold, so that in the first place we shall treat of ignorance, which is the cause of sin on the part of reason; secondly, of weakness or passion, which is the cause of sin on the part of the sensitive appetite (Q. LXXVII); thirdly, of malice, which is the cause of sin on the part of the will (Q. LXXVIII).

Under the first head there are four points of inquiry: (1) Whether ignorance is a cause of sin? (2) Whether ignorance is a sin? (3) Whether it excuses from sin altogether? (4) Whether it diminishes sin?

ARTICLE 1. *Whether Ignorance Can Be a Cause of Sin?*

We proceed thus to the First Article: It would seem that ignorance cannot be a cause of sin.

Objection 1. For that which does not exist is not the cause of anything. Now ignorance is a non-being, since it is a privation of knowledge. Therefore ignorance is not a cause of sin.

Obj. 2. Further, causes of sin should be taken in respect of sin being a turning to something, as was stated above (Q. LXXV, A. 1). Now ignorance seems to have reference to a turning away from something. Therefore it should not be accounted a cause of sin.

Obj. 3. Further, every sin is seated in the will as we have said above (Q. LXXIV, A. 1). Now the will does not turn to that which is not known, because its object is the good apprehended. Therefore ignorance cannot be a cause of sin.

On the contrary, Augustine says (*De Nat. et Grat.* lxvii)[1] that some sin through ignorance.

I answer that, According to the Philosopher[2] a moving cause is twofold, direct and accidental. A direct cause is one that moves by its own power, as the generating principle is the moving cause of heavy and light things. An accidental cause is either one that removes an impediment, or the removal itself of an impediment. It is in this way that ignorance can be the cause of a sinful act; for it is a privation of knowledge perfecting the reason that forbids the act of sin, in so far as the reason directs human acts.

Now we must observe that the reason directs human acts in accordance with a twofold knowledge, universal and particular. For in conferring about what is to be done, it employs a syllogism, the conclusion of which is an act of judgment, or of choice, or an operation. Now actions are about singulars. Therefore the conclusion of a practical syllogism is a singular proposition. But a singular proposition does not follow from a universal proposition, except through the medium of a particular proposition; thus a man is restrained from an act of parricide by the knowledge that it is wrong to kill one's father, and that this man is his father. Hence ignorance about either of these two propositions, namely of the universal principle which is a rule of reason, or of the particular circumstance, could cause an act of parricide. Hence it is clear that not every kind of ignorance is the cause of a sin, but that alone which removes the knowledge

which would prevent the sinful act. Consequently if a man's will be so disposed that he would not be restrained from the act of parricide, even though he recognized his father, his ignorance about his father is not the cause of his committing the sin, but is concomitant with the sin. Therefore such a man sins, "not through ignorance but in ignorance," as the Philosopher states.[3]

Reply Obj. 1. Non-being cannot be the direct cause of anything; but it can be an accidental cause, as being the removal of an impediment.

Reply Obj. 2. As knowledge, which is removed by ignorance, regards sin as turning towards something, so too, ignorance of this respect of a sin is the cause of that sin, as removing its impediment.

Reply Obj. 3. The will cannot turn to that which is absolutely unknown; but if something be known in one respect, and unknown in another, the will can will it. It is thus that ignorance is the cause of sin; for instance, when a man knows that what he is killing is a man, but not that it is his own father, or when one knows that a certain act is pleasurable, but not that it is a sin.

ARTICLE 2. *Whether Ignorance Is a Sin?*

We proceed thus to the Second Article: It would seem that ignorance is not a sin.

Objection 1. For sin is a word, deed or desire contrary to God's law, as stated above (Q. LXXI, A. 6). Now ignorance does not denote an act, either internal or external. Therefore ignorance is not a sin.

Obj. 2. Further, sin is more directly opposed to grace than to knowledge. Now privation of grace is not a sin, but a punishment resulting from sin. Therefore ignorance, which is privation of knowledge, is not a sin.

Obj. 3. Further, if ignorance is a sin, this can only be in so far as it is voluntary. But if ignorance is a sin through being voluntary, it seems that the sin will consist in the act itself of the will, rather than in the ignorance. Therefore the ignorance will not be a sin, but rather a result of sin.

Obj. 4. Further, every sin is taken away by repentance, nor does any sin, except only original sin, pass as to guilt, yet remain in act. Now ignorance is not removed by repentance, but remains in act, all its guilt being removed by repentance. Therefore ignorance is not a sin, unless perhaps it be original sin.

Obj. 5. Further, if ignorance itself be a sin,

[1] PL 44, 287; cf. *De Lib. Arb.*, III, 18 (PL 32, 1295).
[2] *Physics*, VIII, 4 (254b7).
[3] *Ethics*, III, 1 (1110b25).

then a man will be sinning as long as he remains in ignorance. But ignorance is continual in the one who is ignorant. Therefore a person in ignorance would be continually sinning, which is clearly false, for thus ignorance would be a most grievous sin. Therefore ignorance is not a sin.

On the contrary, Nothing but sin deserves punishment. But ignorance deserves punishment, according to I Cor. 14. 38: *If any man know not, he shall not be known.* Therefore ignorance is a sin.

I answer that, Ignorance differs from nescience in that nescience denotes mere absence of knowledge. Therefore whoever lacks knowledge about anything can be said to be nescient about it, in which sense Dionysius puts nescience in the angels (*Cæl. Hier.* vii).[1] On the other hand, ignorance denotes privation of knowledge, that is, lack of knowledge of those things that one has a natural aptitude to know. Some of these we are under an obligation to know, those, namely without the knowledge of which we are unable to accomplish a due act rightly. Therefore all are bound in common to know the articles of faith, and the universal precepts of law, and each individual is bound to know matters regarding his duty or state. Meanwhile there are other things which a man may have a natural aptitude to know, yet he is not bound to know them, such as the geometrical theorems, and contingent particulars, except in some individual case. Now it is evident that whoever neglects to have or do what he ought to have or do, commits a sin of omission. Therefore on account of negligence, ignorance of what one is bound to know, is a sin; it is not however imputed as a sin to man if he fails to know what he is unable to know. Consequently ignorance of such things is called invincible, since it cannot be overcome by study. For this reason such ignorance, not being voluntary, since it is not in our power to be rid of it, is not a sin. Therefore it is evident that no invincible ignorance is a sin. On the other hand, vincible ignorance is a sin, if it be about matters one is bound to know; but not, if it be about things one is not bound to know.

Reply Obj. 1. As stated above (Q. LXXI, A. 6, REPLY 1), when we say that sin is a word, deed or desire, we include the opposite negations, by reason of which omissions have the character of sin. And thus negligence, according as ignorance is a sin, is comprised in the above definition of sin; in so far, that is, as one omits to say what one ought, or to do what one ought, or to desire

what one ought, in order to acquire the knowledge which we ought to have.

Reply Obj. 2. Although privation of grace is not a sin in itself, yet by reason of negligence in preparing oneself for grace, it may have the character of sin, even as ignorance. Nevertheless even here there is a difference, since man can acquire knowledge by his acts, while grace is not acquired by acts, but by God's favour.

Reply Obj. 3. Just as in a sin of transgression, the sin consists not only in the act of the will, but also in the act willed, which is commanded by the will, so in a sin of omission, not only the act of the will is a sin, but also the omission, in so far as it is in some way voluntary. And accordingly, the neglect to know, or even lack of consideration is a sin.

Reply Obj. 4. Although when the guilt has passed away through repentance, the ignorance remains, according as it is a privation of knowledge, nevertheless the negligence does not remain, by reason of which the ignorance is said to be a sin.

Reply Obj. 5. Just as in other sins of omission, man sins actually only at the time at which the affirmative precept is binding, so is it with the sin of ignorance. For the ignorant man sins actually indeed, not continually, but only at the time for acquiring the knowledge that he ought to have.

ARTICLE 3. *Whether Ignorance Excuses From Sin Altogether?*

We proceed thus to the Third Article: It would seem that ignorance excuses from sin altogether.

Objection 1. For as Augustine says[2] "every sin is voluntary." Now ignorance causes involuntariness, as stated above (Q. VI., A. 8). Therefore ignorance excuses from sin altogether.

Obj. 2. Further, that which is done beside the intention, is done accidentally. Now the intention cannot be about what is unknown. Therefore what a man does through ignorance is accidental in human acts. But what is accidental does not give the species. Therefore nothing that is done through ignorance in human acts, should be deemed sinful or virtuous.

Obj. 3. Further, man is the subject of virtue and sin in so far as he is a partaker of reason. Now ignorance excludes knowledge which perfects the reason. Therefore ignorance excuses from sin altogether.

On the contrary, Augustine says (*De Lib. Arb.* iii, 18)[3] that "some things done through

---

[1] Sect. 3 (PG 3, 209); cf. *De Eccl. Hier.,* VI, 3 (PG 3, 537).

[2] *De Vera Relig.,* XIV (PL 34, 133).   [3] PL 32, 1295.

ignorance are rightly reproved." Now those things alone are rightly reproved which are sins. Therefore some things done through ignorance are sins. Therefore ignorance does not altogether excuse from sin.

I answer that, Ignorance, by its very nature, renders the act which it causes involuntary. Now it has already been stated (A. 1) that ignorance is said to cause the act which the contrary knowledge would have prevented; so that this act, if knowledge were to hand, would be contrary to the will, which is the meaning of the word involuntary. If, however the knowledge which is taken away by ignorance would not have prevented the act, on account of the inclination of the will to that act, the lack of this knowledge does not make that man unwilling, but not willing, as stated in the *Ethics*.[1] And ignorance of this kind, which is not the cause of the sinful act, as already stated (since it does not make the act to be involuntary), does not excuse from sin. The same applies to any ignorance that does not cause, but follows or accompanies the sinful act. On the other hand, ignorance which is the cause of the act, since it makes it to be involuntary, of its very nature excuses from sin, because voluntariness is essential to sin.

But it may fail to excuse altogether from sin, and this for two reasons. First, on the part of the thing itself which is not known. For ignorance excuses from sin in so far as something is not known to be a sin. Now it may happen that a person ignores some circumstance of a sin, the knowledge of which circumstance would prevent him from sinning, whether it belong to the substance of the sin, or not, and nevertheless his knowledge is sufficient for him to be aware that the act is sinful. For instance, if a man strike someone, knowing that it is a man (which suffices for it to be sinful) and yet ignorant of the fact that it is his father, (which is a circumstance constituting another species of sin); or, suppose that he is unaware that this man will defend himself and strike him back, and that if he had known this, he would not have struck him (which does not affect the sinfulness of the act). Therefore, though this man sins through ignorance, yet he is not altogether excused, because, notwithstanding, he has knowledge of the sin. Secondly, this may happen on the part of the ignorance itself, because, that is, this ignorance is voluntary, either directly, as when a man wishes of set purpose to be ignorant of certain things that he may sin the more freely; or indirectly, as when a man, through stress of

work or other occupations, neglects to acquire the knowledge which would restrain him from sin. For such negligence renders the ignorance itself voluntary and sinful, provided it be about matters one is bound and able to know. Consequently this ignorance does not altogether excuse from sin. If, however, the ignorance be such as to be entirely involuntary, either through being invincible, or through being of matters one is not bound to know, then such ignorance excuses from sin altogether.

Reply Obj. 1. Not every ignorance causes involuntariness, as stated above (Q. VI, A. 8). Hence not every ignorance excuses from sin altogether.

Reply Obj. 2. So far as voluntariness remains in the ignorant person, the intention of sin remains in him, so that, in this respect, his sin is not accidental.

Reply Obj. 3. If the ignorance be such as to exclude the use of reason entirely, it excuses from sin altogether, as is the case with madmen and imbeciles. But such is not always the ignorance that causes the sin; and so it does not always excuse from sin altogether.

ARTICLE 4. *Whether Ignorance Diminishes a Sin?*

We proceed thus to the Fourth Article: It would seem that ignorance does not diminish a sin.

Objection 1. For that which is common to all sins does not diminish sin. Now ignorance is common to all sins, for the Philosopher says[2] that "every evil man is ignorant." Therefore ignorance does not diminish sin.

Obj. 2. Further, one sin added to another makes a greater sin. But ignorance is itself a sin, as stated above (A. 2). Therefore it does not diminish a sin.

Obj. 3. Further, the same thing does not both aggravate and diminish sin. Now ignorance aggravates sin; for Ambrose commenting on Rom. 2. 4, *Knowest thou not that the benignity of God leadeth thee to penance?* says[3]: "Thy sin is most grievous if thou knowest not." Therefore ignorance does not diminish sin.

Obj. 4. Further, if any kind of ignorance diminishes a sin, this would seem to be chiefly the case as regards the ignorance which removes the use of reason altogether. Now this kind of ignorance does not diminish sin, but increases it; for the Philosopher says[4] that "a drunken

---

[1] Aristotle, III, 1 (1110b23).

[2] *Ethics,* III, 1 (1110b28).
[3] Cf. *Glossa ordin.* (VI, 6F); *Glossa* Lombardi (PL 191, 1338).   [4] *Ethics,* III, 5 (1113b31).

man merits a double punishment." Therefore ignorance does not diminish sin.

On the contrary, Whatever is a reason for sin to be forgiven diminishes sin. Now such is ignorance, as is clear from I Tim. 1. 13: *I obtained ... mercy ... because I did it ignorantly.* Therefore ignorance diminishes or alleviates sin.

I answer that, Since every sin is voluntary, ignorance can diminish sin, in so far as it diminishes its voluntariness; and if it does not render it less voluntary, it in no way alleviates the sin. Now it is evident that the ignorance which excuses from sin altogether (through making it altogether involuntary) does not diminish a sin, but does away with it altogether. On the other hand, ignorance which is not the cause of the sin being committed, but is concomitant with it, neither diminishes nor increases the sin.

Therefore sin cannot be alleviated by any ignorance, but only by such as is a cause of the sin being committed, and yet does not excuse from the sin altogether. Now it happens sometimes that such ignorance is directly and essentially voluntary, as when a man is purposely ignorant that he may sin more freely, and ignorance of this kind seems rather to make the act more voluntary and more sinful, since it is through the will's intention to sin that he is willing to bear the hurt of ignorance, for the sake of freedom in sinning. Sometimes, however, the ignorance which is the cause of a sin being committed is not directly voluntary, but indirectly or accidentally, as when a man is unwilling to work hard at his studies, the result being that he is ignorant, or as when a man wilfully drinks too much wine, the result being that he becomes drunk and indiscreet, and this ignorance diminishes voluntariness and consequently alleviates the sin. For when a thing is not known to be a sin, the will cannot be said to consent to the sin directly and of itself, but only accidentally. Therefore, in that case there is less contempt, and therefore less sin.

Reply Obj. 1. The ignorance by which every evil man is ignorant is not the cause of sin being committed, but something resulting from that cause, namely of the passion or habit inclining to sin.

Reply Obj. 2. One sin added to another makes more sins, but it does not always make a sin greater, since it may be that the two sins do not coincide, but are separate. It may happen, if the first diminishes the second, that the two together have not the same gravity as one of them alone would have; thus murder is a more griev-

ous sin if committed by a man when sober than if committed by a man when drunk, although in the latter case there are two sins, because drunkenness diminishes the sinfulness of the resulting sin more than is implied in the gravity of drunkenness itself.

Reply Obj. 3. The words of Ambrose may be understood as referring absolutely to affected ignorance. Or they may have reference to a species of the sin of ingratitude, the highest degree of which is that man even ignores the benefits he has received. Or again, they may be an allusion to the ignorance of unbelief, which undermines the foundation of the spiritual edifice.

Reply Obj. 4. The drunken man deserves a double punishment for the two sins which he commits, namely drunkenness and the sin which results from his drunkenness. And yet drunkenness, on account of the ignorance connected with it, diminishes the resulting sin, and more, perhaps, than the gravity of the drunkenness itself implies, as stated above (reply 2). It might also be said that the words quoted refer to an ordinance of the legislator named Pittacus, who ordered drunkards to be more severely punished if they assaulted anyone; having an eye, not to the indulgence which the drunkard might claim, but to expediency, since more harm is done by the drunk than by the sober, as the Philosopher observes.[1]

QUESTION LXXVII

OF THE CAUSE OF SIN ON THE PART OF THE SENSITIVE APPETITE

(In Eight Articles)

We must now consider the cause of sin on the part of the sensitive appetite, as to whether a passion of the soul may be a cause of sin. And under this head there are eight points of inquiry: (1) Whether a passion of the sensitive appetite can move or incline the will? (2) Whether it can overcome the reason against the latter's knowledge? (3) Whether a sin resulting from a passion is a sin of weakness? (4) Whether the passion of self-love is the cause of every sin? (5) Of three causes mentioned in I John, 2. 16: *Concupiscence of the eyes, Concupiscence of the flesh, and Pride of life.* (6) Whether the passion which causes a sin diminishes it? (7) Whether passion excuses from sin altogether? (8) Whether a sin committed through passion can be mortal?

[1] *Politics,* II, 12 (1274^{b}18).

ARTICLE 1. *Whether the Will Is Moved by a Passion of the Sensitive Appetite?*

We proceed thus to the First Article: It would seem that the will is not moved by a passion of the sensitive appetite.

Objection 1. For no passive power is moved except by its object. Now the will is a power both passive and active, since it is "mover and moved," as the Philosopher says of the appetitive power in general.[1] Since therefore the object of the will is not a passion of the sensitive appetite, but rather a good of reason, it seems that a passion of the sensitive appetite does not move the will.

Obj. 2. Further, the higher mover is not moved by the lower; thus the soul is not moved by the body. Now the will, which is the rational appetite, is compared to the sensitive appetite as a higher mover to a lower; for the Philosopher says[2] that the rational appetite moves the sensitive appetite, even as in the heavenly bodies one sphere moves another. Therefore the will cannot be moved by a passion of the sensitive appetite.

Obj. 3. Further, nothing immaterial can be moved by that which is material. Now the will is an immaterial power, because it does not use a corporeal organ, since it is in the reason, as stated in the book on the *Soul*.[3] But the sensitive appetite is a material power, since it is seated in an organ of the body. Therefore a passion of the sensitive appetite cannot move the intellectual appetite.

On the contrary, It is written (Dan. 13. 56): *Lust hath perverted thy heart.*

I answer that, A passion of the sensitive appetite cannot draw or move the will directly; but it can do so indirectly, and this in two ways. First, by a kind of distraction. For since all the soul's powers are rooted in the one essence of the soul, it follows of necessity that when one power is intent in its act, another power becomes relaxed, or is even altogether impeded, in its act, both because all power is weakened through being applied to many things, so that, on the contrary, through being centred on one thing, it is less able to be directed to several; and because, in the operations of the soul, a certain attention is requisite, and if this be closely fixed on one thing, less attention is given to another. In this way, by a kind of distraction, when the movement of the sensitive appetite is enforced in re-

spect of any passion whatever, the proper movement of the rational appetite or will must, of necessity, become relaxed or altogether impeded.

Secondly, this may happen on the part of the will's object, which is good apprehended by reason. Because the judgment and apprehension of reason are impeded on account of a vehement and inordinate apprehension of the imagination and judgment of the estimative power, as appears in those who are out of their mind. Now it is evident that the apprehension of the imagination and the judgment of the estimative power follow the passion of the sensitive appetite, even as the verdict of the taste follows the disposition of the tongue. For this reason we observe that those who are in some kind of passion do not easily turn their imagination away from the object of their affection, the result being that the judgment of the reason often follows the passion of the sensitive appetite, and consequently the will's movement follows it also, since it has a natural inclination always to follow the judgment of the reason.

Reply Obj. 1. Although the passion of the sensitive appetite is not the direct object of the will, yet it occasions a certain change in the judgment about the object of the will, as stated.

Reply Obj. 2. The higher mover is not directly moved by the lower; but, in a manner, it can be moved by it indirectly, as stated.

The Third Objection is solved in like manner.

ARTICLE 2. *Whether the Reason Can Be Overcome by a Passion Against Its Knowledge?*

We proceed thus to the Second Article: It would seem that the reason cannot be overcome by a passion against its knowledge.

Objection 1. For the stronger is not overcome by the weaker. Now knowledge, on account of its certitude, is the strongest thing in us. Therefore it cannot be overcome by a passion, which is weak and soon passes away.[4]

Obj. 2. Further, the will is not directed save to the good or the apparent good. Now when a passion draws the will to that which is really good, it does not influence the reason against its knowledge; and when it draws it to that which is good apparently, but not really, it draws it to that which appears good to the reason. But what appears to the reason is in the knowledge of the reason. Therefore a passion never influences the reason against its knowledge.

---

[1] *Soul,* III, 10 (433[b]16).
[2] *Ibid.,* III, 11 (434[a]12).   [3] *Ibid.,* III, 9 (432[b]5).

[4] Aristotle, *Categories,* 8 (9[b]28).

Obj. 3. Further, if it be said that it draws the reason from its knowledge of something in general, to form a contrary judgment about a particular matter,—on the contrary, if a universal and a particular proposition be opposed, they are opposed by contradiction, e.g., Every man, and Not every man. Now if two opinions contradict one another, they are contrary to one another, as stated in the book *Interpretation.*[1] If therefore anyone, while knowing something in general, were to pronounce an opposite judgment in a particular case, he would have two contrary opinions at the same time, which is impossible.

Obj. 4. Further, whoever knows the universal, knows also the particular which he knows to be contained in the universal; thus who knows that every mule is sterile, knows that this particular animal is sterile, provided he knows it to be a mule, as is clear from the *Posterior Analytics.*[2] Now he who knows something in general, e.g., that no fornication is lawful, knows this general proposition to contain, for example, the particular proposition. This is an act of fornication. Therefore it seems that his knowledge extends to the particular.

Obj. 5. Further, according to the Philosopher,[3] "words express the thoughts of the mind." Now it often happens that man, while in a state of passion, confesses that what he has chosen is an evil, even in that particular case. Therefore he has knowledge, even in particular.

Therefore it seems that the passions cannot draw the reason against its universal knowledge; for it is impossible for it to have universal knowledge together with an opposite particular judgment.

On the contrary, The Apostle says (Rom. 7. 23): *I see another law in my members, fighting against the law of my mind, and captivating me in the law of sin.* Now the law that is in the members is concupiscence, of which he had been speaking previously. Since then concupiscence is a passion, it seems that a passion draws the reason counter to its knowledge.

I answer that, As the Philosopher states,[4] the opinion of Socrates was that knowledge can never be overcome by passion; therefore he held every virtue to be a kind of knowledge, and every sin a kind of ignorance. In this he was somewhat right, because, since the object of the will is a good or an apparent good, it is never

moved to an evil unless that which is not good appear good in some respect to the reason; so that the will would never tend to evil, unless there were ignorance or error in the reason. Hence it is written (Prov. 14. 22): *They err that work evil.*

Experience, however, shows that many act contrary to the knowledge that they have, and this is confirmed by Divine authority, according to the words of Luke 12. 47: *The servant who knew the will of his lord . . . and did not . . . shall be beaten with many stripes,* and of James 4. 17: *To him . . . who knoweth to do good, and doth it not, to him it is a sin.* Consequently he was not altogether right, and it is necessary, with the Philosopher[5] to make a distinction.

Since man is directed to right action by a twofold knowledge, namely universal and particular, a defect in either of them suffices to hinder the rectitude of the will and of the deed, as stated above (Q. LXXVI, A. 1). It may happen, then, that a man has some knowledge in general, for example that no fornication is lawful, and yet he does not know in particular that this act, which is fornication, must not be done; and this suffices for the will not to follow the universal knowledge of the reason. Again, it must be observed that nothing prevents a thing which is known habitually from not being considered actually. Therefore it is possible for a man to have correct knowledge not only in general but also in particular, and yet not to consider his knowledge actually. And in such a case it does not seem difficult for a man to act counter to what he does not actually consider.

Now, that a man sometimes fails to consider in particular what he knows habitually may happen through mere lack of attention; for instance, a man who knows geometry may not attend to the consideration of geometrical conclusions, which he is ready to consider at any moment. Sometimes man fails to consider actually what he knows habitually on account of some hindrance supervening, for example some external occupation, or some bodily infirmity; and, in this way, a man who is in a state of passion, fails to consider in particular what he knows in general, in so far as the passions hinder him from considering it.

Now it hinders him in three ways. First, by way of distraction, as explained above (A. 1). Secondly, by way of opposition, because a passion often inclines to something contrary to what man knows in general. Thirdly, by way of bodily change, the result of which is that the

[1] Aristotle, 14 (23ᵇ40).
[2] Aristotle, I, 1 (71ᵃ17).
[3] *Interpretation,* 1 (16ᵃ3).
[4] *Ethics,* VII, 2 (1145ᵇ23); cf. VI, 13 (1144ᵇ19).
[5] *Ibid.,* VII, 3 (1146ᵇ31).

reason is somehow fettered so as not to exercise its act freely; just as sleep or drunkenness, on account of some change wrought on the body, fetters the use of reason. That this takes place in the passions is evident from the fact that sometimes, when the passions are very intense, man loses the use of reason altogether; for many have gone out of their minds through excess of love or anger. It is in this way that passion draws the reason to judge in particular, against the knowledge which it has in general.

Reply Obj. 1. Universal knowledge, which is most certain, does not hold the foremost place in action, but rather particular knowledge, since actions are about singulars. Therefore it is not astonishing that in matters of action passion acts counter to universal knowledge, if the consideration of particular knowledge be lacking.

Reply Obj. 2. The fact that something that is not good appears good in particular to the reason, is due to a passion. And yet this particular judgment is contrary to the universal knowledge of the reason.

Reply Obj. 3. It is impossible for anyone to have an actual knowledge or true opinion about a universal affirmative proposition, and at the same time a false opinion about a particular negative proposition, or vice versa. But it may well happen that a man has true habitual knowledge about a universal affirmative proposition, and actually a false opinion about a particular negative; for an act is directly opposed, not to a habit, but to an act.

Reply Obj. 4. He that has knowledge in universal is hindered, on account of a passion, from reasoning about that universal, so as to draw the conclusion; but he reasons about another universal proposition suggested by the inclination of the passion, and draws his conclusion accordingly. Hence the Philosopher says[1] that the syllogism of an incontinent man has four propositions, two of which are universal, of which one is of the reason, e.g., No fornication is lawful, and the other, of passion, e.g., Pleasure is to be pursued. Hence passion fetters the reason, and hinders it from arguing and concluding under the first proposition, so that while the passion lasts, the reason argues and concludes under the second.

Reply Obj. 5. Even as a drunken man sometimes gives utterance to words of deep signification, of which, however, he is incompetent to judge, his drunkenness hindering him, so a man who is in a state of passion may indeed say in words that he ought not to do so and so, yet his inner thought is that he must do it, as stated in the *Ethics*.[2]

ARTICLE 3. *Whether a Sin Committed through Passion Should Be Called a Sin of Weakness?*

We proceed thus to the Third Article: It would seem that a sin committed through passion should not be called a sin of weakness.

Objection 1. For a passion is a vehement movement of the sensitive appetite, as stated above (A. 1). Now vehemence of movements is evidence of strength rather than of weakness. Therefore a sin committed through passion should not be called a sin of weakness.

Obj. 2. Further, weakness in man regards that which is most fragile in him. Now this is the flesh; and hence it is written (Ps. 77. 39): *He remembered that they are flesh.* Therefore sins of weakness should be those which result from bodily defects, rather than those which are due to a passion.

Obj. 3. Further, man does not seem to be weak in respect of things which are subject to his will. Now it is subject to man's will whether he do or do not the things to which his passions incline him, according to Gen. 4. 7: *Thy appetite shall be under thee (Vulg.,—The lust thereof shall be under thee) and thou shalt have dominion over it.* Therefore sin committed through passion is not a sin of weakness.

On the contrary, Cicero (*De Quæst. Tusc.* iv, 14)[3] calls the passions diseases of the soul. Now weakness is another name for disease. Therefore a sin that arises from passion should be called a sin of weakness.

I answer that, The cause of sin is on the part of the soul, in which, chiefly, sin resides. Now weakness may be applied to the soul by way of likeness to weakness of the body. Accordingly, man's body is said to be weak, when it is disabled or hindered in the execution of its proper action, through some disorder of the body's parts, so that the humours and members of the human body cease to be subject to its governing and moving power. Hence a member is said to be weak when it cannot do the work of a healthy member, the eye, for instance, when it cannot see clearly, as the Philosopher states.[4] Therefore weakness of the soul is when the soul is hindered from fulfilling its proper action on account of a disorder in its parts. Now as the parts of the body are said to be out of order when they fail to comply with the order of nature, so too the

[1] *Ethics*, VII, 3 (1147ª24).

[2] *Ibid.* (1147ª18).
[3] DD IV, 31.
[4] *History of Animals*, X, 1 (633ᵇ20).

parts of the soul are said to be inordinate when they are not subject to the order of reason, for the reason is the ruling power of the soul's parts. Accordingly, when the concupiscible or irascible power is affected by any passion contrary to the order of reason, the result being that an impediment arises in the aforesaid manner to the due action of man, it is said to be a sin of weakness. Hence the Philosopher compares[1] the incontinent man to a paralytic, whose limbs move in a manner contrary to his intention.

Reply Obj. 1. Just as in the body the stronger the movement against the order of nature, the greater the weakness, so likewise, the stronger the movement of passion against the order of reason, the greater the weakness of the soul.

Reply Obj. 2. Sin consists chiefly in an act of the will, which is not hindered by weakness of the body. For he that is weak in body may have a will ready for action, and yet be hindered by a passion, as stated above (A. 1). Hence when we speak of sins of weakness, we refer to weakness of soul rather than of body. And yet even weakness of soul is called weakness of the flesh, in so far as it is owing to a condition of the flesh that the passions of the soul arise in us through the sensitive appetite being a power using a corporeal organ.

Reply Obj. 3. It is in the will's power to give or refuse its consent to what passion inclines us to do, and it is in this sense that our appetite is said to be under us. And yet this consent or dissent of the will is hindered in the way already explained (A. 1).

ARTICLE 4. *Whether Self-Love Is the Source of Every Sin?*

We proceed thus to the Fourth Article: It would seem that self-love is not the source of every sin.

Objection 1. For that which is good and right in itself is not the proper cause of sin. Now love of self is a good and right thing in itself. And therefore man is commanded to love his neighbour as himself (Levit. 19. 18). Therefore self-love cannot be the proper cause of sin.

Obj. 2. Further, the Apostle says (Rom. 7. 8): *Sin taking occasion by the commandment wrought in me all manner of concupiscence;* on which words a gloss says[2] that "the law is good, since by forbidding concupiscence, it forbids all

evils," the reason for which is that concupiscence is the cause of every sin. Now concupiscence is a different passion from love, as stated above (Q. XXIII, A. 4; Q. XXX, A. 2). Therefore self-love is not the cause of every sin.

Obj. 3. Further, Augustine in commenting on Ps. 79. 17, *Things set on fire and dug down,* says that "every sin is due either to love arousing us to undue ardour or to fear inducing false humility."[3] Therefore self-love is not the only cause of sin.

Obj. 4. Further, as man sins at times through inordinate love of self, so does he sometimes through inordinate love of his neighbour. Therefore self-love is not the cause of every sin.

On the contrary, Augustine says[4] that "self-love, amounting to contempt of God, builds up the city of Babylon." Now every sin makes man a citizen of Babylon. Therefore self-love is the cause of every sin.

I answer that, As stated above (Q. LXXV, A. 1), the proper and direct cause of sin is to be considered on the part of the turning to a changeable good; in which respect every sinful act proceeds from inordinate desire for some temporal good. Now the fact that anyone desires a temporal good inordinately, is due to the fact that he loves himself inordinately, for to wish anyone some good is to love him. Therefore it is evident that inordinate love of self is the cause of every sin.

Reply Obj. 1. Well ordered self-love, by which man desires a fitting good for himself, is right and natural; but it is inordinate self-love, leading to the contempt of God, that Augustine puts as the cause of sin.

Reply Obj. 2. Concupiscence, by which a man desires good for himself, is reduced to self-love as to its cause, as we have already stated.

Reply Obj. 3. Man is said to love both the good he desires for himself, and himself, to whom he desires it. Love, in so far as it is directed to the object of desire (for example a man is said to love wine or money) admits, as its cause, fear which pertains to avoidance of evil; for every sin arises either from inordinate desire for some good, or from inordinate avoidance of some evil. But each of these is reduced to self-love, since it is through loving himself that man desires good things, or avoids evil things.

Reply Obj. 4. A friend is like another self. Therefore the sin which is committed through

---

[1] *Ethics,* I, 13 (1102ᵇ18).
[2] *Glossa ordin.* (VI, 16 E); *Glossa interl.* (VI, 16v); *Glossa* Lombardi (PL 191, 1416); cf. Augustine, *De Spir. et Litt.,* IV (PL 44, 204).

[3] PL 36, 1027.
[4] *City of God,* XIV, 28 (PL 41, 436); *Ennar. in Ps.,* Ps. 64.1 (PL 36, 773).

love for a friend seems to be committed through self-love.

ARTICLE 5. *Whether Concupiscence of the Flesh, Concupiscence of the Eyes, and Pride of Life Are Fittingly Described as Causes of Sin?*

We proceed thus to the Fifth Article: It would seem that concupiscence of the flesh, concupiscence of the eyes, and pride of life are unfittingly described as causes of sin.

Objection 1. Because, according to the Apostle (I Tim. 6. 10), *covetousness* (Douay,—*The desire of money) is the root of all evils.* Now pride of life is not included in covetousness. Therefore it should not be reckoned among the causes of sin.

Obj. 2. Further, concupiscence of the flesh is aroused chiefly by what is seen by the eyes, according to Dan. 13. 56: *Beauty hath deceived thee.* Therefore concupiscence of the eyes should not be divided against concupiscence of the flesh.

Obj. 3. Further, concupiscence is desire for pleasure, as stated above (Q. XXX, A. 1). Now objects of pleasure are perceived not only by the sight, but also by the other senses. Therefore concupiscence of the hearing and of the other senses should also have been mentioned.

Obj. 4. Further, just as man is induced to sin through inordinate desire of good things, so is he also through inordinate avoidance of evil things, as stated above (A. 4, Reply 3). But nothing is mentioned here pertaining to avoidance of evil. Therefore the causes of sin are insufficiently described.

On the contrary, It is written (I John 2. 16): *All that is in the world is concupiscence of the flesh, or* (Vulg.,—*and) concupiscence of the eyes, or* (Vulg.,—*and) pride of life.* Now a thing is said to be "in the world" by reason of sin. Therefore it is written (*ibid.* 5. 19): *The whole world is seated in wickedness.* Therefore these three are causes of sin.

I answer that, As stated above (A. 4), inordinate self-love is the cause of every sin. Now self-love includes inordinate desire of good, for a man desires good for the one he loves. Hence it is evident that inordinate desire of good is the cause of every sin. Now good is, in two ways, the object of the sensitive appetite, in which are the passions, which are the cause of sin. First, absolutely, according as it is the object of the concupiscible part. Secondly, under the aspect of difficulty, according as it is the object to the irascible part, as stated above (Q. XXIII, A. 1).

Again, concupiscence is twofold, as stated above (Q. XXX, A. 3). One is natural, and is directed to those things which sustain the nature of the body, whether as regards the preservation of the individual, such as food, drink, and the like, or as regards the preservation of the species, such as sexual matters; and the inordinate appetite of such things is called "concupiscence of the flesh." The other is spiritual concupiscence, and is directed to those things which do not afford support or pleasure through the fleshly senses, but are pleasurable in respect of the apprehension or imagination, or some similar mode of perception; such are money, apparel, and the like; and this spiritual concupiscence is called "concupiscence of the eyes," whether this be taken as referring to the sight itself, of which the eyes are the organ, so as to denote curiosity, according to Augustine's exposition,[1] or to the concupiscence of things which are proposed outwardly to the eyes, so as to denote covetousness, according to the explanation of others. The inordinate appetite of the arduous good pertains to the "pride of life"; for pride is the inordinate appetite of excellence, as we shall state further on (Q. LXXXIV, A. 2; Part II-II, Q. CLXII, A. 1).

It is therefore evident that all passions that are a cause of sin can be reduced to these three. For all the passions of the concupiscible part can be reduced to the first two, and all the irascible passions to the third, which is not divided into two because all the irascible passions conform to spiritual concupiscence.

Reply Obj. 1. "Pride of life" is included in covetousness according as the latter denotes any kind of appetite for any kind of good. How covetousness, as a special vice, which goes by the name of "avarice," is the root of all sins, shall be explained further on (Q. LXXXIV, A. 1).

Reply Obj. 2. "Concupiscence of the eyes" does not mean here the concupiscence for all things that can be seen by the eyes, but only for such things as afford, not carnal pleasure in respect of touch, but in respect of the eyes only, that is, of any apprehensive power.

Reply Obj. 3. The sense of sight is the most excellent of all the senses, and covers a larger ground, as stated in the *Metaphysics;*[2] and so its name is transferred to all the other senses, and even to the inner apprehensions, as Augustine states (*De Verb. Dom.*).[3]

Reply Obj. 4. Avoidance of evil is caused by the appetite for good, as stated above (Q. XXV,

---

[1] *Confessions*, x, 54 (PL 32, 802).
[2] Aristotle, I, 1 (980ᵃ23).
[3] *Serm. ad Popul.*, Serm. CXII, 6 (PL 38, 646).

A. 2; Q. XXIX, A. 2); and so those passions alone are mentioned which incline to good, as being the causes of those which cause inordinately the avoidance of evil.

ARTICLE 6. Whether Sin Is Alleviated on Account of a Passion?

We proceed thus to the Sixth Article: It would seem that sin is not alleviated on account of passion.

Objection 1. For increase of cause adds to the effect; thus if a hot thing causes something to melt, a hotter will do so yet more. Now passion is a cause of sin, as stated above (AA. 1, 2, 3, 4). Therefore the more intense the passion the greater the sin. Therefore passion does not diminish sin, but increases it.

Obj. 2. Further, a good passion stands in the same relation to merit as an evil passion does to sin. Now a good passion increases merit; for a man seems to merit the more, according as he is moved by a greater pity to help a poor man. Therefore an evil passion also increases rather than diminishes a sin.

Obj. 3. Further, a man seems to sin the more grievously according as he sins with a more intense will. But the passion that impels the will makes it tend with greater intensity to the sinful act. Therefore passion aggravates a sin.

On the contrary, The passion of concupiscence is called a temptation of the flesh. But the greater the temptation that overcomes a man, the less grievous his sin, as Augustine states.[1]

I answer that, Sin consists essentially in an act of free choice, which is "a power of the will and reason";[2] while passion is a movement of the sensitive appetite. Now the sensitive appetite can be related to the free choice both antecedently and consequently; antecedently, according as a passion of the sensitive appetite draws or inclines the reason or will, as stated above (AA. 1, 2; Q. IX, A. 2; Q. X, A. 3); and consequently, in so far as the movements of the higher powers, if they are vehement, overflow onto the lower, since it is not possible for the will to be moved to anything intensely without a passion being aroused in the sensitive appetite.

Accordingly if we take passion as preceding the sinful act, it must diminish the sin; for the act is a sin in so far as it is voluntary, and under our control. Now a thing is said to be under our control through the reason and will. And

therefore the more the reason and will do anything of their own accord, and not through the impulse of a passion, the more is it voluntary and under our control. In this respect passion diminishes sin, in so far as it diminishes its voluntariness.

On the other hand, a consequent passion does not diminish a sin, but increases it; or rather it is a sign of its gravity, in so far, namely, as it shows the intensity of the will towards the sinful act; and in this sense it is true that the greater the pleasure or the concupiscence with which anyone sins, the greater the sin.

Reply Obj. 1. Passion is the cause of sin on the part of that to which the sinner turns. But the gravity of a sin is measured on the part of that from which he turns, which results accidentally (that is, beside his intention) from his turning to something else. Now an effect is increased by the increase not of its accidental cause, but of its direct cause.

Reply Obj. 2. A good passion consequent to the judgment of reason increases merit. But if it precede, so that a man is moved to do well rather by his passion than by the judgment of his reason, such a passion diminishes the goodness and praiseworthiness of his action.

Reply Obj. 3. Although the movement of the will incited by the passion is more intense, yet it is not so much the will's own movement as if it were moved to sin by the reason alone.

ARTICLE 7. Whether Passion Excuses from Sin Altogether?

We proceed thus to the Seventh Article: It would seem that passion excuses from sin altogether.

Objection 1. For whatever causes an act to be involuntary, excuses from sin altogether. But concupiscence of the flesh, which is a passion, makes an act to be involuntary, according to Gal. 5. 17: The flesh lusteth against the spirit ...so that you do not the things that you would. Therefore passion excuses from sin altogether.

Obj. 2. Further, passion causes a certain ignorance in a particular case, as stated above (A. 2). But ignorance in a particular case excuses from sin altogether, as stated above (Q. XIX, A. 6). Therefore passion excuses from sin altogether.

Obj. 3. Further, disease of the soul is graver than disease of the body. But bodily disease excuses from sin altogether, as in the case of mad people. Much more, therefore, does passion, which is a disease of the soul.

On the contrary, The Apostle (Rom. 7. 5)

---

[1] City of God, XIV, 12 (PL 41, 420); De Nat. et Grat., XXV (PL 44, 261).

[2] Cf. Peter Lombard, Sent., II, d. 24, chap. 3 (QR I, 421).

speaks of the passions as *passions of sins,* for no other reason than that they cause sin; and this would not be the case if they excused from sin altogether. Therefore passion does not excuse from sin altogether.

I answer that, An act which is evil in its genus, can be excused from sin altogether only by that which renders it altogether involuntary. Consequently, if the passion be such that it renders the subsequent act wholly involuntary, it entirely excuses from sin; otherwise, it does not excuse entirely. In this matter two points apparently should be observed: first, that a thing may be voluntary either in itself, as when the will tends towards it directly; or in its cause, when the will tends towards that cause and not towards the effect, as is the case with one who wilfully gets drunk, for in that case he is considered to do voluntarily whatever he does through being drunk. Secondly, we must observe that a thing is said to be voluntary directly or indirectly; directly, if the will tends towards it; indirectly, if the will could have prevented it, but did not.

Accordingly therefore we must make a distinction. Because a passion is sometimes so strong as to take away the use of reason altogether, as in the case of those who are mad through love or anger. And then if such a passion were voluntary from the beginning, the act is imputed as sin, because it is voluntary in its cause, as we have stated with regard to drunkenness. If, however, the cause be not voluntary but natural, for instance, if anyone through sickness or some such cause fall into such a passion as deprives him of the use of reason, his act is rendered wholly involuntary, and he is entirely excused from sin. Sometimes, however, the passion is not such as to take away the use of reason altogether. And then reason can drive the passion away, by turning to other thoughts; or it can prevent it from having its full effect, since the members are not put to work except by the consent of reason, as stated above (Q. XVII, A. 9). Therefore such a passion does not excuse from sin altogether.

Reply Obj. 1. The words, *So that you do not the things that you would* are not to be referred to outward deeds, but to the inner movement of concupiscence; for a man may wish never to desire evil, in which sense we are to understand the words of Rom. 7. 19: *The evil which I will not, that I do.* Or again they may be referred to the will as preceding the passion, as is the case with the incontinent, who act counter to their resolution on account of their concupiscence.

Reply Obj. 2. The particular ignorance which excuses altogether is ignorance of a circumstance which a man is unable to know even after taking due precautions. But passion causes ignorance of law in a particular case by preventing universal knowledge from being applied to a particular act, which passion the reason is able to drive away, as stated.

Reply Obj. 3. Bodily disease is involuntary. There would be a comparison, however, if it were voluntary, as we have stated about drunkenness, which is a kind of bodily disease.

ARTICLE 8. *Whether a Sin Committed through Passion Can Be Mortal?*

We proceed thus to the Eighth Article: It would seem that sin committed through passion cannot be mortal.

Objection 1. Because venial sin is divided against mortal sin. Now sin committed from weakness is venial, since it has in itself a cause for pardon (*venia*). Since therefore sin committed through passion is a sin of weakness, it seems that it cannot be mortal.

Obj. 2. Further, the cause is more powerful than its effect. But passion cannot be a mortal sin, for there is no mortal sin in the sensuality, as stated above (Q. LXXIV, A. 4). Therefore a sin committed through passion cannot be mortal.

Obj. 3. Further, passion is a hindrance to reason, as explained above (AA. 1, 2). Now it belongs to the reason to turn to God, or to turn away from Him, which is the essence of a mortal sin. Therefore a sin committed through passion cannot be mortal.

On the contrary, The Apostle says (Rom. 7. 5) that *the passions of the sins . . . work* (Vulg., —*did work*) *in our members to bring forth fruit unto death.* Now it is proper to mortal sin to bring forth fruit unto death. Therefore sin committed through passion may be mortal.

I answer that, Mortal sin, as stated above (Q. LXXII, A. 5), consists in turning away from our last end which is God, which turning away pertains to the deliberating reason, whose function it is also to direct towards the end. Therefore that which is contrary to the last end can happen not to be a mortal sin only when the deliberating reason is unable to come to the rescue, which is the case in sudden movements. Now when anyone proceeds from passion to a sinful act, or to a deliberate consent, this does not happen suddenly. And so the deliberating reason can come to the rescue here, since it can drive the passion away, or at least hinder it from having its effect, as stated above. Therefore if it does not come to the rescue, there is a mortal sin; and it is thus, as we see, that many murders and adulteries are committed through passion.

Reply Obj. 1. A sin may be venial in three ways. First, through its cause, that is, through having cause to be forgiven, which cause lessens the sin; thus a sin that is committed through weakness or ignorance is said to be venial. Secondly, through its issue; thus every sin, through repentance, becomes venial, that is, receives pardon (*veniam*). Thirdly, by its genus, for example an idle word. This is the only kind of venial sin that is opposed to mortal sin, but the objection regards the first kind.

Reply Obj. 2. Passion causes sin as regards the turning to something. But that this be a mortal sin regards the turning away, which follows accidentally from the turning to, as stated above (A. 6, Reply 1); hence the argument does not prove.

Reply Obj. 3. Passion does not always hinder the act of reason altogether. Consequently free choice remains to reason, so that it is able to turn away from God, or turn to Him. If, however, the use of reason be taken away altogether, the sin is no longer either mortal or venial.

QUESTION LXXVIII
OF THAT CAUSE OF SIN WHICH IS MALICE
(*In Four Articles*)

WE must now consider the cause of sin on the part of the will, namely malice; and under this head there are four points of inquiry: (1) Whether it is possible for anyone to sin through certain malice, that is, purposely? (2) Whether everyone that sins through habit sins through certain malice? (3) Whether everyone that sins through certain malice sins through habit? (4) Whether it is more grievous to sin through certain malice than through passion?

ARTICLE 1. *Whether Anyone Sins Through Certain Malice?*

We proceed thus to the First Article: It would seem that no one sins purposely, or through certain malice.

Objection 1. Because ignorance is opposed to purpose or certain malice. Now "every evil man is ignorant," according to the Philosopher,[1] and it is written (Prov. 14. 22): *They err that work evil.* Therefore no one sins through certain malice.

[1] *Ethics*, III, 1 (1110b28).

Obj. 2. Further, Dionysius says (*Div. Nom.* iv)[2] that "no one works intending evil." Now to sin through malice seems to denote the intention of doing evil in sinning,[3] because an act is not denominated from that which is unintentional and accidental. Therefore no one sins through malice.

Obj. 3. Further, malice itself is a sin. If therefore malice is a cause of sin, it follows that sin goes on causing sin infinitely, which is absurd. Therefore no one sins through malice.

On the contrary, It is written (Job 34. 27): (*Who*) *as it were on purpose have revolted from God* (Vulg.,—*Him*), *and would not understand all His ways.* Now to revolt from God is to sin. Therefore some sin purposely or through certain malice.

I answer that, Man like any other being has naturally an appetite for the good. And so if his appetite incline away to evil, this is due to corruption or disorder in some one of the principles of man; for it is thus that sin occurs in the actions of natural things. Now the principles of human acts are the intellect, and the appetite, both rational (that is, the will) and sensitive. Therefore just as sin occurs sometimes in human acts through a defect of the intellect, as when anyone sins through ignorance, and sometimes through a defect in the sensitive appetite, as when anyone sins through passion, so too does it occur through a defect consisting in a disorder of the will. Now the will is lacking in order when it loves more the lesser good. But the consequence of loving a thing less is that one chooses to suffer some hurt in its regard, in order to obtain a good that one loves more; as when a man, even knowingly, suffers the loss of a limb that he may save his life, which he loves more. Accordingly when an inordinate will loves some temporal good, for example riches or pleasure, more than the order of reason or Divine law, or Divine charity, or some such thing, it follows that it is willing to suffer the loss of some spiritual good so that it may obtain possession of some temporal good. Now evil is nothing other than the privation of some good; and so a man wishes knowingly a spiritual evil, which is evil absolutely, by which he is deprived of a spiritual good, in order to possess a temporal good. Therefore he is said to sin through certain malice or on purpose, because he chooses evil knowingly.

Reply Obj. 1. Ignorance sometimes excludes

[2] Sect. 19 (PG 3, 716); Sect. 31 (PG 3, 732).
[3] Alluding to the derivation of *Malitia* (malice) from *malum* (evil).

the absolute knowledge that a particular action is evil, and then man is said to sin through ignorance. Sometimes it excludes the knowledge that a particular action is evil at this particular moment, as when he sins through passion. And sometimes it excludes the knowledge that a particular evil is not to be suffered for the sake of possessing a particular good, but not the absolute knowledge that it is an evil. It is thus that a man is ignorant, when he sins through certain malice.

Reply Obj. 2. Evil cannot be intended by anyone for its own sake, but it can be intended for the sake of avoiding another evil, or obtaining another good, as stated above. And in this case anyone would choose to obtain a good intended for its own sake without suffering loss of the other good, even as a lustful man would wish to enjoy a pleasure without offending God; but with the two set before him to choose from, he prefers by sinning to incur God's anger, to being deprived of the pleasure.

Reply Obj. 3. The malice through which anyone sins, may be taken to denote habitual malice, in the sense in which the Philosopher calls[1] an evil habit by the name of malice, just as a good habit is called virtue. And in this way anyone is said to sin through malice when he sins through the inclination of a habit. It may also denote actual malice, whether by malice we mean the choice itself of evil (and thus anyone is said to sin through malice in so far as he sins through making a choice of evil), or whether by malice we mean some previous fault that gives rise to a subsequent fault, as when anyone impugns the grace of his brother through envy. Nor does this imply that a thing is its own cause, for the interior act is the cause of the exterior act. And one sin is the cause of another; not indefinitely, however, since we can trace it back to some previous sin which is not caused by any previous sin, as was explained above (Q. LXXV, A. 4, Reply 3).

ARTICLE 2. *Whether Everyone That Sins through Habit Sins through Certain Malice?*

We proceed thus to the Second Article: It would seem that not everyone who sins through habit sins through certain malice.

Objection 1. Because sin committed through certain malice seems to be most grievous. Now it happens sometimes that a man commits a slight sin through habit, as when he utters an idle word. Therefore sin committed from habit is not always committed through certain malice.

[1] *Ethics,* II, 5 (1105^b19).

Obj. 2. Further, acts proceeding from habits are like the acts by which those habits were formed.[2] But the acts which precede a vicious habit are not committed through certain malice. Therefore the sins that arise from habit are not committed through certain malice.

Obj. 3. Further, when a man commits a sin through certain malice, he rejoices after having done it, according to Prov. 2. 14: *Who are glad when they have done evil, and rejoice in most wicked things;* and this, because it is pleasant to obtain what we desire, and to do those actions which are connatural to us by reason of habit. But those who sin through habit are sorrowful after committing a sin; because "bad men," that is, those who have a vicious habit, "are full of remorse."[3] Therefore sins that arise from habit are not committed through certain malice.

On the contrary, A sin committed through certain malice is one that is done through choice of evil. Now we make choice of those things to which we are inclined by habit, as stated in the *Ethics*[4] with regard to virtuous habits. Therefore a sin that arises from habit is committed through certain malice.

I answer that, There is a difference between a sin committed by one who has the habit, and a sin committed through habit. For it is not necessary to use a habit, since it is subject to the will of the person who has that habit. Hence habit is defined as being something we use when we will. And thus, just as it may happen that one who has a vicious habit may break forth into a virtuous act, because a bad habit does not corrupt reason altogether, something of which remains unimpaired, the result being that a sinner does some works which are generically good; so too it may happen sometimes that one who has a vicious habit, acts, not from that habit, but through the uprising of a passion, or again through ignorance. But whenever he uses the vicious habit he necessarily sins through certain malice. Because to anyone that has a habit whatever is befitting to him in respect of that habit has the aspect of something lovable, since it thereby becomes, in a way, connatural to him, according as custom and habit are a second nature. Now the very thing which befits a man in respect of a vicious habit is something that excludes a spiritual good, the result being that a man chooses a spiritual evil that he may obtain possession of what befits him in respect of that habit. And this is to sin through certain

[2] Aristotle, *Ethics,* II, 2 (1104^a27).
[3] *Ibid.,* IX, 4 (1166^b24).
[4] *Ibid.,* VI, 2 (1139^a32).

malice. Therefore it is evident that whoever sins through habit sins through certain malice.

Reply Obj. 1. Venial sin does not exclude spiritual good, which is the grace of God or charity. Therefore it is an evil, not absolutely, but in a relative sense; and for that reason its habit is not an absolute but a relative evil.

Reply Obj. 2. Acts proceeding from habits are of like species as the acts from which those habits were formed, but they differ from them as perfect from imperfect. Such is the difference between sin committed through certain malice and sin committed through passion.

Reply Obj. 3. He that sins through habit always rejoices for what he does through habit as long as he uses the habit. But since he is able not to use the habit, and to think of something else by means of his reason, which is not altogether corrupted, it can happen that while not using the habit he is sorry for what he has done through the habit. And so it often happens that such a man is sorry for his sin not because sin in itself is displeasing to him, but on account of his reaping some disadvantage from the sin.

ARTICLE 3. *Whether One Who Sins through Certain Malice Sins through Habit?*

We proceed thus to the Third Article: It would seem that whoever sins through certain malice sins through habit.

Objection 1. For the Philosopher says[1] that an unjust action is not done as an unjust man does it, that is, through choice, unless it be done through habit. Now to sin through certain malice is to sin through making a choice of evil, as stated above (A. 1). Therefore no one sins through certain malice unless he has the habit of sin.

Obj. 2. Further, Origen says (*Peri Archon,* 1, iii)[2] that "a man is not suddenly ruined and lost, but necessarily falls away little by little." But the greatest fall seems to be that of the man who sins through certain malice. Therefore a man comes to sin through certain malice, not from the outset, but from inveterate custom, which may engender a habit.

Obj. 3. Further, whenever a man sins through certain malice, his will has to be inclined of itself to the evil he chooses. But by the nature of that power man is inclined not to evil but to good. Therefore if he chooses evil, this must be due to something supervening, which is passion or habit. Now when a man sins through passion, he sins not through certain malice, but

through weakness, as stated (Q. LXXVII, A. 3). Therefore whenever anyone sins through certain malice, he sins through habit.

Obj. 4. *On the contrary,* The good habit stands in the same relation to the choice of something good as the bad habit to the choice of something evil. But it happens sometimes that a man without having the habit of a virtue chooses that which is good according to that virtue. Therefore sometimes also a man, without having the habit of vice, may choose evil, which is to sin through certain malice.

I answer that, The will is related differently to good and to evil. Because from the very nature of the power, it is inclined to the rational good, as its proper object; and therefore every sin is said to be contrary to nature. Hence, if a will be inclined, by its choice, to some evil, this must be occasioned by something else. Sometimes, in fact, this is occasioned through some defect in the reason, as when anyone sins through ignorance; and sometimes this arises through the impulse of the sensitive appetite, as when anyone sins through passion. Yet neither of these amounts to a sin through certain malice; for then alone does anyone sin through certain malice when his will is moved to evil of its own accord. This may happen in two ways. First, through his having a corrupt disposition inclining him to evil, so that, in respect of that disposition, some evil is, as it were, suitable to him and is like him; and to this thing by reason of its suitableness, the will tends as to something good, because everything tends of its own accord to that which is suitable to it. Moreover this corrupt disposition is either a habit acquired by custom and which becomes a second nature, or a sickly condition on the part of the body, as in the case of a man who is naturally inclined to certain sins by reason of some natural corruption in himself. Secondly, the will of its own accord may tend to an evil, through the removal of some obstacle; for instance, if a man be prevented from sinning not through sin being in itself displeasing to him, but through hope of eternal life, or fear of hell, so that if hope gives place to despair, or fear to presumption, he will end in sinning through certain malice, being freed from the bridle, as it were.

It is evident, therefore, that sin committed through certain malice always presupposes some lack of order in man, which, however, is not always a habit; so that it does not follow of necessity, if a man sins through certain malice, that he sins through habit.

---

[1] *Ethics,* v, 6 (1134ª17).
[2] PG 11, 155.

Reply Obj. 1. To do an action as an unjust man does may be not only to do unjust things through certain malice, but also to do them with pleasure, and without any notable resistance on the part of reason, and this occurs only in one who has a habit.

Reply Obj. 2. It is true that a man does not fall suddenly into sin from certain malice, and that something is presupposed; but this something is not always a habit, as stated above.

Reply Obj. 3. That which inclines the will to evil is not always a habit or a passion, but at times is something else.

Reply Obj. 4. There is no comparison between choosing good and choosing evil, because evil is never without some good of nature, while good can be perfectly without the evil of fault.

ARTICLE 4. *Whether It Is More Grievous to Sin through Certain Malice than through Passion?*

We proceed thus to the Fourth Article: It would seem that it is not more grievous to sin through certain malice than through passion.

Objection 1. For ignorance excuses from sin either altogether or in part. Now ignorance is greater in one who sins through certain malice than in one who sins through passion, since he that sins through certain malice suffers from the worst form of ignorance, which according to the Philosopher[1] is ignorance of principle, for he has a false estimation of the end, which is the principle in matters of action. Therefore there is more excuse for one who sins through certain malice than for one who sins through passion.

Obj. 2. Further, the more a man is impelled to sin the less grievous is his sin, as is clear with regard to a man who is thrown headlong into sin by a more impetuous passion. Now he that sins through certain malice is impelled by habit, the impulse of which is stronger than that of passion. Therefore to sin through habit is less grievous than to sin through passion.

Obj. 3. Further, to sin through certain malice is to sin through choosing evil. Now he that sins through passion also chooses evil. Therefore he does not sin less than the man who sins through certain malice.

On the contrary, A sin that is committed on purpose for this very reason deserves heavier punishment, according to Job 34. 26: *He hath struck them as being wicked, in open sight, who, as it were, on purpose, have revolted from Him.* Now punishment is not increased except

[1] *Ethics,* VII, 8 (1151ᵃ16).

for a graver fault. Therefore a sin is aggravated through being done on purpose, that is, through certain malice.

I answer that, A sin committed through certain malice is more grievous than a sin committed through passion for three reasons. First, because, as sin consists chiefly in an act of the will, it follows that, other things being equal, a sin is all the more grievous according as the movement of the sin belongs more to the will. Now when a sin is committed through certain malice the movement of sin belongs more to the will, which is then moved to evil of its own accord, than when a sin is committed through passion, when the will is impelled to sin by something extrinsic, as it were. Hence a sin is aggravated by the very fact that it is committed through certain malice, and so much the more as the malice is greater; but it is diminished by being committed through passion, and so much the more as the passion is stronger. Secondly, because the passion which incites the will to sin, soon passes away, so that man repents of his sin, and soon returns to his good intentions; but the habit through which a man sins by malice is a permanent quality, so that who sins through malice, abides longer in his sin. For this reason the Philosopher compares[2] the intemperate man, who sins through malice, to a sick man who suffers from a chronic disease, while he compares the incontinent man, who sins through passion, to one who suffers intermittently. Thirdly, because he who sins through certain malice is ill-disposed in respect of the end itself, which is the principle in matters of action; and so the defect is more dangerous than in the case of the man who sins through passion, whose purpose tends to a good end, although this purpose is interrupted on account of the passion for the time being. Now the worst of all defects is defect of principle. Therefore it is evident that a sin committed through malice is more grievous than one committed through passion.

Reply Obj. 1. Ignorance of choice, to which the objection refers, neither excuses nor diminishes a sin, as stated above (Q. LXXVI, AA. 3, 4). Therefore neither does a greater ignorance of the kind make a sin to be less grave.

Reply Obj. 2. The impulse due to passion is, as it were, due to a defect which is outside the will; but by a habit, the will is inclined from within. Hence the comparison fails.

Reply Obj. 3. It is one thing to sin while choosing, and another to sin through choosing.

[2] *Ibid.,* VII, 8 (1150ᵇ32).

For he that sins through passion sins while choosing, but not through choosing, because his choosing is not for him the first principle of his sin; for he is induced through the passion to choose what he would not choose were it not for the passion. On the other hand, he that sins through certain malice chooses evil of his own accord, in the way already explained (A. 1), so that his choosing, of which he has full control, is the principle of his sin; and for this reason he is said to sin *through* choosing.

QUESTION LXXIX
OF THE EXTERNAL CAUSES OF SIN
(*In Four Articles*)

WE must now consider the external causes of sin, and (1) on the part of God; (2) on the part of the devil (Q. LXXX); (3) on the part of man (Q. LXXXI).

Under the first head there are four points of inquiry: (1) Whether God is a cause of sin? (2) Whether the act of sin is from God? (3) Whether God is the cause of spiritual blindness and hardness of heart? (4) Whether these things are directed to the salvation of those who are blinded or hardened?

ARTICLE 1. *Whether God Is a Cause of Sin?*

We proceed thus to the First Article: It would seem that God is a cause of sin.

Objection 1. For the Apostle says of certain ones (Rom. 1. 28): *God delivered them up to a reprobate sense, to do those things which are not right* (Douay,—*convenient*), and a gloss comments on this by saying[1] that "God works in men's hearts, by inclining their wills to whatever He wills, whether to good or to evil." Now sin consists in doing what is not right, and in having a will inclined to evil. Therefore God is to man a cause of sin.

Obj. 2. Further, it is written (Wisd. 14. 11): *The creatures of God are turned to an abomination; and a temptation to the souls of men.* But a temptation usually denotes a provocation to sin. Since therefore creatures were made by God alone, as was established in the First Part (Q. XLIV, A. 1), it seems that God is a cause of sin, by provoking man to sin.

Obj. 3. Further, the cause of the cause is the cause of the effect. Now God is the cause of free choice, which itself is the cause of sin. Therefore God is the cause of sin.

Obj. 4. Further, every evil is opposed to good.

But it is not contrary to God's goodness that He should cause the evil of punishment; since of this evil it is written (Isa. 45. 7) that God creates evil, and (Amos 3. 6): *Shall there be evil in the city which God* (Vulg.,—*the Lord*) *hath not done?* Therefore it is not incompatible with God's goodness that He should cause the evil of fault.

On the contrary, It is written (Wisd. 11. 25): *Thou . . . hatest none of the things which Thou hast made.* Now God hates sin, according to Wisd. 14. 9: *To God the wicked and his wickedness are hateful.* Therefore God is not a cause of sin.

I answer that, Man is, in two ways, a cause either of his own or of another's sin. First, directly, namely by inclining his or another's will to sin; secondly, indirectly, namely by not preventing someone from sinning. Hence (Ezech. 3. 18) it is said to the watchman: *If thou say not to the wicked: "Thou shalt surely die"*[2] . . . *I will require his blood at thy hand.* Now God cannot be directly the cause of sin, either in Himself or in another, since every sin is a departure from the order which is to God as to the end; but God inclines and turns all things to Himself as to their last end, as Dionysius states (*Div. Nom.* i),[3] so that it is impossible that He should be either to Himself or to another the cause of departing from the order which is to Himself. Therefore He cannot be directly the cause of sin. In like manner neither can He cause sin indirectly. For it happens that God does not give some the assistance by which they may avoid sin, which assistance were He to give, they would not sin. But He does all this according to the order of His wisdom and justice, since He Himself is Wisdom and Justice. Hence if someone sin it is not ascribed to Him as though He were the cause of that sin; even as a pilot is not said to cause the wrecking of the ship through not steering the ship, unless he cease to steer while able and bound to steer. It is therefore evident that God is in no way a cause of sin.

Reply Obj. 1. As to the words of the Apostle, the solution is clear from the text. For if God delivered some up to a reprobate sense, it follows that they already had a reprobate sense, so as to do what was not right. Accordingly He is said to deliver them up to a reprobate sense in so far as He does not hinder them from following that reprobate sense, even as we are said

[1] *Glossa ordin.* (VI, 5E); Augustine, *De Grat. et Lib. Arb.,* XXI (PL 44, 909).

[2] Vulg.,—*If, when I say to the wicked, "Thou shalt surely die," thou declare it not to him.*
[3] Sect. 5 (PG 3, 593).

to expose a person to danger if we do not protect him. The saying of Augustine[1] from which the gloss quoted[2] is taken, to the effect that "God inclines men's will to good and evil," is to be understood as meaning that He inclines the will directly to good, and to evil, in so far as He does not hinder it, as stated above. And yet even this is due as being deserved through a previous sin.

Reply Obj. 2. When it is said the *creatures of God are turned "to" an abomination, and a temptation to the souls of men,* the preposition "to" does not denote causality but sequel.[3] For God did not make the creatures that they might be an evil to man. This was the result of man's folly, and hence the text goes on to say, *and a snare to the feet of the unwise,* who, that is, in their folly, use creatures for a purpose other than that for which they were made.

Reply Obj. 3. The effect which proceeds from the mediate cause according as it is subordinate to the first cause, is reduced to that first cause; but if it proceed from the mediate cause according as it goes outside the order of the first cause, it is not reduced to that first cause; thus if a servant do any thing contrary to his master's orders, it is not ascribed to the master as though he were its cause. In like manner sin, which free choice commits against the commandment of God is not attributed to God as being its cause.

Reply Obj. 4. Punishment is opposed to the good of the person punished, who is thus deprived of some good or other. But fault is opposed to the good of subordination to God, and so it is directly opposed to the Divine goodness. Consequently there is no comparison between fault and punishment.

ARTICLE 2. *Whether the Act of Sin Is from God?*

We proceed thus to the Second Article: It would seem that the act of sin is not from God.

Objection 1. For Augustine says (*De Perfect. Justit.* ii)[4] that "the act of sin is not a thing." Now whatever is from God is a thing. Therefore the act of sin is not from God.

Obj. 2. Further, man is not said to be the cause of sin except because he is the cause of the sinful act; for "no one works intending

evil," as Dionysius states (*Div. Nom.* iv).[5] Now God is not a cause of sin, as stated above (A. 1). Therefore God is not the cause of the act of sin.

Obj. 3. Further, some actions are evil and sinful in their species, as was shown above (Q. XVIII, A. 5). Now whatever is the cause of a thing causes whatever belongs to it in respect of its species. If therefore God caused the act of sin, He would be the cause of sin, which is false, as was proved above (A. 1). Therefore God is not the cause of the act of sin.

On the contrary, The act of sin is a movement of free choice. Now "the will of God is the cause of every movement," as Augustine declares (*De Trin.* iii, 4).[6] Therefore God's will is the cause of the act of sin.

I answer that, The act of sin is both a being and an act; and in both respects it is from God. Because every being, whatever the mode of its being, must be derived from the First Being, as Dionysius declares (*Div. Nom.* 5).[7] Again every action is caused by something existing in act, since nothing produces an action except in so far as it is in act; and every being in act is reduced to the First Act, namely God, as to its cause, Who is act by His Essence. Therefore God is the cause of every action, in so far as it is an action. But sin denotes a being and an action with a defect. And this defect is from a created cause, namely free choice, as falling away from the order of the First Agent, namely God. Consequently this defect is not reduced to God as its cause, but to free choice, even as the defect of limping is reduced to a crooked leg as its cause, but not to the moving power, which nevertheless causes whatever there is of movement in the limping. Accordingly God is the cause of the act of sin, and yet He is not the cause of sin, because He does not cause the act to have a defect.

Reply Obj. 1. In this passage Augustine calls by the name of thing that which is a thing absolutely, namely, substance; for in this sense the act of sin is not a thing.

Reply Obj. 2. Not only the act but also the defect is reduced to man as its cause, which defect consists in man not being subject to Whom he ought to be, although he does not intend this principally. Therefore man is the cause of the sin, while God is cause of the act, but such that in no way is He the cause of the defect accompanying the act, so that He is not the cause of the sin.

---

[1] *De Grat. et Lib. Arb.,* XXI (PL 44, 909).

[2] *Glossa ordin.* (VI 5E).

[3] This is made clear by the Douay Version: the Latin *factæ sunt in abominationem* admits of the translation *were made to be an abomination,* which might imply causality.

[4] PL 44, 294.

[5] Sect. 19; 31 (PG 3, 716; 732).

[6] PL 42, 873.   [7] Sect. 4 (PG 3, 817).

Reply Obj. 3. As stated above (Q. XVIII, A. 5, REPLY 2; Q. LIV, A. 3, REPLY 2), acts and habits do not take their species from the privation itself, in which consists the nature of evil, but from some object to which that privation is united. And so this defect which consists in not being from God belongs to the species of the act consequently, and not as a specific difference.

ARTICLE 3. *Whether God Is the Cause of Spiritual Blindness and Hardness of Heart?*

We proceed thus to the Third Article: It would seem that God is not the cause of spiritual blindness and hardness of heart.

Objection 1. For Augustine says (QQ. LXXXIII, *qu.* 3)[1] that "God is not the cause of that which makes man worse." Now man is made worse by spiritual blindness and hardness of heart. Therefore God is not the cause of spiritual blindness and hardness of heart.

Obj. 2. Further, Fulgentius says (*De Dupl. Prædest.* i, 19):[2] "God does not punish what He causes." Now God punishes the hardened heart, according to Ecclus. 3. 27: *A hard heart shall fear evil at the last.* Therefore God is not the cause of hardness of heart.

Obj. 3. Further, the same effect is not put down to contrary causes. But the cause of spiritual blindness is said to be the malice of man, according to Wisd. 2. 21: *For their own malice blinded them,* and again, according to II Cor. 4. 4: *The god of this world hath blinded the minds of unbelievers,* which causes seem to be opposed to God. Therefore God is not the cause of spiritual blindness and hardness of heart.

On the contrary, It is written (Isa. 6. 10): *Blind the heart of this people, and make their ears heavy,* and Rom. 9. 18: *He hath mercy on whom He will, and whom He will He hardeneth.*

I answer that, Spiritual blindness and hardness of heart imply two things. One is the movement of the human mind in cleaving to evil and turning away from the Divine light. And as regards this, God is not the cause of spiritual blindness and hardness of heart, just as He is not the cause of sin. The other thing is the withdrawal of grace, the result of which is that the mind is not enlightened by God to see rightly, and man's heart is not softened to live rightly. And as regards this, God is the cause of spiritual blindness and hardness of heart.

Now we must consider that God is the universal cause of the enlightening of souls, ac-

cording to John 1. 9: *That was the true light which enlighteneth every man that cometh into this world,* even as the sun is the universal cause of the enlightening of bodies, though not in the same way; for the sun enlightens by necessity of nature, while God works freely, through the order of His wisdom. Now although the sun, so far as it is concerned, enlightens all bodies, yet if it be encountered by an obstacle in a body it leaves it in darkness, as happens to a house whose window-shutters are closed, although the sun is in no way the cause of the house being darkened, since it does not act of its own accord in failing to light up the interior of the house; and the cause of this is the person who closed the shutters. On the other hand, God of His own accord withholds His grace from those in whom He finds an obstacle, so that the cause of grace being withheld is not only the man who raises an obstacle to grace, but God, Who, of His own accord, withholds His grace. In this way God is the cause of spiritual blindness, deafness of ear, and hardness of heart.

These differ from one another in respect of the effects of grace, which both perfects the intellect by the gift of wisdom, and softens the affections by the fire of charity. And since two of the senses excel in rendering service to the intellect, namely sight and hearing, of which the former assists discovery, and the latter teaching, hence it is that spiritual blindness corresponds to sight, heaviness of the ears to hearing, and hardness of heart to the affections.

Reply Obj. 1. Blindness and hardheartedness, as regards the withholding of grace, are punishments, and therefore, in this respect, they make man no worse. It is because he is already worsened by sin that he incurs them, even as other punishments.

Reply Obj. 2. This argument considers hardheartedness in so far as it is a sin.

Reply Obj. 3. Malice is the cause which deserves blindness just as sin is the cause of punishment; and in this way too, the devil is said to blind, in so far as he induces man to sin.

ARTICLE 4. *Whether Blindness and Hardness of Heart Are Directed to the Salvation of Those Who Are Blinded and Hardened?*

We proceed thus to the Fourth Article: It would seem that blindness and hardness of heart are always directed to the salvation of those who are blinded and hardened.

Objection 1. For Augustine says (*Enchir.* XI)[3] that "as God is supremely good, He would

[1] PL 40, 11.
[2] PL 65, 167.
[3] PL 40, 236.

in no way allow evil to be done, unless He could draw some good from every evil." Much more, therefore, does He direct to some good the evil of which He Himself is the cause. Now God is the cause of blindness and hardness of heart, as stated above (A. 3). Therefore they are directed to the salvation of those who are blinded and hardened.

Obj. 2. Further, it is written (Wisd. 1. 13) that *God hath no pleasure in the destruction of the ungodly.* (Vulg.,—*God made not death, neither hath He pleasure in the destruction of the living.*) Now He would seem to take pleasure in their destruction if He did not turn their blindness to their profit; just as a physician would seem to take pleasure in torturing the invalid if he did not intend to heal the invalid when he prescribes a bitter medicine for him. Therefore God turns blindness to the profit of those who are blinded.

Obj. 3. Further, *God is not a respecter of persons* (Acts 10. 34). Now He directs the blinding of some to their salvation, as in the case of some of the Jews, who were blinded so as not to believe in Christ, and, through not believing, to slay Him, and afterwards were seized with compunction, and converted, as related by Augustine.[1] Therefore God turns all blindness to the spiritual welfare of those who are blinded.

Obj. 4. On the other hand, According to Rom. 3. 8, evil should not be done that good may ensue. Now blindness is an evil. Therefore God does not blind some for the sake of their welfare.

I answer that, Blindness is a kind of preamble to sin. Now sin has a twofold relation,—to one thing directly, namely to the sinner's damnation;—to another by reason of God's mercy or providence, namely that the sinner may be healed, in so far as God permits some to fall into sin, that by acknowledging their sin, they may be humbled and converted, as Augustine states (*De Nat. et Grat.* xxvii).[2] Therefore blindness, of its very nature, is directed to the damnation of those who are blinded, for which reason it is accounted an effect of reprobation. But, through God's mercy, temporary blindness is directed medicinally to the spiritual welfare of those who are blinded. This mercy, however, is not vouchsafed to all those who are blinded, but only to the predestinated, to whom *all things work together unto good* (Rom. 8. 28). Therefore as regards some, blindness is directed to their healing; but as regards others, to their damnation, as Augustine says (*loc. cit.*).

Reply Obj. 1. Every evil that God does or permits to be done is directed to some good; yet not always to the good of those in whom the evil is, but sometimes to the good of others, or of the whole universe. Thus He directs the sin of tyrants to the good of the martyrs, and the punishment of the lost to the glory of His justice.

Reply Obj. 2. God does not take pleasure in the loss of man as regards the loss itself, but by reason of His justice, or of the good that ensues from the loss.

Reply Obj. 3. That God directs the blindness of some to their spiritual welfare is due to His mercy; but that the blindness of others is directed to their loss is due to His justice. And that He vouchsafes His mercy to some, and not to all, does not make God a respecter of persons, as explained in the First Part (Q. XXIII, A. 5, REPLY 3).

Reply Obj. 4. Evil of fault must not be done that good may ensue, but evil of punishment must be inflicted for the sake of good.

QUESTION LXXX

OF THE CAUSE OF SIN AS REGARDS THE DEVIL

(*In Four Articles*)

WE must now consider the cause of sin as regards the devil; and under this head there are four points of inquiry: (1) Whether the devil is directly the cause of sin? (2) Whether the devil induces us to sin, by persuading us inwardly? (3) Whether he can make us sin of necessity? (4) Whether all sins are due to the devil's suggestion?

ARTICLE 1. *Whether the Devil Is Directly the Cause of Man's Sinning?*

We proceed thus to the First Article: It would seem that the devil is directly the cause of man's sinning.

Objection 1. For sin consists directly in an act of the appetite. Now Augustine says (*De Trin.* iv, 12)[3] that "the devil inspires his friends with evil desires"; and Bede, commenting on Acts 5. 3, says[4] that the devil draws the mind to evil desires; and Isidore says[5] that "the devil fills men's hearts with secret lusts." Therefore the devil is directly the cause of sin.

Obj. 2. Further, Jerome says (*Contra Jovin.*

---

[1] *Quaest.* XVII *in Matt.*, Q. XIV, on 13.15 (PL 35, 1372).
[2] PL 44, 262.

[3] PL 42, 897.
[4] PL 92, 954.
[5] *Sent.*, II, 12 (PL 83, 647).

ii. 2)[1] that as God is the perfecter of good, so is the devil the perfecter of evil. But God is directly the cause of our good. Therefore the devil is directly the cause of our sins.

Obj. 3. Further, the Philosopher says in a chapter of the *Eudemian Ethics*[2] that there must be some extrinsic principle of human counsel. Now human counsel is not only about good things but also about evil things. Therefore, as God moves man to take good counsel, and so is the cause of good, so the devil moves him to take evil counsel, and consequently is directly the cause of sin.

On the contrary, Augustine proves (*De Lib. Arb.* i, ii; iii, i)[3] that "nothing else than his own will makes man's mind the slave of his desire." Now man does not become a slave to his desire, except through sin. Therefore the cause of sin cannot be the devil, but man's own will alone.

I answer that, Sin is an action, so that a thing can be directly the cause of sin in the same way as anyone is directly the cause of an action; and this can only happen by moving that action's proper principle to act. Now the proper principle of a sinful action is the will, since every sin is voluntary. Consequently nothing can be directly the cause of sin except that which can move the will to act.

Now the will, as stated above (Q. IX, AA. 1, 4, 6), can be moved by two things: first by its object, in the sense that the apprehended appetible is said to move the appetite; secondly by that agent which moves the will inwardly to will, and this is no other than either the will itself, or God, as was shown above (Q. IX, A. 3). Now God cannot be the cause of sin, as stated above (Q. LXXIX, A. 1). Therefore it follows that in this respect, a man's will alone is directly the cause of his sin.

As regards the object, a thing may be understood as moving the will in three ways. First, the object itself which is proposed to the will; thus we say that food arouses man's desire to eat. Secondly, he that proposes or offers this object. Thirdly, he that persuades the will that the object proposed has an aspect of good, because he also in a fashion offers the will its proper object, which is a real or apparent good of reason. Accordingly, in the first way the sensible things, which approach from without, move a man's will to sin. In the second and third ways, either the devil or a man may incite to sin, either by offering an object of desire to the senses, or by per-

suading the reason. But in none of these three ways can anything be the direct cause of sin, because the will is not of necessity moved by any object except the last end, as stated above (Q. X, A. 2; Part I, Q. CV, A. 4). Consequently neither the thing offered from without, nor he that proposes it, nor he that persuades, is the sufficient cause of sin. Therefore it follows that the devil is a cause of sin neither directly nor sufficiently, but only by persuasion, or by proposing the object of desire.

Reply Obj. 1. All these, and other like authorities, if we meet with them, are to be understood as denoting that the devil induces man to affection for a sin, either by suggesting to him, or by offering him objects of desire.

Reply Obj. 2. This comparison is true in so far as the devil is somewhat the cause of our sins, even as God is in a certain way the cause of our good actions, but does not extend to the mode of causation; for God causes good things in us by moving the will inwardly, while the devil cannot move us in this way.

Reply Obj. 3. God is the universal principle of all inward movements of man; but that the human will be determined to an evil counsel is directly due to the human will, and to the devil as persuading or offering the object of desire.

ARTICLE 2. *Whether the Devil Can Induce Man to Sin by Internal Instigations?*

We proceed thus to the Second Article: It would seem that the devil cannot induce man to sin by internal instigations.

Objection 1. For the internal movements of the soul are vital functions. Now no vital functions can be exercised except by an intrinsic principle, not even those of the vegetal soul, which are the lowest of vital functions. Therefore the devil cannot instigate man to evil through his internal movements.

Obj. 2. Further, all the internal movements arise from the external senses according to the order of nature. Now it belongs to God alone to do anything beside the order of nature, as was stated in the First Part (Q. CX, A. 4). Therefore the devil cannot effect anything in man's internal movements, except in respect of things which are perceived by the external senses.

Obj. 3. Further, the internal acts of the soul are to understand and to imagine. Now the devil can do nothing in connection with either of these, because, as stated in the First Part (Q. CXI, A. 2, Reply 2), the devil cannot put things into the human intellect, nor does it seem possible for him to produce anything in the imagina-

---

[1] PL 23, 299.
[2] VII, 14 (1248[a]22).
[3] PL 32, 1233; 1271.

tion, since imaginary forms, being more spiritual, are more excellent than those which are in sensible matter, which, nevertheless, the devil is unable to produce, as is clear from what we have said in the First Part (Q. CX, A. 2). Therefore the devil cannot through man's internal movements induce him to sin.

On the contrary, According to this the devil would never tempt man unless he appeared visibly, which is evidently false.

I answer that, The interior part of the soul is intellectual and sensitive; and the intellectual part contains the intellect and the will. As regards the will, we have already stated (A. 1) how the devil is related to it. Now the intellect, of its very nature, is moved by that which enlightens it in the knowledge of truth, which the devil has no intention of doing in man's regard; rather does he darken man's reason so that it may consent to sin, which darkness is due to the imagination and sensitive appetite. Consequently the whole inward operation of the devil seems to be confined to the imagination and sensitive appetite, by moving either of which he can induce man to sin. For his operation may result in presenting certain forms to the imagination, and he is also able to incite the sensitive appetite to some passion or other.

The reason of this is, that as stated in the First Part (Q. CX, A. 3), the corporeal nature has a natural aptitude to be moved locally by the spiritual nature, so that the devil can produce all those effects which can result from the local movement of bodies here below, unless he is restrained by the Divine power. Now the representation of forms to the imagination is due sometimes to local movement; for the Philosopher says[1] that "when an animal sleeps, the blood descends in abundance to the sensitive principle, and the movements descend with it," that is, the impressions left by the action of sensible objects, which impressions are preserved by means of sensible species, and continue to move the apprehensive principle, so that they appear just as though the sensitive principles were being affected by them at the time. Hence such a local movement of the vital spirits or humours can be produced by the demons, whether man sleep or wake, and so it happens that man's imagination is brought into play.

In like manner, the sensitive appetite is incited to certain passions according to certain fixed movements of the heart and the vital spirits. Therefore the devil can co-operate in this also. And through certain passions being aroused

in the sensitive appetite, the result is that man more easily perceives the movement or sensible intention which is brought in the manner explained, before the apprehensive principle, since, as the Philosopher observes,[2] "lovers are moved by even a slight likeness to an apprehension of the beloved." It also happens, through the rousing of a passion, that what is put before the imagination is judged as being something to be pursued, because to him who is held by a passion whatever the passion inclines to him seems good. In this way the devil induces man inwardly to sin.

Reply Obj. 1. Although vital functions are always from an intrinsic principle, yet an extrinsic agent can co-operate with them, even as external heat co-operates with functions of the vegetal soul, that food may be more easily digested.

Reply Obj. 2. This apparition of imaginary forms is not altogether outside the order of nature, nor is it due to a command alone, but according to local movement, as explained above. Consequently the *Reply to the Third Objection* is clear, because these forms are received originally from the senses.

ARTICLE 3. *Whether the Devil Can Induce Man to Sin of Necessity?*

We proceed thus to the Third Article: It would seem that the devil can induce man to sin of necessity.

Objection 1. Because the greater can compel the lesser. Now it is said of the devil (Job. 41. 24) that *there is no power on earth that can compare with him.* Therefore he can compel man to sin, while he dwells on the earth.

Obj. 2. Further, man's reason cannot be moved except in respect of things that are offered outwardly to the senses, or are represented to the imagination, because all our knowledge arises from the senses, and "we cannot understand without a phantasm."[3] Now the devil can move man's imagination, as stated above (A. 2), and also the external senses, for Augustine says (QQ. LXXXIII, *qu.* 12)[4] that "this evil," of which, that is, the devil is the cause, "extends gradually through all the approaches to the senses, it adapts itself to shapes, blends with colours, mingles with sounds, seasons every flavour." Therefore it can incline man's reason to sin of necessity.

Obj. 3. Further, Augustine says[5] that "there is some sin when the flesh lusteth against the spir-

---

[1] *Dreams,* 3 (461ᵇ11).

[2] *Ibid.,* 2 (460ᵇ5).   [3] Aristotle, *Soul,* III, 7 (431ᵃ16).
[4] PL 40, 14.   [5] *City of God,* XIX, 4 (PL 41, 629).

it." Now the devil can cause concupiscence of the flesh, even as other passions, in the way explained above (A. 2). Therefore he can induce man to sin of necessity.

On the contrary, It is written (I Pet. 5. 8): *Your adversary the devil, as a roaring lion, goeth about seeking whom he may devour.* Now it would be useless to admonish thus if it were true that man were under the necessity of succumbing to the devil. Therefore he cannot induce man to sin of necessity.

I answer that, The devil by his own power, unless he is restrained by God, can compel anyone to do an act which, in its genus, is a sin; but he cannot bring about the necessity of sinning. This is evident from the fact that man does not resist that which moves him to sin except by his reason, the use of which the devil is able to impede altogether by moving the imagination and the sensitive appetite, as is the case with one who is possessed. But then, the reason being thus fettered, whatever man may do it is not imputed to him as a sin. If, however, the reason is not altogether fettered, then, in so far as it is free, it can resist sin, as stated above (Q. LXXVII, A. 7). It is consequently evident that the devil can in no way compel man to sin.

Reply Obj. 1. Not every power that is greater than man can move man's will. God alone can do this, as stated above (Q. IX, A. 6).

Reply Obj. 2. That which is apprehended by the senses or the imagination does not move the will of necessity, so long as man has the use of reason; nor does such an apprehension always fetter the reason.

Reply Obj. 3. The lusting of the flesh against the spirit, when the reason actually resists it, is not a sin, but is matter for the exercise of virtue. That reason does not resist is not in the devil's power. Therefore he cannot bring about the necessity of sinning.

ARTICLE 4. *Whether All the Sins of Men Are Due to the Devil's Suggestion?*

We proceed thus to the Fourth Article: It would seem that all the sins of men are due to the devil's suggestion.

Objection 1. For Dionysius says (*Div. Nom.* iv)[1] that "the crowd of demons are the cause of all evils, both to themselves and to others."

Obj. 2. Further, whoever sins mortally becomes the slave of the devil, according to John 8. 34: *Whosoever committeth sin is the slave* (Douay,—*servant*) *of sin.* Now *by whom a man is overcome, of the same also he is the slave* (2

Pet. 2. 19). Therefore whoever commits a sin, has been overcome by the devil.

Obj. 3. Further, Gregory says (*Moral.* iv, 3)[2] the sin of the devil is irreparable, because he sinned at no other's suggestion. Therefore, if any men were to sin of their own free choice and without suggestion from any other, their sin would be irremediable, which is clearly false. Therefore all the sins of men are due to the devil's suggestion.

On the contrary, It is written (*De Eccl. Dogm.* lxxxii):[3] "Not all our evil thoughts are incited by the devil; sometimes they are due to a movement of our choice."

I answer that, the devil is the occasional and indirect cause of all our sins in so far as he induced the first man to sin, by reason of whose sin human nature is so infected that we are all prone to sin, even as the burning of wood might be imputed to the man who dried the wood so as to make it easily inflammable. He is not, however, the direct cause of all the sins of men, as though each were the result of his suggestion. Origen proves this (*Peri Archon*, iii, 3)[4] from the fact that even if the devil were no more, men would still have the desire for food, sexual pleasures and the like, which desire might be inordinate, unless it were subordinate to reason, a matter that is subject to free choice.

Reply Obj. 1. The crowd of demons are the cause of all our evils as regards their original cause, as we have said.

Reply Obj. 2. A man becomes another's slave not only by being overcome by him but also by subjecting himself to him voluntarily; it is thus that one who sins of his own accord becomes the slave of the devil.

Reply Obj. 3. The devil's sin was irremediable, not only because he sinned without another's suggestion, but also because he was not already prone to sin on account of any previous sin. And this cannot be said of any sin of man.

QUESTION LXXXI
OF THE CAUSE OF SIN ON THE PART OF MAN
(In Five Articles)

WE must now consider the cause of sin on the part of man. Now, while man, like the devil, is the cause of another's sin by outward suggestion, he has a certain special manner of causing sin in another, by way of origin. Therefore we must speak about original sin, the consideration of

---

[1] Sect. 18 (PG 3, 716).

[2] PL 75, 642.

[3] Gennadius (PL 58, 999).   [4] PG 11, 305.

which will be threefold: (1) Of its transmission; (2) of its essence (Q. LXXXII); (3) of its subject (Q. LXXXIII).

Under the first head there are five points of inquiry: (1) Whether man's first sin is transmitted by way of origin to his descendants? (2) Whether all the other sins of our first parent, or of any other parents, are transmitted to their descendants by way of origin? (3) Whether original sin is contracted by all those who are begotten of Adam by way of seminal generation? (4) Whether it would be contracted by anyone formed miraculously from some part of the human body? (5) Whether original sin would have been contracted if the woman, and not the man, had sinned?

ARTICLE 1. *Whether the First Sin of Our First Parent Is Contracted by His Descendants by Way of Origin?*

We proceed thus to the First Article: It would seem that the first sin of our first parent is not contracted by others by way of origin.

Objection 1. For it is written (Ezech. 18. 20): *The son shall not bear the iniquity of the father.* But he would bear the iniquity if he contracted it from him. Therefore no one contracts any sin from one of his parents by way of origin.

Obj. 2. Further, an accident is not transmitted by way of origin, unless its subject be also transmitted, since accidents do not pass from one subject to another. Now the rational soul which is the subject of sin, is not transmitted by way of origin, as was shown in the First Part (Q. CXVIII, A. 2). Therefore neither can any sin be transmitted by way of origin.

Obj. 3. Further, whatever is transmitted by way of human origin is caused by the semen. But the semen cannot cause sin, because it lacks the rational part of the soul, which alone can be a cause of sin. Therefore no sin can be contracted by way of origin.

Obj. 4. Further, that which is more perfect in nature is more powerful in action. Now perfect flesh cannot infect the soul united to it, for otherwise the soul could not be cleansed of original sin, so long as it is united to the body. Much less, therefore, can the semen infect the soul.

Obj. 5. Further, the Philosopher says:[1] "No one finds fault with those who are ugly by nature, but only those who are so through want of exercise and through carelessness." Now those are said to be naturally ugly who are so from their origin. Therefore nothing which comes by way of origin is blameworthy or sinful.

[1] *Ethics*, III, 5 (1114ª23).

On the contrary, The Apostle says (Rom. 5. 12): *By one man sin entered into this world, and by sin death.* Nor can this be understood as denoting imitation or suggestion, since it is written (Wisd. 2. 24): *By the envy of the devil, death came into the world.* It follows therefore that through origin from the first man sin entered into the world.

I answer that, According to the Catholic Faith we are bound to hold that the first sin of the first man is transmitted to his descendants, by way of origin.[2] For this reason children are taken to be baptized soon after their birth, to show that they have to be washed from some uncleanness. The contrary is part of the Pelagian heresy, as is clear from Augustine in many of his books.[3]

In endeavouring to explain how the sin of our first parent could be transmitted by way of origin to his descendants, various writers have gone about it in various ways. For some,[4] considering that the subject of sin is the rational soul, maintained that the rational soul is transmitted with the semen, so that thus an infected soul would seem to produce other infected souls. Others,[5] rejecting this as erroneous, endeavoured to show how the guilt of the parent's soul can be transmitted to the children, even though the soul be not transmitted, from the fact that defects of the body are transmitted from parent to child; thus a leper may beget a leper, or a gouty man may be the father of a gouty son, on account of some seminal corruption, although this corruption is not leprosy or gout. Now since the body is proportioned to the soul, and since the soul's defects flow over into the body, and vice versa, in like manner, say they, a culpable defect of the soul is passed on to the child, through the transmission of the semen, although the semen itself is not the subject of guilt.

But all these explanations are insufficient. Because, granted that some bodily defects are transmitted by the way of origin from parent to child, and granted that even some defects of the soul are transmitted in consequence, on account of a defect in the bodily habit, as in the case of

[2] See the Council of Carthage, XVI, anno 418, can. 2 (MA IV, 327; cf. MA III, 811; DZ 102); Conc. Arausic, II, anno 529, can. 2 (MA VIII, 712; DZ 175).

[3] *Retract.*, I, 9 (PL 32, 598); *De Pecc. Remiss. et Bapt. Parv.*, II, 9 (PL 44, 158); *Cont. Julian.*, III, 1 (PL 44, 703); *De Dono Persev.*, II, XI (PL 45, 996; 1008).

[4] Anonymously referred to in Peter Lombard, *Sent.*, II, d. 31, chap. 2 (QR 1, 468); cf. Augustine, *Contra Julian.*, V, 4 (PL 44, 794); cf. Kors, *La Justice Primitive* (p. 21 and *passim*); cf. also DTC, art. *Péché originel* (XII. 450).

[5] Peter Lombard, *Sent.*, II, d. 31, chaps. 3–6 (QR 1, 469–472); cf. Kors, *La Justice Primitive* (p. 55); and also DTC, art. *Péché originel* (XII, 450).

idiots begetting idiots, nevertheless the fact of having a defect by the way of origin seems to exclude the notion of guilt, which is essentially something voluntary. Therefore granted that the rational soul were transmitted, from the very fact that the stain on the child's soul is not in its will, it would cease to be a guilty stain binding its subject to punishment; for, as the Philosopher says,[1] "no one reproaches a man born blind; one rather takes pity on him."

Therefore we must explain the matter otherwise by saying that all men born of Adam may be considered as one man, since they have one common nature, which they receive from their first parents;[2] even as in civil matters, all who are members of one community are reputed as one body, and the whole community as one man. Indeed Porphyry says[3] that "by sharing the same species, many men are one man." Accordingly the multitude of men born of Adam are as so many members of one body. Now the action of one member of the body, of the hand for instance, is voluntary not by the will of that hand but by the will of the soul, the first mover of the members. Hence a murder which the hand commits would not be imputed as a sin to the hand, considered by itself as apart from the body, but is imputed to it as something belonging to man and moved by man's first moving principle. In this way then, the disorder which is in this man born of Adam, is voluntary not by his will, but by the will of his first parent, who, by the movement of generation, moves all who originate from him, even as the soul's will moves all the members to their actions. Hence the sin which is thus transmitted by the first parent to his descendants is called original, just as the sin which flows from the soul into the bodily members is called actual. And just as the actual sin that is committed by a member of the body is not the sin of that member, except in so far as that member is a part of the man, for which reason it is called a human sin, so original sin is not the sin of the person, except in so far as this person receives his nature from his first parent, for which reason it is called the sin of nature, according to Eph. 2. 3: We . . . were by nature children of wrath.

Reply Obj. 1. The son is said not to bear the iniquity of his father because he is not punished for his father's sin, unless he share in his guilt. It is thus in the case before us, because guilt is transmitted by the way of origin from father to son, even as actual sin is transmitted through being imitated.

Reply Obj. 2. Although the soul is not transmitted, because the power in the semen is not able to cause the rational soul, nevertheless the motion of the semen is a disposition to the transmission of the rational soul, so that the semen by its own power transmits the human nature from parent to child, and with that nature, the stain which infects it; for he that is born is associated with his first parent in his guilt through the fact that he inherits his nature from him by a kind of movement which is that of generation.

Reply Obj. 3. Although the guilt is not actually in the semen, yet human nature is there virtually, accompanied by that guilt.

Reply Obj. 4. The semen is the principle of generation, which is an act proper to nature, by helping it to propagate itself. Hence the soul is more infected by the semen than by the flesh which is already perfect, and already determined to a certain person.

Reply Obj. 5. A man is not blamed for that which he has from his origin, if we consider the man born in himself. But if we consider him as referred to a principle, then he may be reproached for it; thus a man may from his birth be under a family disgrace, on account of a crime committed by one of his forbears.

ARTICLE 2. Whether Also Other Sins of the First Parent or of Nearer Ancestors Are Transmitted to Their Descendants?

We proceed thus to the Second Article: It would see that also other sins, whether of the first parent or of nearer ancestors, are transmitted to their descendants.

Objection 1. For punishment is never due unless for fault. Now some are punished by the judgment of God for the sin of their immediate parents, according to Exod. 20. 5: I am . . . God, . . . jealous, visiting the iniquity of the fathers upon the children, unto the third and fourth generation. Furthermore, according to human law, the children of those who are guilty of high treason are disinherited. Therefore the guilt of nearer ancestors is also transmitted to their descendants.

Obj. 2. Further, a man can better transmit to another that which he has of himself than that which he has received from another; thus fire heats better than hot water does. Now a man

---

[1] Ethics, III, 5 (1114ᵃ26).

[2] Cf. St. Augustine, passim, and especially, De Nupt. et Concupisc., II, 5 (PL 44, 444); cf. DTC, art. Péché Originel (XII, 395). See also Anselm, De Conceptu Virginali, XXIII (PL 158, 454); cf. Kors, La Justice Primitive (p. 33; p. 147); DTC, loc. cit., pp. 475–478.

[3] Isagoge, trans. of Boëthius, chap. De Specie. (PL 64, 111).

transmits to his children, by the way of origin, the sin which he has from Adam. Much more therefore should he transmit the sin which he has contracted of himself.

Obj. 3. Further, the reason why we contract original sin from our first parent is because we were in him as in the principle of our nature, which he corrupted. But we were likewise in our nearer ancestors as in principles of our nature, which however it be corrupt, can be corrupted yet more by sin, according to Apoc. 22. 11: *He that is filthy, let him be filthier still.* Therefore children contract, by the way of origin, the sins of their nearer ancestors, even as they contract the sin of their first parent.

On the contrary, Good is more self-diffusive than evil. But the merits of the nearer ancestors are not transmitted to their descendants. Much less therefore are their sins.

I answer that, Augustine puts this question in the *Enchiridion,* xlvi, xlvii,[1] and leaves it unsolved. Yet if we look into the matter carefully we shall see that it is impossible for the sins of the nearer ancestors, or even any other but the first sin of our first parent to be transmitted by the way of origin. The reason is that a man begets his like in species but not in individual. Consequently those things that pertain directly to the individual, such as personal actions and matters affecting them, are not transmitted by parents to their children; for a grammarian does not transmit to his son the knowledge of grammar that he has acquired by his own studies. On the other hand, those things that concern the nature of the species are transmitted by parents to their children, unless there be a defect of nature; thus a man with eyes begets a son having eyes, unless nature fails. And if nature be strong, even certain accidents of the individual pertaining to natural disposition, are transmitted to the children, for example fleetness of body, acuteness of intellect, and so forth; but in no way those that are purely personal, as stated above.

Now just as something may belong to the person as such, and also something through the gift of grace, so may something belong to the nature as such, namely whatever is caused by the principles of nature, and something too through the gift of grace. In this way original justice, as stated in the First Part (Q. C, A. 1), was a gift of grace, conferred by God on all human nature in our first parent. This gift the first man lost by his first sin. Therefore as that original justice together with the nature was to

have been transmitted to his posterity, so also was its disorder. Other actual sins, however, whether of the first parent or of others, do not corrupt the nature as nature, but only as the nature of that person, that is, in respect of the proneness to sin. And consequently other sins are not transmitted.

Reply Obj. 1. According to Augustine in his letter to Avitus,[2] children are never inflicted with spiritual punishment on account of their parents, unless they share in their guilt, either in their origin, or by imitation, because every soul is God's immediate property, as stated in Ezech. 18. 4. Sometimes, however, by Divine or human judgment, children receive bodily punishment on their parents' account, since the child, as to its body, is part of its father.

Reply Obj. 2. A man can more easily transmit that which he has of himself, provided it be transmissible. But the actual sins of our nearer ancestors are not transmissible, because they are purely personal, as stated above.

Reply Obj. 3. The first sin infects nature with a human corruption pertaining to nature; but other sins infect it with a corruption pertaining only to the person.

ARTICLE 3. *Whether the Sin of the First Parent Is Transmitted by the Way of Origin to All Men?*

We proceed thus to the Third Article: It would seem that the sin of the first parent is not transmitted, by the way of origin, to all men.

Objection 1. For death is a punishment consequent upon original sin. But not all those who are born of the seed of Adam will die, since those who will be still living at the coming of our Lord, will never die, as it seems from 1 Thessal. 4. 14: *We who are alive . . . unto the coming of the Lord, shall not prevent them who have slept.* Therefore they do not contract original sin.

Obj. 2. Further, no one gives another what he has not himself. Now a man who has been baptized has not original sin. Therefore he does not transmit it to his children.

Obj. 3. Further, the gift of Christ is greater than the sin of Adam, as the Apostle declares (Rom. 5. 15, *sqq.*). But the gift of Christ is not transmitted to all men. Neither, therefore, is the sin of Adam.

On the contrary, The Apostle says (Rom. 5. 12): *Death passed upon all men in whom all have sinned.*

I answer that, According to the Catholic

---

[1] PL 40, 254, 255.

[2] *Ep. ad Auxilium,* 250 (PL 33, 1066).

Faith we must firmly believe that, Christ alone excepted, all men descended from Adam contract original sin from him; otherwise all would not need redemption which is through Christ, and this is erroneous. The reason for this may be gathered from what has been stated (A. 1), namely that original sin, in virtue of the sin of our first parent, is transmitted to his posterity, just as, from the soul's will, actual sin is transmitted to the members of the body, through their being moved by the will. Now it is evident that actual sin can be transmitted to all such members as have an inborn aptitude to be moved by the will. Therefore original sin is transmitted to all those who are moved by Adam by the movement of generation.

Reply Obj. 1. It is held with greater probability and more commonly that all those that are alive at the coming of our Lord will die and rise again shortly, as we shall state more fully in the Third Part (Suppl., Q. LXXVIII, A. 1, obj. 1). If, however, it be true, as others hold, that they will never die, (an opinion which Jerome mentions among others in a letter to Minerius, on the Resurrection of the Body—*Ep.* cxix),[1] then we must say in reply to the objection, that although they are not to die, the debt of death is none the less in them, and that the punishment of death will be remitted by God, since He can also forgive the punishment due for actual sins.

Reply Obj. 2. Original sin is taken away by Baptism as to the guilt, in so far as the soul recovers grace as regards the mind. Nevertheless original sin remains in its effect as regards the "fomes," which is the disorder of the lower parts of the soul and of the body itself, in respect of which, and not of the mind, man exercises his power of generation. Consequently those who are baptized transmit original sin; for parents do not beget as being renewed in Baptism, but as still retaining something of the oldness of the first sin.

Reply Obj. 3. Just as Adam's sin is transmitted to all who are born of Adam corporally, so is the grace of Christ transmitted to all that are begotten of Him spiritually, by faith and Baptism; and this, not only as to the removal of the sin of their first parent, but also to the removal of actual sins, and the obtaining of glory.

ARTICLE 4. *Whether Original Sin Would Be Contracted by a Person Formed Miraculously from Human Flesh?*

We proceed thus to the Fourth Article: It

would seem that original sin would be contracted by a person formed miraculously from human flesh.

Objection 1. For a gloss on Gen. 4. 1 says[2] that "Adam's entire posterity was corrupted in his loins, because they were not severed from him in the place of life before he sinned, but in the place of exile after he had sinned." But if a man were to be formed in the above manner, his flesh would be severed in the place of exile. Therefore it would contract original sin.

Obj. 2. Further, original sin is caused in us by the soul being infected through the flesh. But man's flesh is entirely corrupted. Therefore a man's soul would contract the infection of original sin from whatever part of the flesh it was formed.

Obj. 3. Further, original sin comes upon all from our first parent, in so far as we were all in him when he sinned. But those who might be formed out of human flesh would have been in Adam. Therefore they would contract original sin.

On the contrary, They would not have been in Adam according to seminal principle, which alone is the cause of the transmission of original sin, as Augustine states (*Gen. ad lit.* x, 18, 20).[3]

I answer that, As stated above (AA. 1, 3), original sin is transmitted from the first parent to his posterity, in so far as they are moved by him through generation, even as the members are moved by the soul to actual sin. Now there is no movement to generation except by the active power of generation, so that those alone contract original sin who are descended from Adam through the active power of generation originally derived from Adam, that is, who are descended from him through the seminal principle; for the seminal principle is nothing else than the active power of generation. But if anyone were to be formed by God out of human flesh, it is evident that the active power would not be derived from Adam. Consequently he would not contract original sin, even as a hand would have no part in a human sin if it were moved, not by the man's will, but by some external mover.

Reply Obj. 1. Adam was not in the place of exile until after his sin. Consequently it is not on account of the place of exile, but on account of the sin, that original sin is trans-

[1] PL 22, 971.

[2] *Glossa ordin.* (I, 44F); Augustine, *De Gen. ad lit.*, IX, 4 (PL 34, 396).

[3] PL 34, 422, 424.

mitted to those to whom his active generation extends.

Reply Obj. 2. The flesh does not corrupt the soul except in so far as it is the active principle in generation, as we have stated.

Reply Obj. 3. If a man were to be formed from human flesh, he would have been in Adam by way of bodily substance, but not according to seminal principle, as stated above. Therefore he would not contract original sin.

ARTICLE 5. *Whether if Eve, and Not Adam, Had Sinned, Their Children Would Have Contracted Original Sin?*

We proceed thus to the Fifth Article: It would seem that if Eve, and not Adam, had sinned, their children would have contracted original sin.

Objection 1. Because we contract original sin from our parents, in so far as we were once in them, according to the word of the Apostle (Rom. 5. 12): *In whom all have sinned.* Now a man pre-exists in his mother as well as in his father. Therefore a man would have contracted original sin from his mother's sin as well as from his father's.

Obj. 2. Further, if Eve, and not Adam, had sinned, their children would have been born liable to suffering and death, since "it is the mother that provides the matter in generation" as the Philosopher states,[1] while death and liability to suffering are the necessary results of matter. Now liability to suffering and the necessity of dying are punishments of original sin. Therefore if Eve, and not Adam, had sinned, their children would contract original sin.

Obj. 3. Further, Damascene says (*De Fide Orthod.* iii, 2)[2] that the Holy Ghost came upon the Virgin, (of whom Christ was to be born without original sin) purifying her. But this purification would not have been necessary, if the infection of original sin were not contracted from the mother. Therefore the infection of original sin is contracted from the mother, so that if Eve had sinned, her children would have contracted original sin, even if Adam had not sinned.

On the contrary, The Apostle says (Rom. 5, 12): *By one man sin entered into this world.* Now, if the woman would have transmitted original sin to her children, he should have said that it entered by two, since both of them sinned, or rather that it entered by a woman, since she sinned first. Therefore original sin is

transmitted to the children not by the mother, but by the father.

I answer that, The solution of this question is made clear by what has been said. For it has been stated (A. 1) that original sin is transmitted by the first parent in so far as he is the mover in the begetting of his children. Therefore it has been said (A. 4) that if anyone were begotten materially only, of human flesh, they would not contract original sin. Now it is evident that in the opinion of philosophers, the active principle of generation is from the father, while the mother provides the matter.[3] Therefore original sin is contracted, not from the mother, but from the father, so that, accordingly, if Eve, and not Adam, had sinned, their children would not contract original sin. On the other hand, however, if Adam, and not Eve, had sinned, they would contract it.

Reply Obj. 1. The child pre-exists in its father as in its active principle, and in its mother as in its material and passive principle. Consequently the comparison fails.

Reply Obj. 2. Some hold that if Eve, and not Adam, had sinned, their children would be immune from the sin, but would have been subject to the necessity of dying and to other forms of suffering that are a necessary result of the matter which is provided by the mother, not as punishments, but as actual defects.[4] This, however, seems unreasonable. Because, as stated in the First Part (Q. XCVII, AA. 1, 2, REPLY 4), immortality and impassibility, in the original state, were a result, not of the condition of matter, but of original justice, by which the body was subjected to the soul, so long as the soul remained subject to God. Now privation of original justice is original sin. If, therefore, supposing Adam had not sinned, original sin would not have been transmitted to posterity on account of Eve's sin, it is evident that the children would not have been deprived of original justice; and consequently they would not have been liable to suffer and subject to the necessity of dying.

Reply Obj. 3. This prevenient purification in the Blessed Virgin was not needed to hinder the transmission of original sin, but because it was proper that the Mother of God shine with the greatest purity. For nothing is worthy to receive God unless it be pure, according to Ps. 92. 5: *Holiness becometh Thy House, O Lord.*

---

[1] *Generation of Animals,* II, 4 (738[b]20).
[2] PG 94, 985.

[3] Aristotle, *Generation of Animals,* II, 4 (738[b]20); Avicenna, *De Nat. Anim.,* IX, 1 (41 ra); IX, 3 (42 r).
[4] Albert the Great, *In Sent.,* IV, d. 1, A. 21 (BO XXIX, 37).

QUESTION LXXXII
Of original sin, as to its essence
(*In Four Articles*)

WE must now consider original sin as to its essence, and under this head there are four points of inquiry: (1) Whether original sin is a habit? (2) Whether there is but one original sin in each man? (3) Whether original sin is concupiscence? (4) Whether original sin is equally in all?

ARTICLE 1. *Whether Original Sin Is a Habit?*

We proceed thus to the First Article: It would seem that original sin is not a habit.

Objection 1. For original sin is the absence of original justice, as Anselm states (*De Concep. Virg.* ii, iii),[1] so that original sin is a privation. But privation is opposed to habit. Therefore original sin is not a habit.

Obj. 2. Further, actual sin has the nature of fault more than original sin, in so far as it is more voluntary. Now the habit of actual sin has not the nature of a fault, for otherwise it would follow that a man while asleep would be guilty of sin. Therefore no original habit has the nature of a fault.

Obj. 3. Further, in wickedness act always precedes habit, because evil habits are not infused but acquired. Now original sin is not preceded by an act. Therefore original sin not a habit.

On the contrary, Augustine says in his book on the Baptism of infants (*De Pecc. Merit. et Remiss.* i, 39)[2] that on account of original sin little children have the aptitude of concupiscence though they have not the act. Now aptitude denotes some kind of habit. Therefore original sin is a habit.

I answer that, As stated above (Q. XLIX, A. 4; Q. L, A. 1), habit is twofold. The first is a habit whereby power is inclined to an act; thus science and virtue are called habits. In this way original sin is not a habit. The second kind of habit is the disposition of a complex nature, according to which that nature is well or ill disposed to something, chiefly when such a disposition has become like a second nature, as in the case of sickness or health. In this sense original sin is a habit. For it is a disordered disposition, arising from the destruction of the harmony which was essential to original justice, even as bodily sickness is a disordered disposition of

the body, by reason of the destruction of that equilibrium which is essential to health. Hence it is that original sin is called the "languor of nature."[3]

Reply Obj. 1. As bodily sickness is partly a privation, in so far as it denotes the destruction of the equilibrium of health, and partly something positive, namely the very humours that are disposed in a disordered way, so too original sin denotes the privation of original justice, and besides this, the disordered disposition of the parts of the soul. Consequently it is not a pure privation, but a corrupt habit.

Reply Obj. 2. Actual sin is a lack of order in an act. But original sin, being the sin of nature, is an inordinate disposition of nature, and has the character of fault through being transmitted from our first parent, as stated above (Q. LXXXI, A. 1). Now this inordinate disposition of nature is a kind of habit, while the inordinate disposition of an act is not, and for this reason original sin can be a habit, although actual sin cannot.

Reply Obj. 3. This objection considers the habit which inclines a power to an act. But original sin is not this kind of habit. Nevertheless a certain disposition to an inordinate act does follow from original sin, not directly, but indirectly, namely by the removal of the obstacle, that is, original justice, which hindered inordinate movements; just as disposition to inordinate bodily movements results indirectly from bodily sickness. Nor is it necessary to say that original sin is a habit infused, or a habit acquired (except by the act of our first parent, but not by our own act); but it is a habit inborn due to our corrupt origin.

ARTICLE 2. *Whether There Are Several Original Sins in One Man?*

We proceed thus to the Second Article: It would seem that there are many original sins in one man.

Objection 1. For it is written (Ps. 50. 7): *Behold I was conceived in iniquities, and in sins did my mother conceive me.* But the sin in which a man is conceived is original sin. Therefore there are several original sins in man.

Obj. 2. Further, one and the same habit does not include its subject to contraries, since the inclination of habit is like that of nature which tends to one thing. Now original sin, even in one man, inclines to various and contrary sins. Therefore original sin is not one habit, but several.

---

[1] PL 158, 434, 435.

[2] PL 44, 150; cf. Peter Lombard, *Sent.*, II, d. 30, chap. 6 (QR 1, 465).

[3] Cf. Peter Lombard, *Sent.*, II, d. 30, chap. 8 (QR 1, 464).

Obj. 3. Further original sin infects every part of the soul. Now the different parts of the soul are different subjects of sin, as shown above (Q. LXXIV). Since then one sin cannot be in different subjects, it seems that original sin is not one but several.

On the contrary, It is written (John 1. 29): *Behold the Lamb of God, behold Him Who taketh away the sin of the world;* and the reason for the employment of the singular is that the *sin of the world,* which is original sin, is one, as a gloss expounds this passage.[1]

I answer that, In one man there is one original sin. Two reasons may be assigned for this. The first is on the part of the cause of original sin. For it has been stated (Q. LXXXI, A. 2) that the first sin alone of our first parent was transmitted to his posterity. Therefore in one man original sin is one in number; and in all men, it is one in proportion, that is, in relation to its first principle. The second reason may be taken from the very essence of original sin. Because in every inordinate disposition unity of species depends on the cause, while the unity of number is derived from the subject. For example, take bodily sickness. Various species of sickness proceed from different causes, for example from excessive heat or cold, or from a lesion in the lung or liver; while one specific sickness in one man will be one in number. Now the cause of this corrupt disposition that is called original sin, is one only, namely the privation of original justice, removing the subjection of man's mind to God. Consequently original sin is specifically one, and in one man can be only one in number; in different men, however, it is one in species and in proportion, but is numerically many.

Reply Obj. 1. The employment of the plural, —*in sins,* may be explained by the custom of the Divine Scriptures in the frequent use of the plural for the singular, for example, *They are dead that sought the life of the child;* or by the fact that all actual sins virtually pre-exist in original sin, as in a principle, so that it is virtually many; or by the fact of there being many deformities in the sin of our first parent, namely pride, disobedience, gluttony, and so forth; or by several parts of the soul being infected by original sin.

Reply Obj. 2. Of itself and directly, that is, by its own form, one habit cannot incline its subject to contraries. But there is no reason why it should not do so, indirectly and accidentally, that is, by the removal of an obstacle;

[1] *Glossa ordin.* (v, 189F).

thus, when the harmony of a mixed body is destroyed, the elements have tendencies to contrary places. In like manner, when the harmony of original justice is destroyed, the various powers of the soul have various opposite tendencies.

Reply Obj. 3. Original sin infects the different parts of the soul in so far as they are the parts of one whole, even as original justice held all the soul's parts together in one. Consequently there is but one original sin, just as there is but one fever in one man, although the various parts of the body are affected.

ARTICLE 3. *Whether Original Sin Is Concupiscence?*

We proceed thus to the Third Article: It would seem that original sin is not concupiscence.

Objection 1. For every sin is contrary to nature, according to Damascene (*De Fide Orthod.* ii, 4, 30).[2] But concupiscence is in accordance with nature, since it is the proper act of the concupiscible power, which is a natural power. Therefore concupiscence is not original sin.

Obj. 2. Further, through original sin *the passions of sins* are in us, according to the Apostle (Rom. 7. 5). Now there are several other passions besides concupiscence, as stated above (Q. XXIII, A. 4). Therefore original sin is not concupiscence any more than another passion.

Obj. 3. Further, by original sin, all the parts of the soul are disordered, as stated above (A. 2). But the intellect is the highest of the soul's parts, as the Philosopher states.[3] Therefore original sin is ignorance rather than concupiscence.

On the contrary, Augustine says (*Retract.* i, 15):[4] "Concupiscence is the guilt of original sin."

I answer that, Everything takes its species from its form, and it has been stated (A. 2) that the species of original sin is taken from its cause. Consequently the formal element of original sin must be considered in respect of the cause of original sin. But contraries have contrary causes. Therefore the cause of original sin must be considered with respect to the cause of original justice, which is opposed to it. Now the whole order of original justice consists in man's will being subject to God, which subjection, first and chiefly, was in the will, whose function it is to move all the other parts to the end, as stated

[2] PG 94, 876, 976; also IV, 20 (PG 94, 1196).
[3] *Ethics,* X, 7 (1177ᵃ20).
[4] PL 32, 608; cf. *De Pecc. Remiss et Bapt. Parv.,* I, 29 (PL 44, 142); *De Nupt. et Concupisc.,* I, 25 (PL 44, 430).

above (Q. IX, A. I), so that the will being turned away from God, all the other powers of the soul become disordered. Accordingly the privation of original justice, by which the will was made subject to God, is the formal element in original sin, while every other disorder of the soul's powers is a kind of material element in respect of original sin. Now the lack of order of the other powers of the soul consists chiefly in their turning inordinately to changeable good, which lack of order may be called by the general name of concupiscence. Hence original sin is concupiscence, materially, but privation of original justice, formally.

Reply Obj. 1. Since, in man, the concupiscible power is naturally governed by reason, the act of concupiscence is so far natural to man as it is in accord with the order of reason; while, in so far as it trespasses beyond the bounds of reason, it is, for a man, contrary to reason. Such is the concupiscence of original sin.

Reply Obj. 2. As stated above (Q. XXV, A. I), all the irascible passions are reducible to concupiscible passions, as holding the principal place; and of these, concupiscence is the most impetuous in moving, and is felt most, as stated above (*ibid.*, A. 2, REPLY I). Therefore original sin is ascribed to concupiscence, as being the chief passion, and as in a fashion including all the others.

Reply Obj. 3. As in good things the intellect and reason stand first, so conversely in evil things the lower part of the soul is found to take precedence, for it clouds and draws the reason, as stated above (Q. LXXVII, AA. I, 2; Q. LXXX, A. 2). Hence original sin is called concupiscence rather than ignorance,[1] although ignorance is comprised among the material defects of original sin.

ARTICLE 4. *Whether Original Sin Is Equally in All?*

We proceed thus to the Fourth Article: It would seem that original sin is not equally in all.

Objection 1. Because original sin is inordinate concupiscence, as stated above (A. 3). Now all are not equally prone to acts of concupiscence. Therefore original sin is not equally in all.

Obj. 2. Further, original sin is an inordinate disposition of the soul, just as sickness is an inordinate disposition of the body. But sickness

is subject to degrees. Therefore original sin is subject to degrees.

Obj. 3. Further, Augustine says (*De Nup. et Concup.* i, 23, 24)[2] that "lust transmits original sin to the child." But the act of generation may be more lustful in one than in another. Therefore original sin may be greater in one than in another.

On the contrary, Original sin is the sin of nature, as stated above (Q. LXXXI, A. I). But nature is equally in all. Therefore original sin is too.

I answer that, There are two things in original sin. One is the privation of original justice, the other is the relation of this privation to the sin of our first parent, from whom it is transmitted to man through his corrupt origin. As to the first, original sin has no degrees, since the gift of original justice is taken away entirely; and privations that remove something entirely, such as death and darkness, cannot be more or less, as stated above (Q. LXXIII, A. 2). In like manner, neither is this possible as to the second, since all are related equally to the first principle of our corrupt origin, from which principle original sin takes the nature of guilt; for relations cannot be more or less. Consequently it is evident that original sin cannot be more in one than in another.

Reply Obj. 1. Through the bond of original justice being broken, which held together all the powers of the soul in a certain order, each power of the soul tends to its own proper movement, and the more impetuously as it is stronger. Now it happens that some of the soul's powers are stronger in one man than in another, on account of the different bodily temperaments. Consequently if one man is more prone than another to acts of concupiscence, this is not due to original sin, because the bond of original justice is equally broken in all, and the lower parts of the soul are, in all, left to themselves equally; but it is due to the various dispositions of the powers, as stated.

Reply Obj. 2. Sickness of the body, even sickness of the same species, has not an equal cause in all; for instance if a fever be caused by corruption of the bile, the corruption may be greater or lesser, and nearer to, or further from a vital principle. But the cause of original sin is equal in all, so that there is no comparison.

Reply Obj. 3. It is not the actual lust that transmits original sin, for supposing God were to grant to a man to feel no inordinate lust in

---

[1] Cf. Peter Lombard, *Sent.*, II, d. 30, chap. 8 (QR I, 464); cf. also Hugh of St. Victor, *De Sacram.*, I, pt. VII, chap. 26 (PL 176, 298). See also Lottin, RT (1932) pp. 635-641.

[2] PL 44, 428, 429; cf. Fulgentius, *De Fide*, II (PL 65, 679).

the act of generation, he would still transmit original sin. We must understand this to be habitual lust, according to which the sensitive appetite is not kept subject to reason by the bonds of original justice. This lust is equally in all.

QUESTION LXXXIII
OF THE SUBJECT OF ORIGINAL SIN
(*In Four Articles*)

WE must now consider the subject of original sin, under which head there are four points of inquiry: (1) Whether the subject of original sin is the flesh rather than the soul? (2) If it be the soul, whether this be through its essence or through its powers? (3) Whether the will prior to the other powers is the subject of original sin? (4) Whether certain powers of the soul are specially infected, namely the generative power, the concupiscence part, and the sense of touch?

ARTICLE 1. *Whether Original Sin Is More in the Flesh than in the Soul?*

We proceed thus to the First Article: It would seem that original sin is more in the flesh than in the soul.

Objection 1. For the rebellion of the flesh against the mind arises from the corruption of original sin. Now the root of this rebellion is seated in the flesh, for the Apostle says (Rom. 7. 23): *I see another law in my members fighting against the law of my mind.* Therefore original sin is seated chiefly in the flesh.

Obj. 2. Further, a thing is more in its cause than in its effect; thus heat is in the heating fire more than in the hot water. Now the soul is infected with the corruption of original sin by the carnal semen. Therefore original sin is in the flesh rather than in the soul.

Obj. 3. Further, we contract original sin from our first parent in so far as we were in him by reason of seminal principle. Now our souls were not in him thus, but only our flesh. Therefore original sin is not in the soul, but in the flesh.

Obj. 4. Further, the rational soul created by God is infused into the body. If therefore the soul were infected with original sin, it would follow that it is corrupted in its creation or infusion; and thus God would be the cause of sin, since He is the author of the soul's creation and infusion.

Obj. 5. Further, no wise man pours a precious liquid into a vessel knowing that the vessel will corrupt the liquid. But the rational soul

is more precious than any liquid. If therefore the soul, by being united with the body, could be corrupted with the infection of original sin, God, Who is wisdom itself, would never infuse the soul into such a body. But He does infuse the soul into the body. Therefore it is not corrupted by the flesh. Therefore original sin is not in the soul but in the flesh.

On the contrary, The subject of a virtue and of the vice or sin contrary to that virtue is the same. But the flesh cannot be the subject of virtue. For the Apostle says (Rom. 7. 18): *I know that there dwelleth not in me, that is to say, in my flesh, that which is good.* Therefore the flesh cannot be the subject of original sin, but only the soul.

I answer that, One thing can be in another in two ways. First, as in its cause, either principal, or instrumental; secondly, as in its subject. Accordingly the original sin of all men was in Adam indeed, as in its principal cause, according to the words of the Apostle (Rom. 5. 12): *In whom all have sinned.* But it is in the bodily semen as in its instrumental cause, since it is by the active power of the semen that original sin together with human nature is transmitted to the child. But original sin can in no way be in the flesh as its subject, but only in the soul.

The reason for this is that, as stated above (Q. LXXXI, A. 1), original sin is transmitted from the will of our first parent to his posterity by a certain movement of generation, in the same way as actual sin is transmitted from any man's will to his other parts. Now in this transmission it is to be observed that whatever accrues from the motion of the will consenting to sin, to any part of man that can in any way share in that guilt, either as its subject or as its instrument, has the character of sin. Thus from the will consenting to gluttony, concupiscence of food accrues to the concupiscible faculty, and partaking of food accrues to the hand and the mouth, which, in so far as they are moved by the will to sin, are the instruments of sin. But that further action is evoked in the nutritive power and the internal members, which have no natural aptitude for being moved by the will, does not bear the character of guilt.

Accordingly, since the soul can be the subject of guilt, while the flesh, of itself, cannot be the subject of guilt, whatever accrues to the soul from the corruption of the first sin has the character of guilt, while whatever accrues to the flesh has the character not of guilt but of punishment, so that, therefore, the soul is the subject of original sin, and not the flesh.

Reply Obj. 1. As Augustine says (*Retract.* i, 26),[1] the Apostle is speaking, in that passage, of man already redeemed, who is delivered from guilt but is still liable to punishment, by reason of which sin is stated to dwell *in the flesh.* Consequently it follows that the flesh is the subject not of guilt but of punishment.

Reply Obj. 2. Original sin is caused by the semen as instrumental cause. Now there is no need for anything to be more in the instrumental cause than in the effect, but only in the principal cause; and, in this way original sin was in Adam more fully, since in him it had the nature of actual sin.

Reply Obj. 3. The soul of any individual man was in Adam in respect of his seminal principle, not indeed as in its effective principle, but as in a pre-disposing principle. Because the bodily semen, which is transmitted from Adam, does not of its own power produce the rational soul, but disposes the matter for it.

Reply Obj. 4. The corruption of original sin is in no way caused by God, but by the sin alone of our first parent through carnal generation. And so, since creation implies a relation in the soul to God alone, it cannot be said that the soul is tainted through being created. On the other hand, infusion implies relation both to God infusing and to the flesh into which the soul is infused. And so, with regard to God infusing, it cannot be said that the soul is stained through being infused, but only with regard to the body into which it is infused.

Reply Obj. 5. The common good takes precedence of private good. Therefore God, according to His wisdom, does not set aside the universal order of things, (which is that such a soul be infused into such a body), in order to prevent the particular corruption of this soul; all the more so, seeing that the nature of the soul demands that it should not exist prior to its infusion into the body, as stated in the First Part (Q. XC, A. 4; Q. CXVIII, A. 3). And it is better for the soul to be thus, according to its nature, than not to be at all, especially since it can avoid damnation by means of grace.

ARTICLE 2. *Whether Original Sin Is in the Essence of the Soul Rather than in the Powers?*

We proceed thus to the Second Article: It would seem that original sin is not in the essence of the soul rather than in the powers.

Objection 1. For the soul is naturally apt to be the subject of sin in respect of those parts which can be moved by the will. Now the soul is

[1] PL 32, 629.

not moved by the will as to its essence but only as to the powers. Therefore original sin is in the soul, not according to its essence, but only according to the powers.

Obj. 2. Further, original sin is opposed to original justice. Now original justice was in a power of the soul, because power is the subject of virtue. Therefore original sin also is in a power of the soul rather than in its essence.

Obj. 3. Further, just as original sin is derived by the soul from the flesh, so is it derived by the powers from the essence. But original sin is more in the soul than in the flesh. Therefore it is more in the powers than in the essence of the soul.

Obj. 4. Further, original sin is said to be concupiscence, as stated (Q. LXXXII, A. 3). But concupiscence is in the powers of the soul. Therefore original sin is also.

On the contrary, Original sin is called the sin of nature, as stated above (Q. LXXXI, A. 1). Now the soul is the form and nature of the body in respect of its essence, and not in respect of its powers, as stated in the First Part (Q. LXXVI, A. 6). Therefore the soul is the subject of original sin chiefly in respect of its essence.

I answer that, The subject of a sin is chiefly that part of the soul to which the moving cause of that sin primarily pertains; thus if the moving cause of a sin is sensual pleasure, which pertains to the concupiscible power through being its proper object, it follows that the concupiscible power is the proper subject of that sin. Now it is evident that original sin is caused through our origin. Consequently that part of the soul which is first reached by man's origin is the primary subject of original sin. Now the origin reaches the soul as the term of generation according as it is the form of the body; and this belongs to the soul in respect of its own essence, as was proved in the First Part (Q. LXXVI, A. 6). Therefore the soul, in respect of its essence, is the primary subject of original sin.

Reply Obj. 1. As the motion of the will of an individual reaches to the soul's powers and not to its essence, so the motion of the will of the first generator, through the channel of generation, reaches first of all to the essence of the soul, as stated.

Reply Obj. 2. Even original justice pertained primordially to the essence of the soul, because it was God's gift to human nature, to which the essence of the soul is related before the powers. For the powers seem rather to regard the person, in so far as they are the principles of personal acts. Hence they are the proper subjects of actual sins, which are the sins of the person.

Reply Obj. 3. The body is related to the soul as matter to form, which though it comes after in order of generation nevertheless comes first in the order of perfection and nature. But the essence of the soul is related to the powers as a subject to its proper accidents, which follow their subject both in the order of generation and in that of perfection. Consequently the comparison fails.

Reply Obj. 4. Concupiscence, in relation to original sin, holds the position of matter and effect, as stated above (Q. LXXXII, A. 3).

ARTICLE 3. *Whether Original Sin Infects the Will Before the Other Powers?*

We proceed thus to the Third Article: It would seem that original sin does not infect the will before the other powers.

Objection 1. For every sin belongs chiefly to that power by whose act it was caused. Now original sin is caused by an act of the generative power. Therefore it seems to belong to the generative power more than to the others.

Obj. 2. Further, original sin is transmitted through the carnal semen. But the other powers of the soul are more akin to the flesh than the will is, as is evident with regard to all the sensitive powers, which use a bodily organ. Therefore original sin is in them more than in the will.

Obj. 3. Further, the intellect precedes the will, for the object of the will is only the good understood. If therefore original sin infects all the powers of the soul, it seems that it must first of all infect the intellect, as preceding the others.

On the contrary, Original justice has a prior relation to the will, because it is "rectitude of the will," as Anselm states (*De Concep. Virg.* iii).[1] Therefore original sin, which is opposed to it, also has a prior relation to the will.

I answer that, Two things must be considered in the infection of original sin. First, its inherence to its subject; and in this respect it regards first the essence of the soul, as stated above (A. 2). In the second place we must consider its inclination to act; and in this way it regards the powers of the soul. It must therefore regard first of all that power in which is seated the first inclination to commit a sin, and this is the will, as stated above (Q. LXXIV, AA. 1, 2). Therefore original sin regards first of all the will.

Reply Obj. 1. Original sin, in man, is not caused by the generative power of the child, but by the act of the parental generative power. Consequently it does not follow that the child's generative power is the subject of original sin.

Reply Obj. 2. Original sin spreads in two ways: from the flesh to the soul, and from the essence of the soul to the powers. The former follows the order of generation, the latter follows the order of perfection. Therefore, although the other, namely the sensitive powers, are more akin to the flesh, yet, since the will, being the higher power, is more akin to the essence of the soul, the infection of original sin reaches it first.

Reply Obj. 3. The intellect precedes the will in one way, by proposing its object to it. In another way the will precedes the intellect, in the order of motion to act, which motion pertains to sin.

ARTICLE 4. *Whether the Powers Mentioned Above Are More Infected Than the Others?*

We proceed thus to the Fourth Article: It would seem that the powers mentioned above are not more infected than the others.

Objection 1. For the infection of original sin seems to pertain more to that part of the soul which can be first the subject of sin. Now this is the rational part, and chiefly the will. Therefore that power is most infected by original sin.

Obj. 2. Further, no power of the soul is infected by guilt except in so far as it can obey reason. Now the generative power cannot obey reason, as stated in the *Ethics.*[2] Therefore the generative power is not the most infected by original sin.

Obj. 3. Further, of all the senses the sight is the most spiritual and the nearest to reason, in so far as "it shows us how a number of things differ."[3] But the infection of guilt is first of all in the reason. Therefore the sight is more infected than touch.

On the contrary, Augustine says[4] that "the infection of original sin is most apparent in the movements of the members of generation, which are not subject to reason." Now those members serve the generative power in the mingling of sexes, in which there is the pleasure of touch, which is the most powerful incentive to concupiscence. Therefore the infection of original sin regards these three chiefly, namely the generative power, the concupiscible power and the sense of touch.

I answer that, Those corruptions especially are said to be infectious which are of such a nature as to be transmitted from one subject to

---

[1] PL 158, 436.

[2] Aristotle, I, 13 (1102b29).
[3] Aristotle, *Metaphysics,* I, 1 (980a27).
[4] *City of God,* XIV, 20 (PL 41, 428).

another; hence contagious diseases, such as leprosy and mange and the like, are said to be infectious. Now the corruption of original sin is transmitted by the act of generation, as stated above (Q. LXXXI, A. I). Therefore the powers which concur in this act are chiefly said to be infected. Now this act serves the generative power, in so far as it is directed to generation; and it includes pleasure of the touch, which is the most powerful object of the concupiscible power. Consequently, while all the parts of the soul are said to be corrupted by original sin, these three are said specially to be corrupted and infected.

Reply Obj. 1. Original sin, in so far as it inclines to actual sins, belongs chiefly to the will, as stated above (A. 3). But in so far as it is transmitted to the offspring, it belongs to the aforesaid powers proximately, and to the will, remotely.

Reply Obj. 2. The infection of actual sin belongs only to the powers which are moved by the will of the sinner. But the infection of original sin is not derived from the will of him who contracts it, but through his natural origin, which is effected by the generative power. Hence it is this power that is infected by original sin.

Reply Obj. 3. Sight is not related to the act of generation except in respect of remote disposition, in so far as the concupiscible likeness is seen through the sight. But the pleasure is completed in the touch. Therefore this infection is ascribed to the touch rather than to the sight.

QUESTION LXXXIV

OF THE CAUSE OF SIN, IN RESPECT OF ONE SIN BEING THE CAUSE OF ANOTHER

(In Four Articles)

WE must now consider the cause of sin, in so far as one sin can be the cause of another. Under this head there are four points of inquiry: (1) Whether covetousness is the root of all sins? (2) Whether pride is the beginning of every sin? (3) Whether other special sins should be called capital vices, besides pride and covetousness? (4) How many capital vices there are, and which are they?

ARTICLE 1. *Whether Covetousness Is the Root of All Sins?*

We proceed thus to the First Article: It would seem that covetousness is not the root of all sins.

Objection 1. For covetousness, which is immoderate desire for riches, is opposed to the virtue of liberality. But liberality is not the root of all virtues. Therefore covetousness is not the root of all sins.

Obj. 2. Further, the desire for the means proceeds from desire for the end. Now riches, the desire for which is called covetousness, are not desired except as being useful for some end, as stated in the *Ethics*.[1] Therefore covetousness is not the root of all sins, but proceeds from some deeper root.

Obj. 3. Further, it often happens that avarice, which is another name for covetousness, arises from other sins; as when a man desires money through ambition, or in order to sate his gluttony. Therefore it is not the root of all sins.

On the contrary, The Apostle says (I Tim. 6. 10): *The desire of money is the root of all evil.*

I answer that, According to some,[2] covetousness may be understood in different ways. First, as denoting inordinate desire for riches, and thus it is a special sin. Secondly, as denoting inordinate desire for any temporal good; and thus it is a genus comprising all sins, because every sin includes an inordinate turning to a changeable good, as stated above (Q. LXXII, A. 2). Thirdly, as denoting an inclination of a corrupt nature to desire corruptible goods inordinately; and they say that in this sense covetousness is the root of all sins, comparing it to the root of a tree, which draws its sustenance from earth, just as every sin grows out of the love of temporal things.[3]

Now, though all this is true, it does not seem to explain the mind of the Apostle when he states that covetousness is the root of all sins. For in that passage he clearly speaks against those who, because they *will become rich, fall into temptation, and into the snare of the devil . . . for covetousness is the root of all evils.* Hence it is evident that he is speaking of covetousness as denoting the inordinate desire for riches. Accordingly, we must say that covetousness, as denoting a special sin, is called the root of all sins, in likeness to the root of a tree, in furnishing sustenance to the whole tree. For we see that by riches man acquires the means of committing any sin whatever, and of sating his desire for any sin whatever, since money helps man to obtain all manner of temporal goods, according to Eccles. 10. 19: *All things obey money.* So that in this sense desire for riches is the root of all sins.

Reply Obj. 1. Virtue and sin do not arise from the same source. For sin arises from the desire

---

[1] Aristotle, I, 5 (1096ª7).

[2] Cf. Albert, *In Sent.*, II, d. 42, A. 8 (BO XXVII, 668).

[3] Cf. Albert, *Ibid.;* also Peter Lombard, *Sent.*, II, d. 42, chap. 8 (QR I, 532).

of changeable good; and consequently the desire of that good which helps one to obtain all temporal goods, is called the root of all sins. But virtue arises from the desire for the immutable Good; and consequently charity, which is the love of God, is called the root of the virtues, according to Eph. 3. 17: *Rooted and founded in charity.*

Reply Obj. 2. The desire of money is said to be the root of sins, not as though riches were sought for their own sake, as being the last end, but because they are much sought after as useful for any temporal end. And since a universal good is more desirable than a particular good, they move the appetite more than any individual goods, which along with many others can be procured by means of money.

Reply Obj. 3. Just as in natural things we do not ask what always happens, but what happens most frequently, for the reason that the nature of corruptible things can be hindered, so as not always to act in the same way; so also in moral matters we consider what happens in the majority of cases, not what happens invariably, for the reason that the will does not act of necessity. So when we say that covetousness is the root of all evils, we do not assert that no other evil can be its root, but that other evils more frequently arise from it, for the reason given.

ARTICLE 2. *Whether Pride Is the Beginning of Every Sin?*

We proceed thus to the Second Article: It would seem that pride is not the beginning of every sin.

Objection 1. For the root is a beginning of a tree, so that the beginning of a sin seems to be the same as the root of sin. Now covetousness is the root of every sin, as stated above (A. 1). Therefore it is also the beginning of every sin, and not pride.

Obj. 2. Further, it is written (Ecclus. 10. 14): *The beginning of the pride of man is apostasy* (Douay,—*to fall off*) *from God.* But apostasy from God is a sin. Therefore another sin is the beginning of pride, so that the latter is not the beginning of every sin.

Obj. 3. Further, the beginning of every sin would seem to be that which causes all sins. Now this is inordinate self-love, which, according to Augustine,[1] "builds up the city of Babylon." Therefore self-love, and not pride, is the beginning of every sin.

On the contrary, It is written (Ecclus. 10.

15): *Pride is the beginning of all sin.*

I answer that, Some say pride is to be taken in three ways.[2] First, as denoting inordinate desire to excel; and thus it is a special sin. Secondly, as denoting actual contempt of God, to the effect of not being subject to His commandment; and thus, they say, it is a general sin. Thirdly, as denoting an inclination to this contempt, owing to the corruption of nature; and in this sense they say that it is the beginning of every sin, and that it differs from covetousness, because covetousness regards sin as turning towards the changeable good by which sin is, as it were, nourished and fostered, for which reason covetousness is called the "root"; pride however regards sin as turning away from God, to Whose commandment man refuses to be subject, for which reason it is called the "beginning," because the beginning of evil consists in turning away from God.

Now though all this is true, but nevertheless it does not explain the mind of the wise man who said (*loc. cit.*): *Pride is the beginning of all sin.* For it is evident that he is speaking of pride as denoting inordinate desire to excel, as is clear from what follows (*verse* 17): *God hath overturned the thrones of proud princes;* indeed this is the point of nearly the whole chapter. We must therefore say that pride, even as denoting a special sin, is the beginning of every sin. For we must take note that, in voluntary actions, such as sins, there is a twofold order, of intention, and of execution. In the former order, the principle is the end, as we have stated many times before (Q. I, A. 1; Reply 1; Q. XVIII, A. 7, Reply 2; Q. XXV, A. 2). Now man's end in acquiring all temporal goods is that, through their means, he may have some perfection and excellence. Therefore, from this point of view, pride, which is the desire to excel, is said to be the *beginning* of every sin. On the other hand, in the order of execution, the first place belongs to that which by furnishing the opportunity of fulfilling all desires of sin, has the character of a root, and such are riches; so that, from this point of view, covetousness is said to be the *root* of all evils, as stated above (A. 1).

This suffices for the *Reply to the First Objection.*

Reply Obj. 2. Apostasy from God is stated to be the beginning of pride in so far as it denotes a turning away from God, because from the fact that man wishes not to be subject to God it follows that he desires inordinately his own excellence in temporal things. Therefore, in the pas-

---

[1] *City of God,* XIV, 28 (PL 41, 436); cf. *Enarr. in Ps.,* Ps. 64.1 (PL 36, 773).

[2] Cf. Albert, *In Sent.,* II, d. 42, A. 8 (BO XXVII, 668).

sage quoted, apostasy from God does not denote the special sin, but rather that general condition of every sin, consisting in its turning away from unchangeable good. It may also be said that apostasy from God is said to be the beginning of pride because it is the first species of pride. For it is characteristic of pride to be unwilling to be subject to any superior, and especially to God, the result being that a man is unduly lifted up, in respect of the other species of pride.

Reply Obj. 3. In desiring to excel, man loves himself, for to love oneself is the same as to desire some good for oneself. Consequently it amounts to the same whether we put pride or self-love as the beginning of every evil.

ARTICLE 3. *Whether Any Other Special Sins, Besides Pride and Avarice Should Be Called Capital?*

We proceed thus to the Third Article: It would seem that no other special sins, besides pride and avarice, should be called capital.

Objection 1. For "the head seems to be to an animal what the root is to a plant," as stated in the treatise on the *Soul*,[1] because the roots are like a mouth. If therefore covetousness is called the *root of all evils,* it seems that it alone, and no other sin, should be called a capital vice.

Obj. 2. Further, the head bears a certain relation of order to the other members, in so far as sensation and movement follow from the head. But sin implies privation of order. Therefore sin has not the character of head, so that no sins should be called capital.

Obj. 3. Further, capital crimes are those which receive capital punishment. But every kind of sin comprises some that are punished thus. Therefore the capital sins are not certain specific sins.

On the contrary, Gregory (*Moral.* xxxi, 45)[2] enumerates certain special vices under the name of capital.

I answer that, The word capital is derived from *caput* (a head). Now the head, properly speaking, is that part of an animal's body which is the principle and director of the whole animal. Hence, metaphorically speaking, every directing principle is called a head, and even men who direct and govern others are called heads. Accordingly a capital vice is so called, in the first place, from head taken in the proper sense, and thus the name capital is given to a sin for which capital punishment is inflicted. It is not in this sense that we are now speaking of capi-

tal sins, but in another sense, in which the term capital is derived from head, taken metaphorically for a principle or director of others. In this way a capital vice is one from which other vices arise, chiefly by being their final cause, which origin is formal, as stated above (Q. LXXII, A. 6). Therefore a capital vice is not only the principle of others, but is also their director and, in a way, their leader; because the art or habit, to which the end belongs, is always the principle and the commander in matters concerning the means. Hence Gregory (*Moral.* xxxi, 45)[3] compares these capital vices to the "leaders of an army."

Reply Obj. 1. The term capital is taken from *caput* and applied to something connected with, or partaking of the head, as having some property of the head, but not as being the head taken literally. And therefore the capital vices are not only those which have the character of primary origin, as covetousness which is called the root, and pride which is called the beginning, but also those which have the character of proximate origin in respect of several sins.

• *Reply Obj.* 2. Sin lacks order in so far as it turns away from God, for in this respect it is an evil, and evil, according to Augustine (*De Natura Boni*, iv),[4] is "the privation of mode, species and order." But in so far as sin implies a turning to something, it regards some good. Therefore, in this respect, there can be order in sin.

Reply Obj. 3. This objection considers capital sin as so called from the punishment it deserves, in which sense we are not taking it here.

ARTICLE 4. *Whether the Seven Capital Vices Are Suitably Enumerated?*

We proceed thus to the Fourth Article: It would seem that we ought not to enumerate seven capital vices, namely vainglory, envy, anger, covetousness, sadness (*tristitia*), gluttony, lust.

Objection 1. For sins are opposed to virtues. But there are four principal virtues, as stated above (Q. LXI, A. 2). Therefore there are only four principal or capital vices.

Obj. 2. Further, the passions of the soul are causes of sin, as stated above (Q. LXXVII). But there are four principal passions of the soul, two of which, namely hope and fear, are not mentioned among the above sins, while certain vices are mentioned to which pleasure and sadness belong, since pleasure belongs to gluttony and lust, and sadness to acedia and envy. There-

---

[1] Aristotle, II, 4 (416ᵃ4).
[2] PL 76, 621.

[3] PL 76, 620.　　　[4] PL 42, 553.

fore the principal sins are unfittingly enumerated.

Obj. 3. Further, anger is not a principal passion. Therefore it should not be placed among the principal vices.

Obj. 4. Further, just as covetousness or avarice is the root of sin, so is pride the beginning of sin, as stated above (A. 2). But avarice is put as one of the capital vices. Therefore pride also should be placed among the capital vices.

Obj. 5. Further, some sins are committed which cannot be caused through any of these; as for instance when one sins through ignorance, or when one commits a sin with a good intention, for example steals in order to give an alms. Therefore the capital vices are insufficiently enumerated.

On the contrary stands the authority of Gregory who enumerates them in this way (*Moral.* xxxi, 45).[1]

I answer that, As stated above (A. 3), the capital vices are those which give rise to others, especially by way of final cause. Now this kind of origin may take place in two ways. First, on account of the condition of the sinner, who is disposed so as to have a strong inclination for one particular end, the result being that he frequently goes forward to other sins. But this kind of origin does not come under the consideration of art, because man's particular dispositions are infinite in number. Secondly, on account of a natural relationship of the ends to one another. And it is in this way that most frequently one vice arises from another, so that this kind of origin can come under the consideration of art.

Accordingly therefore, those vices are called capital whose ends have certain fundamental reasons for moving the appetite; and it is in respect of these fundamental reasons that the capital vices are differentiated. Now a thing moves the appetite in two ways. First, directly and of its very nature; thus good moves the appetite to seek it, while evil, for the same reason, moves the appetite to avoid it. Secondly, indirectly and on account of something else, as it were; thus one seeks an evil on account of some attendant good, or avoids a good on account of some attendant evil.

Again, man's good is threefold. For, in the first place, there is a certain good of the soul, which derives its aspect of desirability merely through being apprehended, namely the excellence of honour and praise, and this good is sought inordinately by vainglory. Secondly, there is the good of the body, and this regards either the preservation of the individual, for example meat and drink, which good is pursued inordinately by gluttony, or the preservation of the species, for example, sexual intercourse, which good is sought inordinately by lust. Thirdly, there is external good, namely riches, to which covetousness is referred. These same four vices avoid inordinately the contrary evils.

Or again, good moves the appetite chiefly through possessing some property of happiness, which all men seek naturally. Now in the first place happiness implies perfection, since happiness is a perfect good, to which belongs excellence or renown, which is desired by pride or vainglory. Secondly, it implies satiety, which covetousness seeks in the promise of riches. Thirdly, it implies pleasure, without which happiness is impossible, as stated in the *Ethics*,[2] and this gluttony and lust pursue.

On the other hand, avoidance of good on account of an attendant evil occurs in two ways. For this happens either in respect of one's own good, and thus we have acedia, which is sadness about one's spiritual good, on account of the attendant bodily labour; or else it happens in respect of another's good, and this, if it be without recrimination, belongs to envy, which is sadness about another's good as being a hindrance to one's own excellence, while if it be with recrimination with a view to vengeance, it is anger. Again, these same vices seek the contrary evils.

Reply Obj. 1. Virtue and vice do not originate in the same way, since virtue is caused by the subordination of the appetite to reason, or to the unchangeable good, which is God, while vice arises from the appetite for changeable good. Therefore there is no need for the principal vices to be contrary to the principal virtues.

Reply Obj. 2. Fear and hope are irascible passions. Now all the passions of the irascible part arise from passions of the concupiscible part; and these are all, in a way, directed to pleasure or sorrow. Hence pleasure and sorrow have a prominent place among the capital sins as being the most important of the passions, as stated above (Q. XXV, A. 4).

Reply Obj. 3. Although anger is not a principal passion, yet it has a distinct place among the capital vices, because it implies a special kind of movement in the appetite, in so far as recrimination against another's good has the aspect of a virtuous good, that is, of the right to vengeance.

---

[1] PL 76, 621.

[2] Aristotle, I, 8 (1099ᵃ7); X, 7 (1177ᵃ22).

Reply Obj. 4. Pride is said to be the beginning of every sin in the order of the end, as stated above (A. 2), and it is in the same order that we are to consider the capital sin as being principal. Therefore pride, like a universal vice, is not counted along with the others, but is reckoned as the "queen of them all," as Gregory states (*Moral.* xxxi, 45).[1] But covetousness is said to be the root from another point of view, as stated above (AA. 1, 2,).

Reply Obj. 5. These vices are called capital because others most frequently arise from them. Hence nothing prevents some sins from arising out of other causes. Nevertheless we might say that all the sins which are due to ignorance can be reduced to acedia, to which pertains the negligence of a man who declines to acquire spiritual goods on account of the attendant labour; for the ignorance that can cause sin is due to negligence, as stated above (Q. LXXVI, A. 2). That a man commit a sin with a good intention seems to point to ignorance in so far as he does not know that evil should not be done that good may come of it.

QUESTION LXXXV
OF THE EFFECTS OF SIN
(*In Six Articles*)

WE must now consider the effects of sin; and (1) The corruption of the good of nature; (2) The stain on the soul (Q. LXXXVI); (3) The debt of punishment (Q. LXXXVII).

Under the first head there are six points of inquiry: (1) Whether the good of nature is diminished by sin? (2) Whether it can be taken away altogether? (3) Of the four wounds, mentioned by Bede, with which human nature is stricken in consequence of sin. (4) Whether privation of mode, species and order is an effect of sin? (5) Whether death and other bodily defects are the result of sin? (6) Whether they are, in any way, natural to man?

ARTICLE I. *Whether Sin Diminishes the Good of Nature?*

We proceed thus to the First Article: It would seem that sin does not diminish the good of nature.

Objection 1. For man's sin is no worse than the devil's. But natural good remains unimpaired in devils after sin, as Dionysius states (*Div. Nom.* iv).[2] Therefore neither does sin diminish the good of human nature.

[1] PL 76, 620.
[2] Sect. 23 (PG 3, 725).

Obj. 2. Further, when that which follows is changed, that which precedes remains unchanged since substance remains the same when its accidents are changed. But nature exists before the voluntary action. Therefore, when sin has caused a disorder in a voluntary act, nature is not changed on that account, so that the good of nature be diminished.

Obj. 3. Further, sin is an action, while diminution is a passion. Now no agent is passive by the very reason of its acting, although it is possible for it to act on one thing, and to be passive as regards another. Therefore he who sins does not by his sin diminish the good of his nature.

Obj. 4. Further, no accident acts on its subject, because that which is patient is a potential being, while that which is subjected to an accident is already an actual being as regards that accident. But sin is in the good of nature as an accident in a subject. Therefore sin does not diminish the good of nature, since to diminish is to act.

On the contrary, A certain man going down from Jerusalem to Jericho (Luke 10. 30), that is, to the corruption of sin, *was stripped of his gifts, and wounded in his nature,* as Bede expounds the passage.[3] Therefore sin diminishes the good of nature.

I answer that, The good of human nature is threefold. First, there are the principles of which nature is constituted, and the properties that flow from them, such as the powers of the soul, and so forth. Secondly, since man has from nature an inclination to virtue, as stated above (Q. LI, A. 1; Q. LXIII, A. 1), this inclination to virtue is a good of nature. Thirdly, the gift of original justice, conferred on the whole human nature in the person of the first man, may be called a good of nature.

Accordingly, the first-mentioned good of nature is neither destroyed nor diminished by sin. The third good of nature was entirely destroyed through the sin of our first parent. But the second good of nature, namely the natural inclination to virtue, is diminished by sin. Because human acts produce an inclination to like acts, as stated above (Q. L, A. 1). Now from the very fact that a thing becomes inclined to one of two contraries, its inclination to the other contrary must be diminished. Therefore as sin is opposed to virtue, from the very fact that a man sins there results a diminution of that good of nature which is the inclination to virtue.

Reply Obj. 1. Dionysius is speaking of the first-mentioned good of nature, which consists

[3] *Glossa ordin.* (v, 153A).

in being, living and understanding, as anyone may see who examines his words closely.

Reply Obj. 2. Although nature precedes the voluntary action, it has an inclination to a certain voluntary action. Therefore nature is not changed in itself through a change in the voluntary action; rather it is the inclination that is changed in so far as it is directed to its term.

Reply Obj. 3. A voluntary action proceeds from various powers, active and passive. The result is that through voluntary actions something is caused or taken away in the man who acts, as we stated when treating of the production of habits (Q. LI, A. 2).

Reply Obj. 4. An accident does not act on its subject as an efficient cause, but it acts on it formally, in the same sense as when we say that whiteness makes a thing white. In this way there is nothing to hinder sin from diminishing the good of nature; but only in so far as sin is itself a diminution of the good of nature, through being a disorderly action. But as regards the lack of order of the agent, we must say that such lack of order is caused by the fact that in the acts of the soul there is an active and a passive element; thus the sensible object moves the sensitive appetite, and the sensitive appetite inclines the reason and will, as stated above (Q. LXXVII, AA. 1, 2). The result of this is the lack of order, not as though an accident acted on its own subject, but in so far as the object acts on the power, and one power acts on another and puts it out of order.

ARTICLE 2. *Whether the Entire Good of Human Nature Can Be Destroyed by Sin?*

We proceed thus to the Second Article: It would seem that the entire good of human nature can be destroyed by sin.

Objection 1. For the good of human nature is finite, since human nature itself is finite. Now any finite thing is entirely taken away if the subtraction be continuous. Since therefore the good of nature can be continually diminished by sin, it seems that in the end it can be entirely taken away.

Obj. 2. Further, in a thing of one nature, the whole and the parts are uniform, as is evidently the case with air, water, flesh and all bodies with similar parts. But the good of nature is wholly uniform. Since therefore a part of it can be taken away by sin, it seems that the whole can also be taken away by sin.

Obj. 3. Further, the good of nature that is weakened by sin is aptitude for virtue. Now this aptitude is destroyed entirely in some on ac-

count of sin; thus the lost cannot be restored to virtue any more than the blind can to sight. Therefore sin can take away the good of nature entirely.

On the contrary, Augustine says (*Enchirid.* xiv)[1] that "evil does not exist except in some good." But the evil of sin cannot be in the good of virtue or of grace, because they are contrary to it. Therefore it must be in the good of nature, and consequently it does not destroy it entirely.

I answer that, As stated above (A. 1), the good of nature, that is diminished by sin, is the natural inclination to virtue, which is befitting to man from the very fact that he is a rational being; for it is due to this that he performs actions in accord with reason, which is to act virtuously. Now sin cannot entirely take away from man the fact that he is a rational being, for then he would no longer be capable of sin. Therefore it is not possible for this good of nature to be destroyed entirely.

Since, however, this same good of nature may be continually diminished by sin, some,[2] in order to illustrate this, have made use of the example of a finite thing being diminished indefinitely without being entirely destroyed. For the Philosopher says that if from a finite magnitude a continual subtraction be made in the same quantity, it will at last be entirely destroyed; for instance if from any finite length I continue to subtract the length of a span. If, however, the subtraction be made each time in the same proportion, and not in the same quantity, it may go on indefinitely, as, for instance, if a quantity be halved, and one half be diminished by half, it will be possible to go on thus indefinitely, provided that what is subtracted in each case be less than what was subtracted before. But this does not apply to the question at issue, since a subsequent sin does not diminish the good of nature less than a previous sin, but perhaps more, if it be a more grievous sin.

We must, therefore, explain the matter otherwise by saying that the inclination referred to above is to be considered as a middle term between two others, for it is based on the rational nature as on its root, and tends to the good of virtue as to its term and end. Consequently its diminution may be understood in two ways: first, on the part of its root; secondly, on the part of its term. In the first way it is not diminished by sin, because sin does not diminish nature, as stated above (A. 1). But it is diminished

[1] PL 40, 238.
[2] Cf. William of Auxerre, *Summa Aurea,* Pt. II, tr. 26, Q. 5 (fol. 87a).

in the second way in so far as an obstacle is placed against its attaining its term. Now if it were diminished in the first way, it would have to be entirely destroyed at last by the rational nature being entirely destroyed. Since, however, it is diminished on the part of the obstacle which is placed against its attaining its term, it is evident that it can be diminished indefinitely, because obstacles can be placed indefinitely, according as man can go on indefinitely adding sin to sin; and yet it cannot be destroyed entirely, because the root of this inclination always remains. An example of this may be seen in a transparent body, which has an inclination to receive light from the very fact that it is transparent; yet this inclination or aptitude is diminished on the part of supervening clouds, although it always remains rooted in the nature of the body.

Reply Obj. 1. This objection avails when diminution is made by subtraction. But here the diminution is made by raising obstacles, and this neither diminishes nor destroys the root of the inclination, as stated above.

Reply Obj. 2. The natural inclination is indeed wholly uniform. Nevertheless it stands in relation both to its principle and to its term, and in respect of this diversity of relation, it is in one way diminished and in another is not.

Reply Obj. 3. Even in the lost the natural inclination to virtue remains, for otherwise they would have no remorse of conscience. That it is not reduced to act is owing to their being deprived of grace by Divine justice. Thus even in a blind man the aptitude to see remains in the very root of his nature, in so far as he is an animal naturally endowed with sight; yet this aptitude is not reduced to act, for the lack of a cause capable of reducing it, by forming the organ needed for sight.

ARTICLE 3. *Whether Weakness, Ignorance, Malice, and Concupiscence Are Suitably Reckoned as the Wounds of Nature Consequent upon Sin?*

We proceed thus to the Third Article: It would seem that weakness, ignorance, malice and concupiscence are not suitably reckoned as the wounds of nature consequent upon sin.

Objection 1. For one same thing is not both effect and cause of the same thing. But these are considered to be causes of sin, as appears from what has been said above (Q. LXXVI, A. 1; Q. LXXVII, AA. 3, 5; Q. LXXVIII, A. 1). Therefore they should not be considered as effects of sin.

Obj. 2. Further, malice is the name of a sin.

Therefore it should have no place among the effects of sin.

Obj. 3. Further, concupiscence is something natural, since it is the act of the concupiscible power. But that which is natural should not be considered a wound of nature. Therefore concupiscence should not be considered a wound of nature.

Obj. 4. Further, it has been stated (Q. LXXVII, A. 3) that to sin from weakness is the same as to sin from passion. But concupiscence is a passion. Therefore it should not be divided against weakness.

Obj. 5. Further, Augustine (*De Nat. et Grat.* lxvii)[1] accounts "two things as punishments inflicted on the soul of the sinner," namely "ignorance and difficulty," from which arise "error and vexation," which four do not coincide with the four in question. Therefore it seems that one or the other reckoning is incomplete.

On the contrary, The authority of Bede suffices.[2]

I answer that, As a result of original justice, the reason had perfect hold over the lower parts of the soul, while reason itself was perfected by God and was subject to Him. Now this same original justice was forfeited through the sin of our first parent, as already stated (Q. LXXXI, A. 2), so that all the powers of the soul are left, as it were, destitute of their proper order, by which they are naturally directed to virtue, and this destitution is called a wounding of nature.

Again, there are four of the soul's powers that can be the subject of virtue, as stated above (Q. LXI, A. 2), namely the reason, where prudence resides, the will, where justice is, the irascible power, the subject of fortitude, and the concupiscible power, the subject of temperance. Therefore in so far as the reason is deprived of its order to the true, there is the wound of ignorance; in so far as the will is deprived of its order to the good, there is the wound of malice; in so far as the irascible power is deprived of its order to the arduous, there is the wound of weakness; and in so far as the concupiscible power is deprived of its order to the delectable, moderated by reason, there is the wound of concupiscence.

Accordingly these are the four wounds inflicted on the whole of human nature as a result of our first parent's sin. But since the inclination to the good of virtue is diminished in each individual on account of actual sin, as was explained above (AA. 1, 2), these four wounds are also the

[1] PL 44, 287; *De Lib. Arb.*, III, 18 (PL 32, 1296).
[2] Cf. above, Part I, Q. CI, A. 1, obj. 2.

result of other sins, in so far as, through sin, the reason is obscured, especially in practical matters, the will hardened to evil, good actions become more difficult, and concupiscence more inflamed.

Reply Obj. 1. There is no reason why the effect of one sin should not be the cause of another, because the soul, from the very fact that it is thrown into disorder by sinning once, is more easily inclined to sin again.

Reply Obj. 2. Malice is not to be taken here as a sin, but as a certain proneness of the will to evil, according to the words of Gen. 8. 21: *Man's senses are prone to evil from his youth.* (Vulg.,—*The imagination and thought of man's heart are prone to evil from his youth.*)

Reply Obj. 3. As stated above (Q. LXXXII, A. 3, REPLY 1), concupiscence is natural to man in so far as it is subject to reason; but, in so far as it goes beyond the bounds of reason, it is unnatural to man.

Reply Obj. 4. Speaking in a general way, every passion can be called a weakness, in so far as it weakens the soul's strength and impedes the reason. Bede, however, took weakness in the strict sense, as contrary to fortitude which pertains to the irascible power.

Reply Obj. 5. The difficulty which is mentioned in this book of Augustine includes the three wounds affecting the appetitive powers, namely malice, weakness and concupiscence, for it is owing to these three that a man finds it difficult to tend to the good. Error and vexation are consequent wounds, since a man is vexed through being weakened in respect of the objects of his concupiscence.

ARTICLE 4. *Whether Privation of Mode, Species, and Order Is the Effect of Sin?*

We proceed thus to the Fourth Article: It would seem that privation of mode, species and order is not the effect of sin.

Objection 1. For Augustine says (*De Natura Boni*, iii)[1] that "where these three abound, the good is great; where they are less, there is less good; where they are not, there is no good at all." But sin does not cancel out the good of nature. Therefore it does not take away mode, species and order.

Obj. 2. Further, nothing is its own cause. But sin itself is "the privation of mode, species and order," as Augustine states (*De Natura Boni*, iv).[2] Therefore privation of mode, species and order is not the effect of sin.

Obj. 3. Further, different effects result from

different sins. Now since mode, species and order are diverse, their corresponding privations must be diverse also, and, consequently, must be the result of different sins. Therefore privation of mode, species and order is not the effect of each sin.

On the contrary, Sin is to the soul what weakness is to the body, according to Ps. 6. 3, *Have mercy on me, O Lord, for I am weak.* Now weakness deprives the body of mode, species and order. Therefore sin deprives the soul of mode, species and order.

I answer that, As stated in the First Part (Q. V, A. 5), mode, species and order are consequent upon every created good, as such, and also upon every being. Because every being and every good as such depends on its form from which it derives its species. Again, any kind of form, whether substantial or accidental, of anything whatever, is according to some measure, and so it is stated in the *Metaphysics*[3] that "the forms of things are like numbers," so that a form has a certain mode corresponding to its measure. Lastly, owing to its form, each thing has a relation of order to something else.

Accordingly there are different grades of mode, species and order, corresponding to the different degrees of good. For there is a good belonging to the very substance of nature, which good has its mode, species and order, and is neither destroyed nor diminished by sin. There is again the good of the natural inclination, which also has its mode, species and order; and this is diminished by sin, as stated above (AA. 1, 2), but is not entirely destroyed. Again, there is the good of virtue and grace; this too has its mode, species and order, and is entirely taken away by sin. Lastly, there is a good consisting in the ordered act itself, which also has its mode, species and order, the privation of which is essentially sin. Hence it is clear both how sin is privation of mode, species and order, and how it destroys or diminishes mode, species and order.

This suffices for the *Replies to the first two Objections.*

Reply Obj. 3. Mode, species and order follow one from the other, as explained above. And so they are destroyed or diminished together.

ARTICLE 5. *Whether Death and Other Bodily Defects Are the Result of Sin?*

We proceed thus to the Fifth Article: It would seem that death and other bodily defects are not the result of sin.

---

[1] PL 42, 553.   [2] PL 42, 553.

[3] Aristotle, VIII, 3 (1043[b]33).

Objection 1. Because equal causes have equal effects. Now these defects are not equal in all, but abound in some more than in others, although original sin, from which especially these defects seem to result, is equal in all, as stated above (Q. LXXXII, A. 4). Therefore death and such defects are not the result of sin.

Obj. 2. Further, if the cause is removed, the effect is removed. But these defects are not removed when all sin is removed by baptism or penance. Therefore they are not the effect of sin.

Obj. 3. Further, actual sin has more of the character of guilt than original sin has. But actual sin does not change the nature of the body by subjecting it to some defect. Much less, therefore, does original sin. Therefore death and other bodily defects are not the result of sin.

On the contrary, The Apostle says (Rom. 5. 12): *By one man sin entered into this world, and by sin death.*

I answer that, One thing causes another in two ways: first, directly; secondly, accidentally. Directly, one thing is the cause of another if it produces its effect by reason of the power of its nature or form, from which it follows that the effect is directly intended by the cause. Consequently, as death and such defects are beside the intention of the sinner, it is evident that sin is not, of itself, the cause of these defects. Accidentally, one thing is the cause of another if it causes it by removing an obstacle; thus it is stated in the *Physics*[1] that "by displacing a pillar a man moves accidentally the stone resting thereon." In this way the sin of our first parent is the cause of death and all such defects in human nature, in so far as by the sin of our first parent original justice was taken away, by which not only were the lower powers of the soul held together under the control of reason, without any disorder whatever, but also the whole body was held together in subjection to the soul, without any defect, as stated in the First Part (Q. XCVII, A. 1). Therefore, original justice being forfeited through the sin of our first parent, just as human nature was stricken in the soul by the disorder among the powers, as stated above (A. 3; Q. LXXXII, A. 3), so also it became subject to corruption, by reason of disorder in the body.

Now the withdrawal of original justice has the character of punishment, even as the withdrawal of grace has. Consequently, death and all consequent bodily defects are punishments of

original sin. And although these defects are not intended by the sinner, nevertheless they are ordered according to the justice of God Who inflicts them as punishments.

Reply Obj. 1. Causes that produce their effects directly, if equal, produce equal effects; for if such causes be increased or diminished, the effect is increased or diminished. But equal causes of an obstacle being removed do not point to equal effects. For supposing a man employs equal force in displacing two columns, it does not follow that the movements of the stones resting on them will be equal, but that one will move with the greater velocity which has the greater weight according to the property of its nature, to which it is abandoned when the obstacle to its falling is removed. Accordingly, when original justice is removed, the nature of the human body is left to itself, so that according to different natural temperaments some men's bodies are subject to more defects, some to fewer, although original sin is equal in all.

Reply Obj. 2. Both original and actual sin are removed by the same cause that removes these defects, according to the Apostle (Rom. 8. 11): *He . . . shall quicken . . . your mortal bodies, because of His Spirit that dwelleth in you,* but each is done according to the order of Divine wisdom, at a fitting time. Because it is right that we should first of all be conformed to Christ's sufferings before attaining to the immortality and impassibility of glory, which was begun in Him, and by Him acquired for us. Hence, it is necessary that our bodies should remain, for a time, subject to suffering, in order that we may merit the impassibility of glory, in conformity with Christ.

Reply Obj. 3. Two things may be considered in actual sin, the substance of the act, and the aspect of fault. As regards the substance of the act, actual sin can cause a bodily defect; thus some sicken and die through eating too much. But as regards the fault, it deprives us of grace which is given to us that we may regulate the acts of the soul, but not that we may ward off defects of the body, as original justice did. Therefore actual sin does not cause those defects, as original sin does.

ARTICLE 6. *Whether Death and Other Defects Are Natural to Man?*

We proceed thus to the Sixth Article: It would seem that death and such defects are natural to man.

Objection 1. For "the corruptible and the in-

---

[1] Aristotle, VIII, 4 (255ᵇ25).

corruptible differ generically,"¹ But man is of the same genus as other animals, which are naturally corruptible. Therefore man is naturally corruptible.

Obj. 2. Further, whatever is composed of contraries is naturally corruptible, as having within itself the cause of its corruption. But such is the human body. Therefore it is naturally corruptible.

Obj. 3. Further, a hot thing naturally consumes moisture. Now human life is preserved by hot and moist elements. Since therefore the vital functions are fulfilled by the action of natural heat, as stated in the book on the *Soul*,² it seems that death and such defects are natural to man.

On the contrary, 1. God made in man whatever is natural to him. Now *God made not death* (Wisd. 1. 13). Therefore death is not natural to man.

2. Further, that which is natural cannot be called either a punishment or an evil, since what is natural to a thing is suitable to it. But death and such defects are the punishment of original sin, as stated above (A. 5). Therefore they are not natural to man.

3. Further, matter is proportionate to form, and everything to its end. Now man's end is everlasting Happiness, as stated above (Q. II, A. 7; Q. V, AA. 3, 4). And the form of the human body is the rational soul, which is incorruptible, as was proved in the First Part (Q. LXXV, A. 6). Therefore the human body is naturally incorruptible.

I answer that, We may speak of any corruptible thing in two ways; first, in respect of its universal nature, secondly, as regards its particular nature. A thing's particular nature is its own power of action and self-preservation. And in respect of this nature, "every corruption and defect is contrary to nature," as stated in the book on the *Heavens*,³ since this power tends to the being and preservation of the thing to which it belongs.

On the other hand, the universal nature is an active power in some universal principle of nature, for instance in some heavenly body; or again belonging to some superior substance, in which sense God is said by some to be "the Nature Who makes nature."⁴ This power intends

the good and the preservation of the universe, for which alternate generation and corruption in things are requisite. And in this respect corruption and defect in things are natural, not indeed as regards the inclination of the form, which is the principle of being and perfection, but as regards the inclination of matter, which is allotted proportionately to its particular form according to the regulation of the universal agent. And although every form intends perpetual being as far as it can, yet no form of a corruptible being can achieve its own perpetuity, except the rational soul, for the reason that the latter is not entirely subject to matter, as other forms are; indeed it has an immaterial operation of its own, as stated in the First Part (Q. LXXV, A. 2). Consequently as regards his form, incorruption is more natural to man than to other corruptible things. But since that very form has a matter composed of contraries, from the inclination of that matter there results corruptibility in the whole. In this respect man is naturally corruptible as regards the nature of his matter left to itself, but not as regards the nature of his form.

The *first three objections* argue on the side of the matter, while *the other three* argue on the side of the form. Therefore in order to solve them, we must observe that the form of man, which is the rational soul, in respect of its incorruptibility is proportioned to its end, which is everlasting Happiness. But the human body, which is corruptible, considered in respect of its nature, is in a way proportioned to its form, and in another way it is not. For we may note a twofold condition in any matter, one which the agent chooses, and another which is not chosen by the agent, and is a natural condition of matter. Thus, a smith in order to make a knife chooses a matter both hard and flexible, which can be sharpened so as to be useful for cutting, and in respect of this condition iron is a matter adapted for a knife; but that iron is breakable and inclined to rust results from the natural disposition of iron, nor does the workman choose this in the iron, but rather would do without it if he could. Therefore this disposition of matter is not proportioned to the workman's intention, nor to the purpose of his art. In like manner the human body is the matter chosen by nature, in respect of its being of a mixed temperament, in order that it may be most suitable as an organ of touch and of the other sensitive and moving powers. But the fact that it is corruptible is due to a condition of matter, and is not chosen by nature; indeed nature would

---

¹ Aristotle, *Metaphysics*, x, 10 (1058ᵇ28).

² Aristotle, II, 4 (416ᵇ29).

³ Aristotle, II, 6 (288ᵇ14).

⁴ Cf. Averroes, *In de Cælo* I, comm. 2 (v, 3A), where the expression *Natura naturans* is found; see also in Averroes, *In Phys.*, II, comm. 11. (IV, 52C). *Natura naturans* occurs in Bonaventure, *In Sent.*, III, d. 8, d. 2 (QR III, 197).

choose an incorruptible matter if it could. But God, to Whom every nature is subject, in forming man supplied the defect of nature, and by the gift of original justice, gave the body a certain incorruptibility, as was stated in the First Part (Q. XCVII, A. 1). It is in this sense that it is said that *God made not death,* and that death is the punishment of sin.

This suffices for the *Replies to the Objections.*

QUESTION LXXXVI

OF THE STAIN OF SIN

(*In Two Articles*)

WE must now consider the stain of sin, under which head there are two points of inquiry: (1) Whether an effect of sin is a stain on the soul? (2) Whether it remains in the soul after the act of sin?

ARTICLE 1. *Whether Sin Causes a Stain on the Soul?*

We proceed thus to the First Article: It would seem that sin causes no stain on the soul.

Objection 1. For a higher nature cannot be defiled by contact with a lower nature; hence the sun's ray is not defiled by contact with tainted bodies, as Augustine says (*Contra Quinque Hæreses,* v).[1] Now the human soul is of a much higher nature than changeable things, to which it turns by sinning. Therefore it does not contract a stain from them by sinning.

Obj. 2. Further, sin is chiefly in the will, as stated above (Q. LXXIV, AA. 1, 2). Now "the will is in the reason," as stated in the book on the *Soul.*[2] But the reason or intellect is not stained by considering anything whatever; rather indeed is it perfected thereby. Therefore neither is the will stained by sin.

Obj. 3. Further, if sin causes a stain, this stain is either something positive or a pure privation. If it be something positive, it can only be either a disposition or a habit, for it seems that nothing else can be caused by an act. But it is neither disposition nor habit, for it happens that a stain remains even after the removal of a disposition or habit; for instance, in a man who after committing a mortal sin of prodigality, is so changed as to fall into a sin of the opposite vice. Therefore the stain does not denote anything positive in the soul. Again, neither is it a pure privation. For all sins agree on the part of

turning away and privation of grace; and so it would follow that there is but one stain caused by all sins. Therefore the stain is not the effect of sin.

On the contrary, It was said to Solomon (Ecclus. 47, 22): *Thou hast stained thy glory;* and it is written (Ephes. 5. 27): *That He might present it to Himself a glorious church not having spot or wrinkle;* and in each case it is question of the stain of sin. Therefore a stain is the effect of sin.

I answer that, A stain is properly ascribed to corporeal things, when a bright body loses its brightness through contact with another body, for example, a garment, gold, or silver, or the like. Accordingly a stain is ascribed to spiritual things in like manner. Now man's soul has a twofold brightness; one from the refulgence of the natural light of reason, by which he is directed in his actions; the other, from the refulgence of the Divine light, namely of wisdom and grace, by which man is also perfected for the purpose of doing good and fitting actions. Now, when the soul cleaves to things by love, there is a kind of contact in the soul, and when man sins, he cleaves to certain things against the light of reason and of the Divine law, as shown above (Q. LXXI, A. 6). Therefore the loss of brightness occasioned by this contact is metaphorically called a stain on the soul.

Reply Obj. 1. The soul is not defiled by inferior things by their own power, as though they acted on the soul; on the contrary, the soul, by its own action, defiles itself, through cleaving to them inordinately, against the light of reason and of the Divine law.

Reply Obj. 2. The action of the intellect is accomplished by the intelligible thing being in the intellect according to the mode of the intellect, so that the intellect is not defiled, but perfected, by it. On the other hand, the act of the will consists in a movement towards things themselves so that love attaches the soul to the thing loved. Thus it is that the soul is stained when it cleaves inordinately, according to Osee 9. 10: *They . . . became abominable as those things were which they loved.*

Reply Obj. 3. The stain is neither something positive in the soul, nor does it denote a pure privation. It denotes a privation of the soul's brightness in relation to its cause, which is sin; therefore different sins occasion different stains. It is like a shadow, which is the privation of light through the interposition of a body, and which varies according to the diversity of the interposed bodies.

[1] Contained among the works of Augustine. (PL 42, 1107).
[2] Aristotle, III, 9 (432^{b}5).

ARTICLE 2. *Whether the Stain Remains in the Soul After the Act of Sin?*

We proceed thus to the Second Article: It would seem that the stain does not remain in the soul after the act of sin.

Objection 1. For after an action, nothing remains in the soul except habit or disposition. But the stain is not a habit or disposition, as stated above (A. 1, obj. 3). Therefore the stain does not remain in the soul after the act of sin.

Obj. 2. Further, the stain is to the sin what the shadow is to the body, as stated above (A. 1, reply 3). But the shadow does not remain when the body has passed by. Therefore the stain does not remain in the soul when the act of sin is past.

Obj. 3. Further, every effect depends on its cause. Now the cause of the stain is the act of sin. Therefore when the act of sin is no longer there, neither is the stain in the soul.

On the contrary, It is written (Jos. 22. 17): *Is it a small thing to you that you sinned with Beelphegor, and the stain of that crime remaineth in you* (Vulg.,—*us*) *to this day?*

I answer that, The stain of sin remains in the soul even when the act of sin is past. The reason for this is that the stain, as stated above (A. 1), denotes a blemish in the brightness of the soul, on account of its withdrawing from the light of reason or of the Divine law. And therefore so long as man remains out of this light, the stain of sin remains in him. But as soon as, moved by grace, he returns to the Divine light and to the light of reason, the stain is removed. For although the act of sin ceases, whereby man withdrew from the light of reason and of the Divine law, man does not at once return to the state in which he was before, and it is necessary that his will should have a movement contrary to the previous movement. Thus if one man be parted from another on account of some kind of movement, he is not reunited to him as soon as the movement ceases, but he needs to draw near to him and to return by a contrary movement.

Reply Obj. 1. Nothing positive remains in the soul after the act of sin, except the disposition or habit; but there does remain something privative, namely the privation of union with the Divine light.

Reply Obj. 2. After the interposed body has passed by, the transparent body remains in the same position and relation as regards the illuminating body, and so the shadow passes at once. But when the sin is past, the soul does not re-

main in the same relation to God. And so there is no comparison.

Reply Obj. 3. The act of sin parts man from God, which parting causes the defect of brightness, just as local movement causes local parting. Therefore, just as when movement ceases, local distance is not removed, so neither, when the act of sin ceases, is the stain removed.

QUESTION LXXXVII
OF THE DEBT OF PUNISHMENT
(*In Eight Articles*)

WE must now consider the debt of punishment. We shall consider (1) The debt itself; (2) Mortal and venial sin, which differ in respect of the punishment due to them (Q. LXXXVIII).

Under the first head there are eight points of inquiry: (1) Whether the debt of punishment is an effect of sin? (2) Whether one sin can be the punishment of another? (3) Whether any sin incurs a debt of eternal punishment? (4) Whether sin incurs a debt of punishment that is infinite in quantity? (5) Whether every sin incurs a debt of eternal and infinite punishment? (6) Whether the debt of punishment can remain after sin? (7) Whether every punishment is inflicted for a sin? (8) Whether one person can incur punishment for another's sin?

ARTICLE 1. *Whether the Debt of Punishment Is an Effect of Sin?*

We proceed thus to the First Article: It would seem that the debt of punishment is not an effect of sin.

Objection 1. For that which is accidentally related to a thing does not seem to be its proper effect. Now the debt of punishment is accidentally related to sin, for it is beside the intention of the sinner. Therefore the debt of punishment is not an effect of sin.

Obj. 2. Further, evil is not the cause of good. But punishment is good, since it is just, and is from God. Therefore it is not an effect of sin, which is evil.

Obj. 3. Further, Augustine says[1] that "every inordinate affection is its own punishment." But punishment does not incur a further debt of punishment, because then it would go on infinitely. Therefore sin does not incur the debt of punishment.

On the contrary, It is written (Rom. 2. 9): *Tribulation and anguish upon every soul of man that worketh evil.* But to work evil is to sin. Therefore sin incurs a punishment which is sig-

[1] *Confessions,* i, 19 (PL 32, 670).

nified by the words *tribulation and anguish.*

I answer that, The fact that whenever one thing rises up against another it suffers some detriment from it, passes over from natural things to human affairs. For we observe in natural things that when one contrary supervenes, the other acts with greater energy, for which reason "hot water freezes more rapidly," as stated in the treatise on *Meteorology.*[1] And so we find that the natural inclination of man is to repress those who rise up against him. Now it is evident that all things contained in an order, are, in a manner, one, in relation to the principle of that order. Consequently, whatever rises up against an order is put down by that order or by the principle of that order. And because sin is an inordinate act, it is evident that whoever sins commits an offence against an order. And therefore he is put down, in consequence, by that same order, which repression is punishment.

Accordingly, man can be punished with a threefold punishment corresponding to the three orders to which the human will is subject. In the first place a man's nature is subjected to the order of his own reason; secondly, it is subjected to the order of another man who governs him either in spiritual or in temporal matters, as a member either of the state or of the household; thirdly, it is subjected to the universal order of the Divine government. Now each of these orders is disturbed by sin, for the sinner acts against his reason, and against human and Divine law. Hence he incurs a threefold punishment; one, inflicted by himself, namely remorse of conscience; another, inflicted by man; and a third, inflicted by God.

Reply Obj. 1. Punishment follows sin, in so far as sin is an evil by reason of its lack of order. Therefore just as evil is accidental to the sinner's act, being beside his intention, so also is the debt of punishment.

Reply Obj. 2. A just punishment may be inflicted either by God or by man. Hence the punishment itself is the effect of sin, not directly but dispositively. Sin, however, makes man deserving of punishment, and that is an evil; for Dionysius says (*Div. Nom.* iv)[2] that "punishment is not an evil, but to deserve punishment is." Consequently the debt of punishment is considered to be directly the effect of sin.

Reply Obj. 3. This punishment of the inordinate affection is due to sin as overturning the order of reason. Nevertheless sin incurs a further punishment, through disturbing the order of the Divine or human law.

Article 2. *Whether Sin Can Be the Punishment of Sin?*

We proceed thus to the Second Article: It would seem that sin cannot be the punishment of sin.

Objection 1. For the purpose of punishment is to bring man back to the good of virtue, as the Philosopher declares.[3] Now sin does not bring man back to the good of virtue, but leads him in the opposite direction. Therefore sin is not the punishment of sin.

Obj. 2. Further, just punishments are from God, as Augustine says (QQ. LXXXIII, *qu.* 82).[4] But sin is not from God, and is an injustice. Therefore sin cannot be the punishment of sin.

Obj. 3. Further, the nature of punishment is to be something against the will. But sin is something from the will, as shown above (Q. LXXIV, AA. 1, 2). Therefore sin cannot be the punishment of sin.

On the contrary, Gregory says (*Hom.* xi *in Ezech.*)[5] that "some sins are punishments of others."

I answer that, We may speak of sin in two ways: first, in its essence; secondly, as to that which is accidental to it. Sin as such can in no way be the punishment of another. For sin considered in its essence is something proceeding from the will, for it is from this that it derives the character of guilt. But punishment is essentially something against the will, as stated in the First Part (Q. XLVIII, A. 5). Consequently it is evident that sin, regarded in its essence, can in no way be the punishment of sin.

On the other hand, sin can be the punishment of sin accidentally in three ways. First, when one sin is the cause of another by removing an impediment to it. For passions, temptations of the devil, and the like are causes of sin, but are impeded by the help of Divine grace which is withdrawn on account of sin. Therefore since the withdrawal of grace is a punishment, and is from God, as stated above (Q. LXXIX, A. 3), the result is that the sin which ensues from this is also a punishment accidentally. It is in this sense that the Apostle speaks (Rom. 1. 24) when he says: *Wherefore God gave them up to the desires of their heart,* namely to their passions; because, that is, when men are deprived of the help of Divine grace, they are overcome

---

[1] Aristotle, I, 12 (348b32).
[2] Sect. 22 (PG 3, 724).

[3] *Ethics,* X, 9 (1180a4).
[4] PL 40, 98.
[5] PL 76, 915.

by their passions. In this way sin is always said to be the punishment of a preceding sin. Secondly, by reason of the substance of the act, which is such as to cause pain, whether it be an interior act, as is clearly the case with anger or envy, or an exterior act, as is the case with one who endures considerable trouble and loss in order to achieve a sinful act, according to Wisd. 5. 7: *We wearied ourselves in the way of iniquity.* Thirdly, on the part of the effect, so that one sin is said to be a punishment by reason of its effect. In the last two ways, a sin is a punishment not only in respect of a preceding sin, but also with regard to itself.

Reply Obj. 1. Even when God punishes men by permitting them to fall into sin, this is directed to the good of virtue. Sometimes indeed it is for the good of those who are punished, when, that is, men arise from sin more humble and more cautious. But it is always for the amendment of others, who seeing some men fall from sin to sin, are the more fearful of sinning. With regard to the other two ways, it is evident that the punishment is intended for the sinner's amendment, since the very fact that man endures toil and loss in sinning is of a nature to withdraw man from sin.

Reply Obj. 2. This objection considers sin essentially as such; and the same answer applies *to the third objection.*

ARTICLE 3. *Whether Any Sin Incurs a Debt of Eternal Punishment?*

We proceed thus to the Third Article: It would seem that no sin incurs a debt of eternal punishment.

Objection 1. For a just punishment is equal to the fault, since justice is equality. Hence it is written (Isa. 27. 8): *In measure against measure, when it shall be cast off, thou shalt judge it.* Now sin is temporal. Therefore it does not incur a debt of eternal punishment.

Obj. 2. Further, "punishments are a kind of medicine."[1] But no medicine should be infinite, because it is directed to an end, and "what is directed to an end is not infinite," as the Philosopher states.[2] Therefore no punishment should be infinite.

Obj. 3. Further, no one does a thing always unless he delights in it for its own sake. But *God hath not pleasure in the destruction of men* (Vulg.,—*of the living*). Therefore He will not inflict eternal punishment on man.

Obj. 4. Further, nothing accidental is infinite.

But punishment is accidental, for it is not natural to the one who is punished. Therefore it cannot be of infinite duration.

On the contrary, It is written (Matt. 25. 46): *These shall go into everlasting punishment;* and (Mark 3. 29): *He that shall blaspheme against the Holy Ghost, shall never have forgiveness, but shall be guilty of an everlasting sin.*

I answer that, As stated above (A. 1), sin incurs a debt of punishment through disturbing an order. But the effect remains so long as the cause remains. Therefore so long as the disturbance of the order remains the debt of punishment must remain also. Now disturbance of an order is sometimes reparable, sometimes irreparable. For a defect which destroys the principle is always irreparable, although if the principle be saved, defects can be repaired by virtue of that principle. For instance, if the principle of sight be destroyed, sight cannot be restored except by Divine power; but, if the principle of sight is preserved, while there arise certain impediments to the use of sight, these can be remedied by nature or by art. Now in every order there is a principle by which one takes part in that order. Consequently if a sin destroys the principle of the order by which man's will is subject to God, the disorder will be such as to be considered in itself, irreparable, although it is possible to repair it by the power of God. Now the principle of this order is the last end, to which man adheres by charity. Therefore whatever sins turn man away from God, so as to destroy charity, considered in themselves, incur a debt of eternal punishment.

Reply Obj. 1. Punishment is proportionate to sin in point of severity both in Divine and in human judgments. In no judgment, however, as Augustine says,[3] is it requisite for punishment to equal fault in point of duration. For the fact that adultery or murder is committed in a moment does not call for a momentary punishment; in fact they are punished sometimes by imprisonment or banishment for life,—sometimes even by death. In such a case account is not taken of the time occupied in killing, but rather of the expediency of removing the murderer from the fellowship of the living, so that this punishment, in its own way, represents the eternity of punishment inflicted by God. Now according to Gregory[4] "it is just that he who has sinned against God in his own eternity should be punished in God's eternity." A man is

---

[1] Aristotle, *Ethics*, II, 3 (1104[b]17).
[2] *Politics*, I, 9 (1257[b]27).

[3] *City of God*, XXI, 11 (PL 41, 725).
[4] *Moral.*, XXXIV, 19 (PL 76, 738).

said to have sinned in his own eternity not only as regards continual sinning throughout his whole life, but also because, from the very fact that he fixes his end in sin, he has the will to sin everlastingly. Hence Gregory says (*ibid.*) that "the wicked would wish to live without end, that they might abide in their sins for ever."

Reply Obj. 2. Even the punishment that is inflicted according to human laws is not always intended as a medicine for the one who is punished, but sometimes only for others; thus when a thief is hanged, this is not for his own amendment, but for the sake of others, that at least they may be deterred from crime through fear of the punishment, according to Prov. 19. 25: *The wicked man being scourged, the fool shall be wiser.* Accordingly the eternal punishments inflicted by God on the reprobate are medicinal punishments for those who refrain from sin through the thought of those punishments, according to Ps. 59. 6: *Thou hast given a warning to them that fear Thee, that they may flee from before the bow, that Thy beloved may be delivered.*

Reply Obj. 3. God does not delight in punishments for their own sake; but He does delight in the order of His justice, which requires them.

Reply Obj. 4. Although punishment is related indirectly to nature, nevertheless it is essentially related to the lack of the order, and to God's justice. Therefore, so long as the lack of order lasts, the punishment endures.

ARTICLE 4. *Whether Sin Incurs a Debt of Punishment Infinite in Quantity?*

We proceed thus to the Fourth Article: It would seem that sin incurs a debt of punishment infinite in quantity.

Objection 1. For it is written (Jerem. 10. 24): *Correct me, O Lord, but yet with judgment: and not in Thy fury, lest Thou bring me to nothing.* Now God's anger or fury signifies metaphorically the vengeance of Divine justice; and to be brought to nothing is an infinite punishment, even as to make a thing out of nothing denotes infinite power. Therefore according to God's vengeance, sin is awarded a punishment infinite in quantity.

Obj. 2. Further, quantity of punishment corresponds to quantity of fault, according to Deut. 25. 2: *According to the measure of the sin shall the measure also of the stripes be.* Now a sin which is committed against God, is infi-

nite, because the gravity of a sin increases according to the greatness of the person sinned against (thus it is a more grievous sin to strike the sovereign than a private individual), and God's greatness is infinite. Therefore an infinite punishment is due for a sin committed against God.

Obj. 3. Further, a thing may be infinite in two ways, in duration, and in quantity. Now the punishment is infinite in duration. Therefore it is infinite in quantity also.

On the contrary, If this were the case, the punishments of all mortal sins would be equal, because one infinite is not greater than another.

I answer that, Punishment is proportionate to sin. Now sin comprises two things. First, there is the turning away from the unchangeable good, which is infinite, and therefore, in this respect, sin is infinite. Secondly, there is the inordinate turning to changeable good. In this respect sin is finite, both because the changeable good itself is finite, and because the movement of turning towards it is finite, since the acts of a creature cannot be infinite. Accordingly, in so far as sin consists in turning away from something, its corresponding punishment is the pain of loss, which also is infinite, because it is the loss of the infinite good, that is, God. But in so far as sin turns inordinately to something, its corresponding punishment is the pain of sense, which also is finite.

Reply Obj. 1. It would be inconsistent with Divine justice for the sinner to be brought to nothing absolutely, because this would be incompatible with the perpetuity of punishment that Divine justice requires, as stated above (A. 3). The expression "to be brought to nothing" is applied to one who is deprived of spiritual goods, according to I Cor. 13. 2: *If I . . . have not charity, I am nothing.*

Reply Obj. 2. This argument considers sin as turning away from something, for it is thus that man sins against God.

Reply Obj. 3. Duration of punishment corresponds to duration of fault, not indeed as regards the act, but on the part of the stain, for as long as this remains, the debt of punishment remains. But punishment corresponds to fault in the point of severity. And a fault which is irreparable, is such that, of itself, it lasts for ever; and therefore it incurs an everlasting punishment. But it is not infinite as regards the thing it turns to; and therefore, in this respect, it does not incur punishment of infinite quantity.

ARTICLE 5. *Whether Every Sin Incurs a Debt of Eternal Punishment?*

We proceed thus to the Fifth Article: It would seem that every sin incurs a debt of eternal punishment.

Objection 1. For punishment, as stated above (A. 4), is proportionate to the fault. Now eternal punishment differs infinitely from temporal punishment. But no sin, apparently, differs infinitely from another, since every sin is a human act, which cannot be infinite. Since therefore some sins incur a debt of everlasting punishment, as stated above (A. 4), it seems that no sin incurs a debt of temporal punishment only.

Obj. 2. Further, original sin is the least of all sins; hence Augustine says (*Enchir.* xciii)[1] that "the lightest punishment is incurred by those who are punished for original sin alone." But original sin incurs everlasting punishment, since children who have died in original sin through not being baptized, will never see the kingdom of God, as is shown by our Lord's words (John 3.3): *Unless a man be born again, he cannot see the kingdom of God.* Much more, therefore, will the punishments of all other sins be everlasting.

Obj. 3. Further, a sin does not deserve greater punishment through being united to another sin, for Divine justice has allotted its punishment to each sin. Now a venial sin deserves eternal punishment if it be united to a mortal sin in a lost soul, because in hell there is no remission of sins. Therefore venial sin by itself deserves eternal punishment. Therefore temporal punishment is not due for any sin.

On the contrary, Gregory says (*Dial.* iv, 39),[2] that certain slighter sins are remitted after this life. Therefore all sins are not punished eternally.

I answer that, As stated above (A. 3), a sin incurs a debt of eternal punishment in so far as it causes an irreparable disorder in the order of Divine justice, through being contrary to the very principle of that order, which is the last end. Now it is evident that in some sins there is disorder indeed, but such as not to involve contrariety in respect of the last end, but only in respect of the means to the end, in so far as one is too much or too little intent on them without prejudicing the order to the last end, as, for instance, when a man is too fond of some temporal thing, yet would not offend God for its sake by breaking one of His commandments.

[1] PL 40, 275.
[2] PL 77, 396.

Consequently such sins do not incur everlasting, but only temporal punishment.

Reply Obj. 1. Sins do not differ infinitely from one another in respect of their turning towards changeable good, which constitutes the substance of the sinful act; but they do differ infinitely in respect of their turning away from something. Because some sins consist in turning away from the last end, and some in a disorder affecting the means to the end; and the last end differs infinitely from the means to that end.

Reply Obj. 2. Original sin incurs everlasting punishment not on account of its gravity but by reason of the condition of the subject, namely a human being deprived of grace, without which there is no remission of sin.

The same answer applies to the *Third Objection* about venial sin. Because eternity of punishment does not correspond to the quantity of the sin, but to its irremissibility, as stated above (A. 3).

ARTICLE 6. *Whether the Debt of Punishment Remains After Sin?*

We proceed thus to the Sixth Article: It would seem that there remains no debt of punishment after sin.

Objection 1. For if the cause be removed the effect is removed. But sin is the cause of the debt of punishment. Therefore, when the sin is removed, the debt of punishment ceases also.

Obj. 2. Further, sin is removed by man returning to virtue. Now a virtuous man deserves, not punishment, but reward. Therefore, when sin is removed, the debt of punishment no longer remains.

Obj. 3. Further, "Punishments are a kind of medicine."[3] But a man is not given medicine after being cured of his disease. Therefore, when sin is removed, the debt of punishment does not remain.

On the contrary, It is written (II Kings 12, 13, 14): *David said to Nathan: I have sinned against the Lord. And Nathan said to David: The Lord also hath taken away thy sin; thou shalt not die. Nevertheless because thou hast given occasion to the enemies of the Lord to blaspheme . . . the child that is born to thee shall die.* Therefore a man is punished by God even after his sin is forgiven. And so the debt of punishment remains, when the sin has been removed.

I answer that, Two things may be considered in sin: the guilty act, and the consequent stain. Now it is evident that in all actual sins,

[3] Aristotle, *Ethics*, ii, 3 (1104[b]17).

when the act of sin has ceased, the guilt remains; because the act of sin makes man deserving of punishment in so far as he transgresses the order of Divine justice, to which he cannot return except he pay some sort of penal compensation, which restores him to the equality of justice. And so according to the order of Divine justice, he who has been too indulgent to his will, by transgressing God's commandment, suffers, either willingly or unwillingly, something contrary to what he would wish. This restoration of the equality of justice by penal compensation is also to be observed in injuries done to one's fellow men. Consequently it is evident that when the sinful or injurious act has ceased there still remains the debt of punishment.

But if we speak of the removal of sin as to the stain, it is evident that the stain of sin cannot be removed from the soul, without the soul being united to God, since it was through being separated from Him that it suffered the loss of its brightness, in which the stain consists, as stated above (Q. LXXXVI, A. 1). Now man is united to God by his will. Therefore the stain of sin cannot be removed from man unless his will accept the order of Divine justice, that is to say, unless either of his own accord he take upon himself the punishment of his past sin, or bear patiently the punishment which God inflicts on him; and in both ways punishment avails for satisfaction. Now when punishment is satisfactory, it loses somewhat of the nature of punishment; for the nature of punishment is to be against the will, and although satisfactory punishment, absolutely speaking, is against the will, nevertheless in this particular case and for this particular purpose, it is voluntary. Consequently it is voluntary absolutely, but involuntary in a certain respect, as we have explained when speaking of the voluntary and the involuntary (Q. VI, A. 6). We must, therefore, say that, when the stain of sin has been removed, there may remain a debt of punishment, not indeed of punishment absolutely, but of satisfactory punishment.

Reply Obj. 1. Just as after the act of sin has ceased, the stain remains, as stated above (Q. LXXXVI, A. 2), so the debt of punishment also can remain. But when the stain has been removed, the debt of punishment does not remain in the same way, as stated.

Reply Obj. 2. The virtuous man does not deserve punishment absolutely, but he may deserve it as satisfactory, because his very virtue

demands that he should do satisfaction for his offences against God or man.

Reply Obj. 3. When the stain is removed, the wound of sin is healed as regards the will. But punishment is still requisite in order that the other powers of the soul be healed, since they were disordered by the sin committed (so that, namely, the disorder may be remedied by the contrary of that which caused it). Moreover punishment is requisite in order to restore the equality of justice, and to remove the scandal given to others, so that those who were scandalized at the sin may be edified by the punishment, as may be seen in the example of David quoted above.

ARTICLE 7. *Whether Every Punishment Is Inflicted for a Sin?*

We proceed thus to the Seventh Article: It would seem that not every punishment is inflicted for a sin.

Objection 1. For it is written (John 9. 3, 2) about the man born blind: *Neither hath this man sinned, nor his parents . . . that he should be born blind.* In like manner we see that many children, those also who have been baptized, suffer grievous punishments, fevers, for instance, diabolical possession, and so forth, and yet there is no sin in them after they have been baptized. Moreover before they are baptized, there is no more sin in them than in the other children who do not suffer such things. Therefore not every punishment is inflicted for a sin.

Obj. 2. Further, that sinners should thrive and that the innocent should be punished seem to come under the same head. Now each of these is frequently observed in human affairs, for it is written about the wicked (Ps. 72. 5): *They are not in the labour of men: neither shall they be scourged like other men;* and (Job 21. 7): *(Why then do) the wicked live, are (they) advanced, and strengthened with riches (?);*[1] and (Habac. 1. 13): *Why lookest Thou upon the contemptuous* (Vulg.,—*them that do unjust things), and holdest Thy peace, when the wicked man oppresseth* (Vulg.,—*devoureth), the man that is more just than himself?* Therefore not every punishment is inflicted for a sin.

Obj. 3. Further, it is written of Christ (I Pet. 2. 22) that *He did no sin, nor was guile found in His mouth.* And yet it is said (*ibid.*, 21) that *He suffered for us.* Therefore punishment is not always inflicted by God for sin.

[1] The words in parenthesis show the readings of the Vulgate.

On the contrary, It is written (Job 4. 7, sqq.): *Who ever perished innocent? Or when were the just destroyed? On the contrary, I have seen those who work iniquity . . . perishing by the blast of God;* and Augustine writes (*Retract.* i, 9)[1] that all "punishment is just, and is inflicted for a sin."

I answer that, As already stated (A. 6), punishment can be considered in two ways,—either absolutely, or as being satisfactory. A satisfactory punishment is, in a way, voluntary. And since those who differ as to the debt of punishment may be one in will by the union of love, it happens that one who has not sinned bears willingly the punishment for another, just as even in human affairs we see men take the debts of another upon themselves. If, however, we speak of punishment absolutely, in respect of its being something penal, it has always a relation to a sin in the one punished. Sometimes this is a relation to actual sin, as when a man is punished by God or man for a sin committed by him. Sometimes it is a relation to original sin; and this, either principally or consequently, —principally, the punishment of original sin is that human nature is left to itself, and deprived of the help of original justice. All the penalties which result from the defect in human nature follow from this.

Nevertheless we must observe that sometimes a thing seems penal, and yet is not so absolutely. Because punishment is a species of evil, as stated in the First Part (Q. XLVIII, A. 5). Now evil is privation of good. And since man's good is manifold, namely good of the soul, good of the body, and external goods, it happens sometimes that man suffers the loss of a lesser good that he may profit in a greater good, as when he suffers loss of money for the sake of bodily health, or loss of both of these for the sake of his soul's health and the glory of God. In such cases the loss is an evil to man not absolutely but relatively; hence it does not answer to the name of punishment absolutely, but of medicinal punishment, because a medical man prescribes bitter potions to his patients that he may restore them to health. And since such are not punishments, properly speaking, they are not referred to sin as their cause, except in a restricted sense; because the very fact that human nature needs a treatment of penal medicines is due to the corruption of nature which is itself the punishment of original sin. For there was no need, in the state of innocence, for penal exercises in order to make progress in virtue, so that whatever is penal in the exercise of virtue is reduced to original sin as its cause.

Reply Obj. 1. Defects of this kind of those who are born with them, or which children suffer from, are the effects and the punishments of original sin, as stated above (ANS. Q. LXXXV, A. 5). And they remain even after baptism, for the cause stated above (*ibid.,* REPLY 2); and that they are not equally in all, is due to the diversity of nature, which is left to itself, as stated above (*ibid.,* REPLY 1). Nevertheless, they are directed by Divine providence to the salvation of men, either of those who suffer, or of others who are admonished by their means— and also to the glory of God.

Reply Obj. 2. Temporal and bodily goods are indeed goods of man, but they are of small account; spiritual goods however are man's chief goods. Consequently it belongs to Divine justice to give spiritual goods to the virtuous, and to award them as much temporal goods or evils as suffices for virtue. For, as Dionysius says (*Div. Nom.* viii),[2] "Divine justice does not enfeeble the fortitude of the best men by material gifts." The very fact that others receive temporal goods is detrimental to their spiritual good; therefore the psalm quoted concludes (*verse* 6): *Therefore pride hath held them fast.*

Reply Obj. 3. Christ bore a satisfactory punishment, not for His, but for our sins.

ARTICLE 8. *Whether Anyone is Punished for Another's Sin?*

We proceed thus to the Eighth Article: It would seem that one may be punished for another's sin.

Objection 1. For it is written (*Exod.* 20. 5): *I am . . . God . . . jealous, visiting the iniquity of the fathers upon the children, unto the third and fourth generation of them that hate Me;* and (Matt. 23. 35): *That upon you may come all the just blood that hath been shed upon the earth.*

Obj. 2. Further, human justice springs from Divine justice. Now, according to human justice, children are sometimes punished for their parents, as in the case of high treason. Therefore also according to Divine justice, one is punished for another's sin.

Obj. 3. Further, if it be replied that the son is punished not for the father's sin, but for his own, in so far as he imitates his father's wickedness, this would not be said of the children rather than of outsiders, who are punished in like manner as those whose crimes they imitate.

[1] PL 32, 598; *De Lib. Arb.,* III, 18 (PL 32, 1296).

[2] Sect. 8 (PG 3, 896).

It seems, therefore, that children are punished not for their own sins, but for those of their parents.

On the contrary, It is written (Ezech. 18. 20): *The son shall not bear the iniquity of the father.*

I answer that, If we speak of that satisfactory punishment which one takes upon oneself voluntarily, one may bear another's punishment, in so far as they are, in some way, one, as stated above (A. 7). If, however, we speak of punishment inflicted on account of sin, in so far as it is penal, then each one is punished for his own sin only, because the sinful act is something personal. But if we speak of a punishment that is medicinal, in this way it does happen that one is punished for another's sin. For it has been stated (A. 7) that ills sustained in bodily goods or even in the body itself, are medicinal punishments intended for the health of the soul. Therefore there is no reason why one should not have such punishments inflicted on one for another's sin, either by God or by man; for example on children for their parents, or on servants for their masters, in so far as they are their property so to speak; in such a way, however, that, if the children or the servants take part in the sin, this penal ill has the character of punishment in regard to both the one punished and the one he is punished for. But if they do not take part in the sin, it has the character of punishment in regard to the one for whom the punishment is borne, while, in regard to the one who is punished, it is merely medicinal (except accidentally, if he consent to the other's sin), since it is intended for the good of his soul, if he bears it patiently.

With regard to spiritual punishments, these are not merely medicinal, because the good of the soul is not directed to a yet higher good. Consequently no one suffers loss in the goods of the soul without some fault of his own. Therefore, as Augustine says,[1] such punishments are not inflicted on one for another's sin, because, as regards the soul, the son is not the father's property. Hence the Lord assigns the reason for this by saying (Ezech. 18. 4): *All souls are mine.*

Reply Obj. 1. Both the passages quoted should, it seems, be referred to temporal or bodily punishments, in so far as children are the property of their parents, and posterity of their forefathers. Or otherwise, if they be referred to spiritual punishments, they must be understood in reference to the imitation of sin. Hence in

[1] *Ep. ad Auxilium,* CCL. (PL 33, 1066).

Exodus these words are added: *Of them that hate Me,* and in the chapter quoted from Matthew(*verse* 32) we read: *Fill ye up then the measure of your fathers.*

The sins of the fathers are said to be punished in their children because the latter are the more prone to sin through being brought up amid their parents' crimes, both by becoming accustomed to them, and by imitating their parents' example, conforming to their authority as it were. Moreover they deserve heavier punishment if, seeing the punishment of their parents, they fail to mend their ways. The text adds, *to the third and fourth generation,* because usually men live long enough to see the third and fourth generation, so that both the children can witness their parents' sins so as to imitate them, and the parents can see their children's punishments so as to grieve for them.

Reply Obj. 2. The punishments which human justice inflicts on one for another's sin are bodily and temporal. They are also remedies or medicines against future sins, in order that either they who are punished, or others, may be restrained from similar faults.

Reply Obj. 3. Those who are near of kin are said to be punished, rather than outsiders, for the sins of others, both because the punishment of kindred overflows somewhat upon those who sinned, as stated above, in so far as the child is the father's property, and because the examples and the punishments that occur in one's own household are more moving. Consequently when a man is brought up amid the sins of his parents, he is more eager to imitate them, and if he is not deterred by their punishments, he would seem to be the more obstinate, and, therefore, to deserve more severe punishment.

QUESTION LXXXVIII
OF VENIAL AND MORTAL SIN
(*In Six Articles*)

In the next place, since venial and mortal sins differ in respect of the debt of punishment, we must consider them. First, we shall consider venial sin as compared with mortal sin; secondly, we shall consider venial sin in itself (Q. LXXXIX).

Under the first head there six points of inquiry: (1) Whether venial sin is fittingly divided against mortal sin? (2) Whether they differ generically? (3) Whether venial sin is a disposition to mortal sin? (4) Whether a venial sin can become mortal? (5) Whether a venial sin can become mortal by reason of an aggravating circumstance? (6) Whether a mortal sin can become venial?

Article 1. *Whether Venial Sin Is Fittingly Divided Against Mortal Sin?*

We proceed thus to the First Article: It would seem that venial sin is unfittingly divided against mortal sin.

Objection 1. For Augustine says (*Contra Faust.* xxii, 27):[1] "Sin is a word, deed or desire contrary to the eternal law." But the fact of being against the eternal law makes a sin to be mortal. Consequently every sin is mortal. Therefore venial sin is not divided against mortal sin.

Obj. 2. Further, the Apostle says (I Cor. 10. 31): *Whether you eat or drink, or whatever else you do; do all to the glory of God.* Now whoever sins breaks this commandment, because sin is not done for God's glory. Consequently, since to break a commandment is to commit a mortal sin, it seems that whoever sins, sins mortally.

Obj. 3. Further, whoever cleaves to a thing by love, cleaves either as enjoying it, or as using it, as Augustine states.[2] But no person, in sinning, cleaves to a changeable good as using it, because he does not refer it to that good which gives us happiness, which, properly speaking, is to use, according to Augustine.[3] Therefore whoever sins enjoys a changeable good. Now "to enjoy what we should use is human perverseness," as Augustine again says (QQ. LXXXIII, qu. 30).[4] Therefore, since "perverseness" denotes a mortal sin,[5] it seems that whoever sins, sins mortally.

. *Obj.* 4. Further, whoever approaches one term, from that very fact turns away from the opposite. Now whoever sins approaches a changeable good, and, consequently turns away from the unchangeable good, so that he sins mortally. Therefore venial sin is unfittingly divided against mortal sin.

On the contrary, Augustine says (*Tract.* xli *in Joann.*),[6] that "a crime is one that merits damnation, and a venial sin, one that does not." But a crime denotes a mortal sin. Therefore venial sin is fittingly divided against mortal sin.

I answer that, Certain terms do not appear to be mutually opposed, if taken in their proper

[1] PL 42, 418.
[2] *Christian Doctrine,* I, 3 (PL 34, 20).
[3] *Ibid.*
[4] PL 40, 19.
[5] The Latin *pervertere* means to overthrow, to destroy, hence *perversion* of God's law is a mortal sin.
[6] PL 35, 1697; cf. Peter Lombard, *Sent.,* II, d. 42, chap. 3 (QR I, 529).

sense, while they are opposed if taken metaphorically. Thus to smile is not opposed to being dry; but if we speak of the smiling meadows when they are decked with flowers and fresh with green hues this is opposed to drought. In like manner if mortal be taken literally as referring to the death of the body, it does not imply opposition to venial, nor belong to the same genus. But if mortal be taken metaphorically, as applied to sin, it is opposed to that which is venial.

For sin, being a sickness of the soul, as stated above (Q. LXXI, A. 1, Reply 3; Q. LXXII, A. 5; Q. LXXIV, A. 9, Reply 2), is said to be mortal by comparison with a disease, which is said to be mortal through causing an irreparable defect consisting in the corruption of a principle, as stated above (Q. LXXII, A. 5). Now the principle of the spiritual life, which is a life in accord with virtue, is the order to the last end, as stated above (*ibid.*; Q. LXXXVII, A. 3); and if this order be corrupted, it cannot be repaired by any intrinsic principle, but by the power of God alone, as stated above (Q. LXXXVII, A. 3). because disorders in things referred to the end are repaired through the end, even as an error about conclusions can be repaired through the truth of the principles. Hence the defect of order to the last end cannot be repaired through something else as a higher principle, as neither can an error about principles. Therefore such sins are called mortal, as being irreparable. On the other hand, sins which imply a disorder in things referred to the end, the order to the end itself being preserved, are reparable. These sins are called venial; for a sin receives its acquittal (*veniam*) when the debt of punishment is taken away, and this ceases when the sin ceases, as explained above (Q. LXXXVII, A. 6).

Accordingly, mortal and venial are opposed as reparable and irreparable. And I say this with reference to the intrinsic principle, but not to the Divine power, which can repair all diseases, whether of the body or of the soul. Therefore venial sin is fittingly divided against mortal sin.

Reply Obj. 1. The division of sin into venial and mortal is not a division of a genus into its species which have an equal share of the generic notion; but it is the division of an analogous term into its parts, of which it is predicated, of the one first, and of the other afterwards. Consequently the perfect notion of sin, which Augustine gives, applies to mortal sin. On the other hand, venial sin is called a sin in reference to an imperfect notion of sin, and in relation to mortal sin; even as an accident is called a being, in relation to substance, in reference to the imperfect notion of being. For it is not *against* the law, since he who sins venially neither does what the law forbids, nor omits what the law prescribes to be done; but he acts *beside* the law, through not observing the mode of reason, which the law intends.

Reply Obj. 2. This precept of the Apostle is affirmative, and so it does not bind for all times. Consequently everyone who does not actually refer all his actions to the glory of God does not therefore act against this precept. In order, therefore, to avoid mortal sin each time that one fails actually to refer an action to God's glory, it is enough to refer oneself and all that one has to God habitually. Now venial sin excludes only actual reference of the human act to God's glory, and not habitual reference, because it does not exclude charity, which refers man to God habitually. Therefore it does not follow that he who sins venially, sins mortally.

Reply Obj. 3. He that sins venially, cleaves to temporal good not as enjoying it, because he does not fix his end in it, but as using it, by referring it to God, not actually but habitually.

Reply Obj. 4. Mutable good is not considered to be a term in contraposition to the immutable good, unless one's end is fixed in it, because what is referred to the end has not the character of end.

ARTICLE 2. *Whether Mortal and Venial Sin Differ Generically?*

We proceed thus to the Second Article: It would seem that venial and mortal sin do not differ generically, so that some sins are generically mortal, and some generically venial.

Objection 1. For human acts are considered to be generically good or evil according to their matter or object, as stated above (Q. XVIII, A. 2). Now either mortal or venial sin may be committed in regard to any object or matter, since man can love any mutable good, either less than God, which may be a venial sin, or more than God, which is a mortal sin. Therefore venial and mortal sin do not differ generically.

Obj. 2. Further, as stated above (A. 1; Q. LXXII, A. 5; Q. LXXXVII, A. 3), a sin is called mortal when it is irreparable, venial when it can be repaired. Now irreparability belongs to sin committed out of malice, which, according to some, is irremissible; but reparability belongs to sins committed through weakness or ignorance, which are remissible. Therefore mortal and venial sin differ as sin committed

through malice differs from sin committed through weakness or ignorance. But, in this respect, sins differ not in genus but in cause, as stated above (Q. LXXVII, A. 8, Reply 1). Therefore venial and mortal sin do not differ generically.

Obj. 3. Further, it was stated above (Q. LXXIV, A. 3, Reply 3; A. 10) that sudden movements both of the sensuality and of the reason are venial sins. But sudden movements occur in every kind of sin. Therefore no sins are generically venial.

On the contrary, Augustine, in a sermon on Purgatory[1] enumerates certain generic venial sins, and certain generic mortal sins.

I answer that, Venial sin is so called from *venia* (*pardon*). Consequently a sin may be called venial, first of all, because it has been pardoned; thus Ambrose says[2] that penance makes every sin venial. And this is called venial from the result. Secondly, a sin is called venial because it does not contain anything either partially or totally to prevent its being pardoned. Partially, as when a sin contains something diminishing its guilt, for example a sin committed through weakness or ignorance; and this is called venial from the cause. Totally, through not destroying the order to the last end, so that it deserves temporal, but not everlasting punishment. It is of this venial sin that we wish to speak now.

For as regards the first two, it is evident that they have no determinate genus. But venial sin taken in the third sense can have a determinate genus, so that one sin may be venial generically, and another generically mortal, according as the genus or species of an act is determined by its object. For when the will is directed to a thing that is in itself contrary to charity, by which man is directed to his last end, the sin is mortal by reason of its object. Consequently it is a mortal sin generically, whether it be contrary to the love of God, for example blasphemy, perjury, and the like, or against the love of one's neighbour, for example murder, adultery, and the like. And so such sins are mortal by reason of their genus. Sometimes, however, the sinner's will is directed to a thing containing a certain lack of order, but which is not contrary to the love of God and one's neighbour, for example an idle word, excessive laughter, and so forth. And such sins are venial by reason of their genus.

---

[1] Contained among the works of Augustine, *Serm.*, CIV (PL 39, 1946).

[2] *De Parad.*, XIV (PL 14, 327).

Nevertheless, since moral acts derive their character of goodness and malice not only from their objects but also from some disposition of the agent, as stated above. (Q. XVIII, AA. 4, 6), it happens sometimes that a sin which is venial generically by reason of its object becomes mortal on the part of the agent, either because he fixes his last end therein, or because he directs it to something that is a mortal sin in its own genus; for example, if a man direct an idle word to the commission of adultery. In like manner it may happen, on the part of the agent, that a sin generically mortal becomes venial, by reason of the act being imperfect, that is not deliberated by reason, which is the proper principle of an evil act, as we have said above (Q. LXXIV, A. 10) in reference to sudden movements of unbelief.

Reply Obj. 1. The very fact that anyone chooses something that is contrary to divine charity proves that he prefers it to the love of God, and consequently, that he loves it more than he loves God. Hence it belongs to the genus of some sins, which are of themselves contrary to charity, that something is loved more than God. And so they are mortal by reason of their genus.

Reply Obj. 2. This argument considers those sins which are venial from their cause.

Reply Obj. 3. This argument considers those sins which are venial by reason of the imperfection of the act.

ARTICLE 3. *Whether Venial Sin Is a Disposition to Mortal Sin?*

We proceed thus to the Third Article: It would seem that venial sin is not a disposition to mortal sin.

Objection 1. For one contrary does not dispose to another. But venial and mortal sin are divided as contrary to one another, as stated above. (A. 1). Therefore venial sin is not a disposition to mortal sin.

Obj. 2. Further, an act disposes to something of like species, and so it is stated in the *Ethics*,[1] that from like acts like dispositions and habits are engendered. But mortal and venial sin differ in genus or species, as stated above (A. 2). Therefore venial sin does not dispose to mortal sin.

Obj. 3. Further, if a sin is called venial because it disposes to mortal sin, it follows that whatever disposes to mortal sin is a venial sin. Now every good work disposes to mortal sin; for Augustine says in his Rule (*Ep.* ccxi)[2] that

"pride lies in wait for good works that it may destroy them." Therefore even good works would be venial sins, which is absurd.

On the contrary. It is written (Ecclus. 19. 1): *He that contemneth small things shall fall by little and little.* Now he that sins venially seems to contemn small things. Therefore by little and little he is disposed to fall away altogether into mortal sin.

I answer that, A disposition is a kind of cause. Therefore since there is a twofold manner of cause, so is there a twofold manner of disposition. For there is a cause which moves directly to the production of the effect, as a hot thing heats. And there is a cause which moves indirectly, by removing an obstacle, as he who displaces a pillar is said to displace the stone that rests on it. Accordingly an act of sin disposes to something in two ways. First, directly, and thus it disposes to an act of like species. In this way, a sin generically venial does not, primarily and of its nature, dispose to a sin generically mortal, for they differ in species. Nevertheless, in this same way, a venial sin can dispose, by way of consequence, to a sin which is mortal on the part of the agent. For the disposition or habit may be so far strengthened by acts of venial sin that the lust of sinning increases, and the sinner fixes his end in that venial sin, since the end for one who has a habit, as such, is to work according to that habit; and the consequence will be that, by sinning often venially, he becomes disposed to a mortal sin. Secondly, a human act disposes to something by removing an obstacle to it. In this way a sin generically venial can dispose to a sin generically mortal. Because he that commits a sin generically venial turns aside from some particular order; and through accustoming his will not to be subject to the due order in lesser matters, is disposed not to subject his will even to the order of the last end, by choosing something that is a mortal sin in its genus.

Reply Obj. 1. Venial and mortal sin are not divided in contrariety to one another, as though they were species of one genus, as stated above (A. 1, REPLY 1), but as an accident is divided against substance. Therefore just as an accident can be a disposition to a substantial form, so can a venial sin dispose to mortal.

Reply Obj. 2. Venial sin is not like mortal sin in species; but it is in genus, since they both imply a defect of due order, although in different ways, as stated (AA. 1, 2).

Reply Obj. 3. A good work is not, of itself, a disposition to mortal sin; but it can be the mat-

---

[1] Aristotle, II, 1 (1103ª26).   [2] PL 33, 960.

ter or occasion of mortal sin accidentally. But a venial sin, of its very nature, disposes to mortal sin, as stated.

ARTICLE 4. *Whether a Venial Sin Can Become Mortal?*

We proceed thus to the Fourth Article: It would seem that a venial sin can become a mortal sin.

Objection 1. For Augustine in explaining the words of John 3. 36, *He that believeth not the Son, shall not see life,* says (*Tract.* xii *in Joann.*):[1] "The slightest," that is venial, "sins kill if we make little of them." Now a sin is called mortal through causing the spiritual death of the soul. Therefore a venial sin can become mortal.

Obj. 2. Further, a movement in the sensuality before the consent of reason is a venial sin, but after consent is a mortal sin, as stated above (Q. LXXIV, A. 8, Reply 2). Therefore a venial sin can become mortal.

Obj. 3. Further, venial and mortal sin differ as curable and incurable disease, as stated above (A. 1). But a curable disease may become incurable. Therefore a venial sin may become mortal.

Obj. 4. Further, a disposition may become a habit. Now venial sin is a disposition to mortal, as stated (A. 3). Therefore a venial sin can become mortal.

On the contrary, Things that differ infinitely are not changed into one another. Now venial and mortal sin differ infinitely, as is evident from what has been said above (Q. LXXII, A. 5, Reply 1; Q. LXXVII, A. 5, Reply 1). Therefore a venial sin cannot become mortal.

I answer that, The fact of a venial sin becoming a mortal sin may be understood in three ways. First, so that the same identical act be at first a venial, and then a mortal sin. This is impossible. Because a sin, like any moral act, consists chiefly in an act of the will, so that an act is not one morally, if the will is changed, even though the act is continuous physically. If, however, the will is not changed, it is not possible for a venial sin to become mortal.

Secondly, this may be taken to mean that a sin generically venial becomes mortal. This is possible, in so far as one may fix one's end in that venial sin, or direct it to some mortal sin as end, as stated above (A. 2).

Thirdly, this may be understood in the sense of many venial sins constituting one mortal sin. If this be taken as meaning that many venial

[1] PL 35, 1492.

sins added together make one mortal sin, it is false, because all the venial sins in the world cannot incur a debt of punishment equal to that of one mortal sin. This is evident as regards the duration of the punishment, since mortal sin incurs a debt of eternal punishment, while venial sin incurs a debt of temporal punishment, as stated above (Q. LXXXVIII, AA. 3, 5).—It is also evident as regards the pain of loss, because mortal sins deserve to be punished by the privation of seeing God, to which no other punishment is comparable, as Chrysostom states (*Hom.* xxiii *in Matt.*).[2] It is also evident as regards the pain of sense, as to the remorse of conscience; although as to the pain of fire, the punishments may perhaps not be improportionate to one another.

If, however, this be taken as meaning that many venial sins make one mortal sin dispositively, it is true, as was shown above (A. 3) with regard to the two different manners of disposition, by which venial sin disposes to mortal sin.

Reply Obj. 1. Augustine is referring to the fact of many venial sins making one mortal sin dispositively.

Reply Obj. 2. That same movement of the sensuality which preceded the consent of reason can never become a mortal sin; but the movement of the reason in consenting is a mortal sin.

Reply Obj. 3. Disease of the body is not an act, but an abiding disposition; therefore, while remaining the same disease, it may undergo change. On the other hand, venial sin is a transient act, which cannot be taken up again, so that in this respect the comparison fails.

Reply Obj. 4. A disposition that becomes a habit is like an imperfect thing in the same species; thus imperfect science, by being perfected, becomes a habit. On the other hand, venial sin is a disposition to something differing generically, even as an accident which disposes to a substantial form, into which it is never changed.

ARTICLE 5. *Whether a Circumstance Can Make a Venial Sin to Be Mortal?*

We proceed thus to the Fifth Article: It would seem that a circumstance can make a venial sin be mortal.

Objection 1. For Augustine says in a sermon on Purgatory[3] that "if anger continue for a long time, or if drunkenness be frequent, they be-

[2] PG 57, 317.
[3] Found among the works of Augustine, *Serm. ad Popul.*, serm., CIV (PL 39, 1946).

come mortal sins." But anger and drunkenness are not mortal but venial sins generically, for otherwise they would always be mortal sins. Therefore a circumstance makes a venial sin to be mortal.

Obj. 2. Further, the Master says (2 *Sent.*, D. XXIV, 12)[1] that pleasure, if lingering, is a mortal sin, but that if it be not lingering, it is a venial sin. Now lingering is a circumstance. Therefore a circumstance makes a venial sin to be mortal.

Obj. 3. Further, evil and good differ more than venial and mortal sin, both of which are generically evil. But a circumstance makes a good act to be evil, as when a man gives an alms for vainglory. Much more, therefore, can it make a venial sin to be mortal.

On the contrary, Since a circumstance is an accident, its quantity cannot exceed that of the act itself, which it has from the act's genus, because the subject always excels its accident. If, therefore, an act be venial by reason of its genus, it cannot become mortal by reason of a circumstance, since, in a way, mortal sin infinitely surpasses the quantity of venial sin, as is evident from what has been said (Q. LXXII, A. 5, Reply 1; Q. LXXXVII, A. 5, Reply 1).

I answer that, As stated above (Q. VII, A. 1; Q. XVIII, A. 5, Reply 4; AA. 10, 11), when we were treating of circumstances, a circumstance, as such, is an accident of the moral act. And yet a circumstance may happen to be taken as the specific difference of a moral act, and then it loses its nature of circumstance, and constitutes the species of the moral act. This happens in sins when a circumstance adds the deformity of another genus; thus when a man has knowledge of another woman than his wife, the deformity of his act is opposed to chastity. But if this other be another man's wife, there is an additional deformity opposed to justice, which forbids one to take what belongs to another; and accordingly this circumstance constitutes a new species of sin known as adultery.

It is, however, impossible for a circumstance to make a venial sin become mortal, unless it adds the deformity of another species. For it has been stated above (A. 1) that the deformity of a venial sin consists in a disorder affecting things that are referred to the end, while the deformity of a mortal sin consists in a disorder about the last end. Consequently it is evident that a circumstance cannot make a venial sin to be mortal, so long as it remains a circum-

[1] QR I, 245.

stance, but only when it transfers the sin to another species, and becomes, as it were, the specific difference of the moral act.

Reply Obj. 1. Length of time is not a circumstance that draws a sin to another species, nor is frequency or custom, except perhaps by something accidental supervening. For an action does not acquire a new species through being repeated or prolonged, unless by chance something supervene in the repeated or prolonged act to change its species, for example disobedience, contempt, or the like.

We must therefore reply to the objection by saying that since anger is a movement of the soul tending to the hurt of one's neighbour, if the angry movement tend to a hurt which is a mortal sin generically, such as murder or robbery, that anger will be a mortal sin generically. And if it be a venial sin, this will be due to the imperfection of the act, in so far as it is a sudden movement of the sensuality. But, if it last a long time, it returns to its generic nature, through the consent of reason. If, on the other hand, the hurt to which the angry movement tends is a sin generically venial, for instance, if a man be angry with someone so as to wish to say some trifling word in jest that would hurt him a little, the anger will not be a mortal sin, however long it last, unless perhaps accidentally; for instance, if it were to give rise to great scandal or something of the kind.

With regard to drunkenness we reply that it is a mortal sin by reason of its genus; for, that a man without necessity, and through the mere lust of wine, make himself unable to use his reason, by which he is directed to God and avoids committing many sins, is expressly contrary to virtue. That it be a venial sin, is due to some sort of ignorance or weakness, as when a man is ignorant of the strength of the wine, or of his own unfitness, so that he has no thought of getting drunk, for in that case the drunkenness is not imputed to him as a sin, but only the excessive drink. If, however, he gets drunk frequently, this ignorance no longer avails as an excuse, for his will seems to choose to give way to drunkenness rather than to refrain from excess of wine. And so the sin returns to its own nature.

Reply Obj. 2. Lingering pleasure is not a mortal sin except in those matters which are mortal sins generically. In such matters, if the pleasure is not lingering there is a venial sin through imperfection of the act, as we have said with regard to anger (Reply 1). For anger is said to be lasting, and pleasure to be lingering, on account of the approval of the deliberating reason.

Reply Obj. 3. A circumstance does not make a good act to be evil, unless it constitute the species of a sin, as we have stated above (Q. XVIII, A. 5, Reply 4).

ARTICLE 6. *Whether a Mortal Sin Can Become Venial?*

We proceed thus to the Sixth Article: It would seem that a mortal sin can become venial.

Objection 1. Because venial sin is equally distant from mortal as mortal sin is from venial. But a venial sin can become mortal, as stated above (A. 4). Therefore also a mortal sin can become venial.

Obj. 2. Further, venial and mortal sin are said to differ in this, that he who sins mortally loves a creature more than God, while he who sins venially loves the creature less than God. Now it may happen that a person in committing a sin generically mortal loves a creature less than God; for instance, if anyone being ignorant that simple fornication is a mortal sin, and contrary to the love of God, commits the sin of fornication, yet so as to be ready, for the love of God, to refrain from that sin if he knew that by committing it he was acting counter to the love of God. Therefore his will be a venial sin, and accordingly a mortal sin can become venial.

Obj. 3. Further, as stated above (A. 5, obj. 3), good is more distant from evil than venial from mortal sin. But an act which is evil in itself can become good; thus to kill a man may be an act of justice, as when a judge condemns a thief to death. Much more therefore can a mortal sin become venial.

On the contrary, An eternal thing can never become temporal. But mortal sin deserves eternal punishment, and venial sin deserves temporal punishment. Therefore a mortal sin can never become venial.

I answer that, Venial and mortal differ as perfect and imperfect in the genus of sin, as stated above (A. 1, Reply 1). Now the imperfect can become perfect by some sort of addition. And, consequently, a venial sin can become mortal by the addition of some deformity pertaining to the genus of mortal sin, as when a man utters an idle word for the purpose of fornication. On the other hand, the perfect cannot become imperfect by addition; and so a mortal sin cannot become venial by the addition of a deformity pertaining to the genus of venial sin, for the sin is not diminished if a man commit fornication in order to utter an

idle word; rather is it aggravated by the additional deformity.

Nevertheless a sin which is generically mortal can become venial by reason of the imperfection of the act, because then it does not completely fulfil the conditions of a moral act, since it is not a deliberate, but a sudden act, as is evident from what we have said above (A. 2). This happens by a kind of subtraction, namely, of deliberate reason. And since a moral act takes its species from deliberate reason, the result is that by such a subtraction the species of the act is destroyed.

Reply Obj. 1. Venial differs from mortal as imperfect from perfect, even as a boy differs from a man. But the boy becomes a man and not vice versa. Hence the argument does not prove.

Reply Obj. 2. If the ignorance be such as to excuse sin altogether, as the ignorance of a madman or an imbecile, then he that commits fornication in a state of such ignorance commits no sin either mortal or venial. But if the ignorance be not invincible, then the ignorance itself is a sin, and contains within itself the lack of the love of God, in so far as a man neglects to learn those things whereby he can safeguard himself in the love of God.

Reply Obj. 3. As Augustine says (*Contra Mendacium*, vii),[1] "those things which are evil in themselves cannot be well done for any good end." Now murder is the slaying of the innocent, and this can in no way be well done. But, as Augustine states (*De Lib. Arb.* i, 4, 5),[2] "the judge who sentences a thief to death, or the soldier who slays the enemy of the common weal, are not murderers."

QUESTION LXXXIX

OF VENIAL SIN IN ITSELF

(*In Six Articles*)

WE must now consider venial sin in itself, and under this head there are six points of inquiry: (1) Whether venial sin causes a stain in the soul? (2) Of the different kinds of venial sin, as denoted by *wood, hay, stubble* (I Cor. 3. 12). (3) Whether man could sin venially in the state of innocence? (4) Whether a good or a wicked angel can sin venially (5) Whether the first movements of unbelievers are venial sins? (6) Whether venial sin can be in a man with original sin alone?

[1] PL 40, 528.
[2] PL 32, 1226; 1227.

ARTICLE 1. *Whether Venial Sin Causes a Stain in the Soul?*

We proceed thus to the First Article: It would seem that venial sin causes a stain in the soul.

Objection 1. For Augustine says (*De Pænit.*),[1] that "if venial sins are multiplied, they destroy the beauty of our souls so as to deprive us of the embraces of our heavenly spouse." But the stain of sin is nothing else but the loss of the soul's beauty. Therefore venial sins cause a stain in the soul.

Obj. 2. Further, mortal sin causes a stain in the soul, on account of the lack of order of the act and of the sinner's affections. But in venial sin there is a lack of order of the act and of the affections. Therefore venial sin causes a stain in the soul.

Obj. 3. Further, the stain on the soul is caused by contact with a temporal thing, through love for it, as stated above (Q. LXXXVI, A. 1). But in venial sin the soul is in contact with a temporal thing through a disordered love. Therefore venial sin brings a stain on to the soul.

On the contrary, It is written (Eph. 5. 27): *That He might present it to Himself a glorious church, not having spot or wrinkle*, on which the gloss says[2]: "that is, some grievous sin." Therefore it seems proper to mortal sin to cause a stain in the soul.

I answer that, As stated above (Q. LXXXVI, A. 1), a stain denotes a loss of brightness due to contact with something, as may be seen in corporeal matters, from which the term has been transferred to the soul by way of likeness. Now just as in the body there is a twofold beauty, one resulting from the inward disposition of the members and colours, the other resulting from the outward radiance which follows, so too, in the soul, there is a twofold beauty, one habitual, and, so to speak, intrinsic, the other, actual, like an outward splendor. Now venial sin is a hindrance to actual beauty, but not to habitual beauty, because it neither destroys nor diminishes the habit of charity and of the other virtues, as we shall show further on (Part II-II, Q. XXIV, A. 10; Q. CXXXIII, A. 1, reply 2), but only hinders their acts. On the other hand, a stain denotes something permanent in the thing stained and so it seems in the nature of a loss of habitual rather than of actual beauty. Therefore, prop-

erly speaking, venial sin does not cause a stain in the soul. If, however, we find it stated anywhere that it does induce a stain, this is in a restricted sense, in so far as it hinders the beauty that results from acts of virtue.

Reply Obj. 1. Augustine is speaking of the case in which many venial sins lead to mortal sin by way of disposition. For otherwise they would not sever the soul from the embrace of its heavenly spouse.

Reply Obj. 2. In mortal sin, the lack of order in the act destroys the habit of virtue, but not in venial sin.

Reply Obj. 3. In mortal sin the soul comes into contact with a temporal thing as its end, so that the influx of the light of grace, which accrues to those who, by charity, cleave to God as their last end, is entirely cut off. On the contrary, in venial sin, man does not cleave to a creature as his last end. Hence there is no comparison.

ARTICLE 2. *Whether Venial Sins Are Suitably Designated as Wood, Hay, and Stubble?*

We proceed thus to the Second Article: It would seem that venial sins are unsuitably designated as *wood, hay*, and *stubble* (I Cor. 3. 12).[3]

Objection 1. For wood, hay, and stubble are said (*ibid.*) to be built on a spiritual foundation. Now venial sins are something outside a spiritual foundation, even as false opinions are outside the pale of science. Therefore venial sins are not suitably designated as wood, hay, and stubble.

Obj. 2. Further, he who builds wood, hay, and stubble, *shall be saved yet so as by fire* (*verse* 15). But sometimes the man who commits a venial sin, will not be saved, even by fire, for instance when venial sins are found in a man who dies in mortal sin. Therefore venial sins are unsuitably designated by wood, hay, and stubble.

Obj. 3. Further, according to the Apostle (*verse* 12), those who build *gold, silver, precious stones*, that is, love of God and our neighbour, and good works, are others from those who build wood, hay, stubble. But those even who love God and their neighbour, and do good works, commit venial sins for it is written (I John 1. 8): *If we say that we have no sin, we deceive ourselves.* Therefore venial sins are not suitably designated by these three.

---

[1] Among the works of Augustine, *Serm. ad Popul.*, serm., CIV (PL 39, 1947).

[2] *Glossa* Lombardi (PL 192, 214); cf. *Glossa interl.* (VI, 96r).

[3] Cf. Augustine, *City of God*, XXI, 26 (PL 41, 744). *Enchir.*, LXVIII (PL 40, 265); cf. also Peter Lombard, *Sent.*, IV, d. 21, chap. 4 (QR II, 881).

Obj. 4. Further, there are many more than three differences and degrees of venial sins. Therefore they are unsuitably comprised under these three.

On the contrary, The Apostle says (I Cor. 3. 15) that the man who builds up wood, hay, stubble, *shall be saved yet so as by fire,* so that he will suffer punishment but not everlasting punishment. Now the debt of temporal punishment belongs properly to venial sin, as stated above (Q. LXXXVII, A. 5). Therefore these three signify venial sins.

I answer that, Some have understood the foundation to be dead faith, upon which some build good works, signified by gold, silver, and precious stones, while others build mortal sins, which according to them are designated by wood hay, and stubble. But Augustine disapproves of this explanation (*De Fide et Oper.* xv),[1] because, as the Apostle says (Gal. 5. 21), he who does the works of the flesh, *shall not obtain the kingdom of God,* which signifies to be saved; but the Apostle says that he who builds wood, hay, and stubble *shall be saved yet so as by fire.* Consequently wood, hay, stubble cannot be understood to denote mortal sins.

Others say[2] that wood, hay, stubble designate good works, which are indeed built upon the spiritual edifice, but are mixed with venial sins; as when a man is charged with the care of a family, which is a good thing, excessive love of his wife, or of his children or of his possessions insinuates itself into his life, under God however, so that, namely, for the sake of these things he would be unwilling to do anything in opposition to God. But neither does this seem to be reasonable. For it is evident that all good works are referred to the love of God and one's neighbour, and so they are designated by *gold, silver,* and *precious stones,* and consequently not by *wood, hay,* and *stubble.*

We must therefore say that the very venial sins that insinuate themselves into those who have a care for earthly things are designated by wood, hay, and stubble. For just as these are gathered together in a house without belonging to the substance of the house, and can be burnt, while the house is saved, so also venial sins are multiplied in a man, while the spiritual edifice remains, and for them man suffers fire, either of temporal trials in this life, or of purgatory after this life, and yet he is saved for ever.

Reply Obj. 1. Venial sins are not said to be built upon the spiritual foundation, as though

they were laid directly upon it, but because they are laid beside it; in the same sense as it is written (Ps. 136. 1): *Upon the waters of Babylon,* i.e., *beside the waters,* because venial sins do not destroy the spiritual edifice.

Reply Obj. 2. It is not said that everyone who builds wood, hay, and stubble, shall be saved as by fire, but only those who build *upon the foundation.* And this foundation is not dead faith, as some have thought,[3] but faith formed by charity, according to Eph. 3. 17: *Rooted and founded in charity.* Accordingly, he that dies in mortal sin with venial sins, has indeed wood, hay, and stubble, but not built upon the spiritual edifice; and consequently he will not be thus saved as by fire.

Reply Obj. 3. Although those who are withdrawn from the care of temporal things sin venially sometimes, yet they commit but slight venial sins, and in most cases they are cleansed by the fervour of charity; therefore they do not build up venial sins, because these do not remain long in them. But the venial sins of those who are busy about earthly things remain longer, because they are unable to have such frequent recourse to the fervour of charity in order to remove them.

Reply Obj. 4. As the Philosopher says,[4] "all things are comprised under three, the beginning, the middle, and the end." Accordingly all degrees of venial sins are reduced to three, namely to *wood,* which remains longer in the fire; *stubble,* which is burnt up at once; and *hay,* which is between these two. For venial sins are removed by fire, quickly or slowly, according as man is more or less attached to them.

ARTICLE 3. *Whether Man Could Commit a Venial Sin in the State of Innocence?*

We proceed thus to the Third Article: It would seem that man could commit a venial sin in the state of innocence.

Objection 1. Because on I Tim. 2. 14. *Adam was not seduced,* a gloss says:[5] "Having had no experience of God's severity, it was possible for him to be so mistaken as to think that what he had done was a venial sin." But he would not have thought this unless he could have committed a venial sin. Therefore he could commit a venial sin without sinning mortally.

Obj. 2. Further, Augustine says (*Gen. ad lit.* xi, 5):[6] "We must not suppose that the

---

[1] PL 40, 213.
[2] Peter Lombard, *Sent.,* IV, d. 21, chap. 5 (QR II, 882).
[3] Cf. Augustine, *De Fide et Oper.,* XV (PL 40, 213).
[4] *Heavens,* I, 1 (268ª12).
[5] *Glossa ordin.* (VI, 119B); *Glossa* Lombardi (PL 192, 341); Augustine, *City of God,* XIV, 11 (PL 41, 420).
[6] PL 34, 432.

tempter would have overcome man, unless first of all there had arisen in man's soul a movement of vainglory which should have been checked." Now the vainglory which preceded man's defeat, which was accomplished through his falling into mortal sin, could be nothing more than a venial sin.—In like manner, Augustine says[1] that "man was allured by a certain desire of making the experiment, when he saw that the woman did not die when she had taken the forbidden fruit." Again, there seems to have been a certain movement of unbelief in Eve, since she doubted what the Lord had said, as appears from her saying (Gen. 3. 3): *Lest perhaps we die.* Now these apparently were venial sins. Therefore man could commit a venial sin before he committed a mortal sin.

Obj. 3. Further, mortal sin is more opposed to the integrity of the original state than venial sin is. Now man could sin mortally notwithstanding the integrity of the original state. Therefore he could also sin venially.

On the contrary, Every sin deserves some punishment. But nothing penal was possible in the state of innocence, as Augustine declares.[2] Therefore he could not commit a sin that would not deprive him of that state of integrity. But venial sin does not change man's state. Therefore he could not sin venially.

I answer that, It is generally admitted that man could not commit a venial sin in the state of innocence.[3] This, however, is not to be understood as though on account of the perfection of his state, the sin which is venial for us would have been mortal for him if he had committed it.[4] Because the dignity of a person is a circumstance that aggravates a sin, although it does not transfer it to another species, unless there is an additional deformity by reason of disobedience, or vow or the like, which does not apply to the question in point. Consequently what is venial in itself could not be changed into mortal by reason of the excellence of the original state. We must therefore understand this to mean that he could not sin venially, because it was impossible for him to commit a sin which was venial in itself, before losing the integrity of the original state by sinning mortally.

The reason for this is because venial sin occurs in us, either through the imperfection

of the act, as in the case of sudden movements in a genus of mortal sin, or through some lack of order in respect of things referred to the end, the due order to the end being safeguarded. Now each of these happens on account of some defect of order, by reason of the lower powers not being checked by the higher. Because the sudden rising of a movement of the sensuality in us is due to the sensuality not being perfectly subject to reason; and the sudden rising of a movement in the reason itself is due, in us, to the fact that the execution of the act of reason is not subject to the act of deliberation which proceeds from a higher good, as stated above (Q. LXXIV, A. 10); and that the human soul is out of order as regards things directed to the end, the due order to the end being safeguarded, is due to the fact that the things referred to the end are not infallibly directed under the end, which holds the highest place, being the beginning, as it were, in matters concerning the appetite, as stated above (Q. X, AA. 1, 2, Reply 3; Q. LXXII, A. 5). Now, in the state of innocence, as stated in the First Part (Q. XCV, A. 1), there was an unerring stability of order, so that the lower powers were always subjected to the higher so long as the highest part of man remained subject to God, as Augustine says.[5] Hence there could be no lack of order in man, unless first of all the highest part of man were not subject to God, which constitutes a mortal sin. From this it is evident that, in the state of innocence, man could not commit a venial sin before committing a mortal sin.

Reply Obj. 1. In the passage quoted, venial is not taken in the same sense as we take it now; but by venial sin we mean that which is easily forgiven.

Reply Obj. 2. This vainglory which preceded man's downfall was his first mortal sin, for it is stated to have preceded his downfall into the outward act of sin. This vainglory was followed, in the man, by the desire to make an experiment, and, in the woman, by doubt, for she gave way to vainglory merely through hearing the serpent mention the precept, as though she refused to be held in check by the precept.

Reply Obj. 3. Mortal sin is opposed to the integrity of the original state in the fact of its destroying that state, which a venial sin cannot do. And because the integrity of the primitive state is incompatible with any lack of order whatever, the result is that the first man could not sin venially before committing a mortal sin.

---

[1] *Gen. ad. lit.,* XI, 42 (PL 34, 454).

[2] *City of God,* XIV, 10 (PL 41, 417).

[3] See Albert, *In Sent.,* II, d. 21, A. 10 (BO XXVII, 369) Bonaventure, *In Sent.,* II, d. 21, A. 3, Q. 1 (QR II, 505).

[4] Cf. Bonaventure, *In Sent.,* II, BK. II, d. 21, A. 3, Q. 1 (QR II, 505).

[5] *City of God,* XIV, 17 (PL 41, 425); XIV, 23 (PL 41, 431); XIII, 13 (PL 41, 386).

ARTICLE 4. *Whether a Good or Wicked Angel Can Sin Venially?*

We proceed thus to the Fourth Article: It would seem that a good or a wicked angel can sin venially.

Objection 1. Because man agrees with the angels in the higher part of his soul which is called the mind, according to Gregory, who says (*Hom.* 29 *in Ev.*)[1] that "man understands in common with the angels." But man can commit a venial sin in the higher part of his soul. Therefore an angel can commit a venial sin also.

Obj. 2. Further, he that can do more, can do less. But an angel could love a created good more than God, and he did, by sinning mortally. Therefore he could also inordinately love a creature less than God, by sinning venially.

Obj. 3. Further, wicked angels seem to do certain things which are venial sins generically, by provoking man to laughter, and other like frivolities. Now the circumstance of the person does not make a mortal sin to be venial, as stated above (A. 3), unless there be a special prohibition, which is not the case in point. Therefore an angel can sin venially.

On the contrary, The perfection of an angel is greater than that of man in the primitive state. But man could not sin venially in the primitive state, and much less, therefore, can an angel.

I answer that, An angel's intellect, as stated in the First Part (Q. LVIII, A. 3; Q. LXXIX, A. 8), is not discursive, that is, it does not proceed from principles to conclusions, so as to understand both separately, as we do. Consequently, whenever the angelic intellect considers a conclusion, it must, of necessity, consider it in its principles. Now in matters of appetite, as we have often stated (Q. VIII, A. 2; Q. X, A. 1; Q. LXXII, A. 5), ends are like principles, while the means are like conclusions. Therefore an angel's mind is not directed to the means except as they stand under the order to the end. Consequently, from their very nature, they can have no lack of order in respect of the means, unless at the same time they have a lack of order in respect of the end, and this is a mortal sin. Now good angels are not moved to the means except in subordination to the due end which is God. And therefore all their actions are acts of charity, so that no venial sin can be in them. On the other hand, wicked angels are moved to nothing except in subordination to the end which is their sin of pride. Therefore they sin mortally in

everything that they do of their own will. This does not apply to the natural desire for good, which desire we have stated to be in them (Part I, Q. LXIII, A. 4; Q. LXIV, A. 2, reply 5).

Reply Obj. 1. Man does indeed agree with the angels in the mind or intellect, but he differs in his mode of understanding, as stated above.

Reply Obj. 2. An angel could not love a creature less than God, without, at the same time, either referring it to God, as the last end, or to some inordinate end, for the reason given above.

Reply Obj. 3. The demons incite man to all such things which seem to be venial that he may become used to them, so as to lead him on to mortal sin. Consequently in all such things they sin mortally, on account of the end they intend.

ARTICLE 5. *Whether the First Movements of the Sensuality in Unbelievers Are Mortal Sins?*

We proceed thus to the Fifth Article: It would seem that the first movements of the sensuality in unbelievers are mortal sins.

Objection 1. For the Apostle says (Rom. 8. 1) that *there is . . . no condemnation to them that are in Christ Jesus, who walk not according to the flesh:* and he is speaking there of the concupiscence of the sensuality, as appears from the context. (ch. 7.) Therefore the reason why concupiscence is not a matter of condemnation to those who walk not according to the flesh, that is, by consenting to concupiscence, is because they are in Christ Jesus. But unbelievers are not in Christ Jesus. Therefore in unbelievers this is a matter of condemnation. Therefore the first movements of unbelievers are mortal sins.

Obj. 2. Further, Anselm says (*De Gratia et Lib. Arb.* vii)[2] that *those who are not in Christ, when they feel the sting of the flesh, follow the road of damnation, even if they walk not according to the flesh.* But damnation is not due save to mortal sin. Therefore, since man feels the sting of the flesh in the first movements of concupiscence, it seems that the first movements of concupiscence in unbelievers are mortal sins.

Obj. 3. Further, Anselm says (*ibid.*): "Man was so made that he ought not to feel concupiscence." Now being answerable for this seems to be remitted to man by the grace of baptism, which the unbeliever has not. Therefore every act of concupiscence in an unbeliever, even without his consent, is a mortal sin, because he acts against his duty.

[1] PL 76, 1214.

[2] PL 158, 530.

On the contrary, It is stated in Acts 10. 34 that *God is not a respecter of persons.* Therefore He does not impute to one to condemnation, what He does not impute to another. But He does not impute first movements to believers, to condemnation. Neither therefore does He impute them to unbelievers.

I answer that, It is unreasonable to say that the first movements of unbelievers are mortal sins, when they do not consent to them. This is evident for two reasons. First, because the sensuality itself cannot be the subject of mortal sin, as stated above (Q. LXXIV, A. 4). Now the sensuality has the same nature in unbelievers as in believers. Therefore it is not possible for the mere movements of the sensuality in unbelievers to be mortal sins.

Secondly, from the state of the sinner. For excellence of the person never diminishes sin, but, on the contrary, increases it, as stated above (Q. LXXIII, A. 10). Therefore a sin is not less grievous in a believer than in an unbeliever, but much more so. For the sins of an unbeliever are more deserving of forgiveness, on account of his ignorance, according to I Tim. 1. 13: *I obtained the mercy of God, because I did it ignorantly in* my *unbelief;* but the sins of believers are more grievous on account of the sacraments of grace, according to Heb. 10. 29: *How much more, do you think, he deserveth worse punishments . . . who hath esteemed the blood of the testament unclean, by which he was sanctified?*

Reply Obj. 1. The Apostle is speaking of the condemnation due to original sin, which condemnation is remitted by the grace of Jesus Christ, although the *fomes* of concupiscence remain. Therefore the fact that believers are subject to concupiscence is not in them a sign of the condemnation due to original sin, as it is in unbelievers.

In this way also is to be understood the saying of Anselm, and so the *Reply to the Second Objection* is evident.

Reply Obj. 3. This duty not to yield to concupiscence was a result of original justice. Therefore that which is opposed to such a duty pertains not to actual but to original sin.

ARTICLE 6. *Whether Venial Sin Can Be in Anyone with Original Sin Alone?*

We proceed thus to the Sixth Article: It would seem that venial sin can be in a man with original sin alone.

Objection 1. For disposition precedes habit. Now venial sin is a disposition to mortal sin,

as stated above (Q. LXXXVIII, A. 3). Therefore in an unbeliever, in whom original sin is not remitted, venial sin exists before mortal sin. And so sometimes unbelievers have venial together with original sin, and without mortal sins.

Obj. 2. Further, venial sin has less in common and less connection with mortal sin than one mortal sin has with another. But an unbeliever in the state of original sin can commit one mortal sin without committing another. Therefore he can also commit a venial sin without committing a mortal sin.

Obj. 3. Further, it is possible to fix the time at which a child is first able to commit an actual sin. And when the child comes to that time, it can stay a short time at least, without committing a mortal sin, because this happens even in the worst criminals. Now it is possible for the child to sin venially during that space of time, however short it may be. Therefore venial sin can be in anyone with original sin alone and without mortal sin.

On the contrary, Man is punished for original sin in the limbo of children, where there is no pain of sense, as we shall state further on (Suppl., Q. LXIX, A. 6); but men are punished in hell for no other than mortal sin. Therefore there will be no place where a man can be punished for venial sin with no other than original sin.

I answer that, It is impossible for venial sin to be in anyone with original sin alone, and without mortal sin. The reason for this is because before a man comes to the age of discretion, the lack of years hinders the use of reason and excuses him from mortal sin, and so much more does it excuse him from venial sin, if he does anything which is such generically. But when he begins to have the use of reason, he is not entirely excused from the guilt of venial or mortal sin. Now the first thing that occurs to a man to think about then, is to deliberate about himself. And if he then direct himself to the due end, he will, by means of grace, receive the remission of original sin; but if he does not then direct himself to the due end, as far as he is capable of discretion at that particular age, he will sin mortally, through not doing that which is in his power to do. Accordingly from that time onward there cannot be venial sin in him without mortal, until afterwards all sin shall have been remitted to him through grace.

Reply Obj. 1. Venial sin precedes mortal sin not as a necessary but as a contingent disposition, just as work sometimes disposes to fever, but not in the way that heat disposes to the form of fire.

Reply Obj. 2. Venial sin is prevented from being with original sin alone not on account of its want of connection or likeness, but on account of the lack of use of reason, as stated above.

Reply Obj. 3. The child that is beginning to have the use of reason can refrain from other mortal sins for a time, but it is not free from the above-mentioned sin of omission, unless it

turn to God as soon as possible. For the first thing that occurs to a man who has discretion is to think of himself, and to direct other things to himself as to their end, since the end is the first thing in the intention. Therefore this is the time when man is bound by God's affirmative precept, which the Lord expressed by saying (Zach. i., 3): *Turn ye to Me . . . and I will turn to you.*

TREATISE ON LAW

1. In General

QUESTION XC

Of the essence of law

(In Four Articles)

WE have now to consider the extrinsic principles of acts. Now the extrinsic principle inclining to evil is the devil, of whose temptations we have spoken in the First Part (Q. CXIV). But the extrinsic principle moving to good is God, Who both instructs us by means of His Law, and assists us by His Grace. Therefore in the first place we must speak of law; in the second place, of grace (Q. CIX).

Concerning law, we must consider: (1) Law itself in general; (2) its parts (Q. XCIII). Concerning law in general three points offer themselves for our consideration: (1) Its essence; (2) The different kinds of law (Q. XCI); (3) The effects of law (Q. XCII).

Under the first head there are four points of inquiry: (1) Whether law is something pertaining to reason? (2) Concerning the end of law. (3) Its cause. (4) The promulgation of law.

ARTICLE 1. Whether Law Is Something Pertaining to Reason?

We proceed thus to the First Article: It would seem that law is not something pertaining to reason.

Objection 1. For the Apostle says (Rom. 7. 23): *I see another law in my members,* etc. But nothing pertaining to reason is in the members, since the reason does not make use of a bodily organ. Therefore law is not something pertaining to reason.

Obj. 2. Further, in the reason there is nothing else but power, habit, and act. But law is not the power itself of reason. In like manner, neither is it a habit of reason, because the habits of reason are the intellectual virtues of which we have spoken above (Q. LVII). Nor again is it an act of reason, because then law would cease when the act of reason ceases, for instance, while we are asleep. Therefore law is nothing pertaining to reason.

Obj. 3. Further, the law moves those who are subject to it to act rightly. But it belongs properly to the will to move to act, as is evident from what has been said above (Q. IX, A. 1). Therefore law pertains, not to the reason, but to the will, according to the words of the Jurist (*Lib.* i. *ff.*, *De Const. Prin.* leg. i):[1] "Whatsoever pleaseth the sovereign has force of law."

On the contrary, It pertains to the law to command and to forbid. But it pertains to reason to command, as stated above (Q. XVII, A. 1). Therefore law is something pertaining to reason.

I answer that, Law is a rule and measure of acts, by which man is induced to act or is restrained from acting; for *lex* (law) is derived from *ligare* (to bind), because it obliges (*obligare*) one to act. Now the rule and measure of human acts is the reason, which is the first principle of human acts, as is evident from what has been stated above (Q. I, A. 1, Reply 3); for it belongs to the reason to direct to the end, which is the first principle in all matters of action, according to the Philosopher.[2] Now that which is the principle in any genus, is the rule and measure of that genus; for instance, unity in the genus of numbers, and the first movement in the genus of movements. Consequently it follows that law is something pertaining to reason.

Reply Obj. 1. Since law is a kind of rule and measure, it may be in something in two ways. First, as in that which measures and rules. And since this is proper to reason, it follows that, in this way law is in the reason alone. Secondly, as in that which is measured and ruled. In this way law is in all those things that are inclined to something by reason of some law, so that any inclination arising from a law may be called a law, not essentially but by participation as it were. And thus the inclination of the members to concupiscence is called the law of the members.[3]

[1] *Digest.* (KR 1, 35a).
[2] *Physics,* II, 9 (200ᵃ22); *Ethics,* VII, 8 (1151ᵃ16).
[3] Cf. Rom. 7.23; Peter Lombard, *Sent.,* II, d. 30, chap. 8 (QR 1, 464).

Reply Obj. 2. Just as in external action we may consider the work and the work done, for instance the work of building and the house built, so in the acts of reason, we may consider the act itself of reason, that is, to understand and to reason, and something produced by this act. With regard to the speculative reason, this is first of all the definition; secondly, the proposition; thirdly, the syllogism or argument. And since also the practical reason makes use of a syllogism in respect of the work to be done, as stated above (Q. XIII, A. 3; Q. LXXVI, A. 1) and as the Philosopher teaches,[1] hence we find in the practical reason something that holds the same position in regard to operations as, in the speculative intellect, the proposition holds in regard to conclusions. And universal propositions of this kind of the practical intellect that are directed to actions have the nature of law. And these propositions are sometimes under our actual consideration, while sometimes they are retained in the reason by means of a habit.

Reply Obj. 3. Reason has its power of moving from the will, as stated above (Q. XVII, A. 1); for it is due to the fact that one wills the end that the reason issues its commands as regards things ordered to the end. But in order that the volition of what is commanded may have the nature of law, it needs to be in accord with some rule of reason. And in this sense is to be understood the saying that the will of the sovereign has the force of law; otherwise the sovereign's will would savour of lawlessness rather than of law.

ARTICLE 2. *Whether the Law Is Always Directed to the Common Good?*

We proceed thus to the Second Article: It would seem that the law is not always directed to the common good as to its end.

Objection 1. For it belongs to law to command and to forbid. But commands are directed to certain individual goods. Therefore the end of the law is not always the common good.

Obj. 2. Further, the law directs man in his actions. But human actions are concerned with particular matters. Therefore the law is directed to some particular good.

Obj. 3. Further, Isidore says (*Etym.* v, 3):[2] "If the law is based on reason, whatever is based on reason will be a law." But reason is the foundation not only of what is ordered to the common good, but also of that which is directed to

private good. Therefore the law is not only directed to the good of all, but also to the private good of an individual.

On the contrary, Isidore says (*Etym.* v, 21)[3] that "laws are enacted for no private profit, but for the common benefit of the citizens."

I answer that, As stated above (A. 1), the law belongs to that which is a principle of human acts, because it is their rule and measure. Now as reason is a principle of human acts, so in reason itself there is something which is the principle in respect of all the rest. Hence to this principle chiefly and above all law must be referred. Now the first principle in practical matters, which are the object of the practical reason, is the last end; and the last end of human life is happiness or beatitude, as stated above (Q. II, A. 7; Q. III, A. 1; Q. LXIX, A. 1). Consequently the law must regard principally the relationship to happiness. Moreover, since every part is ordered to the whole, as imperfect to perfect, and since one man is a part of the perfect community, the law must properly look to the relationship to universal happiness. Hence the Philosopher, in the above definition of legal matters mentions both happiness and the body politic; for he says[4] that "we call those legal matters just which are adapted to produce and preserve happiness and its parts for the body politic," since the state is a perfect community, as he says in the *Politics*.[5]

Now in every genus, that which belongs to it chiefly is the principle of the others, and the others belong to that genus in subordination to that thing; thus fire, which is chief among hot things, is the cause of heat in mixed bodies, and these are said to be hot in so far as they have a share of fire. Consequently, since the law is chiefly ordered to the common good, any other precept in regard to some individual work, must be empty of the nature of a law, save in so far as it regards the common good. Therefore every law is ordered to the common good.

Reply Obj. 1. A command denotes an application of a law to matters regulated by the law. Now the order to the common good, at which the law aims, is applicable to particular ends. And in this way commands are given even concerning particular matters.

Reply Obj. 2. Actions are indeed concerned with particular matters; but those particular matters are referrible to the common good not as to a common genus or species, but as to a

---

[1] *Ethics*, VII, 3 (1147ª24).
[2] PL 82, 199; II, 10 (PL 82, 130).
[3] PL 82, 203.
[4] *Ethics*, V, 1 (1129ᵇ17).
[5] I, 1 (1252ª5).

common final cause, according as the common good is said to be the common end.

Reply Obj. 3. Just as nothing stands firm with regard to the speculative reason except that which is resolved into the first indemonstrable principles, so nothing stands firm with regard to the practical reason unless it be directed to the last end, which is the common good. And whatever is established by reason in this sense has the nature of a law.

ARTICLE 3. *Whether the Reason of Any Man is Able to Make Laws?*

We proceed thus to the Third Article: It would seem that the reason of any man is able to make laws.

Objection 1. For the Apostle says (Rom. 2. 14) that *when the Gentiles, who have not the law, do by nature those things that are of the law, ... they are a law to themselves.* Now he says this of all in general. Therefore anyone can make a law for himself.

Obj. 2. Further, as the Philosopher says,[1] "the intention of the lawgiver is to lead men to virtue." But every man can lead another to virtue. Therefore the reason of any man is able to make laws.

Obj. 3. Further, just as the sovereign of a state governs the state, so every father of a family governs his household. But the sovereign of a state can make laws for the state. Therefore every father of a family can make laws for his household.

On the contrary, Isidore says (*Etym.* v, 10)[2] and it is contained also in the *Decretals:*[3] "A law is an ordinance of the people, whereby something is sanctioned by the Elders together with the Commonalty." Therefore it does not pertain to everyone to make laws.

I answer that, A law, properly speaking, regards first and foremost the order to the common good. Now to order anything to the common good belongs either to the whole people, or to someone who is the vicegerent of the whole people. And therefore the making of a law belongs either to the whole people or to a public personage who has care of the whole people; for in all other fields the directing of anything to the end concerns him to whom the end belongs.

Reply Obj. 1. As stated above (A. 1, Reply 1), a law is in a person not only as in one that rules, but also by participation, as in one that is ruled.

In the latter way each one is a law to himself, in so far as he shares the order that he receives from one who rules him. Hence the same text goes on: *Who show the work of the law written in their hearts.*

Reply Obj. 2. A private person cannot lead another to virtue efficaciously; for he can only advise, and if his advice be not taken, it has no coercive power, such as the law should have, in order to prove an efficacious inducement to virtue, as the Philosopher says.[4] But this coercive power is vested in the whole people or in some public personage, to whom it belongs to inflict penalties, as we shall state further on (Q. XCII, A. 2, Reply 3; Part II-II, Q. LXIV, A. 3). Therefore the framing of laws belongs to him alone.

Reply Obj. 3. As one man is a part of the household, so a household is a part of the state, and the state is a perfect community, according to the *Politics.*[5] And therefore, as the good of one man is not the last end, but is ordered to the common good, so too the good of one household is ordered to the good of a single state, which is a perfect community. Consequently he that governs a family can indeed make certain commands or ordinances, but not such as to have properly the force of law.

ARTICLE 4. *Whether Promulgation Is Essential to a Law?*

We proceed thus to the Fourth Article: It would seem that promulgation is not essential to a law.

Objection 1. For the natural law above all has the character of law. But the natural law needs no promulgation. Therefore it is not essential to a law that it be promulgated.

Obj. 2. Further, it belongs properly to a law to bind one to do or not to do something. But the obligation of fulfilling a law touches not only those in whose presence it is promulgated, but also others. Therefore promulgation is not essential to a law.

Obj. 3. Further, the binding force of a law extends even to the future, since "laws are binding in matters of the future," as the jurists say (*Cod* 1, tit. *De lege et constit.* leg. vii).[6] But promulgation concerns those who are present. Therefore it is not essential to a law.

On the contrary, It is laid down in the *Decretals,* dist. 4,[7] that "laws are established when they are promulgated."

---

[1] *Ethics,* II, 1 (1103^{b}3).
[2] PL 82, 200.
[3] Gratian, *Decretum,* PT. I, d. II, can. I (RF I, 3).

[4] *Ethics,* X, 9 (1180^{a}20).
[5] Aristotle, I, 1 (1252^{a}5).
[6] Justinian, II, 68^a.
[7] Gratian, PT. I, d. IV, append. ad can. 3 (RF I, 6).

I answer that, As stated above (A. 1), a law is imposed on others by way of a rule and measure. Now a rule or measure is imposed by being applied to those who are to be ruled and measured by it. Therefore, in order that a law obtain the binding force which is proper to a law, it must be applied to the men who have to be ruled by it. Such application is made by its being notified to them by promulgation. Therefore promulgation is necessary for the law to obtain its force.

Thus from the four preceding articles, the definition of law may be gathered; and it is nothing other than an ordinance of reason for the common good, made by him who has care of the community, and promulgated.

Reply Obj. 1. The natural law is promulgated by the very fact that God instilled it into man's mind so as to be known by him naturally.

Reply Obj. 2. Those who are not present when a law is promulgated are bound to observe the law in so far as it is notified or can be notified to them by others, after it has been promulgated.

Reply Obj. 3. The promulgation that takes place now extends to future time by reason of the durability of written characters, by which means it is continually promulgated. Hence Isidore says (*Etym.* ii, 10)[1] that *"lex* (law) is derived from *legere* (to read) because it is written."

QUESTION XCI

Of the various kinds of law
(*In Six Articles*)

We must now consider the various kinds of law, under which head there are six points of inquiry: (1) Whether there is an eternal law? (2) Whether there is a natural law? (3) Whether there is a human law? (4) Whether there is a Divine law? (5) Whether there is one Divine law, or several? (6) Whether there is a law of sin?

Article 1. *Whether There Is an Eternal Law?*

We proceed thus to the First Article: It would seem that there is no eternal law.

Objection 1. Because every law is imposed on someone. But there was not someone from eternity on whom a law could be imposed, since God alone was from eternity. Therefore no law is eternal.

Obj. 2. Further, promulgation is essential to law. But promulgation could not be from eternity because there was no one to whom it could

be promulgated from eternity. Therefore no law can be eternal.

Obj. 3. Further, a law implies order to an end. But nothing ordered to an end is eternal, for the last end alone is eternal. Therefore no law is eternal.

On the contrary, Augustine says (*De Lib. Arb.* i, 6):[2] "That Law which is the Supreme Reason cannot be understood to be otherwise than unchangeable and eternal."

I answer that, As stated above (Q. XC, A. 1, Reply 2; AA. 3, 4), a law is nothing else but a dictate of practical reason emanating from the ruler who governs a perfect community. Now it is evident, granted that the world is ruled by Divine Providence, as was stated in the First Part (Q. XXII, AA. 1, 2), that the whole community of the universe is governed by Divine Reason. Therefore the very Idea of the government of things in God, the Ruler of the universe, has the nature of a law. And since the Divine Reason's conception of things is not subject to time but is eternal, according to Prov. 8. 23, hence it is that this kind of law must be called eternal.

Reply Obj. 1. Those things that are not in themselves exist with God, since they are foreknown and preordained by Him, according to Rom. 4. 17: *Who calls those things that are not, as those that are.* Accordingly the eternal concept of the Divine law bears the character of an eternal law, in so far as it is ordained by God to the government of things foreknown by Him.

Reply Obj. 2. Promulgation is made by word of mouth or in writing, and in both ways the eternal law is promulgated, because both the Divine Word and the writing of the Book of Life are eternal. But the promulgation cannot be from eternity on the part of the creature that hears or reads.

Reply Obj. 3. The law implies order to the end actively, in so far, that is, as it directs certain things to the end; but not passively—that is to say, the law itself is not ordered to the end—except accidentally, in a governor whose end is extrinsic to him, and to which end his law must be ordered. But the end of the Divine government is God Himself, and His law is not distinct from Himself. Therefore the eternal law is not ordained to another end.

Article 2. *Whether There Is in Us a Natural Law?*

We proceed thus to the Second Article: It would seem that there is no natural law in us.

[1] PL 82, 130.   [2] PL 32, 1229.

Objection 1. Because man is governed sufficiently by the eternal law, for Augustine says (*De Lib. Arb.* i, 6)[1] that "the eternal law is that by which it is right that all things should be most orderly." But nature does not abound in superfluities as neither does she fail in necessaries. Therefore no law is natural to man.

Obj. 2. Further, by the law man is ordered in his acts to the end, as stated above (Q. XC, A. 2). But the ordering of human acts to their end is not a function of nature, as is the case in irrational creatures, which act for an end solely by their natural appetite; but man acts for an end by his reason and will. Therefore no law is natural to man.

Obj. 3. Further, the more a man is free, the less is he under the law. But man is freer than all the animals, on account of free choice, with which he is endowed above all other animals. Since therefore other animals are not subject to a natural law, neither is man subject to a natural law.

On the contrary, A gloss on Rom. 2. 14: *When the Gentiles, who have not the law, do by nature those things that are of the law,* comments as follows:[2] "Although they have no written law, yet they have the natural law, whereby each one knows, and is conscious of, what is good and what is evil."

I answer that, As stated above (Q. XC, A. 1, Reply 1), law, being a rule and measure, can be in a person in two ways: in one way as in him that rules and measures; in another way, as in that which is ruled and measured, since a thing is ruled and measured in so far as it partakes of the rule or measure. Therefore, since all things subject to Divine providence are ruled and measured by the eternal law, as was stated above (A. 1), it is evident that all things partake somewhat of the eternal law, in so far as, namely, from its being imprinted on them, they derive their respective inclinations to their proper acts and ends. Now among all others, the rational creature is subject to Divine providence in the most excellent way, in so far as it partakes of a share of providence, by being provident both for itself and for others. Therefore it has a share of the Eternal Reason, by which it has a natural inclination to its due act and end; and this participation of the eternal law in the rational creature is called the natural law. Hence the Psalmist after saying (Ps. 4. 6): *Offer up the sacrifice of justice,* as though someone asked

what the works of justice are, adds: *Many say, Who showeth us good things?* in answer to which question he says: *The light of Thy countenance, O Lord, is signed upon us,* thus implying that the light of natural reason, by which we discern what is good and what is evil, which is the function of the natural law, is nothing else than an imprint on us of the Divine light. It is therefore evident that the natural law is nothing else than the rational creature's participation of the eternal law.

Reply Obj. 1. This argument would hold if the natural law were something different from the eternal law. But it is nothing other than a participation of the eternal law, as stated above.

Reply Obj. 2. Every operation of reason and will in us is based on that which is according to nature, as stated above (Q. X, A. 1), for every act of reasoning is based on principles that are known naturally, and every act of appetite in respect of the means is derived from the natural appetite in respect of the last end. And so also the first direction of our acts to their end must be in virtue of the natural law.

Reply Obj. 3. Even irrational animals partake in their own way of the Eternal Reason, just as the rational creature does. But because the rational creature partakes of it in an intellectual and rational manner, therefore the participation of the eternal law in the rational creature is properly called a law, since a law is something pertaining to reason, as stated above (Q. XC, A. 1). Irrational creatures, however, do not partake of it in a rational manner, and so there is no participation of the eternal law in them, except by way of likeness.

ARTICLE 3. *Whether There Is a Human Law?*

We proceed thus to the Third Article: It would seem that there is not a human law.

Objection 1. For the natural law is a participation of the eternal law, as stated above (A. 2). Now through the eternal law "all things are most orderly," as Augustine states (*De Lib. Arb.* i, 6).[3] Therefore the natural law suffices for the ordering of all human affairs. Consequently there is no need for a human law.

Obj. 2. Further, a law bears the character of a measure, as stated above (Q. XC, A. 1). But human reason is not a measure of things, but rather vice versa, as stated in the *Metaphysics.*[4] Therefore no law can emanate from human reason.

Obj. 3. Further, a measure should be most cer-

---

[1] PL 32, 1229.
[2] *Glossa ordin.* (VI, 7E); *Glossa* Lombardi (PL 191, 1345).

[3] PL 32, 1229.
[4] Aristotle, X, 1 (1053ª31).

tain, as stated in the *Metaphysics*.[1] But the dictates of human reason in matters of conduct are uncertain, according to Wisd. 9. 14: *The thoughts of mortal men are fearful, and our counsels uncertain.* Therefore no law can emanate from human reason.

On the contrary, Augustine (*De Lib. Arb.* i, 6)[2] distinguishes two kinds of law, the one eternal, the other temporal, which he calls human.

I answer that, As stated above (Q. XC, A. 1, REPLY 2), a law is a dictate of the practical reason. Now it is to be observed that the same procedure takes place in the practical and in the speculative reason, for each proceeds from principles to conclusions, as stated above (*ibid.*). Accordingly we conclude that just as, in the speculative reason, from naturally known indemonstrable principles we draw the conclusions of the various sciences, the knowledge of which is not imparted to us by nature, but acquired by the efforts of reason, so too it is from the precepts of the natural law, as from general and indemonstrable principles, that the human reason needs to proceed to the more particular determination of certain matters. These particular determinations, devised by human reason, are called human laws, provided the other essential conditions of law be observed, as stated above (Q. XC). Hence Tully says in his *Rhetoric* (*De Invent. Rhet.* ii, 53)[3] that "justice has its source in nature; thence certain things came into custom by reason of their utility; afterwards these things which emanated from nature and were approved by custom, were sanctioned by fear and reverence for the law."

Reply Obj. 1. The human reason cannot have a full participation of the dictate of the Divine Reason, but according to its own mode, and imperfectly. Consequently, as on the part of the speculative reason, by a natural participation of Divine Wisdom, there is in us the knowledge of certain general principles, but not a proper knowledge of each single truth, such as that contained in the Divine Wisdom; so too, on the part of the practical reason, man has a natural participation of the eternal law, according to certain general principles but not as regards the particular determinations of individual cases, which are, however, contained in the eternal law. Hence the need for human reason to proceed further to sanction them by law.

Reply Obj. 2. Human reason is not, of itself, the rule of things; but the principles impressed on it by nature, are general rules and measures of all things relating to human conduct, of which the natural reason is the rule and measure, although it is not the measure of things that are from nature.

Reply Obj. 3. The practical reason is concerned with practical matters, which are singular and contingent, but not with necessary things, with which the speculative reason is concerned. Therefore human laws cannot have that inerrancy that belongs to the demonstrated conclusions of sciences. Nor is it necessary for every measure to be altogether unerring and certain, but according as it is possible in its own particular genus.

ARTICLE 4. *Whether There Was Any Need for a Divine Law?*

We proceed thus to the Fourth Article: It would seem that there was no need for a Divine law.

Objection 1. For, as stated above (A. 2), the natural law is a participation in us of the eternal law. But the eternal law is a Divine law, as stated above (A. 1). Therefore there is no need for a Divine law in addition to the natural law, and human laws derived from the natural law.

Obj. 2. Further, it is written (Ecclus. 15. 14) that *God left man in the hand of his own counsel.* Now counsel is an act of reason, as stated above (Q. XIV, A. 1). Therefore man was left to the direction of his reason. But a dictate of human reason is a human law, as stated above (A. 3). Therefore there is no need for man to be governed also by a Divine law.

Obj. 3. Further, human nature is more self-sufficing than irrational creatures. But irrational creatures have no Divine law besides the natural inclination impressed on them. Much less, therefore, should the rational creature have a Divine law in addition to the natural law.

On the contrary, David prayed God to set His law before him, saying (Ps. 118. 33): *Set before me for a law the way of Thy justifications, O Lord.*

I answer that, Besides the natural and the human law it was necessary for the directing of human conduct to have a Divine law. And this for four reasons. First, because it is by law that man is directed how to perform his proper acts in view of his last end. And indeed if man were ordained to no other end than that which is proportionate to his natural power, there would be no need for man to have any further direction on the part of his reason besides the natural law and human law which is derived from it. But since man is ordained to an end of eternal happiness which is inproportionate to man's natural faculty, as stated above (Q. V, A. 5), therefore it was necessary that, besides the natural and the human law, man should be directed to his end by a law given by God.

Secondly, because, on account of the uncertainty of human judgment, especially on contingent and particular matters, different people form different judgments on human acts; and from this also different and contrary laws result. In order, therefore, that man may know without any doubt what he ought to do and what he ought to avoid, it was necessary for man to be directed in his proper acts by a law given by God, for it is certain that such a law cannot err.

Thirdly, because man can make laws in those matters of which he is able to judge. But man is not able to judge of interior movements, which are hidden, but only of exterior acts, which appear. And yet for the perfection of virtue it is necessary for man to conduct himself rightly in both kinds of acts. Consequently human law could not sufficiently curb and direct interior acts, and it was necessary, for this purpose that a Divine law should supervene.

Fourthly, because, as Augustine says (De Lib. Arb. i, 5),[1] human law cannot punish or forbid all evil deeds, since while aiming at doing away with all evils, it would do away with many good things, and would hinder the advance of the common good, which is necessary for human intercourse. In order, therefore, that no evil might remain unforbidden and unpunished, it was necessary for the Divine law to supervene, by which all sins are forbidden.

And these four causes are touched upon in Ps. 118. 8, where it is said: The law of the Lord is unspotted, that is, allowing no foulness of sin; converting souls, because it directs not only exterior, but also interior acts; the testimony of the Lord is faithful, because of the certainty of what is true and right; giving wisdom to little ones, by directing man to an end supernatural and Divine.

Reply Obj. 1. By the natural law the eternal law is participated proportionately to the capacity of human nature. But to his supernatural end man needs to be directed in a yet higher way. Hence the additional law given by God, by which man shares more perfectly in the eternal law.

Reply Obj. 2. Counsel is a kind of inquiry, and hence it must proceed from some principles. Nor is it enough for it to proceed from princi-

[1] PL 32, 1228.

ples implanted by nature, which are the precepts of the natural law, for the reasons given above, but there is need for certain additional principles, namely, the precepts of the Divine law.

Reply Obj. 3. Irrational creatures are not ordered to an end higher than that which is proportionate to their natural powers. Consequently the comparison fails.

ARTICLE 5. Whether There Is But One Divine Law?

We proceed thus to the Fifth Article: It would seem that there is but one Divine law.

Objection 1. Because, where there is one king in one kingdom there is but one law. Now the whole of mankind is compared to God as to one king, according to Ps. 46. 8: God is the King of all the earth. Therefore there is but one Divine law.

Obj. 2. Further, every law is directed to the end which the lawgiver intends for those for whom he makes the law. But God intends one and the same thing for all men, since according to I Tim. 2. 4: He will have all men to be saved, and to come to the knowledge of the truth. Therefore there is but one Divine law.

Obj. 3. Further, the Divine law seems to be more akin to the eternal law, which is one, than the natural law, according as the revelation of grace is of a higher order than natural knowledge. Therefore much more is the Divine law but one.

On the contrary, The Apostle says (Heb. 7. 12): The priesthood being translated, it is necessary that a translation also be made of the law. But the priesthood is twofold, as stated in the same passage, namely, the levitical priesthood, and the priesthood of Christ. Therefore the Divine law is twofold, namely, the Old Law and the New Law.

I answer that, As stated in the First Part (Q. XXX, A. 3), distinction is the cause of number. Now things may be distinguished in two ways. First, as those things that are altogether different in species, for example, a horse and an ox. Secondly, as perfect and imperfect in the same species, for example, a boy and a man; and in this way the Divine law is divided into Old and New. Hence the Apostle (Gal. 3. 24, 25) compares the state of man under the Old Law to that of a child under a pedagogue; but the state under the New Law, to that of a full grown man, who is no longer under a pedagogue.

Now the perfection and imperfection of these two laws is to be taken in connection with the three conditions pertaining to law, as stated above. For, in the first place, it pertains to law to be directed to the common good as to its end, as stated above (Q. XC, A. 2). This good may be twofold. It may be a sensible and earthly good; and to this, man was directly ordained by the Old Law. Therefore, at the very outset of the law, the people were invited to the earthly kingdom of the Chananæans (Exod. 3. 8, 17). Again it may be an intelligible and heavenly good; and to this, man is ordained by the New Law. Therefore, at the very beginning of His preaching, Christ invited men to the kingdom of heaven, saying (Matt. 4. 17): *Do penance, for the kingdom of heaven is at hand.* Hence Augustine says (*Contra Faust.* iv, 2)[1] that "promises of temporal things are contained in the Old Testament, for which reason it is called old; but the promise of eternal life belongs to the New Testament."

Secondly, it pertains to the law to direct human acts according to the order of justice. In this also the New Law surpasses the Old Law, since it directs our internal acts, according to Matt. 5. 20: *Unless your justice abound more than that of the Scribes and Pharisees, you shall not enter into the kingdom of heaven.* Hence the saying that the Old Law restrains the hand, but the New Law controls the soul (3 *Sentent.*, D. xl).[2]

Thirdly, it pertains to the law to induce men to observe its commandments. This the Old Law did by the fear of punishment, but the New Law, by love, which is poured into our hearts by the grace of Christ, bestowed in the New Law, but foreshadowed in the Old. Hence Augustine says (*Contra Adimant. Manich. discip.* xvii)[3] that "there is little difference between the Law and the Gospel—fear and love."[4]

Reply Obj. 1. As the father of a family issues different commands to the children and to the adults, so also the one King, God, in His one kingdom, gave one law to men while they were yet imperfect, and another more perfect law, when, by the preceding law, they had been led to a greater capacity for Divine things.

Reply Obj. 2. The salvation of man could not be achieved otherwise than through Christ, according to Acts 4. 12: *There is no other name . . . given to men, whereby we must be saved.* Consequently the law that brings all in a perfect way to salvation could not be given until

after the coming of Christ. But before His coming it was necessary to give to the people, of whom Christ was to be born, a law containing certain rudiments of saving justice, in order to prepare them to receive Him.

Reply Obj. 3. The natural law directs man by way of certain general precepts, common to both the perfect and the imperfect: wherefore it is one and the same for all. But the Divine law directs man also in certain particular matters, to which the perfect and imperfect do not stand in the same relation. Hence the necessity for the Divine law to be twofold, as already explained.

ARTICLE 6. *Whether There Is a Law in the Fomes of Sin?*

We proceed thus to the Sixth Article: It would seem that there is no law of the "fomes" of sin.[5]

Objection 1. For Isidore says (*Etym.* v)[6] that the "law is based on reason." But the "fomes" of sin is not based on reason, but deviates from it. Therefore the "fomes" has not the nature of a law.

Obj. 2. Further, every law is binding, so that those who do not obey it are called transgressors. But man is not called a transgressor from not following the instigations of the "fomes," but rather from his following them. Therefore the "fomes" has not the nature of a law.

Obj. 3. Further, the law is ordered to the common good, as stated above (Q. XC, A. 2). But the "fomes" inclines us not to the common good, but to our own private good. Therefore the "fomes" has not the nature of a law.

On the contrary, The Apostle says (Rom. 7. 23): *I see another law in my members, fighting against the law of my mind.*

I answer that, As stated above (A. 2; Q. XC, A. 1, reply 1), the law, as to its essence, resides in him that rules and measures, but by way of participation in that which is ruled and measured, so that every inclination or ordination which may be found in things subject to the law, is called a law by participation, as stated above (*ibid.*). Now those who are subject to a law may receive a twofold inclination from the lawgiver. First, in so far as he directly inclines his subjects to something—sometimes indeed different subjects to different acts; in this way we may say that there is a military law and a mercantile law. Secondly, indirectly. Thus by

---

[1] PL 42, 217.   [2] Peter Lombard (QR II, 734).
[3] PL 42, 159.
[4] Augustine is referring to the difference between the Latin words for fear and love, *timor* and *amor*.

[5] Cf. Peter Lombard, *Sent.*, II, d. 30, chap. 8 (QR I, 464); also John Damascene, *De Fide Orth.*, IV, 22 (PG 94, 1200).
[6] Chap. 3 (PL 82, 199).

the very fact that a lawgiver deprives a subject of some dignity, the latter passes into another order, so as to be under another law, as it were; thus if a soldier be turned out of the army, he becomes a subject of rural or of mercantile legislation.

Accordingly under the Divine Lawgiver various creatures have various natural inclinations, so that what is, as it were, a law for one, is against the law for another; thus I might say that fierceness is, in a way, the law of a dog, but against the law of a sheep or another meek animal. And so the law of man, which, by the Divine ordinance, is allotted to him according to his proper natural condition, is that he should act in accordance with reason; and this law was so effective in the primitive state that nothing either beside or against reason could take man unawares. But when man turned his back on God, he fell under the influence of his sensual impulses; in fact this happens to each one individually, the more he deviates from the path of reason, so that, after a fashion, he is likened to the beasts that are led by the impulse of sensuality, according to Ps. 48. 21: *Man, when he was in honour, did not understand: he hath been compared to senseless beasts, and made like to them.*

So, then, this very inclination of sensuality which is called the "fomes," in other animals has the nature of a law absolutely, yet only in so far as a law may be said to be in such things, by reason of a direct inclination following from a law. But in man, it has not the nature of law in this way, rather is it a deviation from the law of reason. But since, by the just sentence of God, man is destitute of original justice and his reason bereft of its vigour, this impulse of sensuality by which he is led, in so for as it is a penalty following from the Divine law depriving man of his proper dignity, has the nature of a law.

Reply Obj. 1. This argument considers the "fomes" in itself, as an incentive to evil. It is not thus that it has the nature of a law, as stated above, but according as it results from the justice of the Divine law; it is as though we were to say that the law allows a nobleman to be condemned to hard labour for some misdeed.

Reply Obj. 2. This argument considers law in the light of a rule or measure, for it is in this sense that those who deviate from the law become transgressors. But the "fomes" is not a law in this respect, but by a kind of participation, as stated above.

Reply Obj. 3. This argument considers the "fomes" as to its proper inclination, and not as to its origin. And yet if the inclination of sensuality be considered as it is in other animals, thus it is ordained to the common good, namely, to the preservation of nature in the species or in the individual. And this is in man also, in so far as sensuality is subject to reason. But it is called the "fomes" in so far as it strays from the order of reason.

QUESTION XCII
OF THE EFFECTS OF LAW
(*In Two Articles*)

WE must now consider the effects of law, under which head there are two points of inquiry: (1) Whether an effect of law is to make men good? (2) Whether "the effects of law are to command, to forbid, to permit, and to punish," as the Jurist states?[1]

ARTICLE 1. *Whether an Effect of Law Is to Make Men Good?*

We proceed thus to the First Article: It seems that it is not an effect of law to make men good.

Objection 1. For men are good through virtue, since virtue, as stated in the *Ethics,*[2] is "that which makes its subject good." But virtue is in man from God alone, because He it is Who works virtue in us without us, as we stated above (Q. LV, A. 4) in giving the definition of virtue. Therefore the law does not make men good.

Obj. 2. Further, Law does not profit a man unless he obeys it. But the very fact that a man obeys a law is due to his being good. Therefore in man goodness is presupposed to the law. Therefore the law does not make men good.

Obj. 3. Further, Law is ordered to the common good, as stated above (Q. XC, A. 2). But some behave well in things regarding the community, who behave ill in things regarding themselves. Therefore it is not the business of the law to make men good.

Obj. 4. Further, some laws are tyrannical, as the Philosopher says.[3] But a tyrant does not intend the good of his subjects, but considers only his own profit. Therefore law does not make men good.

On the contrary, The Philosopher says[4] that "the intention of every lawgiver is to make good citizens."

---

[1] *Dig.* I, III, 7 (KR I, 34a).
[2] Aristotle, II, 6 (1106ª15).
[3] *Politics,* III, 11 (1282ᵇ12).   [4] *Ethics,* II, 1 (1103ᵇ3).

I answer that, As stated above (Q. XC, A. 1, REPLY 2; AA. 3, 4), a law is nothing else than a dictate of reason in the ruler, by whom his subjects are governed. Now the virtue of any subordinate thing consists in its being well subordinated to that by which it is regulated. Thus we see that the virtue of the irascible and concupiscible faculties consists in their being obedient to reason; and accordingly the virtue of every subject consists in his being well subjected to his ruler, as the Philosopher says.[1] But every law aims at being obeyed by those who are subject to it. Consequently it is evident that the proper effect of law is to lead its subjects to their proper virtue; and since virtue is "that which makes its subject good," it follows that the proper effect of law is to make those to whom it is given, good, either absolutely or in some particular respect. For if the intention of the lawgiver is fixed on true good, which is the common good regulated according to Divine justice, it follows that the effect of the law is to make men good absolutely. If, however, the intention of the lawgiver is fixed on that which is not good absolutely, but useful or pleasurable to himself, or in opposition to Divine justice, then the law does not make men good absolutely, but relatively, that is, in respect to that particular government. In this way good is found even in things that are bad of themselves; thus a man is called a good robber, because he works in a way that is adapted to his end.

Reply Obj. 1. Virtue is twofold, as explained above (Q. LXIII, A. 2), namely, acquired and infused. Now the fact of being accustomed to an action contributes to both, but in different ways; for it causes the acquired virtue, while it disposes to infused virtue, and preserves and fosters it when it already exists. And since law is given for the purpose of directing human acts, in so far as human acts conduce to virtue, to that extent does law make men good. Hence the Philosopher says in the second book of the *Politics*[2] that "lawgivers make men good by habituating them to good works."

Reply Obj. 2. It is not always through perfect goodness of virtue that one obeys the law, but sometimes it is through fear of punishment, and sometimes from the mere dictate of reason, which is a kind of beginning of virtue, as stated above (Q. LXIII, A. 1).

Reply Obj. 3. The goodness of any part is considered in comparison with its whole; hence Augustine says[3] that "unseemly is the part that harmonizes not with its whole." Since then every man is a part of the state, it is impossible that a man be good, unless he be well proportioned to the common good; nor can the whole be well made up unless its parts be proportioned to it. Consequently the common good of the state cannot flourish unless the citizens be virtuous, at least those whose business it is to govern. But it is enough for the good of the community that the other citizens be so far virtuous that they obey the commands of their rulers. Hence the Philosopher says[4] that "the virtue of a sovereign is the same as that of a good man, but the virtue of any common citizen is not the same as that of a good man."

Reply Obj. 4. A tyrannical law, since it is not in accordance with reason, is not a law, absolutely speaking, but rather a perversion of law; and yet in so far as it is something in the nature of a law, it aims at the citizens being good. For all it has in the nature of a law consists in its being an ordinance made by a superior to his subjects, and aims at being obeyed by them, which is to make them good, not absolutely, but with respect to that particular government.

ARTICLE 2. *Whether the Acts of Law Are Suitably Assigned?*

We proceed thus to the Second Article: It would seem that the acts of law are not suitably assigned as consisting in command, prohibition, permission and punishment.[5]

Objection 1. For "every law is a general precept," as the jurist states.[6] But command and precept are the same. Therefore the other three are superfluous.

Obj. 2. Further, the effect of a law is to induce its subjects to be good, as stated above (A. 1). But counsel aims at a higher good than a command does. Therefore it belongs to law to counsel rather than to command.

Obj. 3. Further, just as punishment stirs a man to good deeds, so does reward. Therefore if to punish is put as an effect of law, so also is to reward.

Obj. 4. Further, the intention of a lawgiver is to make men good, as stated above (A. 1). But he that obeys the law merely through fear of being punished is not good; because "although a good deed may be done through servile fear, that is, fear of punishment, it is not done well," as Augustine says (*Contra duas*

---

[1] *Politics*, I, 13 (1260ᵃ20).   [2] Cf. *Ethics*, II, 1 (1103ᵇ3).
[3] *Confessions*, III, 15 (PL 32, 689).

[4] *Politics*, III, 4 (1277ᵃ20).
[5] Gratian, *Decretum*, PT. I, d. 3, can. 4 (RF I, 5); cf. Isidore, *Etymol.*, V, 19 (PL 82, 202).
[6] *Dig.*, I, tit, III, leg. I (KR I, 33b).

Epist.Pelag. ii, 9).[1] Therefore punishment is not a proper effect of law.

On the contrary, Isidore says (*Etym.* v, 19):[2] "Every law either permits something, as: 'A brave man may demand his reward'; or forbids something, as: 'No man may ask a consecrated virgin in marriage'; or punishes, as: 'Let him that commits a murder be put to death.'"

I answer that, Just as an enunciation is a dictate of reason asserting something, so is a law a dictate of reason commanding something. Now it is proper to reason to lead from one thing to another. Therefore just as in demonstrative sciences the reason leads us from principles to assent to the conclusion, so it induces us by some means to assent to the precept of the law.

Now the precepts of law are concerned with human acts, in which the law directs, as stated above (Q. XC, AA. 1, 2; Q. XCI, A. 4). Again, there are three kinds of human acts. For, as stated above (Q. XVIII, A. 8), some acts are good generically, namely, acts of virtue, and in respect of these the act of the law is a precept or command, for the law commands all acts of virtue.[3] Some acts are evil generically, namely, acts of vice, and in respect of these the law forbids. Some acts are generically indifferent, and

in respect of these the law permits; and all acts that are either not distinctly good or not distinctly bad may be called indifferent. And it is the fear of punishment that law makes use of in order to ensure obedience, in which respect punishment is an effect of law.

Reply Obj. 1. Just as to cease from evil is a kind of good, so a prohibition is a kind of precept; and accordingly, taking precept in a wide sense, every law is a kind of precept.

Reply Obj. 2. To advise is not a proper act of law, but may pertain even to a private person, who cannot make a law. Hence too the Apostle, after giving a certain counsel (I Cor. 7. 12) says: *I speak, not the Lord.* Consequently it is not reckoned as an effect of law.

Reply Obj. 3. To reward may also pertain to anyone, but to punish pertains to none but the framer of the law, by whose authority the pain is inflicted. Therefore to reward is not put as an effect of law, but only to punish.

Reply Obj. 4. From becoming accustomed to avoid evil and fulfil what is good, through fear of punishment, one is sometimes led on to do so likewise with delight and of one's own will. Accordingly, law, even by punishing, leads men on to being good.

2. IN PARTICULAR

QUESTION XCIII
OF THE ETERNAL LAW
(*In Six Articles*)

WE must now consider each law by itself; and (1) The eternal law; (2) The natural law (Q. XCIV); (3) The human law (Q. XCV); (4) The old law (Q. XCVIII); (5) The new law, which is the law of the Gospel (Q. CVI). Of the sixth law which is the law of the "fomes," we will let suffice what we have said when treating of original sin (Q. LXXXI; Q. LXXXIII).

Concerning the first there are six points of inquiry: (1) What is the eternal law? (2) Whether it is known to all? (3) Whether every law is derived from it? (4) Whether necessary things are subject to the eternal law? (5) Whether natural contingents are subject to the eternal law? (6) Whether all human things are subject to it?

ARTICLE 1. *Whether the Eternal Law Is a Supreme Type Existing in God?*

We proceed thus to the First Article: It would

seem that the eternal law is not a supreme type (*ratio*) existing in God.

Objection 1. For there is only one eternal law. But there are many types of things in the Divine mind; for Augustine says (QQ. LXXXIII, qu. 46)[4] that "God made each thing according to its type." Therefore the eternal law does not seem to be a type existing in the Divine mind.

Obj. 2. Further, it is of the very character of a law that it be promulgated by word, as stated above (Q. XC, A. 4; Q. XCI, A. 1, Reply 2). But Word is a Personal name in God, as stated in the First Part (Q. XXXIV, A. 1), while type refers to the Essence. Therefore the eternal law is not the same as a Divine type.

Obj. 3. Further, Augustine says (*De Vera Relig.* xxx):[5] "We see a law above our minds, which is called truth." But the law which is above our minds is the eternal law. Therefore truth is the eternal law. But the idea of truth is not the same as the idea of a type. Therefore the eternal law is not the same as the sovereign type.

On the contrary, Augustine says (*De Lib.*

---

[1] PL 44, 586.   [2] PL 82, 202.
[3] Aristotle, *Ethics,* v, 1 (1129[b]19).

[4] PL 40, 30.
[5] PL 34, 147.

Arb. i, 6)[1] that "the eternal law is the sovereign type, to which we must always conform."

I answer that, Just as in every artificer there pre-exists a type of the things that are made by his art, so too in every governor there must pre-exist the type of the order of those things that are to be done by those who are subject to his government. And just as the type of the things to be made by an art is called the art or exemplar of the products of that art, so too the type in him who governs the acts of his subjects bears the character of a law, provided the other conditions be present which we have mentioned above (Q. XC). Now God, by His wisdom, is the Creator of all things, in relation to which He stands as the artificer to the products of his art, as stated in the First Part (Q. XIV, A. 8). Moreover He governs all the acts and movements that are to be found in each single creature, as was also stated in the First Part (Q. CIII, A. 5). Therefore as the type of the Divine Wisdom, in so far as by It all things are created, has the character of art, exemplar or idea, so the type of Divine Wisdom as moving all things to their due end bears the character of law. Accordingly the eternal law is nothing else than the type of Divine Wisdom, as directing all actions and movements.

Reply Obj. 1. Augustine is speaking in that passage of the ideal types which concern the proper nature of each single thing, so that there is in them a certain distinction and plurality, according to their different relations to things, as stated in the First Part (Q. XV, A. 2). But law is said to direct human acts by ordering them to the common good, as stated above (Q. XC, A. 2). And things which are in themselves different may be considered as one, according as they are ordered to one common thing. Therefore the eternal law is one since it is the type of this order.

Reply Obj. 2. With regard to any sort of word, two points may be considered, namely, the word itself, and that which is expressed by the word. For the spoken word is something uttered by the mouth of man, and expresses that which is signified by the human word. The same applies to the human mental word, which is nothing else than something conceived by the mind, by which man expresses mentally the things of which he is thinking. So also in God the Word conceived by the intellect of the Father is the name of a Person; but all things that are in the Father's knowledge, whether they refer to the Essence or to the Persons, or to the works of

God, are expressed by this Word, as Augustine declares (*De Trin.* xv, 14).[2] And among other things expressed by this Word is expressed the eternal law itself. Nor does it follow that the eternal law is a Personal name in God. Nevertheless it is appropriated to the Son, on account of the kinship between type and word.

Reply Obj. 3. The types of the Divine intellect do not stand in the same relation to things as the types of the human intellect. For the human intellect is measured by things, so that a human concept is not true by reason of itself but by reason of its being consonant with things, since an opinion is true or false according as the thing is or is not. But the Divine intellect is the measure of things, since each thing has truth in it to the extent that it imitates the Divine intellect, as was stated in the First Part (Q. XVI, A. 1). Consequently the Divine intellect is true in itself, and its type is truth itself.

ARTICLE 2. *Whether the Eternal Law Is Known to All?*

We proceed thus to the Second Article: It would seem that the eternal law is not known to all.

Objection 1. Because as the Apostle says (I Cor. 2. 11), *the things that are of God no man knoweth, but the Spirit of God.* But the eternal law is a type existing in the Divine mind. Therefore it is unknown to all save God alone.

Obj. 2. Further, as Augustine says (*De Lib. Arb.* i, 6)[3] "the eternal law is that by which it is right that all things should be most orderly." But all do not know how all things are most orderly. Therefore all do not know the eternal law.

Obj. 3. Further, Augustine says (*De Vera Relig.* XXXI)[4] that "the eternal law is not subject to the judgment of man." But according to the *Ethics,*[5] "any man can judge well of what he knows." Therefore the eternal law is not known to us.

On the contrary, Augustine says (*De Lib. Arb.* i, 6)[6] that "knowledge of the eternal law is imprinted in us."

I answer that, A thing may be known in two ways: first, in itself; secondly, in its effect, in which some likeness of that thing is found. Thus someone not seeing the sun in its substance, may know it by its rays. So then we

---

[1] PL 32, 1229.

[2] PL 42, 1076; VI, 10 (PL 42, 931).

[3] PL 32, 1229.

[4] PL 34, 148.

[5] Aristotle, I, 3 (1094[b]27).

[6] PL 32, 1229. Cf. Plotinus, I *Ennead,* i, 8 (BU I, 44); II, iii, 17 (BU II, 43); IV, iii, 17 (BU IV, 84).

must say that no one can know the eternal law as it is in itself, except God Himself and the blessed who see God in His Essence. But every rational creature knows it in its reflection, greater or less. For every knowledge of truth is a kind of reflection and participation of the eternal law, which is the unchangeable truth, as Augustine says (*De Vera Relig.* xxxi).[5] Now all men know the truth to a certain extent, at least as to the common principles of the natural law. And as to the others, they partake of the knowledge of truth, some more, some less; and in this respect they know the eternal law more or less.

Reply Obj. 1. We cannot know the things that are of God, as they are in themselves; but they are made known to us in their effects, according to Rom. 1. 20: *The invisible things of God . . . are clearly seen, being understood by the things that are made.*

Reply Obj. 2. Although each one knows the eternal law according to his own capacity, in the way explained above, yet none can comprehend it, for it cannot be made perfectly known by its effects. Therefore it does not follow that anyone who knows the eternal law in the above way knows also the whole order of things, by which all things are most orderly.

Reply Obj. 3. To judge of a thing may be understood in two ways. First, as when a knowing power judges of its proper object, according to Job 12. 11: *Doth not the ear discern words, and the palate of him that eateth, the taste?* It is to this kind of judgment that the Philosopher alludes when he says that anyone can judge well of what he knows, by judging, namely, whether what is put forward is true. In another way we speak of a superior judging of a subordinate by a kind of practical judgment, as to whether he should be such and such or not. And thus none can judge of the eternal law.

ARTICLE 3. *Whether Every Law Is Derived from the Eternal Law?*

We proceed thus to the Third Article: It would seem that not every law is derived from the eternal law.

Objection 1. For there is a law of the "fomes," as stated above (Q. XCI, A. 6), which is not derived from that Divine law which is the eternal law, since to it pertains the prudence of the flesh, of which the Apostle says (Rom. 8. 7), that *it cannot be subject to the law of God.* Therefore not every law is derived from the eternal law.

Obj. 2. Further, nothing unjust can be derived from the eternal law, because, as stated above (A. 2, obj. 2), "the eternal law is that according to which it is right that all things should be most orderly." But some laws are unjust, according to Isa. 10. 1: *Woe to them that make wicked laws.* Therefore not every law is derived from the eternal law.

Obj. 3. Further, Augustine says (*De Lib. Arb.* i, 5)[1] that "the law which is framed for ruling the people, rightly permits many things which are punished by Divine providence." But the type of Divine providence is the eternal law, as stated above (A. 1). Therefore not even every good law is derived from the eternal law.

On the contrary, Divine Wisdom says (Prov. 8, 15): *By Me kings reign, and lawgivers decree just things.* But the type of Divine Wisdom is the eternal law, as stated above (A. 1). Therefore all laws proceed from the eternal law.

I answer that, As stated above (Q. XC, AA. 1, 2), law denotes a kind of principle (*ratio*) directing acts towards an end. Now wherever there are movers ordered to one another, the power of the second mover has to be derived from the power of the first mover, since the second mover does not move except in so far as it is moved by the first. Hence we observe the same in all those who govern, so that the plan (*ratio*) of government is derived by secondary governors from the governor in chief; thus the plan of what is to be done in a state flows from the king's command to his inferior administrators. And again in things of art the plan of whatever is to be done by art flows from the chief craftsman to the under-craftsmen who work with their hands. Since then the eternal law is the plan of government in the Chief Governor, all the plans of government in the inferior governors must be derived from the eternal law. But these plans of inferior governors are all other laws besides the eternal law. Therefore all laws, in so far as they partake of right reason, are derived from the eternal law. Hence Augustine says (*De Lib. Arb.* i, 6)[2] that "in temporal law there is nothing just and lawful but what man has drawn from the eternal law."

Reply Obj. 1. The "fomes" has the nature of law in man, in so far as it is a punishment resulting from Divine justice; and in this respect it is evident that it is derived from the eternal law. But in so far as it denotes a proneness to sin, it is contrary to the Divine law, and has not the nature of law, as stated above (Q. XCI, A. 6).

[1] PL 32, 1228.   [2] PL 32, 1229.

Reply Obj. 2. Human law has the nature of law in so far as it partakes of right reason; and it is clear that, in this respect, it is derived from the eternal law. But in so far as it deviates from reason, it is called an unjust law, and has the nature not of law but of violence. Nevertheless even an unjust law, in so far as it retains some appearance of law, though being framed by one who is in power, is derived from the eternal law, since all power is from the Lord God, according to Rom. 13. 1.

Reply Obj. 3. Human law is said to permit certain things not as approving of them, but as being unable to direct them. And many things are directed by the Divine law, which human law is unable to direct, because more things are subject to a higher than to a lower cause. Hence the very fact that human law does not meddle with matters it cannot direct comes under the ordination of the eternal law. It would be different were human law to sanction what the eternal law condemns. Consequently it does not follow that human law is not derived from the eternal law, but that it is not on a perfect equality with it.

ARTICLE 4. *Whether Necessary and Eternal Things Are Subject to the Eternal Law?*

We proceed thus to the Fourth Article: It would seem that necessary and eternal things are subject to the eternal law.

Objection 1. For whatever is reasonable is subject to reason. But the Divine will is reasonable, for it is just. Therefore it is subject to reason. But the eternal law is the Divine reason. Therefore God's will is subject to the eternal law. But God's will is eternal. Therefore eternal and necessary things are subject to the eternal law.

Obj. 2. Further, whatever is subject to the King, is subject to the King's law. Now the Son, according to I Cor. 15. 28, 24, *shall be subject . . . to God and the Father, . . . when He shall have delivered up the Kingdom to Him.* Therefore the Son, Who is eternal, is subject to the eternal law.

Obj. 3. Further, the eternal law is the type of the Divine providence. But many necessary things are subject to Divine providence, for instance, the stability of incorporeal substances and of the heavenly bodies. Therefore even necessary things are subject to eternal law.

On the contrary, Things that are necessary cannot be otherwise, and consequently need no restraining. But laws are imposed on men in order to restrain them from evil, as explained above (Q. XCII, A. 2). Therefore necessary things are not subject to the eternal law.

I answer that, As stated above (A. 1), the eternal law is the type of the Divine government. Consequently whatever is subject to the Divine government is subject to the eternal law, while if anything is not subject to the Divine government, neither is it subject to the eternal law. The application of this distinction may be gathered by looking around us. For those things are subject to human government which can be done by man, but what pertains to the nature of man is not subject to human government; for instance, that he should have a soul, hands, or feet. Accordingly all that is in things created by God, whether it be contingent or necessary, is subject to the eternal law, while things pertaining to the Divine Nature or Essence are not subject to the eternal law, but are the eternal law itself.

Reply Obj. 1. We may speak of God's will in two ways. First, as to the will itself; and thus, since God's will is His very Essence, it is subject neither to the Divine government nor to the eternal law, but is the same thing as the eternal law. Secondly, we may speak of God's will as to the things themselves that God wills about creatures, which things are subject to the eternal law in so far as they are planned by Divine Wisdom. In reference to these things God's will is said to be reasonable (*rationalis*), though regarded in itself, it should rather be called their type (*ratio*).

Reply Obj. 2. God the Son was not made by God, but was naturally begotten of God. Consequently He is not subject to Divine providence or to the eternal law but rather is Himself the eternal law by a kind of appropriation, as Augustine explains (*De Vera Relig.* xxxi).[1] But He is said to be subject to the Father by reason of His human nature, in respect of which also the Father is said to be greater than He (John 14. 28).

The third objection we grant, because it deals with those necessary things that are created.

Reply Obj. 4. As the Philosopher says,[2] some necessary things have a cause of their necessity, and thus they derive from something else the fact that they cannot be otherwise. And this is in itself a most effective restraint; for whatever is restrained is said to be restrained in so far as it cannot do otherwise than it is allowed to.

[1] PL 34, 147.
[2] *Metaphysics,* v, 5 (1015ᵇ10).

ARTICLE 5. *Whether Natural Contingents
Are Subject to the Eternal Law?*

We proceed thus to the Fifth Article: It
would seem that natural contingents are not subject to the eternal law.

Objection 1. Because promulgation is essential to law, as stated above (Q. XC, A. 4). But
a law cannot be promulgated except to rational
creatures, to whom it is possible to make an
announcement. Therefore none but rational
creatures are subject to the eternal law, and
consequently natural contingents are not.

Obj. 2. Further, "Whatever obeys reason partakes somewhat of reason," as stated in the
Ethics.[1] But the eternal law is the supreme type,
as stated above (A. 1). Since then natural contingents do not partake of reason in any way,
but are altogether void of reason, it seems that
they are not subject to the eternal law.

Obj. 3. Further, the eternal law is most efficacious. But in natural contingents defects occur. Therefore they are not subject to the eternal law.

On the contrary, It is written (Prov. 8. 29):
*When He compassed the sea with its bounds,
and set a law to the waters, that they should
not pass their limits.*

I answer that, We must speak otherwise of
the law of man than of the eternal law which is
the law of God. For the law of man extends
only to rational creatures subject to man. The
reason of this is because law directs the actions
of those that are subject to the government of
someone; therefore, properly speaking, none
imposes a law on his own actions. Now whatever is done regarding the use of irrational
things subject to man is done by the act of man
himself moving those things, for these irrational
creatures do not move themselves but are moved
by others, as stated above (Q. I, A. 2). Consequently man cannot impose laws on irrational
beings, however much they may be subject to
him. But he can impose laws on rational beings
subject to him, in so far as by his command or
pronouncement of any kind he imprints on their
minds a rule which is a principle of action.

Now just as man, by such pronouncement,
impresses a kind of inward principle of action
on the man that is subject to him, so God imprints on the whole of nature the principles of
its proper actions. And so, in this way, God is
said to command the whole of nature, according to Ps. 148. 6: *He hath made a decree, and
it shall not pass away.* And thus all actions and

movements of the whole of nature are subject
to the eternal law. Consequently irrational creatures are subject to the eternal law through
being moved by Divine providence, but not, as
rational creatures are, through understanding
the Divine commandment.

Reply Obj. 1. The impression of an inward
active principle is to natural things what the
promulgation of law is to men, because law, by
being promulgated, imprints on man a directive principle of human actions, as stated above.

Reply Obj. 2. Irrational creatures neither
partake of nor are obedient to human reason,
but they do partake of the Divine Reason by
obeying it; because the power of Divine Reason
extends over more things than human reason
does. And as the members of the human body
are moved at the command of reason, and yet
do not partake of reason, since they have no apprehension subordinate to reason, so too irrational creatures are moved by God, without, on
that account, being rational.

Reply Obj. 3. Although the defects which occur in natural things are outside the order of
particular causes, they are not outside the order
of universal causes, especially of the First
Cause, which is God, from Whose providence
nothing can escape, as stated in the First Part
(Q. XXII, A. 2). And since the eternal law is the
type of Divine providence, as stated above
(A. 1), hence the defects of natural things are
subject to the eternal law.

ARTICLE 6. *Whether All Human Affairs Are
Subject to the Eternal Law?*

We proceed thus to the Sixth Article: It
would seem that not all human affairs are subject to the eternal law.

Objection 1. For the Apostle says (Gal. 5.
18). *If you are led by the spirit you are not
under the law.* But just men, who are the sons of
God by adoption, are led by the spirit of God,
according to Rom. 8. 14: *Whosoever are led by
the Spirit of God, they are the sons of God.*
Therefore not all men are under the eternal
law.

Obj. 2. Further, the Apostle says (Rom. 8.
7): *The prudence* (Vulg.,—*wisdom*) *of the flesh
is an enemy to God: for it is not subject to the
law of God.* But many are those in whom the
prudence of the flesh dominates. Therefore all
men are not subject to the eternal law which
is the law of God.

Obj. 3. Further, Augustine says (*De Lib. Arb.*
i, 6)[2] that the eternal law "is that by which the

[1] Aristotle, I, 13 (1102[b]25).   [2] PL 32, 1229.

wicked deserve misery, the good a life of blessedness." But those who are already blessed, and those who are already lost, are not in the state of merit. Therefore they are not under the eternal law.

On the contrary, Augustine says:[1] "Nothing evades the laws of the most high Creator and Governor, for by Him the peace of the universe is administered."

I answer that, There are two ways in which a thing is subject to the eternal law, as explained above (A. 5). First, by partaking of the eternal law by way of knowledge; secondly, by way of action and passion, that is by partaking of the eternal law by way of an inward moving principle. And in this second way, irrational creatures are subject to the eternal law, as stated above (*ibid.*). But since the rational nature, together with that which it has in common with all creatures, has something proper to itself in so far as it is rational, consequently it is subject to the eternal law in both ways; because while each rational creature has some knowledge of the eternal law, as stated above (A. 2), it also has a natural inclination to that which is in harmony with the eternal law; for we are naturally adapted to be the receivers of virtue.[2]

Both ways, however, are imperfect, and to a certain extent destroyed, in the wicked, because in them the natural inclination to virtue is corrupted by vicious habits, and, moreover, the natural knowledge of good is darkened by passions and habits of sin. But in the good both ways are found more perfect, because in them, besides the natural knowledge of good, there is the added knowledge of faith and wisdom; and again, besides the natural inclination to good, there is the added interior motive of grace and virtue.

Accordingly, the good are perfectly subject to the eternal law, as always acting according to it. But the wicked are subject to the eternal law, imperfectly as to their actions, indeed, since both their knowledge of good and their inclination to it are imperfect; but this imperfection on the part of action is supplied on the part of passion, in so far as they suffer what the eternal law decrees concerning them, according as they fail to act in harmony with that law. Hence Augustine says (*De Lib. Arb.* i, 15):[3] "I esteem that the just act according to the eternal law"; and (*De Catech. Rud.* xviii):[4] "Out of the just misery of the souls which deserted Him, God knew how to furnish the inferior parts of His creation with most suitable laws."

Reply Obj. 1. This saying of the Apostle may be understood in two ways. First, so that a man is said to be under the law through being pinned down by it against his will, as though he were weighed down under a burden. Hence, on the same passage a gloss says[5] that "he is under the law who refrains from evil deeds through fear of the punishment threatened by the law, and not from love of justice." In this way the spiritual man is not under the law, because he fulfils the law willingly through charity which is poured into his heart by the Holy Ghost. Secondly, it can be understood as meaning that the works of a man who is led by the Holy Ghost are the works of the Holy Ghost rather than his own. Therefore, since the Holy Ghost is not under the law, as neither is the Son, as stated above (A. 4, reply 2), it follows that such works, in so far as they are of the Holy Ghost, are not under the law. The Apostle witnesses to this when he says (II Cor. 3. 17): *Where the Spirit of the Lord is, there is liberty.*

Reply Obj. 2. The prudence of the flesh cannot be subject to the law of God as regards action, since it inclines to actions contrary to the Divine law; yet it is subject to the law of God, as regards passion, since it deserves to suffer punishment according to the law of Divine justice. Nevertheless in no man does the prudence of the flesh dominate so far as to destroy the whole good of his nature. And consequently there remains in man the inclination to act in accordance with the eternal law. For we have seen above (Q. LXXXV, A. 2) that sin does not destroy entirely the good of nature.

Reply Obj. 3. A thing is maintained in the end and moved towards the end by one and the same cause; thus gravity which makes a heavy body rest in the lower place is also the cause of its being moved there. We therefore reply that as it is according to the eternal law that some deserve happiness, others unhappiness, so is it by the eternal law that some are maintained in a happy state, others in an unhappy state. Accordingly both the blessed and the damned are under the eternal law.

QUESTION XCIV
OF THE NATURAL LAW
(*In Six Articles*)

We must now consider the natural law, concerning which there are six points of inquiry:

---

[1] *City of God*, XIX, 12 (PL 41, 640).
[2] Aristotle, *Ethics*, II, 1 (1103^{a}25).
[3] PL 32, 1238.   [4] PL 40, 333.

[5] *Glossa* Lombardi (PL 192, 158); cf. *Glossa ordin.* (VI, 87E).

(1) What is the natural law? (2) What are the precepts of the natural law? (3) Whether all acts of virtue are prescribed by the natural law? (4) Whether the natural law is the same in all? (5) Whether it is changeable? (6) Whether it can be abolished from the heart of man?

ARTICLE 1. *Whether the Natural Law Is a Habit?*

We proceed thus to the First Article: It would seem that the natural law is a habit.

Objection 1. Because, as the Philosopher says,[1] "there are three things in the soul, power, habit, and passion." But the natural law is not one of the soul's powers, nor is it one of the passions, as we may see by going through them one by one. Therefore the natural law is a habit.

Obj. 2. Further, Basil says[2] that the "conscience or synderesis is the law of our mind," which can only apply to the natural law. But synderesis is a habit, as was shown in the First Part (Q. LXXIX, A. 12). Therefore the natural law is a habit.

Obj. 3. Further, the natural law remains in man always, as will be shown further on (A. 6). But man's reason, which the law regards, does not always think about the natural law. Therefore the natural law is not an act, but a habit.

On the contrary, Augustine says (*De Bono Conjug.* xxi)[3] that "a habit is that whereby something is done when necessary." But such is not the natural law, since it is in infants and in the damned who cannot act by it. Therefore the natural law is not a habit.

I answer that, A thing may be called a habit in two ways. First, properly and essentially, and thus the natural law is not a habit. For it has been stated above (Q. XC, A. 1, reply 2) that the natural law is something appointed by reason, just as a proposition is a work of reason. Now that which a man does is not the same as that by which he does it; for example, it is by the habit of grammar that a man speaks correctly. Since then a habit is that by which we act, a law cannot be a habit properly and essentially.

Secondly, the term habit may be applied to that which we hold by a habit; thus faith may mean that which we hold by faith. And accordingly, since the precepts of the natural law are

sometimes considered by reason actually, while sometimes they are in the reason only habitually, in this way the natural law may be called a habit. Thus, in speculative matters, the indemonstrable principles are not the habit itself by which we hold those principles, but are the principles of which we possess the habit.

Reply Obj. 1. The Philosopher proposes there to discover the genus of virtue; and since it is evident that virtue is a principle of action, he mentions only those things which are principles of human acts, namely, powers, habits and passions. But there are other things in the soul besides these three, such as certain acts; thus to will is in the one that wills; again, things known are in the knower; moreover its own natural properties are in the soul, such as immortality and the like.

Reply Obj. 2. Synderesis is said to be the law of our intellect because it is a habit containing the precepts of the natural law, which are the first principles of human actions.

Reply Obj. 3. This argument proves that the natural law is held habitually, and this is granted.

To the argument advanced in the contrary sense we reply that sometimes a man is unable to make use of that which is in him habitually on account of some impediment; thus, on account of sleep, a man is unable to use the habit of science. In like manner, through the deficiency of his age, a child cannot use the habit of understanding of principles, or even the natural law, which is in him habitually.

ARTICLE 2. *Whether the Natural Law Contains Several Precepts, or One Only?*

We proceed thus to the Second Article: It would seem that the natural law contains not several precepts, but one only.

Objection 1. For law is a kind of precept, as stated above (Q. XCII, A. 2). If therefore there were many precepts of the natural law, it would follow that there are also many natural laws.

Obj. 2. Further, the natural law is consequent to human nature. But human nature, as a whole, is one, though as to its parts it is manifold. Therefore, either there is but one precept of the law of nature, on account of the unity of nature as a whole, or there are many by reason of the number of parts of human nature. The result would be that even things relating to the inclination of the concupiscible faculty belong to the natural law.

Obj. 3. Further, law is something pertaining to reason, as stated above (Q. XC, A. 1). Now

[1] *Ethics*, II, 5 (1105[b]20).
[2] Cf. *In Hexaëm.*, hom. VII (PG 29, 158); hom. XII *in Princ. Prov.* (PG 31, 406); cf. also Damascene, *De Fide Orth.*, IV, 22 (PG 94, 1200).
[3] PL 40, 390.

reason is but one in man. Therefore there is only one precept of the natural law.

On the contrary, The precepts of the natural law in man stand in relation to practical matters as the first principles to matters of demonstration. But there are several first indemonstrable principles. Therefore there are also several precepts of the natural law.

I answer that, As stated above (Q. XCI, A. 3), the precepts of the natural law are to the practical reason what the first principles of demonstrations are to the speculative reason; because both are self-evident principles. Now a thing is said to be self-evident in two ways: first, in itself; secondly, in relation to us. Any proposition is said to be self-evident in itself if its predicate is contained in the notion of the subject, although to one who does not know the definition of the subject it happens that such a proposition is not self-evident. For instance, this proposition, Man is a rational being, is, in its very nature, self-evident, since who says man, says a rational being; and yet to one who does not know what a man is this proposition is not self-evident. Hence it is that, as Boëthius says (*De Hebdom.*),[1] certain axioms or propositions are universally self-evident to all; and such are those propositions whose terms are known to all, as, Every whole is greater than its part, and, Things equal to one and the same are equal to one another. But some propositions are self-evident only to the wise, who understand the meaning of the terms of such propositions: thus to one who understands that an angel is not a body, it is self-evident that an angel is not circumscriptively in a place; but this is not evident to the unlearned, for they cannot grasp it.

Now a certain order is to be found in those things that are apprehended by man. For that which, before anything else falls under apprehension, is being, the understanding of which is included in all things whatsoever a man apprehends. Therefore the first indemonstrable principle is that the same thing cannot be affirmed and denied at the same time, which is based on the notion of being and not-being; and on this principle all others are based, as is stated in the *Metaphysics.*[2] Now as being is the first thing that falls under the apprehension absolutely, so good is the first thing that falls under the apprehension of the practical reason, which is directed to action; for every agent acts for an end, which has the aspect of good. Consequently the first principle in the practical

reason is one founded on the notion of good, namely, that the good is what all desire. Hence this is the first precept of law, that good is to be pursued and done, and evil is to be avoided. All other precepts of the natural law are based upon this, so that whatever the practical reason naturally apprehends as man's good belongs to the precepts of the natural law as something to be done or avoided.

Since, however, good has the nature of an end, and evil, the nature of a contrary, hence it is that all those things to which man has a natural inclination are naturally apprehended by reason as being good, and consequently as objects of pursuit, and their contraries as evil, and objects of avoidance. Therefore the order of the precepts of the natural law is according to the order of natural inclinations. Because in man there is first of all an inclination to good in accordance with the nature which he has in common with all substances; that is, every substance seeks the preservation of its own being, according to its nature. And by reason of this inclination, whatever is a means of preserving human life and of warding off its obstacles belongs to the natural law. Secondly, there is in man an inclination to things that pertain to him more specially, according to that nature which he has in common with other animals. And in virtue of this inclination, those things are said to belong to the natural law "which nature has taught to all animals,"[3] such as sexual intercourse, education of offspring and so forth. Thirdly, there is in man an inclination to good, according to the nature of his reason, which nature is proper to him; thus man has a natural inclination to know the truth about God, and to live in society. And in this respect, whatever pertains to this inclination belongs to the natural law; for instance, to shun ignorance, to avoid offending those among whom one has to live, and other such things regarding the above inclination.

Reply Obj. 1. All these precepts of the law of nature have the character of one natural law because they flow from one first precept.

Reply Obj. 2. All the inclinations of any parts whatsoever of human nature, for example, of the concupiscible and irascible parts, in so far as they are ruled by reason, belong to the natural law, and are reduced to one first precept, as stated above, so that the precepts of the natural law are many in themselves, but are based on one common foundation.

[1] PL 64, 1311.
[2] Aristotle, IV, 3 (1005ᵇ29).

[3] *Dig.,* I, I, leg., I (KR I, 29a); cf. Lottin, *Le Droit Naturel* (p. 78; p. 34).

Reply Obj. 3. Although reason is one in itself, yet it directs all things regarding man, so that whatever can be ruled by reason is contained under the law of reason.

ARTICLE 3. *Whether All Acts of Virtue Are Prescribed by the Natural Law?*

We proceed thus to the Third Article: It would seem that not all acts of virtue are prescribed by the natural law.

Objection 1. Because, as stated above (Q. XC, A. 2) it is essential to a law that it be ordered to the common good. But some acts of virtue are ordered to the private good of the individual, as is evident especially in regard to acts of temperance. Therefore not all acts of virtue are the subject of natural law.

Obj. 2. Further, every sin is opposed to some virtuous act. If therefore all acts of virtue are prescribed by the natural law, it seems to follow that all sins are against nature which, however, applies especially to certain sins.

Obj. 3. Further, those things which are according to nature are common to all. But acts of virtue are not common to all, since a thing is virtuous in one and vicious in another. Therefore not all acts of virtue are prescribed by the natural law.

On the contrary, Damascene says (*De Fide Orthod.* iii, 14)[1] that "virtues are natural." Therefore virtuous acts also fall under the natural law.

I answer that, We may speak of virtuous acts in two ways: first, under the aspect of virtuous; secondly, as such and such acts considered in their proper species. If then we speak of acts of virtue considered as virtuous, thus all virtuous acts belong to the natural law. For it has been stated (A. 2) that to the natural law belongs everything to which a man is inclined according to his nature. Now each thing is inclined naturally to an operation that is suitable to it according to its form; thus fire is inclined to give heat. Therefore, since the rational soul is the proper form of man, there is in every man a natural inclination to act according to reason, and this is to act according to virtue. Consequently, considered thus, all acts of virtue are prescribed by the natural law; for each one's reason naturally requires him to act virtuously. But if we speak of virtuous acts, considered in themselves, that is, in their proper species, in this way not all virtuous acts are prescribed by the natural law. For many things are done virtuously to which nature does not incline at first, but which,

through the inquiry of reason, have been found by men to be conducive to well-living.

Reply Obj. 1. Temperance is about the natural concupiscences of food, drink and sexual matters, which are indeed ordered to the natural common good, just as other matters of law are ordered to the moral common good.

Reply Obj. 2. By human nature we may mean either that which is proper to man—and in this sense all sins, as being against reason, are also against nature, as Damascene states (*De Fide Orthod.* ii, 30).[2] Or we may mean that nature which is common to man and other animals, and in this sense, certain special sins are said to be against nature; thus contrary to sexual intercourse, which is natural to all animals, is unisexual lust, which has received the special name of the unnatural vice.

Reply Obj. 3. This argument considers acts in themselves. For it is owing to the various conditions of men that certain acts are virtuous for some, as being proportionate and fitting to them, while they are vicious for others, as being not proportioned to them.

ARTICLE 4. *Whether the Natural Law Is the Same in all Men?*

We proceed thus to the Fourth Article: It would seem that the natural law is not the same in all.

Objection 1. For it is stated in the Decretals (*Dist.* i)[3] that "the natural law is that which is contained in the Law and the Gospel." But this is not common to all men, because, as it is written (Rom. 10. 16), *all do not obey the gospel.* Therefore the natural law is not the same in all men.

Obj. 2. Further, "Things which are according to the law are said to be just," as stated in the *Ethics.*[4] But it is stated in the same book[5] that nothing is so just for everybody as not to be subject to change in regard to some men. Therefore even the natural law is not the same in all men.

Obj. 3. Further, as stated above (AA. 2, 3), to the natural law pertains everything to which a man is inclined according to his nature. Now different men are naturally inclined to different things; some to the desire of pleasures, others to the desire of honours, and other men to other things. Therefore there is not one natural law for all.

---

[1] PG 94, 1045.

[2] PG 94, 976; chap. 4 (PG 94, 876); IV, 20 (PG 94, 1196).

[3] Gratian, Pt. I, Prol. (RF. I, 1).

[4] Aristotle, v, 1 (1129^{b}12).   [5] *Ethics*, v, 7 (1134^{b}32).

On the contrary, Isidore says (*Etym.* v, 4):[1] "The natural law is common to all nations."

I answer that, As stated above (AA. 2, 3), those things to which a man is inclined naturally pertain to the natural law, and among these it is proper to man to be inclined to act according to reason. Now the process of reason is from the common to the proper, as stated in the *Physics*.[2] The speculative reason, however, is differently situated in this matter from the practical reason. For, since the speculative reason is busied chiefly with necessary things which cannot be otherwise than they are, its proper conclusions, like the common principles, contain the truth without fail. The practical reason, on the other hand, is busied with contingent matters, about which human actions are concerned; and consequently, although there is necessity in the general principles, the more we descend to matters of detail the more frequently we encounter defects. Accordingly then in speculative matters truth is the same in all men, both as to principles and as to conclusions, although the truth is not known to all as regards the conclusions, but only as regards the principles which are called "common notions."[3] But in matters of action, truth or practical rectitude is not the same for all as to matters of detail, but only as to the common principles; and where there is the same rectitude in matters of detail, it is not equally known to all.

It is therefore evident that as regards the common principles, whether of speculative or of practical reason, truth or rectitude is the same for all, and is equally known by all. As to the proper conclusions of the speculative reason, the truth is the same for all, but is not equally known to all; thus it is true for all that the three angles of a triangle are together equal to two right angles, although it is not known to all. But as to the proper conclusions of the practical reason, neither is the truth or rectitude the same for all, nor, where it is the same, is it equally known by all. Thus it is right and true for all to act according to reason. And from this principle it follows as a proper conclusion that goods entrusted to another should be restored to their owner. Now this is true for the majority of cases, but it may happen in a particular case that it would be injurious, and therefore unreasonable, to restore goods held in trust; for instance if they are claimed for the purpose of fighting against one's country. And this principle will be found to fail the more according as we descend further into detail, for example if one were to say that goods held in trust should be restored with such and such a guarantee, or in such and such a way; because the greater the number of conditions added, the greater the number of ways in which the principle may fail, so that it be not right to restore or not to restore.

Consequently we must say that the natural law, as to first common principles, is the same for all, both as to rectitude and as to knowledge. But as to certain matters of detail, which are conclusions, as it were of those common principles, it is the same for all in the majority of cases, both as to rectitude and as to knowledge; and yet in some few cases it may fail, both as to rectitude, by reason of certain obstacles (just as natures subject to generation and corruption fail in some few cases on account of some obstacle), and as to knowledge, since in some the reason is perverted by passion, or evil habit, or an evil disposition of nature. Thus formerly, theft, although it is expressly contrary to the natural law, was not considered wrong among the Germans, as Julius Cæsar relates (*De Bello Gall.* vi).[4]

Reply Obj. 1. The meaning of the sentence quoted is not that whatever is contained in the Law and the Gospel belongs to the natural law, since they contain many things that are above nature, but that whatever belongs to the natural law is fully contained in them. Therefore Gratian, after saying that "the natural law is what is contained in the Law and the Gospel," adds at once, by way of example, "by which everyone is commanded to do to others as he would be done by."

Reply Obj. 2. The saying of the Philosopher is to be understood of things that are naturally just not as common principles, but as conclusions drawn from them, having rectitude in the majority of cases, but failing in a few.

Reply Obj. 3. As in man reason rules and commands the other powers, so all the natural inclinations belonging to the other powers must be directed according to reason. Therefore it is universally right for all men that all their inclinations should be directed according to reason.

ARTICLE 5. *Whether the Natural Law Can be Changed?*

We proceed thus to the Fifth Article: It would seem that the natural law can be changed.

---

[1] PL 82, 199.   [2] Aristotle, I, I (184ª16).
[3] Boëthius, *De Hebdom.* (PL 64, 1311); cf. Arnim, *Fragmenta*, Vol. III, v, 2 (III, 51).
[4] Chap. 23 (DD 270).

Objection 1. Because on Ecclus. 17. 9, *He gave them instructions, and the law of life,* the gloss says:[1] "He wished the law of the letter to be written, in order to correct the law of nature." But that which is corrected is changed. Therefore the natural law can be changed.

Obj. 2. Further, the slaying of the innocent, adultery, and theft are against the natural law. But we find these things changed by God, as when God commanded Abraham to slay his innocent son (Gen. 22. 2); and when He ordered the Jews to borrow and purloin the vessels of the Egyptians (Exod. 12. 35); and when He commanded Osee to take to himself a *wife of fornications* (Osee 1. 2). Therefore the natural law can be changed.

Obj. 3. Further, Isidore says (*Etym.* v, 4)[2] that "the possession of all things in common, and a uniform freedom, are matters of natural law." But these things are seen to be changed by human laws. Therefore it seems that the natural law is subject to change.

On the contrary, It is said in the Decretals (*Dist.* v):[3] "The natural law dates from the creation of the rational creature. It does not vary according to time, but remains unchangeable."

I answer that, A change in the natural law may be understood in two ways. First, by way of addition. In this sense nothing hinders the natural law from being changed, since many things for the benefit of human life have been added over and above the natural law, both by the Divine law and by human laws.

Secondly, a change in the natural law may be understood by way of subtraction, so that what previously was according to the natural law ceases to be so. In this sense, the natural law is altogether unchangeable in its first principles. But in its secondary principles, which, as we have said (A. 4), are certain detailed proximate conclusions drawn from the first principles, the natural law is not changed so that what it prescribes be not right in most cases. But it may be changed in some particular cases of rare occurrence, through some special causes hindering the observance of such precepts, as stated above (A. 4).

Reply Obj. 1. The written law is said to be given for the correction of the natural law, either because it supplies what was wanting to the natural law, or because the natural law was perverted in the hearts of some men, as to certain matters, so that they thought those things good which are naturally evil, which perversion stood in need of correction.

Reply Obj. 2. All men alike, both guilty and innocent, die the death of nature, which death of nature is inflicted by the power of God on account of original sin, according to I Kings 2. 6: *The Lord killeth and maketh alive.* Consequently, by the command of God, death can be inflicted on any man, guilty or innocent, without any injustice whatever. In like manner adultery is intercourse with another's wife, who is allotted to him by the law emanating from God. Consequently intercourse with any woman, by the command of God, is neither adultery nor fornication. The same applies to theft, which is the taking of another's property. For whatever is taken by the command of God, to Whom all things belong, is not taken against the will of its owner, which is what theft is. Nor is it only in human things that whatever is commanded by God is right; but also in natural things, whatever is done by God, is, in some way, natural, as stated in the First Part (Q. CV, A. 6, reply 1).

Reply Obj. 3. A thing is said to belong to the natural law in two ways. First, because nature inclines there; for example, that one should not do harm to another. Secondly, because nature did not bring in the contrary; thus we might say that for man to be naked is of the natural law, because nature did not give him clothes, but art invented them. In this sense, "the possession of all things in common, and uniform freedom" are said to be of the natural law, because, that is, the distinction of possessions and slavery were not brought in by nature, but devised by human reason for the benefit of human life. Accordingly the law of nature was not changed in this respect, except by addition.

ARTICLE 6. *Whether the Law of Nature Can Be Abolished from the Heart of Man?*

We proceed thus to the Sixth Article: It would seem that the natural law can be abolished from the heart of man.

Objection 1. Because on Rom. 2. 14, *When the Gentiles who have not the law,* etc., a gloss says[4] that "the law of justice, which sin had blotted out, is graven on the heart of man when he is restored by grace." But the law of justice is the law of nature. Therefore the law of nature can be blotted out.

Obj. 2. Further, the law of grace is more efficacious than the law of nature. But the law of

---

[1] *Glossa ordin.* (III, 403E); Rabanus Maurus, IV, 5 (PL 109, 876).
[2] PL 82, 199.   [3] Gratian, Pt. I, Prol. (RF I, 7).

[4] *Glossa ordin.* (VI, 7E); *Glossa* Lombardi (PL 191, 1345).

grace is blotted out by sin. Much more therefore can the law of nature be blotted out.

Obj. 3. Further, that which is established by law is imposed as just. But many things are enacted by men which are contrary to the law of nature. Therefore the law of nature can be abolished from the heart of man.

On the contrary, Augustine says:[1] "Thy law is written in the hearts of men, which iniquity itself effaces not." But the law which is written in men's hearts is the natural law. Therefore the natural law cannot be blotted out.

I answer that, As stated above (AA. 4, 5), there belong to the natural law, first, certain most common precepts, that are known to all; and secondly, certain secondary and more detailed precepts, which are, as it were, conclusions following closely from first principles. As to those common principles, the natural law, in its universal character, can in no way be blotted out from men's hearts. But it is blotted out in the case of a particular action, in so far as reason is hindered from applying the common principle to a particular point of practice, on account of concupiscence or some other passion, as stated above (Q. LXXVII, A. 2). But as to the other, that is, the secondary precepts, the natural law can be blotted out from the human heart, either by evil persuasions, just as in speculative matters errors occur in respect of necessary conclusions; or by vicious customs and corrupt habits, as among some men, theft, and even unnatural vices, as the Apostle states (Rom. 1), were not considered sinful.

Reply Obj. 1. Sin blots out the law of nature in particular cases, not universally, except perhaps in regard to the secondary precepts of the natural law, in the way stated above.

Reply Obj. 2. Although grace is more efficacious than nature, yet nature is more essential to man, and therefore more enduring.

Reply Obj. 3. This argument is true of the secondary precepts of the natural law, against which some legislators have framed certain enactments which are unjust.

QUESTION XCV
OF HUMAN LAW
(In Four Articles)

WE must now consider human law; and (1) this law considered in itself; (2) its power (Q. XCVI); (3) its mutability (Q. XCVII). Under the first head there are four points of inquiry: (1)

[1] *Confessions,* II. 9 (PL 32, 678).

Its utility. (2) Its origin. (3) Its quality. (4) Its division.

ARTICLE 1. *Whether It was Useful for Laws to Be Framed by Men?*

We proceed thus to the First Article: It would seem that it was not useful for laws to be framed by men.

Objection 1. For the purpose of every law is that man be made good thereby, as stated above (Q. XCII, A. 1). But men are more induced to be good willingly by means of admonitions, than against their will by means of laws. Therefore there was no need to frame laws.

Obj. 2. Further, As the Philosopher says,[2] "men have recourse to a judge as to animate justice." But animate justice is better than inanimate justice, which is contained in laws. Therefore it would have been better for the execution of justice to be entrusted to the decision of judges than to frame laws in addition.

Obj. 3. Further, every law is framed for the direction of human actions, as is evident from what has been stated above (Q. XC, AA. 1, 2). But since human actions are about singulars, which are infinite in number, matters pertaining to the direction of human actions cannot be taken into sufficient consideration except by a wise man, who looks into each one of them. Therefore it would have been better for human acts to be directed by the judgment of wise men than by the framing of laws. Therefore there was no need of human laws.

On the contrary, Isidore says (*Etym.* v, 20):[3] "Laws were made so that in fear of them human audacity might be held in check, that innocence might be safeguarded in the midst of wickedness, and that the dread of punishment might prevent the wicked from doing harm." But these things are most necessary to mankind. Therefore it was necessary that human laws should be made.

I answer that, As stated above (Q. LXIII, A. 1; Q. XCIV, A. 3), man has a natural aptitude for virtue; but the perfection itself of virtue must be acquired by man by means of some kind of training. Thus we observe that man is helped by industry in his necessities, for instance, in food and clothing. Certain beginnings of these he has from nature, that is, his reason and his hands; but he has not the full complement, as other animals have, to whom nature has given sufficient covering and food. Now it is difficult to see how man could suffice for himself in the

[2] *Ethics,* v, 4 (1132ᵃ22). [3] PL 82, 202.

matter of this training; for the perfection of virtue consists chiefly in withdrawing man from undue pleasures, to which above all man is inclined, and especially the young, who are more capable of being trained. Consequently a man needs to receive this training from another, through which to arrive at the perfection of virtue. And as to those young people who are inclined to acts of virtue by their good natural disposition, or by custom, or rather by the gift of God, paternal training suffices, which is by admonitions. But since some are found to be depraved, and prone to vice, and not easily amenable to words, it was necessary for such to be restrained from evil by force and fear, in order that at least they might cease from evil-doing and leave others in peace, and that they themselves, by being accustomed in this way, might be brought to do willingly what hitherto they did from fear, and thus become virtuous. Now this kind of training, which compels through fear of punishment, is the discipline of laws. Therefore, in order that man might have peace and virtue, it was necessary for laws to be framed; for, as the Philosopher says,[1] "as man is the most noble of animals if he be perfect in virtue, so is he the lowest of all if he be severed from law and justice," because man is armed with reason, as the other animals are not, to sate his lust and ferocity.

Reply Obj. 1. Men who are well disposed are led willingly to virtue by being admonished better than by coercion; but men who are evilly disposed are not led to virtue unless they are compelled.

Reply Obj. 2. As the Philosopher says,[2] "it is better that all things be regulated by law than left to be decided by judges," and this for three reasons. First, because it is easier to find a few wise men competent to frame right laws than to find the many who would be necessary to judge rightly of each single case. Secondly, because those who make laws consider long beforehand what laws to make; but judgment on each single case has to be pronounced as soon as it arises. And it is easier for man to see what is right by taking many instances into consideration, than by considering one solitary fact. Thirdly, because lawgivers judge universally and of future events, while those who sit in judgment judge of things present, towards which they are affected by love, hatred, or some kind of cupidity, so that their judgment is perverted. Since then the animated justice of the judge is

not found in every man, and since it can be deflected, therefore it was necessary, whenever possible, for the law to determine how to judge, and for very few matters to be left to the decision of men.

Reply Obj. 3. Certain individual facts which cannot be covered by the law "have necessarily to be committed to judges," as the Philosopher says in the same passage; for instance, "concerning something that has happened or not happened," and the like.

ARTICLE 2. *Whether Every Human Law Is Derived from the Natural Law?*

We proceed thus to the Second Article: It would seem that not every human law is derived from the natural law.

Objection 1. For the Philosopher says[3] that "the legal just is that which originally was a matter of indifference." But those things which arise from the natural law are not matters of indifference. Therefore the enactments of human laws are not all derived from the natural law.

Obj. 2. Further, positive law is contrasted with natural law, as stated by Isidore (*Etym.* v, 4)[4] and the Philosopher.[5] But those things which flow as conclusions from the common principles of the natural law belong to the natural law, as stated above (Q. XCIV, A. 4). Therefore that which is established by human law does not belong to the natural law.

Obj. 3. Further, the law of nature is the same for all; since the Philosopher says[6] that "the natural just is that which is equally valid everywhere." If therefore human laws were derived from the natural law, it would follow that they too are the same for all, which is clearly false.

Obj. 4. Further, it is possible to give a reason for things which are derived from the natural law. But "it is not possible to give the reason for all the legal enactments of the lawgivers," as the Jurist says.[7] Therefore not all human laws are derived from the natural law.

On the contrary, Tully says (*Rhetor.* ii, 53)[8]: "Things which emanated from nature and were approved by custom, were sanctioned by fear and reverence for the laws."

I answer that, As Augustine says (*De Lib. Arb.* i, 5),[9] "that which is not just seems to be no law at all"; therefore the force of a law depends on the extent of its justice. Now in human affairs a thing is said to be just from being

---

[1] *Politics,* I, 2 (1253[a]31).   [2] *Rhetoric,* I, 1 (1354[a]31).

[3] *Ethics,* V, 7 (1134[b]20).   [4] PL 82, 199.
[5] *Loc. cit.*   [6] *Ibid.*   [7] *Dig.,* I, III, leg., 20 (KR I, 34[a]).
[8] DD I, 165.   [9] PL 32, 1227.

right according to the rule of reason. But the first rule of reason is the law of nature, as is clear from what has been stated above (Q. XCI, A. 2, REPLY 2). Consequently every human law has just so much of the character of law as it is derived from the law of nature. But if in any point it differs from the law of nature, it is no longer a law but a corruption of law.

But it must be noted that something may be derived from the natural law in two ways: first, as a conclusion from premises, secondly, by way of determination of certain generalities. The first way is like that by which, in the sciences, demonstrated conclusions are drawn from the principles, while the second mode is like that whereby, in the arts, common forms are determined to something particular; thus the craftsman needs to determine the common form of a house to the shape of this or that house. Some things are therefore derived from the common principles of the natural law by way of conclusions; for instance, that one must not kill may be derived as a conclusion from the principle that one should do harm to no man. But some are derived from these principles by way of determination; for instance, the law of nature has it that the evil-doer should be punished, but that he be punished in this or that way is a determination of the law of nature.

Accordingly both modes of derivation are found in the human law. But those things which are derived in the first way are contained in human law not as emanating from it exclusively, but have some force from the natural law also. But those things which are derived in the second way have no other force than that of human law.

Reply Obj. 1. The Philosopher is speaking of those enactments which are by way of determination or specification of the precepts of the natural law.

Reply Obj. 2. This argument avails for those things that are derived from the natural law, by way of conclusions.

Reply Obj. 3. The common principles of the natural law cannot be applied to all men in the same way on account of the great variety of human affairs, and from this arises the diversity of positive laws among various people.

Reply Obj. 4. These words of the Jurist are to be understood as referring to decisions of rulers in determining particular points of the natural law, on which determinations the judgment of expert and prudent men is based as on its principles; in so far, that is, as they see at once what is the best thing to decide. Hence

the Philosopher says[1] that in such matters "we ought to pay as much attention to the indemonstrable sayings and opinions of persons who surpass us in experience, age and prudence, as to their demonstrations."

ARTICLE 3. *Whether Isidore's Description of the Quality of Positive Law Is Appropriate?*

We proceed thus to the Third Article: It would seem that Isidore's description of the quality of positive law is not appropriate, when he says (*Etym.* v, 21):[2] "Law shall be honest (*honesta*), just, possible according to nature, in harmony with the custom of the country, suitable to place and time, necessary, useful; clearly expressed, lest by its obscurity it lead to misunderstanding; framed for no private benefit, but for the common good of the citizens."

Objection 1. For he had previously expressed the quality of law in three conditions, saying that "law is anything founded on reason, provided that it foster religion, be helpful to discipline, and further the common weal."[3] Therefore it was needless to add any further conditions to these.

Obj. 2. Further, justice is included in honesty, as Tully says (*De Offic.* vii).[4] Therefore after saying honest it was superfluous to add just.

Obj. 3. Further, written law is divided against custom, according to Isidore (*Etym.* ii, 10).[5] Therefore it should not be stated in the definition of law that it is "in harmony with the custom of the country."

Obj. 4. Further, a thing may be necessary in two ways. It may be necessary absolutely, because it cannot be otherwise, and that which is necessary in this way is not subject to human judgment; and so human law is not concerned with necessity of this kind. Again a thing may be necessary for an end, and this necessity is the same as usefulness. Therefore it is superfluous to say both "necessary" and "useful."

On the contrary stands the authority of Isidore.

I answer that, Whenever a thing is for an end, its form must be determined proportionately to that end, just as the form of a saw is such as to be suitable for cutting.[6] Again, everything that is ruled and measured must have a form proportionate to its rule and measure. Now both these conditions are verified of human law, since it is both something ordered to an end, and is a rule

---

[1] *Ethics*, VI, 11 (1143^{b}11).   [2] PL 82, 203.
[3] Chap. 3 (PL 82, 199).   [4] DD IV, 430.
[5] PL 82, 131; V, 3 (PL 82, 199).
[6] Aristotle, *Physics*, II, 9 (200^{a}10).

or measure ruled or measured by a higher measure. And this higher measure is twofold, namely, the Divine law and the natural law, as explained above (A. 2; Q. XCIII, A. 3). Now the end of human law is to be useful to man, as the Jurist states.[1] Therefore Isidore in determining the nature of law, lays down, at first, three conditions: namely, that it foster religion, in so far as it is proportionate to the Divine law: that it be helpful to discipline, in so far as it is proportionate to the natural law; and that it further the common weal, in so far as it is proportionate to the utility of mankind.

All the other conditions afterwards mentioned by him are reduced to these three. For it is called honest because it fosters religion. And when he goes on to say that it should be "just, possible according to nature, in harmony with the customs of the country, adapted to place and time," he implies that it should be helpful to discipline. For human discipline depends first on the order of reason, to which he refers by saying just; secondly, it depends on the ability of the agent, because discipline should be adapted to each one according to his ability, taking also into account the ability of nature (for the same burdens should be not laid on children as on adults); and it should be according to human customs, since man cannot live alone in society, paying no heed to others; thirdly, it depends on certain circumstances, in respect of which he says, "adapted to place and time." The remaining words "necessary, useful," etc., mean that law should further the common weal, so that necessity refers to the removal of evils, usefulness to the attainment of good, clearness of expression to the need of preventing any harm ensuing from the law itself. And since, as stated above (Q. XC, A. 2), law is ordered to the common good, this is expressed in the last part of the description.

This suffices for the Replies to the Objections.

ARTICLE 4. *Whether Isidore's Division of Human Laws Is Appropriate?*

We proceed thus to the Fourth Article: It would seem that Isidore wrongly divided human statutes or human law.

Objection 1. For under this law he includes the "law of nations," so called, because, as he says, "nearly all nations use it."[2] But as he says, natural law "is that which is common to all nations."[3] Therefore the law of nations is

not contained under positive human law, but rather under natural law.

Obj. 2. Further, those laws which have the same force, seem to differ not formally but only materially. But statutes, decrees of the commonalty, senatorial decrees, and the like which he mentions[4] all have the same force. Therefore it seems that they do not differ, except materially. But art takes no notice of such a distinction, since it may go on to infinity. Therefore this division of human laws is not appropriate.

Obj. 3. Further, just as in the state there are princes, priests and soldiers, so are there other human offices. Therefore it seems that as this division includes "military law," and "public law,"[5] referring to priests and magistrates, so also it should include other laws pertaining to other offices of the state.

Obj. 4. Further, those things that are accidental should be passed over. But it is accidental to law that it be framed by this or that man. Therefore it is unreasonable to divide laws according to the names of lawgivers, so that one be called the Cornelian law, another the Falcidian law, etc.[6]

On the contrary, The authority of Isidore suffices.

I answer that, A thing can of itself (*per se*) be divided in respect of something contained in the notion of that thing. Thus a soul, either rational or irrational, is contained in the notion of animal, and therefore animal is divided properly and of itself in respect of its being rational or irrational; but not in the point of its being white or black, which are entirely beside the notion of animal. Now, in the notion of human law many things are contained, in respect of any of which, human law can be divided properly and of itself. For in the first place it belongs to the notion of human law to be derived from the law of nature, as explained above (A. 2). In this respect positive law is divided into the law of nations and civil law, according to the two ways in which something may be derived from the law of nature, as stated above (A. 2). Because to the law of nations belong those things which are derived from the law of nature as conclusions from premises, for example, just buyings and sellings, and the like, without which men cannot live together, which is a point of the law of nature, since man is by nature a social animal, as is proved in the *Poli-*

---

[1] *Dig.*, I, III, leg., 25 *Nulla juris.* (KR_I, 34b).
[2] *Etym.*, v, 6 (PL 82, 200).
[3] *Ibid.*, v, 4 (PL 82, 199).

[4] *Ibid.*, v, 9 (PL 82, 200).
[5] *Ibid.*, v, 7, 8 (PL 82, 200).
[6] *Ibid.*, v, 15 (PL 82, 201).

tics.[1] But those things which are derived from the law of nature by way of particular determination belong to the civil law, according as each state decides on what is best for itself.

Secondly, it belongs to the notion of human law to be ordered to the common good of the state. In this respect human law may be divided according to the different kinds of men who work in a special way for the common good; for example, priests, by praying to God for the people; princes, by governing the people; soldiers, by fighting for the safety of the people. Therefore certain special kinds of law are adapted to these men.

Thirdly, it belongs to the notion of human law to be framed by that one who governs the community of the state, as shown above (Q. XC, A. 3). In this respect there are various human laws according to the various forms of government. Of these, according to the Philosopher,[2] one is monarchy, that is, when the state is governed by one; and then we have Royal Ordinances. Another form is aristocracy, that is, government by the best men or men of highest rank; and then we have the Authoritative legal opinions (*Responsa Prudentum*) and Decrees of the Senate (*Senatus consulta*). Another form is oligarchy, that is, government by a few rich and powerful men; and then we have Prætorian, also called Honorary, law. Another form of government is that of the people, which is called democracy, and there we have Decrees of the commonalty (*Plebiscita*). There is also tyrannical government, which is altogether corrupt, and which, therefore, has no corresponding law. Finally, there is a form of government made up of all these, and which is the best: and in this respect we have law "sanctioned by the Lords and Commons," as stated by Isidore.[3]

Fourthly, it belongs to the notion of human law to direct human actions. In this respect, according to the various matters of which the law treats, there are various kinds of laws which are sometimes named after their authors. Thus we have the *Lex Julia* about adultery,[4] the *Lex Cornelia*[5] concerning assassins, and so on, differentiated in this way not on account of the authors, but on account of the matters to which they refer.

Reply Obj. 1. The law of nations is indeed in some way natural to man, in so far as he is a reasonable being, because it is derived from the natural law by way of a conclusion that is not very remote from its premisses. Therefore men easily agreed on it. Nevertheless it is distinct from the natural law, especially from that natural law which is common to all animals.

The Replies to the other Objections are evident from what has been said.

QUESTION XCVI

OF THE POWER OF HUMAN LAW

(*In Six Articles*)

WE must now consider the power of human law. Under this head there are six points of inquiry: (1) Whether human law should be framed in a general way? (2) Whether human law should repress all vices? (3) Whether human law should direct all acts of virtue? (4) Whether it binds man in conscience? (5) Whether all men are subject to human law? (6) Whether those who are under the law may act beside the letter of the law?

ARTICLE 1. *Whether Human Law Should Be Framed in a General Way Rather than for the Particular Case?*

We proceed thus to the First Article: It would seem that human law should be framed not in a general way but rather for the particular case.

Objection 1. For the Philosopher says[6] that "the legal just ... includes all particular acts of legislation ... and all those matters which are the subject of decrees," which are also individual matters, since decrees are framed about individual actions. Therefore law is framed not only for general questions, but also for the particular.

Obj. 2. Further, law is the director of human acts, as stated above (Q. XC, AA. 1, 2). But human acts are about individual matters. Therefore human laws should be framed, not in a general way, but rather for the particular case.

Obj. 3. Further, law is a rule and measure of human acts, as stated above (Q. XC, AA. 1, 2). But a measure should be most certain as stated in the *Metaphysics*.[7] Since therefore in human acts no general proposition can be so certain as not to fail in some individual cases, it seems that laws should be framed not in general but for individual cases.

On the contrary, The Jurist says (*Dig.* lib. 1, tit. iii, 3, 4)[8] that "laws should be made to suit the majority of instances; and they are not

[1] Aristotle, I, 2 (1253ª2).
[2] *Politics*, III, 7 (1279ª32).
[3] *Etym.*, V, 10 (PL 82, 200); II, 10 (PL 82, 130).
[4] *Dig.*, Bk. XLVIII, 5 (KR I, 845a).
[5] *Dig.*, Bk. XLVIII, 8 (KR I, 852b).
[6] *Ethics*, V, 7 (1134ᵇ23).
[7] Aristotle, X, 1 (1053ª1).
[8] KR I, 34a.

framed according to what may possibly happen in an individual case."

I answer that, Whatever is for an end should be proportionate to that end. Now the end of law is the common good; because, as Isidore says (*Etym.* v, 21)[1] "law should be framed not for any private benefit, but for the common good of all the citizens." Hence human laws should be proportionate to the common good. Now the common good comprises many things. Therefore law should take account of many things, as to persons, as to matters, and as to times. Because the community of the state is composed of many persons, and its good is procured by many actions; nor is it established to endure for only a short time, but to last for all time by the citizens succeeding one another, as Augustine says.[2]

Reply Obj. 1. The Philosopher divides the legal just, that is, positive law, into three parts.[3] For some things are laid down absolutely in a general way, and these are the general laws. Of these he says that "the legal is that which originally was a matter of indifference, but which, when enacted, is so no longer"; for instance the fixing of the ransom of a captive. Some dispositions however are general in one respect and particular in another. These are called privileges, i.e., "private laws,"[4] because they regard private persons, although their power extends to many matters; and in regard to these, he adds, "and further, all particular acts of legislation." Other matters are legal not through being laws, but through being applications of general laws to particular cases; such are decrees which have the force of law, and in regard to these he adds "all matters subject to decrees."

Reply Obj. 2. A principle of direction should be applicable to many; therefore the Philosopher says[5] that all things belonging to one genus are measured by some one thing which is first in that genus. For if there were as many rules or measures as there are things measured or ruled, they would cease to be of use, since their use consists in being applicable to many things. Hence law would be of no use if it did not extend further than to one single act. Because the decrees of prudent men are made for the purpose of directing individual actions; law, however, is a general precept, as stated above (Q. XCII, A. 2, obj. 1).

Reply Obj. 3. "We must not seek the same degree of certainty in all things."[6] Consequently in contingent matters, such as natural and human things, it is enough for a thing to be certain as being true in the greater number of instances, though at times and less frequently it fail.

ARTICLE 2. *Whether It Pertains to Human Law to Repress All Vices?*

We proceed thus to the Second Article: It would seem that it pertains to human law to repress all vices.

Objection 1. For Isidore says (*Etym.* v, 20)[7] that "laws were made in order that, in fear thereof, man's audacity might be held in check." But it would not be held in check sufficiently, unless all evils were repressed by law. Therefore human law should repress all evils.

Obj. 2. Further, the intention of the lawgiver is to make the citizens virtuous. But a man cannot be virtuous unless he restrains himself from all kinds of vice. Therefore it pertains to human law to repress all vices.

Obj. 3. Further, human law is derived from the natural law, as stated above (Q. XCV, A. 2). But all vices are contrary to the law of nature. Therefore human law should repress all vices.

On the contrary, We read in *De Lib. Arb.* i, 5:[8] "It seems to me that the law which is written for the governing of the people rightly permits these things, and that Divine providence punishes them." But Divine providence punishes nothing but vices. Therefore human law rightly allows some vices, by not repressing them.

I answer that, As stated above (Q. XC, AA. 1, 2), law is framed as a rule or measure of human acts. Now a measure should be homogeneous with that which it measures, as stated in the *Metaphysics,*[9] since different things are measured by different measures. Therefore laws imposed on men should also be in keeping with their condition, for, as Isidore says (*Etym.* v, 21),[10] law should be "possible both according to nature, and according to the customs of the country." Now a power or faculty of action is due to an interior habit or disposition, since the same thing is not possible to one who has not a virtuous habit as is possible to one who has. Thus the same is not possible to a child as to a full-grown man, for which reason the law for

[1] PL 82, 203; II, 10 (PL 82, 131).
[2] *City of God,* XXII, 6 (PL 41, 759).
[3] *Ethics,* v, 7 (1134[b]20).
[4] Gratian, *Decretum,* I, 3, can. 3 (RF I, 5); cf. Isidore, *Etym.,* v, 18 (PL 82, 202).
[5] *Metaphysics,* X, I (1052[b]18).

[6] Aristotle, *Ethics,* I, 3 (1094[b]13).
[7] PL 82, 202.
[8] PL 32, 1228.
[9] Aristotle, X, I (1053[a]24).
[10] PL 82, 203; II, 10 (PL 82, 131).

children is not the same as for adults, since many things are permitted to children which in an adult are punished by law or at any rate are open to blame. In like manner many things are permissible to men not perfect in virtue which would be intolerable in a virtuous man.

Now human law is framed for a number of human beings, the majority of whom are not perfect in virtue. Therefore human laws do not forbid all vices, from which the virtuous abstain, but only the more grievous vices, from which it is possible for the majority to abstain, and chiefly those that are to the hurt of others, without the prohibition of which human society could not be maintained; thus human law prohibits murder, theft and the like.

Reply Obj. 1. Audacity seems to refer to the assailing of others. Consequently it pertains to those sins chiefly by which one's neighbour is injured; and these sins are forbidden by human law, as stated.

Reply Obj. 2. The purpose of human law is to lead men to virtue not suddenly, but gradually. Therefore it does not lay upon the multitude of imperfect men the burdens of those who are already virtuous, namely, that they should abstain from all evil. Otherwise these imperfect ones, being unable to bear such precepts, would break out into yet greater evils; thus it is written (Prov. 30. 33): *He that violently bloweth his nose, bringeth out blood;* and (Matt. 9. 17) that if *new wine,* that is, precepts of a perfect life, is *put into old bottles,* that is, into imperfect men, *the bottles break, and the wine runneth out,* that is, the precepts are despised, and those men, from contempt, break out into evils worse still.

Reply Obj. 3. The natural law is a participation in us of the eternal law, while human law falls short of the eternal law. Now Augustine says (*De Lib. Arb.* 1, 5):[1] "The law which is framed for the government of states allows and leaves unpunished many things that are punished by Divine providence. Nor, if this law does not attempt to do everything, is this a reason why it should be blamed for what it does." Therefore, too, human law does not prohibit everything that is forbidden by the natural law.

ARTICLE 3. *Whether Human Law Prescribes Acts of All the Virtues?*

We proceed thus to the Third Article: It would seem that human law does not prescribe acts of all the virtues.

[1] PL 32, 1228.

Objection 1. For vicious acts are contrary to acts of virtue. But human law does not prohibit all vices, as stated above (A. 2). Therefore neither does it prescribe all acts of virtue.

Obj. 2. Further, a virtuous act proceeds from a virtue. But virtue is the end of law, so that whatever is from a virtue cannot come under a precept of law. Therefore human law does not prescribe all acts of virtue.

Obj. 3. Further, law is ordered to the common good, as stated above (Q. XC, A. 2). But some acts of virtue are ordered not to the common good, but to private good. Therefore the law does not prescribe all acts of virtue.

On the contrary, The Philosopher says[2] that the law "prescribes the performance of the acts of a brave man, . . . and the acts of the temperate man, . . . and the acts of the meek man; and in like manner as regards the other virtues and vices, prescribing the former, forbidding the latter."

I answer that, The species of virtues are distinguished by their objects, as explained above (Q. LIV, A. 2; Q. LX, A. 1; Q. LXII, A. 2). Now all the objects of virtues can be referred either to the private good of an individual, or to the common good of the multitude; thus matters of fortitude may be achieved either for the safety of the state, or for upholding the rights of a friend, and in like manner with the other virtues. But law, as stated above (Q. XC, A. 2) is ordered to the common good. Therefore there is no virtue whose acts cannot be prescribed by the law. Nevertheless human law does not prescribe concerning all the acts of every virtue, but only in regard to those that can be ordered to the common good—either immediately, as when certain things are done directly for the common good, or mediately, as when a lawgiver prescribes certain things pertaining to good order, by which the citizens are directed in the upholding of the common good of justice and peace.

Reply Obj. 1. Human law does not forbid all vicious acts by the obligation of a precept, as neither does it prescribe all acts of virtue. But it forbids certain acts of each vice, just as it prescribes some acts of each virtue.

Reply Obj. 2. An act is said to be an act of virtue in two ways. First, from the fact that a man does something virtuous; thus the act of justice is to do what is right, and an act of fortitude is to do brave things, and in this way law prescribes certain acts of virtue. Secondly an act of virtue is when a man does a virtuous

[2] *Ethics,* V, 1 (1129[b]19).

thing in a way in which a virtuous man does it. Such an act always proceeds from virtue, and it does not come under a precept of law but is the end at which the lawgiver aims.

Reply Obj. 3. There is no virtue whose act cannot be ordered to the common good, as stated above, either mediately or immediately.

ARTICLE 4. *Whether Human Law Binds a Man in Conscience?*

We proceed thus to the Fourth Article: It would seem that human law does not bind a man in conscience.

Objection 1. For an inferior power has no jurisdiction in a court of higher power. But the power of man, which frames human law, is beneath the Divine power. Therefore human law cannot impose its precept in a Divine court, such as is the court of conscience.

Obj. 2. Further, the judgment of conscience depends chiefly on the commandments of God. But sometimes God's commandments are made void by human laws, according to Matt. 15.6: *You have made void the commandment of God for your tradition.* Therefore human law does not bind a man in conscience.

Obj. 3. Further, human laws often bring loss of character and injury on man, according to Isa. 10. 1 *et seq.:* *Woe to them that make wicked laws, and when they write, write injustice; to oppress the poor in judgment, and do violence to the cause of the humble of My people.* But it is lawful for anyone to avoid oppression and violence. Therefore human laws do not bind man in conscience.

On the contrary, It is written (I Pet. 2. 19): *This is thanksworthy, if for conscience . . . a man endure sorrows, suffering wrongfully.*

I answer that, Laws framed by man are either just or unjust. If they are just they have the power of binding in conscience, from the eternal law from which they are derived, according to Prov. 8. 15: *By Me kings reign, and lawgivers decree just things.* Now laws are said to be just both from the end, when, that is, they are ordered to the common good; and from their author, that is to say, when the law that is made does not exceed the power of the lawgiver; and from their form, when, that is, burdens are laid on the subjects according to an equality of proportion and with a view to the common good. For, since one man is a part of the community, each man, in all that he is and has, belongs to the community; just as a part, in all that it is, belongs to the whole. Thus also nature inflicts a loss on the part in order to

save the whole, so that on this account such laws as these, which impose proportionate burdens, are just and binding in conscience, and are legal laws.

On the other hand laws may be unjust in two ways. First, by being contrary to human good, through being opposed to the things mentioned above: either in respect of the end, as when an authority imposes on his subjects burdensome laws, conducive not to the common good but rather to his own cupidity or vainglory; or in respect of the author, as when a man makes a law that goes beyond the power committed to him; or in respect of the form, as when burdens are imposed unequally on the community, although with a view to the common good. The like are acts of violence rather than laws, because, as *Augustine says* (*De Lib. Arb.* i, 5),[1] "a law that is not just seems to be no law at all." Therefore such laws do not bind in conscience, except perhaps in order to avoid scandal or disturbance, for which cause a man should even yield his right, according to Matt. 5. 40, 41: *If a man . . . take away thy coat, let go thy cloak also unto him; and whosoever will force thee one mile, go with him other two.*

Secondly, laws may be unjust through being opposed to the Divine good. Such are the laws of tyrants inducing to idolatry, or to anything else contrary to the Divine law; and laws of this kind must in no way be observed, because, as stated in Acts 5. 29, *we ought to obey God rather than men.*

Reply Obj. 1. As the Apostle says (Rom. 13. 1, 2), all human power is from God . . . *therefore he that resisteth the power,* in matters that are within its scope, *resisteth the ordinance of God,* so that he becomes guilty according to his conscience.

Reply Obj. 2. This argument is true of laws that are contrary to the commandments of God, which is beyond the scope of (human) power. Therefore in such matters human law should not be obeyed.

Reply Obj. 3. This argument is true of a law that inflicts unjust hurt on its subjects. The power that man holds from God does not extend to this. Therefore neither in such matters is man bound to obey the law, provided he avoid giving scandal or inflicting a more grievous hurt.

ARTICLE 5. *Whether All Are Subject to the Law?*

We proceed thus to the Fifth Article: It would seem that not all are subject to the law.

[1] PL 32, 1227.

Objection 1. For those alone are subject to a law for whom a law is made. But the Apostle says (I Tim. 1. 9): *The law is not made for the just man*. Therefore the just are not subject to the law of man.

Obj. 2. Further, Pope Urban says:[1] "He that is guided by a private law need not for any reason be bound by the public law." Now all spiritual men are led by the private law of the Holy Ghost, for they are the sons of God, of whom it is said (Rom. 8. 14): *Whosoever are led by the Spirit of God, they are the sons of God*. Therefore not all men are subject to human law.

Obj. 3. Further, the jurist says that "the sovereign is exempt from the laws."[2] But he that is exempt from the law is not bound by it. Therefore not all are subject to the law.

On the contrary, The Apostle says (Rom. 13. 1): *Let every soul be subject to the higher powers*. But subjection to a power seems to imply subjection to the laws framed by that power. Therefore all men should be subject to the law.

I answer that, As stated above (Q. XC, AA. 1, 2; A. 3, reply 2), the notion of law contains two things: first, that it is a rule of human acts; secondly, that it has coercive power. Hence a man may be subject to law in two ways. First, as the regulated is subject to the regulator, and in this way whoever is subject to a power is subject to the law framed by that power. But it may happen in two ways that one is not subject to a power. In one way, by being altogether free from its authority. Hence the subjects of one city or kingdom are not bound by the laws of the sovereign of another city or kingdom, since they are not subject to his authority. In another way by being under a yet higher law. Thus the subject of a proconsul should be ruled by his command, but not in those matters in which the subject receives his orders from the emperor; for in these matters he is not bound by the mandate of the lower authority, since he is directed by that of a higher. In this way, one who is subject absolutely to a law may not be subject to it in certain matters, in respect of which he is ruled by a higher law.

Secondly, a man is said to be subject to a law as the coerced is subject to the coercer. In this way the virtuous and the just are not subject to the law, but only the wicked. Because coercion and violence are contrary to the will;

but the will of the good is in harmony with the law, while the will of the wicked is discordant from it. Therefore in this sense the good are not subject to the law, but only the wicked.

Reply Obj. 1. This argument is true of subjection by way of coercion, for, in this way, *the law is not made for the just men*, because *they are a law to themselves*, since they *shew the work of the law written in their hearts*, as the Apostle says (Rom. 2. 14, 15). Consequently the law does not enforce itself upon them as it does on the wicked.

Reply Obj. 2. The law of the Holy Ghost is above all law framed by man, and therefore spiritual men, in so far as they are led by the law of the Holy Ghost, are not subject to the law in those matters that are inconsistent with the guidance of the Holy Ghost. Nevertheless the very fact that spiritual men are subject to law is due to the leading of the Holy Ghost, according to I Pet. 2. 13: *Be ye subject . . . to every human creature for God's sake*.

Reply Obj. 3. The sovereign is said to be exempt from the law as to its coercive power, since, properly speaking, no man is coerced by himself, and law has no coercive power save from the authority of the sovereign. In this way then is the sovereign said to be exempt from the law, because no one is able to pass sentence on him if he acts against the law. Hence on Ps. 50. 6: *To Thee only have I sinned*, a gloss says[3] that "there is no man who can judge the deeds of a king." But as to the directive force of law, the sovereign is subject to the law by his own will, according to the statement (*Extra, De Constit.* cap. *Cum omnes*)[4] that "whatever law a man makes for another he should keep himself." And a wise authority says:[5] "Obey the law that thou makest thyself." Moreover the Lord reproaches those who *say and do not*, and who *bind heavy burdens and lay them on men's shoulders, but with a finger of their own they will not move them* (Matt. 23. 3, 4). Hence, in the judgment of God, the sovereign is not exempt from the law as to its directive force, but he should fulfil it voluntarily and not from constraint. Again the sovereign is above the law in so far as, when it is expedient, he can change the law, and dispense in it according to time and place.

---

[1] Gratian, *Decret.*, II, causa XIX, Q. 2, can., 2 (RF 1, 840).
[2] *Dig.*, I, tit. III, leg. 31 (KR 1, 34b).
[3] *Glossa* Lombardi (PL 191, 486); cf. *Glossa ordin.* (III, 157E); Cassiodorus, *In Psalm.* 50.6 (PL 70, 361).
[4] *Decretal Greg.*, IX, BK. I, tit. II, chap. 6 (RF II, 8).
[5] Decius Ausonius, *Sent.*, Pittacus, verse 5 (PL 19, 876).

ARTICLE 6. *Whether He Who Is Under a Law May Act Beside the Letter of the Law?*

We proceed thus to the Sixth Article: It seems that he who is subject to a law may not act beside the letter of the law.

Objection 1. For Augustine says (*De Vera Relig.* xxxi):[1] "Although men judge about temporal laws when they make them, yet when once they are made they must pass judgment not on them, but according to them." But if anyone disregard the letter of the law, saying that he observes the intention of the lawgiver, he seems to pass judgment on the law. Therefore it is not right for one who is under a law to disregard the letter of the law in order to observe the intention of the lawgiver.

Obj. 2. Further, to interpret the law pertains to him alone who can make the law. But those who are subject to the law cannot make the law. Therefore they have no right to interpret the intention of the lawgiver, but should always act according to the letter of the law.

Obj. 3. Further, every wise man knows how to explain his intention by words. But those who framed the laws should be accounted wise, for Wisdom says (Prov. 8. 15): *By Me kings reign, and lawgivers decree just things.* Therefore we should not judge of the intention of the lawgiver otherwise than by the words of the law.

On the contrary, Hilary says (*De Trin.* iv):[2] "The meaning of what is said is according to the motive for saying it, because things are not subject to speech, but speech to things." Therefore we should take account of the motive of the lawgiver rather than to his very words.

I answer that, As stated above (A. 4), every law is directed to the common welfare of men, and derives the force and nature of law accordingly. Hence the jurist says:[3] "By no reason of law, or favour of equity, is it allowable for us to interpret harshly, and render burdensome, those useful measures which have been enacted for the welfare of man." Now it happens often that the observance of some point of law conduces to the common good in the majority of instances, and yet, in some cases, is very hurtful. Since then the lawgiver cannot have in view every single case, he shapes the law according to what happens most frequently, by directing his attention to the common good. Therefore if a case arise in which the observance of that law would be hurtful to the general welfare, it should not be observed. For instance, if in a be-

sieged city it be an established law that the gates of the city are to be kept closed, this is good for public welfare as a general rule; but if it were to happen that the enemy are in pursuit of certain citizens who are defenders of the city, it would be a great injury to the city, if the gates were not opened to them, and so in that case the gates ought to be opened, contrary to the letter of the law, in order to maintain the common good, which the lawgiver had in view.

Nevertheless it must be noted that if the observance of the law according to the letter does not involve any sudden risk needing instant remedy, it is not the business of anyone whatsoever to expound what is useful and what is not useful to the state. Those alone can do this who are in authority, and who, on account of such cases, have the power to dispense from the laws. If, however, the peril be so sudden as not to allow of the delay involved by referring the matter to authority, the necessity itself carries with it a dispensation, since necessity knows no law.

Reply Obj. 1. He who in a case of necessity acts beside the letter of the law does not judge of the law, but of a particular case in which he sees that the letter of the law is not to be observed.

Reply Obj. 2. He who follows the intention of the lawgiver does not interpret the law absolutely, but in a case in which it is evident, by reason of the manifest harm, that the lawgiver intended otherwise. For if it be a matter of doubt, he must either act according to the letter of the law or consult those in power.

Reply Obj. 3. No man is so wise as to be able to take account of every single case, and therefore he is not able sufficiently to express in words all those things that are suitable for the end he has in view. And even if a lawgiver were able to take all the cases into consideration, he ought not to mention them all, in order to avoid confusion, but should frame the law according to that which is of most common occurrence.

QUESTION XCVII
OF CHANGE IN LAWS
(*In Four Articles*)

WE must now consider change in laws, under which head there are four points of inquiry: (1) Whether human law is changeable? (2) Whether it should be always changed whenever anything better occurs? (3) Whether it is abolished by custom, and whether custom obtains the force of law? (4) Whether the application

---

[1] PL 34, 148. [2] PL 10, 107.
[3] *Dig.*, I, tit. III, leg. 25 (KR I, 34b).

of human law should be changed by dispensation of those in authority?

ARTICLE 1. *Whether Human Law Should Be Changed in Any Way?*

We proceed thus to the First Article: It would seem that human law should not be changed in any way at all.

Objection 1. For human law is derived from the natural law, as stated above (Q. XCV, A. 2). But the natural law endures unchangeably. Therefore human law should also remain without any change.

Obj. 2. Further, as the Philosopher says,[1] a measure should be absolutely stable. But human law is the measure of human acts, as stated above (Q. XC, AA. 1, 2). Therefore it should remain without change.

Obj. 3. Further, it is of the essence of law to be just and right, as stated above (Q. XCV, A. 2). But that which is right once is right always. Therefore that which is law once should be always law.

On the contrary, Augustine says (*De Lib. Arb.* i, 6):[2] "A temporal law, however just, may be justly changed in course of time."

I answer that, As stated above (Q. XCI, A. 3), human law is a dictate of reason, by which human acts are directed. Thus there may be two causes for the just change of human law: one on the part of reason; the other on the part of man whose acts are regulated by law. The cause on the part of reason is that it seems natural to human reason to advance gradually from the imperfect to the perfect. Hence, in speculative sciences, we see that the teaching of the early philosophers was imperfect, and that it was afterwards perfected by those who succeeded them. So also in practical matters. For those who first endeavoured to discover something useful for the human community, not being able by themselves to take everything into consideration, set up certain institutions which were deficient in many ways; and these were changed by subsequent lawgivers who made institutions that might prove less frequently deficient in respect of the common weal.

On the part of man, whose acts are regulated by law, the law can be rightly changed on account of the changed condition of man, to whom different things are expedient according to the difference of his condition. An example is proposed by Augustine (*De Lib. Arb.* i, 6):[3] "If

[1] *Ethics,* v, 5 (1133ᵃ25).　　[2] PL 32, 1229.
[3] PL 32, 1229.

the people have a sense of moderation and responsibility, and are most careful guardians of the common weal, it is right to enact a law allowing such a people to choose their own magistrates for the government of the commonwealth. But if, as time goes on, the same people become so corrupt as to sell their votes, and entrust the government to scoundrels and criminals, then the right of appointing their public officials is rightly forfeit to such a people, and the choice devolves to a few good men."

Reply Obj. 1. The natural law is a participation of the eternal law, as stated above (Q. XCI, A. 2), and therefore endures without change, owing to the unchangeableness and perfection of the Divine Reason, the Author of nature. But the reason of man is changeable and imperfect, and therefore his law is subject to change. Moreover the natural law contains certain universal precepts, which are everlasting, while human law contains certain particular precepts, according to various emergencies.

Reply Obj. 2. A measure should be as enduring as possible. But nothing can be absolutely unchangeable in things that are subject to change. And therefore human law cannot be altogether unchangeable.

Reply Obj. 3. In corporal things, right is predicated absolutely, and therefore, as far as itself is concerned, always remains right. But right is predicated of law with reference to the common weal, to which one and the same thing is not always adapted, as stated above. Therefore rectitude of this kind is subject to change.

ARTICLE 2. *Whether Human Law Should Always Be Changed Whenever Something Better Occurs?*

We proceed thus to the Second Article: It would seem that human law should be changed whenever something better occurs.

Objection 1. Because human laws are devised by human reason, like other arts. But in the other arts, the tenets of former times give place to others if something better occurs. Therefore the same should apply to human laws.

Obj. 2. Further, by taking note of the past we can provide for the future. Now unless human laws had been changed when it was found possible to improve them, considerable inconvenience would have ensued, because the laws of old were crude in many points. Therefore it seems that laws should be changed whenever anything better occurs to be enacted.

Obj. 3. Further, human laws are enacted about single acts of man. But we cannot acquire perfect knowledge in singular matters, except by experience, which requires time, as stated in the *Ethics*.[1] Therefore it seems that as time goes on it is possible for something better to occur for legislation.

On the contrary, It is stated in the Decretals (*Dist.* xii, 5):[2] "It is absurd, and a detestable shame, that we should suffer those traditions to be changed which we have received from the fathers of old."

I answer that, As stated above (A. 1), human law is rightly changed in so far as such change is conducive to the common weal. But, to a certain extent, the mere change of law is of itself prejudicial to the common good, because custom avails much for the observance of laws, seeing that what is done contrary to general custom, even in slight matters, is looked upon as grave. Consequently, when a law is changed, the binding power of the law is diminished, in so far as custom is abolished. Therefore human law should never be changed, unless, in some way or other, the common welfare be compensated according to the extent of the harm done in this respect. Such compensation may arise either from some very great and very evident benefit conferred by the new enactment, or from the extreme urgency of the case, due to the fact that either the existing law is clearly unjust, or its observance extremely harmful. Therefore the jurist says[3] that "in establishing new laws, there should be evidence of the benefit to be derived, before departing from a law which has long been considered just."

Reply Obj. 1. Rules of art derive their force from reason alone, and therefore whenever something better occurs, the rule followed previously should be changed. But laws derive very great force from custom, as the Philosopher states.[4] Consequently they should not be easily changed.

Reply Obj. 2. This argument proves that laws ought to be changed not in view of any improvement, but for the sake of a great benefit or in a case of great urgency, as stated above. This answer applies also to the Third Objection.

ARTICLE 3. *Whether Custom Can Obtain Force of Law?*

We proceed thus to the Third Article: It would seem that custom cannot obtain force of law, nor abolish a law.

Objection 1. Because human law is derived from the natural law and from the Divine law, as stated above (Q. XCIII, A. 3; Q. XCV, A. 2). But human custom cannot change either the law of nature or the Divine law. Therefore neither can it change human law.

Obj. 2. Further, many evils cannot make one good. But he who first acted against the law did evil. Therefore by multiplying such acts, nothing good is the result. Now a law is something good, since it is a rule of human acts. Therefore law is not abolished by custom, so that the custom itself should obtain force of law.

Obj. 3. Further, the framing of laws belongs to those public men whose business it is to govern the community. Therefore private individuals cannot make laws. But custom grows by the acts of private individuals. Therefore custom cannot obtain force of law, so as to abolish the law.

On the contrary, Augustine says (*Ep. ad Casulan.* xxxvi):[5] "The customs of God's people and the institutions of our ancestors are to be considered as laws." And those who throw contempt on the customs of the Church ought to be punished as those who disobey the law of God.[6]

I answer that, All law proceeds from the reason and will of the lawgiver: the Divine and natural laws from the reasonable will of God; the human law from the will of man, regulated by reason. Now just as human reason and will, in practical matters, may be made manifest by speech, so may they be made known by deeds, since a man apparently chooses as good that which he carries into execution. But it is evident that by human speech law can be both changed and even expounded, in so far as it manifests the interior movement and concept of human reason. Therefore by actions also, especially if they be repeated, so as to make a custom, law can be changed and expressed; and also something can be established which obtains force of law, in so far as by repeated external actions the inward movement of the will, and concepts of reason are most effectually declared. For when a thing is done again and again, it seems to proceed from a deliberate judgment of reason. Accordingly, custom has the force of a law, abolishes law, and is the interpreter of law.

Reply Obj. 1. The natural and Divine laws proceed from the Divine will, as stated above.

---

[1] Aristotle, II, 1 (1103ª16).   [2] Gratian, pt. I (RFI, 28).
[3] *Dig.*, I, tit. IV, leg. 2 (KR I, 35ª).
[4] *Politics*, II, 8 (1269ª20).

[5] PL 33, 136.
[6] Cf. Gratian, *Decret.*, pt. I, d. XI, can. 7 (RF I, 25).

Therefore they cannot be changed by a custom proceeding from the will of man, but only by Divine authority. Hence it is that no custom can prevail over the Divine or natural laws; for Isidore says (*Synon.* ii, 80):[1] "Let custom yield to authority; evil customs should be eradicated by law and reason."

Reply Obj. 2. As stated above (Q. XCVI, A. 6), human laws fail in some cases. Therefore it is possible sometimes to act beside the law, namely, in a case where the law fails, and yet the act will not be evil. And when such cases are multiplied by reason of some change in man, then custom shows that the law is no longer useful, just as it might be declared by the verbal promulgation of a law to the contrary. If, however, the same reason remains, for which the law was previously useful, then it is not the custom that prevails against the law, but the law that overcomes the custom; unless perhaps the sole reason for the apparent uselessness of the law is that it is not "possible according to the custom of the country," which has been stated to be one of the conditions of law.[2] For it is not easy to set aside the custom of a whole people.

Reply Obj. 3. The people among whom a custom is introduced may be of two conditions. For if they are free, and able to make their own laws, the consent of the whole people expressed by a custom counts far more in favour of a particular observance than does the authority of the sovereign, who has not the power to frame laws except as representing the people. Therefore although each individual cannot make laws, yet the whole people can. If however the people have not the free power to make their own laws, or to abolish a law made by a higher authority, nevertheless with such a people a prevailing custom obtains force of law, in so far as it is tolerated by those to whom it belongs to make laws for that people. Because by the very fact that they tolerate it they seem to approve of that which is introduced by custom.

ARTICLE 4. *Whether the Rulers of the People Can Dispense From Human Laws?*

We proceed thus to the Fourth Article: It would seem that the rulers of the people cannot dispense from human laws.

Objection 1. For the law is established "for the common good," as Isidore says (*Etym.* v, 21.).[3] But the common good should not be set aside for the private convenience of an individ-

ual, because, as the Philosopher says,[4] "the good of the nation is more godlike than the good of one man." Therefore it seems that a man should not be dispensed from acting in compliance with the general law.

Obj. 2. Further, those who are placed over others are commanded as follows (Deut. 1. 17): *You shall hear the little as well as the great; neither shall you respect any man's person, because it is the judgment of God.* But to allow one man to do that which is equally forbidden to all seems to be respect of persons. Therefore the rulers of a community cannot grant such dispensations, since this is against a precept of the Divine law.

Obj. 3. Further, human law, in order to be right, should accord with the natural and Divine laws: else it would not "foster religion," nor be "helpful to discipline," which is requisite to the nature of law, as laid down by Isidore (*Etym.* v, 3).[5] But no man can dispense from the Divine and natural laws. Neither, therefore, can he dispense from the human law.

On the contrary, The Apostle says (I Cor. 9. 17): *A dispensation is committed to me.*

I answer that, Dispensation, properly speaking, denotes a measuring out to individuals of some common goods; thus the head of a household is called a dispenser, because to each member of the household he distributes work and necessaries of life in due weight and measure. Accordingly in every community a man is said to dispense, from the very fact that he directs how some general precept is to be fulfilled by each individual. Now it happens at times that a precept which is conducive to the common good as a general rule is not good for a particular individual, or in some particular case, either because it would hinder some greater good, or because it would be the occasion of some evil, as explained above (Q. XCVI, A. 6). But it would be dangerous to leave this to the discretion of each individual, except perhaps by reason of an evident and sudden emergency, as stated above (*ibid.*). Consequently he who is placed over a community is empowered to dispense from a human law that rests upon his authority, so that, when the law fails in its application to persons or circumstances, he may allow the precept of the law not to be observed. If however he grant this permission without any such reason, and of his mere will, he will be an unfaithful or an imprudent dispenser: unfaithful, if he has not the common good in view;

---

[1] PL 83, 863.   [2] Isidore, *Etymol.*, v, 21 (PL 82, 203).
[3] PL 82, 203; II, 10 (PL 82, 131).

[4] *Ethics*, I, 2 (1094[b]10).
[5] PL 82, 199; II, 10 (PL 82, 131).

imprudent, if he ignores the reasons for granting dispensations. Hence Our Lord says (Luke 12. 42): *Who, thinkest thou, is the faithful and wise dispenser* (Douay,—steward), *whom his lord setteth over his family?*

Reply Obj. 1. When a person is dispensed from observing the general law, this should not be done to the prejudice of, but with the intention of benefiting, the common good.

Reply Obj. 2. It is not respect of persons if unequal measures are served out to those who are themselves unequal. Therefore when the condition of any person requires that he should reasonably receive special treatment, it is not respect of persons if he be the object of special favour.

Reply Obj. 3. Natural law, so far as it contains general precepts, which never fail, does not allow of dispensation. In the other precepts, however, which are as conclusions of the general precepts, man sometimes grants a dispensation; for instance, that a loan should not be paid back to the betrayer of his country, or something similar. But to the Divine law each man stands as a private person to the public law to which he is subject. Therefore just as none can dispense from public human law except the man from whom the law derives its authority, or his delegate, so, in the precepts of the Divine law, which are from God, none can dispense but God, or the man to whom He may give special power for that purpose.

QUESTION XCVIII

OF THE OLD LAW

(In Six Articles)

In due sequence we must now consider the Old Law; and (1) The Law itself; (2) its precepts (Q. XCIX). Under the first head there are six points of inquiry: (1) Whether the Old Law was good? (2) Whether it was from God? (3) Whether it came from Him through the angels? (4) Whether it was given to all? (5) Whether it was binding on all? (6) Whether it was given at a suitable time?

ARTICLE 1. *Whether the Old Law Was Good?*

We proceed thus to the First Article: It would seem that the Old Law was not good.

Objection 1. For it is written (Ezech. 20. 25): *I gave them statutes that were not good, and judgments in which they shall not live.* But a law is not said to be good except on account of the goodness of the precepts that it contains. Therefore the Old Law was not good.

Obj. 2. Further, it belongs to the goodness of a law that it conduce to the common welfare, as Isidore says (*Etym.* v, 21).[1] But the Old Law was not salutary; rather was it deadly and hurtful. For the Apostle says (Rom. 7. 8, seq.): *Without the law sin was dead. And I lived some time without the law. But when the commandment came sin revived; and I died.* Again he says (Rom. 5. 20): *Law entered in that sin might abound.* Therefore the Old Law was not good.

Obj. 3. Further, it belongs to the goodness of the law that it should be possible to obey it, both according to nature, and according to human custom. But the Old Law was not such, since Peter said (Acts. 15. 10): *Why tempt you (God) to put a yoke on the necks of the disciples, which neither our fathers nor we have been able to bear?* Therefore it seems that the Old Law was not good.

On the contrary, The Apostle says (Rom. 7. 12): *Wherefore the law indeed is holy, and the commandment holy, and just, and good.*

I answer that, Without any doubt, the Old Law was good. For just as a doctrine is shown to be good by the fact that it accords with right reason, so is a law proved to be good if it accords with reason. Now the Old Law was in accordance with reason. Because it repressed concupiscence, which is in conflict with reason, as evidenced by the commandment, *Thou shalt not covet thy neighbour's goods* (Exod. 20. 17). Moreover the same law forbade all kinds of sin, and these too are contrary to reason. Consequently it is evident that it was a good law. The Apostle argues in the same way (Rom. 7): *I am delighted,* says he (*verse* 22), *with the law of God, according to the inward man;* and again (*verse* 16): *I consent to the law, that is good.*

But it must be noted that the good has various degrees, as Dionysius states (*Div. Nom.* iv);[2] for there is a perfect good, and an imperfect good. In things ordered to an end, there is perfect goodness when a thing is such that it is sufficient in itself to conduce to the end, while there is imperfect goodness when a thing is of some assistance in attaining the end, but is not sufficient for its realization. Thus a medicine is perfectly good if it gives health to a man; but it is imperfect if it helps to cure him without being able to bring him back to health. Again it must be observed that the end of human law is different from the end of Divine law. For the end of human law is the temporal tranquillity of

---

[1] PL 82, 203; II, 10 (PL 82, 131).

[2] Sect. 20 (PG 3, 720).

the state, which end law effects by constraining external actions, as regards those evils which might disturb the peaceful condition of the state. On the other hand, the end of the Divine law is to bring man to that end which is everlasting happiness, which end is hindered by any sin, and not only of external, but also of internal action. Consequently that which suffices for the perfection of human law, namely, the prohibition and punishment of sin, does not suffice for the perfection of the Divine law, but it has to make man altogether fit to partake of everlasting happiness. Now this cannot be done save by the grace of the Holy Ghost, whereby *charity, which fulfilleth the law, . . . is spread abroad in our hearts* (Rom. 5. 5), since *the grace of God is life everlasting* (ibid. 6. 23). But the Old Law could not confer this grace, for this was reserved to Christ; because, as it is written (John 1. 17), the law was given *by Moses, grace and truth came by Jesus Christ.* Consequently the Old Law was good indeed, but imperfect, according to Heb. 7. 19: *The law brought nothing to perfection.*

Reply Obj. 1. The Lord refers there to the ceremonial precepts, which are said not to be good because they did not confer grace for the remission of sins, although by fulfilling these precepts man confessed himself a sinner. Hence it is said pointedly, *and judgments in which they shall not live;* that is, by which they are unable to obtain life; and so the text goes on: *And I polluted them,* that is, showed them to be polluted, *in their own gifts, when they offered all that opened the womb, for their offences.*

Reply Obj. 2. The law is said to have been deadly, as being not the cause but the occasion of death, on account of its imperfection, in so far as it did not confer grace enabling man to fulfil what it prescribed, and to avoid what it forbade. Hence this occasion was not given to men, but taken by them. Therefore the Apostle says (ibid. 11): *Sin, taking occasion by the commandment, seduced me, and by it killed me.* In the same sense when it is said that *the law entered in that sin might abound,* the conjunction "that" must be taken as consecutive and not causally, in so far as men, taking occasion from the law, sinned all the more, both because a sin became more grievous after law had forbidden it, and because concupiscence increased, since we desire a thing the more from its being forbidden.

Reply Obj. 3. The yoke of the law could not be borne without the help of grace, which the law did not confer; for it is written (Rom. 9. 16): *It is not of him that willeth, nor of him that runneth,* namely, that he wills and runs in the commandments of God, *but of God that showeth mercy.* Therefore it is written (Ps. 118. 32): *I have run the way of Thy commandments, when Thou didst enlarge my heart,* that is, by giving me grace and charity.

ARTICLE 2. *Whether the Old Law Was From God?*

We proceed thus to the Second Article: It would seem that the Old Law was not from God.

Objection 1. For it is written (Deut. 32. 4): *The works of God are perfect.* But the Law was imperfect, as stated above (A. 1; Q. XCI, A. 5). Therefore the Old Law was not from God.

Obj. 2. Further, it is written (Ecclus. 3. 14): *I have learned that all the works which God hath made continue for ever.* But the Old Law does not continue for ever, since the Apostle says (Heb. 7. 18): *There is indeed a setting aside of the former commandment, because of the weakness and unprofitableness thereof.* Therefore the Old Law was not from God.

Obj. 3. Further, a wise lawgiver should remove not only evil, but also the occasions of evil. But the Old Law was an occasion of sin, as stated above (A. 1, Reply 2). Therefore the giving of such a law does not pertain to God, to Whom *none is like among the lawgivers* (Job 36. 22).

Obj. 4. Further, it is written (I Tim. 2. 4) that God *will have all men to be saved.* But the Old Law did not suffice to save man, as stated above (A. 1; Q. XCI, A. 5, Reply 2). Therefore the giving of such a law did not pertain to God. Therefore the Old Law was not from God.

On the contrary, Our Lord said (Matt. 15. 6) while speaking to the Jews, to whom the Law was given; *You have made void the commandment of God for your tradition.* And shortly before (verse 4) He had said: *Honour thy father and mother,* which is clearly contained in the Old Law (Exod. 20. 12; Deut. 5. 16). Therefore the Old Law was from God.

I answer that, The Old Law was given by the good God, Who is the Father of Our Lord Jesus Christ. For the Old Law ordered men to Christ in two ways. First by bearing witness to Christ; hence He Himself says (Luke 24. 44): *All things must needs be fulfilled, which are written in the law . . ., and in the prophets, and in the psalms, concerning Me;* and (John 5. 46): *If you did believe Moses, you would per-*

haps believe Me also; for he wrote of Me. Secondly, as a kind of disposition, since by withdrawing men from idolatrous worship, it enclosed (*concludebat*) them in the worship of one God, by Whom the human race was to be saved through Christ. Therefore the Apostle says (Gal. 3. 23): *Before the faith came, we were kept under the law shut up* (*conclusi*), *unto that faith which was to be revealed*. Now it is evident that it is the same thing which gives a disposition to the end and which brings to the end; and when I say "the same," I mean that it does so either by itself or through its subjects. For the devil would not make a law by which men would be led to Christ, Who was to cast him out, according to Matt. 12. 26: *If Satan cast out Satan, his kingdom is divided* (Vulg., —*he is divided against himself*). Therefore the Old Law was given by the same God from Whom came salvation to man, through the grace of Christ.

Reply Obj. 1. Nothing prevents a thing being not perfect absolutely, and yet perfect in respect of time; thus a boy is said to be perfect, not absolutely, but with regard to the condition of time. So, too, precepts that are given to children are perfect in comparison with the condition of those to whom they are given, although they are not perfect absolutely. Hence the Apostle says (Gal. 3. 24): *The law was our pedagogue in Christ*.

Reply Obj. 2. Those works of God endure for ever which God so made that they would endure for ever; and these are His perfect works. But the Old Law was set aside when there came the perfection of grace; not as though it were evil, but as being weak and useless for this time, because, as the Apostle goes on to say, *the law brought nothing to perfection*; hence he says (Gal. 3. 25): *After the faith is come, we are no longer under a pedagogue*.

Reply Obj. 3. As stated above (Q. LXXIX, A. 4), God sometimes permits certain ones to fall into sin that they may thereby be humbled. So also did He wish to give such a law as men by their own forces could not fulfil, so that, while presuming on their own powers, they might find themselves to be sinners, and being humbled might have recourse to the help of grace.

Reply Obj. 4. Although the Old Law did not suffice to save man, yet another help from God besides the Law was available for man, namely, faith in the Mediator, by which the fathers of old were justified even as we are. Accordingly God did not fail man by giving him insufficient aids to salvation.

ARTICLE 3. *Whether the Old Law Was Given Through the Angels?*

We proceed thus to the Third Article: It seems that the Old Law was not given through the angels, but immediately by God.

Objection 1. For an angel means a messenger, so that the word angel denotes ministry, not lordship, according to Ps. 102. 20, 21: *Bless the Lord all ye His angels . . . you ministers of His*. But the Old Law is related to have been given by the Lord, for it is written (Exod. 20. 1): *And the Lord spoke . . . these words*, and further on: *I am the Lord Thy God*. Moreover the same expression is often repeated in Exodus, and in the later books of the Law. Therefore the Law was given by God immediately.

Obj. 2. Further, according to John 1. 17, *the Law was given by Moses*. But Moses received it from God immediately, for it is written (Exod. 33. 11): *The Lord spoke to Moses face to face, as a man is wont to speak to his friend*. Therefore the Old Law was given by God immediately.

Obj. 3. Further, it belongs to the sovereign alone to make a law, as stated above (Q. XC, A. 3). But God alone is Sovereign as regards the salvation of souls, while the angels are the *ministering spirits*, as stated in Heb. 1. 14. Therefore it was not right for the Law to be given through the angels, since it is ordered to the salvation of souls.

On the contrary, The Apostle said (Gal. 3. 19) that the Law was *given* (Vulg.,—*ordained*) *by angels in the hand of a Mediator*. And Stephen said (Acts 7. 53): (*Who*) *have received the Law by the disposition of angels*.

I answer that, The Law was given by God through the angels. And besides the general reason given by Dionysius (*Cæl. Hier.* iv),[1] namely, that the gifts of God should be brought to men by means of the angels, there is a special reason why the Old Law should have been given through them. For it has been stated (AA. 1, 2) that the Old Law was imperfect, and yet disposed man to that perfect salvation of the human race which was to come through Christ. Now it is to be observed that wherever there is an order of powers or arts, he that holds the highest place, himself exercises the principal and perfect acts, while those things which dispose to the ultimate perfection are effected by him through his subordinates; thus the shipbuilder himself rivets the planks together, but prepares the material by means of the workmen

[1] Sect. 2 (PG 3, 180).

who assist him under his direction. Consequently it was fitting that the perfect law of the New Testament should be given by the incarnate God immediately, but that the Old Law should be given to men by the ministers of God, that is, by the angels. It is thus that the Apostle at the beginning of his epistle to the Hebrews (1. 2) proves the excellence of the New Law over the Old; because in the New Testament *God . . . hath spoken to us by His Son,* while in the Old Testament *the word* was *spoken by angels* (2. 2).

Reply Obj. 1. As Gregory says at the beginning of his *Morals* (*Præf., chap.* i),[1] "the angel who is described to have appeared to Moses, is sometimes mentioned as an angel, sometimes as the Lord: an angel, in truth, in respect of that which was subservient to the external delivery; and the Lord, because He was the ruler within, Who granted the power of speaking." Hence also it is that the angel spoke as though in the person of the Lord.

Reply Obj. 2. As Augustine says (*Gen. ad lit.* 12, 27),[2] "it is stated in Exodus that the Lord spoke to Moses face to face; and shortly afterwards we read: 'Show me Thy glory.' Therefore he perceived what he saw and he desired what he saw not." Hence he did not see the very Essence of God, and consequently he was not taught by Him immediately. Accordingly when Scripture states that *He spoke to him face to face,* this is to be understood as expressing the opinion of the people, who thought that Moses was speaking with God mouth to mouth, when God spoke and appeared to him by means of a subordinate creature, that is, an angel and a cloud. Again we may say that this vision *face to face* means some kind of sublime and familiar contemplation, inferior to the vision of the Divine Essence.

Reply Obj. 3. It is for the sovereign alone to make a law by his own authority, but sometimes after making a law, he promulgates it through others. Thus God made the Law by His own authority, but He promulgated it through the angels.

ARTICLE 4. *Whether the Old Law Should Have Been Given to the Jews Alone?*

We proceed thus to the Fourth Article: It would seem that the Old Law should not have been given to the Jews alone.

Objection 1. For the Old Law disposed men for the salvation which was to come through

Christ, as stated above (AA. 2, 3). But that salvation was to come not to the Jews alone but to all nations, according to Isa. 49. 6: *It is a small thing that thou shouldst be my servant to raise up the tribes of Jacob, and to convert the dregs of Israel. Behold I have given thee to be the light of the Gentiles, that thou mayest be My salvation, even to the farthest part of the earth.* Therefore the Old Law should have been given to all nations, and not to one people only.

Obj. 2. Further, according to Acts 10. 34, 35, *God is not a respecter of persons: but in every nation, he that feareth Him, and worketh justice, is acceptable to Him.* Therefore the way of salvation should not have been opened to one people more than to another.

Obj. 3. Further, the law was given through the angels, as stated above (A. 3). But God always vouchsafed the ministrations of the angels not to the Jews alone, but to all nations, for it is written (Ecclus. 17. 14): *Over every nation He set a ruler.* Also on all nations He bestows temporal goods, which are of less account with God than spiritual goods. Therefore He should have given the Law also to all peoples.

On the contrary, It is written (Rom. 3. 1, 2): *What advantage then hath the Jew? . . . Much every way. First indeed, because the words of God were committed to them;* and (Ps. 147. 9): *He hath not done in like manner to every nation: and His judgments He hath not made manifest unto them.*

I answer that, It might be assigned as a reason for the Law being given to the Jews rather than to other peoples that the Jewish people alone remained faithful to the worship of one God, while the others turned away to idolatry; hence the latter were unworthy to receive the Law, lest a holy thing should be given to dogs.

But this reason does not seem fitting, because that people turned to idolatry even after the Law had been made, which was more grievous, as is clear from Exod. 32 and from Amos 5. 25, 26: *Did you offer victims and sacrifices to Me in the desert for forty years, O house of Israel? But you carried a tabernacle for your Moloch, and the image of your idols, the star of your god, which you made to yourselves.* Moreover it is stated expressly (Deut. 9. 6): *Know therefore that the Lord thy God giveth thee not this excellent land in possession for thy justices, for thou art a very stiff-necked people:* but the real reason is given in the preceding verse: *That the Lord might accomplish His word, which He*

---

[1] PL 75, 517.

[2] PL 34, 477.

promised by oath to thy fathers Abraham, Isaac, and Jacob.

What this promise was is shown by the Apostle, who says (Gal. 3. 16) that *to Abraham were the promises made and to his seed. He saith not, "And to his seeds," as of many: but as of one, "And to thy seed, which is Christ."* And so God vouchsafed both the Law and other special boons to that people, on account of the promise made to their fathers that Christ should be born of them. For it was fitting that the people of whom Christ was to be born should be signalized by a special sanctification, according to the words of Levit. 19. 2: *Be ye holy, because I . . . am holy.* Nor again was it on account of the merit of Abraham himself that this promise was made to him, namely, that Christ should be born of his seed, but of gratuitous election and calling of God. Hence it is written (Isa. 41. 2): *Who hath raised up the just one from the east, hath called him to follow him?*

It is therefore evident that it was merely from gratuitous election that the patriarchs received the promise, and that the people sprung from them received the law, according to Deut. 4. 36, 37, *Ye did* (Vulg.,—*Thou didst*) *hear His words out of the midst of the fire, because He loved thy fathers, and chose their seed after them.* And if again it be asked why He chose this people, and not another, that Christ might be born of them, a fitting answer is given by Augustine (*Tract. super Joann.* xxvi):[1] Why He draweth one and draweth not another, seek not thou to judge, if thou wish not to err."

Reply Obj. 1. Although the salvation which was to come through Christ was prepared for all nations, yet it was necessary that Christ should be born of one people, which, for this reason, was privileged above other peoples, according to Rom. 9. 4: *To whom,* namely the Jews, *belongeth the adoption as of children (of God), . . . and the testament, and the giving of the Law; . . . whose are the fathers, and of whom is Christ according to the flesh.*

Reply Obj. 2. Respect of persons takes place in those things which are given according to due; but it has no place in those things which are bestowed gratuitously. Because he who, out of generosity, gives of his own to one and not to another, is not a respecter of persons; but if he were a dispenser of goods held in common, and were not to distribute them according to personal merits, he would be a respecter of persons. Now God bestows the benefits of salvation

on the human race gratuitously; therefore He is not a respecter of persons if He gives them to some rather than to others. Hence Augustine says (*De Prædest. Sanct.* viii):[2] "All whom God teaches, He teaches out of pity; but whom He teaches not, out of justice He teaches not"; for this is due to the condemnation of the human race for the sin of the first parent.

Reply Obj. 3. The benefits of grace are forfeited by man on account of sin, but not the benefits of nature. Among the latter are the ministries of the angels, which the very order of various natures demands, namely, that the lowest beings be governed through the intermediate beings; and also bodily aids, which God vouchsafes not only to men but also to beasts, according to Ps. 35. 7: *Men and beasts Thou wilt preserve, O Lord.*

ARTICLE 5. *Whether All Men Were Bound To Observe the Old Law?*

We proceed thus to the Fifth Article: It would seem that all men were bound to observe the Old Law.

Objection 1. Because whoever is subject to the king must be subject to his law. But the Old Law was given by God, Who is *King of all the earth* (Ps. 46. 8). Therefore all the inhabitants of the earth were bound to observe the Law.

Obj. 2. Further, the Jews could not be saved without observing the Old Law, for it is written (Deut. 27. 26): *Cursed be he that abideth not in the words of this law, and fulfilleth them not in work.* If therefore other men could be saved without the observance of the Old Law, the Jews would be in a worse condition than other men.

Obj. 3. Further, the Gentiles were admitted to the Jewish ritual and to the observances of the Law, for it is written (Exod. 12. 48): *If any stranger be willing to dwell among you, and to keep the Phase of the Lord, all his males shall first be circumcised, and then shall he celebrate it according to the manner; and he shall be as he that is born in the land.* But it would have been useless to admit strangers to the legal observances according to the Divine ordinance if they could have been saved without the observance of the Law. Therefore none could be saved without observing the Law.

On the contrary, Dionysius says (*Cæl. Hier.* ix)[3] that many of the Gentiles were brought back to God by the angels. But it is clear that

---

[1] PL 35, 1607.

[2] PL 44, 971.

[3] Sect. 4 (PG 3, 261).

the Gentiles did not observe the Law. Therefore some could be saved without observing the Law.

I answer that, The Old Law showed forth the precepts of the natural law, and added certain precepts of its own. Accordingly, as to those precepts of the natural law contained in the Old Law all were bound to observe the Old Law; not because they belonged to the Old Law, but because they belonged to the natural law. But as to those precepts which were added by the Old Law, they were not binding on any save the Jewish people alone.

The reason of this is because the Old Law, as stated above (A. 4), was given to the Jewish people that it might receive a prerogative of holiness, in reverence for Christ Who was to be born of that people. Now whatever laws are enacted for the special sanctification of certain ones are binding on them alone; thus clerics who are set aside for the service of God are bound to certain obligations to which the laity are not bound; likewise religious are bound by their profession to certain works of perfection, to which people living in the world are not bound. In like manner this people was bound to certain special observances, to which other peoples were not bound. Hence it is written (Deut. 18. 13): *Thou shalt be perfect and without spot before the Lord thy God;* and for this reason they used a kind of form of profession, as appears from Deut. 26. 3: *I profess this day before the Lord thy God,* etc.

Reply Obj. 1. Whoever are subject to a king are bound to observe his law which he makes for all in general. But if he orders certain things to be observed by the servants of his household, others are bound to them.

Reply Obj. 2. The more a man is united to God, the better his state becomes. Therefore the more the Jewish people were bound to the worship of God, the greater their excellence over other peoples. Hence it is written (Deut. 4. 8): *What other nation is there so renowned that hath ceremonies and just judgments, and all the law?* In like manner, from this point of view, the state of clerics is better than that of the laity, and the state of religious than that of those living in the world.

Reply Obj. 3. The Gentiles obtained salvation more perfectly and more securely under the observances of the Law than under the natural law alone, and for this reason they were admitted to them. So too the laity are now admitted to the ranks of the clergy, and secular persons to those of the religious, although they can be saved without this.

ARTICLE 6. *Whether the Old Law Was Suitably Given at the Time of Moses?*

We proceed thus to the Sixth Article: It would seem that the Old Law was not suitably given at the time of Moses.

Objection 1. Because the Old Law disposed man for the salvation which was to come through Christ, as stated above (AA. 2, 3). But man needed this saving remedy immediately after he had sinned. Therefore the Law should have been given immediately after sin.

Obj. 2. Further, the Old Law was given for the sanctification of those from whom Christ was to be born. Now the promise concerning the *seed, which is Christ* (Gal. 3. 16) was first made to Abraham, as related in Gen. 12. 7. Therefore the Law should have been given at once at the time of Abraham.

Obj. 3. Further, as Christ was born of those alone who descended from Noe through Abraham, to whom the promise was made, so was He born of no other of the descendants of Abraham but David, to whom the promise was renewed, according to II Kings 23. 1: *The man to whom it was appointed concerning the Christ of the God of Jacob . . . said.* Therefore the Old Law should have been given after David, just as it was given after Abraham.

On the contrary, The Apostle says (Gal. 3. 19) that the Law *was set because of transgressions, until the seed should come, to whom He made the promise, being ordained by angels in the hand of a Mediator;* ordained, that is "given in orderly fashion," as the gloss explains.[1] Therefore it was fitting that the Old Law should be given in this order of time.

I answer that, It was most fitting for the Law to be given at the time of Moses. The reason for this may be taken from two things in respect of which every law is imposed on two kinds of men. Because it is imposed on some men who are hard-hearted and proud, whom the law restrains and tames; and it is imposed on good men, who, through being instructed by the law, are helped to fulfil what they desire to do. Hence it was fitting that the Law should be given at such a time as would be appropriate for the overcoming of man's pride. For man was proud of two things, namely, of knowledge and of power. He was proud of his knowledge, as though his natural reason could suffice him for salvation; and accordingly, in order that his pride might be overcome in this matter, man

[1] *Glossa* Lombardi (PL 192, 127); cf. *Glossa ordin.* (VI, 83B).

was left to the guidance of his reason without the help of a written law. And man was able to learn from experience that his reason was deficient, since about the time of Abraham man had fallen headlong into idolatry and the most shameful vices. Therefore, after those times, it was necessary for a written law to be given as a remedy for human ignorance, because *by the Law is the knowledge of sin* (Rom. 3, 20). But, after man had been instructed by the Law, his pride was convinced of his weakness through his being unable to fulfil what he knew. Hence, as the Apostle concludes (Rom. 8. 3, 4), *what the Law could not do in that it was weak through the flesh, God sent* (Vulg.,—*sending*) *His own Son, . . . that the justification of the Law might be fulfilled in us.*

With regard to good men, the Law was given to them as a help, which was most needed by the people, at the time when the natural law began to be obscured on account of the rank growth of sin; for it was fitting that this help should be bestowed on men in an orderly manner, so that they might be led from imperfection to perfection. Therefore it was becoming that the Old Law should be given between the law of nature and the law of grace.

Reply Obj. 1. It was not fitting for the Old Law to be given at once after the sin of the first man: both because man was so confident in his own reasons that he did not acknowledge his need of the Old Law, and because as yet the dictate of the natural law was not darkened by habitual sinning.

Reply Obj. 2. A law should not be given save to the people, since it is a general precept, as stated above (Q. XCVI, AA. 2, 3). Therefore at the time of Abraham God gave men certain familiar, and, as it were, household precepts. But when Abraham's descendants had multiplied, so as to form a people, and when they had been freed from slavery, it was fitting that they should be given a law; for slaves are not that part of the people or state to which it is fitting for the law to be directed, as the Philosopher says.[1]

Reply Obj. 3. Since the Law had to be given to the people, not only those of whom Christ was born received the Law, but the whole people, who were marked with the seal of circumcision, which was the sign of the promise made to Abraham, and in which he believed, according to Rom. 4. 11. Hence even before David, the Law had to be given to that people as soon as they were collected together.

[1] *Politics*, III, 9 (1280ª32); cf. IV, 4 (1291ª9).

QUESTION XCIX

Of the Precepts of the Old Law

(In Six Articles)

We must now consider the precepts of the Old Law; and (1) how they are distinguished from one another; (2) each kind of precept (Q. C). Under the first head there are six points of inquiry: (1) Whether the Old Law contained several precepts or only one? (2) Whether the Old Law contains any moral precepts? (3) Whether it contains ceremonial precepts in addition to the moral precepts? (4) Whether besides these it contains judicial precepts? (5) Whether it contains any others besides these? (6) How the Old Law induced men to keep its precepts.

ARTICLE 1. *Whether the Old Law Contains Only One Precept?*

We proceed thus to the First Article: It would seem that the Old Law contains but one precept.

Objection 1. Because a law is nothing else than a precept, as stated above (Q. XCII, A. 2, reply 1). Now there is but one Old Law. Therefore it contains but one precept.

Obj. 2. Further, the Apostle says (Rom 13. 9): *If there be any other commandment, it is comprised in this word: Thou shalt love thy neighbour as thyself.* But this is only one commandment. Therefore the Old Law contained but one commandment.

Obj. 3. Further, it is written (Matt. 7. 12): *All things . . . whatsoever you would that men should do to you, do you also to them. For this is the Law and the prophets.* But the whole of the Old Law is comprised in the Law and the prophets. Therefore the whole of the Old Law contains but one commandment.

On the contrary, The Apostle says (Ephes. 2. 15): *Making void the Law of commandments contained in decrees,* where he is referring to the Old Law, as the gloss comments on the passage.[2] Therefore the Old Law comprises many commandments.

I answer that, Since a precept of law is binding, it is about something which must be done: and, that a thing must be done arises from the necessity of some end. Hence it is evident that a precept implies, in its very idea, relation to an end, in so far as a thing is commanded as being

[2] *Glossa ordin.* (VI, 91F); *Glossa interl.* (V, 91V); *Glossa Lombardi* (PL 192, 185); cf. Ambrosiaster, *In Ephes.* 2.15 (PL 17, 401).

necessary or expedient to an end. Now many things may happen to be necessary or expedient to an end, and, accordingly, precepts may be given about various things as being ordered to one end. Consequently we must say that all the precepts of the Old Law are one in respect of their relation to one end, and yet they are many in respect of the diversity of those things that are ordered to that end.

Reply Obj. 1. The Old Law is said to be one as being ordered to one end; yet it comprises various precepts, according to the diversity of the things which it directs to the end. Thus also the art of building is one according to the unity of its end, because it aims at the building of a house; and yet it contains various rules, according to the variety of acts ordered to this.

Reply Obj. 2. As the Apostle says (I. Tim. 1. 5), *the end of the commandment is charity* since every law aims at establishing friendship, either between man and man, or between man and God. Therefore the whole Law is comprised in this one commandment, *Thou shalt love thy neighbour as thyself,* as expressing the end of all commandments, because love of one's neighbour includes love of God, when we love our neighbour for God's sake. Hence the Apostle puts this commandment in place of the two which are about the love of God and of one's neighbour, and of which Our Lord said (Matt. 22. 40): *On these two commandments dependeth the whole Law and the prophets.*

Reply Obj. 3. As stated in the *Ethics,*[1] "friendship towards another arises from friendship towards oneself," in so far as man looks on another as on himself. Hence when it is said, *All things whatsoever you would that men should do to you, do you also to them,* this is an explanation of the rule of neighbourly love contained implicitly in the words, *Thou shalt love thy neighbour as thyself,* so that it is an explanation of this commandment.

ARTICLE 2. *Whether the Old Law Contains Moral Precepts?*

We proceed thus to the Second Article: It would seem that the Old Law contains no moral precepts.

Objection 1. For the Old Law is distinct from the law of nature, as stated above (Q. XCI, AA. 4, 5; Q. XCVIII, A. 5). But the moral precepts belong to the law of nature. Therefore they do not belong to the Old Law.

Obj. 2. Further, the Divine law should have come to man's assistance where human reason

fails him, as is evident in regard to things that are of faith, which are above reason. But man's reason seems to suffice for the moral precepts. Therefore the moral precepts do not belong to the Old Law, which is a Divine law.

Obj. 3. Further, the Old Law is said to be *the letter* that *killeth* (II Cor. 3. 6). But the moral precepts do not kill, but quicken, according to Ps. 118. 93: *Thy justifications I will never forget, for by them Thou hast given me life.* Therefore the moral precepts do not belong to the Old Law.

On the contrary, It is written (Ecclus. 17. 9): *Moreover, He gave them discipline* (Douay,— *instructions*) *and the law of life for an inheritance.* Now discipline belongs to morals; for the gloss on Heb. 12. 11: *Now all chastisement* (*disciplina*), etc., says:[2] "Discipline is an exercise in morals by means of difficulties." Therefore the Law which was given by God comprised moral precepts.

I answer that, The Old Law contained some moral precepts, as is evident from Exod. 20. 13, 15: *Thou shalt not kill, Thou shalt not steal.* This was reasonable, because just as the principal intention of human law is to create friendship between man and man, so the chief intention of the Divine law is to establish man in friendship with God. Now since likeness is the reason of love, according to Ecclus. 13. 19: *Every beast loveth its like,* there cannot possibly be any friendship of man to God, Who is supremely good, unless man becomes good. Therefore it is written (Levit. 19. 2; cf. 11. 45): *You shall be holy, for I am holy.* But the goodness of man is virtue, which makes its possessor good. Therefore it was necessary for the Old Law to include precepts about acts of virtue, and these are the moral precepts of the Law.

Reply Obj. 1. The Old Law is distinct from the natural law not as being altogether different from it, but as something added to it. For just as grace presupposes nature, so must the Divine law presuppose the natural law.

Reply Obj. 2. It was fitting that the Divine law should come to man's assistance not only in those things for which reason is insufficient, but also in those things in which human reason may happen to be impeded. Now human reason could not go astray in the universal principle, that is, as to the most common principles of the natural law; but through being habituated to sin, it became obscured in the point of things to be done in detail. But with regard to the other

---

[1] Aristotle, IX, 4 (1166ᵃ1).

[2] *Glossa ordin.* (VI, 159B); *Glossa* Lombardi (PL 192, 503).

moral precepts, which are like conclusions drawn from the common principles of the natural law, the reason of many men went astray, to the extent of judging to be lawful things that are evil in themselves. Hence there was need for the authority of the Divine law to rescue man from both these defects. Thus among the articles of faith not only are those things set forth to which reason cannot reach, such as the Trinity of the Godhead, but also to which right reason can attain, such as the Unity of the Godhead, in order to remove the manifold errors to which reason is liable.

Reply Obj. 3. As Augustine proves (*De Spiritu et Litera*, xiv),[1] even the letter of the law is said to be the occasion of death, as to the moral precepts; in so far as, that is, it prescribes what is good without furnishing the aid of grace for its fulfilment.

ARTICLE 3. *Whether the Old Law Comprises Ceremonial, Besides Moral, Precepts?*

We proceed thus to the Third Article: It would seem that the Old Law does not comprise ceremonial, besides moral, precepts.

Objection 1. For every law that is given to man is for the purpose of directing human actions. Now human actions are called moral, as stated above (Q. I, A. 3). Therefore it seems that the Old Law given to men should not comprise other than moral precepts.

Obj. 2. Further, those precepts that are styled ceremonial seem to refer to the Divine worship. But Divine worship is the act of a virtue, namely, religion, which, as Tully says (*De Invent.* ii, 53)[2] "offers worship and ceremony to the divine nature." Since, then, the moral precepts are about acts of virtue, as stated above (A. 2), it seems that the ceremonial precepts should not be distinct from the moral.

Obj. 3. Further, the ceremonial precepts seem to be those which signify something figuratively. But, as Augustine observes,[3] "of all signs employed by men words hold the first place." Therefore there was no need for the Law to contain ceremonial precepts about certain figurative actions.

On the contrary, It is written (Deut. 4. 13, 14): *Ten words . . . He wrote in two tables of stone; and He commanded me at that time that I should teach you the ceremonies and judgments which you shall do.* But the ten commandments of the Law are moral precepts. Therefore

besides the moral precepts there are others which are ceremonial.

I answer that, As stated above (A. 2), the Divine law is instituted chiefly in order to direct men to God, while human law is instituted chiefly in order to direct men in relation to one another. Hence human laws have not concerned themselves with the institution of anything relating to Divine worship except as affecting the common good of mankind. And for this reason they have devised many institutions relating to Divine matters, according as it seemed expedient for the formation of human morals, as may be seen in the rites of the Gentiles. On the other hand the Divine law directed men to one another according to the demands of that order by which man is directed to God, which order was the chief aim of that law. Now man is directed to God not only by the interior acts of the mind, which are faith, hope, and love, but also by certain external works, whereby man makes profession of his subjection to God, and it is these works that are said to belong to the Divine worship. This worship is called ceremony,— the *munia*, that is, gifts of *Ceres* (who was the goddess of fruits), as some say,[4] because at first offerings were made to God from the fruits; or because, as Valerius Maximus states,[5] the word ceremony was introduced among the Latins to signify the Divine worship, being derived from a town near Rome called *Caere*, since, when Rome was taken by the Gauls, the sacred chattels of the Romans were taken there and most carefully preserved. Accordingly those precepts of the Law which refer to the Divine worship are specially called ceremonial.

Reply Obj. 1. Human acts extend also to the Divine worship, and therefore the Old Law given to man contains precepts about these matters also.

Reply Obj. 2. As stated above (Q. XCI, A. 3), the precepts of the natural law are general, and require to be determined: and they are determined both by human law and by Divine law. And just as these very determinations which are made by human law are said to be not of natural, but of positive law, so the determinations of the precepts of the natural law effected by the Divine law are distinct from the moral precepts which belong to the natural law. Therefore to worship God, since it is an act of virtue, belongs to a moral precept; but the determination of this precept, namely that He is to be worshipped by such and such sacrifices, and

---

[1] PL 44, 216.
[2] DD 1, 165.
[3] *Christian Doctrine*, II, 3 (PL 34, 37).
[4] Albert the Great, *In Sent.*, IV, d. 1, A. 7 (BO XXIX, 19).
[5] *Fact. et Dict. Memor.*, I. 1. (DD 565).

such and such offerings, belongs to the ceremonial precepts. Consequently the ceremonial precepts are distinct from the moral precepts.

Reply Obj. 3. As Dionysius says (*Cæl. Hier.* i),[1] the things of God cannot be manifested to men except by means of sensible likenesses. Now these likenesses move the soul more when they are not only expressed in words, but also offered to the senses. Therefore the things of God are set forth in the Scriptures not only by likenesses expressed in words, as in the case of metaphorical expressions, but also by likenesses of things set before the eyes, which pertains to the ceremonial precepts.

ARTICLE 4. *Whether, Besides the Moral and Ceremonial Precepts, There are Also Judicial Precepts?*

We proceed thus to the Fourth Article: It would seem that there are no judicial precepts in addition to the moral and ceremonial precepts in the Old Law.

Objection 1. For Augustine says (*Contra Faust.* vi, 2)[2] that in the Old Law there are "precepts concerning the life we have to lead, and precepts regarding the life that is foreshadowed." Now the precepts of the life we have to lead are moral precepts, and the precepts of the life that is foreshadowed are ceremonial. Therefore besides these two kinds of precepts we should not put any judicial precepts in the Law.

Obj. 2. Further, a gloss on Ps. 118. 102, *I have not declined from Thy judgments, says,*[3]—that is, "from the rule of life Thou hast set for me." But a rule of life belongs to the moral precepts. Therefore the judicial precepts should not be considered as distinct from the moral precepts.

Obj. 3. Further, judgment seems to be an act of justice, according to Ps. 93. 15: *Until justice be turned into judgment.* But acts of justice, like the acts of other virtues, belong to the moral precepts. Therefore the moral precepts include the judicial precepts, and consequently should not be held as distinct from them.

On the contrary, It is written (Deut. 6. 1): *These are the precepts, and ceremonies, and judgments,* where precepts stands for moral precepts antonomastically. Therefore there are judicial precepts besides moral and ceremonial precepts.

¹ Sect. 3 (PG 3, 121).

² PL 42, 228; x, 2 (PL 42, 243).

³ *Glossa ordin.* (III, 269A); *Glossa* Lombardi (PL 191, 1095).

I answer that, As stated above (AA. 2. 3), it pertains to the Divine law to direct men to one another and to God. Now each of these belongs in a general way to the dictates of the natural law, to which dictates the moral precepts are to be referred; yet each of them has to be determined by Divine or human law, because naturally known principles are general, both in speculative and in practical matters. Accordingly just as the determination of the general precept about Divine worship is effected by the ceremonial precepts, so the determination of the general precepts of that justice which is to be observed among men is effected by the judicial precepts.

We must therefore distinguish three kinds of precept in the Old Law; namely moral precepts, which are dictated by the natural law; ceremonial precepts, which are determinations of the Divine worship; and judicial precepts, which are determinations of the justice to be maintained among men. Therefore the Apostle (Rom. 7. 12) after saying that the *Law is holy,* adds that *the commandment is just, and holy, and good:* just, in respect of the judicial precepts; holy, with regard to the ceremonial precepts (since the word *sanctus*—holy—is applied to that which is consecrated to God); and good, that is, conducive to virtue, as to the moral precepts.

Reply Obj. 1. Both the moral and the judicial precepts aim at the ordering of human life, and consequently they are both comprised under one of the heads mentioned by Augustine, namely, under the precepts of the life we have to lead.

Reply Obj. 2. Judgment denotes execution of justice, by an application of the reason to individual cases in a determinate way. Hence the judicial precepts have something in common with the moral precepts in that they are derived from reason, and something in common with the ceremonial precepts in that they are determinations of general precepts. This explains why sometimes "judgments" comprises both judicial and moral precepts, as in Deut. 5 1: *Hear, O Israel, the ceremonies and judgments;* and sometimes judicial and ceremonial precepts, as in Levit. 18. 4: *You shall do My judgments, and shall observe My precepts,* where "precepts" denotes moral precepts, while "judgments" refers to judicial and ceremonial precepts.

Reply Obj. 3. The act of justice, in general, pertains to the moral precepts, but its determination to some special kind of act pertains to the judicial precepts.

ARTICLE 5. *Whether the Old Law Contains Any Others Besides the Moral, Judicial, and Ceremonial Precepts?*

We proceed thus to the Fifth Article: It would seem that the Old Law contains others besides the moral, judicial, and ceremonial precepts.

Objection 1. Because the judicial precepts belong to the act of justice, which is between man and man, while the ceremonial precepts belong to the act of religion, whereby God is worshipped. Now besides these there are many other virtues, namely, temperance, fortitude, liberality, and several others, as stated above (Q. LX, A. 5). Therefore besides these precepts, the Old Law should comprise others.

Obj. 2. Further, it is written (Deut. 11. 1): *Love the Lord thy God, and observe His precepts and ceremonies, His judgments and commandments.* Now precepts concern moral matters, as stated above (A. 4). Therefore besides the moral, judicial, and ceremonial precepts, the Law contains others which are called "commandments (*mandata*)".

Obj. 3. Further, it is written (Deut 6. 17): *Keep the precepts of the Lord thy God, and the testimonies and ceremonies which I have* (Vulg., —*He hath*) *commanded thee.* Therefore in addition to the above, the Law comprises "testimonies."

Obj. 4. Further, it is written (Ps. 118. 93): *Thy justifications* (that is, "Thy Law," according to a gloss)[1] *I will never forget.* Therefore in the Old Law there are not only moral, ceremonial, and judicial precepts, but also others, called "justifications."

On the contrary, It is written (Deut. 6. 1.): *These are the precepts and ceremonies and judgments which the Lord your God commanded . . . you.* And these words are placed at the beginning of the Law. Therefore all the precepts of the Law are included under them.

I answer that, Some things are included in the Law by way of precept; other things, as being ordained to the fulfilment of the precepts. Now the precepts refer to things which have to be done, and to their fulfilment man is induced by two considerations, namely, the authority of the lawgiver, and the benefit derived from the fulfilment, which benefit consists in the attainment of some good, useful, pleasurable or virtuous, or in the avoidance of some contrary evil. Hence it was necessary that in the Old Law

certain things should be set forth to indicate the authority of God the lawgiver: for example, Deut. 6. 4: *Hear, O Israel, the Lord our God is one Lord;* and Gen. 1. 1.: *In the beginning God created heaven and earth;* and these are called "testimonies." Again it was necessary that in the Law certain rewards should be appointed for those who observe the Law and punishments for those who transgress, as may be seen in Deut. 28.: *If thou wilt hear the voice of the Lord Thy God . . . He will make thee higher than all the nations,* etc.; and these are called "justifications," according as God punishes or rewards certain ones justly.

The things that have to be done do not come under the precept except in so far as they have the character of a duty. Now a duty is twofold: one according to the rule of reason, the other according to the rule of a law which prescribes that duty; thus the Philosopher distinguishes a twofold just—moral and legal.[2]

Moral duty is twofold: for reason dictates that something must be done either as being so necessary that without it the order of virtue would be destroyed, or as being useful for the better maintaining of the order of virtue. And in this sense some of the moral precepts are expressed by way of absolute command or prohibition, as *Thou shalt not kill, Thou shalt not steal;* and these are properly called *precepts.* Other things are prescribed or forbidden not as an absolute duty, but as something better to be done. These may be called "commandments (*mandata*)," because they are expressed by way of inducement and persuasion; an example of this is seen in Exod. 22. 26: *If thou take of thy neighbour a garment in pledge, thou shalt give it him again before sunset,* and in other like cases. Therefore Jerome (*Præfat. in Comment. super Marc.*)[3] says that "justice is in the precepts, charity in the commandments." Duty as fixed by the Law belongs to the judicial precepts as regards human affairs, to the ceremonial precepts as regards Divine matters.

Nevertheless those ordinances also which refer to punishments and rewards may be called testimonies, in so far as they testify to the Divine justice. Again all the precepts of the Law may be styled justifications, as being executions of legal justice. Furthermore the commandments may be distinguished from the precepts, so that those things be called precepts which God Himself prescribed, and those things com-

---

[1] *Glossa interl.* (III, 268v); *Glossa* Lombardi (PL 191, 1090).

[2] *Ethics*, v, 7 (1134^{b}18).

[3] Cf. Pelagius, *In Marc.,* proem. (PL 30, 610); cf. *Glossa ordin.,* on the beginning of Mark (v, 88E).

mandments which He enjoined (*mandavit*) through others, as the very word seems to denote.

From this it is clear that all the precepts of the Law are either moral, ceremonial, or judicial, and that other ordinances have not the character of a precept, but are directed to the observance of the precepts, as stated above.

Reply Obj. 1. Justice alone, of all the virtues, implies the notion of duty. Consequently moral matters are determinable by law in so far as they belong to justice, of which virtue religion is a part, as Tully says (*De Invent.* ii, 53).[1] Therefore the legal just cannot be anything foreign to the ceremonial and judicial precepts.

The Replies to the other Objections are clear from what has been said.

ARTICLE 6. *Whether the Old Law Should Have Induced Men to the Observance of Its Precepts By Means of Temporal Promises and Threats?*

We proceed thus to the Sixth Article: It would seem that the Old Law should not have induced men to the observance of its precepts by means of temporal promises and threats.

Objection 1. For the purpose of the Divine law is to subject man to God by fear and love; hence it is written (Deut. 10. 12): *And now, Israel, what doth the Lord thy God require of thee, but that thou fear the Lord thy God, and walk in His ways, and love Him?* But the desire for temporal goods leads man away from God; for Augustine says (QQ. lxxxiii *qu.* 36),[2] that "covetousness is the bane of charity." Therefore temporal promises and threats seem to be contrary to the intention of a lawgiver; and this makes a law worthy of rejection, as the Philosopher declares.[3]

Obj. 2. Further, the Divine law is more excellent than human law. Now, in sciences, we notice that the loftier the science, the higher the means that it employs. Therefore, since human law employs temporal threats and promises, as means of persuading man, the Divine law should have used, not these, but more lofty means.

Obj. 3. Further, the reward of justice and the punishment of guilt cannot be that which befalls equally the good and the wicked. But as stated in Ecclus. 9. 2, *all* temporal *things equally happen to the just and to the wicked, to the good and to the evil, to the clean and to the unclean, to him that offereth victims, and to him that despiseth sacrifices.* Therefore temporal goods or evils are not suitably set forth as punishments

or rewards of the commandments of the Divine law.

On the contrary, It is written (Isa. 1. 19, 20): *If you be willing, and will hearken to Me, you shall eat the good things of the land. But if you will not, and will provoke Me to wrath: the sword shall devour you.*

I answer that, As in speculative sciences men are led to assent to the conclusions by means of syllogistic arguments, so too in every law, men are led to observe its precepts by means of punishments and rewards. Now it is to be observed that in speculative sciences the means are adapted to the conditions of the hearer. Therefore just as in the sciences we should proceed in an orderly way so that the instruction is based on principles more generally known, so also he who would persuade a man to the observance of any precepts needs to move him at first by things for which he has an affection; just as children are induced to do something, by means of little childish gifts. Now it has been said above (Q. XCVIII, AA. 1, 2, 3) that the Old Law disposed men to Christ as the imperfect disposes to the perfect. Hence it was given to a people as yet imperfect in comparison to the perfection which was to result from Christ's coming, and for this reason, that people is compared to a child that is still under a pedagogue (Gal. 3. 24). But the perfection of man consists in his despising temporal things and cleaving to things spiritual, as is clear from the words of the Apostle (Phil. 3. 13, 15): *Forgetting the things that are behind, I stretch* (Vulg.,—*and stretching*) *forth myself to those that are before. . . . Let us therefore, as many as are perfect, be thus minded.* Those who are yet imperfect desire temporal goods, although in subordination to God. The perverse however place their end in temporalities. It was therefore fitting that the Old Law should conduct men to God by means of temporal goods for which the imperfect have an affection.

Reply Obj. 1. Covetousness, by which man places his end in temporalities, is the bane of charity. But the attainment of temporal goods which man desires in subordination to God is a road leading the imperfect to the love of God, according to Ps. 48. 19: *He will praise Thee, when Thou shalt do well to him.*

Reply Obj. 2. Human law persuades men by means of temporal rewards or by punishments to be inflicted by men; but the Divine law persuades men by means of rewards or punishments to be received from God. In this respect it employs higher means.

Reply Obj. 3. As anyone can see who reads

---

[1] DD I, 165.   [2] PL 40, 25.
[3] Cf. *Politics* VII, 2 (1324[b]23).

carefully the story of the Old Testament, the common state of the people prospered under the Law as long as they obeyed it; and as soon as they departed from the precepts of the Law they were overtaken by many calamities. But certain individuals, although they observed the justice of the Law, met with misfortunes—either because they had already become spiritual (so that misfortune might withdraw them all the more from attachment to temporal things, and that their virtue might be tried); or because, while outwardly fulfilling the works of the Law, their heart was altogether fixed on temporal goods, and far removed from God, according to Isa. 29. 13 (Matt. 15. 8): *This people honoureth Me with their lips; but their heart is far from Me.*

QUESTION C

Of the Moral Precepts of the Old Law

(In Twelve Articles)

We must now consider each kind of precept of the Old Law: and (1) the moral precepts, (2) the ceremonial precepts (Q. CI), (3) the judicial precepts (Q. CIV). Under the first head there are twelve points of inquiry: (1) Whether all the moral precepts of the Old Law belong to the law of nature? (2) Whether the moral precepts of the Old Law are about the acts of all the virtues? (3) Whether all the moral precepts of the Old Law are reducible to the ten precepts of the decalogue? (4) How the precepts of the decalogue are distinguished from one another; (5) Their number; (6) Their order; (7) The manner in which they were given; (8) Whether they are dispensable? (9) Whether the mode of observing a virtue comes under the precept of the Law? (10) Whether the mode of charity comes under the precept? (11) The distinction of other moral precepts. (12) Whether the moral precepts of the Old Law justified man?

Article 1. *Whether All the Moral Precepts of the Old Law Belong to the Law of Nature?*

We proceed thus to the First Article: It would seem that not all the moral precepts belong to the law of nature.

Objection 1. For it is written (Ecclus. 17. 9): *Moreover He gave them instructions, and the law of life for an inheritance.* But instruction is in contradistinction to the law of nature, since the law of nature is not learnt, but held by natural instinct. Therefore not all the moral precepts belong to the natural law.

Obj. 2. Further, the Divine law is more perfect than human law. But human law adds certain things concerning good morals to those that belong to the law of nature, as is evidenced by the fact that the natural law is the same in all men, while these moral institutions are various for various people. Much more reason therefore was there why the Divine law should add to the law of nature ordinances pertaining to good morals.

Obj. 3. Further, just as natural reason leads to good morals in certain matters, so does faith; hence it is written (Gal. 5. 6) that faith *worketh by charity.* But faith is not included in the law of nature, since that which is of faith is above natural reason. Therefore not all the moral precepts of the Divine law belong to the law of nature.

On the contrary, The Apostle says (Rom. 2. 14) that *the Gentiles, who have not the Law, do by nature those things that are of the Law,* which must be understood of things pertaining to good morals. Therefore all the moral precepts of the Law belong to the law of nature.

I answer that, The moral precepts, distinct from the ceremonial and judicial precepts, are about things pertaining of their very nature to good morals. Now since human morals depend on their relation to reason, which is the proper principle of human acts, those morals are called good which accord with reason, and those are called bad which are discordant from reason. And as every judgment of speculative reason proceeds from the natural knowledge of first principles, so every judgment of practical reason proceeds from principles known naturally, as stated above (Q. XCIV, AA. 2, 4), from which principles one may proceed in various ways to judge of various matters. For some matters connected with human actions are so evident that after very little consideration one is able at once to approve or disapprove of them by means of these general first principles. But some matters cannot be the subject of judgment without much consideration of the various circumstances, which all are not able to do carefully, but only those who are wise, just as it is not possible for all to consider the particular conclusions of sciences, but only for those who are versed in philosophy. And lastly there are some matters of which man cannot judge unless he be helped by Divine instruction, such as the articles of faith.

It is therefore evident that since the moral precepts are about matters which concern good morals, and since good morals are those which are in accord with reason, and since also every judgment of human reason must be derived in some way from natural reason, it follows, of necessity, that all of the moral precepts belong to the law of nature, but not all in the same way. For there are certain things which the natural reason of every man, of its own accord and at once, judges to be done or not to be done: for example, Honour thy father and thy mother, and, Thou shalt not kill, Thou shalt not steal; and these belong to the law of nature absolutely. And there are certain things which, after a more careful consideration, wise men judge to be obligatory. Such belong to the law of nature, yet so that they need to be inculcated, the wiser teaching the less wise: for example, *Rise up before the hoary head, and honour the person of the aged man* (Lev. 19. 32), and the like. And there are some things to judge of which human reason needs Divine instruction, by which we are taught about things of God: for example, *Thou shalt not make to thyself a graven thing, nor the likeness of anything; Thou shalt not take the name of the Lord thy God in vain* (Exod. 20. 4, 7).

This suffices for the Replies to the Objections.

ARTICLE 2. *Whether the Moral Precepts of the Law Are About All the Acts of Virtue?*

We proceed thus to the Second Article: It would seem that the moral precepts of the Law are not about all the acts of virtue.

Objection 1. For observance of the precepts of the Old Law is called justification, according to Ps. 118. 8: *I will keep Thy justifications.* But justification is the execution of justice. Therefore the moral precepts are only about acts of justice.

Obj. 2. Further, that which comes under a precept has the character of a duty. But the character of duty belongs to justice alone and to none of the other virtues, for the proper act of justice consists in rendering to each one his due. Therefore the precepts of the moral law are not about the acts of the other virtues, but only about the acts of justice.

Obj. 3. Further, every law is made for the common good, as Isidore says (*Etym.* v, 21).[1] But of all the virtues justice alone regards the common good, as the Philosopher says.[2] Therefore the moral precepts are only about the acts of justice.

On the contrary, Ambrose says (*De Paradiso*

viii)[3] that "a sin is a transgression of the Divine law, and a disobedience to the commandments of heaven." But there are sins contrary to all the acts of virtue. Therefore it belongs to the Divine law to direct all the acts of virtue.

I answer that, Since the precepts of the Law are ordered to the common good, as stated above (Q. XC, A. 2), the precepts of the Law must be diversified according to the various kinds of community; hence the Philosopher teaches[4] that the laws which are made in a state which is ruled by a king must be different from the laws of a state which is ruled by the people, or by a few powerful men in the state. Now human law is ordained for one kind of community, and the Divine law for another kind. Because human law is ordained for the civil community, implying mutual duties of man and his fellows, and men are ordered to one another by outward acts, by which men live in communion with one another. This life in common of man with man pertains to justice, whose proper function consists in directing the human community. Therefore human law makes precepts only about acts of justice; and if it commands acts of other virtues, this is only in so far as they assume the nature of justice, as the Philosopher explains.[5]

But the community for which the Divine law is ordained is that of men in relation to God, either in this life or in the life to come. And therefore the Divine law proposes precepts about all those matters by which men are well ordered in their relations to God. Now man is united to God by his reason, or mind, in which is God's image. Therefore the Divine law proposes precepts about all those matters by which human reason is well ordered. But this is effected by the acts of all the virtues, since the intellectual virtues set in good order the acts of the reason in themselves, while the moral virtues set in good order the acts of the reason in reference to the interior passions and exterior actions. It is therefore evident that the Divine law fittingly proposes precepts about the acts of all the virtues, yet so that certain matters, without which the order of virtue, which is the order of reason, cannot even exist, come under an obligation of precept, while other matters, which pertain to the well-being of perfect virtue, come under an admonition of counsel.

Reply Obj. 1. The fulfillment of the commandments of the Law, even of those which are about the acts of the other virtues, has the

[1] PL 82, 203; II, 10 (PL 82, 131).
[2] *Ethics,* v, 1 (1130ª4).
[3] PL 14, 309.   [4] *Politics,* IV, 1 (1289ª11).
[5] *Ethics,* v, 1 (1129ᵇ23).

character of justification, since it is just that man should obey God; or again, because it is just that all that belongs to man should be subject to reason.

Reply Obj. 2. Justice properly so called regards the duty of one man to another; but all the other virtues regard the duty of the lower powers to reason. It is in relation to this latter duty that the Philosopher speaks of a kind of metaphorical justice.[1]

The Reply to the Third Objection is clear from what has been said about the different kinds of community.

ARTICLE 3. *Whether All the Moral Precepts of the Old Law Are Reducible to the Ten Precepts of the Decalogue?*

We proceed thus to the Third Article: It would seem that not all the moral precepts of the Old Law are reducible to the ten precepts of the decalogue.

Objection 1. For the first and principal precepts of the Law are, *Thou shalt love the Lord thy God,* and, *Thou shalt love thy neighbour,* as stated in Matt. 22. 37, 39. But these two are not contained in the precepts of the decalogue. Therefore not all the moral precepts are contained in the precepts of the decalogue.

Obj. 2. Further, the moral precepts are not reducible to the ceremonial precepts, but rather contrariwise. But among the precepts of the decalogue, one is ceremonial, namely, *Remember that thou keep holy the Sabbath-day* (Exod. 20.8). Therefore the moral precepts are not reducible to all the precepts of the decalogue.

Obj. 3. Further, the moral precepts are about all the acts of virtue. But among the precepts of the decalogue are only such as regard acts of justice, as may be seen by going through them all. Therefore the precepts of the decalogue do not include all the moral precepts.

On the contrary, The gloss on Matt. 5. 11. *Blessed are ye when they shall revile you,* etc., says that "Moses, after propounding the ten precepts, set them out in detail."[2] Therefore all the precepts of the Law are so many parts of the precepts of the decalogue.

I answer that, The precepts of the decalogue differ from the other precepts of the Law in the fact that God Himself is said to have given the precepts of the decalogue, while He gave the other precepts to the people through Moses. Therefore the decalogue includes those precepts the knowledge of which man has immediately from God. Such are those which with but slight

[1] *Ethics,* v, 11 (1138^{b}5).   [2] *Glossa ordin.* (v, 19B).

reflection can be gathered at once from the first general principles, and those also which become known to man immediately through divinely infused faith. Consequently two kinds of precepts are not reckoned among the precepts of the decalogue. First, general principles, for they need no further promulgation after being once inscribed on the natural reason to which they are self-evident; as, for instance, that one should do evil to no man, and other similar principles. And again, those which the careful reflection of wise men shows to be in accord with reason, since the people receive these principles from God through being taught by wise men. Nevertheless both kinds of precepts are contained in the precepts of the decalogue, yet in different ways. For the first general principles are contained in them as principles in their proximate conclusions; but those which are known through wise men are contained, conversely, as conclusions in their principles.

Reply Obj. 1. Those two principles are the first general principles of the natural law, and are self-evident to human reason, either through nature or through faith. Therefore all the precepts of the decalogue are referred to these, as conclusions to general principles.

Reply Obj. 2. The precept of the Sabbath observance is moral in one respect, in so far as it commands man to give some time to the things of God, according to Ps. 45. 11: *Be still and see that I am God.* In this respect it is placed among the precepts of the decalogue, but not as to the fixing of the time, in which respect it is a ceremonial precept.

Reply Obj. 3. The notion of duty is not so patent in the other virtues as it is in justice. Hence the precepts about the acts of the other virtues are not so well known to the people as are the precepts about acts of justice. Therefore the acts of justice especially come under the precepts of the decalogue, which are the primary elements of the Law.

ARTICLE 4. *Whether the Precepts of the Decalogue Are Suitably Distinguished From One Another?*

We proceed thus to the Fourth Article: It would seem that the precepts of the decalogue (Exod. 20) are unsuitably distinguished from one another.

Objection 1. For worship is a virtue distinct from faith. Now the precepts are about acts of virtue. But that which is said at the beginning of the decalogue, *Thou shalt not have strange gods before Me,* belongs to faith, and that which is added, *Thou shalt not make . . . any graven thing,* etc., belongs to worship. Therefore these are not one precept, as Augustine asserts (QQ. *in Exod., qu.* lxxi),[1] but two.

Obj. 2. Further, the affirmative precepts in the Law are distinct from the negative precepts; for example, *Honour thy father and thy mother,* and, *Thou shalt not kill.* But this, *I am the Lord thy God,* is affirmative; and that which follows, *Thou shalt not have strange gods before Me,* is negative. Therefore these are two precepts, and do not, as Augustine says (*loc. cit.*) make one.

Obj. 3. Further, the Apostle says (Rom. 7. 7): *I had not known concupiscence, if the Law did not say: "Thou shalt not covet."* Hence it seems that this precept, *Thou shalt not covet,* is one precept, and, therefore should not be divided into two.

On the contrary stands the authority of Augustine, who in commenting on Exodus (*loc. cit.*)[2] distinguishes three precepts as referring to God, and seven as referring to our neighbour.

I answer that, The precepts of the decalogue are differently divided by different authorities. For Hesychius commenting on Levit. 26. 26, *Ten women shall bake your bread in one oven,* says that the precept of the Sabbath-day observance is not one of the ten precepts, because its observance, in the letter, is not binding for all time.[3] But he distinguishes four precepts pertaining to God, the first being, *I am the Lord thy God;* the second, *Thou shalt not have strange gods before Me,* (thus also Jerome distinguishes these two precepts, in his commentary on Osee 10. 10,[4] *On thy*—Vulg., *their*—*two iniquities*); the third precept according to him is, *Thou shalt not make to thyself any graven thing;* and the fourth, *Thou shalt not take the name of the Lord thy God in vain.* He states that there are six precepts pertaining to our neighbour; the first, *Honour thy father and thy mother;* the second, *Thou shalt not kill;* the third, *Thou shalt not commit adultery;* the fourth, *Thou shalt not steal;* the fifth, *Thou shalt not bear false witness;* the sixth, *Thou shalt not covet.*

But, in the first place, it seems unfitting for the precept of the Sabbath-day observance to be put among the precepts of the decalogue, if it did not in any way belong to the decalogue. Secondly, because, since it is written (Matt.

6. 24), *No man can serve two masters,* the two statements, *I am the Lord thy God,* and, *Thou shalt not have strange gods before Me* seem to be of the same nature and to form one precept. Hence Origen (*Hom.* vii *in Exod.*),[5] who also distinguishes four precepts as referring to God, unites these two under one precept; and puts in the second place, *Thou shalt not make . . . any graven thing;* as third, *Thou shalt not take the name of the Lord thy God in vain;* and as fourth, *Remember that thou keep holy the Sabbath-day.* The other six he puts in the same way as Hesychius.

Since, however, the making of graven things or the likeness of anything is not forbidden except as to the point of their being worshipped as gods—for God commanded an image of the Seraphim (Vulg.,—Cherubim) to be made and placed in the tabernacle, as related in Exod. 25. 18—Augustine more fittingly unites these two, *Thou shalt not have strange gods before Me,* and, *Thou shalt not make . . . any graven thing,* into one precept. Likewise to covet another's wife, for the purpose of carnal knowledge, belongs to the concupiscence of the flesh; but to covet other things, which are desired for the purpose of possession, belongs to the concupiscence of the eyes. Therefore Augustine puts (*ibid.*) as distinct precepts, that which forbids the coveting of another's goods and that which prohibits the coveting of another's wife. Thus he distinguishes three precepts as referring to God, and seven as referring to our neighbour. And this is better.

Reply Obj. 1. Worship is merely a declaration of faith, and therefore the precepts about worship should not be given as distinct from those about faith. Nevertheless precepts should be given about worship rather than about faith, because the precept about faith is presupposed to the precepts of the decalogue, as is also the precept of love. For just as the first general precepts of the natural law are self-evident to a subject having natural reason, and need no promulgation, so also to believe in God is a first and self-evident principle to a subject possessed of faith: *for he that cometh to God, must believe that He is* (Heb. 11. 6). Hence it needs no other promulgation than the infusion of faith.

Reply Obj. 2. The affirmative precepts are distinct from the negative when one is not comprised in the other; thus that man should honour his parents does not include that he should not kill another man, nor does the latter in-

---

[1] PL 34, 621.

[2] PL 34, 620; Cf. *Glossa ordin.,* super Exod. 20.1 (I, 163 B).

[3] PG 93, 1150.   [4] Bk. III (PL 25, 952).   [5] PG 12, 351.

clude the former. But when an affirmative precept is included in a negative, or vice versa, we do not find that two distinct precepts are given; thus there is not one precept saying that *Thou shalt not steal*, and another binding one to keep another's property intact, or to give it back to its owner. In the same way there are not different precepts about believing in God, and about not believing in strange gods.

Reply Obj. 3. All covetousness has one common notion, and therefore the Apostle speaks of the commandment about covetousness as though it were one. But because there are various special kinds of covetousness, therefore Augustine distinguishes different prohibitions against coveting; for covetousness differs specifically in respect of the diversity of actions or things coveted, as the Philosopher says.[1]

ARTICLE 5. *Whether the Precepts of the Decalogue Are Suitably Set Forth?*

We proceed thus to the Fifth Article: It would seem that the precepts of the decalogue (Exod. 20) are unsuitably set forth.

Objection 1. Because sin, as stated by Ambrose (*De Paradiso* viii),[2] is "a transgression of the Divine law and a disobedience to the commandments of heaven." But sins are distinguished according as man sins against God, or his neighbour, or himself. Since, then, the decalogue does not include any precepts directing man in his relations to himself, but only such as direct him in his relations to God and his neighbour, it seems that the precepts of the decalogue are insufficiently enumerated.

Obj. 2. Further, just as the Sabbath-day observance pertained to the worship of God, so also did the observance of other solemnities, and the offering of sacrifices. But the decalogue contains a precept about the Sabbath-day observance. Therefore it should contain others also, pertaining to the other solemnities, and to the sacrificial rite.

Obj. 3. Further, as sins against God include the sin of perjury, so also do they include blasphemy, or other ways of lying against the teaching of God. But there is a precept forbidding perjury. *Thou shalt not take the name of the Lord thy God in vain.* Therefore there should be also a precept of the decalogue, forbidding blasphemy and false doctrine.

Obj. 4. Further, just as man has a natural love for his parents, so has he also for his children. Moreover the commandment of charity extends to all our neighbours. Now the precepts

of the decalogue are ordered to charity, according to I Tim. 1. 5: *The end of the commandment is charity.* Therefore as there is a precept referring to parents, so should there have been some precepts referring to children and other neighbours.

Obj. 5. Further, in every kind of sin, it is possible to sin in thought or in deed. But in some kinds of sin, namely in theft and adultery, the prohibition of sins of deed, when it is said, *Thou shalt not commit adultery, Thou shalt not steal*, is distinct from the prohibition of the sin of thought, when it is said, *Thou shalt not covet thy neighbour's goods*, and, *Thou shalt not covet thy neighbour's wife.* Therefore the same should have been done in regard to the sins of homicide and false witness.

Obj. 6. Further, just as sin happens through disorder of the concupiscible part, so does it arise through disorder of the irascible part. But some precepts forbid inordinate concupiscence, when it is said, *Thou shalt not covet.* Therefore the decalogue should have included some precepts forbidding the disorders of the irascible part. Therefore it seems that the ten precepts of the decalogue are unfittingly enumerated.

On the contrary, It is written (Deut. 4. 13): *He shewed you His covenant, which He commanded you to do, and the ten words that He wrote in two tables of stone.*

I answer that, As stated above (A. 2), just as the precepts of human law direct man in his relations to the human community, so the precepts of the Divine law direct man in his relations to a community or commonwealth of men under God. Now in order that any man may dwell rightly in a community, two things are required: the first is that he behave well to the head of the community; the other is that he behave well to those who are his fellows and partners in the community. It is therefore necessary that the Divine law should contain in the first place precepts ordering man in his relations to God, and in the second place other precepts ordering man in his relations to other men who are his neighbours and live with him under God.

Now man owes three things to the head of the community: first, fidelity; secondly, reverence; thirdly, service. Fidelity to his master consists in his not giving sovereign honour to another, and this is the sense of the first commandment, in the words, *Thou shalt not have strange gods.* Reverence to his master requires that he should do nothing injurious to him, and this is conveyed by the second commandment,

[1] *Ethics*, x, 5 (1175[b]28).   [2] PL 14, 309.

Thou shalt not take the name of the Lord thy God in vain. Service is due to the master in return for the benefits which his subjects receive from him and to this belongs the third commandment of the sanctification of the Sabbath in memory of the creation of all things.

To his neighbours a man behaves himself well both in particular and in general. In particular, as to those to whom he is indebted by paying his debts, and in this sense is to be taken the commandment about honouring one's parents. In general, as to all men by doing harm to none, either by deed, or by word, or by thought. By deed harm is done to one's neighbour sometimes in his person, that is, to his personal existence, and this is forbidden by the words, *Thou shalt not kill;* sometimes in a person united to him as to the propagation of offspring, and this is prohibited by the words, *Thou shalt not commit adultery;* sometimes in his possessions, which are directed to both of these, and with regard to this it is said, *Thou shalt not steal.* Harm done by word is forbidden when it is said, *Thou shalt not bear false witness against thy neighbour;* harm done by thought is forbidden in the words, *Thou shalt not covet.*

The three precepts that direct man in his behaviour towards God may also be differentiated in this same way. For the first refers to deeds, and therefore it is said, *Thou shalt not make . . . a graven thing;* the second, to words, and therefore it is said, *Thou shalt not take the name of the Lord thy God in vain;* the third, to thoughts, because the sanctification of the Sabbath, as the subject of a moral precept, requires repose of the heart in God. Or, according to Augustine (*In Ps.* 32. 2),[1] by the first commandment we reverence the unity of the First Principle; by the second, the Divine truth; by the third, His goodness by which we are sanctified, and in which we rest as in our last end.

Reply Obj. 1. This objection may be answered in two ways. First, because the precepts of the decalogue can be reduced to the precepts of charity. Now there was need for man to receive a precept about loving God and his neighbour, because in this respect the natural law had become obscured on account of sin, but not about the duty of loving oneself, because in this respect the natural law retained its vigour. Or again, because love of oneself is contained in the love of God and of one's neighbour, since true self-love consists in directing oneself to God. And for this reason the decalogue includes

[1] PL 36, 281.

those precepts only which refer to our neighbour and to God.

Secondly, it may be answered that the precepts of the decalogue are those which the people received from God immediately; hence it is written (Deut. 10. 4): *He wrote in the tables, according as He had written before, the ten words, which the Lord spoke to you.* And so the precepts of the decalogue need to be such as the people can understand at once. Now a precept implies the notion of duty. But it is easy for a man, especially for a believer, to understand that, of necessity, he owes certain duties to God and to his neighbour. But that in matters which regard himself and not another, man has of necessity certain duties to himself, is not so evident; for, at first glance, it seems that everyone is free in matters that concern himself. And therefore the precepts which prohibit disorders of a man with regard to himself reach the people through the instruction of men who are versed in such matters. Consequently, they are not contained in the decalogue.

Reply Obj. 2. All the solemnities of the Old Law were instituted in celebration of some Divine favour, either in memory of past favours, or in sign of some favour to come, and in like manner all the sacrifices were offered up with the same purpose. Now of all the Divine favours to be commemorated the chief was that of the Creation, which was called to mind by the sanctification of the Sabbath; therefore the reason for this precept is given in Exod. 20. 11: *In six days the Lord made heaven and earth,* etc. And of all future blessings, the chief and final was the repose of the mind in God, either, in the present life, by grace, or in the future life, by glory; and this repose was also foreshadowed in the Sabbath-day observance; hence it is written (Isa. 58. 13): *If thou turn away thy foot from the Sabbath from doing thy own will in My holy day, and call the Sabbath delightful, and the holy of the Lord glorious.* For these favours first and chiefly are borne in mind by men, especially by the faithful. But other solemnities were celebrated on account of certain particular favours which were temporal and transitory, such as the celebration of the Passover in memory of the past favour of the delivery from Egypt, and as a sign of the future Passion of Christ, which though temporal and transitory, brought us to the repose of the spiritual Sabbath. Consequently, the Sabbath alone, and none of the other solemnities and sacrifices, is mentioned in the precepts of the decalogue.

Reply Obj. 3. As the Apostle says (Heb. 6. 16), *men swear by one greater than themselves; and an oath for confirmation is the end of all their controversy.* Hence, since oaths are common to all, inordinate swearing is the matter of a special prohibition by a precept of the decalogue. According to one interpretation, however, the words, *Thou shalt not take the name of the Lord thy God in vain* are a prohibition of false doctrine, for one gloss expounds them thus: "Thou shalt not say that Christ is a creature."[1]

Reply Obj. 4. That a man should not do harm to anyone is an immediate dictate of his natural reason, and therefore the precepts that forbid the doing of harm are binding on all men. But it is not an immediate dictate of natural reason that a man should do one thing in return for another, unless he happen to be indebted to someone. Now a son's debt to his father is so evident that one cannot get away from it by denying it, since the father is the principle of generation and being, and also of upbringing and teaching. Therefore the decalogue does not prescribe deeds of kindness or service to be done to anyone except to one's parents. On the other hand parents do not seem to be indebted to their children for any favours received, but rather the reverse is the case. Again, a child is a part of his father, and "parents love their children as being a part of themselves," as the Philosopher states.[2] Hence, just as the decalogue contains no ordinance as to man's behaviour towards himself, so, for the same reason, it includes no precept about loving one's children.

Reply Obj. 5. The pleasure of adultery and the usefulness of wealth, in so far as they have the character of pleasurable or useful good, are, of themselves, objects of appetite; and for this reason they needed to be forbidden not only in the deed but also in the desire. But murder and falsehood are, of themselves, objects of repulsion (since it is natural for man to love his neighbour and the truth), and are desired only for the sake of something else. Consequently with regard to sins of murder and false witness, it was necessary to proscribe, not sins of thought, but only sins of deed.

Reply Obj. 6. As stated above (Q. XXV, A. 1), all the passions of the irascible part arise from the passions of the concupiscible part. Hence,

as the precepts of the decalogue are, as it were, the first elements of the Law, there was no need for mention of the irascible passions, but only of the concupiscible passions.

ARTICLE 6. *Whether the Ten Precepts of the Decalogue Are Set in Proper Order?*

We proceed thus to the Sixth Article: It would seem that the ten precepts of the decalogue are not set in proper order.

Objection 1. Because love of one's neighbour seems to be prior to love of God, since our neighbour is better known to us than God is, according to I John 4. 20: *He that loveth not his brother, whom he seeth, how can he love God, Whom he seeth not?* But the first three precepts belong to the love of God, while the other seven pertain to the love of our neighbour. Therefore the precepts of the decalogue are not set in proper order.

Obj. 2. Further, acts of virtue are prescribed by the affirmative precepts, and acts of vice are forbidden by the negative precepts. But according to Boethius in his commentary on the *Categories*,[3] vices should be uprooted before virtues are sown. Therefore among the precepts concerning our neighbour, the negative precepts should have preceded the affirmative.

Obj. 3. Further, the precepts of the Law are about men's actions. But actions of thought precede actions of word or outward deed. Therefore the precepts about not coveting, which regard our thoughts, are unsuitably placed last in order.

On the contrary, The Apostle says (Rom. 13. 1): *The things that are of God, are well ordered* (Vulg.,—*Those that are, are ordained of God*). But the precepts of the decalogue were given immediately by God, as stated above (A. 3). Therefore they are arranged in fitting order.

I answer that, As stated above (AA. 3, 5, Reply 1), the precepts of the decalogue are such as the mind of man is ready to grasp at once. Now it is evident that a thing is so much the more easily grasped by the reason as its contrary is more grievous and repugnant to reason. Moreover it is clear that since the order of reason begins with the end, that, for a man to be inordinately disposed towards his end, is supremely contrary to reason. Now the end of human life and society is God. Consequently it was necessary for the precepts of the decalogue first of all, to direct man to God, since the contrary to this is most grievous. Thus also, in an army, which is ordered to the com-

---

[1] *Glossa ordin.,* on Deut. 5. 11 (I, 337A); *Glossa interl.,* on Exod. 20.7 (I, 164r); Isidore, *Quaest. in Vet. Test., In Exod.,* chap. 29, on 20.7 (PL 83, 301).

[2] *Ethics,* VIII, 12 (1161^{b}19).

[3] *In Cat. Arist.,* IV (PL 64, 277).

mander as to its end, it is requisite first that the soldier should be subject to the commander, and the opposite of this is most grievous; and secondly it is requisite that he should be in co-ordination with the other soldiers.

Now among those things by which we are ordered to God, the first is that man should be subjected to Him faithfully, by having nothing in common with His enemies. The second is that he should show Him reverence. The third that he should offer Him his service. Thus, in an army, it is a greater sin for a soldier to act treacherously and make a compact with the foe than to be insolent to his commander; and this last is more grievous than if he be found wanting in some point of service to him.

As to the precepts that direct man in his behaviour towards his neighbor, it is evident that it is more contrary to reason, and a more grievous sin, if man does not observe the due order as to those persons to whom he is most indebted. Consequently, among those precepts that direct man in his relations to his neighbour the first place is given to that one which regards his parents. Among the other precepts we again find the order to be according to the gravity of sin. For it is more grave and more contrary to reason to sin by deed than by word and by word than by thought. And among sins of deed, murder which destroys life in one already living is more grievous than adultery, which imperils the life of the unborn child; and adultery is more grave than theft, which regards external goods.

Reply Obj. 1. Although our neighbour is better known than God by the way of the senses, nevertheless the love of God is the reason for the love of our neighbour, as shall be declared later on (Part II-II, Q. XXV, A. 1; Q. XXVI, A. 2). Hence the precepts ordering man to God demanded precedence of the others.

Reply Obj. 2. Just as God is the universal principle of being in respect of all things, so is a father a principle of being in respect of his son. Therefore the precept regarding parents was fittingly placed after the precepts regarding God. This argument holds in respect of affirmative and negative precepts about the same kind of deed, although even then it is not altogether cogent. For although in the order of execution, vices should be uprooted before virtues are sown, according to Ps. 33. 15: *Turn away from evil, and do good,* and Isa. 1. 16, 17: *Cease to do perversely; learn to do well,* yet in the order of knowledge, virtue precedes vice, because "the crooked line is known by the

straight";[1] and *by the law is the knowledge of sin* (Rom. 3. 20). Hence the affirmative precept demanded the first place. However, this is not the reason for the order, but that which is given above. Because in the precepts regarding God, which belong to the first table, an affirmative precept is placed last, since its transgression implies a less grievous sin.

Reply Obj. 3. Although sin of thought stands first in the order of execution, yet its prohibition holds a later position in the order of reason.

ARTICLE 7. *Whether the Precepts of the Decalogue Are Suitably Formulated?*

We proceed thus to the Seventh Article: It would seem that the precepts of the decalogue are unsuitably formulated.

Objection 1. For the affirmative precepts direct man to acts of virtue, while the negative precepts withdraw him from acts of vice. But in every matter there are virtues and vices opposed to one another. Therefore in whatever matter there is an ordinance of a precept of the decalogue, there should have been an affirmative and a negative precept. Therefore it was unfitting that affirmative precepts should be framed in some matters, and negative precepts in others.

Obj. 2. Further, Isidore says (*Etym.* ii, 10)[2] that every law is based on reason. But all the precepts of the decalogue belong to the Divine law. Therefore the reason should have been pointed out in each precept, and not only in the first and third.

Obj. 3. Further, by observing the precepts man deserves to be rewarded by God. But the Divine promises concern the rewards of the precepts. Therefore the promise should have been included in each precept, and not only in the second and fourth.

Obj. 4. Further, the Old Law is called "the law of fear,"[3] in so far as it induced men to observe the precepts by means of the threat of punishments. But all the precepts of the decalogue belong to the Old Law. Therefore a threat of punishment should have been included in each, and not only in the first and second.

Obj. 5. Further, all the commandments of God should be retained in the memory, for it is written (Prov. 3. 3): *Write them in the tables of thy heart.* Therefore it was not fitting

---

[1] Aristotle, *Soul,* I, 5 (411ᵃ5).
[2] PL 82, 130; v, 3 (PL 82, 199).
[3] Cf. Augustine, *De Mor. Eccl.,* I, 28 (PL 32, 1334); *Contra Adimant.,* VII (PL 42, 159).

that mention of the memory should be made in the third commandment only. Consequently it seems that the precepts of the decalogue are unsuitably formulated.

On the contrary, It is written (Wisd. 11. 21) that *God made all things, in measure, number and weight.* Much more therefore did He observe a suitable manner in formulating His Law.

I answer that, The highest wisdom is contained in the precepts of the Divine law; hence it is written (Deut. 4. 6): *This is your wisdom and understanding in the sight of nations.* Now it belongs to wisdom to arrange all things in due manner and order. Therefore it must be evident that the precepts of the Law are suitably set forth.

Reply Obj. 1. Affirmation of one thing always leads to the denial of its opposite, but the denial of one opposite does not always lead to the affirmation of the other. For it follows that if a thing is white, it is not black, but it does not follow that if it is not black, it is white, because negation extends further than affirmation. And hence too, that one ought not to do harm to another, which pertains to the negative precepts, extends to more persons, as a primary dictate of reason, than that one ought to do someone a service or kindness. Nevertheless it is a primary dictate of reason that man is a debtor in the point of rendering a service or kindness to those from whom he has received kindness, if he has not yet repaid the debt. Now there are two whose favours no man can sufficiently repay, namely, God and man's father, as stated in the *Ethics.*[1] Therefore it is that there are only two affirmative precepts, one about the honour due to parents, the other about the celebration of the Sabbath in memory of the Divine favour.

Reply Obj. 2. The reasons for the purely moral precepts are manifest; hence there was no need to add the reason. But some of the precepts include ceremonial matter, or a determination of a general moral precept; thus the first precept includes the determination, *Thou shalt not make a graven thing;* and in the third precept the Sabbath-day is fixed. Consequently there was need to state the reason in each case.

Reply Obj. 3. Generally speaking men direct their actions to some point of utility. Consequently in those precepts in which it seemed that there would be no useful result, or that some utility might be hindered, it was necessary to add a promise of reward. And since parents are already on the way to depart from us, no benefit is expected from them; therefore a promise of reward is added to the precept about honouring one's parents. The same applies to the precept forbidding idolatry, since thereby it seemed that men were hindered from receiving the apparent benefit which they think they can get by entering into a compact with the demons.

Reply Obj. 4. Punishments are necessary against those who are prone to evil, as stated in the *Ethics.*[2] Therefore a threat of punishment is only affixed to those precepts of the law which forbade evils to which men were prone. Now men were prone to idolatry by reason of the general custom of the nations. Likewise men are prone to perjury on account of the frequent use of oaths. Hence it is that a threat is affixed to the first two precepts.

Reply Obj. 5. The commandment about the Sabbath was made in memory of a past blessing. Therefore special mention of the memory is made in it. Or again, the commandment about the Sabbath has a determination joined to it that does not belong to the natural law, and therefore this precept needed a special admonition.

ARTICLE 8. *Whether the Precepts of the Decalogue Are Dispensable?*

We proceed thus to the Eighth Article: It would seem that the precepts of the decalogue are dispensable.

Objection 1. For the precepts of the decalogue belong to the natural law. But the natural law fails in some cases and is changeable, like human nature, as the Philosopher says.[3] Now the failure of law to apply in certain particular cases is a reason for dispensation, as stated above (Q. XCVI, A. 6; Q. XCVII, A. 4). Therefore a dispensation can be granted in the precepts of the decalogue.

Obj. 2. Further, man stands in the same relation to human law as God does to Divine law. But man can dispense with the precepts of a law made by man. Therefore, since the precepts of the decalogue are ordained by God, it seems that God can dispense with them. Now our superiors are God's vicegerents on earth; for the Apostle says (II Cor. 2. 10): *For what I have pardoned, if I have pardoned anything, for your sakes have I done it in the person of Christ.* Therefore superiors can dispense with the precepts of the decalogue.

[1] Aristotle, VIII, 14 (1163ᵇ15).

[2] *Ibid.,* x, 9 (1180ᵃ4).

[3] *Ethics,* V, 7 (1134ᵇ29).

Obj. 3. Further, among the precepts of the decalogue is one forbidding murder. But it seems that a dispensation is given by men in this precept, for instance, when according to the prescription of human law, such men as evil-doers or enemies are lawfully slain. Therefore the precepts of the decalogue are dispensable.

Obj. 4. Further, the observance of the Sabbath is ordained by a precept of the decalogue. But a dispensation was granted in this precept, for it is written (I Machab. 2. 4): *And they determined in that day, saying: Whosoever shall come up to fight against us on the Sabbath-day, we will fight against him.* Therefore the precepts of the decalogue are dispensable.

On the contrary are the words of Isa. 24. 5, where some are reproved for that *they have changed the ordinance, they have broken the everlasting covenant,* which, it seems, applies principally to the precepts of the decalogue. Therefore the precepts of the decalogue cannot be changed by dispensation.

I answer that, As stated above (*loc. cit.* cf. obj. 1), precepts admit of dispensation when there occurs a particular case in which, if the letter of the law be observed, the intention of the lawgiver is frustrated. Now the intention of every lawgiver is directed first and chiefly to the common good; secondly, to the order of justice and virtue, whereby the common good is preserved and attained. If therefore there be any precepts which contain the very preservation of the common good, or the very order of justice and virtue, such precepts contain the intention of the lawgiver, and therefore are indispensable. For instance, if in some community a law were enacted, such as this,— that no man should work for the destruction of the commonwealth, or betray the state to its enemies, or that no man should do anything unjust or evil, such precepts would not admit of dispensation. But if other precepts were enacted, subordinate to the above, and determining certain special modes of procedure, these latter precepts would admit of dispensation, in so far as the omission of these precepts in certain cases would not be prejudicial to the former precepts which contain the intention of the lawgiver. For instance if, for the safeguarding of the commonwealth, it were enacted in some city that from each ward some men should keep watch as sentries in case of siege, some might be dispensed from this on account of some greater utility.

Now the precepts of the decalogue contain the very intention of the lawgiver, who is God. For the precepts of the first table, which direct us to God, contain the very order to the common and final good, which is God; while the precepts of the second table contain the order of justice to be observed among men, that nothing undue be done to anyone, and that each one be given his due; for it is in this sense that we are to take the precepts of the decalogue. Consequently the precepts of the decalogue admit of no dispensation whatever.

Reply Obj. 1. The Philosopher is not speaking of the natural law which contains the very order of justice, for it is a never-failing principle that justice should be preserved. But he is speaking in reference to certain fixed modes of observing justice, which fail to apply in certain cases.

Reply Obj. 2. As the Apostle says (II Tim. 2. 13), God *continueth faithful, He cannot deny Himself.* But He would deny Himself if He were to do away with the very order of His own justice, since He is justice itself. Therefore God cannot dispense a man so that it be lawful for him not to direct himself to God, or not to be subject to His justice, even in those matters in which men are directed to one another.

Reply Obj. 3. The slaying of a man is forbidden in the decalogue in so far as it bears the character of something undue, for in this sense the precept contains the very essence of justice. Human law cannot make it lawful for a man to be slain unduly. But it is not undue for evil-doers or foes of the commonwealth to be slain; hence this is not contrary to the precept of the decalogue, and such a killing is no murder as forbidden by that precept, as Augustine observes (*De Lib. Arb.* i, 4).[1] In like manner when a man's property is taken from him, if it be due that he should lose it this is not theft or robbery as forbidden by the decalogue.

Consequently when the children of Israel, by God's command, took away the spoils of the Egyptians (Exod. 12. 35), this was not theft, since it was due to them by the sentence of God.—Likewise when Abraham consented to slay his son (Gen. 22), he did not consent to murder, because his son was due to be slain by the command of God, Who is Lord of life and death. For He it is Who inflicts the punishment of death on all men, both godly and ungodly, on account of the sin of our first parent, and if a man be the executor of that sentence by Divine authority, he will be no mur-

[1] PL 32, 1226.

derer any more than God would be. Again Osee, by taking unto himself a wife of fornications, or an adulterous woman (Osee 1, 2), was not guilty either of adultery or of fornication, because he took unto himself one who was his by command of God, Who is the Author of the institution of marriage.

Accordingly, therefore, the precepts of the decalogue, as to the notion of justice which they contain, are unchangeable; but as to any determination by application to individual actions—for instance that this or that be murder, theft, or adultery, or not—in this point they admit of change; sometimes by Divine authority alone, namely, in such matters as are exclusively of Divine institution, as marriage and the like; sometimes also by human authority, namely in such matters as are subject to human jurisdiction; for in this respect men stand in the place of God, but not in all respects.

Reply Obj. 4. This determination was an interpretation rather than a dispensation. For a man is not taken to break the Sabbath if he does something necessary for human welfare, as Our Lord proves (Matt. 12. 3 *seq.*).

ARTICLE 9. *Whether the Mode of Virtue Falls Under the Precept of the Law?*

We proceed thus to the Ninth Article: It would seem that the mode of virtue falls under the precept of the law.

Objection 1. For the mode of virtue is that deeds of justice should be done justly, that deeds of fortitude should be done bravely, and in like manner as to the other virtues. But it is commanded (Deut. 16. 20) that *thou shalt follow justly after that which is just.* Therefore the mode of virtue falls under the precept.

Obj. 2. Further, that which belongs to the intention of the lawgiver comes chiefly under the precept. But the intention of the lawgiver is directed chiefly to make men virtuous, as stated in the *Ethics,*[1] and it belongs to a virtuous man to act virtuously. Therefore the mode of virtue falls under the precept.

Obj. 3. Further, the mode of virtue seems to consist properly in working willingly and with pleasure. But this falls under a precept of the Divine law, for it is written (Ps. 99. 2): *Serve ye the Lord with gladness;* and (II Cor. 9. 7): *Not with sadness or necessity: for God loveth a cheerful giver;* on which the gloss says:[2] "Whatever ye do, do gladly, and then you will

do it well; but if you do it sorrowfully, it is done in thee, not by thee." Therefore the mode of virtue falls under the precept of the law.

On the contrary, No man can act as a virtuous man acts unless he has the habit of virtue, as the Philosopher explains.[3] Now whoever transgresses a precept of the law deserves to be punished. Hence it would follow that a man who has not the habit of virtue would deserve to be punished, whatever he does. But this is contrary to the intention of the law, which aims at leading man to virtue, by habituating him to good works. Therefore the mode of virtue does not fall under the precept.

I answer that, As stated above (Q. XC, A. 3, REPLY 2), a precept of law has constraining power. Hence that on which the compulsion of the law is brought to bear falls directly under the precept of the law. Now the law compels through fear of punishment, as stated in the *Ethics,*[4] because that properly falls under the precept of the law for which the penalty of the law is inflicted. But Divine law and human law are differently situated as to the appointment of penalties, since the penalty of the law is inflicted only for those things which come under the judgment of the lawgiver; for the law punishes in accordance with the verdict given. Now man, the framer of human law is able to judge only of outward acts, because *man seeth those things that appear,* according to I Kings 16. 7; but God alone, the framer of the Divine law, is able to judge of the inward movements of wills, according to Ps. 7. 10: *The searcher of hearts and reins is God.*

Accordingly, therefore, we must say that the mode of virtue is in some sort regarded both by human and by Divine law; in some respect it is regarded by the Divine, but not by the human law; and in another way, it is regarded neither by the human nor by the Divine law. Now the mode of virtue consists in three things, as the Philosopher states in the *Ethics.*[5] The first is that man should act "knowingly", and this is subject to the judgment of both Divine and human law, because what a man does in ignorance he does accidentally. Hence according to both human and Divine law, certain things are judged in respect of ignorance to be punishable or pardonable.

The second point is that a man should act "deliberately, that is, from choice, choosing that particular action for its own sake," where a

---

[1] Aristotle, II, 1 (1103ᵇ3).
[2] *Glossa ordin.* (III 226A); on II Cor. 9.7 (VI, 72A); Augustine, *Ennar. in Psalm.* (PL 37, 1174).

[3] *Ethics,* II, 4 (1105ᵃ17); V, 8 (1135ᵇ24).
[4] Aristotle, X, 9 (1179ᵇ11).
[5] Aristotle, II, 4 (1105ᵃ31).

twofold internal movement is implied, of volition and of intention, about which we have spoken above (QQ. VIII, XII); and concerning these two, Divine law alone, and not human law, is able to judge. For human law does not punish the man who wishes to slay but slays not, whereas the Divine law does, according to Matt. 5. 22: *Whosoever is angry with his brother, shall be in danger of the judgment.*

The third point is that he should "act from a firm and immovable principle," which firmness belongs properly to a habit, and implies that the action proceeds from a rooted habit. In this respect, the mode of virtue does not fall under the precept either of Divine or of human law, since neither by man nor by God is he punished as breaking the law who gives due honour to his parents and yet has not the habit of filial piety.

Reply Obj. 1. The mode of doing acts of justice, which falls under the precept, is that they be done in accordance with right, but not that they be done from the habit of justice.

Reply Obj. 2. The intention of the lawgiver is twofold. His aim, in the first place, is to lead men to something by the precepts of the law, and this is virtue. Secondly, his intention is brought to bear on the matter itself of the precept, and this is something leading or disposing to virtue, namely, an act of virtue. For the end of the precept and the matter of the precept are not the same, just as neither in other things is the end the same as the means to the end.

Reply Obj. 3. That works of virtue should be done without sadness falls under the precept of the Divine law, for whoever works with sadness works unwillingly. But to work with pleasure, that is, joyfully or cheerfully, in one respect falls under the precept, namely, in so far as pleasure ensues from the love of God and one's neighbour (which love falls under the precept), and love causes pleasure; and in another respect it does not fall under the precept, in so far as pleasure ensues from a habit; for "pleasure taken in a work proves the existence of a habit," as stated in the *Ethics*.[1] For an act may give pleasure either on account of its end, or through its proceeding from an appropriate habit.

ARTICLE 10. *Whether the Mode of Charity Falls Under the Precept of the Divine Law?*

We proceed thus to the Tenth Article: It would seem that the mode of charity falls under the precept of the Divine law.

[1] Aristotle, II, 3 (1104[b]3).

Objection 1. For it is written (Matt. 19. 17): *If thou wilt enter into life, keep the commandments.* From this it seems to follow that the observance of the commandments suffices for entrance into life. But good works do not suffice for entrance into life unless they are done from charity, for it is written (I Cor. 13. 3): *If I should distribute all my goods to feed the poor, and if I should deliver my body to be burned, and have not charity, it profiteth me nothing.* Therefore the mode of charity is included in the commandment.

Obj. 2. Further, the mode of charity consists, properly speaking, in doing all things for God. But this falls under the precept, for the Apostle says (I Cor. 10. 31): *Do all to the glory of God.* Therefore the mode of charity falls under the precept.

Obj. 3. Further, if the mode of charity does not fall under the precept, it follows that one can fulfil the precepts of the law without having charity. Now what can be done without charity can be done without grace, which is always united with charity. Therefore one can fulfil the precepts of the law without grace. But this is the error of Pelagius, as Augustine declares (*De Hæres.* lxxxviii).[2] Therefore the mode of charity is included in the commandment.

On the contrary, Whoever breaks a commandment sins mortally. If therefore the mode of charity falls under the precept, it follows that whoever acts otherwise than from charity sins mortally. But whoever has not charity acts otherwise than from charity. Therefore it follows that whoever has not charity sins mortally in whatever he does, however good this may be in itself, which is absurd.

I answer that, Opinions have been contrary on this question.[3] For some have said absolutely that the mode of charity comes under the precept, and yet that it is possible for one not having charity to fulfil this precept, because he can dispose himself to receive charity from God. Nor (they say) does it follow that a man not having charity sins mortally whenever he does something good of its kind, because it is an affirmative precept that binds one to act from charity, and is binding not for all time, but only for such time as one is in a state of charity. On the other hand, some have said that the mode of charity is altogether outside the precept.

Both these opinions are true up to a certain point. Because the act of charity can be consid-

[2] PL 42, 47.
[3] Cf. Albert the Great, *In Sent.*, III, d. 36, A. 6 (BO XXVIII, 677).

ered in two ways. First, as an act by itself, and thus it falls under the precept of the law which specially prescribes it, namely, *Thou shalt love the Lord thy God, and Thou shalt love thy neighbour.* In this sense, the first opinion is true. Because it is not impossible to observe this precept which regards the act of charity, since man can dispose himself to possess charity, and when he possesses it, he can use it. Secondly, the act of charity can be considered as being the mode of the acts of the other virtues, that is, according as the acts of the other virtues are ordered to charity, which is *the end of the commandment,* as stated in I Tim. 1. 5; for it has been said above (Q. XXI, A. 1, Reply 3; A. 4, Reply 3) that the intention of the end is a formal mode of the act ordered to that end. In this sense the second opinion is true in saying that the mode of charity does not fall under the precept, that is to say that this commandment, *Honour thy father,* does not mean that a man must honour his father from charity, but merely that he must honour him. Therefore he that honours his father, yet has not charity, does not break this precept, although he does break the precept concerning the act of charity, for which reason he deserves to be punished.

Reply Obj. 1. Our Lord did not say, *If thou wilt enter into life, keep one commandment,* but *keep* all *the commandments,* among which is included the commandment concerning the love of God and our neighbour.

Reply Obj. 2. The precept of charity contains the injunction that God should be loved from our whole heart, which means that all things would be referred to God. Consequently man cannot fulfil the precept of charity unless he also refer all things to God. Therefore he that honours his father and mother is bound to honour them from charity, not in virtue of the precept, *Honour thy father and mother,* but in virtue of the precept, *Thou shalt love the Lord thy God with thy whole heart.* And since these are two affirmative precepts not binding for all times, they can be binding each one at a different time, so that it may happen that a man fulfils the precept of honouring his father and mother without at the same time breaking the precept concerning the omission of the mode of charity.

Reply Obj. 3. Man cannot fulfil all the precepts of the law unless he fulfil the precept of charity, which is impossible without charity. Consequently it is not possible, as Pelagius maintained, for man to fulfil the law without grace.

ARTICLE 11. *Whether It Is Right to Distinguish Other Moral Precepts of the Law Besides the Decalogue?*

We proceed thus to the Eleventh Article: It would seem that it is wrong to distinguish other moral precepts of the law besides the decalogue.

Objection 1. Because, as Our Lord declared (Matt. 21. 40), *on these two commandments* of charity *dependeth the whole law and the prophets.* But these two commandments are explained by the ten commandments of the decalogue. Therefore there is no need for other precepts.

Obj. 2. Further, the moral precepts are distinct from the judicial and ceremonial precepts, as stated above (Q. XCIX, AA. 3, 4). But the determinations of the general moral precepts pertain to the judicial and ceremonial precepts, and the general moral precepts are contained in the decalogue, or are even presupposed to the decalogue, as stated above (A. 3). Therefore it was unsuitable to lay down other moral precepts besides the decalogue.

Obj. 3. Further, the moral precepts are about the acts of all the virtues, as stated above (A. 2). Therefore, as the Law contains, besides the decalogue, moral precepts pertaining to religion, liberality, mercy, and chastity, so there should have been added some precepts pertaining to the other virtues, for instance, fortitude, sobriety, and so forth. And yet such is not the case. It is therefore not right to distinguish other moral precepts in the Law besides those of the decalogue.

On the contrary, It is written (Ps. 18. 8): *The law of the Lord is unspotted, converting souls.* But man is preserved from the stain of sin and his soul is converted to God by other moral precepts besides those of the decalogue. Therefore it was right for the Law to include other moral precepts.

I answer that, As is evident from what has been stated (Q. XCIX, A. 3), the judicial and ceremonial precepts derive their force from their institution alone, since before they were instituted it seemed of no consequence whether things were done in this or that way. But the moral precepts derive their efficacy from the very dictate of natural reason, even if they were never included in the Law. Now of these there are three grades: for some are most certain, and so evident as to need no promulgation. Such as the commandments of the love of God and our neighbour, and others like these, as stated above (A. 3, A. 4, Reply 1), which are, as it were, the ends of the commandments. Hence no man can have an erroneous judgment about them. Some precepts are more detailed, the reason of which even an uneducated man can easily grasp. And yet they need to be promulgated, because human judgment, in a few instances, happens to be led astray concerning them. These are the precepts of the decalogue. Again, there are some precepts the reason of which is not so evident to everyone, but only to the wise. These are moral precepts added to the decalogue, and given to the people by God through Moses and Aaron.

But since the things that are evident are the principles by which we know those that are not evident, these other moral precepts added to the decalogue are reducible to the precepts of the decalogue, as so many corollaries. Thus the first commandment of the decalogue forbids the worship of strange gods, and to this are added other precepts forbidding things relating to the worship of idols; thus it is written (Deut. 18. 10, 11): *Neither let there be found among you anyone that shall expiate his son or daughter, making them to pass through the fire: . . . neither let there be any wizard nor charmer, nor anyone that consulteth pythonic spirits, or fortune-tellers, or that seeketh the truth from the dead*. The second commandment forbids perjury. To this is added the prohibition of blasphemy (Levit. 24. 15 *seq*.) and the prohibition of false doctrine (Deut. 13.). To the third commandment are added all the ceremonial precepts. To the fourth commandment prescribing the honour due to parents is added the precept about honouring the aged, according to Levit. 19. 32: *Rise up before the hoary head, and honour the person of the aged man*, and likewise all precepts prescribing the reverence to be observed towards our betters, or kindliness towards our equals or inferiors. To the fifth commandment, which forbids murder, is added the prohibition of hatred and of any kind of violence inflicted on our neighbour, according to Levit. 19. 16: *Thou shalt not stand against the blood of thy neighbour; likewise* the prohibition against hating one's brother (*ibid*. 17): *Thou shalt not hate thy brother in thy heart*. To the sixth commandment which forbids adultery, is added the prohibition about whoredom, according to Deut. 23. 17: *There shall be no whore among the daughters of Israel, nor whoremonger among the sons of Israel;* and the prohibition against unnatural sins, according to Levit 18. 22, 23: *Thou shalt not lie with mankind . . . thou shalt not copulate with any beast*.

To the seventh commandment which prohibits theft, is added the precept forbidding usury, according to Deut. 23. 19: *Thou shalt not lend to thy brother money to usury;* and the prohibition against fraud, according to Deut. 25. 13: *Thou shalt not have divers weights in thy bag;* and universally all prohibitions relating to peculations and larceny. To the eighth commandment, forbidding false testimony, is added the prohibition against false judgment, according to Exod. 23. 2: *Neither shalt thou yield in judgment, to the opinion of the most part, to stray from the truth;* and the prohibition against lying (*ibid*. 7): *Thou shalt fly lying;* and the prohibition against detraction, according to Levit. 19. 16: *Thou shalt not be a detractor, nor a whisperer among the people*. To the other two commandments no further precepts are added, because they forbid all kinds of evil desires.

Reply Obj. 1. The precepts of the decalogue are ordered to the love of God and our neighbour as pertaining evidently to our duty towards them; but the other precepts are so ordered as pertaining to them less evidently.

Reply Obj. 2. It is in virtue of their institution that the ceremonial and judicial precepts are determinations of the precepts of the decalogue, not by reason of a natural instinct, as in the case of the superadded moral precepts.

Reply Obj. 3. The precepts of a law are ordered for the common good, as stated above (Q. XC, A. 2). And since those virtues which direct our conduct towards others pertain directly to the common good, as also does the virtue of chastity, in so far as the generative act conduces to the common good of the species, hence precepts bearing directly on these virtues are given, both in the decalogue and in addition to it. As to the act of fortitude there are the orders to be given by the commanders in the war, which is undertaken for the common good, as is clear from Deut. 20. 3, where the priest is commanded (to speak thus): *Be not afraid, do not give back*. In like manner the prohibition of acts of gluttony is left to paternal admonition, since it is contrary to the good of the household; hence it is said (Deut. 21. 20) in the person of parents: *He slighteth hearing our admonitions, he giveth himself to revelling, and to debauchery and banquetings*.

ARTICLE 12. *Whether the Moral Precepts of the Old Law Justified Man?*

We proceed thus to the Twelfth Article: It would seem that the moral precepts of the Old Law justified man.

Objection 1. Because the Apostle says (Rom. 2. 13): *For not the hearers of the Law are justified before God, but the doers of the Law shall be justified.* But the doers of the Law are those who fulfil the precepts of the Law. Therefore the fulfilling of the precepts of the Law was a cause of justification.

Obj. 2. Further, it is written (Levit. 18. 5): *Keep My laws and My judgments, which if a man do, he shall live in them.* But the spiritual life of man is through justice. Therefore the fulfilling of the precepts of the Law was a cause of justification.

Obj. 3. Further, the Divine law is more efficacious than human law. But human law justifies man, since there is a kind of justice consisting in fulfilling the precepts of law. Therefore the precepts of the Law justified man.

On the contrary, The Apostle says (II Cor. 3. 6): *The letter killeth,* which, according to Augustine (*De Spir. et Lit.* xiv),[1] refers even to the moral precepts. Therefore the moral precepts did not cause justice.

I answer that, Just as healthy is said properly and first of that which is possessed of health, and secondarily of that which is a sign or a safeguard of health, so justification means first and properly the causing of justice, while secondarily and improperly, as it were, it may denote a sign of justice or a disposition to justice. If justice be taken in the last two ways it is evident that it was conferred by the precepts of the Law, in so far, that is, as they disposed men to the justifying grace of Christ, which they also signified, because as Augustine says (*Contra Faust.* xxii, 24),[2] "even the life of that people foretold and foreshadowed Christ."

But if we speak of justification properly so called, then we must notice that it can be considered as it exists in the habit or in the act, so that accordingly justification may be taken in two ways. First, according as man is made just by becoming possessed of the habit of justice; secondly, according as he does works of justice, so that in this sense justification is nothing else than the execution of justice. Now justice, like the other virtues, may denote either the acquired or the infused virtue, as is clear from what has been stated (Q. LXIII, A. 4). The acquired virtue is caused by works; but the infused virtue is caused by God Himself through His grace. The latter is true justice, of which we are speaking now, and in respect of which a man is said to be just before God, according

to Rom. 4. 2: *If Abraham were justified by works, he hath whereof to glory, but not before God.* Hence this justice could not be caused by the moral precepts, which are about human actions. Therefore the moral precepts could not justify man by causing justice.

If, on the other hand, by justification we understand the execution of justice, thus all the precepts of the Law justified man, but in various ways. For the ceremonial precepts taken as a whole contained something just in itself, in so far as they aimed at offering worship to God; but taken individually they contained that which is just, not in itself, but by being a determination of the Divine law. Hence it is said of these precepts that they did not justify man save through the devotion and obedience of those who complied with them. On the other hand the moral and judicial precepts, either in general or also in particular, contained that which is just in itself; but the moral precepts contained that which is just in itself according to that general justice which is every virtue according to the *Ethics*,[3] while the judicial precepts pertained to special justice, which is about contracts connected with the human mode of life, between one man and another.

Reply Obj. 1. The Apostle takes justification for the execution of justice.

Reply Obj. 2. The man who fulfilled the precepts of the Law is said to live in them because he did not incur the penalty of death, which the Law inflicted on its transgressors. The Apostle quotes this passage in this sense (Gal. 3. 12).

Reply Obj. 3. The precepts of human law justify man by acquired justice; it is not about this that we are inquiring now, but only about that justice which is before God.

QUESTION CI

OF THE CEREMONIAL PRECEPTS IN THEMSELVES

(In Four Articles)

WE must now consider the ceremonial precepts. And first we must consider them in themselves; secondly, their cause (Q. CII); thirdly, their duration (Q. CIII). Under the first head there are four points of inquiry: (1) The nature of the ceremonial precepts; (2) Whether they are figurative? (3) Whether there should have been many of them? (4) Of their various kinds.

---

[1] PL 44, 215.
[2] PL 42, 417.

[3] Aristotle, v, 1 (1129[b]30).

ARTICLE 1. *Whether the Nature of the Ceremonial Precepts Consists in Their Pertaining to the Worship of God?*

We proceed thus to the First Article: It would seem that the nature of the ceremonial precepts does not consist in their pertaining to the worship of God.[1]

Objection 1. Because, in the Old Law, the Jews were given certain precepts about abstinence from food (Levit. 11.) and about refraining from certain kinds of clothes, for example (Levit. 19. 19): *Thou shalt not wear a garment that is woven of two sorts;* and again (Num. 15. 38): *To make to themselves fringes in the corners of their garments.* But these are not moral precepts, since they do not remain in the New Law. Nor are they judicial precepts, since they do not pertain to the pronouncing of judgment between man and man. Therefore they are ceremonial precepts. Yet they seem in no way to pertain to the worship of God. Therefore the nature of the ceremonial precepts does not consist in their pertaining to Divine Worship.

Obj. 2. Further, some state that the ceremonial precepts are those which pertain to solemnities, as though they were so called from the *cerei* (candles) which are lit up on those occasions.[2] But many other things besides solemnities pertain to the worship of God. Therefore it does not seem that the ceremonial precepts are so called from their pertaining to the Divine worship.

Obj. 3. Further, some say that the ceremonial precepts are norms, that is, rules, of salvation, because the Greek χαίρε is the same as the Latin *salve.* But all the precepts of the Law are rules of salvation, and not only those that pertain to the worship of God. Therefore not only those precepts which pertain to the Divine worship are called ceremonial.

Obj. 4. Further, Rabbi Moses says (*Doct. Perplex.* iii)[3] that "the ceremonial precepts are those for which there is no evident reason." But there is evident reason for many things pertaining to the worship of God, such as the observance of the Sabbath, the feasts of the Passover and of the Tabernacles, and many other things, the reason for which is set down in the Law. Therefore the ceremonial precepts

are not those which pertain to the worship of God.

On the contrary, It is written (Exod. 18. 19, 20): *Be thou to the people in those things that pertain to God . . . and . . . shew the people the ceremonies and the manner of worshipping.*

I answer that, As stated above (Q. XCIX, A. 4), the ceremonial precepts are determinations of the moral precepts by which man is directed to God, just as the judicial precepts are determinations of the moral precepts by which he is directed to his neighbour. Now man is directed to God by the worship due to Him. Therefore those precepts are properly called ceremonial which pertain to the Divine worship. The reason for their being called so was given above (*ibid.,* A. 3), when we established the distinction between the ceremonial and the other precepts.

Reply Obj. 1. The Divine worship includes not only sacrifices and the like, which seem to be directed to God immediately, but also those things by which His worshippers are duly prepared to worship Him; thus too in other matters, whatever is preparatory to the end comes under the science whose object is the end. Accordingly those precepts of the Law which regard the clothing and food of God's worshippers, and other such matters, pertain to a certain preparation of the ministers, with the view of fitting them for the Divine worship, just as those who administer to a king make use of certain special observances. Consequently such are contained under the ceremonial precepts.

Reply Obj. 2. The alleged explanation of the name does not seem very probable, especially as the Law does not contain many instances of the lighting of candles in solemnities, since even the lamps of the Candlestick were furnished with *oil of olives,* as stated in Levit. 24. 2. Nevertheless we may say that all things pertaining to the Divine worship were more carefully observed on solemn festivals, so that all ceremonial precepts may be included under the observance of solemnities.

Reply Obj. 3. Neither does this explanation of the name appear to be very much to the point, since the word "ceremony" is not Greek but Latin. We may say, however, that, since man's salvation is from God those precepts above all seem to be rules of salvation which direct man to God. And accordingly those which refer to Divine worship are called ceremonial precepts.

Reply Obj. 4. This explanation of the ceremonial precepts has a certain amount of prob-

---

[1] Cf. Albert the Great, *In Sent.,* IV, d. 1, A. 7 (BO XXIX, 19); Cicero, *De Nat. Deor.,* II, 28 (DD IV, 124); *De Invent.,* II, 53 (DD I, 165).

[2] Albert, *In Sent.,* IV, d. 1, A. 7 (BO XXIX, 18).

[3] Chap. 28 (FR 314).

ability; not that they are called ceremonial precisely because there is no evident reason for them, but rather this is a kind of consequence. For since the precepts referring to the Divine worship must be figurative, as we shall state further on (A. 2), the consequence is that the reason for them is not so very evident.

ARTICLE 2. *Whether the Ceremonial Precepts Are Figurative?*

We proceed thus to the Second Article: It would seem that the ceremonial precepts are not figurative.

Objection 1. For it is the duty of every teacher to express himself in such a way as to be easily understood, as Augustine states,[1] and this seems very necessary in the framing of a law because precepts of law are proposed to the populace, for which reason "a law should be manifest," as Isidore declares (*Etym.* v, 21).[2] If therefore the precepts of the Law were given as figures of something, it seems unfitting that Moses should have delivered these precepts without explaining what they signified.

Obj. 2. Further, whatever is done for the worship of God, should be entirely free from unfittingness. But the performance of actions in representation of others seems to savour of the theatre or of poetry, because formerly the actions performed in theatres were done to represent the actions of others. Therefore it seems that such things should not be done for the worship of God. But the ceremonial precepts are ordained to the Divine worship, as stated above (A. 1). Therefore they should not be figurative.

Obj. 3. Further, Augustine says (*Enchirid.* iii, iv)[3] that "God is worshipped chiefly by faith, hope, and charity." But the precepts of faith, hope and charity are not figurative. Therefore the ceremonial precepts should not be figurative.

Obj. 4. Further, Our Lord said (John 4. 24): *God is a spirit, and they that adore Him, must adore Him in spirit and in truth.* But a figure is not the very truth: in fact one is divided against the other. Therefore the ceremonial precepts, which refer to the Divine worship, should not be figurative.

On the contrary, The Apostle says (Coloss. 2. 16, 17): *Let no man . . . judge you in meat or in drink, or in respect of a festival day, or of the new moon, or of the sabbaths, which are a shadow of things to come.*

I answer that, As stated above (A. 1; Q. XCIX, AA. 3, 4), the ceremonial precepts are those which refer to the worship of God. Now the Divine worship is twofold: interior, and external. For since man is composed of soul and body, each of these should be applied to the worship of God, the soul by an interior worship, the body by an outward worship; hence it is written (Ps. 83. 3): *My heart and my flesh have rejoiced in the living God.* And as the body is ordered to God through the soul so the outward worship is ordered to the internal worship. Now interior worship consists in the soul being united to God by the intellect and affections. Therefore according to the various ways in which the intellect and affections of the man who worships God are rightly united to God, his external actions are applied in various ways to the Divine worship.

For in the state of future happiness, the human intellect will gaze on the Divine Truth in Itself. Therefore the external worship will not consist in anything figurative, but solely in the praise of God, proceeding from the inward knowledge and affection, according to Isa. 51. 3: *Joy and gladness shall be found therein, thanksgiving and the voice of praise.*

But in the present state of life we are unable to gaze upon the Divine Truth in Itself, and we need the ray of Divine light to shine upon us under the form of certain sensible figures, as Dionysius states; in various ways, however, according to the various states of human knowledge. For under the Old Law, neither was the Divine Truth manifest in Itself, nor was the way leading to that manifestation as yet opened out, as the Apostle declares (Heb. 9. 8). Hence the external worship of the Old Law needed to be figurative not only of the future truth to be manifested in our heavenly country, but also of Christ, Who is the way leading to that heavenly truth. But under the New Law this way is already revealed, and therefore it needs no longer to be foreshadowed as something future, but to be brought to our minds as something past or present; and the truth of the glory to come, which is not yet revealed, alone needs to be foreshadowed. This is what the Apostle says (Heb. 10. 1): *The Law has* (Vulg., —*having*) *a shadow of the good things to come, not the very image of the things,* for a shadow is less than an image, so that the image belongs to the New Law, but the shadow to the Old.

---

[1] *Christian Doctrine,* IV, 8, 10 (PL 34, 98, 99).
[2] PL 82, 203; II, 10 (PL 82, 131).
[3] PL 40, 232, 233.

Reply Obj. 1. The things of God are not to be revealed to man except in proportion to his capacity, otherwise he would be in danger of downfall, were he to despise what he cannot grasp. Hence it was more beneficial that the Divine mysteries should be revealed to primitive people under a veil of figures that thus they might know them at least implicitly by using those figures to the honour of God.

Reply Obj. 2. Just as human reason fails to grasp poetical expressions because they are lacking in truth, so does it fail to grasp Divine things perfectly on account of the sublimity of the truth they contain. And therefore in both cases there is need of signs by means of sensible figures.

Reply Obj. 3. Augustine is speaking there of internal worship, to which, however, external worship should be ordered, as stated above.

The same answer applies to the *Fourth Objection,* because men were taught by Christ to practise more perfectly the spiritual worship of God.

ARTICLE 3. *Whether There Should Have Been Many Ceremonial Precepts?*

We proceed thus to the Third Article: It would seem that there should not have been many ceremonial precepts.

Objection 1. For those things which lead to an end should be proportionate to that end. But the ceremonial precepts, as stated above (AA. 1, 2), are ordered to the worship of God, and to the foreshadowing of Christ. Now *there is but one God, of Whom are all things, . . . and one Lord Jesus Christ, by Whom are all things* (I Cor. 8. 6). Therefore there should not have been many ceremonial precepts.

Obj. 2. Further, the great number of the ceremonial precepts was an occasion of transgression, according to the words of Peter (Acts 15. 10): *Why tempt you God, to put a yoke upon the necks of the disciples, which neither our fathers nor we have been able to bear?* Now the transgression of the Divine precepts is an obstacle to man's salvation. Since, therefore, every law should conduce to man's salvation, as Isidore says (*Etym.* v, 3),[1] it seems that the ceremonial precepts should not have been given in great number.

Obj. 3. Further, the ceremonial precepts referred to the outward and bodily worship of God, as stated above (A. 2). But the Law should have lessened this bodily worship: since it directed men to Christ, Who taught them to

[1] PL 82, 199; II, 10 (PL 82, 199).

worship God *in spirit and in truth,* as stated in John 4. 23. Therefore there should not have been many ceremonial precepts.

On the contrary, It is written (Osee 8. 12): *I shall write to them* (Vulg.,—*him*) *My manifold laws;* and (Job 11. 6): *That He might show thee the secrets of His wisdom, and that His Law is manifold.*

I answer that, As stated above (Q. XCVI., A. 1) every law is given to a people. Now a people contains two kinds of men. Some are prone to evil, and have to be coerced by the precepts of the law, as stated above (Q. XCV, A. 1); some are inclined to good, either from nature or from custom, or rather from grace, and these have to be taught and improved by means of the precepts of the law. Accordingly, with regard to both kinds of men it was expedient that the Old Law should contain many ceremonial precepts. For in that people there were many prone to idolatry, and therefore it was necessary to recall them by means of ceremonial precepts from the worship of idols to the worship of God. And since men served idols in many ways, it was necessary on the other hand to devise many means of repressing every single one; and again, to lay many obligations on such men in order that being burdened, as it were, by their duties to the Divine worship, they might have no time for the service of idols. As to those who were inclined to good, it was again necessary that there should be many ceremonial precepts; both because thus their mind was turned to God in many ways, and more diligently, and because the mystery of Christ, which was foreshadowed by these ceremonial precepts, brought many benefits to the world, and afforded men many considerations, which needed to be signified by various ceremonies.

Reply Obj. 1. When that which is ordered to an end is sufficient to lead to it, then one such thing suffices for one end; thus one remedy, if it be efficacious, suffices sometimes to restore man to health, and then the remedy needs not to be repeated. But when that which conduces to an end is weak and imperfect, it needs to be multiplied: thus many remedies are given to a sick man when one is not enough to heal him. Now the ceremonies of the Old Law were weak and imperfect, both for representing the mystery of Christ, on account of its surpassing excellence, and for subjugating men's minds to God. Hence the Apostle says (Heb. 7. 18, 19): *There is a setting aside of the former commandment because of the weakness and unprofitableness thereof, for the law brought nothing to perfection.* Consequently these ceremonies needed to be in great number.

Reply Obj. 2. A wise lawgiver should suffer lesser transgressions that the greater may be avoided. And therefore, in order to avoid the sin of idolatry, and the pride which would arise in the hearts of the Jews were they to fulfil all the precepts of the Law, the fact that they would in consequence find many occasions of disobedience did not prevent God from giving them many ceremonial precepts.

Reply Obj. 3. The Old Law lessened bodily worship in many ways. Thus it forbade sacrifices to be offered in every place and by any person. Many such things did it enact for the lessening of bodily worship, as Rabbi Moses, the Egyptian testifies (*Doct. Perplex.* iii).[1] Nevertheless it was necessary not to attenuate the bodily worship of God so much as to allow men to fall away into the worship of idols.

ARTICLE 4. *Whether the Ceremonies of the Old Law Are Suitably Divided into Sacrifices, Sacred Things, Sacraments, and Observances?*

We proceed thus to the Fourth Article: It would seem that the ceremonies of the Old Law are unsuitably divided into *sacrifices, sacred things, sacraments and observances.*[2]

Objection 1. For the ceremonies of the Old Law foreshadowed Christ. But this was done only by the sacrifices, which foreshadowed the sacrifice in which Christ *delivered Himself an oblation and a sacrifice to God* (Eph. 5. 2). Therefore none but the sacrifices were ceremonies.

Obj. 2. Further, the Old Law was ordered to the New. But in the New Law the sacrifice is the Sacrament of the Altar. Therefore in the Old Law there should be no distinction between sacrifices and sacraments.

Obj. 3. Further, a sacred thing is something dedicated to God, in which sense the tabernacle and its vessels were said to be consecrated. But all the ceremonial precepts were ordained to the worship of God, as stated above (A. 1). Therefore all ceremonies were sacred things. Therefore sacred things should not be taken as a part of the ceremonies.

Obj. 4. Further, Observances are so called from having to be observed. But all the precepts of the Law had to be observed, for it is written (Deut. 8. 11): *Observe* (Douay,—*Take heed*) *and beware lest at any time thou forget the Lord thy God, and neglect His commandments*

and *judgments and ceremonies.* Therefore the observances should not be considered as a part of the ceremonies.

Obj. 5. Further, the solemn festivals are reckoned as part of the ceremonial, since they were a shadow of things to come (Coloss. 2. 16, 17): and the same may be said of the oblations and gifts, as appears from the words of the Apostle (Heb. 9. 9); and yet these do not seem to be included in any of those mentioned above. Therefore the above division of ceremonies is unsuitable.

On the contrary, In the Old Law each of the above is called a ceremony. For the sacrifices are called ceremonies (Num. 15. 24): *They shall offer a calf . . . and the sacrifices and libations thereof, as the ceremonies require.* Of the sacrament of Order it is written (Levit. 7. 35): *This is the anointing of Aaron and his sons in the ceremonies.* Of sacred things also it is written (Exod. 38. 21): *These are the instruments of the tabernacle of the testimony . . . in the ceremonies of the Levites.* And again of the observances it is written (III Kings 9. 6): *If you . . . shall turn away from following Me, and will not observe* (Douay,—*keep*) *My . . . ceremonies which I have set before you.*

I answer that, As stated above (AA. 1, 2), the ceremonial precepts are ordered to the Divine worship. Now in this worship we may consider the worship itself, the worshippers, and the instruments of worship. The worship consists specially in sacrifices, which are offered up in honour of God. The instruments of worship refer to the sacred things, such as the tabernacle, the vessels and so forth. With regard to the worshippers two points may be considered. The first point is their preparation for Divine worship, which is effected by a sort of consecration either of the people or of the ministers; and to this the sacraments refer. The second point is their particular mode of life, whereby they are distinguished from those who do not worship God, and to this pertain the observances; for instance, in matters of food, clothing, and so forth.

Reply Obj. 1. It was necessary for the sacrifices to be offered both in some certain place and by some certain men, and all this pertained to the worship of God. Therefore just as their sacrifices signified Christ the victim, so too their sacraments and sacred things foreshadowed the sacraments and sacred things of the New Law, while their observances foreshadowed the mode of life of the people under the New Law—all of which things pertain to Christ.

---

[1] Chap. 32 (FR 325).

[2] Cf. Peter Lombard, *Sent.*, IV, d. 1, chap. 6 (QR II, 748), chap. 4 (QR II, 746).

Reply Obj. 2. The sacrifice of the New Law, namely, the Eucharist, contains Christ Himself, the Author of our Sanctification; for *He* sanctified *the people by His own blood* (Heb. 13. 12). Hence this Sacrifice is also a sacrament. But the sacrifices of the Old Law did not contain Christ, but foreshadowed Him; hence they are not called sacraments. In order to signify this there were certain sacraments apart from the sacrifices of the Old Law, which sacraments were figures of the sanctification to come. Nevertheless to certain consecrations certain sacrifices were united.

Reply Obj. 3. The sacrifices and sacraments were of course sacred things. But certain things were sacred through being dedicated to the Divine worship, and yet were not sacrifices or sacraments. Therefore they retained the common designation of sacred things.

Reply Obj. 4. Those things which pertained to the mode of life of the people who worshipped God retained the common designation of observances, in so far as they fell short of the above. For they were not called sacred things because they had no immediate connection with the worship of God, such as the tabernacle and its vessels had. But by a sort of consequence they were matters of ceremony, in so far as they affected the fitness of the people who worshipped God.

Reply Obj. 5. Just as the sacrifices were offered in a fixed place, so were they offered at fixed times, for which reason the solemn festivals seem to be reckoned among the sacred things. The oblations and gifts are counted together with the sacrifices; hence the Apostle says (Heb. 5. 1): *Every high-priest taken from among men, is ordained for men in things that appertain to God, that he may offer up gifts and sacrifices.*

QUESTION CII

OF THE CAUSES OF THE CEREMONIAL PRECEPTS

(*In Six Articles*)

WE must now consider the causes of the ceremonial precepts, under which head there are six points of inquiry: (1) Whether there was any cause for the ceremonial precepts? (2) Whether the cause of the ceremonial precepts was literal or figurative? (3) The causes of the sacrifices. (4) The causes of the sacraments. (5) The causes of the sacred things. (6) The causes of the observances.

ARTICLE 1. *Whether There Was Any Cause for the Ceremonial Precepts?*

We proceed thus to the First Article: It would seem that there was no cause for the ceremonial precepts.

Objection 1. Because on Ephes. 2. 15, *Making void the law of the commandments,* the gloss says,[1] "that is, making void the Old Law as to the carnal observances, by substituting decrees, that is, evangelical precepts, which are based on reason." But if the observances of the Old Law were based on reason, it would have been useless to void them by the reasonable decrees of the New Law. Therefore there was no reason for the ceremonial observances of the Old Law.

Obj. 2. Further, the Old Law succeeded the law of nature. But in the law of nature there was a precept for which there was no reason save that man's obedience might be tested, as Augustine says (*Gen. ad lit.* viii, 6, 13),[2] concerning the prohibition about the tree of life. Therefore in the Old Law there should have been some precepts for the purpose of testing man's obedience, having no reason in themselves.

Obj. 3. Further, man's works are called moral according as they proceed from reason. If therefore there is any reason for the ceremonial precepts, they would not differ from the moral precepts. It seems therefore that there was no cause for the ceremonial precepts, for the reason of a precept is taken from some cause.

On the contrary, It is written (Ps. 18. 9): *The commandment of the Lord is lightsome, enlightening the eyes.* But the ceremonial precepts are commandments of God. Therefore they are lightsome, and yet they would not be so, if they had no reasonable cause. Therefore the ceremonial precepts have a reasonable cause.

I answer that, Since, according to the Philosopher,[3] it is the function of a wise man to set things in order, those things which proceed from the Divine wisdom must be well ordered, as the Apostle states (Rom. 13. 1). Now there are two conditions required for things to be well ordered. First, that they be ordered to their due end, which is the principle of the whole order in matters of action, since those things that happen by chance outside the intention of the end, or which are not done seriously but for

---

[1] *Glossa interl.* (VI, 91v); *Glossa* Lombardi (PL 192, 185).

[2] PL 34, 377; 383.

[3] *Metaphysics*, I, 2 (982ª18).

fun, are said to be lacking in order. Secondly, that which is done in view of the end should be proportionate to the end. From this it follows that the reason for whatever leads to the end is taken from the end; thus the reason for the disposition of a saw is taken from cutting, which is its end, as stated in the *Physics*.[1] Now it is evident that the ceremonial precepts, like all the other precepts of the Law, were institutions of Divine wisdom; hence it is written (Deut. 4. 6): *This is your wisdom and understanding in the sight of nations.* Consequently we must say that the ceremonial precepts were ordered to a certain end, from which their reasonable causes can be gathered.

Reply Obj. 1. It may be said that there was no reason for the observances of the Old Law, in the sense that there was no reason in the very nature of the thing done; for instance that a garment should not be made of wool and linen. But there could be a reason for them in their relation to something else, namely, in so far as something was signified or excluded thereby. On the other hand, the decrees of the New Law, which refer chiefly to faith and the love of God, are reasonable from the very nature of the act.

Reply Obj. 2. The reason for the prohibition concerning the tree of the knowledge of good and evil was not that this tree was naturally evil. And yet this prohibition was reasonable in its relation to something else, since it signified something. And so also the ceremonial precepts of the Old Law were reasonable on account of their relation to something else.

Reply Obj. 3. The moral precepts in their very nature have reasonable causes, as for instance, Thou shalt not kill, Thou shalt not steal. But the ceremonial precepts have a reasonable cause in their relation to something else, as stated above.

ARTICLE 2. *Whether the Ceremonial Precepts Have a Literal Cause or Merely a Figurative Cause?*

We proceed thus to the Second Article: It would seem that the ceremonial precepts have not a literal but merely a figurative cause.

Objection 1. For among the ceremonial precepts the chief were circumcision and the sacrifice of the paschal lamb. But neither of these had any but a figurative cause, because each was given as a sign. For it is written (Gen. 17. 11): *You shall circumcise the flesh of your foreskin, that it may be for a sign of the covenant between Me and you;* and of the celebration of

the Passover it is written (Exod. 13. 9): *It shall be as a sign in thy hand, and as a memorial before thy eyes.* Therefore much more did the other ceremonial precepts have none but a figurative reason.

Obj. 2. Further, an effect is proportionate to its cause. But all the ceremonial precepts are figurative, as stated above (Q. CI, A. 2). Therefore they have no other than a figurative cause.

Obj. 3. Further, if it be a matter of indifference whether a certain thing, considered in itself, be done in a particular way or not, it seems that it has not a literal cause. Now there are certain points in the ceremonial precepts which appear to be a matter of indifference as to whether they be done in one way or in another; for instance, the number of animals to be offered, and other such particular circumstances. Therefore there is no literal cause for the precepts of the Old Law.

On the contrary, Just as the ceremonial precepts foreshadowed Christ, so did the stories of the Old Testament: for it is written (I Cor. 10. 11) that *all (these things) happened to them in figure.* Now in the stories of the Old Testament, besides the mystical or figurative, there is the literal sense. Therefore the ceremonial precepts had also literal, besides their figurative causes.

I answer that, As stated above (A. 1), the reason for whatever leads to an end must be taken from that end. Now the end of the ceremonial precepts was twofold, for they were ordered to the Divine worship, for that particular time, and to the foreshadowing of Christ, just as the words of the prophets regarded the time being in such a way as to be utterances figurative of the time to come, as Jerome says on Osee 1. 3.[2] Accordingly the reasons for the ceremonial precepts of the Old Law can be taken in two ways. First, in respect of the Divine worship which was to be observed for that particular time. And these reasons are literal, whether they refer to the shunning of idolatry, or recall certain Divine benefits, or remind men of the Divine excellence, or point out the disposition of mind which was then required in those who worshipped God. Secondly, their reasons can be gathered from the point of view of their being ordained to foreshadow Christ. And thus their reasons are figurative and mystical, whether they be taken from Christ Himself and the Church, which pertains to the allegorical sense, or to the morals of the Christian people, which pertains to the moral sense, or to the state of fu-

[1] Aristotle, II, 9 (200^{n}10).   [2] PL 25, 364.

ture glory, according as we are brought there by Christ, which refers to the anagogical sense.

Reply Obj. 1. Just as the use of metaphorical expressions in Scripture belongs to the literal sense because the words are employed in order to convey that particular meaning, so also the meaning of those legal ceremonies which commemorated certain Divine benefits, on account of which they were instituted, and of others similar which belonged to that time, does not go beyond the order of literal causes. Consequently when we assert that the cause of the celebration of the Passover was its signification of the delivery from Egypt, or that circumcision was a sign of God's covenant with Abraham, we assign the literal cause.

Reply Obj. 2. This argument would avail if the ceremonial precepts had been given merely as figures of things to come, and not for the purpose of worshipping God then and there.

Reply Obj. 3. As we stated when speaking of human laws (Q. XCVI, AA. 1, 6), there is a reason for them in a universal way, but not in regard to particular conditions, which depend on the judgment of those who frame them; so also many particular determinations in the ceremonies of the Old Law have no literal cause, but only a figurative cause. But taken in general they have a literal cause.

ARTICLE 3. *Whether a Suitable Cause Can Be Assigned for the Ceremonies Which Pertained to Sacrifices?*

We proceed thus to the Third Article: It would seem that no suitable cause can be assigned for the ceremonies pertaining to sacrifices.

Objection 1. For those things which were offered in sacrifice are those which are necessary for sustaining human life, such as certain animals and certain loaves. But God needs no such sustenance, according to Ps. 49. 13: *Shall I eat the flesh of bullocks? Or shall I drink the blood of goats?* Therefore such sacrifices were unfittingly offered to God.

Obj. 2. Further, only three kinds of quadrupeds were offered in sacrifice to God, namely, oxen, sheep and goats; of birds, generally the turtledove and the dove; but specially, in the cleansing of a leper, an offering was made of sparrows. Now many other animals are more noble than these. Since therefore whatever is best should be offered to God, it seems that not only of these three should sacrifices have been offered to Him.

Obj. 3. Further, just as man has received from God the dominion over birds and beasts, so also has he received dominion over fishes. Consequently it was unfitting for fishes to be excluded from the divine sacrifices.

Obj. 4. Further, turtledoves and doves indifferently are commanded to be offered up. Since then the young of the dove are commanded to be offered, so also should the young of the turtledove.

Obj. 5. Further, God is the Author of life, not only of men, but also of animals, as is clear from Gen. 1. 20, *seq.* Now death is opposed to life. Therefore it was fitting that living animals rather than slain animals should be offered to God; especially as the Apostle admonishes us (Rom. 12. 1), to present our bodies *a living sacrifice, holy, pleasing unto God.*

Obj. 6. Further, if none but slain animals were offered in sacrifice to God, it seems that it mattered not how they were slain. Therefore it was unfitting that the manner of immolation should be determined, especially as regards birds (Levit. 1. 15, *seq.*).

Obj. 7. Further, every defect in an animal is a step towards corruption and death. If therefore slain animals were offered to God, it was unreasonable to forbid the offering of an imperfect animal, for example, a lame, or a blind, or otherwise defective animal.

Obj. 8. Further, those who offer victims to God should partake of them, according to the words of the Apostle (I Cor. 10. 18): *Are not they that eat of the sacrifices partakers of the altar?* It was therefore unfitting for the offerers to be denied certain parts of the victims, namely, the blood, the fat, the breast-bone and the right shoulder.

Obj. 9. Further, just as holocausts were offered up in honour of God, so also were the peace-offerings and sin-offerings. But no female animal was offered up to God as a holocaust, although holocausts were offered of both quadrupeds and birds. Therefore it was inconsistent that female animals should be offered up in peace-offerings and sin-offerings, and that nevertheless birds should not be offered up in peace-offerings.

Obj. 10. Further, all the peace-offerings seem to be of one kind. Therefore it was unfitting to make a distinction among them, so that it was forbidden to eat the flesh of certain peace-offerings on the following day, while it was allowed to eat the flesh of other peace-offerings, as laid down in Levit. 7. 15, *seq.*

Obj. 11. Further, all sins agree in turning us from God. Therefore, in order to reconcile us to God, one kind of sacrifice should have been offered up for all sins.

Obj. 12. Further, all animals that were offered up in sacrifice, were offered up in one way, namely, slain. Therefore it does not seem to be suitable that products of the soil should be offered up in various ways; for sometimes an offering was made of ears of corn, sometimes of flour, sometimes of bread, this being baked sometimes in an oven, sometimes in a pan, sometimes on a gridiron.

Obj. 13. Further, whatever things are serviceable to us should be recognized as coming from God. It was therefore unfitting that besides animals, nothing but bread, wine, oil, incense, and salt should be offered to God.

Obj. 14. Further, bodily sacrifices denote the inward sacrifice of the heart, by which man offers his soul to God. But in the inward sacrifice, the sweetness, which is denoted by honey, surpasses the pungency which salt represents; for it is written (Ecclus 24. 27): *My spirit is sweet above honey.* Therefore it was unfitting that the use of honey, and of leaven which makes bread savoury, should be forbidden in a sacrifice, while the use was prescribed, of salt which is pungent, and of incense which has a bitter taste. Consequently it seems that things pertaining to the ceremonies of the sacrifices have no reasonable cause.

On the contrary, It is written (Levit. 1. 13): *The priest shall offer it all and burn it all upon the altar, for a holocaust, and most sweet savour to the Lord.* Now according to Wisd. 7. 28, *God loveth none but him that dwelleth with wisdom.* From this it seems to follow that whatever is acceptable to God is wisely done. Therefore these ceremonies of the sacrifices were wisely done, as having reasonable causes.

I answer that, As stated above (A. 2), the ceremonies of the Old Law had a twofold cause, namely, a literal cause, according as they were intended for Divine worship, and a figurative or mystical cause, according as they were intended to foreshadow Christ; and on either hand the ceremonies pertaining to the sacrifices can be assigned to a fitting cause.

For, according as the ceremonies of the sacrifices were intended for the divine worship, the causes of the sacrifices can be taken in two ways. First, in so far as the sacrifice represented the directing of the mind to God, to which the offerer of the sacrifice was stimulated. Now in order to direct his mind to God rightly, man must recognize that whatever he has is from God as from its first principle, and direct it to God as its last

end. This was denoted in the offerings and sacrifices by the fact that man offered some of his own belongings in honour of God, as though in recognition of his having received them from God, according to the saying of David (1 Paral. 29. 14): *All things are Thine: and we have given Thee what we received of Thy hand.* Therefore in offering up sacrifices man made protestation that God is the first principle of the creation of all things, and their last end, to which all things must be ordered.

And since for the human mind to be directed to God rightly it must recognize no first author of things other than God, nor place its end in any other, for this reason it was forbidden in the Law to offer sacrifice to any other but God, according to Exod. 22. 20: *He that sacrificeth to gods, shall be put to death, save only to the Lord.* Therefore another reasonable cause may be assigned to the ceremonies of the sacrifices, from the fact that thereby men were withdrawn from offering sacrifices to idols. Hence too it is that the precepts about the sacrifices were not given to the Jewish people until after they had fallen into idolatry, by worshipping the molten calf, as though those sacrifices were instituted, that the people, being ready to offer sacrifices, might offer those sacrifices to God rather than to idols. Thus it is written (Jer. 7. 22): *I spake not to your fathers and I commanded them not, in the day that I brought them out of the land of Egypt, concerning the matter of burnt-offerings and sacrifices.*

Now of all the gifts which God vouchsafed to mankind after they had fallen away by sin, the chief is that He gave His Son; and so it is written (John 3. 16): *God so loved the world, as to give His only-begotten Son; that whosoever believeth in Him, may not perish, but may have life everlasting.* Consequently the chief sacrifice is that by which Christ Himself *delivered Himself . . . to God for an odour of sweetness* (Eph. 5. 2). And for this reason all the other sacrifices of the Old Law were offered up in order to foreshadow this one individual and paramount sacrifice—the imperfect forecasting the perfect. Hence the Apostle says (Heb. 10. 11) that the priest of the Old Law *often* offered the *same sacrifices, which can never take away sins: but* Christ offered *one sacrifice for sins, for ever.* And since the reason of the figure is taken from that which the figure represents, therefore the reasons of the figurative sacrifices of the Old Law should be taken from the true sacrifice of Christ.

Reply Obj. 1. God did not wish these sacrifices

to be offered to Him on account of the things themselves that were offered, as though He stood in need of them; hence it is written (Isa. 1. 11): *I desire not holocausts of rams, and fat of fatlings, and blood of calves and lambs and buckgoats.* But, as stated above, He wished them to be offered to Him in order to prevent idolatry; in order to signify the right ordering of man's mind to God; and in order to represent the mystery of the Redemption of man by Christ.

Reply Obj. 2. In all the respects mentioned above (reply 1), there was a suitable reason for these animals, rather than others, being offered up in sacrifice to God. First, in order to prevent idolatry. Because idolaters offered all other animals to their gods, or made use of them in their sorceries, while the Egyptians (among whom the people had been dwelling) considered it abominable to slay these animals, and so they used not to offer them in sacrifice to their gods. Hence it is written (Exod. 8. 26): *We shall sacrifice the abominations of the Egyptians to the Lord our God.* For they worshipped the sheep, they reverenced the ram (because demons appeared under their form), while they employed oxen for agriculture, which was held by them as something sacred.

Secondly, this was suitable for the previously mentioned right ordering of man's mind to God, and in two ways. First, because it is chiefly by means of these animals that human life is sustained, and moreover they are most clean, and partake of a most clean food. But other animals are either wild, and not appointed to ordinary use among men; or, if they be tame, they have unclean food, as pigs and geese, and nothing but what is clean should be offered to God. These birds especially were offered in sacrifice because there were plenty of them in the land of promise. Secondly, because the sacrificing of these animals represented purity of heart. Because as the gloss says on Levit. 1.,[1] "We offer a calf when we overcome the pride of the flesh; a lamb when we restrain our unreasonable motions; a goat when we conquer our wantonness; a turtledove when we keep chaste; unleavened bread when we feast on the unleavened bread of sincerity." And it is evident that the dove denotes charity and simplicity of heart.

Thirdly, it was fitting that these animals should be offered that they might foreshadow Christ. Because, as the same gloss observes,[2]

---

[1] *Glossa ordin.*, Prol. (1, 214B); Isidore, *Quaest. in Vet. Test., In Lev.* 1 (PL 83, 321).
[2] *Ibid.*

"Christ is offered in the calf to denote the strength of the cross; in the lamb to signify His innocence; in the ram to foreshadow His headship; in the goat to signify the likeness of 'sinful flesh.' The turtledove and dove denoted the union of the two natures"; or else the turtledove signified chastity, while the dove was a figure of charity. "The wheat-flour foreshadowed the sprinkling of believers with the water of Baptism."

Reply Obj. 3. Fish through living in water are further removed from man than other animals, which, like man, live in the air. Again, fish die as soon as they are taken out of water; hence they could not be offered in the temple like other animals.

Reply Obj. 4. Among turtledoves the older ones are better than the young, while with doves the case is the reverse. Therefore, as Rabbi Moses observes (*Doct. Perplex.* iii),[3] "turtledoves and young doves are commanded to be offered because nothing should be offered to God but what is best."

Reply Obj. 5. The animals which were offered in sacrifice were slain because it is by being killed that they become useful to man, since God gave them to man for food. Therefore also they were burnt with fire, because it is by being cooked that they are made fit for human consumption. Moreover the slaying of the animals signified the destruction of sins, and also that man deserved death on account of his sins, as though those animals were slain in man's stead, in order to betoken the expiation of sins. Again the slaying of these animals signified the slaying of Christ.

Reply Obj. 6. The Law fixed the special manner of slaying the sacrificial animals in order to exclude other ways of killing, by which idolaters sacrificed animals to idols. Or again, as Rabbi Moses says (*loc. cit.*),[4] "the Law chose that manner of slaying which was least painful to the slain animal." This excluded cruelty on the part of the offerers, and any mangling of the animals slain.

Reply Obj. 7. It is because unclean animals are accustomed to be held in contempt among men that it was forbidden to offer them in sacrifice to God; and for this reason too they were forbidden (Deut 23. 18) to offer *the hire of a strumpet or the price of a dog in the house of . . . God.* For the same reason they did not offer animals before the seventh day, because such were abortive as it were, the flesh being not yet firm on account of its exceeding softness.

---

[3] Chap. 46 (FR 360).   [4] Chap. 48 (FR 371).

Reply Obj. 8. There were three kinds of sacrifices. There was one in which the victim was entirely consumed by fire, and this was called a holocaust, that is, all burnt. For this kind of sacrifice was offered to God specially to show reverence to His majesty, and love of His goodness, and typified the state of perfection as regards the fulfilment of the counsels. Therefore the whole was burnt up, so that as the whole animal by being dissolved into vapour soared aloft, so it might denote that the whole man, and whatever belongs to him, are subject to the authority of God, and should be offered to Him.

Another sacrifice was the sin-offering, which was offered to God on account of man's need for the forgiveness of sin, and this typifies the state of penitents in satisfying for sins. It was divided into two parts; for one part was burnt, while the other was granted to the use of the priests to signify that remission of sins is granted by God through the ministry of His priests. When, however, this sacrifice was offered for the sins of the whole people, or specially for the sin of the priest, the whole victim was burnt up. For it was not fitting that the priests should have the use of that which was offered for their own sins, to signify that nothing sinful should remain in them. Moreover, this would not be satisfaction for sin, for if the offering were granted to the use of those for whose sins it was offered, it would seem to be the same as if it had not been offered.

The third kind of sacrifice was called the peace-offering, which was offered to God, either in thanksgiving, or for the welfare and prosperity of the offerers, in acknowledgment of benefits already received or yet to be received; and this typifies the state of those who are proficient in the observance of the commandments. These sacrifices were divided into three parts; for one part was burnt in honour of God, another part was allotted to the use of the priests, and the third part to the use of the offerers, in order to signify that man's salvation is from God, by the direction of God's ministers, and through the co-operation of those who are saved.

But it was the universal rule that the blood and fat were not allotted to the use either of the priests or of the offerers, the blood being poured out at the foot of the altar, in honour of God, while the fat was burnt upon the altar (Levit. 9. 9, 10). The reason for this was, first, in order to prevent idolatry, because idolaters used to drink the blood and eat the fat of the victims, according to Deut. 32. 38: *Of whose victims they eat the fat, and drank the wine of their drink-offerings.* Secondly, in order to form them to a right way of living. For they were forbidden the use of the blood that they might abhor the shedding of human blood; hence it is written (Gen. 9. 4, 5): *Flesh with blood you shall not eat: for I will require the blood of your lives.* And they were forbidden to eat the fat in order to withdraw them from lasciviousness; hence it it written (Ezech. 34. 3): *You have killed that which was fat.* Thirdly, on account of the reverence due to God, because blood is most necessary for life, for which reason *life* is said to be *in the blood* (Levit. 17. 11, 14), while fat is a sign of abundant nourishment. Therefore, in order to show that to God we owe both life and a sufficiency of all good things, the blood was poured out, and the fat burnt up in His honour. Fourthly, in order to foreshadow the shedding of Christ's blood, and the abundance of His charity, whereby He offered Himself to God for us.

In the peace-offerings, the breast-bone and the right shoulder were allotted to the use of the priest in order to prevent a certain kind of divination which is known as *spatulamantia,* so called because it was customary in divining to use the shoulder-blade (*spatula*) and the breast-bone of the animals offered in sacrifice; therefore these things were taken away from the offerers. This also denoted the priest's need of wisdom in the heart, to instruct the people (this was signified by the breast-bone, which covers the heart), and his need of fortitude in order to bear with human frailty—and this was signified by the right shoulder.

Reply Obj. 9. Because the holocaust was the most perfect kind of sacrifice, therefore none but a male was offered for a holocaust, because the female is an imperfect animal. The offering of turtledoves and doves was on account of the poverty of the offerers, who were unable to offer bigger animals. And since peace-victims were offered freely, and no one was bound to offer them against his will, hence these birds were offered not among the peace-victims, but among the holocausts and victims for sin, which man was obliged to offer at times. Moreover these birds, on account of their lofty flight, were befitting the perfection of the holocausts, and were suitable for sin-offerings, because their song is doleful.

Reply Obj. 10. The holocaust was the chief of all the sacrifices because the whole was burnt in honour of God, and nothing of it was eaten. The second place in holiness belongs to the sacrifice for sins, which was eaten by the priests in the court only, and on the very day of the sacrifice (Lev. 7. 6, 15). The third place must be given to the peace-offerings of thanksgiving, which were eaten on the same day, but anywhere in Jerusalem. Fourth in order were the *ex-voto* peace-offerings, the flesh of which could be eaten even on the morrow. The reason for this order is that man is bound to God chiefly on account of His majesty; secondly, on account of the sins he has committed; thirdly, because of the benefits he has already received from Him; fourthly, by reason of the benefits he hopes to receive from Him.

Reply Obj. 11. Sins are more grievous by reason of the state of the sinner, as stated above (Q. LXXIII, A. 10). Therefore different victims are commanded to be offered for the sin of a priest, or of a prince, or of some other private individual. "But," as Rabbi Moses says (*loc. cit.*),[1] "we must take note that the more grievous the sin, the lower the species of animal offered for it. Therefore the goat, which is a very base animal, was offered for idolatry, which is the most grievous sin, while a calf was offered for a priest's ignorance, and a ram for the negligence of a prince."

Reply Obj. 12. In the matter of sacrifices the Law had in view the poverty of the offerers, so that those who could not have a four-footed animal at their disposal might at least offer a bird; and that he who could not have a bird might at least offer bread; and that if a man had not even bread he might offer flour or ears of corn.

The figurative cause is that the bread signifies Christ Who is the *living bread* (John 6. 41, 51). He was indeeed an ear of corn, as it were, during the state of the law of nature, in the faith of the patriarchs; He was like flour in the doctrine of the Law of the prophets; and He was like perfect bread after He had taken human nature; baked in the fire, that is, formed by the Holy Ghost in the oven of the virginal womb; baked again in a pan by the toils which He suffered in the world; and consumed by fire on the cross as on a gridiron.

Reply Obj. 13. The products of the soil are useful to man, either as food, and of these bread was offered; or as drink, and of these wine was offered; or as seasoning, and of these oil and salt were offered; or as healing, and of these they offered incense, which both smells sweetly and binds easily together.

Now the bread foreshadowed the flesh of Christ; and the wine, His blood, by which we

[1] Chap. 46 (FR 363).

were redeemed; oil signifies the grace of Christ; salt, His knowledge; incense, His prayer.

Reply Obj. 14. Honey was not offered in the sacrifices to God, both because it was accustomed to be offered in the sacrifices to idols, and in order to denote the absence of all carnal sweetness and pleasure from those who intend to sacrifice to God. Leaven was not offered to denote the exclusion of corruption. Perhaps too, it was accustomed to be offered in the sacrifices to idols.

Salt, however, was offered, because it wards off the corruption of putrefaction, for sacrifices offered to God should be incorrupt. Moreover, salt signifies the discretion of wisdom, or again, mortification of the flesh.

Incense was offered to denote devotion of the heart, which is necessary in the offerer; and again, to signify the odour of a good name, for incense is composed of matter both rich and fragrant. And since the sacrifice of jealousy did not proceed from devotion, but rather from suspicion, therefore incense was not offered there (Num. 5. 15).

ARTICLE 4. *Whether Sufficient Reason Can Be Assigned for the Ceremonies Pertaining to Holy Things?*

We proceed thus to the Fourth Article: It would seem that no sufficient reason can be assigned for the ceremonies of the Old Law that pertain to holy things.

Objection 1. For Paul said (Acts 17. 24): *God Who made the world and all things therein; He being Lord of heaven and earth, dwelleth not in temples made by hands.* It was therefore unfitting that in the Old Law a tabernacle or temple should be set up for the worship of God.

Obj. 2. Further, the state of the Old Law was not changed except by Christ. But the tabernacle denoted the state of the Old Law. Therefore it should not have been changed by the building of a temple.

Obj. 3. Further, the Divine law, more than any other indeed, should lead man to the worship of God. But an increase of divine worship requires multiplication of altars and temples, as is evident in regard to the New Law. Therefore it seems that also under the Old Law there should have been not only one tabernacle or temple, but many.

Obj. 4. Further, the tabernacle or temple was ordained to the worship of God. But in God we should worship above all His unity and simplicity. Therefore it seems unbecoming for the tabernacle or temple to be divided by means of veils.

Obj. 5. Further, the power of the First Mover, that is, God, appears first of all in the east, for it is in that quarter that the first movement begins. But the tabernacle was set up for the worship of God. Therefore it should have been built so as to point to the east rather than the west.

Obj. 6. Further, the Lord commanded (Exod. 20. 4) that they should *not make . . . a graven thing, nor the likeness of anything.* It was therefore unfitting for graven images of the cherubim to be set up in the tabernacle or temple. In like manner the ark, the propitiatory, the candlestick, the table, the two altars, seem to have been placed there without reasonable cause.

Obj. 7. Further, the Lord commanded (Exod. 20. 24): *You shall make an altar of earth unto Me:* and again (*ibid.,* 26): *Thou shalt not go up by steps unto My altar.* It was therefore unfitting that subsequently they should be commanded to make an altar of wood laid over with gold or brass, and of such a height that it was impossible to go up to it except by steps. For it is written (Exod. 27. 1, 2): *Thou shalt make also an altar of setim wood, which shall be five cubits long, and as many broad, . . . and three cubits high . . . and thou shalt cover it with brass;* and (Exod. 30. 1, 3): *Thou shalt make . . . an altar to burn incense, of setim wood . . . and thou shalt overlay it with the purest gold.*

Obj. 8. Further, in God's works nothing should be superfluous; for not even in the works of nature is anything superfluous to be found. But one cover suffices for one tabernacle or house. Therefore it was unfitting to furnish the tabernacle with many coverings, namely, curtains, curtains of goats' hair, rams' skins dyed red, and violet-coloured skins (Exod. 26).

Obj. 9. Further, exterior consecration signifies interior holiness, the subject of which is the soul. It was therefore unsuitable for the tabernacle and its vessels to be consecrated, since they were inanimate bodies.

Obj. 10. Further, it is written (Ps. 33. 2): *I will bless the Lord at all times, His praise shall always be in my mouth.* But the solemn festivals were instituted for the praise of God. Therefore it was not fitting that certain days should be fixed for keeping solemn festivals, so that it seems that there was no suitable cause for the ceremonies relating to holy things.

On the contrary, The Apostle says (Heb. 8. 4) that those who *offer gifts according to the law, . . . serve unto the example and shadow of heavenly things.* As it was answered to Moses, when he was to finish the tabernacle: *See, says He, that thou make all things according to the pattern which was shown thee on the mount.* But that is most reasonable, which presents a likeness to heavenly things. Therefore the ceremonies relating to holy things had a reasonable cause.

I answer that, The chief purpose of the whole external worship is that man may give worship to God. Now man's tendency is to reverence less those things which are common and indistinct from other things; but he admires and reveres those things which are distinct from others in some point of excellence. Hence too it is customary among men for kings and princes, who ought to be reverenced by their subjects, to be clothed in more precious garments, and to possess vaster and more beautiful abodes. And for this reason special times, a special abode, special vessels, and special ministers had to be appointed for the divine worship, so that thereby the soul of man might be brought to greater reverence for God.[1]

In like manner the state of the Old Law, as observed above (A. 2; Q. C, A. 12; Q. CI, A. 2), was instituted that it might foreshadow the mystery of Christ. Now that which foreshadows something should be determinate, so that it may present some likeness to it. Consequently, certain special points had to be observed in matters pertaining to the worship of God.

Reply Obj. 1. The divine worship regards two things: namely, God Who is worshipped; and men, who worship Him. Accordingly God, Who is worshipped, is confined to no bodily place. Therefore there was no need, on His part, for a tabernacle or temple to be set up. But men, who worship Him, are corporeal beings, and for their sake there was need for a special tabernacle or temple to be set up for the worship of God, for two reasons. First, that through coming together with the thought that the place was set aside for the worship of God, they might approach there with greater reverence. Secondly, that certain things relating to the excellence of Christ's Divine or human nature might be signified by the arrangement of various details in such temple or tabernacle.

To this Solomon refers (III Kings 8. 27) when he says: *If heaven and the heavens of heavens cannot contain Thee, how much less this house which I have built for Thee?* And further on (*ibid.* 29, 30) he adds: *That Thy eyes may be open upon this house . . . of which Thou hast said: My name shall be there; . . . that Thou*

---

[1] Cf. Maimonides, *Guide,* III, 45 (FR 357).

mayest hearken to the supplication of Thy servant and of Thy people Israel. From this it is evident that the house of the sanctuary was set up, not in order to contain God, as abiding there locally, but that God's name might dwell there, that is, that God might be made known there by means of things done and said there; and that those who prayed there might, through reverence for the place, pray more devoutly, so as to be heard more readily.

Reply Obj. 2. Before the coming of Christ, the state of the Old Law was not changed as regards the fulfilment of the Law, which was effected in Christ alone; but it was changed as regards the condition of the people that were under the Law. Because, at first, the people were in the desert, having no fixed abode; afterwards they were engaged in various wars with the neighbouring nations; and lastly, at the time of David and Solomon, the state of that people was one of great peace. And then for the first time the temple was built in the place which Abraham, instructed by God, had chosen for the purpose of sacrifice. For it is written (Gen. 22. 2) that the Lord commanded Abraham to *offer* his son *for a holocaust upon one of the mountains which I will show thee;* and it is related further on (*ibid.* 14) that *he called the name of that place, The Lord seeth,* as though, according to the Divine prevision, that place were chosen for the worship of God. Hence it is written (Deut. 12. 5, 6): *You shall come to the place which the Lord your God shall choose . . . and you shall offer . . . your holocausts and victims.*

Now it was not right for that place to be pointed out by the building of the temple before the aforesaid time, for three reasons assigned by Rabbi Moses.[1] First, lest the Gentiles might seize hold of that place. Secondly, lest the Gentiles might destroy it. The third reason is lest each tribe might wish that place to fall to their lot, and strifes and quarrels be the result. Hence the temple was not built until they had a king who would be able to quell such quarrels. Until that time a portable tabernacle was employed for divine worship, no place being as yet fixed for the worship of God. This is the literal reason for the distinction between the tabernacle and the temple.

The figurative reason may be assigned to the fact that they signify a twofold state. For the tabernacle, which was changeable, signifies the state of the present changeable life. But the temple, which was fixed and stable, signifies the

[1] *Guide,* III, 45 (FR 355).

state of future life which is altogether unchangeable. For this reason it is said that in the building of the temple no sound was heard of hammer or saw, to signify that all movements of disturbance will be far removed from the future state. Or else the tabernacle signifies the state of the Old Law, while the temple built by Solomon signifies the state of the New Law. Hence the Jews alone worked at the building of the tabernacle, but the temple was built with the co-operation of the Gentiles, namely, the Tyrians and Sidonians.

Reply Obj. 3. The reason for the unity of the temple or tabernacle may be either literal or figurative. The literal reason was the exclusion of idolatry. For the Gentiles put up various temples to various gods, and so, to strengthen in the minds of men their belief in the unity of the Godhead, God wished sacrifices to be offered to Him in one place only. Another reason was in order to show that bodily worship is not acceptable of itself, and so they were restrained from offering sacrifices anywhere and everywhere. But the worship of the New Law, in whose sacrifice spiritual grace is contained, is of itself acceptable to God; and consequently the multiplication of altars and temples is permitted in the New Law.

As to those matters that regarded the spiritual worship of God, consisting in the teaching of the Law and the Prophets, there were, even under the Old Law, various places, called synagogues, appointed for the people to gather together for the praise of God, just as now there are places called churches in which the Christian people gather together for the divine worship. Thus our church takes the place of both temple and synagogue, since the very sacrifice of the Church is spiritual, and so with us the place of sacrifice is not distinct from the place of teaching. The figurative reason may be that the unity of the Church, whether militant or triumphant, is signified by this.

Reply Obj. 4. Just as the unity of the temple or tabernacle represented the unity of God, or the unity of the Church, so also the division of the tabernacle or temple signified the distinction of those things that are subject to God, and from which we rise to the worship of God. Now the tabernacle was divided into two parts. One was called the "Holy of Holies," and was placed to the west. The other was called the "Holy Place," which was situated to the east. Moreover there was a court facing the tabernacle. Accordingly there are two reasons for this distinction. One is in respect of the tabernacle being ordained to the worship of God. Because the different parts of the world are thus betokened by the division of the tabernacle. For that part which was called the Holy of Holies signified the higher world, which is that of spiritual substances, while that part which is called the Holy Place signified the corporeal world. Hence the Holy Place was separated from the Holy of Holies by a veil, which was of four different colours (denoting the four elements), namely, of linen, signifying earth, because linen, that is, flax, grows out of the earth; purple, signifying water, because the purple tint was made from certain shells found in the sea; violet, signifying air, because it has the colour of the air; and scarlet twice dyed, signifying fire. And this because matter composed of the four elements is a veil between us and incorporeal substances. Hence the high-priest alone, and that once a year, entered into the inner tabernacle, that is, the Holy of Holies, by which we are taught that man's final perfection consists in his entering into that world. But into the outward tabernacle, that is, the Holy Place, the priests entered every day, though the people were only admitted to the court; because the people are able to perceive material things, the inner nature of which only wise men by dint of study are able to discover.

But with regard to the figurative reason, the outward tabernacle, which was called the Holy Place, signified the state of the Old Law, as the Apostle says (Heb. 9. 6, *seq.*), because into that tabernacle *the priests always entered accomplishing the offices of sacrifices.* But the inner tabernacle, which was called the Holy of Holies, signified either the glory of heaven or the spiritual state of the New Law, which is a kind of beginning of the glory to come. To the latter state Christ brought us; and this was signified by the high-priest entering alone, once a year, into the Holy of Holies. The veil betokened the concealing of the spiritual sacrifices under the sacrifices of old. This veil was adorned with four colours: namely, that of linen, to designate purity of the flesh; purple, to denote the sufferings which the saints underwent for God; scarlet twice dyed, signifying the twofold love of God and our neighbour; and violet, in token of heavenly contemplation. With regard to the state of the Old Law the people and the priests were situated differently from one another. For the people saw the corporeal sacrifices themselves which were offered in the court; but the priests were intent on the inner meaning of the sacrifices, because their faith in the mysteries of Christ was more explicit. Hence they entered

into the outer tabernacle. This outer tabernacle was divided from the court by a veil, because some matters relating to the mystery of Christ were hidden from the people, while they were known to the priests, though they were not fully revealed to them, as they were subsequently in the New Testament (cf. Ephes. 3. 5).

Reply Obj. 5. Worship towards the west was introduced in the Law to the exclusion of idolatry because all the Gentiles, in reverence to the sun, worshipped towards the east; hence it is written (Ezech. 8. 16) that certain men *had their backs towards the temple of the Lord, and their faces to the east, and they adored towards the rising of the sun.* Accordingly, in order to prevent this, the tabernacle had the Holy of Holies to westward, that they might adore toward the west. A figurative reason may also be found in the fact that the whole state of the first tabernacle was ordained to foreshadow the death of Christ, which is signified by the west, according to Ps. 67. 5: *Who ascendeth unto the west; the Lord is His name.*

Reply Obj. 6. Both literal and figurative reasons may be assigned for the things contained in the tabernacle. The literal reason is in connection with the divine worship. And because, as already observed (ʀᴇᴘʟʏ 4), the inner tabernacle, called the Holy of Holies, signified the higher world of spiritual substances, hence that tabernacle contained three things, namely, *the ark of the testament in which was a golden pot that had manna, and the rod of Aaron that had blossomed, and the tables* (Heb. 9. 4) on which were written the ten commandments of the Law. Now the ark stood between two cherubim that looked one towards the other; and over the ark was a table, called the propitiatory, raised above the wings of the cherubim, as though it were held up by them, and appearing, to the imagination, to be the very seat of God. For this reason it was called the propitiatory, as though the people received propitiation thence at the prayers of the high-priest. And so it was held up, so to speak, by the cherubim, in obedience, as it were, to God, while the ark of the testament was like the foot-stool to Him that sat on the propitiatory. These three things denote three things in that higher world. First, God Who is above all, and incomprehensible to any creature. Hence no likeness of Him was set up, in order to denote His invisibility. But there was something to represent His seat, since, that is, the creature, which is beneath God, as the seat is under the one sitting on it, is comprehensible. Again in that higher world there are spiritual substances called angels. These are signified by the two cherubim, looking one towards the other, to show that they are at peace with one another, accoring to Job 25:2: *Who maketh peace in . . . high places.* For this reason, too, there was more than one cherub, to betoken the multitude of heavenly spirits, to prevent their receiving worship from those who had been commanded to worship but one God. Moreover there are, enclosed as it were in that spiritual world, the intelligible types of whatsoever takes place in this world, just as in every cause are enclosed the types of its effects, and in the craftsman the types of the works of his craft. This was signified by the ark, which represented, by means of the three things it contained, the three things of greatest import in human affairs. These are wisdom, signified by the tables of the testament; the power of governing, represented by the rod of Aaron; and life, denoted by the manna which was the means of sustenance. Or else these three signified the three Divine attributes, namely, wisdom, in the tables; power, in the rod, goodness, in the manna—both by reason of its sweetness, and because it was through the goodness of God that it was granted to man, so that therefore it was preserved as a memorial of the Divine mercy. Again, these three things were represented in Isaias' vision. For he *saw the Lord sitting upon a throne high and elevated;* and the seraphim standing by; and that the house was filled with the glory of the Lord; and so the seraphim cried out: *All the earth is full of His glory* (Isa. 6. 1, 3). And thus the images of the seraphim were set up, not to be worshipped, for this was forbidden by the first commandment, but as a sign of their function, as stated above.

The outer tabernacle, which denotes this present world, also contained three things, namely, the altar of incense, which was directly opposite the ark; the table of proposition, with the twelve loaves of proposition on it, which stood on the northern side; and the candlestick, which was placed towards the south. These three things seem to correspond to the three which were enclosed in the ark; and they represented the same things as the latter, but more clearly, because, in order that wise men, denoted by the priests entering the temple, might grasp the meaning of these types, it was necessary to express them more manifestly than they are in the Divine or angelic mind. Accordingly the candlestick signified, as its sensible sign, the wisdom which was expressed on the tables in intelligible words. The altar of incense signified the office of the priest, whose duty it was to

bring the people to God. And this was signified also by the rod, because on that altar the sweet-smelling incense was burnt, signifying the holiness of the people acceptable to God; for it is written (Apoc. 8. 3) that the smoke of the sweet-smelling spices signifies the *justifications of the saints* (*cf. ibid.* 19. 8). Moreover it was fitting that the dignity of the priesthood should be denoted, in the ark, by the rod, and, in the outer tabernacle, by the altar of incense, because the priest is the mediator between God and the people, governing the people by Divine power, denoted by the rod, and offering to God the fruit of His government, that is, the holiness of the people, on the altar of incense, so to speak. The table signified the sustenance of life, just as the manna did; but the former, a more general and a coarser kind of nourishment, the latter, a sweeter and more delicate. Again, the candlestick was fittingly placed on the southern side, while the table was placed to the north, because the south is the right-hand side of the world, while the north is the left-hand side, as stated in the book on the *Heavens;*[1] and wisdom, like other spiritual goods, belongs to the right hand, while temporal nourishment belongs to the left, according to Prov. 3. 16: *In her left hand (are) riches and glory.* And the priestly power is midway between temporal goods and spiritual wisdom, because thereby both spiritual wisdom and temporal goods are dispensed.

Another literal signification may be assigned. For the ark contained the tables of the Law in order to prevent forgetfulness of the Law, and so it is written (Exod. 24. 12): *I will give thee two tables of stone, and the Law, and the commandments which I have written: that thou mayest teach them* to the children of Israel. The rod of Aaron was placed there to restrain the people from insubordination to the priesthood of Aaron; hence it is written (Num. 17. 10): *Carry back the rod of Aaron into the tabernacle of the testimony, that it may be kept there for a token of the rebellious children of Israel.* The manna was kept in the ark to remind them of the benefit conferred by God on the children of Israel in the desert; therefore it is written (Exod. 16. 32): *Fill a gomor of it, and let it be kept unto generations to come hereafter, that they may know the bread wherewith I fed you in the wilderness.* The candlestick was set up to enhance the beauty of the temple, for the magnificence of a house depends on its being well lighted. Now the candlestick had seven branches,

---

[1] Aristotle, II, 2 (285^{b}16).

as Josephus observes (*Antiquit.* iii, 7),[1] to signify the seven planets with which the whole world is illuminated. Hence the candlestick was placed towards the south, because for us the course of the planets is from that quarter. The altar of incense was instituted that there might always be in the tabernacle a sweet-smelling smoke, both through respect for the tabernacle, and as a remedy for the stenches arising from the shedding of blood and the slaying of animals. For men despise evil-smelling things as being vile, but sweet-smelling things are much appreciated. The table was placed there to signify that the priests who served the temple should take their food in the temple; therefore, as stated in Matt. 12. 4, it was lawful for none but the priests to eat the twelve loaves which were put on the table in memory of the twelve tribes. And the table was not placed in the middle directly in front of the propitiatory, in order to exclude an idolatrous rite; for the Gentiles, on the feasts of the moon, set up a table in front of the idol of the moon, and so it is written (Jerem. 7.18): *The women knead the dough, to make cakes to the queen of heaven.*

In the court outside the tabernacle was the altar of holocausts, on which sacrifices of those things which the people possessed were offered to God. And therefore the people who offered these sacrifices to God by the hands of the priest could be present in the court. But the priests alone, whose function it was to offer the people to God, could approach the inner altar, on which the very devotion and holiness of the people was offered to God. And this altar was put up outside the tabernacle and in the court, to the exclusion of idolatrous worship; for the Gentiles placed altars inside the temples to offer up sacrifices on them to idols.

The figurative reason for all these things may be taken from the relation of the tabernacle to Christ, Who was foreshadowed therein. Now it must be observed that to show the imperfection of the figures of the Law, various figures were instituted in the temple to signify Christ. For He was foreshadowed by the propitiatory, since He is *a propitiation for our sins* (I John 2. 2). This propitiatory was fittingly carried by cherubim, since of Him it is written (Heb. 1.6): *Let all the angels of God adore Him.* He is also signified by the ark, because just as the ark was made of setim-wood, so was Christ's body composed of most pure members. Moreover it was gilded; for Christ was full of wisdom and charity, which are signified by gold. And in

[1] Sect. 8 (TK IV, 405).

the ark was a golden pot, that is, His holy soul, having manna, that is, *all the fulness of the Godhead* (Coloss. 2. 9). Also there was a rod in the ark, that is, His priestly power; for *He was made a . . . priest for ever* (Heb. 6. 20). And therein were the tables of the Testament, to denote that Christ Himself is a lawgiver. Again, Christ was signified by the candlestick, for He said Himself (John 8. 12): *I am the Light of the world;* while the seven lamps denoted the seven gifts of the Holy Ghost. He is also signified in the table, because He is our spiritual food, according to John 6. 41, 51: *I am the living bread;* and the twelve loaves signified the twelve apostles, or their teaching. Or again, the candlestick and table may signify the Church's teaching, and faith, which also enlightens and refreshes. Again, Christ is signified by the two altars of holocausts and incense. Because all works of virtue must be offered by us to God through Him; both those by which we afflict the body, which are offered, as it were, on the altar of holocausts, and those which, with greater perfection of mind, are offered to God in Christ by the spiritual desires of the perfect, on the altar of incense, as it were, according to Heb. 13 15: *By Him therefore let us offer the sacrifice of praise always to God.*

Reply Obj. 7. The Lord commanded an altar to be made for the offering of sacrifices and gifts in honour of God, and for the upkeep of the ministers who served the tabernacle. Now concerning the construction of the altar the Lord issued a twofold precept. One was at the beginning of the Law (Exod. 20. 24, *seq.*) when the Lord commanded them to make *an altar of earth,* or at least *not of hewn stones;* and again, not to make the altar high, so as to make it necessary to *go up* to it *by steps.* This was in detestation of idolatrous worship, for the Gentiles made their altars ornate and high, thinking that there was something holy and divine in such things. For this reason, too, the Lord commanded (Deut. 16. 21): *Thou shalt plant no grove, nor any tree near the altar of the Lord thy God,* since idolaters were accustomed to offer sacrifices beneath trees, on account of the pleasantness and shade afforded by them. There was also a figurative reason for these precepts. Because we must confess that in Christ, Who is our altar, there is the true nature of flesh, as regards His humanity—and this is to make an altar of earth; and again, in regard to His Godhead, we must confess His equality with the Father,—and this is *not to go up* to the altar by steps. Moreover we should not couple the doctrine of Christ to that of the Gentiles, which provokes men to lewdness.

But when once the tabernacle had been constructed to the honour of God, there was no longer reason to fear these occasions of idolatry. Therefore the Lord commanded the altar of holocausts to be made of brass, and to be conspicuous to all the people; and the altar of incense, which was visible to none but the priests. Nor was brass so precious as to give the people an occasion for idolatry.

Since, however, the reason for the precept, *Thou shalt not go up by steps unto My altar* (Exod. 20. 26) is stated to have been *lest thy nakedness be discovered*, it should be observed that this too was instituted with the purpose of preventing idolatry, for in the feasts of Priapus the Gentiles uncovered their nakedness before the people.[1] But later on the priests were prescribed the use of loin-cloths for the sake of decency, so that without any danger the altar could be placed so high that the priests when offering sacrifices would go up by steps of wood, not fixed but moveable.

Reply Obj. 8. The body of the tabernacle consisted of boards placed on end, and covered on the inside with curtains of four different colours, namely, twisted linen, violet, purple, and scarlet twice dyed. These curtains, however, covered the sides only of the tabernacle; and the roof of the tabernacle was covered with violet-coloured skins; and over this there was another covering of rams' skins dyed red; and over this there was a third curtain made of goats' hair, which covered not only the roof of the tabernacle, but also reached to the ground and covered the boards of the tabernacle on the outside. The literal reason of these coverings taken altogether was the adornment and protection of the tabernacle, that it might be an object of respect. Taken singly, according to some,[2] "the curtains denoted the starry heaven, which is adorned with various stars; the curtain (of goats' skin) signified the waters which are above the firmament; the skins dyed red denoted the empyrean heaven, where the angels are; the violet skins, the heaven of the Blessed Trinity."

The figurative meaning of these things is that the boards of which the tabernacle was constructed signify the faithful of Christ, who compose the Church. The boards were covered on the inner side by curtains of four colours, be-

cause the faithful are inwardly adorned with the four virtues; for "the twisted linen," as the gloss observes,[3] "signifies the flesh refulgent with purity; violet signifies the mind desirous of heavenly things; purple denotes the flesh subject to passions; the twice dyed scarlet betokens the mind in the midst of the passions enlightened by the love of God and our neighbour." The coverings of the building designate prelates and doctors, who ought to be conspicuous for their heavenly manner of life, signified by the violet coloured skins; and who should also be ready to suffer martyrdom, denoted by the skins dyed red; and austere of life and patient in adversity, signified by the curtains of goats' hair, which were exposed to wind and rain, as the gloss observes.[4]

Reply Obj. 9. The literal reason for the sanctification of the tabernacle and vessels was that they might be treated with greater reverence, being assigned, as it were, to the divine worship by this consecration. The figurative reason is that this sanctification signified the sanctification of the living tabernacle, that is, the faithful of whom the Church of Christ is composed.

Reply Obj. 10. Under the Old Law there were seven temporal solemnities, and one continual solemnity, as may be gathered from Num. 28, 29. There was a continual feast, since the lamb was sacrificed every day, morning and evening; and this continual feast of an abiding sacrifice signified the perpetuity of Divine happiness. Of the temporal feasts the first was that which was repeated every week. This was the solemnity of the Sabbath, celebrated in memory of the work of the creation of the universe. Another solemnity, namely, the New Moon, was repeated every month, and was observed in memory of the work of the Divine government. For the things of this lower world owe their variety chiefly to the movement of the moon; therefore this feast was kept at the new moon, and not at the full moon, to avoid the worship of idolaters who used to offer sacrifices to the moon at that particular time. These two blessings are bestowed in common on the whole human race, and hence they were repeated more frequently.

The other five feasts were celebrated once a year, and they commemorated the benefits which had been conferred especially on that people. For there was the feast of the Passover

---

[1] Cf. Maimonides, *Guide*, III, 45 (FR 357).
[2] Peter the Eater, *Hist. Schol.*, Lib. Exod., chap. 58 (PL 198, 1179).

[3] *Glossa ordin.* (I, 180 F); Bede, *De Tabernaculo*, II, 2, super Exod. 26.1 (PL 91, 425).
[4] Cf. *Glossa ordin.*, super Exod. 26.7, 14 (I, 181C; 182 E); See Bede, *De Tabernaculo*, II, 3 (PL 91, 430).

in the first month to commemorate the blessing of being delivered out of Egypt. The feast of Pentecost was celebrated fifty days later, to recall the blessing of the giving of the Law. The other three feasts were kept in the seventh month, nearly the whole of which was solemnized by them, just as the seventh day. For on the first of the seventh month was the feast of Trumpets, in memory of the delivery of Isaac, when Abraham found the ram caught by its horns, which they represented by the horns which they blew. The feast of Trumpets was a kind of invitation whereby they prepared themselves to keep the following feast which was kept on the tenth day. This was the feast of Expiation, in memory of the blessing whereby, at the prayer of Moses, God forgave the people's sin of worshipping the calf. After this was the feast of Scenopegia or of Tents, which was kept for seven days, to commemorate the blessing of being protected and led by God through the desert, where they lived in tents. Hence during this feast they had to take *the fruits of the fairest tree,* that is, the citron, *and trees of dense foliage,* that is, the myrtle, which is fragrant, *and branches of palm-trees, and willows of the brook,* which retain their greenness a long time. And these are to be found in the Land of promise, to signify that God had brought them through the arid land of the wilderness to a land of delights. On the eighth day another feast was observed, of Assembly and Congregation, on which the people collected the expenses necessary for the divine worship, and it signified the uniting of the people and the peace granted to them in the Land of promise.

The figurative reason for these feasts was that the continual sacrifice of the lamb foreshadowed the perpetuity of Christ, Who is the *Lamb of God,* according to Heb. 13. 8: *Jesus Christ yesterday and to-day, and the same for ever.* The Sabbath signified the spiritual rest bestowed by Christ, as stated in Heb. 4. The Neomenia, which is the beginning of the new moon, signified the enlightening of the primitive Church by Christ's preaching and miracles. The feast of Pentecost signified the Descent of the Holy Ghost on the apostles. The feast of Trumpets signified the preaching of the apostles. The feast of Expiation signified the cleansing of the Christian people from sins. And the feast of Tabernacles signified their pilgrimage in this world, where they walk by advancing in virtue. The feast of Assembly or Congregation foreshadowed the assembly of the faithful in the kingdom of heaven, and therefore this feast is

described as most holy (Levit. 23. 36). These three feasts followed immediately on one another, because those who expiate their vices should advance in virtue, until they come to see God, as stated in Ps. 83. 8.

ARTICLE 5. *Whether There Can Be Any Suitable Cause for the Sacraments of the Old Law?*

We proceed thus to the Fifth Article: It would seem that there can be no suitable cause for the sacraments of the Old Law.

Objection 1. For those things that are done for the purpose of divine worship should not be like the observances of idolaters, since it is written (Deut. 12. 31): *Thou shalt not do in like manner to the Lord thy God; for they have done to their gods all the abominations which the Lord abhorreth.* Now worshippers of idols used to cut themselves even to the shedding of blood; for it is related (III Kings 18. 28) that they *cut themselves after their manner with knives and lancets, till they were all covered with blood.* For this reason the Lord commanded (Deut. 14. 1): *You shall not cut yourselves nor make any baldness for the dead.* Therefore it was unfitting for circumcision to be prescribed by the Law (Levit. 12. 3).

Obj. 2. Further, those things which are done for the worship of God should be marked with decorum and gravity, according to Ps. 34. 18: *I will praise Thee in a grave* (Douay,—*strong*) *people.* But it seems to savour of levity for a man to eat with haste. Therefore it was unfittingly commanded (Exod. 12. 11) that they should eat the Paschal lamb *in haste.* Other things too relative to the eating of the lamb were prescribed, which seem altogether unreasonable.

Obj. 3. Further, the sacraments of the Old Law were figures of the sacraments of the New Law. Now the Paschal lamb signified the sacrament of the Eucharist, according to I Cor. 5. 7: *Christ our Pasch is sacrificed.* Therefore there should also have been some sacraments in the Old Law to foreshadow the other sacraments of the New Law, such as Confirmation, Extreme Unction, and Matrimony, and so forth.

Obj. 4. Further, purification can scarcely be done except by removing something impure. But as far as God is concerned, no bodily thing is accounted impure, because all bodies are God's creatures; and *every creature of God is good, and nothing to be rejected that is received with thanksgiving* (I Tim. 4. 4). It was therefore unfitting for them to be purified after contact with a corpse, or any similar corporeal infection.

Obj. 5. Further, it is written (Ecclus. 34. 4): *What can be made clean by the unclean?* But the ashes of the red heifer which was burnt were unclean, since they made a man unclean; for it is stated (Num. 19. 7, *seq.*) that the priest who immolated her was rendered unclean *until the evening;* likewise he that burnt her, and he that gathered up her ashes. Therefore it was unfittingly prescribed there that the unclean should be purified by being sprinkled with those ashes.

Obj. 6. Further, sins are not something corporeal that can be carried from one place to another, nor can man be cleansed from sin by means of something unclean. It was therefore unfitting for the purpose of expiating the sins of the people that the priest should confess the sins of the children of Israel on one of the buck-goats, that it might carry them away into the wilderness; but they were rendered unclean by the other, which they used for the purpose of purification, by burning it together with the calf outside the camp, so that they had to wash their clothes and their bodies with water (Levit. 16.).

Obj. 7. Further, what is already cleansed should not be cleansed again. It was therefore unfitting to apply a second purification to a man cleansed from leprosy, or to a house; as laid down in Levit. 14.

Obj. 8. Further, spiritual uncleanness cannot be cleansed by material water or by shaving the hair. Therefore it seems unreasonable that the Lord ordered (Exod. 30. 18, *seq.*) the making of a brazen laver with its pedestal, that the priests might wash their hands and feet before entering the temple; and that He commanded (Num. 8. 7) the Levites to be sprinkled with the water of purification, and to shave all the hairs of their flesh.

Obj. 9. Further, that which is greater cannot be cleansed by that which is less. Therefore it was unfitting that, in the Law, the higher and lower priests, as stated in Levit. 8., and the Levites, according to Num. 8., should be consecrated with any bodily anointing, bodily sacrifices, and bodily oblations.

Obj. 10. Further, as stated in I Kings 16, 7, *Man seeth those things that appear, but the Lord beholdeth the heart.* But those things that appear outwardly in man are the disposition of his body and his clothes.[1] Therefore it was unfitting for certain special garments to be appointed to the higher and lower priests, as re-

[1] Maimonides, *Guide*, III, 45 (FR 357).

lated in Exod. 28. It seems, moreover, unreasonable that anyone should be debarred from the priesthood on account of defects in the body, as stated in Levit. 21. 17, *seq.: Whosoever of thy seed throughout their families, hath a blemish, he shall not offer bread to his God . . . if he be blind, if he be lame,* etc. It seems therefore, that the sacraments of the Old Law were unreasonable.

On the contrary, It is written (Levit. 20. 8): *I am the Lord that sanctify you.* But nothing unreasonable is done by God, for it is written (Ps. 103. 24): *Thou hast made all things in wisdom.* Therefore there was nothing without a reasonable cause in the sacraments of the Old Law, which were ordained to the sanctification of man.

I answer that, As stated above (Q. CI, A. 4), the sacraments are, properly speaking, things applied to the worshippers of God for their consecration so as, in some way, to appoint them to the worship of God. Now the worship of God belonged in a general way to the whole people; but in a special way, it belonged to the priests and Levites, who were the ministers of divine worship. Consequently, in these sacraments of the Old Law, certain things concerned the whole people in general, while others belonged to the ministers.

In regard to both, three things were necessary. The first was to be established in the state of worshipping God; and this institution was brought about for all in general by circumcision, without which no one was admitted to any of the legal observances, and for the priests by their consecration. The second thing required was the use of those things that pertain to divine worship. And thus, as to the people, there was the partaking of the paschal banquet, to which no uncircumcised man was admitted, as is clear from Exod. 12. 43, *seq.*; and, as to the priests, the offering of the victims, and the eating of the loaves of proposition and of other things that were allotted to the use of the priests. The third thing required was the removal of all impediments to divine worship, namely, of uncleannesses. And so, as to the people, certain purifications were instituted for the removal of certain external uncleannesses, and also expiations from sins; while as to the priests and Levites, the washing of hands and feet and the shaving of the hair were instituted.

And all these things had reasonable causes, both literal, in so far as they were ordained to the worship of God for the time being, and figurative, in so far as they were ordained to foreshadow Christ, as we shall see by taking them one by one.

Reply Obj. 1. The chief literal reason for circumcision was in order that man might profess his belief in one God. And because Abraham was the first to sever himself from the infidels, by going out from his house and kindred, for this reason he was the first to receive circumcision. This reason is set forth by the Apostle (Rom. 4. 9, *seq.*) thus: *He received the sign of circumcision, a seal of the justice of the faith which he had, being uncircumcised;* because, that is, we are told that *unto Abraham faith was reputed to justice,* for the reason that *against hope he believed in hope,* that is, against the hope that is of nature he believed in the hope that is of grace, *that he might be made the father of many nations,* when he was an old man, and his wife an old and barren woman. And in order that this declaration and imitation of Abraham's faith might be fixed firmly in the hearts of the Jews, they received in their flesh such a sign as they could not forget, and so it is written (Gen. 17. 13): *My covenant shall be in your flesh for a perpetual covenant.* This was done on the eighth day, because until then a child is very tender, and so might be seriously injured, and is considered as something not yet consolidated; therefore neither are animals offered before the eighth day. And it was not delayed after that time, lest some might refuse the sign of circumcision on account of the pain, and also lest the parents, whose love for their children increases as they become used to their presence and as they grow older, should withdraw their children from circumcision. A second reason may have been the weakening of concupiscence in that member. A third motive may have been to revile the worship of Venus and Priapus, which gave honour to that part of the body. The Lord's prohibition extended only to the cutting of oneself in honour of idols, and such was not the circumcision of which we have been speaking.

The figurative reason for circumcision was that it foreshadowed the removal of corruption, which was to be brought about by Christ, and will be perfectly fulfilled in the eighth age, which is the age of those who rise from the dead. And since all corruption of guilt and punishment comes to us through our carnal origin, from the sin of our first parent, therefore circumcision was applied to the generative member. Hence the Apostle says (Coloss. 2. 11): *You are circumcised* in Christ *with circumcision not made by hand in despoiling of the body of the flesh, but in the circumcision of* Our Lord Jesus *Christ.*

Reply Obj. 2. The literal reason of the paschal banquet was to commemorate the blessing of being led by God out of Egypt. Hence by celebrating this banquet they declared that they belonged to that people which God had taken to Himself out of Egypt. For when they were delivered from Egypt, they were commanded to sprinkle the lamb's blood on the upper door-posts of their houses; as though declaring that they were averse to the rites of the Egyptians who worshipped the ram. Therefore they were delivered by the sprinkling or rubbing of the blood of the lamb on the door-posts from the danger of extermination which threatened the Egyptians.

Now two things are to be observed in their departure from Egypt: namely, their haste in going, for the Egyptians pressed them to go forth speedily, as related in Exod. 12. 33; and there was the danger that anyone who did not hasten to go with the crowd might be slain by the Egyptians. Their haste was shown in two ways. First by what they ate. For they were commanded to eat unleavened bread, as a sign *that it could not be leavened, the Egyptians pressing them to depart;* and to eat roast meat, for this took less time to prepare; and that they should not break a bone thereof, because in their haste there was no time to break bones. Secondly, as to the manner of eating. For it is written: *You shall gird your reins, and you shall have shoes on your feet, holding staves in your hands, and you shall eat in haste,* which clearly designates men at the point of starting on a journey. To this also is to be referred the command: *In one house shall it be eaten, neither shall you carry forth of the flesh thereof out of the house;* because, that is, on account of their haste, they could not send any gifts of it. The stress they suffered while in Egypt was denoted by the wild lettuces.

The figurative reason is evident, because the sacrifice of the paschal lamb signified the sacrifice of Christ according to I Cor. 5. 7: *Christ our pasch is sacrificed.* The blood of the lamb, which ensured deliverance from the destroyer by being sprinkled on the upper door-posts signified faith in Christ's Passion, in the hearts and on the lips of the faithful, by which same Passion we are delivered from sin and death, according to I Pet. 1. 18: *You were . . . redeemed . . . with the precious blood . . . of a lamb unspotted.* The partaking of its flesh signified the eating of Christ's body in the Sacrament; and the flesh was roasted at the fire to signify Christ's Passion or charity. And it was eaten with unleavened bread to signify the blameless life of the faithful who partake of Christ's body, according to I Cor. 5. 8: *Let us feast . . . with the unleavened bread of sincerity and truth*. The wild lettuces were added to denote repentance for sins, which is rquired of those who receive the body of Christ. Their loins were girt in sign of chastity and the shoes of their feet are the examples of our dead ancestors. The staves they were to hold in their hands denoted pastoral authority, and it was commanded that the paschal lamb should be eaten in one house, that is, in a catholic church, and not in the conventicles of heretics.

Reply Obj. 3. Some of the sacraments of the New Law had corresponding figurative sacraments in the Old Law. For Baptism, which is the sacrament of Faith, corresponds to circumcision. Hence it is written (Col. 2. 11, 12): *You are circumcised . . . in the circumcision of* Our Lord Jesus *Christ; buried with Him in Baptism*. In the New Law the sacrament of the Eucharist corresponds to the banquet of the paschal lamb. The sacrament of Penance in the New Law corresponds to all the purifications of the Old Law. The sacrament of Orders corresponds to the consecration of the pontiff and of the priests. To the sacrament of Confirmation, which is the sacrament of the fulness of grace, there would be no corresponding sacrament of the Old Law, because the time of fulness had not yet come, since *the Law brought no man* (Vulg.,—*nothing*) *to perfection* (Heb. 7. 19). The same applies to the sacrament of Extreme Unction, which is an immediate preparation for entrance into glory, to which the way was not yet opened out in the Old Law, since the price had not yet been paid. Matrimony did indeed exist under the Old Law, as a function of nature, but not as the sacrament of the union of Christ with the Church, for that union was not as yet brought about. Hence under the Old Law it was allowable to give a bill of divorce, which is contrary to the nature of a sacrament.

Reply Obj. 4. As already stated, the purifications of the Old Law were ordained for the removal of impediments to the divine worship, which worship is twofold; namely, spiritual, consisting in devotion of the mind to God, and corporal, consisting in sacrifices, oblations, and so forth. Now men are hindered in the spiritual worship by sins, by which men were said to be polluted, for instance, by idolatry, murder,

adultery, or incest. From such pollutions men were purified by certain sacrifices, offered either for the whole community in general, or also for the sins of individuals; not that those carnal sacrifices had of themselves the power of expiating sin, but that they signified that expiation of sins which was to be effected by Christ, and of which those of old became partakers by protesting their faith in the Redeemer, while taking part in the figurative sacrifices.

The impediments to external worship consisted in certain bodily uncleannesses, which were considered in the first place as existing in man, and consequently in other animals also, and in man's clothes, dwelling-place, and vessels. In man himself uncleanness was considered as arising partly from himself and partly from contact with unclean things. Anything proceeding from man was accounted unclean that was already subject to corruption, or exposed to it; and consequently since death is a kind of corruption, the human corpse was considered unclean. In like manner, since leprosy arises from corruption of the humours, which break out externally and infect other persons, therefore were lepers also considered unclean; and, again, women suffering from a flow of blood, whether from weakness, or from nature (either at the monthly course or at the time of conception); and, for the same reason, men were reputed unclean if they suffered from a flow of seed, whether due to weakness, to nocturnal pollution, or to sexual intercourse. Because every humour issuing from man in the above ways involves some unclean infection. Again, man contracted uncleanness by touching any unclean thing whatever.

Now there was both a literal and a figurative reason for these uncleannesses. The literal reason was taken from the reverence due to those things that belong to the divine worship; both because men are not accustomed, when unclean, to touch precious things, and in order that by rarely approaching sacred things they might have greater respect for them. For since man could seldom avoid all these uncleannesses, the result was that men could seldom approach to touch things belonging to the worship of God, so that when they did approach, they did so with greater reverence and humbleness of mind.[1] Moreover, in some of these the literal reason was that men should not be kept away from worshipping God through fear of coming in contact with lepers and others similarly afflicted with loathsome and contagious diseases. In

---

[1] Maimonides, *Guide*, III, 47 (FR 367).

others, again, the reason was to avoid idolatrous worship, because in their sacrificial rites the Gentiles sometimes employed human blood and seed. All these bodily uncleannesses were purified either by the mere sprinkling of water, or, in the case of those which were more grievous, by some sacrifice of expiation for the sin which was the occasion of the uncleanness in question.

The figurative reason for these uncleannesses was that they were figures of various sins. For the uncleanness of any corpse signifies the uncleanness of sin, which is the death of the soul. The uncleanness of leprosy signified the uncleanness of heretical doctrine; both because heretical doctrine is contagious just as leprosy is, and because no doctrine is so false as not to have some truth mingled with error, just as on the surface of a leprous body one may distinguish the healthy parts from those that are infected. The uncleanness of a woman suffering from a flow of blood denotes the uncleanness of idolatry, on account of the blood which is offered up. The uncleanness of the man who has suffered seminal loss signifies the uncleanness of empty words, for *the seed is the word of God.* (Luke 8, 11) The uncleanness of sexual intercourse and of the woman in child-birth signifies the uncleanness of original sin. The uncleanness of the woman in her periods signifies the uncleanness of a mind that is sensualized by pleasure. Speaking generally, the uncleanness contracted by touching an unclean thing denotes the uncleanness arising from consent in another's sin, according to II Cor. 6. 17: *Go out from among them, and be ye separate . . . and touch not the unclean thing.*

Moreover, this uncleanness arising from the touch was contracted even by inanimate objects; for whatever was touched in any way by an unclean man, became itself unclean. In this the Law attenuated the superstition of the Gentiles, who held that uncleanness was contracted not only by touch, but also by speech or looks, as Rabbi Moses states (*Doct. Perplex.* iii)[1] of a woman in her periods. The mystical sense of this was that to *God the wicked and his wickedness are hateful alike* (Wisd. 14. 9).

There was also an uncleanness of inanimate things considered in themselves, such as the uncleanness of leprosy in a house or in clothes. For just as leprosy occurs in men through a corrupt humour causing putrefaction and corruption in the flesh, so, too, through some corruption and excess of humidity or dryness,

there arises sometimes a kind of corruption in the stones with which a house is built, or in clothes. Hence the Law called this corruption by the name of leprosy, whereby a house or a garment was deemed to be unclean; both because all corruption savoured of uncleanness, as stated above, and because the Gentiles worshipped their household gods as a preservative against this corruption. Hence the Law prescribed such houses, where this kind of corruption was of a lasting nature, to be destroyed, and such garments to be burnt, in order to avoid all occasion of idolatry. There was also an uncleanness of vessels, of which it is written (Num. 19. 15): *The vessel that hath no cover, and binding over it, shall be unclean.* The cause of this uncleanness was that anything unclean might easily drop into such vessels, so as to render them unclean. Moreover, this command aimed at the prevention of idolatry. For idolaters believed that if mice, lizards, or the like, which they used to sacrifice to the idols, fell into the vessels or into the water, these became more pleasing to the gods. Even now some women let down uncovered vessels in honour of the nocturnal deities which they call "*Janæ.*"

The figurative reason of these uncleannesses is that the leprosy of a house signified the uncleanness of the assembly of heretics; the leprosy of a linen garment signified an evil life arising from bitterness of mind; the leprosy of a woollen garment denoted the wickedness of flatterers; leprosy in the warp signified the vices of the soul; leprosy on the woof denoted sins of the flesh, for as the warp is in the woof, so is the soul in the body. The vessel that has neither cover nor binding, betokens a man who lacks the veil of taciturnity, and who is unrestrained by any severity of discipline.

Reply Obj. 5. As stated above (reply 4), there was a twofold uncleanness in the Law: one by way of corruption in the mind or in the body, and this was the graver uncleanness; the other was by mere contact with an unclean thing, and this was less grave, and was more easily expiated. For the former uncleanness was expiated by sacrifices for sins, since all corruption is due to sin, and signifies sin; but the latter uncleanness was expiated by the mere sprinkling of a certain water, of which water we read in Num. 19. For there God commanded them to take a red cow in memory of the sin they had committed in worshipping a calf. And a cow is mentioned rather than a calf, because it was thus that the Lord was accustomed to

---

[1] Chap. 47 (FR 368).

designate the synagogue, according to Osee 4. 16: *Israel hath gone astray like a wanton heifer;* and this was, perhaps, because they worshipped heifers after the custom of Egypt, according to Osee 10. 5: *(They) have worshipped the kine of Bethaven.* And in detestation of the sin of idolatry it was sacrificed outside the camp; in fact, whenever sacrifice was offered up in expiation of the multitude of sins, it was all burnt outside the camp. Moreover, in order to show that this sacrifice cleansed the people from all their sins, *the priest* dipped *his finger in her blood,* and sprinkled *it over against the door of the tabernacle seven times;* for the number seven signifies universality. Further, the very sprinkling of blood pertained to the detestation of idolatry, in which the blood that was offered up was not poured out, but was collected together, and men gathered round it to eat in honour of the idols. Likewise it was burnt by fire, either because God appeared to Moses in a fire, and the Law was given from the midst of fire, or to denote that idolatry, together with all that was connected therewith, was to be extirpated altogether; just as the cow was burnt *with her skin and her flesh, her blood and dung being delivered to the flames.* To this burning were added *cedar-wood, and hyssop, and scarlet twice dyed,* to signify that just as cedar-wood is not liable to putrefaction, and scarlet twice dyed does not easily lose its colour, and hyssop retains its odour after it has been dried, so also was this sacrifice for the preservation of the whole people, and for their good behaviour and devotion. Hence it is said of the ashes of the cow: *That they may be reserved for the multitude of the children of Israel.* Or, according to Josephus,[1] the four elements are indicated here, for cedar-wood was added to the fire to signify the earth, on account of its earthiness; hyssop to signify the air, on account of its smell; scarlet twice dyed to signify water, for the same reason as purple, on account of the dyes which are taken out of the water,—thus denoting the fact that this sacrifice was offered to the Creator of the four elements. And since this sacrifice was offered for the sin of idolatry, both *he that burned her,* and *he that gathered up the ashes,* and *he that sprinkled the water* in which the ashes were placed, were accounted unclean in detestation of that sin, in order to show that whatever was in any way connected with idolatry should be cast aside as being unclean. From this unclean-

[1] The reference is uncertain; possibly *De Bello Judaico,* V, V, 4 (TK III, 265).

ness they were purified by the mere washing of their clothes; nor did they need to be sprinkled with the water on account of this kind of uncleanness, because otherwise the process would have been unending, since he that sprinkled the water became unclean, so that if he were to sprinkle himself he would remain unclean; and if another were to sprinkle him, that one would have become unclean, and in like manner, whoever might sprinkle him, and so on indefinitely.

The figurative reason of this sacrifice was that the red cow signified Christ in respect of his assumed weakness, denoted by the female sex; while the colour of the cow designated the blood of His Passion. And the *red cow was of full age,* because all Christ's works are perfect, *in which there* was *no blemish; and which* had *not carried the yoke,* because Christ was innocent, nor did He carry the yoke of sin. It was commanded to be taken to Moses, because they blamed Him for transgressing the law of Moses by breaking the Sabbath. And it was commanded to be delivered *to Eleazar the priest,* because Christ was delivered into the hands of the priests to be slain. It was immolated *without the camp,* because Christ *suffered outside the gate* (Heb. 13. 12). And the priest dipped *his finger in her blood,* because the mystery of Christ's Passion should be considered and imitated.

It was sprinkled *over against . . . the tabernacle,* which denotes the synagogue, to signify either the condemnation of the unbelieving Jews, or the purification of believers; and this *seven times,* in token either of the seven gifts of the Holy Ghost, or of the seven days wherein all time is comprised. Again, all things that pertain to the Incarnation of Christ should be burnt with fire, that is, they should be understood spiritually; for the skin and flesh signified Christ's outward works; the blood denoted the subtle inward force which quickened His external deeds; the dung signified His weariness, His thirst, and all such things pertaining to His weakness. Three things were added, namely, cedar-wood, which denotes the height of hope or contemplation; hyssop, in token of humility or faith; scarlet twice dyed, which denotes twofold charity; for it is by these three that we should cling to Christ suffering. The ashes of this burning were gathered by *a man that is clean,* because the relics of the Passion came into the possession of the Gentiles, who were not guilty of Christ's death. The ashes were put into water for the purpose of expiation, because Baptism receives from Christ's Passion the power of washing away sins. The priest who immolated and burned the cow, and he who burned, and he who gathered together the ashes, were unclean, as also he that sprinkled the water; either because the Jews became unclean through putting Christ to death, whereby our sins are expiated, and this, until the evening, that is, until the end of the world, when the remnants of Israel will be converted; or else because they who handle sacred things with a view to the cleansing of others contract certain uncleannesses, as Gregory says (*Pastor.* 2, 5);[1] and this until evening, that is, until the end of this life.

Reply Obj. 6. As stated above (ʀᴇply 5), an uncleanness which was caused by corruption either of mind or of body was expiated by sin-offerings. Now special sacrifices used to be offered for the sins of individuals. But since some were neglectful about expiating such sins and uncleannesses, or, through ignorance, failed to offer this expiation, it was laid down that once a year, on the tenth day of the seventh month, a sacrifice of expiation should be offered for the whole people. And because, as the Apostle says (Heb. 7. 28), *the Law maketh men priests, who have infirmity,* the priest first of all had to offer a calf for his own sins, in memory of Aaron's sin in fashioning the molten calf, and besides, to offer a ram for a holocaust, which signified that the priestly sovereignty denoted by the ram, who is the head of the flock, was to be ordained to the glory of God. Then he offered two he-goats for the people, one of which was offered in expiation of the sins of the multitude. For the he-goat is an evil-smelling animal, and from its skin clothes are made having a pungent odour; thus is signified the stench, uncleanness and the sting of sin. After this he-goat had been immolated, its blood was taken, together with the blood of the calf, into the Holy of Holies, and the entire sanctuary was sprinkled with it, to signify that the tabernacle was cleansed from the uncleannesses of the children of Israel. But the corpses of the he-goat and calf which had been offered up for sin had to be burnt, to denote the destruction of sins. They were not, however, burnt on the altar, since none but holocausts were burnt thereon; but it was prescribed that they should be burnt without the camp, in detestation of sin, for this was done whenever sacrifice was offered for a grievous sin, or for the multitude of sins. The other goat was let loose into the wilderness; not indeed to offer it to the demons, whom the Gentiles worshipped in desert places, because it was unlawful to offer

[1] PL 77, 34.

anything to them, but in order to point out the effect of the sacrifice which had been offered up. Hence the priest put his hand on its head while confessing the sins of the children of Israel, as though that goat were to carry them away into the wilderness, where it would be devoured by wild beasts, because it bore the punishment of the people's sins. And it was said to bear the sins of the people either because the forgiveness of the people's sins was signified by its being let loose, or because on its head written lists of sins were fastened.

The figurative reason of these things was that Christ was foreshadowed both by the calf, on account of His power, and by the ram, because He is the Head of the faithful, and by the he-goat, on account of *the likeness of sinful flesh* (Rom. 8. 3). Moreover, Christ was sacrificed for the sins of both priests and people, since both those of high and those of low degree are cleansed from sin by His Passion. The blood of the calf and of the goat was brought into the Holies by the priest, because the entrance to the kingdom of heaven was opened to us by the blood of Christ's Passion. Their bodies were burnt without the camp, because *Christ suffered without the gate,* as the Apostle declares (Heb. 13. 12). The scape-goat may denote either Christ's divinity, Which went away into solitude when the Man Christ suffered, not by going to another place, but by restraining His power; or it may signify the base concupiscence which we ought to cast away from ourselves, while we offer up to Our Lord acts of virtue.

With regard to the uncleanness contracted by those who burnt these sacrifices, the reason is the same as that which we assigned (ʀᴇply 5) to the sacrifice of the red heifer.

Reply Obj. 7. The legal rite did not cleanse the leper of his deformity, but declared him to be cleansed. This is shown by the words of Lev. 14. 3, *seq.,* where it is said that the priest, *when he shall find that the leprosy is cleansed,* shall command *him that is to be purified;* consequently, the leper was already healed. But he was said to be purified in so far as the verdict of the priest restored him to the society of men and to the worship of God. It happened sometimes, however, that bodily leprosy was miraculously cured by the legal rite, when the priest erred in his judgment.

Now this purification of a leper was twofold. For, in the first place, he was declared to be clean; and, secondly, he was restored, as clean, to the society of men and to the worship of God, namely, after seven days. At the first purification the leper who sought to be cleansed offered for himself *two living sparrows, . . . cedar-wood, and scarlet, and hyssop,* in such wise that a sparrow and the hyssop should be tied to the cedarwood with a scarlet thread, so that the cedarwood was like the handle of an aspersory, while the hyssop and sparrow were that part of the aspersory which was dipped into the blood of the other sparrow which was *immolated . . . over living waters.* These things he offered as an antidote to the four defects of leprosy: for cedarwood, which is not subject to putrefaction, was offered against the putrefaction; hyssop, which is a sweet-smelling herb, was offered up against the stench; a living sparrow was offered up against numbness; and scarlet, which has a vivid colour, was offered up against the repulsive colour of leprosy. The living sparrow was let loose to fly away into the plain, because the leper was restored to his former liberty.

On the eighth day he was admitted to divine worship, and was restored to the society of men; but only after having shaved all the hair of his body, and washed his clothes, because leprosy rots the hair, infects the clothes, and gives them an evil smell. Afterwards a sacrifice was offered for his sin, since leprosy was frequently a result of sin, and some of the blood of the sacrifice was put on the tip of the ear of the man that was to be cleansed, *and on the thumb of his right hand, and the great toe of his right foot;* because it is in these parts that leprosy is first diagnosed and felt. In this rite, moreover, three liquids were employed: namely, blood, against the corruption of the blood; oil, to denote the healing of the disease; and living waters, to wash away the filth.

The figurative reason was that the Divine and human natures in Christ were denoted by the two sparrows, one of which, in likeness of His human nature, was offered up in an earthen vessel over living waters, because the waters of Baptism are sanctified by Christ's Passion. The other sparrow, in token of His impassible divinity, remained living, because divinity cannot die; hence it flew away, for divinity could not be encompassed by the Passion. Now this living sparrow, together with the cedar-wood and scarlet or cochineal, and hyssop, that is, faith, hope, and charity, as stated above (Reply 5), was put into the water for the purpose of sprinkling, because we are baptized in the faith of the Godhead. By the waters of Baptism or of his tears man washes his clothes, that is, his works, and all his hair, that is, his thoughts. The tip of the right ear of the man to be cleansed is moistened

with some of the blood and oil in order to strengthen his hearing against harmful words, and the thumb and toe of his right hand and foot are moistened that his deeds may be holy. Other matters pertaining to this purification, or to that also of any other uncleannesses, call for no special remark, beyond what applies to other sacrifices, whether for sins or for trespasses.

Reply Objs. 8 *and* 9. Just as the people were initiated by circumcision to the divine worship, so were the ministers by some special purification or consecration. Therefore they are commanded to be separated from other men, as being specially appointed, rather than others, to the ministry of the divine worship. And all that was done touching them in their consecration or institution was with a view to show that they were in possession of a prerogative of purity, power, and dignity. Hence three things were done in the institution of ministers. For first, they were purified; secondly, they were adorned[1] and consecrated; thirdly, they were employed in the ministry. All in general used to be purified by washing in water, and by certain sacrifices; but the Levites in particular shaved all the hair of their bodies, as stated in Lev. 8. (cf. Num. 8.).

With regard to the high-priests and priests the consecration was performed as follows. First, when they had been washed, they were clothed with certain special garments in designation of their dignity. In particular, the highpriest was anointed on the head with the oil of unction, to denote that the power of consecration was poured forth by him on to others, just as oil flows from the head on to the lower parts of the body; according to Ps. 132. 2: *Like the precious ointment on the head that ran down upon the beard, the beard of Aaron.* But the Levites received no other consecration besides being offered to the Lord by the children of Israel through the hands of the high-priest, who prayed for them. The lesser priests were consecrated on the hands only, which were to be employed in the sacrifices. The tip of their right ear and the thumb of their right hand, and the great toe of their right foot were tinged with the blood of the sacrificial animal, to denote that they should be obedient to God's law in offering the sacrifices (this is denoted by touching their right ear); and that they should be careful and ready in performing the sacrifices (this is signified by the moistening of the right foot and hand). They themselves and their garments were sprinkled with the blood of the ani-

[1] Cf. Lev. 8. 7–9.

mal that had been sacrificed, in memory of the blood of the lamb by which they had been delivered in Egypt. At their consecration the following sacrifices were offered: a calf, for sin, in memory of Aaron's sin in fashioning the molten calf; a ram, for a holocaust, in memory of the sacrifice of Abraham, whose obedience the high-priest was obliged to imitate; again, a ram of consecration, which was as a peace-offering, in memory of the delivery from Egypt through the blood of the lamb; and a basket of bread, in memory of the manna vouchsafed to the people.

In reference to their being destined to the ministry, the fat of the ram, one roll of bread, and the right shoulder were placed on their hands, to show that they received the power of offering these things to the Lord, while the Levites were initiated to the ministry by being brought into the tabernacle of the covenant, as being destined to the ministry touching the vessels of the sanctuary.

The figurative reason of these things was that those who are to be consecrated to the spiritual ministry of Christ should be first of all purified by the waters of Baptism, and by the waters of tears, in their faith in Christ's Passion, which is a sacrifice both of expiation and of purification. They have also to shave all the hair of their body, that is, all evil thoughts. They should, moreover, be decked with virtues, and be consecrated with the oil of the Holy Ghost, and with the sprinkling of Christ's blood. And thus they should be intent on the fulfilment of their spiritual ministry.

Reply Obj. 10. As already stated (A. 4), the purpose of the Law was to induce men to have reverence for the divine worship, and this in two ways. First, by excluding from the worship of God whatever might be an object of contempt; secondly, by introducing into the divine worship all that seemed to savour of reverence. And, indeed, if this was observed in regard to the tabernacle and its vessels, and in the animals to be sacrificed, much more was it to be observed in the very ministers. Therefore, in order to obviate contempt for the ministers, it was prescribed that they should have no bodily stain or defect, since men so deformed are accustomed to be despised by others. For the same reason it was also commanded that the choice of those who were to be destined to the service of God was not to be made in a broadcast manner from any family, but according to their descent from one particular stock, thus giving them distinction and nobility.

In order that they might be revered, special ornate vestments were appointed for their use, and a special form of consecration. This indeed is the general reason of ornate garments. But the high-priest in particular had eight vestments. First, he had a linen tunic. Secondly, he had a purple tunic, round the bottom of which were placed *little bells* and *pomegranates of violet, and purple, and scarlet twice dyed.* Thirdly, he had the ephod, which covered his shoulders and his breast down to the girdle; and it was made of gold, and violet and purple, and scarlet twice dyed and twisted linen, and on his shoulders he bore two onyx stones, on which were graven the names of the children of Israel. Fourthly, he had the rational, made of the same material; it was square in shape, and was worn on the breast, and was fastened to the ephod. On this rational there were twelve precious stones set in four rows, on which also were graven the names of the children of Israel, in token that the priest bore the burden of the whole people, since he bore their names on his shoulders; and that it was his duty ever to think of their welfare, since he wore them on his breast, bearing them in his heart, so to speak. And the Lord commanded the *Doctrine and Truth* to be put in the rational, for certain matters regarding moral and dogmatic truth were written on it. The Jews indeed pretend that on the rational was placed a stone which changed colour according to the various things which were about to happen to the children of Israel, and this they call the *Truth and Doctrine.* Fifthly, he wore a belt or girdle made of the four colours mentioned above. Sixthly, there was the tiara or mitre which was made of linen. Seventhly, there was the golden plate which hung over his forehead; on it was inscribed the Lord's name. Eighthly, there were *the linen breeches to cover the flesh of their nakedness,* when they went up to the sanctuary or altar. Of these eight vestments the lesser priests had four, namely, the linen tunic and breeches, the belt and the tiara.

According to some,[1] the literal reason for these vestments was that they denoted the disposition of the terrestrial globe, as though the high-priest confessed himself to be the minister of the Creator of the world; thus it is written (Wisd. 18. 24): *In the robe* of Aaron *was the whole world* described. For the linen breeches signified the earth out of which the flax grows. The surrounding belt signified the ocean which

---

[1] *Glossa ordin.* (III, 385E); Rabanus Maurus, *In Sap.*, 3.17 (PL 109, 758); cf. Josephus, *Antiqu.*, III, VII, 7 (TK IV, 405).

surrounds the earth. The violet tunic denoted the air by its colour; its little bells betoken the thunder; the pomegranates, the lightning. The ephod, by its many colours, signified the starry heaven; the two onyx stones denoted the two hemispheres, or the sun and moon. The twelve precious stones on the breast are the twelve signs of the zodiac, and they are said to have been placed on the rational, because in heaven are the types (*rationes*) of earthly things, according to Job 38. 33: *Dost thou know the order of heaven, and canst thou set down the reason (rationem) thereof on the earth?* The turban or tiara signified the empyrean; the golden plate was a token of God, the governor of the universe.

The figurative reason is evident. Because bodily stains or defects from which the priests had to be immune signify the various vices and sins from which they should be free. Thus it is forbidden that he should be blind, that is, he ought not to be ignorant; he must not be lame, that is, vacillating and uncertain of purpose; that he must not have *a little, or a great, or a crooked nose*, that is, that he should not, from lack of discretion, exceed in one direction or in another, or even exercise some base occupation, for the nose signifies discretion, because it discerns odours. It is forbidden that he should have *a broken foot* or *hand*, that is, he should not lose the power of doing good works or of advancing in virtue. He is rejected, too, if he have a swelling either in front or behind (Vulg., —*if he be crookbacked*), by which is signified too much love of earthly things; if he be bleareyed, that is, if his mind is darkened by carnal affections, for running of the eyes is caused by a flow of matter. He is also rejected if he have *a pearl in his eye*, that is, if he presumes in his own estimation that he is clothed in the white robe of justice. Again, he is rejected *if he have a continued scab*, that is, lustfulness of the flesh; also, if he have *a dry scurf*, which covers the body without giving pain, and is a blemish on the comeliness of the members, which denotes avarice. Lastly, he is rejected *if he have a rupture* or hernia, through baseness rending his heart, though it appear not in his deeds.

The vestments denote the virtues of God's ministers. Now there are four things that are necessary to all His ministers, namely, chastity denoted by the breeches; a pure life, signified by the linen tunic; the moderation of discretion, signified by the girdle; and rectitude of purpose, denoted by the mitre covering the head. But the high-priests needed four other things in addition

to these. First, a continual recollection of God in their thoughts; and this was signified by the golden plate worn over the forehead, with the name of God engraved thereon. Secondly, they had to bear with the shortcomings of the people; this was denoted by the ephod which they bore on their shoulders. Thirdly, they had to carry the people in their mind and heart by the solicitude of charity, in token of which they wore the rational. Fourthly, they had to lead a godly life by performing works of perfection, and this was signified by the violet tunic. Hence little golden bells were fixed to the bottom of the violet tunic, which bells signified the teaching of divine things united in the high-priest to his godly mode of life. In addition to these were the pomegranates, signifying unity of faith and concord in good morals, because his doctrine should hold together in such a way that it should not rend asunder the unity of faith and peace.

ARTICLE 6. *Whether There Was Any Reasonable Cause for the Ceremonial Observances?*

We proceed thus to the Sixth Article: It would seem that there was no reasonable cause for the ceremonial observances.

Objection 1. For as the Apostle says (I Tim. 4. 4), *every creature of God is good, and nothing to be rejected that is received with thanksgiving*. It was therefore unfitting that they should be forbidden to eat certain foods, as being unclean according to Lev. 11.

Obj. 2. Further, just as animals are given to man for food, so also are herbs; hence it is written (Gen. 9. 3): *As the green herbs have I delivered all* flesh *to you*. But the Law did not distinguish any herbs from the rest as being unclean, although some are most harmful, for instance, those that are poisonous. Therefore it seems that neither should any animals have been prohibited as being unclean.

Obj. 3. Further, if the matter from which a thing is generated be unclean, it seems that likewise the thing generated from it is unclean. But flesh is generated from blood. Since therefore all flesh was not prohibited as unclean, it seems that in like manner neither should blood have been forbidden as unclean, nor the fat which is engendered from blood.

Obj. 4. Further, Our Lord said (Matt. 10. 28; cf. Luke 12. 4), that those should not be feared *that kill the body*, since after death they *have no more that they can do*, which would not be true if after death harm might come to man through anything done with his body. Much less therefore does it matter to an animal already dead how its flesh be cooked. Consequently there seems to be no reason in what is said, Exod. 23. 19: *Thou shalt not boil a kid in the milk of its dam.*

Obj. 5. Further, all that is first brought forth of man and beast, as being most perfect, is commanded to be offered to the Lord (Exod. 13.). Therefore it is an unfitting command that is set forth in Lev. 19. 23: *when you shall be come into the land, and shall have planted in it fruit trees, you shall take away the uncircumcision* (Douay,—*first fruits) of them,* that is, the first crops, and they *shall be unclean to you, neither shall you eat of them.*

Obj. 6. Further, clothing is something extraneous to man's body. Therefore certain kinds of garments should not have been forbidden to the Jews; for instance (Lev. 19. 19): *Thou shalt not wear a garment that is woven of two sorts;* and (Deut. 22. 5): *A woman shall not be clothed with man's apparel, neither shall a man use woman's apparel;* and further on (verse 11): *Thou shalt not wear a garment that is woven of woollen and linen together.*

Obj. 7. Further, to be mindful of God's commandments concerns not the body but the heart. Therefore it is unsuitably prescribed (Deut. 6. 8, *seq.*) that they should *bind* the commandments of God *as a sign* on their hands; and that they should *write them in the entry;* and (Num 15. 38, *seq.*) that they should *make to themselves fringes in the corners of their garments, putting in them ribands of blue, that . . . they may remember . . . the commandments of the Lord.*

Obj. 8. Further, the Apostle says (I Cor. 9. 9) that God doth not *take care for oxen,* and, therefore, neither of other irrational animals. Therefore without reason is it commanded (Deut. 22. 6): *If thou find, as thou walkest by the way, a bird's nest in a tree . . . thou shalt not take the dam with her young;* and (Deut. 25. 4): *Thou shalt not muzzle the ox that treadeth out thy corn;* and (Lev. 19. 19): *Thou shalt not make thy cattle to gender with beasts of any other kind.*

Obj. 9. Further, no distinction was made between clean and unclean plants. Much less therefore should any distinction have been made about the cultivation of plants. Therefore it was unfittingly prescribed (Lev. 19. 19): *Thou shalt not sow thy field with different seeds;* and (Deut. 22. 9, *seq.*): *Thou shalt sow thy vineyard with divers seeds;* and: *Thou shalt not plough with an ox and an ass together.*

Obj. 10. Further, it is apparent that inanimate things are most of all subject to the power of man. Therefore it was unfitting to debar man from taking the silver and gold of which idols were made, or anything they found in the houses of idols, as expressed in the commandment of the Law (Deut. 7. 25, *seq.*). It also seems an absurd commandment set forth in Deut. 23. 13, that they should *dig round about and . . . cover with earth that which they were eased of.*

Obj. 11. Further, piety is required especially in priests. But it seems to be an act of piety to assist at the burial of one's friends; hence, too, Tobias is commended for so doing (Tob. 1. 20. *seqq.*). In like manner it is sometimes an act of piety to marry a loose woman, because she is thus delivered from sin and infamy. Therefore it seems inconsistent for these things to be forbidden to priests (Lev. 21.).

On the contrary, It is written (Deut. 18. 14): *But thou art otherwise instructed by the Lord thy God,* from which words we may gather that these observances were instituted by God to be a special prerogative of that people. Therefore they are not without reason or cause.

I answer that, The Jewish people, as stated above (A. 5), were specially chosen for the worship of God, and among them the priests themselves were specially set apart for that purpose. And just as other things that are applied to the divine worship need to be marked in some particular way so that they be worthy of the worship of God, so too in that people's, and specially the priests', mode of life, there needed to be certain special things befitting the divine worship, whether spiritual or corporal. Now the worship prescribed by the Law foreshadowed the mystery of Christ, so that whatever they did was a figure of things pertaining to Christ, according to I Cor. 10. 11: *All these things happened to them in figures.* Consequently the reasons for these observances may be taken in two ways, first according to their fittingness to the worship of God; secondly, according as they foreshadow something touching the Christian mode of life.

Reply Obj. 1. As stated above (A. 5, Reply 4, 5), the Law distinguished a twofold pollution or uncleanness: one, that of sin, whereby the soul was defiled; and another consisting in some kind of corruption, whereby the body was in some way infected. Speaking then of the first-mentioned uncleanness, no kind of food is unclean, or can defile a man, by reason of its nature; hence we read (Matt. 15. 11): *Not that which goeth into the mouth defileth a man;*

but what cometh out of the mouth, this defileth a man, which words are explained (verse 17) as referring to sins. Yet certain foods can defile the soul accidentally in so far as man partakes of them against obedience or a vow, or from excessive concupiscence, or through their being an incentive to lust, for which reason some refrain from wine and flesh-meat.

If, however, we speak of bodily uncleanness, consisting in some kind of corruption, the flesh of certain animals is unclean, either because like the pig they feed on unclean things, or because their life is among unclean surroundings; thus certain animals, like moles and mice and the like, live underground, from which they contract a certain unpleasant smell; or because their flesh, through being too moist or too dry, engenders corrupt humours in the human body.[1] Hence they were forbidden to eat the flesh of flat-footed animals, that is, animals having an uncloven hoof, on account of their earthiness; and in like manner they were forbidden to eat the flesh of animals that have many clefts in their feet, because such are very fierce and their flesh is very dry, such as the flesh of lions and the like. For the same reason they were forbidden to eat certain birds of prey the flesh of which is very dry, and certain water-fowl on account of their exceeding humidity. In like manner certain fish lacking fins and scales were prohibited on account of their excessive moisture, such as eels and the like. They were, however, allowed to eat ruminants and animals with a divided hoof, because in such animals the humours are well absorbed, and their nature well balanced; for neither are they too moist, as is indicated by the hoof, nor are they too earthy, which is shown by their having not a flat but a cloven hoof. Of fishes they were allowed to partake of the drier kinds, of which the fins and scales are an indication, because thereby the moist nature of the fish is tempered. Of birds they were allowed to eat the tamer kinds, such as hens, partridges, and the like. Another reason was detestation of idolatry: because the Gentiles, and especially the Egyptians, among whom they had grown up, offered up these forbidden animals to their idols, or employed them for the purpose of sorcery; but they did not eat those animals which the Jews were allowed to eat, but worshipped them as gods, or abstained, for some other motive, from eating them, as stated above (A. 3, Reply 2). The third reason was to prevent excessive care about food; hence they were allowed to eat those animals which could be procured easily and promptly.

With regard to blood and fat, they were forbidden to partake of those of any animal whatever without exception. Blood was forbidden both in order to avoid cruelty, that they might abhor the shedding of human blood, as stated above (A. 3, Reply 8); and in order to shun the idolatrous rite whereby it was customary for men to collect the blood and to gather together around it for a banquet in honour of the idols, to whom they held the blood to be most acceptable. Hence the Lord commanded the blood to be poured out and to be covered with earth (Lev. 17. 13). For the same reason they were forbidden to eat animals that had been suffocated or strangled, because the blood of these animals would not be separated from the body or because this form of death is very painful to the victim; and the Lord wished to withdraw them from cruelty even in regard to irrational animals, so as to be less inclined to be cruel to other men, through being used to be kind to beasts. They were forbidden to eat the fat, both because idolaters ate it in honour of their gods and because it used to be burnt in honour of God; and, again, because blood and fat are not nutritious, which is the cause assigned by Rabbi Moses (*Doct. Perplex.* iii).[2] The reason why they were forbidden to eat the sinews is given in Gen. 32. 32, where it is stated that *the children of Israel . . . eat not the sinew . . . because he touched the sinew of* Jacob's *thigh and it shrank.*

The figurative reason for these things is that all these animals signified certain sins, in token of which those animals were prohibited. Hence Augustine says (*Contra Faust.* vi, 7):[3] "If the swine and lamb be called in question, both are clean by nature, because all God's creatures are good; yet the lamb is clean, and the pig is unclean in a certain signification. Thus if you speak of a foolish, and of a wise man, each of these expressions is clean considered in the nature of the sound, letters and syllables of which it is composed; but in signification, the one is clean, the other unclean." The animal that chews the cud and has a divided hoof is clean in signification. Because division of the hoof is a figure of the two Testaments; or of the Father and Son; or of the two natures in Christ; of the distinction of good and evil. But chewing the cud signifies meditation on the Scriptures and a sound understanding of them, and who-

---

[1] Maimonides, *Guide*, iii, 48 (FR 370).

[2] Chap. 48 (FR 371).

[3] PL 42, 233.

ever lacks either of these is spiritually unclean. In like manner those fish that have scales and fins are clean in signification. Because fins signify the heavenly or contemplative life, while scales signify a life of trials, each of which is required for spiritual cleanness.

Of birds certain special kinds were forbidden.[1] In the eagle which flies at a great height, pride is forbidden: in the griffon which is hostile to horses and men, cruelty of powerful men is prohibited. The osprey, which feeds on very small birds, signifies those who oppress the poor. The kite, which is full of cunning, denotes those who are fraudulent in their dealings. The vulture, which follows an army, expecting to feed on the carcases of the slain, signifies those who like others to die or to fight among themselves that they may gain thereby. Birds of the raven kind signify those who are blackened by their lusts; or those who lack kindly feelings, for the raven did not return when once it had been let loose from the ark. The ostrich which, though a bird, cannot fly, and is always on the ground, signifies those who fight for God's cause, and at the same time are taken up with worldly business. The owl, which sees clearly at night, but cannot see in daytime, denotes those who are clever in temporal affairs, but dull in spiritual matters. The gull, which both flies in the air and swims in the water, signifies those who are partial both to Circumcision and to Baptism; or else it denotes those who would fly by contemplation, yet dwell in the waters of sensual delights. The hawk, which helps men to seize the prey, is a figure of those who assist the strong to prey on the poor.[2] The screech-owl, which seeks its food by night but hides by day, signifies the lustful man who seeks to lie hidden in his deeds of darkness.[3] The cormorant, so constituted that it can stay a long time under water, denotes the glutton who plunges into the waters of pleasure. The ibis is an African bird with a long beak, and feeds on snakes; and perhaps it is the same as the stork.[4] It signifies the envious man, who refreshes himself with the ills of others, as with snakes. The swan is bright in colour, and by the aid of its long neck extracts its food from deep places on land or water: it may denote those who seek earthly profit through an external brightness of virtue. The bittern is a bird of the East. It has

a long beak, and its jaws are furnished with follicules, in which it stores its food at first, after a time proceeding to digest it;[5] it is a figure of the miser, who is excessively careful in hoarding up the necessities of life. The coot (Douay, —*porphyrion*) has this peculiarity apart from other birds, that it has a webbed foot for swimming, and a cloven foot for walking, for it swims like a duck in the water, and walks like a partridge on land. It drinks only when it bites, since it dips all its food in water[6]; it is a figure of the man who will not take advice, and does nothing but what is soaked in the water of his own will. The heron, commonly called a falcon, signifies those whose *feet are swift to shed blood* (Ps. 13. 3). The plover, which is a garrulous bird, signifies the gossip. The hoopoe, which builds its nest on dung, feeds on fœtid ordure, and whose song is like a groan, denotes worldly grief which works death in those who are unclean. The bat, which flies near the ground, signifies those who being gifted with worldly knowledge, seek none but earthly things. Of fowls and quadrupeds those alone were permitted which have the hind-legs longer than the fore-legs, so that they can leap; but those were forbidden which cling rather to the earth, because those who abuse the doctrine of the four Evangelists, so that they are not lifted up thereby, are reputed unclean. By the prohibition of blood, fat and nerves, we are to understand the forbidding of cruelty, lust, and bravery in committing sin.

Reply Obj. 2. Men were accustomed to eat plants and other products of the soil even before the deluge, but the eating of flesh seems to have been introduced after the deluge; for it is written (Gen. 9. 3): *Even as the green herbs have I delivered . . . all* flesh *to you.* The reason for this was that the eating of the products of the soil savours rather of a simple life, while the eating of flesh savours of delicate and overcareful living. For the soil gives birth to the herb of its own accord, and such products of the earth may be had in great quantities with very little effort, while no small trouble is necessary either to rear or to catch an animal. Consequently God being wishful to bring His people back to a more simple way of living, forbade them to eat many kinds of animals, but not those things that are produced by the soil. Another reason may be that animals were offered to idols, while the products of the soil were not.

---

[1] Cf. Rabanus Maurus, *De Univ.*, VIII, I (PL III, 222A); chap. 6 (PL III, 240–255); Isidore, *Etym.*, XII, 2, 7 (PL 82, 436, 459).

[2] Albert, *In De An.*, XXIII, I, 22 (BO XII, **482**).

[3] *Op. cit.*, chap. 24 (BO XII, 493).

[4] *Op. cit.*, VIII, I, 2 (BO XI, 427).

[5] *Op. cit.*, XXIII, I, 24 (BO XII, **497**).

[6] *Ibid.* (BO XII, 501).

The Reply to the Third Objection is clear from what has been said (REPLY 1).

Reply Obj. 4. Although the kid that is slain has no perception of the manner in which its flesh is cooked, yet it would seem to savour of heartlessness if the dam's milk, which was intended for the nourishment of her offspring, were served up on the same dish. It might also be said that the Gentiles in celebrating the feasts of their idols prepared the flesh of kids in this manner for the purpose of sacrifice or banquet; hence (Exod. 23.) after the solemnities to be celebrated under the Law had been foretold, it is added: *Thou shalt not boil a kid in the milk of its dam.* The figurative reason for this prohibition is this: the kid, signifying Christ, on account of *the likeness of sinful flesh* (Rom. 8. 3), was not to be seethed, that is, slain, by the Jews, *in the milk of its dam,* that is, during His infancy. Or else it signifies that the kid, that is, the sinner, should not be boiled in the milk of its dam, that is, should not be cajoled by flattery.

Reply Obj. 5. The Gentiles offered their gods the first-fruits, which they held to bring them good luck; or they burnt them for the purpose of sorcery.[1] Consequently (the Israelites) were commanded to look upon the fruits of the first three years as unclean. For in that country nearly all trees bear fruit in three years' time; those trees, namely, that are cultivated either from seed, or from a graft or from a cutting; but it seldom happens that the fruit-stones or seeds encased in a pod are sown, since it would take a longer time for these to bear fruit, and the Law considered what happened most frequently. The fruits, however, of the fourth year, as being the firstlings of clean fruits, were offered to God, and from the fifth year onward they were eaten.

The figurative reason was that this foreshadowed the fact that after the three states of the Law (the first lasting from Abraham to David, the second until they were carried away to Babylon, the third until the time of Christ), the Fruit of the Law, that is, Christ, was to be offered to God. Or again, that we should mistrust our first efforts, on account of their imperfection.

Reply Obj. 6. It is said of a man in Ecclus. 19. 27, that *the attire of the body . . . shows what he is.* Hence the Lord wished His people to be distinguished from other nations, not only by the sign of circumcision, which was in the flesh, but also by a certain difference of attire. Therefore they were forbidden to wear garments woven of woollen and linen together, and for a woman to be clothed with man's apparel, or *vice versa,* for two reasons. First, to avoid idolatrous worship. Because the Gentiles, in their religious rites, used garments of this sort, made of various materials. Moreover in the worship of Mars, women put on men's armour, while, conversely, in the worship of Venus men donned women's attire.[2] The second reason was to preserve them from lust, because the employment of various materials in the making of garments signified inordinate union of sexes, while the use of male attire by a woman, or *vice versa,* has an incentive to evil desires, and offers an occasion of lust. The figurative reason is that the prohibition of wearing a garment woven of woollen and linen signified that it was forbidden to unite the simplicity of innocence, denoted by wool, with the duplicity of malice, signified by linen. It also signifies that woman is forbidden to presume to teach, or perform other duties of men, or that man should not adopt the effeminate manners of a woman.

Reply Obj. 7. As Jerome says on Matt. 23. 6, "the Lord commanded them to make violet-coloured fringes in the four corners of their garments so that the Israelites might be distinguished from other nations."[3] Hence, in this way, they professed to be Jews, and consequently the very sight of this sign reminded them of their Law.

When we read: *Thou shalt bind them on thy hand, and they shall be ever before thy eyes* (Vulg.,—*they shall be and shall move between thy eyes*), "the Pharisees gave a false interpretation to these words, and wrote the decalogue of Moses on a parchment, and tied it on their foreheads like a wreath, so that it moved in front of their eyes[4]; but the intention of the Lord in giving this commandment was that they should be bound in their hands, that is, in their works and that they should be before their eyes, that is, in their thoughts. The violet-coloured fillets which were inserted in their cloaks signify the heavenly intention which should accompany our every deed. It may, however, be said that, because they were a carnal-minded and stiff-necked people, it was necessary for them to be stirred by these sensible things to the observance of the Law.

Reply Obj. 8. Affection in man is twofold: it may be an affection of reason, or it may be an

---

[1] Cf. Maimonides, *Guide*, III, 37 (FR 334).

[2] Cf. Maimonides, *Guide*, III, 37 (FR 335).
[3] PL 26, 175.
[4] Jerome, *In Matt.* 23.6 (PL 26, 174).

affection of passion. If a man's affection be one of reason, it matters not how man behaves to animals, because God has subjected all things to man's power, according to Ps. 8. 8: *Thou hast subjected all things under his feet;* and it is in this sense that the Apostle says that *God has no care for oxen,* because God does not ask of man what he does with oxen or other animals.

But if man's affection be one of passion, then it is moved also in regard to other animals, for since the passion of pity is caused by the afflictions of others, and since it happens that even irrational animals are sensible to pain, it is possible for the affection of pity to arise in a man with regard to the sufferings of animals. Now it is evident that if a man practise a pitiful affection for animals, he is all the more disposed to take pity on his fellow-men; therefore it is written (Prov. 12. 10): *The just regardeth the lives of his beasts: but the bowels of the wicked are cruel.* Consequently the Lord, in order to inculcate pity to the Jewish people, who were prone to cruelty, wished them to practise pity even with regard to dumb animals, and forbade them to do certain things savouring of cruelty to animals. Hence He prohibited them to *boil a kid in the milk of its dam;* and to *muzzle the ox that treadeth out the corn;* and to slay *the dam with her young.* It may, nevertheless, be also said that these prohibitions were made in hatred of idolatry. For the Egyptians held it to be wicked to allow the ox to eat of the grain while threshing the corn. Moreover certain sorcerers were accustomed to ensnare the mother bird with her young during incubation, and to employ them for the purpose of securing fruitfulness and good luck in bringing up children; and also because it was held to be a good omen to find the mother sitting on her young.

As to the mingling of animals of various species, the literal reason may have been threefold. The first was to show detestation for the idolatry of the Egyptians, who employed various mixtures in worshipping the planets, which produce various effects, and on various kinds of things according to their various conjunctions.[1] The second reason was in condemnation of unnatural sins. The third reason was the entire removal of all occasions of concupiscence. Because animals of different species do not easily breed, unless this be brought about by man, and movements of lust are aroused by seeing such things. Therefore in the Jewish traditions we

find it prescribed, as stated by Rabbi Moses, that men shall turn away their eyes from such sights.[2]

The figurative reason for these things is that the necessities of life should not be withdrawn from the ox that treadeth the corn, that is, from the preacher bearing the sheaves of doctrine, as the Apostle states (I Cor. 9. 4, *seqq.*). Again, we should not take the dam with her young, because in certain things we have to keep the spiritual senses, that is, the offspring and set aside the observance of the letter, that is, the mother, for instance in all the ceremonies of the Law. It is also forbidden that beasts of burden, that is, any of the common people, should be allowed to engender, that is, to have any connection, with animals of another kind, that is, with Gentiles or Jews.

Reply Obj. 9. All these minglings were forbidden in agriculture; literally, in detestation of idolatry. For the Egyptians in worshipping the stars employed various combinations of seeds, animals and garments, in order to represent the various conjunctions of the stars.[3] Or else all these minglings were forbidden in detestation of the unnatural vice.

They have, however, a figurative reason. For the prohibition: *Thou shalt not sow thy field with different seeds,* is to be understood, in the spiritual sense, of the prohibition to sow strange doctrine in the Church, which is a spiritual vineyard. Likewise *the field,* that is, the Church, must not be sown *with different seeds,* that is, with Catholic and heretical doctrines. Neither is it allowed to plough *with an ox and an ass together;* thus a fool should not accompany a wise man in preaching, for one would hinder the other.

[The *reply to Obj. 10* is missing from the manuscripts.]

Reply Obj. 11. Sorcerers and idolatrous priests made use, in their rites, of the bones and flesh of dead men. Therefore, in order to extirpate the customs of idolatrous worship, the Lord commanded that the priests of inferior degree, who at fixed times served in the temple, should not *incur an uncleanness at the death* of anyone except of those who were closely related to them, namely, their father or mother, and others thus near of kin to them. But the high-priest had always to be ready for the service of the sanctuary; therefore he was absolutely forbidden to approach the dead, however nearly related to him. They were also forbidden to

[1] Cf. Maimonides, *Guide*, III, 37 (FR 337).

[2] *Op. cit.,* III, 49 (FR 377).
[3] Cf. Maimonides, *Guide*, III, 37 (FR 337).

marry *a harlot* or *one that has been put away*, or any other than a virgin; both on account of the reverence due to the priesthood, the honour of which would seem to be tarnished by such a marriage, and for the sake of the children who would be disgraced by the mother's shame, which was most of all to be avoided when the priestly dignity was passed on from father to son. Again, they were commanded to shave neither head nor beard, and not to make incisions in their flesh, in order to exclude the rites of idolatry. For the priests of the Gentiles shaved both head and beard, and so it is written (Baruch 6. 30): *Priests sit in their temples having their garments rent, and their heads and beards shaven.* Moreover, in worshipping their idols *they cut themselves with knives and lancets* (III Kings 18. 28). For this reason the priests of the Old Law were commanded to do the contrary.

The spiritual reason for these things is that priests should be entirely free from dead works, that is, sins. And they should not shave their heads, that is, set wisdom aside; nor should they shave their beards, that is, set aside the perfection of wisdom; nor rend their garments or cut their flesh, that is, they should not incur the sin of schism.

QUESTION CIII

OF THE DURATION OF THE CEREMONIAL PRECEPTS

(In Four Articles)

WE must now consider the duration of the ceremonial precepts, under which head there are four points of inquiry: (1) Whether the ceremonial precepts were in existence before the Law? (2) Whether at the time of the Law the ceremonies of the Old Law had any power of justification? (3) Whether they ceased at the coming of Christ? (4) Whether it is a mortal sin to observe them after the coming of Christ?

ARTICLE 1. *Whether the Ceremonies of the Law Were in Existence Before the Law?*

We proceed thus to the First Article: It would seem that the ceremonies of the Law were in existence before the Law.

Objection 1. For sacrifices and holocausts were ceremonies of the Old Law, as stated above (Q. CI, A. 4). But sacrifices and holocausts preceded the Law, for it is written (Gen. 4. 3, 4) that *Cain offered, of the fruits of the earth, gifts to the Lord,* and that *Abel offered of the firstlings of his flock, and of their fat.*

Noe also *offered holocausts* to the Lord (Gen. 18. 20), and Abraham did in like manner (Gen. 22. 13). Therefore the ceremonies of the Old Law preceded the Law.

Obj. 2. Further, the erecting and consecrating of the altar were part of the ceremonies relating to holy things. But these preceded the Law. For we read (Gen. 13. 18) that *Abraham . . . built . . . an altar to the Lord;* and (Gen. 28. 18) that *Jacob . . . took the stone . . . and set it up for a title, pouring oil upon the top of it.* Therefore the legal ceremonies preceded the Law.

Obj. 3. Further, the first of the legal sacraments seems to have been circumcision. But circumcision preceded the Law, as appears from Gen. 17. In like manner the priesthood preceded the Law; for it is written (Gen. 14. 18) that *Melchisedech . . . was the priest of the most high God.* Therefore the sacramental ceremonies preceded the Law.

Obj. 4. Further, the distinction of clean from unclean animals belongs to the ceremonies of observances, as stated above (Q. CII, A. 6, Reply 1). But this distinction preceded the Law; for it is written (Gen. 7. 2, 3): *Of all clean beasts take seven and seven . . . but of the beasts that are unclean, two and two.* Therefore the legal ceremonies preceded the Law.

On the contrary, It is written (Deut. 6. 1): *These are the precepts, and ceremonies . . . which the Lord your God commanded that I should teach you.* But they would not have needed to be taught about these things, if the above mentioned ceremonies had been already in existence. Therefore the legal ceremonies did not precede the Law.

I answer that, As is clear from what has been said (Q. CI, Q. 2; Q. CII, A. 2), the legal ceremonies were ordained for a double purpose, the worship of God, and the foreshadowing of Christ. Now whoever worships God must worship Him by means of certain fixed things pertaining to external worship. But the fixing of the divine worship belongs to the ceremonies, just as the determining of our relations with our neighbour is a matter determined by the judicial precepts, as stated above (Q. XCIX, A. 4). Consequently, as among men in general there were certain judicial precepts, not indeed established by Divine authority, but ordained by human reason, so also there were some ceremonies fixed, not by the authority of any law, but according to the will and devotion of those that worship God. Since, however, even before the Law some of the leading men were gifted with the spirit of prophecy, it is to be believed that a heavenly instinct, like a private law, prompted them to worship God in a certain definite way, which would be both in keeping with the interior worship, and a suitable token of Christ's mysteries, which were foreshadowed also by other things that they did, according to I Cor. 10. 11: *All ... things happened to them in figure.* Therefore there were some ceremonies before the Law, but they were not legal ceremonies, because they were not as yet established by legislation.

Reply Obj. 1. The patriarchs offered up these oblations, sacrifices and holocausts previously to the Law out of a certain devotion of their own will, according as it seemed proper to them to offer up in honour of God those things which they had received from Him, and thus to testify that they worshipped God Who is the beginning and end of all.

Reply Obj. 2. They also established certain sacred things, because they thought that the honour due to God demanded that certain places should be set apart from others for the purpose of divine worship.

Reply Obj. 3. The sacrament of circumcision was established by command of God before the Law. Hence it cannot be called a sacrament of the Law as though it were an institution of the Law, but only as an observance included in the Law. Hence Our Lord said (John 7. 22) that circumcision was *not of Moses, but of his fathers.* Again, among those who worshipped God, the priesthood was in existence before the Law by human appointment, for the Law allotted the priestly dignity to the firstborn.

Reply Obj. 4. The distinction of clean from unclean animals was in vogue before the Law, not with regard to eating them, since it is written (Gen. 9. 3): *Everything that moveth and liveth shall be meat for you,* but only as to the offering of sacrifices, because they used only certain animals for that purpose. If, however, they did make any distinction in regard to eating, it was not that it was considered illegal to eat such animals, since this was not forbidden by any law, but from dislike or custom; thus even now we see that certain foods are looked upon with disgust in some countries, while people partake of them in others.

ARTICLE 2. *Whether, at the Time of the Law, the Ceremonies of the Old Law Had Any Power of Justification?*

We proceed thus to the Second Article: It would seem that the ceremonies of the Old Law had the power of justification at the time of the Law.

Objection 1. Because expiation from sin and consecration pertains to justification. But it is written (Exod. 29. 21) that the priests and their apparel were consecrated by the sprinkling of blood and the anointing of oil; and (Levit. 16. 16) that, by sprinkling the blood of the calf, the priest expiated *the sanctuary from the uncleanness of the children of Israel, and from their transgressions and ... their sins.* Therefore the ceremonies of the Old Law had the power of justification.

Obj. 2. Further, that by which man pleases God pertains to justification, according to Ps. 10. 8: *The Lord is just and hath loved justice.* But some pleased God by means of ceremonies, according to Levit. 10. 19: *How could I ... please the Lord in the ceremonies, having a sorrowful heart?* Therefore the ceremonies of the Old Law had the power of justification.

Obj. 3. Further, things relating to the divine worship regard the soul rather than the body, according to Ps. 18. 8: *The Law of the Lord is unspotted, converting souls.* But the leper was cleansed by means of the ceremonies of the Old Law, as stated in Lev. 14. Much more therefore could the ceremonies of the Old Law cleanse the soul by justifying it.

On the contrary, The Apostle says (Gal. 2):[1] *If there had been a law given which could justify* (Vulg.,—*give life*), *Christ died in vain,* that is, without cause. But this is inadmissible. Therefore the ceremonies of the Old Law did not confer justice.

In answer that, As stated above (Q. CII, A. 5, Reply 4), a twofold uncleanness was distinguished in the Old Law. One was spiritual and is the uncleanness of sin. The other was corporal, which rendered a man unfit for divine worship; thus a leper, or anyone that touched carrion, was said to be unclean. And thus uncleanness was nothing but a kind of irregularity. From this uncleanness, then, the ceremonies of the Old Law had the power to cleanse, because they were ordered by the Law to be employed as remedies for the removal of these uncleannesses which were contracted in consequence of the prescription of the Law. Hence the Apostle says (Heb. 9. 13) that *the blood of goats and of oxen, and the ashes of a heifer, being sprinkled, sanctify such as are defiled, to the cleansing of the flesh.* And just as this uncleanness which was washed away by such ceremonies affected the flesh rather than the soul, so also the ceremonies

[1] Cf. Gal. 3.21.

themselves are called by the Apostle shortly before (verse 10) justices of the flesh: *justices of the flesh*, says he, *being laid on them until the time of correction*.

On the other hand, they had no power of cleansing from uncleanness of the soul, that is, from the uncleanness of sin. The reason of this was that at no time could there be expiation from sin, except through Christ, *Who taketh away the sins* (Vulg.,—*sin*) *of the world* (John 1. 29). And since the mystery of Christ's Incarnation and Passion had not yet really taken place, those ceremonies of the Old Law could not really contain in themselves a power flowing from Christ already incarnate and crucified, such as the sacraments of the New Law contain. Consequently they could not cleanse from sin; thus the Apostle says (Heb. 10. 4) that *it is impossible that with the blood of oxen and goats sin should be taken away*. And for this reason he calls them (Gal. 4. 9) *weak and needy elements*, weak indeed, because they cannot take away sin; but this weakness results from their being needy, that is, from the fact that they do not contain grace within themselves.

However, it was possible at the time of the Law for the minds of the faithful to be united by faith to Christ incarnate and crucified, so that they were justified by faith in Christ, of which faith the observance of these ceremonies was a sort of profession, in so far as they foreshadowed Christ. Hence in the Old Law certain sacrifices were offered up for sins, not as though the sacrifices themselves washed sins away, but because they were professions of faith which cleansed from sin. In fact, the Law itself implies this in the terms employed, for it is written (Lev. 4. 26; 5. 16) that in offering the sacrifice for sin *the priest shall pray for him . . . and it shall be forgiven him*, as though the sin were forgiven not in virtue of the sacrifices but through the faith and devotion of those who offered them. It must be observed, however, that the very fact that the ceremonies of the Old Law washed away uncleanness of the body was a figure of that expiation from sins which was effected by Christ.

It is therefore evident that under the state of the Old Law the ceremonies had no power of justification.

Reply Obj. 1. That sanctification of priests and their sons, and of their apparel or of anything else belonging to them, by sprinkling them with blood, had no other effect but to appoint them to the divine worship, and to remove impediments from them, *to the cleansing of the flesh*, as the Apostle states (Heb. 9. 13), in token of that sanctification whereby *Jesus* sanctified *the people by His own blood* (*ibid.* 13. 12). Moreover, the expiation must be understood as referring to the removal of these bodily uncleannesses, not to the forgiveness of sin. Hence even the sanctuary which could not be the subject of sin is stated to be expiated.

Reply Obj. 2. The priests pleased God in the ceremonies by their obedience and devotion, and by their faith in the reality foreshadowed, not by reason of the things considered in themselves.

Reply Obj. 3. Those ceremonies which were prescribed in the cleansing of a leper were not ordained for the purpose of taking away the defilement of leprosy. This is clear from the fact that these ceremonies were not applied to a man until he was already healed; hence it is written (Lev. 14. 3, 4) that the priest, *going out of the camp, when he shall find that the leprosy is cleansed, shall command him that is to be purified to offer*, etc.; from this it is evident that the priest was appointed the judge of leprosy not before, but after cleansing. But these ceremonies were employed for the purpose of taking away the uncleanness of irregularity. They say, however, that if a priest were to err in his judgment, the leper would be cleansed miraculously by the power of God, but not in virtue of the sacrifice. Thus also it was by miracle that the thigh of the adulterous woman rotted when she had drunk the water *on which* the priest had *heaped curses*, as stated in Num. 5. 19-27.

ARTICLE 3. *Whether the Ceremonies of the Old Law Ceased at the Coming of Christ?*

We proceed thus to the Third Article: It would seem that the ceremonies of the Old Law did not cease at the coming of Christ.

Objection 1. For it is written (Baruch 4. 1): *This is the book of the commandments of God, and the law that is for ever*. But the legal ceremonies were part of the Law. Therefore the legal ceremonies were to last for ever.

Obj. 2. Further, the offering made by a leper after being cleansed was a ceremony of the Law. But the Gospel commands the leper, who has been cleansed, to make this offering (Matt. 8. 4). Therefore the ceremonies of the Old Law did not cease at Christ's coming.

Obj. 3. Further, as long as the cause remains, the effect remains. But the ceremonies of the Old Law had certain reasonable causes, since they were ordained to the worship of God, besides the fact that they were intended to be figures of Christ. Therefore the ceremonies of the Old Law should not have ceased.

Obj. 4. Further, circumcision was instituted as a sign of Abraham's faith, the observance of the sabbath to recall the blessing of creation, and other solemnities in memory of other Divine favours, as stated above (Q. CII, A. 4, reply 10; A. 5, reply 1). But Abraham's faith is ever to be imitated even by us, and the blessing of creation and other Divine favours should never be forgotten. Therefore at least circumcision and the other legal solemnities should not have ceased.

On the contrary, The Apostle says (Coloss. 2. 16, 17): *Let no man . . . judge you in meat or in drink, or in respect of a festival day, or of the new moon, or of the sabbaths, which are a shadow of things to come;* and (Heb. 8. 13): *In saying a new (testament), he hath made the former old: and that which decayeth and groweth old, is near its end.*

I answer that, All the ceremonial precepts of the Old Law were ordained to the worship of God, as stated above (Q. CI, AA. 1, 2). Now external worship should be in proportion to the internal worship, which consists in faith, hope, and charity. Consequently exterior worship had to be subject to variations according to the variations in the internal worship, in which a threefold state may be distinguished. One state was in respect of faith and hope, both in heavenly goods, and in the means of obtaining them—in both of these considered as things to come. Such was the state of faith and hope in the Old Law. Another state of the interior worship is that in which we have faith and hope in heavenly goods as things to come, but in the means of obtaining heavenly goods as in things present or past. Such is the state of the New Law. The third state is that in which both are possessed as present, in which nothing is believed in as lacking, nothing hoped for as being yet to come. Such is the state of the Blessed.

In this state of the Blessed, then, nothing in regard to the worship of God will be figurative; there will be only *thanksgiving and voice of praise* (Isa. 51. 3). Hence it is written concerning the city of the Blessed (Apoc. 21. 22): *I saw no temple therein: for the Lord God Almighty is the temple thereof, and the Lamb.* Proportionately, therefore, the ceremonies of the first-mentioned state which foreshadowed the second and third states, had need to cease at the advent of the second state; and other ceremonies had to be introduced which would be in keeping with the state of divine worship for that particular

time, in which heavenly goods are a thing of the future, but the Divine favours by which we obtain the heavenly boons are a thing of the present.

Reply Obj. 1. The Old Law is said to be "for ever" simply and absolutely, as regards its moral precepts; but as regards the ceremonial precepts it lasts for ever in respect of the reality which those ceremonies foreshadowed.

Reply Obj. 2. The mystery of the redemption of the human race was fulfilled in Christ's Passion; hence Our Lord said then: *It is consummated* (John 19. 30). Consequently the prescriptions of the Law must have ceased then altogether, through their reality being fulfilled. As a sign of this, we read that at the Passion of Christ *the veil of the temple was rent* (Matt. 27. 51). Hence, before Christ's Passion, while Christ was preaching and working miracles, the Law and the Gospel were concurrent, since the mystery of Christ had already begun, but was not as yet consummated. And for this reason Our Lord, before His Passion, commanded the leper to observe the legal ceremonies.

Reply Obj. 3. The literal reasons already given (Q. CII) for the ceremonies refer to the divine worship, which was founded on faith in that which was to come. Hence, at the advent of Him Who was to come, both that worship ceased, and all the reasons referring to it.

Reply Obj. 4. The faith of Abraham was commended in that he believed in God's promise concerning his seed to come, in which all nations were to be blessed. Therefore, as long as this seed was yet to come, it was necessary to make profession of Abraham's faith by means of circumcision. But now that it is consummated, the same thing needs to be declared by means of another sign, namely, Baptism, which, in this respect, took the place of circumcision, according to the saying of the Apostle (Coloss. 2. 11, 12): *You are circumcised with circumcision not made by hand, in despoiling of the body of the flesh, but in the circumcision of Christ, buried with Him in Baptism.*

As to the sabbath, which was a sign recalling the first creation, its place is taken by the Lord's Day, which recalls the beginning of the new creature in the Resurrection of Christ. In like manner other solemnities of the Old Law are supplanted by new solemnities, because the blessings vouchsafed to that people foreshadowed the favours granted us by Christ. Hence the feast of the Passover gave place to the feast of Christ's Passion and Resurrection; the feast of Pentecost when the Old Law was given, to the feast of Pentecost on which was given the Law of the living spirit; the feast of the New Moon, to the feast of the Blessed Virgin, when appeared the first rays of the sun, that is, Christ, by the fulness of grace; the feast of Trumpets, to the feasts of the Apostles; the feast of Expiation, to the feasts of Martyrs and Confessors; the feast of Tabernacles, to the feast of the Church Dedication; the feast of the Assembly and Collection, to feast of the Angels, or else to the feast of All Saints.

ARTICLE 4. *Whether since Christ's Passion the Legal Ceremonies Can Be Observed Without Committing Mortal Sin?*

We proceed thus to the Fourth Article: It would seem that since Christ's Passion the legal ceremonies can be observed without committing mortal sin.

Objection 1. For we must not believe that the apostles committed mortal sin after receiving the Holy Ghost, since by His fulness they were *endued with power from on high* (Luke 24. 49). But the apostles observed the legal ceremonies after the coming of the Holy Ghost; for it is stated (Acts 16. 3) that Paul circumcised Timothy, and (Acts 21. 26) that Paul, at the advice of James, *took the men, and . . . being purified with them, entered into the temple, giving notice of the accomplishment of the days of purification, until an oblation should be offered for every one of them.* Therefore the legal ceremonies can be observed since the Passion of Christ without committing mortal sin.

Obj. 2. Further, one of the legal ceremonies consisted in shunning the fellowship of Gentiles. But the first Pastor of the Church complied with this observance; for it is stated (Gal. 2. 12) that, *when* certain men *had come* to Antioch, Peter *withdrew and separated himself* from the Gentiles. Therefore the legal ceremonies can be observed since Christ's Passion without committing mortal sin.

Obj. 3. Further, the commands of the apostles did not lead men into sin. But it was commanded by apostolic decree that the Gentiles should observe certain ceremonies of the Law: for it is written (Acts 15. 28, 29): *It hath seemed good to the Holy Ghost and to us, to lay no further burden upon you than these necessary things: that you abstain from things sacrificed to idols, and from blood, and from things strangled, and from fornication.* Therefore the legal ceremonies can be observed since Christ's Passion without committing mortal sin.

On the contrary, The Apostle says (Gal. 5. 2):

If you be circumcised, Christ shall profit you nothing. But nothing save mortal sin hinders us from receiving Christ's fruit. Therefore since Christ's Passion it is a mortal sin to be circumcised, or to observe the other legal ceremonies.

I answer that, All ceremonies are professions of faith, in which the interior worship of God consists. Now man can make profession of his inward faith, by deeds as well as by words, and in either profession if he makes a false declaration, he sins mortally. Now though our faith in Christ is the same as that of the fathers of old yet, since they came before Christ, while we come after Him, the same faith is expressed in different words by us and by them. For by them was it said (Isa. 7. 14): *Behold a virgin shall conceive and bear a son,* where the verbs are in the future tense; but we express the same by means of verbs in the past tense, and say that she conceived and bore. In like manner the ceremonies of the Old Law signified Christ as having yet to be born and to suffer, but our sacraments signify Him as already born and having suffered. Consequently, just as it would be a mortal sin now for anyone, in making a profession of faith, to say that Christ is yet to be born, which the fathers of old said devoutly and truthfully, so too it would be a mortal sin now to observe those ceremonies which the fathers of old fulfilled with devotion and fidelity. Such is the teaching of Augustine (*Contra Faust.* xix, 16),[1] who says: "It is no longer promised that He shall be born, shall suffer and rise again, truths of which their sacraments were a kind of image; but it is declared that He is already born, has suffered and risen again, of which our sacraments, in which Christians share, are the actual representation."

Reply Obj. 1. On this point there seems to have been a difference of opinion between Jerome and Augustine. For Jerome (*Super Galat.* ii, 11, *seq.*)[2] distinguished two periods of time. One was the time previous to Christ's Passion, during which the legal ceremonies were neither dead, since they were obligatory, and did expiate in their own fashion, nor deadly, because it was not sinful to observe them. But immediately after Christ's Passion they began to be not only dead, so as no longer to be either effectual or binding, but also deadly, so that whoever observed them was guilty of mortal sin. Hence he maintained that after the Passion the apostles

[1] PL 42, 357.
[2] PL 26, 364; *Epist.,* CXII (PL 22, 921); see Hugh of St. Victor, *De Sacram.,* II, VI, 4 (PL 176, 449); Bonaventure, *In Sent.,* IV, d. 3, pt. 3, Q. 2 (QR IV, 87).

never observed the legal ceremonies in real earnest, but only by a kind of pious pretence, lest, that is, they should scandalize the Jews and hinder their conversion. This pretence, however, is to be understood, not as though they did not in reality perform those actions, but in the sense that they performed them without the mind to observe the ceremonies of the Law; thus a man might cut away his foreskin for health's sake, not with the intention of observing legal circumcision.

But since it seems unfitting that the apostles, in order to avoid scandal, should have hidden things pertaining to the truth of life and doctrine, and that they should have made use of pretence in things pertaining to the salvation of the faithful, therefore Augustine (*Epist.* lxxxii)[1] more fittingly distinguished three periods of time. One was the time that preceded the Passion of Christ, during which the legal ceremonies were neither deadly nor dead; another period was after the publication of the Gospel, during which the legal ceremonies are both dead and deadly. The third is a middle period, namely, from the Passion of Christ until the publication of the Gospel, during which the legal ceremonies were dead indeed, because they had neither effect nor binding force, but were not deadly, because it was lawful for the Jewish converts to Christianity to observe them, provided they did not put their trust in them so as to hold them to be necessary unto salvation, as though faith in Christ could not justify without the legal observances. On the other hand, there was no reason why those who were converted from heathendom to Christianity should observe them. Hence Paul circumcised Timothy, who was born of a Jewish mother, but was unwilling to circumcise Titus, who was born of Gentiles.

The reason why the Holy Ghost did not wish the converted Jews to be debarred at once from observing the legal ceremonies, while converted heathens were forbidden to observe the rites of heathendom, was in order to show that there is a difference between these rites. For heathenish ceremonial was rejected as absolutely unlawful, and as prohibited by God for all time; but the legal ceremonial ceased as being fulfilled through Christ's Passion, since it had been instituted by God as a figure of Christ.

Reply Obj. 2. According to Jerome,[2] Peter withdrew himself from the Gentiles by pretence, in order to avoid giving scandal to the Jews, of whom he was the Apostle. Hence he did not sin

at all in acting thus. On the other hand, Paul in like manner made a pretence of blaming him, in order to avoid scandalizing the Gentiles, whose Apostle he was. But Augustine disapproves of this solution,[3] because in the canonical Scripture (viz., Gal. 2. 11), wherein we must not hold anything to be false, Paul says that Peter *was to be blamed*. Consequently it is true that Peter sinned, and Paul blamed him in very truth and not with pretence. Peter, however, did not sin by observing the legal ceremonial for the time being, because this was lawful for him who was a converted Jew. But he did sin by excessive minuteness in the observance of the legal rites lest he should scandalize the Jews, the result being that he gave scandal to the Gentiles.

Reply Obj. 3. Some have held[4] that this prohibition of the apostles is not to be taken literally, but spiritually: namely, that the prohibition of blood signifies the prohibition of murder; the prohibition of things strangled, that of violence and rapine; the prohibition of things offered to idols, that of idolatry; while fornication is forbidden as being evil in itself. This opinion they gathered from certain glosses, which expound these prohibitions in a mystical sense. Since, however, murder and rapine were held to be unlawful even by the Gentiles, there would have been no need to give this special commandment to those who were converted to Christ from heathendom. Hence others maintain that those foods were forbidden literally not to prevent the observance of legal ceremonies, but in order to prevent gluttony.[5] Thus Jerome says on Ezech. 44. 31[6] (*The priest shall not eat of anything that is dead*): "He condemns those priests who from gluttony did not keep these precepts." But since certain foods are more delicate than these and more conducive to gluttony, there seems no reason why these should have been forbidden more than the others.

We must therefore follow a third opinion, and hold that these foods were forbidden literally, not with the purpose of enforcing compliance with the legal ceremonies, but in order to further the union of Gentiles and Jews living side by side. Because blood and things strangled were loathsome to the Jews by ancient custom, while the Jews might have suspected the Gentiles of relapse into idolatry if the latter had partaken of things offered to idols. Hence these things

---

[1] PL 33, 281.   [2] *In Gal.* I, super 2.14 (PL 26, 367).

[3] Augustine, *Epist.*, LXXXII, 2 (PL 33, 280).

[4] William of Auxerre, *Summa Aurea*, IV, I, Q. 2 (244 v^b).

[5] Cf. Jerome, *In Ezech.*, BK XIII, super 44.31 (PL 25, 464); *Glossa ordin.*, super Rom. 14.2 (VI, 29A).

[6] Bk. XIII (PL 25, 464).

were prohibited for the time being, during which the Gentiles and Jews were to become united together. But as time went on, with the lapse of the cause, the effect lapsed also, when the truth of the Gospel teaching was divulged, wherein Our Lord taught that *not that which entereth into the mouth defileth a man* (Matt. 15. 11), and that *nothing is to be rejected that is received with thanksgiving* (I Tim. 4. 4). With regard to fornication a special prohibition was made, because the Gentiles did not hold it to be sinful.

QUESTION CIV
OF THE JUDICIAL PRECEPTS
(In Four Articles)

WE must now consider the judicial precepts, and first of all we shall consider them in general; in the second place we shall consider their reasons (Q. CV). Under the first head there are four points of inquiry: (1) What is meant by the judicial precepts? (2) Whether they are figurative? (3) Their duration. (4) Their division.

ARTICLE 1. *Whether the Judicial Precepts Were Those Which Directed Man in Relation to His Neighbour?*

We proceed thus to the First Article: It would seem that the judicial precepts were not those which directed man in his relations to his neighbour.

Objection 1. For judicial precepts take their name from judgment. But there are many things that direct man as to his neighbour which are not subordinate to judgment. Therefore the judicial precepts were not those which directed man in his relations to his neighbour.

Obj. 2. Further, the judicial precepts are distinct from the moral precepts, as stated above (Q. XCIX, A. 4). But there are many moral precepts which direct man as to his neighbour, as is evidently the case with the seven precepts of the second table. Therefore the judicial precepts are not so called from directing man to his neighbour.

Obj. 3. Further, as the ceremonial precepts relate to God, so do the judicial precepts relate to one's neighbour, as stated above (Q. XCIX, A. 4; Q. CI, A. 1). But among the ceremonial precepts there are some which concern man himself, such as observances in matter of food and apparel, of which we have already spoken (Q. CII, A. 6, reply 1, 6). Therefore the judicial precepts are not so called from directing man to his neighbour.

On the contrary, It is accounted (Ezech. 18. 8) among other works of a good and just man, that *he hath executed true judgment between man and man.* But judicial precepts are so called from judgment. Therefore it seems that the judicial precepts were those which directed the relations between man and man.

I answer that, As is evident from what we have stated above (Q. XCV, A. 2; Q. XCIX, A. 4), in every law some precepts derive their binding force from the dictate of reason itself, because natural reason dictates that something ought to be done or to be avoided. These are called moral precepts, since human morals are based on reason. At the same time there are other precepts which derive their binding force not from the very dictate of reason (because considered in themselves they do not imply an obligation of something due or undue), but from some institution, Divine or human; and such are certain determinations of the moral precepts. When therefore the moral precepts are fixed by Divine institution in matters relating to man's subordination to God, they are called ceremonial precepts; but when they refer to man's relations to other men, they are called judicial precepts. Hence there are two conditions attached to the judicial precepts, namely, first, that they refer to man's relations to other men; secondly, that they derive their binding force not from reason alone, but in virtue of their institution.

Reply Obj. 1. Judgments emanate through the official pronouncement of certain men who are at the head of affairs, and in whom the judicial power is vested. Now it belongs to those who are at the head of affairs to regulate not only litigious matters, but also voluntary contracts which are concluded between man and man, and whatever matters concern the community at large and its government. Consequently the judicial precepts are not only those which concern actions at law, but also all those that are directed to the ordering of one man in relation to another, which ordering is subject to the direction of the sovereign as supreme judge.

Reply Obj. 2. This argument holds in respect of those precepts which direct man in his relations to his neighbour, and derive their binding force from the mere dictate of reason.

Reply Obj. 3. Even in those precepts which direct us to God, some are moral precepts, which the reason itself dictates when it is informed by faith; such as that God is to be loved and worshipped. There are also ceremonial precepts, which have no binding force except in virtue of their Divine institution. Now God is concerned not only with the sacrifices that are offered to Him, but also with whatever relates to the fitness of those who offer sacrifices to Him and worship Him. Because men are ordered to God as to their end and therefore it concerns God and, consequently, is a matter of ceremonial precept, that man should show some fitness for the divine worship. On the other hand, man is not ordered to his neighbour as to his end, so as to need to be disposed in himself with regard to his neighbour, for such is the relationship of a slave to his master, since a slave is his master's in all that he is, as the Philosopher says.[1] Hence there are no judicial precepts ordering man in himself. All such precepts are moral, because the reason, which is the principle in moral matters, holds the same position in man with regard to things that concern him as a prince or judge holds in the state. Nevertheless we must take note that, since the relations of man to his neighbour are more subject to reason than the relations of man to God, there are more precepts by which man is directed in his relations to his neighbour than precepts by which he is directed to God. For the same reason there had to be more ceremonial than judicial precepts in the Law.

ARTICLE 2. *Whether the Judicial Precepts Were Figurative?*

We proceed thus to the Second Article: It would seem that the judicial precepts were not figurative.

Objection 1. Because it seems proper to the ceremonial precepts to be instituted as figures of something else. Therefore, if the judicial precepts are figurative, there will be no difference between the judicial and ceremonial precepts.

Obj. 2. Further, just as certain judicial precepts were given to the Jewish people, so also were some given to other heathen peoples. But the judicial precepts given to other peoples were not figurative, but stated what had to be done. Therefore it seems that neither were the judicial precepts of the Old Law figures of anything.

Obj. 3. Further, those things which relate to the divine worship had to be taught under certain figures because the things of God are above our reason, as stated above (Q. CI, A. 2, Reply 2). But things concerning our neighbour are not above our reason. Therefore the judicial precepts which direct us in relation to our neighbour should not have been figurative.

On the contrary, The judicial precepts are ex-

pounded both in the allegorical and in the moral sense (Exod. 21).

I answer that, A precept may be figurative in two ways. First, primarily and in itself, because, that is, it is instituted principally that it may be the figure of something. In this way the ceremonial precepts are figurative, since they were instituted for the very purpose that they might foreshadow something relating to the worship of God and the mystery of Christ. But some precepts are figurative not primarily and in themselves, but consequently. In this way the judicial precepts of the Old Law are figurative. For they were not instituted for the purpose of being figurative, but in order that they might regulate the state of that people according to justice and equity. Nevertheless they did foreshadow something consequently, since, namely, the entire state of that people, who were directed by these precepts, was figurative, according to I Cor. 10. 11: *All . . . things happened to them in figure.*

Reply Obj. 1. The ceremonial precepts are not figurative in the same way as the judicial precepts, as explained above.

Reply Obj. 2. The Jewish people were chosen by God that Christ might be born of them. Consequently the entire state of that people had to be prophetic and figurative, as Augustine states (*Contra Faust.* 22, 24).[2] For this reason even the judicial precepts that were given to this people were more figurative than those which were given to other nations. Thus, too, the wars and deeds of this people are expounded in the mystical sense, but not the wars and deeds of the Assyrians or Romans, although the latter are more famous in the eyes of men.

Reply Obj 3. In this people the direction of man in regard to his neighbour, considered in itself, was subject to reason. But in so far as it was referred to the worship of God, it was above reason, and in this respect it was figurative.

ARTICLE 3. *Whether the Judicial Precepts of the Old Law Bind For Ever?*

We proceed thus to the Third Article: It would seem that the judical precepts of the Old Law bind for ever.

Objection 1. Because the judicial precepts relate to the virtue of justice, since a judgment is an execution of justice. Now *justice is perpetual and immortal* (Wisd. 1. 15). Therefore the judicial precepts bind for ever.

Obj. 2. Further, Divine institutions are more enduring than human institutions. But the judicial precepts of human laws bind for ever.

---

[1] *Politics,* I, 4 (1254ª12).

[2] PL 42, 417.

Therefore much more do the judicial precepts of the Divine Law.

Obj. 3. Further, the Apostle says (Heb. 7. 18) that *there is a setting aside of the former commandment, because of the weakness and unprofitableness thereof.* Now this is true of the ceremonial precept, which *could* (Vulg.,—*can*) *not, as to the conscience, make him perfect that serveth only in meats and in drinks, and divers washings and justices of the flesh,* as the Apostle declares (Heb. 9. 9, 10). On the other hand, the judicial precepts were useful and efficacious in respect of the purpose for which they were instituted, namely, to establish justice and equity among men. Therefore the judicial precepts of the Old Law are not set aside, but still retain their efficacy.

On the contrary, The Apostle says (Heb. 7. 12) that *the priesthood being translated it is necessary that a translation also be made of the Law.* But the priesthood was transferred from Aaron to Christ. Therefore the entire Law was also transferred. Therefore the judicial precepts are no longer in force.

I answer that, The judicial precepts did not bind for ever, but were annulled by the coming of Christ, yet not in the same way as the ceremonial precepts. For the ceremonial precepts were annulled so far as to be not only "dead," but also "deadly"[1] to those who observe them since the coming of Christ, especially since the promulgation of the Gospel. On the other hand, the judicial precepts are dead indeed, because they have no binding force, but they are not deadly. For if a sovereign were to order these judicial precepts to be observed in his kingdom, he would not sin; unless perhaps they were observed, or ordered to be observed, as though they derived their binding force through being institutions of the Old Law, for it would be a deadly sin to intend to observe them thus.

The reason for this difference may be gathered from what has been said above (A. 2). For it has been stated that the ceremonial precepts are figurative primarily and in themselves, as being instituted chiefly for the purpose of foreshadowing the mysteries of Christ to come. On the other hand, the judicial precepts were not instituted that they might be figures, but that they might shape the state of that people who were ordered to Christ. Consequently, when the state of that people changed with the coming of Christ, the judicial precepts lost their binding force; for the Law was a pedagogue, leading men

to Christ, as stated in Gal. 3. 24. Since, however, these judicial precepts are instituted not for the purpose of being figures, but for the performance of certain deeds, the observance of them is not prejudicial to the truth of faith. But the intention of observing them as though one were bound by the Law is prejudicial to the truth of faith, because it would follow that the former state of the people still lasts, and that Christ has not yet come.

Reply Obj. 1. The obligation of observing justice is indeed perpetual. But the determination of those things that are just according to human or Divine institution must be different, according to the different states of mankind.

Reply Obj. 2. The judicial precepts established by men retain their binding force for ever, so long as the state of government remains the same. But if the state or nation pass to another form of government, the laws must be changed. For democracy, which is government by the people, demands different laws from those of oligarchy, which is government by the rich, as the Philosopher shows.[2] Consequently when the state of that people changed, the judicial precepts had to be changed also.

Reply Obj. 3. Those judicial precepts directed the people to justice and equity in keeping with the demands of that state. But after the coming of Christ, there had to be a change in the state of that people, so that in Christ there was no distinction between Gentile and Jew, as there had been before. For this reason the judicial precepts needed to be changed also.

ARTICLE 4. *Whether It Is Possible To Assign a Distinct Division of the Judicial Precepts?*

We proceed thus to the Fourth Article: It would seem that it is impossible to assign a distinct division of the judicial precepts.

Objection 1. Because the judicial precepts order men in their relations to one another. But those things which need to be ordered, as pertaining to the relationship between man and man, and which are made use of by men, are not subject to division, since they are infinite in number. Therefore it is not possible to assign a distinct division of the judicial precepts.

Obj. 2. Further, the judicial precepts are decisions on moral matters. But moral precepts do not seem to be capable of division except in so far as they are reducible to the precepts of the decalogue. Therefore there is no distinct division of the judicial precepts.

Obj. 3. Further, because there is a division of

---

[1] Cf. Augustine, *Epist.*, LXXXII, 2 (PL 33, 283); also Albert the Great, *In Sent.*, IV, d. 3, A. 6 (BO XXIX, 73).

[2] *Politics*, IV, 1 (1289ª11, 22).

the ceremonial precepts that is certain, the Law alludes to this division by describing some as sacrifices, others as observances. But the Law contains no allusion to a division of the judicial precepts. Therefore it seems that they have no distinct division.

On the contrary, Wherever there is order there must be division. But the notion of order is especially applicable to the judicial precepts, since thereby that people was ordered. Therefore it is most necessary that they should have a distinct division.

I answer that, Since law is the art, as it were, of directing or ordering the life of man, just as in every art there is a distinct division in the rules of art, so, in every law, there must be a distinct division of precepts; otherwise the law would be rendered useless by confusion. We must therefore say that the judicial precepts of the Old Law, by which men were ordered in their relations to one another, are subject to division according to the various ways in which man is ordered.

Now in every people a fourfold order is to be found: one, of the people's sovereign to his subjects; a second, of the subjects among themselves; a third, of the citizens to foreigners; a fourth, of members of the same household, such as the order of the father to his son, of the wife to her husband, of the master to his servant. And according to these four orders we may distinguish different kinds of judicial precepts in the Old Law. For certain precepts are laid down concerning the institution of the sovereign and relating to his office, and about the respect due to him; this is one part of the judicial precepts. Again, certain precepts are given in respect of a man to his fellow citizens, for instance, about buying and selling, judgments and penalties; this is the second part of the judicial precepts. Again, certain precepts are enjoined with regard to foreigners, for instance, about wars waged against their foes, and about the way to receive travellers and strangers; this is the third part of the judicial precepts. Lastly, certain precepts are given relating to home life, for instance, about servants, wives and children; this is the fourth part of the judicial precepts.

Reply Obj. 1. Things pertaining to the ordering of relations between one man and another are indeed infinite in number, yet they are reducible to certain distinct heads, according to the different relations in which one man stands to another, as stated above.

Reply Obj. 2. The precepts of the decalogue

held the first place in the moral order, as stated above (Q. C, A. 3), and consequently it is fitting that other moral precepts should be distinguished in relation to them. But the judicial and ceremonial precepts have a different binding force, derived not from natural reason, but from their institution alone. Hence there is a distinct reason for distinguishing them.

Reply Obj. 3. The Law alludes to the division of the judicial precepts in the very things themselves which are prescribed by the judicial precepts of the Law.

QUESTION CV
OF THE REASON FOR THE JUDICIAL PRECEPTS
(In Four Articles)

WE must now consider the reason for the judicial precepts, under which head there are four points of inquiry: (1) Concerning the reason for the judicial precepts relating to the rulers. (2) Concerning the precepts which pertain to the fellowship of one man with another. (3) Concerning those which pertain to foreigners. (4) Concerning those relating to domestic matters.

ARTICLE 1. *Whether the Old Law Enjoined Fitting Precepts Concerning Rulers?*

We proceed thus to the First Article: It would seem that the Old Law made unfitting precepts concerning rulers.

Objection 1. Because, as the Philosopher says,[1] the ordering of the people depends mostly on the chief ruler. But the Law contains no precept relating to the institution of the chief ruler. And yet we find in it prescriptions concerning the inferior rulers; first (Exod. 18. 21): *Provide out of all the people wise* (Vulg.,— *able*) *men,* etc.; again (Num. 11. 16): *Gather unto Me seventy men of the ancients of Israel;* and again (Deut. 1. 13): *Let me have from among you wise and understanding men,* etc. Therefore the Law provided insufficiently in regard to the rulers of the people.

Obj. 2. Further, "The best gives of the best," as Plato states.[2] Now the best ordering of a state or of any nation is to be ruled by a king, because this kind of government approaches nearest in resemblance to the Divine government, by which God rules the world from the beginning. Therefore the Law should have set a king over the people, and they should not

---

[1] *Politics,* III, 6 (1278^b8).
[2] *Timaeus,* 9, 10 (trans. of Chalcidius—DD 157–158); cf. *Timaeus* (29).

have been allowed a choice in the matter, as indeed they were allowed (Deut. 17. 14, 15): *When thou . . . shalt say: I will set a king over me . . . thou shalt set him*, etc.

Obj. 3. Further, according to Matt. 12. 25: *Every kingdom divided against itself shall be made desolate*, a saying which was verified in the Jewish people, whose destruction was brought about by the division of the kingdom. But the Law should aim chiefly at things pertaining to the general well-being of the people. Therefore it should have forbidden the kingdom to be divided under two kings; nor should this have been introduced even by Divine authority, as we read of its being introduced by the authority of the prophet Ahias the Silonite (III Kings 11. 29 *seq.*).

Obj. 4. Further, just as priests are instituted for the benefit of the people in things concerning God, as stated in Heb. 5. 1, so are rulers set up for the benefit of the people in human affairs. But certain things were allotted as a means of livelihood for the priests and Levites of the Law, such as the tithes and first-fruits, and many like things. Therefore in like manner certain things should have been determined for the livelihood of the rulers of the people, especially since they were forbidden to accept presents, as is clearly stated in Exod. 23. 8: *You shall not* (Vulg.,—*Neither shalt thou*) *take bribes, which even blind the wise, and pervert the words of the just.*

Obj. 5. Further, as a kingdom is the best form of government, so is tyranny the most corrupt. But when the Lord appointed the king, He established a tyrannical law; for it is written (I Kings 8. 11): *This will be the right of the king, that shall reign over you: He will take your sons*, etc. Therefore the Law made unfitting provision with regard to the institution of rulers.

On the contrary, The people of Israel is commended for the beauty of its order (Num. 24. 5): *How beautiful are thy tabernacles, O Jacob, and thy tents, O Israel.* But the beautiful ordering of a people depends on the right establishment of its rulers. Therefore the Law made right provision for the people with regard to its rulers.

I answer that, Two points are to be observed concerning the right ordering of rulers in a state or nation. One is that all should take some share in the government, for this form of constitution ensures peace among the people, commends itself to all, and is guarded by all, as stated in the *Politics.*[1] The other point is to be observed

in respect of the kinds of government, or the different ways in which the constitutions are established. For although these differ in kind, as the Philosopher states,[2] nevertheless the first place is held by the kingdom, where the power of government is vested in one, and aristocracy, which signifies government by the best, where the power of government is vested in a few. Accordingly, the best form of government is in a state or kingdom, where one is given the power to preside over all, while under him are others having governing powers; and yet a government of this kind is shared by all, both because all are eligible to govern, and because the rulers are chosen by all. For this is the best form of polity, being partly kingdom, since there is one at the head of all; partly aristocracy, in so far as a number of persons are set in authority; partly democracy, that is, government by the people, in so far as the rulers can be chosen from the people, and the people have the right to choose their rulers.

Such was the form of government established by the Divine Law. For Moses and his successors governed the people in such a way that each of them was ruler over all, so that there was a kind of kingdom. Moreover, seventy-two men were chosen, who were elders in virtue; for it is written (Deut. 1. 15): *I took out of your tribes men wise and honourable, and appointed them rulers*, so that there was an element of aristocracy. But it was a democratical government in so far as the rulers were chosen from all the people; for it is written (Exod. 18. 21): *Provide out of all the people wise* (Vulg.,—*able*) *men*, etc.; and, again, in so far as they were chosen by the people; hence it is written (Deut. 1. 13): *Let me have from among you wise* (Vulg.,—*able*) *men*, etc. Consequently it is evident that the ordering of the rulers was well provided for by the Law.

Reply Obj. 1. This people was governed under the special care of God: hence it is written (Deut. 7. 6): *The Lord thy God hath chosen thee to be His peculiar people.* And this is why the Lord reserved to Himself the institution of the chief ruler. For this too did Moses pray (Num. 27. 16): *May the Lord the God of the spirits of all the flesh provide a man, that may be over this multitude.* Thus by God's orders Josue was set at the head in place of Moses; and we read about each of the judges who succeeded Josue, that God *raised . . . up a saviour* for the people, and that *the spirit of the Lord was* in them (Judges 3. 9, 10, 15). Hence the

---

[1] Aristotle, II, 9 (1270ᵇ17).

[2] *Ibid.*, III, 7 (1279ᵃ32).

Lord did not leave the choice of a king to the people, but reserved this to Himself, as appears from Deut. 17. 15: *Thou shalt set him whom the Lord thy God shall choose.*

Reply Obj. 2. A kingdom is the best form of government of the people, so long as it is not corrupt. But since the power granted to a king is so great, it easily degenerates into tyranny, unless he to whom this power is given be a very virtuous man; for "it is only the virtuous man that conducts himself well in the midst of prosperity," as the Philosopher observes.[1] Now perfect virtue is to be found in few; and the Jews were especially inclined to cruelty and avarice, which vices above all turn men into tyrants. Hence from the very first the Lord did not set up the kingly authority with full power, but gave them judges and governors to rule them. But afterwards when the people asked Him to do so, being indignant with them, so to speak, He granted them a king, as is clear from His words to Samuel (I Kings 8. 7): *They have not rejected thee, but Me, that I should not reign over them.*

Nevertheless, as regards the appointment of a king, He did establish the manner of election from the very beginning (Deut. 17. 14, *seqq.*); and then He determined two points: first, that in choosing a king they should wait for the Lord's decision, and that they should not make a man of another nation king, because such kings are accustomed to take little interest in the people they are set over, and consequently to have no care for their welfare. Secondly, He prescribed how the king after his appointment should behave, in regard to himself; namely, that he should not accumulate chariots and horses, nor wives, nor immense wealth, because through craving for such things princes become tyrants and forsake justice. He also appointed the manner in which they were to conduct themselves towards God: namely, that they should continually read and ponder on God's Law, and should ever fear and obey God. Moreover, He decided how they should behave towards their subjects: namely, that they should not proudly despise them, or ill-treat them, and that they should not depart from the paths of justice.

Reply Obj. 3. The division of the kingdom, and the multitude of kings was rather a punishment inflicted on that people for their many dissensions, specially against the just rule of David, than a benefit conferred on them for their profit. Hence it is written (Osee 13. 11): *I will give thee a king in My wrath;* and (*ibid.*

8. 4): *They have reigned, but not by Me: they have been princes, and I knew not.*

Reply Obj. 4. The priestly office was bequeathed by succession from father to son; and this, in order that it might be held in greater respect, if not any man from the people could become a priest, since honour was given to them out of reverence for the divine worship. Hence it was necessary to put aside certain things for them both as to tithes and as to first-fruits, and, again, as to oblations and sacrifices, that they might be afforded a means of livelihood. On the other hand, the rulers, as stated above, were chosen from the whole people. Therefore they had their own possessions from which to derive a living, and so much the more, since the Lord forbade even a king to have superabundant wealth or to make too much show of magnificence, both because he could scarcely avoid the excesses of pride and tyranny arising from such things, and because, if the rulers were not very rich, and if their office involved much work and anxiety, it would not tempt the ambition of the common people, and would not become an occasion of sedition.

Reply Obj. 5. That right was not given to the king by Divine institution; rather was it foretold that kings would usurp that right, by framing unjust laws, and by degenerating into tyrants who preyed on their subjects. This is clear from the context that follows: *And you shall be his slaves* (Douay,—*servants*), which pertains to tyranny, since a tyrant rules his subjects as though they were his slaves. Hence Samuel spoke these words to deter them from asking for a king, since the narrative continues: *But the people would not hear the voice of Samuel.* It may happen, however, that even a good king, without being a tyrant, may take away the sons, and make them tribunes and centurions, and may take many things from his subjects in order to secure the common good.

ARTICLE 2. *Whether the Judicial Precepts Were Suitably Framed As to the Relations of One Man With Another?*

We proceed thus to the Second Article: It would seem that the judicial precepts were not suitably framed as regards the relations of one man with another.

Objection 1. For men cannot live together in peace if one man takes what belongs to another. But this seems to have been approved by the Law, since it is written (Deut. 23. 24): *Going into thy neighbour's vineyard, thou mayst eat as many grapes as thou pleasest.* Therefore

[1] *Ethics,* IV, 3 (1124^{a}30).

the Old Law did not make suitable provisions for man's peace.

Obj. 2. Further, one of the chief causes of the downfall of states has been the holding of property by women, as the Philosopher says.[1] But this was introduced by the Old Law, for it is written (Num. 27. 8): *When a man dieth without a son, his inheritance shall pass to his daughter.* Therefore the Law made unsuitable provision for the welfare of the people.

Obj. 3. Further, it is most conducive to the preservation of human society that men may provide themselves with necessaries by buying and selling, as stated in the *Politics.*[2] But the Old Law took away the force of sales, since it prescribes that in the 50th year of the jubilee all that is sold shall return to the vendor (Levit. 25. 28). Therefore in this matter the Law gave the people an unfitting command.

Obj. 4. Further, man's needs require that men should be ready to lend, which readiness ceases if the creditors do not return the pledges; hence it is written (Ecclus. 29. 10): *Many have refused to lend, not out of wickedness, but they were afraid to be defrauded without cause.* And yet this was encouraged by the Law. First, because it is prescribed (Deut. 15. 2): *He to whom any thing is owing from his friend or neighbour or brother, cannot demand it again, because it is the year of remission of the Lord;* and (Exod. 22. 15) it is stated that if a borrowed animal should die while the owner is present, the borrower is not bound to make restitution. Secondly, because the security acquired through the pledge is lost; for it is written (Deut. 24. 10): *When thou shalt demand of thy neighbour any thing that he oweth thee, thou shalt not go into his house to take away a pledge;* and again (verses 12, 13): *The pledge shall not lodge with thee that night, but thou shalt restore it to him presently.* Therefore the Law made insufficient provision in the matter of loans.

Obj. 5. Further, considerable risk attaches to goods deposited with a fraudulent depositary, and therefore great caution should be observed in such matters; hence it is stated in II Mach. 3. 15 that *the priests . . . called upon Him from heaven, Who made the law concerning things given to be kept, that He would preserve them safe, for them that had deposited them.* But the precepts of the Old Law observed little caution in regard to deposits, since it is prescribed (Exod. 22. 10, 11) that when goods deposited

are lost, the owner is to stand by the oath of the depositary. Therefore the Law made unsuitable provision in this matter.

Obj. 6. Further, just as a workman offers his work for hire, so do men let houses and so forth. But there is no need for the tenant to pay his rent as soon as he takes a house. Therefore it seems an unnecessarily hard prescription (Lev. 19. 13) that *the wages of him that hath been hired by thee shall not abide with thee until the morning.*

Obj. 7. Further, since there is often pressing need for a judge, it should be easy to gain access to one. It was therefore unfitting that the Law (Deut. 17. 8, 9) should command them to go to a fixed place to ask for judgment on doubtful matters.

Obj. 8. Further, it is possible that not only two, but three or more, should agree to tell a lie. Therefore it is unreasonably stated (Deut. 19. 15) that *in the mouth of two or three witnesses every word shall stand.*

Obj. 9. Further, punishment should be fixed according to the gravity of the fault; for which reason also it is written (Deut. 25. 2): *According to the measure of the sin, shall the measure also of the stripes be.* Yet the Law fixed unequal punishments for certain faults, for it is written (Exod. 22. 1) that the thief *shall restore five oxen for one ox, and four sheep for one sheep.* Moreover, certain slight offences are severely punished; thus (Num. 15. 32, *seqq.*) a man is stoned for gathering sticks on the sabbath day, and (Deut. 21. 18, *seqq.*) the unruly son is commanded to be stoned on account of certain small transgressions, namely, because *he gave himself to revelling . . . and banquetings.* Therefore the Law prescribed punishments in an unreasonable manner.

Obj. 10. Further, as Augustine says,[3] "Tully writes that the laws recognize eight forms of punishment, indemnity, prison, stripes, retaliation, public disgrace, exile, death, slavery." Now some of these were prescribed by the Law. Indemnity, as when a thief was condemned to make restitution fivefold or fourfold. Prison, as when (Num. 15. 34) a certain man is ordered to be imprisoned. Stripes were prescribed thus (Deut. 25. 2): *if they see that the offender be worthy of stripes; they shall lay him down, and shall cause him to be beaten before them.* Public disgrace was brought on to him who refused to take to himself the wife of his deceased brother, for she took off *his shoe from his foot, and* did *spit in his face (ibid.* 9). It prescribed

---

[1] *Politics,* II, 9 (1270ª23).
[2] Aristotle, I, 9 (1257ª14).

[3] *City of God,* XXI, 11 (PL 41, 725).

the death penalty, as is clear from Lev. 20. 9: *He that curseth his father, or mother, dying let him die.* The Law also recognized the *lex talionis*, by prescribing (Exod. 21. 24): *Eye for eye, tooth for tooth.* Therefore it seems unreasonable that the Law should not have inflicted the two other punishments, namely, exile and slavery.

Obj. 11. Further, no punishment is due except for a fault. But dumb animals cannot commit a fault. Therefore the Law is unreasonable in punishing them (Exod. 21. 29): *If the ox ... shall kill a man or a woman, it shall be stoned;* and (Lev. 20. 16): *The woman that shall lie under any beast, shall be killed together with the same.* Therefore it seems that matters pertaining to the relations of one man with another were unsuitably regulated by the Law.

Obj. 12. Further, the Lord commanded (Exod. 21. 12) a murderer to be punished with death. But the death of a dumb animal is reckoned of much less account than the slaying of a man. Hence murder cannot be sufficiently punished by the slaying of a dumb animal. Therefore it is unfittingly prescribed (Deut. 21. 1, 4) that *when there shall be found ... the corpse of a man slain, and it is not known who is guilty of the murder ... the ancients* of the nearest city *shall take a heifer of the herd, that hath not drawn in the yoke, nor ploughed the ground, and they shall bring her into a rough and stony valley, that never was ploughed, nor sown; and there they shall strike off the head of the heifer.*

On the contrary, It is recalled as a special blessing (Ps. 147. 20) that *He hath not done in like manner to every nation; and His judgments He hath not made manifest to them.*

I answer that, As Augustine says,[1] quoting Tully,[2] "a nation is a body of men united together by consent to the law and by community of welfare." Consequently it pertains to the very notion of a nation that the mutual relations of the citizens be ordered by just laws. Now the relations of one man with another are twofold: some are effected under the guidance of those in authority, others are effected by the will of private persons. And since whatever is subject to the power of an individual can be disposed of according to his will, hence it is that the decision of matters between one man and another and the punishment of evildoers depend on the direction of those in authority, to whom men are subject. On the other hand, the power of private persons is exercised over

the things they possess, and consequently their dealings with one another as regards such things depend on their own will, for instance in buying, selling, giving, and so forth.

Now the Law provided sufficiently in respect of each of these relations between one man and another. For it established judges, as is clearly indicated in Deut. 16. 18: *Thou shalt appoint judges and magistrates in all its* (Vulg.,—*thy*) *gates, ... that they may judge the people with just judgment.* It also directed the manner of pronouncing just judgments, according to Deut. 1. 16, 17: *Judge that which is just, whether he be one of your own country or a stranger: there shall be no difference of persons.* It also removed an occasion of pronouncing unjust judgment, by forbidding judges to accept bribes (Exod. 23. 8; Deut. 16. 19). It prescribed the number of witnesses, namely, two or three; and it appointed certain punishments to certain crimes, as we shall state farther on (Reply 10).

But with regard to possessions, it is a very good thing, says the Philosopher,[3] that the things possessed should be distinct, and that their use should be partly common, and partly granted to others by the will of the possessors. These three points were provided for by the Law. Because, in the first place, the possessions themselves were divided among individuals; for it is written (Num. 33. 53, 54): *I have given you the land for a possession: and you shall divide it among you by lot.* And since many states have been ruined through want of regulations in the matter of possessions, as the Philosopher observes,[4] therefore the Law provided a threefold remedy against the irregularity of possessions. The first was that they should be divided equally according to the number of men, and so it is written (Num. 33. 54): *To the more you shall give a larger part, and to the fewer, a lesser.* A second remedy was that possessions could not be alienated for ever, but after a certain lapse of time should return to their former owner, so as to avoid confusion of possessions (cf. Reply 3). The third remedy aimed at the removal of this confusion, and provided that the dead should be succeeded by their next of kin: in the first place, the son; secondly, the daughter; thirdly, the brother; fourthly, the father's brother; fifthly, any other next of kin. Furthermore, in order to preserve the distinction of property, the Law enacted that heiresses should marry within their own tribe, as recorded in Num. 36. 6.

---

[1] *City of God*, II, 21 (PL 41, 67); cf. XIX, 21 (PL 41, 649).
[2] *De Republica*, I, 25 (DD IX, 292).

[3] *Politics*, II, 5 (1263ᵃ25).
[4] *Ibid.*, II, 9 (1270ᵃ23).

Secondly, the Law commanded that, in some respects, the use of things should belong to all in common. Firstly, as regards the care of them; for it was prescribed (Deut. 22. 1-4). *Thou shalt not pass by, if thou seest thy brother's ox or his sheep go astray; but thou shalt bring them back to thy brother,* and in like manner as to other things. Secondly, as regards fruits. For all alike were allowed on entering a friend's vineyard to eat of the fruit, but not to take any away. And, specially, with respect to the poor, it was prescribed that the forgotten sheaves, and the bunches of grapes and fruit, should be left behind for them (Lev. 19. 9; Deut. 24. 19). Moreover, whatever grew in the seventh year was common property, as stated in Exod. 23. 11 and Lev. 25. 4.

Thirdly, the law recognized the transference of goods by the owner. There was a purely gratuitous transfer; thus it is written (Deut. 14. 28, 29): *The third day thou shalt separate another tithe . . . and the Levite . . . and the stranger, and the fatherless, and the widow . . . shall come and shall eat and be filled.* And there was a transfer for a consideration, for instance, by selling and buying, by letting out and hiring, by loan and also by deposit, concerning all of which we find that the Law made ample provision. Consequently it is clear that the Old Law provided sufficiently concerning the mutual relations of one man with another.

Reply Obj. 1. As the Apostle says (Rom. 13. 8), *he that loveth his neighbour hath fulfilled the Law;* because, namely, all the precepts of the Law, chiefly those concerning our neighbour, seem to aim at the end that men should love one another. Now it is an effect of love that men give their own goods to others, because, as stated in I John 3. 17: *He that . . . shall see his brother in need, and shall shut up his bowels from him: how doth the charity of God abide in him?* Hence the purpose of the Law was to accustom men to give of their own to others readily; thus the Apostle (I Tim. 6. 18) commands the rich *to give easily and to communicate to others.* Now a man does not give easily to others if he will not suffer another man to take some little thing from him without any great injury to him. And so the Law laid down that it should be lawful for a man, on entering his neighbour's vineyard, to eat of the fruit there, but not to carry any away, lest this should lead to the infliction of a grievous harm, and cause a disturbance of the peace; for among a disciplined people the taking of a little does not disturb the peace; in fact, it rather strength-

ens friendship and accustoms men to share with one another.

Reply Obj. 2. The Law did not prescribe that women should succeed to their father's estate except in default of male issue, failing which it was necessary that succession should be granted to the female line in order to comfort the father, who would have been sad to think that his estate would pass to strangers. Nevertheless the Law observed due caution in the matter, by providing that those women who succeeded to their father's estate should marry within their own tribe, in order to avoid confusion of tribal possessions, as stated in Num. 36. 7, 8.

Reply Obj. 3. As the Philosopher says,[1] the regulation of possessions conduces much to the preservation of a state or nation. Consequently, as he himself observes, it was forbidden by the law in some of the heathen states, that anyone should sell his possessions, except to avoid a manifest loss. For if possessions were to be sold indiscriminately, they might happen to come into the hands of a few, so that it might become necessary for a state or country to become empty of inhabitants. Hence the Old Law, in order to remove this danger, ordered things in such a way that while provision was made for men's needs by allowing the sale of possessions to avail for a certain period; but at the same time the said danger was removed by prescribing the return of those possessions after that period had elapsed. The reason for this law was to prevent confusion of possessions, and to ensure the continuance of a definite distinction among the tribes.

But as the town houses were not allotted to distinct estates, therefore the Law allowed them to be sold in perpetuity, like moveable goods. For the number of houses in a town was not fixed, while there was a fixed limit to the amount of estates, which could not be exceeded, although the number of houses in a town could be increased. On the other hand, houses situated not in a town but *in a village that hath no walls,* could not be sold in perpetuity, because such houses are built merely with a view to the cultivation and care of possessions. Therefore the Law rightly made the same prescription in regard to both (Lev. 25.).

Reply Obj. 4. As stated above (reply 1), the purpose of the Law was to accustom men to its precepts, so as to be ready to come to one another's assistance, because this is a very great incentive to friendship. The Law granted these facilities for helping others in the matter

[1] *Politics,* II, 7 (1266ᵇ14).

not only of gratuitous and absolute donations, but also of mutual transfers, because the latter kind of succour is more frequent and benefits the greater number, and it granted facilities for this purpose in many ways. First of all by prescribing that men should be ready to lend, and that they should not be less inclined to do so as the year of remission drew nigh, as stated in Deut. 15. 7, *seqq.* Secondly, by forbidding them to burden a man to whom they might grant a loan, either by exacting usury, or by accepting necessities of life in security, and by prescribing that when this had been done they should be restored at once. For it is written (Deut. 23. 19): *Thou shalt not lend to thy brother money for usury; and* (24. 6): *Thou shalt not take the nether nor the upper millstone to pledge; for he hath pledged his life to thee;* and (Exod. 22. 26): *If thou take of thy neighbour a garment in pledge, thou shalt give it him again before sunset.* Thirdly, by forbidding them to be importunate in exacting payment. Hence it is written (Exod. 22. 25): *If thou lend money to any of my people that is poor that dwelleth with thee, thou shalt not be hard upon them as an extortioner.* For this reason, too, it is enacted (Deut. 24. 10, 11): *When thou shalt demand of thy neighbour anything that he oweth thee, thou shalt not go into his house to take away a pledge, but thou shalt stand without, and he shall bring out to thee what he hath;* both because a man's house is his surest refuge, and therefore it is offensive to a man to be set upon in his own house, and because the Law does not allow the creditor to take away whatever he likes in security, but rather permits the debtor to give what he needs least. Fourthly, the Law prescribed that debts should cease altogether after the lapse of seven years. For it was probable that those who could conveniently pay their debts would do so before the seventh year, and would not defraud the lender without cause. But if they were altogether insolvent, there was the same reason for remitting the debt from love for them as there was for renewing the loan on account of their need.

As regards animals granted in loan, the Law enacted that if through the neglect of the person to whom they were lent they perished or deteriorated in his absence, he was bound to make restitution. But if they perished or deteriorated while he was present and taking proper care of them, he was not bound to make restitution, especially if they were hired for a consideration, because they might have died or de-

teriorated in the same way if they had remained in possession of the lender, so that if the animal had been saved through being lent, the lender would have gained something by the loan which would no longer have been gratuitous. And especially was this to be observed when animals were hired for a consideration, because then the owner received a certain price for the use of the animals and therefore he had no right to any profit by receiving indemnity for the animal, unless the person who had charge of it were negligent. In the case, however, of animals not hired for a consideration, equity demanded that he should receive something by way of restitution at least to the value of the hire of the animal that had perished or deteriorated.

Reply Obj. 5. The difference between a loan and a deposit is that a loan is in respect of goods transferred for the use of the person to whom they are transferred, while a deposit is for the benefit of the depositor. Hence in certain cases there was a stricter obligation of returning a loan than of restoring goods held in deposit. Because the latter might be lost in two ways. First, unavoidably: that is, either through a natural cause, for instance if an animal held in deposit were to die or depreciate in value, or through an extrinsic cause, for instance, if it were taken by an enemy, or devoured by a beast (in which case, however, a man was bound to restore to the owner whatever was left of the animal thus slain); but in the other cases mentioned above he was not bound to make restitution, but only to take an oath in order to clear himself of suspicion. Secondly, the goods deposited might be lost through an avoidable cause, for instance by theft; and then the depositary was bound to restitution on account of his neglect. But, as stated above (reply 4), he who held an animal on loan was bound to restitution even if he were absent when it depreciated or died, because he was held responsible for less negligence than a depositary, who was only held responsible in case of theft.

Reply Obj. 6. Workmen who offer their labour for hire are poor men who toil for their daily bread, and therefore the Law commanded wisely that they should be paid at once, lest they should lack food. But they who offer other commodities for hire are usually rich, nor are they in such need of their price in order to gain a livelihood. And consequently the comparison does not hold.

Reply Obj. 7. The purpose for which judges are appointed among men is that they may decide doubtful points in matters of justice. Now a matter may be doubtful in two ways. First, among simple-minded people, and in order to remove doubts of this kind, it was prescribed (Deut. 16. 18) that *judges and magistrates should be appointed in each tribe, to judge the people with just judgment.* Secondly, a matter may be doubtful even among experts, and therefore, in order to remove doubts of this kind, the Law prescribed that all should foregather in some chief place chosen by God, where there would be both the High-Priest, who would decide doubtful matters relating to the ceremonies of divine worship, and the chief judge of the people, who would decide matters relating to the judgments of men; just as even now cases are taken from a lower to a higher court either by appeal or by consultation. Hence it is written (Deut. 17. 8, 9): *If thou perceive that there be among you a hard and doubtful matter in judgment, . . . and thou see that the words of the judges within thy gates do vary; arise and go up to the place, which the Lord thy God shall choose; and thou shalt come to the priests of the Levitical race, and to the judge that shall be at that time.* But such doubtful matters did not often occur for judgment, and therefore the people were not burdened on this account.

Reply Obj. 8. In the business affairs of men, there is no such thing as demonstrative and infallible proof, and we must be content with a certain conjectural probability, such as that which an orator employs to persuade. Consequently, although it is quite possible for two or three witnesses to agree to a falsehood, yet it is neither easy nor probable that they succeed in so doing; therefore their testimony is taken as being true, especially·if they do not waver in giving it, or are not otherwise suspect. Moreover, in order that witnesses might not easily depart from the truth, the Law commanded that they should be most carefully examined, and that those who were found untruthful should be severely punished, as stated in Deut. 19. 16, *seqq.*

There was, however, a reason for fixing on this particular number, in token of the unerring truth of the Divine Persons, Who are sometimes mentioned as two, because the Holy Ghost is the bond of the other two Persons, and sometimes as three, as Augustine observes[1] on John 8. 17: *In your law it is written that the testimony of two men is true.*

Reply Obj. 9. A severe punishment is inflicted not only on account of the gravity of a fault,

[1] *Tract.*, XXXVI (PL 35, 1669).

but also for other reasons. First, on account of the greatness of the sin, because a greater sin, other things being equal, deserves a greater punishment. Secondly, on account of a habitual sin, since men are not easily cured of habitual sin except by severe punishments. Thirdly, on account of a great desire for or a great pleasure in the sin; for men are not easily deterred from such sins unless they be severely punished. Fourthly, on account of the facility of committing a sin and of concealing it; for such sins, when discovered, should be more severely punished in order to deter others from committing them.

Again, with regard to the greatness of a sin, four degrees may be observed, even in respect of one single deed. The first is when a sin is committed unwillingly, because then, if the sin be altogether involuntary, man is altogether excused from punishment; for it is written (Deut. 22. 25, *seqq.*) that a damsel who suffers violence in a field is not guilty of death, because *she cried, and there was no man to help her.* But if a man sinned in any way voluntarily, and yet through weakness, as for instance when a man sins from passion, the sin is diminished, and the punishment, according to true judgment, should be diminished also; unless perhaps the common good requires that the sin be severely punished in order to deter others from committing such sins, as stated above. The second degree is when a man sins through ignorance, and then he was held to be guilty to a certain extent, on account of his negligence in acquiring knowledge; yet he was not punished by the judges but expiated his sin by sacrifices. Hence it is written (Lev. 4. 2): *The soul that sinneth through ignorance*, etc. This is, however, to be taken as applying to ignorance of fact, and not to ignorance of the Divine precept, which all were bound to know. The third degree was when a man sinned from pride, that is, through deliberate choice or malice, and then he was punished according to the greatness of the sin. The fourth degree was when a man sinned from stubbornness or obstinacy, and then he was to be utterly cut off as a rebel and a destroyer of the commandment of the Law.

Accordingly we must say that, in appointing the punishment for theft the Law considered what would be likely to happen most frequently (Exod. 22. 1-9). Therefore, as regards theft of other things which can easily be safeguarded from a thief, the thief restored only twice their value. But sheep cannot be easily safeguarded from a thief, because they graze in the fields, and therefore it happened more frequently that sheep were stolen in the fields. Consequently the Law inflicted a heavier penalty, by ordering four sheep to be restored for the theft of one. As to cattle, they were yet more difficult to safeguard, because they are kept in the fields, and do not graze in flocks as sheep do; therefore a yet more heavy penalty was inflicted in their regard, so that five oxen were to be restored for one ox. And this I say unless by chance the animal itself were discovered in the thief's possession, because in that case he had to restore only twice the number, as in the case of other thefts; for there was reason to presume that he intended to restore the animal, since he kept it alive. Again, we might say, according to a gloss,[1] that "a cow is useful in five ways: it may be used for sacrifice, for ploughing, for food, for milk, and its hide is employed for various purposes"; and therefore for one cow five had to be restored. But the sheep was useful in four ways: "for sacrifice, for meat, for milk, and for its wool."[2] The unruly son was slain, not because he ate and drank, but on account of his stubbornness and rebellion, which was always punished by death, as stated above. As to the man who gathered sticks on the sabbath, he was stoned as a breaker of the Law, which commanded the sabbath to be observed in commemoration of the belief in the newness of the world, as stated above (Q. C, A. 5). Therefore he was slain as an unbeliever.

Reply Obj. 10. The Old Law inflicted the death penalty for the more grievous crimes, namely, for those which are committed against God, and for murder, for stealing a man, irreverence towards one's parents, adultery and incest. In the case of theft of other things it inflicted punishment by indemnification, while in the case of blows and mutilation it authorized punishment by retaliation; and likewise for the sin of bearing false witness. In other faults of less degree it prescribed the punishment of stripes or of public disgrace.

The punishment of slavery was prescribed by the Law in two cases. First, in the case of a slave who was unwilling to avail himself of the privilege granted by the Law, whereby he was free to depart in the seventh year of remission. He was therefore punished by remaining a slave for ever. Secondly, in the case of a thief who had not wherewith to make restitution, as stated in Exod. 22. 3.

The punishment of absolute exile was not prescribed by the Law because God was worshipped by that people alone, while all other nations were given to idolatry; therefore if any man were exiled from that people absolutely, he would be in danger of falling into idolatry. For this reason it is related (I Kings 26. 19) that David said to Saul: *They are cursed in the sight of the Lord, who have cast me out this day, that I should not dwell in the inheritance of the Lord, saying: Go, serve strange gods.* There was, however, a restricted sort of exile, for it is written in Deut. 19. 4 that *he that striketh* (Vulg.,—*killeth*) *his neighbour ignorantly, and is proved to have had no hatred against him, shall flee to one of the cities* of refuge and *abide there until the death of the high-priest.* For then it became lawful for him to return home, because when the whole people thus suffered a loss they forgot their private quarrels, so that the next of kin of the slain were not so eager to kill the slayer.

Reply Obj. 11. Dumb animals were ordered to be slain not on account of any fault of theirs, but as a punishment to their owners, who had not safeguarded their beasts from these offences. Hence the owner was more severely punished if his ox had butted anyone *yesterday or the day before* (in which case steps might have been taken to avoid the danger), than if it had taken to butting suddenly. Or again, the animal was slain in detestation of the sin, and lest men should be horrified at the sight of it.

Reply Obj. 12. The literal reason for this commandment, as Rabbi Moses declares (*Doct. Perplex.* iii),[3] was "because the slayer was frequently from the nearest city." Therefore the slaying of the calf was a means of investigating the hidden murder. This was brought about in three ways. In the first place the elders of the city swore that they had taken every measure for safeguarding the roads. Secondly, the owner of the heifer was indemnified for the slaying of his beast, and if the murder were previously discovered, the beast was not slain. Thirdly, the place where the heifer was slain remained uncultivated. Therefore, in order to avoid this twofold loss, the men of that city would readily make known the murderer if they knew who he was; and it would seldom happen but that some word or sign would escape about the matter. Or again, this was done in order to frighten people, in detestation of murder. Because the slaying of a heifer, which is a useful animal and full of strength, especially before it has been put under the yoke, signified that whoever

---

[1] *Glossa ordin.,* super Exod. 22.1 (I, 169F).
[2] *Ibid.* (I, 170A).

[3] Chap. 40 (FR 343).

committed murder, however useful and strong he might be, was to forfeit his life, and that by a cruel death, which was implied by the striking off of its head; and that the murderer, as vile and abject, was to be cut off from the fellowship of men, which was betokened by the fact that the heifer after being slain was left to rot in a rough and uncultivated place.

Mystically, the heifer taken from the herd signifies "the flesh of Christ, which had not drawn a yoke, since it had done no sin; nor did it plough the ground, that is, it never knew the stain of revolt."[1] The fact of the heifer being killed in an uncultivated valley signified the despised death of Christ, whereby all sins are washed away, and the devil is shown to be the arch-murderer.

ARTICLE 3. Whether the Judicial Precepts Regarding Foreigners Were Framed in a Suitable Manner?

We proceed thus to the Third Article: It would seem that the judicial precepts regarding foreigners were not suitably framed.

Objection 1. For Peter said (Acts 10. 34, 35): In very deed I perceive that God is not a respecter of persons, but in every nation, he that feareth Him and worketh justice is acceptable to Him. But those who are acceptable to God should not be excluded from the Church of God. Therefore it is unsuitably commanded (Deut. 23. 3) that the Ammonite and the Moabite, even after the tenth generation, shall not enter into the church of the Lord for ever; on the other hand, however, it is prescribed (ibid. 7) to be observed with regard to certain other nations: Thou shalt not abhor the Edomite, because he is thy brother; nor the Egyptian because thou wast a stranger in his land.

Obj. 2. Further, we do not deserve to be punished for those things which are not in our power. But it is not in a man's power to be an eunuch, or born of a prostitute. Therefore it is unsuitably commanded (Deut. 23. 1, 2) that an eunuch and one born of a prostitute shall not enter into the church of the Lord.

Obj. 3. Further, the Old Law mercifully forbade strangers to be molested; for it is written (Exod. 22. 21): Thou shalt not molest a stranger, nor afflict him; for yourselves also were strangers in the land of Egypt; and (23. 9): Thou shalt not molest a stranger, for you know the hearts of strangers, for you also were strangers in the land of Egypt. But it is an affliction to be burdened with usury. Therefore the Law

unsuitably permitted them (Deut. 23. 19, 20) to lend money to the stranger for usury.

Obj. 4. Further, men are much more akin to us than trees. But we should show greater care and love for these things that are nearest to us, according to Ecclus. 13. 19: Every beast loveth its like: so also every man him that is nearest to himself. Therefore the Lord unsuitably commanded (Deut. 20. 13-19) that all the inhabitants of a captured hostile city were to be slain, but that the fruit-trees should not be cut down.

Obj. 5. Further, every one should prefer the common good of virtue to the good of the individual. But the common good is sought in a war which men fight against their enemies. Therefore it is unsuitably commanded (Deut. 20. 5-7) that certain men should be sent home, for instance a man that had built a new house, or who had planted a vineyard, or who had married a wife.

Obj. 6. Further, no man should profit by his own fault. But it is a man's fault if he be timid or faint-hearted, since this is contrary to the virtue of fortitude. Therefore the timid and faint-hearted are unfittingly excused from the toil of battle (Deut. 20. 8).

On the contrary, Divine Wisdom declares (Prov. 8. 8): All my words are just, there is nothing wicked nor perverse in them.

I answer that, Man's relations with foreigners are twofold: peaceful, and hostile. And in directing both kinds of relation the Law contained suitable precepts. For the Jews were offered three opportunities of peaceful relations with foreigners. First, when foreigners passed through their land as travellers. Secondly, when they came to dwell in their land as new-comers. And in both these respects the Law made kind provision in its precepts: for it is written (Exod. 22. 21): Thou shalt not molest a stranger (advenam); and again (ibid. 23. 9): Thou shalt not molest a stranger (peregrino). Thirdly, when any foreigners wished to be admitted entirely to their fellowship and mode of worship. With regard to these a certain order was observed. For they were not at once admitted to citizenship, just as it was the law with some nations that no one was deemed a citizen except after two or three generations, as the Philosopher says.[2] The reason for this was that if foreigners were allowed to meddle with the affairs of a nation as soon as they settled down in its midst, many dangers might occur, since the foreigners not yet having the common good

---

[1] Glossa ordin., super Deut. 21.1 (I, 354A).

[2] Politics, III, 2 (1275^b23).

firmly at heart might attempt something hurtful to the people. Hence it was that the Law prescribed in respect of certain nations that had close relations with the Jews (namely, the Egyptians among whom they were born and educated, and the Idumeans, the children of Esau, Jacob's brother), that they should be admitted to the fellowship of the people after the third generation; but others (with whom their relations had been hostile, such as the Ammonites and Moabites) were never to be admitted to citizenship; while the Amalekites, who were yet more hostile to them, and had no fellowship of thought with them, were to be held as foes in perpetuity; for it is written (Exod. 17. 16): *The war of the Lord shall be against Amalec from generation to generation.*

In like manner with regard to hostile relations with foreigners, the Law contained suitable precepts. For, in the first place, it commanded that war should be declared for a just cause; thus it is commanded (Deut. 20. 10) that when they advanced to besiege a city, they should at first make an offer of peace. Secondly, it enjoined that when once they had entered on a war they should undauntedly persevere in it, putting their trust in God. And in order that they might be the more heedful of this command, it ordered that on the approach of battle the priest should hearten them by promising them God's aid. Thirdly, it prescribed the removal of whatever might prove an obstacle to the fight, and that certain men, who might be in the way, should be sent home. Fourthly, it enjoined that they should use moderation in pursuing the advantage of victory, by sparing women and children, and by not cutting down the fruit-trees of that country.

Reply Obj. 1. The Law excluded the men of no nation from the worship of God and from things pertaining to the welfare of the soul; for it is written (Exod. 12. 48): *If any stranger be willing to dwell among you, and to keep the Phase of the Lord; all his males shall first be circumcised, and then shall he celebrate it according to the manner, and he shall be as that which is born in the land.* But in temporal matters concerning the public life of the people, admission was not granted to everyone at once, for the reason given above: but to some, that is, the Egyptians and Idumeans, in the third generation; while others were excluded in perpetuity, in detestation of their past offence, that is, the peoples of Moab, Ammon, and Amalec. For just as one man is punished for a sin committed by him in order that others

seeing this may be deterred and refrain from sinning, so too may one nation or city be punished for a crime that others may refrain from similar crimes.

Nevertheless it was possible by dispensation for a man to be admitted to citizenship on account of some act of virtue; thus it is related (Judith 14. 6) that Achior, the captain of the children of Ammon, *was joined to the people of Israel, with all the succession of his kindred.* The same applies to Ruth the Moabite, who was *a virtuous woman* (Ruth 3. 11), although it may be said that this prohibition regarded men and not women, who are not able to be citizens absolutely speaking.

Reply Obj. 2. As the Philosopher says,[1] a man is said to be a citizen in two ways: first, absolutely; secondly, in a restricted sense. A man is a citizen absolutely if he has all the rights of citizenship, for instance, the right of debating or voting in the popular assembly. On the other hand, any man may be called citizen in a restricted sense only, if he dwells within the state —even common people or children or old men, who are not fit to enjoy power in matters pertaining to the common good. For this reason bastards, by reason of their base origin, were excluded from the *ecclesia*, that is, from the popular assembly, down to the tenth generation. The same applies to eunuchs, who were not able to receive the honour due to a father, especially among the Jews, where the divine worship was continued through carnal generation; for even among the heathens, those who had many children were marked with special honour, as the Philosopher remarks.[2] Nevertheless, in matters pertaining to the grace of God, eunuchs were not discriminated from others, as neither were strangers, as already stated; for it is written (Isa. 56. 3): *Let not the son of the stranger that adhereth to the Lord speak, saying: The Lord will divide and separate me from His people. And let not the eunuch say: Behold I am a dry tree.*

Reply Obj. 3. It was not the intention of the Law to sanction the acceptance of usury from strangers, but only to tolerate it on account of the proneness of the Jews to avarice, and in order to promote a more peaceful feeling towards those out of whom they made a profit.

Reply Obj. 4. A distinction was observed with regard to hostile cities. For some of them were far distant, and were not among those which had been promised to them. When they

[1] *Politics,* III, 5 (1278ª2).
[2] *Ibid.,* II, 9 (1270ᵇ1).

had taken these cities, they killed all the men who had fought against God's people, but the women and children were spared. But in the neighbouring cities which had been promised to them, all were ordered to be slain, on account of their former crimes, to punish which God sent the Israelites as executor of Divine justice; for it is written (Deut. 9. 5): *Because they have done wickedly, they are destroyed at thy coming in.* The fruit-trees were commanded to be left untouched for the use of the people themselves, to whom the city with its territory was destined to be subjected.

Reply Obj. 5. The builder of a new house, the planter of a vineyard, the newly married husband, were excluded from fighting, for two reasons. First, because man is accustomed to give all his affection to those things which he has lately acquired, or is on the point of having, and consequently he is apt to dread the loss of these above other things. Therefore it was likely enough that on account of this affection they would fear death all the more, and be so much the less brave in battle. Secondly, because, as the Philosopher says,[1] it is a misfortune for a man if he is prevented from obtaining something good when it is within his grasp. And so lest the surviving relations should be the more grieved at the death of these men who had not entered into the possession of the good things prepared for them, and also lest the people should be horror-stricken at the sight of their misfortune, these men were taken away from the danger of death by being removed from the battle.

Reply Obj. 6. The timid were sent back home not that they might be the gainers thereby but lest the people might be the losers by their presence, since their timidity and flight might cause others to be afraid and run away.

ARTICLE 4. *Whether the Old Law Set Forth Suitable Precepts About the Members of the Household?*

We proceed thus to the Fourth Article: It would seem that the Old Law set forth unsuitable precepts about the members of the household.

Objection 1. For "a slave is in every respect his master's property," as the Philosopher states.[2] But that which is a man's property should be his always. Therefore it was unfitting for the Law to command (Exod. 21. 2) that slaves should *go out free* in the seventh year.

Obj. 2. Further, a slave is his master's property, just as an animal, for example, an ass or an ox. But it is commanded (Deut. 22. 1-3) with regard to animals, that they should be brought back to the owner if they be found going astray. Therefore it was unsuitably commanded (Deut. 23. 15): *Thou shalt not deliver to his master the servant that is fled to thee.*

Obj. 3. Further, the Divine Law should encourage mercy more even than the human law. But according to human laws those who illtreat their servants and maidservants are severely punished, and the worse treatment of all seems to be that which results in death. Therefore it is unfittingly commanded (Exod. 21. 20, 21) that *he that striketh his bondman or bondwoman with a rod, and they die under his hands . . . if the party remain alive a day . . . he shall not be subject to the punishment, because it is his money.*

Obj. 4. Further, the dominion of a master over his slave differs from that of the father over his son.[3] But the dominion of master over slave gives the former the right to sell his slave or maidservant. Therefore it was unfitting for the Law to allow a man to sell his daughter to be a servant or handmaid (Exod. 21. 7).

Obj. 5. Further, a father has power over his son. But he who has power over the sinner has the right to punish him for his offences. Therefore it is unfittingly commanded (Deut. 21. 18 *seqq.*) that a father should bring his son to the ancients of the city for punishment.

Obj. 6. Further, the Lord forbade them (Deut. 7. 3, *seqq.*) to make marriages with strange nations, and commanded the dissolution of such as had been contracted (1 Esdras 10.). Therefore it was unfitting to allow them to marry captive women from strange nations (Deut. 21. 10 *seqq.*)

Obj. 7. Further, the Lord forbade them to marry within certain degrees of consanguinity and affinity, according to Levit. 18. Therefore it was unsuitably commanded (Deut. 25. 5) that if any man died without issue, his brother should marry his wife.

Obj. 8. Further, as there is the greatest familiarity between man and wife, so should there be the staunchest fidelity. But this is impossible if the marriage bond can be dissolved. Therefore it was unfitting for the Lord to allow (Deut. 24. 1-4) a man to put his wife away, by writing a bill of divorce; and besides, that he could not take her again to wife.

---

[1] *Physics,* II, 5 (197ª27).
[2] *Politics,* I, 4 (1254ª12).

[3] Aristotle, *Politics,* I, 12 (1259ª37); I, 3 (1253ᵇ8); III, 6 (1278ᵇ32).

Obj. 9. Further, just as a wife can be faithless to her husband, so can a slave be to his master, and a son to his father. But the Law did not command any sacrifice to be offered in order to investigate the injury done by a servant to his master, or by a son to his father. Therefore it seems to have been superfluous for the Law to prescribe the *sacrifice of jealousy* in order to investigate a wife's adultery (Num. 5. 12 *seqq.*). Consequently it seems that the Law put forth unsuitable judicial precepts about the members of the household.

On the contrary, It is written (Ps. 18. 10): *The judgments of the Lord are true, justified in themselves.*

I answer that, The mutual relations of the members of a household regard every-day actions directed to the necessities of life, as the Philosopher states.[1] Now the preservation of man's life may be considered from two points of view. First, from the point of view of the individual, that is, in so far as man preserves his individuality; and for the purpose of the preservation of life, considered from this standpoint, man has at his service external goods, by means of which he provides himself with food and clothing and other such necessaries of life, in the handling of which he has need of servants. Secondly, man's life is preserved from the point of view of the species, by means of generation, for which purpose man needs a wife, that she may bear him children. Accordingly the mutual relations of the members of a household admit of a threefold combination: namely, those of master and servant, those of husband and wife, and those of father and son. And in respect of all these relationships the Old Law contained fitting precepts.

Thus, with regard to servants, it commanded them to be treated with moderation—both as to their work, lest, that is, they should be burdened with excessive labour, for which reason the Lord commanded (Deut. 5. 14) that on the Sabbath day *thy manservant and thy maidservant* should *rest even as thyself;* and also as to the infliction of punishment, for it ordered those who maimed their servants to set them free (Exod. 21. 26, 27). Similar provision was made in favour of a maidservant when married to anyone (*ibid.* 7, *seqq.*). Moreover, with regard to those servants in particular who were taken from among the people, the Law prescribed that they should go out free in the seventh year, taking whatever they brought with them, even their clothes (*ibid.* 2, *seqq.*); and

furthermore it was commanded (Deut. 15. 13) that they should be given provision for the journey.

With regard to wives the Law made certain prescriptions as to those who were to be taken in marriage; for instance, that they should marry a wife from their own tribe (Num. 26. 6), and this lest confusion should ensue in the property of various tribes. Also that a man should marry the wife of his deceased brother when the latter died without issue, as prescribed in Deut. 25. 5, 6, and this in order that he who could not have successors according to carnal origin, might at least have them by a kind of adoption, and that thus the deceased might not be entirely forgotten. It also forbade them to marry certain women; namely, women of strange nations, through fear of their losing their faith, and those of their near kindred, on account of the natural respect due to them. Furthermore it prescribed in what way wives were to be treated after marriage; namely, that they should not be slandered without grave reason, for which reason it ordered punishment to be inflicted on the man who falsely accused his wife of a crime (Deut. 22. 13, *seqq.*). Also that a man's hatred of his wife should not be detrimental to his son (Deut. 21. 15, *seqq.*). Again, that a man should not ill-use his wife through hatred of her, but rather that he should write a bill of divorce and send her away (Deut. 24. 1). Furthermore, in order to foster conjugal love from the very outset, it was prescribed that no public duties should be laid on a recently married man, so that he might be free to rejoice with his wife.

With regard to children, the Law commanded parents to educate them by instructing them in the faith; hence it is written (Exod. 12. 26 *seqq.*): *When your children shall say to you: What is the meaning of this service? you shall say to them: It is the victim of the passage of the Lord.* Moreover, they are commanded to teach them the rules of right conduct; therefore it is written (Deut. 21. 20) that the parents had to say: *He slighteth hearing our admonitions, he giveth himself to revelling and to debauchery.*

Reply Obj. 1. As the children of Israel had been delivered by the Lord from slavery, and for this reason were bound to the service of God, He did not wish them to be slaves in perpetuity. Hence it is written (Lev. 25. 39, *seqq.*): *If thy brother, constrained by poverty, sell himself to thee, thou shalt not oppress him with the service of bondservants: but he shall*

---

[1] *Politics,* I, 2 (1252[b]13).

be as a hireling and a sojourner . . . for they are My servants, and I brought them out of the land of Egypt: let them not be sold as bond-men; and consequently, since they were slaves not absolutely but in a restricted sense, after a lapse of time they were set free.

Reply Obj. 2. This commandment is to be understood as referring to a servant whom his master seeks to kill, or to help him in committing some sin.

Reply Obj. 3. With regard to the ill-treatment of servants, the Law seems to have taken into consideration whether it was certain or not, since, if it were certain, the Law fixed a penalty; for maiming, the penalty was forfeiture of the servant, who was ordered to be given his liberty, while for slaying the punishment was that of a murderer, when the servant died under the blow of his master. If, however, the hurt were not certain, but only probable, the Law did not impose any penalty as regards a man's own servant; for instance if the servant did not die at once after being struck, but after some days, for it would be uncertain whether he died as a result of the blows he received. For when a man struck a free man, yet so that he did not die at once, but *walked abroad again upon his staff,* he that struck him was not guilty of murder, even though afterwards he died. Nevertheless he was bound to pay the doctor's fees incurred by the victim of his assault. But this was not the case if a man killed his own servant, because whatever the servant had, even his very person, was the property of his master. Hence the reason for his not being subject to a pecuniary penalty is set down as being *because it is his money.*

Reply Obj. 4. As stated above (reply 1), no Jew could own a Jew as a slave absolutely, but only in a restricted sense, as a hireling for a fixed time. And in this way the Law permitted that through stress of poverty a man might sell his son or daughter. This is shown by the very words of the Law, where we read: *If any man sell his daughter to be a servant, she shall not go out as bondwomen are wont to go out.* Moreover, in this way a man might sell not only his son, but even himself, rather as a hireling than as a slave, according to Lev. 25. 39, 40: *If thy brother, constrained by poverty, sell himself to thee, thou shalt not oppress him with the service of bondservants: but he shall be as a hireling and a sojourner.*

Reply Obj. 5. As the Philosopher says,[1] the paternal authority has the power only of ad-

monition, but not that of coercion, by which rebellious and headstrong persons can be compelled. Hence in this case the Lord commanded the stubborn son to be punished by the rulers of the city.

Reply Obj. 6. The Lord forbade them to marry strange women on account of the danger of seduction, lest they should be led astray into idolatry. And specially did this prohibition apply with respect to those nations who dwelt near them, because it was more probable that they would hold fast to their religious practices. When, however, the woman was willing to renounce idolatry and become an adherent of the Law, it was lawful to take her in marriage, as was the case with Ruth whom Boaz married. Hence she said to her mother-in-law (Ruth 1. 16): *Thy people shall be my people, and thy God my God.* Accordingly it was not permitted to marry a captive woman unless she first shaved her hair, and pared her nails, and put off the raiment in which she was taken, and mourned for her father and mother, in token that she renounced idolatry for ever.

Reply Obj. 7. As Chrysostom says (*Hom.* xlviii, *super Matt.*),[2] "because death was an unmitigated evil for the Jews, who did everything with a view to the present life, it was ordained that children should be born to the dead man through his brother, thus affording a certain mitigation to his death. It was not, however, ordained that any other than his brother or one next of kin should marry the wife of the deceased, because (the offspring of this union) would not be looked upon as that of the deceased; and, moreover, a stranger would not be under the obligation to support the household of the deceased, as his brother would be bound to do from motives of justice on account of his relationship." Hence it is evident that in marrying the wife of his dead brother, he took his dead brother's place.

Reply Obj. 8. The Law permitted a wife to be divorced not as though it were just absolutely speaking, but on account of the Jew's hardness of heart, as Our Lord declared (Matt. 19. 8). Of this, however, we must speak more fully in the treatise on Matrimony (Suppl., Q. LXVII.).

Reply Obj. 9. Wives break their conjugal faith by adultery, both easily, for motives of pleasure, and hiddenly, since *the eye of the adulterer observeth darkness* (Job 24. 15). But this does not apply to a son in respect of his father, or to a servant in respect of his master,

---

[1] *Ethics,* x, 9 (1180ᵃ18).

[2] PG 58, 489.

because the latter infidelity is not the result of the lust of pleasure, but rather of malice; nor can it remain hidden like the infidelity of an adulterous woman.

QUESTION CVI
OF THE LAW OF THE GOSPEL, CALLED THE NEW LAW, CONSIDERED IN ITSELF
(In Four Articles)

IN proper sequence we have to consider now the Law of the Gospel, which is called the New Law. And in the first place we must consider it in itself; secondly, in comparison with the Old Law (Q. CVII); thirdly, we shall treat of those things that are contained in the New Law (Q. CVIII). Under the first head there are four points of inquiry: (1) What kind of law is it? that is, is it a written law or is it instilled in the heart? (2) Of its power, that is, does it justify? (3) Of its beginning—should it have been given at the beginning of the world? (4) Of its end—whether it will last until the end, or will another law take its place?

ARTICLE 1. *Whether the New Law Is a Written Law?*

We proceed thus to the First Article: It would seem that the New Law is a written law.[1]

Objection 1. For the New Law is just the same as the Gospel. But the Gospel is set forth in writing, according to John 20. 31: *But these are written that you may believe.* Therefore the New Law is a written law.

Obj. 2. Further, the law that is instilled in the heart is the natural law, according to Rom. 2. 14, 15: *(The Gentiles) do by nature those things that are of the law . . . who have* (Vulg., —*show*) *the word of the law written in their hearts.* If therefore the law of the Gospel were instilled in our hearts, it would not be distinct from the law of nature.

Obj. 3. Further, the law of the Gospel is proper to those who are in the state of the New Testament. But the law that is instilled in the heart is common to those who are in the New Testament and to those who are in the Old Testament; for it is written (Wisd. 7. 27) that Divine Wisdom *through nations conveyeth herself into holy souls, she maketh the friends of God and prophets.* Therefore the New Law is not instilled in our hearts.

On the contrary, The New Law is the law of the New Testament. But the law of the New Testament is instilled in our hearts. For the Apostle, quoting the authority of Jeremias 31. 31, 33: *Behold the days shall come, saith the Lord; and I will perfect unto the house of Israel, and unto the house of Juda, a new testament,* says, explaining what this testament is (Heb. 8. 8, 10): *For this is the testament which I will make to the house of Israel . . . by giving* (Vulg.,—*I will give*) *My laws into their mind, and in their heart will I write them.* Therefore the New Law is instilled in our hearts.

I answer that, "Each thing appears to be that which preponderates in it," as the Philosopher states.[2] Now that which is preponderant in the law of the New Testament and on which all its efficacy is based is the grace of the Holy Ghost, which is given through faith in Christ. Consequently the New Law is chiefly the grace itself of the Holy Ghost, which is given to those who believe in Christ. This is manifestly stated by the Apostle who says (Rom. 3. 27): *Where is . . . thy boasting? It is excluded. By what law? Of works? No, but by the law of faith,* for he calls the grace itself of faith "a law." And still more clearly it is written (Rom. 8. 2): *The law of the spirit of life, in Christ Jesus, hath delivered me from the law of sin and of death.* Hence Augustine says (*De Spir. et Lit.* xxiv)[3] that "as the law of deeds was written on tables of stone, so is the law of faith inscribed on the hearts of the faithful"; and elsewhere, in the same book (xxi):[4] "What else are the Divine laws written by God Himself on our hearts, but the very presence of His Holy Spirit?"

Nevertheless the New Law contains certain things that dispose us to receive the grace of the Holy Ghost, and pertaining to the use of that grace; such things are of secondary importance, so to speak, in the New Law, and the faithful needed to be instructed concerning them, both by word and writing, both as to what they should believe and as to what they should do. Consequently we must say that the New Law is in the first place a law that is inscribed on our hearts, but that secondarily it is a written law.

Reply Obj. 1. The Gospel writings contain only such things as pertain to the grace of the Holy Ghost, either by disposing us to it, or by directing us to its use. Thus with regard to the intellect, the Gospel contains certain matters pertaining to the manifestation of Christ's God-

---

[1] According to the Abbot Joachim. Cf. Denifle, *Chartularium*, n. 257 (I, 297), note 1.

[2] *Ethics*, IX, 8 (1169ᵃ2).
[3] PL 44, 225; also chaps. 17, 26 (PL 44, 218, 227).
[4] PL 44, 222.

head or humanity, which dispose us by means of faith through which we receive the grace of the Holy Ghost; and with regard to the affections it contains matters touching the contempt of the world, whereby man is rendered fit to receive the grace of the Holy Ghost; for the world, that is worldly men, cannot receive the Holy Ghost (John 14. 17). As to the use of spiritual grace, this consists in works of virtue to which the writings of the New Testament exhort men in divers ways.

Reply Obj. 2. There are two ways in which a thing may be instilled into man. First, through being part of his nature, and thus the natural law is instilled into man. Secondly, a thing is instilled into man by being, as it were, added on to his nature by a gift of grace. In this way the New Law is instilled into man, not only by indicating to him what he should do, but also by helping him to accomplish it.

Reply Obj. 3. No man ever had the grace of the Holy Ghost except through faith in Christ either explicit or implicit; and by faith in Christ man belongs to the New Testament. Consequently whoever had the law of grace instilled into them belonged to the New Testament.

ARTICLE 2. *Whether the New Law Justifies?*

We proceed thus to the Second Article: It would seem that the New Law does not justify.

Objection 1. For no man is justified unless he obey God's law, according to Heb. 5. 9. *He,* that is, Christ, *became to all that obey Him the cause of eternal salvation.* But the Gospel does not always cause men to believe in it, for it is written (Rom. 10. 16): *All do not obey the Gospel.* Therefore the New Law does not justify.

Obj. 2. Further, the Apostle proves in his epistle to the Romans that the Old Law did not justify, because transgression increased at its advent; for it is stated (Rom. 4. 15): *The Law worketh wrath: for where there is no law, neither is there transgression.* But much more did the New Law increase transgression, since he who sins after the giving of the New Law deserves greater punishment, according to Heb. 10. 28, 29: *A man making void the Law of Moses dieth without any mercy under two or three witnesses. How much more, do you think, he deserveth worse punishments, who hath trodden under-foot the Son of God,* etc.? Therefore the New Law, like the Old Law, does not justify.

Obj. 3. Further, justification is an effect proper to God, according to Rom. 8. 33: *God that justifieth.* But the Old Law was from God just as the New Law. Therefore the New Law does not justify any more than the Old Law.

On the contrary, The Apostle says (Rom. 1. 16): *I am not ashamed of the Gospel: for it is the power of God unto salvation to everyone that believeth.* But there is no salvation but to those who are justified. Therefore the Law of the Gospel justifies.

I answer that, As stated above (A. 1), there is a twofold element in the Law of the Gospel. There is the chief element, namely, the grace of the Holy Ghost bestowed inwardly. And as to this, the New Law justifies. Hence Augustine says (*De Spir. et Lit.* xvii):[1] "There (that is, in the Old Testament), the Law was set forth in an outward fashion, that the ungodly might be afraid; here (that is, in the New Testament) it is given in an inward manner, that they may be justified." The other element of the Evangelical Law is secondary: namely, the teachings of faith, and those commandments which direct human affections and human actions. And as to this, the New Law does not justify. Hence the Apostle says (II Cor. 3. 6): *The letter killeth, but the spirit quickeneth,* and Augustine explains this (*De Spir. et Lit.* xiv, xvii)[2] by saying that the letter denotes any writing that is external to man, even that of the moral precepts such as are contained in the Gospel. Therefore the letter, even of the Gospel would kill, unless there were the inward presence of the healing grace of faith.

Reply Obj. 1. This argument is true of the New Law, not as to its principal, but as to its secondary element, that is, as to the dogmas and precepts outwardly put before man either in words or in writing.

Reply Obj. 2. Although the grace of the New Testament helps man to avoid sin, yet it does not so confirm man in good that he is not able to sin, for this belongs to the state of glory. Hence if a man sin after receiving the grace of the New Testament he deserves greater punishment, as being ungrateful for greater benefits, and as not using the help given to him. And this is why the New Law is not said to "work wrath," because as far as it is concerned it gives man sufficient help to avoid sin.

Reply Obj. 3. The same God gave both the New and the Old Law, but in different ways. For He gave the Old Law written on tables of stone, but the New Law He gave written *in the fleshly tables of the heart,* as the Apostle

[1] PL 44, 218.
[2] PL 44, 215; 219.

expresses it (II Cor. 3. 3). Therefore, as Augustine says (*De Spir. et Lit.* xviii),[1] "the Apostle calls this letter which is written outside man, a ministration of death and a ministration of condemnation; but he calls the other letter, that is, the Law of the New Testament, the ministration of the spirit and the ministration of justice, because through the gift of the Spirit we work justice, and are delivered from the condemnation due to transgression."

ARTICLE 3. *Whether the New Law Should Have Been Given from the Beginning of the World?*

We proceed thus to the Third Article: It would seem that the New Law should have been given from the beginning of the world.

Objection 1. *For there is no respect of persons with God* (Rom. 2. 11). But *all men have sinned and do need the glory of God* (*ibid.* 3. 23). Therefore the Law of the Gospel should have been given from the beginning of the world, in order that it might bring succour to all.

Obj. 2. Further, as men dwell in various places, so do they live in various times. But God, *Who will have all men to be saved* (I Tim. 2. 4), commanded the Gospel to be preached in all places, as may be seen in the last chapters of Matthew and Mark. Therefore the Law of the Gospel should have been at hand for all times, so as to be given from the beginning of the world.

Obj. 3. Further, man needs to save his soul, which is for all eternity, more than to save his body, which is a temporal matter. But God provided man from the beginning of the world with things that are necessary for the health of his body, by subjecting to his power whatever was created for the sake of man (Gen. 1. 26-29). Therefore the New Law also, which is very necessary for the health of the soul, should have been given to man from the beginning of the world.

On the contrary, The Apostle says (I Cor. 15. 46): *That was not first which is spiritual, but that which is natural.* But the New Law is in the highest degree spiritual. Therefore it was not fitting for it to be given from the beginning of the world.

I answer that, Three reasons may be assigned why it was not fitting for the New Law to be given from the beginning of the world. The first is because the New Law, as stated above (A.

1), consists chiefly in the grace of the Holy Ghost, which ought not to have been given abundantly until sin, which is an obstacle to grace, had been cast out of man through the accomplishment of his redemption by Christ. Therefore it is written (John 7. 39): *As yet the Spirit was not given, because Jesus was not yet glorified.* This reason the Apostle states clearly (Rom. 8. 2, *seqq.*) where, after speaking of *the Law of the Spirit of life,* he adds: *God sending His own Son, in the likeness of sinful flesh, of sin*[2] *hath condemned sin in the flesh, that the justification of the Law might be fulfilled in us.*

A second reason may be taken from the perfection of the New Law. Because a thing is not brought to perfection at once from the outset, but through an orderly succession of time; thus one is at first a boy, and then a man. And this reason is stated by the Apostle (Gal. 3. 24, 25): *The Law was our pedagogue in Christ that we might be justified by faith. But after the faith is come, we are no longer under a pedagogue.*

The third reason is found in the fact that the New Law is the law of grace. Therefore man ought first of all to be left to himself under the state of the Old Law, so that through falling into sin, he might realize his weakness, and acknowledge his need of grace. This reason is set down by the Apostle (Rom. 5. 20): *The Law entered in, that sin might abound: and when sin abounded grace did more abound.*

Reply Obj. 1. Mankind on account of the sin of our first parents deserved to be deprived of the aid of grace, and so "from whom it is withheld it is justly withheld, and to whom it is given, it is mercifully given," as Augustine states (*De Perfect. Justit.* iv).[3] Consequently it does not follow that there is respect of persons with God from the fact that He did not offer the Law of grace to all from the beginning of the world, which Law was to be published in due course of time, as stated above.

Reply Obj. 2. The state of mankind does not vary according to diversity of place, but according to succession of time. Hence the New Law avails for all places, but not for all times, although at all times there have been some persons belonging to the New Testament, as stated above (A. 1, REPLY 3).

Reply Obj. 3. Things pertaining to the health of the body are of service to man as regards his nature, which sin does not destroy; but

---

[1] PL 44, 219.

[2] The text quoted should read thus,—*in the likeness of sinful flesh, and a sin offering* (περὶ ἁμαρτίας), *hath,* etc.

[3] *Cf. Epist.,* CCVII (PL 33, 984); *De Pecc. Mer. et Rem.,* II 19. (PL 44, 170).

things pertaining to the health of the soul are ordered to grace, which is forfeit through sin. Consequently the comparison will not hold.

Article 4. *Whether the New Law Will Last Till the End of the World?*

We proceed thus to the Fourth Article: It would seem that the New Law will not last till the end of the world.

Objection 1. Because, as the Apostle says (I Cor. 13. 10), *when that which is perfect is come, that which is in part shall be done away.* But the New Law is *in part*, since the Apostle says (*ibid.* 9): *We know in part and we prophesy in part.* Therefore the New Law is to be done away, and will be succeeded by a more perfect state.[1]

Obj. 2. Further, Our Lord (John 16. 13) promised His disciples the knowledge of all truth when the Holy Ghost, the Comforter, should come. But the Church does not yet know all truth in the state of the New Testament. Therefore we must look forward to another state, in which all truth will be revealed by the Holy Ghost.[2]

Obj. 3. Further, just as the Father is distinct from the Son and the Son from the Father, so is the Holy Ghost distinct from the Father and the Son. But there was a state corresponding with the Person of the Father, namely, the state of the Old Law, wherein men were intent on begetting children; and likewise there is a state corresponding to the Person of the Son, namely, the state of the New Law, wherein the clergy who are intent on wisdom (which is appropriated to the Son) hold a prominent place. Therefore there will be a third state corresponding to the Holy Ghost, wherein spiritual men will hold the first place.[3]

Obj. 4. Further, Our Lord said (Matt. 24. 14): *This Gospel of the kingdom shall be preached in the whole world . . . and then shall the consummation come.* But the Gospel of Christ is already preached throughout the whole world, and yet the consummation has not yet come. Therefore the Gospel of Christ is not the Gospel of the kingdom, but another Gospel, that of the Holy Ghost, is to come yet, as another Law.

On the contrary, Our Lord saith (Matt. 24. 34: *I say to you that this generation shall not pass till all (these) things be done,* which passage Chrysostom (*Hom.* lxxviii)[4] explains as referring to the generation of those that believe

in Christ. Therefore the state of those who believe in Christ will last until the consummation of the world.

I answer that, The state of the world may change in two ways. In one way, according to a change of law, and thus no other state will succeed this state of the New Law. Because the state of the New Law succeeded the state of the Old Law, as a more perfect law a less perfect one. Now no state of the present life can be more perfect than the state of the New Law, since nothing can approach nearer to the last end than that which is the immediate cause of our being brought to the last end. But the New Law does this; hence the Apostle says (Heb. 10. 19-22): *Having therefore, brethren, a confidence in the entering into the Holies by the blood of Christ, a new . . . way which He hath dedicated for us . . . let us draw near.* Therefore no state of the present life can be more perfect than that of the New Law, since the nearer a thing is to the last end the more perfect it is.

In another way the state of mankind may change according as man stands in relation to one and the same law more or less perfectly. And thus the state of the Old Law underwent frequent changes, since at times the laws were very well kept, and at other times were altogether unheeded. Thus, too, the state of the New Law is subject to change with regard to various places, times, and persons, according as the grace of the Holy Ghost dwells in man more or less perfectly. Nevertheless we are not to look forward to a state wherein man is to possess the grace of the Holy Ghost more perfectly than he has possessed it hitherto, especially the apostles who *received the firstfruits of the Spirit,* that is, "sooner and more abundantly than others," as a gloss expounds on Rom. 8. 23.[5]

Reply Obj. 1. As Dionysius says (*Eccl. Hier.* v)[6] there is a threefold state of mankind: the first was under the Old Law, the second is that of the New Law, the third will take place not in this life, but in heaven. But as the first state is figurative and imperfect in comparison with the state of the Gospel, so is the present state figurative and imperfect in comparison with the heavenly state, with the advent of which the present state will be done away as expressed in that very passage (*verse* 12): *We see now through a glass in a dark manner; but then face to face.*

---

[1] Cf. Denifle, *Chartularium,* n. 243 (I, 272).
[2] Cf. *Ibid.* (I, 274).　[3] Cf. *Ibid.* (I, 274).　[4] PG 58, 702.

[5] *Glossa interl.*(VI, 19r); *Glossa* Lombardi (PL 191,1444).
[6] PG 3, 501.

Reply Obj. 2. As Augustine says[1] Montanus and Priscilla pretended that Our Lord's promise to give the Holy Ghost was fulfilled not in the apostles, but in themselves. In like manner the Manicheans maintained that it was fulfilled in Manes whom they held to be the Paraclete.[2] Hence none of the above received the *Acts of the Apostles*, where it is clearly shown that this promise was fulfilled in the apostles; just as Our Lord promised them a second time (Acts 1. 5): *You shall be baptized with the Holy Ghost, not many days hence*, which we read as having been fulfilled in Acts ii. However, these foolish notions are refuted by the statement (John 7. 39) that *as yet the Spirit was not given, because Jesus was not yet glorified*, from which we gather that the Holy Ghost was given as soon as Christ was glorified in His Resurrection and Ascension. Moreover, this puts out of court the senseless idea that the Holy Ghost is to be expected to come at some other time.[3]

Now the Holy Ghost taught the apostles all truth in respect of matters necessary for salvation; those things, namely, that we are bound to believe and to do. But he did not teach them about all future events, for this did not pertain to them according to Acts 1. 7: *It is not for you to know the times or moments which the Father hath put in His own power.*

Reply Obj. 3. The Old Law corresponded not only to the Father, but also to the Son, because Christ was foreshadowed in the Old Law. Hence Our Lord said (John 5. 46): *If you did believe Moses, you would perhaps believe Me also; for he wrote of Me.* In like manner the New Law corresponds not only to Christ, but also to the Holy Ghost, according to Rom. 8. 2: *The law of the Spirit of life in Christ Jesus*, etc. Hence we are not to look forward to another law corresponding to the Holy Ghost.

Reply Obj. 4. Since Christ said at the very outset of the preaching of the Gospel: *The kingdom of heaven is at hand* (Matt. 4. 17), it is most absurd to say that the Gospel of Christ is not the Gospel of the kingdom. But the preaching of the Gospel of Christ may be understood in two ways. First, as denoting the spreading abroad of the knowledge of Christ; and thus the Gospel was preached throughout the whole world even at the time of the apostles, as Chrysostom states (*Hom.* lxxv *in Matt.*).[4] And in this sense the words that follow,—*and then shall*

the consummation come, refer to the destruction of Jerusalem, of which He was speaking literally. Secondly, the preaching of the Gospel may be understood as extending throughout the world and producing its full effect, so that, namely, the Church would be founded in every nation. And in this sense, as Augustine writes to Hesychius (*Epist.* cxcix),[5] the Gospel is not preached to the whole world yet, but, when it is, the consummation of the world will come.

QUESTION CVII

OF THE NEW LAW AS COMPARED WITH THE OLD

(In Four Articles)

WE must now consider the New Law as compared with the Old, under which head there are four points of inquiry: (1) Whether the New Law is distinct from the Old Law? (2) Whether the New Law fulfils the Old? (3) Whether the New Law is contained in the Old? (4) Which is the more burdensome, the New or the Old Law?

ARTICLE 1. *Whether the New Law Is Distinct From the Old Law?*

We proceed thus to the First Article: It would seem that the New Law is not distinct from the Old.

Objection 1. Because both these laws were given to those who believe in God, since *without faith it is impossible to please God*, according to Heb. 11. 6. But the faith of olden times and of nowadays is the same, as the gloss says on Matt. 21. 9.[6] Therefore the law is the same also.

Obj. 2. Further, Augustine says (*Contra Adamant. Manich, discip.* xvii)[7] that "the slight difference between the Law and Gospel is fear and love." But the New and Old Laws cannot be differentiated in respect of these two things, since even the Old Law comprised precepts of charity: *Thou shalt love thy neighbour* (Lev. 19. 18), and: *Thou shalt love the Lord thy God* (Deut. 6. 5). In like manner neither can they differ according to the other difference which Augustine assigns (*Contra Faust.* iv, 2),[8] namely, that "the Old Testament contained temporal promises, while the New Testament contains spiritual and eternal promises," since even the

---

[1] Cf. *De Hæres.*, XXVI (PL 42, 30).

[2] Cf. Augustine, *De Hæres.*, XLVI (PL 42, 38).

[3] The Abbot Joachim; cf. Denifle, *Chartularium*, n. 243 (I, 272).

[4] PG 58, 688.

[5] Chap. 12 (PL 33, 923).

[6] *Glossa ordin.*, super II Cor. 4.13 (VI, 66A); *Glossa interl.* (VI, 66r); *Glossa* Lombardi (PL 192, 33); cf. Augustine, *Enarr. in Ps.*, Ps. 50.14 (PL 36, 596); *Serm.*, XIX (PL 38, 134).

[7] PL 42, 159.

[8] PL 42, 217.

New Testament contains temporal promises, according to Mark 10. 30: *He shall receive a hundred times as much . . . in this time, houses and brethren,* etc., while in the Old Testament they hoped in promises spiritual and eternal, according to Heb. 11. 16: *But now they desire a better, that is to say, a heavenly country,* which is said of the patriarchs. Therefore it seems that the New Law is not distinct from the Old.

Obj. 3. Further, the Apostle seems to distinguish both laws by calling the Old Law *a law of works,* and the New Law *a law of faith* (Rom. 3. 27). But the Old Law was also a law of faith, according to Heb. 11. 39: *All were* (Vulg.,—*All these being*) *approved by the testimony of faith,* which he says of the fathers of the Old Testament. In like manner the New Law is a law of works, since it is written (Matt. 5. 44): *Do good to them that hate you;* and (Luke 22. 19): *Do this for a commemoration of Me.* Therefore the New Law is not distinct from the Old.

On the contrary, the Apostle says (Heb. 7. 12): *The priesthood being translated it is necessary that a translation also be made of the Law.* But the priesthood of the New Testament is distinct from that of the Old, as the Apostle shows in the same place. Therefore the Law is also distinct.

I answer that, As stated above (Q. XC, A. 2; Q. XCI, A. 4), every law orders human conduct to some end. Now things ordered to an end may be divided in two ways, considered from the point of view of the end. First, through being ordered to different ends, and this difference will be specific, especially if such ends are proximate. Secondly, by reason of being closely or remotely connected with the end. Thus it is clear that movements differ in species through being directed to different terms, while according as one part of a movement is nearer to the term than another part, the difference of perfect and imperfect movement is assessed.

Accordingly then two laws may be distinguished from one another in two ways. First, through being altogether different, from the fact that they are ordered to different ends; thus a law of the state ordained to democratic government, would differ specifically from a law ordained to government by the aristocracy. Secondly, two laws may be distinguished from one another through one of them being more closely connected with the end and the other more remotely; thus in one and the same state there is one law enjoined on men of mature age, who can immediately accomplish that which pertains to the common good, and another law regulating the education of children who need to be taught how they are to achieve manly deeds later on.

We must therefore say that, according to the first way the New Law is not distinct from the Old Law, because they both have the same end, namely, man's subjection to God; and there is but one God of the New and of the Old Testament, according to Rom. 3. 30: *It is one God that justifieth circumcision by faith, and uncircumcision through faith.* According to the second way, the New Law is distinct from the Old Law, because the Old Law is like a pedagogue of children, as the Apostle says (Gal. 3. 24), while the New Law is the law of perfection, since it is the law of charity, of which the Apostle says (Coloss. 3. 14) that it is *the bond of perfection.*

Reply Obj. 1. The unity of faith under both Testaments witnesses to the unity of end; for it has been stated above (Q. LXII, A. 2) that the object of the theological virtues, among which is faith, is the last end. Yet faith had a different state in the Old and in the New Law, since what they believed as future, we believe as fact.

Reply Obj. 2. All the differences assigned between the Old and New Laws are gathered from their relative perfection and imperfection. For the precepts of every law prescribe acts of virtue. Now the imperfect, who as yet are not possessed of a virtuous habit, are directed in one way to perform virtuous acts, while those who are perfected by the possession of virtuous habits are directed in another way. For those who as yet are not endowed with virtuous habits are directed to the performance of virtuous acts by reason of some outward cause; for instance, by the threat of punishment, or the promise of some extrinsic rewards, such as honour, riches, or the like. Hence the Old Law, which was given to men who were imperfect, that is, who had not yet received spiritual grace, was called the law of fear, since it induced men to observe its commandments by threatening them with penalties, and is spoken of as containing temporal promises. On the other hand, those who are possessed of virtue are inclined to do virtuous deeds through love of virtue, not on account of some extrinsic punishment or reward. Hence the New Law which derives its pre-eminence from the spiritual grace instilled into our hearts, is called the Law of Love, and it is described as containing spiritual and eternal promises, which are objects of the virtues, chiefly of charity. Accordingly such persons are inclined of themselves to those objects, not as to something foreign but as to something of their own.—For this reason, too, the Old Law is described as "restraining the hand, not the mind,"[1] since when a man re-frains from some sins through fear of being punished his will does not shrink absolutely from sin, as does the will of a man who refrains from sin through love of justice. And hence the New Law, which is the Law of love, is said to "restrain the soul."

Nevertheless there were some in the state of the Old Testament who, having charity and the grace of the Holy Ghost, looked chiefly to spirit-ual and eternal promises, and in this respect they belonged to the New Law. In like manner in the New Testament there are some carnal men who have not yet attained to the perfection of the New Law; and these it was necessary, even under the New Testament, to lead to vir-tuous action by the fear of punishment and by temporal promises.

But although the Old Law contained precepts of charity, nevertheless it did not confer the Holy Ghost by Whom *charity . . . is spread abroad in our hearts* (Rom. 5. 5).

Reply Obj. 3. As stated above (Q. CVI, AA. 1, 2), the New Law is called the law of faith, in so far as its preeminence is derived from that very grace which is given inwardly to believers, and for this reason is called the grace of faith. Nevertheless it consists secondarily in certain deeds, moral and sacramental; but the New Law does not consist chiefly in these latter things, as did the Old Law. As to those under the Old Tes-tament who through faith were acceptable to God, in this respect they belonged to the New Testament, for they were not justified except through faith in Christ, Who is the Author of the New Testament. Hence of Moses the Apostle says (Heb. 11. 26) that he esteemed *the reproach of Christ greater riches than the treasure of the Egyptians.*

ARTICLE 2. *Whether the New Law Fulfils the Old?*

We proceed thus to the Second Article: It would seem that the New Law does not fulfil the Old.

Objection 1. For to fulfil and to make void are contrary. But the New Law voids or excludes the observances of the Old Law, for the Apostle says (Gal. 5. 2): *If you be circumcised, Christ shall profit you nothing.* Therefore the New Law is not a fulfilment of the Old.

Obj. 2. Further, one contrary is not the fulfil-ment of another. But our Lord propounded in the New Law precepts that were contrary to precepts of the Old Law. For we read (Matt.

[1] Peter Lombard, *Sent.*, III, d. 40, chap. 1 (QR II, 734).

5. 27-32): *You have heard that it was said to them of old: . . . Whosoever shall put away his wife, let him give her a bill of divorce. But I say to you that whosoever shall put away his wife . . . maketh her to commit adultery.* Further-more, the same evidently applies to the pro-hibition against swearing, against retaliation, and against hating one's enemies. In like man-ner Our Lord seems to have done away with the precepts of the Old Law relating to the different kinds of foods (Matt. 15. 11): *Not that which goeth into the mouth defileth a man: but what cometh out of the mouth, this defileth a man.* Therefore the New Law is not a fulfilment of the Old.

Obj. 3. Further, whoever acts against a law does not fulfil the law. But Christ in certain cases acted against the Law. For He touched the leper (Matt. 8. 3), which was contrary to the Law. Likewise He seems to have frequently broken the sabbath, since the Jews used to say of Him. (John 9. 16.): *This man is not of God, who keepeth not the sabbath.* Therefore Christ did not fulfil the Law, and so the New Law giv-en by Christ is not a fulfilment of the Old.

Obj. 4. Further, the Old Law contained pre-cepts, moral, ceremonial, and judicial, as stated above (Q. XCIX, A. 4). But Our Lord (Matt. 5.) fulfilled the Law in some respects, but with-out mentioning the judicial and ceremonial pre-cepts. Therefore it seems that the New Law is not a complete fulfilment of the Old.

On the contrary, Our Lord said (Matt. 5. 17): *I am not come to destroy, but to fulfil;* and went on to say (*verse* 18): *One jot or one tittle shall not pass of the Law till all be fulfilled.*

I answer that, As stated above (A. 1), the New Law is compared to the Old as the perfect to the imperfect. Now everything perfect fulfils that which is lacking in the imperfect. And ac-cordingly the New Law fulfils the Old by sup-plying that which was lacking in the Old Law.

Now two things in the Old Law offer them-selves to our consideration: namely, the end, and the precepts contained in the Law. The end of every law is to make men just and virtuous, as was stated above (Q. XCII, A. 1), and conse-quently the end of the Old Law was the justifica-tion of men. The Law, however, could not ac-complish this, but foreshadowed it by certain ceremonial actions, and promised it in words. And in this respect, the New Law fulfils the Old by justifying men through the power of Christ's Passion. This is what the Apostle says (Rom. 8. 3, 4): *What the Law could not do . . . God sending His own Son in the likeness of sin-*

ful flesh . . .hath condemned sin in the flesh, that the justification of the Law might be fulfilled in us. And in this respect, the New Law gives what the Old Law promised, according to II Cor. 1. 20: *Whatever are the promises of God, in Him,* that is, in Christ, *they are "Yea."*[1] Again in this respect, it also fulfils what the Old Law foreshadowed. Hence it is written (Coloss. 2. 17) concerning the ceremonial precepts that they were *a shadow of things to come, but the body is of Christ;* in other words, the truth is found in Christ. Therefore the New Law is called the law of truth while the Old Law is called the law of shadow or of figure.

Now Christ fulfilled the precepts of the Old Law both in His works and in His doctrine. In His works, because He was willing to be circumcised and to fulfil the other legal observances, which were binding for the time being; according to Gal. 4. 4: *Made under the Law.* In His doctrine He fulfilled the precepts of the Law in three ways. First, by explaining the true sense of the Law. This is clear in the case of murder and adultery, the prohibition of which the Scribes and Pharisees thought to refer only to the exterior act; and so Our Lord fulfilled the Law by showing that the prohibition extended also to the interior acts of sins. Secondly, Our Lord fulfilled the precepts of the Law by prescribing the safest way of complying with the statutes of the Old Law. Thus the Old Law forbade perjury, and this is more safely avoided by abstaining altogether from swearing, save in cases of urgency. Thirdly, Our Lord fulfilled the precepts of the Law by adding some counsels of perfection; this is clearly seen in Matt. 19. 21, where our Lord said to the man who affirmed that he had kept all the precepts of the Old Law: *One thing is wanting to thee: If thou wilt be perfect, go, sell whatsoever thou hast,* etc.[2]

Reply Obj. 1. The New Law does not void observance of the Old Law except in the point of ceremonial precepts, as stated above (Q. CIII, AA. 3, 4). Now the latter were figurative of something to come. Therefore from the very fact that the ceremonial precepts were fulfilled when those things were accomplished which they foreshadowed, it follows that they are no longer to be observed, for if they were to be observed, this would mean that something is still to be accomplished and is not yet fulfilled. Thus the promise of a future gift holds no longer when it has been fulfilled by the presentation of the gift. In this way the legal ceremonies are abolished by being fulfilled.

Reply Obj. 2. As Augustine says (*Contra Faust. xix, 26*),[3] those precepts of Our Lord are not contrary to the precepts of the Old Law. For what Our Lord commanded about a man not putting away his wife is not contrary to what the Law prescribed. "For the Law did not say: 'Let him that wills, put his wife away', the contrary of which would be not to put her away. On the contrary, the Law was unwilling that a man should put away his wife, since it prescribed a delay, so that excessive eagerness for divorce might cease through being weakened during the writing of the bill. Hence Our Lord, in order to impress the fact that a wife ought not easily to be put away, allowed no exception save in the case of fornication."[4] The same applies to the prohibition about swearing as stated above. The same is also clear with respect to the prohibition of retaliation. For the Law fixed a limit to revenge, by forbidding men to seek vengeance unreasonably, while Our Lord deprived them of vengeance more completely by commanding them to abstain from it altogether. With regard to the hatred of one's enemies, He dispelled the false interpretation of the Pharisees, by admonishing us to hate, not the person, but his sin. As to discriminating between various foods, which was a ceremonial matter, Our Lord did not forbid this to be observed, but He showed that no foods are naturally unclean, but only in token of something else, as stated above (Q. CII, A. 6, REPLY 1).

Reply Obj. 3. It was forbidden by the Law to touch a leper because by doing so man incurred a certain uncleanness of irregularity, as also by touching the dead, as stated above (Q. CII, A. 5, REPLY 4). But Our Lord, Who healed the leper, could not contract an uncleanness. By those things which He did on the sabbath, He did not break the sabbath in reality, as the Master Himself shows in the Gospel; both because He worked miracles by His Divine power, which is always active among things, and because His works were concerned with the salvation of man, while the Pharisees were concerned for the well-being of animals even on the sabbath; and again because by reason of necessity He excused His disciples for gathering the ears of corn on the sabbath. But He did seem to break the sabbath according to the superstitious interpretation of the Pharisees, who thought that man ought to abstain from doing even

---

[1] The Douay version reads thus: *All the promises of God are in Him, "It is."*

[2] S. Thomas combines Matt. 19.21 with Mark 10.21.

[3] PL 42, 364.

[4] Cf. Augustine, *De Serm. Dom.*, I, 14 (PL 34, 1248).

works of kindness on the sabbath, which was contrary to the intention of the Law.

Reply Obj. 4. The reason why the ceremonial precepts of the Law are not mentioned in Matt. 5. is because, as stated above (REPLY 1), their observance was abolished by their fulfilment. But of the judicial precepts He mentioned that of retaliation, so that what He said about it should refer to all the others. With regard to this precept, He taught that the intention of the Law was that retaliation should be sought out of love of justice, and not as a punishment out of revengeful spite, which He forbade, admonishing man to be ready to suffer yet greater insults; and this remains still in the New Law.

ARTICLE 3. *Whether the New Law Is Contained in the Old?*

We proceed thus to the Third Article: It would seem that the New Law is not contained in the Old.

Objection 1. For the New Law consists chiefly in faith, and therefore it is called the *law of faith* (Rom. 3. 27). But many points of faith are set forth in the New Law which are not contained in the Old. Therefore the New Law is not contained in the Old.

Obj. 2. Further, a gloss says on Matt. 5. 19, *He that shall break one of these least commandments,* that "the lesser commandments are those of the Law, and the greater commandments, those contained in the Gospel."[1] Now the greater cannot be contained in the lesser. Therefore the New Law is not contained in the Old.

Obj. 3. Further, who holds the container holds the contents. If, therefore, the New Law is contained in the Old, it follows that whoever had the Old Law had the New: so that it was superfluous to give men a New Law when once they had the Old. Therefore the New Law is not contained in the Old.

On the contrary, As expressed in Ezech. 1. 16, there was *a wheel in the midst of a wheel,* that is, "the New Testament within the Old," according to Gregory's exposition.[2]

I answer that, One thing may be contained in another in two ways. First, actually, as a located thing is in a place. Secondly, virtually, as an effect in its cause, or as the complement in that which is incomplete; thus a genus contains its species, and a seed contains the whole tree, virtually. It is in this way that the New Law is

contained in the Old: for it has been stated (A. 1) that the New Law is compared to the Old as perfect to imperfect. Hence Chrysostom, expounding Mark 4. 28, *The earth of itself bringeth forth fruit, first the blade, then the ear, afterwards the full corn in the ear,* expresses himself as follows.[3] "He brought forth first the blade, that is, the Law of Nature; then the ear, that is, the Law of Moses; lastly, the full corn, that is, the Law of the Gospel." Hence then the New Law is in the Old as the corn in the ear.

Reply Obj. 1. Whatsoever is set down in the New Testament explicitly and openly as a point of faith is contained in the Old Testament as a matter of belief, but implicitly, under a figure. And accordingly, even as to those things which we are bound to believe, the New Law is contained in the Old.

Reply Obj. 2. The precepts of the New Law are said to be greater than those of the Old Law, in the point of their being set forth explicitly. But as to the substance itself of the precepts of the New Testament, they are all contained in the Old. Hence Augustine says (*Contra Faust.* xix, 23, 28)[4] that "nearly all Our Lord's admonitions or precepts, where He expressed Himself by saying: 'But I say unto you,' are to be found also in those ancient books." Yet, "since they thought that murder was only the slaying of the human body, Our Lord declared to them that every wicked impulse to hurt our brother is to be looked on as a kind of murder." And it is in the point of declarations of this kind that the precepts of the New Law are said to be greater than those of the Old. Nothing, however, prevents the greater from being contained in the lesser virtually, just as a tree is contained in the seed.

Reply Obj. 3. What is set forth implicitly needs to be declared explicitly. Hence after the publishing of the Old Law, a New Law also had to be given.

ARTICLE 4. *Whether the New Law Is More Burdensome Than the Old?*

We proceed thus to the Fourth Article: It would seem that the New Law is more burdensome than the Old.

Objection 1. For Chrysostom (*Opus Imp. in Matt.,* Hom. x)[5] says: "The commandments given to Moses are easy to obey: Thou shalt not kill; Thou shalt not commit adultery: but the

---

[1] Cf. Augustine, *De Serm. Dom.,* i, 1 (PL 34, 1231); *Glossa ordin.* (v, 20A).

[2] *In Ezech.* i. 6 (PL 76, 834).

[3] Reference unknown.

[4] PL 42, 361, 366.

[5] Pseudo-Chrysostom (PG 56, 687).

commandments of Christ are difficult to accomplish, for instance: Thou shalt not give way to anger, or to lust." Therefore the New Law is more burdensome than the Old.

Obj. 2. Further, it is easier to make use of earthly prosperity than to suffer tribulations. But in the Old Testament observance of the Law was followed by temporal prosperity, as may be gathered from Deut. 28. 1-14; while many kinds of trouble ensue to those who observe the New Law, as stated in II Cor. 6. 4-10: *Let us exhibit ourselves as the ministers of God, in much patience, in tribulation, in necessities, in distresses,* etc. Therefore the New Law is more burdensome than the Old.

Obj. 3. The more one has to do, the more difficult it is. But the New Law is something added to the Old. For the Old Law forbade perjury, while the New Law proscribed even swearing; and the Old Law forbade a man to cast off his wife without a bill of divorce, while the New Law forbade divorce altogether, as is clearly stated in Matt. 5. 31, *seqq.,* according to Augustine's expounding.[1] Therefore the New Law is more burdensome than the Old.

On the contrary, It is written (Matt. 11. 28): *Come to Me, all you that labour and are burdened,* which words are expounded by Hilary thus: *"He calls to Himself all those that labour under the difficulty of observing the Law, and are burdened with the sins of this world."*[2] And further on He says of the yoke of the Gospel: *For My yoke is sweet and My burden light.* Therefore the New Law is a lighter burden than the Old.

I answer that, A twofold difficulty may attach to works of virtue with which the precepts of the Law are concerned. One is on the part of the outward works, which of themselves are, in a way, difficult and burdensome. And in this respect the Old Law is a much heavier burden than the New, since the Old Law by its numerous ceremonies prescribed many more outward acts than the New Law, which, in the teaching of Christ and the apostles, added very few precepts to those of the natural law, although afterwards some were added through being instituted by the holy Fathers. Even in these Augustine says that moderation should be observed, lest good conduct should become a burden to the faithful. For he says in reply to the queries of Januarius (*Ep.* lv)[3] that,

"whereas God in His mercy wished religion to be a free service rendered by the public solemnization of a small number of most manifest sacraments, certain persons make it a slave's burden; so much so that the state of the Jews who were subject to the sacraments of the Law, and not to the presumptuous devices of man, was more tolerable."

The other difficulty attaches to works of virtue as to interior acts; for instance, that a virtuous deed be done with promptitude and pleasure. It is this difficulty that virtue solves, because to act thus is difficult for a man without virtue, but through virtue it becomes easy to him. In this respect the precepts of the New Law are more burdensome than those of the Old, because the New Law prohibits certain interior movements of the soul, which were not expressly forbidden in the Old Law in all cases, although they were forbidden in some, without, however, any punishment being attached to the prohibition. Now this is very difficult to a man without virtue; thus even the Philosopher states[4] that it is easy to do what a just man does, but that to do it in the same way, that is, with pleasure and promptitude, is difficult to a man who is not just. Accordingly we read also (I John 5. 3) that *His commandments are not heavy,* which words Augustine expounds by saying that "they are not heavy to the man that loveth; but they are a burden to him that loveth not."[5]

Reply Obj. 1. The passage quoted speaks expressly of the difficulty of the New Law as to the deliberate curbing of interior movements.

Reply Obj. 2. The tribulations suffered by those who observe the New Law are not imposed by the Law itself. Moreover they are easily borne, on account of the love in which the same Law consists; because, as Augustine says (*De Verb. Dom., Serm.* lxx),[6] "love makes light and nothing of things that seem arduous and beyond our power."

Reply Obj. 3. The object of these additions to the precepts of the Old Law was to render it easier to do what it prescribed, as Augustine states.[7] Accordingly this does not prove that the New Law is more burdensome, but rather that it is a lighter burden.

---

[1] *De Serm. Dom.,* I, 14 (PL 34, 1248); chap. 17 (PL 34, 1255); *Cont. Faust.,* XIX, 23, 26 (PL 42, 361, 364).
[2] PL 9, 984.
[3] Chap. 19 (PL 33, 221).

[4] *Ethics,* V, 9 (1137^{a}5).
[5] *De Nat. et Grat.,* 69 (PL 44, 289); *De Pert. Just.,* 10 (PL 44, 302); *Serm. ad Popul.,* LXX, 3 (PL 38, 444).
[6] Chap. 3 (PL 38, 444).
[7] *De Serm. Dom.,* I, 17, 21 (PL 34, 1256; 1265); *Contra Faust.,* XIX, 23, 26 (PL 42, 365).

QUESTION CVIII

OF THE THINGS THAT ARE CONTAINED
IN THE NEW LAW

(*In Four Articles*)

WE must now consider those things that are contained in the New Law, under which head there are four points of inquiry: (1) Whether the New Law ought to prescribe or to forbid any outward works? (2) Whether the New Law makes sufficient provision in prescribing and forbidding external acts? (3) Whether in the matter of internal acts it directs man sufficiently? (4) Whether it fittingly adds counsels to precepts?

ARTICLE 1. *Whether the New Law Ought to Prescribe or Prohibit Any External Acts?*

We proceed thus to the First Article: It would seem that the New Law should not prescribe or prohibit any external acts.

Objection 1. For the New Law is the Gospel of the kingdom, according to Matt. 24. 14: *This Gospel of the kingdom shall be preached in the whole world*. But the kingdom of God consists not in exterior but only in interior acts, according to Luke 17. 21: *The kingdom of God is within you;* and Rom. 14. 17: *The kingdom of God is not meat and drink; but justice and peace and joy in the Holy Ghost*. Therefore the New Law should not prescribe or forbid any external acts.

Obj. 2. Further, the New Law is *the law of the Spirit* (Rom. 8. 2). But *where the Spirit of the Lord is, there is liberty* (II Cor. 3. 17). Now there is no liberty when man is bound to do or avoid certain external acts. Therefore the New Law does not prescribe or forbid any external acts.

Obj. 3. Further, all external acts are understood as referrible to the hand, just as interior acts belong to the mind. But this is assigned as the difference between the New and Old Laws that the *Old Law restrains the hand, while the New Law curbs the mind.*[1] Therefore the New Law should not contain prohibitions and commands about exterior deeds, but only about interior acts.

On the contrary, Through the New Law, men are made *children of light;* hence it is written (John 12. 36): *Believe in the light that you may be the children of light*. Now it is fitting that children of the light should do deeds of light and cast aside deeds of darkness, according to

[1] Peter Lombard, *Sent.*, III, d. 40, chap. 1 (QR II, 734).

Ephes. 5. 8: *You were heretofore darkness, but now light in the Lord. Walk . . . as children of the light*. Therefore the New Law had to forbid certain external acts and prescribe others.

I answer that, As stated above (Q. CVI, AA. 1, 2), the New Law consists chiefly in the grace of the Holy Ghost, which is shown forth by faith working through love. Now men become receivers of this grace through God's Son made man, Whose humanity grace filled first, and from there flowed forth to us. Hence it is written (John 1. 14): *The Word was made flesh,* and afterwards: *full of grace and truth;* and further on: *Of His fulness we all have received, and grace for grace*. Hence it is added that *grace and truth came by Jesus Christ*. Consequently it was fitting that the grace which flows from the incarnate Word should be given to us by means of certain external sensible objects; and that from this inward grace, by which the flesh is subjected to the Spirit, certain external works should ensue.

Accordingly external acts may have a twofold connection with grace. In the first place, as leading in some way to grace. Such are the sacramental acts which are instituted in the New Law, for example, Baptism, the Eucharist, and the like. In the second place there are those external acts which ensue from the promptings of grace, and in these we must observe a difference. For there are some which are necessarily in keeping with, or in opposition to inward grace consisting in faith working through love. Such external works are prescribed or forbidden in the New Law; thus confession of faith is prescribed, and denial of faith is forbidden, for it is written (Matt. 10. 32, 33): (*Every one*) *that shall confess Me before men, I will also confess him before My Father . . . But he that shall deny Me before men, I will also deny him before My Father*. On the other hand, there are works which are not necessarily opposed to, or in keeping with faith working through love. Such works are not prescribed or forbidden in the New Law by virtue of its primitive institution, but have been left by the Lawgiver, that is, Christ, to the discretion of each individual. And so to each one it is free to decide what he should do or avoid; and to each superior, to direct his subjects in such matters as regards what they must do or avoid. Therefore also in this respect the Gospel is called the law of liberty, since the Old Law decided many points and left few to man to decide as he chose.

Reply Obj. 1. The kingdom of God consists

chiefly in internal acts; but as a consequence all things that are essential to internal acts belong also to the kingdom of God. Thus if the kingdom of God is internal justice, peace, and spiritual joy, all external acts that are incompatible with justice, peace, and spiritual joy, are in opposition to the kingdom of God, and consequently should be forbidden in the Gospel of the kingdom. On the other hand, those things that are indifferent as regards these, for instance, to eat of this or that food, are not part of the kingdom of God; therefore the Apostle says before the words quoted: *The kingdom of God is not meat and drink.*

Reply Obj. 2. According to the Philosopher,[1] "what is free is cause of itself." Therefore he acts freely who acts of his own accord. Now man does of his own accord that which he does from a habit that is suitable to his nature, since a habit inclines one as a second nature. If, however, a habit were in opposition to nature, man would not act according to his nature, but according to some corruption affecting that nature. Since then the grace of the Holy Ghost is like an interior habit bestowed on us and inclining us to act rightly, it makes us do freely those things that are in keeping with grace, and shun what is opposed to it.

Accordingly the New Law is called the law of liberty in two respects. First, because it does not bind us to do or avoid certain things except such as are of themselves necessary or opposed to salvation, and come under the prescription or prohibition of the law. Secondly, because it also makes us comply freely with these precepts and prohibitions, since we do so through the promptings of grace. It is for these two reasons that the New Law is called *the law of perfect liberty* (James 1. 25).

Reply Obj. 3. The New Law, by restraining the mind from inordinate movements, must also restrain the hand from inordinate acts, which ensue from inward movements.

ARTICLE 2. *Whether the New Law Made Sufficient Ordinations About External Acts?*

We proceed thus to the Second Article: It would seem that the New Law made insufficient ordinations about external acts.

Objection 1. For faith working through charity seems chiefly to belong to the New Law, according to Gal. 5. 6: *In Christ Jesus neither circumcision availeth anything, nor uncircumcision: but faith that worketh through charity.* But the New Law declared explicitly certain

points of faith which were not set forth explicitly in the Old Law; for instance, belief in the Trinity. Therefore it should also have added certain outward moral deeds which were not fixed in the Old Law.

Obj. 2. Further, in the Old Law not only were sacraments instituted, but also certain sacred things, as stated above (Q. CI, A. 4; Q. CII, A. 4). But in the New Law, although certain sacraments are instituted, yet no sacred things seem to have been instituted by Our Lord; for instance, pertaining either to the sanctification of a temple or of the vessels, or to the celebration of some particular feast. Therefore the New Law made insufficient ordinations about external matters.

Obj. 3. Further, in the Old Law, just as there were certain observances pertaining to God's ministers, so also were there certain observances pertaining to the people, as was stated above when we were treating of the ceremonial of the Old Law (Q. CI, A. 4; Q. CII, A. 6). Now in the New Law certain observances seem to have been prescribed to the ministers of God, as may be gathered from Matt. 10. 9: *Do not possess gold, nor silver, nor money in your purses,* nor other things which are mentioned here and Luke 9., 10. Therefore certain observances pertaining to the faithful should also have been instituted in the New Law.

Obj. 4. Further, in the Old Law, besides moral and ceremonial precepts, there were certain judicial precepts. But in the New Law there are no judicial precepts. Therefore the New Law made insufficient ordinations about external works.

On the contrary, Our Lord said (Matt. 7. 24): *Every one . . . that heareth these My words, and doeth them, shall be likened to a wise man that built his house upon a rock.* But a wise builder leaves out nothing that is necessary to the building. Therefore Christ's words contain all things necessary for man's salvation.

I answer that, As stated above (A. 1), the New Law had to make such prescriptions or prohibitions alone as are essential for the reception or right use of grace. And since we cannot of ourselves obtain grace, but through Christ alone, hence Christ of Himself instituted the sacraments whereby we obtain grace: namely, Baptism, Eucharist, Orders of the ministers of the New Law, by the institution of the apostles and seventy-two disciples, Penance, and indissoluble Matrimony. He also promised Confirmation through the sending of the Holy

---

[1] *Metaphysics,* I, 2 (982b26).

Ghost, and we read that by His institution the apostles healed the sick by anointing them with oil (Mark 6. 13). These are the sacraments of the New Law.

The right use of grace is by means of works of charity. These, in so far as they are essential to virtue, pertain to the moral precepts, which also formed part of the Old Law. Hence, in this respect, the New Law had nothing to add as regards external action. The determination of these works in their relation to the divine worship belongs to the ceremonial precepts of the Law; and, in relation to our neighbour, to the judicial precepts, as stated above (Q. XCIX, A. 4). And therefore, since these determinations are not in themselves necessarily connected with inward grace in which the Law consists, they do not come under a precept of the New Law but are left to the decision of man; some relating to inferiors, as when a precept is given to an individual; others relating to superiors, temporal or spiritual, referring, namely, to the common good.

Accordingly the New Law had no other external works to determine, by prescribing or forbidding, except the sacraments, and those moral precepts which have a necessary connection with virtue, for instance, that one must not kill, or steal, and so forth.

Reply Obj. 1. Matters of faith are above human reason, and so we cannot attain to them except through grace. Consequently, when grace came to be bestowed more abundantly, the result was an increase in the number of explicit points of faith. On the other hand, it is through human reason that we are directed to works of virtue, for it is the rule of human action, as stated above (Q. XIX, A. 3; Q. LXIII, A. 2). Therefore in such matters as these there was no need for any precepts to be given besides the moral precepts of the Law, which proceed from the dictate of reason.

Reply Obj. 2. In the sacraments of the New Law grace is bestowed, which cannot be received except through Christ; consequently they had to be instituted by Him. But in the sacred things no grace is given; for instance, in the consecration of a temple, an altar or the like, or, again, in the celebration of feasts. Therefore Our Lord left the institution of such things to the discretion of the faithful, since they have not of themselves any necessary connection with inward grace.

Reply Obj. 3. Our Lord gave the apostles those precepts not as ceremonial observances, but as moral statutes. And they can be under-

stood in two ways. First, following Augustine (*De Consensu Evang.* 30),[1] as being not commands, but permissions. For He permitted them to set forth to preach without scrip or stick, and so on, since they were empowered to accept their livelihood from those to whom they preached; hence He goes on to say: *For the labourer is worthy of his hire.* Nor is it a sin, but a work of supererogation for a preacher to take means of livelihood with him, without accepting supplies from those to whom he preaches; as Paul did (I Cor. 9. 4, *seqq.*).

Secondly, according to the explanation of other holy men,[2] they may be considered as temporal commands laid upon the apostles for the time during which they were sent to preach in Judea before Christ's Passion. For the disciples, being yet as little children under Christ's care, needed to receive some special commands from Christ, such as all subjects receive from their superiors; and especially so since they were to be accustomed little by little to renounce the care of temporalities, so as to become fitted for the preaching of the Gospel throughout the whole world. Nor must we wonder if He established certain fixed modes of life, as long as the state of the Old Law endured and the people had not as yet achieved the perfect liberty of the Spirit. These statutes He abolished shortly before His Passion, as though the disciples had by their means become sufficiently practised. Hence He said (Luke 22. 35, 26): *When I sent you without purse and scrip and shoes, did you want anything? But they said: Nothing. Then said He unto them: But now, he that hath a purse, let him take it, and likewise a scrip.* Because the time of perfect liberty was already at hand, when they would be left entirely to their own judgment in matters not necessarily connected with virtue.

Reply Obj. 4. Judicial precepts also, considered in themselves, are not essential to virtue in respect of any particular determination, but only in regard to the common notion of justice. Consequently Our Lord left the judicial precepts to the discretion of those who were to have spiritual or temporal charge of others. But as regards the judicial precepts of the Old Law, some of them He explained, because they were misunderstood by the Pharisees, as we shall state later on (A. 3, REPLY 2).

[1] PL 34, 1114.
[2] See Chrysostom, *Hom.*, II, *In Rom.* 16.3 (PG 51, 199); Bede, *In Luc.*, VI, super 22.35 (PL 92, 601); cf. St. Thomas, *Cat. Aurea, In Matt.*, chap. 10, sect. 3; *In Luc.* 22, chap. 10, 35.

ARTICLE 3. *Whether the New Law Directed Man Sufficiently As Regards Interior Actions?*

We proceed thus to the Third Article: It would seem that the New Law directed man insufficiently as regards interior actions.

Objection 1. For there are ten commandments of the decalogue ordering man to God and his neighbour. But Our Lord partly fulfilled only three of them; as regards, namely, the prohibition of murder, of adultery, and of perjury. Therefore it seems that, by omitting to fulfill the other precepts He directed man insufficiently.

Obj. 2. Further, as regards the judicial precepts, Our Lord ordained nothing in the Gospel, except in the matter of divorcing a wife, of punishment by retaliation, and of persecuting one's enemies. But there are many other judicial precepts of the Old Law, as stated above (Q. CIV, A. 4; Q. CV). Therefore, in this respect, He directed human life insufficiently.

Obj. 3. Further, in the Old Law, besides moral and judicial, there were ceremonial precepts about which Our Lord made no ordination. Therefore it seems that He ordained insufficiently.

Obj. 4. Further, in order that the mind be inwardly well disposed, man should do no good deed for any temporal end whatever. But there are many other temporal goods besides the favour of man, and there are many other good works besides fasting, alms-deeds, and prayer. Therefore our Lord unfittingly taught that only in respect of these three works, and of no other earthly goods ought we to shun the glory of human favour.

Obj. 5. Further, solicitude for the necessary means of livelihood is by nature instilled into man, and this solicitude even other animals share with man; hence it is written (Prov. 6. 6, 8): *Go to the ant, O sluggard, and consider her ways . . . she provideth her meat for herself in the summer, and gathereth her food in the harvest.* But every command issued against the inclination of nature is an unjust command, since it is contrary to the law of nature. Therefore it seems that Our Lord unfittingly forbade solicitude about food and raiment.

Obj. 6. Further, no act of virtue should be the subject of a prohibition. Now judgment is an act of justice, according to Ps. 93. 15: *Until justice be turned into judgment.* Therefore it seems that Our Lord unfittingly forbade judgment, and consequently that the New Law directed man insufficiently in the matter of interior acts.

On the contrary, Augustine says (*De Serm. Dom. in Monte.* i, 1):[1] "We should take note that, when He said: 'He that heareth these My words,' He indicates clearly that this sermon of the Lord is replete with all the precepts whereby a Christian's life is formed."

I answer that, As is evident from Augustine's words just quoted, the sermon which Our Lord delivered on the mountain contains the whole process of forming the life of a Christian. Therein man's interior movements are ordered perfectly. For after declaring that his end is Happiness, and after commending the authority of the apostles, through whom the teaching of the Gospel was to be promulgated, He orders man's interior movements, first in regard to man himself, secondly in regard to his neighbour.

This he does in regard to man himself, in two ways, corresponding to man's two interior movements in respect of any prospective action namely, volition of what has to be done, and intention of the end. Therefore, in the first place, He directs man's will in respect of the various precepts of the Law by prescribing that man should refrain not merely from those external works that are evil in themselves, but also from internal acts, and from the occasions of evil deeds. In the second place He directs man's intention, by teaching that in our good works we should seek neither human praise, nor worldly riches, which is to lay up treasures on earth.

Afterwards He directs man's interior movement in respect of his neighbour, by forbidding us, on the one hand, to judge him rashly, unjustly, or presumptuously, and, on the other, to entrust him too readily with sacred things if he be unworthy.

Lastly, He teaches us how to fulfil the teaching of the Gospel; namely, by imploring the help of God, by striving to enter by the narrow door of perfect virtue, and by being wary lest we be led astray by evil influences. Moreover He declares that we must observe His commandments, and that it is not enough to make profession of faith, or to work miracles, or merely to hear His words.

Reply Obj. 1. Our Lord explained the manner of fufilling those precepts of the Law which the Scribes and Pharisees did not rightly understand, and this affected chiefly those precepts of the decalogue. For they thought that the prohibition of adultery and murder covered the external act only, and not the internal desire. And

[1] PL 34, 1231.

they held this opinion about murder and adultery rather than about theft and false witness because the movement of anger tending to murder, and the movement of desire tending to adultery seem to be in us from nature somewhat, but not the desire of stealing or of bearing false witness. They held a false opinion about perjury, for they thought that perjury indeed was a sin, but that oaths were of themselves to be desired, and to be taken frequently, since they seem to proceed from reverence to God. Hence Our Lord shows that an oath is not desirable as a good thing, and that it is better to speak without oaths, unless necessity forces us to have recourse to them.

Reply Obj. 2. The Scribes and Pharisees erred about the judicial precepts in two ways. First, because they considered certain matters contained in the Law of Moses by way of permission to be right in themselves; namely, divorce of a wife, and the taking of usury from strangers. Therefore Our Lord forbade a man to divorce his wife (Matt. 5. 32), and to receive usury (Luke 6. 35), when He said: *Lend, hoping for nothing thereby.*

In another way they erred by thinking that certain things which the Old Law commanded to be done for justice' sake should be done out of desire for revenge, or out of lust for temporal goods, or out of hatred of one's enemies; and this in respect of three precepts. For they thought that desire for revenge was lawful on account of the precept concerning punishment by retaliation, which precept, however, was given that justice might be safeguarded, not that man might seek revenge. Therefore, in order to do away with this, Our Lord teaches that man should be prepared in his mind to suffer yet more if necessary. They thought that movements of covetousness were lawful on account of those judicial precepts which prescribed restitution of what had been purloined, together with something added thereto, as stated above (Q. CV, A. 2, Reply 9); but the Law commanded this to be done in order to safeguard justice, not to encourage covetousness. Therefore Our Lord teaches that we should not demand our goods from motives of cupidity, and that we should be ready to give yet more if necessary. They thought that the movement of hatred was lawful on account of the commandments of the Law about the slaying of one's enemies; but the Law ordered this for the fulfilment of justice, as stated above (Q. CV, A. 3, Reply 4), not to satisfy hatred. Therefore Our Lord teaches us that we ought to love

our enemies, and to be ready to do good to them if necessary. For these precepts are to be taken "according to readiness of the mind," as Augustine says (*De Serm. Dom. in Monte,* i, 19).[1]

Reply Obj. 3. The moral precepts necessarily retained their force under the New Law because they pertain of themselves to the notion of virtue. But the judicial precepts did not necessarily continue to bind in exactly the same way as had been fixed by the Law; this was left to man to decide in one way or another. Hence Our Lord directed us fittingly with regard to these two kinds of precepts. On the other hand, the observance of the ceremonial precepts was totally abolished by the advent of the reality. Therefore in regard to these precepts He commanded nothing on this occasion when He was giving the general points of His doctrine. Elsewhere, however, He makes it clear that the entire bodily worship which was fixed by the Law was to be changed into a spiritual worship as is evident from John 4. 21, 23, where He says: *The hour cometh when you shall neither on this mountain, nor in Jerusalem adore the Father . . . but . . . the true adorers shall adore the Father in spirit and in truth.*

Reply Obj. 4. All worldly goods may be reduced to three—honours, riches, and pleasures, according to I John 2. 16: *All that is in the world is the concupiscence of the flesh,* which refers to pleasures of the flesh, *and the concupiscence of the eyes,* which refers to riches, *and the pride of life,* which refers to ambition for renown and honour. Now the Law did not promise an abundance of carnal pleasures; on the contrary, it forbade them. But it did promise exalted honours and abundant riches; for it is written in reference to the former (Deut. 28. 1): *If thou wilt hear the voice of the Lord thy God . . . He will make thee higher than all the nations;* and in reference to the latter, we read a little further on (*verse* 11): He *will make thee abound with all goods.* But the Jews so distorted the true meaning of these promises as to think that we ought to serve God with these things as the end in view. Therefore Our Lord set this aside by teaching, first of all, that works of virtue should not be done for human glory. And He mentions three works, to which all others may be reduced, since whatever a man does in order to curb his desires comes under the head of fasting; and whatever a man does for the love of his neighbour comes under the head of alms-deeds; and whatever a man does for the worship of God comes under the head

[1] PL 34, 1260.

of prayer. And He mentions these three specially, as they hold the principal place, and are
most often used by men in order to gain glory.
In the second place He taught us that we must
not place our end in riches, when He said: *Lay
not up to yourselves treasures on earth* (Matt.
6. 19).

Reply Obj. 5. Our Lord forbade not necessary
but inordinate solicitude. Now there is a fourfold solicitude to be avoided in temporal matters. First, we must not place our end in them,
nor serve God for the sake of the necessities of
food and raiment. Therefore He says: *Lay not
up for yourselves*, etc. Secondly, we must not
be so anxious about temporal things as to
despair of God's help; therefore Our Lord says
(*ibid.* 32): *Your Father knoweth that you have
need of all these things.* Thirdly, we must not
add presumption to our solicitude; in other
words, we must not be confident of getting the
necessaries of life by our own efforts without
God's help; such solicitude Our Lord sets aside
by saying that a man cannot add anything to his
stature (*ibid.* 27). We must not anticipate the
time of anxiety; namely, by being solicitous
now for the needs, not of the present, but of a
future time; hence He says (*ibid.* 34): *Be not
. . . solicitous for to-morrow.*

Reply Obj. 6. Our Lord did not forbid the
judgment of justice, without which holy things
could not be withdrawn from the unworthy. But
he forbade inordinate judgment, as stated above.

ARTICLE 4. *Whether Certain Definite Counsels
Are Fittingly Proposed in the New Law?*

We proceed thus to the Fourth Article: It
would seem that certain definite counsels are
not fittingly proposed in the New Law.

Objection 1. For counsels are given about
that which is expedient for an end, as we stated
above, when treating of counsel (Q. XIV, A. 2).
But the same things are not expedient for all.
Therefore certain definite counsels should not
be proposed to all.

Obj. 2. Further, counsels are given about a
greater good. But there are no definite degrees
of the greater good. Therefore definite counsels
should not be given.

Obj. 3. Further, counsels pertain to the life
of perfection. But obedience pertains to the life
of perfection. Therefore it was unfitting that
no counsel of obedience should be contained in
the Gospel.

Obj. 4. Further, many matters pertaining to
the life of perfection are found among the commandments, as, for instance, *Love your enemies*

(Matt. 5. 44), and those precepts which Our
Lord gave His Apostles (*ibid.* x.). Therefore the
counsels are unfittingly given in the New Law,
both because they are not all mentioned, and
because they are not distinguished from the
commandments.

On the contrary, The counsels of a wise friend
are of great use, according to Prov. 27. 9:
*Ointment and perfumes rejoice the heart: and
the good counsels of a friend rejoice the soul.*
But Christ is our wisest and greatest friend.
Therefore His counsels are supremely useful
and becoming.

I answer that, The difference between a counsel and a commandment is that a commandment
implies necessity, while a counsel is left to the
choice of the one to whom it is given. Consequently in the New Law, which is the law of
liberty, counsels are added to the commandments, and not in the Old Law, which is the
law of bondage. We must therefore understand
the commandments of the New Law to have
been given about matters that are necessary to
gain the end of eternal Happiness, to which end
the New Law brings us immediately, but that
the counsels are about matters that render the
gaining of this end more assured and expedi-
tious.

Now man is placed between the things of this
world, and spiritual goods in which eternal happiness consists, so that the more he cleaves to
the one, the more he withdraws from the other,
and conversely. Therefore he that cleaves wholly to the things of this world, so as to make
them his end, and to look upon them as the reason and rule of all he does, falls away altogether
from spiritual goods. Hence this disorder is
removed by the commandments. Nevertheless,
for man to gain the above mentioned end, he
does not need to renounce the things of the
world altogether, since he can while using the
things of this world attain to eternal happiness,
provided he does not place his end in them; but
he will attain more speedily to that end by giving up the goods of this world entirely. And
so the evangelical counsels are given for this
purpose.

Now the goods of this world which come into
use in human life consist in three things:
namely, in external wealth pertaining to the
concupiscence of the eyes; carnal pleasures
pertaining to the concupiscence of the flesh;
and honours, which pertain to the pride of life,
according to I John 2. 16; and it is in renouncing these altogether, as far as possible, that the
evangelical counsels consist. Moreover, every

form of the religious life that professes the state of perfection is based on these three, since riches are renounced by poverty, carnal pleasures by perpetual chastity, and the pride of life by the bondage of obedience.

Now if a man observe these absolutely, this is in accordance with the counsels as they stand. But if a man observe any one of them in a particular case, this is taking that counsel in a restricted sense, namely, as applying to that particular case. For instance, when anyone gives an alms to a poor man, not being bound so to do, he follows the counsels in that particular case. In like manner, when a man for some fixed time refrains from carnal pleasures that he may give himself to prayer, he follows the counsel for that particular time. And again, when a man follows not his will as to some deed which he might do lawfully, he follows the counsel in that particular case; for instance, if he do good to his enemies when he is not bound to, or if he forgive an injury of which he might justly seek to be avenged. In this way, too, all particular counsels may be reduced to these three general and perfect counsels.

Reply Obj. 1. The above counsels, considered in themselves, are expedient to all, but owing to some people being ill-disposed, it happens that some of them are inexpedient, because their affection is not inclined to such things. Hence Our Lord, in proposing the evangelical counsels, always makes mention of man's fitness for observing the counsels. For in giving the counsel of perpetual poverty (Matt. 19. 21), He begins with the words: *If thou wilt be perfect,* and then He adds: *Go, sell all* (Vulg.,— *what*) *thou hast.* In like manner when He gave the counsel of perpetual chastity, saying (*ibid.,*

12): *There are eunuchs who have made themselves eunuchs for the kingdom of heaven,* He adds straightway: *He that can take, let him take it.* And, again, the Apostle (I Cor. 7. 35), after giving the counsel of virginity, says: *And this I speak for your profit; not to cast a snare upon you.*

Reply Obj. 2. The greater goods are not definitely fixed in the individual; but those which are simply and absolutely the greater good in general are fixed, and to these all the above particular goods may be reduced, as stated above.

Reply Obj. 3. Even the counsel of obedience is understood to have been given by Our Lord in the words: *And* (let him) *follow Me.* For we follow Him not only by imitating His works, but also by obeying His commandments, according to John 10. 27: *My sheep hear My voice . . . and they follow Me.*

Reply Obj. 4. Those things which Our Lord prescribed about the true love of our enemies and other similar sayings (Matt. 5.; Luke 6.), may be referred to the preparation of the mind, and then they are necessary for salvation; for instance, that man be prepared to do good to his enemies, and other similar actions, when there is need. Hence these things are placed among the precepts. But that anyone should actually and promptly behave thus towards an enemy when there is no special need, is to be referred to the particular counsels, as stated above. As to those matters which are set down in Matt. 10. and Luke 9. and 10., they were either disciplinary commands for that particular time, or concessions, as stated above (A. 2, REPLY 3). Hence they are not set down among the counsels.

TREATISE ON GRACE

QUESTION CIX

OF THE NECESSITY OF GRACE

(In Ten Articles)

WE must now consider the exterior principle of human acts, that is, God, in so far as through grace we are helped by Him to do right; and, first, we must consider the grace of God; secondly, its cause (Q. CXII); thirdly, its effects (Q. CXIII).

The first point of consideration will be three-fold, for we shall consider (1) The necessity of grace; (2) grace itself, as to its essence (Q. CX); (3) its division (Q. CXI).

Under the first head there are ten points of inquiry. (1) Whether without grace man can know any truth? (2) Whether without God's grace man can do or wish any good? (3) Whether without grace man can love God above all things? (4) Whether without grace man by his own natural powers can keep the commandments of the Law? (5) Whether without grace he can merit eternal life? (6) Whether without grace man can prepare himself for grace? (7) Whether without grace he can rise from sin? (8) Whether without grace man can avoid sin? (9) Whether man having received grace can do good and avoid sin without any further Divine help? (10) Whether he can of himself persevere in good?

ARTICLE 1. Whether Without Grace Man Can Know Any Truth?

We proceed thus to the First Article: It would seem that without grace man can know no truth.

Objection 1. For, on I Cor. 12. 3: *No man can say, the Lord Jesus, but by the Holy Ghost,* a gloss of Ambrose says:[1] "Every truth, by whomsoever spoken is from the Holy Ghost." Now the Holy Ghost dwells in us by grace. Therefore we cannot know truth without grace.

Obj. 2. Further, Augustine says (*Solil.* i, 6)[2] that "the most certain sciences are like things lit up by the sun so as to be seen. Now God Himself is He Who sheds the light. And reason is in the mind as sight is in the eye. And the eyes of the mind are the senses of the soul." Now the bodily senses, however pure, cannot see any visible object without the sun's light. Therefore the human mind, however perfect, cannot, by reasoning, know any truth without Divine light. And this pertains to the aid of grace.

Obj. 3. Further, the human mind can only understand truth by thinking, as is clear from Augustine (*De Trin.* xiv, 7).[3] But the Apostle says (II Cor. 3. 5): *Not that we are sufficient to think anything of ourselves, as of ourselves; but our sufficiency is from God.* Therefore man cannot, of himself, know truth without the help of grace.

On the contrary, Augustine says (*Retract.* i, 4).[4] "I do not approve having said in the prayer O God, Who dost wish the clean alone to know the truth; for it may be answered that many who are unclean know many truths." Now man is cleansed by grace, according to Ps. 50. 12: *Create a clean heart in me, O God, and renew a right spirit within my bowels.* Therefore without grace man of himself can know truth.

I answer that, To know truth is a use or act of intellectual light, since, according to the Apostle (Eph. 5. 13): *All that is made manifest is light.* Now every use implies movement, taking movement broadly, so as to call thinking and willing movements, as is clear from the Philosopher.[5] Now in corporeal things we see that for movement there is required not merely the form which is the principle of the movement or action, but there is also required the motion of the first mover. Now the first mover in the order of corporeal things is the heavenly body. Hence no matter how perfectly fire has heat, it would not bring about alteration except by the motion of the heavenly body. But it is clear that as all corporeal movements are reduced to the motion of the heavenly body as to the first corporeal mover, so all movements, both corporeal and spiritual, are reduced to the absolutely First Mover, Who is God. And hence no matter how perfect a corporeal or spiritual nature is supposed to be, it cannot proceed to its act unless it be moved by God; but this motion is ac-

---

[1] *Glossa* Lombardi (PL 191, 1651); cf. *Glossa ordin.*, (VI, 52A); cf. Ambrosiaster (PL 17, 258).
[2] PL 32, 875.
[3] PL 42, 1043.
[4] PL 32, 589.
[5] *Soul*, III, 4 (429^{b}25); III, 7 (431^{a}4).

cording to the plan of His providence, and not by a necessity of nature, as the motion of the heavenly body. Now not only is every motion from God as from the First Mover, but all formal perfection is from Him as from the First Act. And thus the act of the intellect or of any created being whatsoever depends upon God in two ways; first, in so far as it is from Him that it has the perfection or form by which it acts; secondly, in so far as it is moved by Him to act.

Now every form bestowed on created things by God has power for a determined act, which it can bring about in proportion to its own proper endowment, and beyond which it is powerless, except by a superadded form, as water can only heat when heated by the fire. And thus the human understanding has a form, namely, intelligible light itself, which of itself is sufficient for knowing certain intelligible things, namely, those we can come to know through the senses. Higher intelligible things the human intellect cannot know, unless it be perfected by a stronger light, namely, the light of faith or prophecy which is called the light of grace, since it is added to nature.

Hence we must say that for the knowledge of any truth whatsoever man needs Divine help, in order that the intellect may be moved by God to its act. But he does not need a new light added to his natural light in order to know the truth in all things, but only in some that surpass his natural knowledge. And yet at times God miraculously instructs some by His grace in things that can be known by natural reason, even as He sometimes brings about miraculously what nature can do.

Reply Obj. 1. Every truth by whomsoever spoken is from the Holy Ghost as bestowing the natural light and moving us to understand and speak the truth, but not as dwelling in us by sanctifying grace, or as bestowing any habitual gift superadded to nature. For this only takes place with regard to certain truths that are known and spoken, and especially in regard to such as pertain to faith, of which the Apostle speaks.

Reply Obj. 2. The bodily sun sheds its light outside us, but the intelligible Sun, Who is God, shines within us. Hence the natural light itself bestowed upon the soul is God's enlightenment, whereby we are enlightened to see what pertains to natural knowledge; and for this there is required no further knowledge, but only for such things as surpass natural knowledge.

Reply Obj. 3. We always need God's help for every thought in so far as He moves the under-

standing to act; for actually to understand anything is to think, as is clear from Augustine (*De Trin.* xiv, *loc. cit.*).

ARTICLE 2. *Whether Man Can Will or Do Any Good Without Grace?*

We proceed thus to the Second Article: It would seem that man can will and do good without grace.

Objection 1. For that of which he is master is in man's power. Now man is master of his acts, and especially of his willing, as stated above (Q. I, A. I; Q. XIII, A. 6). Hence man, of himself, can will and do good without the help of grace.

Obj. 2. Further, man has more power over what is according to his nature than over what is beyond his nature. Now sin is against his nature, as Damascene says (*De Fide Orthod.* ii, 30):[1] while deeds of virtue are according to his nature, as stated above (Q. LXXI, A. I). Therefore since man can sin of himself, much more would it seem that of himself he can will and do good.

Obj. 3. Further, the good of the intellect is truth, as the Philosopher says.[2] Now the intellect can of itself know truth, even as every other thing can work its own natural operation of itself. Therefore, much more can man of himself do and will good.

On the contrary, The Apostle says (Rom. 9. 16): *It is not of him that willeth,* namely, to will, *nor of him that runneth,* namely, to run, *but of God that showeth mercy.* And Augustine says (*De Corrept. et Gratia,* ii)[3] that without grace men do nothing good when they either think or wish or love or act.

I answer that, Man's nature may be looked at in two ways: first, in its integrity, as it was in our first parent before sin; secondly, as it is corrupted in us after the sin of our first parent. Now in both states human nature needs the help of God as First Mover, to do or will any good whatsoever, as stated above (A. I). But in the state of integrity of nature, as regards the sufficiency of the operative power, man by his natural endowments could will and do the good proportionate to his nature, such as the good of acquired virtue, but not surpassing good, as the good of infused virtue. But in the state of corrupt nature, man falls short even of what he could do by his nature, so that he

[1] PG 94, 976; cf. chap. 4 (PG 94, 876); IV, 20 (PG 94, 1196).
[2] *Ethics,* VI, 2 (1139ᵃ27).
[3] PL 44, 917.

is unable to fulfil it by his own natural powers. Yet because human nature is not altogether corrupted by sin, so as to be shorn of every natural good, even in the state of corrupted nature it can, by virtue of its natural endowments, work some particular good, as to build dwellings, plant vineyards, and the like; yet it cannot do all the good natural to it, so as to fall short in nothing, just as a sick man can of himself make some movements, yet he cannot be perfectly moved with the movements of one in health, unless by the help of medicine he be cured.

And thus in the state of perfect nature man needs a gratuitous strength superadded to natural strength for one reason, that is, in order to do and will supernatural good; but for two reasons, in the state of corrupt nature, namely, in order to be healed, and beyond this in order to carry out works of supernatural virtue, which are meritorious. Furthermore, in both states man needs the Divine help, that he may be moved to act well.

Reply Obj. 1. Man is master of his acts and of his willing or not willing, because of the deliberation of reason, which can be bent to one side or another. And although he is master of his deliberating or not deliberating, yet this can only be by a previous deliberation; and since this cannot go on to infinity, we must come at length to this, that man's free choice is moved by an extrinsic principle, which is above the human mind, namely, by God, as the Philosopher proves in the chapter *on Good Fortune.*[1] Hence the mind of man still healthy is not so much master of its act that it does not need to be moved by God; and much more the free choice of man weakened by sin, by which it is hindered from good by the corruption of the nature.

Reply Obj. 2. To sin is nothing else than to fail in the good which belongs to any being according to its nature. Now as every created thing has its being from another, and considered in itself is nothing, so does it need to be preserved by another in the good which pertains to its nature. For it can of itself fail in good, even as of itself it can fall into non-being, unless it is upheld by God.

Reply Obj. 3. Man cannot even know truth without Divine help, as stated above (A. 1). And yet human nature is more corrupt by sin in regard to the desire for good, than in regard to the knowledge of truth.

[1] *Eudemian Ethics*, VII, 14 (1248ª14).

ARTICLE 3. *Whether By His Own Natural Powers and Without Grace Man Can Love God Above All Things?*

We proceed thus to the Third Article: It would seem that without grace man cannot love God above all things by his own natural powers.

Objection 1. For to love God above all things is the proper and principal act of charity. Now man cannot of himself possess charity, since the *charity of God is poured forth in our hearts by the Holy Ghost Who is given to us,* as is said Rom. 5. 5. Therefore man by his natural powers alone cannot love God above all things.

Obj. 2. Further, no nature can rise above itself. But to love God above all things is to tend above oneself. Therefore without the help of grace no created nature can love God above itself.

Obj. 3. Further, to God, Who is the Highest Good, is due the best love, which is that He be loved above all things. Now without grace man is not capable of giving God the best love, which is His due; otherwise it would be useless to add grace. Hence man, without grace and with his natural powers alone, cannot love God above all things.

On the contrary, As some maintain,[2] man was first made with only natural endowments, and in this state it is manifest that he loved God to some extent. But he did not love God equally with himself, or less than himself, otherwise he would have sinned. Therefore he loved God above himself. Therefore man, by his natural powers alone, can love God more than himself and above all things.

I answer that, As was said above (Part I., Q. LX, A. 5), where the various opinions concerning the natural love of the angels were set forth, man in a state of integral nature, could by his natural power do the good natural to him without the addition of any gratuitous gift, though not without the help of God moving him. Now to love God above all things is natural to man and to every nature, not only rational but irrational, and even to inanimate nature according to the manner of love which can belong to each creature. And the reason of this is that it is natural to all to seek and love things according as they are naturally fit (to be sought and loved) since "all things act according as they are naturally fit" as stated in

[2] Cf. above, Part I, Q. XCV, A. 1.

the *Physics*.[1] Now it is manifest that the good of the part is for the good of the whole. Hence each particular thing, by its natural appetite or love, loves its own proper good on account of the common good of the whole universe, which is God. Hence Dionysius says (*Div. Nom.* iv)[2] that God "turns everything to love of Himself." Hence in the state of original nature man referred the love of himself and of all other things to the love of God as to its end; and thus he loved God more than himself and above all things. But in the state of corrupt nature man falls short of this in the appetite of his rational will, which, unless it is cured by God's grace, follows its private good, on account of the corruption of nature. And hence we must say that in the state of integral nature man did not need the gift of grace added to his natural endowments in order to love God above all things naturally, although he needed God's help to move him to it; but in the state of corrupt nature man needs, even for this, the help of grace which heals his nature.

Reply Obj. 1. Charity loves God above all things in a higher way than nature does. For nature loves God above all things according as He is the beginning and the end of natural good; charity however loves Him as He is the object of Happiness, and according as man has a spiritual fellowship with God. Moreover charity adds to natural love of God a certain quickness and joy, in the same way that every habit of virtue adds to the good act which is done merely by the natural reason of a man who has not the habit of virtue.

Reply Obj. 2. When it is said that nature cannot rise above itself, we must not understand this as if it could not be drawn to any object above itself, for it is clear that our intellect by its natural knowledge can know things above itself, as is shown in our natural knowledge of God. But we are to understand that nature cannot rise to an act exceeding the proportion of its strength. Now to love God above all things is not such an act, for it is natural to every creature, as was said above.

Reply Obj. 3. Love is said to be best not only with respect to the degree of love but also with regard to the motive of loving, and the mode of love. And thus the highest degree of love is that by which charity loves God as the giver of Happiness, as was said above (reply 1).

ARTICLE 4. *Whether Man Without Grace and By His Own Natural Powers Can Fulfil the Commandments of the Law?*

We proceed thus to the Fourth Article: It would seem that man without grace, and by his own natural powers, can fulfil the commandments of the Law.

Objection 1. For the Apostle says (Rom. 2. 14) that *the Gentiles who have not the law, do by nature those things that are of the Law.* Now what a man does naturally he can do of himself without grace. Hence a man can fulfil the commandments of the Law without grace.

Obj. 2. Further, Jerome says (*Expos. Cathol. Fid.*)[3] that they are anathema who say God has laid impossibilities upon man. Now what a man cannot fulfil by himself is impossible to him. Therefore a man can fulfil all the commandments of the Law by himself.

Obj. 3. Further, of all the commandments of the Law, the greatest is this, *Thou shalt love the Lord thy God with thy whole heart* (Matt. 22. 37). Now man with his natural endowments can fulfil this command by loving God above all things, as stated above (A. 3). Therefore man can fulfil all the commandments of the Law without grace.

On the contrary, Augustine says (*De Hæres*, lxxxviii)[4] that it is part of the Pelagian heresy that "they believe that without grace man can fulfil all the Divine commandments."

I answer that, There are two ways of fulfilling the commandments of the Law. The first regards the substance of the works, as when a man does works of justice, fortitude, and of other virtues. And in this way man in the state of integral nature could fulfil all the commandments of the Law; otherwise he would have been unable to sin in that state, since to sin is nothing else than to transgress the Divine commandments. But in the state of corrupted nature man cannot fulfil all the Divine commandments without healing grace. Secondly, the commandments of the law can be fulfilled not merely as regards the substance of the act, but also as regards the mode of acting, that is, their being done out of charity. And in this way, neither in the state of integral nature, nor in the state of corrupt nature can man fulfil the commandments of the law without grace. Hence, Augustine (*De Corrept. et Grat.* ii)[5] having stated that "without grace men can do

---

[1] Aristotle, II, 8 (199ª10).
[2] Sect. 10 (PG 3 708).

[3] Cf. Pelagius, *Epist.*, I, 16 (PL 30, 32).
[4] PL 42, 47.   [5] PL 44, 917.

no good whatever," adds: "Not only do they know by its light what to do, but by its help they do lovingly what they know." Beyond this, in both states they need the help of God's motion in order to fulfil the commandments, as stated above (AA. 2, 3).

Reply Obj. 1. As Augustine says (*De Spir. et Lit.* xxvii),[1] "do not be disturbed at his saying that they do by nature those things that are of the Law; for the Spirit of grace works this, in order to restore in us the image of God, after which we were naturally made."

Reply Obj. 2. What we can do with the Divine assistance is not altogether impossible to us, according to the Philosopher:[2] "What we can do through our friends, we can do, in some sense, by ourselves." Hence Jerome concedes[3] that "our choice is in such a way free that we must confess we still require God's help."

Reply Obj. 3. Man cannot, with his purely natural endowments, fulfil the precept of the love of God through charity, as stated above (A. 3).

ARTICLE 5. *Whether Man Can Merit Everlasting Life Without Grace?*

We proceed thus to the Fifth Article: It would seem that man can merit everlasting life without grace.

Objection 1. For Our Lord says (Matt. 19. 17): *If thou wilt enter into life, keep the commandments*, from which it would seem that to enter into everlasting life rests with man's will. But what rests with our will, we can do of ourselves. Hence it seems that man can merit everlasting life of himself.

Obj. 2. Further, eternal life is the wage or reward bestowed by God on men, according to Matt. 5. 12: *Your reward is very great in heaven.* But wage or reward is meted by God to everyone according to his works, according to Ps. 61. 12: *Thou wilt render to every man according to his works.* Hence, since man is master of his works, it seems that it is within his power to reach everlasting life.

Obj. 3. Further, everlasting life is the last end of human life. Now every natural thing by its natural endowments can attain its end. Much more, therefore, may man attain to life everlasting by his natural endowments, without grace.

On the contrary, The Apostle says (Rom. 6. 23): *The grace of God is life everlasting.* And

as a gloss says,[4] this is said "that we may understand that God, of His own mercy, leads us to everlasting life."

I answer that, Acts conducing to an end must be proportioned to the end. But no act exceeds the proportion of its active principle; and hence we see in natural things that nothing can by its operation bring about an effect which exceeds its active force, but only such as is proportionate to its power. Now everlasting life is an end exceeding the proportion of human nature, as is clear from what we have said above (Q. v, A. 5). Hence man, by his natural endowments, cannot produce meritorious works proportionate to everlasting life, but for this a higher power is needed, namely, the power of grace. And thus without grace man cannot merit everlasting life. Yet he can perform works conducing to a good which is natural to man, as to toil in the fields, to drink, to eat, or to have friends, and the like, as Augustine says in his third *Reply to the Pelagians.*[5]

Reply Obj. 1. Man, by his will, does works meritorious of everlasting life, but, as Augustine says, in the same book,[6] for this it is necessary that the will of man should be prepared with grace by God.

Reply Obj. 2. As the gloss upon Rom. 6. 23, *The grace of God is life everlasting,* says,[7] "It is certain that everlasting life is bestowed for good works; but the works for which it is bestowed, belong to God's grace." And it has been said (A. 4), that to fulfil the commandments of the Law in their due way, by which their fulfilment may be meritorious, requires grace.

Reply Obj. 3. This objection has to do with the natural end of man. Now human nature, since it is nobler, can be raised by the help of grace to a higher end, which lower natures can in no way reach; even as a man who can recover his health by the help of medicines is better disposed to health than one who can in no way recover it, as the Philosopher observes.[8]

ARTICLE 6. *Whether a Man, by Himself and Without the External Aid of Grace, Can Prepare Himself for Grace?*

We proceed thus to the Sixth Article: It would seem that man, by himself and without the external help of grace, can prepare himself for grace.

---

[1] PL 44, 229.   [2] *Ethics,* III, 3 ($1112^{b}27$).
[3] Cf. Pelagius, *Libellus Fidei ad Innocentium* (PL 45, 1718).

[4] *Glossa ordin.* (VI, 15F); *Glossa* Lombardi (PL 191, 1412); cf. Augustine, *Enchir.,* CVII (PL 40, 282).
[5] *Hypognosticon,* III, among the spurious works of Augustine. (PL 45, 1624).   [6] *Ibid.*
[7] Cf. note 4.
[8] *Heavens,* II, 12 ($292^{b}13$).

Objection 1. For nothing impossible is laid upon man, as stated above (A. 4, REPLY 2). But it is written (Zach. 1. 3): *Turn ye to Me . . . and I will turn to you.* Now to prepare for grace is nothing more than to turn to God. Therefore it seems that man of himself, and without the external help of grace, can prepare himself for grace.

Obj. 2. Further, man prepares himself for grace by doing what is in him to do, since if man does what is in him to do God will not deny him grace, for it is written (Matt. 7. 11) that God gives His good Spirit *to them that ask Him.* But what is in our power is said to be in us. Therefore it seems to be in our power to prepare ourselves for grace.

Obj. 3. Further, if a man needs grace in order to prepare for grace, with equal reason will he need grace to prepare himself for the first grace; and thus to infinity, which is impossible. Hence it seems that we must not go beyond what was said first, namely, that man, of himself and without grace, can prepare himself for grace.

Obj. 4. Further, it is written (Prov. 16. 1) that *it is the part of man to prepare the soul.* Now an action is said to be the part of a man when he can do it by himself. Hence it seems that man by himself can prepare himself for grace.

On the contrary, It is written (John 6. 44): *No man can come to Me except the Father, Who hath sent Me, draw him.* But if man could prepare himself, he would not need to be drawn by another. Hence man cannot prepare himself without the help of grace.

I answer that, The preparation of the human will for good is twofold. The first, by which it is prepared to operate rightly and to enjoy God; and this preparation of the will cannot take place without the habitual gift of grace, which is the principle of meritorious works, as stated above (A. 5). There is a second way in which the human will may be taken to be prepared for the gift of habitual grace itself. Now in order that man prepare himself to receive this gift, it is not necessary to presuppose any further habitual gift in the soul, for thus we should go on to infinity. But we must presuppose a gratuitous help from God, Who moves the soul inwardly or inspires the good wish. For in these two ways do we need the Divine assistance, as stated above (AA. 2, 3). Now that we need the help of God to move us is manifest. For since every agent acts for an end, every cause must direct its effect to its end,

and hence since the order of ends is according to the order of agents or movers, man must be directed to the last end by the motion of the first mover, and to the proximate end by the motion of any of the subordinate movers; as the spirit of the soldier is bent towards seeking the victory by the motion of the leader of the army—and towards following the standard of a regiment by the motion of the standard-bearer. And thus since God is the first Mover absolutely, it is by His motion that everything seeks Him under the common intention of good, by which everything seeks to be likened to God in its own way. Hence Dionysius says (*Div. Nom.* iv)[1] that "God turns all to Himself." But He directs just men to Himself as to a special end, which they seek, and to which they wish to cling, according to Ps. 72. 28, *it is good for Me to adhere to my God.* And that they are turned to God can only spring from God's having turned them. Now to prepare oneself for grace is, as it were, to be turned to God, just as whoever has his eyes turned away from the light of the sun prepares himself to receive the sun's light by turning his eyes towards the sun. Hence it is clear that man cannot prepare himself to receive the light of grace except by the gratuitous help of God moving him inwardly.

Reply Obj. 1. Man's turning to God is by free choice; and thus man is bidden to turn himself to God. But free choice can only be turned to God when God turns it, according to Jer. 31. 18: *Convert me and I shall be converted, for Thou art the Lord, my God;* and Lament. 5. 21: *Convert us, O Lord, to Thee, and we shall be converted.*

Reply Obj. 2. Man can do nothing unless moved by God, according to John 15. 5: *Without Me, you can do nothing.* Hence when a man is said to do what is in him to do, this is said to be in his power according as he is moved by God.

Reply Obj. 3. This objection regards habitual grace, for which some preparation is required, since every form requires a disposition in that which is to be its subject. But in order that man should be moved by God, no further motion is presupposed, since God is the First Mover. Hence we need not go to infinity.

Reply Obj. 4. It is the part of man to prepare his soul, since he does this by his free choice. And yet he does not do this without the help of God moving him, and drawing him to Himself, as was said above.

[1] Sect. 10 (PG 3, 708).

ARTICLE 7. *Whether Man Can Rise from Sin Without the Help of Grace?*

We proceed thus to the Seventh Article: It would seem that man can rise from sin without the help of grace.

Objection 1. For what is presupposed to grace takes place without grace. But to rise from sin is presupposed to the enlightenment of grace, since it is written (Eph. 5. 14): *Arise from the dead and Christ shall enlighten thee.* Therefore man can rise from sin without grace.

Obj. 2. Further, sin is opposed to virtue as illness to health, as stated above (Q. LXXI, A. 1, REPLY 3). Now, man, by the power of his nature, can rise from illness to health without the external help of medicine, since there still remains in him the principle of life, from which the natural operation proceeds. Hence it seems that, with equal reason, man may be restored by himself, and return from the state of sin to the state of justice without the help of external grace.

Obj. 3. Further, every natural thing can return by itself to the act befitting its nature, as hot water returns by itself to its natural coldness, and a stone cast upwards returns by itself to its natural movement. Now a sin is an act against nature, as is clear from Damascene (*De Fide Orthod.* ii, 30).[1] Hence it seems that man by himself can return from sin to the state of justice.

On the contrary, The Apostle says (Gal. 2. 21; cf. 3. 21): *For if there had been a law given which could give life—then Christ died in vain,* that is, to no purpose. Hence with equal reason if man has a nature by which he can be justified, *Christ died in vain,* that is, to no purpose. But this cannot fittingly be said. Therefore by himself he cannot be justified, that is, he cannot return from a state of sin to a state of justice.

I answer that, Man by himself can in no way rise from sin without the help of grace. For since sin is transient as to the act and abiding in its guilt, as stated above (Q. LXXXVII, A. 6), to rise from sin is not the same as to cease the act of sin; but to rise from sin means that man has restored to him what he lost by sinning. Now man incurs a triple loss by sinning, as was clearly shown above (Q. LXXXV, A. 1; Q. LXXXVI, A. 1; Q. LXXXVII, A. 1), namely, stain, corruption of natural good, and debt of punishment. He incurs a stain because he forfeits the lustre of grace through the deformity of sin.

[1] PG 94, 976; II, 4; IV, 20 (PG 94, 876, 1196).

Natural good is corrupted, because man's nature is disordered by man's will not being subject to God's; and this order being overthrown, the consequence is that the whole nature of sinful man remains disordered. Lastly, there is the debt of punishment, since by sinning man deserves everlasting damnation.

Now it is manifest that none of these three can be restored except by God. For since the lustre of grace springs from the shedding of Divine light, this lustre cannot be brought back, unless God sheds His light anew; hence a habitual gift is necessary, and this is the light of grace. Likewise, the order of nature can only be restored, that is, man's will can only be subject to God, when God draws man's will to Himself, as stated above (A. 6). So, too, the guilt of eternal punishment can be remitted by God alone, against Whom the offence was committed and Who is man's Judge. And thus in order that man rise from sin there is required the help of grace, both as regards a habitual gift, and as regards the internal motion of God.

Reply Obj. 1. To man is bidden that which pertains to the act of free choice, as this act is required in order that man should rise from sin. Hence when it is said, *Arise, and Christ shall enlighten thee,* we are not to think that the complete rising from sin precedes the enlightenment of grace; but that when man by his free choice, moved by God, strives to rise from sin, he receives the light of justifying grace.

Reply Obj. 2. The natural reason is not the sufficient principle of the health that is in man by justifying grace. This principle is grace which is taken away by sin. Hence man cannot be restored by himself, but he requires the light of grace to be poured upon him anew, as if the soul were infused into a dead body for its resurrection.

Reply Obj. 3. When nature is perfect, it can be restored by itself to its befitting and proportionate condition; but without exterior help it cannot be restored to what surpasses its measure. And thus human nature undone by reason of the act of sin, remains no longer whole, but corrupted, as stated above; nor can it be restored, by itself, to its natural good, much less to the supernatural good of justice.

ARTICLE 8. *Whether Man Without Grace Can Avoid Sin?*

We proceed thus to the Eighth Article: It would seem that without grace man can avoid sin.

Objection 1. For "no one sins in what he cannot avoid," as Augustine says (*De Duab. Anim.* x, xi; *De Libero Arbit.* iii, 18).[1] Hence if a man in mortal sin cannot avoid sin, it would seem that in sinning he does not sin, which is unreasonable.

Obj. 2. Further, men are corrected that they may not sin. If therefore a man in mortal sin cannot avoid sin, correction would seem to be given to no purpose, which is not admissible.

Obj. 3. Further, it is written (Ecclus. 15. 18): *Before man is life and death, good and evil; that which he shall choose shall be given him.* But by sinning no one ceases to be a man. Hence it is still in his power to choose good or evil, and thus man can avoid sin without grace.

On the contrary, Augustine says (*De Perfect. Just.* xxi):[2] "Whoever denies that we ought to say the prayer 'Lead us not into temptation' (and they deny it who maintain that the help of God's grace is not necessary to man for salvation, but that the gift of the law is enough for the human will) ought without doubt to be removed beyond all hearing, and to be anathematized by the tongues of all."

I answer that, We may speak of man in two ways: first, in the state of whole nature, secondly, in the state of corrupted nature. Now in the state of whole nature, man, without habitual grace, could avoid sinning either mortally or venially, since to sin is nothing else than to stray from what is according to our nature—and in the state of integral nature man could avoid this. Nevertheless he could not have done it without God's help to uphold him in good, since if this had been withdrawn, even his nature would have fallen back into nothingness.

But in the state of corrupt nature man needs grace to heal his nature in order that he may entirely abstain from sin. And in the present life this healing is wrought in the mind—the carnal appetite being not yet restored. Hence the Apostle (Rom. 7. 25) says in the person of one who is restored: *I myself, with the mind, serve the law of God, but with the flesh, the law of sin.* And in this state man can abstain from all mortal sin, which has its seat in his reason, as stated above (Q. LXXIV, A. 5); but man cannot abstain from all venial sin on account of the corruption of his lower appetite of sensuality. For the reason can, indeed, repress each of its movements (and hence they are sinful and voluntary), but not all, because whilst it is resisting one, another may arise,

and also because the reason is not always alert to avoid these movements, as was said above (Q. LXXIV, A. 3, REPLY 2).

So, too, before man's reason, where mortal sin is, is restored by justifying grace, he can avoid each mortal sin, and for a time, since it is not necessary that he should be always actually sinning. But it cannot be that he remains for a long time without mortal sin. Hence Gregory says (*Super Ezech. Hom.* ii)[3] that "a sin not at once taken away by repentance, by its weight drags us down to other sins"; and this because, as the lower appetite ought to be subject to the reason, so should the reason be subject to God, and should place in Him the end of its will. Now it is by the end that all human acts ought to be regulated, even as it is by the judgment of the reason that the movements of the lower appetite should be regulated. And thus, even as inordinate movements of the sensitive appetite cannot help occurring, since the lower appetite is not subject to reason, so likewise, since man's reason is not entirely subject to God, the consequence is that many disorders occur in the reason. For when man's heart is not so fixed on God as to be unwilling to be parted from Him for the sake of finding any good or avoiding any evil, many things happen for the achieving or avoiding of which a man strays from God and breaks His commandments, and thus sins mortally, especially since, when surprised, a man acts according to his preconceived end and his pre-existing habits, as the Philosopher says,[4] although with premeditation of his reason a man may do something outside the order of his preconceived end and the inclination of his habit. But because a man cannot always have this premeditation, it cannot help occurring that he acts in accordance with his will turned aside from God, unless, by grace, he is quickly brought back to the due order.

Reply Obj. 1. Man can avoid each but not every act of sin, except by grace, as stated above. Nevertheless, since it is by his own shortcoming that he does not prepare himself to have grace, the fact that he cannot avoid sin without grace does not excuse him from sin.

Reply Obj. 2. Correction is useful "in order that out of the sorrow of correction may spring the will to be regenerate; if indeed he who is corrected is a son of promise, in such sort that whilst the noise of correction is outwardly resounding and punishing, God by hidden inspirations is inwardly causing him to will," as

---

[1] PL 42, 103, 105; PL 32, 1295.
[2] PL 44, 317.
[3] Bk. I (PL 76, 915).   [4] *Ethics*, III, 8 (1117ª18).

Augustine says (*De Corr. et Gratia*).[1] Correction is therefore necessary, from the fact that man's will is required in order to abstain from sin; yet it is not sufficient without God's help. Hence it is written (Ecclus. 7. 14): *Consider the works of God that no man can correct whom He hath despised.*

Reply Obj. 3. As Augustine says (*Hypognostic.* iii),[2] this saying is to be understood of man in the state of integral nature, when as yet he was not a slave of sin. Hence he was able to sin and not to sin. Now, too, whatever a man wills, is given to him. But that he wills good he has by God's assistance.

ARTICLE 9. *Whether One Who Has Already Obtained Grace, Can, Of Himself and Without Further Help of Grace, Do Good and Avoid Sin?*

We proceed thus to the Ninth Article: It would seem that whoever has already obtained grace, can by himself and without further help of grace, do good and avoid sin.

Objection 1. For a thing is useless or imperfect, if it does not fulfil what it was given for. Now grace is given to us that we may do good and keep from sin. Hence if with grace man cannot do this, it seems that grace is either useless or imperfect.

Obj. 2. Further, by grace the Holy Spirit dwells in us, according to I Cor. 3. 16: *Know you not that you are the temple of God, and that the Spirit of God dwelleth in you?* Now since the Spirit of God is omnipotent, He is sufficient to ensure our doing good and to keep us from sin. Hence a man who has obtained grace can do these things without any further assistance of grace.

Obj. 3. Further, if a man who has obtained grace needs further aid of grace in order to live rightly and to keep from sin, with equal reason will he need yet another grace, even though he has obtained this first help of grace. Therefore we must go on to infinity, which is unreasonable. Hence whoever is in grace needs no further help of grace in order to do well and to keep from sin.

On the contrary, Augustine says (*De Natura et Gratia*, xxvi)[3] that "as the eye of the body though most healthy cannot see unless it is helped by the brightness of light, so, neither can a man, even if he is most justified, live rightly unless he be helped by the eternal light

[1] Chap. 1 (PL 44, 921).
[2] Among the spurious works of Augustine (PL 45, 1621).
[3] PL 44, 261.

of justice." But justification is by grace, according to Rom. 3. 24: *Being justified freely by His grace.* Hence even a man who already possesses grace needs a further assistance of grace in order to live rightly.

I answer that, As stated above (AA. 2, 3, 6), in order to live rightly a man needs a twofold help of God—first, a habitual gift whereby corrupted human nature is healed, and after being healed is lifted up so as to work deeds meritorious of everlasting life, which exceed the proportion of nature. Secondly, man needs the help of grace in order to be moved by God to act.

Now with regard to the first kind of help, man in the state of grace does not need a further help of grace, a further infused habit, as it were. Yet he needs the help of grace in another way, that is, in order to be moved by God to act rightly, and this for two reasons: first, for the general reason that no created thing can put forth any act, unless by virtue of the Divine motion. Secondly, for this special reason—the condition of the state of human nature. For although healed by grace as to the mind, yet it remains corrupted and poisoned in the flesh, whereby it serves *the law of sin,* Rom. 7. 25. In the intellect, too, there remains the darkness of ignorance, according to which, as is written (Rom. 8. 26): *We know not what we should pray for as we ought;* since on account of the various turns of circumstances, and because we do not know ourselves perfectly, we cannot fully know what is for our good, according to Wisd. 9. 14: *For the thoughts of mortal men are fearful and our counsels uncertain.* Hence we must be guided and guarded by God, Who knows and can do all things. For this reason also it is fitting in those who have been born again as sons of God, to say: *Lead us not into temptation,* and *Thy Will be done on earth as it is in heaven,* and whatever else is contained in the Lord's Prayer pertaining to this.

Reply Obj. 1. The gift of habitual grace is not given to us for the reason that we may no longer need the Divine help, for every creature needs to be preserved in the good received from Him. Hence if after having received grace man still needs the Divine help, it cannot be concluded that grace is given to no purpose, or that it is imperfect, since man will need the Divine help even in the state of glory, when grace shall be fully perfected. But here grace is to some extent imperfect, in so far as it does not completely heal man, as stated above.

Reply Obj. 2. The operation of the Holy Ghost, which moves and protects us, is not circumscribed by the effect of habitual grace which it causes in us; but beyond this effect He, together with the Father and the Son, moves and protects us.

Reply Obj. 3. This argument merely proves that man needs no further habitual grace.

ARTICLE 10. *Whether Man Possessed of Grace Needs the Help of Grace in Order to Persevere?*

We proceed thus to the Tenth Article: It would seem that man possessed of grace needs no help of grace to persevere.

Objection 1. For perseverance is something less than virtue, even as continence is, as is clear from the Philosopher.[1] Now since man is justified by grace, he needs no further help of grace in order to have the virtues. Much less, therefore, does he need the help of grace to have perseverance.

Obj. 2. Further, all the virtues are infused at once. But perseverance is put down as a virtue. Hence it seems that, together with grace, perseverance is given to the other infused virtues.

Obj. 3. Further, as the Apostle says (Rom. 5. 20) more was restored to man by Christ's gift than he had lost by Adam's sin. But Adam received what enabled him to persevere; and thus man does not need grace in order to persevere.

On the contrary, Augustine says (*De Persev.* ii):[2] "Why is perseverance besought of God, if it is not bestowed by God? For is it not a mocking request to seek what we know He does not give, and what is in our power without His giving it?" Now perseverance is sought even by those who are hallowed by grace; and this is seen, when we say *Hallowed be Thy name,* which Augustine confirms by the words of Cyprian (*De Correp. et Grat.* vi).[3] Hence man, even when possessed of grace, needs perseverance to be given to him by God.

I answer that, Perseverance is taken in three ways. First, to signify a habit of the mind whereby a man stands steadfastly, lest he be moved by the assault of sadness from what is virtuous. And thus perseverance is to sadness as continence is to concupiscence and pleasure, as the Philosopher says.[4] Secondly, perseverance may be called a habit whereby a man has

the purpose of persevering in good to the end. And in both these ways perseverance is infused together with grace, even as continence and the other virtues are. Thirdly, perseverance is called the abiding in good to the end of life. And in order to have this perseverance man does not, indeed, need another habitual grace, but he needs the Divine assistance guiding and guarding him against the attacks of temptations, as appears from the preceding article. And hence after anyone has been justified by grace, he still needs to beseech God for this gift of perseverance, that he may be kept from evil till the end of his life. For to many grace is given to whom perseverance in grace is not given.

Reply Obj. 1. This objection regards the first mode of perseverance, as the second objection regards the second.

Hence the solution of the second objection is clear.

Reply Obj. 3. As Augustine says (*De Natura et Gratia*),[5] "in the original state man received a gift whereby he could persevere, but to persevere was not given him. But now, by the grace of Christ, many receive both the gift of grace whereby they may persevere, and the further gift of persevering," and thus Christ's gift is greater than Adam's fault. Nevertheless it was easier for man to persevere with the gift of grace in the state of innocence in which the flesh was not rebellious against the spirit, than it is now. For the restoration by Christ's grace, although it is already begun in the mind, is not yet completed in the flesh, as it will be in heaven, where man will not merely be able to persevere but will be unable to sin.

QUESTION CX
OF THE GRACE OF GOD AS REGARDS ITS ESSENCE
(In Four Articles)

WE must now consider the grace of God as regards its essence; and under this head there are four points of inquiry: (1) Whether grace implies something in the soul? (2) Whether grace is a quality? (3) Whether grace differs from infused virtue? (4) Of the subject of grace.

ARTICLE 1. *Whether Grace Implies Anything in the Soul?*

We proceed thus to the First Article: It would seem that grace does not imply anything in the soul.

[1] *Ethics,* VII, 1, 9 (1145^{b}1; 1151^{b}32).
[2] PL 45, 996.
[3] PL 44, 992; *De Dono Persev.,* 2 (PL 45, 996).
[4] *Ethics,* VII, 7 (1150^{a}13).

[5] Cf. *De Correp. et Grat.,* XII (PL 44, 937).

Objection 1. For man is said to have the grace of God even as the grace of man. Hence it is written (Gen. 39. 21) that the Lord gave to Joseph *grace* (Douay,—*favour*) *in the sight of the chief keeper of the prison.* Now when we say that a man has the favour of another, nothing is implied in him who has the favour of the other, but an acceptance is implied in him whose favour he has. Hence when we say that a man has the grace of God, nothing is implied in his soul, but we merely signify the Divine acceptance.

Obj. 2. Further, as the soul quickens the body so does God quicken the soul; hence it is written (Deut. 30. 20): *He is thy life.* Now the soul quickens the body immediately. Therefore nothing can come as a medium between God and the soul. Hence grace implies nothing created in the soul.

Obj. 3. Further, on Rom. 1. 7, *Grace to you and peace,* the gloss says:[1] "Grace, that is, the remission of sins." Now the remission of sin implies nothing in the soul, but only in God, Who does not impute the sin, according to Ps. 31, 2: *Blessed is the man to whom the Lord hath not imputed sin.* Hence neither does grace imply anything in the soul.

On the contrary, Light implies something in what is enlightened. But grace is a light of the soul; hence Augustine says (*De Natura et Gratia,* xxii):[2] "The light of truth rightly deserts the prevaricator of the law, and those who have been thus deserted become blind." Therefore grace implies something in the soul.

I answer that, According to the common manner of speech, grace is usually taken in three ways, First, for anyone's love, as we are accustomed to say that the soldier is in the good graces of the king, that is, the king looks on him with favour. Secondly, it is taken for any gift freely bestowed, as we are accustomed to say: I do you this act of grace. Thirdly, it is taken for the recompense of a gift given gratis, according to which we are said to be "grateful" for benefits. Of these three the second depends on the first, since one bestows something on another gratis from the love with which he receives him into his good "graces." And from the second proceeds the third, since from benefits bestowed gratis arises "gratitude."

Now as regards the last two, it is clear that grace implies something in him who receives grace: first, the gift given gratis; secondly, the acknowledgement of the gift. But as regards

the first, a difference must be noted between the grace of God and the grace of man; for since the creature's good springs from the Divine will, therefore from God's love, by which He wishes the good of the creature, some good flows into the creature. On the other hand, the will of man is moved by the good pre-existing in things, and hence man's love does not wholly cause the good of the thing, but pre-supposes it either in part or wholly. Therefore it is clear that every love of God is followed at some time by a good caused in the creature, but not co-eternal with the eternal love. And according to this difference of good the love of God to the creature is looked at differently. For one is common, by which He loves *all things that are* (Wisd. 11. 25), and thereby gives things their natural being. But the second is a special love, by which He draws the rational creature above the condition of its nature to a participation of the Divine good; and according to this love He is said to love anyone absolutely, since it is by this love that God absolutely wishes the eternal good, which is Himself, for the creature.

Accordingly when a man is said to have the grace of God, there is signified something bestowed on man by God. Nevertheless the grace of God sometimes signifies God's eternal love, and then we speak of the grace of predestination, since God gratuitously and not from merits predestines or elects some; for it is written (Eph. 1. 5): He *hath predestinated us into the adoption of children . . . unto the praise of the glory of His grace.*

Reply Obj. 1. Even when a man is said to be in another's good graces, it is understood that there is something in him pleasing to the other; even as anyone is said to have God's grace—with this difference, that what is pleasing to a man in another is presupposed to his love, but whatever is pleasing to God in a man is caused by the Divine love, as was said above.

Reply Obj. 2. God is the life of the soul after the manner of an efficient cause; but the soul is the life of the body after the manner of a formal cause. Now there is no medium between form and matter, since the form, of itself, informs the matter or subject; but the agent informs the subject not by its substance, but by the form which it causes in the matter.

Reply Obj. 3. Augustine says (*Retract.* i, 25):[3] "When I said that grace was for the remission of sins, and peace for our reconciliation with God, you must not take it to mean that peace and reconciliation do not pertain to gen-

[1] *Glossa interl.* (VI, 4r); *Glossa* Lombardi (PL 191, 1316).
[2] PL 44, 258.
[3] PL 32, 624.

eral grace, but that the special name of grace signifies the remission of sins." Not only grace, therefore, but many other of God's gifts pertain to grace. And hence the remission of sins does not take place without some effect divinely caused in us, as will appear later (Q. CXIII, A. 2).

ARTICLE 2. Whether Grace Is a Quality of the Soul?

We proceed thus to the Second Article: It would seem that grace is not a quality of the soul.

Objection 1. For no quality acts on its subject, since the action of a quality is not apart from the action of its subject, and thus the subject would necessarily act upon itself. But grace acts upon the soul, by justifying it. Therefore grace is not a quality.

Obj. 2. Furthermore, substance is nobler than quality. But grace is nobler than the nature of the soul, since we can do many things by grace to which nature is not equal, as stated above (Q. CIX, AA. 1, 2, 3). Therefore grace is not a quality.

Obj. 3. Furthermore, no quality remains after it has ceased to be in its subject. But grace remains, since it is not corrupted, for thus it would be reduced to nothing, just as it was created from nothing; hence it is called a *new creature* (Gal. 6. 15).

On the contrary, on Ps. 103. 15, *That he may make the face cheerful with oil,* the gloss says:[1] "Grace is a certain beauty of soul, which wins the Divine love." But beauty of soul is a quality, even as beauty of body. Therefore grace is a quality.

I answer that, as stated above (A. 1), there is understood to be an effect of God's gratuitous will in whoever is said to have God's grace. Now it was stated (Q. CIX, AA. 1, 2, 5) that man is aided by God's gratuitous will in two ways: First, in so far as man's soul is moved by God to know or will or do something, and in this way the gratuitous effect in man is not a quality, but a movement of the soul; for "motion is the act of the mover in the moved," as is stated in the *Physics.*[2] Secondly, man is helped by God's gratuitous will, in so far as a habitual gift is infused by God into the soul; and this because it is not fitting that God should provide less for those whom His love calls to supernatural good, than for creatures whom

He loves that they may acquire natural good. Now He so provides for natural creatures that not merely does He move them to their natural acts, but He bestows upon them certain forms and powers, which are the principles of acts, in order that they may of themselves be inclined to these movements, and thus the movements whereby they are moved by God become natural and easy to creatures, according to Wisd. 8. 1: *she ... ordereth all things sweetly.* Much more therefore does He infuse into such as He moves towards the acquisition of supernatural good, certain forms or supernatural qualities whereby they may be moved by Him sweetly and promptly to acquire eternal good; and thus the gift of grace is a quality.

Reply Obj. 1. Grace, as a quality, is said to act upon the soul not after the manner of an efficient cause, but after the manner of a formal cause, as whiteness makes a thing white, and justice, just.

Reply Obj. 2. Every substance is either the nature of the thing of which it is the substance, or is a part of the nature, in the same way that matter and form are called substance. And because grace is above human nature, it cannot be a substance or a substantial form, but is an accidental form of the soul. Now what is substantially in God becomes accidental in the soul participating the Divine goodness, as is clear in the case of knowledge. And thus because the soul participates in the Divine goodness imperfectly, the participation of the Divine goodness, which is grace, has its being in the soul in a less perfect way than the soul subsists in itself. Nevertheless, in so far as it is the expression or participation of the Divine goodness, it is nobler than the nature of the soul, though not in its mode of being.

Reply Obj. 3. As Boëthius says,[3] the being of an accident is to inhere. Hence no accident is called being as if it had being, but because by it something is; hence it is said to belong to a being rather than to be a being.[4] And because to become and to be corrupted belong to what is, properly speaking no accident comes into being or is corrupted, but is said to come into being and to be corrupted according as its subject begins or ceases to be in act with this accident. And thus grace is also said to be created because men are created with reference to it, that is, are given a new being out of nothing, that is, not from merits, according to Eph. 2. 10, *created in Jesus Christ in good works.*

[1] *Glossa ordin.* (III, 240E); *Glossa* Lombardi (PL 191, 936).
[2] Aristotle, III, 3 (202ª13).
[3] Cf. Pseudo-Bede, *Sent.,* sect. 1, A (PL 90, 968).
[4] Aristotle, *Metaphysics,* VII, 1 (1028ª18).

ARTICLE 3. *Whether Grace Is the Same as Virtue?*

We proceed thus to the Third Article: It would seem that grace is the same as virtue.

Objection 1. For Augustine says (*De Spir. et Litt.* xiv)[1] that "operating grace is faith that worketh by charity." But faith that worketh by charity is a virtue. Therefore grace is a virtue.

Obj. 2. Further, what fits the definition, fits the defined. But the definitions of virtue given by saints and philosophers fit grace, since "it makes its subject good, and his work good,"[2] and "it is a good quality of the mind, whereby we live righteously," etc.[3] Therefore grace is virtue.

Obj. 3. Further, grace is a quality. Now it is clearly not in the fourth species of quality; namely, form, which is the abiding figure of things, since it does not belong to bodies. Nor is it in the third, since it is not a passion nor a passion-like quality, which is in the sensitive part of the soul, as is proved in the *Physics*;[4] grace itself, however, is principally in the mind. Nor is it in the second species, which is natural power or impotence, because grace is above nature and does not regard good and evil, as does natural power. Therefore it must be in the first species which is habit or disposition. Now habits of the mind are virtues, since even knowledge itself is a virtue after a manner, as stated above (Q. LVII, Q. LVI, A. 3; AA. 1, 2). Therefore grace is the same as virtue.

On the contrary, If grace is virtue, it would seem before all to be one of the three theological virtues. But grace is neither faith nor hope, for these can be without sanctifying grace. Nor is it charity, since "grace foreruns charity," as Augustine says in his book on the Predestination of the Saints (*De Dono Persev.* xvi).[5] Therefore grace is not virtue.

I answer that, Some held that grace and virtue were identical in essence, and differed only logically,—in the sense that we speak of grace in so far as it makes man pleasing to God, or is given gratuitously;—and of virtue in so far as it empowers us to act rightly. And the Master seems to have thought this (*Sent.* ii, D. 27).[6]

But if anyone rightly considers the nature of virtue, this cannot hold, since, as the Philosopher says,[7] "virtue is a disposition of what is perfect,—and I call perfect what is disposed according to its nature." Now from this it is clear that the virtue of a thing has reference to some pre-existing nature, from the fact that everything is disposed with reference to what befits its nature. But it is manifest that the virtues acquired by human acts of which we spoke above (Q. LV.) are dispositions whereby a man is fittingly disposed with reference to the nature by which he is a man; infused virtues however dispose man in a higher manner and towards a higher end, and consequently in relation to some higher nature, that is, in relation to a participation of the Divine Nature, according to II Pet. 1. 4: *He hath given us most great and most precious promises; that by these you may be made partakers of the Divine Nature.* And it is in respect of receiving this nature that we are said to be born again sons of God.

And thus, even as the natural light of reason is something besides the acquired virtues, which are spoken of in relation to this natural light, so also the light of grace which is a participation of the Divine Nature is something besides the infused virtues which are derived from and are ordered to this light; hence the Apostle says (Eph. 5. 8): *For you were heretofore darkness, but now light in the Lord. Walk then as children of the light.* For as the acquired virtues enable a man to walk in accordance with the natural light of reason, so do the infused virtues enable a man to walk as befits the light of grace.

Reply Obj. 1. Augustine calls *faith that worketh by charity* grace since the act of faith of him that worketh by charity is the first act by which sanctifying grace is manifested.

Reply Obj. 2. Good is placed in the definition of virtue with reference to its fitness with some pre-existing nature essential or participated. Now good is not attributed to grace in this manner, but as to the root of goodness in man, as stated above.

Reply Obj. 3. Grace is reduced to the first species of quality; and yet it is not the same as virtue, but is a certain disposition which is presupposed to the infused virtues, as their principle and root.

---

[1] PL 44, 217; chap. XXXII (PL 44, 237); cf. Peter Lombard, *Sent.*, II, d. 26, chap. 4 (QR I, 440).

[2] Cf. Aristotle, *Ethics*, II, 6 (1106ª15).

[3] Cf. above, Q. LV, A. 4.   [4] Aristotle, VII, 3 (245ᵇ3).

[5] PL 45, 1018.

[6] Peter Lombard (QR I, 447); cf. Bonaventure, *In Sent.*, II, d. 27, A. 1, Q. 2 (QR II, 657).

ARTICLE 4. *Whether Grace Is in the Essence of the Soul, as in a Subject, or in One of the Powers?*

We proceed thus to the Fourth Article: It would seem that grace is not in the essence of

[7] *Physics*, VII, 3 (246ª13).

the soul, as in a subject, but in one of the powers.

Objection 1. For Augustine says (*Hypognost. iii*)[1] that grace is related to the will or to free choice "as a rider to his horse." Now the will, or free choice, is a power, as stated above (Part I, Q. LXXXIII, A. 2). Hence grace is in a power of the soul, as in a subject.

Obj. 2. Further, "Man's merit springs from grace," as Augustine says (*De Gratia et Lib. Arbit.* vi).[2] Now merit consists in acts, which proceed from a power. Hence it seems that grace is a perfection of a power of the soul.

Obj. 3. Further, if the essence of the soul is the proper subject of grace, the soul, since it has an essence, must be capable of grace. But this is false, since it would follow that every soul would be capable of grace. Therefore the essence of the soul is not the proper subject of grace.

Obj. 4. Further, the essence of the soul is prior to its powers. Now what is prior may be understood without what is posterior. Hence it follows that grace may be taken to be in the soul, although we suppose no part or power of the soul—namely, neither the will, nor the intellect, nor anything else; which is impossible.

On the contrary, By grace we are born again sons of God. But generation terminates at the essence prior to the powers. Therefore grace is in the soul's essence prior to being in the powers.

I answer that, This question depends on the preceding. For if grace is the same as virtue, it must necessarily be in the powers of the soul as in a subject, since the soul's powers are the proper subject of virtue as stated above (Q. LVI, A. 1). But if grace differs from virtue, it cannot be said that a power of the soul is the subject of grace, since every perfection of the soul's powers has the nature of virtue, as stated above (Q. LV, A. 1; Q. LVI, A. 1). Hence it remains that grace, just as it is prior to virtue, so also it has a subject prior to the powers of the soul, so that, namely, it is in the essence of the soul. For as man in his intellectual power participates in the Divine knowledge through the virtue of faith, and in his power of will participates in the Divine love through the virtue of charity, so also in the nature of the soul does he participate in the Divine Nature, after the manner of a likeness, through a certain regeneration or re-creation.

Reply Obj. 1. As from the essence of the soul

flow its powers, which are the principles of deeds, so likewise the virtues, whereby the powers are moved to act, flow into the powers of the soul from grace. And thus grace is compared to the will as the mover to the moved, which is the same comparison as that of a horseman to the horse—but not as an accident to a subject.

And from this is made clear the *Reply to the second objection.* For grace is the principle of meritorious works through the medium of virtues, just as the essence of the soul is the principle of vital deeds through the medium of the powers.

Reply Obj. 3. The soul is the subject of grace as being in the species of intellectual or rational nature. But the soul is not classed in a species by any of its powers, since the powers are natural properties of the soul following upon the species. Hence the soul differs specifically in its essence from other souls, namely, of dumb animals and of plants. Consequently it does not follow that if the essence of the human soul is the subject of grace every soul may be the subject of grace, since it belongs to the essence of the soul, because it is of such a species.

Reply Obj. 4. Since the powers of the soul are natural properties following upon the species, the soul cannot be without them. Yet, granted that it was without them, the soul would still be called intellectual or rational in its species, not that it would actually have these powers, but on account of the species of such an essence, from which these powers naturally flow.

QUESTION CXI
Of the division of grace
(*In Five Articles*)

WE must now consider the division of grace, under which head there are five points of inquiry: (1) Whether grace is fittingly divided into gratuitous grace and sanctifying grace? (2) Of the division into operating and co-operating grace. (3) Of the division of it into prevenient and subsequent grace. (4) Of the division of gratuitous grace. (5) Of the comparison between sanctifying and gratuitous grace.

ARTICLE 1. *Whether Grace Is Fittingly Divided into Sanctifying Grace and Gratuitous Grace?*

We proceed thus to the First Article: It would seem that grace is not fittingly divided into sanctifying grace and gratuitous grace.

Objection 1. For grace is a gift of God, as is

---

[1] Contained among the works of Augustine (PL 45, 1632).

[2] PL 44, 889.

clear from what has been already stated (Q. CX,
A. I). But man is not therefore pleasing to God
because something is given him by God, but
rather on the contrary, since something is freely
given by God, because man is pleasing to Him.
Hence there is no sanctifying grace.

Obj. 2. Further, whatever is not given on account of preceding merits is given gratis. Now
even natural good is given to man without preceding merit, since nature is presupposed to
merit. Therefore nature itself is given gratuitously by God. But nature is divided against
grace. Therefore to be gratuitously given is not
fittingly set down as a difference of grace, since
it is found outside the genus of grace.

Obj. 3. Further, members of a division are
mutually opposed. But even sanctifying grace,
by which we are justified, is given to us gratuitously, according to Rom. 3. 24: *Being justified
freely (gratis) by His grace.* Hence sanctifying
grace ought not to be divided against gratuitous
grace.

On the contrary, The Apostle attributes both
to grace, namely, to sanctify and to be gratuitously given. For with regard to the first he says
(Eph. 1. 6): *He hath graced us in His beloved
Son.* And with regard to the second (Rom. 2. 6):
*And if by grace, it is not now by works, other-
wise grace is no more grace.* Therefore grace can
be distinguished by its having one only or both.

I answer that, As the Apostle says (Rom. 13.
1), *those things that are of God are well ordered*
(Vulg.,—*those that are, are ordained by God*).
Now the order of things consists in this, that
things are led to God by other things, as Dionysius says (*Cæl. Hier.* iv).[1] And hence since grace
is ordained to lead men to God, this takes place
in a certain order, so that some are led to God
by others.

And thus there is a twofold grace: one whereby man himself is united to God, and this is
called sanctifying grace; the other is that whereby one man co-operates with another in leading
him to God, and this gift is called gratuitous
grace, since it is bestowed on a man beyond the
capability of nature, and beyond the merit
of the person. But whereas it is bestowed on a
man not to justify him, but rather that he may
co-operate in the justification of another, it is
not called sanctifying grace. And it is of this
that the Apostle says (I Cor. 12. 7): *And the
manifestation of the Spirit is given to every
man unto utility,* that is, of others.

Reply Obj. 1. Grace is said to make pleasing,
not efficiently, but formally, that is, because

[1] Sect. 3 (PG 3, 181).

thereby a man is justified, and is made worthy
to be called pleasing to God, according to Col.
1. 21. He *hath made us worthy to be made partakers of the lot of the saints in light.*

Reply Obj. 2. Grace, according as it is gratuitously given, excludes the notion of debt. Now
debt may be taken in two ways: first, as arising
from merit; and this regards the person who
does meritorious works, according to Rom. 4.
4: *Now to him that worketh, the reward is
not reckoned according to grace, but according
to debt.* The second debt regards the condition
of nature. Thus we say it is due to a man to have
reason, and whatever else belongs to human nature. Yet in neither way is debt taken to mean
that God is under an obligation to His creature,
but rather that the creature ought to be subject
to God, that the Divine ordination may be fulfilled in it, which is that a certain nature should
have certain conditions or properties, and that
by doing certain works it should attain to something further. And hence natural endowments
are not a debt in the first sense but in the second.
But supernatural gifts are due in neither sense.
Hence they especially merit the name of grace.

Reply Obj. 3. Sanctifying grace adds to the
notion of gratuitous grace something pertaining
to the nature of grace, since it makes man pleasing to God. And hence gratuitous grace which
does not do this keeps the common name, as
happens in many other cases; and thus the two
parts of the division are opposed as sanctifying
and non-sanctifying grace.

ARTICLE 2. *Whether Grace Is Fittingly Divided
into Operating and Co-Operating Grace?*

We proceed thus to the Second Article: It
would seem that grace is not fittingly divided
into operating and co-operating grace.

Objection 1. For grace is an accident, as stated
above (Q. CX, A. 2, REPLY 2). Now no accident
can act upon its subject. Therefore no grace
can be called operating.

Obj. 2. Further, if grace operates anything in
us it especially brings about justification. But
not only grace works this. For Augustine, on
John 14. 12, *the works that I do he also shall
do,* says (*Serm.* clxix):[2] "He Who created thee
without thyself will not justify thee without
thyself." Therefore no grace ought to be called
absolutely operating.

Obj. 3. Further, to co-operate seems to pertain to the inferior agent, and not to the principal agent. But grace works in us more than free
choice, according to Rom. 9, 16: *It is not of him*

[2] Chap. 11 (PL 38, 923).

that willeth, nor of him that runneth, but of God that sheweth mercy. Therefore no grace ought to be called co-operating.

Obj. 4. Further, division ought to rest on opposition. But to operate and to co-operate are not opposed; for one and the same thing can both operate and co-operate. Therefore grace is not fittingly divided into operating and co-operating.

On the contrary, Augustine says (*De Gratia et Lib. Arbit.* xvii):[1] "God by co-operating with us, perfects what He began by operating in us, since He who perfects by co-operation with such as are willing begins by operating that they may will." But the operations of God whereby He moves us to good pertain to grace. Therefore grace is fittingly divided into operating and co-operating.

I answer that, As stated above (Q. CIX, AA. 2, 3, 6, 9; Q. CX, A. 2) grace may be taken in two ways: first, as a Divine help, whereby God moves us to will and to act; secondly, as a habitual gift divinely bestowed on us.

Now in both these ways grace is fittingly divided into operating and co-operating. For the operation of an effect is not attributed to the thing moved but to the mover. Hence in that effect in which our mind is moved and does not move, but in which God is the sole mover, the operation is attributed to God, and it is with reference to this that we speak of operating grace. But in that effect in which our mind both moves and is moved, the operation is not only attributed to God, but also to the soul; and it is with reference to this that we speak of co-operating grace.

Now there is a twofold act in us. First, there is the interior act of the will, and with regard to this act the will is a thing moved, and God is the mover; and especially when the will which hitherto willed evil begins to will good. And hence, according as God moves the human mind to this act, we speak of operating grace. But there is another, exterior act; and since it is commanded by the will, as was shown above (Q. XVII, A. 9) the operation of this act is attributed to the will. And because God assists us in this act, both by strengthening our will interiorly so as to attain to the act, and by granting outwardly the capability of operating, it is with respect to this that we speak of co-operating grace. Hence after the aforesaid words Augustine adds: "He operates that we may will; and when we will, He co-operates that we may perfect." And thus if grace is taken for God's gratuitous

[1] PL 44, 901.

motion whereby He moves us to meritorious good, it is fittingly divided into operating and co-operating grace.

But if grace is taken for the habitual gift, then again there is a double effect of grace, even as of every other form, the first of which is being, and the second, operation; thus the work of heat is to make its subject hot, and to give heat outwardly. And thus habitual grace in so far as it heals and justifies the soul, or makes it pleasing to God, is called operating grace; but in so far as it is the principle of meritorious works, which spring from the free choice, it is called co-operating grace.

Reply Obj. 1. According as grace is a certain accidental quality, it does not act upon the soul efficiently, but formally, just as whiteness is said to make a surface white.

Reply Obj. 2. God does not justify us without ourselves, because whilst we are being justified we consent to God's justice by a movement of our free choice. Nevertheless this movement is not the cause of grace, but the effect; hence the whole operation pertains to grace.

Reply Obj. 3. One thing is said to co-operate with another not merely when it is a secondary agent under a principal agent, but when it helps to the end intended. Now man is helped by God to will the good, through the means of operating grace. And hence, the end being already presupposed, grace co-operates with us.

Reply Obj. 4. Operating and co-operating grace are the same grace, but are distinguished by their different effects, as is plain from what has been said.

ARTICLE 3. *Whether Grace Is Fittingly Divided into Prevenient and Subsequent Grace?*

We proceed thus to the Third Article: It would seem that grace is not fittingly divided into prevenient and subsequent.

Objection 1. For grace is an effect of the Divine love. But God's love is never subsequent, but always prevenient, according to I John 4. 10: *Not as though we had loved God, but because He hath first loved us.* Therefore grace ought not to be divided into prevenient and subsequent.

Obj. 2. Further, there is but one sanctifying grace in man, since it is sufficient, according to II Cor. 12. 9: *My Grace is sufficient for thee.* But the same thing cannot be before and after. Therefore grace is not fittingly divided into prevenient and subsequent.

Obj. 3. Further, grace is known by its effects. Now there are an infinite number of effects,—

one preceding another. Hence if with regard to these, grace must be divided into prevenient and subsequent, it would seem that there are infinite species of grace. Now no art takes note of the infinite in number. Hence grace is not fittingly divided into prevenient and subsequent.

On the contrary, God's grace is the outcome of His mercy. Now both are said in Ps. 58. 11: *His mercy shall prevent me,* and again, Ps. 22. 6: *Thy mercy will follow me.* Therefore grace is fittingly divided into prevenient and subsequent.

I answer that, As grace is divided into operating and co-operating, with regard to its various effects, so also is it divided into prevenient and subsequent, in whatever we consider grace. Now there are five effects of grace in us: of these, the first is, to heal the soul; the second, to desire good; the third, to carry into effect the good proposed; the fourth, to persevere in good; the fifth, to reach glory. And hence grace, according as it causes the first effect in us, is called prevenient with respect to the second, and according as it causes the second, it is called subsequent with respect to the first effect. And as one effect is posterior to this effect, and prior to that, so may grace be called prevenient and subsequent on account of the same effect viewed with respect to different others. And this is what Augustine says (*De Natura et Gratia,* xxxi):[1] "It precedes in order that we might be healed, it follows in order that, being healed, we might dwell in life; it precedes that we might be called, it follows that we might be glorified."

Reply Obj. 1. God's love signifies something eternal, and hence can never be called anything but prevenient. But grace signifies a temporal effect, which can precede and follow another; and thus grace may be both prevenient and subsequent.

Reply Obj. 2. The division into prevenient and subsequent grace does not divide grace in its essence, but only in its effects, as was already said of operating and co-operating grace. For subsequent grace, according as it pertains to glory, is not numerically distinct from prevenient grace whereby we are at present justified. For even as the charity of earth is not voided in heaven, so must the same be said of the light of grace, since the notion of neither implies imperfection.

Reply Obj. 3. Although the effects of grace may be infinite in number, even as human acts are infinite, nevertheless all are reduced to some of a determinate species, and moreover all coincide in this,—that one precedes another.

[1] PL 44, 264.

ARTICLE 4. *Whether Gratuitous Grace Is Rightly Divided by the Apostle?*

We proceed thus to the Fourth Article: It would seem that gratuitous grace is not rightly divided by the Apostle.

Objection 1. For every gift given to us by God may be called a gratuitous grace. Now there are an infinite number of gifts freely bestowed on us by God as regards both the good of the soul and the good of the body—and yet they do not make us pleasing to God. Hence gratuitous graces cannot be contained under any certain division.

Obj. 2. Further, gratuitous grace is distinguished from sanctifying grace. But faith pertains to sanctifying grace, since we are justified by it, according to Rom. 5. 1: *Being justified therefore by faith.* Hence it is not right to place faith amongst the gratuitous graces, especially since the other virtues are not so placed, as hope and charity.

Obj. 3. Further, the operation of healing, and speaking divers tongues are miracles. Again, the interpretation of speeches pertains either to wisdom or to knowledge, according to Dan. 1. 17: *And to these children God gave knowledge and understanding in every book and wisdom.* Hence it is not correct to divide the grace of healing and kinds of tongues against the working of miracles, and the interpretation of speeches against the word of wisdom and knowledge.

Obj. 4. Further, as wisdom and knowledge are gifts of the Holy Ghost, so also are understanding, counsel, piety, fortitude, and fear, as stated above (Q. LXVIII, A. 4). Therefore these also ought to be placed amongst the gratuitous gifts.

On the contrary, The Apostle says (I Cor. 12. 8, 9, 10): *To one indeed by the Spirit is given the word of wisdom; and to another the word of knowledge, according to the same Spirit, to another, the working of miracles; to another, prophecy; to another, the discerning of spirits; to another divers kinds of tongues; to another interpretation of speeches.*

I answer that, As was said above (A. 1), gratuitous grace is ordered to this, namely, that a man may help another to be led to God. Now no man can help in this by moving interiorly (for this belongs to God alone), but only exteriorly by teaching or persuading. Hence gratuitous grace embraces whatever a man needs in order to instruct another in Divine things which are above reason. Now for this three things are required. First, a man must possess the fulness of knowledge of Divine things, so as to be capable of teaching others. Secondly, he must be able to confirm or prove what he says, otherwise his words would have no weight. Thirdly, he must be capable of fittingly presenting to his hearers what he knows.

Now as regards the first, three things are necessary, as may be seen in human teaching. For whoever would teach another in any science must first be certain of the principles of the science, and with regard to this there is "faith," which is certitude of invisible things, the principles of Catholic doctrine. Secondly, the teacher must know the principal conclusions of the science, and hence we have "the word of wisdom," which is the knowledge of Divine things. Thirdly, he ought to abound with examples and a knowledge of effects, whereby at times he needs to manifest causes; and thus we have "the word of knowledge," which is the knowledge of human things, since *the invisible things of Him . . . are clearly seen, being understood by the things that are made* (Rom. 1. 20).

Now the confirmation of such things as are within reason rests upon arguments, but the confirmation of what is above reason rests on what is proper to the Divine power, and this in two ways. First when the teacher of sacred doctrine does what God alone can do, in miraculous deeds, whether with respect to bodily health— and thus there is "the grace of healing," or merely for the purpose of manifesting the Divine power; for instance, that the sun should stand still or darken, or that the sea should be divided—and thus there is "the working of miracles." Secondly when he can manifest what God alone can know, and these are either future contingents—and thus there is "prophecy," or also the secrets of hearts, and thus there is "the discerning of spirits."

But the capability of speaking can regard either the idiom in which a person can be understood, and thus there is "kinds of tongues"; or it can regard the sense of what is said, and thus there is "the interpretation of speeches."

Reply Obj. 1. As stated above (A. 1), not all the benefits divinely conferred upon us are called gratuitous graces, but only those that surpass the power of nature—for example, that a fisherman should be replete with the word of wisdom and of knowledge and the like. And such as these are here set down as gratuitous graces.

Reply Obj. 2. Faith is enumerated here under the gratuitous graces, not as a virtue justifying man in himself, but as implying a super-eminent certitude of faith, whereby a man is fitted for instructing others concerning such things as belong to the faith. With regard to hope and charity, they belong to the appetitive power, according as man is ordered by it to God.

Reply Obj. 3. The grace of healing is distinguished from the general working of miracles because it has a special reason for inducing one to the faith, since a man is all the more ready to believe when he has received the gift of bodily health through the virtue of faith. So, too, to speak with divers tongues and to interpret speeches have special efficacy in bestowing faith. Hence they are set down as special gratuitous graces.

Reply Obj. 4. Wisdom and knowledge are not numbered among the gratuitous graces in the same way as they are numbered among the gifts of the Holy Ghost, that is in so far as man's mind is rendered easily movable by the Holy Ghost to the things of wisdom and knowledge; for thus they are gifts of the Holy Ghost, as stated above (Q. LXVIII, AA. 1, 4). But they are numbered amongst the gratuitous graces in so far as they imply such a fulness of knowledge and wisdom that a man may not merely think rightly of Divine things, but may instruct others and overpower adversaries. Hence it is significant that it is "the word of wisdom" and "the word of knowledge" that are placed in the gratuitous graces, since, as Augustine says (*De Trin.* xiv, 1),[1] "It is one thing merely to know what a man must believe in order to reach everlasting life, and another thing to know how this may benefit the godly and may be defended against the ungodly."

ARTICLE 5. *Whether Gratuitous Grace is Nobler Than Sanctifying Grace?*

We proceed thus to the Fifth Article: It would seem that gratuitous grace is nobler than sanctifying grace.

Objection 1. For the "people's good is better than the individual good," as the Philosopher says.[2] Now sanctifying grace is ordered to the good of one man alone, while gratuitous grace is ordered to the common good of the whole Church, as stated above (AA. 1, 4). Hence gratuitous grace is nobler than sanctifying grace.

Obj. 2. Further, it is a greater power that is able to act upon another than that which is confined to itself, even as the brightness of the body that can illuminate other bodies is greater than of that which can only shine but cannot illuminate; and hence the Philosopher says[3] that "jus-

---

[1] PL 42, 1037. [2] *Ethics*, I, 2 (1094b8).
[3] *Ibid.*, V, 1 (1129b27).

tice is the most excellent of the virtues," since by it a man bears himself rightly towards others. But by sanctifying grace a man is perfected only in himself, while by gratuitous grace a man works for the perfection of others. Hence gratuitous grace is nobler than sanctifying grace.

Obj. 3. Further, what is proper to the best is nobler than what is common to all; thus to reason, which is proper to man, is nobler than to feel, which is common to all animals. Now sanctifying grace is common to all members of the Church, but gratuitous grace is the proper gift of the more exalted members of the Church. Hence gratuitous grace is nobler than sanctifying grace.

On the contrary, The Apostle (I Cor. 12. 31), having enumerated the gratuitous graces, adds: *And I shew unto you yet a more excellent way;* and as the sequel proves he is speaking of charity, which pertains to sanctifying grace. Hence sanctifying grace is more noble than gratuitous grace.

I answer that, The higher the good to which a virtue is ordered, the more excellent is the virtue. Now the end is always greater than the means. But sanctifying grace directs a man immediately to a union with his last end, whereas gratuitous grace directs a man to what is preparatory to the end; that is, by prophecy and miracles and so forth, men are induced to unite themselves to their last end. And hence sanctifying grace is nobler than gratuitous grace.

Reply Obj. 1. As the Philosopher says,[1] a multitude, as an army, has a twofold good. The first is in the multitude itself, namely, the order of the army; the second is separate from the multitude, namely, the good of the leader—and this is the better good, since the other is ordered to it. Now gratuitous grace is ordered to the common good of the Church, which is ecclesiastical order, while sanctifying grace is ordered to the separate common good, which is God. Hence sanctifying grace is the nobler.

Reply Obj. 2. If gratuitous grace could cause a man to have sanctifying grace, it would follow that gratuitous grace was the nobler, even as the brightness of the sun that enlightens is more excellent than that of an object that is lit up. But by gratuitous grace a man cannot cause another to have union with God, which he himself has by sanctifying grace; but he causes certain dispositions towards it. Hence gratuitous grace needs not to be the more excellent, even as in fire, the heat, manifesting its species whereby it acts to produce heat in other things, is not

[1] *Metaphysics,* XII, 10 (1075^{a}11).

more excellent than the substantial form of the fire itself.

Reply Obj. 3. Feeling is ordered to reason, as to an end, and thus, to reason is nobler. But here it is the contrary, for what is proper is ordered to what is common as to an end. Hence there is no comparison.

QUESTION CXII
OF THE CAUSE OF GRACE
(*In Five Articles*)

WE must now consider the cause of grace, and under this head there are five points of inquiry: (1) Whether God alone is the efficient cause of grace? (2) Whether any disposition towards grace is needed on the part of the recipient, by an act of free choice? (3) Whether such a disposition can make grace follow of necessity? (4) Whether grace is equal in all? (5) Whether anyone may know that he has grace?

ARTICLE 1. *Whether God Alone Is the Cause of Grace?*

We proceed thus to the First Article: It would seem that God alone is not the cause of grace.

Objection 1. For it is written (John 1. 17): *Grace and truth came by Jesus Christ.* Now, by the name Jesus Christ is understood not merely the Divine Nature assuming, but also the created nature assumed. Therefore a creature may be the cause of grace.

Obj. 2. Further, there is this difference between the sacraments of the New Law and those of the Old, that the sacraments of the New Law cause grace, whereas the sacraments of the Old Law merely signify it. Now the sacraments of the New Law are certain visible elements. Therefore God is not the only cause of grace.

Obj. 3. Further, according to Dionysius (*Cœl. Hier.* iii, iv, vii, viii),[2] "Angels cleanse, enlighten, and perfect both lesser angels and men." Now the rational creature is cleansed, enlightened, and perfected by grace. Therefore God is not the only cause of grace.

On the contrary, It is written (Ps. 83. 12): *The Lord will give grace and glory.*

I answer that, Nothing can act beyond its species, since the cause must always be more powerful than its effect. Now the gift of grace surpasses every capability of created nature, since it is nothing of a partaking of the Divine Nature, which exceeds every other nature. And

[2] PG 3, 165, 180, 209, 240.

thus it is impossible that any creature should cause grace. For it is as necessary that God alone should deify, bestowing a partaking of the Divine Nature by a participated likeness, as it is impossible that anything save fire should enkindle.

Reply Obj. 1. Christ's humanity is "an organ of His Godhead," as Damascene says (*De Fide Orthod.* iii, 19).[1] Now an instrument does not bring forth the action of the principal agent by its own power, but in virtue of the principal agent. Hence Christ's humanity does not cause grace by its own power, but by virtue of the Divine Nature joined to it, whereby the actions of Christ's humanity are saving actions.

Reply Obj. 2. As in the person of Christ the humanity causes our salvation by grace, the Divine power being the principal agent, so likewise in the sacraments of the New Law, which are derived from Christ, grace is instrumentally caused by the sacraments, and principally by the power of the Holy Ghost working in the sacraments, according to John 3. 5: *Unless a man be born again of water and the Holy Ghost he cannot enter into the kingdom of God.*

Reply Obj. 3. Angels cleanse, enlighten, and perfect angels or men, by instruction, and not by justifying them through grace. Hence Dionysius says (*Cæl. Hier.* vii)[2] that "this cleansing and enlightenment and perfecting is nothing else than the assumption of Divine knowledge."

ARTICLE 2. *Whether Any Preparation and Disposition for Grace Is Required on Man's Part?*

We proceed thus to the Second Article: It would seem that no preparation or disposition for grace is required on man's part.

Objection 1. For, as the Apostle says (Rom. 4. 4), *To him that worketh, the reward is not reckoned according to grace, but according to debt.* Now a man's preparation by free choice can only be through some operation. Hence it would do away with the notion of grace.

Obj. 2. Further, whoever is going on sinning is not preparing himself to have grace. But to some who are going on sinning grace is given, as is clear in the case of Paul, who received grace whilst he was *breathing out threatenings and slaughter against the disciples of the Lord* (Acts 9. 1). Hence no preparation for grace is required on man's part.

Obj. 3. Further, an agent of infinite power needs no disposition in matter, since it does not even require matter, as appears in creation, to

which grace is compared, which is called a *new creature* (Gal. 6. 15). But only God, Who has infinite power, causes grace, as stated above (A. 1). Hence no preparation is required on man's part to obtain grace.

On the contrary, It is written (Amos 4. 12): *Be prepared to meet thy God, O Israel,* and (I Kings 7. 3): *Prepare your hearts unto the Lord.*

I answer that, As stated above (Q. CXI, A. 2, 3, 6, 9; Q. CX, A. 2; Q. CXI, A. 2), grace is taken in two ways: Sometimes as a habitual gift of God; sometimes, as a help from God, Who moves the soul to good. Now taking grace in the first sense, a certain preparation of grace is required for it, since a form can only be in disposed matter. But if we speak of grace as it signifies a help from God to move us to good, that, as it were, anticipates the Divine help, but rather, every preparation in man must be by the help of God moving the soul to good. And thus even the good movement of free choice, whereby anyone is prepared for receiving the gift of grace is an act of free choice moved by God. And thus man is said to prepare himself, according to Prov. 16. 1. *It is the part of man to prepare the soul;* yet it is principally from God, Who moves free choice. Hence it is said that man's will is prepared by God, and that man's steps are guided by God.

Reply Obj. 1. A certain preparation of man for grace is simultaneous with the infusion of grace; and this operation is meritorious, not indeed of grace, which is already possessed,— but of glory which is not yet possessed. But there is another imperfect preparation, which sometimes precedes the gift of sanctifying grace, and yet it is from God's motion. But it does not suffice for merit, since man is not yet justified by grace, and merit can only arise from grace, as will be seen farther on (Q. CXIV, A. 2).

Reply Obj. 2. Since a man cannot prepare himself for grace unless God go before and move him to good, it is of no account whether anyone arrive at perfect preparation instantaneously, or step by step. For it is written (Ecclus. 11. 23): *It is easy in the eyes of God on a sudden to make the poor man rich.* Now it sometimes happens that God moves a man to good, but not perfect good, and this preparation precedes grace. But He sometimes moves him suddenly and perfectly to good, and man receives grace suddenly, according to John 6. 45: *Every one that hath heard of the Father, and hath learned, cometh to Me.* And thus it happened to Paul, since, suddenly when he was in the midst of sin,

---

[1] PG 94, 1080.   [2] Sect. 3 (PG 3 209).

his heart was perfectly moved by God to hear, to learn, to come; and hence he received grace suddenly.

Reply Obj. 3. An agent of infinite power needs no matter or disposition of matter, brought about by the action of another cause; and yet, looking to the condition of the thing caused, it must cause, in the thing caused, both the matter and the due disposition for the form. So likewise, when God infuses grace into a soul, no preparation is required which He Himself does not bring about.

ARTICLE 3. *Whether Grace is Necessarily Given to Whoever Prepares Himself for It, or to Whoever Does What He Can?*

We proceed thus to the Third Article: It would seem that grace is necessarily given to whoever prepares himself for grace, or to whoever does what he can.

Objection 1. For, on Rom. 5. 1, *Being justified ... by faith, let us have peace*, etc., the gloss says:[1] "God welcomes whoever flies to Him, otherwise there would be injustice with Him." But it is impossible for injustice to be with God. Therefore it is impossible for God not to welcome whoever flies to Him. Hence he receives grace of necessity.

Obj. 2. Further, Anselm says (*De Casu Diaboli.* iii)[2] that the reason why God does not bestow grace on the devil is that he did not wish, nor was he prepared, to receive it. But if the cause be removed, the effect must be removed also. Therefore, if anyone is willing to receive grace it is bestowed on them of necessity.

Obj. 3. Further, good shares itself, as appears from Dionysius (*Div. Nom.* iv).[3] Now the good of grace is better than the good of nature. Hence, since natural forms necessarily come to disposed matter, much more does it seem that grace is necessarily bestowed on whoever prepares himself for grace.

On the contrary, Man is compared to God as clay to the potter, according to Jer. 18. 6: *As clay is in the hand of the potter, so are you in My hand.* But however much the clay is prepared, it does not necessarily receive its shape from the potter. Hence, however much a man prepares himself, he does not necessarily receive grace from God.

I answer that, As stated above (A. 2), man's preparation for grace is from God, as Mover, and from free choice, as moved. Hence the preparation may be looked at in two ways. First, as it is from free choice, and thus there is no necessity that it should obtain grace, since the gift of grace exceeds every preparation of human power. But it may be considered, secondly, as it is from God the Mover, and thus it has a necessity—not indeed of coercion, but of infallibility—as regards what it is ordered to by God, since God's intention cannot fail, according to the saying of Augustine in his book on the Predestination of the Saints (*De Dono Persev.* xiv)[4] that "by God's good gifts whoever is liberated, is most certainly liberated." Hence if God intends, while moving, that the one whose heart He moves should attain to grace, he will infallibly attain to it, according to John 6. 45: *Every one that hath heard of the Father, and hath learned, cometh to Me.*

Reply Obj. 1. This gloss is speaking of such as fly to God by a meritorious act of their free choice, already informed with grace; for if they did not receive grace, it would be against the justice which He Himself established. Or if it refers to the movement of free choice before grace, it is speaking in the sense that man's flight to God is by a Divine motion, which ought not, in justice, to fail.

Reply Obj. 2. The first cause of the defect of grace is on our part, but the first cause of the bestowal of grace is on God's according to Osee 13. 9: *Destruction is thy own, O Israel; thy help is only in Me.*

Reply Obj. 3. Even in natural things, the form does not necessarily follow on the disposition of the matter, except by the power of the agent that causes the disposition.

ARTICLE 4. *Whether Grace Is Greater in One Than in Another?*

We proceed thus to the Fourth Article: It would seem that grace is not greater in one than in another.

Objection 1. For grace is caused in us by the Divine love, as stated above (Q. CX, A. 1). Now it is written (Wisd. 6. 8): *He made the little and the great and He hath equally care of all.* Therefore all obtain grace from Him equally.

Obj. 2. Further, whatever is the greatest possible cannot be more or less. But grace is the greatest possible, since it joins us with our last end. Therefore there is no greater or less in it. Hence it is not greater in one than in another.

Obj. 3. Further, grace is the soul's life, as

---

[1] *Glossa ordin.*, on Rom. 3.22 (Cf. PL 114, 480); *Glossa Lombardi*, on Rom. 3.21 (PL 191, 1360). Cf. Rabanus Maurus, *Enarr. in Epist. Pauli*, ii, 3, on Rom. 3.21 (PL 111, 1341).

[2] PL 158, 328.

[3] Sect. 20 (PG 3, 719); cf. Sect. 1 4 (PG 3, 694, 698).

[4] PL 45, 1014.

stated above (Q. CX, A. 1, Reply 2). But there is no greater or less in life. Hence, neither is there in grace.

On the contrary, It is written (Eph. 4. 7): *But to every one of us is given grace according to the measure of the giving of Christ.* Now what is given in measure is not given to all equally. Hence all have not an equal grace.

I answer that, As stated above (Q. LII, AA. 1, 2; Q. LXVI, AA. 1, 2), habits can have a double magnitude: one with respect to the end or object, as when a virtue is said to be more noble through being ordered to a greater good; the other on the part of the subject, which more or less participates in the habit inhering to it.

Now as regards the first magnitude, sanctifying grace cannot be greater or less, since, of its nature, grace joins man to the Highest Good, which is God. But as regards the subject, grace can receive more or less, since one may be more perfectly enlightened by grace than another. And a certain reason for this is on the part of him who prepares himself for grace, since he who is better prepared for grace receives more grace. Yet it is not here that we must seek the first cause of this diversity, since man prepares himself, only in so far as his free choice is prepared by God. Hence the first cause of this diversity is to be sought on the part of God, Who dispenses His gifts of grace variously, in order that the beauty and perfection of the Church may result from these various degrees; even as He instituted the various conditions of things, that the universe might be perfect. Hence after the Apostle had said (Eph. 4. 7): *To every one of us is given grace according to the measure of the giving of Christ,* having enumerated the various graces, he adds (*verse* 12): *For the perfecting of the saints . . . for the edifying of the body of Christ.*

Reply Obj. 1. The Divine care may be looked at in two ways. First, as regards the Divine act, which is simple and uniform; and thus His care looks equally to all, since by one simple act He administers great things and little. But, secondly, it may be considered in those things which come to creatures by the Divine care; and thus, inequality is found, in so far, that is, as God by His care provides greater gifts for some, and lesser gifts for others.

Reply Obj. 2. This objection is based on the first kind of magnitude of grace. For grace cannot be greater by ordering to a greater good, but in so far as it more or less orders to a greater or less participation of the same good. For there may be diversity of intensity and remissness,

both in grace and in final glory as regards the subjects' participation.

Reply Obj. 3. Natural life pertains to man's substance, and hence cannot be more or less; but man partakes of the life of grace accidentally, and hence man may possess it more or less.

ARTICLE 5. *Whether Man Can Know That He Has Grace?*

We proceed thus to the Fifth Article: It would seem that man can know that he has grace.

Objection 1. For grace by its physical reality is in the soul. Now the soul has most certain knowledge of those things that are in it by their physical reality, as appears from Augustine (*Gen. ad lit.* xii, 25, 31).[1] Hence grace may be known most certainly by one who has grace.

Obj. 2. Further, as knowledge is a gift of God, so is grace. But whoever receives knowledge from God knows that he has knowledge, according to Wis. 7. 17: *The Lord hath given me the true knowledge of the things that are.* Hence, with equal reason, whoever receives grace from God, knows that he has grace.

Obj. 3. Further, light is more knowable than darkness, since, according to the Apostle (Eph. 5. 13), *all that is made manifest is light.* Now sin, which is spiritual darkness, may be known with certainty by one that is in sin. Much more, therefore, may grace, which is spiritual light, be known.

Obj. 4. Further, the Apostle says (I Cor. 2. 12): *Now we have received not the Spirit of this world, but the Spirit that is of God; that we may know the things that are given us from God.* Now grace is God's first gift. Hence, the man who receives grace by the Holy Spirit, by the same Holy Spirit knows the grace given to him.

Obj. 5. Further, it was said by the Lord to Abraham (Gen. 22. 12): *Now I know that thou fearest God,* that is, I have made thee know. Now He is speaking there of chaste fear, which is not apart from grace. Hence a man may know that he has grace.

On the contrary, It is written (Ecclus. 9. 1): *Man knoweth not whether he be worthy of love or hatred.* Now sanctifying grace makes a man worthy of God's love. Therefore no one can know whether he has sanctifying grace.

I answer that, There are three ways of knowing a thing. First, by revelation, and thus anyone may know that he has grace, for God by a special privilege reveals this at times to some, in order that the joy of safety may begin in

[1] PL 34, 475, 479.

them even in this life, and that they may carry on toilsome works with greater trust and greater energy, and may bear the evils of this present life, as when it was said to Paul (II Cor. 12, 9): *My grace is sufficient for thee.*

Secondly, a man may, of himself, know something, and with certainty; and in this way no one can know that he has grace. For certitude about a thing can only be had when we may judge of it by its proper principle. Thus it is by undemonstrable universal principles that certitude is obtained concerning demonstrative conclusions. Now no one can know he has the knowledge of a conclusion if he does not know its principle. But the principle of grace and its object is God, Who by reason of His very excellence is unknown to us, according to Job 36. 26: *Behold God is great, exceeding our knowledge.* And hence His presence in us and His absence cannot be known with certainty, according to Job 9. 11: *If He come to me, I shall not see Him; if He depart I shall not understand.* And hence man cannot judge with certainty that he has grace, according to I Cor. 4. 3, 4: *But neither do I judge my own self . . . but He that judgeth me is the Lord.*

Thirdly, things are known conjecturally by signs; and thus anyone may know he has grace when he is conscious of delighting in God and of despising worldly things, and in so far as a man is not conscious of any mortal sin. And thus it is written (Apoc. 2. 17): *To him that overcometh I will give the hidden manna . . . which no man knoweth, but he that receiveth it,* because whoever receives it knows, by experiencing a certain sweetness, which he who does not receive it does not experience. Yet this knowledge is imperfect; hence the Apostle says (I Cor. 4. 4): *I am not conscious to myself of anything, yet am I not hereby justified,* since, according to Ps. 18. 13: *Who can understand sins? From my secret ones cleanse me, O Lord, and from those of others spare Thy servant.*

Reply Obj. 1. Those things which are in the soul by their essence are known through experimental knowledge, in so far as through acts man has experience of their inward principles; thus when we wish, we perceive that we have a will, and when we exercise the functions of life, we observe that there is life in us.

Reply Obj. 2. It is of the very character of knowledge that a man should have certitude of the objects of knowledge; and likewise, it is of the very character of faith that a man should be certain of the things of faith, and this because certitude pertains to the perfection of the

intellect, in which these gifts exist. Hence, whoever has knowledge or faith is certain that he has them. But it is otherwise with grace and charity and other things of this kind, which perfect the appetitive power.

Reply Obj. 3. Sin has for its principle and its object changeable good, which is known to us. But the object or end of grace is unknown to us on account of the greatness of its light, according to I Tim. 6. 16: *Who . . . inhabiteth light inaccessible.*

Reply Obj. 4. The Apostle is here speaking of the gifts of glory, which have been given to us in hope, and these we know most certainly by faith, although we do not know for certain that we have grace to enable us to merit them. Or it may be said that he is speaking of the privileged knowledge which comes of revelation. Hence he adds (*verse* 10): *But to us God hath revealed them by His Spirit.*

Reply Obj. 5. What was said to Abraham may refer to experimental knowledge which springs from the manifesting of deeds. For in the deed that Abraham had just wrought he could know experimentally that he had the fear of God. Or it may refer to a revelation.

QUESTION CXIII
Of the Effects of Grace
(In Ten Articles)

We have now to consider the effect of grace; and first, the justification of the ungodly, which is the effect of operating grace; and secondly merit, which is the effect of co-operating grace (Q. CXIV). Under the first head there are ten points of inquiry: (1) What is the justification of the ungodly? (2) Whether grace is required for it? (3) Whether any movement of free choice is required? (4) Whether a movement of faith is required? (5) Whether a movement of free choice against sin is required? (6) Whether the remission of sins is to be reckoned with the foregoing? (7) Whether the justification of the ungodly is a work of time or is sudden? (8) Of the natural order of the things concurring to justification. (9) Whether the justification of the ungodly is God's greatest work? (10) Whether the justification of the ungodly is miraculous?

ARTICLE 1. *Whether the Justification of the Ungodly Is the Remission of Sins?*

We proceed thus to the First Article: It would seem that the justification of the ungodly is not the remission of sins.

Objection 1. For sin is opposed not only to justice, but to all the other virtues, as stated above (Q. LXXI, A. 1). Now justification signifies a certain movement towards justice. Therefore not even remission of sin is justification, since movement is from one contrary to the other.

Obj. 2. Further, everything ought to be named from what is predominant in it, according to the book on the *Soul*.[1] Now the remission of sins is brought about chiefly by faith, according to Acts 15. 9: *Purifying their hearts by faith*; and by charity, according to Prov. 10. 12: *Charity covereth all sins*. Therefore the remission of sins ought to be named after faith or charity rather than justice.

Obj. 3. Further, the remission of sins seems to be the same as being called, for whoever is called is afar off, and we are afar off from God by sin. But one is called before being justified according to Rom. 8. 30: *And whom He called, them He also justified*. Therefore justification is not the remission of sins.

On the contrary, On Rom. 8. 30, *Whom He called, them He also justified*, the gloss says,[2] that is, "by the remission of sins." Therefore the remission of sins is justification.

I answer that, Justification taken passively implies a movement towards justice, as heating implies a movement towards heat. But since justice, by its nature, implies a certain rectitude of order, it may be taken in two ways. First, according as it implies a right order in man's act, and thus justice is placed amongst the virtues,—either as particular justice, which directs a man's acts by regulating them in relation to his fellow-man,—or as legal justice, which directs a man's acts by regulating them in their relation to the common good of society, as appears from the *Ethics*.[3]

Secondly, justice is so-called according as it implies a certain rectitude of order in the interior disposition of a man, in so far as what is highest in man is subject to God, and the inferior powers of the soul are subject to the superior, that is, to the reason; and this disposition the Philosopher calls justice metaphorically speaking.[4] Now this justice may be in man in two ways. First, by simple generation, which is from privation to form; and thus justification may belong even to such as are not in sin, when

they receive this justice from God, as Adam is said to have received original justice. Secondly, this justice may be brought about in man by a movement from one contrary to the other, and thus justification implies a transmutation from the state of injustice to the aforesaid state of justice. And it is thus we are now speaking of the justification of the ungodly, according to the Apostle (Rom. 4. 5): *But to him that worketh not, yet believeth in Him that justifieth the ungodly*, etc. And because movement is named after its term to which rather than from its term from which, the transmutation whereby anyone is changed by the remission of sins from the state of ungodliness to the state of justice, borrows its name from its term to which, and is called justification of the ungodly.

Reply Obj. 1. Every sin, according as it implies the disorder of a mind not subject to God, may be called injustice as being contrary to the aforesaid justice, according to I John 3. 4: *Whosoever committeth sin, committeth also iniquity; and sin is iniquity*. And thus the removal of any sin is called the justification of the ungodly.

Reply Obj. 2. Faith and charity imply a special ordering of the human mind to God by the intellect and will; but justice implies a general rectitude of order. Hence this transmutation is named after justice rather than after charity or faith.

Reply Obj. 3. Being called refers to God's inward help moving and exciting our mind to give up sin, and this motion of God is not the remission of sins, but its cause.

ARTICLE 2. *Whether the Infusion of Grace Is Required for the Remission of Guilt, That Is, For the Justification of the Ungodly?*

We proceed thus to the Second Article: It would seem that for the remission of guilt, which is the justification of the ungodly, no infusion of grace is required.

Objection 1. For anyone may be moved from one contrary without being led to the other, if the contraries are not immediate. Now the state of guilt and the state of grace are not immediate contraries, for there is the middle state of innocence wherein a man has neither grace nor guilt. Hence a man may be pardoned his guilt without his being brought to a state of grace.

Obj. 2. Further, the remission of guilt consists in the Divine imputation, according to Ps. 31. 2: *Blessed is the man to whom the Lord hath not imputed sin*. Now the infusion of grace puts something into our soul, as stated above (Q.

---

[1] Aristotle, II 4 (416ᵇ23).

[2] *Glossa interl.* (VI, 20r); *Glossa* Lombardi (PL 191, 1450).

[3] Aristotle, V, 1, 2 (1129ᵇ13; 1130ᵃ14).

[4] *Ibid.*, V, 11 (1138ᵇ5).

cx, A. 1). Hence the infusion of grace is not required for the remission of guilt.

Obj. 3. Further, no one can be subject to two contraries at once. Now some sins are contraries, as wastefulness and miserliness. Hence whoever is subject to the sin of wastefulness is not simultaneously subject to the sin of miserliness, yet it may happen that he has been previously subject to it. Hence by sinning with the vice of wastefulness he is freed from the sin of miserliness. And thus a sin is remitted without grace.

On the contrary, It is written (Rom. 3. 24): *Justified freely by His grace.*

I answer that, By sinning a man offends God, as stated above (Q. LXXI, A. 6). Now an offence is remitted to anyone only when the soul of the offender is at peace with the offended. Hence sin is remitted to us when God is at peace with us, and this peace consists in the love whereby God loves us. Now God's love, considered on the part of the Divine act, is eternal and unchangeable; but as regards the effect it imprints on us, it is sometimes interrupted, since we sometimes fall short of it and once more require it. Now the effect of the Divine love in us, which is taken away by sin, is grace, whereby a man is made worthy of eternal life, from which sin shuts him out. Hence we could not conceive the remission of guilt, without the infusion of grace.

Reply Obj. 1. More is required for an offender to pardon an offence than for one who has committed no offence not to be hated. For it may happen amongst men that one man neither hates nor loves another. But if the other offends him, then the forgiveness of the offence can only spring from a special good-will. Now God's good-will is said to be restored to man by the gift of grace; and hence although a man before sinning may be without grace and without guilt, yet that he is without guilt after sinning can only be because he has grace.

Reply Obj. 2. As God's love consists not merely in the act of the Divine will but also implies a certain effect of grace, as stated above (Q. cx, A. 1), so likewise, when God does not impute sin to a man there is implied a certain effect in him to whom the sin is not imputed; for it proceeds from the Divine love that sin is not imputed to a man by God.

Reply Obj. 3. As Augustine says (*De Nup. et Concup.* i, 26),[1] "If to leave off sinning was the same as to have no sin, it would be enough if Scripture warned us thus (Ecclus. 21. 1): '*My son, hast thou sinned? do so no more?*' Now this

is not enough, but it is added: '*But for thy former sins also pray that they may be forgiven thee.*' " For the act of sin passes, but the guilt remains, as stated above (Q. LXXXVII, A. 6). Hence when anyone passes from the sin of one vice to the sin of a contrary vice, he ceases to have the act of the former sin, but he does not cease to have the guilt, and hence he may have the guilt of both sins at once. For sins are not contrary to each other on the part of their turning from God, wherein sin has its guilt.

ARTICLE 3. *Whether for the Justification of the Ungodly Is Required a Movement of Free Choice?*

We proceed thus to the Third Article: It would seem that no movement of free choice is required for the justification of the ungodly.

Objection 1. For we see that by the sacrament of Baptism infants and sometimes adults are justified without a movement of free choice; for Augustine says[2] that when one of his friends was taken with a fever, "he lay for a long time senseless and in a deadly sweat, and when he was despaired of, he was baptized without his knowing, and was regenerated"; which is effected by sanctifying grace. Now God does not confine His power to the sacraments. Hence He can justify a man without the sacraments, and without any movement of free choice.

Obj. 2. Further, a man has not the use of reason when asleep, and without it there can be no movement of the free choice. But Solomon received from God the gift of wisdom when asleep, as related in III Kings 3. and 2 Paral. 1. Hence with equal reason the gift of sanctifying grace is sometimes bestowed by God on man without the movement of free choice.

Obj. 3. Further, grace is preserved by the same cause as brings it into being, for Augustine says (*Gen. ad lit.* viii, 12)[3] that "so ought man to turn to God as he is ever made just by Him." Now grace is preserved in man without a movement of free choice. Hence it can be infused in the beginning without a movement of free choice.

On the contrary, It is written (John 6. 45): *Every one that hath heard of the Father, and hath learned, cometh to Me.* Now to learn cannot be without a movement of free choice, since the learner assents to the teacher. Hence no one comes to the Father by justifying grace without a movement of free choice.

I answer that, The justification of the un-

---

[1] PL 44, 430.

[2] *Confessions,* IV, 8 (PL 32, 696).

[3] PL 34, 382.

godly is brought about by God moving man to justice. For He it is *that justifieth the ungodly* according to Rom. 4. 5. Now God moves everything in its own manner, just as we see that in natural things what is heavy and what is light are moved differently on account of their diverse natures. Hence He moves man to justice according to the condition of his human nature. But it is man's proper nature to have free choice. Hence in him who has the use of free choice, God's motion to justice does not take place without a movement of free choice; but He so infuses the gift of justifying grace that at the same time He moves free choice to accept the gift of grace, in such as are capable of being moved thus.

Reply Obj. 1. Infants are not capable of the movement of free choice; hence it is by only the informing of their souls that God moves them to justice. Now this cannot be brought about without a sacrament, because as original sin, from which they are justified, does not come to them from their own will, but by carnal generation, so also is grace given them by Christ through spiritual regeneration. And the same reason holds good with madmen and idiots, that have never had the use of free choice. But in the case of one who has had the use of free choice and afterwards has lost it either through sickness or sleep, he does not obtain justifying grace by the exterior rite of Baptism, or of any other sacrament, unless he intended to make use of this sacrament, and this can only be by the use of free choice. And it was in this way that he of whom Augustine speaks was regenerated, because both previously and afterwards he assented to the Baptism.

Reply Obj. 2. Solomon neither merited nor received wisdom whilst asleep, but it was declared to him in his sleep that on account of his previous desire wisdom would be infused into him by God. Hence it is said in his person (Wisd. 7. 7): *I wished, and understanding was given unto me.*

Or it may be said that his sleep was not natural, but was the sleep of prophecy, according to Num. 12. 6: *If there be among you a prophet of the Lord, I will appear to him in a vision, or I will speak to him in a dream.* In such cases the use of free choice remains.

And yet it must be observed that the comparison between the gift of wisdom and the gift of justifying grace does not hold. For the gift of justifying grace especially ordains a man to good, which is the object of the will; and hence a man is moved to it by a movement of the will which is a movement of free choice. But wisdom perfects the intellect which precedes the will; hence without any complete movement of free choice, the intellect can be enlightened with the gift of wisdom, even as we see that things are revealed to men in sleep, according to Job 33. 15, 16: *When deep sleep falleth upon men and they are sleeping in their beds, then He openeth the ears of men, and teaching, instructeth them in what they are to learn.*

Reply Obj. 3. In the infusion of justifying grace there is a certain transmutation of the human soul, and hence a proper movement of the human soul is required in order that the soul may be moved in its own manner. But the conservation of grace is without transmutation, and so no movement on the part of the soul is required but only a continuation of the Divine influx.

ARTICLE 4. *Whether a Movement of Faith Is Required for the Justification of the Ungodly?*

We proceed thus to the Fourth Article: It would seem that no movement of faith is required for the justification of the ungodly.

Objection 1. For as a man is justified by faith, so also by other things, namely, by fear, of which it is written (Ecclus. 1. 27): *The fear of the Lord driveth out sin, for he that is without fear cannot be justified;* and again by charity, according to Luke 7. 47: *Many sins are forgiven her because she hath loved much;* and again by humility, according to James 4. 6: *God resisteth the proud and giveth grace to the humble:* and again by mercy, according to Prov. 15. 27: *By mercy and faith sins are purged away.* Hence the movement of faith is no more required for the justification of the ungodly than the movements of the aforesaid virtues.

Obj. 2. Further, the act of faith is required for justification only in so far as a man knows God by faith. But a man may know God in other ways, namely, by natural knowledge, and by the gift of wisdom. Hence no act of faith is required for the justification of the ungodly.

Obj. 3. Further, there are several articles of faith. Therefore if the act of faith is required for the justification of the ungodly, it would seem that a man ought to think on every article of faith when he is first justified. But this seems inconvenient, since such thought would require a long delay of time. Hence it seems that an act of faith is not required for the justification of the ungodly.

On the contrary, It is written (Rom. 5. 1):

Being justified therefore by faith, let us have peace with God.

I answer that, As stated above (A. 3) a movement of free choice is required for the justification of the ungodly, since man's mind is moved by God. Now God moves man's soul by turning it to Himself according to Ps. 84. 7 (Septuagint): *Thou wilt turn us, O God, and bring us to life.* Hence for the justification of the ungodly a movement of the mind is required, by which it is turned to God. Now the first turning to God is by faith, according to Heb. 11. 6: *He that cometh to God must believe that He is.* Hence a movement of faith is required for the justification of the ungodly.

Reply Obj. 1. The movement of faith is not perfect unless it is quickened by charity; hence in the justification of the ungodly, a movement of charity is infused together with the movement of faith. Now free choice is moved to God by being subject to Him; hence an act of filial fear and an act of humility also concur. For it may happen that one and the same act of free choice springs from different virtues, when one commands and another is commanded, according as the act may be ordered to various ends. But the act of mercy counteracts sin either by way of satisfying for it, and thus it follows justification; or by way of preparation, in so far as the merciful obtain mercy,[1] and thus it can either precede justification, or concur with the other virtues towards justification, since mercy is included in the love of our neighbour.

Reply Obj. 2. By natural knowledge a man is not turned to God according as He is the object of Happiness and the cause of justification. Hence such knowledge does not suffice for justification. But the gift of wisdom presupposes the knowledge of faith, as stated above (Q. LXVIII, A. 4, REPLY 3).

Reply Obj. 3. As the Apostle says (Rom. 4. 5), *to him that . . . believeth in Him that justifieth the ungodly his faith is reputed to justice, according to the purpose of the grace of God.* Hence it is clear that in the justification of the ungodly an act of faith is required in order that a man may believe that God justifies man through the mystery of Christ.

ARTICLE 5. *Whether for the Justification of the Ungodly There Is Required a Movement of Free Choice Towards Sin?*

We proceed thus to the Fifth Article: It would seem that no movement of the free choice

[1] Matt. 5.7.

towards sin is required for the justification of the ungodly.

Objection 1. For charity alone suffices to take away sin, according to Prov. 10. 12: *Charity covereth all sins.* Now the object of charity is not sin. Therefore for this justification of the ungodly no movement of free choice towards sin is required.

Obj. 2. Further, whoever is tending onward ought not to look back, according to Philip. 3. 13, 14: *Forgetting the things that are behind, and stretching forth myself to those that are before, I press towards the mark, to the prize of the supernal vocation.* But whoever is stretching forth to justice has his sins behind him. Hence he ought to forget them, and not stretch forth to them by a movement of free choice.

Obj. 3. Further, in the justification of the ungodly one sin is not remitted without another, for it is irreverent to expect half a pardon from God. Hence, in the justification of the ungodly, if free choice must move against sin, a man ought to think of all his sins. But this is unfitting, both because a great space of time would be required for such thought, and because a man could not obtain the forgiveness of such sins as he had forgotten. Hence for the justification of the ungodly no movement of free choice is required.

On the contrary, It is written (Ps. 31. 5): *I will confess against myself my injustice to the Lord; and Thou hast forgiven the wickedness of my sin.*

I answer that, As stated above (A. 1), the justification of the ungodly is a certain movement whereby the human mind is moved by God from the state of sin to the state of justice. Hence it is necessary for the human mind to regard both extremes according to a movement of free choice, as a body in local movement is related to both terms of the movement. Now it is clear that in local movement the moving body leaves the term from which and nears the term to which. Hence the human mind whilst it is being justified, must, by a movement of free choice withdraw from sin and draw near to justice.

Now to withdraw from sin and to draw near to justice, in the movement of free choice, means detestation and desire. For Augustine says on the words *the hireling fleeth,* etc. (John 10. 12):[2] "Our affections are the movements of our soul; joy is the soul's outpouring; fear is the soul's flight; your soul goes forward when you seek; your soul flees, when you are afraid."

[2] *Tract.*, XLVI (PL 35, 1732).

Hence in the justification of the ungodly there must be two movements of free choice—one, whereby it tends to God's justice, the other whereby it hates sin.

Reply Obj. 1. It pertains to the same virtue to seek one contrary and to avoid the other; and hence, as it pertains to charity to love God, so likewise does it pertain to detest sin whereby the soul is separated from God.

Reply Obj. 2. A man ought not to return to those things that are behind by loving them, but in this matter, he ought to forget them, lest he be drawn to them. Yet he ought to recall them to mind in order to detest them, for this is to fly from them.

Reply Obj. 3. Previous to justification a man must detest each sin he remembers to have committed, and from this remembrance the soul goes on to have a general movement of detestation with regard to all sins committed, in which are included such sins as have been forgotten. For a man is then in such a frame of mind that he would be sorry even for those he does not remember, if they were present to his memory. And this movement co-operates in his justification.

ARTICLE 6. *Whether the Remission of Sins Ought To Be Accounted Amongst the Things Required for Justification?*

We proceed thus to the Sixth Article: It would seem that the remission of sins ought not to be accounted amongst the things required for justification.

Objection 1. For the substance of a thing is not reckoned together with those that are required for a thing; thus a man is not reckoned together with his body and soul. But the justification of the ungodly is itself the remission of sins, as stated above (A. 1). Therefore the remission of sins ought not to be accounted amongst the things required for the justification of the ungodly.

Obj. 2. Further, infusion of grace and remission of sins are the same, just as illumination and expulsion of darkness are the same. But a thing ought not to be reckoned together with itself, for unity is opposed to multitude. Therefore the remission of sins ought not to be reckoned with the infusion of grace.

Obj. 3. Further, the remission of sin follows as effect from cause, from the movement of free choice towards God and sin, since it is by faith and contrition that sin is forgiven. But an effect ought not to be reckoned with its cause, since things thus enumerated together, and, as it were,

condivided, are by nature simultaneous. Hence the remission of sins ought not to be reckoned with the things required for the justification of the ungodly.

On the contrary, In reckoning what is required for a thing we ought not to pass over the end, which is the chief part of everything. Now the remission of sins is the end of the justification of the ungodly; for it is written (Isa. 27. 9): *This is all the fruit, that the sin thereof should be taken away.* Hence the remission of sins ought to be numbered amongst the things required for justification.

I answer that, There are four things which are accounted to be necessary for the justification of the ungodly,[1] namely, the infusion of grace, the movement of free choice towards God by faith, the movement of free choice towards sin, and the remission of sins. The reason for this is that, as stated above (A. 1), the justification of the ungodly is a movement whereby the soul is moved by God from a state of sin to a state of justice. Now in the movement whereby one thing is moved by another, three things are required: first, the motion of the mover; secondly, the movement of the moved; thirdly, the consummation of the movement, or the attainment of the end. On the part of the Divine motion, there is the infusion of grace; on the part of free choice which is moved, there are two movements,—of departure from the term from which, and of approach to the term to which; but the consummation of the movement or the attainment of the end of the movement is implied in the remission of sins, for in this is the justification of the ungodly completed.

Reply Obj. 1. The justification of the ungodly is called the remission of sins, according as every movement has its species from its term. Nevertheless many other things are required in order to reach the term, as stated above (A. 5).

Reply Obj. 2. The infusion of grace and the remission of sin may be considered in two ways. First, with respect to the substance of the act, and thus they are the same; for by the same act God bestows grace and remits sin. Secondly, they may be considered on the part of the objects, and thus they differ by the difference between guilt, which is taken away, and grace, which is infused; just as in natural things generation and corruption differ, although the generation of one thing is the corruption of another.

[1] Cf. Albert, *In Sent.*, IV, d. XVII, A. 10–11 (BO XXIX, 673–679); Bonaventure, *In Sent.*, IV d. XVII, Pt. I, A. 1, QQ. 1–4 (QR IV, 418–424).

Reply Obj. 3. This enumeration is not the division of a genus into its species, in which the things enumerated must be simultaneous, but it is a division of the things required for the completion of anything; and in this enumeration we may have what precedes and what follows, since some of the principles and parts of a composite thing may precede and some follow.

ARTICLE 7. *Whether the Justification of the Ungodly Takes Place in an Instant or Successively?*

We proceed thus to the Seventh Article: It would seem that the justification of the ungodly does not take place in an instant, but successively.

Objection 1. Since as already stated (A. 3), for the justification of the ungodly there is required a movement of free choice. Now the act of free choice is to choose (*eligere*) which requires the deliberation of counsel, as stated above (Q. XV, A. 3). Hence, since deliberation implies a certain discursion, and this implies succession, the justification of the ungodly would seem to be successive.

Obj. 2. Further, the movement of free choice is not without actual consideration. But it is impossible to understand many things actually and at once, as stated above (Part I, Q. LXXXV, A. 4). Hence, since for the justification of the ungodly there is required a movement of free choice towards several things, namely, towards God and towards sin, it would seem impossible for the justification of the ungodly to be in an instant.

Obj. 3. Further, a form that may be greater or less, for example, blackness or whiteness, is received successively by its subject. Now grace may be greater or less, as stated above (Q. CXII., A. 4). Hence it is not received suddenly by its subject. Therefore, seeing that the infusion of grace is required for the justification of the ungodly, it would seem that the justification of the ungodly cannot be in an instant.

Obj. 4. Further, the movement of free choice, which cooperates in justification, is meritorious; and hence it must proceed from grace, without which there is no merit, as we shall state further on (Q. CXIV, A. 2). Now a thing receives its form before operating by this form. Hence grace is first infused, and then free choice is moved towards God and to detest sin. Hence justification is not all at once.

Obj. 5. Further, if grace is infused into the soul, there must be an instant when it first

dwells in the soul; so, too, if sin is forgiven there must be a last instant that man is in sin. But it cannot be the same instant, otherwise opposites would be in the same simultaneously. Hence they must be two successive instants, between which there must be time, as the Philosopher says.[1] Therefore the justification of the ungodly takes place not all at once, but successively.

On the contrary, The justification of the ungodly is caused by the justifying grace of the Holy Spirit. Now the Holy Spirit comes to men's minds suddenly, according to Acts 2. 2: *And suddenly there came a sound from heaven as of a mighty wind coming,* upon which the gloss says[2] that "the grace of the Holy Ghost knows no tardy efforts." Hence the justification of the ungodly is not successive, but instantaneous.

I answer that, The entire justification of the ungodly consists as to its origin in the infusion of grace. For it is by grace that free choice is moved and sin is remitted. Now the infusion of grace takes place in an instant and without succession. And the reason of this is that if a form be not suddenly impressed upon its subject, it is either because that subject is not disposed or because the agent needs time to dispose the subject. Hence we see that immediately the matter is disposed by a preceding alteration, the substantial form accrues to the matter; thus because the atmosphere of itself is disposed to receive light, it is suddenly illuminated by a body actually luminous. Now it was stated (Q. CXII, A. 2) that God, in order to infuse grace into the soul, needs no disposition, save what He Himself has made. And sometimes this sufficient disposition for the reception of grace He makes suddenly, sometimes gradually and successively, as stated above (Q. CXII, A. 2, REPLY 2). For the reason why a natural agent cannot suddenly dispose matter is that in the matter there is a resistant which has some disproportion with the power of the agent; and hence we see that the stronger the agent, the more speedily is the matter disposed. Therefore, since the Divine power is infinite, it can suddenly dispose any matter whatsoever to its form; and much more man's free choice whose movement is by nature instantaneous. Therefore the justification of the ungodly by God takes place in an instant.

Reply Obj. 1. The movement of free choice which concurs in the justification of the un-

[1] *Physics,* VI, 1 (231^{b}6).
[2] *Glossa interl.* (VI, 166v).

godly, is a consent to detest sin, and to draw near to God; and this consent takes place suddenly. Sometimes, indeed, it happens that deliberation precedes, yet this is not of the substance of justification, but a way to justification; as local movement is a way to illumination, and alteration to generation.

Reply Obj. 2. As stated above (Part I, Q. LXXXV, A. 5; Q. LVIII, A. 2), there is nothing to prevent two things being understood at once, according as they are somehow one; thus we understand the subject and predicate together, since they are united in the order of one affirmation. And in the same manner can free choice be moved to two things at once in so far as one is ordered to the other. Now the movement of free choice towards sin is ordered to the movement of free choice towards God, since a man detests sin as contrary to God, to Whom he wishes to cling. Hence in the justification of the ungodly free choice simultaneously detests sin and turns to God, even as a body approaches one point and withdraws from another simultaneously.

Reply Obj. 3. The reason why a form is not received instantaneously in the matter is not the fact that it can inhere more or less; for thus the light would not be suddenly received in the air, which can be illumined more and less. But the reason is to be sought on the part of the disposition of the matter or subject, as stated above.

Reply Obj. 4. The same instant the form is acquired, the thing begins to operate with the form; as fire, the instant it is generated moves upwards, and if its movement was instantaneous, it would be terminated in the same instant. But the movement of free choice, which is to will, is not successive, but instantaneous. Hence the justification of the ungodly does not have to be successive.

Reply Obj. 5. The succession of opposites in the same subject must be looked at differently in the things that are subject to time and in those that are above time. For in those that are in time, there is no last instant in which the previous form inheres in the subject, but there is the last time, and the first instant that the subsequent form inheres in the matter or subject; and this for the reason that in time we are not to consider one instant as immediately preceding another instant, since neither do instants succeed each other immediately in time, nor points in a line, as is proved in the *Physics*.[1] But time is terminated by an instant. Hence in

[1] Aristotle, VI, 1 (231^{b}6).

the whole of the previous time in which anything is moving towards its form, it is under the opposite form; but in the last instant of this time, which is the first instant of the subsequent time, it has the form which is the term of the movement.

But in those things that are above time it is otherwise. For if there be any succession of affections or intellectual conceptions in them (as in the angels), such succession is not measured by continuous time, but by discrete time, even as the things measured are not continuous, as stated above (Part I, Q. LIII, A. 3). In these, therefore, there is a last instant in which the preceding is, and a first instant in which the subsequent is. Nor must there be time in between, since there is no continuity of time, which this would necessitate.

Now the human mind, which is justified, is, in itself, above time, but is subject to time accidentally, in so far, that is, as it understands with continuity and time, with respect to the phantasms in which it considers the intelligible species, as stated above (Part I, Q. LXXXIV, A. 7). We must, therefore, decide from this about its change as regards the condition of temporal movements, that is, we must say that there is no last instant that sin inheres, but a last time; there is however a first instant that grace inheres, and in all the time previous sin inhered.

ARTICLE 8. *Whether the Infusion of Grace Is Naturally the First of the Things Required for the Justification of the Ungodly?*

We proceed thus to the Eighth Article: It would seem that the infusion of grace is not what is naturally required first for the justification of the ungodly.

Objection 1. For we withdraw from evil before drawing near to good, according to Ps. 33. 15: *Turn away from evil, and do good.* Now the remission of sins pertains to the turning away from evil, and the infusion of grace pertains to the turning to good. Hence the remission of sin is naturally before the infusion of grace.

Obj. 2. Further, the disposition naturally precedes the form to which it disposes. Now the movement of free choice is a disposition for the reception of grace. Therefore it naturally precedes the infusion of grace.

Obj. 3. Further, sin hinders the soul from tending freely to God. Now a hindrance to movement must be removed before the movement takes place. Hence the remission of sin and the movement of free choice towards sin are naturally before the movement of free choice towards God and the infusion of grace.

On the contrary, The cause is naturally prior to its effect. Now the infusion of grace is the cause of whatever is required for the justification of the ungodly, as stated above (A. 7). Therefore it is naturally prior to it.

I answer that, The aforesaid four things required for the justification of the ungodly are simultaneous in time, since the justification of the ungodly is not successive, as stated above (A. 7). But in the order of nature, one is prior to another; and in their natural order the first is the infusion of grace, the second, the movement of free choice towards God, the third, the movement of free choice towards sin, the fourth, the remission of sin.

The reason for this is that in every movement the motion of the mover is naturally first; the disposition of the matter, or the movement of the moved, is second; the end or term of the movement in which the motion of the mover rests, is last. Now the motion of God the mover is the infusion of grace, as stated above (A. 6); the movement or disposition of the moved is the twofold movement of free choice; and the term or end of the movement is the remission of sin, as stated above (AA. 1, 6). Hence in their natural order the first in the justification of the ungodly is the infusion of grace; the second is the movement of free choice towards God; the third is the movement of free choice towards sin, for he who is being justified detests sin because it is against God, and thus the movement of free choice towards God naturally precedes the movement of free choice towards sin, since it is its cause and reason; the fourth and last is the remission of sin, to which this transmutation is ordered as to an end, as stated above (AA. 1, 6).

Reply Obj. 1. The withdrawal from one term and approach to another may be looked at in two ways. First, on the part of the thing moved, and thus the withdrawal from a term naturally precedes the approach to a term, since in the subject of movement the opposite which is put away is prior to the opposite which the subject moved attains to by its movement. But on the part of the agent it is the other way about, since the agent, by the form pre-existing in it, acts for the removal of the opposite form; as the sun by its light acts for the removal of darkness, and hence on the part of the sun, illumination is prior to the removal of darkness, but on the part of the atmosphere to be illuminated, to be freed from darkness is, in the order of na-

ture, prior to being illuminated, although both are simultaneous in time. And since the infusion of grace and the remission of sin regard God Who justifies, hence in the order of nature the infusion of grace is prior to the freeing from sin. But if we look at what is on the part of the man justified, it is the other way about, since in the order of nature the being freed from sin is prior to the obtaining of justifying grace. Or it may be said that the term *from which* of justification is sin, and the term *to which* is justice; and that grace is the cause of the forgiveness of sin and of the obtaining of justice.

Reply Obj. 2. The disposition of the subject precedes the reception of the form in the order of nature; yet it follows the action of the agent, by which the subject is disposed. And hence the movement of free choice precedes the reception of grace in the order of nature, and follows the infusion of grace.

Reply Obj. 3. As the Philosopher says,[1] in movements of the soul the movement toward the speculative principle or the practical end is the very first, but in exterior movements the removal of the impediment precedes the attainment of the end. And as the movement of free choice is a movement of the soul, in the order of nature it moves towards God as to its end before removing the impediment of sin.

ARTICLE 9. *Whether the Justification of the Ungodly Is God's Greatest Work?*

We proceed thus to the Ninth Article: It would seem that the justification of the ungodly is not God's greatest work.

Objection 1. For it is by the justification of the ungodly that we attain the grace of a wayfarer. Now by glorification we receive heavenly grace, which is greater. Hence the glorification of angels and men is a greater work than the justification of the ungodly.

Obj. 2. Further, the justification of the ungodly is ordered to the particular good of one man. But the good of the universe is greater than the good of one man, as is plain from the *Ethics.*[2] Hence the creation of heaven and earth is a greater work than the justification of the ungodly.

Obj. 3. Further, to make something from nothing, where there is nothing to co-operate with the agent, is greater than to make something with the co-operation of the recipient. Now in the work of creation something is

[1] *Physics,* II, 9 (200ᵃ19).
[2] Aristotle, I, 2 (1094ᵇ10).

made from nothing, and hence nothing can co-operate with the agent; but in the justification of the ungodly God makes something from something, that is, a just man from a sinner, and there is a co-operation on man's part, since there is a movement of free choice, as stated above (A. 3). Hence the justification of the ungodly is not God's greatest work.

On the contrary, It is written (Ps. 144. 9): *His tender mercies are over all His works,* and in a Collect[1] we say: "O God, Who dost show forth Thine all-mightiness most by pardoning and having mercy"; and Augustine, expounding the words, *greater than these shall he do* (John 14. 12), says[2] that "for a just man to be made from a sinner is greater than to create heaven and earth."

I answer that, A work may be called great in two ways: first, on the part of the mode of action, and thus the work of creation is the greatest work, wherein something is made from nothing; secondly, a work may be called great on account of what is made, and thus the justification of the ungodly, which terminates at the eternal good of a share in the Godhead, is greater than the creation of heaven and earth, which terminates at the good of changeable nature. Hence, Augustine, after saying that "for a just man to be made from a sinner is greater than to create heaven and earth," adds, "for heaven and earth shall pass away, but the justification of the ungodly shall endure."

Again, we must bear in mind that a thing is called great in two ways. First, in absolute quantity, and thus the gift of glory is greater than the gift of grace that sanctifies the ungodly; and in this respect the glorification of the just is greater than the justification of the ungodly. Secondly, a thing may be said to be great in proportionate quantity, and thus the gift of grace that justifies the ungodly is greater than the gift of glory that beatifies the just, for the gift of grace exceeds the worthiness of the ungodly, who are worthy of punishment, more than the gift of glory exceeds the worthiness of the just, who by the fact of their justification are worthy of glory. Hence Augustine says (*ibid.*): "Let him that can, judge whether it is greater to create the angels just, than to justify the ungodly. Certainly, if they both betoken equal power, one betokens greater mercy."

And thus the *reply to the first* is clear.

Reply Obj. 2. The good of the universe is greater than the particular good of one if we consider both in the same genus. But the good of grace in one is greater than the good of nature in the whole universe.

Reply Obj. 3. This objection rests on the manner of acting, in which way creation is God's greatest work.

ARTICLE 10. *Whether the Justification of the Ungodly Is a Miraculous Work?*

We proceed thus to the Tenth Article: It would seem that the justification of the ungodly is a miraculous work.

Objection 1. For miraculous works are greater than non-miraculous. Now the justification of the ungodly is greater than the other miraculous works, as is clear from the quotation from Augustine (A. 9). Hence the justification of the ungodly is a miraculous work.

Obj. 2. Further, the movement of the will in the soul is like the natural inclination in natural things. But when God works in natural things against the inclination of their nature, it is a miraculous work, as when He gave sight to the blind or raised the dead. Now the will of the ungodly is bent on evil. Hence, since God in justifying a man moves him to good, it would seem that the justification of the ungodly is miraculous.

Obj. 3. Further, as wisdom is a gift of God, so also is justice. Now it is miraculous that anyone should suddenly obtain wisdom from God without study. Therefore it is miraculous that the ungodly should be justified by God.

On the contrary, Miraculous works are above natural power. Now the justification of the ungodly is not above natural power; for Augustine says (*De Præd. Sanct.* v)[3] that "to be capable of having faith and to be capable of having charity belongs to man's nature; but to have faith and charity belongs to the grace of the faithful." Therefore the justification of the ungodly is not miraculous.

I answer that, In miraculous works it is usual to find three things.[4] The first is on the part of the power of the agent, because they can only be performed by Divine power; and they are wondrous absolutely, since their cause is hidden, as stated above (Part I, Q. CV, A. 7). And thus both the justification of the ungodly and the creation of the world, and, generally speaking, every work that can be done by God alone, is miraculous.

Secondly, in certain miraculous works it is found that the form introduced is beyond the natural power of such matter, as in the resurrection of the dead life is above the natural power of such a body. And thus the justification of the ungodly is not miraculous, because the soul is naturally capable of grace, "since from its having been made to the likeness of God, it is fit to receive God by grace," as Augustine says.[1]

Thirdly, in miraculous works something is found besides the usual and customary order of causing an effect, as when a sick man suddenly and beyond the usual course of healing by nature or art receives perfect health; and thus the justification of the ungodly is sometimes miraculous and sometimes not. For the common and usual course of justification is that God moves the soul interiorly and that man is converted to God, first by an imperfect conversion, that it may afterwards become perfect; because "charity begun merits increase, and when increased merits perfection," as Augustine says.[2] Yet God sometimes moves the soul so vehemently that it reaches the perfection of justice at once, as took place in the conversion of Paul, which was accompanied at the same time by a miraculous external prostration. Hence the conversion of Paul is commemorated in the Church as miraculous.

Reply Obj. 1. Certain miraculous works, although they are less than the justification of the ungodly as regards the good caused, are beyond the usual order of such effects, and thus have more of the nature of a miracle.

Reply Obj. 2. It is not a miraculous work whenever a natural thing is moved contrary to its inclination; otherwise it would be miraculous for water to be heated, or for a stone to be thrown upwards; but only whenever this takes place beyond the order of the proper cause, which naturally does this. Now no other cause save God can justify the ungodly, even as nothing save fire can heat water. Hence the justification of the ungodly by God is not miraculous in this respect.

Reply Obj. 3. A man naturally acquires wisdom and knowledge from God by his own talent and study. Hence it is miraculous when a man is made wise or learned outside this order. But a man does not naturally acquire justifying grace by his own operation, but by God's. Hence there is no likeness.

[1] *De Trin.*, XIV, 8 (PL 42, 1044).
[2] *Epist.*, CLXXXVI, 3 (PL 33, 819).

QUESTION CXIV

OF MERIT, WHICH IS THE EFFECT OF CO-OPERATING GRACE

(*In Ten Articles*)

WE must now consider merit, which is the effect of co-operating grace; and under this head there are ten points of inquiry: (1) Whether a man can merit anything from God? (2) Whether without grace anyone can merit eternal life? (3) Whether anyone with grace may merit eternal life condignly? (4) Whether it is chiefly through the instrumentality of charity that grace is the principle of merit? (5) Whether a man may merit the first grace for himself? (6) Whether he may merit it for someone else? (7) Whether anyone can merit restoration after sin? (8) Whether he can merit for himself an increase of grace or charity? (9) Whether he can merit final perseverance? (10) Whether temporal goods fall under merit?

ARTICLE 1. *Whether a Man May Merit Anything from God?*

We proceed thus to the First Article: It would seem that a man can merit nothing from God.

Objection 1. For no one, it would seem, merits by giving another his due. But by all the good we do, we cannot make sufficient return to God, since yet more is His due, as also the Philosopher says.[3] Hence it is written (Luke 17. 10): *When you have done all these things that are commanded you, say: We are unprofitable servants; we have done that which we ought to do.* Therefore a man can merit nothing from God.

Obj. 2. Further, it would seem that a man merits nothing from God by what profits himself only and profits God nothing. Now by acting well a man profits himself or another man, but not God, for it is written (Job. 35. 7): *If thou do justly, what shalt thou give Him, or what shall He receive of thy hand.* Hence a man can merit nothing from God.

Obj. 3. Further, whoever merits anything from another makes him his debtor; for a man's wage is a debt due to him. Now God is no one's debtor; hence it is written (Rom. 11. 35): *Who hath first given to Him, and recompense shall be made him?* Hence no one can merit anything from God.

On the contrary, It is written (Jer. 31. 16): *There is a reward for thy work.* Now a reward

[3] *Ethics*, VIII, 14 (1163[b]15).

means something bestowed by reason of merit. Hence it would seem that a man may merit from God.

I answer that, Merit and reward refer to the same, for a reward means something given anyone in return for work or toil, as a price for it. Hence, as it is an act of justice to give a just price for anything received from another, so also is it an act of justice to make a return for work or toil. Now "justice is a kind of equality," as is clear from the Philosopher,[1] and hence absolutely justice is between those that are absolutely equal; but where there is no absolute equality between them, neither is there absolute justice, but there may be a certain manner of justice, as when we speak of a father's or a master's right, as the Philosopher says.[2] And hence where there is justice absolutely, there is the character of merit and reward absolutely. But where there is no absolute right, but only relative, there is no character of merit absolutely, but only relatively, in so far as the character of justice is found there; it is in this way, for example, the child merits something from his father and the slave from his lord.

Now it is clear that between God and man there is the greatest inequality, for they are infinitely apart, and all man's good is from God. Hence there can be no justice of absolute equality between man and God, but only of a certain proportion, in so far as both operate after their own manner. Now the manner and measure of human virtue is in man from God. Hence man's merit with God only exists on the presupposition of the Divine ordination, so that man obtains from God, as a reward of his operation, what God gave him the power of operation for, even as natural things by their proper movements and operations obtain that to which they were ordained by God; differently, indeed, since the rational creature moves itself to act by free choice and so its action has the character of merit, which is not so in other creatures.

Reply Obj. 1. Man merits in so far as he does what he ought by his own will; otherwise the act of justice whereby anyone discharges a debt would not be meritorious.

Reply Obj. 2. God seeks from our goods not profit, but glory, that is, the manifestation of His goodness; even as He seeks it also in His own works. Now nothing accrues to Him, but only to ourselves, by our worship of Him. Hence we merit from God, not that by our works any-

thing accrues to Him, but in so far as we work for His glory.

Reply Obj. 3. Since our action has the character of merit only on the presupposition of the Divine ordination, it does not follow that God is made our debtor absolutely, but His own, in so far as it is due that His will should be carried out.

ARTICLE 2. *Whether Anyone Without Grace Can Merit Eternal Life?*

We proceed thus to the Second Article: It would seem that without grace anyone can merit eternal life.

Objection 1. For man merits from God what he is divinely ordained to, as stated above (A. 1). Now man by his nature is ordained to happiness as his end; hence, too, he naturally wishes to be blessed. Hence man by his natural endowments and without grace can merit beatitude which is eternal life.

Obj. 2. Further, the less a work is due, the more meritorious it is. Now, less due is that work which is done by one who has received fewer benefits. Hence, since he who has only natural endowments has received fewer gifts from God than he who has gratuitous gifts as well as nature, it would seem that his works are more meritorious with God. And thus if he who has grace can merit eternal life to some extent, much more may he who has no grace.

Obj. 3. Further, God's mercy and liberality infinitely surpass human mercy and liberality. Now a man may merit from another, even though he has not hitherto had his grace. Much more, therefore, would it seem that a man without grace may merit eternal life.

On the contrary, The Apostle says (Rom. 6. 23): *The grace of God, life everlasting.*

I answer that, Man without grace may be looked at in two states, as was said above (Q. CIX, A. 2): the first, a state of integral nature, in which Adam was before his sin; the second, a state of corrupt nature, in which we are before being restored by grace. Therefore, if we speak of man in the first state, there is only one reason why man cannot merit eternal life without grace, by his purely natural endowments, namely, because man's merit depends on the Divine pre-ordination. Now no act of anything whatsoever is divinely ordained to anything exceeding the proportion of the powers which are the principles of its act; for it is a law of Divine providence that nothing shall act beyond its powers. Now everlasting life is a good exceed-

---

[1] *Ethics,* v, 3 (1131ᵃ12).

[2] *Ibid.,* v, 6 (1134ᵃ25).

ing the proportion of created nature, since it exceeds its knowledge and desire, according to I Cor. 2. 9: *Eye hath not seen, nor ear heard, neither hath it entered into the heart of man.* And hence it is that no created nature is a sufficient principle of an act meritorious of eternal life, unless there is added a supernatural gift, which we call grace. But if we speak of man as existing in sin, a second reason is added to this, namely, the impediment of sin. For since sin is an offence against God, excluding us from eternal life, as is clear from what has been said above (Q. LXXXVII, A. 3; Q. CXIII, A. 2), no one existing in a state of mortal sin can merit eternal life unless first he be reconciled to God, through his sin being forgiven, which is brought about by grace. For the sinner deserves not life, but death, according to Rom. 6. 23: *The wages of sin is death.*

Reply Obj. 1. God ordained human nature to attain the end of eternal life not by its own strength, but by the help of grace, and in this way its act can be meritorious of eternal life.

Reply Obj. 2. Without grace a man cannot have a work equal to a work proceeding from grace, since the more perfect the principle, the more perfect the action. But the objection would hold good if we supposed the operations equal in both cases.

Reply Obj. 3. With regard to the first reason advanced, the case is different in God and in man. For a man receives all his power of well-doing from God, and not from man. Hence a man can merit nothing from God except by His gift, which the Apostle expresses aptly saying (Rom. 11. 35): *Who hath first given to Him, and recompense shall be made to him?* But man may merit from man before he has received anything from him, by what he has received from God.

But as regards the second proof taken from the impediment of sin, the case is similar with man and God, since one man cannot merit from another whom he has offended unless he makes satisfaction to him and is reconciled.

ARTICLE 3. *Whether a Man in Grace Can Merit Eternal Life Condignly?*

We proceed thus to the Third Article: It would seem that a man in grace cannot merit eternal life condignly.

Objection 1. For the Apostle says (Rom. 8. 18): *The sufferings of this time are not worthy (condignae) to be compared with the glory to come, that shall be revealed in us.* But of all meritorious works, the sufferings of the saints would seem the most meritorious. Therefore no works of men are meritorious of eternal life condignly.

Obj. 2. Further, on Rom. 6. 23, *The grace of God, life everlasting,* a gloss says:[1] "He might have truly said: 'The wages of justice, life everlasting'; but He preferred to say 'The grace of God, life everlasting,' that we may know that God leads us to life everlasting of His own mercy and not by our merits." Now when anyone merits something condignly he receives it not from mercy but from merit. Hence it would seem that a man with grace cannot merit life everlasting condignly.

Obj. 3. Further, merit that equals the reward would seem to be condign. Now no act of the present life can equal everlasting life, which surpasses our knowledge and our desire, and, moreover, surpasses the charity or love of the wayfarer, even as it exceeds nature. Therefore with grace a man cannot merit eternal life condignly.

On the contrary, What is granted in accordance with a just judgment would seem a condign reward. But life everlasting is granted by God in accordance with the judgment of justice, according to II Tim. 4. 8: *As to the rest, there is laid up for me a crown of justice, which the Lord, the just judge, will render to me in that day.* Therefore man merits everlasting life condignly.

I answer that, Man's meritorious work may be considered in two ways: first, as it proceeds from free choice; secondly, as it proceeds from the grace of the Holy Ghost. If it is considered as regards the substance of the work, and according as it springs from free choice, there can be no condignity because of the very great inequality. But there is congruity on account of an equality of proportion: for it seems congruous that, if a man does what he can, God should reward him according to the excellence of His power.

If, however, we speak of a meritorious work according as it proceeds from the grace of the Holy Ghost moving us to life everlasting, it is meritorious of life everlasting condignly. For thus the value of its merit depends upon the power of the Holy Ghost moving us to life everlasting according to John 4. 14: *Shall become in him a fount of water springing up into life everlasting.* And the worth of the work depends on the dignity of grace, whereby a man, being made a partaker of the Divine Nature is adopt-

[1] *Glossa ordin.* (VI, 15F); *Glossa* Lombardi (PL 191, 1412); cf. Augustine, *Enchir.,* chap. CVII (PL 40, 282).

ed as a son of God, to whom the inheritance is due by right of adoption, according to Rom. 8. 17: *If sons, heirs also.*

Reply Obj. 1. The Apostle is speaking of the substance of these sufferings.

Reply Obj. 2. This saying is to be understood of the first cause of our reaching everlasting life, namely, God's mercy. But our merit is a subsequent cause.

Reply Obj. 3. The grace of the Holy Ghost which we have at present, although unequal to glory in act, is equal to it virtually as the seed of a tree, wherein the whole tree is virtually. So likewise by grace the Holy Ghost dwells in man, and He is a sufficient cause of life everlasting; hence, II Cor. 1. 22, He is called the *pledge* of our inheritance.

ARTICLE 4. *Whether Grace Is the Principle of Merit Through Charity Rather Than the Other Virtues?*

We proceed thus to the Fourth Article: It would seem that grace is not the principle of merit through charity rather than the other virtues.

Objection 1. For wages are due to work, according to Matt. 20. 8: *Call the labourers and pay them their hire.* Now every virtue is a principle of some operation, since virtue is an operative habit, as stated above (Q. LV, A. 2). Hence every virtue is equally a principle of merit.

Obj. 2. Further, the Apostle says (I Cor. 3. 8): *Every man shall receive his own reward according to his labour.* Now charity lessens rather than increases the labour, because as Augustine says (*De Verbis Dom., Serm.* lxx),[1] "love makes all hard and repulsive tasks easy and next to nothing." Hence charity is no greater principle of merit than any other virtue.

Obj. 3. Further, the greatest principle of merit would seem to be the one whose acts are most meritorious. But the acts of faith and patience or fortitude would seem to be the most meritorious, as appears in the martyrs, who strove for the faith patiently and bravely even till death. Hence other virtues are a greater principle of merit than charity.

On the contrary, Our Lord said (John 14. 21): *He that loveth Me, shall be loved of My Father; and I will love him and will manifest Myself to him.* Now everlasting life consists in the manifest knowledge of God, according to John 17. 3: *This is eternal life: that they may know Thee, the only true* and living *God.*

Hence the merit of eternal life rests chiefly with charity.

I answer that, As we may gather from what has been stated above (A. 1) human acts have the nature of merit from two causes. First and chiefly from the Divine ordination, according as acts are said to merit that good to which man is divinely ordained. Secondly, on the part of free choice, according as man, above other creatures, has the power of voluntary acts by acting of himself. And in both these ways does merit chiefly rest with charity. For we must first bear in mind that everlasting life consists in the enjoyment of God. Now the human mind's movement to the enjoyment of the Divine good is the proper act of charity, by which all the acts of the other virtues are ordered to this end, since all the other virtues are commanded by charity. Hence the merit of life everlasting pertains first to charity, and secondly, to the other virtues, according as their acts are commanded by charity. So, likewise, is it manifest that what we do out of love we do most willingly. Hence, even according as merit depends on voluntariness, merit is chiefly attributed to charity.

Reply Obj. 1. Charity, in so far as it has the last end for object, moves the other virtues to act. For the habit to which the end pertains always commands the habits to which the means pertain, as was said above (Q. IX, A. 1).

Reply Obj. 2. A work can be toilsome and difficult in two ways. First, from the greatness of the work, and thus the greatness of the work pertains to the increase of merit; and thus charity does not lessen the toil—rather, it makes us undertake the greatest toils, "for it does great things, if it exists," as Gregory says (*Hom. in Evang.* xxx).[2] Secondly, from the defect of the operator; for what is not done with a ready will is hard and difficult to all of us, and this toil lessens merit and is removed by charity.

Reply Obj. 3. The act of faith is not meritorious unless *faith . . . worketh by charity* (Gal. 5. 6). So, too, the acts of patience and fortitude are not meritorious unless a man does them out of charity, according to I Cor. 13. 3: *If I should deliver my body to be burned, and have not charity, it profiteth me nothing.*

ARTICLE 5. *Whether a Man May Merit For Himself the First Grace?*

We proceed thus to the Fifth Article: It would seem that a man may merit for himself the first grace.

---

[1] PL 38, 444.

[2] PL 76, 1221.

Objection 1. Because, as Augustine says (*Ep.* clxxxvi),[1] "faith merits justification." Now a man is justified by the first grace. Therefore a man may merit the first grace.

Obj. 2. Further, God gives grace only to the worthy. Now, no one is said to be worthy of some good unless he has merited it condignly. Therefore we may merit the first grace condignly.

Obj. 3. Further, with men we may merit a gift already received. Thus if a man receives a horse from his master, he merits it by a good use of it in his master's service. Now God is much more bountiful than man. Much more, therefore, may a man, by subsequent works, merit the first grace already received from God.

On the contrary, The nature of grace is contrary to reward of works, according to Rom. 4. 4: *Now to him that worketh, the reward is not reckoned according to grace but according to debt.* Now a man merits what is reckoned to him according to debt as the reward of his works. Hence a man may not merit the first grace.

I answer that, The gift of grace may be considered in two ways. First in the nature of a gratuitous gift, and thus it is manifest that all merit is contrary to grace, since as the Apostle says (Rom. 11. 6), *if by grace, it is not now by works.* Secondly, it may be considered as regards the nature of the thing given, and thus, also, it cannot come under the merit of him who has not grace, both because it exceeds the proportion of nature, and because previous to grace a man in the state of sin has an obstacle to his meriting grace, namely, sin. But when anyone has grace, the grace already possessed cannot come under merit, since reward is the term of the work, but grace is the principle of all our good works, as stated above (Q. CIX). But if anyone merits a further gratuitous gift by virtue of the preceding grace, it would not be the first grace. Hence it is manifest that no one can merit for himself the first grace.

Reply Obj. 1. As Augustine says (*Retract.* i, 23),[2] he was deceived on this point for a time, believing the beginning of faith to be from us, and its consummation to be granted us by God; and this he here retracts. And it seems to be in this sense that he speaks of faith as meriting justification. But if we suppose, as indeed it is a truth of faith, that the beginning of faith is in us from God, the first act must flow from

grace, and thus it cannot be meritorious of the first grace. Therefore man is justified by faith not as though man, by believing, were to merit justification, but that he believes whilst he is being justified; because a movement of faith is required for the justification of the ungodly, as stated above (Q. CXIII, A. 4).

Reply Obj. 2. God gives grace to none but to the worthy, not that they were previously worthy, but that by His grace He makes them worthy, Who alone *can make him clean that is conceived of unclean seed* (Job 14. 4).

Reply Obj. 3. Man's every good work proceeds from the first grace as from its principle, but not from any gift of man. Consequently, there is no comparison between gifts of grace and gifts of men.

ARTICLE 6. *Whether a Man Can Merit the First Grace for Another?*

We proceed thus to the Sixth Article: It would seem that a man can merit the first grace for another.

Objection 1. Because on Matt. 9. 2, *Jesus seeing their faith,* etc., a gloss says:[3] "How much is our personal faith worth with God, Who set such a price on another's faith as to heal the man both inwardly and outwardly!" Now inward healing is brought about by grace. Hence a man can merit the first grace for another.

Obj. 2. Further, the prayers of the just are not void, but efficacious, according to James 5. 16: *The continued prayer of a just man availeth much.* Now he had previously said: *Pray one for another, that you may be saved.* Hence, since man's salvation can only be brought about by grace, it seems that one man may merit for another his first grace.

Obj. 3. Further, it is written (Luke 16. 9): *Make unto you friends of the mammon of iniquity, that when you shall fail they may receive you into everlasting dwellings.* Now it is through grace alone that anyone is received into everlasting dwellings, for by it alone does anyone merit everlasting life as stated above (A. 2; Q. CIX, A. 5). Hence one man may by merit obtain for another his first grace.

On the contrary, It is written (Jer. 15. 1): *If Moses and Samuel shall stand before Me, My soul is not towards this people*—yet they had very great merit with God. Hence it seems that no one can merit the first grace for another.

I answer that, As shown above (AA. 1, 3, 4),

---

[1] Chap. 3 (PL 33, 818); cf. Conc. Arausic, II, anno 529, can. 5 (MA VIII, 713; DZ 178).

[2] PL 32, 621.

[3] *Glossa ordin.* (v, 32E).

our works are meritorious from two causes: first, by virtue of the Divine motion, and thus we merit condignly; secondly, according as they proceed from free choice in so far as we do them willingly, and thus they have congruous merit, since it is congruous that when a man makes good use of his power, God should by His super-excellent power work still higher things. And therefore it is clear that no one can merit condignly for another his first grace, save Christ alone, since each one of us is moved by God to reach life everlasting through the gift of grace; hence condign merit does not reach beyond this motion. But Christ's soul is moved by God through grace not only so as to reach the glory of life everlasting, but so as to lead others to it, inasmuch as He is the Head of the Church and the Author of human salvation, according to Heb. 2. 10: *Who hath brought many children into glory (to perfect) the Author of their salvation.*

But one may merit the first grace for another congruously, because a man in grace fulfils God's will, and it is congruous and in harmony with friendship that God should fulfil man's desire for the salvation of another, although sometimes there may be an impediment on the part of him whose salvation the just man desires. And it is in this sense that the passage from Jeremias speaks.

Reply Obj. 1. A man's faith avails for another's salvation by congruous and not by condign merit.

Reply Obj. 2. The entreaty of prayer rests on mercy, whereas condign merit rests on justice; hence a man may entreat many things from the Divine mercy in prayer, which he does not merit in justice, according to Dan. 9. 18: *For it is not for our justifications that we present our prayers before Thy face, but for the multitude of Thy tender mercies.*

Reply Obj. 3. The poor who receive alms are said to receive others into everlasting dwellings either by entreating their forgiveness in prayer, or by meriting congruously by other good works, or even materially speaking because by these works of mercy exercised towards the poor we merit to be received into everlasting dwellings.

ARTICLE 7. *Whether a Man May Merit Restoration after a Fall?*

We proceed thus to the Seventh Article: It would seem that anyone may merit for himself restoration after a fall.

Objection 1. For what a man may justly ask of God he may justly merit. Now nothing may more justly be besought of God than to be restored after a fall, as Augustine says, according to Ps. 70. 9: *When my strength shall fail, do not Thou forsake me.* Hence a man may merit to be restored after a fall.

Obj. 2. Further, a man's works benefit himself more than another. Now a man is able, to some extent, to merit for another his restoration after a fall, even as his first grace. Much more, therefore, may he merit for himself restoration after a fall.

Obj. 3. Further, when a man is once in grace he merits life everlasting by the good works he does, as was shown above (A. 2; Q. CIX, A. 5). Now no one can attain life everlasting unless he is restored by grace. Hence it would seem that he merits for himself restoration.

On the contrary, It is written (Ezech. 18. 24): *If the just man turn himself away from his justice and do iniquity . . . all his justices which he hath done shall not be remembered.* Therefore his previous merits will in no way help him to rise again. Hence no one can merit for himself restoration after a fall.

I answer that, No one can merit for himself restoration after a future fall, either condignly or congruously. He cannot merit for himself condignly, since the reason of this merit depends on the motion of Divine grace, and this motion is interrupted by the subsequent sin. Hence all benefits which he afterwards obtains from God, by which he is restored, do not fall under merit—the motion of the preceding grace not extending to them. Again, congruous merit, by which one merits the first grace for another, is prevented from having its effect on account of the impediment of sin in the one for whom it is merited. Much more, therefore, is the efficacy of such merit impeded by the obstacle which is in him who merits, and in him for whom it is merited; for both these are in the same person. And therefore a man can in no way merit for himself restoration after a fall.

Reply Obj. 1. The desire whereby we seek for restoration after a fall is called just, and likewise the prayer whereby this restoration is besought is called just, because it tends to justice; not however that it depends on justice by way of merit, but only on mercy.

Reply Obj. 2. Anyone may congruously merit for another his first grace, because there is no impediment (at least, on the part of him who merits), such as is found when anyone recedes from justice after the merit of grace.

Reply Obj. 3. Some have said[1] that no one absolutely merits life everlasting except by the act of final grace, but only conditionally, that is, if he perseveres. But it is unreasonable to say this, for sometimes the act of the last grace is not more, but less meritorious than preceding acts, on account of the prostration of illness. Hence it must be said that every act of charity merits eternal life absolutely; but by subsequent sin, there arises an impediment to the preceding merit, so that it does not obtain its effect, just as natural causes fail of their effects on account of a supervening impediment.

ARTICLE 8. *Whether a Man May Merit the Increase of Grace or Charity?*

We proceed thus to the Eighth Article: It would seem that a man cannot merit an increase of grace or charity.

Objection 1. For when anyone receives the reward he merited, no other reward is due to him; thus it was said of some (Matt. 6. 2): *They have received their reward.* Hence, if anyone were to merit the increase of charity or grace, it would follow that, when his grace has been increased he could not expect any further reward, which is unfitting.

Obj. 2. Further, nothing acts beyond its species. But the principle of merit is grace or charity, as was shown above (AA. 2, 4). Therefore no one can merit greater grace or charity than he has.

Obj. 3. Further, what falls under merit a man merits by every act flowing from grace or charity, as by every such act a man merits life everlasting. If, therefore, the increase of grace or charity falls under merit, it would seem that by every act quickened by charity a man would merit an increase of charity. But what a man merits, he infallibly receives from God, unless hindered by subsequent sin; for it is written (II Tim. 1. 12): *I know Whom I have believed, and I am certain that He is able to keep that which I have committed unto Him.* Hence it would follow that grace or charity is increased by every meritorious act. And this would seem impossible since at times meritorious acts are not very fervent, and would not suffice for the increase of charity. Therefore the increase of charity does not come under merit.

On the contrary, Augustine says[2] that "charity merits increase, and being increased merits to be perfected." Hence the increase of grace or charity falls under merit.

I answer that, As stated above (AA. 3, 6, 7), whatever the motion of grace reaches to, falls under condign merit. Now the motion of a mover extends not merely to the last term of the movement, but to the whole progress of the movement. But the term of the movement of grace is eternal life, and progress in this movement is by the increase of charity or grace according to Prov. 4. 18: *But the path of the just as a shining light, goeth forward and increaseth even to perfect day*, which is the day of glory. And thus the increase of grace falls under condign merit.

Reply Obj. 1. Reward is the term of merit. But there is a double term of movement, namely, the last, and the intermediate, this latter is both beginning and term, and this term is the reward of increase. Now the reward of human favour is as the last end to those who place their end in it; hence such as these receive no other reward.

Reply Obj. 2. The increase of grace is not above the power of the pre-existing grace, although it is above its quantity, even as a tree is not above the power of the seed, although above its quantity.

Reply Obj. 3. By every meritorious act a man merits the increase of grace, equally with the consummation of grace which is eternal life. But just as eternal life is not given at once, but in its own time, so neither is grace increased at once, but in its own time, namely, when a man is sufficiently disposed for the increase of grace.

ARTICLE 9. *Whether a Man May Merit Perseverance?*

We proceed thus to the Ninth Article: It would seem that anyone may merit perseverance.

Objection 1. For what a man obtains by asking can come under the merit of anyone that is in grace. Now men obtain perseverance by asking it of God; otherwise it would be useless to ask it of God in the petitions of the Lord's Prayer, as Augustine says (*De Dono Persev.* ii).[3] Therefore perseverance may come under the merit of whoever has grace.

Obj. 2. Further, it is more not to be able to sin, than not to sin. But not to be able to sin comes under merit, for we merit eternal life, of which impeccability is an essential mark. Much more, therefore, may we merit not to sin, that is, to persevere.

---

[1] Bonaventure, *In Sent.*, III, d. 28, dub. 2 (QR II, 691); bk. III, d. 24, A. 1, Q. 1 (QR III. 511); bk. IV, d. 14, Pt. 2, A. 2, Q. 1, concl. (QR IV, 336).
[2] Cf. *Epist.*, CLXXXVI, 3 (PL 33, 819).
[3] PL 45, 996; *De Corrept. et Grat.*, VI (PL 44, 922).

Obj. 3. Further, increase of grace is greater than perseverance in the grace we already possess. But a man may merit an increase of grace, as was stated above (A. 8). Much more, therefore, may he merit perseverance in the grace he has already.

On the contrary, What we merit, we obtain from God, unless it is hindered by sin. Now many have meritorious works who do not obtain perseverance. Nor can it be urged that this takes place because of the impediment of sin, since sin itself is opposed to perseverance. And thus if anyone were to merit perseverance, God would not permit him to fall into sin. Hence perseverance does not come under merit.

I answer that, Since man's free choice is naturally flexible towards good and evil, there are two ways of obtaining from God perseverance in good. First, through free choice being determined to good by consummate grace, which will be in glory; secondly, on the part of the Divine motion, which inclines man to good unto the end. Now, as explained above (AA. 5, 8), that which is related as a term to the movement of free choice directed by God the mover, falls under human merit, but not what is related to the aforesaid movement as principle. Hence it is clear that the perseverance of glory which is the term of the aforesaid movement falls under merit. But perseverance of the wayfarer does not fall under merit, since it depends solely on the Divine motion, which is the principle of all merit. Now God freely bestows the good of perseverance on whomsoever He bestows it.

Reply Obj. 1. We entreat in prayer things that we do not merit, since "God hears sinners who beseech the pardon of their sins, which they do not merit," as appears from Augustine[1] on John 9. 31, *Now we know that God doth not hear sinners,* otherwise it would have been useless for the publican to say: *O God, be merciful to me a sinner,* Luke 18. 13. So too may we entreat of God in prayer the grace of perseverance either for ourselves or for others, although it does not fall under merit.

Reply Obj. 2. The perseverance which is in heaven is compared as term to the movement of free choice; but not so the perseverance of the wayfarer, for the reason given in the body of the article.

In the same way may we answer *the third objection* which concerns the increase of grace, as was explained above.

[1] *In Joann.,* tract. XLIV (PL 35, 1718).

ARTICLE 10. *Whether Temporal Goods Fall Under Merit?*

We proceed thus to the Tenth Article: It would seem that temporal goods fall under merit.

Objection 1. For what is promised to some as a reward of justice, falls under merit. Now, temporal goods were promised in the Old Law as the reward of justice, as appears from Deut. 28. Hence it seems that temporal goods fall under merit.

Obj. 2. Further, that would seem to fall under merit which God bestows on anyone for a service done. But God sometimes bestows temporal goods on men for services done for Him. For it is written (Exod. 1. 21): *And because the midwives feared God, He built them houses;* on which a gloss of Gregory (*Moral.* xviii, 3)[2] says that "life everlasting might have been awarded them as the fruit of their good-will, but on account of their sin of falsehood they received an earthly reward." And it is written (Ezech. 29. 18): *The King of Babylon hath made his army to undergo hard service against Tyre . . . and there hath been no reward given him,* and further on: *And it shall be wages for his army. . . . I have given him the land of Egypt because he hath laboured for me.* Therefore temporal goods fall under merit.

Obj. 3. Further, as good is to merit so is evil to demerit. But on account of the demerit of sin some are punished by God with temporal punishments, as appears from the Sodomites, Gen. 19. Hence temporal goods falls under merit.

Obj. 4. *On the contrary,* What falls under merit does not come upon all alike. But temporal goods regard the good and the wicked alike, according to Ecclus. 9. 2; *All things equally happen to the just and the wicked, to the good and to the evil, to the clean and to the unclean, to him that offereth victims and to him that despiseth sacrifices.* Therefore temporal goods do not fall under merit.

I answer that, What falls under merit is the reward or wage, which is a kind of good. Now man's good is twofold—the first, absolute; the second, relative. Now man's good absolutely is his last end, (according to Ps. 72. 27: *But it is good for me to adhere to my God*), and consequently what is ordered to and leads to this end; and these fall absolutely under merit. But the relative, not the absolute, good of man is what is good to him now, or what is a good to

[2] PL 76, 41; cf. *Glossa ordin.* (I, 124E).

him under a certain respect; and this does not fall under merit absolutely, but relatively.

Hence we must say that if temporal goods are considered as they are useful for virtuous works, whereby we are led to heaven, they fall directly and absolutely under merit, even as increase of grace, and everything whereby a man is helped to attain Happiness after the first grace. For God gives men, both just and wicked, enough temporal goods to enable them to attain to everlasting life; and thus these temporal goods are absolutely good. Hence it is written in this respect (Ps. 33. 10): *For there is no want to them that fear Him,* and again, Ps. 36. 25: *I have not seen the just forsaken,* etc.

But if these temporal goods are considered in themselves, they are not man's good absolutely, but relatively, and thus they do not fall under merit absolutely, but relatively, in so far, that is, as men are moved by God to do temporal works, in which with God's help they reach their purpose. And thus as life everlasting is the reward absolutely of the works of justice in relation to the Divine motion, as stated above (A. 3), so have temporal goods, considered in themselves, the nature of reward with respect to the Divine motion, whereby men's wills are moved to undertake these works, even though, sometimes, men have not a right intention in them.

Reply Obj. 1. As Augustine says (*Contra Faust.* iv, 2),[1] "in these temporal promises were figures of spiritual things to come. For the carnal people were adhering to the promises of the present life; and not merely their speech but even their life was prophetic."

Reply Obj. 2. These rewards are said to have been divinely brought about in relation to the Divine motion, and not in relation to the malice of their wills, especially as regards the King of Babylon, since he did not besiege Tyre as if wishing to serve God, but rather in order to usurp dominion. So, too, although the midwives had a good will with regard to saving the children, yet their will was not right, since they framed falsehoods.

Reply Obj. 3. Temporal evils are imposed as a punishment on the wicked, since they are not thereby helped to reach life everlasting. But to the just who are aided by these evils they are not punishments but rather medicines as stated above (Q. LXXXVII, A. 7).

Reply Obj. 4. All things happen equally to the good and the wicked as regards the substance of temporal good or evil, but not as regards the end, since the good are led to Happiness by them, not, however, the wicked.

And now enough has been said regarding morals in general.

[1] PL 42, 218.

Part II of the Second Part

PROLOGUE

AFTER the general treatise of virtues and vices, and other things connected with the matter of morals, we must now consider each of these things in particular. For there is less use in speaking about moral matters in general, since actions are about particular things. Now moral matters can be considered in particular from two points of view. First, from the point of view of the moral matter itself, for instance by considering a particular virtue or a particular vice. Secondly, from the point of view of the special states of man, for instance by considering subjects and superiors, active life and contemplative life, or any other differences among men. Accordingly, we shall treat first in a special way of those matters which pertain to all the states of man, secondly in a special way, of those matters which pertain to particular states (Q. CLXXI).

As to the first, we must observe that if we were to treat of each virtue, gift, vice and precept separately, we should have to say the same thing over and over again. For if one wished to treat adequately of this precept: *Thou shalt not commit adultery,* he would have to inquire about adultery which is a sin, the knowledge about which depends on his knowledge of the opposite virtue. The shorter and quicker way, therefore, will be if we include the consideration of each virtue, together with its corresponding gift, opposite vice, and affirmative and negative precepts, in the same treatise. Moreover this way of treatment will be suitable to the vices according to their proper species. For it has been shown above (Part I-II, Q. LXXII) that vices and sins differ in species according to the matter or object, and not according to other differences of sins, for instance, in respect of being sins of thought, word and deed, or committed through weakness, ignorance or malice, and other like differences. Now the matter about which a virtue works what is right, and about which the opposite vice deviates from the right, is the same.

Accordingly we may reduce the whole of moral matters to the consideration of the virtues, which themselves may be reduced to seven in number. Three of these are theological, and of these we must treat first, while the other four are the cardinal virtues, of which we shall treat afterwards (Q. XLVII). Of the intellectual virtues there is one, prudence, which is included and numbered among the cardinal virtues. Art, however, does not pertain to moral science, which is concerned with things to be done, for art is right reason about things to be made, as stated above (Part I-II, Q. LVII, AA. 3, 4). The other three intellectual virtues, namely, wisdom, understanding and knowledge agree, even in name, with some of the gifts of the Holy Ghost. Therefore we shall consider them while considering the gifts corresponding to those virtues. The other moral virtues are all in some way reducible to the cardinal virtues, as was explained above (Part I-II, Q. LXI, A. 3). Hence in treating about each cardinal virtue we shall treat also of all the virtues which, in any way whatever, belong to that virtue, as also of the opposite vices. In this way no matter pertaining to morals will be overlooked.

TREATISE ON FAITH, HOPE, AND CHARITY

QUESTION I

OF FAITH

(*In Ten Articles*)

HAVING to treat now of the theological virtues, we shall begin with Faith, secondly we shall speak of Hope (Q. XVII), and thirdly, of Charity (Q. XXIII).

The treatise on Faith will be fourfold: (1) Of faith itself; (2) Of the corresponding gifts, knowledge and understanding (Q. VIII); (3) Of the opposite vices (Q. X); (4) Of these precepts pertaining to this virtue (Q. XVI).

About faith itself we shall consider: (1) its object; (2) its act (Q. II); (3) the habit of faith (Q. IV).

Under the first head there are ten points of inquiry: (1) Whether the object of faith is the First Truth? (2) Whether the object of faith is something complex or incomplex, that is, whether it is a thing or a proposition? (3) Whether anything false can come under faith? (4) Whether the object of faith can be anything seen? (5) Whether it can be anything known? (6) Whether the things to be believed should be divided into a certain number of articles? (7) Whether the same articles are of faith for all times? (8) Of the number of articles. (9) Of the manner of embodying the articles in a creed. (10) Who has the right to propose a creed of faith?

ARTICLE 1. *Whether the Object of Faith Is the First Truth?*

We proceed thus to the First Article: It would seem that the object of faith is not the First Truth.

Objection 1. For it seems that the object of faith is that which is proposed to us to be believed. Now not only things pertaining to the Godhead, that is, the First Truth, are proposed to us to be believed, but also things concerning Christ's human nature, and the sacraments of the Church, and the condition of creatures. Therefore the object of faith is not only the First Truth.

Obj. 2. Further, Faith and unbelief have the same object since they are opposed to one an-

other. Now unbelief can be about all things contained in Holy Writ, for whichever one of them a man denies, he is considered an unbeliever. Therefore faith also is about all things contained in Holy Writ. But there are many things there concerning man and other creatures. Therefore the object of faith is not only the First Truth, but also created truth.

Obj. 3. Further, Faith is divided with charity, as stated above (Part I-II, Q. LXII, A. 3). Now by charity we love not only God, who is the sovereign Good, but also our neighbour. Therefore the object of Faith is not only the First Truth.

On the contrary, Dionysius says (*Div. Nom.* vii)[1] that "faith is about the simple and everlasting truth." Now this is the First Truth. Therefore the object of faith is the First Truth.

I answer that, The object of every knowing habit includes two things: first, that which is known materially, and is the material object, so to speak, and, secondly, that by which it is known, which is the formal aspect of the object. Thus in the science of geometry, the conclusions are what is known materially, while the formal aspects of the science are the means of demonstration, through which the conclusions are known.

Accordingly if we consider, in faith, the formal aspect of the object, it is nothing else than the First Truth. For the faith of which we are speaking does not assent to anything except because it is revealed by God. Hence faith is based on the Divine Truth itself, as on the means. If, however, we consider materially the things to which faith assents, they include not only God, but also many other things, which, nevertheless, do not come under the assent of faith except as bearing some relation to God, in so far as, namely, through certain effects of the Divine operation, man is helped on his journey towards the enjoyment of God. Consequently from this point of view also the object of faith is, in a way, the First Truth, since nothing comes under faith except in relation to God, even as the object of the medical art is health, for it considers nothing except in relation to health.

[1] Sect. 4 (PG 3, 872).

Reply Obj. 1. Things concerning Christ's human nature, and the sacraments of the Church, or any creatures whatever, come under faith, in so far as by them we are directed to God, and in as much as we assent to them on account of the Divine Truth.

The same answer applies to *the Second Objection,* as regards all things contained in Holy Writ.

Reply Obj. 3. Charity also loves our neighbour on account of God, so that its object, properly speaking, is God, as we shall show further on (Q. XXV., A. 1).

ARTICLE 2. *Whether the Object of Faith Is Something Complex, by Way of a Proposition?*

We proceed thus to the Second Article: It seems that the object of faith is not something complex, by way of a proposition.

Objection 1. For the object of faith is the First Truth, as stated above (A. 1). Now the First Truth is something simple. Therefore the object of faith is not something complex.

Obj. 2. Further, The exposition of faith is contained in the creed. Now the creed does not contain propositions, but things, for it is not stated therein that God is almighty, but: "I believe in God . . . almighty." Therefore the object of faith is not a proposition but a thing.

Obj. 3. Further, Faith is succeeded by vision, according to I Cor. 13. 12: *We see now through a glass in a dark manner: but then face to face. Now I know in part; but then I shall know even as I am known.* But the object of the heavenly vision is something incomplex, for it is the Divine Essence Itself. Therefore the faith of the wayfarer is also.

On the contrary, Faith is a mean between science and opinion. Now the mean is in the same genus as the extremes. Since, then, science and opinion are about propositions, it seems that faith is likewise about propositions, so that its object is something complex.

I answer that, The thing known is in the knower according to the mode of the knower. Now the mode proper to the human intellect is to know the truth by composition and division, as stated in the First Part (Q. LXXXV, A. 5). Hence things that are simple in themselves are known by the intellect according to a certain complexity, just as on the other hand, the Divine intellect knows, without any complexity, things that are complex in themselves.

And so, therefore, the object of faith may be considered in two ways. First, as regards the thing itself which is believed, and thus the object of faith is something incomplex, namely the thing itself about which we have faith. Secondly, on the part of the believer, and in this respect the object of faith is something complex, by way of a proposition. Hence in the past both opinions have been held with a certain amount of truth.[1]

Reply Obj. 1. This argument considers the object of faith on the part of the thing believed.

Reply Obj. 2. The creed mentions the things about which faith is, in so far as the act of the believer is terminated in them, as is evident from the manner of speaking about them. Now the act of the believer does not terminate in a proposition, but in a thing. For as in science we do not form propositions except in order to have knowledge about things through their means, so is it in faith.

Reply Obj. 3. The object of the heavenly vision will be the First Truth seen in itself, according to I John 3. 2: *We know that when He shall appear, we shall be like to Him: because we shall see Him as He is.* Hence that vision will not be by way of a proposition but by way of simple understanding. On the other hand, by faith, we do not apprehend the First Truth as it is in itself. Hence the comparison fails.

ARTICLE 3. *Whether Anything False Can Come Under Faith?*

We proceed thus to the Third Article: It seems that something false can come under faith.

Objection 1. For faith is divided with hope and charity. Now something false can come under hope, since many hope to have eternal life who will not obtain it. The same may be said of charity, for many are loved as being good who nevertheless are not good. Therefore something false can be the object of faith.

Obj. 2. Further, Abraham believed that Christ would be born, according to John 8. 56: *Abraham your father rejoiced that he might see My day: he saw it, and was glad.* But after the time of Abraham, God might not have taken flesh, for it was merely because He willed that He did, so that what Abraham believed about Christ would have been false. Therefore the object of faith can be something false.

Obj. 3. Further, The ancients believed in the future birth of Christ, and many continued so

[1] Cf. Wm. of Auxerre, *Summa Aurea*, III, 3, 2, Q. 2 (134vb); also Philip the Chancellor, *Summa de Bono* (fol. 118vb). Texts quoted by Chenu, RSPT (1928), p. 85.

to believe, until they heard the preaching of the Gospel. Now, when once Christ was born, even before He began to preach, it was false that Christ was yet to be born. Therefore something false can come under faith.

Obj. 4. Further It is a matter of faith that one should believe that the true Body of Christ is contained in the Sacrament of the altar. But it might happen that the bread was not rightly consecrated, and that there was not Christ's true Body there, but only bread. Therefore something false can come under faith.

On the contrary, No virtue that perfects the intellect is related to the false, considered as the evil of the intellect, as the Philosopher declares.[1] Now faith is a virtue that perfects the intellect, as we shall show further on (Q. IV, AA. 2, 5). Therefore nothing false can come under it.

I answer that, Nothing comes under any power, habit or act, except by means of the formal aspect of the object. Thus, colour cannot be seen except by means of light, and a conclusion cannot be known save through the mean of demonstration. Now it has been stated (A. 1) that the formal aspect of the object of faith is the First Truth. And so nothing can come under faith, save in so far as it stands under the First Truth, under which nothing false can stand, as neither can non-being stand under being, nor evil under goodness. It follows therefore that nothing false can come under faith.

Reply Obj. 1. Since the true is the good of the intellect, but not of the appetitive power, it follows that all virtues which perfect the intellect exclude the false altogether, because it is of the nature of a virtue to bear relation to the good alone. On the other hand those virtues which perfect the appetitive part do not entirely exclude the false, for it is possible to act in accordance with justice or temperance, while having a false opinion about what one is doing. Therefore, as faith perfects the intellect, but hope and charity the appetitive part, the comparison between them fails.

Nevertheless neither can anything false come under hope, for a man hopes to obtain eternal life, not by his own power (since this would be an act of presumption), but with the help of grace; and if he perseveres in grace he will obtain eternal life surely and infallibly.

In like manner it pertains to charity to love God, wherever He may be, so that it matters not to charity, whether God be in the individual whom we love for God's sake.

[1] *Ethics,* VI, 2 (1139^{b}13).

Reply Obj. 2. That God would not take flesh, considered in itself was possible even after Abraham's time, but in so far as it stands in God's foreknowledge, it has a certain necessity of infallibility, as explained in the First Part (Q. XIV, A. 13), and it is thus that it comes under faith. Hence in so far as it comes under faith, it cannot be false.

Reply Obj. 3. After Christ's birth, to believe in Him was to believe in Christ's birth at some time or other. The fixing of the time, in which some were deceived, was not due to their faith, but to a human conjecture. For it is possible for a believer to have a false opinion through a human conjecture, but it is impossible for a false opinion to be the outcome of faith.

Reply Obj. 4. The faith of the believer is not directed to such and such species of bread, but to the fact that the true Body of Christ is under the species of sensible bread, when it is rightly consecrated. Hence if it is not rightly consecrated, it does not follow that anything false comes under faith.

ARTICLE 4. *Whether the Object of Faith Can Be Something Seen?*

We proceed thus to the Fourth Article: It seems that the object of faith is something seen.

Objection 1. For Our Lord said to Thomas (John 20. 29): *Because thou hast seen Me, Thomas, thou hast believed.* Therefore vision and faith regard the same object.

Obj. 2. Further, The Apostle, while speaking of the knowledge of faith, says (I Cor. 13. 12): *We see now through a glass in a dark manner.* Therefore what is believed is seen.

Obj. 3. Further, Faith is a spiritual light. Now something is seen under every light. Therefore faith is of things seen.

Obj. 4. Further, Every sense is a kind of sight, as Augustine states (*De Verb. Domini*).[2] But faith is of things heard, according to Rom. 10. 17: *Faith . . . cometh by hearing.* Therefore faith is of things seen.

On the contrary, The Apostle says (Heb. 11. 1) that *faith is the evidence of things that appear not.*

I answer that, Faith implies assent of the intellect to that which is believed. Now the intellect assents to a thing in two ways. First, through being moved to assent by its very object, which is known either by itself (as in the case of first principles, which are held by the habit of understanding), or through something else already known (as in the case of conclusions

[2] *Serm. ad Popul.,* CXII, 6 (PL 38, 646).

which are held by the habit of science). Secondly the intellect assents to something, not because it is sufficiently moved to this assent by its proper object, but through an act of choice, by which it turns voluntarily to one side rather than to the other. And if this be accompanied by doubt and fear of the opposite side, there will be opinion, while, if there be certainty and no fear of the other side, there will be faith.

Now those things are said to be seen which, of themselves, move the intellect or the senses to knowledge of them. Hence it is evident that neither faith nor opinion can be of things seen either by the senses or by the intellect.

Reply Obj. 1. Thomas saw one thing, and believed another. He saw the Man, and believing Him to be God, he made profession of his faith, saying: *My Lord and my God.*[1]

Reply Obj. 2. Those things which come under faith can be considered in two ways. First, in particular; and thus they cannot be seen and believed at the same time, as shown above. Secondly, in general, that is, under the common aspect of credibility; and in this way they are seen by the believer. For he would not believe unless, on the evidence of signs, or of something similar, he saw that they ought to be believed.

Reply. Obj. 3. The light of faith makes us see what we believe. For just as, by the habits of the other virtues, man sees what is fitting to him in respect of that habit, so, by the habit of faith, the human mind is directed to assent to such things as are fitting to a right faith, and not to assent to others.

Reply Obj. 4. Hearing is of words signifying what is of faith, but not of the things themselves that are believed. Hence it does not follow that these things are seen.

ARTICLE 5. *Whether Those Things That Are Of Faith Can Be an Object of Science?*

We proceed thus to the Fifth Article: It would seem that those things that are of faith can be an object of science.

Objection 1. For where science is lacking there is ignorance, since ignorance is the opposite of science. Now we are not in ignorance of those things we have to believe, since ignorance of such things pertains to unbelief, according to I Tim. 1. 13: *I did it ignorantly in unbelief.* Therefore things that are of faith can be an object of science.

Obj. 2. Further, Science is acquired by reasons. Now sacred writers employ reasons to inculcate things that are of faith. Therefore such things can be an object of science.

Obj. 3. Further, Things which are demonstrated are an object of science, since a demonstration is a syllogism that produces science. Now certain matters of faith have been demonstrated by the philosophers such as the Existence and Unity of God, and so forth. Therefore things that are of faith can be an object of science.

Obj. 4. Further, Opinion is further from science than faith is, since faith is said to stand between opinion and science. Now "opinion and science can, in a way, be about the same object," as stated in the *Posterior Analytics.*[2] Therefore faith and science can be about the same object also.

On the contrary, Gregory says (*Hom.* xxvi *in Ev.*)[3] that "when a thing is manifest, it is the object, not of faith, but of perception." Therefore things that are of faith are not the object of perception, but what is an object of science is the object of perception. Therefore there can be no faith about things which are an object of science.

I answer that, All science is derived from principles self-evident and therefore seen; and therefore all objects of science must be, in a fashion, seen.

Now as stated above (A. 4) it is impossible that one and the same thing should be believed and seen by the same person. Hence it is equally impossible for one and the same thing to be an object of science and of belief for the same person. It may happen, however, that a thing which is an object of vision or science for one, is believed by another; for we hope to see some day what we now believe about the Trinity, according to I Cor. 13. 12: *We see now through a glass in a dark manner; but then face to face.* This vision the angels possess already, so that what we believe, they see. In like manner it may happen that what is an object of vision or scientific knowledge for one man, even in the state of a wayfarer, is, for another man, an object of faith, because he does not know it by demonstration.

Nevertheless that which is proposed to be believed equally by all, is equally unknown by all as an object of science; such are the things which are of faith absolutely. Consequently faith and science are not about the same things.

Reply Obj. 1. Unbelievers are in ignorance of things that are of faith, for neither do they see

---

[1] Gregory, *In Evang.*, BK. II, hom. XXVI (PL 76, 1202).

[2] Aristotle, I, 33 (89ª25).

[3] PL 76, 1202.

or know them in themselves, nor do they know them to be credible. The faithful, on the other hand, know them, not as by demonstration, but by the light of faith which makes them see that they ought to believe them, as stated above (A. 4, Reply 2, 3).

Reply Obj. 2. The reasons employed by holy men to prove things that are of faith, are not demonstrations. They are either persuasive arguments showing that what is proposed to our faith is not impossible, or else they are proofs drawn from the principles of faith, that is, from the authority of Holy Writ, as Dionysius declares (*Div. Nom.* ii).[1] Whatever is based on these principles is as well proved in the eyes of the faithful, as a conclusion drawn from self-evident principles is in the eyes of all. Hence again, theology is a science, as we stated at the outset of this work (Part I, Q. I, A. 2).

Reply Obj. 3. Things which can be proved by demonstration are accounted among the articles of faith, not because they are believed absolutely by all, but because they are a necessary prerequisite to matters of faith, so that they must at least be pre-supposed by faith in those who do not know them by demonstration.

Reply Obj. 4. As the Philosopher says,[2] science and opinion about the same object can certainly be in different men, as we have stated above about science and faith. Yet it is possible for one and the same man to have science and faith about the same thing relatively, that is, in relation to the subject, but not in the same respect. For it is possible for the same person, about one and the same thing, to know one thing and to think another. And, in like manner, one may know by demonstration the unity of God, and believe that He is a Trinity. On the other hand, in one and the same man, about the same thing, and in the same respect, science is incompatible with either opinion or faith, yet for different reasons. Because science is incompatible with opinion about the same thing absolutely, for the notion of science demands that what is known should be thought impossible to be otherwise, but the notion of opinion demands that the thing of which there is opinion may be thought possible to be otherwise. Yet that which is held by faith, on account of the certainty of faith, is also thought impossible to be otherwise; and the reason why science and faith cannot be about the same object and in the same respect is because the object of science is something seen, while the object of faith is the unseen, as stated above.

[1] Sect. 2 (PG 3, 640).　　[2] *Op. cit.*, I, 33 (89ᵇ2).

ARTICLE 6. *Whether Those Things That Are of Faith Should Be Divided Into Certain Articles?*

We proceed thus to the Sixth Article: It seems that those things that are of faith should not be divided into certain articles.

Objection 1. For all things contained in Holy Writ are matters of faith. But these, by reason of their multitude, cannot be reduced to a certain number. Therefore it seems superfluous to distinguish certain articles of faith.

Obj. 2. Further, Material differences can be multiplied indefinitely, and therefore art should take no notice of them. Now the formal aspect of the object of faith is one and indivisible, as stated above (A. 1), namely, the First Truth, so that matters of faith cannot be distinguished in respect of their formal object. Therefore no notice should be taken of a material division of matters of faith into articles.

Obj. 3. Further, It has been said by some[3] that an article is an indivisible truth concerning God, exacting (*arctans*) our belief. Now belief is a voluntary act, since, as Augustine says (*Tract.* xxvi *in Joann.*),[4] "no man believes against his will." Therefore it seems that matters of faith should not be divided into articles.

On the contrary, Isidore says:[5] "An article is a glimpse of Divine truth, tending thereto." Now we can only get a glimpse of Divine truth by way of distinguishing, since things which in God are one, are many in our intellect. Therefore matters of faith should be divided into articles.

I answer that, The word article is apparently derived from the Greek, for the Greek ἄρθρον, which the Latin renders *articulus*, signifies a fitting together of distinct parts. And therefore the small parts of the body which fit together are called the articulations of the limbs. Likewise, in the Greek grammar, articles are parts of speech which are affixed to words to show their gender, number or case. Again in rhetoric, articles are parts that fit together in a sentence, for Tully says (*Rhet.* iv)[6] that an article is composed of words each pronounced singly and separately, for example, "Your passion, your voice, your look, have struck terror into your foes."

[3] For the origin of this definition cf. Parent, EHLD (I, 149).　　[4] PL 35, 1607.

[5] Cf. Albert, *In Sent.*, III, d. 24, A. 4 (BO XXVIII, 449) and Bonaventure, *In Sent.*, III, d. 24, A. 3, Q. 2 (QR III, 527). Philip the Chancellor also refers to the same definition without naming the author (*Summa de Bono,* fol. 85va); cf. also Parent, EHLD (I, 149).

[6] *Rhetor. ad Herenn.*, Chap. 19 (DD I, 60).

Hence matters of Christian faith are said to be distinguished into articles in so far as they are divided into parts which fit together. Now the object of faith is something unseen relating to God, as stated above (A. 4). Consequently any matter that, for a special reason, is unseen, is a special article, but when several matters are known or not known, under the same aspect, we are not to distinguish various articles. Thus one encounters one difficulty in seeing that God suffered, and another in seeing that He rose again from the dead, and therefore the article of the Resurrection is distinct from the article of the Passion. But that He suffered, died and was buried, present the same difficulty, so that if one be accepted it is not difficult to accept the others; therefore all these belong to one article.

Reply Obj. 1. Some things proposed to our belief are in themselves of faith, while others are of faith, not in themselves but only in relation to others, even as in the other sciences certain propositions are put forward on their own account, while others are put forward in order to manifest others. Now, since faith is principally of those things which we hope to see in heaven, according to Heb. 11. 1: *Faith is the substance of things to be hoped for*, it follows that those things are in themselves of faith which order us directly to eternal life. Such are the Trinity of Persons in Almighty God,[1] the mystery of Christ's Incarnation, and the like; and these are distinct articles of faith. On the other hand certain things in Holy Writ are proposed to our belief not chiefly on their own account but for the manifestation of those mentioned above; for instance, that Abraham had two sons, that a dead man rose again at the touch of Eliseus' bones, and the like, which are related in Holy Writ for the purpose of manifesting the Divine majesty or the Incarnation of Christ. And such things should not form distinct articles.

Reply Obj. 2. The formal aspect of the object of faith can be taken in two ways. First, on the part of the thing believed, and thus there is one formal aspect of all matters of faith, namely, the First Truth. And from this point of view there is no distinction of articles. Secondly, the formal aspect of matters of faith can be considered from our point of view; and thus the formal aspect of a matter of faith is that it is something unseen. And from this point of view there are various distinct articles of faith, as we saw above.

[1] The reading of the Piana text. The Leonine Edition reads: The three Persons, the omnipotence of God, etc.

Reply Obj. 3. This definition of an article is taken from an etymology of the word as derived from the Latin, rather than in accordance with its real meaning, as derived from the Greek. Hence it does not carry much weight. Yet even then it could be said that although faith is exacted of no man by a necessity of coercion, since belief is a voluntary act, yet it is exacted of him by a necessity of end, since *he that cometh to God must believe that He is*, and *without faith it is impossible to please God*, as the Apostle declares (Heb. 11. 6).

ARTICLE 7. *Whether the Articles of Faith Have Increased in Course of Time?*

We proceed thus to the Seventh Article: It would seem that the articles of faith have not increased in course of time.

Objection 1. Because, as the Apostle says (Heb. 11. 1), *faith is the substance of things to be hoped for*. Now the same things are to be hoped for at all times. Therefore, at all times, the same things are to be believed.

Obj. 2. Further, Development has taken place in sciences devised by man on account of the lack of knowledge in those who discovered them, as the Philosopher observes.[2] Now the doctrine of faith was not discovered by man but was delivered to us by God, as stated in Eph. 2. 8: *It is the gift of God*. Since then there can be no lack of knowledge in God, it seems that knowledge of matters of faith was perfect from the beginning, and did not increase as time went on.

Obj. 3. Further, The operation of grace proceeds in orderly fashion no less than the operation of nature. Now nature always makes a beginning with perfect things, as Boëthius states (*De Consol.* iii, 10).[3] Therefore it seems that the operation of grace also began with perfect things, so that those who were the first to deliver the faith knew it most perfectly.

Obj. 4. Further, Just as the faith of Christ was delivered to us through the apostles, so too, in the Old Testament, the knowledge of faith was delivered by the early fathers to those who came later, according to Deuter. 32. 7: *Ask thy father, and he will declare to thee*. Now the apostles were most fully instructed about the mysteries, for "they received them more fully than others, even as they received them earlier," as a gloss says on Rom. 8. 23: *Ourselves also who have the first fruits of the Spirit.*[4]

[2] *Metaphysics*, II, 1 (993ª30).
[3] PL 63, 764.
[4] *Glossa interl.*, (VI, 19r); *Glossa* Lombardi (PL 191, 1444).

Therefore it seems that knowledge of matters of faith has not increased as time went on.

On the contrary, Gregory says (*Hom.* xvi *in Ezech.*)[1] that "the knowledge of the holy fathers increased as time went on . . .; and the nearer they were to Our Saviour's coming, the more fully did they receive the mysteries of salvation."

I answer that, The articles of faith stand in the same relation to the doctrine of faith, as self-evident principles to a teaching based on natural reason. Among these principles there is a certain order, so that some are contained implicitly in others; thus all principles are reduced, as to their first principle, to this one: "The same thing cannot be affirmed and denied at the same time," as the Philosopher states.[2] In like manner all the articles are contained implicitly in certain primary matters of faith, such as God's existence, and His providence over the salvation of man, according to Heb. 11.6: *He that cometh to God, must believe that He is, and is a rewarder to them that seek Him.* For the being of God includes all that we believe to exist in God eternally, and in these our Happiness consists; while belief in His providence includes all those things which God dispenses in time, for man's salvation, and which are the way to that Happiness. And in this way, again, some of those articles which follow from these are contained in others. Thus faith in the Redemption of mankind includes belief in the Incarnation of Christ, His Passion and so forth.

Accordingly we must conclude that, as regards the substance of the articles of faith, they have not received any increase as time went on, since whatever those who lived later have believed, was contained, although implicitly, in the faith of those Fathers who preceded them. But there was an increase in the number of articles believed explicitly, since to those who lived in later times some were known explicitly which were not known explicitly by those who lived before them. Hence the Lord said to Moses (Exod. 6. 2, 3): *I am the God of Abraham, the God of Isaac, the God of Jacob* (Vulg.,—*I am the Lord that appeared to Abraham, to Isaac, and to Jacob.*) . . . *and My name Adonai I did not show them:* David also said (Ps. 118. 100): *I have had understanding above ancients:* and the Apostle says (Eph. 3. 5) that the mystery of Christ, *in other generations was not known, as it is now revealed to His holy apostles and prophets.*

[1] PL 76, 980.　　　[2] *Metaphysics,* IV, 6 (1011b20).

Reply Obj. 1. Among men the same things were always to be hoped for from Christ. But as they did not acquire this hope save through Christ, the further they were removed from Christ in point of time, the further they were from obtaining what they hoped for. Hence the Apostle says (Heb. 11. 13): *All these died according to faith, not having received the promises, but beholding them afar off.* Now the further off a thing is the less distinctly is it seen. And therefore those who were near to Christ's advent had a more distinct knowledge of the good things to be hoped for.

Reply Obj. 2. Progress in knowledge occurs in two ways. First, on the part of the teacher, be he one or many, who makes progress in knowledge as time goes on. And this is the kind of progress that takes place in sciences devised by man. Secondly, on the part of the learner; thus the master, who has perfect knowledge of the art, does not deliver it all at once to his disciple from the very outset, for he would not be able to take it all in, but he condescends to the disciple's capacity and instructs him little by little. It is in this way that men made progress in the knowledge of faith as time went on. Hence the Apostle (Gal. 3. 24) compares the state of the Old Testament to childhood.

Reply Obj. 3. Two causes are requisite before actual generation can take place, an agent, namely, and matter. In order of the active cause, therefore, the more perfect is naturally first. And in this way nature makes a beginning with perfect things, since the imperfect is not brought to perfection, except by something perfect already in existence. On the other hand, in the order of the material cause, the imperfect comes first, and in this way nature proceeds from the imperfect to the perfect. Now in the manifestation of faith, God is the active cause, having perfect knowledge from all eternity, while man is likened to matter in receiving the influx of God's action. Hence, among men, the knowledge of faith had to proceed from imperfection to perfection. And, although some men have been after the manner of active causes, through being doctors of the faith, nevertheless the manifestation of the Spirit is given to such men for the common good, according to I Cor. 12. 7. And therefore the knowledge of faith was imparted to the Fathers who were instructors in the faith, so far as was necessary at the time for the instruction of the people, either openly or in figures.

Reply Obj. 4. The ultimate consummation of grace was effected by Christ, and so the time of His coming is called the *time of fulness* (Gal. 4. 4) Vulg.,—*fulness of time*. Hence those who were nearest to Christ, whether before, like John the Baptist, or after, like the apostles, had a fuller knowledge of the mysteries of faith. For even with regard to man's state we find that the perfection of manhood comes in youth, and that a man's state is all the more perfect, whether before or after, the nearer it is to the time of his youth.

Article 8. *Whether the Articles of Faith Are Suitably Enumerated?*

We proceed thus to the Eighth Article: It seems that the articles of faith are unsuitably enumerated.

Objection 1. For those things, which can be known by demonstration, do not belong to the faith as to an object of belief for all, as stated above (A. 5). Now it can be known by demonstration that there is one God. Hence the Philosopher proves this,[1] and many other philosophers demonstrated the same truth. Therefore that there is one God should not be set down as an article of faith.

Obj. 2. Further, Just as it is necessary to faith that we should believe God to be almighty, so is it too that we should believe Him to be all-knowing and provident for all, about both of which points some have erred.[2] Therefore, among the articles of faith, mention should have been made of God's wisdom and providence, even as of His omnipotence.

Obj. 3. Further, To know the Father is the same thing as to know the Son, according to John 14. 9: *He that seeth Me, seeth the Father also.* Therefore there ought to be but one article about the Father and Son, and, for the same reason, about the Holy Ghost.

Obj. 4. Further, The Person of the Father is no less than the Person of the Son, and of the Holy Ghost. Now there are several articles about the Person of the Holy Ghost, and likewise about the Person of the Son. Therefore there should be several articles about the Person of the Father.

Obj. 5. Further, Just as certain things are said by appropriation, of the Person of the Father and of the Person of the Holy Ghost, so too is something appropriated to the Person of the Son, in respect of His Godhead. Now, among the articles of faith, a place is given to a work appropriated to the Father, namely the creation, and likewise, a work appropriated to the

Holy Ghost, namely that He spoke by the prophets. Therefore the articles of faith should contain some work appropriated to the Son in respect of His Godhead.

Obj. 6. Further, The sacrament of the Eucharist presents a special difficulty over and above the other articles. Therefore it should have been mentioned in a special article. Consequently it seems that there is not a sufficient number of articles.

On the contrary stands the authority of the Church who formulates the articles thus.[3]

I answer that, As stated above (A. 6, Reply 1), those things in themselves belong to faith, the sight of which we shall enjoy in eternal life, and by which we are brought to eternal life. Now two things are proposed to us to be seen in eternal life: namely, the secret of the Godhead, to see which is to possess Happiness; and the mystery of Christ's humanity, *by Whom we have access* to the glory of the sons of God, according to Rom. 5. 2. Hence it is written (John 17. 3): *This is eternal life: that they may know Thee, the . . . true God, and Jesus Christ Whom Thou hast sent.* Therefore the first distinction in matters of faith is that some concern the majesty of the Godhead, while others pertain to the mystery of Christ's human nature, which is the *mystery of godliness* (I Tim. 3. 16).

Now with regard to the majesty of the Godhead, three things are proposed to our belief. First the unity of the Godhead, to which the first article refers. Secondly, the trinity of the Persons, to which three articles refer, corresponding to the three Persons. And thirdly the works proper to the Godhead: the first of which refers to the order (*esse*) of nature, in relation to which the article about the creation is proposed to us; the second refers to the order (*esse*) of grace, in relation to which all matters concerning the sanctification of man are included in one article; while the third refers to the order (*esse*) of glory, and in relation to this another article is proposed to us concerning the resurrection of the dead and life everlasting. Thus there are seven articles referring to the Godhead.

In like manner, with regard to Christ's human nature, there are seven articles, the first of which refers to Christ's incarnation or conception; the second, to His virginal birth; the third, to His Passion, death and burial; the fourth, to His descent into hell; the fifth, to His resurrection; the sixth, to His ascension; the seventh, to His coming for the judgment, so

---

[1] *Metaphysics*, XII, 10 (1076a4).
[2] Cf. Part I, Q. XIV, A. 6; Q. XXII, A. 2.

[3] The Nicene-Constantinople Creed (MA III, 565; DZ 86).

that in all there are fourteen articles.

Some, however, distinguish twelve articles, six pertaining to the Godhead, and six to the humanity.[1] For they include in one article the three about the three Persons, because we have one knowledge of the three Persons. But they divide the article referring to the work of glorification into two, namely, the resurrection of the body, and the glory of the soul. Likewise they unite the conception and nativity into one article.

Reply Obj. 1. By faith we hold many truths about God, which the philosophers were unable to discover by natural reason, for instance His providence and omnipotence, and that He alone is to be worshipped, all of which are contained in the one article of the unity of God.

Reply Obj. 2. The very name of the Godhead implies a kind of watching over things, as stated in the First Part (Q. XIII, A. 8). Now in beings having an intellect, power does not operate except by the will and knowledge. Hence God's omnipotence includes, in a way, universal knowledge and providence. For He would not be able to do all He wills in things here below unless He knew them and exercised His providence over them.

Reply Obj. 3. We have but one knowledge of the Father, Son, and Holy Ghost, as to the unity of the Essence, to which the first article refers. But as to the distinction of the Persons, which is by the relations of origin, knowledge of the Father does indeed, in a way, include knowledge of the Son, for He would not be Father had He not a Son, the bond between Them being the Holy Ghost. From this point of view there was a sufficient motive for those who referred one article to the three Persons. Since, however, with regard to each Person, certain points have to be observed, about which some happen to fall into error, looking at it in this way, we may distinguish three articles about the three Persons. For Arius believed in the omnipotence and eternity of the Father, but did not believe the Son to be co-equal and consubstantial with the Father; hence the need for an article about the Person of the Son in order to settle this point. In like manner it was necessary to appoint a third article about the Person of the Holy Ghost, against Macedonius. In the same way Christ's conception and birth, just as the resurrection and life everlasting, can from one point of view be united together in one article, in so far as they are ordered to one end; while, from another point of view they can be distinct articles, in so far as each one separately presents a special difficulty.

Reply Obj. 4. It belongs to the Son and Holy Ghost to be sent to sanctify the creature, and about this several things have to be believed. Hence it is that there are more articles about the Persons of the Son and Holy Ghost than about the Person of the Father, Who is never sent, as we stated in the First Part (Q. XLIII, A. 4).

Reply Obj. 5. The sanctification of a creature by grace, and its consummation by glory, is also effected by the gift of charity, which is appropriated to the Holy Ghost, and by the gift of wisdom, which is appropriated to the Son. And therefore each work belongs by appropriation, but under different aspects, both to the Son and to the Holy Ghost.

Reply Obj. 6. Two things may be considered in the sacrament of the Eucharist. One is the fact that it is a sacrament, and in this respect it is like the other effects of sanctifying grace. The other is that Christ's body is miraculously contained there, and thus it is included under God's omnipotence, like all other miracles which are ascribed to God's almighty power.

ARTICLE 9. *Whether It Is Suitable for the Articles of Faith To Be Embodied in a Creed?*

We proceed thus to the Ninth Article: It seems that it is unsuitable for the articles of faith to be embodied in a creed.

Objection 1. Because Holy Writ is the rule of faith, to which no addition or subtraction can lawfully be made, since it is written (Deut. 4. 2): *You shall not add to the word that I speak to you, neither shall you take away from it.* Therefore it was unlawful to make a creed as a rule of faith, after Holy Writ had once been published.

Obj. 2. Further, According to the Apostle (Eph. 4. 5) there is but *one faith.* Now the creed is a profession of faith. Therefore it is not fitting that there should be many creeds handed down.

Obj. 3. Further, The confession of faith, which is contained in the creed, concerns all the faithful. Now the faithful are not all able to believe in God, but only those who have faith that is formed. Therefore it is unfitting for the creed of faith to be expressed in the words: *I believe in one God.*

Obj. 4. Further, The descent into hell is one of the articles of faith, as stated above (A. 8). But the descent into hell is not mentioned in the creed of the early Fathers. Therefore the latter is expressed inadequately.

[1] Cf. Bonaventure, *In Hexaëm,* VIII (QRV, 371).

Obj. 5. Further, Augustine (*Tract.* xxix *in Joann.*)[1] expounding the passage, *You believe in God, believe also in Me* (John 14. 1) says: "We believe Peter or Paul, but we speak only of believing 'in' God." Since then the Catholic Church is merely a created being, it seems unfitting to say: "In the One, Holy, Catholic and Apostolic Church."

Obj. 6. Further, A creed is drawn up that it may be a rule of faith. Now a rule of faith ought to be proposed to all, and that publicly. Therefore every creed, besides the creed of the Fathers, should be sung at Mass. Therefore it seems unfitting to publish the articles of faith in a creed.

On the contrary, The universal Church cannot err, since she is governed by the Holy Ghost Who is the Spirit of truth: for such was Our Lord's promise to His disciples (John 16. 13): *When He, the Spirit of truth, is come, He will teach you all truth.* Now the creed is published by the authority of the universal Church. Therefore it contains nothing unfitting.

I answer that, As the Apostle says (Heb. 11. 6), *he that cometh to God, must believe that He is.* Now a man cannot believe, unless the truth be proposed to him that he may believe it. Hence the need for the truth of faith to be collected together, so that it might the more easily be proposed to all, lest anyone might stray from the truth through ignorance of the faith. It is from its being a collection of propositions of faith that the symbol (the Greek *συμβάλλειν*) takes it name.

Reply Obj. 1. The truth of faith is spread throughout Holy Writ, under various modes of expression, and sometimes obscurely, so that, in order to gather the truth of faith from Holy Writ, one needs long study and practice, which are unattainable by all those who require to know the truth of faith, many of whom have no time for study, being busy with other affairs. And so it was necessary to gather together a clear summary from the sayings of Holy Writ, to be proposed to the belief of all. This indeed was no addition to Holy Writ, but something taken from it.

Reply Obj. 2. The same truth of faith is taught in all the creeds. Nevertheless, the people need more careful instruction about the truth of faith, when errors arise, lest the faith of simple-minded persons be corrupted by heretics. It was this that gave rise to the necessity of formulating several creeds, which in no way differ from one another, save that on account

of the obstinacy of heretics, one contains more explicitly what another contains implicitly.

Reply Obj. 3. The confession of faith is drawn up in a creed in the person, as it were, of the whole Church, which is united together by faith. Now the faith of the Church is a formed faith, since such is the faith to be found in all those who are of the Church outwardly and by merit. Hence the confession of faith is expressed in a creed, in a manner that is in keeping with a formed faith, so that even if some of the faithful lack a formed faith, they should endeavour to acquire it.

Reply Obj. 4. No error about the descent into hell had arisen among heretics, so that there was no need to be more explicit on that point. For this reason it is not repeated in the creed of the Fathers, but is supposed as already settled in the creed of the Apostles. For a subsequent creed does not cancel a preceding one but rather expounds it, as stated above (REPLY 2).

Reply Obj. 5. If we say: "In" the holy Catholic Church, this must be taken as verified in so far as our faith is directed to the Holy Ghost, Who sanctifies the Church, so that the sense is: I believe in the Holy Ghost sanctifying the Church. But it is better and more in keeping with the common use to omit the "in," and say simply, the holy Catholic Church, as Pope Leo observes[2]

Reply Obj. 6. Since the creed of the Fathers is an explanation of the Apostles' Creed, and was drawn up after the faith was already spread abroad, and when the Church was already at peace, it is sung publicly in the Mass. On the other hand the Apostles' Creed, which was drawn up at the time of persecution, before the faith was made public, is said secretly at Prime and Compline, as though it were against the darkness of past and future errors.

ARTICLE 10. *Whether it Pertains to the Sovereign Pontiff To Draw Up a Creed of Faith?*

We proceed thus to the Tenth Article: It would seem that it does not pertain to the Sovereign Pontiff to draw up a creed of faith.

Objection 1. For a new version of the creed becomes necessary in order to explain the articles of faith, as stated above (A. 9, REPLY 2). Now, in the Old Testament, the articles of faith were more and more explained as time went on, by reason of the truth of faith becoming clearer through greater nearness to Christ, as stated above (A. 7). Since then this reason ceased with

[1] PL 35, 1631.

[2] Rufinus, *Comm. in Sym. Apost.* (PL 21, 373).

the advent of the New Law, there is no need for the articles of faith to be more and more explicit. Therefore it does not seem to pertain to the authority of the Sovereign Pontiff to draw up a new version of the creed.

Obj. 2. Further, No man has the power to do what is forbidden under pain of anathema by the universal Church. Now it was forbidden under pain of anathema by the universal Church to make a new version of the creed. For it is stated in the acts of the first[1] council of Ephesus (P. II, ACT. 6)[2] that after the creed of the Nicene council had been read through, "the holy synod decreed that it was unlawful to utter, write or draw up any other creed, than that which was defined by the Fathers assembled at Nicæa together with the Holy Ghost," and this under pain of anathema. The same was repeated in the acts of the council of Chalcedon (P. II, ACT. 5).[3] Therefore it seems that the Sovereign Pontiff has no authority to publish a new version of the creed.

Obj. 3. Further, Athanasius was not the Sovereign Pontiff, but patriarch of Alexandria, and yet he published a creed which is sung in the Church. Therefore it does not seem to pertain to the Sovereign Pontiff any more than to other bishops, to publish a new version of the creed.

On the contrary, The creed was drawn up by a general council. Now such a council cannot be convoked otherwise than by the authority of the Sovereign Pontiff, as stated in the Decretals (Dist. xvii, cap. 4, 5).[4] Therefore to draw up a creed pertains to the authority of the Sovereign Pontiff.

I answer that, As stated above (A. 9, REPLY 2), a new version of the creed becomes necessary in order to set aside the errors that may arise. Consequently to publish a new version of the creed pertains to that authority which is empowered to decide matters of faith finally, so that they may be held by all with unshaken faith. Now this pertains to the authority of the Sovereign Pontiff, "to whom the more important and more difficult questions that arise in the Church are referred," as stated in the Decretals.[5] Hence Our Lord said to Peter whom he made Sovereign Pontiff (Luke 22. 32): *I have prayed for thee, Peter, that thy faith fail*

not, and thou, being once converted, confirm thy brethren. The reason of this is that there should be but one faith of the whole Church, according to I Cor. 1. 10: *That you all speak the same thing, and that there be no schisms among you,* and this could not be secured unless any question of faith that may arise be decided by him who presides over the whole Church, so that the whole Church may hold firmly to his decision. Consequently it pertains to the sole authority of the Sovereign Pontiff to publish a new version of the creed, as do all other matters which concern the whole Church, such as to convoke a general council and so forth.

Reply Obj. 1. The truth of faith is sufficiently explicit in the teaching of Christ and the apostles. But since, according to II Pet. 3. 16, some men are so evil-minded as to pervert the apostolic teaching and other doctrines and Scriptures to their own destruction, it was necessary as time went on to express the faith more explicitly against the errors which arose.

Reply Obj. 2. This prohibition and sentence of the council was intended for private individuals, who have no business to decide matters of faith. For this decision of the general council did not take away from a subsequent council the power of drawing up a new version of the creed, containing not indeed a new faith, but the same faith with greater explicitness. For every council has taken into account that a subsequent council would expound matters more fully than the preceding council, if this became necessary through some heresy arising. Consequently this pertains to the Sovereign Pontiff, by whose authority the council is convoked, and its decision confirmed.

Reply Obj. 3. Athanasius drew up a declaration of faith, not under the form of a creed, but rather by way of an exposition of doctrine, as appears from his way of speaking. But since it contained briefly the whole truth of faith, it was accepted by the authority of the Sovereign Pontiff, so as to be considered as a rule of faith.

QUESTION II
OF THE ACT OF FAITH
(*In Ten Articles*)

WE must now consider the act of faith, and (1) the internal act, (2) the external act (Q. III.).

Under the first head there are ten points of inquiry: (1) What is "to believe," which is the inward act of faith? (2) In how many ways is it expressed? (3) Whether it is necessary for sal-

---

[1] S. Thomas wrote "first" to distinguish it from the other council, A.D. 451, known as the *Latrocinium* and condemned by the Pope.

[2] MA IV, 1362; DZ 125.

[3] MA VII, 109.

[4] Gratian, *Decretum* (RF I, 51).

[5] *Ibid.,* PT. I, d. XVII, 5 (RF I, 52); cf. *Decretal. Gregor.,* IX, III, XLII, 3 (RF II, 644).

vation to believe in anything above natural reason? (4) Whether it is necessary to believe those things that are attainable by natural reason? (5) Whether it is necessary for salvation to believe certain things explicitly? (6) Whether all are equally bound to explicit faith? (7) Whether explicit faith in Christ is always necessary for salvation? (8) Whether it is necessary for salvation to believe in the Trinity explicitly? (9) Whether the act of faith is meritorious? (10) Whether human reason diminishes the merit of faith?

ARTICLE 1. *Whether To Believe Is To Think With Assent?*

We proceed thus to the First Article: It seems that to believe is not to think with assent.

Objection 1. Because the Latin word *cogitatio* (thought) implies a searching, for *cogitare* (to think) seems to be equivalent to *coagitare,* that is, to discuss together. Now Damascene says (*De Fide Orthod.* iv)[1] that faith is "an assent without searching." Therefore thinking has no place in the act of faith.

Obj. 2. Further, Faith resides in the reason, as we shall show further on (Q. IV., A. 2). Now to think is an act of the cogitative faculty, which belongs to the sensitive faculty, as stated in the First Part (Q. LXXVIII., A. 4). Therefore thought has nothing to do with faith.

Obj. 3. Further, To believe is an act of the intellect, since its object is truth. But assent seems to be an act not of the intellect, but of the will, even as consent is, as stated above (Q. I, A. 4; Part I-II, Q. XV, A. 1, Reply 3). Therefore to believe is not to think with assent.

On the contrary, This is how "to believe" is defined by Augustine (*De Prædest. Sanct.* ii).[2]

I answer that, "To think" can be taken in three ways. First, in a general way for any kind of actual consideration of the intellect, as Augustine observes (*De Trin.* xiv, 7):[3] "By understanding I mean now the power whereby we understand when thinking." Secondly, "to think" is more strictly taken for that consideration of the intellect which is accompanied by some kind of inquiry, and which precedes the intellect's arrival at the stage of perfection that comes with the certitude of sight. In this sense Augustine says (*De Trin.* xv, 16)[4] that "the Son of God is not called the Thought, but the Word of God. When our thought realizes what we know and takes form from it, it becomes our

word. Hence the Word of God must be understood without any thinking on the part of God, for there is nothing there that can take form, or be unformed." In this way thought is, properly speaking, the movement of the mind while yet deliberating, and not yet perfected by the full vision of truth. Since, however, such a movement of the mind may be one of deliberation either about universal intentions, which pertains to the intellectual part, or about particular intentions, which pertains to the sensitive part, hence "to think" is taken secondly for an act of the deliberating intellect, and thirdly for an act of the cogitative power.

Accordingly, if "to think" be understood broadly according to the first sense, then "to think with assent" does not express completely what is meant by "to believe", since, in this way a man thinks with assent even when he considers what he knows by science, or understands. If, on the other hand, "to think" be understood in the second way, then this expresses completely the nature of the act of believing. For among the acts belonging to the intellect, some have a firm assent without any such kind of thinking, as when a man considers the things that he knows by science, or understands, for this consideration is already formed. But some acts of the intellect have unformed thought lacking a firm assent, whether they incline to neither side, as in one who doubts; or incline to one side rather than the other, but on account of some slight motive, as in one who suspects; or incline to one side yet with fear of the other, as in one who holds an opinion. But this act "to believe," cleaves firmly to one side, in which respect belief has something in common with science and understanding; yet its knowledge does not attain the perfection of clear vision, in which respect it agrees with doubt, suspicion and opinion. Hence it is proper to the believer to think with assent, so that the act of believing is distinguished from all the other acts of the intellect, which are about the true or the false.

Reply Obj. 1. Faith has not that searching of natural reason which demonstrates what is believed, but a searching into those things through which a man is led to believe, for instance that such things have been uttered by God and confirmed by miracles.

Reply Obj. 2. "To think" is not taken here for the act of the cogitative power, but according as it pertains to the intellect, as explained above.

Reply Obj. 3. The intellect of the believer is determined to one object, not by the reason, but

---

[1] Chap. 11 (PG 94, 1128).
[2] PL 44, 963. Cf. Chenu, EHLD (II, 163).
[3] PL 42, 1044.   [4] PL 42, 1079.

by the will, and so assent is taken here for an act of the intellect as determined to one object by the will.

ARTICLE 2. *Whether the Act of Faith Is Suitably Distinguished as Believing God, Believing in a God, and Believing in God?*

We proceed thus to the Second Article: It would seem that the act of faith is not suitably distinguished as believing God, believing in a God, and believing in God.

Objection 1. For one habit has but one act. Now faith is one habit since it is one virtue. Therefore it is unreasonable to say that there are several acts of faith.

Obj. 2. Further, That which is common to all acts of faith should not be considered as a particular kind of act of faith. Now to "believe God" is common to all acts of faith, since faith is founded on the First Truth. Therefore it seems unreasonable to distinguish it from certain other acts of faith.

Obj. 3. Further, That which can be said of unbelievers, cannot be called an act of faith. Now unbelievers can be said to believe in a God. Therefore it should not be considered an act of faith.

Obj. 4. Further, Movement towards the end pertains to the will, whose object is the good and the end. Now to believe is an act, not of the will, but of the intellect. Therefore *to believe in God,* which implies movement towards an end, should not be considered as a species of that act.

On the contrary is the authority of Augustine who makes this distinction.[1]

I answer that, The act of any power or habit depends on the relation of that power or habit to its object. Now the object of faith can be considered in three ways. For, since "to believe" is an act of the intellect, in so far as the will moves it to assent, as stated above (A. 1, REPLY 3), the object of faith can be considered either on the part of the intellect, or on the part of the will that moves the intellect.

If it be considered on the part of the intellect, then two things can be observed in the object of faith, as stated above (Q. 1, A. 1). One of these is the material object of faith, and in this way an act of faith is "to believe in a God" because, as stated above (*ibid.*) nothing is proposed to our belief, except according as it pertains to God. The other is the formal aspect of the object, for it is as the medium on account

of which we assent to such and such a point of faith; and thus an act of faith is "to believe God," since, as stated above (*ibid.*) the formal object of faith is the First Truth, to Whom man adheres, so as to assent for Its sake to whatever he believes. Thirdly, if the object of faith be considered in so far as the intellect is moved by the will, an act of faith is "to believe in God." For the First Truth is referred to the will, through having the aspect of an end.

Reply Obj. 1. These three do not denote different acts of faith, but one and the same act having different relations to the object of faith.

This suffices for the *Reply to the Second Objection.*

Reply Obj. 3. Unbelievers cannot be said "to believe in a God" as we understand it in relation to the act of faith. For they do not believe that God exists under the conditions that faith determines. Hence they do not truly believe in a God, since, as the Philosopher observes,[2] to know simple things defectively is not to know them at all.

Reply Obj. 4. As stated above (Part I-II, Q. IX, A. 1) the will moves the intellect and the other powers of the soul to the end. And in this respect an act of faith is *to believe in God.*

ARTICLE 3. *Whether It Is Necessary for Salvation to Believe Anything Above the Natural Reason?*

We proceed thus to the Third Article: It seems unnecessary for salvation to believe anything above the natural reason.

Objection 1. For the salvation and perfection of a thing seem to be sufficiently insured by its natural endowments. Now matters of faith, surpass man's natural reason, since they are things unseen as stated above (Q. 1, A. 4). Therefore to believe seems unnecessary for salvation.

Obj. 2. Further, It is dangerous for man to assent to matters of which he cannot judge whether that which is proposed to him be true or false, according to Job 12. 11: *Doth not the ear discern words?* Now a man cannot form a judgment of this kind in matters of faith, since he cannot trace them back to first principles, by which all our judgments are guided. Therefore it is dangerous to believe in such matters. Therefore to believe is not necessary for salvation.

Obj. 3. Further, Man's salvation rests on God, according to Ps. 36. 39: *But the salvation of the just is from the Lord.* Now *the invisible things*

---

[1] *Serm.,* CXLIV, 2 (PL 38, 788); *Tract.,* XXIX, super *Joann.,* 7.17 (PL 35, 1631).

[2] *Metaphysics,* IX, 10 (1051ᵇ25).

of God *are clearly seen, being understood by the things that are made; His eternal power also and Divinity,* according to Rom. 1. 20. And those things which are clearly seen by the understanding are not an object of belief. Therefore it is not necessary for man's salvation, that he should believe certain things.

On the contrary, It is written (Heb. 11. 6): *Without faith it is impossible to please God.*

I answer that, Wherever one nature is subordinate to another, we find that two things concur towards the perfection of the lower nature, one of which is in respect of that nature's proper movement, while the other is in respect of the movement of the higher nature. Thus water by its proper movement moves towards the centre (of the earth), while according to the movement of the moon, it moves round that centre by ebb and flow. In like manner the planets have their proper movements from west to east, while in accordance with the movement of the first heaven, they have a movement from east to west. Now the created rational nature alone is immediately subordinate to God, since other creatures do not attain to the universal, but only to something particular, while they partake of the Divine goodness either in being only, as inanimate things, or also in living and in knowing singulars, as plants and animals. But the rational nature, in so far as it apprehends the universal notion of good and being, is immediately related to the universal principle of being.

Consequently the perfection of the rational creature consists not only in what belongs to it in respect of its nature, but also in that which it acquires through a supernatural participation of Divine goodness. Hence it was said above (Part I-II, Q. III, A. 8) that man's ultimate happiness consists in a supernatural vision of God, to which vision man cannot attain unless he be taught by God, according to John 6. 45: *Every one that hath heard of the Father and hath learned cometh to Me.* Now man acquires a share of this learning, not all at once, but by little and little, according to the mode of his nature. And every one who learns thus must believe, in order that he may acquire science in a perfect degree. Thus also the Philosopher says that "it is necessary for a learner to believe."[1]

Hence, in order that a man arrive at the perfect vision of heavenly happiness, he must first of all believe God, as a disciple believes the master who is teaching him.

[1] *Sophistical Refutations,* 2 (165b3).

Reply Obj. 1. Since man's nature is dependent on a higher nature, natural knowledge does not suffice for its perfection, and some supernatural knowledge is necessary, as stated above.

Reply Obj. 2. Just as man assents to first principles by the natural light of his intellect, so does a virtuous man, by the habit of virtue, judge rightly of things concerning that virtue. And in this way, by the light of faith which God bestows on him, a man assents to matters of faith and not to those which are against faith. Consequently *there is no* danger or *condemnation to them that are in Christ Jesus* (Rom. 8. 1), and whom He has enlightened by faith.

Reply Obj. 3. In many respects faith perceives the invisible things of God in a higher way than natural reason does in proceeding to God from His creatures. Hence it is written (Ecclus. 3. 25): *Many things are shown to thee above the understanding of man.*

ARTICLE 4. *Whether It Is Necessary To Believe Those Things Which Can Be Proved by Natural Reason?*

We proceed thus to the Fourth Article: It would seem unnecessary to believe those things which can be proved by natural reason.

Objection 1. For nothing is superfluous in God's works, much less even than in the works of nature. Now it is superfluous to employ other means, where one already suffices. Therefore it would be superfluous to receive by faith things that can be known by natural reason.

Obj. 2. Further, Those things must be believed, which are the object of faith. Now science and faith are not about the same object, as stated above (Q. I, A. 5). Since therefore all things that can be known by natural reason are an object of science, it seems that there is no need to believe what can be proved by natural reason.

Obj. 3. Further, All things knowable by science seem to be of one nature. If therefore some of them are proposed to man as objects of faith, in like manner the others should also be believed. But this is not true. Therefore it is not necessary to believe those things which can be proved by natural reason.

On the contrary, It is necessary to believe that God is one and incorporeal, which philosophers prove by natural reason.

I answer that, It is necessary for man to accept by faith not only things which are above reason, but also those which can be known by reason, and this for three reasons. First, in order that man may arrive more quickly at the knowledge of Divine truth. Because the science to which it pertains to prove the existence of God is the last of all to offer itself to human inquiry, since it presupposes many other sciences so that it would not be until late in life that man would arrive at the knowledge of God. The second reason is, in order that the knowledge of God may be more general. For many are unable to make progress in the study of science, either through dulness of mind, or through having a number of occupations and temporal needs, or even through laziness in learning, all of whom would be altogether deprived of the knowledge of God, unless Divine things were brought to their knowledge after the manner of faith. The third reason is for the sake of certitude. For human reason is very deficient in things concerning God. A sign of this is that philosophers in their researches, by natural investigation, into human affairs, have fallen into many errors, and have disagreed among themselves. And consequently, in order that men might have knowledge of God, free of doubt and uncertainty, it was necessary for Divine matters to be delivered to them by way of faith, being told to them, as it were, by God Himself Who cannot lie.

Reply Obj. 1. The searchings of natural reason do not suffice mankind for the knowledge of Divine matters, even of those that can be proved by reason, and so it is not superfluous if these others be believed.

Reply Obj. 2. Science and faith cannot be in the same subject and about the same object, but what is an object of science for one, can be an object of faith for another, as stated above (Q. I., A. 5).

Reply Obj. 3. Although all things that can be known by science agree in the character of science, they do not all alike lead man to happiness. Hence they are not all equally proposed to our belief.

ARTICLE 5. *Whether Man Is Bound To Believe Anything Explicitly?*

We proceed thus to the Fifth Article: It seems that man is not bound to believe anything explicitly.

Objection 1. For no man is bound to do what is not in his power. Now it is not in man's power to believe a thing explicitly, for it is written (Rom. 10. 14, 15): *How shall they believe Him, of whom they have not heard? And how shall they hear without a preacher? And how shall they preach unless they be sent?* There-

fore man is not bound to believe anything explicitly.

Obj. 2. Further, Just as we are directed to God by faith, so are we by charity. Now man is not bound to keep the precepts of charity, but it is enough if he be ready to fulfil them, as is evidenced by the precept of Our Lord (Matt. 5. 39): *If one strike thee on one* (Vulg.,—*thy right*) *cheek, turn to him also the other;* and by others of the same kind, according to Augustine's exposition (*De Serm. Dom. in Monte,* xix).[1] Therefore neither is man bound to believe anything explicitly, and it is enough if he be ready to believe whatever God proposes to be believed.

Obj. 3. Further, The good of faith consists in obedience, according to Rom. 1. 5: *For obedience to the faith in all nations.* Now the virtue of obedience does not require man to keep certain fixed precepts, but it is enough that his mind be ready to obey, according to Ps. 118. 60: *I am ready and am not troubled; that I may keep Thy commandments.* Therefore it seems enough for faith too, that man should be ready to believe whatever God may propose, without his believing anything explicitly.

On the contrary, It is written (Heb. 11. 6): *He that cometh to God, must believe that He is, and is a rewarder to them that seek Him.*

I answer that, The precepts of the Law, which man is bound to fulfil, concern acts of virtue which are the means of attaining salvation. Now an act of virtue, as stated above (Q. II., A. 2) depends on the relation of the habit to its object. Again two things may be considered in the object of any virtue; namely, that which is the proper and direct object of that virtue, which necessarily exists in every act of virtue, and that which is accidental and consequent to the object properly so called. Thus it pertains properly and directly to the object of fortitude to face the dangers of death, and to charge at the foe with danger to oneself, for the sake of the common good; yet that, in a just war, a man be armed, or strike another with his sword, and so forth, is reduced to the object of fortitude, but accidentally.

Accordingly, just as a virtuous act is required for the fulfilment of a precept, so is it necessary that the virtuous act should terminate in its proper and direct object. But, on the other hand, the fulfilment of the precept does not require that a virtuous act should terminate in those things which have an accidental or secondary relation to the proper and direct object

1 PL 34, 1260.

of that virtue, except in certain places and at certain times. We must, therefore, say that the direct object of faith is that whereby man is made one of the Blessed, as stated above (Q. I, A. 6, REPLY I), while the indirect and secondary object comprises all things delivered by God to us in Holy Writ, for instance that Abraham had two sons, that David was the son of Jesse, and so forth.

Therefore, as regards the primary points or articles of faith, man is bound to believe them, just as he is bound to have faith; but as to other points of faith, man is not bound to believe them explicitly, but only implicitly, or to be ready to believe them, in so far as he is prepared to believe whatever is contained in the Divine Scriptures. Then alone is he bound to believe such things explicitly, when it is clear to him that they are contained in the doctrine of faith.

Reply Obj. 1. If we understand those things alone to be in a man's power which we can do without the help of grace, then we are bound to do many things which we cannot do without the aid of healing grace, such as to love God and our neighbour, and likewise to believe the articles of faith. But with the help of grace we can do this, for this help to whomsoever it is given from above it is mercifully given; and from whom it is withheld it is justly withheld, as a punishment of a previous, or at least of original, sin, as Augustine states (*De Corr. et Grat.*).[1]

Reply Obj. 2. Man is bound to love, definitely those lovable things which are properly and directly the objects of charity, namely, God and our neighbour. The objection refers to those precepts of charity which belong, as a consequence, to the object of charity.

Reply Obj. 3. The virtue of obedience is seated, properly speaking, in the will. Hence promptness of the will subject to authority, suffices for the act of obedience, because it is the proper and direct object of obedience. But this or that precept is accidental or consequent to that proper and direct object.

ARTICLE 6. *Whether All Are Equally Bound To Have Explicit Faith?*

We proceed thus to the Sixth Article: It would seem that all are equally bound to have explicit faith.

Objection 1. For all are bound to those things which are necessary for salvation, as is evi-

denced by the precepts of charity. Now it is necessary for salvation that certain things should be believed explicitly as we have said (A. 5). Therefore all are equally bound to have explicit faith.

Obj. 2. Further, No one should be put to test in matters that he is not bound to believe. But simple persons are sometimes tested in reference to the slightest articles of faith. Therefore all are bound to believe everything explicitly.

Obj. 3. Further, If the simple are bound to have, not explicit but only implicit faith, their faith must be implied in the faith of the learned. But this seems unsafe, since it is possible for the learned to err. Therefore it seems that the simple should also have explicit faith; so that all are, therefore, equally bound to have explicit faith.

On the contrary, It is written (Job. I. 14): *The oxen were ploughing, and the asses feeding beside them,* because, as Gregory expounds this passage (*Moral.* ii, 30),[2] the simple, who are signified by the asses, ought, in matters of faith, to stay by the learned, who are denoted by the oxen.

I answer that, The unfolding of matters of faith is the result of Divine revelation, for matters of faith surpass natural reason. Now Divine revelation reaches those of lower degree through those who are over them, in a certain order; to men, for instance, through the angels, and to the lower angels through the higher, as Dionysius explains (*Cæl. Hier.* iv, vii).[3] In like manner, therefore, the unfolding of faith must reach men of lower degree through those of higher degree. Consequently, just as the higher angels, who enlighten those who are below them, have a fuller knowledge of Divine things than the lower angels, as Dionysius states (*ibid.* xii.),[4] so too, men of higher degree, whose business it is to teach others, are under obligation to have fuller knowledge of matters of faith, and to believe them more explicitly.

Reply Obj. 1. The unfolding of the articles of faith is not equally necessary for the salvation of all, since those of higher degree, whose duty it is to teach others, are bound to believe explicitly more things than others are.

Reply Obj. 2. Simple persons should not be put to the test about subtle questions of faith, unless they be suspected of having been corrupted by heretics, who are accustomed to corrupt the faith of simple people in such ques-

---

[1] Cf. *Epist.*, cxc, 3 (PL 33, 860); *De Praedest. Sanct.*, 8 (PL 44, 971).

[2] PL 75, 578.

[3] PG 3, 180, 209; cf. also chap. 8, sect. 2 (PG 3, 240).

[4] Sect. 2 (PG 3, 292).

tions. If, however, it is found that they are free from obstinacy in their perverse doctrine, and that it is due to their simplicity, it is no fault of theirs.

Reply Obj. 3. The simple have no faith implied in that of the learned, except in so far as the latter adhere to the Divine teaching. And so the Apostle says (I Cor. 4. 16): *Be ye followers of me, as I also am of Christ.* Hence it is not human knowledge, but the Divine truth that is the rule of faith. And if any of the learned stray from this rule, he does not harm the faith of the simple ones, who think that the learned believe rightly, unless the simple hold obstinately to their individual errors against the faith of the universal Church, which cannot err, since Our Lord said: (Luke 22. 32): *I have prayed for thee,* Peter, *that thy faith fail not.*

ARTICLE 7. *Whether It Is Necessary for the Salvation of All, That They Should Believe Explicitly in the Mystery of the Incarnation of Christ?*

We proceed thus to the Seventh Article: It would seem that it is not necessary for the salvation of all that they should believe explicitly in the mystery of the Incarnation of Christ.

Objection 1. For man is not bound to believe explicitly what the angels are ignorant about, since the unfolding of faith is the result of Divine revelation, which reaches man by means of the angels, as stated above (A. 6; Part I, Q. CXI, A. 1). Now even the angels were in ignorance of the mystery of the Incarnation. Hence, according to the commentary of Dionysius (*Cæl. Hier.* vii),[1] it is they who ask (Ps. 23. 8): *Who is this king of glory?* and (Isa. 63. 1): *Who is this that cometh from Edom?* Therefore men were not bound to believe explicitly in the mystery of Christ's Incarnation.

Obj. 2. Further, It is evident that John the Baptist was one of the teachers, and nearest to Christ, Who said of him (Matt. 11. 11) that *there hath not risen among them that are born of women, a greater than* he. Now John the Baptist does not appear to have known the mystery of Christ explicitly, since he asked Christ (Matt. 11. 3): *Art Thou He that art to come, or look we for another?* Therefore even the teachers were not bound to explicit faith in Christ.

Obj. 3. Further, Many gentiles obtained sal-

vation through the ministry of the angels, as Dionysius states (*Cæl. Hier.* ix).[2] Now it would seem that the gentiles had neither explicit nor implicit faith in Christ, since they received no revelation. Therefore it seems that it was not necessary for the salvation of all to believe explicitly in the mystery of the Incarnation of Christ.

On the contrary, Augustine says (*De Corr. et Gratia,* vii):[3] "Our faith is sound if we believe that no man, old or young, is delivered from the contagion of death and the bonds of sin, except by the one Mediator of God and men, Jesus Christ."

I answer that, As stated above (A. 5; Q. I, A. 6, REPLY 1), the object of faith includes, properly and directly, that thing through which man obtains Happiness. Now the mystery of Christ's Incarnation and Passion is the way by which men obtain Happiness; for it is written (Acts 4. 12): *There is no other name under heaven given to men, whereby we must be saved.* Therefore belief of some kind in the mystery of Christ's Incarnation was necessary at all times and for all persons, but this belief differed according to differences of times and persons. The reason of this is that before the state of sin, man believed explicitly in Christ's Incarnation, in so far as it was intended for the consummation of glory, but not as it was intended to deliver man from sin by the Passion and Resurrection, since man had no foreknowledge of his future sin. He does, however, seem to have had foreknowledge of the Incarnation of Christ, from the fact that he said (Gen. 2. 24): *Wherefore a man shall leave father and mother, and shall cleave to his wife,* of which the Apostle says (Eph. 5. 32) that *this is a great sacrament . . . in Christ and the Church,* and it is incredible that the first man was ignorant about this sacrament.

But after sin, man believed explicitly in the mystery of the Incarnation of Christ, not only as to the Incarnation, but also as to the Passion and Resurrection, by which the human race is delivered from sin and death. For otherwise they would not have foreshadowed Christ's Passion by certain sacrifices both before and after the Law, the meaning of which sacrifices was known by the learned explicitly, while the simple folk, under the veil of those sacrifices, believed them to be ordained by God in reference to Christ's coming, and thus their knowledge was covered with a veil, so to speak. And,

[1] Sect. 3 (PG 3, 209).

[2] Sect. 4 (PG 3, 261).
[3] Cf. *Epist.,* CXC, 2 (PL 33, 858).

as stated above (Q. I., A. 7), the further they were from Christ, the more difficult was their knowledge of Christ's mysteries, and the nearer they were to Christ, the more distinct was their knowledge of Christ's mysteries.

After grace had been revealed, both learned and simple folk are bound to explicit faith in the mysteries of Christ, chiefly as regards those which are observed throughout the Church, and publicly proclaimed, such as the articles which refer to the Incarnation, of which we have spoken above (Q. I, A. 8). As to other minute points in reference to the articles of the Incarnation, men have been bound to believe them more or less explicitly according to each one's state and office.

Reply Obj. 1. "The mystery of the Kingdom of God was not entirely hidden from the angels," as Augustine observes (*Gen. ad. lit.* v, 19),[1] yet certain aspects of the mystery were better known to them when Christ revealed them to them.

Reply Obj. 2. It was not through ignorance that John the Baptist inquired of Christ's advent in the flesh, since he had clearly professed his belief therein, saying: *I saw, and I gave testimony, that this is the Son of God* (John 1. 34). Hence he did not say: *Art Thou He that hast come?* but *Art Thou He that art to come?* thus asking about the future, not about the past. Likewise it is not to be believed that he was ignorant of Christ's future Passion, for he had already said (*ibid.* 29): *Behold the Lamb of God, behold Him who taketh away the sins* (Vulg.,—*sin*) *of the world,* thus foretelling His future immolation; and since other prophets had foretold it, as may be seen especially in Isaias 53. We may therefore say with Gregory (*Hom.* vi *in Ev.*)[2] that he asked this question, being in ignorance as to whether Christ would descend into hell in His own Person. But he did know that the power of Christ's Passion would be extended to those who were detained in Limbo, according to Zach. 9. II: *Thou also, by the blood of Thy testament hast sent forth Thy prisoners out of the pit, wherein is no water.* Nor was he bound to believe explicitly, before its fulfilment, that Christ was to descend there Himself.

It may also be replied that, as Ambrose observes in his commentary on Luke 7. 19,[3] he made this inquiry, not from doubt or ignorance but from devotion; or again, with Chrysostom (*Hom.* xxxvi *in Matt.*),[4] that he inquired, not

as though ignorant himself, but because he wished his disciples to be satisfied on that point, through Christ. Hence Christ framed His answer so as to instruct the disciples, by pointing to the signs of His works.

Reply Obj. 3. Many of the gentiles received revelations of Christ, as is clear from their predictions. Thus we read (Job 19. 25): *I know that my Redeemer liveth.* The Sibyl too foretold certain things about Christ, as Augustine relates (*Contra Faust.*).[5] Moreover we read in the history of the Romans,[6] that at the time of Constantine Augustus and his mother Irene a tomb was discovered, in which there lay a man on whose breast was a golden plate with the inscription: "Christ shall be born of a virgin, and in Him I believe. O sun, during the lifetime of Irene and Constantine, thou shalt see me again." If, however, some were saved without receiving any revelation, they were not saved without faith in a Mediator, for, though they did not believe in Him explicitly, they did, nevertheless, have implicit faith through believing in Divine providence, since they believed that God would deliver mankind in whatever way was pleasing to Him, and according to the revelation of the Spirit, to those who knew the truth, as stated in Job 35. II: *Who teacheth us more than the beasts of the earth.*

ARTICLE 8. *Whether It Is Necessary for Salvation To Believe Explicitly in the Trinity?*

We proceed thus to the Eighth Article: It seems that it was not necessary for salvation to believe explicitly in the Trinity.

Objection 1. For the Apostle says (Heb. 11. 6): *He that cometh to God must believe that He is and is a rewarder to them that seek Him.* Now one can believe this without believing in the Trinity. Therefore it was not necessary to believe explicitly in the Trinity.

Obj. 2. Further, Our Lord said (John 17. 5, 6): *Father, . . . I have manifested Thy name to men,* which words Augustine expounds (*Tract.* cvi)[7] as follows: "Not the name by which Thou are called God, but the name whereby Thou art called My Father," and further on he adds: "In that He made this world, God is known to all nations; in that He is not to be worshipped together with false gods, 'God is known in Judea'; but, in that He is the Father of this Christ, through Whom He takes

[1] PL 34, 334.   [2] PL 76, 1095.
[3] PL 15, 1748.   [4] PG 57, 418.

[5] Bk. XIII, chap. 15 (PL 42, 290).
[6] Theophanes, *Chronographia*, A.C. 773 (PG 108, 918).
[7] PL 35, 1909.

away the sin of the world, He now makes known to men this name of His, which hitherto they knew not." Therefore before the coming of Christ it was not known that Fatherhood and Sonship were in the Godhead. And so the Trinity was not believed explicitly.

Obj. 3. Further, That which we are bound to believe explicitly of God is the object of heavenly Happiness. Now the object of heavenly Happiness is the sovereign good, which can be understood to be in God, without any distinction of Persons. Therefore it was not necessary to believe explicitly in the Trinity.

On the contrary, In the Old Testament the Trinity of Persons is expressed in many ways. Thus at the very outset of Genesis it is written in manifestation of the Trinity: *Let Us make man to Our image and likeness* (Gen. 1. 26). Therefore from the very beginning it was necessary for salvation to believe in the Trinity.

I answer that, It is impossible to believe explicitly in the mystery of Christ without faith in the Trinity, since the mystery of Christ includes that the Son of God took flesh, that He renewed the world through the grace of the Holy Ghost, and again, that He was conceived by the Holy Ghost. Therefore just as, before Christ, the mystery of Christ was believed explicitly by the learned, but implicitly and under a veil, so to speak, by the simple, so too was it with the mystery of the Trinity. And consequently, when once grace had been revealed, all were bound to explicit faith in the mystery of the Trinity. And all who are born again in Christ, have this bestowed on them by the invocation of the Trinity, according to Matt. 28. 19: *Going therefore teach ye all nations, baptizing them in the name of the Father, and of the Son and of the Holy Ghost.*

Reply Obj. 1. Explicit faith in those two things was necessary at all times and for all people; but it was not sufficient at all times and for all people.

Reply Obj. 2. Before Christ's coming, faith in the Trinity lay hidden in the faith of the learned, but through Christ and the apostles it was shown to the world.

Reply Obj. 3. God's sovereign goodness as we understand it now through its effects, can be understood without the Trinity of Persons. But as understood in itself, and as seen by the Blessed, it cannot be understood without the Trinity of Persons. Moreover the mission of the Divine Persons leads us to heavenly happiness.

ARTICLE 9. *Whether To Believe Is Meritorious?*

We proceed thus to the Ninth Article: It seems that to believe is not meritorious.

Objection 1. For the principle of all merit is charity, as stated above (Part I-II, Q. CXIV, A. 4). Now faith, like nature, is a preamble to charity. Therefore, just as an act of nature is not meritorious, since we do not merit by our natural gifts, so neither is an act of faith.

Obj. 2. Further, Belief is a mean between opinion and scientific knowledge or the consideration of things known by science. Now the considerations of science are not meritorious, nor on the other hand is opinion. Therefore belief is not meritorious.

Obj. 3. Further, He who assents to a point of faith, either has a sufficient motive for believing, or he has not. If he has a sufficient motive for his belief, this does not seem to imply any merit on his part, since he is no longer free to believe or not to believe. But if he has not a sufficient motive for believing, to believe is a mark of levity, according to Ecclus. 19. 4: *He that is hasty to give credit, is light of heart,* and this does not seem to be meritorious. Therefore to believe is by no means meritorious.

On the contrary, It is written (Heb. 11. 33) that the saints *by faith . . . obtained promises,* which would not be the case if they did not merit by believing. Therefore to believe is meritorious.

I answer that, As stated above (Part I-II, Q. CXIV, AA. 3, 4), our actions are meritorious in so far as they proceed from free choice moved with grace by God. Therefore every human act proceeding from free choice, if it be referred to God, can be meritorious. Now the act of believing is an act of the intellect assenting to the Divine truth at the command of the will moved by the grace of God, so that it falls under free choice in relation to God. And consequently the act of faith can be meritorious.

Reply Obj. 1. Nature is related to charity which is the principle of merit, as matter to form. But faith is related to charity as the disposition which precedes the ultimate form. Now it is evident that the subject or the matter cannot act save by virtue of the form, nor can a preceding disposition, before the advent of the form. But after the advent of the form, both the subject and the preceding disposition act by virtue of the form, which is the chief principle of action, even as the heat of fire acts by virtue of the substantial form of fire. Accordingly neither nature nor faith can, without charity, produce a meritorious act; but, when accompanied by charity, the act of faith is made meritorious by charity, even as an act of nature, and a natural act of free choice.

Reply Obj. 2. Two things may be considered in science; namely, the assent of the knower to the thing known, and his consideration of the thing known. Now the assent of science is not subject to free choice, because the knower is obliged to assent by the force of the demonstration. And so assent of science is not meritorious. But the actual consideration of what a man knows by science is subject to his free choice, for it is in his power to consider or not to consider. Hence consideration of a thing known by science may be meritorious if it be referred to the end of charity, that is, to the honour of God or the good of our neighbour. On the other hand, in the case of faith, both these things are subject to free choice, so that in both respects the act of faith can be meritorious. But in the case of opinion, there is no firm assent, since it is weak and infirm, as the Philosopher observes,[1] and so it does not seem to proceed from a perfect act of the will. And for this reason, as regards the assent, it does not appear to be very meritorious, though it can be as regards the actual consideration.

Reply Obj. 3. The believer has sufficient motive for believing, for he is moved by the authority of Divine teaching confirmed by miracles, and, what is more, by the inward impulse of the Divine invitation. Hence he does not believe lightly. He has not, however, sufficient reason for scientific knowledge, and hence he does not lose the merit.

ARTICLE 10. *Whether Reasons in Support of What We Believe Lessen the Merit of Faith?*

We proceed thus to the tenth Article: It seems that reasons in support of what we believe lessen the merit of faith.

Objection 1. For Gregory says (*Hom.* xxvi in *Ev.*)[2] that "there is no merit in believing what is shown by reason." If, therefore, human reason provides sufficient proof, the merit of faith is taken away altogether. Therefore it seems that any kind of human reasoning in support of matters of faith, diminishes the merit of believing.

Obj. 2. Further, Whatever lessens the measure of virtue, lessens the amount of merit, since "happiness is the reward of virtue," as the Philosopher states.[3] Now human reasoning seems to diminish the measure of the virtue of faith, since it is of the very notion of faith to be about the unseen, as stated above (Q. I, AA. 4, 5). Now the more a thing is supported by reasons the less is it unseen. Therefore human reasons in support of matters of faith diminish the merit of faith.

Obj. 3. Further, Contrary things have contrary causes. Now what leads to the opposite of faith increases the merit of faith—whether it consist in persecution inflicted by one who endeavours to force a man to renounce his faith, or in an argument persuading him to do so. Therefore reasons in support of faith diminish the merit of faith.

On the contrary, It is written (I Pet. 3. 15): *Being ready always to satisfy every one that asketh you a reason of that faith and hope which is in you.*[4] Now the Apostle would not give this advice if it would imply a diminution in the merit of faith. Therefore reason does not diminish the merit of faith.

I answer that, As stated above (A. 9), the act of faith can be meritorious, in so far as it is subject to the will, not only as to the use, but also as to the assent. Now human reason in support of what we believe may stand in a twofold relation to the will of the believer. First, as preceding the act of the will; as, for instance, when a man either has not the will, or not a prompt will, to believe, unless he be moved by human reasons, and in this way human reason diminishes the merit of faith. In this sense it has been said above (Part I-II, Q. XXIV, A. 3, Reply 1; Q. LXXVII, A. 6, Reply 2) that, in moral virtues, a passion which precedes choice makes the virtuous act less praiseworthy. For just as a man ought to perform acts of moral virtue on account of the judgment of his reason, and not on account of a passion, so ought he to believe matters of faith, not on account of human reason, but on account of the Divine authority. Secondly, human reasons may be consequent to the will of the believer. For when a man's will is ready to believe, he loves the truth he believes, he thinks out and takes to heart whatever reasons he can find in its support; and in this way, human reason does not exclude the merit of faith, but is a sign of greater merit. Thus again, in moral virtues, a consequent passion, is the sign of a more

[1] *Posterior Analytics,* I, 33 (89ª5).
[2] PL 76, 1197.

[3] *Ethics,* I, 9 (1099ᵇ16).
[4] Vulg.,—*Of that hope which is in you.* S. Thomas's reading is apparently taken from Bede.

prompt will, as stated above (Part I-II, Q. XXIV, A. 3, Reply I). We have an indication of this in the words of the Samaritans to the woman, who is a type of human reason: *We now believe, not for thy saying* (John 4. 42).

Reply Obj. I. Gregory is referring to the case of a man who has no will to believe what is of faith, unless he be induced by reasons. But when a man has the will to believe what is of faith, on the authority of God alone, although he may have reasons in demonstration of some of them, for example of the existence of God, the merit of his faith is not, for that reason, lost or diminished.

Reply Obj. 2. The reasons which are brought forward in support of the authority of faith, are not demonstrations which can bring intellectual vision to the human intellect, and therefore they do not cease to be unseen. But they remove obstacles to faith, by showing that what faith proposes is not impossible. Hence such reasons do not diminish the merit or the measure of faith. On the other hand, though demonstrative reasons in support of the preambles of faith, but not of the articles of faith, diminish the measure of faith,[1] since they make the thing believed to be seen, yet they do not diminish the measure of charity, which makes the will ready to believe them, even if they were unseen. And so the measure of merit is not diminished.

Reply Obj. 3. Whatever is in opposition to faith, whether it consist in a man's thoughts, or in outward persecution, increases the merit of faith, in so far as the will is shown to be more prompt and firm in believing. Hence the martyrs had more merit of faith, through not renouncing faith on account of persecution; and even the wise have greater merit of faith, through not renouncing their faith on account of the reasons brought forward by philosophers or heretics in opposition to faith. On the other hand things that are favourable to faith, do not always diminish the promptness of the will to believe, and therefore they do not always diminish the merit of faith.

QUESTION III
OF THE OUTWARD ACT OF FAITH
(*In Two Articles*)

WE must now consider the outward act, namely the confession of faith, under which head

there are two points of inquiry: (1) Whether confession is an act of faith? (2) Whether confession of faith is necessary for salvation?

ARTICLE I. *Whether Confession Is an Act of Faith?*

We proceed thus to the First Article: It would seem that confession is not an act of faith.

Objection 1. For the same act does not pertain to different virtues. Now confession pertains to penance of which it is a part. Therefore it is not an act of faith.

Obj. 2. Further, Man is sometimes deterred by fear or some kind of confusion, from confessing his faith. Therefore the Apostle (Eph. 6. 19) asks for prayers that it may be granted him *with confidence, to make known the mystery of the gospel.* Now it pertains to fortitude, which moderates daring and fear, not to be deterred from doing good on account of confusion or fear. Therefore it seems that confession is not an act of faith, but rather of fortitude or constancy.

Obj. 3. Further, Just as the ardour of faith makes one confess one's faith outwardly, so does it make one do other external good works, for it is written (Gal. 5. 6) that *faith . . . worketh by charity.* But other external works are not held to be acts of faith. Therefore neither is confession an act of faith.

On the contrary, A gloss explains the words of II Thess. I. 11, *and the work of faith in power* as referring to "confession which is a work proper to faith."[2]

I answer that, Outward actions belong properly to the virtue to whose end they are specifically referred. Thus fasting is referred specifically to the end of abstinence, which is to tame the flesh, and consequently it is an act of abstinence.

Now confession of those things that are of faith is referred specifically as to its end to that which concerns faith, according to II Cor. 4. 13: *Having the same spirit of faith, . . . we believe, and therefore we speak also.* For the outward utterance is intended to signify the inward thought. Therefore, just as the inward concept of matters of faith is properly an act of faith, so too is the outward confession of them.

Reply Obj. 1. A threefold confession is commended by the Scriptures. One is the confession of matters of faith, and this is a proper act of faith, since it is referred to the end of

---

[1] The reading of the Piana text. The Leonine edition reads: in support of matters of faith which are, however, preambles to the articles of faith, diminish, etc.

[2] *Glossa ordin.* (VI, 114B); *Glossa* Lombardi (PL 192, 315).

faith, as stated above. Another is the confession of thanksgiving or praise, and this is an act of adoration (*latria*), for its purpose is to give outward honour to God, which is the end of adoration (*latria*). The third is the confession of sins, which is ordained to the blotting out of sins, which is the end of penance, to which virtue it therefore belongs.

Reply Obj. 2. That which removes an obstacle is not an essential, but an accidental cause, as the Philosopher proves.[1] Hence fortitude which removes an obstacle to the confession of faith, for instance, fear or shame, is not the proper and essential cause of confession, but an accidental cause so to speak.

Reply Obj. 3. Inward faith, with the aid of charity, causes all outward acts of virtue, by means of the other virtues, commanding, but not eliciting them. But it produces the act of confession as its proper act, without the help of any other virtue.

ARTICLE 2. *Whether Confession of Faith Is Necessary for Salvation?*

We proceed thus to the Second Article: It would seem that confession of faith is not necessary for salvation.

Objection 1. For a thing seems to be sufficient for salvation if it is a means of attaining the end of virtue. Now the proper end of faith is the joining of the human mind with Divine truth, and this can be realized without any outward confession. Therefore confession of faith is not necessary for salvation.

Obj. 2. Further, By outward confession of faith, a man reveals his faith to another man. But this is unnecessary except for those who have to instruct others in the faith. Therefore it seems that ordinary people are not bound to confess the faith.

Obj. 3. Further, Whatever may tend to scandalize and disturb others, is not necessary for salvation, for the Apostle says (I Cor. 10. 32): *Be without offence to the Jews and to the gentiles, and to the Church of God.* Now confession of the faith sometimes causes a disturbance among unbelievers. Therefore it is not necessary for salvation.

On the contrary, The Apostle says (Rom. 10. 10): *With the heart we believe unto justice; but with the mouth, confession is made unto salvation.*

I answer that, Things that are necessary for salvation come under the precepts of the Divine law. Now since confession of faith is some-

thing affirmative, it can only fall under an affirmative precept. Hence its necessity for salvation depends on how it falls under an affirmative precept of the Divine law. Now affirmative precepts as stated above (Part I-II, Q. LXXI, A. 5, Reply 3; Q. C, A. 10) do not bind for always, although they are always binding; but they bind as to place and time according to other due circumstances, in respect of which human acts have to be regulated in order to be acts of virtue.

Thus then it is not necessary for salvation to confess one's faith at all times and in all places, but in certain places and at certain times, when, namely, by omitting to do so, we would deprive God of due honour, or our neighbour of a service that we ought to render him; for instance, if a man, on being asked about his faith were to remain silent, so as to make people believe either that he is without faith, or that the faith is false, or so as to turn others away from the faith. For in such cases as these, confession of faith is necessary for salvation.

Reply Obj. 1. The end of faith, even as of the other virtues, must be referred to the end of charity, which is the love of God and our neighbour. Consequently when God's honour and our neighbour's good demand, man should not be contented with being united by faith to God's truth, but ought to confess his faith outwardly.

Reply Obj. 2. In cases of necessity where faith is in danger, every one is bound to proclaim his faith to others, either to give good example and encouragement to the rest of the faithful, or to check the attacks of unbelievers. But at other times it is not the duty of all the faithful to instruct others in the faith.

Reply Obj. 3. There is nothing commendable in making a public confession of one's faith if it cause a disturbance among unbelievers, without any profit either to the faith or to the faithful. Hence Our Lord said (Matt. 7. 6): *Give not that which is holy to dogs, neither cast ye your pearls before swine . . . lest turning upon you, they tear you.* Yet, if there is hope of profit to the faith, or if there be urgency, a man should disregard the disturbance of unbelievers, and confess his faith in public. Hence it is written (Matt. 15. 12) that when the disciples had said to Our Lord that *the Pharisees, when they heard this word, were scandalized,* He answered: *Let them alone, they are blind, and leaders of the blind.*

[1] *Physics,* VIII, 4 (255ᵇ24).

QUESTION IV

OF THE VIRTUE ITSELF OF FAITH

(In Eight Articles)

WE must now consider the virtue itself of faith, and, in the first place, faith itself; secondly, those who have faith (Q. V); thirdly, the cause of faith (Q. VI); fourthly, its effects (Q. VII).

Under the first head there are eight points of inquiry: (1) What is faith? (2) In what power of the soul does it reside? (3) Whether its form is charity? (4) Whether formed (*formata*) faith and formless (*informis*) faith are one identically? (5) Whether faith is a virtue? (6) Whether it is one virtue? (7) Of its relation to the other virtues. (8) Of its certitude as compared with the certitude of the intellectual virtues.

ARTICLE 1. *Whether This Is a Fitting Definition of Faith: "Faith Is the Substance of Things To Be Hoped For, the Evidence of Things That Appear Not"?*

We proceed thus to the First Article: It would seem that the Apostle gives an unfitting definition of faith (Heb. 11. 1) when he says: *Faith is the substance of things to be hoped for, the evidence of things that appear not.*

Objection 1. For no quality is a substance, whereas faith is a quality, since it is a theological virtue, as stated above (Part I-II, Q. LXII, A. 3). Therefore it is not a substance.

Obj. 2. Further, Different virtues have different objects. Now things to be hoped for are the object of hope. Therefore they should not be included in a definition of faith, as though they were its object.

Obj. 3. Further, Faith is perfected by charity rather than by hope, since charity is the form of faith, as we shall state further on (A. 3). Therefore the definition of faith should have included the thing to be loved rather than the thing to be hoped for.

Obj. 4. Further, The same thing should not be placed in different genera. Now substance and evidence are different genera, and neither is subalternate to the other. Therefore it is unfitting to state that faith is both substance and evidence.

Obj. 5. Further, Evidence manifests the truth of the matter for which it is adduced. Now a thing is said to be apparent when its truth is already manifest. Therefore it seems to imply a contradiction to speak of *evidence of things that appear not*. And so faith is unfittingly defined.

On the contrary, The authority of the Apostle suffices.

I answer that, Though some say[1] that the above words of the Apostle are not a definition of faith because "the definition makes known the quiddity and essence of a thing," as the *Metaphysics* says.[2] Yet if we consider the matter rightly, this definition overlooks none of the points in reference to which faith can be defined, although the words themselves are not arranged in the form of a definition, just as the philosophers touch on the principles of the syllogism without employing the syllogistic form.

In order to make this clear, we must observe that since habits are known by their acts, and acts by their objects, faith, being a habit, should be defined by its proper act in relation to its proper object. Now the act of faith is to believe, as stated above (Q. II, AA. 2, 9), which is an act of the intellect determined to one object by the will's command. Hence an act of faith is related both to the object of the will, that is, to the good and the end, and to the object of the intellect, that is, to the true. And since faith, since it is a theological virtue, as stated above (Part I-II, Q. LXII, A. 3), has one same thing for object and end, its object and end must, of necessity, be in proportion to one another. Now it has been already stated (Q. I, AA. 1, 4) that the object of faith is the First Truth, as unseen, and whatever we hold on account of it. And thus it must be under the aspect of something unseen that the First Truth is the end of the act of faith, which aspect is that of a thing hoped for, according to the Apostle (Rom. 8. 25): *We hope for that which we see not,* because to see the truth is to possess it. Now no one hopes for what he has already, but for what he does not have, as stated above (Part I-II, Q. LXVII, A. 4).

Accordingly the relation of the act of faith to its end, which is the object of the will, is indicated by the words: *Faith is the substance of things to be hoped for.* For we are accustomed to call by the name of substance the first beginning of a thing, especially when the whole subsequent thing is virtually contained in the first beginning. For instance, we might say that the first indemonstrable principles are the substance of science, because, namely, these principles are in us the first beginnings of science, the whole of which is itself contained in them virtually. In this way then faith is said

[1] Cf. Hugh of S. Victor, *De Sacram.*, I, X, 2 (PL 176, 330).

[2] Aristotle, VII, 4, 5, 12 (1030^a6; 1031^a12; 1037^b25).

to be the *substance of things to be hoped for*, for the reason that in us the first beginning of things to be hoped for is brought about by the assent of faith, which contains virtually all things to be hoped for. Because we hope to be made happy through seeing the unveiled truth to which our faith cleaves, as was made evident when we were speaking of happiness (Part I-II, Q. III, A. 8; Q. IV, A. 3).

The relationship of the act of faith to the object of the intellect, considered as the object of faith, is indicated by the words, *evidence of things that appear not*, where "evidence" is taken for the result of evidence. For evidence induces the intellect to adhere to a truth, and so the firm adhering of the intellect to the non-apparent truth of faith is called evidence here. Hence another reading has "conviction," because, namely, the intellect of the believer is convinced by Divine authority, so as to assent to what it sees not.

Accordingly if anyone would reduce the foregoing words to the form of a definition, he may say that faith is a habit of the mind, whereby eternal life is begun in us, making the intellect assent to what is non-apparent. In this way faith is distinguished from all other things pertaining to the intellect. For when we describe it as "evidence," we distinguish it from opinion, suspicion and doubt, which do not make the intellect adhere to anything firmly; when we go on to say, "of things that appear not," we distinguish it from science and understanding, the object of which is something apparent; and when we say that it is "the substance of things to be hoped for," we distinguish the virtue of faith from faith commonly so called, which has no reference to the Happiness we hope for.

Whatever other definitions are given of faith, are explanations of this one given by the Apostle. For when Augustine says (*Tract.* xl *in Joann.*)[1] that "faith is a virtue whereby we believe what we do not see," and when Damascene says (*De Fide Orthod.* iv)[2] that "faith is an assent without inquiry," and when others say[3] that faith is that certainty of the mind about absent things which surpasses opinion but falls short of science, these all amount to the same as the Apostle's words: *Evidence of things that appear not.* And when Dionysius says (*Div.*

Nom. vii)[4] that "faith is the solid foundation of the believer, establishing him in the truth, and showing forth the truth in him," this comes to the same as *substance of things to be hoped for*.

Reply Obj. 1. Substance, here, does not stand for the supreme genus divided against the other genera, but for that likeness to substance which is found in each genus, according as namely the first thing in a genus contains the others virtually and is said to be the substance of it.

Reply Obj. 2. Since faith pertains to the intellect as commanded by the will, it must be directed, as to its end, to the objects of those virtues which perfect the will, among which is hope, as we shall prove further on (Q. XVIII, A. 1). For this reason the definition of faith includes the object of hope.

Reply Obj. 3. Love may be of the seen and of the unseen, of the present and of the absent. Consequently a thing to be loved is not so properly adapted to faith, as a thing to be hoped for, since hope is always of the absent and the unseen.

Reply Obj. 4. Substance and evidence as included in the definition of faith, do not denote various genera of faith, nor different acts, but different relationships of one act to different objects, as is clear from what has been said.

Reply Obj. 5. Evidence taken from the proper principles of a thing make it apparent, but evidence taken from Divine authority does not make a thing apparent in itself, and such is the evidence referred to in the definition of faith.

ARTICLE 2. *Whether Faith Resides in the Intellect?*

We proceed thus to the Second Article: It would seem that faith does not reside in the intellect.

Objection 1. For Augustine says (*De Prædest. Sanct.* v)[5] that "faith resides in the believer's will." Now the will is a power distinct from the intellect. Therefore faith does not reside in the intellect.

Obj. 2. Further, The assent of faith to believe anything proceeds from the will obeying God. Therefore it seems that faith owes all its praise to obedience. Now obedience is in the will. Therefore faith is in the will, and not in the intellect.

Obj. 3. Further, The intellect is either speculative or practical. Now faith is not in the speculative intellect, since "this is not concerned with things to be sought or avoided," as stated

---

[1] PL 35, 1690; cf. also *Tract.*, LXXIX, on 14.29 (PL 35, 1837); *Quaest. Evang.*, II, Q. XXXIX super Luc. 17.5 (PL 35, 1352).

[2] Chap. 11 (PG 94, 1128).

[3] Cf. Hugh of S. Victor, *De Sacram.*, I, X, 1 (PL 176, 330).

[4] Sect. 4 (PG 3, 872).   [5] PL 44, 968.

in the book on the *Soul*,[1] so that it is not a principle of operation, whereas *faith . . . worketh by charity* (Gal. 5. 6). Likewise, neither is it in the practical intellect, the object of which is some true, contingent thing, that can be made or done. For the object of faith is the Eternal Truth, as was shown above (Q. I, A. I). Therefore faith does not reside in the intellect.

On the contrary, Faith is succeeded by the heavenly vision, according to I Cor. 13. 12: *We see now through a glass in a dark manner; but then face to face.* Now vision is in the intellect. Therefore faith is likewise.

I answer that, Since faith is a virtue, its act must be perfect. Now, for the perfection of an act proceeding from two active principles, each of these principles must be perfect; for it is not possible for a thing to be sawn well, unless the sawyer possess the art, and the saw be well fitted for sawing. Now, a disposition to act well in a power of the soul which is related to opposite objects, is a habit, as stated above (Part I-II, Q. XLIX, A. 4, Reply 1, 2, 3). Therefore an act that proceeds from two such powers must be perfected by a habit residing in each of them. Again, it has been stated above (A. 1; Q. II, AA. 1, 2) that to believe is an act of the intellect, according as the will moves it to assent. And this act proceeds both from the will and the intellect, both of which have a natural aptitude to be perfected by a habit, as we have said above (Part I-II, Q. L, AA. 4, 5). Consequently, if the act of faith is to be perfect, there needs to be a habit in the will as well as in the intellect, even as there needs to be the habit of prudence in the reason, besides the habit of temperance in the concupiscible part, in order that the act of that part be perfect. Now, to believe is immediately an act of the intellect, because the object of that act is the true, which pertains properly to the intellect. Consequently faith, which is the proper principle of that act, must reside in the intellect.

Reply Obj. 1. Augustine takes faith for the act of faith, which is described as depending on the believer's will, in so far as his intellect assents to matters of faith at the command of the will.

Reply Obj. 2. Not only does the will need to be ready to obey, but also the intellect needs to be well disposed to follow the command of the will, even as the concupiscible part needs to be well disposed in order to follow the command of reason; hence there needs to be a habit of virtue not only in the commanding will but also in the assenting intellect.

[1] Aristotle, III, 9 (432ᵇ28).

Reply Obj. 3. Faith resides in the speculative intellect as evidenced by its object. But since this object, which is the First Truth, is the end of all our desires and actions, as Augustine shows (*De Trin.* i, 8),[2] it follows that faith works by charity just as the speculative intellect becomes practical by extension.[3]

ARTICLE 3. *Whether Charity Is the Form of Faith?*

We proceed thus to the Third Article: It would seem that charity is not the form of faith.

Objection 1. For each thing derives its species from its form. When, therefore, two things are opposite members of a division as different species of the one genus, one cannot be the form of the other. Now faith and charity are stated to be opposite members of a division, as different species of virtue (I Cor. 13. 13). Therefore charity cannot be the form of faith.

Obj. 2. Further, A form and the thing of which it is the form are in one subject, since together they make up one thing absolutely. Now faith is in the intellect, while charity is in the will. Therefore charity is not the form of faith.

Obj. 3. Further, The form of a thing is its principle. Now obedience, rather than charity, seems to be the principle of believing, on the part of the will, according to Rom. 1. 5: *For obedience to the faith in all nations.* Therefore obedience rather than charity, is the form of faith.

On the contrary, Each thing works through its form. Now *faith works through charity* (Gal. 5. 6). Therefore the love of charity is the form of faith.

I answer that, As appears from what has been said above (Part I-II, Q. I, A. 3; Q. XVIII, A. 6), voluntary acts take their species from their end which is the will's object. Now that which gives a thing its species, is after the manner of a form in natural things. Therefore the form of any voluntary act is, in a manner, the end to which that act is directed, both because it takes its species from it, and because the mode of an action should correspond proportionately to the end. Now it is evident from what has been said (A. 1), that the act of faith is directed to the object of the will, that is, the good, as to its end. And this good which is the end of faith, namely, the Divine Good, is the proper object of charity. Therefore charity is called the form of faith, in so far as the act of faith is perfected and formed by charity.

[2] PL 42, 831; also chap. 10 (PL 42, 834).
[3] Aristotle, *Soul*, III, 10 (433ᵃ15).

Reply Obj. 1. Charity is called the form of faith because it forms the act of faith. Now nothing hinders one act from being formed by different habits, so as to be reduced to various species in a certain order, as stated above (Part I-II, Q. XVIII, A. 7, Reply 1) when we were treating of human acts in general.

Reply Obj. 2. This objection is true of an intrinsic form. But it is not thus that charity is the form of faith, but in the sense that it forms the act of faith, as explained above.

Reply Obj. 3. Even obedience, and hope likewise, and whatever other virtue might precede the act of faith, is formed by charity, as we shall show further on (Q. XXIII, A. 8), and consequently charity is spoken of as the form of faith.

ARTICLE 4. *Whether Formless Faith Can Become Formed, or Formed Faith Formless?*

We proceed thus to the Fourth Article: It seems that faith without form does not become formed, or formed faith formless.

Objection 1. For, according to I Cor. 13. 10, *when that which is perfect is come, that which is in part shall be done away.* Now formless faith is imperfect in comparison with formed faith. Therefore when formed faith comes, formless faith is done away, so that they are not one identical habit.

Obj. 2. Further, A dead thing does not become a living thing. Now formless faith is dead, according to James 2. 20: *Faith without works is dead.* Therefore formless faith cannot become formed.

Obj. 3. Further, God's grace, by its advent has no less effect in a believer than in an unbeliever. Now by coming to an unbeliever it causes the habit of faith. Therefore when it comes to a believer, who hitherto had the habit of formless faith, it causes another habit of faith in him.

Obj. 4. Further, as Boëthius says (*In Categ. Arist.* i),[1] accidents cannot be altered. Now faith is an accident. Therefore the same faith cannot be at one time formed, and at another formless.

On the contrary, A gloss on the words, *Faith without works is dead* (James 2. 20) adds, "by which it lives once more."[2] Therefore faith which was lifeless and without form hitherto, becomes formed and living.

I answer that, There have been various opinions on this question. For some have said[3] that

formed and formless faith are distinct habits, but that when formed faith comes, formless faith is done away, and that, in like manner, when a man sins mortally after having formed faith, a new habit of formless faith is infused into him by God. But it seems unfitting that grace should deprive man of a gift of God by coming to him, and that a gift of God should be infused into man on account of a mortal sin.

Consequently others have said[4] that formed and formless faith are indeed distinct habits, but that, all the same, when formed faith comes the habit of formless faith is not taken away, and that it remains together with the habit of formed faith in the same object. Yet again it seems unreasonable that the habit of formless faith should remain inactive in a person having formed faith.

We must therefore hold differently that formed and formless faith are one and the same habit. The reason is that a habit is differentiated by that which directly pertains to that habit. Now since faith is a perfection of the intellect, that pertains directly to faith which pertains to the intellect. Again, what pertains to the will does not pertain directly to faith, so as to be able to differentiate the habit of faith. But the distinction of formed from formless faith is in respect of something pertaining to the will, that is, charity, and not in respect of something pertaining to the intellect. Therefore formed and formless faith are not distinct habits.

Reply Obj. 1. The saying of the Apostle refers to those imperfect things from which imperfection is inseparable, for then, when the perfect comes the imperfect must be done away. Thus with the advent of clear vision, faith is done away, because its very notion is *of the things that appear not.* When, however, imperfection is not inseparable from the imperfect thing, the same identical thing which was imperfect becomes perfect. Thus childhood is not of the very notion of man, and consequently the same identical subject who was a child, becomes a man. Now formlessness is not of the very notion of faith, but is accidental to it, as stated above. Therefore unformed faith itself becomes formed.

Reply Obj. 2. That which makes an animal live is inseparable from an animal, because it is its essential form, namely the soul. Consequently a dead thing cannot become a living thing, and a living and a dead thing differ specifically. On the other hand, that which gives faith

---

[1] Chap. *De Subst.* (PL 64, 198).
[2] *Glossa interl.* (VI, 212v).
[3] William of Auxerre, *Sum. Aur.*, III, 15. Q. 2 (208vb).

[4] Cf. Bonaventure, *In Sent.*, III, d. XXIII, A. 2, Q. 4 (QR III, 496).

its form, or makes it live, is not of the essence of faith. Hence there is no comparison.

Reply Obj. 3. Grace causes faith not only when faith begins anew to be in a man, but also as long as faith lasts. For it has been said above (Part I, Q. CIV, A. 1; Part I-II, Q. CIX, A. 9), that God is always working man's justification, even as the sun is always lighting up the air. Hence grace is not less effective when it comes to a believer than when it comes to an unbeliever, since it causes faith in both, in the former by confirming and perfecting it, in the latter by creating it anew.

We might also reply that it is accidental, namely, on account of the disposition of the subject, that grace does not cause faith in one who has it already; just as, on the other hand, a second mortal sin does not take away grace from one who has already lost it through a previous mortal sin.

Reply Obj. 4. When formed faith becomes unformed, faith is not changed, but rather its subject, the soul, which at one time has faith without charity, and at another time, with charity.

ARTICLE 5. *Whether Faith Is a Virtue?*

We proceed thus to the Fifth Article: It seems that faith is not a virtue.

Objection 1. For virtue is ordered to the good, since "it is virtue that makes its subject good," as the Philosopher states.[1] But faith is ordered to the true. Therefore faith is not a virtue.

Obj. 2. Further, Infused virtue is more perfect than acquired virtue. Now faith, on account of its imperfection, is not placed among the acquired intellectual virtues, as the Philosopher states.[2] Much less, therefore, can it be considered an infused virtue.

Obj. 3. Further, formed and formless faith are of the same species, as stated above (A. 4). Now formless faith is not a virtue, since it is not connected with the other virtues. Therefore neither is formed faith a virtue.

Obj. 4. Further, The gratuitous graces and the fruits are distinct from the virtues. But faith is numbered among the gratuitous graces (I Cor. 12. 9) and likewise among the fruits (Gal. 5. 23). Therefore faith is not a virtue.

On the contrary, Man is justified by the virtues, since "justice is all virtue" as the Philosopher states.[3] Now man is justified by faith according to Rom. 5. 1: *Being justified therefore*

by faith let us have peace, etc. Therefore faith is a virtue.

I answer that, As shown above (Part I-II, Q. LVI, A. 3), it is by human virtue that human acts are rendered good. Hence, any habit that is always the principle of a good act, may be called a human virtue. Such a habit is formed faith. For since to believe is an act of the intellect assenting to the truth at the command of the will, two things are required that this act may be perfect, one of which is that the intellect should infallibly tend to its object, which is the true, while the other is that the will should be infallibly directed to the last end, on account of which it assents to the true. And both of these are to be found in the act of formed faith. For it is of the very notion of faith that the intellect should always tend to the true, since nothing false can be the object of faith, as proved above (Q. 1, A. 3); while the effect of charity, which is the form of faith, is that the soul has its will always directed to a good end. Therefore formed faith is a virtue.

On the other hand, unformed faith is not a virtue, because, though the act of unformed faith has its due perfection on the part of the intellect, it has not its due perfection as regards the will; just as, if temperance is in the concupiscible part, without prudence being in the rational part, temperance is not a virtue, as stated above (Part I-II, Q. LXV, A. 1), because the act of temperance requires both an act of reason, and an act of the concupiscible part, even as the act of faith requires an act of the will, and an act of the intellect.

Reply Obj. 1. The truth is itself the good of the intellect, since it is its perfection, and consequently faith has a relation to some good in so far as it determines the intellect to the true. Furthermore, it has a relation to the good considered as the object of the will, in so far as it is formed by charity.

Reply Obj. 2. The faith of which the Philosopher speaks is based on human reasoning in a conclusion which does not follow of necessity from its premises; and which can be false. Hence faith of this kind is not a virtue. On the other hand, the faith of which we are speaking is based on the Divine Truth, which is infallible, and consequently its object cannot be anything false. And therefore faith of this kind can be a virtue.

Reply Obj. 3. Formed and formless faith do not differ specifically, as though they belonged to different species. But they differ as perfect and imperfect within the same species. Hence

---

[1] *Ethics,* II, 6 (1106ª15).
[2] *Ibid.,* VI, 3 (1139ᵇ15).
[3] *Ibid.,* V, 1 (1130ª9).

formless faith, being imperfect, does not satisfy the conditions of a perfect virtue, for "virtue is a kind of perfection."[1]

Reply Obj. 4. Some say that faith which is numbered among the gratuitous graces is unformed faith.[2] But this is said without reason, since the gratuitous graces, which are mentioned in that passage, are not common to all the members of the Church. Hence the Apostle says: *There are diversities of graces,* and again: *To one is given* this grace and *to another* that (I Cor. 12. 4). Now formless faith is common to all the members of the Church, because formlessness is not part of its substance, if we consider it as a gratuitous gift. We must, therefore, say that in that passage, faith denotes a certain excellence of faith for instance, "constancy in faith," according to a gloss,[3] or the *word of faith.*

Faith is numbered among the fruits, in so far as it gives a certain pleasure in its act by reason of its certainty, and so the gloss on the fifth chapter to the Galatians, where the fruits are enumerated, explains faith as being "certainty about the unseen."[4]

ARTICLE 6. *Whether Faith Is One Virtue?*

We proceed thus to the Sixth Article: It would seem that faith is not one.

Objection 1. For just as faith is a gift of God according to Eph. 2. 8, so also wisdom and knowledge are numbered among God's gifts according to Isa. 11. 2. Now wisdom and knowledge differ in this, that wisdom is about eternal things, and knowledge about temporal things, as Augustine states (*De Trin.* xii, 14, 15).[5] Since then, faith is about eternal things, and also about some temporal things, it seems that faith is not one virtue but divided into several parts.

Obj. 2. Further, Confession is an act of faith, as stated above (Q. III, A. 1). Now confession of faith is not one and the same for all, since what we confess as past, the fathers of old confessed as yet to come, as appears from Isa. 7. 14: *Behold a virgin shall conceive.* Therefore faith is not one.

Obj. 3. Further, Faith is common to all be-

lievers in Christ. But one accident cannot be in many subjects. Therefore all cannot have one faith.

On the contrary, The Apostle says (Eph. 4. 5): *One Lord, one faith.*

I answer that, If we take faith as a habit, we can consider it in two ways. First on the part of the object, and thus there is one faith. Because the formal object of faith is the First Truth, by adhering to which we believe whatever is contained in the faith. Secondly, on the part of the subject, and thus faith is differentiated according as it is in various subjects. Now it is evident that faith, just as any other habit, takes its species from the formal aspect of its object, but is individualized by its subject. Hence if we take faith for the habit by which we believe, it is one specifically, but differs numerically according to its various subjects. If, on the other hand, we take faith for that which is believed, then, again, there is one faith, since what is believed by all is one thing, for though the things believed, which all agree in believing, may be different from one another, yet they are all reduced to one.

Reply Obj. 1. Temporal matters which are proposed to be believed do not pertain to the object of faith, except in relation to something eternal, namely the First Truth, as stated above (Q. I, A. I). Hence there is one faith of things both temporal and eternal. It is different with wisdom and knowledge, which consider temporal and eternal matters under the proper aspects of each.

Reply Obj. 2. This difference of past and future arises, not from any difference in the thing believed, but from the different relationships of believers to the one thing believed, as also we have mentioned above (Part I-II, Q. CIII, A. 4).

Reply Obj. 3. This objection considers numerical diversity of faith.

ARTICLE 7. *Whether Faith Is the First of the Virtues?*

We proceed thus to the Seventh Article: It would seem that faith is not the first of the virtues.

Objection 1. For a gloss on Luke 12. 4, *I say to you My friends,* says that "fortitude is the foundation of faith."[6] Now the foundation precedes that which is founded on it. Therefore faith is not the first of the virtues.

Obj. 2. Further, A gloss on Psalm 36., *Be not*

---

[1] *Physics,* VII, 3 (246ᵃ13).

[2] Bonaventure, *In Sent.,* III, d. XXIII, A. 2, Q. 4 (QR III, 494); Albert, *In Sent.,* III,, d. XXIII, A. 5, ad 5 (BO XXVIII, 414); also A. 9, Arg. 5 (BO XXVIII, 421).

[3] *Glossa interl.* (VI, 52v); *Glossa* Lombardi (PL 191, 1653).

[4] *Glossa interl.,* on Gal. 5.22 (VI, 87v); *Glossa* Lombardi, on Gal. 5.22 (PL 192, 160).

[5] PL 42, 1009, 1012.

[6] *Glossa ordin.* (V, 157A); Ambrose, *In Luc.,* on 12.4 (PL 15, 1817).

emulous, says that "hope leads on to faith."[1] Now hope is a virtue, as we shall state further on (Q. XVII, A. 1). Therefore faith is not the first of the virtues.

Obj. 3. Further, It was stated above (A. 2) that the intellect of the believer is moved, out of obedience to God, to assent to matters of faith. Now obedience also is a virtue. Therefore faith is not the first virtue.

Obj. 4. Further, Not formless but formed faith is the foundation, as a gloss remarks on I Cor. 3. 11.[2] Now faith is formed by charity, as stated above (A. 3). Therefore it is owing to charity that faith is the foundation. And so charity is the foundation even more than faith is (for the foundation is the first part of a building) and consequently it seems to precede faith.

Obj. 5. Further, The order of habits is taken from the order of acts. Now, in the act of faith, the act of the will which is perfected by charity, precedes the act of the intellect, which is perfected by faith, as the cause which precedes its effect. Therefore charity precedes faith. Therefore faith is not the first of the virtues.

On the contrary, The Apostle says (Heb. 11. 1) that *faith is the substance of things to be hoped for.* Now the substance of a thing is that which comes first. Therefore faith is first among the virtues.

I answer that, One thing can precede another in two ways: first, by its very nature; secondly, by accident. Faith, by its very nature, precedes all other virtues. For since the end is the principle in matters of action, as stated above (Part I-II, Q. XIII, A. 3; Q. XXXIV, A. 4, Reply 1), the theological virtues, the object of which is the last end, must precede all the others. Again, the last end must of necessity be present to the intellect before it is present to the will, since the will has no inclination for anything except in so far as it is apprehended by the intellect. Hence, as the last end is present in the will by hope and charity, and in the intellect, by faith, the first of all the virtues must, of necessity, be faith, because natural knowledge cannot reach God as the object of heavenly bliss, which is the aspect under which hope and charity tend towards Him.

On the other hand, some virtues can precede

faith accidentally. For an accidental cause precedes its effect accidentally. Now that which removes an obstacle is a kind of accidental cause, according to the Philosopher,[3] and in this sense certain virtues may be said to precede faith accidentally, in so far as they remove obstacles to belief. Thus fortitude removes the inordinate fear that hinders faith; humility removes pride, by which a man refuses to submit himself to the truth of faith. The same may be said of some other virtues, although there are no real virtues, unless faith be presupposed, as Augustine states (*Contra Julian.* iv).[4]

This suffices for the *Reply to the First Objection.*

Reply Obj. 2. Hope cannot lead to faith absolutely. For one cannot hope to obtain eternal happiness, unless one believes this possible, since hope does not tend to the impossible, as stated above (Part I-II, Q. XL, A. 1). It is, however, possible for one to be led by hope to persevere in faith, or to hold firmly to faith; and it is in this sense that hope is said to lead to faith.

Reply Obj. 3. Obedience is twofold. Sometimes it denotes the inclination of the will to fulfil God's commandments. In this way it is not a special virtue, but is a general condition of every virtue, since all acts of virtue come under the precepts of the Divine law, as stated above (Part I-II, Q. C, A. 2); and thus it is requisite for faith. In another way, obedience denotes an inclination to fulfil the commandments considered as a duty. In this way it is a special virtue, and a part of justice, for a man does his duty towards his superior when he obeys him; and thus obedience follows faith, by which man knows that God is his superior, Whom he ought to obey.

Reply Obj. 4. To be a foundation a thing requires not only to come first, but also to be joined to the other parts of the building, since the building would not be founded on it unless the other parts were connected to it. Now the connecting bond of the spiritual edifice is charity, according to Coloss. 3. 14: *Above all ... things have charity which is the bond of perfection.* Consequently faith without charity cannot be the foundation. And yet it does not follow that charity precedes faith.

Reply Obj. 5. Some act of the will is required before faith, but not an act of the will moulded by charity. This latter act presupposes faith,

---

[1] *Glossa interl.* (III, 136v); *Glossa* Lombardi (PL 191, 368). Cf. Cassiodorus, *Expos. in Psalt.*, super Ps. 36.3 (PL 70, 258).

[2] *Glossa ordin.* (VI, 37E); *Glossa* Lombardi (PL 191, 1566). Augustine, *Enchir.*, 4 (PL 40, 233).

[3] *Physics,* VIII, 4 (255^b24).

[4] Chap. 3 (PL 44, 750).

because the will cannot tend to God with perfect love, unless the intellect possesses right faith about Him.

ARTICLE 8. *Whether Faith Is More Certain Than Science and the Other Intellectual Virtues?*

We proceed thus to the Eighth Article: It would seem that faith is not more certain than science and the other intellectual virtues.

Objection 1. For doubt is opposed to certitude, and so a thing would seem to be the more certain through being less doubtful, just as a thing is the whiter, the less it has of an admixture of black. Now understanding, science and also wisdom are free of any doubt about their objects; but the believer may sometimes suffer a movement of doubt, and doubt about matters of faith. Therefore faith is no more certain than the intellectual virtues.

Obj. 2. Further, Sight is more certain than hearing. But *faith is through hearing* according to Rom. 10. 17; but understanding, science, and wisdom imply some kind of intellectual sight. Therefore science and understanding are more certain than faith.

Obj. 3. Further, In matters concerning the intellect, the more perfect is the more certain. Now understanding is more perfect than faith, since faith is the way to understanding, according to another version of Isa. 7. 9:[1] *If you will not believe, you shall not understand* (Vulg.,— continue): and Augustine says (*De Trin.* xiv)[2] that faith is strengthened by science. Therefore it seems that science or understanding is more certain than faith.

On the contrary, The Apostle says (I Thess. 2. 15): *When you had received of us the word of the hearing,* that is, by faith . . . *you received it not as the word of men, but, as it is indeed, the word of God.* Now nothing is more certain than the word of God. Therefore science is not more certain than faith; nor is anything else.

I answer that, As stated above (Part I-II, Q. LVII, A. 4, Reply 2; A. 5, Reply 3), two of the intellectual virtues are about contingent matter, namely prudence and art. Faith comes before these in point of certitude, by reason of its matter, since it is about eternal things, which never change. But the other three intellectual virtues, namely wisdom, science and understanding, are about necessary things, as stated above (Part I-II, Q. LVII, A. 5, Reply 3). But it must be observed that wisdom, science and understanding

may be taken in two ways; first, as intellectual virtues, according to the Philosopher;[3] secondly, as gifts of the Holy Ghost. If we consider them in the first way, we must note that certitude can be looked at in two ways. First, on the part of its cause, and thus a thing which has a more certain cause, is itself more certain. In this way faith is more certain than those three virtues, because it is founded on the Divine truth, while the above three virtues are based on human reason. Secondly, certitude may be considered on the part of the subject, and thus the more a man's intellect lays hold of a thing, the more certain it is. In this way, faith is less certain, because matters of faith are above the human intellect, while the objects of the above three virtues are not. Since, however, a thing is judged absolutely with regard to its cause, but relatively, with respect to a disposition on the part of the subject, it follows that faith is more certain absolutely, while the others are more certain relatively, that is, for us. Likewise if these three be taken as gifts received in this present life, they are related to faith as to their principle which they presuppose, so that again, in this way, faith is more certain.

Reply Obj. 1. This doubt is not on the part of the cause of faith, but on our part, in so far as we do not fully grasp matters of faith with our intellect.

Reply Obj. 2. Other things being equal sight is more certain than hearing. But if (the authority of) the person from whom we hear greatly surpasses that of the seer's sight, hearing is more certain than sight. Thus a man of little science is more certain about what he hears on the authority of an expert in science, than about what is apparent to him according to his own reason. And much more is a man certain about what he hears from God, Who cannot be deceived, than about what he sees with his own reason, which can be mistaken.

Reply Obj. 3. The gifts of understanding and knowledge are more perfect than the knowledge of faith in the point of their greater clearness, but not in regard to more certain adhering, because the whole certitude of the gifts of understanding and knowledge, arises from the certitude of faith, even as the certitude of the knowledge of conclusions arises from the certitude of the principles. But in so far as science, wisdom and understanding are intellectual virtues, they are based upon the natural light of reason, which falls short of the certitude of God's word, on which faith is founded.

[1] The Septuagint.
[2] Chap. 1 (PL 42, 1037).

[3] *Ethics,* VI, 3 (1139[b]15).

QUESTION V

OF THOSE WHO HAVE FAITH

(In Four Articles)

WE must now consider those who have faith, under which head there are four points of inquiry: (1) Whether there was faith in the angels, or in man, in their original state? (2) Whether the demons have faith? (3) Whether those heretics who err in one article, have faith in the others? (4) Whether among those who have faith, one has it more than another?

ARTICLE 1. *Whether There was Faith in the Angels, or in Man, in Their Original State?*

We proceed thus to the First Article: It seems that there was no faith, either in the angels, or in man, in their original state.

Objection 1. For Hugh of S. Victor says in his Sentences (*De Sacram.* i)[1] that "man cannot see God or things that are in God, because he closes his eyes to contemplation." Now the angels, in their original state, before they were either confirmed in grace, or had fallen from it, had their eyes opened to contemplation, since they saw things in the Word, according to Augustine (*Gen. ad lit.* ii, 8).[2] Likewise the first man, while in the state of innocence, seemingly had his eyes open to contemplation; for Hugh of S. Victor says[3] that in his original state "man knew his Creator, not by the mere outward perception of hearing, but by inward inspiration, not as now believers seek an absent God by faith, but by seeing Him clearly present to his contemplation." Therefore there was no faith in the angels and man in their original state.

Obj. 2. Further, The knowledge of faith is dark and obscure, according to I Cor. 13. 12: *We see now through a glass in a dark manner.* Now in their original state there was no obscurity either in the angels or in man, because darkness is a punishment of sin. Therefore there could be no faith in the angels or in man, in their original state.

Obj. 3. Further, The Apostle says (Rom. 10. 17) that *faith . . . cometh by hearing.* Now this could not apply to angels and man in their original state, for then they could not hear anything from another. Therefore, in that state, there was no faith either in man or in the angels.

On the contrary, It is written (Heb. 11. 6): *He that cometh to God, must believe.* Now the original state of angels and man was one of ap-

proach to God. Therefore they had need of faith.

I answer that, Some say that there was no faith in the angels before they were confirmed in grace or fell from it, and in man before he sinned, by reason of the manifest contemplation that they had of Divine things.[4] Since, however, *faith is the evidence of things that appear not,* according to the Apostle (Heb. 11. 1), and since "by faith we believe what we see not," according to Augustine (*Tract.* xl *in* Joann.; *QQ. Evang.* ii, *qu.* 39),[5] that manifestation alone excludes faith, which renders apparent or seen the principal object of faith. Now the principal object of faith is the First Truth, the sight of which gives the happiness of heaven and takes the place of faith. Consequently, as the angels before their confirmation in grace, and man before sin, did not possess the happiness by which God is seen in His Essence, it is evident that the knowledge they possessed was not such as to exclude faith.

It follows, then, that the absence of faith in them could only be explained by their being altogether ignorant of the object of faith. And if man and the angels were created in a purely natural state, as some hold,[6] perhaps one might hold that there was no faith in the angels before their confirmation in grace, or in man before sin, because the knowledge of faith surpasses not only a man's but even an angel's natural knowledge about God.

Since, however, we stated in the First Part (Q. LXII, A. 3; Q. XCV, A. 1) that man and the angels were created with the gift of grace, we must say that there was in them a certain beginning of hoped-for happiness, by reason of grace received but not yet consummated, which happiness was begun in their will by hope and charity, and in the intellect by faith, as stated above (Q. IV, A. 7). Consequently we must hold that the angels had faith before they were confirmed, and man, before he sinned.

Nevertheless we must observe that in the object of faith, there is something formal, as it were, namely the First Truth surpassing all the natural knowledge of a creature, and something material, namely, the thing to which we assent while adhering to the First Truth. With regard to the former, before obtaining the happiness to come, faith is common to all who have knowledge of God, by adhering to the First Truth.

---

[4] Hugh of S. Victor, *De Sacram.*, I, VI, 14 (PL 176, 271); cf. Peter Lombard, *Sent.*, IV, d. 1 chap. 5 (QR II, 747).

[5] PL 35, 1690; PL 35, 1352.

[6] Cf. Part I, Q. XCV, A. 1.

[1] PL 176, 330. [2] PL 34, 270. [3] *Op. cit.*, I, VI, 14 (PL 176, 271).

But with regard to the things which are proposed as the material object of faith, some are believed by one, and known plainly by another, even in the present state, as we have shown above (Q. I, A. 5). In this respect, too, it may be said that the angels before being confirmed, and man, before sin, possessed clear knowledge about certain points in the Divine mysteries, which now we cannot know except by believing them.

Reply Obj. 1. Although the words of Hugh of S. Victor are those of a master, and have the force of an authority, yet it may be said that the contemplation which removes the need of faith, is heavenly contemplation, by which the supernatural truth is seen in its essence. Now the angels did not possess this contemplation before they were confirmed, nor did man before he sinned. Yet their contemplation was of a higher order than ours, for by its means they approached nearer to God, and had manifest knowledge of more of the Divine effects and mysteries than we can have knowledge of. Hence faith was not in them so that they sought an absent God as we seek Him, since by the light of wisdom He was more present to them than He is to us, although He was not so present to them as He is to the Blessed by the light of glory.

Reply Obj. 2. There was no darkness of sin or punishment in the original state of man and the angels, but there was a certain natural obscurity in the human and angelic intellect, in so far as every creature is darkness in comparison with the immensity of the Divine light. And this obscurity suffices for the notion of faith.

Reply Obj. 3. In the original state there was no hearing anything from man speaking outwardly, but there was from God inspiring inwardly; thus the prophets heard, as expressed by the Psalm (84. 9): *I will hear what the Lord God will speak in me.*

ARTICLE 2. *Whether in the Demons There Is Faith?*

We proceed thus to the Second Article: It would seem that the demons have no faith.

Objection 1. For Augustine says (*De Prædest. Sanct.* v)[1] that "faith depends on the believer's will." But this is a good will, since by it man wishes to believe in God. Since then no deliberate will of the demons is good, as stated above (Part I, Q. LXIV, A. 2, Reply 5), it seems that in the demons there is no faith.

Obj. 2. Further, Faith is a gift of Divine

grace, according to Eph. 2. 8: *By grace you are saved through faith, . . . for it is the gift of God.* Now, according to a gloss on Osee 3. 1, *They look to strange gods, and love the husks of the grapes,* the demons lost their gifts of grace by sinning.[2] Therefore faith did not remain in the demons after they sinned.

Obj. 3. Further, Unbelief would seem to be graver than other sins, as Augustine observes (*Tract.* lxxxix *in Joann.*)[3] on John 15. 22, *If I had not come and spoken to them, they would not have sin: but now they have no excuse for their sin.* Now the sin of unbelief is in some men. Consequently, if the demons have faith, some men would be guilty of a sin graver than that of the demons, which seems unreasonable. Therefore in the demons there is no faith.

On the contrary, It is written (James 2. 19): *The devils . . . believe and tremble.*

I answer that, As stated above (Q. I, A. 4; Q. II, A. 1), the believer's intellect assents to that which he believes, not because he sees it either in itself, or by resolving it to first self-evident principles, but because his will commands his intellect to assent. Now, that the will moves the intellect to assent, may be due to two causes. First, through the will being directed to the good, and in this way, to believe is a praiseworthy action. Secondly, because the intellect is convinced that it ought to believe what is said, though that conviction is not based on the evidence of the thing. Thus if a prophet, while preaching the word of God, were to foretell something, and were to give a sign, by raising a dead person to life, the intellect of a witness would be convinced so as to recognize clearly that God, Who does not lie, was speaking, although the thing itself foretold would not be evident in itself, and consequently the character of faith would not be removed.

Accordingly we must say that faith is commended in the first sense in the faithful of Christ. And in this way faith is not in the demons, but only in the second way, for they see many evident signs, by which they recognize that the teaching of the Church is from God, although they do not see the things themselves that the Church teaches, for instance that there are three Persons in God, and so forth.

Reply Obj. 1. The demons are, in a way, compelled to believe, by the evidence of signs, and so their will deserves no praise for their belief.

Reply Obj. 2. Faith, which is a gift of grace,

[1] PL 44, 968.

[2] *Glossa ordin.* (IV, 336E); Jerome *In Osee,* super, 3.1 (PL 25, 833).   [3] PL 35, 1856.

inclines man to believe by giving him a certain affection for the good, even when that faith is formless. Consequently the faith which the demons have, is not a gift of grace. Rather are they compelled to believe through their natural intellectual acumen.

Reply Obj. 3. The very fact that the signs of faith are so evident, that the demons are compelled to believe, is displeasing to them, so that their malice is by no means diminished by their belief.

ARTICLE 3. *Whether a Man Who Disbelieves One Article of Faith, Can Have Formless Faith in the Other Articles?*

We proceed thus to the Third Article: It would seem that a heretic who disbelieves one article of faith, can have formless faith in the other articles.

Objection 1. For the natural intellect of a heretic is not more able than that of a catholic. Now a catholic's intellect needs the aid of the gift of faith in order to believe any article whatever of faith. Therefore it seems that heretics cannot believe any articles of faith without the gift of formless faith.

Obj. 2. Further, Just as faith contains many articles, so does one science, namely geometry, contain many conclusions. Now a man may possess the science of geometry as to some geometrical conclusions, and yet be ignorant of other conclusions. Therefore a man can believe some articles of faith without believing the others.

Obj. 3. Further, Just as man obeys God in believing the articles of faith, so does he also in keeping the commandments of the Law. Now a man can obey some commandments, and disobey others. Therefore he can believe some articles, and disbelieve others.

On the contrary, Just as mortal sin is contrary to charity, so is disbelief in one article of faith contrary to faith. Now charity does not remain in a man after one mortal sin. Therefore neither does faith, after a man disbelieves one article.

I answer that, Neither formed nor formless faith remains in a heretic who disbelieves one article of faith. The reason of this is that the species of every habit depends on the formal character of the object, without which the species of the habit cannot remain. Now the formal object of faith is the First Truth, as manifested in Holy Writ and the teaching of the Church, which proceeds from the First Truth. Consequently whoever does not adhere, as to an infallible and Divine rule, to the teaching of the Church, which proceeds from the First Truth

manifested in Holy Writ, has not the habit of faith but holds that which is of faith otherwise than by faith. In the same way, for example, it is evident that a man whose mind holds a conclusion without knowing how it is proved, has not scientific knowledge, but merely an opinion about it. Now it is manifest that he who adheres to the teaching of the Church, as to an infallible rule, assents to whatever the Church teaches. Otherwise, if, of the things taught by the Church, he holds what he chooses to hold, and rejects what he chooses to reject, he no longer adheres to the teaching of the Church as to an infallible rule, but to his own will. Hence it is evident that a heretic who obstinately disbelieves one article of faith is not prepared to follow the teaching of the Church in all things. But if he is not obstinate, he is no longer in heresy but only in error. Therefore it is clear that such a heretic with regard to one article has no faith in the other articles, but only a kind of opinion in accordance with his own will.

Reply Obj. 1. A heretic does not hold the other articles of faith, about which he does not err, in the same way as one of the faithful does, namely by adhering simply to the Divine Truth, because in order to do so, a man needs the help of the habit of faith. But he holds the things that are of faith, by his own will and judgment.

Reply Obj. 2. The various conclusions of a science have their respective means of demonstration, one of which may be known without another, so that we may know some conclusions of a science without knowing the others. On the other hand faith adheres to all the articles of faith by reason of one means, namely, on account of the First Truth proposed to us in the Scriptures, according to the teaching of the Church who has the right understanding of them. Hence whoever abandons this means is altogether lacking in faith.

Reply Obj. 3. The various precepts of the Law may be referred either to their respective proximate motives, and thus one can be kept without another or to one primary motive, which is perfect obedience to God, in which a man fails whenever he breaks one commandment, according to James 2. 10: *Whosoever shall . . . offend in one point is become guilty of all.*

ARTICLE 4. *Whether Faith Can Be Greater in One Man Than in Another?*

We proceed thus to the Fourth Article: It would seem that faith cannot be greater in one man than in another.

Objection 1. For the quantity of a habit is taken from its object. Now whoever has faith believes everything that is of faith, since by failing in one point, a man loses his faith altogether, as stated above (A. 3). Therefore it seems that faith cannot be greater in one than in another.

Obj. 2. Further, Those things which consist in something supreme cannot be *more* or *less*. Now faith consists in something supreme, because it requires that man should adhere to the First Truth above all things. Therefore faith canot be more or less.

Obj. 3. Further, Faith is to knowledge by grace as the understanding of principles is to natural knowledge, since the articles of faith are the first principles of knowledge by grace, as was shown above (Q. 1, A. 7). Now the understanding of principles is possessed in equal degree by all men. Therefore faith is possessed in equal degree by all the faithful.

On the contrary, Wherever we find great and little, there we find more and less. Now in the matter of faith we find great and little, for Our Lord said to Peter (Matt. 14. 31): *O thou of little faith, why didst thou doubt?* And to the woman he said (Matt. 15. 28): *O woman, great is thy faith!* Therefore faith can be greater in one than in another.

I answer that, As stated above (Part I-II, Q. LII, AA. 1, 2; Q. CXII, A. 4), the quantity of a habit may be considered from two points of view: first, on the part of the object; secondly, on the part of its participation by the subject. Now the object of faith may be considered in two ways: first, in respect of its formal aspect, secondly, in respect of the material object which is proposed to be believed. Now the formal object of faith is one and simple, namely the First Truth, as stated above (Q. 1, A. 1). Hence in this respect there is no diversity of faith among believers, but it is specifically one in all, as stated above (Q. IV, A. 6). But the things which are proposed as the matter of our belief are many and can be received more or less explicitly. And in this respect one man can believe explicitly more things than another, so that faith can be greater in one man on account of its being more explicit.

If, on the other hand, we consider faith from the point of view of its participation by the subject, this happens in two ways, since the act of faith proceeds both from the intellect and from the will, as stated above (A. 2; Q. 1, A. 4; Q. IV, AA. 1, 2). Consequently a man's faith may be described as being greater, in one way, on the

part of his intellect, on account of its greater certitude and firmness, and, in another way, on the part of his will, on account of his greater promptitude, devotion, or confidence.

Reply Obj. 1. A man who obstinately disbelieves a thing that is of faith, has not the habit of faith, and yet he who does not explicitly believe all, while he is prepared to believe all, has that habit. In this respect, one man has greater faith than another, on the part of the object, in so far as he believes more things, as stated above.

Reply Obj. 2. It is of the notion of faith that one should give the first place to the First Truth. But among those who do this, some submit to it with greater certitude and devotion than others. And in this way faith is greater in one than in another.

Reply Obj. 3. The understanding of principles results from man's very nature, which is equally shared by all. But faith results from the gift of grace, which is not equally in all, as explained above (Part I-II, Q. CXII, A. 4). Hence the comparison fails. Nevertheless the truth of principles is more known to one than to another, according to the greater capacity of intellect.

QUESTION VI
OF THE CAUSE OF FAITH
(*In Two Articles*)

WE must now consider the cause of faith, under which head there are two points of inquiry: (1) Whether faith is infused into man by God? (2) Whether formless faith is a gift of God?

ARTICLE 1. *Whether Faith Is Infused into Man by God?*

We proceed thus to the First Article: It seems that faith is not infused into man by God.

Objection 1. For Augustine says (*De Trin.* XIV. 1)[1] that science "begets faith in us, and nourishes, defends and strengthens it." Now those things which science begets in us seem to be acquired rather than infused. Therefore faith does not seem to be in us by Divine infusion.

Obj. 2. Further, That to which man attains by hearing and seeing, seems to be acquired by him. Now man attains to belief both by seeing miracles and by hearing the teachings of faith. For it is written (John 4. 53): *The father . . . knew that it was at the same hour, that Jesus said to him, Thy son liveth; and himself be-*

[1] PL 42, 1037.

lieved, and his whole house; and (Rom. 10. 17) it is said that *faith is through hearing.* Therefore man attains to faith by acquiring it.

Obj. 3. Further, That which depends on a man's will can be acquired by him. But "faith depends on the believer's will," according to Augustine (*De Prædest. Sanct.* v).[1] Therefore faith can be acquired by man.

On the contrary, It is written (Eph. 2. 8, 9): *By grace you are saved through faith, and that not of yourselves . . . that no man may glory . . . for it is the gift of God.*

I answer that, Two things are requisite for faith. First, that the things which are of faith should be proposed to man. This is necessary in order that man believe anything explicitly. The second thing requisite for faith is the assent of the believer to the things which are proposed to him. Accordingly, as regards the first of these, faith must be from God. Because those things which are of faith surpass human reason, and hence they do not come to man's knowledge unless God reveal them. To some, indeed, they are revealed by God immediately, as those things which were to the apostles and prophets, while to some they are proposed by God in sending preachers of the faith, according to Rom. 10. 15: *How shall they preach, unless they be sent?*

As regards the second, namely, man's assent to the things which are of faith, we may observe a twofold cause, either one of external inducement, such as seeing a miracle, or being persuaded by someone to embrace the faith. Neither of these is a sufficient cause, since of those who see the same miracle, or who hear the same sermon, some believe, and some do not. Hence we must assert another interior cause, which moves man inwardly to assent to matters of faith.

The Pelagians held[2] that this cause was nothing else than man's free choice. And consequently they said that the beginning of faith is from ourselves, in so far as, namely, it is in our power to be ready to assent to things which are of faith, but that the consummation of faith is from God, Who proposes to us the things we have to believe. But this is false, for, since man, by assenting to matters of faith, is raised above his nature, this must exist in him from some supernatural principle moving him inwardly, and this is God. Therefore faith, as regards the assent which is the chief act of faith, is from God moving man inwardly by grace.

Reply Obj. 1. Science begets and nourishes faith, by way of the external persuasion afforded by science. But the chief and proper cause of faith is that which moves man inwardly to assent.

Reply Obj. 2. This argument again refers to the cause that proposes outwardly the things that are of faith, or persuades man to believe by words or deeds.

Reply Obj. 3. To believe does indeed depend on the will of the believer. But man's will needs to be prepared by God with grace, in order that he may be raised to things which are above his nature, as stated above.

ARTICLE 2. *Whether Formless Faith Is a Gift of God?*

We proceed thus to the Second Article: It seems that formless faith is not a gift of God.

Objection 1. For it is written (Deut. 32. 4) that *the works of God are perfect.* Now formless faith is something imperfect. Therefore it is not the work of God.

Obj. 2. Further, Just as an act is said to be deformed through lacking its due form, so too is faith called formless when it lacks the form due to it. Now the deformed act of sin is not from God, as stated above (Part I-II, Q. LXXIX, A. 2. REPLY 2). Therefore neither is formless faith from God.

Obj. 3 Further, Whomsoever God heals, He heals wholly, for it is written (John 7. 23): *If a man receive circumcision on the sabbath-day, that the law of Moses may not be broken; are you angry at Me because I have healed the whole man on the sabbath-day?* Now faith heals man from unbelief. Therefore whoever receives from God the gift of faith is at the same time healed from all his sins. But this is not done except by formed faith. Therefore formed faith alone is a gift of God, and consequently formless faith is not from God.

On the contrary, A gloss on I Cor. 13. 2 says[3] that "the faith which lacks charity is a gift of God." Now this is formless faith. Therefore formless faith is a gift of God.

I answer that, Formlessness is a privation. Now it must be noted that privation sometimes pertains to the notion of the species, and sometimes not, but comes to a thing already possessed of its proper species. Thus privation of the due equilibrium of the humours is of the very notion of the species of sickness, while darkness

---

[1] PL 44, 968.   [2] Cf. Conc. Arausic. II, anno 529, can. 5 (MA VIII, 712; DZ 178).

[3] Cf. Peter Lombard, *Sent.,* III, d. 23, chap. 4. (QR II, 657); also, *Glossa ordin.,* on I Cor. 13.2 (VI, 54A); *Glossa* Lombardi, on I Cor. 13.2 (PL 191, 1659).

is not of the notion of a diaphanous body, but comes to it. Since, therefore, when we assign the cause of a thing, we intend to assign the cause of that thing as existing in its proper species, it follows that what is not the cause of a privation cannot be assigned as the cause of the thing to which that privation belongs as existing in the very notion of its species. For we cannot assign as the cause of a sickness something which is not the cause of a disturbance in the humours, though we can assign as cause of a diaphanous body something which is not the cause of the darkness, which is not in the notion of the diaphanous body.

Now the formlessness of faith does not pertain to the notion of the species of faith, since faith is said to be formless through lack of an extrinsic form, as stated above (Q. IV, A. 4). Consequently the cause of formless faith is that which is the cause of faith absolutely so called, and this is God, as stated above (A. 1). It follows, therefore, that formless faith is a gift of God.

Reply Obj. 1. Formless faith, though it is not absolutely perfect with the perfection of a virtue, is, nevertheless, perfect with a perfection that suffices for the notion of faith.

Reply Obj. 2. The deformity of an act is of the notion of the act's species, considered as a moral act, as stated above (Part I, Q. XLVIII, A. 1, Reply 2; Part I-II, Q. XVIII, A. 5). For an act is said to be deformed through being deprived of an intrinsic form, namely the due commensuration of the act's circumstances. Hence we cannot say that God is the cause of a deformed act, for He is not the cause of its deformity, though He is the cause of the act as such.

We may also reply that deformity denotes not only privation of a due form, but also a contrary disposition; and thus deformity is compared to the act as falsehood is to faith. Hence, just as the deformed act is not from God, so neither is a false faith. And as formless faith is from God, so too, acts that are good generically, though not formed by charity, as is frequently the case in sinners, are from God.

Reply Obj. 3. He who receives faith from God without charity, is healed from unbelief, not absolutely (because the sin of his previous unbelief is not removed) but in part, namely, in the point of ceasing from committing such and such a sin. Thus it happens frequently that a man ceases from one act of sin through God causing him thus to cease without ceasing from another act of sin, through the suggestion of his own malice. And in this way sometimes it

is granted by God to a man to believe, and yet he is not granted the gift of charity, just as also the gift of prophecy, or the like, is given to some without charity.

QUESTION VII
Of the effects of faith
(*In Two Articles*)

We must now consider the effects of faith, under which head there are two points of inquiry: (1) Whether fear is an effect of faith? (2) Whether the heart is purified by faith?

ARTICLE 1. *Whether Fear Is an Effect of Faith?*

We proceed thus to the First Article: It would seem that fear is not an effect of faith.

Objection 1. For an effect does not precede its cause. Now fear precedes faith, for it is written (Ecclus. 2. 8): *Ye that fear the Lord, believe in Him.* Therefore fear is not an effect of faith.

Obj. 2. Further, The same thing is not the cause of contraries. Now fear and hope are contraries, as stated above (Part I-II, Q. XXIII, A. 2), and faith begets hope, as a gloss observes on Matt. 1. 2.[1] Therefore fear is not an effect of faith.

Obj. 3. Further, One contrary does not cause another. Now the object of faith is a good, which is the First Truth, while the object of fear is an evil, as stated above (Part I-II, Q. XLII, A. 1). Again, acts take their species from the object, according to what was stated above (Part I-II, Q. XVIII, A. 2). Therefore faith is not a cause of fear.

On the contrary, It is written (James 2. 19): *The devils . . . believe and tremble.*

I answer that, Fear is a movement of the appetitive power, as stated above (Part I-II, Q. XLI, A. 1). Now the principle of all appetitive movements is good or evil apprehended, and consequently the principle of fear and of every appetitive movement must be an apprehension. Again, through faith there arises in us an apprehension of certain punishments for evils, which are inflicted in accordance with the Divine judgment. In this way, then, faith is a cause of the fear by which one dreads to be punished by God. And this is servile fear.

It is also a cause of filial fear, according to which one dreads to be separated from God, or by which one shrinks from equalling oneself to Him, and holds Him in reverence, in so far as faith makes us appreciate God as an unfathom-

[1] *Glossa interl.* (v, 5n).

able and supreme good, separation from which is the greatest evil, and to which it is wicked to wish to be equalled. Of the first fear, namely, servile fear, formless faith is the cause, while formed faith is the cause of the second, namely filial fear, because it makes man adhere to God and to be subject to Him by charity.

Reply Obj. 1. Fear of God cannot universally precede faith, because if we knew nothing at all about Him, with regard to rewards and punishments, concerning which faith teaches us, we should in no way fear Him. If, however, faith be presupposed in reference to certain articles of faith, for example the Divine excellence, then reverential fear follows, the result of which is that man submits his intellect to God, so as to believe in all the Divine promises. Hence the text quoted continues: *And your reward shall not be made void.*

Reply Obj. 2. The same thing in respect of contraries can be the cause of contraries, but not under the same aspect. Now faith begets hope, in so far as it enables us to appreciate the prize which God awards to the just, while it is the cause of fear, in so far as it makes us appreciate the punishments which He intends to inflict on sinners.

Reply Obj. 3. The primary and formal object of faith is the good which is the First Truth. But the material object of faith includes also certain evils; for instance, that it is an evil either not to submit to God, or to be separated from Him, and that sinners will suffer evils of punishment from God. In this way faith can be the cause of fear.

ARTICLE 2. *Whether Faith Has the Effect of Purifying the Heart?*

We proceed thus to the Second Article: It would seem that faith does not purify the heart.

Objection 1. For purity of the heart pertains chiefly to the affections, while faith is in the intellect. Therefore faith has not the effect of purifying the heart.

Obj. 2. Further, That which purifies the heart is incompatible with impurity. But faith is compatible with the impurity of sin, as may be seen in those who have formless faith. Therefore faith does not purify the heart.

Obj. 3 Further, If faith were to purify the human heart in any way, it would chiefly purify the intellect of man. Now it does not purify the intellect from obscurity, since it is a veiled knowledge. Therefore faith in no way purifies the heart.

On the contrary, Peter said (Acts 15. 9): *Purifying their hearts by faith.*

I answer that, A thing is impure through being mixed with baser things; for silver is not called impure, when mixed with gold, which betters it, but when mixed with lead or tin. Now it is evident that the rational creature is more excellent than all transient and corporeal creatures; so that it becomes impure through subjecting itself to transient things by loving them. From this impurity the rational creature is purified by means of a contrary movement, when it tends to that which is above it, namely, God. The first beginning of this movement is faith, since *he that cometh to God must believe that He is,* according to Heb. 11. 6. Hence the first beginning of the heart's purifying is faith. And if faith is perfected through being formed by charity, the heart will thus be perfectly purified.

Reply Obj. 1. Things that are in the intellect are the principles of those which are in the affection, in so far as the apprehended good moves the appetite.

Reply Obj. 2. Even formless faith excludes a certain impurity which is contrary to it, namely that of error, and which consists in the human intellect adhering inordinately to things below itself, through wishing to measure Divine things by the rule of sensible things. But when it is formed by charity, then it is incompatible with any kind of impurity, because *charity covereth all sins* (Prov. 10. 12).

Reply Obj. 3. The obscurity of faith does not pertain to the impurity of sin, but rather to the natural defect of the human intellect, according to the present state of life.

QUESTION VIII

OF THE GIFT OF UNDERSTANDING

(*In Eight Articles*)

WE must now consider the gifts of understanding and knowledge, which correspond to the virtue of faith. With regard to the gift of understanding there are eight points of inquiry: (1) Whether understanding is a gift of the Holy Ghost? (2) Whether it can be together with faith in the same person? (3) Whether the understanding which is a gift of the Holy Ghost, is only speculative, or practical also? (4) Whether all who are in a state of grace have the gift of understanding? (5) Whether this gift is to be found in those who are without grace? (6) Of the relationship of the gift of understanding to the other gifts. (7) Which of the beatitudes corresponds to this gift? (8) Which of the fruits?

ARTICLE 1. *Whether Understanding Is a Gift of the Holy Ghost?*

We proceed thus to the First Article: It would seem that understanding is not a gift of the Holy Ghost.

Objection 1. For the gifts of grace are distinct from the gifts of nature, since they are given in addition to the latter. Now understanding is a natural habit of the soul, by which self-evident principles are known, as stated in the *Ethics*.[1] Therefore it should not be counted among the gifts of the Holy Ghost.

Obj. 2. Further, The Divine gifts are shared by creatures according to their proportion and mode, as Dionysius states (*Div. Nom.* iv).[2] Now the mode of human nature is to know the truth, not absolutely (which pertains to the notion of understanding), but discursively (which is proper to reason), as Dionysius explains (*Div. Nom.* vii).[3] Therefore the Divine knowledge which is bestowed on man should be called a gift of reason rather than a gift of understanding.

Obj. 3. Further, In the powers of the soul the understanding is divided against the will.[4] Now no gift of the Holy Ghost is called after the will. Therefore no gift of the Holy Ghost should receive the name of understanding.

On the contrary, It is written (Isa. 11. 2): *The Spirit of the Lord shall rest upon him, the Spirit of wisdom and of understanding.*

I answer that, The word *intellectus* (understanding) implies an innermost knowledge, for *intelligere* (to understand) is the same as *intus legere* (to read inwardly). This is clear to anyone who considers the difference between intellect and sense, because sensitive knowledge is concerned with external sensible qualities, while intellectual knowledge penetrates into the very essence of a thing, because "the object of the intellect is what a thing is," as stated in the book on the *Soul*.[5]

Now there are many kinds of things that are hidden within, to find which human knowledge has to penetrate within so to speak. Thus, under the accidents lies hidden the nature of the substantial thing, under words lies hidden their meaning, under likenesses and figures the truth they denote lies hidden (because intelligible things are in a certain way inward as compared with sensible things which are perceived externally), and effects lie hidden in their causes, and vice versa. Hence we may speak of understanding with regard to all these things.

Since, however, human knowledge begins with sense, from the outside of things as it were, it is evident that the stronger the light of the understanding, the further can it penetrate into the heart of things. Now the natural light of our understanding is of finite power. And so it can reach just to a certain fixed point. Consequently man needs a supernatural light, in order to penetrate further still so as to know what it cannot know by its natural light. And this supernatural light which is bestowed on man is called the gift of understanding.

Reply Obj. 1. The natural light instilled within us manifests only certain common principles, which are known naturally. But since man is ordained to supernatural happiness, as stated above (Q. 11, A. 3; Part I-II, Q. 111, A. 8), man needs to reach to certain higher truths, for which he requires the gift of understanding.

Reply Obj. 2. The discourse of reason always begins from an understanding and ends at an understanding, because we reason by proceeding from certain understood principles, and the discourse of reason is perfected when we come to understand what we did not know before. Hence the act of reasoning proceeds from something previously understood. Now a gift of grace does not proceed from the light of nature, but is added to it as perfecting it. Therefore this addition is not called reason but rather understanding, since the superadded light is, in comparison with what we know supernaturally, what the natural light is, in regard to those things which we know from the first.

Reply Obj. 3. Will denotes absolutely a movement of the appetite without the determination of any excellence. But understanding denotes a certain excellence of a knowledge that penetrates into the heart of things. Hence the supernatural gift is called after the understanding rather than after the will.

ARTICLE 2. *Whether the Gift of Understanding Is Compatible With Faith?*

We proceed thus to the Second Article: It would seem that the gift of understanding is incompatible with faith.

Objection 1. For Augustine says (QQ. lxxxiii, *qu.* 15)[6] that "the thing which is understood is bounded by the comprehension of

[1] Aristotle, vi, 6 (1140^{b}31).
[2] Sect. 20 (PG 3, 720).
[3] Sect. 2 (PG 3, 869).
[4] Aristotle, *Soul*, iii, 9, 10 (432^{b}5; 433^{a}21).
[5] Aristotle, iii, 6 (430^{b}27).
[6] PL 40, 14.

him who understands it." But the thing which is believed is not comprehended, according to the word of the Apostle to the Philippians (3. 12): *Not as though I had already comprehended* (Douay,—*attained*), *or were already perfect.* Therefore it seems that faith and understanding are incompatible in the same subject.

Obj. 2. Further, Whatever is understood is seen by the understanding. But faith is of things that appear not, as stated above (Q. I, A. 4; Q. IV, A. I). Therefore faith is incompatible with understanding in the same subject.

Obj. 3. Further, Understanding is more certain than science. But science and faith are incompatible in the same subject, as stated above (Q. I, A. 5). Much less, therefore, can understanding and faith be in the same subject.

On the contrary, Gregory says (*Moral.* i)[1] that "understanding enlightens the mind concerning the things it has heard." Now one who has faith can be enlightened in his mind concerning what he has heard; thus it is written (Luke 24. 27, 32) that Our Lord opened the scriptures to His disciples, that they might understand them. Therefore understanding is compatible with faith.

I answer that, We need to make a twofold distinction here: one on the side of faith, the other on the part of understanding. On the side of faith the distinction to be made is that certain things, of themselves, come directly under faith, because they surpass natural reason, such as the mystery of three Persons in one God, and the incarnation of God the Son. But other things come under faith through being subordinate, in one way or another, to those just mentioned; for instance, all that is contained in the Divine Scriptures. On the part of understanding the distinction to be observed is that there are two ways in which we may be said to understand. In one way, we understand a thing perfectly, when we arrive at knowing the essence of the thing we understand, and the very truth considered in itself of the proposition understood. In this way, so long as the state of faith lasts, we cannot understand those things which fall directly under faith, although certain other things that are subordinate to faith can be understood even in this way.

In another way we understand a thing imperfectly, when the essence of a thing or the truth of a proposition is not known as to its quiddity or mode of being, and yet we know that according to the outward appearances, they do not contradict the truth; in so far,

namely, as we understand that on account of the things that appear externally, we should not depart from matters of faith. In this way, even during the state of faith, nothing hinders us from understanding even those things which fall directly under faith.

This suffices for the *Replies to the Objections;* for the first three argue in reference to perfect understanding, while the last refers to the understanding of matters subordinate to faith.

ARTICLE 3. *Whether the Gift of Understanding Is Speculative Only, or Also Practical?*

We proceed thus to the Third Article: It would seem that understanding, considered as a gift of the Holy Ghost, is not practical, but only speculative.

Objection 1. For, according to Gregory (*Moral.* i, 32),[2] understanding "penetrates certain more exalted things." But the practical intellect is occupied, not with exalted, but with lowly things, namely singulars, about which actions are concerned. Therefore understanding, considered as a gift, is not practical.

Obj. 2. Further, The gift of understanding is something more excellent than the intellectual virtue of understanding. But the intellectual virtue of understanding is concerned with none but necessary things according to the Philosopher.[3] Much more, therefore, is the gift of understanding concerned with none but necessary matters. Now the practical intellect is not about necessary things, but about things which may be otherwise than they are, and which may result from man's activity. Therefore the gift of understanding is not practical.

Obj. 3. Further, The gift of understanding enlightens the mind in matters which surpass natural reason. Now human activities, with which the practical intellect is concerned, do not surpass natural reason, which directs in matters of action, as was made clear above (Part I-II, Q. LVIII, A. 2; Q. LXXI, A. 6). Therefore the gift of understanding is not practical.

On the contrary, It is written (Ps. 110. 10): *A good understanding to all that do it.*

I answer that, As stated above (A. 2), the gift of understanding is not only about those things which come under faith first and principally, but also about all things subordinate to faith. Now good actions have a certain relationship to faith, for *faith worketh through charity,* according to the Apostle (Gal. 5. 6). Hence the gift of understanding extends also

[1] PL 75, 547.

[2] PL 75, 547.   [3] *Ethics,* VI, 6 (1140ᵇ31).

to certain actions, not as though it turned about them principally, but in so far as the rule of our actions are the eternal ideas, to which the higher reason, which is perfected by the gift of understanding, adheres, by contemplating and consulting them, as Augustine states (*De Trin.* xii, 7).[1]

Reply Obj. 1. The things with which human actions are concerned are not surpassingly exalted considered in themselves, but, as referred to the rule of the eternal law, and to the end of Divine happiness, they are exalted so that they can be the matter of understanding.

Reply Obj. 2. The excellence of the gift of understanding consists precisely in its considering eternal or necessary intelligibles not only as they are in themselves, but also as they are rules of human actions, because a knowing power is the more excellent, according to the greater number of things to which it extends.

Reply Obj. 3. The rule of human actions is the human reason and the eternal law, as stated above (Part I-II, Q. LXXI, A. 6). Now the eternal law surpasses human reason, so that the knowledge of human actions, as ruled by the eternal law, surpasses the natural reason, and requires the supernatural light of a gift of the Holy Ghost.

ARTICLE 4. *Whether the Gift of Understanding Is in All Who Are in a State of Grace?*

We proceed thus to the Fourth Article: It would seem that the gift of understanding is not in all who are in a state of grace.

Objection 1. For Gregory says (*Moral.* ii, 49)[2] that "the gift of understanding is given as a remedy against dulness of the mind." Now many who are in a state of grace suffer from dulness of the mind. Therefore the gift of understanding is not in all who are in a state of grace.

Obj. 2. Further, Of all things that are connected with knowledge, faith alone seems to be necessary for salvation, since by faith Christ dwells in our hearts, according to Eph. 3. 17. Now the gift of understanding is not in everyone that has faith; indeed, those who have faith ought to pray that they may understand, as Augustine says (*De Trin.* xv, 26).[3] Therefore the gift of understanding is not necessary for salvation, and, consequently, is not in all who are in a state of grace.

Obj. 3. Further, Those things which are

common to all who are in a state of grace are never withdrawn from them. Now the grace of understanding and of the other gifts "sometimes withdraws itself profitably, for, at times, when the mind is puffed up with understanding sublime things, it becomes sluggish and dull in base and vile things," as Gregory observes (*Moral.* ii, 49).[4] Therefore the gift of understanding is not in all who are in a state of grace.

On the contrary, It is written (Ps. 81. 5): *They have not known or understood, they walk on in darkness.* But no one who is in a state of grace walks in darkness, according to John 8. 12: *He that followeth Me, walketh not in darkness.* Therefore no one who is in a state of grace is without the gift of understanding.

I answer that, In all who are in a state of grace, there must be rectitude of the will, since "grace prepares man's will for good," according to Augustine (*Contra Julian. Pelag.* iv, 3).[5] Now the will cannot be rightly directed to good unless there be already some knowledge of the truth, since the object of the will is the good understood, as stated in the book on the *Soul.*[6] Again, just as the Holy Ghost directs man's will by the gift of charity, so as to move it directly to some supernatural good, so also, by the gift of understanding He enlightens the human mind so that it knows some supernatural truth, to which the right will needs to tend. Therefore, just as the gift of charity is in all those who have sanctifying grace, so also is the gift of understanding.

Reply Obj. 1. Some who have sanctifying grace may suffer dullness of mind with regard to things that are not necessary for salvation; but with regard to those that are necessary for salvation, they are sufficiently instructed by the Holy Ghost, according to I John 2. 27: *His unction teacheth you of all things.*

Reply Obj. 2. Although not all who have faith understand fully the things that are proposed to be believed, yet they understand that they ought to believe them, and that they ought in no way to deviate from them.

Reply Obj. 3. With regard to things necessary for salvation, the gift of understanding never withdraws from holy persons. But, in order that they may have no incentive to pride, it does withdraw sometimes with regard to other things, so that their intellect is unable to penetrate all things clearly.

1 PL 42, 1005; cf. XII, 2 (PL 42, 999).
2 PL 75, 592.
3 PL 42, 1096.
4 PL 75, 593.
5 PL 44, 744.
6 Aristotle, III, 10 (433ᵃ21).

Article 5. *Whether the Gift of Understanding Is Found Also in Those Who Have Not Sanctifying Grace?*

We proceed thus to the Fifth Article: It would seem that the gift of understanding is found also in those who have not sanctifying grace.

Objection 1. For Augustine, in expounding the words of Ps. 118. 20: *My soul hath coveted to long for Thy justifications,* says: "Understanding flies ahead, and man's will is weak and slow to follow."[1] But in all who have sanctifying grace, the will is prompt on account of charity. Therefore the gift of understanding can be in those who have not sanctifying grace.

Obj. 2. Further, It is written (Dan. 10. 1) that *there is need of understanding in a* (prophetic) *vision,* and thus it seems that there is no prophecy without the gift of understanding. But there can be no prophesy without sanctifying grace, as evidenced by Matt. 7. 22, where those who say: *We have prophesied in Thy name,* (Vulg.,—*Have we not prophesied in Thy name?*) are answered with the words: *I never knew you.* Therefore the gift of understanding can be without sanctifying grace.

Obj. 3. Further, The gift of understanding corresponds to the virtue of faith, according to Isa. 7. 9, following another reading:[2] *If you will not believe you shall not understand.* Now faith can be without sanctifying grace. Therefore the gift of understanding can be without it.

On the contrary, Our Lord said (John 6. 45): *Every one that hath heard of the Father, and hath learned, cometh to Me.* Now it is by the intellect, as Gregory observes (*Moral.* i, 32),[3] that we learn or understand what we hear. Therefore whoever has the gift of understanding comes to Christ, which is impossible without sanctifying grace. Therefore the gift of understanding cannot be without sanctifying grace.

I answer that, As stated above (Part I-II, Q. LXVIII, AA. 1, 2, 3) the gifts of the Holy Ghost perfect the soul, according as it is amenable to the motion of the Holy Ghost. Accordingly, then, the intellectual light of grace is called the gift of understanding, in so far as man's understanding is easily moved by the Holy Ghost, the consideration of which movement consists in a true apprehension of the end. Therefore unless the human intellect is moved by the Holy Ghost so far as to have a right estimation of the end, it has not yet obtained the gift of understanding, however much the Holy Ghost may have enlightened it in regard to other truths that are preambles to the faith.

Now to have a right estimation about the last end one must not be in error about the end, and must adhere to it firmly as to the greatest good. And no one can do this without sanctifying grace, even as in moral matters a man has a right estimate about the end through a habit of virtue. Therefore no one has the gift of understanding without sanctifying grace.

Reply Obj. 1. By understanding Augustine means any kind of intellectual light. However this does not extend to the perfect notion of a gift, unless the mind of man be led so far as to have a right estimate about the end.

Reply Obj. 2. The understanding that is requisite for prophecy is a kind of enlightenment of the mind with regard to the things revealed to the prophet. But it is not an enlightenment of the mind with regard to a right estimate about the last end, which belongs to the gift of understanding.

Reply Obj. 3. Faith implies only assent to what is proposed, but understanding implies a certain perception of the truth, which perception, except in one who has sanctifying grace, cannot regard the end, as stated above. Hence the comparison between understanding and faith fails.

Article 6. *Whether the Gift of Understanding Is Distinct From the Other Gifts?*

We proceed thus to the Sixth Article: It would seem that the gift of understanding is not distinct from the other gifts.

Objection 1. For there is no distinction between things whose opposites are not distinct. Now wisdom is contrary to folly, understanding is contrary to dulness, counsel is contrary to rashness, knowledge is contrary to ignorance, as Gregory states (*Moral.* ii, 49).[4] But there would seem to be no difference between folly, dulness, ignorance and rashness. Therefore neither does understanding differ from the other gifts.

Obj. 2. Further, The intellectual virtue of understanding differs from the other intellectual virtues in that it is proper to it to be about self-evident principles. But the gift of understanding is not about any self-evident principles, since the natural habit of first principles suffices in respect of those matters which are naturally self-evident. But with respect of such things as are supernatural, faith is sufficient

[1] *Ennar. in Psalm.,* Ps. 118.20 (PL 37, 1522).
[2] The Septuagint.   [3] PL 75, 547.
[4] PL 75, 592.

since the articles of faith are like first principles in supernatural knowledge, as stated above (Q. I, A. 7). Therefore the gift of understanding does not differ from the other intellectual gifts.

Obj. 3. Further, All intellectual knowledge is either speculative or practical. Now the gift of understanding is related to both, as stated above (A. 3). Therefore it is not distinct from the other intellectual gifts, but comprises them all.

On the contrary, When several things are enumerated together they must be, in some way, distinct from one another, because distinction is the principle of number. Now the gift of understanding is enumerated together with the other gifts, as appears from Isa. 11. 2. Therefore the gift of understanding is distinct from the other gifts.

I answer that, The difference between the gift of understanding and three of the others, namely piety, fortitude, and fear, is evident, since the gift of understanding pertains to the cognitive power, while the three others pertain to the appetitive power. But the difference between this gift of understanding and the remaining three, namely wisdom, knowledge, and counsel, which also pertain to the cognitive power, is not so evident.

To some,[1] it seems that the gift of understanding differs from the gifts of knowledge and counsel, in that these two pertain to practical knowledge, while the gift of understanding pertains to speculative knowledge; and that it differs from the gift of wisdom, which also pertains to speculative knowledge, in that wisdom is concerned with judgment, while understanding renders the mind apt to grasp the things that are proposed, and to penetrate into their very heart. And in this sense we have assigned the number of the gifts, above (Part I-II, Q. LXVIII, A. 4).

But if we consider the matter carefully, the gift of understanding is concerned not only with speculative, but also with practical matters, as stated above (A. 3), and, likewise, the gift of knowledge regards both matters, as we shall show further on (Q. IX, A. 3). And, consequently, we must take their distinction in some other way. For all these four gifts are ordered to supernatural knowledge, which, in us, takes its foundation from faith. Now *faith is through hearing* (Rom. 10. 17). Hence some things must be proposed to be believed by man, not as seen, but as heard, to which he assents by faith. Now faith, first and principally, is about the First

[1] William of Auxerre, *Summa Aurea,* III, 8, Q. I (181rb).

Truth, secondarily, about certain considerations concerning creatures, and furthermore extends to the direction of human actions, in so far as it works through charity, as appears from what has been said above (A. 3; Q. IV, A. 2, Reply 3).

Accordingly on the part of the things proposed to faith for belief, two things are requisite on our part. First, that they be penetrated or grasped by the intellect, and this pertains to the gift of understanding. Secondly, it is necessary that man should judge these things rightly, that he should esteem that he ought to adhere to these things, and to withdraw from their opposites. And this judgment, with regard to Divine things pertains to the gift of wisdom, but with regard to created things, pertains to the gift of knowledge, and as to its application to individual works, pertains to the gift of counsel.

Reply Obj. 1. The foregoing difference between those four gifts is clearly in agreement with the distinction of those things which Gregory assigns as their opposites. For dulness is contrary to sharpness, since an intellect is said, by a figure, to be sharp, when it is able to penetrate into the heart of the things that are proposed to it. Hence it is dulness of mind that renders the mind unable to pierce into the heart of a thing. A man is said to be a fool if he judges wrongly about the common end of life, and so folly is properly opposed to wisdom, which makes us judge rightly about the universal cause. Ignorance implies a defect in the mind, even about any particular things whatever, so that it is contrary to knowledge, which gives man a right judgment about particular causes, namely about creatures. Rashness is clearly opposed to counsel, by which man does not proceed to action before deliberating with his reason.

Reply Obj. 2. The gift of understanding is about the first principles of that knowledge which is conferred by grace; but otherwise than faith, because it pertains to faith to assent to them, while it pertains to the gift of understanding to pierce with the mind the things that are said.

Reply Obj. 3. The gift of understanding pertains to both kinds of knowledge, namely, speculative and practical, not as to the judgment, but as to apprehension, by grasping what is said.

ARTICLE 7. *Whether the Sixth Beatitude,
"Blessed Are the Clean of Heart," etc.,
Corresponds to the Gift of Understanding?*

We proceed thus to the Seventh Article: It seems that the sixth beatitude, *Blessed are the*

clean of heart, for they shall see God, does not correspond to the gift of understanding.

Objection 1. Because cleanness of heart seems to pertain chiefly to the appetite. But the gift of understanding pertains, not to the appetite, but rather to the intellectual power. Therefore this beatitude does not correspond to the gift of understanding.

Obj. 2. Further, It is written (Acts 15. 9): *Purifying their hearts by faith.* Now cleanness of heart is acquired by the heart being purified. Therefore this beatitude is related to the virtue of faith rather than to the gift of understanding.

Obj. 3. Further, The gifts of the Holy Ghost perfect man in the present state of life. But the sight of God does not belong to the present life, since it is that which gives happiness to the Blessed, as stated above (Part I-II, Q. III, A. 8). Therefore the sixth beatitude which comprises the sight of God, does not correspond to the gift of understanding.

On the contrary, Augustine says (*De Serm. Dom. in Monte*, i, 4):[1] "The sixth work of the Holy Ghost which is understanding, is applicable to the clean of heart, whose eye being purified, they can see what eye hath not seen."

I answer that, Two things are contained in the sixth beatitude, as also in the others, one by way of merit, namely, cleanness of heart; the other by way of reward, namely, the sight of God, as stated above (Part I-II, Q. LXIX, A. 2), and each of these, in some way, corresponds to the gift of understanding.

For cleanness is twofold. One is a preamble and a disposition to seeing God, and consists in the heart being cleansed of inordinate affections. And this cleanness of heart is effected by the virtues and gifts belonging to the appetitive power. The other cleanness of heart is a kind of complement to the sight of God; such is the cleanness of the mind that is purged of phantasms and errors, so as to receive the truths which are proposed to it about God, no longer by way of corporeal phantasms, nor infected with heretical misrepresentations. And this cleanness is the result of the gift of understanding.

Again, the sight of God is twofold. One is perfect, by which God's Essence is seen. The other is imperfect, by which, though we do not see what God is, yet we see what He is not and by which, the more perfectly we know God in this life, the more we understand that He surpasses all that the mind comprehends. Each of these visions of God pertains to the gift of

[1] PL 34, 1235.

understanding; the first, to the gift of understanding in its state of perfection, as possessed in heaven; the second, to the gift of understanding in its state of origin, as possessed by wayfarers.

This suffices for the *Replies to the Objections*. For the first two arguments refer to the first kind of cleanness; while the third refers to the perfect vision of God. Moreover the gifts both perfect us in this life by kind of beginning, and will be fulfilled, as stated above (cf. Part I-II, Q. LXIX, A. 2).

ARTICLE 8. *Whether Faith, Among the Fruits, Corresponds to the Gift of Understanding?*

We proceed thus to the Eighth Article: It would seem that, among the fruits, faith does not correspond to the gift of understanding.

Objection 1. For understanding is the fruit of faith, since it is written (Isa. 7. 9) according to another reading:[2] *If you will not believe you shall not understand,* where our version has: *If you will not believe, you shall not continue.* Therefore faith is not the fruit of understanding.

Obj. 2. Further, That which precedes is not the fruit of what follows. But faith seems to precede understanding, since it is the foundation of the entire spiritual edifice, as stated above (Q. IV, A. 7; Part I-II, Q. LXVII, A. 2, REPLY 2). Therefore faith is not the fruit of understanding.

Obj. 3. Further, More gifts pertain to the intellect than to the appetite. Now, among the fruits, only one pertains to the intellect, namely, faith, while all the others pertain to the appetite. Therefore faith, it seems, does not pertain to understanding more than to wisdom, knowledge or counsel.

On the contrary, The end of a thing is its fruit. Now the gift of understanding seems to be ordered chiefly to the certitude of faith, which certitude is counted as a fruit. For a gloss on Gal. 5. 22 says that the faith which is a fruit, is certitude about the unseen.[3] Therefore faith, among the fruits, corresponds to the gift of understanding.

I answer that, The fruits of the Spirit, as stated above (Part I-II, Q. LXX, A. 1), when we were discussing them, are so called because they are something ultimate and delightful, produced in us by the power of the Holy Ghost. Now the ultimate and delightful has the nature

[2] The Septuagint.
[3] *Glossa interl.* (VI, 87v); *Glossa* Lombardi (PL 192, 160).

of an end, which is the proper object of the will. And consequently that which is ultimate and delightful with regard to the will, must be, after a fashion, the fruit of all the other things that pertain to the other powers. According, therefore, to this kind of gift or virtue that perfects a power, we may distinguish a double fruit: one, pertaining to the same power; the other, the last of all as it were, pertaining to the will. In this way we must conclude that the fruit which properly corresponds to the gift of understanding is faith, that is, the certitude of faith; while the fruit that corresponds to it last of all is joy, which pertains to the will.

Reply Obj. 1. Understanding is the fruit of faith, taken as a virtue. But we are not taking faith in this sense here, but for a kind of certitude of faith, to which man attains by the gift of understanding.

Reply Obj. 2. Faith cannot altogether precede understanding, for it would be impossible to assent by believing what is proposed to be believed without understanding it in some way. However, the perfection of understanding follows the virtue of faith, which perfection of understanding is itself followed by a kind of certainty of faith.

Reply Obj. 3. The fruit of practical knowledge cannot consist in that very knowledge, since knowledge of that kind is known not for its own sake, but for the sake of something else. On the other hand, speculative knowledge has its fruit in its very self, which fruit is the certitude about the thing known. Hence the gift of counsel, which pertains only to practical knowledge, has no corresponding fruit of its own; while the gifts of wisdom, understanding and knowledge, which can pertain also to speculative knowledge, have but one corresponding fruit, which is certainly denoted by the name of faith. The reason why there are several fruits pertaining to the appetitive faculty, is because, as already stated, the character of end, which the word fruit implies, pertains to the appetitive rather than to the intellective part.

QUESTION IX
OF THE GIFT OF KNOWLEDGE
(*In Four Articles*)

WE must now consider the gift of knowledge, under which head there are four points of inquiry: (1) Whether knowledge is a gift? (2) Whether it is about Divine things? (3) Whether it is speculative or practical? (4) Which beatitude corresponds to it?

ARTICLE 1. *Whether Knowledge Is a Gift?*

We proceed thus to the First Article: It seems that knowledge is not a gift.

Objection 1. For the gifts of the Holy Ghost surpass the natural faculty. But knowledge implies an effect of natural reason; for the Philosopher says[1] that "a demonstration is a syllogism which produces knowledge." Therefore knowledge is not a gift of the Holy Ghost.

Obj. 2. Further, The gifts of the Holy Ghost are common to all holy persons, as stated above (Part I-II, Q. LXVIII, A. 5). Now Augustine says (*De Trin.* xiv, 1)[2] that "many of the faithful lack knowledge though they have faith." Therefore knowledge is not a gift.

Obj. 3. Further, The gifts are more perfect than the virtues, as stated above (Part I-II, Q. LXVIII, A. 8). Therefore one gift suffices for the perfection of one virtue. Now the gift of understanding corresponds to the virtue of faith, as stated above (Q. VIII, A. 5, REPLY 3). Therefore the gift of knowledge does not correspond to that virtue, nor does it appear to what other virtue it can correspond. Since, then, the gifts are perfections of virtues, as stated above (Part I-II, Q. LXVIII, AA. 1, 2), it seems that knowledge is not a gift.

On the contrary Knowledge is counted among the seven gifts, Isa. 11. 2.

I answer that, Grace is more perfect than nature, and, therefore, does not fail in those things in which man can be perfected by nature. Now, when a man, by his natural reason, assents by his intellect to some truth, he is perfected in two ways in respect of that truth: first, because he grasps it, secondly, because he has a sure judgment of it. Accordingly, two things are requisite in order that the human intellect may perfectly assent to the truth of the faith: one of these is that he should have a sound grasp of the things that are proposed to be believed, and this pertains to the gift of understanding, as stated above (Q. VIII, A. 6); while the other is that he should have a sure and right judgment on them, so as to discern what is to be believed from what is not to be believed, and for this the gift of knowledge is required.

Reply Obj. 1. Certitude of knowledge varies in various natures, according to the various conditions of each nature. For man forms a sure judgment about a truth by the discursive process of his reason, and so human knowledge is acquired by means of demonstrative reason-

[1] *Posterior Analytics,* I, 2 (71ᵇ18).
[2] PL 42, 1037.

ing. On the other hand, in God, there is a right judgment of truth, without any discursive process, by simple intuition, as was stated in the First Part (Q. XIV, A. 7); therefore God's knowledge is not discursive, or argumentative, but absolute and simple; and to this knowledge is likened that which is a gift of the Holy Ghost, since it is a participated likeness of it.

Reply Obj. 2. A twofold knowledge may be had about matters of belief. One is the knowledge of what one ought to believe, by discerning things to be believed from things not to be believed. In this way knowledge is a gift and is common to all holy persons. The other is a knowledge about matters of belief, by which one knows not only what one ought to believe, but also how to make the faith known, how to induce others to believe, and confute those who deny the faith. This knowledge is numbered among the gratuitous graces, which are not given to all, but to some. Hence Augustine, after the words quoted, adds: "It is one thing for a man merely to know what he ought to believe, and another to know how to dispense what he believes to the godly, and to defend it against the ungodly."

Reply Obj. 3. The gifts are more perfect than the moral and intellectual virtues. They are not more perfect than the theological virtues, but rather all the gifts are ordered to the perfection of the theological virtues, as to their end. Hence it is not unreasonable if several gifts are ordered to one theological virtue.

ARTICLE 2. *Whether the Gift of Knowledge Is About Divine Things?*

We proceed thus to the Second Article: It seems that the gift of knowledge is about Divine things.

Objection 1. For Augustine says (*De Trin.* xiv, 1)[1] that "knowledge begets, nourishes and strengthens faith." Now faith is about Divine things, because its object is the First Truth, as stated above (Q. I, A. 1). Therefore the gift of knowledge also is about Divine things.

Obj. 2. Further, The gift of knowledge is more excellent than acquired knowledge. But there is an acquired knowledge about Divine things, for instance, the science of metaphysics. Much more therefore is the gift of knowledge about Divine things.

Obj. 3. Further, According to Rom. 1. 20, *the invisible things of God . . . are clearly seen, being understood by the things that are made.* If therefore there is knowledge about created things, it seems that there is also knowledge of Divine things.

On the contrary, Augustine says[2]: "The knowledge of Divine things may be properly called wisdom, and the knowledge of human affairs may properly receive the name of knowledge."

I answer that, A sure judgment about a thing is formed chiefly from its cause, and so the order of judgments should be according to the order of causes. For just as the first cause is the cause of the second, so ought the judgment about a second cause be formed through the first cause. Nor is it possible to judge of the first cause through any other cause. Therefore the judgment which is formed through the first cause is the first and most perfect judgment.

Now in those things where we find something most perfect, the common name of the genus is appropriated for those things which fall short of the most perfect, and some special name is adapted to the most perfect thing, as is the case in Logic. For in the genus of convertible terms, that which signifies "what a thing is," is given the special name of "definition," but the convertible terms which fall short of this, retain the common name, and are called "proper" terms.

Accordingly, since the word knowledge implies certitude of judgment, as stated above (A. 1, REPLY 1), if this certitude of the judgment is derived from the highest cause, the knowledge has a special name, which is wisdom. For a wise man in any branch of knowledge is one who knows the highest cause of that kind of knowledge, and is able to judge of all matters by that cause; and a wise man absolutely, is one who knows the cause which is absolutely highest, namely God. Hence the knowledge of Divine things is called wisdom, while the knowledge of human things is called knowledge (*scientia*), this being the common name denoting certitude of judgment, and appropriated to the judgment which is formed through second causes. Accordingly, if we take knowledge in this way, it is a distinct gift from the gift of wisdom, so that the gift of knowledge is only about human or created things.

Reply Obj. 1. Although matters of faith are Divine and eternal, yet faith itself is something temporal in the mind of the believer. Hence to know what one ought to believe, pertains to the gift of knowledge, but to know in themselves the very things we believe, by a kind of union with them, pertains to the gift of wisdom.

[1] PL 42, 1037.

[2] *Ibid.*

Therefore the gift of wisdom corresponds more to charity which unites man's mind to God.

Reply Obj. 2. This argument takes knowledge in the generic acceptation of the term. It is not thus that knowledge is a special gift, but according as it is restricted to judgments formed through created things.

Reply Obj. 3. As stated above (Q. I, A. I), every cognitive habit regards formally the means through which things are known, and materially, the things that are known through the means. And since that which is formal is of most account, it follows that those sciences which draw conclusions about physical matter (*materia naturalis*) from mathematical principles, are counted rather among the mathematical sciences as being more like to them, though as to their matter they have more in common with the natural sciences; and for this reason it is stated in the *Physics*[1] that they are "more akin to physics (*magis naturales*)." Accordingly, since man knows God through His creatures, this seems to pertain to knowledge, to which it belongs formally, rather than to wisdom, to which it belongs materially; and, conversely, when we judge of creatures according to Divine things, this pertains to wisdom rather than to knowledge.

ARTICLE 3. *Whether the Gift of Knowledge Is Practical Knowledge?*

We proceed thus to the Third Article: It seems that the knowledge which is numbered among the gifts is practical knowledge.

Objection 1. For Augustine says (*De Trin.* xii, 14)[2] that "knowledge is concerned with the actions in which we make use of external things." But the knowledge which is concerned about actions is practical. Therefore the knowledge which is a gift is practical.

Obj. 2. Further, Gregory says (*Moral.* i, 32):[3] "Knowledge is nought if it hath not its use for piety, ... and piety is very useless if it lacks the discernment of knowledge." Now it follows from this authority that knowledge directs piety. But this cannot apply to a speculative science. Therefore the knowledge which is a gift is not speculative but practical.

Obj. 3. Further, The gifts of the Holy Ghost are only in the just, as stated above (Part I-II, Q. LXXXVIII, A. 5). But speculative knowledge can be also in the unjust, according to James 4. 17: *To him ... who knoweth to do good, and doth it not, to him it is a sin.* Therefore the

[1] Aristotle, II, 2 (194ª7).
[2] PL 42, 1009.   [3] PL 75, 547.

knowledge which is a gift is not speculative but practical.

On the contrary, Gregory says (*Moral.* i, *loc. cit.*): "Knowledge on her own day prepares a feast, because she overcomes the fast of ignorance in the mind." Now ignorance is not entirely removed, except by both kinds of knowledge, namely, speculative and practical. Therefore the knowledge which is a gift is both speculative and practical.

I answer that, As stated above(A. I), the gift of knowledge, like the gift of understanding, is ordered to the certitude of faith. Now faith consists primarily and principally in speculation, in so far, namely, as it is founded on the First Truth. But since the First Truth is also the last end for the sake of which our works are done, hence it is that faith extends to works, according to Gal. 5. 6: *Faith ... worketh by charity.* The consequence is that the gift of knowledge also, primarily and principally indeed, regards speculation, in so far, namely, as man knows what he ought to hold by faith; yet, secondarily, it extends to works, since we are directed in our actions by the knowledge of matters of faith, and of conclusions drawn from them.

Reply Obj. 1. Augustine is speaking of the gift of knowledge in so far as it extends to works; for action is ascribed to knowledge, yet not action solely, nor primarily; and in this way it directs piety.

Hence the *Reply to the Second Objection* is clear.

Reply Obj. 3. As we have already stated (Q. VIII, A. 5) about the gift of understanding, not everyone who understands, has the gift of understanding, but only he that understands through a habit of grace. And so we must take note, with regard to the gift of knowledge, that they alone have the gift of knowledge, who judge rightly about matters of faith and action, through the grace bestowed on them, so as never to wander from the rectitude of justice. And this is the knowledge of holy things, according to Wisd. 10. 10: *She conducted the just ... through the right ways ... and gave him the knowledge of holy things.*

ARTICLE 4. *Whether the Third Beatitude, "Blessed Are They That Mourn," etc., Corresponds to the Gift of Knowledge?*

We proceed thus to the Fourth Article: It seems that the third beatitude, *Blessed are they that mourn* (Matt. 5. 5), does not correspond to the gift of knowledge.

Objection 1. For, even as evil is the cause of sorrow and grief, so is good the cause of joy. Now knowledge brings to light good rather than evil, since the latter is known through evil: for "the straight line rules both itself and the crooked line."[1] Therefore this beatitude does not suitably correspond to the gift of knowledge.

Obj. 2. Further, Consideration of truth is an act of knowledge. Now there is no sadness in the consideration of truth, but rather joy, since it is written (Wisd. 8. 16): *Her conversation hath no bitterness, nor her company any tediousness, but joy and gladness.* Therefore this beatitude does not suitably correspond with the gift of knowledge.

Obj. 3. Further, The gift of knowledge consists in speculation, before operation. Now, in so far as it consists in speculation, sorrow does not correspond to it, since "the speculative intellect is not concerned about things to be sought or avoided."[2] Therefore the aforesaid beatitude is not suitably reckoned to correspond with the gift of knowledge.

On the contrary, Augustine says (*De Serm. Dom. in Monte,* iv).[3] "Knowledge befits the mourner, who has discovered that he has been mastered by the evil which he coveted as though it were good."

I answer that, Right judgment about creatures belongs properly to knowledge. Now it is through creatures that man's turning away from God is occasioned, according to Wisd. 14. 11: *Creatures . . . are turned to an abomination . . . and a snare to the feet of the unwise,* of those, namely, who do not judge rightly about creatures, since they deem the perfect good to consist in them. Hence they sin by placing their last end in them, and lose the true good. It is by forming a right judgment of creatures that man becomes aware of this loss, which judgment he exercises through the gift of knowledge. Hence the beatitude of sorrow is said to correspond to the gift of knowledge.

Reply Obj. 1. Created goods do not cause spiritual joy, except in so far as they are referred to the Divine good, which is the proper cause of spiritual joy. Hence spiritual peace and the resulting joy correspond directly to the gift of wisdom. But to the gift of knowledge there corresponds, in the first place, sorrow for past errors, and, in consequence, consolation, since, by his right judgment, man directs creatures to the Divine good. For this reason sor-row is set forth in this beatitude, as the merit, and the resulting consolation, as the reward. And this is begun in this life, and is perfected in the life to come.

Reply Obj. 2. Man rejoices in the very consideration of truth; and yet he may sometimes grieve for the thing, the truth of which he considers. It is thus that sorrow is ascribed to knowledge.

Reply Obj. 3. No beatitude corresponds to knowledge, in so far as it consists in speculation, because man's happiness consists, not in considering creatures, but in contemplating God. But man's happiness does consist somewhat in the right use of creatures, and in well-ordered love of them; and this I say with regard to the happiness of a wayfarer. Hence happiness relating to contemplation is not ascribed to knowledge, but to understanding and wisdom, which are about Divine things.

QUESTION X

OF UNBELIEF IN GENERAL

(In Twelve Articles)

In due sequence we must consider the contrary vices. And first, unbelief, which is contrary to faith; secondly, blasphemy, which is opposed to confession of faith (Q. XIII); thirdly, ignorance and dulness of mind, which are contrary to knowledge and understanding (Q. XV).

As to the first, we must consider (1) Unbelief in general; (2) heresy (Q. XI), (3) apostasy from the faith (Q. XII).

Under the first head there are twelve points of inquiry: (1) Whether unbelief is a sin? (2) What is its subject? (3) Whether it is the greatest of sins? (4) Whether every action of unbelievers is a sin? (5) Of the species of unbelief. (6) Of their comparison, one with another. (7) Whether we ought to dispute about faith with unbelievers? (8) Whether they ought to be compelled to the faith? (9) Whether we ought to have communication with them? (10) Whether unbelievers can have authority over Christians? (11) Whether the rites of unbelievers should be tolerated? (12) Whether the children of unbelievers are to be baptized against their parents' will?

ARTICLE 1. *Whether Unbelief Is a Sin?*

We proceed thus to the First Article: It would seem that unbelief is not a sin.

Objection 1. For every sin is contrary to nature, as Damascene proves (*De Fide Orthod.*

---

[1] Aristotle, *Soul,* I, 5 (411ª5).
[2] Aristotle, *Soul,* III, 9 (432ᵇ27).   [3] PL 34, 1234.

ii, 4).[1] Now unbelief seems not to be contrary to nature; for Augustine says (*De Prædest. Sanct.* v)[2] that "to be capable of having faith, just as to be capable of having charity, is natural to all men; whereas to have faith, even as to have charity, belongs to the grace of the faithful." Therefore not to have faith, which is to be an unbeliever, is not a sin.

Obj. 2. Further, No one sins in that which he cannot avoid, since every sin is voluntary. Now it is not in a man's power to avoid unbelief, for he cannot avoid it unless he have faith, because the Apostle says ((Rom. 10. 14): *How shall they believe in Him, of Whom they have not heard? And how shall they hear without a preacher?* Therefore unbelief does not seem to be a sin.

Obj. 3. Further, As stated above (Part I-II, Q. LXXXIV, A. 4), there are seven capital sins, to which all sins are reduced. But unbelief does not seem to be comprised under any of them. Therefore unbelief is not a sin.

On the contrary, Vice is opposed to virtue. Now faith is a virtue, and unbelief is opposed to it. Therefore unbelief is a sin.

I answer that, Unbelief may be taken in two ways. First, by way of pure negation, so that a man be called an unbeliever merely because he has not the faith. Secondly, unbelief may be taken by way of opposition to the faith, in which sense a man refuses to hear the faith, or despises it, according to Isa. 53. 1: *Who hath believed our report?* It is this that realizes the notion of unbelief, and it is in this sense that unbelief is a sin.

If, however, we take it by way of pure negation, as we find it in those who have heard nothing about the faith, it bears the character, not of sin, but of punishment, because such an ignorance of Divine things is a result of the sin of our first parent. If unbelievers of this kind are damned, it is on account of other sins, which cannot be taken away without faith, but not on account of their sin of unbelief. Hence Our Lord said (John 15. 22): *If I had not come, and spoken to them, they would not have sin;* which Augustine expounds (*Tract.* lxxxix *in Joann.*)[3] as referring to "the sin whereby they believed not in Christ."

Reply Obj. 1. To have the faith is not part of human nature, but it is part of human nature that man's mind should not go against his inner instinct, and the outward preaching of

the truth. Hence, in this way, unbelief is contrary to nature.

Reply Obj. 2. This argument takes unbelief as denoting a simple negation.

Reply Obj. 3. Unbelief, in so far as it is a sin, arises from pride, through which man is unwilling to subject his intellect to the rules of faith, and to sound interpretation of the Fathers. Hence Gregory says (*Moral.* xxxi, 45)[4] that "presumptuous innovations arise from vainglory."

It might also be replied that just as the theological virtues are not reduced to the cardinal virtues, but precede them, so too, the vices opposed to the theological virtues are not reduced to the capital vices.

ARTICLE 2. *Whether Unbelief Is in the Intellect As Its Subject?*

We proceed thus to the Second Article: It would seem that unbelief is not in the intellect as its subject.

Objection 1. For every sin is in the will, according to Augustine (*De Duabus Anim.* x, xi.).[5] Now unbelief is a sin, as stated above (A. 1). Therefore unbelief resides in the will and not in the intellect.

Obj. 2. Further, Unbelief is sinful through contempt of the preaching of faith. But contempt pertains to the will. Therefore unbelief is in the will.

Obj. 3. Further, A gloss on II Cor. 11. 14, *Satan . . . transformeth himself into an angel of light,* says that "if a wicked angel pretend to be a good angel, and be taken for a good angel, it is not a dangerous or an unhealthy error, if he does or says what is becoming to a good angel."[6] This seems to be because of the rectitude of the will of the man who adheres to the angel, since his intention is to adhere to a good angel. Therefore the sin of unbelief seems to consist entirely in a perverse will. Consequently, it does not reside in the intellect.

On the contrary, Things which are contrary to one another are in the same subject. Now faith, to which unbelief is opposed, resides in the intellect. Therefore unbelief also is in the intellect.

I answer that, As stated above (Part I-II, Q. LXXIV, AA. 1, 2), sin is said to be in the power which is the principle of the sinful act. Now a sinful act may have two principles. One is its first and universal principle, which commands all acts of sin; and this is the will, be-

[1] PG 94, 876; chap. 30 (PG 94, 976); cf. also IV, 20 (PG 94, 1196).
[2] PL 44, 968.   [3] PL 35, 1857.

[4] PL 76, 621.   [5] PL 42, 103, 105.
[6] *Glossa ordin.* (VI, 74E); *Glossa* Lombardi (PL 192, 74); Augustine, *Enchir.*, chap. 60 (PL 40, 260).

cause every sin is voluntary. The other principle of the sinful act is the proper and proximate principle which elicits the sinful act; thus the concupiscible part is the principle of gluttony and lust, and so these sins are said to be in the concupiscible part. Now dissent, which is the act proper to unbelief, is an act of the intellect, moved, however, by the will, just as assent is. Therefore unbelief, like faith, is in the intellect as its proximate subject. But it is in the will as its first moving principle, in which way every sin is said to be in the will.

Hence the *Reply to the First Objection* is clear.

Reply Obj. 2. The will's contempt causes the intellect's dissent, which completes the notion of unbelief. Hence the cause of unbelief is in the will, while unbelief itself is in the intellect.

Reply Obj. 3. He that believes a wicked angel to be a good one does not dissent from a matter of faith, because "his bodily senses are deceived, while his mind does not depart from a true and right judgment," as the gloss observes (*ibid.*). But, according to the same authority, to adhere to Satan when he begins to invite one to his state, that is, wickedness and error, is not without sin.

ARTICLE 3. *Whether Unbelief Is the Greatest of Sins?*

We proceed thus to the Third Article: It would seem that unbelief is not the greatest of sins.

Objection 1. For Augustine says (*De Bapt. contra. Donat.* iv, 20):[1] "I should hesitate to decide whether a very wicked catholic ought to be preferred to a heretic, in whose life one finds nothing reprehensible beyond the fact that he is a heretic." But a heretic is an unbeliever. Therefore we ought not to say absolutely that unbelief is the greatest of sins.

Obj. 2. Further, That which diminishes or excuses a sin, is not, it seems, the greatest of sins. Now unbelief excuses or diminishes sin, for the Apostle says (I Tim. 1. 12, 13): *I . . . before was a blasphemer, and a persecutor, and contumelious; but I obtained . . . mercy . . ., because I did it ignorantly in my unbelief.* Therefore unbelief is not the greatest of sins.

Obj. 3. Further, The greater sin deserves the greater punishment, according to Deut. 25. 2: *According to the measure of the sin shall the measure also of the stripes be.* Now a greater punishment is due to believers than to unbelievers, according to Heb. 10. 29: *How much*

more, do you think, he deserveth worse punishments, who hath trodden under foot the Son of God, and hath esteemed the blood of the testament unclean, by which he was sanctified? Therefore unbelief is not the greatest of sins.

On the contrary, Augustine, commenting on John 15. 22, *If I had not come, and spoken to them, they would not have sin,* says (*Tract.* lxxxix *in Joann.*):[2] "Under the general name, He refers to a singularly great sin. For this, namely, infidelity, is the sin to which all others may be traced." Therefore unbelief is the greatest of sins.

I answer that, Every sin consists formally in turning away from God, as stated above (Part I-II, Q. LXXI, A. 6; Q. LXXIII, A. 3). Hence the more a sin severs man from God, the graver it is. Now man is most separated from God by unbelief, because he has not even true knowledge of God; and by false knowledge of God, man does not approach Him, but is severed from Him. Nor is it possible for one who has a false opinion of God to know Him in any way at all, because the object of his opinion is not God. Therefore it is clear that the sin of unbelief is greater than any sin that occurs in the perversion of morals. This does not apply to the sins that are opposed to the theological virtues, as we shall state further on (Q. XXXIV, A. 2, Reply 2; XXXIX, A. 2, Reply 3).

Reply Obj. 1. Nothing hinders a sin that is more grave in its genus from being less grave in respect of some circumstances. Hence Augustine hesitated to decide between a bad catholic, and a heretic not sinning otherwise, because, although the heretic's sin is more grave generically, it can be lessened by a circumstance; and, conversely, the sin of the catholic can, by some circumstance, be aggravated.

Reply Obj. 2. Unbelief includes both ignorance, as an accessory, and resistance to matters of faith, and in the latter respect it is a most grave sin. In respect, however, of this ignorance, it has a certain reason for excuse, especially when a man does not sin from malice, as was the case with the Apostle.

Reply Obj. 3. An unbeliever is more severely punished for his sin of unbelief than another sinner is for any sin whatever, if we consider the kind of sin. But in the case of another sin, for example, adultery, committed by a believer, and by an unbeliever, the believer, other things being equal, sins more gravely than the unbeliever, both on account of his knowledge of the truth through faith, and on account of the

---

[1] PL 43, 171.

[2] PL 35, 1856.

sacraments of faith with which he has been imbued, and which he insults by committing sin.

ARTICLE 4. *Whether Every Act of an Unbeliever Is a Sin?*

We proceed thus to the Fourth Article: It seems that each act of an unbeliever is a sin.

Objection 1. Because a gloss on Rom. 14. 23, *All that is not of faith is sin*, says: "The whole life of unbelievers is a sin."[1] Now the life of unbelievers consists of their actions. Therefore every action of an unbeliever is a sin.

Obj. 2. Further, Faith directs the intention. Now there can be no good save what comes from a right intention. Therefore, among unbelievers, no action can be good.

Obj. 3. Further, When that which precedes is corrupted, that which follows is corrupted also. Now an act of faith precedes the acts of all the virtues. Therefore, since there is no act of faith in unbelievers, they can do no good work, but sin in their every action.

On the contrary, It is said of Cornelius, while yet an unbeliever (Acts 10. 4, 31), that his alms were acceptable to God. Therefore not every action of an unbeliever is a sin, but some of his actions are good.

I answer that, As stated above (Part I-II, Q. LXXXV, AA. 2, 4) mortal sin takes away sanctifying grace, but does not wholly corrupt the good of nature. Since therefore, unbelief is a mortal sin, unbelievers are without grace indeed, yet some good of nature remains in them. Consequently it is evident that unbelievers cannot do those good works which proceed from grace, namely, meritorious works. Yet they can, to a certain extent, do those good works for which the good of nature suffices. Hence it does not follow that they sin in everything they do. But whenever they do anything out of their unbelief, then they sin. For even as one who has the faith, can commit an actual sin, venial or even mortal, which he does not refer to the end of faith, so too, an unbeliever can do a good deed in a matter which he does not refer to the end of his unbelief.

Reply Obj. 1. The words quoted must be taken to mean either that the life of unbelievers cannot be sinless, since without faith no sin is taken away, or that whatever they do out of unbelief, is a sin. Hence the same authority adds: "Because every one that lives or acts according to his unbelief, sins grievously (*ibid.*)."

Reply Obj. 2. Faith directs the intention with regard to the supernatural last end: but even the light of natural reason can direct the intention in respect of a connatural good.

Reply Obj. 3. Unbelief does not so wholly destroy natural reason in unbelievers but that some knowledge of the truth remains in them, which enables them to do deeds that are generically good. With regard, however, to Cornelius, it is to be observed that he was not an unbeliever; otherwise his works would not have been acceptable to God, Whom none can please without faith. Now he had implicit faith, as the truth of the Gospel was not yet made manifest. Hence Peter was sent to him to give him fuller instruction in the faith.

ARTICLE 5. *Whether There Are Several Species of Unbelief?*

We proceed thus to the Fifth Article: It seems that there are not several species of unbelief.

Objection 1. For, since faith and unbelief are contrary to one another, they must be about the same thing. Now the formal object of faith is the First Truth, from which it derives its unity, although its matter contains many points of belief. Therefore the object of unbelief also is the First Truth, while the things which an unbeliever disbelieves are the matter of his unbelief. Now the specific difference depends not on material but on formal principles. Therefore there are not several species of unbelief, according to the various points which the unbeliever disbelieves.

Obj. 2. Further, It is possible to stray from the truth of faith in an infinite number of ways. If therefore the various species of unbelief correspond to the number of various errors, it would seem to follow that there is an infinite number of species of unbelief, and consequently, that we ought not to make these species the object of our consideration.

Obj. 3. Further, The same thing does not belong to different species. Now a man may be an unbeliever through erring about different points of faith. Therefore diversity of errors does not make a diversity of species of unbelief. And so there are not several species of unbelief.

On the contrary, Several species of vice are opposed to each virtue, because "good happens in one way, but evil in many ways," according to Dionysius (*Div. Nom.* iv)[2] and the Philosopher.[3] Now faith is a virtue. Therefore several species of vice are opposed to it.

---

[1] *Glossa ordin.* (VI, 30B); *Glossa* Lombardi (PL 191, 1520); Prosper of Aquitaine, *Sent.*, 106 (PL 51, 441).

[2] Sec. 31 (PG 3, 732).   [3] *Ethics*, II, 6 (1106ᵇ35).

I answer that, As stated above (Part I-II, Q. LXIV), every virtue consists in following some rule of human knowledge or operation. Now conformity to a rule happens one way in one matter, but a deviation from the rule happens in many ways, so that many vices are opposed to one virtue. The diversity of the vices that are opposed to each virtue may be considered in two ways. First, with regard to their different relations to the virtue, and in this way there are determinate species of vices contrary to a virtue. Thus to a moral virtue one vice is opposed by exceeding the virtue, and another, by falling short of the virtue. Secondly, the diversity of vices opposed to one virtue may be considered in respect of the corruption of the various conditions required for that virtue. In this way an infinite number of vices are opposed to one virtue, for example, temperance or fortitude, according to the infinite number of ways in which the various circumstances of a virtue may be corrupted, so that the rectitude of virtue is forsaken. For this reason the Pythagoreans held evil to be infinite.[1]

Accordingly we must say that if unbelief be considered in relation to faith, there are several species of unbelief, determinate in number. For, since the sin of unbelief consists in resisting the faith, this may happen in two ways: either the faith is resisted before it has been accepted, and such is the unbelief of pagans or gentiles; or the Christian faith is resisted after it has been accepted, and this either in the figure, and such is the unbelief of the Jews, or in the very manifestation of truth, and such is the unbelief of heretics. Hence we may, in a general way, reckon these three as species of unbelief.

If, however, the species of unbelief be distinguished according to the various errors that occur in matters of faith, there are not determinate species of unbelief, for errors can be multiplied indefinitely, as Augustine observes (*De Hæresibus*).[2]

Reply Obj. 1. The formal aspect of a sin can be considered in two ways. First, according to the intention of the sinner, in which case the thing to which the sinner turns is the formal object of his sin, and determines the various species of that sin. Secondly, it may be considered as an evil, and in this case the good which is forsaken is the formal object of the sin, which, however, does not derive its species from this point of view; on the contrary it is a privation of a species. We must therefore reply that the object of unbelief is the First Truth considered as that which unbelief forsakes, but its formal object, considered as that to which unbelief turns, is the false opinion that it follows; and it is from this point of view that unbelief derives its various species. Hence, even as charity is one, because it adheres to the Sovereign Good, yet there are various species of vice opposed to charity, which turn away from the Sovereign Good by turning to various temporal goods, and also in respect of various inordinate relations to God; so too, faith is one virtue through adhering to the one First Truth, yet there are many species of unbelief, because unbelievers follow many false opinions.

Reply Obj. 2. This argument considers the various species of unbelief according to various points in which errors occur.

Reply Obj. 3. Since faith is one because it believes in many things in relation to one, so may unbelief, although it errs in many things, be one in so far as all those things are related to one. Yet nothing hinders one man from erring in various species of unbelief, even as one man may be subject to various vices, and to various bodily diseases.

ARTICLE 6. *Whether the Unbelief of Pagans or Heathens Is Graver Than Other Kinds?*

We proceed thus to the Sixth Article: It seems that the unbelief of heathens or pagans is graver than other kinds.

Objection 1. For just as bodily disease is graver according as it endangers the health of a more important member of the body, so does sin appear to be graver, according as it is opposed to that which holds a more important place in virtue. Now that which is most important in faith, is belief in the unity of God, from which the heathens deviate by believing in many gods. Therefore their unbelief is the gravest of all.

Obj. 2. Further, Among heresies, the more detestable are those which contradict the truth of faith in more numerous and more important points. Thus the heresy of Arius, who separated the Godhead, was more detestable than that of Nestorius who severed the humanity of Christ from the Person of God the Son. Now the gentiles deny the faith in more numerous and important points than Jews and heretics, since they do not accept the faith at all. Therefore their unbelief is the gravest.

Obj. 3. Further, Every good diminishes evil.

---

[1] Cf. Aristotle, *Metaphysics*, I, 5 (986ª 22).
[2] Sect. 88 (PL 42, 50).

Now there is some good in the Jews, since they believe in the Old Testament as being from God, and there is some good in heretics, since they venerate the New Testament. Therefore they sin less grievously than gentiles, who receive neither Testament.

On the contrary, It is written (II Pet. 2. 21): *It had been better for them not to have known the way of justice, than after they have known it, to turn back.* Now the gentiles have not known the way of justice, but heretics and Jews have abandoned it after knowing it in some way. Therefore theirs is the graver sin.

I answer that, As stated above (A. 5), two things may be considered in unbelief. One of these is its relation to faith, and from this point of view, he who resists the faith after accepting it, sins more grievously against faith than he who resists it without having accepted it, just as he who fails to fulfil what he has promised, sins more grievously than if he had never promised it. In this way the unbelief of heretics, who confess their belief in the Gospel, and resist that faith by corrupting it, is a more grievous sin than that of the Jews, who have never accepted the Gospel faith. Since, however, they accepted the figure of that faith in the Old Law, which they corrupt by their false interpretations, their unbelief is a more grievous sin than that of the heathens, because the latter have not accepted the Gospel faith in any way at all.

The second thing to be considered in unbelief is the corruption of matters of faith. In this respect, since heathens err on more points than Jews, and these in more points than heretics, the unbelief of heathens is more grievous than the unbelief of the Jews, and that of the Jews than that of heretics, except perhaps in such cases as that of the Manichees, who, in matters of faith, err even more than heathens do.

Of these two gravities the first surpasses the second from the point of view of guilt, since, as stated above (A. 1) unbelief has the character of guilt, from its resisting faith, rather than from the mere absence of faith; for the latter, as was stated (A. 1) seems rather to bear the character of punishment. Hence, speaking absolutely, the unbelief of heretics is the worst.

This suffices for the *Replies to the objections.*

ARTICLE 7. *Whether One Ought To Dispute With Unbelievers in Public?*

We proceed thus to the Seventh Article: It seems that one ought not to dispute with unbelievers in public.

Objection 1. For the Apostle says (II Tim. 2. 14): *Contend not in words, for it is to no profit, but to the subverting of the hearers.* But it is impossible to dispute with unbelievers publicly without contending in words. Therefore one ought not to dispute publicly with unbelievers.

Obj. 2. Further, The law of Martianus Augustus[1] confirmed by the canons (*De Sum. Trin.* Cod. lib. i, leg. *Nemo*)[2] expresses itself thus: "It is an insult to the judgment of the most religious synod, if anyone ventures to debate or dispute in public about matters which have once been judged and disposed of." Now all matters of faith have been decided by the holy councils. Therefore it is an insult to the councils, and consequently a grave sin to presume to dispute in public about matters of faith.

Obj. 3. Further, Disputations are conducted by means of arguments. But an argument is a reason in settlement of a dubious matter. But things that are of faith, being most certain, ought not to be a matter of doubt. Therefore one ought not to dispute in public about matters of faith.

On the contrary, It is written (Acts 9. 22, 29) that *Saul increased much more in strength, and confounded the Jews,* and that *he spoke . . . to the gentiles and disputed with the Greeks.*

I answer that, In disputing about the faith, two things must be observed, one on the part of the disputant, the other on the part of his hearers. On the part of the disputant, we must consider his intention. For if he were to dispute as though he had doubts about the faith, and did not hold the truth of faith for certain, and as though he intended to probe it with arguments, without doubt he would sin, as being doubtful of the faith and an unbeliever. On the other hand, it is praiseworthy to dispute about the faith in order to confute errors, or even for practice.

On the part of the hearers we must consider whether those who hear the disputation are instructed and firm in the faith, or simple and wavering. As to those who are well instructed and firm in the faith, there can be no danger in disputing about the faith in their presence. But as to simple-minded people, we must make a distinction. For either they are provoked and molested by unbelievers, for instance Jews or heretics, or pagans, who strive to corrupt the faith in them, or else they are not subject to provocation in this matter, as in those countries where there are no unbelievers. In the first case it is necessary to dispute in public about

[1] Cf. *Conc. Chalced.* (MA VII, 475). [2] Justinian, KR II, 6a.

the faith, provided there be those who are equal and adapted to the task of confuting errors, since in this way simple people are strengthened in the faith, and unbelievers are deprived of the opportunity to deceive, while if those who ought to withstand the perverters of the truth of faith were silent, this would tend to strengthen error. Hence Gregory says (*Pastor.* ii, 4):[1] "Even as a thoughtless speech gives rise to error, so does an indiscreet silence leave those in error who might have been instructed." On the other hand, in the second case it is dangerous to dispute in public about the faith, in the presence of simple people, whose faith for this very reason is more firm, that they have never heard anything differing from what they believe. Hence it is not expedient for them to hear what unbelievers have to say against the faith.

Reply Obj. 1. The Apostle does not entirely forbid disputations, but such as are disorderly, and consist of contentious words rather than of sound speeches.

Reply Obj. 2. That law forbade those public disputations about the faith which arise from doubting the faith, but not those which are for its safeguarding.

Reply Obj. 3. One ought to dispute about matters of faith not as though one doubted about them, but in order to make the truth known, and to confute errors. For, in order to confirm the faith, it is necessary sometimes to dispute with unbelievers, sometimes by defending the faith, according to I Pet. 3. 15: *Being ready always to satisfy everyone that asketh you a reason of that hope and faith which is in you.* (Vulg.,—*Of that hope which is in you.*) Sometimes again, it is necessary, in order to convince those who are in error, according to Tit. 1. 9: *That he may be able to exhort in sound doctrine and to convince the gainsayers.*

ARTICLE 8. *Whether Unbelievers Ought To Be Compelled to the Faith?*

We proceed thus to the Eighth Article: It seems that unbelievers ought by no means to be compelled to the faith.

Objection 1. For it is written (Matt. 13. 28) that the servants of the householder, in whose field cockle had been sown, asked him: *Wilt thou that we go and gather it up?* and that he answered: *No, lest perhaps gathering up the cockle, you root up the wheat also together with it;* on which passage Chrysostom says (*Hom.* xlvi *in Matt.*):[2] "Our Lord says this so as to forbid the slaying of men. For it is not right to

slay heretics, because if you do you will necessarily slay many innocent persons." Therefore it seems that for the same reason unbelievers ought not to be compelled to the faith.

Obj. 2. Further, We read in the Decretals (Dist. xlv, can., *De Judæis*)[3]: "The holy synod prescribes, with regard to the Jews, that for the future, none are to be compelled to believe." Therefore, in like manner, neither should unbelievers be compelled to the faith.

Obj. 3. Further, Augustine says (*Tract.* xxvi *in Joann.*)[4] that it is possible for a man to do other things against his will, "but he cannot believe unless he is willing." But the will cannot be compelled. Therefore it seems that unbelievers ought not to be compelled to the faith.

Obj. 4. It is said in God's person (Ezech. 18. 32): *I desire not the death of the sinner* (Vulg., —*of him that dieth*). Now we ought to conform our will to the Divine will, as stated above (Part I-II, Q. XIX, AA. 9, 10). Therefore we should not even wish unbelievers to be put to death.

On the contrary, It is written (Luke 14. 23): *Go out into the highways and hedges; and compel them to come in.* Now men enter into the house of God, that is, into Holy Church, by faith. Therefore some ought to be compelled to the faith.

I answer that, Among unbelievers there are some who have never received the faith, such as the heathens and the Jews, and these are by no means to be compelled to the faith, in order that they may believe, because to believe depends on the will. Nevertheless they should be compelled by the faithful, if it be possible to do so, so that they do not hinder the faith, by their blasphemies, or by their evil persuasions, or even by their open persecutions. It is for this reason that Christ's faithful often wage war with unbelievers, not indeed for the purpose of forcing them to believe, because even if they were to conquer them, and take them prisoners, they should still leave them free to believe, if they will, but in order to prevent them from hindering the faith of Christ. On the other hand, there are unbelievers who at some time have accepted the faith, and professed it, such as heretics and all apostates. Such should be submitted even to bodily compulsion, that they may fulfil what they have promised, and hold what they at one time received.

Reply Obj. 1. Some have understood the authority quoted to forbid, not the excommunication but the slaying of heretics, as appears from the words of Chrysostom. Augustine too, says

[1] PL 77, 30.   [2] PG 58, 477.   [3] Gratian, *Decretum.* (RF I, 161).   [4] PL 35, 1607.

(*Ep. ad Vincentian.* xciii, 5)[1] of himself: "It was once my opinion that none should be compelled to union with Christ, that we should deal in words, and fight with arguments. However this opinion of mine is undone, not by words of contradiction, but by convincing examples. Because fear of the law was so profitable, that many say: Thanks be to the Lord Who has broken our chains asunder." Accordingly the meaning of Our Lord's words, *Suffer both to grow until the harvest,* must be gathered from those which precede, *lest perhaps gathering up the cockle, you root up the wheat also together with it.* For, as Augustine says (*Contra Ep. Parmen.* iii, 2)[2] these words show that "when this is not to be feared, that is to say, when a man's crime is so publicly known, and so hateful to all, that he has no defenders, or none such as might cause a schism, the severity of discipline should not slacken."

Reply Obj. 2. Those Jews who have in no way received the faith, ought by no means to be compelled to the faith. If, however, they have received it, they ought to be compelled to keep it, as is stated in the same chapter.

Reply Obj. 3. Just as taking a vow is a matter of will, and keeping a vow, a matter of obligation, so acceptance of the faith is a matter of the will, and keeping the faith, when once one has received it, is a matter of obligation. Therefore heretics should be compelled to keep the faith. Thus Augustine says to the Count Boniface (*Ep.* clxxxv):[3] "What do these people mean by crying out continually: 'We may believe or not believe just as we choose. Whom did Christ compel?' They should remember that Christ at first compelled Paul and afterwards taught him."

Reply Obj. 4. As Augustine says in the same letter, "None of us wishes any heretic to perish. But the house of David did not deserve to have peace, unless his son Absalom had been killed in the war which he had raised against his father. Thus if the Catholic Church gathers together some to the perdition of others, she heals the sorrow of her maternal heart by the delivery of so many nations."[4]

ARTICLE 9. *Whether it is Lawful to Communicate with Unbelievers?*

We proceed thus to the Ninth Article: It would seem that it is lawful to communicate with unbelievers.

Objection 1. For the Apostle says (I Cor. 10. 27): *If any of them that believe not, invite you, and you be willing to go, eat of anything that is set before you.* And Chrysostom says (*Hom.* xxv *super Epist. ad Heb.*):[5] "If you wish to go to dine with pagans, we permit it without any reservation." Now to sit at table with anyone is to communicate with him. Therefore it is lawful to communicate with unbelievers.

Obj. 2. Further, The Apostle says (I Cor. 5. 12): *What have I to do to judge them that are without?* Now unbelievers are without. When, therefore, the Church forbids the faithful to communicate with certain people, it seems that they ought not to be forbidden to communicate with unbelievers.

Obj. 3. Further, A master cannot employ his servant, unless he communicate with him, at least by word, since the master moves his servant by command. Now Christians can have unbelievers, either Jews, or pagans, or Saracens, for servants. Therefore they can lawfully communicate with them.

On the contrary, It is written (Deut. 7. 2, 3): *Thou shalt make no league with them, nor show mercy to them; neither shalt thou make marriages with them:* and a gloss on Levit. 15. 19, *The woman who at the return of the month,* etc., says: "It is so necessary to shun idolatry, that we should not come in touch with idolaters or their disciples, nor have any dealings with them."[6]

I answer that, Communication with a particular person is forbidden to the faithful, in two ways: first, as a punishment of the person with whom they are forbidden to communicate; secondly, for the safety of those who are forbidden to communicate with others. Both motives can be gathered from the Apostle's words (I Cor. 5. 6). For after he had pronounced sentence of excommunication, he adds as his reason *Know you not that a little leaven corrupts the whole lump?* and afterwards he adds the reason on the part of the punishment inflicted by the sentence of the Church when he says (*verse* 12): *Do not you judge them that are within?*

Accordingly, in the first way the Church does not forbid the faithful to communicate with unbelievers, who have not in any way received the Christian faith, namely, with pagans and Jews, because she has not the right to exercise spiritual judgment over them, but only temporal judgment, in the case when, while dwelling among Christians they are guilty of

---

[1] PL 33, 329. [2] PL 43, 92.
[3] Chap. 6 (PL 33, 803.) [4] Chap. 8 (PL 33, 807).
[5] PG 63, 176; Cf. Gratian, *Decretum,* II, causa XI, Q.3, can. 24 *Admensam.* (RF I, 650). [6] *Glossa ordin.* (I, 241B).

some misdemeanour, and are condemned by the faithful to some temporal punishment. But in this way, (that is, as a punishment), the Church forbids the faithful to communicate with those unbelievers who have forsaken the faith they once received, either by corrupting the faith, as heretics, or by entirely renouncing the faith, as apostates, because the Church pronounces sentence of excommunication on both.

With regard to the second way, it seems that one ought to distinguish according to the various conditions of persons, circumstances and time. For if some are firm in the faith so that it is to be hoped that their communicating with unbelievers will lead to the conversion of the latter rather than to the turning away of the faithful from the faith, these are not to be forbidden to communicate with unbelievers who have not received the faith, such as pagans or Jews, especially if there be some urgent necessity for so doing. But in the case of simple people and those who are weak in the faith, whose perversion is to be feared as a probable result, they should be forbidden to communicate with unbelievers, and especially to be on very familiar terms with them, or to communicate with them without necessity.

This suffices for the *Reply to the First Objection.*

Reply Obj. 2. The Church does not exercise judgment against unbelievers in the point of inflicting spiritual punishment on them, but she does exercise judgment over some of them in the matter of temporal punishment. It is under this head that sometimes the Church, for certain special sins, withdraws the faithful from communication with certain unbelievers.

Reply Obj. 3. There is more probability that a servant who is ruled by his master's commands will be converted to the faith of his master who is a believer, than if the case were the reverse, and so the faithful are not forbidden to have unbelieving servants. If, however, the master were in danger, through communicating with such a servant, he should send him away, according to Our Lord's command (Matt. 18. 8): *If . . . thy foot scandalize thee, cut it off, and cast it from thee.*

With regard to the argument in the contrary sense, the reply is that the Lord gave this command in reference to those nations into whose territory the Jews were about to enter. For the Jews were inclined to idolatry, so that it was to be feared lest, through frequent dealings with those nations, they should be estranged from the faith. Hence the text goes on (*verse* 4): *For she will turn away thy son from following Me.*

ARTICLE 10. *Whether Unbelievers May Have Authority or Dominion over the Faithful?*

We proceed thus to the Tenth Article: It seems that unbelievers may have authority or dominion over the faithful.

Objection 1. For the Apostle says (I Tim. 6. 1): *Whosoever are servants under the yoke, let them count their masters worthy of all honour,* and it is clear that he is speaking of unbelievers, since he adds (*verse* 2): *But they that have believing masters, let them not despise them.* Moreover it is written (I Pet. 2. 18): *Servants be subject to your masters with all fear, not only to the good and gentle, but also to the froward.* Now this command would not be contained in the apostolic teaching, unless unbelievers could have authority over the faithful. Therefore it seems that unbelievers can have authority over the faithful.

Obj. 2. Further, All the members of a prince's household are his subjects. Now some of the faithful were members of unbelieving princes' households, for we read in the Epistle to the Philippians (4. 22): *All the saints salute you, especially they that are of Cæsar's household,* referring to Nero, who was an unbeliever. Therefore unbelievers can have authority over the faithful.

Obj. 3. Further, According to the Philosopher[1] a slave is his master's instrument in human affairs, even as a craftsman's labourer is his instrument in matters concerning the working of his art. Now, in such matters, a believer can be subject to an unbeliever, for he may work on an unbeliever's farm. Therefore unbelievers may have authority over the faithful even as to dominion.

On the contrary, Those who are in authority can pronounce judgment on those over whom they are placed. But unbelievers cannot pronounce judgment on the faithful, for the Apostle says (I Cor. 6. 1): *Dare any of you, having a matter against another, go to be judged before the unjust,* that is, unbelievers, *and not before the saints?* Therefore it seems that unbelievers cannot have authority over the faithful.

I answer that, That this question may be considered in two ways. First, we may speak of dominion or authority of unbelievers over the faithful as of a thing to be established for the first time. This ought by no means to be allowed, since it would provoke scandal and endanger the faith, for subjects are easily influ-

[1] *Politics,* I, 4 (1253b32).

enced by their superiors to comply with their commands, unless the subjects are of great virtue; moreover unbelievers hold the faith in contempt, if they see the faithful fall away. Hence the Apostle forbade the faithful to go to law before an unbelieving judge. And so the Church altogether forbids unbelievers to acquire dominion over believers, or to have authority over them in any capacity whatever.

Secondly, we may speak of dominion or authority, as already in force. And here we must observe that dominion and authority are institutions of human law, while the distinction between faithful and unbelievers arises from the Divine law. Now the Divine law which is the law of grace, does not do away with human law which is the law of natural reason. Therefore the distinction between faithful and unbelievers, considered in itself, does not do away with dominion and authority of unbelievers over the faithful. Nevertheless this right of dominion or authority can be justly done away with by the sentence or ordination of the Church which has the authority of God, since unbelievers in virtue of their unbelief deserve to forfeit their power over the faithful who are converted into children of God.

This the Church does sometimes, and sometimes not. For among those unbelievers who are subject, even in temporal matters, to the Church and her members, the Church made the law that if the slave of a Jew became a Christian, he should forthwith receive his freedom, without paying any price, if he should be a *vernaculus*, that is, born in slavery; and likewise if, when yet an unbeliever, he had been bought for his service. If, however, he had been bought for sale, then he should be offered for sale within three months. Nor does the Church harm them in this, because since those Jews themselves are subject to the Church, she can dispose of their possessions, even as secular princes have enacted many laws to be observed by their subjects, in favour of liberty. On the other hand, the Church has not applied the above law to those unbelievers who are not subject to her or her members in temporal matters, although she has the right to do so: and this, in order to avoid scandal, for as Our Lord showed (Matt. 17. 25, 26) that He could be excused from paying the tribute, because *the children are free*, yet He ordered the tribute to be paid in order to avoid giving scandal. Thus Paul too, after saying that servants should honour their masters, adds, *lest the name of the Lord and His doctrine be blasphemed*.

This suffices for the *Reply to the First Objection.*

Reply Obj. 2. The authority of Cæsar preceded the distinction of faithful from unbelievers. Hence it was not cancelled by the conversion of some to the faith. Moreover it was a good thing that there should be some of the faithful in the emperor's household, that they might defend the rest of the faithful. Thus the Blessed Sebastian strengthened the hearts of Christians whom he saw faltering under torture, and, the while, remained hidden under the military cloak in the palace of Diocletian.

Reply Obj. 3. Slaves are subject to their masters for their whole lifetime, and are subject to their overseers in everything, while the craftsman's labourer is subject to him for certain special works. Hence it would be more dangerous for unbelievers to have dominion or authority over the faithful than that they should be allowed to employ them in some craft. Therefore the Church permits Christians to work on the land of Jews, because this does not entail their living together with them. Thus Solomon besought the King of Tyre to send master workmen to hew the trees, as related in III Kings 5. Yet, if there be reason to fear that the faithful will be perverted by such communications and dealings, they should be absolutely forbidden.

ARTICLE 11. *Whether the Rites of Unbelievers Ought To Be Tolerated?*

We proceed thus to the Eleventh Article: It would seem that rites of unbelievers ought not to be tolerated.

Objection 1. For it is evident that unbelievers sin in observing their rites, and not to prevent a sin, when one can, seems to imply consent therein, as a gloss observes[1] on Rom. 1. 32: *Not only they that do them, but they also that consent to them that do them.* Therefore it is a sin to tolerate their rites.

Obj. 2. Further, The rites of the Jews are compared to idolatry, because a gloss on Gal. 5. 1, *Be not held again under the yoke of bondage*, says: "The bondage of that law was not lighter than that of idolatry."[2] But it would not be allowable for anyone to observe the rites of idolatry; in fact Christian princes at first caused the temples of idols to be closed, and afterwards, to be destroyed, as Augustine relates.[3] There-

---

[1] *Glossa ordin.* (VI, 6E); *Glossa* Lombardi (PL 191, 1336); cf. Ambrosiaster, *In Rom.* 1. 32 (PL 17, 66).
[2] *Glossa interl.* (VI, 86v); *Glossa* Lombardi (PL 192, 152). Cf. Augustine, *Contra Faust.*, IX, 18 (PL 42, 358).
[3] *City Of God*, XVIII, 54 (PL 41, 620).

fore it follows that even the rites of Jews ought not to be tolerated.

Obj. 3. Further, Unbelief is the greatest of sins, as stated above (A. 3). Now other sins such as adultery, theft and the like, are not tolerated, but are punishable by law. Therefore neither ought the rites of unbelievers to be tolerated.

On the contrary, Gregory says, speaking of the Jews:[1] "They should be allowed to observe all their feasts, just as hitherto they and their fathers have for ages observed them."

I answer that, Human government is derived from the Divine government, and should imitate it. Now although God is all-powerful and supremely good, nevertheless He allows certain evils to take place in the universe, which He might prevent, lest, without them, greater goods might be forfeited, or greater evils ensue. Accordingly in human government also, those who are in authority, rightly tolerate certain evils, lest certain goods be lost, or certain greater evils be incurred; thus Augustine says (*De Ordine,* ii, 4):[2] "If you do away with harlots, the world will be convulsed with lust." Hence, though unbelievers sin in their rites, they may be tolerated, either on account of some good that ensues therefrom, or because of some evil avoided. Thus from the fact that the Jews observe their rites, which, of old, foreshadowed the truth of the faith which we hold, there follows this good—that our very enemies bear witness to our faith, and that our faith is represented in a figure, so to speak. For this reason they are tolerated in the observance of their rites. On the other hand, the rites of other unbelievers, which are neither truthful nor profitable are by no means to be tolerated, except perhaps in order to avoid an evil, for instance the scandal or disturbance that might ensue, or some hindrance to the salvation of those who if they were unmolested might gradually be converted to the faith. For this reason the Church, at times, has tolerated the rites even of heretics and pagans, when unbelievers were very numerous.

This suffices for the *Replies to the Objections.*

ARTICLE 12. *Whether the Children of Jews and of Other Unbelievers Ought To Be Baptized Against Their Parents' Will?*

We proceed thus to the Twelfth Article: It seems that the children of Jews and of other

unbelievers ought to be baptized against their parents' will.

Objection 1. For the bond of marriage is stronger than the right of parental authority over children, since the right of parental authority can be made to cease when a son is set at liberty, while the marriage bond cannot be severed by man, according to Matt. 19. 6: *What . . . God hath joined together let no man put asunder.* And yet the marriage bond is broken on account of unbelief, for the Apostle says (I Cor. 7. 15): *If the unbeliever depart, let him depart. For a brother or sister is not under servitude in such cases:* and a canon says[3] that if the unbelieving partner is unwilling to abide with the other without insult to their Creator, then the other partner is not bound to cohabitation. Much more, therefore, does unbelief abrogate the right of unbelieving parents' authority over their children, and consequently their children may be baptized against their parents' will.

Obj. 2. Further, One is more bound to succour a man who is in danger of everlasting death, than one who is in danger of temporal death. Now it would be a sin if one saw a man in danger of temporal death and failed to go to his aid. Since, then, the children of Jews and other unbelievers are in danger of everlasting death should they be left to their parents who would imbue them with their unbelief, it seems that they ought to be taken way from them and baptized, and instructed in the faith.

Obj. 3. Further, The children of a bondsman are themselves bondsmen, and under the power of his master. Now the Jews are bondsmen of kings and princes; therefore their children are also. Consequently kings and princes have the power to do what they will with Jewish children. Therefore no injustice is committed if they baptize them against their parents' wishes.

Obj. 4. Further, Every man belongs more to God, from Whom he has his soul, than to his carnal father, from whom he has his body. Therefore it is not unjust if Jewish children be taken away from their parents, and consecrated to God in Baptism.

Obj. 5. Further, Baptism avails for salvation more than preaching does, since Baptism removes immediately the stain of sin and the debt of punishment, and opens the gate of heaven. Now if danger ensue through not preaching, it is imputed to him who omitted to preach, according to the words of Ezech. 33. 6 about the man who *sees the sword coming and sounds not*

---

[1] Gratianus, *Decretum,* I, d. 45, can. 3 *Qui sincera.* (RF I, 161). Cf. Gregory, *Registrum,* XIII, 6, *Epist.,* XII (PL 67, 1267).   [2] PL 32, 1000.

[3] Gratianus, *Decretum,* II, XXVIII, Q. 1, can. 4 *Uxor legitima* (RF I, 1080); Q. 2, can. 2 *Si infidelis* (RF I, 1090).

the trumpet. Much more therefore, if Jewish children are lost through not being baptized are they accounted guilty of sin, who could have baptized them and did not.

On the contrary, Injustice should be done to no man. Now it would be an injustice to Jews if their children were to be baptized against their will, since they would lose the rights of parental authority over their children as soon as these were Christians. Therefore these should not be baptized against their parents' will.

I answer that, The custom of the Church has very great authority and ought to be jealously observed in all things, since the very doctrine of catholic doctors derives its authority from the Church. Hence we ought to abide by the authority of the Church rather than by that of an Augustine or a Jerome or of any doctor whatever. Now it was never the custom of the Church to baptize the children of Jews against the will of their parents, although in times past there have been many very powerful catholic princes like Constantine and Theodosius, with whom most holy bishops have been on most friendly terms, as Sylvester with Constantine, and Ambrose with Theodosius, who would certainly not have failed to obtain this favour from them if it had been at all reasonable. It seems therefore dangerous to repeat this assertion, that the children of Jews should be baptized against their parents' wishes, in contradiction to the custom of the Church observed up to this time.

There are two reasons for this custom. One is on account of the danger to faith. For children baptized before coming to the use of reason, afterwards when they come to perfect age, might easily be persuaded by their parents to renounce what they had unknowingly embraced. And this would be detrimental to the faith.

The other reason is that it is against natural justice. For a child is by nature part of its father. Thus, at first, it is not distinct from its parents as to its body, so long as it is enfolded within its mother's womb; and later on after birth, and before it has the use of its free choice, it is enfolded in the care of its parents, which is like a spiritual womb, for so long as a child does not have the use of reason, he does not differ from an irrational animal. Thus even as an ox or a horse belongs to someone who, according to the civil law, can use them when he likes, as his own instrument, so, according to the natural law, a son, before coming to the use of reason, is under his father's care. Hence it would be contrary to natural justice, if a child, before coming to the use of reason, were to be taken away from its parents' custody, or anything done to it against its parents' wish. As soon, however, as it begins to have the use of its free choice, it begins to belong to itself, and is able to look after itself, in matters concerning the Divine or the natural law; and then it should be induced, not by compulsion but by persuasion, to embrace the faith. It can then consent to the faith, and be baptized, even against its parents' wish; but not before it comes to the use of reason. Hence it is said[1] of the children of the fathers of old that they were saved in the faith of their parents; by which we are given to understand that it is the parents' duty to look after the salvation of their children, especially before they come to the use of reason.

Reply Obj. 1. In the marriage bond, both husband and wife have the use of the free choice, and each can assent to the faith without the other's consent. But this does not apply to a child before it comes to the use of reason. Yet the comparison holds good after the child has come to the use of reason, if it is willing to be converted.

Reply Obj. 2. No one should be snatched from natural death against the order of civil law; for instance, if a man were condemned by the judge to temporal death, nobody ought to rescue him by violence. Hence no one ought to break the order of the natural law, by which a child is in the custody of its father, in order to rescue it from the danger of everlasting death.

Reply Obj. 3. Jews are bondsmen of princes by civil bondage, which does not exclude the order of natural or Divine law.

Reply Obj. 4. Man is directed to God by his reason, through which he can know Him. Hence a child before coming to the use of reason, in the natural order of things, is directed to God by its parents' reason, under whose care it lies by nature. And it is for them to dispose of the child in all matters relating to God.

Reply Obj. 5. The peril that ensues from the omission of preaching threaten only those who are entrusted with the duty of preaching. Hence it had already been said (Ezech. 3. 17): *I have made thee a watchman to the children* (Vulg.,—house) *of Israel*. On the other hand, to provide the sacraments of salvation for the children of unbelievers is the duty of their parents. Hence it is they whom the danger threatens, if through being deprived of the sacraments their children fail to obtain salvation.

[1] Peter Lombard, *Sent.*, IV, d. 1, chap. 8 (QR II, 749).

QUESTION XI

OF HERESY

(In Four Articles)

WE must now consider heresy: under which head there are four points of inquiry: (1) Whether heresy is a species of unbelief? (2) Of the matter about which it is. (3) Whether heretics should be tolerated? (4) Whether those who return from heresy should be received?

ARTICLE 1. Whether Heresy Is a Species of Unbelief?

We proceed thus to the First Article: It would seem that heresy is not a species of unbelief.

Objection 1. For unbelief is in the understanding, as stated above (Q. X, A. 2). Now heresy would seem not to pertain to the understanding, but rather to the appetitive power; for Jerome says on Gal. 5. 19 and is quoted in the Decretals,[1] The works of the flesh are manifest: "Heresy is derived from a Greek word meaning choice, whereby a man makes choice of that school which he deems best." But choice is an act of the appetitive power, as stated above (Part I-II, Q. XIII, A. 1). Therefore heresy is not a species of unbelief.

Obj. 2. Further, Vice takes its species chiefly from its end; hence the Philosopher says[2] that "he who commits adultery that he may steal, is a thief rather than an adulterer." Now the end of heresy is temporal profit, especially lordship and glory, which pertain to the vice of pride or covetousness; for Augustine says (De Util. Credendi, i)[3] that "a heretic is one who either devises or follows false and new opinions, for the sake of some temporal profit, especially that he may lord and be honoured above others." Therefore heresy is a species of pride rather than of unbelief.

Obj. 3. Further, Since unbelief is in the understanding, it would seem not to pertain to the flesh. Now heresy belongs to the works of the flesh, for the Apostle says (Gal. 5. 19): The works of the flesh are manifest, which are fornication, uncleanness, and among the others, he adds, dissensions, sects, which are the same as heresies. Therefore heresy is not a species of unbelief.

On the contrary, Falsehood is contrary to truth. Now "a heretic is one who devises or fol-lows false or new opinions." Therefore heresy is opposed to the truth, on which faith is founded; and consequently it is a species of unbelief.

I answer that, The word heresy as stated in the first objection denotes a choosing. Now choice as stated above (Part I-II, Q. XIII, A. 3) is about things directed to the end, the end being presupposed. Now, in matters of faith, the will assents to some truth, as to its proper good, as was shown above (Q. IV, A. 3). Therefore that which is the chief truth, has the character of last end, while those which are secondary truths have the character of being directed to the end.

Now, whoever believes, assents to someone's words; so that, in every form of belief, the person to whose words assent is given seems to hold the chief place and to be the end as it were; while the things comprising the assent to that person hold a secondary place. Consequently he that holds the Christian faith rightly, assents, by his will, to Christ, in those things which truly pertain to His doctrine.

Accordingly there are two ways in which a man may deviate from the rectitude of the Christian faith. First, because he is unwilling to assent to Christ Himself; and such a man has an evil will, so to say, in respect of the very end. This pertains to the species of unbelief in pagans and Jews. Secondly, because, though he intends to assent to Christ, yet he fails in his choice of those things by which he assents to Christ, because he chooses, not what Christ really taught, but the suggestions of his own mind. Therefore heresy is a species of unbelief pertaining to those who profess the Christian faith, but corrupt its dogmas.

Reply Obj. 1. Choice pertains to unbelief in the same way as the will pertains to faith, as stated above.

Reply Obj. 2. Vices take their species from their proximate end, while, from their remote end, they take their genus and cause. Thus in the case of adultery committed for the sake of theft, there is there the species of adultery taken from its proper end and object; but the ultimate end shows that the act of adultery is both the result of the theft, and is included under it, as an effect under its cause, or a species under its genus, as appears from what we have said about acts in general (Part I-II, Q. XVIII, A. 7). Therefore, as to the case in point also, the proximate end of heresy is adherence to one's own false opinion, and from this it derives its species, while its remote end reveals its cause, namely, that it arises from pride or covetousness.

---

[1] Gratian, Decretum, II, causa XXIV, Q. 3, can. 27 (RF I, 997).

[2] Ethics, V, 2 (1130a24).   [3] PL 42, 65.

Reply Obj. 3. Just as heresy is so called from its being a choosing[1] so does sect derive its name from its being a cutting off (*secando*), as Isidore states (*Etym.* viii, 3).[2] And so heresy and sect are the same thing, and each pertains to the works of the flesh, not indeed by reason of the act itself of unbelief in respect of its proximate object, but by reason of its cause, which is either the desire of an undue end, in which way it arises from pride or covetousness, as stated in the second objection, or some illusion of the imagination (which is the principle of error, as the Philosopher states in the *Metaphysics*),[3] for the imagination has a certain connection with the flesh, in so far as its act is dependent on a bodily organ.

ARTICLE 2. *Whether Heresy Is Properly About Matters of Faith?*

We proceed thus to the Second Article: It seems that heresy is not properly about matters of faith.

Objection 1. For just as there are heresies and sects among Christians, so were there among the Jews and Pharisees, as Isidore observes (*Etym.* viii, 3).[4] Now their dissensions were not about matters of faith. Therefore heresy is not about matters of faith, as though they were its proper matter.

Obj. 2. Further, The matter of faith is the thing believed. Now heresy is not only about things, but also about words, and about interpretations of Holy Writ. For Jerome says on Gal. 5. 20[5] that "whoever expounds the Scriptures in any sense but that of the Holy Ghost by Whom they were written, may be called a heretic, though he may not have left the Church"; and elsewhere he says[6] that "heresies spring up from words spoken amiss." Therefore heresy is not properly about the matter of faith.

Obj. 3. Further, We find the holy doctors differing even about matters pertaining to the faith, for example Augustine[7] and Jerome,[8] on the question about the cessation of the legal observances. And yet this was without any heresy on their part. Therefore heresy is not properly about the matter of faith.

On the contrary, Augustine says in his book against the Manichees:[9] "In Christ's Church, those are heretics, who hold mischievous and erroneous opinions, and when rebuked that they may think soundly and rightly, offer a stubborn resistance, and, refusing to mend their pernicious and deadly doctrines, persist in defending them." Now pernicious and deadly doctrines are none but those which are contrary to the dogmas of faith by which *the just man liveth* (Rom. 1. 17). Therefore heresy is about matters of faith, as about its proper matter.

I answer that, We are speaking of heresy now as denoting a corruption of the Christian faith. Now it does not imply a corruption of the Christian faith if a man has a false opinion in matters that are not of faith, for instance, in questions of geometry and so forth, which cannot belong to the faith by any means; but only when a person has a false opinion about things belonging to the faith. Now a thing may be of faith in two ways, as stated above (Part I, Q. XXXII, A. 4), in one way, directly and principally, for instance, the articles of faith; in another way, indirectly and secondarily, for example those matters, the denial of which leads to the corruption of some article of faith. And there may be heresy in either way, even as there can be faith.

Reply Obj. 1. Just as the heresies of the Jews and Pharisees were about opinions relating to Judaism or Pharisaism, so also heresies among Christians are about matters touching the Christian faith.

Reply Obj. 2. A man is said to expound Holy Writ in another sense than that required by the Holy Ghost when he so distorts the meaning of Holy Writ that it is contrary to what the Holy Ghost has revealed. Hence it is written (Ezech. 13. 6) about the false prophets: *They have persisted to confirm what they have said,* namely by false interpretations of Scripture. Moreover a man professes his faith by the words that he utters, since confession is an act of faith, as stated above (Q. III, A. 1). Therefore inordinate words about matters of faith may lead to corruption of the faith; and hence it is that Pope Leo says in a letter to Proterius, Bishop of Alexandria[10]: "The enemies of Christ's cross lie in wait for our every deed and word, so that, if we but give them the slightest pretext, they may accuse us mendaciously of agreeing with Nestorius."

Reply Obj. 3. As Augustine says (*Ep.* xliii),[11] and we find it stated in the *Decretals* (xxiv,

[1] From the Greek αἱρεῖν, to cut off.
[2] PL 82, 296.   [3] IV, 5 (1010[b]1).
[4] PL 82, 297.   [5] PL 26, 443.
[6] *Glossa ordin.,* on Osee 2.16 (IV, 336A). Cf. Peter Lombard, *Sent.,* IV, d. 13, chap. 2 (QR II, 818).
[7] *Epist.,* LXXXII, 2 (PL 33, 281).
[8] *Epist.,* CXII (PL 22, 921).

[9] Cf. *City of God,* XVIII, 51 (PL 41, 613).
[10] *Epist.,* CXXIX, chap. 2 (PL 54, 1076).   [11] PL 33, 160.

qu. 3, can. *Dixit Apostolus*):[1] "By no means should we accuse of heresy those who, however false and perverse their opinion may be, defend it without obstinate fervour, and seek the truth with careful anxiety, ready to mend their opinion, when they have found the truth," because, namely, they do not make a choice in contradiction to the doctrine of the Church. Accordingly, certain doctors seem to have differed either in matters the holding of which in this or that way is of no consequence, so far as faith is concerned, or even in matters of faith which were not as yet defined by the Church; although if anyone were obstinately to deny them after they had been defined by the authority of the universal Church, he would be accounted a heretic. This authority resides chiefly in the Sovereign Pontiff. For we read (*Decret.* xxiv, qu. 1, cap. 12):[2] "Whenever a question of faith is in dispute, I think that all our brethren and fellow bishops ought to refer the matter to none other than Peter, as being the source of their name and honour," against whose authority neither Jerome nor Augustine nor any of the holy doctors defended their opinion. Hence Jerome (Pelagius) says to Pope Damasus:[3] "This, most blessed Pope, is the faith that we have been taught in the Catholic Church. If anything therein has been incorrectly or carelessly expressed, we beg that it may be set aright by you who hold the faith and see of Peter. If however this, our profession, be approved by the judgment of your apostleship, whoever may blame me, will prove that he himself is ignorant, or malicious, or even not a catholic but a heretic."

ARTICLE 3. *Whether Heretics Ought To Be Tolerated?*

We proceed thus to the Third Article: It seems that heretics ought to be tolerated.

Objection 1. For the Apostle says (II Tim. 2. 24, 25): *The servant of the Lord must not wrangle, . . . with modesty admonishing them that resist the truth, if peradventure God may give them repentance to know the truth, and they may recover themselves from the snares of the devil.* Now if heretics are not tolerated but put to death, they lose the opportunity of repentance. Therefore it seems contrary to the Apostle's command.

Obj. 2. Further, Whatever is necessary in the Church should be tolerated. Now heresies are necessary in the Church, since the Apostle says (I Cor. 11. 19): *There must be . . . heresies, that they . . . , who are reproved, may be manifest among you.* Therefore it seems that heretics should be tolerated.

Obj. 3. Further, The Master commanded his servants (Matt. 13. 30) to suffer the cockle *to grow until the harvest,* that is, the end of the world, as the same text explains. Now holy men explain that the cockle denotes heretics.[4] Therefore heretics should be tolerated.

On the contrary, The Apostle says (Tit. 3. 10, 11): *A man that is a heretic, after the first and second admonition, avoid: knowing that he, that is such an one, is subverted.*

I answer that, With regard to heretics two points must be observed: one, on their own side, the other, on the side of the Church. On their own side there is the sin, by which they deserve not only to be separated from the Church by excommunication, but also to be severed from the world by death. For it is a much graver matter to corrupt the faith which quickens the soul, than to forge money, which supports temporal life. Therefore if forgers of money and other evil-doers are condemned to death at once by the secular authority, much more reason is there for heretics, as soon as they are convicted of heresy, to be not only excommunicated but even put to death.

On the part of the Church, however, there is mercy which looks to the conversion of the wanderer, and therefore she condemns not at once, but *after the first and second admonition,* as the Apostle directs. After that, if he is yet stubborn, the Church no longer hoping for his conversion, looks to the salvation of others, by excommunicating him and separating him from the Church, and furthermore delivers him to the secular tribunal to be exterminated from the world by death. For Jerome commenting on Gal. 5. 9, *A little leaven,* says,[5] and we find it in the *Decretals,*[6] "Cut off the decayed flesh, expel the mangy sheep from the fold, lest the whole house, the whole paste, the whole body, the whole flock, burn, perish, rot, die. Arius was but one spark in Alexandria, but as that spark was not at once put out, the whole earth was laid waste by its flame."

Reply Obj. 1. This very modesty demands that the heretic should be admonished a first and second time; and if he be unwilling to re-

---

[1] Gratian, (RF I, 998).   [2] Gratian (RF I, 970).
[3] Cf. Pelagius, *Libellus Fidei ad Innocentium* (PL 45, 1718).
[4] Cf. Chrysostom, *In Matt.*, hom. XLVI (PG 58, 475).
[5] PL 26, 430.
[6] Gratian, *Decretum,* II, causa XXIV, Q. 3, can. 16 (RF I, 995).

tract he must be reckoned as already subverted, as we may gather from the words of the Apostle quoted above.

Reply Obj. 2. The profit that ensues from heresy is beside the intention of heretics, for it consists in the constancy of the faithful being put to the test as the Apostle says, and "makes us shake off our sluggishness, and search the Scriptures more carefully," as Augustine states (*De Gen. cont. Manich.* i).[1] What they really intend is the corruption of the faith, which is to inflict the very greatest harm. Consequently we should consider what they directly intend, and expel them, rather than what is beside their intention, and so, tolerate them.

Reply Obj. 3. According to *Decret.* xxiv (qu. iii., can. *Notandum*),[2] "to be excommunicated is not to be uprooted." A man is excommunicated, as the Apostle says (I Cor. 5. 5) that his *spirit may be saved in the day of Our Lord.* Yet if heretics be altogether uprooted by death, this is not contrary to Our Lord's command, which is to be understood as referring to the case when the cockle cannot be plucked up without plucking up the wheat, as we explained above (Q. X, A. 8, Reply 1), when treating of unbelievers in general.

ARTICLE 4. *Whether the Church Should Receive Those Who Return From Heresy?*

We proceed thus to the Fourth Article: It seems that the Church ought in all cases to receive those who return from heresy.

Objection 1. For it is written (Jerem. 3. 1) in the person of the Lord. *Thou hast prostituted thyself to many lovers; nevertheless return to Me saith the Lord.* Now the sentence of the Church is God's sentence, according to Deut. 1. 17: *You shall hear the little as well as the great: neither shall you respect any man's person, because it is the judgment of God.* Therefore even those who are guilty of the prostitution of unbelief which is spiritual prostitution, should be received all the same.

Obj. 2. Further, Our Lord commanded Peter (Matt. 18. 22) to forgive his offending brother *not* only *till seven times, but till seventy times seven times,* which Jerome expounds as meaning that a man should be forgiven, as often as he has sinned.[3] Therefore he ought to be received by the Church as often as he has sinned by falling back into heresy.

Obj. 3. Further, Heresy is a kind of unbelief. Now other unbelievers who wish to be converted are received by the Church. Therefore heretics also should be received.

On the contrary, The Decretal *Ad abolendam* (*De Hæreticis,* cap. ix)[4] says that "those who are found to have relapsed into the error which they had already abjured, must be left to the secular tribunal." Therefore they should not be received by the Church.

I answer that, In obedience to Our Lord's institution, the Church extends her charity to all, not only to friends, but also to foes who persecute her, according to Matt. 5. 44: *Love your enemies; do good to them that hate you.* Now it is part of charity that we should both wish and work our neighbour's good. Again, good is twofold. One is spiritual, namely the health of the soul, which good is chiefly the object of charity, since it is this chiefly that we should wish for one another. Consequently, from this point of view, heretics who return after falling no matter how often, are admitted by the Church to Penance by which the way of salvation is opened to them.

The other good is that which charity considers secondarily, namely, temporal good, such as the life of the body, worldly possessions, good repute, ecclesiastical or secular dignity, for we are not bound by charity to wish others this good, except in relation to the eternal salvation of them and of others. Hence if the presence of one of these goods in one individual might be an obstacle to eternal salvation in many, we are not bound out of charity to wish such a good to that person, rather should we desire him to be without it, both because eternal salvation takes precedence of temporal good, and because the good of the many is to be preferred to the good of one. Now if heretics were always received on their return, in order to save their lives and other temporal goods, this might be prejudicial to the salvation of others, both because they would infect others if they relapsed again, and because, if they escaped without punishment, others would feel more assured in lapsing into heresy. For it is written (Eccles. 8. 11): *For because sentence is not speedily pronounced against the evil, the children of men commit evils without any fear.*

For this reason the Church not only admits to Penance those who return from heresy for the first time, but also safeguards their lives, and sometimes by dispensation, restores them to the ecclesiastical dignities which they may have had before, should their conversion appear to be sincere: we read of this as having

[1] PL 34, 173.   [2] Gratian (RF I, 1000).
[3] PL 26, 137.

[4] *Decretal. Gregor.,* IX, v, tit. 7, chap. 9 (RF II, 781).

frequently been done for the good of peace. But when they fall again, after having been received, this seems to prove them to be inconstant in faith, and therefore when they return again, they are admitted to Penance, but are not delivered from the pain of death.

Reply Obj. 1. In God's tribunal, those who return are always received, because God is a searcher of hearts, and knows those who return in sincerity. But the Church cannot imitate God in this, for she presumes that those who relapse after being once received, are not sincere in their return; hence she does not debar them from the way of salvation, but neither does she protect them from the sentence of death.

Reply Obj. 2. Our Lord was speaking to Peter of sins committed against oneself, for one should always forgive such offences and spare our brother when he repents. These words are not to be applied to sins committed against one's neighbor or against God, for "it is not left to our discretion to forgive such offences," as Jerome says on Matt. 18. 15. *If thy brother shall offend against thee.*[1] Yet even in this matter the law prescribes limits according as God's honour or our neighbour's good demands.

Reply Obj. 3. When other unbelievers who have never received the faith are converted, they do not as yet show signs of inconstancy in faith, as relapsed heretics do. Hence the comparison fails.

QUESTION XII
OF APOSTASY
(In Two Articles)

WE must now consider apostasy; about which there are two points of inquiry: (1) Whether apostasy pertains to unbelief? (2) Whether, on account of apostasy from the faith, subjects are absolved from allegiance to an apostate prince?

ARTICLE 1. *Whether Apostasy Pertains to Unbelief?*

We proceed thus to the First Article: It seems that apostasy does not pertain to unbelief.

Objection 1. For that which is the origin of all sins does not seem to pertain to unbelief, since there are many sins without unbelief. Now apostasy seems to be the origin of every sin, for it is written (Ecclus. 10. 14): *The beginning of the pride of man is apostasy* (Douay,—*to fall off*) *from God*, and further on (*verse* 15):

[1] *Glossa ordin.* (v, 56F).

Pride is the beginning of all sin. Therefore apostasy does not pertain to unbelief.

Obj. 2. Further, Unbelief is an act of the understanding. But apostasy seems rather to consist in some outward deed or utterance, or even in some inward act of the will, for it is written (Prov. 6. 12-14): *A man that is an apostate, an unprofitable man walketh with a perverse mouth. He winketh with the eyes, presseth with the foot, speaketh with the finger. With a wicked heart he deviseth evil, and at all times he soweth discord.* Moreover if anyone were to have himself circumcised, or to worship at the tomb of Mahomet, he would be deemed an apostate. Therefore apostasy does not pertain to unbelief.

Obj. 3. Further, Heresy, since it pertains to unbelief, is a determinate species of unbelief. If then, apostasy pertained to unbelief, it would follow that it is a determinate species of unbelief which does not seem to agree with what has been said (Q. X, A. 5). Therefore apostasy does not pertain to unbelief.

On the contrary, It is written (John 6. 67): *Many of His disciples went back*, that is, apostatized, of whom Our Lord had said previously (*verse* 65): *There are some of you that believe not.* Therefore apostasy pertains to unbelief.

I answer that, Apostasy denotes a backsliding from God. This may happen in various ways according to the different kinds of union between man and God. For, in the first place, man is united to God by faith; secondly, by having his will duly submissive in obeying His commandments; thirdly, by certain special things pertaining to supererogation such as the religious life, the clerical state, or holy Orders. Now if that which follows be removed, that which precedes, remains, but the converse does not hold. Accordingly a man may apostatize from God by withdrawing from the religious life which he had professed, or from the holy Order which he had received; and this is called apostasy from religious life or Orders. A man may also apostatize from God, by rebelling in his mind against the Divine commandments. And though man may apostatize in both the above ways, he may still remain united to God by faith. But if he give up the faith, then he seems to turn away from God altogether, and consequently, apostasy simply and absolutely is that by which a man withdraws from the faith, and is called apostasy of perfidy. In this way apostasy, absolutely so called, pertains to unbelief.

Reply Obj. 1. This objection refers to the

second kind of apostasy, which denotes an act of the will in rebellion against God's commandments, an act that is to be found in every mortal sin.

Reply Obj. 2. It pertains to faith not only that the heart should believe, but also that external words and deeds should bear witness to the inward faith, for confession is an act of faith. In this way too, certain external words or deeds pertain to unbelief, in so far as they are signs of unbelief, even as a sign of health is said itself to be healthy. Now although the authority quoted may be understood as referring to every kind of apostate, yet it applies most truly to an apostate from the faith. For since faith is the first foundation of things to be hoped for, and since, without faith it is *impossible to please God* (Heb. 11. 6), when once faith is removed, man retains nothing that may be useful for the obtaining of eternal salvation, for which reason it is written (Prov. 6. 12): *A man that is an apostate, an unprofitable man.* For faith is the life of the soul, according to Rom. 1. 17: *The just man liveth by faith.* Therefore, just as when the life of the body is taken away, man's every member and part loses its due disposition, so, when the life of justice, which is by faith, is done away, disorder appears in all his members. First, in his mouth, through which chiefly his heart stands revealed; secondly, in his eyes; thirdly, in the instrument of movement; fourthly, in his will, which tends to evil. The result is that *he sows discord,* endeavouring to sever others from the faith even as he severed himself.

Reply Obj. 3. The species of a quality or form is not diversified by the fact of its being the term from which or to which of movement; on the contrary, it is the movement that takes its species from the terms. Now apostasy regards unbelief as the term to which of the movement of withdrawal from the faith. And so apostasy does not imply a special kind of unbelief, but an aggravating circumstance of unbelief, according to II Pet. 2. 21: *It had been better for them not to know the truth* (Vulg.,—*the way of justice*), *than after they had known it, to turn back.*

ARTICLE 2. *Whether a Prince Forfeits His Dominion over His Subjects, on Account of Apostasy from the Faith, So That They No Longer Owe Him Allegiance?*

We proceed thus to the Second Article: It would seem that a prince does not so forfeit his dominion over his subjects, on account of apostasy from the faith, so that they no longer owe him allegiance.

Objection 1. For Ambrose says[1] that "the Emperor Julian, though an apostate, nevertheless had under him Christian soldiers, who when he said to them, 'Fall into line for the defence of the republic,' were bound to obey." Therefore subjects are not absolved from their allegiance to their prince on account of his apostasy.

Obj. 2. Further, An apostate from the faith is an unbeliever. Now we find that certain holy men served unbelieving masters; thus Joseph served Pharaoh, Daniel served Nabuchodonosor, and Mardochai served Assuerus. Therefore apostasy from the faith does not release subjects from allegiance to their sovereign.

Obj. 3. Further, Just as by apostasy from the faith, a man turns away from God, so does every sin. Consequently if, on account of apostasy from the faith, princes were to lose their right to command those of their subjects who are believers, they would equally lose it on account of other sins. But this seems to be false. Therefore we ought not to refuse allegiance to a sovereign on account of his apostatizing from the faith.

On the contrary, Gregory VII says:[2] "Holding to the institutions of our holy predecessors, we, by our apostolic authority, absolve from their oath those who through loyalty or through the sacred bond of an oath owe allegiance to excommunicated persons: and we absolutely forbid them to continue their allegiance to such persons, until these shall have made amends." Now apostates from the faith, like heretics, are excommunicated, according to the Decretal (Extra, *De Hæreticis,* cap. *Ad abolendam*).[3] Therefore princes should not be obeyed when they have apostatized from the faith.

I answer that, As stated above (Q. X, A. 10), unbelief, in itself, is not inconsistent with dominion, since dominion is a device of the law of nations which is a human law; but the distinction between believers and unbelievers is of Divine law, which does not annul human law. Nevertheless a man who sins by unbelief may be sentenced to the loss of his right of dominion, as also, sometimes, on account of other sins.

Now it does not pertain to the Church to punish unbelief in those who have never received

---

[1] Augustine, *Enarr. in Ps.,* CXXIV, 3 (PL 37, 1654).

[2] Cf. Gratian, *Decretum,* PT. II, causa XV, Q. 6 can. 4 (RF I, 756). See also Synodum Romanum, IV, 1078 (MA XX, 506; cf. 514).

[3] *Decretal Gregor.,* IX, BK. V, VII, chap. 9 (RF II, 780).

the faith, according to the saying of the Apostle (I Cor. 5. 12): *What have I to do to judge them that are without?* She can, however, pass sentence of punishment on the unbelief of those who have received the faith. And it is fitting that they should be punished by being deprived of the allegiance of their subjects, for this same allegiance might conduce to great corruption of the faith, since, as was stated above (A. 1., obj. 2), "a man that is an apostate . . . with a wicked heart deviseth evil, and . . . soweth discord," in order to sever others from the faith. Consequently, as soon as sentence of excommunication is passed on a man on account of apostasy from the faith, his subjects are *ipso facto* absolved from his authority and from the oath of allegiance by which they were bound to him.

Reply Obj. 1. At that time the Church was but recently instituted, and had not, as yet, the power of curbing earthly princes; and so she allowed the faithful to obey Julian the apostate in matters that were not contrary to the faith, in order to avoid incurring a yet greater danger.

Reply Obj. 2. As stated in the article, it is not a question of those unbelievers who have never received the faith.

Reply Obj. 3. Apostasy from the faith severs man from God altogether, as stated above (A. 1), which is not the case in any other sin.

QUESTION XIII
Of the sin of blasphemy, in general
(In Four Articles)

We must now consider the sin of blasphemy, which is opposed to the confession of faith; and (1) blasphemy in general, (2) that blasphemy which is called the sin against the Holy Ghost (Q. xiv).

Under the first head there are four points of inquiry: (1) Whether blasphemy is opposed to the confession of faith? (2) Whether blasphemy is always a mortal sin? (3) Whether blasphemy is the most grievous sin? (4) Whether blasphemy is in the damned?

Article 1. *Whether Blasphemy Is Opposed to the Confession of Faith?*

We proceed thus to the First Article: It would seem that blasphemy is not opposed to the confession of faith.

Objection 1. Because to blaspheme is to utter an affront or insult against the Creator. Now this pertains to ill-will against God rather

than to unbelief. Therefore blasphemy is not opposed to the confession of faith.

Obj. 2. Further, On Eph. 4. 31, *Let blasphemy . . . be put away from you,* a gloss says,[1] that which is committed "against God or the saints." But confession of faith seems to be only about those things which pertain to God, Who is the object of faith. Therefore blasphemy is not always opposed to the confession of faith.

Obj. 3. Further, According to some,[2] there are three kinds of blasphemy. The first of these is when something unfitting is affirmed of God; the second is when something fitting is denied of Him; and the third, when something proper to God is ascribed to a creature, so that it seems blasphemy is not only about God, but also about His creatures. Now the object of faith is God. Therefore blasphemy is not opposed to confession of faith.

On the contrary, The Apostle says (I Tim. 1. 12, 13): *I . . . before was a blasphemer and a persecutor,* and afterwards, *I did it ignorantly in my unbelief.* Hence it seems that blasphemy pertains to unbelief.

I answer that, The word blasphemy seems to denote the disparagement of some surpassing goodness, especially that of God. Now God, as Dionysius says (*Div. Nom.* i),[3] "is the very essence of true goodness." Hence whatever befits God, pertains to His goodness, and whatever does not befit Him, is far removed from the notion of perfect goodness which is His Essence. Consequently whoever either denies anything befitting God, or affirms anything unbefitting Him, disparages the Divine goodness. Now this may happen in two ways. In the first way it may happen merely in respect of the opinion in the intellect; in the second way this opinion is united to a certain detestation in the affections, even as, on the other hand, faith in God is perfected by love of Him. Accordingly this disparagement of the Divine goodness is either in the intellect alone, or in the affections also. If it is in thought only, it is blasphemy of the heart, while if it issues forth outwardly in speech it is blasphemy of the tongue. It is in this sense that blasphemy is opposed to confession of faith.

Reply Obj. 1. He that speaks against God, with the intention of reviling Him, disparages the Divine goodness, not only in respect of the vanity of his intellect, but also by reason of

---

[1] *Glossa* Lombardi (PL 192, 208); cf. *Glossa ordin.* (vi, 107E).
[2] Alexander of Hales, *Summa Theol.*, ii, n. 474 (QR iii, 464). [3] Sect. 5 (PG 3, 593).

the wickedness of his will, by which he detests and strives to hinder the honour due to God, and this is perfect blasphemy.

Reply Obj. 2. Even as God is praised in His saints, in so far as praise is given to the works which God does in His saints, so does blasphemy against the saints, redound, as a consequence, against God.

Reply Obj. 3. Properly speaking, the sin of blasphemy is not in this way divided into three species, since to affirm unfitting things, or to deny fitting things of God, differ merely as affirmation and negation. For this diversity does not cause distinct species of habits, since the falsehood of affirmations and negations is made known by the same knowledge, and it is the same ignorance which errs in either way, since "negatives are proved by affirmatives," according to the *Posterior Analytics.*[1] Again to ascribe to creatures things that are proper to God, seems to amount to the same as affirming something unfitting of Him, since whatever is proper to God is God Himself; and to ascribe to a creature, that which is proper to God, is to assert that God is the same as a creature.

ARTICLE 2. *Whether Blasphemy Is Always a Mortal Sin?*

We proceed thus to the Second Article: It would seem that blasphemy is not always a mortal sin.

Objection 1. Because a gloss on the words, *Now lay you also all away*, etc. (Coloss. 3. 8) says:[2] "After prohibiting greater crimes he forbids lesser sins"; and yet among the latter he includes blasphemy. Therefore blasphemy is comprised among the lesser, that is, venial, sins.

Obj. 2. Further, Every mortal sin is opposed to one of the precepts of the decalogue. But blasphemy does not seem to be contrary to any of them. Therefore blasphemy is not a mortal sin.

Obj. 3. Further, Sins committed without deliberation, are not mortal; hence first movements are not mortal sins, because they precede the deliberation of the reason, as was shown above (Part I-II, Q. LXXIV, AA. 3, 10). Now blasphemy sometimes occurs without deliberation of the reason. Therefore it is not always a mortal sin.

On the contrary, It is written (Lev. 24. 16): *He that blasphemeth the name of the Lord, dying let him die.* Now the punishment of death

is not inflicted except for a mortal sin. Therefore blasphemy is a mortal sin.

I answer that, As stated above (Part I-II, Q. LXXII, A. 5), a mortal sin is one by which a man is severed from the first principle of spiritual life, which principle is the love of God. Therefore whatever things are contrary to charity are mortal sins in respect of their genus. Now blasphemy, as to its genus, is opposed to Divine charity, because, as stated above (A. 1), it disparages the Divine goodness, which is the object of charity. Consequently blasphemy is a mortal sin, by reason of its genus.

Reply Obj. 1. This gloss is not to be understood as meaning that all the sins which follow are mortal, but that although all those mentioned previously are more grievous sins, some of those mentioned afterwards are less grievous; and yet among the latter some more grievous sins are included.

Reply Obj. 2. Since, as stated above (A. 1), blasphemy is contrary to the confession of faith, its prohibition is reduced to the prohibition of unbelief, expressed by the words: *I am the Lord thy God*, etc. (Exod. 20. 1). Or else, it is forbidden by the words: *Thou shalt not take the name of . . . God in vain (ibid. 7).* Because he who asserts something false about God, takes His name in vain even more than he who uses the name of God in confirmation of a falsehood.

Reply Obj. 3. There are two ways in which blasphemy may occur unawares and without deliberation. In the first way, by a man failing to direct his mind to the blasphemous nature of his words, and this may happen through his being moved suddenly by passion so as to break out into words suggested by his imagination, without heeding to the meaning of those words. This is a venial sin, and is not a blasphemy properly so called. In the second way, by turning his mind to the meaning of his words, and to their blasphemous nature. In this case he is not excused from mortal sin, even as neither is he who, in a sudden movement of anger, kills one who is sitting beside him.

ARTICLE 3. *Whether the Sin of Blasphemy Is the Greatest Sin?*

We proceed thus to the Third Article: It would seem that the sin of blasphemy is not the greatest sin.

Objection 1. For, according to Augustine (*Enchirid.* xii),[3] "a thing is said to be evil be-

---

[1] Aristotle, I, 25 (86^{b}28).
[2] *Glossa* Lombardi (PL192, 281); cf. *Glossa ordin.* (VI, 107E); cf. Ambrosiaster, *In Coloss.* 3.8 (PL 17, 462).
[3] PL 40, 237; *De Mor. Eccl.*, II, 3 (PL 32, 1346).

cause it does harm." Now the sin of murder, since it destroys a man's life, does more harm than the sin of blasphemy, which can do no harm to God. Therefore the sin of murder is more grievous than that of blasphemy.

Obj. 2. Further, A perjurer calls upon God to witness to a falsehood, and thus seems to assert that God is false. But not every blasphemer goes so far as to say that God is false. Therefore perjury is a more grievous sin than blasphemy.

Obj. 3. Further, On Ps. 74. 6, *Lift not up your horn on high,* a gloss says: "To excuse oneself for sin is the greatest sin of all."[1] Therefore blasphemy is not the greatest sin.

On the contrary, On Isa. 18. 2, *To a terrible people,* etc. a gloss says: "In comparison with blasphemy, every sin is slight."[2]

I answer that, As stated above (A. 1), blasphemy is opposed to the confession of faith, so that it contains the gravity of unbelief. And the sin is aggravated if the will's detestation is added to it, and yet more, if it breaks out into words, even as love and confession add to the praise of faith. Therefore, since, as stated above (Q. X, A. 3), unbelief is the greatest of sins in respect of its genus, it follows that blasphemy also, is a very great sin, through belonging to the same genus as unbelief and being an aggravated form of that sin.

Reply Obj. 1. If we compare murder and blasphemy as regards the objects of those sins, it is clear that blasphemy, which is a sin committed directly against God, is more grave than murder, which is a sin against one's neighbour. On the other hand, if we compare them in respect of the harm wrought by them, murder is the graver sin, for murder does more harm to ones neighbour than blasphemy does to God. Since, however, the gravity of a sin depends on the intention of the perverse will, rather than on the effect of the deed, as was shown above (Part I-II, Q. LXXIII, A. 8), it follows that, as the blasphemer intends to do harm to God's honour, absolutely speaking he sins more grievously than the murderer. Nevertheless murder takes precedence, as to punishment, among sins committed against our neighbour.

Reply Obj. 2. A gloss on the words, *Let . . . blasphemy be put away from you* (Eph. 4. 31) says: "Blasphemy is worse than perjury."[3] The

reason is that the perjurer does not say or think something false about God, as the blasphemer does, but he calls God to witness to a falsehood, not that he thinks God to be a false witness, but in the hope, as it were, that God will not testify to the matter by some evident sign.

Reply Obj. 3. To excuse oneself for sin is a circumstance that aggravates every sin, even blasphemy itself. And it is called the most grievous sin, because it makes every sin more grievous.

ARTICLE 4. *Whether the Damned Blaspheme?*

We proceed thus to the Fourth Article: It seems that the damned do not blaspheme.

Objection 1. Because some wicked men are deterred from blaspheming now, on account of the fear of future punishment. But the damned are undergoing these punishments, so that they abhor them yet more. Therefore, much more are they restrained from blaspheming.

Obj. 2. Further, Since blasphemy is a most grievous sin, it is most demeritorious. Now in the life to come there is no state of meriting or demeriting. Therefore there will be no place for blasphemy.

Obj. 3. Further, It is written (Eccles. 11. 3) that *the tree, . . . in what place soever it shall fall, there shall it be:* from which it is clear that, after this life, man acquires neither merit nor sin which he did not already possess in this life. Now many will be damned who were not blasphemous in this life. Neither, therefore, will they blaspheme in the life to come.

On the contrary, It is written (Apoc. 16. 9): *The men were scorched with great heat, and they blasphemed the name of God, Who hath power over these plagues,* and a gloss on these words says[4] that "those who are in hell, though aware that they are deservedly punished, will nevertheless complain that God is so powerful as to torture them thus." Now this would be blasphemy in their present state, and consequently it will also be in their future state.

I answer that, As stated above (AA. 1, 3), detestation of the Divine goodness is necessary to the notion of blasphemy. Now those who are in hell retain their perverse will which is turned away from God's justice, since they love the things for which they are punished, would wish to use them if they could, and hate the punishments inflicted on them for those same sins. They regret indeed the sins which they have committed, not because they hate them, but because they are punished for them. According-

---

[1] *Glossa ordin.* (III, 193B); *Glossa* Lombardi (PL 191, 700); Cassiodorus, *Expos. in Psalt.*, super Ps. 74.4 (PL 70, 537).

[2] *Glossa ordin.* (IV, 38E).

[3] *Glossa ordin.* (VI, 95B); Augustine, *Contra Mendac.*, Chap. 19 (PL 40, 545).

[4] *Glossa ordin.* (VI, 266A).

ly this detestation of the Divine justice is, in them, the interior blasphemy of the heart. And it is credible that after the resurrection they will blaspheme God with the tongue, even as the saints will praise Him with their voices.

Reply Obj. 1. In the present life men are deterred from blasphemy through fear of punishment which they think they can escape. But in hell the damned have no hope of escape, so that, in despair, they are borne towards whatever their perverse will suggests to them.

Reply Obj. 2. Merit and demerit pertain to the state of a wayfarer, and so good is meritorious in them, while evil is demeritorious. In the blessed, on the other hand, good is not meritorious but is part of their reward of Happiness. And, in like manner, in the damned, evil is not demeritorious, but is part of the punishment of damnation.

Reply Obj. 3. Whoever dies in mortal sin bears with him a will that detests the Divine justice with regard to a certain thing, and in this respect there can be blasphemy in him.

QUESTION XIV

OF BLASPHEMY AGAINST THE HOLY GHOST

(*In Four Articles*)

WE must now consider in particular blasphemy against the Holy Ghost, under which head there are four points of inquiry: (1) Whether blasphemy or the sin against the Holy Ghost is the same as the sin committed through certain malice? (2) Of the species of this sin. (3) Whether it cannot be forgiven? (4) Whether it is possible to begin by sinning against the Holy Ghost before committing other sins?

ARTICLE 1. *Whether the Sin Against the Holy Ghost Is the Same as the Sin Committed Through Certain Malice?*

We proceed thus to the First Article: It would seem that the sin against the Holy Ghost is not the same as the sin committed through certain malice.

Objection 1. Because the sin against the Holy Ghost is the sin of blasphemy, according to Matt. 12. 32. But not every sin committed through certain malice is a sin of blasphemy, since many other kinds of sin may be committed through certain malice. Therefore the sin against the Holy Ghost is not the same as the sin committed through certain malice.

Obj. 2. Further, The sin committed through

certain malice is divided against sin committed through ignorance, and sin committed through weakness; but the sin against the Holy Ghost is divided against the sin against the Son of Man (Matt. 12. 32). Therefore the sin against the Holy Ghost is not the same as the sin committed through certain malice, since things whose opposites differ, are themselves different.

Obj. 3. Further, The sin against the Holy Ghost is itself a generic sin, having its own determinate species. But sin committed through certain malice is not a special kind of sin, but a condition or general circumstance of sin, which can affect any kind of sin at all. Therefore the sin against the Holy Ghost is not the same as the sin committed through certain malice.

On the contrary, The Master says (2 *Sent., d.* 43)[1] that to sin against the Holy Ghost is "to take pleasure in the malice of sin for its own sake." Now this is to sin through certain malice. Therefore it seems that the sin committed through certain malice is the same as the sin against the Holy Ghost.

I answer that, Three meanings have been given to the sin or blasphemy against the Holy Ghost. For the earlier doctors, namely Athanasius (*Super Matt.* 12. 32),[2] Hilary (*Can. xii in Matt.*),[3] Ambrose (*Super Luc.* 12. 10, *Whosoever speaketh a word,* etc.),[4] Jerome (*Super Matt.* 12),[5] and Chrysostom (*Hom.* xli *in Matt.*),[6] say that the sin against the Holy Ghost is literally to utter a blasphemy against the Holy Spirit, whether by Holy Spirit we understand the essential name applicable to the whole Trinity, each Person of which is a Spirit and is holy, or the personal name of one of the Persons of the Trinity. In the latter sense blasphemy against the Holy Ghost is distinct from blasphemy against the Son of Man (Matt. 12. 32), for Christ did certain things in respect of His human nature, by eating, drinking, and the like actions, while He did others in respect of His Godhead, by casting out devils, raising the dead, and the like, which things He did both by the power of His own Godhead and by the operation of the Holy Ghost, of Whom He was full, according to His human nature. Now the Jews began by speaking blasphemy against the Son of Man, when they said (Matt. 11. 19) that He was *a glutton, . . . a wine drinker,* and a *friend of publicans;* but afterwards they blasphemed against the Holy Ghost, when they ascribed to the prince of devils those works which Christ

[1] Chap. 1 (QR 1, 533).   [2] PG 27, 1386.
[3] PL 9, 980.   [4] PL 15, 1817.
[5] PL 26, 83.   [6] PG 57, 449.

did by the power of His own Divine Nature and by the operation of the Holy Ghost.

Augustine, however (*De Verb. Dom.*, Serm. lxxi),[1] says that blasphemy or the sin against the Holy Ghost, is final impenitence, when, namely, a man perseveres in mortal sin until death, and that it is not confined to utterance by word of mouth, but extends to words in thought and deed, not to one word only, but to many. Now this word, in this sense, is said to be uttered against the Holy Ghost, because it is contrary to the remission of sins, which is the work of the Holy Ghost, Who is the love both of the Father and of the Son. Nor did Our Lord say this to the Jews, as though they had sinned against the Holy Ghost, since they were not yet guilty of final impenitence, but He warned them, lest by similar utterances they should come to sin against the Holy Ghost; and it is in this sense that we are to understand Mark 3. 29, 30, where after Our Lord had said: *But he that shall blaspheme against the Holy Ghost*, etc. the Evangelist adds, *because they said: He hath an unclean spirit.*

But others understand it differently,[2] and say that the sin or blasphemy against the Holy Ghost, is a sin committed against that good which is appropriated to the Holy Ghost, because goodness is appropriated to the Holy Ghost, just as power is appropriated to the Father, and wisdom to the Son. Hence they say that when a man sins through weakness, it is a sin against the Father; that when he sins through ignorance, it is a sin against the Son; and that when he sins through certain malice, that is, through the very choosing of evil, as explained above (Part. I-II, Q. LXXVIII, AA. 1, 3), it is a sin against the Holy Ghost.

Now this may happen in two ways. First by reason of the very inclination of a vicious habit which we call malice, and in this way to sin through malice is not the same as to sin against the Holy Ghost. In another way it happens that, by reason of contempt, that which might have prevented the choosing of evil is rejected or removed; thus hope is removed by despair, and fear by presumption, and so on, as we shall explain further on (A. 2). Now all these things which prevent the choosing of sin are effects of the Holy Ghost in us, so that, in this sense, to sin through malice is to sin against the Holy Ghost.

Reply Obj. 1. Just as the confession of faith consists in a protestation not only of words but also of deeds, so blasphemy against the Holy Ghost can be uttered in word, thought and deed.

Reply Obj. 2. According to the third interpretation, blasphemy against the Holy Ghost is distinguished against blasphemy against the Son of Man, according as He is also the Son of God, that is, the *power of God and the wisdom of God* (I Cor. 1. 24). Therefore, in this sense, the sin against the Son of Man will be that which is committed through ignorance, or through weakness.

Reply Obj. 3. Sin committed through certain malice, in so far as it results from the inclination of a habit, is not a special sin, but a general condition of sin. But in so far as it results from a special contempt of an effect of the Holy Ghost in us, it has the character of a special sin. According to this interpretation the sin against the Holy Ghost is a special kind of sin, as also according to the first interpretation. But according to the second, it is not a species of sin, because final impenitence may be a circumstance of any kind of sin.

ARTICLE 2. *Whether It Is Fitting To Distinguish Six Kinds of Sin against the Holy Ghost?*

We proceed thus to the Second Article: It seems unfitting to distinguish six kinds of sin against the Holy Ghost, namely, despair, presumption, impenitence, obstinacy, resisting the known truth, envy of our brother's spiritual good, which are assigned by the Master (2 *Sent.*, d. 43).[3]

Objection 1. For to deny God's justice or mercy pertains to unbelief. Now, by despair, a man rejects God's mercy, and by presumption, His justice. Therefore each of these is a kind of unbelief rather than of the sin against the Holy Ghost.

Obj. 2. Further, Impenitence, it seems, looks to past sins, while obstinacy looks to future sins. Now past and future time do not diversify the species of virtues or vices, since the faith by which we believe that Christ was born, is the same as that by which those of old believed that He would be born. Therefore obstinacy and impenitence should not be reckoned as two species of the sin against the Holy Ghost.

Obj. 3. Further, *Grace and truth came by Jesus Christ* (John 1. 17). Therefore it seems that resistance of the known truth, and envy of a brother's spiritual good, pertain to blasphemy against the Son rather than against the Holy Ghost.

---

[1] Chap. 12 (PL 38, 445).

[2] Richard of St. Victor, *De Spir. Blasphemiae* (PL 196, 1187).

[3] Chap. 1 (QR 1, 536).

Obj. 4. Further, Bernard says (*De Dispens. et Præcept.* xi)[1] that "to refuse to obey is to resist the Holy Ghost." Moreover a gloss on Lev. 10. 16, says that a feigned repentance is a blasphemy against the Holy Ghost.[2] Again, schism also seems to be directly opposed to the Holy Ghost by Whom the Church is united together. Therefore it seems that the species of sins against the Holy Ghost are insufficiently enumerated.

On the contrary, Augustine (*De Fide ad Petrum* iii)[3] says that those who despair of pardon for their sins, or who without merits presume on God's mercy, sin against the Holy Ghost, and (*Enchirid.* lxxxiii)[4] that "he who dies in a state of obstinacy is guilty of the sin against the Holy Ghost," and (*De Verb. Dom.,* Serm. lxxi)[5] that "impenitence is a sin against the Holy Ghost," and (*De Serm. Dom. in Monte* xxii),[6] that "to resist fraternal goodness with the brands of envy is to sin against the Holy Ghost," and in his book *De unico Baptismo* (*De Bap. contra Donat.* vi, 35)[7] he says that "a man who spurns the truth, is either envious of his brethren to whom the truth is revealed, or ungrateful to God by Whose inspiration the Church is taught," and therefore, seemingly, sins against the Holy Ghost.

I answer that, The above species are fittingly assigned to the sin against the Holy Ghost taken in the third sense, because they are distinguished in respect of the removal or contempt of those things by which a man can be prevented from sinning through choice. These things are either on the part of God's judgment, or on the part of His gifts, or on the part of sin. For, by the consideration of the Divine judgment, where justice is accompanied with mercy, man is hindered from sinning through choice, both by hope, arising from the consideration of the mercy that pardons sins and rewards good deeds, which hope is removed by despair; and by fear, arising from the consideration of the Divine justice that punishes sins, which fear is removed by presumption, when, namely, a man presumes that he can obtain glory without merits or pardon without repentance.

God's gifts by which we are withdrawn from sin, are two: one is the acknowledgment of the truth, against which there is the resistance of the known truth, when, namely, a man resists the truth which he has acknowledged, in order to sin more freely; while the other is the assistance of inward grace, against which there is envy of a brother's spiritual good, when, namely, a man is envious not only of his brother's person, but also of the increase of Divine grace in the world.

On the part of sin, there are two things which may withdraw man from sin: one is the disorder and shamefulness of the act, the consideration of which usually arouses man to repentance for the sin he has committed; and against this there is impenitence, not as denoting permanence in sin until death, in which sense it was taken above (A. 1) (for thus it would not be a special sin, but a circumstance of sin), but as denoting the purpose of not repenting. The other thing is the smallness and brevity of the good which is sought in sin, according to Rom. 6. 21: *What fruit had you therefore then in those things, of which you are now ashamed?* The consideration of this usually prevents man's will from being hardened in sin; and this is removed by obstinacy, by which man hardens his purpose by clinging to sin. Of these two it is written (Jerem. 8. 6): *There is none that doth penance for his sin, saying: What have I done?* as regards the first; and, *They are all turned to their own course, as a horse rushing to the battle,* as regards the second.

Reply Obj 1. The sins of despair and presumption consist, not in disbelieving in God's justice and mercy, but in despising them.

Reply Obj. 2. Obstinacy and impenitence differ not only in respect of past and future time, but also in respect of certain formal aspects by reason of the diverse consideration of those things which may be considered in sin, as explained above.

Reply Obj. 3. Grace and truth were the work of Christ through the gifts of the Holy Ghost which He gave to men.

Reply Obj. 4. To refuse to obey belongs to obstinacy, while a feigned repentance belongs to impenitence, and schism to the envy of a brother's spiritual good, by which the members of the Church are united together.

ARTICLE 3. *Whether the Sin against the Holy Ghost Can Be Forgiven?*

We proceed thus to the Third Article: It would seem that the sin against the Holy Ghost can be forgiven.

Objection 1. For Augustine says (*De Verb.*

---

[1] PL 182, 876.
[2] *Glossa ordin.* (I, 232C)—Hesychius, *In Lev.* II, super 10.16 (PG 49, 456).
[3] Fulgentius, chap. 3 (PL 65, 690).
[4] PL 40, 272.
[5] Chap. 12, 13, 21 (PL 38, 455, 457, 464).
[6] PL 34, 1266.
[7] PL 43, 219.

Dom. Serm. lxxi):[1] "We should despair of no man, so long as Our Lord's patience brings him back to repentance." But if any sin cannot be forgiven, it would be possible to despair of some sinners. Therefore the sin against the Holy Ghost can be forgiven.

Obj. 2. Further, No sin is forgiven except through the soul being healed by God. But "no disease is incurable to an all-powerful physician," as a gloss says[2] on Ps. 102. 3, *Who healeth all thy diseases*. Therefore the sin against the Holy Ghost can be forgiven.

Obj 3. Further, Free choice is related to both good or evil. Now, so long as man is a wayfarer, he can fall away from any virtue, since even an angel fell from heaven, so that it is written (Job. 4. 18, 19): *In His angels He found wickedness: how much more shall they that dwell in houses of clay?* Therefore, in like manner, a man can return from any sin to the state of justice. Therefore the sin against the Holy Ghost can be forgiven.

On the contrary, It is written (Matt. 12. 31): *He that shall speak against the Holy Ghost, it shall not be forgiven him, neither in this world, nor in the world to come;* and Augustine says (*De verb. Dom.* i)[3] that "so great is the downfall of this sin that it cannot submit to the humiliation of asking for pardon."

I answer that, According to the various interpretations of the sin against the Holy Ghost, there are various ways in which it may be said that it cannot be forgiven. For if by the sin against the Holy Ghost we understand final impenitence, it is said to be unpardonable, since it is in no way pardoned, because the mortal sin in which a man perseveres until death will not be forgiven in the life to come, since it was not remitted by repentance in this life.

According to the other two interpretations, it is said to be unpardonable, not as though it is no way forgiven, but because, considered in itself, it deserves not to be pardoned, and this in two ways. First, as regards the punishment, since he that sins through ignorance or weakness, deserves less punishment, while he that sins through certain malice, can offer no excuse in alleviation of his punishment. Likewise those who blasphemed against the Son of Man before His Godhead was revealed, could have some excuse, on account of the weakness of the flesh which they perceived in Him, and hence,

they deserved less punishment; but those who blasphemed against His very Godhead, by ascribing to the devil the works of the Holy Ghost, had no excuse in diminution of their punishment. Therefore, according to Chrysostom's commentary (*Hom.* xlii *in Matt.*),[4] the Jews are said not to be forgiven this sin, neither in this world nor in the world to come, because they were punished for it, both in the present life, through the Romans, and in the life to come, in the pains of hell. Thus also Athanasius[5] adduces the example of their forefathers who, first of all, wrangled with Moses on account of the shortage of water and bread; and this the Lord bore with patience, because they were to be excused on account of the weakness of the flesh. But afterwards they sinned more grievously, when, by ascribing to an idol the favours bestowed by God Who had brought them out of Egypt, they blasphemed, so to speak, against the Holy Ghost, saying (Exod. 32. 4): *These are thy gods, O Israel, that have brought thee out of the land of Egypt*. Therefore the Lord both inflicted temporal punishment on them, since *there were slain on that day about three and twenty thousand men* (*ibid.* 28), and threatened them with punishment in the life to come, saying, (*ibid.* 34): *I, in the day of revenge, will visit this sin . . . of theirs*.

Secondly, this may be understood to refer to the guilt. Thus a disease is said to be incurable in respect of the nature of the disease, which removes whatever might be a means of cure, as when it takes away the power of nature, or causes loathing for food and medicine, although God is able to cure such a disease. So too, the sin against the Holy Ghost is said to be unpardonable, by reason of its nature, in so far as it removes those things which are a means towards the pardon of sins. This does not, however, close the way of forgiveness and healing to an all-powerful and merciful God, Who, sometimes, by a miracle, so to speak, restores spiritual health to such men.

Reply Obj. 1. We should despair of no man in this life, considering God's omnipotence and mercy. But if we consider the circumstances of sin, some are called (Eph. 2. 2) *children of despair*.[6]

Reply Obj. 2. This argument considers the question on the part of God's omnipotence, not on that of the circumstances of sin.

[1] Chap. 13 (PL 38, 457).
[2] *Glossa* Lombardi (PL 191, 920); Augustine, *Enarr. in Ps.* 102.3 (PL 37, 1319).
[3] Chap. 22 (PL 34, 1266).

[4] PG 57, 449.
[5] *Epist.*, IV, *Ad Serapionem* (PG 26, 662).
[6] *Filios diffidentiae*, which the Douay version renders *children of unbelief*.

Reply Obj. 3. In this life free choice does indeed ever remain subject to change. Yet sometimes it rejects that by which, so far as it is concerned, it can be turned to good. Hence considered in itself this sin is unpardonable, although God can pardon it.

ARTICLE 4. Whether a Man Can Sin First of All against the Holy Ghost?

We proceed thus to the Fourth Article: It seems that a man cannot sin first of all against the Holy Ghost, without having previously committed other sins.

Objection 1. For the natural order requires that one should be moved to perfection from imperfection. This is evident as regards good things, according to Prov. 4. 18: The path of the just, as a shining light, goeth forwards and increases even to perfect day. Now, in evil things, the perfect is the greatest evil, as the Philosopher states.[1] Since then the sin against the Holy Ghost is the most grievous sin, it seems that man comes to commit this sin through committing lesser sins.

Obj. 2. Further, To sin against the Holy Ghost is to sin through certain malice, or through choice. Now man cannot do this until he has sinned many times; for the Philosopher says[2] that although a man is able to do unjust deeds, yet he cannot all at once do them as an unjust man does, that is, from choice. Therefore it seems that the sin against the Holy Ghost cannot be committed except after other sins.

Obj. 3. Further, Repentance and impenitence are about the same object. But there is no repentance, except about past sins. Therefore the same applies to impenitence which is a species of the sin against the Holy Ghost. Therefore the sin against the Holy Ghost presupposes other sins.

On the contrary, It is easy in the eyes of God on a sudden to make a poor man rich (Ecclus. 11. 23). Therefore, conversely, it is possible for a man, according to the malice of the devil who tempts him, to be led to commit the most grievous of sins which is that against the Holy Ghost.

I answer that, As stated above (A. 1), in one way, to sin against the Holy Ghost is to sin through certain malice. Now one may sin through certain malice in two ways, as stated in the same place: first, through the inclination of a habit; but this is not, properly speaking, to sin against the Holy Ghost, nor does a man come

to commit this sin all at once, in as much as sinful acts must precede so as to cause the habit that induces to sin. Secondly, one may sin through certain malice, by contemptuously rejecting the things by which a man is withdrawn from sin. This is, properly speaking, to sin against the Holy Ghost, as stated above (A. 1); and this also, for the most part, presupposes other sins, for it is written (Prov. 18. 3) that the wicked man, when he is come into the depth of sins, contemneth.

Nevertheless it is possible for a man, in his first sinful act, to sin against the Holy Ghost by contempt, both on account of his free choice, and on account of the many previous dispositions, or again, through being vehemently moved to evil, while but feebly attached to good. Hence never or scarcely ever does it happen that the perfect sin all at once against the Holy Ghost. Hence Origen says (Peri Archon, i, 3):[3] "I do not think that anyone who stands on the highest step of perfection, can fail or fall suddenly; this can only happen by degrees and bit by bit."

The same applies, if the sin against the Holy Ghost be taken literally for blasphemy against the Holy Ghost. For such blasphemy as Our Lord speaks of always proceeds from contemptuous malice.

If, however, with Augustine we understand the sin against the Holy Ghost to denote final impenitence, it does not regard the question in point, because this sin against the Holy Ghost requires persistence in sin until the end of life.

Reply Obj. 1. Movement both in good and in evil is made, for the most part, from imperfect to perfect, according as man progresses in good or evil. And yet in both cases, one man can begin from a greater (good or evil) than another man does. Consequently, that from which a man begins can be perfect in good or evil according to its genus, although it may be imperfect as regards the series of good or evil actions by which a man progresses in good or evil.

Reply Obj. 2. This argument considers the sin which is committed through certain malice, when it proceeds from the inclination of a habit.

Reply Obj. 3. If by impenitence we understand with Augustine persistence in sin until the end, it is clear that it presupposes sin, just as repentance does. If, however, we take it for habitual impenitence, in which sense it is a sin against the Holy Ghost, it is evident that it can precede sin, for it is possible for a man who has never sinned to have the purpose either of re-

---

[1] Metaphysics, v, 16 (1021^{b}25).
[2] Ethics, v, 6 (1134^{a}17).
[3] Chap. 3 (PG 11, 155).

penting or of not repenting, if he should happen to sin.

QUESTION XV
OF THE VICES OPPOSED TO KNOWLEDGE AND UNDERSTANDING
(*In Three Articles*)

WE must now consider the vices opposed to knowledge and understanding. Since, however, we have treated of ignorance which is opposed to knowledge, when we were discussing the causes of sins (Part I-II, Q. LXXVI), we must now inquire about blindness of mind and dulness of sense, which are opposed to the gift of understanding; and under this head there are three points of inquiry: (1) Whether blindness of mind is a sin? (2) Whether dulness of sense is a sin distinct from blindness of mind? (3) Whether these vices arise from sins of the flesh?

ARTICLE 1. *Whether Blindness of Mind Is a Sin?*

We proceed thus to the First Article: It would seem that blindness of mind is not a sin.

Objection 1. Because, it seems that that which excuses from sin is not itself a sin. Now blindness of mind excuses from sin; for it is written (John 9. 41): *If you were blind, you should not have sin.* Therefore blindness of mind is not a sin.

Obj. 2. Further, Punishment differs from guilt. But blindness of mind is a punishment, as appears from Isa. 6. 10, *Blind the heart of this people,* for, since it is an evil, it could not be from God, were it not a punishment. Therefore blindness of mind is not a sin.

Obj. 3. Further, Every sin is voluntary, according to Augustine (*De Vera Relig.* xiv).[1] Now blindness of mind is not voluntary, since, as Augustine says,[2] "all love to know the resplendent truth," and as we read in Eccles. 11. 7, *the light is sweet and it is delightful for the eyes to see the sun.* Therefore blindness of mind is not a sin.

On the contrary, Gregory (*Moral.* xxxi, 45)[3] puts blindness of mind among the vices arising from lust.

I answer that, Just as bodily blindness is the privation of the principle of bodily sight, so blindness of mind is the privation of the principle of mental or intellectual sight. Now this has a threefold principle. One is the light of nat-

ural reason, which light, since it pertains to the species of the rational soul, is never forfeit from the soul, and yet, at times, it is prevented from exercising its proper act, through being hindered by the lower powers, which the human intellect needs in order to understand; for instance in the case of imbeciles and madmen, as stated in the First Part (Q. LXXXIV, AA. 7, 8).

Another principle of intellectual sight is a certain habitual light superadded to the natural light of reason, which light is sometimes forfeit from the soul. This privation is blindness, and is a punishment, in so far as the privation of the light of grace is a punishment. Hence it is written concerning some (Wisd. 2. 21): *Their own malice blinded them.*

A third principle of intellectual sight is an intelligible principle, through which a man understands other things, to which principle a man may attend or not attend. That he does not attend to it happens in two ways. Sometimes it is due to the fact that a man's will is deliberately turned away from the consideration of that principle, according to Ps. 35. 5, *He would not understand, that he might do well.* Sometimes it is due to the mind being more busy about things which it loves more, so as to be hindered thus from considering this principle, according to Ps. 57. 9, *Fire,* that is of concupiscence, *hath fallen on them and they shall not see the sun.* In either of these ways blindness of mind is a sin.

Reply Obj. 1. The blindness that excuses from sin is that which arises from the natural defect of one who cannot see.

Reply Obj. 2. This argument considers the second kind of blindness which is a punishment.

Reply Obj. 3. To understand the truth is, in itself, something loved by all; and yet, accidentally it may be hateful to someone, in so far as a man is hindered thereby from having what he loves yet more.

ARTICLE 2. *Whether Dulness of Sense Is a Sin Distinct from Blindness of Mind?*

We proceed thus to the Second Article: It seems that dulness of sense is not a distinct sin from blindness of the mind.

Objection 1. Because one thing has one contrary. Now dulness is opposed to the gift of understanding, according to Gregory (*Moral.* ii, 49);[4] and so is blindness of mind, since understanding denotes a principle of sight. Therefore dulness of sense is the same as blindness of mind.

---

[1] PL 34, 133.
[2] *Confessions,* X, 33 (PL 32, 794).   [3] PL 76, 621.

[4] PL 75, 592.

Obj. 2. Further, Gregory (*Moral.* xxxi, 45)[1] in speaking of dulness describes it as "dulness of sense in respect of understanding." Now dulness of sense in respect of understanding seems to be the same as a defect in understanding, which pertains to blindness of mind. Therefore dulness of sense is the same as blindness of mind.

Obj. 3. Further, If they differ at all, it seems to be chiefly in the fact that blindness of mind is voluntary, as stated above (A. 1), while dulness of sense is a natural defect. But a natural defect is not a sin, so that, accordingly, dulness of sense would not be a sin, which is contrary to what Gregory says (*loc. cit.*), where he reckons it among the sins arising from gluttony.

On the contrary, Different causes produce different effects. Now Gregory says (*Moral.* xxxi, *ibid.*) that "dulness of sense arises from gluttony, and that blindness of mind arises from lust." Now these others are different vices. Therefore those are different vices also.

I answer that, Dull is opposed to sharp: and a thing is said to be sharp because it can pierce, so that a thing is called dull through being obtuse and unable to pierce. Now a bodily sense, by a kind of likeness, is said to pierce the medium, in so far as it perceives its object from a distance, or is able by penetration as it were to perceive the smallest details or the inmost parts of a thing. Hence in corporeal things the senses are said to be acute when they can perceive a sensible object from afar, by sight, hearing, or scent, while on the other hand they are said to be dull, through being unable to perceive, except sensible objects that are near at hand, or of great power.

Now, by way of likeness to bodily sense, we speak of sense in connection with the intellect; and this latter sense is in respect of certain primals and extremes, as stated in the *Ethics*,[2] even as the senses are cognizant of sensible objects as of certain principles of knowledge. Now this sense which is connected with understanding, does not perceive its object through a medium of corporeal distance, but through certain other media, as, for instance, when it perceives a thing's essence through a property and a cause through its effect. Consequently a man is said to have an acute sense in connection with his understanding, if, as soon as he apprehends a property or effect of a thing, he understands the nature of the thing itself, and if he attains to the consideration of its slightest details. But

a man is said to have a dull sense in connection with his understanding, if he cannot arrive at knowing the truth about a thing, without many explanations; in which case, moreover, he is unable to reach to a perfect consideration of everything pertaining to the nature of that thing.

Accordingly dulness of sense in connection with understanding denotes a certain weakness of the mind as to the consideration of spiritual goods, while blindness of mind implies the complete privation of the knowledge of such things. Both are opposed to the gift of understanding, by which a man knows spiritual goods by apprehending them, and has a subtle penetration of their inmost nature. This dulness has the character of sin, just as blindness of mind has, that is, in so far as it is voluntary, as evidenced in one who, owing to his affection for carnal things, dislikes or neglects the careful consideration of spiritual things.

This suffices for the *Replies to the Objections.*

ARTICLE 3. *Whether Blindness of Mind and Dulness of Sense Arise From Sins of the Flesh?*

We proceed thus to the Third Article: It would seem that blindness of mind and dulness of sense do not arise from sins of the flesh.

Objection 1. For Augustine (*Retract.* i, 4)[3] retracts what he had said in his *Soliloquies* (i, 1),[4] "God Who didst wish none but the clean to know the truth," and says that one might reply that "many, even those who are unclean, know many truths." Now men become unclean chiefly by sins of the flesh. Therefore blindness of mind and dulness of sense are not caused by sins of the flesh.

Obj. 2. Further, Blindness of mind and dulness of sense are defects in connection with the intellective part of the soul, but carnal sins pertain to the corruption of the flesh. But the flesh does not act on the soul, but rather the reverse. Therefore the sins of the flesh do not cause blindness of mind and dulness of sense.

Obj. 3. Further, All things are more acted upon by what is near them than to what is remote. Now spiritual vices are nearer the mind than carnal vices are. Therefore blindness of mind and dulness of sense are caused by spiritual rather than by carnal vices.

On the contrary, Gregory says (*Moral.* xxxi, 45)[5] that "dulness of sense arises from gluttony, and blindness of mind from lust."

I answer that, The perfect intellectual operation in man consists in an abstraction from sen-

---

[1] PL 76, 621.
[2] Aristotle, VI, 8 (1142ᵃ26).

[3] PL 32, 589.   [4] PL 32, 870.
[5] PL 76, 621.

sible phantasms, and therefore the more a man's intellect is freed from those phantasms, the more thoroughly will it be able to consider things intelligible, and to set in order all things sensible. Thus Anaxagoras stated that the intellect requires to be detached in order to command, and that the agent must have power over matter, in order to be able to move it as the Philosopher relates.[1] Now it is evident that pleasure fixes a man's attention on that which he takes pleasure in; and so the Philosopher says[2] that we all do best that which we take pleasure in doing, while as to other things, we do them either not at all, or in a faint-hearted fashion.

Now carnal vices, namely gluttony and lust, are concerned with pleasures of touch in matters of food and sex; and these are the most impetuous of all pleasures of the body. For this reason these vices cause man's attention to be very firmly fixed on corporeal things, so that in consequence man's operation in regard to intelligible things is weakened, more, however, by lust than by gluttony, in so far as sexual pleasures are more vehement than those of the table. Therefore lust gives rise to blindness of mind, which excludes almost entirely the knowledge of spiritual things, while dulness of sense arises from gluttony, which makes a man weak in regard to the same intelligible things. On the other hand, the contrary virtues, namely abstinence and chastity, dispose man very much to the perfection of intellectual operation. Hence it is written (Dan. 1. 17) that *to these children on account of their abstinence and continency, God gave knowledge and understanding in every book, and wisdom.*

Reply Obj. 1. Although some who are the slaves of carnal vices are at times capable of subtle considerations about intelligible things, on account of the perfection of their natural genius, or of some superadded habit, nevertheless, on account of the pleasures of the body, it must happen that their attention is frequently withdrawn from this subtle contemplation. Therefore the unclean can know some truths, but their uncleanness is a clog on their knowledge.

Reply Obj. 2. The flesh acts on the intellectual part not by altering it, but by impeding its operation in the above mentioned manner.

Reply Obj. 3. It is owing to the fact that the carnal vices are further removed from the mind, that they distract the mind's attention to more remote things, so that they hinder the mind's contemplation all the more.

QUESTION XVI
OF THE PRECEPTS OF FAITH,
KNOWLEDGE, AND UNDERSTANDING
(In Two Articles)

WE must now consider the precepts pertaining to the above, and under this head there are two points of inquiry: (1) The precepts concerning faith: (2) The precepts concerning the gifts of knowledge and understanding.

ARTICLE 1. *Whether in the Old Law There Should Have Been Given Precepts of Faith?*

We proceed thus to the First Article: It seems that, in the Old Law there should have been given precepts of faith.

Objection 1. Because a precept is about something due and necessary. Now it is most necessary for man that he should believe, according to Heb. 11. 6, *Without faith it is impossible to please God.* Therefore there was very great need for precepts of faith to be given.

Obj. 2. Further, The New Testament is contained in the Old, as the reality in the figure, as stated above (Part I-II, Q. CVII, A. 3). Now the New Testament contains explicit precepts of faith, for instance John 14. 1: *You believe in God; believe also in Me.* Therefore it seems that some precepts of faith ought to have been given in the Old Law also.

Obj. 3. Further, To prescribe the act of a virtue comes to the same as to forbid the opposite vices. Now the Old Law contained many precepts forbidding unbelief: thus (Exod. 20. 3): *Thou shalt not have strange gods before Me,* and (Deut. 13. 1-3) they were forbidden to hear the words of the prophet or dreamer who might wish to turn them away from their faith in God. Therefore precepts of faith should have been given in the Old Law also.

Obj. 4. Further, Confession is an act of faith, as stated above (Q. III, A. 1). Now the Old Law contained precepts about the confession and the promulgation of faith: for they were commanded (Exod. 12. 27) that, when their children should ask them, they should tell them the meaning of the paschal observance, and (Deut. 13. 9) they were commanded to slay anyone who disseminated doctrine contrary to faith. Therefore the Old Law should have contained precepts of faith.

Obj. 5. Further, All the books of the Old Testament are contained in the Old Law; therefore

---

[1] *Physics,* VIII, 5 (256ᵇ24).
[2] *Ethics,* X, 5 (1175ᵃ30).

Our Lord said (John 15. 25) that it was written in the Law: *They have hated Me without cause*, although this is found written in Ps. 34. and 68. Now it is written (Ecclus. 2. 8): *Ye that fear the Lord, believe Him*. Therefore the Old Law should have contained precepts of faith.

On the contrary, The Apostle (Rom. 3. 27) calls the Old Law the *law of works* which he contrasts with the *law of faith*. Therefore the Old Law ought not have contained precepts of faith.

I answer that, A master does not impose laws on others than his subjects, and therefore the precepts of a law presuppose that everyone who receives the law is subject to the giver of the law. Now the primary subjection of man to God is by faith, according to Heb. 11. 6: *He that cometh to God, must believe that He is*. Hence faith is presupposed to the precepts of the Law. For this reason (Exod. 20. 2) that which is of faith is set down before the legal precepts, in the words, *I am the Lord thy God, Who brought thee out of the land of Egypt,* and, likewise (Deut. 6. 4), the words, *Hear, O Israel, the Lord thy* (Vulg.,—*our*) *God is one,* precede the recording of the precepts.

Since, however, faith contains many things subordinate to the faith by which we believe that God is, which is the first and chief of all articles of faith, as stated above (Q. 1, A. 7), it follows that, if we presuppose faith in God, by which man's mind is subjected to Him, it is possible for precepts to be given about other articles of faith. Thus Augustine expounding the words: *This is My commandment* (John 15. 12) says (*Tract. lxxxiii in Joann.*)[1] that "we have received many precepts of faith." In the Old Law, however, the secret things of faith were not to be set before the people, and thus, presupposing their faith in one God, no other precepts of faith were given in the Old Law.

Reply Obj. 1. Faith is necessary as being the principle of spiritual life, and therefore it is presupposed before the receiving of the Law.

Reply Obj. 2. Even then Our Lord both presupposed something of faith, namely belief in one God, when He said: *You believe in God*, and commanded something, namely, belief in the Incarnation, by which one Person is God and man. This explanation of faith pertains to the faith of the New Testament. And therefore He added: *Believe also in Me*.

Reply Obj. 3. The prohibitive precepts con-

[1] PL 35, 1846.

cern sins, which corrupt virtue. Now virtue is corrupted by any particular defect, as stated above (Q. X, A. 5). Therefore faith in one God being presupposed, prohibitive precepts had to be given in the Old Law, so that men might be warned of those particular defects by which their faith might be corrupted.

Reply Obj. 4. Confession of faith and its teaching also presuppose man's submission to God by faith, so that the Old Law could contain precepts relating to the confession and teaching of faith, rather than to faith itself.

Reply Obj. 5. In this passage, again, that faith is presupposed by which we believe that God is; hence it begins, *Ye that fear the Lord,* which is not possible without faith. The words which follow,—*believe Him,* must be referred to certain special articles of faith, chiefly to those things which God promises to them that obey Him, and so the passage concludes,—*and your reward shall not be made void.*

ARTICLE 2. *Whether the Precepts Referring to Knowledge and Understanding Were Fittingly Set Down in the Old Law?*

We proceed thus to the Second Article: It would seem that the precepts referring to knowledge and understanding were unfittingly set down in the Old Law.

Objection 1. For knowledge and understanding pertain to cognition. Now cognition precedes and directs action. Therefore the precepts referring to knowledge and understanding should precede the precepts of the Law referring to action. Since, then, the first precepts of the Law are those of the decalogue, it seems that precepts of knowledge and understanding should have been given a place among the precepts of the decalogue.

Obj. 2. Further, Learning precedes teaching, for a man must learn from another before he teaches another. Now the Old Law contains precepts about teaching,—both affirmative precepts, as, for example (Deut. 4. 9), *Thou shalt teach them to thy sons, and to thy grandsons,—* and prohibitive precepts, as, for instance (Deut. 4. 2), *You shall not add to the word that I speak to you, neither shall you take away from it.* Therefore it seems that man ought to have been given also some precepts directing him to learn.

Obj. 3. Further, Knowledge and understanding seem more necessary to a priest than to a king, and so it is written (Malach. 2. 7): *The lips of the priest shall keep knowledge, and they shall seek the law at his mouth,* and (Osee 4. 6): *Because thou hast rejected knowledge, I will reject thee, that thou shalt not do the office of priesthood to Me.* Now the king is commanded to learn knowledge of the Law (Deut. 17. 18, 19). Much more, therefore, should the Law have commanded the priests to learn the Law.

Obj. 4. Further, It is not possible while asleep to meditate on things pertaining to knowledge and understanding; and also it is hindered by extraneous occupations. Therefore it is unfittingly commanded (Deut. 6. 7): *Thou shalt meditate upon them sitting in thy house, and walking on thy journey, sleeping and rising.* Therefore the precepts relating to knowledge and understanding are unfittingly set down in the Law.

On the contrary, It is written (Deut. 4. 6): *That, hearing all these precepts, they may say, Behold a wise and understanding people.*

I answer that, Three things may be considered in relation to knowledge and understanding: first, their reception; secondly, their use; and thirdly, their preservation. Now the reception of knowledge or understanding is by means of teaching and learning, and both are prescribed in the Law. For it is written (Deut. 6. 6): *These words which I command thee . . ., shall be in thy heart.* This pertains to learning, since it is the duty of a disciple to apply his mind to what is said, while the words that follow,—*and thou shalt tell them to thy children,* refer to teaching.

The use of knowledge and understanding is the meditation on those things which one knows or understands. In reference to this, the text goes on,—*thou shalt meditate upon them sitting in thy house,* etc.

Their preservation is effected by the memory, and, as regards this, the text continues,—*and thou shalt bind them as a sign on thy hand, and they shall be and shall move between thy eyes. And thou shalt write them in the entry, and on the doors of thy house.* Thus the continual remembrance of God's commandments is signified, since it is impossible for us to forget those things which are continually attracting the notice of our senses, whether by touch, as those things we hold in our hands, or by sight, as those things which are ever before our eyes, or to which we are continually returning, for instance, to the house door. Moreover it is clearly stated (Deut. 4. 9): *Forget not the words that thy eyes have seen and let them not go out of thy heart all the days of thy life.* We read of these things also being commanded more notably in the New Testament, both in the teaching of the Gospel and in that of the apostles.

Reply Obj. 1. According to Deut. 4. 6, *this is your wisdom and understanding in the sight of the nations.* By this we are given to understand that the wisdom and understanding of those who believe in God consist in the precepts of the Law. Therefore the precepts of the Law had to be given first, and afterwards men had to be led to know and understand them, and so it was not fitting that the precepts referred to above should be placed among the precepts of the decalogue which take the first place.

Reply Obj. 2. There are also in the Law precepts relating to learning, as stated above. Nevertheless teaching was commanded more expressly than learning, because it concerned the learned, who were not under any other authority, but were immediately under the law, and to them the precepts of the Law were given. On the other hand learning concerned the people of lower degree, and these the precepts of the Law have to reach through the learned.

Reply Obj. 3. Knowledge of the Law is so closely bound up with the priestly office that being charged with the office implies being charged to know the Law. Hence there was no need for special precepts to be given about the training of the priests. On the other hand, the doctrine of God's law is not so bound up with the kingly office, because a king is placed over his people in temporal matters. Hence it is especially commanded that the king should be instructed by the priests about things pertaining to the law of God.

Reply Obj. 4. That precept of the Law does not mean that man should meditate on God's law by sleeping, but during sleep, that is, that he should meditate on the law of God when he is preparing to sleep, because this leads to his having better phantasms while asleep, in so far as our movements pass from the state of vigil to the state of sleep, as the Philosopher explains.[1] In like manner we are commanded to meditate on the Law in every action of ours, not that we are bound to be always actually thinking about the Law, but that we should regulate all our actions according to it.

QUESTION XVII
OF HOPE
(*In Eight Articles*)

AFTER treating of faith, we must consider hope, and (1) hope itself; (2) the gift of fear (Q.

[1] *Ethics,* I, 13 (1102ᵇ9).

XIX); (3) the contrary vices (Q. XX); (4) the corresponding precepts (Q. XXII). The first of these points gives rise to a twofold consideration (1) Hope, considered in itself: (2) Its subject (Q. XVIII).

Under the first head there are eight points of inquiry: (1) Whether hope is a virtue? (2) Whether its object is eternal happiness? (3) Whether, by virtue of hope, one man may hope for another's happiness? (4) Whether a man may lawfully hope in man? (5) Whether hope is a theological virtue? (6) Of its distinction from the other theological virtues: (7) Of its relation to faith: (8) Of its relation to charity.

ARTICLE 1. *Whether Hope Is a Virtue?*

We proceed thus to the First Article: It seems that hope is not a virtue.

Objection 1. For "no man makes ill use of a virtue," as Augustine states (*De Lib. Arb.* ii).[1] But one may make ill use of hope, since the passion of hope, like the other passions, is subject to a mean and extremes. Therefore hope is not a virtue.

Obj. 2. Further, No virtue results from merits, since "God works virtue in us without us," as Augustine states (*De Grat. et Lib. Arb.* xvii).[2] But hope is caused by grace and merits, according to the Master (3 *Sent., d.* 26).[3] Therefore hope is not a virtue.

Obj. 3. Further, "Virtue is the disposition of a perfect thing."[4] But hope is the disposition of an imperfect thing, of one, namely, that lacks what it hopes to have. Therefore hope is not a virtue.

On the contrary, Gregory says (*Moral.* i, 27)[5] that the three daughters of Job signify these three virtues, faith, hope and charity. Therefore hope is a virtue.

I answer that, According to the Philosopher,[6] "virtue in each thing is that which makes its subject good, and its work good likewise." Consequently wherever we find a good human act, it must correspond to some human virtue. Now in all things measured and ruled, the good is that which attains its proper rule; thus we say that a coat is good if it neither exceeds nor falls short of its proper measurement. But, as we stated above (Part I-II, Q. LXXI, A. 6), human acts have a twofold measure; one is proximate and homogeneous, namely, the rea-

son, while the other is supreme and excelling, namely, God. Therefore every human act is good which attains reason or God Himself. Now the act of hope, of which we speak now, attains God. For, as we have already stated (Part I-II, Q. XL, A. 1), when we were treating of the passion of hope, the object of hope is a future good, difficult but possible to obtain. Now a thing is possible to us in two ways: first, by ourselves, secondly, by means of others, as stated in the *Ethics.*[7] Therefore, in so far as we hope for anything as being possible to us by means of the Divine assistance, our hope attains God Himself, on Whose help it leans. It is therefore evident that hope is a virtue, since it causes a human act to be good and to attain its due rule.

Reply Obj. 1. In the passions, the mean of virtue depends on right reason being attained, and in this also consists the notion of virtue. Therefore in hope too, the good of virtue depends on a man's attaining, by hoping, the due rule, namely, God. Consequently man cannot make ill use of hope which attains God, as neither can he make ill use of moral virtue which attains the reason, because to attain thus is to make good use of virtue. Nevertheless, the hope of which we speak now, is not a passion but a habit of the mind, as we shall show further on (Q. XVIII, A. 1).

Reply Obj. 2. Hope is said to arise from merits, as regards the thing hoped for, in so far as we hope to obtain happiness by means of grace and merits; or as regards the act of formed hope. The habit itself of hope, by which we hope to obtain Happiness, does not flow from our merits, but from grace alone.

Reply Obj. 3. He who hopes is indeed imperfect in relation to that which he hopes to obtain, but has not as yet; yet he is perfect in so far as he already attains his proper rule, namely God, on Whose help he leans.

ARTICLE 2. *Whether Eternal Happiness Is the Proper Object of Hope?*

We proceed thus to the Second Article: It seems that eternal happiness is not the proper object of hope.

Objection 1. For a man does not hope for that which surpasses every movement of his soul, since hope itself is a movement of the soul. Now eternal happiness surpasses every movement of the human soul, for the Apostle says (I Cor. 2. 9) that it hath not *entered into the heart of man.* Therefore happiness is not the proper object of hope.

---

[1] Chap. 18, 19 (PL 32, 1267, 1268).
[2] PL 44, 901; cf. Also Peter Lombard, *Sent.,* II, d. 26, chap. 5 (QR I, 446).
[3] Chap. 1 (QR I, 670).
[4] Aristotle, *Physics,* VII, 3 (246ᵃ13).
[5] PL 75, 544.   [6] *Ethics,* II, 6 (1106ᵃ15).
[7] *Ibid.,* III, 3 (1112ᵇ27).

Obj. 2. Further, Prayer is an expression of hope, for it is written (Ps. 36. 5): *Commit thy way to the Lord, and trust in Him, and He will do it.* Now it is lawful for man to pray God not only for eternal happiness, but also for the goods, both temporal and spiritual, of the present life, and, as evidenced by the Lord's prayer, to be delivered from evils which will no longer be in eternal happiness. Therefore eternal happiness is not the proper object of hope.

Obj. 3. Further, The object of hope is something difficult. Now many things besides eternal happiness are difficult to man. Therefore eternal happiness is not the proper object of hope.

On the contrary, The Apostle says (Heb. 6. 19) that we have hope *which entereth in,* that is, maketh us to enter, . . . *within the veil,* that is, into the happiness of heaven, according to the interpretation of a gloss on these words.[1] Therefore the object of hope is eternal happiness.

I answer that, As stated above (A. 1), the hope of which we speak now, attains God by leaning on His help in order to obtain the hoped for good. Now an effect must be proportionate to its cause. Therefore the good which we ought to hope for from God properly and chiefly, is the infinite good, which is proportionate to the power of our divine helper, since it is proper to an infinite power to lead anyone to an infinite good. Such a good is eternal life, which consists in the enjoyment of God Himself. For we should hope from Him for nothing less than Himself, since His goodness, by which he imparts good things to His creature, is no less than His Essence. Therefore the proper and principal object of hope is eternal happiness.

Reply Obj. 1. Eternal happiness does not enter into the heart of man perfectly, that is so that it be possible for a wayfarer to know its nature and quality; yet, under the common notion, that of the perfect good, it is possible for it to be apprehended by a man, and it is in this way that the movement of hope towards it arises. Hence the Apostle says pointedly (Heb. 6. 19) that hope *enters in, even within the veil,* because that which we hope for is as yet veiled so to speak.

Reply Obj. 2. We ought not to pray God for any other goods except in reference to eternal happiness. Hence hope looks to eternal happiness chiefly, and other things, for which we pray God, it looks to secondarily and as referred to eternal happiness: just as faith looks to God

principally, and, secondarily, those things which are referred to God, as stated above (Q. 1, A. 1).

Reply Obj. 3. To him that longs for something great, all lesser things seem small; therefore to him that hopes for eternal happiness, nothing else appears arduous, as compared with that hope; although, as compared with the capability of the man who hopes, other things besides may be arduous to him, so that he may have hope for such things in reference to its principal object.

ARTICLE 3. *Whether One Man May Hope for Another's Eternal Happiness?*

We proceed thus to the Third Article: It seems that one may hope for another's eternal happiness.

Objection 1. For the Apostle says (*Philip.* 1. 6): *Being confident of this very thing, that He Who hath begun a good work in you, will perfect it unto the day of Jesus Christ.* Now the perfection of that day will be eternal happiness. Therefore one man may hope for another's eternal happiness.

Obj. 2. Further, Whatever we ask of God, we hope to obtain from Him. But we ask God to bring others to eternal happiness, according to James 5. 16: *Pray for one another that you may be saved.* Therefore we can hope for another's eternal happiness.

Obj. 3. Further, Hope and despair are about the same object. Now it is possible to despair of another's eternal happiness, since otherwise Augustine would have no reason for saying that "we should not despair of anyone so long as he lives" (*Serm.* LXXI, 13).[2] Therefore one can also hope for another's eternal salvation.

On the contrary, Augustine says (*Enchirid.* viii)[3] that "hope is only of such things as belong to him who is supposed to hope for them."

I answer that, We can hope for something in two ways: first, absolutely, and thus the object of hope is always something arduous and pertaining to the person who hopes. Secondly, we can hope for something through something else being presupposed, and in this way its object can be something pertaining to someone else. In order to explain this we must observe that love and hope differ in this, that love denotes union between lover and beloved, while hope denotes a movement or a stretching forth of the appetite towards an arduous good. Now union is of things that are distinct, and therefore love can directly regard the other, whom a man unites to himself by love, looking upon him as his other self. But

---

[1] *Glossa interl.* (VI, 144v); *Glossa* Lombardi (PL 192, 446).

[2] PL 38, 456.   [3] PL 40, 235.

movement is always towards its own term which is proportionate to the subject moved. Therefore hope regards directly one's own good, and not that which pertains to another. Yet if we presuppose the union of love with another, a man can hope for and desire something for another man, as for himself; and, accordingly, he can hope for another's eternal life, in so far as is united to him by love, and just as it is the same virtue of charity by which a man loves God, himself, and his neighbour, so too it is the same virtue of hope by which a man hopes for himself and for another.

This suffices for the *Replies to the Objections*.

ARTICLE 4. *Whether a Man Can Lawfully Hope in Man?*

We proceed thus to the Fourth Article: It would seem that one may lawfully hope in man.

Objection 1. For the object of hope is eternal happiness. Now we are helped to obtain eternal happiness by the patronage of the saints, for Gregory says (*Dialog*. i, 8)[1] that "predestination is furthered by the saints' prayers." Therefore one may hope in man.

Obj. 2. Further, If a man may not hope in another man, it ought not to be reckoned a sin in a man, that one should not be able to hope in him. Yet this is reckoned a vice in some, as appears from Jer. 9. 4: *Let every man take heed of his neighbour, and let him not trust in any brother of his*. Therefore it is lawful to trust in a man.

Obj. 3. Further, Prayer is the expression of hope, as stated above (A. 2, obj. 2). But it is lawful to pray to a man for something. Therefore it is lawful to hope in him.

On the contrary, It is written (Jer. 17. 5): *Cursed be the man that trusteth in man*.

I answer that, Hope, as stated above (Part I-II, Q. XL, A. 7; Q. XLII, A. 1), regards two things, namely, the good which it intends to obtain, and the help by which that good is obtained. Now the good which a man hopes to obtain, has the aspect of a final cause, while the help by which one hopes to obtain that good, has the character of an efficient cause. Now in each of these kinds of cause we find a principal and a secondary cause. For the principal end is the last end, while the secondary end is that which is referred to an end. In like manner the principal agent cause is the first agent, while the secondary efficient cause is the secondary and instrumental agent. Now hope regards eternal happiness as its last end, and the Divine assistance as the first cause leading to happiness.

[1] PL 77, 188.

Accordingly, just as it is not lawful to hope for any good save happiness, as one's last end, but only as something referred to final happiness, so too, it is unlawful to hope in any man, or any creature, as though it were the first cause of movement towards happiness. It is, however, lawful to hope in a man or a creature as being the secondary and instrumental agent, through whom one is helped to obtain any goods that are ordered to happiness. It is in this way that we turn to the saints, and that we ask men also for certain things, and for this reason some are blamed in that they cannot be trusted to give help.

This suffices for the *Replies to the Objections*.

ARTICLE 5. *Whether Hope Is a Theological Virtue?*

We proceed thus to the Fifth Article: It seems that hope is not a theological virtue.

Objection 1. For a theological virtue is one that has God for its object. Now hope has for its object not only God but also other goods which we hope to obtain from God. Therefore hope is not a theological virtue.

Obj. 2. Further, A theological virtue is not a mean between two vices, as stated above (Part I-II, Q. LXIV, A. 4). But hope is a mean between presumption and despair. Therefore hope is not a theological virtue.

Obj. 3. Further, Expectation pertains to longanimity which is a species of fortitude. Since, then, hope is a kind of expectation, it seems that hope is not a theological but a moral virtue.

Obj. 4. Further, The object of hope is something arduous. But it pertains to magnanimity, which is a moral virtue, to tend to the arduous. Therefore hope is a moral, and not a theological, virtue.

On the contrary, Hope is enumerated (I Cor. 13.) together with faith and charity, which are theological virtues.

I answer that, Since specific differences, by their very nature, divide a genus, in order to decide under what division we must place hope, we must observe whence it derives its character of virtue. Now it has been stated above (A. 1) that hope has the character of virtue from the fact that it attains the supreme rule of human actions: and this it attains both as its first efficient cause, in so far as it leans on its assistance, and as its final cause, in so far as it expects happiness from its enjoyment. Hence it is evident that God is the principal object of hope, considered as a virtue. Since, then, the very notion of a theological virtue is one that has God for its object, as stated above (Part I-II, Q. LXII, A. 1), it is evident that hope is a theological virtue.

Reply Obj. 1. Whatever else hope expects to obtain, it hopes for it in reference to God as the last end, or as the first efficient cause, as stated above (A. 4).

Reply Obj. 2. In things measured and ruled the mean consists in the measure or rule being attained; if we go beyond the rule, there is excess, if we fall short of the rule, there is deficiency. But in the rule or measure itself there is no such thing as a mean or extremes. Now a moral virtue is concerned with things ruled by reason, and these things are its proper object; and hence it is proper to it to follow the mean as regards its proper object. On the other hand, a theological virtue is concerned with the First Rule not ruled by another rule, and that Rule is its proper object. Therefore it is not proper for a theological virtue, with regard to its proper object, to follow the mean, although this may happen to it accidentally with regard to something that is referred to its principal object. Thus faith can have no mean or extremes in the point of trusting to the First Truth, in which it is impossible to trust too much; but on the part of the things believed, it may have a mean and extremes, just as one truth is a mean between two falsehoods. So too, hope has no mean or extremes, as regards its principal object, since it is impossible to trust too much in the Divine assistance; yet it may have a mean and extremes as regards those things a man trusts to obtain, in so far as he either presumes above his capability, or despairs of things of which he is capable.

Reply Obj. 3. The expectation which is mentioned in the definition of hope does not imply delay, as does the expectation which pertains to longanimity. It implies a reference to the Divine assistance, whether that which we hope for be delayed or not.

Reply Obj. 4. Magnanimity tends to something arduous in the hope of obtaining something that is within one's power, and so its proper object is the doing of great things. On the other hand hope, as a theological virtue, looks to something arduous, to be obtained by another's help, as stated above (A. 1).

ARTICLE 6. *Whether Hope Is Distinct from the Other Theological Virtues?*

We proceed thus to the Sixth Article: It seems that hope is not distinct from the other theological virtues.

Objection 1. For habits are distinguished by

their objects, as stated above (Part I-II, Q. LIV, A. 2). Now the object of hope is the same as of the other theological virtues. Therefore hope is not distinct from the other theological virtues.

Obj. 2. Further, In the Creed of faith, in which we make profession of faith, we say: "I expect the resurrection of the dead and the life of the world to come."[1] Now expectation of future happiness pertains to hope, as stated above (A. 5). Therefore hope is not distinct from faith.

Obj. 3. Further, By hope man tends to God. But this pertains properly to charity. Therefore hope is not distinct from charity.

On the contrary, There cannot be number without distinction. Now hope is numbered with the other theological virtues, for Gregory says (*Moral.* i, 27)[2] that the three virtues are faith, hope, and charity. Therefore hope is distinct from the theological virtues.

I answer that, A virtue is said to be theological from having God for the object to which it adheres. Now one may adhere to a thing in two ways: first, for its own sake, secondly, because something else is attained through it. Accordingly charity makes us adhere to God for His own sake, uniting our minds to God by the emotion of love. On the other hand, hope and faith make man adhere to God as to a principle from which certain things accrue to us. Now we derive from God both knowledge of truth and the attainment of perfect goodness. Accordingly faith makes us adhere to God, as the source from which we derive the knowledge of truth, since we believe that what God tells us is true. But hope makes us adhere to God, as the source from which we derive perfect goodness, that is, in so far as, by hope, we trust to the Divine assistance for obtaining Happiness.

Reply Obj. 1. God is the object of these virtues under different aspects as stated above; and a different aspect of the object suffices for the distinction of habits, as stated above (Part I-II, Q. LIV, A. 2).

Reply Obj. 2. Expectation is mentioned in the creed of faith, not as though it were the proper act of faith, but because the act of hope presupposes the act of faith, as we shall state further on (A. 7). Hence an act of faith is expressed in the act of hope.

Reply Obj. 3. Hope makes us tend to God, as to a good to be obtained finally, and as to a helper strong to assist. But charity, properly

[1] *Nicaeno-Cpolit. Creed* (MA III, 565; DZ 86).
[2] PL 75, 544.

speaking, makes us tend to God by uniting our affections to Him, so that we live, not for ourselves, but for God.

Article 7. *Whether Hope Precedes Faith?*

We proceed thus to the Seventh Article: It seems that hope precedes faith.

Objection 1. Because a gloss on Ps. 36. 3, *Trust in the Lord, and do good,* says: "Hope is the entrance to faith and the beginning of salvation."[1] But salvation is by faith whereby we are justified. Therefore hope precedes faith.

Obj. 2. Further, That which is included in a definition should precede the thing defined and be more known. But hope is included in the definition of faith (Heb. 11. 1): *Faith is the substance of things to be hoped for.* Therefore hope precedes faith.

Obj. 3. Further, Hope precedes a meritorious act, for the Apostle says (I Cor. 9. 10): *He that plougheth should plough in hope . . . to receive fruit.* But the act of faith is meritorious. Therefore hope precedes faith.

On the contrary, It is written (Matt. 1. 2): *Abraham begot Isaac,* that is, Faith begot hope, according to a gloss.[2]

I answer that, Absolutely speaking, faith precedes hope. For the object of hope is a future good, arduous but possible to obtain. In order, therefore, that we may hope, it is necessary for the object of hope to be proposed to us as possible. Now the object of hope is, in one way, eternal happiness, and, in another way, the Divine assistance, as explained above (A. 2; A. 6, Reply 3), and both of these are proposed to us by faith, by which we come to know that we are able to obtain eternal life, and that for this purpose the Divine assistance is ready for us, according to Heb. 11. 6: *He that cometh to God, must believe that He is, and is a rewarder to them that seek Him.* Therefore it is evident that faith precedes hope.

Reply Obj. 1. As the same gloss observes further on, *hope* is called the entrance to faith, that is, of the thing believed, "because by hope we enter in to see what we believe."—Or we may reply that it is called the entrance to faith, because by hope man begins to be established and perfected in faith.

Reply Obj 2. The thing to be hoped for is included in the definition of faith because the proper object of faith is something not apparent in itself. Hence it was necessary to express it in

a circumlocution by something resulting from faith.

Reply Obj. 3. Hope does not precede every meritorious act; but it suffices for it to accompany or follow it.

Article 8. *Whether Charity Precedes Hope.*

We proceed thus to the Eighth Article: It would seem that charity precedes hope.

Objection 1. For Ambrose says on Luke 17. 6, *If you had faith like to a grain of mustard-seed,* etc.: "Charity flows from faith, and hope from charity."[3] But faith precedes charity. Therefore charity precedes hope.

Obj. 2. Further, Augustine says[4] that "good emotions and affections proceed from love and holy charity." Now to hope, considered as an act of hope, is a good movement of the soul. Therefore it flows from charity.

Obj. 3. Further, The Master says (*Sent.* iii, d. 26)[5] that "hope proceeds from merits, which precede not only the thing hoped for, but also hope itself, which, in the order of nature, is preceded by charity." Therefore charity precedes hope.

On the contrary, The Apostle says (I Tim. 1. 5): *The end of the commandment is charity from a pure heart, and a good conscience,* that is, *from hope,* according to a gloss.[6] Therefore hope precedes charity.

I answer that, Order is twofold. One is the order of generation and of matter, in respect of which the imperfect precedes the perfect: the other is the order of perfection and form, in respect of which the perfect naturally precedes the imperfect. In respect of the first order hope precedes charity, and this is clear from the fact that hope and all movements of the appetite flow from love, as stated above (Part I-II, Q. XXVII, A. 4; Q. XXVIII, A. 6, Reply 2; Q. XL, A. 7) in the treatise on the passions.

Now there is a perfect, and an imperfect love. Perfect love is that by which a man is loved in himself, as when someone wishes a person some good for his own sake; thus a man loves his friend. Imperfect love is that by which a man loves something, not for its own sake, but that he may obtain that good for himself; thus a man loves what he desires. The first love pertains to charity, which adheres to God for His own sake; while hope pertains to the second love, since he that hopes, intends to obtain possession of something for himself.

---

[1] *Glossa interl.* (III, 136v); *Glossa* Lombardi (PL 191, 368); Cassiodorus, *Expos. in Psalt.,* super Ps. 36.3 (PL 70, 258). [2] *Glossa interl.* (V, 51).

[3] Bk. VIII (PL 15, 1865).
[4] *City of God,* XIV, 9 (PL 41, 414). [5] Chap. 1 (QR II, 670).
[6] *Glossa interl.* (VI, 116v); *Glossa* Lombardi (PL 192,329).

Hence in the order of generation, hope precedes charity. For just as a man is led to love God through fear of being punished by Him for his sins, as Augustine states in his commentary on the First canonical epistle of John (*Tract.* ix),[1] so too, hope leads to charity, in so far as a man through hoping to be rewarded by God, is encouraged to love God and obey His commandments. On the other hand, in the order of perfection charity naturally precedes hope. And therefore, with the advent of charity, hope is made more perfect, because we hope chiefly in our friends. It is in this sense that Ambrose states (obj. 1) that charity flows from hope.

From this appears the *Reply to the First Objection.*

Reply Obj. 2. Hope and every movement of the appetite proceed from some kind of love, by which the expected good is loved. But not every kind of hope proceeds from charity, but only the movement of formed hope, namely, that by which man hopes to obtain good from God, as from a friend.

Obj. 3. The Master is speaking of formed hope, which is naturally preceded by charity and the merits caused by charity.

QUESTION XVIII
OF THE SUBJECT OF HOPE
(*In Four Articles*)

WE must now consider the subject of hope, under which head there are four points of inquiry: (1) Whether the virtue of hope is in the will as its subject? (2) Whether it is in the blessed? (3) Whether it is in the damned? (4) Whether there is certainty in the hope of a wayfarer?

ARTICLE 1. *Whether Hope Is in the Will as Its Subject?*

We proceed thus to the First Article: It would seem that hope is not in the will as its subject.

Objection 1. For the object of hope is an arduous good, as stated above (Q. XVII, A. 1; Part I-II, Q. XL, A. 1). Now the arduous is the object, not of the will, but of the irascible part. Therefore hope is not in the will but in the irascible part.

Obj. 2. Further, Where one suffices it is superfluous to add another. Now charity, which is the most perfect of the virtues, suffices for the perfecting of the will. Therefore hope is not in the will.

Obj. 3. Further, The one same power cannot exercise two acts at the same time; thus the in-

tellect cannot understand many things simultaneously. Now the act of hope can be at the same time as an act of charity. Since, then, the act of charity evidently pertains to the will, it follows that the act of hope does not pertain to that power. Thus, therefore, hope is not in the will.

On the contrary, The soul is not capable of God except as regards the mind in which is memory, intellect and will, as Augustine declares (*De Trin.* xiv).[2] Now hope is a theological virtue having God for its object. Since therefore it is neither in the memory, nor in the intellect, which belong to the cognitive power, it follows that it is in the will as its subject.

I answer that, As shown above (Part I, Q. LXXXVII, A. 2), habits are known by their acts. Now the act of hope is a movement of the appetitive part, since its object is a good. And, since there is a twofold appetite in man, namely, the sensitive which is divided into irascible and concupiscible, and the intellectual appetite, called the will, as stated in the First Part (Q. LXXXII, A. 5), those movements which occur in the lower appetite are accompanied by passion, while those in the higher appetite are without passion, as shown above (*ibid.,* Reply 1; Part I-II, Q. XXII, A. 3, Reply 3). Now the act of the virtue of hope cannot belong to the sensitive appetite, since the good which is the principal object of this virtue is not a sensible good but a Divine good. Therefore hope resides in the higher appetite, called the will, and not in the lower appetite, of which the irascible is a part.

Reply Obj. 1. The object of the irascible is an arduous sensible, but the object of the virtue of hope is an arduous intelligible, or rather supra-intelligible.

Reply Obj. 2. Charity perfects the will sufficiently with regard to one act, which is the act of loving; but another virtue is required in order to perfect it with regard to its other act, which is that of hoping.

Reply Obj. 3. The movement of hope and the movement of charity are mutually related, as was shown above (Q. XVII, A. 8). Hence there is no reason why both movements should not belong at the same time to the same power, even as the intellect can understand many things at the same time if they are related to one another, as stated in the First Part (Q. LXXXV, A. 4).

ARTICLE 2. *Whether in the Blessed There Is Hope?*

We proceed thus to the Second Article: It would seem that in the blessed there is hope.

Objection 1. For Christ was a perfect comprehensor from the first moment of his conception. Now He had hope, since, according to a gloss, the words of Ps. 30, 2, *In Thee, O Lord, have I hoped* are said in His person.[1] Therefore in the blessed there can be hope.

Obj. 2. Further, Even as the obtaining of happiness is an arduous good, so is its continuation. Now, before they obtain happiness, men hope to obtain it. Therefore, after they have obtained it, they can hope to continue in its possession.

Obj. 3. Further, By the virtue of hope, a man can hope for happiness, not only for himself, but also for others, as stated above (Q. XVII, A. 3). But the blessed who are in heaven hope for the happiness of others, or they would not pray for them. Therefore there can be hope in them.

Obj. 4. Further, The happiness of the saints implies not only glory of the soul but also glory of the body. Now the souls of the saints in heaven, look yet for the glory of their bodies (Apoc. 6. 10; Augustine,—*Gen. ad. lit.* xii, 35).[2] Therefore in the blessed there can be hope.

On the contrary, The Apostle says (Rom. 8. 24): *What a man seeth, why doth he hope for?* Now the blessed enjoy the sight of God. Therefore hope has no place in them.

I answer that, If what gives a thing its species be removed, the species is destroyed, and that thing cannot remain the same; just as when a natural body loses its form it does not remain the same specifically. Now hope takes its species from its principal object, even as the other virtues do, as was shown above (Q. XVII, AA. 5, 6), and its principal object is eternal happiness according as it is possible of attainment by the assistance of God, as stated above (Q. XVII, A. 2). Since then the arduous possible good cannot be an object of hope except in so far as it is something future, it follows that when happiness is no longer future, but present, it is incompatible with the virtue of hope. Consequently hope, like faith, is voided in heaven, and neither of them can be in the blessed.

Reply Obj. 1. Although Christ was a comprehensor and therefore blessed as to the enjoyment of God, nevertheless He was, at the same time, a wayfarer, as regards the passibility of nature, to which He was still subject. Hence it was possible for Him to hope for the glory of impassibility and immortality, yet not so as to have the virtue of hope, the principal object of which is not the glory of the body but the enjoyment of God.

[1] *Glossa interl.* (III, 125v); *Glossa* Lombardi (PL 191, 300).   [2] PL 34, 483.

Reply Obj. 2. The Happiness of the saints is called eternal life, because through enjoying God they become partakers, as it were, of God's eternity which surpasses all time, so that the continuation of Happiness does not differ in respect of present, past and future. Hence the blessed do not hope for the continuation of their Happiness (for as regards this there is no future), but are in actual possession of it.

Reply Obj. 3. So long as the virtue of hope lasts, one hopes for one's own happiness, and for that of others by the same hope. But when hope in the blessed, by which they hoped for their own Happiness, is voided, they hope for the Happiness of others indeed, yet not by the virtue of hope, but rather by the love of charity. Even so, he that has Divine charity, by that same charity loves his neighbour, and yet a man may love his neighbour, without having the virtue of charity, but by some other love.

Reply Obj. 4. Since hope is a theological virtue having God for its object, its principal object is the glory of the soul, which consists in the enjoyment of God, and not the glory of the body. Moreover, although the glory of the body is something arduous in comparison with human nature, yet it is not so for one who has the glory of the soul, both because the glory of the body is a very small thing as compared with the glory of the soul, and because one who has the glory of the soul has already the sufficient cause of the glory of the body.

ARTICLE 3. *Whether Hope Is in the Damned?*

We proceed thus to the Third Article: It would seem that there is hope in the damned.

Objection 1. For the devil is damned and prince of the damned, according to Matt. 25. 41: *Depart . . . you cursed, into everlasting fire, which was prepared for the devil and his angels.* But the devil has hope, according to Job 40. 28, *Behold his hope shall fail him.* Therefore it seems that the damned have hope.

Obj. 2. Further, Just as faith is either formed or unformed, so is hope. But unformed faith can be in the devils and the damned, according to James 2. 19: *The devils . . . believe and tremble.* Therefore it seems that unformed hope also can be in the damned.

Obj. 3. Further, After death there accrues to man no merit or demerit that he had not before, according to Eccl. 11. 3, *If the tree fall to the south, or to the north, in what place soever it shall fall, there shall it be.* Now many who are damned, in this life hoped and never despaired. Therefore they will hope in the future life also.

On the contrary, Hope causes joy, according to Rom. 12. 12, *Rejoicing in hope.* Now the damned have no joy, but sorrow and grief, according to Isa. 65. 14, *My servants shall praise for joyfulness of heart, and you shall cry for sorrow of heart, and shall howl for grief of spirit.* Therefore no hope is in the damned.

I answer that, Just as it is of the very notion of happiness that the will should find rest therein, so is it of the very notion of punishment that what is inflicted in punishment should go against the will. Now that which is not known can neither be restful nor contrary to the will. Therefore Augustine says (*Gen. ad lit.* xi, 17)[1] that the angels could not be perfectly happy in their first state before their confirmation, or unhappy before their fall, since they had no foreknowledge of what would happen to them. For perfect and true happiness requires that one should be certain of being happy for ever; otherwise the will would not rest.

In like manner, since the everlastingness of damnation pertains to the punishment of the damned, it would not be truly penal unless it went against the will; and this would be impossible if they were ignorant of the everlastingness of their damnation. Hence it pertains to the unhappy condition of the damned, that they should know that they cannot by any means escape from damnation and obtain happiness. Therefore it is written (Job. 15. 22): *He believeth not that he may return from darkness to light.* It is, therefore, evident that they cannot apprehend happiness as a possible good, as neither can the blessed apprehend it as a future good. Consequently there is no hope either in the blessed or in the damned. On the other hand, hope can be in wayfarers, whether of this life or in purgatory, because in either case they apprehend happiness as a future possible thing.

Reply Obj. 1. As Gregory says (*Moral.* xxxiii, 20)[2] this is said of the devil as regards his members, whose hope will fail utterly. Or, if it be understood of the devil himself, it may refer to the hope by which he expects to vanquish the saints, in which sense we read just before (*verse* 18): *He trusteth that the Jordan may run into his mouth.* This is not, however, the hope of which we are speaking.

Reply Obj. 2. As Augustine says (*Enchirid.* viii),[3] "faith is about things, bad or good, past, present or future, one's own or another's; but hope is only about good things, future and concerning oneself." Hence it is possible for unformed faith to be in the damned, but not hope,

since the Divine goods are not for them future possible things, but far removed from them.

Reply Obj. 3. Lack of hope in the damned does not change their demerit, as neither does the voiding of hope in the blessed increase their merit; but both these things are due to the change in their respective states.

ARTICLE 4. *Whether There Is Certainty in the Hope of a Wayfarer?*

We proceed thus to the Fourth Article: It would seem that there is no certainty in the hope of a wayfarer.

Objection 1. For hope resides in the will. But certainty pertains not to the will but to the intellect. Therefore there is no certainty in hope.

Obj. 2. Further, Hope is based on grace and merits, as stated above (Q. XVII, A. 1). Now it is impossible in this life to know for certain that we are in a state of grace, as stated above (Part I-II, Q. CXII, A. 5). Therefore there is no certainty in the hope of a wayfarer.

Obj. 3. Further, There can be no certainty about that which may fail. Now many a hopeful wayfarer fails to obtain Happiness. Therefore the wayfarer's hope has no certainty.

On the contrary, "Hope is the certain expectation of future happiness," as the Master states (*Sent.* iii, d. 26);[4] and this may be gathered from II Tim. 1. 12, *I know Whom I have believed, and I am certain that He is able to keep that which I have committed to Him.*

I answer that, Certainty is found in a thing in two ways, essentially and by participation. It is found essentially in the cognitive power; by participation, in whatever is moved infallibly to its end by the cognitive power. In this way we say that nature works with certainty, since it is moved by the Divine intellect which moves everything with certainty to its end. In this way too, the moral virtues are said to work with greater certainty than art, since, like a second nature, they are moved to their acts by the reason.[5] And thus too, hope tends to its end with certainty, as though sharing in the certainty of faith which is in the cognitive power.

This suffices for the *Reply to the First Objection.*

Reply Obj. 2. Hope is not founded chiefly in grace already received, but on God's omnipotence and mercy, by which even he that does not have grace can obtain it, so as to come to eternal life. Now whoever has faith is certain of God's omnipotence and mercy.

[1] PL 34, 438.   [2] PL 76, 697.   [3] PL 40, 234.

[4] Chap. 1 (QR II, 670).
[5] Aristotle, *Ethics*, II, 6 (1106[b]14).

Reply Obj. 3. That some who have hope fail to obtain Happiness is due to a fault of free choice in placing the obstacle of sin, but not to any deficiency in God's power or mercy, on which hope is based. Hence this does not prejudice the certainty of hope.

QUESTION XIX
OF THE GIFT OF FEAR
(In Twelve Articles)

WE must now consider the gift of fear, about which there are twelve points of inquiry: (1) Whether God is to be feared? (2) Of the division of fear into filial, initial, servile and worldly. (3) Whether worldly fear is always evil? (4) Whether servile fear is good? (5) Whether it is substantially the same as filial fear? (6) Whether servile fear departs when charity comes? (7) Whether fear is the beginning of wisdom? (8) Whether initial fear is substantially the same as filial fear? (9) Whether fear is a gift of the Holy Ghost? (10) Whether it grows when charity grows? (11) Whether it remains in heaven? (12) Which of the beatitudes and fruits correspond to it?

ARTICLE 1. *Whether God Can Be Feared?*

We proceed thus to the First Article: It would seem that God cannot be feared.

Objection 1. For the object of fear is a future evil, as stated above (Part I-II, Q. XLI, A. 2). But God is free of all evil, since He is goodness itself. Therefore God cannot be feared.

Obj. 2. Further, Fear is opposed to hope. Now we hope in God. Therefore we cannot fear Him at the same time.

Obj. 3. Further, As the Philosopher states,[1] "we fear those things whence evil comes to us." But evil comes to us, not from God, but from ourselves, according to Osee 13. 9: *Destruction is thy own, O Israel: thy help is . . . in Me.* Therefore God is not to be feared.

On the contrary, It is written (Jer. 10. 7): *Who shall not fear Thee, O King of nations?* and (Malach. 1. 6): *If I be a master, where is My fear?*

I answer that, Just as hope has two objects, one of which is the future good itself that one expects to obtain, while the other is someone's help, through whom one expects to obtain what one hopes for, so, too, fear may have two objects, one of which is the very evil which a man shrinks from, while the other is that from which the evil may come. Accordingly in the first way

[1] *Rhetoric,* II, 5 (1382^{b}32).

God, Who is goodness itself, cannot be an object of fear; but He can be an object of fear in the second way, in so far as there may come to us some evil either from Him or in relation to Him.

From Him there comes the evil of punishment, but this is evil not absolutely but relatively, and, absolutely speaking, is a good. Because, since a thing is said to be good through being ordered to an end, while evil implies lack of this order, that which excludes the order to the last end is altogether evil, and such is the evil of fault. On the other hand the evil of punishment is indeed an evil, in so far as it is the privation of some particular good, yet absolutely speaking it is a good, in so far as it is ordered to the last end.

In relation to God the evil of fault can come to us if we be separated from Him; and in this way God can and ought to be feared.

Reply Obj. 1. This objection considers the object of fear as being the evil which a man shuns.

Reply Obj. 2. In God, we may consider both His justice, in respect of which He punishes those who sin, and His mercy, in respect of which He sets us free. The consideration of His justice gives rise to fear in us, but the consideration of His mercy gives rise to hope, so that, accordingly, God is the object of both hope and fear, but under different aspects.

Reply Obj. 3. The evil of fault is not from God as its author, but from us, in so far as we forsake God. But the evil of punishment is from God as its author, in so far as it has the character of a good, since it is something just, through being inflicted on us justly, although originally this is due to the demerit of sin. Thus it is written (Wisd. 1. 13, 16): *God made not death . . . but the wicked with works and words have called it to them.*

ARTICLE 2. *Whether Fear Is Fittingly Divided into Filial, Initial, Servile and Worldly Fear?*

We proceed thus to the Second Article: It would seem that fear is unfittingly divided into filial, initial, servile and worldly fear.

Objection 1. For Damascene says (*De Fide Orthod.* ii, 15)[2] that there are six kinds of fear, namely, laziness, shamefacedness, etc., of which we have treated above (Part I-II, Q. XLI, A. 4), and which are not mentioned in the division in question. Therefore this division of fears seems unfitting.

Obj. 2. Further, Each of these fears is either good or evil. But there is a fear, namely, natural fear, which is neither morally good, since it is in

[2] PG 94, 932.

the demons, according to James 2. 19, *The devils . . . believe and tremble,* nor evil, since it is in Christ, according to Mark 14. 33, Jesus *began to fear and be heavy.* Therefore the above division of fear is insufficient.

Obj. 3. Further, The relation of son to father differs from that of wife to husband, and this again from that of servant to master. Now filial fear, which is that of the son in comparison with his father, is distinct from servile fear, which is that of the servant in comparison with his master. Therefore chaste fear, which seems to be that of the wife in relation to her husband, ought to be distinguished from all these other fears.

Obj. 4. Further, Even as servile fear fears punishment, so do initial and worldly fear. Therefore no distinction should be made between them.

Obj. 5. Further, Even as concupiscence is about some good, so is fear about some evil. Now concupiscence of the eyes, which is the desire for things of this world, is distinct from concupiscence of the flesh, which is the desire for one's own pleasure. Therefore worldly fear, by which one fears to lose external goods, is distinct from human fear, by which one fears harm to one's own person.

On the contrary stands the authority of the Master (3 *Sent.,* d. 34).[1]

I answer that, We are speaking of fear now, in so far as it makes us in some way turn to God or away from Him. For, since the object of fear is an evil, sometimes, on account of the evils he fears, man withdraws from God, and this is called human or worldly fear; while sometimes, on account of the evils he fears, he turns to God and adheres to Him. This latter evil is twofold, namely evil of punishment, and evil of fault.

Accordingly if a man turn to God and adhere to Him, through fear of punishment, it will be servile fear; but if it be on account of fear of committing a fault, it will be filial fear, for it becomes a child to fear offending its father. If, however, it be on account of both, it will be initial fear, which is between both these fears. As to whether it is possible to fear the evil of fault the question has been treated above (Part I-II, Q. XLII, A. 3) when we were considering the passion of fear.

Reply Obj. 1. Damascene divides fear as a passion of the soul; but this division of fear is taken from its relation to God, as explained above.

Reply Obj. 2. Moral good consists chiefly

[1] Chap. 4 (QR II, 701).

in turning to God, while moral evil consists chiefly in turning away from Him; and therefore all the moral fears mentioned above imply either moral evil or moral good. Now natural fear is presupposed to moral good and evil, and so it is not numbered among these kinds of fear.

Reply Obj. 3. The relation of servant to master is based on the power which the master exercises over the servant, while, on the contrary, the relation of a son to his father or of a wife to her husband is based on the son's affection towards his father to whom he submits himself, or on the wife's affection towards her husband to whom she binds herself in the union of love. Hence filial and chaste fear amount to the same, because by the love of charity God becomes our Father, according to Rom. 8. 15, *You have received the spirit of adoption of sons, whereby we cry: Abba Father;* and by this same charity He is called our spouse, according to II Cor. 11. 2, *I have espoused you to one husband, that I may present you as a chaste virgin to Christ.* But servile fear does not pertain to these, since it does not include charity in its definition.

Reply Obj. 4. These three fears regard punishment but in different ways. For worldly or human fear regards a punishment which turns man away from God, and which God's enemies sometimes inflict or threaten; but servile and initial fear regard a punishment by which men are drawn to God, and which is inflicted or threatened by God. Servile fear regards this punishment chiefly, while initial fear regards it secondarily.

Reply Obj. 5. It amounts to the same whether man turns away from God through fear of losing his worldly goods, or through fear of forfeiting the well-being of his body, since external goods pertain to the body. Hence both these fears are reckoned as one here, although they fear different evils, even as they correspond to the desire of different goods. This diversity causes a specific diversity of sins, all of which alike however lead man away from God.

ARTICLE 3. *Whether Worldly Fear Is Always Evil?*

We proceed thus to the Third Article: It would seem that worldly fear is not always evil.

Objection 1. Because regard for men seems to be a kind of human fear. Now some are blamed for having no regard for man, for instance, the unjust judge of whom we read (Luke 18. 2) that he *feared not God, nor regarded man*. Therefore it seems that worldly fear is not always evil.

Obj. 2. Further, Worldly fear seems to have reference to the punishments inflicted by the secular power. Now punishments of this kind incite us to good actions, according to Rom. 13. 3, *Wilt thou not be afraid of the power? Do that which is good, and thou shalt have praise from the same*. Therefore worldly fear is not always evil.

Obj. 3. Further, It seems that what is in us naturally, is not evil, since our natural gifts are from God. Now it is natural to man to fear detriment to his body, and loss of his worldly goods, by which the present life is supported. Therefore it seems that worldly fear is not always evil.

On the contrary, Our Lord said (Matt. 10. 28): *Fear ye not them that kill the body*, thus forbidding worldly fear. Now nothing but what is evil is forbidden by God. Therefore worldly fear is evil.

I answer that, As shown above (Part I-II, Q. XVIII, A. 2; Q. LIV, A. 2) moral acts and habits take their name and species from their objects. Now the proper object of the appetite's movement is the final good, so that, in consequence, every appetitive movement is both specified and named from its proper end. For if anyone were to describe covetousness as love of work because men work on account of covetousness, this description would be incorrect, since the covetous man seeks work not as end but as a means. The end that he seeks is wealth, and so covetousness is rightly described as the desire or the love of wealth, and this is evil. Accordingly worldly love is, properly speaking, the love by which a man trusts in the world as his end, so that worldly love is always evil. Now fear is born of love, "since man fears the loss of what he loves," as Augustine states.[1] Hence worldly fear is that which arises from worldly love as from an evil root, for which reason worldly fear is always evil.

Reply Obj. 1. One may have regard for men in two ways. First, in so far as there is in them something divine, for instance the good of grace or of virtue, or at least of the natural image of God; and in this way those are blamed who have no regard for man. Secondly, one may have regard for men as being in opposition to God, and thus it is praiseworthy to have no regard for men, according as we read of Elias or Eliseus (Ecclus. 48. 13): *In his days he feared not the prince*.

[1] QQ. LXXXIII, Qu. 33 (PL 40, 22).

Reply Obj. 2. When the secular power inflicts punishment in order to withdraw men from sin, it is acting as God's minister, according to Rom. 13. 4, *For he is God's minister, an avenger to execute wrath upon him that doth evil*. To fear the secular power in this way is part, not of worldly fear, but of servile or initial fear.

Reply Obj. 3. It is natural for man to shrink from detriment to his own body and loss of worldly goods, but to forsake justice on that account is contrary to natural reason. Hence the Philosopher says[2] that there are certain things, namely sinful deeds, which no fear should drive us to do, since to do such things is worse than to suffer any punishment whatever.

ARTICLE 4. *Whether Servile Fear Is Good?*

We proceed thus to the Fourth Article: It would seem that servile fear is not good.

Objection 1. For if the use of a thing is evil, the thing itself is evil. Now the use of servile fear is evil, for according to a gloss on Rom. 8. 15, *if a man do anything through fear, although the deed be good, it is not well done*.[3] Therefore servile fear is not good.

Obj. 2. Further, No good grows from a sinful root. Now servile fear grows from a sinful root, because when commenting on Job 3. 11, *Why did I not die in the womb?* Gregory says (*Moral.* iv, 27);[4] "When a man dreads the punishment which confronts him for his sin and no longer loves the friendship of God which he has lost, his fear is born of fear, not of humility." Therefore servile fear is evil.

Obj. 3. Further, Just as mercenary love is opposed to the love of charity, so is servile fear, apparently, opposed to chaste fear. But mercenary love is always evil. Therefore servile fear is also.

On the contrary, Nothing evil is from the Holy Ghost. But servile fear is from the Holy Ghost, since a gloss on Rom. 8. 15, *You have not received the spirit of bondage*, etc., says: "It is the one same spirit that bestows two fears,"[5] namely, servile and chaste fear. Therefore servile fear is not evil.

I answer that, It is owing to its servility that servile fear may be evil. For servitude is op-

[2] *Ethics*, III, 1 (1110^a26).
[3] *Glossa* Lombardi (PL 191, 1439); cf. *Glossa ordin.* (VI, 18F).
[4] PL 75, 662.
[5] *Glossa ordin.* (VI, 18F); *Glossa* Lombardi (PL 191, 1439); cf. Augustine, *In Joann.*, tract LXXXV, on 15.15 (PL 35, 1849).

posed to freedom. Since, then, "what is free is cause of itself,"[1] a slave is one who does not act as cause of his own action, but as though moved from without. Now whoever does a thing through love, does it of himself so to speak, because it is by his own inclination that he is moved to act, so that it is contrary to the very notion of servility that one should act from love. Consequently servile fear as such is contrary to charity. If therefore servility were essential to fear, servile fear would be evil absolutely, even as adultery is evil absolutely, because that which makes it contrary to charity belongs to its very species.

This servility, however, does not belong to the species of servile fear, even as neither does formlessness to the species of unformed faith. For the species of a moral habit or act is taken from the object. Now the object of servile fear is punishment, and it is by accident that, either the good to which the punishment is contrary is loved as the last end, and that consequently the punishment is feared as the greatest evil, which is the case with one who does not have charity, or that the punishment is directed to God as its end, and that, consequently, it is not feared as the greatest evil, which is the case with one who has charity. For the species of a habit is not destroyed through its object or end being ordered to a further end. Consequently servile fear is substantially good, but its servility is evil.

Reply Obj. 1. This saying of Augustine is to be applied to a man who does something through servile fear as such, so that he loves not justice, and fears nothing but the punishment.

Reply Obj. 2. Servile fear as to its substance is not born of fear, but its servility is, in so far, that is, as man is unwilling, by love to subject his affections to the yoke of justice.

Reply Obj. 3. Mercenary love is that by which God is loved for the sake of worldly goods and this is, of itself, contrary to charity, so that mercenary love is always evil. But servile fear, as to its substance, implies merely fear of punishment, whether or not this be feared as the principal evil.

ARTICLE 5. *Whether Servile Fear Is Substantially the Same as Filial Fear?*

We proceed thus to the Fifth Article: It would seem that servile fear is substantially the same as filial fear.

Objection 1. For filial fear is to servile fear the same apparently as formed faith is to unformed faith, since the one is accompanied by mortal sin and the other not. Now formed faith and unformed faith are substantially the same. Therefore servile and filial fear are substantially the same.

Obj. 2. Further, Habits are diversified by their objects. Now the same thing is the object of servile and of filial fear, since they both fear God. Therefore servile and filial fear are substantially the same.

Obj. 3. Further, Just as man hopes to enjoy God and to obtain favours from Him, so does he fear to be separated from God and to be punished by Him. Now the hope by which we hope to enjoy God, and to receive other favours from Him is the same, as stated above (Q. XVII, A. 2, REPLY 2). Therefore filial fear, by which we fear separation from God, is the same as servile fear by which we fear His punishments.

On the contrary, Augustine (*In prim. canon. Joan., Tract,* ix)[2] says that there are two fears, one servile, another filial or chaste fear.

I answer that, The proper object of fear is evil. And since acts and habits are diversified by their objects, as shown above (Part I-II, Q. LIV, A. 2), it follows of necessity that different kinds of fear correspond to different kinds of evil. Now the evil of punishment, from which servile fear shrinks, differs specifically from evil of fault, which filial fear shuns, as shown above (Part I, Q. XLVIII, A. 5). Hence it is evident that servile and filial fear are not the same substantially but differ specifically.

Reply Obj. 1. Formed and unformed faith differ, not as regards the object, since each of them believes God and believes in a God, but in respect of something extrinsic, namely the presence or absence of charity, and so they do not differ substantially. On the other hand, servile and filial fear differ as to their objects, and hence the comparison fails.

Reply Obj. 2. Servile fear and filial fear do not have the same relationship to God. For servile fear looks upon God as the cause of the infliction of punishment, while filial fear looks upon Him, not as the active cause of guilt, but rather as the term from which it shrinks to be separated by guilt. Consequently the identity of object, namely God, does not prove a specific identity of fear, since also natural movements differ specifically according to their different relationships to some one term, for movement from whiteness is not specifically the same as movement towards whiteness.

---

[1] Aristotle, *Metaphysics,* I, 2 (982^{b}26).   [2] PL 35, 2049.

Reply Obj. 3. Hope looks upon God as the principle not only of the enjoyment of God, but also of any other favour whatever. This cannot be said of fear, and so there is no comparison.

ARTICLE 6. *Whether Servile Fear Remains with Charity?*

We proceed thus to the Sixth Article: It seems that servile fear does not remain with charity.

Objection 1. For Augustine says in his commentary on the First Canonical epistle of John (*Tract.* ix)[1] that "when charity takes up its abode, it drives away fear which had prepared a place for it."

Obj. 2. Further, *The charity of God is poured forth in our hearts, by the Holy Ghost, Who is given to us* (Rom. 5. 5). Now *where the Spirit of the Lord is, there is liberty* (II Cor. 3. 17). Since then freedom excludes servitude, it seems that servile fear is driven away when charity comes.

Obj. 3. Further, Servile fear is caused by self-love, in so far as punishment diminishes one's own good. Now love of God drives away self-love, for it makes us despise ourselves; thus Augustine testifies[2] that "the love of God unto the contempt of self builds up the city of God." Therefore it seems that servile fear is driven out when charity comes.

On the contrary, Servile fear is a gift of the Holy Ghost, as stated above (A. 4). Now the gifts of the Holy Ghost are not forfeited through the advent of charity, by which the Holy Ghost dwells in us. Therefore servile fear is not driven out when charity comes.

I answer that, Servile fear proceeds from self-love, because it is fear of punishment which is detrimental to one's own good. Hence the fear of punishment is consistent with charity, in the same way as self-love is, because it comes to the same thing that a man love his own good and that he fear to be deprived of it.

Now self-love may stand in a threefold relationship to charity. In one way it is contrary to charity, when a man places his end in the love of his own good. In another way it is included in charity, when a man loves himself for the sake of God and in God. In a third way, it is indeed distinct from charity, but is not contrary to it, as when a man loves himself from the point of view of his own good, yet not so as to place his end in this his own good, just as one may have another special love for one's

[1] PL 35, 2047.   [2] *City of God,* XIV, 28 (PL 41, 436).

neighbour, besides the love of charity which is founded on God, when we love him by reason of usefulness, consanguinity, or some other human consideration, which, however, is referable to charity.

Accordingly fear of punishment is, in one way, included in charity, because separation from God is a punishment, which charity shuns exceedingly. Hence this belongs to chaste fear. In another way it is contrary to charity, when a man shrinks from the punishment that is opposed to his natural good, as being the chief evil in opposition to the good which he loves as an end; and in this way fear of punishment is not consistent with charity. In another way fear of punishment is indeed substantially distinct from chaste fear, when, that is, a man fears a penal evil, not because it separates him from God, but because it is hurtful to his own good; and yet he does not place his end in this good, so that neither does he dread this evil as being the principal evil. Such fear of punishment is consistent with charity; but it is not called servile, except when punishment is dreaded as a principal evil, as explained above (AA. 2, 4). Hence fear considered as servile, does not remain with charity, but the substance of servile fear can remain with charity, even as self-love can remain with charity.

Reply Obj. 1. Augustine is speaking of fear, considered as servile. And such is the sense of the two *other* objections.

ARTICLE 7. *Whether Fear is the Beginning of Wisdom?*

We proceed thus to the Seventh Article: It seems that fear is not the beginning of wisdom.

Objection 1. For the beginning of a thing is a part of it. But fear is not a part of wisdom, since fear is seated in the appetitive power, while wisdom is in the intellect. Therefore it seems that fear is not the beginning of wisdom.

Obj. 2. Further, Nothing is the beginning of itself. Now *fear of the Lord, that is wisdom,* according to Job. 28. 28. Therefore it seems that fear of God is not the beginning of wisdom.

Obj. 3. Further, Nothing is prior to the beginning. But something is prior to fear, since faith precedes fear. Therefore it seems that fear is not the beginning of wisdom.

On the contrary, It is written in the Psalm (110. 10): *The fear of the Lord is the beginning of wisdom.*

I answer that, A thing may be called the beginning of wisdom in two ways: in one way, because it is the beginning of wisdom itself as to its essence; in another way, as to its effect. Thus the beginning of an art as to its essence consists in the principles from which that art proceeds, while the beginning of an art as to its effect is that from which it begins to operate: for instance we might say that the beginning of the art of building is the foundation, because that is where the builder begins his work.

Now, since wisdom is the knowledge of Divine things, as we shall state further on (Q. XLV, A. 1), it is considered by us in one way, and in another way by philosophers. For, seeing that our life is ordered to the enjoyment of God, and is directed to this according to a participation of the Divine Nature, conferred on us through grace, wisdom, as we look at it, is considered not only as making us know God, as it is with the philosophers, but also as directing human conduct; since this is directed not only by the human law, but also by the Divine law, as Augustine shows (De Trin. xii, 13).[1]

Accordingly the beginning of wisdom as to its essence consists in the first principles of wisdom, which are the articles of faith, and in this sense faith is said to be the beginning of wisdom. But as regards the effect, the beginning of wisdom is the point where wisdom begins to work, and in this way fear is the beginning of wisdom, yet servile fear in one way, and filial fear, in another. For servile fear is like a principle disposing a man to wisdom from without, in so far as he refrains from sin through fear of punishment, and is thus fashioned for the effect of wisdom, according to Ecclus. 1. 27, The fear of the Lord driveth out sin. On the other hand, chaste or filial fear is the beginning of wisdom, as being the first effect of wisdom. For since the regulation of human conduct by the Divine law belongs to wisdom, in order to make a beginning, man must first of all fear God and submit himself to Him; thus the result will be that in all things he will be ruled by God.

Reply Obj. 1. This argument proves that fear is not the beginning of wisdom as to the essence of wisdom.

Reply Obj. 2. The fear of God is compared to a man's whole life that is ruled by God's wisdom, as the root to the tree; hence it is written (Ecclus. 1. 25): The root of wisdom is to fear the Lord, for (Vulg.,—and) the branches thereof are longlived. Consequently, as the root is said to be virtually the tree, so the fear of God is said to be wisdom.

[1] PL 42, 1009.

Reply Obj. 3. As stated above, faith is the beginning of wisdom in one way, and fear, in another. Hence it is written (Ecclus. 25. 16): The fear of God is the beginning of love: and the beginning of faith is to be fast joined to it.

ARTICLE 8. Whether Initial Fear Differs Substantially From Filial Fear?

We proceed thus to the Eighth Article: It seems that initial fear differs substantially from filial fear.

Objection 1. For filial fear is caused by love. Now initial fear is the beginning of love, according to Ecclus. 25. 16, The fear of God is the beginning of love. Therefore initial fear is distinct from filial fear.

Obj. 2. Further, Initial fear dreads punishment, which is the object of servile fear, so that initial and servile fear would seem to be the same. But servile fear is distinct from filial fear. Therefore initial fear also is substantially distinct from filial fear.

Obj. 3. Further, A mean differs in the same ratio from both the extremes. Now initial fear is the mean between servile and filial fear. Therefore it differs from both filial and servile fear.

On the contrary, Perfect and imperfect do not diversify the substance of a thing. Now initial and filial fear differ in respect of perfection and imperfection of charity, as Augustine states in his commentary on the First Canonical Epistle of John (Tract. ix).[2] Therefore initial fear does not differ substantially from filial fear.

I answer that, Initial fear is so called because it is a beginning (initium). Since, however, both servile and filial fear are, in some way, the beginning of wisdom, each may be called in some way, initial. It is not in this sense, however, that we are to understand initial fear in so far as it is distinct from servile and filial fear, but in the sense according to which it belongs to the state of beginners, in whom there is a beginning of filial fear resulting from a beginning of charity, although they do not possess the perfection of filial fear, because they have not yet attained to the perfection of charity. Consequently initial fear stands in the same relation to filial fear as imperfect to perfect charity. Now perfect and imperfect charity differ, not as to essence but as to state. Therefore we must conclude that initial fear, as we understand it here, does not differ essentially from filial fear.

[2] PL 35, 2049.

Reply Obj. 1. The fear which is a beginning of love is servile fear, which "introduces charity, just as the bristle introduces the thread," as Augustine states (*Tract.* ix *in Ep.* 1. *Joann.*).[1] Or else, if it be referred to initial fear, this is said to be the beginning of love, not absolutely, but relatively to the state of perfect charity.

Reply Obj. 2. Initial fear does not dread punishment as its proper object, but as having something of servile fear connected with it. For this servile fear, as to its substance, remains indeed, with charity, its servility being cast aside; but its act remains with imperfect charity in the man who is moved to perform good actions not only through love of justice, but also through fear of punishment, though this same act ceases in the man who has perfect charity, which *casteth out fear,* according to I John 4. 18.

Reply Obj. 3. Initial fear is a mean between servile and filial fear, not as between two things of the same genus, but as the imperfect is a mean between a perfect being and a non-being, as stated in the *Metaphysics,*[2] for it is the same substantially as the perfect being, while it differs altogether from non-being.

ARTICLE 9. *Whether Fear Is a Gift of the Holy Ghost?*

We proceed thus to the Ninth Article: It seems that fear is not a gift of the Holy Ghost.

Objection 1. For no gift of the Holy Ghost is opposed to a virtue, which is also from the Holy Ghost; otherwise the Holy Ghost would be in opposition to Himself. Now fear is opposed to hope, which is a virtue. Therefore fear is not a gift of the Holy Ghost.

Obj. 2. Further, It is proper to a theological virtue to have God for its object. But fear has God for its object, in so far as God is feared. Therefore fear is not a gift, but a theological virtue.

Obj. 3. Further, Fear arises from love. But love is counted as a theological virtue. Therefore fear also is a theological virtue, being connected with the same matter, as it were.

Obj. 4. Further, Gregory says (*Moral.* ii, 49)[3] that fear is bestowed as a remedy against pride. But the virtue of humility is opposed to pride. Therefore again, fear is a kind of virtue.

Obj. 5. Further, The gifts are more perfect than the virtues, since they are bestowed in support of the virtues as Gregory says (*Moral.* ii, 49).[4] Now hope is more perfect than fear, since hope regards good, while fear regards evil. Since, then, hope is a virtue, it should not be said that fear is a gift.

On the contrary, The fear of the Lord is numbered among the seven gifts of the Holy Ghost (Isa. 11. 3).

I answer that, Fear is of several kinds, as stated above (A. 2). Now it is not human fear, according to Augustine (*De Gratia et Lib. Arb.* xviii),[5] that is a gift of God,—for it was by this fear that Peter denied Christ,—but that fear of which it was said (Matt. 10. 28): *Fear Him that can destroy both soul and body into hell.*

Again servile fear is not to be reckoned among the seven gifts of the Holy Ghost, though it is from Him, because, according to Augustine (*De Nat. et Grat.* lvii)[6] it is compatible with the will to sin; but the gifts of the Holy Ghost are incompatible with the will to sin, as they are inseparable from charity, as stated above (Part I-II, Q. LXVIII, A. 5).

It follows, therefore, that the fear of God, which is numbered among the seven gifts of the Holy Ghost, is filial or chaste fear. For it was stated above (Part I-II, Q. LXVIII, AA. 1, 3) that the gifts of the Holy Ghost are certain habitual perfections of the soul's powers, by which these are rendered amenable to the motion of the Holy Ghost, just as, by the moral virtues, the appetitive powers are rendered amenable to the motion of reason. Now for a thing to be amenable to the motion of a certain mover, the first condition required is that it be a non-resistant subject of that mover, because resistance of the movable subject to the mover hinders the movement. This is what filial or chaste fear does, since thus we revere God and avoid separating ourselves from Him. Hence, according to Augustine (*De Serm. Dom. in Monte,* i, 4)[7] filial fear holds the first place, as it were, among the gifts of the Holy Ghost, in the ascending order, and the last place, in the descending order.

Reply Obj. 1. Filial fear is not opposed to the virtue of hope, since thus we fear, not that we may fail of what we hope to obtain by God's help, but lest we withdraw ourselves from this help. Therefore filial fear and hope cling together, and perfect one another.

Reply Obj. 2. The proper and principal object of fear is the evil shunned, and in this way, as stated above (A. 1), God cannot be an object of fear. Yet He is, in this way, the object of hope and the other theological virtues,

[1] PL 35, 2047.   [2] Aristotle, 11, 2 (994ª28).

[3] PL 75, 593.   [4] PL 75, 592.   [5] PL 44, 904.   [6] PL 44, 280.   [7] PL 34, 1234.

since, by the virtue of hope, we trust in God's help, not only to obtain any other goods, but, chiefly, to obtain God Himself, as the principal good. The same evidently applies to the other theological virtues.

Reply Obj. 3. From the fact that love is the principle of fear, it does not follow that the fear of God is of a distinct habit from charity, which is the love of God, since love is the principle of all the emotions, and yet we are perfected by different habits in respect of different emotions. Therefore love has more of the character of a virtue than fear has because love regards good, to which virtue is principally directed according to its very notion, as was shown above (Part I-II, Q. LV, AA. 3, 4); for this reason hope also is counted as a virtue; but fear principally regards evil, the avoidance of which it denotes, and so it is something less than a theological virtue.

Reply Obj. 4. According to Ecclus. 10. 14, *the beginning of the pride of man is to fall off from God,* that is, to refuse submission to God, and this is opposed to filial fear, which reveres God. Thus fear cuts off the source of pride, for which reason it is bestowed as a remedy against pride. Yet it does not follow that it is the same as the virtue of humility, but that it is its principle. For the gifts of the Holy Ghost are the principles of the intellectual and moral virtues, as stated above (Part I-II, Q. LXVIII, A. 4), while the theological virtues are the principles of the gifts, as stated above (Part I-II, Q. LXIX, A. 4, Reply 3).

This suffices for the *Reply to the Fifth Objection.*

ARTICLE 10. *Whether Fear Decreases When Charity Increases?*

We proceed thus to the Tenth Article: It seems that fear decreases when charity increases.

Objection 1. For Augustine says in his commentary on the First Canonical Epistle of John (*Tract.* ix):[1] "The more charity increases, the more fear decreases."

Obj. 2. Further, Fear decreases when hope increases. But charity increases when hope increases, as stated above (Q. XVII, A. 8). Therefore fear decreases when charity increases.

Obj. 3. Further, Love implies union, but fear implies separation. Now separation decreases when union increases. Therefore fear decreases when the love of charity increases.

On the contrary, Augustine says (QQ. LXXXIII,

qu. 36)[2] that "the fear of God not only begins but also perfects wisdom, whereby we love God above all things, and our neighbour as ourselves."

I answer that, Fear is twofold, as stated above (A. 2): one is filial fear, by which a son fears to offend his father or to be separated from him; the other is servile fear, by which one fears punishment. Now filial fear must increase when charity increases, even as an effect increases with the increase of its cause. For the more one loves a man, the more one fears to offend him and to be separated from him. On the other hand servile fear, as regards its servility, is entirely cast out when charity comes, although the fear of punishment remains as to its substance, as stated above (A. 6). This fear decreases as charity increases, chiefly as regards its act, since the more a man loves God, the less he fears punishment; first, because he thinks less of his own good, to which punishment is opposed; secondly, because, the faster he clings, the more confident he is of the reward, and, consequently, the less fearful of punishment.

Reply Obj. 1. Augustine speaks there of the fear of punishment.

Reply Obj. 2. It is fear of punishment that decreases when hope increases; but with the increase of the latter filial fear increases, because the more certainly a man expects to obtain a good by another's help, the more he fears to offend him or to be separated from him.

Reply Obj. 3. Filial fear does not imply separation from God, but submission to Him, and shuns separation from that submission. Yet, in a way, it implies separation, in the point of not presuming to equal oneself to Him, and of submitting to Him, which separation is to be found even in charity, in so far as a man loves God more than himself and more than anything else. Hence the increase of the love of charity implies not a decrease but an increase in the reverence of fear.

ARTICLE 11. *Whether Fear Remains in Heaven?*

We proceed thus to the Eleventh Article: It seems that fear does not remain in heaven.

Objection 1. For it is written (Prov. 1. 33): *He ... shall enjoy abundance, without fear of evils,* which is to be understood as referring to those who already enjoy wisdom in everlasting happiness. Now every fear is about some evil, since evil is the object of fear, as stated above

[1] PL 35, 2047.

[2] PL 40, 26.

(AA. 2, 5; Part I-II, Q. XLII, A. 1). Therefore there will be no fear in heaven.

Obj. 2. Further, In heaven men will be conformed with God, according to I John 3. 2, *When He shall appear, we shall be like to Him.* But God fears nothing. Therefore, in heaven, men will have no fear.

Obj. 3. Further, Hope is more perfect than fear, since hope concerns good, and fear, evil. Now hope will not be in heaven. Therefore neither will there be fear in heaven.

On the contrary, It is written (Ps. 18. 10): *The fear of the Lord is holy, enduring for ever and ever.*

I answer that, Servile fear, or fear of punishment, will by no means be in heaven, since such a fear is excluded by the security which is essential to everlasting happiness, as stated above (Part I-II, Q. V, A. 4). But with regard to filial fear, as it increases with the increase of charity, so is it perfected when charity is made perfect; hence, in heaven, it will not have quite the same act as it has now.

In order to make this clear, we must observe that the proper object of fear is a possible evil, just as the proper object of hope is a possible good. And since the movement of fear is like one of avoidance, fear implies avoidance of a possible arduous evil, for little evils inspire no fear. Now as a thing's good consists in its staying in its own order, so a thing's evil consists in its forsaking its order. Again, the order of a rational creature is that it should be under God and above other creatures. Hence, just as it is an evil for a rational creature to submit, by love, to a lower creature, so too is it an evil for it if it does not submit to God, but presumptuously revolts against Him or contemns Him. Now this evil is possible to a rational creature considered as to its nature, on account of the natural flexibility of the free choice; but in the blessed, it becomes impossible, by reason of the perfection of glory. Therefore the avoidance of this evil that consists in non-subjection to God, and is possible to nature, but impossible in the state of bliss, will be in heaven; while in this life there is avoidance of this evil as of something altogether possible.

Hence Gregory, expounding the words of Job (26. 11), *The pillars of heaven tremble, and dread at His beck,* says (*Moral.* xvii, 29):[1] "The heavenly powers that gaze on Him without ceasing, tremble while contemplating: but their awe, lest it should be of a penal nature, is one

[1] PL 76, 31.

not of fear but of wonder," because, that is, they wonder at God's supereminence and incomprehensibility. Augustine also[2] in this sense, admits fear in heaven, although he leaves the question doubtful. "If," he says, "this chaste fear that endureth for ever and ever is to be in the future life, it will not be a fear that is afraid of an evil which might possibly occur, but a fear that holds fast to a good which we cannot lose. For when we love the good which we have acquired, with an unchangeable love, without doubt, if it is allowable to say so, our fear is sure of avoiding evil. Because chaste fear denotes a will that cannot consent to sin, and whereby we avoid sin without trembling lest, in our weakness, we fall, and possess ourselves in the tranquillity born of charity. But, if no kind of fear is possible there, perhaps fear is said to endure for ever and ever, because that which fear will lead us to, will be everlasting."

Reply Obj. 1. The passage quoted excludes from the blessed the fear that denotes solicitude, and anxiety about evil, but not the fear which is accompanied by security.

Reply Obj. 2. As Dionysius says (*Div. Nom.* ix),[3] "the same things are both like and unlike God. They are like by reason of a variable imitation of the Inimitable,"—that is because, so far as they can, they imitate God, Who cannot be imitated perfectly,—"they are unlike because they are the effects of a Cause of Whom they fall short infinitely and immeasurably." Hence, if there be no fear in God (since there is none above Him to whom He may be subject) it does not follow that there is none in the blessed, whose happiness consists in perfect subjection to God.

Reply Obj. 3. Hope implies a certain defect, namely the futurity of happiness, which ceases when happiness is present. But fear implies a natural defect in a creature, in so far as it is infinitely distant from God, and this defect will remain even in heaven. Hence fear will not be cast out altogether.

ARTICLE 12. *Whether Poverty of Spirit Is the Beatitude Corresponding to the Gift of Fear?*

We proceed thus to the Twelfth Article: It seems that poverty of spirit is not the beatitude corresponding to the gift of fear.

Objection 1. For fear is the beginning of the spiritual life, as explained above (A. 7); but poverty pertains to the perfection of the spiritual life, according to Matt. (19. 21), *If thou*

[2] *City of God,* XIV, 9 (PL 41, 416).   [3] Sect. 7 (PG 3, 916).

wilt be perfect, go sell what thou hast, and give to the poor. Therefore poverty of spirit does not correspond to the gift of fear.

Obj. 2. Further, It is written (Ps. 118. 120): *Pierce Thou my flesh with Thy fear,* from which it seems to follow that it pertains to fear to restrain the flesh. But the curbing of the flesh seems to pertain rather to the beatitude of mourning. Therefore the beatitude of mourning corresponds to the gift of fear, rather than the beatitude of poverty.

Obj. 3. Further, The gift of fear corresponds to the virtue of hope, as stated above (A. 9, REPLY 1). Now the last beatitude which is, *Blessed are the peacemakers, for they shall be called the children of God,* seems above all to correspond to hope, because according to Rom. 5. 2, *we . . . glory in the hope of the glory of the sons of God.* Therefore that beatitude corresponds to the gift of fear, rather than poverty of spirit.

Obj. 4. Further, It was stated above (Part I-II, Q. LXX, A. 2) that the fruits correspond to the beatitudes. Now none of the fruits correspond to the gift of fear. Neither, therefore, does any of the beatitudes.

On the contrary, Augustine says (*De Serm. Dom. in Monte,* i, 4):[1] "The fear of the Lord is befitting the humble of whom it is said: Blessed are the poor in spirit."

I answer that, Poverty of spirit properly corresponds to fear. Because, since it pertains to filial fear to show reverence and submission to God, whatever results from this submission pertains to the gift of fear. Now from the very fact that a man submits to God, it follows that he ceases to seek greatness either in himself or in another but seeks it only in God. For that would be inconsistent with perfect subjection to God; hence it is written (Ps. 19. 8): *Some trust in chariots and some in horses; but we will call upon the name of . . . our God.* It follows that if a man fear God perfectly, he does not, by pride, seek greatness either in himself or in external goods, namely honours and riches. In either case this pertains to poverty of spirit, in so far as the latter denotes either the voiding of a puffed up and proud spirit, according to Augustine's interpretation (*loc. cit.*),[2] or the renunciation of worldly goods which is done in spirit, that is, by one's own will, through the instigation of the Holy Spirit, according to the expounding of Ambrose on Luke 6. 20[3] and Jerome on Matt. 5. 3.[4]

[1] PL 34, 1234.   [2] PL 34, 1231.   [3] PL 15, 1735.   [4] PL 26, 34.

Reply Obj. 1. Since a beatitude is an act of perfect virtue, all the beatitudes pertain to the perfection of spiritual life. And this perfection seems to require that whoever would strive to obtain a perfect share of spiritual goods, needs to begin by despising earthly goods, so that fear holds the first place among the gifts. Perfection, however, does not consist in the renunciation itself of temporal goods, but rather this is the way to perfection. Filial fear, however, to which the beatitude of poverty corresponds, is consistent with the perfection of wisdom, as stated above (A. 7).

Reply Obj. 2. The undue exaltation of man either in himself or in other things is more directly opposed to that submission to God which is the result of filial fear, than is external pleasure. Yet this is, in consequence, opposed to fear, since whoever fears God and is subject to Him, takes no delight in things other than God. Nevertheless, pleasure is not concerned, as exaltation is, with the arduous character of a thing which fear regards; and so the beatitude of poverty corresponds to fear directly, and the beatitude of mourning, consequently.

Reply Obj. 3. Hope denotes a movement and a relationship of tendency to a term, while fear implies movement by way of a relation of withdrawal from a term. Therefore the last beatitude which is the term of spiritual perfection, fittingly corresponds to hope, by way of ultimate object; but the first beatitude, which implies withdrawal from external things which hinder submission to God, fittingly corresponds to fear.

Reply Obj. 4. As regards the fruits, it seems that those things correspond to the gift of fear, which pertain to the moderate use of temporal things or to abstinence from them; such are modesty, continency and chastity.

QUESTION XX

OF DESPAIR

(*In Four Articles*)

WE must now consider the contrary vices; (1) Despair; (2) Presumption (Q. XXI). Under the first head there are four points of inquiry: (1) Whether despair is a sin? (2) Whether it can be without unbelief? (3) Whether it is the greatest of sins? (4) Whether it arises from sloth?

ARTICLE 1. *Whether Despair Is a Sin?*

We proceed thus to the First Article: It would seem that despair is not a sin.

Objection 1. For every sin includes a turning to a changeable good, together with a turning away from the immutable good, as Augustine states (*De Lib. Arb.* ii, 19).[1] But despair includes no turning to a changeable good. Therefore it is not a sin.

Obj. 2. Further, That which grows from a good root seems to be no sin, because *a good tree cannot bring forth evil fruit* (Matt. 7. 18). Now despair seems to grow from a good root, namely, fear of God, or from horror at the greatness of one's own sins. Therefore despair is not a sin.

Obj. 3. Further, If despair were a sin, it would be a sin also for the damned to despair. But this is not imputed to them as their fault but as part of their damnation. Therefore neither is it imputed to wayfarers as their fault, so that it is not a sin.

On the contrary, That which leads men to sin, seems not only to be a sin itself, but a principle of sins. Now such is despair, for the Apostle says of certain men. (Eph. 4, 19): *Who, despairing, have given themselves up to lasciviousness, unto the working of all uncleanness and* (Vulg.,—*unto*) *covetousness.* Therefore despair is not only a sin but also the principle of other sins.

I answer that, According to the Philosopher,[2] "affirmation and negation in the intellect correspond to search and avoidance in the appetite," while truth and falsehood in the intellect correspond to good and evil in the appetite. Consequently every appetitive movement which is conformed to a true intellect, is good in itself, while every appetitive movement which is conformed to a false intellect is evil in itself and sinful. Now the true opinion of the intellect about God is that from Him comes salvation to mankind, and pardon to sinners, according to Ezech. 18. 23, *I desire not the death of the sinner, but that he should be converted, and live.* (Vulg.,—*Is it My will that a sinner should die . . . and not that he should be converted and live?*) But it is a false opinion that He refuses pardon to the repentant sinner, or that He does not turn sinners to Himself by sanctifying grace. Therefore, just as the movement of hope, which is in conformity with the true opinion, is praiseworthy and virtuous, so the contrary movement of despair, which is in conformity with the false opinion about God, is vicious and sinful.

Reply Obj. 1. In every mortal sin there is, in some way, turning away from the immutable good, and turning to a changeable good, but not always in the same way. Because, since the theological virtues have God for their object, the sins which are contrary to them, such as hatred of God, despair and unbelief, consist principally in turning away from the immutable good; but, consequently, they imply turning to a changeable good, in so far as the soul that is a deserter from God, must necessarily turn to other things. Other sins, however, consist principally in turning to a changeable good, and, consequently, in turning away from the immutable good; for the fornicator intends, not to depart from God, but to enjoy carnal pleasure, the result of which is that he departs from God.

Reply Obj. 2. A thing may grow from a virtuous root in two ways. First, directly and on the part of the virtue itself, just as an act proceeds from a habit; and in this way no sin can grow from a virtuous root, for in this sense Augustine declared (*De Lib. Arb.* ii, 18, 19)[3] that "no man makes evil use of virtue." Secondly, a thing proceeds from a virtue indirectly, or is occasioned by a virtue, and in this way nothing hinders a sin proceeding from a virtue; thus sometimes men pride themselves of their virtues, according to Augustine (*Ep.* ccxi):[4] "Pride lies in wait for good works that they may die." In this way fear of God or horror of one's own sins may lead to despair, in so far as man makes evil use of those good things, by allowing them to be an occasion of despair.

Reply Obj. 3. The damned are outside the pale of hope on account of the impossibility of returning to happiness; hence it is not imputed to them that they hope not, but it is a part of their damnation. Just as also, it would be no sin for a wayfarer to despair of obtaining that which he had no natural capacity for obtaining, or which was not due to be obtained by him; for instance, if a physician were to despair of healing some sick man, or if anyone were to despair of ever becoming rich.

ARTICLE 2. *Whether There Can Be Despair Without Unbelief?*

We proceed thus to the Second Article: It would seem that there can be no despair without unbelief.

Objection 1. For the certainty of hope is derived from faith, and so long as the cause remains the effect is not done away. Therefore

---

[1] PL 32, 1269; cf. Chap. 16 (PL 32, 1269).
[2] *Ethics,* VI, 2 (1139ª27).
[3] PL 32, 1267, 1268.
[4] PL 33, 960.

a man cannot lose the certainty of hope, by despairing, unless his faith be removed.

Obj. 2. Further, To prefer one's own guilt to God's mercy and goodness is to deny the infinity of God's goodness and mercy, and so, pertains to unbelief. But whoever despairs, prefers his own guilt to the Divine mercy and goodness, according to Gen. 4. 13: *My iniquity is greater than that I may deserve pardon.* Therefore whoever despairs, is an unbeliever.

Obj. 3. Further, Whoever falls into a condemned heresy, is an unbeliever. But he that despairs seems to fall into a condemned heresy, namely, that of the Novatians, who say that there is no pardon for sins after Baptism. Therefore it seems that whoever despairs is an unbeliever.

On the contrary, To remove that which follows is not to remove that which precedes. But hope follows faith, as stated above (Q. XVII, A. 7). Therefore when hope is removed, faith can remain. Therefore not everyone who despairs, is an unbeliever.

I answer that, Unbelief pertains to the intellect, but despair, to the appetite. And the intellect is about universals, while the appetite is moved in connection with particulars, since the appetitive movement is from the soul towards things, which, in themselves, are particular. Now it may happen that a man, while having a right opinion in the universal, is not rightly disposed as to his appetitive movement, his estimation being corrupted in a particular matter, because, in order to pass from the universal estimation to the appetite for a particular thing, it is necessary to have a particular estimate,[1] just as it is impossible to infer a particular conclusion from an universal proposition, except through the holding of a particular proposition. Hence it is that a man, while having right faith, in the universal, fails in an appetitive movement, in regard to some particular, his particular estimation being corrupted by a habit or a passion, just as the fornicator, by choosing fornication as a good for himself at this particular moment, has a corrupt estimation in a particular matter, although he retains the true universal estimation according to faith, namely that fornication is a mortal sin. In the same way, a man, while retaining in the universal the true estimation of faith, that is, that there is in the Church the power of forgiving sins, may suffer a movement of despair, namely, that for him, being in such a state, there is no hope of pardon, his estimation being corrupted

in a particular matter. In this way there can be despair, just as there can be other mortal sins, without unbelief.

Reply Obj. 1. The effect is done away not only when the first cause is removed, but also when the secondary cause is removed. Hence the movement of hope can be done away not only by the removal of the universal estimation of faith, which is, so to say, the first cause of the certainty of hope, but also by the removal of the particular estimation, which is the secondary cause, as it were.

Reply Obj. 2. If anyone were to judge, in universal, that God's mercy is not infinite, he would be an unbeliever. But he who despairs does not judge thus, but that, for him in that state, on account of some particular disposition, there is no hope of the Divine mercy.

The same answer applies to the *Third Objection,* since the Novatians denied, in universal, that there is remission of sins in the Church.

ARTICLE 3. *Whether Despair Is the Greatest of Sins?*

We proceed thus to the Third Article: It would seem that despair is not the greatest of sins.

Objection 1. For there can be despair without unbelief, as stated above (A. 2). But unbelief is the greatest of sins, because it overthrows the foundation of the spiritual edifice. Therefore despair is not the greatest of sins.

Obj. 2. Further, A greater evil is opposed to a greater good, as the Philosopher states.[2] But charity is greater than hope, according to I Cor. 13. 13. Therefore hatred is a greater sin than despair.

Obj. 3. Further, In the sin of despair there is nothing but inordinate turning away from God; but in other sins there is not only inordinate turning away from God, but also an inordinate turning (to creatures). Therefore the sin of despair is not more but less grave than other sins.

On the contrary, An incurable sin seems to be most grievous, according to Jerem. 30. 12: *Thy bruise is incurable, thy wound is very grievous.* Now the sin of despair is incurable, according to Jerem. 15. 18: *My wound is desperate so as to refuse to be healed* (Vulg.,— *Why is my wound,* etc.). Therefore despair is a most grievous sin.

I answer that, Those sins which are contrary to the theological virtues are generically more grievous than others because, since the theo-

---

[1] *Soul,* III, 11 (434ª19).

[2] *Ethics,* VIII, 10 (1160ᵇ9).

logical virtues have God for their object, the sins which are opposed to them imply turning away from God directly and principally. Now every mortal sin takes its principal malice and gravity from the fact of its turning away from God, for if it were possible to turn to a changeable good, even inordinately, without turning away from God, it would not be a mortal sin. Consequently a sin which, first and of its very nature, includes turning away from God, is most grievous among mortal sins.

Now unbelief, despair and hatred of God are opposed to the theological virtues; and among them, if we compare hatred of God and unbelief to despair, we shall find that, in themselves, that is, in respect of their proper species, they are more grievous. For unbelief is due to a man not believing God's own truth, while the hatred of God arises from man's will being opposed to God's goodness itself; but despair consists in a man ceasing to hope for a share of God's goodness. Hence it is clear that unbelief and hatred of God are against God as He is in Himself, while despair is against Him according as His good is shared in by us. Therefore strictly speaking it is a more grievous sin to disbelieve God's truth or to hate God than not to hope to receive glory from Him.

If, however, despair be compared to the other two sins from man's point of view, then despair is more dangerous, since hope withdraws us from evils and induces us to seek for good things, so that when hope is given up, men rush headlong into sin, and are drawn away from good works. And so a gloss on Prov. 24. 10, *If thou lose hope being weary in the day of distress, thy strength shall be diminished*, says:[1] "Nothing is more hateful than despair, for the man that has it loses his constancy both in the every day toils of this life, and, what is worse, in the battle of faith." And Isidore says (*De Sum. Bono*, ii, 14):[2] "To commit a crime is to kill the soul, but to despair is to fall into hell."

ARTICLE 4. *Whether Despair Arises From Sloth?*

We proceed thus to the Fourth Article: It would seem that despair does not arise from sloth.

Objection 1. Because different causes do not give rise to one same effect. "Now despair of the future life arises from lust," according to Gregory (*Moral.* xxxi, 45),[3] Therefore it does not arise from sloth.

Obj. 2. Further, Just as despair is contrary to hope, so is sloth contrary to spiritual joy. But spiritual joy arises from hope, according to Rom. 12. 12, *rejoicing in hope*. Therefore sloth arises from despair, and not vice versa.

Obj. 3. Further, Contrary effects have contrary causes. Now hope, the contrary of which is despair, seems to proceed from the consideration of Divine favours, especially the Incarnation, for Augustine says (*De Trin.* xiii, 10):[4] "Nothing was so necessary to raise our hope, than that we should be shown how much God loves us. Now what greater proof could we have of this than that God's Son should deign to unite Himself to our nature?" Therefore despair arises rather from the neglect of the above consideration than from sloth.

On the contrary, Gregory (*Moral.* xxxi, *loc. cit.*) reckons despair among the effects of sloth.

I answer that, As stated above (Q. XVII, A. 1; Part I-II, Q. XL, A. 1), the object of hope is a good, difficult but possible to obtain by oneself or by another. Consequently the hope of obtaining happiness may be lacking in a person in two ways: first, through his not considering it an arduous good, secondly, through his considering it impossible to obtain either by himself, or by another. Now, the fact that spiritual goods taste good to us no more, or seem to be goods of no great account, is chiefly due to our affections being infected with the love of bodily pleasures, among which sexual pleasures hold the first place; for the love of those pleasures leads man to have a distaste for spiritual things, and not to hope for them as arduous goods. In this way despair is caused by lust.

On the other hand, the fact that a man considers an arduous good impossible to obtain, either by himself or by another, is due to his being over downcast, because when this state of mind dominates his affections, it seems to him that he will never be able to rise to any good. And since sloth is a sadness that casts down the spirit, in this way despair is born of sloth.

Now this is the proper object of hope,—that the thing is possible, because the good and the arduous pertain to other passions also. Hence despair is born of sloth in a more special way, though it may arise from lust, for the reason given above.

This suffices for the *Reply to the First Objection*.

Reply Obj. 2. According to the Philosopher,[5] just as hope gives rise to joy, so, when a man

[1] *Glossa ordin.* (III, 332A).
[2] PL 83, 617.   [3] PL 76, 621.
[4] PL 42, 1024.
[5] *Rhetoric*, I, 11 (1370^{a}30); cf. II, 2, 12 (1378^{b}2; 1389^{a}19).

is joyful he has greater hope; and, accordingly, those who are sorrowful fall the more easily into despair, according to II Cor. 2. 7: *Lest . . . such an one be swallowed up by overmuch sorrow.* Yet, since the object of hope is good, to which the appetite tends naturally, and which it shuns not naturally but only on account of some supervening obstacle, it follows that, more directly, hope gives birth to joy, while on the contrary despair is born of sorrow.

Reply Obj. 3. This very neglect to consider the Divine favours arises from sloth. For when a man is influenced by a certain passion he considers chiefly the things which pertain to that passion, so that a man who is full of sorrow does not easily think of great and joyful things, but only of sad things, unless by a great effort he turn his thoughts away from sadness.

QUESTION XXI
OF PRESUMPTION
(In Four Articles)

WE must now consider presumption, under which head there are four points of inquiry: (1) What is the object on which presumption is based? (2) Whether presumption is a sin? (3) To what is it opposed? (4) From what vice does it arise?

ARTICLE 1. *Whether Presumption Is Based on God, or in Our Own Power?*

We proceed thus to the First Article: It would seem that presumption, which is a sin against the Holy Ghost, is based, not in God, but on our own power.

Objection 1. For the lesser the power, the more grievously does he sin who leans too much on it. But man's power is less than God's. Therefore it is a more grievous sin to presume on human power than to presume on the power of God. Now the sin against the Holy Ghost is most grievous. Therefore presumption, which is counted as a species of sin Against the Holy Ghost, clings to human rather than to Divine power.

Obj. 2. Further, Other sins arise from the sin against the Holy Ghost, for this sin is called malice which is a source from which sins arise. Now other sins seem to arise from the presumption by which man presumes on himself, rather than from the presumption by which he presumes on God, since self-love is the origin of sin, according to Augustine.[1] Therefore it seems that presumption which is a sin against the Holy Ghost, relies chiefly on human power.

[1] *City of God*, XIV, 28 (PL 41, 436).

Obj. 3. Further, Sin arises from the inordinate turning to a changeable good. Now presumption is a sin. Therefore it arises from turning to human power, which is a changeable good, rather than from turning to the power of God, which is an immutable good.

On the contrary, Just as, through despair, a man despises the Divine mercy, on which hope relies, so, through presumption, he despises the Divine justice, which punishes the sinner. Now justice is in God even as mercy is. Therefore, just as despair consists in turning from God, so presumption consists in an inordinate turning to Him.

I answer that, Presumption seems to imply immoderate hope. Now the object of hope is an arduous possible good, and a thing is possible to a man in two ways, first by his own power, secondly by the power of God alone. With regard to either hope there may be presumption owing to lack of moderation. As to the hope with which a man relies on his own power, there is presumption if he tends to a good which surpasses his powers as though it were possible to him, according to Judith 6. 15: *Thou humblest them that presume of themselves.* This presumption is contrary to the virtue of magnanimity which holds to the mean in this kind of hope.

But as to the hope with which a man relies on the power of God, there may be presumption through immoderation, in the fact that a man tends to some good which is not possible as though it were possible by the power and mercy of God, for instance, if a man hope to obtain pardon without repenting, or glory without merits. This presumption is, properly, a species of sin against the Holy Ghost, because, namely, by presuming thus a man removes or despises the assistance of the Holy Spirit, by which he is withdrawn from sin.

Reply Obj. 1. As stated above (Q. XX, A. 3; Part I-II, Q. LXXIII, A. 3) a sin which is against God is, in its genus, graver than other sins. Hence presumption by which a man relies on God inordinately is a more grievous sin than the presumption of leaning on one's own power, since to rely on the Divine power for obtaining what is unbecoming to God, is to depreciate the Divine power, and it is evident that it is a graver sin to detract from the Divine power than to exaggerate one's own.

Reply Obj. 2. The presumption by which a man presumes inordinately on God includes self-love, by which he loves his own good inordinately. For when we desire a thing very much, we think we can easily procure it through others, even though we cannot.

Reply Obj. 3. Presumption on God's mercy implies both turning to a changeable good, in so far as it arises from an inordinate desire of one's own good, and turning away from the immutable good, in as much as it ascribes to the Divine power that which is unbecoming to it, for thus man turns away from God's power.

ARTICLE 2. *Whether Presumption Is a Sin?*

We proceed thus to the Second Article: It would seem that presumption is not a sin.

Objection 1. For no sin is a reason why man should be heard by God. Yet, through presumption some are heard by God, for it is written (Judith 9. 17): *Hear me a poor wretch making supplication to Thee, and presuming of Thy mercy.* Therefore presumption on God's mercy is not a sin.

Obj. 2. Further, Presumption denotes excessive hope. But there cannot be excess of that hope which is in God, since His power and mercy are infinite. Therefore it seems that presumption is not a sin.

Obj. 3. Further, That which is a sin does not excuse from sin. But presumption excuses from sin; for the Master says (*Sent.* ii, *d.* 22)[1] that Adam sinned less, because he sinned in the hope of pardon, which seems to indicate presumption. Therefore presumption is not a sin.

On the contrary, It is counted as a species of sin against the Holy Ghost.

I answer that, As stated above (Q. XX, A. 1) with regard to despair, every appetitive movement that is conformed to a false intellect, is evil in itself and sinful. Now presumption is an appetitive movement, since it denotes an inordinate hope. Moreover it is conformed to a false intellect, just as despair is; for just as it is false that God does not pardon the repentant, or that He does not turn sinners to repentance, so is it false that He grants forgiveness to those who persevere in their sins, and that He gives glory to those who cease from good works. And it is to this opinion that the movement of presumption is conformed. Consequently presumption is a sin, but less grave than despair, since, on account of His infinite goodness, it is more proper to God to have mercy and to spare, than to punish; for the former becomes God in Himself, the latter becomes Him by reason of our sins.

Reply Obj. 1. Presumption sometimes stands for hope, because even the right hope which

[1] Chap. 4 (QR 1, 412).

we have in God seems to be presumption, if it be measured according to man's estate. Yet it is not presumption if we look at the immensity of the goodness of God.

Reply Obj. 2. Presumption does not denote excessive hope, as though man hoped too much in God, but through man hoping to obtain from God something unbecoming to Him, which is the same as to hope too little in Him, since it implies a depreciation of His power, as stated above (A. 1, REPLY 1).

Reply Obj. 3. To sin with the intention of persevering in sin and through the hope of being pardoned, is presumptuous, and this does not diminish, but increases sin. To sin, however, with the hope of obtaining pardon some time, and with the intention of refraining from sin and of repenting of it, is not presumptuous, but diminishes sin, because this seems to indicate a will less hardened in sin.

ARTICLE 3. *Whether Presumption Is More Opposed to Fear Than to Hope?*

We proceed thus to the Third Article: It would seem that presumption is more opposed to fear than to hope.

Objection 1. Because inordinate fear is opposed to right fear. Now presumption seems to pertain to inordinate fear, for it is written (Wisd. 17. 10): *A troubled conscience always presumes* (Douay,—forecasteth) *grievous things,* and (*ibid.* 11) *that fear is a help to presumption.* (Vulg.,—*Fear is nothing else but a yielding up of the succours from thought.*) Therefore presumption is opposed to fear rather than to hope.

Obj. 2. Further, Contraries are most distant from one another. Now presumption is more distant from fear than from hope, because presumption implies movement to something, just as hope does, while fear denotes movement from a thing. Therefore presumption is more contrary to fear than to hope.

Obj. 3. Further, Presumption excludes fear altogether, while it does not exclude hope altogether, but only the rectitude of hope. Since therefore opposites destroy one another, it seems that presumption is opposed to fear rather than to hope.

On the contrary, When two vices are opposed to one another they are contrary to the same virtue, as timidity and audacity are opposed to fortitude. Now the sin of presumption is contrary to the sin of despair, which is directly opposed to hope. Therefore it seems that presumption also is more directly opposed to hope.

I answer that, As Augustine states (*Contra Julian.* iv, 3),[1] "every virtue not only has a contrary vice manifestly distinct from it, as temerity is opposed to prudence, but also a sort of kindred vice, alike, not in truth but only in its deceitful appearance, as cunning is opposed to prudence." This agrees with the Philosopher who says[2] that a virtue seems to have more in common with one of the opposite vices than with the other, as temperance with insensibility, and fortitude with audacity. Accordingly presumption appears to be manifestly opposed to fear, especially servile fear, which looks to the punishment arising from God's justice, the remission of which presumption hopes for; yet by a kind of false likeness it is more opposed to hope, since it denotes an inordinate hope in God. And since things are more directly opposed when they belong to the same genus than when they belong to different genera, it follows that presumption is more directly opposed to hope than to fear. For they both look to and rely on the same object, hope in an orderly way, presumption inordinately.

Reply Obj. 1. Just as hope is misused in speaking of evils, and properly applied in speaking of good, so is presumption; it is in this way that inordinate fear is called presumption.

Reply Obj. 2. Contraries are things that are most distant from one another within the same genus. Now presumption and hope denote a movement of the same genus, which can be either ordered or inordinate. Hence presumption is more directly contrasted to hope than to fear, since it is contrasted to hope by reason of a proper difference, as an inordinate thing to an ordinate one, while it is contrasted to fear in respect of its generic difference, which is the movement of hope.

Reply Obj. 3. Presumption is contrasted to fear by a generic contrariety, and to the virtue of hope by a contrariety of difference. Hence presumption excludes fear altogether even generically; but it does not exclude hope except by reason of its difference, by excluding its ordinateness.

ARTICLE 4. *Whether Presumption Arises From Vainglory?*

We proceed thus to the Fourth Article: It seems that presumption does not arise from vainglory.

Objection 1. For presumption seems to rely most of all on the Divine mercy. Now mercy (*misericordia*) regards unhappiness (*miseriam*)

which is contrary to glory. Therefore presumption does not arise from vainglory.

Obj. 2. Further, Presumption is opposed to despair. Now despair arises from sorrow, as stated above (Q. XX, A. 4, Reply 2). Since therefore opposites have opposite causes, presumption would seem to arise from pleasure, and consequently from sins of the flesh, which give the most absorbing pleasure.

Obj. 3. Further, The vice of presumption consists in tending to some impossible good as though it were possible. Now it is owing to ignorance that one thinks an impossible thing to be possible. Therefore presumption arises from ignorance rather than from vainglory.

On the contrary, Gregory says (*Moral.* xxxi, 45)[3] that "presumption of novelties is a daughter of vainglory."

I answer that, As stated above (A. 1), presumption is twofold. One by which a man leans on his own power, when he attempts something beyond his power, as though it were possible to him. And presumption of this kind clearly arises from vainglory, for it is owing to a great desire for glory that a man attempts things beyond his power, and especially novelties which call for greater admiration. Hence Gregory states explicitly that presumption of novelties is a daughter of vainglory. The other presumption is an inordinate trust in the Divine mercy or power, consisting in the hope of obtaining glory without merits, or pardon without repentance. Such-like presumption seems to arise directly from pride, as though man thought so much of himself as to think that God would not punish him or exclude him from glory, however much he might be a sinner.

This suffices for the *Replies to the Objections.*

QUESTION XXII

OF THE PRECEPTS RELATING TO HOPE AND FEAR

(*In Two Articles*)

We must now consider the precepts relating to hope and fear, under which head there are two points of inquiry: (1) The precepts relating to hope; (2) The precepts relating to fear.

ARTICLE 1. *Whether There Should Be a Precept of Hope?*

We proceed thus to the First Article: It seems that no precept should be given relating to the virtue of hope.

Objection 1. For when an effect is sufficiently

procured by one cause, there is no need to induce it by another. Now man is sufficiently induced by his natural inclination to hope for good. Therefore there is no need of a precept of the Law to induce him to do this.

Obj. 2. Further, Since precepts are given about acts of virtue, the chief precepts are about the acts of the chief virtues. Now the chief of all the virtues are the three theological virtues, namely, hope, faith and charity. Consequently, as the chief precepts of the Law are those of the decalogue, to which all others may be reduced, as stated above (Part I-II, Q. C, A. 3), it seems that if any precept of hope were given, it should be found among the precepts of the decalogue. But it is not to be found there. Therefore it seems that the Law should contain no precept of hope.

Obj. 3. Further, To prescribe an act of virtue is equivalent to a prohibition of the act of the opposite vice. Now no precept is to be found forbidding despair which is contrary to hope. Therefore it seems unfitting for a precept of hope to be given.

On the contrary, Augustine says on John 15. 12, *This is My commandment, that you love one another* (*Tract.* lxxxiii *in Joann.*):[1] "How many things are commanded us about faith! How many relating to hope!" Therefore it is fitting that some precepts should be given about hope.

I answer that, Among the precepts contained in Holy Writ, some belong to the substance of the Law, others are preambles to the Law. The preambles to the Law are those without which no law is possible; such are the precepts relating to the act of faith and the act of hope, because the act of faith inclines man's mind so that he recognizes the Author of the Law to be One to Whom he owes submission, while, by the hope of a reward, he is induced to observe the precepts. The precepts that belong to the substance of the Law are those which relate to right conduct and are imposed on man already subject and ready to obey. And therefore when the Law was given these precepts were set forth from the very outset under the form of a command.

Yet the precepts of hope and faith were not to be given under the form of a command, since, unless man already believed and hoped, it would be useless to give him the Law. But, just as the precept of faith had to be given under the form of an announcement or reminder, as stated above (Q. XVI, A. 1), so too, the precept of hope, in the first promulgation of the Law, had

to be given under the form of a promise. For he who promises rewards to them that obey him, by that very fact, urges them to hope. Hence all the promises contained in the Law are incitements to hope.

Since, however, when once the Law has been given, it is for a wise man to induce men not only to observe the precepts, but also, and much more, to safeguard the foundation of the Law, therefore, after the first promulgation of the Law, Holy Writ holds out to man many inducements to hope, even by way of warning or command, and not merely by way of promise, as in the Law; for instance in the Psalm (61. 9): *Hope* (Douay,—*Trust*) *in Him all ye congregation of the people,* and in many other passages of the Scriptures.

Reply Obj. 1. Nature inclines us to hope for the good which is proportionate to human nature; but for man to hope for a supernatural good he had to be induced by the authority of the Divine law, partly by promises, partly by admonitions and commands. Nevertheless there was need for precepts of the Divine law to be given even for those things to which natural reason inclines us, such as the acts of the moral virtues, for the sake of insuring a greater stability, especially since the natural reason of man was clouded by the lusts of sin.

Reply Obj. 2. The precepts of the law of the decalogue belong to the first promulgation of the Law. Hence there was no need for giving a precept of hope among the precepts of the decalogue, and it was enough to induce men to hope by the inclusion of certain promises, as in the case of the first and fourth commandments.

Reply Obj. 3. In those observances to which man is bound as under a duty, it is enough that he receive an affirmative precept as to what he has to do, in which is implied the prohibition of what he must avoid doing. Thus he is given a precept concerning the honour due to parents, but not a prohibition against dishonouring them, except by the law inflicting punishment on those who dishonour their parents. And since in order to be saved it is man's duty to hope in God, he had to be induced to do so by one of the above ways, affirmatively, so to speak, and in which is implied the prohibition of the opposite.

ARTICLE 2. *Whether There Should Have Been Given a Precept of Fear?*

We proceed thus to the Second Article: It would seem that, in the Law, there should not have been given a precept of fear.

Objection 1. For the fear of God is about things which are a preamble to the Law, since it is the *beginning of wisdom* (Ps. 110. 10). Now things which are a preamble to the Law do not come under a precept of the Law. Therefore no precept of fear should be given in the Law.

Obj. 2. Further, Given the cause, the effect is also given. Now love is the cause of fear, since every fear proceeds from some kind of love, as Augustine states (QQ. LXXXIII, *qu.* 33).[1] Therefore given the precept of love, it would have been superfluous to command fear.

Obj. 3. Further, Presumption, in a way, is opposed to fear. But the Law contains no prohibition against presumption. Therefore it seems that neither should any precept of fear have been given.

On the contrary, It is written (Deut. 10. 12): *And now, Israel, what doth the Lord thy God require of thee, but that thou fear the Lord thy God?* But He requires of us that which He commands us to do. Therefore it is a matter of precept that man should fear God.

I answer that, Fear is twofold, servile and filial. Now just as man is induced, by the hope of rewards, to observe precepts of law, so too is he induced thereto by the fear of punishment, which fear is servile. And just as according to what has been said (A. 1), in the promulgation of the Law there was no need for a precept of the act of hope, and men were to be induced to hope by promises, so neither was there need for a precept, under form of command, of fear which regards punishment, and men were to be induced to this fear by the threat of punishment. And this was realized both in the precepts of the decalogue, and afterwards, in due sequence, in the secondary precepts of the Law. Yet, just as the wise men and the prophets who, consequently, strove to strengthen man in the observance of the Law, delivered their teaching about hope under the form of admonition or command, so too did they in the matter of fear.

On the other hand filial fear which shows reverence to God, is a sort of genus in respect of the love of God, and a kind of principle of all observances connected with reverence for God. Hence precepts of filial fear are given in the Law, even as precepts of love, because each is a preamble to the external acts prescribed by the Law and to which the precepts of the decalogue pertain. Hence in the passage quoted in the argument *On the contrary,* man is required to have fear, and *to walk in God's ways,* by worshipping Him, and *to love Him.*

Reply Obj. 1. Filial fear is a preamble to the Law, not as though it were extrinsic to it, but as being a principle of the Law, just as love is. Hence precepts are given of both, since they are like general principles of the whole Law.

Reply Obj. 2. From love proceeds filial fear, as also other good works that are done from charity. Hence, just as after the precept of charity, precepts are given of the other acts of virtue, so at the same time precepts are given of fear and of the love of charity, just as, in demonstrative sciences, it is not enough to lay down the first principles, unless the conclusions also are given which follow from them proximately or remotely.

Reply Obj. 3. Inducement to fear suffices to exclude presumption, even as inducement to hope suffices to exclude despair, as stated above (A. 1, REPLY 3).

QUESTION XXIII
OF CHARITY, CONSIDERED IN ITSELF
(*In Eight Articles*)

IN proper sequence, we must consider charity; and (1) charity itself; (2) the corresponding gift of wisdom (Q. XLV). The first consideration will be fivefold: (1) Charity itself; (2) The object of charity (Q. XXV); (3) Its acts (Q. XXVII); (4) The opposite vices (Q. XXXIV); (5) The precepts relating to charity (Q. XLIV);

The first of these considerations will be twofold: (1) Charity, considered in itself; (2) Charity, considered in its relation to its subject (Q. XXIV). Under the first head there are eight points of inquiry: (1) Whether charity is friendship? (2) Whether it is something created in the soul? (3) Whether it is a virtue? (4) Whether it is a special virtue? (5) Whether it is one virtue? (6) Whether it is the greatest of the virtues? (7) Whether any true virtue is possible without it? (8) Whether it is the form of the virtues?

ARTICLE 1. *Whether Charity Is Friendship?*

We proceed thus to the First Article: It would seem that charity is not friendship.

Objection 1. "For nothing is so proper to friendship as to dwell with one's friend," according to the Philosopher.[2] Now charity is of man towards God and the angels, *whose dwelling* (Douay,—*conversation*) *is not with men* (Dan. 2. 11). Therefore charity is not friendship.

Obj. 2. Further, There is no friendship without return of love.[3] But charity extends even to

---

[1] PL 40, 22.

[2] *Ethics*, VIII, 5 (1157[b]19).   [3] *Ibid.*, VIII, 2 (1155[b]28).

one's enemies, according to Matt. 5. 44: *Love your enemies.* Therefore charity is not friendship.

Obj. 3. Further, According to the Philosopher[1] there are three kinds of friendship, directed respectively towards the delightful, the useful, or the virtuous. Now charity is not friendship for the useful or delightful; for Jerome says in his letter to Paulinus[2] which is to be found at the beginning of the Bible: "True friendship cemented by Christ, is where men are drawn together, not by household interests, not by mere bodily presence, not by crafty and cajoling flattery, but by the fear of God, and the study of the Divine Scriptures." No more is it friendship for the virtuous, since by charity we love even sinners, while friendship based on the virtuous is only for virtuous men.[3] Therefore charity is not friendship.

On the contrary, It is written (John 15. 15): *I will not now call you servants . . . but* My *friends.* Now this was said to them by reason of nothing else than charity. Therefore charity is friendship.

I answer that, According to the Philosopher,[4] not every love has the character of friendship, but that love which is together with benevolence, when, that is, we love someone so as to wish good to him. If, however, we do not wish good to what we love, but wish its good for ourselves, (thus we are said to love wine, or a horse, or the like) it is love not of friendship, but of a kind of concupiscence. For it would be absurd to speak of having friendship for wine or for a horse. Yet neither does well-wishing suffice for friendship, for a certain mutual love is requisite, since friendship is between friend and friend: and this mutual well-wishing is founded on some kind of communication. Accordingly, since there is a communication between man and God, in so far as He communicates His happiness to us, there must be some kind of friendship based on this same communication, of which it is written (I Cor. 1. 9): *God is faithful: by Whom you are called unto the fellowship of His Son.* The love which is based on this communication, is charity. And so it is evident that charity is the friendship of man for God.

Reply Obj. 1. Man's life is twofold. There is his outward life in respect of his sensitive and corporeal nature, and with regard to this life there is no communication or fellowship be-

tween us and God or the angels. The other is man's spiritual life in respect of his mind, and with regard to this life there is fellowship between us and both God and the angels, imperfectly indeed in this present state of life, and so it is written (Phil. 3. 20): *Our conversation is in heaven.* But this "conversation" will be perfected in heaven, when *His servants shall serve Him, and they shall see His face* (Apoc. 22. 3, 4). Therefore charity is imperfect here, but will be perfected in heaven.

Reply Obj. 2. Friendship extends to a person in two ways: first in respect of himself, and in this way friendship never extends but to one's friend; secondly, it extends to someone in respect of another, as, when a man has friendship for a certain person, for his sake he loves all belonging to him, be they children, servants, or connected with him in any way. Indeed, so much do we love our friends, that for their sake we love all who belong to them, even if they hurt or hate us. And in this way, the friendship of charity extends even to our enemies, whom we love out of charity in relation to God, to Whom the friendship of charity is chiefly directed.

Reply Obj. 3. The friendship that is based on the virtuous is directed to none but a virtuous man as the principal person, but for his sake we love those who belong to him, even though they be not virtuous. In this way charity, which above all is friendship based on the virtuous, extends to sinners, whom, out of charity, we love for God's sake.

ARTICLE 2. *Whether Charity Is Something Created in the Soul?*

We proceed thus to the Second Article: It would seem that charity is not something created in the soul.

Objection 1. For Augustine says (*De Trin.* viii, 7):[5] "He that loves his neighbour, consequently, loves love itself. Now God is love. Therefore it follows that he loves God principally." Again he says (*De Trin.* xv, 17):[6] "It was said: God is charity, even as it was said: God is a Spirit." Therefore charity is not something created in the soul, but in God Himself.

Obj. 2. Further, God is the life of the soul spiritually, just as the soul is the life of the body, according to Deut. 30. 20: *He is thy life.* Now the soul by itself quickens the body. Therefore God quickens the soul by Himself. But He quickens it by charity, according to I John 3. 14: *We know that we have passed from death*

---

[1] *Ethics,* VIII, 2, 3(1155^{b}21; 1156^{a}7).
[2] *Epist.,* LIII (PL 22, 540).
[3] Aristotle, *Ethics,* VIII, 4 (1157^{a}18).
[4] *Ibid.,* VIII, 2 (1155^{b}31).

[5] PL 42, 957.
[6] PL 42, 1080.

to life, because we love the brethren. Therefore God is charity itself.

Obj. 3. Further, No created thing is of infinite power; on the contrary every creature is vanity. But charity is not vanity, but rather is opposed to vanity; and it is of infinite power, since it brings the human soul to the infinite good. Therefore charity is not something created in the soul.

On the contrary, Augustine says:[1] "By charity I mean the movement of the soul towards the enjoyment of God for His own sake." But a movement of the soul is something created in the soul. Therefore charity is something created in the soul.

I answer that, The Master looks thoroughly into this question in Q. XVII. of the First Book of the Sentences,[2] and concludes that charity is not something created in the soul, but is the Holy Ghost Himself dwelling in the mind. Nor does he mean to say that this movement of love by which we love God is the Holy Ghost Himself, but that this movement of love is from the Holy Ghost without any intermediary habit, while other virtuous acts are from the Holy Ghost by means of the habits of other virtues, for instance the habit of faith or hope or of some other virtue. And this he said on account of the excellence of charity.

But if we consider the matter rightly this would be, on the contrary, detrimental to charity. For when the Holy Ghost moves the human mind the movement of charity does not proceed from this motion in such a way that the human mind is merely moved, without being the principle of this movement, as when a body is moved by some extrinsic motive power. For this is contrary to the notion of a voluntary act, whose principle needs to be in itself, as stated above (Part I-II, Q. VI, A. 1), so that it would follow that to love is not a voluntary act, which involves a contradiction, since love, of its very notion, implies an act of the will.

Likewise, neither can it be said that the Holy Ghost moves the will in such a way to the act of loving, as though the will were an instrument, for an instrument, though it is a principle of action, nevertheless has not the power to act or not to act, for then again the act would cease to be voluntary and meritorious, although it has been stated above (Part I-II, Q. CXIV, A. 4) that the love of charity is the root of merit. The will must be so moved by the Holy Ghost

to the act of love, that the will itself also is the efficient cause of that act.

Now no act is perfectly produced by an active power, unless it be of the very nature of that power by reason of some form which is the principle of that action. Therefore God, Who moves all things to their due ends, bestowed on each thing the form by which it is inclined to the end appointed to it by Him; and in this way He *ordereth all things sweetly* (Wisd. 8. 1). But it is evident that the act of charity surpasses the nature of the power of the will, so that, therefore, unless some form be superadded to the natural power, inclining it to the act of love, this same act would be less perfect than the natural acts and the acts of the other powers; nor would it be easy and pleasurable to perform. And this is evidently untrue, since no virtue has such a strong inclination to its act as charity has, nor does any virtue perform its act with so great pleasure. Therefore it is most necessary that, for us to perform the act of charity, there should be in us some habitual form superadded to the natural power, inclining that power to the act of charity, and causing it to act with ease and pleasure.

Reply Obj. 1. The Divine Essence Itself is charity, even as It is wisdom, and goodness. Therefore just as we are said to be good with the goodness which is God, and wise with the wisdom which is God (since the goodness by which we are formally good is a participation of Divine goodness, and the wisdom by which we are formally wise, is a share of Divine wisdom), so too, the charity by which formally we love our neighbour is a participation of Divine charity. For this manner of speaking is common among the Platonists, with whose doctrines Augustine was imbued; and the failure to refer to this has been to some an occasion of error.[3]

Reply Obj. 2. God is effectively the life both of the soul by charity, and of the body by the soul; but formally charity is the life of the soul, even as the soul is the life of the body. Consequently we may conclude from this that just as the soul is immediately united to the body, so is charity to the soul.

Reply Obj. 3. Charity works formally. Now the efficacy of a form depends on the power of the agent, who instils the form, and therefore it is evident that charity is not vanity. But because it produces an infinite effect, since, by justifying the soul, it unites it to God, this proves the infinity of the Divine power, which is the author of charity.

---

[1] *Christian Doctrine,* III, 10 (PL 34, 72).
[2] Dist. 1, chap. 1 (QR 1, 106).

[3] Peter Lombard, *Sent.,* 1, d. 17, chap. 1 (QR 1, 106).

ARTICLE 3. *Whether Charity Is a Virtue?*

We proceed thus to the Third Article: It would seem that charity is not a virtue.

Objection 1. For charity is a kind of friendship. Now philosophers do not count friendship a virtue, as may be gathered from the *Ethics*;[1] nor is it numbered among the virtues whether moral or intellectual. Neither, therefore, is charity a virtue.

Obj. 2. Further, "Virtue is the ultimate limit of power."[2] But charity is not something ultimate, for it applies rather to joy and peace. Therefore it seems that charity is not a virtue, but rather is joy and peace.

Obj. 3. Further, Every virtue is an accidental habit. But charity is not an accidental habit, since it is a more excellent thing than the soul itself. But no accident is more excellent than its subject. Therefore charity is not a virtue.

On the contrary, Augustine says (*De Moribus Eccl.* xi):[3] "Charity is a virtue which, when our affections are perfectly ordered, unites us to God, for by it we love Him."

I answer that, Human acts are good according as they are regulated by their due rule and measure. Therefore human virtue which is the principle of all man's good acts consists in following the rule of human acts, which is twofold, as stated above (Q. XVII, A. 1), namely, human reason and God. Consequently just as moral virtue is defined as being in accord with right reason, as stated in the *Ethics*,[4] so too the nature of virtue consists in attaining God, as also stated above with regard to faith (Q. IV, A. 3) and hope (Q. XVII, A. 1). Therefore, it follows that charity is a virtue, for, since charity attains God, it unites us to God, as evidenced by the authority of Augustine quoted above.

Reply Obj. 1. The Philosopher does not deny that friendship is a virtue, but affirms that it is "either a virtue or with a virtue."[5] For we might say that it is a moral virtue about works done in respect of another person, but under a different aspect from justice. For justice is about works done in respect of another person under the aspect of the legal due, while friendship considers the aspect of a friendly and moral duty, or rather that of a gratuitous favour, as the Philosopher explains.[6] Nevertheless it may

be admitted that it is not a virtue distinct of itself from the other virtues. For its praiseworthiness and virtuousness are derived merely from its object, in so far, that is, as it is based on the moral goodness of the virtues. This is evident from the fact that not every friendship is praiseworthy and virtuous, as in the case of friendship based on pleasure or utility. Therefore friendship for the virtuous is something consequent to virtue rather than a virtue. Moreover there is no comparison with charity since it is not founded principally on the virtue of a man, but on the goodness of God.

Reply Obj. 2. It belongs to the same virtue to love a man and to rejoice about him, since joy results from love, as stated above (Part I-II, Q. XXV, A. 2) in the treatise on the passions. And therefore love is considered a virtue, rather than joy, which is an effect of love. And when virtue is described as being something ultimate, we mean that it is last, not in the order of effect, but in the order of excess, just as one hundred pounds exceed forty.

Reply Obj. 3. Every accident is inferior to substance if we consider its being, since substance is a being in itself, while an accident has its being in another. But considered as to its species, an accident which results from the principles of its subject is inferior to its subject, even as an effect is inferior to its cause. But an accident that results from a participation of some higher nature is more excellent than its subject, in so far as it is a likeness of that higher nature, even as light is superior to the diaphanous body. In this way charity is more excellent than the soul, since it is a participation of the Holy Ghost.

ARTICLE 4. *Whether Charity is a Special Virtue?*

We proceed thus to the Fourth Article: It would seem that charity is not a special virtue.

Objection 1. For Jerome says: "Let me briefly define all virtue as the charity with which we love God and our neighbour";[7] and Augustine says (*De Moribus Eccl.*)[8] that virtue is "the order of love." Now no special virtue is included in the definition of virtue in general. Therefore charity is not a special virtue.

Obj. 2. Further, That which extends to all works of virtue, cannot be a special virtue. But charity extends to all works of virtue, according to I Cor. 13. 4: *Charity is patient, is kind*, etc.; indeed it extends to all human works according

---

[1] Aristotle, VIII, 1 (1155ᵃ3).
[2] Aristotle, *Heavens*, I, 11 (281ᵃ11). Cf. Thomas, *In De Cælo*, I, 25.
[3] PL 32, 1319.
[4] Aristotle, II, 6 (1107ᵃ1); Cf. II, 2 (1103ᵇ31).
[5] *Ethics*, VIII, 1 (1155ᵃ3).
[6] *Ibid.*, VIII, 13 (1162ᵇ21).

[7] Cf. Augustine, *Epist.*, CLXVII *Ad Hieron.*, 4 (PL 33, 739).
[8] Cf. *City of God*, XV, 22 (PL 41, 467).

to I Cor. 16. 14: *Let all your things be done in charity*. Therefore charity is not a special virtue.

Obj. 3 Further, The precepts of the Law refer to acts of virtue. Now Augustine says (*De Perfect. Human. Justit.* v, 5)[1] that, " 'Thou shalt love' is a general commandment, and 'Thou shalt not covet,' a general prohibition." Therefore charity is a general virtue.

On the contrary, Nothing general is enumerated together with what is special. But charity is enumerated together with special virtues, namely hope and faith, according to I Cor. 13. 13: *And now there remains faith, hope, charity, these three*. Therefore charity is a special virtue.

I answer that, Acts and habits are specified by their objects, as shown above (Part I-II, Q. XVIII, A. 2; Q. LIV, A. 2). Now the proper object of love is the good, as stated above (Part I-II, Q. XXVII, A. 1), so that wherever there is a special aspect of good, there is a special kind of love. But the Divine good, in so far as it is the object of happiness, has a special aspect of good. And so the love of charity, which is the love of that good, is a special kind of love. Therefore charity is a special virtue.

Reply Obj. 1. Charity is included in the definition of every virtue, not as being essentially every virtue, but because every virtue depends on it in a way, as we shall state further on (A. 7). In this same way prudence is included in the definition of the moral virtues, as explained in the *Ethics*,[2] from the fact that they depend on prudence.

Reply Obj. 2. The virtue or art which is concerned about the last end, commands the virtues or arts which are concerned about other ends which are secondary, just as the military art commands the art of horse-riding.[3] Accordingly since charity has for its object the last end of human life, namely everlasting happiness, it follows that it extends to the acts of a man's whole life, by commanding them, not by eliciting immediately all acts of virtue.

Reply Obj. 3. The precept of love is said to be a general command because all other precepts are reduced to it as to their end, according to I Tim. 1. 5: *The end of the commandment is charity*.

ARTICLE 5. *Whether Charity Is One Virtue?*

We proceed thus to the Fifth Article: It seems that charity is not one virtue.

Objection 1. For habits are distinct according to their objects. Now there are two objects of

charity,—God and our neighbour, which are infinitely distant from one another. Therefore charity is not one virtue.

Obj. 2. Further, Different aspects of the object diversify a habit, even though that object be one in reality, as shown above (Q. XVII, A. 6; Part I-II, Q. LIV, A. 2, Reply 1). Now there are many aspects under which God is an object of love, because we are debtors to His love by reason of each one of His favours. Therefore charity is not one virtue.

Obj. 3. Further, Charity comprises friendship for our neighbour. But the Philosopher posits several species of friendship.[4] Therefore charity is not one virtue, but is multiplied in different species.

On the contrary, Just as God is the object of faith, so is He the object of charity. Now faith is one virtue by reason of the unity of the Divine truth, according to Eph. 4. 5: *One faith*. Therefore charity also is one virtue by reason of the unity of the Divine goodness.

I answer that, Charity, as stated above (A. 1) is a kind of friendship of man for God. Now the different species of friendship are differentiated, first of all, in respect of a diversity of end, and in this way there are three species of friendship, namely friendship for the useful, for the delightful, and for the virtuous; secondly, in respect of the different kinds of communion on which friendships are based; thus there is one species of friendship between kinsmen, and another between fellow citizens or fellow travellers, the former being based on natural communion, the latter on civil communion or on the comradeship of the road, as the Philosopher explains.[5] Now charity cannot be differentiated in either of these ways. For the end of charity is one, namely the goodness of God; and the fellowship of everlasting happiness, on which this friendship is based, is also one. Hence it follows that charity is one virtue absolutely and not divided into several species.

Reply Obj. 1. This argument would hold if God and our neighbour were equally objects of charity. But this is not true, for God is the principal object of charity, while our neighbour is loved out of charity for God's sake.

Reply Obj. 2. God is loved by charity for His own sake; hence charity regards principally but one aspect of lovableness, namely God's goodness, which is His substance, according to Ps. 105. 1: *Give glory to the Lord for He is good*. Other reasons that inspire us with love

---

[1] PL 44, 297.   [2] Aristotle, II, 6 (1107[a]1); VI, 13 (1144[b]26).
[3] *Ibid.*, I, 1 (1094[a]12).

[4] *Ibid.*, VIII, 3, 11 (1156[a]7; 1161[a]10).
[5] *Ethics*, VIII, 12 (1161[b]11).

for Him, or which make it our duty to love Him, are secondary and result from the first.

Reply Obj. 3. Human friendship of which the Philosopher treats has various ends and various forms of fellowship. This does not apply to charity, as stated above. Therefore the comparison fails.

ARTICLE 6. *Whether Charity Is the Most Excellent of the Virtues?*

We proceed thus to the Sixth Article: It seems that charity is not the most excellent of the virtues.

Objection 1. Because the higher power has the higher virtue even as it has a higher operation. Now the intellect is higher than the will, since it directs the will. Therefore faith, which is in the intellect, is more excellent than charity which is in the will.

Obj. 2. Further, The thing by which another works seems the less excellent of the two, even as a servant, by whom his master works, is beneath his master. Now *faith . . . worketh by charity,* according to Gal. 5. 6. Therefore faith is more excellent than charity.

Obj. 3. Further, That which is by way of addition to another seems to be the more perfect of the two. Now hope seems to be something additional to charity, for the object of charity is good, while the object of hope is an arduous good. Therefore hope is more excellent than charity.

On the contrary, It is written (I Cor. 13. 13): *The greater of these is charity.*

I answer that, Since good, in human acts, depends on their being regulated by the due rule, it is necessary that human virtue, which is a principle of good acts, consist in attaining the rule of human acts. Now the rule of human acts is twofold, as stated above (A. 3), namely, human reason and God. Yet God is the first rule, by which even human reason must be regulated. Consequently the theological virtues which consist in attaining this first rule, since their object is God, are more excellent than the moral, or the intellectual virtues, which consist in attaining human reason: and it follows that among the theological virtues themselves, the first place belongs to that which attains God most.

Now that which is of itself always ranks before that which is by another. But faith and hope attain God indeed in so far as we derive from Him the knowledge of truth or the acquisition of good; but charity attains God Himself that it may rest in Him, but not that something may accrue to us from Him. Hence charity is

more excellent than faith or hope, and, consequently, than all the other virtues, just as prudence, which by itself attains reason, is more excellent than the other moral virtues, which attain reason in so far as it appoints the mean in human operations or passions.

Reply Obj. 1. The operation of the intellect is completed by the thing understood being in the understanding subject, so that the excellence of the intellectual operation is assessed according to the measure of the intellect. On the other hand, the operation of the will and of every appetitive power is completed in the tendency of the appetite towards a thing as its term, and therefore the excellence of the appetitive operation is gauged according to the thing which is the object of the operation. Now those things which are beneath the soul are more excellent in the soul than they are in themselves, because a thing is contained according to the mode of the container (*De Causis,* xii).[1] On the other hand, things that are above the soul, are more excellent in themselves than they are in the soul. Consequently it is better to know than to love the things that are beneath us; for which reason the Philosopher gave the preference to the intellectual virtues over the moral virtues;[2] but the love of the things that are above us, especially of God, ranks before the knowledge of such things. Therefore charity is more excellent than faith.

Reply Obj. 2. Faith works by love, not instrumentally, as a master by his servant, but as by its proper form; hence the argument does not prove.

Reply Obj. 3. The same good is the object of charity and of hope; but charity implies union with that good, while hope implies distance from it. Hence charity does not regard that good as being arduous, as hope does, since what is already united has not the character of arduous; and this shows that charity is more perfect than hope.

ARTICLE 7. *Whether Any True Virtue Is Possible Without Charity?*

We proceed thus to the Seventh Article: It seems that there can be true virtue without charity.

Objection 1. For it is proper to virtue to produce a good act. Now those who have not charity do some good actions, as when they clothe the naked, or feed the hungry and so forth. Therefore true virtue is possible without charity.

Obj. 2. Further, Charity is not possible with-

---

[1] Sect. 11 (BA 175.11).
[2] *Ethics,* x, 7, 8 ($1177^a 12$; $1178^a 9$).

out faith, since it comes of *an unfeigned faith,* as the Apostle says (I Tim. 1. 5). Now, in unbelievers, there can be true chastity, if they curb their concupiscences, and true justice, if they judge rightly. Therefore true virtue is possible without charity.

Obj. 3. Further, Science and art are virtues, according to the *Ethics.*[1] But they are to be found in sinners who lack charity. Therefore true virtue can be without charity.

On the contrary, The Apostle says (I Cor. 13. 3): *If I should distribute all my goods to the poor, and if I should deliver my body to be burned, and have not charity, it profiteth me nothing.* And yet true virtue is very profitable, according to Wisd. 8. 7: *She teacheth temperance, and prudence, and justice, and fortitude, which are such things as men can have nothing more profitable in life.* Therefore no true virtue is possible without charity.

I answer that, Virtue is ordered to the good, as stated above (Part I-II, Q. LV, A. 4). Now the good is chiefly an end, for things directed to the end are not said to be good except in relation to the end. Accordingly, just as the end is twofold, the last end, and the proximate end, so also, is good twofold, one, the ultimate and universal good, the other proximate and particular. The ultimate and principal good of man is the enjoyment of God, according to Ps. 72. 28: *It is good for me to adhere to God,* and to this good man is ordered by charity. Man's secondary and, as it were, particular good may be twofold: one is truly good, because, considered in itself, it can be directed to the principal good, which is the last end; while the other is good apparently and not truly, because it leads us away from the final good. Accordingly it is evident that absolutely true virtue is that which is directed to man's principal good; thus also the Philosopher says[2] that "virtue is the disposition of a perfect thing to that which is best"; and in this way no true virtue is possible without charity.

If, however, we take virtue as being ordered to some particular end, then we may speak of virtue being where there is no charity, in so far as it is directed to some particular good. But if this particular good is not a true, but an apparent good, it is not a true virtue that is ordered to such a good, but a false likeness to virtue. Even so, as Augustine says (*Contra Julian.* iv, 3),[3] "the prudence of the miser, whereby he devises various roads to gain, is no true virtue;

nor the miser's justice, whereby he scorns the property of another through fear of severe punishment; nor the miser's temperance, whereby he curbs his desire for expensive pleasures; nor the miser's fortitude, whereby as Horace says, 'he braves the sea, he crosses mountains, he goes through fire, in order to avoid poverty' (*Epist.* lib. i, *Ep.* i, 45)." If, on the other hand, this particular good be a true good, for instance the welfare of the state, or the like, it will indeed be a true virtue, imperfect, however, unless it be referred to the final and perfect good. Accordingly no strictly true virtue is possible without charity.

Reply Obj. 1. The act of one lacking charity may be of two kinds. One is in accordance with his lack of charity, as when he does something that is referred to that by which he lacks charity. Such an act is always evil; thus Augustine says (*Contra Julian.* iv, 3)[4] that the actions which an unbeliever performs as an unbeliever, are always sinful, even when he clothes the naked, or does any like thing, and directs it to his unbelief as end.

There is, however, another act of one lacking charity, not in accordance with his lack of charity, but in accordance with his possession of some other gift of God, whether faith, or hope, or even his natural good, which is not completely taken away by sin, as stated above (Q. X, A. 4; Part I-II, Q. LXXXV, A. 2). In this way it is possible for an act, without charity, to be generically good, but not perfectly good, because it lacks its due order to the last end.

Reply Obj. 2. Since the end is in practical matters what the principle is in speculative matters, just as there can be no absolutely true science if a right estimation of the first indemonstrable principle be lacking, so, there can be no absolutely true justice, or chastity, without that due ordering to the end, which is effected by charity, however rightly a man may be affected about other matters.

Reply Obj. 3. Science and art of their very notion imply a relation to some particular good, and not to the ultimate good of human life, as do the moral virtues, which make man good absolutely, as stated above (Part I-II, Q. LVI, A. 3). Hence the comparison fails.

ARTICLE 8. *Whether Charity Is the Form of the Virtues?*

We proceed thus to the Eighth Article: It seems that charity is not the form of the virtues.

---

[1] Aristotle, VI, 3, 4, 5 (1139^b15; 1140^a20; 1140^b4).
[2] *Physics,* VII, 3 (246^a13).   [3] PL 44, 748.
[4] PL 44, 750.

Objection 1. Because the form of a thing is either exemplary or essential. Now charity is not the exemplary form of the other virtues, since it would follow that the other virtues are of the same species as charity; nor is it the essential form of the other virtues, since then it would not be distinct from them. Therefore it is in no way the form of the virtues.

Obj. 2. Further, Charity is compared to the other virtues as their root and foundation, according to Eph. 3. 17: *Rooted and founded in charity*. Now a root or foundation is not the form, but rather the matter of a thing, since it is the first part in the making. Therefore charity is not the form of the virtues.

Obj. 3. Further, Formal, final, and efficient causes do not coincide with one another.[1] Now charity is called the end and the mother of the virtues (I Tim. 1. 5). Therefore it should not be called their form.

On the contrary, Ambrose says that charity is the form of the virtues.[2]

I answer that, In morals the form of an act is taken chiefly from the end. The reason of this is that the principle of moral acts is the will, whose object and form, so to speak, are the end. Now the form of an act always follows from a form of the agent. Consequently, in morals, that which gives an act its order to the end, must give the act its form. Now it is evident, in accordance with what has been said (A. 7), that it is charity which directs the acts of all other virtues to the last end, and which, consequently, also gives the form to all other acts of virtue; and it is precisely in this sense that charity is called the form of the virtues, for these are called virtues in relation to "formed" acts.

Reply Obj. 1. Charity is called the form of the other virtues not as being their exemplary or their essential form, but rather by way of effective cause, in so far as it sets the form on all, in the aforesaid manner.

Reply Obj. 2. Charity is compared to the foundation or root in so far as all other virtues draw their sustenance and nourishment from it, and not in the sense that the foundation and root have the character of a material cause.

Reply Obj. 3. Charity is said to be the end of other virtues, because it directs all other virtues to its own end. And since a mother is one who conceives within herself and by another, charity is called the mother of the other virtues, because, by commanding them, it conceives the acts of the other virtues, by the desire of the last end.

QUESTION XXIV

OF THE SUBJECT OF CHARITY

(*In Twelve Articles*)

WE must now consider charity in relation to its subject, under which head there are twelve points of inquiry: (1) Whether charity is in the will as its subject? (2) Whether charity is caused in man by preceding acts or by a Divine infusion? (3) Whether it is infused according to our natural capactiy? (4) Whether it increases in the person who has it? (5) Whether it increases by addition? (6) Whether it increases by every act? (7) Whether it increases without limit? (8) Whether the charity of a wayfarer can be perfect? (9) Of the various degrees of charity. (10) Whether charity can diminish? (11) Whether charity can be lost after it has been possessed? (12) Whether it is lost through one mortal sin?

ARTICLE 1. *Whether the Will Is the Subject of Charity?*

We proceed thus to the First Article: It seems that the will is not the subject of charity.

Objection 1. For charity is a kind of love. Now, according to the Philosopher[3] "love is in the concupiscible part." Therefore charity is also in the concupiscible part and not in the will.

Obj. 2. Further, Charity is the foremost of the virtues, as stated above (Q. XXIII, A. 6). But the reason is the subject of virtue. Therefore it seems that charity is in the reason and not in the will.

Obj. 3. Further, Charity extends to all human acts, according to I Cor. 16. 14: *Let all your things be done in charity*. Now the principle of human acts is free choice. Therefore it seems that charity is chiefly in free choice as its subject, and not in the will.

On the contrary, The object of charity is the good, which is also the object of the will. Therefore charity is in the will as its subject.

I answer that, Since as stated in the First Part (Q. LXXX, A. 2), the appetite is twofold, namely the sensitive, and the intellectual which is called the will, the object of each is the good, but in different ways. For the object of the sensitive appetite is a good apprehended by sense, but the object of the intellectual appetite or will is good under the universal aspect of good, according as it can be apprehended by the intellect. Now the object of charity is not a sensible

---

[1] Aristotle, *Physics*, II, 7 (198ª24).

[2] Cf. Ambrosiaster, *In I Cor.*, on 7.2 (PL 17, 239); see also Peter Lombard, *Sent.*, III, d. 23, chap. 3 (QR II, 655).

[3] *Topics*, II, 7 (113ᵇ2).

good, but the Divine good which is known by the intellect alone. Therefore the subject of charity is not the sensitive, but the intellectual appetite, that is, the will.

Reply Obj. 1. The concupiscible part is a part of the sensitive, not of the intellectual appetite, as proved in the First Part (Q. LXXXI, A. 2). Therefore the love which is in the concupiscible, is the love of sensible good. Nor can the concupiscible reach to the Divine good which is an intelligible good, but the will alone can. Consequently the concupiscible part cannot be the subject of charity.

Reply Obj. 2. According to the Philosopher,[1] the will also is in the reason. And therefore charity is not excluded from the reason through being in the will. Yet charity is regulated, not by the reason, as human virtues are, but by God's wisdom, and transcends the rule of human reason, according to Eph. 3. 19: *The charity of Christ, which surpasseth all knowledge.* Hence it is not in the reason, either as its subject, like prudence is, or as its rule, like justice and temperance are, but only by a certain kinship of the will to the reason.

Reply Obj. 3. As stated in the First Part (Q. LXXXIII, A. 4), the free choice is not a distinct power from the will. Yet charity is not in the will considered as free choice, the act of which is to choose. "For choice is of things directed to the end, whereas the will is of the end itself."[2] Hence charity, whose object is the last end, should be described as residing in the will rather than in free choice.

ARTICLE 2. *Whether Charity Is Caused in Us by Infusion?*

We proceed thus to the Second Article: It seems that charity is not caused in us by infusion.

Objection 1. For that which is common to all creatures, is in man naturally. Now, according to Dionysius (*Div. Nom.* iv),[3] the Divine good, which is the object of charity, "is for all an object of dilection and love." Therefore charity is in us naturally, and not by infusion.

Obj. 2. Further, The more lovable a thing is, the easier it is to love it. Now God is supremely lovable, since He is supremely good. Therefore it is easier to love Him than other things. But we need no infused habit in order to love other things. Neither, therefore, do we need one in order to love God.

Obj. 3. Further, The Apostle says (I Tim. 1. 5): *The end of the commandment is charity from a pure heart, and a good conscience, and an unfeigned faith.* Now these three have reference to human acts. Therefore charity is caused in us from preceding acts, and not from infusion.

On the contrary, The Apostle says (Rom. 5. 5): *The charity of God is poured forth in our hearts by the Holy Ghost, Who is given to us.*

I answer that, As stated above (Q. XXIII, A. 1), charity is a friendship of man for God, founded upon the fellowship of everlasting happiness. Now this fellowship is in respect, not of natural, but of gratuitous gifts, for, according to Rom. 6. 23, *the grace of God is life everlasting.* Therefore charity itself surpasses our natural powers. Now that which surpasses the power of nature cannot be natural or acquired by the natural powers, since a natural effect does not transcend its cause. Therefore charity can be in us neither naturally, nor through acquisition by the natural powers, but by the infusion of the Holy Ghost, Who is the love of the Father and the Son, and the participation of Whom in us is caused charity, as stated above (Q. XXIII, A. 2, REPLY 1).

Reply Obj. 1. Dionysius is speaking of the love of God, which is founded on the fellowship of natural goods, and is therefore in all naturally. On the other hand, charity is founded on a supernatural fellowship, so that the comparison fails.

Reply Obj. 2. Just as God is supremely knowable in Himself yet not to us, on account of a defect in our knowledge which depends on sensible things, so too, God is supremely lovable in Himself, in as much as He is the object of happiness. But He is not supremely lovable to us in this way, on account of the inclination of our affection towards visible goods. Hence it is evident that for us to love God above all things in this way, it is necessary that charity be infused into our hearts.

Reply Obj. 3. When it is said that in us charity proceeds from *a pure heart, and a good conscience, and an unfeigned faith,* this must be referred to the act of charity which is aroused by these things.—Or again, this is said because these acts dispose man to receive the infusion of charity. The same remark applies to the saying of Augustine (*Tract. ix. in prim. canon. Joann.*):[4] "Fear leads to charity," and of a gloss on Matt. 1. 2: "Faith begets hope, and hope charity."[5]

---

[1] *Soul*, III, 9 (432ᵇ5).
[2] Aristotle, *Ethics*, III, 2 (1111ᵇ26).
[3] Sect. 10 (PG 3, 708).

[4] PL 35, 2048.
[5] *Glossa interl.* (v, 51).

ARTICLE 3. *Whether Charity Is Infused According to Our Natural Capacity?*

We proceed thus to the Third Article: It would seem that charity is infused according to our natural capacity.

Objection 1. For it is written (Matt. 25. 15) that *He gave to every one according to his own virtue* (Douay,—*proper ability*). Now, in man, none but natural virtue precedes charity, since there is no virtue without charity, as stated above (Q. XXIII, A. 7). Therefore God infuses charity into man according to the measure of his natural virtue.

Obj. 2. Further, Among things ordered towards one another, the second is proportioned to the first; thus we find in natural things that the form is proportioned to the matter, and in gratuitous gifts, that glory is proportioned to grace. Now, since charity is a perfection of nature, it is compared to the capacity of nature as second to first. Therefore it seems that charity is infused according to the capacity of nature.

Obj. 3. Further, Men and angels partake of happiness according to the same measure, since happiness is alike in both, according to Matt. 22. 30 and Luke 20. 36. Now charity and other gratuitous gifts are bestowed on the angels, according to their natural capacity, as the Master teaches (*Sent.* ii, d. 3).[1] Therefore the same apparently applies to man.

On the contrary, It is written (John 3. 8): *The Spirit breatheth where He will,* and (I Cor. 12. 11): *All these things one and the same Spirit worketh, dividing to every one according as He will.* Therefore charity is given, not according to our natural capacity, but according as the Spirit wills to distribute His gifts.

I answer that, The quantity of a thing depends on the proper cause of that thing, since the more universal cause produces a greater effect. Now, since charity surpasses the proportion of human nature, as stated above (A. 2) it depends, not on any natural virtue, but on the sole grace of the Holy Ghost Who infuses charity. Therefore the quantity of charity depends neither on the condition of nature nor on the capacity of natural virtue, but only on the will of the Holy Ghost Who *divides* His gifts *according as He will.* Hence the Apostle says (Eph. 4. 7): *To every one of us is given grace according to the measure of the giving of Christ.*

Reply Obj. 1. The virtue in accordance with

[1] Chap. 2 (QR I, 318).

which God gives His gifts to each one, is a disposition or previous preparation or effort of the one who receives grace. But the Holy Ghost forestalls even this disposition or effort, by moving man's mind either more or less, according as He will. Wherefore the Apostle says (Coloss. 1. 12): *Who hath made us worthy to be partakers of the lot of the saints in light.*

Reply Obj. 2. The form does not surpass the proportion of the matter, but both of the same genus. In like manner grace and glory are referred to the same genus, for grace is nothing else than a beginning of glory in us. But charity and nature do not belong to the same genus, so that the comparison fails.

Reply Obj. 3. The angel's is an intellectual nature, and it is consistent with his condition that he should be borne wholly wheresoever he is borne, as stated in the First Part (Q. LXI, A. 6). Hence there was a greater effort in the higher angels, both for good in those who persevered, and for evil in those who fell, and consequently those of the higher angels who remained steadfast became better than the others, and those who fell became worse. But man's is a rational nature, to which it pertains to be sometimes in potency and sometimes in act, so that it is not necessarily borne wholly wherever it is borne, and where there are greater natural gifts there may be less effort, and vice versa. Thus the comparison fails.

ARTICLE 4. *Whether Charity Can Increase?*

We proceed thus to the Fourth Article: It seems that charity cannot increase.

Objection 1. For nothing increases save what has quantity. Now quantity is twofold, namely dimensive and virtual. The former does not befit charity which is a spiritual perfection, while virtual quantity regards the objects in respect of which charity does not increase, since the slightest charity loves all that is to be loved out of charity. Therefore charity does not increase.

Obj. 2. Further, That which is at the term receives no increase. But charity is at the term, being the greatest of the virtues, and the supreme love of the greatest good. Therefore charity cannot increase.

Obj. 3. Further, Increase is a kind of movement. Therefore wherever there is increase there is movement, and if there be increase of essence there is movement of essence. Now there is no movement of essence save either by corruption or generation. Therefore charity cannot increase essentially, unless it happen to be generated anew or corrupted, which is unreasonable.

On the contrary, Augustine says (*Tract.* lxxiv *in Joann.*)[1] that "charity merits increase that by increase it may merit perfection."

I answer that, The charity of a wayfarer can increase. For we are called wayfarers by reason of our being on the way to God, Who is the last end of our happiness. On this way we advance as we draw near to God, Who is approached not by steps of the body but by the affections of the mind; and this approach is the result of charity, since it unites man's mind to God. Consequently it pertains to the very notion of the charity of a wayfarer that it can increase, for if it could not, all further advance along the way would cease. Hence the Apostle calls charity the way, when he says (I Cor. 12. 31): *I show unto you yet a more excellent way.*

Reply Obj. 1. Charity is not subject to dimensive, but only to virtual quantity; and the latter depends not only on the number of objects, namely whether they be in greater number or of greater excellence, but also on the intensity of the act, namely whether a thing is loved more, or less. It is in this way that the virtual quantity of charity increases.

Reply Obj. 2. Charity is at a summit with regard to its object, in so far as its object is the Supreme Good, and from this it follows that charity is the most excellent of the virtues. Yet not every charity is at a summit as regards the intensity of the act.

Reply Obj. 3. Some have said that charity does not increase in its essence, but only as to its radication in its subject, or according to its fervour.[2] But these people did not know what they were talking about. For since charity is an accident, its being is to be in something. So that an essential increase of charity means nothing else but that it is yet more in its subject, which implies a greater radication in its subject. Furthermore charity is essentially a virtue directed to act, so that an essential increase of charity is the same as ability to produce an act of more fervent love. Hence charity increases essentially, not by beginning to be, or ceasing to be in its subject, as the objection imagines, but by beginning to be more and more in its subject.

ARTICLE 5. *Whether Charity Increases by Addition?*

We proceed thus to the Fifth Article: It seems that charity increases by addition.

Objection 1. For just as increase may be in respect of bodily quantity, so may it be according to virtual quantity. Now increase in bodily quantity results from addition; for the Philosopher says[3] that "increase is addition to a pre-existing magnitude." Therefore the increase of charity which is according to virtual quantity is by addition.

Obj. 2. Further, Charity is a kind of spiritual light in the soul, according to I John 2. 10: *He that loveth his brother abideth in the light.* Now light increases in the air by addition; thus the light in a house increases when another candle is lit. Therefore charity also increases in the soul by addition.

Obj. 3. Further, The increase of charity is God's work, even as the causing of it, according to II Cor. 9. 10: *He will increase the growth of the fruits of your justice.* Now when God first infuses charity, He puts something in the soul that was not there before. Therefore also, when He increases charity, He puts something there which was not there before. Therefore charity increases by addition.

On the contrary, Charity is a simple form. Now nothing greater results from the addition of one simple thing to another, as proved in the *Physics*[4] and the *Metaphysics*.[5] Therefore charity does not increase by addition.

I answer that, Every addition is of something to something else, so that in every addition we must at least presuppose that the things added together are distinct before the addition. Consequently if charity be added to charity, the added charity must be presupposed as distinct from the charity to which it is added, not necessarily by a distinction of reality, but at least by a distinction of thought. For God is able to increase a bodily quantity by adding a magnitude which did not exist before, but was created at that very moment; which magnitude, though not pre-existent in reality, is nevertheless capable of being distinguished from the quantity to which it is added. Therefore if charity be added to charity we must presuppose the distinction, at least logical, of the one charity from the other.

Now distinction among forms is twofold, specific and numeric. Specific distinction of habits follows diversity of objects, while numeric distinction follows distinction of subjects. Consequently a habit may receive increase through extending to objects to which it did not extend before; thus the science of geom-

---

[1] PL 35, 1827; *Epist.*, CLXXXVI, chap. 3 (PL 33, 819).
[2] William of Auxerre, *Summa Aurea,* III, 5, Q. 4 (146va).

[3] *Generation and Corruption,* I, 5 (320^{b}30).
[4] Aristotle, VI, 2 (232^{a}23).　　[5] Aristotle, III, 4 (1001^{b}8).

etry increases in one who acquires knowledge of geometrical matters which he did not know hitherto. But this cannot be said of charity, for even the slightest charity extends to all that we have to love by charity. Hence the addition which causes an increase of charity cannot be understood as though the added charity were presupposed to be distinct specifically from that to which it is added.

It follows therefore that if charity be added to charity, we must presuppose a numerical distinction between them, which follows a distinction of subjects; thus whiteness receives an increase when one white thing is added to another, although such an increase does not make a thing whiter. This, however, does not apply to the case in point, since the subject of charity is none other than the rational mind, so that an increase of charity of such a kind could only take place by one rational mind being added to another; which is impossible. Moreover, even if it were possible, the result would be a greater lover, but not a more loving one. It follows, therefore, that charity can by no means increase by the addition of charity to charity, as some have held to be the case.[1]

Accordingly charity increases only by its subject partaking of charity more and more, that is, by being more reduced to its act and more subject to it. For this is the proper mode of increase in a form that is intensified, since the being of such a form consists wholly in its adhering to its subject. Consequently, since the magnitude of a thing follows on its being, to say that a form is greater is the same as to say that it is more in its subject, and not that another form is added to it; for this would be the case if the form, of itself, had any quantity, and not in comparison with its subject. Therefore charity increases by being intensified in its subject, and this is for charity to increase according to essence, and not by charity being added to charity.

Reply Obj. 1. Bodily quantity has something as quantity, and something else, in so far as it is an accidental form. As quantity, it is distinguishable in respect of position or number, and in this way we have the increase of magnitude by addition, as may be seen in animals. But in so far as it is an accidental form, it is distinguishable only in respect of its subject, and in this way it has its proper increase, like other accidental forms, by way of intensity in its subject, for instance in things subject to

rarefaction, as is proved in the *Physics*.[2] In like manner science, as a habit, has its quantity from its objects, and accordingly it increases by addition, when a man knows more things; and again, as an accidental form, it has a certain quantity through being in its subject, and in this way it increases in a man who knows the same scientific truths with greater certainty now than before. In the same way charity has a twofold quantity; but with regard to that which it has from its object, it does not increase, as stated above. Hence it follows that it increases solely by being intensified.

Reply Obj. 2. The addition of light to light can be understood through the light being intensified in the air on account of there being several luminaries giving light; but this distinction does not apply to the case in point, since there is but one luminary shedding forth the light of charity.

Reply Obj. 3. The infusion of charity denotes a change to the state of having charity from the state of not having it, so that something must come which was not there before. On the other hand, the increase of charity denotes a change to "more having" from "less having," so that there is need, not for anything to be there that was not there before, but for something to be more there that previously was less there. This is what God does when He increases charity, that is He makes it to have a greater hold on the soul, and the likeness of the Holy Ghost to be more perfectly participated by the soul.

ARTICLE 6. *Whether Charity Increases Through Every Act of Charity?*

We proceed thus to the Sixth Article: It seems that charity increases through every act of charity.

Objection 1. For that which can do what is more, can do what is less. But every act of charity can merit everlasting life; and this is more than a simple addition of charity, since it includes the perfection of charity. Much more, therefore, does every act of charity increase charity.

Obj. 2. Further, Just as the habits of acquired virtue are engendered by acts, so too an increase of charity is caused by an act of charity. Now each virtuous act conduces to the engendering of virtue. Therefore also each virtuous act of charity conduces to the increase of charity.

Obj. 3. Further, Gregory says[3] that "to stand

---

[1] Albert, *In Sent.*, I, d. 17, A. 10 (BO xxv, 482); Bonaventure, *In Sent.*, I, d. 17, A. 1, Q. 2 (QR I, 311).

[2] Aristotle, IV, 9 (217ª14).

[3] *Reg. Pastor.*, III, I (PL 77, 51).

still in the way to God is to go back." Now no man goes back when he is moved by an act of charity. Therefore whoever is moved by an act of charity goes forward in the way to God. Therefore charity increases through every act of charity.

On the contrary, The effect does not surpass the power of its cause. But an act of charity is sometimes done with tepidity or slackness. Therefore it does not conduce to a more excellent charity, rather does it dispose one to a lower degree.

I answer that, The spiritual increase of charity is somewhat like the increase of a body. Now bodily increase in animals and plants is not a continuous movement, so that if a thing increase so much in so much time, it needs to increase proportionally in each part of that time, as happens in local movement; but for a certain space of time nature works by disposing for the increase, without causing any actual increase, and afterwards brings into effect that to which it had disposed, by giving the animal or plant an actual increase. In like manner charity does not actually increase through every act of charity, but each act of charity disposes to an increase of charity, in so far as one act of charity makes man more ready to act again according to charity, and this readiness increasing, man breaks out into an act of more fervent love, and strives to advance in charity, and then his charity increases actually.

Reply Obj. 1. Every act of charity merits everlasting life, which, however, is not to be bestowed then and there, but at its proper time. In like manner every act of charity merits an increase of charity; yet this increase does not take place at once, but when we strive for that increase.

Reply Obj. 2. Even when an acquired virtue is being engendered, each act does not complete the formation of the virtue, but conduces towards that effect by disposing to it, while the last act, which is the most perfect, and acts in virtue of all those that preceded it, reduces the virtue into act, just as when many drops hollow out a stone.

Reply Obj. 3. Man advances in the way to God, not merely by actual increase of charity, but also by being disposed to that increase.

ARTICLE 7. *Whether Charity Increases Without Limit?*

We proceed thus to the Seventh Article: It would seem that charity does not increase without limit.

Objection 1. For every movement is towards some end and term, as stated in the *Metaphysics*.[1] But the increase of charity is a movement. Therefore it tends to an end and term. Therefore charity does not increase without limit.

Obj. 2. Further, No form surpasses the capacity of its subject. But the capacity of the rational creature who is the subject of charity is finite. Therefore charity cannot increase without limit.

Obj. 3. Further, Every finite thing can, by continual increase, attain to the quantity of another finite thing however much greater, unless the amount of its increase be ever less and less. Thus the Philosopher states[2] that if we divide a given line into an infinite number of parts, and take these parts away and add them to another line, we shall never arrive at any definite quantity resulting from those two lines, namely the one from which we subtracted and the one to which we added what was subtracted. But this does not occur in the case in point, because there is no need for the second increase of charity to be less than the first, since rather is it probable that it would be equal or greater. As, therefore, the charity of the blessed is something finite, if the charity of the wayfarer can increase without limit, it would follow that the charity of the way can equal the charity of heaven, which is unreasonable. Therefore the wayfarer's charity cannot increase without limit.

On the contrary, The Apostle says (Philip. 3. 12): *Not as though I had already attained, or were already perfect; but I follow after, if I may, by any means apprehend,* on which words a gloss says:[3] "Even if he has made great progress, let none of the faithful say: 'Enough.' For whosoever says this, leaves the road before coming to his destination." Therefore the wayfarer's charity can ever increase more and more.

I answer that, A term to the increase of a form may be fixed in three ways. First by reason of the form itself having a fixed measure, and when this has been reached it is no longer possible to go any further in that form, but if any further advance is made, another form is attained. An example of this is paleness, the bounds of which may, by continual alteration, be passed, either so that whiteness ensues, or so that blackness results. Secondly, on the

---

[1] Aristotle, II, 2 (994[b]13).   [2] *Physics*, III, 6 (266[b]16). [3] *Glossa* Lombardi (PL 192, 246). Cf. *Glossa ordin.* (VI, 101F); Prosper of Aquitaine, *Sent.*, sent. 235 (PL 51, 460).

part of the agent, whose power does not extend to a further increase of the form in its subject. Thirdly, on the part of the subject, which is not capable of further perfection.

Now, in none of these ways is a limit imposed to the increase of man's charity, while he is in the state of a wayfarer. For charity itself considered as such has no limit to its increase, since it is a participation of the infinite charity which is the Holy Ghost. In like manner the cause of the increase of charity, namely God, is possessed of infinite power. Furthermore, on the part of its subject, no limit to this increase can be fixed, because whenever charity increases there is a corresponding increased ability to receive a further increase. It is therefore evident that it is not possible to fix any limits to the increase of charity in this life.

Reply Obj. 1. The increase of charity is directed to an end which is not in this but in a future life.

Reply Obj. 2. The capacity of the rational creature is increased by charity, because the heart is enlarged by it, according to II Cor. 6. 11: *Our heart is enlarged.* And therefore it still remains capable of receiving a further increase.

Reply Obj. 3. This argument holds good in those things which have the same kind of quantity, but not in those which have different kinds; thus however much a line may increase it does not reach the quantity of a surface. Now the quantity of a wayfarer's charity which follows the knowledge of faith, is not of the same kind as the quantity of the charity of the blessed, which follows open vision. Hence the argument does not prove.

ARTICLE 8. *Whether Charity Can Be Perfect in This Life?*

We proceed thus to the Eighth Article: It seems that charity cannot be perfect in this life.

Objection 1. For this would have been the case with the apostles before all others. Yet it was not so, since the Apostle says (Philip. 3. 11): *Not as though I had already attained, or were already perfect.* Therefore charity cannot be perfect in this life.

Obj. 2. Further, Augustine says[1] that "whatever kindles charity quenches cupidity, but where charity is perfect, cupidity is done away altogether." But this cannot be in this world, where it is impossible to live without sin, according to 1 John 1. 8: *If we say that we have*

no sin, we deceive ourselves. Now all sin arises from some inordinate cupidity. Therefore charity cannot be perfect in this life.

Obj. 3. Further, What is already perfect cannot be perfected any more. But in this life charity can always increase, as stated above (A. 7). Therefore charity cannot be perfect in this life.

On the contrary, Augustine says in his commentary on the First Canonical Epistle of John (*Tract.* v):[2] "Charity is perfected by being strengthened; and when it has been brought to perfection, it exclaims: 'I desire to be dissolved and to be with Christ.' " Now this is possible in this life, as in the case of Paul. Therefore charity can be perfect in this life.

I answer that, The perfection of charity may be understood in two ways: first with regard to the object loved, secondly with regard to the person who loves. With regard to the object loved, charity is perfect if the object be loved as much as it is lovable. Now God is as lovable as He is good, and His goodness is infinite, and therefore He is infinitely lovable. But no creature can love Him infinitely since all created power is finite. Consequently no creature's charity can be perfect in this way; the charity of God alone can, by which He loves Himself.

On the part of the person who loves, charity is perfect when he loves as much as he can. This happens in three ways. First, so that a man's whole heart is always actually borne towards God. This is the perfection of the charity of heaven, and is not possible in this life, where, by reason of the weakness of human life, it is impossible to think always actually of God, and to be moved by love towards Him. Secondly, so that man makes an earnest endeavour to give his time to God and Divine things, while scorning other things except in so far as the needs of the present life demand. This is the perfection of charity that is possible to a wayfarer; but it is not common to all who have charity. Thirdly, so that a man gives his whole heart to God habitually, that is, by neither thinking nor desiring anything contrary to the love of God. And this perfection is common to all who have charity.

Reply Obj. 1. The Apostle denies that he has the perfection of heaven, and hence a gloss on the same passage says[3] that "he was a

---

[1] QQ. LXXXIII, qu. 36 (PL 40, 25).

[2] PL 35, 2014.

[3] *Glossa ordin.* (VI, 101F); *Glossa* Lombardi (PL 192-247), Cf. Augustine, *Enarr. in Psalm.*, Ps. 88.5 (PL 36, 417).

perfect wayfarer, but had not yet achieved the perfection to which the way leads."

Reply Obj. 2. This is said on account of venial sins, which are contrary, not to the habit, but to the act of charity; hence they are incompatible, not with the perfection of the way, but with that of heaven.

Reply Obj. 3. The perfection of the way is not perfection absolutely, and so it can always increase.

ARTICLE 9. *Whether Charity Is Rightly Distinguished into Three Degrees, Beginning, Progress and Perfection?*

We proceed thus to the Ninth Article: It would seem unfitting to distinguish three degrees of charity, beginning, progress and perfection.

Objection 1. For there are many degrees between the beginning of charity and its ultimate perfection. Therefore it is not right to put only one.

Obj. 2. Further, Charity begins to progress as soon as it begins to be. Therefore we ought not to distinguish between charity as progressing and as beginning.

Obj. 3. Further, In this world, however perfect a man's charity may be, it can increase, as stated above (A. 7). Now for charity to increase is to progress. Therefore perfect charity ought not to be distinguished from progressing charity. And so the above degrees are unsuitably assigned to charity.

On the contrary, Augustine says (*In prim. canon. Joann., Tract.* v):[1] "As soon as charity is born it takes food," which refers to beginners; "after taking food, it waxes strong," which refers to those who are progressing; "and when it has become strong it is perfected," which refers to the perfect. Therefore there are three degrees of charity.

I answer that, The spiritual increase of charity may be considered in respect of a certain likeness to the growth of the human body. For although this latter growth may be divided into many parts, yet it has certain fixed divisions according to those particular actions or pursuits to which man is brought by this same growth. Thus we speak of a man being an infant until he has the use of reason, after which we distinguish another state of man when he begins to speak and to use his reason, while there is again a third state, that of puberty, when he begins to acquire the power of generation, and so on until he arrives at perfection.

[1] PL 35, 2014.

In like manner the different degrees of charity are distinguished according to the different pursuits to which man is brought by the increase of charity. For at first it is incumbent on man to occupy himself chiefly with avoiding sin and resisting his concupiscences, which move him in opposition to charity; and this concerns beginners, in whom charity has to be fed or fostered lest it be destroyed. In the second place man's chief pursuit is to aim at progress in good, and this is the pursuit of the proficient, whose chief aim is to strengthen their charity by adding to it. Man's third pursuit is to aim chiefly at union with and enjoyment of God, and this pertains to the perfect who *desire to be dissolved and to be with Christ.*

In like manner we observe in local motion that at first there is withdrawal from one term, then approach to the other term, and thirdly, rest in his term.

Reply Obj. 1. All these distinct degrees which can be discerned in the increase of charity, are comprised in the above three, even as every division of continuous things is included in these three,—the beginning, the middle, and the end, as the Philosopher states.[2]

Reply Obj. 2. Although those who are beginners in charity may progress, yet the chief care that besets them is to resist the sins which disturb them by their onslaught. Afterwards, however, when they come to feel this onslaught less, they begin to tend to perfection with greater security; yet with one hand doing the work, and with the other holding the sword as related in 2 Esdr. 4. 17 about those who built up Jerusalem.

Reply Obj. 3. Even the perfect make progress in charity; yet this is not their chief care, but their aim is principally directed towards union with God. And though both the beginner and the proficient seek this, yet their solicitude is chiefly about other things, with the beginner, about avoiding sin, with the proficient, about progressing in virtue.

ARTICLE 10. *Whether Charity Can Decrease?*

We proceed thus to the Tenth Article: It seems that charity can decrease.

Objection 1. For contraries by their nature affect the same subject. Now increase and decrease are contraries. Since then charity increases, as stated above (A. 4), it seems that it can also decrease.

Obj. 2. Further, Augustine, speaking to God,

[2] *Heavens*, I, 1 (268[a]12).

says[1]: "He loves Thee less, who loves aught beside Thee"; and (QQ. LXXXIII, qu. 36)[2] he says that "what kindles charity quenches cupidity." From this it seems to follow that, on the contrary, what arouses cupidity quenches charity. But cupidity, by which a man loves something beside God, can increase in man. Therefore charity can decrease.

Obj. 3. Further, As Augustine says (*Gen. ad lit.* viii, 12)[3] "God makes the just man, by justifying him, but in such a way, that if the man turns away from God, he no longer retains the effect of the Divine operation." From this we may gather that when God preserves charity in man, He works in the same way as when He first infuses charity into him. Now at the first infusion of charity God infuses less charity into him that prepares himself less. Therefore also in preserving charity, He preserves less charity in him that prepares himself less. Therefore charity can decrease.

On the contrary, In Scripture, charity is compared to fire, according to Cant. 8. 6: *The lamps thereof,* that is, of charity, *are fire and flames.* Now fire always mounts upward so long as it lasts. Therefore as long as charity endures, it can ascend, but cannot descend, that is, decrease.

I answer that, The quantity which charity has in comparison with its proper object cannot decrease, even as neither can it increase, as stated above (A. 4, Reply 1; A. 5.). Since, however, it increases in that quantity which it has in comparison with its subject, we must consider whether here it can decrease in this way. Now, if it decreases, this must be either through an act, or by the mere cessation from act. It is true that virtues acquired through acts decrease and sometimes cease altogether through cessation from act, as stated above (Part I-II, Q. LIII, A. 3). Therefore the Philosopher says,[4] in reference to friendship, "that want of intercourse," that is, the neglect to call upon or speak with one's friends, "has destroyed many a friendship." Now this is because the preservation of a thing depends on its cause, and the cause of an acquired virtue is a human act, so that when human acts cease, the acquired virtue decreases and at last ceases altogether. Yet this does not occur to charity, because it is not the result of human acts, but is caused by God alone, as stated above (A. 2). Hence it follows that even when its act ceases, it does not for this reason decrease, or cease altogether, unless the cessation involves a sin.

The consequence is that a decrease of charity cannot be caused except either by God or by some sin. Now no defect is caused in us by God, except by way of punishment, in so far as He withdraws His grace in punishment of sin. Hence He does not diminish charity except by way of punishment, and this punishment is due on account of sin.

It follows, therefore, that if charity decrease, the cause of this decrease must be sin either effectively or by way of merit. But mortal sin does not diminish charity in either of these ways, but destroys it entirely, both effectively, because every mortal sin is contrary to charity, as we shall state further on (A. 12), and by way of merit, since when, by sinning mortally, a man acts against charity, he deserves that God should withdraw charity from him.

In like manner, neither can venial sin diminish charity either effectively or by way of merit. Not effectively, because it does not touch charity, since charity is about the last end, while venial sin is a disorder about things directed to the end; and a man's love for the end is none the less through his committing an inordinate act as regards the things directed to the end. Thus sick people sometimes, though they love health much, are irregular in keeping to their diet; and thus again, in speculative sciences, the false opinions that are deduced from the principles do not diminish the certitude of the principles. So too, venial sin does not merit a diminution of charity; for when a man offends in a small matter he does not deserve to suffer loss in a great matter. For God does not turn away from man more than man turns away from Him. Therefore he that is out of order in respect of things directed to the end, does not deserve to suffer loss of charity by which he is ordered to the last end.

The consequence is that charity can by no means be diminished, if we speak of direct causality, yet whatever disposes to its corruption may be said to conduce indirectly to its diminution, and such are venial sins, or even the cessation from the practice of works of charity.

Reply Obj. 1. Contraries affect the same subject when that subject stands in equal relation to both. But charity does not stand in equal relation to increase and decrease. For it can have a cause of increase, but not of decrease, as stated above. Hence the argument does not prove.

Reply Obj. 2. Cupidity is twofold, one by which man places his end in creatures, and this

[1] *Confessions,* X, 40 (PL 32, 796).   [2] PL 40, 25.
[3] PL 34, 383.   [4] *Ethics,* VIII, 5 (1157[b]13).

kills charity altogether, since it is its poison, as Augustine states.[1] This makes us love God less (that is, less than we ought to love Him by charity), not indeed by diminishing charity but by destroying it altogether. It is thus that we must understand the saying: "He loves Thee less, who loves aught beside Thee," for he adds these words,—"which he loveth not for Thee." This does not apply to venial sin, but only to mortal sin, since that which we love in venial sin, is loved for God's sake habitually though not actually.—There is another cupidity, that of venial sin, which is always diminished by charity; and yet this cupidity cannot diminish charity, for the reason given above.

Reply Obj. 3. A movement of free choice is requisite in the infusion of charity, as stated above (Part I-II, Q. CXIII, A. 3). Therefore that which diminishes the intensity of free choice conduces dispositively to a diminution in the charity to be infused. On the other hand, no movement of free choice is required for the preservation of charity; otherwise it would not remain in us while we sleep. Hence charity does not decrease on account of an obstacle on the part of the intensity of the movement of free choice.

ARTICLE 11. *Whether We Can Lose Charity When Once We Have It?*

We proceed thus to the Eleventh Article: It would seem that we cannot lose charity when once we have it.

Objection 1. For if we lose it, this can only be through sin. Now he who has charity cannot sin, for it is written (I John 3. 9): *Whosoever is born of God, committeth not sin; for His seed abideth in him, and he cannot sin, because he is born of God.* But none save the children of God have charity, "for it is this which distinguishes the children of God from the children of perdition," as Augustine says (*De Trin.* xv, 18).[2] Therefore he that has charity cannot lose it.

Obj. 2. Further, Augustine says (*De Trin.* viii, 7)[3] that "if love be not true, it should not be called love." Now, as he says again in a letter to Count Julian, "charity which can fail was never true."[4] Therefore it was no charity at all.

Therefore, when once we have charity, we cannot lose it.

Obj. 3. Further, Gregory says in a homily for Pentecost (*In Evang.* xxx)[5] that "God's love works great things where it is; if it ceases to work it is not charity." Now no man loses charity by doing great things. Therefore if charity be there, it cannot be lost.

Obj. 4. Further, Free choice is not inclined to sin unless by some motive for sinning. Now charity excludes all motives for sinning, both self-love and cupidity, and all such things. Therefore charity cannot be lost.

On the contrary, It is written (Apoc. 2. 4): *I have somewhat against thee, because thou hast left thy first charity.*

I answer that, The Holy Ghost dwells in us by charity, as shown above (A. 2; Q. XXIII, A. 2). We can, accordingly, consider charity in three ways: first on the part of the Holy Ghost, Who moves the soul to love God, and in this respect charity is incompatible with sin through the power of the Holy Ghost, Who does unfailingly whatever He wills to do. Hence it is impossible for these two things to be true at the same time,—that the Holy Ghost should will to move a certain man to an act of charity, and that this man, by sinning, should lose charity. For the gift of perseverance is counted among "the blessings of God by which whoever is delivered, is most certainly delivered," as Augustine says in his book on the Predestination of the saints (*De Dono Persev.* xiv).[6]

Secondly charity may be considered as such, and thus it is incapable of anything that is against its notion. Therefore charity cannot sin at all, even as neither can heat cool, nor injustice do good, as Augustine says (*De Serm. Dom. in Monte,* ii, 24).[7]

Thirdly charity can be considered on the part of its subject, which is changeable on account of free choice. Moreover charity may be compared with this subject, both from the general point of view of form in comparison with matter, and from the special point of view of habit as compared with power. Now it is of the very notion of a form to be in its subject in such a way that it can be lost, when it does not entirely fill the potentiality of matter; this is evident in the forms of things generated and corrupted, because the matter of such things receives one form in such a way, that it retains within it the potency to another form, as though its potentiality were not completely satisfied with the one form. Hence the one form may be lost

[1] QQ. LXXXIII, Q. 36, PL 40, 25.
[2] PL 42, 1082.   [3] PL 42, 956.
[4] Cf. Paulinus Aquiliensis, *De Salutaribus ad Henricum Comitem,* VII (PL 99, 202; Cf. PL 40, 1049). See Gratian, *Decretum,* II, causa 33, Q. 3 De Poenit., d. 2, can. 2 (RF 1, 1190); Lombard, *Sent.,* III, d. 31, chap. 1 (QR II, 690); Jerome, *Epist.,* III (PL 22, 335); Alcuin, *Epist.,* XLI (PL 100, 203).

[5] PL 76, 1221.   [6] PL 45, 1014.   [7] PL 34, 1305.

by the other being received. On the other hand the form of a celestial body which entirely fills the potentiality of its matter, so that the latter does not retain the potency to another form, is in its subject inseparably. Accordingly the charity of the blessed, because it entirely fills the potentiality of the rational mind, since every actual movement of that mind is directed to God, is possessed by its subject inseparably. But the charity of the wayfarer does not so fill the potentiality of its subject, because the latter is not always actually directed to God. Hence when it is not actually directed to God, something may occur by which charity is lost.

It is proper to a habit to incline a power to act, and this belongs to a habit, in so far as it makes whatever is suitable to it to seem good, and whatever is unsuitable, to seem evil. For as the taste judges of savours according to its disposition, even so does the human mind judge of things to be done according to its habitual disposition. Hence the Philosopher says[1] that "such as a man is, so does the end appear to him." Accordingly charity is inseparable from its possessor, where that which pertains to charity cannot appear otherwise than good, and that is in heaven, where God is seen in His Essence, which is the very essence of goodness. Therefore the charity of heaven cannot be lost, although the charity of the way can, because in this state God is not seen in His Essence, which is the essence of goodness.

Reply Obj. 1. The passage quoted speaks from the point of view of the power of the Holy Ghost, by Whose preservation those whom He wills to move are rendered immune from sin, as much as He wills.

Reply Obj. 2. The charity which comprises in its very notion the possibility of failure is no true charity; for this would be the case were its love given only for a time, and afterwards were to cease, which would be inconsistent with true love. If, however, charity be lost through the changeableness of the subject, and against the purpose of charity included in its act, this is not contrary to true charity.

Reply Obj. 3. The love of God always works great things in its purpose, which pertains to the notion of charity; but it does not always work great things in its act, on account of the condition of its subject.

Reply Obj. 4. Charity according to the character of its act excludes every motive

[1] *Ethics,* III, 5 (1114ª32).

for sinning. But it happens sometimes that charity is no acting actually, and then it is possible for a motive to intervene for sinning, and if we consent to this motive, we lose charity.

ARTICLE 12. *Whether Charity Is Lost Through One Mortal Sin?*

We proceed thus to the Twelfth Article: It seems that charity is not lost through one mortal sin.

Objection 1. For Origen says (*Peri Archon,* i):[2] "When a man who has mounted to the stage of perfection, is satiated, I do not think that he will become empty or fall away suddenly; but he must do so gradually and by little and little." But man falls away by losing charity. Therefore charity is not lost through only one mortal sin.

Obj. 2. Further, Pope Leo in a sermon on the Passion[3] addresses Peter thus: "Our Lord saw in thee not a conquered faith, not an averted love, but constancy shaken. Tears abounded where love never failed, and the words uttered in trepidation were washed away by the fount of charity." From this Bernard drew his assertion[4] that charity in Peter was not quenched but cooled. But Peter sinned mortally in denying Christ. Therefore charity is not lost through one mortal sin.

Obj. 3. Further, Charity is stronger than an acquired virtue. Now a habit of acquired virtue is not destroyed by one contrary sinful act. Much less, therefore, is charity destroyed by one contrary mortal sin.

Obj. 4. Further, Charity denotes love of God and our neighbour. Now it seems that one may commit a mortal sin, and yet retain the love of God and one's neighbour; because an inordinate affection for things directed to the end does not remove the love for the end, as stated above (A. 10). Therefore charity towards God can endure, though there be a mortal sin through an inordinate affection for some temporal good.

Obj. 5. Further, The object of a theological virtue is the last end. Now the other theological virtues, namely faith and hope, are not done away by one mortal sin; in fact they remain though unformed. Therefore charity can remain without a form, even though one mortal sin has been committed.

[2] Chap. 3 (PG 11, 155).
[3] *Serm.,* LX, chap. 4 (PL 54, 345).
[4] Cf. William of St. Thierry, *De Nat. et Dign. Amor.,* chap. 6 (PL 184, 390).

On the contrary, By mortal sin man becomes deserving of eternal death, according to Rom. 6. 23: *The wages of sin is death.* On the other hand whoever has charity is deserving of eternal life, for it is written (John 14. 21): *He that loveth Me, shall be loved by My Father: and I will love Him, and will manifest Myself to him,* in which manifestation everlasting life consists, according to John 17. 3: *This is eternal life; that they may know Thee the . . . true God, and Jesus Christ Whom Thou hast sent.* Now no man can be worthy, at the same time, of eternal life and of eternal death. Therefore it is impossible for a man to have charity with a mortal sin. Therefore charity is destroyed by one mortal sin.

I answer that, That one contrary is removed by the other contrary supervening. Now every mortal sin is contrary to charity by its very notion, which consists in man's loving God above all things, and subjecting himself to Him entirely, by referring all that is his to God. It is therefore of the very notion of charity that man should so love God as to wish to submit to Him in all things, and always to follow the rule of His commandments; for whatever is contrary to His commandments is manifestly contrary to charity, and therefore by its very nature is capable of destroying charity.

If indeed charity were an acquired habit dependent on the power of its subject, it would not necessarily be removed by one mortal sin, for act is directly contrary, not to habit but to act. Now the endurance of a habit in its subject does not require the endurance of its act, so that when a contrary act supervenes, the acquired habit is not at once done away. But charity, being an infused habit, depends on the action of God Who infuses it, Who stands in relation to the infusion and preservation of charity, as the sun does to the diffusion of light in the air, as stated above (A. 10, obj. 3; Q. IV, A. 4, Reply 3). Consequently, just as the light would cease at once in the air, were an obstacle placed to its being lit up by the sun, even so charity ceases at once to be in the soul through the placing of an obstacle to the outpouring of charity by God into the soul.

Now it is evident that through every mortal sin which is contrary to God's commandments, an obstacle is placed to the outpouring of charity, since from the very fact that a man chooses to prefer sin to God's friendship, which requires that we should follow His will, it follows that the habit of charity is lost at once through one mortal sin. Hence Augustine says (*Gen. ad lit.* viii, 12)[1] that "man is enlightened by God's presence, but he is darkened at once by God's absence, because distance from Him is effected not by change of place but by aversion of the will."

Reply Obj. 1. This saying of Origen may be understood, in one way, that a man who is in the state of perfection does not suddenly go so far as to commit a mortal sin, but is disposed to this by some previous negligence, for which reason venial sins are said to be dispositions to mortal sin, as stated above (Part I-II, Q. LXXXVIII, A. 3). Nevertheless he falls, and loses charity through the one mortal sin if he commits it.

Since, however, he adds: "If some slight slip should occur, and he recover himself quickly, he does not appear to fall altogether," we may reply in another way, that when he speaks of a man being emptied and falling away altogether, he means one who falls so as to sin through malice; and this does not occur in a perfect man all at once.

Reply Obj. 2. Charity may be lost in two ways; first, directly, by actual contempt, and, in this way, Peter did not lose charity. Secondly, indirectly, when a sin is committed against charity, through some passion of desire or fear. It was by sinning against charity in this way, that Peter lost charity, although he soon recovered it.

The *Reply to the Third Objection* is evident from what has been said.

Reply Obj. 4. Not every inordinate affection for things directed to the end, that is, for created goods, constitutes a mortal sin, but only such as is directly contrary to the Divine will; and then the inordinate affection is contrary to charity, as stated in this article.

Reply Obj. 5. Charity denotes union with God, but faith and hope do not. Now every mortal sin consists in turning away from God, as stated above (Q. XX, A. 3). Consequently every mortal sin is contrary to charity, but not to faith or hope, but only certain determinate sins, which destroy the habit of faith or of hope, even as charity is destroyed by every mortal sin. Hence it is evident that charity cannot remain without form, since it is itself the ultimate form of the virtues, by reason of its looking to God under the aspect of last end, as stated above (Q. XXIII, A. 8).

[1] PL 34, 383.

QUESTION XXV

OF THE OBJECT OF CHARITY

(*In Twelve Articles*)

WE must now consider the object of charity; which consideration will be twofold: (1) The things we ought to love out of charity: (2) The order in which they ought to be loved (Q. XXVI).

Under the first head there are twelve points of inquiry: (1) Whether we should love God alone, out of charity, or should we love our neighbour also? (2) Whether charity should be loved out of charity? (3) Whether irrational creatures ought to be loved out of charity? (4) Whether one may love oneself out of charity? (5) Whether one's own body? (6) Whether sinners should be loved out of charity? (7) Whether sinners love themselves? (8) Whether we should love our enemies out of charity? (9) Whether we are bound to show them tokens of friendship? (10) Whether we ought to love the angels out of charity? (11) Whether we ought to love the demons? (12) How to enumerate the things we are bound to love out of charity.

ARTICLE 1. *Whether the Love of Charity Stops at God, or Extends to Our Neighbour?*

We proceed thus to the First Article: It seems that the love of charity stops at God and does not extend to our neighbour.

Objection 1. For as we owe God love, so do we owe Him fear, according to Deut. 10. 12: *And now Israel, what doth the Lord thy God require of thee, but that thou fear . . . and love Him?* Now the fear with which we fear man, and which is called human fear, is distinct from the fear with which we fear God, and which is either servile or filial, as is evident from what has been stated above (Q. XIX, A. 2). Therefore also the love with which we love God, is distinct from the love with which we love our neighbour.

Obj. 2. Further, The Philosopher says[1] that "to be loved is to be honoured." Now the honour due to God, which is known as *latria*, is distinct from the honour due to a creature, and known as *dulia*. Therefore again the love with which we love God is distinct from that with which we love our neighbour.

Obj. 3. Further, Hope begets charity, as a gloss states[2] on Matt. 1. 2. Now hope is so due to God that it is reprehensible to hope in man,

[1] *Ethics*, VIII, 8 (1159ᵃ16).   [2] *Glossa interl.* (v, 51).

according to Jerem. 17. 5: *Cursed be the man that trusteth in man.* Therefore charity is so due to God as not to extend to our neighbour.

On the contrary, It is written (I John 4. 21): *This commandment we have from God, that he, who loveth God, love also his brother.*

I answer that, As stated above (Part I-II, Q. LIV, A. 3) habits are not differentiated unless their acts are of different species. For every act of the one species belongs to the same habit. Now since the species of an act is derived from its object, considered under its formal aspect, it follows of necessity that it is specifically the same act that tends to an aspect of the object and that tends to the object under that aspect; thus the visual act by which we see the light, and by which we see the colour under the aspect of light is specifically the same.

Now the aspect under which our neighbour is to be loved, is God, since what we ought to love in our neighbour is that he may be in God. Hence it is clear that the act by which we love God, and by which we love our neighbour is specifically the same. Consequently the habit of charity extends not only to the love of God, but also to the love of our neighbour.

Reply Obj. 1. We may fear our neighbour, even as we may love him, in two ways: first, on account of something that is proper to him, as when a man fears a tyrant on account of his cruelty, or loves him by reason of his own desire to get something from him. And human fear of this kind is distinct from the fear of God, and the same applies to love. Secondly, we fear a man or love him on account of what he has of God; as when we fear the secular power by reason of its exercising the ministry of God for the punishment of evil-doers, and love it for its justice. Fear of man of this kind is not distinct from fear of God, as neither is love of this kind.

Reply Obj. 2. Love looks to good in general, but honour looks to the honoured person's own good, for it is given to a person in recognition of his own virtue. Hence love is not differentiated specifically on account of the various degrees of goodness in various persons so long as it is referred to one good common to all; but honour is distinguished according to the good belonging to individuals. Consequently we love all our neighbours with the same love of charity, in so far as they are referred to one good common to them all, which is God; but we give various honours to various people according to each one's own virtue, and likewise to

God we give the unique honour of latria on account of His unique virtue.

Reply Obj. 3. It is wrong to hope in man as though he were the principal author of salvation, but not to hope in man as helping us ministerially under God. In like manner it would be wrong if a man loved his neighbour as though he were his last end, but not if he loved him for God's sake; and this is what charity does.

ARTICLE 2. *Whether We Should Love Charity out of Charity?*

We proceed thus to the Second Article: It would seem that charity need not be loved out of charity.

Objection 1. For the things to be loved out of charity are contained in the two precepts of charity (Matt. 22. 37-39), and neither of them includes charity, since charity is neither God nor our neighbour. Therefore charity need not be loved out of charity.

Obj. 2. Further, Charity is founded on the fellowship of happiness, as stated above (Q. XXIII, A. 1). But charity cannot participate in happiness. Therefore charity need not be loved out of charity.

Obj. 3. Further, Charity is a kind of friendship, as stated above (*ibid.*). But no man can have friendship for charity or for an accident, since such things cannot return love for love, which pertains to the notion of friendship, as stated in the *Ethics*.[1] Therefore charity need not be loved out of charity.

On the contrary, Augustine says (*De Trinit.* viii, 7):[2] "He that loves his neighbour, must, in consequence, love love itself." But we love our neighbour out of charity. Therefore it follows that charity also is loved out of charity.

I answer that, Charity is love. Now love, by reason of the nature of the power whose act it is, is capable of reflecting on itself; for since the object of the will is the universal good, whatever has the aspect of good, can fall under the act of the will, and since to will is itself a good, man can will himself to will. Even so the intellect, whose object is the true, understands that it understands, because this again is something true. But love also, by reason of its own species, is capable of reflecting on itself, because it is a spontaneous movement of the lover towards the beloved, and so from the very fact that a man loves, he loves himself to love.

Yet charity is not absolute love, but has the character of friendship, as stated above (Q. XXIII, A. 1). Now by friendship a thing is loved in two ways: first, as the friend for whom we have friendship, and to whom we wish good things; secondly, as the good which we wish to a friend. It is in the latter and not in the former way that charity is loved out of charity, because charity is the good which we desire for all those whom we love out of charity. The same applies to happiness, and to the other virtues.

Reply Obj. 1. God and our neighbour are those with whom we are friends, but love of them includes the loving of charity, since we love both God and our neighbour, in so far as we love ourselves and our neighbour to love God, and this is to have charity.

Reply Obj. 2. Charity is the fellowship itself of the spiritual life, by which we arrive at happiness; hence it is loved as the good which we desire for all whom we love out of charity.

Reply Obj. 3. This argument considers friendship as referred to those with whom we are friends.

ARTICLE 3. *Whether Irrational Creatures Also Ought To Be Loved out of Charity?*

We proceed thus to the Third Article: It seems that irrational creatures also ought to be loved out of charity.

Objection 1. For it is chiefly by charity that we are conformed to God. Now God loves irrational creatures out of charity, for He loves *all things that are* (Wisd. 11. 25), and whatever He loves, He loves by Himself Who is charity. Therefore we also should love irrational creatures out of charity.

Obj. 2. Further, Charity is referred to God principally, and extends to other things as referable to God. Now just as the rational creature is referable to God, in so far as it bears the likeness of image, so too, are the irrational creatures, in as much as they bear the likeness of a trace. Therefore charity extends also to irrational creatures.

Obj. 3. Further, Just as the object of charity is God, so is the object of faith. Now faith extends to irrational creatures, since we believe that heaven and earth were created by God, that the fishes and birds were brought forth out of the waters, and animals that walk, and plants, out of the earth. Therefore charity extends also to irrational creatures.

On the contrary, The love of charity extends to none but God and our neighbour. But the word neighbour cannot be extended to irrational

---

[1] Aristotle, VIII, 2 (1155^{b}29).　　　[2] PL 42, 957.

creatures, since they have no fellowship with man in the rational life. Therefore charity does not extend to irrational creatures.

I answer that, According to what has been stated above (Q. XXIII, A. 1) charity is a kind of friendship. Now the love of friendship is twofold. First, there is the love for the friend to whom our friendship is given, secondly, the love for those good things which we desire for our friend. With regard to the first, no irrational creature can be loved out of charity, and for three reasons. Two of these reasons refer in a general way to friendship, which cannot have an irrational creature for its object. First because friendship is towards one to whom we wish good things, while, properly speaking, we cannot wish good things to an irrational creature, because it is not able, properly speaking, to possess good, this being proper to the rational creature which, through its free choice, is the master of its disposal of the good it possesses. Hence the Philosopher says[1] that "we do not speak of good or evil happening to such things, except metaphorically." Secondly, because all friendship is based on some fellowship in life "for nothing is so proper to friendship as to live together," as the Philosopher proves.[2] Now irrational creatures can have no fellowship in human life which is regulated by reason. Hence friendship with irrational creatures is impossible, except metaphorically speaking. The third reason is proper to charity, for charity is based on the fellowship of everlasting happiness, to which the irrational creature cannot attain. Therefore we cannot have the friendship of charity towards an irrational creature.

Nevertheless we can love irrational creatures out of charity, if we regard them as the good things that we desire for others, in so far, namely, as we wish for their preservation, to God's honour and man's use. Thus too does God love them out of charity.

Thus the *Reply to the First Objection* is evident.

Reply Obj. 2. The likeness by way of trace does not confer the capacity for everlasting life, but the likeness of image does, and so the comparison fails.

Reply Obj. 3. Faith can extend to all that is in any way true, but the friendship of charity extends only to such things as have a natural capacity for everlasting life. Therefore the comparison fails.

ARTICLE 4. *Whether a Man Ought To Love Himself out of Charity?*

We proceed thus to the Fourth Article: It seems that a man is not bound to love himself out of charity.

Objection 1. For Gregory says in a homily (*In Evang.* xvii)[3] that "there can be no charity between less than two." Therefore no man has charity towards himself.

Obj. 2. Further, Friendship, of its very notion, implies mutual love and equality,[4] which cannot be of one man towards himself. But charity is a kind of friendship, as stated above (Q. XXIII, A. 1). Therefore a man cannot have charity towards himself.

Obj. 3. Further, Anything relating to charity cannot be blameworthy, since charity *dealeth not perversely* (I Cor. 13. 4). Now a man deserves to be blamed for loving himself, since it is written (II Tim. 3. 1, 2): *In the last days shall come dangerous times, men shall be lovers of themselves.* Therefore a man cannot love himself out of charity.

On the contrary, It is written (Levit. 19. 18): *Thou shalt love thy friend as thyself.* Now we love our friends out of charity. Therefore we should love ourselves too out of charity.

I answer that, Since charity is a kind of friendship, as stated above (Q. XXIII, A. 1), we may consider charity from two standpoints. First, under the common notion of friendship, and in this way we must hold that, properly speaking, a man is not a friend to himself, but something more than a friend, since friendship implies union, for Dionysius says (*Div. Nom.* iv)[5] that love is "a unitive force"; but a man is one with himself, which is more than being united to another. Hence, just as unity is the principle of union, so the love with which a man loves himself is the form and root of friendship. For if we have friendship with others it is because we do unto them as we do unto ourselves, hence we read in the *Ethics,*[6] that "the origin of friendly relations with others lies in our relations to ourselves." Thus too, with regard to principles, we have something greater than science, namely understanding.

Secondly, we may speak of charity in respect of its proper notion, namely as denoting man's friendship with God in the first place, and, consequently, with the things of God, among which

[1] *Physics,* II, 6 (197^{b}8).
[2] *Ethics,* VIII, 5 (1157^{b}19).
[3] PL 76, 1139.
[4] Aristotle, *Ethics,* VIII, 2 (1155^{b}28); cf. VIII, 7 (1158^{b}28).
[5] Sect. 12 (PG 3, 709).
[6] Aristotle, IX, 4, 8 (1166^{a}1; 1168^{b}5).

things is man himself who has charity. Hence, among these other things which he loves out of charity because they pertain to God, he loves also himself out of charity.

Reply Obj. 1. Gregory speaks there of charity under the common notion of friendship; and the *Second Objection* is to be taken in the same sense.

Reply Obj. 3. Those who love themselves are to be blamed in so far as they love themselves as regards their sensitive nature, which they indulge. This is not to love oneself truly according to one's rational nature, so as to desire for oneself the good things which pertain to the perfection of reason: and in this way chiefly it is through charity that a man loves himself.

ARTICLE 5. Whether a Man Ought To Love His Body out of Charity?

We proceed thus to the Fifth Article: It seems that a man ought not to love his body out of charity.

Objection 1. For we do not love one with whom we are unwilling to associate. But those who have charity shun the society of the body, according to Rom. 7. 24: *Who shall deliver me from the body of this death?* and Philip. 1. 23: *Having a desire to be dissolved and to be with Christ.* Therefore our bodies are not to be loved out of charity.

Obj. 2. Further, The friendship of charity is based on fellowship in the enjoyment of God. But the body can have no share in that enjoyment. Therefore the body is not to be loved out of charity.

Obj. 3. Further, Since charity is a kind of friendship it is towards those who are capable of loving in return. But our body cannot love us out of charity. Therefore it should not be loved out of charity.

On the contrary, Augustine says[1] that there are four things that we should love out of charity, and among them he counts our own body.

I answer that, Our bodies can be considered in two ways, first, in respect of their nature, secondly, in respect of the corruption of sin and its punishment. Now the nature of our body was created, not by an evil principle, as the Manicheans pretend, but by God. Hence we can use it for God's service, according to Rom. 6. 13: *Present . . . your members as instruments of justice unto God.* Consequently, out of the love of charity with which we love God, we ought to love our bodies also. But we ought not to love the evil effects of sin and the cor-

ruption of punishment; we ought rather, by the desire of charity, to long for the removal of such things.

Reply Obj. 1. The Apostle did not shrink from the society of his body, as regards the nature of the body; on the contrary, in this respect he was loth to be deprived of it, according to II Cor. 5, 4: *We would not be unclothed, but clothed over.* He did, however, wish to escape from the taint of concupiscence, which remains in the body, and from the corruption of the body which weighs down the soul, so as to hinder it from seeing God. Hence he says expressly: *From the body of this death.*

Reply Obj. 2. Although our bodies are unable to enjoy God by knowing and loving Him, yet by the works which we do through the body, we are able to attain to the perfect enjoyment of God. Hence from the enjoyment in the soul there overflows a certain happiness into the body, namely, "the vigor of health and incorruption," as Augustine states (*Ep. ad Dioscor.* cxviii).[2] Hence, since the body has, in a fashion, a share of happiness, it can be loved with the love of charity.

Reply Obj. 3. Mutual love is found in the friendship which is for another, but not in that which a man has for himself, either in respect of his soul or in respect of his body.

ARTICLE 6. Whether We Ought To Love Sinners out of Charity?

We proceed thus to the Sixth Article: It would seem that we ought not to love sinners out of charity.

Objection 1. For it is written (Ps. 118. 113): *I have hated the unjust.* But David had perfect charity. Therefore sinners should be hated rather than loved, out of charity.

Obj. 2. Further, "Love is proved by deeds," as Gregory says in a homily for Pentecost (*In Evang.* xxx).[3] But just men do no works of love for the unjust; on the contrary, they do such as would appear to be works of hate, according to Ps. 100. 8: *In the morning I put to death all the wicked of the land;* and God commanded (Exod. 22. 18): *Wizards thou shalt not suffer to live.* Therefore sinners should not be loved out of charity.

Obj. 3. Further, It is part of friendship that one should desire and wish good things for one's friends. Now the saints, out of charity, desire evil things for the wicked, according to Ps. 9. 18: *May the wicked be turned into hell.*

---

[1] *Christian Doctrine,* I, 23, 26 (PL 34, 27; 29).

[2] Chap. 3 (PL 33, 439).
[3] PL 76, 1220.

Therefore sinners should not be loved out of charity.

Obj. 4. Further, It is proper to friends to rejoice in, and will the same things. Now charity does not make us will what sinners will, nor to rejoice in what gives them joy, but rather the contrary. Therefore sinners should not be loved out of charity.

Obj. 5. Further "It is proper to friends to associate together," according to the *Ethics*.[1] But we ought not to associate with sinners, according to II Cor. 6. 17: *Go ye out from among them.* Therefore we should not love sinners out of charity.

On the contrary, Augustine says[2] that when it is said: *Thou shalt love thy neighbour,* "it is evident that we ought to look upon every man as our neighbour." Now sinners do not cease to be men, for sin does not destroy nature. Therefore we ought to love sinners out of charity.

I answer that, Two things may be considered in the sinner, his nature and his guilt. According to his nature, which he has from God, he has a capacity for happiness, on the fellowship of which charity is based, as stated above (A. 3; Q. XXIII, AA. 1, 5); therefore we ought to love sinners, out of charity, in respect of their nature. On the other hand their guilt is opposed to God, and is an obstacle to happiness. Therefore, in respect of their guilt by which they are opposed to God, all sinners are to be hated, even one's father or mother or kindred, according to Luke 14. 26. For it is our duty to hate, in the sinner, his being a sinner, and to love in him, his being a man capable of bliss. And this is to love him truly, out of charity, for God's sake.

Reply Obj. 1. The prophet hated the unjust, as such, and the object of his hate was their iniquity, which was their evil. Such hatred is perfect, of which he himself says (Ps. 138. 22): *I have hated them with a perfect hatred.* Now hatred of a person's evil is equivalent to love of his good. Hence also this perfect hatred belongs to charity.

Reply Obj. 2. As the Philosopher observes,[3] when our friends fall into sin, we ought not to deny them the benefits of friendship so long as there is hope of their mending their ways, and we ought to help them more readily to regain virtue than to recover money, had they lost it, since virtue is more akin than money

to friendship. When, however, they fall into very great wickedness, and become incurable, we ought no longer to show them friendliness. It is for this reason that both Divine and human laws command such sinners to be put to death, because there is greater likelihood of their harming others than of their mending their ways. Nevertheless the judge puts this into effect not out of hatred for the sinners, but out of the love of charity, by reason of which he prefers the public good to the life of the individual. Moreover the death inflicted by the judge profits the sinner, if he be converted, for the expiation of his crime; and if he be not converted, it profits so as to put an end to the sin, because the sinner is thus deprived of the power to sin any more.

Reply Obj. 3. Imprecations of this kind which we come across in Holy Writ, may be understood in three ways. First, by way of prediction, not by way of wish, so that the sense is: *May the wicked be,* that is, *The wicked shall be, turned into hell.* Secondly, by way of wish, yet so that the desire of the wisher is not referred to the man's punishment, but to the justice of the punisher, according to Ps. 57. 11: *The just shall rejoice when he shall see the revenge,* since, according to Wisd. 1. 13, not even God *hath pleasure in the destruction of the wicked* (Vulg.,—*living*) when He punishes them, but He rejoices in His justice, according to Ps. 10. 8: *The Lord is just and hath loved justice.* Thirdly, so that this desire is referred to the removal of the sin, and not to the punishment itself, to the effect, namely, that the sin be destroyed, but that the man may live.

Reply Obj. 4. We love sinners out of charity, not so as to will what they will, or to rejoice in what gives them joy, but so as to make them will what we will, and rejoice in what rejoices us. Hence it is written (Jerem. 15. 19): *They shall be turned to thee, and thou shalt not be turned to them.*

Reply Obj. 5. The weak should avoid associating with sinners, on account of the danger in which they stand of being perverted by them. But it is commendable for the perfect, of whose corruption there is no fear, to associate with sinners that they may convert them. For thus did Our Lord eat and drink with sinners as related by Matthew (9. 11-13). Yet all should avoid the society of sinners, as regards fellowship in sin; in this sense it is written (II Cor. 6. 17): *Go out from among them . . . and touch not the unclean thing,* that is, by consenting to sin.

---

[1] Aristotle, VIII, 5 (1157ᵇ19).
[2] *Christian Doctrine,* I, 30 (PL 34, 31).
[3] *Ethics,* IX, 3 (1165ᵇ13).

ARTICLE 7. *Whether Sinners Love Themselves?*

We proceed thus to the Seventh Article: It seems that sinners love themselves.

Objection 1. For that which is the principle of sin, is most of all in the sinner. Now love of self is the principle of sin since Augustine says[1] that it builds up the city of Babylon. Therefore sinners most of all love themselves.

Obj. 2. Further, Sin does not destroy nature. Now it is in keeping with nature that every man should love himself, and so even irrational creatures naturally desire their own good, for instance, the preservation of their being, and so forth. Therefore sinners love themselves.

Obj. 3. Further, Good is beloved by all, as Dionysius states (*Div. Nom.* iv).[2] Now many sinners consider themselves to be good. Therefore many sinners love themselves.

On the contrary, It is written (Ps. 10. 6): *He that loveth iniquity, hateth his own soul.*

I answer that, Love of self is common to all, in one way; in another way it is proper to the good; in a third way, it is proper to the wicked. For it is common to all for each one to love what he thinks himself to be. Now a man is said to be a thing, in two ways: first, in respect of his substance and nature, and this way all think themselves to be what they are, that is, composed of a soul and body. In this way too, all men, both good and wicked, love themselves, in so far as they love their own preservation.

Secondly, a man is said to be something in respect of some predominance, as the sovereign of a state is spoken of as being the state, and so, what the sovereign does, the state is said to do. In this way, all do not think themselves to be what they are. For the reasoning mind is the predominant part of man, while the sensitive and corporeal nature takes the second place, the former of which the Apostle calls the *inward man,* and the latter, the *outward man* (II Cor. 4. 16). Now the good look upon their rational nature or the inward man as being the chief thing in them, and so in this way they think themselves to be what they are. On the other hand, the wicked consider their sensitive and corporeal nature, or the outward man, to hold the first place. Therefore, since they do not know themselves rightly, they do not truly love themselves, but love what they think themselves to be. But the good know themselves truly, and therefore truly love themselves.

The Philosopher proves this from five things that are proper to friendship.[3] For in the first place, every friend wishes his friend to be and to live; secondly, he desires good things for him; thirdly, he does good things to him; fourthly, he takes pleasure in his company; fifthly, he is of one mind with him, rejoicing and sorrowing in almost the same things. In this way the good love themselves, as to the inward man, because they wish his preservation in his integrity, they wish good things for him, namely spiritual goods, indeed they do their best to obtain them, and they take pleasure in entering into their own hearts, because they find there good thoughts in the present, the memory of past good, and the hope of future good, all of which are sources of pleasure. Likewise they experience no clashing of wills, since their whole soul tends to one thing.

On the other hand, the wicked have no wish to be preserved in the integrity of the inward man, nor do they desire spiritual goods for him, nor do they work for that end, nor do they take pleasure in their own company by entering into their own hearts, because they find there evils present, past and future, which they shrink from; nor do they agree with themselves, on account of the gnawings of conscience, according to Ps. 49. 21: *I will reprove thee and set before thy face.* And in the same manner it may be shown that the wicked love themselves as regards the corruption of the outward man, but the good do not love themselves thus.

Reply Obj. 1. The love of self which is the principle of sin is that which is proper to the wicked, and reaches "to the contempt of God," as stated in the passage quoted, because the wicked so desire external goods as to despise spiritual goods.

Reply Obj. 2. Although natural love is not altogether forfeited by wicked men, yet it is perverted in them, as explained above.

Reply Obj. 3. The wicked have some share of self-love, in so far as they think themselves good. Yet such love of self is not true but apparent; and even this is not possible in those who are very wicked.

ARTICLE 8. *Whether Charity Requires That We Should Love Our Enemies?*

We proceed thus to the Eighth Article: It seems that charity does not require us to love our enemies.

Objection 1. For Augustine says (*Enchirid.* lxxiii)[4] that "this great good, namely, the love

---

[1] *City of God,* XIV, 28 (PL 41, 436).   [2] Sect. 10 (PG 3, 708).   [3] *Ethics,* IX, 4 (1166ᵃ3).   [4] PL 40, 266.

of our enemies, is not so universal in its application as the object of our petition when we say: 'Forgive us our trespasses.'" Now no one is forgiven sin unless he has charity, because, according to Prov. 10, 12, *charity covereth all sins.* Therefore charity does not require that we should love our enemies.

Obj. 2. Further, Charity does not do away with nature. Now everything, even an irrational being, naturally hates its contrary, as a lamb hates a wolf, and water, fire. Therefore charity does not make us love our enemies.

Obj. 3. Further, Charity *doth nothing perversely* (I Cor. 13. 4). Now it seems perverse to love one's enemies, as it would be to hate one's friends; hence Joab upbraided David by saying (II Kings 19. 6): *Thou lovest them that hate thee, and thou hatest them that love thee.* Therefore charity does not make us love our enemies.

On the contrary, Our Lord said (Matt. 5. 44): *Love your enemies.*

I answer that, Love of one's enemies may be understood in three ways. First, as though we were to love our enemies as enemies; this is perverse, and contrary to charity, since it implies love of that which is evil in another.

Secondly love of one's enemies may mean that we love them as to their nature, but in a universal way, and in this sense charity requires that we should love our enemies, namely, that in loving God and our neighbour, we should not exclude our enemies from the love given to our neighbour in general.

Thirdly love of one's enemies may be considered as specially directed to them, namely, that we should have a special movement of love towards our enemies. Charity does not require this absolutely, because it does not require that we should have a special movement of love to every individual man, since this would be impossible. Nevertheless charity does require this, in respect of our being prepared in mind, namely that we should be ready to love our enemies individually, if the necessity were to occur.

That man should actually do so, and love his enemy for God's sake, without it being necessary for him to do so, belongs to the perfection of charity. For since man loves his neighbour out of charity for God's sake, the more he loves God the more he puts enmities aside and shows love towards his neighbour; thus if we loved a certain man very much, we would love his children though they were unfriendly towards us. This is the sense in which Augustine speaks in the passage quoted in the

First Objection, the *Reply* to which is therefore evident.

Reply Obj. 2. Everything naturally hates its contrary as such. Now our enemies are contrary to us, as enemies, and so this fact should be hateful to us, for their enmity should displease us. They are not, however, contrary to us as men and capable of happiness; and it is as such that we are bound to love them.

Reply Obj. 3. It is wrong to love one's enemies as enemies; and charity does not do this, as stated above.

ARTICLE 9. *Whether It Is Necessary for Salvation That We Should Show Our Enemies the Signs and Effects of Love?*

We proceed thus to the Ninth Article: It seems that charity demands of a man to show his enemy the signs or effects of love.

Objection 1. For it is written (I John 3. 18): *Let us not love in word nor in tongue, but in deed and in truth.* Now a man loves in deed by showing the one he loves signs and effects of love. Therefore charity requires that a man show his enemies such signs and effects of love.

Obj. 2. Further, Our Lord said in the same breath (Matt. 5. 44): *Love your enemies,* and, *Do good to them that hate you.* Now charity demands that we love our enemies. Therefore it demands also that we should do good to them.

Obj. 3. Further, Not only God but also our neighbour is the object of charity. Now Gregory says in a homily for Pentecost (*In Evang.* xxx),[1] that "love of God cannot be idle, for wherever it is it does great things, and if it ceases to work, it is no longer love." Hence charity towards our neighbour cannot be without producing works. But charity requires us to love our neighbour without exception, even though he be an enemy. Therefore charity requires us to show the signs and effects of love towards our enemies.

On the contrary, A gloss on Matt. 5. 44, *Do good to them that hate you,* says:[2] "To do good to one's enemies is the height of perfection." Now charity does not require us to do that which pertains to its perfection. Therefore charity does not require us to show the signs and effects of love to our enemies.

I answer that, The effects and signs of charity are the result of inward love, and are in proportion with it. Now it is absolutely necessary, for the fulfilment of the precept, that we should inwardly love our enemies in general, but not individually, except as regards the

[1] PL 76, 1221.   [2] *Glossa ordin.* (v, 23B).

mind being prepared to do so, as explained above (A. 8). We must accordingly apply this to the showing of the effects and signs of love. For some of the signs and favours of love are shown to our neighbours in general, as when we pray for all the faithful, or for a whole people, or when anyone bestows a favour on a whole community, and the fulfilment of the precept requires that we should show the like favours or signs of love towards our enemies. For if we did not so, it would be a proof of vengeful spite, and contrary to what is written (Levit. 19. 18): *Seek not revenge, nor be mindful of the injury of thy citizens.*

But there are other favours or signs of love, which one shows to certain persons in particular, and it is not necessary for salvation that we show our enemies such favours and signs of love, except as regards being ready in our minds, for instance to come to their assistance in a case of urgency, according to Prov. 25. 21: *If thy enemy be hungry, give him to eat; if he thirst, give him . . . drink.* Outside cases of urgency, to show such favours to an enemy belongs to the perfection of charity, by which we not only beware, as in duty bound, of being overcome by evil, but also wish to overcome evil by good, which belongs to perfection; for then we not only beware of being drawn into hatred on account of the hurt done to us, but purpose to induce our enemy to love us on account of our kindliness.

This suffices for the *Replies to the Objections.*

ARTICLE 10. *Whether We Ought To Love the Angels out of Charity?*

We proceed thus to the Tenth Article: It seems that we are not bound to love the angels out of charity.

Objection 1. For, as Augustine says,[1] "charity is a twofold love,—the love of God and of our neighbour." Now love of the angels is not contained in the love of God, since they are created substances; nor does it seem to be contained in the love of our neighbour, since they do not belong with us to a common species. Therefore we are not bound to love them out of charity.

Obj. 2. Further, Dumb animals have more in common with us than the angels have, since they belong to the same proximate genus as we do. But we do not have charity towards dumb animals, as stated above (A. 3). Neither, therefore, have we towards the angels.

Obj. 3. Further, "Nothing is so proper to friends as companionship with one another."[2] But the angels are not our companions; we cannot even see them. Therefore we are unable to give them the friendship of charity.

On the contrary, Augustine says:[3] "If the name of neighbour is given either to those whom we pity, or to those who pity us, it is evident that the precept binding us to love our neighbour includes also the holy angels from whom we receive many merciful favours."

I answer that, As stated above (Q. XXIII, AA. 1, 5), the friendship of charity is founded upon the fellowship of everlasting happiness, in which men share in common with the angels. For it is written (Matt. 22. 30) that *in the resurrection . . . men shall be as the angels of God in heaven.* It is therefore evident that the friendship of charity extends also to the angels.

Reply Obj. 1. Our neighbour is not only one who is united to us in a common species, but also one who is united to us by sharing in the blessings pertaining to everlasting life, and it is on the latter fellowship that the friendship of charity is founded.

Reply Obj. 2. Dumb animals are united to us in the proximate genus by reason of their sensitive nature; but we are partakers of everlasting happiness, by reason not of our sensitive nature but of our rational mind, wherein we associate with the angels.

Reply Obj. 3. The companionship of the angels does not consist in outward conversation, which we have in respect of our sensitive nature; it consists in a fellowship of the mind, imperfect indeed in this life, but perfect in heaven, as stated above (Q. XXIII, A. 1, Reply 1).

ARTICLE 11. *Whether We Are Bound To Love the Demons out of Charity?*

We proceed thus to the Eleventh Article: It would seem that we ought to love the demons out of charity.

Objection 1. For the angels are our neighbours by reason of their fellowship with us in a rational mind. But the demons also share in our fellowship thus, since natural gifts, such as life and understanding, remain in them unimpaired, as Dionysius states (*Div. Nom.* iv)[4] Therefore we ought to love the demons out of charity.

Obj. 2. Further, The demons differ from the blessed angels in the matter of sin, even as sin-

---

[1] *Christian Doctrine,* I, 26 (PL 34, 29).

[2] *Ethics,* VIII, 5 (1157[b]19).
[3] *Op. cit.,* I, 30 (PL 34, 31).   [4] Sect. 23 (PG 3, 725).

ners from just men. Now the just man loves the sinner out of charity. Therefore he ought to love the demons also out of charity.

Obj. 3. Further, We ought, out of charity, to love, as being our neighbours, those from whom we receive favours, as appears from the passage of Augustine quoted above (A. 10, *on the contrary*). Now the demons are useful to us in many things, for "by tempting us they work crowns for us," as Augustine says.[1] Therefore we ought to love the demons out of charity.

On the contrary, It is written (Isa. 28. 18): *Your league with death shall be abolished, and your covenant with hell shall not stand.* Now the perfection of a peace and covenant is through charity. Therefore we ought not to have charity for the demons who live in hell and administer death.

I answer that, As stated above (A. 6), in the sinner, we are bound, out of charity, to love his nature, but to hate his sin. But the name of demon is given to designate a nature deformed by sin, and therefore demons should not be loved out of charity. Without however laying stress on the word, the question as to whether the spirits called demons ought to be loved out of charity must be answered in accordance with the statement made above (AA. 2, 3), that a thing may be loved out of charity in two ways. First, a thing may be loved as the person who is the object of friendship, and thus we cannot have the friendship of charity towards the demons. For it pertains to the notion of friendship that one should be a well-wisher towards one's friend; and it is impossible for us, out of charity, to desire the good of everlasting life, to which charity is referred, for those spirits whom God has condemned eternally, since this would be in opposition to our charity towards God by which we approve of His justice.

Secondly, we love a thing as being that which we desire to be enduring as another's good. In this way we love irrational creatures out of charity, since we wish them to endure to give glory to God and be useful to man, as stated above (A. 3); and in this way too we can love the nature of the demons even out of charity, in so far as we desire those spirits to be preserved, as to their natural gifts, for God's glory.

Reply Obj. 1. The possession of everlasting happiness is not impossible for the angelic mind as it is for the mind of a demon; consequently the friendship of charity which is based on the fellowship of everlasting life rather than on the fellowship of nature, is possible towards

the angels, but not towards the demons.

Reply Obj. 2. In this life, men who are in sin retain the possibility of obtaining everlasting happiness. This is not so of those who are lost in hell, who, in this respect, are in the same case as the demons.

Reply Obj. 3. That the demons are useful to us is due not to their intention but to the ordering of Divine providence; hence this leads us to be friends, not with them, but with God, Who turns their perverse intention to our profit.

ARTICLE 12. *Whether Four Things Are Rightly Enumerated As To Be Loved out of Charity, Namely, God, Our Neighbour, Our Body, and Ourselves?*

We proceed thus to the Twelfth Article: It would seem that these four things are not rightly enumerated as to be loved out of charity, namely, God, our neighbour, our body, and ourselves.

Objection 1. For, as Augustine states (*Tract. super Joann.* lxxxiii),[2] "he that loveth not God, loveth not himself." Hence love of oneself is included in the love of God. Therefore love of oneself is not distinct from the love of God.

Obj. 2. Further, A part ought not to be divided against the whole. But our body is part of ourselves. Therefore it ought not to be divided from ourselves as a distinct object of love.

Obj. 3. Further, Just as a man has a body, so has his neighbour. Since then the love with which a man loves his neighbour is distinct from the love with which a man loves himself, so the love with which a man loves his neighbour's body ought to be distinct from the love with which he loves his own body. Therefore these four things are not rightly distinguished as objects to be loved out of charity.

On the contrary, Augustine says:[3] "There are four things to be loved; one which is above us," namely God; "another, which is ourselves, a third which is next to us," namely our neighbour; "and a fourth which is beneath us," namely our own body.

I answer that, As stated above (Q. XXIII, AA. 1, 5), the friendship of charity is based on the fellowship of happiness. Now, in this fellowship, one thing is considered as the principle from which happiness flows, namely God; a second is that which directly partakes of happiness, namely men and angels; a third is a thing to which happiness comes by a kind of

---

[1] Cf. Bernard, *In Cant.*, serm. XVII (PL 183, 858).

[2] PL 35, 1846.

[3] *Christian Doctrine*, I, 23 (PL 34, 27).

overflow, namely the human body. Now the source from which happiness flows is lovable by reason of its being the cause of happiness. But that which is a partaker of happiness can be an object of love for two reasons, either through being one with ourselves, or through being associated with us in the sharing of happiness, and in this respect, there are two things to be loved out of charity, according as man loves both himself and his neighbour.

Reply Obj. 1. The different relations between a lover and the various things loved makes a different kind of lovableness. Accordingly, since the relation between the human lover and God is different from his relation to himself, these two are considered as distinct objects of love, for the love of the one is the cause of the love of the other, so that the former love being removed the latter is taken away.

Reply Obj. 2. The subject of charity is the rational mind that can be capable of obtaining happiness, to which the body does not reach directly, but only by a kind of overflow. Hence, by his reasonable mind which holds the first place in him, man, out of charity, loves himself in one way, and his own body in another.

Reply Obj. 3. Man loves his neighbour, both as to his soul and as to his body, by reason of a certain fellowship in happiness. Therefore, on the part of his neighbour, there is only one reason for loving him, and our neighbour's body is not counted as a special object of love.

QUESTION XXVI
OF THE ORDER OF CHARITY
(In Thirteen Articles)

WE must now consider the order of charity, under which head there are thirteen points of inquiry: (1) Whether there is an order in charity? (2) Whether man ought to love God more than his neighbour? (3) Whether more than himself? (4) Whether he ought to love himself more than his neighbour? (5) Whether man ought to love his neighbour more than his own body? (6) Whether he ought to love one neighbour more than another? (7) Whether he ought to love more, a neighbor who is better, or one who is more closely united to him? (8) Whether he ought to love more, one who is akin to him by blood, or one who is united to him by other ties? (9) Whether, out of charity, a man ought to love his son more than his father? (10) Whether he ought to love his mother more than his father? (11) Whether he ought to love his wife more than his father or mother? (12)

Whether we ought to love those who are kind to us more than those whom we are kind to? (13) Whether the order of charity endures in heaven?

ARTICLE 1. *Whether There Is Order in Charity?*

We proceed thus to the First Article: It would seem that there is no order in charity.

Objection 1. For charity is a virtue. But no order is assigned to the other virtues. Neither, therefore, should any order be assigned to charity.

Obj. 2. Further, Just as the object of faith is the First Truth, so is the object of charity the Sovereign Good. Now no order is appointed for faith, but all things are believed equally. Neither, therefore, ought there to be any order in charity.

Obj. 3. Further, Charity is in the will. But ordering belongs, not to the will, but to the reason. Therefore no order should be ascribed to charity.

On the contrary, It is written (Cant. 2. 4): *He brought me into the cellar of wine, he set in order charity in me.*

I answer that, As the Philosopher says,[1] "the terms before and after are used in reference to some principle." Now order implies that certain things are, in some way, before and after. Hence wherever there is a principle, there must be also order of some kind. But it has been said above (Q. XXIII, A. 1; Q. XXV, A. 12) that the love of charity tends to God as to the principle of happiness, on the fellowship of which the friendship of charity is based. Consequently there must be some order in things loved out of charity, which order is in reference to the first principle of that love, which is God.

Reply Obj. 1. Charity tends towards the last end considered as last end, and this does not apply to any other virtue, as stated above (Q. XXIII, A. 6). Now the end has the character of principle in matters of appetite and action, as was shown above (Q. XXIII, A. 7; Part I-II, Q. XIII, A. 3). Therefore charity, above all, implies relation to the First Principle, and consequently, in charity above all, we find an order in reference to the First Principle.

Reply Obj. 2. Faith pertains to the cognitive power, whose operation depends on the thing known being in the knower. On the other hand, charity is in an affective power, whose operation consists in the soul tending to things themselves. Now order is to be found more especially

[1] *Metaphysics,* V, 11 (1018b9).

in things themselves, and flows from them into our knowledge. Hence order is more appropriate to charity than to faith. And yet there is a certain order in faith, in so far as it is chiefly about God, and secondarily about things referred to God.

Reply Obj. 3. Order belongs to reason as the power that orders, and to the appetitive power as to the power which is ordered. It is in this way that order is stated to be in charity.

ARTICLE 2. *Whether God Ought To Be Loved More Than Our Neighbour?*

We proceed thus to the Second Article: It would seem that God ought not to be loved more than our neighbour.

Objection 1. For it is written (I John 4. 20): *He that loveth not his brother whom he seeth, how can he love God, Whom he seeth not?* From which it seems to follow that the more a thing is visible the more lovable it is, since "loving begins with seeing," according to the *Ethics.*[1] Now God is less visible than our neighbour. Therefore He is less lovable, out of charity, than our neighbour.

Obj. 2. Further, Likeness causes love, according to Ecclus. 13. 19: *Every beast loveth its like.* Now man bears more likeness to his neighbour than to God. Therefore man loves his neighbour, out of charity, more than he loves God.

Obj. 3. Further, What charity loves in a neighbour, is God, according to Augustine.[2] Now God is not greater in Himself than He is in our neighbour. Therefore He is not more to be loved in Himself than in our neighbour. Therefore we ought not to love God more than our neighbour.

On the contrary, A thing ought to be loved more if others ought to be hated on its account. Now we ought to hate our neighbour for God's sake, if, that is, he leads us astray from God, according to Luke 14. 26: *If any man come to Me and hate not his father, and mother, and wife, and children, and brethren, and sisters . . . he cannot be My disciple.* Therefore we ought to love God, out of charity, more than our neighbour.

I answer that, Each kind of friendship regards chiefly the subject in which we chiefly find the good on the fellowship of which that friendship is based; thus civil friendship regards chiefly the ruler of the state, on whom the entire common good of the state depends; hence to him

before all, the citizens owe fidelity and obedience. Now the friendship of charity is based on the fellowship of happiness, which consists essentially in God, as the First Principle, from whom it flows to all who are capable of happiness. Therefore God ought to be loved chiefly and before all out of charity, for He is loved as the cause of happiness, while our neighbour is loved as receiving together with us a share of happiness from Him.

Reply Obj. 1. A thing is a cause of love in two ways. First, as being the reason for loving, and in this way good is the cause of love, since each thing is loved according to its measure of goodness. Secondly, a thing causes love, as being a way to acquire love. It is in this way that seeing is the cause of loving, not as though a thing were lovable according as it is visible, but because by seeing a thing we are led to love it. Hence it does not follow that what is more visible is more lovable, but that as an object of love we meet with it before others; and that is the sense of the Apostle's argument. For, since our neighbour is more visible to us, he is the first lovable object we meet with, because "the soul learns, from those things it knows, to love what it knows not," as Gregory says in a homily (*In Evang.* xi).[3] Hence it can be argued that, if any man does not love his neighbour, neither does he love God, not because his neighbour is more lovable, but because he is the first thing to demand our love. But God is more lovable by reason of His greater goodness.

Reply Obj. 2. The likeness we have to God precedes and causes the likeness we have to our neighbour, because from the very fact that we share along with our neighbour in something received from God, we become like to our neighbour. Hence by reason of this likeness we ought to love God more than we love our neighbour.

Reply Obj. 3. Considered in His substance, God is equally in all, in whomsoever He may be, for He is not lessened by being in anything. And yet our neighbour does not possess God's goodness equally with God, for God has it essentially, and our neighbour by participation.

ARTICLE 3. *Whether, out of Charity, Man Is Bound To Love God More Than Himself?*

We proceed thus to the Third Article: It would seem that man is not bound, out of charity, to love God more than himself.

Objection 1. For the Philosopher says[4] that "a man's friendly relations with others arise from his friendly relations with himself." Now

---

[1] Aristotle, IX, 5, 12 (1167ᵃ4; 1171ᵇ29).
[2] *Christian Doctrine,* I, 22, 27 (PL 34, 26; 29).
[3] PL 76, 1114.   [4] *Ethics,* IX, 4, 10 (1166ᵃ1; 1168ᵇ5).

the cause is stronger than its effect. Therefore man's friendship towards himself is greater than his friendship for anyone else. Therefore he ought to love himself more than God.

Obj. 2. Further, One loves a thing in so far as it is one's own good. Now the reason for loving a thing is more loved than the thing itself which is loved for that reason, even as the principles which are the reason for knowing a thing are more known. Therefore man loves himself more than any other good loved by him. Therefore he does not love God more than himself.

Obj. 3. Further, A man loves God as much as he loves to enjoy God. But a man loves himself as much as he loves to enjoy God, since this is the highest good a man can wish for himself. Therefore man is not bound, out of charity, to love God more than himself.

On the contrary, Augustine says:[1] "If thou oughtest to love thyself, not for thy own sake, but for the sake of Him in Whom is the rightest end of thy love, let no other man take offence if him also thou lovest for God's sake." Now the cause of a thing being such is yet more so. Therefore man ought to love God more than himself.

I answer that, The good we receive from God is twofold, the good of nature, and the good of grace. Now the fellowship of natural goods bestowed on us by God is the foundation of natural love, in virtue of which not only man, so long as his nature remains unimpaired, loves God above all things and more than himself, but also every single creature, each in its own way, that is, either by an intellectual, or by a rational, or by an animal, or at least by a natural love, as stones do, for instance, and other things bereft of knowledge, because each part naturally loves the common good of the whole more than its own particular good. This is evidenced by its operation, since the principal inclination of each part is towards common action conducive to the usefulness of the whole. It may also be seen in political virtues according to which sometimes the citizens suffer damage even to their own property and persons for the sake of the common good. And so much more is this realized with regard to the friendship of charity which is based on the fellowship of the gifts of grace. Therefore man ought, out of charity, to love God, Who is the common good of all, more than himself, since happiness is in God as in the universal and fountain-head principle of all who are able to have a share of that happiness.

[1] *Christian Doctrine,* I, 22 (PL 34, 27).

Reply Obj. 1. The Philosopher is speaking of friendly relations towards another person in whom the good, which is the object of friendship, resides in some particular way, and not of friendly relations with another in whom the aforesaid good resides in totality.

Reply Obj. 2. The part does indeed love the good of the whole, as becomes a part, not however so as to refer the good of the whole to itself, but rather itself to the good of the whole.

Reply Obj. 3. That a man wishes to enjoy God pertains to that love of God which is love of concupiscence. Now we love God with the love of friendship more than with the love of concupiscence, because the Divine good is greater in itself than our share of good in enjoying Him. Hence, absolutely, out of charity, man loves God more than himself.

ARTICLE 4. *Whether out of Charity, Man Ought To Love Himself More Than His Neighbour?*

We proceed thus to the Fourth Article: It would seem that a man ought not, out of charity, to love himself more than his neighbour.

Objection 1. For the principal object of charity is God, as stated above (A. 2). Now sometimes our neighbour is more closely united to God than we ourselves. Therefore we ought to love such a one more than ourselves.

Obj. 2. Further, The more we love a person, the more we avoid injuring him. Now a man, out of charity, submits to injury for his neighbour's sake, according to Prov. 12. 26: *He that neglecteth a loss for the sake of a friend, is just.* Therefore a man ought, out of charity, to love his neighbour more than himself.

Obj. 3. Further, It is written (I Cor. 13: 5) that *charity seeketh not its own.* Now the thing we love most is the one whose good we seek most. Therefore a man does not, out of charity, love himself more than his neighbour.

On the contrary, It is written (Lev. 19. 18, Matt. 22. 39): *Thou shalt love thy neighbour* (Lev. *loc. cit.,—friend*) *as thyself.* From this it seems to follow that man's love for himself is the exemplar of his love for another. But the exemplar exceeds the copy. Therefore, out of charity, a man ought to love himself more than his neighbour.

I answer that, There are two things in man, his spiritual nature and his corporeal nature. And a man is said to love himself by reason of his loving himself with regard to his spiritual nature, as stated above (Q. XXV, A. 7), so that accordingly, a man ought, out of charity, to love himself more than he loves any other person. This is evident from the very reason for loving, since, as stated above (A. 2; Q. XXV, A. 12), God is loved as the principle of good, on which the love of charity is founded; while man, out of charity, loves himself by reason of his being a partaker of that good, and loves his neighbour by reason of his fellowship in that good. Now fellowship is a reason for love according to a certain union in relation to God. Therefore just as unity surpasses union, the fact that man himself has a share of the Divine good is a more potent reason for loving than that another should be a partner with him in that share. Therefore man, out of charity, ought to love himself more than his neighbour. And a sign of this is that a man ought not to give way to any evil of sin which counteracts his share of happiness, not even that he may free his neighbour from sin.

Reply Obj. 1. The love of charity takes its quantity not only from its object which is God, but also from the lover, who is the man that has charity, even as the quantity of any action depends in some way on the subject. Therefore, though a better neighbour is nearer to God, yet because he is not as near to the man who has charity as this man is to himself, it does not follow that a man is bound to love his neighbour more than himself.

Reply Obj. 2. A man ought to bear bodily injury for his friend's sake, and in this very thing he loves himself more as regards his spiritual mind, because it pertains to the perfection of virtue, which is a good of the mind. In spiritual matters, however, man ought not to suffer injury by sinning in order to free his neighbour from sin, as stated above.

Reply Obj. 3. As Augustine says in his Rule,[1] "the saying, 'charity seeks not her own,' means that it prefers the common to the private good." Now the common good is always more lovable to the individual than his private good, even as the good of the whole is more lovable to the part than the latter's own partial good, as stated above (A. 3).

ARTICLE 5. *Whether a Man Ought To Love His Neighbour More Than His Own Body?*

We proceed thus to the Fifth Article: It would seem that a man is not bound to love his neighbour more than his own body.

Objection 1. For his neighbour includes his

[1] *Epist.*, CCXI (PL 33, 963).

neighbour's body. If therefore a man ought to love his neighbour more than his own body, it follows that he ought to love his neighbour's body more than his own.

Obj. 2. Further, A man ought to love his own soul more than his neighbour's, as stated above (A. 4). Now a man's own body is nearer to his soul than his neighbour. Therefore we ought to love our body more than our neighbour.

Obj. 3. Further, A man imperils that which he loves less for the sake of what he loves more. Now every man is not bound to imperil his own body for his neighbour's safety; rather this belongs to the perfect, according to John 15. 13: *Greater love than this no man hath, that a man lay down his life for his friends.* Therefore a man is not bound, out of charity, to love his neighbour more than his own body.

On the contrary, Augustine says[2] that "we ought to love our neighbour more than our own body."

I answer that, Out of charity we ought to love more that which has more fully the reason for being loved out of charity, as stated above (AA. 2, 4). Now fellowship in the full participation of happiness which is the reason for loving one's neighbour, is a greater reason for loving than the participation of happiness by way of overflow, which is the reason for loving one's own body. Therefore, as regards the welfare of the soul we ought to love our neighbour more than our own body.

Reply Obj. 1. According to the Philosopher[3] "a thing seems to be that which is predominant in it," so that when we say that we ought to love our neighbour more than our own body, this refers to his soul, which is his predominant part.

Reply Obj. 2. Our body is nearer to our soul than our neighbour as regards the constitution of our own nature; but as regards the participation of happiness, our neighbour's soul is more closely associated with our own soul than even our own body is.

Reply Obj. 3. Every man is immediately concerned with the care of his own body, but not with his neighbour's welfare, except perhaps in cases of urgency. Therefore charity does not necessarily require a man to imperil his own body for his neighbour's welfare except in a case where he is under obligation to do so; and if a man of his own accord offer himself for that purpose, this belongs to the perfection of charity.

[2] *Christian Doctrine*, I, 27 (PL 34, 29).
[3] *Ethics*, IX, 8 (1169ᵃ2).

ARTICLE 6. *Whether We Ought To Love One Neighbour More Than Another?*

We proceed thus to the Sixth Article: It would seem that we ought not to love one neighbour more than another.

Objection 1. For Augustine says:[1] "One ought to love all men equally. Since, however, one cannot do good to all, we ought to consider those chiefly who by reason of place, time or any other circumstance, by a kind of chance, are more closely united to us." Therefore one neighbour ought not to be loved more than another.

Obj. 2. Further, Where there is one and the same reason for loving several, there should be no inequality of love. Now there is one and the same reason for loving all one's neighbours, which reason is God, as Augustine states.[2] Therefore we ought to love all our neighbours equally.

Obj. 3. Further, To love a man is to wish him good things, as the Philosopher states.[3] Now to all our neighbours we wish an equal good, namely everlasting life. Therefore we ought to love all our neighbours equally.

On the contrary, One's obligation to love a person is proportionate to the gravity of the sin one commits in acting against that love. Now it is a more grievous sin to act against the love of certain neighbours, than against the love of others. Hence the commandment of Lev. 20. 9),—*He that curseth his father or mother, dying let him die,* which does not apply to those who cursed others than these. Therefore we ought to love some neighbours more than others.

I answer that, There have been two opinions on this question. For some have said[4] that we ought, out of charity, to love all our neighbours equally as regards our affection, but not as regards the outward effect. They held that the order of love is to be understood as applying to outward favours, which we ought to confer on those who are close to us in preference to those who are distant, and not to the inward affection, which ought to be given equally to all including our enemies.

But this is unreasonable. For the affection of charity, which is the inclination of grace, is not less orderly than the natural appetite, which is the inclination of nature, for both inclinations flow from Divine wisdom. Now we observe in the physical order that the natural inclination in each thing is proportioned to the act or move-

---

[1] *Christian Doctrine,* I, 28 (PL 34, 30).

[2] *Ibid.,* I, 27 (PL 34, 29); I, 22 (PL 34, 29).

[3] *Rhetoric.* II, 4 (1380ᵇ35; 1381ᵃ19).

[4] The unknown author of *Tractatus Theologiae,* cited by Lombard, *Sent.,* III, d. 29, chap. 2 (QR II, 682).

ment that is fitting to the nature of that thing; thus in earth the inclination of gravity is greater than in water, because it is fitting to earth to be beneath water. Consequently the inclination also of grace which is the affection of charity, must be proportioned to those actions which have to be performed outwardly, so that, namely, the affection of our charity be more intense towards those to whom we ought to behave with greater kindness.

We must, therefore, say that, even as regards the affection we ought to love one neighbour more than another. The reason is that, since the principle of love is God and the person himself who loves, it must be that the affection of love increases in proportion to the nearness to one or the other of those principles. For as we stated above (A. 1), wherever we find a principle, order depends on relation to that principle.

Reply Obj. 1. Love can be unequal in two ways. First, on the part of the good we wish our friend. In this respect we love all men equally out of charity, because we wish them all one same generic good, namely everlasting happiness. Secondly love is said to be greater through its action being more intense. And in this way we ought not to love all equally.

Or we may reply that we have unequal love for certain persons in two ways. First, through our loving some and not loving others. As regards beneficence we are bound to observe this inequality, because we cannot do good to all; but as regards benevolence, love ought not to be thus unequal. The other inequality arises from our loving some more than others; and Augustine does not mean to exclude the latter inequality, but the former, as is evident from what he says of beneficence.

Reply Obj. 2. Our neighbours are not all equally related to God. Some are nearer to Him by reason of their greater goodness, and those we ought, out of charity, to love more than those who are not so near to Him.

Reply Obj. 3. This argument considers the quantity of love on the part of the good which we wish our friends.

ARTICLE 7. *Whether We Ought To Love Those Who Are Better More Than Those Who Are More Closely United To Us?*

We proceed thus to the Seventh Article: It seems that we ought to love those who are better more than those who are more closely united to us.

Objection 1. For that which is in no way hateful seems more lovable than that which is hateful for some reason, just as a thing is all the whiter for having less black mixed with it. Now those who are connected with us are hateful for some reason, according to Luke 14. 26: *If any man come to Me, and hate not his father,* etc. On the other hand good men are not hateful for any reason. Therefore it seems that we ought to love those who are better more than those who are more closely connected with us.

Obj. 2. Further, By charity above all, man is likened to God. But God loves more the better man. Therefore man also, out of charity, ought to love the better man more than one who is more closely united to him.

Obj. 3. Further, In every friendship that ought to be loved most which has most to do with the foundation of that friendship: for, by natural friendship we love most those who are connected with us by nature, our parents for instance, or our children. Now the friendship of charity is founded upon the fellowship of happiness, which has more to do with better men than with those who are more closely united to us. Therefore, out of charity, we ought to love better men more than those who are more closely connected with us.

On the contrary, It is written (I Tim. 5. 8): *If any man have not care of his own, and especially of those of his house, he hath denied the faith, and is worse than an infidel.* Now the inward affection of charity ought to correspond to the outward effect. Therefore charity regards those who are nearer to us before those who are better.

I answer that, Every act should be proportionate both to its object and to the agent. But from its object it takes its species, while from the power of the agent it takes the mode of its intensity; thus movement has its species from the term to which it tends, while the intensity of its speed arises from the disposition of the thing moved and the power of the mover. Accordingly love takes its species from its object, but its intensity is due to the lover.

Now the object of charity's love is God, and man is the lover. Therefore the specific diversity of the love which is in accordance with charity, as regards the love of our neighbour, depends on his relation to God, so that, out of charity, we should wish a greater good to one who is nearer to God; for though the good which charity wishes to all, namely everlasting happiness, is one in itself, yet it has various degrees according to various shares of happiness, and it belongs to charity to wish God's justice to be maintained, in accordance with which better

men have a fuller share of happiness. And this pertains to the species of love; for there are different species of love according to the different goods that we wish for those whom we love.

On the other hand, the intensity of love is measured with regard to the man who loves, and accordingly man loves those who are more closely united to him with more intense affection as to the good he wishes for them, than he loves those who are better as to the greater good he wishes for them.

Again a further difference must be observed here. For some neighbours are near to us by their natural origin, a nearness which cannot be lessened, since that origin makes them to be what they are. But the goodness of virtue, according to which some are close to God, can come and go, increase and decrease, as was shown above (Q. XXIV, AA. 4, 10, 11). Hence it is possible for one, out of charity, to wish this man who is more closely united to one to be better than another, and so reach a higher degree of happiness.

Moreover there is yet another reason for which, out of charity, we love more those who are more nearly connected with us, since we love them in more ways. For, towards those who are not connected with us we have no other friendship than charity, but for those who are connected with us we have certain other friendships, according to the way in which they are connected. Now since the good on which every other friendship of the virtuous is based is directed, as to its end, to the good on which charity is based, it follows that charity commands each act of another friendship, even as the art which is about the end commands the art which is about the means. Consequently this very act of loving someone because he is akin or connected with us, or because he is a fellow-countryman or for any like reason that is referable to the end of charity, can be commanded by charity, so that, out of charity both eliciting and commanding, we love in more ways those who are more nearly connected with us.

Reply Obj. 1. We are commanded to hate, in our kindred, not their kinship, but only the fact of their being an obstacle between us and God. In this respect they are not akin but hostile to us, according to Micah. 7. 6: *A man's enemies are they of his own household.*

Reply Obj. 2. Charity conforms man to God proportionately, by making man comport himself towards what is his, as God does towards what is His. For we may, out of charity, will certain things as fitting to us which God does not will, because it is fitting to Him not to will them, as stated above (Part I-II, Q. XIX, A. 10), when we were treating of the goodness of the will.

Reply Obj. 3. Charity elicits the act of love not only as regards the object, but also as regards the lover, as stated above. The result is that the man who is more nearly united to us is more loved.

ARTICLE 8. *Whether We Ought To Love More Those Who Are Connected with Us by Ties of Blood?*

We proceed thus to the Eighth Article: It would seem that we ought not to love more those who are more closely united to us by ties of blood.

Objection 1. For it is written (Prov. 18. 24): *A man amiable in society, shall be more friendly than a brother.* Again, Valerius Maximus says (*Fact. et Dict. Memor.* iv, 7):[1] "The ties of friendship are most strong and in no way yield to the ties of blood. Moreover it is quite certain and undeniable, that as to the latter, the lot of birth is fortuitous, whereas we contract the former by an untrammelled will, and a solid pledge." Therefore we ought not to love more than others those who are united to us by ties of blood.

Obj. 2. Further, Ambrose says (*De Officiis,* i, 7):[2] "I love not less you whom I have begotten in the Gospel, than if I had begotten you in wedlock, for nature is no more eager to love than grace. Surely we ought to love those whom we expect to be with us for ever more than those who will be with us only in this world." Therefore we should not love our kindred more than those who are otherwise connected with us.

Obj. 3. Further, "Love is proved by deeds," as Gregory states (*Hom. in Ev.* xxx).[3] Now we are bound to do acts of love to others than our kindred; thus in the army a man must obey his officer rather than his father. Therefore we are not bound to love our kindred most of all.

On the contrary, The commandments of the decalogue contain a special precept about the honour due to our parents (Exod. 20. 12). Therefore we ought to love more specially those who are united to us by ties of blood.

I answer that, As stated above (A. 7), we ought out of charity to love those who are more closely united to us more, both because our love for them is more intense, and because there are more reasons for loving them. Now intensity of love arises from the union of lover and beloved,

and therefore we should measure the love of different persons according to the different kinds of union, so that a man is more loved in matters touching that particular union in respect of which he is loved. And, again, in comparing love to love we should compare one union with another.

Accordingly we must say that friendship among blood relations is based upon their connection by natural origin, the friendship of fellow-citizens on their civic fellowship, and the friendship of those who are fighting side by side on the comradeship of battle. Therefore in matters pertaining to nature we should love our kindred most, in matters concerning relations between citizens, we should prefer our fellow-citizens, and on the battlefield our fellow-soldiers. Hence the Philosopher says[4] that "it is our duty to render to each class of people such respect as is natural and appropriate. This is in fact the principle upon which we seem to act, for we invite our relations to a wedding. . . . It would seem to be a special duty to afford our parents the means of living . . . and to honour them." And the same applies to other kinds of friendship.

If however we compare union with union, it is evident that the union arising from natural origin is prior to, and more stable than, all others, because it is something affecting the very substance, while other unions are something added above and may cease altogether. Therefore the friendship of kindred is more stable, while other friendships may be stronger in respect of that which is proper to each of them.

Reply Obj. 1. Because the friendship of comrades originates through their own choice, love of this kind takes precedence of the love of kindred in matters where we are free to do as we choose, for instance in matters of action. Yet the friendship of kindred is more stable, since it is more natural, and preponderates over others in matters touching nature. Consequently we are more bound to them in the providing of necessaries.

Reply Obj. 2. Ambrose is speaking of love with regard to favours respecting the fellowship of grace, namely, moral instruction. For in this matter, a man ought to provide for his spiritual children whom he has begotten spiritually, more than for the sons of his body, whom he is bound to support in bodily sustenance.

Reply Obj. 3. The fact that in the battle a man obeys his officer rather than his father proves that he loves his father less, not absolute-

---

[1] DD 664.   [2] PL 16, 34.   [3] PL 76, 1220.   [4] *Ethics,* IX, 2 (1165[a]17).

ly but relatively, that is, as regards the love which is based on fellowship in battle.

ARTICLE 9. *Whether a Man Ought, out of Charity, To Love His Children More Than His Father?*

We proceed thus to the Ninth Article: It seems that a man ought, out of charity, to love his children more than his father.

Objection 1. For we ought to love those more to whom we are bound to do good. Now we are more bound to do good to our children than to our parents, since the Apostle says (II Cor. 12. 14): *Neither ought the children to lay up for the parents, but the parents for the children.* Therefore a man ought to love his children more than his parents.

Obj. 2. Further, Grace perfects nature. But parents naturally love their children more than these love them, as the Philosopher states.[1] Therefore a man ought to love his children more than his parents.

Obj. 3. Further, Man's affections are conformed to God by charity. But God loves His children more than they love Him. Therefore we also ought to love our children more than our parents.

On the contrary, Ambrose says[2] that we ought to love God first, then our parents, then our children, and lastly those of our household.

I answer that, As stated above (A. 4, Reply 1, A. 7), the degrees of love may be thought of from two standpoints. First, from that of the object. In this respect the more a thing has the aspect of good, and the more like to God, the more is it to be loved. And in this way a man ought to love his father more than his children, because, namely, he loves his father as his principle, in which respect he is a more exalted good and more like God.

Secondly, the degrees of love may be measured from the standpoint of the lover, and in this respect a man loves more that which is more closely connected with him. In this way a man's children are more lovable to him than his father, as the Philosopher states.[3] First, because parents love their children as being part of themselves; but the father is not part of his son, so that the love of a father for his children, is more like a man's love for himself. Secondly, because parents know better that so and so is their child than vice versa. Thirdly, because children are nearer to their parents, as being part of them than their parents are to them to

whom they stand in the relation of a principle. Fourthly, because parents have loved longer, for the father begins to love his child at once, while the child begins to love his father after a lapse of time; and the longer love lasts, the stronger it is, according to Ecclus. 9. 14: *Forsake not an old friend, for the new will not be like to him.*

Reply Obj. 1. The debt due to a principle is submission of respect and honour, while that due to the effect proportionately on the part of the principle is one of influence and care. Hence the duty of children to their parents consists chiefly in honour, while that of parents to their children is especially one of care.

Reply Obj. 2. It is natural for a man as father to love his children more, if we consider them as closely connected with him; but if we consider which is the more exalted good, the son naturally loves his father more.

Reply Obj. 3. As Augustine says,[4] "God loves us for our good and for His honour." Therefore since our father is related to us as principle, even as God is, it belongs properly to the father to receive honour from his children, and to the children to be provided by their parents with what is good for them. Nevertheless in cases of necessity the child is bound out of the favours received to provide for his parents before all.

ARTICLE 10. *Whether a Man Ought To Love His Mother More Than His Father?*

We proceed thus to the Tenth Article: It would seem that a man ought to love his mother more than his father.

Objection 1. For, as the Philosopher says,[5] "the female produces the body in generation." Now man receives his soul, not from his father, but from God by creation, as stated in the First Part (Q. XC, A. 2; Q. CXVIII, A. 2). Therefore a man receives more from his mother than from his father, and consequently he ought to love her more than him.

Obj. 2. Further, Where greater love is given, greater love is due. Now a mother loves her child more than the father does, for the Philosopher says[6] that "mothers have greater love for their children. For the mother labours more in child-bearing, and she knows more surely than the father who are her children." Therefore a man ought to love his mother more than his father.

Obj. 3. Further, Love should be more fond towards those who have laboured for us more,

---

[1] *Ethics,* VIII, 12 (1161[b]21).   [2] Cf. Origen, *In Cant.,* hom. II, on 2.4 (PG 13, 64).   [3] *Ethics,* VIII, 12 (1161[b]19).

[4] *Christian Doctrine,* I, 32 (PL 34, 32).
[5] *Generation of Animals,* I, 20 (729[a]10); II, 4 (738[b]23).
[6] *Ethics,* IX, 7 (1168[a]25).

according to Rom. 16. 6: *Salute Mary, who hath laboured much among you.* Now the mother labours more than the father in giving birth and education to her child; hence it is written (Ecclus. 7. 29): *Forget not the groanings of thy mother.* Therefore a man ought to love his mother more than his father.

On the contrary, Jerome says on Ezech. 44. 24[1] that a man ought to love God the Father of all, and then his own father, and mentions the mother afterwards.

I answer that, In making such comparisons as this, we must take the answer in the strict sense, so that the present question is whether the father as father, ought to be loved more than the mother as mother. The reason is that virtue and vice may make such a difference in these matters that friendship may be diminished or destroyed, as the Philosopher remarks.[2] Hence Ambrose says that good servants should be preferred to wicked children.[3]

Strictly speaking, however, the father should be loved more than the mother. For father and mother are loved as principles of our natural origin. Now the father is principle in a more excellent way than the mother, because he is the active principle, while the mother is a passive and material principle. Consequently, strictly speaking, the father is to be loved more.

Reply Obj. 1. In the begetting of man, the mother supplies the formless matter of the body, and the latter receives its form through the formative power that is in the semen of the father. And though this power cannot create the rational soul, yet it disposes the matter of the body to receive that form.

Reply Obj. 2. This applies to another kind of love. For the friendship between lover and lover differs specifically from the friendship between child and parent. But the friendship we are speaking of here, is that which a man owes his father and mother through being begotten of them.

The *Reply to the Third Objection* is evident.

ARTICLE 11. *Whether a Man Ought To Love His Wife More Than His Father and Mother?*

We proceed thus to the Eleventh Article: It would seem that a man ought to love his wife more than his father and mother.

Objection 1. For no man leaves a thing for another unless he love the latter more. Now it is written (Gen. 2. 24) that *a man shall leave father and mother* on account of his wife.

Therefore a man ought to love his wife more than his father and mother.

Obj. 2. Further, The Apostle says (Eph. 5. 33) that a husband should *love his wife as himself.* Now a man ought to love himself more than his parents. Therefore he ought to love his wife also more than his parents.

Obj. 3. Further, Love should be greater where there are more reasons for loving. Now there are more reasons for love in the friendship of a man towards his wife. For the Philosopher says[4] that "in this friendship there are the motives of utility, pleasure, and also of virtue, if husband and wife are virtuous." Therefore a man's love for his wife ought to be greater than his love for his parents.

On the contrary, According to Eph. 5. 28, *men ought to love their wives as their own bodies.* Now a man ought to love his body less than his neighbour, as stated above (A. 5), and among his neighbours he should love his parents most. Therefore he ought to love his parents more than his wife.

I answer that, As stated above (AA. 7, 9), the degrees of love may be taken from the aspect of good or from the union between those who love. From the aspect of good, which is on the part of the object loved, a man should love his parents more than his wife, because he loves them as his principles and considered as a more exalted good. But on the part of the union, the wife ought to be loved more, because she is united to her husband as one flesh, according to Matt. 19. 6: *Therefore now they are not two, but one flesh.* Consequently a man loves his wife more intensely, but greater reverence should be shown to his parents.

Reply Obj. 1. A man does not in all respects leave his father and mother for the sake of his wife, for in certain cases a man ought to succour his parents rather than his wife. He does however leave all his kinsfolk, and cleaves to his wife as regards the union of carnal connection and cohabitation.

Reply Obj. 2. The words of the Apostle do not mean that a man ought to love his wife equally with himself, but that a man's love for himself is the reason for his love of his wife, since she is one with him.

Reply Obj. 3. There are also several reasons for a man's love for his father; and these, in a certain respect, namely, as regards good, are more weighty than those for which a man loves his wife; although the latter outweigh the former as regards the closeness of union.

---

[1] Bk. XIII (PL 25, 462).   [2] *Ethics,* VIII, 7 (1158[b]33).
[3] Cf. Origen, *In Cant.,* hom., II, on 2.4 (PG 13, 54).

[4] *Ethics,* VIII, 12 (1162[a]24).

As to *the argument in the contrary sense*, it must be observed that in the words quoted, the particle "as" denotes not equality of love but the reason of love. For the principal reason why a man loves his wife is her being united to him in the flesh.

ARTICLE 12. *Whether a Man Ought To Love More His Benefactor Than One He Has Benefited?*

We proceed thus to the Twelfth Article: It seems that a man ought to love his benefactor more than one he has benefited.

Objection 1. For Augustine says (*De Catech. Rud.* iv)[1] "Nothing will incite another more to love you than that you love him first: for he must have a hard heart indeed, who not only refuses to love, but declines to return love already given." Now a man's benefactor forestalls him in the kindly deeds of charity. Therefore we ought to love our benefactors above all.

Obj. 2. Further, The more grievously we sin by ceasing to love a man or by working against him, the more ought we to love him. Now it is a more grievous sin to cease loving a benefactor or to work against him than to cease loving one to whom one has hitherto done kindly actions. Therefore we ought to love our benefactors more than those to whom we are kind.

Obj. 3. Further, Of all things lovable, God is to be loved most, and then one's father, as Jerome says.[2] Now these are our greatest benefactors. Therefore a benefactor should be loved above all others.

On the contrary. The Philosopher says[3] that "benefactors seem to love the recipients of their benefactions, rather than vice versa."

I answer that, As stated above (AA. 7, 9, 11), a thing is loved more in two ways: first because it has the character of a more excellent good, secondly by reason of a closer connection. In the first way we ought to love our benefactor most, because, since he is a principle of good to the man he has benefited, he has the character of a more excellent good, as stated above with regard to one's father (A. 9).

In the second way, however, we love those more who have received benefactions from us, as the Philosopher proves[4] by four arguments. First because the recipient of benefactions is in a sense the handiwork of the benefactor, so that we are accustomed to say of a man: He was made by so and so. Now it is natural to a man

to love his own work (thus it is to be observed that poets love their own poems); and the reason is that we love to be and to live, and these are made manifest especially in our action. Secondly, because we all naturally love that in which we see our own good. Now it is true that the benefactor has some good of his in the recipient of his benefaction, and the recipient some good in the benefactor; but the benefactor sees his virtuous good in the recipient, while the recipient sees his useful good in the benefactor. Now it gives more pleasure to see one's virtuous good than one's useful good, both because it is more enduring,—for usefulness quickly passes, and the pleasure of calling a thing to mind is not like the pleasure of having it present,—and because it is more pleasant to recall virtuous goods than the profit we have derived from others. Thirdly, because it is the lover's part to act, since he wills and works the good of the beloved, while the beloved takes a passive part in receiving good, so that to love surpasses being loved, for which reason the greater love is on the part of the benefactor. Fourthly because it is more difficult to give than to receive favours, and we are most fond of things which have cost us most trouble, while in a sense we despise what comes easy to us.

Reply Obj. 1. It is something in the benefactor that incites the recipient to love him, while the benefactor loves the recipient not through being incited by him, but through being moved to this of his own accord. And what we do of our own accord surpasses what we do through another.

Reply Obj. 2. The love of the beneficiary for the benefactor is more of a duty, and therefore the contrary is the greater sin. On the other hand, the love of the benefactor for the beneficiary is more spontaneous, and therefore it is quicker to act.

Reply Obj. 3. God also loves us more than we love Him, and parents love their children more than these love them. Yet it does not follow that we love all who have received good from us more than any of our benefactors. For we prefer such benefactors as God and our parents from whom we have received the greatest favours to those on whom we have bestowed lesser benefits.

ARTICLE 13. *Whether the Order of Charity Endures in Heaven?*

We proceed thus to the Thirteenth Article: It would seem that the order of charity does not endure in heaven.

---

[1] PL 40, 314.
[2] *Comment. in Ezechiel.*, XLIV. 25. (PL 25, 462).
[3] *Ethics*, IX, 7 (1167^{b}17). [4] *Ibid.*

Objection 1. For Augustine says (*De Vera Relig.* xlviii):[1] "Perfect charity consists in loving greater goods more, and lesser goods less." Now charity will be perfect in heaven. Therefore a man will love those who are better more than either himself or those who are connected with him.

Obj. 2. Further, We love more him to whom we wish a greater good. Now each one in heaven wishes a greater good for those who have more good; otherwise his will would not be conformed in all things to God's will, and to be better in heaven is to have more good. Therefore in heaven each one loves more those who are better, and consequently he loves others more than himself, and one who is not connected with him more than one who is.

Obj. 3. Further, In heaven love will be entirely for God's sake, for then will be fulfilled the words of I Cor. 15. 28: *That God may be all in all.* Therefore he who is nearer God will be loved more, so that a man will love a better man more than himself, and one who is not connected with him, more than one who is.

On the contrary, Nature is not done away, but perfected, by glory. Now the order of charity given above (AA. 3, 6, 7, 8) is derived from nature, since all things naturally love themselves more than others. Therefore this order of charity will endure in heaven.

I answer that, The order of charity as regards the love of God above all things must remain in heaven. For this will be realized absolutely when man shall enjoy God perfectly. But, as regards the order between man himself and other men, a distinction seems to be necessary, because, as we stated above (A. 7), the degrees of love may be distinguished either in respect of the good which a man desires for another, or according to the intensity of love itself. In the first way a man will love better men than himself, and those who are less good, less than himself, because, by reason of the perfect conformity of the human to the Divine will, each of the blessed will desire everyone to have what is due to him according to Divine justice. Nor will that be a time for advancing by means of merit to a yet greater reward, as happens now while it is possible for a man to desire both the virtue and the reward of a better man; but then the will of each one will rest within the limits determined by God.

In the second way however a man will love himself more than even his better neighbours, because the intensity of the act of love arises on the part of the person who loves, as stated

[1] PL 34, 164.

above (A. 7). Moreover it is for this that the gift of charity is bestowed by God on each one, namely, that he may first of all direct his mind to God, and this pertains to a man's love for himself, and that, in the second place, he may wish other things to be directed to God, and even work for that end according to his capacity.

As to the order to be observed among our neighbours, a man will love absolutely those who are better, according to the love of charity. Because the entire life of the blessed consists in directing their minds to God, and so the entire ordering of their love will be ruled with respect to God, so that each one will love more and regard as nearer to himself those who are nearer to God. For then one man will no longer succour another, as he needs to in the present life, in which each man has to succour those who are closely connected with him rather than those who are not, no matter what be the nature of their distress; hence it is that in this life, a man, by the inclination of charity, loves more those who are more closely united to him, for he is under a greater obligation to bestow on them the effect of charity. It will however be possible in heaven for a man to love in several ways one who is connected with him, since the causes of virtuous love will not be banished from the mind of the blessed. Yet all these reasons are incomparably surpassed by that which is taken from nearness to God.

Reply Obj. 1. This argument should be granted as to those who are joined together; but as regards man himself, he ought to love himself so much the more than others as his charity is more perfect, since perfect charity orders man to God perfectly, and this pertains to love of oneself, as stated above.

Reply Obj. 2. This argument considers the order of love in respect of the degree of good one wills the person one loves.

Reply Obj. 3. God will be to each one the entire reason of his love, for God is man's entire good. For if we make the impossible supposition that God were not man's good, He would not be man's reason for loving. Hence it is that in the order of love man should love himself more than all else after God.

QUESTION XXVII

OF THE PRINCIPAL ACT OF CHARITY, WHICH IS LOVE

(In Eight Articles)

WE must now consider the act of charity, and (1) the principal act of charity, which is love,

(2) the other acts or effects which follow from that act (Q. XXVIII).

Under the first head there are eight points of inquiry: (1) Which is the more proper to charity, to love or to be loved? (2) Whether to love considered as an act of charity is the same as goodwill? (3) Whether God should be loved for His own sake? (4) Whether God can be loved immediately in this life? (5) Whether God can be loved wholly? (6) Whether the love of God is according to measure? (7) Which is the better, to love one's friend, or one's enemy? (8) Which is the better, to love God, or one's neighbour?

ARTICLE 1. *Whether To Be Loved Is More Proper to Charity Than To Love*

We proceed thus to the First Article: It would seem that it is more proper to charity to be loved than to love.

Objection 1. For the better charity is to be found in those who are themselves better. But those who are better should be more loved. Therefore to be loved is more proper to charity.

Obj. 2. Further, That which is to be found in more subjects seems to be more in keeping with nature, and, for that reason, better. Now, as the Philosopher says,[1] "many would rather be loved than love, and lovers of flattery always abound." Therefore it is better to be loved than to love, and consequently it is more in keeping with charity.

Obj. 3. Further, The cause of anything being such is yet more so. Now men love because they are loved, for Augustine says (*De Catech. Rud.* iv)[2] that "nothing incites another more to love you than that you love him first." Therefore charity consists in being loved rather than in loving.

On the contrary, The Philosopher says[3] that "friendship consists in loving rather than in being loved." Now charity is a kind of friendship. Therefore it consists in loving rather than in being loved.

I answer that, To love belongs to charity as charity. For, since charity is a virtue, by its very essence it has an inclination to its proper act. Now to be loved is not the act of the charity of the person loved; for this act is to love, but to be loved belongs to him as coming under the common notion of good, in so far as another is moved towards the good of the person loved by an act of charity. Hence it is clear that to love is more proper to charity than to

be loved, for that which befits a thing substantially and by reason of itself pertains to it more than that which is befitting to it by reason of something else. This can be exemplified in two ways. First, in the fact that friends are more commended for loving than for being loved; indeed, if they be loved and yet love not, they are blamed. Secondly, because a mother, whose love is the greatest, seeks rather to love than to be loved; "for some women," as the Philosopher observes,[4] "entrust their children to a nurse; they do love them indeed, yet seek not to be loved in return, if they happen not to be loved."

Reply Obj. 1. A better man, through being better, is more lovable, but through having more perfect charity, loves more. He loves more, however, in proportion to the person he loves. For a better man does not love that which is beneath him less than it can be loved, while he who is less good fails to love one who is better as much as he can be loved.

Reply Obj. 2. As the Philosopher says,[5] men wish to be loved in so far as they wish to be honoured. For just as honour is bestowed on a man in order to bear witness to the good which is in him, so by being loved a man is shown to have some good, since good alone is lovable. Accordingly men seek to be loved and to be honoured, for the sake of something else, namely to make known the good which is in the person loved. On the other hand, those who have charity seek to love for the sake of loving, as though this were itself the good of charity, even as the act of any virtue is that virtue's good. Hence it is more proper to charity to wish to love than to wish to be loved.

Reply Obj. 3. Some love on account of being loved, not so that to be loved is the end of their loving, but because it is a kind of way leading a man to love.

ARTICLE 2. *Whether To Love Considered As an Act of Charity Is the Same As Goodwill?*

We proceed thus to the Second Article: It would seem that to love, considered as an act of charity, is nothing else than goodwill.

Objection 1. For the Philosopher says[6] that "to love is to wish a person well." But this is goodwill. Therefore the act of charity is nothing but goodwill.

Obj. 2. Further, The act belongs to the same subject as the habit. Now the habit of charity is in the power of the will, as stated above (Q. XXIV, A. 1). Therefore the act of charity is

---

[1] *Ethics,* VIII, 8 (1159ª12).
[2] PL 40, 314.   [3] *Ethics,* VIII, 8 (1159ª27).
[4] *Ibid.* [5] *Ibid.* (1159ª16). [6] *Rhetoric,* II, 4 (1380ᵇ35; 1381ª19).

also an act of the will. But it tends to good only, and this is goodwill. Therefore the act of charity is nothing else than goodwill.

Obj. 3. Further, The Philosopher reckons five things pertaining to friendship,[1] the first of which is that a man should wish his friend well; the second, that he should wish him to be and to live; the third, that he should take pleasure in his company; the fourth, that he should make choice of the same things; the fifth, that he should grieve and rejoice with him. Now the first two pertain to goodwill. Therefore goodwill is the first act of charity.

On the contrary, The Philosopher says in the same book[2] that "goodwill is neither friendship nor love, but the beginning of friendship." Now charity is friendship, as stated above (Q. XXIII, A. 1). Therefore goodwill is not the same as to love considered as an act of charity.

I answer that, Goodwill properly speaking is that act of the will by which we wish well to another. Now this act of the will differs from actual love, considered not only as being in the sensitive appetite but also as being in the intellective appetite or will. For the love which is in the sensitive appetite is a passion. Now every passion seeks its object with a certain eagerness. And the passion of love is not aroused suddenly, but is born of an earnest consideration of the object loved; hence the Philosopher, showing the difference between goodwill and the love which is a passion, says[3] that "goodwill does not imply impetuosity or desire," that is to say, does not have an eager inclination, because it is by the sole judgment of his reason that one man wishes another well. Again love of this kind arises from familiarity, but goodwill sometimes arises suddenly, as happens to us if we look at men fighting, and we wish one of the fighters to win. But the love, which is in the intellective appetite also differs from goodwill, because it denotes a certain union of affections between the lover and the beloved, in so far as the lover thinks of the beloved as in some way united to him, or belonging to him, and so tends towards him. On the other hand, goodwill is a simple act of the will by which we wish a person well, even without presupposing the above mentioned union of the affections with him. Accordingly, to love, considered as an act of charity, includes goodwill, but such dilection or love adds union of affections, and so the Philosopher says[4] that "goodwill is a beginning of friendship."

Reply Obj. 1. The Philosopher, by thus defining "to love," does not describe it fully, but mentions only that part of its definition in which the act of love is chiefly manifested.

Reply Obj. 2. To love is indeed an act of the will tending to the good, but it adds a certain union with the beloved, which union is not denoted by goodwill.

Reply Obj. 3. These things mentioned by the Philosopher belong to friendship because they arise from a man's love for himself, as he says in the same passage, in so far as a man does all these things in respect of his friend, even as he does them to himself; and this belongs to the aforesaid union of the affections.

ARTICLE 3. *Whether out of Charity God Ought To Be Loved for Himself?*

We proceed thus to the Third Article: It seems that God is loved out of charity, not for Himself but for the sake of something else.

Objection 1. For Gregory says in a homily (*In Evang.* xi):[5] "The soul learns from the things it knows to love those it knows not," where by things unknown he means the intelligible and the Divine, and by things known he indicates the objects of the senses. Therefore God is to be loved for the sake of something else.

Obj. 2. Further, Love follows knowledge. But God is known through something else, according to Rom. 1. 20: *The invisible things of God are clearly seen, being understood by the things that are made.* Therefore He is also loved on account of something else and not for Himself.

Obj. 3. Further, Hope begets charity as a gloss says[6] on Matt. 1. 1, and "fear leads to charity," according to Augustine in his commentary on the First Canonical Epistle of John (*Tract.* ix).[7] Now hope looks forward to obtain something from God, while fear shuns something which can be inflicted by God. Therefore it seems that God is to be loved on account of some good we hope for, or some evil to be feared. Therefore He is not to be loved for Himself.

On the contrary, According to Augustine,[8] "to enjoy is to cleave to something for its own sake." Now God is to be enjoyed as he says in the same book.[9] Therefore God is to be loved for Himself.

I answer that, The preposition "for" denotes

---

[1] *Ethics,* IX, 4 (1166ª3).   [2] *Ibid.,* 5 (1166ᵇ30; 1167ª3).   [3] *Ibid.,* IX, 5 (1166ᵇ33).   [4] *Ibid.* (1167ª3).

[5] PL 76, 1114.   [6] *Glossa interl.* (v, 51).   [7] PL 35, 2048.   [8] *Christian Doctrine,* I, 5 (PL 34, 21).   [9] *Ibid.,* I, 4 (PL 34, 20).

a relation of causality. Now there are four kinds of cause, namely final, formal, efficient, and material, to which a material disposition also is to be reduced, though it is not a cause absolutely but relatively. According to these four kinds of causes one thing is said to be loved for another. In respect of the final cause, we love medicine, for instance, for health; in respect of the formal cause, we love a man for his virtue, because, that is, by his virtue he is formally good and therefore lovable; in respect of the efficient cause, we love certain men because, for instance, they are the sons of such and such a father; and in respect of the disposition which is reducible to the genus of a material cause, we speak of loving something for that which disposed us to love it, for example we love a man for the favours received from him, although after we have begun to love our friend, we no longer love him for his favours, but for his virtue.

Accordingly, as regards the first three ways, we love God, not for anything else, but for Himself. For He is not ordered to anything else as to an end, but is Himself the last end of all things; nor does He require to receive any form in order to be good, for His very substance is His goodness, which is itself the exemplar of all other good things; nor again does goodness accrue to Him from anything else, but from Him to all other things.

In the fourth way, however, He can be loved for something else, because we are disposed by certain things to advance in His love, for instance, by favours bestowed by Him, by the rewards we hope to receive from Him, or even by the punishments which we are minded to avoid through Him.

Reply Obj. 1. "From the things it knows the soul learns to love what it knows not," not as though the things it knows were the reason for its loving things it knows not, through being the formal, final, or efficient cause of this love, but because this knowledge disposes man to love the unknown.

Reply Obj. 2. Knowledge of God is indeed acquired through other things, but after He is known, He is no longer known through them, but through Himself, according to John 4. 42: *We now believe, not for thy saying: for we ourselves have heard Him, and know that this is indeed the Saviour of the world.*

Reply Obj. 3. Hope and fear lead to charity by way of a certain disposition, as was shown above (Q. XVII, A. 8; Q. XIX, AA. 4, 7, 10; also above, Ans.).

ARTICLE 4. *Whether God Can Be Loved Immediately in This Life?*

We proceed thus to the Fourth Article: It seems that God cannot be loved immediately in this life.

Objection 1. For "the unknown cannot be loved" as Augustine says (*De Trin.* x, 1, 2).[1] Now we do not know God immediately in this life, since *we see now through a glass, in a dark manner* (I Cor. 13. 12). Neither, therefore, do we love Him immediately.

Obj. 2. Further, He who cannot do what is less, cannot do what is more. Now it is more to love God than to know Him, since *he who is joined* to God by love, *is one spirit* with Him (I Cor. 6. 17). But man cannot know God immediately. Therefore much less can he love Him immediately.

Obj. 3. Further, Man is severed from God by sin, according to Isa. 59. 2: *Your iniquities have divided between you and your God.* Now sin is in the will rather than in the intellect. Therefore man is less able to love God immediately than to know Him immediately.

On the contrary, Knowledge of God, because it is mediate, is said to be *enigmatic,* and *falls away* in heaven, as stated in I Cor. 13. 12. But charity *does not fall* away as stated in the same passage (*verse* 8). Therefore the charity of the way adheres to God immediately.

I answer that, As stated above (Q. XXVI, A. 1, REPLY 2), the act of a cognitive power is completed by the thing known being in the knower, while the act of an appetitive power consists in the appetite being inclined towards the thing in itself. Hence it follows that the movement of the appetitive power is towards things in respect of their own condition, while the act of a cognitive power follows the mode of the knower.

Now in itself the very order of things is such that God is knowable and lovable for Himself, since He is essentially truth and goodness itself, by which other things are known and loved. But with regard to us, since our knowledge is derived through the senses, those things are knowable first, which are nearer to our senses, and the last term of knowledge is that which is most remote from our senses.

Accordingly, we must assert that to love, which is an act of the appetitive power, tends, even in this state of life, to God first, and flows on from Him to other things, and in this sense charity loves God immediately, and other things

[1] PL 42, 974, 975.

through God. On the other hand, with regard to knowledge, it is the reverse, since we know God through other things, either as a cause through its effects, or by way of pre-eminence or negation as Dionysius states (*Div. Nom.* i).[1]

Reply Obj. 1. Although the unknown cannot be loved, it does not follow that the order of knowledge is the same as the order of love, since love is the term of knowledge, and consequently, love can begin at once where knowledge ends, namely in the thing itself which is known through another thing.

Reply Obj. 2. Since to love God is something greater than to know Him, especially in this state of life, it follows that love of God presupposes knowledge of God. And because this knowledge does not rest in creatures, but, through them, tends to something else, love begins there, and thence goes on to other things by a kind of circular movement; for knowledge begins from creatures, tends to God, and love begins with God as the last end, and passes on to creatures.

Reply Obj. 3. Turning away from God, which is brought about by sin, is removed by charity, but not by knowledge alone; hence charity, by loving God, unites the soul immediately to Him with a chain of spiritual union.

ARTICLE 5. *Whether God Can Be Loved Wholly?*

We proceed thus to the Fifth Article: It seems that God cannot be loved wholly.

Objection 1. For love follows knowledge. Now God cannot be wholly known by us, since this would imply comprehension of Him. Therefore He cannot be wholly loved by us.

Obj. 2. Further, Love is a kind of union, as Dionysius shows (*Div. Nom.* iv).[2] But the heart of man cannot be wholly united to God, because *God is greater than our heart* (I John 3. 20). Therefore God cannot be loved wholly.

Obj. 3. Further, God loves Himself wholly. If therefore He be loved wholly by another, this one will love Him as much as God loves Himself. But this is unreasonable. Therefore God cannot be wholly loved by a creature.

On the contrary, It is written (Deut. 6. 5): *Thou shalt love the Lord thy God with thy whole heart.*

I answer that, Since love may be understood as something between lover and beloved, when we ask whether God can be wholly loved the question may be understood in three ways.

First so that the mode "wholly" be referred to the thing loved, and thus God is to be loved wholly, since man should love all that pertains to God. Secondly, it may be understood as though "wholly" referred to the lover and thus again God ought to be loved wholly, since man ought to love God with all his might, and to order all he has to the love of God, according to Deut. 6. 5: *Thou shalt love the Lord thy God with thy whole heart.* Thirdly, it may be understood by way of comparison of the lover to the thing loved, so that the mode of the lover equal the mode of the thing loved. This is impossible: for, since a thing is lovable in proportion to its goodness, God is infinitely lovable, since His goodness is infinite. Now no creature can love God infinitely, because all power of creatures, whether it be natural or infused, is finite.

This suffices for the *Replies to the Objections,* because the first three objections consider the question in this third sense, while the last takes it in the second sense.

ARTICLE 6. *Whether in Loving God We Ought To Observe Any Mode?*

We proceed thus to the Sixth Article: It would seem that we ought to observe some mode in loving God.

Objection 1. For the notion of good consists in "mode, species and order," as Augustine states (*De Nat. Boni,* iii).[3] Now the love of God is the best thing in man, according to Coloss. 3. 14: *Above all . . . things, have charity.* Therefore there ought to be a mode of the love of God.

Obj. 2. Further, Augustine says (*De Morib. Eccl.* viii):[4] "Prithee, tell me which is the mode of love. For I fear lest I burn with the desire and love of my Lord, more or less than I ought." But it would be useless to seek the mode of the Divine love unless there were one. Therefore there is a mode of the love of God.

Obj. 3. Further, As Augustine says (*Gen. ad lit.* iv, 3),[5] "the measure which is appointed to each thing, is its mode." Now the measure of the human will, as also of external action, is the reason. Therefore just as it is necessary for the reason to appoint a mode to the exterior effect of charity, according to Rom. 12. 1: *Your reasonable service,* so also the interior love of God requires a mode.

On the contrary, Bernard says (*De Dilig. Deum,* 1)[6] that "God is the cause of our loving

---

[1] Sect. 5 (PG 3, 593).   [2] Sect. 12 (PG 3, 709).

[3] PL 42, 553.   [4] PL 32, 1316.
[5] PL 34, 299.   [6] PL 182, 974.

God; the measure is to love Him without measure."

I answer that, As appears from the words of Augustine quoted above (obj. 3) mode signifies a determination of measure, which determination is to be found both in the measure and in the thing measured, but not in the same way. For it is found in the measure essentially, because a measure is of itself the determining and modifying rule of other things; but in the things measured, it is found relatively, that is in so far as they attain to the measure. Hence there can be nothing unmodified in the measure; but the thing measured is unmodified if it fails to attain to the measure, whether by deficiency or by excess.

Now in all matters of appetite and action the measure is the end, because the proper reason for all that we desire or do should be taken from the end, as the Philosopher proves.[1] Therefore the end has a mode by itself, while the means take their mode from being proportionate to the end. Hence, according to the Philosopher,[2] in every art, the desire for the end is endless and unlimited, while there is a limit to the means. Thus the physician does not put limits to health, but makes it as perfect as he possibly can; but he puts a limit to medicine, for he does not give as much medicine as he can, but according as health demands, so that if he give too much or too little, the medicine would be immoderate.

Again, the end of all human actions and affections is the love of God, by which we attain principally to our last end, as stated above (Q. XXIII, A. 6), and therefore the mode in the love of God must not be taken as in a thing measured where we find too much or too little, but as in the measure itself, where there cannot be excess, and where the more the rule is attained the better it is, so that the more we love God the better our love is.

Reply Obj. 1. That which is so by its essence takes precedence of that which is so through another, and therefore the goodness of the measure which has the mode essentially, takes precedence of the goodness of the thing measured, which has its mode through something else; and so too, charity, which has a mode as a measure has, is above the other virtues, which have a mode through being measured.

Reply Obj. 2. As Augustine adds in the same passage, the measure of our love for God, is to love Him with our whole heart, that is, to love Him as much as He can be loved, and this pertains to the mode which is proper to the measure.

Reply Obj. 3. An affection whose object is subject to reason's judgment, should be measured by reason. But the object of the Divine love which is God surpasses the judgment of reason, and therefore it is not measured by reason but exceeds it. Nor is there parity between the interior act and external acts of charity. For the interior act of charity has the character of an end, since man's ultimate good consists in his soul cleaving to God, according to Ps. 72. 28: *It is good for me to adhere to my God;* but the exterior acts are as means to the end, and so have to be measured both according to charity and according to reason.

ARTICLE 7. *Whether It Is More Meritorious To Love an Enemy Than To Love a Friend?*

We proceed thus to the Seventh Article: It seems more meritorious to love an enemy than to love a friend.

Objection 1. For it is written (Matt. 5. 46): *If you love them that love you, what reward shall you have?* Therefore it is not deserving of reward to love one's friend. But, as the same passage proves, to love one's enemy is deserving of a reward. Therefore it is more meritorious to love one's enemy than to love one's friend.

Obj. 2. Further, An act is the more meritorious through proceeding from a greater charity. But it belongs "to the perfect children of God" to love their enemies as Augustine says,[3] while those also who have imperfect charity love their friends. Therefore it is more meritorious to love one's enemy than to love one's friend.

Obj. 3. Further, Where there is more effort for good, there seems to be more merit, since *every man shall receive his own reward according to his own labour* (I Cor. 3. 8). Now a man has to make a greater effort to love his enemy than to love his friend, because it is more difficult. Therefore it seems more meritorious to love one's enemy than to love one's friend.

Obj. 4. *On the contrary,* The better an action is, the more meritorious it is. Now it is better to love one's friend, since it is better to love a better man, and the friend who loves you is better than the enemy who hates you. Therefore it is more meritorious to love one's friend than to love one's enemy.

I answer that, God is the reason for our lov-

---

[1] *Physics,* II, 9 (200ᵃ32).
[2] *Politics,* I, 9 (1257ᵇ26).
[3] *Enchiridion,* LXXIII (PL 40, 266).

ing our neighbour out of charity, as stated above (Q. XXV, A. I). When therefore it is asked which is better or more meritorious, to love one's friend or one's enemy, these two loves may be compared in two ways: first, on the part of our neighbour whom we love, secondly, on the part of the reason for which we love him.

In the first way, love of one's friend surpasses love of one's enemy, because a friend is both better and more closely united to us, so that he is a more suitable matter of love, and consequently the act of love pervading this matter is better, and therefore its opposite is worse, for it is worse to hate a friend than an enemy.

In the second way, however, it is better to love one's enemy than one's friend, and this for two reasons. First, because it is possible to love one's friend for another reason than God, whereas God is the only reason for loving one's enemy. Secondly, because if we suppose that both are loved for God, our love for God is proved to be all the stronger through carrying a man's affections to things which are furthest from him, that is, even to the love of his enemies, just as the power of a fire is proved to be the stronger according as it throws its heat to more distant objects. Hence our love for God is proved to be so much the stronger, as the things we accomplish for its sake are the more difficult, just as the power of fire is so much the stronger, as it is able to set fire to a less inflammable matter.

Yet just as the same fire acts with greater force on what is near than on what is distant, so too, charity loves with greater fervour those who are united to us than those who are far removed; and in this respect the love of friends, considered in itself, is more ardent and better than the love of one's enemy.

Reply Obj. 1. The words of Our Lord must be taken in their strict sense, because the love of one's friends is not meritorious in God's sight when we love them merely because they are our friends; and this would seem to be the case when we love our friends in such a way that we love not our enemies. On the other hand the love of our friends is meritorious if we love them for God's sake, and not merely because they are our friends.

The *Reply to the other objections* is evident from what has been said in the article, because the two arguments that follow consider the reason for loving, while the last considers the question on the part of those who are loved.

ARTICLE 8. *Whether It Is More Meritorious To Love One's Neighbour Than to Love God?*

We proceed thus to the Eighth Article: It would seem that it is more meritorious to love one's neighbour than to love God.

Objection 1. For the more meritorious thing would seem to be what the Apostle preferred. Now the Apostle preferred the love of our neighbour to the love of God, according to Rom. 9. 3; *I wished myself to be an anathema from Christ, for my brethren.* Therefore it is more meritorious to love one's neighbour than to love God.

Obj. 2. Further, In a certain sense it seems to be less meritorious to love one's friend, as stated above (A. 7). Now God is our chief friend, since *He hath first loved us* (I John 4. 10). Therefore it seems less meritorious to love God.

Obj. 3. Further, Whatever is more difficult seems to be more virtuous and meritorious, since virtue is about that which is difficult and good.[1] Now it is easier to love God than to love one's neighbour, both because all things love God naturally, and because there is nothing unlovable in God, and this cannot be said of one's neighbour. Therefore it is more meritorious to love one's neighbour than to love God.

On the contrary, That on account of which a thing is such, is yet more so. Now the love of one's neighbour is not meritorious except by reason of his being loved for God's sake. Therefore the love of God is more meritorious than the love of our neighbour.

I answer that, This comparison may be taken in two ways. First, by considering both loves separately; and then, without doubt, the love of God is the more meritorious, because a reward is due to it for its own sake, since the ultimate reward is the enjoyment of God, to Whom the movement of the love of God tends. Hence a reward is promised to him that loves God (John 14. 21): *He that loveth Me, shall be loved of My Father, and I will . . . manifest Myself to him.* Secondly, the comparison may be understood to be between the love of God alone on the one side, and the love of one's neighbour for God's sake, on the other. In this way love of our neighbour includes love of God, while love of God does not include love of our neighbour. Hence the comparison will be between perfect love of God, extending also to our neighbour, and inadequate and imperfect

---

[1] *Ethics*, II, 3 (1105ᵃ9).

love of God, for *this commandment we have from God, that he, who loveth God, love also his brother* (I John 4. 21).

Reply Obj. 1. According to one gloss,[1] the Apostle did not desire this, that is, to be severed from Christ for his brethren, when he was in a state of grace, but had formerly desired it when he was in a state of unbelief, so that we should not imitate him in this respect.

We may also reply, with Chrysostom (*De Compunct.* 1)[2] that this does not prove the Apostle to have loved his neighbour more than God, but that he loved God more than himself. For he wished to be deprived for a time of the Divine enjoyment which pertains to love of oneself in order that God might be honoured in his neighbour, which pertains to the love of God.

Reply Obj. 2. A man's love for his friends is sometimes less meritorious in so far as he loves them for their sake, so as to fall short of the true reason for the friendship of charity, which is God. Hence that God be loved for His own sake does not diminish the merit, but is the entire reason for merit.

Reply Obj. 3. The "good" has, more than the "difficult," to do with the reason of merit and virtue. Therefore it does not follow that whatever is more difficult is more meritorious, but only what is more difficult and at the same time better.

QUESTION XXVIII
OF JOY
(In Four Articles)

WE must now consider the effects which result from the principal act of charity which is love, and (1) the interior effects, (2) the exterior effects (Q. XXXI). As to the first, three things have to be considered: (1) Joy, (2) Peace (Q. XXIX), (3) Mercy (Q. XXX).

Under the first head there are four points of inquiry, (1) Whether joy is an effect of charity? (2) Whether this kind of joy is compatible with sorrow (3) Whether this joy can be full? (4) Whether it is a virtue?

ARTICLE 1. *Whether Joy Is an Effect in Us of Charity?*

We proceed thus to the First Article: It would seem that joy is not an effect in us of charity.

Objection 1. For the absence of what we love

[1] *Glossa ordin.* (VI, 20E); *Glossa* Lombardi (PL 191, 1454). [2] PG 47, 406; *In Rom.*, hom., XVI (PG 60, 599).

causes sorrow rather than joy. But God, Whom we love by charity, is absent from us, so long as we are in this state of life, since *while we are in the body, we are absent from the Lord* (II Cor. 5. 6). Therefore charity causes sorrow in us rather than joy.

Obj. 2. Further, It is chiefly through charity that we merit happiness. Now mourning, which pertains to sorrow, is put among those things by which we merit happiness, according to Matt. 5. 5: *Blessed are they that mourn, for they shall be comforted.* Therefore sorrow, rather than joy, is an effect of charity.

Obj. 3. Further, Charity is a virtue distinct from hope, as shown above (Q. XVII, A. 6). Now joy is caused by hope, according to Rom. 12. 12: *Rejoicing in hope.* Therefore it is not caused by charity.

On the contrary, It is written (Rom. 5. 5): *The charity of God is poured forth in our hearts by the Holy Ghost, Who is given to us.* But joy is caused in us by the Holy Ghost according to Rom. 14. 17: *The kingdom of God is not meat and drink, but justice and peace, and joy in the Holy Ghost.* Therefore charity is a cause of joy.

I answer that, As stated above (Part I-II, Q. XXV, A. 3; Q. XXVI, A. 1, REPLY 2), when we were treating of the passions, joy and sorrow proceed from love, but in contrary ways. For joy is caused by love either through the presence of the thing loved or because the proper good of the thing loved exists and endures in it; and the latter is the case chiefly in the love of benevolence, whereby a man rejoices in the well-being of his friend, even though he be absent. On the other hand sorrow arises from love either through the absence of the thing loved, or because the loved object to which we wish well is deprived of its good or afflicted with some evil. Now charity is love of God, Whose good is unchangeable, since He is His goodness; and from the very fact that He is loved, He is in those who love Him by His most excellent effect, according to I John 4. 16: *He that abideth in charity. abideth in God, and God in him.* Therefore spiritual joy, which is about God, is caused by charity.

Reply Obj. 1. So long as we are in the body, we are said to be *absent from the Lord*, in comparison with that presence by which He is present to some by the vision of sight; hence the Apostle goes on to say (*ibid.*): *For we walk by faith and not by sight.* Nevertheless, even in this life, He is present to those who love Him, by the indwelling of His grace.

Reply Obj. 2. The mourning that merits happiness is about those things that are contrary to happiness. Therefore it amounts to the same that charity causes this mourning, and this spiritual joy about God, since to rejoice in a certain good amounts to the same as to grieve for things that are contrary to it.

Reply Obj. 3. There can be spiritual joy about God in two ways. First, when we rejoice in the Divine good considered in itself; secondly, when we rejoice in the Divine good as participated by us. The former joy is the better, and proceeds from charity chiefly. But the latter joy proceeds also from hope, by which we look forward to enjoy the Divine good, although this enjoyment itself, whether perfect or imperfect, is obtained according to the measure of one's charity.

ARTICLE 2. *Whether the Spiritual Joy, Which Is Caused by Charity, Is Compatible With an Admixture of Sorrow?*

We proceed thus to the Second Article: It would seem that the spiritual joy that is caused by charity is compatible with an admixture of sorrow.

Objection 1. For it pertains to charity to rejoice in our neighbour's good, according to I Cor. 13. 4, 6: *Charity . . . rejoiceth not in iniquity, but rejoiceth with the truth.* But this joy is compatible with an admixture of sorrow, according to Rom. 12. 15: *Rejoice with them that rejoice, weep with them that weep.* Therefore the spiritual joy of charity is compatible with an admixture of sorrow.

Obj. 2. Further, According to Gregory (*Hom. in Evang.* xxxiv),[1] penance consists in "deploring past sins, and in not committing again those we have deplored." But there is no true penance without charity. Therefore the joy of charity has an admixture of sorrow.

Obj. 3. Further, It is through charity that man desires to be with Christ according to Philip 1. 23: *Having a desire to be dissolved and to be with Christ.* Now this desire gives rise, in man, to a certain sadness, according to Ps. 119. 5: *Woe is me that my sojourning is prolonged!* Therefore the joy of charity admits of a seasoning of sorrow.

On the contrary, The joy of charity is joy about the Divine wisdom. Now this kind of joy has no admixture of sorrow, according to Wisd. 8. 16: *Her conversation hath no bitterness.* Therefore the joy of charity is incompatible with an admixture of sorrow.

[1] PL 76, 1256.

I answer that, As stated above (A. 1, reply 3), a twofold joy in God arises from charity. One, the more excellent, is proper to charity; and with this joy we rejoice in the Divine good considered in itself. This joy of charity is incompatible with an admixture of sorrow, even as the good which is its object is incompatible with any admixture of evil: hence the Apostle says (Philip. 4. 4): *Rejoice in the Lord always.*

The other is the joy of charity by which we rejoice in the Divine good as participated by us. This participation can be hindered by anything contrary to it, and therefore, in this respect, the joy of charity is compatible with an admixture of sorrow, in so far as a man grieves for that which hinders the participation of the Divine good, either in us or in our neighbour, whom we love as ourselves.

Reply Obj. 1. Our neighbour does not weep save on account of some evil. Now every evil implies lack of participation in the sovereign good. Hence charity makes us weep with our neighbour is so far as he is hindered from participating in the Divine good.

Reply Obj. 2. Our sins divide between us and God, according to Isa. 59. 2; therefore this is the reason why we grieve for our past sins, or for those of others, in so far as they hinder us from participating in the Divine good.

Reply Obj. 3. Although in this unhappy abode we participate, after a fashion, in the Divine good, by knowledge and love, yet the unhappiness of this life is an obstacle to a perfect participation in the Divine good such as will exist in heaven. Hence this very sorrow, by which a man grieves for the delay of glory, is connected with the hindrance to a participation of the Divine good.

ARTICLE 3. *Whether the Spiritual Joy Which Is Caused by Charity Can Be Filled?*

We proceed thus to the Third Article: It seems that the spiritual joy which is caused by charity cannot be filled.

Objection 1. For the more we rejoice in God, the more is our joy in Him filled. But we can never rejoice in Him as much as it is fitting that we should rejoice in God, since His goodness which is infinite, surpasses the creature's joy which is finite. Therefore joy in God can never be filled.

Obj. 2. Further, That which is filled cannot be increased. But the joy, even of the blessed, can be increased, since one's joy is greater than another's. Therefore joy in God cannot be filled in a creature.

Obj. 3. Further, Comprehension seems to be nothing else than the fulness of knowledge. Now, just as the cognitive power of a creature is finite, so is its appetitive power. Since therefore God cannot be comprehended by any creature, it seems that no creature's joy in God can be filled.

On the contrary, Our Lord said to His disciples (John 15. 11): *That My joy may be in you, and your joy may be filled.*

I answer that, Fulness of joy can be understood in two ways. First, on the part of the thing rejoiced in, so that one rejoice in it as much as it is fitting that one should rejoice in it, and thus God's joy alone in Himself is filled, because it is infinite, and this is wholly fitting to the infinite goodness of God; but the joy of any creature must be finite. Secondly, fulness of joy may be understood on the part of the one who rejoices. Now joy is compared to desire as rest to movement, as stated above (Part I-II, Q. XXV, AA. 1, 2), when we were treating of the passions, and rest is full when there is no more movement. Hence joy is full, when there remains nothing to be desired. But as long as we are in this world, the movement of desire does not cease in us, because it still remains possible for us to approach nearer to God by grace, as was shown above (Q. XXIV, AA. 4, 7). When once, however, perfect happiness has been attained, nothing will remain to be desired because then there will be full enjoyment of God, in which man will obtain whatever he had desired, even with regard to other goods, according to Ps. 102. 5: *Who satisfieth thy desire with good things.* Hence desire will be at rest, not only our desire for God, but all our desires, so that the joy of the blessed is full to perfection, —indeed over-full, since they will obtain more than they were capable of desiring: for *neither hath it entered into the heart of man, what things God hath prepared for them that love Him* (I Cor. 2. 9). This is what is meant by the words of Luke 6. 38: *Good measure and pressed down, and shaken together, and running over shall they give into your bosom.* Yet, since no creature is capable of the joy wholly fitting to God, it follows that this perfectly full joy is not taken into man, but, on the contrary, man enters into it, according to Matt. 25. 21: *Enter into the joy of thy Lord.*

Reply Obj. 1. This argument takes the fulness of joy in reference to the thing in which we rejoice.

Reply Obj. 2. When each one attains to Happiness he will reach the term appointed to him by Divine predestination, and nothing further

will remain to which he may tend, although by reaching that term, some will approach nearer to God than others. Hence each one's joy will be full with regard to himself, because his desire will be fully set at rest; yet one's joy will be greater than another's, on account of a fuller participation of the Divine happiness.

Reply Obj. 3. Comprehension denotes fulness of knowledge in respect of the thing known, so that it is known as much as it can be. There is however a fulness of knowledge in respect of the knower, just as we have said of joy. Hence the Apostle says (Coloss. 1. 9): *That you may be filled with the knowledge of His will, in all wisdom and spiritual understanding.*

ARTICLE 4. *Whether Joy Is a Virtue?*

We proceed thus to the Fourth Article: It seems that joy is a virtue.

Objection 1. For vice is contrary to virtue. Now sorrow is set down as a vice, as in the case of acedia and envy. Therefore joy also should be accounted a virtue.

Obj. 2. Further, As love and hope are passions, the object of which is the good, so also is joy. Now love and hope are considered to be virtues. Therefore joy also should be considered a virtue.

Obj. 3. Further, The precepts of the Law are about acts of virtue. But we are commanded to rejoice in the Lord, according to Philip. 4. 4: *Rejoice in the Lord always.* Therefore joy is a virtue.

On the contrary, It is not numbered among the theological virtues, nor among the moral, nor among the intellectual virtues, as is evident from what has been said above (Part I-II, Q. LVII, A. 2; Q. LX, A. 3; Q. LXII, A. 3).

I answer that, As stated above (Part I-II, Q. LV, A. 2), virtue is an operative habit, and so by its very notion it has an inclination to a certain act. Now it may happen that from the same habit there proceed several ordered acts of the same character, each of which follows from another. And since the subsequent acts do not proceed from the virtuous habit except through the preceding act, hence it is that the virtue is defined and named in reference to that preceding act, although those other acts also proceed from the virtue. Now it is evident from what we have said about the passions (Part I-II, Q. XXV, AA. 1, 2, 3; Q. XXVII, A. 4) that love is the first affection of the appetitive power, and that both desire and joy follow from it. Hence the same virtuous habit inclines us to love and desire the beloved good, and to rejoice in it. But because love is the first of these acts, that virtue takes its name, not from joy, nor from desire, but from love, and is called charity. Hence joy is not a virtue distinct from charity, but an act, or effect, of charity. And for this reason it is numbered among the Fruits (Gal. 5. 22).

Reply Obj. 1. The sorrow which is a vice is caused by inordinate self-love, and this is not a special vice but a general source of the vices, as stated above (Part I-II, Q. LXXVII, A. 4); and so it was necessary to account certain particular sorrows as special vices, because they do not arise from a special, but from a general vice. On the other hand love of God is accounted a special virtue, namely charity, to which joy is reduced, as its proper act, as stated above (here and A. 2).

Reply Obj. 2. Hope proceeds from love even as joy does, but hope adds, on the part of the object, a special character, namely difficult, and possible to obtain; for which reason it is accounted a special virtue. On the other hand joy does not add to love any special aspect that might cause a special virtue.

Reply Obj. 3. The Law prescribes joy as being an act of charity, although it is not its first act.

QUESTION XXIX
OF PEACE
(In Four Articles)

WE must now consider peace, under which head there are four points of inquiry: (1) Whether peace is the same as concord? (2) Whether all things desire peace? (3) Whether peace is an effect of charity? (4) Whether peace is a virtue?

ARTICLE 1. *Whether Peace Is the Same as Concord?*

We proceed thus to the First Article: It would seem that peace is the same as concord.

Objection 1. For Augustine says:[1] "Peace among men is well ordered concord." Now we are speaking here of no other peace than that of men. Therefore peace is the same as concord.

Obj. 2. Further, Concord is union of wills. Now the notion of peace consists in such union, for Dionysius says (*Div. Nom.* xi)[2] that "peace unites all, and makes them of one mind." Therefore peace is the same as concord.

Obj. 3. Further, Things whose opposites are identical are themselves identical. Now the one same thing is opposed to concord and peace, namely dissension; hence it is written (I Cor. 14. 33): *God is not the God of dissension but of peace*. Therefore peace is the same as concord.

On the contrary, There can be concord in evil between wicked men. But *there is no peace to the wicked* (Isa. 48. 22). Therefore peace is not the same as concord.

I answer that, Peace includes concord and adds something to it. Hence wherever peace is, there is concord, but there is not peace wherever there is concord, if we give peace its proper meaning. For concord, properly speaking, is between one man and another, in so far as the wills of various hearts agree together in consenting to the same thing. Now the heart of one man may happen to tend to different things, and this in two ways. First, in respect of the different appetitive powers; thus the sensitive appetite very often tends to that which is opposed to the rational appetite, according to Gal. 5. 17: *The flesh lusteth against the spirit.* Secondly, in so far as one and the same appetitive power tends to different objects of appetite, which it cannot obtain all at the same time, so that there is of necessity a clashing of the movements of the appetite. Now the union of such movement is of the very notion of peace, because man's heart is not at peace so long as he does not have what he wants, or if, having what he wants, there still remains something for him to want, and which he cannot have at the same time. On the other hand this union does not belong to the notion of concord; and so concord denotes union of appetites among various persons, while peace denotes, in addition to this union, the union of the appetites even in one man.

Reply Obj. 1. Augustine is speaking there of that peace which is between one man and another, and he says that this peace is concord, not indeed any kind of concord, but that which is well ordered, through one man agreeing with another in respect of something befitting to both of them. For if one man concord with another, not by a spontaneous will but through being forced, as it were, by the fear of some evil that threatens him, such concord is not really peace, because the order of each concordant is not observed, but is disturbed by some fear-inspiring cause. For this reason he premises that "peace is tranquillity of order," which tranquillity consists in all the appetitive movements in one man being set at rest together.

Reply Obj. 2. If one man consent to the same thing together with another man, his consent is nevertheless not entirely united to himself, unless at the same time all his appetitive movements be in agreement.

[1] *City of God*, XIX, 13 (PL 41, 640).
[2] Sect. 1 (PG 3, 948).

Reply Obj. 3. A twofold dissension is opposed to peace, namely dissension between a man and himself, and dissension between one man and another. The latter alone is opposed to concord.

ARTICLE 2. *Whether All Things Desire Peace?*

We proceed thus to the Second Article: It seems that not all things desire peace.

Objection 1. For, according to Dionysius (*Div. Nom.* xi),[1] peace "unites consent." But there cannot be unity of consent in things which lack knowledge. Therefore such things cannot desire peace.

Obj. 2. Further, The appetite does not tend to opposite things at the same time. Now many desire war and dissension. Therefore all men do not desire peace.

Obj. 3. Further, Good alone is an object of appetite. But a certain peace is, it seems, evil, for otherwise Our Lord would not have said (Matt. 10. 34): *I came not to send peace.* Therefore all things do not desire peace.

Obj. 4. Further, That which all desire would seem to be the sovereign good which is the last end. But this is not true of peace, since it is attainable even by a wayfarer; otherwise Our Lord would in vain command (Mark 9. 49): *Have peace among you.* Therefore all things do not desire peace.

On the contrary, Augustine says[2] that all things desire peace and Dionysius says the same (*Div. Nom.* xi).[3]

I answer that, From the very fact that a man desires a certain thing it follows that he desires to obtain what he desires, and, in consequence, to remove whatever may be an obstacle to his obtaining it. Now a man may be hindered from obtaining the good he desires by a contrary desire either of his own or of some other, and both are removed by peace, as stated above (A. 1). Hence it follows of necessity that whoever desires anything desires peace, in so far as he who desires anything desires to attain, with tranquillity and without hindrance, to that which he desires; and this is what is meant by peace which Augustine defines "the tranquillity of order."[4]

Reply Obj. 1. Peace denotes union not only of the intellectual or rational appetite, or of the animal appetite, in both of which consent may be found, but also of the natural appetite.

Hence Dionysius says (*ibid.*) that "peace is the cause of consent and of connaturalness," where consent denotes the union of appetites proceeding from knowledge, and connaturalness, the union of natural appetites.

Reply Obj. 2. Even those who seek war and dissension desire nothing but peace, which they do not consider themselves to have. For as we stated above (A. 1, Reply 1), there is no peace when a man agrees with another man counter to what he would prefer. Consequently men seek by means of war to break this concord, because it is a defective peace, in order that they may obtain a peace in which nothing is contrary to their will. Hence all wars are waged that men may find a more perfect peace than that which they had before.

Reply Obj. 3. Peace gives calm and unity to the appetite. Now just as the appetite may tend to what is good absolutely, or to what is good apparently, so too, peace may be either true or apparent. There can be no true peace except where the appetite is directed to what is truly good, since every evil, though it may appear good in a way, so as to calm the appetite in some respect, has, nevertheless many defects, which cause the appetite to remain restless and disturbed. Hence true peace is only in good men and about good things. The peace of the wicked is not a true peace but a semblance of peace, and so it is written (Wisd. 14. 22): *Whereas they lived in a great war of ignorance, they call so many and so great evils peace.*

Reply Obj. 4. Since true peace is only about good things, as the true good is possessed in two ways, perfectly and imperfectly, so there is a twofold true peace. One is perfect peace. It consists in the perfect enjoyment of the supreme good, and unites all one's desires by giving them rest in one object. This is the last end of the rational creature, according to Ps. 147. 14: *Who hath placed peace in thy borders.* The other is imperfect peace, which may be had in this world, for though the chief movement of the soul finds rest in God, yet there are certain things within and without which disturb that peace.

ARTICLE 3. *Whether Peace Is the Proper Effect of Charity?*

We proceed thus to the Third Article: It seems that peace is not the proper effect of charity.

Objection 1. For one cannot have charity without sanctifying grace. But some have peace who have not sanctifying grace; for instance

1 Sect. 1 (PG 3, 948).
2 *City of God,* XIX, 12 (PL 41, 638).
3 Sect. 1 (PG 3, 948).
4 *City of God,* XIX, 13 (PL 41, 640).

the gentiles sometimes have peace. Therefore peace is not the effect of charity.

Obj. 2. Further, If a certain thing is caused by charity, its contrary is not compatible with charity. But dissension, which is contrary to peace, is compatible with charity, for we find that even holy doctors, such as Jerome and Augustine, dissented in some of their opinions.[1] We also read that Paul and Barnabas dissented from one another (Acts 15.). Therefore it seems that peace is not the effect of charity.

Obj. 3. Further, The same thing is not the proper effect of different things. Now peace is the effect of justice, according to Isa. 32. 17: *And the work of justice shall be peace.* Therefore it is not the effect of charity.

On the contrary, It is written (Ps. 118. 165): *Much peace have they that love Thy Law.*

I answer that, Peace implies a twofold union, as stated above (A. 1). The first is the result of one's own appetites being directed to one object, while the other results from one's own appetite being united with the appetite of another. And each of these unions is effected by charity. The first, in so far as man loves God with his whole heart, by referring all things to Him, so that all his desires tend to one object. The second, in so far as we love our neighbour as ourselves, the result being that we wish to fulfil our neighbour's will as though it were ours; hence it is reckoned a sign of friendship if people make choice of the same things,[2] and Tully says (*De Amicitia*)[3] that friends like and dislike the same things.

Reply Obj. 1. Without sin no one falls from a state of sanctifying grace, for it turns man away from his due end by making him place his end in something undue, so that his appetite does not cleave chiefly to the true final good, but to some apparent good. Hence, without sanctifying grace, peace is not real but only apparent.

Reply Obj. 2. As the Philosopher says,[4] friends need not agree in opinion, but only upon such goods as conduce to life, and especially upon such as are important; because dissension in small matters is scarcely accounted dissension. Hence nothing hinders those who have charity from holding different opinions. Nor is this an obstacle to peace, because opinions concern the intellect, which precedes the appetite that is united by peace. In like manner if there be con-

cord as to goods of importance, dissension with regard to some that are of little account is not contrary to charity. For such a dissension proceeds from a difference of opinion, because one man thinks that the particular good, which is the object of dissension, belongs to the good about which they agree, while the other thinks that it does not. Accordingly such dissension about very slight matters and about opinions is inconsistent with a state of perfect peace, in which the truth will be known fully, and every desire fulfilled, but it is not inconsistent with the imperfect peace of the wayfarer.

Reply Obj. 3. Peace is the work of justice indirectly, in so far as justice removes the obstacles to peace; but it is the work of charity directly, since charity, according to its very notion, causes peace. For love is "a unitive force" as Dionysius says (*Div. Nom.* iv),[5] and peace is the union of the appetite's inclinations.

ARTICLE 4. *Whether Peace Is a Virtue?*

We proceed thus to the Fourth Article: It seems that peace is a virtue.

Objection 1. For nothing is a matter of precept, unless it is an act of virtue. But there are precepts about keeping peace, for example: *Have peace among you* (Mark 9. 49). Therefore peace is a virtue.

Obj. 2. Further, We do not merit except by acts of virtue. Now it is meritorious to keep peace, according to Matt. 5. 9: *Blessed are the peacemakers, for they shall be called the children of God.* Therefore peace is a virtue.

Obj. 3. Further, Vices are opposed to virtues. But dissensions, which are contrary to peace, are numbered among the vices (Gal. 5. 20). Therefore peace is a virtue.

On the contrary, Virtue is not the last end, but the way to it. But peace is the last end, after a fashion, as Augustine says.[6] Therefore peace is not a virtue.

I answer that, As stated above (Q. XXVIII, A. 4), when a number of acts all proceeding uniformly from an agent follow one from the other, they all arise from the same virtue, nor do they each have a virtue from which they proceed, as may be seen in corporeal things. For, though fire by heating, both liquefies and rarefies, there are not two powers in fire, one of liquefaction, the other of rarefaction, but fire produces all such actions by its one power of heating.

Since then peace is caused by charity from

---

[1] See Augustine, *Epist.,* 28, (PL 33, 111; cf. PL 22, 565); *Epist.,* 40 (PL 33, 154; cf. PL 22, 647); *Epist.,* 82 (PL 33, 275; cf. PL 22, 936); See Jerome, *Epist.,* 112 (PL 22, 916; cf. PL 33, 251); *In Gal.* 1, super 2.11 (PL 26, 364).

[2] Aristotle, *Ethics,* IX, 4 (1166ᵃ7).

[3] DD IV, 552.   [4] *Ethics,* IX, 6 (1167ᵃ22).

[5] Sect. 12 (PG 3, 709).

[6] *City of God,* XIX, 11 (PL 41, 637).

its very character of being love of God and of our neighbour, as shown above (A. 3), there is no other virtue except charity whose proper act is peace, as we have also said in reference to joy (Q. XXVIII, A. 4).

Reply Obj. 1. We are commanded to keep peace because it is an act of charity; and for this reason too it is a meritorious act. Hence it is placed among the beatitudes, which are acts of perfect virtue, as stated above (Part I-II, Q. LXIX, AA. 1, 3). It is also numbered among the fruits, in so far as it is a final good, having spiritual sweetness.

This suffices for the *Reply to the Second Objection.*

Reply Obj. 3. Several vices are opposed to one virtue in respect of its various acts, so that not only is hatred opposed to charity, in respect of its act which is love, but also acedia and envy, in respect of joy, and dissension in respect of peace.

QUESTION XXX
OF MERCY
(*In Four Articles*)

WE must now go on to consider Mercy,[1] under which head there are four points of inquiry: (1) Whether evil is the cause of mercy on the part of the person pitied? (2) To whom does it belong to pity? (3) Whether mercy is a virtue? (4) Whether it is the greatest of virtues?

ARTICLE 1. *Whether Evil Is Properly the Motive of Mercy?*

We proceed thus to the First Article: It would seem that, properly speaking, evil is not the motive of mercy.

Objection 1. For, as shown above (Q. XIX, A. 1; Part I, Q. XLVIII, A. 6), fault is an evil rather than punishment. Now fault provokes indignation rather than mercy. Therefore evil does not excite mercy.

Obj. 2. Further, Cruelty and harshness seem to excel other evils. Now the Philosopher says[2] that "harshness does not call for pity but drives it away." Therefore evil, as such, is not the motive of mercy.

Obj. 3. Further, Signs of evils are not true evils. But signs of evils excite one to mercy, as the Philosopher states.[3] Therefore evil, properly speaking, is not an incentive to mercy.

[1] The one Latin word *misericordia* signifies either pity or mercy. The distinction between these two is that pity may stand either for the act or for the virtue, whereas mercy stands only for the virtue.

[2] *Rhetoric*, II, 8 (1386ª22).   [3] *Ibid.* (1386ᵇ2).

On the contrary, Damascene says (*De Fide Orthod.* ii, 14)[4] that "mercy is a kind of sorrow." Now evil is the motive of sorrow. Therefore it is the motive of mercy.

I answer that, As Augustine says,[5] "mercy is heartfelt sympathy for another's distress, impelling us to succour him if we can." For mercy takes its name *misericordia* from denoting a man's compassionate heart (*miserum cor*) for another's unhappiness. Now unhappiness is opposed to happiness. And it is of the very notion of happiness or felicity that one should obtain what one wishes and what pertains to justice; for, according to Augustine (*De Trin.* xiii, 5),[6] happy is he "who has whatever he desires, and desires nothing amiss." Hence, on the other hand, it belongs to unhappiness that a man should suffer what he wishes not.

Now a man wishes a thing in three ways: first, by his natural appetite; thus all men naturally wish to be and to live. Secondly, a man wishes a thing from deliberate choice. Thirdly, a man wishes a thing, not in itself, but in its cause; thus, if a man wishes to eat what is harmful for him, we say that, in a way, he wishes to be ill.

Accordingly the motive of mercy, being something pertaining to misery, is, in the first way, anything contrary to the will's natural appetite, namely corruptive or distressing evils, the contrary of which man desires naturally. Hence the Philosopher says[7] that "pity is sorrow for a visible evil, whether corruptive or distressing." Secondly, such evils are yet more provocative of pity if they are contrary to deliberate choice, and so the Philosopher says[8] that those evils excite our pity "when they are the result of an accident, as when something turns out ill, whereas we hoped well of it." Thirdly, they cause yet greater pity, if they are entirely contrary to the will, as when evil befalls a man who has always striven to do well. And so the Philosopher says[9] that "we pity most the distress of one who suffers undeservedly."

Reply Obj. 1. It is of the very notion of fault that it be voluntary; and in this respect it deserves punishment rather than mercy. Since, however, fault may be, in a way, a punishment, through having something connected with it that is against the sinner's will, it may, in this respect, call for mercy. It is in this sense that we pity and commiserate sinners. Thus Gregory says in a homily (*Hom. in Ev.* xxxiv)[10] that

[4] PG 94, 932.   [5] *City of God*, IX, 5 (PL 41, 261).
[6] PL 42, 1020.   [7] *Rhetoric*, II, 8 (1385ᵇ13).
[8] *Ibid.* (1386ª5, 11).   [9] *Ibid.* (1386ᵇ6).   [10] PL 76, 1246.

"true justice is not disdainful," that is, towards sinners, "but compassionate," and again it is written (Matt. 9. 36) that Jesus *seeing the multitudes, had compassion on them: because they were distressed, and lying like sheep that have no shepherd.*

Reply Obj. 2. Since pity is compassion for another's distress, it is directed, properly speaking, towards another, and not to oneself, except figuratively, like justice, according as a man is considered to have various parts.[1] Thus it is written (Ecclus. 30. 24): *Have pity on thy own soul, pleasing God.* Accordingly just as, properly speaking, a man does not pity himself, but suffers in himself, as when we suffer cruel treatment in ourselves, so too, in the case of those who are so closely united to us as to be as it were part of ourselves, such as our children or our parents, we do not pity their distress, but suffer as for our own wounds; in this sense the Philosopher says that "harshness drives pity away."

Reply Obj. 3. Just as pleasure results from hope and memory of good things, so does sorrow arise from the prospect or the recollection of evil things; though not so keenly as when they are present to the senses. Hence the signs of evil move us to pity, in so far as they represent as present the evil that excites our pity.

ARTICLE 2. *Whether the Reason for Taking Pity Is a Defect in the Person Who Pities?*

We proceed thus to the Second Article: It seems that the reason for taking pity is not a defect in the person who takes pity.

Objection 1. For it is proper to God to be merciful, wherefore it is written (Ps. 144. 9): *His tender mercies are over all His works.* But there is no defect in God. Therefore a defect cannot be the reason for taking pity.

Obj. 2. Further, If a defect is the reason for taking pity, those in whom there is most defect, must take most pity. But this is false, for the Philosopher says[2] that "those who are completely ruined are pitiless." Therefore it seems that the reason for taking pity is not a defect in the person who pities.

Obj. 3. Further, To be treated with contempt pertains to defect. But the Philosopher says[3] that "those who are disposed to contumely are pitiless." Therefore the reason for taking pity is not a defect in the person who pities.

On the contrary, Pity is a kind of sorrow. But a defect is the reason of sorrow; hence those

who are in bad health give way to sorrow more easily, as we have said (Part I-II, Q. XLVII, A. 3). Therefore the reason why one takes pity is a defect in oneself.

I answer that, Since pity is grief for another's distress, as stated above (A. 1), from the very fact that a person takes pity on anyone, it follows that another's distress grieves him. And since sorrow or grief is about one's own ills, one grieves or sorrows for another's distress in so far as one looks upon another's distress as one's own. Now this happens in two ways: first, through union of the affections, which is the effect of love. For, since he who loves another looks upon his friend as another self, he counts his friend's hurt as his own, so that he grieves for his friend's hurt as though he were hurt himself. Hence the Philosopher[4] accounts "grieving with one's friend" as being one of the signs of friendship, and the Apostle says (Rom. 12. 15): *Rejoice with them that rejoice, weep with them that weep.*

Secondly, it happens through real union, for instance when another's evil comes near to us, so as to pass to us from him. Hence the Philosopher says[5] that men pity such as are akin to them, and like them, because it makes them realize that the same may happen to themselves. This also explains why the old and the wise who consider that they may fall upon evil times, as also feeble and timorous persons, are more inclined to pity. On the contrary, however, those who consider themselves happy, and so far powerful as to think themselves in no danger of suffering any hurt, are not so inclined to pity. Accordingly a defect is always the reason for taking pity, either because one looks upon another's defect as one's own, through being united to him by love, or on account of the possibility of suffering like things.

Reply Obj. 1. God takes pity on us through love alone, in so far as He loves us as belonging to Him.

Reply Obj. 2. Those who are already in infinite distress do not fear to suffer more, and therefore they are without pity. In like manner this applies to those also who are in great fear, for they are so intent on their own passion, that they pay no attention to the suffering of others.

Reply Obj. 3. Those who are disposed to contumely, whether through having been despised, or because they wish to despise others, are incited to anger and daring, which are manly passions and arouse the human spirit to attempt

---

[1] Aristotle, *Ethics*, v, 11 (1138^{b}8).
[2] *Rhetoric*, ii, 8 (1385^{b}19).   [3] *Ibid.* (1385^{b}31).

[4] *Ethics*, ix, 4 (1166^{a}7).
[5] *Rhetoric*, ii, 8 (1385^{b}16).

difficult things. Hence they make a man think that he is going to suffer something in the future, so that while they are disposed in that way they are pitiless, according to Prov. 27. 4: *Anger hath no mercy, nor fury when it breaketh forth.* For a like reason the proud are without pity, because they despise others, and think them wicked, so that they account them as suffering deservedly whatever they suffer. Hence Gregory says (*Hom. in Ev.* xxxiv)[1] that "false godliness, that is, of the proud, is not compassionate but disdainful."

Article 3. *Whether Mercy Is a Virtue?*

We proceed thus to the Third Article: It seems that mercy is not a virtue.

Objection 1. For the chief part of virtue is choice as the Philosopher states.[2] Now "choice is the desire of what has been already counselled."[3] Therefore whatever hinders counsel cannot be called a virtue. But mercy hinders counsel, according to the saying of Sallust (*Catilin.*),[4] "All those that take counsel about matters of doubt, should be free from . . . anger . . . and mercy, because the mind does not easily see the truth when these things stand in the way." Therefore mercy is not a virtue.

Obj. 2. Further, Nothing contrary to virtue is praiseworthy. But "nemesis is contrary to mercy," as the Philosopher states,[5] and yet it is a praiseworthy passion.[6] Therefore mercy is not a virtue.

Obj. 3. Further, Joy and peace are not special virtues, because they result from charity, as stated above (Q. XXVIII, A. 4; Q. XXIX, A. 4). Now mercy, also, results from charity; for it is out of charity that we weep with them that weep, as we rejoice with them that rejoice. Therefore mercy is not a special virtue.

Obj. 4. Further, Since mercy belongs to the appetitive power, it is not an intellectual virtue, and, since it has not God for its object, neither is it a theological virtue. Moreover it is not a moral virtue, because neither is it about operations, for this belongs to justice; nor is it about passions, since it is not reduced to one of the twelve means mentioned by the Philosopher.[7] Therefore mercy is not a virtue.

On the contrary, Augustine says:[8] "Cicero in praising Cæsar expresses himself much better and in a fashion at once more humane and more in accordance with religious feeling, when he says: 'Of all thy virtues none is more marvellous or more graceful than thy mercy.' " Therefore mercy is a virtue.

I answer that, Mercy signifies grief for another's distress. Now this grief may denote, in one way, a movement of the sensitive appetite, in which case mercy is not a virtue but a passion. But, in another way, it may denote a movement of the intellectual appetite, according as one person's evil is displeasing to another. This movement may be ruled in accordance with reason, and in accordance with this movement regulated by reason, the movement of the lower appetite may be regulated. Hence Augustine says[9] that "this movement of the mind" namely mercy, "obeys the reason, when mercy is vouchsafed in such a way that justice is safeguarded, whether we give to the needy or forgive the repentant." And since it belongs to the notion of human virtue that the movements of the soul should be regulated by reason, as was shown above (Part I-II, Q. LVI, A. 4; Q. LIX, A. 4; Q. LX, A. 5), it follows that mercy is a virtue.

Reply Obj. 1. The words of Sallust are to be understood as applying to the mercy which is a passion unregulated by reason; for thus it impedes the counselling of reason, by making it wander from justice.

Reply Obj. 2. The Philosopher is speaking there of pity and nemesis considered both as passions. They are contrary to one another on the part of their respective estimation of another's evils, for which pity grieves in so far as it esteems someone to suffer undeservedly, while nemesis rejoices, in so far as it esteems someone to suffer deservedly, and grieves if things go well with the undeserving; "both of these are praiseworthy and come from the same disposition of character."[10] Properly speaking, however, it is envy which is opposed to pity, as we shall state further on (Q. XXXVI, A. 3, Reply 3).

Reply Obj. 3. Joy and peace add nothing to the aspect of good which is the object of charity, and so they do not require any other virtue besides charity. But mercy regards a certain special aspect, namely the misery of the person pitied.

Reply Obj. 4. Mercy, considered as a virtue, is a moral virtue having relation to the passions, and it is reduced to the mean called nemesis, because "they both proceed from the same character."[11] Now the Philosopher proposes these

[1] PL 76, 1246.
[2] *Ethics,* II, 5 (1106ª3); cf. III, 2 (1111ᵇ5).
[3] *Ibid.,* III, 2 (1112ª14); cf. VI, 2 (1139ª23).
[4] Chap. 51 (BU 52).   [5] *Rhetoric,* II, 9 (1386ᵇ9).
[6] *Ethics,* II, 7 (1108ª35).   [7] *Ibid.* (1107ª28).
[8] *City of God,* IX, 5 (PL 41, 260).

[9] *Ibid.* (PL 41, 261).
[10] Aristotle, *Rhetoric,* II, 9 (1386ᵇII).   [11] *Ibid.*

means not as virtues, but as passions, because, even as passions, they are praiseworthy. Yet nothing prevents them from proceeding from some elective habit, in which case they assume the character of a virtue.

ARTICLE 4. Whether Mercy Is the Greatest of the Virtues?

We proceed thus to the Fourth Article: It would seem that mercy is the greatest of the virtues.

Objection 1. For the worship of God seems a most virtuous act. But mercy is preferred before the worship of God, according to Os. 6. 6 and Matt. 12. 7: I have desired mercy and not sacrifice. Therefore mercy is the greatest virtue.

Obj. 2. Further, On the words of I Tim. 4. 8: Godliness is profitable to all things, a gloss says:[1] "The sum total of a Christian's rule of life consists in mercy and godliness." Now the Christian rule of life embraces every virtue. Therefore the sum total of all virtues is contained in mercy.

Obj. 3. Further, Virtue is that which makes its subject good. Therefore the more a virtue makes a man like God, the better is that virtue: since man is the better for being more like God. Now this is chiefly the result of mercy, since of God is it said (Ps. 144. 9) that His tender mercies are over all His works, and (Luke 6. 36) Our Lord said: Be ye . . . merciful, as your Father also is merciful. Therefore mercy is the greatest of virtues.

On the contrary, The Apostle after saying (Col. 3. 12): Put ye on . . . as the elect of God . . . the bowels of mercy, etc., adds (verse 14): Above all things have charity. Therefore mercy is not the greatest of virtues.

I answer that, A virtue may take precedence of others in two ways: first, in itself; secondly, in relation to its subject. In itself, mercy takes precedence of other virtues, for it pertains to mercy to be bountiful to others, and, what is more, to succour others in their wants, which pertains chiefly to one who stands above. Hence mercy is accounted as being proper to God, His omnipotence is declared to be chiefly manifested in this.

On the other hand, with regard to its subject, mercy is not the greatest virtue, unless that subject be greater than all others, surpassed by none and excelling all; since for him that has anyone above him it is better to be

[1] Glossa ordin. (VI, 120E); Glossa Lombardi (PL 192, 348). Ambrosiaster, In I Tim., on 4.8 (PL 17, 500).

united to that which is above than to supply the defect of that which is beneath. Hence, as regards man, who has God above him, charity which unites him to God is greater than mercy, by which he supplies the defects of his neighbour. But of all the virtues which relate to our neighbour, mercy is the greatest, even as its act surpasses all others, since it belongs to one who is higher and better to supply the defect of another, in so far as the latter is deficient.

Reply Obj. 1. We worship God by external sacrifices and gifts, not for His own profit, but for that of ourselves and our neighbour. For He does not need our sacrifices, but wishes them to be offered to Him in order to arouse our devotion and to profit our neighbour. Hence mercy, by which we supply others' defects is a sacrifice more acceptable to Him, as conducing more directly to our neighbour's well-being, according to Heb. 13. 16: Do not forget to do good and to impart, for by such sacrifices God's favour is obtained.

Reply Obj. 2. The sum total of the Christian religion consists in mercy, as regards external works; but the inward love of charity by which we are united to God preponderates over both love and mercy for our neighbour.

Reply Obj. 3. Charity likens us to God by uniting us to Him in the bond of love. And therefore it surpasses charity which likens us to God as regards similarity of works.

QUESTION XXXI
OF BENEFICENCE
(In Four Articles)

WE must now consider the outward acts or effects of charity, (1) Beneficence, (2) Almsdeeds, which are a part of beneficence (Q. XXXII), (3) Fraternal correction, which is a kind of alms (Q. XXXIII).

Under the first head there are four points of inquiry: (1) Whether beneficence is an act of charity? (2) Whether we ought to be beneficent to all? (3) Whether we ought to be more beneficent to those who are more closely united to us? (4) Whether beneficence is a special virtue?

ARTICLE 1. Whether Beneficence Is an Act of Charity?

We proceed thus to the First Article: It would seem that beneficence is not an act of charity.

Objection 1. For charity is chiefly directed to God. Now we cannot benefit God, according to Job 35. 7: What shalt thou give Him? or what *shall He receive of thy hand?* Therefore beneficence is not an act of charity.

Obj. 2. Further, Beneficence consists chiefly in making gifts. But this belongs to liberality. Therefore beneficence is an act of liberality and not of charity.

Obj. 3. Further, What a man gives, he gives either as being due, or as not due. But a benefit conferred as being due belongs to justice, while a benefit conferred as not due, is given freely, and in this respect is an act of mercy. Therefore every benefit conferred is either an act of justice, or an act of mercy. Therefore it is not an act of charity.

On the contrary, Charity is a kind of friendship, as stated above (Q. XXIII, A. 1). Now the Philosopher places among the acts of friendship doing good, that is, being beneficent, to one's friends.[1] Therefore it is an act of charity to do good to others.

I answer that, Beneficence simply means doing good to someone. This good may be considered in two ways. First under the general aspect of good, and this belongs to beneficence in general, and is an act of friendship, and, consequently, of charity. For the act of love includes goodwill by which a man wishes his friend well, as stated above (Q. XXIII, A. 1; Q. XXVII, A. 2). Now the will carries into effect if possible, the things it wills, so that, consequently, the result of an act of love is that a man is beneficent to his friends. Therefore beneficence in its general notion is an act of friendship or charity.

But if the good which one man does another, be considered under some special aspect of good, then beneficence will assume a special character and will belong to some special virtue.

Reply Obj. 1. According to Dionysius (*Div. Nom.* iv),[2] "love moves those whom it orders, to a mutual relationship: it turns the inferior to the superior to be perfected by them; it moves the superior to watch over the inferior"; and in this respect beneficence is an effect of love. Hence it is not for us to benefit God, but to honour Him by obeying Him, while it is for Him, out of His love, to bestow good things on us.

Reply Obj. 2. Two things must be observed in the bestowal of gifts. One is the thing given outwardly, while the other is the inward passion that a man has in the delight of riches. It pertains to liberality to moderate this inward passion, so as to avoid excessive desire and love for riches; for this makes a man more ready

to part with his wealth. Hence, if a man makes some great gift, while yet desiring to keep it for himself, his is not a liberal giving. On the other hand, as regards the outward gift, the act of beneficence belongs in general to friendship or charity. Hence it does not detract from a man's friendship, if, through love, he give his friend something he would like to keep for himself; rather does this prove the perfection of his friendship.

Reply Obj. 3. Just as friendship or charity sees, in the benefit bestowed, the general aspect of good, so does justice see therein the aspect of debt, while pity considers the relieving of distress or defect.

ARTICLE 2. *Whether We Ought to Do Good to All?*

We proceed thus to the Second Article: It would seem that we are not bound to do good to all.

Objection 1. For Augustine says[3] that "we are unable to do good to everyone." Now virtue does not incline one to the impossible. Therefore it is not necessary to do good to all.

Obj. 2. Further, It is written (Ecclus. 12. 5): *Give to the good, and receive not a sinner.* But many men are sinners. Therefore we need not do good to all.

Obj. 3. Further, *Charity dealeth not perversely* (I Cor. 13. 4). Now to do good to some is to deal perversely; for instance if one were to do good to an enemy of the common weal, or if one were to do good to an excommunicated person, since, by doing so, he would be holding communion with him. Therefore, since beneficence is an act of charity, we ought not to do good to all.

On the contrary, The Apostle says (Gal. 6. 10): *Whilst we have time, let us work good to all men.*

I answer that, As stated above (A. 1, Reply 1), beneficence follows on love in so far as love moves the superior to watch over the inferior. Now degrees among men are not unchangeable as among angels, because men are subject to many failings, so that he who is superior in one respect, is or may be inferior in another. Therefore, since the love of charity extends to all, beneficence also should extend to all, but according as time and place require; for all acts of virtue must be modified with a view to their due circumstances.

Reply Obj. 1. Absolutely speaking it is impossible to do good to every single one; yet it

---

[1] *Ethics,* IX, 4 (1166ª3).   [2] Sect. 12 (PG 3, 709).   [3] *Christian Doctrine,* I, 28 (PL 34, 30).

is true of each individual that one may be bound to do good to him in some particular case. Hence charity binds us, though not actually doing good to someone, to be prepared in mind to do good to anyone if we have time to spare. There is however a good that we can do to all, if not to each individual, at least to all in general, as when we pray for all, for unbelievers as well as for the faithful.

Reply Obj. 2. In a sinner there are two things, his guilt and his nature. Accordingly we are bound to succour the sinner as to the maintenance of his nature, but not so as to abet his sin, for this would be to do evil rather than good.

Reply Obj. 3. The excommunicated and the enemies of the commonweal are deprived of all beneficence, in so far as this prevents them from doing evil deeds. Yet if their nature be in urgent need of succour lest it fail, we are bound to help them; for instance, if they be in danger of death through hunger or thirst, or suffer some like distress, unless this be according to the order of justice.

ARTICLE 3. *Whether We Ought to Do Good to Those Rather Who Are More Closely United to Us?*

We proceed thus to the Third Article: It seems that we are not bound to do good to those rather who are more closely united to us.

Objection 1. For it is written (Luke 14. 12): *When thou makest a dinner or a supper, call not thy friends, nor thy brethren, nor thy kinsmen.* Now these are the most closely united to us. Therefore we are not bound to do good to those rather who are more closely united to us, but preferably to strangers and to those who are in want; hence the text goes on: *But, when thou makest a feast, call the poor, the maimed,* etc.

Obj. 2. Further, To help another in the battle is an act of very great goodness. But a soldier on the battlefield is bound to help a fellow-soldier who is a stranger rather than a kinsman who is a foe. Therefore in doing acts of kindness we are not bound to give the preference to those who are most closely united to us.

Obj. 3. Further, We should pay what is due before conferring gratuitous favours. But it is a man's duty to be good to those who have been good to him. Therefore we ought to do good to our benefactors rather than to those who are closely united to us.

Obj. 4. Further, A man ought to love his parents more than his children, as stated above

(Q. XXVI, A. 9). Yet a man ought to be more beneficent to his children, since *neither ought the children to lay up for the parents,* according to II Cor. 12. 14. Therefore we are not bound to be more beneficent to those who are more closely united to us.

On the contrary, Augustine says:[1] "Since one cannot do good to all, we ought to consider those chiefly who by reason of place, time or any other circumstance, by a kind of chance are more closely united to us."

I answer that, Grace and virtue imitate the order of nature, which is established by Divine wisdom. Now the order of nature is such that every natural agent pours forth its activity first and most of all on the things which are nearest to it; thus fire heats most what is next to it. In like manner God pours forth the gifts of His goodness first and most plentifully on the substances which are nearest to Him, as Dionysius declares (*Cæl. Hier.* vii).[2] But the bestowal of benefits is an act of charity towards others. Therefore we ought to be most beneficent towards those who are most closely connected with us.

Now one man's nearness to another may be measured in reference to the various matters in which men are engaged together; (thus the intercourse of kinsmen is in natural matters, that of fellow-citizens is in civic matters, that of the faithful is in spiritual matters, and so forth); and various benefits should be conferred in various ways according to these various fellowships, because we ought in preference to bestow on each one such benefits as pertain to the matter in which, speaking absolutely, he is most closely joined to us. And yet this may vary according to the various requirements of time, place, or matter in hand, because in certain cases one ought, for instance, to succour a stranger, in extreme necessity, rather than one's own father, if he is not in such urgent need.

Reply Obj. 1. Our Lord did not absolutely forbid us to invite our friends and kinsmen to eat with us, but to invite them so that they may invite us in return, since that would be an act not of charity but of cupidity. The case may occur, however, that one ought rather to invite strangers, on account of their greater want. For it must be understood that, other things being equal, one ought to succour those rather who are most closely connected with us. And if of two, one be more closely connected and the other in greater want, it is not possible to de-

[1] *Christian Doctrine*, I, 28 (PL 34, 30).
[2] Sect. 3 (PG 3, 209).

cide by any general rule which of them we ought to help rather than the other, since there are various degrees of want as well as of connection, and the matter requires the judgment of a prudent man.

Reply Obj. 2. The common good of many is more Godlike than the good of an individual. Therefore it is a virtuous action for a man to endanger even his own life, either for the spiritual or for the temporal common good of his country. Since therefore men engage together in warlike acts in order to safeguard the common weal, the soldier who with this in view succours his comrade, succours him not as a private individual, but with a view to the welfare of his country as a whole. Therefore it is not a matter for wonder if a stranger be preferred to one who is a blood relation.

Reply Obj. 3. A thing may be due in two ways. There is one which should be numbered, not among the goods of the debtor, but rather as belonging to the person to whom it is due; for instance, a man may have another's goods, whether in money or in kind, either because he has stolen them, or because he has received them on loan or in deposit, or in some other way. In this case a man ought to pay what he owes, rather than benefit his connections out of it, unless perhaps, the case be so urgent that it would be lawful for him to take another's property in order to relieve the one who is in need. Yet, again, this would not apply if the creditor were in equal distress. In such a case, however, the claims on either side would have to be weighed with regard to such other conditions as a prudent man would take into consideration, because, on account of the different particular cases, as the Philosopher states,[1] it is impossible to lay down a general rule.

The other kind of due is one which is counted among the goods of the debtor and not of the creditor; for instance, a thing may be due not because justice requires it, but on account of a certain moral equity, as in the case of benefits received freely. Now no benefactor confers a benefit equal to that which a man receives from his parents, and therefore in paying back benefits received, we should give the first place to our parents before all others, unless, on the other side, there be such weightier motives as need or some other circumstance, for instance the common good of the Church or state. In other cases we must take into account the connection and the benefit received; and here again no general rule can be laid down.

[1] *Ethics*, IX, 2 (1164[b]27).

Reply Obj. 4. Parents are like superiors, and so a parent's love tends to conferring benefits, while the children's love tends to honour their parents. Nevertheless in a case of extreme urgency it would be lawful to abandon one's children rather than one's parents, to abandon whom it is by no means lawful, on account of the obligation we lie under towards them for the benefits we have received from them, as the Philosopher states.[2]

ARTICLE 4. *Whether Beneficence Is a Special Virtue?*

We proceed thus to the Fourth Article: It seems that beneficence is a special virtue.

Objection 1. For precepts are directed to virtue, since "lawgivers purpose to make men virtuous."[3] Now beneficence and love are prescribed as distinct from one another, for it is written (Matt. 5. 44): *Love your enemies, do good to them that hate you*. Therefore beneficence is a virtue distinct from charity.

Obj. 2. Further, Vices are opposed to virtues. Now there are opposed to beneficence particular vices by which a hurt is inflicted on our neighbour, for instance, rapine, theft and so forth. Therefore beneficence is a special virtue.

Obj. 3. Further, Charity is not divided into many species. But there would seem to be many kinds of beneficence, according to the various kinds of benefits. Therefore beneficence is a distinct virtue from charity.

On the contrary, The internal and the external act do not require different virtues. Now beneficence and goodwill differ only as external and internal act, since beneficence is the execution of goodwill. Therefore as goodwill is not a distinct virtue from charity, so neither is beneficence.

I answer that, Virtues differ according to the different aspects of their objects. Now the formal aspect of the object of charity and of beneficence is the same, since both virtues look to the common aspect of good, as explained above (A. 1). Therefore beneficence is not a distinct virtue from charity, but denotes an act of charity.

Reply Obj. 1. Precepts are given, not about habits but about acts of virtue. Therefore distinction of precept denotes distinction, not of habits, but of acts.

Reply Obj. 2. Even as all benefits conferred on our neighbour, if we consider them under the common aspect of good, are to be traced

[2] *Ibid.*, VIII, 14 (1163[b]18).
[3] Aristotle, *Ethics*, II, 1 (1103[b]3); cf. I, 13 (1102[a]9).

to love, so all hurts, considered under the common aspect of evil, are to be traced to hatred. But if we consider these same things under certain special aspects of good or of evil, they are to be traced to certain special virtues or vices, and in this way also there are various kinds of benefits.

Hence the *Reply to the Third Objection* is evident.

QUESTION XXXII
OF ALMSDEEDS
(*In Ten Articles*)

WE must now consider almsdeeds, under which head there are ten points of inquiry: (1) Whether almsgiving is an act of charity? (2) Of the different kinds of alms. (3) Which alms are of greater account, spiritual or corporal? (4) Whether corporal alms have a spiritual effect? (5) Whether the giving of alms is a matter of precept? (6) Whether corporal alms should be given out of the things we need? (7) Whether corporal alms should be given out of ill-gotten goods? (8) Who can give alms? (9) To whom should we give alms? (10) How should alms be given?

ARTICLE I. *Whether Almsgiving Is an Act of Charity?*

We proceed thus to the First Article: It seems that almsgiving is not an act of charity.

Objection 1. For without charity one cannot do acts of charity. Now it is possible to give alms without having charity, according to I Cor. 13. 3: *If I should distribute all my goods to feed the poor . . . and have not charity, it profiteth me nothing.* Therefore almsgiving is not an act of charity.

Obj. 2. Further, Almsdeeds are counted among works of satisfaction, according to Dan. 4. 24: *Redeem thou thy sins with alms.* Now satisfaction is an act of justice. Therefore almsgiving is an act of justice and not of charity.

Obj. 3. Further, The offering of sacrifices to God is an act of worship. But almsgiving is offering a sacrifice to God, according to Heb. 13. 16: *Do not forget to do good and to impart, for by such sacrifices God's favour is obtained.* Therefore almsgiving is not an act of charity, but of worship.

Obj. 4. Further, The Philosopher says[1] that to give for a good purpose is an act of liberality. Now this is especially true of almsgiving. Therefore almsgiving is not an act of charity.

[1] *Ethics,* IV, I (1120[a]24).

On the contrary, It is written (I John 3. 17): *He that hath the substance of this world, and shall see his brother in need, and shall put up his bowels from him, how doth the charity of God abide in him?*

I answer that, External acts belong to that virtue to which the motive for doing those acts pertains. Now the motive for giving alms is to relieve one who is in need. Therefore some have defined alms as being "a deed whereby something is given to the needy, out of compassion and for God's sake,"[2] which motive belongs to mercy, as stated above (Q. XXX, A. 4). Hence it is clear that almsgiving is, properly speaking, an act of mercy. This appears in its very name, for in Greek (ἐλεημοσύνη) it is derived from having mercy (ἐλεειν) even as the Latin *miseratio* is. And since mercy is an effect of charity, as shown above (Q. XXX, A. 2; A. 3, obj. 3), it follows that almsgiving is an act of charity through the medium of mercy.

Reply Obj. 1. An act of virtue may be taken in two ways. First materially, and thus an act of justice is to do what is just; and such an act of virtue can be without the virtue, since many, without having the habit of justice, do what is just, led by the natural light of reason, or through fear, or in the hope of gain. Secondly, we speak of a thing being an act of justice formally, and thus an act of justice is to do what is just, in the same way as a just man, that is, with readiness and delight, and such an act of virtue cannot be without the virtue. Accordingly almsgiving can be materially without charity, but to give alms formally, that is, for God's sake, with delight and readiness, and altogether as one ought, is not possible without charity.

Reply Obj. 2. Nothing hinders the proper elicited act of one virtue being attributed to another virtue as commanding it and directing it to this other virtue's end. It is in this way that almsgiving is placed among works of satisfaction in so far as pity for the one in distress is directed to the satisfaction for his sin. And in so far as it is directed to placate God, it has the character of a sacrifice, and thus it is commanded by worship.

Hence the *Reply to the Third Objection* is evident.

Reply Obj. 4. Almsgiving pertains to liberality in so far as liberality removes an obstacle

[2] Albert, *In Sent.,* IV, d. XV, A. 15 (BO XXIX, 492); Alexander of Hales, *Summa Theol.,* IV, Q. CV, m. 1, A. 2 (IV, 406vb). Cf. Bonaventure, *In Sent.,* IV, d. 15, Pt. II, A. 1, Q. 4 (QR IV, 368). Cf. also William of Auxerre, *Summa Aurea,* Pt. III, tr. 7, chap. 7, Q. 1 (162rb).

to that act, which might arise from excessive love of riches, the result of which is that one clings to them more than one ought.

ARTICLE 2. *Whether the Different Kinds of Almsdeeds Are Suitably Enumerated?*

We proceed then to the Second Article: It seems that the different kinds of almsdeeds are unsuitably enumerated.

Objection 1. For we count seven corporal almsdeeds, namely, to feed the hungry, to give drink to the thirsty, to clothe the naked, to harbour the harbourless, to visit the sick, to ransom the captive, to bury the dead; all of which are expressed in the following verse:

"To visit, to quench or to feed, to ransom, clothe, harbour or bury."[1]

Again we count also seven spiritual alms, namely, to instruct the ignorant, to counsel the doubtful, to comfort the sorrowful, to reprove the sinner, to forgive injuries, to bear with those who trouble and annoy us, and to pray for all, which are all contained in the following verse:

"To counsel, reprove or console, to pardon, forbear, or to pray."[2] Yet so that counsel includes both advice and instruction.

And it seems that these various almsdeeds are unsuitably enumerated. For the purpose of almsdeeds is to succour our neighbour. But a dead man profits nothing by being buried; otherwise Our Lord would not have spoken truly when He said (Matt. 10. 28):[3] *Be not afraid of them who kill the body, and after that have no more that they can do.* This explains why Our Lord, in enumerating the works of mercy, made no mention of the burial of the dead (Matt. 25. 35, 36). Therefore it seems that these almsdeeds are unsuitably enumerated.

Obj. 2. Further, As stated above (A. 1), the purpose of giving alms is to relieve our neighbour's need. Now there are many needs of human life other than those mentioned above, for instance, a blind man needs a leader, a lame man needs someone to lean on, a poor man needs riches. Therefore these almsdeeds are unsuitably enumerated.

Obj. 3. Further, Almsgiving is a work of mercy. But the reproof of the wrong-doer pertains, apparently, to severity rather than to

mercy. Therefore it ought not to be counted among the spiritual almsdeeds.

Obj. 4. Further, Almsgiving is intended for the supply of a defect. But no man is without the defect of ignorance in some matter or other. Therefore, apparently, each one ought to instruct anyone who is ignorant of what he knows himself.

On the contrary, Gregory says (*Hom. in Ev.* ix):[4] "Let him that hath understanding beware lest he withhold his knowledge; let him that hath abundance of wealth, watch lest he slacken his merciful bounty; let him who is a servant to art be most solicitous to share his skill and profit with his neighbour; let him who has an opportunity of speaking with the wealthy, fear lest he be condemned for retaining his talent, if when he has the chance he plead not with him the cause of the poor." Therefore the above mentioned almsdeeds are suitably enumerated in respect of those things of which men have abundance or insufficiency.

I answer that, The above mentioned distinction of almsdeeds is suitably taken from the various needs of our neighbour, some of which affect the soul, and are relieved by spiritual almsdeeds, while others affect the body, and are relieved by corporal almsdeeds. For corporal need occurs either during this life or afterwards. If it occurs during this life, it is either a common need in respect of things needed by all, or it is a special need occurring through some accident supervening. In the first case, the need is either internal or external. Internal need is twofold: one which is relieved by solid food, namely hunger, in respect of which we have to feed the hungry; while the other is relieved by liquid food, namely thirst, and in respect of this we have to give drink to the thirsty. The common need with regard to external help is twofold: one in respect of clothing, and as to this we have to clothe the naked; while the other is in respect of a dwelling place, and as to this we have to harbour the harbourless. Again if the need be special, it is either the result of an internal cause, like sickness, and then we have to visit the sick, or it results from an external cause, and then we have to ransom the captive. After this life we give burial to the dead.

In like manner spiritual needs are relieved by spiritual acts in two ways: first by asking for help from God, and in this respect we have prayer, by which one man prays for others; secondly, by giving human assistance, and this in

---

[1] Quoted also by Albert, *In Sent.,* IV, d. 15, A. 23 (BO XXIX, 505); Alexander of Hales, *Summa Theol.,* IV, Q. CV, m. 1, A. 2 (IV, 407vb); Bonaventure, *In Sent.,* IV, d. 15, Pt. II, dub. 2 (QR IV, 376).

[2] See note 1.

[3] The quotation is from Luke 12.4.

[4] PL 76, 1109.

three ways. First, in order to relieve a deficiency on the part of the intellect, and if this deficiency be in the speculative intellect, the remedy is applied by instructing, and if in the practical intellect, the remedy is applied by counselling. Secondly, there may be a deficiency on the part of the appetitive power, especially by way of sorrow, which is remedied by comforting. Thirdly, the deficiency may be due to a disordered act, and this may be the subject of a threefold consideration. First, in respect of the sinner, since sin proceeds from his disordered will, and thus the remedy takes the form of reproof. Secondly, in respect of the person sinned against; and if the sin be committed against ourselves, we apply the remedy by pardoning the injury, while, if it be committed against God or our neighbour, "it is not in our choice to pardon," as Jerome observes (*Super Matt.* 18, 15).[1] Thirdly, in respect of the result of the disordered act, on account of which the sinner is an annoyance to those who live with him, even apart from the sinner's intention, in which case the remedy is applied by bearing with him, especially with regard to those who sin out of weakness, according to Rom. 15. 1: *We that are stronger, ought to bear the infirmities of the weak*, and not only as regards their being infirm and consequently troublesome on account of their unruly actions, but also by bearing any other burdens of theirs with them, according to Gal. 6. 2: *Bear ye one another's burdens*.

Reply Obj. 1. Burial does not profit a dead man as though his body could be capable of perception after death. In this sense Our Lord said that those who kill the body *have no more that they can do;* and for this reason He did not mention the burial of the dead with the other works of mercy, but those only which are more clearly necessary. Nevertheless it does concern the deceased what is done with his body, both that he may live in the memory of man whose respect he forfeits if he remain without burial, and as regards a man's fondness for his own body while he was yet living, a fondness which kindly persons should imitate after his death. It is thus that some are praised for burying the dead, as Tobias, and those who buried Our Lord, as Augustine says (*De Cura pro Mort.* iii).[2]

Reply Obj. 2. All other needs are reduced to these, for blindness and lameness are kinds of sickness, so that to lead the blind, and to support the lame, come to the same as visiting the

sick. In like manner to assist a man against any distress that is due to an extrinsic cause comes to the same as the ransom of captives. And the wealth with which we relieve the poor is sought merely for the purpose of relieving those needs; hence there was no reason for special mention of this particular need.

Reply Obj. 3. The reproof of the sinner, as to the exercise of the act of reproving, seems to imply the severity of justice, but, as to the intention of the reprover, who wishes to free a man from the evil of sin, it is an act of mercy and lovingkindness, according to Prov. 27. 6: *Better are the wounds of a friend, than the deceitful kisses of an enemy.*

Reply Obj. 4. Nescience is not always a defect, but only when it is about what one ought to know, and it is a part of almsgiving to supply this defect by instruction. In doing this however we should observe the due circumstances of persons, place and time, even as in other virtuous acts.

ARTICLE 3. *Whether Corporal Alms Are of More Account Than Spiritual Alms?*

We proceed thus to the Third Article: It seems that corporal alms are of more account than spiritual alms.

Objection 1. For it is more praiseworthy to give an alms to one who is in greater want, since an almsdeed is to be praised because it relieves one who is in need. Now the body which is relieved by corporal alms, is by nature more needy than the spirit which is relieved by spiritual alms. Therefore corporal alms are of more account.

Obj. 2. Further, an alms is less praiseworthy and meritorious if the kindness is compensated, and so Our Lord says (Luke 14. 12): *When thou makest a dinner or a supper, call not thy neighbours who are rich, lest perhaps they also invite thee again.* Now there is always compensation in spiritual almsdeeds, since he who prays for another, profits thereby, according to Ps. 35. 13: *My prayer shall be turned into my bosom;* and he who teaches another, makes progress himself in knowledge, which cannot be said of corporal almsdeeds. Therefore corporal almsdeeds are of more account than spiritual almsdeeds.

Obj. 3. Further, an alms is to be commended if the needy one is comforted by it; hence it is written (Job 31. 20): *If his sides have not blessed me,* and the Apostle says to Philemon (*verse* 7): *The bowels of the saints have been refreshed by thee, brother.* Now a corporal alms

---

[1] PL 26, 136.   [2] PL 40, 595.

is sometimes more welcome to a needy man than a spiritual alms. Therefore bodily almsdeeds are of more account than spiritual almsdeeds.

On the contrary, Augustine says (*De Serm. Dom. in Monte,* i, 20)[1] on the words, *Give to him that asketh of thee* (Matt. 5. 42): "You should give so as to injure neither yourself nor another, and when you refuse what another asks, you must not lose sight of the claims of justice, and send him away empty; at times indeed you will give what is better than what is asked for, if you reprove him that asks unjustly." Now reproof is a spiritual alms. Therefore spiritual almsdeeds are preferable to corporal almsdeeds.

I answer that, There are two ways of comparing these almsdeeds. First, speaking absolutely, and in this respect, spiritual almsdeeds hold the first place, for three reasons. First, because the offering is more excellent, since it is a spiritual gift, which surpasses a corporal gift, according to Prov. 4. 2: *I will give you a good gift, forsake not My Law.* Secondly, on account of what is succoured, because the spirit is more excellent than the body, and so, even as a man in looking after himself, ought to look to his soul more than to his body, so ought he in looking after his neighbour, whom he ought to love as himself. Thirdly, as regards the acts themselves by which our neighbour is succoured, because spiritual acts are more excellent than corporal acts, which are, in a fashion, servile.

Secondly, we may compare them with regard to some particular case, when some corporal alms excels some spiritual alms; for instance, a man in hunger is to be fed rather than instructed, and as the Philosopher observes,[2] for a needy man money is better than philosophy, although the latter is better absolutely.

Reply Obj. 1. It is better to give to one who is in greater want, other things being equal, but if he who is less needy is better, and is in want of better things, it is better to give to him; and it is thus in the case in point.

Reply Obj. 2. Compensation does not detract from the merit and praise of almsgiving if it be not intended, even as human glory, if not intended, does not detract from virtue. Thus Sallust says of Cato (*Catilin.*)[3] that "the less he sought fame, the more he became famous"; and thus it is with spiritual almsdeeds. Nevertheless the intention of gaining spiritual goods

does not detract from merit, as the intention of gaining corporal goods.

Reply Obj. 3. The merit of an almsgiver depends on that in which the will of the recipient should rest reasonably, and not on that in which it rests when it is disordered.

ARTICLE 4. *Whether Corporal Almsdeeds Have a Spiritual Effect?*

We proceed thus to the Fourth Article: It seems that corporal almsdeeds have not a spiritual effect.

Object 1. For no effect exceeds its cause. But spiritual goods exceed corporal goods. Therefore corporal almsdeeds have no spiritual effect.

Obj. 2. Further, the sin of simony consists in giving the corporal for the spiritual, and it is to be utterly avoided. Therefore one ought not to give alms in order to receive a spiritual effect.

Obj. 3. Further, to multiply the cause is to multiply the effect. If therefore corporal almsdeeds cause a spiritual effect, the greater the alms, the greater the spiritual profit, which is contrary to what we read (Luke 21.) of the widow who cast two brass mites into the treasury, and in Our Lord's own words *cast in more than . . . all.* Therefore bodily almsdeeds have no spiritual effect.

On the contrary, It is written (Ecclus. 17. 18): *The alms of a man . . . shall preserve the grace of a man as the apple of the eye.*

I answer that, Corporal almsdeeds may be considered in three ways. First, with regard to their substance, and in this way they have merely a corporal effect, in so far, namely, as they supply our neighbour's corporal needs. Secondly, they may be considered with regard to their cause, in so far as a man gives a corporal alms out of love for God and his neighbour, and in this respect, they bring forth a spiritual fruit, according to Ecclus. 29. 13, 14: *Lose thy money for thy brother . . . place thy treasure in the commandments of the Most High, and it shall bring thee more profit than gold.*

Thirdly, with regard to the effect, and in this way again, they have a spiritual fruit, in so far as our neighbour, who is succoured by a corporal alms, is moved to pray for his benefactor; hence the above text goes on (*verse* 15): *Shut up alms in the heart of the poor, and it shall obtain help for thee from all evil.*

Reply Obj. 1. This argument considers corporal almsdeeds as to their substance.

Reply Obj. 2. He who gives an alms does not intend to buy a spiritual thing with a corporal

[1] PL 34, 1264.
[2] *Topics,* III, 2 (118ª10).   [3] Chap. 54 (DD 58).

thing, for he knows that spiritual things infinitely surpass corporal things, but he intends to merit a spiritual fruit through the love of charity.

Reply Obj. 3. The widow who gave less in quantity gave more in proportion; and thus we gather that the fervour of her charity, from which corporal almsdeeds derive their spiritual efficacy, was greater.

ARTICLE 5. *Whether Almsgiving Is a Matter of Precept?*

We proceed thus to the Fifth Article: It would seem that almsgiving is not a matter of precept.

Objection 1. For the counsels are distinct from the precepts. Now almsgiving is a matter of counsel, according to Dan. 4. 24: *Let my counsel be acceptable to the King;* (Vulg.,— *to thee, and*) *redeem thou thy sins with alms.* Therefore almsgiving is not a matter of precept.

Obj. 2. Further, it is lawful for everyone to use and to keep what is his own. Yet by keeping it he will not give alms. Therefore it is lawful not to give alms, and consequently almsgiving is not a matter of precept.

Obj. 3. Further, whatever is a matter of precept binds the transgressor at some time or other under pain of mortal sin, because positive precepts are binding for some fixed time. Therefore, if almsgiving were a matter of precept, it would be possible to point to some fixed time when a man would commit a mortal sin unless he gave an alms. But it does not appear how this can be so, because it can always be deemed probable that the person in need can be relieved in some other way, and that what we would spend in almsgiving might be needful to ourselves either now or in some future time. Therefore it seems that almsgiving is not a matter of precept.

Obj. 4. Further, Every commandment is reducible to the precepts of the Decalogue. But these precepts contain no reference to almsgiving. Therefore almsgiving is not a matter of precept.

On the contrary, No man is punished eternally for omitting to do what is not a matter of precept. But some are punished eternally for omitting to give alms, as is clear from Matt. 25. 41-43. Therefore almsgiving is a matter of precept.

I answer that, As love of our neighbour is a matter of precept, whatever is a necessary condition to the love of our neighbour is a matter

of precept also. Now the love of our neighbour requires that not only should we be our neighbour's well-wishers, but also his well-doers, according to I John 3. 18: *Let us not love in word, nor in tongue, but in deed, and in truth.* And in order to be a person's well-wisher and welldoer, we ought to succour his needs: this is done by almsgiving. Therefore almsgiving is a matter of precept.

Since, however, precepts are about acts of virtue, it follows that all almsgiving must be a matter of precept in so far as it is necessary to virtue, namely, in so far as it is demanded by right reason. Now right reason demands that we should take into consideration something on the part of the giver, and something on the part of the recipient. On the part of the giver, it must be noted that he should give of his surplus, according to Luke 11. 41: *That which remaineth, give alms.* This surplus is to be taken in reference not only to himself, so as to denote what is unnecessary to the individual, but also in reference to those of whom he has charge, because each one must first of all look after himself and then after those over whom he has charge, and afterwards with what remains relieve the needs of others (in respect of these things we have the expression necessary to the person taking the word person as expressive of dignity). Thus nature first, by its nutritive power, takes what it requires for the upkeep of one's own body, and afterwards yields the residue for the formation of another by the power of generation.

On the part of the recipient it is requisite that he should be in need, for otherwise there would be no reason for giving him alms; yet since it is not possible for one individual to relieve the needs of all, we are not bound to relieve all who are in need, but only those who could not be succoured if we did not succour them. For in such cases the words of Ambrose apply, "Feed him that dies of hunger; if thou hast not fed him, thou hast slain him."[1]

Accordingly we are bound to give alms of our surplus, as also to give alms to one whose need is extreme; otherwise almsgiving, like any other greater good, is a matter of counsel.

Reply Obj. 1. Daniel spoke to a king who was not subject to God's Law, and therefore such things as were prescribed by the Law which he did not profess, had to be counselled to him. Or he may have been speaking in ref-

[1] *Sermones,* serm. LXXXI or LXIV (III, 377). Cf. PL 17, 613, 614. Cf. also Gratian, *Decretum,* I, d. 86, can. 21, *Pasce* (RF II, 302).

erence to a case in which almsgiving was not a matter of precept.

Reply Obj. 2. The temporal goods which God grants us are ours as to the ownership, but as to the use of them, they belong not to us alone but also to such others as we are able to succour out of what we have over and above our needs. Hence Basil says:[1] "If you acknowledge them," namely, your temporal goods, "as coming from God, is He unjust because He apportions them unequally? Why are you rich while another is poor, unless it be that you may have the merit of a good stewardship, and he the reward of patience? It is the hungry man's bread that you withhold, the naked man's cloak that you have stored away, the shoe of the barefoot that you have left to rot, the money of the needy that you have buried underground: and so you injure as many as you might help." Ambrose expresses himself in the same way,[2] as he is quoted in the Decretals.[3]

Reply Obj. 3. There is a time when we sin mortally if we omit to give alms; on the part of the recipient when we see that his need is evident and urgent, and that he is not likely to be succoured otherwise—on the part of the giver, when he has superfluous goods, which he does not need for the time being, as far as he can judge with probability. Nor need he consider every case that may possibly occur in the future, for this would be to think about the morrow, which Our Lord forbade us to do (Matt. 6. 34), but he should judge what is superfluous and what necessary, according as things probably and generally occur.

Reply Obj. 4. All succour given to our neighbour is reduced to the precept about honouring our parents. For thus does the Apostle interpret it (I Tim. 4. 8) where he says: *Dutifulness*[4] (Douay,—*Godliness*) *is profitable to all things, having promise of the life that now is, and of that which is to come,* and he says this because the precept about honouring our parents contains the promise, *that thou mayest be longlived upon the land* (Exod. 20. 12); and dutifulness comprises all kinds of almsgiving.

ARTICLE 6. *Whether One Ought To Give Alms Out of What One Needs?*

We proceed thus to the Sixth Article: It would seem that one ought not to give alms out of what one needs.

Objection 1. For the order of charity should

be observed not only as regards the effect of our benefactions but also as regards our interior affections. Now it is a sin to invert the order of charity, because this order is a matter of precept. Since, then, the order of charity requires that a man should love himself more than his neighbour, it seems that he would sin if he deprived himself of what he needed, in order to succour his neighbour.

Obj. 2. Further, Whoever gives away what he needs himself, squanders his own substance, and that is to be a prodigal, according to the Philosopher.[5] But no vicious deed should be done. Therefore we should not give alms out of what we need.

Obj. 3. Further, The Apostle says (I Tim. 5. 8): *If any man have not care of his own, and especially of those of his house, he hath denied the faith, and is worse than an infidel.* Now if a man gives of what he needs for himself or for his charge, he seems to detract from the care he should have for himself or his charge. Therefore it seems that whoever gives alms from what he needs, sins gravely.

On the contrary, Our Lord said (Matt. 19. 21):*If thou wilt be perfect, go, sell what thou hast, and give to the poor.* Now he that gives all he has to the poor, gives not only what he needs not, but also what he needs. Therefore a man may give alms out of what he needs.

I answer that, A thing is necessary in two ways: first, because without it something is impossible, and it is altogether wrong to give alms out of what is necessary to us in this sense; for instance, if a man found himself in the presence of a case of urgency, and had merely sufficient to support himself and his children, or others under his charge, he would be throwing away his life and that of others if he were to give away in alms what was then necessary to him. Yet I say this without prejudice to such a case as might happen, supposing that by depriving himself of necessaries a man might help a great personage, and a support of the Church or State, since it would be a praiseworthy act to endanger one's life and the lives of those who are under our charge for the delivery of such a person, since the common good is to be preferred to one's own.

Secondly, a thing is said to be necessary, if a man cannot without it live in keeping with the condition or state either of his own person or the persons of whom he has charge. The "necessary" considered thus is not an invariable quantity, for one might add much more to

---

[1] *Hom super Luc.* 12.18 (PG 31, 275).
[2] *Ibid.* Cf. Basil, hom. III, *In Luc.* 12.16 (PG 31, 1752).
[3] Gratian, *Decretum,* pt. i. d. XLVII, can. 8, *Sicut* II (RF I, 171).   [4] *Pietas,* from which comes our English word *Pity.*
[5] *Ethics,* IV, I (1121ª17).

a man's property, and yet not go beyond what he needs in this way, or one might take much from him, and he would still have sufficient for the decencies of life in keeping with his own position. Accordingly it is good to give alms of this kind of "necessary"; and it is a matter not of precept but of counsel. Yet it would be inordinate to deprive oneself of one's own in order to give to others to such an extent that the remainder would be insufficient for one to live in keeping with one's station and the ordinary occurrences of life; for no man ought to live unbecomingly.

There are, however, three exceptions to the above rule. The first is when a man changes his state of life, for instance, by entering religion, for then he gives away all his possessions for Christ's sake, and performs the work of perfection by transferring himself to another state. Secondly, when that which he deprives himself of, though it be required for the decencies of life, can nevertheless easily be recovered, so that he does not suffer extreme inconvenience. Thirdly, when he is in presence of extreme indigence in a private person, or great need on the part of the common weal. For in such cases it would seem praiseworthy to forego the requirement of one's station, in order to provide for a greater need.

The objections may be easily solved from what has been said.

ARTICLE 7. *Whether One May Give Alms Out of Ill-Gotten Goods?*

We proceed thus to the Seventh Article: It seems that one may give alms out of ill-gotten goods.

Objection 1. For it is written (Luke 16. 9): *Make unto you friends of the mammon of iniquity.* Now mammon signifies riches. Therefore it is lawful to make spiritual friends for oneself by giving alms out of ill-gotten riches.

Obj. 2. Further, All filthy lucre seems to be ill-gotten. But the profits from whoredom are filthy lucre; therefore it was forbidden (Luke 23. 18) to offer therefrom sacrifices or oblations to God: *Thou shalt not offer the hire of a strumpet . . . in the house of . . . thy God.* In like manner gains from games of chance are ill-gotten, for, as the Philosopher says,[1] "we take such gains from our friends to whom we ought rather to give." And most of all are the profits from simony ill-gotten, since thereby the Holy Ghost is wronged. Nevertheless out of such gains it is lawful to give alms. There-

fore one may give alms out of ill-gotten goods.

Obj. 3. Further, Greater evils should be avoided more than lesser evils. Now it is less sinful to keep back another's property than to commit murder of which a man is guilty if he fails to succour one who is in extreme need, as appears from the words of Ambrose who says (*loc. cit.* A. 5): "Feed him that dies of hunger, if thou hast not fed him, thou hast slain him." Therefore, in certain cases, it is lawful to give alms of ill-gotten goods.

On the contrary, Augustine says (*Serm.* CXIII, 2):[2] "Give alms from your just labours. For you will not bribe Christ your judge, not to hear you with the poor whom you rob . . . . Give not alms from interest and usury: I speak to the faithful to whom we dispense the Body of Christ."

I answer that, A thing may be ill-gotten in three ways. In the first place a thing is ill-gotten if it be due to the person from whom it is gotten, and may not be kept by the person who has obained possession of it; as in the case of rapine, theft and usury, and of such things a man may not give alms since he is bound to restore them.

Secondly, a thing is ill-gotten, when he that has it may not keep it and yet he may not return it to the person from whom he received it, because he received it unjustly, while the latter gave it unjustly. This happens in simony, where both giver and receiver act against the justice of the Divine Law, so that restitution is to be made not to the giver, but by giving alms. The same applies to all similar cases of illegal giving and receiving.

Thirdly, a thing is ill-gotten not because the taking was unlawful, but because it is the outcome of something unlawful, as in the case of a woman's profits from whoredom. This is filthy lucre properly so called, because the practice of whoredom is filthy and against the Law of God, yet the woman does not act unjustly or unlawfully in taking money. Consequently it is lawful to keep and to give in alms what is thus acquired by an unlawful action.

Reply Obj. 1. As Augustine says,[3] "Some have misunderstood this saying of Our Lord, so as to take another's property and give thereof to the poor, thinking that they are fulfilling the commandment by so doing. This interpretation must be amended." Yet "all riches are called riches of iniquity," as stated in *De Quœst. Ev.* ii.,[4] because "riches are not unjust

---

[1] *Ethics*, IV, I (1122ª10).

[2] PL 38, 649.   [3] (PL 38, 648).
[4] Q. XXXIV (PL 35, 1349).

save for those who are themselves unjust, and put all their trust in them." Or, according to Ambrose in his commentary on Luke 16. 9, "*Make unto yourselves friends*, etc., He calls mammon unjust, because it draws our affections by the various allurements of wealth[1]— Or, because "among the many ancestors whose property you inherit, there is one who took the property of others unjustly, although you know nothing about it," as Basil says in a homily.[2]— Or, all riches are styled riches of iniquity, that is, of inequality, because they are not distributed equally among all, one being in need, and another in affluence.

Reply Obj. 2. We have already explained how alms may be given out of the profits of whoredom. Yet sacrifices and oblations were not made from these at the altar, both on account of the scandal, and through reverence for sacred things. It is also lawful to give alms out of the profits of simony, because they are not due to him who paid, but rather he deserves to lose them. But as to the profits from games of chance, there would seem to be something unlawful as being contrary to the Divine Law, when a man wins from one who cannot alienate his property, such as minors, lunatics and so forth, or when a man, with the desire of making money out of another man, entices him to play, and wins from him by cheating. In these cases he is bound to restitution, and consequently cannot give away his gains in alms. Then again there would seem to be something unlawful as being against the positive civil law, which altogether forbids any such profits.[3] Since, however, a civil law does not bind all, but only those who are subject to that law, and moreover may be abrogated through desuetude, it follows that all such as are bound by these laws are bound to make restitution of such gains, unless perhaps the contrary custom prevail, or unless a man win from one who enticed him to play, in which case he is not bound to restitution, because the loser does not deserve to be paid back; and yet he cannot lawfully keep what he has won, so long as that positive law is in force, and so in this case he ought to give it away in alms.

Reply Obj. 3. All things are common property in a case of extreme necessity. Hence one who is in such dire straits may take another's goods in order to succour himself, if he can find no one who is willing to give him something. For the same reason a man may retain what belongs to another, and give alms of them; or even take something if there be no other way of succouring the one who is in need. If however this be possible without danger, he must ask the owner's consent, and then succour the poor man who is in extreme necessity.

ARTICLE 8. *Whether One Who Is Under Another's Power Can Give Alms?*

We proceed thus to the Eighth Article: It would seem that one who is under another's power can give alms.

Objection 1. For religious are under the power of their prelates to whom they have vowed obedience. Now if it were unlawful for them to give alms, they would lose by entering the state of religion, for as Ambrose says[4] on I Tim. 4. 8: *Dutifulness* (Douay—*Godliness*) *is profitable to all things:* "The sum total of the Christian religion consists in dutiful conduct," and the most creditable form of this is to give alms. Therefore those who are in another's power can give alms.

Obj. 2. Further, A wife is under her husband's power (Gen. 3. 16). But a wife can give alms since she is her husband's partner; hence it is related of the Blessed Lucy that she gave alms without the knowledge of her betrothed.[5] Therefore a person is not prevented from giving alms, by being under another's power.

Obj. 3. Further, The subjection of children to their parents is founded on nature, and so the Apostle says (Eph. 6. 1): *Children, obey your parents in the Lord.* But, apparently, children may give alms out of their parents' property. For it is in a way their own, since they are the heirs; therefore, since they can employ it for some bodily use it seems that much more can they use it in giving alms so as to profit their souls. Therefore those who are under another's power can give alms.

Obj. 4. Further, Servants are under their master's power, according to Tit. 2. 9: *Exhort servants to be obedient to their masters.* Now they may lawfully do anything that will profit their masters, and this would be especially the case if they gave alms for them. Therefore those who are under another's power can give alms.

On the contrary, Alms should not be given out of another's property, "but each one should

---

[1] PL 15, 1854.

[2] Cf. Simeonem Logothetam, serm VI, among the works of St. Basil (PG 32, 1190), cf. Thomas, *Cat. Aurea, In Luc.*, chap. 16, 2.

[3] Codex, III, tit. XLIII *De aleatoribus* (KR II, 147ᵇ).

[4] Cf. Ambrosiaster, *In I Tim.* 4.8 (PL 17, 500).

[5] Mombritius, *Sanctuarium, Passio S. Luciae* (II, 107.53).

give alms out of the just profit of his own labour," as Augustine says (*De Verb. Dom.*).[1] Now if those who are subject to anyone were to give alms, this would be out of another's property. Therefore those who are under another's power cannot give alms.

I answer that, Anyone who is under another's power must, as such, be ruled in accordance with the power of his superior; for the natural order demands that the inferior should be ruled according to its superior. Therefore in those matters in which the inferior is subject to his superior, his ministrations must be subject to the superior's permission. Accordingly he that is under another's power must not give alms of anything in respect of which he is subject to that other, except in so far as he has been commissioned by his superior. But if he has something in respect of which he is not under the power of his superior, he is no longer subject to another in its regard, being independent in respect of that particular thing, and he can give alms from it.

Reply Obj. 1. If a monk be dispensed through being commissioned by his superior, he can give alms from the property of his monastery, in accordance with the terms of his commission; but if he has no such dispensation, since he has nothing of his own, he cannot give alms without his abbot's permission either express or presumed for some probable reason, except in a case of extreme necessity, when it would be lawful for him to commit a theft in order to give an alms. Nor does it follow that he is worse off than before, because, as stated in *De Eccles. Dogm.* (lxxi),[2] "it is a good thing to give one's property to the poor little by little, but it is better still to give all at once in order to follow Christ, and being freed from care, to be needy with Christ."

Reply Obj. 2. A wife, who has other property besides her dowry which is for the support of the burdens of marriage, whether that property be gained by her own industry or by any other lawful means, can give alms out of that property without asking her husband's permission; yet such alms should be moderate, lest through giving too much she impoverish her husband. Otherwise she ought not to give alms without the express or presumed consent of her husband, except in cases of necessity, as stated, in the case of a monk, in the preceding Reply. For though the wife be her husband's equal in the marriage act, yet in matters of

housekeeping, the head of the woman is the man, as the Apostle says (I Cor. 11. 3). As regards Blessed Lucy, she had a betrothed, not a husband, and so she could give alms with her mother's consent.

Reply Obj. 3. What belongs to the children belongs also to the father. Therefore the child cannot give alms, except in such small quantity that one may presume the father to be willing, unless, as might happen, the father authorize his child to dispose of any particular property. The same applies to servants. Hence the *Reply to the Fourth Objection* is clear.

ARTICLE 9. *Whether One Ought To Give Alms to Those Rather Who Are More Closely United to Us?*

We proceed thus to the Ninth Article: It seems that one ought not to give alms to those rather who are more closely united to us.

Objection 1. For it is written (Ecclus. 12. 4, 6): *Give to the merciful and uphold not the sinner . . . Do good to the humble and give not to the ungodly.* Now it happens sometimes that those who are closely united to us are sinful and undutiful. Therefore we ought not to give alms to them in preference to others.

Obj. 2. Further, Alms should be given that we may receive an eternal reward in return, according to Matt. 6. 18: *And thy Father Who seeth in secret, will repay thee.* Now the eternal reward is gained chiefly by the alms which are given to the saints, according to Luke 16. 9: *Make unto you friends of the mammon of iniquity, that when you shall fail, they may receive you into everlasting dwellings,* which passage Augustine expounds (*De Verb. Dom.* xxxv):[3] "Who shall have everlasting dwellings unless the saints of God? And who are they that shall be received by them into their dwellings, if not those who succour them in their needs?" Therefore alms should be given to the more holy persons rather than to those who are more closely united to us.

Obj. 3. Further, Man is more closely united to himself. But a man cannot give himself an alms. Therefore it seems that we are not bound to give alms to those who are most closely united to us.

On the contrary, The Apostle says (I Tim. 5. 8): *If any man have not care of his own, and especially of those of his house, he hath denied the faith, and is worse than an infidel.*

I answer that, As Augustine says,[4] it falls to

---

[1] *Serm.,* CXIII, 2 (PL 38, 649).
[2] Gennadius (PL 58, 997).

[3] *Serm.,* CXIII, 1 (PL 38, 648).
[4] *Christian Doctrine,* I, 28 (PL 34, 30).

us by lot, as it were, to have to look to the welfare of those who are more closely united to us. Nevertheless in this matter we must employ discretion, according to the various degrees of connection, holiness and utility. For we ought to give alms to one who is much holier and in greater want, and to one who is more useful to the common good, rather than to one who is more closely united to us, especially if the latter be not very closely united, and has no special claim on our care then and there, and who is not in very urgent need.

Reply Obj. 1. We ought not to help a sinner as such, that is by encouraging him to sin, but as man, that is by supporting his nature.

Reply Obj. 2. Almsdeeds deserve on two counts to receive an eternal reward. First because they are rooted in charity, and in this respect an almsdeed is meritorious in so far as it observes the order of charity, which requires that, other things being equal, we should, in preference, help those who are more closely connected with us. Therefore Ambrose says (*De Officiis,* i, 30):[1] "It is with commendable liberality that you forget not your kindred, if you know them to be in need, for it is better that you should yourself help your own family, who would be ashamed to beg help from others." Secondly, almsdeeds deserve to be rewarded eternally through the merit of the recipient, who prays for the giver, and it is in this sense that Augustine is speaking.

Reply Obj. 3. Since almsdeeds are works of mercy, just as a man does not, properly speaking, pity himself, but only by a kind of comparison, as stated above (Q. XXX, A. 1, Reply 2), so too, properly speaking, no man gives himself an alms, unless he act in another's person; thus when a man is appointed to distribute alms, he can take something for himself, if he be in want, on the same ground as when he gives to others.

ARTICLE 10. *Whether Alms Should Be Given in Abundance?*

We proceed thus to the Tenth Article: It would seem that alms should not be given in abundance.

Objection 1. For we ought to give alms to those chiefly who are most closely connected with us. But we ought not to give to them in such a way that they are likely to become richer thereby, as Ambrose says (*De Offic.* i, 30).[2] Therefore neither should we give abundantly to others.

Obj. 2. Further, Ambrose says (*ibid.*): "We should not lavish our wealth on others all at once, we should dole it out by degrees." But to give abundantly is to give lavishly. Therefore alms should not be given in abundance.

Obj. 3. Further, The Apostle says (II Cor. 8. 13): *Not that others should be eased,* that is, should live on you without working themselves, *and you burthened,* that is, impoverished. But this would be the result if alms were given in abundance. Therefore we ought not to give alms abundantly.

On the contrary, It is written (Tob. 4. 9): *If thou have much, give abundantly.*

I answer that, Alms may be considered abundant in relation either to the giver, or to the recipient; in relation to the giver, when that which a man gives is great as compared with his means. To give thus is praiseworthy, and so Our Lord (Luke 21. 3, 4) commended the widow because *of her want, she cast in all the living that she had.* Nevertheless those conditions must be observed which were laid down when we spoke of giving alms out of one's necessary goods (A. 6).

On the part of the recipient, an alms may be abundant in two ways. First, by relieving his need sufficiently, and in this sense it is praiseworthy to give alms. Secondly, by relieving his need more than sufficiently; this is not praiseworthy, and it would be better to give to several that are in need. Hence the Apostle says (I Cor. 13. 3): *If I should distribute . . . to feed the poor,* on which words a gloss comments:[3] "Thus we are warned to be careful in giving alms, and to give, not to one only, but to many, that we may profit many."

Reply Obj. 1. This argument considers abundance of alms as exceeding the needs of the recipient.

Reply Obj. 2. The passage quoted considers abundance of alms on the part of the giver; but the sense is that God does not wish a man to lavish all his wealth at once, except when he changes his state of life, and so he goes on to say: "Except we imitate Eliseus who slew his oxen and fed the poor with what he had, so that no household cares might keep him back."

Reply Obj. 3. In the passage quoted the words, *not that others should be eased* or refreshed, refer to that abundance of alms which surpasses the need of the recipient, to whom one should give alms not that he may have an easy life, but that he may have relief. Never-

---

[1] PL 16, 72.   [2] PL 16, 72.

[3] *Glossa* Lombardi (PL 191, 1660); cf. *Glossa interl.* (VI, 54r).

theless we must bring discretion to bear on the matter, on account of the various conditions of men, some of whom are more daintily nurtured, and need finer food and clothing. Hence Ambrose says (*De Offic.* i, 30):[1] "When you give an alms to a man, you should take into consideration his age and his weakness; and sometimes the shame which proclaims his good birth; and again that perhaps he has fallen from riches to indigence through no fault of his own."

With regard to the words that follow, *and you burthened,* they refer to abundance on the part of the giver. Yet, as a gloss says on the same passage,[2] "he says this, not because it would be better to give in abundance, but because he fears for the weak, and he admonishes them so to give that they lack not for themselves."

QUESTION XXXIII
Of fraternal correction
(*In Eight Articles*)

We must now consider Fraternal Correction, under which head there are eight points of inquiry: (1) Whether fraternal correction is an act of charity? (2) Whether it is a matter of precept? (3) Whether this precept binds all, or only superiors? (4) Whether this precept binds the subject to correct his superior? (5) Whether a sinner may correct anyone? (6) Whether one ought to correct a person who becomes worse through being corrected? (7) Whether secret correction should precede denouncement? (8) Whether witnesses should be called before denouncement?

ARTICLE 1. *Whether Fraternal Correction Is an Act of Charity?*

We proceed thus to the First Article: It seems that fraternal correction is not an act of charity.

Objection 1. For a gloss on Matt. 18. 15, *If thy brother shall offend against thee,* says that a man should reprove his brother out of zeal for justice.[3] But justice is a distinct virtue from charity. Therefore fraternal correction is an act, not of charity, but of justice.

Obj. 2. Further, Fraternal correction is given by secret admonition. Now admonition is a kind of counsel, which is an act of prudence, for "a prudent man is one who is of good coun-

sel."[4] Therefore fraternal correction is an act, not of charity, but of prudence.

Obj. 3. Further, Contrary acts do not belong to the same virtue. Now it is an act of charity to bear with a sinner, according to Gal. 6. 2: *Bear ye one another's burdens and so you shall fulfil the law of Christ,* which is the law of charity. Therefore it seems that the correction of a sinning brother, which is contrary to bearing with him, is not an act of charity.

On the contrary, To correct the wrongdoer is a spiritual almsdeed. But almsdeeds are works of charity, as stated above (Q. XXXII, A. 1). Therefore fraternal correction is an act of charity.

I answer that, The correction of the wrongdoer is a remedy which should be employed against a man's sin. Now a man's sin may be considered in two ways: first as being harmful to the sinner; secondly as conducing to the harm of others, by hurting or scandalizing them, or by being detrimental to the common good, the justice of which is disturbed by that man's sin.

Consequently the correction of a wrongdoer is twofold. One applies a remedy to the sin considered as an evil of the sinner himself. This is fraternal correction properly so called, which is directed to the amendment of the sinner. Now to do away with anyone's evil is the same as to procure his good, and to procure a person's good is an act of charity, by which we wish and do our friend well. Consequently fraternal correction also is an act of charity, because thereby we drive out our brother's evil, namely sin, the removal of which pertains to charity even more than the removal of an external loss, or of a bodily injury, by so much the more as the contrary good of virtue is more akin to charity than the good of the body or of external things. Therefore fraternal correction is an act of charity rather than the healing of a bodily infirmity, or the relieving of an external bodily need.

There is another correction which applies a remedy to the sin of the wrongdoer, considered as hurtful to others, and especially to the common good. This correction is an act of justice, whose concern it is to safeguard the rectitude of justice between one man and another.

Reply Obj. 1. This gloss speaks of the second correction which is an act of justice. Or if it speaks of the first correction, then it takes justice as denoting a general virtue, as we shall state further on (Q. LVIII, A. 5), in which sense

---

[1] PL 16, 74.
[2] *Glossa* Lombardi on II Cor. 8.13 (PL 192, 58); cf. *Glossa interl.,* on II Cor. 8.13 (VI, 71V).
[3] *Glossa ordin.* (V, 56F).

[4] Aristotle, *Ethics,* VI, 5, 7, 9(1140ᵃ25; 1141ᵇ8; 1142ᵇ31).

again all *sin is iniquity* (I John 3. 4), through being contrary to justice.

Reply Obj. 2. According to the Philosopher,[1] "prudence regulates whatever is directed to the end," about which things counsel and choice are concerned. Nevertheless when, guided by prudence, we perform rightly some action which is directed to the end of some virtue, such as temperance or fortitude, that action belongs chiefly to the virtue to whose end it is directed. Since, then, the admonition which is given in fraternal correction is directed to the removal of a brother's sin, which removal pertains to charity, it is evident that this admonition is chiefly an act of charity, which virtue commands it, so to speak, but secondarily an act of prudence, which executes and directs the action.

Reply Obj. 3. Fraternal correction is not opposed to forbearance with the weak, but on the contrary it results from it. For a man bears with a sinner, in so far as he is not disturbed against him, and retains his goodwill towards him, the result being that he strives to make him do better.

ARTICLE 2. *Whether Fraternal Correction Is a Matter of Precept?*

We proceed thus to the Second Article: It would seem that fraternal correction is not a matter of precept.

Objection 1. For nothing impossible is a matter of precept, according to the saying of Jerome:[2] "Accursed be he who says that God has commanded anything impossible." Now it is written (Ecclus. 7. 14): *Consider the works of God, that no man can correct whom He hath despised.* Therefore fraternal correction is not a matter of precept.

Obj. 2. Further, All the precepts of the Divine law are reduced to the precepts of the Decalogue. But fraternal correction does not come under any precept of the Decalogue. Therefore it is not a matter of precept.

Obj. 3. Further, The omission of a Divine precept is a mortal sin, which has no place in a holy man. Yet holy and spiritual men are found to omit fraternal correction: since Augustine says:[3] "Not only those of low degree, but also those of high position, refrain from reproving others, moved by a guilty cupidity, not by the claims of charity." Therefore fraternal correction is not a matter of precept.

Obj. 4. Further, Whatever is a matter of precept is something due. If, therefore fraternal correction is a matter of precept, it is due to our brethren that we correct them when they sin. Now when a man owes anyone a corporal due, such as the payment of a sum of money, he must not be content that his creditor come to him, but he should seek him out, that he may pay him his due. Hence we should have to go seeking for those who need correction, in order that we might correct them; which appears to be unfitting, both on account of the great number of sinners, for whose correction one man could not suffice, and because religious would have to leave the cloister in order to reprove men, which would be unbecoming. Therefore fraternal correction is not a matter of precept.

On the contrary, Augustine says (*De Verb. Dom.* i):[4] "You become worse than the sinner if you fail to correct him." But this would not be so unless, by this neglect, one omitted to observe some precept. Therefore fraternal correction is a matter of precept.

I answer that, Fraternal correction is a matter of precept. We must observe, however, that while the negative precepts of the Law forbid sinful acts, the positive precepts inculcate acts of virtue. Now sinful acts are evil in themselves, and cannot become good, no matter how, or when, or where, they are done, because of themselves they are connected with an evil end, as stated in the *Ethics*,[5] therefore negative precepts bind always and for all times. On the other hand acts of virtue must not be done anyhow, but by observing the due circumstances which are required in order that an act be virtuous; namely, that it be done where, when, and how it ought to be done. And since the disposition of whatever is directed to the end depends on the character of the end, the chief of these circumstances of a virtuous act is this aspect of the end, which in this case is the good of virtue. If therefore such a circumstance be omitted from a virtuous act as entirely takes away the good of virtue, such an act is contrary to a precept. If, however, the circumstance omitted from a virtuous act be such as not to destroy the virtue altogether, though it does not perfectly attain the good of virtue, it is not against a precept. Hence the Philosopher says[6] that if we depart but little from the mean, it is not contrary to the virtue, but if we depart much from the mean, virtue is

---

[1] *Ethics*, VI, 12 (1144ᵃ8).
[2] Cf. Pelagius, *Epist.*, 1 *Ad Demetr.*, chap. 16 (PL 30, 32); *Libellus Fidei ad Innocentium* (PL 45, 1718).
[3] *City of God*, I, 9 (PL 41, 22).

[4] *Serm.*, LXXXII, 4 (PL 38, 508).
[5] Aristotle, II, 6 (1107ᵃ12).
[6] *Ethics*, II, 9 (1109ᵇ18).

destroyed in its act. Now fraternal correction is directed to a brother's amendment, so that it is a matter of precept in so far as it is necessary for that end, but not so that we have to correct our erring brother at all places and times.

Reply Obj. 1. In all good deeds man's action is not efficacious without the Divine assistance, and yet man must do what is in his power. Hence Augustine says (*De Correp. et Gratia,* xv):[1] "Since we do not know who is predestined and who is not, charity should so guide our feelings, that we wish all to be saved." Consequently we ought to do our brethren the kindness of correcting them, with the hope of God's help.

Reply Obj. 2. As stated above (Q. XXXII, A. 5, Reply 4) all the precepts about rendering service to our neighbour are reduced to the precept about the honour due to parents.

Reply Obj. 3. Fraternal correction may be omitted in three ways. First, meritoriously, when out of charity one omits to correct someone. For Augustine says:[2] "If a man refrains from chiding and reproving wrongdoers, because he awaits a suitable time for so doing, or because he fears lest, if he does so, they may become worse, or hinder, oppress, or turn away from the faith, others who are weak and need to be instructed in a life of goodness and virtue, this does not seem to result from covetousness, but to be counselled by charity."

Secondly, fraternal correction may be omitted in such a way that one commits a mortal sin, namely, "when (as he says in the same passage) one fears what people may think, or lest one may suffer grievous pain or death"; provided, however, that the mind is so dominated by such things, that it gives them the preference to fraternal charity. This would seem to be the case when a man thinks that he might probably withdraw some wrongdoer from sin, and yet omits to do so, through fear or covetousness.

Thirdly, such an omission is a venial sin, when through fear or covetousness, a man is reluctant to correct his brother's faults, and yet not to such a degree that if he saw clearly that he could withdraw him from sin, he would still forbear from so doing, through fear or covetousness, because in his own mind he prefers fraternal charity to these things. It is in this way that holy men sometimes omit to correct wrongdoers.

Reply Obj. 4. We are bound to pay that

[1] PL 44, 944.　　　[2] *City of God,* I, 9 (PL 41, 22).

which is due to some fixed and certain person, whether it be a corporal or a spiritual good, without waiting for him to come to us, but by taking proper steps to find him. Therefore just as he that owes money to a creditor should seek him, when the time comes, so as to pay him what he owes, so he that has spiritual charge of some person is bound to seek him out, in order to reprove him for a sin. On the other hand we are not bound to seek someone on whom to bestow such favours as are due not to any certain person but to all our neighbours in general, whether those favours be material or spiritual goods, but it suffices that we bestow them when the opportunity occurs; because, as Augustine says,[3] we must look upon this "as a matter of chance." For this reason he says (*De Verb. Dom.* xvi, 1)[4] that "Our Lord warns us not to be listless in regard of one another's sins; not indeed by being on the look out for something to denounce, but by correcting what we see"; otherwise we should become spies on the lives of others, which is against the saying of Prov. 24. 15: *Lie not in wait, nor seek after wickedness in the house of the just, nor spoil his rest.* It is evident from this that there is no need for religious to leave their cloister in order to rebuke evil-doers.

ARTICLE 3. *Whether Fraternal Correction Belongs Only to Prelates?*

We proceed thus to the Third Article: It seems that fraternal correction belongs to prelates alone.

Objection 1. For Jerome says (cf. Origen, *Hom.* vii *in Jos.*)[5] to let priests endeavour to fulfil this saying of the Gospel: *"If thy brother sin against thee,"* etc. Now prelates having charge of others were usually designated under the name of priests. Therefore it seems that fraternal correction belongs to prelates alone.

Obj. 2. Further, Fraternal correction is a spiritual alms. Now corporal almsgiving belongs to those who are placed above others in temporal matters, that is, to the rich. Therefore fraternal correction belongs to those who are placed above others in spiritual matters, that is, to prelates.

Obj. 3. Further, When one man reproves another he moves him by his rebuke to something better. Now in natural things the inferior is moved by the superior. Therefore in the order of virtue also, which follows the order of na-

[3] *Christian Doctrine,* I, 28 (PL 34, 30).
[4] *Serm.,* LXXXII, 1 (PL 38, 506).
[5] PG 12, 861.

ture, it belongs to prelates alone to correct inferiors.

On the contrary, It is written (XXIV, Q. III, can. *Tam Sacerdotes*):[1] "Both priests and all the rest of the faithful should be most solicitous for those who perish, so that their reproof may either correct their sinful ways, or, if they be incorrigible, cut them off from the Church."

I answer that, As stated above (A. 1), correction is twofold. One is an act of charity, which seeks in a special way the recovery of an erring brother by means of a simple warning. And such correction belongs to anyone who has charity, be he subject or prelate. But there is another correction which is an act of justice purposing the common good, which is procured not only by warning one's brother, but also, sometimes, by punishing him, that others may, through fear, desist from sin. Such a correction belongs only to prelates, whose business it is not only to admonish, but also to correct by means of punishments.

Reply Obj. 1. Even as regards that fraternal correction which is common to all, prelates have a more grave responsibility, as Augustine says;[2] for just as a man ought to bestow temporal favours on those especially of whom he has temporal care, so too ought he to confer spiritual favours, such as correction, teaching and the like, on those who are entrusted to his spiritual care. Therefore Jerome does not mean that the precept of fraternal correction concerns priests only, but that it concerns them in a special way.

Reply Obj. 2. Just as he who has the means with which to give corporal assistance is rich in this respect, so he whose reason is gifted with a sane judgment, so as to be able to correct another's wrong-doing, is, in this respect, to be looked on as a superior.

Reply Obj. 3. Even in the physical order certain things act mutually on one another, through being in some respect higher than one another, in so far as each is somewhat in act, and somewhat in potency with regard to another. In like manner one man can correct another in so far as he has a sane judgment in a matter in which the other is lacking, though he is not his superior absolutely.

ARTICLE 4. *Whether a Man Is Bound To Correct His Prelate?*

We proceed thus to the Fourth Article: It would seem that no man is bound to correct his prelate.

Objection 1. For it is written (Exod. 19. 12): *The beast that shall touch the mount shall be stoned* (Vulg.,—*Everyone that shall touch the mount, dying he shall die.*), and (II Kings 6. 7) it is related that the Lord struck Oza for touching the ark. Now the mount and the ark signify our prelates. Therefore prelates should not be corrected by their subjects.

Obj. 2. Further, A gloss on Gal. 2. 11, *I withstood him to the face*, adds: "as an equal."[3] Therefore, since a subject is not equal to his prelate, he ought not to correct him.

Obj. 3. Further, Gregory says (*Moral.* xxiii)[4] that "one ought not to presume to reprove the conduct of holy men, unless one thinks better of oneself." But one ought not to think better of oneself than of one's prelate. Therefore one ought not to correct one's prelate.

On the contrary, Augustine says in his Rule:[5] "Show mercy not only to yourselves, but also to him who (that is, prelates), being in the higher position among you, is therefore in greater danger." But fraternal correction is a work of mercy. Therefore prelates also ought to be corrected.

I answer that, A subject is not able to administer to his prelate the correction which is an act of justice through the coercive nature of punishment; but the fraternal correction which is an act of charity pertains to everyone in respect of any person towards whom he is bound by charity, provided there be something in that person which requires correction. Now an act which proceeds from a habit or power extends to whatever is contained under the object of that power or habit; thus vision extends to all things comprised in the object of sight. Since, however, a virtuous act needs to be moderated by due circumstances, it follows that when a subject corrects his prelate, he ought to do so in a becoming manner, not with impudence and harshness, but with gentleness and respect. Hence the Apostle says (I Tim. 5. 1): *An ancient man rebuke not, but entreat him as a father*. Hence Dionysius finds fault with the monk Demophilus[6] for rebuking a priest with insolence, by striking and turning him out of the church.

Reply Obj. 1. It would seem that a subject touches his prelate inordinately when he upbraids him with insolence, as also when he speaks ill of him; and this is signified by God's

---

[1] Gratian, *Decretum* (RF I, 994).
[2] *City of God*, I, 9 (PL 41, 23).
[3] *Glossa interl.* (VI, 80v); *Glossa Lombardi* (PL 192, 108).   [4] Bk. 5, chap. 10 (PL 75, 692).
[5] *Epist.*, CCXI (PL 33, 965).
[6] *Epist.*, VIII, 1 (PG 3, 1088).

condemnation of those who touched the mount and the ark.

Reply Obj. 2. To withstand anyone in public exceeds the mode of fraternal correction, and so Paul would not have withstood Peter then, unless he were in some special way his equal as regards the defence of the faith. But even one who is not an equal can reprove privately and respectfully. Hence the Apostle in writing to the Colossians (4. 17) tells them to admonish their prelate: *Say to Archippus: Fulfil thy ministry.*[1] It must be observed, however, that if the faith were endangered, a subject ought to rebuke his prelate even publicly. Hence Paul, who was under Peter, rebuked him in public, on account of the imminent danger of scandal concerning faith, and, as the gloss of Augustine says[2] on Gal. 2. 11, "Peter gave an example to superiors that if at any time they should happen to stray from the straight path, they should not disdain to be reproved by their subjects."

Reply Obj. 3. To presume oneself to be better absolutely than one's prelate, would seem to be presumptuous pride; but there is no presumption in thinking oneself better in some respect, because, in this life no man is without some fault. We must also remember that when a man reproves his prelate charitably, it does not follow that he thinks himself any better, but merely that he offers his help to one who, "being in the higher position among you, is therefore in greater danger," as Augustine observes in his Rule quoted above.

ARTICLE 5. *Whether a Sinner Ought To Reprove a Wrongdoer?*

We proceed thus to the Fifth Article: It would seem that a sinner ought to reprove a wrongdoer.

Objection 1. For no man is excused from obeying a precept by having committed a sin. But fraternal correction is a matter of precept, as stated above (A. 2). Therefore it seems that a man ought not to forbear from such correction for the reason that he has committed a sin.

Obj. 2. Further, Spiritual almsdeeds are of more account than corporal almsdeeds. Now one who is in sin ought not to abstain from administering corporal alms. Much less therefore ought he, on account of a previous sin, to refrain from correcting wrongdoers.

Obj. 3. Further, It is written (I John 1. 8):

If we say that we have no sin, we deceive ourselves. Therefore if, on account of a sin, a man is hindered from reproving his brother, there will be none to reprove the wrongdoer. But the latter proposition is unreasonable, and so therefore is the former also.

On the contrary, Isidore says (*De Summo Bono,* iii):[3] "He that is subject to vice should not correct the vices of others." Again it is written (Rom. 2. 1): *Wherein thou judgest another, thou condemnest thyself. For thou dost the same things which thou judgest.*

I answer that, As stated above (A. 3, Reply 2), to correct a wrongdoer belongs to a man, in so far as his reason is gifted with right judgment. Now sin, as stated above (Part I-II, Q. LXXXV, A. 2), does not destroy the good of nature so as to deprive the sinner's reason of all right judgment, and in this respect he may be competent to find fault with others for committing sin. Nevertheless a previous sin proves somewhat of a hindrance to this correction, for three reasons. First because this previous sin renders a man unworthy to rebuke another; and especially is he unworthy to correct another for a lesser sin, if he himself has committed a greater. Hence Jerome says on the words, *Why seest thou the mote?* etc. (Matt. 7. 3): "He is speaking of those who, while they are themselves guilty of mortal sin, have no patience with the lesser sins of their brethren."[4]

Secondly, such correction becomes unfitting on account of the scandal which ensues if the corrector's sin be well known, because it would seem that he corrects, not out of charity, but more for the sake of ostentation. Hence the words of Matt. 7. 4, *How sayest thou to thy brother?* etc. are expounded by Chrysostom thus:[5] "That is,—'With what object?' Out of charity, think you, that you may save your neighbour? No, because you would look after your own salvation first. What you want is, not to save others, but to hide your evil deeds with good teaching, and to seek to be praised by men for your knowledge."

Thirdly, on account of the rebuker's pride; when, for instance, a man thinks lightly of his own sins, and, in his own heart, sets himself above his neighbour, judging the latter's sins with harsh severity, as though he himself were a just man. Hence Augustine says (*De Serm. Dom. in Monte,* ii, 19):[6] "To reprove the faults

---

[1] Vulg.,—*Take heed to the ministry which thou hast received in the Lord, that thou fulfil it.* Cf. II Tim. 4.5.
[2] *Glossa ordin.* (VI, 81B); *Glossa* Lombardi (PL 192, 109); cf. Augustine, *Epist.,* LXXXII, 2 (PL 33, 278).

[3] *Sent.,* III, 32 (PL 83, 704).   [4] PL 26, 48.
[5] *Hom.,* XVII in the *Opus Imperfectum,* falsely ascribed to S. John Chrysostom. (PG 56, 727).
[6] PL 34, 1298.

of others is the duty of good and kindly men; when a wicked man rebukes anyone, his rebuke is the latter's acquittal." And so, as Augustine says (*ibid.*): "When we have to find fault with anyone, we should think whether we were never guilty of his sin; and then we must remember that we are men, and might have been guilty of it; or that we once had it on our conscience, but have it no longer; and then we should bethink ourselves that we are all weak, in order that our reproof may be the outcome, not of hatred, but of pity. But if we find that we are guilty of the same sin, we must not rebuke him, but groan with him, and invite him to repent with us."

It appears from this that, if a sinner reprove a wrongdoer with humility, he does not sin, nor does he bring a further condemnation on himself, although thereby he proves himself deserving of condemnation, either in his brother's or in his own conscience, on account of his previous sin.

Hence the *Replies to the Objections* are clear.

ARTICLE 6. *Whether One Ought To Forbear From Correcting Someone, Through Fear Lest He Become Worse?*

We proceed thus to the Sixth Article: It would seem that one ought not to forbear from correcting someone through fear lest he become worse.

Objection 1. For sin is weakness of the soul, according to Ps. 6. 3: *Have mercy on me, O Lord, for I am weak.* Now he that has charge of a sick person, must not cease to take care of him, even if he be fractious or contemptuous, because then the danger is greater, as in the case of madmen. Much more, therefore should one correct a sinner, no matter how badly he takes it.

Obj. 2. Further, According to Jerome vital truths are not to be foregone on account of scandal.[1] Now God's commandments are vital truths. Since, therefore, fraternal correction is a matter of precept, as stated above (A. 2), it seems that it should not be foregone for fear of scandalizing the person to be corrected.

Obj. 3. Further, According to the Apostle (Rom. 3. 8) we should not do evil that good may come of it. Therefore, in like manner, good should not be omitted lest evil befall. Now fraternal correction is a good thing. Therefore it

should not be omitted for fear lest the person corrected become worse.

On the contrary It is written (Prov. 9. 8): *Rebuke not a scorner lest he hate thee,* where a gloss remarks:[2] "You must not fear lest the scorner insult you when you rebuke him: rather should you bear in mind that by making him hate you, you may make him worse." Therefore one ought to forego fraternal correction, when we fear lest we may make a man worse.

I answer that, As stated above (A. 3) the correction of the wrongdoer is twofold. One, which belongs to prelates, and is directed to the common good, has coercive force. Such correction should not be omitted for fear that the person corrected be disturbed, both because if he is unwilling to amend his ways of his own accord he should be made to cease sinning by being punished, and because, if he be incorrigible, the common good is safeguarded in this way, since the order of justice is observed, and others are deterred by one being made an example of. Hence a judge does not forbear from pronouncing sentence of condemnation against a sinner for fear of disturbing him or his friends.

The other fraternal correction is directed to the amendment of the wrongdoer, whom it does not coerce, but merely admonishes. Consequently when it is thought probable that the sinner will not take the warning, and will become worse, such fraternal correction should be foregone, because the means should be regulated according to the requirements of the end.

Reply Obj. 1. The doctor uses force towards a madman who is unwilling to submit to his treatment; and this may be compared with the correction administered by prelates, which has coercive power, but not with simple fraternal correction.

Reply Obj. 2. Fraternal correction is a matter of precept in so far as it is an act of virtue, and it will be a virtuous act in so far as it is proportionate to the end. Consequently whenever it is a hindrance to the end, for instance when a man becomes worse through it, it is no longer a vital truth, nor is it a matter of precept.

Reply Obj. 3. Whatever is directed to an end becomes good through being directed to the end. Hence whenever fraternal correction hinders the end, namely the amendment of our brother, it is no longer good, so that when such a correction is omitted, good is not omitted lest evil should befall.

---

[1] Cf. Hugh of St. Cher, *In Univ. Test.*, on Matt. 18.7 (VI, 61); Alexander of Hales, *Summa Theol.*, II, n. 862 (QR III, 821).

[2] *Glossa ordin.* (III, 318A); Gregory, *Moral.*, VIII, 42 (PL 75, 842).

ARTICLE 7. *Whether the Precept of Fraternal Correction Demands That a Private Admonition Should Precede Denunciation?*

We proceed thus to the Seventh Article: It would seem that the precept of fraternal correction does not demand that a private admonition should precede denunciation.

Objection 1. For, in works of charity, we should above all follow the example of God, according to Eph. 5. 1, 2: *Be ye followers of God, as most dear children, and walk in love.* Now God sometimes punishes a man for a sin, without previously warning him in secret. Therefore it seems that there is no need for a private admonition to precede denunciation.

Obj. 2. Further, According to Augustine (*De Mendacio*, xv),[1] "we learn from the deeds of holy men how we ought to understand the commandments of Holy Writ." Now among the deeds of holy men we find that a hidden sin is publicly denounced, without any previous admonition in private. Thus we read (Gen. 37. 2) that *Joseph accused his brethren to his father of a most wicked crime;* and (Acts 5. 4, 9) that Peter publicly denounced Ananias and Saphira who had secretly *by fraud kept back the price of the land,* without beforehand admonishing them in private; nor do we read that Our Lord admonished Judas in secret before denouncing him. Therefore the precept does not require that secret admonition should precede public denunciation.

Obj. 3. Further, It is a graver matter to accuse than to denounce. Now one may go to the length of accusing a person publicly, without previously admonishing him in secret; for it is decided in the Decretal (Cap. *Qualiter, De Accusationibus*)[2] that "nothing else need precede accusation except inscription."[3] Therefore it seems that the precept does not require that a secret admonition should precede public denunciation.

Obj. 4. Further, It does not seem probable that the customs observed by religious in general are contrary to the precepts of Christ. Now it is customary among religious orders to proclaim in chapter this or that one for a fault, without any previous secret admonition. There-

fore it seems that this admonition is not required by the precept.

Obj. 5. Further, Religious are bound to obey their prelates. Now a prelate sometimes commands either all in general, or someone in particular, to tell him if they know of anything that requires correction. Therefore it would seem that they are bound to tell them this, even before any secret admonition. Therefore the precept does not require secret admonition before public denunciation.

On the contrary, Augustine says (*De Verb. Dom.* xvi)[4] on the words, *Rebuke him between thee and him alone* (Matt. 18. 15): "Aiming at his amendment, while avoiding his disgrace. For perhaps from shame he might begin to defend his sin; and him whom you thought to make a better man, you make worse." Now we are bound by the precept of charity to beware lest our brother become worse. Therefore the order of fraternal correction comes under the precept.

I answer that, With regard to the public denunciation of sins it is necessary to make a distinction, because sins may be either public or secret. In the case of public sins, a remedy is required not only for the sinner, that he may become better, but also for others, who know of his sin, lest they be scandalized. Therefore such sins should be denounced in public, according to the saying of the Apostle (I Tim. 5. 20): *Them that sin reprove before all, that the rest also may have fear,* which is to be understood as referring to public sins, as Augustine states (*De Verb. Dom.*).[5]

On the other hand, in the case of secret sins, the words of Our Lord seem to apply (Matt. 18. 15): *If thy brother shall offend against thee,* etc. For if he offend thee publicly in the presence of others, he no longer sins against thee alone, but also against others whom he disturbs. Since, however, a man's neighbour may take offence even at his secret sins, it seems that we must make yet a further distinction. For certain secret sins are hurtful to our neighbour either in his body or in his soul, as, for instance, when a man plots secretly to betray his country to its enemies, or when a heretic secretly turns other men away from the faith. And since he that sins thus in secret, sins not only against you in particular, but also against others, it is necessary to take steps to denounce him at once, in order to prevent him doing such harm, unless by chance you were firmly persuaded

---

[1] PL 40, 506.

[2] *Decretal. Gregor.,* IX, v, 1, chap. 24 (RF II, 746).

[3] The accuser was bound by Roman Law to endorse (*se inscribere*) the writ of accusation. The effect of this endorsement or inscription was that the accuser bound himself, if he failed to prove the accusation, to suffer the same punishment as the accused would have to suffer if proved guilty.

[4] *Serm.,* LXXXII, 4 (PL 38, 509).

[5] *Ibid.,* 7 (PL 38, 510).

that this evil result would be prevented by admonishing him secretly.

On the other hand there are other sins which injure none but the sinner, and the person sinned against, either because he alone is hurt by the sinner, or at least because he alone knows about his sin, and then our one purpose should be to succour our sinning brother; and just as the physician of the body restores the sick man to health, if possible, without cutting off a limb, but, if this be unavoidable, cuts off a limb which is least indispensable, in order to preserve the life of the whole body, so too he who desires his brother's amendment should, if possible, so amend him as regards his conscience that he keep his good name.

For a good name is useful, first of all to the sinner himself, not only in temporal matters, wherein a man suffers many losses if he lose his good name, but also in spiritual matters, because many are restrained from sinning through fear of dishonour, so that when a man finds his good name lost, he puts no curb on his sinning. Hence Jerome says[1] on Matt. 18. 15: "If he sin against thee, thou shouldst rebuke him in private, lest he persist in his sin if he should once become shameless or unabashed." Secondly, we ought to safeguard our sinning brother's good name, first because the dishonour of one leads to the dishonour of others, according to the saying of Augustine (*Ep. ad pleb. Hipponens.* lxxviii):[2] "When a few of those who bear a name for holiness are reported falsely or proved in truth to have done anything wrong, people will seek by busily repeating it to make it believed of all"; and also when one man's sin is made public others are incited to sin likewise.

Since, however, one's conscience should be preferred to a good name, Our Lord wished that we should publicly denounce our brother and so deliver his conscience from sin, even though he should forfeit his good name. Therefore it is evident that the precept may require a secret admonition to precede public denunciation.

Reply Obj. 1. Whatever is hidden, is known to God, and so hidden sins are to the judgment of God just what public sins are to the judgment of man. Nevertheless God does rebuke sinners often by secretly admonishing them, so to speak, with an inward inspiration, either while they wake or while they sleep, according to Job 33. 15-37: *By a dream in a vision by night, when deep sleep falleth upon men . . . then He openeth the ears of men, and teaching instruct-*

[1] PL 26, 136.   [2] PL 33, 271.

eth them in what they are to learn, that He may withdraw a man from the things he is doing.

Reply Obj. 2. Our Lord as God knew the sin of Judas as though it were public, and so He could have made it known at once. Yet He did not, but warned Judas of his sin in words that were obscure. The sin of Ananias and Saphira was denounced by Peter acting for God, by Whose revelation he knew of their sin. With regard to Joseph it is probable that he warned his brethren, though Scripture does not say so. Or we may say that the sin was public with regard to his brethren, and so it is stated in the plural that he accused *his brethren.*

Reply Obj. 3. When there is danger to a great number of people, those words of Our Lord do not apply, because then your brother does not sin against you alone.

Reply Obj. 4. Proclamations made in the chapter of religious are about little faults which do not affect a man's good name. Hence they are reminders of forgotten faults rather than accusations or denunciations. If, however, they should be of such a nature as to injure our brother's good name, it would be contrary to Our Lord's precept to denounce a brother's fault in this manner.

Reply Obj. 5. A prelate is not to be obeyed contrary to a Divine precept, according to Acts 5. 29: *We ought to obey God rather than men.* Therefore when a prelate commands anyone to tell him anything that he knows to need correction, the command rightly understood supports the safeguarding of the order of fraternal correction, whether the command be addressed to all in general, or to some particular individual. If, on the other hand, a prelate were to issue a command in express opposition to this order instituted by Our Lord, both would sin, the one commanding, and the one obeying him, as disobeying Our Lord's command. Consequently he ought not to be obeyed, because a prelate is not the judge of secret things, but God alone is; hence he has no power to command anything in respect of hidden matters, except in so far as they are made known through certain signs, as by ill repute or suspicion; in which case a prelate can command just as a judge, whether secular or ecclesiastical, can bind a man under oath to tell the truth.

ARTICLE 8. *Whether Before the Public Denunciation Witnesses Ought To Be Brought Forward?*

We proceed thus to the Eighth Article: It seems that before the public denunciation witnesses ought not to be brought forward.

Objection 1. For secret sins ought not to be made known to others, because by so doing a man would betray his brother's sins instead of correcting them, as Augustine says (*De Verb. Dom.* xvi).[1] Now by bringing forward witnesses one makes known a brother's sin to others. Therefore in the case of secret sins one ought not to bring witnesses forward before the public denunciation.

Obj. 2. Further, Man should love his neighbour as himself. Now no man brings in witnesses to prove his own secret sin. Neither therefore ought one to bring forward witnesses to prove the secret sin of our brother.

Obj. 3. Further, Witnesses are brought forward to prove something. But witnesses afford no proof in secret matters. Therefore it is useless to bring witnesses forward in such cases.

Obj. 4. Further, Augustine says in his Rule that "before bringing it to the notice of witnesses . . . . it should be put before the superior."[2] Now to bring a matter before a superior or a prelate is to tell the Church. Therefore witnesses should not be brought forward before the public denunciation.

On the contrary, Our Lord said (Matt. 18. 16): *Take with thee one or two more, that in the mouth of two,* etc.

I answer that, The right way to go from one extreme to another is to pass through the middle space. Now Our Lord wished the beginning of fraternal correction to be hidden, when one brother corrects another between this one and himself alone, while He wished the end to be public, when such a one would be denounced to the Church. Consequently it is befitting that witnesses should be brought between the two extremes, so that at first the brother's sin be indicated to a few, who will be of use without being a hindrance, and thus his sin be amended without dishonouring him before the public.

Reply Obj. 1. Some have understood the order of fraternal correction to demand that we should first of all rebuke our brother secretly, and that if he listens, it is well; but if he listen not, and his sin be altogether hidden, they say that we should go no further in the matter, but if it has already begun to reach the notice of several by various signs, we ought to procede further, according to Our Lord's command.[3] But this is contrary to what Augustine says in his rule[4] that we are bound to reveal a brother's sin,

"lest it cause corruption in the heart." Therefore we must say otherwise that when the secret admonition has been given once or several times, as long as there is probable hope of his amendment, we must continue to admonish him in private, but as soon as we are able to judge with any probability that the secret admonition is of no avail, we must take further steps, however secret the sin may be, and call witnesses, unless perhaps it were thought probable that this would not conduce to our brother's amendment, and that he would become worse; because on that account one ought to abstain altogether from correcting him, as stated above (A. 6).

Reply Obj. 2. A man needs no witnesses that he may amend his own sin; yet they may be necessary that we may amend a brother's sin. Hence the comparison fails.

Reply Obj. 3. There may be three reasons for bringing in witnesses. First, to show that the deed in question is a sin, as Jerome says;[5] secondly, to prove that the deed was done, if it is repeated, as Augustine says (*loc. cit.*); thirdly, to prove that the man who rebuked his brother has done what he could, as Chrysostom says (*Hom. in Matt.* lx).[6]

Reply Obj. 4. Augustine means that the matter ought to be made known to the prelate before it is stated to the witnesses, in so far as the prelate is a private individual who is able to be of more use than others, but not that it is to be told him as to the Church, that is, as holding the position of judge.

QUESTION XXXIV
OF HATRED
(*In Six Articles*)

WE must now consider the vices opposed to charity: (1) hatred, which is opposed to love; (2) acedia and envy, which are opposed to the joy of charity (Q. XXXV); (3) discord and schism, which are contrary to peace (Q. XXXVII); (4) offence and scandal, which are contrary to beneficence and fraternal correction (Q. XLIII).

Under the first head there are six points of inquiry: (1) Whether it is possible to hate God? (2) Whether hatred of God is the greatest of sins? (3) Whether hatred of one's neighbour is always a sin? (4) Whether it is the greatest of all sins against our neighbour? (5) Whether it

---

[1] *Serm.*, LXXXVII, chap. 7 (PL 38, 510).
[2] *Epist.*, CCXI (PL 33, 962).
[3] William of Auxerre, *Summa Aurea*, PT. III, TR. 24, Q. 5, A. 2 (239va); Albert, *In Sent.*, IV, d. XIV, A. 21 (BO XXIX, 827).   [4] *Epist.*, CCXI (PL 33, 962).

[5] *Glossa interl.*, on Matt. 18. 16 (v, 57r); Jerome, *In Matt.* III, on 18. 16 (PL 26,136).
[6] *In Matt.*, hom., LX (PG58, 586).

is a capital sin? (6) From what capital sin does it arise?

ARTICLE 1. Whether It Is Possible for Anyone To Hate God?

We proceed thus to the First Article: It seems that no man can hate God.

Objection 1. For Dionysius says (Div. Nom. iv)[1] that "the first good and beautiful is an object of love and dilection to all." But good is goodness and beauty itself. Therefore He is hated by none.

Obj. 2. Further, In the Apocryphal books of Esdras (3. 4., 36, 39) it is written that all things call upon truth . . . and (all men) do well like of her works. Now God is the very truth according to John 14. 6. Therefore all love God, and none can hate Him.

Obj. 3. Further, Hatred is a kind of aversion. But according to Dionysius (Div. Nom. i.)[2] God draws all things to Himself. Therefore none can hate Him.

On the contrary, It is written (Ps. 73. 23): The pride of them that hate Thee ascendeth continually, and (John 15. 24): But now they have both seen and hated both Me and My Father.

I answer that, As shown above (Part I-II, Q. XXIX, A. 1), hatred is a movement of the appetitive power, which power is not set in motion save by something apprehended. Now God can be apprehended by man in two ways: first, in Himself, as when He is seen in His Essence; secondly, in His effects, when, that is, the invisible things of God . . . are clearly seen, being understood by the things that are made (Rom. 1. 20). Now God in His Essence is goodness itself, which no man can hate—for it is of the character of good to be loved. Hence it is impossible for one who sees God in His Essence, to hate Him.

Moreover some of His effects are such that they can in no way be contrary to the human will, since to be, to live, to understand, which are effects of God, are desirable and lovable to all. Therefore again God cannot be an object of hatred if we consider Him as the Author of such effects. Some of God's effects, however, are contrary to a disordered will, such as the infliction of punishment, and the prohibition of sin by the Divine Law. Such effects are repugnant to a will debased by sin, and as regards the consideration of them God may be an object of hatred to some, in so far as they look upon Him as forbidding sin, and inflicting punishment.

Reply Obj. 1. This argument is true of those who see God's Essence, which is the very essence of goodness.

Reply Obj. 2. This argument is true in so far as God is apprehended as the cause of such effects as are naturally loved of all, among which are the works of Truth who reveals herself to men.

Reply Obj. 3. God draws all things to Himself, in so far as He is the source of being, since all things, in as much as they are, tend to be like God, Who is Being itself.

ARTICLE 2. Whether Hatred of God Is the Greatest of Sins?

We proceed thus to the Second Article: It seems that hatred of God is not the greatest of sins.

Objection 1. For the most grievous sin is the sin against the Holy Ghost, since it cannot be forgiven, according to Matt. 12. 32. Now hatred of God is not counted among the various kinds of sin against the Holy Ghost, as may be seen from what has been said above (Q. XIV, A. 2). Therefore hatred of God is not the most grievous sin.

Obj. 2. Further, Sin consists in withdrawing oneself from God. Now an unbeliever who has not even knowledge of God seems to be further away from Him than a believer, who though he hate God, nevertheless knows Him. Therefore it seems that the sin of unbelief is graver than the sin of hatred against God.

Obj. 3. Further, God is an object of hatred only by reason of those of His effects that are contrary to the will, the chief of which is punishment. But hatred of punishment is not the most grievous sin. Therefore hatred of God is not the most grievous sin.

On the contrary, "The best is opposite to the worst," according to the Philosopher.[3] But hatred of God is opposed to the love of God, in which man's best consists. Therefore hatred of God is man's worst sin.

I answer that, That the defect in sin consists in its turning away from God, as stated above (Q. X, A. 3), and this turning away would not have the character of guilt, were it not voluntary. Hence the nature of guilt consists in a voluntary turning away from God.

Now this voluntary turning away from God is directly implied in the hatred of God, but in other sins, by participation and relatively. For just as the will cleaves directly to what it loves, so does it directly shun what it hates. Hence

---

[1] Sect. 10 (PG 3, 708).   [2] Sect. 4 (PG 3, 697).   [3] Ethics, VIII, 10 (1160ᵇ9).

when a man hates God, his will is directly turned away from God, while in other sins, fornication for instance, a man turns away from God, not directly but indirectly, in so far, namely, as he desires an inordinate pleasure, to which turning away from God is connected. Now that which is so by itself always takes precedence of that which is so by another. Therefore hatred of God is more grievous than other sins.

Reply Obj. 1. According to Gregory (*Moral.* xxv, 11),[1] "it is one thing not to do good things, and another to hate the giver of good things, even as it is one thing to sin without deliberation and another to sin deliberately." This implies that to hate God, the giver of all good things, is to sin deliberately, and this is a sin against the Holy Ghost. Hence it is evident that hatred of God is chiefly a sin against the Holy Ghost, in so far as the sin against the Holy Ghost denotes a special kind of sin. And yet it is not reckoned among the kinds of sin against the Holy Ghost because it is found generally in every species of that sin.

Reply Obj. 2. Even unbelief is not sinful unless it be voluntary; and therefore the more voluntary it is, the more it is sinful. Now it becomes voluntary by the fact that a man hates the truth that is proposed to him. Therefore it is evident that unbelief derives sinfulness from hatred of God, Whose truth is the object of faith; and hence just as a cause is greater than its effect, so hatred of God is a greater sin than unbelief.

Reply Obj. 3. Not everyone who hates his punishment, hates God the author of punishments. For many hate the punishments inflicted on them, and yet they bear them patiently out of reverence for the Divine justice. Therefore Augustine says[2] that God commands us to bear with penal evils, not to love them. On the other hand, to break out into hatred of God when He inflicts those punishments is to hate God's very justice, and that is a most grievous sin. Hence Gregory says (*Moral.* xxv, *loc cit.*): "Even as sometimes it is more grievous to love sin than to do it, so is it more wicked to hate justice than not to have done it."

ARTICLE 3. *Whether Hatred of One's Neighbour Is Always a Sin?*

We proceed thus to the Third Article: It seems that hatred of one's neighbour is not always a sin.

Objection 1. For no sin is commanded or counselled by the law of God, according to

Prov. 8. 8: *All my words are just, there is nothing wicked nor perverse in them.* Now, it is written (Luke 14. 26): *If any man come to Me, and hate not his father and mother . . . he cannot be My disciple.* Therefore hatred of one's neighbour is not always a sin.

Obj. 2. Further, Nothing wherein we imitate God can be a sin. But it is in imitation of God that we hate certain people; for it is written (Rom. 1. 30): *Detractors, hateful to God.* Therefore it is possible to hate certain people without committing a sin.

Obj. 3. Further, Nothing that is natural is a sin, for sin is a wandering away from what is according to nature, according to Damascene (*De Fide Orthod.* ii).[3] Now it is natural to a thing to hate whatever is contrary to it, and to aim at its undoing. Therefore it seems that it is not a sin to hate one's enemy.

On the contrary, It is written (I John 2. 9): *He that . . . hateth his brother, is in darkness.* Now spiritual darkness is sin. Therefore there cannot be hatred of one's neighbour without sin.

I answer that, Hatred is opposed to love, as stated above (Part I-II, Q. XXIX, AA. 1, 2); so that hatred of a thing is evil according as the love of that thing is good. Now love is due to our neighbour in respect of what he holds from God, that is, in respect of nature and grace, but not in respect of what he has of himself and from the devil, that is, in respect of sin and lack of justice. Consequently it is lawful to hate the sin in one's brother, and whatever pertains to the defect of Divine justice, but we cannot hate our brother's nature and grace without sin. Now it is part of our love for our brother that we hate the fault and the lack of good in him, since desire for another's good is equivalent to hatred of his evil. Consequently the hatred of one's brother, if we consider it absolutely, is always sinful.

Reply Obj. 1. By the commandment of God (Exod. 20. 12) we must honour our parents—as united to us in nature and kinship. But we must hate them in so far as they prove an obstacle to our attaining the perfection of Divine justice.

Reply Obj. 2. God hates the sin which is in the detractor, not his nature. And so we can hate detractors without committing a sin.

Reply Obj. 3. Men are not opposed to us in respect of the goods which they have received from God; therefore, in this respect, we should love them. But they are opposed to us in so far as they show hostility towards us, and this is

---

[1] PL 76, 399.   [2] *Confessions*, x, 28 (PL 32, 795).   [3] Chap. 4, 30 (PG 94, 876, 976); IV, 20 (PG 94, 1196).

sinful in them. In this respect we should hate them, for we should hate in them the fact that they are hostile to us.

ARTICLE 4. *Whether Hatred of Our Neighbour Is the Most Grievous Sin against Our Neighbour?*

We proceed thus to the Fourth Article: It would seem that hatred of our neighbour is the most grievous sin against our neighbour.

Objection 1. For it is written (I John 3. 15): *Whosoever hateth his brother is a murderer.* Now murder is the most grievous of sins against our neighbour. Therefore hatred is also.

Obj. 2. Further, Worst is opposed to best. Now the best thing we give our neighbour is love, since all other things come back to love. Therefore hatred is the worst.

On the contrary, A thing is said to be evil, "because it hurts," as Augustine observes (*Enchir.* xii).[1] Now there are sins by which a man hurts his neighbour more than by hatred, for instance, theft, murder and adultery. Therefore hatred is not the most grievous sin.

Moreover, Chrysostom commenting on Matt. 5. 19, *He that shall break one of these least commandments,* says:[2] "The commandments of Moses, Thou shalt not kill, Thou shalt not commit adultery, count for little in their reward, but they count for much if they be disobeyed. On the other hand the commandments of Christ such as, Thou shalt not be angry, Thou shalt not desire, are great in their reward, but little in the transgression." Now hatred is an internal movement like anger and concupiscence. Therefore hatred of one's brother is a less grievous sin than murder.

I answer that, Sins committed against our neighbour are evil on two counts: first by reason of the disorder in the person who sins, secondly by reason of the hurt inflicted on the person sinned against. On the first count, hatred is a more grievous sin than external actions that hurt our neighbour, because hatred is a disorder of man's will, which is the chief part of man, and in which is the root of sin, so that if a man's outward actions were to be inordinate, without any disorder in his will, they would not be sinful; for instance, if he were to kill a man through ignorance or out of zeal for justice. And if there be anything sinful in a man's outward sins against his neighbour, it is all to be traced to his inward hatred. On the other hand, as regards the hurt inflicted on his neighbour, a man's

outward sins are worse than his inward hatred. This suffices for the *Replies to the Objections.*

ARTICLE 5. *Whether Hatred Is a Capital Sin?*

We proceed thus to the Fifth Article: It seems that hatred is a capital sin.

Objection 1. For hatred is directly opposed to charity. Now charity is the foremost among the virtues, and the mother of all others. Therefore hatred is the chief of the capital sins, and the origin of all others.

Obj. 2. Further, Sins arise in us on account of the inclinations of our passions, according to Rom. 7. 5: *The passions of sins . . . did work in our members, to bring forth fruit unto death.* Now all other passions of the soul seem to arise from love and hatred, as was shown above (Part I-II, Q. XXVII, A. 4; Q. XXVIII, A. 6, Reply 2). Therefore hatred should be put among the capital sins.

Obj. 3. Further, Vice is a moral evil. Now hatred regards evil more than any other passion does. Therefore it seems that hatred should be reckoned a capital sin.

On the contrary, Gregory (*Moral.* xxxi, 45)[3] does not number hatred among the seven capital sins.

I answer that, As stated above (Part I-II, Q. LXXXIV, AA. 3, 4), a capital vice is one from which other vices arise most frequently. Now vice is contrary to man's nature, in so far as he is a rational animal; and when a thing acts contrary to its nature, that which is natural to it is corrupted little by little. Consequently it must first of all fail in that which is less in accordance with its nature, and last of all in that which is most in accordance with its nature, since what is first in construction is last in destruction. Now that which, first and foremost, is most natural to man, is the love of what is good, and especially love of the Divine good, and of his neighbour's good. Therefore hatred, which is opposed to this love, is not the first but the last thing in the downfall of virtue resulting from vice; and therefore it is not a capital vice.

Reply Obj. 1. As stated in the *Physics,*[4] "the virtue of a thing consists in its being well disposed in accordance with its nature." Hence what is first and foremost in the virtues must be first and foremost in the natural order. Hence charity is put among the foremost of the virtues, and for the same reason hatred cannot be first among the vices, as stated above.

Reply Obj. 2. Hatred of the evil that is contrary to one's natural good is the first of the

---

[1] PL 40, 237.   [2] *Hom.,* x in the *Opus Imperfectum,* falsely ascribed to S. John Chrysostom. (PG 56, 688).

[3] PL 76, 621.   [4] Aristotle, VII, 3 (246ª13).

soul's passions, even as love of one's natural good is. But hatred of one's connatural good cannot be first, but is something last, because such hatred is a proof of an already corrupted nature, even as love of an extraneous good.

Reply Obj. 3. Evil is twofold. One is a true evil, for the reason that it is incompatible with one's natural good, and the hatred of such an evil may have priority over the other passions. There is, however, another which is not a true, but an apparent evil, which, namely, is a true and connatural good, and yet is reckoned evil on account of the corruption of nature; and the hatred of such an evil must come last. This hatred is vicious, but the former is not.

ARTICLE 6. *Whether Hatred Arises From Envy?*

We proceed thus to the Sixth Article: It seems that hatred does not arise from envy.

Objection 1. For envy is sorrow for another's good. Now hatred does not arise from sorrow, for, on the contrary, we grieve for the presence of the evil we hate. Therefore hatred does not arise from envy.

Obj. 2. Further, Hatred is opposed to love. Now love of our neighbour is referred to our love of God, as stated above (Q. XXV, A. 1; Q. XXVI, A. 2). Therefore hatred of our neighbour is referred to our hatred of God. But hatred of God does not arise from envy, for we do not envy those who are very far removed from us, but rather those who seem to be near us, as the Philosopher states.[1] Therefore hatred does not arise from envy.

Obj. 3. Further, To one effect there is one cause. Now hatred is caused by anger, for Augustine says in his Rule[2] that "anger grows into hatred." Therefore hatred does not arise from envy.

On the contrary, Gregory says (*Moral.* xxxi, 45)[3] that "out of envy cometh hatred."

I answer that, As stated above (A. 5), hatred of his neighbour is a man's last step in the path of sin, because it is opposed to the love which he naturally has for his neighbour. Now if a man declines from that which is natural, it is because he intends to avoid that which is naturally an object to be shunned. Now every animal naturally avoids sorrow, just as it desires pleasure, as the Philosopher states.[4] Accordingly just as love arises from pleasure, so does hatred arise from sorrow. For just as we are moved to love whatever gives us pleasure, because, for that very reason it assumes the aspect of good,

so we are moved to hate whatever displeases us, in so far as for this reason it assumes the aspect of evil. Therefore, since envy is sorrow for our neighbour's good, it follows that our neighbour's good becomes hateful to us, so that out of envy hatred arises.

Reply Obj. 1. Since the appetitive power, like the apprehensive power, reflects on its own acts, it follows that there is a kind of circular movement in the actions of the appetitive power. And so according to the first forward course of the appetitive movement, love gives rise to desire, from which follows pleasure when one has obtained what one desired. And since the very fact of taking pleasure in the good one loves has the aspect of good, it follows that pleasure causes love. And in the same way sorrow causes hatred.

Reply Obj. 2. Love and hatred have different aspects, for the object of love is good, which flows from God to creatures, and so love is due to God in the first place, and to our neighbour afterwards. On the other hand, hatred is of evil, which has no place in God Himself, but only in His effects, for which reason it has been stated above (A. 1), that God is not an object of hatred, except in so far as He is considered in relation to His effects, and consequently hatred is directed to our neighbour before being directed to God. Therefore, since envy of our neighbour is the mother of hatred of our neighbour, it becomes, in consequence, the cause of hatred towards God.

Reply Obj. 3. Nothing prevents a thing arising from various causes in various respects, and accordingly hatred may arise both from anger and from envy. However it arises more directly from envy, which looks upon the very good of our neighbour as displeasing and therefore hateful, while hatred arises from anger by way of increase. For at first, through anger, we desire our neighbour's evil according to a certain measure, that is in so far as that evil has the aspect of vengeance; but afterwards, through the continuance of anger, man goes so far as absolutely to desire his neighbour's evil, which desire is part of hatred. Hence it is evident that hatred is caused by envy formally as regards the aspect of the object, but dispositively by anger.

QUESTION XXXV

OF ACEDIA

(*In Four Articles*)

WE must now consider the vices opposed to the joy of charity. This joy is either about the Di-

---

[1] *Rhetoric,* II, 10 (1387^{b}22). [2] *Epist.,* CCXI (PL 33, 964).
[3] PL 76, 621. [4] *Ethics,* VII, 13 (1153^{b}1); X, 2 (1172^{b}9).

vine good, and then its contrary is acedia,[1] or about our neighbour's good, and then its contrary is envy. Therefore we must consider (1) Acedia and (2) Envy (Q. XXXVI).

Under the first head there are four points of inquiry: (1) Whether acedia is a sin? (2) Whether it is a special vice? (3) Whether it is a mortal sin? (4) Whether it is a capital sin?

ARTICLE 1. *Whether Acedia Is a Sin?*

We proceed thus to the First Article: It seems that acedia is not a sin.

Objection 1. For we are neither praised nor blamed for our passions, according to the Philosopher.[2] Now acedia is a passion, since it is a kind of sorrow, according to Damascene (*De Fide Orthod.* ii),[3] and as we stated above (Part I-II, Q. XXXV, A. 8). Therefore acedia is not a sin.

Obj. 2. Further, No bodily failing that occurs at fixed times is a sin. But acedia is like this, for Cassian says (*De Instit. Monast.* x):[4] "The monk is troubled with acedia chiefly about the sixth hour; it is like an intermittent fever, and inflicts the soul of the one it lays low with burning fires at regular and fixed intervals." Therefore acedia is not a sin.

Obj. 3. Further, That which proceeds from a good root does not seem to be a sin. Now acedia proceeds from a good root, for Cassian says[5] that acedia arises from the fact that "we sigh at being deprived of spiritual fruit, and think that other monasteries and those which are a long way off are much better than the one we dwell in"; all of which seems to point to humility. Therefore acedia is not a sin.

Obj. 4. Further, All sin is to be avoided, according to Ecclus. 21. 2: *Flee from sins as from the face of a serpent.* Now Cassian says:[6] "Experience shows that the onslaught of acedia is not to be evaded by flight but to be conquered by resistance." Therefore acedia is not a sin.

On the contrary, Whatever is forbidden in Holy Writ is a sin. Now such is acedia, for it is written (Ecclus. 6. 26): *Bow down thy shoulder, and bear her,* namely spiritual wisdom, *and be not grieved (acedieris) with her bands.* Therefore acedia is a sin.

I answer that, Acedia, according to Damascene (*loc. cit.*) is "an oppressive sorrow," which, namely, so weighs upon man's mind, that he wants to do nothing (thus acid things (*acida*)

are also cold). Hence acedia implies a certain weariness of work, as appears from a gloss[7] on Ps. 106. 18, *Their soul abhorred all manner of meat,* and from the definition of some who say that acedia is a sluggishness of the mind which neglects to begin good.[8]

Now this kind of sorrow is always evil, sometimes in itself, sometimes in its effect. For sorrow is evil in itself when it is about that which is apparently evil but good in reality, even as, on the other hand, pleasure is evil if it is about that which seems to be good but is, in truth, evil. Since, then, spiritual good is a good in very truth, sorrow about spiritual good is evil in itself. And yet that sorrow also which is about a real evil is evil in its effect, if it so oppresses man as to draw him away entirely from good deeds. Hence the Apostle (II Cor. 2. 7) did not wish those who repented to be *swallowed up with overmuch sorrow.*

Accordingly, since acedia, as we understand it here, denotes sorrow for spiritual good, it is evil on two counts, both in itself and in point of its effect. Consequently it is a sin, for by sin we mean an evil movement of the appetite, as appears from what has been said above (Q. X., A. 2; Part I-II, Q. LXXIV, A. 3).

Reply Obj. 1. Passions are not sinful in themselves; but they are blameworthy in so far as they are applied to something evil, just as they deserve praise in so far as they are applied to something good. Therefore sorrow, in itself, calls neither for praise nor for blame; but moderate sorrow for evil calls for praise, while sorrow for good, and again immoderate sorrow for evil, calls for blame. It is in this sense that acedia is said to be a sin.

Reply Obj. 2. The passions of the sensitive appetite may either be venial sins in themselves, or incline the soul to mortal sin. And since the sensitive appetite has a bodily organ, it follows that on account of some bodily change a man becomes more apt to commit some particular sin. Hence it may happen that certain sins may become more insistent, through certain bodily changes occurring at certain fixed times. Now all bodily effects, of themselves, dispose one to sorrow; and thus it is that those who fast are harassed by acedia towards mid-day, when they begin to feel the want of food, and to be oppressed by the sun's heat.

Reply Obj. 3. It is a sign of humility if a man

---

[1] Sometimes translated as 'sloth.'
[2] *Ethics,* II, 5 (1105^{b}31).   [3] PG 94, 932.
[4] *De Institutione Cœnob.,* Chap. 1 (PL 49, 363).
[5] *Ibid.,* X, 2 (PL 49, 366).
[6] *Ibid.,* X, 25 (PL 49, 398).

[7] *Glossa ordin.* (III, 247A); *Glossa* Lombardi (PL 191, 977); Cf. Augustine, *Enarr. in Ps.,* Ps. 106, 18 (PL 37, 1425).
[8] Rhabanus Maurus, *De Ecclesiast. Discip.,* III, *De acedia* (PL 112, 1251).

does not think too much of himself, through observing his own faults; but if a man contemns the good things he has received from God, this, far from being a proof of humility, shows him to be ungrateful; and from such contempt results acedia, because we sorrow for things that we consider evil and worthless. Accordingly we ought to think much of the goods of others, in such a way as not to disparage those we have received ourselves from God, because if we did they would give us sorrow.

Reply Obj. 4. Sin is always to be shunned, but the assaults of sin should be overcome sometimes by flight, sometimes by resistance; by flight when a continued thought increases the incentive to sin, as in lust, for which reason it is written (I Cor. 6. 18): *Fly fornication;* by resistance, when perseverance in the thought diminishes the incentive to sin, which incentive arises from some trivial consideration. This is the case with acedia, because the more we think about spiritual goods, the more pleasing they become to us, and with this acedia dies away.

ARTICLE 2. *Whether Acedia Is a Special Vice?*

We proceed thus to the Second Article: It seems that acedia is not a special vice.

Objection 1. For that which belongs to all vices does not constitute a special kind of vice. But every vice makes a man sorrowful about the opposite spiritual good; for the lustful man is sorrowful about the good of continence, and the glutton about the good of abstinence. Since then acedia is sorrow for spiritual good, as stated above (A. 1), it seems that acedia is not a special sin.

Obj. 2. Further, Acedia, through being a kind of sorrow, is opposed to joy. Now joy is not accounted one special virtue. Therefore acedia should not be considered a special vice.

Obj. 3. Further, Since spiritual good is a kind of common object, which virtue seeks, and vice shuns, it does not constitute a special virtue or vice, unless it be limited by some addition. Now nothing, it seems, except toil, can narrow it to acedia, if this is a special vice, because the reason why a man shuns spiritual goods is that they are toilsome, and so acedia is a kind of weariness. But to shun toil and seek bodily repose seem to be due to the same cause, namely, idleness (*pigritia*). Hence acedia would be nothing but laziness, which seems untrue, for idleness is opposed to carefulness, while acedia is opposed to joy. Therefore acedia is not a special vice.

On the contrary, Gregory (*Moral.* xxxi, 45)[1] distinguishes acedia from the other vices. Therefore it is a special vice.

I answer that, Since acedia is sorrow for spiritual good, if we take spiritual good in a general way, acedia will not be a special vice, because, as stated above (A. 1), every vice shuns the spiritual good of its opposite virtue. Again it cannot be said that acedia is a special vice in so far as it shuns spiritual good as toilsome, or troublesome to the body, or as a hindrance to the body's pleasure, for this again would not sever acedia from carnal vices, by which a man seeks bodily comfort and pleasure.

Therefore we must say that a certain order exists among spiritual goods; for all the spiritual goods that are in the acts of each virtue are ordered to one spiritual good, which is the Divine good, about which there is a special virtue, namely, charity. Hence it pertains to each virtue to rejoice in its own spiritual good, which consists in its own act, while it pertains specially to charity to have that spiritual joy by which one rejoices in the Divine good. In like manner the sorrow by which one is displeased at the spiritual good which is in each act of virtue, belongs, not to any special vice, but to every vice; but sorrow in the Divine good about which charity rejoices belongs to a special vice, which is called acedia. This suffices for the *Replies to the Objections*

ARTICLE 3. *Whether Acedia Is a Mortal Sin?*

We proceed thus to the Third Article: It would seem that acedia is not a mortal sin.

Objection 1. For every mortal sin is contrary to a precept of the Divine Law. But acedia seems contrary to no precept, as one may see by going through the precepts of the Decalogue. Therefore acedia is not a mortal sin.

Obj. 2. Further, In the same genus, a sin of deed is no less grievous than a sin of thought. Now it is not a mortal sin to refrain in deed from some spiritual good which leads to God; otherwise it would be a mortal sin not to observe the counsels. Therefore it is not a mortal sin to refrain in thought from such spiritual works. Therefore acedia is not a mortal sin.

Obj. 3. Further, No mortal sin is to be found in a perfect man. But acedia is to be found in a perfect man; for Cassian says (*De Instit. Cænob* x, 2)[2] that acedia is "well known to the solitary, and is a most vexatious and persistent foe to the hermit." Therefore acedia is not always a mortal sin.

[1] PL 76, 621.   [2] PL 49, 363.

On the contrary, It is written (II Cor. 7. 20): *The sorrow of the world worketh death.* But such is acedia; for it is not sorrow *according to God,* which is contrasted with sorrow of the world. Therefore it is a mortal sin.

I answer that, As stated above (Part I-II, Q. LXXXVIII, AA. 1, 2), mortal sin is so called because it destroys the spiritual life which is the effect of charity, according to which God dwells in us. Therefore any sin which by its very character is contrary to charity is a mortal sin by reason of its genus. And such is acedia, because the proper effect of charity is joy in God, as stated above (Q. XXVIII, A. 1), while acedia is sorrow about spiritual good in so far as it is a Divine good. Therefore acedia is a mortal sin in respect of its genus.

But is must be observed with regard to all sins that are mortal in respect of their genus, that they are not mortal except when they attain to their perfection. For the consummation of sin is in the consent of reason; for we are speaking now of human sins consisting in human acts, the principle of which is the reason. Therefore if the sin be a mere beginning of sin in the sensuality alone, without attaining to the consent of reason, it is a venial sin on account of the imperfection of the act. Thus in the genus of adultery, the concupiscence that goes no further than the sensuality is a venial sin, but if it reach to the consent of reason, it is a mortal sin. So too, the movement of acedia is sometimes in the sensuality alone, by reason of the opposition of the flesh to the spirit, and then it is a venial sin; but sometimes it reaches to the reason, which consents in the flight from horror and detestation of the Divine good, on account of the flesh utterly prevailing over the spirit. In this case it is clear that acedia is a mortal sin.

Reply Obj. 1. Acedia is opposed to the precept about keeping holy the Sabbath-day. For this precept, in so far as it is a moral precept, implicitly commands the mind to rest in God; and sorrow of the mind about Divine good is contrary to this.

Reply Obj. 2. Acedia is not a withdrawal of the mind from any spiritual good, but from the Divine good, to which the mind is obliged to adhere. Therefore if a man is sorry because someone forces him to do acts of virtue that he is not bound to do, this is not a sin of acedia, but rather when he is sorry to have to do something for God's sake.

Reply Obj. 3. Imperfect movements of acedia are to be found in holy men, but they do not reach to the consent of reason.

ARTICLE 4. *Whether Acedia Should Be Accounted a Capital Vice?*

We proceed thus to the Fourth Article: It would seem that acedia ought not to be accounted a capital vice.

Objection 1. For a capital vice is one that moves a man to sinful acts, as stated above (Q. XXXIV, A. 5). Now acedia does not move one to action, but on the contrary withdraws one from it. Therefore it should not be accounted a capital sin.

Obj. 2. Further, A capital sin is one to which daughters are assigned. Now Gregory (*Moral* XXXI, 45)[1] assigns six daughters to acedia, namely "malice, spite, faint-heartedness, despair, sluggishness in regard to the commandments, wandering of the mind after unlawful things." Now these do not seem in reality to arise from acedia. For spite seems to be the same as hatred, which arises from envy, as stated above (Q. XXXIV, A. 6); malice is a genus which contains all vices, and, in like manner, a wandering of the mind after unlawful things is to be found in every vice; sluggishness about the commandments seems to be the same as acedia, while faint-heartedness and despair may arise from any sin. Therefore acedia is not rightly accounted a capital sin.

Obj. 3. Further, Isidore distinguishes the vice of acedia from the vice of sorrow, saying[2] that in so far as a man shirks his duty because it is distasteful and burdensome, it is sorrow, and in so far as he is inclined to undue repose, it is acedia; and of sorrow he says that it gives rise to spite, faint-heartedness, bitterness, despair; but he states that from acedia seven things arise, namely, "idleness, drowsiness, uneasiness of the mind, restlessness of the body, instability, loquacity, curiosity."[3] Therefore it seems that either Gregory or Isidore has wrongly assigned acedia as a capital sin together with its daughters.

On the contrary, The same Gregory (*loc. cit.*) states that acedia is a capital sin, and has the daughters mentioned above.

I answer that, As stated above (Part I-II, Q. LXXXIV, AA. 3, 4), a capital vice is one which easily gives rise to others as being their final cause. Now just as we do many things on account of pleasure, both in order to obtain it, and through being moved to do something under the impulse of pleasure, so again we do

[1] PL 76, 621.   [2] *Sent.*, II, 37 (PL 83, 638).
[3] *Quaest. in Vet. Test., In Deut.*, XVI, on 7.1 (PL 83, 366).

many things on account of sorrow, either that we may avoid it, or through being exasperated into doing something under its pressure. Therefore, since acedia is a kind of sorrow, as stated above (A. 1), it is fittingly accounted a capital sin.

Reply Obj. 1. Acedia by weighing on the mind, hinders us from doing things that cause sorrow. Nevertheless it induces the mind to do certain things, either because they are in harmony with sorrow, such as weeping, or because they are a means of avoiding sorrow.

Reply Obj 2. Gregory fittingly assigns the daughters of acedia. For since, according to the Philosopher,[1] "no man can be a long time in company with what is painful and unpleasant," it follows that something arises from sorrow in two ways: first, that man shuns whatever causes sorrow; secondly, that he passes to other things that give him pleasure; thus those who find no joy in spiritual pleasures have recourse to pleasures of the body, according to the Philosopher.[2] Now in the avoidance of sorrow the order observed is that man at first flies from unpleasant things, and secondly he struggles against such things as cause sorrow. Now spiritual goods which are the object of the sorrow of acedia are both end and means. Avoidance of the end is the result of despair, while avoidance of those goods which are the means to the end, in matters of difficulty which come under the counsels, is the effect of faint-heartedness, and in matters of common justice, is the effect of sluggishness about the commandments. The struggle against spiritual goods that cause sorrow is sometimes with men who lead others to spiritual goods, this is called spite; and sometimes it extends to the spiritual goods themselves, when a man goes so far as to detest them, and this is properly called malice. In so far as a man turns from spiritual things to external objects of pleasure, the daughter of acedia is called wandering after unlawful things. From this it is clear how to reply to the objections against each of the daughters, for malice does not denote here that which is generic to all vices, but must be understood as explained. Nor is spite taken as synonymous with hatred, but for a kind of indignation, as stated above; and the same applies to the others.

Reply Obj. 3. This distinction between sorrow and acedia is also given by Cassian (*De Instit. Cænob.* x. 1).[3] But Gregory more fittingly (*loc. cit.*) calls acedia a kind of sorrow, because, as stated above (A. 2), sorrow is not a distinct vice, in so far as a man shirks a distasteful and burdensome work, or sorrows on account of any other cause whatever, but only in so far as he is sorry on account of the Divine good, which sorrow belongs to the notion of acedia, since acedia seeks undue rest in so far as it spurns the Divine good. Moreover the things which Isidore lists as arising from acedia and sorrow, are reduced to those mentioned by Gregory; for bitterness which Isidore states to be the result of sorrow, is an effect of spite. Idleness and drowsiness are reduced to sluggishness about the precepts, for some are idle and omit them altogether, while others are drowsy and fulfil them with negligence. All the other five which he accounts as effects of acedia belong to the wandering of the mind after unlawful things. This tendency to wander, if it reside in the mind itself that is desirous of rushing importunately after various things is called uneasiness of the mind, but if it pertains to the knowledge, it is called curiosity; if it affect the speech it is called loquacity; and in so far as it affects a body that changes place, it is called restlessness of the body, when, namely, a man shows the unsteadiness of his mind by the disordered movements of members of his body; while if it causes the body to move from one place to another, it is called instability; or instability may denote changeableness of purpose.

QUESTION XXXVI
Of Envy
(In Four Articles)

WE must now consider envy, and under this head there are four points of inquiry: (1) What is envy? (2) Whether it is a sin? (3) Whether it is a mortal sin? (4) Whether it is a capital sin, and which are its daughters?

ARTICLE 1. *Whether Envy Is a Kind of Sorrow?*

We proceed thus to the First Article: It would seem that envy is not a kind of sorrow.

Objection 1. For the object of sorrow is an evil. But the object of envy is a good, for Gregory says (*Moral.* v, 46)[4] of the envious man that "self-inflicted pain wounds the mind consumed by envy, which is racked by the prosperity of another." Therefore envy is not a kind of sorrow.

Obj. 2. Further, Likeness is a cause, not of sorrow but rather of pleasure. But likeness is a

---

[1] *Ethics*, VIII, 5, 6 (1157^{b}15; 1158^{a}23).
[2] *Ibid.*, x, 6 (1176^{b}19); cf. VII, 14 (1154^{b}2).
[3] PL 49, 359.
[4] PL 75, 728.

cause of envy; for the Philosopher says:[1] "Men are envious of such as are like them in genus, in knowledge, in stature, in habit, or in reputation." Therefore envy is not a kind of sorrow.

Obj. 3. Further, Sorrow is caused by a defect, and therefore those who are in great defect are inclined to sorrow, as stated above (Part I-II, Q. XLVII, A. 3) when we were treating of the passions. Now those "who lack little, and who love honours, and who are considered wise," are envious, according to the Philosopher.[2] Therefore envy is not a kind of sorrow.

Obj. 4. Further, Sorrow is opposed to pleasure. Now opposite effects do not have one and the same cause. Therefore, since the recollection of goods once possessed is a cause of pleasure, as stated above (Part I-II, Q. XXXII, A. 3) it will not be a cause of sorrow. But it is a cause of envy; for the Philosopher says[3] that we envy those "who have or have had things that befitted ourselves, or which we possessed at some time." Therefore envy is not a kind of sorrow.

On the contrary, Damascene (*De Fide Orthod.* ii, 14)[4] calls envy a species of sorrow, and says that envy is sorrow "for another's good."

I answer that, The object of a man's sorrow is his own evil. Now it may happen that another's good is apprehended as one's own evil, and in this way sorrow can be about another's good. But this happens in two ways: first, when a man is sorry about another's good in so far as it threatens to be an occasion of harm to himself, as when a man grieves for his enemy's prosperity, for fear lest he may do him some harm. Such sorrow is not envy, but rather an effect of fear, as the Philosopher states.[5]

Secondly, another's good may be thought of as being one's own evil in so far as it conduces to the lessening of one's own good name or excellence. It is in this way that envy grieves for another's good; and consequently men are envious especially of those goods in which glory consists, and about which men like to be honoured and esteemed, as the Philosopher remarks.[6]

Reply Obj. 1. Nothing hinders what is good for one from being apprehended as evil for another; and in this way it is possible for sorrow to be about good, as stated above.

Reply Obj. 2. Since envy is about another's glory in so far as it diminishes the glory a man desires to have, it follows that a man is envious of those only whom he wishes to rival or sur-

pass in glory. But this does not apply to people who are far removed from one another; for no man, unless he be out of his mind, endeavours to rival or surpass in glory those who are far above him. Thus a commoner does not envy the king, nor does the king envy a commoner whom he is far above. Therefore a man does not envy those who are far removed from him, whether in place, time, or station, but those who are near him, and whom he strives to rival or surpass. For it is against our will that these should be in greater glory than we are, and that gives rise to sorrow. On the other hand, likeness causes pleasure in so far as it is in agreement with the will.

Reply Obj. 3. A man does not strive for mastery in matters where he is very deficient; and so he does not envy one who surpasses him in such matters, unless he surpass him by little, for then it seems to him that this is not beyond him and so he makes an effort. Hence, if his effort fails through the other's glory surpassing his, he grieves. And thus it is that those who love to be honoured are more envious; and in like manner the fainthearted are envious, because all things are great to them, and whatever good may befall another, they reckon that they themselves have been bested in something great. Hence it is written (Job 5. 2): *Envy slayeth the little one,* and Gregory says (*Moral.* v)[7] that "we can envy those only whom we think better in some respect than ourselves."

Reply Obj 4. Recollection of past goods in so far as we have had them, causes pleasure; in so far as we have lost them, causes sorrow; and in so far as others have them, causes envy; because that, above all, seems to take away from our own glory. Hence the Philosopher says[8] that "the old envy the young, and those who have spent much in order to get something, envy those who have got it by spending little," because they grieve that they have lost their goods, and that others have acquired goods.

Article 2. *Whether Envy Is a Sin?*

We proceed thus to the Second Article: It seems that envy is not a sin.

Objection 1. For Jerome says to Laeta about the education of her daughter (*Ep.* cvii):[9] "Let her have companions, so that she may learn together with them, envy them, and be nettled when they are praised." But no one should be advised to commit a sin. Therefore envy is not a sin.

---

[1] *Rhetoric,* II, 10 (1387[b]22).   [2] *Ibid.* (1387[b]27, 31).
[3] *Rhetoric* (1388[a]20).   [4] PG 94, 932.
[5] *Ibid.,* II, 9 (1386[b]22).   [6] *Ibid.,* II, 10 (1387[b]5).
[7] Chap. 46 (PL 75, 727).   [8] *Rhetoric,* II, 10 (1388[a]22).
[9] PL 22, 871.

Obj. 2. Further, "Envy is sorrow for an-other's good," as Damascene says (*De Fide Orthod.* ii, 14).[1] But this is sometimes praise-worthy, for it is written (Prov. 29. 2): *When the wicked shall bear rule, the people shall mourn.* Therefore envy is not always a sin.

Obj. 3. Further, Envy denotes a kind of zeal. But there is a good zeal, according to Ps. 68. 10: *The zeal of Thy house hath eaten me up.* Therefore envy is not always a sin.

Obj. 4. Further, Punishment is divided against fault. But envy is a kind of punishment; for Gregory says (*Moral.* v, 46):[2] "When the foul sore of envy corrupts the vanquished heart, the very exterior itself shows how forcibly the mind is urged by madness. For paleness seizes the complexion, the eyes are weighed down, the spirit is inflamed, while the limbs are chilled, there is frenzy in the heart, there is gnashing with the teeth." Therefore envy is not a sin.

On the contrary, It is written (Gal 5. 26): *Let us not be made desirous of vainglory, pro-voking one another, envying one another.*

I answer that, As stated above (A. 1), envy is sorrow for another's good. Now this sorrow may come about in four ways. First, when a man grieves for another's good through fear that it may cause harm either to himself, or to some other goods. This sorrow is not envy, as stated above (A. 1), and may be without sin. Hence Gregory says (*Moral.* xxii, 11):[3] "It very often happens that without charity being lost, both the destruction of an enemy rejoices us, and again his glory, without any sin of envy, saddens us, since, when he falls, we be-lieve that some are deservedly set up, and when he prospers, we dread lest many suffer unjust-ly."

Secondly, we may grieve over another's good, not because he has it, but because the good which he has we have not; and this, properly speaking is zeal, as the Philosopher says.[4] And if this zeal be about virtuous goods, it is praise-worthy, according to I Cor. 14. 1: *Be zealous for spiritual gifts,* while, if it be about temporal goods, it may be either sinful or sinless.

Thirdly, one may grieve over another's good, because he who happens to have that good is unworthy of it. Such sorrow as this cannot be occasioned by virtuous goods, which make a man just, but, as the Philosopher states,[5] is about riches, and those things which can accrue to the worthy and the unworthy; and he calls

this sorrow nemesis (νέμεσις),[6] saying that it belongs to good morals. But he says this because he considered temporal goods in themselves, in so far as they may seem great to those who look not to eternal goods; but, according to the teaching of faith, temporal goods that accrue to those who are unworthy are so disposed accord-ing to God's just ordering, either for the correc-tion of those men, or for their condemnation, and such goods are as nothing in comparison with the goods to come, which are prepared for good men. Therefore sorrow of this kind is for-bidden in Holy Writ, according to Ps. 36. 1: *Be not emulous of evil doers, nor envy them that work iniquity,* and elsewhere (Ps. 72. 2, 3): *My steps had well nigh slipped, for I was envious of the wicked, when I saw the prosperity of sinners.* (Douay,—*because I had a zeal on occasion of the wicked, seeing the prosperity of sinners.*)

Fourthly, we grieve over a man's good, and in so far as his good surpasses ours; this is envy properly speaking, and is always sinful, as also the Philosopher states,[7] because to do so is to grieve over what should make us rejoice, name-ly, over our neighbour's good.

Reply Obj. 1. Envy there denotes the zeal with which we ought to strive to progress with those who are better than we are.

Reply Obj. 2. This argument considers sorrow for another's good in the first sense given above.

Reply Obj. 3. Envy differs from zeal, as stated above. Hence a certain zeal may be good, while envy is always evil.

Reply Obj. 4. Nothing hinders a sin from be-ing penal because of something joined to it as stated above (Part I-II, Q. LXXXVII, A. 2) when we were treating sins.

ARTICLE 3. *Whether Envy Is a Mortal Sin?*

We proceed thus to the Third Article: It would seem that envy is not a mortal sin.

Objection 1. For since envy is a kind of sor-row, it is a passion of the sensitive appetite. Now there is no mortal sin in the sensuality, but only in the reason, as Augustine declares (*De Trin.* xii, 12).[8] Therefore envy is not a mortal sin.

Obj. 2. Further, There cannot be mortal sin in infants. But envy can be in them, for Au-gustine says:[9] "I myself have seen and known even a baby envious, it could not speak, yet it turned pale and looked bitterly on its foster-

[6] The nearest equivalent is "indignation." The use of the word "nemesis" to signify "revenge" does not represent the original Greek. Cf. *Rhetoric*, II, 9 (1386ᵇ12; 1387ᵃ8).
[7] *Rhetoric*, II, 11 (1388ᵃ34).
[8] PL 42, 1007.   [9] *Confessions*, I, 11 (PL 32, 665).

[1] PG 94, 932.   [2] PL 75, 728.
[3] PL 76, 226.   [4] *Rhetoric*, II, 11 (1388ᵃ30).
[5] *Ibid.*, 9 (1387ᵃ11).

brother." Therefore envy is not a mortal sin.

Obj. 3. Further, Every mortal sin is contrary to some virtue. But envy is contrary, not to a virtue but to nemesis (νέμεσις), which is a passion, according to the Philosopher.[1] Therefore envy is not a mortal sin.

On the contrary, It is written (Job. 5. 2): *Envy slayeth the little one.* Now nothing slays spiritually, except mortal sin. Therefore envy is a mortal sin.

I answer that, Envy is a mortal sin, in respect of its genus. For the genus of a sin is taken from its object; and envy according to the aspect of its object is contrary to charity, from which the soul derives its spiritual life, according to I John 3. 14, *We know that we have passed from death to life, because we love the brethren.* Now the object both of charity and of envy is our neighbour's good, but by contrary movements, since charity rejoices in our neighbour's good, while envy grieves over it, as stated above (A. 1). Therefore it is evident that envy is a mortal sin in respect of its genus

Nevertheless, as stated above (Q. XXXV, A. 3; Part I-II, Q. LXXII, A. 5, Reply 1), in every kind of mortal sin we find certain imperfect movements in the sensuality, which are venial sins; such are the first movement of concupiscence, in the genus of adultery, and the first movement of anger, in the genus of murder; and so in the genus of envy we find sometimes even in perfect men certain first movements, which are venial sins.

Reply Obj. 1. The movement of envy in so far as it is a passion of the sensuality, is an imperfect thing in the genus of human acts, the principle of which is the reason, so that envy of that kind is not a mortal sin. The same applies to the envy of little children who have not the use of reason. From this the *Reply to the Second Objection* is manifest.

Reply Obj. 3. According to the Philosopher,[2] envy is contrary both to nemesis and to pity, but for different reasons. For it is directly contrary to pity, their principal objects being contrary to one another, since the envious man grieves over his neighbour's good, while the pitiful man grieves over his neighbour's evil, so that the envious have no pity, as he states in the same passage, nor is the pitiful man envious. On the other hand, envy is contrary to nemesis on the part of the man whose good grieves the envious man, for nemesis is sorrow for the good of the undeserving according to Ps. 72.

3: *I was envious of the wicked, when I saw the prosperity of sinners,* while the envious grieves over the good of those who are deserving of it. Hence it is clear that the former contrariety is more direct than the latter. Now pity is a virtue, and an effect proper to charity, so that envy is contrary to pity and charity.

ARTICLE 4. *Whether Envy Is a Capital Vice?*

We proceed thus to the Fourth Article: It seems that envy is not a capital vice.

Objection 1. For the capital vices are distinct from their daughters. Now envy is the daughter of vainglory; for the Philosopher says[3] that "those who love honour and glory are more envious." Therefore envy is not a capital vice.

Obj. 2. Further, The capital vices seem to be less grave than the other vices which arise from them. For Gregory says (*Moral.* xxxi, 45):[4] "The leading vices seem to worm their way into the deceived mind under some kind of pretext, but those which follow them provoke the soul to all kinds of outrage, and confuse the mind with their wild outcry." Now envy seems to be a most grave sin, for Gregory says (*Moral.* v, 46):[5] "Though in every evil thing that is done, the venom of our old enemy is infused into the heart of man, yet in this wickedness the serpent stirs his whole bowels and discharges the bane of spite fitted to enter deep into the mind." Therefore envy is not a capital sin.

Obj. 3. Further, It seems that its daughters are unfittingly assigned by Gregory (*Moral.* xxxi, 45),[6] who says that "from envy arise hatred, tale-bearing, detraction, joy at our neighbour's misfortunes, and grief for his prosperity." For joy at our neighbour's misfortunes and grief for his prosperity seem to be the same as envy, as appears from what has been said above (A. 3). Therefore these should not be assigned as daughters of envy.

On the contrary stands the authority of Gregory (*Moral.* xxxi, 45)[7] who states that envy is a capital sin and assigns to it the daughters mentioned above.

I answer that, Just as acedia is grief for a Divine spiritual good, so envy is grief for our neighbour's good. Now it has been stated above (Q. XXXV, A. 4) that acedia is a capital vice for the reason that it incites man to do certain things, with the purpose either of avoiding sorrow or of satisfying its demands. Therefore envy is accounted a capital vice for the same reason.

---

[1] *Rhetoric,* II, 9 (1386^{b}16).
[2] *Ibid.,* (1386^{b}9).
[3] *Ibid.,* II, 10 (1387^{b}31).   [4] PL 76, 622.
[5] PL 76, 728.   [6] PL 76, 621.   [7] PL 76, 621.

Reply Obj. 1. As Gregory says (*Moral.* xxxi, 45),[1] "the capital vices are so closely akin to one another that one springs from the other. For the first offspring of pride is vainglory, which by corrupting the mind it occupies begets envy, since while it craves for the power of an empty name, it repines for fear lest another should acquire that power." Consequently the notion of a capital vice does not exclude its originating from another vice, but it demands that it should have some principal reason for being itself the origin of several kinds of sin. However it is perhaps because envy manifestly arises from vainglory, that it is not reckoned a capital sin, either by Isidore[2] or by Cassian (*De Instit. Cœnob.* v. 1).[3]

Reply Obj. 2. It does not follow from the passage quoted that envy is the greatest of sins, but that when the devil tempts us to envy, he is enticing us to that which has its chief place in his heart, for as stated further on in the same passage, by the envy of the devil, death came into the world.

There is, however, a kind of envy which is accounted among the most grievous sins, namely envy of another's spiritual good, which envy is a sorrow for the increase of God's grace, and not merely for our neighbour's good. Hence it is accounted a sin against the Holy Ghost, because thereby a man envies, as it were, the Holy Ghost Himself, Who is glorified in His works.

Reply Obj. 3. The number of envy's daughters may be understood for the reason that in the struggle aroused by envy there is something by way of beginning, something by way of middle, and something by way of term. The beginning is that a man strives to lower another's reputation, and this either secretly, and then we have tale-bearing, or openly, and then we have detraction.—The middle consists in the fact that when a man aims at defaming another, he is either able to do so, and then we have joy at another's misfortune, or he is unable, and then we have grief at another's prosperity. —The term is hatred itself, because just as good which delights causes love, so does sorrow cause hatred, as stated above (Q. XXXIV, A. 6). —Grief at another's prosperity is in one way the very same as envy, when, that is, a man grieves over another's prosperity, in so far as it gives the latter glory, but in another way it is a daughter of envy, in so far as the envious man sees his neighbour prosper notwithstanding his efforts to prevent it. On the other hand, joy at

[1] PL 76, 621. [2] *Sent.*, II, 37 (PL 83, 638); cf. *Quaest. in Vet. Test., In Deut.* XVI, super 7.1 (PL 83, 366). [3] PL 49, 201.

another's misfortune is not directly the same as envy, but is a result of it, because grief over our neighbour's good which is envy, gives rise to joy in his evil.

QUESTION XXXVII
OF THE SINS WHICH ARE CONTRARY TO PEACE
(*In Two Articles*)

WE must now consider the sins contrary to peace, and first we shall consider discord which is in the heart; secondly contention, which is on the lips (Q. XXXVIII); thirdly, those things which consist in deeds; namely schism (Q. XXXIX); quarrelling (Q. XLI), war (Q. XL), and sedition (Q. XLII.). Under the first head there are two points of inquiry: (1) Whether discord is a sin? (2) Whether it is a daughter of vainglory?

ARTICLE 1. *Whether Discord Is a Sin?*

We proceed thus to the First Article: It would seem that discord is not a sin.

Objection 1. For to be in disaccord with man is to sever oneself from another's will. But this does not seem to be a sin, because God's will alone, and not our neighbour's, is the rule of our own will. Therefore discord is not a sin.

Obj. 2 Further, Whoever induces another to sin, sins also himself. But it appears not to be a sin to incite others to discord, for it is written (Acts 23. 6) that Paul, knowing that the one part were Sadducees, and the other Pharisees, cried out in the council: *Men brethren, I am a Pharisee, the son of Pharisees, concerning the hope and resurrection of the dead I am called in question. And when he had so said, there arose a dissension between the Pharisees and the Sadducees.* Therefore discord is not a sin.

Obj. 3. Further, Sin, especially mortal sin, is not to be found in a holy man. But discord is to be found even among holy men, for it is written (Acts 15. 39): *There arose a dissension between Paul and Barnabas, so that they departed one from another.* Therefore discord is not a sin, and least of all a mortal sin.

On the contrary, Dissensions, that is, discords, are reckoned among the works of the flesh (Gal. 5. 20), of which it is said afterwards (*verse* 21) that *they who do such things shall not obtain the kingdom of God.* Now nothing, save mortal sin, excludes man from the kingdom of God. Therefore discord is a mortal sin.

I answer that, Discord is opposed to concord.

Now, as stated above (Q. XXIX, A. 3) concord results from charity, in so far as charity joins many hearts together in one thing, which is chiefly the Divine good, secondarily, the good of our neighbour. Therefore discord is a sin, in so far as it is opposed to this concord.

But it must be observed that this concord is destroyed by discord in two ways: first, directly, secondly, accidentally. Now, human acts and movements are said to be direct (*per se*) when they are according to one's intention. Therefore a man directly is in disaccord with his neighbour when he knowingly and intentionally dissents from the Divine good and his neighbour's good, to which he ought to consent. This is a mortal sin in respect of its genus, because it is contrary to charity, although the first movements of such discord are venial sins by reason of their being imperfect acts.

The accidental in human acts is that which occurs beside the intention. Hence when, several intend a good pertaining to God's honour, or our neighbour's profit, while one thinks a certain thing good, and another thinks contrariwise, the discord is in this case accidentally contrary to the Divine good or that of our neighbour. Such discord is neither sinful nor against charity, unless it be accompanied by an error about things necessary to salvation, or by undue obstinacy, since it has also been stated above (Q. XXIX, AA. 1, 3, Reply 2) that the concord which is an effect of charity is union of wills, not of opinions. It follows from this that discord is sometimes the sin of one party only, for instance, when one wills a good which the other knowingly resists; while sometimes it implies sin in both parties, as when each dissents from the other's good, and loves his own.

Reply Obj. 1. One man's will considered in itself is not the rule of another man's will; but in so far as our neighbour's will adheres to God's will, it becomes in consequence, a rule regulated according to its proper measure. Therefore it is a sin to be in disaccord with such a will, because by that very fact one is in disaccord with the Divine rule.

Reply Obj. 2. Just as a man's will that adheres to God is a right rule, to disaccord with which is a sin, so too a man's will that is opposed to God is a perverse rule, to disaccord with which is good. Hence to cause a discord by which a good concord resulting from charity is destroyed, is a grave sin; hence it is written (Prov. 6. 16): *Six things there are, which the Lord hateth, and the seventh His soul detesteth*, which seventh is stated (*verse* 19) to be *him that soweth discord among brethren.* On the other hand, to arouse a discord by which an evil concord (that is, concord in an evil will) is destroyed, is praiseworthy. In this way Paul was to be commended for sowing discord among those who agreed together in evil, because Our Lord also said of Himself (Matt. 10. 34): *I came not to send peace, but the sword.*

Reply Obj. 3. The discord between Paul and Barnabas was accidental and not direct, because each intended some good, yet the one thought one thing good, while the other thought something else, which was owing to human deficiency; for that controversy was not about things necessary to salvation. Moreover all this was ordained by Divine providence on account of the good which would ensue.

ARTICLE 2. *Whether Discord Is a Daughter of Vainglory?*

We proceed thus to the Second Article: It seems that discord is not a daughter of vainglory.

Objection 1. For anger is a vice distinct from vainglory. Now discord is apparently the daughter of anger, according to Prov. 15. 18: *A passionate man stirreth up strifes.* Therefore it is not a daughter of vainglory.

Obj. 2. Further, Augustine expounding the words of John 7. 39, *As yet the Spirit was not given*, says (*Tract.* xxxii)[1] "Malice severs, charity unites." Now discord is none other than a separation of wills. Therefore discord arises from malice, that is, envy, rather than from vainglory.

Obj. 3. Further, Whatever gives rise to many evils, would seem to be a capital vice. Now such is discord, because Jerome in commenting on Matt. 12. 25, *Every kingdom divided against itself shall be made desolate*, says:[2] "Just as concord makes small things thrive, so discord brings the greatest things to ruin." Therefore discord should itself be accounted a capital vice, rather than a daughter of vainglory.

On the contrary stands the authority of Gregory (*Moral.* xxxi, 45).[3]

I answer that, Discord denotes a certain disunion of wills, in so far, namely, as one man's will holds fast to one thing, while the other man's will holds fast to something else. Now if a man's will holds fast to its own ground, this is due to the fact that he prefers what is his own to that which belongs to others, and if he do this inordinately, it is due to pride and

1 PL 35, 1646.   2 PL 26, 82; cf. Sallust, *Jugurth.*
3 PL 76, 621.

vainglory. Therefore discord, whereby a man holds to his own way of thinking, and departs from that of others, is reckoned to be a daughter of vainglory.

Reply Obj. 1. Strife is not the same as discord, for strife consists in external deeds, and so it is fitting that it should arise from anger, which incites the mind to hurt one's neighbour; discord however consists in a divergence in the movements of wills, which arises from pride or vainglory, for the reason given above.

Reply Obj. 2. In discord we may consider that which is the term from which, that is, another's will from which we recede, and in this respect it arises from envy; and again we may consider that which is the term to which, that is, something of our own to which we cling, and in this respect it is caused by vainglory. And since in every moment the term to which is more important than the term from which (because the end is of more account than the beginning), discord is accounted a daughter of vainglory rather than of envy, though it may arise from both for different reasons, as stated.

Reply Obj. 3. The reason why concord makes small things thrive, while discord brings the greatest to ruin, is because the more united a force is, the stronger it is, while the more disunited it is the weaker it becomes (*De Causis.* xvii).[1] Hence it is evident that this is part of the proper effect of discord which is a disunion of wills, and in no way indicates that other vices arise from discord, as though it were a capital vice.

QUESTION XXXVIII
Of contention
(*In Two Articles*)

We must now consider contention, in respect of which there are two points of inquiry: (1) Whether contention is a mortal sin? (2) Whether it is a daughter of vainglory?

ARTICLE 1. *Whether Contention Is a Mortal Sin?*

We proceed thus to the First Article: It seems that contention is not a mortal sin.

Objection 1. For there is no mortal sin in spiritual men, and yet contention is to be found in them, according to Luke 22. 24: *And there was also a strife amongst* the disciples of Jesus, *which of them should . . . be the greatest.* Therefore contention is not a mortal sin.

Obj. 2. Further, No well disposed man should

be pleased that his neighbour commit a mortal sin. But the Apostle says (Philip. 1. 17): *Some out of contention preach Christ,* and afterwards he says (*verse* 18): *In this also I rejoice, yea, and will rejoice.* Therefore contention is not a mortal sin.

Obj. 3. Further, It happens that people contend either in the courts or in disputations, without any spiteful purpose, and with a good intention, as, for example, those who contend by disputing with heretics. Hence a gloss on I Kings 14. 1. *It come to pass one day,* etc. says.[2] "Catholics do not raise contentions with heretics unless they are first challenged to dispute." Therefore contention is not a mortal sin.

Obj. 4. Further, Job seems to have contended with God, according to Job 39. 32: *Shall he that contendeth with God be so easily silenced?* And yet Job was not guilty of mortal sin, since the Lord said of him (*ibid.* 42. 7): *You have not spoken the thing that is right before me, as my servant Job hath.* Therefore contention is not always a mortal sin.

On the contrary, It is against the precept of the Apostle who says (II Tim. 2. 14): *Contend not in words.* Moreover (Gal. 5. 20) contention is included among the works of the flesh, and as stated there (*verse* 21) *they who do such things shall not obtain the kingdom of God.* Now whatever excludes a man from the kingdom of God and is against a precept, is a mortal sin. Therefore contention is a mortal sin.

I answer that, To contend is to tend against some one. Therefore just as discord denotes a contrariety of wills, so contention signifies contrariety of speech. For this reason when a man contrasts various contrary things in a speech, this is called "*contentio,*" which Tully calls one of the rhetorical colours (*Rhet. ad Heren.* iv, 15),[3] where he says that "it consists in developing a speech from contrary things, for instance: Adulation has a pleasant beginning, and a most bitter end."

Now contrariety of speech may be looked at in two ways: first with regard to the intention of the contentious party; secondly, with regard to the manner of contending. As to the intention, we must consider whether he contends against the truth, and then he is to be blamed, or against falsehood, and then he should be praised. As to the manner, we must consider whether his manner of contending is in keeping with the persons and the matter in dispute, for then it would be praiseworthy; hence Tully

---

[1] Sect. 16 (BA 179.13).
[2] *Glossa ordin.* (II, 77A).
[3] DD I, 57.

says (*Rhet. ad Heren.* iii, 13)[1] that "contention is a sharp speech suitable for proof and refutation"; or whether it exceeds the demands of the persons and matter in dispute, in which case it is blameworthy.

Accordingly if we take contention as denoting a disclaimer of the truth and an inordinate manner, it is a mortal sin. Thus Ambrose defines contention: "Contention is a disclaimer of the truth with clamorous confidence." If, however, contention denote a disavowal of what is false, with the proper measure of acrimony, it is praiseworthy; but if it denote a disavowal of falsehood, together with an inordinate manner, it can be a venial sin, unless perhaps the contention be conducted so inordinately as to give scandal to others. Hence the Apostle after saying (II Tim. 2. 14): *Contend not in words,* adds, *for it is to no profit, but to the subverting of the hearers.*

Reply Obj. 1. The disciples of Christ did not contend together with the intention of disclaiming the truth, since each one stood up for what he thought was true. Yet there was inordinateness in their contention, because they contended about a matter which they ought not to have contended about, namely the primacy of honour; for they were not spiritual men as yet, as a gloss says on the same passage;[2] and for this reason Our Lord checked them.

Reply Obj. 2. Those who preached Christ *out of contention* were to be blamed, because, although they did not gainsay the truth of faith, but preached it, yet they did gainsay the truth by the fact that they thought they would *raise affliction* to the Apostle who was preaching the truth of faith. Hence the Apostle rejoiced not in their contention, but in the fruit that would result from it, namely that Christ would be made known; for evil is sometimes the occasion of good results.

Reply Obj. 3. Contention is complete and is a mortal sin when, in contending before a judge, a man gainsays the truth of justice, or in a disputation, intends to impugn the true doctrine. In this sense Catholics do not contend against heretics, but the reverse. But when, whether in court or in a disputation, it is incomplete, that is, in respect of the acrimony of speech, it is not always a mortal sin.

Reply Obj. 4. Contention here denotes an ordinary dispute. For Job had said (13. 3): *I will speak to the Almighty, and I desire to rea-*

son *with God;* yet he intended not to impugn the truth, but to defend it, and in seeking the truth thus, he had no wish to be inordinate in mind or in speech.

ARTICLE 2. *Whether Contention Is a Daughter of Vainglory?*

We proceed thus to the Second Article: It seems that contention is not a daughter of vainglory.

Objection 1. For contention is akin to zeal, and hence it is written (I Cor. 3. 3): *Whereas there is among you zeal* (Douay,—*envying*) *and contention, are you not carnal, and walk according to men?* Now zeal pertains to envy. Therefore contention arises rather from envy.

Obj. 2. Further, Contention is accompanied by raising of the voice. But "the voice is raised on account of anger," as Gregory declares (*Moral.* xxxi, 45).[3] Therefore contention too arises from anger.

Obj. 3. Further, Among other things knowledge seems to be the matter of pride and vainglory, according to I Cor. 8. 1: *Knowledge puffeth up.* Now contention is often due to lack of knowledge, and by knowledge we do not impugn the truth, we know it. Therefore contention is not a daughter of vainglory.

On the contrary stands the authority of Gregory (*Moral.* xxxi).[4]

I answer that, As stated above (Q. XXXVII, A. 2), discord is a daughter of vainglory, because each of the parties in disaccord clings to his own opinion, rather than acquiesce with the other. Now it is proper to pride and vainglory to seek one's own glory. And just as people are discordant when they hold to their own opinion in their hearts, so are they contentious when each defends his own opinion by words. Consequently contention is reckoned a daughter of vainglory for the same reason as discord.

Reply Obj. 1. Contention, like discord, is akin to envy in so far as a man severs himself from the one with whom he is discordant, or with whom he contends, but in so far as a contentious man holds to something, it is akin to pride and vainglory, because, namely, he clings to his own opinion, as stated above.

Reply Obj. 2. The contention of which we are speaking puts on a loud voice for the purpose of impugning the truth, so that it is not the chief part of contention. Hence it does not follow that contention arises from the same source as the raising of the voice.

Reply Obj. 3 Pride and vainglory are occa-

---

[1] DD 1, 40.
[2] *Glossa ordin.*, super Luc. 22.24 (v, 177B); Bede, *In Luc.*, bk. VI, super 22.24 (PL 92, 598).
[3] PL 76, 621.   [4] Ibid.

sioned chiefly by goods, even those that are contrary to them, for instance, when a man is proud of his humility; for when a thing arises in this way, it does so not directly but accidentally, in which way nothing hinders one contrary from arising out of another. Hence there is no reason why the *per se* and direct effects of pride or vainglory, should not result from the contraries of those things which are the occasion of pride.

QUESTION XXXIX
OF SCHISM
(*In Four Articles*)

WE must now consider the vices contrary to peace, which belong to deeds; such as schism, strife (Q. XLI), sedition (Q. XLII), and war (Q. XL). In the first place, then, about schism, there are four points of inquiry: (1) Whether schism is a special sin? (2) Whether it is graver than unbelief? (3) Of the power exercised by schismatics; (4) Of the punishment inflicted on them.

ARTICLE 1. *Whether Schism Is a Special Sin?*

We proceed thus to the First Article: It seems that schism is not a special sin.

Objection 1. For schism, as Pope Pelagius I. says (*Epist. ad Viator. et Pancrat.*),[1] "denotes a division." But every sin causes a division, according to Isa. 59. 2: *Your sins have divided between you and your God.* Therefore schism is not a special sin.

Obj. 2. Further, A man is apparently a schismatic if he disobeys the Church. But every sin makes a man disobey the commandments of the Church, because sin, according to Ambrose (*De Parad.* viii)[2] is "disobedience against the heavenly commandments." Therefore every sin is a schism.

Obj. 3. Further, Heresy also divides a man from the unity of faith. If, therefore, the word schism denotes a division, it would seem not to differ, as a special sin, from the sin of unbelief.

On the contrary, Augustine (*Contra Faust.* xx),[3] distinguishes between schism and heresy, for he says that "a schismatic is one who holds the same faith, and practises the same worship, as others, and takes pleasure in the mere disunion of the community; but a heretic is one who holds another faith from that of the Catholic Church." Therefore schism is not a general sin.

[1] MA IX, 731; cf. Gratian, *Decretum*, Pt. II, causa XXIV, Q. 1, can. 34, *Schisma*. (RF I, 979).
[2] PL 14, 309.
[3] Chap. 3 (PL 42, 369); cf. *Contra Crescon.*, II, 3 (PL 43, 469).

I answer that, As Isidore says (*Etym.* viii, 3),[4] schism "takes its name from being a scission of minds," and scission is opposed to unity. Therefore the sin of schism is one that is directly and per se opposed to unity. For in the moral as in the physical order, the species is not constituted by that which is accidental. Now, in the moral order, the essential is that which is intended, and that which results beside the intention, is, as it were, accidental. Hence the sin of schism is, properly speaking, a special sin, for the reason that the schismatic intends to sever himself from that unity which is the effect of charity; because charity unites not only one person to another with the bond of spiritual love, but also the whole Church in unity of spirit.

Accordingly schismatics properly so called are those who, wilfully and intentionally separate themselves from the unity of the Church; for this is the chief unity, and the particular unity of several individuals among themselves is subordinate to the unity of the Church, even as the mutual adaptation of each member of a natural body is subordinate to the unity of the whole body. Now the unity of the Church consists in two things: namely, in the mutual connection or communion of the members of the Church, and again in the subordination of all the members of the Church to the one head, according to Coloss. 2. 18, 19:*Puffed up by the sense of his flesh, and not holding the Head, from which the whole body, by joints and bands, being supplied with nourishment and compacted, groweth unto the increase of God.* Now this Head is Christ Himself, Whose vicegerent in the Church is the Sovereign Pontiff. Therefore schismatics are those who refuse to submit to the Sovereign Pontiff, and to hold communion with those members of the Church who acknowledge his supremacy.

Reply Obj. 1. The division between man and God that results from sin is not intended by the sinner; it happens beside his intention as a result of his turning inordinately to a changeable good, and so it is not schism properly so called.

Reply Obj. 2. The essence of schism consists in rebelliously disobeying the commandments; and I say "rebelliously," since a schismatic both obstinately scorns the commandments of the Church, and refuses to submit to her judgment. But every sinner does not do this, and so every sin is a schism.

Reply Obj. 3. Heresy and schism are distinguished in respect of those things to which each

[4] PL 82, 297.

is opposed per se and directly. For heresy is per se opposed to faith, while schism is per se opposed to the unity of ecclesiastical charity. Therefore just as faith and charity are different virtues, although whoever lacks faith lacks charity, so too schism and heresy are different vices, although whoever is a heretic is also a schismatic, but not conversely. This is what Jerome says in his commentary on the Epistle to Titus (3. 10):[1] "I consider the difference between schism and heresy to be that heresy holds false doctrine while schism severs a man from the Church." Nevertheless, just as the loss of charity is the road to the loss of faith, according to I Tim. 1. 6: *From which things*, that is, charity and the like, *some going astray, are turned aside into vain babbling*, so too, schism is the road to heresy. Therefore Jerome adds (*ibid.*) that "at the outset it is possible, in a certain respect, to find a difference between schism and heresy; yet there is no schism that does not devise some heresy for itself, that it may appear to have had a reason for separating from the Church."

ARTICLE 2. *Whether Schism Is a Graver Sin Than Unbelief?*

We proceed thus to the Second Article: It seems that schism is a graver sin than unbelief.

Objection 1. For the graver sin meets with a graver punishment, according to Deut. 25. 2: *According to the measure of the sin shall the measure also of the stripes be.* Now we find the sin of schism punished more severely than even the sin of unbelief or idolatry for we read (Exod. 32. 28), that some were slain by the swords of their fellow men on account of idolatry; but of the sin of schism we read (Num. 16. 30): *If the Lord do a new thing, and the earth opening her mouth swallow them down, and all things that belong to them, and they go down alive into hell, you shall know that they have blasphemed the Lord* God. Moreover the ten tribes who were guilty of schism in revolting from the rule of David were most severely punished (IV Kings 17). Therefore the sin of schism is graver than the sin of unbelief.

Obj. 2. Further, "The good of the multitude is greater and more godlike than the good of the individual," as the Philosopher states.[2] Now schism is opposed to the good of the multitude, namely, ecclesiastical unity, while unbelief is contrary to the particular good of one man, namely the faith of an individual. Therefore it seems that schism is a graver sin than unbelief.

Obj. 3. Further, A greater good is opposed to a greater evil, according to the Philosopher.[3] Now schism is opposed to charity, which is a greater virtue than faith to which unbelief is opposed, as shown above (Q. XXIII, A. 6). Therefore schism is a graver sin than unbelief.

On the contrary, That which results from an addition to something else surpasses that thing either in good or in evil. Now heresy results from something being added to schism, for it adds corrupt doctrine, as Jerome declares in the passage quoted above (A. 1, REPLY 3). Therefore schism is a less grievous sin than unbelief.

I answer that, The gravity of a sin can be considered in two ways: first, according to the species of that sin, secondly, according to its circumstances. And since particular circumstances are infinite in number, so too they can be varied in an infinite number of ways. Therefore if one were to ask in general which of two sins is the graver, the question must be understood to refer to the gravity derived from the sin's genus. Now the genus or species of a sin is taken from its object, as shown above (Part I-II, Q. LXXII, A. 1; Q. LXXIII, A. 3). Therefore the sin which is opposed to the greater good is, in respect of its genus, more grievous, for instance a sin committed against God is graver than a sin committed against one's neighbour.

Now it is evident that unbelief is a sin committed against God Himself, according as He is in Himself the First Truth, on which faith is founded; but schism is opposed to ecclesiastical unity, which is a participated good, and a lesser good than God Himself. Therefore it is manifest that the sin of unbelief is generically more grievous than the sin of schism, although it may happen that a particular schismatic sins more grievously than a particular unbeliever, either because his contempt is greater, or because his sin is a source of greater danger, or for some similar reason.

Reply Obj. 1. It had already been declared to that people by the law which they had received that there was one God, and that no other God was to be worshipped by them; and the same had been confirmed among them by many kinds of signs. Consequently there was no need for those who sinned against this faith by falling into idolatry, to be punished in an unusual manner; it was enough that they should be punished in the usual way. On the other hand, it was not so well known among them that

---

[1] PL 26, 633.   [2] *Ethics*, I, 2 (1094[b]10).   [3] *Ibid.*, VIII, 10 (1160[b]9).

Moses was always to be their ruler, and so it was necessary for those who rebelled against his authority to be punished in a miraculous and unusual manner.

We may also reply by saying that the sin of schism was sometimes more severely punished in that people, because they were inclined to seditions and schisms. For it is written (I Esd. 4. 15): *This city since days gone by has rebelled against its kings; and seditions and wars were raised therein* (Vulg.,—*This city is a rebellious city, and hurtful to the kings and provinces, and . . . wars were raised therein of old.*). Now sometimes a more severe punishment is inflicted for a frequently repeated sin (as stated above, Part I-II, Q. CV, A. 2, Reply 9), because punishments are medicines intended to keep man away from sin, so that where there is greater proneness to sin, a more severe punishment ought to be inflicted. As regards the ten tribes, they were punished not only for the sin of schism, but also for that of idolatry, as stated in the passage quoted.

Reply Obj. 2. Just as the good of the multitude is greater than the good of a unit in that multitude, so is it less than the extrinsic good to which that multitude is directed, even as the good of a rank of soldiers in the army is less than the good of the commander-in-chief. In like manner the good of ecclesiastical unity, to which schism is opposed, is less than the good of Divine truth, to which unbelief is opposed.

Reply Obj. 3. Charity has two objects; one is its principal object and is the Divine goodness, the other is its secondary object and is our neighbour's good. Now schism and other sins against our neighbour, are opposed to charity in respect of its secondary good, which is less than the object of faith, for this is God Himself; and so these sins are less grievous than unbelief. On the other hand, hatred of God, which is opposed to charity in respect of its principal object, is not less grievous than unbelief. Nevertheless of all sins committed by man against his neighbour, the sin of schism would seem to be the greatest, because it is opposed to the spiritual good of the multitude.

ARTICLE 3. *Whether Schismatics Have Any Power?*

We proceed thus to the Third Article: It would seem that schismatics have some power.

Objection 1. For Augustine says (*Contra Donat.* i, 1):[1] "Just as those who come back to the Church after being baptized, are not bap-

[1] PL 43, 109.

tized again, so those who return after being ordained, are not ordained again." Now Order is a kind of power. Therefore schismatics have some power since they retain their Orders.

Obj. 2. Further, Augustine says (*De Unico Bapt.*):[2] "One who is separated can confer a sacrament even as he can have it." But the power of conferring a sacrament is a very great power. Therefore schismatics who are separated from the Church, have a spiritual power.

Obj. 3. Further, Pope Urban II says:[3] "We command that persons consecrated by bishops who were themselves consecrated according to the Catholic rite, but have separated themselves by schism from the Roman Church, should be received mercifully and that their Orders should be acknowledged, when they return to the unity of the Church, provided they be of commendable life and knowledge." But this would not be so, unless spiritual power were retained by schismatics. Therefore schismatics have spiritual power.

On the contrary, Cyprian says in a letter (*Ep.* lii):[4] which is quoted in the Decretals:[5] "He who observes neither unity of spirit nor the concord of peace, and severs himself from the bonds of the Church, and from the fellowship of her priests, cannot have episcopal power or honour."

I answer that, Spiritual power is twofold, the one sacramental, the other a power of jurisdiction. The sacramental power is one that is conferred by some kind of consecration. Now all the consecrations of the Church are immovable so long as the consecrated thing remains, as appears even in inanimate things, since an altar, once consecrated, is not consecrated again unless it has been broken up. Consequently such a power as this remains, as to its essence, in the man who has received it by consecration, as long as he lives, even if he fall into schism or heresy; and this appears from the fact that if he come back to the Church, he is not consecrated again. Since, however, the lower power ought not to exercise its act except in so far as it is moved by the higher power, as may be seen even in natural things, it follows that such persons lose the use of their power, so that it is not lawful for them to use it. Yet if they use

[2] Cf. *De Bap. contra Donat.*, VI 5. (PL 43, 200).
[3] Council of Piacenza, X (MA XX, 806); cf. Gratian, *Decretum*, II, causa IX, Q. 1, can. 5, *Ordinationse* (RF I, 602).
[4] Cf. PL 4, 355; the text of this letter is also given as one of the letters of St. Cornelius (*Epist.*, X, PL 3, 816).
[5] Gratian, *Decretum*, II, causa VII, Q. 1, can. 6, *Novatianus* (RF I, 568).

it, this power has its effect in sacramental acts, because in these things man acts only as God's instrument, so that sacramental effects are not precluded on account of any fault whatever in the person who confers the sacrament.

On the other hand, the power of jurisdiction is that which is conferred by a mere human appointment. Such a power as this does not stay with the recipient immovably, so that it does not remain in heretics and schismatics; and consequently they neither absolve nor excommunicate, nor grant indulgence, nor do anything of the kind, and if they do, it is invalid.

Accordingly when it is said that such persons have no spiritual power, it is to be understood as referring either to the second power, or if it be referred to the first power, not as referring to the essence of the power, but to its lawful use.

This suffices for the *Replies to the Objections.*

ARTICLE 4. *Whether It Is Right That Schismatics Should Be Punished With Excommunication?*

We proceed thus to the Fourth Article: It would seem that schismatics are not rightly punished with excommunication.

Objection 1. For excommunication deprives a man chiefly of a share in the sacraments. But Augustine says (*Contra Donat.* vi, 5)[1] that Baptism can be received from a schismatic. Therefore it seems that excommunication is not a fitting punishment for schismatics.

Obj. 2. Further, It is the duty of Christ's faithful to lead back those who have gone astray, and so it is written against certain persons (Ezech. 34. 4): *That which was driven away you have not brought again, neither have you sought that which was lost.* Now schismatics are more easily brought back by such as may hold communion with them. Therefore it seems that they ought not to be excommunicated.

Obj. 3. Further, A double punishment is not inflicted for one and the same sin, according to Nahum 1. 9: *God will not judge the same twice* (Septuagint Version.). Now some receive a temporal punishment for the sin of schism, according to XXIII, Q. v.,[2] where it is stated: "Both divine and earthly laws have laid down that those who are severed from the unity of the Church, and disturb her peace, must be punished by the secular power." Therefore they ought not to be punished with excommunication.

¹ PL 43, 200.
² Gratian, *Decretum,* can. 44, *Qualinos.* (RF I, 943).

On the contrary, It is written (Num. 16. 26): *Depart from the tents of these wicked men,* those, namely, who had caused the schism, *and touch nothing of theirs, lest you be involved in their sins.*

I answer that, According to Wisd. 11. 17, *By what things a man sinneth, by the same also he should be punished* (Vulg.,—*he is tormented*). Now a schismatic, as shown above (A. 1), commits a twofold sin: first by separating himself from communion with the members of the Church, and in this respect the fitting punishment for schismatics is that they be excommunicated. Secondly, they refuse submission to the head of the Church, and therefore, since they are unwilling to be controlled by the Church's spiritual power, it is just that they should be compelled by the secular power.

Reply Obj. 1. It is not lawful to receive Baptism from a schismatic save in a case of necessity, since it is better for a man to quit this life marked with the sign of Christ, no matter from whom he may receive it, whether from a Jew or a pagan, than deprived of that mark, which is bestowed in Baptism.

Reply Obj. 2. Excommunication does not forbid the intercourse by which a person by salutary admonitions leads back to the unity of the Church those who are separated from her. Indeed this very separation brings them back somewhat, because through confusion at their separation, they are sometimes led to do penance.

Reply Obj. 3. The punishments of the present life are medicinal, and therefore when one punishment does not suffice to compel a man, another is added, just as physicians employ several bodily medicines when one has no effect. In like manner the Church, when excommunication does not sufficiently restrain certain men, employs the compulsion of the secular arm. If, however, one punishment suffices, another should not be employed.

QUESTION XL

OF WAR

(*In Four Articles*)

WE must now consider war, under which head there are four points of inquiry: (1) Whether some kind of war is lawful? (2) Whether it is lawful for clerics to fight? (3) Whether it is lawful for belligerents to lay ambushes? (4) Whether it is lawful to fight on holy days?

ARTICLE I. *Whether It is Always Sinful To Wage War?*

We proceed thus to the First Article: It seems that it is always sinful to wage war.

Objection 1. Because punishment is not inflicted except for sin. Now those who wage war are threatened by Our Lord with punishment, according to Matt. 26. 52: *All that take the sword shall perish with the sword.* Therefore all wars are unlawful.

Obj. 2. Further, Whatever is contrary to a Divine precept is a sin. But war is contrary to a Divine precept, for it is written (Matt. 5. 39): *But I say to you not to resist evil;* and (Rom. 12. 19): *Not revenging yourselves, my dearly beloved, but give place unto wrath.* Therefore war is always sinful.

Obj. 3. Further, Nothing, except sin, is contrary to an act of virtue. But war is contrary to peace. Therefore war is always a sin.

Obj. 4. Further, The exercise of a lawful thing is itself lawful, as is evident in exercises of the sciences. But warlike exercises which take place in tournaments are forbidden by the Church, since those who are slain in these trials are deprived of ecclesiastical burial. Therefore it seems that war is a sin absolutely.

On the contrary, Augustine says in a sermon on the son of the centurion:[1] "If the Christian Religion forbade war altogether, those who sought salutary advice in the Gospel would rather have been counselled to cast aside their arms, and to give up soldiering altogether. On the contrary, they were told: 'Do violence to no man; . . . and be content with your pay' (Luke 3. 14). If he commanded them to be content with their pay, he did not forbid soldiering."

I answer that, In order for a war to be just, three things are necessary. First, the authority of the sovereign by whose command the war is to be waged. For it is not the business of a private person to declare war, because he can seek for redress of his rights from the tribunal of his superior. Moreover it is not the business of a private person to summon together the people, which has to be done in wartime. And as the care of the common weal is committed to those who are in authority, it is their business to watch over the common weal of the city, kingdom or province subject to them. And just as it is lawful for them to have re-

course to the material sword in defending that common weal against internal disturbances, when they punish evil-doers, according to the words of the Apostle (Rom. 13. 4): *He beareth not the sword in vain: for he is God's minister, an avenger to execute wrath upon him that doth evil;* so too, it is their business to have recourse to the sword of war in defending the common weal against external enemies. Hence it is said to those who are in authority (Ps. 81. 4): *Rescue the poor: and deliver the needy out of the hand of the sinner;* and for this reason Augustine says (*Contra Faust.* xxii, 75):[2] "The natural order conducive to peace among mortals demands that the power to declare and counsel war should be in the hands of those who hold the supreme authority."

Secondly, a just cause is required, namely that those who are attacked should be attacked because they deserve it on account of some fault. Therefore Augustine says (Q. x, *super Jos.*):[3] "A just war is usually described as one that avenges wrongs, when a nation or state has to be punished, for refusing to make amends for the wrongs inflicted by its subjects, or to restore what it has seized unjustly."

Thirdly, it is necessary that the belligerents should have a right intention, so that they intend the advancement of good, or the avoidance of evil. Hence Augustine says (*De Verb. Dom.*):[4] "True religion does not look upon as sinful those wars that are waged not for motives of aggrandisement, or cruelty, but with the object of securing peace, of punishing evil-doers, and of uplifting the good." For it may happen that the war is declared by the legitimate authority, and for a just cause, and yet be rendered unlawful through a wicked intention. Hence Augustine says (*Contra Faust.* xxii):[5] "The passion for inflicting harm, the cruel thirst for vengeance, an unpacific and relentless spirit, the fever of revolt, the lust of power, and such things, all these are rightly condemned in war."

Reply Obj. 1. As Augustine says (*Contra Faust.* xxii):[6] "To take the sword is to arm oneself in order to take the life of anyone, without the command or permission of superior or lawful authority." On the other hand, to have recourse to the sword (as a private person) by the authority of the sovereign or judge, or (as

---

[1] *Ep. ad Marcel.*, CXXXVIII, chap. 2 (PL 33, 531). Cf. Gratian, *Decretum*, PT. II, causa XXIII, Q. I, can. 2 *Paratus* (RF I, 891).

[2] PL 42, 448.   [3] *Quaest. in Hept.*, VI (PL 34, 781).

[4] Cf. Gratian, *Decretum*, PT. II, causa XXIII, Q. I, can. 6, *Apud veros* (RF I, 893); see Augustine, *City of God*, XIX, 12 (PL 41, 637).

[5] Chap. 74 (PL 42, 447).

[6] Chap. 70 (PL 42, 444).

a public person) through zeal for justice, and by the authority, so to speak, of God, is not to *take the sword,* but to use it as commissioned by another, and so it does not deserve punishment. And yet even those who make sinful use of the sword are not always slain with the sword, but they always perish with their own sword, because, unless they repent, they are punished eternally for their sinful use of the sword.

Reply Obj. 2. Precepts of this kind, as Augustine observes (*De Serm. Dom. in Monte,* i),[1] should always be borne in readiness of mind, so that we be ready to obey them, and, if necessary, to refrain from resistance or self-defence. Nevertheless it is necessary sometimes for a man to act otherwise for the common good, or for the good of those with whom he is fighting. Hence Augustine says (*Ep. ad Marcellin.*):[2] "Those whom we have to punish with a kindly severity, it is necessary to handle in many ways against their will. For when we are stripping a man of the lawlessness of sin, it is good for him to be vanquished, since nothing is more hopeless than the happiness of sinners, whence arises a guilty impunity, and an evil will, like an internal enemy."

Reply Obj. 3. Those who wage war justly aim at peace, and so they are not opposed to peace, except to the evil peace, which Our Lord *came not to send upon earth* (Matt. 10. 34). Hence Augustine says (*Ep. ad Bonif.* clxxxix):[3] "We do not seek peace in order to be at war, but we go to war that we may have peace. Be peaceful, therefore, in warring, so that you may vanquish those whom you war against, and bring them to the prosperity of peace."

Reply Obj. 4. Manly exercises in warlike feats of arms are not all forbidden, but those which are inordinate and perilous, and end in slaying or plundering. In olden times warlike exercises presented no such danger, and hence they were called exercises of arms or bloodless wars, as Jerome states in an epistle (cf. Veget., —*De Re Milit.* i).[4]

ARTICLE 2. *Whether It Is Lawful for Clerics and Bishops To Fight?*

We proceed thus to the Second Article: It seems lawful for clerics and bishops to fight.

Objection 1. For, as stated above (A. 1), wars are lawful and just in so far as they protect the poor and the entire common weal from suffering at the hands of the foe. Now this seems to be above all the duty of prelates, for Gregory says (*Hom. in Ev.* xiv):[5] "The wolf comes upon the sheep, when any unjust and rapacious man oppresses those who are faithful and humble. But he who was thought to be the shepherd, and was not, leaveth the sheep, and flieth, for he fears lest the wolf hurt him, and dares not stand up against his injustice." Therefore it is lawful for prelates and clerics to fight.

Obj. 2. Further, Pope Leo IV writes (xxiii, qu. 8, can. *Igitur*):[6] "As adverse tidings had frequently come from the Saracen side, some said that the Saracens would come to the port of Rome secretly and covertly; for which reason we commanded our people to gather together, and ordered them to go down to the sea-shore." Therefore it is lawful for bishops to fight.

Obj. 3. Further, It seems to be the same whether a man does a thing himself, or consents to its being done by another, according to Rom. 1. 32: *They who do such things, are worthy of death, and not only they that do them, but they also that consent to them that do them.* Now those, above all, seem to consent to a thing, who induce others to do it. But it is lawful for bishops and clerics to induce others to fight, for it is written (xxiii, qu. 8, can. *Hortatu*)[7] that "Charles went to war with the Lombards at the instance and entreaty of Adrian, bishop of Rome." Therefore they also are allowed to fight.

Obj. 4. Further, Whatever is right and meritorious in itself is lawful for prelates and clerics. Now it is sometimes right and meritorious to make war, for it is written (xxiii, qu. 8, can. *Omni timore*)[8] that "if a man die for the true faith, or to save his country, or in defence of Christians, God will give him a heavenly reward." Therefore it is lawful for bishops and clerics to fight.

On the contrary, It was said to Peter as representing bishops and clerics (Matt. 26. 52): *Put up again thy sword into the scabbard* (Vulg., —*its place*). Therefore it is not lawful for them to fight.

I answer that, Several things are requisite for the good of a human society, and a number of things are done better and quicker by a number of persons than by one, as the Philosopher observes,[9] while certain occupations are so inconsistent with one another, that they cannot be

---

[1] Chap. 19 (PL 34, 1260); cf. *Epist.,* 138. 2 (PL 33, 531).
[2] *Epist.,* 138.2 (PL 33, 531).   [3] PL 33, 856.
[4] Chaps. 9–28 (DD 664–672); II, 23 (DD 684).
[5] PL 76, 1128.
[6] Gratian, *Decretum* (RF I, 954); cf. Leo IV, *Epist. Ad Ludovicum Augustum* (MA XIV, 888).
[7] Gratian, *Decretum,* (RF I, 955).
[8] *Ibid.*
[9] *Politics,* I, 2 (1252[b]3).

fittingly exercised at the same time; hence those who are assigned to important duties are forbidden to occupy themselves with things of small importance. Thus according to human laws, soldiers who are assigned to warlike pursuits are forbidden to engage in commerce.

Now warlike pursuits are altogether incompatible with the duties of a bishop and a cleric for two reasons. The first reason is a general one, because, namely, warlike pursuits are full of unrest, so that they hinder the mind very much from the contemplation of Divine things, the praise of God, and prayers for the people, which belong to the duties of a cleric. Therefore just as commercial enterprises are forbidden to clerics, because they entangle the mind too much, so too are warlike pursuits, according to II Tim. 2. 4: *No man being a soldier to God, entangleth himself with secular business.* The second reason is a special one, because, namely, all the clerical Orders are directed to the ministry of the altar, on which the Passion of Christ is represented sacramentally, according to I Cor. 11. 26: *As often as you shall eat this bread, and drink the chalice, you shall show the death of the Lord, until He come.* Therefore it is unbecoming for them to slay or shed blood, and it is more fitting that they should be ready to shed their own blood for Christ, so as to imitate in deed what they portray in their ministry. For this reason it has been decreed[1] that those who shed blood, even without sin, become irregular. Now no man who has a certain duty to perform can lawfully do that which renders him unfit for that duty. Therefore it is altogether unlawful for clerics to fight, because war is directed to the shedding of blood.

Reply Obj. 1. Prelates ought to withstand not only the wolf who brings spiritual death upon the flock, but also the pillager and the oppressor who work bodily harm; not, however, by having recourse themselves to material arms, but by means of spiritual weapons, according to the saying of the Apostle (II Cor. 10. 4): *The weapons of our warfare are not carnal, but mighty through God.* Such are salutary warnings, devout prayers, and, for those who are obstinate, the sentence of excommunication.

Reply Obj. 2. Prelates and clerics may, by the authority of their superiors, take part in wars, not indeed by taking up arms themselves, but by affording spiritual help to those who fight justly, by exhorting and absolving them, and by other like spiritual helps. Thus in the Old Testament (Jos. 6. 4) the priests were commanded to sound the sacred trumpets in the battle. It was for this purpose that bishops or clerics were first allowed to go to war; and it is an abuse of this permission, if any of them take up arms themselves.

Reply Obj. 3. As stated above (Q. XXIII, A. 4, REPLY 2) every power, art or virtue that pertains to the end, has to dispose that which is directed to the end. Now, among the faithful, carnal wars should be considered as having for their end the Divine spiritual good to which clerics are deputed. Therefore it is the duty of clerics to dispose and counsel other men to engage in just wars. For they are forbidden to take up arms, not as though it were a sin, but because such an occupation is unbecoming their persons.

Reply Obj. 4. Although it is meritorious to wage a just war, nevertheless it is rendered unlawful for clerics, by reason of their being assigned to works more meritorious still. Thus the marriage act may be meritorious; and yet it becomes reprehensible in those who have vowed virginity, because they are bound to a yet greater good.

ARTICLE 3. *Whether It Is Lawful To Lay Ambushes in War?*

We proceed thus to the Third Article: It seems that it is unlawful to lay ambushes in war.

Objection 1. For it is written (Deut. 16. 20): *Thou shalt follow justly after that which is just.* But ambushes, since they are a kind of deception, seem to pertain to injustice. Therefore it is unlawful to lay ambushes even in a just war.

Obj. 2. Further, Ambushes and deception seem to be opposed to faithfulness even as lies are. But since we are bound to keep faith with all men, it is wrong to lie to anyone, as Augustine states (*Contra Mend.* xv).[2] Therefore, as "one is bound to keep faith with one's enemy," as Augustine states (*Ep. ad Bonifac.* clxxxix),[3] it seems that it is unlawful to lay ambushes for one's enemies.

Obj. 3. *Further,* It is written (Matt. 7. 12): *Whatsoever you would that men should do to you, do you also to them;* and we ought to observe this in all our dealings with our neighbour. Now our enemy is our neighbour. Therefore, since no man wishes ambushes or deceptions to be prepared for himself, it seems that no one ought to carry on war by laying ambushes.

---

[1] Gratian, *Decretum,* PT. I, d. L, can. 4, *Miror.* (RF I, 178).

[2] PL 40, 530.   [3] PL 33, 856.

On the contrary, Augustine says (*QQ. in Heptateuch., qu.* x, *super Jos.*):[1] "Provided the war be just, it is no concern of justice whether it be carried on openly or by ambushes," and he proves this by the authority of the Lord, Who commanded Joshua to lay ambushes for the city of Hai (*Jos.* 8. 2).

I answer that, The object of laying ambushes is in order to deceive the enemy. Now a man may be deceived by another's word or deed in two ways. First, through being told something false, or through the breaking of a promise, and this is always unlawful. No one ought to deceive the enemy in this way, for there are certain rights of war and convenants, which ought to be observed even among enemies, as Ambrose states (*De Offic.* i, 29).[2]

Secondly, a man may be deceived by what we say or do, because we do not declare our purpose or meaning to him. Now we are not always bound to do this, since even in the Sacred Doctrine many things have to be concealed, especially from unbelievers, lest they deride it, according to Matt. 7. 6: *Give not that which is holy, to dogs.* Therefore much more ought the plan of campaign to be hidden from the enemy. For this reason among other things that a soldier has to learn is the art of concealing his purpose lest it come to the enemy's knowledge, as stated in the Book on *Strategy* by Frontinus.[3] Concealment of this kind is what is meant by an ambush which may be lawfully employed in a just war. Nor can these ambushes be properly called deceptions, nor are they contrary to justice or to a well-ordered will. For a man would have an inordinate will if he were unwilling that others should hide from him.

This suffices for the *Replies to the Objections.*

ARTICLE 4. *Whether It is Lawful To Fight on Holy Days?*

We proceed thus to the Fourth Article: It seems unlawful to fight on holy days.

Objection 1. For holy days are instituted that we may give our time to the things of God. Hence they are included in the keeping of the Sabbath prescribed Exod. 20. 8, for Sabbath is interpreted rest. But wars are full of unrest. Therefore by no means is it lawful to fight on holy days.

Obj. 2. Further, Certain persons are reproached (Isa. 58. 3) because on fast-days they exacted what was owing to them, were guilty of strife, and of striking with their fists. Much more,

therefore, is it unlawful to fight on holy days.

Obj. 3. Further, No inordinate deed should be done to avoid temporal harm. But fighting on a holy day seems in itself to be an inordinate deed. Therefore no one should fight on a holy day even through the need of avoiding temporal harm.

On the contrary, It is written (I Machab. 2. 41): *The Jews rightly determined . . . saying: Whosoever shall come up against us to fight on the Sabbath-day, we will fight against him.*

I answer that, The observance of holy days is no hindrance to those things which are ordered to man's safety, even that of his body. Hence Our Lord argued with the Jews, saying (John 7. 23): *Are you angry at Me because I have healed the whole man on the Sabbath-day?* Hence physicians may lawfully attend to their patients on holy days. Yet much more reason is there for safeguarding the common weal (by which many are saved from being slain, and innumerable evils both temporal and spiritual prevented), than the bodily safety of an individual. Therefore, for the purpose of safeguarding the common weal of the faithful, it is lawful to carry on a war on holy days, provided there be need for doing so; because it would be to tempt God, if notwithstanding such a need, one were to choose to refrain from fighting. However, as soon as the need ceases, it is no longer lawful to fight on a holy day, for the reasons given. And this suffices for the *Replies to the Objections.*

QUESTION XLI
OF STRIFE
(*In Two Articles*)

WE must now consider strife,[4] under which head there are two points of inquiry: (1) Whether strife is a sin? (2) Whether it is a daughter of anger?

ARTICLE 1. *Whether Strife Is Always a Sin?*

We proceed thus to the First Article: It seems that strife is not always a sin.

Objection 1. For strife seems a kind of contention; hence Isidore says (*Etym.* x)[5] that the word "*rixosus* (quarrelsome) is derived from the snarling (*rictu*) of a dog, because the quarrelsome man is ever ready to contradict; he delights in brawling, and provokes contention." Now contention is not always a sin. Neither, therefore, is strife.

---

[1] PL 34, 781. [2] PL 16, 68.
[3] *Stratagematum.*, I 1. (DD 504).

[4] Strife here denotes fighting between individuals.
[5] PL 82, 392.

Obj. 2. Further, It is related (Gen. 26. 21) that the servants of Isaac *digged* another well, *and for that they quarrelled likewise.* Now it is not credible that the household of Isaac quarrelled publicly, without being reproved by him, supposing it were a sin. Therefore strife is not a sin.

Obj. 3. Further, Strife seems to be a war between individuals. But war is not always sinful. Therefore strife is not always a sin.

On the contrary, Strifes[1] are reckoned among the works of the flesh (Gal. 5. 20), and *they who do such things shall not obtain the kingdom of God.* Therefore strifes are not only sinful, but they are even mortal sins.

I answer that, While contention implies a contradiction of words, strife denotes a certain contradiction of deeds. Hence a gloss on Gal. 5. 20 says[2] that strifes are "when persons strike one another through anger." Hence strife is a kind of private war, because it takes place between private persons, being declared not by public authority, but rather by a disordered will. Therefore strife is always sinful. In fact it is a mortal sin in the man who attacks another unjustly, for it is not without mortal sin that one inflicts harm on another even if the deed be done by the hands. But in him who defends himself, it may be without sin, or it may sometimes involve a venial sin, or sometimes a mortal sin; and this depends on his purpose and on his manner of defending himself. For if his sole purpose be to withstand the injury done to him, and he defend himself with due moderation, it is no sin, and one cannot say properly that there is strife on his part. But if, on the other hand, his self-defence be inspired by vengeance and hatred, it is always a sin. It is a venial sin, if a slight movement of hatred or vengeance obtrude itself, or if he does not much exceed moderation in defending himself; but it is a mortal sin if he makes for his assailant with the fixed intention of killing him, or inflicting grievous harm on him.

Reply Obj. 1. Strife is not just the same as contention, and there are three things in the passage quoted from Isidore, which express the inordinate nature of strife. First, the quarrelsome man is always ready to fight, and this is conveyed by the words, "ever ready to contradict," that is to say, whether the other man says or does well or ill. Secondly, he delights in quarrelling itself, and so the passage proceeds,

"and delights in brawling." Thirdly, he provokes others to quarrel, and thus it goes on, "and provokes contention."

Reply Obj. 2. The sense of the text is not that the servants of Isaac quarrelled, but that the inhabitants of that country quarrelled with them. Therefore these sinned, and not the servants of Isaac, who bore the calumny (cf. Gen. 21. 20).

Reply Obj. 3. In order for a war to be just it must be declared by authority of the governing power, as stated above (Q. XL, A. 1), strife however proceeds from a private feeling of anger or hatred. For if the servants of a sovereign or judge, in virtue of their public authority, attack certain men and these defend themselves, it is not the former who are said to be guilty of strife, but those who resist the public authority. Hence it is not the assailants in this case who are guilty of strife and commit sin, but those who defend themselves beyond order.

ARTICLE 2. *Whether Strife Is a Daughter of Anger?*

We proceed thus to the Second Article: It seems that strife is not a daughter of anger.

Objection 1. For it is written (James 4. 1): *Whence are wars and contentions? Are they not . . . from your concupiscences, which war in your members?* But anger is not in the concupiscible part. Therefore strife is a daughter, not of anger, but of concupiscence.

Obj. 2. Further, It is written (Prov. 28. 25): *He that boasteth and puffeth up himself, stirreth up quarrels.* Now strife is apparently the same as quarrel. Therefore it seems that strife is a daughter of pride or vainglory which make a man boast and puff himself up.

Obj. 3. Further, It is written (Prov. 18. 6): *The lips of a fool intermeddle with strife.* Now folly differs from anger, for it is opposed, not to meekness, but to wisdom or prudence. Therefore strife is not a daughter of anger.

Obj. 4. Further, It is written (Prov. 10. 12): *Hatred stirreth up strifes.* But "hatred arises from envy," according to Gregory (*Moral.* xxxi, 45).[3] Therefore strife is not a daughter of anger, but of envy.

Obj. 5. Further, It is written (Prov. 17. 19): *He that studieth discords, soweth* (Vulg.,— *loveth*) *quarrels.* But discord is a daughter of vainglory, as stated above (Q. XXXVII, A. 2). Therefore strife is also.

On the contrary, Gregory says (*Moral.* xxxi, 45)[4] that "anger gives rise to strife"; and it

---

[1] The Douay Version has "quarrels."

[2] *Glossa interl.* (VI, 87v); *Glossa Lombardi* (PL 192, 159).

[3] PL 76, 621.   [4] PL 76, 621.

is written (Prov. 15. 18; 29. 22): *A passionate man stirreth up strifes.*

I answer that, As stated above (A. 1), strife denotes an antagonism extending to deeds, when one man designs to harm another. Now there are two ways in which one man may intend to harm another. In one way it is as though he intended absolutely the other's hurt, which in this case is the outcome of hatred, for the intention of hatred is directed to the hurt of one's enemy either openly or secretly. In another way a man intends to hurt another who knows and withstands his intention. This is what we mean by strife, and it belongs properly to anger which is the desire of vengeance, for the angry man is not content to hurt secretly the object of his anger, he even wishes him to feel the hurt and know that what he suffers is in revenge for what he has done, as may be seen from what has been said above about the passion of anger (Part I-II, Q. XLVI, A. 6, Reply 2). Therefore, properly speaking, strife arises from anger.

Reply Obj. 1. As stated above (Part I-II, Q. XXV, AA. 1, 2), all the irascible passions arise from those of the concupiscible part, so that whatever is the immediate outcome of anger, arises also from concupiscence as from its first root.

Reply Obj. 2. Boasting and puffing up of self which are the result of anger or vainglory, are not the direct but the occasional cause of quarrels or strife, because, when a man resents another being preferred to him, his anger is aroused, and then his anger results in quarrel and strife.

Reply Obj. 3. Anger, as stated above (Part I-II, Q. XLVIII, A. 3) hinders the judgment of the reason, so that it bears a likeness to folly. Hence they have a common effect, since it is due to a defect in the reason that a man designs to hurt another inordinately.

Reply Obj. 4. Although strife sometimes arises from hatred, it is not the proper effect of hate, because when one man hates another it is beside his intention to hurt him in a quarrelsome and open manner, since sometimes he seeks to hurt him secretly. When, however, he sees himself prevailing, he endeavours to harm him with strife and quarrel. But to hurt a man in a quarrel is the proper effect of anger, for the reason given above.

Reply Obj. 5. Strifes give rise to hatred and discord in the hearts of those who are guilty of strife, and so he that "studies," that is intends to sow discord among others, causes them to

quarrel among themselves. Even so any sin may command the act of another sin, by directing it to its own end. This does not, however, prove that strife is the daughter of vainglory properly and directly.

QUESTION XLII
OF SEDITION
(*In Two Articles*)

WE must now consider sedition, under which head there are two points of inquiry: (1) Whether it is a special sin? (2) Whether it is a mortal sin?

ARTICLE 1. *Whether Sedition Is a Special Sin Distinct from Other Sins?*

We proceed thus to the First Article: It seems that sedition is not a special sin distinct from other sins.

Objection 1. For, according to Isidore (*Etym.* x),[1] "a seditious man is one who sows dissent among minds, and begets discord." Now, by provoking the commission of a sin, a man sins by no other kind of sin than that which he provoked. Therefore it seems that sedition is not a special sin distinct from discord.

Obj. 2. Further, Sedition denotes a kind of division. Now schism takes its name from scission, as stated above (Q. XXXIX, A. 1). Therefore it seems that the sin of sedition is not distinct from that of schism.

Obj. 3. Further, Every special sin that is distinct from other sins, is either a capital vice, or arises from some capital vice. Now sedition is reckoned neither among the capital vices, nor among those vices which arise from them, as appears from *Moral.* xxxi,[2] where both kinds of vice are enumerated. Therefore sedition is not a special sin, distinct from other sins.

On the contrary, Seditions are mentioned as distinct from other sins (II Cor. 12. 20).

I answer that, Sedition is a special sin, having something in common with war and strife, and differing somewhat from them. It has something in common with them, in so far as it implies a certain antagonism, and it differs from them in two points. First, because war and strife denote actual aggression on either side, while sedition may be said to denote either actual aggression, or the preparation for such aggression. Hence a gloss on II Cor. 12. 20 says[3] that "seditions are tumults tending to fight," when, that is, a number of people make preparations with the

---

[1] PL 82, 394.   [2] Chap. 45 (PL 76, 621).
[3] *Glossa interl.* (VI, 771); *Glossa* Lombardi (PL 192, 89).

intention of fighting. Secondly, they differ in that war is, properly speaking, carried on against external foes, being as it were between one people and another, while strife is between one individual and another, or between few people on one side and few on the other, while sedition, in its proper sense, is between the mutually dissentient parts of one people, as when one part of the state rises in tumult against another part. Therefore, since sedition is opposed to a special kind of good, namely the unity and peace of a people, it is a special kind of sin.

Reply Obj. 1. A seditious man is one who incites others to sedition, and since sedition denotes a kind of discord, it follows that a seditious man is one who creates discord, not of any kind, but between the parts of a multitude. And the sin of sedition is not only in him who sows discord, but also in those who dissent from one another inordinately.

Reply Obj. 2. Sedition differs from schism in two respects. First, because schism is opposed to the spiritual unity of the multitude, namely ecclesiastical unity, while sedition is contrary to the temporal or secular unity of the multitude, for instance of a city or kingdom. Secondly, schism does not imply any preparation for a bodily fight as sedition does, but only a spiritual dissent.

Reply Obj. 3. Sedition, like schism, is contained under discord, since each is a kind of discord, not between individuals, but between the parts of a multitude.

ARTICLE 2. *Whether Sedition Is Always a Mortal Sin?*

We proceed thus to the Second Article: It seems that sedition is not always a mortal sin.

Objection 1. For sedition denotes "a tumult tending to fight," according to the gloss quoted above (A. 1). But fighting is not always a mortal sin; indeed it is sometimes just and lawful, as stated above (Q. XL, A. 1; Q. XLI, A. 1). Much more, therefore, can sedition be without a mortal sin.

Obj. 2. Further, Sedition is a kind of discord, as stated above (A. 1, REPLY 3). Now discord can be without mortal sin, and sometimes without any sin at all. Therefore sedition can be also.

Obj. 3. Further, It is praiseworthy to deliver a multitude from a tyrannical rule. Yet this cannot easily be done without some dissension in the multitude, if one part of the multitude seeks to retain the tyrant, while the rest strive to dethrone him. Therefore there can be sedition without mortal sin.

On the contrary, The Apostle forbids seditions together with other things that are mortal sins (II Cor. 12. 20).

I answer that, As stated above (A. 1), sedition is contrary to the unity of the multitude, that is, the people of a city or kingdom. Now Augustine says[1] that wise men understand the word people to designate "not any crowd of persons, but the assembly of those who are united together in fellowship recognized by law and for the common good." Therefore it is evident that the unity to which sedition is opposed is the unity of law and common good; hence it follows manifestly that sedition is opposed to justice and the common good. Therefore by reason of its genus it is a mortal sin, and its gravity will be all the greater according as the common good which it assails surpasses the private good which is assailed by strife.

Accordingly the sin of sedition is first and chiefly in its authors, who sin most grievously; and secondly it is in those who are led by them to disturb the common good. Those, however, who defend the common good, and withstand the seditious party, are not themselves seditious, even as neither is a man to be called quarrelsome because he defends himself, as stated above (Q. XLI, A. 1).

Reply Obj. 1. It is lawful to fight, provided it be for the common good, as stated above (Q. XL, A. 1). But sedition runs counter to the common good of the multitude, so that it is always a mortal sin.

Reply Obj. 2. Discord from what is not evidently good may be without sin, but discord from what is evidently good cannot be without sin; and sedition is discord of this kind, for it is contrary to the unity of the multitude, which is a manifest good.

Reply Obj. 3. A tyrannical government is not just, because it is directed, not to the common good, but to the private good of the ruler, as the Philosopher states.[2] Consequently there is no sedition in disturbing a government of this kind, unless indeed the tyrant's rule be disturbed so inordinately that his subjects suffer greater harm from the consequent disturbance than from the tyrant's government. Indeed it is the tyrant rather that is guilty of sedition, since he encourages discord and sedition among his subjects, that he may lord over them more securely; for this is tyranny, since it is ordered to the private good of the ruler and to the injury of the multitude.

[1] *City of God,* II, 21 (PL 41, 67).
[2] *Politics,* III, 7 (1279^{b}6); *Ethics,* VIII, 10 (1160^{b}8).

QUESTION XLIII

Of scandal

(*In Eight Articles*)

It remains for us to consider the vices which are opposed to beneficence, among which some come under the head of injustice, those, namely, whereby one harms one's neighbour unjustly. But scandal seems to be specially opposed to charity. Accordingly we must here consider scandal, under which head there are eight points of inquiry: (1) What is scandal? (2) Whether scandal is a sin? (3) Whether it is a special sin? (4) Whether it is a mortal sin? (5) Whether the perfect can be scandalized? (6) Whether they can give scandal? (7) Whether spiritual goods are to be given up on account of scandal? (8) Whether temporal things are to be given up on account of scandal?

ARTICLE 1. *Whether Scandal Is Fittingly Defined As Being Something Less Rightly Said or Done That Occasions Spiritual Downfall?*

We proceed thus to the First Article: It seems that scandal is unfittingly defined as "something less rightly said or done that occasions spiritual downfall."

Objection 1. For scandal is a sin as we shall state further on (A. 2). Now, according to Augustine (*Contra Faust.* xxii, 27),[1] "a sin is a word, deed, or desire contrary to the law of God." Therefore the definition given above is insufficient, since it omits thought or desire.

Obj. 2. Further, Since among virtuous or right acts one is more virtuous or more right than another, that one alone which has perfect rectitude would not seem to be a less right one. If, therefore, scandal is something less rightly said or done, it follows that every virtuous act except the best of all, is a scandal.

Obj. 3. Further, An occasion is an accidental cause. But nothing accidental should enter a definition, because it does not specify the thing defined. Therefore it is unfitting, in defining scandal, to say that it is an occasion.

Obj. 4. Further, Whatever a man does may be the occasion of another's spiritual downfall, because accidental causes are indeterminate. Consequently, if scandal is something that occasions another's spiritual downfall, any deed or word can be a scandal. And this seems unreasonable.

Obj. 5. Further, A man occasions his neighbour's spiritual downfall when he offends or weakens him. Now scandal is divided against offence and weakness, for the Apostle says (Rom. 14. 21): *It is good not to eat flesh, and not to drink wine, nor anything whereby thy brother is offended, or scandalized, or weakened.* Therefore the above definition of scandal is unfitting.

On the contrary, Jerome in expounding Matt. 15. 12, *Dost thou know that the Pharisees, when they heard this word,* etc., says:[2] "When we read 'Whosoever shall scandalize,' the sense is 'Whosoever shall, by deed or word, occasion another's downfall.'"

I answer that, As Jerome observes (*ibid.*) "the Greek σκάνδαλον may be rendered offence, downfall, or a stumbling against something." For when a body, while moving along a path, meets with an obstacle, it may happen to stumble against it, and be disposed to fall down; such an obstacle is a σκάνδαλον. In like manner, while going along the spiritual way, a man may be disposed to a spiritual downfall by another's word or deed, in so far, that is, as one man by his injunction, inducement or example, moves another to sin; and this is scandal properly so called. Now nothing by its very nature disposes a man to spiritual downfall except that which has some lack of rectitude, since what is perfectly right secures man against a fall, instead of conducing to his downfall. Scandal is, therefore, fittingly defined as "something less rightly done or said, that occasions another's spiritual downfall."[3]

Reply Obj. 1. The thought or desire of evil lies hidden in the heart, and therefore it does not suggest itself to another man as an obstacle conducing to his spiritual downfall; hence it cannot come under the head of scandal.

Reply Obj. 2. A thing is said to be less right, not because something else surpasses it in rectitude, but because it has some lack of rectitude, either through being evil in itself, such as sin, or through having an appearance of evil. Thus, for instance, if a man were to *sit at meat in the idol's temple* (I Cor. 8. 10), though this is not sinful in itself, provided it be done with no evil intention, yet, since it has a certain appearance of evil, and a semblance of worshipping the idol, it might occasion another man's spiritual downfall. Hence the Apostle says (I Thessal. 5. 22): *From all appearance of evil refrain yourselves.* Scandal is therefore fittingly described as something done "less rightly," so as to com-

---

[1] PL 42, 418.
[2] PL 26, 111; cf. *Glossa interl.*, on Matt. 18.8 (v, 56r).
[3] *Glossa interl.* on Matt. 18.8 (v, 56r).

prise both whatever is sinful in itself, and all that has an appearance of evil.

Reply Obj. 3. As stated above (Part I-II, Q. LXXV, AA. 2, 3; Q. LXXX, A. 1), nothing can be a sufficient cause of a man's spiritual downfall, which is sin, save his own will. Therefore another man's words or deeds can only be an imperfect cause, conducing somewhat to that downfall. For this reason scandal is said to afford not a cause, but an occasion, which is an imperfect, and not always an accidental cause. Nor is there any reason why certain definitions should not make mention of things that are accidental, since what is accidental to one may be proper to something else; thus the accidental cause is mentioned in the definition of chance.[1]

Reply Obj. 4. Another's word or deed may be the cause of another's sin in two ways, directly and accidentally. Directly, when a man either intends, by his evil word or deed, to lead another man into sin, or, if he does not so intend, when his deed is of such a character as to lead another into sin; for instance, when a man publicly commits a sin or does something that has an appearance of sin. In this case he that does such an act does, properly speaking, afford an occasion of another's spiritual downfall, and so his act is called "active scandal."—One man's word or deed is the accidental cause of another's sin, when he neither intends to lead him into sin, nor does what is of a nature to lead him into sin, and yet this other one, through being ill-disposed, is led into sin, for instance, into envy of another's good, and then he who does this righteous act, does not, so far as he is concerned, afford an occasion of the other's downfall, but it is this other one who takes the occasion according to Rom. 7. 8: *Sin taking occasion by the commandment wrought in me all manner of concupiscence.* Therefore this is passive, without active scandal, since he that acts rightly does not, for his own part, afford the occasion of the other's downfall. Sometimes therefore it happens that there is active scandal in the one together with passive scandal in the other, as when one commits a sin being induced to it by another; sometimes there is active without passive scandal, for instance when one, by word or deed, provokes another to sin, and the latter does not consent; and sometimes there is passive without active scandal, as we have already said.

Reply Obj. 5. Weakness denotes proneness to scandal; while offence signifies resentment against the person who commits a sin, which

resentment may be sometimes without spiritual downfall; and scandal is the stumbling that results in downfall.

ARTICLE 2. *Whether Scandal Is a Sin?*

We proceed thus to the Second Article: It would seem that scandal is not a sin.

Objection 1. For sins do not occur from necessity, since all sin is voluntary, as stated above (Part I-II, Q. LXXIV, A. 1; Q. LXXX, A. 1). Now it is written (Matt. 18. 7): *It must needs be that scandals come.* Therefore scandal is not a sin.

Obj. 2. Further, No sin arises from a sense of dutifulness, because a *good tree cannot bring forth evil fruit* (Matt. 7. 18). But scandal may come from a sense of dutifulness, for Our Lord said to Peter (Matt. 16. 23): *Thou art a scandal unto Me,* in reference to which words Jerome says[2] that "the Apostle's error was due to his sense of dutifulness, and such is never inspired by the devil." Therefore scandal is not always a sin.

Obj. 3. Further, Scandal denotes a stumbling. But he that stumbles does not always fall. Therefore scandal, which is a spiritual fall, can be without sin.

On the contrary, Scandal is "something less rightly said or done."[3] Now anything that lacks rectitude is a sin. Therefore scandal is always with sin.

I answer that, As already stated (A. 1, Reply 4), scandal is of two kinds, passive scandal in the person scandalized, and active scandal in the person who gives scandal, and so occasions a downfall. Accordingly passive scandal is always a sin in the person scandalized; for he is not scandalized except in so far as he succumbs to a spiritual downfall, and that is a sin.

Yet there can be passive scandal without sin on the part of the person whose action has occasioned the scandal, as for instance, when a person is scandalized at another's good deed. In like manner active scandal is always a sin in the person who gives scandal, since either what he does is a sin, or if it only have the appearance of sin, it should always be left undone out of that love for our neighbour which binds each one to be solicitous for his neighbour's salvation, so that if he persists in doing it he acts against charity. Yet there can be active scandal without sin on the part of the person scandalized, as stated above (A. 1, Reply 4).

Reply Obj. 1. These words, *It must needs be*

[1] Aristotle, *Physics*, II, 5 (197ᵃ5).

[2] *In Matt.*, Bk. III, super 16.23 (PL 26, 124).
[3] Cf. *Glossa interl.*, super Matt. 18.8 (V, 56r).

that scandals come, are to be understood to convey not the absolute, but the conditional necessity of scandal; in which sense it is necessary that whatever God foresees or foretells must happen, provided it be taken together with such foreknowledge, as explained in the First Part (Q. XIV, A. 13, REPLY 3; Q. XXIII, A. 6, REPLY 2).

Or we may say that the necessity of scandals occurring is a necessity of end, because they are useful in order that *they . . . who are reproved may be made manifest* (I Cor. 11. 19).

Or scandals must occur because of the condition of man who fails to shield himself from sin. Thus a physician on seeing a man partaking of unsuitable food might say that such a man must injure his health, which is to be understood on the condition that he does not change his diet. In like manner it must be that scandals come so long as men fail to change their evil mode of living.

Reply Obj. 2. In that passage scandal is taken in the wide sense for any kind of hindrance. For Peter wished to hinder Our Lord's Passion out of a sense of dutifulness towards Christ.

Reply Obj. 3. No man stumbles spiritually, without being kept back somewhat from advancing in God's way, and that is at least a venial sin.

ARTICLE 3. *Whether Scandal Is a Special Sin?*

We proceed thus to the Third Article: It would seem that scandal is not a special sin.

Objection 1. For scandal is "something said or done less rightly."[1] But this applies to every kind of sin. Therefore every sin is a scandal, and consequently, scandal is not a special sin.

Obj. 2. Further, Every special kind of sin, or every special kind of injustice, may be found separately from other kinds, as stated in the *Ethics.*[2] But scandal is not to be found separately from other sins. Therefore it is not a special kind of sin.

Obj. 3. Further, Every special sin is constituted by something which specifies the moral act. But the notion of scandal consists in its being something done in the presence of others, and the fact of a sin being committed openly, though it is an aggravating circumstance, does not seem to constitute the species of a sin. Therefore scandal is not a special sin.

On the contrary, A special virtue has a special sin opposed to it. But scandal is opposed to a special virtue, namely charity. For it is written (Rom. 14. 15): *If, because of thy meat, thy*

brother *be grieved, thou walkest not now according to charity.* Therefore scandal is a special sin.

I answer that, As stated above (A. 1, REPLY 4; A. 2), scandal is twofold, active and passive. Passive scandal cannot be a special sin, because through another's word or deed a man may fall into any kind of sin; and the fact that a man takes occasion to sin from another's word or deed does not constitute a special kind of sin, because it does not imply a special deformity in opposition to a special virtue.

On the other hand, active scandal may be understood in two ways, directly and accidentally. The scandal is accidental when it is beside the agent's intention, as when a man does not intend, by his inordinate deed or word, to occasion another's spiritual downfall, but merely to satisfy his own will. In such a case even active scandal is not a special sin, because a species is not constituted by that which is accidental.

Active scandal is direct when a man intends, by his inordinate word or deed, to draw another into sin, and then it becomes a special kind of sin on account of the intention of a special kind of end, because moral actions take their species from their end, as stated above (Part I-II, Q. I, A. 3; Q. XVIII, A. 6). Hence, just as theft and murder are special kinds of sin, on account of their denoting the intention of doing a special injury to one's neighbour, so too, scandal is a special kind of sin, because thereby a man intends a special harm to his neighbour, and it is directly opposed to fraternal correction, by which a man intends the removal of a special kind of harm.

Reply Obj. 1. Any sin may be the matter of active scandal, but it may derive the formal aspect of a special sin from the end intended, as stated above.

Reply Obj. 2. Active scandal can be found separate from other sins, as when a man scandalizes his neighbour by a deed which is not a sin in itself, but has an appearance of evil.

Reply Obj. 3. Scandal does not derive the species of a special sin from the circumstance in question, but from the intention of the end, as stated above.

ARTICLE 4. *Whether Scandal Is a Mortal Sin?*

We proceed thus to the Fourth Article: It would seem that scandal is a mortal sin.

Objection 1. For every sin that is contrary to charity is a mortal sin, as stated above (Q. XXXV, A. 3; Part I-II, Q. LXXXVIII, A. 2). But scandal is contrary to charity, as stated above

---

[1] Cf. *Glossa Inter.,* super Matt. 18.8 (v, 56r).
[2] Aristotle, v, 2 (1130ᵃ19).

(AA. 2, 3): Therefore scandal is a mortal sin.

Obj. 2. Further, No sin except mortal sin deserves the punishment of eternal damnation. But scandal deserves the punishment of eternal damnation, according to Matt. 18. 6: *He that shall scandalize one of these little ones, that believe in Me, it were better for him that a millstone should be hanged about his neck, and that he should be drowned in the depth of the sea.* For, as Jerome says on this passage,[1] "it is much better to receive a brief punishment for a fault, than to await everlasting torments." Therefore scandal is a mortal sin.

Obj. 3. Further, Every sin committed against God is a mortal sin, because mortal sin alone turns man away from God. Now scandal is a sin against God, for the Apostle says (I Cor. 8. 12): *When you wound the weak conscience of the brethren,* (Vulg.,—*When you sin thus against the brethren and wound their weak conscience.*) *you sin against Christ.* Therefore scandal is always a mortal sin.

On the contrary, It may be a venial sin to lead a person into venial sin, and yet this would be to give scandal. Therefore scandal may be a venial sin.

I answer that, As stated above (A. 1), scandal denotes a stumbling by which a person is disposed to a spiritual downfall. Consequently passive scandal may sometimes be a venial sin, when it consists in a stumbling and nothing more, for instance, when a person is disturbed by a movement of venial sin occasioned by another's inordinate word or deed. But sometimes it is a mortal sin, when the stumbling results in a downfall, for instance when a person goes so far as to commit a mortal sin through another's inordinate word or deed.

Active scandal, if it be accidental, may sometimes be a venial sin; for instance, when, through a slight indiscretion, a person either commits a venial sin, or does something that is not a sin in itself, but has some appearance of evil. On the other hand, it is sometimes a mortal sin, either because a person commits a mortal sin, or because he has such contempt for his neighbour's spiritual welfare that he declines, for the sake of procuring it, to forego doing what he wishes to do. But in the case of active direct scandal, as when a person intends to lead another into sin, if he intends to lead him into mortal sin, his own sin will be mortal; and in like manner if he intends by committing a mortal sin himself to lead another into venial sin. But if he intends, by committing a venial

[1] PL 26, 133.

sin, to lead another into venial sin, there will be a venial sin of scandal.

And this suffices for the *Replies to the Objections.*

ARTICLE 5. *Whether Passive Scandal May Happen Even to the Perfect?*

We proceed thus to the Fifth Article: It seems that passive scandal may happen even to the perfect.

Objection 1. For Christ was supremely perfect; and yet He said to Peter (Matt. 16. 23): *Thou art a scandal to Me.* Much more therefore can other perfect men suffer scandal.

Obj. 2. Further, Scandal denotes an obstacle which is brought into a person's spiritual life. Now even perfect men can be hindered in their progress along the spiritual life, according to I Thess. 2. 18: *We would have come to you. I Paul indeed, once and again; but Satan hath hindered us.* Therefore even perfect men can suffer scandal.

Obj. 3. Further, Even perfect men are liable to venial sins, according to I John 1. 8: *If we say that we have no sin, we deceive ourselves.* Now passive scandal is not always a mortal sin, but is sometimes venial, as stated above (A. 4). Therefore passive scandal may be found in perfect men.

On the contrary, Jerome, in commenting on Matt. 18. 6, *He that shall scandalize one of these little ones,* says:[2] "Observe that it is the little one that is scandalized, for the elders do not take scandal."

I answer that, Passive scandal implies that the mind of the person who takes scandal is unsettled in its adherence to good. Now no man can be unsettled who adheres firmly to something immovable. The elders, that is, the perfect, adhere to God alone, Whose goodness is unchangeable, for though they adhere to their superiors, they do so only in so far as these adhere to Christ, according to I Cor. 4. 16: *Be ye followers of me, as I also am of Christ.* Therefore, however much others may appear to them to conduct themselves ill in word and deed, they themselves do not stray from their righteousness, according to Ps. 124. 1: *They that trust in the Lord shall be as Mount Sion: he shall not be moved for ever that dwelleth in Jerusalem.* Therefore scandal is not found in those who adhere to God perfectly by love, according to Ps. 118. 165: *Much peace have they that love Thy law, and to them there is no stumbling-block* (*scandalum*).

[2] PL 26, 133.

Reply Obj. 1. As stated above (A. 2, reply 2), in this passage, scandal is used in a broad sense to denote any kind of hindrance. Hence Our Lord said to Peter: *Thou art a scandal to Me,* because he was endeavouring to weaken Our Lord's purpose of undergoing His Passion.

Reply Obj. 2. Perfect men may be hindered in the performance of external actions. But they are not hindered by the words or deeds of others from tending to God in the internal acts of the will, according to Rom. 8. 38, 39: *Neither death, nor life . . . shall be able to separate us from the love of God.*

Reply Obj. 3. Perfect men sometimes fall into venial sins through the weakness of the flesh; but they are not scandalized (taking scandal in its true sense), by the words or deeds of others, although there can be an approach to scandal in them, according to Ps. 72. 2: *My feet were almost moved.*

ARTICLE 6. *Whether Active Scandal Can Be Found in the Perfect?*

We proceed thus to the Sixth Article: It seems that active scandal can be found in the perfect.

Objection 1. For passion is the effect of action. Now some are scandalized passively by the words or deeds of the perfect, according to Matt. 14. 12: *Dost thou know that the Pharisees, when they heard this word, were scandalized?* Therefore active scandal can be found in the perfect.

Obj. 2. Further, Peter, after receiving the Holy Ghost, was in the state of the perfect. Yet afterwards he scandalized the gentiles, for it is written (Gal. 2. 14): *When I saw that they walked not uprightly unto the truth of the Gospel, I said to Cephas,* that is, Peter, *before them all: If thou being a Jew, livest after the manner of the gentiles, and not as the Jews do, how dost thou compel the gentiles to live as do the Jews?* Therefore active scandal can be in the perfect.

Obj. 3. Further, Active scandal is sometimes a venial sin. But venial sins may be in perfect men. Therefore active scandal may be in perfect men.

On the contrary, Active scandal is more opposed to perfection than passive scandal. But passive scandal cannot be in the perfect. Much less, therefore, can active scandal be in them.

I answer that, Active scandal, properly so called, occurs when a man says or does a thing which in itself is of a nature to occasion another's downfall, and that is only when what he says or does is inordinate. Now it belongs to the perfect to order all their actions according to the rule of reason, as stated in I Cor. 14. 40: *Let all things be done decently and according to order;* and they are careful to do this especially in those matters in which not only would they do wrong, but would also be to others an occasion of wrong-doing. And if indeed they fail in this moderation in such words or deeds as come to the knowledge of others, this has its origin in human weakness because of which they fall short of perfection. Yet they do not fall short so far as to stray far from the order of reason, but only a little and in some slight matter, and this is not so grave that anyone can reasonably take from it an occasion for committing sin.

Reply Obj. 1. Passive scandal is always due to some active scandal; yet this active scandal is not always in another, but in the very person who is scandalized, because, that is, he scandalizes himself.

Reply Obj. 2. In the opinion of Augustine[1] and of Paul also, Peter sinned and was to be blamed in withdrawing from the gentiles in order to avoid the scandal of the Jews, because he did this somewhat incautiously, so that the gentiles who had been converted to the faith were scandalized. Nevertheless Peter's action was not so grave a sin as to give others sufficient ground for scandal. Hence they were guilty of passive scandal, while there was no active scandal in Peter.

Reply Obj. 3. The venial sins of the perfect consist chiefly in sudden movements, which being hidden cannot give scandal. If, however, they commit any venial sins even in their external words or deeds, these are so slight as to be insufficient in themselves to give scandal.

ARTICLE 7. *Whether Spiritual Goods Should Be Given Up on Account of Scandal?*

We proceed thus to the Seventh Article: It seems that spiritual goods ought to be given up on account of scandal.

Objection 1. For Augustine (*Contra Ep. Parmen.* iii, 2)[2] teaches that punishment for sin should cease when the peril of schism is feared. But punishment of sins is a spiritual good, since it is an act of justice. Therefore a spiritual good is to be given up on account of scandal.

Obj. 2. Further, The Sacred Doctrine is a most spiritual thing. Yet one ought to desist from it on account of scandal, according to

---

[1] *Epist.,* XXVIII, 3 (PL 33, 113); *Epist.,* XL, 3 (PL 33, 156); *Epist.,* LXXXII, 2 (PL 33, 277).   [2] PL 43, 92.

Matt. 7. 6: *Give not that which is holy, to dogs, neither cast ye your pearls before swine lest . . . turning upon you, they tear you.* Therefore a spiritual good should be given up on account of scandal.

Obj. 3. Further, Since fraternal correction is an act of charity, it is a spiritual good. Yet sometimes it is omitted out of charity, in order to avoid giving scandal to others, as Augustine observes.[1] Therefore a spiritual good should be given up on account of scandal.

Obj. 4. Further, Jerome says[2] that in order to avoid scandal we should give up whatever it is possible to omit without prejudice to the threefold truth, that is, the truth of life, of justice and of doctrine. Now the observance of the counsels, and the bestowal of alms may often be omitted without prejudice to this threefold truth; otherwise whoever omitted them would always be guilty of sin, and yet such things are the greatest of spiritual works. Therefore spiritual works should be omitted on account of scandal.

Obj. 5. Further, The avoidance of any sin is a spiritual good, since any sin brings spiritual harm to the sinner. Now it seems that one ought sometimes to commit a venial sin in order to avoid scandalizing one's neighbour, for instance when by sinning venially one would prevent someone else from committing a mortal sin; for one is bound to hinder the damnation of one's neighbour as much as one can without prejudice to one's own salvation, which is not precluded by a venial sin. Therefore one ought to give up a spiritual good in order to avoid scandal.

On the contrary, Gregory says (*Hom. Super Ezech.* vii):[3] "If people are scandalized at the truth, it is better to allow the birth of scandal, than to abandon the truth." Now spiritual goods belong, above all others, to the truth. Therefore spiritual goods are not to be given up on account of scandal.

I answer that, Although scandal is twofold, active and passive, the present question does not apply to active scandal, for since active scandal is something said or done less rightly, nothing ought to be done that implies active scandal.

The question does, however, apply to passive scandal, and accordingly we have to see what ought to be given up in order to avoid scandal.

[1] *City of God,* I, 9 (PL 41, 22).

[2] Cf. Wm. of Auxerre, *Summa Aurea,* III, tr. 24, Q. 4 (236v[b]); also Hugh of St. Cher, *In Matt.* 18.7 (VI, 61); cf. also Gregory the Great, *In Ezech.,* hom., VII (PL 76, 842). [3] PL 76, 842.

Now a distinction must be made in spiritual goods. For some of them are necessary for salvation, and cannot be omitted without mortal sin, and it is evident that no man ought to commit a mortal sin in order to prevent another from sinning, because according to the order of charity a man ought to love his own spiritual welfare more than another's. Therefore one ought not to give up that which is necessary for salvation, in order to avoid giving scandal.

Again a distinction seems necessary among spiritual things which are not necessary for salvation, because the scandal which arises from such things sometimes proceeds from malice; for instance when a man wishes to hinder those spiritual goods by stirring up scandal. This is the scandal of the Pharisees, who were scandalized at Our Lord's teaching, and Our Lord teaches (Matt. 15. 14) that we ought to treat suchlike scandal with contempt.

Sometimes scandal proceeds from weakness or ignorance, and such is the scandal of little ones. In order to avoid this kind of scandal, spiritual goods ought to be either concealed, or sometimes even deferred (if this can be done without incurring immediate danger), until the matter being explained the scandal cease. If, however, the scandal continue after the matter has been explained, it would seem to be due to malice, and then it would no longer be right to omit that spiritual good in order to avoid suchlike scandal.

Reply Obj. 1. In the infliction of punishment it is not the punishment itself that is the end in view but its medicinal properties in checking sin; therefore punishment partakes of the nature of justice, in so far as it checks sin. But if it is evident that the infliction of punishment will result in more numerous and more grievous sins being committed, the infliction of punishment will no longer be a part of justice. It is in this sense that Augustine is speaking, when, that is, the excommunication of a few threatens to bring about the danger of a schism, for in that case it would not pertain to the truth of justice to pronounce excommunication.

Reply Obj. 2. With regard to a man's doctrine two points must be considered, namely, the truth which is taught, and the act of teaching. The first of these is necessary for salvation, that, namely, he whose duty it is to teach should not teach what is contrary to the truth, and that he should teach the truth according to the requirements of times and persons; therefore on no account ought he to suppress the truth and teach error in order to avoid any scandal that might ensue.—But the act itself of teaching is one of the spiritual almsdeeds, as stated above (Q. XXXII, A. 2), and so the same is to be said of it as of the other works of mercy, of which we shall speak further on (REPLY 4).

Reply Obj. 3. As stated above (Q. XXXIII, A. 1), fraternal correction aims at the correction of a brother, and therefore it is to be counted among spiritual goods in so far as this end can be obtained, which is not the case if the brother be scandalized through being corrected. And so, if the correction be omitted in order to avoid scandal, no spiritual good is given up.

Reply Obj. 4. The truth of life, of doctrine, and of justice comprises not only whatever is necessary for salvation, but also whatever is a means of obtaining salvation more perfectly, according to I Cor. 12. 31: *Be zealous for the better gifts.* Therefore neither the counsels nor even the works of mercy are to be altogether omitted in order to avoid scandal; but sometimes they should be concealed or deferred, on account of the scandal of the little ones, as stated above. Sometimes, however, the observance of the counsels and the fulfilment of the works of mercy are necessary for salvation. This may be seen in the case of those who have vowed to keep the counsels, and of those whose duty it is to relieve the wants of others, either in temporal matters (as by feeding the hungry), or in spiritual matters (as by instructing the ignorant), whether such duties arise from their being enjoined as in the case of prelates, or from the need on the part of the person in want; and then the same applies to these things as to others that are necessary for salvation.

Reply Obj. 5. Some have said that one ought to commit a venial sin in order to avoid scandal.[1] But this implies a contradiction, since if it ought to be done, it is no longer evil or sinful, for a sin cannot be a matter of choice. It may happen however that, on account of some circumstance, something is not a venial sin, though it would be were it not for that circumstance; thus an idle word is a venial sin, when it is uttered uselessly, yet if it be uttered for a reasonable cause, it is neither idle nor sinful. And though venial sin does not deprive a man of grace which is his means of salvation, yet, in so far as it disposes him to mortal sin, it tends to the loss of salvation.

[1] Cassianus, *Collationes*, Coll. XVII, chap. 17 (PL 49, 1063).

ARTICLE 8. *Whether Temporal Goods Should Be Given Up on Account of Scandal?*

We proceed thus to the Eighth Article: It would seem that temporal goods should be given up on account of scandal.

Objection 1. For we ought to love our neighbour's spiritual welfare which is hindered by scandal more than any temporal goods whatever. But we give up what we love less for the sake of what we love more. Therefore we should give up temporal goods in order to avoid scandalizing our neighbour.

Obj. 2. Further, According to Jerome's rule,[2] whatever can be given up without prejudice to the threefold truth should be given up in order to avoid scandal. Now temporal goods can be given up without prejudice to the threefold truth. Therefore they should be given up in order to avoid scandal.

Obj. 3. Further, No temporal good is more necessary than food. But we ought to give up taking food on account of scandal, according to Rom. 14. 15: *Destroy not him with thy meat for whom Christ died.* Much more therefore should all other temporal goods be given up on account of scandal.

Obj. 4. Further, The most fitting way of safeguarding and recovering temporal goods is the court of justice. But it is unlawful to have recourse to justice, especially if scandal ensues, for it is written (Matt. 5. 40): *If a man will contend with thee in judgment, and take away thy coat, let go thy cloak also unto him;* and (I Cor. 6. 7): *Already indeed there is plainly a fault among you, that you have lawsuits one with another. Why do you not rather take wrong? why do you not rather suffer yourselves to be defrauded?* Therefore it seems that we ought to forego temporal goods on account of scandal.

Obj. 5. Further, We ought, it seems, to give up least of all those temporal goods which are connected with spiritual goods, and yet we ought to give them up on account of scandal. For the Apostle while sowing spiritual things did not accept a temporal stipend lest he *should give any hindrance to the Gospel of Christ* as we read I Cor. 9. 12. For a like reason the Church does not demand tithes in certain countries, in order to avoid scandal. Much more, therefore, ought we to give up other temporal goods in order to avoid scandal.

On the contrary, Blessed Thomas of Canter-

[2] Cf. Hugh of St. Cher, *In Univ. Test.*, super Matt. 18.7 (VI, 61); Alexander of Hales, *S. T.*, II–II, n. 862 (QR III, 821).

bury demanded the restitution of Church property, notwithstanding that the king took scandal from his doing so.[1]

I answer that, A distinction must be made in temporal goods, for either they are ours, or they are committed to us to take care of them for someone else; thus the goods of the Church are committed to prelates, and the goods of the community are entrusted to all such persons as have authority over the common weal. In this latter case the care of such things (as of things held in deposit) devolves of necessity on those persons to whom they are entrusted, and therefore, even as other things that are necessary for salvation, they are not to be given up on account of scandal. On the other hand, as regards those temporalities of which we have the dominion, sometimes, on account of scandal, we are bound to give them up, and sometimes we are not so bound, whether we abandon them by giving them up, if we have them in our possession, or by omitting to claim them, if they are in the possession of others. For if the scandal arise from this through the ignorance or weakness of others (in which case, as stated above, A. 7, it is scandal of the little ones) we must either give up such temporalities altogether, or the scandal must be abated by some other means, namely, by some kind of admonition. Hence Augustine says (*De Serm. Dom. in Monte,* i, 20):[2] "Thou shouldst give so as to injure neither thyself nor another, as much as thou canst lend, and if thou refusest what is asked, thou must yet be just to him, indeed thou wilt give him something better than he asks, if thou reprove him that asks unjustly." Sometimes, however, scandal arises from malice. This is scandal of the Pharisees, and we ought not to give up temporal goods for the sake of those who stir up scandals of this kind, for this would both be harmful to the common good, since it would give wicked men an opportunity of plunder, and would be injurious to the plunderers themselves, who would remain in sin as long as they were in possession of another's property. Hence Gregory says (*Moral.* xxxi, 13):[3] "Sometimes we ought to suffer those who rob us of our temporalities, while sometimes we should resist them, as far as equity allows, in the hope not only that we may safeguard our property, but also lest those who take what is not theirs may lose themselves."

This suffices for the *Reply to the First Objection.*

Reply Obj. 2. If it were permissible for wicked men to rob other people of their property, this would tend to the detriment of the truth of life and justice. Therefore we are not always bound to give up our temporal goods in order to avoid scandal.

Reply Obj. 3. The Apostle had no intention of counselling total abstinence from food on account of scandal, because our welfare requires that we should take food, but he intended to counsel abstinence from a particular kind of food, in order to avoid scandal, according to I Cor. 8. 13: *I will never eat flesh, lest I should scandalize my brother.*

Reply Obj. 4. According to Augustine (*De Serm. Dom. in Monte,* i, 19)[4] this precept of Our Lord is to be understood of "the preparedness of the mind," namely, that man should be prepared, if it be expedient, to suffer being harmed or defrauded, rather than go to law. But sometimes it is not expedient, as stated above (REPLY 2). The same applies to the saying of the Apostle.

Reply Obj. 5. The scandal which the Apostle avoided arose from an error of the gentiles who were not used to this payment. Hence he was obliged to give it up for the time being, so that they might be taught first of all that such a payment was a duty. For a like reason the Church refrains from demanding tithes in those countries where it is not customary to pay them.

QUESTION XLIV
OF THE PRECEPTS OF CHARITY
(*In Eight Articles*)

WE must now consider the Precepts of Charity, under which head there are eight points of inquiry: (1) Whether precepts should be given about charity? (2) Whether there should be one or two? (3) Whether two suffice? (4) Whether it is fittingly prescribed that we should love God, *with thy whole heart?* (5) Whether it is fittingly added: *With thy whole mind,* etc.? (6) Whether it is possible to fulfil this precept in this life? (7) Of the precept: *Thou shalt love thy neighbour as thyself:* (8) Whether the order of charity is included in the precept?

ARTICLE I. *Whether Any Precept Should Be Given about Charity?*

We proceed thus to the First Article: It would seem that no precept should be given about charity.

[1] Cf. John of Salisbury, *vita S. Thomae* (PL 190, 200).
[2] PL 34, 1264.   [3] PL 76, 586.   [4] PL 34, 1260.

Objection 1. For charity imposes the manner on all acts of virtue, since it is the form of the virtues as stated above (Q. XXIII, A. 8), while the precepts are about the virtues themselves. Now, according to the common saying, the manner is not included in the precept. Therefore no precepts should be given about charity.

Obj. 2. Further, Charity, which *is poured forth in our hearts by the Holy Ghost* (Rom. 5. 5), makes us free, since *where the Spirit of the Lord is, there is liberty* (II Cor. 3. 17). Now the obligation that arises from a precept is opposed to liberty, since it imposes a necessity. Therefore no precept should be given about Charity.

Obj. 3. Further, Charity is the foremost among all the virtues, to which the precepts are ordered, as shown above (Part I-II, Q. C, A. 9, reply 2). If, therefore, any precepts were given about charity, they should have a place among the chief precepts which are those of the decalogue. But they have no place there. Therefore no precepts should be given about charity.

On the contrary, Whatever God requires of us is included in a precept. Now God requires that man should love Him, according to Deut. 10. 12. Therefore precepts had to be given about the love of charity, which is the love of God.

I answer that, As stated above (Part I-II, Q. XCIX, AA. 1, 5; Q. C, A. 5, reply 1), a precept implies the notion of something due. Hence a thing is a matter of precept in so far as it is something due. Now a thing is due in two ways: for its own sake, and for the sake of something else. In every affair, it is the end that is due for its own sake, because it has the character of a good for its own sake, while that which is directed to the end is due for the sake of something else; thus for a physician, it is due for its own sake that he should heal, while it is due for the sake of something else that he should give a medicine in order to heal. Now the end of the spiritual life is that man be united to God, and this union is effected by charity, while all things pertaining to the spiritual life are ordered to this union, as to their end. Hence the Apostle says (I Tim. 1, 5): *The end of the commandment is charity from a pure heart, and a good conscience, and an unfeigned faith.* For all the virtues, about whose acts the precepts are given, are directed either to the freeing of the heart from the whirl of the passions—such as the virtues that regulate the passions—or at least to the possession of a good conscience—such as the virtues that regulate oper-

ations—or to the having of a right faith—such as those which pertain to the worship of God; and these three things are required of man that he may love God. For an impure heart is withdrawn from loving God on account of the passion that inclines it to earthly things; an evil conscience gives man a horror for God's justice, through fear of His punishments; and an untrue faith draws man's affections to an untrue representation of God, and separates him from the divinity and from the truth of God. Now in every genus that which is for its own sake takes precedence of that which is for the sake of another, therefore the greatest precept is that of charity, as stated in Matt. 22. 39.

Reply Obj. 1. As stated above (Part I-II, Q. C, A. 10) when we were treating of the commandments, the mode of love does not come under those precepts which are about the other acts of virtue; for instance, this precept, *Honour thy father and thy mother* does not prescribe that this should be done out of charity. The act of love does, however, fall under special precepts.

Reply Obj. 2. The obligation of a precept is not opposed to liberty except in one whose mind is turned away from that which is prescribed, as may be seen in those who keep the precepts through fear alone. But the precept of love cannot be fulfilled save of one's own will, and therefore it is not opposed to charity.

Reply Obj. 3. All the precepts of the decalogue are directed to the love of God and of our neighbour, and therefore the precepts of charity had not to be enumerated among the precepts of the decalogue, since they are included in all of them.

ARTICLE 2. *Whether There Should Have Been Given Two Precepts of Charity?*

We proceed thus to the Second Article: It seems that there should not have been given two precepts of charity.

Objection 1. For the precepts of the Law are directed to virtue, as stated above (A. 1, obj. 3). Now charity is one virtue, as shown above (Q. XXIII, A. 5). Therefore only one precept of charity should have been given.

Obj. 2. Further, As Augustine says,[1] charity loves none but God in our neighbour. Now we are sufficiently directed to love God by the precept, *Thou shalt love the Lord thy God.* Therefore there was no need to add the precept about loving our neighbour.

Obj. 3. Further, Different sins are opposed to

[1] *Christian Doctrine,* I, 22, 27 (PL 34, 27; 29).

different precepts. But it is not a sin to put aside the love of our neighbour, provided we do not put aside the love of God; indeed, it is written (Luke 14. 26): *If any man come to Me, and hate not his father, and mother, . . . he cannot be My disciple*. Therefore the precept of the love of God is not distinct from the precept of the love of our neighbour.

Obj. 4. Further, The Apostle says (Rom. 13. 8): *He that loveth his neighbour hath fulfilled the Law*. But a law is not fulfilled unless all its precepts be observed. Therefore all the precepts are included in the love of our neighbour, and consequently the one precept of the love of our neighbour suffices. Therefore there should not be two precepts of charity.

On the contrary, It is written (I John 4. 21): *This commandment we have from God, that he who loveth God, love also his brother*.

I answer that, As stated above (Part I-II, Q. XCI, A. 3; Q. C, A. 1) when we were treating of the commandments, the precepts are to the Law what propositions are to speculative sciences, for in these latter, the conclusions are contained virtually in the first principles. Hence whoever knows the principles as to their entire virtual content has no need to have the conclusions put separately before him. Since, however, some who know the principles are unable to consider all that is virtually contained in them, it is necessary, for their sake, that in the sciences conclusions should be deduced from their principles. Now in practical matters in which the precepts of the Law direct us, the end has the character of principle, as stated above (Q. XXIII, A. 7, Reply 2; Q. XXVI, A. 1, Reply 1), and the love of God is the end to which the love of our neighbour is directed. Therefore we had to receive precepts not only of the love of God but also of the love of our neighbour, on account of those who are less intelligent, who do not easily understand that one of these precepts is included in the other.

Reply Obj. 1. Although charity is one virtue, yet it has two acts, one of which is directed to the other as to its end. Now precepts are given about acts of virtue, and so there had to be several precepts of charity.

Reply Obj. 2. God is loved in our neighbour, as the end is loved in that which is directed to the end; and yet there was need for an explicit precept about both, for the reason given above.

Reply Obj. 3. The means derive their goodness from their relation to the end, and accordingly turning from the means derives its malice from the same source and from no other.

Reply Obj. 4. Love of our neighbour includes love of God, as the end is included in the means, and vice versa. And yet each precept had to be given explicitly, for the reason given above.

ARTICLE 3. *Whether Two Precepts of Charity Suffice?*

We proceed thus to the Third Article: It would seem that two precepts of charity do not suffice.

Objection 1. For precepts are given about acts of virtue. Now acts are distinguished by their objects. Since, then, man is bound to love four things out of charity, namely, God, himself, his neighbour and his own body, as shown above (Q. XXV, A. 12), it seems that there ought to be four precepts of charity, so that two are not sufficient.

Obj. 2. Further, Love is not the only act of charity, but also joy, peace and beneficence. But precepts should be given about the acts of the virtues. Therefore two precepts of charity do not suffice.

Obj. 3. Further, Virtue consists not only in doing good but also in avoiding evil. Now we are led by the positive precepts to do good, and by the negative precepts to avoid evil. Therefore there ought to have been not only positive, but also negative precepts about charity; and so two precepts of charity are not sufficient.

On the contrary, Our Lord said (Matt. 22. 40): *On these two commandments dependeth the whole Law and the prophets*.

I answer that, Charity, as stated above (Q. XXIII, A. 1), is a kind of friendship. Now friendship is between one person and another, and so Gregory says (*Hom. in Ev.* xvii):[1] "Charity is not possible between less than two," and it has been explained how one may love oneself out of charity (Q. XXV, A. 4). Now since good is the object of dilection and love, and since good is either an end or a means, it is fitting that there should be two precepts of charity, one by which we are induced to love God as our end, and another by which we are led to love our neighbour for God's sake, for the sake of our end.

Reply Obj. 1. As Augustine says,[2] "though four things are to be loved out of charity, there was no need of a precept as regards the second and fourth, that is, love of oneself and of one's body. For however much a man may stray from the truth, the love of himself and of his own body always remains in him." And yet the mode of this love had to be prescribed to man, name-

---

[1] PL 76, 1139.

[2] *Christian Doctrine*, i, 23 (PL 34, 27).

ly, that he should love himself and his own body in an ordered manner, and this is done by his loving God and his neighbour.

Reply Obj. 2. As stated above (Q. XXVIII, AA. 1, 4; Q. XXIX, A. 3), the other acts of charity result from the act of love as effects from their cause. Hence the precepts of love virtually include the precepts about the other acts. And yet we find that, for the sake of the laggards, special precepts were given about each act:— about joy (Philip. 4. 4): *Rejoice in the Lord always;* about peace (Heb. 12. 14): *Follow peace with all men;* about beneficence (Gal. 6. 10): *Whilst we have time, let us work good to all men;* and Holy Writ contains precepts about each of the parts of beneficence, as may be seen by anyone who considers the matter carefully.

Reply Obj. 3. To do good is more than to avoid evil, and therefore the positive precepts virtually include the negative precepts. Nevertheless we find explicit precepts against the vices contrary to charity, for, against hatred it is written (Levit. 19. 17): *Thou shalt not hate thy brother in thy heart;* against acedia (Ecclus. 6. 26): *Be not grieved with her bands;* against envy (Gal. 5. 26): *Let us not be made desirous of vainglory, provoking one another, envying one another;* against discord (I Cor. 1. 10): *That you all speak the same thing, and that there be no schisms among you;* and against scandal (Rom. 14. 13): *That you put not a stumbling-block or a scandal in your brother's way.*

ARTICLE 4. *Whether It Is Fittingly Commanded That Man Should Love God With His Whole Heart?*

We proceed thus to the Fourth Article: It would seem that it is unfittingly commanded that man should love God with his whole heart.

Objection 1. For the mode of a virtuous act is not a matter of precept, as shown above (Part I-II, Q. C, A. 9). Now the words *with thy whole heart* signify the mode of the love of God. Therefore it is unfittingly commanded that man should love God with his whole heart.

Obj. 2. Further, "A thing is whole and perfect when it lacks nothing."[1] If therefore it is a matter of precept that God be loved with the whole heart, whoever does something not pertaining to the love of God acts counter to the precept, and consequently sins mortally. Now a venial sin does not pertain to the love of God. Therefore a venial sin is a mortal sin, which is absurd.

[1] Aristotle, *Physics*, III, 6 (207ª9).

Obj. 3. Further, To love God with one's own heart belongs to perfection, since according to the Philosopher,[2] "to be whole is to be perfect." But that which belongs to perfection is not a matter of precept, but a matter of counsel. Therefore we ought not to be commanded to love God with our whole heart.

On the contrary, It is written (Deut. 6. 5): *Thou shalt love the Lord thy God with thy whole heart.*

I answer that, Since precepts are given about acts of virtue, an act is a matter of precept according as it is an act of virtue. Now it is requisite for an act of virtue that not only should it fall on its own matter, but also that it should be clothed with its due circumstances, by which it is proportioned to that matter. But God is to be loved as the last end, to which all things are to be referred. Therefore some kind of totality had to be designated in connection with the precept of the love of God.

Reply Obj. 1. The commandment that prescribes an act of virtue does not prescribe the mode which that virtue derives from another and higher virtue, but it does prescribe the mode which belongs to its own proper virtue, and this mode is signified in the words *with thy whole heart.*

Reply Obj. 2. To love God with one's whole heart happens in two ways. First, actually, so that a man's whole heart is always actually directed to God, and this is the perfection of heaven. Secondly, in the sense that a man's whole heart is habitually directed to God, so that it consents to nothing contrary to the love of God, and this is the perfection of the way. Venial sin is not contrary to this latter perfection, because it does not destroy the habit of charity, since it does not tend to a contrary object but merely hinders the use of charity.

Reply Obj. 3. That perfection of charity to which the counsels are directed is between the two perfections mentioned in the preceding reply: and it consists in man renouncing, as much as possible, temporal things, even such as are lawful, because they occupy the mind and hinder the actual movement of the heart towards God.

ARTICLE 5. *Whether to the Words, "Thou Shalt Love the Lord Thy God With Thy Whole Heart," It Was Fitting To Add "and With Thy Whole Soul, and With Thy Whole Strength"?*

We proceed thus to the Fifth Article: It would seem that it was unfitting to the words, *Thou*

[2] *Ibid.*

shalt love the Lord thy God, with thy whole heart, to add, *and with thy whole soul, and with thy whole strength* (Deut. 6. 5).

Objection 1. For heart does not mean here a part of the body, since to love God is not a bodily action, and therefore heart is to be taken here in a spiritual sense. Now the heart understood spiritually is either the soul itself or part of the soul. Therefore it is superfluous to mention both heart and soul.

Obj. 2. Further, A man's strength whether spiritual or corporal depends on the heart. Therefore after the words, *Thou shalt love the Lord thy God with thy whole heart,* it was unnecessary to add, *with all thy strength.*

Obj. 3. Further, Matt. 22. 37 we read: *With all thy mind,* which words do not occur here. Therefore it seems that this precept is unfittingly worded in Deut. 6.

On the contrary stands the authority of Scripture.

I answer that, This precept is differently worded in various places. For, as we said in the first objection, in Deut. 6. three points are mentioned, *with thy whole heart,* and *with thy whole soul,* and *with thy whole strength.* In Matt. 22. we find two of these mentioned, namely *with thy whole heart* and *with thy whole soul,* while *with thy whole strength* is omitted, but *with thy whole mind* is added. Yet in Mark 12 we find all four, namely *with thy whole heart,* and *with thy whole soul,* and *with thy whole mind,* and *with thy whole force* which is the same as strength. Moreover, these four are indicated in Luke 10., where in place of *strength* or *force* we read *with all thy might.*[1]

Accordingly these four have to be explained, since the fact that one of them is omitted here or there is due to one implying another. We must therefore observe that love is an act of the will which is here denoted by the heart, because just as the bodily heart is the principle of all the movements of the body, so too the will, especially as regards the intention of the last end which is the object of charity, is the principle of all spiritual movements. Now there are three principles of action that are moved by the will, namely, the intellect which is signified by "the mind," the lower appetitive power, signified by "the soul"; and the exterior executive power signified by "strength," "force" or "might". Accordingly we are commanded to

direct our whole intention to God, and this is signified by the words *with thy whole heart;* to submit our intellect to God, and this is expressed in the words *with thy whole mind;* to regulate our appetite according to God, in the words *with thy whole soul;* and to obey God in our external actions, and this is to love God with our whole *strength, force* or *might.*

Chrysostom, on the other hand, takes heart and soul in the contrary sense;[2] and Augustine[3] refers heart to the thought, soul to the manner of life, and mind to the intellect. Again some explain *with thy whole heart* as denoting the intellect, *with thy whole soul* as signifying the will, *with thy mind* as pointing to the memory.[4] And again, according to Gregory of Nyssa (*De Hom. Opif.* viii),[5] "heart" signifies the vegetative soul, "soul" the sensitive soul, and "mind" the intellectual soul, because our nourishment, sensation, and understanding ought all to be referred by us to God.

This suffices for the *Replies to the Objections.*

ARTICLE 6. *Whether It Is Possible in This Life To Fulfil This Precept of the Love of God?*

We proceed thus to the Sixth Article: It would seem that in this life it is possible to fulfil this precept of the love of God.

Objection 1. For according to Jerome[6] "accursed is he who says that God has commanded anything impossible." But God gave this commandment, as is clear from Deut. 6. 5. Therefore it is possible to fulfil this precept in this life.

Obj. 2. Further, Whoever does not fulfil a precept sins mortally, since according to Ambrose (*De Parad.* viii)[7] sin is nothing else than "a transgression of the Divine Law, and disobedience of the heavenly commandments." If therefore this precept cannot be fulfilled by wayfarers, it follows that in this life no man can be without mortal sin, and this is against the saying of the Apostle (I Cor. 1. 8): (*Who also*) *will confirm you unto the end without crime,* and (I Tim. 3. 10): *Let them minister, having no crime.*

Obj. 3. Further, Precepts are given in order to direct man in the way of salvation, according to Ps. 18. 9: *The commandment of the Lord is lightsome, enlightening the eyes.* Now it is

---

[1] St. Thomas is explaining the Latin text which reads *ex tota fortitudine tua* (Deut.), *ex tota virtute tua* (Mark) and *ex omnibus viribus tuis* (Luke), although the Greek in all three cases has ἐξ ὅλης τῆς ἰσχύος σου, which the Douay renders *with thy whole strength.*

[2] Cf. Ps. Chrysostom, *opus imperf.,* hom. XLII in Matt. 22.37 (PG 56, 873).

[3] *Christian Doctrine,* I, 22 (PL 34, 27).

[4] Cf. *Glossa interl.,* on Matt. 22.37 (v, 70r).

[5] PG 44, 145.

[6] Cf. Pelagius, *Libellus Fidei ad Innocentium* (PL 45, 1718); *Epist.,* I, chap. 16 (PL 30, 32).   [7] PL 14, 309.

useless to direct anyone to what is impossible. Therefore it is not impossible to fulfil this precept in this life.

On the contrary, Augustine says (*De Perfect. Justit.* viii):[1] "In the fulness of heavenly charity this precept will be fulfilled: Thou shalt love the Lord thy God, etc. For as long as any carnal concupiscence remains that can be restrained by continence, man cannot love God with all his heart."

I answer that, A precept can be fulfilled in two ways perfectly, and imperfectly. A precept is fulfilled perfectly when the end intended by the author of the precept is reached; yet it is fulfilled, imperfectly however, when although the end intended by its author is not reached, nevertheless the order to that end is not departed from. Thus if the commander of an army order his soldiers to fight, his command will be perfectly obeyed by those who fight and conquer the foe, which is the commander's intention; yet it is fulfilled, although imperfectly, by those who fight without gaining the victory, provided they do nothing contrary to military discipline. Now God intends by this precept that man should be wholly united to Him, and this will be realized in heaven, when God will be *all in all,* according to I Cor. 15. 28. Hence this precept will be observed fully and perfectly in heaven; yet it is fulfilled, though imperfectly, on the way. Nevertheless on the way the more one man fulfils it more perfectly than another, the more he approaches by some kind of likeness to the perfection of heaven.

Reply Obj. 1. This argument proves that the precept can be fulfilled after a fashion on the way, but not perfectly.

Reply Obj. 2. Even as the soldier who fights legitimately without conquering is not blamed nor deserves to be punished for this, so too he that does not fulfil this precept on the way, but does nothing against the love of God, does not sin mortally.

Reply Obj. 3. As Augustine says (*De Perfect. Justit.* viii),[2] "why should not this perfection be prescribed to man, although no man attains it in this life? For one cannot run straight unless one knows where to run. And how would one know this if no precept pointed it out."

ARTICLE 7. *Whether the Precept of the Love of Our Neighbour Is Fittingly Expressed?*

We proceed thus to the Seventh Article: It seems that the precept of the love of our neighbour is unfittingly expressed.

[1] PL 44, 300.   [2] PL 44, 301.

Objection 1. For the love of charity extends to all men, even to our enemies, as may be seen in Matt. 5. 44. But the word "neighbour" denotes a kind of nearness which does not seem to exist towards all men. Therefore it seems that this precept is unfittingly expressed.

Obj. 2. Further, According to the Philosopher[3] the origin of our friendly relations with others lies in our relation to ourselves," from which it seems to follow that love of self is the principle of one's love for one's neighbour. Now the principle is greater than that which results from it. Therefore man ought not to love his neighbour as himself.

Obj. 3. Further, Man loves himself, but not his neighbour, naturally. Therefore it is unfitting that he should be commanded to love his neighbour as himself.

On the contrary, It is written (Matt. 22. 39): *The second commandment is like to this: Thou shalt love thy neighbour as thyself.*

I answer that, This precept is fittingly expressed, for it indicates both the reason for loving and the mode of love.

The reason for loving is indicated in the word "neighbour," because the reason why we ought to love others out of charity is because they are near to us, both as to the natural image of God, and as to the capacity for glory. Nor does it matter whether we say *neighbour,* or *brother* according to I John 4. 21, or *friend,* according to Levit. 19. 18, because all these words express the same affinity.

The mode of love is indicated in the words "as thyself." This does not mean that a man must love his neighbour equally as himself, but in like manner as himself, and this in three ways. First, as regards the end, namely, that he should love his neighbour for God's sake, even as he loves himself for God's sake, so that his love for his neighbour may be a holy love. Secondly, as regards the rule of love, namely, that a man should not give way to his neighbour in evil, but only in good things, even as he ought to gratify his own will in good things alone, so that his love for his neighbour may be a just love. Thirdly, as regards the reason for loving, namely, that a man should love his neighbour not for his own profit or pleasure, but in the sense of wishing his neighbour well, even as he wishes himself well, so that his love for his neighbour may be a true love, for when a man loves his neighbour for his own profit or pleasure, he does not love his neighbour truly, but loves himself.

[3] *Ethics,* IX, 4 (1166ᵃ1); IX, 8 (1168ᵇ5).

This suffices for the *Replies to the Objections.*

ARTICLE 8. *Whether the Order of Charity Is Included in the Precept?*

We proceed thus to the Eighth Article: It seems that the order of charity is not included in the precept.

Objection 1. For whoever transgresses a precept does a wrong. But if man loves some one as much as he ought, and loves any other man more, he wrongs no man. Therefore he does not transgress the precept. Therefore the order of charity is not included in the precept.

Obj. 2. Further, Whatever is a matter of precept is sufficiently delivered to us in Holy Writ. Now the order of charity which was given above (Q. XXVI) is nowhere indicated in Holy Writ. Therefore it is not included in the precept.

Obj. 3. Further, Order implies some kind of distinction. But the love of our neighbour is prescribed without any distinction, in the words, *Thou shalt love thy neighbour as thyself.* Therefore the order of charity is not included in the precept.

On the contrary, Whatever God works in us by His grace, He teaches us first of all by the precepts of His Law, according to Jerem. 31. 33: *I will give My Law in their heart* (Vulg.,— *in their bowels, and I will write it in their heart*). Now God causes in us the order of charity, according to Cant. 2. 4: *He set in order charity in me.* Therefore the order of charity comes under the precept of the Law.

I answer that, As stated above (A. 4, Reply 1), the mode which is essential to an act of virtue comes under the precept which prescribes that virtuous act. Now the order of charity is essential to the virtue, since it is based on the proportion of love to the thing loved, as shown above (Q. XXVI, A. 4, Reply 1; AA. 7, 9). It is therefore evident that the order of charity must come under the precept.

Reply Obj. 1. A man gratifies more the person he loves more, so that if he loved less one whom he ought to love more, he would wish to gratify more one whom he ought to gratify less, and so he would do an injustice to the one he ought to love more.

Reply Obj. 2. The order of those four things we have to love out of charity is expressed in Holy Writ. For when we are commanded to love God with our *whole heart,* we are given to understand that we must love Him above all things. When we are commanded to love our neighbour *as ourselves,* the love of self is set before love of our neighbour. In like manner where we are commanded (I John 3. 16) *to lay down our souls,* that is, the life of our bodies, *for the brethren,* we are given to understand that a man ought to love his neighbour more than his own body; and again when we are commanded (Gal. 6. 10) to *work good . . . especially to those who are of the household of the faith,* and when a man is blamed (I Tim. 5. 8) if he *have not care of his own, and especially of those of his house,* it means that we ought to love most those of our neighbours who are more virtuous or more closely united to us.

Reply Obj. 3. It follows from the very words, *Thou shalt love thy neighbour* that those who are nearer to us are to be loved more.

QUESTION XLV
OF THE GIFT OF WISDOM
(*In Six Articles*)

WE must now consider the gift of wisdom which corresponds to charity; and first, wisdom itself, secondly, the opposite vice (Q. XLIV.). Under the first head there are six points of inquiry: (1) Whether wisdom should be numbered among the gifts of the Holy Ghost? (2) What is its subject? (3) Whether wisdom is only speculative or also practical? (4) Whether the wisdom that is a gift is compatible with mortal sin? (5) Whether it is in all those who have sanctifying grace? (6) Which beatitude corresponds to it?

ARTICLE 1. *Whether Wisdom Should Be Counted Among the Gifts of the Holy Ghost?*

We proceed thus to the First Article: It seems that wisdom ought not to be counted among the gifts of the Holy Ghost.

Objection 1. For the gifts are more perfect than the virtues, as stated above (Part I-II, Q. LXVIII, A. 8). Now virtue is directed to the good alone, and so Augustine says (*De Lib. Arb.* ii, 19)[1] that "no man makes bad use of the virtues." Much more therefore are the gifts of the Holy Ghost directed to the good alone. But wisdom is directed to evil also, for it is written (James 3. 15) that a certain wisdom is *earthly, sensual, devilish.* Therefore wisdom should not be counted among the gifts of the Holy Ghost.

Obj. 2. Further, According to Augustine (*De Trin.* xiv, 11.)[2] "wisdom is the knowledge of Divine things." Now that knowledge of Divine things which man can acquire by his natural endowments belongs to the wisdom which is an intellectual virtue, while the supernatural

---

[1] PL 32, 1268.　　　　[2] PL 42, 1037.

knowledge of Divine things belongs to faith which is a theological virtue, as explained above (Q. I, A. I; Q. IV, A. 5; Part I-II, Q. LXII, A. 2). Therefore wisdom should be called a virtue rather than a gift.

Obj. 3. Further, It is written (Job. 28. 28): *Behold the fear of the Lord, that is wisdom, and to depart from evil, that is understanding.* And in this passage according to the rendering of the Septuagint which Augustine follows (*De Trin.* xii, 14; xiv, 1)[1] we read: *Behold piety, that is wisdom.* Now both fear and piety are gifts of the Holy Ghost. Therefore wisdom should not be numbered among the gifts of the Holy Ghost as though it were distinct from the others.

On the contrary, Is is written (Isa. 11. 2): *The Spirit of the Lord shall rest upon Him; the spirit of wisdom and of understanding.*

I answer that, According to the Philosopher,[2] it pertains to wisdom to consider the highest cause. By means of that cause we are able to form a most certain judgment about other causes, and according to it all things should be set in order. Now the highest cause may be understood in two ways, either absolutely or in some genus. Accordingly he that knows the highest cause in any genus, and by its means is able to judge and set in order all the things that belong to that genus, is said to be wise in that genus, for instance in medicine or architecture, according to I Cor. 3. 10: *As a wise architect, I have laid a foundation.* On the other hand, he who knows the cause that is the highest absolutely, which is God, is said to be wise absolutely, because he is able to judge and set in order all things according to Divine rules.

Now man obtains this judgment through the Holy Ghost, according to I Cor. 2. 15: *The spiritual man judgeth all things,* because as stated in the same chapter (*verse* 10), *the Spirit searcheth all things, yea the deep things of God.* Therefore it is evident that wisdom is a gift of the Holy Ghost.

Reply Obj. 1. A thing is said to be good in two ways: first in the sense that it is good truly and perfect absolutely, secondly, by a kind of likeness, being perfect in wickedness; thus we speak of a good or a perfect thief, as the Philosopher observes.[3] And just as with regard to those things which are truly good, we find a highest cause, namely the sovereign good which is the last end, by knowing which man is said to be truly wise, so too in evil things something is to be found to which all others are to be re-

ferred as to a last end, by knowing which man is said to be wise for the doing of evil, according to Jerem. 4. 22: *They are wise to do evils, but to do good they have no knowledge.* Now whoever turns away from his due end must fix on some undue end, since every agent acts for an end. Hence, if he fixes his end in external earthly things, his wisdom is called earthly, if in the goods of the body, it is called sensual wisdom, if in some excellence, it is called devilish wisdom, because it imitates the devil's pride, of which it is written (Job. 41. 25): *He is king over all the children of pride.*

Reply Obj. 2. The wisdom which is called a gift of the Holy Ghost differs from that which is an acquired intellectual virtue, for the latter is attained by human effort, while the former is *descending from above* (James 3. 15.). In like manner it differs from faith, since faith assents to the Divine truth in itself, while it belongs to the gift of wisdom to judge according to the Divine truth. Hence the gift of wisdom presupposes faith, because "a man judges well what he knows."[4]

Reply Obj. 3. Just as piety, which pertains to the worship of God, is a manifestation of faith, in so far as we make profession of faith by worshipping God, so too, piety manifests wisdom. For this reason piety is stated to be wisdom, and so is fear, for the same reason, because if a man fear and worship God, this shows that he has a right judgment about Divine things.

ARTICLE 2. *Whether Wisdom Is in the Intellect As in a Subject?*

We proceed thus to the Second Article: It would seem that wisdom is not in the intellect as in a subject.

Objection 1. For Augustine says (*Ep.* CXL)[5] that "wisdom is the charity of God." Now charity is in the will as its subject, and not in the intellect, as stated above (Q. XXIV, A. 1). Therefore wisdom is not in the intellect as its subject.

Obj. 2. Further, It is written (Ecclus. 6. 23): *The wisdom of doctrine is according to her name,* for wisdom (*sapientia*) may be described as "sweet-tasting science" (*sapida scientia*), and this seems to pertain to the affections, to which it pertains to taste spiritual pleasure or sweetness. Therefore wisdom is in the affections rather than in the intellect.

Obj. 3. Further, The intellectual power is

---

[1] PL 42, 1010; 1036.
[2] *Metaphysics,* I, 2 (928ᵃ8).   [3] *Ibid.,* V, 16 (1021ᵇ17).

[4] Aristotle, *Ethics,* I, 3 (1094ᵇ27).
[5] Chap. 18 (PL 33, 557).

sufficiently perfected by the gift of understanding. Now it is superfluous to require two things where one suffices for the purpose. Therefore wisdom is not in the intellect.

On the contrary, Gregory says (*Moral.* ii, 49)[1] that wisdom is contrary to folly. But folly is in the intellect. Therefore wisdom is also.

I answer that, As stated above (A. 1, Q. viii, A. 6), wisdom denotes a certain rectitude of judgment according to the Eternal Law. Now rectitude of judgment is twofold: first, on account of perfect use of reason, secondly, on account of a certain connaturality with the matter about which one has to judge in a given instance. Thus, about matters of chastity, a man after inquiring with his reason forms a right judgment if he has learnt the science of morals, while he who has the habit of chastity judges rightly of such matters by a kind of connaturality.

Accordingly it pertains to the wisdom that is an intellectual virtue to pronounce right judgment about Divine things after reason has made its inquiry, but it pertains to wisdom as a gift of the Holy Ghost to judge rightly about them on account of a certain connaturality with them; thus Dionysius says (*Div. Nom. ii*)[2] that Hierotheus is perfect in Divine things, for he not only learns, but also suffers Divine things." Now this sympathy or connaturality for Divine things is the result of charity, which unites us to God, according to I Cor. 6. 17: *He who is joined to the Lord, is one spirit.* Consequently wisdom which is a gift, has its cause in the will, which cause is charity, but it has its essence in the intellect, whose act is to judge rightly, as stated above (Part I, Q. LXXIX, A. 3).

Reply Obj. 1. Augustine is speaking of wisdom as to its cause, from which also wisdom (*sapientia*) takes its name, in so far as it denotes a certain sweetness (*saporem*).

Hence the *Reply to the Second Objection* is evident, that is if this be the true meaning of the text quoted. For, apparently this is not the case, because such an exposition of the text would only fit the Latin word for wisdom, while it does not apply to the Greek, and perhaps not in other languages. Hence it would seem that in the text quoted wisdom stands for the renown of doctrine, for which it is praised by all.

Reply Obj. 3. The intellect exercises a twofold act, perception and judgment. The gift of understanding regards the former; the gift of wisdom regards the latter according to the Divine ideas, the gift of knowledge, according to human ideas.

ARTICLE 3. *Whether Wisdom Is Merely Speculative, or Practical Also?*

We proceed thus to the Third Article: It seems that wisdom is not practical but merely speculative.

Objection 1. For the gift of wisdom is more excellent than the wisdom which is an intellectual virtue. But wisdom as an intellectual virtue is merely speculative. Much more therefore is wisdom, as a gift, speculative and not practical.

Obj. 2. Further, The practical intellect is about matters of operation which are contingent. But wisdom is about Divine things which are eternal and necessary. Therefore wisdom cannot be practical.

Obj. 3. Further, Gregory says (*Moral.* vi, 37)[3] that "in contemplation we seek the Beginning which is God, but in action we labour under a mighty bundle of wants." Now wisdom pertains to the vision of Divine things, in which there is no toiling under a load, since according to Wis. 8. 16, *her conversation hath no bitterness, nor her company any tediousness.* Therefore wisdom is merely contemplative, and not practical or active.

On the contrary, It is written (Coloss. 4. 5): *Walk with wisdom towards them that are without.* Now this pertains to action. Therefore wisdom is not merely speculative, but also practical.

I answer that, As Augustine says (*De Trin.* xii, 14),[4] the higher part of the reason is the province of wisdom, while the lower part is the domain of knowledge. Now the higher reason according to the same authority (*ibid.* 7)[5] is "intent on the consideration and consultation of the heavenly (that is, Divine) types." It considers them in so far as it contemplates Divine things in themselves, and it consults them in so far as it judges of human acts by Divine things, directing human acts according to Divine rules. Accordingly wisdom as a gift is not merely speculative but also practical.

Reply Obj. 1. The higher a virtue is the greater the number of things to which it extends, as stated in *De Causis.*[6] Therefore from the very fact that wisdom as a gift is more excellent than wisdom as an intellectual virtue, since it attains to God more intimately by a kind of union

[1] PL 75, 592.
[2] Sect. 9 (PG 3, 648).

[3] PL 75, 764.   [4] PL 42, 1009.
[5] PL 42, 1005.   [6] Sects. 9, 16 (BA 174.15; 179.5).

of the soul with Him, it is able to direct us not only in contemplation but also in action.

Reply Obj. 2. Divine things are indeed necessary and eternal in themselves, yet they are the rules of the contingent things which are the subject-matter of human actions.

Reply Obj. 3. A thing is considered in itself before being compared with something else. Therefore to wisdom belongs first of all contemplation of Divine things which is the vision of the Beginning, and afterwards the direction of human act according to the Divine rules. Nor from the direction of wisdom does there result any bitterness or toil in human acts, but rather the result of wisdom is to make the bitter sweet, and labour a rest.

ARTICLE 4. *Whether Wisdom Can Be Without Grace and With Mortal Sin?*

We proceed thus to the Fourth Article: It seems that wisdom can be without grace and with mortal sin.

Objection 1. For saints glory chiefly in such things as are incompatible with mortal sin, according to II Cor. 1. 12: *Our glory is this, the testimony of our conscience.* Now one ought not to glory in one's wisdom, according to Jerem. 9. 23: *Let not the wise man glory in his wisdom.* Therefore wisdom can be without grace and with mortal sin.

Obj. 2. Further, wisdom denotes knowledge of Divine things, as stated above (AA. 1, 3). Now one in mortal sin may have knowledge of the Divine truth, according to Rom. 1. 18: *(Those men that) detain the truth of God in injustice.* Therefore wisdom is compatible with mortal sin.

Obj. 3. Further, Augustine says (*De Trin.* xv, 18)[1] while speaking of charity: "Nothing surpasses this gift of God; it is this alone that divides the children of the eternal kingdom from the children of eternal perdition." But wisdom is distinct from charity. Therefore it does not divide the children of the kingdom from the children of perdition. Therefore it is compatible with mortal sin.

On the contrary, It is written (Wisd. 1. 4): *Wisdom will not enter into a malicious soul, nor dwell in a body subject to sins.*

I answer that, The wisdom which is a gift of the Holy Ghost, as stated above (AA. 2, 3), enables us to judge rightly of Divine things, or of other things according to Divine rules, by reason of a certain connaturalness or union with Divine things, which is the effect of charity, as

stated above (A. 2). Hence the wisdom of which we are speaking presupposes charity. Now charity is incompatible with mortal sin, as shown above (Q. XXIV, A. 12). Therefore it follows that the wisdom of which we are speaking cannot be together with mortal sin.

Reply Obj. 1. These words are to be understood as referring to worldly wisdom, or to wisdom in Divine things acquired through human reasons. In such wisdom the saints do not glory, according to Prov. 30. 2: *The wisdom of men is not with Me:* But they do glory in Divine wisdom according to I Cor. 1. 30: *(Who) of God is made unto us wisdom.*

Reply Obj. 2. This argument considers not the wisdom of which we speak but that which is acquired by the study and searching of reason, and is compatible with mortal sin.

Reply Obj. 3. Although wisdom is distinct from charity it presupposes it, and for that very reason divides the children of perdition from the children of the kingdom.

ARTICLE 5. *Whether Wisdom Is in All Who Have Grace?*

We proceed thus to the Fifth Article: It would seem that wisdom is not in all who have grace.

Objection 1. For it is greater to have wisdom than to hear wisdom. Now it is only for the perfect to hear wisdom, according to I Cor. 2. 6: *We speak wisdom among the perfect.* Since then not all who have grace are perfect, it seems that much less all who have grace have wisdom.

Obj. 2. Further, "The wise man sets things in order," as the Philosopher states;[2] and it is written (James 3. 17) that the wise man *judges without dissimulation* (Vulg.,—*The wisdom that is from above . . . is . . . without judging, without dissimulation*). Now it is not for all that have grace to judge, or put others in order, but only for those in authority. Therefore wisdom is not in all that have grace.

Obj. 3. Further, "Wisdom is a remedy against folly," as Gregory says (*Moral.* ii, 49).[3] Now many that have grace are naturally foolish, for instance madmen who are baptized or those who without being guilty of mortal sin have become insane. Therefore wisdom is not in all that have grace.

On the contrary, Whoever is without mortal sin is beloved of God, since he has charity, by which he loves God, and God loves them that love Him (Prov. 8. 17). Now it is written (Wis. 7. 28) that God *loveth none but him that dwell-*

---

[1] PL 42, 1082.

[2] *Metaphysics,* I, 2 (982[a]18).   [3] PL 75, 592.

eth with wisdom. Therefore wisdom is in all those who have charity and are without mortal sin.

I answer that, The wisdom of which we are speaking, as stated above (AA. 1, 3), denotes a certain rectitude of judgment in the contemplation and consultation of Divine things, and as to both of these men obtain various degrees of wisdom through union with Divine things. For the measure of right judgment attained by some, whether in the contemplation of Divine things or in directing human affairs according to Divine rules, is no more than suffices for their salvation. This měasure is wanting to none who is without mortal sin through having sanctifying grace, since if nature does not fail in necessary things, much less does grace fail. Therefore it is written (I John 2. 27): (*His*) *unction teacheth you of all things.*

Some, however, receive a higher degree of the gift of wisdom, both as to the contemplation of Divine things (by both knowing more exalted mysteries and being able to impart this knowledge to others) and as to the direction of human affairs according to Divine rules (by being able to direct not only themselves but also others according to those rules). This degree of wisdom is not common to all that have sanctifying grace, but belongs rather to the gratuitous graces, which the Holy Ghost dispenses as He wills, according to I Cor. 12. 8: *To one indeed by the Spirit is given the word of wisdom,* etc.

Reply Obj. 1. The Apostle speaks there of wisdom as extending to the hidden mysteries of Divine things, as indeed he says himself (*ibid.* 7): *We speak the wisdom of God in a mystery, a wisdom which is hidden.*

Reply Obj. 2. Although it belongs to those alone who are in authority to direct and judge other men, yet it pertains to every man to direct and judge his own actions, as Dionysius declares (*Ep. ad Demophil.*).[1]

Reply Obj. 3. Baptized idiots, like little children, have the habit of wisdom, which is a gift of the Holy Ghost, but they do not have the act, on account of the bodily impediment which hinders the use of reason in them.

ARTICLE 6. *Whether the Seventh Beatitude Corresponds to the Gift of Wisdom?*

We proceed thus to the Sixth Article: It seems that the seventh beatitude does not correspond to the gift of wisdom.

Objection 1. For the seventh beatitude is:

[1] *Epist.,* VIII, 3 (PG 3, 1093).

Blessed are the peacemakers, for they shall be called the children of God. Now both these things belong immediately to charity, since of peace it is written (Ps. 118. 165): *Much peace have they that love Thy law,* and, as the Apostle says (Rom. 5. 5), *the charity of God is poured forth in our hearts by the Holy Ghost Who is given to us,* and Who is *the Spirit of adoption of sons, whereby we cry: Abba (Father)* (*ibid.* 8, 15). Therefore the seventh beatitude ought to be ascribed to charity rather than to wisdom.

Obj. 2. Further, A thing is declared by its proximate effect rather than by its remote effect. Now the proximate effect of wisdom seems to be charity, according to Wisd. 7. 27: *Through nations she conveyeth herself into holy souls; she maketh the friends of God and prophets,* while peace and the adoption of sons seem to be remote effects, since they result from charity, as stated above (Q. XXIX, A. 3). Therefore the beatitude corresponding to wisdom should be determined according to the love of charity rather than according to peace.

Obj. 3. Further. It is written (James 3. 17): *The wisdom, that is from above, first indeed is chaste, then peaceable, modest, easy to be persuaded, consenting to the good, full of mercy and good fruits, judging without dissimulation* (Vulg.,—*without judging, without dissimulation.*). Therefore the beatitude corresponding to wisdom should not refer to peace rather than to the other effects of heavenly wisdom.

On the contrary, Augustine says (*De Serm. Dom. in Monte,* i, 4)[2] that "wisdom is becoming to peacemakers, in whom there is no movement of rebellion, but only obedience to reason."

I answer that, The seventh beatitude is fittingly ascribed to the gift of wisdom, both as to the merit and as to the reward. The merit is denoted in the words, *Blessed are the peacemakers.* Now a peacemaker is one who makes peace, either in himself, or in others, and in both cases this is the result of setting in due order those things in which peace is established; for "peace is the tranquillity of order," according to Augustine.[3] Now "it pertains to wisdom to set things in order," as the Philosopher declares;[4] therefore to be peaceful is fittingly ascribed to wisdom. The reward is expressed in the words, *they shall be called the children of God.* Now men are called the children of God in so far as they participate in the likeness of the only begotten and natural Son

[2] PL 34, 1235.   [3] *City of God,* XIX, 13 (PL 41, 640).
[4] *Metaphysics,* I, 2 (982ᵃ18).

of God, according to Rom. 8. 29, *Whom He foreknew . . . to be made conformable to the image of His Son, Who* is Wisdom Begotten. Hence by participating in the gift of wisdom, man attains to the sonship of God.

Reply Obj. 1. It belongs to charity to be at peace, but it belongs to wisdom to make peace by setting things in order. Likewise the Holy Ghost is called the "Spirit of adoption" in so far as we receive from Him the likeness of the natural Son, Who is the Begotten Wisdom.

Reply Obj. 2. These words refer to the Uncreated Wisdom, which in the first place unites itself to us by the gift of charity, and consequently reveals to us the mysteries, the knowledge of which is infused wisdom. Hence, the infused wisdom which is a gift is not the cause but the effect of charity.

Reply Obj. 3. As stated above (A. 3) it belongs to wisdom, as a gift not only to contemplate Divine things, but also to regulate human acts. Now the first thing to be effected in this direction of human acts is the removal of evils opposed to wisdom; therefore fear is said to be *the beginning of wisdom* (Ps. 110. 10), because it makes us shun evil, while the last thing is like an end, by which all things are reduced to their right order; and it is this that constitutes peace. Hence James said with reason that *the wisdom that is from above* (and this is the gift of the Holy Ghost) *first indeed is chaste*, because it avoids the corruption of sin, and *then peaceable*, wherein lies the ultimate effect of wisdom, for which reason peace is numbered among the beatitudes. As to the things that follow, they declare in becoming order the means by which wisdom leads to peace. For when a man, by modesty, avoids the corruption of sin, the first thing he has to do is, as far as he can, to be moderate in all things, and in this respect wisdom is said to be "modest." Secondly, in those matters in which he is not sufficient by himself, he should be guided by the advice of others, and as to this we are told further that wisdom is "easy to be persuaded." These two are conditions required that man may be at peace with himself. But in order that man may be at peace with others it is furthermore required, first that he should not be opposed to their good; this is what is meant by "consenting to the good." Secondly, that he should bring to his neighbour's deficiencies, sympathy in his heart, and succour in his actions, and this is denoted by the words "full of mercy and good fruits." Thirdly, he should strive in all charity to correct the sins of others, and this

is indicated by the words "judging without dissimulation," lest he should purpose to sate his hatred under cover of correction.

QUESTION XLVI

OF FOLLY, WHICH IS OPPOSED TO WISDOM

(*In Three Articles*)

WE must now consider folly, which is opposed to wisdom; and under this head there are three points of inquiry: (1) Whether folly is contrary to wisdom? (2) Whether folly is a sin? (3) To which capital sin is it reducible?

ARTICLE 1. *Whether Folly Is Contrary to Wisdom?*

We proceed thus to the First Article: It seems that folly is not contrary to wisdom.

Objection 1. For it seems that unwisdom is directly opposed to wisdom. But folly does not seem to be the same as unwisdom, for the latter is apparently about Divine things alone, while folly is about both Divine and human things. Therefore folly is not contrary to wisdom.

Obj. 2. Further, One contrary is not the way to arrive at the other. But folly is the way to arrive at wisdom, for it is written (I Cor. 3. 18): *If any man among you seem to be wise in this world, let him become a fool, that he may be wise.* Therefore folly is not opposed to wisdom.

Obj. 3. Further, One contrary is not the cause of the other. But wisdom is the cause of folly; for it is written (Jerem. 10. 14): *Every man is become a fool for knowledge*, and wisdom is a kind of knowledge. Moreover it is written (Isa. 47. 10): *Thy wisdom and thy knowledge, this hath deceived thee.* Now to be deceived pertains to folly. Therefore folly is not contrary to wisdom.

Obj. 4. Further, Isidore says (*Etym.* x, under the letter S)[1] that "a fool is one whom shame does not incite to sorrow, and who is unconcerned when he is injured." But this pertains to spiritual wisdom, according to Gregory (*Moral.* x, 29).[2] Therefore folly is not opposed to wisdom.

On the contrary, Gregory says (*Moral.* ii, 49)[3] that "the gift of wisdom is given as a remedy against folly."

I answer that, Folly (*Stultitia*) seems to take its name from "stupor"; and so Isidore says (*loc. cit.*): "A fool is one who through dulness (*stuporem*) remains unmoved." And folly differs from fatuity, according to the same au-

[1] PL 82, 393.   [2] PL 75, 947.   [3] PL 75, 592.

thority (*ibid.*),[1] in that folly implies apathy in the heart and dulness in the senses while fatuity denotes entire privation of the spiritual sense. Therefore folly is fittingly opposed to wisdom.

For *sapiens* (wise) as Isidore says (*ibid.*) "is so named from *sapor* (savour), because just as the taste is quick to distinguish between savours of meats, so is a wise man in discerning things and causes." Therefore it is manifest that folly is opposed to wisdom as its contrary, while fatuity is opposed to it is a pure negation, for the fatuous man lacks the sense of judgment; the fool has the sense, though dulled, and the wise man has the sense acute and penetrating.

Reply Obj. 1. According to Isidore (*ibid.*) unwisdom is contrary to wisdom because it lacks the savour of discretion and sense, so that unwisdom seems to be the same as folly. Yet a man would appear to be a fool chiefly through some deficiency in the verdict of that judgment which is according to the highest cause, for if a man fails in judgment about some trivial matter, he is not for that reason called a fool.

Reply Obj. 2. Just as there is an evil wisdom, as stated above (Q. XLV, A. 1, REPLY 1), which is called worldly wisdom, because it takes for the highest cause and last end some worldly good, so too there is a good folly opposed to this evil wisdom, by which man despises worldly things; and it is of this folly that the Apostle speaks.

Reply Obj. 3. It is the wisdom of the world that deceives and makes us foolish in God's sight, as is evident from the Apostle's words (I Cor. 3. 19).

Reply Obj. 4. To be unconcerned when one is injured is sometimes due to the fact that one has no taste for worldly things, but only for heavenly things. Hence this belongs not to worldly but to Divine wisdom, as Gregory declares (*ibid.*). Sometimes however it is the result of a man's being stupid absolutely about everything, as may be seen in idiots, who do not discern what is injurious to them, and this belongs to folly absolutely.

ARTICLE 2. *Whether Folly Is a Sin?*

We proceed thus to the Second Article: It seems that folly is not a sin.

Objection 1. For no sin arises in us from nature. But some are fools naturally. Therefore folly is not a sin.

Obj. 2. Further, "Every sin is voluntary," according to Augustine (*De Vera Relig.* xiv).[2] But folly is not voluntary. Therefore it is not a sin.

Obj. 3. Further, Every sin is contrary to a Divine precept. But folly is not contrary to any precept. Therefore folly is not a sin.

On the contrary, It is written (Prov. 1. 32): *The prosperity of fools shall destroy them.* But no man is destroyed save for sin. Therefore folly is a sin.

I answer that, Folly, as stated above (A. 1), denotes dulness of sense in judging, and chiefly as regards the highest cause, which is the last end and the sovereign good. Now a man may in this respect contract dulness in judgment in two ways. First, from a natural indisposition, as in the case of idiots, and such folly is no sin. Secondly, by plunging his sense into earthly things, by which his sense is rendered incapable of perceiving Divine things, according to I Cor. 2. 14. *The sensual man perceiveth not these things that are of the Spirit of God,* even as sweet things have no savour for a man whose taste is infected with an evil humour; and such folly is a sin.

This suffices for the *Reply to the First Objection.*

Reply Obj. 2. Though no man wishes to be a fool, yet he wishes those things of which folly is a consequence, namely to withdraw his sense from spiritual things and to plunge it into earthly things. The same thing happens in regard to other sins; for the lustful man desires pleasure, without which there is no sin, although he does not desire sin absolutely, for he would wish to enjoy the pleasure without sin.

Reply Obj. 3. Folly is opposed to the precepts about the contemplation of truth, of which we have spoken above (Q. XVI) when we were treating of knowledge and understanding.

ARTICLE 3. *Whether Folly Is a Daughter of Lust?*

We proceed thus to the Third Article: It would seem that folly is not a daughter of lust.

Objection 1. For Gregory (*Moral.* xxxi, 45)[3] enumerates the daughters of lust, among which however he makes no mention of folly. Therefore folly does not proceed from lust.

Obj. 2. Further, The Apostle says (I Cor. 3. 19): *The wisdom of this world is foolishness with God.* Now, according to Gregory (*Moral.* x, 29)[4] "the wisdom of this world consists in covering the heart with crafty devices"; and this pertains to duplicity. Therefore folly is a daughter of duplicity rather than of lust.

Obj. 3. Further, Anger especially is the cause of fury and madness in some persons, and this pertains to folly. Therefore folly arises from anger rather than from lust.

On the contrary, It is written (Prov. 7. 22): *Immediately he followeth her,* that is, the harlot . . . *not knowing that he is drawn like a fool to bonds.*

I answer that, As already stated (A. 2), folly, in so far as it is a sin, is caused by the spiritual sense being dulled, so as to be incapable of judging spiritual things. Now man's sense is plunged into earthly things chiefly by lust, which is about the greatest pleasures; and these absorb the mind more than any others. Therefore the folly which is a sin arises chiefly from lust.

Reply Obj. 1. It is part of folly that a man should have a distaste for God and His gifts. Hence Gregory mentions two daughters of lust, pertaining to folly, namely, "hatred of God and despair of the life to come"; thus he divides folly into two parts as it were.

Reply Obj. 2. These words of the Apostle are to be understood, not causally but essentially, because, namely, worldly wisdom itself is folly with God. Hence it does not follow that whatever belongs to worldly wisdom is a cause of this folly.

Reply Obj. 3. Anger by reason of its keenness, as stated above (Part I-II, Q. XLVIII, A. 2), produces a great change in the nature of the body, and therefore it conduces very much to the folly which results from a bodily impediment. On the other hand the folly which is caused by a spiritual impediment, namely by the mind being plunged into earthly things, arises chiefly from lust, as stated above.

TREATISE ON ACTIVE AND CONTEMPLATIVE LIFE

QUESTION CLXXIX

OF THE DIVISION OF LIFE INTO ACTIVE AND CONTEMPLATIVE

(In Two Articles)

WE must next consider active and contemplative life. This consideration will be fourfold: (1) Of the division of life into active and contemplative; (2) Of the contemplative life (Q. CLXXX); (3) Of the active life (Q. CLXXXI); (4) Of the comparison between the active and the contemplative life (Q. CLXXXII).

Under the first head there are two points of inquiry: (1) Whether life is fittingly divided into active and contemplative? (2) Whether this is an adequate division?

ARTICLE 1. *Whether Life Is Fittingly Divided into Active and Contemplative?*

We proceed thus to the First Article: It seems that life is not fittingly divided into active and contemplative.

Objection 1. For the soul is the principle of life by its essence; for the Philosopher says[1] that "in living things to live is to be." Now the soul is the principle of action and contemplation by its powers. Therefore it would seem that life is not fittingly divided into active and contemplative.

Obj. 2. Further, The division of that which comes afterwards is unfittingly applied to that which comes first. Now active and contemplative, or speculative and practical, are differences of the intellect,[2] while "to live" comes before "to understand," since "to live" comes first to living things through the vegetative soul, as the Philosopher states.[3] Therefore life is unfittingly divided into active and contemplative.

Obj. 3. Further, The word "life" implies movement, according to Dionysius (*Div. Nom.* iv);[4] but contemplation consists rather in rest, according to Wisd. 8. 16: *When I enter into my house, I shall repose myself with her.* Therefore it would seem that life is unfittingly divided into active and contemplative.

On the contrary, Gregory says (*Hom.* ii, *super Ezech.*):[5] "There is a twofold life wherein Almighty God instructs us by His holy word, the active life and the contemplative."

I answer that, Properly speaking, those things are said to live whose movement or operation is from within themselves. Now that which is proper to a thing and to which it is most inclined, is that which is most becoming to it from itself; and so every living thing gives proof of its life by that operation which is most proper to it, and to which it is most inclined. Thus the life of plants is said to consist in nourishment and generation; the life of animals in sensation and movement; and the life of men in their understanding and acting according to reason. Therefore also in men the life of every man would seem to be that in which he delights most, and on which he is most intent, and that in which especially they wish to pass their time with their friends, as stated in the *Ethics*.[6] Accordingly since certain men are especially intent on the contemplation of truth, while others are especially intent on external actions, it follows that man's life is fittingly divided into active and contemplative.

Reply Obj. 1. Each thing's proper form that makes it actually to be is the principle of operation proper to that thing. Hence to live is, in living things, to be, because living things through having being from their form, act in such and such a way.

Reply Obj. 2. Life in general is not divided into active and contemplative, but the life of man, who derives his species from having an intellect, and therefore the same division applies to intellect and human life.

Reply Obj. 3. It is true that contemplation enjoys rest from external movements. Nevertheless to contemplate is itself a movement of the intellect, in so far as every operation is described as a movement; in which sense the Phi-

---

[1] *Soul*, II, 4 (415^{b}13).
[2] *Ibid.*, III, 10 (433^{a}14).   [3] *Ibid.*, II, 4 (415^{a}24).
[4] Sect. 10 (PG 3, 705); cf. VI, 2 (PG 3, 857).
[5] PL 76, 952.
[6] Aristotle, IX, 12 (1172^{a}5).

losopher says[1] that sensation and understanding are movements of a kind, in so far as the act of a perfect thing is a movement. In this way Dionysius (*Div. Nom.* iv)[2] ascribes three movements to the soul in contemplation, namely straight, circular, and oblique.

ARTICLE 2. *Whether Life Is Adequately Divided into Active and Contemplative?*

We proceed thus to the Second Article: It seems that life is not adequately divided into active and contemplative.

Objection 1. For the Philosopher says[3] that "there are three most excellent kinds of life," the life of pleasure, the civil which would seem to be the same as the active, and the contemplative life. Therefore the division of life into active and contemplative would seem to be inadequate.

Obj. 2. Further, Augustine mentions[4] three kinds of life, namely the life of "leisure" which pertains to the contemplative, the "busy" life which pertains to the active, and a third "composed of both." Therefore it would seem that life is inadequately divided into active and contemplative.

Obj. 3. Further, Man's life is diversified according to the different actions in which men are occupied. Now there are more than two occupations of human actions. Therefore it would seem that life should be divided into more kinds than the active and the contemplative.

On the contrary, These two lives are signified by the two wives of Jacob (Gen. 19): the active by Lia, and the contemplative by Rachel; and by the two hostesses of our Lord: the contemplative life by Mary, and the active life by Martha (Luke 10. 38), as Gregory declares (*Moral* vi, 37).[5] Now this signification would not be fitting if there were more than two lives. Therefore life is adequately divided into active and contemplative.

I answer that, As stated in the foregoing Article (reply 2), this division applies to the human life as derived from the intellect. Now the intellect is divided into active and contemplative, since the end of intellectual knowledge is either the knowledge itself of truth, which pertains to the contemplative intellect, or some external action, which pertains to the practical or active intellect. Therefore life too is adequately divided into active and contemplative.

Reply Obj. 1. The life of pleasure places its end in pleasures of the body, which are common to us and dumb animals; therefore as the Philosopher says,[6] it is the life of a beast. Hence it is not included in this division of the life of a man into active and contemplative.

Reply Obj. 2. A mean is a combination of extremes, and therefore it is virtually contained in them, as tepid in hot and cold, and pale in white and black. In like manner active and contemplative comprise that which is composed of both. Nevertheless as in every mixture one of the absolutes predominates, so too, in the mean state of life sometimes the contemplative, sometimes the active element, abounds.

Reply Obj. 3. All the occupations of human actions, if directed to the requirements of the present life in accord with right reason, belong to the active life which provides for the necessities of the present life by means of well-ordered activity. If, on the other hand, they minister to any concupiscence whatever, they belong to the life of pleasure, which is not comprised under the active life. Those human occupations that are directed to the consideration of truth belong to the contemplative life.

QUESTION CLXXX
OF THE CONTEMPLATIVE LIFE
(In Eight Articles)

WE must now consider the contemplative life, under which head there are eight points of inquiry: (1) Whether the contemplative life pertains to the intellect only, or also to the affections? (2) Whether the moral virtues pertain to the contemplative life? (3) Whether the contemplative life consists in one action or in several? (4) Whether the consideration of any truth whatever pertains to the contemplative life? (5) Whether the contemplative life of man in this state can arise to the vision of God? (6) Of the movements of contemplation assigned by Dionysius (*Div. Nom.* iv). (7) Of the pleasure of contemplation. (8) Of the duration of contemplation.

ARTICLE 1. *Whether the Contemplative Life Has Nothing To Do With the Affections, and Pertains Wholly to the Intellect?*

We proceed thus to the First Article: It seems that the contemplative life has nothing to do with the affections and pertains wholly to the intellect.

Objection 1. For the Philosopher says[7] that

[1] *Soul,* III, 7 (431ª4).   [2] Sect. 8 (PG 3, 704).
[3] *Ethics,* I, 5 (1095ᵇ17).
[4] *City of God,* XIX, 2, 3, 19 (PL 41, 624; 627; 647).
[5] PL 75, 764.
[6] *Loc. cit.*   [7] *Metaphysics,* II, 1 (993ᵇ20).

"the end of contemplation is truth." Now truth pertains wholly to the intellect. Therefore it would seem that the contemplative life wholly regards the intellect.

Obj. 2. Further, Gregory says (*Moral.* vi, 37)[1] that "Rachel, which is interpreted 'vision of the principle,' signifies the contemplative life." Now the vision of a principle belongs properly to the intellect. Therefore the contemplative life belongs properly to the intellect.

Obj. 3. Further, Gregory says (*Hom.* ii *in Ezech.*)[2] that it pertains to the contemplative life "to rest from external action." Now the affective or appetitive power inclines to external actions. Therefore it would seem that the contemplative life has nothing to do with the appetitive power.

On the contrary, Gregory says (*ibid.*) that "the contemplative life is to cling with our whole mind to the love of God and our neighbour, and to desire nothing beside our Creator." Now desire and love pertain to the affective or appetitive power, as stated above (Part I-II, Q. XXV, A. 2). Therefore the contemplative life has also something to do with the affective or appetitive power.

I answer that, As stated above (Q. CLXXIX, A. 1) the contemplative life is said of those who are chiefly intent on the contemplation of truth. Now intention is an act of the will, as stated above (Part I-II, Q. XII, A. 1), because intention is of the end which is the object of the will. Consequently the contemplative life, as regards the essence of the action, pertains to the intellect, but as regards what moves to the exercise of that action it belongs to the will, which moves all the other powers, even the intellect, to their actions, as stated above (Part I-II, Q. IX, A. 1).

Now the appetitive power moves one to observe things either with the senses or with the intellect, sometimes for love of the thing seen because, as it is written (Matt. 6. 21), *where thy treasure is, there is thy heart also,* sometimes for love of the very knowledge that one acquires by observation. Hence Gregory makes the contemplative life to consist in "the love of God," in so far as through loving God we are aflame to gaze on His beauty. And since everyone delights when he obtains what he loves, it follows that the contemplative life terminates in delight, which is seated in the affective power, the result being that love also becomes more intense.

Reply Obj. 1. From the very fact that truth is the end of contemplation, it has the aspect

of an appetible good, both lovable and delightful, and in this respect it pertains to the appetitive power.

Reply Obj. 2. We are urged to the vision of the first principle, namely God, by the love for it; hence Gregory says (*Hom.* ii *in Ezech.*)[3] that "the contemplative life tramples on all cares and longs to see the face of its Creator."

Reply Obj. 3. The appetitive power moves not only the bodily members to perform external actions, but also the intellect to practise the act of contemplation, as stated in the *Article.*

ARTICLE 2. *Whether the Moral Virtues Pertain to the Contemplative Life?*

We proceed thus to the Second Article: It seems that the moral virtues pertain to the contemplative life.

Objection 1. For Gregory says (*Hom.* ii *in Ezech.*)[4] that "the contemplative life is to cling to the love of God and our neighbour with the whole mind." Now all the moral virtues, whose acts are prescribed by the precepts of the Law, are reducible to the love of God and of our neighbour, for *love . . . is the fulfilling of the Law* (Rom. 13. 10). Therefore it would seem that the moral virtues belong to the contemplative life.

Obj. 2. Further, The contemplative life is chiefly directed to the contemplation of God; for Gregory says (*Hom.* ii *in Ezech.*)[5] that "the mind tramples on all cares and longs to gaze on the face of its Creator." Now no one can accomplish this without cleanness of heart, which is a result of moral virtue. For it is written (Matt. 5. 8): *Blessed are the clean of heart, for they shall see God;* and (Heb. 12. 14): *Follow peace with all men, and holiness, without which no man shall see God.* Therefore it would seem that the moral virtues pertain to the contemplative life.

Obj. 3. Further, Gregory says (*Hom.* ii *in Ezech.*)[6] that "the contemplative life gives beauty to the soul," and so it is signified by Rachel, of whom it is said (Gen. 29. 17) that she was *of a beautiful countenance.* Now the beauty of the soul consists in the moral virtues, especially temperance, as Ambrose says (*De Offic.* i, 43).[7] Therefore it seems that the moral virtues pertain to the contemplative life.

On the contrary, The moral virtues are directed to external actions. Now Gregory says (*Hom.* ii *in Ezech.*)[8] that it belongs to the con-

[1] PL 75, 764.   [2] PL 76, 953.

[3] PL 76, 953.   [4] *Ibid.*   [5] *Ibid.*   [6] *Ibid.*
[7] PL 16, 93.   [8] *Loc. cit.*

templative life "to rest from external action." Therefore the moral virtues do not pertain to the contemplative life.

I answer that, A thing may belong to the contemplative life in two ways, essentially or as a predisposition. The moral virtues do not belong to the contemplative life essentially, because the end of the contemplative life is the consideration of truth. And as the Philosopher states,[1] "knowledge," which pertains to the consideration of truth, "has little influence on the moral virtues"; hence he declares[2] that the moral virtues pertain to active but not to contemplative happiness.

On the other hand, the moral virtues belong to the contemplative life as a predisposition. For the act of contemplation, in which the contemplative life essentially consists is hindered both by the impetuosity of the passions which withdraw the soul's intention from intelligible to sensible things, and by outward disturbances. Now the moral virtues curb the impetuosity of the passions, and quell the disturbance of outward occupations. Hence moral virtues belong dispositively to the contemplative life.

Reply Obj. 1. As stated in the foregoing Article, the contemplative life has its moving cause on the part of the affections, and in this respect the love of God and our neighbour is requisite to the contemplative life. Now moving causes do not enter into the essence of a thing, but dispose and perfect it. Therefore it does not follow that the moral virtues belong essentially to the contemplative life.

Reply Obj. 2. Holiness, that is, cleanness of heart, is caused by the virtues that are concerned with the passions which hinder the purity of the reason; and peace is caused by justice which is about operations, according to Isa. 32. 17, *The work of justice shall be peace,* since he who refrains from wronging others lessens the occasions of quarrels and disturbances. Hence the moral virtues dispose one to the contemplative life by causing peace and cleanness of heart.

Reply Obj. 3. Beauty, as stated above (Q. CXLV, A. 2), consists in a certain clarity and due proportion. Now each of these has its roots in the reason, because both the light that makes beauty seen, and the establishing of due proportion among things belong to reason. Hence since the contemplative life consists in an act of the reason, there is beauty in it *per se* and essentially; therefore it is written (Wis. 8. 2) of the contemplation of wisdom: *I became a*

lover of her beauty. On the other hand, beauty is in the moral virtues by participation, in so far that is as they share the order of reason; and above all is it in temperance, which restrains the concupiscences which especially darken the light of reason. Hence it is that the virtue of chastity most of all makes man apt for contemplation, since sexual pleasures most of all weigh the mind down to sensible objects, as Augustine says (*Soliloq.* i, 10).[3]

ARTICLE 3. *Whether There Are Various Actions Pertaining to the Contemplative Life?*

We proceed thus to the Third Article: It seems that there are various actions pertaining to the contemplative life.

Objection 1. For Richard of S. Victor[4] distinguishes between contemplation, meditation, and cogitation. Yet all these apparently pertain to the contemplative life. Therefore it would seem that there are various actions pertaining to the contemplative life.

Obj. 2. Further, The Apostle says (II Cor. 3. 18): *But we . . . beholding (speculantes) the glory of the Lord with open face, are transformed into the same clarity.* (Vulg.,—*into the same image from glory to glory.*) Now this belongs to the contemplative life. Therefore in addition to the three mentioned above, vision (*speculatio*) belongs to the contemplative life.

Obj. 3. Further, Bernard says (*De Consid.* v, 14)[5] that "the first and greatest contemplation is admiration of the Majesty." Now according to Damascene (*De Fide Orthod.* ii, 15)[6] admiration is a kind of fear. Therefore it would seem that several acts are requisite for the contemplative life.

Obj. 4. Further, Prayer, reading, and meditation, are said to belong to the contemplative life.[7] Again, hearing belongs to the contemplative life, since it is stated that Mary (by whom the contemplative life is signified) *sitting . . . at the Lord's feet, heard His word* (Luke 10. 39). Therefore it would seem that several acts are requisite for the contemplative life.

On the contrary, Life signifies here the operation on which a man is chiefly intent. Therefore if there are several operations of the contemplative life, there will be, not one, but several contemplative lives.

I answer that, We are now speaking of the contemplative life as it pertains to man. Now

---

[1] *Ethics,* II, 4 (1105^{b}2).   [2] *Ibid.,* X, 8 (1178^{a}9).

[3] PL 32, 878.

[4] *De Grat. Contemplativa,* I, 4 (PL 196, 66).

[5] PL 182, 806.   [6] PG 94, 932.

[7] Cf. Hugh of St. Victor, *Allegor. in N.T.,* III, 3 (PL 175, 805).

according to Dionysius (*Div. Nom.* vii)[1] between man and angel there is this difference, that an angel has an insight of the truth by simple apprehension, while as man arrives at the insight of a simple truth by a process from several things. Accordingly, then, the contemplative life has one act in which it is finally completed, namely the contemplation of truth, and from this act it derives its unity. Yet it has many acts by which it arrives at this final act. Some of these pertain to the reception of principles, from which it proceeds to the contemplation of truth; others are concerned with deducing from the principles, the truth the knowledge of which is sought; and the last and crowning act is the contemplation itself of the truth.

Reply Obj. 1. According to Richard of S. Victor (*loc. cit.*) cogitation would seem to pertain to the consideration (*inspectio*) of the many things from which a person intends to gather one simple truth. Hence cogitation may comprise not only the perceptions of the senses in the knowing of certain effects, but also the data of the imagination, and again the discourse of reason about the various signs or of anything that conduces to the truth in view, although, according to Augustine, (*De Trin.* xiv, 7),[2] cogitation may signify any actual operation of the intellect. Meditation would seem to be the process of reason from certain principles that lead to the contemplation of some truth; and consideration has the same meaning, according to Bernard (*De Consid.* ii, 2),[3] although, according to the Philosopher,[4] every operation of the intellect may be called consideration. But contemplation regards the simple act of gazing (*intuitio*) on the truth; hence Richard says again[5] that "contemplation is the soul's clear and free dwelling (*contuitus*) upon the object of its gaze; meditation is the survey (*intuitio*) of the mind while occupied in searching for the truth; and cogitation is the mind's glance which is prone to wander."

Reply Obj. 2. According to a gloss of Augustine on his passage (*De Trin.* xv, 8),[6] "beholding (*speculatio*) denotes seeing in a mirror (*speculo*), not from a watch-tower (*specula*)." Now to see a thing in a mirror is to see a cause in its effect in which its likeness is reflected. Hence "beholding" would seem to be reducible to meditation.

Reply Obj. 3. Admiration is a kind of fear

[1] Sect. 2 (PG 3, 869).   [2] PL 42, 1042.
[3] PL 182, 745.   [4] *Soul*, II, 1 (412ª11).
[5] *De Grat. Contempl.*, I, 3, 4 (PL 196, 66; 67).
[6] PL 42, 1067; cf. *Glossa ordin.* (VI, 65E); *Glossa* Lombardi (PL 192, 28).

resulting from the apprehension of a thing that surpasses our power. Hence it results from the contemplation of the sublime truth. For it was stated above (A. 1) that contemplation terminates in the affections.

Reply Obj. 4. Man reaches the knowledge of truth in two ways. First, by means of things received from another. In this way, as regards the things he receives from God, he needs prayer, according to Wisd. 7. 7, *I called upon God, and the spirit of wisdom came upon me*, while as regards the things he receives from man, he needs hearing, in so far as he receives from the spoken word, and reading, in so far as he receives from the tradition of Holy Writ. Secondly, he needs to apply himself by his personal study, and thus he requires meditation.

ARTICLE 4. *Whether the Contemplative Life Consists in the Contemplation of God Alone, or Also in the Consideration of Any Truth Whatever?*

We proceed thus to the fourth Article: It seems that the contemplative life consists not only in the contemplation of God, but also in the consideration of any truth.

Objection 1. For it is written (Ps. 138. 14): *Wonderful are Thy works, and my soul knoweth right well.* Now the knowledge of God's works is effected by any contemplation of the truth. Therefore it would seem that it pertains to the contemplative life to contemplate not only the divine truth, but also any other.

Obj. 2. Further, Bernard says (*De Consid.* v, 14)[7] that "contemplation consists in admiration first of God's majesty, secondly of His judgments, thirdly of His benefits, fourthly of His promises." Now of these four the first alone regards the divine truth, and the other three pertain to His effects. Therefore the contemplative life consists not only in the contemplation of the divine truth, but also in the consideration of truth regarding the divine effects.

Obj. 3. Further, Richard of S. Victor (*De Contempl.* i, 6)[8] distinguishes six species of contemplation. The first belongs to "the imagination alone," and consists in thinking of corporeal things. The second is in "the imagination guided by reason," and consists in considering the order and disposition of sensible objects. The third is in the "reason based on the imagination"; when, that is, from the consideration of the visible we rise to the invisible. The fourth is "in the reason and according to reason," when the mind is intent on things invisible

[7] PL 182, 806.   [8] PL 196, 70.

of which the imagination has no knowledge. The fifth is "above the reason," when by divine revelation we know things that cannot be comprehended by the human reason. The sixth is "above reason and against reason"; when, that is, by the divine enlightening we know things that seem contrary to human reason, such as the doctrine of the mystery of the Trinity. Now only the last of these would seem to pertain to the divine truth. Therefore the contemplation of truth regards not only the divine truth, but also that which is considered in creatures.

Obj. 4. Further, In the contemplative life the contemplation of truth is sought as being the perfection of man. Now any truth is a perfection of the human intellect. Therefore the contemplative life consists in the contemplation of any truth.

On the contrary, Gregory says (*Moral.* vi, 37)[1] that "in contemplation we seek the principle, which is God."

I answer that, As stated above (A. 2), a thing may belong to the contemplative life in two ways: principally, and secondarily or as a predisposition. That which belongs principally to the contemplative life is the contemplation of the divine truth, because this contemplation is the end of the whole human life. Hence Augustine says (*De Trin.* i, 8)[2] that "the contemplation of God is promised us as being the goal of all our actions and the everlasting perfection of our joys." This contemplation will be perfect in the life to come, when we shall see God face to face, and it will make us perfectly happy. But now the contemplation of the divine truth is open to us imperfectly, namely *through a glass* and *in a dark manner* (I Cor. 13. 12). Hence it bestows on us a certain beginning of happiness, which starts now and will be continued in the life to come; hence the Philosopher[3] places man's ultimate happiness in the contemplation of the supreme intelligible object.

Since, However, God's effects show us the way to the contemplation of God Himself, according to Rom. 1. 20, *The invisible things of God . . . are clearly seen, being understood by the things that are made,* it follows that the contemplation of the divine effects also belongs in a secondary way to the contemplative life, according, that is, as man is guided in this way to the knowledge of God. Hence Augustine says (*De Vera Relig.* xxix)[4] that "in the study of creatures we must not exercise an empty and futile curiosity, but should make them the step-ping-stone to things unperishable and everlasting."

Accordingly it is clear from what has been said (AA. 2, 3) that four things pertain, in a certain order, to the contemplative life: first, the moral virtues; secondly, other acts apart from contemplation; thirdly, contemplation of the divine effects; fourthly, the complement of all, which is the contemplation of the divine truth itself.

Reply Obj. 1. David sought the knowledge of God's works so that he might be led by them to God; hence he says elsewhere (Ps. 142. 5, 6): *I meditated on all Thy works: I meditated upon the works of Thy hands: I stretched forth my hands to Thee.*

Reply Obj. 2. By considering the divine judgments man is guided to the consideration of the divine justice; and by considering the divine benefits and promises, man is led to the knowledge of God's mercy or goodness, as by effects already manifested or yet to be vouchsafed.

Reply Obj. 3. These six denote the steps by which we ascend by means of creatures to the contemplation of God. For the first step consists in the perception of sensible things themselves; the second step consists in going forward from sensible to intelligible things; the third step is to judge of sensible things according to intelligible things; the fourth is the absolute consideration of the intelligible things to which one has attained by means of sensibles; the fifth is the contemplation of those intelligible things that are unattainable by means of sensibles, but which the reason is able to grasp; the sixth step is the consideration of such intelligible things as the reason can neither discover nor grasp, which pertain to the sublime contemplation of divine truth, in which contemplation is ultimately perfected.

Reply Obj. 4. The ultimate perfection of the intellect is the divine truth; and other truths perfect the intellect in relation to the divine truth.

ARTICLE 5. *Whether in the Present State of Life the Contemplative Life Can Reach to the Vision of the Divine Essence?*

We proceed thus to the Fifth Article: It seems that in the present state of life the contemplative life can reach to the vision of the Divine essence.

Objection 1. For, as stated in Gen. 32. 30, Jacob said: *I have seen God face to face, and my soul has been saved.* Now the vision of God's face is the vision of the Divine essence. There-

---

[1] PL 75, 764.　　[2] PL 42, 831.
[3] *Ethics*, X, 7 (1177ᵃ17).　　[4] PL 34, 145.

fore it would seem that in the present life one may come, by means of contemplation, to see God in His essence.

Obj. 2. Further, Gregory says (*Moral.* vi, 37)[1] that contemplative men "withdraw within themselves in order to explore spiritual things, nor do they ever carry with them the shadows of things corporeal, or if these follow them they prudently drive them away; but being desirous of seeing the boundless light, they suppress all the images by which they tend to circumscribe themselves, and through longing to reach what is above them, they overcome that which they are." Now man is not hindered from seeing the Divine essence, which is the boundless light, save by the necessity of turning to corporeal phantasms. Therefore it would seem that the contemplation of the present life can extend to the vision of the boundless light in its essence.

Obj. 3. Further, Gregory says (*Dial.* ii, 35):[2] "All creatures are small to the soul that sees its Creator; therefore when the man of God, (the blessed Benedict, namely), saw a fiery globe in the tower and angels returning to heaven, without doubt he could only see such things by the light of God." Now the blessed Benedict was still in this life. Therefore the contemplation of the present life can extend to the vision of the essence of God.

On the contrary, Gregory says (*Hom.* ii *in Ezech.*):[3] "As long as we live in this mortal flesh, no one reaches such a height of contemplation as to fix the eyes of his mind on the ray itself of boundless light."

I answer that, As Augustine says (*Gen. ad Lit.* xii, 27),[4] "no one seeing God lives this mortal life wherein the bodily senses have their play; and unless in some way he depart this life, whether by going altogether out of his body, or by withdrawing from his carnal senses, he is not caught up into that vision." This has been carefully discussed above (Q. CLXXV, AA. 4, 5), where we spoke of rapture, and in the First Part (Q. XII, A. 11), where we treated of the vision of God.

Accordingly we must state that one may be in this life in two ways. First, with regard to act, that is to say by actually making use of the bodily senses, and thus contemplation in the present life can in no way attain to the vision of God's essence. Secondly, one may be in this life potentially and not with regard to act, that is to say, when the soul is united to the mortal body as its form, yet so as to make

use neither of the bodily senses, nor even of the imagination, as happens in rapture; and in this way the contemplation of the present life can attain to the vision of the Divine essence. Consequently the highest degree of contemplation in the present life is that which Paul had in rapture, in which he was in a middle state between the present life and the life to come.

Reply Obj. 1. As Dionysius says in a letter to the monk Caius,[5] "if anyone seeing God, understood what he saw, he saw not God Himself, but something belonging to God." And Gregory says (*Hom.* ii *in Ezech.*);[6] "By no means is God seen now in His glory; but the soul sees something of lower degree, and therefore advances along the straight road and afterwards attains to the glory of vision." Accordingly the words of Jacob, *I saw God face to face* do not imply that he saw God's essence, but that he saw some shape, imaginary of course, in which God spoke to him; or, "since we know a man by his face, by the face of God he signified his knowledge of Him," according to a gloss of Gregory on the same passage (*Moral.* xxiv, 6).[7]

Reply Obj. 2. In the present state of life human contemplation is impossible without phantasms, because it is connatural to man to see the intelligible species in the phantasms, as the Philosopher states.[8] Yet the knowledge of our intellect does not rest in the phantasms themselves, but contemplates in them the purity of the intelligible truth; and this not only in natural knowledge, but also in that which we obtain by revelation. For Dionysius says (*Cæl. Hier.* ii)[9] that "the Divine glory shows us the angelic hierarchies under certain symbolic figures, and by its power we are brought back to the single ray of light," that is, to the simple knowledge of the intelligible truth. It is in this sense that we must understand the statement of Gregory that "contemplatives do not carry along with them the shadows of things corporeal," since their contemplation is not fixed on them but on the consideration of the intelligible truth.

Reply Obj. 3. By these words Gregory does not imply that the blessed Benedict in that vision saw God in His essence, but he wishes to show that because "all creatures are small to him that see God," it follows that all things can easily be seen through the enlightenment of the

---

[1] PL 75, 763.   [2] PL 66, 200.   [3] PL 76, 956.
[4] PL 34, 477.

[5] *Epist.*, 1 (PG 3, 1065).
[6] PL 76, 953.
[7] PL 76, 293; Cf. *Glossa ordin.*, on Gen. 32. 30 (I, 96 F).
[8] *Soul*, III, 7 (431ᵃ16).
[9] Sect. 2 (PG 3, 121).

Divine light. Therefore he adds (*ibid.*): "For however little he may see of the Creator's light, all created things become petty to him."

ARTICLE 6. *Whether the Operation of Contemplation Is Fittingly Divided Into a Threefold Movement, Circular, Straight, and Oblique?*

We proceed thus to the Sixth Article: It seems that the operation of contemplation is unfittingly divided into a threefold movement, circular, straight, and oblique (*Div. Nom.* iv).[1]

Objection 1. For contemplation pertains exclusively to rest, according to Wisd. 8. 16, *When I go into my house, I shall repose myself with her.* Now movement is opposed to rest. Therefore the operations of the contemplative life should not be described as movements.

Obj. 2. Further, The action of the contemplative life pertains to the intellect, according to which man is like the angels. Now Dionysius describes these movements as being different in the angels from what they are in the soul. For he says (*loc. cit.*) that the circular movement in the angel is "according to his enlightenment by the beautiful and the good." On the other hand, he assigns the circular movement of the soul to several things: The first of which is "the withdrawal of the soul into itself from externals"; the second is "a certain concentration of its powers," by which it is rendered free of error and of outward occupation; and the third is "union with those things that are above it." Again, he describes differently their respective straight movements. For he says that the straight movement of the angel is "that by which he proceeds to the care of those things that are beneath him." On the other hand, he describes the straight movement of the soul as being twofold: first, "its progress towards things that are near it"; secondly, "its uplifting from external things to simple contemplation." Further, he assigns a different oblique movement to each. For he assigns the oblique movement of the angels to the fact that "while providing for those who have less they remain unchanged in relation to God"; but he assigns the oblique movement of the soul to the fact that "the soul is enlightened in Divine knowledge by reasoning and discoursing." Therefore it would seem that the operations of contemplation are unfittingly assigned according to the ways mentioned above.

Obj. 3. Further, Richard of S. Victor (*De Contempl.* i, 5)[2] mentions many other different movements in likeness to the birds of the air.

For some of these rise at one time to a great height, at another swoop down to earth, and they do so repeatedly; others fly now to the right, now to the left again and again; others go forwards or lag behind many times; others fly in a circle now more now less extended; and others remain suspended almost immovably in one place. Therefore it would seem that there are only three movements of contemplation.

On the contrary, stands the authority of Dionysius (*loc. cit.*).

I answer that, As stated above (Q. CLXXIX, A. 1, REPLY 3), the operation of the intellect, in which contemplation essentially consists, is called a movement in so far as movement is the act of a perfect thing, according to the Philosopher.[3] Since, however, it is through sensible things that we come to the knowledge of intelligible things, and since sensible operations do not take place without movement, the result is that even intelligible operations are described as movements, and are differentiated in likeness to various movements. Now of bodily movements, local movements are the most perfect and come first, as proved in the *Physics*;[4] therefore the foremost among intelligible operations are described by being likened to them. These movements are of three kinds; for there is the circular movement, by which a thing moves uniformly round one point as centre, another is the straight movement, by which a thing goes from one point to another; the third is oblique, being composed as it were of both the others. Consequently, in intelligible operations, that which is absolutely uniform is compared to circular movement; the intelligible operation by which one proceeds from one point to another is compared to the straight movement; while the intelligible operation which unites something of uniformity with progress to various points is compared to the oblique movement.

Reply Obj. 1. External bodily movements are opposed to the rest of contemplation, which consists in rest from outward occupations; but the movements of intellectual operations belong to the rest of contemplation.

Reply Obj. 2. Man is like the angels in intellect generically, but the intellectual power is much higher in the angel than in man. Consequently these movements must be ascribed to men and angels in different ways, according as they are differently related to uniformity. For the angelic intellect has uniform knowledge in two respects. First, because it does not require intelligible truth from the variety of composite

---

[1] Sect. 8 (PG 3, 704).   [2] PL 196, 68.   [3] *Soul,* III, 7 (431ª4).   [4] Aristotle, VIII, 7 (260ª26).

things; secondly, because it understands the truth of intelligible things not discursively, but by simple intuition. On the other hand, the intellect of the soul acquires intelligible truth from sensible things, and understands it by a certain discourse of the reason.

Therefore Dionysius assigns the circular movement of the angels to the fact that their intuition of God is uniform and unceasing, having neither beginning nor end; even as a circular movement having neither beginning nor end is uniformly around the one same centre. But on the part of the soul, before it can arrive at this uniformity, its twofold lack of uniformity needs to be removed. First, that which arises from the variety of external things, and this is removed by the soul withdrawing from externals, and so the first thing he mentions regarding the circular movement of the soul is "the soul's withdrawal into itself from external objects." Secondly, another lack of uniformity requires to be removed from the soul, and this is owing to the discourse of reason. This is done by directing all the soul's operations to the simple contemplation of the intelligible truth, and this is indicated by his saying in the second place that "the soul's intellectual powers must be uniformly concentrated," in other words that discourse must be laid aside and the soul's gaze fixed on the contemplation of the one simple truth. In this operation of the soul there is no error, even as there is clearly no error in the understanding of first principles which we know by simple intuition. Afterwards, these two things being presupposed, he mentions thirdly the uniformity which is like that of the angels, for then all things being laid aside, the soul continues in the contemplation of God alone. This he expresses by saying: " Then being thus made uniform, by being brought to unity (that is, conformity) and with its powers united, it is conducted to the good and the beautiful."

The straight movement of the angel cannot apply to his proceeding from one thing to another by considering them, but only to the order of his providence, namely to the fact that the higher angel enlightens the lower angels through the angels that are intermediate. He indicates this when he says: "The angel's movement takes a straight line when he proceeds to the care of things subject to him, taking in his course whatever things are direct," that is, in keeping with the dispositions of the direct order. The straight movement in the soul he ascribes however to the soul's proceeding from exterior sensibles to the knowledge of intelligible objects.

The oblique movement in the angels he describes as being composed of the straight and circular movements, in so far as their care for those beneath them is in accordance with their contemplation of God. The oblique movement in the soul he also declares to be partly straight and partly circular, in so far as in reasoning it makes use of the light received from God.

Reply Obj. 3. These varieties of movement that are taken from the distinction between above and below, right and left, forwards and backwards, and from varying circles, are all comprised under either straight and oblique movement, because they all denote the discourse of reason. For if the reason pass from the genus to the species, or from the part to the whole, it will be, as he explains, from above to below; if from one opposite to another, it will be from right to left; if from the cause to the effect, it will be backwards and forwards; if it be about accidents that surround a thing, near at hand or far remote, the movement will be circular. The discourse of reason from sensible to intelligible objects, if it be according to the order of natural reason, belongs to the straight movement; but if it be according to the Divine enlightenment, it will belong to the oblique movement as explained above (REPLY 2). That alone which he describes as immobility belongs to the circular movement.

Hence it is evident that Dionysius describes the movement of contemplation with much greater fulness and depth.

ARTICLE 7. *Whether There Is Delight in Contemplation?*

We proceed thus to the Seventh Article: It seems that there is no delight in contemplation.

Objection 1. For delight belongs to the appetitive power; but contemplation resides chiefly in the intellect. Therefore it would seem that there is no delight in contemplation.

Obj. 2. Further, All strife and struggle is a hindrance to delight. Now there is strife and struggle in contemplation. For Gregory says (*Hom.* ii *in Ezech.*)[1] that "when the soul strives to contemplate God, it is in a state of struggle; at one time it almost overcomes, because by understanding and feeling it tastes something of the unbounded light, and at another time it almost succumbs, because even while tasting it fails." Therefore there is no delight in contemplation.

Obj. 3. Further, Delight is the result of a perfect operation, as stated in the *Ethics.*[2] Now

[1] PL 76, 955.   [2] Aristotle, x, 4 (1174[b]23).

the contemplation of wayfarers is imperfect, according to I Cor. 13. 12, *We see now through a glass in a dark manner*. Therefore it seems that there is no delight in the contemplative life.

Obj. 4. Further, A lesion of the body is an obstacle to delight. Now contemplation causes a lesion of the body; thus it is stated (Gen. 32.) that after Jacob had said (*verse* 30) *I have seen God face to face, he halted on his foot, . . . because he touched the sinew of his thigh and it shrank*. Therefore it seems that there is no delight in contemplation.

On the contrary, It is written of the contemplation of wisdom (Wisd. 8. 16): *Her conversation hath no bitterness, nor her company any tediousness, but joy and gladness;* and Gregory says (*Hom.* ii *in Ezech.*)[1] that "the contemplative life is sweetness exceedingly lovable."

I answer that, There may be delight in any particular contemplation in two ways. First by reason of the operation itself, because each individual delights in the operation which befits him according to his own nature or habit. Now contemplation of the truth befits a man according to his nature as a rational animal, the result being that all men naturally desire to know, so that consequently they delight in the knowledge of truth. And more delightful still does this become to one who has the habit of wisdom and science, the result of which is that he contemplates without difficulty. Secondly, contemplation may be delightful on the part of its object, in so far as one contemplates that which one loves; even as bodily vision gives pleasure not only because to see is pleasurable in itself, but because one sees a person whom one loves. Since, then, the contemplative life consists chiefly in the contemplation of God, to which charity moves us, as stated above (AA. 1, 2, Reply 1), it follows that there is delight in the contemplative life, not only by reason of the contemplation itself, but also by reason of the Divine love.

In both respects the delight surpasses all human delight, both because spiritual delight is greater than carnal pleasure, as stated above (Part I-II, Q. XXXI, A. 5), when we were treating of the passions, and because the love itself by which God is loved out of charity surpasses all love. Hence it is written (Ps. 33. 9): *O taste and see that the Lord is sweet.*

Reply Obj. 1. Although the contemplative life consists essentially in an act of the intellect, it has its beginning in the appetite, since it is through charity that one is urged to the con-

templation of God. And since the end corresponds to the beginning, it follows that the term also and the end of the contemplative life has its being in the affections, since one delights in seeing the object loved, and the very delight in the object seen arouses a yet greater love. Hence Gregory says (*Hom.* ii *in Ezech.*)[2] that "when we see one whom we love, we are so aflame as to love him more." And this is the ultimate perfection of the contemplative life, namely that the Divine truth be not only seen but also loved.

Reply Obj. 2. Strife or struggle arising from the opposition of an external thing hinders delight in that thing. For a man delights not in a thing against which he strives. But in that for which he strives he delights yet more when he has obtained it, other things being equal. Therefore Augustine says[3] that "the more peril there was in the battle, the greater the joy in the triumph." But there is no strife or struggle in contemplation from the truth which we contemplate being contrary to us, though there is on the part of our defective understanding and our corruptible body which drags us down to lower things, according to Wisd. 9. 15, *The corruptible body is a load upon the soul, and the earthly habitation presseth down the mind that museth upon many things*. Hence it is that when man attains to the contemplation of truth, he loves it yet more, while he hates the more his own deficiency and the weight of his corruptible body, so as to say with the Apostle (Rom. 7. 24): *Unhappy man that I am, who shall deliver me from the body of this death?* Therefore Gregory says (*Hom.* ii *in Ezech.*):[4] "When God is once known by desire and understanding, He withers all carnal pleasure in us."

Reply Obj. 3. The contemplation of God in this life is imperfect in comparison with the contemplation in heaven; and in like manner the delight of the wayfarer's contemplation is imperfect as compared with the delight of contemplation in heaven, of which it is written (Ps. 35. 9):*Thou shalt make them drink of the torrent of Thy pleasure*. Yet, though the contemplation of Divine things which is to be had by wayfarers is imperfect, it is more delightful than all other contemplation however perfect, on account of the excellence of that which is contemplated. Hence the Philosopher says:[5] "It happens that these substances, excellent beyond compare, and divine, are less accessible to our knowledge, and though we grasp them but feebly, nevertheless from their excellence that

[1] PL 76, 956.

[2] PL 76, 954.   [3] *Confessions*, VIII, 7 (PL 32, 752).
[4] PL 76, 955.   [5] *Parts of Animals*, I, 5 (644[b]24).

knowledge gives us more delight than any of those things that are round about us"; and Gregory says in the same sense (*loc. cit.*): "The contemplative life is sweetness exceedingly lovable; for it carries the soul away above itself, it opens heaven and discovers the spiritual world to the eyes of the mind."

Reply Obj. 4. After contemplation Jacob halted with one foot, "because we need to grow weak in the love of the world before we wax strong in the love of God," as Gregory says (*loc. cit.*). Therefore, as he goes on to say, "when we have known the sweetness of God, we have one foot sound while the other halts; since every one who halts on one foot leans only on that foot which is sound."

ARTICLE 8. *Whether the Contemplative Life Is Continuous?*

We proceed thus to the Eighth Article: It seems that the contemplative life is not continuous.

Objection 1. For the contemplative life consists essentially in things pertaining to the intellect. Now all the intellectual perfections of this life will be made void, according to I Cor. 13. 8, *Whether prophecies shall be made void, or tongues shall cease, or knowledge shall be destroyed.* Therefore the contemplative life is made void.

Obj. 2. Further, A man tastes the sweetness of contemplation by snatches and for a short time only. Hence Augustine says,[1] "Thou admittest me to a most unwonted affection in my inmost soul, to a strange sweetness, . . . yet through my grievous weight I sink down again." Again, Gregory commenting on the words of Job 4. 15, *When a spirit passed before me,* says:[2] "The mind does not remain long at rest in the sweetness of inward contemplation, for it is recalled to itself and beaten back by the very immensity of the light." Therefore the contemplative life is not continuous.

Obj. 3. Further, That which is not connatural to man cannot be continuous. Now "the contemplative life," according to the Philosopher,[3] "is better than the life which is according to man." Therefore it seems that the contemplative life is not continuous.

On the contrary, Our Lord said (Luke 10. 42): *Mary hath chosen the best part, which shall not be taken away from her,* since as Gregory says (*Hom.* ii *in Ezech.*),[4] "the contempla-

tive life begins here so as it may be perfected in our heavenly home."

I answer that, A thing may be described as continuous in two ways: first, in regard to its nature; secondly, in regard to us. It is evident that in regard to itself contemplative life is continuous for two reasons: first, because it is about incorruptible and unchangeable things; secondly, because it has no contrary, for "there is nothing contrary to the pleasure of contemplation," as stated in the *Topics*.[5] But even in our regard contemplative life is continuous,—both because it belongs to us in respect of the activity of the incorruptible part of the soul, namely the intellect, so that it can endure after this life, —and because in the works of the contemplative life we do not work with our bodies, so that we are the more able to persevere in this kind of work, as the Philosopher observes.[6]

Reply Obj. 1. The manner of contemplation is not the same here as in heaven; yet the contemplative life is said to remain by reason of charity, in which it has both its beginning and its end. Gregory speaks in this sense (*Hom.* ii *in Ezech.*):[7] "The contemplative life begins here, so as to be perfected in our heavenly home, because the fire of love which begins to burn here is aflame with a yet greater love when we see Him Whom we love."

Reply Obj. 2. No action can last long at its highest pitch. Now the highest point of contemplation is to reach the uniformity of Divine contemplation, according to Dionysius (*Div. Nom.* iv)[8] and as we have stated above (A. 6, REPLY 2). Hence although contemplation cannot last long in this respect, it can be of long duration as regards the other contemplative acts.

Reply Obj. 3. The Philosopher declares the contemplative life to be above man because it befits us "so far as there is in us something divine," namely the intellect, which is incorruptible and impassible in itself, so that its act can endure longer.

QUESTION CLXXXI
OF THE ACTIVE LIFE
(In Four Articles)

WE must now consider the active life, under which head there are four points of inquiry: (1) Whether all the works of the moral virtues pertain to the active life? (2) Whether prudence pertains to the active life? (3) Whether teach-

[1] *Confessions,* X, 65 (PL 32, 807).
[2] PL 75, 711.
[3] *Ethics,* X, 7 (1177b26).   [4] PL 76, 954.
[5] Aristotle, I, 13 (106a38).
[6] *Ethics,* X, 7 (1177a21).   [7] PL 76, 954.
[8] Sect. 9 (PG 3, 705); cf. *De Cæl. Hier.,* III, 2 (PG 3, 165).

ing pertains to the active life? (4) Of the duration of the active life.

ARTICLE 1. *Whether All the Acts of the Moral Virtues Pertain to the Active Life?*

We proceed thus to the First Article: It seems that the acts of the moral virtues do not all pertain to the active life.

Objection 1. For the active life seems to regard only our relations with other persons. Hence Gregory says (*Hom.* ii *in Ezech.*)[1] that "the active life is to give bread to the hungry," and after mentioning many things that regard our relations with other people he adds finally, "and to give to each and every one whatever he needs." Now we are not directed in our relations to others by all the acts of moral virtues, but only by those of justice and its parts, as stated above (Q. LVIII, AA. 2, 8; Part I-II, Q. LX, AA. 2, 3). Therefore the acts of the moral virtues do not all pertain to the active life.

Obj. 2. Further, Gregory says (*Hom.* ii *in Ezech.*):[2] "Lia who was blear-eyed but fruitful signifies the active life, which being occupied with works, sees less, and yet since it urges one's neighbour both by word and example to its imitation it begets a numerous offspring of good deeds." Now this would seem to belong to charity, by which we love our neighbour, rather than to the moral virtues. Therefore it seems that the acts of moral virtue do not pertain to the active life.

Obj. 3. Further, As stated above (Q. CLXXX, A. 2), the moral virtues dispose one to the contemplative life. Now disposition and perfection belong to the same thing. Therefore it would seem that the moral virtues do not pertain to the active life.

On the contrary, Isidore says (*De Summo Bono,* iii, 15):[3] "In the active life all vices must first of all be extirpated by the practice of good works, in order that in the contemplative life the mind's eye being purified one may advance to the contemplation of the Divine light." Now all vices are not extirpated save by the acts of the moral virtues. Therefore the acts of the moral virtues pertain to the active life.

I answer that, As stated above (Q. CLXXIX, A. 1) the active and the contemplative life differ according to the different occupations of men intent on different ends. One of these occupations is the consideration of the truth; and this is the end of the contemplative life, while the other is external work to which the active life is directed. Now it is evident that the moral

virtues are chiefly directed not to the contemplation of truth but to operation. Hence the Philosopher says[4] that "for virtue knowledge is of little or no avail." And so it is clear that the moral virtues belong essentially to the active life; for which reason the Philosopher[5] subordinates the moral virtues to the happiness of the active life.

Reply Obj. 1. The chief of the moral virtues is justice by which one man is directed in his relations towards another, as the Philosopher proves.[6] Hence the active life is described with reference to our relations with other people, because it consists in these things, not exclusively, but principally.

Reply Obj. 2. It is possible by the acts of all the moral virtues for one to direct one's neighbour to good by example, and this is what Gregory here ascribes to the active life.

Reply Obj. 3. Even as the virtue that is directed to the end of another virtue passes, in a certain way, into the species of the latter virtue, so again when a man makes use of things pertaining to the active life merely as dispositions to contemplation, such things are comprised under the contemplative life. On the other hand, when we practise the works of the moral virtues as being good in themselves, and not as dispositions to the contemplative life, the moral virtues belong to the active life.

It may also be replied, however, that the active life is a disposition to the contemplative life.

ARTICLE 2. *Whether Prudence Pertains to the Active Life?*

We proceed thus to the Second Article: It seems that prudence does not pertain to the active life.

Objection 1. For just as the contemplative life pertains to the cognitive power, so the active life pertains to the appetitive power. Now prudence belongs not to the appetitive but to the cognitive power. Therefore prudence does not belong to the active life.

Obj. 2. Further, Gregory says (*Hom.* ii *in Ezech.*)[7] that "the active life being occupied with work, sees less," and therefore it is signified by Lia who was blear-eyed. But prudence requires clear eyes, so that one may judge rightly of what has to be done. Therefore it seems that prudence does not pertain to the active life.

Obj. 3. Further, Prudence stands between the moral and the intellectual virtues. Now just as

---

[1] PL 76, 953.   [2] *Ibid.*   [3] PL 83, 690.

[4] *Ethics,* II, 4 (1105^{b}2).   [5] *Ibid.,* X, 8 (1178^{a}9).
[6] *Ibid.,* V, 1 (1129^{b}27).   [7] Bk. II (PL 76, 954).

the moral virtues belong to the active life, as stated in the foregoing Article, so do the intellectual virtues pertain to the contemplative life. Therefore it would seem that prudence pertains neither to the active nor to the contemplative life, but to an intermediate kind of life, of which Augustine make mention.[1]

On the contrary, The Philosopher says[2] that prudence pertains to active happiness, to which the moral virtues belong.

I answer that, As stated above (A. 1, Reply 3; Part I-II, Q. XVIII, A. 6), if one thing be directed to another as its end, it is drawn, especially in moral matters, to the species of the thing to which it is directed; for instance "he who commits adultery that he may steal, is a thief rather than an adulterer," according to the Philosopher.[3] Now it is evident that the knowledge of prudence is directed to the works of the moral virtues as its end, since it is "right reason about things to be done,[4] so that the ends of the moral virtues are the principles of prudence, as the Philosopher says in the same book.[5] Accordingly, just as it was stated above (A. 1, Reply 3) that the moral virtues in one who directs them to the quiet of contemplation belong to the contemplative life, so the knowledge of prudence, which is of itself directed to the works of the moral virtues, belongs directly to the active life, provided we take prudence in its proper sense as the Philosopher speaks of it.

If however we take it in a more general sense, as comprising any kind of human knowledge, then prudence, as regards a certain part of it, belongs to the contemplative life. In this sense Tully (*De Offic.* i)[6] says that "the man who is able most clearly and quickly to grasp the truth and to unfold his reasons, is usually considered to be most prudent and wise."

Reply Obj. 1. Moral works take their species from their end, as stated above (Part I-II, Q. XVIII, AA. 4, 6), and therefore the knowledge pertaining to the contemplative life is that which has its end in the very knowledge of truth; but the knowledge of prudence, through having its end in an act of the appetitive power, belongs to the active life.

Reply Obj. 2. Being occupied with external things makes a man see less in intelligible things, which are separated from sensible objects with which the works of the active life are concerned. Nevertheless the external occupa-

tion of the active life enables a man to see more clearly in judging of what is to be done, which belongs to prudence, both on account of experience, and on account of the mind's attention, since "when the mind is attentive it takes on all its force," as Sallust observes (*Conjur. Catil.*).[7]

Reply Obj. 3. Prudence is said to be intermediate between the intellectual and the moral virtues because it resides in the same subject as the intellectual virtues, but accords wholly with the moral virtues as to matter. But this third kind of life is intermediate between the active and the contemplative life as regards the things about which it is occupied, because it is occupied sometimes with the contemplation of the truth, sometimes with external things.

ARTICLE 3. *Whether Teaching Is a Work of the Active or of the Contemplative Life?*

We proceed thus to the Third Article: It seems that teaching is a work not of the active but of the contemplative life.

Objection 1. For Gregory says (*Hom.* v *in Ezech.*)[8] that "the perfect who have been able to contemplate heavenly goods proclaim them to their brethren, whose souls they inflame with love for their hidden beauty." But this pertains to teaching. Therefore teaching is a work of the contemplative life.

Obj. 2. Further, Act and habit would seem to be brought back to the same kind of life. Now teaching is an act of wisdom, for the Philosopher says that "to be able to teach is an indication of knowledge."[9] Therefore since wisdom or knowledge pertain to the contemplative life, it would seem that teaching also belongs to the contemplative life.

Obj. 3. Further, Prayer, no less than contemplation, is an act of the contemplative life. Now even the prayer by which one prays for another belongs to the contemplative life. Therefore it would seem that it belongs also to the contemplative life to acquaint another, by teaching him, of the truth we have meditated.

On the contrary, Gregory says (*Hom.* ii *in Ezech.*):[10] "The active life is to give bread to the hungry, to teach the ignorant the words of wisdom."

I answer that, The act of teaching has a twofold object. For teaching is conveyed by speech, and speech is the audible sign of the interior concept. Accordingly one object of teaching is the matter or object of the interior concept; and as to this object teaching belongs some-

---

[1] *City of God,* XIX, 2, 3, 19 (PL 41, 624; 625; 647).
[2] *Ethics,* x, 8 (1178a16).   [3] *Ibid.,* v, 2 (1130a24).
[4] *Ibid.,* VI 5 (1140b20).   [5] *Ibid.,* x, 8 (1178a17).
[6] DD IV, 428.

[7] Chap. 51 (BU 47).   [8] Bk. I (PL 76, 827).
[9] *Metaphysics,* I, 1 (981b7).   [10] Bk. II (PL 76, 953).

times to the active, sometimes to the contemplative life. It belongs to the active life when a man conceives a truth inwardly so as to be directed by it in his outward action; but it belongs to the contemplative life when a man conceives inwardly an intelligible truth in whose consideration and love he delights. Hence Augustine says:[1] "Let them choose for themselves the better part," namely the contemplative life; "let them be busy with the word, long for the sweetness of teaching, occupy themselves with the knowledge that saves," thus stating clearly that teaching belongs to the contemplative life.

The other object of teaching is on the part of the speech heard, and thus the object of teaching is the hearer. As to this object all teaching belongs to the active life to which external actions pertain.

Reply Obj. 1. The authority quoted speaks expressly of doctrine as to its matter, in so far as it is concerned with the consideration and love of truth.

Reply Obj. 2. Habit and act have a common object. Hence this argument clearly considers the matter of the interior concept. For it pertains to the man having wisdom and knowledge to be able to teach in so far as he is able to express his interior concept in words, so as to bring another man to understand the truth.

Reply Obj. 3. He who prays for another does nothing towards the man for whom he prays, but only towards God Who is the intelligible truth; but he who teaches another does something in his regard by external action. Hence the comparison fails.

ARTICLE 4. *Whether the Active Life Remains After This Life?*

We proceed thus to the Fourth Article: It seems that the active life remains after this life.

Objection 1. For the acts of the moral virtues belong to the active life, as stated above (A. 1). But the moral virtues endure after this life according to Augustine (*De Trin.* xiv, 9).[2] Therefore seemingly the active life remains after this life.

Obj. 2. Further, Teaching others belongs to the active life, as stated in the foregoing Article. But in the life to come when we shall be like the angels, teaching will be possible, even as apparently it is in the angels of whom one enlightens, cleanses, and perfects another, which refers to the receiving of knowledge, according

to Dionysius (*Cæl. Hier.* vii).[3] Therefore it would seem that the active life remains after this life.

Obj. 3. Further, The more lasting a thing is in itself, the more it seems to be able to endure after this life. But the active life seems to be more lasting in itself; for Gregory says (*Hom.* v *in Ezech.*)[4] that "we can remain fixed in the active life, whereas we are in no way able to maintain an attentive mind in the contemplative life." Therefore the active life is much more able than the contemplative to endure after this life.

On the contrary, Gregory says (*Hom.* ii *in Ezech.*):[5] "The active life ends with this world, but the contemplative life begins here, to be perfected in our heavenly home."

I answer that, As stated above (A. 1), the active life has its end in external actions; and if these are referred to the quiet of contemplation, for that very reason they belong to the contemplative life. But in the future life of the blessed the occupation of external actions will cease, and if there be any external actions at all, these will be referred to contemplation as their end. For, as Augustine says at the end of the *City of God*,[6] "there we shall rest and we shall see, we shall see and love, we shall love and praise." And he had said before[7] that there God "will be seen without end, loved without wearying, praised without tiring: such will be the occupation of all, the common love, the universal activity."

Reply Obj. 1. As stated above (Q. CXXXVI, A. 1, REPLY 1), the moral virtues will remain not as to those actions which are about the means, but as to the actions which are about the end. Such acts are those that conduce to the quiet of contemplation, which in the words quoted above Augustine denotes by "rest," and this rest excludes not only outward disturbance but also the inward disturbance of the passions.

Reply Obj. 2. The contemplative life, as stated above (Q. CLXXX, A. 4), consists chiefly in the contemplation of God, and as to this, one angel does not teach another, since according to Matt. 18. 10, *the little one's angels,* who belong to the lower order, *always see the face of the Father;* and so, in the life to come, no man will teach another of God, but *we shall* all *see Him as He is* (I *John* 3. 2), This is in keeping with the saying of Jeremias (31. 34): *They shall teach no more every man his neighbour, ...*

---

[1] *Serm. ad Popul.,* serm. CIV, 1 (PL 38, 616).
[2] PL 42, 1046.

[3] Sect. 3 (PG 3, 209).
[4] Bk. I (PL 76, 825).   [5] Bk. II (PL 76, 954).
[6] XXII, 30 (PL 41, 804).   [7] *Ibid.* (PL 41, 802).

saying: Know the Lord: for all shall know me, from the least of them even to the greatest.

But as regards things pertaining to the dispensation of the mysteries of God, one angel teaches another by cleansing, enlightening, and perfecting him; and thus they have something of the active life so long as the world lasts, from the fact that they are occupied in administering to the creatures below them. This is signified by the fact that Jacob saw angels ascending the ladder (Gen. 28. 12),—which refers to contemplation,—and descending,—which refers to action. Nevertheless, as Gregory remarks (*Moral.* ii, 3),[1] "they do not wander abroad from the Divine vision in such a way as to be deprived of the joys of inward contemplation." Hence in them the active life does not differ from the contemplative life as it does in us for whom the works of the active life are a hindrance to contemplation.

Nor is the likeness to the angels promised to us as regards the administering to lower creatures, for this does not belong to us not by reason of our natural order, as it is to the angels, but by reason of our seeing God.

Reply Obj. 3. That the durability of the active life in the present state surpasses the durability of the contemplative life arises not from any property of either life considered in itself, but from our own deficiency, since we are withheld from the heights of contemplation by the weight of the body. Hence Gregory adds (*ibid.*) that "the mind through its very weakness being repelled from that immense height recoils on itself."

QUESTION CLXXXII

OF THE ACTIVE LIFE IN COMPARISON WITH THE CONTEMPLATIVE LIFE

(In Four Articles)

WE must now consider the active life in comparison with the contemplative life, under which head there are four points of inquiry: (1) Which of them is greater import or excellence? (2) Which of them has the greater merit? (3) Whether the contemplative life is hindered by the active life? (4) Of their order.

ARTICLE 1. *Whether the Active Life Is More Excellent Than the Contemplative?*

We proceed thus to the First Article: It seems that the active life is more excellent than the contemplative.

Objection 1. For "that which belongs to better men would seem to be worthier and better," as the Philosopher says.[2] Now the active life belongs to persons of higher rank, namely prelates, who are placed in a position of honour and power; hence Augustine says[3] that "in our actions we must not love honour or power in this life." Therefore it would seem that the active life is more excellent than the contemplative.

Obj. 2. Further, In all habits and acts, commanding belongs to the more excellent; thus the military art, being the more excellent, commands the art of the bridle-maker. Now it belongs to the active life to direct and command the contemplative, as appears from the words addressed to Moses (Exod. 19. 21), *Go down and charge the people, lest they should have a mind to pass the fixed limits to see the Lord.* Therefore the active life is more excellent than the contemplative.

Obj. 3. Further, No man should be taken away from a greater thing in order to be occupied with lesser things, for the Apostle says (I Cor. 12. 31): *Be zealous for the better gifts.* Now some are taken away from the state of the contemplative life to the occupations of the active life, as in the case of those who are transferred to the state of prelacy. Therefore it would seem that the active life is more excellent than the contemplative.

On the contrary, Our Lord said (Luke 10. 42): *Mary hath chosen the best part, which shall not be taken away from her.* Now Mary is a figure of the contemplative life. Therefore the contemplative life is more excellent than the active.

I answer that, Nothing prevents certain things being more excellent in themselves which nevertheless are surpassed by another in some respect. Accordingly we must reply that the contemplative life absolutely is more excellent than the active; and the Philosopher proves this by eight reasons.[4] The first is because the contemplative life befits man according to that which is best in him, namely the intellect, and according to its proper objects, namely intelligibles; the active life however is occupied with externals. Hence Rachel, by whom the contemplative life is signified, is interpreted "the vision of the principle," whereas as Gregory says (*Moral.* vi, 37)[5] the active life is signified by Lia who was "blear-eyed." The second reason is because the contemplative life can be

---

[1] PL 75, 556.
[2] *Topics,* III, 1 (116ᵇ12).
[3] *City of God,* XIX, 19 (PL 41, 647).
[4] *Ethics,* X, 7, 8 (1177ᵃ12; 1178ᵃ9).   [5] PL 75, 764.

more continuous, although not as regards the highest degree of contemplation, as stated above (Q. CLXXX, A. 8; Q. CLXXXI, A. 4, REPLY 3), and so Mary, by whom the contemplative life is signified, is described as sitting all the time at the Lord's feet. Thirdly, because the contemplative life is more delightful than the active; hence Augustine says[1] that "Martha was troubled, but Mary feasted." Fourthly, because in the contemplative life man is more self-sufficient, since he needs fewer things for that purpose; therefore it was said (Luke 10. 41): *Martha, Martha, thou art careful and art troubled about many things.* Fifthly, because the contemplative life is loved more for its own sake, while the active life is directed to something else. Hence it is written (Ps. 26. 4): *One thing I have asked of the Lord, this will I seek after, that I may dwell in the house of the Lord all the days of my life, that I may see the delight of the Lord.* Sixthly, because the contemplative life consists in leisure and rest, according to Ps. 45. 11, *Be still and see that I am God.* Seventhly, because the contemplative life is according to Divine things, while active life is according to human things; hence Augustine says:[2] " 'In the beginning was the Word': to Him was Mary hearkening; 'The word was made flesh': Him was Martha serving." Eighthly, because the contemplative life is according to that which is most proper to man, namely his intellect; in the works of the active life however the lower powers also, which are common to us and brutes, have their part; hence (Ps. 35. 8) after the words, *Men and beasts thou wilt preserve, O Lord,* that which is special to man is added (*verse* 10): *In Thy light we shall see light.*

Our Lord adds a ninth reason (Luke 10. 42) when He says: *Mary hath chosen the best part, which shall not be taken away from her,* which words Augustine expounds thus:[3] "Not,—Thou hast chosen badly but,—She has chosen better. Why better? Listen,—Because it shall not be taken away from her. But the burden of necessity shall at length be taken from thee; but the sweetness of truth is eternal."

Yet in a restricted sense and in a particular case one should prefer the active life on account of the needs of the present life. Thus too the Philosopher says:[4] "It is better to philosophize than to be rich, yet for one who is in need, it is better to be rich."

Reply Obj. 1. Not only the active life concerns prelates, but they should also excel in the contemplative life; hence Gregory says (*Pastor.* ii, 1):[5] "A prelate should be foremost in action, more uplifted than others in contemplation."

Reply Obj. 2. The contemplative life consists in a certain liberty of mind. For Gregory says (*Hom.* iii *in Ezech.*)[6] that "the contemplative life obtains a certain freedom of mind, for it thinks not of temporal but of eternal things." And Boethius says (*De Consol.* v, 2):[7] "The soul of man must be more free while it continues to gaze on the Divine mind, and less so when it stoops to bodily things." Therefore it is evident that the active life does not directly command the contemplative life, but prescribes certain works of the active life as dispositions to the contemplative life, which it accordingly serves rather than commands. Gregory refers to this when he says (*loc. cit. in Ezech.*)[8] that "the active life is bondage, but the contemplative life is freedom."

Reply Obj. 3. Sometimes a man is called away from the contemplative life to the works of the active life on account of some necessity of the present life, yet not so as to be compelled to forsake contemplation altogether. Hence Augustine says:[9] "The love of truth seeks a holy leisure, the demands of charity undertake an honest toil," the work namely of the active life. "If no one imposes this burden upon us we must devote ourselves to the search for and contemplation of truth, but if it be imposed on us, we must bear it because charity demands it of us. Yet even then we must not altogether forsake the delights of truth, lest we deprive ourselves of its sweetness, and this burden overwhelm us." Hence it is clear that when a person is called from the contemplative to the active life, this is done by way not of taking away but of addition.

ARTICLE 2. *Whether the Active Life Is of Greater Merit Than the Contemplative?*

We proceed thus to the Second Article: It would seem that the active life is of greater merit than the contemplative.

Objection 1. For merit implies relation to reward; and reward is due to labour, according to I Cor. 3. 8, *Every man shall receive his own reward according to his own labour.* Now labour is ascribed to the active life, and rest to the contemplative life; for Gregory says (*Hom.* ii

---

[1] *Serm. ad Popul.*, serm. CIII, 4 (PL 38, 615).
[2] *Ibid.*, CIV, 2 (PL 38, 617).
[3] *Ibid.*, CIII, 4 (PL 38, 615).   [4] *Topics*, III, 2 (118ᵃ10).

[5] PL 77, 26.   [6] PL 76, 812.   [7] PL 63, 836.
[8] PL 76, 809.   [9] *City of God*, XIX, 19 (PL 41, 647).

in Ezech.):[1] "Whosoever is converted to God must first of all sweat from labour, that is, he must take Lia, that afterwards he may rest in the embraces of Rachel so as to see the principle." Therefore the active life is of greater merit than the contemplative.

Obj. 2. Further, The contemplative life is a certain beginning of the happiness to come; therefore Augustine commenting on John 21. 22, *So I will have him to remain till I come,* says (*Tract.* cxxiv *in Joann.*):[2] "This may be expressed more clearly: Let perfect works follow Me conformed to the example of My passion, and let contemplation begun here remain until I come, that it may be perfected when I shall come." And Gregory says (*loc. cit. in Ezech.*) that "the life of contemplation begins here, so as to be perfected in our heavenly home." Now the life to come will be a state not of meriting but of receiving the reward of our merits. Therefore the contemplative life would seem to have less of the character of merit than the active, but more of the character of reward.

Obj. 3. Further, Gregory says (*Hom.* xii *in Ezech.*)[3] that "no sacrifice is more acceptable to God than zeal for souls." Now by the zeal for souls a man turns to the occupations of the active life. Therefore it would seem that the contemplative life is not of greater merit than the active.

On the contrary, Gregory says (*Moral.* vi):[4] "Great are the merits of the active life, but greater still those of the contemplative."

I answer that, As stated above (Part I-II, Q. CXIV, A. 4), the root of merit is charity; and, while, as stated above (Q. XXV, A. 1), charity consists in the love of God and our neighbour, the love of God is by itself the more meritorious than the love of our neighbour, as stated above (Q. XXVII, A. 8). Therefore that which pertains more directly to the love of God is of its very genus more meritorious than that which pertains directly to the love of our neighbour for God's sake. Now the contemplative life pertains directly and immediately to the love of God; for Augustine says[5] that "the love of truth seeks a holy leisure," namely of the contemplative life, for it is that truth above all which the contemplative life seeks, as stated above (Q. CLXXX, A. 4; Q. CLXXXI, A. 4, Reply 2). On the other hand, the active life is more directly concerned with the love of our neighbour, be-

cause it is *busy about much serving* (Luke 10. 40). Therefore the contemplative life is generically of greater merit than the active life. This is moreover asserted by Gregory (*Hom.* iii *in Ezech.*):[6] "The contemplative life surpasses in merit the active life, because the latter labours under the stress of present work," by reason of the necessity of assisting our neighbour, "while the former with heartfelt relish has a foretaste of the coming rest," that is the contemplation of God.

Nevertheless it may happen that one man merits more by the works of the active life than another by the works of the contemplative life. For instance through excess of Divine love a man may now and then suffer separation from the sweetness of Divine contemplation for the time being, that God's will may be done and for His glory's sake. Thus the Apostle said (Rom. 9. 3): *I wished myself to be an anathema from Christ, for my brethren;* which words Chrysostom expounds as follows (*De Compunct.* i):[7] "His mind was so steeped in the love of Christ that, although he desired above all to be with Christ, he despised even this, because thus he pleased Christ."

Reply Obj. 1. External labour conduces to the increase of the accidental reward, but the increase of merit with regard to the essential reward consists chiefly in charity, a sign of which is external labour borne for Christ's sake. Yet a much more expressive sign of this is shown when a man, renouncing whatsoever pertains to this life, delights to occupy himself entirely with Divine contemplation.

Reply Obj. 2. In the state of future happiness man has arrived at perfection, and therefore there is no room for advancement by merit; and if there were, the merit would be more efficacious by reason of the greater charity. But in the present life contemplation is not without some imperfection, and can always become more perfect; therefore it does not remove the idea of merit, but causes a yet greater merit on account of the practice of greater Divine charity.

Reply Obj. 3. A sacrifice is rendered to God spiritually when something is offered to Him; and of all man's goods, God specially accepts that of the human soul when it is offered to Him in sacrifice. Now a man ought to offer to God, in the first place, his soul, according to Ecclus. 30. 24, *Have pity on thy own soul, pleasing God;* in the second place, the souls of others, according to Apoc. 22. 17, *He that hear-*

---

[1] Bk. II (PL 76, 954). [2] PL 35, 1974.
[3] Bk. I (PL 76, 932). [4] Chap. 37 (PL 75, 764).
[5] *City of God,* XIX, 19 (PL 41, 647).
[6] Bk. I (PL 76, 809). [7] PG 47, 405.

eth, let him say: Come. And the more closely a man unites his own or another's soul to God, the more acceptable is his sacrifice to God; therefore it is more acceptable to God that one apply one's own soul and the souls of others to contemplation than to action. Consequently the statement that "no sacrifice is more acceptable to God than zeal for souls," does not mean that the merit of the active life is preferable to the merit of the contemplative life, but that it is more meritorious to offer to God one's own soul and the souls of others, than any other external gifts.

ARTICLE 3. *Whether the Contemplative Life Is Hindered By the Active Life?*

We proceed thus to the Third Article: It would seem that the contemplative life is hindered by the active life.

Objection 1. For the contemplative life requires a certain stillness of mind, according to Ps. 45. 2, *Be still, and see that I am God;* but the active life involves restlessness, according to Luke 10. 41, *Martha, Martha, thou art careful and troubled about many things.* Therefore the active life hinders the contemplative.

Obj. 2. Further, Clearness of vision is a requisite for the contemplative life. Now active life is a hindrance to clear vision; for Gregory says (*Hom.* ii *in Ezech.*)[1] that "Lia is bleareyed and fruitful, because the active life, being occupied with works, sees less." Therefore the active life hinders the contemplative.

Obj. 3. Further, One contrary hinders the other. Now the active and the contemplative life are apparently contrary to one another, since the active life is busy about many things, while the contemplative life attends to the contemplation of one; therefore they differ in opposition to one another. Therefore it would seem that the contemplative life is hindered by the active.

On the contrary, Gregory says (*Moral.* vi, 37):[2] "Those who wish to hold the fortress of contemplation must first of all train in the camp of action."

I answer that, The active life may be considered from two points of view. First, as regards the attention to and practice of external works; and thus it is evident that the active life hinders the contemplative, in so far as it is impossible for one to be busy with external action and at the same time give oneself to Divine contemplation. Secondly, active life may be considered as quieting and putting in order the in-

ternal passions of the soul; and from this point of view the active life is a help to the contemplative, since the latter is hindered by the lack of order of the internal passions. Hence Gregory says (*loc. cit.*): "Those who wish to hold the fortress of contemplation must first of all train in the camp of action. Thus after careful study they will learn whether they no longer wrong their neighbour, whether they bear with equanimity the wrongs their neighbours do to them, whether their soul is neither overcome with joy in the presence of temporal goods, nor cast down with too great a sorrow when those goods are withdrawn. In this way they will know when they withdraw within themselves, in order to explore spiritual things, whether they no longer carry with them the shadows of the things corporeal or, if these follow them, whether they prudently drive them away." Hence the work of the active life conduces to the contemplative, by quelling the interior passions which give rise to the phantasms by which contemplation is hindered. And this suffices for the *Replies to the Objections;* for these arguments consider the occupation itself of external actions, and not the effect which is the moderation of the passions.

ARTICLE 4. *Whether the Active Life Precedes the Contemplative?*

We proceed thus to the Fourth Article: It seems that the active life does not precede the contemplative.

Objection 1. For the contemplative life pertains directly to the love of God, while the active life pertains to the love of our neighbour. Now the love of God precedes the love of our neighbour, since we love our neighbour for God's sake. It seems therefore the contemplative life also precedes the active life.

Obj. 2. Further, Gregory says (*Hom.* ii *in Ezech.*):[3] "It should be observed that while a well-ordered life proceeds from action to contemplation, sometimes it is useful for the soul to turn from the contemplative to the active life." Therefore the active life is not absolutely prior to the contemplative.

Obj. 3. Further, It would seem that there is not necessarily any order between things that are suitable to different subjects. Now the active and the contemplative life are suitable to different subjects; for Gregory says (*Moral.* vi, 37):[4] "Often those who were able to contemplate God so long as they were undisturbed have fallen when pressed with occupation; and

---

[1] Bk. II (PL 76, 954).   [2] PL 75, 763.   [3] PL 76, 954.   [4] PL 75, 761.

frequently they who might live advantageously occupied with the service of their fellow-creatures are killed by the sword of their inaction."

On the contrary, Gregory says (*Hom.* iii *in Ezech.*):[1] "The active life precedes in time the contemplative life, for it is from good works that we tend to contemplation."

I answer that, A thing is said to precede in two ways. First, with regard to its nature; and in this way the contemplative life precedes the active, in so far as it applies itself to things which precede and are better than others. And for this reason it moves and directs the active life. For the higher reason which is assigned to contemplation is compared to the lower reason which is assigned to action, and the husband is compared to his wife, who should be ruled by her husband, as Augustine says (*De Trin.* xii, 12).[2]

Secondly, a thing precedes with regard to us, because it comes first in the order of generation. In this way the active precedes the contemplative life, because it disposes one to it, as stated above (A. 3; Q. CLXXXI, A. 1, Reply 3); and, in the order of generation, disposition precedes form, although the latter precedes absolutely and according to its nature.

Reply Obj. 1. The contemplative life is directed to the love of God, not of any degree, but to that which is perfect; but the active life is necessary for any degree of the love of our neighbour. Hence Gregory says (*loc. cit. in Ezech.*): "Without the contemplative life it is possible to enter the heavenly kingdom, provided one omit not the good actions we are able to do; but we cannot enter therein without the active life, if we neglect to do the good we can do."

From this it is also evident that the active precedes the contemplative life as that which is common to all precedes, in the order of generation, that which is proper to the perfect.

Reply Obj. 2. Progress from the active to the contemplative life is according to the order of generation; but the return from the contemplative life to the active is according to the order of direction, in so far, that is, as the active life is directed by the contemplative. Even thus habit is acquired by acts, and by the acquired habit one acts yet more perfectly, as stated in the *Ethics.*[3]

Reply Obj. 3. He that is prone to yield to his passions on account of his impulse to action is likewise more apt for the active life by reason of his restless spirit. Hence Gregory says (*Moral.* vi, 37) that "there are some so restless that when they are free from labour they labour all the more, because the more leisure they have for thought, the worse interior turmoil they have to bear." Others, on the contrary, have a mind naturally pure and restful, so that they are apt for contemplation, and if they were to apply themselves wholly to action, this would be detrimental to them. Hence Gregory says (*loc. cit., Moral.* vi) that "some are so slothful of mind that if they chance to have any hard work to do they give way at the very outset." Yet, as he adds further on,[4] "often . . . love stimulates slothful souls to work, and fear restrains souls that are disturbed in contemplation." Consequently those who are more adapted to the active life can prepare themselves for the contemplative by the practice of the active life; while, none the less, those who are more adapted to the contemplative life can take upon themselves the works of the active life, so as to become yet more apt for contemplation.

[1] Bk. I (PL 76, 809).
[2] PL 42, 1007; cf. also chaps. 3, 7 (PL 42, 999, 1003).

[3] Aristotle, II, 1 (1103ª14); also II, 2, 4 (1103ᵇ26; 1105ª 17).   [4] PL 75, 762.

TREATISE ON THE STATES OF LIFE

QUESTION CLXXXIII
Of man's various duties and states in general
(In Four Articles)

WE must next consider man's various states and duties. We shall consider (1) man's duties and states in general; (2) the state of the perfect in particular (Q. CLXXXIV).

Under the first head there are four points of inquiry: (1) What constitutes a state among men? (2) Whether among men there should be various states and duties? (3) Of the diversity of duties. (4) Of the diversity of states.

ARTICLE 1. *Whether the Notion of a State Denotes a Condition of Freedom or Servitude?*

We proceed thus to the First Article: It seems that the notion of a state does not denote a condition of freedom or servitude.

Objection 1. For state (*status*) takes its name from standing (*stando*). Now a person is said to stand on account of his being upright, and so it is said (Ezech. 2. 1), *Son of man, stand (sta) upon thy feet;* and Gregory says (*Moral.* vii):[1] "To fall by speaking harmful words is to forfeit entirely the state of rectitude." But a man acquires spiritual uprightness by submitting his will to God; therefore a gloss on Ps. 32. 1, *Praise becometh the upright,* says:[2] "The upright are those who direct their heart according to God's will." Therefore it would seem that obedience to the Divine commandments suffices alone for the notion of a state.

Obj. 2. Further, The word state seems to denote immobility, according to 1 Cor. 15. 58, *Be ye steadfast (stabiles) and immovable;* hence Gregory says (*Hom.* ix *in Ezech.*).[3] "The stone is foursquare, and is stable on all sides, if no disturbance will make it fall." Now it is virtue that "enables us to act with immobility," according to the *Ethics.*[4] Therefore it would seem that a state is acquired by every virtuous action.

Obj. 3. Further, The word state seems to indicate height of a kind, because to stand is to be raised upwards. Now one man is made higher than another by various duties; and in like manner men are raised upwards in various ways by various grades and orders. Therefore the mere difference of grades, orders, or duties suffices for a difference of states.

On the contrary, It is thus laid down in the Decretals (Part II, Q. VI, cap. 40):[5] "Whenever anyone intervenes in a cause where life or state is at stake he must do so not by a proxy, but in his own person"; and state here has reference to freedom or servitude. Therefore it would seem that nothing differentiates a man's state except that which refers to freedom or servitude.

I answer that, State, properly speaking, denotes a kind of position according to which a thing is disposed with a certain immobility in a manner according with its nature. For it is natural to man that his head should be directed upwards, his feet set firmly on the ground, and his other intermediate members disposed in fitting order; and this is not the case if he lie down, sit, or recline, but only when he stands upright. Nor again is he said to stand if he moves, but only when he is still. Hence it is again that even in human acts, a matter is said to have stability (*statum*) in reference to its own disposition in the point of a certain immobility or rest. Consequently matters which easily change and are extrinsic to them do not constitute a state among men, for instance that a man be rich or poor, of high or low rank, and so forth. Therefore in the civil law (Lib. *Cassius* ff *de Senatoribus*)[6] it is said that if a man be removed from the senate, he is deprived of his dignity rather than of his state. But that alone seems to pertain to a man's state, which regards an obligation binding his person, in so far, that is, as a man is his own master or subject to another, not indeed from any slight or unstable cause, but from one that is firmly established; and this is something pertaining to the nature of freedom or servitude. Therefore state properly regards freedom or servitude, whether in spiritual or in civil matters.

---

[1] Chap. 37 (PL 75, 800).
[2] *Glossa ordin.* (III, 130A); *Glossa* Lombardi (PL 191, 325); Augustine, *Enarr. in Ps., Ennar.* 2, serm. 1 (PL 36, 277).   [3] Bk. II (PL 76, 1044).
[4] Aristotle, II, 4 (1105ª32).

[5] Gratian (RF I, 481).
[6] *Digest.*, Bk. I, IX, 3 (KR I, 40ª).

Reply Obj. 1. Uprightness as such does not pertain to the notion of state, except in so far as it is connatural to man with the addition of a certain being at rest. Hence other animals are said to stand without its being required that they should be upright; nor again are men said to stand, however upright their position be, unless they be still.

Reply Obj. 2. Immobility does not suffice for the notion of state; for even one who sits or lies down is still, and yet he is not said to stand.

Reply Obj. 3. Duty implies relation to act, while grades denote an order of superiority and inferiority. But state requires immobility in that which regards a condition of the person himself.

ARTICLE 2. *Whether There Should Be Different Duties or States in the Church?*

We proceed thus to the Second Article: It seems that there should not be different duties or states in the Church.

Objection 1. For difference is opposed to unity. Now the faithful of Christ are called to unity according to John 21. 22: *That they . . . may be one in Us . . . as We also are one.* Therefore there should not be a difference of duties and states in the Church.

Obj. 2. Further, Nature does not employ many means where one suffices. But the working of grace is much more orderly than the working of nature. Therefore it would be more fitting for things pertaining to the operations of grace to be administered by the same persons, in such a way that there would not be a distinction of duties and states in the Church.

Obj. 3. Further, The good of the Church seems to consist chiefly in peace, according to Ps. 147. 3, *Who hath placed peace in thy borders,* and II Cor. 13. 11, *Have peace, and the God of peace . . . shall be with you.* Now distinction is a hindrance to peace, for peace would seem to result from likeness, according to Ecclus. 13. 19, *Every beast loveth its like,* while the Philosopher says[1] that a little difference causes dissension in a state. Therefore it would seem that there ought not to be a distinction of states and duties in the Church.

On the contrary, It is written in praise of the Church (Ps. 44. 10) that she is *surrounded with variety;* and a gloss on these words says[2] that "the Queen," namely the Church," is bedecked

[1] *Politics,* v, 3 (1303^{b}14).
[2] *Glossa ordin.* (III, 150A); *Glossa* Lombardi (PL 191, 444); cf. Cassiodorus, *Expos. in Psalt.,* on Ps. 44.10 (PL 70, 524).

with the teaching of the apostles, the confession of martyrs, the purity of virgins, the sorrowings of penitents."

I answer that, The difference of states and duties in the Church regards three things. In the first place it regards the perfection of the Church. For even as in the order of natural things, perfection, which in God is simple and uniform, is not to be found in the created universe except in a multiform and manifold manner, so too, the fulness of grace, which is centred in Christ as head, flows forth to His members in various ways, for the perfecting of the body of the Church. This is the meaning of the Apostle's words (Eph. 4. 11, 12): *He gave some apostles, and some prophets and other some evangelists, and other some pastors and doctors for the perfecting of the saints.* Secondly, it regards the need of those actions which are necessary in the Church. For a diversity of actions requires a diversity of men appointed to them, in order that all things may be accomplished without delay or confusion; and this is indicated by the Apostle (Rom. 12. 4, 5), *As in one body we have many members, but all the members have not the same office, so we being many are one body in Christ.* Thirdly, this belongs to the dignity and beauty of the Church, which consist in a certain order; hence it is written (III Kings 10. 4, 5) that *when the queen of Saba saw all the wisdom of Solomon . . . and the apartments of his servants, and the order of his ministers . . . she had no longer any spirit in her.* Hence the Apostle says (II Tim. 2. 20) that *in a great house there are not only vessels of gold and silver, but also of wood and of earth.*

Reply Obj. 1. The distinction of states and duties is not an obstacle to the unity of the Church, for this results from the unity of faith, charity, and mutual service, according to the saying of the Apostle (Eph. 4. 16): *From Whom the whole body being compacted,* namely by faith, *and fitly joined together,* namely by charity, *by what every joint supplieth,* namely by one man serving another.

Reply Obj. 2. Just as nature does not employ many means where one suffices, so neither does it confine itself to one where many are required, according to the saying of the Apostle (I Cor. 12. 17), *If the whole body were the eye, where would be the hearing?* Hence there was need in the Church, which is Christ's body, for the members to be differentiated by various duties, states, and grades.

Reply Obj. 3. Just as in the natural body the

various members are held together in unity by the power of the quickening spirit, and are dissociated from one another as soon as that spirit departs, so too in the Church's body the peace of the various members is preserved by the power of the Holy Spirit, Who quickens the body of the Church, as stated in John 6. Hence the Apostle says (Eph. 4. 3): *Careful to keep the unity of the Spirit in the bond of peace.* Now a man departs from this unity of spirit when he seeks his own, just as in an earthly kingdom peace ceases when the citizens seek each man his own. Besides, the peace both of mind and of an earthly commonwealth is the better preserved by a distinction of duties and states, since thereby the greater number have a share in public actions. Therefore the Apostle says (I Cor. 12. 24, 25) that *God hath tempered us* (Vulg.,—*the body*) *together that there might be no schism in the body, but the members might be mutually careful one for another.*

ARTICLE 3. *Whether Duties Differ According to Their Actions?*

We proceed thus to the Third Article: It seems that duties do not differ according to their actions.

Objection 1. For there are infinite varieties of human acts both in spiritual things and in temporal. Now there can be no certain distinction among things that are infinite in number. Therefore human duties cannot be differentiated according to a difference of acts.

Obj. 2. Further, The active and the contemplative life differ according to their acts, as stated above (Q. CLXXIX, A. 1). But the distinction of duties seems to be other than the distinction of lives. Therefore duties do not differ according to their acts.

Obj. 3. Further, Even ecclesiastical orders, states, and grades seem to differ according to their acts. If, then, duties differ according to their acts it would seem that duties, grades, and states differ in the same way. Yet this is not true, since they are divided into their respective parts in different ways. Therefore duties do not differ according to their acts.

On the contrary, Isidore says (*Etym.* vi, 19)[1] that "duty (*officium*) takes its name from to effect (*efficere*), as though it were instead of '*efficium*,' by the change of one letter for the sake of the sound." But effecting pertains to action. Therefore duties differ according to their acts.

I answer that, As stated above (A. 2), differ-

ence among the members of the Church is directed to three things: perfection, action, and beauty; and according to these three we may distinguish a threefold distinction among the faithful. One, with regard to perfection, and thus we have the difference of states, in reference to which some persons are more perfect than others. Another distinction regards action and this is the distinction of duties; for persons are said to have various duties when they are appointed to various actions. A third distinction regards the order of ecclesiastical beauty; and thus we distinguish various grades according as in the same state or duty one person is above another. Hence according to a variant text (Septuagint) it is written (Ps. 47. 3): *In her grades shall God be known.*

Reply Obj. 1. The material diversity of human acts is infinite. It is not thus that duties differ, but by their formal diversity which results from diverse species of acts, and in this way human acts are not infinite.

Reply Obj. 2. Life is predicated of a thing absolutely. Therefore diversity of lives results from a diversity of acts which are fitting to man considered in himself. But efficient, from which we have the word office (as stated in the argument, *On the contrary*), denotes action tending to something else according to the *Metaphysics.*[2] Hence offices differ properly in respect of acts that are referred to other persons; thus a teacher is said to have an office, and so is a judge, and so forth. Therefore Isidore says (*loc. cit.*) that to have an office "is to be officious," that is harmful "to no one, but to be useful to all."

Reply Obj. 3. Differences of state, offices and grades are taken from different things, as stated above. Yet these three things may concur in the same subject; thus when a person is appointed to a higher action, he attains thereby both office and grade and at the same time a certain state of perfection, on account of the sublimity of the act, as in the case of a bishop. The ecclesiastical orders are particularly distinct according to various offices. For Isidore says (*Etym.* vi, 19):[3] "There are various kinds of offices; but the foremost is that which relates to sacred and Divine things."

ARTICLE 4. *Whether the Difference of States Applies to Those Who Are Beginning, Progressing, or Perfect?*

We proceed thus to the Fourth Article: It seems that the difference of states does not ap-

---

[1] PL 82, 252.   [2] Aristotle, IX, 8 (1050ª30).   [3] PL 82, 252.

ply to those who are beginning, progressing, or perfect.

Objection 1. For different things have diverse species and differences. Now this difference of beginning, progress, and perfection is applied to the degrees of charity, as stated above (Q. XXIV, A. 9), where we were treating of charity. Therefore it would seem that the differences of states should not be assigned in this manner.

Obj. 2. Further, As stated above (A. 1) state regards a condition of servitude or freedom, which apparently has no connection with the above mentioned difference of beginning, progress, and perfection. Therefore it is unfitting to divide state in this way.

Obj. 3. Further, The distinction of beginning, progress, and perfection seems to refer to more and less, and this seems to imply the notion of grades. But the distinction of grades differs from that of states, as we have said above (A. 3). Therefore state is unfittingly divided according to beginning, progress, and perfection.

On the contrary, Gregory says (*Moral.* xxiv, 11).[1] "There are three states of the converted, the beginning, the middle, and the perfection"; and (*Hom.* iii *in Ezech.*):[2] "Other is the beginning of virtue, other its progress, and other still its perfection."

I answer that, As stated above (A. 1) state regards freedom or servitude. Now in spiritual things there is a twofold servitude and a twofold freedom; for there is the servitude of sin and the servitude of justice. And there is likewise a twofold freedom: from sin, and from justice, as appears from the words of the Apostle (Rom. 6. 20, 22), *When you were the servants of sin, you were free men to justice;* . . . *but now being made free from sin,* you are . . . *become servants to God.*

Now the servitude of sin or justice consists in being inclined to evil by a habit of sin, or inclined to good by a habit of justice. And in like manner freedom from sin is not to be overcome by the inclination to sin, and freedom from justice is not to be held back from evil for the love of justice. Nevertheless, since man, by his natural reason, is inclined to justice, while sin is contrary to natural reason, it follows that freedom from sin is true freedom which is united to the servitude of justice, since they both incline man to that which is fitting to him. In like manner true servitude is the servitude of sin, which is connected with freedom from justice, because man is thereby hindered

from attaining that which is proper to him. That man becomes the servant of justice or sin results from man's efforts, as the Apostle declares (*ibid., verse* 16): *To whom you yield yourselves servants to obey, his servants you are whom you obey, whether it be of sin unto death, or of obedience unto justice.* Now in every human effort we can distinguish a beginning, a middle, and a term. And consequently the state of spiritual servitude and freedom is differentiated according to these things, namely the beginning,—to which pertains the state of beginners,—the middle, to which pertains the state of the proficient,—and the term, to which belongs the state of the perfect.

Reply Obj. 1. Freedom from sin results from charity which *is poured forth in our hearts by the Holy Ghost, Who is given to us* (Rom. 5. 5). Hence it is written (II Cor. 3. 17): *Where the Spirit of the Lord is, there is liberty.* Therefore the same division applies to charity as to the state of those who enjoy spiritual freedom.

Reply Obj. 2. Men are said to be beginners, proficient, and perfect (so far as these terms indicate different states), not in relation to any occupation whatever, but in relation to such occupations as pertain to spiritual freedom or servitude, as stated above in this Article and A. 1.

Reply Obj. 3. As already observed (A. 3, Reply 3), nothing hinders grade and state from concurring in the same subject. For even in earthly affairs those who are free not only belong to a different state from those who are slaves, but are also of a higher grade.

QUESTION CLXXXIV

OF THINGS PERTAINING TO THE STATE OF PERFECTION IN GENERAL

(In Eight Articles)

WE must now consider those things that pertain to the state of perfection to which the other states are ordered. For the consideration of offices in relation to other acts belongs to the legislator; and in relation to the sacred ministry, it comes under the consideration of Orders, of which we shall treat in the Third Part (Suppl., Q. XXXIV). Concerning the state of the perfect, a threefold consideration presents itself: (1) The state of perfection in general; (2) things relating to the perfection of bishops (Q. CLXXXV); (3) things relating to the perfection of religious (Q. CLXXXVI).

Under the first head there are eight points of inquiry: (1) Whether perfection bears any

---

[1] PL 76, 302.   [2] Bk. II (PL 76, 960).

relation to charity? (2) Whether one can be perfect in this life? (3) Whether the perfection of this life consists chiefly in observing the counsels or in observing the commandments? (4) Whether whoever is perfect is in the state of perfection? (5) Whether especially prelates and religious are in the state of perfection? (6) Whether all prelates are in the state of perfection? (7) Which is the more perfect, the episcopal or the religious state? (8) The comparison between religious and parish priests and archdeacons.

Article 1. *Whether the Perfection of the Christian Life Consists Especially in Charity?*

We proceed thus to the First Article: It seems that the perfection of the Christian life does not consist especially in charity.

Objection 1. For the Apostle says (I Cor. 14. 20): *In malice be children, but in sense be perfect.* But charity regards not the senses but the affections. Therefore it would seem that the perfection to the Christian life does not chiefly consist in charity.

Obj. 2. Further, It is written (Eph. 6. 13): *Take unto you the armour of God, that you may be able to resist in the evil day, and to stand in all things perfect;* and the text continues (verses 14, 16) speaking of the armour of God: *Stand therefore having your loins girt about with truth, and having on the breastplate of justice . . . in all things taking the shield of faith.* Therefore the perfection of the Christian life consists not only in charity, but also in other virtues.

Obj. 3. Further, Virtues, like other habits, are specified by their acts. Now it is written (James 1. 4) that *patience hath a perfect work.* Therefore it seems that the state of perfection consists more specially in patience.

On the contrary, It is written (Col. 3. 14): *Above all things have charity, which is the bond of perfection,* because it binds, as it were, all the other virtues together in perfect unity.

I answer that, A thing is said to be perfect in so far as it attains its proper end, which is its ultimate perfection. Now it is charity that unites us to God, Who is the last end of the human mind, since *he that abideth in charity abideth in God, and God in him* (I John 4. 16). Therefore the perfection of the Christian life consists especially in charity.

Reply Obj. 1. The perfection of the human senses would seem to consist chiefly in their concurring together in the unity of truth, according to I Cor. 1. 10. *That you be perfect in the same mind (sensu), and in the same judgment.* Now this is effected by charity which operates consent in us men. Therefore even the perfection of the senses has its roots in the perfection of charity.

Reply Obj. 2. A man may be said to be perfect in two ways. First, absolutely. And this perfection regards that which belongs to a thing's nature; for instance an animal may be said to be perfect when it lacks nothing in the disposition of its members and in such things as are necessary for an animal's life. Secondly, a thing is said to be perfect relatively. And this perfection regards something connected with the thing externally, such as whiteness or blackness or something of the kind. Now the Christian life consists especially in charity, by which the soul is united to God; and so it is written (I John 3. 14): *He that loveth not abideth in death.* Hence the perfection of the Christian life consists absolutely in charity, but in the other virtues relatively. And since that which is absolutely, is paramount and greatest in comparison with other things, it follows that the perfection of charity is paramount in relation to the perfection that regards the other virtues.

Reply Obj. 3. Patience is stated to have a perfect work in relation to charity, in so far as it is an effect of the abundance of charity that a man bears hardships patiently, according to Rom. 8. 35, *Who . . . shall separate us from the love of Christ? Shall tribulation? or distress?* etc.

Article 2. *Whether Any One Can Be Perfect in This Life?*

We proceed thus to the Second Article: It seems that none can be perfect in this life.

Objection 1. For the Apostle says (I Cor. 13. 10): *When that which is perfect is come, that which is in part shall be done away.* Now in this life that which is in part is not done away; for in this life faith and hope, which are in part, remain. Therefore none can be perfect in this life.

Obj. 2. Further, The perfect is that which lacks nothing, according to the *Physics.*[1] Now there is no one in this life who lacks nothing; for it is written (James 3. 2): *In many things we all offend;* and (Ps. 138. 16): *Thy eyes did see my imperfect being.* Therefore none is perfect in this life.

[1] Aristotle, III, 6 (207ª8).

Obj. 3. Further, The perfection of the Christian life, as stated in the foregoing Article, relates to charity, which comprises the love of God and of our neighbour. Now, neither as to the love of God can one have perfect charity in this life, since according to Gregory (*Hom.* ii *in Ezech.*)[1] "the furnace of love which begins to burn here will burn more fiercely when we see Him Whom we love"; nor as to the love of our neighbour, since in this life we cannot love all our neighbours actually, even though we love them habitually; and habitual love is imperfect. Therefore it seems that no one can be perfect in this life.

On the contrary, The Divine law does not prescribe the impossible. Yet it prescribes perfection according to Matt. 5. 48, *Be you . . . perfect, as also your heavenly Father is perfect.* Therefore it seems that one can be perfect in this life.

I answer that, As stated in the foregoing Article, the perfection of the Christian life consists in charity. Now perfection implies a certain universality, because according to the *Physics,*[2] "the perfect is that which lacks nothing." Hence we may consider a threefold perfection. One is absolute, and answers to a totality not only on the part of the lover, but also on the part of the thing loved, so that God be loved as much as He is lovable. Such perfection as this is not possible to any creature, but belongs to God alone, in Whom good is wholly and essentially.

Another perfection answers to an absolute totality on the part of the lover, so that the affective power always actually tends to God as much as it possibly can; and such perfection as this is not possible so long as we are on the way, but we shall have it in heaven.

The third perfection answers to a totality neither on the part of the thing loved, nor on the part of the lover as regards his always actually tending to God, but on the part of the lover as regards the removal of obstacles to the movement of love towards God, in which sense Augustine says[3] that "carnal desire is the bane of charity; to have no carnal desires is the perfection of charity." Such perfection as this can be had in this life, and in two ways. First, by the removal from man's affections of all that is contrary to charity, such as mortal sin; and there can be no charity apart from this perfection. Hence it is necessary for salvation. Secondly, by the removal from man's affections not

only of whatever is contrary to charity, but also of whatever hinders the mind's affections from tending wholly to God. Charity is possible apart from this perfection, for instance in those who are beginners and in those who are making progress.

Reply Obj. 1. The Apostle is speaking there of heavenly perfection which is not possible to those who are on the way.

Reply Obj. 2. Those who are perfect in this life are said to "offend in many things" with regard to venial sins, which result from the weakness of the present life; and in this respect they have an "imperfect being" in comparison with the perfection of heaven.

Reply Obj. 3. As the state of the present life does not allow of a man always tending actually to God, so neither does it allow of his always tending actually to each individual neighbour; but it suffices for him to tend to all in common and collectively, and to each individual habitually and according to the preparedness of his mind.

Now in the love of our neighbour, as in the love of God, we may observe a twofold perfection: one without which charity is impossible, and consisting in one's having in one's affections nothing that is contrary to the love of one's neighbour; and another without which it is possible to have charity. The latter perfection may be considered in three ways. First, as to the extent of love, through a man loving not only his friends and acquaintances but also strangers and even his enemies, for as Augustine says (*Enchir.* lxxiii)[4] this is a mark of the perfect children of God. Secondly, as to the intensity of love, which is shown by the things which man despises for his neighbour's sake, through his despising not only external goods for the sake of his neighbour, but also bodily hardships and even death, according to John. 15. 13, *Greater love than this no man hath, that a man lay down his life for his friends.* Thirdly, as to the effect of love, so that a man will pour out not only temporal but also spiritual goods and even himself, for his neighbour's sake, according to the words of the Apostle (II Cor. 12. 15), *But I most gladly will spend and be spent myself for your souls.*

ARTICLE 3. *Whether Perfection Consists in the Observance of the Commandments or of the Counsels?*

We proceed thus to the Third Article: It seems that perfection consists in the observance

---

[1] Bk. II (PL 76, 954).   [2] Aristotle, III, 6 (207ᵃ8).
[3] QQ. LXXXIII, Qu. 36 (PL 40, 25).   [4] PL 40, 266.

not of the commandments but of the counsels.

Objection 1. For our Lord said (Matt. 19. 21): *If thou wilt be perfect, go sell all* (Vulg.,— *what) thou hast, and give to the poor . . . and come, follow Me.* Now this is a counsel. Therefore perfection regards the counsels and not the precepts.

Obj. 2. Further, All are bound to the observance of the commandments, since this is necessary for salvation. Therefore, if the perfection of the Christian life consists in observing the commandments, it follows that perfection is necessary for salvation, and that all are bound to it. And this is evidently false.

Obj. 3. Further, The perfection of the Christian life is gauged according to charity, as stated above (A. 1). Now the perfection of charity, seemingly, does not consist in the observance of the commandments, since the perfection of charity is preceded both by its increase and by its beginning, as Augustine says on the canonical epistles of St. John (*Tract.* ix).[1] But the beginning of charity cannot precede the observance of the commandments, since according to John 14. 23, *If any one love Me, he will keep My word.* Therefore the perfection of life regards not the commandments but the counsels.

On the contrary, It is written (Deut. 6. 5): *Thou shalt love the Lord thy God with thy whole heart,* and (Lev. 19. 18): *Thou shalt love thy neighbour* (Vulg.,—*friend) as thyself;* and these are the commandments of which our Lord said (Matt. 22. 40): *On these two commandments dependeth the whole law and the prophets.* Now the perfection of charity, in respect of which the Christian life is said to be perfect, consists in our loving God with our whole heart, and our neighbour as ourselves. Therefore it would seem that perfection consists in the observance of the precepts.

I answer that, Perfection is said to consist in a thing in two ways: in one way, in itself and essentially; in another, secondarily and accidentally. In itself and essentially the perfection of the Christian life consists in charity, principally as to the love of God, secondarily as to the love of our neighbour, both of which are the matter of the chief commandments of the Divine law, as stated above (*On the contrary;* Part I-II, Q. C, A. 3, Reply 1; A. 2). Now the love of God and of our neighbour is not commanded according to a measure, so that what is in excess of the measure be a matter of counsel. This is evident from the very form of the commandment, pointing, as it does, to perfection,—for

instance in the words, *Thou shalt love the Lord thy God with thy whole heart,* since "the whole is the same as the perfect," according to the Philosopher,[2]—and in the words, *Thou shalt love thy neighbour as thyself,* since every one loves himself most. The reason of this is that *the end of the commandment is charity* according to the Apostle (I Tim. 1. 5). And the end is not subject to a measure, but only such things as are directed to the end, as the Philosopher observes;[3] thus a physician does not measure the amount of his healing, but how much medicine or diet he shall employ for the purpose of healing. Consequently it is evident that perfection consists essentially in the observance of the commandments; hence Augustine says (*De Perf. Justit.* viii):[4] "Why then should not this perfection be prescribed to man, although no man has it in this life?"

Secondarily and instrumentally, however, perfection consists in the observance of the counsels, all of which, like the commandments, are directed to charity; yet not in the same way. For the commandments, other than the precepts of charity, are directed to the removal of things contrary to charity, with which, namely, charity is incompatible. But the counsels are directed to the removal of things that hinder the act of charity, and yet are not contrary to charity, such as marriage, the occupation of worldly business, and so forth. Hence Augustine says (*Enchir.* cxxi):[5] "Whatever things God commands, for instance, 'Thou shalt not commit adultery,' and whatever are not commanded, yet suggested by a special counsel, for instance, 'It is good for a man not to touch a woman,' are then done rightly when they are referred to the love of God, and of our neighbour for God's sake, both in this world and in the world to come." Hence it is that in the Conferences of the Fathers (*Coll.* i, cap. vii)[6] the abbot Moses says: "Fastings, watchings, meditating on the Scriptures, penury and loss of all one's wealth, these are not perfection but means to perfection, since not in them does the school of perfection find its end, but through them it achieves its end," and he had already said that "we endeavour to ascend by these steps to the perfection of charity."

Reply Obj. 1. In this saying of our Lord something is indicated as being the way to perfection by the words, *Go, sell all thou hast, and give to the poor;* and something else is added

---

[1] PL 35, 2047.

[2] *Physics,* III, 6 (207ª13).   [3] *Politics,* I, 9 (1257ᵇ26).
[4] PL 44, 301.   [5] PL 40, 288.
[6] Cassianus (PL 49, 490).

in which consists perfection, when He said, *And follow Me*. Hence Jerome in his commentary on Matt. 19. 27, *Behold we have left all things*, says[1] that "since it is not enough merely to leave, Peter added that which is perfect: 'And have followed Thee'"; and Ambrose, commenting on Luke 5. 27, *Follow Me*, says:[2] "He commands him to follow, not with steps of the body, but with devotion of the soul," which is the effect of charity. Therefore it is evident from the very way of speaking that the counsels are means of attaining to perfection, since it is thus expressed: *If thou wilt be perfect, go, sell*, etc., as though He said: "By so doing thou shalt accomplish this end."

Reply Obj. 2. As Augustine says (*De Perf. Justit.* viii)[3] the perfection of charity is prescribed to man in this life because "one runs not right unless one knows whither to run. And how shall we know this if no commandment declares it to us?" And since that which is a matter of precept can be fulfilled variously, one does not break a commandment through not fulfilling it in the best way, but it is enough to fulfil it in any way whatever. Now the perfection of Divine love is a matter of precept for all without exception, so that even the perfection of heaven is not excepted from this precept, as Augustine says (*loc. cit.*),[4] and one escapes transgressing the precept, in whatever measure one attains to the perfection of Divine love. The lowest degree of Divine love is to love nothing more than God, or contrary to God, or equally with God, and whoever fails from this degree of perfection in no way fulfils the precept. There is another degree of the Divine love, which cannot be fulfilled so long as we are on the way, as stated in the foregoing Article, and it is evident that to fail from this is not to be a transgressor of the precept; and in like manner one does not transgress the precept, if one does not attain to the intermediate degrees of perfection, provided one attain to the lowest.

Reply Obj. 3. Just as man has a certain perfection of his nature as soon as he is born, which perfection belongs to the very essence of his species, while there is another perfection which he acquires by growth, so again there is a perfection of charity which belongs to the very species of charity, namely that man love God above all things, and love nothing contrary to God; while there is another perfection of charity even in this life, to which a man attains by a kind of spiritual growth, for instance when a man refrains even from lawful things, in order more freely to give himself to the service of God.

ARTICLE 4. *Whether Whoever Is Perfect Is in the State of Perfection?*

We proceed thus to the Fourth Article: It seems that whoever is perfect is in the state of perfection.

Objection 1. For, as stated in the foregoing Article, (REPLY 3), just as bodily perfection is reached by bodily growth, so spiritual perfection is acquired by spiritual growth. Now after bodily growth one is said to have reached the state of perfect age. Therefore it seems also that after spiritual growth, when one has already reached spiritual perfection, one is in the state of perfection.

Obj. 2. Further, According to the *Physics*,[5] movement from one contrary to another has the same character as movement from less to more. Now when a man is changed from sin to grace he is said to change his state, in so far as the state of sin differs from the state of grace. Therefore it would seem that in the same manner, when one progresses from a lesser to a greater grace so as to reach the perfect degree, one is in the state of perfection.

Obj. 3. Further, A man acquires a state by being freed from servitude. But one is freed from the servitude of sin by charity, because *charity covereth all sins* (Prov. 10. 12). Now one is said to be perfect on account of charity, as stated above (A. 1). Therefore, it seems that whoever has perfection, for this very reason has the state of perfection.

On the contrary, Some are in the state of perfection who are wholly lacking in charity and grace, for instance wicked bishops or religious. Therefore it would seem that on the other hand some have the perfection of life who nevertheless have not the state of perfection.

I answer that, As stated above (Q. CLXXXIII, A. 1), state properly regards a condition of freedom or servitude. Now spiritual freedom or servitude may be considered in man in two ways: first, with respect to his internal actions; secondly, with respect to his external actions. And since according to I Kings 16. 7, *man seeth those things that appear, but the Lord beholdeth the heart*, it follows that with regard to man's internal disposition we consider his spiritual state in relation to the Divine judgment, while with regard to his external actions we consider man's spiritual state in relation to the Church.

---

[1] Bk. II (PL 26, 144).   [2] Bk. v (PL 15, 1724).
[3] PL 44, 302.   [4] PL 44, 301.
[5] Aristotle, v, 2 (226^{b}1).

It is in this latter sense that we are now speaking of states, namely in so far as the Church derives a certain beauty from the variety of states.

Now it must be observed that so far as men are concerned, in order that any one attain to a state of freedom or servitude there is required first of all an obligation or a release. For the mere fact of serving someone does not make a man a slave, since even the free serve, according to Gal. 5. 13, *By charity of the spirit serve one another;* nor again does the mere fact of ceasing to serve make a man free, as in the case of a runaway slave. But properly speaking a man is a slave if he be bound to serve, and a man is free if he be released from service. Secondly, it is required that the above obligation be imposed with a certain solemnity, even as a certain solemnity is observed in other matters which among men obtain a settlement in perpetuity. Accordingly, properly speaking, one is said to be in the state of perfection not through having the act of perfect love, but through binding himself in perpetuity and with a certain solemnity to those things that pertain to perfection.

Moreover it happens that some persons bind themselves to that which they do not keep, and some fulfil that to which they have not bound themselves, as in the case of the two sons (Matt. 21. 28, 30), one of whom when his father said: *Work in my vineyard,* answered: *I will not, and afterwards . . . he went,* while the other *answering said: I go . . . and he went not.* Therefore nothing hinders some from being perfect without being in the state of perfection, and some in the state of perfection without being perfect.

Reply Obj. 1. By bodily growth a man progresses in things pertaining to nature, and therefore he attains to the state of nature; especially since what is according to nature is, in a way, unchangeable, in so far as nature is determined to one thing. In like manner by inward spiritual growth a man reaches the state of perfection in relation to the Divine judgment. But as regards the distinctions of ecclesiastical states, a man does not reach the state of perfection except by growth in respect of external actions.

Reply Obj. 2. This argument also regards the interior state. Yet when a man passes from sin to grace, he passes from servitude to freedom; and this does not result from a mere progress in grace, except when a man binds himself to things pertaining to grace.

Reply Obj. 3. Again this argument considers the interior state. Nevertheless, although charity causes the change of condition from spiritual servitude to spiritual freedom, an increase of charity has not the same effect.

ARTICLE 5. *Whether Religious and Prelates Are in the State of Perfection?*

We proceed thus to the Fifth Article: It seems that prelates and religious are not in the state of perfection.

Objection 1. For the state of perfection differs from the state of the beginners and the proficient. Now no class of men is specially assigned to the state of the proficient or of the beginners. Therefore it would seem that neither should any class of men be assigned to the state of perfection.

Obj. 2. Further, The outward state should answer to the inward, for otherwise one is guilty of lying, "which consists not only in false words, but also in deceitful deeds," according to Ambrose in one of his sermons (xxx. *de Tempore*).[1] Now there are many prelates and religious who have not the inward perfection of charity. Therefore, if all religious and prelates are in the state of perfection, it would follow that all of them that are not perfect are in mortal sin, as deceivers and liars.

Obj. 3. Further, As stated above (A. 1), perfection is measured according to charity. Now the most perfect charity would seem to be in the martyrs, according to John. 15. 13, *Greater love than this no man hath, that a man lay down his life for his friends;* and a gloss on Heb. 12. 4, *For you have not yet resisted unto blood,* says:[2] "In this life no love is more perfect than that to which the holy martyrs attained, who strove against sin even unto blood." Therefore it would seem that the state of perfection should be ascribed to the martyrs rather than to religious and bishops.

On the contrary, Dionysius (*Eccl. Hier.* v)[3] ascribes perfection to bishops as being perfecters, and (*ibid.* vi)[4] to religious (whom he calls monks or θεράπευται, i.e. servants of God) as being perfected.

I answer that, As stated in the foregoing Article, there is required for the state of perfection a perpetual obligation to things pertaining to perfection, together with a certain solemnity. Now both these conditions apply to religious and bishops. For religious bind themselves by vow to refrain from wordly affairs, which they

---

[1] PL 17, 688.
[2] *Glossa* Lombardi (PL 192, 501); Augustine, *Serm.,* CLIX, 1 (PL 38, 868).   [3] Sects. 5, 7 (PG 3, 505, 508).
[4] Sect. 3 (PG 3, 532).

might lawfully use, in order more freely to give themselves to God, in which consists the perfection of the present life. Hence Dionysius says (*Eccl. Hier.* vi.),[1] speaking of religious: "Some call them θεράπευται, i.e. servants of God, on account of their pure service and bondage, others call them monks on account of the indivisible and single-minded life which unites them in a Godlike union and a perfection beloved of God, through their envelopment in, that is, contemplation of, indivisible things." Moreover, the obligation in both cases is undertaken with a certain solemnity of profession and consecration, and therefore Dionysius adds (*ibid.*): "Hence the holy legislation in bestowing perfect grace on them accords them a hallowing invocation."

In like manner bishops bind themselves to things pertaining to perfection when they take up the pastoral duty, to which it pertains that a shepherd *lay down his life for his sheep,* according to John 10. 15. Therefore the Apostle says (I Tim. 6. 12): *Thou . . . hast confessed a good confession before many witnesses,* that is to say, "when he was ordained," as a gloss says on this passage.[2] Again, a certain solemnity of consecration is employed together with this profession, according to II Tim. 1. 6: *Stir up the grace of God which is in thee by the imposition of my hands,* which the gloss ascribes to the grace of the episcopate.[3] And Dionysius says (*Eccl. Hier.* v)[4] that "when the high priest," that is, the bishop, "is ordained, he receives on his head the most holy imposition of the sacred oracles, whereby it is signified that he is a participator in the whole and entire hierarchical power, and that not only is he the enlightener of all (which pertains to his holy discourses and actions), but that he also confers this on others."

Reply Obj. 1. Beginning and increase are sought not for their own sake, but for the sake of perfection; hence it is only to the state of perfection that some are admitted under certain obligations and with solemnity.

Reply Obj. 2. Those who enter the state of perfection do not profess to be perfect, but to tend to perfection. Hence the Apostle says (Phil. 3. 12): *Not as though I had already attained, or were already perfect; but I follow after, if I may by any means apprehend:* and afterwards

(verse 15): *Let us therefore as many as are perfect, be thus minded.* Hence a man who takes up the state of perfection is not guilty of lying or deceit through not being perfect, but through withdrawing his mind from the intention of reaching perfection.

Reply Obj. 3. Martyrdom represents the most perfect act of charity. But an act of perfection is not enough to establish a state of perfection, as we have said (A. 4).

ARTICLE 6. *Whether All Ecclesiastical Prelates Are in the State of Perfection?*

We proceed thus to the Sixth Article: It seems that all ecclesiastical prelates are in the state of perfection.

Objection 1. For Jerome commenting on Tit. 1. 5, *Ordain . . . in every city,* etc., says:[5] "Formerly priest was the same as bishop," and afterwards he adds: "Just as priests know that by the custom of the Church they are subject to the one who is placed over them, so too, bishops should recognize that, by custom rather than by the very ordinance of our Lord, they are above the priests, and are together the rightful governors of Church." Now bishops are in the state of perfection. Therefore those priests also are who have the care of souls.

Obj. 2. Further, Just as bishops together with their consecration receive the care of souls, so also do parish priests and archdeacons, of whom a gloss on Acts 6. 3, *Brethren, look ye out . . . seven men of good reputation,* says:[6] "The apostles decided here to appoint throughout the Church seven deacons, who were to be of a higher degree, and as it were the supports of that which is nearest to the altar." Therefore it would seem that these also are in the state of perfection.

Obj. 3. Further, Just as bishops are bound to *lay down their life for their sheep,* so too are parish priests and archdeacons. But this belongs to the perfection of charity, as stated above (A. 2, REPLY 3; A. 5). Therefore it would seem that parish priests and archdeacons also are in the state of perfection.

On the contrary, Dionysius says (*Eccl. Hier.* v):[7] *The order of pontiffs is consummative and perfecting, that of the priests is illuminative and light-giving, that of the ministers is cleansing and discriminative.* Hence it is evident that perfection is ascribed to bishops only.

---

[1] PG 3, 532.

[2] *Glossa interl.* (VI, 123M); *Glossa* Lombardi (PL 192, 360).

[3] *Glossa interl.* (VI, 124r); *Glossa* Lombardi (PL 192, 365).

[4] Pt. III, sect. 7 (PG 3, 513).

[5] PL 26, 598.

[6] *Glossa ordin.* (VI, 174E); cf. Bede, *In Act.* 6.3 (PL 92, 956).

[7] Pt. I, sect. 7 (PG 3, 508); cf. sect. 6 (PG 3, 505).

I answer that, In priests and deacons having care of souls two things may be considered, namely their order and their charge. Their order is directed to some act in the Divine offices. Hence it has been stated above (Q. CLXXXIII, A. 3, REPLY 3) that the distinction of orders is comprised under the distinction of offices. And so by receiving a certain order a man receives the power of exercising certain sacred acts, but he is not bound on this account to things pertaining to perfection, except in so far as in the Western Church the receiving of a sacred order includes the taking of a vow of continence, which is one of the things pertaining to perfection, as we shall state further on (Q. CLXXXVI, A. 4). Therefore it is clear that from the fact that a man receives a sacred order a man is not placed absolutely in the state of perfection, although inward perfection is required in order that one exercise such acts worthily.

In like manner, neither are they placed in the state of perfection on the part of the charge which they take upon themselves. For they are not bound by this very fact under the obligation of a perpetual vow to retain the care of souls, but they can surrender it,—either by entering religion, even without their bishop's permission (Cf. Decret. xix, qu. 2, cap. *Duæ sunt*),[1]—or again an archdeacon may with his bishop's permission resign his archdeaconry or parish, and accept a simple prebend without cure, which would be in no way lawful if he were in the state of perfection; for *no man putting his hand to the plough and looking back is fit for the kingdom of God* (Luke 9. 62). On the other hand bishops, since they are in the state of perfection, cannot abandon the episcopal charge save by the authority of the Sovereign Pontiff (to whom alone it belongs also to dispense from perpetual vows), and this for certain causes, as we shall state further on (Q. CLXXXV, A. 4). Therefore it is manifest that not all prelates are in the state of perfection, but only bishops.

Reply Obj. 1. We may speak of priest and bishop in two ways. First, with regard to the name; and thus formerly bishops and priests were not distinct. For bishops are so called "because they watch over others," as Augustine observes,[2] while the priests according to the Greek are elders.[3] Hence the Apostle employs the term "priests" in reference to both, when he says (I Tim. 5. 17): *Let the priests that rule*

well be esteemed worthy of double honour;* and again he uses the term "bishops" in the same way, and so, addressing the priests of the Church of Ephesus he says (Acts 20. 28): *Take heed to yourselves and to the whole flock, wherein the Holy Ghost hath placed you bishops, to rule the church of God.*

But as regards the thing signified by these terms, there was always a difference between them, even at the time of the apostles. This is clear on the authority of Dionysius (*Eccl. Hier.* v),[4] and of a gloss on Luke 10. 1, *After these things the Lord appointed,* etc., which says:[5] "Just as the apostles were made bishops, so the seventy-two disciples were made priests of the second order." Subsequently, however, in order to avoid schism, it became necessary to distinguish even the terms, by calling the higher ones bishops and the lower ones priests.

But to assert that priests in no way differ from bishops is reckoned by Augustine among heretical doctrines (*De Hæres.* liii),[6] where he says that the Arians maintained that "no distinction should be proclaimed between a priest and a bishop."

Reply Obj. 2. Bishops have the chief care of the sheep of their diocese, while parish priests and archdeacons exercise an inferior ministry under the bishops. Hence a gloss on I Cor. 12. 28, *to one, helps, to another, governments,* (Vulg.,—*God hath set some in the church . . . helps, governments,* etc.) says: Helps, that is, "assistants to those who are in authority, as Titus was to the Apostle, or as archdeacons to the bishop"; governments, namely "persons of lesser authority, such as priests who have to instruct the people"; and Dionysius says (*Eccl. Hier.* v)[7] that "just as we see the whole hierarchy culminating in Jesus, so each office culminates in its respective godlike hierarch or bishop." Also it is said (XVI, Q. 1, cap. *Cunctis*):[8] "Priests and deacons must all take care not to do anything without their bishop's permission." Therefore it is evident that they stand in relation to their bishop as wardens or mayors to the king; and for this reason, just as in earthly governments the king alone receives a solemn blessing, while others are appointed by simple commission, so too in the Church the episcopal charge is conferred with the solemnity of consecration, while the archdeacon or parish priest receives his charge by simple appointment, al-

---

[1] Gratian (RF I, 839).
[2] *City of God,* XIX, 19 (PL 41, 647).
[3] Referring to the Greek ἐπίσκοπος and πρεσβύτερος from which the English "bishop" and "priest" are derived.

[4] PG 3, 500.
[5] *Glossa ordin.* (v, 151E); cf. Bede (PL 92, 461).
[6] PL 42, 40.   [7] Sect. 5 (PG 3, 512).
[8] Gratian, *Decretum,* pt. II, can. 41 (RF I, 773).

though he is consecrated in receiving orders before having a charge.

Reply Obj. 3. As parish priests and arch-deacons have not the chief charge, but a certain ministry as committed to them by the bishop, so the pastoral office does not belong to them in chief, nor are they bound to lay down their life for the sheep, except in so far as they have a share in their charge. Hence we should say that they have an office pertaining to perfection rather than that they attain the state of perfection.

ARTICLE 7. *Whether the Religious State Is More Perfect Than That of Prelates?*

We proceed thus to the Seventh Article: It seems that the religious state is more perfect than that of prelates.

Objection 1. For our Lord said (Matt. 19. 21): *If thou wilt be perfect, go* and *sell all* (Vulg.,—*what*) *thou hast, and give to the poor;* and religious do this. But bishops are not bound to do so, for it is said (XII, Q. I, cap. 19):[1] "Bishops, if they wish, may bequeath to their heirs their personal or acquired property, and whatever belongs to them personally." There-fore religious are in a more perfect state than bishops.

Obj. 2. Further, Perfection consists more es-pecially in the love of God than in the love of our neighbour. Now the religious state is directly ordered to the love of God, and therefore it takes "its name from the divine service and bondage," as Dionysius says (*Eccl. Hier.* vi);[2] but the bishop's state would seem to be ordered to the love of our neighbour, of whose care he is the warden, and from this he takes his name, as Augustine observes.[3] Therefore it would seem that the religious state is more perfect than that of bishops.

Obj. 3. Further, The religious state is directed to the contemplative life, which is more excel-lent than the active life to which the episcopal state is directed. For Gregory says (*Pastor.* ii, 1)[4] that "Isaias wishing to be of profit to his neighbour by means of the active life desired the office of preaching, whereas Jeremias, who was fain to hold fast to the love of his Creator, exclaimed against being sent to preach." There-fore it would seem that the religious state is more perfect than the episcopal state.

On the contrary, It is not lawful for anyone to pass from a more excellent to a less excellent

state, for this would be to look back.[5] Yet a man may pass from the religious to the episcopal state, for it is said (XVIII, Q. I, cap. *Statutum*)[6] that "the holy ordination makes a monk to be a bishop." Therefore the episcopal state is more perfect than the religious.

I answer that, As Augustine says (*Gen. ad Lit.* xii, 16),[7] "the agent is ever more excellent than the patient." Now in the genus of perfec-tion according to Dionysius (*Eccl. Hier.* v, vi),[8] bishops are in the position of perfecters, while religious are in the position of being perfected, the former of which pertains to action, and the latter to passion. From this it is evident that the state of perfection is more excellent in bishops than in religious.

Reply Obj. 1. Renunciation of one's posses-sions may be considered in two ways. First, as being actual, and thus it is not essential, but a means, to perfection, as stated above (A. 3). Hence nothing hinders the state of perfection from being without renunciation of one's pos-sessions, and the same applies to other outward practices. Secondly, it may be considered in re-lation to one's preparedness, in the sense of being prepared to renounce or give away all, and this belongs directly to perfection. Hence Augustine says (*De QQ. Evang.* ii, 11).[9] "Our Lord shows that the children of wisdom under-stand righteousness to consist neither in eating nor in abstaining, but in bearing want patient-ly." Hence the Apostle says (Phil. 4. 12): *I know . . . both to abound and to suffer need.* Now bishops especially are bound to despise all things for the honour of God and the spiritual welfare of their flock, when it is necessary for them to do so, either by giving to the poor of their flock, or by suffering with joy the being stripped of their own goods.[10]

Reply Obj. 2. That bishops are busy about things pertaining to the love of their neighbour arises out of the abundance of their love of God. Hence our Lord asked Peter first of all whether he loved Him, and afterwards commit-ted the care of His flock to him. And Gregory says (*Pastor.* i, 5):[11] "If the pastoral care is a proof of love, he who refuses to feed God's flock, though having the means to do so, is con-victed of not loving the supreme Pastor." And it is a sign of greater love if a man devotes

---

[1] Gratian, *Decretum,* PT. II (RF I, 684).
[2] Sect. 3 (PG 3, 534).
[3] *City of God,* XIX, 19 (PL 41, 647).   [4] PL 77, 20.

[5] Cf. Luke, 9.62.
[6] Gratian, *Dectretum,* PT. II (RF I, 828).
[7] PL 34, 467.
[8] PG 3, 505; 532.
[9] On Luke, 7.35 (PL 35, 1337).
[10] Cf. Heb. 10.34.
[11] PL 77, 19.

himself to others for his friend's sake, than if he be willing only to serve his friend.

Reply Obj. 3. As Gregory says (*Pastor.* ii, 1),[1] "a prelate should be foremost in action, and more uplifted than others in contemplation," because it is incumbent on him to contemplate not only for his own sake, but also for the purpose of instructing others. Hence Gregory applies (*Hom.* v *in Ezech.*)[2] the words of Ps. 144. 7, *They shall publish the memory . . . of Thy sweetness,* to perfect men returning after their contemplation.

ARTICLE 8. *Whether Parish Priests and Archdeacons Are More Perfect Than Religious?*

We proceed thus to the Eighth Article: It seems that also parish priests and archdeacons are more perfect than religious.

Objection 1. For Chrysostom says in his Dialogue, (*De Sacerdot.*, vi):[3] "Take for example a monk, such as Elias, if I may exaggerate somewhat; he is not to be compared with one who, cast among the people and compelled to carry the sins of many, remains firm and strong." A little further on he says: "If I were given the choice, where would I prefer to please, in the priestly office, or in the monastic solitude, without hesitation I should choose the former." Again in the same book he says:[4] "If you compare the toils of this project, namely of the monastic life, with a well-employed priesthood, you will find them as far distant from one another as a common citizen is from a king." Therefore it would seem that priests who have the care of souls are more perfect than religious.

Obj. 2. Further, Augustine says in a letter to Valerius (*Ep.* xxi):[5] "Let thy religious prudence observe that in this life, and especially at these times, there is nothing so difficult, so onerous, so perilous as the office of bishop, priest, or deacon; while in God's sight there is no greater blessing, if one engage in the fight as ordered by our Commander-in-chief." Therefore religious are not more perfect than priests or deacons.

Obj. 3. Further, Augustine says (*Ep.* lx *ad Aurel.*):[6] "It would be most regrettable were we to exalt monks to such a disastrous degree of pride, and deem the clergy deserving of such a grievous insult, as to assert that a bad monk is a good clerk, since sometimes even a good monk makes a bad clerk." And a little before this he says[7] that "God's servants," that is

monks, "must not be allowed to think that they may easily be chosen for something better," namely the clerical state, "if they should thereby become worse," namely by leaving the monastic state. Therefore it would seem that those who are in the clerical state are more perfect than religious.

Obj. 4. Further, It is not lawful to pass from a more perfect to a less perfect state. Yet it is lawful to pass from the monastic state to a priestly office with a charge attached, as appears (XVI, Q. I, cap. 28)[8] from a decree of Pope Gelasius, who says:[9] "If there be a monk, who by the merit of his exemplary life is worthy of the priesthood, and the abbot under whose authority he fights for Christ his King ask that he be made a priest, the bishop shall take him and ordain him in such place as he shall choose fitting." And Jerome says (*Ad Rustic. Monach., Ep.* cxxv):[10] "In the monastery so live as to deserve to be a clerk." Therefore parish priests and archdeacons are more perfect than religious.

Obj. 5. Further, Bishops are in a more perfect state than religious, as shown in the foregoing Article. But parish priests and archdeacons, through having care of souls, are more like bishops than religious are. Therefore they are more perfect.

Obj. 6. Further, virtue is concerned with the difficult and the good, according to the *Ethics.*[11] Now it is more difficult to lead a good life in the office of parish priest or archdeacon than in the religious state. Therefore parish priests and archdeacons have more perfect virtue than religious.

On the contrary, It is stated (XIX, Q. II, cap. *Duæ*):[12] "If a man while governing the people in his church under the bishop and leading a secular life is inspired by the Holy Ghost to desire to work out his salvation in a monastery or under some canonical rule, since he is led by a private law, there is no reason why he should be constrained by a public law." Now a man is not led by the law of the Holy Ghost, which is here called a private law, except to something more perfect. Therefore it would seem that religious are more perfect than archdeacons or parish priests.

I answer that, When we compare things in the point of supereminence, we look not at that in which they agree, but at that in which they

---

[1] PL 77, 26. [2] Bk. I (PL 76, 826).
[3] PG 48, 683. [4] PG 48, 682. [5] PL 33, 88.
[6] PL 33, 228. [7] PL 33, 227.

[8] Gratian, *Decretum* (RF I, 768).
[9] Pseudo-Gelasius, n. 9 (Thiel 613).
[10] PL 22, 1082.
[11] Aristotle, II, 3 (1105[b]9).
[12] Gratian, *Decretum* (RF I, 839).

differ. Now in parish priests and archdeacons three things may be considered, their state, their order, and their office. It belongs to their state that they are seculars, to their order that they are priests or deacons, to their office that they have the care of souls committed to them.

Accordingly, if we compare these with one who is a religious by state, a deacon or priest by order, having the care of souls by office, as many monks and canons regular have, this one will excel in the first point, and in the other points he will be equal. But if the latter differ from the former in state and office, but agree in order, such as religious priests and deacons not having the care of souls, it is evident that the latter will be more excellent than the former in state, less excellent in office, and equal in order.

We must therefore consider which is the greater, pre-eminence of state or of office; and here, it seems, we should take note of two things, goodness and difficulty. Accordingly, if we make the comparison with a view to goodness, the religious state surpasses the office of parish priest or archdeacon, because a religious pledges his whole life to the quest of perfection, while the parish priest or archdeacon does not pledge his whole life to the care of souls, as a bishop does, nor does it belong to him, as it does to a bishop, to exercise the care of souls in chief, but only in certain particulars regarding the care of souls committed to his charge, as stated above (A. 6, Reply 2). Therefore the comparison of their religious state with their office is like the comparisons of the universal with the particular, and of a holocaust with a sacrifice, which is less than a holocaust according to Gregory (*Hom.* viii *in Ezech.*).[1] Hence it is said (xix, Q. I, cap. 1):[2] "Clerics who wish to take the monastic vows through being desirous of a better life must be allowed by their bishops the free entrance into the monastery."

This comparison, however, must be considered as regarding the genus of the deed; for as regards the charity of the doer it happens sometimes that a deed which is of less account in its genus is of greater merit if it be done out of greater charity.

On the other hand, if we consider the difficulty of leading a good life in religion and in the office of one having the care of souls, in this way it is more difficult to lead a good life together with the exercise of the care of souls, on account of outward dangers, although the re-

ligious life is more difficult as regards the genus of the deed, by reason of the strictness of religious observance.

If, however, the religious is also without orders, as in the case of religious lay brethren, then it is evident that the pre-eminence of order excels in the point of dignity, since by holy orders a man is appointed to the most august ministry of serving Christ Himself in the sacrament of the altar. For this requires a greater inward holiness than that which is requisite for the religious state, since as Dionysius says (*Eccles. Hier.* vi)[3] "the monastic order must follow the priestly orders, and ascend to Divine things in imitation of them." Hence, other things being equal, a cleric who is in holy orders sins more grievously if he does something contrary to holiness than a religious who is not in holy orders, although a religious who is not in orders is bound to regular observance to which persons in holy orders are not bound.

Reply Obj. 1. We might answer briefly these quotations from Chrysostom by saying that he does not speak of a priest of lesser order who has the care of souls, but of a bishop, who is called a high-priest; and this agrees with the purpose of that book in which he consoles himself and Basil in that they were chosen to be bishops.

We may, however, pass this over and reply that he speaks in view of the difficulty. For he had already said (cap. 6):[4] "When the pilot is surrounded by the stormy sea and is able to bring the ship safely out of the tempest, then he deserves to be acknowledged by all as a perfect pilot"; and afterwards he concludes, as quoted above in the objection, with regard to the monk, "who is not to be compared with one who, cast among the people, . . . remains firm"; and he gives the reason why, because "both in the calm and in the storm he piloted himself to safety." This proves nothing more than that the state of one who has the cure of souls is fraught with more danger than the monastic state; and to keep oneself innocent in face of a greater peril is proof of greater virtue. On the other hand, it also indicates greatness of virtue if a man avoid dangers by entering religion; hence he does not say that he would prefer to have the priestly office to being in the monastic solitude, but that he would rather please in the former than in the latter, since this is a proof of greater virtue.

Reply Obj. 2. This passage quoted from Au-

---

[1] PL 76, 1037.
[2] Gratian, *Decretum* (RF I, 839).
[3] Sect. I (PG 3, 533).
[4] PG 48, 683.

gustine also clearly refers to the question of difficulty which proves the greatness of virtue in those who lead a good life, as stated above (reply 1).

Reply Obj. 3. Augustine there compares monks with clerics as regards the pre-eminence of order, not as regards the distance between religious and secular life.

Reply Obj. 4. Those who are taken from the religious state to receive the care of souls, being already in sacred orders, attain to something they had not hitherto, namely the office of the care of souls, yet they do not put aside what they had already. For it is said in the *Decretals* (XVI, Q. 1, cap. 3):[1] "With regard to those monks who after long residence in a monastery attain to the order of clerics, we bid them not to lay aside their former purpose."

On the other hand, parish priests and archdeacons, when they enter religion, resign their charge, in order to attain to the state of perfection. This very fact shows the excellence of the religious life. When religious who are not in orders are admitted to the clerical state and to the sacred orders, they are clearly promoted to something better, as stated in the Fourth Objection; this is indicated by the very way in which Jerome expresses himself: "So live in the monastery as to deserve to be a clerk."

Reply Obj. 5. Parish priests and archdeacons are more like bishops than religious are, in a certain respect, namely as regards the care of souls which they have in a secondary way; but as regards the obligation in perpetuity, religious are more like a bishop, as appears from what we have said above (AA. 5. 6).

Reply Obj. 6. The difficulty that arises from the arduousness of the deed adds to the perfection of virtue; but the difficulty that results from outward obstacles sometimes lessens the perfection of virtue,—for instance when a man does not love virtue so much as to wish to avoid the obstacles to virtue, according to the saying of the Apostle (I Cor. 9. 25), *Everyone that striveth for the mastery refraineth himself from all things;* and sometimes it is a sign of more perfect virtue,—for instance when a man does not forsake virtue, although he is hindered in the practice of virtue unawares or by some unavoidable cause. In the religious state there is greater difficulty arising from the arduousness of deeds; but for those who in any way at all live in the world, there is greater difficulty resulting from obstacles to virtue, which obstacles the religious has had the foresight to avoid.

[1] Gratian, *Decretum* (RF 1, 762).

QUESTION CLXXXV
Of things pertaining to the
EPISCOPAL STATE
(*In Eight Articles*)

We must now consider things pertaining to the episcopal state. Under this head there are eight points of inquiry: (1) Whether it is lawful to desire the office of a bishop? (2) Whether it is lawful to refuse the office of bishop definitively? (3) Whether the better man should be chosen for the episcopal office? (4) Whether a bishop may pass over to the religious state? (5) Whether he may lawfully abandon his subjects in a bodily manner? (6) Whether he can have anything of his own? (7) Whether he sins mortally by not distributing ecclesiastical goods to the poor? (8) Whether religious who are appointed to the episcopal office are bound to religious observances?

ARTICLE 1. *Whether It Is Lawful To Desire the Office of a Bishop?*

We proceed thus to the First Article: It seems that it is lawful to desire the office of a bishop.

Objection 1. For the Apostle says (I Tim. 3. 1): *He that desires* (Vulg., —*If a man desire*) *the office of a bishop, he desireth a good work.* Now it is lawful and praiseworthy to desire a good work. Therefore it is even praiseworthy to desire the office of a bishop.

Obj. 2. Further, The episcopal state is more perfect than the religious, as we have said above (Q. CLXXXIV, A. 7). But it is praiseworthy to desire to enter the religious state. Therefore it is also praiseworthy to desire promotion to the episcopal state.

Obj. 3. Further, It is written (Prov. 11. 26): *He that hideth up corn shall be cursed among the people; but a blessing upon the head of them that sell.* Now a man who is apt, both in manner of life and by knowledge, for the episcopal office, would seem to hide up the spiritual wheat, if he shuns the episcopal state, but by accepting the episcopal office he enters the state of a dispenser of spiritual wheat. Therefore it would seem praiseworthy to desire the office of a bishop, and blameworthy to refuse it.

Obj. 4. Further, The deeds of the saints related in Holy Writ are set before us as an example, according to Rom. 15. 4, *What things soever were written, were written for our learning.* Now we read (Isa. 6. 8) that Isaias offered himself for the office of preacher, which belongs chiefly to bishops. Therefore it would seem praiseworthy to desire the office of a bishop.

On the contrary, Augustine says:[1] "The higher place, without which the people cannot be ruled, though it be filled becomingly, is unbecomingly desired."

I answer that, Three things may be considered in the episcopal office. One is principal and final, namely the bishop's work, by which the good of our neighbour is intended, according to John 21. 17, *Feed My sheep.* Another thing is the height of degree, for a bishop is placed above others, according to Matt. 24. 45, *A faithful and a wise servant, whom his lord hath appointed over his family.* The third is something resulting from these, namely reverence, honour, and a sufficiency of temporalities, according to I Tim. 5. 17, *Let the priests that rule well be esteemed worthy of double honour.*

Accordingly, to desire the episcopal office on account of these incidental goods is manifestly unlawful, and pertains to covetousness or ambition. Therefore our Lord said against the Pharisees (Matt. 23. 6, 7): *They love the first places at feasts, and the first chairs in the synagogues, and salutations in the market-place, and to be called by men, Rabbi.* As regards the second, namely the height of degree, it is presumptuous to desire the episcopal office. Hence our Lord reproved His disciples for seeking precedence, by saying to them (Matt. 20. 25): *You know that the princes of the gentiles lord it over them.* Here Chrysostom says (*Hom.* LXV *in Matt.*)[2] that in these words He points out that it is heathenish to seek precedence; and thus by comparing them to the gentiles He converted their impetuous soul.

On the other hand, to desire to do good to one's neighbour is in itself praiseworthy, and virtuous. Nevertheless, since considered as an episcopal act it has height of degree attached to it, it would seem that, unless there be manifest and urgent reason for it, it would be presumptuous for any man to desire to be set over others in order to do them good. Thus Gregory says (*Pastor.* i, 8)[3] that "it was praiseworthy to seek the office of a bishop when it was certain to bring one into graver dangers." Therefore it was not easy to find a person to accept this burden, especially seeing that it is through the zeal of charity that one is divinely instigated to do so, according to Gregory, who says (*Pastor.* i, 7)[4] that "Isaias being desirous of

profiting his neighbour, commendably desired the office of preacher."

Nevertheless anyone may, without presumption, desire to do such works if he should happen to be in that office, or to be worthy of doing them, so that the object of his desire is the good work and not the precedence in dignity. Hence Chrysostom says:[5] "It is indeed good to desire a good work, but to desire the primacy of honour is vanity. For primacy seeks one that shuns it, and abhors one that desires it."

Reply Obj. 1. As Gregory says (*Pastor.* i, 8),[6] "when the Apostle said this he who was set over the people was the first to be dragged to the torments of martyrdom," so that there was nothing to be desired in the episcopal office, save the good work. Therefore Augustine says[7] that when the Apostle said, "Whoever desireth the office of bishop, desireth a good work," he wished to explain that "the episcopacy signifies work and not honour. For it is a Greek word, ἐπί denoting 'over' and σκόπος 'watching.' Therefore if we like we may render ἐπισκοπεῖν by the Latin 'superintendere' (to watch over), that a man may know himself to be no bishop if he loves to precede rather than to profit others." For, as he observed shortly before, "in our actions we should seek, not honour nor power in this life, since all things beneath the sun are vanity, but the work itself which that honour or power enables us to do." Nevertheless, as Gregory says (*Pastor., loc. cit.*), "the Apostle while praising the desire (namely of the good work) forthwith turns this object of praise into one of fear, when he adds: *It behoveth . . . a bishop to be blameless,*" as though to say: "I praise what you seek, but learn first what it is you seek."

Reply Obj. 2. There is no parity between the religious and the episcopal state, for two reasons. First because perfection of life is a prerequisite of the episcopal state, as appears from our Lord asking Peter if he loved Him more than the others, before committing the pastoral office to him, while perfection is not a prerequisite of the religious state, since the latter is the way to perfection. Hence our Lord did not say (Matt. 19. 21): *If thou art perfect, go, sell all* (Vulg.,—*what*) *thou hast,* but *If thou wilt be perfect.* The reason for this difference is because, according to Dionysius

---

[1] *City of God,* XIX, 19 (PL 41, 647).
[2] PG 58, 622.
[3] PL 77, 21.   [4] PL 77, 20.

[5] The quotation is from the *Opus Imperf. In Matt., Hom.* XXXV. (PG 56, 830), falsely ascribed to St. John Chrysostom.   [6] PL 77, 21.
[7] *City of God,* XIX, 19 (PL 41, 647).

(*Eccles. Hier.* v),[1] perfection pertains actively to the bishop, as the perfecter, but to the monk passively as one who is perfected; and one needs to be perfect in order to bring others to perfection, but not in order to be brought to perfection. Now it is presumptuous to think oneself perfect, but it is not presumptuous to tend to perfection.

Secondly, because he who enters the religious state subjects himself to others for the sake of a spiritual profit, and anyone may lawfully do this. Therefore Augustine says:[2] "No man is debarred from striving for the knowledge of truth, since this pertains to a praiseworthy ease." On the other hand, he who enters the episcopal state is raised up in order to watch over others, and no man should seek to be raised thus, according to Heb. 5. 4. *Neither doth any man take the honour to himself, but he that is called by God;* and Chrysostom says:[3] "To desire supremacy in the Church is neither just nor useful. For what wise man seeks of his own accord to submit to such servitude and peril, as to have to render an account of the whole Church? None save him who fears not God's judgment, and makes a secular abuse of his ecclesiastical authority, by turning it to secular uses."

Reply Obj. 3. The dispensing of spiritual wheat is not to be carried on in an arbitrary fashion, but chiefly according to the appointment and disposition of God, and in the second place according to the appointment of the higher prelates, in whose person it is said (I Cor. 4. 1): *Let a man so account of us as of the ministers of Christ, and the dispensers of the mysteries of God.* Therefore a man is not understood to hide spiritual wheat if he avoids governing or correcting others, and is not able to do so, neither in virtue of his office nor of his superior's command; thus alone is he understood to hide it when he neglects to dispense it while under obligation to do so in virtue of his office, or obstinately refuses to accept the office when it is imposed on him. Hence Augustine says:[4] "The love of truth seeks a holy leisure, the demands of charity undertake an honest labour. If no one imposes this burden upon us, we must devote ourselves to the research and contemplation of truth, but if it be imposed on us, we must bear it because charity demands it of us."

[1] Sect. 6 (PG 3, 513); cf. VI, 3 (PG 3, 532).
[2] *Loc. cit.*
[3] *Opus Imperf. in Matt.,* Hom., XXXV, (PG 56, 830) falsely ascribed to St. John Chrysostom.
[4] *Loc. cit.*

Reply Obj. 4. As Gregory says (*Pastor.* i, 7),[5] "Isaias, who wishing to be sent, knew himself to be already cleansed by the live coal taken from the altar, shows us that no one should dare uncleansed to approach the sacred ministry. Since then it is very difficult for anyone to be able to know that he is cleansed, it is safer to decline the office of preacher."

ARTICLE 2. *Whether It Is Lawful for a Man To Refuse Absolutely an Appointment to the Episcopate?*

We proceed thus to the Second Article: It seems that it is lawful to refuse absolutely an appointment to the episcopate.

Objection 1. For as Gregory says (*Pastor.* i, 7),[6] "Isaias wishing to be of profit to his neighbour by means of the active life, desired the office of preaching, but Jeremias who was fain to hold fast to the love of his Creator exclaimed against being sent to preach." Now no man sins by being unwilling to forgo better things in order to adhere to things that are not so good. Since then the love of God surpasses the love of our neighbour, and the contemplative life is preferable to the active, as shown above (Q. XXVI, A. 2; CLXXXII, A. 1) it would seem that a man does not sin if he refuse absolutely the episcopal office.

Obj. 2. Further, As Gregory says (*Pastor.* i, 7),[7] "it is very difficult for anyone to be able to know that he is cleansed; nor should anyone uncleansed approach the sacred ministry." Therefore if a man perceives that he is not cleansed, however urgently the episcopal office be enjoined him, he ought not to accept it.

Obj. 3. Further, Jerome, in the prologue to his Commentary on Mark, says that "it is related of the Blessed Mark that after receiving the faith he cut off his thumb that he might be excluded from the priesthood."[8] Likewise some take a vow never to accept a bishopric. Now to place an obstacle to a thing amounts to the same as refusing it altogether. Therefore it would seem that one may, without sin, refuse the episcopal office absolutely.

On the contrary, Augustine says (*Ep.* xlviii, *ad Eudox.*):[9] "If Mother Church requires your

[5] PL 77, 20.   [6] PL 77, 20.
[7] PL 77, 20.
[8] From a prologue to the gospel of St. Mark preceding a gloss (v, 89r); cf. *Monarchianische Prologe zu den vier Evangelien,* Corssen, p. 10. For the author cf. Martin, *Historisches Jahrbuch* (1927) pp. 237–257. Cf. Lagrange, *Evangile Selon S. Marc,* pp. 25, 26. For the authenticity of the fact cf. *Acta Sanctorum,* Acta S. Marci, 23 April, prol. (BL XII, 349C).   [9] PL 33, 188.

service, neither accept with greedy conceit, nor refuse with fawning indolence"; and afterwards he adds: "Nor prefer your ease to the needs of the Church; for if no good men were willing to assist her in her labour, you would seek in vain how we could be born of her."

I answer that, Two things have to be considered in the acceptance of the episcopal office: first, what a man may fittingly desire according to his own will; secondly, what is proper for a man to do according to the will of another. As regards his own will it becomes a man to look chiefly to his own spiritual welfare, but that he look to the spiritual welfare of others becomes a man according to the appointment of another having authority, as stated above (A. I, Reply 3). Hence just as it is a mark of an inordinate will that a man of his own choice incline to be appointed to the government of others, so too it indicates an inordinate will if a man definitively refuse that office of government in direct opposition to the appointment of his superior, and this for two reasons.

First, because this is contrary to the love of our neighbour, for whose good a man should offer himself according as place and time demand; hence Augustine says[1] that "the demands of charity undertake an honest labour." Secondly, because this is contrary to humility, by which a man submits to his superior's commands; hence Gregory says (*Pastor.* i, 6):[2] "In God's sight humility is true when it does not obstinately refuse to submit to what is usefully prescribed."

Reply Obj. I. Although simply and absolutely speaking the contemplative life is more excellent than the active, and the love of God better than the love of our neighbour, yet, on the other hand, the good of the many should be preferred to the good of the individual. Therefore Augustine says in the passage quoted above: "Nor prefer your own ease to the needs of the Church," and all the more since it belongs to the love of God that a man undertake the pastoral care of Christ's sheep. Hence Augustine, commenting on John 21. 17, *Feed My sheep,* says (*Tract.* cxxiii *in Joann.*):[3] "Be it the task of love to feed the Lord's flock, even as it was the mark of fear to deny the Shepherd."

Moreover prelates are not transferred to the active life, so as to forsake the contemplative; and so Augustine says[4] that "if the burden of the pastoral office be imposed, we must not

abandon the delights of truth," which are derived from contemplation.

Reply Obj. 2. No one is bound to obey his superior by doing what is unlawful, as appears from what was said above concerning obedience (Q. CIV, A. 5). Accordingly it may happen that he who is appointed to the office of prelate perceives something in himself on account of which it is unlawful for him to accept a prelacy. But this obstacle may sometimes be removed by the very person who is appointed to the pastoral cure—for instance, if he have a purpose to sin, he may abandon it—and for this reason he is not excused from being bound to obey definitely the superior who has appointed him.

Sometimes, however, he is unable himself to remove the impediment that makes the pastoral office unlawful to him, yet the prelate who appoints him can do so—for instance, if he be irregular or excommunicate. In such a case he ought to make known his defect to the prelate who has appointed him, and if the latter be willing to remove the impediment, he is bound humbly to obey. Hence when Moses had said (Exod. 4. 10): *I beseech thee, Lord, I am not eloquent from yesterday, and the day before,* the Lord answered (*verse* 12): *I will be in thy mouth, and I will teach thee what thou shalt speak.*

At other times the impediment cannot be removed, neither by the person appointing nor by the one appointed—for instance, if an archbishop be unable to dispense from an irregularity. Therefore a subject, if irregular, would not be bound to obey him by accepting the episcopate or even sacred orders.

Reply Obj. 3. It is not in itself necessary for salvation to accept the episcopal office, but it becomes necessary by reason of the superior's command. Now one may lawfully place an obstacle to things thus necessary for salvation before the command is given; otherwise it would not be lawful to marry a second time, lest one should thus incur an impediment to the episcopate or holy orders. But this would not be lawful in things necessary for salvation. Hence the Blessed Mark did not act against a precept by cutting off his finger, although it is credible that he did this by the instigation of the Holy Ghost, without which it would be unlawful for anyone to lay hands on himself.

If a man take a vow not to accept the bishop's office, and by this intend to bind himself not even to accept it in obedience to his superior prelate, his vow is unlawful. But if he intend to bind himself so far as it lies with him

---

[1] *City of God,* XIX, 19 (PL 41, 647).　　[2] PL 77, 19.
[3] PL 35, 1967.　　[4] *Op. cit.,* XIX, 19 (PL 41, 648).

not to seek the episcopal office, nor to accept it except under urgent necessity, his vow is lawful, because he vows to do what it becomes a man to do.

ARTICLE 3. *Whether He That Is Appointed to the Episcopate Ought To Be Better Than Others?*

We proceed thus to the Third Article: It seems that one who is appointed to the episcopate ought to be better than others.

Objection 1. For our Lord, when about to commit the pastoral office to Peter, asked him if he loved Him more than the others. Now a man is the better through loving God the more. Therefore it would seem that one ought not to be appointed to the episcopal office except he be better than others.

Obj. 2. Further, Pope Symmachus says (cap. *Vilissimus*, i, qu. 1):[1] "A man is of very little worth who though excelling in dignity, excels not in knowledge and holiness." Now he who excels in knowledge and holiness is better. Therefore a man ought not to be appointed to the episcopate unless he be better than others.

Obj. 3. Further, In every genus the lesser are governed by the greater, as corporeal things are governed by things spiritual, and the lower bodies by the higher, as Augustine says (*De Trin.* iii, 4).[2] Now a bishop is appointed to govern others. Therefore he should be better than others.

On the contrary, The Decretal says (cap *Cum dilectus, de electione,* etc.)[3] that "it suffices to choose a good man, nor is it necessary to choose the better man."

I answer that, In designating a man for the episcopal office, something has to be considered on the part of the person designate, and something on the part of the designator. For on the part of the designator, whether by election or by appointment, it is required that he choose such a one as will dispense the divine mysteries faithfully. These should be dispensed for the good of the Church, according to I Cor. 14. 12, *Seek to abound unto the edifying of the Church,* and the divine mysteries are not committed to men for their own reward, which they should await in the life to come. Consequently he who has to choose or appoint one for a bishop, is not bound to take one who is best absolutely, that is, according to charity, but one who is best for governing the Church, one namely who is able to

instruct, defend, and govern the Church peacefully. Hence Jerome, commenting on Tit. 1. 5, *Ordain . . . in every city,* says against certain persons that "some seek to erect as pillars of the Church, not those whom they know to be more useful to the Church, but those whom they love more, or those by whose obsequiousness they have been cajoled or undone, or for whom some person in authority has spoken, and, not to say worse than this, have succeeded by means of gifts in being made clerics."[4]

Now this pertains to the receiving of persons, which in such matters is a grave sin. Hence a gloss on James 2. 1, *Brethren, have not . . . with respect of persons,* says: "If this distinction of sitting and standing be referred to ecclesiastical honours, we must not deem it a slight sin to 'have the faith of the Lord of glory with respect of persons.' For who would suffer a rich man to be chosen for the Church's seat of honour, in despite of a poor man who is better instructed and holier?"[5]

On the part of the person appointed, it is not required that he esteem himself better than others, for this would be proud and presumptuous, but it suffices that he perceive nothing in himself which would make it unlawful for him to take up the office of prelate. Hence although Peter was asked by our Lord if he loved Him more than the others, he did not, in his reply, set himself before the others, but answered simply that he loved Christ.

Reply Obj. 1. Our Lord knew that, by His own bestowal, Peter was in other respects fitted to govern the Church, and therefore He questioned him about his greater love, to show that when we find a man otherwise fitted for the government of the Church, we must look chiefly to his pre-eminence in the love of God.

Reply Obj. 2. This statement refers to the pursuits of the man who is placed in authority. For he should aim at showing himself to be more excellent than others in both knowledge and holiness. Therefore Gregory says (*Pastor.* ii, 1)[6] "the occupations of a prelate ought to excel those of the people as much as the shepherd's life excels that of his flock." But he is not to be blamed and looked upon as worthless if he excelled not before being raised to the prelacy.

Reply Obj. 3. According to I Cor. 12. 4 *seq., there are diversities of graces, . . . and . . . of*

---

[1] Gratian, *Decretum,* PT. II (RF I, 376).
[2] PL 42, 873.
[3] *Decretal. Gregor.,* IX, BK. I, VI, 32 (RF II, 78).

[4] PL 26, 596; Cf. Gratian, *Decretum,* II, VIII, Q. I, 6 RF I, 591).
[5] *Glossa ordin.* (VI, 212A); Augustine, *Epist.,* CLXVII, 5 (PL 33, 740).   [6] PL 77, 20.

ministries . . . and . . . of operations. Hence nothing hinders one from being more fitted for the office of governing who does not excel in the grace of holiness. It is otherwise in the government of the natural order, where that which is higher in the natural order is for that very reason more fitted to dispose of those that are lower.

ARTICLE 4. *Whether a Bishop May Lawfully Forsake the Episcopal Charge in Order To Enter Religion?*

We proceed thus to the Fourth Article: It seems that a bishop cannot lawfully forsake his episcopal charge in order to enter religion.

Objection 1. For no one can lawfully pass from a more perfect to a less perfect state, since this is to look back, which is condemned by the words of our Lord (Luke 9. 62), *No man putting his hand to the plough, and looking back, is fit for the kingdom of God.* Now the episcopal state is more perfect than the religious, as shown above (Q. CLXXXIV, A. 7). Therefore just as it is unlawful to return to the world from the religious state, so is it unlawful to pass from the episcopal to the religious state.

Obj. 2. Further, The order of grace is more congruous than the order of nature. Now according to nature a thing is not moved in contrary directions; thus if a stone be naturally moved downwards, it cannot naturally return upwards from below. But according to the order of grace it is lawful to pass from the religious to the episcopal state. Therefore it is not lawful to pass contrariwise from the episcopal to the religious state.

Obj. 3. Further, In the works of grace nothing should be inoperative. Now when once a man is consecrated bishop he retains in perpetuity the spiritual power of giving orders and doing like things that pertain to the episcopal office, and this power would seem to remain inoperative in one who gives up the episcopal charge. Therefore it would seem that a bishop may not forsake the episcopal charge and enter religion.

On the contrary, No man is compelled to do what is in itself unlawful. Now those who seek to resign their episcopal charge are compelled to resign (Extrav. *de Renunt.,* cap. *Quidam*).[1] Therefore apparently it is not unlawful to give up the episcopal charge.

I answer that, The perfection of the episcopal state consists in this that for love of God a man binds himself to work for the salvation of his neighbour, and therefore he is bound to retain the pastoral charge so long as he is able to procure the spiritual welfare of the subjects entrusted to his care, a matter which he must not neglect—neither for the sake of the quiet of divine contemplation, since the Apostle, on account of the needs of his subjects, suffered patiently to be delayed even from the contemplation of the life to come, according to Philip 1. 22-25, *What I shall choose I know not, but I am straitened between two, having a desire to be dissolved, and to be with Christ, a thing by far better. But to abide still in the flesh is needful for you. And having this confidence, I know that I shall abide;* nor for the sake of avoiding any hardships or of acquiring any gain whatsoever, because as it is written (John 10. 11), *the good shepherd giveth his life for his sheep.*

At times, however, it happens in several ways that a bishop is hindered from procuring the spiritual welfare of his subjects. Sometimes on account of his own defect, either of conscience (for instance if he be guilty of murder or simony), or of body (for example if he be old or infirm), or of irregularity arising, for instance, from bigamy. Sometimes he is hindered through some defect in his subjects, whom he is unable to profit. Hence Gregory says (*Dial.* ii, 3):[2] "The wicked must be borne patiently, when there are some good who can be succoured, but when there is no profit at all for the good, it is sometimes useless to labour for the wicked. Therefore the perfect when they find that they labour in vain are often minded to go elsewhere in order to labour with fruit." Sometimes again this hindrance arises on the part of others, as when scandal results from a certain person being in authority, for the Apostle says (I Cor. 8. 13): *If meat scandalize my brother, I will never eat flesh:* provided, however the scandal is not caused by the wickedness of persons desirous of subverting the faith or the justice of the Church, because the pastoral charge is not to be laid aside on account of scandal of this kind, according to Matt. 15. 14, *Let them alone,* those namely who were scandalized at the truth of Christ's teaching, *they are blind, and leaders of the blind.*

Nevertheless just as a man takes upon himself the charge of authority at the appointment of a higher superior, so too he should be subject to the latter's authority in laying aside the accepted charge for the reasons given above.

---

[1] *Decretal. Gregor.,* IX, I, V, chap. 12 (RF II, 113).   [2] PL 66, 138.

Hence Innocent III. says (Extrav. *de Renunt.*, cap. *Nisi cum pridem*):[1] "Though thou hast wings wherewith thou art anxious to fly away into solitude, they are so tied by the bonds of authority that thou art not free to fly without our permission." For the Pope alone can dispense from the perpetual vow, by which a man binds himself to the care of his subjects, when he took upon himself the episcopal office.

Reply Obj. 1. The perfection of religious and that of bishops are gauged from different standpoints. For it pertains to the perfection of a religious to occupy oneself in working out one's own salvation, while it pertains to the perfection of a bishop to occupy oneself in working for the salvation of others. Hence so long as a man can be useful to the salvation of his neighbour, he would be going back if he wished to pass to the religious state, to busy himself only with his own salvation, since he has bound himself to work not only for his own but also for others' salvation. Therefore Innocent III. says in the Decretal quoted above[2] that "it is more easily allowable for a monk to ascend to the episcopacy than for a bishop to descend to the monastic life." If, however, he be unable to procure the salvation of others it is proper that he should seek his own.

Reply Obj. 2. On account of no obstacle should a man forego the work of his own salvation, which pertains to the religious state. But there may be an obstacle to the procuring of another's salvation, and therefore a monk may be raised to the episcopal state in which he is able also to work out his own salvation. And a bishop, if he be hindered from procuring the salvation of others, may enter the religious life, and may return to his bishopric should the obstacle cease, for instance by the correction of his subjects, cessation of the scandal, healing of his infirmity, removal of his ignorance by sufficient instruction. Again, if he owed his promotion to simony of which he was in ignorance, and resigning his episcopate entered the religious life, he can be reappointed to another bishopric. On the other hand, if a man be deposed from the episcopal office for some sin and confined in a monastery that he may do penance, he cannot be reappointed to a bishopric. Hence it is stated (VII, Q. I, cap. *Hoc nequaquam*):[3] "The holy synod orders that any man who has been degraded from the episcopal dignity to the monastic life and a

place of repentance, should by no means rise again to the episcopate."

Reply Obj. 3. Even in natural things power remains inactive on account of a supervening obstacle, for instance the act of sight ceases through an affliction of the eye. So neither is it unreasonable if, on account of a supervening impediment, the episcopal power remain without the exercise of its act.

ARTICLE 5. *Whether It Is Lawful for a Bishop on Account of Bodily Persecution To Abandon the Flock Committed to His Care?*

We proceed thus to the Fifth Article: It seems that it is unlawful for a bishop, on account of some temporal persecution, to withdraw his bodily presence from the flock committed to his care.

Objection 1. For our Lord said (John 10. 12) that he is a hireling and no true shepherd, who *seeth the wolf coming, and leaveth the sheep and flieth;* and Gregory says (*Hom.* xiv *in Ev.*)[4] that "the wolf comes upon the sheep when any man by his injustice and robbery oppresses the faithful and the humble." Therefore if, on account of the persecution of a tyrant, a bishop withdraws his bodily presence from the flock entrusted to his care, it would seem that he is a hireling and not a shepherd.

Obj. 2. Further, It is written (Prov. 6. 1): *My son, if thou be surety for thy friend, thou hast engaged fast thy hand to a stranger,* and afterwards (*verse* 3): *Run about, make haste, stir up thy friend.* Gregory expounds these words and says (*Pastor.* iii, 4):[5] "To be surety for a friend, is to come to the aid of the soul in danger. And whoever is put forward as an example to the lives of others, is warned not only to watch but also to support his friend." Now he cannot do this if he withdraw his bodily presence from his flock. Therefore it would seem that a bishop should not on account of persecution withdraw his bodily presence from his flock.

Obj. 3. Further, it belongs to the perfection of the bishop's state that he devote himself to the care of his neighbour. Now it is unlawful for one who has professed the state of perfection to forsake altogether the things that pertain to perfection. Therefore it would seem unlawful for a bishop to withdraw his bodily presence from the execution of his office, except perhaps for the purpose of devoting himself to works of perfection in a monastery.

On the contrary, Our Lord commanded the

---

[1] Cf. *Decretal Gregor.*, IX, I, 9, chap. 10 (RF II, 112).
[2] RF II, 111.
[3] Gratian, *Decretum.*, PT. II (RF I, 585).

[4] Bk. I (PL 76, 1128).   [5] PL 77, 54.

apostles, whose successors bishops are (Matt. 10. 23): *When they shall persecute you in this city, flee into another.*

I answer that, In any obligation the chief thing to be considered is the end of the obligation. Now bishops bind themselves to fulfil the pastoral office for the sake of the salvation of their subjects. Consequently when the salvation of his subjects demands the personal presence of the pastor, the pastor should not withdraw his personal presence from his flock, neither for the sake of some temporal advantage nor even on account of some impending danger to his person, since the good shepherd is bound to lay down his life for his sheep.

On the other hand, if the salvation of his subjects can be sufficiently provided for by another person in the absence of the pastor, it is lawful for the pastor to withdraw his bodily presence from his flock, either for the sake of some advantage to the Church, or on account of some danger to his person. Hence Augustine says (*Ep.* ccxxviii, *ad Honorat.*):[1] "Christ's servants may flee from one city to another when one of them is specially sought out by persecutors, in order that the Church be not abandoned by others who are not so sought for. When, however, the same danger threatens all, those who stand in need of others must not be abandoned by those whom they need." For "if it is dangerous for the helmsman to leave the ship when the sea is calm, how much more so when it is stormy," as Pope Nicholas I. says[2] and it is repeated in VII, 1 can. 47.[3]

Reply Obj. 1. To flee as a hireling is to prefer temporal advantage or one's bodily welfare to the spiritual welfare of one's neighbour. Hence Gregory says (*loc. cit.*): "A man cannot endanger himself for the sake of his sheep if he uses his authority over them not through love of them but for the sake of earthly gain; and so he fears to stand in the way of danger lest he lose what he loves." But he who, in order to avoid danger, leaves the flock without endangering the flock, does not flee as a hireling.

Reply Obj. 2. If he who is surety for another be unable to fulfil his engagement, it suffices that he fulfil it through another. Hence if a superior is hindered from attending personally to the care of his subjects, he fulfils his obligation if he do so through another.

Reply Obj. 3. When a man is appointed to a bishopric he embraces the state of perfection

as regards one kind of perfection; and if he be hindered from its practice he is not bound to another kind of perfection, so as to be obliged to enter the religious state. Yet he is under the obligation of retaining the intention of devoting himself to his neighbour's salvation, should an opportunity offer, and necessity require it of him.

ARTICLE 6. *Whether It Is Lawful for a Bishop To Have Property of His Own?*

We proceed thus to the Sixth Article: It seems that it is not lawful for a bishop to have property of his own.

Objection 1. For our Lord said (Matt. 19. 21): *If thou wilt be perfect, go sell all* (Vulg., —what) *thou hast, and give to the poor . . . and come, follow Me;* hence it would seem to follow that voluntary poverty is requisite for perfection. Now bishops are in the state of perfection. Therefore it would seem unlawful for them to possess anything as their own.

Obj. 2. Further, Bishops take the place of the apostles in the Church, according to a gloss on Luke 10. 1.[4] Now our Lord commanded the apostles to possess nothing of their own, according to Matt. 10. 9, *Do not possess gold, nor silver, nor money in your purses;* hence Peter said for himself and the other apostles (Matt. 19. 27): *Behold we have left all things and have followed Thee.* Therefore it would seem that bishops are bound to keep this command, and to possess nothing of their own.

Obj. 3. Further, Jerome says (*Ep. ad Nepotian.*):[5] "The Greek κλῆρος denotes the Latin '*sors.*' Hence clerics are so called either they are of the Lord's estate, or because the Lord Himself is the estate, that is, portion of clerics. Now he that possesses the Lord can have nothing beside God; and if he have gold and silver, possessions, and chattels of all kinds, with such a portion the Lord does not vouchsafe to be his portion also." Therefore it would seem that not only bishops but even clerics should have nothing of their own.

On the contrary, It is stated (XII, Q. 1, cap. 19):[6] "Bishops, if they wish, may bequeath to their heirs their personal or acquired property, and whatever belongs to them personally."

I answer that, No one is bound to works of supererogation, unless he binds himself specially thereto by vow. Hence Augustine says (*Ep.* cxxvii, *ad Paulin. et Arment.*):[7] "Since

---

[1] PL 33, 1014.
[2] *Epist. Ad Huntfridum Episc.* (MA xv, 399).
[3] Gratian, *Decretum.* pt. ii (RF i, 586).

[4] *Glossa ordin.* (v, 151E); Bede (PL 92, 461).
[5] *Epist.*, lii (PL 22, 531).
[6] Gratian, *Decretum.*, pt. ii (RF i, 684).   [7] PL 33, 487.

you have taken the vow you have already bound yourself, you can no longer do otherwise. Before you were bound by the vow you were free to submit." Now it is evident that to live without possessing anything is a work of supererogation, for it is a matter not of precept but of counsel. Therefore our Lord after saying to the young man: *If thou wilt enter into life, keep the commandments*, said afterwards by way of addition: *If thou wilt be perfect go sell all that thou hast, and give to the poor* (Matt. 19. 17, 21). Bishops, however, do not bind themselves at their ordination to live without possessions of their own; nor indeed does the pastoral office, to which they bind themselves, make it necessary for them to live without anything of their own. Therefore bishops are not bound to live without possessions of their own.

Reply Obj. 1. As stated above (Q. CLXXXIV, A. 3, REPLY 1) the perfection of the Christian life does not essentially consist in voluntary poverty, but voluntary poverty conduces instrumentally to the perfection of life. Hence it does not follow that where there is greater poverty there is greater perfection; indeed the highest perfection is compatible with great wealth, since Abraham, to whom it was said (Gen. 17. 1): *Walk before Me and be perfect*, is stated to have been rich (*ibid.* 13. 2).

Reply Obj. 2. This saying of our Lord can be understood in three ways. First, mystically, that we should possess neither gold nor silver means that the preacher should not rely chiefly on temporal wisdom and eloquence; thus Jerome expounds the passage in commenting on Matt. 10. 10, *Nor two coats.*[1]

Secondly, according to Augustine's explanation (*De Consens. Ev.* ii, 30),[2] we are to understand that our Lord said this not in command but in permission. For He permitted them to go preaching without gold or silver or other means, since they were to receive the means of livelihood from those to whom they preached; and so He added: *For the workman is worthy of his meat*. And yet if anyone were to use his own means in preaching the Gospel, this would be a work of supererogation, as Paul says in reference to himself (I Cor. 9. 12, 15).

Thirdly, according to the exposition of Chrysostom (*Hom.* ii *in Rom.* 16. 3, *Salute Prisca*),[3] we are to understand that our Lord laid these commands on His disciples in reference to the mission on which they were sent to preach to the Jews, so that they might be encouraged to trust in His power, seeing that He provided for their wants without their having means of their own. But it does not follow from this that they, or their successors, were obliged to preach the Gospel without having means of their own, since we read of Paul (II Cor. 11. 8) that he *received wages* of other churches for preaching to the Corinthians, and therefore it is clear that he possessed something sent to him by others. And it seems foolish to say that so many holy bishops as Athanasius, Ambrose, and Augustine would have disobeyed these commandments if they believed themselves bound to observe them.

Reply Obj. 3. Every part is less than the whole. Accordingly a man has other portions together with God if he becomes less intent on things pertaining to God by occupying himself with things of the world. Now neither bishops nor clerics ought thus to possess means of their own that while busy with their own they neglect those that concern the worship of God.

ARTICLE 7. *Whether Bishops Sin Mortally If They Do Not Distribute to the Poor the Ecclesiastical Goods Which Accrue to Them?*

We proceed thus to the Seventh Article: It seems that bishops sin mortally if they do not distribute to the poor the ecclesiastical goods which they acquire.

Objection 1. For Ambrose expounding Luke 12. 16, *The land of a certain . . . man brought forth plenty of fruits*, says (*Serm.* lxiv, *de Temp.*):[4] "Let no man claim as his own that which he has taken and obtained by violence from the common property in excess of his requirements"; and afterwards he adds: "It is not less criminal to take from him who has, than, when you are able and have plenty, to refuse him who has not." Now it is a mortal sin to take another's property by violence. Therefore bishops sin mortally if they give not to the poor that which they have in excess.

Obj. 2. Further, A gloss of Jerome on Isa. 3. 14, *The spoil of the poor is in your house*, says that ecclesiastical goods belong to the poor.[5] Now whoever keeps for himself or gives to others that which belongs to another, sins mortally and is bound to restitution. Therefore if bishops keep for themselves, or give to their relations or friends, their surplus of ecclesiastical goods, it would seem that they are bound to restitution.

---

[1] PL 26, 65.   [2] PL 34, 1114.   [3] PG 51, 197.

[4] *Serm. Dom.*, VIII *post Pent.* Cf. PL 17, 613–614; cf. Basil, (translation of Rufinus), PG 31, 1752; cf. Gratian, *Decretum*, Pt. I, d. 47, can. 8 (RF I, 171).

[5] *Glossa ordin.* (IV, 12A); Jerome (PL 24, 69).

Obj. 3. Further, Much more may one take what is necessary for oneself from the goods of the Church, than accumulate a surplus from them. Yet Jerome says in a letter to Pope Damasus:[1] "It is right that those clerics who receive no goods from their parents and relations should be supported from the funds of the Church. But those who have sufficient income from their parents and their own possessions, if they take what belongs to the poor, they commit and incur the guilt of sacrilege." Therefore the Apostle says (I Tim. 5. 16): *If any of the faithful have widows, let him minister to them, and let not the Church be charged, that there may be sufficient for them that are widows indeed.* Much more therefore do bishops sin mortally if they give not to the poor the surplus of their ecclesiastical goods.

On the contrary, Many bishops do not give their surplus to the poor, but would seem commendably to lay it out so as to increase the revenue of the Church.

I answer that, The same is not to be said of their own goods which bishops may possess and of ecclesiastical goods. Because they have real dominion over their own goods; therefore from the very nature of the case they are not bound to give these things to others, and may either keep them for themselves or bestow them on others at will. Nevertheless they may sin in this disposal by inordinate affection, which leads them either to accumulate more than they should, or not to assist others in accordance with the demands of charity; yet they are not bound to restitution, because such things are entrusted to their ownership.

On the other hand, they hold ecclesiastical goods as dispensers or trustees. For Augustine says (*Ep.* clxxxv, *ad Bonif.*):[2] "If we possess privately what is enough for us, other things belong not to us but to the poor, and we have the dispensing of them; but we can claim ownership of them only by wicked theft." Now dispensing requires good faith, according to I Cor. 4. 2, *Here now it is required among the dispensers that a man be found faithful.*

Moreover ecclesiastical goods are to be applied not only to the good of the poor, but also to the divine worship and the needs of its ministers. Hence it is said (XII, Q. II, cap. 28):[3] "Of the Church's revenues or the offerings of the faithful only one part is to be assigned to .

the bishop, two parts are to be used by the priest, under pain of suspension, for the ecclesiastical fabric, and for the benefit of the poor; the remaining part is to be divided among the clergy according to their respective merits."

Accordingly if the goods which are assigned to the use of the bishop are distinct from those which are appointed for the use of the poor, or the ministers, or for the ecclesiastical worship, and if the bishop keeps back for himself part of that which should be given to the poor, or to the ministers for their use, or expended on the divine worship, without doubt he is an unfaithful dispenser, sins mortally, and is bound to restitution. But as regards those goods which are deputed to his private use, the same apparently applies as to his own property, namely that he sins through immoderate attachment or use of them if he exceeds moderation in what he keeps for himself, and fails to assist others according to the demands of charity.

On the other hand, if no distinction is made in these goods, their distribution is entrusted to his good faith; and if he fail or exceed in a slight degree, this may happen without prejudice to his good faith, because in such matters a man cannot possibly decide precisely what ought to be done. On the other hand, if the excess be very great he cannot be ignorant of the fact, and consequently he would seem to be lacking in good faith, and is guilty of mortal sin. For it is written (Matt. 24. 48-51) that *if that evil servant shall say in his heart: My lord is long acoming,* which shows contempt of God's judgment, *and shall begin to strike his fellow-servants,* which is a sign of pride, *and shall eat and drink with drunkards,* which proceeds from lust, *the lord of that servant shall come in a day that he hopeth not . . . and shall separate him,* namely from the fellowship of good men, *and appoint his portion with hypocrites,* namely in hell.

Reply Obj. 1. This saying of Ambrose refers to the administration not only of ecclesiastical things but also of any goods whatever from which a man is bound, as a duty of charity, to provide for those who are in need. But it is not possible to state definitely when this need is such as to impose an obligation under pain of mortal sin, as is the case in other points of detail that have to be considered in human acts; for the decision in such matters is left to human prudence.

Reply Obj. 2. As stated in the Article the goods of the Church have to be employed not only for the use of the poor, but also for other

---

[1] Cf. Gratian, *Decretum,* II, I, Q. 2, can. 6 (RF I, 409); causa 16, Q. I, can. 68 (RF I, 785); cf. among the works of Jerome, *Reg. Mon.,* IV (PL 30, 344).
[2] PL 33, 809. [3] Gratian, *Decretum,* PT. II (RF I, 697).

purposes. Hence if a bishop or cleric wish to deprive himself of that which is assigned to his own use and give it to his relations or others, he does not sin so long as he observes moderation, so that, namely, they cease to be in want without thus becoming the richer. Hence Ambrose says (*De Offic.* i, 30):[1] "It is a commendable liberality if you overlook not your kindred when you know them to be in want; yet not so as to wish to make them rich with what you can give to the poor."

Reply Obj. 3. The goods of churches should not all be given to the poor, except in a case of necessity; for then, as Ambrose says (*De Offic.* ii, 28),[2] even the vessels consecrated to the divine worship are to be sold for the ransom of prisoners, and other needs of the poor. In such a case of necessity a cleric would sin if he chose to maintain himself on the goods of the Church, always supposing him to have a patrimony of his own on which to support himself.

Reply Obj. 4. The goods of the churches should be employed for the good of the poor. Consequently a man is to be commended if, there being no present necessity for helping the poor, he spends the surplus from the Church revenue in buying property, or lays it by for some future use connected with the Church or the needs of the poor. But if there be a pressing need for helping the poor, to lay by for the future is a superfluous and inordinate saving, and is forbidden by our Lord Who said (Matt. 6. 34): *Be . . . not solicitous for the morrow.*

ARTICLE 8. *Whether Religious Who Are Raised to the Episcopate Are Bound to Religious Observances?*

We proceed thus to the Eighth Article: It seems that religious who are raised to the episcopate are not bound to religious observances.

Objection 1. For it is said (XVIII, Q. 1, cap, *Statutum*)[3] that "a canonical election loosens a monk from the yoke imposed by the rule of the monastic profession, and the holy ordination makes of a monk a bishop." Now the regular observances pertain to the yoke of the rule. Therefore religious who are appointed bishops are not bound to religious observances.

Obj. 2. Further, He who ascends from a lower to a higher degree does not seem to be bound to those things which pertain to the lower degree; thus it was stated above (Q. LXXXVIII, A.

12, Reply 1) that a religious is not bound to keep the vows he made in the world. But a religious who is appointed to the episcopate ascends to something greater, as stated above (Q. CLXXXIV, A. 7). Therefore it would seem that a bishop is not bound to those things to which he was bound in the state of religion.

Obj. 3. Further, Religious would seem to be bound above all to obedience, and to live without property of their own. But religious who are appointed bishops are not bound to obey the superiors of their order, since they are above them; nor apparently are they bound to poverty, since according to the decree quoted above (obj. 1) "when the holy ordination has made of a monk a bishop he enjoys the right, as the lawful heir, of claiming his paternal inheritance." Moreover they are sometimes allowed to make a will. Much less therefore are they bound to other regular observances.

On the contrary, It is said in the Decretals (XVI, Q. 1, cap. 3):[4] "With regard to those who after long residence in a monastery attain to the order of clerics, we bid them not to lay aside their former purpose."

I answer that, As stated above (A. 1, Reply 2) the religious state pertains to perfection, as a way of tending to perfection, while the episcopal state pertains to perfection as a kind of teacher of perfection. Hence the religious state is compared to the episcopal state as the state of the disciple to that of the master, and as disposition to perfection. Now the disposition is not voided at the advent of perfection, except perhaps as regards what is incompatible with perfection, while as to that in which it is in accord with perfection it is confirmed the more. Thus when the disciple has become a master it is no longer appropriate to him to be a listener, but it is fitting to him to read and meditate even more than before.

Accordingly we must assert that if there be among religious observances any that instead of being an obstacle to the episcopal office are a safeguard of perfection, such as continence, poverty, and so forth, a religious, even after he has been made a bishop, remains bound to observe these, and consequently to wear the habit of his order, which is a sign of this obligation.

On the other hand, a man is not bound to keep such religious observances as may be incompatible with the episcopal office, for instance solitude, silence, and certain severe abstinences or watchings and such as would render him bodily unable to exercise the episcopal office.

---

[1] PL 16, 72; Cf. Gratian, *Decretum,* pt. I. d. 86, can. 16 (RF I, 301).   [2] PL 16, 148; cf. Gratian, *Decretum,* pt. II, causa XII, Q. 2, can. 70 (RF I, 710).
[3] Gratian, *Decretum,* pt. II (RF I, 828).

[4] Gratian, pt. II (RF I, 762).

For the rest he may dispense himself from them, according to the needs of his person or office, and the manner of life of those among whom he dwells, in the same way as religious superiors dispense themselves in such matters.

Reply Obj. 1. He who from being a monk becomes a bishop is loosened from the yoke of the monastic profession not in everything, but in those that are incompatible with the episcopal office, as stated in the Article.

Reply Obj. 2. The vows of those who are living in the world are compared to the vows of religion as the particular to the universal, as stated above (obj. 2). But the vows of religion are compared to the episcopal dignity as disposition to perfection. Now the particular is superfluous when one has the universal, but the disposition is still necessary when perfection has been attained.

Reply Obj. 3. It is accidental that religious who are bishops are not bound to obey the superiors of their order, because, that is, they have ceased to be subjects, even as the latter have ceased to be their religious superiors. Nevertheless the obligation of the vow remains virtually, so that if any person be lawfully set above them they would be bound to obey them, since they are bound to obey both the statutes of their rule in the way mentioned above, and their superiors if they have any.

As to property they cannot in any way have it. For they claim their paternal inheritance not as their own, but as due to the Church. Hence it is added (*ibid.*) that "after he has been ordained bishop at the altar to which he is consecrated and appointed according to the holy canons, he must restore whatever he may acquire."

Nor can he make any will at all, because he is entrusted solely with the administration of things ecclesiastical, and this ends with his death, after which a will comes into force according to the Apostle (Heb. 9. 17). If, however, by the Pope's permission he make a will, he is not to be understood to bequeath property of his own, but we are to understand that by apostolic authority the power of his administration has been prolonged so as to remain in force after his death.

QUESTION CLXXXVI

OF THOSE THINGS IN WHICH THE
RELIGIOUS STATE PROPERLY CONSISTS

(In Ten Articles)

WE must now consider things pertaining to the religious state, which consideration will be four-

fold. In the first place we shall consider those things in which the religious state consists chiefly; secondly, those things which are lawfully befitting to religious (Q. CLXXXVII); thirdly, the different kinds of religious orders (Q. CLXXXVIII); fourthly, the entrance into the religious state (Q. CLXXXIX).

Under the first head there are ten points of inquiry: (1) Whether the religious state is perfect? (2) Whether religious are bound to all the counsels? (3) Whether voluntary poverty is required for the religious state? (4) Whether continence is necessary? (5) Whether obedience is necessary? (6) Whether it is necessary that these should be the matter of a vow? (7) Of the sufficiency of these vows. (8) Of their comparison one with another. (9) Whether a religious sins mortally whenever he transgresses a statute of his rule? (10) Whether, other things being equal, a religious sins more grievously by the same kind of sin than a secular person?

ARTICLE 1. *Whether Religion Implies a State of Perfection?*

We proceed thus to the First Article: It would seem that religion does not imply a state of perfection.

Objection 1. For that which is necessary for salvation does not seem to pertain to perfection. But religion is necessary for salvation, whether because "thereby we are bound (*religamur*) to the one true God," as Augustine says (*De Vera Relig.* 55),[1] or because it takes its name from "our returning (*religimus*) to God Whom we had lost by neglecting Him," according to Augustine.[2] Therefore it would seem that religion does not denote the state of perfection.

Obj. 2. Further, Religion according to Tully (*De Inv. Rhet.* ii, 53)[3] is that "which offers worship and ceremony to the divine nature." Now the offering of worship and ceremony to God would seem to pertain to the ministry of holy orders rather than to the diversity of states, as stated above (Q. XL, A. 2; Q. CLXXXIII, A. 3). Therefore it would seem that religion does not denote the state of perfection.

Obj. 3. Further, The state of perfection is distinct from the state of beginners and that of the proficient. But in religion also some are beginners, and some are proficient. Therefore religion does not denote the state of perfection.

Obj. 4. Further, Religion would seem a place of repentance; for it is said in the Decrees (VII, Q. I, cap. *Hoc nequaquam*):[4] "The holy

[1] PL 34, 172. [2] *City of God*, X, 3 (PL 41, 280).
[3] DD I, 165. [4] Gratian, *Decretum*, pt. II (RF I, 585).

synod orders that any man who has been degraded from the episcopal dignity to the monastic life and a place of repentance should by no means rise again to the episcopate." Now a place of repentance is opposed to the state of perfection; hence Dionysius (*Eccl. Hier.* vi)[1] places penitents in the lowest place, namely among those who are to be cleansed. Therefore it would seem that religion is not the state of perfection.

On the contrary, In the *Conferences of the Fathers* (*Collat.* i. 7)[2] abbot Moses speaking of religious says: "We must recognize that we have to undertake the hunger of fasting, watchings, bodily toil, privation, reading and other acts of virtue in order by these degrees to mount to the perfection of charity." Now things pertaining to human acts are specified and named from the intention of the end. Therefore religious belong to the state of perfection. Moreover Dionysius says (*Eccl. Hier.* vi)[3] that those who are called servants of God by reason of their rendering pure service and subjection to God, are united to the perfection beloved of Him.

I answer that, As stated above (Q. CXLI, A. 2) that which is applicable to many things in common is ascribed antonomastically to that to which it is applicable by way of excellence. Thus the name of fortitude is claimed by the virtue which preserves the firmness of the mind in regard to most difficult things, and the name of temperance by that virtue which tempers the greatest pleasures. Now religion as stated above (Q. LXXXI, A. 2; A. 3, Reply 2) is a virtue by which a man offers something to the service and worship of God. Therefore those who give themselves up entirely to the divine service, as offering a holocaust to God, are called religious antonomastically. Hence Gregory says (*Hom.* viii *in Ezech.*):[4] "Some there are who keep nothing for themselves, but sacrifice to almighty God their tongue, their senses, their life, and the property they possess." Now the perfection of man consists in adhering wholly to God, as stated above (Q. CLXXXIV, A. 2), and in this sense religion denotes the state of perfection.

Reply Obj. 1. To offer something to the worship of God is necessary for salvation, but to offer oneself wholly, and one's possessions, to the worship of God belongs to perfection.

Reply Obj. 2. As stated above (Q. LXXXI, A. 1, Reply 1; A. 4, Reply 1 and 2) when we were

treating of the virtue of religion, religion has reference not only to the offering of sacrifices and other like things that are proper to religion, but also to the acts of all the virtues which, in so far as these are referred to God's service and honour, become acts of religion. Accordingly if a man devotes his whole life to the divine service, his whole life belongs to religion, and thus by reason of the religious life that they lead, those who are in the state of perfection are called religious.

Reply Obj. 3. As stated above (*On the contrary*) religion denotes the state of perfection by reason of the end intended. Hence it does not follow that whoever is in the state of perfection is already perfect, but that he tends to perfection. Hence Origen commenting on Matt. 19. 21, *If thou wilt be perfect*, etc., says (*Tract.* xv *in Matt.*)[5] that "he who has exchanged riches for poverty in order to become perfect does not become perfect at the very moment of giving his goods to the poor; but from that day the contemplation of God will begin to lead him to all the virtues." Thus all are not perfect in religion, but some are beginners, some proficient.

Reply Obj. 4. The religious state was instituted chiefly that we might obtain perfection by means of certain exercises by means of which the obstacles to perfect charity are removed. By the removal of the obstacles of perfect charity, much more are the occasions of sin cut off, for sin destroys charity altogether. Therefore since it pertains to penance to cut out the causes of sin, it follows that the religious state is a most fitting place for penance. Hence (XXXIII, Q. II, cap. *Admonere*)[6] a man who had killed his wife is counselled to enter a monastery which is described as "better and lighter," rather than to do public penance while remaining in the world.

ARTICLE 2. *Whether Every Religious Is Bound To Keep All the Counsels?*

We proceed thus to the Second Article: It would seem that every religious is bound to keep all the counsels.

Objection 1. For whoever professes a certain state of life is bound to observe whatever belongs to that state. Now each religious professes the state of perfection. Therefore every religious is bound to keep all the counsels that pertain to the state of perfection.

Obj. 2. Further, Gregory says (*Hom.* viii *in Ezech.*)[7] that "he who renounces this world, and

---

[1] Sect. 1 (PG 3, 529).   [3] Sect. 3 (PG 3, 532).
[2] Cassianus (PL 49, 489).   [4] Bk. II (PL 76, 1037).

[5] PG 13, 1301.
[6] Gratian, *Decretum*, pt. II. (RF I, 1152).
[7] Bk. II (PL 76, 1038).

does all the good he can, is like one who has gone out of Egypt and offers sacrifice in the wilderness." Now it pertains specially to religious to renounce the world. Therefore it pertains to them also to do all the good they can, and so it would seem that each of them is bound to fulfil all the counsels.

Obj. 3. Further, If it is not requisite for the state of perfection to fulfil all the counsels, it would seem enough to fulfil some of them. But this is false, since some who lead a secular life fulfil some of the counsels, for instance those who observe continence. Therefore it would seem that every religious who is in the state of perfection is bound to fulfil whatever pertains to perfection; and such are the counsels.

On the contrary, One is not bound, unless one bind oneself, to do works of supererogation. But every religious does not bind himself to keep all the counsels, but to certain definite ones, some to some, others to others. Therefore all are not bound to keep all of them.

I answer that, A thing pertains to perfection in three ways. First, essentially, and thus, as stated above (Q. CLXXXIV, A. 3) the perfect observance of the precepts of charity belongs to perfection. Secondly, a thing belongs to perfection as a consequence; such are those things that result from the perfection of charity, for instance to bless them that curse you (Luke 6. 27), and to keep counsels of a like kind, which though they are binding as regards the preparedness of the mind, so that one has to fulfil them when necessity requires, yet are sometimes fulfilled without there being any necessity, through superabundance of charity. Thirdly, a thing pertains to perfection instrumentally and by way of disposition, as poverty, continence, abstinence, and the like.

Now it has been stated (A. 1) that the perfection of charity is the end of the religious state. And the religious state is a school or exercise for the attainment of perfection, which men strive to reach by various practices, just as a physician may use various remedies in order to heal. But it is evident that for him who works for an end it is not necessary that he should already have attained the end, but it is requisite that he should tend to it by some path. Hence he who enters the religious state is not bound to have perfect charity, but he is bound to tend to this, and use his endeavours to have perfect charity.

For the same reason he is not bound to fulfil those things that result from the perfection of charity, although he is bound to intend to fulfil

them. He acts against this intention if he contemns them, however, and so he sins not by omitting them but by contempt of them.

In like manner he is not bound to observe all the practices by which perfection may be attained, but only those which are definitely prescribed to him by the rule which he has professed.

Reply Obj. 1. He who enters religion does not make profession to be perfect, but he professes to endeavour to attain perfection; even as he who enters the schools does not profess to have knowledge, but to study in order to acquire knowledge. Therefore as Augustine says,[1] Pythagoras was unwilling to profess to be a wise man, but acknowledged himself "a lover of wisdom." Hence a religious does not violate his profession if he be not perfect, but only if he despises to tend to perfection.

Reply Obj. 2. Just as, though all are bound to love God with their whole heart, yet there is a certain wholeness of perfection which cannot be omitted without sin, and another wholeness which can be omitted without sin, provided there be no contempt, as stated above (REPLY 1) so too, all, both religious and seculars, are bound in a certain measure to do whatever good they can, for to all without exception it is said (Eccles. 9. 10): *Whatsoever thy hand is able to do, do it earnestly.* Yet there is a way of fulfilling this precept so as to avoid sin, namely if one do what one can as required by the conditions of one's state of life, provided there be no contempt of doing better things, which contempt sets the mind against spiritual progress.

Reply Obj. 3. There are some counsels such that if they are omitted, man's whole life would be taken up with secular business; for instance if he have property of his own, or enter the married state, or do something of the kind that pertains to the essential vows of religion themselves. Therefore religious are bound to keep all such counsels. Other counsels there are, however, about certain particular better actions, which can be omitted without one's life being taken up with secular actions. Therefore there is no need for religious to be bound to fulfil all of them.

ARTICLE 3. *Whether Poverty Is Required for Religious Perfection?*

We proceed thus to the Third Article: It seems that poverty is not required for religious perfection.

[1] *City of God,* VIII, 2 (PL 41, 225); cf. Cicero, *Tuscul.,* V, 3 (DD IV, 47).

Objection 1. For that which it is unlawful to do does not apparently belong to the state of perfection. But it would seem to be unlawful for a man to give up all he possesses, since the Apostle (II Cor. 8. 12) lays down the way in which the faithful are to give alms, saying: *If the will be forward, it is accepted according to that which a man hath,* that is, "you should keep back what you need,"[1] and afterwards he adds (*verse* 13): *For I mean not that others should be eased, and you burthened,* that is "with poverty," according to a gloss.[2] Moreover a gloss on I Tim. 6. 8, *Having food, and wherewith to be covered,* says: "Though we brought nothing, and will carry nothing away, we must not give up these temporal things altogether."[3] Therefore it seems that voluntary poverty is not requisite for religious perfection.

Obj. 2. Further, Whosoever exposes himself to danger sins. But he who renounces all he has and embraces voluntary poverty exposes himself to danger—not only spiritual, according to Prov. 30. 9, *Lest perhaps . . . being compelled by poverty, I should steal and forswear the name of my God,* and Ecclus. 27. 1, *Through poverty many have sinned,*—but also corporal, for it is written (Eccl. 7. 13): *As wisdom is a defence, so money is a defence,* and the Philosopher says[4] that "the waste of property appears to be a sort of ruining of one's self, since thereby man lives." Therefore it would seem that voluntary poverty is not requisite for the perfection of religious life.

Obj. 3. Further, Virtue observes the mean, as stated in the *Ethics.*[5] But he who renounces all by voluntary poverty seems to go to the extreme rather than to observe the mean. Therefore he does not act virtuously, and so this does not pertain to the perfection of life.

Obj. 4. Further, The ultimate perfection of man consists in happiness. Now riches conduce to happiness; for it is written (Ecclus. 31. 8): *Blessed is the rich man that is found without blemish,* and the Philosopher says[6] that riches contribute instrumentally to happiness. Therefore voluntary poverty is not requisite for religious perfection.

Obj. 5. Further, The episcopal state is more perfect than the religious state. But bishops may have property, as stated above (Q. CLXXXV., A. 6). Therefore religious may also.

Obj. 6. Further, Almsgiving is a work most acceptable to God, and as Chrysostom says (*Hom.* ix *in Ep. ad Hebr.*)[7] "is a most effective remedy in repentance." Now poverty excludes almsgiving. Therefore it would seem that poverty does not pertain to religious perfection.

On the contrary, Gregory says (*Moral.* viii, 26):[8] "There are some of the just who bracing themselves up to lay hold of the very height of perfection, while they aim at higher objects within abandon all things without." Now, as stated above, (AA. 1, 2) it pertains properly to religious to brace themselves up in order to lay hold of the very height of perfection. Therefore it belongs to them to abandon all outward things by voluntary poverty.

I answer that, As stated above (A. 2), the religious state is an exercise and a discipline for attaining to the perfection of charity. For this it is necessary that a man wholly withdraw his affections from worldly things, since Augustine says,[9] speaking to God: "Too little doth he love Thee who loves anything with Thee, which he loveth not for Thee." Therefore he says (QQ. LXXXIII, qu. 36)[10] that "charity is nourished by the lessening of cupidity, and is perfect when cupidity is no more." Now the possession of worldly things draws a man's mind to the love of them; hence Augustine says (*Ep. ad Paulin. et Theras.* xxxi)[11] that "we are more firmly attached to earthly things when we have them than when we desire them; for why did that young man go away sad, save because he had great wealth? For it is one thing not to wish to lay hold of what one has not, and another to renounce what one already has; the former are rejected as foreign to us, the latter are cut off as a limb." And Chrysostom says (*Hom.* lxiii *in Matt.*)[12] that "the possession of wealth kindles a greater flame and the desire for them becomes stronger."

Hence it is that in the attainment of the perfection of charity the first foundation is voluntary poverty, whereby a man lives without property of his own, according to the saying of our Lord (Matt. 19. 21), *If thou wilt be perfect, go, sell all* (Vulg.,—*what*) *thou hast, and give to the poor, . . . and come, follow Me.*

Reply Obj. 1. As the gloss adds (*ibid.*),[13] the Apostle said "not that we (you) should be burthened," that is with poverty, "not as though it were not better to give all; but he feared for

---

[1] *Glossa interl.* (VI, 711); *Glossa* Lombardi (PL 192, 58).
[2] *Glossa interl.* (VI, 71v); *Glossa* Lombardi (PL 192, 58).
[3] *Glossa* Lombardi (PL 192, 358); cf. *Glossa interl.,* on II Cor. 8.13 (VI, 122v).   [4] *Ethics,* IV, I (1120ᵃ2).
[5] Aristotle, II, 6 (1106ᵇ36).
[6] *Ethics,* I, 8 (1099ᵇI).

[7] PG 63, 81.   [8] PL 75, 829.
[9] *Confessions,* X, 40 (PL 32, 796).
[10] PL 40, 25.   [11] PL 33, 124.   [12] PG 58, 605.
[13] *Glossa* Lombardi, on II Cor. 8.13 (PL 192, 58); cf. *Glossa interl.* (VI, 122v).

the weak, whom he admonished so to give as not to suffer privation." Hence in like manner the other gloss[1] means not that it is unlawful to renounce all one's temporal goods, but that this is not required of necessity. Therefore Ambrose says (*De Offic.* i):[2] "Our Lord does not wish," namely does not command us "to pour out our wealth all at once, but to dispense it; or perhaps to do as did Eliseus who slew his oxen, and fed the poor with that which was his own so that no household care might hold him back."

Reply Obj. 2. He who renounces all his possessions for Christ's sake exposes himself to no danger, neither spiritual nor corporal. For spiritual danger ensues from poverty when the latter is not voluntary, because those who are unwillingly poor, through the desire of money-getting, fall into many sins, according to I Tim. 9, *They that will become rich, fall into temptation and into the snare of the devil.* This affection is put away by those who embrace voluntary poverty, but it gathers strength in those who have wealth, as stated in the Article. Again bodily danger does not threaten those who, intent on following Christ, renounce all their possessions and entrust themselves to divine providence. Hence Augustine says (*De Serm. Dom. in Monte,* ii, 17):[3] "Those who seek first the kingdom of God and His justice are not weighed down by anxiety lest they lack what is necessary."

Reply Obj. 3. According to the Philosopher[4] the mean of virtue is taken according to right reason, not according to the quantity of a thing. Consequently whatever may be done in accordance with right reason is not rendered sinful by the greatness of the quantity, but all the more virtuous. It would, however, be against right reason to throw away all one's possessions through intemperance, or without any useful purpose; but it is in accordance with right reason to renounce wealth in order to devote oneself to the contemplation of wisdom. Even certain philosophers are said to have done this; for Jerome says (*Ep. ad Paulin.*):[5] "That famous Theban, Crates, once a very wealthy man, when he was going to Athens to study philosophy, cast away a large amount of gold; for he considered that he could not possess both gold and virtue at the same time." Much more therefore is it according to right reason for a man to renounce all he has in order perfectly

to follow Christ. Therefore Jerome says (*Ep. ad Rust. Monach.*):[6] "Poor thyself, follow Christ poor."

Reply Obj. 4. Happiness or felicity is twofold. One is perfect, to which we look forward in the life to come; the other is imperfect, in respect of which some are said to be happy in this life. The happiness of this life is twofold, one is according to the active life, the other according to the contemplative life, as the Philosopher asserts.[7] Now wealth conduces instrumentally to the happiness of the active life which consists in external actions, because as the Philosopher says,[8] "we do many things by friends, by riches, by political influence, as it were by instruments." On the other hand, it does not conduce to the happiness of the contemplative life, but rather is it an obstacle to it, in so far as the anxiety it involves disturbs the quiet of the soul, which is most necessary to one who contemplates. Hence it is that the Philosopher asserts[9] that "for actions many things are needed, but the contemplative man needs no such things," namely external goods, "for his operation, but they are impediments to his contemplation."

Man is directed to future happiness by charity; and since voluntary poverty is an efficacious exercise for the attaining of perfect charity, it follows that it is of great avail in acquiring the happiness of heaven. Therefore our Lord said (Matt. 19. 21): *Go, sell all* (Vulg.,—*what*) *thou hast, and give to the poor, and thou shalt have treasure in heaven.* Now riches once they are possessed are in themselves of a nature to hinder the perfection of charity, especially by enticing and distracting the mind. Hence it is written (Matt. 13. 22) that *the care of this world and the deceitfulness of riches choketh up the word* of God, for as Gregory says (*Hom.* xv *in Ev.*)[10] *by preventing the good desire from entering into the heart, they destroy life at its very outset.* Consequently it is difficult to safeguard charity amidst riches; hence our Lord said (Matt. 19. 23) that *a rich man shall hardly enter into the kingdom of heaven,* which we must understand as referring to one who actually has wealth, since He says that this is impossible for him who places his affection in riches, according to the explanation of Chrysostom (*Hom.* lxiii *in Matt.*),[11] for He adds (*verse*

---

[1] *Glossa ordin.*, on I Tim. 6.8 (VI, 122F); *Glossa Lombardi* (PL 192, 358).
[2] Chap. 30 (PL 16, 72).   [3] PL 34, 1293.
[4] *Ethics,* II, 6 (1107[a]1).   [5] *Epist.*, LVIII (PL 22, 580).

[6] *Epist.,* CXXV (PL 22, 1085).
[7] *Ethics,* X, 7, 8 (1177[a]12; 1178[a]9).
[8] *Ibid.,* I, 8 (1099[n]33).
[9] *Ibid.,* X, 8 (1178[b]1).
[10] Bk. I (PL 76, 1133).
[11] PG 58, 605.

24): *It is easier for a camel to pass through the eye of a needle, than for a rich man to enter into the kingdom of heaven.*

Hence it is not said absolutely that the *rich man* is blessed, but *the rich man that is found without blemish, and that hath not gone after gold,* and this because he has done a difficult thing, and so the text continues (*verse* 9): *Who is he? and we will praise him; for he hath done wonderful things in his life,* namely by not loving riches though placed in the midst of them.

Reply Obj. 5. The episcopal state is not directed to the attainment of perfection, but rather to the effect that, in virtue of the perfection which he already has, a man may govern others, by administering not only spiritual but also temporal things. This belongs to the active life, wherein many occur that may be done by means of wealth as an instrument, as stated in the preceding Reply. Therefore it is not required of bishops, who make profession of governing Christ's flock, that they have nothing of their own, as it is required of religious who make profession of learning to obtain perfection.

Reply Obj. 6. The renouncement of one's own wealth is compared to almsgiving as the universal to the particular, and as the holocaust to the sacrifice. Hence Gregory says (*Hom.* viii *in Ezech.*)[1] that "those who assist the needy with the things they possess, by their good deeds offer sacrifice, since they offer up something to God and keep back something for themselves; but those who keep nothing for themselves offer a holocaust which is greater than a sacrifice." Therefore Jerome also says (*Contra Vigilant.* v):[2] "When you declare that those do better who retain the use of their possessions, and dole out the fruits of their possessions to the poor, it is not I but the Lord Who answers you; If thou wilt be perfect, etc"., and afterwards he goes on to say: "This man whom you praise belongs to the second and third degree, and we too commend him; provided we acknowledge the first as to be preferred to the second and third." For this reason in order to exclude the error of Vigilantius it is said (*De Eccl. Dogm.* 71):[3] It is a good thing to give away one's goods by dispensing them to the poor; it is better to give them away once for all with the intention of following the Lord, and, free of solicitude, to be poor with Christ."

ARTICLE 4. *Whether Perpetual Continence Is Required for Religious Perfection?*

We proceed thus to the Fourth Article: It seems that perpetual continence is not required for religious perfection.

Objection 1. For all perfection of the Christian life began with Christ's apostles. Now the apostles do not appear to have observed continence, as evidenced by Peter, of whose mother-in-law we read Matt. 8. 14. Therefore it would seem that perpetual continence is not requisite for religious perfection.

Obj. 2. Further, The first example of perfection is shown to us in the person of Abraham, to whom the Lord said (*Gen.* 17. 1): *Walk before Me, and be perfect.* Now the copy should not surpass the example. Therefore perpetual continence is not requisite for religious perfection.

Obj. 3. Further, That which is required for religious perfection is to be found in every religious order. Now there are some religious who lead a married life. Therefore religious perfection does not require perpetual continence.

On the contrary, The Apostle says (II Cor. 7. 1): *Let us cleanse ourselves from all defilement of the flesh and of the spirit, perfecting sanctification in the fear of God.* Now cleanness of flesh and spirit is safeguarded by continence, for it is said (I Cor. 7. 34): *The unmarried woman and the virgin thinketh on the things of the Lord that she may be holy both in spirit and in body* (Vulg.,—*both in body and in spirit*). Therefore religious perfection requires continence.

I answer that, The religious state requires the removal of whatever hinders man from devoting himself entirely to God's service. Now the use of sexual union hinders the mind from giving itself wholly to the service of God, and this for two reasons. First, on account of its vehement pleasure, which by frequent repetition increases concupiscence, as also the Philosopher observes;[4] and hence it is that the use of sexual intercourse withdraws the mind from that perfect intentness on tending to God. Augustine expresses this when he says (*Solil.* i, 10):[5] "I consider that nothing so casts down the manly mind from its height as the fondling of women, and those bodily contacts which belong to the married state." Secondly, because it involves man in solicitude for the control of his wife, his children, and his temporalities which serve

---

[1] Bk. II (PL 76, 1037).
[2] PL 23, 366.
[3] Gennadius (PL 58, 997).

[4] *Ethics*, III, 12 (1119[b]9).
[5] PL 32, 876.

for their upkeep. Hence the Apostle says (I Cor. 7. 32, 33): *He that is without a wife is solicitous for the things that belong to the Lord, how he may please God: but he that is with a wife is solicitous for the things of the world, how he may please his wife.*

Therefore perpetual continence, as well as voluntary poverty, is requisite for religious perfection. Therefore just as Vigilantius was condemned for equalling riches to poverty,[1] so was Jovinian condemned for equalling marriage to virginity.[2]

Reply Obj. 1. The perfection not only of poverty but also of continence was introduced by Christ Who said (Matt. 19. 12): *There are eunuchs who have made themselves eunuchs, for the kingdom of heaven,* and then added: *He that can take, let him take it.* And lest anyone should be deprived of the hope of attaining perfection, he admitted to the state of perfection those even who were married. Now the husbands could not without committing an injustice forsake their wives, although all could without injustice renounce riches. Therefore Peter whom He found married, He severed not from his wife, while He withheld from marriage John who wished to marry.

Reply Obj. 2. As Augustine says (*De Bono Conjug.* 22),[3] "the chastity of celibacy is better than the chastity of marriage, one of which Abraham had in use, both of them in habit. For he lived chastely, and he might have been chaste without marrying, but it was not requisite then." Nevertheless if the patriarchs of old had perfection of mind together with wealth and marriage, which is a mark of the greatness of their virtue, this is no reason why any weaker person should presume to have such great virtue that he can attain to perfection though rich and married; as neither does a man unarmed presume to attack his enemy because Samson slew many foes with the jaw-bone of an ass. For those fathers, had it been seasonable to observe continence and poverty, would have been most careful to observe them.

Reply Obj. 3. Such ways of living as admit of the use of marriage are not the religious life simply and absolutely speaking, but in a restricted sense, in so far as they have a certain share in those things that belong to the religious state.

[1] Cf. Jerome, *Contra Vigilant.* (PL 23, 366).

[2] Cf. Siricius, *Epist.*, VII (PL 13, 1168; cf. PL 16, 1169); Jerome, *Adv. Jovin.*, I (PL 23, 224); Augustine, *De Haeres.*, 82 (PL 42, 46); Isidore, *Etymol.*, VIII, 5 (PL 82, 303).

[3] PL 40, 392.

ARTICLE 5. *Whether Obedience Belongs to Religious Perfection?*

We proceed thus to the Fifth Article: It seems that obedience does not belong to religious perfection.

Objection 1. For those things seem to belong to religious perfection which are works of supererogation and are not binding upon all. But all are bound to obey their superiors, according to the saying of the Apostle (Heb. 13. 17), *Obey your prelates, and be subject to them.* Therefore it would seem that obedience does not belong to religious perfection.

Obj. 2. Further, Obedience would seem to belong properly to those who have to be guided by the sense of others, that is persons who are lacking in discernment. Now the Apostle says (Heb. 5. 14) that *strong meat is for the perfect, for them who by custom have their senses exercised to the discerning of good and evil.* Therefore it would seem that obedience does not belong to the state of the perfect.

Obj. 3. Further, If obedience were requisite for religious perfection, it would follow that it is fitting for all religious. But it is not fitting for all, since some religious lead a solitary life, and have no superior whom they obey. Again religious superiors apparently are not bound to obedience. Therefore obedience would seem not to pertain to religious perfection.

Obj. 4. Further, If the vow of obedience were requisite for religion, it would follow that religious are bound to obey their superiors in all things, just as they are bound to abstain from all sexual intercourse by their vow of continence. But they are not bound to obey their superiors in all things, as stated above (Q. CIV., A. 5), when we were treating of the virtue of obedience. Therefore the vow of obedience is not requisite for religion.

Obj. 5. Further, Those services are most acceptable to God which are done freely and not of necessity, according to II Cor. 9. 7, *Not with sadness or of necessity.* Now that which is done out of obedience is done of necessity of precept. Therefore those good works are more deserving of praise which are done of one's own accord. Therefore the vow of obedience is unbecoming to religion whereby men seek to attain to that which is better.

On the contrary, Religious perfection consists chiefly in the imitation of Christ, according to Matt. 19. 21, *If thou wilt be perfect,* etc. . . . *follow Me.* Now in Christ obedience is commended above all according to Philip. 2.

8, *He became* (Vulg.,—*becoming*) *obedient unto death*. Therefore it seems that obedience belongs to religious perfection.

I answer that, As stated above (AA. 2, 3) the religious state is a discipline and exercise for tending to perfection. Now those who are being instructed or exercised in order to attain a certain end must follow the direction of someone under whose control they are instructed or exercised so as to attain that end as disciples under a master. Hence religious need to be placed under the instruction and command of someone as regards things pertaining to the religious life; hence it is said (VII, Q. I, cap. *Hoc nequaquam*):[1] "The monastic life denotes subjection and discipleship." Now one man is subjected to another's command and instruction by obedience, and consequently obedience is requisite for religious perfection.

Reply Obj. 1. To obey one's superiors in matters that are necessary to virtue is not a work of supererogation, but is common to all; but to obey in matters pertaining to the practice of perfection belongs properly to religious. This latter obedience is compared to the former as the universal to the particular. For those who live in the world keep something for themselves, and offer something to God, and in the latter respect they are under obedience to their superiors; while those who live in religion give themselves wholly and their possessions to God, as stated above (AA. I, 3). Hence their obedience is universal.

Reply Obj. 2. As the Philosopher says,[2] by performing actions we contract certain habits, and when we have acquired the habit we are best able to perform the actions. Accordingly those who have not attained to perfection acquire perfection by obeying, while those who have already acquired perfection are most ready to obey, not as though they need to be directed to the acquisition of perfection, but as maintaining themselves by this means in that which belongs to perfection.

Reply Obj. 3. The subjection of religious is chiefly in reference to bishops, who are compared to them as perfectors to perfected, as Dionysius states (*Eccl. Hier.* vi),[3] where he also says that "the monastic order is subjected to the perfecting virtues of the bishops, and is taught by their godlike enlightenment." Hence neither hermits nor religious superiors are exempt from obedience to bishops; and if they be

wholly or partly exempt from obedience to the bishop of the diocese, they are nevertheless bound to obey the Sovereign Pontiff, not only in matters affecting all in common, but also in those which pertain specially to religious discipline.

Reply Obj. 4. The vow of obedience taken by religious, extends to the disposition of a man's whole life, and in this way it has a certain universality, although it does not extend to all individual acts. For some of these do not belong to religion, through not being of those things that concern the love of God and of our neighbour, such as rubbing one's beard, lifting a stick from the ground and so forth, which do not come under a vow nor under obedience; some are also contrary to religion. Nor is there any comparison with continence whereby acts are excluded which are altogether contrary to religion.

Reply Obj. 5. The necessity of coercion makes an act involuntary and consequently deprives it of the character of praise or merit. But the necessity which is consequent upon obedience is a necessity not of coercion but of a free will, in so far as a man is willing to obey, although perhaps he would not be willing to do the thing commanded considered in itself. Therefore since by vow of obedience a man lays himself under the necessity of doing for God's sake certain things that are not pleasing in themselves, for this very reason that which he does is the more acceptable to God, though it be of less account, because man can give nothing greater to God, than by subjecting his will to another man's for God's sake. Hence in the Conferences of the Fathers (*Coll.* xviii, 7)[4] it is stated that the Sarabaitæ are the worst class of monks, because through providing for their own needs without being subject to superiors, they are free to do as they will; and yet day and night they are more busily occupied in work than those who live in monasteries.

ARTICLE 6. *Whether It is Requisite for Religious Perfection That Poverty, Continence, and Obedience Should Come Under a Vow?*

We proceed thus to the Sixth Article: It seems that it is not requisite for religious perfection that the three aforesaid, namely poverty, continence, and obedience, should come under a vow.

Objection 1. For the discipline of perfection is founded on the principles laid down by our Lord. Now our Lord in formulating perfection

---

[1] Gratian, *Decretum*, PT. II (RF 1, 585).
[2] *Ethics*, II, 1, 2 (1103ª14; 1103ᵇ26).
[3] Sect. 3 (PG 3, 532).
[4] Cassian (PL 49, 1102).

(Matt. 19. 21) said: *If thou wilt be perfect, go, sell all* (Vulg.,—*what*) *thou hast, and give to the poor,* without any mention of a vow. Therefore it would seem that a vow is not necessary for the discipline of religion.

Obj. 2. Further, A vow is a promise made to God, and so (Eccl. 5. 3) the wise man after saying: *If thou hast vowed anything to God, defer not to pay it,* adds at once, *for an unfaithful and foolish promise displeaseth Him.* But when a thing is being actually given there is no need for a promise. Therefore it suffices for religious perfection that one keep poverty, continence, and obedience without vowing them.

Obj. 3. Further, Augustine says (*De Adult. Conjug.* i, 14):[1] "The services we render are more pleasing when we might lawfully not render them, yet do so out of love." Now it is lawful not to render a service which we have not vowed, whereas it is unlawful if we have vowed to render it. Therefore it seems that it is more pleasing to God to keep poverty, continence, and obedience without a vow. Therefore a vow is not requisite for religious perfection.

On the contrary, In the Old Law the Nazareans were consecrated by vow according to Num. 6. 2, *When a man or woman shall make a vow to be sanctified and will consecrate themselves to the Lord,* etc. Now these were a figure of those *who attain the summit of perfection,* as Gregory says (*Moral.* ii, 52).[2] Therefore a vow is requisite for religious perfection.

I answer that, It pertains to religious to be in the state of perfection, as shown above (Q. CLXXXIV, A. 5). Now the state of perfection requires an obligation to whatever belongs to perfection, and this obligation consists in binding oneself to God by means of a vow. But it is evident from what has been said (AA. 3, 4, 5) that poverty, continence, and obedience belong to the perfection of the Christian life. Consequently the religious state requires that one be bound to these three by vow. Hence Gregory says (*Hom.* viii *in Ezech.*):[3] "When a man vows to almighty God all his possessions, all his life, all his knowledge, it is a holocaust"; and afterwards he says that this refers to those who renounce the present world.

Reply Obj. 1. Our Lord declared that it belongs to the perfection of life that a man follow Him, not anyhow, but in such a way as not to turn back. Therefore He says again (Luke 9. 62): *No man putting his hand to the plough,* and looking back, *is fit for the kingdom of God.* And though some of His disciples went back, yet when our Lord asked (John 6. 68, 69), *Will you also go away?* Peter answered for the others: *Lord, to whom shall we go?* Hence Augustine says (*De Consensu Ev.* ii, 17)[4] that "as Matthew and Mark relate, Peter and Andrew followed Him after drawing their boats on to the beach, not as though they purposed to return, but as following Him at His command." Now this unwavering following of Christ is made fast by a vow, and therefore a vow is requisite for religious perfection.

Reply Obj. 2. As Gregory says (*loc. cit.*) religious perfection requires that a man give God whatever he has vowed. But a man cannot actually give God his whole life, because that life taken as a whole is not simultaneous but successive. Hence a man cannot give his whole life to God otherwise than by the obligation of a vow.

Reply Obj. 3. Among other services that we can lawfully give, is our own liberty, which is dearer to man than anything else. Consequently when a man of his own accord deprives himself by vow of the liberty of abstaining from things pertaining to God's service, this is most acceptable to God. Hence Augustine says (*Ep.* cxxvi, *ad Paulin. et Arment.*):[5] "Repent not of thy vow; rejoice rather that thou canst no longer do lawfully, what thou mightest have done lawfully but to thy own cost. Happy the necessity that compels to better things."

ARTICLE 7. *Whether It Is Right To Say That Religious Perfection Consists in These Three Vows?*

We proceed thus to the Seventh Article: It seems that it is not right to say that religious perfection consists in these three vows.

Objection 1. For the perfection of life consists of inward rather than of outward acts, according to Rom. 14. 17, *The kingdom of God is not meat and drink, but justice and peace and joy in the Holy Ghost.* Now the religious vow binds a man to things belonging to perfection. Therefore vows of inward actions, such as contemplation, love of God and our neighbour, and so forth, should pertain to the religious state, rather than the vows of poverty, continence, and obedience which refer to outward actions.

Obj. 2. Further, The above three things come under the religious vow in so far as they belong to the practice of tending to perfection. But there are many other things that religious prac-

[1] PL 40, 459.
[2] PL 75, 596; cf. *Glossa ordin.* (1, 275B).
[3] Bk. II (PL 76, 1037).
[4] PL 34, 1097.　　　[5] PL 33, 487.

tise, such as abstinence, watchings, and the like. Therefore it would seem that these three vows are incorrectly described as pertaining to the state of perfection.

Obj. 3. Further, By the vow of obedience a man is bound to do according to his superior's command whatever pertains to the practice of perfection. Therefore the vow of obedience suffices without the two other vows.

Obj. 4. Further, External goods comprise not only riches but also honours. Therefore, if religious, by the vow of poverty, renounce earthly riches, there should be another vow whereby they may despise worldly honours.

On the contrary, It is stated (*Extrav. de Statu Monach.*, cap. *Cum ad monasterium*)[1] that "the keeping of chastity and the renouncing of property are joined to the monastic rule."

I answer that, The religious state may be considered in three ways. First, as being a practice of tending to the perfection of charity; secondly, as quieting the human mind from outward solicitude, according to I Cor. 7. 32: *I would have you to be without solicitude;* thirdly, as a holocaust whereby a man offers himself and his possessions wholly to God. And in corresponding manner the religious state is constituted by these three vows.

First, as regards the practice of perfection, a man is required to remove from himself whatever may hinder his affections from tending wholly to God, for it is in this that the perfection of charity consists. Such hindrances are of three kinds. First, the attachment to external goods, which is removed by the vow of poverty; secondly, the concupiscence of sensible pleasures, chief among which are sexual pleasures, and these are removed by the vow of continence; thirdly, the want of order in the human will, and this is removed by the vow of obedience.

In like manner the disquiet of worldly solicitude is aroused in man in reference especially to three things. First, as regards the dispensing of external things, and this solicitude is removed from man by the vow of poverty; secondly, as regards the control of wife and children, which is cut away by the vow of continence; thirdly, as regards the disposal of one's own actions, which is eliminated by the vow of obedience, whereby a man commits himself to the disposal of another.

Again, a holocaust is the offering to God of all that one has, according to Gregory (*Hom. viii in Ezech.*).[2] Now man has a threefold good,

according to the Philosopher.[3] First, the good of external things, which he wholly offers to God by the vow of voluntary poverty; secondly, the good of his own body, and this good he offers to God especially by the vow of continence, whereby he renounces the greatest bodily pleasures; the third is the good of the soul, which man wholly offers to God by the vow of obedience, whereby he offers God his own will by which he makes use of all the powers and habits of the soul.

Therefore the religious state is fittingly constituted by the three vows.

Reply Obj. 1. As stated above (AA. 1, 2), the end to which the religious vow is directed is the perfection of charity, since all the interior acts of virtue belong to charity as to their mother, according to I Cor. 13. 4, *Charity is patient, is kind*, etc. Hence the interior acts of virtue, for instance humility, patience, and so forth, do not come under the religious vow, but this is directed to them as its end.

Reply Obj. 2. All other religious observances are directed to the above three principal vows; for if any of them are instituted for the purpose of procuring a livelihood, such as labour, begging, and so on, they are to be referred to poverty, for the safeguarding of which religious seek a livelihood by these means. Other observances whereby the body is chastised, such as watching, fasting, and the like, are directly ordered to the observance of the vow of continence. And such religious observances as regard human actions whereby a man is directed to the end of religion, namely the love of God and his neighbour (such as reading, prayer, visiting the sick, and the like), are comprised under the vow of obedience that applies to the will, which directs its actions to the end according to the ordering of another person. The distinction of habit belongs to all three vows, as a sign of being bound by them. Hence the religious habit is given or blessed at the time of profession.

Reply Obj. 3. By obedience a man offers to God his will, to which though all human affairs are subject, yet some are subject to it alone in a special manner, namely human actions, since passions belong also to the sensitive appetite. Therefore in order to restrain the passions of carnal pleasures and of external objects of appetite, which hinder the perfection of life, there was need for the vows of continence and poverty; but for the ordering of one's own actions according as the state of perfection re-

---

[1] *Decretal. Gregor.*, IX, III, tit. 35, chap. 6 (RF II, 599).
[2] Bk. II (PL 76, 1037).

[3] *Ethics*, I, 8 (1098[b]12).

quires, there was need for the vow of obedience.

Reply Obj. 4. As the Philosopher says,[1] strictly and truly speaking honour is not due save to virtue. Since, however, external goods serve instrumentally for certain acts of virtue, the consequence is that a certain honour is given to their excellence especially by the common people who acknowledge none but outward excellence. Therefore since religious tend to the perfection of virtue it becomes them not to renounce the honour which is given to God and all the saints on account of virtue, according to Ps. 138. 17, *But to me thy friends, O God, are made exceedingly honourable.* On the other hand, they renounce the honour that is given to outward excellence by the very fact that they withdraw from a worldly life. Hence no special vow is needed for this.

ARTICLE 8. *Whether the Vow of Obedience Is the Chief of the Three Religious Vows?*

We proceed thus to the Eighth Article: It seems that the vow of obedience is not the chief of the three religious vows.

Objection 1. For the perfection of the religious life was inaugurated by Christ. Now Christ gave a special counsel of poverty, but He is not stated to have given a special counsel of obedience. Therefore the vow of poverty is greater than the vow of obedience.

Obj. 2. Further, It is written (Ecclus. 26. 20) that *no price is worthy of a continent soul.* Now the vow of that which is more worthy is itself more excellent. Therefore the vow of continence is more excellent than the vow of obedience.

Obj. 3. Further, The greater a vow the more indispensable it would seem to be. Now the vows of poverty and continence are so inseparable from the monastic rule that not even the Sovereign Pontiff can allow them to be broken, according to a Decretal (*De Statu Monach.*, cap. *Cum ad monasterium*);[2] yet he can dispense a religious from obeying his superior. Therefore it would seem that the vow of obedience is less than the vow of poverty and continence.

On the contrary, Gregory says (*Moral.* xxxv. 45):[3] Obedience is rightly placed before victims, since by victims another's flesh, but by obedience one's own will, is sacrificed." Now the religious vows are holocausts, as stated above (AA. 1, 7). Therefore the vow of obedience is the chief of all religious vows.

I answer that, The vow of obedience is the

chief of the three religious vows, and this for three reasons.

First, because by the vow of obedience man offers God something greater, namely his own will; for this is of more account than his own body, which he offers God by continence, and than external things, which he offers God by the vow of poverty. Therefore that which is done out of obedience is more acceptable to God than that which is done of one's own will, according to the saying of Jerome to the monk Rusticus:[4] "My words are intended to teach you not to rely on your own judgment"; and a little further on he says: "You may not do what you will; you must eat what you are bidden to eat, you may possess as much as you receive, clothe yourself with what is given to you." Hence fasting is not acceptable to God if it is done of one's own will, according to Isa. 58. 3, *Behold in the day of your fast your own will is found.*

Secondly, because the vow of obedience includes the other vows, but not *vice versa;* for a religious, though bound by vow to observe continence and poverty, yet these also come under obedience, as well as many other things besides the keeping of continence and poverty.

Thirdly, because the vow of obedience extends properly to those acts that are closely connected with the end of religion; and the more closely a thing is connected with the end, the better it is.

It follows from this that the vow of obedience is more essential to the religious life. For if a man without taking a vow of obedience were to observe, even by vow, voluntary poverty and continence, he would not therefore belong to the religious state, which is to be preferred to virginity observed even by vow; for Augustine says (*De Virgin.* xlvi):[5] "No one, I think would dare to prefer virginity to the monastic life."

Reply Obj. 1. The counsel of obedience was included in the very following of Christ, since to obey is to follow another's will. Consequently it is more pertinent to perfection than the vow of poverty, because as Jerome, commenting on Matt. 19. 27, *Behold we have left all things,* observes,[6] "Peter added that which is perfect when he said: And have followed Thee."

Reply Obj. 2. The words quoted mean that continence is to be preferred not to all other

---

[1] *Ethics,* IV, 3 (1123[b]35).
[2] *Decretal. Gregor.,* IX, III, tit. 35, chap. 6 (RF II, 599).
[3] PL 76, 621.

[4] *Epist.,* CXXV (PL 22, 1080).
[5] PL 40, 424. S. Augustine wrote not *monasterio* but *martyrio*—"to martyrdom"; and S. Thomas quotes the passage correctly, Q. CXXIV, A. 3, and Q. CLII, A. 5.
[6] Bk. III (PL 26, 144).

acts of virtue, but to conjugal chastity, or to external riches of gold and silver which are measured by weight.[1] Or again continence is taken in a general sense for abstinence from all evil, as stated above (Q. CLV, A. 4, Reply 1).

Reply Obj. 3. The Pope cannot dispense a religious from his vow of obedience so as to release him from obedience to every superior in matters relating to the perfection of life, for he cannot exempt him from obedience to himself. He can, however, exempt him from subjection to a lower superior, but this is not to dispense him from his vow of obedience.

ARTICLE 9. *Whether a Religious Sins Mortally Whenever He Transgresses the Things Contained in His Rule?*

We proceed thus to the Tenth Article: It seems that a religious sins mortally whenever he transgresses the things contained in his rule.

Objection 1. For to break a vow is a sin worthy of condemnation, as appears from I Tim. 5. 11, 12, where the Apostle says that widows who *will marry have* (Vulg.,—*having*) *damnation, because they have made void their first faith.* But religious are bound to a rule by the vows of their profession. Therefore they sin mortally by transgressing the things contained in their rule.

Obj. 2. Further, The rule is enjoined upon a religious in the same way as a law. Now he who transgresses a precept of law sins mortally. Therefore it would seem that a monk sins mortally if he transgress the things contained in his rule.

Obj. 3. Further, Contempt involves a mortal sin. Now whoever repeatedly does what he ought not to do seems to sin from contempt. Therefore it would seem that a religious sins mortally by frequently transgressing the things contained in his rule.

On the contrary, The religious state is safer than the secular state; hence Gregory (*Ep. ad Leand. Episc.,* cap. i.)[2] compares the secular life to the stormy sea, and the religious life to the calm port. But if every transgression of the things contained in his rule were to involve a religious in mortal sin, the religious life would be fraught with danger on account of its multitude of observances. Therefore not every transgression of the things contained in the rule is a mortal sin.

I answer that, As stated above (A. 2; A. 7,

[1] *Pondere,* referring to the Latin *ponderatio* in the Vulgate, which the Douay version renders "price."
[2] PL 75, 511.

reply 1 and 2), a thing is contained in the rule in two ways. First, as the end of the rule, for instance things that pertain to the acts of the virtues; and the transgression of these, as regards those which come under a common precept, involves a mortal sin. But as regards those which go beyond the common obligation of a precept, their transgression does not involve a mortal sin, except by reason of contempt, because, as stated above (A. 2), a religious is not bound to be perfect, but to tend to perfection, to which the contempt of perfection is opposed. Secondly, a thing is contained in the rule through pertaining to the outward practice, such as all external observances, to some of which a religious is bound by the vow of his profession. Now the vow of profession regards chiefly the three things mentioned before, namely poverty, continence, and obedience, and all others are directed to these. Consequently the transgression of these three involves a mortal sin, while the transgression of the others does not involve a mortal sin, except either by reason of contempt of the rule (since this is directly contrary to the profession whereby a man vows to live according to the rule), or by reason of a precept, whether given orally by a superior, or expressed in the rule, since this would be to act contrary to the vow of obedience.

Reply Obj. 1. He who professes a rule does not vow to observe all the things contained in the rule, but he vows the regular life which consists essentially in the three previously mentioned things. Hence in certain religious orders precaution is taken to profess, not the rule, but to live according to the rule, that is to tend to form one's conduct in accordance with the rule as a kind of model; and this is set aside by contempt. Yet greater precaution is observed in some religious orders by professing obedience according to the rule, so that only that which is contrary to a precept of the rule is contrary to the profession, while the transgression or omission of other things binds only under pain of venial sin, because, as stated above (A. 7, Reply 2), such things are disposition to the chief vows. And venial sin is a disposition to mortal, as stated above (Part I-II Q. LXXXVIII, A. 3), since it hinders those things whereby a man is disposed to keep the chief precepts of Christ's law, namely the precepts of charity.

There is also a religious order, that of the Friars Preachers, where such transgressions or omissions do not, by their very nature, involve sin, either mortal or venial; but they bind one to suffer punishment attached to them, because it is in this way that they are bound to observe such things. Nevertheless they may sin venially or mortally through neglect, concupiscence, or contempt.

Reply Obj. 2. Not all the contents of the law are set forth by way of precept, for some are expressed under the form of ordinance or statute binding under pain of a fixed punishment. Accordingly, just as in the civil law the transgression of a legal statute does not always render a man deserving of bodily death, so neither in the law of the Church does every ordinance or public statute bind under mortal sin. And the same applies to the statutes of the rule.

Reply Obj. 3. An action or transgression proceeds from contempt when a man's will refuses to submit to the ordinance of the law or rule, and from this he proceeds to act against the law or rule. On the other hand, he does not sin from contempt, but from some other cause, when he is led to do something against the ordinance of the law or rule through some particular cause such as concupiscence or anger, even though he often repeat the same kind of sin through the same or some other cause. Thus Augustine says (*De Nat. et Grat.* xxix)[1] that not all sins are committed through proud contempt. Nevertheless the frequent repetition of a sin leads to contempt by way of disposition, according to the words of Prov. 18. 3, *The wicked man, when he is come into the depth of sins, contemneth.*

ARTICLE 10. *Whether a Religious Sins More Grievously Than a Secular by the Same Kind of Sin?*

We proceed thus to the Tenth Article: It would seem that a religious does not sin more grievously than a secular by the same kind of sin.

Objection 1. For it is written (2 Paralip. 30. 18, 19): *The Lord Who is good will show mercy to all them who with their whole heart seek the Lord the God of their fathers, and will not impute it to them that they are not sanctified.* Now religious apparently follow the Lord the God of their fathers with their whole heart rather than seculars, who partly give themselves and their possessions to God and reserve part for themselves, as Gregory says (*Hom.* viii *in Ezech.*).[2] Therefore it

[1] PL 44, 263.
[2] Bk. II (PL 76, 1037).

would seem that it is less imputed to them if they fall short somewhat of their sanctification.

Obj. 2. Further, God is less angered at a man's sins if he does some good deeds, according to 2 Paralip. 19. 2, 3, *Thou helpest the ungodly, and thou art joined in friendship with them that hate the Lord, and therefore thou didst deserve indeed the wrath of the Lord: but good works are found in thee.* Now religious do more good works than seculars. Therefore if they commit any sins, God is less angry with them.

Obj. 3. Further, This present life is not carried through without sin, according to Jas. 3. 2, *In many things we all offend.* Therefore if the sins of religious were more grievous than those of seculars it would follow that religious are worse off than seculars, and consequently it would not be a wholesome counsel to enter religion.

On the contrary, The greater the evil the more it would seem to be deplored. But the sins of those who are in the state of holiness and perfection seem to be the most deplorable, for it is written (Jer. 23. 9): *My heart is broken within me,* and afterwards (*verse* 9): *For the prophet and the priest are defiled; and in My house I have found their wickedness.* Therefore religious and others who are in the state of perfection, other things being equal, sin more grievously.

I answer that, A sin committed by a religious may be in three ways more grievous than a like sin committed by a secular. First, if it be against his religious vow; for instance if he be guilty of fornication or theft, because by fornication he acts against the vow of continence, and by theft against the vow of poverty, and not merely against a precept of the divine law. Secondly, if he sin out of contempt, because thereby he would seem to be the more ungrateful for the divine favours which have raised him to the state of perfection. Thus the Apostle says (Heb. 10. 29) that the believer *deserveth worse punishments* who through contempt tramples under foot the Son of God. Hence the Lord complains (Jer. 11. 15): *What is the meaning that My beloved hath wrought much wickedness in My house?* Thirdly, the sin of a religious may be greater on account of scandal, because many take note of his manner of life. Hence it is written (Jer. 23. 14): *I have seen the likeness of adulterers, and the way of lying in the Prophets of Jerusalem; and they strengthened the hands of the wicked, that no man should return from his evil doings.*

On the other hand, if a religious, not out of contempt, but out of weakness or ignorance, commit a sin that is not against the vow of his profession, without giving scandal (for instance if he commit it in secret) he sins less grievously in the same kind of sin than a secular, because his sin if slight is absorbed as it were by his many good works, and if it be mortal, he more easily recovers from it. First, because he has a right intention towards God, and though it be intercepted for the moment, it is easily restored to its former state. Hence Origen commenting on Ps. 36. 24, *When he shall fall he shall not be bruised,* says (*Hom.* iv *in Ps.* 36):[1] "The wicked man, if he sin, repents not, and fails to make amends for his sin. But the just man knows how to make amends and recover himself; even as he who had said: 'I know not the man,' shortly afterwards when the Lord had looked on him, knew to shed most bitter tears, and he who from the roof had seen a woman and desired her knew to say: 'I have sinned and done evil before Thee.' "[2] Secondly, he is assisted by his fellow-religious to rise again, according to Eccles. 4. 10, *If one fall he shall be supported by the other: woe to him that is alone, for when he falleth he hath none to lift him up.*

Reply Obj. 1. The words quoted refer to things done through weakness or ignorance, but not to those that are done out of contempt.

Reply Obj. 2. Josaphat also, to whom these words were addressed, sinned not out of contempt, but out of a certain weakness of human affection.

Reply Obj. 3. The just sin not easily out of contempt; but sometimes they fall into a sin through ignorance or weakness from which they easily arise. If, however, they go so far as to sin out of contempt, they become most wicked and incorrigible, according to the word of Jeremias (2. 20) *Thou hast broken My yoke, thou hast burst My bands, and thou hast said: 'I will not serve.' For on every high hill, and under every green tree thou didst prostitute thyself.* Hence Augustine says (*Ep.* lxxviii, *ad Pleb. Hippon.*):[3] "From the time I began to serve God, even as I scarcely found better men than those who made progress in monasteries, so have I not found worse than those who in the monastery have fallen."

[1] PG 12, 1353.
[2] Cf. II Kings, 11.2; Ps. 50.6.
[3] PL 33, 272.

QUESTION CLXXXVII

OF THOSE THINGS THAT ARE APPROPRIATE TO RELIGIOUS

(In Six Articles)

WE must now consider the things that are appropriate to religious; and under this head there are six points of inquiry: (1) Whether it is lawful for them to teach, preach, and do like things? (2) Whether it is lawful for them to meddle in secular business? (3) Whether they are bound to manual labour? (4) Whether it is lawful for them to live on alms? (5) Whether it is lawful for them to beg? (6) Whether it is lawful for them to wear coarser clothes than other persons?

ARTICLE 1. *Whether It Is Lawful for Religious to Teach, Preach, and the Like?*

We proceed thus to the First Article: It would seem unlawful for religious to teach, preach, and the like.

Objection 1. For it is said (VII, Q. 1, cap. *Hoc nequaquam*)[4] in an ordinance of a synod of Constantinople:[5] "The monastic life is one of subjection and discipleship, not of teaching, authority, or pastoral care." And Jerome says to Riparius and Desiderius (*Contra Vigilant.* vi):[6] "A monk's duty is not to teach but to lament." Again Pope Leo says (*Ep.* cxx, *ad Theodoret,* cf. XVI, Q. 1, cap. *Adjicimus*):[7] "Let none dare to preach save the priests of the Lord, be he monk or layman, and no matter what knowledge he may boast of having." Now it is not lawful to exceed the bounds of one's office or transgress the ordinance of the Church. Therefore it seems that it is unlawful for religious to teach, preach, and the like.

Obj. 2. Further, In an ordinance of the Council of Nicea (cf. XVI, Q. 1, cap. *Placuit*)[8] it is laid down as follows: "It is our absolute and peremptory command addressed to all, that monks shall not hear confessions except of one another, as is right, that they shall not bury the dead except those dwelling with them in the monastery, or if by chance a brother happen to die while on a visit." But just as the above

[4] Gratian, *Decretum,* pt. II (RF I, 585).
[5] *Pseudo-Synod* Photiano, anno 879, actio v (MA XVIIA, 503).
[6] PL 23, 367; cf. Gratian, *Decretum,* pt. II, causa XVI, Q. 1, can. 4 (RF I, 762).
[7] *Epist.* cxx, chap. 6 (MA VI, 250; cf. PL 54, 1054); Gratian, *Decretum,* pt. II (RF I, 765).
[8] Gratian, *Decretum,* pt. II (RF I, 761). This chapter is not found in the Nicaean Council; cf. Note of the Editors of Gratian, *ibid.*

belong to the duty of clerics, so also do preaching and teaching. Therefore since "the business of a monk differs from that of a cleric," as Jerome says (*Ep.* i, *ad Heliod.*),[1] it would seem unlawful for religious to preach, teach, and the like.

Obj. 3. Further, Gregory says (*Regist.* v):[2] "No man can fulfil ecclesiastical duties and keep consistently to the monastic rule," and this is quoted XVI, Q. I, cap. 2.[3] Now monks are bound to keep consistently to the monastic rule. Therefore it would seem that they cannot fulfil ecclesiastical duties, of which teaching and preaching are a part. Therefore apparently it is unlawful for them to preach, teach, and do similar things.

On the contrary, Gregory is quoted (XVI, Q. I, cap. 24)[4] as saying: "By authority of this decree framed in virtue of our apostolic power and the duty of our office, be it lawful to monk priests who represent the apostles, to preach, baptize, give communion, pray for sinners, impose penance, and absolve from sin."

I answer that, A thing is declared to be unlawful to a person in two ways. First, because there is something in him contrary to that which is declared unlawful to him; thus to no man is it lawful to sin, because each man has in himself reason and an obligation to God's law, to which things sin is contrary. And in this way it is said to be unlawful for a person to preach, teach, or do like things, because there is in him something incompatible with these things, either by reason of a precept,—thus those who are irregular by ordinance of the Church may not be raised to the sacred orders—or by reason of sin, according to Ps. 49. 16, *But to the sinner God hath said: Why dost thou declare My justice?*

In this way it is not unlawful for religious to preach, teach, and do like things, both because they are bound neither by vow nor by precept of their rule to abstain from these things, and because they are not rendered less apt for these things by any sin committed, but on the contrary they are the more apt through having taken upon themselves the practice of holiness.

For it is foolish to say that a man is rendered less fit for spiritual duties through advancing himself in holiness; and consequently it is a foolish opinion of those who declare that the religious state is an obstacle to the fulfilment of such duties.[5] The opinion of these persons is confuted by Pope Boniface IV. by the reasons given above.[6] His words which are quoted (XVI, Q. I, cap. 25)[7] are these: "There are some who without any dogmatic proof, and with extreme daring, inspired with a zeal rather of bitterness than of love, assert that monks though they be dead to the world and live to God, are unworthy of the power of the priestly office, and that they cannot confer penance, nor christen, nor absolve in virtue of the power divinely bestowed on them in the priestly office. But they are altogether deceived." He proves this first because it is not contrary to the rule; thus he continues: "For neither did the Blessed Benedict the saintly teacher of monks forbid this in any way," nor is it forbidden in other rules. Secondly, he refutes the above error from the usefulness of the monks, when he adds at the end of the same chapter: "The more perfect a man is, the more effective is he in these," namely in spiritual works.

Secondly, a thing is said to be unlawful for a man not on account of there being in him something contrary thereto, but because he lacks that which enables him to do it; thus it is unlawful for a deacon to say mass, because he is not in priestly orders, and it is unlawful for a priest to deliver judgment because he lacks the episcopal authority. Here, however, a distinction must be made. Because those things which are a matter of an order cannot be deputed to one who has not the order, while matters of jurisdiction can be deputed to those who have not ordinary jurisdiction; thus the delivery of a judgment is deputed by the bishop to a simple priest.

In this sense it is said to be unlawful for monks and other religious to preach, teach, and so forth, because the religious state does not give them the power to do these things. They can, however, do them if they receive orders, or ordinary jurisdiction, or if matters of jurisdiction be delegated to them.

---

[1] *Epist.*, XIV (PL 22, 352).

[2] Indict. XIII, *Epist.*, I (PL 77, 722).

[3] Gratian, *Decretum*, PT. II (RF I, 761).

[4] Gratian, *Decretum*, PT. II (RF I, 767). Cf. Conc. Nemausensi, anno 1096, can. 3 (MA XX, 935).

[5] St. Thomas seems to have in mind the adversaries of the Mendicant Orders, especially William of St. Amour (*De Periculis Novissimorum Temporum*) and Gerard of Abbeville (*Quod.*, XLV, A. I, 1269). Against the former St. Thomas wrote opusculum XIX, *Contra Impugnantes*, and against the latter opusculum XVIII, *De Perf. Vitae Spir.*, Nicholas of Lisieux replied against Thomas with the work *De Perf. Status Cleric.*, in *Collectione* XXIII *Errorum.* See Glorieux, *Mél. Mandonnet* (I, 51); RTAM (1934) p. 5; RTAM (1935) p. 129.

[6] Boniface IV. See Richter and Friedberg, *Decretum Magistri Gratiani*, PT. II, causa XVI, Q. I, n. 166 (I, 767).

[7] Gratian, *Decretum*, PT. II, causa XVI, Q. I, can. 25 (RF I, 767).

Reply Obj. 1. It results from the words quoted that the fact of their being monks does not give monks the power to do these things, yet it does not involve in them anything contrary to the performance of these acts.

Reply Obj. 2. Again, this ordinance of the Council of Nicea forbids monks to claim the power of exercising those acts on the ground of their being monks, but it does not forbid those acts being delegated to them.

Reply Obj. 3. These two things are incompatible, namely, the ordinary cure of ecclesiastical duties, and the observance of the monastic rule in a monastery. But this does not prevent monks and other religious from being sometimes occupied with ecclesiastical duties through being deputed to them by superiors having ordinary cure, especially members of religious orders that are especially instituted for that purpose, as we shall say further on (Q. CLXXXVIII., A. 4).

ARTICLE 2. *Whether It Is Lawful for Religious to Occupy Themselves With Secular Business?*

We proceed thus to the Second Article: It would seem unlawful for religious to occupy themselves with secular business.

Objection 1. For in the above mentioned decree of Pope Boniface IV it is said (XVI, Q. I, cap. *Sunt nonnulli*)[1] that "the Blessed Benedict bade them to be altogether free from secular business; and this is most explicitly prescribed by the apostolic doctrine and the teaching of all the Fathers, not only to religious, but also to all the canonical clergy," according to II Tim. 2. 4, *No man being a soldier to God, entangleth himself with secular business.* Now it is the duty of all religious to be soldiers to God. Therefore it is unlawful for them to occupy themselves with secular business.

Obj. 2. Further, The Apostle says (I Thess. 4. 11): *That you use your endeavour to be quiet, and that you do your own business,* which a gloss[2] explains thus,—"by refraining from other people's affairs, so as to be the better able to attend to the amendment of your own life." Now religious devote themselves in a special way to the amendment of their life. Therefore they should not occupy themselves with secular business.

Obj. 3. Further, Jerome, commenting on

Matt. 11. 8, *Behold they that are clothed in soft garments are in the houses of kings,* says: "Hence we gather that an austere life and severe preaching should avoid the palaces of kings and the mansions of the voluptuous."[3] But the needs of secular business induce men to frequent the palaces of kings. Therefore it is unlawful for religious to occupy themselves with secular business.

On the contrary, The Apostle says (Rom. 16. 1): *I commend to you Phœbe our sister,* and further on (*verse* 2), *that you assist her in whatsoever business she shall have need of you.*

I answer that, As stated above (Q. CLXXXVI, AA. 1, 7), the religious state is directed to the attainment of the perfection of charity, consisting principally in the love of God and secondarily in the love of our neighbour. Consequently that which religious intend chiefly and for its own sake is to give themselves to God. Yet if their neighbour be in need, they should attend to his affairs out of charity, according to Gal. 6. 2, *Bear ye one another's burdens: and so you shall fulfil the law of Christ,* since through serving their neighbour for God's sake, they are obedient to the divine love. Hence it is written (Jas. 1. 27): *Religion clean and undefiled before God and the Father, is this: to visit the fatherless and widows in their tribulation,* which means, according to a gloss,[4] "to assist the helpless in their time of need." We must conclude therefore that it is unlawful for both monks and clerics to carry on secular business from motives of avarice; but from motives of charity, and with their superior's permission, they may occupy themselves with due moderation in the administration and direction of secular business. Hence it is said in the Decretals (Dist. lxxxviii, cap. 1):[5] "The holy synod decrees that henceforth no cleric shall buy property or occupy himself with secular business, save with a view to the care of the fatherless, orphans, or widows, or when the bishop of the city commands him to take charge of the business connected with the Church." And the same applies to religious as to clerics, because they are both debarred from secular business on the same grounds, as stated in the Article.

Reply Obj. 1. Monks are forbidden to occupy themselves with secular business from motives of avarice, but not from motives of charity.

Reply Obj. 2. To occupy oneself with secular

---

[1] Cf. Gratian, *Decretum,* pt. II (RF I, 767); see above, A. I.

[2] *Glossa interl.* (VI, IIIV); *Glossa* Lombardi (PL 192, 300).

[3] PL 26, 73.

[4] *Glossa interl.* (VI, 211V).

[5] Gratian, pt. I (RF I, 306).

business on account of another's need is not officiousness but charity.

Reply Obj. 3. To haunt the palaces of kings from motives of pleasure, glory, or avarice is not appropriate to religious, but there is nothing unseemly in their visiting them from motives of piety. Hence it is written (IV Kings 4. 13): *Hast thou any business, and wilt thou that I speak to the king or to the general of the army?* Likewise it is fitting for religious to go to the palaces of kings to rebuke and guide them, even as John the Baptist rebuked Herod, as related in Matt. 14. 4.

ARTICLE 3. *Whether Religious Are Bound to Manual Labour?*

We proceed thus to the Third Article: It would seem that religious are bound to manual labor.

Objection 1. For religious are not exempt from the observance of precepts. Now manual labour is a matter of precept according to I Thess. 4. 11, *Work with your own hands as we commanded you.* Hence Augustine says (*De Oper. Monach.* 30):[1] "But who can allow these insolent men," namely religious that do no work, of whom he is speaking there, "who disregard the most salutary admonishment of the Apostle, not merely to be borne with as being weaker than others, but even to preach as though they were holier than others." Therefore it would seem that religious are bound to manual labour.

Obj. 2. Further A gloss[2] on II Thess. 3. 10, *If any man will not work, neither let him eat,* says: "Some say that this command of the Apostle refers to spiritual works, and not to the bodily labour of the farmer or craftsman"; and further on: "But it is useless for them to try to hide from themselves and from others the fact that they are unwilling not only to fulfil, but even to understand the useful admonishments of charity"; and again further on: "He wishes God's servants to employ themselves in corporal works that they may gain a livelihood." Now religious especially are called servants of God, because they give themselves entirely to the service of God, as Dionysius asserts (*Eccl. Hier.* vi).[3] Therefore it would seem that they are bound to manual labour.

Obj. 3. Further, Augustine says (*De Oper. Monach.* 17):[4] "I would like to know how they

[1] PL 40, 577.

[2] *Glossa ordin.* (VI, 115F); *Glossa* Lombardi (PL 192, 324). Cf. Augustine. *De Oper. Mon.*, I (PL 40, 549).

[3] Pt. I, Sect. 3 (PG 3, 532).

[4] PL 40, 564.

would occupy themselves, who are unwilling to work with their body. We occupy our time, say they, with prayers, psalms, reading, and the word of God." Yet these things are no excuse, and he proves this, as regards each in particular. For in the first place, as to prayer, he says: "One prayer of the obedient man is sooner granted than ten thousand prayers of the contemptuous," meaning that those are contemptuous and unworthy to be heard who work not with their hands. Secondly, as to the divine praises he adds: "Even while working with their hands they can easily sing hymns to God." Thirdly, with regard to reading, he goes on to say: "Those who say they are occupied in reading, do they not find there what the Apostle commanded? What sort of perverseness is this, to wish to read but not to obey what one reads?" Fourthly, he adds in reference to preaching (chap. 18): "If one has to speak, and is so busy that he cannot spare time for manual work, can all in the monastery do this? And since all cannot do this, why should all make this a pretext for being exempt? And even if all were able, they should do so by turns, not only so that the others may be occupied in other works, but also because it suffices that one speak while many listen." Therefore it would seem that religious should not desist from manual labour on account of spiritual works of this kind to which they devote themselves.

Obj. 4. Further, A gloss[5] on Luke 12. 33, *Sell what you possess,* says: "Not only give your clothes to the poor, but sell what you possess, that having once for all renounced all your possessions for the Lord's sake, you may henceforth work with the labour of your hands, so as to have wherewith to live or to give alms." Now it belongs properly to religious to renounce all they have. Therefore it would seem likewise to belong to them to live and give alms through the labour of their hands.

Obj. 5. Further, Religious especially would seem to be bound to imitate the life of the apostles, since they profess the state of perfection. Now the apostles worked with their own hands, according to I Cor. 4. 12: *We labour, working with our own hands.* Therefore it would seem that religious are bound to manual labour.

On the contrary, Those precepts that are commonly enjoined upon all are equally binding on religious and seculars. But the precept of manual labour is enjoined upon all in common, as appears from II Thess. 3. 6, *Withdraw yourselves from every brother walking disorderly,*

[5] *Glossa ordin.* (V, 158B).

etc. (for by brother he signifies every Christian, according to I Cor. 7. 12, *If any brother have a wife that believeth not*). Now it is written in the same passage (II Thess. 3. 10): *If any man will not work, neither let him eat.* Therefore religious are not bound to manual labour any more than seculars are.

I answer that, Manual labour is directed to four things. First and principally to obtain food; hence it was said to the first man (Gen. 3. 19): *In the sweat of thy face shalt thou eat bread,* and it is written (Ps. 132. 2): *For thou shalt eat the labours of thy hands.* Secondly, it is directed to the removal of idleness from which arise many evils; hence it is written (Ecclus. 33. 28, 29): *Send thy slave to work, that he be not idle, for idleness hath taught much evil.* Thirdly, it is directed to the curbing of concupiscence, in so far as it is a means of afflicting the body; hence it is written (II Cor. 6. 5, 6): *In labours, in watchings, in fastings, in chastity.* Fourthly, it is directed to almsgiving, and so it is written (Eph. 4. 28): *He that stole, let him now steal no more; but rather let him labour, working with his hands the thing which is good, that he may have something to give to him that suffereth need.*

Accordingly, in so far as manual labour is directed to obtaining food, it comes under a necessity of precept in so far as it is necessary for that end, since that which is directed to an end derives its necessity from that end, being, in effect, so far necessary as the end cannot be obtained without it. Consequently he who has no other means of livelihood is bound to work with his hands, whatever his condition may be. This is signified by the words of the Apostle: *If any man will not work, neither let him eat,* as though to say: "The necessity of manual labour is the necessity of meat." So that if one could live without eating, one would not be bound to work with one's hands. The same applies to those who have no other lawful means of livelihood, since a man is understood to be unable to do what he cannot do lawfully. Therefore we find that the Apostle prescribed manual labour merely as a remedy for the sin of those who gained their livelihood by unlawful means. For the Apostle ordered manual labour first of all in order to avoid theft, as appears from Eph. 4. 28, *He that stole, let him now steal no more; but rather let him labour, working with his hands.* Secondly, to avoid the coveting of others' property, so that it is written (I Thess. 4. 11): *Work with your own hands, as we commanded you, and that you walk hon-*

estly towards them that are without. Thirdly, to avoid the discreditable pursuits whereby some seek a livelihood. Hence he says (II Thess. 3. 10-12): *When we were with you, this we declared to you: If any man will not work, neither let him eat. For we have heard that there are some among you who walk disorderly, working not at all, but curiously meddling* (namely, as a gloss explains it,[1] "who make a living by meddling in unlawful things"). *Now we charge them that are such, and beseech them . . . that working with silence, they would eat their own bread.* Hence Jerome states in the preface to the second book of his commentary on the epistle to the Galatians[2] that the Apostle said this "not so much in his capacity of teacher as on account of the faults of the people."

It must, however, be observed that under manual labour are comprised all those human occupations whereby man can lawfully gain a livelihood, whether by using his hands, his feet, or his tongue. For watchmen, couriers, and the like who live by their labour, are understood to live by their handiwork, because, since the hand is the organ of organs, handiwork denotes all kinds of work by which a man may lawfully gain a livelihood.

In so far as manual labour is directed to the removal of idleness, or the affliction of the body, it does not come under a necessity of precept if we consider it in itself, since there are many other means besides manual labour of afflicting the body or of removing idleness, for the flesh is afflicted by fastings and watchings, and idleness is removed by meditation on the holy scriptures and by the divine praises. Hence a gloss[3] on Ps. 118. 82, *My eyes have failed for Thy word,* says: "He is not idle who meditates on God's word; nor is he who works abroad any better than he who devotes himself to the study of knowing the truth." Consequently for these reasons religious are not bound to manual labour, as neither are seculars, except when they are so bound by the statutes of their order. Thus Jerome says (*Ep. iv, ad Rustic. Monach.*):[4] "The Egyptian monasteries are accustomed to admit none unless they work or labour, not so much for the necessities of life, as for the welfare of the soul, lest it be led astray by wicked thoughts."

[1] *Glossa ordin.* (VI, 116A); *Glossa* Lombardi (PL 192, 325).   [2] PL 26, 382.

[3] *Glossa ordin.* (III, 267F); *Glossa* Lombardi (PL 191, 1085). Cf. Ambrose, *In Psalm.* 118.82 (PL 15, 1423).

[4] *Epist.,* cxxv (PL 22, 1079); cf. Gratian, *Decretum,* pt. III, d. v, can. 34 (RF I, 1421).

But in so far as manual labour is directed to almsgiving, it does not come under the necessity of precept, save perhaps in some particular case, when a man is under an obligation to give alms, and has no other means of having the wherewithal to assist the poor: for in such a case religious would be bound as well as seculars to do manual labour.

Reply Obj. 1. This command of the Apostle is of natural law. Hence a gloss[1] on II Thess. 3. 6, *That you withdraw yourselves from every brother walking disorderly*, says, "otherwise than the natural order requires," and he is speaking of those who abstained from manual labour. Hence nature has provided man with hands instead of arms and clothes with which she has provided other animals, in order that with his hands he may obtain these and other necessaries. From this it is clear that this precept, even as all the precepts of the natural law, is binding on both religious and seculars alike. Yet not everyone sins that works not with his hands, because those precepts of the natural law which regard the good of the many are not binding on each individual, but it suffices that one person apply himself to this business and another to that; for instance, that some be craftsmen, others husbandmen, others judges, and others teachers, and so forth, according to the words of the Apostle (I Cor. 12. 17), *If the whole body were the eye, where would be the hearing? If the whole were the hearing, where would be the smelling?*

Reply Obj. 2. This gloss is taken from Augustine's book, *De Operibus Monachorum,*[2] where he speaks against certain monks who declared it to be unlawful for the servants of God to work with their hands, on account of our Lord's saying (Matt. 6. 25): *Be not solicitous for your life, what you shall eat.* Nevertheless his words do not imply that religious are bound to work with their hands, if they have other means of livelihood. This is clear from his adding: "He wishes the servants of God to work with their bodies for their livelihood."[3] Now this does not apply to religious any more than to seculars, which is evident for two reasons. First, on account of the way in which the Apostle expresses himself, by saying: *That you withdraw yourselves from every brother walking disorderly* (II Thess. 3. 6). For he calls all Christians brothers, since at that time religious orders were not as yet founded.

Secondly, because religious have no other obligations than what seculars have, except as required by the rule they profess. Therefore if their rule contain nothing about manual labour, religious are not otherwise bound to manual labour than seculars are.

Reply Obj. 3. A man may devote himself in two ways to all the spiritual works mentioned by Augustine in the passage quoted: in one way with a view to the common good, in another with a view to his private advantage. Accordingly those who devote themselves publicly to these spiritual works are thereby exempt from manual labour for two reasons: first, because they are obliged to be occupied exclusively with such works; secondly, because those who devote themselves to such works have a claim to be supported by those for whose advantage they work.

On the other hand, those who devote themselves to such works not publicly but privately at it were, ought not on that account to be exempt from manual labour, nor have they a claim to be supported by the offerings of the faithful, and it is of these that Augustine is speaking. For when he says: "They can sing divine hymns even while working with their hands, like the craftsmen who give tongue to fable telling without withdrawing their hands from their work," it is clear that he cannot refer to those who sing the canonical hours in the church, but to those who tell psalms or hymns as private prayers. Likewise what he says of reading and prayer is to be referred to the private prayer and reading which even lay people do at times, and not to those who perform public prayers in the church, or give public lectures in the schools. Hence he does not say: "Those who say they are occupied in teaching and instructing," but: "Those who say they are occupied in reading." Again he speaks of that preaching which is addressed, not publicly to the people, but to one or a few in particular by way of private admonishment. Hence he says expressly: "If one has to speak." For according to a gloss on I Cor. 2. 4, "Speech is addressed privately, preaching to many."[4]

Reply Obj. 4. Those who despise all for God's sake are bound to work with their hands when they have no other means of livelihood, or of almsgiving (should the case occur where almsgiving were a matter of precept), but not otherwise, as stated in the Article. It is in this sense that the gloss quoted is to be understood.

¹ *Glossa interl.* (VI, 115v); *Glossa* Lombardi (PL 192, 324).　　² Chaps. 1, 2, 3 (PL 40, 549, 550, 551).　　³ Chap. 3 (PL 40, 551).

⁴ *Glossa interl.* (VI, 35v); *Glossa* Lombardi (PL 191, 1548).

Reply Obj. 5. That the apostles worked with their hands was sometimes a matter of necessity, sometimes a work of supererogation. It was of necessity when they failed to receive a livelihood from others. Hence a gloss[1] on I Cor. 4. 12, *We labour, working with our own hands*, adds "because no man giveth to us." It was of supererogation, as appears from I Cor. 9. 12, where the Apostle says that he did not use the power he had of living by the Gospel. The Apostle had recourse to this supererogation for three motives. First, in order to deprive the false apostles of the pretext for preaching, for they preached merely for a temporal advantage; hence he says (II Cor. 11. 12): *But what I do, that I will do that I may cut off the occasion from them*, etc. Secondly, in order to avoid burdening those to whom he preached; hence he says (II Cor. 12. 13): *What is there that you have had less than the other churches, but that I myself was not burthensome to you?* Thirdly, in order to give an example of work to the idle; hence he says (II Thess. 3. 8, 9): *We worked night and day . . . that we might give ourselves a pattern unto you, to imitate us.* However, the Apostle did not do this in those places like Athens where he had facilities for preaching, as Augustine observes (*De Oper. Monach.* 18).[2]

Yet religious are not for this reason bound to imitate the Apostle in this matter, since they are not bound to all works of supererogation. Hence neither did the other apostles work with their hands.

ARTICLE 4. *Whether It Is Lawful for Religious to Live on Alms?*

We proceed thus to the Fourth Article: It would seem unlawful for religious to live on alms.

Objection 1. For the Apostle (I Tim. 5. 16) forbids those widows who have other means of livelihood to live on the alms of the Church, so that the Church may have *sufficient for them that are widows indeed.* And Jerome says to Pope Damasus[3] that "those who have sufficient income from their parents and their own possessions, if they take what belongs to the poor they commit and incur the guilt of sacrilege, and by the abuse of such things they eat and drink judgment to themselves." Now religious

if they be able-bodied can support themselves by the work of their hands. Therefore it would seem that they sin if they consume the alms belonging to the poor.

Obj. 2. Further, To live at the expense of the faithful is the stipend appointed to those who preach the Gospel in payment of their labour or work, according to Matt. 10. 10: *The workman is worthy of his meat.* Now it pertains not to religious to preach the Gospel, but chiefly to prelates who are pastors and teachers. Therefore religious cannot lawfully live on the alms of the faithful.

Obj. 3. Further, Religious are in the state of perfection. But it is more perfect to give than to receive alms, for it is written (Acts 20. 35): *It is a more blessed thing to give, rather than to receive.* Therefore they should not live on alms, but rather should they give alms of their handiwork.

Obj. 4. Further, It pertains to religious to avoid obstacles to virtue and occasions of sin. Now the receiving of alms offers an occasion of sin, and hinders an act of virtue; hence a gloss[4] on II Thess. 3. 9, *That we might give ourselves a pattern unto you,* says: "He who through idleness eats often at another's table, must flatter the one who feeds him." It is also written (Exod. 23. 8): *Neither shalt thou take bribes which . . . blind the wise, and pervert the words of the just,* and (Prov. 22. 7): *The borrower is servant to him that lendeth.* This is contrary to religion, and so a gloss[5] on II Thess. 3. 9, *That we might give ourselves a pattern,* etc., says, "Our religion calls men to liberty." Therefore it would seem that religious should not live on alms.

Obj. 5. Further, Religious especially are bound to imitate the perfection of the apostles; hence the Apostle says (Phil. 3. 15): *Let us . . . as many as are perfect, be thus minded.* But the Apostle was unwilling to live at the expense of the faithful, either in order to cut off the occasion from the false apostles as he himself says (II Cor. 11. 12), or to avoid giving scandal to the weak, as appears from I Cor. 9. 12. It would seem therefore that religious ought for the same reasons to refrain from living on alms. Hence Augustine says (*De Oper. Monach.* 28):[6] "Cut off the occasion of disgraceful marketing whereby you lower yourselves in the esteem of others, and give scandal

---

[1] *Glossa interl.* (VI, 39r); *Glossa* Lombardi (PL 191, 1569).

[2] PL 40, 566.

[3] Cf. *Reg. Mon.*, chap. 4, among the works of Jerome (PL 30, 344). Cf. also Gratian, *Decretum*, pt. II, I, Q. 2, can. 6 (RF I, 409); causa XVI, Q. 1, can. 68 (RF I, 785).

[4] *Glossa ordin.* (VI, 115F); *Glossa* Lombardi (PL 192, 324).

[5] *Glossa ordin.* (VI, 115F); *Glossa* Lombardi (PL 192, 324).   [6] PL 40, 576.

to the weak; and show men that you seek not an easy livelihood in idleness, but the kingdom of God by the narrow and strait way."

On the contrary, Gregory says (Dial. ii, 1):[1] "The Blessed Benedict after leaving his home and parents dwelt for three years in a cave, and while there lived on the food brought to him by a monk of Rome." Nevertheless, although he was able-bodied, we do not read that he sought to live by the labour of his hands. Therefore religious may lawfully live on alms.

I answer that, A man may lawfully live on what is his or due to him. Now that which is given out of liberality becomes the property of the person to whom it is given. Therefore religious and clerics whose monasteries or churches have received from the munificence of princes or of any of the faithful any endowment whatsoever for their support, can lawfully live on such endowment without working with their hands, and yet without doubt they live on alms. Therefore in like manner if religious receive movable goods from the faithful they can lawfully live on them. For it is absurd to say that a person may accept an alms of some great property but not bread or some small sum of money. Nevertheless since these gifts would seem to be bestowed on religious in order that they may have more leisure for religious works, in which the donors of temporal goods wish to have a share, the use of such gifts would become unlawful for them if they abstained from religious works, because in that case, so far as they are concerned, they would be thwarting the intention of those who bestowed those gifts.

A thing is due to a person in two ways. First, on account of necessity, which makes all things common, as Ambrose asserts (cf. *Serm. de Temp.* lxiv).[2] Consequently if religious be in need they can lawfully live on alms. Such necessity may occur in three ways. First, through weakness of body, the result being that they are unable to make a living by working with their hands. Secondly, because that which they gain by their handiwork is insufficient for their livelihood; hence Augustine says (*De Oper. Monach.* 17)[3] that "the good works of the faithful should not leave God's servants who work with their hands without a supply of necessaries, that when the hour comes for them to nourish their souls, so as to make it impossible for them to do these corporal works, they

be not oppressed by want." Thirdly, because of the former mode of life of those who were unaccustomed to work with their hands; hence Augustine says[4] that "if they had in the world the wherewithal easily to support this life without working, and gave it to the needy when they were converted to God, we must believe their weakness and bear with it. For those who have thus been delicately brought up are wont to be unable to bear the toil of bodily labour."

In another way a thing becomes due to a person through his affording others something whether temporal or spiritual, according to I Cor. 9. 11, *If we have sown unto you spiritual things, is it a great matter if we reap your carnal things?* And in this sense religious may live on alms as being due to them in four ways. First, if they preach by the authority of the prelates. Secondly, if they be ministers of the altar, according to I Cor. 9. 13, 14, *They that serve the altar partake with the altar. So also the Lord ordained that they who preach the Gospel should live by the Gospel.* Hence Augustine says (*De Oper. Monach.* 21):[5] "If they are preachers of the gospel, I allow, they have a claim to live at the charge of the faithful; if they be ministers of the altar and dispensers of the sacraments, this claim is no pretence but theirs by perfect right." The reason for this is because the sacrifice of the altar wherever it be offered is common to all the faithful. Thirdly, if they devote themselves to the study of Holy Writ to the common profit of the whole Church. Therefore Jerome says (*Contra Vigil.* v):[6] "It is still the custom in Judea, not only among us but also among the Hebrews, for those who meditate on the law of the Lord day and night, and have no other share on earth but God alone, to be supported by the subscriptions of the synagogues and of the whole world." Fourthly, if they have endowed the monastery with the goods they possessed, they may live on the alms given to the monastery. Hence Augustine says (*De Oper. Monach.* 25)[7] that "those who renouncing or distributing their means, whether ample or of any amount whatever, have desired with pious and salutary humility to be numbered among the poor of Christ, have a claim on the community and on brotherly love to receive a livelihood in return. They are to be commended indeed if they work with their hands, but if they be unwilling, who will dare to force them? Nor does it matter," as he goes

---

[1] PL 66, 128.

[2] Cf. PL 17, 613–614. Cf. Basil. hom. III *In Luc.* 12.16 (PG 31, 1747).　　　[3] PL 40, 565.

[4] *Op. cit.,* chap. 21 (PL 40, 567).　　　[5] PL 40, 567.

[6] PL 23, 365.

[7] PL 40, 573.

on to say, "to which monasteries, or in what place any one of them has bestowed his goods on his needy brethren; for all Christians belong to one commonwealth."

On the other hand, in the default of any necessity, or of their affording any profit to others, it is unlawful for religious to wish to live in idleness on the alms given to the poor. Hence Augustine says (*De Oper. Monach.* 22):[1] "Sometimes those who enter the profession of God's service come from a servile condition of life, from tilling the soil or working at some trade or lowly occupation. In their case it is not so clear whether they came with the purpose of serving God, or of evading a life of want and toil with a view to being fed and clothed in idleness, and furthermore to being honoured by those by whom they were accustomed to be despised and downtrodden. Such persons surely cannot excuse themselves from work on the score of bodily weakness, for their former mode of life is evidence against them." And he adds further on (25):[2] "If they be unwilling to work, neither let them eat. For if the rich humble themselves to piety, it is not that the poor may be exalted to pride; since it is altogether unseemly that in a life wherein senators become labourers, labourers should become idle, and that where the lords of the manor have come after renouncing their ease, the serfs should live in comfort."

Reply Obj. 1. These authorities must be understood as referring to cases of necessity, that is to say, when there is no other means of succouring the poor, for then they would be bound not only to refrain from accepting alms, but also to give what they have for the support of the needy.

Reply Obj. 2. Prelates are able to preach in virtue of their office, but religious may be able to do so in virtue of delegation; and thus when they work in the field of the Lord, they may make their living thereby, according to II Tim. 2. 6, *The husbandman that laboureth must first partake of the fruits,* which a gloss explains thus, "that is to say, the preacher, who in the field of the Church tills the hearts of his hearers with the plough of God's word."[3] Those also who minister to the preachers may live by the gospel. Hence a gloss on Rom. 15. 27, *If the Gentiles have been made partakers of their spiritual things, they ought also in carnal things to minister to them,* says, "namely, to the Jews

who sent preachers from Jerusalem."[4] There are moreover other reasons for which a person has a claim to live at the charge of the faithful, as stated in the Article.

Reply Obj. 3. Other things being equal, it is more perfect to give than to receive. Nevertheless to give or to give up all one's possessions for Christ's sake, and to receive a little for one's livelihood is better than to give to the poor part by part, as stated above (Q. CLXXXVI, A. 3, Reply 6).

Reply Obj. 4. To receive gifts so as to increase one's wealth, or to accept a livelihood from another without having a claim to it, and without profit to others or being in need oneself, affords an occasion of sin. But this does not apply to religious, as stated above in the Article.

Reply Obj. 5. Whenever there is evident necessity for religious living on alms without doing any manual work, as well as an evident profit to be derived by others, it is not the weak who are scandalized, but those who are full of malice like the Pharisees, whose scandal our Lord teaches us to despise (Matt. 15. 12-14). If, however, these motives of necessity and profit be lacking, the weak might possibly be scandalized thereby; and this should be avoided. Yet the same scandal might be occasioned through those who live in idleness on the common revenues.

ARTICLE 5. *Whether It Is Lawful for Religious To Beg?*

We proceed this to the Fifth Article: It seems unlawful for religious to beg.

Objection 1. For Augustine says (*De Oper. Monach.* 28):[5] "The most cunning foe has scattered on all sides a great number of hypocrites wearing the monastic habit, who go wandering about the country," and afterwards he adds: "They all ask, they all demand to be supported in their profitable penury, or to be paid for a pretended holiness." Therefore it would seem that the life of mendicant religious is to be condemned.

Obj. 2. Further, It is written (I Thess. 4. 11): *That you . . . work with your own hands as we commanded you, and that you walk honestly towards them that are without: and that you want nothing of any man's;* and a gloss on this passage says: "You must work and not be idle, because work is both honourable and a light to the unbeliever; and you must not covet that which belongs to another, and much less beg

---

[1] PL 40, 568. [2] PL 40, 573.
[3] *Glossa ordin.* (VI, 124E); *Glossa* Lombardi (PL 192, 368).
[4] *Glossa interl.* (VI, 31v); *Glossa* Lombardi (PL 191, 1526). [5] PL 40, 575.

or take anything."[1] Again a gloss on II Thess. 3. 10, *If any man will not work*, etc., says: "He wishes the servants of God to work with the body, so as to gain a livelihood, and not be compelled by want to ask for necessaries."[2] Now this is to beg. Therefore it would seem unlawful to beg while omitting to work with one's hands.

Obj. 3. Further, That which is forbidden by law and contrary to justice, is unbecoming to religious. Now begging is forbidden in the divine law, for it is written (Deut. 15. 4): *There shall be no poor nor beggar among you*, and (Ps. 36. 25): *I have not seen the just forsaken, nor his seed seeking bread*. Moreover an able-bodied mendicant is punished by civil law, according to the law *Of able-bodied mendicants*.[3] Therefore it is unfitting for religious to beg.

Obj. 4. Further, "Shame is about an uncomely action," as Damascene says (*De Fide Orthod.* ii, 15).[4] Now Ambrose says (*De Offic.* i, 30)[5] that "to be ashamed to ask is a sign of good birth." Therefore it is disgraceful to beg, and consequently this is unbecoming to religious.

Obj. 5. Further, According to our Lord's command it is especially becoming to preachers of the Gospel to live on alms, as stated above (A. 4). Yet it is not becoming that they should beg, since a gloss on II Tim. 2. 6, *The husbandman, that laboureth*, etc., says:[6] "The Apostle wishes the evangelist to understand that to accept necessaries from those among whom he labours is not mendicancy but a right." Therefore it would seem unbecoming for religious to beg.

On the contrary, It becomes religious to live in imitation of Christ. Now Christ was a mendicant, according to Ps. 39. 18, *But I am a beggar and poor;* where a gloss says:[7] "Christ said this of Himself as bearing the 'form of a servant,'" and further on: "A beggar is one who entreats another, and a poor man is one who has not enough for himself." Again it is written (Ps. 69. 6): *I am needy and poor;* where a gloss says:[8] "'Needy,' that is a suppliant; 'and poor,'

that is, not having enough for myself, because I have no worldly wealth." And Jerome says in a letter:[9] "Beware lest whereas thy Lord," that is Christ, "begged, thou amass other people's wealth." Therefore it becomes religious to beg.

I answer that, Two things may be considered in reference to mendicancy. The first is on the part of the act itself of begging, which has a certain abasement attaching to it, since of all men those would seem most abased who are not only poor, but are so needy that they have to receive their meat from others. In this way some deserve praise for begging out of humility, just as they abase themselves in other ways, as being the most efficacious remedy against pride which they desire to quench either in themselves or in others by their example. For just as a disease that arises from excessive heat is most efficaciously healed by things that excel in cold, so proneness to pride is most efficaciously healed by those things which savour most of abasement. Hence it is said in the Decretal on Penance (D. 11, cap. *Si quis semel*):[10] "To condescend to the humblest duties, and to devote oneself to the lowliest service is an exercise of humility; for thus one is able to heal the disease of pride and human glory." Hence Jerome praises Fabiola (*Ep. ad Ocean.*)[11] for that "she desired to receive alms, having poured forth all her wealth for Christ's sake." The Blessed Alexis acted in like manner, for, having renounced all his possessions for Christ's sake he rejoiced in receiving alms even from his own servants. It is also related of the Blessed Arsenius in the Lives of the Fathers (v. 6)[12] that he gave thanks because he was forced by necessity to ask for alms. Hence it is enjoined to some people as a penance for grievous sins to go on a pilgrimage begging. Since, however, humility like the other virtues should not be without discretion, one should be discreet in becoming a mendicant for the purpose of humiliation, lest a man thereby incur the mark of covetousness or of anything else unbecoming.

Secondly, mendicancy may be considered on the part of that which one gets by begging: and thus a man may be led to beg by a twofold motive. First, by the desire to have wealth or meat without working for it, and such mendicancy is unlawful; secondly, by a motive of necessity or usefulness. The motive is one of

---

[1] *Glossa ordin.* (VI, 111E); *Glossa* Lombardi (PL 192, 300).
[2] *Glossa ordin.* (VI, 116A); *Glossa* Lombardi (PL 192, 325). Cf. Augustine, *De Oper. Mon.*, 3 (PL 40, 551).
[3] *Codex*, XI, tit. XXVI, leg. 1 (KR II, 435ᵇ).
[4] PG 94, 932; Cf. Nemesius, *De Nat. Hom.*, XX (PG 40, 688).
[5] PL 16, 74.
[6] *Glossa ordin.* (VI, 124E); *Glossa* Lombardi (PL 192, 368); cf. Augustine, *De Oper. Mon.*, XV (PL 40, 561).
[7] *Glossa* Lombardi (PL 191, 406); cf. *Glossa ordin.* (III, 143, E).
[8] *Glossa* Lombardi (PL 191, 645); cf. *Glossa interl.* (III, 184r).

[9] Cf. *Epist.*, LVIII (PL 22, 584).
[10] Gratian, PT. II, causa XXXIII, Q. 3 (RF I, 1190).
[11] *Epist.* LXXVII (PL 22, 696).   [12] PL 73, 888.

necessity if a man has no other means of livelihood save begging, and it is a motive of usefulness if he wishes to accomplish something useful, and is unable to do so without the alms of the faithful. And so alms are besought for the building of a bridge, or church, or for any other work whatever that is conducive to the common good; thus scholars may seek alms that they may devote themselves to the study of wisdom. In this way mendicancy is lawful to religious no less than to seculars.

Reply Obj. 1. Augustine is speaking there explicitly of those who beg from motives of covetousness.

Reply Obj. 2. The first gloss speaks of begging from motives of covetousness, as appears from the words of the Apostle, while the second gloss speaks of those who without effecting any useful purpose, beg their livelihood in order to live in idleness. On the other hand, he lives not idly who in any way lives usefully.

Reply Obj. 3. This precept of the divine law does not forbid anyone to beg, but it forbids the rich to be so stingy that some are compelled by necessity to beg. The civil law imposes a penalty on able-bodied mendicants who beg from motives neither of utility nor of necessity.

Reply Obj. 4. Uncomeliness is twofold. One arises from lack of virtue (*inhonestas*), the other from an external defect; thus it is uncomely for a man to be sick or poor. Such uncomeliness of mendicancy does not pertain to sin, but it may pertain to humility, as stated in the Article.

Reply Obj. 5. Preachers have the right to be fed by those to whom they preach; yet if they wish to seek this by begging so as to receive it as a free gift and not as a right this will be a mark of greater humility.

ARTICLE 6. *Whether It Is Lawful for Religious To Wear Coarser Clothes Than Others?*

We proceed thus to the Sixth Article: It would seem unlawful for religious to wear coarser clothes than others.

Objection 1. For according to the Apostle (I Thess. 5. 22) we ought to *refrain from all appearance of evil.* Now coarseness of clothes has an appearance of evil, for our Lord said (Matt. 7. 15): *Beware of false prophets who come to you in the clothing of sheep;* and a gloss on Apoc. 6. 8, *Behold a pale horse,* says:[1] "The devil finding that he cannot succeed, neither by outward afflictions nor by manifest heresies, sends in advance false brethren, who

---

under the guise of religion assume the characteristics of the black and red horses by corrupting the faith." Therefore it would seem that religious should not wear coarse clothes.

Obj. 2. Further, Jerome says to Nepotian:[2] "Avoid sombre," that is, black, "equally with glittering apparel. Fine and coarse clothes are equally to be shunned, for the one exhales pleasure, the other vainglory." Therefore, since vainglory is a graver sin than the use of things which give pleasure, it would seem that religious who should tend to perfection ought to avoid coarse rather than fine clothes.

Obj. 3. Further, Religious should aim especially at doing works of penance. Now in works of penance we should use not outward signs of sorrow, but rather signs of joy; for our Lord said (Matt. 6. 16): *When you fast, be not, as the hypocrites, sad,* and afterwards He added: *But thou, when thou fastest, anoint thy head and wash thy face.* Augustine commenting on these words (*De Serm. Dom. in Monte,* ii, 12).[3] "In this chapter we must observe that not only the glare and pomp of outward things, but even the weeds of mourning may be a subject of ostentation, all the more dangerous as being a decoy under the guise of God's service." Therefore it seems that religious ought not to wear coarse clothes.

On the contrary, The Apostle says (Heb. 11. 37): *They wandered about in sheep-skins, in goat-skins,* and a gloss adds,[4]—"as Elias and others." Moreover it is said in the Decretal XXI, Q. IV, cap. *Omnis jactantia:*[5] "If any persons be found to deride those who wear coarse and religious apparel they must be reproved. For in the early times all those who were consecrated to God went about in common and coarse apparel."

I answer that, As Augustine says[6] that in all external things, "it is not the use but the intention of the user that is at fault." In order to judge of this it is necessary to observe that coarse and homely apparel may be considered in two ways. First, as being a sign of a man's disposition or condition, because according to Ecclus. 19. 27, *the attire . . . of the man* shows *what he is.* In this way coarseness of attire is sometimes a sign of sorrow. Hence those who are beset with sorrow are accustomed to wear coarser clothes, just as on the other hand in

---

[1] *Glossa ordin.* (VI, 249F).

[2] *Epist.,* LII (PL 22, 535).

[3] PL 34, 1287.

[4] *Glossa interl.* (VI, 157v); *Glossa* Lombardi (PL 191, 499).

[5] Gratian, pt. II (RF I, 857).

[6] *Christian Doctrine,* III, 12 (PL 34, 73).

times of festivity and joy they wear finer clothes. Hence penitents make use of coarse apparel, for example, the king (Jonas 3. 6) who *was clothed with sack-cloth,* and Achab (III Kings 21. 27) who *put hair-cloth upon his flesh.*

Sometimes, however, it is a sign of the contempt of riches and worldly ostentation. Hence Jerome says to the monk Rusticus:[1] "Let your sombre attire indicate your purity of mind, your coarse robe prove your contempt of the world, yet so that your mind be not inflated withal, lest your speech belie your habit." In both these ways it is becoming for religious to wear coarse attire, since religion is a state of penance and of contempt of worldly glory.

But that a person wish to signify this to others arises from three motives. First, in order to humble himself; for just as a man's mind is uplifted by fine clothes, so is it humbled by lowly apparel. Hence speaking of Achab who *put hair-cloth on his flesh,* the Lord said to Elias: *Hast thou seen Achab humbled before Me?* (III Kings 21. 29). Secondly, in order to set an example to others; hence a gloss on Matt. 3. 4 (*John*) *had his garments of camel's hair,* says: "He who preaches penance is clothed in the habit of penance."[2] Thirdly, on account of vainglory; thus Augustine says (*De Serm. Dom. in Monte,* ii, 12)[3] that "even the weeds of mourning may be a subject of ostentation."

Accordingly in the first two ways it is praiseworthy to wear humble apparel, but in the third way it is sinful.

Secondly, coarse and homely attire may be considered as the result of covetousness or negligence, and thus also it is sinful.

Reply Obj. 1. Coarseness of attire has not of itself the appearance of evil; indeed it has more the appearance of good, namely of the contempt of worldly glory. Hence it is that wicked persons hide their wickedness under coarse clothing. And so Augustine says (*De Serm. Dom. in Monte,* ii, 24)[4] that "the sheep should not dislike their clothing for the reason that the wolves sometimes hide themselves under it."

Reply Obj. 2. Jerome is speaking there of the coarse attire that is worn on account of human glory.

Reply Obj. 3. According to our Lord's teaching men should do no deed of holiness for the sake of show; and this is especially the case when one does something strange. Hence Chry-

sostom says:[5] "While praying a man should do nothing strange, so as to draw the gaze of others, either by shouting or striking his breast, or casting up his hands," because the very strangeness draws people's attention to him. Yet blame does not attach to all strange behaviour that draws people's attention, for it may be done well or ill. Hence Augustine says (*De Serm. Dom. in Monte,* ii, 12)[6] that "in the practice of the Christian religion when a man draws attention to himself by unwonted squalor and shabbiness, since he acts thus voluntarily and not of necessity, we can gather from his other deeds whether his behaviour is motived by contempt of excessive dress or by affectation." Religious, however, would especially seem not to act thus from affectation, since they wear a coarse habit as a sign of their profession whereby they profess contempt of the world.

QUESTION CLXXXVIII
OF THE DIFFERENT KINDS OF RELIGIOUS LIFE
(*In Eight Articles*)

WE must now consider the different kinds of religious life, and under this head there are eight points of inquiry: (1) Whether there are different kinds of religious life or only one? (2) Whether a religious order can be established for the works of the active life? (3) Whether a religious order can be directed to soldiering? (4) Whether a religious order can be established for preaching and the exercise of like works? (5) Whether a religious order can be established for the study of science? (6) Whether a religious order that is directed to the contemplative life is more excellent than one that is directed to the active life? (7) Whether religious perfection is diminished by possessing something in common? (8) Whether the religious life of solitaries is to be preferred to the religious life of those who live in community.

ARTICLE 1. *Whether There Is Only One Religious Order?*

We proceed thus to the First Article: It would seem that there is but one religious order.

Objection 1. For there can be no diversity in that which is possessed wholly and perfectly; therefore there can be only one first and sovereign good, as stated in the First Part (Q. XI, A. 3). Now as Gregory says (*Hom.* viii *in Ezech.*),[7] "when a man vows to Almighty God

[1] *Epist.,* CXXV (PL 22, 1075).
[2] *Glossa ordin.* (V, 13E).
[3] PL 34, 520.   [4] PL 34, 1306.

[5] Pseudo-Chrysostom, *Op. Imperf. in Matt.,* hom. XIII, on 5.5 (PG 56, 709). [6] PL 34, 1287. [7] Bk. II (PL 76, 1037).

all that he has, all his life, all his knowledge, it is a holocaust," without which there is no religious life. Therefore it would seem that there are not many religious orders but only one.

Obj. 2. Further, Things which agree in essentials differ only accidentally. Now there is no religious order without the three essential vows of religion, as stated above (Q. CLXXXVI, AA. 6, 7). Therefore it would seem that religious orders differ not specifically, but only accidentally.

Obj. 3. Further, The state of perfection belongs both to religious and to bishops, as stated above (Q. CLXXXIV, A. 5). Now the episcopate is not diversified specifically, but is one wherever it may be; hence Jerome says to Bishop Evagrius:[1] "Wherever a bishop is, whether at Rome, or Gubbio, or Constantinople, or Reggio, he has the same excellence, the same priesthood." Therefore in like manner there is but one religious order.

Obj. 4. Further, Anything that may lead to confusion should be removed from the Church. Now it would seem that a diversity of religious orders might confuse the Christian people, as a Decretal states (Cap. *Ne Nimia:* de Relig. Dom.).[2] Therefore it seems that there ought not to be different religious orders.

On the contrary, It is written (Ps. 44. 10) that it pertains to the adornment of the queen that she is *surrounded with variety.*

I answer that, As stated above (Q. CLXXXVI, A. 7; Q. CLXXXVII, A. 2), the religious state is a training school wherein one aims by practice at the perfection of charity. Now there are various works of charity to which a man may devote himself, and there are also various kinds of exercise. Therefore religious orders may be differentiated in two ways. First, according to the different things to which they may be directed; thus one may be directed to the lodging of pilgrims, another to visiting or ransoming captives. Secondly, there may be various religious orders according to the diversity of practices; thus in one religious order the body is chastised by abstinence in food, in another by the practice of manual labour, scantiness of clothes, or the like.

Since, however, the end imports most in every matter, religious orders differ more especially according to their various ends than according to their various practices.

[1] *Epist.,* CXLVI (PL 22, 1194); cf. Gratian, *Decretum,* Pt. I, d. 93, can. 24 (RF I, 328).

[2] *Decretal. Gregor.,* IX, BK. III, tit. XXXVI, chap. 9 (RF II, 607).

Reply Obj. 1. The obligation to devote oneself wholly to God's service is common to every religious order; hence religious do not differ in this respect, as though in one religious order a person retained some one thing of his own, and in another order some other thing. But the difference is in respect of the different things wherein one may serve God, and whereby a man may dispose himself to the service of God.

Reply Obj. 2. The three essential vows of religion pertain to the practice of religion as principles to which all other matters are reduced, as stated above (Q. CLXXXVI, A. 7, REPLY 2). But there are various ways of disposing oneself to the observance of each of them. For instance one disposes oneself to observe the vow of continence, by solitude of place, by abstinence, by mutual fellowship, and by many like means. Accordingly it is evident that the community of the essential vows is compatible with diversity of religious life, both on account of the different dispositions and on account of the different ends, as explained above in this Article.

Reply Obj. 3. In matters relating to perfection, the bishop stands in the position of agent, and the religious as passive, as stated above (Q. CLXXXIV, A. 7). Now the agent, even in natural things, the higher it is, is so much the more one, while the things that are passive are various. Hence with reason the episcopal state is one, while religious orders are many.

Reply Obj. 4. Confusion is opposed to distinction and order. Accordingly the multitude of religious orders would lead to confusion if different religious orders were directed to the same end and in the same way, without necessity or utility. Therefore to prevent this happening it has been wholesomely forbidden to establish a new religious order without the authority of the Sovereign Pontiff.

ARTICLE 2. *Whether a Religious Order Should Be Established for the Works of the Active Life?*

We proceed thus to the Second Article: It seems that no religious order should be established for the works of the active life.

Objection 1. For every religious order belongs to the state of perfection, as stated above (Q. CLXXXIV, A. 5). Now the perfection of the religious state consists in the contemplation of divine things. For Dionysius says (*Eccles. Hier.* vi)[3] that "they are called servants of God by reason of their rendering pure service and subjection to God, and on account of the in-

[3] Sect. 3 (PG 3, 532).

divisible and singular life which unites them by holy reflections," that is, contemplations, "on invisible things, to the Godlike unity and the perfection beloved of God." Therefore it seems that no religious order should be established for the works of the active life.

Obj. 2. Further, It seems that the same judgment applies to canons regular as to monks, according to Extrav. *De Postul.,* cap. *Ex parte,*[1] and *De Statu monach.,* cap. *Quod Dei timorem,*[2] for it is stated that "they are not considered to be separated from the fellowship of holy monks," and the same would seem to apply to all other religious. Now the monastic rule was established for the purpose of the contemplative life; therefore Jerome says to Paulinus (*Ep.* lviii).[3] "If you wish to be what you are called, a monk, that is, a solitary, what business have you in a city?" The same is found stated in Extrav. *De Renuntiatione,* cap. *Nisi cum pridem,*[4] and *De Regular.,* cap. *Licet quibusdam.*[5] Therefore it would seem that every religious order is directed to the contemplative life, and none to the active life.

Obj. 3. Further, The active life is concerned with the present world. Now all religious are said to renounce the world; therefore Gregory says (*Hom.* viii *in Ezech.*):[6] "He who renounces this world, and does all the good he can, is like one who has gone out of Egypt and offers sacrifices in the wilderness." Therefore it would seem that no religious order can be directed to the active life.

On the contrary, It is written (James i. 27): *Religion clean and undefiled before God and the Father, is this: to visit the fatherless and widows in their tribulation.* Now this belongs to the active life. Therefore religious life can be fittingly directed to the active life.

I answer that, As stated above (Q. CLXXXVII, A. 2), the religious state is directed to the perfection of charity, which extends to the love of God and of our neighbour. Now the contemplative life which seeks to devote itself to God alone belongs directly to the love of God, while the active life, which ministers to our neighbour's needs, belongs directly to the love of one's neighbour. And just as out of charity we love our neighbour for God's sake, so the services we render our neighbour rebound to God, according to Matt. 25. 40, *What you*

have done (Vulg.,—*As long as you did it*) *to one of these My least brethren, you did it to Me.* Consequently those services which we render our neighbour, in so far as we refer them to God, are described as sacrifices, according to Heb. 13. 16, *Do not forget to do good and to impart, for by such sacrifices God's favour is obtained.* And since it belongs properly to religion to offer sacrifice to God, as stated above (Q. LXXXI, A. 1, REPLY 1), it follows that certain religious orders are fittingly directed to the works of the active life. Hence in the *Conferences of the Fathers* (*Coll.* xiv, 4)[7] the Abbot Nesteros in distinguishing the various aims of religious orders says: "Some direct their intention exclusively to the hidden life of the desert and purity of heart, some are occupied with the instruction of the brethren and the care of the monasteries, while others delight in the service of the guest-house," that is, in hospitality.

Reply Obj. 1. Service and subjection rendered to God are not precluded by the works of the active life, whereby a man serves his neighbour for God's sake, as stated in the Article. Nor do these works preclude singularity of life; not that they involve man's living apart from his fellowmen, but in the sense that each man individually devotes himself to things pertaining to the service of God; and since religious occupy themselves with the works of the active life for God's sake, it follows that their action results from their contemplation of divine things. Hence they are not entirely deprived of the fruit of the contemplative life.

Reply Obj. 2. The same judgment applies to monks and to all other religious, as regards things common to all religious orders, for instance as regards their devoting themselves wholly to the divine service, their observance of the essential vows of religion, and their refraining from worldly business. But it does not follow that this likeness extends to other things that are proper to the monastic profession, and are directed especially to the contemplative life. Hence in the aforesaid Decretal, *De Postulando,* it is not stated absolutely that "the same judgment applies to canons regular as to monks," but that it applies "in matters already mentioned," namely that "they are not to act as advocates in lawsuits." Again the Decretal quoted, referring to the monastic state, after the statement that "canons regular are not considered to be separated from the fellowship of monks," goes on to say: "Nevertheless they obey an easier rule." Hence it is evident that

---

[1] *Decretal. Gregor.,* IX, BK. I, tit. 37, chap. 2 (RF II, 211).
[2] *Ibid.,* BK. III, tit. 35, chap. 5 (RF II, 599).
[3] PL 22, 583.
[4] *Decretal. Gregor.,* IX, BK. I, tit. IX, chap. 10 (RF II, 107).
[5] *Decretal Gregor.,* IX, BK. III, tit. 31, chap. 18 (RF II, 575).　　[6] BK. II (PL 76, 1038).
[7] Cassian (PL 49, 957).

they are not bound to all that monks are bound.

Reply Obj. 3. A man may be in the world in two ways: in one way by his bodily presence, in another way by the bent of his mind. Hence our Lord said to His disciples (John 15. 19): *I have chosen you out of the world,* and yet speaking of them to His Father He said (*ibid.* 17. 11): *These are in the world, and I come to Thee.* Although, then, religious who are occupied with the works of the active life are in the world as to the presence of the body, they are not in the world as regards their bent of mind, because they are occupied with external things, not as seeking anything of the world, but merely for the sake of serving God; for *they . . . use this world, as if they used it not,* to quote I Cor. 7. 31. Hence (James 1. 27) after it is stated that *religion clean and undefiled . . . is . . . to visit the fatherless and widows in their tribulation,* it is added, *and to keep one's self unspotted from this world,* namely to avoid being attached to worldly things.

ARTICLE 3. *Whether a Religious Order Can Be Directed to Soldiering?*

We proceed thus to the Third Article: It would seem that no religious order can be directed to soldiering.

Objection 1. For all religious orders belong to the state of perfection. Now our Lord said with reference to the perfection of Christian life (Matt. 5. 39): *I say to you not to resist evil; but if one strike thee on the right cheek, turn to him also the other,* which is inconsistent with the duties of a soldier. Therefore no religious order can be established for soldiering.

Obj. 2. Further, The bodily encounter of the battlefield is more grievous than the encounter in words that takes place between counsel at law. Yet religious are forbidden to plead at law, as appears from the Decretal *De Postulando quoted above* (A. 2, obj. 2). Therefore much less may a religious order be established for soldiering.

Obj. 3. Further, The religious state is a state of penance, as we have said above (Q. CLXXXVII, A. 6). Now according to the code of laws soldiering is forbidden to penitents; for it is said in the Decretal *De Pœnit.,* Dist. v, cap. 3:[1] "It is altogether opposed to the rules of the Church, to return to worldly soldiering after doing penance." Therefore it is unfitting for any religious order to be established for soldiering.

Obj. 4. Further, No religious order may be established for an unjust aim. But as Isidore says (*Etym.* xviii),[2] a just war is one that is waged by order of the emperor. Since then religious are private individuals, it would seem unlawful for them to wage war; and consequently no religious order may be established for this purpose.

On the contrary, Augustine says to Boniface (*Ep.* clxxxix):[3] "Beware of thinking that none of those can please God who handle warlike weapons. Of such was holy David to whom the Lord gave great testimony." Now religious orders are established in order that men may please God. Therefore nothing hinders the establishing of a religious order for the purpose of soldiering.

I answer that, As stated above (A. 2), a religious order may be established not only for the works of the contemplative life, but also for the works of the active life, in so far as they are concerned in helping our neighbour and in the service of God, but not in so far as they are directed to a worldly aim. Now the occupation of soldiering may be directed to the assistance of our neighbour, not only as regards private individuals, but also as regards the defence of the whole commonwealth. Hence it is said of Judas Machabeus (I Mach. 3. 2, 3) that *he* (Vulg.,—*they*) *fought with cheerfulness the battle of Israel, and he got his people great honour.* It can also be directed to the upkeep of divine worship, and hence (*ibid.* 21) Judas is stated to have said: *We will fight for our lives and our laws,* and further on (13. 3) Simon said: *You know what great battles I and my brethren, and the house of my father, have fought for the laws and the sanctuary.*

Hence a religious order may be fittingly established for soldiering, not indeed for any worldly purpose, but for the defence of divine worship and public safety, or also of the poor and oppressed, according to Ps. 81. 4: *Rescue the poor, and deliver the needy out of the hand of the sinner.*

Reply Obj. 1. Not to resist evil may be understood in two ways. First, in the sense of forgiving the wrong done to oneself, and thus it may pertain to perfection, when it is expedient to act thus for the spiritual welfare of others. Secondly, in the sense of tolerating patiently the wrongs done to others; and this pertains to imperfection, or even to vice, if one be able to resist the wrongdoer in a becoming manner.

[1] Gratian, pt. II, causa XXXIII, Q. 3 (RF I, 1240).

[2] Chap. I (PL 82, 639).
[3] PL 33, 855; Cf. Gratian, *Decretum,* pt. II, causa XXIII, Q. I, can. 3 (RF I, 892).

Hence Ambrose says (*De Offic.* i, 27).[1] "The courage whereby a man in battle defends his country against barbarians, or protects the weak at home, or his friends against robbers is full of justice, even as our Lord says in the passage quoted, . . . *thy goods, ask them not again.*[2] If, however, a man were not to demand the return of that which belongs to another, he would sin if it were his business to do so; for it is praiseworthy to give away one's own, but not another's property. And much less should the things of God be neglected, for as Chrysostom says,[3] "it is most wicked to overlook the wrongs done to God."

Reply Obj. 2. It is inconsistent with any religious order to act as counsel at law for a worldly end, but it is not inconsistent to do so at the orders of one's superior and in favour of one's monastery, as stated in the same Decretal or for the defence of the poor and widows. Therefore it is said in the Decretals (Dist. lxxxviii, cap. 1):[4] "The holy synod has decreed that henceforth no cleric is to buy property or occupy himself with secular business, save with a view to the care of the fatherless . . . and widows." Likewise to be a soldier for the sake of some worldly purpose is contrary to all religious life, but this does not apply to those who are soldiers for the sake of God's service.

Reply Obj. 3. Worldly soldiering is forbidden to penitents, but the soldiering which is directed to the service of God is imposed as a penance on some people, as in the case of those upon whom it is enjoined to take arms in defence of the Holy Land.

Reply Obj. 4. The establishment of a religious order for the purpose of soldiering does not imply that the religious can wage war on their own authority; but they can do so only on the authority of the sovereign or of the Church.

ARTICLE 4. *Whether a Religious Order Can Be Established for Preaching or Hearing Confessions?*

We proceed thus to the Fourth Article: It would seem that no religious order may be established for preaching, or hearing confessions.

Objection 1. For it is said (VII, Q. 1, cap. *Hoc nequaquam*):[5] "The monastic life is one

of subjection and discipleship, not of teaching, authority, or pastoral care." and the same apparently applies to religious. Now preaching and hearing confessions are the actions of a pastor and teacher. Therefore a religious order should not be established for this purpose.

Obj. 2. Further, The purpose for which a religious order is established would seem to be something most proper to the religious life, as stated above (AA. 2, 3). Now the aforesaid actions are not proper to religious but to bishops. Therefore a religious order should not be established for the purpose of such actions.

Obj. 3. Further, It seems unfitting that the authority to preach and hear confessions should be committed to an unlimited number of men; and there is no fixed number of those who are received into a religious order. Therefore it is unfitting for a religious order to be established for the purpose of the aforesaid actions.

Obj. 4. Further, Preachers have a right to receive their livelihood from the faithful of Christ, according to I Cor. 9. If then the office of preaching be committed to a religious order established for that purpose, it follows that the faithful of Christ are bound to support an unlimited number of persons, which would be a heavy burden on them. Therefore a religious order should not be established for the exercise of these actions.

Obj. 5. Further, The organization of the Church should be in accordance with Christ's institution. Now Christ sent first the twelve apostles to preach, as related in Luke 9., and afterwards He sent the seventy-two disciples, as stated in Luke 10. Moreover, according to the gloss of Bede[6] on *And after these things* (Luke 10. 1), "the apostles are represented by the bishops, the seventy-two disciples by the lesser priests," that is, the parish priests. Therefore in addition to bishops and parish priests, no religious order should be established for the purpose of preaching and hearing confessions.

On the contrary, In the *Conferences of the Fathers* (*Coll.* xiv, 4)[7] Abbot Nesteros, speaking of the various kinds of religious orders, says: "Some choosing the care of the sick, others devoting themselves to the relief of the afflicted and oppressed, or applying themselves to teaching, or giving alms to the poor, have been most highly esteemed on account of their devotion and piety." Therefore just as a religious order may be established for the care of the sick, so also may one be established for

---

[1] PL 16, 66.

[2] Luke 6. 30: *Of him that taketh away thy goods, ask them not again.* Cf. Matt. 5. 40.

[3] Pseudo-Chrysostom, *op. imperf. in Matt.,* hom. v, on 4.10 (PG 56, 668).   [4] Gratian, PT. I (RF I, 306).

[5] Gratian, *Decretum,* PT. II, causa VII, Q. I, can. 45 (RF I, 585).

[6] *Glossa ordin.* (V, 151E); Bede, PL 92, 461.

[7] Cassian (PL 49, 959).

teaching the people by preaching and like works.

I answer that, As stated above (A. 2), it is fitting for a religious order to be established for the works of the active life, in so far as they are directed to the good of our neighbour, the service of God, and the upkeep of divine worship. Now the good of our neighbour is advanced by things pertaining to the spiritual welfare of the soul rather than by things pertaining to the supplying of bodily needs, in proportion to the excellence of spiritual over corporal things. Hence it was stated above (Q. XXXII, A. 3) that spiritual works of mercy surpass corporal works of mercy. Moreover this is more pertinent to the service of God, to Whom no sacrifice is more acceptable than zeal for souls, as Gregory says (*Hom.* xii *in Ezech.*).[1] Furthermore, it is a greater thing to employ spiritual arms in defending the faithful against the errors of heretics and the temptations of the devil, than to protect the faithful by means of bodily weapons. Therefore it is most fitting for a religious order to be established for preaching and similar works pertaining to the salvation of souls.

Reply Obj. 1. He who works by virtue of another acts as an instrument. And "a minister is like an animated instrument," as the Philosopher says.[2] Hence if a man preach or do something similar by the authority of his superiors, he does not rise above the degree of discipleship or subjection, which is appropriate to religious.

Reply Obj. 2. Some religious orders are established for soldiering, to wage war not indeed on their own authority, but on that of the sovereign or of the Church who are able to wage war by virtue of their office, as stated above (A. 3, Reply 4). In the same way certain religious orders are established for preaching and hearing confessions, not indeed by their own authority, but by the authority of the higher and lower superiors, to whom these things belong by virtue of their office. Consequently to be subject to one's superiors in such a ministry is proper to a religious order of this kind.

Reply Obj. 3. Bishops do not allow these religious severally and indiscriminately to preach or hear confessions, but according to the discretion of the religious superiors, or according to their own appointment.

Reply Obj. 4. The faithful are not bound by law to contribute to the support of other than their ordinary prelates, who receive the tithes

and offerings of the faithful for that purpose, as well as other ecclesiastical revenues. But if some men are willing to minister to the faithful by exercising the aforesaid acts gratuitously, and without demanding payment as of right, the faithful are not burdened thereby because their temporal contributions can be liberally repaid by those men, nor are they bound by law to contribute, but by charity, and yet not so that they be burdened thereby and others eased, as stated in II Cor. 8. 13. If, however, none be found to devote themselves gratuitously to services of this kind, the ordinary prelate is bound, if he cannot suffice by himself, to seek other suitable persons and support them himself.

Reply Obj. 5. The seventy-two disciples are represented not only by the parish priests, but by all those of lower order who in any way assist the bishops in their office. For we do not read that our Lord appointed the seventy-two disciples to certain fixed parishes, but that *He sent them two and two before His face into every city and place whither He Himself was to come.* It was fitting, however, that in addition to the ordinary prelates others should be chosen for these duties on account of the multitude of the faithful, and the difficulty of finding a sufficient number of persons to be appointed to each locality, just as it was necessary to establish religious orders for military service, on account of the secular princes being unable to cope with unbelievers in certain countries.

ARTICLE 5. *Whether a Religious Order Should Be Established for the Purpose of Study?*

We proceed thus to the Fifth Article: It would seem that a religious order should not be established for the purpose of study.

Objection 1. For it is written (Ps. 70. 15, 16): *Because I have not known letters* (Douay,— *learning*), *I will enter into the powers of the Lord,* that is, "Christian virtue," according to a gloss.[3] Now the perfection of Christian virtue seems to pertain especially to religious. Therefore it is not for them to apply themselves to the study of letters.

Obj. 2. Further, That which is a source of dissent is unbecoming to religious, who are gathered together in the unity of peace. Now study leads to dissent; hence also different schools of thought arose among the philosophers. And so Jerome in his commentary on the epistle to Titus i. 5, *and shouldst ordain . . . in every city,* says:[4] "Before a diabolical

[1] Bk. 1 (PL 76, 932).
[2] *Politics,* 1, 4 (1253[b]29); *Ethics,* VIII, 11 (1161[b]4).

[3] *Glossa interl.* (III, 185r); *Glossa* Lombardi (PL 191, 653).   [4] PL 26, 597.

instinct brought study into religion, and people said: I am of Paul, I of Apollo, I of Cephas," etc. Therefore it would seem that no religious order should be established for the purpose of study.

Obj. 3. Further, Those who profess the Christian religion should profess nothing in common with the Gentiles. Now among the Gentiles were some who professed philosophy, and even now some secular persons are known as professors of certain sciences. Therefore the study of letters does not become religious.

On the contrary, Jerome in his letter to Paulinus[1] urges him to acquire learning in the monastic state, saying: "Let us learn on earth those things the knowledge of which will remain in heaven," and further on: "Whatever you seek to know, I will endeavor to know with you."

I answer that, As stated above (AA. 2, 3), religion may be ordered to the active and to the contemplative life. Now chief among the works of the active life are those which are directly ordered to the salvation of souls, such as preaching and the like. Accordingly the study of letters is becoming to religious in three ways. First, as regards that which is proper to the contemplative life, to which the study of learning helps in a twofold manner. In one way by helping directly to contemplate, namely by enlightening the intellect. For the contemplative life of which we are now speaking is directed chiefly to the consideration of divine things, as stated above (Q. CLXXX, A. 4), to which consideration man is directed by study; for which reason it is said in praise of the righteous (Ps. 1, 2) that *he shall meditate day and night* on the law of the Lord, and (Ecclus. 39. 1): *The wise man will seek out the wisdom of all the ancients, and will be occupied in the prophets.* In another way the study of letters is a help to the contemplative life indirectly, by removing the obstacles to contemplation, namely the errors which in the contemplation of divine things frequently beset those who are ignorant of the scriptures. Thus we read in the *Conferences of the Fathers (Coll.* x, 3)[2] that the Abbot Serapion through simplicity fell into the error of the Anthropomorphites, who thought that God had a human shape. Hence Gregory says (*Moral.* vi, 37)[3] that "some through seeking in contemplation more than they are able to grasp, fall away into perverse doctrines, and by failing to be the humble disciples of truth become

the masters of error." Hence it is written (Eccles. 2. 3): *I thought in my heart to withdraw my flesh from wine, that I might turn my mind to wisdom and might avoid folly.*

Secondly, the study of letters is necessary to religious institutions for preaching and other like works; therefore the Apostle (Tit. 1. 9), speaking of bishops to whose office these acts belong, says: *Embracing that faithful word which is according to doctrine, that he may be able to exhort in sound doctrine and to convince the gainsayers.* Nor does it matter that the apostles were sent to preach without having studied letters, because, as Jerome says in his letter to Paulinus,[4] "whatever others acquire by exercise and daily meditation in God's law, was taught them by the Holy Ghost."

Thirdly, the study of letters is becoming to religious as regards that which is common to all religious orders. For it helps us to avoid the lusts of the flesh; therefore Jerome says to the monk Rusticus:[5] "Love the science of the Scriptures and thou shalt have no love for carnal vice." For it turns the mind away from lustful thoughts, and tames the flesh on account of the toil that study entails according to Ecclus. 31. 1, *Watching for riches consumeth the flesh.* It also helps to remove the desire of riches, and therefore it is written (Wisd. 7. 8): *I . . . esteemed riches nothing in comparison with her,* and (I Mach. 12. 9): *We needed none of these things,* namely assistance from without, *having for our comfort the holy books that are in our hands.* It also helps to teach obedience, and so Augustine says (*De Oper. Monach.* 17):[6] "What sort of perverseness is this, to wish to read, but not to obey what one reads?" Hence it is clearly fitting that a religious order be established for the study of letters.

Reply Obj. 1. This commentary of the gloss is an exposition of the Old Law of which the Apostle says (II Cor. 3. 6): *The letter killeth.* Hence not to know letters is to disapprove of the circumcision of the letter and other carnal observances.

Reply Obj. 2. Study is directed to knowledge which, without charity, *puffeth up,* and consequently leads to dissent, according to Prov. 13. 10, *Among the proud there are always dissensions;* but, with charity, it *edifieth* and begets concord. Hence the Apostle after saying (I Cor. 1. 5): *You are made rich . . . in all utterance and in all knowledge,* adds (*verse* 10):

---

[1] *Epist.,* LIII (PL 22, 549).
[2] Cassian (PL 49, 823).   [3] PL 75, 761.

[4] *Epist.,* LIII (PL 22, 543).
[5] *Epist.,* CXXV (PL 22, 1078).   [6] PL 40, 565.

That you all speak the same thing, and that there be no schisms among you. But Jerome is not speaking here of the study of letters, but of the study of dissensions which heretics and schismatics have brought into the Christian religion.

Reply Obj. 3. The philosophers professed the study of letters in the matter of secular learning; but it becomes religious to devote themselves chiefly to the study of letters in reference to the doctrine that is *according to godliness* (Tit. I. I). It becomes not religious, whose whole life is devoted to the service of God, to seek for other learning, save in so far as it is referred to the sacred doctrine. Hence Augustine says at the end of his work *On Music*:[1] "Whilst we think that we should not overlook those whom heretics delude by the deceitful assurance of reason and knowledge, we are slow to advance in the consideration of their methods. Yet we should not be praised for doing this, were it not that many holy sons of their most loving mother the Catholic Church had done the same under the necessity of confounding heretics."

ARTICLE 6. *Whether a Religious Order That Is Devoted to the Contemplative Life Is More Excellent Than One That Is Given to the Active Life?*

We proceed thus to the Sixth Article: It seems that a religious order which is devoted to the contemplative life is not more excellent than one which is given to the active life.

Objection I. For it is said (Extrav. *de Regular. et Transeunt. ad Relig.,* cap *Licet*),[2] "Even as a greater good is preferred to a lesser, so the common profit takes precedence of private profit; and in this case teaching is rightly preferred to silence, responsibility to contemplation, work to rest." Now the religious order which is directed to the greater good is better. Therefore it would seem that those religious orders that are directed to the active life are more excellent than those which are directed to the contemplative life.

Obj. 2. Further, Every religious order is directed to the perfection of charity, as stated above (AA. I, 2). Now a gloss on Heb. 12. 4, *For you have not yet resisted unto blood,* says:[3] "In this life there is no more perfect love than that to which the holy martyrs attained, who

¹ Bk. VI, chap. 17 (PL 32, 1194).
² *Decretal. Gregor.,* IX, Bk. III, tit. 31, chap. 18 (RF II, 575).
³ *Glossa* Lombardi (PL 192, 501); Augustine, *Serm. ad Popul.,* CLIX, I (PL 38, 868).

fought against sin unto blood." Now to fight unto blood is becoming those religious who are directed to military service, and yet this pertains to the active life. Therefore it would seem that religious orders of this kind are the most excellent.

Obj. 3. Further, It seems that the stricter a religious order is, the more excellent it is. But there is no reason why certain religious orders directed to the active life should not be of stricter observance than those directed to the contemplative life. Therefore they are more excellent.

On the contrary, Our Lord said (Luke 10. 42) that the *best part* was Mary's, by whom the contemplative life is signified.

I answer that, As stated above (A. I), the difference between one religious order and another depends chiefly on the end, and secondarily on the exercise. And since one thing cannot be said to be more excellent than another save in respect of that in which it differs from it, it follows that the excellence of one religious order over another depends chiefly on their ends, and secondarily on their respective exercises. Nevertheless each of these comparisons is considered in a different way. For the comparison with respect to the end is absolute, since the end is sought for its own sake; but the comparison with respect to exercise is relative, since exercise is sought not for its own sake, but for the sake of the end. Hence a religious order is preferable to another if it be directed to an end that is absolutely more excellent either because it is a greater good or because it is directed to more goods. If, however, the end be the same, the excellence of one religious order over another depends secondarily, not on the amount of exercise, but on the proportion of the exercise to the end in view. Therefore in the *Conferences of the Fathers* (*Coll.* ii, 2)[4] Blessed Antony is quoted as preferring discretion whereby a man moderates all his actions, to fastings, watchings, and all such observances.

Accordingly we must say that the work of the active life is twofold. One proceeds from the fulness of contemplation, such as teaching and preaching. Therefore Gregory says (*Hom.* v *in Ezech.*)[5] that the words of Ps. 144. 7, *They shall publish the memory of . . . Thy sweetness,* refer "to perfect men returning from their contemplation." And this work is more excellent than simple contemplation. For even as it is better to enlighten than merely to shine,

⁴ Cassian (PL 49, 525).
⁵ Bk. II (PL 76, 826).

so is it better to give to others the fruits of one's contemplation than merely to contemplate. The other work of the active life consists entirely in outward occupation, for instance almsgiving, receiving guests, and the like, which are less excellent than the works of contemplation, except in cases of necessity, as stated above (Q. CLXXXII, A. 1).

Accordingly the highest place in religious orders is held by those which are directed to teaching and preaching, which, moreover, are nearest to the episcopal perfection, even as in other things "the end of that which is first is in conjunction with the beginning of that which is second," as Dionysius states (*Div. Nom.* vii).[1] The second place belongs to those which are directed to contemplation, and the third to those which are occupied with external actions. Moreover, in each of these degrees it may be noted that one religious order excels another through being directed to a higher action in the same genus; thus among the works of the active life it is better to ransom captives than to receive guests, and among the works of the contemplative life prayer is better than study. Again one will excel another if it be directed to more of these actions than another, or if it have statutes more adapted to the attainment of the end in view.

Reply Obj. 1. This Decretal refers to the active life as directed to the salvation of souls.

Reply Obj. 2. Those religious orders that are established for the purpose of military service aim more directly at shedding the enemy's blood than at the shedding of their own, which latter belongs more properly to martyrs. Yet there is no reason why religious of this description should not acquire the merit of martyrdom in certain cases, and in this respect stand higher than other religious; even as in some cases the works of the active life take precedence of contemplation.

Reply Obj. 3. Strictness of observances, as the Blessed Antony remarks in the *Conferences of the Fathers* (*Coll.* ii, 2)[2] is not the chief object of commendation in a religious order; and it is written (Isa. 58. 5): *Is this such a fast as I have chosen, for a man to afflict his soul for a day?* Nevertheless it is adopted in religious life as being necessary for taming the flesh, which if done without discretion, is liable to make us fail altogether, as the Blessed Antony observes.[3] Therefore a religious order is not more excellent through having stricter observ-

ances, but because its observances are directed by greater discretion to the end of religion. Thus the taming of the flesh is more efficaciously directed to continence by means of abstinence in meat and drink, which pertain to hunger and thirst, than by the privation of clothing, which pertains to cold and nakedness, or by bodily labour.

ARTICLE 7. *Whether Religious Perfection Is Diminished By Possessing Something in Common?*

We proceed thus to the Seventh Article: It would seem that religious perfection is diminished by possessing something in common.

Objection 1. For our Lord said (Matt. 19. 21): *If thou wilt be perfect, go sell all* (Vulg., —*what*) *thou hast and give to the poor.* Hence it is clear that to lack worldly wealth belongs to the perfection of Christian life. Now those who possess something in common do not lack worldly wealth. Therefore it would seem that they do not quite reach to the perfection of Christian life.

Obj. 2. Further, The perfection of the counsels requires that one should be without worldly solicitude; therefore the Apostle in giving the counsel of virginity said (I Cor. 7. 32): *I would have you to be without solicitude.* Now it belongs to the solicitude of the present life that certain people keep something to themselves for the morrow, and this solicitude was forbidden His disciples by our Lord (Matt. 6. 34) saying: *Be not . . . solicitous for to-morrow.* Therefore it would seem that the perfection of Christian life is diminished by having something in common.

Obj. 3. Further, Possessions held in common belong in some way to each member of the community; therefore Jerome (*Ep.* lx., *ad Heliod.*)[4] says in reference to certain people "They are richer in the monastery than they had been in the world; though serving the poor Christ they have wealth, which they had not while serving the rich devil; the Church rejects them now that they are rich, who in the world were beggars." But it is derogatory to religious perfection that one should possess wealth of one's own. Therefore it is also derogatory to religious perfection to possess anything in common.

Obj. 4. Further, Gregory (*Dial.* iii, 14)[5] relates of a very holy man named Isaac, that "when his disciples humbly signified that he should accept the possessions offered to him for

---

[1] Sect. 3 (PG 3, 872).
[2] Cassian (PL 49, 526).　　　[3] Cassian, *Ibid.*
[4] PL 22, 596.　　　[5] PL 77, 245.

the use of the monastery, he being solicitous for the safeguarding of his poverty, held firmly to his opinion, saying, 'A monk who seeks earthly possessions is no monk at all' "; and this refers to possessions held in common, and which were offered him for the common use of the monastery. Therefore it would seem destructive of religious perfection to possess anything in common.

Obj. 5. Further, Our Lord in prescribing religious perfection to His disciples, said (Matt. 10. 9, 10): *Do not possess gold, nor silver, nor money in your purses, nor scrip for your journey.* By these words, as Jerome says in his commentary,[1] "He reproves those philosophers who are commonly called Bactroperatæ[2] who as despising the world and valuing all things at naught carried their pantry about with them." Therefore it would seem derogatory to religious perfection that one should keep something whether for oneself or for the common use.

On the contrary, Prosper says (*De Vita Contempl.*)[3] and it is quoted in the Decretals:[4] "It is sufficiently clear both that for the sake of perfection one should renounce having anything of one's own, and that the possession of revenues, which are of course common property, is no hindrance to the perfection of the Church."

I answer that, As stated above (Q. CLXXXIV, A. 3; Q. CLXXXV, A. 6, REPLY 1), perfection consists, essentially, not in poverty, but in following Christ according to the saying of Jerome (in his commentary on Matt. 19. 27, and *have followed Thee*):[5] "Since it is not enough to leave all, Peter adds that which is perfect, namely, 'We have followed Thee.'" Poverty, however, is like an instrument or exercise for the attainment of perfection. Hence in the *Conferences of the Fathers* (*Coll.* i, 7)[6] the abbot Moses says: "Fastings, watchings, meditating on the Scriptures, poverty, and privation of all one's possessions are not perfection, but means of perfection." Now the privation of one's possessions, or poverty, is a means of perfection, since by doing away with riches we remove certain obstacles to charity; and these are chiefly three. The first is the cares which riches bring with them; therefore our Lord said (Matt. 13. 22): *That which was sown* (Vulg.,—*He that received the seed*) *among thorns, is he that heareth the word, and the*

care of this world, and the deceitfulness of riches, choketh up the word. The second is the love of riches, which increases with the possession of wealth; therefore Jerome says (in his commentary on Matt. 19. 24, *It is easier for a camel*)[7] that "since it is difficult to despise riches when we have them, our Lord did not say: It is impossible for a rich man to enter the kingdom of heaven, but: It is difficult." The third is vainglory or elation which results from riches, according to Ps. 48. 7, *They that trust in their own strength, and glory in the multitude of their riches.*

Accordingly the first of these three cannot be altogether separated from riches whether great or small. For man must take a certain amount of care in acquiring or keeping external things. But so long as external things are sought or possessed only in a small quantity, and as much as is required for a mere livelihood, such care does not hinder one much, and consequently is not inconsistent with the perfection of Christian life. For our Lord did not forbid all care, but only such as is excessive and hurtful; therefore Augustine, commenting on Matt. 6. 25, *Be not solicitous for your life, what you shall eat,* says,[8] "In saying this He does not forbid them to procure these things in so far as they needed them, but to be intent on them, and for their sake to do whatever they are bidden to do in preaching the Gospel." Yet the possession of much wealth increases the weight of care, which is a great distraction to man's mind and hinders him from giving himself wholly to God's service. The other two, however, namely the love of riches and taking pride or glorying in riches, result only from an abundance of wealth.

Nevertheless it makes a difference in this matter if riches, whether abundant or moderate, be possessed in private or in common. For the care that one takes of one's own wealth pertains to love of self, whereby a man loves himself in temporal matters; but the care that is given to things held in common pertains to the love of charity which *seeketh not her own,* but looks to the common good. And since religion is directed to the perfection of charity, and charity is perfected in the love of God extending to contempt of self, it is contrary to religious perfection to possess anything in private. But the care that is given to common goods may pertain to charity, although it may prove an obstacle to some higher act of char-

---

[1] PL 26, 64.   [2] i.e., staff and scrip bearers.
[3] Julianus Pomerius, Bk. II, chap. 9 (PL 59, 453).
[4] Gratian, Pt. II, causa XII, Q. 1, can. 13 (RF I, 681).
[5] PL 26, 144.   [6] Cassian (PL 49, 490).
[7] PL 26, 143.
[8] Cf. *De Oper. Mon.* 26 (PL 40, 573).

ity, such as divine contemplation or the instructing of one's neighbour.

Hence it is evident that to have excessive riches in common, whether in movable or in immovable property, is an obstacle to perfection, though not absolutely incompatible with it. But it is not an obstacle to religious perfection to have enough external things, whether movables or immovables, as suffice for a livelihood, if we consider poverty in relation to the common end of religious orders, which is to devote oneself to the service of God. But if we consider poverty in relation to the special end of any religious order, then this end being presupposed, a greater or lesser degree of poverty is adapted to that religious order; and each religious order will be the more perfect in respect of poverty according as it professes a poverty more adapted to its end. For it is evident that for the purpose of the outward and bodily works of the active life a man needs the assistance of outward things, whereas few are required for contemplation. Hence the Philosopher says[1] that "many things are needed for action, and the more so the greater and nobler the actions are. But the contemplative man requires no such things for the exercise of his act: he needs only the necessaries; other things are an obstacle to his contemplation." Accordingly it is clear that a religious order directed to the bodily actions of the active life, such as soldiering or the lodging of guests, would be imperfect if it lacked common riches; but those religious orders which are directed to the contemplative life are the more perfect according as the poverty they profess burdens them with less care for temporal things. And the care of temporal things is so much a greater obstacle to religious life as the religious life requires a greater care of spiritual things.

Now it is manifest that a religious order established for the purpose of contemplating and of giving to others the fruits of one's contemplation by teaching and preaching requires greater care of spiritual things than one that is established for contemplation only. Therefore it becomes a religious order of this kind to embrace a poverty that burdens one with the least amount of care. Again it is clear that to keep what one has acquired at a fitting time for one's necessary use involves the least burden of care. Therefore a threefold degree of poverty corresponds to the three aforesaid degrees of religious life. For it is fitting that a religious order which is directed to the bodily actions of the

active life should have an abundance of riches in common; that the common possession of a religious order directed to contemplation should be more moderate, unless the said religious be bound, either themselves or through others, to give hospitality or to assist the poor; and that those who aim at giving the fruits of their contemplation to others should have their life most exempt from external cares, this being accomplished by their laying up the necessaries of life procured at a fitting time. This, our Lord, the Founder of poverty, taught by His example. For He had a purse which He entrusted to Judas, and in which were kept the things that were offered to Him, as related in John 12. 6.

Nor should it be argued that Jerome (*Comment. in Matt.* 17)[2] says: "If anyone object that Judas carried money in the purse, we answer that He deemed it unlawful to spend the property of the poor on His own uses," namely by paying the tax, because among those poor His disciples held a foremost place, and the money in Christ's purse was spent chiefly on their needs. For it is stated (John 4. 8) that *His disciples were gone into the city to buy meats,* and (John 13. 29) that the disciples *thought, because Judas had the purse, that Jesus had said to him: Buy those things which we have need of for the festival day, or that he should give something to the poor.* From this it is evident that to keep money by, or any other common property for the support of religious of the same order, or of any other poor, is in accordance with the perfection which Christ taught by His example. Moreover, after the resurrection, the disciples from whom all religious orders took their origin kept the price of the lands, and distributed it according as each one had need (Acts 4. 34, 35).

Reply Obj. 1. As stated above (Q. CLXXXIV, A. 3), this saying of our Lord does not mean that poverty itself is perfection, but that it is the means of perfection. Indeed, as shown above (Q. CLXXXVI, A. 8), it is the least of the three chief means of perfection, since the vow of continence excels the vow of poverty, and the vow of obedience excels them both. Since, however, the means are sought not for their own sake, but for the sake of the end, a thing is better not for being a greater instrument, but for being more adapted to the end. Thus a physician does not heal the more, the more medicine he gives, but the more the medicine is adapted to the disease. Accordingly it

---

[1] *Ethics,* X, 8 (1178[b]1).

[2] Bk. III (PL 26, 132).

does not follow that a religious order is the more perfect according as the poverty it professes is more perfect, but according as its poverty is more adapted to the end both common and special.

Granted even that the religious order which exceeds others in poverty be more perfect in so far as it is poorer, this would not make it more perfect absolutely. For possibly some other religious order might surpass it in matters relating to continence, or obedience, and thus be more perfect absolutely, since to excel in better things is to be better absolutely.

Reply Obj. 2. Our Lord's words (*Matt.* 6. 34), *Be not solicitous for to-morrow,* do not mean that we are to keep nothing for the morrow; for the Blessed Antony shows the danger of so doing, in the *Conferences of the Fathers* (*Coll.* ii, 2),[1] where he says: "It has been our experience that those who have attempted to practise the privation of all means of livelihood, so as not to have the wherewithal to procure themselves food for one day, have been deceived so unawares that they were unable to finish properly the work they had undertaken." And, as Augustine says (*De Oper. Monach.* 23),[2] "if this saying of our Lord, 'Be not solicitous for to-morrow,' means that we are to lay nothing by for the morrow, those who shut themselves up for many days from the sight of men, and apply their whole mind to a life of prayer, will be unable to provide themselves with these things." Again he adds afterwards: "Are we to suppose that the more holy they are, the less do they resemble the birds?" And further on: "For if it be argued from the Gospel that they should lay nothing by, they answer rightly: Why then did our Lord have a purse, wherein He kept the money that was collected? Why, in days long gone by, when famine was imminent, was grain sent to the holy fathers? Why did the apostles thus provide for the needs of the saints?" Accordingly the saying: *Be not solicitous for to-morrow,* according to Jerome in his commentary on this passage,[3] is to be rendered thus: "It is enough that we think of the present; the future being uncertain, let us leave it to God";—according to Chrysostom,[4] "It is enough to endure the toil for necessary things, labour not in excess for unnecessary things";—according to Augustine (*De Serm. Dom. in Monte,* ii, 17):[5]

"When we do any good action, we should bear in mind not temporal things which are denoted by the morrow, but eternal things."

Reply Obj. 3. The saying of Jerome applies where there are excessive riches, possessed in private as it were, or by the abuse of which even the individual members of a community wax proud and wanton. But they do not apply to moderate wealth, set by for the common use, merely as a means of livelihood of which each one stands in need. For it amounts to the same that each one makes use of things pertaining to the necessaries of life, and that these things be set by for the common use.

Reply Obj. 4. Isaac refused to accept the offer of possessions because he feared lest this should lead him to have excessive wealth, the abuse of which would be an obstacle to religious perfection. Hence Gregory adds (*ibid.*): "He was as afraid of forfeiting the security of his poverty as the rich miser is careful of his perishable wealth." It is not, however, related that he refused to accept such things as were necessary for the upkeep of community life.

Reply Obj. 5. The Philosopher says[6] that bread, wine, and the like are natural riches, while money is artificial riches. Hence it is that certain philosophers declined to make use of money, and employed other things, living according to nature. Therefore Jerome shows (*ibid.*) by the words of our Lord, Who equally forbade both, that it comes to the same to have money and to possess other things necessary for life. And though our Lord commanded those who were sent to preach not to carry these things on the way, He did not forbid them to be possessed in common. How these words of our Lord should be understood has been shown above (Q. CLXXXV, A. 6, REPLY 2; Part I-II, Q. CVIII, A. 2, REPLY 3).

ARTICLE 8. *Whether the Religious Life of Those Who Live in Community Is More Perfect Than That of Those Who Lead a Solitary Life?*

We proceed thus to the Eighth Article: It would seem that the religious life of those who live in community is more perfect than that of those who lead a solitary life.

Objection 1. For it is written (Eccles. 4. 9): *It is better . . . that two should be together, than one; for they have the advantage of their society.* Therefore the religious life of those who live in community would seem to be more perfect.

---

[1] PL 49, 526.
[2] PL 40, 570.   [3] PL 26, 47.
[4] Pseudo-Chrysostom, *op. Imperf. in Matt.* (PG 56 724).   [5] PL 34, 1294.
[6] *Politics,* I, 9 (1257ª25;ᵇ10).

Obj. 2. Further, It is written (Matt. 18. 20): *Where there are two or three gathered together in My name, there am I in the midst of them.* But nothing can be better than the fellowship of Christ. Therefore it would seem better to live in community than in solitude.

Obj. 3. Further, The vow of obedience is more excellent than the other religious vows; and humility is most acceptable to God. Now obedience and humility are better observed in company than in solitude; for Jerome says to the monk Rusticus (*Ep.* cxxv).[1] "In solitude pride quickly takes man unawares, he sleeps as much as he will, he does what he likes"; while he says when instructing one who lives in community, these words: "You may not do what you will, you must eat what you are bidden to eat, you may possess so much as you receive, you must obey one you prefer not to obey, you must be a servant to your brethren, you must fear the superior of the monastery as God, love him as a father."[2] Therefore it would seem that the religious life of those who live in community is more perfect than that of those who lead a solitary life.

Obj. 4. Further, Our Lord said (Luke 11. 33): *No man lighteth a candle and putteth it in a hidden place, nor under a bushel.* Now those who lead a solitary life would seem to be in a hidden place, and to be doing no good to any man. Therefore it would seem that their religious life is not more perfect.

Obj. 5. Further, That which is in accord with man's nature is apparently more pertinent to the perfection of virtue. But man is naturally a social animal, as the Philosopher says.[3] Therefore it would seem that to lead a solitary life is not more perfect than to lead a community life.

On the contrary, Augustine says (*De Oper. Monach.* 23)[4] that "those are holier who keep themselves aloof from the approach of all, and give their whole mind to a life of prayer."

I answer that, Solitude, like poverty, is not the essence of perfection, but a means to it. Hence in the *Conferences of the Fathers* (*Coll.* i, 7)[5] the Abbot Moses says that "solitude," even as fasting and other like things, "is a sure means of acquiring purity of heart." Now it is evident that solitude is a means adapted not to action but to contemplation, according to Osee 2. 14, *I . . . will lead her into solitude* (Douay,—*the wilderness*); *and I will speak

to her heart.* Therefore it is not suitable to those religious orders that are directed to the works whether corporal or spiritual of the active life, except perhaps for a time, after the example of Christ, Who as Luke relates (6. 12), *went out into a mountain to pray; and He passed the whole night in the prayer of God.*

On the other hand, it is suitable to those religious orders that are directed to contemplation. It must, however, be observed that what is solitary should be self-sufficing by itself. Now such a thing is one that lacks nothing, and this pertains to the idea of a perfect thing. Therefore solitude befits the contemplative who has already attained to perfection. This happens in two ways:—in one way by the gift only of God, as in the case of John the Baptist, who was *filled with the Holy Ghost even from his mother's womb* (Luke 1. 11), so that he was in the desert even as a boy; in another way by the practice of virtuous action, according to Heb. 5. 14: *Strong meat is for the perfect; for them who by custom have their senses exercised to the discerning of good and evil.*

Now man is assisted in this practice by the fellowship of others in two ways. First, as regards his intellect, to the effect of his being instructed in that which he has to contemplate; therefore Jerome says to the monk Rusticus (*loc. cit.*): "It pleases me that you have the fellowship of holy men, and teach not yourself." Secondly, as regards the affections, seeing that man's noisome affections are restrained by the example and reproof which he receives from others; for as Gregory says (*Moral.* xxx, 23),[6] commenting on the words, *To whom I have given a house in the wilderness* (Job 39. 6), "What profits solitude of the body, if solitude of the heart be lacking?" Hence a social life is necessary for the practice of perfection. Now solitude befits those who are already perfect; therefore Jerome says to the monk Rusticus (*loc. cit.*): "Do we condemn the solitary life? Not at all; indeed we have often commended it. But we wish the soldiers who pass from the monastic school to be such as not to be deterred by the hard noviciate of the desert, and such as have given proof of their conduct for a considerable time."

Accordingly, just as that which is already perfect surpasses that which is being schooled in perfection, so the life of the solitaries, if duly practised, surpasses the community life. But if it be undertaken without the aforesaid practice, it is fraught with very great danger,

[1] PL 22, 1077. [2] *Epist.*, cxxv (PL 22, 1080).
[3] *Politics*, 1, 2 (1253ª2).
[4] PL 40, 570. [5] Cassian (PL 49, 489). [6] PL 76, 561.

unless the grace of God supply that which others acquire by practice, as in the case of the Blessed Antony and the Blessed Benedict.

Reply Obj. 1. Solomon shows that two are better than one on account of the help which one affords the other either in lifting him up, or in warning him, or giving him spiritual heat (Eccles. 4. 10, 11). But those who have already attained to perfection do not require this help.

Reply Obj. 2. According to I John 4. 16, *He that abideth in charity abideth in God and God in him.* Therefore just as Christ is in the midst of those who are united together in the fellowship of brotherly love, so does He dwell in the heart of the man who devotes himself to divine contemplation through love of God.

Reply Obj. 3. Actual obedience is required of those who need to be schooled according to the direction of others in the attainment of perfection; but those who are already perfect are sufficiently led by the spirit of God so that they need not to obey others actually. Nevertheless they have obedience in the preparedness of the mind.

Reply Obj. 4. As Augustine says,[1] "no one is forbidden to seek the knowledge of truth, for this pertains to a praiseworthy leisure." That a man be placed on a *candlestick,* does not concern him but his superiors, and "if this burden is not placed on us," as Augustine goes on to say,[2] "we must devote ourselves to the contemplation of truth," for which purpose solitude is most helpful. Nevertheless, those who lead a solitary life are most useful to mankind. Hence, referring to them, Augustine says (*De Morib. Eccl.* xxxi):[3] "They dwell in the most lonely places, content to live on water and the bread that is brought to them from time to time, enjoying colloquy with God to whom they have adhered with a pure mind. To some they seem to have renounced human intercourse more than is right; but these understand not how much such men profit us by the spirit of their prayers, what an example to us is the life of those whom we are forbidden to see in the body."

Reply Obj. 5. A man may lead a solitary life for two motives. One is because he is unable, as it were, to bear with human fellowship on account of his uncouthness of mind; and this is beast-like. The other is with a view to adhering wholly to divine things; and this is

[1] *City of God,* XIX, 19 (PL 41, 647).
[2] *Ibid.*
[3] PL 32, 1337.

superhuman. Hence the Philosopher says[4] that "he who associates not with others is either a beast or a god," that is, a godly man.

QUESTION CLXXXIX
OF THE ENTRANCE INTO RELIGIOUS LIFE
(*In Ten Articles*)

WE must now consider the entrance into religious life. Under this head there are ten points of inquiry: (1) Whether those who are not practised in the observance of the commandments should enter religion? (2) Whether it is lawful for a person to be bound by vow to enter religion? (3) Whether those who are bound by vow to enter religion are bound to fulfil their vow? (4) Whether those who vow to enter religion are bound to remain there in perpetuity? (5) Whether children should be received into religion? (6) Whether one should be withheld from entering religion through deference to one's parents? (7) Whether parish priests or archdeacons may enter religion? (8) Whether one may pass from one religious order to another? (9) Whether one ought to induce others to enter religion? (10) Whether serious deliberation with one's relations and friends is requisite for entrance into religion?

ARTICLE 1. *Whether Those Who Are Not Practised in Keeping the Commandments Should Enter Religion?*

We proceed thus to the First Article: It seems that none should enter religion but those who are practised in the observance of the commandments.

Objection 1. For our Lord gave the counsel of perfection to the young man who said that he had kept the commandments from his youth (Matt. 19. 20). Now all religious orders originate from Christ. Therefore it would seem that none should be allowed to enter religion but those who are practised in the observance of the commandments.

Obj. 2. Further, Gregory says (*Hom.* iii *in Ezech.*):[5] "No one comes suddenly to the summit; but he must make a beginning of a good life in the smallest matters, so as to accomplish great things." Now the great things are the counsels which pertain to the perfection of life, while the lesser things are the commandments which belong to common justice. Therefore it would seem that one ought not to enter religion for the purpose of keeping the

[4] *Politics,* I, 2 (1253ª27).   [5] PL 76, 959.

counsels unless one be already practised in the observance of the precepts.

Obj. 3. Further, The religious state, like the holy orders, has a place of eminence in the Church. Now, as Gregory writes to Syagrius, a bishop of Gaul (*Regist.* ix *Ep.* cvi),[1] and it is quoted in the Decretals,[2] "order should be observed in ascending to orders. For he seeks a fall who aspires to mount to the summit by overpassing the steps. And we are well aware that walls when built receive not the weight of the beams until the new fabric is rid of its moisture, lest if they should be burdened with weight before they are seasoned they bring down the whole building." Therefore it would seem that one should not enter religion unless one be practised in the observance of the precepts.

Obj. 4. Further, A gloss on Ps. 130. 2, *As a child that is weaned is towards his mother,* says.[3] "First we are conceived in the womb of Mother Church, by being taught the rudiments of faith. Then we are nourished as it were in her womb, by progressing in those same elements. Afterwards we are brought forth to the light by being regenerated in baptism. Then the Church bears us as it were in her hands and feeds us with milk, when after baptism we are instructed in good works and are nourished with the milk of simple doctrine while we progress; until having grown out of infancy we leave our mother's milk for a father's control, that is to say, we pass from simple doctrine, by which we are taught the Word made flesh, to the Word that was in the beginning with God." Afterwards he goes on to say: "For those who are just baptized on Holy Saturday are borne in the hands of the Church as it were and fed with milk until Pentecost, during which time nothing arduous is prescribed, no fasts, no rising at midnight. Afterwards they are confirmed by the Paraclete Spirit, and being weaned so to speak, begin to fast and keep other difficult observances. Many, like the heretics and schismatics, have perverted this order by being weaned before the time. Hence they have come to naught." Now this order is apparently perverted by those who enter religion, or induce others to enter religion, before they are practised in the easier observance of the commandments. Therefore they would seem to be heretics or schismatics.

[1] PL 77, 1031; the latter part of the text is from *Epist.*, LIII (PL 77, 784).

[2] Gratian, pt. I, d. 48, can. 2 (RF I, 174).

[3] *Glossa ordin.* (III, 284A); *Glossa* Lombardi (PL 191, 1172).

Obj. 5. Further, One should proceed from that which precedes to that which follows after. Now the commandments precede the counsels, because they are more universal, for the implication of the one by the other is not convertible, since whoever keeps the counsels keeps the commandments, but the converse does not hold. Seeing then that the right order requires one to pass from that which comes first to that which comes after, it follows that one ought not to pass to the observance of the counsels in religion without being first of all practised in the observance of the commandments.

On the contrary, Matthew the publican who was not practised in the observance of the commandments was called by our Lord to the observance of the counsels. For it is stated (Luke 5. 28) that *leaving all things he . . . followed Him.* Therefore it is not necessary for a person to be practised in the observance of the commandments before passing to the perfection of the counsels.

I answer that, As shown above (Q. CLXXXVIII, A. I), the religious state is a spiritual exercising for the attainment of the perfection of charity. This is accomplished through the removal of the obstacles to perfect charity by religious observances; and these obstacles are those things which attach man's affections to earthly things. Now the attachment of man's affections to earthly things is not only an obstacle to the perfection of charity, but sometimes leads to the loss of charity when through turning inordinately to temporal goods man turns away from the immutable good by sinning mortally. Hence it is evident that the observances of the religious state, while removing the obstacles to perfect charity, remove also the occasions of sin; for instance, it is clear that fasting, watching, obedience, and the like withdraw man from sins of gluttony and lust and all other manner of sins.

Consequently it is right that not only those who are practised in the observance of the commandments should enter religion in order to attain to yet greater perfection, but also those who are not practised, in order the more easily to avoid sin and attain to perfection.

Reply Obj. 1. Jerome commenting on Matt. 19. 20, *All these have I kept,* says:[4] "The young man lies when he says: All these have I kept from my youth. For if he had fulfilled this one of the commandments: Thou shalt love thy neighbour as thyself, why did he go away sad when he heard: Go, sell all that thou hast and

[4] PL 26, 142.

give to the poor?" But this means that he lied as to the perfect observance of this commandment. Hence Origen says (*Tract.* viii, *super Matt.*)[1] that "it is written in the Gospel according to the Hebrews that when our Lord had said to him: 'Go, sell all thou hast,' the rich man began to scratch his head; and that our Lord said to him: How sayest thou: I have fulfilled the law and the prophets, seeing that it is written in the law: Thou shalt love thy neighbour as thyself? Behold many of thy brethren, children of Abraham, are clothed in filth, and die of hunger, whilst thy house is full of all manner of good things, and nothing whatever hath passed thence to them. And thus our Lord reproves him saying: If thou wilt be perfect, go, etc. For it is impossible to fulfil the commandment which says, Thou shalt love thy neighbour as thyself, and to be rich, especially to have such great wealth." This also refers to the perfect fulfilment of this precept. On the other hand, it is true that he kept the commandments imperfectly and in a general way. For perfection consists chiefly in the observance of the precepts of charity, as stated above (Q. CLXXXIV, A. 3). Therefore in order to show that the perfection of the counsels is useful both to the innocent and to sinners, our Lord called not only the innocent youth but also the sinner Matthew. Yet Matthew obeyed His call, and the youth obeyed not, because sinners are converted to the religious life more easily than those who presume on their innocency. It is to the former that our Lord says (Matt. 21. 31): *The publicans and the harlots shall go into the kingdom of God before you.*

Reply Obj. 2. The highest and the lowest place can be taken in three ways. First, in reference to the same state and the same man; and thus it is evident that no one comes to the summit suddenly, since every man that lives rightly, progresses during the whole course of his life, so as to arrive at the summit. Secondly, in comparison with various states, and thus he who desires to reach a higher state need not begin from a lower state; for instance, if a man wish to be a cleric he need not first of all be practised in the life of a layman. Thirdly, in comparison with different persons; and in this way it is clear that one man begins straightway not only from a higher state, but even from a higher degree of holiness, than the highest degree to which another man attains throughout his whole life. Hence Gregory says (*Dial.* ii, 1):[2] "*All are agreed that the boy Benedict*

began at a high degree of grace and perfection in his daily life."

Reply Obj. 3. As stated above (Q. CLXXXIV, AA. 6, 8) holiness is a prerequisite to holy orders, but the religious state is a school for the attainment of holiness. Hence the burden of orders should be laid on the walls when these are already seasoned with holiness, whereas the burden of religion seasons the walls, that is men, by drawing out the damp of vice.

Reply Obj. 4. It is manifest from the words of this gloss that it is chiefly a question of the order of doctrine, in so far as one has to pass from easy matter to that which is more difficult. Hence it is clear from what follows that the statement that certain heretics and schismatics have perverted this order refers to the order of doctrine. For it continues thus: "But he says that he has kept these things," namely the aforesaid order, "binding himself by an oath. Thus I was humble not only in other things but also in knowledge, for 'I was humbly minded'; because I was first of all fed with milk, which is the Word made flesh, so that I grew up to partake of the bread of angels, namely the Word that is in the beginning with God." The example which is given in proof, of the newly baptized not being commanded to fast until Pentecost, shows that no difficult things are to be laid on them as an obligation before the Holy Ghost inspires them inwardly to take upon themselves difficult things of their own choice. Hence after Pentecost and the receiving of the Holy Ghost the Church observes a fast. Now the Holy Ghost (according to Ambrose in his commentary on Luke 1. 15, *He shall be filled with the Holy Ghost*)[3] "is not confined to any particular age; He ceases not when men die, He is not excluded from the maternal womb." Gregory also in a homily for Pentecost (xxx *in Ev.*)[4] says: "He fills the boy harpist and makes him a psalmist; He fills the boy abstainer and makes him a wise judge."[5] and afterwards he adds: "No time is needed to learn whatsoever He will, for He teaches the mind by the merest touch." Again it is written (Eccles. 8. 8), *It is not in man's power to stop the Spirit,* and the Apostle admonishes us (I Thess. 5. 19): *Extinguish not the Spirit,* and (Acts 7. 51) it is said against certain persons: *You always resist the Holy Ghost.*

Reply Obj. 5. There are certain chief precepts which are the ends, so to say, of the com-

[1] PG 13, 1293–1294.   [2] PL 66, 128.

[3] PL 15, 1627.   [4] PL 76, 1225.

[5] Cf. Daniel 1.8–17.

mandments and counsels. These are the precepts of charity, and the counsels are directed to them, not that these precepts cannot be observed without keeping the counsels, but that the keeping of the counsels conduces to the better observance of the precepts. The other precepts are secondary and are directed to the precepts of charity, in such a way that unless one observe them it is altogether impossible to keep the precepts of charity.

Accordingly in the intention the perfect observance of the precepts of charity precedes the counsels, and yet sometimes it follows them in point of time. For such is the order of the end in relation to things directed to the end. But the observance in a general way of the precepts of charity together with the other precepts is compared to the counsels as the common to the proper, because one can observe the precepts without observing the counsels, but not vice versa. Hence the common observance of the precepts precedes the counsels in the order of nature; but it does not follow that it precedes them in point of time, for a thing is not in the genus before being in one of the species. But the observance of the precepts apart from the counsels is directed to the observance of the precepts together with the counsels, just as an imperfect to a perfect species, even as the irrational to the rational animal. Now the perfect is naturally prior to the imperfect, since nature as Boëthius says (*De Consol.* iii, 10)[1] begins with perfect things. And yet it is not necessary for the precepts first of all to be observed without the counsels, and afterwards with the counsels, just as it is not necessary for one to be an ass before being a man, or married before being a virgin. In like manner it is not necessary for a person first of all to keep the commandments in the world before entering religion; especially as the worldly life does not dispose one to religious perfection, but is rather an obstacle to it.

ARTICLE 2. *Whether One Ought To Be Bound by Vow To Enter Religion?*

We proceed thus to the Second Article: It seems that one ought not to be bound by vow to enter religion.

Objection 1. For in making his profession a man is bound by the religious vow. Now before profession a year of probation is allowed, according to the rule of the Blessed Benedict (cap. 58),[2] and according to the decree of Innocent III. (cap. *Nullus, de Regular. et Tran-*

seunt, etc.),[3] who moreover forbade anyone to be bound to the religious life by profession before completing the year of probation. Therefore it would seem that much less ought anyone while yet in the world to be bound by vow to enter religion.

Obj. 2. Further, Gregory says,[4] and it is quoted in the Decretals,[5] that Jews "should be persuaded to be converted, not by compulsion but of their own free will." Now one is compelled to fulfil what one has vowed. Therefore no one should be bound by vow to enter religion.

Obj. 3. Further, No one should give another an occasion of falling; therefore it is written (Exod. 21. 33, 34): *If a man open a pit . . . and an ox or an ass fall into it, the owner of the pit shall pay the price of the beasts.* Now through being bound by vow to enter religion it often happens that people fall into despair and various sins. Therefore it would seem that one ought not to be bound by vow to enter religion.

On the contrary, It is written (Ps. 75. 12): *Vow ye, and pay to the Lord your God;* and a gloss says[6] that "some vows concern the individual, such as vows of chastity, virginity, and the like." Consequently Holy Scripture invites us to vow these things. But Holy Scripture invites us only to that which is better. Therefore it is better to bind oneself by vow to enter religion.

I answer that, As stated above (Q. LXXXVIII, A. 6), when we were treating of vows, one and the same work done in fulfilment of a vow is more praiseworthy than if it be done apart from a vow, both because to vow is an act of religion, which has a certain pre-eminence among the virtues, and because a vow strengthens a man's will to do good; and just as a sin is more grievous through proceeding from a will obstinate in evil, so a good work is more praiseworthy through proceeding from a will confirmed in good by means of a vow. Therefore it is in itself praiseworthy to bind oneself by vow to enter religion.

Reply Obj. 1. The religious vow is twofold. One is the solemn vow which makes a man a monk or a brother in some other religious or-

---

[1] PL 63, 734.   [2] *Reg. ad Mon.* (PL 66, 803).

[3] Cf. Bremond, *Bull. Ord. Praed.*, Innocentius IV, diplom. 74, anno 1244, 17 Junii (I, 144).

[4] Cf. Conc. Toletano IV, chap. 57 (MA x, 633); Gregory the Great, *Registrum*, BK. I, indict. IX, epist. XLVII (PL 77, 509).

[5] Gratian, pt. I, d. 45, can. 5 (RF I, 162).

[6] *Glossa ordin.* (III, 194F); cf. Augustine, *Enarr in Ps.* 75.12 (PL 36, 967).

der. This is called the profession, and such a vow should be preceded by a year's probation, as the Objection proves. The other is the simple vow which does not make a man a monk or a religious, but only binds him to enter religion, and such a vow need not be preceded by a year's probation.

Reply Obj. 2. The words quoted from Gregory must be understood as referring to absolute violence. But the compulsion arising from the obligation of a vow is not absolute necessity, but a necessity of end, because after such a vow one cannot attain to the end of salvation unless one fulfil that vow. Such a necessity is not to be avoided; indeed, as Augustine says to Armentarius and Paulina (*Ep.* cxxvii),[1] "happy is the necessity that compels us to better things."

Reply Obj. 3. The vow to enter religion is a strengthening of the will for better things, and consequently, considered in itself, instead of giving a man an occasion of falling, withdraws him from it. But if one who breaks a vow falls more grievously, this does not derogate from the goodness of the vow, as neither does it derogate from the goodness of Baptism that some sin more grievously after being baptized.

ARTICLE 3. *Whether One Who Is Bound by a Vow To Enter Religion Is Under an Obligation of Entering Religion?*

We proceed thus to the Third Article: It would seem that one who is bound by the vow to enter religion is not under an obligation of entering religion.

Objection 1. For it is said in the Decretals (XVII, Q. II, cap. 1):[2] "Gonsaldus, a priest under pressure of sickness and emotional fervour, promised to become a monk. He did not, however, bind himself to a monastery or abbot; nor did he commit his promise to writing, but he renounced his benefice in the hands of a notary; and when he was restored to health he refused to become a monk." And afterwards it is added "We adjudge and by apostolic authority we command that the aforesaid priest be admitted to his benefice and sacred duties, and that he be allowed to retain them in peace." Now this would not be if he were bound to enter religion. Therefore it would seem that one is not bound to keep one's vow of entering religion.

Obj. 2. Further, No one is bound to do what is not in his power. Now it is not in a person's power to enter religion, since this depends on

the consent of those whom he wishes to join. Therefore it would seem that a man is not obliged to fulfil the vow by which he bound himself to enter religion.

Obj. 3. Further, A less useful vow cannot remit a more useful one. Now the fulfilment of a vow to enter religion might hinder the fulfilment of a vow to take up the cross in defence of the Holy Land; and the latter apparently is the more useful vow, since thereby a man obtains the forgiveness of his sins. Therefore it would seem that the vow by which a man has bound himself to enter religion is not necessarily to be fulfilled.

On the contrary, It is written (Eccles. 5. 3): *If thou hast vowed anything to God, defer not to pay it, for an unfaithful and foolish promise displeaseth him;* and a gloss on Ps. 75. 12, *Vow ye, and pay to the Lord your God,* says:[3] "To vow depends on the will; but after the vow has been taken the fulfilment is of obligation."

I answer that, As stated above (Q. LXXXVIII, A. 1), when we were treating of vows, a vow is a promise made to God in matters concerning God. Now, as Gregory says in his letter to Boniface:[4] "If among men of good faith contracts are wont to be absolutely irrevocable, how much more shall the breaking of this promise given to God be deserving of punishment!" Therefore a man is under an obligation to fulfil what he has vowed, provided this be something pertaining to God.

Now it is evident that entrance into religion pertains very much to God, since thereby man devotes himself entirely to the divine service, as stated above (Q. CLXXXVI, A. 1). Hence it follows that he who binds himself to enter religion is under an obligation to enter religion according as he intends to bind himself by his vow, so that if he intend to bind himself absolutely, he is obliged to enter as soon as he can, through the cessation of a lawful impediment; but if he intend to bind himself to a certain fixed time, or under a certain fixed condition, he is bound to enter religion when the time comes or the condition is fulfilled.

Reply Obj. 1. This priest had made not a solemn, but a simple vow. Hence he was not a monk in effect, so as to be bound by law to dwell in a monastery and renounce his cure. However, in the court of conscience one ought to advise him to renounce all and enter religion.

---

[1] PL 33, 487.   [2] Gratian, pt. II (RF I, 813).

[3] *Glossa* Lombardi (PL 191, 709); cf. *Glossa interl.* (III 19v); *Glossa ordin.* (III, 194F).

[4] Cf. Gratian, *Decretum,* pt. II, XXVII, Q. I, can. 2 (RF I. 1048); see Innocent I, *Epist.,* II, can. 13 (MA III, 1036), or chap. 14 (PL 20, 479).

Hence (Extrav., *De Voto et Voti Redemptione*, cap. *Per tuas*)[1] the Bishop of Grenoble, who had accepted the episcopate after vowing to enter religion, without having fulfilled his vow, is counselled that "if he wish to heal his conscience he should renounce the government of his see and pay his vows to the Most High."

Reply Obj. 2. As stated above (Q. LXXXVIII, A. 3, Reply 2), when we were treating of vows, he who has bound himself by vow to enter a certain religious order is bound to do what is in his power in order to be received in that order; and if he intend to bind himself absolutely to enter the religious life, if he be not admitted to one he is bound to go to another; but if he intend to bind himself only to one particular order, he is bound only according to the measure of the obligation to which he has engaged himself.

Reply Obj. 3. The vow to enter religion being perpetual is greater than the vow of pilgrimage to the Holy Land, which is a temporal vow; and as Alexander III. says,[2] "he who exchanges a temporary service for the perpetual service of religion is in no way guilty of breaking his vow." Moreover it may be reasonably stated that also by entrance into religion a man obtains remission of all his sins. For if by giving alms a man may at once satisfy for his sins, according to Dan. 4. 24, *Redeem thou thy sins with alms,* much more does it suffice to satisfy for all his sins that a man devote himself wholly to the divine service by entering religion, for this surpasses all manner of satisfaction, even that of public penance, according to the Decretals (XXXIII, Q. I, cap. *Admonere*)[3] just as a holocaust exceeds a sacrifice, as Gregory declares (*Hom.* viii *in Ezech.*).[4] Hence we read in the *Lives of the Fathers* (VI., 1. No. 9)[5] that by entering religion one receives the same grace as by being baptized. And yet even if one were not thereby absolved from all debt of punishment, nevertheless the entrance into religion is more profitable than a pilgrimage to the Holy Land, which, as regards the advancement in good, is preferable to absolution from punishment.

ARTICLE 4. *Whether He Who Has Vowed To Enter Religion Is Bound To Remain in Religion in Perpetuity?*

We proceed thus to the Fourth Article: It would seem that he who has vowed to enter

religion is bound in perpetuity to remain in religion.

Objection 1. For it is better not to enter religion than to leave after entering, according to II Pet. 2. 21, *It had been better for them not to have known the way of justice, than after they have known it to turn back,* and Luke 9. 62, *No man putting his hand to the plough, and looking back, is fit for the kingdom of God.* But he who bound himself by the vow to enter religion, is under the obligation to enter, as stated above (A. 3). Therefore he is also bound to remain for always.

Obj. 2. Further, Everyone is bound to avoid that which gives rise to scandal, and is a bad example to others. Now by leaving after entering religion a man gives a bad example and is an occasion of scandal to others, who are thereby withdrawn from entering or incited to leave. Therefore it seems that he who enters religion in order to fulfil a vow which he had previously taken, is bound to remain evermore.

Obj. 3. Further, The vow to enter religion is accounted a perpetual vow; hence it is preferred to temporal vows, as stated above (A. 3, Reply 3; Q. LXXXVIII, A. 12, Reply 1). But this would not be so if a person after vowing to enter religion were to enter with the intention of leaving. It seems, therefore, that he who vows to enter religion is bound also to remain in perpetuity.

On the contrary, the vow of profession, for the reason that it binds a man to remain in religion for evermore, prerequires a year of probation; but this is not required previously to the simple vow whereby a man binds himself to enter religion. Therefore it seems that he who vows to enter religion is not for that reason bound to remain there in perpetuity.

I answer that, The obligation of a vow proceeds from the will, because to vow is an act of the will according to Augustine (*super Ps.* 75).[6] Consequently the obligation of a vow extends as far as the will and intention of the person who takes the vow. Accordingly if in vowing he intend to bind himself not only to enter religion, but also to remain there evermore, he is bound to remain in perpetuity. If, on the other hand, he intend to bind himself to enter religion for the purpose of trial, while retaining the freedom to remain or not remain,

---

[1] *Decretal. Gregor.*, IX, Bk. III, tit. 34, chap. 10 (RF II, 595).   [2] *Ibid.*, chap. 4 (RF II, 590).
[3] Gratian, Pt. II, causa 33, Q. 2, can. 8 (RF I, 1152).
[4] PL 76, 1038.   [5] PL 73, 994.

[6] PL 36, 967; cf. *Epist.*, CXXVII, PL 33, 487; this text is quoted also by Albert the Great, *In Sent.*, IV. d. 38, A. 1 (BO XXX, 396); cf. Wm. of Auxerre, *Summa Aurea*, Pt. III, tr. 22, chap. 1, Q. 1 (230vb); Bonaventure, *In Sent.*, IV, d. 38, A. 1, Q. 2, Arg. 1 (QR IV, 816); *Glossa* Lombardi (PL 191, 709).

it is clear that he is not bound to remain. If, however, in vowing he thought merely of entering religion, without thinking of being free to leave, or of remaining in perpetuity, it would seem that he is bound to enter religion according to the form prescribed by common law, which is that those who enter should be given a year's probation. Therefore he is not bound to remain for ever.

Reply Obj. 1. It is better to enter religion with the purpose of making a trial than not to enter at all, because by so doing one disposes oneself to remain always. Nor is a person accounted to turn or to look back save when he omits to do that which he engaged to do; otherwise whoever does a good work for a time would be unfit for the kingdom of God unless he did it always, which is evidently false.

Reply Obj. 2. A man who has entered religion gives neither scandal nor bad example by leaving, especially if he do so for a reasonable motive; and if others are scandalized, it will be passive scandal on their part, and not active scandal on the part of the person leaving, since in doing so, he has done what was lawful, and expedient on account of some reasonable motive, such as sickness, weakness, and the like.

Reply Obj. 3. He who enters with the purpose of leaving immediately does not seem to fulfil his vow, since this was not his intention in vowing. Hence he must change that purpose, at least so as to wish to try whether it is good for him to remain in religion, but he is not bound to remain for evermore.

ARTICLE 5. *Whether Children Should Be Received in Religion?*

We proceed thus to the Fifth Article: It would seem that children ought not to be received in religion.

Objection 1. Because it is said (Extrav., *De Regular. et Transeunt. ad Relig.*, cap. 1):[1] "No one should be tonsured unless he be of legal age and willing." But children, it seems, are not of legal age, nor have they a will of their own, not having perfect use of reason. Therefore it seems that they ought not to be received in religion.

Obj. 2. Further, The state of religion would seem to be a state of repentance; hence religion is derived from *religare* (*to bind*) or from *re-eligere* (*to choose again*), as Augustine says.[2]

But repentance does not befit children. Therefore it seems that they should not enter religion.

Obj. 3. Further, The obligation of a vow is like that of an oath. But children under the age of fourteen ought not to be bound by oath (*Decret.* XXII, Q. V, cap. *Pueri* and cap. *Honestum.*).[3] Therefore it would seem that neither should they be bound by vow.

Obj. 4. Further, It seems to be unlawful to bind a person to an obligation that can be justly cancelled. Now if any persons of unripe age bind themselves to religion they can be withdrawn by their parents or guardians. For it is written in the Decretals (XX, Q. II, cap. 2)[4] that "if a maid under twelve years of age shall take the sacred veil of her own accord, her parents or guardians, if they choose, can at once declare the deed null and void." It is therefore unlawful for children, especially of unripe age, to be admitted or bound to religion.

On the contrary, Our Lord said (Matt. 19. 14): *Suffer the little children, and forbid them not to come to Me.* Expounding these words Origen says (*Tract.* XV *in Matt.*)[5] that the disciples of Jesus before they have been taught the conditions of justice rebuke those who offer children and babes to Christ, but our Lord urges His disciples to stoop to the service of children. We must therefore take note of this, lest deeming ourselves to excel in wisdom we despise the Church's little ones, as though we were great, and forbid the children to come to Jesus.

I answer that, As stated above (A. 2, reply 1) the religious vow is twofold. One is the simple vow consisting in a mere promise made to God, and proceeding from the interior deliberation of the mind. Such a vow derives its efficacy from the divine law. Nevertheless it may encounter a twofold obstacle. First, through lack of deliberation, as in the case of the insane, whose vows are not binding, as stated in Extrav., *De Regular. et Transeunt. ad Relig.*, cap. *Sicut tenor.*[6] The same applies to children who have not reached the required use of reason, so as to be capable of guile, which use boys attain, as a rule, at about the age of fourteen, and girls at the age of twelve, this being what is called the age of puberty, although in some it comes earlier and in others it is delayed, according to the various dispositions of nature. Secondly, the efficacy of a simple vow encounters an ob-

---

[1] *Decretal Gregor.*, IX, BK. III, tit. 31, chap. 1 (RF II, 569).

[2] *City of God*, X, 3 (PL 41, 280); cf. *De Vera Relig.*, 55 (PL 40, 172); *Retract.*, I, 13 (PL 32, 605).

[3] Gratian, PT. II, can. 15, 16 (RF I, 887).

[4] Gratian, PT. II, can. 2 (RF I, 847).

[5] PG 13, 1269.

[6] *Decretal. Gregor.*, IX, BK. III, tit. 31, chap. 15 (RF II, 574).

stacle if the person who makes a vow to God is not his own master; for instance, if a slave, though having the use of reason, vows to enter religion, or even is ordained, without the knowledge of his master; for his master can annul this, as stated in the Decretals (Dist. LIV, cap. *Si servus*).[1] And since boys and girls under the age of puberty are naturally in their father's power as regards the disposal of their manner of life, their father may either cancel or approve their vow, if it please him to do so, as it is expressly said with regard to a woman (Num. 30. 4).

Accordingly if before reaching the age of puberty a child makes a simple vow, not yet having full use of reason, he is not bound in virtue of the vow; but if he has the use of reason before reaching the age of puberty, he is bound, so far as he is concerned, by his vow; yet this obligation may be removed by his father's authority, under whose control he still remains, because the ordinance of the law whereby one man is subject to another considers what happens in the majority of cases. If, however, the child has passed the age of puberty, his vow cannot be annulled by the authority of his parents, though if he has not the full use of reason, he would not be bound in the sight of God.

The other is the solemn vow which makes a man a monk or a religious. Such a vow is subject to the ordinance of the Church, on account of the solemnity attached to it. And since the Church considers what happens in the majority of cases, a profession made before the age of puberty, however much the person who makes profession may have the use of reason, or be capable of guile, does not take effect so as to make him a religious. Nevertheless, although they cannot be professed before the age of puberty, they can, with the consent of their parents, be received into religion to be educated there; thus it is related of John the Baptist (Luke 1. 80) that *the child grew and was strengthened in spirit, and was in the deserts.* Hence, as Gregory states (*Dial.* ii, 3),[2] "the Roman nobles began to give their sons to the blessed Benedict to be nurtured for Almighty God"; and this is most fitting, according to Lament. 3. 27, *It is good for a man when he has borne the yoke from his youth.* It is for this reason that by common custom children are made to apply themselves to those duties or arts with which they are to pass their lives.

Reply Obj. 1. The legal age for receiving the

tonsure and taking the solemn vow of religion is the age of puberty, when a man is able to make use of his own will; but before the age of puberty it is possible to have reached the lawful age to receive the tonsure and be educated in a religious house.

Reply Obj. 2. The religious state is chiefly directed to the attainment of perfection, as stated above (Q. CLXXXVI, A. 1, Reply 4); and accordingly it is befitting to children, who are easily drawn to it. But as a consequence it is called a state of repentance, since occasions of sin are removed by religious observances, as stated above (Q. CLXXXVI, A. 1, Reply 4).

Reply Obj. 3. Even as children are not bound to take oaths (as the canon states), so are they not bound to take vows. If, however, they bind themselves by vow or oath to do something, they are bound in God's sight if they have the use of reason, but they are not bound in the sight of the Church before reaching the age of fourteen.

Reply Obj. 4. A woman who has not reached the age of puberty is not rebuked (Num. 30. 4) for taking a vow without the consent of her parents. Hence it is evident that she does not sin in vowing. But we are given to understand that she binds herself by vow, so far as she is concerned, without prejudice to her parents' authority.

ARTICLE 6. *Whether One Ought To Be Withdrawn from Entering Religion through Deference to One's Parents?*

We proceed thus to the Sixth Article: It would seem that one ought to be withdrawn from entering religion through deference to one's parents.

Objection 1. For it is not lawful to omit that which is of obligation in order to do that which is of free choice. Now deference to one's parents comes under an obligation of the precept concerning the honouring of our parents (Exod. 20. 12); hence the Apostle says (I Tim. 5. 4): *If any widow have children or grandchildren, let her learn first to govern her own house, and to make a return of duty to her parents.* But the entrance to religion is of free choice. Therefore it would seem that one ought not to omit deference to one's parents for the sake of entering religion.

Obj. 2. Further, the subjection of a son to his father seems to be greater than that of a slave to his master, since sonship is natural, while slavery results from the curse of sin, as appears from Gen. 9. 25. Now a slave cannot set aside

---

[1] Gratian, pt. I, can. 20 (RF I, 213).   [2] PL 66, 140.

the service of his master in order to enter religion or take holy orders, as stated in the Decretals (Dist. LIV., cap. *Si servus*).[1] Much less therefore can a son set aside the deference due to his father in order to enter religion.

Obj. 3. Further, A man is more indebted to his parents than to those to whom he owes money. Now persons who owe money to anyone cannot enter religion. For Gregory says (*Regist.* viii, *Indict.* i, *Ep.* 5)[2] and it is quoted in the Decretals,[3] that "those who are engaged in public business must by no means be admitted into a monastery, when. they seek admittance, unless first of all they withdraw from public traffic." Therefore it seems that much less may children enter religion in despite of their duty to their parents.

On the contrary, It is related (Matt. 4. 22) that James and John *left their nets and father, and followed* our Lord. "By this," says Hilary (*Can.* iii *in Matt.*)[4] "we learn that we who intend to follow Christ are not bound by the cares of the secular life, and by the ties of home."

I answer that, As stated above (Q. CI, A. 2, REPLY 2) when we were treating of piety, parents as such have the character of a principle, and therefore it belongs to them as such to have the care of their children. Hence it is unlawful for a person having children to enter religion so as altogether to set aside the care for their children, namely without providing for their education. For it is written (I Tim. 5. 8) that *if any man have not care of his own . . . he hath denied the faith, and is worse than an infidel.*

However it accidentally belongs to parents to be assisted by their children, in so far, that is, as they are placed in a condition of necessity. Consequently we must say that when their parents are in such need that they cannot fittingly be supported otherwise than by the help of their children, these latter may not lawfully enter religion in despite of their duty to their parents. If, however, the parents' necessity be not such as to stand in great need of their children's assistance, the latter may, in despite of the duty they owe their parents, enter religion even against their parents' command, because after the age of puberty every freeman enjoys freedom in things concerning the disposition of his state of life, especially in such as belong to the service of God, and we should

more obey the Father of spirits that we may live, as says the Apostle (Heb. 12. 9), than obey our parents. Hence as we read (Matt. 8. 22; Luke 9. 62) our Lord rebuked the disciple who was unwilling to follow him at once on account of his father's burial, for there were others who could see to this, as Chrysostom remarks (*Hom.* xxvii *in Matt.*).[5]

Reply Obj. 1. The commandment of honouring our parents extends not only to bodily but also to spiritual service, and to the paying of deference. Hence even those who are in religion can fulfil the commandment of honouring their parents, by praying for them and by revering and assisting them, as becomes religious, since even those who live in the world honour their parents in different ways as befits their condition.

Reply Obj. 2. Since slavery was imposed in punishment of sin, it follows that by slavery man forfeits something which otherwise would belong to him, namely the free disposal of his person, for a slave, as regards what he is, belongs to his master. On the other hand, the son, through being subject to his father, is not hindered from freely disposing of his person by transferring himself to the service of God, which is most conducive to man's good.

Reply Obj. 3. He who is under a certain fixed obligation cannot lawfully set it aside so long as he is able to fulfil it. Therefore if a person is under an obligation to give an account to someone or to pay a certain fixed debt, he cannot lawfully evade this obligation in order to enter religion. If, however, he owes a sum of money, and has not wherewithal to pay the debt, he must do what he can, namely by surrendering his goods to his creditor. According to civil law (Lib. *Ob Æs*)[6] money lays an obligation not on the person of a freeman, but on his property, because the person of a freeman is above all valuation in money. Hence, after surrendering his property, he may lawfully enter religion, nor is he bound to remain in the world in order to earn the means of paying the debt. On the other hand, he does not owe his father a special debt, except as may arise in a case of necessity, as stated above.

ARTICLE 7. *Whether Parish Priests May Lawfully Enter Religion?*

We proceed thus to the Seventh Article: It would seem that parish priests cannot lawfully enter religion.

---

[1] Gratian, Pt. I, can. 20 (RF I, 213).
[2] PL 77, 910.
[3] Gratian, Pt. I, d. LIII, can. 1 (RF I, 206).
[4] PL 9, 931.
[5] PG 57, 348.
[6] *Codex*, Bk. IV, tit. x, leg. 12.

Objection 1. For Gregory says (*Past.* iii)[1] that he who undertakes the cure of souls, "receives an awful warning in the words: '*My son, if thou be surety for thy friend, thou hast engaged fast thy hand to a stranger*'" (Prov. 6. 1); and he goes on to say, "because to be surety for a friend is to take charge of the soul of another on the surety of one's own behaviour." Now he who is under an obligation to a man for a debt cannot enter religion, unless he pay what he owes, if he can (A. 6, obj. 3). Since then a priest is able to work for the care of souls, to which obligation he has pledged his soul, it would seem unlawful for him to lay aside the care of souls in order to enter religion.

Obj. 2. Further, What is lawful to one is likewise lawful to all. But if all priests having care of souls were to enter religion, the people would be left without a pastor's care, which would be unfitting. Therefore it seems that parish priests cannot lawfully enter religion.

Obj. 3. Further, Chief among the acts to which religious orders are directed are those whereby a man gives to others the fruit of his contemplation. Now such acts are appropriate to parish priests and archdeacons, to whom it pertains by virtue of their office to preach and hear confessions. Therefore it would seem unlawful for a parish priest or archdeacon to pass over to religion.

On the contrary, It is said in the Decretals (XIX, Q. II, cap. *Duæ sunt leges.*):[2] "If a man, while governing the people in his church under the bishop and leading a secular life, is inspired by the Holy Ghost to desire to work out his salvation in a monastery or under some canonical rule, even though his bishop withstand him, we authorize him to go freely."

I answer that, As stated above (A. 3, Reply 3; Q. LXXXVIII, A. 12, Reply 1), the obligation of a perpetual vow stands before every other obligation. Now it belongs properly to bishops and religious to be bound by perpetual vow to devote themselves to the divine service, while parish priests and archdeacons are not, as bishops are, bound by a perpetual and solemn vow to retain the care of souls. Therefore bishops cannot lay aside their bishopric for any pretext whatever, without the authority of the Roman Pontiff (Extrav., *De Regular. et Transeunt., ad Relig.*, cap. *Licet.*);[3] archdeacons and parish priests however are free to renounce in the hands of the bishop the care entrusted to

them, without the Pope's special permission, who alone can dispense from perpetual vows. Therefore it is evident that archdeacons and parish priests may lawfully enter religion.

Reply Obj. 1. Parish priests and archdeacons have bound themselves to the care of their subjects as long as they retain their archdeaconry or parish, but they did not bind themselves to retain their archdeaconry or parish forever.

Reply Obj. 2. As Jerome says (*Contra Vigil.* vi, *Multa in Orbe*):[4] "Although they," namely religious, "are sorely smitten by thy poisonous tongue, about whom you argue, saying: 'If all shut themselves up and live in solitude, who will go to church? who will convert worldlings? who will be able to urge sinners to virtue?' If this holds true, if all are fools with thee, who can be wise? Nor will virginity be commendable, for if all be virgins, and none marry, the human race will perish. Virtue is rare, and is not desired by many." It is therefore evident that this is a foolish fear; thus might a man fear to draw water lest the river run dry.

ARTICLE 8. *Whether It Is Lawful To Pass from One Religious Order to Another?*

We proceed thus to the Eighth Article: It seems unlawful to pass from one religious order to another, even a stricter one.

Objection 1. For the Apostle says (Heb. 10. 25): *Not forsaking our assembly, as some are accustomed;* and a gloss observes:[5] "Those namely who yield through fear of persecution, or who presuming on themselves withdraw from the company of sinners or of the imperfect, that they may appear to be righteous." Now those who pass from one religious order to another more perfect one would seem to do this. Therefore it seems that this is unlawful.

Obj. 2. Further, The profession of monks is stricter than that of canons regular (Extrav., *De Statu Monach.* and Canon Reg., cap. *Quod Dei timorem*).[6] But it is unlawful for anyone to pass from the state of canon regular to the monastic state. For it is said in the Decretals (XIX, Q. III, 2):[7] "We ordain and without any exception forbid any professed canon regular to become a monk, unless (which God forbid) he have fallen into public sin." Therefore it would seem unlawful for anyone to pass from one religious order to another of higher rank.

---

[1] Chap. 4 (PL 77, 54).   [2] Gratian, pt. II (RF I, 840).
[3] *Decretal Gregor.*, IX, Bk. III, tit. XXXI, chap. 18 (RF II, 576).

[4] PL 23, 366.
[5] *Glossa interl.* (VI, 1531); *Glossa* Lombardi (PL 192, 484).
[6] *Decretal Gregor.*, IX, Bk. III, tit. XXXV, chap. 5 (RF II, 599).   [7] Gratian, pt. II, causa XIX, Q. 3, can. 2 (RF I, 840).

Obj. 3. Further, A person is bound to fulfil what he has vowed, as long as he is able lawfully to fulfil it; thus if a man has vowed to observe continence, he is bound, even after contracting marriage by words in the present tense, to fulfil his vow so long as the marriage is not consummated, because he can fulfil the vow by entering religion. Therefore if a person may lawfully pass from one religious order to another he will be bound to do so if he vowed it previously while in the world. But this would seem objectionable, since in many cases it might give rise to scandal. Therefore a religious may not pass from one religious order to another stricter one.

On the contrary, It is said in the Decretals (xx, Q. IV, 1):[1] "If holy virgins design for the good of their soul to pass to another monastery on account of a stricter life, and decide to remain there, the holy synod allows them to do so"; and the same would seem to apply to any religious. Therefore one may lawfully pass from one religious order to another.

I answer that, It is not commendable to pass from one religious order to another apart from the case of great usefulness or necessity: both because this frequently gives scandal to those who remain; and because, other things being equal, it is easier to make progress in a religious order to which one is accustomed than in one to which one is not habituated. Hence in the *Conferences of the Fathers (Coll.* xiv, 5)[2] Abbot Nesteros says: "It is best for each one that he should, according to the resolve he has made, hasten with the greatest zeal and care to reach the perfection of the work he has undertaken, and in no way forsake the profession he has chosen." And further on he adds (cap. 6) by way of reason: "For it is impossible that one and the same man should excel in all the virtues at once, since if he endeavour to practise them equally, he will of necessity, while trying to attain them all, end in acquiring none of them perfectly," because the various religious orders excel in respect of various works of virtue.

Nevertheless one may commendably pass from one religious order to another for three reasons. First, through zeal for a more perfect religious life, which excellence depends, as stated above (Q. CLXXXVIII, A. 6), not merely on severity, but chiefly on the end to which a religious order is directed, and secondarily on the discretion whereby the observances are proportionate to the due end. Secondly, on

account of a religious order falling away from the perfection it ought to have; for instance, if in a more severe religious order, the religious begin to live less strictly, it is commendable for one to pass even to a less severe religious order if the observance is better. Hence in the *Conferences of the Fathers (Coll.* xix, 3, 5)[3] Abbot John says of himself that he had passed from the solitary life, in which he was professed, to a less severe life, namely of those who lived in community, because the hermitical life had begun to fall into decline and laxity. Thirdly, on account of sickness or weakness, the result of which sometimes is that one is unable to keep the ordinances of a more severe religious order, though able to observe those of a less strict religion.

There may be, however, a difference in these three cases. For in the first case one ought, on account of humility, to seek permission, which however, cannot be denied, provided it be certain that this other religion is more severe. And if there be a doubt about this, one should ask one's superior to decide (Extrav., *De Regular. et Transeunt, ad Relig.* cap. *Licet).*[4] In like manner the superior's decision should be sought in the second case. In the third case it is also necessary to have a dispensation.

Reply Obj. 1. Those who pass to a stricter religious order, do so not out of presumption that they may appear just, but out of devotion, that they may become more just.

Reply Obj. 2. Religious orders whether of monks or of canons regular are ordered to the works of the contemplative life. Chief among these are those which are performed in the divine mysteries, and these are the direct object of the orders of canons regular, the members of which are essentially religious clerics. On the other hand, monastic religious are not essentially clerics, according to the Decretals (Causa xvi, Q. 1, cap. *Nemo potest* and cap. *Alia causa.*).[5] Hence although monastic orders are more severe, it would be lawful, supposing the members to be lay monks, to pass from the monastic order to an order of canons regular, according to the statement of Jerome to the monk Rusticus:[6] "So live in the monastery as to deserve to become a cleric"; but not conversely, as expressed in the Decretal quoted.[7] If, however, the monks be clerics devoting themselves

---

[1] Gratian, pt. II (RF I, 851).   [2] PL 49, 959.

[3] PL 49, 1129, 1131.

[4] *Decret. Gregor.,* IX, BK. III, tit. XXXI, chap. 18 (RF II, 576).

[5] Gratian, *Decretum,* pt. II (RF I, 762).

[6] *Epist.,* CXXV (PL 22, 1082).

[7] Causa XIX, Q. 3, can. 2 (RF I, 840).

to the sacred ministry, they have this in common with canons regular coupled with greater severity, and consequently it will be lawful to pass from an order of canons regular to a monastic order, provided however that one seek the superior's permission (XIX, Q. III, cap. *Statuimus* ii).[1]

Reply Obj. 3. The solemn vow whereby a person is bound to a less strict order is more binding than the simple vow whereby a person is bound to a stricter order. For if after taking a simple vow a person were to be married, his marriage would not be invalid, as it would be after taking a solemn vow. Consequently a person who is professed in a less severe order is not bound to fulfil a simple vow he has taken on entering a more severe order.

ARTICLE 9. *Whether One Ought To Induce Others To Enter Religion?*

We proceed thus to the Ninth Article: It seems that no one ought to induce others to enter religion.

Objection 1. For the blessed Benedict prescribes in his Rule (cap. 58)[2] that "those who seek to enter religion must not easily be admitted, but spirits must be tested whether they be of God"; and Cassian has the same instruction (*De Inst. Cœnob.* iv, 3).[3] Much less therefore is it lawful to induce anyone to enter religion.

Obj. 2. Further, Our Lord said (Matt. 23. 15): *Woe to you . . . because you go round about the sea and the land to make one proselyte and when he is made you make him the child of hell twofold more than yourselves.* Now thus would seem to do those who induce persons to enter religion. Therefore this would seem blameworthy.

Obj. 3. Further, No one should induce another to do what is to his prejudice. But those who are induced to enter religion sometimes take harm from it, for sometimes they are under obligation to enter a stricter religion. Therefore it would not seem praiseworthy to induce others to enter religion.

On the contrary, It is written (Exod. 26. 3 seqq.): *Let one curtain draw the other.* Therefore one man should draw another to God's service.

I answer that, Those who induce others to enter religion not only do not sin, but merit a great reward. For it is written (James 5. 20): *He who causeth a sinner to be converted from the error of his way, shall save his soul from death, and shall cover a multitude of sins;* and (Dan. 12. 3): *They that instruct many to justice shall be as stars for all eternity.*

Nevertheless such inducement may be affected by a threefold lack of order. First, if one person force another by violence to enter religion, and this is forbidden in the Decretals (XX, Q. III, cap. *Præsens*).[4] Secondly, if one person persuade another simoniacally to enter religion, by giving him presents: and this is forbidden in the same Decretal (Q. II, cap. *Quam pios*).[5] But this does not apply to the case where one provides a poor person with necessaries by educating him in the world for the religious life; or when without any compact one gives a person little presents for the sake of good fellowship. Thirdly, if one person entices another by lies: for it is to be feared that the person thus enticed may turn back on finding himself deceived, and thus *the last state of that man* may become *worse than the first* (Luke 11. 26).

Reply Obj. 1. Those who are induced to enter religion have still a time of probation in which they make a trial of the hardships of religion, so that they are not easily admitted to the religious life.

Reply Obj. 2. According to Hilary (*Can.* xxiv *in Matt.*)[6] this saying of our Lord was a forecast of the wicked endeavours of the Jews, after the preaching of Christ, to draw Gentiles or even Christians to observe the Jewish ritual, thereby making them doubly children of hell, because, namely, they were not forgiven the former sins which they committed while adherents of Judaism, and furthermore they incurred the guilt of Jewish perfidy; and thus interpreted these words have nothing to do with the case in point. According to Jerome, however, in his commentary on this passage of Matthew,[7] the reference is to the Jews even at the time when it was yet lawful to keep the legal observances, in so far as he whom they converted to Judaism "from paganism, was merely misled; but when he saw the wickedness of his teachers, he returned to his vomit, and becoming a pagan deserved a greater punishment for his treachery." Hence it is manifest that it is not blameworthy to draw others to the service of God or to the religious life, but only when one gives a bad example to the person converted whence he becomes worse.

Reply Obj. 3. The lesser is included in the greater. Therefore a person who is bound by

---

[1] Gratian, *Decretum*, PT. II (RF I, 840).
[2] PL 66, 803.　　[3] PL 49, 154.
[4] Gratian, PT. II (RF I, 850).
[5] Gratian, PT. II, causa I (RF I, 408).
[6] PL 9, 1049.　　[7] PL 26, 176.

vow or oath to enter a lesser order may be lawfully induced to enter a greater one, unless there be some special obstacle, such as ill-health, or the hope of making greater progress in the lesser order. On the other hand, one who is bound by vow or oath to enter a greater order cannot be lawfully induced to enter a lesser order, except for some special and evident cause, and then with the superior's dispensation.

ARTICLE 10. *Whether It Is Praiseworthy To Enter Religion Without Taking Counsel of Many, and Previously Deliberating for a Long Time?*

We proceed thus to the Tenth Article: It would not seem praiseworthy to enter religion without taking counsel of many, and previously deliberating for a long time.

Objection 1. For it is written (I John 4. 1): *Believe not every spirit, but try the spirits if they be of God.* Now sometimes a man's purpose of entering religion is not of God, since it often comes to nothing through his leaving the religious life; for it is written (Acts 5. 39): *If this counsel be of God, you cannot overthrow it.* Therefore it would seem that one ought to make a searching inquiry before entering religion.

Obj. 2. Further, It is written (Prov. 25. 9): *Treat thy cause with thy friend.* Now a man's cause would seem to be especially one that concerns a change in his state of life. Therefore it seems that one ought not to enter religion without discussing the matter with one's friends.

Obj. 3. Further, Our Lord (Luke 14. 28) in making a comparison with a man who has a mind to build a tower, says that he doth *first sit down and reckon the charges that are necessary, whether he have wherewithal to finish it,* lest he become an object of mockery, for that *this man began to build and was not able to finish.* Now the wherewithal to build the tower, as Augustine says (*Ep. ad Lætum,* ccxliii),[1] "is nothing less than that each one should renounce all his possessions." Yet it happens sometimes that many cannot do this, nor keep other religious observances; and in figure of this it is stated (I Kings 17. 39) that David could not walk in Saul's armour, for he was not used to it. Therefore it would seem that one ought not to enter religion without long deliberation beforehand and taking counsel of many.

On the contrary, It is stated (Matt. 4. 20) that upon our Lord's calling them, Peter and

Andrew *immediately leaving their nets, followed Him.* Hence Chrysostom says (*Hom.* xiv *in Matt.*).[2] "Such obedience as this does Christ require of us, that we delay not even for a moment."

I answer that, Long deliberation and the advice of many are required in great matters of doubt, as the Philosopher says,[3] while advice is unnecessary in matters that are certain and fixed. Now with regard to entering religion three points may be considered. First, the entrance itself into religion, considered by itself; and thus it is certain that entrance into religion is a greater good, and to doubt about this is to disparage Christ Who gave this counsel. Hence Augustine says (*De Verb. Dom.* vii, 2):[4] "The East, that is Christ, calleth thee, and thou turnest to the West, namely mortal and fallible man." Secondly, the entrance into religion may be considered in relation to the strength of the person who intends to enter. And here again there is no room for doubt about the entrance to religion, since those who enter religion trust not to be able to stay by their own power, but by the assistance of the divine power, according to Isa. 40. 31, *They that hope in the Lord shall renew their strength, they shall take wings as eagles, they shall run and not be weary, they shall walk and not faint.* Yet if there be some special obstacle (such as bodily weakness, a burden of debts, or the like) in such cases a man must deliberate and take counsel with such as are likely to help and not hinder him. Hence it is written (Ecclus. 37. 12): *Treat with a man without religion concerning holiness, with an unjust man concerning justice,*[5] meaning that one should not do so; hence the text goes on (*verses* 14, 15), *Give no heed to these in any matter of counsel, but be continually with a holy man.* In these matters, however, one should not take long deliberation. Therefore Jerome says (*Ep. ad Paulin.* ciii):[6] "Hasten, I pray thee, cut off rather than loosen the rope that holds the boat to the shore." Thirdly, we may consider the way of entering religion, and which order one ought to enter, and about such matters also one may take counsel of those who will not stand in one's way.

Reply Obj. 1. The saying: *Try the spirits, if they be of God,* applies to matters admitting of doubt whether the spirit be of God; thus those who are already in religion may doubt

[1] PL 33, 1055.

[2] PG 57, 219.   [3] *Ethics,* III, 3 (1112ᵇ8).
[4] *Serm. ad Popul.,* serm. c, 2 (PL 38, 604).
[5] The Douay version supplies the negative; *Treat not ... nor with ...*
[6] PL 22, 549.

whether he who offers himself to religion be led by the spirit of God, or be moved by hypocrisy. Therefore they must try the postulant whether he be moved by the divine spirit. But for him who seeks to enter religion there can be no doubt but that the purpose of entering religion to which his heart has given birth is from the spirit of God, for it is His spirit that leads man into the land of uprightness (Ps. 142. 10).

Nor does this prove that it is not of God that some turn back, since not all that is of God is incorruptible; otherwise corruptible creatures would not be of God, as the Manicheans hold, nor could some who have grace from God lose it, which is also heretical. But God's counsel whereby He makes even things corruptible and changeable, is imperishable according to Isa. 46. 10, *My counsel shall stand and all My will shall be done.* Hence the purpose of entering religion needs not to be tried whether it be of God, because it requires no further demonstration, as a gloss says[1] on I Thess. 5. 21, *Prove all things.*

Reply Obj. 2. Even as *the flesh lusteth against the spirit* (Gal. 5. 17), so too carnal friends often thwart our spiritual progress, according to Mic. 7. 6, *A man's enemies are they of his own household.* Therefore Cyril expounding Luke 9. 61, *Let me first take my leave of them that are at my house,* says:[2] "By asking first to take leave of them that were at his house, he shows he was somewhat of two minds. For to communicate with his neighbours, and consult those who are unwilling to relish righteousness, is an indication of weakness and turning back. Hence he hears our Lord say: 'No man putting his hand to the plough, and looking back, is fit for the kingdom of God,' because he looks back who seeks delay in order to go home and confer with his kinsfolk."

Reply Obj. 3. The building of the tower signifies the perfection of Christian life, and the renunciation of one's possessions is the wherewithal to build this tower. Now no one doubts or deliberates about wishing to have the wherewithal, or whether he is able to build the tower if he have the wherewithal, but what does come

under deliberation is whether one has the wherewithal. Again it is not necessarily a matter of deliberation whether one ought to renounce all that one has, or whether by so doing one may be able to attain to perfection, while it is a matter of deliberation whether that which he is doing amounts to the renunciation of all that he has, since unless he does renounce (which is to have the wherewithal) he cannot, as the text goes on to state, be Christ's disciple, and this is to build the tower. The misgiving of those who hesitate as to whether they may be able to attain to perfection by entering religion is shown by many examples to be unreasonable. Hence Augustine says:[3] "On that side whither I had set my face, and whither I trembled to go, there appeared to me the chaste dignity of continency, . . . honestly alluring me to come and doubt not, and stretching forth to receive and embrace me, her holy hands full of multitudes of good examples. There were so many young men and maidens here, a multitude of youth and every age, grave widows and aged virgins. . . . And she smiled at me with a persuasive mockery as though to say: 'Canst not thou what these youths and these maidens can? Or can they either in themselves, and not rather in the Lord their God? . . . Why standest thou in thyself, and so standest not? Cast thyself upon Him; fear not, He will not withdraw Himself that thou shouldst fall. Cast thyself fearlessly upon Him: He will receive and will heal thee.'"

The example quoted of David is not to the point, because the arms of Saul, as a gloss on the passage observes,[4] are "the sacraments of the Law, as being burdensome"; religion however is the sweet yoke of Christ, for as Gregory says (*Moral.* iv),[5] "what burden does He lay on the shoulders of the mind, Who commands us to shun all troublesome desires, Who warns us to turn aside from the rough paths of this world?"

To those indeed who take this sweet yoke upon themselves He promises the refreshment of the divine enjoyment and the eternal rest of their souls; to which may He who made this promise bring us, Jesus Christ our Lord, Who is over all things God blessed for ever. Amen.

[1] *Glossa interl.* (VI, 113r); *Glossa* Lombardi (PL 192, 309).
[2] PG 72, 663.
[3] *Confessions,* VIII, 27 (PL 32, 761).
[4] *Glossa interl.* (II, 82v).
[5] Chap. 33 (PL 75, 673).

THIRD PART

❖❖❖❖❖❖❖❖❖❖❖

PROLOGUE

BECAUSE our Saviour the Lord Jesus Christ, in order to *save His people from their sins* (Matt. 1. 21), as the angel announced, showed to us in His own Person the way of truth, whereby we may attain to the bliss of eternal life by rising again, it is necessary in order to complete the work of theology that after considering the last end of human life, and the virtues and vices, there should follow the consideration of the Saviour of all, and of the benefits bestowed by Him on the human race.

Concerning this we must consider (1) the Saviour Himself; (2) the sacraments by which we attain to our salvation (Q. LX); (3) the end of immortal life to which we attain by the resurrection (Supp. Q. LXIX).

Concerning the first, a twofold consideration arises: the first, about the mystery of the Incarnation itself, whereby God was made man for our salvation; the second, about such things as were done and suffered by our Saviour—that is, God incarnate (Q. XXVII).

TREATISE ON THE INCARNATION

QUESTION I

OF THE FITNESS OF THE INCARNATION

(In Six Articles)

CONCERNING the first, three things present themselves for consideration: first, the fitness of the Incarnation of Christ; secondly, the mode of union of the Word Incarnate (Q. II); thirdly, what follows this union (Q. XVI).

Under the first head there are six points of inquiry: (1) Whether it was fitting for God to become incarnate? (2) Whether it was necessary for the restoration of the human race? (3) Whether if there had been no sin God would have become incarnate? (4) Whether He became incarnate primarily to take away original sin rather than actual? (5) Whether it was fitting for God to become incarnate from the beginning of the world? (6) Whether His Incarnation ought to have been deferred to the end of the world?

ARTICLE 1. *Whether It Was Fitting That God Should Become Incarnate?*

We proceed thus to the First Article: It would seem that it was not fitting for God to become incarnate.

Objection 1. Since God from all eternity is the very essence of goodness, it was best for Him to be as He had been from all eternity. But from all eternity He had been without flesh. Therefore it was most fitting for Him not to be united to flesh. Therefore it was not fitting for God to become incarnate.

Obj. 2. Further, it is not fitting to unite

things that are infinitely apart, even as it would not be a fitting union if one were "to paint a figure in which the neck of a horse was joined to the head of a man."[1] But God and flesh are infinitely apart, since God is most simple, and flesh is most composite,—especially human flesh. Therefore it was not fitting that God should be united to human flesh.

Obj. 3. Further, a body is as distant from the highest spirit as evil is from the highest good. But it was wholly unfitting that God, Who is the highest good, should assume evil. Therefore it was not fitting that the highest uncreated spirit should assume a body.

Obj. 4. Further, it is not becoming that He Who surpassed the greatest things should be contained in the least, and that He upon Whom rests the care of great things should leave them for lesser things. But the whole universe of things cannot contain God Who takes care of the whole world. Therefore it would seem unfitting that "He should be hid under the frail body of a babe in swathing bands, in comparison with Whom the whole universe is accounted as little; and that this Prince should quit His throne for so long, and transfer the government of the whole world to so frail a body," as Volusianus writes to Augustine.[2]

On the contrary, It would seem most fitting that by visible things the invisible things of God should be made known, for to this end was the whole world made, as is clear from the word of the Apostle (Rom. 1. 20): *For the invisible things of God . . . are clearly seen, being understood by the things that are made.* But, as Damascene says in the beginning of the third book,[3] by the mystery of the Incarnation are made known at once the goodness, the wisdom, the justice, and the power or might of God—"His goodness, for He did not despise the weakness of His own handiwork; His justice, since, on man's defeat, He caused the tyrant to be overcome by none other than man, and yet He did not snatch men forcibly from death; His wisdom, for He found a suitable discharge for a most heavy debt; His power, or infinite might, for there is nothing greater than for God to become man." Therefore it was fitting for God to become incarnate.

I answer that, To each thing, that is fitting which belongs to it by reason of its very nature; thus, to reason is proper to man, since

this belongs to him because he is rational by nature. But the very nature of God is the essence of goodness, as is clear from Dionysius.[4] Hence, what belongs to the nature of goodness befits God. But it belongs to the nature of goodness to communicate itself to others, as is plain from Dionysius.[5] Hence it belongs to the nature of the highest good to communicate itself in the highest manner to the creature, and this is brought about chiefly by "His so joining created nature to Himself that one Person is made up of these three—the Word, a soul and flesh," as Augustine says.[6] Hence it is manifest that it was fitting that God should become incarnate.

Reply Obj. 1. The mystery of the Incarnation was not effected through God being changed in any way from the unchanging state in which He had been from eternity, but through His having united Himself to the creature in a new way, or rather through having united it to Himself. But it is fitting that a creature which by nature is changeable should not always be in the same way. And therefore, as the creature began to be, although it had not been before, so likewise, not having been previously united to God in Person, it was afterwards united to Him.

Reply Obj. 2. To be united to God in unity of person was not fitting to human flesh, according to its natural endowments, since it was above its dignity; nevertheless, it was fitting that God, by reason of His infinite goodness, should unite it to Himself for man's salvation.

Reply Obj. 3. Every mode of being wherein any creature whatsoever differs from the Creator has been established by God's wisdom, and is ordained to God's goodness. For God, Who is uncreated, immutable, and incorporeal, produced mutable and corporeal creatures for His own goodness. And so also the evil of punishment was established by God's justice for God's glory. But evil of fault is committed by withdrawing from the art of the Divine wisdom and from the order of the Divine goodness. And therefore it could be fitting to God to assume a nature created, mutable, corporeal, and subject to penalty, but it did not become Him to assume the evil of fault.

Reply Obj. 4. As Augustine replies:[7] "The Christian doctrine nowhere holds that God was

---

[1] Horace, *Ars. Poet.*, line 1.
[2] *Epist.*, CXXXV (PL 33, 512).
[3] *De Fide Orth.*, III, 1 (PG 94, 984).

[4] *De Div. Nom.*, I, 5 (PG 3, 593).
[5] *Ibid.*, IV, 20 (PG 3, 720); cf. IV, 1 (PG 3, 693).
[6] *De Trin.*, XIII, 17 (PL 42, 1031).
[7] *Epist. ad Volusian*, CXXXVII, 2 (PL 33, 517).

so joined to human flesh as either to desert or lose, or to transfer and as it were, contract within this frail body, the care of governing the universe. This is the thought of men unable to see anything but corporeal things. . . . God is great not in mass, but in might. Hence the greatness of His might feels no straits in narrow surroundings. Nor, if the passing word of a man is heard at once by many, and wholly by each, is it incredible that the abiding Word of God should be everywhere at once?" Hence nothing unfitting arises from God becoming incarnate.

ARTICLE 2. *Whether It Was Necessary for the Restoration of the Human Race That the Word of God Should Become Incarnate?*

We proceed thus to the Second Article: It would seem that it was not necessary for the restoration of the human race that the Word of God should become incarnate.

Objection 1. For since the Word of God is perfect God, as has been said (Part I, Q. IV, AA. 1 and 2), no power was added to Him by the assumption of flesh. Therefore, if the incarnate Word of God restored human nature, He could also have restored it without taking on flesh.

Obj. 2. Further, for the restoration of human nature, which had fallen through sin, it would seem that nothing more is required than that man should satisfy for sin. Now man can satisfy, as it would seem, for sin; for God ought not to require from man more than man can do, and since He is more inclined to be merciful than to punish, as He lays the penalty of the act of sin to man's charge, so He ought to credit him with the recompense of the contrary act. Therefore it was not necessary for the restoration of human nature that the Word of God should become incarnate.

Obj. 3. Further, to revere God pertains especially to man's salvation; hence it is written (Mal. 1. 6): *If, then, I be a father, where is my honour? and if I be a master, where is my fear?* But men revere God the more by considering Him as elevated above all, and far beyond man's senses, hence (Ps. 112. 4) it is written: *The Lord is high above all nations, and His glory above the heavens;* and farther on: *Who is as the Lord our God?* which relates to reverence. Therefore it would seem unfitting to man's salvation that God should be made like us by assuming flesh.

On the contrary, What frees the human race from perdition is necessary for the salvation of man. But the mystery of the Incarnation is such, according to John 3. 16: *God so loved the world as to give His only-begotten Son, that whosoever believeth in Him may not perish, but may have life everlasting.* Therefore it was necessary for man's salvation that God should become incarnate.

I answer that, A thing is said to be necessary for a certain end in two ways. First, when the end cannot be without it, as food is necessary for the preservation of human life. Secondly, when the end is attained better and more conveniently, as a horse is necessary for a journey. In the first way it was not necessary that God should become incarnate for the restoration of human nature. For God of His omnipotent power could have restored human nature in many other ways. But in the second way it was necessary that God should become incarnate for the restoration of human nature. Hence Augustine says:[1] "We shall also show that other ways were not wanting to God, to Whose power all things are equally subject, but that there was not a more fitting way of healing our misery."

Now this may be viewed with respect to the furtherance of man in good. First, with regard to faith, which is made more certain by believing God Himself Who speaks; hence Augustine says:[2] "In order that man might journey more trustfully toward the truth, the Truth itself, the Son of God, having assumed human nature, established and founded faith." Secondly, with regard to hope, which is thereby greatly lifted up; hence Augustine says:[3] "Nothing was so necessary for raising our hope as to show us how deeply God loved us. And what could afford us a stronger proof of this than that the Son of God should become a partner with us of human nature?" Thirdly, with regard to charity, which is greatly enkindled by this; hence Augustine says:[4] "What greater cause is there of the Lord's coming than to show God's love for us?" And he afterwards adds: "If we have been slow to love, at least let us hasten to love in return." Fourthly, with regard to right doing, in which He set us an example; hence Augustine says in a sermon:[5] "Man who might be seen was not to be followed; but God was to be followed, Who could not be seen. And therefore God was made man, that He Who might be seen by man, and Whom man might follow, might be shown to man." Fifthly,

[1] *De Trin.,* XIII, 10 (PL 42, 1024).
[2] *City of God,* XI, 2 (PL 41, 318).
[3] *De Trin.,* XIII, 10 (PL 42, 1024).
[4] *De Catech. Rudib.,* IV (PL 40, 314).
[5] *Serm. ad Popul.,* CCCLXXI, 2 (PL 39, 1660).

with regard to the full participation of the Divinity, which is the true happiness of man and end of human life; and this is bestowed upon us by Christ's humanity, for Augustine says in a sermon:[1] "God was made man, that man might be made God."

So also was this useful for our withdrawal from evil. First, because man is taught by it not to prefer the devil to himself, nor to honour him who is the author of sin; hence Augustine says:[2] "Since human nature is so united to God as to become one person, let not these proud spirits dare to prefer themselves to man because they have no bodies." Secondly, because we are thereby taught how great is man's dignity, lest we should sully it with sin; hence Augustine says:[3] "God has proved to us how high a place human nature holds amongst creatures, since He appeared to men as a true man." And Pope Leo says in a sermon on the Nativity:[4] "Learn, O Christian, thy worth; and being made a partner of the Divine nature, refuse to return by evil deeds to your former worthlessness." Thirdly, because, in order to do away with man's presumption, "the grace of God is commended in Jesus Christ, though no merits of ours went before," as Augustine says.[5] Fourthly, because "man's pride, which is the greatest stumbling-block to our clinging to God, can be convinced and cured by humility so great," as Augustine says in the same place. Fifthly, in order to free man from the thraldom of sin, which, as Augustine says,[6] "ought to be done in such a way that the devil should be overcome by the justice of the man Jesus Christ," and this was done by Christ satisfying for us. Now a mere man could not have satisfied for the whole human race, and God was not bound to satisfy; hence it was needful for Jesus Christ to be both God and man. And so Pope Leo says in the same sermon:[7] "Weakness is assumed by strength, lowliness by majesty, in order that one and the same Mediator of God and men might die in one and rise in the other—for this was our fitting remedy. Unless He was true God, He would not have brought a remedy; and unless He was true man, He would not have set an example."

And there are very many other advantages

which accrued, above the apprehension of man's senses.

Reply Obj. 1. This argument has to do with the first kind of necessity, without which we cannot attain to the end.

Reply Obj. 2. Satisfaction may be said to be sufficient in two ways. First, perfectly, in so far as it is completely sufficient, being adequate to make good the fault committed, and in this way the satisfaction of a mere man cannot be sufficient for sin, both because the whole of human nature has been corrupted by sin, whereas the goodness of any person or persons could not make up adequately for the harm done to the whole of the nature, and also because a sin committed against God has a kind of infinity from the infinity of the Divine majesty, because the greater the person we offend, the more grievous the offence. Hence for adequate satisfaction it was necessary that the act of the one satisfying should have an infinite efficacy, as being of God and man.

Secondly, man's satisfaction may be termed sufficient, imperfectly—that is, in the acceptation of him who is content with it, even though it is not adequate, and in this way the satisfaction of a mere man is sufficient. And because everything imperfect presupposes some perfect thing, by which it is sustained, hence it is that the satisfaction of every mere man has its efficacy from the satisfaction of Christ.

Reply Obj. 3. By taking flesh, God did not lessen His majesty, and in consequence did not lessen the reason for reverencing Him, which is increased by the increase of knowledge of Him. But, on the contrary, because He wished to draw near to us by taking flesh, He drew us to know Him the more.

ARTICLE 3. *Whether, If Man Had Not Sinned, God Would Have Become Incarnate?*

We proceed thus to the Third Article: It would seem that if man had not sinned, God would still have become incarnate.

Objection 1. For as long as the cause endures the effect continues. But as Augustine says:[8] "Many other things are to be considered in the Incarnation of Christ besides absolution from sin," and these were discussed above (A.2). Therefore if man had not sinned, God would have become incarnate.

Obj. 2. Further, it belongs to the omnipotence of the Divine power to perfect His works, and to manifest Himself by some infinite effect. But no mere creature can be called an infinite

---

[1] Contained among the works of Augustine, *Serm. suppos.*, serm. CXXVIII (PL 39, 1997).
[2] *De Trin.*, XIII, 17 (PL 42, 1031).
[3] *De Vera Relig.*, 16 (PL 34, 134).
[4] *Serm.*, XXI, 3 (PL 54, 192).
[5] *De Trin.*, XIII, 17 (PL 42, 1031).
[6] *Ibid.*, XIII, 13, 14 (PL 42, 1027; 1028).
[7] Chap. 2 (PL 54, 192).
[8] *De Trin.*, XIII, 17 (PL 42, 1031).

effect, since it is finite of its very essence. Now, it seems that in the work of the Incarnation alone is an infinite effect of the Divine power manifested in a special manner, by which power things infinitely distant are united, since it has been brought about that man is God. And in this work especially the universe would seem to be perfected, according as the last creature— namely, man—is joined to the first principle— namely, God. Therefore, even if man had not sinned God would have become incarnate.

Obj. 3. Further, human nature has not been made more capable of grace by sin. But after sin it is capable of the grace of union, which is the greatest grace. Therefore, if man had not sinned, human nature would have been capable of this grace, nor would God have withheld from human nature any good it was capable of. Therefore, if man had not sinned, God would have become incarnate.

Obj. 4. Further, God's predestination is eternal. But it is said of Christ (Rom. 1. 4): *Who was predestinated the Son of God in power.* Therefore, even before sin it was necessary that the Son of God should become incarnate, in order to fulfil God's predestination.

Obj. 5. Further, the mystery of the Incarnation was revealed to the first man, as is plain from Gen. 2. 23. *This now is bone of my bones,* etc., which the Apostle says is *a great sacrament . . . in Christ and in the Church,* as is plain from Eph. 5. 32. But man could not be foreconscious of his fall, for the same reason that the angels could not, as Augustine proves.[1] Therefore, even if man had not sinned, God would have become incarnate.

On the contrary, Augustine says (*De Verb. Apost.* viii, 2),[2] expounding what is set down in Luke 19. 10, *For the Son of Man is come to seek and to save that which was lost:* "Therefore, if man had not sinned, the Son of Man would not have come." And on I Tim. 1. 15, *Christ Jesus came into this world to save sinners,* a gloss says:[3] "There was no cause of Christ's coming into the world except to save sinners. Take away diseases, take away wounds, and there is no need of medicine."

I answer that, There are different opinions about this question. For some say[4] that even if

man had not sinned the Son of Man would have become incarnate. Others assert the contrary,[5] and it seems that our assent ought rather to be given to this opinion.

For such things as spring from God's will, alone, and beyond the creature's due, can be made known to us only through being revealed in the Sacred Scripture, in which the Divine Will is made known to us. Hence, since everywhere in the Sacred Scripture the sin of the first man is assigned as the reason of the Incarnation, it is more in accordance with this to say that the work of the Incarnation was ordained by God as a remedy for sin, so that, had sin not existed, the Incarnation would not have been. And yet the power of God is not limited to this; even had sin not existed, God could have become incarnate.

Reply Obj. 1. All the other causes which are assigned in the preceding article have to do with a remedy for sin. For if man had not sinned, he would have been imbued with the light of Divine wisdom, and would have been perfected by God with the rectitude of justice in order to know and carry out everything needful. But because man, on deserting God, had fallen to the level of corporeal things, it was necessary that God should take flesh, and by corporeal things should afford him the remedy of salvation. Hence, on John 1. 14, *And the Word was made flesh,* St. Augustine says:[6] "Flesh had blinded thee, flesh heals thee; for Christ came and destroyed the vices of the flesh by the flesh."

Reply Obj. 2. The infinity of Divine power is shown in the mode of production of things from nothing. Again, it suffices for the perfection of the universe that the creature be ordered in a natural manner to God as to an end. But that a creature should be united to God in person exceeds the limits of the perfection of nature.

Reply Obj. 3. A double capability may be remarked in human nature: one, in respect to the order of natural power, and this is always fulfilled by God, Who apportions to each according to its natural capability; the other in respect to the order of the Divine power, which all creatures implicitly obey; and the capability we speak of pertains to this. But God does not fulfil all such capabilities, otherwise God could do only what He has done in creatures, and this is false, as stated above (Part I, Q. XXV, A. 5; Q. CV, A. 6). But there is no reason why human nature should not have been raised to something

---

[1] *De Gen. ad lit.,* XI, 18 (PL 34, 439).

[2] *Serm. ad Popul.,* CLXXIV, 2 (PL 38, 940).

[3] *Glossa ordin.* (VI, 117B); *Glossa Lombardi* (PL 192, 332); Augustine, *Serm. ad Popul.,* CLXXV, 1 (PL 38, 945).

[4] Albert the Great, *In Sent.,* BK. III, d. XX, A. 4 (BO XXVIII, 361); Alexander of Hales, *Summa Theol.,* III, Q. 2, m. 13 (III, 12ra); Rupert, *In Matt.,* BK. XIII (PL 168, 1628); cf. DTC., art. *Incarnation* (VII, 1495, 1501).

[5] Bonaventure, *In Sent.,* III, d. 1, A. 2, Q. 2 (QR III, 24).

[6] *In Joann. Tract.,* II, on 1.14 (PL 35, 1395).

greater after sin. For God allows evils to happen in order to bring a greater good from them; hence it is written (Rom. 5. 20): *Where sin abounded, grace did more abound.* Hence, too, in the blessing of the Paschal candle, we say:[1] "O happy fault, that merited such and so great a Redeemer!"

Reply Obj. 4. Predestination presupposes the foreknowledge of future things; and hence, as God predestines the salvation of anyone to be brought about by the prayers of others, so also He predestined the work of the Incarnation to be the remedy of human sin.

Reply Obj. 5. Nothing prevents an effect from being revealed to one to whom the cause is not revealed. Hence, the mystery of the Incarnation could be revealed to the first man without his being fore-conscious of his fall. For not everyone who knows the effect knows the cause.

ARTICLE 4. *Whether God Became Incarnate Primarily in Order To Take Away Actual Sin, Rather Than To Take Away Original Sin?*

We proceed thus to the Fourth Article: It would seem that God became incarnate primarily as a remedy for actual sins rather than for original sin.

Objection 1. For the more grievous the sin, the more it runs counter to man's salvation, for which God became incarnate. But actual sin is more grievous than original sin, for the lightest punishment is due to original sin, as Augustine says (*Contra Julian.* v, 11).[2] Therefore the Incarnation of Christ is chiefly directed to taking away actual sins, rather than the taking away of original sin.

Obj. 2. Further, pain of sense is not due to original sin, but merely pain of loss, as has been shown (Part I-II, Q. LXXXVII, A. 5). But Christ came to suffer the pain of sense on the Cross in satisfaction for sins—and not the pain of loss, for He did not lack either the beatific vision or the enjoyment of it. Therefore He came chiefly in order to take away actual sin rather than original sin.

Obj. 3. Further, as Chrysostom says (*De Compunctione Cordis,* ii, 3):[3] "This must be the mind of the faithful servant, to account the benefits of his Lord which have been bestowed on all alike as though they were bestowed on himself alone. For as if speaking of himself alone, Paul writes to the Galatians (2. 20): *Christ . . . loved me and delivered Him-*

self for me." But our individual sins are actual sins, for original sin is the common sin. Therefore we ought to have this conviction, to believe that He has come chiefly for actual sins.

On the contrary, It is written (John 1. 29): *Behold the Lamb of God, behold Him Who taketh away the sins* (Vulg., *sin*) *of the world.*

I answer that, It is certain that Christ came into this world not only to take away that sin which is handed on originally to posterity, but also in order to take away all sins subsequently added to it; not that all are taken away (and this is from men's fault, since they do not adhere to Christ, according to John 3. 19: *The light is come into the world, and men loved darkness rather than the light*), but because He offered what was sufficient for blotting out all sins. Hence it is written (Rom. 5. 15-16): *But not as the offence, so also the gift. . . . For judgment indeed was by one unto condemnation, but grace is of many offences unto justification.*

Moreover, the more grievous the sin, the more particularly did Christ come to blot it out. But "greater" is said in two ways: in one way intensively, as a more intense whiteness is said to be greater, and in this way actual sin is greater than original sin, for it has more of the nature of voluntariness, as has been shown (Part I-II, Q. LXXXI, A. 1). In another way a thing is said to be greater extensively, as whiteness on a greater surface is said to be greater; and in this way original sin, whereby the whole human race is infected, is greater than any actual sin, which is proper to one person. And in this respect Christ came principally to take away original sin, since "the good of the race is a more Divine thing than the good of an individual," as is said in the *Ethics.*[4]

Reply Obj. 1. This argument looks to the intensive greatness of sin.

Reply Obj. 2. In the future award the pain of sense will not be meted out to original sin. Yet the penalties such as hunger, thirst, death, and the like, which we suffer sensibly in this life flow from original sin. And hence Christ, in order to satisfy fully for original sin, wished to suffer sensible pain, that He might consume death and the like in Himself.

Reply Obj. 3. Chrysostom says:[5] "The Apostle used these words not as if wishing to diminish Christ's gifts, ample as they are, and spreading throughout the whole world, but that he might account himself alone the occasion of them. For what does it matter that they are given to others, if what are given to you are as

---

[1] Missal, *S.O.P.*, p. 153.
[2] PL 44, 809.　　[3] PG 47, 419.

[4] Aristotle, I, 2 (1094b8).　　[5] *Op. cit.,* II, 6 (PG 47, 419).

complete and perfect as if none of them were given to another than yourself?" And hence, although a man ought to account Christ's gifts as given to himself, yet he ought not to consider them not to be given to others. And thus we do not exclude that He came chiefly to wipe away the sin of the whole nature rather than the sin of one person. But that sin of the nature is as perfectly healed in each one as if it were healed in him alone. Hence, on account of the union of charity, what is vouchsafed to all ought to be accounted his own by each one.

ARTICLE 5. *Whether It Was Fitting That God Should Become Incarnate in the Beginning of the Human Race?*

We proceed thus to the Fifth Article: It would seem that it was fitting that God should become incarnate in the beginning of the human race.

Objection 1. For the work of the Incarnation sprang from the immensity of Divine charity, according to Eph. 2. 4, 5: *But God (Who is rich in mercy), for His exceeding charity wherewith He loved us . . . even when we were dead in sins, hath quickened us together in Christ.* But charity does not tarry in bringing assistance to a friend who is suffering need, according to Prov. 3. 28: *Say not to thy friend: Go, and come again, and to-morrow I will give to thee, when thou canst give at present.* Therefore God ought not to have put off the work of the Incarnation, but ought thereby to have brought relief to the human race from the beginning.

Obj. 2. Further, it is written (I Tim. 1. 15): *Christ Jesus came into this world to save sinners.* But more would have been saved had God become incarnate at the beginning of the human race; for in the various centuries very many, through not knowing God, perished in their sin. Therefore it was fitting that God should become incarnate at the beginning of the human race.

Obj. 3. Further, the work of grace is not less ordered than the work of nature. But nature takes its rise from the perfect, as Boëthius says.[1] Therefore the work of grace ought to have been perfect from the beginning. But in the work of the Incarnation we see the perfection of grace, according to John 1. 14: *The Word was made flesh,* and afterwards it is added: *Full of grace and truth.* Therefore Christ ought to have become incarnate at the beginning of the human race.

[1] *De Consol.,* III, 10 (PL 63, 764).

On the contrary, It is written (Gal. 4. 4): *But when the fulness of the time was come, God sent His Son, made of a woman, made under the law,* upon which a gloss says[2] that "the fulness of the time is when it was decreed by God the Father to send His Son." But God has prescribed everything by His wisdom. Therefore God became incarnate at the most fitting time, and it was not fitting that God should become incarnate at the beginning of the human race.

I answer that, Since the work of the Incarnation is principally ordained to the restoration of the human race by blotting out sin, it is manifest that it was not fitting for God to become incarnate at the beginning of the human race before sin. For medicine is given only to the sick. Hence Our Lord Himself says (Matt. 9. 12, 13): *They that are in health need not a physician, but they that are ill. . . . For I am not come to call the just, but sinners.*

Nor was it fitting that God should become incarnate immediately after sin. First, on account of the manner of man's sin, which had come of pride; hence man was to be liberated in such a manner that he might be humbled, and see how he stood in need of a deliverer. Hence on the words in Gal. 3. 19, *Being ordained by angels in the hand of a mediator,* a gloss says:[3] "With great wisdom was it so ordered by God that the Son of Man should not be sent immediately after man's fall. For first of all God left man under the natural law, with freedom of choice, in order that he might know the powers of his nature; and when he failed in them, he received the law; whereupon, by the fault not of the law, but of his nature, the disease gained strength; so that having recognized his infirmity he might cry out for a physician, and beseech the aid of grace."

Secondly, on account of the order of furtherance in good, whereby we proceed from imperfection to perfection. Hence the Apostle says (I Cor. 15. 46, 47): *Yet that was not first which is spiritual, but that which is natural; afterwards that which is spiritual. . . . The first man was of the earth, earthly; the second man from heaven, heavenly.*

Thirdly, on account of the dignity of the incarnate Word, for on the words (Gal. 4. 4), *But when the fulness of the time was come,* a gloss says:[4] "The greater the judge who was

[2] *Glossa* Lombardi (PL 192, 135); cf. *Glossa ordin.* (VI, 84E).—Ambrosiaster, *In Gal.* (PL 17, 380).
[3] *Glossa ordin.* (VI, 83B); *Glossa* Lombardi (PL 192, 128).
[4] *Glossa* Lombardi (PL 192, 135); cf. *Glossa ordin.* (VI, 684E).—Augustine, *In Joann., tract.,* XXXI (PL 35, 1638).

coming, the more numerous was the band of heralds who ought to have preceded him."

Fourthly, lest the fervour of faith should cool by the length of time, for the charity of many will grow cold at the end of the world. Hence (Luke 18. 8) it is written: *But yet the Son of Man, when He cometh, shall He find think you faith on earth?*

Reply Obj. 1. Charity does not put off bringing assistance to a friend, always bearing in mind the circumstances as well as the state of the persons. For if the physician were to give the medicine at the very outset of the ailment, it would do less good, and would hurt rather than benefit. And hence the Lord did not bestow upon the human race the remedy of the Incarnation in the beginning, lest they should despise it through pride, if they did not already recognize their disease.

Reply Obj. 2. Augustine replies to this (*De Sex Quest Pagan., Ep.* cii), saying (Q. 2)[1] that "Christ wished to appear to man and to have His doctrine preached to them when and where He knew those were who would believe in Him. But in such times and places as His Gospel was not preached He foresaw that not all, indeed, but many would so bear themselves towards His preaching as not to believe in His corporeal presence, even were He to raise the dead." But the same Augustine, taking exception to this reply in his book (*De Perseverantia,* ix),[2] says: "How can we say the inhabitants of Tyre and Sidon would not believe when such great wonders were wrought in their midst, or would not have believed had they been wrought, when God Himself bears witness that they would have done penance with great humility if these signs of Divine power had been wrought in their midst?" And he adds in answer:[3] "Hence, as the Apostle says (Rom. 9. 16), 'it is not of him that willeth nor of him that runneth, but of God that showeth mercy'; Who [succours whom He will of] those who, as He foresaw, would believe in His miracles if wrought amongst them, [while others] He succours not, having judged them in His predestination secretly yet justly. Therefore let us unshrinkingly believe His mercy to be with those who are set free, and His truth with those who are condemned."

Reply Obj. 3. Perfection is prior to imperfection, both in time and nature, in things that are different (for what brings others to perfec-

tion must itself be perfect); but in one and the same thing, imperfection is prior in time though posterior in nature. And thus the eternal perfection of God precedes in duration the imperfection of human nature, but the latter's ultimate perfection in union with God follows.

ARTICLE 6. *Whether the Incarnation Ought To Have Been Put Off Till the End of the World?*

We proceed thus to the Sixth Article: It would seem that the work of the Incarnation ought to have been put off till the end of the world.

Objection 1. For it is written (Ps. 91. 11): *My old age in plentiful mercy*—that is, "in the last days," as a gloss says.[4] But the time of the Incarnation is especially the time of mercy, according to Ps. 101. 14: *For it is time to have mercy on it.* Therefore the Incarnation ought to have been put off till the end of the world.

Obj. 2. Further, as has been said (A. 5, REPLY 3), in the same subject perfection is subsequent in time to imperfection. Therefore what is most perfect ought to be the very last in time. But the highest perfection of human nature is in the union with the Word, because *in Christ it hath pleased the Father that all the fulness of the Godhead should dwell,* as the Apostle says (Col. 1. 19, and 2. 9). Therefore the Incarnation ought to have been put off till the end of the world.

Obj. 3. Further, what can be done by one ought not to be done by two. But the one coming of Christ at the end of the world was sufficient for the salvation of human nature. Therefore it was not necessary for Him to come beforehand in His Incarnation, and hence the Incarnation ought to have been put off till the end of the world.

On the contrary, It is written (Habac. 3. 2): *In the midst of the years Thou shalt make it known.* Therefore the mystery of the Incarnation which was made known to the world ought not to have been put off till the end of the world.

I answer that, As it was not fitting that God should become incarnate at the beginning of the world, so also it was not fitting that the Incarnation should be put off till the end of the world. And this is shown first from the union of the Divine and human nature. For, as it has been said (A. 5, REPLY 3), perfection precedes

---

[1] *Epist.,* CII *Ad Deogratias* (PL 33, 375).
[2] PL 45, 1006.
[3] *De Dono Persev.,* XI (PL 45, 1007).

[4] *Glossa* Lombardi (PL 191, 859); cf. *Glossa interl.* (III, 226v).

imperfection in time in one way, and contrariwise in another way imperfection precedes perfection. For in that which is made perfect from being imperfect imperfection precedes perfection in time, whereas in that which is the efficient cause of perfection, perfection precedes imperfection in time. Now in the work of the Incarnation both concur; for by the Incarnation human nature is raised to its highest perfection, and in this way it was not becoming that the Incarnation should take place at the beginning of the human race. And the Word incarnate is the efficient cause of the perfection of human nature, according to John 1. 16: *Of His fulness we have all received,* and hence the work of the Incarnation ought not to have been put off till the end of the world. But the perfection of glory to which human nature is to be finally raised by the Word Incarnate will be at the end of the world.

Secondly, from the effect of man's salvation; for, as is said *Qq. Vet. et Nov. Test., qu.* 83,[1] "it is in the power of the Giver to have pity when, or as much as, He wills. Hence He came when He knew it was fitting to succour, and when His boons would be welcome. For when by the feebleness of the human race men's knowledge of God began to grow dim and their morals to change, He was pleased to choose Abraham as a standard of the restored knowledge of God and of holy living; and later on when reverence grew weaker, He gave the law to Moses in writing; and because the gentiles despised it and would not submit themselves to it, and they who received it would not keep it, being touched with pity, God sent His Son, to grant to all remission of their sin and to offer them, justified, to God the Father." But if this remedy had been put off till the end of the world, all knowledge and reverence of God and all uprightness of morals would have been swept away from the earth.

Thirdly, this appears fitting to the manifestation of the Divine power, which has saved men in several ways,—not only by faith in some future thing, but also by faith in something present and past.

Reply Obj. 1. This gloss has in view the mercy of God, which leads us to glory. Nevertheless, if it is referred to the mercy shown the human race by the Incarnation of Christ, we must reflect that, as Augustine says (*Retract.* i, 26),[2] the time of the Incarnation may be compared to the youth of the human race, "on account of the strength and fervour of faith,

which works by love"; and to old age—that is, the sixth age—"on account of the number of centuries, for Christ came in the sixth age." And "although youth and old age cannot be together in a body, yet they can be together in a soul, the former on account of ardor, the latter on account of sobriety." And hence Augustine says elsewhere (QQ. lxxxiii, *qu.* 44)[3] that "it was not becoming that the Master by Whose imitation the human race was to be formed to the highest virtue should come from heaven, save in the time of youth." But in another work (*De Gen. cont. Manich.* i, 23)[4] he says that Christ came in the sixth age—that is, in the old age—of the human race.

Reply Obj. 2. The work of the Incarnation is to be viewed not as merely the term of a movement from imperfection to perfection, but also as a principle of perfection in human nature, as has been said.

Reply Obj. 3. As Chrysostom says[5] on John 3, 17, *"For God sent not His Son into the world to judge the world":* "There are two comings of Christ: the first, for the remission of sins; the second, to judge the world. For if He had not done so, all would have perished together, since all have sinned and need the glory of God." Hence it is plain that He ought not to have put off the coming in mercy till the end of the world.

QUESTION II

OF THE MODE OF UNION OF THE WORD INCARNATE

(*In Twelve Articles*)

Now we must consider the mode of union of the Incarnate Word; and, first, the union itself; secondly, the Person assuming (Q. III.); thirdly, the nature assumed (Q. IV.).

Under the first head there are twelve points of inquiry: (1) Whether the union of the Word Incarnate took place in the nature? (2) Whether it took place in the Person? (3) Whether it took place in the suppositum or hypostasis? (4) Whether the Person or hypostasis of Christ is composite after the Incarnation? (5) Whether any union of body and soul took place in Christ? (6) Whether the human nature was united to the Word accidentally? (7) Whether the union itself is something created? (8) Whether it is the same as assumption? (9) Whether the union of the two natures is the greatest union? (10) Whether the union of the

[1] Ambrosiaster (PL 35, 2276).   [2] PL 32, 626.

[3] PL 40, 28.   [4] PL 34, 192.
[5] *In Joann.,* hom. XXVIII (PG 59, 162).

two natures in Christ was brought about by grace? (11) Whether any merits preceded it? (12) Whether the grace of union was natural to the man Christ?

ARTICLE 1. *Whether the Union of the Incarnate Word Took Place in One Nature?*

We proceed thus to the First Article: It would seem that the Union of the Word Incarnate took place in one nature.

Objection 1. For Cyril says[1] (he is quoted in the acts of the Council of Chalcedon, part ii., act. 1):[2] "We must understand not two natures, but one incarnate nature of the Word of God"; and this could not be unless the union took place in the nature. Therefore the union of the Word Incarnate took place in the nature.

Obj. 2. Further, Athanasius says in his Creed[3] that, "as the rational soul and the flesh together are one man, so God and man together are one Christ." Now the rational soul and flesh together form one human nature. Therefore the union took place in the nature.

Obj. 3. Further, of two natures one is not denominated by the other unless they are to some extent mutually changed. But the Divine and human natures in Christ are denominated one by the other; for Cyril says (*loc. cit.*) that "the Divine nature is incarnate," and Gregory Nazianzen says (*Ep.* i. *ad Cledon.*)[4] that "the human nature is deified," as appears from Damascene (*De Fide Orthod.* iii, 6, 11, 17).[5] Therefore from two natures one seems to have resulted.

On the contrary, It is said in the declaration of the Council of Chalcedon:[6] "We confess that in these latter times the only-begotten Son of God appeared in two natures, without mingling, without change, without division, without separation—the distinction of natures not having been taken away by the union." Therefore the union did not take place in the nature.

I answer that, To make this question clear we must consider what is nature. Now it is to be observed that the word nature comes from nativity. Hence this word was used first of all to signify the begetting of living beings, which is called birth or sprouting forth, the word *natura* meaning, as it were, *nascitura*. After-

wards this word nature was taken to signify the principle of this begetting; and because in living things the principle of generation is an intrinsic principle, this word nature was further employed to signify any intrinsic principle of motion; thus the Philosopher says[7] that "nature is the principle of motion in that in which it is *per se* and not accidentally." Now this principle is either form or matter. Hence sometimes form is called nature, and sometimes matter. And because the end of natural generation, in that which is generated, is the essence of the species, which the definition signifies, this essence of the species is called the nature. And thus Boëthius defines nature (*De Duab. Nat.*):[8] "Nature is what informs a thing with its specific difference"—that is, which perfects the specific definition. Therefore we are now speaking of nature as it signifies the essence, or the "what-it-is," or the quiddity of the species.

Now if we take nature in this way it is impossible that the union of the Incarnate Word took place in the nature. For one thing is made of two or more in three ways. First, from two complete things which remain in their perfection. This can only happen to those things whose form is composition, order, or figure, just as a heap is made up of many stones brought together without any order, but solely with juxtaposition, and a house is made of stones and beams arranged in order, and fashioned to a figure. And in this way some said[9] the union was by manner of mingling (*confusio*) (which is without order) or by manner of commensuration (which is with order). But this cannot be. First, because neither composition nor order nor figure is a substantial form, but accidental; and hence it would follow that the union of the Incarnation was not essential (*per se*), but accidental, which will be disproved later on (A. 6). Secondly, because thereby we should not have an absolute unity, but relative only, for there remain several things actually. Thirdly, because the form of such things is not a nature, but rather an art, as the form of a house, and thus one nature would not be constituted in Christ, as they wish.

Secondly, one thing is made up of several things, which are perfect but changed, as a mixture is made up of its elements; and in this way some have said that the union of the Incarnation was brought about by manner of

[1] *Epist.*, XLV (PG 77, 232); *Epist.*, XLVI (PG 77, 240); *Apologeticus adv. Orient. Episc.*, anath. 8 (PG 76, 349); *Orat.* 1 *de Recta Fide ad Religiosissimas Reginas* (PG 76, 1212). [2] MA VI, 675, 683.
[3] Cf. Creed "*Quicumque*" (MA II, 1355; DZ 40).
[4] *Orat.*, XLV (PG 36, 633); cf. *Orat.*, XXXIX (PG 36, 353).
[5] PG 94, 1008, 1024, 1069.
[6] Pt. II, actio 5 (MA VII, 115; DZ 148).
[7] *Physics*, II, 1 (192ᵇ21).
[8] Chap. 1 (PL 64, 1342).
[9] Probably Eutyches; cf. DTC., art. *Eutychès* (V, 1601–1608); cf. St. Thomas, *In Sent.*, III, d. V, Q. 1, A. 2; *Contra Gent.*, IV, 35.

combination.[1] But this cannot be. First, because the Divine Nature is altogether immutable, as has been said (Part I, Q. IX, AA. I and 2), and hence neither can it be changed into something else, since it is incorruptible, nor can anything else be changed into it, for it cannot be generated. Secondly, because what is mixed is of the same species with none of the elements; for flesh differs in species from any of it elements. And thus Christ would be of the same nature neither with His Father nor with His mother. Thirdly, because there can be no mixture of things widely apart, for the species of one of them is absorbed—for example, if we were to put a drop of water in a flagon of wine. And hence, since the Divine Nature infinitely exceeds the human nature, there could be no mixture, but the Divine Nature alone would remain.

Thirdly, a thing is made up of things not mixed nor changed, but which are imperfect, just as man is made up of soul and body, and likewise as one body of various members. But this cannot be said of the mystery of the Incarnation. First, because both natures, that is, the Divine and the human, are perfect—each in its kind. Secondly, because the Divine and human natures cannot constitute anything after the manner of quantitative parts, as the members make up the body, for the Divine Nature is incorporeal; nor after the manner of form and matter, for the Divine Nature cannot be the form of anything, especially of anything corporeal, since it would follow that the species resulting therefrom would be communicable to several, and thus there would be several Christs. Thirdly, because Christ would exist neither in human nature nor in the Divine Nature, since any difference added varies the species, as unity varies number, as it is said.[2]

Reply Obj. 1. This authority of Cyril is expounded in the Fifth Synod (that is, Constantinople II, coll. viii, can. 8)[3] thus: "If anyone proclaiming one nature of the Word of God to be incarnate does not receive it as the Fathers taught—namely, that from the Divine and human natures (a union in subsistence having taken place) one Christ results,—but endeavours from these words to introduce one nature or substance of the Divinity and flesh of Christ:

—let such a one be anathema." Hence the sense is not that from two natures one results, but that the Nature of the Word of God united flesh to Itself in the Person.

Reply Obj. 2. From the soul and body a double unity—namely, of nature and person—results in each of us; of nature according as the soul is united to the body, and formally perfects it, so that one nature springs from the two as from act and potency or from matter and form. But the likeness is not in this sense, for the Divine Nature cannot be the form of a body, as was proved (Part I, Q. III, A. 8). Unity of person results from them, however, since there is a single someone subsisting in flesh and soul, and in this lies the likeness, for the one Christ subsists in the Divine and human natures.

Reply Obj. 3. As Damascene says,[4] the Divine Nature is said to be incarnate because "It is united to flesh personally," and not that It is changed into the nature of flesh. So likewise the flesh is said to be deified, as he also says (*ibid.* 17),[5] not by change, but by union with the Word, its natural properties still remaining, and hence it may be considered as deified because it becomes the flesh of the Word of God, but not that it becomes God.

ARTICLE 2. *Whether the Union of the Incarnate Word Took Place in the Person?*

We proceed thus to the Second Article: It would seem that the union of the Incarnate Word did not take place in the person.

Objection 1. For the Person of God is not distinct from His Nature, as we said (Part I, Q. XXXIX, A. 1). If, therefore, the union did not take place in the nature, it follows that it did not take place in the person.

Obj. 2. Further, Christ's human nature has no less dignity than ours. But personality belongs to dignity, as was stated above (Part I, Q. XXIX, A. 3, REPLY 2). Hence, since our human nature has its proper personality, much more reason was there that Christ's should have its proper personality.

Obj. 3. Further, as Boëthius says (*De Duab. Nat.*),[6] "a person is an individual substance of rational nature." But the Word of God assumed an individual human nature, for "universal human nature does not exist of itself, but is the object of pure thought," as Damascene says (*De Fide Orthod.* iii, 11).[7] Therefore

---

[1] Eutyches; cf. Boëthius, *De Duabus Nat.*, chap. 7 (PL 64, 1351).

[2] Aristotle, *Metaphysics*, VIII, 3 (1043^b36).

[3] MA IX, 382; DZ 220. (the words "one Christ results," which are in the text of the Council, are missing from the *Summa*).

[4] *De Fide Orth.*, III, 17 (PG 94, 1069), cf. chap. 6 (PG 94, 1008). [5] PG 94, 1069.

[6] Chap. 3 (PL 64, 1343). [7] PG 94, 1024.

the human nature of Christ has its personality. Hence it does not seem that the union took place in the person.

On the contrary, We read in the Council of Chalcedon (Part ii, act. 5):[1] "We confess that Our Lord Jesus Christ is not parted or divided into two persons, but is one and the same Only-Begotten Son and Word of God." Therefore the union took place in the person.

I answer that, Person has a different meaning from nature. For nature, as has been said (A. 1), designates the essence of the species which is signified by the definition. And if nothing was found to be added to what belongs to the notion of the species, there would be no need to distinguish the nature from the suppositum of the nature, which is the individual subsisting in this nature, because every individual subsisting in a nature would be altogether one with its nature. Now in certain subsisting things we happen to find what does not belong to the notion of the species—namely, accidents and individuating principles, which appears chiefly in such things as are composed of matter and form. Hence in such as these the nature and the suppositum really differ; not indeed as if they were wholly separate, but because the suppositum includes the nature itself of the species, and in addition certain other things outside the notion of the species. Hence the suppositum is taken to be a whole which has the nature as its formal part to perfect it; and consequently in such beings as are composed of matter and form the nature is not predicated of the suppositum, for we do not say that this man is his manhood. But if there is a thing in which there is nothing outside the species or its nature (as in God), the suppositum and the nature are not really distinct in it, but only in our way of thinking, because it is called nature according as it is an essence, and a suppositum according as it is subsisting. And what is said of a suppositum is to be applied to a person in rational or intellectual creatures, for a person is nothing else than "an individual substance of rational nature," according to Boëthius.[2]

Therefore, whatever is found in a person is united to it in person, whether it belongs to its nature or not. Hence, if the human nature is not united to God the Word in person, it is not united to Him in any way; and thus belief in the Incarnation is altogether done away with, and Christian faith wholly overturned.

Therefore, since the Word has a human nature united to Him, which does not however belong to His Divine Nature, it follows that the union took place in the Person of the Word, and not in the nature.

Reply Obj. 1. Although in God Nature and Person are not really distinct, yet they have distinct meanings, as was said above, because person signifies after the manner of something subsisting. And because human nature is so united to the Word that the Word subsists in it, and not so that His Nature receives from it any addition or change, it follows that the union of human nature to the Word of God took place in the person, and not in the nature.

Reply Obj. 2. Personality pertains of necessity to the dignity of a thing and to its perfection so far as it pertains to the dignity and perfection of that thing to exist by itself (which is understood by the word person). Now it is a greater dignity to exist in something nobler than oneself than to exist by oneself. Hence the human nature of Christ has a greater dignity than ours from this very fact that in us, being as it were existent by itself, it has its own personality, but in Christ it exists in the Person of the Word. Thus to perfect the species belongs to the dignity of a form, yet the sensitive part in man, on account of its union with the nobler form which perfects the species, is more noble than in brutes, where it is itself the form which perfects.

Reply Obj. 3. "The Word of God did not assume human nature in general, but *'in atomo'* "—that is, in an individual—as Damascene says (*De Fide Orthod.* iii, 11),[3] for otherwise every man would be the Word of God, even as Christ was. Yet we must bear in mind that not every individual in the genus of substance, even in rational nature, is a person, but that alone which exists by itself, and not that which exists in some more perfect thing. Hence the hand of Socrates, although it is a kind of individual, is not a person, because it does not exist by itself, but in something more perfect—namely, in the whole. And hence, too, this is signified by a person being defined as an individual substance, for the hand is not a complete substance, but part of a substance. Therefore, although this human nature is a kind of individual in the genus of substance, it has not its own personality, because it does not exist separately, but in something more perfect—namely, in the Person of the Word. Therefore the union took place in the person.

---

[1] MA VII, 115; DZ 148.
[2] *De Duabus Nat.,* 3 (PL 64, 1343).

[3] PG 94, 1024.

ARTICLE 3. *Whether the Union of the Word Incarnate Took Place in the Suppositum or Hypostasis?*

We proceed thus to the Third Article: It would seem that the union of the Word Incarnate did not take place in the suppositum or hypostasis.

Objection 1. For Augustine says (*Enchir.* xxv, xxxviii):[1] "Both the Divine and human substance are one Son of God; but they are one thing (*aliud*) by reason of the Word and another thing (*aliud*) by reason of the man." And Pope Leo says in his letter to Flavian (*Ep.* xxviii):[2] "One of these is glorious with miracles, the other succumbs under injuries." But *one* (*aliud*) and *the other* (*aliud*) differ in suppositum. Therefore the union of the Word Incarnate did not take place in the suppositum.

Obj. 2. Further, "hypostasis is nothing more than a particular substance," as Boëthius says (*De Duab. Nat.*).[3] But it is plain that in Christ there is another particular substance beyond the hypostasis of the Word—namely, the body and the soul and the composite of these. Therefore there is another hypostasis in Him besides the hypostasis of the Word.

Obj. 3. Further, the hypostasis of the Word is not included in any genus or species, as is plain from Part I, Q. III, A. 5; Q. XXX, A. 4, REPLY 3. But Christ, according as He is made man, is contained under the species of man; for Dionysius says (*Div. Nom.* 1):[4] "Within the limits of our nature He came, Who far surpasses the whole order of nature supersubstantially." Now nothing is contained under the human species unless it be a hypostasis of the human species. Therefore in Christ there is another hypostasis besides the hypostasis of the Word of God; and hence the same conclusion follows as above.

On the contrary, Damascene says (*De Fide Orthod.* iii, 4):[5] "In Our Lord Jesus Christ we acknowledge two natures and one hypostasis."

I answer that, Some[6] who did not know the relation of hypostasis to person, although granting that there is but one person in Christ, held, nevertheless, that there is one hypostasis of God and another of man, as if the union took place in the person and not in the hypostasis.

Now this, for three reasons, is clearly erroneous. First, because person only adds to hypostasis a determinate nature—namely, rational—according to what Boëthius says (*De Duab. Nat.*),[7] "a person is an individual substance of rational nature"; and hence it is the same to attribute to the human nature in Christ a proper hypostasis and a proper person. And the holy Fathers, seeing this, condemned both in the Fifth Council held at Constantinople,[8] saying: "If anyone seeks to introduce into the mystery of Christ two subsistences or two persons, let him be anathema. For by the incarnation of one of the Holy Trinity, God the Word, the Holy Trinity received no argument of person or subsistence." Now subsistence is the same as the subsisting thing, which is proper to hypostasis, as is plain from Boëthius (*De Duab. Nat.*).[9]

Secondly, because if it is granted that person adds to hypostasis something in which the union can take place, this something is nothing else than a property pertaining to dignity, according as it is said by some that a person is "a hypostasis distinguished by a property pertaining to dignity."[10] If, therefore, the union took place in the person and not in the hypostasis, it follows that the union only took place in regard to some dignity. And this is what Cyril,[11] with the approval of the Council of Ephesus,[12] condemned in these terms: "If anyone after the uniting divides the subsistences in the one Christ, only joining them in a union of dignity or authority or power, and not rather in a concourse of natural union, let him be anathema."

Thirdly, because to the hypostasis alone are attributed the operations and the natural properties, and whatever belongs to the nature in the concrete; for we say that this man reasons, and is capable of laughter, and is a rational animal. So likewise this man is said to be a suppositum, because he underlies (*supponitur*) whatever belongs to man and receives its predication. Therefore, if there is any hypostasis in Christ besides the hypostasis of the Word, it follows that whatever pertains to man is verified of some other than the Word—for exam-

---

[1] PL 40, 250; PL 40, 251.
[2] Chap. 4 (PL 54, 767).
[3] Chap. 3 (PL 64, 1344).
[4] Sect. 4 (PG 3, 592).
[5] PG 94, 997.
[6] The Archbishop of Sens; cf. William of Auxerre, *Summa Aurea*, PT. III, tr. 1, chap. 1, Q. 8 (113rb).
[7] Chap. 3 (PL 64, 1343).
[8] Coll. VIII, can. 5 (MA IX, 379; DZ 217).
[9] Chap. 3 (PL 64, 1344).
[10] Bonaventure, *In Sent.*, BK. I, d. XXIII, A. 1, Q. 1 (QR I, 405).
[11] *Epist.*, XVII, anath. 3 (PG 77, 120); Mercator's translation, PL 48, 840.
[12] Pt. I, chap. 26, anath. 3 (MA IV, 1082; DZ 115); cf. Council of Constantinople II, coll. VIII, can. 13 (MA IX, 386; DZ 226).

ple, that He was born of a Virgin, suffered, was crucified, was buried. And this, too, was condemned with the approval of the Council of Ephesus (*ibid.* can. 4)[1] in these words: "If anyone ascribes to two persons or subsistences such words as are in the evangelical and apostolic Scriptures, or have been said of Christ by the saints, or by Himself of Himself, and, moreover, applies some of them to the man, taken as distinct from the Word of God, and some of them (as if they could be used of God alone) only to the Word of God the Father, let him be anathema."

Therefore it is plainly a heresy condemned long since by the Church to say that in Christ there are two hypostases, or two supposita, or that the union did not take place in the hypostasis or suppositum. Hence in the same Council (can. 2)[2] it is said: "If anyone does not confess that the Word was united to flesh in subsistence, and that Christ with His flesh is both —namely, God and man—let him be anathema."

Reply Obj. 1. Just as accidental difference makes a thing other (*alterum*), so essential difference makes another thing (*aliud*). Now it is plain that the otherness which springs from accidental difference may pertain to the same hypostasis or suppositum in created things, since the same thing numerically can underlie different accidents. But it does not happen in created things that the same numerically can subsist in divers essences or natures. Hence just as when we speak of other and other in regard to creatures we do not signify diversity of suppositum, but only diversity of accidental forms, so likewise when Christ is said to be one thing or another thing we do not imply diversity of suppositum or hypostasis, but diversity of nature. Hence Gregory Nazianzen says in a letter to Chelidonius (*Ep.* ci):[3] "In the Saviour we may find one thing and another, yet He is not one person and another. And I say 'one thing and another,' whereas, on the contrary, in the Trinity we say one Person and another (so as not to confuse the subsistences), but not one thing and another."

Reply Obj. 2. Hypostasis signifies a particular substance, not in every way, but as it is in its complement. Yet as it is in union with something more complete, it is not said to be a hypostasis, as for instance a hand or a foot. So likewise the human nature in Christ, although it is a particular substance, neverthe-

less cannot be called a hypostasis or suppositum because it is in union with a completed thing—namely, the whole Christ, as He is God and man. But the complete being with which it coincides is said to be a hypostasis or suppositum.

Reply Obj. 3. In created things a singular thing is placed in a genus or species not by reason of what belongs to its individuation, but by reason of its nature, which is determined according to its form, and in composite things individuation is taken rather from matter. Hence we say that Christ is in the human species by reason of the nature assumed, and not by reason of the hypostasis.

ARTICLE 4. *Whether After the Incarnation the Person or Hypostasis of Christ Is Composite?*

We proceed thus to the Fourth Article: It would seem that the Person of Christ is not composite.

Objection 1. For the Person of Christ is not other than the Person or hypostasis of the Word, as appears from what has been said (A. 2). But in the Word, Person and Nature do not differ, as appears from Part I, Q. XXXIX, A. 1. Therefore since the Nature of the Word is simple, as was shown above (Part I, Q. III, A. 7), it is impossible that the Person of Christ be composite.

Obj. 2. Further, all composition requires parts. But the Divine Nature is incompatible with the notion of a part, for every part involves the notion of imperfection. Therefore it is impossible that the Person of Christ be composed of two natures.

Obj. 3. Further, what is composed of others would seem to be homogeneous with them, as from bodies only a body can be composed. Therefore if there is anything in Christ composed of the two natures, it follows that this will not be a person but a nature; and hence the union in Christ will take place in the nature, which is contrary to A. 1.

On the contrary, Damascene says (*De Fide Orthod.* iii, 4),[4] "In the Lord Jesus Christ we acknowledge two natures, but one hypostasis composed from both."

I answer that, The Person or hypostasis of Christ may be viewed in two ways. First as it is in itself, and thus it is altogether simple, even as the Nature of the Word. Secondly, in the aspect of person or hypostasis to which it pertains to subsist in a nature; and from this

---

[1] MA IV, 1082; DZ 116.

[2] MA IV, 1082; DZ 114.　　[3] PG 37, 180.

[4] PG 94, 997.

point of view the Person of Christ subsists in two natures. Hence though there is one subsisting being in Him, yet there are different aspects of subsistence, and hence He is said to be a composite person, in so far as one being subsists in two.

And from this *the solution to the first* is clear.

Reply Obj. 2. This composition of a person from natures is not so called by reason of parts, but by reason of number, even as that in which two things are found together may be said to be composed of them.

Reply Obj. 3. It is not found in every composition that the thing composed is homogeneous with its component parts, but only in the parts of a continuous thing, for the continuous is composed solely of continuous (parts). But an animal is composed of soul and body, and neither of these is an animal.

ARTICLE 5. *Whether in Christ There Is Any Union of Soul and Body?*

We proceed thus to the Fifth Article: It would seem that in Christ there was no union of soul and body.

Objection 1. For from the union of soul and body in us a person or a human hypostasis is caused. Hence if the soul and body were united in Christ, it follows that a hypostasis resulted from their union. But this was not the hypostasis of God the Word, for It is eternal. Therefore in Christ there would be a person or hypostasis besides the hypostasis of the Word, which is contrary to AA. 2 and 3.

Obj. 2. Further, from the union of soul and body results the nature of the human species. But Damascene says (*De Fide Orthod.* iii, 3),[1] that "we must not conceive a common species in the Lord Jesus Christ." Therefore there was no union of soul and body in Him.

Obj. 3. Further, the soul is united to the body for the sole purpose of making it alive. But the body of Christ could be made alive by the Word of God Himself, seeing He is the fount and principle of life. Therefore in Christ there was no union of soul and body.

On the contrary, The body is not said to be animated save from its union with the soul. Now the body of Christ is said to be animated, as the Church chants:[2] "Taking an animate body, He deigned to be born of a Virgin." Therefore in Christ there was a union of soul and body.

I answer that, Christ is called a man univocally with other men, as being of the same species, according to the Apostle (Phil. 2. 7), *being made in the likeness of a man.* Now it belongs to the notion of the human species that the soul be united to the body, for the form does not constitute the species, except through the fact that it becomes the act of matter, and this is the term of generation through which nature intends the species. Hence it must be said that in Christ the soul was united to the body, and the contrary is heretical, since it destroys the truth of Christ's humanity.

Reply Obj. 1. This would seem to be the reason which was of weight with such as denied the union of the soul and body in Christ[3]—namely, lest they should thereby be forced to admit a second person or hypostasis in Christ, since they saw that the union of soul and body in mere men resulted in a person. But this happens in mere men because the soul and body are so united in them as to exist by themselves. But in Christ they are united together so as to be united to something higher, which subsists in the nature composed of them. And hence from the union of the soul and body in Christ a new hypostasis or person does not result, but what is composed of them is united to the already existing hypostasis or Person.

Nor does it therefore follow that the union of the soul and body in Christ is of less effect than in us, for its union with something nobler does not lessen but increases its virtue and worth; just as the sensitive soul in animals constitutes the species, as being considered the ultimate form, yet it does not do so in man, although it is of greater power and dignity, and this because of its union with a further and nobler perfection—namely, the rational soul, as has been said above (A. 2, REPLY 2).

Reply Obj. 2. This saying of Damascene may be taken in two ways. First, as referring to human nature, which, according as it is in one individual alone, has not the nature of a common species, but only according as either it is abstracted from every individual, and considered in bare contemplation or according as it is in all individuals. Now the Son of God did not assume human nature as it exists in the mere consideration of the intellect, since in this way He would not have assumed human nature in reality, unless it be said that human nature is a separate idea, just as the Platonists held man to be without matter.[4] But in this way the Son

[1] PG 94, 993.

[2] Feast of the Circumcision, At Lauds, antiph. 1a (Breviary, *S.O.P.* p. 390).

[3] See below, A6.   [4] Cf. Aristotle, *Metaphysics,* III, 2 (997ᵇ8); see above, Part I, Q. LXXXIV, A. I.

of God would not have assumed flesh, contrary to what is written (Luke 24. 39), *A spirit hath not flesh and bones as you see Me to have.* Neither can it be said that the Son of God assumed human nature as it is in all the individuals of the same species, because otherwise He would have assumed all men. Therefore it remains, as Damascene says further on (*ibid.* 11)[1] that He assumed human nature *in atomo* —that is, in an individual; not, indeed, in another individual which is a suppositum or a person of that nature, but in the Person of the Son of God.

Secondly, this saying of Damascene may be taken not as referring to human nature as if from the union of soul and body one common nature (namely, human) did not result, but as referring to the union of the two natures, Divine and human, which do not combine so as to form a third something that becomes a common nature, for in this way it would become predicable of many, and this is what he is aiming at, since he adds: "For there was not generated, neither will there ever be generated, another Christ, Who from the Godhead and manhood, and in the Godhead and manhood, is perfect God and perfect man."

Reply Obj. 3. There are two principles of corporeal life: one the effecting principle, and in this way the Word of God is the principle of all life; the other, the formal principle of life, for since "in living things to be is to live," as the Philosopher says,[2] just as everything is formally by its form, so likewise the body lives by the soul; in this way a body could not live by the Word, Which cannot be the form of a body.

ARTICLE 6. *Whether the Human Nature Was United to the Word of God Accidentally?*

We proceed thus to the Sixth Article: It would seem that the human nature was united to the Word of God accidentally.

Objection 1. For the Apostle says (Phil. 2. 7) of the Son of God, that He was *in habit found as a man.* But habit is accidentally associated with that to which it pertains, whether habit be taken for one of the ten predicaments or as a species of quality. Therefore human nature is accidentally united to the Son of God.

Obj. 2. Further, whatever comes to a thing that is complete in being comes to it accidentally, for an accident is said to be what can come or go without the subject being corrupted. But human nature came to Christ in time, Who

had perfect being from eternity. Therefore it came to Him accidentally.

Obj. 3. Further, whatever does not pertain to the nature or the essence of a thing is its accident, for whatever is, is either a substance or an accident. But human nature does not pertain to the Divine Essence or Nature of the Son of God, for the union did not take place in the nature, as was said above (A. 1). Hence the human nature must have accrued accidentally to the Son of God.

Obj. 4. Further, an instrument accrues accidentally. But the human nature was the instrument of the Godhead in Christ, for Damascene says (*De Fide Orthod.* iii, 15),[3] that "the flesh of Christ is the instrument of the Godhead." Therefore it seems that the human nature was united to the Son of God accidentally.

On the contrary, Whatever is predicated accidentally, predicates, not substance, but quantity, or quality, or some other mode of being. If therefore the human nature accrues accidentally, when we say Christ is man we do not predicate substance, but quality or quantity, or some other mode of being, which is contrary to the Decretal of Pope Alexander (III.), who says:[4] "Since Christ is perfect God and perfect man, what foolhardiness have some to dare to affirm that Christ as man is not a substance?"

I answer that, In evidence of this question we must know that two heresies have arisen with regard to the mystery of the union of the two natures in Christ. The first confused the natures, as Eutyches and Dioscorus,[5] who held that from the two natures one nature resulted, so that they confessed Christ to be *from* two natures (which were distinct before the union), but not *in* two natures (the distinction of nature coming to an end after the union).

The second was the heresy of Nestorius and Theodore of Mopsuestia,[6] who separated the

---

[1] PG 94, 1024.   [2] *Soul*, II, 4 (415[b]13).

[3] PG 94, 1060.

[4] Fragment of a letter (MA XXII, 457); cf. *Append. Conc. Later.*, p. XLIX, chap. 20 (MA XXII, 426); cf. *Decretal Gregor.* IX, BK. V, tit. VII, chap. 7 (RF II, 779).

[5] See John Damascene, *De Fide Orth.*, III, 3 (PG 94, 993); Conc. Chalced., actio 5 (MA VII, 106). For Eutyches see especially Leo the Great, *Epist.*, XXVIII, chap. 6 (PL 54, 777); Boëthius, *De Duabus Nat.*, chaps. 5–7 (PL 64, 1347–1352).

[6] Cf. John Damascene, *Ibid.;* Conc. of Constant. II, col. VIII, can. 4–5 (MA IX, 378; DZ 216–217); See Theodore of Mopsuestia, *Fragm. De Incarn.*, VII (PG 66, 976); *Frag. Epist. ad Domnum* (PG 66, 1012). On Nestorius cf. Cyril of Alexandria, *Epist.*, II *Ad Nestorium* (PG 77, 41); *Epist.*, IV (PG 77, 45); *Epist.*, XVII (PG 77, 112); anath. 3, 4, 8 (PG 77, 120–121); Nestor, *Epist.*, II *ad Cyrillum* (*Epist.*, v among the works of Cyril—PG 77, 53); Mercator's trans., PL 48, 820.

persons. For they held the Person of the Son of God to be distinct from the Person of the Son of man, and said these were mutually united —first, by indwelling, since the Word of God dwelt in the man as in a temple; secondly, by unity of affection, since the will of the man was always in agreement with the will of the Word of God; thirdly, by operation, according as they said the man was the instrument of the Word of God; fourthly, by greatness of honour, according as all honour shown to the Son of God was equally shown to the Son of man, on account of His Union with the Son of God; fifthly, by equivocation—that is, sharing of names, according as we say that this man is God and the Son of God. Now it is plain that all these modes imply an accidental union.

But some more recent masters, thinking to avoid these heresies, through ignorance fell into them. For some[1] conceded one person in Christ, but maintained two hypostases, or two supposita, saying that a man, composed of body and soul, was from the beginning of his conception assumed by the Word of God. And this is the first opinion set down by the Master (III. *Sent.*, d. 6).[2] But others[3] desirous of keeping the unity of person, held that the soul of Christ was not united to the body, but that these two were mutually separate, and were united to the Word accidentally, so that the number of persons might not be increased. And this is the third opinion which the Master sets down (*ibid.*).[4]

But both of these opinions fall into the heresy of Nestorius; the first, indeed, because to maintain two hypostases or supposita in Christ is the same as to maintain two persons, as was shown above (A. 3). And if stress is laid on the word person, we must have in mind that even Nestorius spoke of unity of person on account of the unity of dignity and honour. Hence the fifth Council (Constantinople II., coll. viii, can. 5)[5] directs an anathema against such a one as holds "one person in dignity, honour and adoration, as Theodore and Nestorius foolishly wrote." But the other opinion falls into the error of Nestorius by maintaining an accidental union. For there is no difference in saying that the Word of God is united to the Man Christ

by indwelling, as in His temple (as Nestorius said), or by putting on man, as a garment, which is the third opinion; rather it says something worse than Nestorius—namely, that the soul and body are not united.

Now the Catholic faith, holding the mean between the above positions, does not affirm that the union of God and man took place in the essence or nature, nor yet in something accidental, but midway, in a subsistence or hypostasis. Hence in the fifth Council (*ibid.*)[6] we read: 'Since the unity may be understood in many ways, those who follow the impiety of Apollinaris and Eutyches, professing the destruction of what came together" (that is, destroying both natures), "confess a union by mingling; but the followers of Theodore and Nestorius, maintaining division, introduce a union of affection. But the Holy Church of God, rejecting the impiety of both these treasons, confesses a union of the Word of God with flesh, by composition, which is in subsistence."

Therefore it is plain that the second of the three opinions mentioned by the Master,[7] which holds one hypostasis of God and man, is not to be called an opinion, but an article of Catholic faith. So likewise the first opinion which holds two hypostases, and the third which holds an accidental union, are not to be styled opinions, but heresies condemned by the Church in Councils.

Reply Obj. 1. As Damascene says (*De Fide Orthod.* iii, 26):[8] "Examples need not be wholly and at all points similar, for what is wholly similar is the same, and not an example, and especially in Divine things, for it is impossible to find a wholly similar example in the Theology"— that is, in the Godhead of Persons—"and in the Dispensation"—that is, the mystery of the Incarnation. Hence the human nature in Christ is likened to a habit—that is, a garment, not indeed in regard to accidental union, but inasmuch as the Word is seen by the human nature, as a man by his garment, and also inasmuch as the garment is changed, for it is shaped according to the figure of him who puts it on, and yet he is not changed from his form on account of the garment. So likewise the human nature assumed by the Word of God is ennobled, but the Word of God is not changed, as Augustine says.[9]

---

[1] The Archbishop of Sens; cf. William of Auxerre *Summa Aurea*, pt. III, tr. I, chap. I, Q. 8 (113rb).
[2] QR II, 574.
[3] Cf. Abelard, *Introd. ad Theol.*, III, 6 (PL 178, 1106); Gerhohum, *Epist.*, VII, VIII (PL 193, 496, 503); condemned by Alexander III, *Epist.*, DCCXLIV (PL 200, 685); cf. William of Auxerre, *Summa Aurea*, BK. III, chap. I, Q. 2 (110va).   [4] QR II, 578.   [5] MA IX, 379; DZ 217.

[6] Can. 4 (MA IX, 778; DZ 216).
[7] *Sent.*, III, dist. VI, chap. 3 (QR II, 576).
[8] PG 94, 1096.
[9] QQ. LXXXIII, Qu. 73.

Reply Obj. 2. Whatever accrues after the completion of the being comes accidentally, unless it be taken into communion with the complete being, just as in the resurrection the body comes to the soul which pre-exists, yet not accidentally, because it is assumed to the same being, so that the body has vital being through the soul; but it is not so with whiteness, for the being of whiteness is other from the being of man to which whiteness comes. But the Word of God from all eternity had complete being in hypostasis or person, while in time the human nature accrued to it, not as if it were assumed to one being according as this is of the nature (even as the body is assumed to the being of the soul), but to one being according as this is of the hypostasis or person. Hence the human nature is not accidentally united to the Son of God.

Reply Obj. 3. Accident is divided against substance. Now substance, as is plain from the *Metaphysics*,[1] is taken in two ways: first, for essence or nature; secondly, for suppositum or hypostasis. Hence the union having taken place in the hypostasis is enough to show that it is not an accidental union, although the union did not take place in the nature.

Reply Obj. 4. Not everything that is assumed as an instrument pertains to the hypostasis of the one who assumes, as is plain in the case of a saw or a sword; yet nothing prevents what is assumed into the unity of the hypostasis from being as an instrument, even as the body of man or his members. Hence Nestorius held that the human nature was assumed by the Word merely as an instrument, and not into the unity of the hypostasis. And therefore he did not concede that the man was really the Son of God, but His instrument. Hence Cyril says (*Epist. ad Monach. Ægyptii*):[2] "The Scripture does not affirm that this Emmanuel"—that is, Christ—"was assumed for the office of an instrument, but as God truly humanized"—that is, made man. But Damascene held[3] that the human nature in Christ is an instrument belonging to the unity of the hypostasis.

ARTICLE 7. *Whether the Union of the Divine and Human Natures Is Anything Created?*

We proceed thus to the Seventh Article: It would seem that the union of the Divine and human natures is not anything created.

Objection 1. For there can be nothing created

---

[1] Aristotle, v, 8 (1017[b]23).
[2] *Epist.*, 1 (PG 77, 29).
[3] *De Fide Orth.*, III, 15 (PG 94, 1060).

in God, because whatever is in God is God. But the union is in God, for God Himself is united to human nature. Therefore it seems that the union is not anything created.

Obj. 2. Further, the end holds first place in everything. But the end of the union is the Divine hypostasis or Person in which the union is terminated. Therefore it seems that this union ought chiefly to be judged with reference to the condition of the Divine hypostasis, which is not anything created. Therefore the union is nothing created.

Obj. 3. Further, "That which is the cause of a thing being such is still more so."[4] But man is said to be the Creator on account of the union. Therefore much more is the union itself nothing created, but the Creator.

On the contrary, Whatever has a beginning in time is created. Now this union was not from eternity, but began to be in time. Therefore the union is something created.

I answer that, The union of which we are speaking is a relation which we consider between the Divine and the human nature, according as they come together in one Person of the Son of God. Now, as was said above (Part I, Q. XIII, A. 7), every relation which we consider between God and the creature is really in the creature, by whose change the relation is brought into being, whereas it is not really in God, but according to reason only, since it does not arise from any change in God. And hence we must say that the union of which we are speaking is not really in God, but only in reason; but in the human nature, which is a creature, it is really. Therefore we must say it is something created.

Reply Obj. 1. This union is not really in God, but only in reason, for God is said to be united to a creature from the fact that the creature is united to God without any change in Him.

Reply Obj. 2. The nature of a relation, as of motion, depends upon the end or term, but its being depends on the subject. And since this union has real being nowhere save in a created nature, as was said above, it follows that it has a created being.

Reply Obj. 3. A man is called Creator and is God because of the union, since it is terminated in the Divine hypostasis; yet it does not follow that the union itself is the Creator or God, because that a thing is said to be created regards its being rather than its relation.

---

[4] Aristotle, *Posterior Analytics*, I, 2 (72[a]29).

ARTICLE 8. *Whether Union Is the Same As Assumption?*

We proceed thus to the Eighth Article: It would seem that union is the same as assumption.

Objection 1. For relations, as motions, are specified by their terms. Now the term of assumption and union is one and the same—namely, the Divine hypostasis. Therefore it seems that union and assumption are not different.

Obj. 2. Further, in the mystery of the Incarnation the same thing seems to be what unites and what assumes, and what is united and what is assumed. But union and assumption seem to follow the action and passion of the thing uniting and the united, of the thing assuming and the assumed. Therefore union seems to be the same as assumption.

Obj. 3. Further, Damascene says (*De Fide Orthod.* iii, 11):[1] "Union is one thing, incarnation is another; for union demands mere joining together, and leaves unsaid the end of the joining; but incarnation and being made human determine the end of joining." But likewise assumption does not determine the end of joining together. Therefore it seems that union is the same as assumption.

On the contrary, The Divine Nature is said to be united, not assumed.

I answer that, As was said above (A. 7), union implies a certain relation of the Divine Nature and the human, according as they come together in one Person. Now all relations which begin to be in time are brought about by some change, and change consists in action and passion. Hence the *first* and principal difference between assumption and union must be said to be that union implies the relation: assumption however implies the action whereby someone is said to assume, or the passion whereby something is said to be assumed.

Now from this difference another *second* difference arises, for assumption implies becoming, whereas union implies having become, and therefore the thing uniting is said to be united, but the thing assuming is not said to be assumed. For the human nature is taken to be in the term of assumption to the Divine hypostasis when man is spoken of, and hence we can truly say that the Son of God, Who assumes human nature unto Himself, is man. But human nature, considered in itself—that is, in the abstract—is viewed as assumed; and we do

[1] PG 94, 1024.

not say the Son of God is human nature.

From this same follows a *third* difference which is that a relation, especially one of equivalence, is no more to one extreme than to the other, whereas action and passion bear themselves differently to the agent and the patient, and to different terms. And hence assumption determines the term from which and the term to which, for assumption means as it were a taking to oneself from another (*ad se sumere*). But union determines none of these things; hence it may be said indifferently that the human nature is united with the Divine, or conversely. But the Divine Nature is not said to be assumed by the human, but conversely, because the human nature is joined to the Divine personality so that the Divine Person subsists in human nature.

Reply Obj. 1. Union and assumption have not the same relation to the term, but a different relation, as was said above.

Reply Obj. 2. What unites and what assumes are not the same. For whatsoever Person assumes unites, and not conversely. For the Person of the Father united the human nature to the Son, but not to Himself; and hence He is said to unite and not to assume. So likewise the united and the assumed are not identical, for the Divine Nature is said to be united, but not assumed.

Reply Obj. 3. Assumption determines with whom the union is made on the part of the one assuming, since assumption means taking unto oneself, whereas incarnation and being made human (determine with whom the union is made) on the part of the thing assumed, which is flesh or human nature. And thus assumption differs logically both from union and from incarnation or being made human.

ARTICLE 9. *Whether the Union of the Two Natures in Christ Is the Greatest of All Unions?*

We proceed thus to the Ninth Article: It would seem that the union of the two natures in Christ is not the greatest of all unions.

Objection 1. For what is united falls short of the unity of what is one, since what is united is by participation, but what is one is one by essence. Now in created things some are said absolutely to be one, as is shown especially in unity itself, which is the principle of number. Therefore the union of which we are speaking does not imply the greatest of all unions.

Obj. 2. Further, the greater the distance between things united, the less the union. Now, the things united by this union are most distant

—namely, the Divine and human natures, for they are infinitely apart. Therefore their union is the least of all.

Obj. 3. Further, from union there results one. But from the union of soul and body in us there arises what is one in person and nature, whereas from the union of the Divine and human nature there results what is one in person only. Therefore the union of soul and body is greater than that of the Divine and human natures; and hence the union of which we speak does not imply the greatest unity.

On the contrary, Augustine says (*De Trin.* i, 10)[1] that "man is in the Son of God more than the Son in the Father." But the Son is in the Father by unity of essence, and man is in the Son by the union of the Incarnation. Therefore the union of the Incarnation is greater than the unity of the Divine Essence, which nevertheless is the greatest union; and thus the union of the Incarnation implies the greatest unity.

I answer that, Union implies the joining of several in some one thing. Therefore the union of the Incarnation may be taken in two ways: first, in regard to the things united; secondly, in regard to that in which they are united. And in this regard this union has a pre-eminence over other unions, for the unity of the Divine Person, in which the two natures are united, is the greatest. But it has no pre-eminence in regard to the things united.

Reply Obj. 1. The unity of the Divine Person is greater than numerical unity, which is the principle of number. For the unity of a Divine Person is an uncreated and self-subsisting unity, not received into another by participation. Also, it is complete in itself, having in itself whatever pertains to the nature of unity; and therefore the nature of a part does not pertain to it, as in numerical unity, which is a part of number, and which is shared in by the things numbered. And hence in this respect the union of the Incarnation is higher than numerical unity by reason of the unity of the Divine Person, and not by reason of the human nature, which is not the unity of the Divine Person, but is united to it.

Reply Obj. 2. This reason regards the things united, and not the Person in Whom the union takes place.

Reply Obj. 3. The unity of the Divine Person is greater than the unity of person and nature in us, and hence the union of the Incarnation is greater than the union of soul and body in us.

[1] PL 42, 834.

And because what is urged in the argument *on the contrary* rests upon what is untrue—namely, that the union of the Incarnation is greater than the unity of the Divine Persons in Essence—we must say to the authority of Augustine that the human nature is not more in the Son of God than the Son of God in the Father, but much less. But the man in some respects is more in the Son than the Son in the Father—namely, in so far as the same suppositum is signified when I say man, meaning Christ, and when I say Son of God; the same suppositum however is not signified by the words Father and Son.

ARTICLE 10. *Whether the Union of the Two Natures in Christ Took Place by Grace?*

We proceed thus to the Tenth Article: It would seem that the union of the Incarnation did not take place by grace.

Objection 1. For grace is an accident, as was shown above (Part I-II, Q. CX, A. 2). But the union of the human nature to the Divine did not take place accidentally, as was shown above (A. 6). Therefore it seems that the union of the Incarnation did not take place by grace.

Obj. 2. Further, the subject of grace is the soul. But it is written (Col. 2. 9): *In Christ* (Vulg., *Him*) *dwelleth all the fulness of the Godhead corporeally.* Therefore it seems that this union did not take place by grace.

Obj. 3. Further, every saint is united to God by grace. If, therefore, the union of the Incarnation was by grace, it would seem that Christ is said to be God no more than other holy men.

On the contrary, Augustine says (*De Praed. Sanct.* x):[2] "By the same grace every man is made a Christian, from the beginning of his faith, as this man from His beginning was made Christ." But this man became Christ by union with the Divine Nature. Therefore this union was by grace.

I answer that, As was said above (Part I-II, Q. CX, A. 1), grace is taken in two ways: first, as the will of God freely giving something; secondly, as the free gift itself of God. Now human nature stands in need of the gratuitous will of God in order to be lifted up to God, since this is above its natural capability. Moreover, human nature is lifted up to God in two ways: first, by operation, by which, for example, the saints know and love God; secondly, by personal being, and this mode belongs exclusively to Christ, in Whom human nature is assumed so as to be in the Person of the Son of God. But

[2] PL 44, 982.

it is plain that for the perfection of operation the power needs to be perfected by a habit, whereas that a nature has being in its own suppositum does not take place by means of a habit.

And hence we must say that if grace be understood as the will of God gratuitously doing something or holding anything as well-pleasing or acceptable to Him, the union of the Incarnation took place by grace, even as the union of the saints with God by knowledge and love. But if grace be taken as the free gift of God, then the fact that the human nature is united to the Divine Person may be called a grace, since it took place without being preceded by any merits—but not as though there were an habitual grace, by means of which the union took place.

Reply Obj. 1. The grace which is an accident is a certain likeness of the Divinity participated by man. But by the Incarnation human nature is not said to have participated a likeness of the Divine Nature, but is said to be united to the Divine Nature itself in the Person of the Son. But the thing itself is greater than a participated likeness of it.

Reply Obj. 2. Habitual grace is only in the soul; but the grace—that is, the free gift of God—of being united to the Divine Person belongs to the whole human nature, which is composed of soul and body. And in this way it is said that the fulness of the Godhead dwelt corporeally in Christ because the Divine Nature is united not merely to the soul, but to the body also. Although it may also be said[1] that it dwelt in Christ corporeally—that is, not as in a shadow, as it dwelt in the sacraments of the old law, of which it is said in the same place (verse 17) that they are the *shadow of things to come, but the body is Christ* (Vulg., *Christ's*), according, that is, as the body is opposed to the shadow.

And some say[2] that the Godhead is said to have dwelt in Christ corporeally—that is, in three ways, just as a body has three dimensions: first, by essence, presence, and power, as in other creatures; secondly, by sanctifying grace, as in the saints; thirdly, by personal union, which is proper to Christ.

Hence the *reply to the third objection* is manifest—namely, because the union of the Incarnation did not take place by habitual grace alone as in the way other saints are joined to God, but according to the subsistence or person.

ARTICLE 11. *Whether Any Merits Preceded the Union of the Word Incarnate?*

We proceed thus to the Eleventh Article: It would seem that the union of the Incarnation followed upon certain merits.

Objection 1. For upon Ps. 32. 22, *Let Thy mercy, O Lord, be upon us, as,* etc., a gloss says:[3] "Here the prophet's desire for the Incarnation and its merited fulfilment are hinted at." Therefore the Incarnation falls under merit.

Obj. 2. Further, whoever merits anything merits that without which it cannot be. But the ancient Fathers merited eternal life, to which they were able to attain only by the Incarnation; for Gregory says (*Moral.* xiii, 43):[4] "Those who came into this world before Christ's coming, whatsoever eminency of justice they may have had, could not, on being divested of the body, at once be admitted into the bosom of the heavenly country, seeing that He had not as yet come Who, by His own descending, should place the souls of the righteous in their everlasting seat." Therefore it would seem that they merited the Incarnation.

Obj. 3. Further, of the Blessed Virgin it is sung that "she merited to bear the Lord of all,[5] and this took place through the Incarnation. Therefore the Incarnation falls under merit.

On the contrary, Augustine says (*De Praed. Sanct.* xv):[6] "Whoever can find merits preceding the singular generation of our Head may also find merits preceding the repeated regeneration of us His members." But no merits preceded our regeneration, according to Titus 3. 5: *Not by the works of justice which we have done, but according to His mercy He saved us, by the laver of regeneration.* Therefore no merits preceded the generation of Christ.

I answer that, With regard to Christ Himself, it is clear from the above (AA. 2, 3, 6) that no merits of His could have preceded the union. For we do not hold that He was first of all a mere man, and that afterwards by the merits of a good life it was granted Him to become the Son of God, as Photinus held,[7] but we hold that from the beginning of His conception this man was truly the Son of God, seeing that He had no other hypostasis but that of the Son of God, according to Luke 1. 35: *The Holy which shall*

---

[1] Cf. Hugh of St. Cher, *In Univ. Test.*, on Col. 2.9 (VII, 191ra).   [2] Hugh of St. Cher, *Ibid.*

[3] *Glossa interl.* (III, 131v); *Glossa* Lombardi (PL 191, 336).
[4] PL 75, 1038.
[5] Little Office of the Blessed Virgin, Dominican Rite, Ant. at *Benedictus.*   [6] PL 44, 983.
[7] Cf. below, Q. XXXV, A. 4. Cf. Vigilius Tapsensus, *Contra Arianos,* I (PL 62, 182).

be born of thee shall be called the Son of God.
And hence every operation of this man followed
the union. Therefore no operation of His could
have been meritorious of the union.

Neither could the deeds of any other man
whatsoever have adequately merited this union.
First, because the meritorious works of man are
properly ordered to happiness, which is the reward of virtue, and consists in the full enjoyment of God. The union of the Incarnation,
however, since it is in the personal being, transcends the union of the beatified mind with God,
which is through the act of possession, and
therefore it cannot fall under merit. Secondly,
because grace cannot fall under merit, for it is
the principle of meriting. Hence, still less does
the Incarnation fall under merit, since it is the
principle of grace, according to John i. 17:
Grace and truth came by Jesus Christ. Thirdly,
because the Incarnation is for the reformation
of the entire human nature, and therefore it
does not fall under the merit of any individual
man, since the goodness of a mere man cannot
be the cause of the good of the entire nature.
Yet the holy Fathers fittingly merited the Incarnation by desiring and beseeching; for it was
becoming that God should hearken to those
who obeyed Him.

And thereby *the reply to the first objection*
is manifest.

Reply Obj. 2. It is false that under merit
falls everything without which there can be no
reward. For there is something pre-required
not merely for reward, but also for merit, as
the Divine goodness and grace and the very
nature of man. And again, the mystery of the
Incarnation is the principle of merit, because
of His fulness we all have received (John i. 16).

Reply Obj. 3. The Blessed Virgin is said to
have merited to bear the Lord of all not because
she merited His Incarnation, but because by the
grace bestowed upon her she merited that grade
of purity and holiness which fitted her to be the
Mother of God.

ARTICLE 12. *Whether the Grace of Union Was Natural to the Man Christ?*

We proceed thus to the Twelfth Article: It
would seem that the grace of union was not
natural to the man Christ.

Objection 1. For the union of the Incarnation
did not take place in the nature, but in the
Person, as was said above (A. 2). Now a thing
is designated according to its end. Therefore
this grace ought rather to be called personal
than natural.

Obj. 2. Further, grace is divided against nature, even as gratuitous things, which are from
God, are distinguished from natural things,
which are from an intrinsic principle. But if
things are divided in opposition to one another,
one is not designated by the other. Therefore
the grace of Christ was not natural to Him.

Obj. 3. Further, natural is that which is according to nature. But the grace of union is
not natural to Christ in regard to the Divine
Nature, otherwise it would belong to the other
Persons; nor is it natural to Him according to
the human nature, otherwise it would belong
to all men, since they are of the same nature
as He. Therefore it would seem that the grace
of union is in no way natural to Christ.

On the contrary, Augustine says (*Enchir.*
xl):[1] "In the assumption of human nature,
grace itself became somewhat natural to that
man, so as to leave no room for sin in Him."

I answer that, According to the Philosopher,[2]
nature designates, in one way, birth itself, in
another, the essence of a thing. Hence natural
may be taken in two ways: first, for what is
only from the essential principles of a thing,
as it is natural to fire to mount upwards; secondly, we call natural to man what he has had
from his birth, according to Eph. 2. 3: *We were
by nature children of wrath;* and Wisd. 12. 10:
*They were a wicked generation, and their mal-
ice natural.* Therefore the grace of Christ,
whether of union or habitual, cannot be called
natural as if caused by the principles of the
human nature of Christ, although it may be
called natural as if coming to the human nature
of Christ by the causality of His Divine Nature. But these two kinds of grace are said to
be natural to Christ in so far as He had them
from His nativity, since from the beginning of
His conception the human nature was united
to the Divine Person, and His soul was filled
with the gift of grace.

Reply Obj. 1. Although the union did not
take place in the nature, yet it was caused by
the power of the Divine Nature, which is truly
the nature of Christ, and it, moreover, belonged
to Christ from the beginning of His nativity.

Reply Obj. 2. The union is not said to be
grace and natural in the same respect; for it
is called a grace in so far as it is not from merit,
and it is said to be natural in so far as by the
power of the Divine Nature it was in the humanity of Christ from His nativity.

Reply Obj. 3. The grace of union is not natural to Christ according to His human nature,

[1] PL 40, 252.　　　[2] *Metaphysics,* v, 4 (1014^{b}16; ^{b}35).

as if it were caused by the principles of the human nature, and hence need not belong to all men. Nevertheless, it is natural to Him in regard to the human nature on account of the *property* of His birth, seeing that He was conceived by the Holy Ghost, so that He might be at the same time the natural Son of God and of man. But it is natural to Him in regard to the Divine Nature, since the Divine Nature is the active principle of this grace; and this belongs to the whole Trinity—namely, to be the active principle of this grace.

QUESTION III

OF THE MODE OF UNION ON THE PART OF THE PERSON ASSUMING

(*In Eight Articles*)

WE must now consider the union on the part of the Person assuming, and under this head there are eight points of inquiry: (1) Whether to assume is befitting to a Divine Person? (2) Whether it is befitting to the Divine Nature? (3) Whether the nature abstracted from the personality can assume? (4) Whether one Person can assume without another? (5) Whether each Person can assume? (6) Whether several Persons can assume one individual nature? (7) Whether one Person can assume two individual natures? (8) Whether it was more fitting for the Person of the Son of God to assume human nature than for another Divine Person?

ARTICLE 1. *Whether It Is Fitting for a Divine Person to Assume a Created Nature?*

We proceed thus to the First Article: It would seem that it is not befitting to a Divine Person to assume a created nature.

Objection 1. For a Divine Person signifies something most perfect. Now no addition can be made to what is perfect. Therefore, since to assume is to take to oneself, so that what is assumed is added to the one who assumes, it does not seem to be befitting to a Divine Person to assume a created nature.

Obj. 2. Further, that to which anything is assumed is communicated in some degree to what is assumed to it, just as dignity is communicated to whosoever is assumed to a dignity. But it is of the nature of a person to be incommunicable, as was said above (Part I, Q. XXIX, A. 3, REPLY 4; Q. XXX, A. 4). Therefore it is not befitting to a Divine Person to assume —that is, to take to Himself.

Obj. 3. Further, person is constituted by nature. But it is not allowable that the thing con-

stituted should assume the constituent, since the effect does not act on its cause. Hence it is not befitting to a Person to assume a nature.

On the contrary, Augustine says (*De Fide ad Petrum,* ii):[1] "This God—that is, the Only-Begotten One—took the form"—that is, the nature—"of a servant to His own Person." But the Only-Begotten God is a Person. Therefore it is befitting to a Person to take—that is, to assume a nature.

I answer that, In the word assumption are implied two things—namely, the principle and the term of the act, for to assume is to take something to oneself. Now of this assumption a Person is both the principle and the term. The principle, because it properly belongs to a person to act, and this assuming of flesh took place by the Divine action. Likewise a Person is the term of this assumption, because, as was said above (Q. II, AA. 1 and 2), the union took place in the Person, and not in the nature. Hence it is plain that to assume a nature is most properly befitting to a Person.

Reply Obj. 1. Since the Divine Person is infinite, no addition can be made to it. Hence Cyril says in a letter to the General Council of Ephesus:[2] "We do not conceive the mode of conjunction to be according to addition," just as in the union of man with God, which is by the grace of adoption, nothing is added to God, but what is Divine is united to man; hence, not God but man is perfected.

Reply Obj. 2. A Person is said to be incommunicable in so far as It cannot be predicated of several supposita, but nothing prevents several things being predicated of the Person. Hence it is not contrary to the nature of person to be communicated so as to subsist in several natures, for even in a created person several natures may concur accidentally, as in the person of one man we find quantity and quality. But this is proper to a Divine Person, on account of its infinity, that there should be a concurrence of natures in it, not accidentally, but in subsistence.

Reply Obj. 3. As was said above (Q. II, A. 6, REPLY 2), the human nature constitutes a Divine Person not absolutely but according as the Person is designated from such a nature. For human nature does not make the Son of Man to be absolutely, since He was from eternity, but only to be man. It is by the Divine Nature that a Divine Person is constituted absolutely.

[1] Fulgentius (PL 65, 680).
[2] *Epist.,* XVII (PG 77, 112); Mercator's translation, PL 48, 835.

Hence the Divine Person is not said to assume the Divine Nature, but to assume the human nature.

ARTICLE 2. *Whether It Is Befitting To the Divine Nature To Assume?*

We proceed thus to the Second Article: It would seem that it is not befitting to the Divine Nature to assume.

Objection 1. Because, as was said above (A. 1), to assume is to take to oneself. But the Divine Nature did not take to Itself human nature, for the union did not take place in the nature but in the person, as was said above (Q. II, AA. 1 and 2). Hence it is not befitting to the Divine Nature to assume human nature.

Obj. 2. Further, the Divine Nature is common to the three Persons. If, therefore, it is befitting to the Divine Nature to assume, it consequently is befitting to the three Persons; and thus the Father assumed human nature even as the Son, which is erroneous.

Obj. 3. Further, to assume is to act. But to act befits a person, not a nature, which is rather taken to be the principle by which the agent acts. Therefore to assume is not befitting to the nature.

On the contrary, Augustine[1] says (*De Fide ad Petrum,* ii): "That nature which remains eternally begotten of the Father (that is, which is received from the Father by eternal generation) took our nature free of sin from His Mother."

I answer that, As was stated above (A. 1), in the word assumption two things are signified—namely, the principle and the term of the action. Now to be the principle of the assumption belongs to the Divine Nature in itself, because the assumption took place by Its power, but to be the term of the assumption does not belong to the Divine Nature in itself, but by reason of the Person in Whom It is considered to be. Hence a Person is primarily and most properly said to assume, but it may be said secondarily that the Nature assumed a nature to Its Person. And after the same manner the Nature is also said to be incarnate, not that it is changed to flesh, but that it assumed the nature of flesh. Hence Damascene says (*De Fide Orthod.* iii, 6):[2] "Following the blessed Athanasius and Cyril we say that the Nature of God is incarnate."

Reply Obj. 1. *Oneself* is reciprocal, and points to the same suppositum. But the Divine Nature does not differ in suppositum from the Person of the Word. Hence, inasmuch as the Divine Nature took human nature to the Person of

the Word, It is said to take it to Itself. But although the Father takes human nature to the Person of the Word, He did not thereby take it to Himself, for the suppositum of the Father and the Son is not the same; and hence it cannot properly be said that the Father assumes human nature.

Reply Obj. 2. What is befitting to the Divine Nature in Itself is befitting to the three Persons, as goodness, wisdom, and the like. But to assume belongs to It by reason of the Person of the Word, as was said above, and hence it is befitting to that Person alone.

Reply Obj. 3. As in God "what is" and "that by which it is" are the same, so likewise in Him "what acts" and "that by which it acts" are the same, since everything acts in so far as it is a being. Hence the Divine Nature is both that by which God acts, and the very God Who acts.

ARTICLE 3. *Whether the Nature Abstracted from the Personality by the Intellect Can Assume?*

We proceed thus to the Third Article: It would seem that if we abstract the Personality by our intellect, the Nature cannot assume.

Objection 1. For it was said above (A. 2) that it belongs to the Nature to assume by reason of the Person. But what belongs to one by reason of another cannot belong to it if the other is removed; just as a body, which is visible by reason of colour, without colour cannot be seen. Hence if the Personality be abstracted by the intellect, the Nature cannot assume.

Obj. 2. Further, assumption implies the term of union, as was said above (A. 1). But the union cannot take place in the nature, but only in the Person. Therefore, if the Personality be abstracted, the Divine Nature cannot assume.

Obj. 3. Further, it has been said above (Part I, Q. XL, A. 3) that in the Godhead if the Personality is abstracted, nothing remains. But the one who assumes is something. Therefore, if the Personality is abstracted, the Divine Nature cannot assume.

On the contrary, In the Godhead Personality signifies a personal property, and this is threefold—namely, Paternity, Sonship and Procession, as was said above (Part I, Q. XXX, A. 2). Now if we take these away by the intellect, there still remains the omnipotence of God, by which the Incarnation was wrought, as the angel says (Luke 1. 37): *No word shall be impossible with God.* Therefore it seems that if the Personality be removed, the Divine Nature can still assume.

---

[1] Fulgentius (PL 65, 678).   [2] PG 94, 1008.

I answer that, The intellect stands in two ways towards God. First, to know God as He is, and in this manner it is impossible for the intellect to circumscribe something in God and leave the rest, for all that is in God is one, except the distinction of Persons; and as regards these, if one is removed the other is taken away, since they are distinguished by relations only which must be together at the same time. Secondly, the intellect stands towards God, not indeed as knowing God as He is, but in its own way—that is, understanding manifoldly and separately what in God is one; and in this way our intellect can understand the Divine goodness and wisdom, and the like, which are called essential attributes, without understanding Paternity or Sonship, which are called Personalities. And hence if we abstract Personality by our intellect, we may still understand the Nature assuming.

Reply Obj. 1. Because in God "what is", and "that by which it is", are one, if any one of the things which are attributed to God in the abstract is considered in itself, separated from all else, it will still be something subsisting, and consequently a Person, since it is an intellectual nature. Hence just as we now say three Persons, on account of holding three personal properties, so likewise if we exclude by our intellect the personal properties there will still remain in our consideration the Divine Nature as subsisting and as a Person. And in this way It may be understood to assume human nature by reason of Its subsistence or Personality.

Reply Obj. 2. Even if the personal properties of the three Persons are circumscribed by the intellect, nevertheless there will remain in our thoughts the one Personality of God, as the Jews understand. And the assumption can be terminated in It, as we now say it is terminated in the Person of the Word.

Reply Obj. 3. If we abstract the Personality by the intellect, it is said that nothing remains by way of resolution—that is, as if the subject of the relation and the relation itself were distinct because all we can think of in God is considered as a subsisting suppositum. However, some of the things predicated of God can be understood without others, not by way of resolution, but by the way mentioned above.

ARTICLE 4. *Whether One Person Without Another Can Assume a Created Nature?*

We proceed thus to the Fourth Article: It would seem that one Person cannot assume a created nature without another assuming it.

Objection 1. For "the works of the Trinity are inseparable," as Augustine says (*Enchir.* xxxviii).[1] But as the three Persons have one essence, so likewise They have one operation. Now to assume is a kind of operation. Therefore it cannot belong to one divine person without belonging to another.

Obj. 2. Further, as we say the Person of the Son became incarnate, so also did the Nature, for "the whole Divine Nature became incarnate in one of Its hypostases," as Damascene says (*De Fide Orthod.* iii, 6).[2] But the Nature is common to the three Persons. Therefore the assumption is.

Obj. 3. Further, as the human nature in Christ is assumed by God, so likewise are men assumed by Him through grace, according to Rom. 14. 3: *God hath taken him to Him.* But this assumption pertains to all the Persons; therefore the first also.

On the contrary, Dionysius says (*Div. Nom.* ii)[3] that the mystery of the Incarnation pertains to discrete theology—that is, according to which something distinct is said of the Divine Persons.

I answer that, As was said above (AA. 1, 2), assumption implies two things—namely, the act of assuming and the term of assumption. Now the act of assumption proceeds from the Divine power, which is common to the three Persons, but the term of the assumption is a Person, as stated above (A. 2). Hence what has to do with action in the assumption is common to the three Persons, but what pertains to the nature of term belongs to one Person in such a manner as not to belong to another; for the three Persons caused the human nature to be united to the one Person of the Son.

Reply Obj. 1. This argument regards the operation, and the conclusion would follow if it implied this operation only, without the term, which is a Person.

Reply Obj. 2. The Nature is said to be incarnate and to assume by reason of the Person in Whom the union is terminated, as stated above (AA. 1 and 2), and not as it is common to the three Persons. Now "the whole Divine Nature" is said to be "incarnate"; not that it is incarnate in all the Persons, but because nothing is wanting to the perfection of the Divine Nature of the Person incarnate.

Reply Obj. 3. The assumption which takes place by the grace of adoption is terminated in a certain participation of the Divine Nature

[1] PL 40, 251.
[2] PG 94, 1005.   [3] Sect. 3, 6 (PG 3, 640, 644).

by an assimilation to Its goodness, according to II Pet. I. 4: *That you may be made partakers of the Divine Nature*, and hence this assumption is common to the three Persons, both in regard to the principle and the term. But the assumption which is by the grace of union is common on the part of the principle, but not on the part of the term, as was said above.

ARTICLE 5. *Whether Each of the Divine Persons Could Have Assumed Human Nature?*

We proceed thus to the Fifth Article: It would seem that no other Divine Person could have assumed human nature except the Person of the Son.

Objection 1. For by this assumption it has been brought about that God is the Son of Man. But it was not becoming that either the Father or the Holy Ghost should be said to be a Son, for this would tend to the confusion of the Divine Persons. Therefore the Father and Holy Ghost could not have assumed flesh.

Obj. 2. Further, by the Divine Incarnation men have come into possession of the adoption of sons, according to Rom. 8. 15: *For you have not received the spirit of bondage again in fear, but the spirit of adoption of sons.* But sonship by adoption is a participated likeness of natural sonship which does not belong to the Father nor the Holy Ghost; hence it is said (Rom. 8. 29): *For whom He foreknew He also predestinated to be made conformable to the image of His Son.* Therefore it seems that no other Person except the Person of the Son could have become incarnate.

Obj. 3. Further, the Son is said to be sent and to be begotten by the temporal nativity, according as He became incarnate. But it does not belong to the Father to be sent, for He is innascible, as was said above (Part I, Q. XXXII, A. 3; Q. XLIII, A. 4). Therefore at least the Person of the Father cannot become incarnate.

On the contrary, Whatever the Son can do, so can the Father and the Holy Ghost, for otherwise the power of the three Persons would not be one. But the Son was able to become incarnate. Therefore the Father and the Holy Ghost were able to become incarnate.

I answer that, As was said above (AA. 1, 2, 4), assumption implies two things—namely, the act of the one assuming and the term of the assumption. Now the principle of the act is the Divine power, and the term is a Person. But the Divine power is indifferently and commonly in all the Persons. Moreover, the nature of Per-

sonality is common to all the Persons, although the personal properties are different. Now whenever a power regards several things indifferently, it can terminate its action in any of them indifferently, as is plain in rational powers, which regard opposites, and can do either of them. Therefore the Divine power could have united human nature to the Person of the Father or of the Holy Ghost, as It united it to the Person of the Son. And hence we must say that the Father or the Holy Ghost could have assumed flesh even as the Son.

Reply Obj. 1. The temporal sonship, whereby Christ is said to be the Son of Man, does not constitute His Person, as does the eternal Sonship, but is something following upon the temporal birth. Hence, if the name of son were transferred to the Father or the Holy Ghost in this manner, there would be no confusion of the Divine Persons.

Reply Obj. 2. Adoptive sonship is a certain participation of natural sonship; but it takes place in us, by appropriation, by the Father, Who is the principle of natural sonship, and by the gift of the Holy Ghost, Who is the love of the Father and Son, according to Gal. 4. 6: *God hath sent the Spirit of His Son into your hearts crying, Abba, Father.* And therefore, even as by the Incarnation of the Son we receive adoptive sonship in the likeness of His natural sonship, so likewise, had the Father become incarnate, we should have received adoptive sonship from Him, as from the principle of the natural sonship, and from the Holy Ghost as from the common bond of Father and Son.

Reply Obj. 3. It belongs to the Father to be innascible as to eternal birth, and the temporal birth would not destroy this. But the Son of God is said to be sent in regard to the Incarnation because He is from another, without which the Incarnation would not suffice for the nature of mission.

ARTICLE 6. *Whether Several Divine Persons Can Assume One and the Same Individual Nature?*

We proceed thus to the Sixth Article: It would seem that two Divine Persons cannot assume one and the same individual nature.

Objection 1. For, this being granted, there would either be several men or one. But not several, for just as one Divine Nature in several Persons does not make several gods, so one human nature in several persons does not make several men. Nor could there be only one man, for one man is *this man*, which signifies one person; and hence the distinction of three Divine Persons would be destroyed, which cannot be allowed. Therefore neither two nor three Persons can take one human nature.

Obj. 2. Further, the assumption is terminated in the unity of Person, as has been said above (A. 4). But the Father, Son, and Holy Ghost are not one Person. Therefore the three Persons cannot assume one human nature.

Obj. 3. Further, Damascene says (*De Fide Orthod.* iii, 3, 4),[1] and Augustine (*De Trin.* i, 13),[2] that from the Incarnation of God the Son it follows that whatever is said of the Son of God is said of the Son of Man, and conversely. Hence, if three Persons were to assume one human nature, it would follow that whatever is said of each of the three Persons would be said of the man; and conversely, what was said of the man could be said of each of the three Persons. Therefore what is proper to the Father —namely, to beget the Son—would be said of the man, and consequently would be said of the Son of God; and this could not be. Therefore it is impossible that the three Persons should assume one human nature.

On the contrary, The Incarnate Person subsists in two natures—namely, the divine and human. But the three Persons can subsist in one Divine Nature. Therefore they can also subsist in one human nature in such a way that the human nature be assumed by the three Persons.

I answer that, As was said above (Q. II, A. 5, REPLY 1), by the union of the soul and body in Christ neither a new person is made nor a new hypostasis, but one human nature is assumed to the Divine Person or hypostasis, which, indeed, does not take place by the power of the human nature, but by the power of the Divine Person. Now such is the characteristic of the Divine Persons that one does not exclude another from communicating in the same nature, but only in the same Person. Hence, since in the mystery of the Incarnation "the whole reason of the deed is the power of the doer," as Augustine says (*Ep. ad Volusianum*, cxxxvii),[3] it is rather to be judged of it in regard to the nature of the Divine Person assuming, and not according to the nature of the human nature assumed. Therefore it is not impossible that two or three Divine Persons should assume one human nature.

But it would be impossible for them to as-sume one human hypostasis or person; thus Anselm says, (*Cur Deus Homo*, ii, 9),[4] that "several Persons cannot assume one and the same man to unity of Person."

Reply Obj. 1. In the hypothesis that three Persons assume one human nature, it would be true to say that the three Persons were one man because of the one human nature. For just as it is now true to say that the three Persons are one God on account of the one Divine Nature, so it would be true to say they are one man on account of the one human nature. Nor would the "one" imply unity of person, but unity in human nature; for it could not be argued that because the three Persons were one man they were one absolutely. For nothing hinders our saying that men, who are many absolutely, are in some respect one—for example, one people—and as Augustine says (*De Trin.* vi, 3):[5] "The Spirit of God and the spirit of man are by nature different, but by inherence one spirit results," according to I Cor. 6. 17: *He who is joined to the Lord is one spirit.*

Reply Obj. 2. In this supposition the human nature would be assumed to the unity not indeed of one Person, but to the unity of each Person, so that even as the Divine Nature has a natural unity with each Person, so also the human nature would have a unity with each Person by assumption.

Reply Obj. 3. In the mystery of the Incarnation, there results a communication of the properties belonging to the nature, because whatever belongs to the nature can be predicated of the Person subsisting in that nature, no matter to which of the natures it may apply. Hence in this hypothesis, of the Person of the Father may be predicated what belongs to the human nature and what belongs to the Divine; and likewise of the Person of the Son and of the Holy Ghost. But what belongs to the Person of the Father by reason of His own Person could not be attributed to the Person of the Son or Holy Ghost on account of the distinction of Persons which would still remain. Therefore it might be said that as the Father was unbegotten, so the man was unbegotten, according as "man" stood for the Person of the Father. But if one were to go on to say, "The man is unbegotten; the Son is man; therefore the Son is unbegotten," it would be the fallacy of figure of speech or of accident; even as we now say God is unbegotten because the Father is unbegotten, yet we cannot conclude that the Son is unbegotten, although He is God.

---

[1] PG 94, 988.   [2] PL 42, 840.
[3] Chap. 2 (PL 33, 519).

[4] PL 158, 407.   [5] PL 42, 926.

ARTICLE 7. *Whether One Divine Person Can Assume Two Human Natures?*

We proceed thus to the Seventh Article: It would seem that one Divine Person cannot assume two human natures.

Objection 1. For the nature assumed in the mystery of the Incarnation has no other suppositum than the suppositum of the Divine Person, as is plain from what has been stated above (Q. II, AA. 3 and 6). Therefore, if we suppose one Person to assume two human natures, there would be one suppositum of two natures of the same species, which would seem to imply a contradiction, for the nature of one species is only multiplied by a distinction of supposita.

Obj. 2. Further, in this hypothesis it could not be said that the Divine Person incarnate was one man, seeing that He would not have one human nature; neither could it be said that there were several, for several men are distinct by suppositum, whereas in this case there would be only one suppositum. Therefore the aforesaid hypothesis is impossible.

Obj. 3. Further, in the mystery of the Incarnation the whole Divine Nature is united to the whole nature assumed—that is, to every part of it—for Christ is "perfect God and perfect man, whole God and whole man," as Damascene says (*De Fide Orthod.* iii, 7).[7] But two human natures cannot be wholly united together, because the soul of one would have to be united to the body of the other, and, again, two bodies would be together, which would give rise to confusion of natures. Together it is not possible for one Divine Person to assume two human natures.

On the contrary, Whatever the Father can do, that also can the Son do. But after the Incarnation the Father can still assume a human nature other in number from that which the Son has assumed, for in nothing is the power of the Father or the Son lessened by the Incarnation of the Son. Therefore it seems that after the Incarnation the Son can assume another human nature distinct from the one He has assumed.

I answer that, What has power for one thing, and no more, has a power limited to one. Now the power of a Divine Person is infinite, nor can it be limited by any created thing. Hence it may not be said that a Divine Person so assumed one human nature as to be unable to assume another. For it would seem to follow from this that the Personality of the Divine

[1] PG 94, 1012.

Nature was so contained by one human nature as to be unable to assume another to its Personality; and this is impossible, for the Uncreated cannot be contained by any creature. Hence it is plain that, whether we consider the Divine Person in regard to His Power, which is the principle of the union, or in regard to His Personality, which is the term of the union, it has to be said that the Divine Person, over and beyond the human nature which He has assumed, can assume a human nature other in number.

Reply Obj. 1. A created nature is perfected in its essentials by its form, which is multiplied according to the division of matter. And hence, if the composition of matter and form constitutes a new suppositum, the consequence is that the nature is multiplied by the multiplication of supposita. But in the mystery of the Incarnation the union of form and matter—that is, of soul and body—does not constitute a new suppositum, as was said above (A. 6). Hence there can be a numerical multitude on the part of the nature, on account of the division of matter, without distinction of supposita.

Reply Obj. 2. It might seem possible to reply that in such a hypothesis it would follow that there were two men by reason of the two natures without there being there two supposita, just as, on the contrary, the three Persons would be called one man on account of the one nature assumed, as was said above (A. 6, REPLY 1). But this does not seem to be true, because we must use words according to the purpose of their meaning, which arises out of a consideration of the things which are around us. Consequently, in order to judge of a word's meaning and co-meanings, we must consider the things which are around us, in which a word derived from some form is never used in the plural unless there are several supposita. For a man who has on two garments is not said to be two persons clothed, but one clothed with two garments; and whoever has two qualities is designated in the singular as such by reason of the two qualities. Now the assumed nature is, as it were, a garment, although this similitude does not fit at all points, as has been said above (Q. II, A. 6, REPLY 1). And hence, if the Divine Person were to assume two human natures, He would be called, on account of the unity of suppositum, one man having two human natures. Now it happens that many men are said to be one people from the fact that they have some one thing in common, and not on account of the unity of suppositum. So likewise, if two Divine Persons were to assume one singular human nature, they would be said to be one man, as stated (A. 6, Reply 1), not from the unity of suppositum, but because they have some one thing in common.

Reply Obj. 3. The Divine and human natures do not bear the same relation to the one Divine Person, but the Divine Nature is related first of all to It since as It is one with It from eternity, and afterwards the human nature is related to the Divine Person, from the fact that it is assumed by the Divine Person in time, not indeed that the nature is the Person, but that the Person subsists in the nature. For the Son of God is His Godhead, but is not His manhood. And hence, in order that the human nature may be assumed by the Divine Person, the Divine Nature must be united by a personal union with the whole nature assumed—that is, in all its parts. Now in the two natures assumed there would be a uniform relation to the Divine Person, nor would one assume the other. Hence it would not be necessary for one of them to be altogether united to the other— that is, all the parts of one with all the parts of the other.

ARTICLE 8. *Whether It Was More Fitting That the Person of the Son Rather Than Any Other Divine Person Should Assume Human Nature?*

We proceed thus to the Eighth Article: It would seem that it was not more fitting that the Son of God should become incarnate than the Father or the Holy Ghost.

Objection 1. For by the mystery of the Incarnation men are led to the true knowledge of God, according to John 18. 37: *For this was I born, and for this came I into the world, to give testimony to the truth.* But by the Person of the Son of God becoming incarnate many have been kept back from the true knowledge of God, since they referred to the very Person of the Son what was said of the Son in His human nature, as Arius, who held[1] an inequality of Persons, according to what is said (John 14. 28): *The Father is greater than I.* Now this error would not have arisen if the Person of the Father had become incarnate, for no one would have taken the Father to be less than the Son. Hence it seems fitting that the Person

of the Father, rather than the Person of the Son, should have become incarnate.

Obj. 2. Further, the effect of the Incarnation would seem to be, as it were a kind of re-creation of human nature, according to Gal. 6. 15: *For in Christ neither circumcision availeth anything, nor uncircumcision, but a new creature.* But the power of creation is appropriated to the Father. Therefore it would have been more becoming to the Father than to the Son to become incarnate.

Obj. 3. Further, the Incarnation is ordained to the remission of sins, according to Matt. 1. 21: *Thou shalt call His name Jesus. For He shall save His people from their sins.* Now the remission of sins is attributed to the Holy Ghost, according to John 20. 22, 23: *Receive ye the Holy Ghost. Whose sins you shall forgive, they are forgiven them.* Therefore it became the Person of the Holy Ghost rather than the Person of the Son to become incarnate.

On the contrary, Damascene says (*De Fide Orthod.* iii, 1):[2] "In the mystery of the Incarnation the wisdom and power of God are made known: the wisdom, for He found a most suitable discharge for a most heavy debt; the power, for He made the conquered conquer." But power and wisdom are appropriated to the Son, according to I Cor. 1. 24: *Christ, the power of God and the wisdom of God.* Therefore it was fitting that the Person of the Son should become incarnate.

I answer that, It was most fitting that the Person of the Son should become incarnate. First, on the part of the union, for such as are similar are fittingly united. Now the Person of the Son, Who is the Word of God, has a certain common agreement with all creatures, because the word of the craftsman—that is, his concept—is an exemplary likeness of whatever is made by him. Hence the Word of God, Who is His eternal concept, is the exemplary likeness of all creatures. And therefore as creatures are established in their proper species, though subject to change, by the participation of this likeness, so by the non-participated but personal union of the Word with a creature it was fitting that the creature should be restored in its order to eternal and unchangeable perfection; for the craftsman by the intelligible form of his art, whereby he fashioned his handiwork, restores it when it has fallen into ruin. Moreover, He has a particular agreement with human nature, since the Word is the concept of the eternal Wisdom, from Whom all man's

[1] Cf. Athanasius, *De Incarn. Verbi et Contra Arianos,* IV (PG 26, 989); Ambrose, *De Fide,* II, 8 (PL 16, 595); V, 18 (PL 16, 724); Augustine, *In Joann.,* tract. LXXVIII (PL 35, 1836); cf. Part I, Q. XLII, A. 4.

[2] PG 94, 984.

wisdom is derived. And hence man is perfected in wisdom (which is his proper perfection, as he is rational) by participating the Word of God, as the disciple is instructed by receiving the word of his master. Hence it is said (Ecclus. 1. 5): *The Word of God on high is the fountain of wisdom.* And hence for the consummate perfection of man it was fitting that the very Word of God should be personally united to human nature.

Secondly, the reason of this fitness may be taken from the end of the union, which is the fulfilling of predestination—that is, of such as are preordained to the heavenly inheritance, which is bestowed only on sons, according to Rom. 8. 17: *If sons, heirs also.* Hence it was fitting that by Him Who is the natural Son men should share this likeness of sonship by adoption, as the Apostle says in the same chapter (8. 29): *For whom He foreknew, He also predestinated to be made conformable to the image of His Son.*

Thirdly, the reason of this fitness may be taken from the sin of our first parent, for which the Incarnation supplied the remedy. For the first man sinned by seeking knowledge, as is plain from the words of the serpent, promising to man *the knowledge of good and evil* (Gen. 3. 5). Hence it was fitting that by the Word of true knowledge man might be led back to God, having wandered from God through an inordinate thirst for knowledge.

Reply Obj. 1. There is nothing which human malice cannot abuse, since it even abuses God's goodness, according to Rom. 2. 4: *Or despisest thou the riches of His goodness?* Hence, even if the Person of the Father had become incarnate, men would have been capable of finding an occasion of error, as though for example the Son were not able to restore human nature.

Reply Obj. 2. The first creation of things was made by the power of God the Father through the Word; hence the second creation ought to have been brought about through the Word, by the power of God the Father, in order that restoration should correspond to creation according to II Cor. 5. 19: *For God indeed was in Christ reconciling the world to Himself.*

Reply Obj. 3. To be the gift of the Father and the Son is proper to the Holy Ghost. But the remission of sins is caused by the Holy Ghost as by the gift of God. And hence it was more fitting to man's justification that the Son should become incarnate, Whose gift the Holy Ghost is.

QUESTION IV

OF THE MODE OF UNION ON THE PART OF THE HUMAN NATURE ASSUMED

(*In Six Articles*)

WE must now consider the union on the part of what was assumed. About which we must consider first what things were assumed by the Word of God; secondly, what were co-assumed, whether perfections or defects (Q. VII).

Now the Son of God assumed human nature and its parts. Hence a threefold consideration arises. First, with regard to the nature; secondly, with regard to its part (Q. V); thirdly, with regard to the order of the assumption (Q. VI).

Under the first head there are six points of inquiry: (1) Whether human nature was more capable of being assumed than any other nature? (2) Whether He assumed a person? (3) Whether He assumed a man? (4) Whether it was becoming that He should assume human nature abstracted from all individuals? (5) Whether it was becoming that He should assume human nature in all its individuals? (6) Whether it was becoming that He should assume human nature in any man begotten of the stock of Adam?

ARTICLE 1. *Whether Human Nature Was More Capable of Being Assumed By the Son of God Than Any Other Nature?*

We proceed thus to the First Article: It would seem that human nature is not more capable of being assumed by the Son of God than any other nature.

Objection 1. For Augustine says (*Ep. ad Volusianum,* cxxxvii):[1] "In deeds wrought miraculously the whole reason of the deed is the power of the doer." Now the power of God Who wrought the Incarnation, which is a most miraculous work, is not limited to one nature, since the power of God is infinite. Therefore human nature is not more capable of being assumed than any other creature.

Obj. 2. Further, likeness is the reason for the fittingness of the Incarnation of the Divine Person, as above stated (Q. III, A. 8). But as in rational creatures we find the likeness of image, so in irrational creatures we find the likeness of trace. Therefore the irrational creature was as capable of assumption as human nature.

Obj. 3. Further, in the angelic nature we find a more perfect likeness of God than in human

[1] Chap. 2 (PL 33, 519).

nature, as Gregory says:[1] where he introduces Ezech. 28. 12: *Thou wast the seal of resemblance.* And sin is found in angels, even as in man, according to Job 4. 18: *And in His angels He found wickedness.* Therefore the angelic nature was as capable of assumption as the nature of man.

Obj. 4. Further, since the highest perfection belongs to God, the more like to God a thing is, the more perfect it is. But the whole universe is more perfect than its parts, amongst which is human nature. Therefore the whole universe is more capable of being assumed than human nature.

On the contrary, It is said (Prov. 8. 31) by the mouth of Begotten Wisdom: *My delights were to be with the children of men,* and hence there would seem some fitness in the union of the Son of God with human nature.

I answer that, A thing is said to be assumable as being capable of being assumed by a Divine Person, and this capability cannot be taken with reference to the natural passive power, which does not extend to what transcends the natural order, as the personal union of a creature with God transcends it. Hence it follows that a thing is said to be assumable according to some fitness for such a union. Now this fitness in human nature may be taken from two things—namely, according to its dignity, and according to its need. According to its dignity, because human nature, as being rational and intellectual, was made for attaining to the Word Itself to some extent by its operation—namely, by knowing and loving Him. According to its need, because it stood in need of restoration, having fallen under original sin. Now these two things belong to human nature alone. For in the irrational creature the fitness of dignity is wanting, and in the angelic nature the aforesaid fitness of need is wanting. Hence it follows that only human nature was assumable.

Reply Obj. 1. Creatures are said to be of such and such a character with reference to their proper causes, not with reference to what belongs to them from their first and universal causes; thus we call a disease incurable not because that it cannot be cured by God, but that it cannot be cured by the proper principles of the subject. Therefore a creature is said to be not capable of being assumed not as if we withdrew anything from the power of God, but in order to show the condition of the creature, which has no capability for this.

Reply Obj. 2. The likeness of image is found in human nature, according as it is capable of God—namely, by attaining to Him through its own operation of knowledge and love. But the likeness of trace regards only a representation by Divine impression, existing in the creature, and does not imply that the irrational creature, in which merely this likeness exists, can attain to God by its own operation alone. For what is wanting in regard to the less has no fitness for the greater; just as a body which is not fitted to be perfected by a sensitive soul is much less fitted for an intellectual soul. Now much greater and more perfect is the union with God in personal being than the union by operation. And hence the irrational creature which falls short of the union with God by operation has no fitness to be united with Him in personal being.

Reply Obj. 3. Some say[2] that angels are not assumable, since they are perfect in their personality from the beginning of their creation, inasmuch as they are not subject to generation and corruption; hence they cannot be assumed to the unity of a Divine Person unless their personality be destroyed, and this does not befit the incorruptibility of their nature nor the goodness of the One assuming, to Whom it does not belong to corrupt any perfection in the creature assumed. But this would not seem totally to disprove the fitness of the angelic nature for being assumed. For God by producing a new angelic nature could join it to Himself in unity of Person, and in this way nothing pre-existing would be corrupted in it. But as was said above, there is wanting the fitness of need, because, although the angelic nature in some is the subject of sin, their sin is irremediable, as stated above (Part I, Q. LXIV, A. 2).

Reply Obj. 4. The perfection of the universe is not the perfection of one person or suppositum, but of something which is one by position or order, of which very many parts are not capable of assumption, as was said above. Hence it follows that only human nature is capable of being assumed.

ARTICLE 2. *Whether the Son of God Assumed a Person?*

We proceed thus to the Second Article: It would seem that the Son of God assumed a person.

Objection 1. For Damascene says (*De Fide Orthod,* iii, 11)[3] that "the Son of God assumed

[1] *In Evang.,* BK. II, hom. XXXIV (PL 76, 1250).

[2] Cf. Albert the Great, *In Sent.,* III, d. II, A. 2 (BO XXVIII, 24).   [3] PG 94, 1024.

human nature '*in atomo*', that is, in an individual." But an individual of rational nature is a person, as is plain from Boëthius (*De Duab. Nat.*).[1] Therefore the Son of God assumed a person.

Obj. 2. Further, Damascene says (*De Fide Orthod.* iii, 6)[2] that "the Son of God assumed what He had sown in our nature." But He sowed our personality there. Therefore the Son of God assumed a person.

Obj. 3. Further, nothing is absorbed unless it exist. But Innocent III. says in a Decretal[3] that the Person of God absorbed the person of man. Therefore it would seem that the person of man existed previous to its being assumed.

On the contrary, Augustine says (*De Fide ad Petrum,* xvii)[4] that "God assumed the nature, not the person, of man."

I answer that, A thing is said to be assumed from the fact that it is taken into another. Hence, what is assumed must be presupposed to the assumption, as what is moved from place to place is presupposed to the motion itself. Now a person in human nature is not presupposed to assumption; rather, it is the term of the assumption, as was said (Q. III, AA. 1 and 2). For if it were presupposed, it must either have been corrupted, in which case it would be assumed in vain, or it remains after the union, and thus there would be two persons, one assuming and the other assumed, which is false, as was shown above (Q. II, A. 6). Hence it follows that the Son of God in no way assumed a human person.

Reply Obj. 1. The Son of God assumed human nature *in atomo,* that is, in an individual, which is no other than the uncreated suppositum, the Person of the Son of God. Hence it does not follow that a person was assumed.

Reply Obj. 2. Its proper personality is not wanting to the nature assumed through the loss of anything pertaining to the perfection of the human nature but through the addition of something which is above human nature—namely, the union with a Divine Person.

Reply Obj. 3. Absorption does not here imply the destruction of anything pre-existing, but the hindering what might otherwise have been. For if the human nature had not been assumed by a Divine Person, the human nature would have had its own personality; and in this way

is it said, although improperly, that the Person absorbed the person, because the Divine Person by His union hindered the human nature from having its own personality.

ARTICLE 3. *Whether the Divine Person Assumed a Man?*

We proceed thus to the Third Article: It would seem that the Divine Person assumed a man.

Objection 1. For it is written (Ps. 64. 5): *Blessed is he whom Thou hast chosen and taken to Thee,* which a gloss expounds of Christ;[5] and Augustine says (*De Agone Christ.* xi):[6] "The Son of God assumed a man, and in him bore things human."

Obj. 2. Further, the word man signifies a human nature. But the Son of God assumed a human nature. Therefore He assumed a man.

Obj. 3. Further, the Son of God is a man. But He is not one of the men He did not assume, for with equal reason He would be Peter or any other man. Therefore He is the man whom He assumed.

On the contrary, Is the authority of Felix, Pope and Martyr, which is quoted by the Council of Ephesus:[7] "We believe in Our Lord Jesus Christ, born of the Virgin Mary, because He is the Eternal Son and Word of God, and not a man assumed by God, in such sort that there is another besides Him."

I answer that, As has been said above (A. 2), what is assumed is not the term of the assumption, but is presupposed to the assumption. Now it was said (Q. III, AA. 1, 2) that the individual to Whom the human nature is assumed is none other than the Divine Person, Who is the term of the assumption. Now this word man signifies human nature according as it is made to be in a suppositum, because, as Damascene says (*De Fide Orthod.* iii, 4, 11),[8] "Just as this word God signifies Him who has divine nature, so also this word man signifies him who has human nature." And hence it cannot properly be said that the Son assumed a man, granted (as it must be, in fact) that in Christ there is but one suppositum and one hypostasis. But according to such as hold that there are two hypostases or two supposita in Christ,[9] it

[1] Chap. 3 (PL 64, 1343). [2] PG 94, 1005.

[3] Cf. Paschas Diac., *De Spir. Sancto,* II, 4 (PL 62, 29); cf. also William of Auxerre, *Summa Aurea,* Pt. III, tr. I, chap. I, Q. 8 (112va); Alexander of Hales, *Summa Theol.,* III, Q. 6, A. 4 (III, 20va); see also Albert, *In Sent.,* III, d. 5, A. 12, arg. I (BO XXVIII, 110).

[4] Fulgentius (PL 65, 698).

[5] *Glossa interl.* (III, 173v); *Glossa* Lombardi (PL 191, 584).

[6] *Enarr. in Ps.,* Ps. 64, on verse 5 (PL 36, 778).

[7] Pt. II, actio I (MA IV, 1187); Cf. Cyril, *Apolog. adv. Orient. Episc.,* anath. 6 (PG 76, 344).

[8] PG 94, 1028.

[9] Cf. Peter Lombard, *Sent.,* III, d. VI, chap. 2. (QR II, 574); see DTC, art. *Science de Jésus-Christ* (XIV, 1649).

may fittingly and properly be said that the Son of God assumed a man. Hence the first opinion quoted in III. *Sent.*,[1] grants that a man was assumed. But this opinion is erroneous, as was said above (Q. II, A. 6).

Reply Obj. 1. These phrases are not to be taken too literally, but are to be explained with reverence wherever they are used by holy doctors; so that we might say that a man was assumed because his nature was assumed, and because the assumption terminated in this, that the Son of God is man.

Reply Obj. 2. The word man signifies human nature in the concrete, according as it is in a suppositum; and hence, since we cannot say a suppositum was assumed, so we cannot say a man was assumed.

Reply Obj. 3. The Son of God is not the man whom He assumed, but the man whose nature He assumed.

ARTICLE 4. *Whether the Son of God Ought To Have Assumed Human Nature Abstracted from All Individuals?*

We proceed thus to the Fourth Article: It would seem that the Son of God ought to have assumed human nature abstracted from all individuals.

Objection 1. For the assumption of human nature took place for the common salvation of all men; hence it is said of Christ (I Tim. 4. 10) that He is *the Saviour of all men, especially of the faithful.* But nature as it is in individuals withdraws from its universality. Therefore the Son of God ought to have assumed human nature as it is abstracted from all individuals.

Obj. 2. Further, what is noblest in all things ought to be attributed to God. But in every genus what is of itself is best. Therefore the Son of God ought to have assumed self-existing (*per se*) man, which, according to Platonists,[2] is human nature abstracted from its individuals. Therefore the Son of God ought to have assumed this.

Obj. 3. Further, human nature was not assumed by the Son of God in the concrete as is signified by the word man, as was said above (A. 3). Now in this way it signifies human nature as it is in individuals, as is plain from what has been said (*ibid.*). Therefore the Son of God assumed human nature as it is separated from individuals.

On the contrary, Damascene says (*De Fide Orthod.* iii, 11):[3] "God the Word incarnate did not assume a nature which exists in pure thought, for this would have been no Incarnation, but a false and fictitious Incarnation." But human nature as it is separated or abstracted from individuals "is taken to be a pure conception, since it does not exist in itself," as Damascene says (*ibid.*). Therefore the Son of God did not assume human nature as it is separated from individuals.

I answer that, The nature of man or of any other sensible thing, beyond the being which it has in individuals, may be taken in two ways: first, as if it had being of itself, apart from matter, as the Platonists held;[4] secondly, as existing in an intellect either human or Divine.

Now it cannot subsist of itself, as the Philosopher proves,[5] because sensible matter belongs to the specific nature of sensible things, and is placed in its definition, as flesh and bones in the definition of man. Hence human nature cannot be apart from sensible matter.

Nevertheless, if human nature were subsistent in this way, it would not be fitting that it should be assumed by the Word of God. First, because this assumption is terminated in a Person, and it is contrary to the nature of a common form to be thus individualized in a person. Secondly, because to a common nature can only be attributed common and universal operations, according to which man neither merits nor demerits, whereas, on the contrary, the assumption took place in order that the Son of God, having assumed our nature, might merit for us. Thirdly, because a nature so existing would not be sensible, but intelligible. But the Son of God assumed human nature in order to show Himself in men's sight, according to Baruch 3. 38: *Afterwards He was seen upon earth, and conversed with men.*

Likewise, neither could human nature have been assumed by the Son of God, as it is in the Divine intellect, since thus it would be none other than the Divine Nature, and, in this way, human nature would be in the Son of God from eternity.

Neither can we say that the Son of God assumed human nature as it is in a human intellect, for this would mean nothing else but that He is understood to assume a human nature. And thus if He did not assume it in reality, this would be a false understanding, nor

---

[1] Dist., II, chap. 2 (QR II, 574).
[2] Cf. Aristotle, *Metaphysics*, III, 2 (997^{b}8); cf. also above, Part I, Q. LXXXIV, A. I.
[3] PG 94, 1024.
[4] Cf. Aristotle, *Loc. cit.*; see also above, Part I, Q. LXXXIV, A. I.
[5] *Metaphysics*, VII, 15 (1039^{b}27).

would this assumption of the human nature be anything but "a fictitious Incarnation," as Damascene says (*loc. cit.*).

Reply Obj. 1. The incarnate Son of God is the common Saviour of all, not by a community of genus or species, such as is attributed to the nature separated from the individuals, but by a community of cause, whereby the incarnate Son of God is the universal cause of human salvation.

Reply Obj. 2. Self-existing (*per se*) man is not to be found in nature in such a way as to be outside the singular, as the Platonists held,[1] although some say Plato believed that the separate man was only in the Divine intellect.[2] And hence it was not necessary for it to be assumed by the Word, since it had been with Him from eternity.

Reply Obj. 3. Although human nature was not assumed in the concrete, as if the suppositum were presupposed to the assumption, nevertheless it is assumed in an individual, since it is assumed so as to be in an individual.

ARTICLE 5. *Whether the Son of God Ought To Have Assumed Human Nature in All Individuals?*

We proceed thus to the Fifth Article: It would seem that the Son of God ought to have assumed human nature in all individuals.

Objection 1. For what is assumed first and by itself is human nature. But what belongs *per se* to a nature belongs to all who exist in the nature. Therefore it was fitting that human nature should be assumed by the Word of God in all its supposita.

Obj. 2. Further, the Divine Incarnation proceeded from Divine Love; hence it is written (John 3. 16): *God so loved the world as to give His only-begotten Son.* But love makes us give ourselves to our friends as much as we can. But it was possible for the Son of God to assume several human natures, as was said above (Q. III, A. 7), and by the same reason all. Hence it was fitting for the Son of God to assume human nature in all its supposita.

Obj. 3. Further, a skilful workman completes his work in the shortest manner possible. But it would have been a shorter way if all men had been assumed to the natural sonship than for one natural Son to lead many to the adoption of sons, as is written Gal. 4. 5 (*cf.* Heb. 2. 10). Therefore human nature ought

to have been assumed by God in all its supposita.

On the contrary, Damascene says (*De Fide Orthod.* iii, 11)[3] that "the Son of God did not assume human nature as a species, nor did He assume all its hypostases."

I answer that, It was unfitting for human nature to be assumed by the Word in all its supposita. First, because the multitude of supposita of human nature, which are natural to it, would have been taken away. For since we must not consider any other suppositum in the assumed nature except the Person assuming, as was said above (A. 3; Q. 2, A. 6), if there was no human nature except what was assumed, it would follow that there was but one suppositum of human nature, which is the Person assuming. Secondly, because this would have taken away from the dignity of the incarnate Son of God, as He is the First-born of many brethren, according to the human nature, even as He is the First-born of all creatures according to the Divine, for then all men would be of equal dignity. Thirdly, because it is fitting that as one Divine suppositum is incarnate so He should assume one human nature only, so that on both sides unity might be found.

Reply Obj. 1. To be assumed belongs to the human nature of itself because it does not belong to it by reason of a person, as it belongs to the Divine Nature to assume by reason of the Person; not, however, that it belongs to it of itself as if belonging to its essential principles, or as its natural property, in which manner it would belong to all its supposita.

Reply Obj. 2. The love of God to men is shown not merely in the assumption of human nature, but especially in what He suffered in human nature for other men, according to Rom. 5. 8: *But God commendeth His charity towards us; because when as yet we were sinners . . . Christ died for us,* which would not have taken place had He assumed human nature in all its supposita.

Reply Obj. 3. In order to shorten the way, which the skilful workman does, what can be done by one must not be done by many. Hence it was most fitting that by one man all the rest should be saved.

ARTICLE 6. *Whether It Was Fitting for the Son of God To Assume Human Nature of the Stock of Adam?*

We proceed thus to the Sixth Article: It would seem that it was not fitting for the Son

---

[1] Cf. Aristotle, *Metaphysics*, III, 2 (997ᵇ8); cf. also above, Part I, Q. LXXXIV, A. 1.

[2] Cf. Augustine, QQ. LXXXIII, qu. 46 (PL 40, 30).

[3] PG 94, 1024.

of God to assume human nature of the stock of Adam.

Objection 1. For the Apostle says (Heb. 7. 26): *For it was fitting that we should have such a high priest, . . . separated from sinners.* But He would have been still further separated from sinners had He not assumed human nature of the stock of Adam, a sinner. Hence it seems that He ought not to have assumed human nature of the stock of Adam.

Obj. 2. Further, in every genus the principle is nobler than what is from the principle. Hence, if He wished to assume human nature, He ought rather to have assumed it in Adam himself.

Obj. 3. Further, the Gentiles were greater sinners than the Jews, as a gloss[1] says on Gal. 2. 15: *For we by nature are Jews, and not of the Gentiles, sinners.* Hence, if He wished to assume human nature from sinners, He ought rather to have assumed it from the Gentiles than from the stock of Abraham, who was just.

On the contrary (Luke 3.), the genealogy of our Lord is traced back to Adam.

I answer that, As Augustine says (*De Trin.* xiii, 18):[2] "God was able to assume human nature elsewhere than from the stock of Adam, who by his sin had fettered the whole human race; yet God judged it better to assume human nature from the vanquished race, and thus to vanquish the enemy of the human race." And this for three reasons: First, because it would seem to belong to justice that he who sinned should make amends; and hence that from the nature which had been corrupted should be assumed that whereby satisfaction was to be made for the whole nature. Secondly, it pertains to man's greater dignity that the conqueror of the devil should spring from the stock conquered by the devil. Thirdly, because God's power is thereby made more manifest, since, from a corrupt and weakened nature He assumed that which was raised to such might and glory.

Reply Obj. 1. Christ ought to be separated from sinners as regards sin, which He came to overthrow, and not as regards nature which He came to save, and in which *it behoved Him in all things to be made like to His brethren,* as the Apostle says (Heb. 2. 17). And in this is His innocence the more wonderful, seeing that though assumed from a mass subject to sin, His nature was endowed with such purity.

Reply Obj. 2. As was said above (reply 1)

it behoved Him Who came to take away sins to be separated from sinners as regards sin, to which Adam was subject, whom Christ *brought out of his sin,* as is written Wisd. 10. 2. For it behoved Him Who came to cleanse all, not to need cleansing Himself; just as in every genus of motion the first mover is immovable as regards that motion, just as the first to alter is itself unalterable. Hence it was not fitting that He should assume human nature in Adam himself.

Reply Obj. 3. Since Christ ought especially to be separated from sinners as regards sin, and to possess the highest innocence, it was fitting that between the first sinner and Christ some just men should stand midway, in whom certain signs of (His) future holiness should shine forth. And hence, even in the people from whom Christ was to be born, God appointed signs of holiness, which began in Abraham, who was the first to receive the promise of Christ, and circumcision, as a sign that the covenant should be kept, as is written Gen. 17. 11.

QUESTION V

Of the Manner of Union with Regard to the Parts of Human Nature

(*In Four Articles*)

We must now consider the assumption of the parts of human nature; and under this head there are four points of inquiry: (1) Whether the Son of God ought to have assumed a true body? (2) Whether He ought to have assumed an earthly body—that is, one of flesh and blood? (3) Whether He ought to have assumed a soul? (4) Whether He ought to have assumed an intellect?

ARTICLE 1. *Whether the Son of God Ought To Have Assumed a True Body?*

We proceed thus to the First Article: It would seem that the Son of God did not assume a true body.

Objection 1. For it is written (Phil. 2. 7), that He was *made in the likeness of men.* But what is something in truth is not said to be in the likeness thereof. Therefore the Son of God did not assume a true body.

Obj. 2. Further, the assumption of a body in no way diminishes the dignity of the Godhead; for Pope Leo says (*Serm. de Nativ.*)[3] that "the glorification did not absorb the lesser nature, nor did the assumption lessen the high-

---

[1] *Glossa interl.* (VI, 811); *Glossa* Lombardi (PL 192, 114).
[2] PL 42, 1032.

[3] *Serm.,* XXI, 2 (PL 54, 192).

er." But it pertains to the dignity of God to be altogether separated from bodies. Therefore it seems that by the assumption God was not united to a body.

Obj. 3. Further, signs ought to correspond to the things signified. But the apparitions of the Old Testament which were signs of the manifestation of Christ were not in a real body, but by visions in the imagination, as is plain from Isa. 60. 1: *I saw the Lord sitting*, etc. Hence it would seem that the apparition of the Son of God in the world was not in a real body, but only in imagination.

On the contrary, Augustine says (QQ. lxxxiii, qu. 14):[1] "If the body of Christ was a phantom, Christ deceived us, and if He deceived us, He is not the Truth. But Christ is the Truth. Therefore His body was not a phantom." Hence it is plain that He assumed a true body.

I answer that, As is said (*De Eccles. Dogm.* ii):[2] "The Son of God was not born in appearance only, as if He had an imaginary body, but His body was real." The proof of this is threefold. First, from the essence of human nature, to which it pertains to have a true body. Therefore granted, as already proved (Q. IV, A. 1), that it was fitting for the Son of God to assume human nature, He must consequently have assumed a real body.

The second reason is taken from what was done in the mystery of the Incarnation. For if His body was not real but imaginary, He neither underwent a real death, nor of those things which the Evangelists recount of Him did He do any in very truth, but only in appearance; and hence it would also follow that the real salvation of man has not taken place; since the effect must be proportionate to the cause.

The third reason is taken from the dignity of the Person assuming, Whom it did not become to have anything fictitious in His work, since He is the Truth. Hence Our Lord Himself deigned to refute this error (Luke 24. 37, 39), when the disciples, *troubled and frighted, supposed that they saw a spirit,* and not a true body; therefore He offered Himself to their touch, saying: *Handle, and see; for a spirit hath not flesh and bones, as you see Me to have.*

Reply Obj. 1. This likeness indicates the truth of the human nature in Christ,—just as all that truly exist in human nature are said to be like in species,—and not a mere imaginary likeness. In proof of this the Apostle adds (Phil. 2. 8) that He became *obedient unto death, even to the death of the cross;* which

would have been impossible, had it been only an imaginary likeness.

Reply Obj. 2. By assuming a true body the dignity of the Son of God is nowise lessened. Hence Augustine says (*De Fid. ad Pet.* ii):[3] "He emptied Himself, taking the form of a servant, that He might become a servant; yet did He not lose the fulness of the form of God." For the Son of God assumed a true body not so as to become the form of a body, which is contrary to the Divine simplicity and purity—for this would be to assume a body to the unity of the nature, which is impossible, as is plain from what has been stated above (Q. II, A. 1), but, the natures remaining distinct, He assumed a body to the unity of Person.

Reply Obj. 3. The figure ought to correspond to the reality as regards the likeness and not as regards the truth of the thing. "For if they were alike in all points, it would no longer be a likeness but the reality itself," as Damascene says (*De Fide Orthod.* iii, 26).[4] Hence it was more fitting that the apparitions of the Old Testament should be in appearance only, being figures; and that the apparition of the Son of God in the world should be in a true body, as the thing prefigured by these figures. Hence the Apostle says (Col. 2. 17): *Which are a shadow of things to come, but the body is Christ's.*

ARTICLE 2. *Whether the Son of God Ought To Have Assumed an Earthly Body— Namely, One of Flesh and Blood?*

We proceed thus to the Second Article: It would seem that Christ had not a carnal or earthly, but a heavenly body.

Objection 1. For the Apostle says (I Cor. 15. 47):*The first man was of the earth, earthy; the second man from heaven, heavenly.* But the first man—that is, Adam—was of the earth as regards his body, as is plain from Gen. 1. Therefore the second man—that is, Christ— was of heaven as regards the body.

Obj. 2. Further, it is said (I Cor. 15. 50): *Flesh and blood shall not* (Vulg., *cannot*) *possess the kingdom of God.* But the kingdom of God is in Christ chiefly. Therefore there is no flesh or blood in Him, but rather a heavenly body.

Obj. 3. Further, whatever is best is to be attributed to God. But of all bodies a heavenly body is the best. Therefore it behoved Christ to assume such a body.

---

[1] PL 40, 14.   [2] Gennadius (PL 58, 981).   [3] Fulgentius (PL 65, 682).   [4] PG 94, 1096.

On the contrary, Our Lord says (Luke 24. 39): *A spirit hath not flesh and bones, as you see Me to have.* Now flesh and bones are not of the matter of heavenly bodies, but are composed of the inferior elements. Therefore the body of Christ was not a heavenly, but a carnal and earthly body.

I answer that, By the same reasons which proved that the body of Christ was not an imaginary one, it may also be shown that it was not a heavenly body.[1] First, because even as the truth of the human nature of Christ would not have been maintained had His body been an imaginary one such as Manes supposed,[2] so likewise it would not have been maintained if we supposed, as did Valentine,[3] that it was a heavenly body. For since the form of man is a natural thing, it requires determinate matter, namely, flesh and bones, which must be placed in the definition of man, as is plain from the Philosopher.[4]

Secondly, because this would lessen the truth of such things as Christ did in the body. For since a heavenly body is impassible and incorruptible, as is proved in the book on the Heavens,[5] if the Son of God had assumed a heavenly body. He would not have truly hungered or thirsted, nor would he have undergone His passion and death.

Thirdly, this would have detracted from God's truthfulness. For since the Son of God showed Himself to men as if He had a carnal and earthly body, the manifestation would have been false had He had a heavenly body. Hence (*De Eccles. Dogm.* ii)[6] it is said: "The Son of God was born, taking flesh of the Virgin's body, and not bringing it with Him from heaven."

Reply Obj. 1. Christ is said in two ways to have come down from heaven. First, by reason of His Divine Nature; not indeed that the Divine Nature ceased to be in heaven, but because He began to be here below in a new way, namely, by His assumed nature, according to John 3. 13: *No man hath ascended into heaven, but He that descended from heaven, the Son of Man, Who is in heaven.* Secondly, by reason of His body, not indeed

that the very substance of the body of Christ descended from heaven, but that His body was formed by a heavenly power, that is, by the Holy Ghost. Hence Augustine, explaining the passage quoted, says (*Ad Orosium*):[7] "I call Christ a heavenly man because He was not conceived of human seed." And Hilary expounds it in the same way (*De Trin.* x).[8]

Reply Obj. 2. Flesh and blood are not taken here for the substance of flesh and blood but for the corruption of flesh, which was not in Christ as far as it was sinful, but as far as it was a punishment; thus, for a time it was in Christ that He might carry through the work of our redemption.

Reply Obj. 3. It pertains to the greatest glory of God to have raised a weak and earthly body to such sublimity. Hence in the General Council of Ephesus (P. II, ACT. 1)[9] we read the saying of St. Theophilus: "Just as the best workmen are esteemed not merely for displaying their skill in precious materials, but very often because by making use of the poorest clay and commonest earth, they show the power of their craft, so the best of all workmen, the Word of God, did not come down to us by taking a heavenly body of some most precious matter, but shewed the greatness of His skill in clay."

ARTICLE 3. *Whether the Son of God Assumed a Soul?*

We proceed thus to the Third Article: It would seem that the Son of God did not assume a soul.

Objection 1. For John has said, teaching the mystery of the Incarnation (John i. 14): *The Word was made flesh*—with no mention being made of a soul. Now it is not said that *the Word was made flesh* as if changed to flesh, but because He assumed flesh. Therefore He seems not to have assumed a soul.

Obj. 2. Further, a soul is necessary to the body, in order to quicken it. But this was not necessary for the body of Christ, as it would seem, for of the Word of God it is written (Ps. 35. 10): *Lord, with Thee is the fountain of life.* Therefore it would seem altogether superfluous for the soul to be there when the Word was present. But "God and nature do nothing in vain," as the Philosopher says.[10] Therefore the Word would seem not to have assumed a soul.

---

[1] See A. 1.   [2] See below, Q. XVI, A. 1.

[3] Cf. Irenaeus, *Adv. Haeres.*, I, 11 (PG 7, 561) V, 1 (PG 7, 1121); Tertullian, *Adv. Valent.*, XXVII (PL 2, 619); Epiphanius, *Adv. Haeres.*, I, 2, haeres. 31 (PG 41, 488); Augustine, *De Haeres.*, XI (PL 42, 27); Isidore, *Etymol.*, VIII, 5 (PL 82, 299); see also John Damascene, *De Fide Ortho.*, III, 12 (PG 94, 1028).

[4] *Metaphysics*, VII, 11 (1036^b3).

[5] Aristotle, I, 3 (270^a12).   [6] Gennadius (PL 58, 981).

[7] *Dial.* QQ. LXV, QU. 4, contained among the works of Augustine (PL 40, 736).

[8] PL 10, 354.   [9] MA IV, 1188.

[10] *Heavens*, I, 4 (271^a33); cf. II, 11 (291^b13).

Obj. 3. Further, by the union of soul and body is constituted the common nature, which is the human species. But "in the Lord Jesus Christ we are not to look for a common species," as Damascene says (*De Fide Orthod.* iii, 3).[1] Therefore He did not assume a soul.

On the contrary, Augustine says (*De Agone Christ.* xxi).[2] "Let us not hearken to such as say that only a human body was assumed by the Word of God, and take 'the Word was made flesh' to mean that the man had no soul nor any other part of a man, save flesh."

I answer that, As Augustine says (*De Haeres.* 49, 55),[3] it was first of all the opinion of Arius[4] and then of Apollinaris[5] that the Son of God assumed only flesh, without a soul, holding that the Word took the place of a soul to the body. And consequently it followed that there were not two natures in Christ, but only one; for from a soul and body one human nature is constituted.

But this opinion cannot hold, for three reasons. First, because it is counter to the authority of Scripture, in which Our Lord makes mention of His soul, Matt. 26. 38: *My soul is sorrowful even unto death;* and John 10. 18: *I have power to lay down My soul (animam meam:* Douay, *My life).* But to this Apollinaris[6] replied that in these words soul is taken metaphorically, in which way mention is made in the Old Testament of the soul of God (Isa. 1. 14): *My soul hateth your new moons and your solemnities.* But, as Augustine says (*Qq.* lxxxiii., qu. 80),[7] the Evangelists relate how Jesus wondered, was angered, sad, and hungry. Now these show that He had a true soul, just as that He ate, slept and was weary shows that He had a true human body; otherwise, if these things are a metaphor, because the like are said of God in the Old Testament, the trustworthiness of the Gospel story is undermined. For it is one thing that things were foretold in a figure and another that historical events were related in very truth by the Evangelists.

Secondly, this error lessens the utility of the Incarnation, which is man's liberation. For Augustine argues thus (*Contra Felician.* xiii):[8] "If the Son of God in taking flesh passed over the soul, either He knew its sinlessness, and trusted it did not need a remedy, or He considered it unsuitable to Him, and did not bestow on it the boon of redemption; or He reckoned it altogether incurable, and was unable to heal it; or He cast it off as worthless and seemingly unfit for any use. Now two of these reasons imply a blasphemy against God. For how shall we call Him omnipotent, if He is unable to heal what is beyond hope? or God of all, if He has not made our soul. And as regards the other two reasons, in one the cause of the soul is ignored, and in the other no place is given to merit. Is He to be considered to understand the cause of the soul Who seeks to separate it from the sin of wilful transgression, enabled as it is to receive the law by the endowment of the habit of reason? Or how can His generosity be known to anyone who says it was despised on account of its ignoble sinfulness? If you look at its origin, the substance of the soul is more precious than the body, but if at the sin of transgression, on account of its understanding it is worse than the body. Now I know and declare that Christ is perfect wisdom, nor have I any doubt that He is most loving; and because of the first of these He did not despise what was better and more capable of prudence; and because of the second He sustained what was most wounded."

Thirdly, this position is against the truth itself of the Incarnation. For flesh and the other parts of man receive their species through the soul. Hence, if the soul is absent, there are no bones nor flesh, except equivocally, as is plain from the Philosopher.[9]

Reply Obj. 1. When we say, *The Word was made flesh,* "flesh" is taken for the whole man, as if we were to say, *The Word was made man,* as Isa. 40. 5: *All flesh together shall see that the mouth of the Lord hath spoken.* And the whole man is signified by flesh, because, as is said in the authority quoted (John 1. 14), the Son of God became visible by flesh; hence it is added: And we saw His glory. Or because, as Augustine says (QQ. lxxxiii, *qu.* 80),[10] "in all that union the Word is the highest, and flesh the last and lowest. Hence, wishing to commend the love of God's humility to us, the

---

[1] PG 94, 993.   [2] PL 40, 302.
[3] PL 42, 39, 40.
[4] Cf. Athanasius, *Contra Apollinarium,* II, 3 (PG 26, 1136); I, 15 (PG 26, 1121); Epiphanius, *Adv. Haeres.,* II, 2, haeres. 69 (PG 42, 232); Augustine, *De Haeres,* XLIX (PL 42, 40).
[5] Cf. Augustine, *De Haeres,* LV (PL 42, 40). Leo the Great, *Serm.,* XXIV, 5 (PL 54, 207).
[6] Cf. Theophilus of Alexandria, *Epist. ad Totius Aegypti Episc.,* anni 402, trans. by Jerome (PL 22, 795); Cyril of Alexandria, *De Incarn. Dom.,* XIX (PG 75, 1453); Augustine, QU. LXXXIII, Qu. 80 (PL 40, 94).
[7] PL 40, 95.

[8] Vigilius Tapsensis, *De Unit. Trin.,* XIX (PL 62, 347); or among the works of Augustine, chap. 13 (PL 42, 1168).
[9] *Soul,* II, 1 (412[b]20); *Metaphysics,* VII, 10 (1035[b]25).
[10] PL 40, 94.

Evangelist mentioned the Word and flesh, leaving the soul on one side, since it is less than the Word and nobler than flesh." Again, it was reasonable to mention flesh, which, as being farther away from the Word, was less assumable, as it would seem.

Reply Obj. 2. The Word is the fountain of life as the first effecting cause of life, but the soul is the principle of the life of the body as its form. Now the form is the effect of the agent. Hence from the presence of the Word it might rather have been concluded that the body was animated, just as from the presence of fire it may be concluded that the body, in which fire adheres, is warm.

Reply Obj. 3. It is not unfitting, indeed it is necessary, to say that in Christ there was a nature which was constituted by the soul coming to the body. But Damascene denied (*ibid.*) that in Jesus Christ there was a common species—that is, a third something resulting from the Godhead and the humanity.

ARTICLE 4. *Whether the Son of God Should Have Assumed an Intellect?*

We proceed thus to the Fourth Article: It would seem that the Son of God did not assume a human mind or intellect.

Objection 1. For where a thing is present, its image is not required. But man is made to God's image, as regards his mind, as Augustine says (*De Trin.* xii, 7).[1] Hence, since in Christ there was the presence of the Divine Word itself, there was no need of a human mind.

Obj. 2. Further, the greater light dims the lesser. But the Word of God, Who is *the light, which enlighteneth every man that cometh into this world,* as is written John 1. 9, is compared to the mind as the greater light to the lesser, since our mind is a kind of light, being as it were a lamp enkindled by the First Light (Prov. 20. 27): *The spirit of a man is the lamp of the Lord.* Therefore in Christ Who is the Word of God there is no need of a human mind.

Obj. 3. Further, the assumption of human nature by the Word of God is called His Incarnation. But the intellect or human mind is neither flesh nor the act of flesh, for it is not the act of a body, as is proved in the book on the *Soul.*[2] Hence it would seem that the Son of God did not assume a human mind.

On the contrary, Augustine says (*De Fid. ad Pet.* xiv):[3] "Firmly hold and nowise doubt that Christ the Son of God has true flesh and a

rational soul of the same kind as ours, since of His flesh He says (Luke 24. 39): 'Handle, and see; for a spirit hath not flesh and bones, as you see Me to have.' And He proves that He has a soul, saying (John 10. 17): 'I lay down my soul (Douay, life) that I may take it again.' And He proves that He has an intellect, saying (Matth. 11. 29): 'Learn of Me, because I am meek and humble of heart.' And God says of Him by the prophet (Isa. 52. 13): 'Behold my servant shall understand.'"

I answer that, As Augustine says (*De Haeres.* 55),[4] "the Apollinarists[5] thought differently from the Catholic Church concerning the soul of Christ, saying with the Arians[6] that Christ God took flesh alone, without a soul; and on being overcome on this point by the Gospel witness, they went on to say that the mind was wanting to Christ's soul, but that the Word Itself supplied its place."

But this position is refuted by the same arguments as the preceding. First, because it runs counter to the Gospel story, which relates how He marvelled (as is plain from Matt. 8. 10). Now marvelling cannot be without reason, since it implies the comparing of effect and cause, according as, that is, when we see an effect and are ignorant of its cause, we seek to know it, as is said in the *Metaphysics.*[7]

Secondly, it is inconsistent with the purpose of the Incarnation, which is the justification of man from sin. For the human soul is not capable of sin nor of justifying grace except through the mind. Hence it was especially necessary for the mind to be assumed. And so Damascene says (*De Fide Orthod.* iii, 6)[8] that "the Word of God assumed a body and an intellectual and rational soul," and adds afterwards: "The whole was united to the whole, that He might bestow salvation on me wholly; for what was not assumed is not curable."

Thirdly, it is against the truth of the Incarnation. For since the body is proportioned to the soul as matter to its proper form, it is not truly human flesh if it is not perfected by a human, that is, a rational, soul. And hence if Christ had had a soul without a mind, He would not have had true human flesh, but irrational flesh, since our soul differs from an animal soul by the mind alone. Hence Augustine says (*QQ.* lxxxiii, *qu.* 80)[9] that from this error it would have followed that the Son of God "took an animal with the form of a human body," which,

---

[1] PL 42, 1004.   [2] Aristotle, III, 4 (429ª24).
[3] Fulgentius (PL 65, 697).

[4] PL 42, 40.   [5] Cf. above, A. 3.
[6] Cf. above, A. 3.   [7] Aristotle, I, 2 (982ᵇ12; 983ª12).
[8] PG 94, 1005.   [9] PL 40, 93.

again, is against the Divine truth, which cannot suffer any fictitious untruth.

Reply Obj. 1. Where a thing is by its presence, its image is not required to supply the place of the thing, as where the emperor is the soldiers do not pay homage to his image. Yet the image of a thing is required together with its presence that it may be perfected by the presence of the thing, just as the image in the wax is perfected by the impression of the seal, and as the image of a man is reflected in the mirror by his presence. Hence in order to perfect the human mind it was necessary that the Word should unite it to Himself.

Reply Obj. 2. The greater light dims the lesser light of another luminous body, but it does not dim, rather it perfects the light of the body illuminated; at the presence of the sun the light of the stars is put out, but the light of the air is perfected. Now the intellect or mind of man is, as it were, a light lit up by the light of the Divine Word; and hence by the presence of the Word the mind of man is perfected rather than overshadowed.

Reply Obj. 3. Although the intellectual power is not the act of a body, nevertheless the essence of the human soul, which is the form of the body, requires that it should be more noble in order that it may have the power of understanding; and hence it is necessary that a better disposed body should correspond to it.

QUESTION VI
OF THE ORDER OF ASSUMPTION
(*In Six Articles*)

WE must now consider the order of the foregoing assumption, and under this head there are six points of inquiry: (1) Whether the Son of God assumed flesh through the medium of the soul? (2) Whether He assumed the soul through the medium of the spirit or mind? (3) Whether the soul was assumed previous to the flesh? (4) Whether the flesh of Christ was assumed by the Word previous to being united to the soul? (5) Whether the whole human nature was assumed through the medium of the parts? (6) Whether it was assumed through the medium of grace?

ARTICLE 1. *Whether the Son of God Assumed Flesh Through the Medium of the Soul?*

We proceed thus to the First Article: It would seem that the Son of God did not assume flesh through the medium of the soul.

Objection 1. For the mode in which the Son of God is united to human nature and its parts is more perfect than the mode whereby He is in all creatures. But He is in all creatures immediately by essence, power and presence. Much more, therefore, is the Son of God united to flesh without the medium of the soul.

Obj. 2. Further, the soul and flesh are united to the Word of God in unity of hypostasis or person. But the body pertains immediately to the person, or hypostasis of man, even as the soul. Indeed, the human body, since it is matter, would rather seem to be nearer the hypostasis than the soul, which is a form, since the principle of individuation, which is implied in the word hypostasis, would seem to be matter. Hence the Son of God did not assume flesh through the medium of the soul.

Obj. 3. Further, take away the medium and you separate what were joined by the medium; for example, if the surface be removed colour would leave the body, since it is in the body through the medium of the surface. But though the soul was separated from the body by death, yet there still remained the union of the Word to the flesh, as will be shown (Q. L, AA. 2 and 3). Hence the Word was not joined to flesh through the medium of the soul.

On the contrary, Augustine says (*Ep. ad Volusianum,* cxxxvii):[1] "The greatness of the Divine power fitted to itself a rational soul, and through it a human body, so as to raise the whole man to something higher."

I answer that, A medium is spoken of in reference to a beginning and an end. Hence just as beginning and end imply order, so also does a medium. Now there is a twofold order: one, of time, the other, of nature. But in the mystery of the Incarnation nothing is said to be a medium in the order of time, for the Word of God united the whole human nature to Himself at the same time, as will appear (AA. 3, 4). An order of nature between things may be taken in two ways: first, as regards rank of dignity, as we say the angels are midway between man and God; secondly, as regards the notion of causality, as we say a cause is midway between the first cause and the last effect. And this second order follows the first to some extent, for as Dionysius says (*Cæl Hier.* xiii),[2] God acts upon the more remote substances through those less remote from Him. Hence if we consider the rank of dignity, the soul is found to be midway between God and flesh; and in this way it may be said that the Son of

[1] Chap. 2 (PL 33, 519).
[2] Sect. 3 (PG 3, 300).

God united flesh to Himself through the medium of the soul. But even as regards the order of causality the soul is to some extent the cause of flesh being united to the Son of God. For the flesh would not have been capable of assumption except by its relation to the rational soul, through which it becomes human flesh. For it was said above (Q. IV, A. I) that human nature was capable of being assumed before all others.

Reply Obj. I. We may consider a twofold order between creatures and God. The first is by reason of creatures being caused by God and depending on Him as on the principle of their being; and thus on account of the infinity of His power God touches each thing immediately, by causing and preserving it, and so it is that God is immediately in all things by essence, presence and power.

But the second order is by reason of things being led back to God as to their end. And it is here that there is a medium between the creature and God, since "lower creatures are led back to God by higher," as Dionysius says,[1] and to this order pertains the assumption of human nature by the Word of God, Who is the term of the assumption. And hence it is united to flesh through the soul.

Reply Obj. 2. If the hypostasis of the Word of God were constituted absolutely by human nature, it would follow that the body was nearer to it, since it is matter which is the principle of individuation; even as the soul, which is the specifying form, would be nearer the human nature. But because the hypostasis of the Word is prior to and more exalted than the human nature, the more exalted any part of the human nature is, the nearer it is to the hypostasis of the Word. And hence the soul is nearer the Word of God than the body is.

Reply Obj. 3. Nothing prevents one thing being the cause of the aptitude and congruity of another, even though if it be taken away the other remains, because although a thing's becoming may depend on another, yet when it is in being it no longer depends on it; just as a friendship brought about by some other may endure when the latter has gone; or as a woman is taken in marriage on account of her beauty, which makes a woman's fittingness for the marriage tie, yet when her beauty passes away, the marriage tie still remains. So likewise, when the soul was separated, the union of the Word with flesh still endured.

[1] *Cæl. Hier.*, IV, 3 (PG 3, 181); cf. *Eccl. Hier.*, V, I (PG 3, 504).

ARTICLE 2. *Whether the Son of God Assumed a Soul Through the Medium of the Spirit or Mind?*

We proceed thus to the Second Article: It would seem that the Son of God did not assume a soul through the medium of the spirit.

Objection I. For nothing is a medium between itself and another. But the spirit or mind is nothing else in essence but the soul itself, as was said above (Part I, Q. LXXVII, A. I, REPLY I). Therefore the Son of God did not assume a soul through the medium of the spirit or mind.

Obj. 2. Further, what is the medium of the assumption is itself more assumable. But the spirit or mind is not more assumable than the soul, which is plain from the fact that angelic spirits are not assumable, as was said above (Q. IV, A. I). Hence it seems that the Son of God did not assume a soul through the medium of the spirit.

Obj. 3. Further, that which comes later is assumed by the first through the medium of what comes before. But soul designates the very essence, which naturally comes before its power, which is the mind. Therefore it would seem that the Son of God did not assume a soul through the medium of the spirit or mind.

On the contrary, Augustine says (*De Agone Christ.* xviii):[2] "The invisible and unchangeable Truth took a soul by means of the spirit, and a body by means of the soul."

I answer that, As stated above (A. I), the Son of God is said to have assumed flesh through the medium of the soul, both on account of the order of dignity, and the fittingness of the assumption. Now both these may be applied to the intellect, which is called the spirit, if we compare it with the other parts of the soul. For the soul is assumed fittingly only through the fact that it has a capacity for God, being in His likeness, which is in respect of the mind, which is called the spirit, according to Eph. 4. 23: *Be renewed in the spirit of your mind.* So, too, the intellect is the highest and noblest of the parts of the soul, and the most like to God, and hence Damascene says (*De Fide Orthod.* iii, 6)[3] that "the Word of God is united to flesh through the medium of the intellect; for the intellect is the purest part of the soul, God Himself being an intellect."

Reply Obj. I. Although the intellect is not distinct from the soul in essence, it is distinct from the other parts of the soul according to

[2] PL 40, 300.
[3] PG 94, 1005.

its aspect as a power; and it is in this way that it has the nature of a medium.

Reply Obj. 2. Fitness for assumption is wanting to the angelic spirits not from any lack of dignity, but because of the irreparable character of their fall, which cannot be said of the human spirit, as is clear from what has been said above (Part I, Q. LXII, A. 8; Q. LXIV, A. 2).

Reply Obj. 3. The soul, between which and the Word of God the intellect is said to be a medium, does not stand for the essence of the soul, which is common to all the powers, but for the lower powers, which are common to every soul.

ARTICLE 3. *Whether the Soul Was Assumed Before the Flesh By the Son of God?*

We proceed thus to the Third Article: It would seem that the soul of Christ was assumed before the flesh by the Word.

Objection 1. For the Son of God assumed flesh through the medium of the soul, as was said above (A. 1). Now the medium is reached before the end. Therefore the Son of God assumed the soul before the body.

Obj. 2. Further, the soul of Christ is nobler than the angels, according to Ps. 96. 8: *Adore Him, all you His angels.* But the angels were created in the beginning, as was said above (Part I, Q. XLVI, A. 3). Therefore the soul of Christ also (was created in the beginning). But it was not created before it was assumed, for Damascene says (*De Fide Orthod.* iii),[1] that "neither the soul nor the body of Christ ever had any hypostasis, save the hypostasis of the Word." Therefore it would seem that the soul was assumed before the flesh, which was conceived in the womb of the Virgin.

Obj. 3. Further, it is written (John 1. 14): *We saw Him* (Vulg., *His glory*) *full of grace and truth,* and it is added afterwards that *of His fulness we have all received* (verse 16)— that is, all the faithful of all time, as Chrysostom expounds it (*Hom.* xiv *in Joann.*).[2] Now this could not have been unless the soul of Christ had all fulness of grace and truth before all the saints, who were from the beginning of the world, for the cause is not subsequent to the effect. Hence since the fulness of grace and truth was in the soul of Christ from union with the Word, according to what is written in the same place: *We saw His glory, the glory as it were of the Only-begotten of the Father, full of grace and truth,* it would seem

in consequence that from the beginning of the world the soul of Christ was assumed by the Word of God.

On the contrary, Damascene says (*De Fide Orthod.* iv, 6):[3] "The intellect was not, as some untruthfully say, united to the true God, and henceforth called Christ, before the Incarnation which was of the Virgin."

I answer that, Origen (*Peri Archon,* i, 7, 8; ii. 8)[4] maintained that all souls, amongst which he placed Christ's soul, were created in the beginning. But this is not fitting, if we suppose that it was first of all created but not at once joined to the Word, since it would follow that this soul once had its own subsistence without the Word; and thus, since it was assumed by the Word, either the union did not take place in the subsistence, or the pre-existing subsistence of the soul was corrupted.

So likewise it is not fitting to suppose that this soul was united to the Word from the beginning and that it afterwards became incarnate in the womb of the Virgin, for thus His soul would not seem to be of the same nature as ours, which are created at the same time that they are infused into bodies. Hence Pope Leo says (*Ep. ad Julian.* xxxv)[5] that "Christ's flesh was not of a different nature to ours, nor was a different soul breathed into it in the beginning than into other men."

Reply Obj. 1. As was said above (A. 1), the soul of Christ is said to be the medium in the union of the flesh with the Word, in the order of nature; but it does not follow from this that it was the medium in the order of time.

Reply Obj. 2. As Pope Leo says in the same Epistle,[6] Christ's soul "excels our soul not by diversity of genus, but by sublimity of power"; for it is of the same genus as our souls, yet excels even the angels in *fulness of grace and truth.* But the mode of creation of the soul is in harmony with its properties; and since it is the form of the body, it is consequently created at the same time that it is united with the body. This does not happen to angels, since they are substances entirely apart from bodies.

Reply Obj. 3. Of the fulness of Christ all men receive according to the faith they have in Him; for it is written (Rom. 3. 22) that *the justice of God is by faith of Jesus Christ unto all and upon all them that believe in Him.* Now just as we believe in Him as already born, so the ancients believed in Him as about to be born, since *having the same spirit of faith* . . . .

[1] Chap. 27 (PG 94, 1097).   [2] PG 59, 91.

[3] PG 94, 1112.   [4] PG 11, 170; PG 11, 178.
[5] Chap. 3 (PL 54, 809).   [6] Chap. 3 (PL 54, 809).

we also believe, as it is written (II Cor. 4. 13). But the faith which is in Christ has the power of justifying by reason of the purpose of the grace of God, according to Rom. 4. 5: *But to him that worketh not, yet believeth in Him that justifieth the ungodly, his faith is reputed to justice according to the purpose of the grace of God.* Hence because this purpose is eternal, there is nothing to hinder some from being justified by the faith of Jesus Christ even before His soul was full of grace and truth.

ARTICLE 4. *Whether the Flesh of Christ Was Assumed By the Word Before Being United to the Soul?*

We proceed thus to the Fourth Article: It would seem that the flesh of Christ was assumed by the Word before being united to the soul.

Objection 1. For Augustine says (*De Fid. ad Pet.* xviii):[1] "Most firmly hold, and nowise doubt that the flesh of Christ was not conceived in the womb of the Virgin without the Godhead, before it was assumed by the Word." But the flesh of Christ would seem to have been conceived before being united to the rational soul, because matter or disposition is prior to the completing form in order of generation. Therefore the flesh of Christ was assumed before being united to the soul.

Obj. 2. Further, as the soul is a part of human nature, so is the body. But the human soul in Christ had no other principle of being than in other men, as is clear from the authority of Pope Leo, quoted above (A. 3). Therefore it would seem that the body of Christ had no other principle of being than we have. But in us the body is begotten before the rational soul comes to it. Therefore it was the same in Christ. And thus the flesh was assumed by the Word before being united to the soul.

Obj. 3. Further, as is said (*De Causis*),[2] "the first cause excels the second in bringing about the effect, and precedes it in its union with the effect." But the soul of Christ is compared to the Word as a second cause to a first. Hence the Word was united to the flesh before it was to the soul.

On the contrary, Damascene says (*De Fide Orthod.* iii, 2):[3] "At the same time the Word of God was made flesh and flesh was united to a rational and intellectual soul." Therefore the union of the Word with the flesh did not precede the union with the soul.

I answer that, The human flesh is capable of being assumed by the Word on account of the order which it has to the rational soul as to its proper form. Now it does not have this order before the rational soul comes to it, because when any matter becomes proper to any form, at the same time it receives that form; hence the alteration is terminated at the same instant in which the substantial form is introduced. And so it is that the flesh ought not to have been assumed before it was human flesh, which happened when the rational soul came to it. Therefore since the soul was not assumed before the flesh, because it is against the nature of the soul to be before it is united to the body, so likewise the flesh ought not to have been assumed before the soul, since it is not human flesh before it has a rational soul.

Reply Obj. 1. Human flesh depends upon the soul for its being; and hence, before the coming of the soul, there is no human flesh, but there may be a disposition towards human flesh. Yet in the conception of Christ, the Holy Ghost, Who is an agent of infinite might, disposed the matter and brought it to its perfection at the same time.

Reply Obj. 2. The form actually gives the species, but the matter in itself is in potency to the species. And hence it would be against the nature of a form to exist before the specific nature, which is brought about through its union with matter; but it is not against the nature of matter to exist prior to the specific nature. And therefore the dissimilarity between our origin and Christ's origin, inasmuch as our flesh is conceived before being animated, and Christ's flesh is not, is by reason of what precedes the perfection of the nature, namely, that we are conceived from the seed of man, and Christ is not. But a difference which would be with reference to the origin of the soul would bespeak a diversity of nature.

Reply Obj. 3. The Word of God is understood to be united to the flesh before the soul by the common mode whereby He is in the rest of creatures by essence, power, and presence. Yet I say *before,* not in time, but in nature; for the flesh is understood as a being, which it has from the Word, before it is understood as animated, which it has from the soul. But by the personal union we understand the flesh as united to the soul before it is united to the Word, for it is from its union with the soul that it is capable of being united to the Word in Person; especially since a person is found only in the rational nature.

---

[1] Fulgentius (PL 65, 698).
[2] Sect. 1 (BA 163).   [3] PG 94, 985.

ARTICLE 5. *Whether the Whole Human Nature Was Assumed Through the Medium of the Parts?*

We proceed thus to the Fifth Article: It would seem that the Son of God assumed the whole human nature through the medium of its parts.

Objection 1. For Augustine says (*De Agone Christ.* xviii)[1] that "the invisible and unchangeable Truth assumed the soul through the medium of the spirit, and the body through the medium of the soul, and in this way the whole man." But the spirit, soul, and body are parts of the whole man. Therefore He assumed all, through the medium of the parts.

Obj. 2. Further, the Son of God assumed flesh through the medium of the soul because the soul is more like to God than the body. But the parts of human nature, since they are simpler than the body, would seem to be more like to God, Who is most simple, than the whole. Therefore He assumed the whole through the medium of the parts.

Obj. 3. Further, the whole results from the union of parts. But the union is taken to be the term of the assumption, and the parts are presupposed to the assumption. Therefore He assumed the whole by the parts.

On the contrary, Damascene says (*De Fide Orthod.* iii, 16):[2] "In Our Lord Jesus Christ we do not behold parts of parts, but such as are immediately joined, that is, the Godhead and the manhood." Now the humanity is a whole, which is composed of soul and body, as out of parts. Therefore the Son of God assumed the parts through the medium of the whole.

I answer that, When anything is said to be a medium in the assumption of the Incarnation, we do not signify order of time, because the assumption of the whole and the parts was simultaneous. For it has been shown (AA. 3, 4) that the soul and body were mutually united at the same time in order to constitute the human nature of the Word. But it is order of nature that is signified. Hence by what is prior in nature is assumed which is posterior in nature. Now a thing is prior in nature in two ways: first on the part of the agent, secondly on the part of the matter, for these two causes exist prior to the thing. On the part of the agent, that is absolutely first which is first included in his intention, but that is relatively first with which his operation begins; and this because the intention is prior to the operation.

On the part of the matter, that is first which exists first in the transmutation of the matter. Now in the Incarnation the order depending on the agent must be particularly considered, because, as Augustine says (*Ep. ad Volusianum,* cxxxvii),[3] "in such things the whole reason of the deed is the power of the doer." But it is manifest that according to the intention of the doer what is complete is prior to what is incomplete, and, consequently, the whole to the parts. Hence it must be said that the Word of God assumed the parts of human nature through the medium of the whole; for even as He assumed the body on account of its relation to the rational soul, so likewise He assumed a body and soul on account of their relation to human nature.

Reply Obj. 1. From these words nothing may be gathered, except that the Word, by assuming the parts of human nature, assumed the whole human nature. And thus the assumption of parts is prior in the order of the intellect, if we consider the operation, but not in order of time; but the assumption of the nature is prior if we consider the intention, and this is to be first absolutely, as was said above.

Reply Obj. 2. God is so simple that He is also most perfect, and hence the whole is more like to God than the parts, since it is more perfect.

Reply Obj. 3. It is a personal union wherein the assumption is terminated, not a union of nature, which springs from a conjunction of parts.

ARTICLE 6. *Whether the Human Nature Was Assumed Through the Medium of Grace?*

We proceed thus to the sixth Article: It would seem that the Son of God assumed human nature through the medium of grace.

Objection 1. For by grace we are united to God. But the human nature in Christ was most closely united to God. Therefore the union took place by grace.

Obj. 2. Further, as the body lives by the soul, which is its perfection, so does the soul by grace. But the human nature was fitted for the assumption by the soul. Therefore the Son of God assumed the soul through the medium of grace.

Obj. 3. Further, Augustine says (*De Trin.* xv, 11)[4] that the incarnate Word is like our spoken word. But our word is united to our speech by means of breathing (*spiritus*). There-

---

[1] PL 40, 300.   [2] PG 94, 1068.

[3] Chap. 2 (PL 33, 519).
[4] PL 42, 1071.

fore the Word of God is united to flesh by means of the Holy Spirit, and hence by means of grace, which is attributed to the Holy Spirit, according to I Cor. 12. 4: *Now there are diversities of graces, but the same Spirit.*

On the contrary, Grace is a kind of accident of the soul, as was shown above (Part I-II, Q. CX, A. 2). Now the union of the Word with human nature took place in the subsistence, and not accidentally, as was shown above (Q. II., A. 6). Therefore the human nature was not assumed by means of grace.

I answer that, In Christ there was the grace of union and habitual grace. Therefore grace cannot be taken to be the medium of the assumption of the human nature whether we speak of the grace of union or of habitual grace. For the grace of union is the personal being itself that is given freely from above to the human nature in the Person of the Word, and is the term of the assumption. But the habitual grace pertaining to the special holiness of that man is an effect following the union, according to John 1. 14: *We saw His glory, . . . as it were of the Only-begotten of the Father, full of grace and truth,*—by which we are given to understand that because this Man (as a result of the union) is the Only-begotten of the Father, He is full of grace and truth. But if by grace we understand the will of God doing or bestowing something freely, the union took place by grace not as a means, but as the efficient cause.

Reply Obj. 1. Our union with God is by operation, in so far, that is, as we know and love Him, and hence this union is by habitual grace, in so far as a perfect operation proceeds from a habit. Now the union of the human nature with the Word of God is in personal being, which depends not on any habit, but immediately on the nature itself.

Reply Obj. 2. The soul is the substantial perfection of the body; grace is but an accidental perfection of the soul. Hence grace cannot order the soul to personal union, which is not accidental, as the soul orders the body.

Reply Obj. 3. Our word is united to our speech by means of breathing (*spiritus*) not as a formal medium, but as a moving medium. For from the word conceived within, the breathing proceeds, from which the speech is formed. And similarly from the eternal Word proceeds the Holy Spirit, Who formed the body of Christ, as will be shown (Q. XXXII, A. 1). But it does not follow from this that the grace of the Holy Spirit is the formal medium in the aforesaid union.

QUESTION VII

OF THE GRACE OF CHRIST AS AN INDIVIDUAL MAN

(*In Thirteen Articles*)

WE must now consider such things as were co-assumed by the Son of God in human nature; and first what belongs to perfection, secondly, what belongs to defect (Q. XIV).

Concerning the first, there are three points of consideration: (1) The grace of Christ; (2) His knowledge (Q. IX); (3) His power (Q. XIII).

With regard to His grace we must consider two things: (1) His grace as He is an individual man; (2) His grace as He is the Head of the Church (Q. VIII.). Of the grace of union we have already spoken (Q. II).

Under the first head there are thirteen points of inquiry: (1) Whether in the soul of Christ there was any habitual grace? (2) Whether in Christ there were virtues? (3) Whether He had faith? (4) Whether He had hope? (5) Whether in Christ there were the gifts? (6) Whether in Christ there was the gift of fear? (7) Whether in Christ there were any gratuitous graces? (8) Whether in Christ there was prophecy? (9) Whether there was the fulness of grace in Him? (10) Whether such fulness was proper to Christ? (11) Whether the grace of Christ was infinite? (12) Whether it could have been increased? (13) How this grace stood towards the union?

ARTICLE 1. *Whether in the Soul of Christ There Was Any Habitual Grace?*

We proceed thus to the First Article: It would seem there was no habitual grace in the soul assumed by the Word.

Objection 1. For grace is a certain partaking of the Godhead by the rational creature, according to II Pet. 1. 4: *By Whom He hath given us most great and precious promises, that by these you may be made partakers of the Divine Nature.* Now Christ is God not by participation, but in truth. Therefore there was no habitual grace in Him.

Obj. 2. Further, grace is necessary to man, that he may operate well, according to I Cor. 15. 10: *I have laboured more abundantly than all they; yet not I, but the grace of God with me;* and in order that he may reach eternal life, according to Rom. 6. 23: *The grace of God (is) life everlasting.* Now the inheritance of everlasting life was due to Christ by the mere fact of His being the natural Son of God; and by the fact of His being the Word, by Whom all things were made, He had the power of doing all things well. Therefore His human nature needed no further grace beyond union with the Word.

Obj. 3. Further, what operates as an instrument does not need a habit for its own operations, since habits are rooted in the principal agent. Now the human nature in Christ was as "the instrument of the Godhead," as Damascene says (*De Fide Orthod.* iii, 15).[1] Therefore there was no need of habitual grace in Christ.

On the contrary, It is written (Isa. 11. 2): *The Spirit of the Lord shall rest upon Him;* which (*Spirit*), indeed, is said to be in man by habitual grace, as was said above (Part I., Q. VIII, A. 3; Q. XLIII, AA. 3, 6). Therefore there was habitual grace in Christ.

I answer that, It is necessary to suppose habitual grace in Christ for three reasons. First, on account of the union of His soul with the Word of God. For the nearer any recipient is to an inflowing cause, the more does it partake of its influence. Now the inflow of grace is from God, according to Ps. 83. 12: *The Lord will give grace and glory.* And hence it was most fitting that His soul should receive the inflow of Divine grace. Secondly, on account of the dignity of this soul, whose operations were to attain so closely to God by knowledge and love, to which it is necessary for human nature to be raised by grace. Thirdly, on account of the relation of Christ to the human race. For Christ, as man, is the *Mediator of God and men,* as is written, I Tim. 2. 5, and hence He had to have grace which would overflow upon others, according to John 1. 10: *And of His fulness we have all received, and grace for grace.*

Reply Obj. 1. Christ is the true God in Divine Person and Divine Nature. Yet because together with unity of person there remains distinction of natures, as stated above (Q. II, AA. 1, 2), the soul of Christ is not Divine through its essence. Hence it has to be made Divine by participation, which is by grace.

Reply Obj. 2. To Christ, since He is the natural Son of God, is due an eternal inheritance, which is the uncreated happiness through the uncreated act of knowledge and love of God—that is, the same whereby the Father knows and loves Himself. Now the soul was not capable of this act, on account of the difference of natures. Hence it had to attain to God by a created act of fruition which could not be without grace.

Likewise, since He was the Word of God, He had the power of doing all things well by the Divine operation. And because it is necessary to admit in Him a human operation, distinct from the Divine operation, as will be shown (Q. XIX, A. 1), it was necessary for Him to have habitual grace whereby this operation might be perfect in Him.

Reply Obj. 3. The humanity of Christ is the instrument of the Godhead—not, indeed, an inanimate instrument, which in no way acts, but is merely acted upon, but an instrument animated by a rational soul, which is so acted upon as to act. And hence the nature of the action demanded that he should have habitual grace.

ARTICLE 2. *Whether in Christ There Were Virtues?*

We proceed thus to the Second Article: It would seem that in Christ there were no virtues.

Objection 1. For Christ had the fulness of grace. Now grace is sufficient for every good act, according to II Cor. 12. 9: *My grace is sufficient for thee.* Therefore there were no virtues in Christ.

Obj. 2. Further, according to the Philosopher,[2] virtue is divided against a certain heroic or godlike habit which is attributed to godlike men. But this belongs chiefly to Christ. Therefore Christ had not virtues, but something higher than virtue.

Obj. 3. Further, as was said above (Part I-II, Q. LXV, AA. 1, 2), all the virtues are bound together. But it was not becoming for Christ to have all the virtues, as is clear in the case of liberality and magnificence, for these have to do with riches, which Christ spurned, according to Matt. 8. 20: *The Son of man hath not where to lay His head.* Temperance and continence also regard wicked desires, from which Christ was free. Therefore Christ had not the virtues.

On the contrary, On Ps. 1. 2, *But His will is in the law of the Lord,* a gloss says:[3] "This refers to Christ, Who is full of all good." But a good quality of the mind is a virtue. Therefore Christ was full of all virtue.

I answer that, As was said above (Part I-II, Q. CX, AA. 3, 4), as grace regards the essence of the soul, so does virtue regard its power. Hence it is necessary that as the powers of the soul flow from its essence, so do the virtues flow from grace. Now the more perfect a principle

---

[1] PG 94, 1049, 1060.

[2] *Ethics,* VII, 1 (1145ᵃ19).

[3] *Glossa* Lombardi (PL 191, 62); cf. *Glossa ordin.* (III, 87A).

is, the more it impresses its effects. Hence, since the grace of Christ was most perfect, there flowed from it, in consequence, the virtues which perfect the several powers of the soul for all the soul's acts; and thus Christ had all the virtues.

Reply Obj. 1. Grace suffices a man for all whereby he is ordered to happiness; nevertheless, it effects some of these immediately by itself, such as to make him pleasing to God, and the like, and some others through the medium of the virtues which proceed from grace.

Reply Obj. 2. A heroic or godlike habit only differs from virtue commonly so called by a more perfect mode, in so far, that is, as one is disposed to good in a higher way than is common to all. Hence it is not thus proved that Christ had not the virtues, but that He had them most perfectly beyond the common mode. In this sense Plotinus gave to a certain sublime degree of virtue the name of "virtue of the purified soul."[1]

Reply Obj. 3. Liberality and magnificence are praiseworthy in regard to riches in so far as anyone does not esteem wealth to the extent of wishing to retain it so as to forego what ought to be done. But he esteems them least who wholly despises them, and casts them aside for love of perfection. And hence by altogether contemning all riches, Christ showed the highest kind of liberality and magnificence, although He also performed the act of liberality, as far as it became Him, by causing to be distributed to the poor what was given to Himself. Hence, when Our Lord said to Judas (John 13. 27), *That which thou dost, do quickly,* the disciples understood Our Lord to have ordered him to give something to the poor.

But Christ had no evil desires whatever, as will be shown (Q. xv, AA. 1, 2); yet He was not thereby prevented from having temperance, which is the more perfect in man as he is without evil desires. Hence, according to the Philosopher,[2] the temperate man differs from the continent in this, that the temperate has not the evil desires which the continent suffers. Hence, taking continence in this sense, as the Philosopher takes it, Christ, from the very fact that He had all virtue, had not continence, since it is not a virtue but something less than virtue.

ARTICLE 3. *Whether in Christ There Was Faith?*

We proceed thus to the Third Article: It would seem that there was faith in Christ.

Objection 1. For faith is a nobler virtue than the moral virtues—for example, temperance and liberality. Now these were in Christ, as stated above (A. 2). Much more, therefore, was there faith in Him.

Obj. 2. Further, Christ did not teach virtues which He had not Himself, according to Acts 1. 1: *Jesus began to do and to teach.* But of Christ it is said (Heb. 12. 2) that He is *the author and finisher of our faith.* Therefore there was faith in Him before all others.

Obj. 3. Further, everything imperfect is excluded from the blessed. But in the blessed there is faith, for on Rom. 1. 17, *the justice of God is revealed therein from faith to faith,* a gloss says:[3] "From the faith of words and hope to the faith of things and sight." Therefore it would seem that in Christ also there was faith, since it implies nothing imperfect.

On the contrary, It is written (Heb. 11. 1): *Faith is the evidence of things that appear not.* But there was nothing that was not manifest to Christ, according to what Peter said to Him (John 21. 17): *Thou knowest all things.* Therefore there was no faith in Christ.

I answer that, As was said above (Part II-II, Q. IV, A. 1), the object of faith is a Divine thing not seen. Now the habit of virtue, as every other habit, takes its species from the object. Hence, if we deny that the Divine thing was not seen, we exclude the very notion of faith. Now from the first moment of His conception Christ saw God's Essence fully, as will be made clear (Q. XXXIV, A. 1). Hence there could be no faith in Him.

Reply Obj. 1. Faith is a nobler virtue than the moral virtues, seeing that it has to do with nobler matter; nevertheless, it implies a certain defect with regard to that matter, and this defect was not in Christ. And hence there could not be faith in Him, although the moral virtues were in Him, since in their nature they imply no defect with regard to their matter.

Reply Obj. 2. The merit of faith consists in this, that man through obedience assents to what things he does not see, according to Rom. 1. 5: *For obedience to the faith in all nations for His name.* Now Christ had most perfect obedience to God, according to Phil. 2. 8: *Becoming obedient unto death.* And hence He taught nothing pertaining to merit which He did not fulfil more perfectly Himself.

Reply Obj. 3. As a gloss says in the same

---

[1] Cf. Part I-II, Q. LXI, A. 5; cf. also Macrobius, *In Somn. Scip.*, I, 8 (DD 32).   [2] *Ethics*, VII, 9 (1152ᵃ1).

[3] *Glossa ordin.* (VI, 5A); *Glossa* Lombardi (PL 191, 1323).

place,[1] faith is that "whereby such things as are not seen are believed." But faith in things seen is improperly so called, and only after a certain similitude with regard to the certainty and firmness of the assent.

ARTICLE 4. *Whether in Christ There Was Hope?*

We proceed thus to the Fourth Article: It would seem that there was hope in Christ.

Objection 1. For it is said "in the Person of Christ," according to a gloss[2] (Ps. 30. 1): *In Thee, O Lord, have I hoped.* But the virtue of hope is that whereby a man hopes in God. Therefore the virtue of hope was in Christ.

Obj. 2. Further, hope is the expectation of future Happiness as was shown above (Part II-II, Q. XVII, A. 1, Reply 2; A. 5, Reply 3). But Christ awaited something pertaining to Happiness—namely the glorifying of His body. Therefore it seems there was hope in Him.

Obj. 3. Further, everyone may hope for what pertains to his perfection, if it has yet to come. But there was something still to come pertaining to Christ's perfection, according to Eph. 4. 12: *For the perfecting of the saints, for the work of the ministry, for the building up* (Douay, *edifying*) *of the body of Christ.* Hence it seems that it befitted Christ to have hope.

On the contrary, It is written (Rom. 8. 24): *What a man seeth, why doth he hope for?* Thus it is clear that as faith is of the unseen, so also is hope. But there was no faith in Christ, as was said above (A. 3). Neither, consequently, was there hope.

I answer that, As it is of the nature of faith that one assents to what one does not see, so is it of the nature of hope that one expects what as yet one has not; and as faith, in so far as it is a theological virtue, does not regard everything unseen, but only God, so likewise hope, as a theological virtue, has God Himself for its object, the enjoyment of Whom man chiefly expects by the virtue of hope; yet, in consequence, whoever has the virtue of hope may expect the Divine aid in other things, even as he who has the virtue of faith believes God not only in Divine things, but even in whatsoever is divinely revealed.

Now from the beginning of His conception Christ had the Divine enjoyment fully, as will be shown (Q. XXXIV, A. 4), and hence he had not the virtue of hope. Nevertheless He had hope as regards such things as He did not yet possess, although He had no faith with regard to anything; because, although He knew all things fully, for which reason faith was altogether wanting to Him, nevertheless He did not as yet fully possess all that pertained to His perfection, namely, immortality and glory of the body, which He could hope for.

Reply Obj. 1. This is said of Christ with reference to hope, not as a theological virtue, but in so far as He hoped for some other things not yet possessed, as was said above.

Reply Obj. 2. The glory of the body does not pertain to Happiness as being that in which Happiness principally consists, but by a certain outpouring from the soul's glory, as was said above (Part I-II, Q. IV, A. 6). Hence hope, as a theological virtue, does not regard the Happiness of the body but the soul's Happiness, which consists in the Divine enjoyment.

Reply Obj. 3. The building up of the Church by the conversion of the faithful does not pertain to the perfection of Christ, by which He is perfect in Himself, but according as it leads others to a sharing of His perfection. And because hope properly regards what is expected by him who hopes, the virtue of hope cannot properly be said to be in Christ, because of the aforesaid reason.

ARTICLE 5. *Whether in Christ There Were the Gifts?*

We proceed thus to the Fifth Article: It would seem that the gifts were not in Christ.

Objection 1. For, as is commonly said, the gifts are given to help the virtues. But what is perfect in itself does not need an exterior help. Therefore, since the virtues of Christ were perfect, it seems there were no gifts in Him.

Obj. 2. Further, to give and to receive gifts would not seem to belong to the same, since to give pertains to one who has, and to receive pertains to one who has not. But it belongs to Christ to give gifts acording to Ps. 67. 19. *Thou hast given gifts to men* (Vulg., *Thou hast received gifts in men*). Therefore it was not becoming that Christ should receive the gifts of the Holy Ghost.

Obj. 3. Further, four gifts would seem to pertain to the contemplation of earth—namely, wisdom, knowledge, understanding, and counsel which pertains to prudence; hence the Philosopher enumerates these with the intellectual virtues.[3] But Christ had the contemplation of heaven. Therefore He had not these gifts.

---

[1] *Ibid.*; cf. Augustine, *Quaest. Evang.*, Qu. 39 (PL 35, 1353).

[2] Cf. *Glossa interl.* (III, 125v).

[3] *Ethics*, VI, 3 (1139^{b}16).

On the contrary, It is written (Is. 4. 1): *Seven women shall take hold of one man,* on which a gloss says:[1] "That is, the seven gifts of the Holy Ghost shall take hold of Christ."

I answer that, As was said above (Part I-II, Q. LXVIII, A. 1), the gifts, properly, are certain perfections of the soul's powers, inasmuch as these are designed to be moved by the Holy Ghost. But it is clear that the soul of Christ is moved in a most perfect manner by the Holy Ghost, according to Luke 4. 1: *And Jesus, being full of the Holy Ghost, returned from the Jordan, and was led by the Spirit into the desert.* Hence it is manifest that in Christ the gifts were in a pre-eminent degree.

Reply Obj. 1. What is perfect in the order of its nature needs to be helped by something of a higher nature; just as man, however perfect, needs to be helped by God. And in this way the virtues, which perfect the powers of the soul, as they are controlled by reason, no matter how perfect they are, need to be helped by the gifts, which perfect the soul's powers, according as these are moved by the Holy Ghost.

Reply Obj. 2. Christ is not a recipient and a giver of the gifts of the Holy Ghost, in the same respect; for He gives them as God and receives them as man. Hence Gregory says (*Moral.* ii, 56)[2] that "the Holy Ghost never quitted the human nature of Christ, from Whose Divine nature He proceedeth."

Reply Obj. 3. In Christ there was not only heavenly knowledge, but also earthly knowledge, as will be said (Q. XV, A. 10). And yet even in heaven the gifts of the Holy Ghost will still exist, in a certain manner, as was said above (Part. I-II, Q. LXVIII, A. 6).

ARTICLE 6. *Whether in Christ There Was the Gift of Fear?*

We proceed thus to the Sixth Article: It would seem that in Christ there was not the gift of fear.

Objection 1. For hope would seem to be stronger than fear, since the object of hope is goodness, and of fear, evil, as was said above (Part I-II, Q. XL, A. 1; Q. XLI, A. 2; Q. XLII, A. 1). But in Christ there was not the virtue of hope, as was said above (A. 4). Hence, likewise, there was not the gift of fear in Him.

Obj. 2. Further, by the gift of fear we fear either to be separated from God, which pertains to chaste fear;—or to be punished by Him, which pertains to servile fear, as Augustine says (*in Joann. Tract.* ix).[3] But Christ did not fear being separated from God by sin, nor being punished by Him on account of a fault, since it was impossible for Him to sin, as will be said (Q. XV, AA. 1 and 2). Now fear is not of the impossible. Therefore in Christ there was not the gift of fear.

Obj. 3. Further, it is written (I John 4. 18) that *perfect charity casteth out fear.* But in Christ there was most perfect charity, according to Eph. 3. 19: *The charity of Christ which surpasseth all knowledge.* Therefore in Christ there was not the gift of fear.

On the contrary, It is written (Isa. 11. 3): *And He shall be filled with the spirit of the fear of the Lord.*

I answer that, As was said above (Part I-II, Q. XLII, A. 1), fear regards two objects, of which one is an evil causing terror; the other is that by whose power an evil can be inflicted, as we fear the king in so far as he has the power of putting to death. Now whoever can hurt would not be feared unless he had a certain greatness of power, to which resistance could not easily be offered; for what we easily repel we do not fear. And hence it is plain that no one is feared except for some pre-eminence.

And in this way it is said that in Christ there was the fear of God, not indeed as it regards the evil of separation from God by fault, nor as it regards the evil of punishment for fault, but according as it regards the Divine eminence, on account of which the soul of Christ, led by the Holy Spirit, was borne towards God in an act of reverence. Hence it is written (Heb. 5, 7) that in all things he *was heard for His reverence.* For Christ as man had this act of reverence towards God in a fuller sense and beyond all others. And hence Scripture attributes to Him the fulness of the fear of the Lord.

Reply Obj. 1. The habits of virtues and gifts regard goodness properly and of themselves, evil, however, consequently, since it pertains to the nature of virtue to render acts good, as is said in the *Ethics.*[4] And hence the nature of the gift of fear regards not that evil which fear is concerned with, but the eminence of that goodness—namely, of God, by Whose power evil may be inflicted. On the other hand, hope, as a virtue, regards not only the author of good, but even the good itself, as far as it is not yet possessed. And hence to Christ, Who already

---

[1] *Glossa ordin.* (IV, 13A); Jerome, *In Isaiam,* II, on 4, 1 (PL 24, 74).   [2] PL 75, 598.

[3] PL 35, 2049; cf. *tract.,* LXXXV, on 15.15 (PL 35, 1849). [4] Aristotle, II, 6 (1106ª18).

possessed the perfect good of Happiness, we do not attribute the virtue of hope, but we do attribute the gift of fear.

Reply Obj. 2. This reason is based on fear in so far as it regards the evil object.

Reply Obj. 3. Perfect charity casts out servile fear, which principally regards punishment. But this kind of fear was not in Christ.

ARTICLE 7. *Whether the Gratuitous Graces Were in Christ?*

We proceed thus to the Seventh Article: It would seem that the gratuitous graces were not in Christ.

Objection 1. For it does not pertain to whoever has anything in its fulness to have it by participation. Now Christ has grace in its fulness, according to John 1. 14: *Full of grace and truth.* But the gratuitous graces would seem to be certain participations, bestowed distributively and particularly upon various subjects, according to I Cor. 12. 4: *Now there are diversities of graces.* Therefore it would seem that there were no gratuitous graces in Christ.

Obj. 2. Further, what is due to anyone would not seem to be gratuitously bestowed on him. But it was due to the man Christ that He should abound in the word of wisdom and knowledge, and to be mighty in doing wonderful works and the like, all of which pertain to gratuitous graces, since He is *the power of God and the wisdom of God,* as is written I Cor. 1. 24. Therefore it was not fitting for Christ to have the gratuitous graces.

Obj. 3. Further, gratuitous graces are ordained to the benefit of the faithful. But it does not seem that a habit or any other disposition which a man does not use is for the benefit of others, according to Ecclus. 20. 32: *Wisdom that is hid and treasure that is not seen: what profit is there in them both?* Now we do not read that Christ made use of these gratuitously given graces, especially as regards the gift of tongues. Therefore not all the gratuitous graces were in Christ.

On the contrary, Augustine says (*Ep. ad Dardan.* cclxxxii)[1] that as in the head are all the senses, so in Christ were all the graces.

I answer that, As was said above (Part I-II, Q. CXI, AA. 1, 4), the gratuitous graces are ordained for the manifestation of faith and spiritual doctrine. For he who teaches has to have the means of making his doctrine clear; otherwise his doctrine would be useless. Now Christ is the first and chief teacher of spiritual

[1] Chap. 13 (PL 33, 847).

doctrine and faith, according to Heb. 2. 3, 4: *Which having begun to be declared by the Lord was confirmed unto us by them that heard Him, God also bearing them witness by signs and wonders,* etc. Hence it is clear that all the gratuitous graces were most excellently in Christ, as in the first and chief teacher of the faith.

Reply Obj. 1. As sanctifying grace is ordained to meritorious acts both interior and exterior, so likewise gratuitous grace is ordained to certain exterior acts manifestive of the faith, as the working of miracles, and the like. Now of both these graces Christ had the fulness, since inasmuch as His soul was united to the Godhead, He had the perfect power of effecting all these acts. But other saints who are moved by God as separated and not united instruments receive power in a particular manner in order to bring about this or that act. And hence in other saints these graces are divided, but not in Christ.

Reply Obj. 2. Christ is said to be *the power of God and the wisdom of God* according as He is the Eternal Son of God. But in this respect it does not pertain to Him to have grace, but rather to be the bestower of grace; but it pertains to Him in His human nature to have grace.

Reply Obj. 3. The gift of tongues was bestowed on the apostles, because they were sent to teach all nations; but Christ wished to preach personally only in the one nation of the Jews, as He Himself says (Matt. 15. 24): *I was not sent but to the sheep that are lost of the house of Israel;* and the Apostle says (Rom. 15. 8): *I say that Christ Jesus was minister of the circumcision.* And hence it was not necessary for Him to speak several languages. Yet was a knowledge of all languages not wanting to Him, since even the secrets of hearts, of which all words are signs, were not hidden from Him, as will be shown (Q. X, A. 2). Nor was this knowledge uselessly possessed, just as it is not useless to have a habit, which we do not use when there is no occasion.

ARTICLE 8. *Whether in Christ There Was the Gift of Prophecy?*

We proceed thus to the Eighth Article: It would seem that in Christ there was not the gift of prophecy.

Objection 1. For prophecy implies a certain obscure and imperfect knowledge, according to Num. 12. 6: *If there be among you a prophet of the Lord, I will appear to him in a vision, or I will speak to him in a dream.* But Christ had full and unveiled knowledge, much more than Moses, of whom it is added that *plainly and not by riddles and figures doth he see God* (verse 8). Therefore we ought not to admit prophecy in Christ.

Obj. 2. Further, as faith has to do with what is not seen, and hope with what is not possessed, so prophecy has to do with what is not present, but distant; for a prophet means, as it were, a teller of far-off things. But in Christ there could be neither faith nor hope, as was said above (AA. 3, 4). Hence prophecy also ought not to be admitted in Christ.

Obj. 3. Further, a prophet is in an inferior order to an angel; hence Moses, who was the greatest of the prophets, as was said above (Part II-II, Q. CLXXIV, A. 4) *is said* (Acts 7, 38) to have spoken with an angel in the desert. But Christ was *made lower than the angels,* not as to the knowledge of His soul, but only as regards the sufferings of His body, as is shown Heb. 2. 9. Therefore it seems that Christ was not a prophet.

On the contrary, It is written of Him (Deut. 18. 15): *Thy God will raise up to thee a prophet of thy nation and of thy brethren,* and He says of Himself (Matt. 13. 57 and John 4. 44): *A prophet is not without honour, save in his own country.*

I answer that, A prophet means, as it were, a teller or seer of far-off things, in so far as he knows and announces what things are far from men's senses, as Augustine says (*Contra Faust.* xvi, 18).[1] Now we must bear in mind that no one can be called a prophet for knowing and announcing what is distant from others, whose life he is not sharing. And this is clear in regard to place and time. For if anyone living in France were to know and announce to others living in France what things were transpiring at the time in Syria, it would be prophetical, as Eliseus told Giezi (IV Kings 5. 26) how the man had leapt down from his chariot to meet him. But if anyone living in Syria were to announce what things were there, it would not be prophetical. And the same appears in regard to time. For it was prophetical of Isaias to announce that Cyrus, King of the Persians, would rebuild the temple of God, as is clear from Isa., 44. 28. But it was not prophetical of Esdras to write it (I Esdras 1, 3), in whose time it took place.

Hence if God or angels, or even the blessed, know and announce what is beyond our know-

[1] PL 42, 327.

ing, this does not pertain to prophecy, since they in no way touch our state. Now Christ before His passion touched our state, since He was not merely a comprehensor, but a wayfarer. Hence it was prophetical in Him to know and announce what was beyond the knowledge of other wayfarers, and for this reason He is called a prophet.

Reply Obj. 1. These words do not prove that enigmatical knowledge—namely, by dream and vision—belongs to the nature of prophecy; but the comparison is drawn between other prophets, who saw Divine things in dreams and visions, and Moses, who saw God plainly and not by riddles—and who is yet called a prophet, according to Deut. 24. 10: *And there arose no more a prophet in Israel like unto Moses.* Nevertheless it may be said that although Christ had full and unveiled knowledge as regards the intellectual part, yet in the imaginative part He had certain likenesses in which Divine things could be viewed, since He was not only a comprehensor, but a wayfarer.

Reply Obj. 2. Faith regards such things as are unseen by him who believes, and hope, too, is of such things as are not possessed by the one who hopes; but prophecy is of such things as are beyond the sense of men, with whom the prophet dwells and converses in this state of pilgrimage. And hence faith and hope are contrary to the perfection of Christ's Happiness, but prophecy is not.

Reply Obj. 3. Angels, being comprehensors, are above prophets, who are merely wayfarers; but not above Christ, Who was both a comprehensor and a wayfarer.

ARTICLE 9. *Whether in Christ There Was the Fulness of Grace?*

We proceed thus to the Ninth Article: It would seem that in Christ there was not the fulness of grace.

Objection 1. For the virtues flow from grace, as was said above (Part I-II, Q. CX, A. 4). But in Christ there were not all the virtues, for there was neither faith nor hope in Him, as was shown above (AA. 3, 4). Therefore in Christ there was not the fulness of grace.

Obj. 2. Further, as is plain from what was said above (Part I-II, Q. CXI, A. 2), grace is divided into operating and co-operating. Now operating grace signifies that whereby the ungodly is justified, which has no place in Christ, Who never lay under any sin. Therefore in Christ there was not the fulness of grace.

Obj. 3. Further, it is written (Jas. 1. 17):

*Every best gift and every perfect gift is from
above, coming down from the Father of lights.*
But what comes thus is possessed partially, and
not fully. Therefore no creature, not even the
soul of Christ, can have the fulness of the gifts
of grace.

On the contrary, It is written (John 1. 14):
We saw Him (Vulg., *His glory*) *full of grace
and truth.*

I answer that, To have fully is to have wholly
and perfectly. Now totality and perfection can
be taken in two ways. First as regards their
intensive quantity; for instance, I may say that
some man has whiteness fully, because he has
as much of it as can naturally be in him. Secondly, as regards power; for instance, if anyone be said to have life fully because he has it
in all the effects or works of life; and thus man
has life fully, but brute animals or plants have
not.

Now in both these ways Christ has the fulness of grace. First, since He has grace in its
highest degree, in the most perfect way it can
be had. And this appears, first, from the nearness of Christ's soul to the cause of grace. For
it was said above (A. 1) that the nearer a recipient is to the inflowing cause, the more
abundantly it receives. And hence the soul of
Christ, which is more closely united to God
than all other rational creatures, receives the
greatest inflowing of His grace. Secondly, in
His relation to the effect. For the soul of Christ
so received grace, that, in a manner, it is
poured out from it upon others. And hence He
had to have the greatest grace; just as fire
which is the cause of heat in other hot things,
is of all things the hottest.

Likewise, as regards the power of grace, He
had grace fully, since He had it for all the
operations and effects of grace; and this, because grace was bestowed on Him as upon a
universal principle in the genus of such as have
grace. Now the power of the first principle of
a genus universally extends itself to all the
effects of that genus; thus the power of the sun,
which is the universal cause of generation, as
Dionysius says (*Div. Nom.* iv),[1] extends to
all things that come under generation. Hence
the second fulness of grace is seen in Christ
in so far as His grace extends to all the effects of
grace, which are the virtues, gifts and the like.

Reply Obj. 1. Faith and hope signify effects
of grace with certain defects on the part of the
recipient of grace, in so far as faith is of the unseen, and hope of what is not yet possessed.

[1] Sect. 4 (PG 3, 700).

Hence it was not necessary that in Christ, Who
is the author of grace, there should be any defects such as faith and hope imply, but whatever perfection is in faith and hope was in
Christ most perfectly; just as in fire there are
not all the modes of heat which are defective
by the subject's defect, but whatever belongs
to the perfection of heat.

Reply Obj. 2. It pertains *per se* to operating
grace to justify; but that it makes the ungodly
to be just is accidental to it on the part of the
subject, in which sin is found. Therefore the
soul of Christ was justified by operating grace,
since it was rendered just and holy by it from
the beginning of His conception, not that it was
until then sinful, or even not just.

Reply Obj. 3. The fulness of grace is attributed to the soul of Christ according to the
capacity of the creature, and not by comparison with the infinite fulness of the Divine goodness.

ARTICLE 10. *Whether the Fulness of Grace Is Proper to Christ?*

We proceed thus to the Tenth Article: It
would seem that the fulness of grace is not
proper to Christ.

Objection 1. For what is proper to anyone
belongs to him alone. But to be full of grace
is attributed to some others; for it was said to
the Blessed Virgin (Luke 1. 28): *Hail, full of
grace;* and again it is written (Acts 6. 8):
Stephen, full of grace and fortitude. Therefore
the fulness of grace is not proper to Christ.

Obj. 2. Further, what can be communicated
to others through Christ does not seem to be
proper to Christ. But the fulness of grace can
be communicated to others through Christ,
since the Apostle says (Eph. 3. 19): *That you
may be filled unto all the fulness of God.*
Therefore the fulness of grace is not proper
to Christ.

Obj. 3. Further, the state of the wayfarer
seems to be proportioned to the state of the
goal. But in the state of our heavenly home
there will be a certain fulness, since in our
heavenly country with its fulness of all good,
although some things are bestowed in a pre-
eminent way, yet nothing is possessed in an
exclusive manner, as is clear from Gregory
(*Hom. De Cent. Ovib.; xxxiv in Ev.*).[2] Therefore in the state of heaven the fulness of grace
is possessed by everyone, and hence the fulness
of grace is not proper to Christ.

On the contrary, The fulness of grace is at-

[2] *In Evang.,* BK. II, hom. XXXIV (PL 76, 1248).

tributed to Christ according as He is the Only-begotten of the Father, according to John 1. 14: *We saw Him* (Vulg., *His glory*) *as it were . . . the Only-begotten of the Father, full of grace and truth*. But to be the Only-begotten of the Father is proper to Christ. Therefore it is proper to Him to be full of grace and truth.

I answer that, The fulness of grace may be taken in two ways: first, on the part of grace itself, or secondly on the part of the one who has grace. Now on the part of grace itself there is said to be the fulness of grace when the highest point of grace is attained, both as to essence and power, because grace is possessed in its highest possible excellence and in its greatest possible extension to all its effects. And this fulness of grace is proper to Christ. But on the part of the subject there is said to be the fulness of grace when anyone fully possesses grace according to his condition; whether as regards intensity, by reason of grace being intense in him to the limit assigned by God, according to Eph. 4. 7: *But to every one of us is given grace according to the measure of the giving of Christ;* or as regards power, by reason of a man having the help of grace for all that belongs to his office or state, as the Apostle says (Eph. 3. 8): *To me, the least of all the saints, is given this grace, . . . to enlighten all men*. And this fulness of grace is not proper to Christ, but is communicated to others by Christ.

Reply Obj. 1. The Blessed Virgin is said to be full of grace not on the part of grace itself —since she had not grace in its greatest possible excellence—nor for all the effects of grace, but she is said to be full of grace in reference to herself, that is, because she had sufficient grace for the state to which God had chosen her, namely, to be the mother of His Only-begotten. So, too, Stephen is said to be full of grace, since he had sufficient grace to be a fit minister and witness of God, to which office he had been called. And the same must be said of others. Of these fulnesses one is more full than another, according as one is divinely pre-ordained to a higher or lower state.

Reply Obj. 2. The Apostle is there speaking of that fulness which has reference to the subject, in comparison with what man is divinely pre-ordained to; and this is either something in common, to which all the saints are pre-ordained, or something special, which pertains to the pre-eminence of some. And in this manner a certain fulness of grace is common to all the saints, namely, to have grace enough to

merit eternal life, which consists in the full enjoyment of God. And this is the fulness of grace which the Apostle desires for the faithful to whom he writes.

Reply Obj. 3. These gifts which are in common in heaven, namely: vision, possession and enjoyment, and the like, have certain gifts corresponding to them in this life which are also common to all the saints. Yet there are certain prerogatives of saints, both in heaven and on earth, which are not possessed by all.

ARTICLE 11. *Whether the Grace of Christ Is Infinite?*

We proceed thus to the Eleventh Article: It would seem that Christ's grace is infinite.

Objection 1. For everything immeasurable is infinite. But the grace of Christ is immeasurable, since it is written (John 3. 34): *For God doth not give the Spirit by measure to His Son,*[1] namely Christ. Therefore the grace of Christ is infinite.

Obj. 2. Further, an infinite effect shows an infinite power which can only spring from an infinite essence. But the effect of Christ's grace is infinite, since it extends to the salvation of the whole human race; for He is *the propitiation for our sins . . . and for those of the whole world, as is said* (I John 2. 2). Therefore the grace of Christ is infinite.

Obj. 3. Further, every finite thing by addition can attain to the quantity of any other finite thing. Therefore if the grace of Christ is finite the grace of any other man could increase to such an extent as to reach to an equality with Christ's grace, against what is written (Job 28. 17): *Gold nor crystal cannot equal it,* as Gregory expounds it (*Moral.* xviii).[2] Therefore the grace of Christ is infinite.

On the contrary, Grace is something created in the soul. But every created thing is finite, according to Wisd. 11, 21: *Thou hast ordered all things in measure and number and weight*. Therefore the grace of Christ is not infinite.

I answer that, As was made clear above (Q. II, A. 10; Q. VI, A. 6), a twofold grace may be considered in Christ. The first is the grace of union, which, as was said (Q. II, A. 10; Q. VI, A. 6), is for Him to be personally united to the Son of God, which is a free grant to human nature; and it is clear that this grace is infinite, as the Person of God is infinite.

The second is habitual grace, which may be taken in two ways: first according as it is a

---

[1] *To His Son* is lacking in the Vulgate.
[2] Chap. 48 (PL 76, 85).

kind of being, and in this way it must be a finite being, since it is in the soul of Christ, as in a subject, and Christ's soul is a creature having a finite capacity; hence the being of grace cannot be infinite, since it cannot exceed its subject. Secondly it may be viewed in its proper nature of grace; and thus the grace of Christ can be termed infinite, since it is not limited, that is, it has whatsoever can pertain to the nature of grace, and what pertains to the nature of grace is not bestowed on Him in a fixed measure, seeing that *according to the purpose* of God to Whom it pertains to measure grace, grace is bestowed on Christ's soul as on a universal principle for bestowing grace on human nature, according to Eph. 1. 5, 6, *He hath graced us in His beloved Son.* Thus we might say that the light of the sun is infinite, not indeed in being, but according to the nature of light, as having whatever can pertain to the nature of light.

Reply Obj. 1. When it is said that the Father *doth not give the Spirit by measure*, it may be expounded of the gift which God the Father from all eternity gave the Son, namely, the Divine Nature, which is an infinite gift. Hence the comment of a certain gloss:[1] *So that the Son may be as great as the Father is.*

Or again, it may be referred to the gift which is given the human nature, namely, that it be united to the Divine Person, and this also is an infinite gift. Hence a gloss[2] says on this text: "As the Father begot a full and perfect Word, it is united thus full and perfect to human nature."

Thirdly, it may be referred to habitual grace, according as the grace of Christ extends to whatever belongs to grace. Hence Augustine expounding this (*Tract. xiv in Joann.*)[3] says: "The division of the gifts is a measurement. . . . for to one indeed by the Spirit is given the word of wisdom, to another . . . the word of knowledge. But Christ the giver does not receive by measure."

Reply Obj. 2. The grace of Christ has an infinite effect, both because of the aforesaid infinity of grace, and because of the unity of the Divine Person, to Whom Christ's soul is united.

Reply Obj. 3. The lesser can attain by increase to the quantity of the greater when both have the same kind of quantity. But the grace of any man is compared to the grace of Christ

as a particular to a universal power; hence as the force of fire, no matter how much it increases, can never equal the sun's strength, so the grace of a man, no matter how much it grows, can never equal the grace of Christ.

ARTICLE 12. *Whether the Grace of Christ Could Increase?*

We proceed thus to the Twelfth Article: It would seem that the grace of Christ could increase.

Objection 1. For to every finite thing addition can be made. But the grace of Christ was finite as we have said (A. 11). Therefore it could increase.

Obj. 2. Further, it is by Divine power that grace is increased, according to II Cor. 9. 8: *And God is able to make all grace abound in you.* But the Divine power, being infinite, is confined by no limits. Therefore it seems that the grace of Christ could have been greater.

Obj. 3. Further, it is written (Luke 2. 52) that the child *Jesus advanced in wisdom and age and grace with God and men.* Therefore the grace of Christ could increase.

On the contrary, It is written (John 1. 14): *We saw Him* (Vulg., *His glory*) *as it were . . . the Only-begotten of the Father, full of grace and truth.* But nothing can be or can be thought greater than that anyone should be the Only-begotten of the Father. Therefore no greater grace can be or can be thought than that of which Christ was full.

I answer that, For a form to be incapable of increase happens in two ways: first on the part of the subject itself; secondly, on the part of the form itself. On the part of the subject, indeed, when the subject reaches the utmost limit wherein it partakes of this form, after its own manner, for example, if we say that air cannot increase in heat when it has reached the utmost limit of heat which can exist in the nature of air, although there may be greater heat in actual existence, namely, the heat of fire. But on the part of the form, the possibility of increase is excluded when a subject reaches the utmost perfection which this form can have; for example, if we say the heat of fire cannot be increased because there cannot be a more perfect grade of heat than that to which fire attains.

Now the proper measure of grace, like that of other forms, is determined by the Divine wisdom, according to Wisd. 11. 21: *Thou hast ordered all things in number, weight and measure.* And it is with reference to its end that a measure is set to every form; just as there

[1] *Glossa interl.* (v, 197r); Augustine, *In Joann.*, tract. xv, on 4.35 (PL 35, 1509).
[2] *Glossa ordin.* (v, 197A).
[3] PL 35, 1509.

is no greater gravity than that of the earth because there is no lower place than that of the earth. Now the end of grace is the union of the rational creature with God. But there can neither be nor be thought a greater union of the rational creature with God than that which is in the Person. And hence the grace of Christ reached the highest measure of grace. And so it is clear that the grace of Christ cannot be increased on the part of grace itself.

But neither can it be increased on the part of the subject, since Christ as man was a true and full comprehensor from the first instant of His conception. Hence there could have been no increase of grace in Him, as there could be none in the rest of the blessed, whose grace could not increase, seeing that they have reached their last end.

But as regards men who are wholly wayfarers, their grace can be increased both on the part of the form, since they have not attained the highest degree of grace, and also on the part of the subject, since they have not yet attained their end.

Reply Obj. 1. If we speak of mathematical quantity, addition can be made to any finite quantity, since there is nothing on the part of finite quantity which is contrary to addition. But if we speak of natural quantity, there may be incompatability on the part of the form to which a determined quantity is due, even as other accidents are determined. Hence the Philosopher says[1] that "there is naturally a term of all fixed things, and a limit of magnitude and increase." And hence to the quantity of the whole there can be no addition. And still more must we suppose a term in the forms themselves, beyond which they may not go. Hence it is not necessary that addition should be capable of being made to Christ's grace, although it is finite in its essence.

Reply Obj. 2. Although the Divine power can make something greater and better than the habitual grace of Christ, yet it could not make it to be ordered to anything greater than the personal union with the only-begotten Son of the Father; and to this union, by the determining of the Divine wisdom, the measure of grace is sufficient.

Reply Obj. 3. Anyone may increase in wisdom and grace in two ways. First according as the very habits of wisdom and grace are increased, and in this way Christ did not increase. Secondly, as regards the effects, that is, in so far as they do wiser and greater works; and in this

way Christ increased in wisdom and grace even as in age, since in the course of time He did more perfect works, to prove Himself true man, both in the things of God and in the things of man.

ARTICLE 13. *In What Way the Habitual Grace of Christ Was Related to the Union?*

We proceed thus to the Thirteenth Article: It would seem that the habitual grace did not follow after the union.

Objection 1. For nothing follows itself. But this habitual grace seems to be the same as the grace of union; for Augustine says (*De Predest. Sanct.* xv):[2] "Every man becomes a Christian from the beginning of his belief, by the same grace whereby this Man from His beginning became Christ," and of these two the first pertains to habitual grace and the second to the grace of union. Therefore it would seem that habitual grace did not follow upon the union.

Obj. 2. Further, disposition precedes perfection if not in time, at least in thought. But the habitual grace seems to be a disposition in human nature for the personal union. Therefore it seems that the habitual grace did not follow but rather preceded the union.

Obj. 3. Further the common precedes the proper. But habitual grace is common to Christ and other men, and the grace of union is proper to Christ. Therefore habitual grace is prior in thought to the union. Therefore it does not follow it.

On the contrary, It is written (Isa. 42. 1): *Behold my servant, I will uphold him . . .* and farther on: *I have given My Spirit upon Him;* and this pertains to the gift of habitual grace. Hence it remains that the assumption of human nature to the unity of the Person preceded the habitual grace of Christ.

I answer that, The union of the human nature with the Divine Person, which, as we have said above (Q. II, A. 10; Q. VI, A. 6), is the grace of union, precedes the habitual grace of Christ not in order of time, but by nature and in thought; and this for a triple reason. First, with reference to the order of the principles of both. For the principle of the union is the Person of the Son assuming human nature, Who is said to be sent into the world (John 3. 17) because He assumed human nature; but the principle of habitual grace, which is given with charity, is the Holy Ghost, Who is said to be sent because He dwells in the mind by charity. Now the mission of the Son is prior, in the

---

[1] *Soul,* II, 4 (416[a]16).

[2] PL 44, 982.

order of nature, to the sending of the Holy Ghost, even as in the order of nature the Holy Ghost proceeds from the Son, and love from wisdom. Hence the personal union, according to which is understood the mission of the Son, is prior in the order of nature to habitual grace, according to which is understood the mission of the Holy Ghost. Secondly, the reason of this order may be taken from the relation of grace to its cause. For grace is caused in man by the presence of the Godhead, as light in the air by the presence of the sun. Hence it is written (Ezech. 43. 2): *The glory of the God of Israel came in by the way of the east; . . . and the earth shone with His majesty.* But the presence of God in Christ is understood according to the union of human nature with the Divine Person. Hence the habitual grace of Christ is understood to follow this union, as light follows the sun.

Thirdly, the reason of this order can be taken from the end of grace, since it is ordained to acting rightly, and actions belong to the suppositum and the individual. Hence action and, in consequence, grace ordering to it, presuppose the hypostasis which operates. Now the hypostasis did not exist in the human nature before the union, as is clear from (Q. IV, A. 3). Therefore the grace of union precedes, in thought, habitual grace.

Reply Obj. 1. Augustine here means by grace the gratuitous will of God, bestowing benefits freely; and hence every man is said to be made a Christian by the same grace whereby a Man became Christ, since both take place by the gratuitous will of God without merits.

Reply Obj. 2. As disposition in the order of generation precedes the perfection to which it disposes, in such things as are successively perfected, so it naturally follows the perfection which one has already obtained; just as heat, which was a disposition to the form of fire, is an effect flowing from the form of already existing fire. Now the human nature in Christ is united to the Person of the Word from the beginning without succession. Hence habitual grace is not understood to have preceded the union, but to have followed it as a kind of natural property. Hence, as Augustine says (*Enchir.* xl):[1] "Grace is in a manner natural to the Man Christ."

Reply Obj. 3. The common precedes the proper when both are of the same genus; but when they are of divers genera, there is nothing to prevent the proper being prior to the com-

mon. Now the grace of union is not in the same genus as habitual grace, but is above all genera even as th Divine Person Himself. Hence there is nothing to prevent this proper from being before the common since it does not result from something being added to the common, but is rather the principle and source of that which is common.

QUESTION VIII

OF THE GRACE OF CHRIST AS HE IS THE HEAD OF THE CHURCH

(In Eight Articles)

WE must now consider the grace of Christ as the Head of the Church; and under this head there are eight points of inquiry: (1) Whether Christ is the Head of the Church? (2) Whether He is the Head of men as regards their bodies or only as regards their souls? (3) Whether He is the Head of all men? (4) Whether He is the Head of the angels? (5) Whether the grace of Christ as Head of the Church is the same as His habitual grace as an individual man? (6) Whether to be Head of the Church is proper to Christ? (7) Whether the devil is the head of all the wicked? (8) Whether Antichrist can also be called the head of all the wicked?

ARTICLE 1. *Whether Christ Is the Head of the Church?*

We proceed thus to the First Article: It would seem that it does not belong to Christ as man to be Head of the Church.

Objection 1. For the head imparts sense and motion to the members. Now spiritual sense and motion which are by grace, are not imparted to us by the Man Christ, because, as Augustine says (*De Trin.* xv, 26),[2] not even Christ, as man, but only as God, bestows the Holy Ghost. Therefore it does not belong to Him as man to be Head of the Church.

Obj. 2. Further, it is not fitting for the head to have a head. But God is the Head of Christ, as man, according to I Cor. 11. 3, *The Head of Christ is God.* Therefore Christ Himself is not a head.

Obj. 3. Furthermore, the head of a man is a particular member, receiving an influx from the heart. But Christ is the universal principle of the whole Church. Therefore He is not the Head of the Church.

On the contrary, It is written (Eph. 1. 22): *And He . . . hath made Him head over all the Church.*

[1] PL 40, 252.   [2] PL 42, 1093.

I answer that, As the whole Church is termed one mystic body from its likeness to the natural body of a man, which in various members has various acts, as the Apostle teaches (Rom. 12.4; I Cor. 12.12), so likewise Christ is called the Head of the Church from a likeness with the human head, in which we may consider three things, namely, order, perfection, and power. Order, because the head is the first part of man, beginning from the higher part; and hence it is that every principle is usually called a head according to Ezech. 16. 24: *At every head of the way, thou hast set up a sign of thy prostitution.* Perfection, because in the head dwell all the senses, both interior and exterior, whereas in the other members there is only touch, and hence it is said (Isa. 9. 15): *The aged and honourable, he is the head.* Power, because the power and movement of the other members, together with the direction of them in their acts, is from the head, by reason of the sensitive and moving power there ruling; hence the ruler is called the head of a people, according to I Kings 15. 17: *When thou wast a little one in thy own eyes, wast thou not made the head of the tribes of Israel?*

Now these three things belong spiritually to Christ.

First, on account of His nearness to God His grace is the highest and first, though not in time, since all have received grace on account of His grace, according to Rom. 8. 29: *For whom He foreknew, He also predestinated to be made conformable to the image of His Son; that He might be the first-born amongst many brethren.* Secondly, He had perfection as regards the fulness of all graces, according to John 1. 14, *We saw Him* (Vulg., *His glory*) . . . *full of grace and truth,* as was shown, Q. VII, A. 9. Thirdly, He has the power of bestowing grace on all the members of the Church, according to John 1. 16: *Of His fulness we have all received.* And thus it is plain that Christ is fittingly called the Head of the Church.

Reply Obj. 1. To give grace or the Holy Ghost belongs to Christ as He is God, as originator; but instrumentally it belongs also to Him as man, since His manhood is the instrument of His Godhead. And hence by the power of the Godhead His actions were health-bringing to us —that is, by causing grace in us, both meritoriously and efficiently. But Augustine denies that Christ as man gives the Holy Ghost as originator. Even other saints are said to give the Holy Ghost instrumentally, or ministerially,

according to Gal 3. 5: *He . . . who giveth to you the Spirit,* etc.

Reply Obj. 2. In metaphorical speech we must not expect a likeness in all respects, for thus there would be not likeness but identity. Accordingly a natural head has not another head because one human body is not part of another; but a metaphorical body—that is, an ordered multitude—is part of another multitude as the domestic multitude is part of the civil multitude; and hence the father who is head of the domestic multitude has a head above him—that is, the civil governor. And so there is no reason why God should not be the Head of Christ, although Christ Himself is Head of the Church.

Reply Obj. 3. The head has a manifest pre-eminence over the other exterior members, but the heart has a certain hidden influence. And hence the Holy Ghost is likened to the heart, since He invisibly quickens and unifies the Church; but Christ is likened to the Head in His visible nature in which man is set over man.

ARTICLE 2. *Whether Christ Is the Head of Men As to Their Bodies or Only As to Their Souls?*

We proceed thus to the Second Article: It would seem that Christ is not the Head of men as to their bodies.

Objection 1. For Christ is said to be the Head of the Church in so far as He bestows spiritual sense and the movement of grace on the Church. But a body is not capable of this spiritual sense and movement. Therefore Christ is not the Head of men as regards their bodies.

Obj. 2. Further, we share bodies with the brutes. If therefore Christ was the Head of men as to their bodies, it would follow that He was the Head of brute animals, and this is not fitting.

Obj. 3. Further, Christ took His body from other men, as is clear from Matt. 1.1 and Luke 3.23. But the head is the first of the members, as was said above (A. 1). Therefore Christ is not the Head of the Church as regards bodies.

On the contrary, It is written (Phil. 3. 21): *Who will reform the body of our lowness, made like to the body of His glory.*

I answer that, The human body has a natural relation to the rational soul, which is its proper form and mover. And in so far as the soul is its form, it receives from the soul life and the other properties which belong to the human body according to its species; but in so far as the soul is its mover, the body serves the soul instrumentally. Therefore we must hold that the manhood of Christ had the power of influence, because it is united to the Word of God, to Whom His body is united through the soul, as stated above (Q. VI, A. I). Hence the whole manhood of Christ—that is, according to soul and body—influences all, both in soul and body; but principally the soul, and secondarily the body. First, in so far as the *members of the body are presented as instruments of justice* in the soul that lives through Christ, as the Apostle says (Rom. 6. 13). Secondly, in so far as the life of glory flows from the soul on to the body, according to Rom. 8. 11: *He that raised up Jesus from the dead shall quicken also your mortal bodies, because of His Spirit that dwelleth in you.*

Reply Obj. 1. The spiritual sense of grace does not reach to the body first and principally, but secondarily and instrumentally, as was said above.

Reply Obj. 2. The body of an animal has no relation to a rational soul, as the human body has. Hence there is no parity.

Reply Obj. 3. Although Christ drew the matter of His body from other men, yet all draw from Him the immortal life of their body, according to I Cor. 15. 22: *And as in Adam all die, so also in Christ all shall be made alive.*

ARTICLE 3. *Whether Christ Is the Head of All Men?*

We proceed thus to the Third Article: It would seem that Christ is not the Head of all men.

Objection 1. For the head has no relation except to the members of its body. Now the unbelievers are in no way members of the Church which is the body of Christ, as it is written (Eph. 1. 23). Therefore Christ is not the Head of all men.

Obj. 2. Further, the Apostle writes to the Ephesians (5. 25, 27): *Christ delivered Himself up for the Church that He might present it to Himself a glorious Church, not having spot or wrinkle or any such thing.* But there are many of the faithful in whom is found the spot or the wrinkle of sin. Therefore Christ is not the Head of all the faithful.

Obj. 3. Further, the sacraments of the Old Law are compared to Christ as the shadow to the body, as is written (Col. 2. 17). But the fathers of the Old Testament in their day served unto these sacraments, according to Heb. 8. 5. *Who serve unto the example and shadow of heavenly things.* Hence they did not pertain to Christ's body, and therefore Christ is not the Head of all men.

On the contrary, It is written (I Tim 4. 10): *Who is the Saviour of all men, especially of the faithful,* and (I John 2. 2): *He is the propitiation for our sins, and not for ours only, but also for those of the whole world.* Now to save men and to be a propitiation for their sins belongs to Christ as Head. Therefore Christ is the Head of all men.

I answer that, This is the difference between the natural body of man and the Church's mystical body, that the members of the natural body are all together and the members of the mystical are not all together; neither as regards the being of nature, since the body of the Church is made up of the men who have been from the beginning of the world until its end; nor as regards the being of grace, since, of those who are at any one time, some there are who are without grace, yet will afterwards obtain it, and some have it already. We must therefore consider the members of the mystical body not only as they are in act, but as they are in potency. Nevertheless, some are in potency who will never be reduced to act, and some are reduced at some time to act; and this according to three degrees, of which the first is by faith, the second by the charity of this life, the third by the fruition of the life to come.

Hence we must say that if we take the whole time of the world in general, Christ is the Head of all men, but according to different degrees. For, first and principally, He is the Head of such as are actually united to Him by glory; secondly, of those who are actually united to Him by charity; thirdly, of those who are actually united to Him by faith; fourthly, of those who are united to Him merely in potency, which is not yet reduced to act, yet will be reduced to act according to Divine predestination; fifthly, of those who are united to Him in potency, which will never be reduced to act; such are those men existing in the world who are not predestined, who, however, on their departure from this world, wholly cease to be members of Christ, as being no longer in potency to be united to Christ.

Reply Obj. 1. Those who are unbelievers, though not actually in the Church, are in the Church potentially. And this potentiality is rooted in two things—first and principally, in the power of Christ, which is sufficient for the salvation of the whole human race; secondly, in the liberty of choice.

Reply Obj. 2. To be *a glorious Church not having spot or wrinkle* is the ultimate end to which we are brought by the Passion of Christ.

Hence this will be in heaven, and not on earth, in which *if we say we have no sin, we deceive ourselves,* as is written (I John 1. 8). Nevertheless, there are some—namely, mortal—sins from which they are free who are members of Christ by the actual union of charity; but such as are tainted with these sins are not members of Christ actually, but potentially; except, perhaps, imperfectly, by formless faith, which unites to God relatively but not absolutely— namely, so that through Christ man partakes of the life of grace. For, as is written (Jas. 2. 20): *Faith without works is dead.* Yet such as these receive from Christ a certain vital act— that is, to believe—as if a lifeless limb were moved by a man to some extent.

Reply Obj. 3. The holy Fathers made use of the sacraments of the Law not as realities, but as images and shadows of what was to come. Now it is the same motion to an image as image, and to the reality, as is clear from the Philosopher.[1] Hence the ancient Fathers, by observing the sacraments of the Law, were borne to Christ by the same faith and love whereby we also are borne to Him, and hence the ancient Fathers belong to the same body of the Church as we.

ARTICLE 4. *Whether Christ Is the Head of the Angels?*

We proceed thus to the Fourth Article: It would seem that Christ as man is not the head of the angels.

Objection 1. For the head and members are of one nature. But Christ as man is not of the same nature with the angels, but only with men, since, as is written (Heb. 2. 16): *For nowhere doth He take hold of the angels; but of the seed of Abraham He taketh hold.* Therefore Christ as man is not the head of the angels.

Obj. 2. Further, Christ is the head of such as belong to the Church, which is His Body, as is written (Eph. 1. 23). But the angels do not belong to the Church. For the Church is the congregation of the faithful, and in the angels there is no faith, for they do not *walk by faith* but *by sight,* otherwise they would be *absent from the Lord,* as the Apostle argues (II Cor. 5. 6). Therefore Christ as man is not head of the angels.

Obj. 3. Further, Augustine says (*Tract.* xix and xxiii *in Joann.*),[2] that as the Word which was in the beginning with the Father quickens souls, so the Word made flesh quickens bodies, which

angels lack. But the Word made flesh is Christ as man. Therefore Christ as man does not give life to angels, and hence as man He is not the head of the angels.

On the contrary, The Apostle says (Col. 2. 10), *Who is the head of all Principality and Power,* and the same reason holds good with the other orders of angels. Therefore Christ is the Head of the angels.

I answer that, As was said above (A. 1, Reply 2), where there is one body we must allow that there is one head. Now a multitude ordered to one end, with distinct acts and duties, may be metaphorically called one body. But it is manifest that both men and angels are ordered to one end, which is the glory of the enjoyment of God. Hence the mystical body of the Church consists not only of men but of angels. Now of all this multitude Christ is the Head, since He is nearer God, and shares His gifts more fully, not only than man, but even than angels; and of His influence not only men but even angels partake, since it is written (Eph. 1. 20-22): that God the Father set *Him,* namely Christ, *on His right hand in the heavenly places, above all Principality and Power and Virtue and Dominion and every name that is named not only in this world, but also in that which is to come. And He hath subjected all things under His feet.* Therefore Christ is not only the Head of men, but of angels. Hence we read (Matt. 4. 11) that *angels came and ministered to Him.*

Reply Obj. 1. Christ's influence over all men is chiefly with regard to their souls, wherein men agree with angels in generic nature, though not in specific nature. By reason of this agreement Christ can be said to be the Head of the angels, although the agreement falls short as regards the body.

Reply Obj. 2. The Church, on earth, is the congregation of the faithful; but, in heaven it is the congregation of comprehensors. Now Christ was not merely a wayfarer, but a comprehensor. And therefore He is the Head not merely of the faithful, but of comprehensors, as having grace and glory most fully.

Reply Obj. 3. Augustine here uses the similitude of cause and effect—according as, namely, corporeal things act on bodies, and spiritual things on spiritual things. Nevertheless, the humanity of Christ, by virtue of the spiritual nature—that is, the Divine— can cause something not only in the spirits of men, but also in the spirits of angels, on account of its most close conjunction with God—that is, by personal union.

---

[1] *Memory and Reminiscence,* 1 (450[b]27).

[2] PL 35, 1552, 1585.

ARTICLE 5. *Whether the Grace of Christ, As Head of the Church, Is the Same As His Habitual Grace, According As He Is Man?*

We proceed thus to the Fifth Article: It would seem that the grace whereby Christ is Head of the Church and the individual grace of the Man are not the same.

Objection 1. For the Apostle says (Rom. 5. 15): *If by the offence of one many died, much more the grace of God and the gift, by the grace of one man, Jesus Christ, hath abounded unto many.* But the actual sin of Adam is distinct from original sin which he transmitted to his posterity. Hence the personal grace which is proper to Christ Himself is distinct from His grace according as He is the Head of the Church, which flows to others from Him.

Obj. 2. Further, habits are distinguished according to acts. But the personal grace of Christ is ordered to one act—namely, the sanctification of His soul; and the grace as head is ordered to another—namely, to sanctifying others. Therefore the personal grace of Christ is distinct from His grace as He is the Head of the Church.

Obj. 3. Further, as was said above (Q. VII, introd.), in Christ we distinguish a threefold grace—namely, the grace of union, the grace as head, and the individual grace of the Man. Now the individual grace of Christ is distinct from the grace of union. Therefore it is also distinct from the grace as head.

On the contrary, It is written (John 1. 16): *Of His fulness we all have received.* Now He is our Head because we receive from Him. Therefore He is our Head because He has the fulness of grace. Now He had the fulness of grace because personal grace was in Him in its perfection, as was said above (Q. VII, A. 9). Therefore He is our head according to personal grace. Hence His grace as head and personal grace are not distinct.

I answer that, Since everything acts in so far as it is a being in act, it must be the same act whereby it is in act and whereby it acts, just as it is the same heat whereby fire is hot and whereby it heats. Yet not every act whereby anything is in act suffices for its being the principle of acting upon others. For since "the agent is nobler than the patient," as Augustine says (*Gen. ad. lit.* xii, 16)[1] and the Philosopher,[2] the agent must act on others by reason of a certain pre-eminence. Now it was said above (Q. VII, AA. 9, 10), grace was received by the soul of

Christ in the highest way; and therefore from this pre-eminence of grace which He received, it is from Him that this grace is bestowed on others,—and this belongs to the nature of head. Hence the personal grace whereby the soul of Christ is justified is essentially the same as His grace as He is the Head of the Church, and justifies others; but there is a distinction of reason between them.

Reply Obj. 1. Original sin in Adam, which is a sin of the nature, is derived from his actual sin, which is a personal sin, because in him the person corrupted the nature; and by means of this corruption the sin of the first man is transmitted to posterity, according as the corrupt nature corrupts the person. Now grace is not vouchsafed to us by Christ by means of human nature, but solely by the personal action of Christ Himself. Hence we must not distinguish a two-fold grace in Christ, one corresponding to the nature, the other to the person, as in Adam we distinguish the sin of the nature and of the person.

Reply Obj. 2. Different acts, one of which is the reason and the cause of the other, do not diversify a habit. Now the act of the personal grace which is formally to sanctify its subject, is the reason of the justification of others, which pertains to the grace of the head. Hence it is that the essence of the habit is not diversified by this difference.

Reply Obj. 3. Personal grace and grace of the head are ordered to an act; but the grace of union is not ordered to an act, but to the personal being. Hence the personal grace and the grace of the head agree in the essence of the habit; but the grace of union does not, although the personal grace can be called in a manner the grace of union, since it brings about a fitness for the union; and thus the grace of union, the grace of the head, and the personal grace are one in essence, though there is a distinction of reason between them.

ARTICLE 6. *Whether It Is Proper to Christ To Be Head of the Church?*

We proceed thus to the Sixth Article: It seems that it is not proper to Christ to be Head of the Church.

Objection 1. For it is written (I Kings 15. 17): *When thou wast a little one in thy own eyes, wast thou not made the head of the tribes of Israel?* Now there is but one Church in the New and the Old Testament. Therefore it seems that with equal reason any other man than Christ might be head of the Church.

---

[1] PL 34, 467.   [2] *Soul,* III, 5 (430ᵃ18).

Obj. 2. Further, Christ is called Head of the Church from His bestowing grace on the Church's members. But it belongs to others also to grant grace to others, according to Eph. 4. 29: *Let no evil speech proceed from your mouth; but that which is good to the edification of faith, that it may administer grace to the hearers.* Therefore it seems to belong also to others than Christ to be head of the Church.

Obj. 3. Further, Christ by His ruling over the Church is not only called Head, but also Shepherd and Foundation. Now Christ did not retain for Himself alone the name of Shepherd, according to I Pet. 5. 4, *And when the prince of pastors shall appear, you shall receive a never-fading crown of glory;* nor the name of Foundation, according to Apoc. 21. 14: *And the wall of the city had twelve foundations.* Therefore it seems that He did not retain the name of Head for Himself alone.

On the contrary, It is written (Col. 2. 19): *The head* of the Church is that *from which the whole body, by joints and bands being supplied with nourishment and compacted, groweth unto the increase of God.* But this belongs only to Christ. Therefore Christ alone is Head of the Church.

I answer that, The head influences the other members in two ways. First, by a certain intrinsic influence, according as moving and sensitive power flow from the head to the other members; secondly, by a certain exterior governance, according as by sight and the senses, which are rooted in the head, man is guided in his exterior acts.

Now the interior inflowing of grace is from no one save Christ, Whose manhood, through its union with the Godhead, has the power of justifying; but the influence over the members of the Church, as regards their exterior governance, can belong to others. And in this way others may be called heads of the Church, according to Amos 6. 1, *Ye great men, heads of the people,* differently, however, from Christ. First, because Christ is the Head of all who pertain to the Church in every place and time and state, but all other men are called heads with reference to certain special places, as bishops of their Churches, or with reference to a determined time, as the Pope is the head of the whole Church—namely, during the time of his Pontificate—and with reference to a determined state, according as they are in the state of wayfarers. Secondly, because Christ is the Head of the Church by His own power and authority, while others are called heads, in so

far as they rule in the place of Christ, according to II Cor. 2. 10, *For what I have pardoned, if I have pardoned anything, for your sakes I have done it in the person of Christ,* and 5. 20. *For Christ therefore we are ambassadors, God, as it were, exhorting by us.*

Reply Obj. 1. The word head is employed in that passage in regard to exterior government, just as a king is said to be the head of his kingdom.

Reply Obj. 2. Man does not distribute grace by an inward inflowing, but by exteriorly persuading to the effects of grace.

Reply Obj. 3. As Augustine says (*Tract.* xlvi *in Joann.*):[1] "If the rulers of the Church are Shepherds, how is there one Shepherd, except that all these are members of one Shepherd?" So likewise others may be called foundations and heads, according as they are members of the one Head and Foundation. Nevertheless, as Augustine says (*Tract.* xlvii),[2] "He gave to His members to be shepherds; yet none of us calleth himself the Door. He kept this for Himself alone." And this because by door is implied the principal authority, since it is by the door that all enter the house, and it is Christ alone by *Whom also we have access . . . into this grace, wherein we stand* (Rom. 5. 2); but by the other names above-mentioned there may be implied not merely the principal but also the secondary authority.

ARTICLE 7. *Whether the Devil Is the Head of All the Wicked?*

We proceed thus to the Seventh Article: It would seem that the devil is not the head of the wicked.

Objection 1. For it belongs to the head to diffuse sense and movement into the members, as a gloss says,[3] on Eph. 1. 22, *And made Him head,* etc. But the devil has no power of insinuating the evil of sin, which proceeds from the will of the sinner. Therefore the devil cannot be called the head of the wicked.

Obj. 2. Further, by every sin a man is made evil. But not every sin is from the devil; and this is plain as regards the sins of the demons, who did not sin through the persuasion of another; so likewise not every sin of man proceeds from the devil, for it is said (*De Eccles. Dogm.* lxxxii):[4] "Not all our wicked thoughts are always raised up by the suggestion of the

---

[1] PL 35, 1730.   [2] PL 35, 1734.
[3] *Glossa ordin.,* super Coloss 1.18 (VI, 90, G); *Glossa* Lombardi, super Coloss. 1.18 (PL 192, 264).
[4] Gennadius, chap. 82 (PL 58, 999).

devil, but sometimes they spring from the movement of our choice." Therefore the devil is not the head of all the wicked.

Obj. 3. Further, one head is placed on one body. But the whole multitude of the wicked do not seem to have anything in which they are united, for evil is contrary to evil and it springs also from divers defects, as Dionysius says (*Div. Nom.* iv).[1] Therefore the devil cannot be called the head of all the wicked.

On the contrary, A gloss[2] on Job 18. 17, *Let the memory of him perish from the earth,* says: "This is said of every evil one, yet so as to be referred to the head—that is, the devil."

I answer that, As was said above (A. 8), the head not only influences the members interiorly, but also governs them exteriorly, directing their actions to an end. Hence it may be said that anyone is the head of a multitude, either as regards both—that is, by interior influence and exterior governance—and thus Christ is the Head of the Church, as was stated (A. 8); or as regards exterior governance, and thus every prince or prelate is head of the multitude subject to him. And in this way the devil is called the head of all the wicked. For, as is written (Job. 41. 25): *He is king over all the children of pride.*

Now it belongs to a governor to lead those whom he governs to their end. But the end of the devil is the turning aside of the rational creature from God; hence from the beginning he has endeavoured to lead man from obeying the Divine precept. But this turning aside from God has the nature of an end, since it is sought for under the appearance of liberty, according to Jer. 2. 20: *Of old time thou hast broken my yoke, thou hast burst my bands, and thou saidst, "I will not serve."* Hence, in so far as some are brought to this end by sinning, they fall under the rule and government of the devil, and therefore he is called their head.

Reply Obj. 1. Although the devil does not influence the rational mind interiorly, yet he leads it to evil by persuasion.

Reply Obj. 2. A governor does not always suggest to individuals to obey his will, but proposes to all the sign of his will, in consequence of which some are incited by persuasion, and some of their own accord, as is plain in the leader of an army, whose standard all the soldiers follow, though no one persuades them. Therefore in the same way, the first sin of the devil,

who *sinneth from the beginning* (I John 3. 8), is held out to all to be followed, and some imitate at his suggestion, and some of their own accord without any suggestion. And hence the devil is the head of all the wicked, inasmuch as they imitate him, according to Wisd. 2. 24, 25: *By the envy of the devil, death came into the world. And they follow him that are of his side.*

Reply Obj. 3. All sins agree in the turning aside from God, although they differ by turning to different changeable goods.

Article 8. *Whether Antichrist May Be Called the Head of All the Wicked?*

We proceed thus to the Eighth Article: It would seem that Antichrist is not the head of the wicked.

Objection 1. For there are not several heads of one body. But the devil is the head of the multitude of the wicked. Therefore Antichrist is not their head.

Obj. 2. Further, Antichrist is a member of the devil. Now the head is distinguished from the members. Therefore Antichrist is not the head of the wicked.

Obj. 3. Further, the head has an influence over the members. But Antichrist has no influence over the wicked who have preceded him. Therefore Antichrist is not the head of the wicked.

On the contrary, A gloss[3] on Job 21. 29, *Ask any of them that go by the way,* says: "Whilst he was speaking of the body of all the wicked, suddenly he turned his speech to Antichrist the head of all evil-doers."

I answer that, As was said above (A. 1), in the head are found naturally three things: order, perfection, and the power of influencing. But as regards the order of time, Antichrist is not said to be the head of the wicked as if his sin had preceded, as the sin of the devil preceded. So likewise he is not called the head of the wicked from the power of influencing, although he will pervert some in his day by exterior persuasion; nevertheless those who were before him were not led into wickedness by him nor have imitated his wickedness. Hence he cannot be called the head of all the wicked in this way, but of some. Therefore it remains to be said that he is the head of all the wicked by reason of the perfection of his wickedness. Hence, on II Thess. 2. 4, *Showing himself as if he were God,* a gloss says:[4] "As in Christ dwelt the fulness of the Godhead, so in Antichrist the

---

[1] Sect. 30 (PG 3, 729).
[2] *Glossa ordin.* (III, 40A); Gregory the Great, *Moral.,* XIV, 21 (PL 75, 1052).

[3] *Glossa ordin.* (III, 45A); Gregory the Great, *Moral.,* XV, 58 (PL 75, 1117).
[4] *Glossa ordin.* (VI, 114F); *Glossa* Lombardi (PL 192, 317).

fulness of all wickedness." Not indeed as if his humanity were assumed by the devil into unity of person, as the humanity of Christ by the Son of God, but that the devil by suggestion infuses his wickedness more copiously into him than into all others. And in this way all the wicked who have gone before are signs of Antichrist, according to II Thess. 2. 7, *For the mystery of iniquity already worketh.*

Reply Obj. 1. The devil and Antichrist are not two heads, but one, since Antichrist is called the head because as the wickedness of the devil is most fully impressed on him. Hence, on II Thess. 2. 4, *Showing himself as if he were God*, a gloss says:[1] "The head of all the wicked, namely the devil, who is king over all the children of pride will be in him." Now he is said to be in him not by personal union, nor by indwelling, since "the Trinity alone dwells in the mind" (as is said *De Eccles. Dogm.* lxxxiii),[2] but by the effect of wickedness.

Reply Obj. 2. As the head of Christ is God, and yet He is the Head of the Church, as was said above (A. 1, Reply 2), so likewise Antichrist is a member of the devil and yet is head of the wicked.

Reply Obj. 3. Antichrist is said to be the head of all the wicked not by a likeness of influence, but by a likeness of perfection. For in him the devil, as it were, brings his wickedness to a head, in the same way that anyone is said to bring his purpose to a head when he executes it.

QUESTION IX

OF CHRIST'S KNOWLEDGE IN GENERAL
(In Four Articles)

WE must now consider Christ's knowledge, concerning which the consideration will be twofold. First, of Christ's knowledge in general; secondly, of each particular kind of knowledge He had (Q. x).

Under the first head there are four points of inquiry: (1) Whether Christ had any knowledge besides the Divine? (2) Whether He had the knowledge which the blessed or comprehensors have? (3) Whether He had an imprinted or infused knowledge? (4) Whether He had any acquired knowledge?

ARTICLE 1. *Whether Christ Had Any Knowledge Besides the Divine?*

We proceed thus to the First Article: It would seem that in Christ there was no knowledge except the Divine.

Objection 1. For knowledge is necessary that things may be known thereby. But by His Divine knowledge Christ knew all things. Therefore any other knowledge would have been superfluous in Him.

Obj. 2. Further, the lesser light is dimmed by the greater. But all created knowledge in comparison with the uncreated knowledge of God is as the lesser to the greater light. Therefore there shone in Christ no other knowledge except the Divine.

Obj. 3. Further, the union of the human nature with the Divine took place in the Person, as is clear from Q. II, A. 2. Now, according to some[3] there is in Christ a certain knowledge of the union, whereby Christ knew what belongs to the mystery of the Incarnation more fully than anyone else. Hence, since the personal union contains two natures, it would seem that there are not two knowledges in Christ, but one only, pertaining to both natures.

On the contrary, Ambrose says (*De Incarnat.* vii):[4] "God assumed the perfection of human nature in the flesh; He took upon Himself the sense of man, but not the swollen sense of the flesh." But created knowledge pertains to the sense of man. Therefore in Christ there was created knowledge.

I answer that, As said above (Q. v), the Son of God assumed an entire human nature—that is, not only a body, but also a soul, and not only a sensitive, but also a rational soul. And therefore He had to have created knowledge, for three reasons. First, on account of the soul's perfection. For the soul, considered in itself, is in potency to knowing intelligible things, since it is like a tablet on which nothing is written, and yet it may be written upon through the possible intellect, whereby it may become all things, as is said in the book on the *Soul*.[5] Now what is in potency is imperfect unless reduced to act. But it was fitting that the Son of God should assume not an imperfect, but a perfect human nature, since the whole human race was to be brought back to perfection by its means. Hence the soul of Christ had to be perfected by a knowledge which would be its proper perfection. And therefore it was necessary that there should be another knowledge in Christ besides the Divine knowledge, otherwise the soul of Christ would have been more imperfect than the souls of the rest of men.

---

[1] Cf. preceding note.   [2] Gennadius (PL 58, 999).

[3] Alexander of Hales, *Summa Theol.*, pt. III, Q. 13, m. 2 (III, 42rb); cf. m. 5 (III, 43rb). Cf. Pergamo, *Studi Franceseani* (1932) pp. 129-163.
[4] PL 16, 872.   [5] Aristotle, III, 4 (430ᵃ1).

Secondly, because, since "everything is on account of its operation," as stated in the book on the Heavens,[1] Christ would have had an intellectual soul to no purpose if He had not understood by it; and this pertains to created knowledge.

Thirdly, because some created knowledge pertains to the nature of the human soul—namely, that whereby we naturally know first principles; since we are here taking knowledge in the wide sense of any cognition of the human intellect. Now nothing natural was wanting to Christ, since He took the whole human nature, as stated above (Q. v). And hence the Sixth Council[2] condemned the opinion of those who denied that in Christ there are two knowledges or two wisdoms.

Reply Obj. 1. Christ knew all things with the Divine knowledge by an uncreated operation which is the very Essence of God, since God's understanding is His substance, as the Philosopher proves.[3] Hence this act could not belong to the human soul of Christ, seeing that it belongs to another nature. Therefore, if there had been no knowledge in the soul of Christ other than the divine it would have known nothing; and thus it would have been assumed to no purpose, since everything is on account of its operation.

Reply Obj. 2. If the two lights are supposed to be in the same order, the lesser is dimmed by the greater, as the light of the sun dims the light of a candle, both being in the class of things giving light. But if we suppose two lights, one of which is in the class of things giving light and the other in the class of things receiving light, the lesser light is not dimmed by the greater, but rather is strengthened, as the light of the air by the light of the sun. And in this manner the light of knowledge is not dimmed, but rather is heightened in the soul of Christ by the light of the Divine knowledge, which is *the true light which enlighteneth every man that cometh into this world*, as is written John 1. 9.

Reply Obj. 3. On the part of what are united we hold there is a knowledge in Christ, both as to His Divine and as to His human nature, so that, by reason of the union whereby there is one hypostasis of God and man, the things of God are attributed to man, and the things of man are attributed to God, as was said above (Q. III AA. 1 and 6). But on the part of the union itself we cannot admit any knowledge in Christ. For this union is in personal being, and knowledge belongs to a person only by reason of a nature.

ARTICLE 2. *Whether Christ Had the Knowledge Which the Blessed or Comprehensors Have?*

We proceed thus to the Second Article: It would seem that in Christ there was not the knowledge of the blessed or comprehensors.

Objection 1. For the knowledge of the blessed is a participation of Divine light, according to Ps. 35. 10: *In Thy light we shall see light.* Now Christ had not the divine light as a participated light, but He had the Godhead Itself substantially abiding in Him, according to Col. 2. 9: *For in Him dwelleth all the fulness of the Godhead corporeally.* Therefore in Christ there was not the knowledge of the blessed.

Obj. 2. Further, the knowledge of the blessed makes them blessed, according to John 17. 3: *This is eternal life: that they may know Thee, the only true God, and Jesus Christ Whom Thou hast sent.* But this Man was blessed through being united to God in person, according to Ps. 64. 5: *Blessed is He Whom Thou hast chosen and taken to Thee.* Therefore it is not necessary to suppose the knowledge of the blessed in Him.

Obj. 3. Further, to man belongs a double knowledge—one by nature, one above nature. Now the knowledge of the blessed, which consists in the vision of God, is not natural to man, but above his nature. But in Christ there was another and much higher supernatural knowledge—that is, the Divine knowledge. Therefore there was no need of the knowledge of the blessed in Christ.

On the contrary, The knowledge of the blessed consists in the knowledge of God. But He knew God fully, even as He was man, according to John 8. 55: *I do know Him, and do keep His word.* Therefore in Christ there was the knowledge of the blessed.

I answer that, What is in potency is reduced to act by what is in act, for that whereby things are heated must itself be hot. Now man is in potency to the knowledge of the blessed, which consists in the vision of God, and is ordered to it as to an end; for man as a rational creature is capable of that blessed knowledge, since he is made in the image of God. Now men are brought to this end of Happiness by the humanity of Christ, according to Heb. 2. 10: *For it became Him, for Whom are all things, and by Whom are all things, Who had brought many children*

[1] Aristotle, II, 3 (286a8).
[2] Actio 4 (MA XI, 274); Agatho, *Epist.*, 1, *Ad Augustos Imperatores* (PL 87, 1161).
[3] *Metaphysics*, XII, 9 (1074b15).

unto glory, to perfect the author of their salvation by His passion. And hence it was necessary that the beatific knowledge, which consists in the vision of God, should belong to the man Christ in a most perfect manner, since the cause ought always to be more powerful than the thing caused.

Reply Obj. 1. The Godhead is united to the manhood of Christ in Person, not in essence or nature; yet with the unity of Person remains the distinction of natures. And therefore the soul of Christ, which is a part of human nature, through a light participated from the Divine Nature, is perfected with the beatific knowledge whereby it sees God in essence.

Reply Obj. 2. By the union this Man is blessed with the uncreated Happiness, even as by the union He is God; yet besides the uncreated Happiness it was necessary that there should be in the human nature of Christ a created Happiness, whereby His soul was established in the last end of human nature.

Reply Obj. 3. The beatific vision or knowledge is to some extent above the nature of the rational soul, since it cannot reach it of its own power; but in another way it is in accordance with its nature, since it is capable of it by nature, having been made to the likeness of God, as stated above. But the uncreated knowledge is in every way above the nature of the human soul.

Article 3. *Whether Christ Had an Imprinted or Infused Knowledge?*

We proceed thus to the Third Article: It would seem that there was not in Christ another infused or imprinted knowledge besides the beatific knowledge.

Objection 1. For all other knowledge compared to the beatific knowledge is like imperfect to perfect. But imperfect knowledge is removed by the presence of perfect knowledge, as the clear *face-to-face* vision removes the enigmatical vision of faith, as is plain from I Cor. 13. 10, 12. Since, therefore, in Christ there was the beatific knowledge, as stated above (A. 2), it would seem that there could not be any other imprinted knowledge.

Obj. 2. Further, an imperfect mode of knowledge disposes towards a more perfect, as opinion, the result of dialectical syllogisms, disposes towards science, which results from demonstrative syllogisms. Now, when perfection is reached, there is no further need of the disposition, even as on reaching the end motion is no longer necessary. Hence, since every created

knowledge is compared to beatific knowledge as imperfect to perfect and as disposition to its term, it seems that since Christ had beatific knowledge, it was not necessary for Him to have any other knowledge.

Obj. 3. Further, as corporeal matter is in potency to the sensible form, so the possible intellect is in potency to the intelligible form. Now coporeal matter cannot receive two sensible forms at once, one more perfect and the other less perfect. Therefore neither can the soul receive a double knowledge at once, one more perfect and the other less perfect. And hence the same conclusion as above.

On the contrary, It is written (Col. 2. 3) that in Christ *are hid all the treasures of wisdom and knowledge.*

I answer that, As stated above (A. 1), it was fitting that the human nature assumed by the Word of God should not be imperfect. Now everything in potency is imperfect unless it be reduced to act. But the possible intellect of man is in potency to all intelligible things, and it is reduced to act by intelligible species, which are its completing forms, as is plain from what is said in the treatise on the *Soul.*[1] And hence we must admit in Christ an infused knowledge, inasmuch as through the Word of God there is imprinted upon the soul of Christ, which is personally united to Him, the intelligible species of all things to which the possible intellect is in potency; even as in the beginning of the creation of things, the Word of God imprinted intelligible species upon the minds of the angels, as is clear from Augustine (*Gen. ad lit.* ii, 8).[2] And therefore, even as in the angels, according to Augustine,[3] there is a double knowledge—one the "morning" knowledge, whereby they know things in the Word, the other the "evening" knowledge, whereby they know things in their proper natures by infused species, so likewise, besides the Divine uncreated knowledge in Christ, there is in His soul a beatific knowledge, whereby He knows the Word, and things in the Word; and an infused or imprinted knowledge, whereby He knows things in their proper nature by intelligible species proportioned to the human mind.

Reply Obj. 1. The imperfect vision of faith of its very nature is opposed to manifest vision, seeing that it is of the essence of faith to have reference to the unseen, as was said above (Part II-II, Q. 1, A. 4). But knowledge by infused

---

[1] Aristotle, III, 8 (431^{b}21).   [2] PL 34, 269.
[3] *De Gen. ad lit.,* IV, 22 (PL 34, 312); *City of God,* XI, 7 (PL 41, 322); cf. above, Part I, Q. LVIII, A. 6.

species includes no opposition to beatific knowledge. Therefore there is no parity.

Reply Obj. 2. Disposition is referred to perfection in two ways: first, as a way leading to perfection, secondly, as an effect proceeding from perfection; thus matter is disposed by heat to receive the form of fire, and, when this comes, the heat does not cease, but remains as an effect of this form. So, too, opinion caused by a dialectical syllogism is a way to science, which is acquired by demonstration; yet, when this has been acquired, there may still remain the knowledge gained by the dialectical syllogism, following, so to say, the demonstrative knowledge, which is through the cause, since he who knows the cause is thereby enabled the better to understand the probable signs from which dialectical syllogisms proceed. So likewise in Christ, together with the beatific knowledge there still remains infused knowledge, not as a way to Happiness, but as strengthened by Happiness.

Reply Obj. 3. The beatific knowledge is not by a species, that is a likeness of the Divine Essence, or of whatever is known in the Divine Essence, as is plain from what has been said in the First Part (Q. XII, AA. 2, 9); but it is a knowledge of the Divine Essence immediately, because the Divine Essence itself is united to the mind of the blessed as an intelligible to an intelligent being; and the Divine Essence is a form exceeding the capacity of any creature whatsoever. Hence, together with this superexceeding form, there is nothing to hinder from being in the rational mind, intelligible species, proportioned to its nature.

ARTICLE 4. *Whether Christ Had Any Acquired Knowledge?*

We proceed thus to the Fourth Article: It would seem that in Christ there was no acquired experimental knowledge (*scientia*).

Objection 1. For whatever befitted Christ, He had most perfectly. Now Christ did not possess acquired knowledge most perfectly, since He did not devote Himself to the study of letters, by which knowledge is acquired in its perfection; for it is said (John 7. 15): *The Jews wondered, saying: How doth this Man know letters, having never learned?* Therefore it seems that in Christ there was no acquired knowledge.

Obj. 2. Further, Nothing can be added to what is full. But the power of Christ's soul was filled with intelligible species divinely infused, as was said above (A. 3). Therefore no acquired species could accrue to His soul.

Obj. 3. Further, he who already has the habit of knowledge acquires no new habit through what he receives from the senses (otherwise two forms of the same species would be in the same thing at the same time), but the habit which previously existed is strengthened and increased. Therefore, since Christ had the habit of infused knowledge, it does not seem that He acquired a new knowledge through what He perceived by the senses.

On the contrary, It is written (Heb. 5. 8): *Whereas . . . He was the Son of God, He learned obedience by the things which He suffered*—that is, "experienced," says a gloss.[1] Therefore there was in the soul of Christ an experimental knowledge, which is acquired knowledge.

I answer that, As is plain from what was said above (Q. IV, A. 2, arg. 2; Q. V), nothing that God planted in our nature was wanting to the human nature assumed by the Word of God. Now it is manifest that God planted in human nature not only a possible, but an agent intellect. Hence it is necessary to say that in the soul of Christ there was not merely a possible, but also an agent intellect. But if in other things God and nature make nothing in vain, as the Philosopher says,[2] still less in the soul of Christ is there anything in vain. Now what has not its proper operation is useless, "since everything exists for the sake of its operation," as is said in the book on the *Heavens*.[3] Now the proper operation of the agent intellect is to make intelligible species in act, by abstracting them from phantasms; hence, it is said[4] that the agent intellect is that by which "everything is made actual." And thus it is necessary to say that in Christ there were intelligible species received in the possible intellect by the action of the agent intellect, which means that there was acquired knowledge in Him, which some call experimental.[5]

And hence, although elsewhere I wrote differently (III, *Sent.* d. XIV, A. 3; d. XVIII, A. 3), it must be said that in Christ there was acquired knowledge, which is properly knowledge in a human manner, both as regards the subject receiving and as regards the active cause. For such knowledge is in Christ according to the light of the agent intellect, which is natural to the human soul. But infused knowledge is attri-

---

[1] *Glossa interl.* (VI, 142v); *Glossa* Lombardi (PL 192, 438).   [2] *Heavens*, I, 4 (271ᵃ33).
[3] Aristotle, II, 3 (286ᵃ8).   [4] *Soul*, III, 5 (430ᵃ15).
[5] Cf. Bonaventure, *In Sent.*, III, d. 14, A. 3, Q. 2 (QR III, 322); cf. also Albert the Great, *In Sent.*, III, d. 13, A. 10 (BO XXVIII, 249).

buted to the soul on account of a light infused from on high, and this manner of knowing is proportioned to the angelic nature. But the beatific knowledge, whereby the very Essence of God is seen, is proper and natural to God alone, as was said in the First Part (Q. XII, A. 4).

Reply Obj. 1. Since there is a twofold way of acquiring knowledge—by discovery and by being taught—the way of discovery is the higher, and the way of being taught is secondary. Hence it is said:[1] "He indeed is the best who knows everything by himself; yet on the other hand he is good who obeys him that speaks rightly." And hence it was more fitting for Christ to possess a knowledge acquired by discovery than by being taught, especially since He was given to be the Teacher of all, according to Joel 2. 23: *Be joyful in the Lord your God, because He hath given you a Teacher of justice.*

Reply Obj. 2. The human mind has two relations. One is to higher things, and in this respect the soul of Christ was full through infused knowledge. The other relation is to lower things—that is, to phantasms, which naturally move the human mind by virtue of the agent intellect. Now it was necessary that even in this respect the soul of Christ should be filled with knowledge, not that the first fulness was insufficient for the human mind in itself, but that it had to be also perfected with regard to phantasms.

Reply Obj. 3. Acquired and infused habits are not to be classed together; for the habit of knowledge is acquired by the relation of the human mind to phantasms, and hence another habit of the same kind cannot be again acquired. But the habit of infused knowledge is of a different nature, as coming down to the soul from on high and not from phantasms. And hence there is no parity between these habits.

QUESTION X

Of the beatific knowledge of
Christ's Soul
(In Four Articles)

Now we must consider each of the above knowledges. Since, however, we have treated of the Divine knowledge in the First Part (Q. XIV), it now remains to speak of the three others: (1) of the beatific knowledge; (2) of the infused knowledge (Q. XI); (3) of the acquired knowledge (Q. XII).

[1] Aristotle, *Ethics*, I, 6 (1095[b]10).

But, again, because much has been said in the First Part (Q. XII) of the beatific knowledge, which consists in the vision of God, we shall speak here only of such things as belong properly to the soul of Christ.

Under this head there are four points of inquiry: (1) Whether the soul of Christ comprehended the Word or the Divine Essence? (2) Whether it knew all things in the Word? (3) Whether the soul of Christ knew the infinite in the Word? (4) Whether it saw the Word or the Divine Essence clearer than did any other creature?

ARTICLE 1. *Whether the Soul of Christ Comprehended the Word or the Divine Nature?*

We proceed thus to the First Article: It would seem that the soul of Christ comprehended and comprehends the Word or Divine Essence.

Objection 1. For Isidore says[2] that the Trinity is known only to Itself and to the Man assumed. Therefore the Man assumed communicates with the Holy Trinity in that knowledge of Itself which is proper to the Holy Trinity. Now this is the knowledge of comprehension. Therefore the soul of Christ comprehends the Divine Essence.

Obj. 2. Further, to be united to God in personal being is greater than to be united by vision. But as Damascene says (*De Fide Orthod.* iii, 6),[3] "the whole Godhead in one Person is united to the human nature in Christ." Therefore much more is the whole Divine Nature seen by the soul of Christ, and hence it would seem that the soul of Christ comprehended the Divine Essence.

Obj. 3. Further, what belongs by nature to the Son of God belongs by grace to the Son of Man, as Augustine says (*De Trin.* i, 13).[4] But to comprehend the Divine Essence belongs by nature to the Son of God. Therefore it belongs by grace to the Son of Man, and thus it seems that the soul of Christ comprehended the Divine Essence by grace.

On the contrary, Augustine says (QQ. lxxxiii, qu. 15):[5] "Whatsoever comprehends itself is finite to itself." But the Divine Essence is not finite with respect to the soul of Christ, since It infinitely exceeds it. Therefore the soul of Christ does not comprehend the Word.

I answer that, As is plain from Q. II, AA. 1, 6, the union of the natures in the Person of Christ

[2] *Sent.*, Bk. I, 3 (PL 83, 543).   [3] PG 94, 1005.
[4] PL 42, 842; cf. *Contra Serm. Arian.*, chap. 8 (PL 42, 688).   [5] PL 40, 14.

took place in such a way that the properties of both natures remained unconfused—in such a way, namely, that, "the uncreated remained uncreated, and the created remained within the limits of the creature," as Damascene says (*De Fide Orthod.* iii, 3).[1] Now it is impossible for any creature to comprehend the Divine Essence, as was shown in the First Part (Q. XII, A. 7), seeing that the infinite is not comprehended by the finite. And hence it must be said that the soul of Christ in no way comprehends the Divine Essence.

Reply Obj. 1. The Man assumed is accounted with the Divine Trinity in the knowledge of Itself, not indeed as regards comprehension, but by reason of a certain most excellent knowledge above the rest of creatures.

Reply Obj. 2. Not even in the union by personal being does the human nature comprehend the Word of God or the Divine Nature, for although it was wholly united to the human nature in the one Person of the Son, yet the whole power of the Godhead was not circumscribed by the human nature. Hence Augustine says (*Ep. ad Volusian.* cxxxvii):[2] "I would have you know that it is not the Christian doctrine that God was united to flesh in such a manner as to quit or lose the care of the world's government, neither did He narrow or reduce it when He transferred it to that little body." So likewise the soul of Christ sees the whole Essence of God, yet does not comprehend it, since it does not see It totally—that is, not as perfectly as it is knowable, as was said in the First Part (Q. XII, A. 7).

Reply Obj. 3. This saying of Augustine is to be understood of the grace of union, by reason of which all that is said of the Son of God in His Divine Nature is also said of the Son of Man on account of the identity of suppositum. And in this way it may be said that the Son of Man is a comprehensor of the Divine Essence, not indeed by His soul, but in His Divine Nature; even as we may also say that the Son of Man is the Creator.

ARTICLE 2. *Whether the Soul of Christ Knew All Things in the Word?*

We proceed thus to the Second Article: It would seem that the soul of Christ does not know all things in the Word.

Objection 1. For it is written (Mark 13. 32): *But of that day or hour no man knoweth, neither the angels in heaven nor the Son, but the Father.* Therefore He does not know all things in the Word.

Obj. 2. Further, the more perfectly anyone knows a principle the more he knows in the principle. But God sees His Essence more perfectly than the soul of Christ does. Therefore He knows more in the Word than the soul of Christ. Therefore the soul of Christ does not know all things in the Word.

Obj. 3. Further, the extent of knowledge depends on the number of things knowable. If, therefore, the soul of Christ knew in the Word all that the Word knows, it would follow that the knowledge of the soul of Christ would equal the Divine knowledge—that is, the created would equal the uncreated, which is impossible.

On the contrary, On Apoc. 5. 12, *The Lamb that was slain is worthy to receive . . . divinity and wisdom,* a gloss says[3]—that is, "the knowledge of all things."

I answer that, When it is inquired whether Christ knows all things in the Word, "all things" may be taken in two ways. First, properly, to stand for all that in any way whatsoever is, will be, or was done, said, or thought, by whomsoever and at any time. And in this way it must be said that the soul of Christ knows all things in the Word. For every created intellect knows in the Word, not all things absolutely, but so many more things the more perfectly it sees the Word. Yet no beatified intellect fails to know in the Word whatever pertains to itself. Now to Christ and to His dignity all things to some extent belong, since all things are subject to Him. Moreover, He has been appointed Judge of all by God, *because He is the Son of Man,* as is said John 5. 27; and therefore the soul of Christ knows in the Word all things existing in whatever time, and the thoughts of men, of which He is the Judge, so that what is said of Him (John 2. 25), *For He knew what was in man,* can be understood not merely of the Divine knowledge, but also of His soul's knowledge, which it had in the Word.

Secondly, "all things" may be taken widely, as extending not merely to such things as are in act at some time, but even to such things as are in potency, and never have been nor ever will be reduced to act. Now some of these are in the Divine power alone, and not all of these does the soul of Christ know in the Word. For this would be to comprehend all that God could do, which would be to comprehend the Divine power, and, consequently, the Divine Essence.

For every power is known from the knowledge of all it can do. Some, however, are not only in the power of God, but also in the power of the creature; and all of these the soul of Christ knows in the Word, for it comprehends in the Word the essence of every creature, and, consequently, its power and virtue, and all things that are in the power of the creature.

Reply Obj. 1. Arius and Eunomius[1] understood this saying not of the knowledge of the soul, which they did not hold to be in Christ, as was said above (Q. V, A. 3), but of the Divine knowledge of the Son, Whom they held to be less than the Father as regards knowledge. But this will not stand, since all things were made by the Word of God, as is said in John 1. 3, and, amongst other things, all times were made by Him. Now He is not ignorant of anything that was made by Him.

He is said, therefore, not to know the day and the hour of the Judgment because He does not make it known, since, on being asked by the apostles (Acts 1. 6), He was unwilling to reveal it; and, on the contrary, we read (Gen. 22. 12): *Now I know that thou fearest God*—that is, Now I have made thee know. But the Father is said to know because He imparted this knowledge to the Son. Hence, by saying *but the Father*, we are given to understand that the Son knows not merely in the Divine Nature, but also in the human, because, as Chrysostom argues (*Hom.* lxxviii *in Matt.*),[2] if it is given to Christ as man to know how to judge —which is greater—much more it is given to Him to know the less—namely, the time of Judgment.

Origen, however,[3] expounds it "of His body, which is the Church, which is ignorant of this time." Lastly, some say[4] this is to be understood of the adoptive, and not of the natural Son of God.

Reply Obj. 2. God knows His Essence so much the more perfectly than the soul of Christ that He comprehends it. And hence He knows

all things, not merely whatever are in act at any time, which things He is said to know by knowledge of vision, but also whatever He Himself can do, which He is said to know by simple intelligence, as was shown in the First Part (Q. XIV, A. 9). Therefore the soul of Christ knows all things that God knows in Himself by the knowledge of vision, but not all that God knows in Himself by knowledge of simple intelligence; and thus in Himself God knows many more things than the soul of Christ.

Reply Obj. 3. The extent of knowledge depends not merely on the number of knowable things, but also on the clearness of the knowledge. Therefore, although the knowledge of the soul of Christ which He has in the Word is equal to the knowledge of vision which God has in Himself as regards the number of things known, nevertheless the knowledge of God infinitely exceeds the knowledge of the soul of Christ in clearness of knowledge, since the uncreated light of the Divine intellect infinitely exceeds any created light received by the soul of Christ; although, absolutely speaking, the Divine knowledge exceeds the knowledge of the soul of Christ not only as regards the mode of knowing, but also as regards the number of things knowable, as was stated above.

ARTICLE 3. *Whether the Soul of Christ Can Know the Infinite in the Word?*

We proceed thus to the Third Article: It would seem that the soul of Christ cannot know the infinite in the Word.

Objection 1. For that the infinite should be known is contrary to the definition of the infinite, which is said to be that "from which, however much we may take, there always remains something to be taken."[5] But it is impossible for the definition to be separated from the thing defined, since this would mean that contradictories exist together. Therefore it is impossible that the soul of Christ knows the infinite.

Obj. 2. Further, the knowledge of the infinite is infinite. But the knowledge of the soul of Christ cannot be infinite, because its capacity is finite, since it is created. Therefore the soul of Christ cannot know the infinite.

Obj. 3. Further, there can be nothing greater than the infinite. But more is contained in the Divine knowledge, absolutely speaking, than in the knowledge of Christ's soul, as stated above (A. 2). Therefore the soul of Christ does not know the infinite.

[1] See Athanasius, *Contra Arianos*, orat. III (PG 26, 380); Hilary, *De Trin.*, X (PL 10, 282); Ambrose, *De Fide*, V, 16 (PL 16, 716); Jerome, *In Matt.*, BK. IV, on 24.36 (PL 26, 188). [2] PG 58, 701.

[3] On Matt. 24.36 (PG 13, 1687).

[4] Gregory of Tours, *Hist. Francorum*, BK. I, prol. (PL 71, 162); cited by Abelard, *Sic et Non*, Sect. 76 (PL 178, 1451); Cf. Rabanus Maurus, *In Matt.*, BK. VII, on 24.36 (PL 107, 1078); cf. Peter the Eater, *Hist. Scholast.*, *In Evang.*, chap. 142 (PL 198, 1611); Alexander of Hales, *Summa Theol.*, PT. III, Q. 13, m. 4, ad 1 (III, 43ra); See also Origen, *In Matt.* 24.36 (PG 13, 1687); Gregory the Great, *Registrum*, BK. X, indict. III, *Epist.* XXXIX (PL 77, 1097); cf. *Glossa ordin.* on Matt. 24.36 (V, 75A); *Glossa interl.* (V, 751).

[5] Aristotle, *Physics*, III, 6 (207ª7).

On the contrary, The soul of Christ knows all its power and all it can do. Now it can cleanse infinite sins, according to I John 2. 2: *He is the propitiation for our sins, and not for ours only, but also for those of the whole world.* Therefore the soul of Christ knows the infinite.

I answer that, Knowledge regards only being, since being and truth are convertible. Now a thing is said to be a being in two ways. First, absolutely—that is, whatever is a being in act; secondly, relatively—that is, whatever is a being in potency. And because, as is said in the *Metaphysics,*[1] everything is known as it is in act, and not as it is in potency, knowledge first and principally regards being in act, and secondarily regards being in potency, which is not knowable of itself, but according as that in whose power it exists is known.

Hence, with regard to the first mode of knowledge, the soul of Christ does not know the infinite. Because there is not an infinity of things in act, even though we were to reckon all that are in act at any time whatsoever, since the state of generation and corruption will not last for ever; consequently there is a certain number not only of things lacking generation and corruption, but also of things subject to generation and corruption. But with regard to the other mode of knowing, the soul of Christ knows infinite things in the Word, for it knows, as stated above (A. 2), all that is in the power of the creature. Hence, since in the power of the creature there is an infinite number of things, it knows the infinite, as it were, by a certain knowledge of simple intelligence, and not by a knowledge of vision.

Reply Obj. 1. As we said in the First Part (Q. VII, A. 1), the infinite is taken in two ways. First, on the part of a form, and thus we have the negatively infinite—that is, a form or act not limited by being received into matter or a subject. And this infinite of itself is most knowable on account of the perfection of the act, although it is not comprehensible by the finite power of the creature; for thus God is said to be infinite. And this infinite the soul of Christ knows, yet does not comprehend.

Secondly, there is the infinite as regards matter which is taken privatively—that is, because it has not the form it ought naturally to have, and in his way we have infinite in quantity. Now this infinite is of its very character unknowable, because it is, as it were, matter with privation of form, as is said in the *Physics.*[2]

But all knowledge is by form or act. Therefore if this infinite is to be known according to its mode of being, it cannot be known. For its mode is that part be taken after part, as is said in the *Physics.*[3] And in this way it is true that, if we take something from it, that is, taking part after part, there always remains something to be taken. But as material things can be received by the intellect immaterially, and many things unitedly, so can infinite things be received by the intellect, not after the manner of infinite, but as it were finitely; and thus what are in themselves infinite are, in the intellect of the knower, finite. And in this way the soul of Christ knows an infinite number of things, in so far as it knows them not by discoursing from one to another, but in some one thing; for example, in any creature in whose potency infinite things exist, and principally in the Word Himself.

Reply Obj. 2. There is nothing to hinder a thing from being infinite in one way and finite in another, as when in quantities we imagine a surface infinite in length and finite in breadth. Hence, if there were an infinite number of men, they would have a relative infinity—that is, in multitude; but, as regards the essence, they would be finite, since the essence of all would be limited to one specific nature. But what is infinite absolutely in its essence is God, as was said in the First Part (Q. VII, A. 2). Now "the proper object of the intellect is what a thing is," as is said in the book on the *Soul,*[4] to which pertains the notion of the species.

And thus the soul of Christ, since it has a finite capacity, attains to, but does not comprehend, what is absolutely infinite in essence, as stated above (A. 1). But the infinite in potency which is in creatures can be comprehended by the soul of Christ, since it is compared to that soul according to its essence, in which respect it is not infinite. For even our intellect understands a universal,—for example, the nature of a genus or species, which in a manner has infinity, in so far as it can be predicated of an infinite number.

Reply Obj. 3. That which is infinite in every way can be but one. Hence the Philosopher says[5] that since bodies have dimensions in every part there cannot be several infinite bodies. Yet if anything were infinite in one way only, nothing would hinder that there be several such infinite things, as if we were to suppose several lines of infinite length drawn on a surface of

---

[1] Aristotle, IX, 9 (1051ᵃ30).
[2] Aristotle, III, 6 (207ᵃ25).
[3] *Ibid.* (206ᵃ25). [4] Aristotle, III, 6 (430ᵇ28).
[5] *Heavens,* I, 7 (274ᵇ19).

finite breadth. Hence, because infinity is not a substance, but is accidental to things that are said to be infinite, as the Philosopher says,[1] just as the infinite is multiplied by different subjects, so, too, a property of the infinite must be multiplied, in such a way that it belongs to each of them according to that particular subject. Now it is a property of the infinite that nothing is greater than it. Hence, if we take one infinite line, there is nothing greater in it than the infinite; so, too, if we take any one of other infinite lines, it is plain that each has infinite parts. Therefore of necessity in this particular line there is nothing greater than all these infinite parts; yet in another or a third line there will be more infinite parts besides these. We observe this in numbers also, for the species of even numbers are infinite, and likewise the species of odd numbers are infinite; yet there are more even and odd numbers than even.

And thus it must be said that nothing is greater than the absolutely and in every way infinite; but than the infinite which is limited in some respect, nothing is greater in that order, although we may suppose something greater outside that order. In this way, therefore, there are infinite things in the power of the creature, and yet there are more in the power of God than in the power of the creature. So, too, the soul of Christ knows infinite things by the knowledge of simple intelligence, yet God knows more by this manner of knowledge or understanding.

ARTICLE 4. *Whether the Soul of Christ Sees the Word or the Divine Essence More Clearly Than Does Any Other Creature?*

We proceed thus to the Fourth Article: It would seem that the soul of Christ does not see the Word more perfectly than does any other creature.

Objection 1. For the perfection of knowledge depends upon the medium of knowing, just as the knowledge we have by means of a demonstrative syllogism is more perfect than that which we have by means of a probable syllogism. But all the blessed see the Word immediately in the Divine Essence Itself, as was said in the First Part (Q. XII, A. 2). Therefore the soul of Christ does not see the Word more perfectly than any other creature.

Obj. 2. Further, the perfection of vision does not exceed the power of seeing. But the rational power of a soul such as is the soul of Christ is below the intellectual power of an angel, as is plain from Dionysius (*Cæl. Hier,* iv).[2] Therefore the soul of Christ did not see the Word more perfectly than the angels.

Obj. 3. Further, God sees His Word infinitely more perfectly than does the soul. Hence there are infinite possible mediate degrees between the manner in which God sees His Word, and the manner in which the soul of Christ sees the Word. Therefore we cannot assert that the soul of Christ sees the Word or the Divine Essence more perfectly than does every other creature.

On the contrary, The Apostle says (Eph. 1. 20, 21) that God set Christ *on His right hand in the heavenly places, above all principality and power and virtue and dominion, and every name that is named not only in this world, but also in that which is to come.* But in that heavenly glory the higher anyone is the more perfectly does he know God. Therefore the soul of Christ sees God more perfectly than does any other creature.

I answer that, The vision of the Divine Essence is granted to all the blessed by a partaking of the Divine light which is shed upon them from the fountain of the Word of God, according to Ecclus. 1. 5: *The Word of God on high is the fountain of Wisdom.* Now the soul of Christ, since it is united to the Word in person, is more closely joined to the Word of God than any other creature. Hence it more fully receives the light in which God is seen by the Word Himself than any other creature. And therefore more perfectly than the rest of creatures it sees the First Truth itself, which is the Essence of God; hence it is written (John 1. 14): *And we saw His glory, the glory as it were of the Only-begotten of the Father, full* not only *of grace* but also of *truth.*

Reply Obj. 1. Perfection of knowledge, on the part of the thing known, depends on the medium; but as regards the knower, it depends on the power or habit. And hence it is that even amongst men one sees a conclusion in a medium more perfectly than another does. And in this way the soul of Christ, which is filled with a more abundant light, knows the Divine Essence more perfectly than do the other blessed, although all see the Divine Essence in itself.

Reply Obj. 2. The vision of the Divine Essence exceeds the natural power of any creature, as was said in the First Part (Q. XII, A. 4). And hence the degrees thereof depend rather on the order of grace in which Christ is supreme, than on the order of nature, in which the angelic nature is placed before the human.

---

[1] *Physics,* III, 5 (204ᵃ20).

[2] Sect. 2 (PG 3, 180).

Reply Obj. 3. As stated above (Q. VII, A. 12), there cannot be a greater grace than the grace of Christ with respect to the union with the Word; and the same is to be said of the perfection of the Divine vision, although, absolutely speaking, there could be a higher and more sublime degree by the infinity of the Divine power.

QUESTION XI
OF THE KNOWLEDGE IMPRINTED OR INFUSED IN THE SOUL OF CHRIST
(In Six Articles)

WE must now consider the knowledge imprinted or infused in the soul of Christ, and under this head there are six points of inquiry: (1) Whether Christ knows all things by this knowledge? (2) Whether He could use this knowledge without turning to phantasms? (3) Whether this knowledge was by way of comparison? (4) Of the comparison of this knowledge with the angelic knowledge. (5) Whether it was a habitual knowledge? (6) Whether it was distinguished by various habits?

ARTICLE 1. *Whether Christ Knew All Things by Imprinted or Infused Knowledge?*

We proceed thus to the First Article: It would seem that by this knowledge Christ did not know all things.

Objection 1. For this knowledge is imprinted upon Christ for the perfection of the possible intellect. Now the possible intellect of the human soul does not seem to be in potency to all things absolutely, but only to those things with regard to which it can be reduced to act by the agent intellect, which is its proper active principle; and these are knowable by natural reason. Therefore by this knowledge Christ did not know what exceeded the natural reason.

Obj. 2. Further, phantasms are to the human intellect as colours to sight, as is said in the book on the *Soul.*[1] But it does not pertain to the perfection of the power of seeing to know what is entirely without colour. Therefore it does not pertain to the perfection of human intellect to know things of which there can be no phantasms, such as separate substances. Hence, since this knowledge was in Christ for the perfection of His intellectual soul, it seems that by this knowledge He did not know separate substances.

Obj. 3. Further, it does not pertain to the perfection of the intellect to know singulars.

[1] Aristotle, III, 7 (431ᵃ14).

Hence it would seem that by this knowledge the soul of Christ did not know singulars.

On the contrary, It is written (Isa. 11. 2) that *the Spirit of wisdom and understanding, of knowledge and counsel shall fill Him,*[2] under which are included all knowable things; for the knowledge of all Divine things belongs to wisdom, the knowledge of all immaterial things to understanding, the knowledge of all conclusions to science, the knowledge of all practical things to counsel. Hence it would seem that by the knowledge infused in Him by the Holy Ghost Christ had the knowledge of all things.

I answer that, As was said above (Q. IX, A. 1), it was fitting that the soul of Christ should be wholly perfected by having each of its potentialities reduced to act. Now it must be borne in mind that in the human soul, as in every creature, there is a twofold passive power: one in relation to a natural agent; the other in relation to the first agent, which can reduce any creature to a higher act than a natural agent can reduce it, and this is usually called the obediential power of a creature. Now both powers of Christ's soul were reduced to act by this divinely imprinted knowledge. And hence, by it the soul of Christ knew first, whatever can be known by the power of the light of the agent intellect— as, for example, whatever pertains to human sciences; secondly, by this knowledge Christ knew all things made known to man by Divine revelation, whether they belong to the gift of wisdom or the gift of prophecy, or any other gift of the Holy Ghost; for the soul of Christ knew these things more fully and completely than others. Yet He did not know the Essence Itself of God by this knowledge, but by the first alone, of which we spoke above (Q. X).

Reply Obj. 1. This argument refers to the natural action of an intellectual soul in comparison with its natural agent, which is the agent intellect.

Reply Obj. 2. The human soul in the state of this life, since it is somewhat fettered by the body, so as to be unable to understand without phantasms, cannot understand separate substances. But after the state of this life the separated soul will be able, in a measure, to know separate substances by itself, as was said in the First Part (Q. LXXXIX, A. 2), and this is especially clear as regards the souls of the blessed. Now before His Passion, Christ was

[2] Vulg.: *The Spirit of the Lord shall rest upon Him, the Spirit of wisdom and understanding, the Spirit of counsel ... the Spirit of knowledge ... Cf.* Ecclus. 15.5.

not merely a wayfarer but also a comprehensor; hence His soul could know separate substances in the same way that a separated soul could.

Reply Obj. 3. The knowledge of singulars pertains to the perfection of the intellectual soul not in speculative knowledge, but in practical knowledge, which is imperfect without the knowledge of singulars, in which operations exist, as is said in the *Ethics.*[1] Hence for prudence are required the remembrance of past things, knowledge of present things, and foresight of future things, as Tully says.[2] Therefore, since Christ had the fulness of prudence by the gift of counsel, He consequently knew all singular things—present, past, and future.

ARTICLE 2. *Whether Christ Could Use This Knowledge Without Turning to Phantasms?*

We proceed thus to the Second Article: It would seem that the soul of Christ could not understand by this knowledge except by turning to phantasms.

Objection 1. For, as is stated in the book on the *Soul,*[3] phantasms are related to man's intellectual soul as colours to sight. But Christ's power of seeing could not become actual save by turning to colours. Therefore His intellectual soul could understand nothing except by turning to phantasms.

Obj. 2. Further, Christ's soul is of the same nature as ours; otherwise He would not be of the same species as we, contrary to what the Apostle says (Phil. 2. 7) . . . *being made in the likeness of men.* But our soul cannot understand except by turning to phantasms. Hence, neither can Christ's soul otherwise understand.

Obj. 3. Further, senses are given to man to help his intellect. Hence, if the soul of Christ could understand without turning to phantasms, which are received by the senses, it would follow that in the soul of Christ the senses were useless, which is not fitting. Therefore it seems that the soul of Christ can only understand by turning to phantasms.

On the contrary, The soul of Christ knew certain things which could not be known through phantasms, namely, separate substances. Therefore it could understand without turning to phantasms.

I answer that, In the state before His Passion Christ was at the same time a wayfarer and a comprehensor, as will be more clearly shown (Q. XV, A. 10). Especially had He the conditions of a wayfarer on the part of the body, which was passible; but the conditions of a comprehensor He had chiefly on the part of the intellectual soul. Now this is the condition of the soul of a comprehensor—namely, that it is in no way subject to its body, or dependent upon it, but wholly dominates it. Hence after the resurrection glory will flow from the soul to the body. But the soul of man on earth needs to turn to phantasms, because it is fettered by the body and in a measure subject to and dependent upon it. And hence the souls of the blessed both before and after the resurrection can understand without turning to phantasms. And this must be said of the soul of Christ, which had fully the capabilities of a comprehensor.

Reply Obj. 1. This likeness which the Philosopher asserts is not with regard to everything. For it is manifest that the end of the power of seeing is to know colours; but the end of the intellectual power is not to know phantasms, but to know intelligible species, which it apprehends from and in phantasms, according to the state of the present life. Therefore there is a likeness in respect of what both powers regard, but not in respect of that in which the condition of both powers is terminated. Now nothing prevents a thing in different states from reaching its end by different ways, although the proper end of a thing is always one. Hence, although the sight knows nothing without colour, nevertheless in a certain state the intellect can know without phantasms, but not without intelligible species.

Reply Obj. 2. Although the soul of Christ was of the same nature as our souls, yet it had a state which our souls have not yet in fact, but only in hope—that is, the state of comprehension.

Reply Obj. 3. Although the soul of Christ could understand without turning to phantasms, yet it could also understand by turning to phantasms. Hence the senses were not useless in it; especially as the senses are not afforded to man solely for intellectual knowledge, but also for the need of animal life.

ARTICLE 3. *Whether This Knowledge Was By Way of Comparison?*

We proceed thus to the Third Article: It would seem that the soul of Christ had not this knowledge by way of comparison.

Objection 1. For Damascene says (*De Fide Orthod.* iii, 14):[4] "We do not uphold counsel

---

[1] Aristotle, VI, 7 (1141^{b}14).
[2] *Rhetoric,* II, 53 (DD 1, 165).
[3] Aristotle, III, 7 (431^{a}14).
[4] PG 94, 1044. Cf. II, 22 (PG 94, 948).

or choice in Christ." Now these things are withheld from Christ only in so far as they imply comparison and discursion. Therefore it seems that there was no knowledge by way of comparison or discursive knowledge in Christ.

Obj. 2. Further, man needs comparison and discursion of reason in order to find out the unknown. But the soul of Christ knew everything, as was said above (Q. X, A. 2). Hence there was no discursive or collative knowledge in Him.

Obj. 3. Further, the knowledge in Christ's soul was like that of comprehensors, who are likened to the angels, according to Matt. 22. 30. Now there is no collative or discursive knowledge in the angels, as Dionysius shows (*Div. Nom.* vii).[1] Therefore there was no discursive or collative knowledge in the soul of Christ.

On the contrary, Christ had a rational soul, as was shown (Q. V, A. 4). Now the proper operation of a rational soul consists in bringing together and discursion from one thing to another. Therefore there was collative or discursive knowledge in Christ.

I answer that, Knowledge may be discursive or collative in two ways. First, in the acquisition of the knowledge, as happens to us, who proceed from one thing to the knowledge of another, as from causes to effects, and conversely. And in this way the knowledge in Christ's soul was not discursive or collative, since this knowledge which we are now considering was divinely infused in Him, and not acquired by the searching of reasoning.

Secondly, knowledge may be called discursive or collative in use, as at times those who know, conclude to the effect from the causes, not in order to learn anew, but wishing to use the knowledge they already have. And in this way the knowledge in Christ's soul could be collative or discursive, since it could conclude one thing from another as it pleased, as in Matt. 17. 24, 25, when Our Lord asked Peter: *Of whom do the kings of the earth receive tribute, of their own children, or of strangers?* on Peter replying: *Of strangers,* He concluded: *Then the children are free.*

Reply Obj. 1. From Christ is excluded that counsel which is with doubt, and consequently choice, which essentially includes such counsel; but the use of counsel is not excluded from Christ.

Reply Obj. 2. This reason rests upon discursion and comparison, as used to acquire knowledge.

Reply Obj. 3. The blessed are likened to the

[1] Sect. 2 (PG 3, 868).

angels in the gifts of graces, yet there still remains the difference of natures. And hence to use comparison and discursion is connatural to the souls of the blessed, but not to angels.

ARTICLE 4. *Whether in Christ This Knowledge Was Greater Than the Knowledge of the Angels?*

We proceed thus to the Fourth Article: It would seem that this knowledge was not greater in Christ than in the angels.

Objection 1. For perfection is proportioned to the thing perfected. But the human soul in the order of nature is below the angelic nature. Therefore since the knowledge we are now speaking of is imprinted upon Christ's soul for its perfection, it seems that this knowledge is less than the knowledge by which the angelic nature is perfected.

Obj. 2. Further, the knowledge of Christ's soul was in a measure comparative and discursive, which cannot be said of the angelic knowledge. Therefore the knowledge of Christ's soul was less than the knowledge of the angels.

Obj. 3. Further, the more immaterial knowledge is, the greater it is. But the knowledge of the angels is more immaterial than the knowledge of Christ's soul, since the soul of Christ is the act of a body, and turns to phantasms, which cannot be said of the angels. Therefore the knowledge of angels is greater than the knowledge of Christ's soul.

On the contrary, The Apostle says (Heb. 2. 9): *For we see Jesus, Who was made a little lower than the angels, for the suffering of death, crowned with glory and honour,* from which it is plain that Christ is said to be lower than the angels only in regard to the suffering of death. And hence, not in knowledge.

I answer that, The knowledge imprinted on Christ's soul may be looked at in two ways: first, as regards what it has from the inflowing cause; secondly, as regards what it has from the subject receiving it. Now with regard to the first, the knowledge imprinted upon the soul of Christ was much more excellent than the knowledge of the angels, both in the number of things known and in the certainty of the knowledge, since the spiritual light, which is imprinted on the soul of Christ, is much more excellent than the light which pertains to the angelic nature. But as regards the second, the knowledge imprinted on the soul of Christ is less than the angelic knowledge, in the manner of knowing that is natural to the human soul—that is, by turning to phantasms, and by comparison and discursion.

And thus the *reply to the objections* is made clear.

ARTICLE 5. *Whether This Knowledge Was Habitual?*

We proceed thus to the Fifth Article: It would seem that in Christ there was no habitual knowledge.

Objection 1. For it has been said (A. 1; Q. IX, A. 1) that the highest perfection of knowledge befitted Christ's soul. But the perfection of an actually existing knowledge is greater than that of a potentially or habitually existing knowledge. Therefore it was fitting for Him to know all things actually. Therefore He had not habitual knowledge.

Obj. 2. Further, since habits are ordered to acts, a habitual knowledge which is never reduced to act would seem in vain. Now, since Christ knew all things, as was said A. 1, He could not have considered all things actually, thinking over one after another, since the infinite cannot be passed over by enumeration. Therefore the habitual knowledge of certain things would have been in vain to Him,—which is unfitting. Therefore He had an actual and not a habitual knowledge of what He knew.

Obj. 3. Further, habitual knowledge is a perfection of the knower. But perfection is more noble than the thing perfected. If, therefore, in the soul of Christ there was any created habit of knowledge, it would follow that this created thing was nobler than the soul of Christ. Therefore there was no habitual knowledge in Christ's soul.

On the contrary, The knowledge of Christ we are now speaking about was univocal with our knowledge, even as His soul was of the same species as ours. But our knowledge is in the genus of habit. Therefore the knowledge of Christ was habitual.

I answer that, As stated above (A. 4), the mode of the knowledge impressed on the soul of Christ befitted the subject receiving it. For the thing received is in the receiver according to the mode of the receiver. Now the connatural mode of the human soul is that it should sometimes be understanding in act, and sometimes in potency. But the medium between a pure power and a completed act is a habit, and extremes and medium are of the same genus. Thus it is plain that it is the connatural mode of the human soul to receive knowledge as a habit. Hence it must be said that the knowledge imprinted on the soul of Christ was habitual, and that He could use it when He pleased.

Reply Obj. 1. In Christ's soul there was a twofold knowledge, each most perfect of its kind. The first exceeded the mode of human nature, as by it He saw the Essence of God, and other things in It, and this was the most perfect, absolutely. Nor was this knowledge habitual, but actual with respect to everything He knew in this way. But the second knowledge was in Christ in a manner proportioned to human nature, that is, according as He knew things by species divinely imprinted upon Him, and of this knowledge we are now speaking. Now this knowledge was not most perfect, absolutely, but merely in the genus of human knowledge; hence it was not necessary for it to be always in act.

Reply Obj. 2. A habit is reduced to act by the command of the will, since a habit is that which we act when we will. Now the will is indeterminate in regard to infinite things. Yet it is not in vain, even when it does not actually tend to all things, provided it actually tends to what is fitting according to the place and time. And hence neither is a habit in vain even if all that it extends to is not reduced to act, provided that that which befits the due end of the will be reduced to act according as the matter in hand and the time require.

Reply Obj. 3. Goodness and being are taken in two ways. First, absolutely, and thus a substance, which subsists in its being and goodness, is a good and a being; secondly, being and goodness are taken relatively, and in this way an accident is a being and a good, not that it has being and goodness, but that its subject is a being and a good. And hence habitual knowledge is not absolutely better or more excellent than the soul of Christ, but relatively, since the whole goodness of habitual knowledge is added to the goodness of the subject.

ARTICLE 6. *Whether This Knowledge Was Distinguished By Divers Habits?*

We proceed thus to the Sixth Article: It would seem that in the soul of Christ there was only one habit of knowledge.

Objection 1. For the more perfect knowledge is, the more united it is; hence the higher angels understand by the more universal forms, as was said in the First Part (Q. LV, A. 3). Now Christ's knowledge was most perfect. Therefore it was most one. Therefore it was not distinguished by several habits.

Obj. 2. Further, our faith is derived from Christ's knowledge; hence it is written (Heb. 12. 2): *Looking on Jesus the author and finisher of faith.* But there is only one habit of faith about all things subject to belief, as was said in the Second Part (II-II, Q. IV, A. 6). Much more, therefore, was there only one habit of knowledge in Christ.

Obj. 3. Further, knowledge is distinguished by the various aspects (*ratio*) of knowable things. But the soul of Christ knew everything under one aspect—that is, by a divinely infused light. Therefore in Christ there was only one habit of knowledge.

On the contrary, It is written (*Zach.* 3. 9) that on *one stone*, that is, Christ, *there are seven eyes.* Now by the eye is understood knowledge. Therefore it would seem that in Christ there were several habits of knowledge.

I answer that, As stated above (A. 4), the knowledge imprinted on Christ's soul has a mode connatural to a human soul. Now it is connatural to a human soul to receive species of a lesser universality than the angels receive, so that it knows different specific natures by different intelligible species. But it so happens that we have different habits of knowledge because there are different genera of knowable things, inasmuch as what are reduced to one genus are known by the same habit of knowledge; thus it is said (*Poster.* i, 28),[1] that "one science is of what falls under one genus." And hence the knowledge imprinted on Christ's soul was distinguished by different habits.

Reply Obj. 1. As was said (A. 4), the knowledge of Christ's soul is most perfect, and exceeds the knowledge of angels with regard to what is in it on the part of God's gift; but it is below the angelic knowledge as regards the mode of the recipient. And it pertains to this mode that this knowledge is distinguished by various habits, as if it existed in more particular species.

Reply Obj. 2. Our faith rests upon the First Truth, and hence Christ is the author of our faith by the Divine knowledge, which is absolutely one.

Reply Obj. 3. The divinely infused light is the common aspect for understanding what is divinely revealed, as the light of the understanding is with regard to what is naturally known. Hence, in the soul of Christ there must be the proper species of singular things, in order to know each with proper knowledge; and in this way there must be various habits of knowledge in Christ's soul, as stated above.

[1] Aristotle, *Posterior Analytics*, I, 28 (87ᵃ38).

QUESTION XII

OF THE ACQUIRED KNOWLEDGE OF CHRIST'S SOUL

(*In Four Articles*)

WE must now consider the acquired or experimental knowledge of Christ's soul; and under this head there are four points of inquiry. (1) Whether Christ knew all things by this knowledge? (2) Whether He advanced in this knowledge? (3) Whether He learnt anything from man? (4) Whether He received anything from angels?

ARTICLE 1. *Whether Christ Knew All Things By this Knowledge?*

We proceed thus to the First Article: It would seem that Christ did not know everything by this knowledge.

Objection 1. For this knowledge is acquired by experience. But Christ did not experience everything. Therefore He did not know everything by this knowledge.

Obj. 2. Further, man acquires knowledge through the senses. But not all sensible things were subjected to Christ's bodily senses. Therefore Christ did not know everything by this knowledge.

Obj. 3. Further, the extent of knowledge depends on the things knowable. Therefore if Christ knew all things by this knowledge, His acquired knowledge would have been equal to His infused and beatific knowledge, which is not fitting. Therefore Christ did not know all things by this knowledge.

On the contrary, Nothing imperfect was in Christ's soul. Now this knowledge of His would have been imperfect if He had not known all things by it, since the imperfect is that to which addition may be made. Hence Christ knew all things by this knowledge.

I answer that, Acquired knowledge is held to be in Christ's soul, as we have said Q. IX, A. 4, by reason of the agent intellect, lest its action, which is to make things intelligible in act, should be useless; even as imprinted or infused knowledge is held to be in Christ's soul for the perfection of the possible intellect. Now "just as the possible intellect is that by which all things are in potency, so the agent intellect is that by which all are in act," as is said in the book on the *Soul.*[2] And hence, as the soul of Christ knew by infused knowledge all things to which the possible intellect is in any

[2] Aristotle, III, 5 (430ᵃ14).

way in potency, so by acquired knowledge it knew whatever can be known by the action of the agent intellect.

Reply Obj. 1. The knowledge of things may be acquired not merely by experiencing the things themselves, but by experiencing other things, since by the power of the light of the agent intellect man can go on to understand effects from causes, and causes from effects, like from like, contrary from contrary. Therefore Christ, though He did not experience all things, came to the knowledge of all things from what He did experience.

Reply Obj. 2. Although all sensible things were not subjected to Christ's bodily senses, yet other sensible things were subjected to His senses, and from this He could come to know other things by the most excellent power of His reason, in the manner described in the previous reply; just as in seeing heavenly bodies He could comprehend their powers and the effects they have upon things here below, which were not subjected to His senses. And for the same reason, from any other things whatsoever, He could come to the knowledge of yet other things.

Reply Obj. 3. By this knowledge the soul of Christ did not know all things absolutely, but all such as are knowable by the light of man's agent intellect. Hence by this knowledge He did not know the essences of separate substances, nor past, present, or future singulars, which, nevertheless, He knew by infused knowledge, as was said above (Q. XI).

ARTICLE 2. *Whether Christ Advanced in This Knowledge?*

We proceed thus to the Second Article: It would seem that Christ did not advance in this knowledge.

Objection 1. For even as Christ knew all things by His beatific and His infused knowledge, so also did He by this acquired knowledge, as is plain from what has been said (A. 1). But He did not advance in these knowledges. Therefore neither in this.

Obj. 2. Further, to advance belongs to the imperfect, since the perfect cannot be added to. Now we cannot suppose an imperfect knowledge in Christ. Therefore Christ did not advance in this knowledge.

Obj. 3. Further, Damascene says (*De Fide Orthod.* iii, 22):[1] "Whoever say that Christ advanced in wisdom and grace, as if receiving additional sensations, do not venerate the union

which is in hypostasis." But it is impious not to venerate this union. Therefore it is impious to say that His knowledge received increase.

On the contrary, It is written (Luke 2. 52): *Jesus advanced in wisdom and age and grace with God and men;* and Ambrose says (*De Incar. Dom.* vii)[2] that He advanced in human wisdom. Now human wisdom is that which is acquired in a human manner—that is, by the light of the agent intellect. Therefore Christ advanced in this knowledge.

I answer that, There is a twofold advancement in knowledge: one in essence, according as the habit of knowledge is increased; the other in effect—for example, if someone were with one and the same habit of knowledge to prove to someone else some minor truths at first, and afterwards greater and more subtle conclusions. Now in this second way it is plain that Christ advanced in knowledge and grace, even as in age, since as His age increased He wrought greater deeds, and showed greater knowledge and grace. But as regards the habit of knowledge, it is plain that His habit of infused knowledge did not increase, since from the beginning He had perfect infused knowledge of all things; and still less could His beatific knowledge increase; while in the First Part (Q. XIV, A. 15; REPLY 2) we have already said that His Divine knowledge could not increase.

Therefore, if in the soul of Christ there was no habit of acquired knowledge, beyond the habit of infused knowledge, as appears to some,[3] and once appeared to me[4], no knowledge in Christ increased in essence, but merely by experience—that is, by the comparison of the infused intelligible species with phantasms. And in this way they maintain that Christ's knowledge grew in experience—for example, by comparing the infused intelligible species with what He received through the senses for the first time.

But because it seems unfitting than any natural intelligible action should be wanting to Christ, and because to extract intelligible species from phantasms is a natural action of man's agent intellect, it seems becoming to place even this action in Christ. And it follows from this that in the soul of Christ there was a habit of

---

[1] PG 94, 1088.

[2] PL 16, 872.

[3] Bonaventure, *In Sent.*, III, d. XIV, A. 3, Q. 2 (QR III, 322); Alexander of Hales, *Summa Theol.*, Pt. III, Q. XIII, m. 2 (III, 42vb); cf. John Damascene, *De Fide Ortho.*, III, 13 (PG 94, 1033); William of Auxerre, *Summa Aurea*, Pt. III, tr. 1, chap. 5, Q. 1 (116vb); Albert, *In Sent.*, III, d. XIII, A. 10 (BO XXVIII, 249).

[4] *In Sent.*, III, d. XIV, A. 3; d. XVIII, A. 3, ad 5.

knowledge which could increase by this abstraction of species, since the agent intellect, after abstracting the first intelligible species from phantasms, could abstract others, and others again.

Reply Obj. 1. Both the infused knowledge and the beatific knowledge of Christ's soul were the effects of an agent of infinite power, which could produce the whole at once; and thus in neither knowledge did Christ advance, since from the beginning He had them perfectly. But the acquired knowledge is caused by the agent intellect which does not produce the whole at once, but successively; and hence by this knowledge Christ did not know everything from the beginning, but step by step, and after a time—that is, in His perfect age; and this is plain from what the Evangelist says, namely, that He increased in knowledge and age together.

Reply Obj. 2. Even this knowledge was always perfect for the time being, although it was not always perfect absolutely and in comparison to the nature; hence it could increase.

Reply Obj. 3. This saying of Damascene regards those[1] who say absolutely that addition was made to Christ's knowledge—that is, as regards any knowledge of His, and especially as regards the infused knowledge which is caused in Christ's soul by union with the Word; but it does not regard the increase of knowledge caused by the natural agent.

ARTICLE 3. *Whether Christ Learned Anything from Man?*

We proceed thus to the Third Article: It would seem that Christ learned something from man.

Objection 1. For it is written (Luke 2. 46, 47) that, *They found Him in the temple in the midst of the doctors, hearing them, and asking them questions.* But to ask questions and to reply pertains to a learner. Therefore Christ learned something from man.

Obj. 2. Further, to acquire knowledge from a man's teaching seems more noble than to acquire it from sensible things, since in the soul of the man who teaches the intelligible species are in act, but in sensible things the intelligible species are only in potency. Now Christ received experimental knowledge from sensible things, as stated above (A. 2; Q. IX,

A. 4). Much more, therefore, could He receive knowledge by learning from men.

Obj. 3. Further, by experimental knowledge Christ did not know everything from the beginning, but advanced in it, as was said above (A. 2). But anyone hearing words which mean something may learn something he does not know. Therefore Christ could learn from men something He did not know by this knowledge.

On the contrary, It is written (Ps. 55. 4): *Behold, I have given Him for a witness to the people, for a leader and a master to the Gentiles.* Now a master is not taught, but teaches. Therefore Christ did not receive any knowledge by the teaching of any man.

I answer that, In any genus that which is the first mover is not moved according to the same species of movement, just as the first principle of change is not itself changed. Now Christ is established by God the Head of the Church—indeed, of all men, as was said above (Q. VIII., A. 3), so that not only all might receive grace through Him, but that all might receive the doctrine of Truth from Him. Hence He Himself says (John 18. 37): *For this was I born, and for this came I into the world; that I should give testimony to the truth.* And thus it did not befit His dignity that He should be taught by any man.

Reply Obj. 1. As Origen says (*Hom. xix in Luc.*):[2] "Our Lord asked questions not in order to learn anything, but in order to teach by questioning. For from the same well of knowledge came the question and the wise reply." Hence the Gospel goes on to say that *all that heard Him were astonished at His wisdom and His answers.*

Reply Obj. 2. Whoever learns from man does not receive knowledge immediately from the intelligible species which are in his mind, but through sensible words, which are signs of intelligible concepts. Now as words formed by a man are signs of his intellectual knowledge, so are creatures, formed by God, signs of His wisdom. Hence it is written (Ecclus. 1. 10) that God *poured* wisdom *out upon all His works.* Hence, just as it is better to be taught by God than by man, so it is better to receive our knowledge from sensible creatures and not by man's teaching.

Reply Obj. 3. Jesus advanced in experimental knowledge, as in age, as stated above (A. 2). Now as a fitting age is required for a man to acquire knowledge by discovery, so also that he may acquire it by being taught. But our

---

[1] Cf. Abelard, *Sic et Non*, Sect. 76 (PL 178, 1451); see DTC, art. *Agnoètes* (I, 589); art. *Jésus-Christ* (VIII, 1259); art. *Science de Jésus-Christ* (XIV, 1635).

[2] Translation of Jerome (PG 13, 1851; cf. PL 26, 240).

Lord did nothing unbecoming to His age, and hence He did not give ear to hearing the lessons of doctrine until such time as He was able to have reached that grade of knowledge by way of experience. Hence Gregory says (*Sup. Ezech.* Lib. i, Hom. ii):[1] "In the twelfth year of His age He deigned to question men on earth, since in the course of reason, the word of doctrine is not vouchsafed before the age of perfection."

ARTICLE 4. *Whether Christ Received Knowledge from the Angels?*

We proceed thus to the Fourth Article: It would seem that Christ received knowledge from the angels.

Objection 1. For it is written (Luke 22. 43) that *there appeared to Him an angel from heaven, strengthening Him.* But we are strengthened by the comforting words of a teacher, according to Job. 4. 3, 4: *Behold thou hast taught many and hast strengthened the weary hand. Thy words have confirmed them that were staggering.* Therefore Christ was taught by angels.

Obj. 2. Further, Dionysius says (*Cæl. Hier.* iv):[2] "For I see that even Jesus,—the supersubstantial substance of supercelestial substances—when without change He took our substance upon Himself, was subject in obedience to the instructions of the Father and God by the angels." Hence it seems that even Christ wished to be subject to the decrees of the Divine law, whereby men are taught by means of angels.

Obj. 3. Further, as in the natural order the human body is subject to the celestial bodies, so likewise is the human mind to angelic minds. Now Christ's body was subject to the impressions of the heavenly bodies, for He felt the heat in summer and the cold in winter, and other human passions. Therefore His human mind was subject to the illuminations of supercelestial spirits.

On the contrary, Dionysius says (*Cæl. Hier.* vii)[3] that "the highest angels question Jesus, and learn the knowledge of His Divine work, and of the flesh assumed for us; and Jesus teaches them directly." Now to teach and to be taught do not belong to the same. Therefore Christ did not receive knowledge from the angels.

I answer that, Since the human soul is midway between spiritual substances and corporeal things, it is perfected naturally in two ways. First by knowledge received from sensible things; secondly, by knowledge imprinted or infused by the illumination of spiritual substances. Now in both these ways the soul of Christ was perfected; first by experimental knowledge of sensible things, for which there is no need of angelic light, since the light of the agent intellect suffices; secondly, by the higher impression of infused knowledge, which He received directly from God. For as His soul was united to the Word above the common mode, in unity of person, so above the common manner of men was it filled with knowledge and grace by the Word of God Himself, and not by the medium of angels, who in their beginning received the knowledge of things by the influence of the Word, as Augustine says (*Gen. ad lit.* ii, 8).[4]

Reply Obj. 1. This strengthening by the angel was for the purpose not of instructing Him, but of proving the truth of His human nature. Hence Bede says (on Luke 22. 43):[5] "In testimony of both natures are the angels said to have ministered to Him and to have strengthened Him. For the Creator did not need help from His creature; but having become man, even as it was for our sake that He was sad, so was it for our sake that He was strengthened"—that is, in order that our faith in the Incarnation might be strengthened.

Reply Obj. 2. Dionysius says that Christ was subject to the angelic instructions not by reason of Himself, but by reason of what happened at His Incarnation, and as regards the care of Him whilst He was a child. Hence in the same place he adds that *Jesus' withdrawal to Egypt decreed by the Father is announced to Joseph by angels, and again His return to Judæa from Egypt.*

Reply Obj. 3. The Son of God assumed a passible body (as will be said hereafter, Q. XIV, A. 1) and a soul perfect in knowledge and grace (Q. XIV, A. 1, reply 1; A. 4). Hence His body was rightly subject to the impression of heavenly bodies; but His soul was not subject to the impression of heavenly spirits.

QUESTION XIII
OF THE POWER OF CHRIST'S SOUL
(*In Four Articles*)

WE must now consider the power of Christ's soul; and under this head there are four points of inquiry: (1) Whether He had omnipotence absolutely? (2) Whether He had omnipotence with regard to corporeal creatures? (3) Wheth-

---

[1] PL 76, 796.
[2] Sect. 4 (PG 3, 181).   [3] Sect. 3 (PG 3, 209).
[4] PL 34, 269.   [5] PL 92, 603.

er He had omnipotence with regard to His own body? (4) Whether He had omnipotence as regards the execution of His own will?

ARTICLE 1. *Whether the Soul of Christ Had Omnipotence Absolutely?*

We proceed thus to the First Article: It would seem that the soul of Christ had omnipotence.

Objection 1. For Ambrose says on Luke 1. 32:[1] "The power which the Son of God had naturally, the Man was about to receive in time." Now this would seem to regard the soul principally, since it is the chief part of man. Hence since the Son of God had omnipotence from all eternity, it would seem that the soul of Christ received omnipotence in time.

Obj. 2. Further, as the power of God is infinite, so is His knowledge. But the soul of Christ in a manner had the knowledge of all that God knows, as was said above (Q. X, A. 2). Therefore He had all power, and thus He was omnipotent.

Obj. 3. Further, the soul of Christ has all knowledge. Now knowledge is either practical or speculative. Therefore He has a practical knowledge of what He knows—that is, He knew how to do what He knows; and thus it seems that He can do all things.

On the contrary, What is proper to God cannot belong to any creature. But it is proper to God to be omnipotent, according to Exod. 15. 2, 3: *He is my God and I will glorify Him,* and further on, *Almighty is His name.* Therefore the soul of Christ, as being a creature, has not omnipotence.

I answer that, As was said above (Q. II, A. 1; Q. X, A. 1) in the mystery of the Incarnation the union in person so took place that there still remained the distinction of natures, each nature still retaining what belonged to it. Now the active power of a thing follows its form, which is the principle of action. But the form is either the very nature of the thing, as in simple things, or is the constituent of the nature of the thing, as in such as are composed of matter and form. Hence it is clear that the active power of anything follows from its nature. And it is in this way that omnipotence is something that follows upon the Divine Nature. For since the Divine Nature is the very uncircumscribed Being of God, as is plain from Dionysius (*Div. Nom.* v),[2] It has an active power over everything that can have the nature of being, and

this is to have omnipotence; just as every other thing has an active power over such things as the perfection of its nature extends to, as for instance what is hot gives heat. Therefore since the soul of Christ is a part of human nature, it cannot possibly have omnipotence.

Reply Obj. 1. By union with the Person, the Man receives omnipotence in time, which the Son of God had from eternity. The result of this union is that as the Man is said to be God, so is He said to be omnipotent; not that the omnipotence of the Man is distinct (as neither is His Godhead) from that of the Son of God, but because there is one Person of God and man.

Reply Obj. 2. According to some,[3] knowledge and active power are not of the same character; for an active power flows from the very nature of the thing, for the reason that action is considered to come forth from the agent; but knowledge is not always possessed by the very essence of the knower, since it may be had by assimilation of the knower to the thing known by the aid of likenesses that are received.

But this reason seems not to be enough, because even as we may understand by a likeness obtained from another, so also may we act by a form obtained from another, as water or iron heats, by heat borrowed from fire. Hence there would be no reason why the soul of Christ, as it can know all things by the likenesses of all things impressed upon it by God, cannot do these things by the same likenesses.

It has, therefore, to be further considered that what is received in the lower nature from the higher is possessed in an inferior manner; for heat is not received by water in the perfection and strength it had in fire. Therefore, since the soul of Christ is of an inferior nature to the Divine Nature, the likenesses of things are not received in the soul of Christ in the perfection and strength they had in the Divine Nature. And hence it is that the knowledge of Christ's soul is inferior to Divine knowledge as regards the manner of knowing, for God knows things more perfectly than the soul of Christ; and also as regards the number of things known, since the soul of Christ does not know all that God can do, and these God knows by the knowledge of simple intelligence (although it knows all things present, past, and future which God knows by the knowledge of vision). So, too, the likenesses of things infused into Christ's soul do not equal the Divine power in acting—that

---

[1] *Glossa ordin.* (v, 125A); cf. Bede, *hom.* 1 (PL 94, 11); See Peter Lombard, *Sent.,* III, d. XIV, chap. 2 (QR II, 610).

[2] Sect. 4 (PG 3, 817).

[3] Peter Lombard, *Sent.,* III, d. XIV, chap. 1(QR II, 608); see William of Auxerre, *Summa Aurea,* III, 1, chap. 5, Q. 1 (117ra).

is, so as to do all that God can do, or to do in the same manner as God does, Who acts with an infinite might wherof the creature is not capable. Now there is no thing to know which in some way an infinite power is needed, although a certain kind of knowledge belongs to an infinite power; yet there are things which can be done only by an infinite power, as creation and the like, as is plain from what has been said in the First Part (Q. XLV, A. 5, Reply 3; Q. LXV, A. 3, Reply 3; Q. XXV, A. 3, Reply 4). Hence Christ's soul which, being a creature, is finite in power, can know, indeed, all things, but not in every way. Yet it cannot do all things, which pertains to the nature of omnipotence; and, amongst other things, it is clear that it cannot create itself.

Reply Obj. 3. Christ's soul has practical and speculative knowledge, yet it is not necessary that it should have practical knowledge of all those things of which it has speculative knowledge. Because for speculative knowledge a mere conformity or assimilation of the knower to the thing known suffices, whereas for practical knowledge it is required that the forms of the things in the intellect should be operative. Now to have a form and to impress this form upon something else is more than merely to have the form; as to shine and to illuminate is more than merely to shine. Hence the soul of Christ has a speculative knowledge of creation (for it knows how God creates), but it has no practical knowledge of this mode, since it has no knowledge operative of creation.

ARTICLE 2. *Whether the Soul of Christ Had Omnipotence With Regard To the Changing of Creatures?*

We proceed thus to the Second Article: It would seem that the soul of Christ had omnipotence with regard to the changing of creatures.

Objection 1. For He Himself says (Matt. 28. 18): *All power is given to Me in heaven and on earth.* Now by the words "heaven and earth" are meant all creatures, as is plain from Gen. 1. 1: *In the beginning God created heaven and earth.* Therefore it seems that the soul of Christ had omnipotence with regard to the changing of creatures.

Obj. 2. Further, the soul of Christ is the most perfect of all creatures. But every creature can be moved by another creature; for Augustine says (*De Trin.* iii, 4)[1] that "even as the denser and lower bodies are ruled in a fixed way by the subtler and stronger bodies, so are all bodies by

the spirit rational of life; and the truant and sinful rational spirit of life by the rational, loyal and righteous spirit of life." But the soul of Christ moves even the highest spirits, enlightening them, as Dionysius says (*Cæl. Hier.* vii)[2] Therefore it seems that the soul of Christ has omnipotence with regard to the changing of creatures.

Obj. 3. Further, Christ's soul had in its highest degree the grace of miracles or works of power as well as the rest of the graces. But every change of the creature can belong to the grace of miracles, since even the heavenly bodies were miraculously changed from their course, as Dionysius proves (*Ep. ad Polycarp.*).[3] Therefore Christ's soul had omnipotence with regard to the changing of creatures.

On the contrary, To transmute creatures belongs to Him Who conserves them. Now this belongs to God alone, according to Heb. 1. 3: *Upholding all things by the word of His power.* Therefore God alone has omnipotence with regard to the changing of creatures. Therefore this does not belong to Christ's soul.

I answer that, Two distinctions are here needed. Of these the first is with respect to the changing of creatures, which is threefold. The first is natural, being brought about by the proper agent according to the order of nature; the second is miraculous, being brought about by a supernatural agent above the accustomed order and course of nature, as to raise the dead; the third is according as every creature may be brought to nothing.

The second distinction has to do with Christ's soul, which may be looked at in two ways: first in its proper nature and with its power of nature or of grace; secondly, as it is the instrument of the Word of God, personally united to Him.

Therefore if we speak of the soul of Christ in its proper nature and with its power whether of nature or of grace, it had power to cause those effects proper to a soul (for example, to rule the body and direct human acts, and also, by the fulness of grace and knowledge to enlighten all rational creatures falling short of its perfection), in a manner befitting a rational creature.

But if we speak of the soul of Christ as it is the instrument of the Word united to Him, it had an instrumental power to effect all the miraculous changes which can be ordered to the end of the Incarnation, which is to re-establish all things that are in heaven and on earth.

But the changings of creatures according as

they may be brought to nothing corresponds to the creation of things, whereby they were brought from nothing. And hence even as God alone can create, so, too, He alone can return creatures to nothing, and He alone upholds them in being, lest they fall back to nothing. And thus it must be said that the soul of Christ had not omnipotence with regard to the changing of creatures.

Reply Obj. 1. As Jerome says:[1] "Power is given Him"—that is, to Christ as man—"Who a little while before was crucified, buried in the tomb, and afterwards rose again." But all power is said to have been given Him by reason of the union, whereby it was brought about that a Man was omnipotent, as was said above (A. 1, Reply 1). And although this was made known to the angels before the Resurrection, yet after the Resurrection it was made known to all men, as Remigius says.[2] Now, things are said to happen when they are made known. Hence after the Resurrection our Lord says *that all power is given* to Him *in heaven and on earth.*

Reply Obj. 2. Although every creature can be changed by some other creature, except, indeed, the highest angel, and even it can be enlightened by Christ's soul, yet not every change that can be made in a creature can be made by a creature, since some changes can be made by God alone. Yet all changes that can be made in creatures can be made by the soul of Christ, as the instrument of the Word, but not in its proper nature and power, since some of these changes pertain to the soul neither in the order of nature nor in the order of grace.

Reply Obj. 3. As was said in the Second Part (II-II, Q. CLXXVIII, A. 1, Reply 1), the grace of mighty works or miracles is given to the soul of a saint, so that these miracles are wrought not by his own, but by Divine power. Now this grace was bestowed on Christ's soul most excellently—that is, not only that He might work miracles, but also that He might communicate this grace to others. Hence it is written (Matt. 10. 1) that, *having called His twelve disciples together, He gave them power over unclean spirits, to cast them out, and to heal all manner of diseases, and all manner of infirmities.*

ARTICLE 3. *Whether the Soul of Christ Had Omnipotence With Regard To His Own Body?*

We proceed thus to the Third Article: It would seem that Christ's soul had omnipotence with regard to His own body.

Objection 1. For Damascene says (*De Fide Orthod.* iii, 20)[3] that all natural things were voluntary to Christ; "He willed to hunger, He willed to thirst, He willed to fear, He willed to die, etc." Now God is called omnipotent because *He hath done all things whatsoever He would* (Ps. 113. 11). Therefore it seems that Christ's soul had omnipotence with regard to the natural operations of His own body.

Obj. 2. Further, human nature was more perfect in Christ than in Adam, who had a body entirely subject to the soul, so that nothing could happen to the body against the will of the soul—and this on account of the original justice which it had in the state of innocence. Much more, therefore, had Christ's soul omnipotence with regard to His body.

Obj. 3. Further, the body is naturally changed by the imagination of the soul, and so much more changed the stronger the soul's imagination, as was said in the First Part (Q. CXVII, A. 3, Reply 2, 3). Now the soul of Christ had most perfect strength as regards both the imagination and the other powers. Therefore the soul of Christ was omnipotent with regard to His own body.

On the contrary, It is written (Heb. 2. 17) that *it behoved Him in all things to be made like unto His brethren,* and especially as regards what belongs to the condition of human nature. But it belongs to the condition of human nature that the health of the body and its nourishment and growth are not subject to the bidding of reason or will, since natural things are subject to God alone Who is the author of nature. Therefore they were not subject in Christ. Therefore Christ's soul was not omnipotent with regard to His own body.

I answer that, As stated above (A. 2), Christ's soul may be viewed in two ways. First, in its proper nature and power; and in this way, as it was incapable of making exterior bodies change from the course and order of nature, so, too, was it incapable of changing its own body from its natural disposition, since the soul, of its own nature, has a determinate relation to its body. Secondly Christ's soul may be viewed as an instrument united in person to God's Word; and thus every disposition of His own body was wholly subject to His power. Nevertheless, since the power of an action is not properly attributed to the instrument, but to the principal agent, this omnipotence is attributed to the Word of God rather than to Christ's soul.

Reply Obj. 1. This saying of Damascene re-

---

[1] *In Matt.*, IV, on 28.18 (PL 26, 226).
[2] Cf. St. Thomas, *Catena Aurea, In Matt.*, 28.18.
[3] PG 94, 1084.

fers to the Divine will of Christ, since, as he says in the preceding chapter (ch. 19, *cf.* 14, 15),[1] "it was by the consent of the Divine will that the flesh was allowed to suffer and do what was proper to it."

Reply Obj. 2. It was no part of the original justice which Adam had in the state of innocence that a man's soul should have the power of changing his own body to any form, but that it should keep it from any hurt. Yet Christ could have assumed even this power if He had wished. But since man has three states—namely, innocence, sin, and glory, even as from the state of glory He assumed comprehension, and from the state of innocence, freedom from sin, so also from the state of sin did He assume the necessity of being under the penalties of this life, as will be said (Q. XIV, A. 2).

Reply Obj. 3. If the imagination be strong, the body obeys naturally in some things—for example, as regards falling from a beam set on high—since the imagination was formed to be a principle of local motion, as is said in the treatise on the *Soul*.[2] So, too, as regards alteration in heat and cold, and their consequences, for the passions of the soul, according to which the heart is moved, naturally follow the imagination, and thus by arousing the spirits the whole body is altered. But the other corporeal dispositions which have no natural relation to the imagination are not changed by the imagination, however strong it is—for example, the shape of the hand, or foot, or such-like.

ARTICLE 4. *Whether the Soul of Christ Had Omnipotence As Regards the Execution of His Will?*

We proceed thus to the Fourth Article: It would seem that the soul of Christ had not omnipotence as regards the execution of His own will.

Objection 1. For it is written (Mark 7. 24) that *entering into a house, He would that no man should know it, and He could not be hid.* Therefore He could not carry out the purpose of His will in all things.

Obj. 2. Further, a command is a sign of will, as was said in the First Part (Q. XIX, A. 12). But our Lord commanded certain things to be done, and the contrary came to pass, for it is written (Matt. 9. 30, 31) that Jesus strictly charged them whose eyes had been opened, saying: *See that no man know this. But they going out spread His fame abroad in all that*

country. Therefore He could not carry out the purpose of His will in everything.

Obj. 3. Further, a man does not ask from another for what he can do himself. But our Lord besought the Father, praying for what He wished to be done, for it is written (Luke 6. 12): *He went out into a mountain to pray, and He passed the whole night in the prayer of God.* Therefore He could not carry out the purpose of His will in all things.

On the contrary, Augustine says (QQ. *Nov. et Vet. Test.*, qu. 77):[3] It is impossible for the will of the Saviour not to be fulfilled: nor is it possible for Him to will what He knows ought not to come to pass.

I answer that, Christ's soul willed things in two ways. First, what was to be brought about by Himself; and it must be said that He was capable of whatever He willed thus, since it would not befit His wisdom if He willed to do anything of Himself that was not subject to His power. Secondly, He wished things to be brought about by the Divine power, as the resurrection of His own body and such miraculous deeds, which He could not effect by His own power, except as the instrument of the Godhead, as was said above (A. 2).

Reply Obj. 1. As Augustine says:[4] "What came to pass, this Christ must be said to have willed. For it must be remarked that this happened in the country of the Gentiles, to whom it was not yet time to preach. Yet it would have been invidious not to welcome such as came spontaneously for the faith. Hence He did not wish to be heralded by His own, and yet He wished to be sought; and so it came to pass." Or it may be said that this will of Christ was not with regard to what was to be carried out by it but with regard to what was to be done by others, which did not come under His human will. Hence in the letter of Pope Agatho,[5] which was approved in the Sixth Council,[6] we read: "When He, the Creator and Redeemer of all, wished to be hid and could not, must not this be referred only to His human will which He deigned to assume in time?"

Reply Obj. 2. As Gregory says (Moral. xix, 23),[7] by the fact that Our Lord charged His mighty works to be kept secret, "He gave an example to His servants coming after Him that they should wish their miracles to be hidden; and yet, that others may profit by their example,

---

[1] PG 94, 1080; Cf. PG 94, 1037; PG 94, 1045.
[2] Aristotle, III, 9, 10 (432[b]13; 433[a]9).
[3] Ambrosiaster (PL 35, 2271).   [4] *Ibid.*
[5] *Epist.*, 1, Ad Augustos Imperatores (PL 87, 1177).
[6] Conc. Cpolit. III, actio 4 (MA XI, 250).
[7] PL 76, 120.

they are made public against their will." And thus this command signified His will to fly from human glory, according to John 8, 50, *I seek not My own glory.* Yet He wished absolutely, and especially by His Divine will, that the miracle wrought should be published for the good of others.

Reply Obj. 3. Christ prayed both for things that were to be brought about by the Divine power, and for what He Himself was to do by His human will, since the power and operation of Christ's soul depended on God, *Who works in all* (Vulg., *you*), *both to will and to accomplish* (Phil. 2. 13).

QUESTION XIV

OF THE DEFECTS OF BODY ASSUMED BY THE SON OF GOD

(In Four Articles)

WE must now consider the defects Christ assumed in the human nature; and, first, of the defects of body; secondly, of the defects of soul (Q. XV.).

Under the first head there are four points of inquiry: (1) Whether the Son of God should have assumed in human nature defects of body? (2) Whether He assumed the necessity of being subject to these defects? (3) Whether He contracted these defects? (4) Whether He assumed all these defects?

ARTICLE 1. *Whether the Son of God in Human Nature Ought To Have Assumed Defects of Body?*

We proceed thus to the First Article: It would seem that the Son of God ought not to have assumed human nature with defects of body.

Objection 1. For as His soul is personally united to the Word of God, so also is His body. But the soul of Christ had every perfection, both of grace and truth, as was said above (Q. VII, A. 9; Q. IX, seqq.). Hence, His body also ought to have been in every way perfect, not having any imperfection in it.

Obj. 2. Further, the soul of Christ saw the Word of God by the vision wherein the blessed see, as was said above (Q. IX, A. 2), and thus the soul of Christ was blessed. Now by the beatification of the soul the body is glorified; since, as Augustine says (*Ep. ad Dios.* cxviii),[1] "God made the soul of a nature so strong that from the fulness of its blessedness there pours over even into the lower nature (that is, the body), not indeed the bliss proper to the beatific frui-

[1] Chap. 3 (PL 33, 439).

tion and vision, but the fulness of health" (that is, the vigour of incorruptibility). Therefore the body of Christ was incorruptible and without any defect.

Obj. 3. Further, penalty is the consequence of fault. But there was no fault in Christ, according to I Pet. 2. 22: *Who did no guile.* Therefore defects of body, which are penalties, ought not have been in Him.

Obj. 4. Further, no reasonable man assumes what keeps him from his proper end. But by such bodily defects the end of the Incarnation seems to be hindered in many ways. First, because by these infirmities men were kept back from knowing Him, according to Isa. 53. 2, 3: [*There was no sightliness*] *that we should be desirous of Him. Despised and the most abject of men, a man of sorrows and acquainted with infirmity, and His look was, as it were, hidden and despised, whereupon we esteemed Him not.* Secondly, because the desire of the holy Fathers would not seem to be fulfilled, in whose person it is written (Isa. 51. 9): *Arise, arise, put on Thy strength, O Thou Arm of the Lord.* Thirdly, because it would seem more fitting for the devil's power to be overcome and man's weakness healed, by strength than by weakness. Therefore it does not seem to have been fitting that the Son of God assumed human nature with infirmities or defects of body.

On the contrary, It is written (Heb. 2. 18): *For in that wherein He Himself hath suffered and been tempted, He is able to succour them also that are tempted.* Now He came to succour us; hence David said of Him (Ps. 120. 1.): *I have lifted up my eyes to the mountains, from whence help shall come to me.* Therefore it was fitting for the Son of God to assume flesh subject to human infirmities, in order to suffer and be tempted in it and so bring succour to us.

I answer that, It was fitting for the body assumed by the Son of God to be subject to human infirmities and defects; and especially for three reasons. First, because it was in order to satisfy for the sin of the human race that the Son of God, having taken flesh, came into the world. Now one satisfies for another's sin by taking on himself the punishment due to the sin of the other. But these bodily defects, namely, death, hunger, thirst, and the like, are the punishment of sin, which was brought into the world by Adam, according to Rom. 5. 12: *By one man sin entered into this world, and by sin death.* Hence it was useful for the end of the Incarnation that He should assume these penalties in our flesh and in our stead, according to Isa. 53. 4, *Surely He hath borne our infirmities.*

Secondly, in order to cause belief in the Incarnation. For since human nature is known to men only as it is subject to these defects, if the Son of God had assumed human nature without these defects, He would not have seemed to be true man, nor to have true, but imaginary, flesh, as the Manicheans held.[1] And so, as is said, Phil. 2. 7: *He . . . emptied Himself, taking the form of a servant, being made in the likeness of men, and in habit found as a man.* Hence, Thomas, by the sight of His wounds, was recalled to the faith, as related John. 20. 26.

Thirdly, in order to show us an example of patience by valiantly bearing up against human sufferings and defects. Hence it said (Heb. 12. 3) that He *endured such opposition from sinners against Himself, that you be not wearied, fainting in your minds.*

Reply Obj. 1. The penalties one suffers for another's sin are the matter, as it were, of the satisfaction for that sin; but the principle is the habit of soul, whereby one is inclined to wish to satisfy for another, and from which the satisfaction has its efficacy, for satisfaction would not be efficacious unless it proceeded from charity, as will be explained (Suppl. Q. XIV, A. 2). Hence, the soul of Christ had to be perfect as regards the habit of knowledge and virtue, in order to have the power of satisfying, but His body was subject to infirmities, that the matter of satisfaction should not be wanting.

Reply Obj. 2. From the natural relationship which is between the soul and the body, glory flows into the body from the soul's glory. Yet this natural relationship in Christ was subject to the will of His Godhead, and thereby it came to pass that the Happiness remained in the soul, and did not flow into the body, but the flesh suffered what belongs to a nature capable of suffering; thus Damascene says (*De Fide Orth.* iii, 19)[2] that, "it was by the consent of the Divine will that the flesh was allowed to suffer and do what was proper to it."

Reply Obj. 3. Punishment always follows sin actual or original, sometimes of the one punished, sometimes of the one for whom he who suffers the punishment satisfies. And so it was with Christ, according to Isa. 53. 5: *He was wounded for our iniquities, He was bruised for our sins.*

Reply Obj. 4. The infirmity assumed by Christ did not impede, but greatly furthered the end

of the Incarnation, as above stated. And although these infirmities concealed His Godhead, they made known His Manhood, which is the way of coming to the Godhead, according to Rom. 5. 1, 2: *By Jesus Christ we have access to God.* Moreover, the ancient Fathers did not desire bodily strength in Christ, but spiritual strength, with which He vanquished the devil and healed human weakness.

ARTICLE 2. *Whether Christ Assumed the Necessity of Being Subject to These Defects.*

We proceed thus to the Second Article: It would seem that Christ was not of necessity subject to these defects.

Objection 1. For it is written (Isa. 53. 7): *He was offered because it was His own will,* and the prophet is speaking of the offering of the Passion. But will is opposed to necessity. Therefore Christ was not of necessity subject to bodily defects.

Obj. 2. Further, Damascene says (*De Fide Orth.* iii, 20):[3] "Nothing forced is seen in Christ: all is voluntary." Now what is voluntary is not necessary. Therefore these defects were not of necessity in Christ.

Obj. 3. Further, necessity is induced by something more powerful. But no creature is more powerful than the soul of Christ, to which it pertained to preserve its own body. Therefore these defects were not of necessity in Christ.

On the contrary, The Apostle says (Rom. 8. 3) that *God sent His own Son in the likeness of sinful flesh.* Now it is a condition of sinful flesh to be under the necessity of dying, and suffering other like passions. Therefore the necessity of suffering these defects was in Christ's flesh.

I answer that, Necessity is twofold. One is a necessity of constraint, brought about by an external agent, and this necessity is contrary to both nature and will, since these flow from an internal principle. The other is natural necessity, resulting from the natural principles—either the form (as it is necessary for fire to heat), or the matter (as it is necessary for a body composed of contraries to be dissolved). Hence, with this necessity, which results from the matter, Christ's body was subject to the necessity of death and other like defects, since, as was said[4] "it was by the consent of the Divine will that the flesh was allowed to do and suffer what was proper to it." And this necessity results from the principles of human flesh, as was said above in this article. But if we speak of necessity of

[1] See below, Q. XVI, A. 1.
[2] PG 94, 1080; cf. III, 14, 15 (PG 94, 1037, 1045).

[3] PG, 94 1084.
[4] John Damascene, *De Fide Orth.*, III, 19 (PG 94, 1080).

constraint, as contrary to the bodily nature, thus again was Christ's body in its own natural condition subject to necessity in regard to the nail that pierced and the scourge that struck. Yet according as such necessity is contrary to the will, it is clear that in Christ these defects were not of necessity as regards either the Divine will, or the human will of Christ considered absolutely, as following the deliberation of reason, but only as regards the natural movement of the will, according as it naturally shrinks from death and bodily hurt.

Reply Obj. 1. Christ is said to be *offered because it was His own will*—that is, Divine will and deliberate human will, although death was contrary to the natural movement of His human will, as Damascene says (*De Fide Orthod.* iii, 23, 24).[1]

Reply Obj. 2. This is plain from what has been said.

Reply Obj. 3. Nothing was more powerful than Christ's soul, absolutely; yet there was nothing to hinder a thing being more powerful in regard to this or that effect, as a nail for piercing. And this I say, in so far as Christ's soul is considered in its own proper nature and power.

ARTICLE 3. *Whether Christ Contracted Bodily Defects?*

We proceed thus to the Third Article: It would seem that Christ contracted bodily defects.

Objection 1. For we are said to contract what we derive with our nature from birth. But Christ, together with human nature, derived His bodily defects and infirmities through His birth from His mother, whose flesh was subject to these defects. Therefore it seems that He contracted these defects.

Obj. 2. Further, what is caused by the principles of nature is derived together with nature, and hence is contracted. Now these penalties are caused by the principles of human nature. Therefore Christ contracted them.

Obj. 3. Further, Christ is likened to other men in these defects, as is written Heb. 2. 17. But other men contract these defects. Therefore it seems that Christ contracted these defects.

On the contrary, These defects are contracted through sin, according to Rom. 5. 12: *By one man sin entered into this world, and by sin, death.* Now sin had no place in Christ. Therefore Christ did not contract these defects.

I answer that, In the verb "to contract" is

understood the order of effect to cause—that is, that is said to be contracted which is derived of necessity together with its cause. Now the cause of death and the like defects in human nature is sin, since *by sin death entered into this world,* according to Rom. 5. 12. And hence they who incur these defects as due to sin, are properly said to contract them. Now Christ had not these defects as due to sin, since, as Augustine, expounding John 3. 31, *He that cometh from above, is above all,* says:[2] "Christ came from above—that is, from the height of human nature, which it had before the fall of the first man." For He received human nature without sin, in the purity which it had in the state of innocence. In the same way He might have assumed human nature without defects. Thus it is clear that Christ did not contract these defects as if taking them upon Himself as due to sin, but by His own will.

Reply Obj. 1. The flesh of the Virgin was conceived in original sin, and therefore contracted these defects. But from the Virgin, Christ's flesh assumed the nature without fault, and He might likewise have assumed the nature without its penalty. But He wished to bear its penalty in order to carry out the work of our redemption, as stated above (A. 1). Therefore He had these defects—not that He contracted them, but that He assumed them.

Reply Obj. 2. The cause of death and other corporeal defects of human nature is twofold: the first is remote, and results from the material principles of the human body, because it is made up of contraries. But this cause was held in check by original justice. Hence the proximate cause of death and other defects is sin, whereby original justice is withdrawn. And thus, because Christ was without sin, He is said not to have contracted these defects, but to have assumed them.

Reply Obj. 3. Christ was made like other men in the quality and not in the cause of these defects; and hence, unlike others, He did not contract them.

ARTICLE 4. *Whether Christ Ought To Have Assumed All the Bodily Defects of Men?*

We proceed thus to the Fourth Article: It would seem that Christ ought to have assumed all the bodily defects of men.

Objection 1. For Damascene says (*De Fide Orthod.* iii, 6, 18):[3] "What is unassumable is

---

[1] PG 94, 1088, 1092.

[2] Cf. Hugh of St. Cher, *In Univ. Test.,* on John 3.31 (VI, 301va).

[3] PG 94, 1005, 1071.

incurable." But Christ came to cure all our defects. Therefore He ought to have assumed all our defects.

Obj. 2. Further, it was said (A. 1, Reply 1), that in order to satisfy for us, Christ ought to have had perfective habits of soul and defects of body. Now as regards the soul, He assumed the fulness of all grace. Therefore as regards the body, He ought to have assumed all defects.

Obj. 3. Further, amongst all bodily defects death holds the chief place. Now Christ assumed death. Much more, therefore, ought He to have assumed other defects.

On the contrary, Contraries cannot take place simultaneously in the same. Now some infirmities are contrary to each other, being caused by contrary principles. Hence it could not be that Christ assumed all human infirmities.

I answer that, As stated above (A. 1), Christ assumed human defects in order to satisfy for the sin of human nature, and for this it was necessary for Him to have the fulness of knowledge and grace in His soul. Hence Christ ought to have assumed those defects which flow from the common sin of the whole nature, yet are not incompatible with the perfection of knowledge and grace.

And thus it was not fitting for Him to assume all human defects or infirmities. For there are some defects that are incompatible with the perfection of knowledge and grace, as ignorance, a proneness towards evil, and an obstinacy toward well-doing.

Some other defects do not flow from the whole of human nature in common on account of the sin of our first parent, but are caused in some men by certain particular causes, as leprosy, epilepsy, and the like; and these defects are sometimes brought about by the fault of the man—for example, from inordinate eating; sometimes by a defect in the formative power. Now neither of these pertains to Christ, since His flesh was conceived of the Holy Ghost, Who has infinite wisdom and power, and cannot err or fail; and He Himself did nothing wrong in the order of His life.

But there are some third defects, to be found amongst all men in common, by reason of the sin of our first parent, as death, hunger, thirst, and the like; and all these defects Christ assumed, which Damascene (*De Fide Orthod.* i, 11; iii, 20)[1] calls "natural and non-detracting passions"—natural, as following all human nature in common; non-detracting, as implying no defect of knowledge or grace.

[1] PG 94, 844, 1081.

Reply Obj. 1. All particular defects of men are caused by the corruptibility and capacity for suffering of the body, some particular causes being added; and hence, since Christ healed the capacity for suffering and corruptibility of our body by assuming it, He consequently healed all other defects.

Reply Obj. 2. The fulness of all grace and knowledge was due to Christ's soul of itself, from the fact of its being assumed by the Word of God; and hence Christ assumed all the fulness of wisdom and grace absolutely. But He assumed our defects as a steward, in order to satisfy for our sin, and not that they belonged to Him of Himself. Hence it was not necessary for Him to assume them all, but only such as sufficed to satisfy for the sin of the whole nature.

Reply Obj. 3. Death comes to all men from the sin of our first parent; but not other defects, although they are less than death. Hence there is no parity.

QUESTION XV

OF THE DEFECTS OF SOUL ASSUMED BY CHRIST

(*In Ten Articles*)

WE must now consider the defects pertaining to the soul; and under this head there are ten points of inquiry: (1) Whether there was sin in Christ? (2) Whether there was the *fomes* of sin in Him? (3) Whether there was ignorance? (4) Whether His soul was passible? (5) Whether in Him there was sensible pain? (6) Whether there was sorrow? (7) Whether there was fear? (8) Whether there was wonder? (9) Whether there was anger? (10) Whether He was at once wayfarer and comprehensor?

ARTICLE 1. *Whether There Was Sin in Christ?*

We proceed thus to the First Article: It would seem that there was sin in Christ.

Objection 1. For it is written (Ps. 21. 2): *O God, My God, look upon me: why hast Thou forsaken Me? Far from My salvation are the words of My sins.* Now these words are said in the person of Christ Himself, as appears from His having uttered them on the cross. Therefore it would seem that in Christ there were sins.

Obj. 2. Further, the Apostle says (Rom. 5. 12) that *in Adam all have sinned*—namely, because all were in Adam by origin. Now Christ also was in Adam by origin. Therefore He sinned in him.

Obj. 3. Further, the Apostle says (Heb. 2. 18) that *in that, wherein He Himself hath suffered and been tempted, He is able to succour them also that are tempted.* Now above all do we require His help against sin. Therefore it seems that there was sin in Him.

Obj. 4. Further, it is written (II Cor. 5. 21) that *Him that knew no sin* (that is, Christ), *for us God hath made sin.* But that really is, which has been made by God. Therefore there was really sin in Christ.

Obj. 5. Further, as Augustine says (*De Agone Christ.* xi),[1] "in the man Christ the Son of God gave Himself to us as a pattern of living." Now man needs a pattern not merely of right living, but also of repentance for sin. Therefore it seems that in Christ there ought to have been sin, that He might repent of His sin, and thus afford us a pattern of repentance.

On the contrary, He Himself says (John 8. 46): *Which of you shall convince Me of sin?*

I answer that, As was said above (Q. XIV, A. 1), Christ assumed our defects that He might satisfy for us, that He might prove the truth of His human nature, and that He might become an example of virtue to us. Now it is plain that by reason of these three things He ought not to have assumed the defect of sin. First, because sin in no way works our satisfaction; rather, it impedes the power of satisfying, since, as it is written (Ecclus. 34. 23), *The Most High approveth not the gifts of the wicked.* Secondly, the truth of His human nature is not proved by sin, since sin does not belong to human nature, of which God is the cause, but rather has been sown in it against its nature by the devil, as Damascene says (*De Fide Orthod.* iii, 20).[2] Thirdly, because by sinning He could afford no example of virtue, since sin is opposed to virtue. Hence Christ in no way assumed the defect of sin—either original or actual—according to what is written (I Pet. 2. 22): *Who did no sin, neither was guile found in His mouth.*

Reply Obj. 1. As Damascene says (*De Fide Orthod.* iii, 25),[3] things are said of Christ in two ways: first, with reference to His natural and hypostatic property, as when it is said that God became man, and that He suffered for us; secondly, with reference to His personal and relative property, when things are said of Him in our person which in no way belong to Him of Himself. Hence, in the seven rules of Tichonius[4]

which Augustine quotes,[5] the first regards "Our Lord and His Body," since "Christ and His Church are taken as one person." And thus Christ, speaking in the person of His members, says (Ps. 21. 2): *The words of My sins*—not that there were any sins in the Head.

Reply Obj. 2. As Augustine says (*Gen. ad lit.* x, 20),[6] Christ was in Adam and the other fathers not altogether as we were. For we were in Adam as regards both seminal principle and bodily substance, since, as he goes on to say: "As in the seed there is a visible bulk and an invisible virtue, both have come from Adam. Now Christ took the visible substance of His flesh from the Virgin's flesh; but the principle of His conception did not spring from the seed of man, but far otherwise—from on high." Hence He was not in Adam according to seminal principle, but only according to bodily substance. And therefore Christ did not receive human nature from Adam actively, but only materially—and from the Holy Ghost actively; even as Adam received his body materially from the slime of the earth, actively from God. And thus Christ did not sin in Adam, in whom He was only as regards His matter.

Reply Obj. 3. In His temptation and passion Christ has succoured us by satisfying for us. Now sin does not further satisfaction, but hinders it, as has been said. Hence, it was not necessary for Him to have sin, but He was wholly free from sin; otherwise the punishment He bore would have been due to Him for His own sin.

Reply Obj. 4. God *made Christ sin*,—not, indeed, in such sort that He had sin in Himself, but that He made Him a victim for sin, even as it is written (Osee 4. 8): *They shall eat the sins of My people*—they —that is, the priests, who by the law ate the victims offered for sin. And in that way it is written (Isa. 53. 6) that *the Lord hath laid on Him the iniquity of us all* (that is, He gave Him up to be a victim for the sins of all men); or *He made Him sin* (that is, made Him to have the likeness of sinful flesh), as is written (Rom. 8. 3), and this on account of the passible and mortal body He assumed.

Reply Obj. 5. A penitent can give a praiseworthy example not by having sinned, but by freely bearing the punishment of sin. And hence Christ set the highest example to penitents, since He willingly bore the punishment, not of His own sin, but of the sins of others.

[1] PL 40, 298.   [2] PG 94, 1081.
[3] PG 94, 1093.
[4] *De Septem Reg.*, 1 (PL 18, 15).
[5] *Christian Doctrine,* III, 31 (PL 34, 82).
[6] PL 34, 424.

ARTICLE 2. *Whether There Was the "Fomes"*
of Sin in Christ?

We proceed thus to the Second Article: It
would seem that in Christ there was the *fomes*
of sin.

Objection 1. For the *fomes* of sin, and the
passibility and mortality of the body spring
from the same principle, namely, from the withdrawal of original justice, whereby the inferior
powers of the soul were subject to the reason,
and the body to the soul. Now passibility and
mortality of body were in Christ. Therefore
there was also the *fomes* of sin.

Obj. 2. Further, as Damascene says (*De Fide
Orthod.* iii, 19),[1] "it was by consent of the Divine will that the flesh of Christ was allowed to
suffer and do what was proper to it." But it is
proper to the flesh to lust after its pleasures.
Now since the *fomes* of sin is nothing more than
concupiscence, as the gloss says[2] on Rom. 7. 8,
it seems that in Christ there was the *fomes* of
sin.

Obj. 3. Further, it is by reason of the *fomes*
of sin that *the flesh lusteth against the spirit*, as
is written (Gal. 5. 17). But the spirit is shown
to be so much the stronger and worthier to be
crowned according as the more completely it
overcomes its enemy—namely, the concupiscence of the flesh, according to II Tim. 2, 5, he
is not crowned except he strive lawfully. Now
Christ had a most valiant and conquering spirit, and one most worthy of a crown, according to Apoc. 6. 2 : *There was a crown given Him,
and He went forth conquering that He might
conquer.* Therefore it would especially seem that
the *fomes* of sin ought to have been in Christ.

On the contrary, It is written (Matt. 1. 20) :
*That which is conceived in her is of the Holy
Ghost.* Now the Holy Ghost drives out sin and
the inclination to sin, which is implied in the
word *fomes.* Therefore in Christ there ought
not to have been the *fomes* of sin.

I answer that, As was said above (Q. VII,
AA. 2, 9), Christ had grace and all the virtues
most perfectly. Now moral virtues, which are
in the irrational part of the soul, make it subject to reason, and so much the more as the
virtue is more perfect; thus, temperance controls the concupiscible appetite, fortitude and
meekness the irascible appetite, as was said in
the Second Part (I-II, Q. LVI, A. 4). But there

belongs to the very nature of the *fomes* of sin
an inclination of the sensual appetite to what is
contrary to reason. And hence it is plain that
the more perfect the virtues are in any man, the
weaker the *fomes* of sin becomes in him. Hence,
since in Christ the virtues were in their highest
degree, the *fomes* of sin was not in Him; because also this defect cannot be ordered to satisfaction, but rather inclined to what is contrary
to satisfaction.

Reply Obj. 1. The inferior powers pertaining
to the sensitive appetite have a natural capacity to be obedient to reason; but not the bodily
powers, nor those of the bodily humours, nor
those of the vegetative soul, as is made plain
in the *Ethics.*[3] And hence perfection of virtue,
which is in accordance with right reason, does
not exclude possibility of body; yet it excludes
the *fomes* of sin, the nature of which consists
in the resistance of the sensitive appetite to
reason.

Reply Obj. 2. The flesh naturally desires what
is pleasing to it by the concupiscence of the sensitive appetite; but the flesh of man, who is a
rational animal, desires this after the manner
and order of reason. And thus with the concupiscence of the sensitive appetite Christ's flesh
naturally sought food, drink, and sleep, and all
else that is sought according to right reason, as
is plain from Damascene (*De Fide Orthod.* iii,
14).[4] Yet it does not therefore follow that in
Christ there was the *fomes* of sin, for this implies the lust after pleasurable things against
the order of reason.

Reply Obj. 3. The spirit gives evidence of
fortitude to some extent by resisting that concupiscence of the flesh which is opposed to it;
yet a greater fortitude of spirit is shown if by
its strength the flesh is thoroughly overcome,
so as to be incapable of lusting against the spirit. And hence this belonged to Christ, whose
spirit reached the highest degree of fortitude.
And although He suffered no internal assault
on the part of the *fomes* of sin, He sustained
an external assault on the part of the world and
the devil, and won the crown of victory by overcoming them.

ARTICLE 3. *Whether in Christ There Was
Ignorance?*

We proceed thus to the Third Article: It
would seem that there was ignorance in Christ.

Objection 1. For that is truly in Christ which
belongs to Him in His human nature, although
it does not belong to Him in His Divine Nature,

---

[1] PG 94, 1080; cf. chap. 14 (PG, 1037); chap. 15 (PG
94, 1045).
[2] *Glossa interl.* (VI, 16v); *Glossa* Lombardi (PL 191,
1416).

[3] Aristotle, I, 13 (1102[b]28).   [4] PG 94, 1036.

as suffering and death. But ignorance belongs to Christ in His human nature; for Damascene says (*De Fide Orthod.* iii, 21)[1] that "He assumed an ignorant and enslaved nature." Therefore ignorance was truly in Christ.

Obj. 2. Further, one is said to be ignorant through defect of knowledge. Now some kind of knowledge was wanting to Christ, for the Apostle says (II Cor. 5. 21) *Him that knew no sin, for us He hath made sin.* Therefore there was ignorance in Christ.

Obj. 3. Further, it is written (Isa. 8. 4): *For before the child know to call his father and his mother, the strength of Damascus . . . shall be taken away.* Therefore in Christ there was ignorance of certain things.

On the contrary, Ignorance is not taken away by ignorance. But Christ came to take away our ignorance; for *He came to enlighten them that sit in darkness and in the shadow of death* (Luke 1. 79). Therefore there was no ignorance in Christ.

I answer that, As there was the fulness of grace and virtue in Christ, so too there was the fulness of all knowledge, as is plain from what has been said above (Q. VII, AA. 2, 5, 7, 8; QQ. IX-XII). Now as the fulness of grace and virtue in Christ excluded the *fomes* of sin, so the fulness of knowledge excluded ignorance, which is opposed to knowledge. Hence, even as the *fomes* of sin was not in Christ, neither was there ignorance in Him.

Reply Obj. 1. The nature assumed by Christ may be viewed in two ways. First, in its specific nature, and thus Damascene calls it "ignorant and enslaved"; hence he adds: "For man's nature is a slave of Him (that is, God) Who made it; and it has no knowledge of future things." Secondly, it may be considered with regard to what it has from its union with the Divine hypostasis, from which it has the fulness of knowledge and grace, according to John 1. 14: *We saw Him* (Vulg., *His glory*) *as it were the Only-begotten of the Father, full of grace and truth;* and in this way the human nature in Christ was not affected with ignorance.

Reply Obj. 2. Christ is said not to have known sin, because He did not know it by experience; but He knew it by simple knowledge.

Reply Obj. 3. The prophet is speaking in this passage of the human knowledge of Christ; for he says: *Before the Child* (that is, in His human nature) *know to call His father* (that is, Joseph, who was His reputed father), *and His mother* (that is, Mary), *the strength of Da-*

mascus . . . *shall be taken away.* Nor are we to understand this as if He had been some time a man without knowing it, but *before He know* (that is, before He is a man having human knowledge),—literally, *the strength of Damascus and the spoils of Samaria shall be taken away* by the King of the Assyrians—or spiritually, "before His birth He will save His people solely by invocation," as a gloss expounds it.[2]

Augustine however says[3] that this was fulfilled in the adoration of the Magi. For he says: "Before He uttered human words in human flesh, He received the strength of Damascus, that is, the riches which Damascus vaunted (for in riches the first place is given to gold). They themselves were the spoils of Samaria. Because Samaria is taken to signify idolatry, since this people, having turned away from the Lord, turned to the worship of idols. Hence these were the first spoils which the child took from the domination of idolatry." And in this way "before the child know" may be taken to mean "before he show himself to know."

ARTICLE 4. *Whether Christ's Soul Was Passible?*

We proceed thus to the Fourth Article: It would seem that the soul of Christ was not passible.

Objection 1. For nothing suffers except by reason of something stronger, since "the agent is greater than the patient," as is clear from Augustine (*Gen. ad lit.* xii, 16),[4] and from the Philosopher.[5] Now no creature was stronger than Christ's soul. Therefore Christ's soul could not suffer at the hands of any creature; and hence it was not passible, for its capability of suffering would have been to no purpose if it could not have suffered at the hands of anything.

Obj. 2. Further, Tully (*De Tusc. Quæs.* III, 10)[6] says that the soul's passions are ailments. But Christ's soul had no ailment; for the soul's ailment results from sin, as is plain from Ps. 40. 5: *Heal my soul, for I have sinned against Thee.* Therefore in Christ's soul there were no passions.

Obj. 3. Further, the soul's passions would seem to be the same as the *fomes* of sin, hence the Apostle (Rom. 7. 5) calls them the *passions of sins.* Now the *fomes* of sin was not in Christ, as was said (A. 2). Therefore it seems that there were no passions in His soul; and hence His soul was not passible.

---

[1] PG 94, 1084.

[2] *Glossa interl.* (IV, 22v); Jerome, *In Isaiam* (PL 24, 118).
[3] *Serm.*, CCII, 2 (PL 38, 1034).   [4] PL 34, 467.
[5] *Soul,* III, 5 (430ª18).   [6] DD IV, 7.

On the contrary, It is written (Ps. 87. 4) in the person of Christ: *My soul is filled with evils* —not sins, indeed, but human evils—that is, "pains," as a gloss expounds it.[1] Hence the soul of Christ was passible.

I answer that, A soul placed in a body may suffer in two ways: first with a bodily passion; secondly, with an animal passion. It suffers with a bodily passion through bodily hurt; for since the soul is the form of the body, soul and body have but one being, and hence, when the body is disturbed by any bodily passion, the soul, too, must be accidentally disturbed—that is, in the being which it has in the body. Therefore, since Christ's body was passible and mortal, as was said above (Q. XIV, AA. 1, 2), His soul also was of necessity passible in like manner.

But the soul is said to suffer with an animal passion in its operation,—either as it is proper to the soul, or as it is of the soul more than of the body. And although the soul is said to suffer in this way through sensation and understanding, as was said in the Second Part (I-II, Q. XXII, A. 3; Q. XLI, A. 1), nevertheless the affections of the sensitive appetite are most properly called passions of the soul. Now these were in Christ, even as all else pertaining to man's nature. Hence Augustine says:[2] "Our Lord having designed to live in the form of a servant, took these upon Himself whenever He judged they ought to be assumed; for there was no false human affection in Him Who had a true body and a true human soul."

Nevertheless we must know that these passions were in Christ otherwise than in us, in three ways. First, as regards the object, since in us these passions very often tend towards what is unlawful, but not so in Christ. Secondly, as regards the principle, since these passions in us frequently forestall the judgment of reason, but in Christ all movements of the sensitive appetite sprang from the disposition of the reason. Hence Augustine says[3] that "Christ assumed these movements in His human soul by an unfailing dispensation, when He willed; even as He became man when He willed." Thirdly, as regards the effect, because in us these movements, at times, do not remain in the sensitive appetite, but deflect the reason; but not so in Christ, since by His disposition the movements that are naturally becoming to human flesh so remained in the sensitive appetite that the reason was in

no way hindered in doing what was right. Hence Jerome says[4] that "Our Lord, in order to prove the reality of the assumed manhood, 'was sorrowful' in very deed; yet lest a passion should hold sway over His soul, it is by a propassion that He is said to have 'begun to grow sorrowful and to be sad' "; so that it is a perfect passion when it dominates the soul—that is, the reason; and a propassion when it has its beginning in the sensitive appetite, but goes no further.

Reply Obj. 1. The soul of Christ could have prevented these passions from coming upon it, and especially by the Divine power; yet of His own will He subjected Himself to these corporeal and animal passions.

Reply Obj. 2. Tully is speaking there according to the opinions of the Stoics,[5] who did not give the name of passions to all but only to the disorderly movements of the sensitive appetite. Now, it is manifest that passions like these were not in Christ.

Reply Obj. 3. The *passions of sins* are movements of the sensitive appetite that tend to unlawful things; and these were not in Christ, as neither was the *fomes* of sin.

ARTICLE 5. *Whether There Was Sensible Pain in Christ?*

We proceed thus to the Fifth Article: It would seem that there was no true sensible pain in Christ.

Objection 1. For Hilary says (*De Trin.* x):[6] "Since with Christ to die was life, what pain may He be supposed to have suffered in the sacrament of His death, Who bestows life on such as die for Him?" And further on he says:[7] "The Only-begotten assumed true man, not ceasing to be God; and although blows struck Him and wounds were inflicted on Him, and scourges fell upon Him, and the cross lifted Him up, yet these wrought in deed the vehemence of the passion, but brought no pain." Hence there was no true pain in Christ.

Obj. 2. Further, it would seem to be proper to flesh conceived in original sin to be subject to the necessity of pain. But the flesh of Christ was not conceived in sin, but of the Holy Ghost in the Virgin's womb. Therefore it lay under no necessity of suffering pain.

Obj. 3. Further, the delight of the contemplation of Divine things dulls the sense of pain; hence the martyrs in their passions bore up more

---

[1] *Glossa interl.* (III, 216r); *Glossa Lombardi* (PL 191, 811); Augustine, *Enarr. in Ps.* (PL 36, 1110).
[2] *City of God,* XIV, 9 (PL 41, 415).
[3] *Ibid.*

[4] On Matt. 26.37 (PL 26, 205).
[5] Cf. Part I–II, Q. XXIV, A. 2.
[6] PL 10, 350.   [7] PL 10, 361.

patiently by thinking of the Divine love. But Christ's soul was in the perfect enjoyment of contemplating God, Whom He saw in essence, as was said above (Q. IX, A. 2). Therefore He could feel no pain.

On the contrary, It is written (Isa. 53. 4): *Surely He hath borne our infirmities and carried our sorrows.*

I answer that, As is plain from what has been said in the Second Part (I-II, Q. XXXV, A. 7), for true bodily pain are required bodily hurt and the sense of hurt. Now Christ's body was able to be hurt, since it was passible and mortal, as above stated (Q. XIV, AA. I, 2); neither was the sense of hurt wanting to it, since Christ's soul possessed perfectly all natural powers. Therefore no one should doubt but that in Christ there was true pain.

Reply Obj. 1. In all these and similar words, Hilary does not intend to exclude the reality of the pain, but the necessity of it. Hence after the foregoing he adds:[1] "Nor, when He thirsted, or hungered, or wept, was the Lord seen to drink, or eat, or grieve. But in order to prove the reality of the body, the body's customs were assumed, so that the custom of our body was atoned for by the custom of our nature. Or when He took drink or food, He acceded, not to the body's necessity, but to its custom." And he uses the word "necessity" in reference to the first cause of these defects, which is sin, as above stated (Q. XIV, AA. I, 3), so that Christ's flesh is said not to have lain under the necessity of these defects, in the sense that there was no sin in it. Hence he adds: "For He (that is, Christ) had a body—one proper to His origin, which did not exist through the unholiness of our conception, but subsisted in the form of our body by the strength of His power." But as regards the proximate cause of these defects, which is composition of contraries, the flesh of Christ lay under the necessity of these defects, as was said above (Q. XIV, A. 2).

Reply Obj. 2. Flesh conceived in sin is subject to pain, not merely on account of the necessity of its natural principles, but from the necessity of the guilt of sin. Now this necessity was not in Christ, but only the necessity of natural principles.

Reply Obj. 3. As was said above (Q. XIV, A. I, Reply 2), by the power of the Godhead of Christ Happiness was kept in the soul, so as not to overflow into the body, lest His passibility and mortality should be taken away; and for the same reason the delight of contemplation

was so kept in the mind as not to overflow into the sensitive powers, lest sensible pain should thereby be prevented.

ARTICLE 6. *Whether There Was Sorrow in Christ?*

We proceed thus to the Sixth Article: It would seem that in Christ there was no sorrow.

Objection 1. For it is written of Christ (Isa. 42. 4): *He shall not be sad nor troublesome.*

Obj. 2. Further, it is written (Prov. 12. 21): *Whatever shall befall the just man, it shall not make him sad.* And the reason of this the Stoics asserted[2] to be that no one is saddened save by the loss of his goods. Now the just man esteems only justice and virtue as his goods, and these he cannot lose; otherwise the just man would be subject to fortune if he was saddened by the loss of the goods fortune has given him. But Christ was most just, according to Jer. 23. 6: *This is the name that they shall call Him: The Lord, our just one.* Therefore there was no sorrow in Him.

Obj. 3. Further, the Philosopher says[3] that "all sorrow is evil, and to be shunned." But in Christ there was no evil to be shunned. Therefore there was no sorrow in Christ.

Obj. 4. Furthermore, as Augustine says:[4] "Sorrow regards the things we suffer unwillingly." But Christ suffered nothing against His will, for it is written (Isa. 53. 7): *He was offered because it was His own will.* Hence there was no sorrow in Christ.

On the contrary, Our Lord said (Matt. 26. 38): *My soul is sorrowful even unto death.* And Ambrose says (*De Trin.* ii, 7)[5] that "as a man He had sorrow; for He bore my sorrow. I call it sorrow, fearlessly, since I preach the cross."

I answer that, As was said above (A. 5, Reply 3), by Divine dispensation the joy of contemplation remained in Christ's mind so as not to overflow into the sensitive powers, and thereby shut out sensible pain. Now even as sensible pain is in the sensitive appetite, so also is sorrow. But there is a difference of motive or object; for the object and motive of pain is hurt perceived by the sense of touch, as when anyone is wounded, but the object and motive of sorrow is anything hurtful or evil interiorly apprehended either by the reason or the imagination, as was said in the Second Part (I-II, Q. XXXV, AA. 2, 7), as when anyone grieves over

[2] Cf. Arnim, *Fragments,* vol. III, chap. 9, sect. 3 (III, 150); cf. below, Q. XLVI, A. 6, Arg. 2.

[3] *Ethics,* VII, 13 (1153^{b}1).

[4] *City of God,* XIV, 6 (PL 41, 409); cf. chap. 15 (PL 41, 424). [5] PL 16, 594.

[1] PL 10, 364

the loss of grace or money. Now Christ's soul could apprehend things inwardly as hurtful either to Himself, as His passion and death,—or to others, as the sin of His disciples, or of the Jews that killed Him. And hence, as there could be true pain in Christ, so too could there be true sorrow; otherwise, indeed, than in us, in the three ways above stated (A. 4), when we were speaking of the passions of Christ's soul in general.

Reply Obj. 1. Sorrow was not in Christ, as a perfect passion; yet is was in Him in a state of beginning as a propassion. Hence it is written (Matt. 26. 37): *He began to grow sorrowful and to be sad.* For "it is one thing to be sorrowful and another to grow sorrowful," as Jerome says, on this text.[1]

Reply Obj. 2. As Augustine says,[2] for the three passions, desire, joy, and fear, the Stoics held three εὐπαθείας —that is, good passions— in the soul of the wise man: namely, for desire, will; for joy, delight; for fear, caution. But as regards sorrow, they denied it could be in the soul of the wise man, for sorrow regards evil already present, and they thought that no evil could befall a wise man; and they denied this because they believed that only the virtuous is good, since it makes men good, and that nothing is evil except what is sinful, whereby men become wicked.

Now although what is virtuous is man's chief good, and what is sinful is man's chief evil, since these pertain to reason, which is supreme in man, yet there are certain secondary goods of man, which pertain to the body, or to the exterior things that minister to the body. And hence in the soul of the wise man there may be sorrow in the sensitive appetite by his apprehending these evils, without this sorrow disturbing the reason. And in this way are we to understand that whatsoever shall befall the just man, it shall not make him sad, because his reason is troubled by no misfortune. And thus Christ's sorrow was a propassion, and not a passion.

Reply Obj. 3. All sorrow is an evil of punishment; but it is not always an evil of fault, except only when it proceeds from an inordinate affection. Hence Augustine says:[3] "Whenever these affections follow reason, and are caused when and where needed, who will dare to call them diseases or vicious passions?"

Reply Obj. 4. There is no reason why a thing may not of itself be contrary to the will, and yet be willed by reason of the end to which it is ordered, as bitter medicine is not of itself desired, but only as it is ordered to health. And thus Christ's death and passion were of themselves involuntary, and caused sorrow, although they were voluntary as ordered to the end, which is the redemption of the human race.

ARTICLE 7. *Whether There Was Fear in Christ?*

We proceed thus to the Seventh Article: It would seem that there was no fear in Christ.

Objection 1. For it is written (Prov. 28. 1): *The just, bold as a lion, shall be without dread.* But Christ was most just. Therefore there was no fear in Christ.

Obj. 2. Further, Hilary says (*De Trin.* x):[4] "I ask those who think thus, does it stand to reason that He should dread to die, Who by expelling all dread of death from the Apostles, encouraged them to the glory of martyrdom?" Therefore it is unreasonable that there should be fear in Christ.

Obj. 3. Further, fear seems only to regard what a man cannot avoid. Now Christ could have avoided both the evil of punishment which He endured, and the evil of fault which befell others. Therefore there was no fear in Christ.

On the contrary, It is written (Mark 14. 33): Jesus *began to fear and to be heavy.*

I answer that, As sorrow is caused by the apprehension of a present evil, so also is fear caused by the apprehension of a future evil. Now the apprehension of a future evil, if the evil be quite certain, does not arouse fear. Hence the Philosopher says[5] that we do not fear a thing unless there is some hope of avoiding it. For when there is no hope of avoiding it the evil is considered present, and thus it causes sorrow rather than fear. Hence fear may be considered in two ways. First, according as the sensitive appetite naturally shrinks from bodily hurt, by sorrow if it is present, and by fear if it is future; and thus fear was in Christ, even as sorrow. Secondly, fear may be considered in the uncertainty of the future event, "as when at night we are frightened at a sound, not knowing what it is"; and in this way there was no fear in Christ, as Damascene says (*De Fide Orthod.* iii, 23).[6]

Reply Obj. 1. The just man is said to be without dread in so far as dread implies a perfect passion drawing man from what reason dictates. And thus fear was not in Christ, but only as a propassion. Hence it is said (Mark 14. 33) that

---

[1] In Matt., IV, on 26.37 (PL 26, 205).
[2] *City of God*, XIV, 8 (PL 41, 411).
[3] *Ibid.*, XIV, 9 (PL 41, 414).

[4] PL 10, 350.
[5] *Rhetoric*, II, 5 (1382ᵇ29).
[6] PG 94, 1089.

Jesus *began to fear and to be heavy,* with a pro-passion, as Jerome expounds.[1]

Reply Obj. 2. Hilary[2] excludes fear from Christ in the same way that he excludes sorrow —that is, as regards the necessity of fearing. And yet to show the reality of His human nature, He voluntarily assumed fear, even as sorrow.

Reply Obj. 3. Although Christ could have avoided future evils by the power of His God-head, yet they were unavoidable, or not easily avoidable by the weakness of the flesh.

ARTICLE 8. *Whether There Was Wonder in Christ?*

We proceed thus to the Eighth Article: It would seem that in Christ there was no wonder.

Objection 1. For the Philosopher says[3] that wonder results when we see an effect without knowing its cause; and thus wonder belongs only to the ignorant. Now there was no igno-rance in Christ, as was said (A. 3). Therefore there was no wonder in Christ.

Obj. 2. Further, Damascene says (*De Fide Orthod.* ii, 15)[4] that "wonder is fear springing from the imagination of something great"; and hence the Philosopher says[5] that "the magnani-mous man does not wonder." But Christ was most magnanimous. Therefore there was no wonder in Christ.

Obj. 3. Further, no man wonders at what he himself can do. Now Christ could do whatsoever was great. Therefore it seems that He wondered at nothing.

On the contrary, It is written (Matt. 8. 10): *Jesus hearing this*—that is, the words of the centurion—*marvelled.*

I answer that, Wonder properly regards what is new and unusual. Now there could be nothing new and unusual as regards Christ's Divine knowledge; nor as regards the human knowl-edge whereby He knew things in the Word, or by which He saw things by infused species. Yet things could be new and unusual with regard to His experimental knowledge, in regard to which new things could occur to Him day by day. Hence, if we speak of Christ with respect to His Divine knowledge, and His beatific and even His infused knowledge, there was no wonder in Christ. But if we speak of Him with respect to experimental knowledge, wonder could be in Him; and He assumed this affection for our in-struction—that is, in order to teach us to won-

der at what He Himself wondered at. Hence Augustine says (*Super Gen. cont. Manich.* i, 8)[6]: "Our Lord wondered in order to show us that we, who still need to be so affected, must wonder. Hence all these emotions are not signs of a disturbed mind, but of a Master teaching."

Reply Obj. 1. Although Christ was ignorant of nothing, yet new things might occur to His experimental knowledge, and thus wonder would be caused.

Reply Obj. 2. Christ did not marvel at the Centurion's faith as if it was great with respect to Himself, but because it was great with respect to others.

Reply Obj. 3. He could do all things by the Divine power, for with respect to this there was no wonder in Him, but only with respect to His human experimental knowledge, as was said above.

ARTICLE 9. *Whether There Was Anger in Christ?*

We proceed thus to the Ninth Article: It would seem that there was no anger in Christ.

Objection 1. For it is written (Jas. 1. 20): *The anger of man worketh not the justice of God.* Now whatever was in Christ pertained to the justice of God, since of Him it is written (I Cor. 1. 30): *For He* (Vulg., *Who*) *of God is made unto us . . . justice.* Therefore it seems that there was no anger in Christ.

Obj. 2. Further, anger is opposed to meekness, as is plain from the *Ethics.*[7] But Christ was meek. Therefore there was no anger in Him.

Obj. 3. Further, Gregory says (*Moral.* v, 45)[8] that "anger that comes of evil blinds the eye of the mind, but anger that comes of zeal disturbs it." Now the mind's eye in Christ was neither blinded nor disturbed. Therefore in Christ there was neither sinful anger nor zealous anger.

On the contrary, It is written (John 2. 17) that the words of Ps. 68. 10, *the zeal of Thy house hath eaten me up,* were fulfilled in Him.

I answer that, As was said in the Second Part (I-II, Q XLVI, A. 3, Reply 3, and II-II, Q. CLVIII, A. 2, Reply 3), anger is an effect of sor-row. For when sorrow is inflicted upon someone, there arises within him a desire of the sensitive appetite to repel this injury brought upon him-self or others. Hence anger is a passion com-posed of sorrow and the desire of revenge. Now it was said (A. 6) that sorrow could be in Christ. As to the desire of revenge it is sometimes with sin—that is, when anyone seeks revenge beyond the order of reason; and in this way anger could

---

[1] *In Matt.,* IV, on 26.37 (PL 26, 205).

[2] *In Matt.,* on 26.37 (PL 9, 1066).

[3] *Metaphysics,* I, 2 (982[b]17; 983[a]12).

[4] PG 94, 982.   [5] *Ethics,* IV, 3 (1125[a]2).

[6] PL 34, 180.   [7] Aristotle, IV, 5 (1125[b]26).

[8] PL 75, 726.

not be in Christ, for this kind of anger is called sinful anger.[1] Sometimes, however, this desire is without sin—indeed is praiseworthy—for example, when anyone seeks revenge according to the order justice, and this is called zealous anger. [2] For Augustine says[3] that "he is eaten up by zeal for the house of God, who seeks to better whatever He sees to be evil in it, and if he cannot right it, bears with it and sighs." Such was the anger that was in Christ.

Reply Obj. 1. As Gregory says (*Moral.* v, 45),[4] anger is in man in two ways,—sometimes it forestalls reason, and causes it to operate, and in this way it is properly said "to work," for operations are attributed to the principal agent. It is in this way that we must understand that *the anger of man worketh not the justice of God.* Sometimes anger follows reason, and is, as it were, its instrument, and then the operation, which pertains to justice, is not attributed to anger but to reason.

Reply Obj. 2. It is the anger which outsteps the bounds of reason that is opposed to meekness, and not the anger which is controlled and brought within its proper bounds by reason, for meekness holds the mean in anger.

Reply Obj. 3. In us the natural order is that the soul's powers mutually impede each other—that is, if the operation of one power is intense, the operation of the other is weakened. This is the reason why any movement whatsoever of anger, even if it be tempered by reason, dims the mind's eye of him who contemplates. But in Christ, by control of the Divine power, every power was allowed to do what was proper to it, and one power was not impeded by another. Hence, as the joy of His mind in contemplation did not impede the sorrow or pain of the inferior part, so, conversely, the passions of the inferior part in no way impeded the act of reason.

ARTICLE 10. *Whether Christ Was At Once a Wayfarer and a Comprehensor?*

We proceed thus to the Tenth Article: It would seem that Christ was not at once a wayfarer and a comprehensor.

Objection 1. For it belongs to a wayfarer to be moving toward the end of Happiness, and to a comprehensor it belongs to be resting in the end. Now to be moving towards the end and to be resting in the end cannot belong to the same. Therefore Christ could not be at once wayfarer and comprehensor.

Obj. 2. Further, to tend to Happiness, or to obtain it, does not pertain to man's body, but to his soul; hence Augustine says (*Ep. ad Dios.* cxviii.)[5] that "upon the inferior nature, which is the body, there overflows, not indeed the Happiness which belongs to such as enjoy and understand, the fulness of health, that is, the vigour of incorruption." Now although Christ had a passible body, He fully enjoyed God in His mind. Therefore Christ was not a wayfarer but a comprehensor.

Obj. 3. Further, the Saints, whose souls are in heaven and whose bodies are in the tomb, enjoy Happiness in their souls, although their bodies are subject to death, yet they are called not wayfarers, but only comprehensors. Hence, with equal reason would it seem that Christ was a pure comprehensor and in no way a wayfarer, since His mind enjoyed God although His body was mortal.

On the contrary, It is written (Jer. 14. 8): *Why wilt Thou be as a stranger in the land, and as a wayfaring man turning in to lodge?*

I answer that, A man is called a wayfarer from tending to Happiness, and a comprehensor from having already obtained Happiness, according to I Cor. 9. 24: *So run that you may comprehend* (Douay, *obtain*); and Phil. 3. 12: *I follow after, if by any means I may comprehend* (Douay, *obtain*). Now man's perfect Happiness consists in both soul and body, as stated in the Second Part (I-II, Q. IV, A. 6). In the soul, as regards what is proper to it, according as the mind sees and enjoys God; in the body, according as the body *will rise spiritual in power and glory and incorruption,* as is written I Cor. 15. 42. Now before His passion Christ's mind saw God fully, and thus He had Happiness as far as it regards what is proper to the soul; but Happiness was wanting with regard to all else, since His soul was passible, and His body both passible and mortal, as is clear from the above (A. 4; Q. XIV, AA. 1, 2). Hence He was at once comprehensor, since He had the Happiness proper to the soul, and at the same time wayfarer, since He was tending to Happiness as regards what was wanting to His Happiness.

Reply Obj. 1. It is impossible to be moving towards the end and resting in the end in the same respect; but there is nothing against this under a different respect, as when a man is at once a knower with regard to what he already knows, and yet is a learner with regard to what he does not know.

Reply Obj. 2. Happiness principally and prop-

---

[1] Gregory, *Ibid.*   [2] *Ibid.*
[3] *Tract.* x, on John 2.17 (PL 35, 1471).   [4] PL 75, 725.
[5] Chap. 3 (PL 33, 439).

erly belongs to the soul with regard to the mind, yet secondarily and, so to say, instrumentally, bodily goods are required for Happiness; thus the Philosopher says[1] that exterior goods minister organically to Happiness.

Reply Obj. 3. There is no parity between the soul of a saint and of Christ, for two reasons: first, because the souls of saints are not passible, as Christ's soul was; secondly, because their bodies do nothing by which they tend to Happiness, as Christ by His bodily sufferings tended to Happiness as regards the glory of His body.

QUESTION XVI
OF THE CONSEQUENCES OF THE UNION WITH REGARD TO THOSE THINGS WHICH ARE APPLICABLE TO CHRIST IN HIS BEING AND BECOMING
(In Twelve Articles)

WE must now consider the consequences of the union: and first as to what belongs to Christ in Himself; secondly, as to what belongs to Christ in relation to God the Father (Q. XX); thirdly, as to what belongs to Christ in relation to us (Q. XXV).

Concerning the first, there occurs a twofold consideration. The first is about such things as belong to Christ according to being and becoming; the second regards such things as belong to Christ by reason of unity (Q. XVII).

Under the first head there are twelve points of inquiry: (1) Whether this is true: God is man? (2) Whether this is true: Man is God? (3) Whether Christ may be called a lordly man? (4) Whether what belongs to the Son of Man may be predicated of the Son of God, and conversely? (5) Whether what belongs to the Son of Man may be predicated of the Divine Nature, and what belongs to the Son of God of the human nature? (6) Whether this is true: The Son of God was made man? (7) Whether this is true: Man was made God? (8) Whether this is true: Christ is a creature? (9) Whether this is true: This man, pointing out Christ, began to be? or always was? (10) Whether this is true: Christ as man is a creature? (11) Whether this is true: Christ as man is God? (12) Whether this is true: Christ as man is a hypostasis or person?

ARTICLE 1. *Whether This Is True: "God Is Man"?*

We proceed thus to the First Article: It would seem that this is false: God is man.

[1] *Ethics,* I, 8 (1099ᵃ30).

Objection 1. For every affirmative proposition in remote matter is false. Now this proposition, God is man, is in remote matter, since the forms signified by the subject and predicate are most widely apart. Therefore, since the aforesaid proposition is affirmative, it would seem to be false.

Obj. 2. Further, the three Divine Persons are in greater mutual agreement than the human nature and the Divine. But in the mystery of the Incarnation one Person is not predicated of another; for we do not say that the Father is the Son, or conversely. Therefore it seems that the human nature ought not to be predicated of God by saying that God is man.

Obj. 3. Further, Athanasius says (*Symb. Fid.*)[2] that, "as the soul and the flesh are one man, so are God and man one Christ." But this is false: The soul is the body. Therefore this also is false: God is man.

Obj. 4. Further, it was said in the First Part (Q. XXXIX, A. 4) that what is predicated of God not relatively but absolutely, belongs to the whole Trinity and to each of the Persons. But this word man is not relative, but absolute. Hence, if it is predicated of God, it would follow that the whole Trinity and each of the Persons is man; and this is clearly false.

On the contrary, It is written (Phil. 2. 6, 7): *Who being in the form of God, . . . emptied Himself, taking the form of a servant, being made in the likeness of man, and in habit found as a man;* and thus He Who is in the form of God is man. Now He Who is in the form of God is God. Therefore God is man.

I answer that, This proposition, God is man, is admitted by all Christians, yet not in the same way by all. For some admit the proposition, but not in the proper acceptation of the terms. Thus the Manicheans say[3] the Word of God is man, not indeed true, but fictitious man, since they say that the Son of God assumed an imaginary body, and thus God is called man as a bronze figure is called man if it has the figure of a man. So, too, those who held that Christ's body and soul were not united[4] could not say that God is true man, but that He is figuratively called man by reason of the parts. Now both these opinions were disproved above (Q. II, A. 5; Q. V, AA. 1, 2).

Some, on the contrary, hold the reality on the part of man, but deny the reality on the part of

[2] Cf. Creed "*Quicumque*" (MA II, 1355; DZ 40).
[3] Cf. Augustine, *Confessions,* V, 20 (PL 32, 716); *De Haeres.,* XLVI (PL 42, 37); cf. above, Q. V, A. 2.
[4] Cf. Q. II, A. 6.

God. For they say[1] that Christ, Who is God and man, is God not naturally, but by participation —that is, by grace, even as all other holy men are called gods, Christ being more excellently so than the rest, on account of His more abundant grace. And thus, when it is said that God is man, God does not stand for the true and natural God. And this is the heresy of Photinus, which was disproved above (Q. II, A. 11).

But some admit this proposition, together with the reality of both terms, holding that Christ is true God and true man; yet they do not preserve the truth of the predication. For they say that man is predicated of God by reason of a certain conjunction either of dignity, or of authority, or of affection or indwelling. It was thus that Nestorius held God to be man,[2] nothing further being meant than that God is joined to man by such a conjunction that man is dwelt in by God, and united to Him in affection, and in a share of the Divine authority and honour. And into the same error fall those who suppose two supposita or hypostases in Christ,[3] since it is impossible to understand how, of two things distinct in suppositum or hypostasis, one can be properly predicated of the other, except by a figurative expression, in so far as they are united in something, as if we were to say that Peter is John because they are somehow mutually joined together. And these opinions also were disproved above (Q. II, AA. 3, 6).

Hence, supposing the truth of the Catholic belief, that the true Divine Nature is united with true human nature not only in person, but also in suppositum or hypostasis, we say that this proposition is true and proper, God is man —not only by the truth of its terms—that is, because Christ is true God and true man, but by the truth of the predication. For a word signifying the common nature in the concrete may stand for all contained in the common nature, as this word man may stand for any individual man. And thus this word God, from its very mode of signification, may stand for the Person of the Son of God, as was said in the First Part (Q. XXXIX, A. 4). Now of every suppositum of any nature we may truly and properly predicate a word signifying that nature in the concrete, as man may properly and truly be predicated of Socrates and Plato. Hence, since the Person of the Son of God for Whom this word God stands, is a suppositum of human nature, this word man may be truly and properly

predicated of this word God, as it stands for the Person of the Son of God.

Reply Obj. 1. When different forms cannot come together in one suppositum, the proposition is necessarily in remote matter, the subject signifying one form and the predicate another. But when two forms can come together in one suppositum, the matter is not remote, but natural or contingent, as when I say: Something white is musical. Now the Divine and human natures, although most widely apart, nevertheless come together by the mystery of the Incarnation in one suppositum, in which neither exists accidentally, but [both] essentially. Hence this proposition, God is man, is neither in remote nor in contingent, but in natural matter; and man is not predicated of God accidentally, but essentially, as being predicated of its hypostasis—not, indeed, by reason of the form signified by this word God, but by reason of the suppositum, which is a hypostasis of human nature.

Reply Obj. 2. The three Divine Persons agree in one Nature, and are distinguished in suppositum; and hence they are not predicated one of another. But in the mystery of the Incarnation the natures, being distinct, are not predicated one of the other in the abstract. For the Divine Nature is not the human nature. But because they agree in suppositum, they are predicated of each other in the concrete.

Reply Obj. 3. "Soul" and "flesh" are taken in the abstract, even as Godhead and manhood; but in the concrete we say "animate" and "carnal" or "corporeal," as, on the other hand, "God" and "man." Hence in both cases the abstract is not predicated of the abstract, but only the concrete of the concrete.

Reply Obj. 4. This word man is predicated of God because of the union in person, and this union implies a relation. Hence it does not follow the rule of those words which are absolutely predicated of God from eternity.

ARTICLE 2. *Whether This Is True:* "*Man Is God*"?

We proceed thus to the Second Article: It would seem that this is false: Man is God.

Objection 1. For God is an incommunicable name; hence (Wisd. 13. 10; 14. 21) idolaters are rebuked for giving the name of God, which is incommunicable, to wood and stones. Hence with equal reason does it seem unbecoming that this word God should be predicated of man.

Obj. 2. Further, whatever is predicated of the predicate may be predicated of the subject. But

---

[1] Cf. Ps. 81.6; John 10.34.
[2] Cf. above, Q. II, A. 6.
[3] The Archbishop of Sens; cf. above, Q. II, A. 6.

this is true: God is the Father, or: God is the Trinity. Therefore, if it is true that Man is God, it seems that this also is true: Man is the Father, or: Man is the Trinity. But these are false. Therefore the first is false.

Obj. 3. Further, it is written (Ps. 80. 10): *There shall be no new God in thee.* But man is something new, for Christ was not always man. Therefore this is false: Man is God.

On the contrary, It is written (Rom. 9. 5): *Of whom is Christ according to the flesh, Who is over all things, God blessed for ever.* Now Christ, according to the flesh, is man. Therefore this is true: Man is God.

I answer that, Granted the reality of both natures—that is, Divine and human—and of the union in person and hypostasis, this is true and proper: Man is God, even as this: God is man. For this word man may stand for any hypostasis of human nature, and thus it may stand for the Person of the Son of God, Whom we say is a hypostasis of human nature. Now it is manifest that the word God is truly and properly predicated of the Person of the Son of God, as was said in the First Part (Q. XXXIX, A. 4). Hence it remains that this is true and proper: Man is God.

Reply Obj. 1. Idolaters attributed the name of the Deity to stones and wood considered in their own nature, because they thought there was something divine in them. But we do not attribute the name of the Deity to the man in His human nature, but in the eternal suppositum, which by union is also a suppositum of human nature, as stated above.

Reply Obj. 2. This word Father is predicated of this word God according as this word God stands for the Person of the Father. And in this way it is not predicated of the Person of the Son, because the Person of the Son is not the Person of the Father. And, consequently, it is not necessary that this word Father be predicated of this word Man, of which the word God is predicated, since Man stands for the Person of the Son.

Reply Obj. 3. Although the human nature in Christ is something new, yet the suppositum of the human nature is not new, but eternal. And because this word God is predicated of man not on account of the human nature, but by reason of the suppositum, it does not follow that we assert a new God. But this would follow, if we held that Man stands for a created suppositum; even as must be said by those who assert that there are two supposita in Christ.[1]

[1] Cf. fn, 1, p. 717 above.

ARTICLE 3. *Whether Christ Can Be Called a Lordly Man?*[2]

We proceed thus to the Third Article: It would seem that Christ can be called a lordly man.

Objection 1. For Augustine says (*Qq.* lxxxiii. *qu.* 36)[3] that "we are to be counselled to hope for the goods that were in the Lordly Man," and he is speaking of Christ. Therefore it seems that Christ was a lordly man.

Obj. 2. Further, as lordship belongs to Christ by reason of His Divine Nature, so does manhood belong to the human nature. Now God is said to be humanized, as is plain from Damascene (*De Fide Orthod.* iii, 11),[4] where he says that "being humanized manifests the conjunction with man." Hence with like reason may it be said denominatively that this man is lordly.

Obj. 3. Further, as lordly is derived from lord, so is Divine derived from *Deus* (God). But Dionysius (*Eccl. Hier.* iv)[5] calls Christ "the most Divine Jesus." Therefore with like reason may Christ be called a lordly man.

On the contrary, Augustine says (*Retract.* i, 19):[6] "I do not see that we may rightly call Jesus Christ a lordly man, since He is the Lord Himself."

I answer that, As was said above (A. 2, REPLY 3), when we say "the Man Christ Jesus," we signify the eternal suppositum, which is the Person of the Son of God, because there is only one suppositum of both natures. Now God and Lord are predicated essentially of the Son of God, and hence they ought not to be predicated denominatively, since this takes away from the truth of the union. Hence, since we say lordly denominatively from lord, it cannot truly and properly be said that this Man is lordly, but rather that He is Lord. But if, when we say "the Man Christ Jesus," we mean a created suppositum, as those who assert two supposita in Christ,[7] this man might be called lordly, since he is assumed to a participation of Divine honour, as the Nestorians said.[8] And, even in this way, the human nature is not called "divine"

[2] The question is hardly apposite in English. S. Thomas explains why we can say in Latin, *e.g., oratio dominica* (the Lord's Prayer) or *passio dominica* (Our Lord's Passion), but not speak of our Lord as *homo dominicus* (a lordly man).
[3] PL 40, 26.　　[4] PG 94, 1024.
[5] Pt. III, sect. 10 (PG 3, 484).
[6] PL 32, 616.
[7] Cf. fn. 1, p. 717 above.
[8] Cf. Nestorius, in Cyril of Alexandria, *Dial. cum Nestorio* (PG 76, 252); John Damascene, *De Fide Orth.,* III, 2 (PG 94, 988).

by essence, but "deified"—not, indeed, by its being converted into the Divine Nature, but by its conjunction with the Divine Nature in one hypostasis, as is plain from Damascene (*De Fide Orthod.* iii, 11, 17).[1]

Reply Obj. 1. Augustine retracts these and the like words (*Retract.* i, 19);[2] hence, after the foregoing words (*Retract. ibid.*), he adds: "Wherever I have said this"—namely, that Christ Jesus is a lordly man—"I wish it unsaid, having afterwards seen that it ought not to be said, although it may be defended with some reason"—that is, because one might say that He was called a lordly man by reason of the human nature, which this word man signifies, and not by reason of the suppositum.

Reply Obj. 2. This one suppositum, which is of the human and Divine natures, was first of the Divine Nature—that is, from eternity. Afterwards in time it was made a suppositum of human nature by the Incarnation. And for this reason it is said to be humanized—not that it assumed a man, but that it assumed human nature. But the converse of this is not true—namely, that a suppositum of human nature assumed the Divine Nature; hence we may not say a deified or lordly man.

Reply Obj. 3. This word Divine is usually predicated even of things of which the word God is predicated essentially; thus we say that "the Divine Essence is God," by reason of identity; and that "the Essence belongs to God," or is "Divine," on account of the different way of signifying; and we speak of the "Divine Word," though the Word is God. So, too, we say "a Divine Person," just as we say "the person of Plato," on account of its different mode of signification. But lordly is not predicated of those of which lord is predicated; for we are not accustomed to call a man who is a lord, lordly, but whatsoever belongs to a lord is called lordly, as the lordly will, or the lordly hand, or the lordly possession. And hence the man Christ, Who is Our Lord, cannot be called lordly; yet His flesh can be called lordly flesh and His passion the lordly passion.

ARTICLE 4. *Whether What Belongs to the Son of Man Can Be Predicated of the Son of God, and Conversely?*

We proceed thus to the Fourth Article: It would seem that what belongs to the human nature cannot be said of God.

Objection 1. For opposites cannot be said of the same. Now, what belongs to human nature

is contrary to what is proper to God, since God is uncreated, immutable, and eternal, and it belongs to the human nature to be created, temporal and mutable. Therefore what belongs to the human nature cannot be said of God.

Obj. 2. Further, to attribute to God what is defective seems to take away from the Divine honour, and to be a blasphemy. Now what pertains to the human nature contains a kind of defect, as to suffer, to die, and the like. Hence it seems that what pertains to the human nature can in no way be said of God.

Obj. 3. Further, to be assumed pertains to the human nature; yet it does not pertain to God. Therefore what belongs to the human nature cannot be said of God.

On the contrary, Damascene says (*De Fide Orthod.* iii, 4)[3] that "God assumed the idioms" that is, the properties—"of flesh, since God is said to be passible, and the God of glory was crucified."

I answer that, On this question there was a difference of opinion between Nestorians and Catholics. The Nestorians wished to divide words predicated of Christ, in this way—namely, that such as pertained to human nature should not be predicated of God, and that such as pertained to the Divine Nature should not be predicated of the Man. Hence Nestorius said:[4] "If anyone attempt to attribute sufferings to the Word, let him be anathema." But if there are any words applicable to both natures, of them they predicated what pertained to both natures, as the name "Christ" or "Lord." Hence they granted that Christ was born of a Virgin, and that He was from eternity, but they did not say that God was born of a Virgin, or that the Man was from eternity.

Catholics on the other hand maintained that words which are said of Christ either in His Divine or in His human nature may be said either of God or of man. Hence Cyril says:[5] "If anyone ascribes to two persons or substances" —that is, hypostases—"such words as are in the evangelical and apostolic Scriptures, or have been said of Christ by the Saints, or by Himself of Himself, and believes that some are to be applied to the Man, and apportions some to the Word alone—let him be anathema." And the reason of this is that, since there is one hypostasis of both natures, the same hypostasis is signified by the name of either nature. Thus

[1] PG 94, 1024; 1069.   [2] PL 32, 616.

[3] PG 94, 1000.

[4] Anathema 12, translation of Mercator (PL 48, 923).

[5] *Epist.*, XVII, *Ad Nestorium*, anath. 4 (PG 77, 120); cf. Council of Ephesus, PT. I, chap. 26 (MA IV, 1082; DZ 116); also Mercator's translation (PL 48, 840).

whether we say man or God, the hypostasis of Divine and human nature is signified. And hence, of the Man may be said what belongs to the Divine Nature, as of a hypostasis of the Divine Nature; and of God may be said what belongs to the human nature, as of a hypostasis of human nature.

Nevertheless, it must be borne in mind that in a proposition in which something is predicated of another, we must not merely consider what the predicate is predicated of, but also the reason of its being predicated. Thus, although we do not distinguish things predicated of Christ, yet we distinguish that by reason of which they are predicated, since those things that belong to the Divine Nature are predicated of Christ in His Divine Nature, and those that belong to the human nature are predicated of Christ in His human nature. Hence Augustine says (*De Trin.* i, 11):[1] "We must distinguish what is said by Scripture in reference to the form of God, and what in reference to the form of a servant"; and further on he says (13):[2] "The prudent, careful, and devout reader will discern the reason and point of view of what is said."

Reply Obj. 1. It is impossible for opposites to be predicated of the same in the same respects, but nothing prevents their being predicated of the same in different aspects. And thus opposites are predicated of Christ, not in the same, but in different natures.

Reply Obj. 2. If the things pertaining to defect were attributed to God in His Divine Nature, it would be a blasphemy, since it would be a lessening of His honour. But there is no kind of wrong done to God if they are attributed to Him in His assumed nature. Hence in a discourse of the Council of Ephesus[3] it is said: "God accounts nothing a wrong which is the occasion of man's salvation. For no lowliness that He assumed for us injures that Nature which can be subject to no injury, yet makes lower things Its own, to save our nature. Therefore, since these lowly and worthless things do no harm to the Divine Nature but bring about our salvation, how dost thou maintain that what was the cause of our salvation was the occasion of harm to God?"

Reply Obj. 3. To be assumed pertains to human nature not in its suppositum, but in itself; and thus it does not belong to God.

[1] PL 42, 836.
[2] PL 42, 840.
[3] Pt. III, chap. 10 (MA v, 205); Theodotus Ancyranus, hom. II (PG 77, 1372).

ARTICLE 5. *Whether What Belongs to the Son of Man Can Be Predicated of the Divine Nature and What Belongs to the Son of God Predicated of the Human Nature?*

We proceed thus to the Fifth Article: It would seem that what belongs to the human nature can be said of the Divine Nature.

Objection 1. For what belongs to the human nature is predicated of the Son of God, and of God. But God is His own Nature. Therefore, what belongs to the human nature may be predicated of the Divine Nature.

Obj. 2. Further, the flesh pertains to human nature. But as Damascene says (*De Fide Orthod.* iii, 6),[4] "we say, after the blessed Athanasius and Cyril, that the Nature of the Word was incarnate." Therefore it would seem with equal reason that what belongs to the human nature may be said of the Divine Nature.

Obj. 3. Further, what belongs to the Divine Nature belongs to Christ's human nature, such as to know future things and to possess saving power. Therefore it would seem with equal reason that what belongs to the human may be said of the Divine Nature.

On the contrary, Damascene says (*De Fide Orthod.* iii, 4):[5] "When we mention the Godhead we do not predicate of it the idioms"— that is, the properties—"of the humanity; for we do not say that the Godhead is passible or creatable." Now the Godhead is the Divine Nature. Therefore what is proper to the human nature cannot be said of the Divine Nature.

I answer that, What belongs to one cannot be said of another, unless they are both the same; thus capable of laughter can be predicated only of man. Now in the mystery of the Incarnation the Divine and human natures are not the same, but the hypostasis of the two natures is the same. And hence what belongs to one nature cannot be predicated of the other if they are taken in the abstract. Now concrete words stand for the hypostasis of the nature; and hence of concrete words we may predicate indifferently what belongs to either nature—whether the word of which they are predicated refers to each nature, as the word Christ, by which is signified "both the Godhead anointing and the manhood anointed"; or to the Divine Nature alone, as this word "God" or "the Son of God"; or to the manhood alone, as this word "Man" or "Jesus." Hence Pope Leo says (*Ep. ad Palæst.* cxxiv):[6] "It is of no consequence from what substance

[4] PG 94, 1008.   [5] PG 94, 997.
[6] Chap. 7 (PL 54, 1066).

we name Christ; because since the unity of person remains inseparably, one and the same is altogether Son of Man by His flesh, and altogether Son of God by the Godhead which He has with the Father."

Reply Obj. 1. In God, Person and Nature are really the same, and by reason of this identity the Divine Nature is predicated of the Son of God. Nevertheless, its mode of predication is different, and hence certain things are said of the Son of God which are not said of the Divine Nature; thus we say that the Son of God is born, yet we do not say that the Divine Nature is born, as was said in the First Part (Q. XXXIX, A. 5). So, too, in the mystery of the Incarnation we say that the Son of God suffered, yet we do not say that the Divine Nature suffered.

Reply Obj. 2. Incarnation implies union with flesh, rather than any property of flesh. Now in Christ each nature is united to the other in person; and by reason of this union the Divine Nature is said to be incarnate and the human nature deified, as stated above (Q. II, A. 1, Reply 3).

Reply Obj. 3. What belongs to the Divine Nature is predicated of the human nature—not, indeed, as it belongs essentially to the Divine Nature, but as it is participated by the human nature. Hence, whatever cannot be participated by the human nature (as to be uncreated and omnipotent), is in no way predicated of the human nature. But the Divine Nature received nothing by participation from the human nature; and hence what belongs to the human nature can in no way be predicated of the Divine Nature.

ARTICLE 6. *Whether This Is True: "God Was Made Man"?*

We proceed thus to the Sixth Article: It would seem that this is false: God was made man.

Objection 1. For since man signifies a substance, to be made man is to be made absolutely. But this is false: "God was made absolutely." Therefore this is false: God was made man.

Obj. 2. Further, to be made man is to be changed. But God cannot be the subject of change, according to Mal. 3. 6: *I am the Lord, and I change not.* Hence this is false: God was made man.

Obj. 3. Further, man as predicated of Christ stands for the Person of the Son of God. But this is false: God was made the Person of the Son of God. Therefore this is false: God was made man.

On the contrary, It is written (John 1. 14): *The Word was made flesh;* and as Athanasius says (*Ep. ad Epictetum*),[1] "when he said, 'The Word was made flesh,' it is as if it were said that God was made man."

I answer that, A thing is said to be made that which begins to be predicated of it for the first time. Now to be man is truly predicated of God, as stated above (A. 1), yet in such sort that it pertains to God to be man, not from eternity, but from the time of His assuming human nature. Hence, this is true, God was made man, though it is understood differently by some, even as this, God is man, as we said above (A. 1).

Reply Obj. 1. To be made man is to be made absolutely in all those in whom human nature begins to be in a newly created suppositum. But God is said to have been made man because the human nature began to be in an eternally pre-existing suppositum of the Divine Nature. And hence for God to be made man does not mean that God was made absolutely.

Reply Obj. 2. As stated above, to be made implies that something is newly predicated of another. Hence, whenever anything is predicated for the first time of another, and there is a change in that of which it is predicated, then to be made is to be changed; and this takes place in whatever is predicated absolutely, for whiteness or greatness cannot newly affect anything, unless it be newly changed to whiteness or greatness. But whatever is predicated relatively can be newly predicated of anything without its change, as a man may be made to be on the right side without being changed, and merely by the change of him on whose left side he was. Hence in such cases not all that is said to be made is changed, since it may happen by the change of something else. And it is thus we say of God: *Lord, Thou art made* (Douay, *hast been*) *our refuge* (Ps. 89. 1). Now to be man belongs to God by reason of the union, which is a relation. And hence to be man is newly predicated of God without any change in Him, by a change in the human nature, which is assumed to a Divine Person. And hence, when it is said, God was made man, we understand no change on the part of God, but only on the part of the human nature.

Reply Obj. 3. Man stands not for the bare Person of the Son of God, but according as it subsists in human nature. Hence, although this is false, "God was made the Person of the Son of God," yet this is true, "God was made man" by being united to human nature.

[1] PG 26, 1061.

ARTICLE 7. *Whether This Is True: "Man Was Made God?"*

We proceed thus to the Seventh Article: It would seem that this is true: Man was made God.

Objection 1. For it is written (Rom. 1. 2, 3): *Which He had promised before by His prophets in the holy Scriptures, concerning His Son Who was made to Him of the seed of David according to the flesh.* Now Christ, as man, is of the seed of David according to the flesh. Therefore man was made the Son of God.

Obj. 2. Further, Augustine says (*De Trin.* i, 13)[1] that "such was this assumption, which made God man, and man God." But by reason of this assumption this is true: God was made man. Therefore, in like manner, this is true: Man was made God.

Obj. 3. Further, Gregory Nazianzen says (*Ep. ad Chelid.* ci):[2] "God was humanized and man was deified, or whatever else one may like to call it." Now God is said to be humanized by being made man. Therefore with equal reason man is said to be deified by being made God; and thus it is true that "Man was made God."

Obj. 4. Further, when it is said that "God was made man," the subject of the making or change is not God, but human nature, which the word man signifies. Now that seems to be the subject of the making to which the making is attributed. Hence Man was made God is truer than God was made man.

On the contrary, Damascene says (*De Fide Orthod.* iii, 2):[3] "We do not say that man was deified, but that God was humanized." Now to be made God is the same as to be deified. Hence this is false: Man was made God.

I answer that, This proposition, Man was made God, may be understood in three ways. First, so that the participle "made" absolutely determines either the subject or the predicate; and in this sense it is false, since neither the Man of Whom it is predicated was made, nor is God made, as will be said (AA. 8, 9). And in the same sense this is false: God was made man. But it is not of this sense that we are now speaking.

Secondly, it may be so understood that the word "made" determines the composition, with this meaning: Man was made God—that is, it was brought about that Man is God. And in this sense both are true—namely, that Man was made God and that God was made Man. But this it not the proper sense of these

phrases; unless, indeed, we are to understand that "man" has not a personal, but a simple supposition. For although "this man" was not made God, because this suppositum—namely, the Person of the Son of God—was eternally God, yet man, speaking commonly, was not always God.

Thirdly, properly understood, this participle "made" attaches making to man with respect to God, as the term of the making. And in this sense, granted that the Person or hypostasis in Christ are the same as the suppositum of God and Man, as was shown (Q. II, AA. 2, 3), this proposition is false, because, when it is said, Man was made God, "man" has a personal suppositum; because to be God is not verified of the Man in His human nature, but in His suppositum. Now the suppositum of human nature, of Whom "to be God" is verified, is the same as the hypostasis or Person of the Son of God, Who was always God. Hence it cannot be said that this Man began to be God, or is made God, or that He was made God.

But if there were a different person or hypostasis of God and man, so that "to be God" was predicated of the man, and, conversely, by reason of a certain conjunction of supposita, or of personal dignity, or of affection or indwelling, as the Nestorians said,[4] then with equal reason might it be said that Man was made God—that is, joined to God—and that God was made Man—that is, joined to man.

Reply Obj. 1. In these words of the Apostle the relative "Who" which refers to the Person of the Son of God ought not to be considered as affecting the predicate, as if someone already existing of the *seed of David according to the flesh* was made the Son of God—and it is in this sense that the objection takes it. But it ought to be taken as affecting the subject, with this meaning—that the *Son of God was made to Him* ("namely, to the honour of the Father," as a gloss expounds it),[5] *being of the seed of David according to the flesh,* as if to say "the Son of God having flesh of the seed of David to the honour of God."

Reply Obj. 2. This saying of Augustine is to be taken in the sense that by the assumption that took place in the Incarnation it was brought about that Man is God and God is Man; and in this sense both sayings are true, as stated above.

The same is to be said in the *reply to the*

[1] PL 42, 840.   [2] PG 37, 180.   [3] PG 94, 988.

[4] See above, Q. II, A. 6.
[5] *Glossa interl.* (VI, 3v); *Glossa* Lombardi (PL 191, 1305).

third, since to be deified is the same as to be made God.

Reply Obj. 4. A term placed in the subject is taken materially—that is, for the suppositum; placed in the predicate it is taken formally—that is, for the nature signified. Hence when it is said that Man was made God, the being made is not attributed to the human nature but to the suppositum of the human nature, Which is God from eternity, and hence it does not befit Him to be made God. But when it is said that God was made Man, the making is taken to be terminated in the human nature. Hence, properly speaking, this is true: God was made Man, and this is false: Man was made God; even as if Socrates, who was already a man, were made white, and were pointed out, this would be true: This man was made white to-day, and this would be false: This white thing was made man to-day.

Nevertheless, if on the part of the subject there is added some word signifying human nature in the abstract, it might be taken in this way for the subject of the making—for example, if it were said that "human nature was made the Son of God's."

ARTICLE 8. *Whether This Is True: "Christ Is a Creature"?*

We proceed thus to the Eighth Article: It would seem that this is true: Christ is a creature.

Objection 1. For Pope Leo says:[1] "A new and unheard of covenant: God Who is and was, is made a creature." Now we may predicate of Christ whatever the Son of God became by the Incarnation. Therefore this is true: Christ is a creature.

Obj. 2. Further, the properties of both natures may be predicated of the common hypostasis of both natures, no matter by what word they are signified, as stated above (A. 5). But it is the property of human nature to be created, as it is the property of the Divine Nature to be Creator. Hence both may be said of Christ—namely, that He is a creature and that he is uncreated and Creator.

Obj. 3. Further, the principal part of a man is the soul rather than the body. But Christ, by reason of the body which He took from the Virgin, is said absolutely to be born of the Virgin. Therefore by reason of the soul which is created by God, it ought to be said absolutely that He is a creature.

On the contrary, Ambrose says:[2] "Was Christ made by a word? Was Christ created by a command?" as if to say: No! Hence he adds: "How can there be a creature in God? For God has a simple not a composite Nature." Therefore it must not be granted that "Christ is a creature."

I answer that, As Jerome says,[3] "words spoken out of order lead to heresy"; hence with us and heretics the very words ought not to be in common, lest we seem to countenance their error. Now the Arian heretics said[4] that Christ was a creature and less than the Father, not only in His human nature, but even in His Divine Person. And hence we must not say absolutely that Christ is a creature or less than the Father, but with a qualification—namely, in His human nature. But such things as could not be considered to belong to the Divine Person in Itself may be predicated absolutely of Christ by reason of His human nature; thus we say absolutely that Christ suffered, died and was buried, even as in corporeal and human beings, things of which we may doubt whether they belong to the whole or the part, if they are observed to exist in a part, are not predicated of the whole absolutely—that is, without qualification, for we do not say that the Ethiopian is white but that he is white as regards his teeth; but we say without qualification that he is curly, since this can only belong to him as regards his hair.

Reply Obj. 1. Sometimes, for the sake of brevity, the holy doctors use the word "creature" of Christ without any qualifying term; we should however take as understood the qualification, "as man."

Reply Obj. 2. All the properties of the human, just as of the Divine Nature, may be predicated equally of Christ. Hence Damascene says (*De Fide Orthod.* iii, 4)[5] that "Christ, Who is God and Man, is called created and uncreated, divisible and indivisible." Nevertheless things of which we may doubt to what nature they belong are not to be predicated without a qualification. Hence he afterwards adds (*De Fide Orthod.* iv, 5)[6] that "the one hypostasis"—that is, of Christ—"is uncreated in its Godhead and created in its manhood"; even so conversely, we may not say

[1] Among the works of Augustine, *Serm. Suppos.*, CXXVIII (PL 39, 1998).

[2] *De Fide*, I, 16 (PL 16, 575).
[3] Cf. *Glossa ordin.*, on Osee 2.16 (IV, 336A); cf. Peter Lombard, *Sent.*, IV, d. XIII, chap. 2 (QR II, 818).
[4] Cf. Athanasius, *Epist. De Synod.*, XVI (PL 26, 708); Epiphanius, *Adv. Haeres.*, II, 2, *haeres.* 69 (PG 42, 213); cf. above, Q. X, A. 2, REPLY 1.
[5] PG 94, 997. [6] PG 94, 1109.

without qualification, "Christ is incorporeal" or "impassible," in order to avoid the error of Manes,[1] who held that Christ had not a true body, nor truly suffered, but we must say, with a qualification, that Christ was incorporeal and impassible in His Godhead.

Reply Obj. 3. There can be no doubt how the birth from the Virgin applies to the Person of the Son of God, as there can be in the case of creation; and hence there is no parity.

ARTICLE 9. *Whether This Is True: "This Man, Pointing Out Christ, Began To Be"?*

We proceed thus to the Ninth Article: It would seem that this Man, pointing out Christ, began to be.

Objection 1. For Augustine says (*Tract.* cv *in Joann.*)[2] that "before the world was, neither were we, nor the Mediator of God and men—the Man Jesus Christ." But what was not always, has begun to be. Therefore this Man, pointing to Christ, began to be.

Obj. 2. Further, Christ began to be Man. But to be man is to be absolutely. Therefore this man began to be, absolutely.

Obj. 3. Further, "man" implies a suppositum of human nature. But Christ was not always a suppositum of human nature. Therefore this Man began to be.

On the contrary, It is written (Heb. 13. 8): *Jesus Christ yesterday and to-day: and the same for ever.*

I answer that, We must not say that "this Man"—pointing to Christ—"began to be," unless we add something. And this for a twofold reason. First, for this proposition is false absolutely, in the judgment of the Catholic Faith, which affirms that in Christ there is one suppositum and one hypostasis, as also one Person. For according to this, when we say "this Man," pointing to Christ, the eternal suppositum is necessarily meant, with Whose eternity to begin to be is incompatible. Hence this is false: *This Man began to be.* Nor does it matter that to begin to be refers to the human nature, which is signified by this word man, because the term placed in the subject is not taken formally so as to signify the nature, but is taken materially so as to signify the suppositum, as was said (A. 7; Reply 4).

Secondly, because even if this proposition were true, it ought not to be made use of without qualification, in order to avoid the heresy of Arius, who, since he pretended that the Person of the Son of God is a creature and less than the Father, so he maintained that He began to be, saying there was a time when He was not.[3]

Reply Obj. 1. The words quoted must be qualified—that is, we must say that the Man Jesus Christ was not, before the world was, in His humanity.

Reply Obj. 2. With this word "begin" we cannot argue from the lower to the higher. For it does not follow if this began to be white, that therefore it began to be coloured. And this because "to begin" implies being now and not before; for it does not follow if This was not white before that therefore it was not coloured before. Now, to be absolutely is higher than to be man. Hence this does not follow: Christ began to be Man—therefore He began to be.

Reply Obj. 3. This word Man, as it is taken for Christ, although it signifies the human nature, which began to be, nevertheless stands for the eternal suppositum which did not begin to be. Hence, since it signifies the suppositum when placed in the subject, and refers to the nature when placed in the predicate, therefore this is false: The Man Christ began to be; but this is true: Christ began to be Man.

ARTICLE 10. *Whether This Is True: "Christ as Man Is a Creature"?*

We proceed thus to the Tenth Article: It would seem that this is false: "Christ as Man is a creature," or "began to be."

Objection 1. For nothing in Christ is created except the human nature. But this is false: Christ as Man is the human nature. Therefore this is also false: Christ as Man is a creature.

Obj. 2. Further, the predicate is predicated of the term placed in reduplication, rather than of the subject of the proposition; as when I say: A body as coloured is visible, if follows that the coloured is visible. But as stated (A. 8,) we must not absolutely grant that the Man Christ is a creature; nor consequently that Christ as Man is a creature.

Obj. 3. Further, whatever is predicated of a man as man is predicated of him *per se* and absolutely, for *per se* is the same as "in virtue of itself," as is said in the *Metaphysics.*[4] But

---

[1] See fn. 3, p. 796 above.   [2] PL 35, 1907.

[3] See above, Q. X, A. 2, Reply 1; Q. XVI, A. 8; also Part I, Q. XLII, A. 2, Reply 4; cf. further, Athanasius, *Epist. encycl. ad Episc. Aegypti* (PG 25, 573); *Epist. ad Jovianum* (PG 26, 810); *Epist. ad Afros Episc.* (PG 26, 1038); Basil, *hom.* XVI (PG 31, 473); Hilary, *De Trin.,* XII (PL 10, 444); cf. Nicaean Creed (MA II, 667; DZ 54).

[4] Aristotle, V, 18 (1022[a]14; [a]25).

this is false: Christ is *per se* and absolutely a creature. Hence this, too, is false: Christ as Man is a creature.

On the contrary, Whatever is, is either Creator or creature. But this is false: Christ as Man is Creator. Therefore this is true: Christ as Man is a creature.

I answer that, When we say "Christ as Man" this word "man" may be added in the reduplication either by reason of the suppositum or by reason of the nature. If it be added by reason of the suppositum, since the suppositum of the human nature in Christ is eternal and uncreated, this will be false: Christ as Man is a creature. But if it be added by reason of the human nature, it is true, since by reason of the human nature or in the human nature, it belongs to Him to be a creature, as was said (A. 8).

It must however be borne in mind that the term thus added by the reduplication signifies the nature rather than the suppositum, since it is added as a predicate, which is taken formally, for it is the same to say Christ as Man and to say Christ as He is a Man. Hence this is to be granted rather than denied: Christ as Man is a creature. But if something further be added whereby [the term covered by the reduplication] is attracted to the suppositum, this proposition is to be denied rather than granted, for instance were one to say: Christ as "this" Man is a creature.

Reply Obj. 1. Although Christ is not the human nature, He has human nature. Now the word creature is naturally predicated not only of abstract but also of concrete things, since we say that manhood is a creature and that man is a creature.

Reply Obj. 2. Man as placed in the subject refers to the suppositum but, as placed in the reduplication refers rather to the nature, as was stated above. And because the nature is created and the suppositum uncreated, therefore, although it is not granted absolutely that "this man is a creature," yet it is granted that "Christ as Man is a creature."

Reply Obj. 3. It belongs to every man who is a suppositum of human nature alone to have his being only in human nature. Hence of every such suppositum it follows that if it is a creature as man, it is a creature absolutely. But Christ is a suppositum not merely of human nature but also of the Divine Nature, in which He has an uncreated being. Hence it does not follow that if He is a creature as Man He is a creature absolutely.

ARTICLE 11. *Whether This Is True: "Christ as Man Is God"?*

We proceed thus to the Eleventh Article: It would seem that Christ, as Man, is God.

Objection 1. For Christ is God by the grace of union. But Christ, as Man, has the grace of union. Therefore Christ as Man is God.

Obj. 2. Further, to forgive sins is proper to God, according to Isa. 43. 25: *I am He that blot out thy iniquities for My own sake.* But Christ as Man forgives sin, according to Matt. 9. 6: *But that you may know that the Son of Man hath power on earth to forgive sins,* etc. Therefore Christ as Man is God.

Obj. 3. Further, Christ is not Man in general, but is this particular Man. Now Christ, as this Man, is God, since by "this Man" we signify the eternal suppositum which is God naturally. Therefore Christ as Man is God.

On the contrary, Whatever belongs to Christ as Man belongs to every man. Now, if Christ as Man is God, it follows that every man is God—which is clearly false.

I answer that, This term man when placed in reduplication may be taken in two ways. First as referring to the nature, and in this way it is not true that Christ as Man is God, because the human nature is distinct from the Divine by a difference of nature. Secondly it may be taken by reason of the suppositum, and in this way, since the suppositum of the human nature in Christ is the Person of the Son of God, to Whom it belongs *per se* to be God, it is true that Christ, as Man, is God. Nevertheless because the term placed in the reduplication signifies the nature rather than the suppositum, as stated above (A. 10), hence this is to be denied rather than granted: Christ as Man is God.

Reply Obj. 1. It is not with regard to the same respect that a thing moves towards, and that it is, something; for to move belongs to a thing by reason of its matter or subject, and to be in act belongs to it by reason of its form. So too it is not with regard to the same respect that it belongs to Christ to be ordered to be God by the grace of union, and to be God. For the first belongs to Him in His human nature, and the second, in His Divine Nature. Hence this is true: Christ as Man has the grace of union; yet not this: Christ as Man is God.

Reply Obj. 2. *The Son of Man has on earth the power of forgiving sins,* not by virtue of the human nature, but by virtue of the Divine Nature, in which Divine Nature resides the power of forgiving sins by authority, whereas in the human nature it resides instrumentally and ministerially. Hence Chrysostom expounding this passage says:[1] "He said pointedly 'on earth to forgive sins,' in order to show that by an indivisible union He united human nature to the power of the Godhead, since although He was made Man, yet He remained the Word of God."

Reply Obj. 3. When we say "this man," the demonstrative pronoun "this" attracts "man" to the suppositum; and hence "Christ as this Man, is God," is a true proposition rather than "Christ as Man is God."

ARTICLE 12. *Whether This Is True: "Christ as Man Is a Hypostasis or Person"?*

We proceed thus to the Twelfth Article: It would seem that Christ as Man is a person.

Objection 1. For what belongs to every man belongs to Christ as Man, since He is like other men according to Phil. 2. 7: *Being made in the likeness of men.* But every man is a person. Therefore Christ as Man is a person.

Obj. 2. Further, Christ as Man is a substance of rational nature. But He is not a universal substance; therefore He is an individual substance. Now a person is nothing else than an individual substance of rational nature, as Boëthius says (*De Duab. Nat.*).[2] Therefore Christ as Man is a person.

Obj. 3. Further, Christ as Man is a being of human nature, and a suppositum and a hypostasis of the same nature. But every hypostasis and suppositum and being of human nature is a person. Therefore Christ as Man is a person.

On the contrary, Christ as Man is not an eternal person. Therefore if Christ as Man is a person it would follow that in Christ there are two persons—one temporal and the other eternal, which is erroneous, as was said above (Q. II, A. 6; Q. IV, A. 2).

I answer that, As was said (AA. 10, 11), the term Man placed in the reduplication may refer either to the suppositum or to the nature. Hence when it is said: Christ as Man is a person, if it is taken as referring to the suppositum, it is clear that Christ as Man is a person, since the suppositum of human nature is nothing else than the Person of the Son of God. But if it be taken as referring to the nature, it may be understood in two ways. First, we may so understand it as if it belonged to human nature to be in a person, and in this way it is true, for whatever subsists in human nature is a person.

Secondly it may be taken that in Christ a proper personality, caused by the principles of the human nature, is due to the human nature; and in this way Christ as Man is not a person, since the human nature does not exist of itself apart from the Divine Nature, and yet the notion of person requires this.

Reply Obj. 1. It belongs to every man to be a person, according as everything subsisting in human nature is a person. Now, this is proper to the Man Christ that the Person subsisting in His human nature is not caused by the principles of the human nature, but is eternal. Hence in one way He is a person, as Man, and in another way He is not, as stated above.

Reply Obj. 2. The individual substance which is included in the definition of a person means a complete substance subsisting of itself and separate from all else. Otherwise, a man's hand might be called a person, since it is a kind of individual substance; nevertheless, because it is an individual substance existing in something else, it cannot be called a person; nor, for the same reason, can the human nature in Christ, although it may be called something individual and singular.

Reply Obj. 3. As a person signifies something complete and self-subsisting in rational nature, so a hypostasis, suppositum, and being of nature in the genus of substance, signify something that subsists of itself. Hence, as human nature is not of itself a person apart from the Person of the Son of God, so likewise it is not of itself a hypostasis or suppositum or a being of nature. Hence in the sense in which we deny that "Christ as Man is a person" we must deny all the other propositions.

QUESTION XVII

OF WHAT PERTAINS TO CHRIST'S UNITY FROM THE STANDPOINT OF BEING

(*In Two Articles*)

WE must now consider what pertains to Christ's unity in general. For, in their proper place, we must determine what pertains to unify and plurality in detail; thus we determined (Q. IX) that there is only one knowledge in Christ, and it will be concluded hereafter (Q. XXXV, A. 2) that there is not only one nativity in Christ.

Hence we must consider Christ's unity (1) of being; (2) of will (Q. XVIII); (3) of operation (Q. XIX).

Under the first head there are two points of inquiry: (1) Whether Christ is one or two? (2) Whether there is only one being in Christ?

---

[1] Cf. Thomas, *Cat. Aurea*, on Mark, 2.10.
[2] Chap. 4 (PL 64, 1343).

ARTICLE 1. *Whether Christ Is One or Two?*

We proceed thus to the First Article: It would seem that Christ is not one, but two.

Objection 1. For Augustine says (*De Trin.* i, 7):[1] "Because the form of God took the form of a servant, both are God by reason of God Who assumed, yet both are Man by reason of the man assumed." Now "both" may only be said when there are two. Therefore Christ is two.

Obj. 2. Further, where there is one thing and another there are two. Now Christ is one thing and another; for Augustine says (*Enchir.* xxxv):[2] "Being in the form of God . . . He took the form of a servant . . . being both in one; but He was one of these as Word, and the other as man." Therefore Christ is two.

Obj. 3. Further, Christ is not only man; for, thus He would be a mere man. Therefore He is something else than man, and thus in Christ there is one thing and another. Therefore Christ is two.

Obj. 4. Further, Christ is something that the Father is, and something that the Father is not. Therefore Christ is one thing and another. Therefore Christ is two.

Obj. 5. Further, as in the mystery of the Trinity there are three Persons in one Nature, so in the mystery of the Incarnation there are two natures in one Person. But on account of the unity of the Nature, notwithstanding the distinction of Person, the Father and Son are one, according to John 10. 30: *I and the Father are one*. Therefore, notwithstanding the unity of Person, Christ is two on account of the duality of nature.

Obj. 6. Further, the Philosopher says[3] that "one" and "two" are predicated denominatively. Now Christ has a duality of nature. Therefore Christ is two.

Obj. 7. "Further, as accidental form makes a thing otherwise (*alterum*) so does substantial form make another thing (*aliud*)" as Porphyry says.[4] Now in Christ there are two substantial natures, the human and the Divine. Therefore Christ is one thing and another. Therefore Christ is two.

On the contrary, Boëthius says (*De Duab. Nat.*):[5] "Whatever is, in so far as it is, is one." But we confess that Christ is. Therefore Christ is one.

I answer that, Nature, considered in itself,

as it is used in the abstract, cannot truly be predicated of the suppositum or person, except in God, in Whom "what it is" and "that by which it is" do not differ, as stated in the First Part (Q. XXIX, A. 4, REPLY 1). But in Christ, since there are two natures—namely, the Divine and the human—one of them—namely, the Divine—may be predicated of Him both in the abstract and in the concrete, for we say that the Son of God, Who is signified by the word Christ, is the Divine Nature and is God. But the human nature cannot be predicated of Christ in the abstract, but only in the concrete —that is, as it is signified by the suppositum. For we cannot truly say that Christ is human nature, because human nature is not naturally predicated of its suppositum. But we say that Christ is a man, even as Christ is God. Now God signifies one having Godhead, and man signifies one having manhood. Yet one having manhood is differently signified by the word man and by the word Jesus or Peter. For this word man implies one having manhood indistinctly, even as the word God implies indistinctly one having the Godhead; but the word Peter or Jesus implies one having manhood distinctly—that is, with its determinate individual properties—as Son of God implies one having the Godhead under a determinate personal property.

Now the dual number is placed in Christ with regard to the natures. Hence, if both the natures were predicated in the abstract of Christ, it would follow that Christ is two. But because the two natures are not predicated of Christ except as they are signified in the suppositum, it must be by reason of the suppositum that "one" or "two" is predicated of Christ. Now some placed two supposita in Christ, and one Person, which, in their opinion, would seem to be the suppositum completed with its final completion.[6] Hence, since they placed two supposita in Christ, they said that God is two, in the neuter. But because they asserted one Person, they said that Christ is one, in the masculine, for the neuter gender signifies something unformed and imperfect, whereas the masculine signifies something formed and perfect.[7] On the other hand, the Nestorians, who asserted two Persons in Christ,[8] said that Christ is two not only in the neuter, but also in the masculine.[9] But since we

[1] PL 42, 829   [2] PL 40, 250.

[3] *Physics*, III, 3 (202ª18).

[4] *Isagoge*, Boëthius' translation (CG IV, 35.6).

[5] Chap. 4 (PL 64, 1346).

[6] See fn. 1, p. 717 above.

[7] Cf. William of Auxerre, *Summa Aurea*, III, tr. 1, chap. 1, Q. 8 (113va).   [8] Cf. Q. II, A. 6.

[9] Cf. Cyril of Alexandria, *Adv. Nestorii Blasphemias*, II, 6 (PG 76, 85); see also DTC, art. *Hypostatique* (*Union*) (VII, 473).

maintain one person and one suppositum in Christ, as is clear from Q. II, AA. 2, 3, it follows that we say that Christ is one not merely in the masculine, but also in the neuter.

Reply Obj. 1. This saying of Augustine is not to be taken as if "both" referred to the predicate, so as to mean that Christ is both, but it refers to the subject. And thus "both" does not stand for two supposita, but for two words signifying two natures in the concrete. For I can say that "both"—namely, God and Man— "are God" on account of God Who assumes; and "both"—namely, God and Man—"are Man on account of the man assumed."

Reply Obj. 2. When it is said that "Christ is one thing and another," this saying is to be explained in this sense—"having this nature and another." And it is in this way that Augustine explains it (Contra Felic. xi),[1] where, after saying, "In the mediator of God and man, the Son of God is one thing, and the Son of Man another," he adds, "I say another thing by reason of the difference of substance, and not another thing by reason of the unity of person." Hence Gregory Nazianzen says (*Ep. ad Chelid.* ci):[2] "If we must speak briefly, that of which the Saviour is, is one thing and another; thus the invisible is not the same as the visible, and what is without time is not the same as what is in time. Yet they are not one and another; far from it. For both these are one."

Reply Obj. 3. This is false: "Christ is only man," because it does not exclude another suppositum, but another nature, since terms placed in the predicate are taken formally. But if anything is added whereby it is drawn to the suppositum, it would be a true proposition—for instance, "Christ is only that which is man." Nevertheless, it would not follow that He is "any other thing than man," because "another thing," since it refers to a diversity of substance, properly refers to the suppositum, even as all relative things bearing a personal relation. But it does follow: Therefore He has another nature.

Reply Obj. 4. When it is said, "Christ is something that the Father is," "something" signifies the Divine Nature, which is predicated even in the abstract of the Father and Son. But when it is said, "Christ is something that is not the Father," "something" signifies not the human nature as it is in the abstract, but as it is

in the concrete; not, indeed, in a distinct, but in an indistinct suppositum—that is, according as it underlies the nature and not the individuating properties. Hence it does not follow that Christ is one thing and another, or that He is two, since the suppositum of the human nature in Christ, which is the Person of the Son of God, is not accounted numerically with the Divine Nature, which is predicated of the Father and Son.

Reply Obj. 5. In the mystery of the Divine Trinity the Divine Nature is predicated even in the abstract of the three Persons; hence it may be said absolutely that the three Persons are one. But in the mystery of the Incarnation both natures are not predicated in the abstract of Christ; hence it cannot be said absolutely that Christ is two.

Reply Obj. 6. Two signifies what has duality, not in another, but in the same thing of which "two" is predicated. Now what is predicated is said of the suppositum, which is implied by the word Christ. Hence, although Christ has duality of nature, yet, because He has not duality of suppositum, it cannot be said that Christ is two.

Reply Obj. 7. "Otherwise" implies diversity of accident. Hence diversity of accident suffices for anything to be called "otherwise" absolutely. But "another thing" implies diversity of substance. Now not merely the nature, but also the suppositum is said to be a substance, as is said in the *Metaphysics*.[3] Hence diversity of nature does not suffice for anything to be called "another thing" absolutely unless there is diversity of suppositum. But diversity of nature makes "another thing" relatively—that is, in nature— if there is no diversity of suppositum.

ARTICLE 2. *Whether There Is Only One Being in Christ?*

We proceed thus to the Second Article: It would seem that in Christ there is not only one being, but two.

Objection 1. For Damascene says (*De Fide Orthod.* iii, 13-15)[4] that whatever follows the nature is doubled in Christ. But being follows the nature, for being is from the form. Hence in Christ there are two beings.

Obj. 2. Further, the being of the Son of God is the Divine Nature itself, and is eternal, whereas the being of the Man Christ is not the Divine Nature, but is a temporal being. Therefore there is not only one being in Christ.

Obj. 3. Further, in the Trinity, although there

[1] Vigilius Tapsensus, *De Unit. Trin.*, chap. 14 (PL 62, 344) or chap. 11 (PL 42, 1166).
[2] PG 37, 180.
[3] Aristotle, v. 8 (1017[b]23).   [4] PG 94, 1033–1061.

are three Persons, yet on account of the unity of nature there is only one being. But in Christ there are two natures, though there is one Person. Therefore in Christ there is not only one being but two.

Obj. 4. Further, in Christ the soul gives some being to the body, since it is its form. But it does not give the Divine being, since this is uncreated. Therefore in Christ there is another being besides the Divine being; and thus in Christ there is not only one being.

On the contrary, Everything is said to be a being, in so far as it is one, for one and being are convertible. Therefore, if there were two beings in Christ and not one only, Christ would be two and not one.

I answer that, Because in Christ there are two natures and one hypostasis, it follows that things belonging to the nature in Christ must be two, and that those belonging to the hypostasis in Christ must be only one. Now being pertains both to nature and to hypostasis; to hypostasis as to that which has being, and to nature as to that by which something has being. For nature is taken after the manner of a form, which is said to be a being because something is by it; as for instance by whiteness a thing is white, and by manhood a thing is man. Now it must be borne in mind that if there is a form or nature which does not pertain to the personal being of the subsisting hypostasis, this being is not said to belong to the person absolutely, but relatively; just as to be white is the being of Socrates not as he is Socrates, but as he is white. And there is no reason why this being should not be multiplied in one hypostasis or person, for the being whereby Socrates is white is distinct from the being whereby he is a musician. But the being which belongs to the very hypostasis or person in itself cannot possibly be multiplied in one hypostasis or person, since it is impossible that there should not be one being for one thing.

If, therefore, the human nature accrued to the Son of God not hypostatically or personally, but accidentally, as some maintained,[1] it would be necessary to assert two beings in Christ —one according as He is God—the other according as He is Man; just as in Socrates we place one being according as he is white, and another according as he is a man, since "being white" does not pertain to the personal being of Socrates. But being possessed of a head, being corporeal, being animated,—all these pertain to

[1] See Q. II, A. 6.

the one person of Socrates, and hence there arises from these only the one being of Socrates. And if it so happened that after the person of Socrates was constituted there accrued to him hands or feet or eyes, as happened to him who was born blind, no new being would be thereby added to Socrates, but only a relation to these—because, that is, he would be said to be not only with reference to what he had previously, but also with reference to what accrued to him afterwards.

And thus, since the human nature is united to the Son of God hypostatically or personally as was said above (Q. II, A. 6), and not accidentally, it follows that by the human nature there accrued to Him no new personal being, but only a new relation of the pre-existing personal being to the human nature, in such a way that the Person is said to subsist not only in the Divine, but also in the human nature.

Reply Obj. 1. Being is consequent upon nature not as upon that which has being but as upon that whereby a thing is, whereas it is consequent upon person or hypostasis as upon that which has being. Hence it has unity from the unity of hypostasis rather than duality from the duality of the nature.

Reply Obj. 2. The eternal being of the Son of God, which is the Divine Nature, becomes the being of man, in so far as the human nature is assumed by the Son of God to unity of Person.

Reply Obj. 3. As was said in the First Part (Q. L, A. 2, Reply 3; Q. LXXV, A. 5, Reply 4), since the Divine Person is the same as the Nature, there is no distinction in the Divine Persons between the being of the Person and the being of the Nature, and, consequently, the three Persons have only one being. But they would have a triple being if the being of the Person were distinct in them from the being of the Nature.

Reply Obj. 4. In Christ the soul gives being to the body, since it makes it actually animated, which is to give it the fulfilment of its nature and species. But if we consider the body perfected by the soul without the hypostasis having both—this whole, composed of soul and body, as signified by the word humanity, does not signify "what is," but "that by which it is." Hence being belongs to the subsisting person, according as it has a relation to such a nature, and of this relation the soul is the cause, in so far as it perfects human nature by informing the body.

QUESTION XVIII

OF WHAT PERTAINS TO THE UNITY IN CHRIST FROM THE STANDPOINT OF WILL

(In Six Articles)

WE must now consider unity as regards the will; and under this head there are six points of inquiry: (1) Whether the Divine will and the human are different in Christ? (2) Whether in Christ's human nature the will of sensuality is distinct from the will of reason? (3) Whether as regards the reason there were several wills in Christ? (4) Whether there was free choice in Christ? (5) Whether Christ's human will was always conformed to the Divine will in the thing willed? (6) Whether there was any contrariety of wills in Christ?

ARTICLE 1. *Whether There Are Two Wills in Christ?*

We proceed thus to the First Article: It would seem that in Christ there are not two wills, one Divine, the other human.

Objection 1. For the will is the first mover and ruler in whoever wills. But in Christ the first mover and ruler was the Divine will, since in Christ everything human was moved by the Divine will. Hence it seems that in Christ there was only one will, namely, the Divine.

Obj. 2. Further, an instrument is not moved by its own will but by the will of its mover. Now the human nature of Christ was the instrument of His Godhead. Hence the human nature of Christ was not moved by its own will, but by the Divine will.

Obj. 3. Further, that alone is multiplied in Christ which belongs to the nature. But the will does not seem to pertain to nature, for natural things are of necessity, whereas what is voluntary is not of necessity. Therefore there is but one will in Christ.

Obj. 4. Further, Damascene says (*De Fide Orthod.* iii, 14)[1] that "to will in this or that way belongs not to our nature but to our intellect—that is, to our personal intellect." But every will is this or that will, since there is nothing in a genus which is not at the same time in some one of its species. Therefore all will belongs to the person. But in Christ there was and is but one person. Therefore in Christ there is only one will.

On the contrary, Our Lord says (Luke 22. 42): *Father if Thou wilt, remove this chalice from Me. But yet not My will but Thine be*

[1] PG 94, 1036.

done. And Ambrose, quoting this to the Emperor Gratian (*De Fide* ii, 7)[2] says: "As He assumed my will, He assumed my sorrow"; and on Luke (*loc. cit.*)[3] he says: "His will He refers to the Man—the Father's, to the Godhead. For the will of man is temporal, and the will of the Godhead eternal."

I answer that, Some placed only one will in Christ, but they seem to have had different motives for holding this. For Apollinaris did not hold an intellectual soul in Christ, but maintained that the Word was in place of the soul,[4] or even in place of the intellect.[5] Hence since "the will is in the reason," as the Philosopher says,[6] it followed that in Christ there was no human will, and thus there was only one will in Him. So, too, Eutyches and all who held one composite nature in Christ[7] were forced to place one will in Him. Nestorius,[8] too, who maintained that the union of God and man was one of affection and will, held only one will in Christ.

But later on, Macarius, Patriarch of Antioch,[9] Cyrus of Alexandria,[10] and Sergius of Constantinople[11] and some of their followers,[12] held that there is one will in Christ, although they held that in Christ there are two natures united in a hypostasis; because they believed that Christ's human nature never moved with its own motion, but only in so far as it was moved by the Godhead, as is plain from the conciliar letter of Pope Agatho.[13] And hence in the sixth Council held at Constantinople[14] it was decreed that it must be said that there are two wills in Christ, in the following passage: "In accordance with what the Prophets of old taught us concerning Christ, and as He taught us Himself, and the Symbol of the Holy Fathers has handed down to us, we confess two natural wills in Him and two natural operations."

[2] PL 16, 594.   [3] Bk. x, on 22.42 (PL 15, 1911).
[4] See above, Q. V, A. 3.
[5] Cf. Athanasius, *Contra Apollinarium*, I, 2 (PG 26, 1096); Gregory of Nazianzus, *Epist.*, CCII (PG 37, 333); Gregory of Nyssa, *Adv. Apoll.*, n. 35 (PG 45, 1201); Theophilus of Alexandria, *Epist. ad Totius Aegypti Episc.,* anni 402, Jerome's translation (PL 22, 795); Augustine, QQ. 83, qu. 80 (PL 40, 93); Socrates, *Hist. Eccl.*, II, 16 (PG 67, 364); Theodore the Nestorian, *Haeret. Fabul. Compend.* IV, 8 (PG 83, 425).   [6] *Soul*, III, 9 (432ᵇ5).
[7] See above, Q. II, A. 6.   [8] See above, Q. II, A. 6.
[9] Cf. Council of Constantinople III, actio 11 (MA XI, 511–518).   [10] *Ibid.*, actio 13 (MA XI, 567).
[11] *Ibid.*, actio 12 (MA XI, 534).
[12] For example, Pyrrhus; cf. Conc. Lateran. Romanum (MA X, 1002); Theodorus Pharanitanus, *Ibid.* (MA X, 959, 962); Paul of Constant., *Ibid.* (MA X, 1023).
[13] *Epist.*, III (PL 87, 1221). Cf. Conc. Cpolit, III, Act. 4 (MA XI, 291).   [14] Actio 18, (MA XI, 638).

And this much it was necessary to say. For it is manifest that the Son of God assumed a perfect human nature, as was shown above (Q. IV, A. 2; Q. V; Q. IX, A. 1). Now the will pertains to the perfection of human nature, being one of its natural powers, even as the intellect, as was stated in the First Part (Q. LXXIX, A. 1, Reply 2; Q. LXXX, A. 2). Hence we must say that the Son of God assumed a human will, together with human nature. Now by the assumption of human nature the Son of God suffered no diminution of what pertains to His Divine Nature, to which it belongs to have a will, as was said in the First Part (Q. XIX, A. 1). Hence it must be said that there are two wills in Christ —that is, one human, the other Divine.

Reply Obj. 1. Whatever was in the human nature of Christ was moved at the bidding of the Divine will; yet it does not follow that in Christ there was no movement of the will proper to human nature, for the good wills of other saints are moved according to the will of God, *Who worketh* in them *both to will and to accomplish*, as is written Phil. 2. 13. For although the will cannot be inwardly moved by any creature, yet it can be moved inwardly by God, as was said in the First Part (Q. CV, A. 4; Q. CVI, A. 2; Q. CXI, A. 2). And thus, too, Christ by His human will followed the Divine will according to Ps. 39. 9; *That I should do Thy will, O my God, I have desired it.* Hence Augustine says (*Contra Maxim.* ii, 20):[1] "Where the Son says to the Father, 'Not what I will, but what Thou willest,' what do you gain by adding your own words and saying 'He shows that His will was truly subject to His Father,' as if we denied that man's will ought to be subject to God's will?"

Reply Obj. 2. It is proper to an instrument to be moved by the principal agent, yet diversely, according to the property of its nature. For an inanimate instrument, as an axe or a saw, is moved by the craftsman with only a corporeal movement; but an instrument animated by a sensitive soul is moved by the sensitive appetite, as a horse by its rider, and an instrument animated with a rational soul is moved by its will, as by the command of his lord the servant is moved to act, the servant being like an animate instrument, as the Philosopher says.[2] And hence it was in this manner that the human nature of Christ was the instrument of the Godhead, and was moved by its own will.

Reply Obj. 3. The power of the will itself is

natural, and necessarily follows upon the nature. But the movement or act of this power— which is also called will—is sometimes natural and necessary—for example, with respect to Happiness; and sometimes springs from the free choice of reason and is neither necessary nor natural, as is plain from what has been stated in the Second Part (I-II, Q. X, AA. 1, 2).[3] And yet even reason itself, which is the principle of this movement, is natural. Hence besides the Divine will it is necessary to place in Christ a human will, not only as a natural power, or a natural movement, but also as a rational movement.

Reply Obj. 4. When we say "to will in a certain way," we signify a determinate mode of willing. Now a determinate mode regards the thing of which it is the mode. Hence since the will pertains to the nature, "to will in a certain way" belongs to the nature, not indeed considered absolutely, but as it is in a hypostasis of such a kind. Hence the human will of Christ had a determinate mode from the fact of being in a Divine hypostasis—that is, it was always moved in accordance with the bidding of the Divine will.

ARTICLE 2. *Whether in Christ There Was Any Will of Sensuality Besides the Will of Reason?*

We proceed thus to the Second Article: It would seem that in Christ there was no will of sensuality besides the will of reason.

Objection 1. For the Philosopher says[4] that "the will is in the reason, and in the sensitive appetite are the irascible and concupiscible parts." Now sensuality signifies the sensitive appetite. Hence in Christ there was no will of sensuality.

Obj. 2. Further, according to Augustine (*De Trin.* xii, 12, 13)[5] the sensuality is signified by the serpent. But there was nothing serpent-like in Christ, for He had the likeness of a venomous animal without the venom, as Augustine says (*De Pecc. Merit. et Remiss.* i, 32)[6] commenting on John 3. 14, *As Moses lifted up the serpent in the desert.* Hence in Christ there was no will of sensuality.

Obj. 3. Further, will is consequent upon nature, as was said (A. 1, Reply 3). But in Christ there was only one nature besides the Divine. Hence in Christ there was only one human will.

On the contrary, Ambrose says (*De Fide* ii, 7):[7] "Mine is the will which He calls His own,

[1] PL 42, 789.
[2] *Politics*, I, 4 (1253ᵇ32); *Ethics*, VIII, 11 (1161ᵇ4).
[3] See also Part I, Q. LXXXII, A. 2.
[4] *Soul*, III, 9 (432ᵇ5).   [5] PL 42, 1007, 1008.
[6] PL 44, 145.   [7] PL 16, 594.

because as Man He assumed my sorrow." From this we are given to understand that sorrow pertains to the human will of Christ. Now sorrow pertains to the sensuality, as was said in the Second Part (I-II, Q. XXIII, A. 1; Q. XXV, A. 1). Therefore it seems, in Christ there is a will of sensuality besides the will of reason.

I answer that, As was said (Q. IV, A. 2; Q. V, A. 9; Q. IX, A. 1), the Son of God assumed human nature together with everything pertaining to the perfection of human nature. Now in human nature is included animal nature, as the genus in its species. Hence the Son of God must have assumed together with the human nature whatever pertains to the perfection of animal nature, one of which things is the sensitive appetite, which is called sensuality. Consequently it must be allowed that there was sensuality in Christ. But it must be borne in mind that sensuality or the sensual appetite, since it is made to obey reason, is said to be rational by participation, as is clear from the Philosopher.[1] And because "the will is in the reason," as stated above (Arg. 1), it may equally be said that the sensuality is a will by participation.

Reply Obj. 1. This argument is based on the will, essentially so called, which is only in the intellectual part; but the will so-called by participation can be in the sensitive part, in so far as it obeys reason.

Reply Obj. 2. Sensuality is signified by the serpent—not as regards the nature of the sensuality, which Christ assumed, but as regards the corruption of the *fomes,* which was not in Christ.

Reply Obj. 3. Where there is one thing on account of another, there seems to be only one; thus a surface which is visible by colour is one visible thing with the colour. So, too, because the sensuality is called the will only because it partakes of the rational will, there is said to be but one human will in Christ, even as there is but one human nature.

ARTICLE 3. *Whether in Christ There Were Two Wills As Regards the Reason?*

We proceed thus to the Third Article: It would seem that in Christ there were two wills as regards the reason.

Objection 1. For Damascene says (*De Fide Orthod.* ii, 22)[2] that there is a double will in man—namely, the natural will which is called θέλησις, and the rational will which is called βούλησις. Now Christ in His human nature had whatever belongs to the perfection of human

nature. Hence both the foregoing wills were in Christ.

Obj. 2. Further, the appetitive power is diversified in man by the difference of the apprehensive power, and hence according to the difference of sense and intellect is the difference of sensitive and intellectual appetite in man. But in the same way as regards man's apprehension, we hold the difference of reason and intellect, both of which were in Christ. Therefore there was a double will in Him, one intellectual and the other rational.

Obj. 3. Further, some[3] ascribe to Christ a will of piety, which can only be on the part of reason. Therefore in Christ on the part of reason there are several wills.

On the contrary, In every order there is one first mover. But the will is the first mover in the genus of human acts. Therefore in one man there is only one will, properly speaking, which is the will of reason. But Christ is one man. Therefore in Christ there is only one human will.

I answer that, As stated above (A. 1, Reply 3), the will is sometimes taken for the power, and sometimes for the act. Hence if the will is taken for the act, it is necessary to place two wills—that is, two species of acts of the will in Christ on the part of the reason. For the will, as was said in the Second Part (I-II, Q. VIII, AA. 2, 3), regards both the end and the means, and is affected differently towards both. For towards the end it is borne simply and absolutely, as towards what is good in itself; but towards the means it is borne under a certain relation, as the goodness of the means depends on something else. Hence the act of the will, according as it is drawn to anything desired of itself, as health, which act is called by Damascene[4] θέλησις—that is, simple will—and by the Masters[5] will as nature, is different from the act of the will as it is drawn to anything that is desired only in order to something else, as to take medicine; and this act of the will Damascene calls[6] βούλησις—that is, counselling will, and the Masters,[7] will as reason. But this diversity of acts does not diversify the power, since both acts regard the one com-

[1] *Ethics,* I, 13 (1102ᵇ30). [2] PG 94, 944.

[3] Hugh of St. Victor, *De Quat. Volunt. Christ.* (PL 176, 841); cf. Bonaventure, *In Sent.,* III, d. XVII, A. 1, Q. 3 (QR III, 369); A. 2, Q. 2. (QR III, 373).
[4] *De Fide Orth.,* II, 22 (PG 94, 944).
[5] Cf. Peter Lombard, *Sent.,* II, d. XXIV, chap. 3 (QR I, 421); Alexander of Hales, *Summa Theol.,* I-II, n. 388 (QR II, 465); Bonaventure, *In Sent.,* II, d. XXIV, PT. I, A. 2, Q. 3 (QR II, 566); Albert the Great, *In Sent.,* III, d. XVII, A. 5 (BO XXVIII, 304).
[6] *Loc. cit.*
[7] Hugh of St. Victor, *Loc. cit.*

mon aspect of the object, which is goodness. Hence we must say that if we are speaking of the power of the will, in Christ there is but one human will, essentially so called and not by participation; but if we are speaking of the will as an act, we thus distinguish in Christ a will as nature, which is called θέλησις, and a will as reason, which is called βούλησις.

Reply Obj. 1. These two wills are not diversified according to the power but only according to the difference of act, as we have said.

Reply Obj. 2. The intellect and the reason are not distinct powers, as was said in the First Part (Q. LXXIX, A. 8).

Reply Obj. 3. The will of piety would not seem to be distinct from the will considered as nature, since it flees from another's evil absolutely considered.

ARTICLE 4. *Whether There Was Free Choice in Christ?*

We proceed thus to the Fourth Article: It would seem that in Christ there was no free choice.

Objection 1. For Damascene says (*De Fide Orthod.* iii, 14)[1] that γνώμη—that is, opinion, thinking or cogitation, and προαίρεσις—that is, election, "cannot possibly be attributed to Our Lord, if we wish to speak with accuracy." But in the things of faith especially we must speak with accuracy. Therefore there was no election in Christ and consequently no free choice, of which election is the act.

Obj. 2. Further, the Philosopher says[2] that "choice is a desire of something after taking counsel." Now counsel does not appear to be in Christ, because we do not take counsel concerning such things as we are certain of. But Christ was certain of everything. Hence there was no counsel and consequently no free choice in Christ.

Obj. 3. Further, free choice is indifferent. But Christ's will was determined to good, since He could not sin, as stated above (Q. XV, AA. 1, 2). Hence there was no free choice in Christ.

On the contrary, It is written (Isa. 7. 15): *He shall eat butter and honey, that He may know to refuse the evil and to choose the good,* which is an act of free choice. Therefore there was free choice in Christ.

I answer that, As was said above (A. 3), there was a twofold act of the will in Christ: one whereby His will was drawn to anything willed in itself, which pertains to the nature of an end;

the other whereby His will was drawn to anything willed on account of its being ordered to another—which pertains to the nature of means. Now, as the Philosopher says[3] choice differs from will in this, that will of itself regards the end, while choice regards the means. And thus simple will is the same as the will as nature, but choice (*electio*) is the same as the will as reason, and is the proper act of free choice (*liberum arbitrium*), as was said in the First Part (Q. LXXXIII, A. 3). Hence, since will as reason is placed in Christ, we must also place choice, and consequently free choice, whose act is choice, as was said in the First Part (*ibid.*; cf. I-II, Q. XIII, A. 1).

Reply Obj. 1. Damascene excludes choice from Christ in so far as he considers that doubt is implied in the word choice. Nevertheless doubt is not necessary to choice, since it belongs even to God Himself to choose, according to Eph. 1. 4: *He chose us in Him before the foundation of the world,* although in God there is no doubt. Yet doubt is accidental to choice when it is in an ignorant nature. We may also say the same of whatever else is mentioned in the authority quoted.

Reply Obj. 2. Choice presupposes counsel, yet it follows counsel only as determined by judgment. For what we judge to be done, we choose, after the inquiry of counsel, as is stated.[4] Hence if anything is judged necessary to be done without any preceding doubt or inquiry, this suffices for choice. Therefore it is plain that doubt or inquiry belong to choice not essentially, but only when it is in an ignorant nature.

Reply Obj. 3. The will of Christ, though determined good, is not determined to this or that good. Hence it pertains to Christ, even as to the blessed, to choose with a free choice confirmed in good.

ARTICLE 5. *Whether the Human Will of Christ Was Altogether Conformed to the Divine Will in the Thing Willed?*

We proceed thus to the Fifth Article: It would seem that the human will in Christ did not will anything except what God willed.

Objection 1. For it is written (Ps. 39. 9) in the person of Christ: *That I should do Thy will: O my God, I have desired it.* Now he who desires to do another's will, wills what the other wills. Hence it seems that Christ's human will willed nothing but what was willed by His Divine will.

Obj. 2. Further, Christ's soul had most per-

---

[1] PG 94, 1044.
[2] *Ethics*, III, 2 (1112ª15); cf. VI, 2 (1139ª23).
[3] *Ibid.*, III, 2 (1111ᵇ26).   [4] *Ibid.*, III, 3 (1113ª9).

fect charity, which, indeed, surpasses the comprehension of all our knowledge, according to Eph. 3. 19, *the charity of Christ, which surpasseth all knowledge.* Now charity makes men will what God wills; hence the Philosopher says[1] that one mark of friendship is to will and choose the same. Therefore the human will in Christ willed nothing else than was willed by His Divine will.

Obj. 3. Further, Christ was a true comprehensor. But the Saints who are comprehensors in heaven will only what God wills, otherwise they would not be happy, because they would not obtain whatever they will, for blessed is he "who has what he wills, and wills nothing amiss," as Augustine says (*De Trin.* xiii, 5).[2] Hence in His human will Christ wills nothing else than does the Divine will.

On the contrary, Augustine says (*Contra Maxim.* ii, 20):[3] "When Christ says 'Not what I will, but what Thou wilt, He shows Himself to have willed something else than did His Father; and this could only have been by His human heart, since He did not transfigure our weakness into His Divine but into His human will."

I answer that, As was said (AA. 2, 3), in Christ according to His human nature there is a manifold will—namely, the will of sensuality, which is called will by participation, and the rational will, whether considered after the manner of nature, or after the manner of reason. Now it was said above (Q. XIII, A. 3, Reply 1; Q. XIV, A. 1, Reply 2) that by a certain dispensation the Son of God before His Passion "allowed His flesh to do and suffer what was proper to it." And in like manner He allowed all the powers of His soul to do and suffer what belonged to them. Now it is clear that the will of sensuality naturally shrinks from sensible pains and bodily hurt. In like manner, the will as nature turns from what is against nature and what is evil in itself, as death and the like; yet the will as reason may at times choose these things in relation to an end, as in a mere man the sensuality and the will absolutely considered shrink from burning, which, nevertheless, the will as reason may choose for the end of health. Now it was the will of God that Christ should undergo pain, suffering, and death, not that these of themselves were willed by God, but for the sake of man's salvation. Hence it is plain that in His will of sensuality and in His rational will considered as nature, Christ could

will what God did not; but in His will as reason He always willed the same as God, which appears from what He says (Matt. 26. 39): *Not as I will, but as Thou wilt.* For He willed in His reason that the Divine will should be fulfilled although He said that He willed something else by another will.

Reply Obj. 1. By His rational will Christ willed the Divine will to be fulfilled; but not by His will of sensuality, the movement of which does not extend to the will of God—nor by His will considered as nature which is borne towards things absolutely considered, and not in relation to the Divine Will.

Reply Obj. 2. The conformity of the human will to the Divine regards the will of reason, according to which the wills even of friends agree, in so far, that is, as reason considers something willed in its relation to the will of a friend.

Reply Obj. 3. Christ was at once comprehensor and wayfarer, since He was enjoying God in His mind and had a passible body. Hence things repugnant to His natural will and to His sensitive appetite could happen to Him in His passible flesh.

ARTICLE 6. *Whether There Was Contrariety of Wills in Christ?*

We proceed thus to the Sixth Article: It would seem that there was contrariety of wills in Christ.

Objection 1. For contrariety of wills regards contrariety of objects, just as contrariety of movements springs from contrariety of terms, as is plain from the Philosopher.[4] Now Christ in His different wills wished contrary things. For in His Divine will He wished for death, from which He shrank in His human will, hence Athanasius says:[5] "When Christ says 'Father, if it be possible, let this chalice pass from Me; yet not My will, but Thine be done,'[6] and again, 'The spirit indeed is willing, but the flesh weak,'[7] He denotes two wills—the human, which through the weakness of the flesh shrank from the passion—and His Divine will eager for the passion." Hence there was contrariety of wills in Christ.

Obj. 2. Further, it is written (Gal. 5. 17) that *the flesh lusteth against the spirit, and the spirit against the flesh.* Now when the spirit desires one thing, and the flesh another, there is con-

---

[1] *Ethics,* IX, 4 (1166ᵃ7).
[2] PL 42, 1020.   [3] PL 42, 789.
[4] *Physics,* v, 5 (229ᵃ25).
[5] *De Incarn. et Cont. Arianos,* written against Apollinarius. n. 21 (PG 26, 1021).
[6] Matt. 26.39; cf. Mark 14.36; Luke 22.42.
[7] Matt. 26.41; Mark 14.38.

trariety of wills. But this was in Christ; for by
the will of charity which the Holy Spirit was
causing in His mind, He willed the passion, according to Isa. 53. 7; *He was offered because
it was His own will,* yet in His flesh He shrank
from the passion. Therefore there was contrariety of wills in Him.

Obj. 3. Further, it is written (Luke 22. 43)
that *being in an agony, He prayed the longer.*
Now agony seems to imply a certain struggle in
a soul drawn to contrary things. Hence it seems
that there was contrariety of will in Christ.

On the contrary, In the decisions of the Sixth
Council[1] it is said: "We confess two natural
wills, not in opposition, as evil-minded heretics
assert,[2] but following His human will, and neither withstanding nor striving against, but
rather being subject to, His Divine and omnipotent will."

I answer that, Contrariety can exist only
where there is opposition in the same and as regards the same. For if the diversity exists as
regards diverse things, and in diverse subjects,
this would not suffice for the nature of contrariety, nor even for the nature of contradiction—for example, if a man were well formed
or healthy as regards his hand, but not as regards his foot.

Hence for there to be contrariety of wills in
anyone it is necessary, first, that the diversity
of wills should regard the same. For if the will
of one regards the doing of something with reference to some universal reason, and the will of
another regards the not doing the same with
reference to some particular reason, there is
not complete contrariety of will—for example,
when a judge wishes a brigand to be hanged for
the good of the commonwealth, and one of the
latter's kindred wishes him not to be hanged on
account of a private love, there is no contrariety
of wills; unless, indeed, the desire of the private good went so far as to wish to hinder the
public good for the private good—in that case
the opposition of wills would regard the same.

Secondly, for contrariety of wills it is necessary that it should be in the same will. For
if a man wishes one thing with his rational appetite and wishes another thing with his sensitive appetite, there is no contrariety, unless the
sensitive appetite so far prevailed as to change
or at least keep back the rational appetite; for
in this case something of the contrary move-

ment of the sensitive appetite would reach the
rational will.

And hence it must be said that although the
natural will and the sensitive will in Christ
wished what the Divine will and His rational
will did not wish, yet there was no contrariety
of wills in Him. First, because neither His natural will nor the will of sensuality rejected the
reason for which the Divine will and the will of
the human reason in Christ wished the passion.
For the absolute will of Christ wished the salvation of the human race, although it did not
pertain to it to will this for the sake of something further, but the movement of sensuality
was not able to extend so far. Secondly, because
neither the Divine will nor the will of reason in
Christ was impeded or retarded by the natural
will or the appetite of sensuality. So, too, on
the other hand, neither the Divine will nor the
will of reason in Christ shrank from or retarded
the movement of the natural human will and
the movement of the sensuality in Christ. For
it pleased Christ, in His Divine will, and also
in His will of reason, that His natural will and
will of sensuality should be moved according
to the order of their nature. Hence it is clear
that in Christ there was no opposition or contrariety of wills.

Reply Obj. 1. The fact of any will in Christ
willing something else than did the Divine will
proceeded from the Divine will itself, by whose
permission the human nature in Christ was
moved by its proper movements, as Damascene
says (*De Fide Orthod.* iii., 14, 19).[3]

Reply Obj. 2. In us the desires of the spirit
are impeded or retarded by the desires of the
flesh; this did not occur in Christ. Hence in
Christ there was no contrariety of flesh and
spirit, as in us.

Reply Obj. 3. The agony in Christ was not
in the rational part of the soul, in as far as it
implies a struggle in the will arising from a diversity of motives, as when anyone, on his reason considering one, wishes one thing, and on its
considering another, wishes the contrary. For
this springs from the weakness of the reason,
which is unable to judge which is the best absolutely. Now this did not occur in Christ, since
by His reason He judged it to be best absolutely that the Divine will regarding the salvation
of the human race should be fulfilled by His
passion. Nevertheless, there was an agony in
Christ as regards the sensitive part, in so far as
it implied a dread of coming trial, as Damascene
says (*De Fide Orthod.* ii, 15; iii, 18, 23)[4]

[1] Actio 18 (MA xi, 638; DZ 291).
[2] Cf. Council of Constantinople, iii, Actio 12, *Epist.* of
Sergius of Constant., ad *Honorium* (MA xi, 534); actio
11, Macarius, *ad Constantinum* (MA xi, 514).
[3] PG 94, 1037; 1080.   [4] PG 94, 932; 1073; 1087.

QUESTION XIX

Of what pertains to the power of Christ with regard to operation

(*In Four Articles*)

WE must now consider the unity of Christ's operation; and under this head there are four points of inquiry: (1) Whether in Christ there was one or several operations of the Godhead and Manhood? (2) Whether in Christ there were several operations of the human nature? (3) Whether Christ by His human operation merited anything for Himself? (4) Whether He merited anything for us by it?

ARTICLE 1. *Whether in Christ There Is Only One Operation of the Godhead and Manhood?*

We proceed thus to the First Article: It would seem that in Christ there is but one operation of the Godhead and the Manhood.

Objection 1. For Dionysius says (*Div. Nom.* ii):[1] "The most loving operation of God is made manifest to us by the supersubstantial Word having taken flesh integrally and truly, and having operated and suffered whatsoever befits His human and Divine operation." But he here mentions only one human and Divine operation, which is called in Greek θεανδρική —that is, God-manlike. Hence it seems that there is but one composite operation in Christ.

Obj. 2. Further, there is but one operation of the principal and instrumental agent. Now the human nature in Christ was the instrument of the Divine, as was said above (Q. VII, A. 1, REPLY 3; Q. VIII, A. 1, REPLY 1; Q. XVIII, A. 1, REPLY 2). Hence the operations of the Divine and human natures in Christ are the same.

Obj. 3. Further, since in Christ there are two natures in one hypostasis or person, whatever pertains to the hypostasis or person is one and the same. But operation pertains to the hypostasis or person, for it is only a subsisting suppositum that operates; hence, according to the Philosopher[2] acts are of singulars. Hence in Christ there is only one operation of the Godhead and the Manhood.

Obj. 4. Further, as being belongs to a subsisting hypostasis, so also does operation. But on account of the unity of hypostasis there is only one being in Christ, as was above stated (Q. XVII, A. 2). Hence, on account of the same unity, there is one operation in Christ.

Obj. 5. Further, where there is one thing op-

erated there is one operation. But the same thing was operated by the Godhead and the Manhood, as the healing of the lepers or the raising of the dead. Hence it seems that in Christ there is but one operation of the Godhead and the Manhood.

On the contrary, Ambrose says (*De Fide* ii, 8):[3] "How can the same operation spring from different powers? Cannot the lesser operate as the greater? And can there be one operation where there are different substances?"

I answer that, The aforesaid heretics (Q. XVIII, A. 1), who placed one will in Christ placed one operation in Christ.[4] Now in order better to understand their erroneous opinion, we must bear in mind that wherever there are several ordered agents, the inferior is moved by the superior, as in man the body is moved by the soul and the lower powers by the reason. And thus the actions and movements of the inferior principle are things operated rather than operations. Now what pertains to the highest principle is properly the operation; thus we say of man that to walk, which belongs to the feet, and to touch, which belongs to the hand, are things operated by the man—one of which is operated by the soul through the feet, the other through the hands. And because it is the same soul that operates through both there is only one indifferent operation, on the part of the thing operating, which is the first moving principle; but difference is found on the part of what is operated. Now, as in a mere man the body is moved by the soul, and the sensitive by the rational appetite, so in the Lord Jesus Christ the human nature is moved and ruled by the Divine. Hence they said that there is one indifferent operation on the part of the Godhead operating, but divers things operated, since the Godhead of Christ did one thing by Itself, as to uphold all things by the word of His power—and another thing by His human nature, as to walk in body. Hence the Sixth Council[5] quotes the words of Severus the heretic,[6] who said: "What things were done and wrought by the one Christ, differ greatly; for some are becoming to God, and some are human, as to walk bodily on the earth is indeed human, but to give hale steps to sickly limbs,

---

[1] Sect. 6 (PG 3, 644).
[2] *Metaphysics*, I, 1 (981[a]16).

[3] PL 16, 598.
[4] Cf. John Damascene, *De Fide Orth.*, III, 15 (PG 94, 1046).
[5] Third Council of Constantinople, Act. 10. (MA XI, 443).
[6] *Epist.*, 1 *Ad Sergium* (Ms. British Museum Addit. 17154); cf. Lebon, *Le Monophysisme sévérien*, p. 447; p. 538.

wholly unable to walk on the ground, is becoming to God. Yet One—that is, the Incarnate Word—wrought one and the other—neither was this from one nature, and that from another; nor can we justly affirm that because there are distinct things operated there are therefore two operating natures and forms."

But they were deceived in this, for what is moved by another has a twofold action: one which it has from its own form; the other, which it has according as it is moved by another; thus the operation of an axe of itself is to cleave, but according as it is moved by the craftsman, its operation is to make benches. Hence the operation which belongs to a thing by its form is proper to it, nor does it belong to the mover, except in so far as he makes use of this kind of thing for his work; thus to heat is the proper operation of fire, but not of a smith, except in so far as he makes use of fire for heating iron. But the operation which belongs to the thing only in so far as it is moved by another, is not different from the operation of the mover; thus to make a bench is not the work of the axe independently of the workman but the axe participates instrumentally in the operation of the workman. Hence, wheresoever the mover and the moved have different forms or operative powers, there must the proper operation of the mover and the proper operation of the moved be distinct, although the moved shares in the operation of the mover, and the mover makes use of the operation of the moved, and, consequently, each acts in communion with the other.

Therefore in Christ the human nature has its proper form and power whereby it acts, and so has the Divine. Hence the human nature has its proper operation distinct from the Divine operation, and conversely. Nevertheless, the Divine Nature makes use of the operation of the human nature, as of the operation of its instrument; and in the same way the human nature shares in the operation of the Divine Nature, as an instrument shares in the operation of the principal agent. And this is what Pope Leo says (*Ep. ad Flavian*, xxviii, 4):[1] "Both forms (that is, both the Divine and the human nature in Christ) do what is proper to each in union with the other—that is, the Word operates what belongs to the Word, and the flesh carries out what belongs to flesh."

But if there were only one operation of the Godhead and manhood in Christ, it would be

necessary to say either that the human nature had not its proper form and power (for this could not possibly be said of the Divine), from which it would follow that in Christ there was only the Divine operation; or it would be necessary to say that from the Divine and human power there was made up in Christ of one power. Now both of these are impossible. For by the first the human nature in Christ is supposed to be imperfect, and by the second a confusion of the natures is supposed. Hence it is with reason that the Sixth Council (Act. 18)[2] condemned this opinion, and decreed as follows: "We glorify two natural, indivisible, unconvertible, unconfused, and inseparable operations in the same Lord Jesus Christ our true God," that is, the Divine operation and the human operation.

Reply Obj. 1. Dionysius places in Christ a theandric—that is, a God-manlike or Divine-human—operation not by any confusion of the operations or powers of both natures, but because His Divine operation employs the human, and His human operation shares in the power of the Divine. Hence, as he says in a certain epistle (*Ad Caium*, iv),[3] "what is of man He works beyond man; and this is shown by the Virgin conceiving supernaturally and by the unstable waters bearing up the weight of bodily feet." Now it is clear that to be begotten belongs to human nature, and likewise to walk; yet both were in Christ supernaturally. So, too, He wrought Divine things humanly, as when He healed the leper with a touch. Hence in the same epistle he adds: "He performed Divine works not as God does, and human works not as man does, but, God having been made man, by a new operation of God and man."

Now, that he understood there to be two operations in Christ, one of the Divine and the other of the human nature, is clear from what he says, *Div. Nom.* ii:[4] "Whatever pertains to His human operation the Father and the Holy Ghost in no way share in, except, as one might say, by their most gracious and merciful will"— that is, in so far as the Father and the Holy Ghost in their mercy wished Christ to do and to suffer human things. And he adds: "He is truly the unchangeable God, and God's Word by the sublime and unspeakable operation of God, which, being made man for us, He wrought." Hence it is clear that the human operation, in which the Father and the Holy Ghost do not share except by Their merciful consent, is dis-

1 PL 54, 767.

2 MA xi, 638; DZ 292. 3 PG 3, 1072.
4 Sect. 6 (PG 3, 644).

tinct from His operation as the Word of God, wherein the Father and the Holy Ghost share.

Reply Obj. 2. The instrument is said to do something through being moved by the principal agent; and yet, besides this, it can have its proper operation through its own form, as stated above of fire. And hence the action of the instrument as instrument is not different from the action of the principal agent; yet it may have another operation, according as it is a thing. Hence the operation of Christ's human nature, as the instrument of the Godhead, is not distinct from the operation of the Godhead, for the salvation with which the manhood of Christ saves us and that with which His Godhead saves us are not distinct; nevertheless, the human nature in Christ, since it is a certain nature, has a certain operation of its own distinct from the Divine, as stated above.

Reply Obj. 3. To operate belongs to a subsisting hypostasis, in accordance, however, with the form and nature from which the operation receives its species. Hence from the diversity of forms or natures spring the various species of operations, but from the unity of hypostasis springs the numerical unity as regards the operation of the species; thus fire has two operations specifically different, namely, to illuminate and to heat, from the difference of light and heat, and yet the illumination of the fire that illuminates at one and the same time is numerically one. So, likewise, in Christ there are necessarily two specifically different operations according to His two natures; nevertheless, each of the operations at one and the same time is numerically one in Christ, as one walking and one healing.

Reply Obj. 4. Being and operation belong to the person by reason of the nature, yet in a different manner. For being belongs to the very constitution of the person, and in this respect it has the nature of a term; consequently, unity of person requires unity of the complete and personal being. But operation is an effect of the person by reason of a form or nature. Hence plurality of operations is not incompatible with personal unity.

Reply Obj. 5. The proper work of the Divine operation is different from the proper work of the human operation. Thus to heal a leper is a proper work of the Divine operation, but to touch him is the proper work of the human operation. Now both these operations concur in one work, since one nature acts in union with the other, as stated above.

ARTICLE 2. *Whether in Christ There Are Several Human Operations?*

We proceed thus to the Second Article: It would seem that in Christ there are several human operations.

Objection 1. For Christ as man communicates with plants in His nutritive nature, with the brutes in His sensitive nature, and with the angels in His intellectual nature, even as other men do. Now the operation of a plant as plant and of an animal as animal are different. Therefore Christ as man has several operations.

Obj. 2. Further, powers and habits are distinguished by their acts. Now in Christ's soul there were various powers and habits; therefore also various operations.

Obj. 3. Further, instruments ought to be proportioned to their operations. Now the human body has various members of different form, and consequently fitted to various operations. Therefore in Christ there are various operations in the human nature.

On the contrary, As Damascene says (*De Fide Orthod.* iii, 15, 16),[1] "operation follows on the nature." But in Christ there is only one human nature. Therefore in Christ there is only one human operation.

I answer that, Since it is by his reason that man is what he is, that operation is called human absolutely which proceeds from the reason through the will, which is the rational appetite. Now if there is any operation in man which does not proceed from the reason and the will, it is not absolutely a human operation, but belongs to man by reason of some part of human nature; sometimes by reason of the nature of elementary bodies, as for example to be borne downwards; sometimes by reason of the force of the vegetative soul, as to be nourished, and to grow; sometimes by reason of the sensitive part, as to see and hear, to imagine and remember, to desire and to be angry. Now between these operations there is a difference. For the operations of the sensitive soul are to some extent obedient to reason, and consequently they are somewhat rational and human in so far as they obey reason, as is clear from the Philosopher.[2] But the operations that spring from the vegetative soul, or from the nature of elemental bodies, are not subject to reason; consequently they are nowise rational; nor simply human, but only as regards a part of human nature.

[1] PG 94, 1048; 1068; cf. II, 16 (PG 94, 949).
[2] *Ethics*, I, 13 (1102[b]30).

Now it was said (A. 1) that when a lower agent acts by its own form, the operations of the inferior and of the superior agent are distinct; but when the inferior agent acts only as moved by the superior agent, then the operation of the superior and the inferior agent is one. And hence in every mere man the operations of the elemental body and of the vegetative soul are distinct from the will's operation, which is properly human; so likewise the operations of the sensitive soul in that it is not moved by reason; but in so far as it is moved by reason, the operations of the sensitive and the rational part are the same. Now there is but one operation of the rational part if we consider the principle of the operation, which is the reason or will; but the operations are many if we consider their relationship to various objects. And there were some[1] who called this a diversity of the things operated rather than of operations, judging the unity of the operation solely from the operative principle. And it is in this respect that we are now considering the unity and plurality of operations in Christ.

Hence in every mere man there is but one operation which is properly called human, but besides this there are in a mere man certain other operations, which are not properly human, as was said above. But in the Man Jesus Christ there was no motion of the sensitive part which was not ordered by reason. Even the natural and bodily operations pertained in some respects to His will, since it was His will that His flesh should do and suffer what was proper to it, as stated above (Q. XVIII, A. 5). Much more, therefore, is there one operation in Christ than in any other man whatsoever.

Reply Obj. 1. The operations of the sensitive and nutritive parts are not strictly human, as stated above; yet in Christ these operations were more human than in others.

Reply Obj. 2. Powers and habits are diversified by comparison with their objects. Hence in this way the diversity of operations corresponds to the various powers and habits, as likewise to the various objects. Now we do not wish to exclude this diversity of operations from Christ's humanity, nor that which springs from a diversity of time, but only that which regards the first active principle, as was said above.

From this may be gathered the *reply to the third objection.*

ARTICLE 3. *Whether the Human Action of Christ Could Be Meritorious to Him?*

We proceed thus to the Third Article: It would seem that the human action of Christ could not be meritorious to Him.

Objection 1. For before His death Christ was a comprehensor even as He is now. But comprehensors do not merit, because the charity of the comprehensor belongs to the reward of Happiness, since enjoyment depends upon it. Hence it does not seem to be the principle of meriting, since merit and reward are not the same. Therefore Christ before His passion did not merit, even as He does not merit now.

Obj. 2. Further, no one merits what is due to him. But because Christ is the Son of God by nature the eternal inheritance is due to Him, which other men merit by their good works. And hence Christ Who from the beginning was the Word of God, could not merit anything for Himself.

Obj. 3. Further, whoever has the principal does not properly merit what flows from its possession. But Christ has the glory of the soul, from which, in the natural course, flowed the glory of the body, as Augustine says (*Ep. ad Dios.* cxviii),[2] though by a dispensation it was brought about that in Christ the glory of the soul should not overflow to the body. Hence Christ did not merit the glory of the body.

Obj. 4. Further, the manifestation of Christ's excellence is a good not of Christ Himself, but of those who know Him. Hence it is promised as a reward to such as love Christ that He will be manifested to them, according to John 14. 21: *He that loveth Me, shall be loved of My Father, and I will love him and will manifest Myself to him.* Therefore Christ did not merit the manifestation of His greatness.

On the contrary, The Apostle says (Phil. 2. 8, 9): *Becoming obedient unto death . . . . For which cause God also hath exalted Him.* Therefore by obeying He merited His exaltation and thus He merited something for Himself.

I answer that, To have any good thing of oneself is more excellent than to have it from another, for "what is of itself a cause is always more excellent than what is a cause through another," as is said in the *Physics.*[3] Now a thing is said to have, of itself, that of which it is to some extent the cause. But God is the first cause of all our goods by authority, and in this way no creature has any good of itself, accord-

---

[1] Cf. Albert the Great, *In Sent.*, III, d. XVII, A. 5, ad 4 (BO XXVIII, 304).

[2] Chap. 3 (PL 33, 439).

[3] Aristotle, VIII, 5 (257ᵃ30).

ing to I Cor. 4. 7: *What hast thou that thou hast not received?* Nevertheless, in a secondary manner anyone may be a cause to himself of having certain good things, in so far, that is, as he co-operates with God in the matter, and thus whoever has anything by his own merit has it, in a manner, of himself. Hence it is better to have a thing by merit than without merit.

Now since all perfection and greatness must be attributed to Christ, consequently He must have by merit what others have by merit, unless it be of such a nature that its want would detract from Christ's dignity and perfection more than would accrue to Him by merit. Hence He merited neither grace nor knowledge nor the Happiness of the soul, nor the Godhead, because, since merit regards only what is not yet possessed, it would be necessary that Christ should have been without these at some time; and to be without them would have diminished Christ's dignity more than His merit would have increased it. But the glory of the body, and the like, are less than the dignity of meriting, which pertains to the virtue of charity. Hence we must say that Christ had, by merit, the glory of His body and whatever pertained to His outward excellence, as His Ascension, veneration, and the rest. And thus it is clear that He could merit for Himself.

Reply Obj. 1. Enjoyment, which is an act of charity, pertains to the glory of the soul, which Christ did not merit. Hence if He merited by charity, it does not follow that the merit and the reward are the same. Nor did He merit by charity according as it was the charity of a comprehensor, but according as it was that of a wayfarer. For He was at once a wayfarer and a comprehensor, as was said above (Q. XV, A. 10). And therefore, since He is no longer a wayfarer, He is not in the state of meriting.

Reply Obj. 2. Because by nature Christ is God and the Son of God, the Divine glory and the lordship of all things are due to Him as to the first and supreme Lord. Nevertheless a glory is due to Him as a beatified man, and this He has partly without merit, and partly with merit, as is clear from what has been said.

Reply Obj. 3. It is by Divine decree that there is an overflow of glory from the soul to the body, in keeping with human merit, so that as man merits by the act of the soul which he performs in the body, so he may be rewarded by the glory of the soul overflowing to the body. And hence not only the glory of the soul, but also the glory of the body falls under merit, according to Rom. 8. 11: *He ... shall quicken also our* (Vulg., *your*) *mortal bodies, because of His Spirit that dwelleth in us* (Vulg., *you*). And thus it could fall under Christ's merit.

Reply Obj. 4. The manifestation of Christ's excellence is His good as regards the being which it has in the knowledge of others, although in regard to the being which they have in themselves it chiefly belongs to the good of those who know Him. Yet even this is referred to Christ according as they are His members.

ARTICLE 4. *Whether Christ Could Merit for Others?*

We proceed thus to the Fourth Article: It would seem that Christ could not merit for others.

Objection 1. For it is written (Ezech. 18. 20): *The soul that sinneth, the same shall die.* Hence, for a like reason, the soul that merits shall be recompensed. Therefore it is not possible that Christ merited for others.

Obj. 2. Further, of the fulness of Christ's grace we all receive, as is written John 1. 16. Now other men having Christ's grace cannot merit for others. For it is written (Ezech. 14. 20) that if *Noe and Daniel and Job be in the city* (Vulg., *in the midst thereof*) ... *they shall deliver neither son nor daughter; but they shall only deliver their own souls by their justice.* Hence Christ could not merit anything for us.

Obj. 3. Further, the *reward* that we merit is due *according to justice* (Vulg., *debt*) *and not according to grace*, as is clear from Rom. 4. 4. Therefore if Christ merited our salvation it follows that our salvation is not by God's grace but by justice, and that He acts unjustly with those whom He does not save, since Christ's merit extends to all.

On the contrary, It is written (Rom. 5. 18): *As by the offence of one, unto all men to condemnation; so also by the justice of one, unto all men to justification of life.* But Adam's demerits reached to the condemnation of others. Much more, therefore, does the merit of Christ reach others.

I answer that, As stated above (Q. VIII, AA. 1, 5), grace was in Christ not merely as in an individual, but also as in the Head of the whole Church, to Whom all are united, as members to a head, who in a mystical fashion constitute one person. And hence it is that Christ's merit extends to others according as they are His members, even as in a man the action of the head reaches in a manner to all his members, since it perceives not merely for itself alone but for all the members.

Reply Obj. 1. The sin of an individual harms himself alone; but the sin of Adam, who was appointed by God to be the principle of the whole nature, is transmitted to others by carnal propagation. So, too, the merit of Christ, Who has been appointed by God to be the head of all men in regard to grace, extends to all His members.

Reply Obj. 2. Others receive of Christ's fulness not indeed the fount of grace, but some particular grace. And hence it need not be that men merit for others, as Christ did.

Reply Obj. 3. As the sin of Adam reaches others only by carnal generation, so, too, the merit of Christ reaches others only by spiritual regeneration, which takes place in baptism; wherein we are incorporated with Christ, according to Gal. 3. 27, *As many of you as have been baptized in Christ, have put on Christ;* and it is by grace that it is granted to man to be regenerated in Christ. And thus man's salvation is from grace.

QUESTION XX
OF CHRIST'S SUBJECTION TO THE FATHER
(In Two Articles)

WE must now consider such things as belong to Christ in relation to the Father. Some of these things are predicated of Him because of His relation to the Father—for example, that He was subject to Him, that He prayed to Him, that He ministered to Him by priesthood. And some are predicated, or may be predicated, of Him because of the Father's relation to Him— for example, that the Father adopted Him and that He predestined Him.

Hence we must consider (1) Christ's subjection to the Father; (2) His prayer (Q. XXI); (3) His priesthood (Q. XXII); (4) Adoption —whether it is becoming to Him (Q. XXIII); (5) His predestination (Q. XXIV).

Under the first head there are two points of inquiry: (1) Whether Christ is subject to the Father? (2) Whether He is subject to Himself?

ARTICLE 1. *Whether We May Say That Christ Is Subject to the Father?*

We proceed thus to the First Article: It would seem that we may not say that Christ was subject to the Father.

Objection 1. For everything subject to the Father is a creature, since, as is said in *De Eccles. Dogm.* iv,[1] "in the Trinity there is no

[1] Gennadius (PL 58, 982).

dependence or subjection." But we cannot say absolutely that Christ is a creature, as was stated above (Q. XVI, A. 8). Therefore we cannot say absolutely that Christ is subject to God the Father.

Obj. 2. Further, a thing is said to be subject to God when it is subservient to His dominion. But we cannot attribute subservience to the human nature of Christ; for Damascene says (*De Fide Orthod.* iii, 21):[2] "We must bear in mind that we may not call it (that is, Christ's human nature) a servant; for the words 'subservience' and 'domination' are not names of the nature, but of relations, as the words 'paternity' and 'filiation.'" Hence Christ in His human nature is not subject to God the Father.

Obj. 3. Further, it is written (I Cor. 15. 28): *And when all things shall be subdued unto Him, then the Son also Himself shall be subject unto Him that put all things under Him.* But, as is written (Heb. 2. 8): *We see not as yet all things subject to Him.* Hence He is not yet subject to the Father, Who has subjected all things to Him.

On the contrary, Our Lord says (John 14. 28), *The Father is greater than I;* and Augustine says (*De Trin.* i, 7):[3] "It is not without reason that the Scripture mentions both, that the Son is equal to the Father and the Father greater than the Son, for the first is said on account of the form of God, and the second on account of the form of a servant, without any confusion." Now the less is subject to the greater. Therefore in the form of a servant Christ is subject to the Father.

I answer that, What is proper to a nature belongs to whoever has that nature. Now human nature from its condition has a threefold subjection to God. The first regards the degree of goodness, according as the Divine Nature is the very essence of goodness, as is clear from Dionysius (*Div. Nom.* i),[4] while a created nature has a participation of the Divine goodness, being subject, so to say, to the rays of this goodness. Secondly, human nature is subject to God as regards God's power, since human nature, even as every creature, is subject to the operation of the Divine ordinance. Thirdly, human nature is especially subject to God through its proper act, in so far, that is, as by its own will it obeys His command.

This threefold subjection to God Christ professes of Himself. The first (Matt. 19. 17): *Why askest thou Me concerning good? One is*

[2] PG 94, 1085.   [3] PL 42, 829.
[4] Sect. 5 (PG 3, 593).

good, God. And on this Jerome remarks:[1] "He who had called Him a good master, and had not confessed Him to be God or the Son of God, is told that no man, however holy, is good in comparison with God." And hereby He gave us to understand that He Himself, in His human nature, did not attain to the height of Divine goodness. And because "in such things as are great, but not in bulk, to be great is the same as to be good," as Augustine says (*De Trin.* vi, 8),[2] for this reason the Father is said to be greater than Christ in His human nature.

The second subjection is attributed to Christ according as all that befell Christ is believed to have happened by Divine appointment; hence Dionysius says (*Cæl. Hier.* iv)[3] that "Christ is subject to the ordinance of God the Father." And this is the subjection of subservience, whereby *every creature serves God* (Judith 16. 17), being subject to His ordinance, according to Wisd. 16. 24: *The creature serving Thee the Creator.* And in this way the Son of God (Phil. 2. 7) is said to have taken *the form of a servant.*

The third subjection He attributes to Himself, saying (John 8. 29): *I do always the things that please Him.* And this is the subjection to the Father of obedience. Hence it is written (Phil. 2. 8) that he became *obedient* to the Father *unto death.*

Reply Obj. 1. As we are not to understand that Christ is a creature absolutely, but only in His human nature, whether this qualification be added or not, as stated above (Q. XVI, A. 8), so also we are to understand that Christ is subject to the Father not absolutely but in His human nature, even if this qualification be not added; and yet it is better to add this qualification in order to avoid the error of Arius, who held the Son to be less than the Father.[4]

Reply Obj. 2. The relation of subservience and dominion is based upon action and passion, since it belongs to a servant to be moved by the command of his master. Now to act is not attributed to the nature as agent, but to the person, since "acts belong to supposita and to singulars," according to the Philosopher.[5] Nevertheless action is attributed to the nature as to that whereby the person or hypostasis acts. Hence, although the nature is not properly said to rule or serve, yet every hypostasis or person may be properly said to be ruling or serving in this or that nature. And in this way nothing

prevents Christ being subject or servant to the Father in human nature.

Reply Obj. 3. As Augustine says (*De Trin.* i, 8):[6] "Christ will give the kingdom to God and the Father, when He has brought the just, over whom He now reigns by faith, to the vision"—that is, to see the essence common to the Father and the Son; and then He will be totally subject to the Father not only in Himself, but also in His members by the full participation of the divine goodness. And then all things will be fully subject to Him by the final accomplishment of His will concerning them; although even now all things are subject to Him as regards His power, according to Matt. 28. 18: *All power is given to Me in heaven and in earth.*

ARTICLE 2. *Whether Christ Is Subject to Himself?*

We proceed thus to the Second Article: It would seem that Christ is not subject to Himself.

Objection 1. For Cyril says in a synodal letter[7] which the Council of Ephesus[8] received: "Christ is neither servant nor master of Himself. It is foolish, or rather impious, to think or say this." And Damascene says the same (*De Fide Orthod.* iii, 21):[9] "The one Being, Christ, cannot be the servant or master of Himself." Now Christ is said to be the servant of the Father in so far as He is subject to Him. Hence Christ is not subject to Himself.

Obj. 2. Further, servant has reference to master. Now nothing has a relation to itself; hence Hilary says (*De Trin.* vii)[10] that nothing is like or equal to itself. And so Christ cannot be said to be the servant of Himself, and consequently to be subject to Himself.

Obj. 3. Further, "as the rational soul and flesh are one man; so God and man are one Christ," as Athanasius says (*Symb. Fid.*).[11] Now man is not said to be subject to himself or servant to himself or greater than himself because his body is subject to his soul. Therefore, Christ is not said to be subject to Himself because His Manhood is subject to His Godhead.

On the contrary, Augustine says (*De Trin.* i, 7):[12] "Truth shows in this way (that is, where-

---

[1] *In Matt.*, bk. III, on 19.17 (PL 26, 141).
[2] PL 42, 929.　　[3] Sect. 4 (PG 3, 181).
[4] See above, Q. X, A2, Reply 1.
[5] *Metaphysics*, I, 1 (981ª16).

[6] PL 42, 831.
[7] *Epist.*, XVII, *Ad Nestorium* (PG 77, 112), or Mercator's trans. (PL 48, 836).
[8] Pt. I, Chap. 26 (MA IV, 1075).　　[9] PG 94, 1085.
[10] PL 10, 211; cf. BK. III (PL 10, 91).
[11] Cf. Creed, "*Quicumque*" (MA II, 1355; DZ 40).
[12] PL 42, 828.

by the Father is greater than Christ in human nature) that the Son is less than Himself."

Further, as he argues (*ibid.*), the form of a servant was so taken by the Son of God that the form of God was not lost. But because of the form of God, which is common to the Father and the Son, the Father is greater than the Son in human nature. Therefore the Son is greater than Himself in human nature.

Further, Christ in His human nature is the servant of God the Father, according to John 20. 17: *I ascend to My Father and to your Father, to My God and your God.* Now whoever is the servant of the Father is the servant of the Son, otherwise not everything that belongs to the Father would belong to the Son. Therefore Christ is His own servant and is subject to Himself.

I answer that, As was said above (A. 1, Reply 2), to be master and servant is attributed to a person or hypostasis according to a nature. Hence when it is said that Christ is the master or servant of Himself, or that the Word of God is the Master of the Man Christ, this may be understood in two ways. First, so that this is understood to be said by reason of another hypostasis or person, as if there was the person of the Word of God ruling and another person of the man serving; and this is the heresy of Nestorius.[1] Hence in the condemnation of Nestorius it is said in the Council of Ephesus[2]: "If anyone say that the Word begotten of God the Father is the God or Lord of Christ, and does not rather confess the same to be at once God and man as the Word made flesh, according to the Scriptures, let him be anathema." And in this sense it is denied by Cyril[3] and Damascene[4] (obj. 1); and in the same sense must it be denied that Christ is less than Himself or subject to Himself.

Secondly, it may be understood of the diversity of natures in the one person or hypostasis. And thus we may say that in one of them, in which He agrees with the Father, He presides and rules together with the Father; and in the other nature, in which He agrees with us, He is subject and serves, and in this sense Augustine says that the Son is less than Himself.

Yet it must be borne in mind that since this

name Christ is the name of a Person, even as the name Son, those things can be predicated *per se* and absolutely of Christ which belong to Him by reason of the Person, Which is eternal; and especially those relations which seem more properly to pertain to the Person or the hypostasis. But whatever pertains to Him in His human nature is rather to be attributed to Him with a qualification, so that we say that Christ is absolutely greatest, Lord, Ruler, whereas to be subject or servant or less is to be attributed to Him with the qualification, in His human nature.

Reply Obj. 1. Cyril and Damascene deny that Christ is the head of Himself because this implies a plurality of supposita, which is required in order that anyone may be the master of another.

Reply Obj. 2. Absolutely speaking it is necessary that the master and the servant should be distinct; yet a certain notion of mastership and subservience may be preserved according as the same one is master of Himself in different respects.

Reply Obj. 3. On account of the various parts of man, one of which is superior and the other inferior, the Philosopher says[5] that there is justice between a man and himself in so far as the irascible and concupiscible powers obey reason. Hence this way a man may be said to be subject and subservient to Himself as regards His different parts.

To the other arguments, the reply is clear from what has been said. For Augustine asserts that the Son is less than or subject to Himself in His human nature, and not by a diversity of supposita.

QUESTION XXI
Of Christ's Prayer
(In Four Articles)

We must now consider Christ's prayer; and under this head there are four points of inquiry: (1) Whether it is becoming that Christ should pray? (2) Whether it pertains to Him in respect of His sensuality? (3) Whether it is becoming to Him to pray for Himself or only for others? (4) Whether every prayer of His was heard?

Article 1. *Whether It Is Becoming to Christ to Pray?*

We proceed thus to the First Article: It would seem unbecoming that Christ should pray.

Objection 1. For, as Damascene says (*De*

---

[1] Cf. above, Q. 11, A. 6.

[2] Pt. 1, Chap. 26, anath. 6 (MA iv, 1083; DZ 118); Cyril of Alexandria, *Epist.*, xvii, anath. 6 (PG 77, 121) or (PL 48, 840).

[3] *Epist.*, xvii (PG 77, 112) or Mercator's trans. (PL 48, 836).

[4] *De Fide Orth.*, iii, 21 (PG 94, 1085).

[5] *Ethics*, v, 11 (1138[b]5).

Fide Orthod. iii, 24),[1] "prayer is the asking for becoming things from God." But since Christ could do all things, it does not seem becoming to Him to ask anything from anyone. Therefore it does not seem fitting that Christ should pray.

Obj. 2. Further, we need not ask in prayer for what we know for certain will happen; thus, we do not pray that the sun may rise to-morrow. Nor is it fitting that anyone should ask for what he knows will not happen. But Christ in all things knew what would happen. Therefore it was not fitting that He should ask anything in prayer.

Obj. 3. Further, Damascene says (*De Fide Orthod.* iii, *loc. cit.*) that "prayer is the raising up of the mind to God." Now Christ's mind needed no uplifting to God, since His mind was always united to God, not only by the union of the hypostasis, but by the enjoyment of beatitude. Therefore it was not fitting that Christ should pray.

On the contrary, It is written (Luke 6. 12) *And it came to pass in those days, that He went out into a mountain, and He passed the whole night in the prayer of God.*

I answer that, As was said in the Second Part (II-II, Q. LXXXIII, AA. 1, 2), prayer is the unfolding of our will to God, that He may fulfil it. If, therefore, there had been but one will in Christ—namely, the Divine—it would in no way be fitting for Him to pray, since the Divine will of itself is effective of whatever He wishes by it, according to Ps. 134. 6: *Whatsoever the Lord pleased, He hath done.* But because the Divine and the human wills are distinct in Christ, and the human will of itself is not efficacious enough to do what it wishes, except by Divine power, hence to pray belongs to Christ as man and as having a human will.

Reply Obj. 1. Christ as God and not as man was able to carry out all He wished, since as man He was not omnipotent, as stated above (Q. XIII, A. 1). Nevertheless being both God and man, He wished to offer prayers to the Father, not as though He were powerless, but for our instruction. First, that He might show Himself to be from the Father; hence He says (John 11. 42): *Because of the people who stand about I have said it* (that is, the words of the prayer) *that they may believe that Thou hast sent Me.* Hence Hilary says (*De Trin.* x):[2] "He did not need prayer. It was for us He prayed, lest the Son should be unknown." Secondly, to give us an example of prayer; hence

Ambrose says (on Luke 6. 12):[3] "Be not deceived, nor think that the Son of God prays as a weakling, in order to beseech what He cannot effect. For the Author of power, the Master of obedience persuades us to the precepts of virtue by His example." Hence Augustine says (*Tract.* civ *in Joann.*):[4] "Our Lord in the form of a servant could have prayed in silence, if need be, but He wished to show Himself a suppliant of the Father, in such sort as to bear in mind that He was our Teacher."

Reply Obj. 2. Amongst the other things which He knew would happen, He knew that some would be brought about by His prayer; and for these He not unbecomingly besought God.

Reply Obj. 3. To rise is nothing more than to move towards what is above. Now movement is taken in two ways, as is said in the book on the *Soul;*[5] first, strictly, according as it implies the passing from potency to act, in so far as it is the act of something imperfect, and thus to rise pertains to what is potentially and not actually above. Now in this sense, as Damascene says (*De Fide Orthod.* iii, *loc. cit.*), "the human intellect of Christ did not need to rise to God, since it was ever united to God both by personal being and by the blessed vision." Secondly, movement signifies the act of something perfect—that is, something existing in act, as to understand and to feel are called movements; and in this sense the mind of Christ was always raised up to God, since He was always contemplating Him as existing above Himself.

ARTICLE 2. *Whether It Pertains to Christ to Pray According to His Sensuality?*

We proceed thus to the Second Article: It would seem that it pertains to Christ to pray according to His sensuality.

Objection 1. For it is written (Ps. 83. 3) in the person of Christ: *My heart and My flesh have rejoiced in the Living God.* Now sensuality is called the appetite of the flesh. Hence Christ's sensuality could ascend to the Living God by rejoicing; and with equal reason by praying.

Obj. 2. Further, prayer would seem to pertain to that which desires what is asked for. Now Christ asked for something that His sensuality desired when He said (Matt. 26. 39): *Let this chalice pass from Me.* Therefore Christ's sensuality prayed.

Obj. 3. Further, it is a greater thing to be

---

[1] PG 94, 1089.   [2] PL 10, 398.

[3] PL 15, 1732.   [4] PL 35, 1902.
[5] Aristotle, III, 7 (431ᵃ6).

united to God in person than to mount to Him in prayer. But the sensuality was assumed by God to the unity of Person, even as every other part of human nature. Much more, therefore, could it mount to God by prayer.

On the contrary, It is written (Phil. 2. 7) that the Son of God in the nature that He assumed was *made in the likeness of men.* But the rest of men do not pray with their sensuality. Therefore, neither did Christ pray according to His sensuality.

I answer that, To pray according to sensuality may be understood in two ways. First as if prayer itself were an act of the sensuality, and in this sense Christ did not pray with His sensuality, since His sensuality was of the same nature and species in Christ as in us. Now in us sensuality cannot pray for two reasons: first because the movement of sensuality cannot transcend sensible things, and, consequently, it cannot mount to God, which is required for prayer; secondly, because prayer implies a certain ordering since we desire something to be fulfilled by God, and this is the work of reason alone. Hence prayer is an act of the reason, as was said in the Second Part (II-II, Q. LXXXIII, A. 1).

Secondly, we may be said to pray according to sensuality when our prayer lays before God what is in our appetite of sensuality; and in this sense Christ prayed with His sensuality, in so far, that is, His prayer expressed the desire of His sensuality, as if it were the advocate of the sensuality—and this, that He might teach us three things. First, to show that He had taken a true human nature, with all its natural affections; secondly, to show that a man may wish with his natural desire what God does not wish; thirdly, to show that man should subject his own will to the Divine will. Hence Augustine says in the Enchiridion:[1] "Christ acting as a man, shows a kind of private human will when He says 'Let this chalice pass from Me' (Matt. 26. 39); for this was the human will desiring something proper to itself and, so to say, private. But because He wishes man to be right and to be directed to God, He adds: 'Nevertheless not as I will but as Thou wilt,' as if to say, 'See thyself in Me, for thou canst desire something proper to thee, even though God wishes something else.' "

Reply Obj. 1. The flesh rejoices in the Living God, not by the act of the flesh mounting to God, but by the out-pouring of the heart into the flesh, in so far as the sensitive appetite follows the movement of the rational appetite.

Reply Obj. 2. Although the sensuality wished what the reason asked for, it did not belong to the sensuality to seek this by praying, but to the reason, as stated above.

Reply Obj. 3. The union in person is according to the personal being, which pertains to every part of the human nature, but the uplifting of prayer is by an act which pertains only to the reason, as stated above. Hence there is no parity.

ARTICLE 3. *Whether It Was Fitting That Christ Should Pray for Himself?*

We proceed thus to the Third Article: It would seem that it was not fitting that Christ should pray for Himself.

Objection 1. For Hilary says (*De Trin.* x).[2] "Although His word of beseeching did not benefit Himself, yet He spoke for the profit of our faith." Hence it seems that Christ prayed not for Himself but for us.

Obj. 2. Further, no one prays save for what He wishes, because, as was said (A. 1), prayer is an unfolding of our will to God that He may fulfil it. Now Christ wished to suffer what He suffered. For Augustine says (*Contra Faust.* xxvi):[3] "A man, though unwilling, often is sad; though unwilling, sleeps; though unwilling, hungers and thirsts. But He (that is, Christ) did all these things, because He wished." Therefore it was not fitting that He should pray for Himself.

Obj. 3. Further, Cyprian says (*De Orat. Dom.*):[4] "The Master of Peace and Unity did not wish prayers to be offered individually and privately, lest when we prayed we should pray for ourselves alone." Now Christ did what He taught, according to Acts 1. 1: *Jesus began to do and to teach.* Therefore Christ never prayed for Himself alone.

On the contrary, Our Lord Himself said while praying (John 17. 1): *Glorify Thy Son.*

I answer that, Christ prayed for Himself in two ways. First, by expressing the desire of His sensuality, as stated above (A. 2); or also of His simple will, considered as a nature, as when He prayed that the chalice of His Passion might pass from Him (Matt. 26. 39). Secondly, by expressing the desire of His deliberate will, which is considered as reason, as when He prayed for the glory of His Resurrection (John

---

[1] *Glossa ordin.,* on Ps. 32.1 (III, 130 A); *Glossa* Lombardi (PL 191, 326); Augustine, *Enarr. in Ps.,* Ps. 32.1 (PL 36, 277).

[2] PL 10, 398.   [3] Chap. 8 (PL 42, 484).
[4] Chap. 8 (PL 4, 510).

17. 1). And this is reasonable. For as we have said above (A. 1, Reply 1) Christ wished to pray to His Father in order to give us an example of praying, and also to show that His Father is the author both of His eternal procession in the Divine Nature, and of all the good that He possesses in the human nature. Now just as in His human nature He had already received certain gifts from His Father, so there were other gifts which He had not yet received, but which He expected to receive. And therefore, as He gave thanks to the Father for gifts already received in His human nature, by acknowledging Him as their author, as we read (Matt. 26. 27 and John 11. 41): so also, in recognition of His Father He besought Him in prayer for those gifts still due to Him in His human nature, such as the glory of His body, and the like. And in this He gave us an example, that we should give thanks for benefits received, and ask in prayer for those we have not as yet.

Reply Obj. 1. Hilary is speaking of vocal prayer, which was not necessary to Him for His own sake, but only for ours. Hence he says pointedly that "His word of beseeching did not benefit Himself." For if *the Lord hears the desire of the poor*, as is said in the Psalm (9. 38), much more the mere will of Christ has the force of a prayer with the Father; hence He Himself said (John 11. 42): *I know that Thou hearest Me always, but because of the people who stand about have I said it, that they may believe that Thou hast sent Me.*

Reply Obj. 2. Christ wished indeed to suffer what He suffered, at that particular time; nevertheless He wished to obtain, after His passion, the glory of His body, which as yet He had not. This glory He expected to receive from His Father as its author, and therefore it was fitting that He should pray to Him for it.

Reply Obj. 3. This very glory which Christ, while praying, besought for Himself, pertained to the salvation of others according to Rom. 4. 25: *He rose again for our justification.* Consequently the prayer which He offered for Himself was also in a manner offered for others. So also anyone that asks a boon of God that he may use it for the good of others prays not only for himself but also for others.

ARTICLE 4. *Whether Christ's Prayer Was Always Heard?*

We proceed thus to the Fourth Article: It would seem that Christ's prayer was not always heard.

Objection 1. For He besought that the chalice of His passion might be taken from Him, as we read (Matt. 26. 39), and yet it was not taken from Him. Therefore it seems that not every prayer of His was heard.

Obj. 2. Further, He prayed that the sin of those who crucified Him might be forgiven, as is related (Luke 23. 34). Yet not all were pardoned this sin, since the Jews were punished on account of it. Therefore it seems that not every prayer of His was heard.

Obj. 3. Further, Our Lord prayed for them *who would believe in Him through the word* of the apostles, that they *might all be one in Him*, and that they might attain to being with Him (John 17. 20, 21, 24). But not all attain to this. Therefore not every prayer of His was heard.

Obj. 4. Further, it is said (Ps. 21. 3) in the person of Christ: *I shall cry by day, and Thou wilt not hear.* Not every prayer of His, therefore, was heard.

On the contrary, The Apostle says (Heb. 5. 7): *With a strong cry and tears offering up prayers . . . He was heard for His reverence.*

I answer that, As stated above (A. 1), prayer is a certain manifestation of the human will. Therefore, the request of one who prays is granted when his will is fulfilled. Now absolutely speaking the will of man is the will of reason, for we will absolutely that which we will in accordance with reason's deliberation. But what we will in accordance with the movement of sensuality, or even of the simple will, which is considered as nature, is willed not absolutely but conditionally (*secundum quid*)— that is, provided no obstacle be discovered by reason's deliberation. Therefore such a will should rather be called a *velleity* than an absolute will, because man would will (*vellet*) this if there were no obstacle.

But according to the will of reason, Christ willed nothing but what He knew God to will. Therefore every absolute will of Christ, even human, was fulfilled, because it was in conformity with God; and consequently His every prayer was fulfilled. For in this respect also is it that other men's prayers are fulfilled, in that their will is in conformity with God, according to Rom. 8. 27: *And He that searcheth the hearts knoweth,* that is, approves of, *what the Spirit desireth,* that is, what the Spirit makes the saints to desire: *because He asketh for the saints according to God,* that is, in conformity with the Divine will.

Reply Obj. 1. This prayer for the passing of the chalice is variously explained by the Saints.

For Hilary (*super Matt.*, 31)[1] says: "When He asks that this may pass from Him, He does not pray that it may pass by Him, but that others may share in that which passes on from Him to them; so that the sense is: As I am partaking of the chalice of the passion, so may others drink of it, with unfailing hope, with unflinching anguish, without fear of death."

Or, according to Jerome (on Matt. 26. 39):[2] "He says pointedly, 'This chalice,' that is of the Jewish people, who cannot allege ignorance as an excuse for putting Me to death, since they have the Law and the Prophets, who foretold concerning Me."

Or, according to Dionysius of Alexandria:[3] "When He says 'Remove this chalice from Me,' He does not mean, 'Let it not come to Me'; for if it come not, it cannot be removed. But, as that which passes is neither untouched nor yet permanent, so the Saviour beseeches that a slightly pressing trial may be repulsed."

Lastly, Ambrose,[4] Origen[5] and Chrysostom[6] say that He prayed thus as man, being reluctant to die according to His natural will.

Thus, therefore, whether we understand, according to Hilary, that He thus prayed that other martyrs might be imitators of His Passion, or that He prayed that the fear of drinking His chalice might not trouble Him, or that death might not deter Him, His prayer was entirely fulfilled. But if we understand that He prayed that He might not drink the chalice of His passion and death, or that He might not drink it at the hands of the Jews, what He besought was not indeed fulfilled, because His reason which formed the petition did not desire its fulfilment, but for our instruction, He wished to make known to us His natural will, and the movement of His sensuality, which was His as man.

Reply Obj. 2. Our Lord did not pray for all those who crucified Him, as neither did He for all those who would believe in Him, but for those only who were predestined to obtain eternal life through Him.

And so the *reply to the third objection* is also manifest.

Reply Obj. 4. When He says: *I shall cry and Thou wilt not hear*, we must take this as referring to the desire of sensuality, which

[1] PL 9, 1068.   [2] PL 26, 206.
[3] *Fragm. in Luc.*, on 22.42 (PG 10, 1589); cf. St. Thomas, *Cat. Aurea*, chap. XXII, 11.
[4] *In Luc.*, bk. X, on 22.42 (PL 15, 1911).
[5] *In Matt.*, comm. series, n. 92, on 26.39 (PG 13, 1123).
[6] *In Matt.*, hom. LXXXIV (PG 58, 752).

shunned death. But He heard as to the desire of His reason, as stated above.

QUESTION XXII
Of the priesthood of Christ
(In Six Articles)

We have now to consider the Priesthood of Christ; and under this head there are six points of inquiry: (1) Whether it is fitting that Christ should be a priest? (2) Of the victim offered by this priest. (3) Of the effect of this priesthood. (4) Whether the effect of His priesthood pertains to Himself, or only to others? (5) Of the eternal duration of His priesthood. (6) Whether He should be called *a priest according to the order of Melchisedech?*

ARTICLE 1. *Whether It Is Fitting That Christ Should Be a Priest?*

We proceed thus to the First Article: It would seem unfitting that Christ should be a priest.

Objection 1. For a priest is less than an angel; hence it is written (Zach. 3. 1): *The Lord showed me the high-priest standing before the angel of the Lord.* But Christ is greater than the angels, according to Heb. 1. 4: *Being made so much better than the angels, as He hath inherited a more excellent name than they.* Therefore it is unfitting that Christ should be a priest.

Obj. 2. Further, things which were in the Old Testament were figures of Christ, according to Col. 2. 17: *Which are a shadow of things to come, but the body is Christ's.* But Christ was not descended in the flesh from the priests of the Old Law, for the Apostle says (Heb. 7. 14): *It is evident that Our Lord sprang out of Juda, in which tribe Moses spoke nothing concerning priests.* Therefore it is not fitting that Christ should be a priest.

Obj. 3. Further, in the Old Law, which is a figure of Christ, the lawgivers and the priests were distinct; hence the Lord said to Moses the lawgiver (Exod. 28. 1): *Take unto thee Aaron, thy brother, . . . that he* (Vulg., *they*) *may minister to Me in the priest's office.* But Christ is the giver of the New Law, according to Jer. 31. 33: *I will give My law in their bowels.* Therefore it is unfitting that Christ should be a priest.

On the contrary, It is written (Heb. 4. 14): *We have* (Vulg., *Having*) *therefore a great high-priest that hath passed into the heavens, Jesus, the Son of God.*

I answer that, properly the office of a priest is to be a mediator between God and the people, in so far, that is, as He bestows Divine things on the people, and therefore *sacerdos* (priest) means a giver of sacred things (*sacra dans*), according to Mal. 2. 7: *They shall seek the law at his*—that is, the priest's—*mouth;* and again, because he offers up the people's prayers to God, and, in a manner, makes satisfaction to God for their sins; therefore the Apostle says (Heb. 5. 1): *Every high-priest taken from among men is ordained for men in the things that appertain to God, that he may offer up gifts and sacrifices for sins.* Now this is most befitting to Christ. For through Him are divine gifts bestowed on men, according to II Pet. 1. 4: *By Whom* (that is, Christ) *He hath given us most great and precious promises, that by these you may be made partakers of the Divine Nature.* Moreover, He reconciled the human race to God, according to Col. 1. 19, 20: *In Him* (that is, Christ) *it hath well pleased* (*the Father*) *that all fulness should dwell, and through Him to reconcile all things unto Himself.* Therefore it is most fitting that Christ should be a priest.

Reply Obj. 1. Hierarchical power does indeed pertain to the angels, since they also are between God and man, as Dionysius explains (*Cæl. Hier.* ix),[1] so that the priest himself, as being between God and man, is called an angel, according to Mal. 2. 7: *He is the angel of the Lord of hosts.* Now Christ was greater than the angels, not only in His Godhead, but also in His humanity, as having the fulness of grace and glory. Therefore also He had the hierarchical or priestly power in a higher degree than the angels, so that even the angels were ministers of His priesthood, according to Matt. 4. 11: *Angels came and ministered unto Him.* But, in regard to His passibility, He *was made a little lower than the angels*, as the Apostle says (Heb. 2. 9), and thus He was conformed to those wayfarers who are established in the priesthood.

Reply Obj. 2. As Damascene says (*De Fide Orthod.* iii, 26):[2] "What is like in every particular must be, of course, identical, and not a copy." Since, therefore, the priesthood of the Old Law was a figure of the priesthood of Christ, He did not wish to be born of the stock of the figurative priests, that it might be made clear that His priesthood is not quite the same as theirs, but differs from theirs as truth from figure.

Reply Obj. 3. As stated above (Q. VII, A. 7, reply 1), other men have certain graces distributed among them, but Christ, as being the Head of all, has the perfection of all graces. Therefore, as to others, one is a lawgiver, another is a priest, another is a king; but all these come together in Christ, as the fount of all grace. Hence it is written (Isa. 33. 22): *The Lord is our Judge, the Lord is our lawgiver, the Lord is our King: He will* come and *save us.*

ARTICLE 2. *Whether Christ Was at the Same Time Priest and Victim?*

We proceed thus to the Second Article: It would seem that Christ Himself was not both priest and victim.

Objection 1. For it is the duty of the priest to slay the victim. But Christ did not kill Himself. Therefore He was not both priest and victim.

Obj. 2. Further, the priesthood of Christ has a greater similarity to the Jewish priesthood, instituted by God, than to the priesthood of the Gentiles, by which the demons were worshipped. Now in the Old Law man was never offered up in sacrifice, whereas this was very much to be reprehended in the sacrifices of the Gentiles, according to Ps. 105. 38: *They shed innocent blood; the blood of their sons and of their daughters, which they sacrificed to the idols of Chanaan.* Therefore in Christ's priesthood the Man Christ should not have been the victim.

Obj. 3. Further, every victim, through being offered to God, is sanctified to God. But the humanity of Christ was from the beginning sanctified and united to God. Therefore it cannot be said fittingly that Christ as man was a victim.

On the contrary, The Apostle says (Eph. 5. 2): *Christ hath loved us, and hath delivered Himself for us, an oblation and a victim* (Douay, *sacrifice*) *to God for an odour of sweetness.*

I answer that, As Augustine says,[3] "Every visible sacrifice is a sacrament, that is a sacred sign, of the invisible sacrifice." Now the invisible sacrifice is that by which a man offers his spirit to God, according to Ps. 50. 19: *A sacrifice to God is an afflicted spirit.* Therefore, whatever is offered to God in order to raise man's spirit to Him may be called a sacrifice.

Now man requires to offer sacrifice for three reasons. First, for the remission of sin, by which he is turned away from God. Hence the Apostle says (Heb. 5. 1) that it pertains to the priest *to offer gifts and sacrifices for sins.* Secondly, that man may be preserved in a state

---

[1] Sect. 2 (PG 3, 257).　　[2] PG 94, 1096.　　[3] *City of God*, x, 5 (PL 41, 282).

of grace, by ever adhering to God, in which consists his peace and salvation. And so under the Old Law the sacrifice of peace-offerings was offered up for the salvation of the offerers, as is prescribed in the third chapter of Leviticus. Thirdly, in order that the spirit of man be perfectly united to God, which will be most perfectly realized in glory. Hence, under the Old Law, the holocaust was offered, so called because the victim was wholly burnt, as we read in the first chapter of Leviticus.

Now these effects were conferred on us by the humanity of Christ. For, in the first place, our sins were blotted out, according to Rom. 4. 25: *Who was delivered up for our sins.* Secondly, through Him we received the grace of salvation, according to Heb. 5. 9: *He became to all that obey Him the cause of eternal salvation.* Thirdly, through Him we have acquired the perfection of glory, according to Heb. 10. 19: *We have* (Vulg., *Having*) *a confidence in the entering into the Holies* (that is, the heavenly glory) *through His Blood.* Therefore Christ Himself, as man, was not only priest, but also a perfect victim, being at the same time victim for sin, victim for a peace-offering, and a holocaust.

Reply Obj. 1. Christ did not slay Himself, but of His own free-will He exposed Himself to death, according to Is. 53. 7: *He was offered because it was His own will.* Thus He is said to have offered Himself.

Reply Obj. 2. The slaying of the Man Christ may be referred to a twofold will. First, to the will of those who slew Him, and in this respect He was not a victim, for the slayers of Christ are not accounted as offering a sacrifice to God, but as guilty of a great crime, a likeness of which was borne by the wicked sacrifices of the Gentiles, in which they offered up men to idols. Secondly, the slaying of Christ may be considered in reference to the will of the Sufferer, Who freely offered Himself to suffering. In this respect He is a victim, and in this He differs from the sacrifices of the Gentiles.

Reply Obj. 3. The fact that Christ's manhood was holy from its beginning does not prevent that same manhood, when it was offered to God in the Passion, being sanctified in a new way—namely, as a victim actually offered then. For it acquired then the actual holiness of a victim from the charity which it had from the beginning and from the grace of union sanctifying it absolutely.[1]

---

[1] The reply to Obj. 3 is missing from the Leonine text; the reply given above is found in the Piana text.

ARTICLE 3. *Whether the Effect of Christ's Priesthood Is the Expiation of Sins?*

We proceed thus to the Third Article: It would seem that the effect of Christ's priesthood is not the expiation of sins.

Objection 1. For it belongs to God alone to blot out sins, according to Isa. 43. 25: *I am He that blot out thy iniquities for My own sake.* But Christ is priest, not as God, but as man. Therefore the priesthood of Christ does not expiate sins.

Obj. 2. Further, the Apostle says (Heb. 10. 1-3) that the victims of the Old Testament could not *make perfect: for then they would have ceased to be offered; because the worshippers once cleansed should have no conscience of sin any longer; but in them there is made a commemoration of sins every year.* But in like manner under the priesthood of Christ a commemoration of sins is made in the words: *Forgive us our trespasses* (Matt. 6. 12). Moreover, the Sacrifice is offered continuously in the Church; therefore again we say: *Give us this day our daily bread.* Therefore sins are not expiated by the priesthood of Christ.

Obj. 3. Further, in the sin-offerings of the Old Law, a he-goat was mostly offered for the sin of a prince, a she-goat for the sin of some private individual, a calf for the sin of a priest, as we gather from Lev. 4. 3, 23, 28. But Christ is compared to none of these, but to the lamb, according to Jer. 11. 19: *I was as a meek lamb, that is carried to be a victim.* Therefore it seems that His priesthood does not expiate sins.

On the contrary, The Apostle says (Heb. 9. 14): *The blood of Christ, Who by the Holy Ghost offered Himself unspotted unto God, shall cleanse our conscience from dead works, to serve the living God.* But dead works denote sins. Therefore the priesthood of Christ has the power to cleanse from sins.

I answer that, Two things are required for the perfect cleansing from sins, corresponding to the two things comprised in sin—namely, the stain of sin and the debt of punishment. The stain of sin is, indeed, blotted out by grace, by which the sinner's heart is turned to God, while the debt of punishment is entirely removed by the satisfaction that man offers to God. Now the priesthood of Christ produces both these effects. For by its power grace is given to us, by which our hearts are turned to God, according to Rom. 3. 24, 25: *Being justified freely by His grace, through the redemp-*

tion that is in Christ Jesus, Whom God hath proposed to be a propitiation, through faith in His blood. Moreover, He satisfied for us fully, since He hath borne our infirmities and carried our sorrows (Isa. 53. 4). Therefore it is clear that the priesthood of Christ has full power to expiate sins.

Reply Obj. 1. Although Christ was a priest not as God, but as man, yet one and the same was both priest and God. Therefore in the Council of Ephesus[1] we read: "If anyone say that the very Word of God did not become our High-Priest and Apostle, when He become flesh and a man like us, but altogether another one, the man born of a woman, let him be anathema." Hence in so far as His humanity operated by virtue of the divinity, that sacrifice was most efficacious for the blotting out of sins. For this reason Augustine says (De Trin. iv, 14):[2] "So that, since four things are to be observed in every sacrifice—to whom it is offered, by whom it is offered, what is offered, for whom it is offered, the same one true Mediator reconciling us to God by the sacrifice of peace, was one with Him to Whom it was offered, united in Himself those for whom it was offered, at the same time offered it Himself, and was Himself that which He offered."

Reply Obj. 2. Sins are commemorated in the New Law, not on account of the inefficacy of the priesthood of Christ, as though sins were not sufficiently expiated by Him, but in regard to those who either are not willing to be participators in His sacrifice, such as unbelievers, for whose sins we pray that they be converted; or who, after taking part in this sacrifice, fall away from it by whatsoever way by sinning. The Sacrifice which is offered every day in the Church is not other than that which Christ Himself offered, but is a commemoration of it. Therefore Augustine says,[3] "Christ Himself both is the priest who offers it and the victim: the sacred token of which He wished to be the daily Sacrifice of the Church."

Reply Obj. 3. As Origen says (Sup. Joann. i, 29),[4] though various animals were offered up under the Old Law, yet the daily sacrifice, which was offered up morning and evening, was a lamb, as appears from Num. 38. 3, 4. By which it was signified that the offering up of the true lamb—that is, Christ—was the culminating sacrifice of all. Hence (John 1. 29)

it is said: Behold the Lamb of God, behold Him Who taketh away the sins (Vulg., sin) of the world.

ARTICLE 4. Whether the Effect of the Priesthood of Christ Pertained Not Only to Others, but Also to Himself?

We proceed thus to the Fourth Article: It would seem that the effect of the priesthood of Christ pertained not only to others, but also to Himself.

Objection 1. For it belongs to the priest's office to pray for the people, according to II Mach. 1. 23: The priests made prayer while the sacrifice was consuming. Now Christ prayed not only for others, but also for Himself, as we have said above (Q. XXI, A. 3), and as expressly stated (Heb. 5. 7): In the days of His flesh, with a strong cry and tears, He offered (Vulg., offering) up prayers and supplications to Him that was able to save Him from death. Therefore the priesthood of Christ had an effect not only in others, but also in Himself.

Obj. 2. Further, in His passion Christ offered Himself as a sacrifice. But by His passion He merited not only for others, but also for Himself, as stated above (Q. XIX, AA. 3, 4). Therefore the priesthood of Christ had an effect not only in others, but also in Himself.

Obj. 3. Further, the priesthood of the Old Law was a figure of the priesthood of Christ. But the priest of the Old Law offered sacrifice not only for others, but also for himself; for it is written (Lev. 16. 17) that the high-priest goeth into the sanctuary to pray for himself and his house, and for the whole congregation of Israel. Therefore the priesthood of Christ also had an effect not merely in others, but also in Himself.

On the contrary, We read in the acts of the Council of Ephesus:[5] "If anyone say that Christ offered sacrifice for Himself, and not rather for us alone (for He Who knew not sin needed no sacrifice), let him be anathema." But the priest's office consists principally in offering sacrifice. Therefore the priesthood of Christ had no effect in Himself.

I answer that, As stated above (A. 1), a priest is set between God and man. Now he needs someone between himself and God, who of himself cannot approach to God; and such a one is subject to the priesthood by sharing in its effect. But this cannot be said of Christ, for the Apostle says (Heb. 7. 25): Coming of Himself to God, always living to make intercession

---

[1] Pt. I, chap. 26, anath. 10 (MA IV, 1083; DZ 122); Cyril of Alexandria, Epist., XVII, anath. 10 (PG 77, 121), or Mercator's trans. (PL 48, 841).

[2] PL 42, 901.

[3] City of God, X, 20 (PL 41, 298).   [4] PG 14, 289.

[5] See note, Q. XXII, A. 3, Reply 1.

for us (Vulg., *He is able to save for ever them that come to God by Him; always living*, etc.). And therefore it is not fitting for Christ to be the recipient of the effect of His priesthood, but rather to communicate it to others. For the influence of the first agent in every genus is such that it receives nothing in that genus; thus the sun gives but does not receive light; fire gives but does not receive heat. Now Christ is the fountain-head of the entire priesthood, for the priest of the Old Law was a figure of Him, while the priest of the New Law works in His person, according to II Cor. 2. 10: *For what I have pardoned, if I have pardoned anything, for your sakes have I done it in the person of Christ*. Therefore it is not fitting that Christ should receive the effect of His priesthood.

Reply Obj. 1. Although prayer is befitting to priests, it is not their proper office, for it is befitting to everyone to pray both for himself and for others, according to Jas. 5. 16: *Pray for one another that you may be saved*. And so we may say that the prayer by which Christ prayed for Himself was not an action of His priesthood.

But this answer seems to be precluded by the Apostle, who, after saying (Heb. 5. 6), *Thou art a priest for ever according to the order of Melchisedech*, adds, *Who in the days of His flesh offering up prayers*, etc., as quoted above (obj. 1), so that it seems that the prayer by which Christ prayed pertained to His priesthood. We must therefore say that other priests partake in the effect of their priesthood not as priests, but as sinners, as we shall state farther on (reply 3). But Christ had, speaking absolutely, no sin, though He had the *likeness of sin in the flesh* (Vulg., *of sinful flesh*), as is written Rom. 8. 3. And, consequently, we must not say absolutely that He partook of the effect of His priesthood but with this qualification—in regard to the passibility of the flesh. Therefore he adds pointedly, *that was able to save Him from death*.

Reply Obj. 2. Two things may be considered in the offering of a sacrifice by any priest—namely, the sacrifice itself which is offered, and the devotion of the offerer. Now the proper effect of priesthood is that which results from the sacrifice itself. But Christ obtained a result from His passion not as by virtue of the sacrifice, which is offered by way of satisfaction, but by the very devotion with which out of charity He humbly endured the passion.

Reply Obj. 3. A figure cannot equal the reality, and therefore the priest of the Old Law who was a figure could not attain to such perfection as not to need a sacrifice of satisfaction. But Christ did not stand in need of this. Consequently, there is no comparison between the two; and this is what the Apostle says (Heb. 7. 28): *The Law maketh men priests, who have infirmity; but the word of the oath, which was since the Law, the Son Who perfected for evermore*.

ARTICLE 5. *Whether the Priesthood of Christ Endures For Ever?*

We proceed thus to the Fifth Article: It would seem that the priesthood of Christ does not endure for ever.

Objection 1. For as stated above (A. 4, Reply 1, 3) those alone need the effect of the priesthood who have the weakness of sin, which can be expiated by the priest's sacrifice. But this will not be for ever. For in the Saints there will be no weakness, according to Isa. 60. 21: *Thy people shall be all just,* while no expiation will be possible for the weakness of sin, since "there is no redemption in hell" (*Office of the Dead,* Resp. vii). Therefore the priesthood of Christ would endure for ever uselessly.

Obj. 2. Further, the priesthood of Christ was made manifest most of all in His passion and death, when *by His own blood He entered into the Holies* (Heb. 9. 12). But the passion and death of Christ will not endure for ever, as stated Rom. 6. 9: *Christ rising again from the dead, dieth now no more*. Therefore the priesthood of Christ will not endure for ever.

Obj. 3. Further, Christ is a priest not as God, but as man. But at one time Christ was not man, namely during the three days He lay dead. Therefore the priesthood of Christ endures not for ever.

On the contrary, It is written (Ps. 109. 4): *Thou art a priest for ever*.

I answer that, In the priestly office, we may consider two things: first, the offering of the sacrifice; secondly, the consummation of the sacrifice, consisting in this, that those for whom the sacrifice is offered obtained the end of the sacrifice. Now the end of the sacrifice which Christ offered consisted not in temporal but in eternal goods, which we obtain through His death, according to Heb. 9. 11: *Christ is* (Vulg., *being come*) *a high-priest of the good things to come,* for which reason the priesthood of Christ is said to be eternal. Now this consummation of Christ's sacrifice was foreshadowed in this, that the high-priest of the

Old Law, once a year, entered into the Holy of Holies with the blood of a he-goat and a calf, as laid down, Lev. 16. 11, and yet he offered up the he-goat and calf not within the Holy of Holies, but without. In like manner Christ entered into the Holy of Holies—that is, into heaven—and prepared the way for us, that we might enter by the virtue of His blood, which He shed for us on earth.

Reply Obj. 1. The Saints who will be in heaven will not need any further expiation by the priesthood of Christ, but having expiated, they will need consummation through Christ Himself, on Whom their glory depends, as is written (Apoc. 21. 23): *The glory of God hath enlightened it*—that is, the city of the Saints—*and the Lamb is the lamp thereof.*

Reply Obj. 2. Although Christ's passion and death are not to be repeated, yet the power of that Victim endures for ever, for, as it is written (Heb. 10. 14), *by one oblation He hath perfected for ever them that are sanctified.*

And so the *reply to the third objection* is clear, because, as it is said in Heb. 10. 14: *For by one oblation he hath perfected for ever them that are sanctified.* But the unity of this sacrifice was foreshadowed in the Law in that, once a year, the high-priest of the Law entered into the Holies, with a solemn oblation of blood, as set down, Lev. 16. 11. But the figure fell short of the reality in this, that the victim had not an everlasting power, for which reason those sacrifices were renewed every year.

ARTICLE 6. *Whether the Priesthood of Christ Was According to the Order of Melchisedech?*

We proceed thus to the Sixth Article: It would seem that Christ's priesthood was not according to the order of Melchisedech.

Objection 1. For Christ is the fountain-head of the entire priesthood, as being the principal priest. Now that which is principal does not follow the order of others, but others follow its order. Therefore Christ should not be called a priest according to the order of Melchisedech.

Obj. 2. Further, the priesthood of the Old Law was more akin to Christ's priesthood than was the priesthood that existed before the Law. But the nearer the sacraments were to Christ, the more clearly they signified Him; as is clear from what we have said in the Second Part (II-II, Q. II, A. 7). Therefore the priesthood of Christ should be denominated after the priesthood of the Law, rather than after the priesthood of Melchisedech, which was before the Law.

Obj. 3. Further, it is written (Heb. 7. 2, 3): *That is "king of peace," without father, without mother, without genealogy; having neither beginning of days nor ending of life,* which can be referred only to the Son of God. Therefore Christ should not be called a priest according to the order of Melchisedech, as of some one else, but according to His own order.

On the contrary, It is written (Ps. 109. 4): *Thou art a priest for ever according to the order of Melchisedech.*

I answer that, As above stated (A. 4, REPLY 3) the priesthood of the Law was a figure of the priesthood of Christ, not as adequately representing the reality, but as falling far short of it; both because the priesthood of the Law did not wash away sins, and because it was not eternal, as the priesthood of Christ. Now the excellence of Christ's over the Levitical priesthood was foreshadowed in the priesthood of Melchisedech, who received tithes from Abraham, in whose loins the priesthood of the Law was tithed. Consequently the priesthood of Christ is said to be *according to the order of Melchisedech* on account of the excellence of the true priesthood over the figural priesthood of the Law.

Reply Obj. 1. Christ is said to be according to the order of Melchisedech not as though the latter were a more excellent priest, but because he foreshadowed the excellence of Christ's over the Levitical priesthood.

Reply Obj. 2. Two things may be considered in Christ's priesthood: namely, the offering made by Christ, and the partaking of it. As to the actual offering, the priesthood of Christ was more distinctly foreshadowed by the priesthood of the Law, by reason of the shedding of blood, than by the priesthood of Melchisedech in which there was no blood-shedding. But if we consider the participation of this sacrifice and its effect, in which the excellence of Christ's priesthood over the priesthood of the Law principally consists, then the former was more distinctly foreshadowed by the priesthood of Melchisedech, who offered bread and wine, signifying, as Augustine says (*Tract.* xxvi *in Joann.*)[1] ecclesiastical unity, which is established by our taking part in the sacrifice of Christ. Therefore also in the New Law the true sacrifice of Christ is presented to the faithful under the form of bread and wine.

Reply Obj. 3. Melchisedech is described as *without father, without mother, without genealogy,* and as *having neither beginning of days*

[1] PL 35, 1614.

nor ending of life, not as though he had not these things, but because these details in his regard are not supplied by Holy Scripture. And in this it is that, as the Apostle says in the same passage, he is *likened unto the Son of God,* Who had no earthly father, no heavenly mother, and no genealogy, according to Isa. 53. 8: *Who shall declare His generation?* and Who in His Godhead has neither beginning nor end of days.

QUESTION XXIII
OF THE ADOPTION OF CHRIST
(*In Four Articles*)

WE now come to consider whether adoption befits Christ, and under this head there are four points of inquiry: (1) Whether it is fitting that God should adopt sons? (2) Whether this is fitting to God the Father alone? (3) Whether it is proper to man to be adopted to the sonship of God? (4) Whether Christ can be called the adopted Son?

ARTICLE 1. *Whether It Is Fitting That God Should Adopt Sons?*

We proceed thus to the First Article: It would seem that it is not fitting that God should adopt sons.

Objection 1. For, as jurists say, no one adopts anyone but a stranger as his son.[1] But no one is a stranger in relation to God, Who is the Creator of all. Therefore it seems unfitting that God should adopt.

Obj. 2. Further, adoption seems to have been introduced in default of natural sonship. But in God there is natural sonship, as set down in the First Part (Q. XXVII, A. 2). Therefore it is unfitting that God should adopt.

Obj. 3. Further, the purpose of adopting anyone is that he may succeed, as heir, the person who adopts him. But it does not seem possible for anyone to succeed God as heir, for He can never die. Therefore it is unfitting that God should adopt.

On the contrary, It is written (Eph. 1. 5) that *He hath predestinated us unto the adoption of children of God.* But the predestination of God is not ineffectual. Therefore God does adopt some as His sons.

I answer that, A man adopts someone as his son because out of his goodness he admits him as heir to his estate. Now God is infinitely good, for which reason He admits His creatures to a

participation of His good things; especially rational creatures, who since they are made to the image of God, are capable of the Divine Happiness. And this consists in the enjoyment of God, by which also God Himself is happy and rich in Himself—that is, in the enjoyment of Himself. Now a man's inheritance is that which makes him rich. Therefore, inasmuch as God, of His goodness, admits men to the inheritance of Happiness, He is said to adopt them. Moreover Divine exceeds human adoption, because God, by bestowing His grace, makes man whom He adopts worthy to receive the heavenly inheritance, whereas man does not make him worthy whom he adopts, but rather in adopting him he chooses one who is already worthy.

Reply Obj. 1. Considered in his nature man is not a stranger in respect to God, as to the natural gifts bestowed on him; but he is as to the gifts of grace and glory, in regard to which he is adopted.

Reply Obj. 2. Man works in order to supply his wants; not however God, Who works in order to communicate the abundance of His perfection. Therefore, as by the act of creation the Divine goodness is communicated to all creatures in a certain likeness, so by the act of adoption the likeness of natural sonship is communicated to men, according to Rom. 8. 29: *Whom He foreknew . . . to be made conformable to the image of His Son.*

Reply Obj. 3. Spiritual goods can be possessed by many at the same time, not however material goods. Therefore none can receive a material inheritance except the successor of a deceased person, whereas all receive the spiritual inheritance at the same time in its entirety without detriment to the ever-living Father. Yet it might be said that God ceases to be, according as He is in us by faith, so as to begin to be in us by vision, as a gloss says[2] on Rom. 8. 17: *If sons, heirs also.*

ARTICLE 2. *Whether It Is Fitting That the Whole Trinity Should Adopt?*

We proceed thus to the Second Article: It would seem unfitting that the whole Trinity should adopt.

Objection 1. For adoption is said of God in likeness to human things. But among men those only adopt who can beget, and in God this can be applied only to the Father. Therefore in God the Father alone can adopt.

[1] This definition is discussed in Part III, Suppl., Q. LVII, A. I.

[2] *Glossa ordin.* (VI, 19A); *Glossa* Lombardi (PL 191, 1441).

Obj. 2. Further, by adoption men become the brethren of Christ, according to Rom. 8. 29: *That He might be the first-born among many brethren.* Now brethren are the sons of the same father; therefore Our Lord says (John 20. 17): *I ascend to My Father and to your Father.* Therefore Christ's Father alone has adopted sons.

Obj. 3. Further, it is written (Gal. 4. 4, 5, 6): *God sent His Son . . . that we might receive the adoption of sons. And because you are sons of God, God hath sent the Spirit of His Son into your hearts, crying: "Abba" ("Father").* Therefore it belongs to Him to adopt Who has the Son and the Holy Ghost. But this belongs to the person of the Father alone. Therefore it befits the Father alone to adopt.

On the contrary, It belongs to Him to adopt us as sons Whom we can call Father; hence it is written (Rom. 8. 15): *You have received the spirit of adoption of sons, whereby we cry: "Abba" ("Father").* But when we say to God, *"Our Father,"* we address the whole Trinity, as is the case with the other names which are said of God in respect of creatures, as stated in the First Part (Q. XXXIII, A. 3, obj. 1; cf. Q. XLV, A. 6). Therefore to adopt is befitting to the whole Trinity.

I answer that, There is this difference between an adopted son of God and the natural Son of God, that the latter is *begotten not made,* whereas the former is made, according to John 1. 12: *He gave them power to be made the sons of God.* Yet sometimes the adopted son is said to be begotten by reason of the spiritual regeneration which is by grace, not by nature; hence it is written (Jas. 1. 18): *Of His own will hath He begotten us by the word of truth.* Now although, in God, to beget belongs to the Person of the Father, yet to produce any effect in creatures is common to the whole Trinity, by reason of the oneness of their Nature, since where there is one nature there must be one power and one operation; hence Our Lord says (John 5. 19): *What things soever* the Father *doth, these the Son also doth in like manner.* Therefore it belongs to the whole Trinity to adopt men as sons of God.

Reply Obj. 1. All human individuals are not of one individual nature, so that there need be one operation and one effect of them all, as is the case in God. Consequently in this respect no comparison is possible.

Reply Obj. 2. By adoption we are made the brethren of Christ, as having with Him the same Father, Who, nevertheless, is the Father of Christ in one way, and ours in another. Hence pointedly Our Lord says, separately, *My Father,* and *Your Father* (John 20. 17). For He is Christ's Father by natural generation, and this is proper to Him, whereas He is our Father by a voluntary operation, which is common to Him and to the Son and Holy Ghost, so that Christ is not the Son of the whole Trinity, as we are.

Reply Obj. 3. As stated above (A. 1, Reply 2), adoptive sonship is a certain likeness of the eternal Sonship, just as all that takes place in time is a certain likeness of what has been from eternity. Now man is likened to the splendour of the Eternal Son by reason of the light of grace which is attributed to the Holy Ghost. Therefore adoption, though common to the whole Trinity, is appropriated to the Father as its author; to the Son, as its exemplar; to the Holy Ghost, as imprinting on us the likeness of this exemplar.

ARTICLE 3. *Whether It Is Proper to the Rational Creature to Be Adopted?*

We proceed thus to the Third Article: It would seem that it is not proper to the rational creature to be adopted.

Objection 1. For God is not said to be the Father of the rational creature, save by adoption. But God is called the Father even of the irrational creature, according to Job 38. 28: *Who is father of the rain? Or who begot the drops of dew?* Therefore it is not proper to the rational creature to be adopted.

Obj. 2. Further, by reason of adoption some are called sons of God. But to be sons of God seems to be properly attributed by the Scriptures to the angels, according to Job 1. 6: *On a certain day when the sons of God came to stand before the Lord.* Therefore it is not proper to the rational creature to be adopted.

Obj. 3. Further, whatever is proper to a nature belongs to all that have that nature, just as being capable of laughter belongs to all men. But to be adopted does not belong to every rational nature. Therefore it is not proper to human nature.

On the contrary, Adopted sons are the *heirs of God,* as is stated Rom. 8. 17. But such an inheritance belongs to none but the rational nature. Therefore it is proper to the rational nature to be adopted.

I answer that, As stated above (A. 1, Reply 3), the sonship of adoption is a certain likeness of natural sonship. Now the Son of God proceeds naturally from the Father as the Intellectual Word, being one with the Father Himself. To this Word, therefore, something may be likened in three ways. First, on the part of the form but not on the part of its intelligibility; thus the form of a house already built is like the mental word of the builder according to the species of the form, but not in intelligibility, because the form of a house in matter is not intelligible, as it was in the mind of the builder. In this way every creature is like the Eternal Word, since it was made through the Word. Secondly, the creature is likened to the Word not only as to its form, but also as to its intelligibility; thus the knowledge which is begotten in the disciple's mind is likened to the word in the mind of the master. In this way the rational creature, even in its nature, is likened to the Word of God. Thirdly, a creature is likened to the Eternal Word as to the oneness of the Word with the Father, which is by reason of grace and charity; therefore Our Lord prays (John 17. 21, 22): *That they may be one in Us . . . as We also are one.* And this likeness perfects the adoption, for to those who are thus like Him the eternal inheritance is due.

It is therefore clear that to be adopted belongs to the rational creature alone; not indeed to all, but only to those who have charity, which is *poured forth in our hearts by the Holy Ghost* (Rom. 5. 5), for which reason (Rom. 8. 15) the Holy Ghost is called *the Spirit of adoption of sons.*

Reply Obj. 1. God is called the Father of the irrational creature, not properly speaking by reason of adoption, but by reason of creation, according to the first-mentioned participation of likeness.

Reply Obj. 2. Angels are called sons of God by adoptive sonship not that it belongs to them first, but because they were the first to receive the adoption of sons.

Reply Obj. 3. Adoption is a property resulting not from nature but from grace, of which the rational nature is capable. Therefore it need not belong to every rational nature; but every rational creature must be capable of adoption.

ARTICLE 4. *Whether Christ As Man Is the Adopted Son of God?*

We proceed thus to the Fourth Article: It would seem that Christ as man is the adopted Son of God.

Objection 1. For Hilary says (*De Trin.* ii)[1] speaking of Christ: "The dignity of power

[1] PL 10, 68.

is not lost when carnal humanity is adopted." Therefore Christ as man is the adopted Son of God.

Obj. 2. Further, Augustine says (*De Prædest. Sanct.* xv)[2] that "by the same grace that Man is Christ, as from the birth of faith every man is a Christian." But other men are Christians by the grace of adoption. Therefore this Man is Christ by adoption, and consequently He would seem to be an adopted son.

Obj. 3. Further, Christ, as man, is a servant. But it is of greater dignity to be an adopted son than to be a servant. Therefore much more is Christ, as man, an adopted Son.

On the contrary, Ambrose says (*De Incarn.* viii):[3] "We do not call an adopted son a natural son; the natural son is a true son." But Christ is the true and natural Son of God, according to I John 5. 20: *That we may . . . be in His true Son,* Jesus Christ. Therefore Christ, as Man, is not an adopted Son.

I answer that, Sonship belongs properly to the hypostasis or person, not to the nature; hence in the First Part (Q. XXXII, A. 3) we have stated that Sonship is a personal property. Now in Christ there is no other than the uncreated person or hypostasis, to Whom it belongs by nature to be the Son. But it has been said above (A. 1, REPLY 2), that the sonship of adoption is a participated likeness of natural sonship, nor can a thing be said to participate in what it has essentially. Therefore Christ, Who is the natural Son of God, can in no way be called an adopted Son. But according to those who suppose two persons or two hypostases or two supposita in Christ, no reason prevents Christ being called the adopted Son of God.[4]

Reply Obj. 1. As sonship does not properly belong to the nature, so neither does adoption. Consequently, when it is said that carnal humanity is adopted, the expression is improper, and adoption is used to signify the union of human nature to the Person of the Son.

Reply Obj. 2. This comparison of Augustine is to be referred to the principle because just as it is granted to any man without meriting it to be a Christian, so did it happen that this man without meriting it was Christ. But there is a difference on the part of the term, because by the grace of union Christ is the natural Son, whereas another man by habitual grace is an adopted son. Yet habitual grace in Christ does not make one who was not a son to be an

[2] PL 44, 982.   [3] PL 16, 875.
[4] See above, Q. II, A. 6.

adopted son, but is a certain effect of Sonship in the soul of Christ, according to John 1. 14: *We saw His glory . . . as it were of the Only-begotten of the Father, full of grace and truth.*

Reply Obj. 3. To be a creature, as also to be a servant or subject to God, regards not only the person, but also the nature; but this cannot be said of sonship. Therefore the comparison does not hold.

QUESTION XXIV

OF THE PREDESTINATION OF CHRIST

(*In Four Articles*)

WE shall now consider the predestination of Christ. Under this head there are four points of inquiry: (1) Whether Christ was predestined? (2) Whether He was predestined as man? (3) Whether His predestination is the exemplar of ours? (4) Whether it is the cause of our predestination?

ARTICLE 1. *Whether It Is Befitting That Christ Should Be Predestined?*

We proceed thus to the First Article: It would seem unfitting that Christ should be predestined.

Objection 1. For the term of predestination seems to be the adoption of sons, according to Ephes. 1. 5: *Who hath predestined us unto the adoption of children.* But it is not befitting to Christ to be an adopted Son, as stated above (Q. XXIII, A. 4). Therefore it is not fitting that Christ be predestined.

Obj. 2. Further, we must consider two things in Christ: His human nature and His person. But it cannot be said that Christ is predestined by reason of His human nature, for this proposition is false—The human nature is Son of God. In like manner neither by reason of the person; for this person is the Son of God, not by grace, but by nature, whereas predestination regards what is of grace, as stated in the First Part (Q. XXIII, AA. 2, 5). Therefore Christ was not predestined to be the Son of God.

Obj. 3. Further, just as that which has been made was not always, so also that which is predestined, since predestination implies a certain antecedence. But because Christ was always God and the Son of God, it cannot be said that that Man was "made the Son of God." Therefore, for a like reason, we ought not to say that Christ was "predestined the Son of God."

On the contrary, The Apostle says, speaking of Christ (Rom. 1. 4): *Who was predestinated the Son of God in power.*

I answer that, As is clear from what has been said in the First Part (Q. XXIII, A. 2), predestination, in its proper sense, is a certain Divine preordination from eternity of those things which are to be done in time by the grace of God. Now, that man is God, and that God is man, is something done in time by God through the grace of union. Nor can it be said that God has not from eternity preordained to do this in time, since it would follow that something would come anew into the Divine Mind. And we must admit that the union itself of natures in the Person of Christ falls under the eternal predestination of God. For this reason do we say that Christ was predestined.

Reply Obj. 1. The Apostle there speaks of that predestination by which we are predestined to be adopted sons. And just as Christ in a singular manner above all others is the natural Son of God, so in a singular manner is He predestined.

Reply Obj. 2. As a gloss[1] says on Rom. 1. 4, some[2] understood predestination to refer to the nature and not to the Person—that is to say, that on human nature was bestowed the grace of being united to the Son of God in unity of Person.

But in that case the phrase of the Apostle would be improper, for two reasons. First, for a general reason: for we do not speak of a person's nature, but of his suppositum, as being predestined, because to be predestined is to be directed towards salvation, which belongs to a suppositum acting for the end of Happiness. Secondly, for a special reason. Because to be Son of God is not befitting to human nature; for this proposition is false: The human nature is the Son of God, unless one were to force from it such an exposition as: Who was predestined the Son of God in power—that is, It was predestined that the Human nature should be united to the Son of God in the Person.

Hence we must attribute predestination to the Person of Christ; not, indeed, in Himself or as subsisting in the Divine Nature, but as subsisting in the human nature. Therefore the Apostle, after saying (Rom. 1. 3), *Who was made to Him of the seed of David according to the flesh,* added, *Who was predestinated the Son of God in power,* so as to give us to understand that in respect of His being of the seed

---

[1] *Glossa ordin.* (VI, 4B); *Glossa* Lombardi (PL 191, 1309).

[2] William of Auxerre, *Summa Aurea,* PT. III, tr. 1, chap. 2, Q. 4 (115ra).

of David according to the flesh, He was predestined the Son of God in power. For although it is natural to that Person, considered in Himself, to be the Son of God in power, yet this is not natural to Him considered in the human nature, in respect of which this befits Him according to the grace of union.

Reply Obj. 3. Origen commenting on Rom. I. 4 says[1] that the true reading of this passage of the Apostle is: *Who was destined to be the Son of God in power,* so that no antecedence is implied. And so there would be no difficulty.

Others refer[2] the antecedence implied in the participle "predestinated" not to the fact of being the Son of God, but to its manifestation, according to the customary way of speaking in Holy Scripture by which things are said to take place when they are made known, so that the sense would be—Christ was predestined to be made known as the Son of God. But this is an improper signification of predestination. For a person is properly said to be predestined by reason of his being directed to the end of Happiness; but the Happiness of Christ does not depend on our knowledge.

It is therefore better to say that the antecedence implied in the participle "predestinated" is to be referred to the Person not in Himself, but by reason of the human nature, since, although that Person was the Son of God from eternity, it was not always true that one subsisting in human nature was the Son of God. Hence Augustine says (*De Prædest. Sanct.* xv):[3] "Jesus was predestined so that He Who according to the flesh was to be the son of David, should be nevertheless Son of God in power."

Moreover, it must be observed that, although the participle "predestined," just as this participle "made," implies antecedence, yet there is a difference. For "to be made" belongs to the thing in itself, whereas "to be predestined" belongs to someone as being in the apprehension of one who preordains. Now that which underlies a form or nature in reality can be apprehended either as under that form or absolutely. And since it cannot be said absolutely of the Person of Christ that He began to be the Son of God, yet this is becoming to Him as understood or apprehended to exist in human nature, because at one time it began to

[1] PG 14, 849.
[2] Hugh of St. Victor, *Quaest. in Epist. Pauli,* In Philipp. Q. 9(PL 175, 578); *Glossa* Lombardi, on Rom. 1. 4 (PL 191, 1310); William of Auxerre, *Summa Aurea,* III, I, chap. 3, Q. 1 (115ra).
[3] PL 44, 982.

be true that one existing in human nature was the Son of God; therefore this proposition—Christ was predestined the Son of God—is truer than this—Christ was made the Son of God.

ARTICLE 2. *Whether This Proposition Is False: Christ As Man Was Predestined To Be the Son of God?*

We proceed thus to the Second Article: It would seem that this proposition is false: "Christ as man was predestined to be the Son of God."

Objection 1. For at some time everyone is that which he was predestined to be, since God's predestination does not fail. If, therefore, Christ as man was predestined to be the Son of God, it seems to follow that as man He is the Son of God. But the latter is false. Therefore the former is false.

Obj. 2. Further, what is befitting to Christ as man is befitting to any man; since He belongs to the same species as other men. If, therefore, Christ, as man, was predestined to be the Son of God, it will follow that this is befitting to any other man. But the latter is false. Therefore the former is false.

Obj. 3. Further, that is predestined from eternity which is to take place at some time. But this proposition, The Son of God was made man, is truer than this, Man was made the Son of God as was held above (Q. XVI, A. 7). Therefore this proposition, Christ, as the Son of God, was predestined to be man, is truer than this, Christ as Man was predestined to be the Son of God.

On the contrary, Augustine (*De Prædest. Sanct.* xv)[4] says: "Because God the Son was made Man, we say that the Lord of Glory was predestined."

I answer that, Two things may be considered in predestination. One on the part of eternal predestination itself, and in this respect it implies a certain antecedence in regard to that which comes under predestination. Secondly, predestination may be considered as regards its temporal effect, which is some gratuitous gift of God. Therefore from both points of view we must say that predestination is ascribed to Christ by reason of His human nature alone; for human nature was not always united to the Word, and it was united in Person to the Son of God by grace bestowed on it. Consequently, only by reason of human nature can predestination be attributed to Christ. Therefore Augus-

[4] PL 44, 982.

tine says (*ibid*): "This human nature of ours was predestined to be raised to so great, so lofty, so exalted a position, that it would be impossible to raise it higher." Now that is said to belong to anyone as man which belongs to him by reason of human nature. Consequently, we must say that Christ, as Man, was predestined to be the Son of God.

Reply Obj. 1. When we say, Christ, as Man, was predestined to be the Son of God, this determination, "as Man," can be referred in two ways to the action signified by the participle. First, as regards what comes under predestination materially, and thus it is false. For the sense would be that it was predestined that Christ, as Man, should be the Son of God. And in this sense the objection takes it.

Secondly, it may be referred to the very nature of the action itself, that is, according as predestination implies antecedence and gratuitous effect. And thus predestination belongs to Christ by reason of His human nature, as stated above. And in this sense He is said to be predestined as Man.

Reply Obj. 2. Something may be befitting to a man by reason of human nature, in two ways. First, so that human nature be its cause; thus being capable of laughter is befitting to Socrates by reason of human nature, being caused by its principles. In this manner to be predestined is not befitting either to Christ or to any other man by reason of human nature. This is the sense of the objection.

Secondly, a thing may be befitting to someone by reason of human nature because human nature is susceptible of it. And in this sense we say that Christ was predestined by reason of human nature; because predestination refers to the exaltation of human nature in Him, as stated above.

Reply Obj. 3. As Augustine says (*loc. cit.*): "The Word of God assumed Man to Himself in such a singular and ineffable manner that at the same time He may be truly and correctly called the Son of Man, because He assumed Man to Himself; and the Son of God, because it was the Only-begotten God Who assumed human nature." Consequently, since this assumption comes under predestination by reason of its being gratuitous, we can say both that the Son of God was predestined to be man, and that the Son of Man was predestined to be the Son of God. But because grace was not bestowed on the Son of God that He might be man, but rather on human nature, that it might be united to the Son of God, it is more proper to say that Christ, as Man, was predestined to be the Son of God, than that, Christ, as Son of God, was predestined to be Man.

ARTICLE 3. *Whether Christ's Predestination Is the Exemplar of Ours?*

We proceed thus to the Third Article: It would seem that Christ's predestination is not the exemplar of ours.

Objection 1. For the exemplar exists before the exemplate. But nothing exists before the eternal. Since, therefore, our predestination is eternal, it seems that Christ's predestination is not the exemplar of ours.

Obj. 2. Further, the exemplar leads us to knowledge of the exemplate. But there was no need for God to be led from something else to knowledge of our predestination, since it is written (Rom. 8. 29): *Whom He foreknew, He also predestinated.* Therefore Christ's predestination is not the exemplar of ours.

Obj. 3. Further, the exemplar is conformed to the exemplate. But Christ's predestination seems to be of a different nature from ours, because we are predestined to the sonship of adoption, whereas Christ was predestined *Son of God in power,* as is written (Rom. 1. 4). Therefore His predestination is not the exemplar of ours.

On the contrary, Augustine says (*De Prædest. Sanct.* xv):[1] "The Saviour Himself, the Mediator of God and men, the Man Christ Jesus is the most splendid light of predestination and grace." Now He is called the light of predestination and grace because our predestination is made manifest by His predestination and grace, and this seems to pertain to the nature of an exemplar. Therefore Christ's predestination is the exemplar of ours.

I answer that, Predestination may be considered in two ways. First, on the part of the act of predestination, and thus Christ's predestination cannot be said to be the exemplar of ours, for in the same way and by the same eternal act God predestined us and Christ.

Secondly, predestination may be considered on the part of that to which anyone is predestined, and this is the term and effect of predestination. In this sense Christ's predestination is the exemplar of ours, and this in two ways. First, in respect of the good to which we are predestined, for He was predestined to be the natural Son of God, whereas we are predestined to the adoption of sons, which is a participated likeness of natural sonship. Hence it is written

[1] PL 44, 981.

(Rom. 8. 29): *Whom he foreknew, He also predestinated to be made conformable to the image of His Son.* Secondly, in respect of the manner of obtaining this good—that is, by grace. This is most manifest in Christ; because human nature in Christ, without any antecedent merits, was united to the Son of God, and of the fulness of His grace we all have received, as it is written (John 1. 16).

Reply Obj. 1. This argument considers the act itself of the predestinator.

The same is to be said of *the second objection.*

Reply Obj. 3. The exemplate need not be conformed to the exemplar in all respects; it is sufficient that it imitate it in some.

ARTICLE 4. *Whether Christ's Predestination Is the Cause of Ours?*

We proceed thus to the Fourth Article: It would seem that Christ's predestination is not the cause of ours.

Objection 1. For that which is eternal has no cause. But our predestination is eternal. Therefore Christ's predestination is not the cause of ours.

Obj. 2. Further, that which depends on the simple will of God has no other cause but God's will. Now, our predestination depends on the simple will of God, for it is written (Eph. 1. 11): *Being predestinated according to the purpose of Him, Who worketh all things according to the counsel of His will.* Therefore Christ's predestination is not the cause of ours.

Obj. 3. Further, if the cause be taken away, the effect is also taken away. But if we take away Christ's predestination, ours is not taken away, since even if the Son of God were not incarnate, our salvation might yet have been achieved in a different manner, as Augustine says (*De Trin.* xiii, 10).[1] Therefore Christ's predestination is not the cause of ours.

On the contrary, It is written (Eph. 1. 5): *(Who) hath predestinated us unto the adoption of children through Jesus Christ.*

I answer that, If we consider predestination on the part of the very act of predestining, then Christ's predestination is not the cause of ours, because by one and the same act God predestined both Christ and us. But if we consider predestination on the part of its term, thus Christ's predestination is the cause of ours, for God, by predestining from eternity, so decreed our salvation that it should be achieved through Jesus Christ. For eternal predestina-

tion covers not only that which is to be accomplished in time, but also the mode and order in which it is to be accomplished in time.

Reply Objs. 1 *and* 2. These arguments consider predestination on the part of the act of the one predestining.

Reply Obj. 3. If Christ were not to have been incarnate, God would have decreed men's salvation by other means. But since He decreed the Incarnation of Christ, He decreed at the same time that He should be the cause of our salvation.

QUESTION XXV

OF THE ADORATION OF CHRIST

(In Six Articles)

WE have now to consider things pertaining to Christ in reference to us; and first, the adoration of Christ, by which we adore Him; secondly, we must consider how He is our Mediator with God (Q. XXVI).

Under the first head there are six points of inquiry: (1) Whether Christ's Godhead and humanity are to be adored with one and the same adoration? (2) Whether the flesh of Christ is to be adored with the adoration of *latria?* (3) Whether the adoration of *latria* is to be given to the image of Christ? (4) Whether *latria* is to be given to the Cross of Christ? (5) Whether to His mother? (6) Concerning the adoration of the relics of Saints.

ARTICLE 1. *Whether Christ's Humanity and Divinity Are To Be Adored with the Same Adoration?*

We proceed thus to the First Article: It would seem that Christ's humanity and divinity are not to be adored with the same adoration.

Objection 1. For Christ's Godhead is to be adored as being common to Father and Son; and thus it is written (John 5. 23): *That all may honour the Son, as they honour the Father.* But Christ's humanity is not common to Him and the Father. Therefore Christ's humanity and divinity are not to be adored with the same adoration.

Obj. 2. Further, "honour is properly the reward of virtue," as the Philosopher says.[2] But virtue merits its reward by action. Since, therefore, in Christ the action of the Divine Nature is distinct from that of the human nature, as stated above (Q. XIX, A. 1), it seems that Christ's humanity is to be adored with a different honour from that which is given to His divinity.

---

[1] PL 42, 1024.

[2] *Ethics,* IV 3 (1123^{b}35).

Obj. 3. Further, if the soul of Christ were not united to the Word, it would have been worthy of veneration on account of the excellence of its wisdom and grace. But by being united to the Word it lost nothing of its worthiness. Therefore human nature in Christ should receive a certain veneration proper to it, besides the veneration which is given to His Godhead.

On the contrary, We read in the chapters of the Fifth Council:[1] "If anyone say that Christ is adored in two natures, so as to introduce two distinct adorations, and does not adore God the Word incarnate with the one and the same adoration as His flesh, as the Church has handed down from the beginning, let such a one be anathema."

I answer that, We may consider two things in a person to whom honour is given: the person himself, and the cause of his being honoured. Now properly speaking honour is given to a subsistent thing in its entirety, for we do not speak of honouring a man's hand, but the man himself. And if at any time it happen that we speak of honouring a man's hand or foot, it is not by reason of these members being honoured of themselves but by reason of the whole being honoured in them. In this way a man may be honoured even in something external; for instance in his vesture, his image, or his messenger. The cause of honour is that by reason of which the person honoured has a certain excellence, for honour is reverence given to something on account of its excellence, as stated in the Second Part (II-II, Q. CIII, A. I). If therefore in one man there are several causes of honour, for instance, rank, knowledge, and virtue, the honour given to him will be one in respect of the person honoured, but several in respect of the causes of honour; for it is the man that is honoured, both on account of knowledge and by reason of his virtue.

Since, therefore, in Christ there is but one Person of the Divine and human natures, and one hypostasis, and one suppositum, He is given one adoration and one honour on the part of the Person adored; but on the part of the cause for which He is honoured we can say that there are several adorations, for instance that He receives one honour on account of His uncreated knowledge, and another on account of His created knowledge. But if it be said that there are several persons or hypostases

in Christ, it would follow that there would be, absolutely speaking, several adorations. And this is what is condemned in the Councils. For it is written in the chapters of Cyril:[2] "If anyone dare to say that the man assumed should be adored besides the Divine Word, as though these were distinct persons, and does not rather honour the Emmanuel with one single adoration, according as the Word was made flesh, let him be anathema."

Reply Obj. 1. In the Trinity there are three Who are honoured, but only one cause of honour. In the mystery of the Incarnation it is the reverse, and therefore only one honour is given to the Trinity and only one to Christ, but in a different way.

Reply Obj. 2. Operation is not the object but the reason of honour. And therefore there being two operations in Christ shows not two adorations but two causes of adoration.

Reply Obj. 3. If the soul of Christ were not united to the Word of God, it would be the principal thing in that Man. Therefore honour would be due to it principally, since man is that which is most excellent in him. But since Christ's soul is united to a Person of greater dignity, to that Person is honour principally due to Whom Christ's soul is united. Nor is the dignity of Christ's soul diminished by this, but rather increased, as stated above (Q. II, A. 2, Reply 2).

ARTICLE 2. *Whether Christ's Humanity Should Be Adored with the Adoration of "Latria"?*

We proceed thus to the Second Article: It would seem that Christ's soul should not be adored with the adoration of *latria.*

Objection 1. For on the words of Ps. 98. 5, *Adore His foot-stool for it is holy,* a gloss says:[3] "The flesh assumed by the Word of God is rightly adored by us, for no one partakes spiritually of His flesh unless he first adore it; but not indeed with the adoration called 'latria,' which is due to the Creator alone." Now the flesh is part of the humanity. Therefore Christ's humanity is not to be adored with the adoration of *latria.*

Obj. 2. Further, the worship of *latria* is not to be given to any creature, since for this reason were the Gentiles reproved, that they *worshipped and served the creature,* as it is written (Rom. 1. 25). But Christ's humanity is a crea-

---

[1] Second Council of Constantinople, coll. VIII., can. 9. (MA IX, 382; DZ 120).

[2] *Epist.,* XVII, *Ad Nestorium,* anath. 8 (PG 77, 121); Mercator's trans., PL 48, 840; also in the Council of Ephesus, PT. I, chap. 26 (MA IV, 1083; DZ 120).

[3] *Glossa ordin.* (III, 233E); *Glossa* Lombardi (PL 191, 895).

ture. Therefore it should not be adored with the adoration of *latria*.

Obj. 3. Further, the adoration of *latria* is due to God in recognition of His supreme dominion, according to Deut. 6. 13: *Thou shalt adore* (Vulg., *fear;* cf. Matt. 4. 10) *the Lord thy God, and shalt serve Him only.* But Christ as man is less than the Father. Therefore His humanity is not to be adored with the adoration of *latria*.

On the contrary, Damascene says (*De Fide Orthod.* iv, 3):[1] "We adore the flesh of Christ, the incarnate Word of God, not for its own sake, but because the Word of God is united thereto in hypostasis." And on Ps. 98. 5, *Adore His foot-stool,* a gloss says:[2] "He who adores the body of Christ regards not the earth, but rather Him whose foot-stool it is, in Whose honour he adores the foot-stool." But the incarnate Word is adored with the adoration of *latria.* Therefore also His body or His humanity.

I answer that, As stated above (A. 1) adoration is properly due to the subsisting hypostasis, yet the reason for honouring may be something non-subsistent, on account of which the person in whom it is is honoured. And so the adoration of Christ's humanity may be understood in two ways. First, so that the humanity is the thing adored, and thus to adore the flesh of Christ is nothing else than to adore the incarnate Word of God, just as to adore a King's robe is nothing else than to adore a robed King. And in this sense the adoration of Christ's humanity is the adoration of *latria.* Secondly, the adoration of Christ's humanity may be taken as given by reason of its being perfected with every gift of grace. And so in this sense the adoration of Christ's humanity is the adoration not of *latria* but of *dulia.* So that one and the same Person of Christ is adored with *latria* on account of His Divinity, and with *dulia* on account of His perfect humanity. Nor is this unfitting. For the honour of *latria* is due to God the Father Himself on account of His Godhead; and the honour of *dulia* on account of the dominion by which He rules over creatures. Therefore on Ps. 7. 1, *O Lord my God, in Thee have I hoped,* a gloss says:[3] "Lord of all by power, to Whom 'dulia' is due: God of all by creation, to Whom 'latria' is due."

Reply Obj. 1. That gloss is not to be understood as though the flesh of Christ were adored

[1] PG 94, 1105.
[2] *Glossa ordin.* (III, 233E); *Glossa* Lombardi (PL 191, 895); Augustine, *Enarr. in Ps.* (PL 37, 1264).
[3] *Glossa interl.* (III, 94V); *Glossa* Lombardi (PL 191, 111).

separately from its Godhead, for this would happen only if there were one hypostasis of God and another of man. But since, as Damascene says (*loc. cit.*): "If by a subtle distinction you divide what is seen from what is understood, it cannot be adored because it is a creature"— that is, with adoration of *latria.* And then thus understood as distinct from the Word of God, it should be adored with the adoration of *dulia;* not any kind of *dulia,* such as is given to other creatures, but with a certain higher adoration, which is called *hyperdulia.*

And from this appear the *answers to the second and third objections.* Because the adoration of *latria* is not given to Christ's humanity by reason of itself, but by reason of the Godhead to which it is united, according to which Christ is not less than the Father.

ARTICLE 3. *Whether the Image of Christ Should Be Adored with the Adoration of Latria?*

We proceed thus to the Third Article: It would seem that Christ's image should not be adored with the adoration of *latria.*

Objection 1. For it is written (Exod. 20. 4): *Thou shalt not make to thyself a graven thing, nor the likeness of anything.* But no adoration should be given against the commandment of God. Therefore Christ's image should not be adored with the adoration of *latria.*

Obj. 2. Further, we should have nothing in common with the works of the Gentiles, as the Apostle says (Eph. 5. 11). But the Gentiles are reproached principally for that *they changed the glory of the incorruptible God into the likeness of the image of a corruptible man,* as is written (Rom. 1. 23). Therefore Christ's image is not to be adored with the adoration of *latria.*

Obj. 3. Further, to Christ the adoration of *latria* is due by reason of His divinity, not of His humanity. But the adoration of *latria* is not due to the image of His divinity, which is imprinted on the rational soul. Much less, therefore, is it due to the material image which represents the humanity of Christ Himself.

Obj. 4. Further, it seems that nothing should be done in the Divine worship that is not instituted by God; therefore the Apostle (I Cor. 11. 23) when about to hand down the doctrine of the sacrifice of the Church, says: *I have received of the Lord that which also I delivered unto you.* But Scripture does not lay down anything concerning the adoration of images. Therefore Christ's image is not to be adored with the adoration of *latria.*

On the contrary, Damascene (*De Fide Or-*

thod. iv, 16)[1] quotes Basil[2] as saying: "The honour given to an image reaches to the prototype"—that is, the exemplar. But the exemplar itself—namely, Christ—is to be adored with the adoration of *latria;* therefore also His image.

I answer that, As the Philosopher says,[3] there is a twofold movement of the mind towards an image: one indeed towards the image itself as a certain thing, another, towards the image in so far as it is the image of something else. And between these movements there is this difference, that the former, by which one is moved towards an image as a certain thing, is different from the movement towards the thing, but the latter movement, which is towards the image as an image, is one and the same as that which is towards the thing. Thus therefore we must say that no reverence is shown to Christ's image as a thing,—for instance, carved or painted wood—because reverence is not due save to a rational creature. It follows therefore that reverence should be shown to it in so far only as it is an image. Consequently the same reverence should be shown to Christ's image as to Christ Himself. Since, therefore, Christ is adored with the adoration of *latria,* it follows that His image should be adored with the adoration of *latria.*

Reply Obj. 1. This commandment does not forbid the making of any graven thing or likeness, but the making of it for the purpose of adoration, and therefore it is added: *Thou shalt not adore them nor serve them.* And because, as stated above, the movement towards the image is the same as the movement towards the thing, its adoration is forbidden in the same way as adoration of the thing whose image it is. Therefore in the passage quoted we are to understand the prohibition to adore those images which the Gentiles made for the purpose of venerating their own gods—that is, the demons—and so it is first said: *Thou shalt not have strange gods before Me.* But no corporeal image could be put for the true God Himself, since He is incorporeal; because, as Damascene observes (*loc. cit.*): "It is the highest absurdity and impiety to fashion a figure of what is Divine." But because in the New Testament God was made man, He can be adored in His corporeal image.

Reply Obj. 2. The Apostle forbids us to have anything in common with the unfruitful works of the Gentiles, but not with their useful works.

Now the adoration of images must be numbered among the unfruitful works in two respects. First, because some of the Gentiles used to adore the images themselves, as things, believing that there was something Divine in them, on account of the answers which the demons used to give in them, and on account of other like wonderful effects. Secondly on account of the things of which they were images, for they set up images to certain creatures, to Whom in these images they gave the veneration of *latria.* Whereas we give the adoration of *latria* to the image of Christ, Who is true God, not for the sake of the image, but for the sake of the thing whose image it is, as stated above.

Reply Obj. 3. Reverence is due to the rational creature for its own sake. Consequently, if the adoration of *latria* were shown to the rational creature in which this image is, there might be an occasion of error—namely, lest the movement of adoration might stop short at the man, as a thing, and not be carried on to God, Whose image he is. This cannot happen in the case of a graven or painted image in insensible material.

Reply Obj. 4. The Apostles, led by the inward stirring of the Holy Ghost, handed down to the churches certain instructions which they did not leave in writing, but which have been ordained in accordance with the observance of the Church as practised by the faithful as time went on. Therefore the Apostle says (II Thess. 2. 14): *Stand fast; and hold the traditions which you have learned, whether by word—* that is by word of mouth—*or by our epistle—* that is by word put into writing. Among these traditions is the worship of Christ's image. Hence, too, it is said that Blessed Luke painted the image of Christ, which is in Rome.

ARTICLE 4. *Whether Christ's Cross Should Be Worshipped with the Adoration of "Latria"?*

We proceed thus to the Fourth Article: It would seem that Christ's cross should not be worshipped with the adoration of *latria.*

Objection 1. For no dutiful son honours that which dishonours his father, as the scourge with which he was scourged, or the gibbet on which he was hanged; rather does he abhor it. Now Christ underwent the most shameful death on the cross, according to Wisd. 2. 20: *Let us condemn Him to a most shameful death.* Therefore we should not venerate the cross but rather we should abhor it.

Obj. 2. Further, Christ's humanity is worshipped with the adoration of *latria* because it is united to the Son of God in Person. But this

[1] PG 94, 1169.   [2] *De Spir. Sancto,* chap. 18 (PG 32, 149).   [3] *Memory and Reminiscence,* 1 (450 [b] 27).

cannot be said of the cross. Therefore Christ's cross should not be worshipped with the adoration of *latria*.

Obj. 3. Further, as Christ's cross was the instrument of His passion and death, so were also many other things, for instance, the nails, the crown, the lance; yet to these we do not show the worship of *latria*. It seems, therefore, that Christ's cross should not be worshipped with the adoration of *latria*.

On the contrary, We show the worship of *latria* to that in which we place our hope of salvation. But we place our hope in Christ's cross, for the Church sings:

Dear Cross, best hope o'er all beside,
That cheers the solemn passion-tide:
Give to the just increase of grace,
Give to each contrite sinner peace.[1]

Therefore Christ's cross should be worshipped with the adoration of *latria*.

I answer that, As stated above (A. 3), honour or reverence is due to a rational creature only, while to an insensible creature, no honour or reverence is due save by reason of a rational nature. And this in two ways. First, in so far as it represents a rational nature; secondly, in so far as it is united to it in any way whatsoever. In the first way men are accustomed to venerate the king's image; in the second way, his robe. And both are venerated by men with the same veneration as they show to the king.

If, therefore, we speak of the cross itself on which Christ was crucified, it is to be venerated by us in both ways—namely, in one way in so far as it represents to us the figure of Christ extended thereon; in the other way, from its contact with the limbs of Christ, and from its being saturated with His blood. Therefore in each way it is worshipped with the same adoration as Christ—namely, the adoration of *latria*. And for this reason also we speak to the cross and pray to it, as to the Crucified Himself. But if we speak of the effigy of Christ's cross in any other material whatever—for instance, in stone or wood, silver or gold—thus we venerate the cross merely as Christ's image, which we worship with the adoration of *latria*, as stated above (A. 3).

Reply Obj. 1. If in Christ's cross we consider the point of view and intention of those who did not believe in Him, it will appear as His shame; but if we consider its effect, which is our salvation, it will appear as endowed with Divine power, by which it triumphed over the enemy, according to Col. 2. 14, 15: *He hath taken the same out of the way, fastening it to the cross, and despoiling the principalities and powers, He hath exposed them confidently, in open show, triumphing over them in Himself.* Therefore the Apostle says (I Cor. 1. 18): *The Word of the cross to them indeed that perish is foolishness; but to them that are saved— that is, to us—it is the power of God.*

Reply Obj. 2. Although Christ's cross was not united to the Word of God in Person, yet it was united to Him in some other way—namely, by representation and contact. And for this sole reason reverence is shown to it.

Reply Obj. 3. By reason of the contact of Christ's limbs we worship not only the cross, but all that belongs to Christ. Hence Damascene says (*De Fid. Orthod.* iv, 11):[2] "The precious wood, as having been sanctified by the contact of His holy body and blood, should be meetly worshipped, as also His nails, His lance, and His sacred dwelling-places, such as the manger, the cave and so forth." Yet these very things do not represent Christ's image as the cross does, which is called *the Sign of the Son of Man that will appear in heaven,* as it is written (Matt. 24. 30). Therefore the angel said to the women (Mark 16. 6): *You seek Jesus of Nazareth, Who was crucified;* he did not say "pierced," but "crucified." For this reason we worship the image of Christ's cross in any material, but not the image of the nails or of any such thing.

ARTICLE 5. *Whether the Mother of God Should Be Worshipped with the Adoration of "Latria"?*

We proceed thus to the Fifth Article: It would seem that the Mother of God is to be worshipped with the adoration of *latria*.

Objection 1. For it seems that the same honour is due to the king's mother as to the king; hence it is written (III Kings 2. 19) that a *throne was set for the king's mother, and she sat on His right hand.* Moreover, Augustine says:[3] "It is right that the throne of God, the resting-place of the Lord of Heaven, the abode of Christ, should be there where He is Himself." But Christ is worshipped with the adoration of *latria*. Therefore His Mother also should be.

Obj. 2. Further, Damascene says (*De Fid. Orth.* iv, 16):[4] "The honour of the Mother re-

---

[1] Hymn *Vexilla Regis;* translation of Father Aylward, O.P. Sung at Vespers on Passion Sunday.

[2] PG 94, 1129.
[3] *Sermon on the Assumption,* work of an anonymous author, contained among the works of Augustine (PL 40, 1146). [4] PG 94, 1172.

flects on the Son." But the Son is worshipped with the adoration of *latria*. Therefore the Mother also.

Obj. 3. Further, Christ's Mother is more akin to Him than the cross. But the cross is worshipped with the adoration of *latria*. Therefore also His Mother is to be worshipped with the same adoration.

On the contrary, The Mother of God is a mere creature. Therefore the worship of *latria* is not due to her.

I answer that, Since *latria* is due to God alone, it is not due to a creature so far as we venerate a creature for its own sake. For though insensible creatures are not capable of being venerated for their own sake, yet the rational creature is capable of being venerated for its own sake. Consequently the worship of *latria* is not due to any mere rational creature for its own sake. Since, therefore, the Blessed Virgin is a mere rational creature, the worship of *latria* is not due to her, but only the veneration of *dulia;* but in a higher degree than to other creatures, since she is the Mother of God. For this reason we say that not any kind of *dulia* is due to her, but *hyperdulia*.

Reply Obj. 1. The honour due to the king's mother is not equal to the honour which is due to the king, but is somewhat like it by reason of a certain excellence on her part. This is what is meant by the authorities quoted.

Reply Obj. 2. The honour given to the Mother reflects on her Son, because the Mother is to be honoured for her Son's sake. But not in the same way as honour given to an image reflects on its exemplar, because the image itself, considered as a thing, is not to be venerated in any way at all.

Reply Obj. 3. The cross, considered in itself, is not a suitable object of veneration, as stated above (A. 4). But the Blessed Virgin is in herself a suitable object of veneration. Hence there is no comparison.

ARTICLE 6. *Whether Any Kind of Worship Is Due to the Relics of the Saints?*

We proceed thus to the Sixth Article: It would seem that the relics of the saints are not to be worshipped at all.

Objection 1. For we should avoid doing what may be the occasion of error. But to worship the relics of the dead seems to savour of the error of the Gentiles, who gave honour to dead men. Therefore the relics of the saints are not to be honoured.

Obj. 2. Further, it seems absurd to venerate what is insensible. But the relics of the saints are insensible bodies. Therefore it is absurd to venerate them.

Obj. 3. Further, a dead body is not of the same species as a living body: consequently it does not seem to be the same in number with it. Therefore, after a saint's death, it seems that his body should not be worshipped.

On the contrary, It is written (*De Eccles. Dogm.*):[1] "We believe that the bodies of the saints, above all the relics of the blessed martyrs, as being the members of Christ, should be worshipped in all sincerity"; and further on: "If anyone holds a contrary opinion, he is not accounted a Christian, but a follower of Eunomius and Vigilantius."

I answer that, As Augustine says:[2] "If a father's coat or ring, or anything else of that kind, is so much more cherished by his children as love for one's parents is greater, in no way are the bodies themselves to be despised, which are much more intimately and closely united to us than any garment; for they belong to man's very nature." It is clear from this that he who has a certain affection for anyone venerates whatever of his is left after his death not only his body and the parts thereof, but even external things, such as his clothes, and the like. Now it is manifest that we should show veneration to the saints of God, as being members of Christ, the children and friends of God, and our intercessors. Therefore in memory of them we ought to venerate any relics of theirs in a fitting manner; and principally their bodies, which were temples, and organs of the Holy Ghost dwelling and operating in them, and are destined to be likened to the body of Christ by the glory of the Resurrection. Hence God Himself fittingly honours such relics by working miracles at their presence.

Reply Obj. 1. This was the argument of Vigilantius, who words are quoted by Jerome in the book he wrote against him as follows:[3] "We see something like a pagan rite introduced under pretext of religion; they worship with kisses I know not what tiny heap of dust in a mean vase surrounded with precious linen." To him Jerome replies (*Ep. ad Ripar.* cix):[4] "We do not adore, I will not say the relics of the martyrs, but either the sun or the moon or even the angels"—that is to say, with the worship of *latria*. "But we honour the martyrs' relics, so

---

[1] Gennadius, chap 73 (PL 58, 997).
[2] *City of God,* I, 13 (PL 41, 27).
[3] *Contra Vigilant.* (PL 23, 357); cf. *Epist.,* CIX (PL 22, 907).   [4] PL 22, 907.

that thereby we give honour to Him Whose martyrs they are; we honour the servants, that the honour shown to them may reflect on their Master." Consequently, by honouring the martyrs' relics we do not fall into the error of the Gentiles, who gave the worship of *latria* to dead men.

Reply Obj. 2. We worship that insensible body not for its own sake, but for the sake of the soul, which was once united to it, and now enjoys God; and for God's sake, whose ministers the saints were.

Reply Obj. 3. The dead body of a saint is not the same in number with that which the saint had during life, on account of the difference of form—namely, the soul; but it is the same by identity of matter, which is destined to be reunited to its form.

QUESTION XXVI
OF CHRIST AS CALLED THE MEDIATOR
OF GOD AND MAN
(*In Two Articles*)

WE have now to consider how Christ is called the Mediator of God and man, and under this head there are two points of inquiry: (1) Whether it is proper to Christ to be the Mediator of God and man? (2) Whether this belongs to Him by reason of His human nature?

ARTICLE 1. *Whether It Is Proper to Christ To Be the Mediator of God and Man?*

We proceed thus to the First Article: It would seem that it is not proper to Christ to be the Mediator of God and man.

Objection 1. For just as a priest, so too, a prophet seems to be mediator between God and man, according to Deut. 5.5: *I was the mediator and stood between God* (Vulg., *the Lord*) *and you at that time.* But it is not proper to Christ to be a priest and a prophet. Neither, therefore, is it proper to Him to be Mediator.

Obj. 2. Further, that which is fitting to angels, both good and bad, cannot be said to be proper to Christ. But to be between God and man is fitting to the good angels, as Dionysius says (*Div. Nom.* iv).[1] It is also fitting to the bad angels—that is, the demons, for they have something in common with God—namely, immortality; and something they have in common with men—namely, passibility of soul and consequently unhappiness, as appears from what Augustine says.[2] Therefore it is not proper to Christ to be a Mediator of God and man.

[1] Sect. 2 (PG 3, 696).
[2] *City of God*, IX, 13, 15 (PL 41, 267; 268).

Obj. 3. Further, it pertains to the office of Mediator to beseech one of those between whom he mediates for the other. But the Holy Ghost, as it is written (Rom. 8. 26), *asketh* God *for us with unspeakable groanings.* Therefore the Holy Ghost is a Mediator between God and man. Therefore this is not proper to Christ.

On the contrary, It is written (I Tim. 2. 5): *There is . . . one Mediator of God and man, the man Christ Jesus.*

I answer that, Properly speaking, the office of a mediator is to join together and unite those between whom he mediates, for extremes are united in the mean (*medio*). Now to unite men to God in a perfecting way belongs to Christ, through Whom men are reconciled to God, according to II Cor. 5. 19: *God was in Christ reconciling the world to Himself.* And, consequently, Christ alone is the perfect Mediator of God and men, since by His death He reconciled the human race to God. Hence the Apostle, after saying, *Mediator of God and man, the man Christ Jesus,* added: *Who gave Himself a redemption for all.*

However, nothing hinders certain others from being called mediators, in some respect, between God and man, according as they co-operate in uniting men to God, in a disposing way or ministerially.

Reply Obj. 1. The prophets and priests of the Old Law were called mediators between God and man, dispositively and ministerially, in so far as they foretold and foreshadowed the true and perfect Mediator of God and men. As to the priests of the New Law, they may be called mediators of God and men in so far as they are the ministers of the true Mediator by administering, in His stead, the saving sacraments to men.

Reply Obj. 2. The good angels, as Augustine says,[3] cannot rightly be called mediators between God and men. "For since, in common with God, they have both Happiness and immortality, and none of these things in common with unhappy and mortal man, how much rather are they not aloof from men and joined to God, than established between them?" Dionysius, however, says that they do occupy a middle place, because, in the order of nature, they are established below God and above man. Moreover they fulfil the office of mediator, not indeed principally and in a perfecting way, but ministerially and in a disposing way; hence (Matt. 4. 11) it is said that *angels came and ministered unto Him*—namely, Christ. As to the demons, it is true that they have immortality in common

[3] *City of God*, IX, 13 (PL 41, 267).

with God, and unhappiness in common with men. "Hence for this purpose does the immortal and unhappy demon intervene, in order that he may hinder men from passing to a happy immortality," and may allure them to an unhappy immortality. And so he is like *an evil mediator, who separates friends.*"[1]

But Christ had Happiness in common with God, mortality in common with men. Hence "for this purpose did He intervene, that having fulfilled the span of His mortality, He might from dead men make immortal,—which He showed in Himself by rising again; and that He might from unhappy men make happy,—for which reason He never forsook us." Therefore He is "the good Mediator, Who reconciles enemies."[2]

Reply Obj. 3. Since the Holy Ghost is in everything equal to God, He cannot be said to be between, or a Mediator of, God and men; but Christ alone, Who, though equal to the Father in His Godhead, yet is less than the Father in His human nature, as stated above (Q. XX, A. 1).[3] Hence on Gal. 3. 20, *Christ is a Mediator* (Vulg., *Now a mediator is not of one, but God is one*), the gloss says:[4] "Not the Father nor the Holy Ghost." The Holy Ghost, however, is said "to ask for us," because He makes us ask.[5]

ARTICLE 2. *Whether Christ, As Man, Is the Mediator of God and Men?*

We proceed thus to the Second Article: It would seem that Christ is not, as man, the Mediator of God and men.

Objection 1. For Augustine says (*Contra Felic.* x):[6] "One is the Person of Christ, lest there be not one Christ, not one substance; lest, the office of Mediator being denied, He be called the Son either of God alone, or merely the Son of a man." But He is the Son of God and man, not as man, but as at the same time God and man. Therefore neither should we say that, as man alone, He is Mediator of God and man.

Obj. 2. Further, just as Christ, as God, has a common nature with the Father and the Holy Ghost, so, as man, He has a common nature with men. But for the reason that, as God, He has the same nature as the Father and the Holy Ghost, He cannot be called Mediator, as God; for on I Tim. 2. 5, *Mediator of God and man,* a gloss says.[7] "As the Word, He is not a Media-

tor, because He is equal to God, and God 'with God,' and at the same time one God." Therefore neither, as man, can He be called Mediator, on account of His having the same nature as men.

Obj. 3. Further, Christ is called Mediator because He reconciled us to God; and this He did by taking away sin, which separated us from God. But to take away sin belongs to Christ not as man but as God. Therefore Christ is our Mediator not as man, but as God.

On the contrary, Augustine says:[8] "Not because He is the Word is Christ Mediator, since He Who is supremely immortal and supremely happy is far from us unhappy mortals, but He is Mediator as man."

I answer that, We may consider two things in a mediator: first, that he is a mean; secondly, that he unites others. Now it is of the nature of a mean to be distant from each extreme, while a mediator unites by communicating to one that which belongs to the other. Now neither of these can be applied to Christ as God, but only as man. For, as God, He does not differ from the Father and the Holy Ghost in nature and power of dominion; nor have the Father and the Holy Ghost anything that the Son has not, so that He be able to communicate to others something belonging to the Father or the Holy Ghost, as though it were belonging to others than Himself. But both can be applied to Him as man. Because, as man, He is distant both from God, by nature, and from man by dignity of both grace and glory. Again, it belongs to Him, to unite men to God, by tendering to men both precepts and gifts, and by offering satisfaction and prayers to God for men. And therefore He is most truly called Mediator as man.

Reply Obj. 1. If we take the Divine Nature from Christ, we consequently take from Him the singular fulness of grace, which belongs to Him as the Only-begotten of the Father, as it is written (John 1. 14). From which fulness it resulted that He was established over all men, and approached nearer to God.

Reply Obj. 2. Christ, as God, is in all things equal to the Father. But even in the human nature He is above all men. Therefore, as man, He can be Mediator, but not as God.

Reply Obj. 3. Although it belongs to Christ as God to take away sin as having the authority, yet it belongs to Him as man to satisfy for the sin of the human race. And in this sense He is called the Mediator of God and men.

[1] Augustine, *Ibid.*, IX, 15 (PL 41, 269).   [2] *Ibid.*
[3] Cf. Creed, "*Quicumque*" (MA II, 1355; DZ 40).
[4] *Glossa Lombardi* (PL 192, 129); cf. *Glossa ordin.* (VI, 83E).   [5] Cf. *Glossa interl.*, on Rom. 8.26 (VI, 19V).
[6] Vigilius Tapsensus, *De Unit. Trin.*, 12 (PL 62, 342).
[7] *Glossa ordin.* (VI, 118F); *Glossa Lombardi* (PL 192, 339); Augustine, *Confessions*, X, 68 (PL 32, 808).
[8] *City of God*, IX, 15 (PL 41, 269).

TREATISE ON THE SACRAMENTS

QUESTION LX

OF THE SACRAMENTS

(*In Eight Articles*)

AFTER considering those things that concern the mystery of the incarnate Word, we must consider the sacraments of the Church which derive their efficacy from the Word incarnate Himself. First we shall consider the sacraments in general; secondly, we shall consider specially each sacrament (Q. LXVI).

Concerning the first our consideration will be fivefold: (1) What is a sacrament? (2) Of the necessity of the sacraments (Q. LXI). (3) Of the effects of the sacraments (Q. LXII). (4) Of their cause (Q. LXIV). (5) Of their number (Q. LXV).

Under the first heading there are eight points of inquiry: (1) Whether a sacrament is a kind of sign? (2) Whether every sign of a sacred thing is a sacrament? (3) Whether a sacrament is a sign of one thing only, or of several? (4) Whether a sacrament is a sign that is a sensible thing? (5) Whether a determinate sensible thing is required for a sacrament? (6) Whether signification expressed by words is necessary for a sacrament? (7) Whether determinate words are required? (8) Whether anything may be added to or subtracted from these words?

ARTICLE 1. *Whether a Sacrament Is a Kind of Sign?*

We proceed thus to the First Article: It seems that a sacrament is not a kind of sign.

Objection 1. For sacrament appears to be derived from making holy (*sacrando*), just as medicament, from healing (*medicando*). But this seems to be of the nature of a cause rather than to the nature of a sign. Therefore a sacrament is in the genus of cause rather than in the genus of sign.

Obj. 2. Further, sacrament seems to signify something hidden, according to Tob. 12. 7: *It is good to hide the secret (sacramentum) of a king;* and Ephes. 3. 9: *What is the dispensation of the mystery (sacramenti) which hath been hidden from eternity in God.* But that which is hidden, seems to be against the nature

of a sign for, "a sign is that which conveys something else to the mind besides the species which it puts into the senses," as Augustine explains.[1] Therefore it seems that a sacrament is not in the genus of sign.

Obj. 3. Further, an oath is sometimes called a sacrament, for it is written in the Decretals:[2] "Children who have not attained the use of reason must not be obliged to swear, and whoever has foresworn himself once, must no more be a witness, nor be allowed to take a sacrament"—that is, an oath. But an oath is not a kind of sign, and therefore it seems that a sacrament is not a kind of sign.

On the contrary, Augustine says:[3] "The visible sacrifice is the sacrament, that is, the sacred sign, of the invisible sacrifice."

I answer that, All things that are ordered to one, even in different ways, can be denominated from it; thus, from health which is in an animal, not only is the animal said to be healthy through being the subject of health, but medicine also is said to be healthy through producing health, diet through preserving it, and urine, through being a sign of health. Consequently, a thing may be called a sacrament either from having a certain hidden sanctity, and in this sense a sacrament is the same as a sacred secret; or from having some relationship to this sanctity, which relationship may be that of a cause, or of a sign or of any other relation. But now we are speaking of sacraments in a special sense, as implying the relationship of sign, and in this way a sacrament is a kind of sign.

Reply Obj. 1. Because medicine is an efficient cause of health, consequently whatever things are denominated from medicine are called so in relation to one first agent, so that a medicament implies a certain causality. But sanctity from which a sacrament is denominated is not there taken as an efficient cause, but rather as a formal or a final cause. Therefore it does not follow that a sacrament need always imply causality.

---

[1] *Christian Doctrine,* II, 1 (PL 34, 35).
[2] Gratian, *Decretum,* II, causa XXII, Q. 5, can. 14 (RF I, 886).
[3] *City of God,* X, 5 (PL 41, 282).

Reply Obj. 2. This argument considers sacrament in the sense of a sacred secret. Now not only God's, but also the king's, secret, is said to be sacred and to be a sacrament, because according to the ancients, whatever it was unlawful to lay violent hands on was said to be holy or sacrosanct,[1] such as the city walls,[2] and persons of high rank. Consequently those secrets, whether Divine or human, which it is unlawful to violate by making them known to anybody whatever, are called sacred secrets or sacraments.

Reply Obj. 3. Even an oath has a certain relation to sacred things, in so far as it consists in calling a sacred thing to witness. And in this sense it is called a sacrament, not in the sense in which we speak of sacraments now, the word sacrament being thus used not equivocally but analogically—that is, by reason of a different relation to the one thing—namely, something sacred.

ARTICLE 2. *Whether Every Sign of a Holy Thing Is a Sacrament?*

We proceed thus to the Second Article: It seems that not every sign of a sacred thing is a sacrament.

Objection 1. For all sensible creatures are signs of sacred things, according to Rom. 1. 20: *The invisible things of God are clearly seen being understood by the things that are made.* And yet all sensible things cannot be called sacraments. Therefore not every sign of a sacred thing is a sacrament.

Obj. 2. Further, whatever was done under the Old Law was a figure of Christ Who is the *Holy of Holies* (Dan. 9. 24), according to I Cor. 10. 11: *All (these) things happened to them in figure;* and Col. 2. 17: *Which are a shadow of things to come, but the body is Christ's.* And yet not all that was done by the Fathers of the old Testament, not even all the ceremonies of the Law, were sacraments, but only in certain special cases, as stated in the Second Part (I-II, Q. CI, A. 4). Therefore it seems that not every sign of a sacred thing is a sacrament.

Obj. 3. Further, even in the New Testament many things are done in sign of some sacred thing, yet they are not called sacraments; such as sprinkling with holy water, the consecration of an altar, and the like. Therefore not every sign of a sacred thing is a sacrament.

On the contrary, A definition is convertible with the thing defined. Now some[3] define a sacrament as being "the sign of a sacred thing"; moreover, this is clear from the passage quoted above (A. 1) from Augustine. Therefore it seems that every sign of a sacred thing is a sacrament.

I answer that, Signs are given to men, to whom it is proper to come to the unknown by means of the known. Consequently a sacrament properly so called is that which is the sign of some sacred thing pertaining to man, so that properly speaking a sacrament, as considered by us now, is defined as being the sign of a holy thing so far as it makes men holy.

Reply Obj. 1. Sensible creatures signify something holy—namely, Divine wisdom and goodness in so far as these are holy in themselves, but not in so far as we are made holy by them. Therefore they cannot be called sacraments as we understand sacraments now.

Reply Obj. 2. Some things pertaining to the Old Testament signified the holiness of Christ considered as holy in Himself. Others signified His holiness considered as the cause of our holiness; thus the sacrifice of the Paschal Lamb signified Christ's Sacrifice whereby we are made holy, and such things are properly styled sacraments of the Old Law.

Reply Obj. 3. Names are given to things considered in reference to their end and state of completeness. Now a disposition is not an end, whereas perfection is. Consequently things that signify disposition to holiness are not called sacraments, and with regard to these the objection is verified: only those are called sacraments which signify the perfection of holiness in man.

ARTICLE 3. *Whether a Sacrament Is a Sign of One Thing Only?*

We proceed thus to the Third Article: It seems that a sacrament is a sign of one thing only.

Objection 1. For that which signifies many things is an ambiguous sign, and consequently occasions deception; this is clearly seen in equivocal words. But all deception should be removed from the Christian religion, according to Col. 2. 8: *Beware lest any man cheat you by*

---

[1] Cf. *Digest,* I, tit. VIII, leg. 8 (KR 1, 40A).
[2] *Ibid.,* leg. 1 (KR 1, 39a).

[3] Cf. Lanfranc, *De Corp. et Sang. Dom.,* XII (PL 150, 422); Hugh of St. Victor, *De Sacr.,* I, IX, 2 (PL 176, 317); Peter Lombard, *Sent.,* IV, d. 1, chap. 2 (QR II, 745); Albert the Great, *In Sent.,* IV, dist. 1, A. 1, Q. 2 (QR IV, 14); Alexander of Hales, *Summa Theol.,* IV, Q. 1, m. 1 (IV, 2ra); Bonaventure, *In Sent.,* IV, d. 1, A. 1, Q. 2 (QR IV, 14).

philosophy and vain deceit. Therefore it seems that a sacrament is not a sign of several things.

Obj. 2. Further, as stated above (A. 2), a sacrament signifies a holy thing in so far as it is a cause of man's holiness. But there is only one cause of man's holiness, namely, the blood of Christ, according to Heb. 13. 12: *Jesus, that He might sanctify the people by His own blood, suffered without the gate.* Therefore it seems that a sacrament does not signify several things.

Obj. 3. Further, it has been said above (A. 2, reply 3) that a sacrament signifies properly the very end of sanctification. Now the end of sanctification is eternal life, according to Rom. 6. 22: *You have your fruit unto sanctification, and the end life everlasting.* Therefore it seems that the sacraments signify one thing only—namely, eternal life.

On the contrary, In the Sacrament of the Altar, two things are signified, namely, Christ's true body, and Christ's mystical body, as Augustine says (*Liber Sent. Prosper.*).[1]

I answer that, As stated above (A. 2) a sacrament properly speaking is that which is ordained to signify our sanctification. In which three things may be considered; namely, the very cause of our sanctification, which is Christ's passion, the form of our sanctification, which is grace and the virtues, and the ultimate end of our sanctification, which is eternal life. And all these are signified by the sacraments. Consequently a sacrament is a sign that is both a reminder of the past, that is, the passion of Christ; and an indication of that which is effected in us by Christ's passion, that is, grace; and a prognostic, that is, a foretelling of future glory.

Reply Obj. 1. A sign is ambiguous and the occasion of deception when it signifies many things not ordered to one another. But when it signifies many things according as through being mutually ordered they form one thing, then the sign is not ambiguous but certain; thus this word "man" signifies the soul and body according as together they form the human nature. In this way a sacrament signifies the three things aforesaid, according as by being in a certain order they are one thing.

Reply Obj. 2. Since a sacrament signifies that which sanctifies, it must signify the effect, which is understood in the sanctifying cause itself according as it is sanctifying.

Reply Obj. 3. It is enough for the nature of a sacrament that it signify that perfection

which consists in the form, nor is it necessary that it should signify only that perfection which is the end.

ARTICLE 4. *Whether a Sacrament Is Always Something Sensible?*

We proceed thus to the Fourth Article: It seems that a sacrament is not always something sensible.

Objection 1. Because, according to the Philosopher,[2] every effect is a sign of its cause. But just as there are certain sensible effects, so are there certain intelligible effects; thus science is the effect of a demonstration. Therefore not every sign is sensible. Now it is enough for the nature of a sacrament that it be a sign of some sacred thing, in so far as by it man is sanctified, as stated above (A. 2). Therefore it is not required for a sacrament that it be some sensible thing.

Obj. 2. Further, sacraments belong to the kingdom of God or the Divine worship. But sensible things do not seem to belong to the Divine worship; for we are told (John 4. 24) that *God is a spirit; and they that adore Him, must adore Him in spirit and in truth,* and (Rom. 14. 17) that *the kingdom of God is not meat and drink.* Therefore sensible things are not required for the sacraments.

Obj. 3. Further, Augustine says (*De Lib. Arb.* ii, 19)[3] that "sensible things are goods of least account, since without them man can live rightly." But the sacraments are necessary for man's salvation, as we shall show farther on (Q. LXI, A. 1), so that man cannot live rightly without them. Therefore sensible things are not required for the sacraments.

On the contrary, Augustine says (*Tract.* lxxx, *sup. Joann.* xv, 3):[4] "The word is added to the element and this becomes a sacrament," and he is speaking there of water which is a sensible element. Therefore sensible things are required for the sacraments.

I answer that, Divine wisdom provides for each thing according to its mode; hence it is written (Wis. 8. 1) that *she . . . ordereth all things sweetly,* and therefore also we are told (Matt. 25. 15) that she *gave to everyone according to his proper ability.* Now it is natural to man to acquire knowledge of the intelligible from the sensible. But a sign is that by means of which one attains to the knowledge of something else. Consequently, since the sacred things which are signified by the sacraments

---

[1] Cf. Lanfranc, *De Corp. et Sang. Dom.*, xiv (PL 150, 424); Gratian, *Decretum*, iii, d. 2, can. 48 (RF 1, 1331).

[2] *Prior Analytics*, ii, 27 (70ª7).
[3] PL 32, 1268.   [4] PL 35, 1840.

are the spiritual and intelligible goods by means of which man is sanctified, it follows that the sacramental signs consist in sensible things, just as in the Divine Scriptures spiritual things are set before us under the likeness of things sensible. And hence it is that sensible things are required for the sacraments, as Dionysius also proves in his book on the heavenly hierarchy (*Cæl. Hier.* i).[1]

Reply Obj. 1. The name and definition of a thing is taken principally from that which belongs to a thing primarily and through itself, and not from that which belongs to it through something else. Now a sensible effect being the primary and direct object of man's knowledge (since all our knowledge springs from the senses) by its very nature leads to the knowledge of something else, whereas intelligible effects are not such as to be able to lead us to the knowledge of something else, except in so far as they are manifested by some other thing, that is, by certain sensibles. It is for this reason that the name sign is given primarily and principally to things which are offered to the senses; hence Augustine says[2] that a sign "is that which brings something else to the mind besides the species which it impresses on the senses." But intelligible effects do not have the nature of a sign except in so far as they are pointed out by certain signs. And in this way, too, certain things which are not sensible are termed sacraments as it were, in so far as they are signified by certain sensible things, of which we shall treat further on (Q. LXIII, A. 1, Reply 2; A. 3, Reply 2; Q. LXXIII, A. 6; Q. LXXXIV, A. 1, Reply 3).

Reply Obj. 2. Sensible things considered in their own nature do not belong to the worship or kingdom of God, but considered only as signs of spiritual things in which the kingdom of God consists.

Reply Obj. 3. Augustine speaks there of sensible things considered in their own nature but not as employed to signify spiritual things, which are the highest goods.

ARTICLE 5. *Whether Determinate Things Are Required for a Sacrament?*

We proceed thus to the Fifth Article: It seems that determinate things are not required for a sacrament.

Objection. 1. For sensible things are required in sacraments for the purpose of signification, as stated above (A. 4). But nothing hinders the

same thing being signified by various sensible things; thus in Holy Scripture God is signified metaphorically, sometimes by a stone (II Kings 22. 2; Zach. 3. 9; I Cor. 10. 4; Apoc. 4. 3), sometimes by a lion (Isa. 31. 4; Apoc. 5. 5), sometimes by the sun (Isa. 60. 19, 20; Malach. 4. 2), or by something similar. Therefore it seems that various things can be suitable to the same sacrament. Therefore determinate things are not required for the sacraments.

Obj. 2. Further, the health of the soul is more necessary than that of the body. But in bodily medicines, which are ordered to the health of the body, one thing can be substituted for another which happens to be wanting. Therefore much more in the sacraments, which are spiritual remedies ordered to the health of the soul, can one thing be substituted for another when this happens to be lacking.

Obj. 3. Further, it is not fitting that the salvation of men be restricted by the Divine Law, still less by the Law of Christ, Who came to save all. But in the state of the Law of nature determinate things were not required in the sacraments, but were put to that use through a vow, as appears from Gen. 28. 20, where Jacob vowed that he would offer to God tithes and peace-offerings. Therefore it seems that man should not have been restricted, especially under the New Law, to the use of any determinate thing in the sacraments.

On the contrary, Our Lord said (John 3. 5); *Unless a man be born again of water and the Holy Ghost, he cannot enter into the kingdom of God.*

I answer that, In the use of the sacraments two things may be considered, namely, the worship of God, and the sanctification of man, the former of which pertains to man in relation to God, and the latter pertains to God in relation to man. Now it is not for anyone to determine that which is in the power of another but only that which is in his own power. Since, therefore, the sanctification of man is in the power of God Who sanctifies, it is not for man to decide what things should be used for his sanctification, but this should be determined by Divine institution. Therefore in the sacraments of the New Law, by which man is sanctified according to I Cor. 6. 11, *You are washed, you are sanctified,* we must use those things which are determined by Divine institution.

Reply Obj. 1. Though the same thing can be signified by various signs, yet to determine which sign must be used belongs to the signifier. Now it is God Who signifies spiritual

[1] Sect. 1 (PG 3, 121); cf. *De Eccl. Hier.*, chap. 2, sect. 2 (PG 3, 417).
[2] *Christian Doctrine,* II, 1 (PL 34, 35).

things to us by means of the sensible things in the sacraments, and of similitudes in the Scriptures. And consequently, just as the Holy Ghost decides by what similitudes spiritual things are to be signified in certain passages of Scripture, so also must it be determined by Divine institution what things are to be employed for the purpose of signification in this or that sacrament.

Reply Obj. 2. Sensible things are endowed with natural powers conducive to the health of the body, and therefore if two of them have the same power it does not matter which we use. Yet they are ordained to sanctification not through any power that they possess naturally, but only in virtue of the Divine institution. And therefore it was necessary that God should determine the sensible things to be employed in the sacraments.

Reply Obj. 3. As Augustine says (*Contra Faust.* xix, 16),[1] various sacraments suit different times, just as different times are signified by different parts of the verb, namely, present, past, and future. Consequently, just as under the state of the Law of nature man was moved by inward instinct and without any outward law, to worship God, so also the sensible things to be employed in the worship of God were determined by inward instinct. But later on it became necessary for a law to be given from without; both because the Law of nature had become obscured by man's sins, and in order to signify more expressly the grace of Christ, by which the human race is sanctified. And hence the need for those things to be determinate, of which men have to make use in the sacraments. Nor is the way of salvation narrowed thereby, because the things which need to be used in the sacraments are either in everyone's possession or can be had with little trouble.

ARTICLE 6. *Whether Words Are Required for the Significance of the Sacraments?*

We proceed thus to the Sixth Article: It seems that words are not required for the signification of the sacraments.

Objection 1. For Augustine says (*Contra Faust.* xix, 16):[2] "What else is a corporal sacrament but a kind of visible word?" Therefore to add words to the sensible things in the sacraments seems to be the same as to add words to words. But this is superfluous. Therefore words are not required besides the sensible things in the sacraments.

Obj. 2. Further, a sacrament is some one thing. But it does not seem possible to make one thing of those that belong to different genera. Since, therefore, sensible things and words are of different genera, for sensible things are the product of nature, but words of reason, it seems that in the sacraments words are not required besides sensible things.

Obj. 3. Further, the sacraments of the New Law succeed those of the Old Law, since "the former were instituted when the latter were abolished," as Augustine says (*Contra Faust.* xix, 13).[3] But no form of words was required in the sacraments of the Old Law. Therefore neither is it required in those of the New Law.

On the contrary, The Apostle says (Eph. 5. 25, 26): *Christ loved the Church, and delivered Himself up for it; that He might sanctify it, cleansing it by the laver of water in the word of life.* And Augustine says (*Tract.* xxx *in Joann.*):[4] "The word is added to the element, and this becomes a sacrament."

I answer that, The sacraments, as stated above (AA. 2, 3), are employed as signs for man's sanctification. Consequently they can be considered in three ways, and in each way it is fitting for words to be added to the sensible signs. For in the first place they can be considered in regard to the cause of sanctification, which is the Word incarnate, to Whom the sacraments have a certain conformity in that the word is joined to the sensible sign, just as in the mystery of the Incarnation the Word of God is united to sensible flesh.

Secondly, sacraments may be considered on the part of man who is sanctified, and who is composed of soul and body, to whom the sacramental remedy is proportioned, since it touches the body through the visible thing, and the soul through faith in the words. Hence Augustine says (*Tract.* lxxx *in Joann.*)[5] on John 15. 3, Now you are clean by reason of the word, etc.: "Whence hath water this so great virtue, to touch the body and wash the heart, but by the word doing it, not because it is spoken, but because it is believed?"

Thirdly, a sacrament may be considered on the part of the sacramental signification. Now Augustine says[6] that "words are the principal signs used by men," because words can be formed in various ways for the purpose of signifying various mental concepts, so that we are able to express what we conceive by the mind with greater distinctness by means of words. And

[1] PL 42, 356. [2] PL 42, 356.

[3] PL 42, 355.
[4] PL 35, 1840. [5] PL 35, 1840.
[6] *Christian Doctrine,* II, 3 (PL 34, 37).

therefore in order to insure the perfection of sacramental signification it was necessary to determine the signification of the sensible things by means of certain words. For water may signify both a cleansing by reason of its wetness, and refreshment by reason of its being cool; but when we say, "I baptize thee," it is clear that we use water in baptism in order to signify a spiritual cleansing.

Reply Obj. 1. The sensible things of the sacraments are called words by way of a certain likeness, in so far as they partake of a certain significative power, which resides principally in the very words, as stated above. Consequently it is not a superfluous repetition to add words to the visible element in the sacraments, because one determines the other, as stated above.

Reply Obj. 2. Although words and other sensible things are not in the same genus, considered in their natures, yet have they something in common as to the things signified by them, which is more perfect in words than in other things. Therefore in the sacraments, words and things, like form and matter, combine in the formation of one thing, in so far as the signification of things is completed by means of words, as above stated. And under words are comprised also sensible actions, such as cleansing and anointing and the like, because they have a like signification with the things.

Reply Obj. 3. As Augustine says (*Contra Faust.* xix, 16),[1] the sacraments of things present should be different from sacraments of things to come. Now the sacraments of the Old Law foretold the coming of Christ. Consequently they did not signify Christ so clearly as the sacraments of the New Law, which flow from Christ Himself, and have a certain likeness to Him, as stated above. Nevertheless in the Old Law, certain words were used in things pertaining to the worship of God, both by the priests, who were the ministers of those sacraments, according to Num. 6. 23, 24: *Thus shall you bless the children of Israel, and you shall say to them: The Lord bless thee,* etc.; and by those who made use of those sacraments, according to Deut. 26. 3: *I profess this day before the Lord thy God,* etc.

ARTICLE 7. *Whether Determinate Words Are Required in the Sacraments?*

We proceed thus to the Seventh Article: It seems that determinate words are not required in the sacraments.

[1] PL 42, 356.

Objection 1. For as the Philosopher says,[2] "words are not the same for all." But salvation, which is sought through the sacraments, is the same for all. Therefore determinate words are not required in the sacraments.

Obj. 2. Further, words are required in the sacraments since they are the principal means of signification, as stated above (A. 6). But it happens that various words mean the same. Therefore determinate words are not required in the sacraments.

Obj. 3. Further, corruption of anything changes its species. But some corrupt the pronunciation of words, and yet it is not credible that the sacramental effect is hindered thereby, for otherwise unlettered men and stammerers, in conferring sacraments, would frequently do so invalidly. Therefore it seems that determinate words are not required in the sacraments.

On the contrary, Our Lord used determinate words in consecrating the sacrament of the Eucharist, when He said (Matt. 26. 26): *This is My Body.* Likewise He commanded His disciples to baptize under a form of determinate words, saying (Matt. 28. 19): *Go ye and teach all nations, baptizing them in the name of the Father, and of the Son, and of the Holy Ghost.*

I answer that, As stated above (A. 6, REPLY 2), in the sacraments the words are as the form, and sensible things are as the matter. Now in all things composed of matter and form, the determining principle is on the part of the form, which is as it were the end and term of the matter. Consequently for the being of a thing the need of a determinate form is prior to the need of determinate matter, for determinate matter is needed that it may be proportioned to the determinate form. Since, therefore, in the sacraments determinate sensible things are required, which are as the sacramental matter, much more is there need in them of a determinate form of words.

Reply Obj. 1. As Augustine says (*Tract.* lxxx *sup. Joann.*),[3] the word operates in the sacraments "not because it is spoken," that is, not by the outward sound of the voice, "but because it is believed," that is, in accordance with the sense of the words which is held by faith. And this sense is indeed the same for all, though the same words as to their sound be not used by all. Consequently no matter in what language this sense is expressed, the sacrament is complete.

[2] *Interpretation,* 1 (16a5).   [3] PL 35, 1840.

Reply Obj. 2. Although it happens in every language that various words signify the same thing, yet one of those words is that which those who speak that language use principally and more commonly to signify that particular thing, and this is the word which should be used for the sacramental signification. So also among sensible things, that one is used for the sacramental signification which is most commonly employed for the action by which the sacramental effect is signified; thus water is most commonly used by men for bodily cleansing, by which the spiritual cleansing is signified, and therefore water is employed as the matter of baptism.

Reply Obj. 3. If he who corrupts the pronunciation of the sacramental words does so on purpose, he does not seem to intend to do what the Church intends, and thus the sacrament seems to be defective.

But if he do this through error or a slip of the tongue, and if he so far mispronounce the words as to deprive them of sense, the sacrament seems to be defective. This would be the case especially if the mispronunciation be in the beginning of a word, for instance, if one were to say *in nomine matris* instead of *in nomine Patris.* If, however, the sense of the words be not entirely lost by this mispronunciation, the sacrament is complete. This would be the case principally if the end of a word be mispronounced; for instance, if one were to say *in nomine patrias et filias.* For although the words thus mispronounced have no appointed meaning, yet we allow them an accommodated meaning corresponding to the usual forms of speech. And so, although the sensible sound is changed, yet the sense remains the same.

What has been said about the various mispronunciations of words, either at the beginning or at the end, holds because with us a change at the beginning of a word changes the meaning, whereas a change at the end generally speaking does not effect such a change; but with the Greeks the sense is changed also in the beginning of words in the conjugation of verbs.

Nevertheless the principle point to observe is the extent of the corruption entailed by mispronunciation, for in either case it may be so little that it does not alter the sense of the words, or so great that it destroys it. But it is easier for the one to happen on the part of the beginning of the words and the other at the end.

ARTICLE 8. *Whether It Is Lawful to Add Anything to the Words in Which the Sacramental Form Consists?*

We proceed thus to the Eighth Article: It seems that it is not lawful to add anything to the words in which the sacramental form consists.

Objection 1. For these sacramental words are not less necessary than are the words of Holy Scripture. But it is not lawful to add anything to, or to take anything from, the words of Holy Scripture; for it is written (Deut. 4. 2): *You shall not add to the word that I speak to you, neither shall you take away from it;* and (Apoc. 22. 18, 19): *I testify to everyone that heareth the words of the prophecy of this book: if any man shall add to these things, God shall add to him the plagues written in this book. And if any man shall take away . . . God shall take away his part out of the book of life.* Therefore it seems that neither is it lawful to add anything to, or to take anything from, the sacramental forms.

Obj. 2. Further, in the sacraments words are by way of form, as stated above (A. 6, REPLY 2; A. 7). But any addition or subtraction in forms changes the species, as also in numbers.[1] Therefore it seems that if anything be added to or subtracted from a sacramental form, it will not be the same sacrament.

Obj. 3. Further, just as the sacramental form demands a certain number of words, so does it require that these words should be pronounced in a certain order and without interruption. If therefore, the sacrament is not rendered invalid by addition or subtraction of words, in like manner it seems that neither is it rendered invalid if the words be pronounced in a different order or with interruptions.

On the contrary, Certain words are inserted by some in the sacramental forms which are not inserted by others; thus the Latins baptize under this form: *I baptize thee in the name of the Father, and of the Son, and of the Holy Ghost,* whereas the Greeks use the following form: *The servant of God, N . . . is baptized in the name of the Father,* etc. Yet both confer the sacrament validly. Therefore it is lawful to add something to, or to take something from, the sacramental forms.

I answer that, With regard to all the variations that may occur in the sacramental forms, two points seem to call for our attention. One is on the part of the person who says the words,

---

[1] Aristotle, *Metaphysics,* VIII, 3 (1043ᵇ36).

and whose intention is essential to the sacrament, as will be explained further on (Q. LXIV, A. 8). Therefore if he intends by such addition or suppression to perform a rite other from that which is recognized by the Church, it seems that the sacrament is invalid, because he seems not to intend to do what the Church does.

The other point to be considered is the meaning of the words. For since in the sacraments, the words produce an effect according to the sense which they convey, as stated above (A. 7, Reply 1), we must see whether the change of words destroys the due sense of the words, because then, the sacrament is clearly rendered invalid. Now it is clear that if any of those things which are of the substance of the sacramental form be suppressed, that the due sense of the words is destroyed, and consequently the sacrament is invalid. Therefore Didymus says (*De Spir. Sanct.* ii):[1] "If anyone attempt to baptize in such a way as to omit one of the aforesaid names," that is, of the Father, Son, and Holy Ghost, "his baptism will be invalid." But if that which is omitted be not a substantial part of the form, such an omission does not destroy the due sense of the words, nor consequently the validity of the sacrament. Thus in the form of the Eucharist, —*For this is My Body*, the omission of the word "for" does not destroy the due sense of the words, nor consequently cause the sacrament to be invalid; although perhaps he who makes the omission may sin from negligence or contempt.

Again, it is possible to add something that destroys the due sense of the words; for instance, if one were to say: "I baptize thee in the name of the Father Who is greater, and of the Son Who is less," with which form the Arians baptized;[2] and consequently such an addition makes the sacrament invalid. But if the addition be such as not to destroy the due sense, the sacrament is not rendered invalid. Nor does it matter whether this addition be made at the beginning, in the middle, or at the end. For instance, if one were to say, "I baptize thee in the name of the Father Almighty, and of the Only Begotten Son, and of the Holy Ghost, the Paraclete," the baptism would be valid; and in like manner if one were to say, "I baptize thee in the name of the Father, and of the Son, and of the Holy Ghost; and may

the Blessed Virgin succour thee," the baptism would be valid.

Perhaps, however, if one were to say, "I baptize thee in the name of the Father, and of the Son, and of the Holy Ghost, and of the Blessed Virgin Mary," the baptism would be void, because it is written (I Cor. 1. 13): *Was Paul crucified for you or were you baptized in the name of Paul?* But this is true if the intention be to baptize in the name of the Blessed Virgin as in the name of the Trinity, by which baptism is consecrated, for such a sense would be contrary to true faith, and would therefore render the sacrament invalid; but if the addition, "and in the name of the Blessed Virgin" be understood not as if the name of the Blessed Virgin effected anything in baptism, but as intimating that her intercession may help the person baptized to preserve the baptismal grace, then the sacrament is not rendered void.

Reply Obj. 1. It is not lawful to add anything to the words of Holy Scripture as regards the sense, but many words are added by Doctors by way of explanation of the Holy Scriptures. Nevertheless, it is not lawful to add even words to Holy Scripture as though such words were a part thereof, for this would amount to forgery. It would amount to the same if anyone were to pretend that something is necessary to a sacramental form which is not so.

Reply Obj. 2. Words belong to a sacramental form by reason of the sense signified by them. Consequently any addition or suppression of words which does not add to or take from the due sense does not destroy the species of the sacrament.

Reply Obj. 3. If the words are interrupted to such an extent that the intention of the speaker is interrupted, the sacramental sense is destroyed, and consequently, the validity of the sacrament. But this is not the case if the interruption is so slight, that the intention of the speaker and the sense of the words is not interrupted.

The same is to be said of a change in the order of the words. Because if this destroys the sense of the phrase, the sacrament is invalidated, as happens when a negation is made to precede or follow a word. But if the order is so changed that the sense of the phrase does not vary, the sacrament is not invalidated, according to the Philosopher's dictum: "Nouns and verbs mean the same though they be transposed."[3]

---

[1] Translation of Jerome (PG 39, 1054); cf. PL 23, 130.
[2] Cf. Athanasius, *Contra Arianos*, orat. 1 (PG 26, 236); *Epist. De Synod.* n. 31 (PG 25, 473); Hilary, *De Trin.*, 2 (PL 10, 53); Ambrose, *De Spir. Sancto*, 1, 3 (PL 16, 337).

[3] *Interpretation*, 10 (20[b]1).

QUESTION LXI

OF THE NECESSITY OF THE SACRAMENTS

(*In Four Articles*)

WE must now consider the necessity of the sacraments, concerning which there are four points of inquiry: (1) Whether sacraments are necessary for man's salvation? (2) Whether they were necessary in the state that preceded sin? (3) Whether they were necessary in the state after sin and before Christ? (4) Whether they were necessary after Christ's coming?

ARTICLE 1. *Whether Sacraments Are Necessary for Man's Salvation?*

We proceed thus to the First Article: It seems that sacraments are not necessary for man's salvation.

Objection 1. For the Apostle says (I Tim. 4. 8): *Bodily exercise is profitable to little.* But the use of sacraments pertains to bodily exercise, because sacraments are perfected in the signification of sensible things and words, as stated above (Q. LX, A. 6). Therefore sacraments are not necessary for the salvation of man.

Obj. 2. Further, the Apostle was told (II Cor. 12. 9): *My grace is sufficient for thee.* But it would not suffice if sacraments were necessary for salvation. Therefore sacraments are not necessary for man's salvation.

Obj. 3. Further, given a sufficient cause, nothing more seems to be required for the effect. But Christ's Passion is the sufficient cause of our salvation, for the Apostle says (Rom. 5. 10): *If, when we were enemies, we were reconciled to God by the death of His Son: much more, being reconciled, shall we be saved by His life.* Therefore sacraments are not necessary for man's salvation.

On the contrary, Augustine says (*Contra Faust.* xix, 11):[1] "It is impossible to keep men together in one religious denomination, whether true or false, except they be united by means of visible signs or sacraments." But it is necessary for salvation that men be united together in the name of the one true religion. Therefore sacraments are necessary for man's salvation.

I answer that, Sacraments are necessary to man's salvation for three reasons. The first is taken from the condition of human nature to which it is proper to be led by things corporeal

[1] PL 42, 355.

and sensible to things spiritual and intelligible. Now it belongs to Divine providence to provide for each thing according as its condition requires. Divine wisdom, therefore, fittingly provides man with means of salvation, in the shape of corporeal and sensible signs that are called sacraments.

The second reason is taken from the state of man who in sinning subjected himself by his affections to corporeal things. Now the healing remedy should be given to a man so as to reach the part affected by disease. Consequently it was fitting that God should provide man with a spiritual medicine by means of certain corporeal signs; for if man were offered spiritual things without a veil, his mind being taken up with the material world would be unable to apply itself to them.

The third reason is taken from the fact that man is prone to direct his activity chiefly towards material things. Lest, therefore, it should be too hard for man to be drawn away entirely from bodily actions, bodily exercise was offered to him in the sacraments, by which he might be trained to avoid superstitious practices, consisting in the worship of demons, and all manner of harmful action, consisting in sinful deeds.

It follows, therefore, that through the institution of the sacraments man, consistently with his nature, is instructed through sensible things; he is humbled, through knowing that he is subject to corporeal things, seeing that he receives assistance through them; and he is even preserved from harmful actions, by the healthy exercise of the sacraments.

Reply Obj. 1. Bodily exercise, as such, is not very profitable, but exercise taken in the use of the sacraments is not merely bodily, but to a certain extent spiritual, namely, in its signification and in its causality.

Reply Obj. 2. God's grace is a sufficient cause of man's salvation. But God gives grace to man in a way which is suitable to him. Hence it is that man needs the sacraments that he may obtain grace.

Reply Obj. 3. Christ's Passion is a sufficient cause of man's salvation. But it does not follow that the sacraments are not also necessary for that purpose, because they obtain their effect through the power of Christ's Passion; and Christ's Passion is, so to say, applied to man through the sacraments according to the Apostle (Rom. 6. 3): *All we who are baptized in Christ Jesus, are baptized in His death.*

ARTICLE 2. *Whether Before Sin Sacraments Were Necessary to Man?*

We proceed thus to the Second Article: It seems that before sin sacraments were necessary to man.

Objection 1. For, as stated above (A. 1, Reply 2) man needs sacraments that he may obtain grace. But man needed grace even in the state of innocence, as we stated in the First Part (Q. XCV, A. 4; cf. I-II, Q. CIX, A. 2; Q. CXIV, A. 2). Therefore sacraments were necessary in that state also.

Obj. 2. Further, sacraments are fitting to man by reason of the conditions of human nature, as stated above (A. 1). But man's nature is the same before and after sin. Therefore it seems that before sin man needed the sacraments.

Obj. 3. Further, matrimony is a sacrament, according to Eph. 5. 32: *This is a great sacrament; but I speak in Christ and in the Church.* But matrimony was instituted before sin, as may be seen in Gen. 2. Therefore sacraments were necessary to man before sin.

On the contrary, None but the sick need remedies, according to Matt. 9. 12: *They that are in health need not a physician.* Now the sacraments are spiritual remedies for the healing of wounds inflicted by sin. Therefore they were not necessary before sin.

I answer that, Sacraments were not necessary in the state of innocence before sin. This can be proved from the rectitude of that state, in which the higher ruled the lower, and in no way depended on them; for just as the mind was subject to God, so were the lower powers of the soul subject to the mind, and the body to the soul. And it would be contrary to this order if the soul were perfected either in knowledge or in grace by anything corporeal, which happens in the sacraments. Therefore in the state of innocence man needed no sacraments, whether as remedies against sin or as means of perfecting the soul.

Reply Obj. 1. In the state of innocence man needed grace; not so that he needed to obtain grace by means of sensible signs, but in a spiritual and invisible manner.

Reply Obj. 2. Man's nature is the same before and after sin, but the state of his nature is not the same. Because after sin, the soul, even in its higher part, needs to receive something from corporeal things in order that it may be perfected, whereas man had no need of this in that state.

Reply Obj. 3. Matrimony was instituted in the state of innocence not as a sacrament, but as a function of nature. Consequently, however, it foreshadowed something in relation to Christ and the Church, just as everything else foreshadowed Christ.

ARTICLE 3. *Whether There Should Have Been Sacraments After Sin, Before Christ?*

We proceed thus to the Third Article: It seems that there should have been no sacraments after sin, before Christ.

Objection 1. For it has been stated (A. 1, Reply 3) that the Passion of Christ is applied to men through the sacraments, so that Christ's Passion is compared to the sacraments as cause to effect. But effect does not precede cause. Therefore there should have been no sacramnts before Christ's coming.

Obj. 2. Further, sacraments should be suitable to the state of the human race, as Augustine declares (*Contra Faust.* xix, 16, 17).[1] But the state of the human race underwent no change after sin until it was repaired by Christ. Neither, therefore, should the sacraments have been changed, so that besides the sacraments of the natural law others should be instituted in the law of Moses.

Obj. 3. Further, the nearer a thing approaches to that which is perfect, the more like it should it be. Now the perfection of human salvation was accomplished by Christ, to Whom the sacraments of the Old Law were nearer than those that preceded the Law. Therefore they should have borne a greater likeness to the sacraments of Christ. And yet it appears the contrary is the case, since it was foretold that the priesthood of Christ would be *according to the order of Melchisedech, and not . . . according to the order of Aaron* (Heb. 7. 11). Therefore sacraments were unsuitably instituted before Christ.

On the contrary, Augustine says (*Contra Faust.* xix, 13)[2] that "the first sacraments which the Law commanded to be solemnized and observed were announcements of Christ's future coming. But it was necessary for man's salvation that Christ's coming should be announced beforehand. Therefore it was necessary that some sacraments should be instituted before Christ.

I answer that, Sacraments are necessary for man's salvation in so far as they are sensible signs of invisible things whereby man is made holy. Now after sin no man can be made holy save through Christ, *Whom God hath pro-*

---

[1] PL 42, 356, 357.   [2] PL 42, 355.

posed to be a propitiation, through faith in His blood, to the showing of His justice . . . that He Himself may be just, and the justifier of him who is of the faith of Jesus Christ (Rom. 3. 25, 26). Therefore before Christ's coming there was need for some visible signs whereby man might testify to his faith in the future coming of a Saviour. And these signs are called sacraments. It is therefore clear that some sacraments were necessary before Christ's coming.

Reply Obj. 1. Christ's Passion is the final cause of the old sacraments, for they were instituted in order to foreshadow it. Now the final cause precedes not in time, but in the intention of the agent. Consequently, it is not unfitting that there should be sacraments before Christ's Passion.

Reply Obj. 2. The state of the human race after sin and before Christ can be considered from two points of view. First, from the nature of faith, and thus it was always one and the same, since men were made righteous through faith in the future coming of Christ. Secondly, according as sin was more or less intense, and knowledge concerning Christ more or less explicit. For as time went on sin began to gain a greater hold on man, so much so that with the clouding of man's reason, the precepts of the natural law were insufficient to make man live rightly, and it became necessary to have a written code of fixed laws, and together with these certain sacraments of faith. For it was necessary, as time went on, that the knowledge of faith should be more and more unfolded, since, as Gregory says (*Hom.* vi *in Ezech.*):[1] "With the advance of time there was an advance in the knowledge of Divine things." Consequently in the Old Law there was also a need for certain fixed sacraments significative of man's faith in the future coming of Christ, which sacraments are compared to those that preceded the Law as something determinate to that which is indeterminate, since before the Law it was not laid down precisely of what sacraments men were to make use, whereas this was prescribed by the Law; and this was necessary both on account of the overclouding of the natural law, and for the clearer signification of faith.

Reply Obj. 3. The sacrament of Melchisedech which preceded the Law is more like the Sacrament of the New Law in its matter, in so far as *he offered bread and wine* (Gen. 14. 18), just as bread and wine are offered in the

[1] PL 76, 980.

sacrifice of the New Testament. Nevertheless, the sacraments of the Mosaic Law are more like the thing signified by the sacrament, that is, the Passion of Christ, as clearly appears in the Paschal Lamb and the like. The reason of this was for fear that if the sacraments retained the same appearance, it might seem, where there was no interruption of time, to be the continuation of one and the same sacrament.

ARTICLE 4. *Whether There Was Need for Any Sacraments After Christ Came?*

We proceed thus to the Fourth Article: It seems that there was no need for any sacraments after Christ came.

Objection 1. For the figure should cease with the advent of the truth. But *grace and truth came by Jesus Christ* (John 1. 17). Since, therefore, the sacraments are signs or figures of the truth, it seems that there was no need for any sacraments after Christ's Passion.

Obj. 2. Further, the sacraments consist in certain elements, as stated above (Q. LX, A. 4). But the Apostle says (Gal. 4. 3, 4) that *when we were children we were serving under the elements of the world,* but that now *when the fulness of time* has *come,* we are no longer children. Therefore it seems that we should not serve God under the elements of this world by making use of corporeal sacraments.

Obj. 3. Further, according to James 1. 17, with God *there is no change, nor shadow of alteration.* But it seems to argue some change in the Divine will that God should give man certain sacraments for his sanctification now during the time of grace, and other sacraments before Christ's coming. Therefore it seems that other sacraments should not have been instituted after Christ.

On the contrary, Augustine says (*Contra Faust.* xix, 13)[2] that the sacraments of the Old Law "were abolished because they were fulfilled; and others were instituted, fewer in number, but more efficacious, more profitable, and of easier accomplishment."

I answer that, As the ancient Fathers were saved through faith in Christ's future coming, so are we saved through faith in Christ's past birth and Passion. Now the sacraments are signs in affirmation of the faith whereby man is justified, and signs should vary according as they signify the future, the past, or the present; for as Augustine says (*Contra Faust.* xix, 16),[3] "the same thing is variously pronounced

[2] PL 42, 355.   [3] PL 42, 356.

as to be done and as having been done; for instance the word *'passurus'* (going to suffer) differs from *'passus'* (having suffered)." Therefore there must be other sacraments of the New Law, that signify Christ in relation to the past, besides those of the Old Law, that foreshadowed the future.

Reply Obj. 1. As Dionysius says (*Eccl. Hier.* v),[1] the state of the New Law is between the state of the Old Law, whose figures are fulfilled in the New, and the state of glory, in which all truth will be openly and perfectly revealed. Therefore then there will be no sacraments. But now, so long as we know *through a glass in a dark manner*, (I Cor. 13. 12) we need sensible signs in order to reach spiritual things, and this pertains to the nature of the sacraments.

Reply Obj. 2. The Apostle calls the sacraments of the Old Law *weak and needy elements* (Gal. 4. 9) because they neither contained nor caused grace. Hence the Apostle says that those who used these sacraments served God *under the elements of this world,* for the very reason that these sacraments were nothing else than the elements of this world. But our sacraments both contain and cause grace. Consequently the comparison does not hold.

Reply Obj. 3. Just as the head of the house is not proved to have a changeable will, through issuing various commands to his household at various seasons, ordering things differently in winter and summer, so it does not follow that there is any change in God because He instituted sacraments of one kind after Christ's coming and of another kind at the time of the Law; because the latter were suitable as foreshadowing grace, the former as signifying the presence of grace.

QUESTION LXII
OF THE SACRAMENTS' PRINCIPAL
EFFECT, WHICH IS GRACE
(*In Six Articles*)

WE have now to consider the effect of the sacraments. First of their principal effect, which is grace; secondly, of their secondary effect, which is a character (Q. LXIII). Concerning the first there are six points of inquiry: (1) Whether the sacraments of the New Law are the cause of grace? (2) Whether sacramental grace confers anything in addition to the grace of the virtues and gifts? (3) Whether the sac-

raments contain grace? (4) Whether there is any power in them for the causing of grace? (5) Whether the sacraments derive this power from Christ's Passion? (6) Whether the sacraments of the Old Law caused grace?

ARTICLE 1. *Whether the Sacraments Are the Cause of Grace?*

We proceed thus to the First Article: It seems that the sacraments are not the cause of grace.

Objection 1. For it seems that the same thing is not both sign and cause, since the nature of sign appears to be more in keeping with an effect. But a sacrament is a sign of grace. Therefore it is not its cause.

Obj. 2. Further, nothing corporeal can act on a spiritual thing, since the agent is more excellent than the patient, as Augustine says (*Gen. ad lit.* xii, 16).[2] But the subject of grace is the human mind, which is a spiritual thing. Therefore the sacraments cannot cause grace.

Obj. 3. Further, what is proper to God should not be ascribed to a creature. But it is proper to God to cause grace, according to Ps. 83. 12: *The Lord will give grace and glory.* Since, therefore, the sacraments consist in certain words and created things, it seems that they cannot cause grace.

On the contrary, Augustine says (*Tract.* lxxx *in Joann.*)[3] that the baptismal water "touches the body and cleanses the heart." But the heart is not cleansed save through grace. Therefore it causes grace, and for like reason so do the other sacraments of the Church.

I answer that, We must say that in some way the sacraments of the New Law cause grace. For it is evident that through the sacraments of the New Law man is incorporated with Christ; thus the Apostle says of Baptism (Gal. 3. 27): *As many of you as have been baptized in Christ have put on Christ.* And man is made a member of Christ through grace alone.

Some, however, say[4] that they are the cause of grace not by their own operation, but in so far as God causes grace in the soul when the sacraments are employed. And they give as an example a man who on presenting a leaden coin, receives, by the king's command, a hundred pounds; not as though the leaden coin, by any

---

[2] PL 34, 467.   [3] PL 35, 1840.

[4] Richard Fishacre, *In Sent.,* IV, dist. 1, and Robert Kilwardby, *In Sent.,* IV, d. 1. (In Simonin and Meersseman, *De Sacram. Efficientia,* pp. 16, 27); cf. Bonaventure, *In Sent.,* IV, d. 1, art. 1, Q. 1 (QR IV, 23).

operation of its own, caused him to be given that sum of money, but this being the effect of the mere will of the king. Hence Bernard says in a sermon on the Lord's Supper:[1] "Just as a canon is invested by means of a book, an abbot by means of a crozier, a bishop by means of a ring, so by the various sacraments various kinds of grace are conferred." But if we examine the question properly, we shall see that according to the above mode the sacraments are mere signs. For the leaden coin is nothing but a sign of the king's command that this man should receive money. In like manner the book is a sign of the conferring of a canonry. Hence, according to this opinion the sacraments of the New Law would be mere signs of grace, whereas we have it on the authority of many saints that the sacraments of the New Law not only signify, but also cause grace.

We must therefore say otherwise, that an agent cause is twofold, principal and instrumental. The principal cause works by the power of its form, to which form the effect is likened; just as fire by its own heat makes something hot. In this way none but God can cause grace, since grace is nothing else than a participated likeness of the Divine Nature, according to II Pet. 1. 4: *He hath given us most great and precious promises; that we may be* (Vulg.,—*you may be made*) *partakers of the Divine Nature.*—But the instrumental cause works not by the power of its form, but only by the motion whereby it is moved by the principal agent, so that the effect is not likened to the instrument but to the principal agent; for instance, the couch is not like the axe, but like the art which is in the craftsman's mind. And it is thus that the sacraments of the New Law cause grace, for they are instituted by God to be employed for the purpose of conferring grace. Hence Augustine says (*Contra Faust.* xix, 16):[2] "All these things," namely, pertaining to the sacraments, "are done and pass away, but the power," namely, of God, "which works by them, remains ever." Now that is, properly speaking, an instrument by which someone works, and so it is written (Tit. 3. 5): *He saved us by the laver of regeneration.*

Reply Obj. 1. The principal cause cannot properly be called a sign of its effect, even though the latter be hidden and the cause itself sensible and manifest. But an instrumental cause, if manifest, can be called a sign of a hidden effect, for this reason that it is not

merely a cause but also in a measure an effect in so far as it is moved by the principal agent. And in this sense the sacraments of the New Law are both cause and signs. Hence, too, is it that, to use the common expression, they effect what they signify. From this it is clear that they have perfectly the nature of a sacrament, being ordered to something sacred not only as a sign, but also as a cause.

Reply Obj. 2. An instrument has a twofold action. One is instrumental, in respect of which it works not by its own power but by the power of the principal agent. The other is its proper action, which belongs to it in respect of its own form; thus it belongs to an axe to cut asunder by reason of its sharpness, but to make a couch in so far as it is the instrument of an art. But it does not accomplish the instrumental action save by exercising its proper action, for it is by cutting that it makes a couch. In like manner the corporeal sacraments by their proper operation, which they exercise on the body that they touch, accomplish through the Divine institution an instrumental operation on the soul; for example, the water of baptism, in respect of its proper power, cleanses the body, and thereby, since it is the instrument of the Divine power, cleanses the soul, since from soul and body one thing is made. And thus it is that Augustine says[3] that it "touches the body and cleanses the heart."

Reply Obj. 3. This argument considers that which causes grace as principal agent; for this belongs to God alone, as stated above.

ARTICLE 2. *Whether Sacramental Grace Confers Anything in Addition to the Grace of the Virtues and Gifts?*

We proceed thus to the Second Article: It seems that sacramental grace confers nothing in addition to the grace of the virtues and gifts.

Objection 1. For the grace of the virtues and gifts perfects the soul sufficiently, both in the essence of the soul and in its powers, as is clear from what was said in the Second Part (I-II, Q. CX, AA. 3, 4). But grace is ordered to the perfecting of the soul. Therefore sacramental grace cannot confer anything in addition to the grace of the virtues and gifts.

Obj. 2. Further, the soul's defects are caused by sin. But all sins are sufficiently removed by the grace of the virtues and gifts, because there is no sin that is not contrary to some virtue. Since, therefore, sacramental grace is ordered to the removal of the soul's defects, it cannot

---

[1] PL 183, 272.   [2] PL 42, 357.

[3] *In Joann.*, tract. LXXX (PL 35, 1840).

confer anything in addition to the grace of the virtues and gifts.

Obj. 3. Further, every addition or subtraction of form varies the species.[1] If, therefore, sacramental grace confers anything in addition to the grace of the virtues and gifts, it follows that it is called grace equivocally, and so we are none the wiser when it is said that the sacraments cause grace.

On the contrary, If sacramental grace confers nothing in addition to the grace of the virtues and gifts, it is useless to confer the sacraments on those who have the virtues and gifts. But there is nothing useless in God's works. Therefore it seems that sacramental grace confers something in addition to the grace of the virtues and gifts.

I answer that, As stated in the Second Part (I-II, Q. CX, AA. 3, 4), grace, considered in itself, perfects the essence of the soul, in so far as it is a certain participated likeness of the Divine Being. And just as the soul's powers flow from its essence, so from grace there flow certain perfections into the powers of the soul, which are called virtues and gifts, whereby the powers are perfected in reference to their actions. Now the sacraments are ordered to certain special effects which are necessary in the Christian life; thus Baptism is ordered to a certain spiritual regeneration, by which man dies to vice and becomes a member of Christ, which effect is something special in addition to the actions of the soul's powers; and the same holds true of the other sacraments. Consequently just as the virtues and gifts confer, in addition to grace commonly so called, a certain special perfection ordered to the powers' proper actions, so does sacramental grace confer, over and above grace commonly so called, and in addition to the virtues and gifts, a certain Divine assistance in obtaining the end of the sacrament. It is thus that sacramental grace confers something in addition to the grace of the virtues and gifts.

Reply Obj. 1. The grace of the virtues and gifts perfects the essence and powers of the soul sufficiently as regards the general ordering of the soul's actions; but as regards certain special effects which are necessary in a Christian life, sacramental grace is needed.

Reply Obj. 2. Vices and sins are sufficiently removed by virtues and gifts as to present and future time, in so far as they prevent man from sinning. But in regard to past sins, the acts of which are transitory whereas their guilt remains, man is provided with a special remedy in the sacraments.

Reply Obj. 3. The notion of Sacramental grace is compared to grace commonly so called, as the notion of species to genus. Therefore just as it is not equivocal to use the term "animal" in its common sense and as applied to a man, so neither is it equivocal to speak of grace commonly so called and of sacramental grace.

ARTICLE 3. *Whether the Sacraments of the New Law Contain Grace?*

We proceed thus to the Third Article: It seems that the sacraments of the New Law do not contain grace.

Objection 1. For it seems that what is contained is in the container. But grace is not in the sacraments; neither as in a subject, because the subject of grace is not a body but a spirit, nor as in a vessel, for according to the *Physics,*[2] "a vessel is a movable place," and an accident cannot be in a place. Therefore it seems that the sacraments of the New Law do not contain grace.

Obj. 2. Further, sacraments are instituted as means whereby men may obtain grace. But since grace is an accident it cannot pass from one subject to another. Therefore it would be of no account if grace were in the sacraments.

Obj. 3. Further, a spiritual thing is not contained by a corporeal, even if it be therein; for the soul is not contained by the body, rather does it contain the body. Since, therefore, grace is something spiritual, it seems that it cannot be contained in a corporeal sacrament.

On the contrary, Hugh of S. Victor says (*De Sacram.* i)[3] that "a sacrament through its being sanctified, contains an invisible grace."

I answer that, A thing is said to be in another in many ways; in two of which grace is said to be in the sacraments. First, as in its sign, for a sacrament is a sign of grace. Secondly, as in its cause, for, as stated above (A. 1) a sacrament of the New Law is an instrumental cause of grace. Therefore grace is in a sacrament of the New Law, not as to the likeness, of species as an effect in its univocal cause, nor as to some proper and permanent form proportioned to such an effect, as effects in non-univocal causes, for instance, as things generated are in the sun, but as to a certain instrumental power transient and incomplete in its natural being, as will be explained later on (A. 4).

---

[1] Aristotle, *Metaphysics,* VIII, 3 (1043[b]36).

[2] Aristotle, IV, 4 (212[a]14).

[3] IX, 2 (PL 176, 317).

Reply Obj. 1. Grace is said to be in a sacrament not as in its subject, nor as in a vessel considered as a place, but according as a vessel is understood as the instrument of some work to be done, according to Ezech. 9. 1: *Everyone hath a destroying vessel* (Douay—*weapon*) *in his hand.*

Reply Obj. 2. Although an accident does not pass from one subject to another, nevertheless in a fashion it does pass from its cause into its subject through the instrument; not so that it be in each of these in the same way, but in each according to its proper nature.

Reply Obj. 3. If a spiritual thing exist perfectly in something, it contains it and is not contained by it. But, in a sacrament, grace has a passing and incomplete mode of being, and consequently it is not unfitting to say that the sacraments contain grace.

ARTICLE 4. *Whether There Be in the Sacraments a Power of Causing Grace?*

We proceed thus to the Fourth Article: It seems that there is not in the sacraments a power of causing grace.

Objection 1. For the power of causing grace is a spiritual power. But a spiritual power is not in a body; neither as proper to it, because power flows from a thing's essence and consequently cannot transcend it; nor as derived from something else, because that which is received into anything follows the mode of the recipient. Therefore in the sacraments there is no power of causing grace.

Obj. 2. Further, whatever exists is reducible to some genus of being and some degree of good. But there is no assignable genus of being to which such a power can belong, as anyone may see by running through them all. Nor is it reducible to some degree of good; for neither is it one of the goods of least account, since sacraments are necessary for salvation, nor is it an intermediate good, such as are the powers of the soul, which are natural powers, nor is it one of the greater goods, for it is neither grace nor a power of the mind. Therefore it seems that in the sacraments there is no power of causing grace.

Obj. 3. Further, if there be such a power in the sacraments, it is caused there by nothing less than a creative act of God. But it seems unbecoming that so excellent a being should cease to exist as soon as the sacrament is complete. Therefore it seems that in the sacraments there is no power for causing grace.

Obj. 4. Further, the same thing cannot be in several. But several things concur in the completion of a sacrament, namely, words and things, while in one sacrament there can be but one power. Therefore it seems that there is no power of causing grace in the sacraments.

On the contrary, Augustine says (*Tract. lxxx in Joann.*):[1] "Whence hath water so great power, that it touches the body and cleanses the heart?" And Bede says[2] that "Our Lord conferred a power of regeneration on the waters by the contact of His most pure body."

I answer that, Those who hold that the sacraments do not cause grace save by a certain concomitance,[3] deny the sacraments any power that is itself productive of the sacramental effect, and hold that the Divine power assists the sacraments and produces their effect. But if we hold that a sacrament is an instrumental cause of grace, we must allow that there is in the sacraments a certain instrumental power of bringing about the sacramental effects. Now such power is proportionate to the instrument, and consequently it stands in comparison to the complete and perfect power of anything as the instrument to the principal agent. For an instrument, as stated above (A. 1), does not work save as moved by the principal agent, which works of itself. And therefore the power of the principal agent exists in nature completely and perfectly, whereas the instrumental power has a being that passes from one thing into another, and is incomplete; just as motion is an imperfect act passing from agent to the thing acted upon.

Reply Obj. 1. A spiritual power cannot be in a corporeal thing after the manner of a permanent and complete power; as the argument proves. But there is nothing to hinder an instrumental spiritual power from being in a body, in so far as a body can be moved by a particular spiritual substance so as to produce a particular spiritual effect; thus in the very voice which is perceived by the senses there is a certain spiritual power, in so far as it proceeds from a mental concept, of arousing the mind of man. It is in this way that a spiritual power is in the sacraments, since they are ordained by God to the production of a spiritual effect.

Reply Obj. 2. Just as motion, through being an imperfect act, is not properly in a genus, but is reducible to a genus of perfect act, for instance, alteration to the genus of quality,

[1] PL 35, 1840.
[2] *In Luc.*, BK. I, on 3.21 (PL 92, 358); cf. Lombard, *Sent.*, BK. IV, d. III, chap. 5 (QR II, 759); Gratian, *Decretum*, Pt. III, d. IV, can. 10 (RF I, 1364).
[3] Cf. fn. 4, p. 858 above.

so, instrumental power, properly speaking, is not in any genus, but is reducible to a genus and species of perfect power.

Reply Obj. 3. Just as an instrumental power accrues to an instrument through its being moved by the principal agent, so does a sacrament receive spiritual power from Christ's blessing and from the action of the minister in applying it to a sacramental use. Hence Augustine says in a sermon on the Epiphany (S. Maximus of Turin, *Serm.* xii):[1] "Nor should you marvel, if we say that water, a corporeal substance, achieves the cleansing of the soul. It does indeed, and penetrates every secret hiding-place of the conscience. For subtle and clear as it is, the blessing of Christ makes it yet more subtle, so that it permeates into the very principles of life and searches the innermost recesses of the heart."

Reply Obj. 4. Just as the one same power of the principal agent is instrumentally in all the instruments that are ordered to the production of an effect, because they are one as being so ordered, so also the one same sacramental power is in both words and things, since words and things combine to form one sacrament.

ARTICLE 5. *Whether the Sacraments of the New Law Derive Their Power from Christ's Passion?*

We proceed thus to the Fifth Article: It seems that the sacraments of the New Law do not derive their power from Christ's Passion.

Objection 1. For the power of the sacraments is in the causing of grace which is the principle of spiritual life in the soul. But as Augustine says (*Tract.* xix *in Joann.*):[2] "The Word, as He was in the beginning with God, quickens souls; as He was made flesh, quickens bodies." Since, therefore, Christ's Passion pertains to the Word as made flesh, it seems that it cannot cause the power of the sacraments.

Obj. 2. Further, the power of the sacraments seems to depend on faith; for as Augustine says (*Tract.* lxxx *in Joann.*),[3] the Divine word perfects the sacrament "not because it is spoken, but because it is believed." But our faith regards not only Christ's Passion but also the other mysteries of His humanity, and in a yet higher measure, His divinity. Therefore it seems that the power of the sacraments is not due specially to Christ's Passion.

Obj. 3. Further, the sacraments are ordered to man's justification, according to I Cor. 6. 11: *You are washed . . . you are justified.* Now jus-

tification is ascribed to the Resurrection, according to Rom. 4. 25: *(Who) rose again for our justification.* Therefore it seems that the sacraments derive their power from Christ's Resurrection rather than from His Passion.

On the contrary, On Rom. 5. 14: *After the similitude of the transgression of Adam,* etc., the gloss says:[4] "From the side of Christ asleep on the Cross flowed the sacraments which brought salvation to the Church." Consequently, it seems that the sacraments derive their power from Christ's Passion.

I answer that, As stated above (A. 1) a sacrament in causing grace works after the manner of an instrument. Now an instrument is twofold: the one, separate, as a stick, for instance; the other, joined, as a hand. Moreover, the separate instrument is moved by means of the joined instrument, as a stick by the hand. Now the principal efficient cause of grace is God Himself, in comparison with Whom Christ's humanity is as a united instrument, whereas the sacrament is as a separate instrument. Consequently, the saving power must be derived by the sacraments from Christ's Godhead through His humanity.

Now sacramental grace seems to be ordained principally to two things: namely, to take away the defects consequent on past sins, in so far as they are transitory in act, but endure in guilt; and, further, to perfect the soul in things pertaining to Divine Worship in regard to the religion of the Christian life. But it is manifest from what has been stated above (Q. XLVIII, AA. 1, 2, 6; Q. XLIX, AA. 1, 3) that Christ delivered us from our sins principally through His Passion, not only by way of efficiency and merit, but also by way of satisfaction. Likewise by His Passion He inaugurated the Rites of the Christian Religion by offering *Himself—an oblation and a sacrifice to God* (Eph. 5. 2). Therefore it is manifest that the sacraments of the Church derive their power specially from Christ's Passion, the Power of which is in a manner united to us by our receiving the sacraments. It was in sign of this that from the side of Christ hanging on the Cross there flowed water and blood, the former of which belongs to Baptism, the latter to the Eucharist, which are the most powerful sacraments.

Reply Obj. 1. The Word, since He was in the beginning with God, quickens souls as principal agent; but His flesh, and the mysteries accomplished therein, are as instrumental causes in

---

[1] PL 57, 557.   [2] PL 35, 1552.
[3] PL 35, 1840.

[4] *Glossa ordin.* (VI, 13B); *Glossa* Lombardi (PL 191, 1392).

the process of giving life to the soul; while in giving life to the body they act not only as instrumental causes, but also to a certain extent as exemplars, as we stated above (Q. LVI, A. I Reply 3).

Reply Obj. 2. Christ dwells in us *by faith* (Eph. 3. 17). Consequently, by faith Christ's power is united to us. Now the power of blotting out sin belongs in a special way to His Passion. And therefore men are delivered from sin especially by faith in His Passion, according to Rom. 3. 25: *Whom God hath proposed to be a propitiation through faith in His Blood*. Therefore the power of the sacraments which is ordered to the remission of sins is derived especially from faith in Christ's Passion.

Reply Obj. 3. Justification is ascribed to the Resurrection by reason of the term to which, which is newness of life through grace. But it is ascribed to the Passion by reason of the term from which, namely, in regard to the forgiveness of sin.

ARTICLE 6. *Whether the Sacraments of the Old Law Caused Grace?*

We proceed thus to the Sixth Article: It seems that the sacraments of the Old Law also caused grace.

Objection 1. For, as stated above (A. 5, Reply 2) the sacraments of the New Law derive their efficacy from faith in Christ's Passion. But there was faith in Christ's Passion under the Old Law, as well as under the New, since we have *the same spirit of faith* (II Cor. 4. 13). Therefore just as the sacraments of the New Law confer grace, so did the sacraments of the Old Law.

Obj. 2. Further, there is no sanctification save by grace. But men were sanctified by the sacraments of the Old Law: for it is written (Lev. 8. 31): *And when he*, that is, Moses, *had sanctified them*, that is, Aaron and his sons, *in their vestments*, etc. Therefore it seems that the sacraments of the Old Law conferred grace.

Obj. 3. Further, Bede says in a homily on the Circumcision:[1] "Under the Law circumcision provided the same health-giving balm against the wound of original sin as baptism in the time of revealed grace." But Baptism confers grace now. Therefore circumcision conferred grace, and in like manner, the other sacraments of the Law; for just as Baptism is the door of the sacraments of the New Law, so was circumcision

the door of the sacraments of the Old Law; hence the Apostle says (Gal. 5. 3): *I testify to every man circumcising himself, that he is a debtor to the whole law.*

On the contrary, it is written (Gal. 4. 9): *Turn you again to the weak and needy elements?* i.e., *to the Law*, the gloss says,[2] "which is called weak, because it does not justify perfectly." But grace justifies perfectly. Therefore the sacraments of the Old Law did not confer grace.

I answer that, It cannot be said that the sacraments of the Old Law conferred justifying grace of themselves, that is, by their own power, since thus Christ's Passion would not have been necessary, according to Gal. 2. 21: *If justice be by the Law, then Christ died in vain.*

But neither can it be said that they derived the power of conferring justifying grace from Christ's Passion. For as it was stated above (A. 5),[3] the power of Christ's Passion is united to us by faith and the sacraments, but in different ways; because the link that comes from faith is produced by an act of the soul, whereas the link that comes from the sacraments is produced by making use of exterior things. Now nothing hinders that which is subsequent in point of time from causing movement, even before it exists in reality, in so far as it pre-exists in an act of the soul; thus the end, which is subsequent in point of time, moves the agent in so far as it is apprehended and desired by him. On the other hand, what does not yet actually exist does not cause movement if we consider the use of exterior things. Consequently, the efficient cause cannot in point of time come into being after causing movement, as does the final cause. It is therefore clear that the sacraments of the New Law do reasonably derive the power of justification from Christ's Passion, which is the cause of man's justification, whereas the sacraments of the Old Law did not.

Nevertheless the Fathers of old were justified by faith in Christ's Passion, just as we are. And the sacraments of the Old Law were a kind of protestation of that faith, in so far as they signified Christ's Passion and its effects. It is therefore manifest that the sacraments of the Old Law were not endowed with any power by which they conduced to the bestowal of justify-

---

[1] *Homilies*, BK. II, hom. X, On the Feast of the Circumcision (PL 94, 54).

[2] *Glossa* Lombardi (PL 192, 141); cf. *Glossa ordin.* (VI, 85A).

[3] See also Q. XLVIII, A 6, reply 2; Q. XLIX, A. I, reply 4, 5.

ing grace, and they merely signified faith by which men were justified.

Reply Obj. 1. The Fathers of old had faith in the future Passion of Christ, which, according as it was apprehended by the soul, was able to justify them. But we have faith in the past Passion of Christ, which is able to justify, also by the real use of sacramental things as stated above.

Reply Obj. 2. That sanctification was a figure, for they were said to be sanctified because they gave themselves up to the Divine worship according to the rite of the Old Law, which was wholly ordered to the foreshadowing of Christ's Passion.

Reply Obj. 3. There have been many opinions about Circumcision. For, according to some,[1] Circumcision conferred no grace, but only remitted sin. But this is impossible, because man is not justified from sin save by grace, according to Rom. 3. 24: *Being justified freely by His grace.*

Therefore others said[2] that by Circumcision grace is conferred, as to the privative effects of sin, but not as to its positive effects. But this also appears to be false, because by Circumcision children received the power of obtaining glory, which is the ultimate positive effect of grace. Moreover, as regards the order of the formal cause, positive effects are naturally prior to privative effects, though according to the order of the material cause, the reverse is the case, for a form does not exclude privation save by informing the subject.

Hence others[3] say that Circumcision conferred grace also as regards a certain positive effect, that is, by making man worthy of eternal life, but not so as to repress concupiscence which makes man prone to sin. And so at one time it seemed to me.[4] But if the matter be considered carefully, this too appears to be untrue, because the very least grace is sufficient to resist any degree of concupiscence, and to merit eternal life.

And therefore it seems better to say that Circumcision, just as also the other sacraments of the Old Law, was merely a sign of justifying faith; and therefore the Apostle says (Rom. 4. 11) that Abraham *received the sign of Circum-*

cision, a seal of the justice of faith. Consequently grace was conferred in Circumcision in so far as it was a sign of Christ's future Passion, as will be made clear further on (Q. LXX, A. 4).

QUESTION LXIII
OF THE OTHER EFFECT OF THE SACRAMENTS WHICH IS A CHARACTER
(*In Six Articles*)

WE have now to consider the other effect of the sacraments, which is a character, and concerning this there are six points of inquiry: (1) Whether by the sacraments a character is produced in the soul? (2) What is this character? (3) Of whom is this character? (4) What is its subject? (5) Is it indelible? (6) Whether every sacrament imprints a character?

ARTICLE 1. *Whether a Sacrament Imprints a Character on the Soul?*

We proceed thus to the First Article: It seems that a sacrament does not imprint a character on the soul.

Objection 1. For the word "character" seems to signify some kind of distinctive sign. But Christ's members are distinguished from others by eternal predestination, which does not imply anything in the predestined, but only in God predestining, as we have stated in the First Part (Q. XXIII, A. 2). For it is written (II Tim. 2. 19): *The sure foundation of God standeth firm, having this seal: The Lord knoweth who are His.* Therefore the sacraments do not imprint a character on the soul.

Obj. 2. Further, a character is a distinctive sign. Now a sign, as Augustine says,[5] "is that which conveys something else to the mind besides the species which it impresses on the senses." But nothing in the soul can impress a species on the senses. Therefore it seems that no character is imprinted on the soul by the sacraments.

Obj. 3. Further, just as the believer is distinguished from the unbeliever by the sacraments of the New Law, so was it under the Old Law. But the sacraments of the Old Law did not imprint a character; hence they are called *justices of the flesh* (Heb. 9. 10) by the Apostle. Therefore neither it seems do the sacraments of the New Law.

On the contrary, The Apostle says (II Cor. 1, 21, 22): *He . . . that hath anointed us is God; Who also hath sealed us, and given the pledge of the spirit in our hearts.* But a character

---

[1] Hugh of St. Victor, *De Sacram.*, II, VI, 3 (PL 176, 448); *Glossa ordin.*, on Rom. 4, 11 (VI, 11B); *Glossa* Lombardi on Rom. 4, 11 (PL 191, 1372).

[2] William of Auxerre, *Summa Aurea*, IV (246ra).

[3] Alexander of Hales, *Summa Theol.*, pt. IV, Q. 7, m. 7, A. 5, sect. 2 (IV, 39vb); Bonaventure, *In Sent.*, IV, d. 1, pt. II, A. 2, Q. 3 (QR IV, 44).

[4] *In Sent.*, IV, d. 1, Q. 2, A. 4, Q. 3.

[5] *Christian Doctrine*, II, 1 (PL 34, 35).

means nothing else than a kind of sealing. Therefore it seems that by the sacraments God imprints His character on us.

I answer that, As is clear from what has been already stated (Q. LXII, A. 5) the sacraments of the New Law are ordained for a twofold purpose: namely, for a remedy against sins, and for the perfecting of the soul in things pertaining to the Divine worship according to the rite of the Christian life. Now whenever anyone is alloted to some definite purpose he is accustomed to receive some outward sign of it; thus in olden times soldiers who enlisted in the ranks used to be marked with certain characters on the body, because they were alloted to a bodily service. Since, therefore, by the sacraments men are alloted to a spiritual service pertaining to the worship of God, it follows that by their means the faithful receive a certain spiritual character. Therefore Augustine says (*Contra Parmen.* ii, 13):[1] "If a deserter from the battle, through dread of the mark of enlistment on his body, throws himself on the emperor's clemency, and having besought and received mercy, return to the fight, is that character renewed, when the man has been set free and reprimanded? is it not rather acknowledged and approved? Are the Christian sacraments, by any chance, of a nature less lasting than this bodily mark?"

Reply Obj. 1. The faithful of Christ are destined to the reward of the glory that is to come, by the seal of Divine Predestination. But they are alloted to acts becoming the Church that is now, by a certain spiritual seal that is set on them, and is called a character.

Reply Obj. 2. The character imprinted on the soul has the nature of a sign in so far as it is imprinted by a sensible sacrament, since we know that a certain one has received the baptismal character through his being cleansed by the sensible water. Nevertheless from a kind of likeness, anything that fashions one thing to another, or discriminates one thing from another, even though it be not sensible, can be called a character or a seal; thus the Apostle calls Christ *the figure* or χαρακτήρ *of the substance* of the Father (Heb. 1. 3).

Reply Obj. 3. As stated above (Q. LXII, A. 6) the sacraments of the Old Law had not in themselves any spiritual power of producing a spiritual effect. Consequently in those sacraments there was no need of a spiritual character, and bodily circumcision sufficed, which the Apostle calls *a seal* (Rom. 4. 11).

[1] PL 43, 71.

ARTICLE 2. *Whether a Character Is a Spiritual Power?*

We proceed thus to the Second Article: It seems that a character is not a spiritual power.

Objection 1. For character seems to be the same thing as figure; hence (Heb. 1. 3), where we read *figure of His substance,* for *figure* the Greek has χαρακτήρ. Now figure is in the fourth species of quality, and thus differs from power which is in the second species of quality. Therefore character is not a spiritual power.

Obj. 2. Further, Dionysius says (*Eccl. Hier.* ii):[2] "The Divine Beatitude admits him that seeks happiness to a share in Itself, and grants this share to him by conferring on him Its own light as a kind of seal." Consequently, it seems that a character is a kind of light. Now light belongs rather to the third species of quality. Therefore a character is not a power, since this seems to belong to the second species.

Obj. 3. Further, character is defined by some[3] thus: "A character is a holy sign of the communion of faith and of the holy ordination, conferred by a hierarch." Now a sign is in the genus of relation, not of power. Therefore a character is not a spiritual power.

Obj. 4. Further, a power has the nature of a cause and principle.[4] But a sign which is placed in the definition of a character is rather in the nature of an effect. Therefore a character is not a spiritual power.

On the contrary, The Philosopher says:[5] "There are three things in the soul, power, habit, and passion." Now a character is not a passion, since a passion passes quickly, whereas a character is indelible, as will be made clear further on (A. 5). In like manner it is not a habit, because no habit is indifferent to acting well or ill, whereas a character is indifferent to either, since some use it well, some ill. Now this cannot occur with a habit, because no one abuses a habit of virtue, or uses well an evil habit. It remains, therefore, that a character is a power.

I answer that, As stated above (A. 1), the sacraments of the New Law produce a character, in so far as by them we are appointed to

[2] Part III, sect. 4 (PG 3, 400).
[3] Dionysius, according to Alexander of Hales, *Summa Theol.*, Pt. IV, Q. 19, m. 1, A. 1 (IV, 86vb) and Bonaventure, *In Sent.*, IV, d. VI, Pt. I, A. 1, Q. 1 (QR IV, 137); see also Albert, *In Sent.*, IV, d. VI, A. 4 (BO XXIX, 123); also Thomas, *In Sent.*, IV, d. IV, Q. 1, A. 2; cf. Dionysius the Areopagite, *De Eccl. Hier.*, 2, Pt. III, 4 (PG 3, 400).
[4] Aristotle, *Metaphysics*, V, 12 (1019^{a}15).
[5] *Ethics*, II, 5 (1105^{b}20).

the worship of God according to the rite of the Christian religion. Therefore Dionysius (*Eccl. Hier.* ii),[1] after saying that God "by a kind of sign grants a share of Himself to those that approach Him through baptism," adds "by making them Godlike and communicators of Divine things." Now the worship of God consists either in receiving Divine things or in bestowing them on others. And for both these purposes some power is needed; for to bestow something on others, active power is necessary, and in order to receive, we need a passive power. Consequently, a character signifies a certain spiritual power ordered to things pertaining to the Divine worship.

But it must be observed that this spiritual power is instrumental, as we have stated above (Q. LXII, A. 4) of the power which is in the sacraments. For to have a sacramental character belongs to God's ministers, and a minister is a kind of instrument, as the Philosopher says.[2] Consequently, just as the virtue which is in the sacraments is not of itself in a genus, but is reducible to a genus, for the reason that it is of a transitory and incomplete nature, so also a character is not properly in a genus or species, but is reducible to the second species of quality.

Reply Obj. 1. Figure is a certain boundary of quantity. Therefore, properly speaking, it is only in corporeal things, and of spiritual things is said metaphorically. But a thing is not put in a genus or species except by that which is properly predicated of it. Consequently, a character cannot be in the fourth species of quality, although some have held this to be the case.[3]

Reply Obj. 2. The third species of quality contains only sensible passions or sensible qualities. Now a character is not a sensible light. Consequently, it is not in the third species of quality as some have maintained.[4]

Reply Obj. 3. The relation signified by the word "sign" must be founded on something. Now the relation of this sign which is a character cannot be founded immediately on the essence of the soul, because then it would belong to every soul naturally. Consequently, there must be something in the soul on which such a relation is founded. And this is the essence of

a character. Therefore it need not be in the genus relation as some have held.[5]

Reply Obj. 4. A character is in the nature of a sign in comparison to the sensible sacrament by which it is imprinted. But considered in itself, it is in the nature of a principle, in the way already explained.

ARTICLE 3. *Whether the Sacramental Character Is the Character of Christ?*

We proceed thus to the Third Article: It seems that the sacramental character is not the character of Christ.

Objection 1. For it is written (Eph. 4. 30): *Grieve not the Holy Spirit of God, whereby you are sealed.* But something that seals is implied in the nature of character. Therefore the sacramental character should be attributed to the Holy Ghost rather than to Christ.

Obj. 2. Further, a character has the nature of a sign. And it is a sign of the grace that is conferred by the sacrament. Now grace is poured forth into the soul by the whole Trinity; hence it is written (Ps. 83. 12): *The Lord will give grace and glory.* Therefore it seems that the sacramental character should not be attributed specially to Christ.

Obj. 3. Further, a man is marked with a character that he may be distinguishable from others. But the saints are distinguishable from others by charity, which, as Augustine says (*De Trin.* xv, 18),[6] "alone separates the children of the kingdom from the children of perdition." Therefore also the children of perdition are said to have *the character of the beast* (Apoc. 13. 16, 17). But charity is not attributed to Christ, but rather to the Holy Ghost according to Rom. 5. 5: *The charity of God is poured forth in our hearts, by the Holy Ghost, Who is given to us;* or even to the Father, according to II Cor. 13. 13: *The grace of Our Lord Jesus Christ and the charity of God.* Therefore it seems that the sacramental character should not be attributed to Christ.

On the contrary, Some[7] define character thus: "A character is a distinctive mark printed on the rational soul by the eternal Character, whereby the created trinity is sealed with the likeness of the creating and re-creating Trinity, and distinguishing him from those who are not so enlikened, according to the state of faith." But the eternal Character is Christ Himself,

---

[1] III, 4 (PG 3, 400).   [2] *Politics,* I, 4 (1253^{b}30).
[3] Referred to by Alexander of Hales, *Summa Theol.,* Pt. IV, Q. XIX, m 1, A. 2 (IV 87vb); also by Bonaventure, *In Sent.,* IV, d. VI, Pt. I, A. 1, Q. 1 (QR IV, 137); Albert, *In Sent.,* IV, d. VI, A. 3 (BO XXIX, 121).
[4] William of Auxerre, *Summa Aurea,* IV (250ra); cf. also preceding note.

[5] Cf. note 3.   [6] PL 42, 1082.
[7] Cf. Albert, *In Sent.,* IV, d. VI, A. 4 (BO XXIX, 123); cf. A. 3 (BO XXIX, 122); Bonaventure, *In Sent.,* IV, d. VI, Pt. I, A. 1, Q. 1 (QR IV, 137).

according to Heb. 1. 3: *Who being the brightness of His glory and the figure,* or character, *of His substance.* It seems, therefore, that the character should properly be attributed to Christ.

I answer that, As has been made clear above (A. 1), a character is properly a kind of seal, whereby something is marked, as being ordered to some end; thus a coin is marked with a character for use in exchange of goods, and soldiers are marked with a character as being assigned to military service. Now the faithful are assigned to a twofold end. First and principally to the enjoyment of glory. And for this purpose they are marked with the seal of grace according to Ezech. 9. 4: *Mark Thou upon the foreheads of the men that sigh and mourn;* and Apoc. 7. 3: *Hurt not the earth, nor the sea, nor the trees, till we sign the servants of our God in their foreheads.*

Secondly, each of the faithful is appointed to receive, or to bestow on others, things pertaining to the worship of God. And to this end, properly speaking, the sacramental character is alloted. Now the whole rite of the Christian religion is derived from Christ's priesthood. Consequently, it is clear that the sacramental character is specially the character of Christ, to Whose priesthood the faithful are made like by reason of the sacramental characters, which are nothing else than certain participations of Christ's Priesthood, flowing from Christ Himself.

Reply Obj. 1. The Apostle speaks there of that sealing by which a man is assigned to future glory, and which is effected by grace, which is attributed to the Holy Ghost, since it is through love that God gives us something freely, which pertains to the nature of grace; for the Holy Ghost is love. Therefore it is written (I Cor. 12. 4): *There are diversities of graces, but the same Spirit.*

Reply Obj. 2. The sacramental character is a thing as regards the exterior sacrament, and a sacrament in regard to the ultimate effect. Consequently, something can be attributed to a character in two ways. First, according to the nature of sacrament, and thus it is a sign of the invisible grace which is conferred in the sacrament. Secondly, according to the proper nature of character. And thus it is a sign conferring on a man a likeness to some principal person in whom is vested the authority over that to which he is assigned; thus soldiers who are assigned to military service are marked with their leader's sign, by which they are, in a

fashion, likened to him. And in this way those who are appointed to the Christian worship, of which Christ is the author, receive a character by which they are likened to Christ. Consequently, properly speaking, this is Christ's character.

Reply Obj. 3. A character distinguishes one from another in relation to some particular end, to which he who receives the character is ordered, as has been stated concerning the military character (A. 1) by which a soldier of the king is distinguished from the enemy's soldier in relation to the battle. In like manner the character of the faithful is that by which the faithful of Christ are distinguished from the servants of the devil, either in relation to eternal life, or in relation to the worship of the Church that now is. Of these the former is the result of charity and grace, as the objection runs, while the latter results from the sacramental character. Therefore the *character of the beast* may be understood by opposition, to mean either the obstinate malice for which some are assigned to eternal punishment, or the profession of an unlawful form of worship.

ARTICLE 4. *Whether the Character Is in the Powers of the Soul As in a Subject?*

We proceed thus to the Fourth Article: It seems that the character is not in the powers of of the soul as in a subject.

Objection 1. For a character is said to be a disposition to grace. But grace is in the essence of the soul as in a subject as we have stated in the Second Part (I-II, Q. CX, A. 4). Therefore it seems that the character is in the essence of the soul and not in the powers.

Obj. 2. Further, a power of the soul does not seem to be the subject of anything save habit and disposition. But a character as stated above (A. 2), is neither habit nor disposition, but rather a power, the subject of which is nothing else than the essence of the soul. Therefore it seems that the character is not in a power of the soul as in a subject, but rather in its essence.

Obj. 3. Further, the powers of the rational soul are divided into those of knowledge and those of appetite. But it cannot be said that a character is only in a knowing power, nor, again, only in an appetitive power, since it is neither ordered to knowledge only, nor to desire only. Likewise, neither can it be said to be in both, because the same accident cannot be in different subjects. Therefore it seems that a character is not in a power of the soul as in a subject, but rather in the essence.

On the contrary, A character, according to its definition given above (A. 3), is imprinted in the rational soul by way of an image. But the image of the Trinity in the soul is seen in the powers. Therefore a character is in the powers of the soul.

I answer that, As stated above (A. 3), a character is a kind of seal by which the soul is marked, so that it may receive, or bestow on others, things pertaining to Divine worship. Now the Divine worship consists in certain actions, and the powers of the soul are properly ordered to actions, just as the essence is ordered to being. Therefore a character is not in the essence of the soul as in a subject, but in its power.

Reply Obj. 1. The subject is ascribed to an accident in respect of that to which the accident disposes it proximately, but not in respect of that to which it disposes it remotely or indirectly. Now a character disposes the soul directly and proximately to the fulfilling of things pertaining to Divine worship, and because such cannot be accomplished suitably without the help of grace, since, according to John 4. 24, *they that adore* God *must adore Him in spirit and in truth,* consequently the Divine bounty bestows grace on those who receive the character, so that they may accomplish worthily the service to which they are appointed. Therefore the subject should be ascribed to a character in respect of those actions that pertain to the Divine worship rather than in respect of grace.

Reply Obj. 2. The essence of the soul is the subject of the natural power, which flows from the principles of the essence. Now a character is not a power of this kind, but a spiritual power coming from without. Therefore, just as the essence of the soul, from which man has his natural life, is perfected by grace by which the soul lives spiritually, so the natural power of the soul is perfected by a spiritual power, which is a character. For habit and disposition belong to a power of the soul, since they are ordered to actions of which the powers are the principles. And in like manner whatever is ordered to action should be attributed to a power.

Reply Obj. 3. As stated above, a character is ordered to things pertaining to the Divine worship, which is a protestation of faith expressed by exterior signs. Consequently, a character needs to be in the soul's knowing power, where also is faith.

ARTICLE 5. *Whether a Character Can Be Blotted Out from the Soul?*

We proceed thus to the Fifth Article: It seems that a character can be blotted out from the soul.

Objection 1. Because the more perfect an accident is, the more firmly does it adhere to its subject. But grace is more perfect than a character, because a character is ordered to grace as to a further end. Now grace is lost through sin. Much more, therefore, is a character so lost.

Obj. 2. Further, by a character a man is assigned to the Divine worship, as stated above (AA. 3, 4). But some pass from the worship of God to a contrary worship by apostasy from the faith. It seems, therefore, that such lose the sacramental character.

Obj. 3. Further, when the end ceases, the means to the end should cease also for otherwise it would remain uselessly; thus after the resurrection there will be no marriage, because begetting will cease, to which marriage is ordered. Now the exterior worship to which a character is ordered will not endure in heaven, where nothing is done in figure, but all will be truth without a veil. Therefore the sacramental character does not last in the soul for ever, and consequently it can be blotted out.

On the contrary, Augustine says (*Contra Parmen.* ii, 13):[1] "The Christian sacraments are not less lasting than the bodily mark" of military service. But the character of military service is not repeated, but is "recognized and approved" in the man who obtains the emperor's forgiveness after offending him. Therefore neither can the sacramental character be blotted out.

I answer that, As stated above (A. 3), in a sacramental character Christ's faithful have a share in His Priesthood, in the sense that as Christ has the full power of a spiritual priesthood, so His faithful are likened to Him by sharing a certain spiritual power with regard to the sacraments and to things pertaining to the Divine worship. For this reason it is unbecoming that Christ should have a character; but His priestly power is compared to a character as that which is complete and perfect is compared to some participation of itself. Now Christ's Priesthood is eternal, according to Ps. 109. 4: *Thou art a priest for ever, according to the order of Melchisedech.* Consequently, every sanctification wrought by His Priesthood, is perpetual, enduring as long as the thing sancti-

[1] PL 43, 72.

fied endures. This is clear even in inanimate things, for the consecration of a church or an altar lasts for ever unless they be destroyed. Since, therefore, the subject of a character is the soul as to its intellectual part, where faith resides, as stated above (A. 4, Reply 3), it is clear that, the intellect being perpetual and incorruptible, a character cannot be blotted out from the soul.

Reply Obj. 1. Grace and character are in the soul in different ways. For grace is in the soul as a form having complete being therein, whereas a character is in the soul as an instrumental power, as stated above (A. 2). Now a complete form is in its subject according to the condition of the subject. And since the soul as long as it is a wayfarer is changeable in respect of free-choice, it results that grace is in the soul in a changeable manner. But an instrumental power follows rather the condition of the principal agent, and consequently a character exists in the soul in an indelible manner, not from any perfection of its own, but from the perfection of Christ's Priesthood, from which the character flows like an instrumental power.

Reply Obj. 2. As Augustine says (*ibid.*), "even apostates are not deprived of their baptism, for when they repent and return to the fold they do not receive it again; from which we conclude that it cannot be lost." The reason of this is that a character is an instrumental power, as stated above (Reply 1), and the nature of an instrument as such is to be moved by another, but not to move itself; this belongs to the will. Consequently, however much the will be moved in the contrary direction, the character is not removed, by reason of the immobility of the principal mover.

Reply Obj. 3. Although external worship does not last after this life, yet its end remains. Consequently, after this life the character remains, both in the good as adding to their glory, and in the wicked as increasing their shame; just as the character of the military service remains in the soldiers after the victory, as the boast of the conquerors, and the disgrace of the conquered.

ARTICLE 6. *Whether a Character Is Imprinted By Each Sacrament of the New Law?*

We proceed thus to the Sixth Article: It seems that a character is imprinted by all the sacraments of the New Law.

Objection 1. For each sacrament of the New Law makes man a participator in Christ's Priesthood. But the sacramental character is nothing but a participation in Christ's Priesthood, as already stated (AA. 3, 5). Therefore it seems that a character is imprinted by each sacrament of the New Law.

Obj. 2. Further, a character is to the soul in which it exists as a consecration to the thing consecrated. But by each sacrament of the New Law man receives sanctifying grace, as stated above (Q. LXII, A. 1). Therefore it seems that a character is imprinted by each sacrament of the New Law.

Obj. 3. Further, a character is a thing and a sacrament. But in each sacrament of the New Law there is something which is only a thing, and something which is only a sacrament, and something which is both thing and sacrament. Therefore a character is imprinted by each sacrament of the New Law.

On the contrary, Those sacraments in which a character is imprinted are not repeated, because a character is indelible, as stated above (A. 5), whereas some sacraments are repeated, for instance, penance and matrimony. Therefore not all the sacraments imprint a character.

I answer that, As stated above (Q. LXII, AA. 1, 5), the sacraments of the New Law are ordained for a twofold purpose, namely, as a remedy for sin, and for the Divine worship. Now all the sacraments, from the fact that they confer grace, have this in common, that they afford a remedy against sin, whereas not all the sacraments are directly ordered to the Divine worship. Thus it is clear that penance, whereby man is delivered from sin, does not afford man any advance in the Divine worship, but restores him to his former state.

Now a sacrament may belong to the Divine worship in three ways: first in regard to the thing done; secondly, in regard to the agent; thirdly, in regard to the recipient. In regard to the thing done, the Eucharist belongs to the Divine worship, for the Divine worship consists principally therein, so far as it is the sacrifice of the Church. And by this same sacrament a character is not imprinted on man, because it does not order man to any further sacramental action or benefit received, since rather is it "the end and consummation of all the sacraments," as Dionysius says (*Eccl. Hier.* iii, 1).[1] But it contains within itself Christ, in Whom there is not the character, but the very plenitude of the Priesthood.

But it is the sacrament of Order that pertains to the sacramental agents, for it is by this sacrament that men are assigned to confer sacra-

[1] PG 3, 424.

ments on others, while the sacrament of Baptism pertains to the recipients, since it confers on man the power to receive the other sacraments of the Church; hence it is called the door of the sacraments. In a way Confirmation also is ordained for the same purpose, as we shall explain in its proper place (Q. LXV, A. 3). Consequently, these three sacraments imprint a character, namely, Baptism, Confirmation, and Order.

Reply Obj. 1. Every sacrament makes man a participator in Christ's Priesthood, from the fact that it confers on him some effect thereof. But every sacrament does not allot a man to do or receive something pertaining to the worship of the priesthood of Christ, while it is just this that is required for a sacrament to imprint a character.

Reply Obj. 2. Man is sanctified by each of the sacraments, according as sanctity means cleansing from sin, which is the effect of grace. But in a special way some sacraments, which imprint a character, sanctify man by a certain consecration, thus assigning him to the Divine worship; just as inanimate things are said to be consecrated because they are assigned to Divine worship.

Reply Obj. 3. Although a character is a thing and a sacrament, it does not follow that everything that is a thing and a sacrament is a character. With regard to the other sacraments we shall explain further on what is the thing and what is the sacrament. (Q. LXXIII, A. 1, Reply 3; Q. LXXXIV, A. 1, Reply 3).

QUESTION LXIV

OF THE CAUSES OF THE SACRAMENTS

(In Ten Articles)

IN the next place we have to consider the causes of the sacraments, both as to authorship and as to ministration. Concerning which there are ten points of inquiry: (1) Whether God alone works inwardly in the sacraments? (2) Whether the institution of the sacraments is from God alone? (3) Of the power which Christ exercised over the sacraments. (4) Whether He could communicate that power to others? (5) Whether the wicked can have the power of administering the sacraments? (6) Whether the wicked sin in administering the sacraments? (7) Whether the angels can be ministers of the sacraments? (8) Whether the minister's intention is necessary in the sacraments? (9) Whether right faith is required therein, so that it be impossible for an unbeliever to confer a sacrament? (10) Whether a right intention is required therein?

ARTICLE 1. *Whether God Alone Works Inwardly Sacramental Effect?*

We proceed thus to the First Article: It seems that not God alone, but also the minister, works inwardly sacramental effect.

Objection 1. For the inward sacramental effect is to cleanse man from sin and enlighten him by grace. But it belongs to the ministers of the Church "to cleanse, enlighten and perfect," as Dionysius explains (*Cæl. Hier.* v).[1] Therefore it seems that the sacramental effect is the work not only of God, but also of the ministers of the Church.

Obj. 2. Further, certain prayers are offered up in conferring the sacraments. But the prayers of the just are more acceptable to God than those of any other, according to John 9. 31: *If a man be a server of God, and doth His will, him He heareth.* Therefore it seems that a man obtains a greater sacramental effect if he receive it from a good minister. Consequently, the interior effect is partly the work of the minister and not of God alone.

Obj. 3. Further, man is of greater account than an inanimate thing. But an inanimate thing contributes something to the interior effect, since "water touches the body and cleanses the heart," as Augustine says (*Tract.* lxxx *in Joann.*).[2] Therefore the interior sacramental effect is partly the work of man and not of God alone.

On the contrary, It is written (Rom. 8. 33): *God that justifieth.* Since, then, the inward effect of all the sacraments is justification, it seems that God alone works the interior sacramental effect.

I answer that, There are two ways of producing an effect: first, as a principal agent; secondly, as an instrument. In the former way the interior sacramental effect is the work of God alone. First, because God alone can enter the soul wherein the sacramental effect takes place, and no agent can operate immediately where it is not. Secondly, because grace which is an interior sacramental effect is from God alone, as we have established in the Second Part (I-II, Q. CXII, A. 1), while the character which is the interior effect of certain sacraments is an instrumental power which flows from the principal agent, which is God.

In the second way, however, the interior sacramental effect can be the work of man, in so far as he works as a minister. For a minister is of the nature of an instrument, since the action of both is applied to something extrinsic, while the interior effect is produced through the power of the principal agent, which is God.

Reply Obj. 1. Cleansing, in so far as it is attributed to the ministers of the Church, is not a washing from sin; deacons are said to cleanse in so far as they remove the unclean from the body of the faithful, or prepare them by their pious admonitions for the reception of the sacraments. In like manner also priests are said to enlighten God's people, not indeed by giving them grace, but by conferring on them the sacraments of grace, as Dionysius explains (*ibid.*).

Reply Obj. 2. The prayers which are said in giving the sacraments are offered to God not on the part of the individual, but on the part of the whole Church, whose prayers are acceptable to God, according to Matt. 18 .19: *If two of you shall consent upon earth, concerning anything whatsoever they shall ask, it shall be done to them by My Father.* Nor is there any reason why the devotion of a just man should not contribute to this effect.

But that which is the sacramental effect is not sought through the prayer of the Church or of the minister, but through the merit of Christ's Passion, the power of which operates in the sacraments, as stated above (Q. LXII, A. 5). Therefore the sacramental effect is made no better by a better minister. And yet something in addition may be asked for for the receiver of the sacrament through the devotion of the minister; but this is not the work of the minister, but the work of God Who hears the minister's prayer.

Reply Obj. 3. Inanimate things do not produce anything towards the inward sacramental effect, except instrumentally, as stated above. In like manner neither do men produce the sacramental effect, except ministerially, as also stated above.

ARTICLE 2. *Whether the Sacraments Are Instituted By God Alone?*

We proceed thus to the Second Article: It seems that the sacraments are not instituted by God alone.

Objection 1. For those things which God has instituted are delivered to us in Holy Scripture. But in the sacraments certain things are done which are nowhere mentioned in Holy Scripture; for instance, the chrism with which men are confirmed, the oil with which priests are

anointed, and many others, both words and actions, which we employ in the sacraments. Therefore the sacraments were not instituted by God alone.

Obj. 2. Further, a sacrament is a kind of sign. Now sensible things have their own natural signification. Nor can it be said that God takes pleasure in certain significations and not in others, because He approves of all that He made. Moreover, it seems to be peculiar to the demons to be enticed to something by means of signs; for Augustine says:[1] "The demons are enticed . . . by means of creatures, which were created not by them but by God, by various means of attraction according to their various natures, not as an animal is enticed by food, but as a spirit is drawn by a sign." It seems, therefore, that there is no need for the sacraments to be instituted by God.

Obj. 3. Further, the apostles were God's vicegerents on earth; hence the Apostle says (II Cor. 2. 10): *For what I have pardoned, if I have pardoned anything, for your sakes have I done it in the person of Christ,* that is, as though Christ Himself had pardoned. Therefore it seems that the apostles and their successors can institute new sacraments.

On the contrary, The institutor of anything is he who gives it strength and power, as in the case of those who institute laws. But the power of a sacrament is from God alone, as we have shown above (A. 1; Q. LXII, A. 1). Therefore God alone can institute a sacrament.

I answer that, As appears from what has been said above (*ibid.*), the sacraments are instrumental causes of spiritual effects. Now an instrument has its power from the principal agent. But an agent in respect of a sacrament is twofold; namely, he who institutes the sacraments, and he who makes use of the sacrament instituted, by applying it for the production of the effect. Now the power of a sacrament cannot be from him who makes use of the sacrament, because he works but as a minister. Consequently, it remains that the power of the sacrament is from the institutor of the sacrament. Since, therefore, the power of the sacrament is from God alone, it follows that God alone can institute the sacraments.

Reply Obj. 1. Human institutions observed in the sacraments are not essential to the sacrament, but belong to the solemnity which is added to the sacraments in order to arouse devotion and reverence in the recipients. But those things that are essential to the sacrament are

[1] *City of God,* XXI, 6 (PL 41, 717).

instituted by Christ Himself, Who is God and man. And though they are not all handed down by the Scriptures, yet the Church holds them from the intimate tradition of the apostles, according to the saying of the Apostle (I Cor. 11. 34): *The rest I will set in order when I come.*

Reply Obj. 2. From their very nature sensible things have a certain aptitude for the signifying of spiritual effects, but this aptitude is fixed by the Divine institution to some special signification. This is what Hugh of S. Victor means by saying (*De Sacram.* i)[1] that "a sacrament owes its signification to its institution." Yet God chooses certain things rather than others for sacramental signification, not as though His operation were restricted to them, but in order that their signification be more suitable to them.

Reply Obj. 3. The apostles and their successors are God's vicars in governing the Church which is built on faith and the sacraments of faith. Therefore, just as they may not institute another Church, so neither may they deliver another faith, nor institute other sacraments; on the contrary, the Church is said to be built up with the sacraments which flowed from the side of Christ while hanging on the Cross.[2]

ARTICLE 3. *Whether Christ As Man Had the Power of Producing the Inward Sacramental Effect?*

We proceed thus to the Third Article: It seems that Christ as man had the power of producing the interior sacramental effect.

Objection 1. For John the Baptist said (John 1. 33): *He, Who sent me to baptize in water, said to me: He upon Whom thou shalt see the Spirit descending and remaining upon Him, He it is that baptizeth with the Holy Ghost.* But to baptize with the Holy Ghost is to confer inwardly the grace of the Holy Ghost. And the Holy Ghost descended upon Christ as man, not as God, for thus He Himself gives the Holy Ghost. Therefore it seems that Christ as man had the power of producing the inward sacramental effect.

Obj. 2. Further, our Lord said (Matt. 9. 6): *That you may know that the Son of Man hath power on earth to forgive sins.* But forgiveness of sins is an inward sacramental effect. Therefore it seems that Christ as man produces the inward sacramental effect.

Obj. 3. Further, the institution of the sacraments belongs to him who acts as principal agent in producing the inward sacramental effect. Now it is clear that Christ instituted the sacraments. Therefore it is He Who produces the inward sacramental effect.

Obj. 4. Further, no one can confer the sacramental effect without conferring the sacrament unless he produces the sacramental effect by his own power. But Christ conferred the sacramental effect without conferring the sacrament, as in the case of Magdalen to whom He said: *Thy sins are forgiven Thee* (Luke 7. 48). Therefore it seems that Christ, as man, produces the inward sacramental effect.

Obj. 5. Further, the principal agent in causing the inward effect is that in virtue of which the sacrament operates. But the sacraments derive their power from Christ's Passion and through the invocation of His Name, according to I Cor. 1. 13: *Was Paul then crucified for you? or were you baptized in the name of Paul?* Therefore Christ, as man, produces the inward sacramental effect.

On the contrary, Augustine (Isidore, *Etymol.* vi, 19)[3] says: "The Divine power in the sacraments works in a hidden way in producing their salutary effect." Now the Divine power is Christ's as God, not as man. Therefore Christ produces the inward sacramental effect not as man but as God.

I answer that, Christ produces the inward sacramental effect both as God and as man, but not in the same way. For, as God, He works in the sacraments by authority, but as man His operation conduces to the inward sacramental effects meritoriously and efficiently, but instrumentally. For it has been stated (Q. XLVIII, AA. 1, 6; Q. XLIX, A. 1) that Christ's Passion which belongs to Him in respect of His human nature, is the cause of our justification, both meritoriously and efficiently, not as the principal agent thereof, or by authority, but as an instrument, in so far as His humanity is the instrument of His Godhead, as stated above (Q. XIII, AA. 2, 3; Q. XIX, A. 1).

Nevertheless, since it is an instrument united to the Godhead in unity of Person, it has a certain headship and causality in regard to extrinsic instruments, which are the ministers of the Church and the sacraments themselves, as has been explained above (A. 1). Consequently, just as Christ, as God, has the power of authority over the sacraments, so, as man, He has the power of ministry in chief, or power

---

[1] IX, 2 (PL 176, 317).
[2] *Glossa ordin.*, on Rom. 5.14 (VI, 13B); *Glossa* Lombardi (PL 191, 1392); Augustine, *Ennar. in Ps.*, Ps. 138, Prol. (PL 37, 1785).
[3] PL 82, 255.

of excellence. And this consists in four things. First in this, that the merit and power of His Passion operates in the sacraments, as stated above (Q. LXII, A. 5). And because the power of the Passion is joined to us by faith, according to Rom. 3. 25: *Whom God hath proposed to be a propitiation, through faith in His blood,* which faith we proclaim by calling on the name of Christ, therefore, secondly, Christ's power of excellence over the sacraments consists in this, that they are sanctified by the invocation of His name. And because the sacraments derive their power from His institution, hence, thirdly, the excellence of Christ's power consists in this, that He, Who gave them their power, could institute the sacraments. And since cause does not depend on effect, but rather conversely, it belongs to the excellence of Christ's power that He could bestow the sacramental effect without conferring the exterior sacrament. Thus it is clear how to solve *the objections,* for the arguments on either side are true to a certain extent, as explained above.

ARTICLE 4. *Whether Christ Could Communicate to Ministers the Power Which He Had in the Sacraments?*

We proceed thus to the Fourth Article: It seems that Christ could not communicate to ministers the power which He had in the sacraments.

Objection 1. For as Augustine argues against Maximin,[1] "if He could, but would not, He was jealous of His power." But jealousy was far from Christ Who had the fulness of charity. Since, therefore, Christ did not communicate His power to ministers, it seems that He could not.

Obj. 2. Further, on John 14. 12: *Greater than these shall he do,* Augustine says (*Tract.* lxxii):[2] "I affirm this to be altogether greater," namely, for a man from being ungodly to be made righteous, "than to create heaven and earth." But Christ could not communicate to His disciples the power of creating heaven and earth; neither, therefore, could He give them the power of justifying the wicked. Since, therefore, the justification of the wicked is effected by the power that Christ has in the sacraments, it seems that He could not communicate that power to ministers.

Obj. 3. Further, it belongs to Christ as Head of the Church that grace should flow from Him to others, according to John 1. 16:

Of His fulness we all have received. But this could not be communicated to others, since then the Church would be deformed, having many heads. Therefore it seems that Christ could not communicate His power to ministers.

On the contrary, On John 1. 31: *I knew Him not,* Augustine says (*Tract.* v)[3] that "he did not know that Our Lord having the authority of baptizing . . . would keep it to Himself." But John would not have been in ignorance of this if such a power were incommunicable. Therefore Christ could communicate His power to ministers.

I answer that, As stated above (A. 3), Christ had a twofold power in the sacraments. One was the power of authority, which belongs to Him as God, and this power He could not communicate to any creature, just as neither could He communicate the Divine Essence. The other was the power of excellence, which belongs to Him as man. This power He could communicate to ministers; namely, by giving them such a fulness of grace that their merits would conduce to the sacramental effect, and that by the invocation of their names, the sacraments would be sanctified, and that they themselves might institute sacraments, and by their mere will confer the sacramental effect without observing the sacramental rite. For an instrument, that is joined, the more powerful it is, the more able is it to lend its power to the separated instrument, as the hand can to a stick.

Reply Obj. 1. It was not through jealousy that Christ refrained from communicating to ministers of the Church His power of excellence, but for the good of the faithful, lest they should put their trust in men, and lest there should be various kinds of sacraments, giving rise to division in the Church, as may be seen in those who said: *I am of Paul, I am of Apollo, and I of Cephas* (I Cor. 1. 12).

Reply Obj. 2. This objection is true of the power of authority, which belongs to Christ as God. At the same time the power of excellence can be called authority in comparison to other ministers. Hence on I Cor. 1. 13: *Is Christ divided?* the gloss says[4] that "He could give power of authority in baptizing to those to whom He gave the power of administering it."

Reply Obj. 3. It was in order to avoid the incongruity of many heads in the Church that Christ was unwilling to communicate to ministers His power of excellence. If, however, He

---

[1] Bk. II, chap. 7 (PL 42, 762).   [2] PL 35, 1823.

[3] PL 35, 1419.   [4] *Glossa* Lombardi (PL 191, 1539); *Glossa ordin.* (VI, 34A).

had done so, He would have been Head in chief, the others secondary to Him.

ARTICLE 5. *Whether the Sacraments Can Be Conferred By Evil Ministers?*

We proceed thus to the Fifth Article: It seems that the sacraments cannot be conferred by evil ministers.

Objection 1. For the sacraments of the New Law are ordained for the purpose of cleansing from sin and for the bestowal of grace. Now evil men, being themselves unclean, cannot cleanse others from sin, according to Ecclus. 34. 4: *Who* (Vulg., *What*) *can be made clean by the unclean?* Moreover, since they have not grace, it seems that they cannot give grace, for no one gives what he has not. It seems, therefore, that the sacraments cannot be conferred by wicked men.

Obj. 2. Further, all the power of the sacraments is derived from Christ, as stated above (A. 3; Q. LXII, A. 5). But evil men are cut off from Christ, because they have not charity, by which the members are united to their Head, according to I John 4. 16: *He that abideth in charity, abideth in God, and God in him.* Therefore it seems that the sacraments cannot be conferred by evil men.

Obj. 3. Further, if anything is wanting that is required for the sacraments, the sacrament is invalid; for instance, if the required matter or required form be wanting. But the minister required for a sacrament is one who is without the stain of sin, according to Lev. 21. 17, 18: *Whosoever of thy seed throughout their families, hath a blemish, he shall not offer bread to his God, neither shall he approach to minister to Him.* Therefore it seems that if the minister be wicked, the sacrament has no effect.

On the contrary, Augustine says on John 1. 33: *He upon Whom thou shalt see the Spirit,* etc. (*Tract.* v *in Joann.*),[1] that "John did not know that Our Lord, having the authority of baptizing, would keep it to Himself, but that the ministry would certainly pass to both good and evil men. . . . What is a bad minister to thee, where the Lord is good?"

I answer that, As stated above (A. 1), the ministers of the Church work instrumentally in the sacraments, because, in a way, a minister is of the nature of an instrument. But, as stated above (Q. LXII, AA. 1, 4), an instrument acts not by reason of its own form, or power, but by the power of the one who moves it. Consequently, whatever form or power an instru-

[1] PL 35, 1419.

ment has in addition to that which it has as an instrument, is suitable to it, for instance, that a physician's body, which is the instrument of his soul, in which is his medical art, be healthy or sickly; or that a pipe through which water passes be of silver or lead. Therefore the ministers of the Church can confer the sacraments, even though they be wicked.

Reply Obj. 1. The ministers of the Church do not by their own power cleanse from sin those who approach the sacraments, nor do they confer grace on them; it is Christ Who does this by His own power while He employs them as instruments. Consequently, those who approach the sacraments receive an effect by which they are likened not to the ministers but to Christ.

Reply Obj. 2. Christ's members are united to their Head by charity, so that they may receive life from Him; for as it is written (I John 3. 14): *He that loveth not abideth in death.* Now it is possible for a man to work with a lifeless instrument, and separated from him as to bodily union, provided it be united to him by some sort of motion; for a workman works in one way with his hand, in another with his axe. Consequently, it is thus that Christ works in the sacraments, both by wicked men as lifeless instruments, and by good men as living instruments.

Reply Obj. 3. A thing is required in a sacrament in two ways. First, as being essential to it, and if this be wanting, the sacrament is invalid; for instance, if the due form or matter be wanting. Secondly, a thing is required for a sacrament by reason of a certain fitness. And in this way good ministers are required for a sacrament.

ARTICLE 6. *Whether Wicked Men Sin in Administering the Sacraments?*

We proceed thus to the Sixth Article: It seems that wicked men do not sin in administering the sacraments.

Objection 1. For just as men serve God in the sacraments, so do they serve Him in works of charity; hence it is written (Heb. 13. 16): *Do not forget to do good and to impart, for by such sacrifices God's favour is obtained.* But the wicked do not sin in serving God by works of charity: indeed, they should be persuaded to do so, according to Dan. 4. 24: *Let my counsel be acceptable* to the king; *Redeem thou thy sins with alms.* Therefore it seems that wicked men do not sin in administering the sacraments.

Obj. 2. Further, whoever co-operates with another in his sin is also guilty of sin, according to Rom. 1. 32: *He is* (Vulg., *They are*) *worthy of death; not only he that commits the sin, but also he who consents to them that do them.* But if wicked ministers sin in administering sacraments, those who receive sacraments from them co-operate in their sin. Therefore they would sin also, which seems unreasonable.

Obj. 3. Further, it seems that no one should act when in doubt, for thus man would be driven to despair, as being unable to avoid sin. But if the wicked were to sin in administering sacraments, they would be in a state of perplexity, since sometimes they would sin also if they did not administer sacraments; for instance, when by reason of their office it is their bounden duty to do so, for it is written (I Cor. 9. 16): *For a necessity lieth upon me: Woe is unto me if I preach not the gospel.* Sometimes also on account of some danger; for instance, if a child in danger of death be brought to a sinner for baptism. Therefore it seems that the wicked do not sin in administering the sacraments.

On the contrary, Dionysius says (*Eccl. Hier.* i)[1] that "it is wrong for the wicked even to touch the symbols," that is, the sacramental signs. And he says in the epistle to Demophilus:[2] "It seems presumptuous for such a man," that is, a sinner, "to lay hands on priestly things; he is neither afraid nor ashamed, all unworthy that he is, to take part in Divine things, with the thought that God does not see what he sees in himself: he thinks, by false pretences, to cheat Him Whom he calls his Father; he dares to utter, in the person of Christ, words polluted by his infamy, I will not call them prayers, over the Divine symbols."

I answer that, A sinful action consists in this, that a man fails to act as he ought to, as the Philosopher explains.[3] Now it has been said (A. 5, REPLY 3) that it is fitting for the ministers of sacraments to be just, because ministers should be like their Lord, according to Lev. 19. 2: *Be ye holy, because I . . . am holy,* and Ecclus. 10. 2: *As the judge of the people is himself, so also are his ministers.* Consequently, there can be no doubt that the wicked sin by exercising the ministry of God and the Church, by conferring the sacraments. And

---

[1] Sect. 5 (PG 3, 377).
[2] *Epist.,* VIII, 2 (PG 3, 1093).
[3] *Ethics,* II, 3, 6 (1104ᵇ21; 1106ᵇ20).

since this sin pertains to irreverence towards God and the defiling of holy things, as far as the man who sins is concerned, although holy things in themselves cannot be defiled, it follows that such a sin is mortal in its genus.

Reply Obj. 1. Works of charity are not made holy by some process of consecration, but they pertain to the holiness of justice, as being in a way parts of justice. Consequently, when a man shows himself as a minister of God, by doing works of charity, if he is just, he will be made yet holier; but if he is a sinner, he is thereby disposed to holiness. On the other hand, the sacraments are holy in themselves owing to their mystical consecration. Therefore the holiness of justice is required in the minister, that he may be suitable for his ministry, for which reason he acts unbecomingly and sins if while in a state of sin he attempts to fulfil that ministry.

Reply Obj. 2. He who approaches a sacrament, receives it from a minister of the Church not because he is such and such a man, but because he is a minister of the Church. Consequently, as long as the latter is tolerated in the ministry, he that receives a sacrament from him does not communicate in his sin, but communicates with the Church from whom he has his ministry. But if the Church, by degrading, excommunicating, or suspending him, does not tolerate him in the ministry, he that receives a sacrament from him sins, because he communicates in his sin.

Reply Obj. 3. A man who is in mortal sin is not perplexed absolutely, if by reason of his office it is his duty to minister sacraments, because he can repent of his sin and so minister lawfully. But there is nothing unreasonable in his being perplexed if we suppose that he wishes to remain in sin.

However, in a case of necessity when even a lay person might baptize, he would not sin in baptizing. For it is clear that then he does not exercise the ministry of the Church, but comes to the aid of one who is in need of his services. It is not so with the other sacraments, which are not so necessary as baptism, as we shall show further on (Q. LXV, AA. 3, 4; Q. LXVII, A. 3).

ARTICLE 7. *Whether Angels Can Administer Sacraments?*

We proceed thus to the Seventh Article: It seems that angels can administer sacraments.

Objection 1. Because a higher minister can do whatever the lower can; thus a priest can do whatever a deacon can, but not conversely. But angels are higher ministers in the hierarchical order than any men whatsoever, as Dionysius says (*Cæl. Hier.* ix).[1] Therefore, since men can be ministers of sacraments, it seems that much more can angels be.

Obj. 2. Further, in heaven holy men are likened to the angels (Matt. 22. 30). But some holy men, when in heaven, can be ministers of the sacraments, since the sacramental character is indelible, as stated above (Q. LXIII, A. 5). Therefore it seems that angels too can be ministers of sacraments.

Obj. 3. Further, as stated above (Q. VIII, A. 7), the devil is head of the wicked, and the wicked are his members. But sacraments can be administered by the wicked. Therefore it seems that they can be administered even by demons.

On the contrary, It is written (Heb. 5. 1): *Every high priest taken from among men, is ordained for men in the things that appertain to God.* But angels whether good or bad are not taken from among men. Therefore they are not ordained ministers in the things that pertain to God, that is, in the sacraments.

I answer that, As stated above (A. 3; Q. LXII, A. 5), the whole power of the sacraments flows from Christ's Passion, which belongs to Him as man. And men, not angels, resemble Him in their very nature; indeed, in respect of His Passion, He is described as being *a little lower than the angels* (Heb. 2. 9). Consequently, it belongs to men, but not to angels, to dispense the sacraments and to take part in their administration.

But it must be observed that as God did not bind His power to the sacraments, so as to be unable to bestow the sacramental effect without conferring the sacrament, so neither did He bind His power to the ministers of the Church so as to be unable to give angels power to administer the sacraments. And since good angels are messengers of truth, if any sacramental rite were performed by good angels, it should be considered valid, because it ought to be evident that this is being done by the will of God; for instance, certain churches are said to have been consecrated by the ministry of the angels. But if demons, who are "lying spirits," were to perform a sacramental rite, it should be pronounced as invalid.

Reply Obj. 1. What men do in a less perfect manner, that is, by sensible sacraments, which are proportionate to their nature, angels also

[1] Sect. 2 (PG 3, 260).

do, as ministers of a higher degree, in a more perfect manner, that is, invisibly,—by cleansing, enlightening, and perfecting.

Reply Obj. 2. The saints in heaven resemble the angels as to their share of glory, but not as to the conditions of their nature, and consequently not in regard to the sacraments.

Reply Obj. 3. Wicked men do not owe their power of conferring sacraments to their being through wickedness members of the devil. Consequently, it does not follow that *a fortiori* the devil, their head, can do so.

ARTICLE 8. *Whether the Minister's Intention Is Required for the Validity of a Sacrament?*

We proceed thus to the Eighth Article: It seems that the minister's intention is not required for the validity of a sacrament.

Objection 1. For the minister of a sacrament works instrumentally. But the perfection of an action does not depend on the intention of the instrument but on that of the principal agent. Therefore the minister's intention is not necessary for the perfecting of a sacrament.

Obj. 2. Further, one man's intention cannot be known to another. Therefore if the minister's intention were required for the validity of a sacrament, he who approaches a sacrament could not know whether he has received the sacrament. Consequently he could have no certainty in regard to salvation; the more that some sacraments are necessary for salvation, as we shall state further on (Q. LXV, A. 4).

Obj. 3. Further, a man's intention cannot bear on that to which he does not attend. But sometimes ministers of sacraments do not attend to what they say or do, through thinking of something else. Therefore in this respect the sacrament would be invalid through want of intention.

On the contrary, What is unintentional happens by chance. But this cannot be said of the sacramental operation. Therefore the sacraments require the intention of the minister.

I answer that, When a thing is indifferent to many uses, it must be determined to one if that one has to be effected. Now those things which are done in the sacraments can be done with various intent; for instance, washing with water, which is done in baptism, may be ordered to bodily cleanliness, to the health of the body, to amusement, and many other similar things. Consequently, it needs to be determined to one purpose, that is, the sacramental effect, by the intention of him who washes. And this intention is expressed by the words which are pronounced in the sacraments; for instance the words, *I baptize thee in the name of the Father*, etc.

Reply Obj. 1. An inanimate instrument has no intention regarding the effect, but instead of the intention there is the motion whereby it is moved by the principal agent. But an animate instrument, such as a minister, is not only moved, but in a sense moves itself, in so far as by his will he moves his members to act. Consequently, his intention is required, whereby he subjects himself to the principal agent; that is, it is necessary that he intend to do that which Christ and the Church do.

Reply Obj. 2. On this point there are two opinions. For some[1] hold that the mental intention of the minister is necessary, in the absence of which the sacrament is invalid, and that this defect in the case of children who have not the intention of approaching the sacrament is made good by Christ, Who baptizes inwardly; but in adults, because they have the intention of receiving the sacrament, this defect is made good by their faith and devotion.

This might be true enough of the ultimate effect, that is, justification from sins, but as to that effect which is both real and sacramental, namely, the character, it does not appear possible for it to be made good by the devotion of the recipient, since a character is never imprinted save by a sacrament.

Consequently, others[2] with better reason hold that the minister of a sacrament acts in the person of the whole Church, whose minister he is, while in the words uttered by him, the intention of the Church is expressed, and that this suffices for the validity of the sacrament, unless the contrary be outwardly expressed on the part either of the minister or of the recipient of the sacrament.

Reply Obj. 3. Although he who thinks of something else has no actual intention, yet he has habitual intention, which suffices for the validity of the sacrament; for instance if, when a priest goes to baptize someone, he intends to do to him what the Church does. Therefore if subsequently during the exercise of the act his mind be distracted by other matters, the sacrament is valid in virtue of his original intention. Nevertheless, the minister of a sacrament should take great care to have actual intention. But this is not entirely in man's power,

because when a man wishes to be very intent on something, he begins unintentionally to think of other things, according to Ps. 39. 13: *My heart hath forsaken me.*

ARTICLE 9. *Whether Faith Is Required of Necessity in the Minister of a Sacrament?*

We proceed thus to the Ninth Article: It seems that faith is required of necessity in the minister of a sacrament.

Objection 1. For, as stated above (A. 8), the intention of the minister is necessary for the validity of a sacrament. But "faith directs the intention," as Augustine says against Julian (In *Psalm* 31. 2, *cf. Contra Julian.* iv, 3).[3] Therefore, if the minister is without the true faith, the sacrament is invalid.

Obj. 2. Further, if a minister of the Church has not the true faith, it seems that he is a heretic. But heretics, it seems, cannot confer sacraments. For Cyprian says in an epistle against heretics:[4] "Everything whatsoever heretics do is carnal, void and counterfeit, so that nothing that they do should receive our approval." And Pope Leo says in his epistle to Leo Augustus (clvi):[5] "It is a matter of notoriety that the light of all the heavenly sacraments is extinguished in the see of Alexandria, by an act of dire and senseless cruelty. The sacrifice is no longer offered, the chrism is no longer consecrated, all the mysteries of religion have fled at the touch of the parricide hands of ungodly men." Therefore a sacrament requires of necessity that the minister should have the true faith.

Obj. 3. Further, those who have not the true faith seem to be separated from the Church by excommunication: for it is written in the second canonical epistle of John (10): *If any man come to you, and bring not this doctrine, receive him not into the house, nor say to him: God speed you;* and (Tit. 3. 10): *A man that is a heretic, after the first and second admonition avoid.* But it seems that an excommunicate cannot confer a sacrament of the Church: since he is separated from the Church, to whose ministry the dispensation of the sacraments belongs. Therefore a sacrament requires of necessity that the minister should have the true faith.

On the contrary, Augustine says against the Donatist Petilian:[6] "Remember that the evil

---

[1] Cf. Bonaventure, *In Sent.,* IV, d. VI, pt. II, A. 3, Q. 1, ad 5 (QR IV, 153); Alexander of Hales, *Summa Theol.,* Pt. IV, Q. 13, m. 1, A. 1, ad 4 (IV, 64ra); cf. St. Thomas, *In Sent.,* IV, d. VI, Q. 1, A. 2.

[2] Albert, *In Sent.,* IV, d. VI, A. 12 (BO XXIX, 140).

[3] PL 36, 259; PL 44, 754.

[4] *Epist.,* LXX (PL 3, 1081); cf. PL 4, 421); Conc. of Carthage 1, anno 255 (MA 1, 924).

[5] Chap. 5 (PL 54, 1131).

[6] Bk. II, Chap. 47 (PL 43, 298).

lives of wicked men are not prejudicial to God's sacraments, by rendering them either invalid or less holy."

I answer that, As stated above (A. 5), since the minister works instrumentally in the sacraments, he acts not by his own but by Christ's power. Now just as charity belongs to a man's own power so also does faith. Therefore, just as the validity of a sacrament does not require that the minister should have charity, and even sinners can confer sacraments, as stated above (*ibid.*), so neither is it necessary that he should have faith, and even an unbeliever can confer a true sacrament, provided that the other essentials be there.

Reply Obj. 1. It may happen that a man's faith is defective in regard to something else, and not in regard to the reality of the sacrament which he confers; for instance, he may believe that it is unlawful to swear in any case whatever, and yet he may believe that baptism is an efficient cause of salvation. And thus such unbelief does not hinder the intention of conferring the sacrament. But if his faith is defective in regard to the very sacrament that he confers, although he believes that no inward effect is caused by the thing done outwardly, yet he does know that the Catholic Church intends to confer a sacrament by that which is outwardly done. Therefore, his unbelief notwithstanding, he can intend to do what the Church does, although he esteems it to be nothing. And such an intention suffices for a sacrament, because as stated above (A. 8, Reply 2) the minister of a sacrament acts in the person of the Church by whose faith any defect in the minister's faith is made good.

Reply Obj. 2. Some heretics[1] in conferring sacraments do not observe the form prescribed by the Church, and these confer neither the sacrament nor the reality of the sacrament. But some[2] do observe the form prescribed by the Church, and these confer indeed the sacra-

[1] The Marcosians: Cf. Irenaeus, *Contra Haeres*, I, 21 (PG 7, 657); Epiphanius, *Adv. Haeres*, I, 3, haeres 34 (PG 41, 621); the Sabellians: Cf. Epihanius, *Adv. Haeres.*, II, 1, haeres. 62; the Eunomians: Cf. Gregory of Nyssa, *Contra Eunom.*, XI (PG 45, 881); the Paulinists: Cf. Innocent I, *Epist.*, XVII, chap. 5 (PL 20, 533); the Montanists: Cf. Gregory the Great, *Registrum*, Bk. XI, indict. III, epist. LXVII (PL 77, 1206); for many others, see Gennadius, *De Eccl. Dogm.*, chap. 52 (PL 58, 993). See Pt. III, Q. LXVI, A. 9, reply 3.
[2] The Arians: Cf. Athanasius, *Contra Arianos*, orat. 1 (PG 26, 236); Ambrose, *De Spir. Sancto*, I, 3 (PL 16, 337); the Novatians: Cf. Innocent I, *Epist.*, XVII, chap. 5 (PL 20, 533); the Monophysites and Nestorians: Cf. Gregory the Great, *Registrum*, Bk. XI, indict. IV, epist. LXVII (PL 77, 1206, 1207).

ment but not the reality. I say this if they are clearly cut off from the Church, because from the very fact that anyone receives the sacraments from them, he sins, and consequently is hindered from receiving the effect of the sacrament. Therefore Augustine (Fulgentius,—*De Fide ad Pet.*)[3] says: "Be well assured and have no doubt whatever that those who are baptized outside the Church, unless they come back to the Church, will reap disaster from their Baptism." In this sense Pope Leo says[4] that "the light of the sacraments was extinguished in the See of Alexandria"; namely, in regard to the reality of the sacrament, not as to the sacrament itself.

Cyprian, however, thought that heretics do not confer even the sacrament, but in this respect we do not follow his opinion. Hence Augustine says (*De unico Baptismo*, xiii):[5] "Though the martyr Cyprian refused to recognize Baptism conferred by heretics or schismatics, yet so great are his merits, culminating in the crown of martyrdom, that the light of his charity dispels the darkness of his fault, and if anything needed pruning, the sickle of his suffering cut it off."

Reply Obj. 3. The power of administering the sacraments belongs to the spiritual character which is indelible, as explained above (Q. LXIII, A. 3). Consequently, if a man be suspended by the Church, or excommunicated or degraded, he does not lose the power of conferring sacraments, but the permission to use this power. Therefore he does indeed confer the sacrament, but he sins in so doing. He also sins that receives a sacrament from such a man, so that he does not receive the reality of the sacrament, unless ignorance excuses him.

ARTICLE 10. *Whether the Validity of a Sacrament Requires a Good Intention in the Minister?*

We proceed thus to the Tenth Article: It seems that the validity of a sacrament requires a good intention in the minister.

Objection 1. For the minister's intention should be in conformity with the Church's intention, as explained above (A. 8, Reply 1). But the intention of the Church is always good. Therefore the validity of a sacrament requires of necessity a good intention in the minister.

Obj. 2. Further, a perverse intention seems worse than a playful one. But a playful inten-

[3] Fulgentius, 36 (PL 65, 703).
[4] *Epist.* CLVI, 5 (PL 54, 1131).   [5] PL 43, 606.

tion destroys a sacrament; for instance, if someone were to baptize anybody not seriously but in fun. Much more, therefore, does a perverse intention destroy a sacrament; for instance, if somebody were to baptize a man in order to kill him afterwards.

Obj. 3. Further, a perverse intention vitiates the whole work, according to Luke 11. 34: *If thy eye be evil, thy whole body will be darksome.* But the sacraments of Christ cannot be contaminated by evil men, as Augustine says against Petilian (*Cont. Litt. Petil.* ii, 39).[1] Therefore it seems that, if the minister's intention is perverse, the sacrament is invalid.

On the contrary, A perverse intention belongs to the wickedness of the minister. But the wickedness of the minister does not annul the sacrament; neither, therefore, does his perverse intention.

I answer that, The minister's intention may be perverted in two ways. First in regard to the sacrament; for instance, when a man does not intend to confer a sacrament, but to make a mockery of it. Such a perverse intention takes away the truth of the sacrament, especially if it be manifested outwardly.

Secondly, the minister's intention may be perverted as to something that follows the sacrament; for instance, a priest may intend to baptize a woman so as to be able to abuse her, or to consecrate the Body of Christ, so as to use it for sorcery. And because that which comes first does not depend on that which follows, consequently such a perverse intention does not annul the sacrament; but the minister himself sins grievously in having such an intention.

Reply Obj. 1. The Church has a good intention both as to the validity of the sacrament and as to its use, but it is the former intention that perfects the sacrament, while the latter conduces to the meritorious effect. Consequently, the minister who conforms his intention to the Church as to the former rectitude, but not as to the latter, perfects the sacrament indeed, but gains no merit for himself.

Reply Obj. 2. The intention of mimicry or fun excludes the first kind of right intention necessary for the validity of a sacrament. Consequently, there is no comparison.

Reply Obj. 3. A perverse intention perverts the action of the one who has such an intention, not the action of another. Consequently, the perverse intention of the minister perverts the sacrament in so far as it is his action, not in so

far as it is the action of Christ, Whose minister he is. It is just as if the servant of some man were to carry alms to the poor with a wicked intention, although his master had commanded him with a good intention to do so.

QUESTION LXV

OF THE NUMBER OF THE SACRAMENTS

(*In Four Articles*)

WE have now to consider the number of the sacraments, and concerning this there are four points of inquiry: (1) Whether there are seven sacraments? (2) The order of the sacraments among themselves. (3) Their mutual comparison. (4) Whether all the sacraments are necessary for salvation?

ARTICLE 1. *Whether There Should Be Seven Sacraments of the Church?*

We proceed thus to the First Article: It seems that there ought not to be seven sacraments.

Objection 1. For the sacraments derive their efficacy from the Divine power and the power of Christ's Passion. But the Divine power is one, and Christ's Passion is one, since *by one oblation He hath perfected for ever them that are sanctified* (Heb. 10. 14). Therefore there should be but one sacrament.

Obj. 2. Further, a sacrament is intended as a remedy for the defect caused by sin. Now this is twofold, punishment and guilt. Therefore two sacraments would be enough.

Obj. 3. Further, sacraments belong to the actions of the ecclesiastical hierarchy, as Dionysius explains (*Eccl. Hier.* v).[2] But, as he says, there are three actions of the ecclesiastical hierarchy, namely, "to cleanse, to enlighten, to perfect." Therefore there should be no more than three sacraments.

Obj. 4. Further, Augustine says (*Contra Faust.* xix, 13)[3] that the sacraments of the New Law are "less numerous" than those of the Old Law. But in the Old Law there was no sacrament corresponding to Confirmation and Extreme Unction. Therefore these should not be counted among the sacraments of the New Law.

Obj. 5. Further, lust is not more grievous than other sins, as we have made clear in the Second Part (I-II, Q. LXXIV, A. 5; II-II, Q. CLIV, A. 3). But there is no sacrament instituted as a remedy for other sins. Therefore neither should matrimony be instituted as a remedy for lust.

[1] PL 43, 293.

[2] Sect. 2 (PG 3, 501).   [3] PL 42, 355.

Obj. 6. *On the other hand,* It seems that there are more than seven sacraments. For sacraments are a kind of sacred sign. But in the Church there are many sanctifications by sensible signs, such as Holy Water, the Consecration of Altars, and the like. Therefore there are more than seven sacraments.

Obj. 7. Further, Hugh of S. Victor (*De Sacram.* i)[1] says that the sacraments of the Old Law were oblations, tithes and sacrifices. But the Sacrifice of the Church is one sacrament, called the Eucharist. Therefore oblations also and tithes should be called sacraments.

Obj. 8. Further, there are three kinds of sin, original, mortal and venial. Now Baptism is intended as a remedy against original sin, and Penance against mortal sin. Therefore besides the seven sacraments, there should be another against venial sin.

I answer that, As stated above (Q. LXII, A. 5; Q. LXIII, A. 1), the sacraments of the Church were instituted for a twofold purpose: namely, in order to perfect man in things pertaining to the worship of God according to the religion of Christian life, and to be a remedy against the defects caused by sin. And in either way it is fitting that there should be seven sacraments.

For spiritual life has a certain conformity with the life of the body, just as other corporeal things have a certain likeness to things spiritual. Now a man attains perfection in the corporeal life in two ways: first, in regard to his own person; secondly, in regard to the whole community of the society in which he lives, for man is naturally a social animal. With regard to himself man is perfected in the life of the body, in two ways; first, through himself (*per se*), that is, by acquiring some vital perfection; secondly, accidentally (*per accidens*), that is, by the removal of hindrances to life, such as ailments, or the like. Now the life of the body is perfected *per se*, in three ways. First, by generation, whereby a man begins to be and to live; and corresponding to this in the spiritual life there is Baptism, which is a spiritual regeneration, according to Tit. 3. 5: *By the laver of regeneration,* etc. Secondly, by growth, whereby a man is brought to perfect size and strength; and corresponding to this in the spiritual life there is Confirmation, in which the Holy Ghost is given to strengthen us. Therefore the disciples who were already baptized were bidden thus: *Stay you in the city till you be endued with power from on high* (Luke 24. 49). Thirdly, by nourishment, whereby life

and strength are preserved to man; and corresponding to this in the spiritual life there is the Eucharist. Therefore it is said (John 6. 54): *Except you eat of the flesh of the Son of Man, and drink His blood, you shall not have life in you.*

And this would be enough for man if he had an impassible life, both corporally and spiritually; but since man is liable at times to both corporal and spiritual infirmity, that is, sin, hence man needs a cure from his infirmity. This cure is twofold. One is the healing, that restores health, and corresponding to this in the spiritual life there is Penance, according to Ps. 40. 5: *Heal my soul, for I have sinned against Thee.* The other is the restoration of former vigour by means of suitable diet and exercise; and corresponding to this in the spiritual life there is Extreme Unction, which removes the remainders of sin, and prepares man for final glory. Therefore it is written (Jas. 5. 15): *And if he be in sins they shall be forgiven him.*

In regard to the whole community, man is perfected in two ways. First, by receiving power to rule the community and to exercise public acts; and corresponding to this in the spiritual life there is the sacrament of Order, according to the saying of Heb. 7. 27, that priests offer sacrifices not for themselves only, but also for the people. Secondly in regard to natural propagation. This is accomplished by Matrimony both in the corporal and in the spiritual life, since it is not only a sacrament but also a function of nature.

We may likewise gather the number of the sacraments from their being instituted as a remedy against the defect caused by sin. For Baptism is intended as a remedy against the lack of spiritual life; Confirmation, against the infirmity of soul found in those of recent birth; the Eucharist, against the soul's proneness to sin; Penance, against actual sin committed after baptism; Extreme Unction against the remainders of sins,—of those sins, namely, which are not sufficiently removed by Penance, whether through negligence or through ignorance; Order, against divisions in the community; Matrimony, as a remedy against concupiscence in the individual, and against the decrease in numbers that results from death.

Some,[2] again, gather the number of sacra-

---

[1] Part XI, chap. 2 (PL 176, 344); XII, 4 (PL 176, 351).

[2] Alexander of Hales, *Summa Theol.,* IV, Q. 8, m. 7, A. 2 (IV, 52rb); Bonaventure, *In Sent.,* IV, d. II, A. 3, Q. 3 (QR IV, 53); Albert, *In Sent.,* IV, d. II, A. 1 (BO XXIX, 43); See Hugh of St. Victor, *De Sacram.,* I, IX, 3 (PL 176, 320).

ments from a certain adaptation to the virtues and to the defects and penal effects resulting from sin. They say that Baptism corresponds to Faith, and is ordained as a remedy against original sin; Extreme Unction, to Hope, being ordained against venial sin; the Eucharist, to Charity, being ordained against the penal effect of malice; Order, to Prudence, being ordained against ignorance; Penance, to Justice, bring ordained against mortal sin; Matrimony, to Temperance, being ordained against concupiscence; Confirmation, to Fortitude, being ordained against infirmity.

Reply Obj. 1. The same principal agent uses various instruments for various effects, in accordance with the thing to be done. In the same way the Divine power and the Passion of Christ work in us through the various sacraments as through various instruments.

Reply Obj. 2. Guilt and punishment are diversified both according to species, since there are various species of guilt and punishment, and according to men's various states and dispositions. And in this respect it was necessary to have a number of sacraments, as explained above.

Reply Obj. 3. In hierarchical actions we must consider the agents, the recipients and the actions. The agents are the ministers of the Church, and to these the sacrament of Order belongs. The recipients are those who approach the sacraments, and these are brought into being by Matrimony. The actions are cleansing, enlightening, and perfecting. Mere cleansing, however, cannot be a sacrament of the New Law, which confers grace; yet it belongs to certain sacramentals, that is, catechism and exorcism. But cleansing coupled with enlightening, according to Dionysius,[1] belongs to Baptism; and, for him who falls back into sin, they belong secondarily to Penance and Extreme Unction. And perfecting, as regards power, which is, as it were, a formal perfection, belongs to Confirmation, while, as regards the attainment of the end, it belongs to the Eucharist.

Reply Obj. 4. In the sacrament of Confirmation we receive the fulness of the Holy Ghost in order to be strengthened, while in Extreme Unction man is prepared for the immediate attainment of glory; and neither of these two purposes was appropriate to the Old Testament. Consequently, nothing in the Old Law could correspond to these sacraments. Nevertheless, the sacraments of the Old Law were more numerous on account of the various kinds of sacrifices and ceremonies.

[1] *Eccl. Hier.*, V, 3 (PG 3, 504).

Reply Obj. 5. There was need for a special sacrament to be applied as a remedy against the concupiscence of sex: first because by this concupiscence not only the person but also the nature is defiled; secondly, by reason of its vehemence which clouds the reason.

Reply Obj. 6. Holy Water and other consecrated things are not called sacraments because they do not produce the sacramental effect, which is the receiving of grace. They are, however, a kind of disposition to the sacraments: either by removing obstacles, as for example Holy Water is ordained against the snares of the demons, and against venial sins; or by making things suitable for the perfection and conferring of a sacrament, as for example the altar and vessels are consecrated through reverence for the Eucharist.

Reply Obj. 7. Oblations and tithes, both in the Law of nature and in the Law of Moses, were ordained not only for the sustenance of the ministers and the poor, but also figuratively; and consequently they were sacraments. But now they remain no longer as figures, and therefore they are not sacraments.

Reply Obj. 8. The infusion of grace is not necessary for the blotting out of venial sin. Therefore, since grace is infused in each of the sacraments of the New Law, none of them was instituted directly against venial sin. This is taken away by certain sacramentals, for instance, Holy Water and the like.—Some,[2] however, hold that Extreme Unction is ordained against venial sin. But of this we shall speak in its proper place (Suppl. XXX, A. 1).

ARTICLE 2. *Whether the Order of the Sacraments, As Given Above, Is Becoming?*

We proceed thus to the Second Article: It seems that the order of the sacraments as given above (A. 1) is unbecoming.

Objection 1. For according to the Apostle (I Cor. 15. 46), *that was . . . first . . . which is natural, afterwards that which is spiritual.* But man is begotten through Matrimony by a first and natural generation, while in Baptism he is regenerated as by a second and spiritual generation. Therefore Matrimony should precede Baptism.

Obj. 2. Further, through the sacrament of Order man receives the power of performing sacramental actions. But the agent precedes his action. Therefore Order should precede

[2] Alexander of Hales, *Summa Theol.*, IV, Q. 8, m. 7, A. 2 (IV, 52rb); Bonaventure, *In Sent.*, IV, d. 11, A. 1, Q. 3 (QR IV, 53).

Baptism and the other sacraments.

Obj. 3. Further, the Eucharist is a spiritual food, while Confirmation is compared to growth. But food causes, and consequently precedes, growth. Therefore the Eucharist precedes Confirmation.

Obj. 4. Further, Penance prepares man for the Eucharist. But a disposition precedes perfection. Therefore Penance should precede the Eucharist.

Obj. 5. Further, that which is nearer the last end comes after other things. But, of all the sacraments, Extreme Unction is nearest to the last end, which is Happiness. Therefore it should be placed last among the sacraments.

On the contrary, The order of the sacraments, as given above (A. 1), is commonly adopted by all.

I answer that, The reason of the order among the sacraments appears from what has been said above (A. 1). For just as unity precedes multitude, so those sacraments which are intended for the perfection of the individual, naturally precede those which are intended for the perfection of the multitude; and consequently the last place among the sacraments is given to Order and Matrimony, which are intended for the perfection of the multitude, while Matrimony is placed after Order, because it has less participation in the nature of the spiritual life, to which the sacraments are ordered. Moreover, among things ordered to the perfection of the individual those naturally come first which are ordered directly (*per se*) to the perfection of the spiritual life, and afterwards, those which are ordered to it indirectly (*per accidens*), namely, by removing some supervening accidental cause of harm; such are Penance and Extreme Unction, while of these Extreme Unction is naturally placed last, for it preserves the healing which was begun by Penance.

Of the remaining three, it is clear that Baptism which is a spiritual regeneration, comes first; then Confirmation, which is ordered to the formal perfection of power; and after these the Eucharist which is ordered to final perfection.

Reply Obj. 1. Matrimony according as it is ordered to animal life, is a function of nature. But in so far as it has something spiritual it is a sacrament. And because it has the least amount of spirituality it is placed last.

Reply Obj. 2. For a thing to be an agent it must first of all be perfect in itself. Therefore those sacraments by which a man is perfected in himself are placed before the sacrament of Order, in which a man is made a perfecter of others.

Reply Obj. 3. Nourishment both precedes growth, as its cause, and follows it, as maintaining the perfection of size and power in man. Consequently, the Eucharist can be placed before Confirmation, as Dionysius places it (*Eccl. Hier.* iii, iv),[1] and can be placed after it, as the Master does.[2]

Reply Obj. 4. This argument would hold if Penance were required of necessity as a preparation to the Eucharist. But this is not true, for if anyone is without mortal sin he does not need Penance in order to receive the Eucharist. Thus it is clear that Penance is an accidental preparation to the Eucharist, that is to say, sin being supposed. Therefore it is written in the last chapter of the second Book of Paralipomenon (*cf.* 2 Paral. 33. 18):[3] "Thou, O Lord of the just, didst not impose penance on just men."

Reply Obj. 5. Extreme Unction, for this very reason, is given the last place among those sacraments which are ordained to the perfection of the individual.

ARTICLE 3. *Whether the Eucharist Is the Greatest of the Sacraments?*

We proceed thus to the Third Article: It seems that the Eucharist is not the greatest of the sacraments.

Objection 1. For the common good is of more account than the good of the individual.[4] But Matrimony is ordered to the common good of the human race by means of generation, whereas the sacrament of the Eucharist is ordered to the private good of the recipient. Therefore it is not the greatest of the sacraments.

Obj. 2. Further, it seems that those sacraments are greater which are conferred by a greater minister. But the sacraments of Confirmation and Order are conferred by a bishop only, who is a greater minister than a simple priest, by whom the sacrament of the Eucharist is conferred. Therefore those sacraments are greater.

Obj. 3. Further, those sacraments are greater that have the greater power. But some of the sacraments imprint a character—namely, Baptism, Confirmation and Order whereas the Eu-

---

[1] PG 3, 424; 472.

[2] *Sent.*, IV, dist. VIII, chap. 1 (QR II, 787).

[3] The words quoted are from the apocryphal Prayer of Manasses, which, before the Council of Trent, was to be found inserted in some Latin copies of the Bible.

[4] Aristotle, *Ethics*, I, 2 (1094b8).

charist does not. Therefore those sacraments are greater.

Obj. 4. Further, that seems to be greater on which others depend without its depending on them. But the Eucharist depends on Baptism, since no one can receive the Eucharist except he has been baptized. Therefore Baptism is greater than the Eucharist.

On the contrary, Dionysius says (*Eccl. Hier.* iii, 1)[1] that "No one receives hierarchical perfection save by the most Godlike Eucharist." Therefore this sacrament is greater than all the others and perfects them.

I answer that, Absolutely speaking, the sacrament of the Eucharist is the greatest of all the sacraments, and this may be shown in three ways. First, from what is contained in the sacrament, for in the sacrament of the Eucharist Christ Himself is contained substantially, whereas the other sacraments contain a certain instrumental power which is a share of Christ's power, as we have shown above (Q. LXII, A. 4 REPLY 3, A. 5). Now, that which is essentially such is always of more account than that which is such by participation.

Secondly, this is made clear by considering the relation of the sacraments to one another. For all the other sacraments seem to be ordered to this one as to their end. For it is manifest that the sacrament of Order is ordered to the consecration of the Eucharist, and the sacrament of Baptism to the reception of the Eucharist, while a man is perfected by Confirmation, so as not to fear to abstain from this sacrament. By Penance and Extreme Unction man is prepared to receive the Body of Christ worthily. And Matrimony, at least in its signification, touches this sacrament, in so far as it signifies the union of Christ with the Church, of which union the Eucharist is a figure; hence the Apostle says (Eph. 5. 32): *This is a great sacrament: but I speak in Christ and in the Church.*

Thirdly, this is made clear by considering the rites of the sacraments. For nearly all the sacraments terminate in the Eucharist, as Dionysius says (*Eccl. Hier.* iii, 1);[2] thus those who have been ordained receive Holy Communion, as also do those who have been baptized, if they be adults.

The remaining sacraments may be compared to one another in several ways. For on the ground of necessity, Baptism is the greatest of the sacraments, while from the point of view of perfection, Order comes first, and Confirma-

tion holds a middle place. The sacraments of Penance and Extreme Unction are on a degree inferior to those mentioned above, because, as stated above (A. 2), they are ordered to the Christian life, not directly (*per se*), but accidentally, as it were, that is to say, as remedies against supervening defects. And among these, Extreme Unction is compared to Penance, as Confirmation to Baptism, in such a way that Penance is more necessary, whereas Extreme Unction is more perfect.

Reply Obj. 1. Matrimony is ordered to the common good as regards the body. But the common spiritual good of the whole Church is contained substantially in the sacrament itself of the Eucharist.

Reply Obj. 2. By Order and Confirmation the faithful of Christ are alloted to certain special duties, and this can be done by the prince alone. Consequently the conferring of these sacraments belongs exclusively to a bishop, who is, as it were, a prince in the Church. But a man is not alloted to any duty by the sacrament of the Eucharist; rather is this sacrament the end of all duties, as stated above.

Reply Obj. 3. The sacramental character, as stated above (Q. LXIII, A. 3), is a kind of participation in Christ's priesthood. Therefore the sacrament that unites man to Christ Himself is greater than a sacrament that imprints Christ's character.

Reply Obj. 4. This argument holds good on the ground of necessity. For thus Baptism, being of the greatest necessity, is the greatest of the sacraments, just as Order and Confirmation have a certain excellence considered in their administration, and Matrimony by reason of its signification. For there is no reason why a thing should not be greater from a certain point of view which is not greater absolutely speaking.

ARTICLE 4. *Whether All the Sacraments Are Necessary for Salvation?*

We proceed thus to the Fourth Article: It seems that all the sacraments are necessary for salvation.

Objection 1. For what is not necessary seems to be superfluous. But no sacrament is superfluous, because God does nothing without a purpose. Therefore all the sacraments are necessary for salvation.

Obj. 2. Further, just as it is said of Baptism (John 3. 5): *Unless a man be born again of water and the Holy Ghost, he cannot enter into the kingdom of God,* so of the Eucharist is it

---

[1] PG 3, 425. [2] PG 3, 424.

said (John 6. 54): *Except you eat of the flesh of the Son of Man, and drink of His blood, you shall not have life in you.* Therefore, just as Baptism is a necessary sacrament, so is the Eucharist.

Obj. 3. Further, a man can be saved without the sacrament of Baptism, provided that some unavoidable obstacle, and not his contempt for religion, debar him from the sacrament, as we shall state further on (Q. LXVIII, A. 2). But contempt of religion in any sacrament is a hindrance to salvation. Therefore, in like manner, all the sacraments are necessary for salvation.

On the contrary, Children are saved by Baptism alone without the other sacraments.

I answer that, Necessity with respect to end, of which we speak now, is twofold. First, a thing may be necessary so that without it the end cannot be attained; thus food is necessary for human life. And this is absolute necessity with respect to end. Secondly, a thing is said to be necessary, if, without it, the end cannot be attained so suitably; thus a horse is necessary for a journey. But this is not absolute necessity with respect to end.

In the first way, three sacraments are necessary for salvation. Two of them are necessary to the individual: Baptism, simply and absolutely; Penance, in the case of mortal sin committed after Baptism. But the sacrament of Order is necessary to the Church, since *where there is no governor the people shall fall* (Prov. 11. 14).

But in the second way the other sacraments are necessary. For in a sense Confirmation perfects Baptism, Extreme Unction perfects Penance, while Matrimony, by multiplying them, preserves the numbers in the Church.

Reply Obj. 1. For a thing not to be superfluous it is enough if it be necessary either in the first or the second way. It is thus that the sacraments are necessary, as stated above.

Reply Obj. 2. These words of Our Lord are to be understood of spiritual, and not of merely sacramental, eating, as Augustine explains.[1]

Reply Obj. 3. Although contempt of any of the sacraments is a hindrance to salvation, yet it does not amount to contempt of the sacrament if anyone does not trouble to receive a sacrament that is not necessary for salvation. Otherwise those who do not receive Orders, and those who do not contract Matrimony, would be guilty of contempt of those sacraments.

[1] *Tract.*, XXVI, *super Joann.* (PL 35, 1614).

Supplement to the Third Part

TREATISE ON THE RESURRECTION

I. BEFORE THE RESURRECTION

OF MATTERS CONCERNING THE
RESURRECTION, AND FIRST, OF THE
PLACE WHERE SOULS ARE AFTER DEATH

(In Seven Articles)

IN sequence to the foregoing we must treat of matters concerning the state of resurrection. For after speaking of the sacraments whereby man is delivered from the death of sin, we must next speak of the resurrection whereby man is delivered from death of punishment. The treatise on the resurrection offers a three-fold consideration, namely the things that precede, those that accompany, and those that follow the resurrection. Consequently we must speak (1) of those things which partly, though not wholly, precede the resurrection; (2) of the resurrection itself and its circumstances (Q. LXXV); (3) of the things which follow it (Q. LXXXVII).

Among the things which precede the resurrection we must consider (1) the places appointed for the reception of bodies after death; (2) the quality of separated souls, and the punishment inflicted on them by fire (Q. LXX); (3) the intercessary prayers (*suffragia*) whereby the souls of the departed are assisted by the living (Q. LXXI); (4) the prayers of the saints in heaven (Q. LXXII); (5) the signs preceding the general judgment (Q. LXXIII); (6) the fire of the world's final conflagration which will precede the appearance of the Judge (Q. LXXIV).

Under the first head there are seven points of inquiry: (1) Whether any places are appointed to receive souls after death? (2) Whether souls are conveyed there immediately after death? (3) Whether they are able to leave those places? (4) Whether the limbo of hell is the same as Abraham's bosom? (5) Whether limbo is the same as the hell of the damned? (6) Whether the limbo of the patri-

archs is the same as the limbo of children? (7) Whether so many places should be distinguished?

ARTICLE 1. *Whether Places Are Appointed
To Receive Souls After Death?*

We proceed thus to the First Article: It would seem that places are not appointed to receive souls after death.

Objection 1. For as Boëthius says (*De Hebdom.*):[1] "Wise men are agreed that incorporeal things are not in a place," and this agrees with the words of Augustine (*Gen. ad Lit.* xii, 32):[2] "We can answer without hesitation that the soul is not conveyed to corporeal places, except with a body, or that it is not conveyed locally." Now the soul separated from the body is without a body, as Augustine also says (*ibid.*). Therefore it is absurd to assign any places for the reception of souls.

Obj. 2. Further, Whatever has a definite place has more in common with that place than with any other. Now separated souls, like certain other spiritual substances, are indifferent to all places; for it cannot be said that they agree with certain bodies and differ from others, since they are utterly removed from all corporeal conditions. Therefore places should not be assigned for their reception.

Obj. 3. Further, Nothing is assigned to separated souls after death except what conduces to their punishment or to their reward. But a corporeal place cannot conduce to their punishment or reward, since they receive nothing from bodies. Therefore definite places should not be assigned to receive them.

On the contrary, The empyrean heaven is a corporeal place, and yet "as soon as it was made it was filled with the holy angels," as Bede says.[3] Since then angels even as separated souls are incorporeal, it would seem that some

[1] PL 64, 1311.   [2] PL 34, 480.
[3] *Hexaëm.*, I, on Gen. 1. 2 (PL 91, 14); cf. *Glossa ordin.* on Gen. 1. 1 (I, 23F).

place should also be assigned to receive separated souls.

Further, this appears from Gregory's statement (*Dial.* iv)[1] that souls after death are conveyed to various corporeal places, as in the case of Paschasius whom Germanus, Bishop of Capua, found at the baths, and of the soul of King Theodoric, which he asserts to have been conveyed to hell.[2] Therefore after death souls have certain places for their reception.

I answer that, Although spiritual substances do not depend on a body in respect of their being, nevertheless the corporeal world is governed by God by means of the spiritual world, as asserted by Augustine (*De Trin.* iii, 4)[3] and Gregory (*Dial.* iv, 6).[4] Hence it is that there is a certain fittingness by way of congruity of spiritual substances to corporeal substances, in that the more noble bodies are adapted to the more noble substances; hence also the philosophers held that the order of separate substances is according to the order of movables.[5] And though after death souls have no bodies assigned to them of which they are the forms or determinate movers, nevertheless certain corporeal places are appointed to them by way of congruity in reference to their degree of nobility (wherein they are as though in a place, after the manner in which incorporeal things can be in a place), according as they more or less approach to the first substance (to which the highest place is fittingly assigned), namely God, whose throne the Scriptures proclaim heaven to be (Isa. 66. 1; Acts 7. 49). Therefore we hold that those souls that have a perfect share of the Godhead are in heaven, and that those souls that are deprived of that share are assigned to a contrary place.

Reply Obj. 1. Incorporeal things are not in place after a manner known and familiar to us, in which way we say that bodies are properly in place, but they are in place after a manner befitting spiritual substances, a manner that cannot be fully manifest to us.

Reply Obj. 2. Things have something in common with or a likeness to one another in two ways. First, by sharing a same quality; thus hot things have something in common. And incorporeal things can have nothing in common with corporeal things in this way. Secondly, by a kind of proportionality, by reason of which the Scriptures apply the corporeal world to the spiritual metaphorically. Thus the Scriptures speak of God as the sun (Wisd. 5. 6; Isa. 60. 19) because He is the principle of spiritual life just as the sun is of corporeal life. In this way certain souls have more in common with certain places; for instance, souls that are spiritually enlightened, with luminous bodies, and souls that are plunged in darkness by sin, with dark places.

Reply Obj. 3. The separated soul receives nothing directly from corporeal places in the same way as bodies which are maintained by their respective places, yet these same souls, through knowing themselves to be appointed to such places, gather joy or sorrow from this; and thus their place conduces to their punishment or reward.

ARTICLE 2. *Whether Souls Are Conveyed to Heaven or Hell Immediately After Death?*

We proceed thus to the Second Article: It would seem that no souls are conveyed to heaven or hell immediately after death.

Objection 1. For a gloss on Ps. 36. 10, *Yet a little while and the wicked shall not be,* says[6] that "the saints are delivered at the end of life; yet after this life they will not yet be where the saints will be when it is said to them: Come ye blessed of My Father." Now those saints will be in heaven. Therefore after this life the saints do not go immediately up to heaven.

Obj. 2. Further, Augustine says (*Enchir.* cix)[7] that "the time which lies between man's death and the final resurrection holds the souls in secret receptacles according as each one is worthy of rest or of suffering." Now these secret abodes cannot denote heaven and hell, since also after the final resurrection the souls will be there together with their bodies, so that he would have no reason to distinguish between the time before and the time after the resurrection. Therefore they will be neither in hell nor in heaven until the day of judgment.

Obj. 3. Further, the glory of the soul is greater than that of bodies. Now the glory of the body is awarded to all at the same time, so that each one may have the greater joy in the common rejoicing of all, as appears from a gloss on Heb. 11. 40, *God providing some better thing for us* —"that the common joy may make each one rejoice the more."[8] Much more, therefore, ought

[1] Chaps. 25, 28, 29 (PL 77, 357, 365, 368).
[2] Cf. Gregory the Great, *Dial.,* IV, 30, 40 (PL 77, 369, 397). [3] PL 42, 873. [4] PL 77, 328.
[5] Cf. Aristotle, *Metaphysics,* XII, 8 (1073ᵃ36).

[6] *Glossa* Lombardi (PL 191, 370); cf. Augustine, *Enarr. in Ps.* (PL 36, 361).
[7] PL 40, 283.
[8] *Glossa interl.* (VI, 157v); *Glossa* Lombardi (PL 192, 500).

the glory of souls to be deferred until the end, so as to be awarded to all at the same time.

Obj. 4. Further, Punishment and reward, being pronounced by the sentence of the judge, should not precede the judgment. Now hell fire and the joys of heaven will be awarded to all by the sentence of Christ judging them, namely at the last judgment, according to Matt. 25. Therefore no one will go up to heaven or down to hell before the day of judgment.

On the contrary, It is written (II Cor. 5. 1): *If our earthly house of this habitation be dissolved, that we have . . . a house not made with hands, but reserved in heaven* (Vulg.,—*eternal in heaven.* Cf. I Pet. 1. 4). Therefore, after the body's dissolution, the soul has an abode, which had been reserved for it in heaven.

Further, the Apostle says (Philip. 1. 23): *I desire* (Vulg.,—*Having a desire*) *to be dissolved and to be with Christ.* From these words Gregory argues as follows (*Dial.* iv, 25):[1] "If there is no doubt that Christ is in heaven, it cannot be denied that Paul's soul is in heaven likewise." Now it cannot be denied that Christ is in heaven, since this is an article of faith.[2] Therefore neither is it to be doubted that the souls of the saints are borne to heaven. That also some souls go down to hell immediately after death is evident from Luke 16. 22, *And the rich man died, and he was buried in hell.*

I answer that, Even as in bodies there is heaviness or lightness whereby they are borne to their own place which is the end of their movement, so in the souls there is merit or demerit whereby they reach their reward or punishment, which are the ends of their deeds. Therefore just as a body is conveyed at once to its place, by its heaviness or lightness, unless there is an obstacle, so too the soul, the bonds of the flesh being broken, by which it was detained in the state of the wayfarer, receives at once its reward or punishment, unless there is an obstacle. Thus sometimes venial sin, though needing first of all to be cleansed, is an obstacle to the receiving of the reward, the result being that the reward is delayed. And since a place is assigned to souls in keeping with their reward or punishment, as soon as the soul is set free from the body it is either plunged into hell or soars to heaven, unless it be held back by some debt, for which its flight must be delayed until the soul is first of all cleansed. This truth is attested by the manifest authority of the canonical Scriptures and the doctrine of the holy Fathers; therefore the contrary must be judged

heretical as stated in *Dial.* iv[3] and in *De Eccl. Dogm.*[4]

Reply Obj. 1. The gloss explains itself, for it expounds the words, *They will not yet be where the saints will be,* etc., by saying immediately afterwards: "That is to say, they will not have the double stole which the saints will have at the resurrection."

Reply Obj. 2. Among the secret abodes of which Augustine speaks, we must also put hell and heaven, where some souls are detained before the resurrection. The reason why a distinction is drawn between the time before and the time after the resurrection is because before the resurrection they are there without the body while afterwards they are with the body, and because in certain places there are souls now which will not be there after the resurrection.

Reply Obj. 3. There is a kind of continuity among men as regards the body, because in this respect is verified the saying of Acts 17. 24, 26, *God . . . hath made of one all mankind.* But He has fashioned souls independently of one another. Consequently it is not so fitting that all men should be glorified together in the soul as that they should be glorified together in the body.

Moreover the glory of the body is not so essential as the glory of the soul. Therefore it would be more derogatory to the saints if the glory of the soul were delayed than that the glory of the body be deferred; nor could this detriment to their glory be compensated on account of the joy of each one being increased by the common joy.

Reply Obj. 4. Gregory proposes and solves this very difficulty (*Dial.* iv, 25):[5] "If then," he says, "the souls of the just are in heaven now, what will they receive in reward for their justice on the judgment day?" And he answers: "Surely it will be a gain to them at the judgment, that whereas now they enjoy only the happiness of the soul, afterwards they will enjoy also that of the body, so as to rejoice also in the flesh wherein they bore sorrow and torments for the Lord." The same is to be said in reference to the damned.

ARTICLE 3. *Whether the Souls Who Are in Heaven or Hell Are Able To Leave Those Places?*

We proceed thus to the Third Article: It would seem that the souls in heaven or hell are unable to leave those places.

---

[1] PL 77, 357.   [2] Cf. Apostles Creed (DZ 6).

[3] Chap. 25, 28 (PL 77, 356, 365).
[4] Gennadius, chap. 79 (PL 58, 998).   [5] PL 77, 357.

Objection 1. For Augustine says (*De Cura pro Mort.* xiii):[1] "If the souls of the dead took any part in the affairs of the living, to say nothing of others, there is myself whom not for a single night would my loving mother fail to visit since she followed me by land and sea in order to abide with me"; and from this he concludes that the souls of the departed do not mingle in the affairs of the living. But they would be able to do so if they were to leave their abode. Therefore they do not go forth from their abode.

Obj. 2. Further, It is written (Ps. 26. 4): *That I may dwell in the house of the Lord all the days of my life,* and (Job. 7. 9): *He that shall go down to hell shall not come up.* Therefore neither the good nor the wicked quit their abode.

Obj. 3. Further, As stated above (A. 2), dwelling places are awarded to souls after death as a reward or punishment. Now after death neither the rewards of the saints nor the punishments of the damned are increased. Therefore they do not leave their abodes.

On the contrary, Jerome writing against Vigilantius addresses him thus:[2] "For thou sayest that the souls of the apostles and martyrs have taken up their abode either in Abraham's bosom or in the place of refreshment, or under the altar of God, and that they are unable to visit their graves when they will. Wouldst thou then lay down the law for God? Wouldst thou put the apostles in chains, imprison them until the day of judgment, and forbid them to be with their Lord, them of whom it is written: *These follow the Lamb whithersoever He goeth?* (Acts, 14. 4) And if the Lamb is everywhere, therefore we must believe that those also who are with Him are everywhere." Therefore it is absurd to say that the souls of the departed do not leave their abode.

Further, Jerome argues as follows (*ibid.*): "Since the devil and the demons wander throughout the whole world, and are everywhere present with wondrous speed, why should the martyrs, after shedding their blood, be imprisoned and unable to go forth?" Hence we may infer that not only the good sometimes leave their abode, but also the wicked, since their damnation does not exceed that of the demons who wander about everywhere.

Further, The same conclusion may be gathered from Gregory (*Dial.* iv),[3] where he relates many cases of the dead having appeared to the living.

I answer that, There are two ways of understanding a person to leave hell or heaven. First, that he goes out of those places absolutely, so that heaven or hell be no longer his place, and in this way no one who is finally consigned to hell or heaven can go out of them, as we shall state further on (Q. LXXI, A. 5, REPLY 5). Secondly, they may be understood to go forth for a time, and here we must distinguish what befits them according to the order of nature and what according to the order of Divine providence, for as Augustine says (*De Cura pro Mort.* xvi):[4] "Human affairs have their limits other than have the wonders of the Divine power, nature's works differ from those which are done miraculously."

Consequently, according to the natural course, the separated souls consigned to their respective abodes are utterly cut off from communion with the living. For according to the course of nature men living in mortal bodies are not immediately united to separate substances, since their entire knowledge arises from the senses; nor would it be fitting for them to leave their abode for any purpose other than to take part in the affairs of the living.

Nevertheless, according to the disposition of Divine providence separated souls sometimes come forth from their abode and appear to men, as Augustine, in the book quoted above,[5] relates of the martyr Felix who appeared visibly to the people of Nola when they were besieged by the barbarians.. It is also credible that this may occur sometimes to the damned, and that for man's instruction and intimidation they be permitted to appear to the living; or again in order to seek our prayers, as to those who are detained in purgatory, as evidenced by many instances related in the fourth book of the *Dialogues.*[6] There is, however, this difference between the saints and the damned, that the saints can appear when they will to the living, but not the damned; for even as the saints while living in the flesh are able by the gifts of gratuitous grace to heal and work wonders, which can only be done miraculously by the Divine power, and cannot be done by those who lack this gift, so it is not unfitting for the souls of the saints to be endowed with a power in virtue of their glory so that they are able to appear wondrously to the living when they will,

[1] PL 40, 604.　　[2] *Contra Vigilant.* (PL 23, 359).
[3] Chaps. 12, 16, 30, 40, 55 (PL 77, 337, 348, 368, 396, 417).

[4] PL 40, 606.
[5] *De Cura pro Mort.,* 16 (PL 40, 606).
[6] Chap. 30, 40, 55 (PL 77, 369, 397, 417).

while others are unable to do so unless they be sometimes permitted.

Reply Obj. 1. Augustine, as may be gathered from what he says afterwards, is speaking according to the common course of nature. And yet it does not follow that even if the dead be able to appear to the living as they will, that they appear as often as when living in the flesh, because when they are separated from the flesh, they are either wholly conformed to the divine will, so that they may do nothing but what they see to be agreeable with the Divine disposition, or else they are so overwhelmed by their punishments that their grief for their unhappiness surpasses their desire to appear to others.

Reply Obj. 2. The authorities quoted speak in the sense that no one comes forth from heaven or hell absolutely, and do not imply that one may not come forth for a time.

Reply Obj. 3. As stated above (A. 1, Reply 3) the soul's place conduces to its punishment or reward in so far as the soul, through being consigned to that place, is affected either by joy or by grief. Now this joy or grief at being consigned to such a place remains in the soul even when it is outside that place. Thus a bishop who is given the honour of sitting on a throne in the church incurs no dishonour when he leaves the throne, for though he sits not there actually, the place remains assigned to him.

We must also *reply to the arguments in the contrary sense.*

Reply Obj. 4. Jerome is speaking of the apostles and martyrs in reference to that which they gain from their power of glory, and not to that which befits them as due to them by nature. And when he says that they are everywhere, he does not mean that they are in several places or everywhere at once, but that they can be wherever they will.

Reply Obj. 5. There is no equivalence between demons and angels on the one hand and the souls of the saints and of the damned on the other. For the good or bad angels have allotted to them the office of presiding over men, to watch over them or to try them; but this cannot be said of the souls of men. Nevertheless, according to the power of glory, it is fitting to the souls of the saints that they can be where they will, and this is what Jerome means to say.

Reply Obj. 6. Although the souls of the saints or of the damned are sometimes actually present where they appear, we are not to believe that this is always so, for sometimes these apparitions occur to persons whether asleep or awake by the activity of good or wicked angels in order to instruct or deceive the living. Thus sometimes even the living appear to others and tell them many things in their sleep, and yet it is clear that they are not present, as Augustine proves from many instances (*De Cura pro Mort.* xi, xii).[1]

ARTICLE 4. *Whether the Limbo of Hell Is the Same As Abraham's Bosom?*

We proceed thus to the Fourth Article: It would seem that the limbo of hell is not the same as Abraham's bosom.

Objection 1. For according to Augustine (*Gen. ad Lit.* xxxiii, 33):[2] "I have not yet found Scripture mentioning hell in a good sense." Now Abraham's bosom is taken in a favourable sense, as Augustine goes on to say (*ibid.*): "Surely no one would be allowed to give an unfavourable signification to Abraham's bosom and the place of rest whither the godly poor man was carried by the angels." Therefore Abraham's bosom is not the same as the limbo of hell.

Obj. 2. Further, Those who are in hell do not see God. Yet God is seen by those who are in Abraham's bosom, as may be gathered from Augustine[3] who, speaking of Nebridius, says: "Whatever that be, which is signified by that bosom, there lives my Nebridius," and further on: "Now lays he not his ear to my mouth, but his spiritual mouth unto Thy fountain, and drinketh as much as he can receive wisdom in proportion to his thirst, endlessly happy." Therefore Abraham's bosom is not the same as the limbo of hell.

Obj. 3. Further, The Church does not pray that a man be taken to hell, and yet she prays that the angels may carry the departed soul to Abraham's bosom. Therefore it would seem that Abraham's bosom is not the same as limbo.

On the contrary, The place where the beggar Lazarus was taken is called Abraham's bosom (Luke, 16. 22). Now he was taken to hell, for as a gloss on Job 30. 23, *Where a house is appointed for every one that liveth,* says,[4] "hell was the house of all the living until the coming of Christ." Therefore Abraham's bosom is the same as limbo.

Further, Jacob said to his sons (Gen. 44. 38): *You will bring down my grey hairs with sorrow*

---

[1] PL 40, 601, 602.   [2] PL 34, 482.
[3] *Confessions,* IX, 6 (PL 32, 765).
[4] *Glossa ordin.* (III, 57F); Gregory the Great, *Moral.,* XX, 34 (PL 76, 177).

to hell, and therefore Jacob knew that he would be taken to hell after his death. Therefore Abraham likewise was taken to hell after his death, and consequently Abraham's bosom would seem to be a part of hell.

I answer that, After death men's souls cannot find rest save by the merit of faith, because *he that cometh to God must believe* (Heb. 11. 6). Now the first example of faith was given to men in the person of Abraham, who was the first to sever himself from the body of unbelievers, and to receive a special sign of faith, for which reason the place of rest given to men after death is called Abraham's bosom, as Augustine declares (*Gen. ad Lit.* xii, 34).[1]

But the souls of the saints have not at all times had the same rest after death, because since Christ's coming they have had complete rest through enjoying the vision of God, whereas before Christ's coming they had rest through being exempt from punishment, but their desire was not set at rest by their attaining their end. Consequently the state of the saints before Christ's coming may be considered both as regards the rest it afforded, and thus it is called Abraham's bosom, and as regards its lack of rest, and thus it is called the limbo of hell.

Accordingly, before Christ's coming the limbo of hell and Abraham's bosom were one place accidentally and not essentially; and consequently, nothing prevents Abraham's bosom from being after Christ's coming, and from being altogether distinct from limbo, since things that are one accidentally may be parted from one another.

Reply Obj. 1. The state of the holy Fathers as regards what was good in it was called Abraham's bosom, but as regards its deficiencies it was called hell. Accordingly, neither is Abraham's bosom taken in an unfavourable sense, nor hell in a favourable sense, although in a way they are one.

Reply Obj. 2. The place of rest of the holy Fathers was called Abraham's bosom before as well as after Christ's coming, but in different ways. For since before Christ's coming the saints' rest had a lack of rest attached to it, it was called both hell and Abraham's bosom, in so far as God was not seen there. But since after the coming of Christ the saints' rest is complete through their seeing God, this rest is called Abraham's bosom, but not hell in any way. It is to this bosom of Abraham that the Church prays for the faithful to be brought.

Hence the *Reply to the Third Objection* is

[1] PL 34, 482; Cf. *De An. et ejus Orig.*, IV, 16 (PL 44, 538).

evident, and the same meaning applies to a gloss on Luke 16. 22, *It came to pass that the beggar died*, etc., which says[2]: "Abraham's bosom is the rest of the blessed poor, whose is the kingdom of heaven."

ARTICLE 5. *Whether Limbo Is the Same As the Hell of the Damned?*

We proceed thus to the Fifth Article: It would seem that the limbo of hell is the same as the hell of the damned.

Objection 1. For Christ is said to have "bitten" hell (Osee, 13. 14), but not to have swallowed it, because He took some but not all from there.[3] Now He would not be said to have bitten hell if those whom He set free were not part of the multitude shut up in hell. Therefore since those whom He set free were shut up in hell, the same were shut up in limbo and in hell. Therefore limbo is either the same as hell, or is a part of hell.

Obj. 2. Further, In the Creed Christ is said to have descended into hell.[4] But He did not descend save to the limbo of the Fathers. Therefore the limbo of the Fathers is the same as hell.

Obj. 3. Further, It is written (Job 17. 16): *All that I have shall go down into the deepest hell* (Douay,—*pit*). Now since Job was a holy and just man, he went down to limbo. Therefore limbo is the same as the deepest hell.

On the contrary, "In hell there is no redemption."[5] But the saints were redeemed from limbo. Therefore limbo is not the same as hell.

Further, Augustine says (*Gen. ad Lit.* xii, 33):[6] "I do not see how we can believe that the rest which Lazarus received was in hell." Now the soul of Lazarus went down into limbo. Therefore limbo is not the same as hell.

I answer that, The abodes of souls after death may be distinguished in two ways: either as to their situation, or as to the quality of the places, according, that is, as souls are punished or rewarded in certain places. If therefore we consider the limbo of the Fathers and hell in respect of the aforesaid quality of the places, there is no doubt that they are distinct, both because in hell there is sensible punishment, which was not in the limbo of the Fathers, and because in hell there is eternal punishment, whereas the saints were detained but temporally in the limbo of the Fathers.

[2] Cf. Bede, *In Luc.*, BK. v, (PL 92, 535).
[3] Cf. Gregory the Great, *In Evang.*, BK. II, hom. XXII (PL 76, 1177).   [4] Apostles Creed (DZ 6).
[5] Office of the Dead, *Resp.* VII.   [6] PL 34, 482.

On the other hand, if we consider them as to the situation of the place, it is probable that hell and limbo are the same place, or that they are continuous as it were, yet so that some higher part of hell be called the limbo of the Fathers. For those who are in hell receive various punishments according to the diversity of their guilt, so that those who are condemned are consigned to darker and deeper parts of hell according as they have been guilty of graver sins, and consequently the holy Fathers in whom there was the least amount of sin were consigned to a higher and less darksome part than all those who were condemned to punishment.

Reply Obj. 1. When Christ, by His descent, delivered the Fathers from limbo, He is said to have bitten hell and to have descended into hell in so far as hell and limbo are the same as to situation.

This suffices for the *Reply to the Second Objection.*

Reply Obj. 3. Job descended, not to the hell of the damned, but to the limbo of the Fathers. the latter is called the deepest place not in reference to the places of punishment, but in comparison with other places, as including all penal places under one head.—Again we may reply with Augustine (*Gen. ad Lit.* xii, 33)[1] who says of Jacob: "When Jacob said to his sons, 'You will bring down my grey hairs with sorrow to hell,' he seems to have feared most, lest he should be troubled with so great a sorrow as to obtain, not the rest of good men, but the hell of sinners." The saying of Job may be expounded in the same way, as being the utterance of one in fear, rather than an assertion.

ARTICLE 6. *Whether the Limbo of Children Is the Same As the Limbo of the Fathers?*

We proceed thus to the Sixth Article: It would seem that the limbo of children is the same as the limbo of the Fathers.

Objection 1. For punishment should correspond to sin. Now the Fathers were detained in limbo for the same sin as children, namely for original sin. Therefore the place of punishment should be the same for both.

Obj. 2. Further, Augustine says (*Enchir.* xciii):[2] "The punishment of children who die in none but original sin is most lenient." But no punishment is more lenient than that of the holy Fathers. Therefore the place of punishment is the same for both.

On the contrary, Even as temporal punishment in purgatory and eternal punishment in

[1] PL 34, 482.   [2] PL 40, 275.

hell are due to actual sin, so temporal punishment in the limbo of the Fathers and eternal punishment in the limbo of the children were due to original sin. If, therefore, hell and purgatory are not the same it would seem that neither are the limbo of children and the limbo of the Fathers the same.

I answer that, The limbo of the Fathers and the limbo of children, without any doubt, differ as to the quality of punishment or reward. For children have no hope of the blessed life, as the Fathers in limbo had, in whom, moreover, shone forth the light of faith and grace. But as regards their situation, there is reason to believe that the place of both is the same, except that the limbo of the Fathers is placed higher than the limbo of children, just as we have stated in reference to limbo and hell (A. 5).

Reply Obj. 1. The Fathers did not stand in the same relation to original sin as children. For in the Fathers original sin was expiated in so far as it infected the person, while there remained an obstacle on the part of nature, on account of which their satisfaction was not yet complete. On the other hand, in children there is an obstacle both on the part of the person and on the part of nature, and for this reason different abodes are appointed to the Fathers and to children.

Reply Obj. 2. Augustine is speaking of punishments due to some one by reason of his person. Of these the most lenient are due to those who are burdened with none but original sin. But lighter still is the punishment due to those who are debarred from the reception of glory by no personal defect but only by a defect of nature, so that this very delay of glory is called a kind of punishment.

ARTICLE 7. *Whether So Many Abodes Should Be Distinguished?*

We proceed thus to the Seventh Article: It would seem that we should not distinguish so many abodes.

Objection 1. For after death, just as abodes are due to souls on account of sin, so are they due on account of merit. Now there is only one abode due on account of merit, namely paradise. Therefore neither should there be more than one abode due on account of sin, namely hell.

Obj. 2. Further, Abodes are appointed to souls after death on account of merits or demerits. Now there is one place where they merit or demerit. Therefore only one abode should be assigned to them after death.

Obj. 3. Further, The places of punishment should correspond to the sins. Now there are only three kinds of sin, namely original, venial, and mortal. Therefore there should only be three penal abodes.

Obj. 4. *On the other hand,* it would seem that there should be many more than those assigned. For this darksome air is the prison house of the demons (II Pet. 2. 17), and yet it is not reckoned among the five abodes which are mentioned by certain authors. Therefore there are more than five abodes.

Obj. 5. Further, The earthly paradise is distinct from the heavenly paradise. Now some were borne away to the earthly paradise after this state of life, as is related of Enoch (Eccl. 44. 16) and Elias (IV Kings, 2. 11). Since then the earthly paradise is not counted among the five abodes, it would seem that there are more than five.

Obj. 6. Further, Some penal place should correspond to each state of sinners. Now if we suppose a person to die in original sin who has committed only venial sins, none of the assigned abodes will be befitting to him. For it is clear that he would not be in heaven, since he would be without grace, and for the same reason neither would he be in the limbo of the Fathers; nor again, would he be in the limbo of children, since there is no sensible punishment there, which is due to such a person by reason of venial sin; nor would he be in purgatory, where there is none but temporal punishment, whereas everlasting punishment is due to him; nor would he be in the hell of the damned, since he is not guilty of actual mortal sin. Therefore a sixth abode should be assigned.

Obj. 7. Further, Rewards and punishments vary in quantity according to the differences of sins and merits. Now the degrees of merit and sin are infinite. Therefore we should distinguish an infinite number of abodes, in which souls are punished or rewarded after death.

Obj. 8. Further, Souls are sometimes punished in the places where they sinned, as Gregory states (*Dial.* iv, 55).[1] But they sinned in the place which we inhabit. Therefore this place should be reckoned among the abodes, especially since some are punished for their sins in this world, as the Master said above (iv. *Sent.* d. 15).[2]

Obj. 9. Further, Just as some die in a state of grace and have some venial sins for which they deserve punishment, so some die in mortal sin and have some good for which they

would deserve a reward. Now to those who die in grace with venial sins an abode is assigned where they are punished before they receive their reward, which abode is purgatory. Therefore, on the other hand, there should be equally an abode for those who die in mortal sin together with some good works.

Obj. 10. Further, Just as the Fathers were delayed from obtaining full glory of the soul before Christ's coming, so are they now detained from receiving the glory of the body. Therefore as we distinguish an abode of the saints before the coming of Christ from the one where they are received now, so ought we to distinguish the one in which they are received now from the one where they will be received after the resurrection.

I answer that, The abodes of souls are distinguished according to the souls' various states. Now the soul united to a mortal body is in the state of meriting, while the soul separated from the body is in the state of receiving good or evil for its merits, so that after death it is either in the state of receiving its final reward, or in the state of being hindered from receiving it. If it is in the state of receiving its final retribution, this happens in two ways: either in the respect of good, and then it is paradise; or in respect of evil, and thus as regards actual sin it is hell, and as regards original sin it is the limbo of children. On the other hand, if it be in the state where it is hindered from receiving its final reward, this is either on account of a defect of the person, and thus we have purgatory where souls are detained from receiving their reward at once on account of the sins they have committed, or else it is on account of a defect of nature, and thus we have the limbo of the Fathers, where the Fathers were detained from obtaining glory on account of the guilt of human nature which could not yet be expiated.

Reply Obj. 1. "Good happens in one way, but evil in many ways," according to Dionysius (*Div. Nom.* iv)[3] and the Philosopher.[4] Therefore it is not unfitting if there be one place of blissful reward and several places of punishment.

Reply Obj. 2. The state of meriting and demeriting is one state, since the same person is able to merit and demerit. Therefore it is fitting that one place should be assigned to all. But of those who receive according to their merits there are various states, and consequently the comparison fails.

---

[1] PL 77, 417. [2] Chap. 3 (QR II, 829). [3] Sect. 30 (PG 3, 729). [4] *Ethics,* II, 6 (1106^{b}34).

Reply Obj. 3. One may be punished in two ways for original sin, as stated above, either in reference to the person, or in reference to nature only. Consequently there is a twofold limbo corresponding to that sin.

Reply Obj. 4. This darksome air is assigned to the demons not as the place where they receive retribution for their merits, but as a place befitting their office, in so far as they are appointed to try us. Hence it is not accounted among the abodes of which we are treating now, since hell fire is assigned to them in the first place (Matt. 25).

Reply Obj. 5. The earthly paradise belongs to the state of the wayfarer rather than to the state of those who receive for their merits, and consequently it is not put among the abodes of which we are treating now.

Reply Obj. 6. This supposition is impossible. If, however, it were possible, such a one would be punished in hell eternally, for that venial sin is punished temporally in purgatory happens to it through its having grace joined to it; therefore if it is joined to a mortal sin, which is without grace, it will be punished eternally in hell. And since this one who dies in original sin has a venial sin without grace, it is not unfitting to suppose that he is punished eternally.

Reply Obj. 7. Diversity of degrees in punishments or rewards does not diversify the state, and it is according to the diversity of state that we distinguish various abodes. Hence the argument does not prove.

Reply Obj. 8. Although separated souls are sometimes punished in the place where we dwell, it does not follow that this is their proper place of punishment, but this is done for our instruction, that seeing their punishment we may be deterred from sin. That souls while yet in the flesh are punished here for their sins has nothing to do with the question, because a punishment of this kind does not place a man outside the state of meriting or demeriting, whereas we are treating now of the abodes to which souls are assigned after the state of merit or demerit.

Reply Obj. 9. It is impossible for evil to be pure and without the admixture of good, just as the supreme good is without any admixture of evil. Consequently those who are to be conveyed to Happiness, which is a supreme good, must be cleansed of all evil; therefore there must be a place where such persons are cleansed if they go from this life without being perfectly clean. But those who will be thrust into hell will not be free from all good, and consequently the comparison fails, since those who are in hell can receive the reward of their goods in so far as their past goods avail for the mitigation of their punishment.

Reply Obj. 10. The essential reward consists in the glory of the soul, but the body's glory, since it overflows from the soul, is entirely founded as it were on the soul, and consequently lack of the soul's glory causes a difference of state, whereas lack of the body's glory does not. For this reason, too, the same place, namely the empyrean, is assigned to the holy souls separated from their bodies and united to glorious bodies; the same place however was not assigned to the souls of the Fathers both before and after the glorification of souls.

QUESTION LXX

Of the Quality of the Soul after Leaving the Body, and the Punishment Inflicted on It by Material Fire

(In Three Articles)

We must next consider the general quality of the soul after leaving the body, and the punishment inflicted on it by material fire. Under this head there are three points of inquiry: (1) Whether the sensitive powers remain in the separated soul? (2) Whether the acts of these powers remain in the soul? (3) Whether the separated soul can suffer from corporeal fire?

ARTICLE 1. *Whether the Sensitive Powers Remain in the Separated Soul?*

We proceed thus to the First Article: It would seem that the sensitive powers remain in the separated soul.

Objection 1. For Augustine says (*De Spir. et Anim.* xv):[1] "The soul withdraws from the body taking all with itself, sense and imagination, reason, understanding and intelligence, the concupiscible and irascible powers." Now sense, imagination, concupiscible and irascible are sensitive powers. Therefore the sensitive powers remain in the separated soul.

Obj. 2. Further, Augustine says (*De Eccl. Dogm.* xvi):[2] "We believe that man alone has a substantial soul, which lives though separated from the body, and keeps alive its senses and understanding." Therefore the soul retains its senses after being separated from the body.

Obj. 3. Further, The soul's powers are either

[1] Alcher of Clairvaux (PL 40, 791).
[2] Gennadius (PL 58, 984).

its essential parts as some maintain, or at least are its natural properties. Now that which is in a thing essentially cannot be separated from it, nor is a subject severed from its natural properties. Therefore it is impossible for the soul to lose any of its powers after being separated from the body.

Obj. 4. Further, A whole is not entire if one of its parts is lacking. Now the soul's powers are called its parts. Therefore, if the soul lose any of its powers after death, it will not be entire after death, and this is unfitting.

Obj. 5. Further, The soul's powers co-operate in merit more even than the body, since the body is a mere instrument of action, while the powers are principles of action. Now the body must of necessity be rewarded together with the soul, since it co-operated in merit. Much more, therefore, is it necessary that the powers of the soul be rewarded together with it. Therefore the separated soul does not lose them.

Obj. 6. Further, If the soul after separation from the body loses its sensitive power, that power must fall back into nothing. For it cannot be said that it falls back into some matter, since it has no matter as a part of itself. Now that which entirely falls back into nothing is not restored in numerical identity; therefore at the resurrection the soul will not have the numerically same sensitive powers. Now according to the Philosopher,[1] as the soul is to the body so are the soul's powers to the parts of the body, for instance the sight to the eye. But if it were not the same soul that returns to the body, it would not be the same man. Therefore for the same reason it would not be the numerically same eye, if the visual power were not numerically the same; and in like manner no other part would rise again the same in number, and consequently neither would the whole man be the same in number. Therefore it is impossible for the separated soul to lose its sensitive powers.

Obj. 7. Further, If the sensitive powers were to be corrupted when the body is corrupted, it would follow that they are weakened when the body is weakened. Yet this is not the case, for according to the book on the *Soul*,[2] "if an old man were given the eye of a young man, he would, without doubt, see as well as a young man." Therefore neither are the sensitive powers corrupted when the body is corrupted.

On the contrary, Augustine says (*De Eccl. Dogm.* xix):[3] "Of two substances alone does man consist, soul and body; the soul with its reason, and the body with its senses." Therefore the sensitive powers belong to the body, and consequently when the body is corrupted the sensitive powers do not remain in the soul.

Further, The Philosopher, speaking of the separation of the soul, expresses himself thus:[4] "If, however, anything remain at last, we must ask what this is, because in certain beings it is not impossible. The soul, for instance, if it be of such a disposition,—not the whole soul but the intellect; for as regards the whole soul this is probably impossible." Hence it seems that the whole soul is not separated from the body, but only the intellectual powers of the soul, and consequently not the sensitive or vegetative powers.

Further, The Philosopher, speaking of the intellect, says:[5] "This alone comes to be separated, as the everlasting from the corruptible; for it is clear from this that the remaining parts are not separable as some maintain." Therefore the sensitive powers do not remain in the separated soul.

I answer that, There are many opinions on this question. For some, holding the view that all the powers are in the soul in the same way as colour is in a body, hold that the soul separated from the body takes all its powers away with it, because, if it lacked any one of them, it would follow that the soul is changed in its natural properties, since these cannot change so long as their subject remains. But this view is false, for since a power is called so because it enables us to do or suffer something, and since to do and to be able belong to the same subject, it follows that the subject of a power is the same as that which is agent or patient. Hence the Philosopher says[6] that "where we find power there we find action." Now it is evident that certain operations, of which the soul's powers are the principles, do not belong to the soul properly speaking but to the soul as united to the body, because they are not performed except through the medium of the body, —such as to see, to hear, and so forth. Hence it follows that such powers belong to the united soul and body as their subject, but to the soul as their quickening (*influens*) principle, just as the form is the principle of the properties of a composite being. Some operations, however, are performed by the soul without a bodily organ,—for instance to understand, to consider,

[1] *Soul*, II, 1 (412b17).   [2] Aristotle, I, 4 (408b21).
[3] Gennadius (PL 58, 985).

[4] *Metaphysics*, XII, 3 (1070a24).
[5] *Soul*, II, 2 (413b26).   [6] *Sleep*, 1 (454a8).

to will; therefore, since these actions are proper to the soul, the powers that are the principles of them belong to the soul not only as their principle but also as their subject. Therefore, since so long as the proper subject remains its proper passions must also remain, and when it is corrupted they also must be corrupted, it follows that these powers which use no bodily organ for their actions must remain in the separated body, while those which use a bodily organ must be corrupted when the body is corrupted; and such are all the powers belonging to the sensitive and the vegetative soul.

On this account some draw a distinction in the sensitive powers of the soul, for they say that they are of two kinds—some being acts of organs and emanating from the soul into the body are corrupted with the body; others, from which the former originate, are in the soul, because by them the soul sensitizes the body for seeing, hearing, and so on, and these primary powers remain in the separated soul. But this statement seems unreasonable, because the soul, by its essence and not through the medium of certain other powers, is the origin of those powers which are the acts of organs, even as any form, from the very fact that by its essence it informs its matter, is the origin of the properties which result naturally in the composite. For were it necessary to suppose other powers in the soul by means of which the powers that perfect the organs may flow from the essence of the soul, for the same reason it would be necessary to suppose other powers by means of which these mean powers flow from the essence of the soul, and so on to infinity, and if we have to stop it is better to do so at the first step.

Hence others say that the sensitive and other like powers do not remain in the separated soul except in a restricted sense, namely as rooted in it, in the same way as a result is in its principle, because there remains in the separated soul the ability to quicken once more these powers if it should be reunited to the body; nor is it necessary for this ability to be anything in addition to the essence of the soul, as stated above. This opinion appears to be the more reasonable.

Reply Obj. 1. This saying of Augustine is to be understood as meaning that the soul takes away with it some of those powers actually, namely understanding and intelligence, and some radically, as stated above.

Reply Obj. 2. The senses which the soul takes away with it are not these external senses, but the internal, those, namely, which pertain to the intellectual part, for the intellect is sometimes called sense, as Basil states in his commentary on the Proverbs,[1] and again the Philosopher.[2] If, however, he means the external senses we must reply as above to the first objection.

Reply Obj. 3. As stated above the sensitive powers are related to the soul not as natural passions to their subject, but as compared to their origin. Therefore the conclusion does not follow.

Reply Obj. 4. The powers of the soul are called its potential parts. Now the nature of such wholes is that the entire power of the whole is found perfectly in one of the parts, but partially in the others; thus in the soul the soul's power is found perfectly in the intellectual part, but partially in the others. Therefore, as the powers of the intellectual part remain in the separated soul, the latter will remain entire and undiminished, although the sensitive powers do not remain actually; just as neither is the king's power decreased by the death of a mayor who shared his authority.

Reply Obj. 5. The body co-operates in merit, as an essential part of the man who merits. The sensitive powers, however, do not co-operate thus, since they are of the genus of accidents. Hence the comparison fails.

Reply Obj. 6. The powers of the sensitive soul are said to be acts of the organs, not as though they were the essential forms of those organs, except in reference to the soul whose powers they are. But they are the acts of the organs by perfecting them for their proper operations, just as heat is the act of fire by perfecting it for the purpose of heating. Therefore, just as a fire would remain numerically the same, although another heat were in it (even so the cold of water that has been heated returns not numerically the same, although the water remains the same in number), so the organs will be the same numerically, although the powers be not numerically the same.

Reply Obj. 7. The Philosopher is speaking there of these powers as being rooted in the soul. This is clear from his saying that "old age is an affection not of the soul, but of that in which the soul is," namely the body. For in this sense the powers of the soul are neither weakened nor corrupted on account of the body.

[1] *Hom.*, XII, *In Princ. Prov.* (PG 31, 412).
[2] *Ethics*, VI, 11 (1143^b5).

ARTICLE 2. *Whether the Acts of the Sensitive Powers Remain in the Separated Soul?*

We proceed thus to the Second Article: It would seem that the acts of the sensitive powers remain in the separated soul.

Objection 1. For Augustine says (*De Spiritu et Anima*, xv):[1] "When the soul leaves the body it derives pleasure or sorrow through being affected with these (namely the imagination, and the concupiscible and irascible powers) according to its merits." But the imagination, the concupiscible, and the irascible are sensitive powers. Therefore the separated soul will be affected as regards the sensitive powers, and consequently will be in some act by reason of them.

Obj. 2. Further, Augustine says (*Gen. ad Lit.* xii, 24)[2] that "the body feels not, but the soul through the body," and further on: "The soul feels certain things, not through the body but without the body." Now that which befits the soul without the body can be in the soul separated from the body. Therefore the soul will then be able to feel actually.

Obj. 3. Further, To see likenesses of bodies, as occurs in sleep, belongs to imaginary vision which is in the sensitive part. Now it happens that the separated soul sees likenesses of bodies in the same way as when we sleep. Thus Augustine says (*Gen. ad Lit.* xii, 32):[3] "For I see not why the soul has a likeness of its own body when, the body lying senseless, yet not quite dead, it sees some things which many have related after returning to life from this suspended animation and yet has it not when it has left the body through death having taken place." For it is unintelligible that the soul should have a likeness of its body, except in so far as it sees that likeness; therefore he said before of those who lie senseless that "they have a certain likeness of their own body, by which they are able to be borne to corporeal places and by means of sensible likenesses to experience such things as they see." Therefore the separated soul can exercise the acts of the sensitive powers.

Obj. 4. Further, The memory is a power of the sensitive part as proved in the book on *Memory and Reminiscence.*[4] Now separated souls will actually remember the things they did in this world. Therefore it is said to the rich glutton (Luke 16. 25): *Remember that thou didst receive good things in thy lifetime.* There-

fore the separated soul will exercise the act of a sensitive power.

Obj. 5. Further, According to the Philosopher,[5] the irascible and concupiscible are in the sensitive part. But joy and sorrow, love and hatred, fear and hope, and similar emotions which according to our faith we hold to be in separated souls, are in the irascible and concupiscible. Therefore separated souls will not be deprived of the acts of the sensitive powers.

On the contrary, That which is common to soul and body cannot remain in the separated soul. Now all the operations of the sensitive powers are common to the soul and body: and this is evident from the fact that no sensitive power exercises an act except through a bodily organ. Therefore the separated soul will be deprived of the acts of the sensitive powers.

Further, The Philosopher says[6] that "when the body is corrupted, the soul neither remembers nor loves," and the same applies to all the acts of the sensitive powers. Therefore the separated soul does not exercise the act of any sensitive power.

I answer that, Some distinguish two kinds of acts in the sensitive powers; external acts which the soul exercises through the body, and these do not remain in the separated soul; and internal acts which the soul performs by itself, and these will be in the separated soul. This statement would seem to have come down from the opinion of Plato, who held that the soul is united to the body as a perfect substance in no way dependant on the body, and merely as a mover is united to the thing moved.[7] This is an evident consequence of transmigration which he held.[8] And since according to him nothing is in motion except what is moved, and lest he should go on infinitely, he said that the first mover moves itself, and he maintained that the soul is the cause of its own movement.[9] Accordingly there would be a twofold movement of the soul, one by which it moves itself, and another whereby the body is moved by the soul, so that this act "to see" is first of all in the soul itself as moving itself, and secondly in the bodily organ in so far as the soul moves the body.

This opinion is refuted by the Philosopher[10]

[1] Alcher of Clairvaux (PL 40, 791).
[2] PL 34, 475; cf. III, 5 (PL 34, 282).
[3] PL 34, 480.   [4] Aristotle, 1 (450ª12).
[5] *Soul*, III, 9 (432ᵇ6).   [6] *Ibid.*, 1, 4 (408ᵇ27).
[7] Cf. Part I, Q. LXXXI, A. 1; Q. LXXVI, A. 1; cf. also Plato, *Alcibiades*, 1 (129); *Epinomis*, x (898c); *Timaeus*, (42); *Phaedrus* (249).
[8] *Republic*, x (618); *Phaedo* (82); *Timaeus* (76, 90); cf. Augustine, *City of God*, XII, 26 (PL 41, 375).
[9] Cf. Aristotle, *Soul*, 1, 3 (406ᵇ26); *Physics*, VIII, 9 (265ᵇ 32).   [10] *Soul*, 1, 3 (405ᵇ31).

who proves that the soul does not move itself, and that it is in no way moved in respect of such operations as seeing, feeling, and the like, but that such operations are movements of the composite only. We must therefore conclude that the acts of the sensitive powers in no way remain in the separated soul, except perhaps as in their remote origin.

Reply Obj. 1. Some deny that this book is Augustine's: for it is ascribed to a Cistercian who compiled it from Augustine's works, and added things of his own. Hence we are not to take what is written there, as having authority. If, however, its authority should be maintained, it must be said that the meaning is that the separated soul is affected with imagination and other like powers, not as though such affection were the act of the aforesaid powers, but in the sense that the soul will be affected in the future life for good or ill according to the things which it committed in the body through the imagination and other like powers, so that the imagination and such powers are not supposed to elicit that affection, but to have elicited in the body the merit of that affection.

Reply Obj. 2. The soul is said to feel through the body not as though the act of feeling belonged to the soul by itself, but as belonging to the whole composite by reason of the soul, just as we say that heat heats. That which is added, namely that the soul feels some things without the body, such as fear and so forth, means that it feels such things without the outward movement of the body that takes place in the acts of the proper senses, since fear and like passions do not occur without any bodily movement.

It may also be replied that Augustine is speaking according to the opinion of the Platonists who maintained this as stated above.[1]

Reply Obj. 3. Augustine speaks there as for the most part throughout that book, as one inquiring and not deciding. For it is clear that there is no comparison between the soul of a sleeper and the separated soul, since the soul of the sleeper uses the organ of imagination wherein corporeal likenesses are impressed; which cannot be said of the separated soul. Or we may reply that likenesses of things are in the soul, both as to the sensitive and imaginative power and as to the intellectual power, with greater or lesser abstraction from matter and material conditions. Therefore Augustine's comparison holds in this respect that just as the images of corporeal things are in the soul of the dreamer or of one who is carried out of his

[1] Cf. also Part I, Q. LXXVII, A. 5, Reply 3.

mind, imaginatively, so are they in the separated soul intellectually, but not that they are in the separated soul imaginatively.

Reply Obj. 4. As stated in the first book of Sentences,[2] memory has a twofold meaning. Sometimes it means a power of the sensitive part, in so far as its gaze extends over past time; and in this way the act of the memory will not be in the separated soul. And so the Philosopher says[3] that "when this," that is the body, "is corrupted, the soul remembers not." In another way memory is used to designate that part of the imagination which pertains to the intellectual part, in so far namely as it abstracts from all differences of time, since it regards not only the past but also the present, and the future as Augustine says (*De Trin.* xiv, 11).[4] Taking memory in this sense the separated soul will remember.[5]

Reply Obj. 5. Love, joy, sorrow, and the like, have a twofold meaning. Sometimes they denote passions of the sensitive appetite, and thus they will not be in the separated soul, because in this way they are not exercised without a definite movement of the heart. In another way they denote acts of the will which is in the intellectual part, and in this way they will be in the separated soul, even as delight will be there without bodily movement, even as it is in God, namely in so far as it is a simple movement of the will. In this sense the Philosopher says[6] that "God's joy is one simple delight."

ARTICLE 3. *Whether the Separated Soul Can Suffer from a Bodily Fire?*

We proceed thus to the Third Article: It would seem that the separated soul cannot suffer from a bodily fire.

Objection 1. For Augustine says:[7] "The things that affect the soul well or ill after its separation from the body are not corporeal but resemble corporeal things." Therefore the separated soul is not punished with a bodily fire.

Obj. 2. Further, Augustine says[8] that the agent is always more excellent than the patient. But it is impossible for any body to be more excellent than the separated soul. Therefore it cannot suffer from a body.

[2] *In Sent.*, d. III, Q. 4, A. 1, ad 2; cf. *Sent.*, III, d. XXVI, Q. 2, A. 5, ad 4.
[3] *Soul*, I, 4 (408^{b}27).
[4] PL 42, 1047.
[5] Cf. Part I, Q. LXXVII, A. 8; Q. LXXXIX, A. 6.
[6] *Ethics*, VII, 14 (1154^{b}26).
[7] *Gen. ad lit.*, XII, 32 (PL 34, 480).
[8] *Ibid.*, XII, 16 (PL 34, 467); cf. *De Musica*, VI, 5 (PL 32, 1168).

Obj. 3. Further, According to the Philosopher[1] and Boëthius (*De Duab. Natur.*)[2] only those things that agree in matter are active and passive in relation to one another. But the soul and corporeal fire do not agree in matter, since there is no matter common to spiritual and corporeal things; and therefore they cannot be changed into one another, as Boëthius says (*ibid.*). Therefore the separated soul does not suffer from a bodily fire.

Obj. 4. Further, Whatsoever is acted upon receives something from the agent. Therefore if the soul suffer from the bodily fire, it will receive something from it. Now whatsoever is received in a thing is received according to the mode of the recipient. Therefore that which is received in the soul from the fire is in it not materially but spiritually. Now the forms of things existing spiritually in the soul are its perfections. Therefore though it be granted that the soul suffer from the bodily fire, this will not conduce to its punishment, but rather to its perfection.

Obj. 5. Further, If it be said that the soul is punished merely by seeing the fire, as Gregory would seem to say (*Dial.* iv, 29),[3] on the contrary,—If the soul sees the fire of hell, it cannot see it save by intellectual vision, since it has not the organs by which sensitive or imaginative vision is effected. But it would seem impossible for intellectual vision to be the cause of sorrow, since "there is no sorrow contrary to the pleasure of considering," according to the Philosopher.[4] Therefore the soul is not punished by that vision.

Obj. 6. Further, If it be said that the soul suffers from the corporeal fire through being held by it, even as now it is held by the body while living in the body, on the contrary,— The soul while living in the body is held by the body in so far as there results one thing from the soul and the body, as from form and matter. But the soul will not be the form of that corporeal fire. Therefore it cannot be held by the fire in the manner spoken of above.

Obj. 7. Further, Every bodily agent acts by contact. But a corporeal fire cannot be in contact with the soul, since contact is only between corporeal things whose bounds come together. Therefore the soul suffers not from that fire.

Obj. 8. Further, An organic agent does not act on a remote object except through acting on the intermediate objects; therefore it is able to act at a fixed distance in proportion to its power. But souls, or at least the demons to whom this equally applies, are sometimes outside the place of hell, since sometimes they appear to men even in this world; and yet they are not then free from punishment, for just as the glory of the saints is never interrupted, so neither is the punishment of the damned. And yet we do not find that all the intermediate things suffer from the fire of hell; nor again is it credible that any corporeal things of an elemental nature has such a power that its action can reach to such a distance. Therefore it does not seem that the pains suffered by the souls of the damned are inflicted by a corporeal fire.

On the contrary, The possibility of suffering from a corporeal fire is equally consistent with separated souls and with demons. Now demons suffer from corporeal fire since they are punished by that fire into which the bodies of the damned will be cast after the resurrection, and which must be as corporeal fire. This is evident from the words of our Lord (Matt. 25. 41), *Depart from Me, you cursed, into everlasting fire, which was prepared for the devil,* etc. Therefore separated souls also can suffer from that fire.

Further, Punishment should correspond to sin. Now in sinning the soul subjected itself to the body by perverse concupiscence. Therefore it is just that it should be punished by being made subject to a bodily thing by suffering from it.

Further, There is greater union between form and matter than between agent and patient. Now the diversity of spiritual and corporeal nature does not hinder the soul from being the form of the body. Therefore neither is it an obstacle to its suffering from a body.

I answer that, Given, from what we have said above[5] that the fire of hell is not called so metaphorically, nor an imaginary fire, but a real corporeal fire, we must say that the soul will suffer punishment from a corporeal fire, since our Lord said (Matt. 25. 41) that this fire was prepared for the devil and his angels, who are incorporeal even as the soul. But how it is that they can thus suffer is explained in many ways.

For some have said that the mere fact that the soul sees the fire makes the soul suffer from the fire; and so Gregory (*Dial.* iv, 29)[6] says: "The soul suffers from the fire by merely seeing it." But this does not seem sufficient, because whatever is seen, from the fact that it is

---

[1] *Generation and Corruption,* I, 10 (328ᵃ19).
[2] Chap. 6 (PL 64, 1350).
[3] PL 77, 368.   [4] *Topics,* I, 13 (106ᵃ38).
[5] Thomas, *In Sent.,* IV, d. XLIV, Q. 3, A. 2, I.
[6] PL 77, 368.

seen, is a perfection of the seer; therefore it cannot conduce to his punishment, as seen. Sometimes, however, it is of a penal or saddening nature accidentally, in so far, that is, as it is apprehended as something hurtful, and consequently, besides the fact that the soul sees the fire, there must be some relation of the soul to the fire, according to which the fire is hurtful to the soul.

Hence others have said that although a corporeal fire cannot burn the soul, the soul nevertheless apprehends it as hurtful to itself, and in consequence of this apprehension is seized with fear and sorrow, in fulfilment of Ps. 13. 5, *They have trembled for fear, where there was no fear.* Hence Gregory says[1] that "the soul burns through seeing itself aflame." But this, again, seems insufficient, because in this case the soul would suffer from the fire not in reality but only in apprehension, for although a real passion of sorrow or pain may result from a false imagination, as Augustine observes (*Gen. ad Lit.* xii, 32),[2] it cannot be said in relation to that passion that one really suffers from the thing, but from the likeness of the thing that is seen. Moreover, this kind of suffering would be more unlike real suffering than that which results from imaginary vision, since the latter is stated to result from real images of things, which images the soul carries about with it, whereas the former results from false conceptions which the erring soul imagines; and furthermore, it is not probable that separated souls or demons, who are endowed with keen intelligence, would think it possible for a corporeal fire to hurt them if they were in no way distressed thereby.

Hence others say that it is necessary to admit that the soul suffers even really from the corporeal fire; and so Gregory says:[3] "We can gather from the words of the Gospel that the soul suffers from the fire not only by seeing it, but also by feeling it." They explain the possibility of this as follows. They say that this corporeal fire can be considered in two ways. First, as a corporeal thing, and thus it has not the power to act on the soul. Secondly, as the instrument of the vengeance of Divine justice. For the order of Divine justice demands that the soul which by sinning subjected itself to corporeal things should be subjected to them also in punishment. Now an instrument acts not only in virtue of its own nature, but also in virtue of the principal agent; therefore it is not unreasonable if that fire, seeing that it acts in

virtue of a spiritual agent, should act on the spirit of a man or demon, in the same way as we have explained the sanctification of the soul by the sacraments.[4]

But, again, this does not seem to suffice, since every instrument, in acting on that on which it is used instrumentally, has its own connatural action besides the action whereby it acts in virtue of the principal agent; in fact it is by fulfilling the former that it effects the latter action, even as, in Baptism, it is by laving the body that water sanctifies the soul, and the saw by cutting wood produces the shape of a house. Hence we must allow the fire to exercise on the soul an action connatural to the fire, in order that it may be the instrument of Divine justice in the punishment of sin, and for this reason we must say that a body cannot naturally act on a spirit, nor in any way be hurtful or distressful to it, except in so far as the latter is in some way united to a body; for thus we observe that *the corruptible body is a load upon the soul* (Wisd. 9. 15). Now a spirit is united to a body in two ways. In one way as form to matter, so that from their union there results one thing absolutely, and the spirit that is thus united to a body both quickens the body and is somewhat burdened by the body; but it is not thus that the spirit of man or demon is united to the corporeal fire. In another way as the mover is united to the things moved, or as a thing placed is united to place, even as incorporeal things are in a place. In this way created incorporeal spirits are confined to a place, being in one place in such a way as not to be in another. Now although of its nature a corporeal thing is able to confine an incorporeal spirit to a place, it is not able of its nature to detain an incorporeal spirit in the place to which it is confined, and so to tie it to that place that it be unable to seek another, since a spirit is not by nature in a place so as to be subject to place. But it is added over and above corporeal fire as the instrument of the vengeance of Divine justice thus to detain a spirit; and thus it has a penal effect on it, by hindering it from fulfilling its own will, that is by hindering it from acting where it will and as it will.

This way is asserted by Gregory (*Ibid.*). For in explaining how the soul can suffer from that fire by feeling it, he expresses himself as follows: "Since Truth declares the rich sinner to be condemned to fire, will any wise man deny that the souls of the wicked are imprisoned in

---

[1] *Ibid.*   [2] PL 34, 480.   [3] *Loc. cit.*

[4] Thomas, *In Sent.*, IV, d. I, Q. I, A. 4; cf. above, Part III, Q. LXII, A. I.

flames?" Julian says the same[1] as quoted by the Master (iv *Sent.* d. 44):[2] "If the incorporeal spirit of a living man is held by the body, why shall it not be held after death by a corporeal fire?" and Augustine says[3] that "just as, although the soul is spiritual and the body corporeal, man is so fashioned that the soul is united to the body as giving it life, and on account of this union conceives a great love for its body, so it is chained to the fire, as receiving punishment from it, and from this union conceives a loathing."

Accordingly we must unite all the above modes together in order to understand perfectly how the soul suffers from a corporeal fire, so as to say that the fire of its nature is able to have an incorporeal spirit united to it as a thing placed is united to a place, that as the instrument of Divine justice it is enabled to detain it enchained as it were, and in this respect this fire is really hurtful to the spirit, and thus the soul seeing the fire as something hurtful to it is tormented by the fire. Hence Gregory (*Ibid.*) mentions all these in order, as may be seen from the above quotations.

Reply Obj. 1. Augustine speaks there as one inquiring, and so he expresses himself otherwise when deciding as quoted above.[4] Or we may reply that Augustine means to say that the things which are the proximate occasion of the soul's pain or sorrow are spiritual, since it would not be distressed unless it apprehended the fire as hurtful to it; and so the fire as apprehended is the proximate cause of its distress, whereas the corporeal fire which exists outside the soul is the remote cause of its distress.

Reply Obj. 2. Although the soul is more excellent absolutely than the fire, the fire is relatively more excellent than the soul, in so far, that is, as it is the instrument of Divine justice.

Reply Obj. 3. The Philosopher and Boëthius are speaking of the action whereby the patient is changed into the nature of the agent. Such is not the action of the fire on the soul, and consequently the argument is not conclusive.

Reply Obj. 4. By acting on the soul the fire bestows nothing on it but detains it, as stated above. Hence the argument is not to the point.

Reply Obj. 5. In intellectual vision sorrow is not caused by the fact that something is seen, since the thing seen as such can in no way be contrary to the intellect. But in the sensible vision the thing seen, by its very action on the

sight so as to be seen, there may be accidentally something corruptive of the sight, in so far as it destroys the harmony of the organ. Nevertheless, intellectual vision may cause sorrow in so far as the thing seen is apprehended as hurtful, not that it hurts through being seen, but in some other way altogether. It is thus that the soul in seeing the fire is distressed.

Reply Obj. 6. The comparison does not hold in every respect, but it does in some, as explained above.

Reply Obj. 7. Although there is no bodily contact between the soul and body, there is a certain spiritual contact between them (even as the mover of the heaven, being spiritual, touches the heaven, when it moves it, with a spiritual contact) in the same way as a painful object is said to touch, as stated in the treatise on *Generation and Corruption.*[5] This mode of contact is sufficient for action.

Reply Obj. 8. The souls of the damned are never outside hell, except by Divine permission, either for the instruction or for the trial of the elect. And wherever they are outside hell they nevertheless always see its fire as prepared for their punishment. Therefore, since this vision is the immediate cause of their distress, as stated above (reply 1), wherever they are, they suffer from hell-fire. Even so prisoners, though outside the prison, suffer somewhat from the prison, seeing themselves condemned to it. Hence just as the glory of the elect is not diminished neither as to the essential nor as to the accidental reward if they happen to be outside the empyrean (in fact this somewhat conduces to their glory), so the punishment of the damned is in no way diminished, if by God's permission they happen to be outside hell for a time. A gloss on James 3. 6, *inflameth the wheel of our nativity,* etc., is in agreement with this, for it is worded thus: "The devil, wherever he is, whether in the air or under the earth, drags with him the torments of his flames."[6] But the objection argues as though the corporeal fire tortured the spirit immediately in the same way as it torments bodies.

QUESTION LXXI
Of Works of Intercession for
THE DEAD
(In Fourteen Articles)

WE must now consider works of intercession for the dead. Under this head there are four-

[1] Julian, Bishop of Toledo, *Prognostic* II, 17 (PL 96, 482).   [2] Chap. 7 (QR II, 1003).
[3] *City of God*, XXI, 10 (PL 41, 725).   [4] *Ibid.*
[5] Aristotle, I, 6 (323ᵃ22).
[6] *Glossa ordin.* (VI, 213F); Bede, *In Jac.* (PL 93, 27).

teen points of inquiry: (1) Whether intercessory works performed by one person can profit others? (2) Whether the dead can be assisted by the works of the living? (3) Whether the intercessory works of sinners profit the dead? (4) Whether intercessory works for the dead profit those who perform them? (5) Whether intercessory works profit those who are in hell? (6) Whether they profit those who are in purgatory? (7) Whether they avail the children in limbo? (8) Whether in any way they profit those who are in heaven? (9) Whether the prayer of the Church, the Sacrament of the altar, and almsgiving profit the departed? (10) Whether indulgences granted by the Church profit them? (11) Whether the burial service profits the departed? (12) Whether intercessory works for one dead person profit that person more than others? (13) Whether intercessory works for many avail each one as much as if they were offered for each individual? (14) Whether general works of intercession avail those for whom special ones are not offered, as much as special and general prayers of intercession together avail those for whom they are offered?

ARTICLE 1. *Whether the Works of Intercession of One Person Can Profit Others?*

We proceed thus to the First Article: It would seem that the works of intercession (*suffragia*) of one person cannot profit others.

Objection 1. For it is written (Gal. 6. 8): *What things a man shall sow, those also shall he reap.* Now if one person reaped fruit from the intercessory works of another, he would reap from another's sowing. Therefore a person receives no fruit from the intercessory works of others.

Obj. 2. Further, It belongs to God's justice that each one should receive according to his merits, and so the psalm (61. 13) says: *Thou wilt render to every man according to his works.* Now it is impossible for God's justice to fail. Therefore it is impossible for one man to be assisted by the works of another.

Obj. 3. Further, A work is meritorious on the same count as it is praiseworthy, namely in so far as it is voluntary. Now one man is not praised for the work of another. Therefore neither can the work of one man be meritorious and fruitful for another.

Obj. 4. Further, It belongs to Divine justice to repay good for good in the same way as evil for evil. But no man is punished for the evil-doings of another; indeed, according to Ezech.

18. 4, *the soul that sinneth, the same shall die.* Therefore neither does one person profit by another's good.

On the contrary, It is written (Ps. 118. 63): *I am a partaker with all them that fear Thee,* etc.

Further, All the faithful united together by charity are members of the one body of the Church. Now one member is assisted by another. Therefore one man can be assisted by the merits of another.

I answer that, Our actions can avail for two purposes. First, for acquiring a certain state; thus by a meritorious work a man obtains the state of Happiness. Secondly, for something consequent upon a state; thus by some work a man merits an accidental reward, or a rebate of punishment. And for both these purposes our actions may avail in two ways: first, by way of merit, secondly, by way of prayer, the difference being that merit relies on justice, and prayer on mercy, since he who prays obtains his petition from the mere liberality of the one he prays.

Accordingly we must say that the work of one person in no way can avail another for acquiring a state by way of merit, so that, namely, a man is able to merit eternal life by the works which I do, because the share of glory is awarded according to the measure of the recipient, and each one is disposed by his own and not by another's actions,—disposed, that is to say, by being worthy of reward. By way of prayer, however, the work of one may profit another while he is a wayfarer, even for acquiring a state; for instance, one man may obtain the first grace for another, and since the answer to prayer depends on the liberality of God, to Whom we pray, it may extend to whatever is subject to the order of the Divine power.

On the other hand, as regards that which is consequent upon or accessory to a state, the work of one may avail another, not only by way of prayer but even by way of merit, and this happens in two ways. First, on account of their communion in the root of the work, which root is charity in meritorious works. Therefore all who are united together by charity acquire some benefit from one another's works, although according to the measure of each one's state, since even in heaven each one will rejoice in the goods of others. Hence it is that the communion of saints is laid down as an article of faith.[1] Secondly, through the in-

[1] Cf. The Apostles Creed (DZ 6).

tention of the doer who does certain works specially for the purpose that they may profit such persons, so that those works become somewhat the works of those for whom they are done, as though they were bestowed on them by the doer. And so they can avail them either for the fulfilment of satisfaction or for some similar purpose that does not change their state.

Reply Obj. 1. This reaping is the receiving of eternal life, as stated in John 4. 36, *And he that reapeth . . . gathereth fruit unto life everlasting.* Now a share of eternal life is not given to a man save for his own works, for although we may petition for another that he obtain life, this never happens except by means of his own works, when namely, at the prayers of one, another is given the grace whereby he merits eternal life.

Reply Obj. 2. The work that is done for another becomes his for whom it is done, and in like manner the work done by a man who is one with me is somewhat mine. Hence it is not contrary to Divine justice if a man receives the fruit of the works done by a man who is one with him in charity, or of works done for him. This also happens according to human justice, so that the satisfaction offered by one is accepted in lieu of another's.

Reply Obj. 3. Praise is not given to a person save according to his relation to an act, and therefore praise is "in relation to something."[1] And since no man is made or shown to be well or ill disposed to something by another's deed, it follows that no man is praised for another's deeds save accidentally, in so far as he is somewhat the cause of those deeds, by giving counsel, assistance, inducement, or by any other means. On the other hand, a work is meritorious to a person not only by reason of his disposition, but also in view of something consequent upon his disposition or state, as appears from what has been said.

Reply Obj. 4. It is directly contrary to justice to take away from a person that which is his due, but to give a person what is not his due is not contrary to justice, but surpasses the bounds of justice, for it is liberality. Now a person cannot be hurt by the ills of another, unless he be deprived of something of his own. Consequently it is not becoming that one should be punished for another's sins, as it is that one should acquire some advantage from the good deeds of another.

[1] *Ethics*, I, 12 (1101[b]12).

ARTICLE 2. *Whether the Dead Can Be Assisted by the Works of the Living?*

We proceed thus to the Second Article: It would seem that the dead cannot be assisted by the works of the living.

Objection 1. First, because the Apostle says (II Cor. 5. 10): *We must all be manifested before the judgment seat of Christ, that every one may receive the proper things of the body, according as he hath done.* Therefore nothing can accrue to a man from the works of others, which are done after his death and when he is no longer in the body.

Obj. 2. Further, This also seems to follow from the words of Apoc. 14. 13, *Blessed are the dead who die in the Lord . . . for their works follow them.*

Obj. 3. Further, It belongs only to one who is on the way to advance on account of some deed. Now after death men are no longer wayfarers, because to them the words of Job 19. 8, refer: *He hath hedged in my path round about, and I cannot pass.* Therefore the dead cannot be assisted by a person's intercessory works.

Obj. 4. Further, No one is assisted by the deed of another unless there be some community of life between them. Now there is no community between the dead and the living, as the Philosopher says.[2] Therefore the intercessions of the living do not profit the dead.

On the contrary are the words of II Machab. 12. 46: *It is . . . a holy and wholesome thought to pray for the dead, that they may be loosed from sins.* But this would not be profitable unless it were a help to them. Therefore the intercessory works of the living profit the dead.

Further, Augustine says (*De Cura pro Mort.* i):[3] "Of no small weight is the authority of the Church whereby she clearly approves of the custom by which a commendation of the dead has a place in the prayers which the priests pour forth to the Lord God at His altar." This custom was established by the apostles themselves according to the Damascene in a sermon on works of intercession for the dead,[4] where he expresses himself thus: "Realizing the nature of the Mysteries the disciples of the Saviour and His holy apostles sanctioned a commemoration of those who had died in the faith, being made in the awe-inspiring and life-giving Mysteries." This is also confirmed by the au-

[2] *Ethics*, I, 11 (1101[a]35).
[3] PL 40, 593.
[4] *De His Qui in Fide Dormierunt*, III (PG 95, 249).

thority of Dionysius (*Hier. Eccl.* vii),[1] where he mentions the rite of the Early Church in praying for the dead, and, moreover, asserts that the works of intercession of the living profit the dead.[2] Therefore we must believe this without any doubt.

I answer that, Charity, which is the bond uniting the members of the Church, extends not only to the living, but also to the dead who die in charity. For charity which is the life of the soul, even as the soul is the life of the body, has no end: *Charity never falleth away* (I Cor. 13. 8). Moreover, the dead live in the memory of the living, and therefore the intention of the living can be directed to them. Hence the intercessory works of the living profit the dead in two ways even as they profit the living, both on account of the bond of charity and on account of the intention being directed to them. Nevertheless, we must not believe that the intercessory works of the living profit them so as to change their state from unhappiness to happiness or conversely; but they avail for the lessening of punishment or something of the kind that involves no change in the state of the dead.

Reply Obj. 1. Man while living in the body merited that such things should avail him after death. Therefore if he is assisted thereby after this life, this is, nevertheless, the result of the things he has done in the body.

Or we may reply, according to John Damascene in the sermon quoted above, that these words refer to the retribution which will be made at the final judgment, of eternal glory or eternal unhappiness; for then each one will receive only according as he himself has done in the body. Meanwhile, however, he can be assisted by the intercessions of the living.

Reply Obj. 2. The words quoted refer expressly to the sequel of eternal retribution as is clear from the opening words: *Blessed are the dead,* etc. Or we may reply that deeds done on their behalf are somewhat their own, as stated above (A. 1).

Reply Obj. 3. Although, strictly speaking, after death souls are not in the state of the way, yet in a certain respect they are still on the way, in so far as they are delayed awhile in their advance towards their final reward. Therefore, strictly speaking, their way is hedged in round about, so that they can no more be changed by any works in respect of the state of happiness or unhappiness. Yet their way is not so hedged around that they cannot

be helped by others in the matter of their being delayed from receiving their final reward, because in this respect they are still wayfarers.

Reply Obj. 4. Although the communion of civic deeds, of which the Philosopher speaks, is impossible between the dead and the living, because the dead are outside civic life, the communication of the spiritual life is possible between them, for that life is founded on charity towards God, to Whom the spirits of the dead live.

ARTICLE 3. *Whether Suffrages Performed by Sinners Profit the Dead?*

We proceed thus to the Third Article: It would seem that intercessory works performed by sinners do not profit the dead.

Objection 1. For, according to John 9. 31, *God doth not hear sinners.* Now if their prayers were to profit those for whom they pray, they would be heard by God. Therefore the intercessory prayers performed by them do not profit the dead.

Obj. 2. Further, Gregory says (*Pastoral,* i, 10)[3] that "when an offensive person is sent to intercede, the wrath of the angered party is provoked to harsher measures." Now every sinner is offensive to God. Therefore God is not inclined to mercy by the intercession of sinners, and consequently their works of intercession are of no avail.

Obj. 3. Further, A person's deed would seem to be more fruitful to the doer than to another. But a sinner merits nothing for himself by his deeds. Much less, therefore, can he merit for another.

Obj. 4. Further, Every meritorious work must be a living work, that is to say, formed by charity. Now works done by sinners are dead. Therefore the dead for whom they are done cannot be assisted thereby.

Obj. 5. *On the contrary,* No man can know for certain about another man whether the latter be in a state of sin or of grace. If, therefore, only those intercessory works were profitable that are done by those who are in a state of grace, a man could not know of whom to ask intercessory works for his dead, and consequently many would be deterred from obtaining works of intercession.

Obj. 6. *Further,* According to Augustine (*Enchir.* cx),[4] as quoted in the text (iv *Sent.* d. 45),[5] the dead are assisted by works of intercession according as while living they merit-

[1] PG 3, 556.   [2] *Ibid.* (PG 3, 560).   [3] PL 77, 23.   [4] PL 40, 283.   [5] Lombard, chap. 2 (QR II, 1006).

ed to be assisted after death. Therefore the worth of prayers of intercession is measured according to the disposition of the person for whom they are performed. Therefore it would appear that it differs not whether they be performed by good or by wicked persons.

I answer that, Two things may be considered in the intercessions performed by the wicked. First, the deed done (*opus operatum*), for instance the sacrifice of the altar. And since our sacraments have their efficacy from themselves independently of the deed of the doer, and are equally efficacious by whomsoever they are performed, in this respect the intercessory works of the wicked profit the departed. Secondly, we may consider the deed of the doer (*opus operans*), and then we must draw a distinction; because the deed of a sinner who offers intercessory works may be considered in one way in so far as it is his own deed, and thus it can in no way be meritorious either to himself or to another; in another way in so far as it is another's deed, and this happens in two ways. First, when the sinner, offering works of intercession, represents the whole Church; for instance a priest when he performs the burial service in church. And since one in whose name or in whose stead a thing is done is understood to do it himself as Dionysius asserts (*Cæl. Hier.* xiii),[1] it follows that the intercessory works of that priest, although a sinner, profit the departed. Secondly, when he acts as the instrument of another, for the work of the instrument belongs more to the principal agent. Therefore, although he who acts as the instrument of another be not in a state of merit, his act may be meritorious on account of the principal agent; for instance if a servant being in sin do any work of mercy at the command of his master who has charity. Hence, if a person dying in charity command works of intercession to be offered for him, or if some other person having charity prescribe them, those works of intercession avail for the departed, even though the persons by whom they are performed be in sin. Nevertheless they would avail more if those persons were in charity, because then those works would be meritorious on two counts.

Reply Obj. 1. The prayer offered by a sinner is sometimes not his but another's, and consequently in this respect is worthy to be heard by God. Nevertheless, God sometimes hears sinners, when, namely, they ask for something acceptable to God. For God dispenses His goods

[1] Sect. 4 (PG 3, 305).

not only to the just but also to sinners (Matt. 5. 45), not indeed on account of their merits, but of His pity. Hence a gloss on John 9. 31, *God doth not hear sinners*, says[2] that he speaks as one "unanointed" and as not seeing clearly.

Reply Obj. 2. Although the sinner's prayer is not acceptable in so far as he is offensive, it may be acceptable to God on account of another in whose stead or at whose command he offers the prayer.

Reply Obj. 3. The reason why the sinner who performs these works of intercession gains nothing thereby is because he is not capable of profiting by reason of his own indisposition. Nevertheless, as stated above, it may in some way profit another, who is disposed.

Reply Obj. 4. Although the sinner's deed is not living in so far as it is his own, it may be living in so far as it is another's, as stated above.

Since, however, *the arguments in the contrary sense* would seem to show that it matters not whether one obtain intercession from good or from evil persons, we must reply to them also.

Reply Obj. 5. Although one cannot know for certain about another whether he be in the state of salvation, one may infer it with probability from what one sees outwardly of a man, for a tree is known by its fruit (Matt. 7. 16).

Reply Obj. 6. In order that intercession avail another, it is requisite that the one for whom it is performed be capable of availing by it, and a man has become capable of this by his own works which he did in his life-time. This is what Augustine means to say. Nevertheless, works must be such that they can profit him, and this depends not on the person for whom the intercession is performed, but rather on the one who offers the intercessory works whether by performing them or by commanding them.

ARTICLE 4. *Whether Intercessory Prayers Offered by the Living for the Dead Profit Those Who Offer Them?*

We proceed thus to the Fourth Article: It would seem that intercessory works offered by the living for the dead do not profit those who offer them.

Objection 1. For according to human justice a man is not absolved from his own debt if he pays a debt for another man. Therefore a man is not absolved from his own debt for the rea-

[2] *Glossa interl.* (v, 215r); Augustine, *In Joann.* (PL 35, 1718).

son that by offering works of intercession he has paid the debt of the one for whom he offered them.

Obj. 2. Further, Whatever a man does, he should do it as best he can. Now it is better to assist two than one. Therefore if one who by works of intercession has paid the debt of a dead person is freed from his own debt, it would seem that one ought never to satisfy for oneself but always for another.

Obj. 3. Further, If the satisfaction of one who satisfies for another profits him equally with the one for whom he satisfies, it will likewise equally profit a third person if he satisfy for him at the same time, and likewise a fourth and so on. Therefore he might satisfy for all by one work of satisfaction, which is absurd.

On the contrary, It is written (Ps. 34. 13): *My prayer shall be turned into my bosom.* Therefore, in like manner, intercessory works that are offered for others profit those who satisfy.

Further, The Damascene says in the sermon *On those who fell asleep in the faith:*[1] "Just as when about to anoint a sick man with the ointment or other holy oil, first of all he," namely the anointer, "shares in the anointing and thus proceeds to anoint the patient, so whoever strives for his neighbour's salvation first of all profits himself and afterwards his neighbour." And thus the question at issue is answered.

I answer that, The work of intercession that is done for another may be considered in two ways. First, as expiating punishment by way of compensation which is a condition of satisfaction, and in this way the work of intercession that is counted as belonging to the person for whom it is done, while absolving him from the debt of punishment, does not absolve the performer from his own debt of punishment, because in this compensation we have to consider the equality of justice, and this work of satisfaction can be equal to the one debt without being equal to the other, for the debts of two sinners require a greater satisfaction than the debt of one. Secondly, it may be considered as meriting eternal life, and this it has as proceeding from its root, which is charity, and in this way it profits not only the person for whom it is done, but also and still more the doer.

This suffices for the *Replies to the Objections;* for the first considered the work of intercession as a work of satisfaction, while the others consider it as meritorious.

[1] Sect. 18 (PG 95, 264).

ARTICLE 5. *Whether Works of Intercession Profit Those Who Are in Hell?*

We proceed thus to the Fifth Article: It would seem that works of intercession profit those who are in hell.

Objection 1. For it is written (II Machab. 12. 40): *They found under the coats of the slain some of the donaries of the idols . . ., which the law forbiddeth to the Jews,* and yet we read further on (*verse* 43) that Judas *sent twelve thousand drachms of silver to Jerusalem . . . to be offered for the sins of the dead.* Now it is clear that they sinned mortally through acting against the Law, and consequently that they died in mortal sin, and were taken to hell. Therefore works of intercession profit those who are in hell.

Obj. 2. Further, The text (iv *Sent.* d. 45)[2] quotes the saying of Augustine (*Enchir.* cx)[3] that "those whom works of intercession profit gain either entire forgiveness, or at least an abatement of their damnation." Now only those who are in hell are said to be damned. Therefore works of intercession profit even those who are in hell.

Obj. 3. Further, Dionysius says (*Eccl. Hier.* cap ult.):[4] "If here the prayers of the just avail those who are alive, how much more do they, after death, profit those alone who are worthy of their holy prayers?" Hence we may gather that intercessory works are more profitable to the dead than to the living. Now they profit the living even though they be in mortal sin, for the Church prays daily for sinners that they be converted to God. Therefore intercessory works avail also for the dead who are in mortal sin.

Obj. 4. Further, In the Lives of the Fathers (iii, 172: vi, 3)[5] we read, and Damascene relates[6] in a sermon of his that Macarius discovered the skull of a dead man on the road, and that after praying he asked whose head it was, and the head replied that it had belonged to a pagan priest who was condemned to hell; and yet he confessed that he and others were assisted by the prayers of Macarius. Therefore the intercessory works of the Church profit even those who are in hell.

Obj. 5. Further, The Damascene in the same sermon[7] relates that Gregory, while praying for Trajan, heard a voice from heaven saying

[2] Lombard, chap. 2 (QR II, 1007).
[3] PL 40, 283.   [4] PG 3, 561.
[5] PL 73, 797; 1013.
[6] *De His Qui in Fide Dormierunt,* 10 (PG 95, 256).
[7] PG 95, 264.

to him: "I have heard thy voice, and I pardon Trajan," and of this fact the Damascene adds in the same sermon (*ibid.*) "the whole East and West are witnesses." Yet it is clear that Trajan was in hell, since "he put many martyrs to a cruel death" (*ibid.*). Therefore the intercessory works of the Church avail even for those who are in hell.

On the contrary, Dionysius says (*Eccl. Hier.* vii):[1] "The high priest prays not for the unclean, because by so doing he would act counter to the Divine order," and a commentator[2] on the same place says that "he prays not that sinners be forgiven, because his prayer for them would not be heard." Therefore works of intercession do not avail those who are in hell.

Further, Gregory says (*Moral.* xxxiv, 19):[3] "There is the same reason for not praying then (namely, after the judgment day) for men condemned to the everlasting fire, as there is now for not praying for the devil and his angels who are sentenced to eternal punishment, and for this same reason the saints pray not for dead unbelieving and wicked men, because, indeed, knowing them to be already condemned to eternal punishment, they shrink from pleading for them by the merit of their prayers before they are summoned to the presence of the just Judge."

Further, The text (iv *Sent.* d. 45)[4] quotes the words of Augustine:[5] "If a man depart this life without the faith that worketh by charity and its sacraments, in vain do his friends have recourse to such acts of kindness." Now all the damned come under that head. Therefore intercessory works do not profit them.

I answer that, There have been three opinions about the damned. For some have said that a twofold distinction must be made in this matter. First, as to time; for they said that after the judgment day no one in hell will be assisted by any intercession, but that before the judgment day some are assisted by the intercessory works of the Church. Secondly, they made a distinction among those who are detained in hell. Some of these, they said, are very bad, those namely who have died without faith and the sacraments, and these, since they were not of the Church, neither by grace nor

by name, the intercessory works of the Church cannot avail; while others are not very bad, those namely who belonged to the Church as actual members, who had the faith, frequented the sacraments and performed works generically good, and for these the intercessory works of the Church ought to avail.

Yet they were confronted with a difficulty which troubled them, for it would seem to follow from this (since the punishment of hell is finite in intensity although infinite in duration) that a multiplicity of intercessory works would take away that punishment altogether, which is the error of Origen,[6] and consequently they endeavoured in various ways to avoid this difficulty.

For Præpositinus said[7] that intercessory works for the damned can be so multiplied that they are entirely freed from punishment, not absolutely as Origen maintained, but for a time, namely till the judgment day, for their souls will be reunited to their bodies, and will be cast back into the punishments of hell without hope of pardon. But this opinion seems incompatible with Divine providence, which leaves nothing unordered in things. For guilt cannot be restored to order save by punishment; therefore it is impossible for punishment to cease, unless first of all guilt be expiated, so that, as guilt remains for ever in the damned, their punishment will in no way be interrupted.

For this reason the followers of Gilbert de la Porrée[8] devised another explanation. These said that the process in the lessening of punishments by intercessory works is as the process in dividing a line, which though finite, is indefinitely divisible, and is never destroyed by division, if it is diminished not by equal but by proportionate quantities, for instance if we begin by taking away a quarter of the whole and, secondly, a quarter of that quarter, and then a quarter of this second quarter, and so on indefinitely. In like manner, they say by the first work of intercession a certain proportion of the punishment is taken away, and by the second an equally proportionate part of the remainder. But this explanation is in many ways defective. First, because it seems that indefinite division which is applicable to continuous quantity cannot be transferred to spiritual

---

[1] PG 3, 564.

[2] Maximus, *In De Eccl. Hier.*, chap. VIII, pt. III, sect. 7 (PG 4, 181); Cf. Albert, *In Sent.*, IV, d. XLV, A. 3, Sed contra 2 (BO XXX, 610).

[3] PL 76, 739.

[4] Peter Lombard, chap. 2 (QR II, 1007).

[5] *Serm. ad Popul.*, Serm. CLXXII, chap. 2 (PL 38, 937).

[6] *Peri Archon,* I, 6 (PG 11, 169); cf. Gregory the Great, *Moral.*, XXXIV, 19 (PL 76, 737).

[7] *Summa,* Pt. IV (fol. 85rb); see William of Auxerre, *Summa Aurea,* Pt. IV (303ra); Bonaventure, *In Sent.*, IV, d. XLVI, Pt. I, Q. I, A. I (QR IV, 957); Albert, *In Sent.*, IV, d. XLVI, A. 2 (BO XXX, 630).

[8] Cf. Albert, *In Sent.*, IV, d. XLVI, A. 2 (BO XXX, 630).

quantity; secondly, because there is no reason why the second work of intercession, if it be of equal worth, should diminish the punishment less than the first; thirdly, because punishment cannot be diminished unless guilt be diminished, even as it cannot be done away unless the guilt be done away; fourthly, because in the division of a line we come at length to something which is not sensible, for a sensible body is not indefinitely divisible, and thus it would follow that after many works of intercession the remaining punishment would be so little as not to be felt, and thus would no longer be a punishment.

Hence others found another explanation. For William of Auxerre said[1] that intercessory works profit the damned not by diminishing or interrupting their punishment, but by fortifying the person punished, even as a man who is carrying a heavy load might bathe his face in water, for thus he would be enabled to carry it better, and yet his load would be none the lighter. But this again is impossible, because according to Gregory (*Moral.* ix)[2] a man suffers more or less from the eternal fire according as his guilt deserves, and consequently some suffer more, some less, from the same fire; therefore since the guilt of the damned remains unchanged, it cannot be that he suffers less punishment. Moreover, this opinion is presumptuous, as being in opposition to the statements of holy men, and groundless as being based on no authority. It is also unreasonable. First, because the damned in hell are cut off from the bond of charity in virtue of which the departed are in touch with the works of the living. Secondly, because they have entirely come to the end of life, and have received the final award for their merits, even as the saints who are in heaven. For the remaining punishment or glory of the body does not make them to be wayfarers, since glory essentially and radically resides in the soul. It is the same with the unhappiness of the damned, and so their punishment cannot be diminished as neither can the glory of the saints be increased as to the essential reward.

However, we may admit, in a certain measure, the manner in which, according to some, intercessory works profit the damned, if it be said that they profit neither by diminishing nor interrupting their punishment, nor again by diminishing their sense of punishment, but

by withdrawing from the damned some matter of sorrow, which matter they might have if they knew themselves to be so outcast as to be a care to no one; and this matter of sorrow is withdrawn from them when intercessory works are offered for them. Yet even this is impossible according to the general law, because as Augustine says (*De Cura pro Mort.* xiii)[3]—and this applies especially to the damned—"the spirits of the departed are where they see nothing of what men do or of what happens to them in this life," and consequently they know not when intercessory works are offered for them, unless this relief be granted from above to some of the damned in despite of the general law. This, however, is a matter of great uncertainty; therefore it is safer to say absolutely that intercessory prayers do not profit the damned, nor does the Church intend to pray for them, as appears from the authors quoted above.[4]

Reply Obj. 1. The donaries to the idols were not found on those dead so that they might be taken as a sign that they were carried off in reverence to the idols, but they took them as conquerors because they were due to them by right of war. They sinned, however, venially by covetousness, and consequently they were not damned in hell, and thus works of intercession could profit them. Or we may say, according to some, that in the midst of fighting, seeing they were in danger, they repented of their sin, according to Ps. 77. 34, *When He slew them, then they sought Him,* and this can be held as a probable opinion. Therefore the offering was made for them.

Reply Obj. 2. In these words damnation is taken in a broad sense for any kind of punishment, so as to include also the punishment of purgatory which is sometimes entirely expiated by works of intercession, and sometimes not entirely, but diminished.

Reply Obj. 3. Intercession for a dead person is more acceptable than for a living person, as regards his being in greater want, since he cannot help himself as a living person can. But a living person is better off in that he can be taken from the state of mortal sin to the state of grace, which cannot be said of the dead. Hence there is not the same reason for praying for the dead as for the living.

Reply Obj. 4. This assistance did not consist in a diminishment of their punishment, but in this alone (as stated in the same place) that when he prayed they were permitted to see one

---

[1] Cf. Albert, *Ibid.*, See also Bonaventure, *In Sent.*, IV, d. XLVI, Pt. I, A. I, Q. I (QR IV, 958).

[2] Chap. 65 (PL 75, 913).

[3] PL 40, 605.   [4] On the Contrary, 1, 2, 3.

another, and in this they had a certain joy, not real but imaginary, in the fulfilment of their desire. Even so the demons are said to rejoice when they draw men into sin, although this in no way diminishes their punishment, as neither is the joy of the angels diminished by the fact that they take pity on our ills.

Reply Obj. 5. Concerning the incident of Trajan it may be supposed with probability that he was recalled to life at the prayers of blessed Gregory, and thus obtained the grace whereby he received the pardon of his sins and in consequence was freed from punishment. The same applies to all those who were miraculously raised from the dead, many of whom were evidently idolaters and damned. For we must say likewise of all such persons that they were consigned to hell, not finally, but as was actually due to their own merits according to justice, and that according to higher causes, in view of which it was foreseen that they would be recalled to life, they were to be disposed of otherwise.

Or we may say with some that Trajan's soul was not freed absolutely from the debt of eternal punishment, but that his punishment was suspended for a time, that is, until the judgment day. Nor does it follow that this is the general result of works of intercession, because things happen differently in accordance with the general law from that which is permitted in particular cases and by privilege. Even so the bounds of human affairs differ from those of the signs of the Divine power as Augustine says (*De Cura pro Mort.* xvi).[1]

ARTICLE 6. Whether Works of Intercession Profit Those Who Are in Purgatory?

We proceed thus to the Sixth Article: It would seem that works of intercession do not profit even those who are in purgatory.

Objection 1. For purgatory is a part of hell. Now "there is no redemption in hell,"[2] and it is written (Ps. 6. 6), *Who shall confess to Thee in hell?* Therefore works of intercession do not profit those who are in purgatory.

Obj. 2. Further, The punishment of purgatory is finite. Therefore if some of the punishment is abated by works of intercession, it would be possible to have such a great number of prayers of intercession that the punishment would be entirely remitted, and consequently the sin entirely unpunished; and this would seem incompatible with Divine justice.

Obj. 3. Further, Souls are in purgatory in

order that they may be purified there, and being pure may come to the kingdom. Now nothing can be purified unless something be done to it. Therefore intercessory works offered by the living do not diminish the punishment of purgatory.

Obj. 4. If intercessory works availed those who are in purgatory, those especially would seem to avail them which are offered at their behest. Yet these do not always avail; for instance, if a person before dying were to provide for so many works of intercession to be offered for him that if they were offered they would suffice for the remission of his entire punishment. Now supposing these works of intercession to be delayed until he is released from punishment, they will profit him nothing. For it cannot be said that they profit him before they are discharged, and after they are fulfilled he no longer needs them, since he is already released. Therefore works of intercession do not avail those who are in purgatory.

On the contrary, As quoted in the text (iv *Sent.* d. 45),[3] Augustine says (*Enchir.* cx)[4] that prayers of intercession profit those who are not very good or not very bad. Now such are those who are detained in purgatory. Therefore, etc.

Further, Dionysius says (*Eccl. Hier.* vii)[5] that "the godlike priest in praying for the departed prays for those who lived a holy life, and yet contracted certain stains through human frailty." Now such persons are detained in purgatory. Therefore, etc.

I answer that, The punishment of purgatory is intended to supplement the satisfaction which was not fully completed in the body. Consequently, since, as stated above (A. 1, REPLY 2; Q. XIII, A. 2), the works of one person can avail for another's satisfaction, whether the latter be living or dead, the intercessory works of the living, without any doubt, profit those who are in purgatory.

Reply Obj. 1. The words quoted refer to those who are in the hell of the damned, where there is no redemption for those who are finally consigned to that punishment. We may also reply with Damascene (*Serm. de Dormientibus*)[6] that such statements are to be explained with reference to the lower causes, that is according to the demands of the merits of those who are consigned to those punishments. But according to the Divine mercy, which transcends human merits, it happens otherwise

---

[1] PL 40, 606. [2] Office of the dead, *Resp.*, VII.

[3] Peter Lombard, chap. 2 (QR II, 1007).
[4] PL 40, 283.   [5] Sect. 4 (PG 3, 560).
[6] Sect. 8 (PG 95, 253); cf. sect. 2 (PG 95, 249).

through the prayers of the just than is implied by the expressions quoted in the authorities above. Now "God changes His sentence but not his counsel," as Gregory says.[1] Hence Damascene (loc. cit.)[2] quotes as instances of this the Ninevites, Achab and Ezechias, in whom it is apparent that the sentence pronounced against them by God was commuted by the Divine mercy.[3]

Reply Obj. 2. It is not unreasonable that the punishment of those who are in purgatory be entirely done away by the multiplicity of intercessions. But it does not follow that the sins remain unpunished, because the punishment of one undertaken in lieu of another is credited to that other.

Reply Obj. 3. The purifying of the soul by the punishment of purgatory is nothing else than the expiation of the guilt that hinders it from obtaining glory. And since, as stated above, the guilt of one person can be expiated by the punishment which another undergoes in his stead, it is not unreasonable that one person be purified by another satisfying for him.

Reply Obj. 4. Intercession avails on two counts, namely the action of the agent and the action done (Ex opere operante and ex opere operato). By action done I mean not only the sacrament of the Church, but the effect incidental to that action,—thus from the giving of alms there follow the relief of the poor and their prayer to God for the deceased. In like manner the action of the agent may be considered in relation either to the principal agent or to the secondary agent. I say, then, that the dying person, as soon as he provides for certain prayers of intercession to be offered for him, receives the full reward of those intercessions, even before they are discharged, as regards the efficacy of the intercessions that results from the action as proceeding from the principal agent. But as regards the efficacy of the intercessions arising from the action done or from the action as proceeding from the secondary agent, he does not receive the fruit before the intercessions are discharged. And if, before this, he happens to be released from his punishment, he will in this respect be deprived of the fruit of the intercessions, and this will fall back upon those by whose fault he was then defrauded. For it is not unreasonable that a person be defrauded in temporal matters by another's fault,—and the punishment of purgatory is temporal,—although as regards the eternal retribution none can be defrauded save by his own fault.

ARTICLE 7. Whether Works of Intercession Avail the Children Who Are in Limbo?

We proceed thus to the Seventh Article: It would seem that works of intercession avail the children who are in limbo.

Objection 1. For they are not detained there except for another's sin. Therefore it is most fitting that they should be assisted by the intercessory prayers of others.

Obj. 2. Further, In the text (iv Sent. d. 45)[4] it is held from the words of Augustine (Enchir. cx.)[5] the intercessory works of the Church obtain forgiveness for those who are not very bad. Now children are not reckoned among those who are very bad, since "their punishment is very light."[6] Therefore the intercessory prayers of the Church avail them.

On the contrary, The text (ibid.) quotes Augustine as saying[7] that intercessory prayers do not avail those who have departed hence without the faith that works by love. Now the children departed thus. Therefore intercessory works do not avail them.

I answer that, Unbaptized children are not detained in limbo save because they lack the state of grace. Hence, since the state of the dead cannot be changed by the works of the living, especially as regards the merit of the essential reward or punishment, the intercessions of the living cannot profit the children in limbo.

Reply Obj. 1. Although original sin is such that one person can be assisted by another on its account, nevertheless the souls of the children in limbo are in such a state that they cannot be assisted, because after this life there is no time for obtaining grace.

Reply Obj. 2. Augustine is speaking of those who are not very bad, but have been baptized. This is clear from what precedes: "Since these sacrifices, whether of the altar or of any alms whatsoever, are offered for those who have been baptized," etc.

ARTICLE 8. Whether Works of Intercession Profit the Saints in Heaven?

We proceed thus to the Eighth Article: It would seem that in some way intercessory works profit the saints in heaven.

[1] Moral. XVI, 37 (PL 75, 1144).
[2] Sect. 14 (PG 95, 261).
[3] Jonas, 3.10; III Kings 21.29; IV Kings 20.5.
[4] Peter Lombard (QR II, 1007).   [5] PL 40, 283.
[6] Op. Cit., chap. XCIII (PL 40, 275).
[7] Serm. ad Pop., serm. CLXXII, 2 (PL 38, 937).

Objection 1. For the words of the collect in the mass say:[1] "Even as they (that is, the sacraments) avail thy saints unto glory, so may they profit us unto healing." Now foremost among all intercessions is the sacrifice of the altar. Therefore intercessions profit the saints in heaven.

Obj. 2. Further, The sacraments cause what they signify. Now the third part of the host, that namely which is dropped into the chalice, signifies those who lead a happy life in heaven. Therefore the intercessions of the Church profit those who are in heaven.

Obj. 3. Further, The saints rejoice in heaven not only in their own goods, but also in the goods of others; hence it is written (Luke 15. 10): *There is* (Vulg.,—*shall be*) *joy before the angels of God upon one sinner doing penance.* Therefore the joy of the saints in heaven increases on account of the good works of the living, and consequently our works of intercession also profit them.

Obj. 4. Further, The Damascene says (*Serm. de Dormient.*)[2] quoting the words of Chrysostom:[3] "For if the heathens," he says, "burn the dead together with what has belonged to them, how much more shouldst thou, a believer, send forth a believer together with what has belonged to him, not that they also may be brought to ashes like him, but that thou mayest surround him with greater glory by so doing; and if he be a sinner who has died, that thou mayest loose him from his sins, and if he be just, that thou mayest add to his meed and reward!" And thus the same conclusion follows.

On the contrary, As quoted in the text (iv *Sent.* d. 45),[4] Augustine says:[5] "It is insulting to pray for a martyr in church, since we ought to commend ourselves to his prayers."

Further, To be assisted belongs to one who is in need. But the saints in heaven are without any need whatever. Therefore they are not assisted by the intercessions of the Church.

I answer that, Intercession by its very nature implies the giving of some assistance, which does not apply to one who suffers no default, since no one is able to be assisted except he who is in need. Hence, as the saints in heaven are free from all need, being inebriated with the plenty of God's house (Ps. 35. 10), they

are not able to be assisted by works of intercession.

Reply Obj. 1. Such expressions do not mean that the saints receive an increase of glory in themselves through our observing their feasts, but that we profit thereby in celebrating their glory with greater solemnity. Thus, through our knowing or praising God, and through His glory thus increasing somewhat in us, there accrues something, not to God, but to us.

Reply Obj. 2. Although the sacraments cause what they signify, they do not produce this effect in respect of everything that they signify; otherwise, since they signify Christ, they would produce something in Christ (which is absurd). But they produce their effect on the recipient of the sacrament in virtue of that which is signified by the sacrament. Thus it does not follow that the sacrifices offered for the faithful departed profit the saints, but that by the merits of the saints which we commemorate, or which are signified in the sacrament, they profit others for whom they are offered.

Reply Obj. 3. Although the saints in heaven rejoice in all our goods, it does not follow that if our joys be increased their joy is also increased formally, but only materially, because every passion is increased formally in respect of the formal aspect of its object. Now the formal aspect of the saints' joy, no matter what they rejoice in, is God Himself, in Whom they cannot rejoice more and less, for otherwise their essential reward, consisting of their joy in God, would vary. Hence from the fact that the goods are multiplied, wherein they rejoice with God as the formal aspect of their joy, it does not follow that their joy is intensified, but that they rejoice in more things. Consequently it does not follow that they are assisted by our works.

Reply Obj. 4. The sense is not that an increase of meed or reward accrues to the saint from the intercessions offered by a person, but that this accrues to the offerer. Or we may reply that the blessed departed may derive a reward from intercessions through having, while living, provided for intercessory works to be offered for himself, and this was meritorious for him.

ARTICLE 9. *Whether the Prayers of the Church, the Sacrifice of the Altar, and Alms Profit the Departed?*

We proceed thus to the Ninth Article: It would seem that the souls of the departed are not assisted only by the prayers of the Church,

---

[1] Postcommunion, Feast of S. Andrew, Apostle. (Nov, 30).   [2] Sect. 6 (PG 95, 252).
[3] *In Matt.*, hom. xxx (PG 57, 375).
[4] QR ii, 1007.
[5] *Serm. ad Pop.*, serm. CLIX, 1 (PL 38, 868).

the sacrifice of the altar and alms, or that they are not assisted by them chiefly.

Objection 1. For punishment should compensate for punishment. Now fasting is more penal than almsgiving or prayer. Therefore fasting profits more as intercession than any of the above.

Obj. 2. Further, Gregory numbers fasting together with these three, as stated in the Decretals (xiii, Q. ii, cap. 22):[1] "The souls of the departed are released in four ways, either by the offerings of priests, or the alms of their friends, or the prayers of the saints, or the fasting of their kinsfolk." Therefore the three mentioned here[2] are insufficiently numbered by Augustine.[3]

Obj. 3. Further, Baptism is the greatest of the sacraments, especially as regards its effect. Therefore Baptism and other sacraments ought to be offered for the departed equally with or more than the sacrament of the altar.

Obj. 4. Further, This would seem to follow from the words of I Cor. 15. 29, *If the dead rise not again at all, why are they then baptized for them?* Therefore Baptism avails as intercession for the dead.

Obj. 5. Further, In different masses there is the same sacrifice of the altar. If, therefore, sacrifice, and not the mass, be counted among the intercessions, it would seem that the effect would be the same whatever mass be said for a deceased person, whether in honour of the Blessed Virgin or of the Holy Ghost, or any other. Yet this seems contrary to the ordinance of the Church which has appointed a special mass for the dead.

Obj. 6. Further, The Damascene (*Serm. de Dormient.*)[4] teaches that candles and oil should be offered for the dead. Therefore not only the offering of the sacrifice of the altar, but also other offerings should be reckoned among intercessions for the dead.

I answer that, The intercessory works of the living profit the dead in so far as the latter are united to the living in charity, and in so far as the intention of the living is directed to the dead. Consequently those works are by nature best adapted to assist the dead which pertain chiefly to the communication of charity, or to the directing of one's intention to another person. Now the sacrament of the Eucharist belongs chiefly to charity, since it is the sacrament of ecclesiastical unity, because it contains Him in Whom the whole Church is united and incorporated, namely Christ; therefore the Eucharist is as it were the origin and bond of charity. Again, chief among the effects of charity is the work of almsgiving. Therefore on the part of charity these two, namely the sacrifice of the Church and almsgiving are the chief helps for the dead. But on the part of the intention directed to the dead the chief help is prayer, because prayer by its very nature implies relation not only to the person who prays, even as other works do, but more directly still to that which we pray for. Hence these three are accounted the principal means of succouring the dead, although we must allow that any other goods whatsoever that are done out of charity for the dead are profitable to them.

Reply Obj. 1. When one person satisfies for another, the point to consider, in order that the effect of his satisfaction reach the other, is the thing whereby the satisfaction of one passes to another, rather than even the punishment undergone by way of satisfaction; although the punishment expiates more the guilt of the one who satisfies, in so far as it is a kind of medicine. And consequently the three previously mentioned are more profitable to the departed than fasting.

Reply Obj. 2. It is true that fasting can profit the departed by reason of charity, and on account of the intention being directed to the departed. Nevertheless, fasting does not by its nature contain anything pertaining to charity or to the directing of the intention, and these things are extrinsic to it as it were, and for this reason Augustine did not number, while Gregory did place, fasting among the suffrages for the dead.

Reply Obj. 3. Baptism is a spiritual regeneration, and therefore just as by generation being does not accrue save to the being generated, so Baptism produces its effect only in the person baptized, as regards the deed done; and yet as regards the deed of the doer, whether of the baptizer or of the baptized, it may profit others even as other meritorious works. On the other hand, the Eucharist is the sign of ecclesiastical unity, and therefore by reason of the deed done its effect can pass to another, which is not the case with the other sacraments.

Reply Obj. 4. According to a gloss[5] this passage may be expounded in two ways. First,

1 RF I, 728.

2 Peter Lombard, *Sent.,* IV, d. 45, chap. 2 (QR II, 1006).

3 *Serm. ad Pop.,* serm. CLXXII, 2 (PL 38, 936); *Enchiridion,* CX (PL 40, 280); cf. *De Cura pro Mort.,* XVIII (PL 40, 609).   4 Sect. 19 (PG 95, 265).

5 *Glossa ordin.* (VI, 58F); *Glossa Lombardi* (PL 191, 1683). Cf. Sedulius Scotus, *In Epist. B. Paul:* (PL 103, 159); Lanfranc, *In D. Pauli Epist.* (PL 150, 210).

thus: "If the dead rise not again, nor did Christ rise again, why are they baptized for them? that is, for sins, since they are not pardoned if Christ rose not again," because in Baptism not only Christ's passion but also His resurrection operates, for the latter is in a sense the cause of our spiritual resurrection. Secondly, thus: "There have been some misguided persons who were baptized for those who had departed this life without baptism, thinking that this would profit them"; and according to this explanation the Apostle is speaking, in the above words, merely according to the opinion of certain persons.

Reply Obj. 5. In the office of the mass there is not only a sacrifice but also prayers. Hence the mass contains two of the things mentioned by Augustine (*loc. cit.*), namely prayer and sacrifice. As regards the sacrifice offered the mass profits equally the departed, no matter in whose honour it be said, and this is the principal thing done in the mass. But as regards the prayers, that mass is most profitable in which the prayers are appointed for this purpose. Nevertheless, this defect may be supplied by the greater devotion, either of the one who says mass, or of the one who orders the mass to be said, or again, by the intercession of the saint whose help is sought in the mass.

Reply Obj. 6. This offering of candles or oil may profit the departed in so far as they are a kind of alms, for they are given for the worship of the Church or for the use of the faithful.

ARTICLE 10. *Whether the Indulgences of the Church Profit the Dead?*

We proceed thus to the Tenth Article: It would seem that the indulgences granted by the Church profit even the dead.

Objection 1. First, on account of the custom of the Church, who orders the preaching of a crusade in order that some one may gain an indulgence for himself and for two or three and sometimes even ten souls, both of the living and of the dead.[1] But this would amount to a deception unless they profited the dead. Therefore indulgences profit the dead.

Obj. 2. Further, The merit of the whole Church is more efficacious than that of one person. Now personal merit serves as an intercession for the departed, for instance in the case of almsgiving. Much more therefore does the merit of the Church on which indulgences are founded.

[1] Cf. Albert, *In Sent.*, IV, d. XX, A. 18, Q. 3, Arg. 1 (BO XXIX, 853).

Obj. 3. Further, The indulgences of the Church profit those who are members of the Church. Now those who are in purgatory are members of the Church, for otherwise the intercessory prayers of the Church would not profit them. Therefore it would seem that indulgences profit the departed.

On the contrary, In order that indulgences may avail a person, there must be a fitting cause for granting the indulgence. Now there can be no such cause on the part of the dead, since they can do nothing that is of profit to the Church, and it is for such a cause that indulgences are chiefly granted. Therefore, it seems, indulgences do not profit the dead.

Further, Indulgences are regulated according to the decision of the party who grants them. If, therefore, indulgences could avail the dead, it would be in the power of the party granting them to release a deceased person entirely from punishment, which seems to be absurd.

I answer that, An indulgence may profit a person in two ways: in one way, principally; in another, secondarily. It profits principally the person who avails himself of an indulgence, who, namely, does that for which the indulgence is granted, for instance one who visits the shrine of some saint. Hence since the dead can do none of those things for which indulgences are granted, indulgences cannot avail them directly.

However, they profit secondarily and indirectly the person for whom one does that which is the cause of the indulgence. This is sometimes feasible and sometimes not, according to the different forms of indulgence. For if the form of indulgence be such as this: "Whosoever does this or that shall gain so much indulgence," he who does this cannot transfer the fruit of the indulgence to another, because it is not in his power to apply to a particular person the intention of the Church who dispenses the common prayers of intercession from which indulgences derive their value, as stated above (Q. XXVII, A. 3, Reply 2). If, however, the indulgence be granted in this form: "Whosoever does this or that, he, his father, or any other person connected with him and detained in purgatory, will gain so much indulgence," an indulgence of this kind will avail not only a living but also a deceased person. For there is no reason why the Church is able to transfer the common merits, on which indulgences are based, to the living and not to the dead.

Nor does it follow that a prelate of the Church can free souls from purgatory at his choice, since for indulgences to avail there must be a fitting cause for granting them, as stated above (Q. XXV, A. 2).

ARTICLE 11. *Whether the Burial Service Profits the Dead?*

We proceed thus to the Eleventh Article: It would seem that the burial service profits the dead.

Objection 1. For Damascene (*Serm. de Dormient.*)[1] quotes Athanasius as saying: "Even though he who has departed in godliness be taken up to heaven, do not hesitate to call upon God and to burn oil and wax at his tomb: for such things are pleasing to God and receive a great reward from Him." Now the like pertain to the burial service. Therefore the burial service profits the dead.

Obj. 2. Further, According to Augustine,[2] "In olden times the funerals of just men were cared for with dutiful piety, their obsequies celebrated, their graves provided, and themselves while living charged their children touching the burial or even the translation of their bodies." But they would not have done this unless the tomb and things of this kind conferred something on the dead. Therefore this kind of thing profits the dead in some way.

Obj. 3. Further, No one does a work of mercy on some one's behalf unless it profit him. Now burying the dead is counted among the works of mercy, and therefore Augustine says:[3] "Tobias, as attested by the angel, is declared to have found favour with God by burying the dead." Therefore such burial observances profit the dead.

Obj. 4. Further, It is unbecoming to assert that the devotion of the faithful is fruitless. Now some, out of devotion, arrange for their burial in some religious locality. Therefore the burial service profits the dead.

Obj. 5. Further, God is more inclined to pity than to condemn. Now burial in a sacred place is hurtful to some if they are unworthy, and therefore Gregory says (*Dial.* iv, 50):[4] "If those who are burdened with grievous sins are buried in the church this will lead to their more severe condemnation rather than to their release." Much more, therefore, should we say that the burial service profits the good.

On the contrary, Augustine says (*De Cura pro Mort.* xviii):[5] "Whatever service is done the body is no aid to salvation, but an office of humanity."

Further, Gregory says:[6] "The funereal equipment, the disposition of the grave, the solemnity of the obsequies are a comfort to the living rather than a help to the dead."

Further, Our Lord said (Luke 12. 4): *Be not afraid of them who kill the body, and after that have no more that they can do.* Now after death the bodies of the saints can be hindered from being buried, as we read of having been done to certain martyrs at Lyons in Gaul (Eusebius, *Eccl. Hist.* vi, 1).[7] Therefore the dead take no harm if their bodies remain unburied, and consequently the burial service does not profit the dead.

I answer that, We have recourse to burial for the sake of both the living and the dead. For the sake of the living, lest their eyes be revolted by the disfigurement of the corpse, and their bodies be infected by the stench, and this as regards the body. But it profits the living also spiritually in so far as our belief in the resurrection is affirmed thereby. It profits the dead in so far as one bears the dead in mind and prays for them through looking on their burial place; hence, too, a monument takes its name from remembrance, for a monument is something that recalls the mind (*monens mentem*), as Augustine observes.[8] It was, however, a pagan error that burial was profitable to the dead by procuring rest for his soul, for they believed that the soul could not be at rest until the body was buried, which is altogether ridiculous and absurd.

That, moreover, burial in a sacred place profits the dead, does not result from the action done, but rather from the action itself of the doer, when, that is, the dead person himself, or another, arranges for his body to be buried in a sacred place, and commends him to the patronage of some saint, by whose prayers we must believe that he is assisted, as well as to the intercessory works of those who serve the holy place, and pray more frequently and more specially for those who are buried in their midst. But such things as are done for the display of the obsequies are profitable to the living as being a consolation to them; and yet they can also profit the dead, not directly but in-

---

[1] Sect. 19 (PG 95, 265).

[2] *City of God*, I, 13 (PL 41, 27); cf. *De Cura pro Mort.*, 3 (PL 40, 595).

[3] *Ibid.*

[4] PL 77, 412.

[5] PL 40, 610.

[6] Cf. Gratian, *Decretum*, II, causa XIII, Q. 2, can. 22 (RF 1, 728). The text is from Augustine, *De Cura pro Mort.*, 2 (PL 40, 594).

[7] PG 20, 433.

[8] *De Cura pro Mort.*, 4 (PL 40, 596).

directly, in so far as men are aroused to pity thereby and consequently to pray, or in so far as the outlay on the burial brings either assistance to the poor or adornment to the church, for it is in this sense that the burial of the dead is accounted among the works of mercy.

Reply Obj. 1. By bringing oil and candles to the tombs of the dead we profit them indirectly, either as offering them to the Church and as giving them to the poor, or as doing this in reverence of God. Hence, after the words quoted we read: "For oil and candles are a holocaust."

Reply Obj. 2. The fathers of old arranged for the burial of their bodies, so as to show that "the bodies of the dead are the object of Divine providence, not that there is any feeling in a dead body, but in order to confirm the belief in the resurrection," as Augustine says.[1] Hence, also, they wished to be buried in the land of promise,[2] where they believed Christ's birth and death would take place, Whose resurrection is the cause of our rising again.

Reply Obj. 3. Since flesh is a part of man's nature, man has a natural affection for his flesh, according to Eph. 5. 29, *No man ever hated his own flesh.* Hence in accordance with this natural affection a man has during life a certain solicitude for what will become of his body after death, and he would grieve if he had a presentiment that some indignity would happen to his body. Consequently those who love a man, through being conformed to the one they love in his affection for himself, treat his body with loving care. For as Augustine says:[3] "If a father's garment and ring, and whatever such like is the more dear to those whom they leave behind the greater their affection is towards their parents, in no way are the bodies themselves to be spurned which truly we wear in more familiar and close conjunction than anything else we put on."

Reply Obj. 4. As Augustine says (*De Cura pro Mort.* iv),[4] the devotion of the faithful is not fruitless when they arrange for their friends to be buried in holy places, since by so doing they commend their dead to the prayers of the saints, as stated above.

Reply Obj. 5. The wicked man dead takes no harm by being buried in a holy place, except in so far as he procured such a burial place, unfitting for him, by reason of human glory.

[1] *City of God,* I, 13 (PL 41, 27); cf. *De Cura pro Mort.,* 3 (PL 40, 595).
[2] Cf. Gen. 23; 25.9; 49.29; 50.24.
[3] *City of God,* I, 13 (PL 41, 27); cf. *De Cura pro Mort.,* 3 (PL 40, 595).　　[4] PL 40, 596.

ARTICLE 12. *Whether Works of Intercession Offered for One Deceased Person Profit the Person for Whom They Are Offered More Than Others?*

We proceed thus to the Twelfth Article: It would seem that works of intercession offered for one deceased person are not more profitable to the one for whom they are offered, than to others.

Objection 1. For spiritual light is more communicable than a material light. Now a material light, for instance of a candle, though kindled for one person only, avails equally all those who are gathered together, though the candle be not lit for them. Therefore, since intercessory works are a kind of spiritual light, though they be offered for one person in particular, do not avail him any more than the others who are in purgatory .

Obj. 2. Further, As stated in the text (iv *Sent.* d. 45),[5] intercessory works avail the dead "in so far as during this life they merited that they might avail them afterwards." Now some merited that works of intercession might avail them more than those for whom they are offered. Therefore they profit more by those works of intercession, for otherwise their merits would be rendered unavailing.

Obj. 3. Further, The poor have not so many works of intercession offered for them as the rich. Therefore if the intercessory works offered for certain people profit them alone, or profit them more than others, the poor would be worse off; yet this is contrary to our Lord's saying (Luke 6. 20): *Blessed are ye poor, for yours is the kingdom of God.*

On the contrary, Human justice is copied from Divine justice. But if a person pay another's debt human justice releases the latter alone. Therefore since he who offers works of intercession for another pays the debt, in a sense, of the person for whom he offers them, they profit this person alone.

Further, just as a man by offering works of intercession satisfies somewhat for a deceased person, so, too, sometimes a person can satisfy for a living person. Now where one satisfies for a living person the satisfaction counts only for the person for whom it is offered. Therefore one also who offers works of intercession profits him alone for whom he offers them.

I answer that, There have been two opinions on this question. For some, like Præpositinus,[6]

[5] Peter Lombard (QR II, 1006); the text is taken from Augustine, *Enchir.,* cx (PL 40, 283).
[6] *Summa,* IV (fol. 85rb).

have said that works of intercession offered for one particular person avail chiefly, not the person for whom they are offered, but those who are most worthy. And they instanced a candle which is lit for a rich man and profits those who are with him no less than the rich man himself, and perhaps even more, if they have keener sight. They also gave the instance of a lesson which profits the person to whom it is given no more than others who listen with him, but perhaps profits these others more, if they be more intelligent. And if it were pointed out to them that in this case the Church's ordinance in appointing certain special prayers for certain persons is futile, they said that the Church did this to excite the devotion of the faithful, who are more inclined to offer special than common works of intercession, and pray more fervently for their kinsfolk than for strangers. Others, on the contrary, said that works of intercession avail more those for whom they are offered. Now both opinions have a certain amount of truth, for the value of intercessory works may be gauged from two sources. For their value is derived in the first place from the virtue of charity, which makes all goods common, and in this respect they avail more the person who is more full of charity, although they are not offered specially for him. In this way the value of works of intercession regards more a certain inward consolation by reason of which one who is in charity rejoices in the goods of another after death in respect of the lessening of punishment; for after death there is no possibility of obtaining or increasing grace, whereas during life the works of others avail for this purpose by the virtue of charity. In the second place intercessory works derive their value from being applied to another person by one's intention. In this way the satisfaction of one person counts for another, and there can be no doubt that thus they avail more the person for whom they are offered; in fact, they avail him alone in this way, because satisfaction, properly speaking, is directed to the remission of punishment. Consequently, as regards the remission of punishment, works of intercession avail chiefly the person for whom they are offered, and accordingly there is more truth in the second opinion than in the first.

Reply Obj. 1. Works of intercession avail after the manner of a light in so far as they reach the dead, who thereby receive a certain amount of consolation, and this is all the greater according as they are endowed with a greater charity. But in so far as intercessory works are a satisfaction applied to another by the intention of the offerer, they do not resemble a light, but rather the payment of a debt; and it does not follow, if one person's debt be paid, that the debt of others is paid likewise.

Reply Obj. 2. Such a merit is conditional, for in this way they merited that works of intercession would profit them if offered for them, and this was merely to render themselves fit recipients of those works of intercession. It is therefore clear that they did not directly merit the assistance of those prayers of intercession, but made themselves fit by their preceding merits to receive the fruit of intercessory works. Hence it does not follow that their merit is rendered unavailing.

Reply Obj. 3. Nothing hinders the rich from being in some respects better off than the poor, for instance as regards the expiation of their punishment. But this is as nothing in comparison with the kingdom of heaven, where the poor are shown to be better off by the authority quoted.

ARTICLE 13. *Whether Works of Intercession Offered for Several Are of As Much Value to Each One As If They Had Been Offered For Each in Particular?*

We proceed thus to the Thirteenth Article: It would seem that works of intercession offered for several are of as much value to each one as if they had been offered for each in particular.

Objection 1. For it is clear that if one person receives a lesson he loses nothing if others receive the lesson with him. Therefore in like manner a person for whom a work of intercession is offered loses nothing if some one else is reckoned together with him; and consequently if it be offered for several, it is of as much value to each one as if it were offered for each in particular.

Obj. 2. Further, It is to be observed that according to the common practice of the Church, when Mass is said for one deceased person, other prayers are added for other deceased persons. Now this would not be done if the dead person for whom the Mass is said were to lose something thereby. Therefore the same conclusion follows as above.

Obj. 3. Further, Intercessions, especially of prayers, rely on the Divine power. But with God, just as it makes no difference whether He helps by means of many or by means of a few, so it differs not whether He assists many or a few. Therefore if the one same prayer be said for many, each one of them will receive as much assistance as one person would if that same prayer were said for him alone.

On the contrary, It is better to assist many than one. If therefore a work of intercession offered for several is of as much value to each one as if it were offered for one alone, it would seem that the Church ought not to have appointed a Mass and prayer to be said for one person in particular, but that Mass ought always to be said for all the faithful departed, and this is evidently false.

Further, A work of intercession has a finite efficiency. Therefore if it be divided among many it avails less for each one than if it were offered for one only.

I answer that, If the value of intercessory works be considered according as it is derived from the virtue of charity uniting the members of the Church together, intercessory works offered for several persons avail each one as much as if they were offered for one alone, because charity is not diminished if its effect be divided among many, in fact rather is it increased; and in like manner joy increases through being shared by many, as Augustine says.[1] Consequently many in purgatory rejoice in one good deed no less than one does. On the other hand, if we consider the value of works of intercession, in so far as they are a kind of satisfaction applied to the dead by the intention of the person offering them, then the prayer of intercession for some person in particular avails him more than that which is offered for him in common with many others; for in this case the effect of the intercessory prayers is divided in virtue of Divine justice among those for whom the intercessions are offered.

Hence it is evident that this question depends on the first;[2] and, moreover, it is made clear why special intercessions are appointed to be offered in the Church.

Reply Obj. 1. Intercessions considered as works of satisfaction do not profit after the manner of an action as teaching does; for teaching, like any other action, produces its effect according to the disposition of the recipient. But they profit after the manner of the payment of a debt, as stated above (A. 12, REPLY 1); and so the comparison fails.

Reply Obj. 2. Since intercessory works offered for one person avail others in a certain way, as stated (A. 12), it follows that when

Mass is said for one person, it is not unfitting for prayers to be said for others also. For these prayers are said, not that the satisfaction offered by one intercession be applied to those others chiefly, but that the prayer offered for them in particular may profit them also.

Reply Obj. 3. Prayers may be considered both on the part of the one who prays, and on the part of the person prayed, and its effect depends on both. Consequently though it is no more difficult to the Divine power to absolve many than to absolve one, nevertheless the prayer of one who prays thus is not as satisfactory for many as for one.

ARTICLE 14. *Whether General Works of Intercession Avail Those for Whom Special Works of Intercession Are Not Offered, As Much As Special Works of Intercession Avail Those For Whom They Are Offered in Addition to General Works of Intercession?*

We proceed thus to the Fourteenth Article: It would seem that general works of intercession avail those for whom special works of intercession are not offered, as much as special works of intercession avail those for whom they are offered in addition to general works of intercession.

Objection 1. For in the life to come each one will be rewarded according to his merits. Now a person for whom no works of intercession are offered merited to be assisted after death as much as one for whom special works of intercession are offered. Therefore the former will be assisted by general works of intercession as much as the latter by special and general works of intercession.

Obj. 3. Further, The Eucharist is the chief of the works of intercession of the Church. Now the Eucharist, since it contains Christ whole, has infinite efficacy so to speak. Therefore one offering of the Eucharist for all in general is of sufficient value to release all who are in purgatory, and consequently general works of intercession alone afford as much assistance as special and general works of intercession together.

On the contrary, Two goods are more eligible than one. Therefore special works of intercession, together with general works of intercession, are more profitable to the person for whom they are offered than general works of intercession alone.

I answer that, The reply to this question depends on that which is given to the twelfth

[1] *Confessions,* VIII, 9 (PL 32, 752).
[2] Cf. A. 12.

inquiry (A. 12), for if the works of intercession offered for one person in particular avail indifferently for all, then all works of intercession are common; and consequently one for whom the special works of intercession are not offered will be assisted as much as the one for whom they are offered, if he be equally worthy. On the other hand, if the works of intercession offered for a person do not profit all indifferently, but those chiefly for whom they are offered, then there is no doubt that general and special works of intercession together avail a person more than general works of intercession alone. Hence the Master, in the text (iv *Sent.* d. 45),[1] mentions two opinions: one, when he says that a rich man derives from general, together with special works of intercession, an equal profit to that which a poor man derives from special works of intercession alone, for although the one receives assistance from more sources than the other, he does not receive a greater assistance; the other opinion he mentions when he says that a person for whom special works of intercession are offered obtains a more speedy but not a more complete release, because each will be finally released from all punishment.

Reply Obj. 1. The assistance derived from works of intercession is not directly and absolutely an object of merit, but conditionally as it were; hence the argument does not prove.

Reply Obj. 2. Although the power of Christ Who is contained in the Sacrament of the Eucharist is infinite, yet there is a definite effect to which that sacrament is directed. Hence it does not follow that the whole punishment of those who are in purgatory is expiated by one sacrifice of the altar; even so, by the one sacrifice which a man offers, he is not released from the whole satisfaction due for his sins, and therefore sometimes several Masses are enjoined in satisfaction for one sin. Nevertheless, if anything from special works of intercession are left over for those for whom they are offered (for instance if they do not need them) we may well believe that by God's mercy this is granted to others for whom those works of intercession are not offered, if they need them, as affirmed by Damascene (*Serm. de Dormient.*)[2] who says: "Truly God, since He is just, will adapt ability to the disabled, and will arrange for an exchange of deficiencies"; and this exchange is effected when what is lacking to one is supplied by another.

[1] QR II, 1009.
[2] Sect. 25 (PG 95, 272).

QUESTION LXXII

OF PRAYERS WITH REGARD TO THE SAINTS IN HEAVEN

(In Three Articles)

WE must now consider prayer with regard to the saints in heaven. Under this head there are three points of inquiry: (1) Whether the saints have knowledge of our prayers? (2) Whether we should beseech them to pray for us? (3) Whether the prayers they pour forth for us are always granted?

ARTICLE 1. *Whether the Saints Have Knowledge of Our Prayers?*

We proceed thus to the First Article: It would seem that the saints have no knowledge of our prayers.

Objection 1. For a gloss on Isa. 63. 16, *Thou art our father and Abraham hath not known us, and Israel hath been ignorant of us,* says[3] that "the dead saints know not what the living, even their own children, are doing." This is taken from Augustine (*De Cura pro Mort.* xiii),[4] where he quotes the above authority, and the following are his words: "If such great men as the patriarchs knew not what was happening to the people begotten of them, how can the dead occupy themselves in watching and helping the affairs and actions of the living?" Therefore the saints cannot know our prayers.

Obj. 2. Further, the following words are addressed to King Joas (IV Kings 22. 20): *Therefore* (that is, because thou hast wept before Me), *I will gather thee to thy fathers . . . that thy eyes may not see all the evils which I will bring upon this place.* But Joas would have gained no such advantage from his death if he were to know after death what was happening to his people. Therefore the saints after death do not know our actions, and thus they do not understand our prayers.

Obj. 3. Further, The more perfect a man is in charity, the more he succours his neighbour when the latter is in danger. Now the saints, in this life, watch over their neighbour, especially their kinsfolk, when these are in danger, and manifestly assist them. Since then, after death, their charity is much greater, if they were aware of our deeds, much more would they watch over their friends and kindred and assist them in their needs; and yet, it seems, they do not. Therefore it would seem

[3] *Glossa interl.* (IV, 102v).   [4] PL 40, 604.

that our deeds and prayers are not known to them.

Obj. 4. Further, Even as the saints after death see the Word, so do the angels of whom it is stated (Matt. 18. 10) that *their angels in heaven always see the face of My Father.* Yet the angels through seeing the Word do not therefore know all things, since the lower angels are cleansed from their lack of knowledge by the higher angels, as Dionysius declares (*Cæl. Hier.* vii).[1] Therefore although the saints see the Word, they do not see therein our prayers and other things that happen in our regard.

Obj. 5. Further, God alone is the searcher of hearts. Now prayer is seated chiefly in the heart. Therefore it belongs to God alone to know our prayers. Therefore our prayers are unknown to the saints.

On the contrary, Gregory, commenting on Job 14. 21, *Whether his children come to honour or dishonour, he shall not understand,* says (*Moral.* xii, 21):[2] "This does not apply to the souls of the saints, for since they have an insight of Almighty God's glory we must in no way believe that anything outside that glory is unknown to them." Therefore they know our prayers.

Further, Gregory says (*Dial.* ii, 35):[3] "All creatures are little to the soul that sees God, because however little it sees of the Creator's light, every created thing appears of little account to it." Now apparently the chief obstacle to the souls of the saints knowing our prayers and other happenings in our regard is that they are far removed from us. Since then distance does not prevent these things, as appears from the authority quoted, it would seem that the souls of the saints know our prayers and what happens here below.

Further, Unless they were aware of what happens in our regard they would not pray for us, since they would be ignorant of our needs. But this is the error of Vigilantius, as Jerome asserts in his letter against him.[4] Therefore the saints know what happens in our regard.

I answer that, The Divine essence is a sufficient medium for knowing all things, and this is evident from the fact that God, by seeing His essence, sees all things. But it does not follow that whoever sees God's essence knows all things, but only those who comprehend the essence of God; even as the knowledge of a principle does not involve the knowledge of all that follows from that principle, unless the whole force of the principle is comprehended. Therefore, since the souls of the saints do not comprehend the Divine essence, it does not follow that they know all that can be known by the Divine essence,—for which reason the lower angels are taught concerning certain matters by the higher angels, though they all see the essence of God; but each of the blessed must see in the Divine essence as many other things as the perfection of his happiness requires. For the perfection of a man's happiness requires him to have whatever he will, and to will nothing out of order, and each one wills with a right will to know what concerns himself. Hence since no rectitude is lacking to the saints, they wish to know what concerns themselves, and consequently it follows that they know it in the Word. Now it pertains to their glory that they assist the needy for their salvation, for thus they become God's co-operators, "than which nothing is more Godlike," as Dionysius declares (*Cæl. Hier.* iii).[5] And so it is evident that the saints know such things as are required for this purpose; and thus it is manifest that they know in the Word the vows, devotions, and prayers of those who have recourse to their assistance.

Reply Obj. 1. The saying of Augustine is to be understood as referring to the natural knowledge of separated souls, which knowledge is devoid of obscurity in holy men. But he is not speaking of their knowledge in the Word, for it is clear that when Isaias said this, Abraham had no such knowledge, since no one had come to the vision of God before the Redemption.

Reply Obj. 2. Although the saints, after this life, know what happens here below, we must not believe that they grieve through knowing the woes of those whom they loved in this world, for they are so filled with heavenly joy that sorrow finds no place in them. Therefore if after death they know the woes of their friends, their grief is forestalled by their removal from this world before their woes occur. Perhaps, however, the non-glorified souls would grieve somewhat, if they were aware of the distress of their dear ones, and since the soul of Josias was not glorified as soon as it went out from his body,[6] it is in this respect that Augustine[7] uses this argument to show that the

---

[1] Sect. 3 (PG 3, 209); cf. *De Eccl. Hier.*, vi, sect. 6 (PG 3, 537).
[2] PL 75, 999.　　[3] PL 66, 200.
[4] *Contra Vigilant.* (PL 23, 359).

[5] Sect. 2 (PG 3, 165).
[6] Cf. Thomas, *In Sent.*, III, d. XXII, Q. 2, A. 2; cf. also Part III, Q. LII, A. 5.
[7] *De Cura pro Mort.*, XIII (PL 40, 604).

souls of the dead have no knowledge of the deeds of the living .

Reply Obj. 3. The souls of the saints have their will fully conformed to the Divine will even as regards the things willed; and consequently, although they retain the love of charity towards their neighbour, they do not succour him otherwise than they see to be in conformity with the disposition of Divine justice. Nevertheless, it is to be believed that they help their neighbour very much by interceding for him to God.

Reply Obj. 4. Although it does not follow that those who see the Word see all things in the Word, they see those things that pertain to the perfection of their happiness, as stated above.

Reply Obj. 5. God alone of Himself knows the thoughts of the heart; yet others know them in so far as these are revealed to them, either by their vision of the Word or by any other means.

ARTICLE 2. *Whether We Ought To Call Upon the Saints To Pray For Us?*

We proceed thus to the Second Article: It would seem that we ought not to call upon the saints to pray for us.

Objection 1. For no man asks anyone's friends to pray for him, except in so far as he believes he will more easily find favour with them. But God is infinitely more merciful than any saint, and consequently His will is more easily inclined to give us a gracious hearing than the will of a saint. Therefore it would seem unnecessary to make the saints mediators between us and God, that they may intercede for us.

Obj. 2. Further, If we ought to beseech them to pray for us, this is only because we know their prayers to be acceptable to God. Now among the saints the holier a man is, the more is his prayer acceptable to God. Therefore we ought always to bespeak the greater saints to intercede for us with God, and never the lesser ones.

Obj. 3. Further, Christ, even as man, is called the *Holy of Holies* (Dan. 9. 24), and, as man, is able to pray. Yet we never call upon Christ to pray for us. Therefore neither should we ask the other saints to do so.

Obj. 4. Further, Whenever one person intercedes for another at the latter's request, he presents his petition to the one with whom he intercedes for him. Now it is unnecessary to present anything to one to whom all things are present. Therefore it is unnecessary to make the saints our intercessors with God.

Obj. 5. Further, It is unnecessary to do a thing if, without doing it, the purpose for which it is done would be achieved in the same way, or else not achieved at all. Now the saints would pray for us just the same, or would not pray for us at all, whether we pray to them or not; for if we be worthy of their prayers, they would pray for us even though we did not pray to them, while if we are unworthy they do not pray for us even though we ask them to. Therefore it seems altogether unnecessary to call on them to pray for us.

On the contrary, It is written (Job. 5. 1): *Call . . . if there be any that will answer thee, and turn to some of the saints.* Now, as Gregory says (*Moral.* v, 43)[1] on this passage, "we call upon God when we beseech Him in humble prayer." Therefore when we wish to pray God, we should turn to the saints, that they may pray God for us.

Further, The saints who are in heaven are more acceptable to God than those who are on the way. Now we should make the saints, who are on the way, our intercessors with God, after the example of the Apostle, who said (Rom. 15. 30): *I beseech you . . . brethren, through our Lord Jesus Christ, and by the charity of the Holy Ghost, that you help me in your prayers for me to God.* Much more, therefore, should we ask the saints who are in heaven to help us by their prayers to God.

Further, An additional argument is provided by the common custom of the Church which asks for the prayers of the saints in the Litany.

I answer that, According to Dionysius (*Eccl. Hier.* v)[2] the order established by God among things is that "the last should be led to God by those that are midway between." Therefore, since the saints who are in heaven are nearest to God, the order of the Divine law requires that we, who while we remain in the body are pilgrims from the Lord, should be brought back to God by the saints who are between us and Him, and this happens when the Divine goodness pours forth its effect into us through them. And since our return to God should correspond to the outflow of His goodness upon us, just as the Divine favours reach us by means of the saints' intercession, so should we, by their means, be brought back to God, that we may receive His favours again. Hence it is that we make them our intercessors with God, and our mediators as it were, when we ask them to pray for us.

Reply Obj. 1. It is not on account of any

---

[1] PL 75, 723.　　[2] Sect. 4 (PG 3, 504).

defect in God's power that He works by means of second causes, but it is for the perfection of the order of the universe, and the more manifold outpouring of His goodness on things, through His bestowing on them not only the goodness which is proper to them, but also that they are the cause of goodness in others. Even so it is not through any defect in His mercy that we need to beseech His clemency through the prayers of the saints, but to the end that the above mentioned order in things be observed.

Reply Obj. 2. Although the greater saints are more acceptable to God than the lesser, it is sometimes profitable to pray to the lesser, and this for five reasons. First, because sometimes one has greater devotion for a lesser saint than for a greater, and the effect of prayer depends very much on one's devotion. Secondly, in order to avoid tediousness, for continual attention to one thing makes a person weary, while by praying to different saints, the fervour of our devotion is aroused anew as it were. Thirdly, because it is granted to some saints to exercise their patronage in certain special cases, for instance to Saint Anthony against the fire of hell.[1] Fourthly, that due honour be given by us to all. Fifthly, because the prayers of several sometimes obtain that which would not have been obtained by the prayers of one.

Reply Obj. 3. Prayer is an act, and acts belong to particular persons (*supposita*). Hence, were we to say: "Christ, pray for us," unless we added something this would seem to refer to Christ's person, and consequently to agree with the error either of Nestorius,[2] who distinguished in Christ the person of the son of man from the person of the Son of God, or of Arius,[3] who asserted that the person of the Son is less than the Father. Therefore to avoid these errors the Church says not: "Christ, pray for us," but "Christ, hear us," or "have mercy on us."

Reply Obj. 4. As we shall state further on (A. 3) the saints are said to present our prayers to God not as though they manifest things unknown to Him, but because they ask God to grant those prayers a gracious hearing, or because they seek the Divine truth about them, namely what ought to be done according to His providence.

Reply Obj. 5. A person is rendered worthy

[1] Cf. *Acta Sanctorum*, 17 Jan., sect. 1 (BL II, 520b); Sect. 2 (BL II, 521b); cf. also DuCange, *Glossarium*, art. *Ignis Infernalis* (III, 1245).
[2] Cf. above, Part III, Q. II, A. 6.
[3] Cf. above, Part I, Q. XXVII, A. 1; Q. XLII, A. 2, Reply 4; Part III, Q. X, A. 2, Reply 1; Q. XVI, AA. 8, 9.

of a saint's prayers for him by the very fact that in his need he has recourse to him with pure devotion. Hence it is not unnecessary to pray to the saints.

ARTICLE 3. *Whether the Prayers Which the Saints Pour Forth To God for Us Are Always Granted?*

We proceed thus to the Third Article: It would seem that the prayers which the saints pour forth to God for us are not always granted.

Objection 1. For if they were always granted, the saints would be heard especially in regard to matters concerning themselves. But they are not heard in reference to these things; hence it is stated in the Apocalypse (6. 11) that on the martyrs beseeching vengeance on them that dwell on earth, *it was said to them that they should rest for a little while till the number of their brethren should be filled up* (Vulg.,—*till their fellow-servants and their brethren . . . should be filled up*). Much less, therefore, are they heard in reference to matters concerning others.

Obj. 2. Further, It is written (Jer. 15. 1): *If Moses and Samuel shall stand before Me, My soul is not towards this people.* Therefore, the saints are not always heard when they pray God for us.

Obj. 3. Further, The saints in heaven are stated to be equal to the angels of God (Matt. 22. 30). But the angels are not always heard in the prayers which they offer up to God. This is evident from Dan. 10. 12, 13, where it is written: *I am come for thy words: but the prince of the kingdom of the Persians resisted me one-and-twenty days.* But the angel who spoke had not come to Daniel's aid except by asking of God to be set free; and yet the fulfilment of his prayer was hindered. Therefore neither are other saints always heard by God when they pray for us.

Obj. 4. Further, Whosoever obtains something by prayer merits it in a sense. But the saints in heaven are not in the state of meriting. Therefore they cannot obtain anything for us from God by their prayers.

Obj. 5. Further, The saints, in all things, conform their will to the will of God. Therefore they will nothing but what they know God to will. But no one prays save for what he wills. Therefore they pray not save for what they know God to will. Now that which God wills would be done even without their praying for it. Therefore their prayers are not efficacious for obtaining anything.

Obj. 6. Further, The prayers of the whole heavenly court, if they could obtain anything, would be more efficacious than all the petitions of the Church here below. Now if the intercessory works of the Church here below for some one in purgatory were to be multiplied, he would be wholly delivered from punishment. Since then the saints in heaven pray for those who are in purgatory on the same account as for us, if they obtain anything for us, their prayers would deliver entirely from punishment those who are in purgatory. But this is not true, because then the Church's intercessory works for the dead would be unnecessary.

On the contrary, It is written (II Machab. 15. 14): *This is he that prayeth much for the people, and for all the holy city, Jeremias the prophet of God,* and that his prayer was granted is clear from what follows (*verse* 15): *Jeremias stretched forth his right hand, and gave to Judas a sword of gold, saying: Take this holy sword, a gift from God,* etc.

Further, Jerome says (*Ep. contra Vigilant.*):[1] "Thou sayest in thy pamphlets, that while we live, we can pray for one another, but that when we are dead no one's prayer for another will be heard"; and afterwards he refutes this in the following words: "If the apostles and martyrs while yet in the body can pray for others, while they are still solicitous for themselves, how much more can they do so when the crown, the victory, the triumph is already theirs!"

Further, This is confirmed by the custom of the Church, which often asks to be assisted by the prayers of the saints.

I answer that, The saints are said to pray for us in two ways. First, by "express" prayer, when by their prayers they seek a hearing of the Divine clemency on our behalf; secondly, by "interpretive" prayer, namely by their merits which, being known to God, avail not only them to glory, but also us as intercessions and prayers, even as the shedding of Christ's blood is said to ask pardon for us (Heb. 12. 24). In both ways the saints' prayers considered in themselves avail to obtain what they ask, yet on our part they may fail so that we obtain not the fruit of their prayers, in so far as they are said to pray for us by reason of their merits availing on our behalf. But in so far as they pray for us by asking something for us in their prayers, their prayers are always granted, since they will only what God wills, nor do they ask save for what they will to be done; and what God wills is always fulfilled,—unless we speak of

His antecedent will, whereby He wills all men to be saved. For this will is not always fulfilled; and therefore it is no wonder if that also which the saints will according to this kind of will is not fulfilled sometimes.

Reply Obj. 1. This prayer of the martyrs is merely their desire to obtain the robe of the body and the fellowship of those who will be saved, and their consent to God's justice in punishing the wicked. Hence a gloss on Apoc. 6. 11, *How long, O Lord,* says:[2] "They desire an increase of joy and the fellowship of the saints, and they consent to God's justice."

Reply Obj. 2. The Lord speaks there of Moses and Samuel according to their state in this life. For we read that they withstood God's anger by praying for the people.[3] And yet even if they had been living at the time in question, they would have been unable to placate God towards the people by their prayers, on account of the wickedness of this same people; and it is thus that we are to understand this passage.

Reply Obj. 3. This dispute among the good angels does not mean that they offered contradictory prayers to God, but that they submitted contrary merits on various sides to the Divine inquiry, with a view of God's pronouncing sentence thereon. This, in fact, is what Gregory says (*Moral.* xvii, 12)[4] in explanation of the aforesaid words of Daniel: "The lofty spirits that are set over the nations never fight in behalf of those that act unjustly, but they justly judge and try their deeds. And when the guilt or innocence of any particular nation is brought into the debate of the court above, the ruling spirit of that nation is said to have won or lost in the conflict. Yet the supreme will of their Maker is victorious over all, for since they have it ever before their eyes, they will not what they are unable to obtain," and therefore neither do they seek for it. And consequently it is clear that their prayers are always heard.

Reply Obj. 4. Although the saints are not in a state to merit for themselves, when once they are in heaven, they are in a state to merit for others, or rather to assist others by reason of their previous merit, for while living they merited that their prayers should be heard after their death.

Or we may reply that prayer is meritorious on one count, and petitionary on another. For merit consists in a certain squaring of the act to the end for which it is intended, and which

---

[1] PL 23, 359.

[2] *Glossa ordin.* (VI, 250A).
[3] Cf. Exod. 17.4; Num. 20.6; I Kings 12.18; cf. *Glossa interl.*, on Jerem. 15.1 (IV, 132V).   [4] PL 76, 20.

is given to it as its reward, while the petition of a prayer depends on the liberality of the person supplicated. Hence prayer sometimes, through the liberality of the person supplicated, obtains that which was not merited either by the suppliant, or by the person supplicated for; and so, although the saints are not in the state of meriting, it does not follow that they are not in the state of being able to petition.

Reply Obj. 5. As appears from the authority of Gregory quoted above (REPLY 3), the saints and angels will nothing but what they see to be in the Divine will, and so neither do they pray for anything else. Nor is their prayer fruitless, since as Augustine says,[1] the prayers of the saints profit the predestined, because it is perhaps preordained that they shall be saved through the prayers of those who intercede for them; and consequently God also wills that what the saints see Him to will shall be fulfilled through their prayers.

Reply Obj. 6. The intercessory works of the Church for the dead are as so many satisfactions of the living in lieu of the dead, and accordingly they free the dead from the punishment which the latter have not paid. But the saints in heaven are not in the state of making satisfaction; and consequently the parallel fails between their prayers and the intercessory works of the Church.

QUESTION LXXIII

OF THE SIGNS THAT WILL PRECEDE THE JUDGMENT

(In Three Articles)

WE must next consider the signs that will precede the judgment, and under this head there are three points of inquiry: (1) Whether any signs will precede the Lord's coming to judgment? (2) Whether in very truth the sun and moon will be darkened? (3) Whether the powers of the heavens will be moved when the Lord shall come?

ARTICLE 1. *Whether Any Signs Will Precede the Lord's Coming to Judgment?*

We proceed thus to the First Article: It would seem that the Lord's coming to judgment will not be preceded by any signs.

Objection 1. Because it is written (I Thess. 5. 3): *When they shall say: Peace and security; then shall sudden destruction come upon them.* Now there would be no peace and security if

[1] *De Praed. Sanct.*, XXII (PL 45, 1030).

men were terrified by previous signs. Therefore signs will not precede that coming.

Obj. 2. Further, Signs are required for the manifestation of something. But His coming is to be hidden; hence it is written (I Thess. 5. 2): *The day of the Lord shall come as a thief in the night.* Therefore signs ought not to precede it.

Obj. 3. Further, The time of His first coming was foreknown by the prophets,[2] which does not apply to His second coming.[3] Now no such signs preceded the first coming of Christ. Therefore neither will they precede the second.

On the contrary, It is written (Luke 21. 25): *There shall be signs in the sun, and in the moon, and in the stars,* etc.

Further, Jerome mentions fifteen signs preceding the judgment.[4] He says that on the first day all the seas will rise fifteen cubits above the mountains; in the second day all the waters will be plunged into the depths, so that scarcely will they be visible; on the third day they will be restored to their previous condition; on the fourth day all the great fishes and other things that move in the waters will gather together and, raising their heads above the sea, roar at one another contentiously; on the fifth day, all the birds of the air will gather together in the fields, wailing to one another, with neither bite nor sup; on the sixth day rivers of fire will arise towards the firmament rushing together from the west to the east; on the seventh day all the stars, both planets and fixed stars, will throw out fiery tails like comets; on the eighth day there will be a great earthquake, and all animals will be laid low; on the ninth day all the plants will be bedewed as it were with blood; on the tenth day all stones, little and great, will be divided into four parts dashing against one another; on the eleventh day all hills and mountains and buildings will be reduced to dust; on the twelfth day all animals will come from forest and mountain to the fields, roaring and tasting of nothing; on the thirteenth day all graves from east to west will open to allow the bodies to rise again; on the fourteenth day all men will leave their abode, neither understanding nor speaking, but rushing hither and thither like madmen; on the fifteenth day all will die

[2] Cf. Gen. 49.10; Dan. 9.24; Agg. 2.8; Luke, 2.26.
[3] Cf. Matt. 24.36; Acts, 1.7.
[4] Referred to by Peter Damian, *De Novissimis et Antichristo*, chap. 4 (PL 145, 840); the reference is not known in St. Jerome; cf. Peter the Eater, *Hist. Schol.*, CXLI (PL 198, 1611); Bonaventure, *In Sent.*, IV, d. XLVIII, dub. 3 (QR IV, 996) comments on the same text without referring to the author.

and will rise again with those who died long before.

I answer that, When Christ shall come to judge He will appear in the form of glory, on account of the authority which is due to a judge. Now it pertains to the dignity of judicial power to have certain signs that induce people to reverence and subjection, and consequently many signs will precede the advent of Christ when He shall come to judgment, in order that the hearts of men be brought to subjection to the coming judge, and be prepared for the judgment, being forewarned by those signs.

But it is not easy to know what these signs may be, for the signs of which we read in the gospels,[1] as Augustine says, writing to Hesychius about the end of the world,[2] refer not only to Christ's coming to judgment, but also to the time of the sack of Jerusalem, and to the coming of Christ in ceaselessly visiting His Church. So that, perhaps, if we consider them carefully, we shall find that none of them refers to the coming advent, as he remarks,[3] because these signs that are mentioned in the gospels, such as wars, fears, and so forth, have been from the beginning of the human race; unless perhaps we say that at that time they will be more prevalent, although it is uncertain in what degree this increase will foretell the imminence of the advent.

The signs mentioned by Jerome are not asserted by him; he merely says that he found them written in the annals of the Hebrews,[4] and, indeed, they contain very little likelihood.

Reply Obj. 1. According to Augustine[5] towards the end of the world there will be a general persecution of the good by the wicked, so that at the same time some will fear, namely the good, and some will be secure, namely the wicked. The words: *When they shall say: Peace and security,* refer to the wicked, who will pay little heed to the signs of the coming judgment, while the words of Luke 21. 26, *men withering away,* etc., should be referred to the good.

We may also reply that all these signs that will happen about the time of the judgment are considered to occur within the time occupied by the judgment, so that the judgment day contains them all. Therefore although men be terrified by the signs appearing about the judgment day, yet before those signs begin to appear the wicked will think themselves to be in peace and security, after the death of Antichrist and before the coming of Christ, seeing that the world is not at once destroyed, as they first thought.

Reply Obj. 2. The day of the Lord is said to come as a thief, because the exact time is not known, since it will not be possible to know it from those signs; although, as we have already said (REPLY 1), all these most manifest signs which will precede the judgment immediately may be comprised under the judgment day.

Reply Obj. 3. At His first advent Christ came secretly, although the appointed time was known beforehand by the prophets. Hence there was no need for such signs to appear at His first coming, as will appear at His second advent, when He will come openly, although the appointed time is hidden.

ARTICLE 2. *Whether Towards the Time of the Judgment the Sun and Moon Will Be Darkened in Very Truth?*

We proceed thus to the Second Article: It would seem that towards the time of the judgment the sun and moon will be darkened in very truth.

Objection 1. For, as Rabanus says,[6] commenting on Matt. 24. 29, "Nothing hinders us from gathering that the sun, moon, and stars will then be deprived of their light, as we know happened to the sun at the time of our Lord's passion."

Obj. 2. Further, The light of the heavenly bodies is directed to the generation of inferior bodies, because by its means and not only by their movement they act upon this lower world, as Averroes says (*De Subst. Orbis.*).[7] But generation will cease then. Therefore neither will light remain in the heavenly bodies.

Obj. 3. Further, According to some the inferior bodies will be cleansed of the qualities by which they act. Now heavenly bodies act not only by movement, but also by light, as stated above (obj. 2). Therefore as the movement of heaven will cease, so will the light of the heavenly bodies.

On the contrary, According to astronomers the sun and moon cannot be eclipsed at the same time. But this darkening of the sun and moon is stated to be simultaneous, when the Lord shall come to judgment. Therefore the darkening will not be in very truth due to a natural eclipse.

---

[1] Matt. 24; Mark 13; Luke 21.
[2] *Epist.,* CXCIX, 9 (PL 33, 914).
[3] *Epist.,* CXCIX, 11 (PL 33, 918).
[4] Cf. Peter the Eater, *Hist. Schol.,* CXLI (PL 198, 1611).
[5] *Epist.,* CXCIX, 11 (PL 33, 918).

[6] Cf. Bede, *In Marc,* BK. IV (PL 92, 263).
[7] Chap. 2 (IX, 8A); cf. *In De Cælo,* BK. II, Comm. 42 (V, 126K).

Further, It is not appropriate for the same thing to be the cause of a thing's failing and increasing. Now when our Lord shall come the light of the luminaries will increase according to Isa. 30. 26, *The light of the moon shall be as the light of the sun, and the light of the sun shall be sevenfold.* Therefore it is unfitting for the light of these bodies to cease when our Lord comes.

I answer that, If we speak of the sun and moon in respect of the very moment of Christ's coming, it is not credible that they will be darkened through being bereft of their light, since when Christ comes and the saints rise again the whole world will be renewed, as we shall state further on, as we have said.[1] If, however, we speak of them in respect of the time immediately preceding the judgment, it is possible that by the Divine power the sun, moon, and other luminaries of the heavens will be darkened, either at various times or all together, in order to inspire men with fear.

Reply Obj. 1. Rabanus is speaking of the time preceding the judgment; therefore he adds that when the judgment day is over the words of Isaias shall be fulfilled.

Reply Obj. 2. Light is in the heavenly bodies not only for the purpose of causing generation in these lower bodies, but also for their own perfection and beauty. Hence it does not follow that where generation ceases the light of the heavenly bodies will cease, but rather that it will increase.

Reply Obj. 3. It does not seem probable that the elemental qualities will be removed from the elements, although some have asserted this. If, however, they are removed, there would still be no parallel between them and light, since the elemental qualities are in opposition to one another, so that their action is corruptive, while light is a principle of action not by way of opposition, but by way of a principle regulating things in opposition to one another and bringing them back to harmony. Nor is there a parallel with the movement of heavenly bodies, for movement is the act of that which is imperfect, and therefore it must cease when the imperfection ceases; this, however, cannot be said of light.

ARTICLE 3. *Whether the Virtues of Heaven Will Be Moved When Our Lord Shall Come?*

We proceed thus to the Third Article: It would seem that the virtues of heaven will not be moved when our Lord shall come.

[1] *In Sent.,* IV, d. XLVII, Q. 2, A. 3; cf. below, Q. LXXIV, A. 7.

Objection 1. For the virtues of heaven can denote only the blessed angels.[2] Now immutability is essential to blessedness. Therefore it will be impossible for them to be moved.

Obj. 2. Further, Ignorance is the cause of wonder.[3] Now ignorance, like fear, is far from the angels, for as Gregory says (*Dial.* iv, 33),[4] "what do they not see, who see Him Who sees all." Therefore it will be impossible for them to be moved with wonder, as stated in the text (iv *Sent.* d. 48).[5]

Obj. 3. Further, All the angels will be present at the Divine judgment; therefore it is stated (Apoc. 7. 11): *All the angels stood round about the throne.* Now the virtues denote one particular order of angels. Therefore it should not be said of them rather than of others, that they are moved.

On the contrary, It is written (Job 26. 11): *The pillars of heaven tremble, and dread at His beck.* Now the pillars of heaven can denote only the virtues of heaven. Therefore the virtues of heaven will be moved.

Further, It is written (Matt. 24. 29): *The stars shall fall from heaven, and the virtues* (Douay,—*powers*) *of heaven shall be moved.*

I answer that, Virtue is twofold as applied to the angels, as Dionysius states (*Cæl. Hier.* xi).[6] For sometimes the name of "virtues" is appropriated to one order, which according to him, is the middle order of the middle hierarchy, but according to Gregory (*Hom. in Ev.* xxxiv)[7] is the highest order of the lowest hierarchy. In another sense it is employed to denote all the heavenly spirits in general. In the question at issue it may be taken either way. For in the text (*loc. cit.*) it is explained according to the second acceptation, so as to denote all the angels, and then they are said to be moved through wonder at the renewing of the world, as stated in the text.

It can also be explained in reference to virtue as the name of a particular order, and then that order is said to be moved more than the others by reason of the effect, since according to Gregory (*loc. cit.*) we ascribe to that order the working of miracles which especially will be worked about that time; or again, because that order—since, according to Dionysius (*loc. cit.*), it belongs to the middle hierarchy—is not limited in its power, and therefore its ministry

[2] Cf. *Glossa interl.* (v, 74v); cf. Bede, *In Matt.* (PL 92, 104).
[3] Aristotle, *Metaphysics,* I, 2 (982^{b}12; 983^{a}12).
[4] PL 77, 376.
[5] Chap. 5 (QR II, 1025).
[6] Sect. 1 (PG 3, 284).   [7] PL 76 1250.

must regard universal causes. Consequently the proper office of the virtues seems to be to move the heavenly bodies which are the cause of what happens in nature here below. And again the very name denotes this, since they are called the *virtues of heaven* (Matt. 24. 29). Accordingly they will be moved then, because they will no more produce their effect, by ceasing to move the heavenly bodies, even as the angels who are appointed to watch over men will no longer fulfil the office of guardians.

Reply Obj. 1. This change alters nothing pertaining to their state, but refers either to their effects which may vary without any change on their part, or to some new consideration of things which hitherto they were unable to see by means of their concreated species, which change of thought is not taken from them by their state of blessedness. Hence Augustine says[1] that "God moves the spiritual creature through time."

Reply Obj. 2. Wonder is usually about things surpassing our condition or power, and accordingly the virtues of heaven will wonder at the Divine power doing such things, in so far as they fail to do or comprehend them. In this sense the blessed Agnes said that "the sun and moon wonder at His beauty,"[2] and this does not imply ignorance in the angels, but removes the comprehension of God from them.

The *Reply to the Third Objection* is clear from what has been said.

QUESTION LXXIV

OF THE FIRE OF THE FINAL CONFLAGRATION

(In Nine Articles)

WE must now consider the fire of the final conflagration, and under this head there are nine points of inquiry: (1) Whether any cleansing of the world is to take place? (2) Whether it will be effected by fire? (3) Whether that fire is of the same species as elemental fire? (4) Whether that fire will cleanse also the higher heavens? (5) Whether that fire will consume the other elements? (6) Whether it will cleanse all the elements? (7) Whether that fire precedes or follows the judgment? (8) Whether men are to be consumed by that fire? (9) Whether the wicked will be involved therein?

ARTICLE 1. *Whether the World Is To Be Cleansed?*

We proceed thus to the First Article: It would seem that there is not to be any cleansing of the world.

Objection 1. For only that which is unclean needs cleansing. Now God's creatures are not unclean, and therefore it is written (Acts 10. 15): *That which God hath cleansed, do not thou call common,* that is, unclean. Therefore the creatures of the world shall not be cleansed.

Obj. 2. Further, According to Divine justice cleansing is directed to the removal of the uncleanness of sin, as instanced in the cleansing after death. But there can be no stain of sin in the elements of this world. Therefore, it seems, they do not need to be cleansed.

Obj. 3. Further, A thing is said to be cleansed when anything extraneous that depreciates it is removed from it, for the removal of that which ennobles a thing is not called a cleansing, but rather a diminishing. Now it pertains to the perfection and nobility of the elements that something of a foreign nature is mingled with them, since the form of a mixed body is more noble than the form of a simple body. Therefore it would seem in no way fitting that the elements of this world can possibly be cleansed.

On the contrary, All renewal is effected by some kind of cleansing. But the elements will be renewed; hence it is written (Apoc. 21. 1): *I saw a new heaven and a new earth: for the first heaven and the first earth was gone.* Therefore the elements shall be cleansed.

Further, a gloss on I Cor. 7. 31, *The fashion of this earth passeth away,* says:[3] "The beauty of this world will perish in the burning of worldly flames." Therefore the same conclusion follows.

I answer that, Since the world was, in a way, made for man's sake, it follows that when man shall be glorified in the body, the other bodies of the world shall also be changed to a better state, so that it is rendered a more fitting place for him and more pleasant to look upon. Now in order that man obtain the glory of the body, it is necessary first of all those things to be removed which are opposed to glory. There are two, namely the corruption and stain of sin,—because according to I Cor. 15. 50, *neither shall corruption possess incorruption,* and all the unclean shall be without the city of glory (Apoc. 22. 15);[4] and again, the elements re-

---

[1] *De Gen. ad Litt.,* VIII, 22 (PL 34, 388).

[2] *Acta Sanctorum,* Life of St. Agnes, by St. Ambrose, chap. 1 (BL II, 715a); cf. Pseudo-Ambrose, *Epist.,* 1 *Ad Virg. Sacras* (PL 17, 814).

[3] *Glossa* Lombardi (PL 191, 1597); cf. *Glossa ordin.* (VI, 44A); Augustine, *City of God,* XX, 16 (PL 41, 682).

[4] Cf. Apoc. 21.27.

quire to be cleansed from the contrary dispositions before they are brought to the newness of glory, proportionately to what we have said with regard to man. Now although, properly speaking, a corporeal thing cannot be the subject of the stain of sin, nevertheless, on account of sin corporeal things contract a certain unfittingness for being appointed to spiritual purposes; and for this reason we find that places where crimes have been committed are considered unfit for the performance of sacred actions therein, unless they are cleansed beforehand. Accordingly that part of the world which is given to our use contracts from men's sins a certain unfitness for being glorified, and therefore in this respect it needs to be cleansed. In like manner with regard to the intervening space, on account of the contact of the elements, there are many corruptions, generations and alterations of the elements, which diminish their purity: therefore the elements need to be cleansed from these also, so that they be fit to receive the newness of glory.

Reply Obj. 1. When it is asserted that every creature of God is clean we are to understand this as meaning that its substance contains no alloy of evil, as the Manichees maintained,[1] saying that evil and good are two substances in some places severed from one another, in others mingled together. But it does not exclude a creature from having an admixture of a foreign nature, which in itself is also good, but is inconsistent with the perfection of that creature. Nor does this prevent evil from being accidental to a creature, although not mingled with it as part of its substance.

Reply Obj. 2. Although corporeal elements cannot be the subject of sin, nevertheless, from the sin that is committed in them they contract a certain unfitness for receiving the perfection of glory.

Reply Obj. 3. The form of a mixed body and the form of an element may be considered in two ways: either as regards the perfection of the species, and thus a mixed body is more perfect; or as regards their continual endurance, and thus the simple body is more noble, because it has not in itself the cause of corruption, unless it be corrupted by something extrinsic, whereas a mixed body has in itself the cause of its corruption, namely the composition of contraries. Therefore a simple body, although it is corruptible in part is incorruptible as a whole, which cannot be said of a mixed body.

[1] Cf. Augustine, *De Haeres.*, XLVI (PL 42, 34); Epiphanius, *Adv. Haeres.*, BK. II, t. II, haeres. 66. n 25 (PG 42, 72).

And since incorruption belongs to the perfection of glory, it follows that the perfection of a simple body is more in keeping with the perfection of glory than the perfection of a mixed body, unless the mixed body has also in itself some principle of incorruption, as the human body has, the form of which is incorruptible. Nevertheless, although a mixed body is somewhat more noble than a simple body, a simple body that exists by itself has a more noble being than if it exist in a mixed body, because in a mixed body simple bodies are in a certain way in potency, while existing by themselves, they are in their ultimate perfection.

ARTICLE 2. *Whether the Cleansing of the World Will Be Effected By Fire?*

We proceed thus to the Second Article: It would seem that this cleansing will not be effected by fire.

Objection 1. For since fire is a part of the world, it needs to be cleansed like the other parts. Now the same thing should not be both cleanser and cleansed. Therefore it would seem that the cleansing will not be by fire.

Obj. 2. Further, Just as fire has a cleansing virtue so has water. Since then all things are not capable of being cleansed by fire, and some need to be cleansed by water,—which distinction is moreover observed by the old law (Num. 31. 22),—it would seem that fire will not at any rate cleanse all things.

Obj. 3. Further, This cleansing would seem to consist in purifying the parts of the world by separating them from one another. Now the separation of the parts of the world from one another at the world's beginning was effected by God's power alone, for the work of distinction was carried out by that power; and so Anaxagoras asserted that the separation was effected by the act of the intellect which moves all things.[2] Therefore it would seem that at the end of the world the cleansing will be done immediately by God and not by fire.

On the contrary, It is written (Ps. 49. 3): *A fire shall burn before Him, and a mighty tempest shall be around Him;* and afterwards in reference to the judgment (*verse* 4): *He shall call heaven from above, and the earth to judge His people.* Therefore it would seem that the final cleansing of the world will be by means of fire.

Further, It is written (II Pet. 3. 12): *The heavens being on fire will be dissolved, and the elements shall melt with the burning heat.*

[2] Cf. Aristotle, *Physics*, III, 4 (203a23); VIII, 9 (265b22).

Therefore this cleansing will be effected by fire.

I answer that, As stated above (A. 1) this cleansing of the world will remove from it the stain contracted from sin, and the impurity resulting from mixture, and will be a disposition to the perfection of glory; and consequently in this threefold respect it will be most fitting for it to be effected by fire. First, because since fire is the most noble of the elements, its natural properties are more like the properties of glory, and this is especially clear in regard to light. Secondly, because fire, on account of the efficacy of its active power, is not as susceptible as the other elements to the admixture of a foreign matter. Thirdly, because the sphere of fire is far removed from our abode; nor are we so familiar with the use of fire as with that of earth, water, and air, so that it is not so liable to depreciation. Moreover, it is most efficacious in cleansing and in separating by a process of rarefaction.

Reply Obj. 1. Fire is not employed by us in its proper matter (since thus it is far removed from us), but only in a foreign matter, and in this respect it will be possible for the world to be cleansed by fire as existing in its pure state.

Reply Obj. 2. The first cleansing of the world by the deluge regarded only the stain of sin. Now the sin which was most prevalent then was the sin of concupiscence, and consequently it was fitting that the cleansing should be by means of its contrary, namely water. But the second cleansing regards both the stain of sin and the impurity of mixture, and in respect of both it is more fitting for it to be effected by fire than by water. For the power of water tends to unite rather than to separate; therefore the natural impurity of the elements could not be removed by water as by fire. Moreover, at the end of the world the prevalent sin will be that of tepidity, as though the world were already growing old, because then, according to Matt. 24. 12, *the charity of many shall grow cold,* and consequently the cleansing will then be fittingly effected by fire. Nor is there any thing that cannot in some way be cleansed by fire; some things, however, cannot be cleansed by fire without being destroyed themselves, such as cloths and wooden vessels, and these the Law ordered to be cleansed with water; yet all these things will be finally destroyed by fire.

Reply Obj. 3. By the work of distinction things received different forms whereby they are distinct from one another, and consequently this could only be done by Him Who is the author of nature. But by the final cleansing things will be restored to the purity in which they were created, and therefore created nature will be able to minister to its Creator to this effect; and for this reason a creature is employed as a minister, because it is thereby ennobled.

ARTICLE 3. *Whether the Fire By Which the World Will Be Cleansed Will Be of the Same Species With Elemental Fire?*

We proceed thus to the Third Article: It would seem that the fire in question is not of the same species as elemental fire.

Objection 1. For nothing consumes itself. But that fire will consume the four elements according to a gloss on II Pet. 3. 12.[1] Therefore that fire will not be of the same species as elemental fire.

Obj. 2. Further, As power is made known by operation, so is nature made known by power. Now that fire will have a different power from the fire which is an element, because it will cleanse the universe, whereas this fire cannot do that. Therefore it will not be of the same species as this.

Obj. 3. Further, In natural bodies those that are of the same species have the same movement. But that fire will have a different movement from the fire that is an element, because it will move in all directions so as to cleanse the whole. Therefore it is not of the same species.

On the contrary, Augustine says,[2] and his words are contained in a gloss[3] on I Cor. 7. 31, that "the fashion of this world will perish in the burning of worldly flames." Therefore that fire will be of the same nature as the fire which is now in the world.

Further, Just as the future cleansing is to be by fire, so was the past cleansing by water; and they are both compared to one another, II Pet. 3. 5. Now in the first cleansing the water was of the same species with elemental water. Therefore in like manner the fire of the second cleansing will be of the same species with elemental fire.

I answer that, We meet with three opinions on this question. For some say that the element of fire which is in its own sphere will come down to cleanse the world, and they explain this descent by way of multiplication, because the fire will spread through finding combustible

---

[1] *Glossa ordin.* (VI, 227B); cf. Bede (PL 93, 82).

[2] *City of God,* XX, 16 (PL 41, 682).

[3] *Glossa* Lombardi (PL 191, 1597); cf. *Glossa ordin.* (VI, 44A).

matter on all sides. And this will result all the more then, since the power of the fire will be raised over all the elements. Against this, however, would seem to be not only the fact that this fire will come down, but also the statement of the saints that it will rise up; thus (II Pet. 3. 10) it is declared that "the fire of the judgment will rise as high as the waters of the deluge";[1] and so it would seem to follow that this fire is situated towards the middle of the place of generation.

Hence others say that this fire will be generated towards the intervening space through the focussing together of the rays of the heavenly bodies, just as we see them focussed together in a burning-glass; for at that time in lieu of glasses there will be concave clouds, on which the rays will strike. But this again does not seem probable, for since the effects of heavenly bodies depend on certain fixed positions and aspects, if this fire resulted from the virtue of the heavenly bodies the time of this cleansing would be known to those who observe the movements of the stars, and this is contrary to the authority of Scripture (Matt. 24. 36).

Consequently others, following Augustine, say that "just as the deluge resulted from an outpouring of the waters of the world, so the fashion of this world will perish by a burning of worldly flames."[2] This burning is nothing else but the assembly of all those lower and higher causes that by their nature have a kindling power, and this assembly will take place not in the ordinary course of things, but by the Divine power; and from all these causes thus assembled the fire that will burn the surface of this world will result.

If we consider these opinions in themselves, we shall find that they differ as to the cause producing this fire and not as to its species. For fire, whether produced by the sun or by some lower heating cause, is of the same species as fire in its own sphere, except in so far as the former has some admixture of foreign matter. And this will of necessity be the case then, since fire cannot cleanse a thing unless this become its matter in some way. Hence we must grant absolutely that the fire in question is of the same species as ours.

Reply Obj. 1. The fire in question, although of the same species as ours, is not numerically the same. Now we see that of two fires of the

same species one destroys the other, namely the greater destroys the lesser, by consuming its matter. In like manner that fire will be able to destroy our fire.

Reply Obj. 2. Just as an operation that proceeds from the power of a thing is an indication of that power, so is its power an indication of its essence or nature, if it proceeds from the essential principles of the thing. But an operation that does not proceed from the power of the operator does not indicate its power. This appears in instruments, for the action of an instrument shows forth the power of the mover rather than that of the instrument, since it shows forth the power of the agent in so far as the latter is the first principle of the action, while it does not show forth the power of the instrument except in so far as it is susceptive of the influence of the principal agent as moving that instrument. In like manner a power that does not proceed from the essential principles of a thing does not indicate the nature of that thing except in the point of susceptibility. Thus the power by which hot water can heat is no indication of the nature of water except in the point of its being receptive of heat. Consequently nothing prevents water that has this power from being of the same species as water that does not have it. In like manner it is not unreasonable that this fire, which will have the power to cleanse the surface of the world, will be of the same species as the fire to which we are used, since the heating power in it arises not from its essential principles, but from the divine power or operation, whether we say that this power is an absolute quality, such as heat in hot water, or a kind of intention as we have ascribed to instrumental power.[3] The latter is more probable since that fire will not act save as the instrument of the Divine power.

Reply Obj. 3. Of its own nature fire tends only upwards; but in so far as it pursues its matter, which it requires when it is outside its own sphere, it follows the site of combustible matter. Accordingly it is not unreasonable for it to take a circular or a downward course, especially in so far as it acts as the instrument of the Divine power.

ARTICLE 4. *Whether That Fire Will Cleanse Also the Higher Heavens?*

We proceed thus to the Fourth Article: It would seem that that fire will cleanse also the higher heavens.

---

[1] Cf. *Glossa interl.* (VI, 227r); Peter Lombard, *Sent.*, IV, d. XLVII, chap. 4 (QR II, 1021).

[2] *City of God*, XX, 16 (PL 41, 682).

[3] Thomas, *In Sent.*, IV, d. 1, Q. 1, A. 4.

Objection 1. For it is written (Ps. 101. 26, 27): *The heavens are the works of Thy hands: they shall perish but Thou remainest.* Now the higher heavens also are the work of God's hands. Therefore they also shall perish in the final burning of the world.

Obj. 2. Further, It is written (II Pet. 3. 12): *The heavens being on fire shall be dissolved, and the elements shall melt with the burning heat of fire.* Now the heavens that are distinct from the elements are the higher heavens, in which the stars are fixed. Therefore it would seem that they also will be cleansed by that fire.

Obj. 3. Further, The purpose of that fire will be to remove from bodies their indisposition to the perfection of glory. Now in the higher heaven we find this indisposition both as regards guilt, since the devil sinned there, and as regards natural deficiency, since a gloss on Rom. 8. 22, *We know that every creature groaneth and is in labour even until now,* says:[1] "All the elements fulfil their duty with labour, even as it is not without labour that the sun and moon travel their appointed course." Therefore the higher heavens also will be cleansed by that fire.

On the contrary, The heavenly bodies are not receptive of impressions from without.

Further, A gloss on II Thess. 1. 8, *In a flame of fire giving vengeance,* says:[2] "There will be in the world a fire that shall precede Him, and shall rise in the air to the same height as did the waters of the deluge." But the waters of the deluge did not rise to the height of the higher heavens but only 15 cubits higher than the mountain summits (Gen. 7. 20). Therefore the higher heavens will not be cleansed by that fire.

I answer that, The cleansing of the world will be for the purpose of removing from bodies the disposition contrary to the perfection of glory, and this perfection is the final consummation of the universe; and this disposition is to be found in all bodies, but differently in different bodies. For in some this indisposition regards something inherent to their substance, as in these lower bodies which by being mixed together fall away from their own purity. In others this indisposition does not regard something inherent to their substance; as in the heavenly bodies, wherein nothing is to be found contrary to the final perfection of the universe, except movement which is the way to perfection, and this not any kind of movement, but

only local movement, which changes nothing intrinsic to a thing, such as its substance, quantity, or quality, but only its place, which is extrinsic to it. Consequently there is no need to take anything away from the substance of the higher heavens, but only to set its movement at rest. Now local movement is brought to rest not by the action of a counter agent, but by the mover ceasing to move; and therefore the heavenly bodies will not be cleansed, neither by fire nor by the action of any creature, but in lieu of being cleansed they will be set at rest by God's will alone.

Reply Obj. 1. As Augustine says,[3] those words of the psalm refer to the aerial heavens which will be cleansed by the fire of the final conflagration. Or we may reply that if they refer also to the higher heavens, these are said to perish as regards their movement whereby now they are moved without cessation.

Reply Obj. 2. Peter explains himself to which heavens he refers. For before the words quoted, he had said (*verses 5-7*): *The heavens . . . first, and the earth . . . through water . . . perished . . . which . . . now, by the same word are kept in store, reserved unto fire unto the day of judgment.*[4] Therefore the heavens to be cleansed are those which before were cleansed by the waters of the deluge, namely the aerial heavens.

Reply Obj. 3. This labour and service of the creature, that Ambrose ascribes to the heavenly bodies, is nothing else than the successive movements whereby they are subject to time, and the lack of that final consummation which they will attain in the end. Nor did the empyrean heaven contract any stain from the sin of the demons, because they were expelled from that heaven as soon as they sinned (Luke 10. 18; Apoc. 12. 7).

ARTICLE 5. *Whether That Fire Will Consume the Other Elements?*

We proceed thus to the Fifth Article: It would seem that the fire in question will consume the other elements.

Objection 1. For a gloss of Bede on II Pet. 3. 12 says:[5] "This exceeding great fire will engulf the four elements whereof the world consists; yet it will not so engulf all things that they will cease to be, but it will consume two of them entirely, and will restore two of them

---

[1] *Glossa* Lombardi (PL 191, 1445); cf. *Glossa ordin.* (VI, 19B); Ambrosiaster (PL 17, 131).

[2] *Glossa ordin.* (VI, 114A); *Glossa* Lombardi (PL 192, 314).

[3] *City of God,* XX, 18, 24 (PL 41, 684, 697).

[4] The entire text differs somewhat from St. Thomas's quotation, but the sense is the same.

[5] *Glossa ordin.* (VI, 227B); Bede, *in II Petr.* (PL 93, 82),

to a better fashion. Therefore it would seem that at least two of the elements are to be entirely destroyed by that fire.

Obj. 2. Further, It is written (Apoc. 21. 1): *The first heaven and the first earth have passed away and the sea is no more.* Now the heaven here denotes the air, as Augustine states,[1] and the sea denotes the gathering together of the waters. Therefore it would seem that these three elements will be wholly destroyed.

Obj. 3. Further, Fire does not cleanse except in so far as other things are made to be its matter. If, then, fire cleanses the other elements, they must become its matter. Therefore they must pass into its nature, and consequently be voided of their own nature.

Obj. 4. Further, The form of fire is the most noble of the forms to which elemental matter can attain. Now all things will be brought to the most noble state by this cleansing. Therefore the other elements will be wholly transformed into fire.

On the contrary, A gloss on I Cor. 7. 31, *The fashion of this world passeth away,* says:[2] "The beauty, not the substance, passeth." But the very substance of the elements belongs to the perfection of the world. Therefore the elements will not be consumed as to their substance.

Further, This final cleansing that will be effected by fire will correspond to the first cleansing which was effected by water. Now the latter did not corrupt the substance of the elements. Therefore neither will the former which will be the work of fire.

I answer that, There are many opinions on this question. For some say that all the elements will remain as to their matter, while all will be changed as regards their imperfection, but that two of them will retain their respective substantial form, namely air and earth, while two of them, namely fire and water, will not retain their substantial form but will be changed to the form of heaven. In this way three elements, namely air, fire, and water, will be called heaven; although air will retain the same substantial form as it has now, since even now it is called heaven. Therefore (Apoc. 21. 1) only heaven and earth are mentioned: *I saw,* says he, *a new heaven and a new earth.*

But this opinion is altogether absurd, for it is opposed both to philosophy—which holds it impossible for the lower bodies to be in potency to the form of heaven, since they have neither

a common matter, nor mutual contrariety; and to theology, since according to this opinion the perfection of the universe with the integrity of its parts will not be assured on account of two of the elements being destroyed.

Consequently heaven is taken to denote the fifth body, while all the elements are designated by earth, as expressed in Ps. 148. 7, 8, *Praise the Lord from the earth* and afterwards, *Fire, hail, snow, ice,* etc.

Hence others say that all the elements will remain as to their substance, but that their active and passive qualities will be taken from them; even as they say too, that in a mixed body the elements retain their substantial form without having their proper qualities, since these are reduced to a mean, and a mean is neither of the extremes. And the following words of Augustine[3] would seem in agreement with this: "In this conflagration of the world the qualities of the corruptible elements that were befitting our corruptible bodies will entirely perish by fire, and the substance itself will have those qualities that become an immortal body."

However, this does not seem probable, for since the proper qualities of the elements are the effects of their substantial form, it seems impossible, as long as the substantial forms remain, for these qualities to be changed, except for a time by some violent action; thus in hot water we see that by virtue of its species it returns to the cold temperature which it had lost by the action of fire, provided the species of water remain. Moreover, these same elemental qualities belong to the second perfection of the elements, as being their proper passions; nor is it probable that in this final consummation the elements will lose anything of their natural perfection.

Therefore it would seem that the reply to this question should be that the elements will remain as to their substance and proper qualities, but that they will be cleansed both from the stain which they contracted from the sins of men, and from the impurity resulting in them through their mutual action and passion; because when once the movement of the first movable body ceases, mutual action and passion will be impossible in the lower elements; and this is what Augustine calls the "qualities of corruptible elements," namely their unnatural dispositions by reason of which they come near to corruption.

Reply Obj. 1. That fire is said to engulf the

---

[1] *City of God,* xx, 18 (PL 41, 684).

[2] *Glossa interl.* (VI, 44r); cf. *Glossa* Lombardi (PL 191, 1597).

[3] *City of God,* xx, 16 (PL 41, 682).

four elements in so far as in some way it will cleanse them. But when it is said further that it will consume two entirely, this does not mean that two of the elements are to be destroyed as to their substance, but that two will be more changed from the property which they have now. Some say that these two are fire and water which excel the others in their active qualities, namely heat and cold, which are the chief principles of corruption in other bodies; and since then there will be no action of fire and water which surpass the others in activity, they would seem especially to be changed from the power which they have now. Others, however, say that these two are air and water, on account of the various movements of these two elements, which movements they derive from the movement of the heavenly bodies. And since these movements will cease (such as the ebb and flow of the sea, and the disturbances of winds and so forth), therefore these elements especially will be changed from the property which they have now.

Reply Obj. 2. As Augustine says,[1] when it is stated: *And the sea is no more,* by the sea we may understand the present world of which he had said previously (Apoc. 20. 13): *The sea gave up the dead that were in it.* If, however, the sea be taken literally we must reply that by the sea two things are to be understood, namely the substance of the waters, and their disposition, as containing salt and as to the movement of the waves. The sea will remain, not as to this second, but as to the first.

Reply Obj. 3. This fire will not act save as the instrument of God's providence and power; therefore it will not act on the other elements so as to consume them but only so as to cleanse them. Nor is it necessary for that which becomes the matter of fire to have its proper species taken away entirely, as appears in incandescent iron, which by virtue of its species that remains returns to its proper and former state as soon as it is taken from the furnace. It will be the same with the elements after they are cleansed by fire.

Reply Obj. 4. In the elemental parts we must consider not only what is befitting a part considered in itself, but also what is befitting it in its relation to the whole. I say, then, that although water would be more noble if it had the form of fire, as likewise would earth and air, yet the universe would be more imperfect if all elemental matter were to assume the form of fire.

[1] *Ibid.*

ARTICLE 6. *Whether All the Elements Will Be Cleansed By That Fire?*

We proceed thus to the Sixth Article: It would seem that neither will all the elements be cleansed by that fire.

Objection 1. Because that fire, as stated already (A. 4. ARG. 2 *on the contrary*), will not rise higher than the waters of the deluge. But the waters of the deluge did not reach to the sphere of fire. Therefore neither will the element of fire be cleansed by the final cleansing.

Obj. 2. Further, A gloss on Apoc. 21. 1, *I saw a new heaven,* etc., says:[2] "There can be no doubt that the transformation of the air and earth will be caused by fire; but it is doubtful about water, since it is believed to have the power of cleansing itself." Therefore at least it is uncertain that all the elements will be cleansed.

Obj. 3. Further, A place where there is an everlasting stain is never cleansed. Now there will always be a stain in hell. Since, then, hell is situated among the elements, it would seem that the elements will not be wholly cleansed.

Obj. 4. Further, The earthly paradise is situated on the earth. Yet it will not be cleansed by fire, since not even the waters of the deluge reached it, as Bede says,[3] as is stated in ii. *Sent.* d. 17.[4] Therefore it would seem that the elements will not all be wholly cleansed.

On the contrary, The gloss quoted above (A. 5, obj. 1) on II Pet. 3. 12 declares[5] that "this fire will engulf the four elements."

I answer that, Some say that the fire in question will rise to the summit of the space containing the four elements, so that the elements would be entirely cleansed both from the stain of sin by which also the higher parts of the elements were infected (as instanced by the smoke of idolatry which stained the higher regions), and again from corruption, since the elements are corruptible in all their parts. But this opinion is opposed to the authority of Scripture, because it is written (II Pet. 3. 7) that those heavens are *kept in store unto fire,* which were cleansed by water; and Augustine says[6] that "the same world which perished in the deluge is reserved unto fire." Now it is clear that the waters of the deluge did not rise to the summit of the space occupied by the elements, but only 15 cubits above the moun-

[2] *Glossa ordin.* (VI, 271A).
[3] Cf. *Hexaëm.*, BK. I, on Gen. 2.8 (PL 91, 44).
[4] Peter Lombard (QR I, 386).
[5] *Glossa ordin.* (VI, 227B); Bede (PL 93, 82); cf. A. 5, obj. 1.   [6] *City of God,* XX, 18 (PL 41, 684).

tain tops; and moreover it is known that vapours or any smoke whatever rising from the earth cannot pierce the entire sphere of fire so as to reach its summit; and so the stain of sin did not reach the aforesaid space. Nor can the elements be cleansed from corruptibility by the removal of something that might be consumed by fire, while it will be possible for the impurities of the elements arising from their mingling together to be consumed by fire. And these impurities are chiefly round about the earth as far as the middle of the air; therefore the fire of the final conflagration will cleanse up to that point, since the waters of the deluge rose to a height which can be approximately calculated from the height of the mountains which they surpassed in a fixed measure.

We therefore grant the *First Objection*.

Reply Obj. 2. The reason for doubt is expressed in the gloss, because, that is, water is believed to have in itself the power of cleansing, yet not such a power as will be sufficient to the future state, as stated above (A. 2, Reply 2).

Reply Obj. 3. The purpose of this cleansing will be chiefly to remove all imperfection from the abode of the saints. Consequently in this cleansing all that is foul will be brought together to the place of the damned; and so hell will not be cleansed, and the dregs of the whole earth will be brought there (Ps. 74. 9).

Reply Obj. 4. Although the sin of the first man was committed in the earthly paradise, this is not the place of sinners, as neither is the empyrean heaven, since from both places man and devil were expelled at once after their sin. Consequently that place needs no cleansing.

Article 7. *Whether the Fire of the Final Conflagration Is To Follow the Judgment?*

We proceed thus to the Seventh Article: It would seem that the fire of the final conflagration is to follow the judgment.

Objection 1. For Augustine[1] gives the following order of the things to take place at the judgment, saying: "At this judgment we have learnt that the following things will occur. Elias the Thesbite will appear, the Jews will believe, Antichrist will persecute, Christ will judge, the dead shall rise again, the good shall be separated from the wicked, the world shall be set on fire and shall be renewed." Therefore the burning will follow the judgment.

Obj. 2. Further, Augustine says:[2] "After the

wicked have been judged, and cast into everlasting fire, the figure of this world will perish in the furnace of worldly flames." Therefore the same conclusion follows.

Obj. 3. Further, When the Lord comes to judgment He will find some men living, as appears from the words of I Thess. 4. 16, where the Apostle speaking in their person, says: *Then we who are alive, who remain unto the coming to the Lord.*[3] But it would not be so if the burning of the world were to come first, since they would be destroyed by the fire. Therefore this fire will follow the judgment.

Obj. 4. Further, It is said that our Lord will come to judge the earth by fire (II Thess. 1. 7), and consequently the final conflagration would seem to be the execution of the sentence of Divine judgment. Now execution follows judgment. Therefore that fire will follow the judgment.

On the contrary, It is written (Ps. 96. 3): *A fire shall go before Him.*

Further, The resurrection will precede the judgment, for otherwise every eye would not see Christ judging. Now the burning of the world will precede the resurrection, for the saints who will rise again will have spiritual and impassible bodies, so that it will be impossible for the fire to cleanse them, and yet the text (iv. *Sent*. d. 47)[4] quotes Augustine[5] as saying that whatever needs cleansing in any way shall be cleansed by that fire. Therefore that fire will precede the judgment.

I answer that, The fire in question will in reality, as regards its beginning, precede the judgment. This can clearly be gathered from the fact that the resurrection of the dead will precede the judgment, since according to I Thess. 4. 13-16, those who have slept *shall be taken up . . . in the clouds . . . into the air . . . to meet Christ* coming to judgment. Now the general resurrection and the glorification of the bodies of the saints will happen at the same time, for the saints in rising again will assume a glorified body, as evidenced by I Cor. 15. 43, *It is sown in dishonour, it shall rise in glory;* and at the same time as the saints' bodies shall be glorified, all creatures shall be renewed, each in its own way, as appears from the statement (Rom. 8. 21) that *the creature . . . itself shall be delivered from the servitude of corruption into the liberty of the glory of the*

---

[1] *City of God*, xx, 30 (PL 41, 708).
[2] *Ibid*., xx, 16 (PL 41, 682).

[3] Vulg.,—*who are left, shall be taken . . . to meet Christ*—the words *who remain*, etc., are from *verse* 14.
[4] Lombard (QR II, 1021).
[5] *City of God*, xx, 18 (PL 41, 684); xvi, 24 (PL 41, 503).

children of God. Since then the burning of the world is a disposition to this renewal, as stated above (AA. 1, 4), it can clearly be gathered that this burning, so far as it shall cleanse the world, will precede the judgment, but as regards a certain action, whereby it will engulf the wicked, it will follow the judgment.

Reply Obj. 1. Augustine is speaking not as one who decides the point, but as expressing an opinion. This is clear from his continuing thus: "That all these things are to happen is a matter of faith, but how and in what order we shall learn more then by experience of the things themselves than now by seeking a definite conclusion by arguing about them. I think, however, they will occur in the order I have given." Hence it is clear that he is speaking as offering his opinion. The same answer applies to the *Second Objection*.

Reply Obj. 3. All men shall die and rise again; yet those are said to be found alive who will live in the body until the time of the conflagration.

Reply Obj. 4. That fire will not carry out the sentence of the judge except as regards the engulfing of the wicked; in this respect it will follow the judgment.

ARTICLE 8. *Whether That Fire Will Have Such an Effect on Men As Is Described?*

We proceed thus to the Eighth Article: It would seem that this fire will not have such an effect on men as is described.[1]

Objection 1. For a thing is said to be consumed when it is reduced to nothing. Now the bodies of the wicked will not be reduced to nothing, but will be kept for eternity, that they may bear an eternal punishment. Therefore this fire will not consume the wicked, as stated in the text.[2]

Obj. 2. Further, If it be said that it will consume the bodies of the wicked by reducing them to ashes, on the contrary: Just as the bodies of the wicked, so will those of the good be brought to ashes, for it is the privilege of Christ alone that His flesh see not corruption. Therefore it will consume also the good who will then be found.

Obj. 3. Further, The stain of sin is more abundant in the elements, which combine together to the formation of the human body in which is the corruption of the fomes even in the good, than in the elements existing outside the human body. Now the elements existing

outside the human body will be cleansed on account of the stain of sin. Much therefore will the elements in the human body whether of the good or of the wicked need to be cleansed, and consequently the bodies of both will need to be destroyed.

Obj. 4. Further, As long as the state of the way lasts the elements act in like manner on the good and the wicked. Now the state of the way will still endure in that conflagration, since after this state of the way death will not be natural, and yet it will be caused by that fire. Therefore that fire will act equally on good and wicked; and consequently it does not seem that any distinction is made between them as to their being affected by that fire, as stated in the text.

Obj. 5. Further, This fire will have done its work in a moment as it were. Yet there will be many among the living in whom there will be many things to be cleansed. Therefore that fire will not suffice for their cleansing.

I answer that, This fire of the final conflagration, in so far as it will precede the judgment, will act as the instrument of Divine justice as well as by the natural power of fire. Accordingly, as regards its natural power, it will act in like manner on the wicked and good who will be alive, by reducing the bodies of both to ashes. But in so far as it acts as the instrument of Divine justice, it will act differently on different people as regards the sense of pain. For the wicked will be tortured by the action of the fire; but the good in whom there will be nothing to cleanse will feel no pain at all from the fire, as neither did the children in the fiery furnace (Dan 3.), although their bodies will not be kept whole, as were the bodies of the children, and it will be possible by God's power for their bodies to be destroyed without their suffering pain. But the good, in whom matter for cleansing will be found, will suffer pain from that fire, more or less according to their different merits.

On the other hand, as regards the action which this fire will have after the judgment, it will act on the damned alone, since the good will all have impassible bodies.

Reply Obj. 1. Consumption there signifies being brought, not to nothing, but to ashes.

Reply Obj. 2. Although the bodies of the good will be reduced to ashes by the fire, they will not suffer pain thereby, as neither did the children in the Babylonian furnace. In this respect a distinction is drawn between the good and the wicked.

---

[1] Peter Lombard, *Sent.*, IV, d. XLVII, chap. 4 (QR,II, 1021).
[2] *Ibid.*

Reply Obj. 3. The elements that are in human bodies, even in the bodies of the elect, will be cleansed by fire. But this will be done, by God's power, without their suffering pain.

Reply Obj. 4. This fire will act not only according to the natural power of the element, but also as the instrument of Divine justice.

Reply Obj. 5. There are three reasons why those who will be found living will be able to be cleansed suddenly. One is because there will be few things in them to be cleansed, since they will be already cleansed by the previous fears and persecutions. The second is because they will suffer pain both while living and of their own will, and pain suffered in this life voluntarily cleanses much more than pain inflicted after death, as in the case of the martyrs, because "if anything needing to be cleansed be found in them, it is cut off by the sickle of suffering," as Augustine says (*De Unic. Bap.* xiii),[1] although the pain of martyrdom is of short duration in comparison with the pain endured in purgatory. The third is because the heat will gain in intensity what it loses in shortness of time.

ARTICLE 9. *Whether That Fire Will Engulf the Wicked?*

We proceed thus to the Ninth Article: It would seem that that fire will not engulf the wicked.

Objection 1. For a gloss on Mal. 3. 3, *He shall purify the sons of Levi,* says that "it is a fire consuming the wicked and refining the good"; and a gloss on I Cor. 3. 13, *Fire shall try every man's work,* says: "We read that there will be a twofold fire, one that will cleanse the elect and will precede the judgment, another that will torture the wicked."[2] Now the latter is the fire of hell that shall engulf the wicked, while the former is the fire of the final conflagration. Therefore the fire of the final conflagration will not be that which will engulf the wicked.

Obj. 2. Further, That fire will obey God in the cleansing of the world. Therefore it should receive its reward like the other elements, especially since fire is the most noble of the elements. Therefore it would seem that it ought not to be cast into hell for the punishment of the damned.

Obj. 3. Further, The fire that will engulf the wicked will be the fire of hell, and this fire was prepared from the beginning of the world for the damned; hence it is written (Matt. 25. 41): *Depart . . . you cursed . . . into everlasting fire which was prepared for the devil,* etc., and (Isa. 30. 33): *Thopheth is prepared from yesterday, prepared by the king,* etc., where a gloss observes:[3] "From yesterday— that is, from the beginning—Thopheth—that is, the valley of hell." But this fire of the final conflagration was not prepared from the beginning, but will result from the meeting together of the fires of the world. Therefore that fire is not the fire of hell which will engulf the wicked.

On the contrary are the words of Ps. 96. 3, where it is said of this fire that it *shall burn His enemies round about.*

Further, It is written (Dan. 7. 10): *A swift stream of fire issued forth from before Him;* and a gloss adds, "to drag sinners into hell."[4] Now the passage quoted refers to that fire of which we are now speaking, as appears from a gloss which observes on the same words:[5] "In order to punish the wicked and cleanse the good." Therefore the fire of the final conflagration will be plunged into hell together with the wicked.

I answer that, The entire cleansing of the world and the renewal for the purpose of cleansing will be directed to the renewal of man, and consequently the cleansing and renewal of the world must correspond with the cleansing and renewal of mankind. Now mankind will be cleansed in one way by the separation of the wicked from the good; therefore it is said (Luke 3. 17): *Whose fan is in His hand, and He will purge His floor, and will gather the wheat,* that is the elect, *into His barn, but the chaff,* that is the wicked, *He will burn with unquenchable fire.* Hence it will be thus with the cleansing of the world, so that all that is ugly and vile will be cast with the wicked into hell, and all that is beautiful and noble will be taken up above for the glory of the elect; and so too will it be with the fire of that conflagration, as Basil says[6] on Ps. 28. 7, *The voice of the Lord divideth the flame of fire,* because whatever fire contains of burning heat and gross matter will go down into hell for the punishment of the wicked, and whatever is subtle and lightsome will remain above for the glory of the elect.

---

[1] PL 43, 606.

[2] *Glossa ordin.* (VI, 37G). Glossa Lombardi (PL 191, 1558).

[3] *Glossa interl.* (IV, 58r).

[4] *Glossa interl.* (IV, 310r); cf. Jerome, *In Dan.* (PL 25, 556). [5] *Ibid.*

[6] *In Psalm.* (PG 29, 297); cf. *In Hexaëm.,* hom. VI (PG 29, 121).

Reply Obj. 1. The fire that will cleanse the elect before the judgment will be the same as the fire that will burn the world, although some say the contrary. For it is fitting that man, being a part of the world, be cleansed with the same fire as the world. They are, however, described as two fires, that will cleanse the good, and torture the wicked, both in reference to their respective offices, and somewhat in reference to their substance, since the substance of the cleansing fire will not all be cast into hell, as stated above.

Reply Obj. 2. This fire will be rewarded because whatever it contains of gross matter will be separated from it, and cast into hell.

Reply Obj. 3. The punishment of the wicked, even as the glory of the elect, will be greater after the judgment than before. Therefore, just as charity will be added to the higher creature in order to increase the glory of the elect, so too whatever is vile in creatures will be thrust down into hell in order to add to the misery of the damned. Consequently it is not unfitting that another fire be added to the fire of the damned that was prepared from the beginning of the world.

2. THE RESURRECTION ITSELF

QUESTION LXXV
OF THE RESURRECTION
(*In Three Articles*)

IN the next place we must consider things connected with and accompanying the resurrection. Of these the first to be considered will be the resurrection itself; the second will be the cause of the resurrection (Q. LXXVI); the third its time and manner (Q. LXXVII); the fourth its term from which (Q. LXXVIII); the fifth the condition of those who rise again (Q. LXXIX).

Under the first head there will be three points of inquiry: (1) Whether there is to be a resurrection of the body? (2) Whether it is generally of all bodies? (3) Whether it is natural or miraculous?

ARTICLE 1. *Whether There Is To Be a Resurrection of the Body?*

We proceed thus to the First Article: It would seem that there is not to be a resurrection of the body.

Objection 1. For it is written (Job 14. 12): *Man when he is fallen asleep, shall not rise again till the heavens be broken.* But the heavens shall never be broken, since the earth, to which it seems this is still less applicable, *standeth for ever* (Eccles. 1. 4). Therefore the man that is dead shall never rise again.

Obj. 2. Further, Our Lord proves the resurrection by quoting the words: *I am the God of Abraham, and the God of Isaac, and the God of Jacob. He is not the God of the dead but of the living* (Matt. 22. 32; Exod. 3. 6). But it is clear that when those words were uttered, Abraham, Isaac, and Jacob lived not in body, but only in the soul. Therefore there will be no resurrection of bodies but only of souls.

Obj. 3. Further, The Apostle (I Cor. 15) seems to prove the resurrection from the reward for labours endured by the saints in this life. For if they trusted in this life alone, they would be the most unhappy of all men. Now there can be sufficient reward for labour in the soul alone, since it is not necessary for the instrument to be repaid together with the worker, and the body is the soul's instrument. Therefore even in purgatory, where souls will be punished for what they did in the body, the soul is punished without the body. Therefore there is no need to hold a resurrection of the body, but it is enough to hold a resurrection of souls, which consists in their being taken from the death of sin and unhappiness to the life of grace and glory.

Obj. 4. Further, The last (state) of a thing is the most perfect, since thereby it attains its end. Now the most perfect state of the soul is to be separated from the body, since in that state it is more conformed to God and the angels, and is more pure, as being separated from any extraneous nature. Therefore separation from the body is its final state, and consequently it does not return from this state to the body, as neither does a man end in becoming a boy.

Obj. 5. Further, Bodily death is the punishment inflicted on man for his own transgression, as appears from Gen. 2, even as spiritual death, which is the separation of the soul from God, is inflicted on man for mortal sin. Now man never returns to life from spiritual death after receiving the sentence of his damnation. Therefore neither will there be any return from bodily death to bodily life, and so there will be no resurrection.

On the contrary, It is written (Job 19. 25-26): *I know that my Redeemer liveth, and in the last day I shall rise out of the earth, and I shall be clothed again with my skin,* etc. Therefore there will be a resurrection of the body.

Further, The gift of Christ is greater than the sin of Adam, as appears from Rom. 5. 15. Now death was brought in by sin, for if sin had not been, there had been no death. Therefore by the gift of Christ man will be restored from death to life.

Further, The members should be conformed to the head. Now our Head lives and will live eternally in body and soul, since *Christ rising again from the dead dieth now no more* (Rom. 6. 8). Therefore men who are His members will live in body and soul; and consequently there must be a resurrection of the body.

I answer that, According to the various opinions about man's last end there have been various opinions holding or denying the resurrection. For man's last end which all men desire naturally is happiness. Some have held that man is able to attain this end in this life; therefore they had no need to admit another life after this, in which man would be able to attain to his perfection, and so they denied the resurrection. But this opinion is confuted with sufficient probability by the changeableness of fortune, the weakness of the human body, the imperfection and instability of knowledge and virtue, all of which are hindrances to the perfection of happiness, as Augustine argues.[1]

Hence others maintained that after this there is another life wherein, after death, man lives according to the soul only, and they held that such a life sufficed to satisfy the natural desire to obtain happiness; therefore Porphyrius said[2] as Augustine states:[3] "The soul, to be happy, must avoid all bodies"; and consequently these did not hold the resurrection. This opinion was based by various people on various false foundations. For certain heretics asserted that all bodily things are from the evil principle, but that spiritual things are from the good principle: and from this it follows that the soul cannot reach the height of its perfection unless it be separated from the body, since the latter withdraws it from its principle, the participation of which makes it happy. Hence all those heretical sects that hold corporeal things to have been created or fashioned by the devil deny the resurrection of the body. The false-

hood of this principle has been shown at the beginning of the second Book.[4]

Others said that the entire nature of man is seated in the soul, so that the soul makes use of the body as an instrument, or as a sailor uses his ship; therefore according to this opinion, it follows that if happiness is attained by the soul alone, man would not be baulked in his natural desire for happiness, and so there is no need to hold the resurrection. But the Philosopher sufficiently destroys this foundation,[5] where he shows that the soul is united to the body as form to matter. Hence it is clear that if man cannot be happy in this life, we must of necessity hold the resurrection.

Reply Obj. 1. The heavens will never be destroyed as to their substance, but as to the effect of their power whereby their movement is the cause of generation and corruption of lower things; for this reason the Apostle says (I Cor. 7. 31): *The fashion of this world passeth away.*

Reply Obj. 2. Abraham's soul, properly speaking, is not Abraham himself, but a part of him (and the same as regards the others). Hence life in Abraham's soul does not suffice to make Abraham a living being, or to make the God of Abraham the God of a living man. But there needs to be life in the whole composite, that is, the soul and body, and although this life was not actually when these words were uttered, it was in each part as ordained to the resurrection. Therefore our Lord proves the resurrection with the greatest subtlety and efficacy.

Reply Obj. 3. The soul is compared to the body, not only as a worker to the instrument with which he works, but also as form to matter; therefore the work belongs to the composite and not to the soul alone, as the Philosopher shows.[6] And since to the worker is due the reward of the work, it is necessary that man himself, who is composed of soul and body, receive the reward of his work. Now as venial offences are called sins as being dispositions to sin, and not as having absolutely and perfectly the character of sin, so the punishment which is awarded to them in purgatory is not a retribution absolutely, but rather a cleansing, which is wrought separately in the body, by death and by its being reduced to ashes, and in the soul by the fire of purgatory.

Reply Obj. 4. Other things being equal, the

---

[1] *City of God,* XXII, 22 (PL 41, 784); cf. XIX, 4 (PL 41, 629).

[2] In the lost work *De Regressu Animae;* cf. also Augustine, *City of God,* XIII, 16 (PL 41, 387).

[3] *City of God,* XXII, 26 (PL 41, 794).

[4] *In Sent.,* d. 1, Pt. I, A. 3.

[5] *Soul,* II, 2 (414^{a}12).

[6] *Ibid.,* I, 4 (408^{b}13).

state of the soul in the body is more perfect than outside the body, because it is a part of the whole composite, and every integral part is material in respect to the whole (although it is more conformed to God relatively). Because, strictly speaking, a thing is more conformed to God when it has all that the condition of its nature requires, since then most of all it imitates the Divine perfection. Hence the heart of an animal is more conformed to an immovable God when it is in movement than when it is at rest, because the pefection of the heart is in its movement, and its rest is its undoing.

Reply Obj. 5. Bodily death was brought about by Adam's sin which was blotted out by Christ's death; hence its punishment does not last for ever. But mortal sin which causes everlasting death through impenitence will not be expiated hereafter. Hence that death will be everlasting.

ARTICLE 2. *Whether the Resurrection Will Be for All Without Exception?*

We proceed thus to the Second Article: It would seem that the resurrection will not be for all without exception.

Objection 1. For it is written (Ps. 1. 5): *The wicked shall not rise again in judgment.* Now men will not rise again except at the time of the general judgment. Therefore the wicked shall in no way rise again.

Obj. 2. Further, It is written (Dan. 12. 2): *Many of those that sleep in the dust of the earth shall awake.* But these words imply a certain restriction. Therefore all will not rise again.

Obj. 3. Further, By the resurrection men are conformed to Christ rising again; therefore the Apostle argues (I Cor. 15. 12, *seqq.*) that if Christ rose again, we also shall rise again. Now those alone should be conformed to Christ rising again who have borne His image, and this belongs to the good alone. Therefore they alone shall rise again.

Obj. 4. Further, Punishment is not remitted unless the fault is condoned. Now bodily death is the punishment of original sin. Therefore, as original sin is not forgiven to all, all will not rise again.

Obj. 5. Further, As we are born again by the grace of Christ, even so shall we rise again by His grace. Now those who die in their mother's womb can never be born again; therefore neither can they rise again, and consequently all will not rise again.

On the contrary, It is said (John 28, 25):

All that are in the graves shall hear the voice of the Son of God, . . . and they that hear shall live. Therefore the dead shall all rise again.

Further, It is written (I Cor. 15. 51): *We shall all indeed rise again,* etc.

Further, The resurrection is necessary in order that those who rise again may receive punishment or reward according to their merits. Now either punishment or reward is due to all, either for their own merits, as to adults, or for others' merits, as to children. Therefore all will rise again.

I answer that, Those things the reason of which comes from the nature of a species must be found in a like manner in all the members of that same species. Now such is the resurrection, because the reason for the resurrection, as stated above (A. 1, Reply 4), is that the soul cannot have the final perfection of the human species so long as it is separated from the body. Hence no soul will remain for ever separated from the body. Therefore it is necessary for all, as well as for one, to rise again.

Reply Obj. 1. As a gloss expounds these words,[1] they refer to the spiritual resurrection whereby the wicked shall not rise again in the particular judgment. Or else they refer to the wicked who are altogether unbelievers, who will not rise again to be judged, since they are already judged (John 3. 18).

Reply Obj. 2. Augustine explains "many" as meaning "all";[2] in fact, this way of speaking is often met with in Holy Writ.[3] Or else the restriction may refer to the children consigned to limbo who, although they shall rise again, are not properly said to awake, since they will have no sense either of pain or of glory, and waking is the unchaining of the senses.

Reply Obj. 3. All, both good and wicked, are conformed to Christ, while living in this life, as regards things pertaining to the nature of the species, but not as regards matters pertaining to grace. Hence all will be conformed to Him in the restoration of natural life, but not in the likeness of glory, except the good alone.

Reply Obj. 4. Those who have died in original sin have, by dying, discharged the obligation of death which is the punishment of original sin. Hence, notwithstanding original sin, they can rise again from death, for the punishment of original sin is to die, rather than to be detained by death.

[1] *Glossa ordin.* (III, 87E); *Glossa* Lombardi (PL 191, 64); Augustine, *Emarr. in Ps.* (PL 36, 69).

[2] *City of God,* XX, 23 (PL 41, 696).

[3] Cf. Matt. 20.28; Rom. 5.15.

Reply Obj. 5. We are born again by the grace of Christ that is given to us, but we rise again by the grace of Christ whereby it came about that He took our nature, since it is by this that we are conformed to Him in natural things. Hence those who die in their mother's womb, although they are not born again by receiving grace, will nevertheless rise again on account of the conformity of their nature with Him, which conformity they acquired by attaining to the perfection of the human species.

ARTICLE 3. *Whether the Resurrection Is Natural?*

We proceed thus to the Third Article: It would seem that the resurrection is natural.

Objection 1. For, as the Damascene says (*De Fide Orthod.* iii, 14),[1] "that which is commonly observed in all, marks the nature of the individuals contained under it." Now resurrection applies commonly to all. Therefore it is natural.

Obj. 2. Further, Gregory says (*Moral.* xiv, 55):[2] "Those who do not hold the resurrection on the principle of obedience ought certainly to hold it on the principle of reason. For what does the world every day but imitate, in its elements, our resurrection?" And he offers as examples the light which as it were dies, and is withdrawn from our sight, and again rises anew, as it were, and is recalled—the shrubs which lose their greenery, and again by a kind of resurrection are renewed—and the seeds which rot and die and then sprout and rise again as it were, which same example is given by the Apostle (I Cor. 15. 36). Now from the works of nature nothing can be known save what is natural. Therefore the resurrection is natural.

Obj. 3. Further, Things that are against nature do not remain for long, because they are violent, so to speak. But the life that is restored by the resurrection will last for ever. Therefore the resurrection will be natural.

Obj. 4. Further, That to which the entire expectation of nature looks forward would seem to be natural. Now such a thing is the resurrection and the glorification of the saints according to Rom. 8. 19. Therefore the resurrection will be natural.

Obj. 5. Further, The resurrection is a kind of movement towards the everlasting union of soul and body. Now movement is natural if it terminates in a natural rest,[3] and the everlast-

ing union of soul and body will be natural, for since the soul is the body's proper mover, it has a body proportionate to it, so that the body is likewise for ever capable of being quickened by it, even as the soul lives for ever. Therefore the resurrection will be natural.

On the contrary, There is no natural return from privation to habit. But death is privation of life. Therefore the resurrection whereby one returns from death to life is not natural.

Further, Things of the one species have one fixed way of origin; hence animals begotten of putrefaction are never of the same species as those begotten of seed, as the Commentator says on the *Physics*.[4] Now the natural way of man's origin is for him to be begotten of a like in species, and such is not the case in the resurrection. Therefore it will not be natural.

I answer that, A movement or an action stands related to nature in three ways. For there is a movement or action of which nature is neither the principle nor the term, and such a movement is sometimes from a principle above nature as in the case of a glorified body, and sometimes from any other principle whatever; for instance, the violent upward movement of a stone which terminates in a violent rest. Again, there is a movement of which nature is both principle and term; for instance, the downward movement of a stone. And there is another movement of which nature is the term, but not the principle, the latter being sometimes something above nature (as in giving sight to a blind man, for sight is natural, but the principle of the sight-giving is above nature), and sometimes something else, as in the forcing of flowers or fruit by artificial process. It is impossible for nature to be the principle and not the term, because natural principles are appointed to definite effects, beyond which they cannot extend.

Therefore the action or movement that is related to nature in the first way can in no way be natural, but is either miraculous if it come from a principle above nature, or violent if from any other principle. The action or movement that is related to nature in the second way is natural absolutely; but the action that is related to nature in the third way cannot be described as natural absolutely, but as natural in a restricted sense, in so far, that is, as it leads to that which is according to nature; but it is called either miraculous or artificial or violent. For, properly speaking, natural is that which is according to nature, and a thing is according

---

[1] PG 94, 1040.   [2] PL 75, 1076.
[3] Aristotle, *Physics*, v, 6 (230^{b}15).   [4] Comm. 46 (IV, 387E).

to nature if it has that nature and whatever results from that nature.[1] Consequently, speaking absolutely, movement cannot be described as natural unless its principle be natural.

Now nature cannot be the principle of resurrection, although resurrection terminates in the life of nature. For nature is the principle of movement in the thing in which nature is,—either the active principle, as in the movement of heavy and light bodies and in the natural alterations of animals,—or the passive principle, as in the generation of simple bodies. The passive principle of natural generation is the natural passive potency which always has an active power corresponding to it in nature, according to the *Metaphysics*;[2] nor as to this does it matter whether the active principle in nature correspond to the passive principle in respect of its ultimate perfection, namely the form; or in respect of a disposition in virtue of which it demands the ultimate form, as in the generation of a man according to the teaching of faith, or in all other generations according to the opinions of Plato[3] and Avicenna.[4] But in nature there is no active principle of the resurrection, neither as regards the union of the soul with the body, nor as regards the disposition which is the demand for that union, since such a disposition cannot be produced by nature except in a definite way by the process of generation from seed. Therefore even granted a passive potency on the part of the body, or any kind of inclination to its union with the soul, it is not such as to suffice for the conditions of natural movement. Therefore the resurrection, strictly speaking, is miraculous and not natural except in a restricted sense, as we have explained.

Reply Obj. 1. Damascene is speaking of those things that are found in all individuals and are caused by the principles of nature. For supposing by a divine operation all men to be made white, or to be gathered together in one place, as happened at the time of the deluge, it would not follow that whiteness or to be in some particular place is a natural property of man.

Reply Obj. 2. From natural things one does not come by a demonstration of reason to know non-natural things, but by a persuasion of rea-

son one may know something above nature, since the natural bears a certain resemblance to the supernatural. Thus the union of soul and body resembles the union of the soul with God by the glory of final enjoyment, as the Master says (ii. *Sent.* d. 1),[5] and in like manner the examples quoted by the Apostle and Gregory are confirmatory evidences of our faith in the resurrection.

Reply Obj. 3. This argument regards an operation which terminates in something that is not natural but contrary to nature. Such is not the resurrection, and hence the argument is not to the point.

Reply Obj. 4. The entire operation of nature is subordinate to the Divine operation, just as the working of a lower art is subordinate to the working of a higher art. Hence just as all the work of a lower art has in view an end unattainable save by the operation of the higher art that produces the form, or makes use of what has been made by art, so the last end which the whole expectation of nature has in view is unattainable by the operation of nature, and for this reason the attaining to it is not natural.

Reply Obj. 5. Although there can be no natural movement terminating in a violent rest, there can be a non-natural movement terminating in a natural rest, as explained above.

QUESTION LXXVI

OF THE CAUSE OF THE RESURRECTION

(*In Three Articles*)

WE must next consider the cause of our resurrection. Under this head there are three points of inquiry: (1) Whether Christ's resurrection is the cause of our resurrection? (2) Whether the sound of the trumpet is? (3) Whether the angels are?

ARTICLE 1. *Whether the Resurrection of Christ Is the Cause of Our Resurrection?*

We proceed thus to the First Article: It would seem that the resurrection of Christ is not the cause of our resurrection.

Objection 1. For, given the cause, the effect follows. Yet given the resurrection of Christ the resurrection of the other dead did not follow at once. Therefore His resurrection is not the cause of ours.

Obj. 2. Further, An effect cannot be unless the cause precedes. But the resurrection of the dead would be even if Christ had not risen

---

[1] Aristotle, *Physics*, II, 1 (192b35).
[2] Aristotle, IX, 1 (1046a19).
[3] Cf. Averroes, *In Meta.*, VII, comm. 31 (VIII, 180K); cf. Chalcidius, *In Timaeum*, 319 (DD 248); see Aristotle, *Metaphysics*, I, 6 (987a29); Plato, *Phaedo* (101); *Timaeus* (50); cf. St. Thomas, *Contra Gent.*, III, 68; cf. also above, Part I, Q. XLV, A. 8.
[4] *Meta.*, IX, 5 (1051rb).

[5] QR I, 311.

again, for God could have delivered man in some other way. Therefore Christ's resurrection is not the cause of ours.

Obj. 3. Further, The same thing produces the one effect throughout the one same species. Now the resurrection will be common to all men. Since then Christ's resurrection is not its own cause, it is not the cause of the resurrection of others.

Obj. 4. Further, An effect retains some likeness to its cause. But the resurrection, at least of some, namely the wicked, bears no likeness to the resurrection of Christ. Therefore Christ's resurrection will not be the cause of theirs.

On the contrary, "In every genus that which is first is the cause of those that come after it."[1] Now Christ, by reason of His bodily resurrection, is called *the firstfruits of them that sleep* (I Cor. 15. 20), and *the first-begotten of the dead* (Apoc. 1. 5). Therefore His resurrection is the cause of the resurrection of others.

Further, Christ's resurrection has more in common with our bodily resurrection than with our spiritual resurrection which is by justification. But Christ's resurrection is the cause of our justification, as appears from Rom. 4. 25, where it is said that He *rose again for our justification.* Therefore Christ's resurrection is the cause of our bodily resurrection.

I answer that, Christ by reason of His human nature is called the mediator of God and men (I Tim. 2. 5); therefore the Divine gifts are bestowed on men by means of Christ's humanity. Now just as we cannot be delivered from spiritual death save by the gift of grace bestowed by God, so neither can we be delivered from bodily death except by resurrection wrought by the Divine power. And therefore as Christ, in respect of His human nature, received the firstfruits of grace from above, and His grace is the cause of our grace, because *of His fulness we all have received . . . grace for grace* (John 1. 16), so in Christ has our resurrection begun, and His resurrection is the cause of ours. Thus Christ as God is, as it were, the equivocal cause of our resurrection, but as God and man rising again, He is the proximate and, so to say, the univocal cause of our resurrection.

Now a univocal agent cause produces its effect in likeness to its own form, so that not only is it an efficient, but also an exemplary cause in relation to that effect. This happens in two ways. For sometimes this very form, whereby the agent is likened to its effect, is the direct principle of the action by which the effect

is produced, as heat in the fire that heats; and sometimes it is not the form in respect of which this likeness is observed, that is primarily and directly the principle of that action, but the principles of that form. For instance, if a white man beget a white man, the whiteness of the begetter is not the principle of active generation, and yet the whiteness of the begetter is said to be the cause of the whiteness of the begotten, because the principles of whiteness in the begetter are the generative principles causing whiteness in the begotten. In this way the resurrection of Christ is the cause of our resurrection, because the same thing that wrought the resurrection of Christ, which is the univocal efficient cause of our resurrection, operates for our resurrection, namely the power of Christ's Godhead which is common to Him and the Father. Hence it is written (Rom. 8. 11): *He that raised up Jesus Christ from the dead shall quicken also your mortal bodies.* And this very resurrection of Christ by virtue of His indwelling Godhead is, as it were, the instrumental cause of our resurrection, since the Divine operations were wrought by means of Christ's flesh as though it were a kind of organ; thus the Damascene instances as an example (*De Fide Orthod.* iii, 15)[2] the touch of His body whereby he healed the leper (Matt. 8. 3).

Reply Obj. 1. A sufficient cause produces at once its effect to which it is immediately ordered but not the effect to which it is ordered by means of something else, no matter how sufficient it may be; thus heat, however intense it be, does not cause heat at once in the first instant, but it begins at once to set up a movement towards heat, because heat is its effect by means of movement. Now Christ's resurrection is said to be the cause of ours in that it works our resurrection not immediately, but by means of its principle, namely the Divine power which will work our resurrection in likeness to the resurrection of Christ. Now God's power works by means of His will which is nearest to the effect; hence it is not necessary that our resurrection should follow at once after He has wrought the resurrection of Christ, but that it should happen at the time which God's will has decreed.

Reply Obj. 2. God's power is not tied to any particular second causes, but that He can produce their effects either immediately or by means of other causes; thus He might work the generation of lower bodies even though there were no movement of the heaven, and yet ac-

---

[1] Aristotle, *Metaphysics*, II, 1 (993^{b}26).

[2] PG 94, 1049.

cording to the order which He has established in things, the movement of the heaven is the cause of the generation of the lower bodies. In like manner according to the order appointed to human things by Divine providence, Christ's resurrection is the cause of ours, and yet He could have appointed another order, and then our resurrection would have had another cause ordained by God.

Reply Obj. 3. This argument holds when all the things of one species have the same order to the first cause of the effect to be produced in the whole of that species. But it is not so in the case in point, because Christ's humanity is nearer to His Godhead, Whose power is the first cause of the resurrection, than is the humanity of others. Hence Christ's Godhead caused His resurrection immediately, but it causes the resurrection of others by means of Christ-man rising again.

Reply Obj. 4. The resurrection of all men will bear some resemblance to Christ's resurrection, as regards that which pertains to the life of nature, in respect of which all were conformed to Christ. Hence all will rise again to immortal life; but in the saints who were conformed to Christ by grace, there will be conformity as to things pertaining to glory.

ARTICLE 2. *Whether the Sound of the Trumpet Will Be the Cause of Our Resurrection?*

We proceed thus to the Second Article: It would seem that the sound of the trumpet will not be the cause of our resurrection.

Objection 1. For the Damascene says (*De Fide Orthod.* iv, 27):[1] "Believe that the resurrection will take place by God's will, power, and nod." Therefore since these are a sufficient cause of our resurrection, we ought not to assign the sound of the trumpet as its cause.

Obj. 2. Further, It is useless to make sounds to one who cannot hear. But the dead will not have hearing. Therefore it is unfitting to make a sound to arouse them.

Obj. 3. Further, If any sound is the cause of the resurrection, this will only be by a power given by God to the sound; therefore a gloss on Ps. 67. 34, *He will give to His voice the voice of power,* says,[2]—"to arouse our bodies." Now from the moment that a power is given to a thing, though it be given miraculously, the act that ensues is natural, as instanced in the man

born blind who, after being restored to sight, saw naturally. Therefore if a sound be the cause of resurrection, the resurrection would be natural, which is false.

On the contrary, It is written (I Thess. 4. 15): *The Lord Himself will come down from heaven . . . with the trumpet of God; and the dead who are in Christ shall rise.*

Further, It is written (John 5. 28) that they *who are in the graves shall hear the voice of the Son of God . . . and (verse 25) they that hear shall live.* Now this voice is called the trumpet, as stated in the text (iv. *Sent.* d. 43).[3] Therefore, etc,

I answer that, Cause and effect must in some way be united together, since mover and moved, maker and made, are simultaneous.[4] Now Christ rising again is the univocal cause of our resurrection; therefore at the resurrection of bodies, Christ must bring about the resurrection at the giving of some common bodily sign.

According to some this sign will be literally Christ's voice commanding the resurrection, even as He commanded the sea and the storm ceased (Matt. 8. 26).

Others say that this sign will be nothing else than the manifest reappearance of the Son of God in the world, according to the words of Matt. 24. 27: *As lightning cometh out of the east, and appeareth even into the west, so shall also the coming of the Son of man be.* These rely on the authority of Gregory who says that "the sound of the trumpet is nothing else but the Son appearing to the world as judge."[5] According to this, the visible presence of the Son of God is called His voice (Ps. 67. 34; John 5. 25), because as soon as He appears all nature will obey His command in restoring human bodies; hence He is described as coming *with commandment* (I Thess. 4. 15). In this way His appearing, in so far as it has the force of a command, is called His voice, which voice, whatever it be, is sometimes called a cry (Matt. 25. 6) as of a crier summoning to judgment; sometimes the sound of a trumpet (I Cor. 15. 52; I Thess. 4. 15), either on account of its distinctness, as stated in the text (iv. *Sent.* d. 43),[6] or as being in keeping with the use of the trumpet in the Old Testament (Num. 10): for by the trumpet they were summoned to the council, stirred to the battle, and called to the feast;

---

[1] PG 94, 1225.
[2] *Glossa ordin.* (III, 179F); *Glossa* Lombardi (PL 191, 618).

[3] Peter Lombard (QR II, 996).
[4] Aristotle, *Physics,* VII, 2 (243ª3).
[5] Quoted by Albert, *In Sent.,* IV, d. XLIII, A. 4 (BO XXX, 510).
[6] Peter Lombard (QR II, 996).

and those who rise again will be summoned to the council of judgment (John 5. 28), to the battle in which *the world shall fight ... against the unwise* (Wisd. 5. 21), and to the feast of everlasting solemnity (Matt. 25. 34).

Reply Obj. 1. In those words Damascene touches on three things respecting the material cause of the resurrection: namely, the Divine will which commands, the power which executes, and the ease of execution, when he adds "nod," in resemblance to our own affairs, since it is very easy for us to do what is done at once at our word. But the ease is much more evident, if before we say a word, our servants execute our will at once at the first sign of our will, which sign is called a nod, and this nod is a kind of cause of that execution, in so far as others are led thereby to accomplish our will. And the Divine nod, at which the resurrection will take place, is nothing but the sign given by God, which all nature will obey by concurring in the resurrection of the dead. This sign is the same as the sound of the trumpet, as explained above.

Reply Obj. 2. As the forms of the Sacrament have the power to sanctify, not through being heard, but through being spoken, so this sound, whatever it be, will have an instrumental efficacy of resuscitation, not through being perceived, but through being uttered. Even so a sound by the pulsation of the air arouses the sleeper, by loosing the organ of perception, and not because it is known, since judgment about the sound that reaches the ears is subsequent to the awakening and is not its cause.

Reply Obj. 3. This argument would avail if the power given to that sound were a complete being in nature, because then that which would proceed from it would have for principle a power already rendered natural. But this power is not of that kind but such as we have ascribed above to the forms of the Sacraments.[1]

ARTICLE 3. *Whether the Angels Will Do Anything Towards the Resurrection?*

We proceed thus to the Third Article: It would seem that the angels will do nothing at all towards the resurrection.

Objection 1. For raising the dead shows a greater power than does begetting men. Now when men are begotten, the soul is not infused into the body by means of the angels. Therefore neither will the resurrection, which is reunion of soul and body, be wrought by the ministry of the angels.

Obj. 2. Further, If this is to be ascribed to the instrumentality of any angels at all, it would seem especially referable to the Virtues, to whom it belongs to work miracles. Yet it is referred not to them, but to the Archangels, according to the text (iv. *Sent.* d. 43).[2] Therefore the resurrection will not be wrought by the ministry of the angels.

On the contrary, It is stated (I Thess. 4. 15) that *the Lord ... shall come down from heaven ... with the voice of an archangel ... and the dead shall rise again.* Therefore the resurrection of the dead will be accomplished by the angelic ministry.

I answer that, According to Augustine (*De Trin.* iii, 4)[3] "just as the grosser and inferior bodies are ruled in a certain order by the more subtle and more powerful bodies, so are all bodies ruled by God by the rational spirit of life"; and Gregory speaks in the same sense (*Dial.* iv, 6).[4] Consequently in all God's bodily works, He employs the ministry of the angels. Now in the resurrection there is something pertaining to the transmutation of the bodies, namely the gathering together of the mortal remains and their disposal for the restoration of the human body; therefore in this respect God will employ the ministry of the angels in the resurrection. But the soul, even as it is immediately created by God, so will it be reunited to the body immediately by God without any operation of the angels, and in like manner He Himself will glorify the body without the ministry of the angels, just as He immediately glorifies man's soul. This ministry of the angels is called their voice, according to one explanation[5] given in the text (iv. *Sent.* d. 43).[6]

Hence the *Reply to the First Objection* is evident from what has been said.

Reply Obj. 2. This ministry will be exercised chiefly by one Archangel, namely Michael, who is the prince of the Church as he was of the Synagogue (Dan. 10. 21).[7] Yet he will act under the influence of the Virtues and the other higher orders, so that what he shall do, the higher orders will, in a way, do also. In like manner the lower angels will cooperate with him as to the resurrection of each individual to whose guardianship they were appointed, so that this voice can be ascribed either "to one or to many angels."[8]

---

[1] *In Sent.*, IV, dist. I, Q. I, A. 4.

[2] Peter Lombard (QR II, 996).
[3] PL 42, 873.   [4] PL 77, 328.
[5] Augustine, *Epist.*, CXL, 34 (PL 33, 573).
[6] Lombard (QR II, 996).
[7] Cf. Dan. 12.1.   [8] Lombard, *loc. cit.*

QUESTION LXXVII

OF THE TIME AND MANNER OF THE RESURRECTION

(In Four Articles)

WE must now consider the time and manner of the resurrection. Under this head there are four points of inquiry: (1) Whether the time of the resurrection should be delayed until the end of the world? (2) Whether that time is hidden? (3) Whether the resurrection will occur at night-time? (4) Whether it will happen suddenly?

ARTICLE 1. *Whether the Time of Our Resurrection Should Be Delayed Till the End of the World?*

We proceed thus to the First Article: It would seem that the time of the resurrection ought not to be delayed till the end of the world, so that all may rise together.

Objection 1. For there is more conformity between head and members than between one member and another, as there is more between cause and effect than between one effect and another. Now Christ, Who is our Head, did not delay His resurrection until the end of the world, so as to rise again together with all men. Therefore there is no need for the resurrection of the early saints to be deferred until the end of the world, so that they may rise again together with the others.

Obj. 2. Further, The resurrection of the Head is the cause of the resurrection of the members. But the resurrection of certain members that desire nobility from their being closely connected with the Head was not delayed till the end of the world, but followed immediately after Christ's resurrection, as is piously believed concerning the Blessed Virgin and John the Evangelist.[1] Therefore the resurrection of others will be so much nearer Christ's resurrection, according as they have been more conformed to Him by grace and merit.

Obj. 3. Further, The state of the New Testament is more perfect, and bears a closer resemblance to Christ, than the state of the Old Testament. Yet some of the fathers of the Old Testament rose again when Christ rose, according to Matt. 27. 52: *Many of the bodies of the saints, that had slept, arose.* Therefore it would seem that the resurrection of the Old Testament saints should not be delayed till the end of the world, so that all may rise together.

[1] Cf. Jerome, *Epist.,* IX (PL 30, 127).

Obj. 4. Further, There will be no numbering of years after the end of the world. Yet after the resurrection of the dead, the years are still reckoned until the resurrection of others, as appears from Apoc. 20. 4, 5. For it is stated there that *I saw . . . the souls of them that were beheaded for the testimony of Jesus, and for the word of God,* and further on: *And they lived and reigned with Christ a thousand years. And the rest of the dead lived not till the thousand years were finished.* Therefore the resurrection of all is not delayed until the end of the world, that all may rise together.

On the contrary, It is written (Job 14. 12): *Man when he is fallen asleep shall not rise again till the heavens be broken, he shall not wake, nor rise out of his sleep,* and it is a question of the sleep of death. Therefore the resurrection of men will be delayed until the end of the world when the heavens shall be destroyed.

Further, It is written (Heb. 11. 39): *All these being approved by the testimony of faith received not the promise,* that is "full happiness of soul and body,"[2] since *God has provided something better for us, lest they should be consummated,* that is "perfected,"[3] *without us,*—"in order that," as a gloss observes,[4] "through all rejoicing each one might rejoice the more." But the resurrection will not precede the glorification of bodies, because *He will reform the body of our lowness made like to the body of His glory* (Phil. 3. 21), and the children of the resurrection will be *as the angels . . . in heaven* (Matt. 22. 30). Therefore the resurrection will be delayed till the end of the world, when all shall rise together.

I answer that, As Augustine states (*De Trin.* iii, 4)[5] Divine providence decreed that "the grosser and lower bodies should be ruled in a certain order by the more subtle and powerful bodies; and therefore the entire matter of the lower bodies is subject to change according to the movement of the heavenly bodies. Hence it would be contrary to the order established in things by Divine providence if the matter of lower bodies were brought to the state of incorruption so long as there remains movement in the higher bodies. And since, according to the teaching of faith, the resurrection will bring men to immortal life conformably to Christ Who *rising again from the dead dieth now no more* (Rom. 6. 9), the resurrection of human bodies will be delayed until the end of

[2] *Glossa interl.* (VI, 157V); *Glossa Lombardi* (PL 192, 500).   [3] *Ibid.*   [4] *Ibid.*   [5] PL 42, 873.

the world when the heavenly movement will cease. For this reason, too, certain philosophers, who held that the movement of the heavens will never cease, maintained that human souls will return to mortal bodies such as we have now,—whether, as Empedocles,[1] they stated that the soul would return to the same body at the end of the great year, or that it would return to another body; thus Pythagoras asserted that "any soul will enter any body,"[2] as stated in the book on the *Soul*.[3]

Reply Obj. 1. Although the head is more conformed to the members by conformity of proportion (which is requisite in order that it have influence over the members) than one member is to another, yet the head has a certain causality over the members which the members have not; and in this the members differ from the head and agree with one another. Hence Christ's resurrection is an exemplar of ours, and through our faith therein there arises in us the hope of our own resurrection. But the resurrection of one of Christ's members is not the cause of the resurrection of other members, and consequently Christ's resurrection had to precede the resurrection of others who have all to rise again at the consummation of the world.

Reply Obj. 2. Although among the members some rank higher than others and are more conformed to the Head, they do not attain to the character of headship so as to be the cause of others. Consequently greater conformity to Christ does not give them a right to rise again before others as though they were exemplar and the others exemplate, as we have said (REPLY 1) in reference to Christ's resurrection; and if it has been granted to others that their resurrection should not be delayed until the general resurrection, this has been by special privilege of grace, and not as due on account of conformity to Christ.

Reply Obj. 3. Jerome, in a sermon on the Assumption,[4] seems to be doubtful of this resurrection of the saints with Christ, namely as to whether, having been witnesses to the resurrection, they died again, so that theirs was a resuscitation (as in the case of Lazarus who died again) rather than a resurrection such as will be at the end of the world,—or really rose again to immortal life, to live for ever in the

body, and to ascend bodily into heaven with Christ, as a gloss says[5] on Matt. 27. 52. The latter seems more probable, because, as Jerome says (*ibid.*), in order that they might bear true witness to Christ's true resurrection, it was fitting that they should truly rise again. Nor was their resurrection hastened for their sake, but for the sake of bearing witness to Christ's resurrection, and that by bearing witness thereto they might lay the foundation of the faith of the New Testament. Therefore it was more fitting that it should be borne by the fathers of the Old Testament than by those who died after the foundation of the New. It must, however, be observed that, although the Gospel mentions their resurrection before Christ's, we must take this statement as made in anticipation, as is often the case with writers of history. For none rose again with a true resurrection before Christ, since He is the *firstfruits of them that sleep* (I Cor. 15. 20), although some were resuscitated before Christ's resurrection, as in the case of Lazarus.

Reply Obj. 4. On account of these words, as Augustine relates,[6] certain heretics asserted that there will be a first resurrection of the dead that they may reign with Christ on earth for a thousand years; hence they were called Chiliasts or Millenarians. Hence Augustine says[7] that these words are to be understood otherwise, namely of the spiritual resurrection, whereby men shall rise again from their sins to the gift of grace, while the second resurrection is of bodies.

The reign of Christ denotes the Church wherein not only martyrs but also the other elect reign, "the part denoting the whole"; or they reign with Christ in glory as regards all, special mention being made of the martyrs, "because they especially reign after death who fought for the truth, even to death."[8]

The number of a thousand years denotes not a fixed number, but the whole of the present time wherein the saints now reign with Christ, because the number 1,000 designates universality more than the number 100, since 100 is the square of 10, whereas 1,000 is a cube resulting from the multiplication of ten by its square, for $10 \times 10 = 100$, and $100 \times 10 = 1,000$. Again in Ps. 104. 8, *The word which He commanded to a thousand*, that is all, *generations*.

---

[1] See Albert, *In Sent.*, IV, d. XLIII, A. 1, sed contra 2 (BO XXX, 501); cf. Empedocles, in Diels, *Die Fragmente*, n. 126 (I, 270); cf. below, Q. XCI, A. 1. obj. 4.

[2] Cf. below, Q. XCVII, A. 5.

[3] Aristotle, I, 3 (407[b]22).

[4] *Epist.*, IX *Ad Paulam et Eustoch.* (PL 30, 127).

[5] *Glossa ordin.* (V, 86A); Rabanus Maurus, BK. VIII (PL 107, 1144).

[6] *City of God*, XX, 7 (PL 41, 667).

[7] *Ibid.*

[8] *Ibid.*, 9 (PL 41, 674).

ARTICLE 2. *Whether the Time of Our Resurrection Is Hidden?*

We proceed thus to the Second Article: It would seem that this time is not hidden.

Objection 1. Because when we know exactly the beginning of a thing, we can know its end exactly, since "all things are measured by a certain period."[1] Now the beginning of the world is known exactly. Therefore its end can also be known exactly. But this will be the time of the resurrection and judgment. Therefore that time is not hidden.

Obj. 2. Further, It is stated (Apoc. 12. 6) that *the woman*, who represents the Church,[2] *had a place prepared by God, that there she might feed* (Vulg.,—*they should feed her*) *a thousand two hundred sixty days*. Again (Dan. 12. 11), a certain fixed number of days is mentioned, which apparently signify years, according to Ezech. 4. 6: *A day for a year, yea a day for a year I have appointed to thee*. Therefore the time of the end of the world and of the resurrection can be known exactly from Holy Writ.

Obj. 3. Further, The state of the New Testament was foreshadowed in the Old Testament. Now we know exactly the time wherein the state of the Old Testament endured. Therefore we can also know exactly the time wherein the state of the New Testament will endure. But the state of the New Testament will last to the end of the world, and therefore it is said (Matt. 28. 20): *Behold I am with you . . . to the consummation of the world*. Therefore the time of the end of the world and of the resurrection can be known exactly.

On the contrary, That which is unknown to the angels will be much more unknown to men, because those things to which men attain by natural reason are much more clearly and certainly known to the angels by their natural knowledge. Moreover revelations are not made to men save by means of the angels as Dionysius asserts (*Cæl. Hier.* iv).[3] Now the angels have no exact knowledge of that time, as appears from Matt. 24. 36: *Of that day and hour no one knoweth, no not the angels of heaven*. Therefore that time is hidden from men.

Further, The apostles were more aware of God's secrets than others who followed them, because they had *the firstfruits of the spirit*

(Rom. 8. 23),—"before others in point of time and more abundantly," as a gloss observes.[4] And yet when they questioned our Lord about this very matter, He answered them (Acts 1. 7): *It is not for you to know the times or moments which the Father hath put in His own power*. Much more, therefore, is it hidden from others.

I answer that, As Augustine says,[5] "as to the last age of the human race, which begins from our Lord's coming and lasts until the end of the world, it is uncertain of how many generations it will consist"; just so old age, which is man's last age, has no fixed time according to the measure of the other ages, since "sometimes alone it lasts as long a time as all the others." The reason of this is because the exact length of future time cannot be known except either by revelation or by natural reason, and the time until the resurrection cannot be reckoned by natural reason, because the resurrection and the end of the heavenly movement will be simultaneous as stated above (A. 1). And all things that are foreseen by natural reason to happen at a fixed time are reckoned by movement, and it is impossible from the movement of the heaven to reckon its end, for since it is circular, it is for this very reason able by its nature to endure for ever, and consequently the time between this and the resurrection cannot be reckoned by natural reason. Again it cannot be known by revelation, so that all may be on the watch and ready to meet Christ, and for this reason when the apostles asked Him about this Christ answered (Acts 1. 7): *It is not for you to know the times or moments which the Father hath put in His own power*, whereby, as Augustine says:[6] "He scatters the fingers of all calculators and bids them be still." For what He refused to tell the apostles, He will not reveal to others; therefore all those who have been misled to reckon this time have so far proved to be untruthful; for some, as Augustine says,[7] stated that from our Lord's Ascension to His last coming 400 years would elapse, others 500, others 1,000. The falseness of these calculators is evident, as will likewise be the falseness of those who even now cease not to calculate.

Reply Obj. 1. When we know a thing's beginning and also its end it follows that its measure is known to us; therefore if we know the beginning of a thing the duration of which is

---

[1] Aristotle, *Generation* and *Corruption*, II, 10 (336[b]12).
[2] Cf. *Glossa interl.*, on Apoc. 12.1 (VI, 257V).
[3] Sect. 2, 3 (PG 3, 180, 181).

[4] *Glossa interl.* (VI, 191); Glossa Lombardi (PL 191, 1444).   [5] QQ. LXXXIII, qu. 58 (PL 40, 43).
[6] *City of God*, XVIII, 53 (PL 41, 617).   [7] *Ibid.*

measured by the movement of the heaven, we are able to know its end, since the movement of heaven is known to us. But the measure of the duration of the heavenly movement is God's ordinance alone, which is unknown to us. Therefore however much we may know its beginning, we are unable to know its end.

Reply Obj. 2. The thousand two hundred sixty days mentioned in the Apocalypse (*loc. cit.*) denote all the time during which the Church endures, and not any definite number of years. The reason of this is because the preaching of Christ on which the Church is built lasted three years and a half, which time contains almost an equal number of days as the above-mentioned number. Again the number of days appointed by Daniel does not refer to a number of years to elapse before the end of the world or until the preaching of Antichrist, but to the time of Antichrist's preaching and the duration of his persecution.

Reply Obj. 3. Although the state of the New Testament in general is foreshadowed by the state of the Old Testament it does not follow that individuals correspond to individuals, especially since all the figures of the Old Testament were fulfilled in Christ. Hence Augustine answers[1] certain persons who wished to liken the number of persecutions suffered by the Church to the number of the plagues of Egypt, in these words: "I do not think that the occurrences in Egypt were in their signification prophetic of these persecutions, although those who think so have shown nicety and ingenuity in adapting them severally the one to the other, not indeed by a prophetic spirit, but by the guess-work of the human mind, which sometimes reaches the truth and sometimes not."

The same remarks would seem applicable to the statements of Abbot Joachim, who by means of such conjectures about the future foretold some things that were true, and in others was deceived.[2]

ARTICLE 3. *Whether the Resurrection Will Take Place at Night-Time?*

We proceed thus to the Third Article: It would seem that the resurrection will not be at night-time.

Objection 1. For the resurrection will not be *till the heavens be broken* (Job 14. 12). Now when the heavenly movement ceases, which is signified by its breaking, there will be no time, neither night nor day. Therefore the resurrection will not be at night-time.

Obj. 2. Further, The end of a thing ought to be most perfect. Now the end of time will be then, and therefore it is said (Apoc. 10. 6) that *time shall be no longer*. Therefore time ought to be then in its most perfect disposition and consequently it should be the daytime.

Obj. 3. Further, The time should be such as to be adapted to what is done therein; therefore (John 13. 30) the night is mentioned as being the time when Judas went out from the fellowship of the light. Now, all things that are hidden at the present time will then be made most manifest, because when the Lord shall come He *will bring to light the hidden things of darkness, and will make manifest the counsels of the hearts* (I Cor. 4. 5). Therefore it ought to be during the day.

On the contrary, Christ's resurrection is the exemplar of ours. Now Christ's resurrection was at night, as Gregory says in a homily for Easter (xxi *in Ev.*).[3] Therefore our resurrection will also be at night-time.

Further, The coming of our Lord is compared to the coming of a thief into the house (Luke 12. 39, 40). But the thief comes to the house at night-time. Therefore our Lord will also come in the night. Now, when He comes the resurrection will take place, as stated above (Q. LXXVI, A. 2). Therefore the resurrection will be at night-time.

I answer that, The exact time and hour at which the resurrection will be cannot be known for certain, as stated in the text (iv. *Sent.* d. 43).[4] Nevertheless some assert with sufficient probability that it will be towards the twilight, the moon being in the east and the sun in the west, because the sun and moon are believed to have been created in these positions, and thus their revolutions will be altogether completed by their return to the same point. Therefore it is said that Christ arose at such an hour.

Reply Obj. 1. When the resurrection occurs, it will not be time but the end of time, because at the very instant that the heavens will cease to move the dead will rise again. Nevertheless the stars will be in the same position as they occupy now at any fixed hour, and accordingly it is said that the resurrection will be at this or that hour.

Reply Obj. 2. The most perfect disposition of time is said to be midday, on account of the light given by the sun. But then the city of God will need neither sun nor moon, because

[1] *City of God,* XVIII, 52 (PL 41, 615).

[2] Cf. DTC, art. *Joachim de Flore* (VIII, 1432); see Grundmann, *Studien,* p. 40.

[3] PL 76, 1173.   [4] Peter Lombard (QR II, 996).

the glory of God will enlighten it. (Apoc. 22. 5). Therefore in this respect it matters not whether the resurrection be in the day or in the night.

Reply Obj. 3. That time should be adapted to manifestation as regards the things that will happen then, and to secrecy as regards the fixing of the time. Hence either may happen fittingly, namely that the resurrection be in the day or in the night.

ARTICLE 4. *Whether the Resurrection Will Happen Suddenly or By Degrees?*

We proceed thus to the Fourth Article: It would seem that the resurrection will not happen suddenly but by degrees.

Objection 1. For the resurrection of the dead is foretold (Ezech. 37. 7, 8) where it is written: *The bones came together . . . and I saw and behold the sinews and the flesh came up upon them, and the skin was stretched out over them, but there was no spirit in them.* Therefore the restoration of the bodies will precede in time their reunion with the souls, and thus the resurrection will not be sudden.

Obj. 2. Further, A thing does not happen suddenly if it require several actions following one another. Now the resurrection requires several actions following one another, namely the gathering of the ashes, the refashioning of the body, the infusion of the soul. Therefore the resurrection will not be sudden.

Obj. 3. Further, All sound is measured by time. Now the sound of the trumpet will be the cause of the resurrection, as stated above (Q. LXXVI, A. 2). Therefore the resurrection will take time and will not happen suddenly.

Obj. 4. Further, No local movement can be sudden as stated in the treatise on the *Sense and the Sensible.*[1] Now the resurrection requires local movement in the gathering of the ashes. Therefore it will not happen suddenly.

On the contrary, It is written (I Cor. 15. 51, 52): *We shall all indeed rise again . . . in a moment, in the twinkling of an eye.* Therefore the resurrection will be sudden.

Further, Infinite power works suddenly. But the Damascene says (*De Fide Orthod.* iv, 27):[2] *Thou shalt believe in the resurrection to be wrought by the power of God,* and it is evident that this is infinite. Therefore the resurrection will be sudden.

I answer that, At the resurrection something will be done by the ministry of the angels, and something immediately by the power of God,

as stated above (Q. LXXVI, A. 3). Accordingly that which is done by the ministry of the angels will not be instantaneous, if by instant we mean an indivisible point of time, but it will be instantaneous if by instant we mean an imperceptible time. But that which will be done immediately by God's power will happen suddenly, namely at the end of the time in which the work of the angels will be done, because the higher power brings the lower to perfection.

Reply Obj. 1. Ezechiel spoke, like Moses, to a rough people, and therefore, just as Moses divided the works of the six days into days, in order that the uncultured people might be able to understand, although all things were made together according to Augustine (*Gen. ad Lit.* iv. 34),[3] so Ezechiel expressed the various things that will happen in the resurrection, although they will all happen together in an instant.

Reply Obj. 2. Although these actions follow one another in nature, they are all together in time, because either they are together in the same instant, or one is in the instant that terminates the other.

Reply Obj. 3. The same would seem to apply to that sound as to the forms of the sacraments, namely that the sound will produce its effect in its last instant.

Reply Obj. 4. The gathering of the ashes which cannot be without local movement will be done by the ministry of the angels. Hence it will be in time though imperceptible on account of the ease of operation which is appropriate to the angels.

QUESTION LXXVIII

OF THE TERM FROM WHICH OF THE RESURRECTION

(In Three Articles)

WE must now consider the term *from which* of the resurrection, and under this head there are three points of inquiry: (1) Whether death is the term from which of the resurrection in every case? (2) Whether ashes are, or dust? (3) Whether this dust has a natural inclination towards the soul?

ARTICLE 1. *Whether Death Will Be the Term From Which of the Resurrection in All Cases?*

We proceed thus to the First Article: It would seem that death will not be the term *from which* of the resurrection in all cases.

Objection 1. Because some shall not die but

---

[1] Aristotle, 6 (446ª29); cf. *Physics,* VI, 3 (234ª24).
[2] PG 94, 1225.
[3] PL 34, 319.

shall be clothed with immortality, for it is said in the creed that our Lord "will come to judge the living and the dead."[1] Now this cannot refer to the time of judgment, because then all will be alive; therefore this distinction must refer to the previous time, and consequently all will not die before the judgment.

Obj. 2. Further, A natural and common desire cannot be empty and vain, but is fulfilled in some cases. Now according to the Apostle (II Cor. 5. 4) it is a common desire that *we would not be unclothed but clothed upon.* Therefore there will be some who will never be stripped of the body by death, but will be arrayed in the glory of the resurrection.

Obj. 3. Further, Augustine says (*Enchir.* cxv)[2] that the four last petitions of the Lord's prayer refer to the present life, and one of them is: *Forgive us our debts* (Douay,—*trespasses*). Therefore the Church prays that all debts may be forgiven her in this life. Now the Church's prayer cannot be void and not granted: *If you ask the Father anything in My name, He will give it you* (John 16. 23). Therefore at some time of this life the Church will receive the remission of all debts, and one of the debts to which we are bound by the sin of our first parent is that we be born in original sin. Therefore at some time God will grant to the Church that men be born without original sin. But death is the punishment of original sin. Therefore at the end of the world there will be some men who will not die, and so the same conclusion follows.

Obj. 4. Further, The wise man should always choose the shortest way. Now the shortest way is for the men who shall be found living to be transferred to the impassibility of the resurrection than for them to die first and afterwards rise again from death to immortality. Therefore God Who is supremely wise will choose this way for those who shall be found living.

On the contrary, It is written (I Cor. 15. 36): *That which thou sowest is not quickened except it die first,* and he is speaking of the resurrection of the body as compared to the seed.

Further, It is written (*ibid.* 22): *As in Adam all die, so also in Christ all shall be made alive.* Now all shall be made alive in Christ. Therefore all shall die in Adam, and so all shall rise again from death.

I answer that, The saints differ in speaking on this question, as may be seen in the text (iv. *Sent.* D. 43).[3] However, the safer and more common opinion is that all shall die and rise again from death, and this for three reasons. First, because it is more in accord with Divine justice, which condemned human nature for the sin of its first parent, that all who by the act of nature derive their origin from him should contract the stain of original sin, and consequently be the debtors of death.

Secondly, because it is more in agreement with Divine Scripture which foretells the resurrection of all;[4] and resurrection is not predicted properly except of "that which has fallen and perished," as the Damascene says (*De Fide Orthod.* iv, 27).[5]

Thirdly, because it is more in harmony with the order of nature where we find that what is corrupted and decayed is not renewed except by means of corruption; thus vinegar does not become wine unless the vinegar be corrupted and pass into the juice of the grape. Therefore since human nature has incurred the defect of the necessity of death, it cannot return to immortality save by means of death. It is also in keeping with the order of nature for another reason, because, as it is stated in the *Physics,*[6] the movement of heaven is as "a kind of life to all existing in nature," just as the movement of the heart is a kind of life of the whole body; therefore even as all the members become dead on the heart ceasing to move, so when the heavenly movement ceases nothing can remain living with that life which was sustained by the influence of that movement. Now such is the life by which we live now, and therefore it follows that those who shall live after the movement of the heaven comes to a standstill must depart from this life.

Reply Obj. 1. This distinction of the dead and the living does not apply to the time itself of the judgment, nor to the whole preceding time, since all who are to be judged were living at some time, and dead at some time; but it applies to that particular time which shall precede the judgment immediately, when, that is, the signs of the judgment shall begin to appear.

Reply Obj. 2. The perfect desire of the saints cannot be in vain, but nothing prevents their conditional desire being in vain. Such is the desire by which we would not be unclothed, but clothed upon, namely if that be possible. And this desire is called by some a "velleity."

---

[1] Apostles Creed (DZ 6).
[2] PL 40, 285.
[3] Lombard (QR II, 998).
[4] John 5.28; I Cor. 15.51.
[5] PG 94, 1220.　　[6] Aristotle, VIII, I (250[b]14).

Reply Obj. 3. It is erroneous to say that any one except Christ is conceived without original sin, because those who would be conceived without original sin would not need the redemption which was wrought by Christ, and thus Christ would not be the Redeemer of all men. Nor can it be said that they did not need this redemption because it was granted to them that they should be conceived without sin. For, this grace was vouchsafed,—either to their parents, that the sin of nature might be healed in them (because so long as that sin remained they were unable to beget without communicating original sin),—or to nature itself which was healed. Now we must allow that every one needs the redemption of Christ personally, and not only by reason of nature, and one cannot be delivered from an evil or absolved from a debt unless one incur the debt or incur the evil; and consequently all could not reap in themselves the fruit of the Lord's prayer unless all were born debtors and subject to evil. Hence the forgiveness of debts or delivery from evil cannot be applied to one who is born without a debt or free from evil, but only to one who is born with a debt and is afterwards delivered by the grace of Christ. Nor does it follow, if it can be asserted without error that some do not die, that they are born without original sin, although death is a punishment of original sin; because God can of His mercy remit the punishment which one has incurred by a past fault, as He forgave the adulterous woman without punishment (John 8.); and in like manner He can deliver from death those who have contracted the debt of death by being born in original sin. And thus it does not follow if they do not die that therefore they were born without original sin.

Reply Obj. 4. The shortest way is not always the one to be chosen, but only when it is more or equally adapted for attaining the end. It is not so here, as is clear from what we have said.

ARTICLE 2. *Whether All Will Rise Again from Ashes?*

We proceed thus to the Second Article: It would seem that all will not rise again from ashes.

Objection 1. For Christ's resurrection is the exemplar of ours. Yet His resurrection was not from ashes, for His flesh saw not corruption according to Ps. 15. 10; Acts 2. 27, 31. Therefore neither will all rise again from ashes.

Obj. 2. Further, The human body is not always burnt. Yet a thing cannot be reduced to ashes unless it be burnt. Therefore not all will rise again from ashes.

Obj. 3. Further, The body of a dead man is not reduced to ashes immediately after death. But some will rise again at once after death, according to the text (iv. *Sent.* d. 43),[1] namely those who will be found living. Therefore all will not rise again from ashes.

Obj. 4. Further, The term from which corresponds to the term to which. Now the term to which of the resurrection is not the same in the good as in the wicked: *We shall all indeed rise again, but we shall not all be changed* (I Cor. 15. 51). Therefore the term from which is not the same. And thus, if the wicked rise again from ashes, the good will not rise again from ashes.

On the contrary, Haymo says (on Rom. 5. 10, *For if when we were enemies*):[2] "All who are born in original sin lie under the sentence: *Earth thou art and into earth shalt thou go.*"[3] Now all who shall rise again at the general resurrection were born in original sin, either at their birth within the womb or at least at their birth from the womb. Therefore all will rise again from ashes.

Further, there are many things in the human body that do not truly belong to human nature. But all these will be removed. Therefore all bodies must be reduced to ashes.

I answer that, The same reasons by which we have shown (A. 1) that all rise again from death prove also that at the general resurrection all will rise again from ashes, unless the contrary, such as the hastening of their resurrection, be vouchsafed to certain persons by a special privilege of grace. For just as holy writ foretells the resurrection, so does it foretell the reformation of bodies (Phil. 3. 21). And thus it follows that even as all die that the bodies of all may be able truly to rise again, so will the bodies of all perish that they may be able to be reformed. For just as death was inflicted by Divine justice as a punishment on man, so was the decay of the body, as appears from Gen. 3. 19, *Earth thou art and into earth shalt thou go* (Vulg.,—*Dust thou art and into dust thou shalt return.*)

Moreover the order of nature requires the dissolution not only of the union of soul and body, but also of the mingling of the elements; even as vinegar cannot be brought back to the

---

[1] Peter Lombard (QR II, 998).
[2] PL 117, 405; cf. Albert, *In Sent.*, IV, d. XLIII, A. 22 (BO XXX, 534), where the same text is quoted.
[3] Gen. 3.19 (Septuagint Version).

quality of wine unless it first be dissolved into the prejacent matter, for the mingling of the elements is both caused and preserved by the movement of the heaven, and when this ceases all mixed bodies will be dissolved into pure elements.

Reply Obj. 1. Christ's resurrection is the exemplar of ours as to the term to which, but not as to the term from which.

Reply Obj. 2. By ashes we mean all the remains that are left after the dissolution of the body,—for two reasons. First, because it was the common custom in olden times to burn the bodies of the dead, and to keep the ashes, and so it became customary to speak of the remains of a human body as ashes. Secondly, on account of the cause of dissolution, which is the flame of the fomes by which the human body is radically infected. Hence, in order to be cleansed of this infection the human body must be dissolved into its primary components, and when a thing is destroyed by fire it is said to be reduced to ashes. Therefore the name of ashes is given to those things into which the human body is dissolved.

Reply Obj. 3. The fire that will cleanse the face of the earth will be able to reduce suddenly to ashes the bodies of those that will be found living, even as it will dissolve other mixed bodies into their prejacent matter.

Reply Obj. 4. Movement does not take its species from its term from which but from its term to which. Hence the resurrection of the saints, which will be glorious must differ from the resurrection of the wicked, which will not be glorious, in respect of the term to which, and not in respect of the term from which. And it often happens that the term to which is not the same, whereas the term from which is the same,—for instance, a thing may be moved from blackness to whiteness and to pallor.

ARTICLE 3. *Whether the Ashes from Which the Human Body Will Be Restored Have Any Natural Inclination towards the Soul Which Will Be United to Them?*

We proceed thus to the Third Article: It would seem that the ashes from which the human body will be restored will have a natural inclination towards the soul which will be united to them.

Objection 1. For if they had no inclination towards the soul, they would stand in the same relation to that soul as other ashes. Therefore it would make no difference whether the body

that is to be united to that soul were restored from those ashes or from others, and this is false.

Obj. 2. Further, The body is more dependent on the soul than the soul on the body. Now the soul separated from the body is still somewhat dependent on the body, and therefore its movement towards God is retarded on account of its desire for the body, as Augustine says (*Gen. ad Lit.* xii, 35).[1] Much more, therefore, has the body when separated from the soul a natural inclination towards that soul.

Obj. 3. Further, It is written (Job 20. 11): *His bones shall be filled with the vices of his youth, and they shall sleep with him in the dust.* But vices are only in the soul. Therefore there will still remain in those ashes a natural inclination towards the soul.

On the contrary, The human body can be dissolved into the very elements, or it can be changed into the flesh of other animals. But the elements are homogeneous, and so is the flesh of a lion or other animal. Since then in the other parts of the elements or animals there is no natural inclination to that soul, neither will there be an inclination towards the soul in those parts into which the human body has been changed. This is made evident on the authority of Augustine (*Enchir.* lxxxviii):[2] "The human body, although changed into the substance of other bodies or even into the elements, although it has become the food and flesh of any animals whatsoever, even of man, will in an instant return to that soul which previously animated it, and made it a living and growing man."

Further, To every natural inclination there corresponds a natural agent; otherwise nature would fail in necessaries. Now the aforesaid ashes cannot be reunited to the same soul by any natural agent. Therefore there is not in them any natural inclination to the aforesaid reunion.

I answer that, Opinion is threefold on this point. For some say that the human body is never dissolved into its very elements, and so there always remains in the ashes a certain force besides the elements, which gives a natural inclination to the same soul. But this assertion is in contradiction with the authority of Augustine quoted above (ARG. *on the contrary,* 1), as well as with the senses and reason, since whatever is composed of contraries can be dissolved into its component parts. And so others say that these parts of the elements into which

[1] PL 34, 483.   [2] PL 40, 273.

the human body is dissolved retain more light, through having been united to the soul, and for this reason have a natural inclination to human souls. But this again is nonsensical, since the parts of the elements are of the same nature and have an equal share of light and darkness. Hence we must say differently that in those ashes there is no natural inclination to resurrection, but only by the ordering of Divine providence, which decreed that those ashes should be reunited to the soul; it is on this account that those parts of the elements shall be reunited and not others.

Hence the *Reply to the First Objection* is clear.

Reply Obj. 2. The soul separated from the body remains in the same nature that it has when united to the body. It is not so with the body, and consequently the comparison fails.

Reply Obj. 3. These words of Job do not mean that the vices actually remain in the ashes of the dead, but that they remain according to the ordering of Divine justice, whereby those ashes are destined to the restoration of the body which will suffer eternally for the sins committed.

QUESTION LXXIX

OF THE CONDITIONS OF THOSE WHO RISE AGAIN, AND FIRST, OF THEIR IDENTITY

(In Three Articles)

IN the next place we must consider the conditions of those who rise again. Here we shall consider: (1) Those which concern the good and wicked in common; (2) those which concern the good only (Q. LXXXII); (3) those which concern only the wicked (Q. LXXXVI). Three things concern the good and wicked in common, namely their identity, their integrity, and their quality, and we shall inquire (1) about their identity; (2) about their integrity (Q. LXXX); (3) about their quality (Q. LXXXI).

Under the first head there are three points of inquiry: (1) Whether the body will rise again identically the same? (2) Whether it will be the selfsame man? (3) Whether it is necessary that the same ashes should return to the same parts in which they were before?

ARTICLE 1. *Whether in the Resurrection the Soul Will Be Reunited to the Same Identical Body?*

We proceed thus to the First Article: It would seem that the soul will not be reunited

to the same identical body at the resurrection.

Objection 1. For *thou sowest not the body that shall be, but bare grain* (1 Cor. 15. 37). Now the Apostle is there comparing death to sowing and resurrection to fructifying. Therefore the same body that is laid aside in death is not resumed at the resurrection.

Obj. 2. Further, To every form some matter is adapted according to its condition, and likewise to every agent some instrument. Now the body is compared to the soul as matter to form, and as instrument to agent. Since then at the resurrection the soul will not be of the same condition as now (for it will be either entirely borne away to the heavenly life to which it adhered while living in the world, or will be cast down into the life of the brutes, if it lived as a brute in this world) it would seem that it will not resume the same body, but either a heavenly or a brutish body.

Obj. 3. Further, After death, as stated above (Q. LXXVIII, A. 3), the human body is dissolved into the elements. Now these elemental parts into which the human body has been dissolved do not agree with the human body dissolved into them, except in primary matter, even as any other elemental parts agree with that same body. But if the body were to be formed from those other elemental parts, it would not be described as identically the same. Therefore neither will it be the selfsame body if it be restored from these parts.

Obj. 4. Further, There cannot be numerical identity where there is numerical distinction of essential parts. Now the form of the mixed body, which form is an essential part of the human body, as being its form, cannot be resumed in numerical identity. Therefore the body will not be identically the same. The minor is proved thus: That which passes away into complete non-being cannot be resumed in identity. This is clear from the fact that there cannot be identity where there is distinction of: and existence, which is the act of a being, is differentiated by being interrupted, as is any interrupted act. Now the form of a mixed body passes away into complete non-being by death, since it is a bodily form, and so also do the contrary qualities from which the mixture results. Therefore the form of a mixed body does not return in identity.

On the contrary, It is written (Job 19. 26): *In my flesh I shall see God my Saviour* (Vulg., —*my God*), where he is speaking of the vision after the resurrection, as appears from the preceding words: *In the last day I shall rise out of the earth.* Therefore the selfsame body will rise again.

Further, Damascene says (*De Fide Orthod.* iv, 27):[1] "Resurrection is the second rising of that which has fallen." But the body which we have now fell by death. Therefore it will rise again the same identically.

I answer that, On this point the philosophers erred and certain modern heretics err. For some of the philosophers allowed that souls separated from bodies are reunited to bodies, yet they erred in this in two ways. First, as to the mode of reunion, for some held the separated soul to be naturally reunited to a body by the way of generation. Secondly, as to the body to which it was reunited, for they held that this second union was not with the selfsame body that was laid aside in death, but with another, sometimes of the same, sometimes of a different species. Of a different species when the soul while existing in the body had led a life contrary to the ordering of reason, so that it passed after death from the body of a man into the body of some other animal to whose manner of living it had conformed in this life, for instance into the body of a dog on account of lust, into the body of a lion on account of robbery and violence, and so forth,— and into a body of the same species when the soul has led a good life in the body, and having after death experienced some happiness, after some centuries began to wish to return to the body; and thus it was reunited to a human body.

But this opinion arises from two false sources. The first of these is that they said that the soul is not united to the body essentially as form to matter, but only accidentally, as mover to the thing moved, or as a man to his clothes. Hence it was possible for them to maintain that the soul pre-existed before being infused into the body begotten of natural generation, as also that it is united to various bodies. The second is that they held intellect not to differ from sense except accidentally, so that man would be said to surpass other animals in intelligence because the sensitive power is more acute in him on account of the excellence of his bodily make-up; and hence it was possible for them to assert that man's soul passes into the soul of a brute animal, especially when the human soul has been habituated to brutish actions. But these two sources are refuted by the Philosopher,[2] and in consequence

of these being refuted, it is clear that the above opinion is false.

In like manner the errors of certain heretics are refuted. Some of them fell into the above opinions of the philosophers, while others held that souls are reunited to heavenly bodies, or again to bodies subtle as the wind, as Gregory relates of a certain Bishop of Constantinople, in his exposition of Job 19. 26, *In my flesh I shall see my God,* etc.[3] Moreover these same errors of heretics may be refuted by the fact that they are prejudicial to the truth of resurrection as witnessed to by Holy Writ. For we cannot call it resurrection unless the soul return to the same body, since resurrection is a second rising, and the same thing rises that falls; therefore resurrection regards the body which after death falls, rather than the soul which after death lives. And consequently if it is not the same body which the soul resumes, it will not be a resurrection, but rather the assuming of a new body.

Reply Obj. 1. A comparison does not apply to every particular, but to some. For in the sowing of grain, the grain sown and the grain that is born of it are neither identical nor of the same condition, since it was first sown without a husk, yet is born with one; and the body will rise again identically the same, but of a different condition, since it was mortal and will rise in immortality.

Reply Obj. 2. The soul rising again and the soul living in this world differ not in essence but in respect of glory and misery, which is an accidental difference. Hence it follows that the body in rising again differs, not in identity, but in condition, so that a difference of bodies corresponds proportionally to the difference of souls.

Reply Obj. 3. That which is understood as though it were in matter before its form remains in matter after corruption, because when that which comes afterwards is removed that which came before may yet remain. Now, as the Commentator observes on the First Book of *Physics*[4] and in *De Substantia Orbis*,[5] in the matter of things subject to generation and corruption, we must presuppose undeterminate dimensions, by reason of which matter is divisible, so as to be able to receive various forms in its various parts. Therefore after the separation of the substantial form from matter, these

[1] PG 94, 1220.
[2] *Soul*, II, 1 (412ᵃ21); III, 3 (414ᵃ31).

[3] *Moral.*, XIV, 56 (PL 75, 1077); the bishop referred to is Eutyches; the work referred to is now unknown.
[4] Comm. 63 (IV, 38D).
[5] Chap. 1 (IX, 4B).

dimensions still remain the same, and consequently the matter existing under those dimensions, whatever form it receive, is more identified with that which was generated from it than any other part of matter existing under any form whatever. Thus the matter that will be brought back to restore the human body will be the same as that body's previous matter.

Reply Obj. 4. Even as a simple quality is not the substantial form of an element, but its proper accident, and the disposition whereby its matter is rendered proper to such a form, so the form of a mixed body, which form is a quality resulting from simple qualities reduced to a mean, is not the substantial form of the mixed body, but its proper accident, and the disposition whereby the matter is in need of the form. Now the human body has no substantial form besides this form of the mixed body, except the rational soul, for if it had any previous substantial form, this would give it substantial being, and would establish it in the genus of substance, so that the soul would be united to a body already established in the genus of substance, and thus the soul would be compared to the body as artificial forms are to their matter, in respect of their being established in the genus of substance by their matter. Hence the union of the soul to the body would be accidental, which is the error of the ancient philosophers refuted by the Philosopher.[1] It would also follow that the human body and each of its parts would not retain their former names in the same sense, which is contrary to the teaching of the Philosopher.[2] Therefore since the rational soul remains, no substantial form of the human body falls away into complete non-being. And the variation of accidental forms does not make a difference of identity. Therefore the selfsame body will rise again, since the selfsame matter is resumed as stated in a previous reply. (REPLY 2).

ARTICLE 2. *Whether It Will Be Identically the Same Man That Shall Rise Again?*

We proceed thus to the Second Article: It would seem that it will not be identically the same man that shall rise again.

Objection 1. For according to the Philosopher:[3] "Whatsoever things are changed in their corruptible substance are not repeated identically." Now such is man's substance in his present state. Therefore after the change

wrought by death the selfsame man cannot be repeated.

Obj. 2. Further, Where there is a distinction of human nature there is not the same identical man; hence Socrates and Plato are two men and not one man, since each has his own distinct human nature. Now the human nature of one who rises again is distinct from that which he has now. Therefore he is not the same identical man. The minor can be proved in two ways. First, because human nature which is the form of the whole is not both form and substance as the soul is, but is a form only. Now such forms pass away into complete non-being, and consequently they cannot be restored. Secondly, because human nature results from union of parts. Now the same identical union as that which existed previously cannot be resumed, because repetition is opposed to identity, since repetition implies number, whereas identity implies unity, and these are incompatible with one another. But resurrection is a repeated union; therefore the union is not the same, and consequently there is not the same human nature nor the same man.

Obj. 3. Further, One same man is not several animals; therefore if it is not the same animal it is not the same identical man. Now where sense is not the same, there is not the same animal, since animal is defined from the primary sense, namely touch, as appears from the book on the *Soul*.[4] But sense, as it does not remain in the separated soul (as some maintain), cannot be resumed in identity. Therefore the man who rises again will not be the same identical animal, and consequently he will not be the same man.

Obj. 4. Further, The matter of a statue ranks higher in the statue than the matter of a man does in man, because artificial things belong to the genus of substance by reason of their matter, but natural things by reason of their form, as appears from the Philosopher,[5] and again from the Commentator (*De Anima*, ii).[6] But if a statue is remade from the same brass, it will not be the same identically. Therefore much less will it be identically the same man if he be reformed from the same ashes.

On the contrary, It is written (Job 19. 27): *Whom I myself shall see . . . and not another,* and he is speaking of the vision after the resurrection. Therefore the same identical man will rise again.

[1] *Soul*, II, 2 (414ᵃ12).
[2] *Ibid.*, II, I (412ᵇ21).
[3] *Generation and Corruption*, II, II (338ᵇ16).
[4] Aristotle, II, 2 (413ᵇ2).
[5] *Physics*, II, I (193ᵇ3).
[6] Comm. 8 (VI, 2, 52E).

Further, Augustine says (*De Trin.* viii, 5)[1] that " to rise again is nothing else but to live again." Now unless the same identical man that died return to life, he would not be said to live again. Therefore he would not rise again, which is contrary to faith.

I answer that, The necessity of holding the resurrection arises from this,—that man may obtain the last end for which he was made, for this cannot be accomplished in this life, nor in the life of the separated soul, as stated above (Q. LXXV, AA. 1, 2); otherwise man would have been made in vain, if he were unable to obtain the end for which he was made. And since it is necessary for the end to be obtained by the selfsame thing that was made for that end, lest it appear to be made without purpose, it is necessary for the selfsame man to rise again; and this is effected by the selfsame soul being united to the selfsame body. For otherwise there would be no resurrection properly speaking, if the same man were not reformed. Hence to maintain that he who rises again is not the selfsame man is heretical, since it is contrary to the truth of Scripture which proclaims the resurrection.

Reply Obj. 1. The Philosopher is speaking of repetition by movement or natural change. For he shows the difference between the recurrence that occurs in generation and corruption and that which is observed in the movement of the heavens. Because the selfsame heaven by local movement returns to the beginning of its movement, since it has a moved incorruptible substance. On the other hand, things subject to generation and corruption return by generation to specific but not numerical identity, because from man blood is engendered, from blood seed, and so on until a man is begotten, not the selfsame man, but the same specifically. In like manner from fire comes air, from air water, from water earth, from which fire is produced, not the selfsame fire, but the same in species. Hence it is clear that the argument, so far as the meaning of the Philosopher is concerned, is not to the point.

We may also reply that the form of other things subject to generation and corruption is not subsistent of itself, so as to be able to remain after the corruption of the composite, as it is with the rational soul. For the soul, even after separation from the body, retains the being which accrues to it when in the body, and the body is made to share that being by the resurrection, since the being of the body and

the being of the soul in the body are not distinct from one another, otherwise the union of soul and body would be accidental. Consequently there has been no interruption in the substantial being of man, such as would make it impossible for the selfsame man to return on account of an interruption in his being, as is the case with other things that are corrupted, the being of which is interrupted altogether, since their form does not remain, and their matter remains under another being. Nevertheless neither does the selfsame man recur by natural generation, because the body of the man begotten is not composed of the whole body of his begetter; hence his body is numerically distinct, and consequently his soul and the whole man.

Reply Obj. 2. There are two opinions about humanity and about any form of a whole. For some say that the form of the whole and the form of the part are really one and the same, but that it is called the form of the part according as it perfects the matter, and the form of the whole according as the whole specific nature results from it. According to this opinion humanity is really nothing else than the rational soul, and so, since the selfsame rational soul is resumed, there will be the same identical humanity, which will remain even after death, although not under the aspect of humanity, because the composite does not derive the specific nature from a separated humanity.

The other opinion, which seems nearer the truth, is Avicenna's,[2] according to whom the form of the whole is not the form of a part only, nor some other form besides the form of the part, but is the whole resulting from the composition of form and matter, embracing both within itself. This form of the whole is called the essence or quiddity. Since then at the resurrection there will be the selfsame body, and the selfsame rational soul, there will be, of necessity, the same humanity. The first argument proving that there will be a distinction of humanity was based on the supposition that humanity is some distinct form, supervening upon form and matter. And this is false. And the second reason does not disprove the identity of humanity, because union implies action or passion, and though there be a different union, this cannot prevent the identity of humanity, because the action and passion from which humanity resulted are not of the essence of humanity, and so a distinction on their part does not involve a distinction of hu-

---

[1] PL 42, 953.

[2] *Meta.*, tr. v, chap. 5 (89va).

manity, for it is clear that generation and resurrection are not the selfsame movement. Yet the identity of the rising man with the begotten man is not hindered for this reason, and in like manner neither is the identity of humanity prevented, if we take union for the relation itself, because this relation is not essential to but concomitant with humanity, since humanity is not one of those forms that are composition or order,[1] as are the forms of things produced by art, so that if there be another distinct composition there is another distinct form of a house.

Reply Obj. 3. This argument affords a very good proof against those who held a distinction between the sensitive and rational souls in man, because in that case the sensitive soul in man would not be incorruptible, as neither is it in other animals; and consequently in the resurrection there would not be the same sensitive soul, and consequently neither the same animal nor the same man. But if we assert that in man the same soul is by its substance both rational and sensitive, we shall encounter no difficulty in this question, because animal is defined from sense, that is, the sensitive soul as from its essential form; but from the sense which means the sensitive power, we know its definition as from an accidental form that contributes more than any other to our knowledge of the quiddity.[2] Accordingly after death there remains the sensitive soul, even as the rational soul, according to its substance; but the sensitive powers, according to some, do not remain. And since these powers are accidental properties, diversity on their part cannot prevent the identity of the whole animal, not even of the animal's parts; nor are powers to be called perfections or acts of organs unless as principles of action, as heat in fire.

Reply Obj. 4. A statue may be considered in two ways, either as a particular substance, or as something artificial. And since it is placed in the genus of substance by reason of its matter, it follows that if we consider it as a particular substance, it is the selfsame statue that is remade from the same matter. On the other hand, it is placed in the genus of artificial things according as it has an accidental form which, if the statue be destroyed, passes away also. Consequently it does not return identically the same, nor can the statue be identically the same. But man's form, namely the soul, re-

mains after the body has perished. Therefore the comparison fails.

ARTICLE 3. *Whether the Ashes of the Human Body Must, by the Resurrection, Return to the Same Parts of the Body That Were Dissolved Into Them?*

We proceed thus to the Third Article: It would seem necessary for the ashes of the human body to return, by the resurrection, to the same parts that were dissolved into them.

Objection 1. For, according to the Philosopher, "as the whole soul is to the whole body, so is a part of the soul to a part of the body, as sight to the pupil."[3] Now it is necessary that after the resurrection the body be resumed by the same soul. Therefore it is also necessary for the same parts of the body to return to the same limbs, in which they were perfected by the same parts of the soul.

Obj. 2. Further, Difference of matter causes difference of identity. But if the ashes do not return to the same parts, each part will not be remade from the same matter of which it consisted before. Therefore they will not be the same identically. Now if the parts are different the whole will also be different, since parts are to the whole as matter is to form.[4] Therefore it will not be the selfsame man, which is contrary to the truth of the resurrection.

Obj. 3. Further, The resurrection is directed to the end that man may receive the wages of his works. Now different parts of the body are employed in different works, whether of merit or of demerit. Therefore at the resurrection each part must return to its former state that it may be rewarded in due measure.

On the contrary, Artificial things are more dependent on their matter than natural things. Now in artificial things, in order that the same artificial thing be remade from the same matter, there is no need for the parts to be brought back to the same position. Neither therefore is it necessary in man.

Further, Change of an accident does not cause a change of identity. Now the situation of parts is an accident. Therefore its change in a man does not cause a change of identity.

I answer that, In this question it makes a difference whether we ask what can be done without prejudice to identity, and what will be done for the sake of what is fitting. As regards the first it must be observed that in man we may speak of parts in two ways: first as of the

[1] Aristotle, *Physics*, II, 1 (193[b]5).
[2] Aristotle, *Soul*, I, 1 (402[b]21).
[3] *Ibid.*, II, 1 (412[b]23).
[4] Aristotle, *Physics*, II, 3 (195[a]19).

various parts of a homogeneous whole, for instance the various parts of flesh, or the various parts of bone; secondly, as of various parts of various species of a heterogeneous whole, for instance bone and flesh. Accordingly if it be said that one part of matter will return to another part of the same species, this causes no change except in the position of the parts, and change of position of parts does not change the species in homogeneous wholes; and so if the matter of one part return to another part, this is in no way prejudicial to the identity of the whole. Thus is it in the example given in the text (iv. *Sent.* d. 44,[1] because a statue, after being remade, is identically the same, not as to its form, but as to its matter, in respect of which it is a particular substance, and in this way a statue is homogeneous, although it is not according to its artificial form.

But if it be said that the matter of one part returns to another part of another species, it follows of necessity that there is a change not only in the position of parts, but also in their identity, yet so that the whole matter, or something belonging to the truth of human nature in one is transferred to another; but not if what was superfluous in one part is transferred to another. Now the identity of parts being taken away, the identity of the whole is removed, if we speak of essential parts, but not if we speak of accidental parts, such as hair and nails, to which apparently Augustine refers.[2] It is thus clear how the transference of matter from one part to another destroys the identity, and how it does not.

But speaking of what is fitting, it is more probable that even the parts will retain their position at the resurrection, especially as regards the essential and organic parts, although perhaps not as regards the accidental parts, such as nails and hair.

Reply Obj. 1. This argument considers organic or heterogeneous parts, but not homogeneous or like parts.

Reply Obj. 2. A change in the position of the parts of matter does not cause a change of identity, although difference of matter does.

Reply Obj. 3. Operation, properly speaking, is not ascribed to the part but to the whole, and therefore the reward is due not to the part but to the whole.

[1] Lombard (QR II, 1001).
[2] *City of God*, XXII, 19 (PL 41, 780); *Enchir.*, LXXXIX (PL 40, 273); cf. Peter Lombard, *Sent.*, IV, d. XLIV, chap. 2 (QR II, 1001).

QUESTION LXXX

OF THE INTEGRITY OF THE BODIES IN THE RESURRECTION

(In Five Articles)

WE must next consider the integrity of the bodies in the resurrection. Under this head there are five points of inquiry: (1) Whether all the members of the human body will rise again in the resurrection? (2) Whether the hair and nails will? (3) Whether the humours will? (4) Whether whatever the body contained belonging to the truth of human nature will rise again? (5) Whether whatever it contained materially will rise again?

ARTICLE 1. *Whether All the Members of the Human Body Will Rise Again?*

We proceed thus to the First Article: It would seem that not all the members of the human body will rise again.

Objection 1. For if the end be done away it is useless to restore the means. Now the end of each member is its act. Since then nothing useless is done in the Divine works, and since the use of certain members is not fitting to man after the resurrection, especially the use of the genital members, for then they *shall neither marry, nor be married* (Matt. 22. 30), it would seem that not all the members shall rise again.

Obj. 2. Further, The entrails are members, and yet they will not rise again. For they can neither rise full, since thus they contain impurities, nor empty, since nothing is empty in nature. Therefore the members shall not all rise again.

Obj. 3. Further, The body shall rise again that it may be rewarded for the works which the soul did through it. Now the member of which a thief has been deprived for theft, and who has afterwards done penance and is saved, cannot be rewarded at the resurrection, neither for any good deed, since it has not co-operated in any, nor for evil deeds, since the punishment of the member would redound to the punishment of the man. Therefore the members will not all rise again with man.

On the contrary, The other members belong more to the truth of human nature than hair and nails. Yet these will be restored to man at the resurrection according to the text (iv. *Sent.* d. 44).[3] Much more therefore does this apply to the other members.

[3] Lombard (QR II, 1001).

Further, The works of God are perfect (Deut. 32. 4). But the resurrection will be the work of God. Therefore man will be remade perfect in all his members.

I answer that, As stated in the book on the *Soul,*[1] the soul stands in relation to the body not only as its form and end, but also as efficient cause. For the soul is compared to the body as art to the thing made by art, as the Philosopher says,[2] and whatever is shown forth explicitly in the product of art is all contained implicitly and originally in the art. In like manner whatever appears in the parts of the body is all contained originally and, in a way, implicitly in the soul. Thus just as the work of an art would not be perfect if its product lacked any of the things contained in the art, so neither could man be perfect, unless the whole that is contained enfolded in the soul be outwardly unfolded in the body, nor would the body correspond in full proportion to the soul. Since then at the resurrection man's body must correspond entirely to the soul, for it will not rise again except according to the relation it bears to the rational soul, it follows that man also must rise again perfect, seeing that he is thereby repaired in order that he may obtain his ultimate perfection. Consequently all the members that are now in man's body must be restored at the resurrection.

Reply Obj. 1. The members may be considered in two ways in relation to the soul: either according to the relation of matter to form, or according to the relation of instrument to agent, since the whole body is compared to the whole soul in the same way as one part is to another.[3] If then the members be considered in the light of the first relationship, their end is not operation, but rather the perfect being of the species, and this is also required after the resurrection; but if they be considered in the light of the second relationship, then their end is operation. And yet it does not follow that when the operation fails the instrument is useless, because an instrument serves not only to accomplish the operation of the agent, but also to show its power. Hence it will be necessary for the virtue of the soul's powers to be shown in their bodily instruments, even though they never proceed to action, so that the wisdom of God be thereby glorified.

Reply Obj. 2. The entrails will rise again in the body even as the other members, and they will be filled not with vile superfluities but with humours of an excellent kind.

Reply Obj. 3. The acts by which we merit are not the acts, properly speaking, of hand or foot but of the whole man, even as the work of art is ascribed not to the instrument but to the craftsman. Therefore though the member which was cut off before a man's repentance did not co-operate with him in the state in which he merits glory, yet man himself merits that the whole man may be rewarded, who with his whole being serves God.

ARTICLE 2. *Whether the Hair and Nails Will Rise Again in the Human Body?*

We proceed thus to the Second Article: It would seem that the hair and nails will not rise again in the human body.

Objection 1. For just as hair and nails result from the surplus of food, so do urine, sweat and other superfluities or dregs. But these will not rise again with the body. Neither therefore will hair and nails.

Obj. 2. Further, Of all the superfluities that are produced from food, seed comes nearest to the truth of human nature, since though superfluous it is needed. Yet seed will not rise again in the human body. Much less therefore will hair and nails.

Obj. 3. Further, Nothing is perfected by a rational soul that is not perfected by a sensitive soul. But hair and nails are not perfected by a sensitive soul, for we do not feel with them according to the book on the *Soul.*[4] Therefore since the human body rises not again except because it is perfected by a rational soul, it would seem that the hair and nails will not rise again.

On the contrary, It is written (Luke 21. 18): *A hair of your head shall not perish.*

Further, Hair and nails were given to man as an ornament. Now the bodies of men, especially of the elect ought to rise again with all their adornment. Therefore they ought to rise again with the hair.

I answer that, The soul is to the animated body as art is to the work of art, and is to the parts of the body as art to its instruments; and so an animated body is called an "organic" body.[5] Now art employs certain instruments for the accomplishment of the work intended, and these instruments belong to the primary intention of art, and it also uses other instruments for the safe-keeping of the principal in-

---

[1] Aristotle, II, 4 (415ᵇ7).
[2] *Generation of Animals,* II, 4 (740ᵇ25).
[3] Aristotle, *Soul,* II, 1 (412ᵇ23).

[4] Aristotle, I, 5 (410ᵃ30).
[5] Cf. Aristotle, *Soul,* II, 1 (412ᵃ28).

struments, and these belong to the secondary intention of art; thus the art of warfare employs a sword for fighting, and a sheath for the safe-keeping of the sword. And so among the parts of an animated body, some are directed to the accomplishment of the soul's operations, for instance the heart, liver, hand, foot, while others are directed to the safe-keeping of the other parts as leaves to cover fruit; and thus hair and nails are in man for the protection of other parts. Consequently, although they do not belong to the primary perfection of the human body, they belong to the secondary perfection, and since man will rise again with all the perfections of his nature, it follows that hair and nails will rise again in him.

Reply Obj. 1. Those superfluities are voided by nature as being useful for nothing. Hence they do not belong to the perfection of the human body. It is not so with those superfluities which nature reserves for the production of hair and nails which she needs for the protection of the members.

Reply Obj. 2. Seed is not required for the perfection of the individual, as hair and nails are, but only for the perfection of the species.

Reply Obj. 3. Hair and nails are nourished and grow, and so it is clear that they share in some operation, which would not be possible unless they were parts in some way perfected by the soul. And since in man there is but one soul, namely the rational soul, it is clear that they are perfected by the rational soul, although not so far as to share in the operation of sense, as neither do bones, and yet it is certain that these will rise again and that they belong to the integrity of the individual.

ARTICLE 3. *Whether the Humours Will Rise Again in the Body?*

We proceed thus to the Third Article: It would seem that the humours will not rise again in the body.

Objection 1. For it is written (I Cor. 15. 50): *Flesh and blood cannot possess the kingdom of God.* Now blood is the chief humour. Therefore it will not rise again in the blessed, who will possess the kingdom of God, and much less in others.

Obj. 2. Further, Humours are intended to make up for waste. Now after the resurrection there will be no waste. Therefore the body will not rise again with humours.

Obj. 3. Further, That which is in process of generation in the human body is not yet perfected by the rational soul. Now the humours

are still in process of generation because they are potentially flesh and bone. Therefore they are not yet perfected by the rational soul. Now the human body is not directed to the resurrection except in so far as it is perfected by the rational soul. Therefore the humours will not rise again.

On the contrary, Whatever enters into the constitution of the human body will rise again with it. Now this applies to the humours, as appears from the statement of Augustine (*De Spir. et Anima,* xv)[1] that "the body consists of functional members; the functional members of homogeneous parts; and the homogeneous parts of humours." Therefore the humours will rise again in the body.

Further, Our resurrection will be conformed to the resurrection of Christ. Now in Christ's resurrection His blood rose again; otherwise the wine would not now be changed into His blood in the Sacrament of the altar. Therefore the blood will rise again in us also, and in like manner the other humours.

I answer that, Whatever belongs to the integrity of human nature in those who take part in the resurrection will rise again, as stated above (AA. 1, 2). Hence whatever humidity of the body belongs to the integrity of human nature must rise again in man. Now there is a threefold humidity in man. There is one which occurs as receding from the perfection of the individual,—either because it is on the way to corruption, and is voided by nature, for instance urine, sweat, matter, and so forth,—or because it is directed by nature to the preservation of the species in some individual, either by the act of the generative power, as seed, or by the act of the nutritive power, as milk. None of these humidities will rise again, because they do not belong to the perfection of the person rising again.

The second kind of humidity is one that has not yet reached its ultimate perfection, which nature achieves in the individual, yet it is directed to it by nature; and this is of two kinds. For there is one kind that has a definite form and is contained among the parts of the body, for instance the blood and the other humours which nature has directed to the members that are produced or nourished from them, and yet they have certain definite forms like the other parts of the body, and consequently will rise again with the other parts of the body. But another kind of humidity is in transition from form to form, namely from the form of hu-

[1] Alcher of Clairvaux (PL 40, 791).

mour to the form of member. Humidities of this kind will not rise again, because after the resurrection each part of the body will be established in its form, so that one will not pass into another. Therefore this humidity that is actually in transition from one form to another will not rise again. Now this humidity may be considered in a twofold state,—either as being at the beginning of its transformation, and thus it is called *ros,* namely the humidity that is found in the cavities of the smaller veins,— or as in the course of transformation and already beginning to undergo alteration, and thus it is called *cambium;* but in neither state will it rise again. The third kind of humidity is that which has already reached its ultimate perfection that nature intends in the body of the individual, and has already undergone transformation and become incorporate with the members. This is called *gluten,* and since it belongs to the substance of the members it will rise again just as the members will.

Reply Obj. 1. In these words of the Apostle flesh and blood do not denote the substance of flesh and blood but deeds of flesh and blood, which are either deeds of sin or the operations of the animal life. Or we may say with Augustine in his letter to Consentius[1] that flesh and blood here signify the corruption which is now predominant in flesh and blood; hence the Apostle's words continue: *Neither shall corruption possess incorruption.*

Reply Obj. 2. Just as the members that serve for generation will be after the resurrection for the integrity of human nature, and not for the operation accomplished now by them, so will the humours be in the body not to make up for waste, but to restore the integrity of human nature and to show forth its natural power.

Reply Obj. 3. Just as the elements are in the course of generation in relation to mixed bodies, because they are their matter, yet not so as to be always in transition when in the mixed body, so too are the humours in relation to the members. And for this reason as the elements in the parts of the universe have definite forms, by reason of which they, like mixed bodies, belong to the perfection of the universe, so too the humours belong to the perfection of the human body, just as the other parts do, although they do not reach its entire perfection, as the other parts do, and although the elements have not perfect forms as mixed bodies have. But as all the parts of the universe receive their perfec-

tion from God, not equally, but each one according to its mode, so too the humours are in some way perfected by the rational soul, yet not in the same measure as the more perfect parts.

ARTICLE 4. *Whether Whatever in the Body Belonged to the Truth of Human Nature Will Rise Again In It?*

We proceed thus to the Fourth Article: It would seem that what was in the body, belonging to the truth of human nature will not all rise again in it.

Objection 1. For food is changed into the truth of human nature. Now sometimes the flesh of the ox or of other animals is taken as food. Therefore if whatever belonged to the truth of human nature will rise again, the flesh of the ox or of other animals will also rise again, which cannot be admitted.

Obj. 2. Further, Adam's rib belonged to the truth of human nature in him, as ours does in us. But Adam's rib will rise again not in Adam but in Eve, for otherwise Eve would not rise again at all since she was made from that rib. Therefore whatever belonged in man to the truth of human nature will not all rise again in him.

Obj. 3. Further, It is impossible for the same thing from different men to rise again. Yet it is possible for something in different men to belong to the truth of human nature, for instance if a man were to partake of human flesh which would be changed into his substance. Therefore there will not rise again in man whatever belonged in him to the truth of human nature.

Obj. 4. Further, If it be said that not all the flesh partaken of belongs to the truth of human nature, and that consequently some of it may possibly rise again in the one man and some in the other,—on the contrary: That which is derived from one's parents would especially seem to belong to the truth of human nature. But if one who partook of nothing but human flesh were to beget children, that which his child derives from him must be of the flesh of other men partaken of by his father, since the seed is from the surplus of food, as the Philosopher proves.[2] Therefore what belongs to the truth of human nature in that child belonged also to the truth of human nature in other men of whose flesh his father had partaken.

Obj. 5. Further, If it be said that what was changed into seed was not that which belonged

[1] *Epist.,* CCV, 2 (PL 33, 943); cf. *Enchir.,* XCI (PL 40, 274).

[2] *Generation of Animals,* I, 18 (726ᵃ26).

to the truth of human nature in the flesh of the men eaten, but something not belonging to the truth of human nature,—on the contrary: Let us suppose that some one is fed entirely on embryos in which there seems to be nothing but what belongs to the truth of human nature, since whatever is in them is derived from the parents. If then the surplus food be changed into seed, that which belonged to the truth of human nature in the embryos—and after these have received a rational soul, the resurrection applies to them—must belong to the truth of human nature in the child begotten of that seed. And thus, since the same being cannot rise again in two subjects, it will be impossible for whatever belonged to the truth of human nature in both to rise again in both of them.

On the contrary, Whatever belonged to the truth of human nature was perfected by the rational soul. Now it is through being perfected by the rational soul that the human body is directed to the resurrection. Therefore whatever belonged to the truth of human nature will rise again in each one.

Further, If anything belonging to the truth of human nature in a man be taken from his body, this will not be the perfect body of a man. Now all imperfection of a man will be removed at the resurrection, especially in the elect, to whom it was promised (Luke 21. 18) that not a hair of their head should perish. Therefore whatever belonged to the truth of human nature in a man will rise again in him.

I answer that, "Everything is related to truth in the same way as to being,"[1] because a thing is true when it is as it appears to him who actually knows it. For this reason Avicenna says[2] that "the truth of anything is a property of the being immutably attached to it." Accordingly a thing is said to belong to the truth of human nature because it belongs properly to the being of human nature, and this is what shares the form of human nature, just as true gold is what has the true form of gold from which gold derives its proper being. In order therefore to see what it is that belongs to the truth of human nature, we must observe that there have been three opinions on that question. For some have maintained that nothing begins anew to belong to the truth of human nature, and that whatever belongs to the truth of human nature, all of it belonged to the truth of human nature when this was cre-

ated; and that this multiplies by itself, so that it is possible for the seed of which the child is begotten to be detached from it by the begetter, and that again the detached part multiplies in the child, so that he reaches perfect quantity by growth, and so on; and that thus was the whole human race multiplied. Therefore according to this opinion, whatever is produced by nourishment, although it seem to have the appearance of flesh and blood, does not belong to the truth of human nature.

Others held that something new is added to the truth of human nature by the natural transformation of the food into the human body if we consider the truth of human nature in the species to the preservation of which the act of the generative power is directed, but that if we consider the truth of human nature in the individual, to the preservation and perfection of which the act of the nutritive power is directed, that which is added by food belongs to the truth of the human nature of the individual, not primarily but secondarily. For they assert that the truth of human nature, first and foremost, consists in the radical humour, that namely which is begotten of the seed of which the human race was originally fashioned, and that what is changed from food into true flesh and blood does not belong principally to the truth of human nature in this particular individual, but secondarily; and that nevertheless this can belong principally to the truth of human nature in another individual who is begotten of the seed of the former. For they assert that seed is the surplus from food, either mingled with something belonging principally to the truth of human nature in the begetter, according to some, or without any such admixture, as others maintain. And thus the nutrimental humour in one becomes the radical humour in another.

The third opinion is that something new begins to belong principally to the truth of human nature even in this individual, because distinction in the human body does not require that any signate material part needs to remain throughout the whole lifetime; any signate part one may take is indifferent to this, whereas it remains always as regards what belongs to the species in it, although as regards what is material in it, it may ebb and flow. And thus the nutrimental humour is not distinct from the radical on the part of its principle (so that it be called radical when begotten of the seed, and nutrimental when produced by the food), but rather on the part of the term, so that it

---

[1] Aristotle, *Metaphysics*, II, 1 (993^{b}30).

[2] *Meta.*, VIII, 6 (1001a).

be called radical when it reaches the term of generation by the act of the generative, or even nutritive power, but nutrimental when it has not yet reached this term, but is still on the way to give nourishment. These three opinions have been more fully exposed and examined in the *Second Book of the Sentences* (ii. *Sent.* d. 30);[1] therefore there is no need for repetition here, except in so far as the question at issue is concerned.

It must accordingly be observed that this question requires different answers according to these opinions. For the first opinion on account of its explanation of the process of multiplication is able to admit perfection of the truth of human nature, both as regards the number of individuals and as regards the due quantity of each individual, without taking into account that which is produced from food; for this is not added except for the purpose of resisting the destruction that might result from the action of natural heat, as lead is added to silver lest it be destroyed in melting. Therefore since at the resurrection human nature must be restored to its perfection, nor does the natural heat tend to destroy the natural humour, there will be no need for anything resulting from food to rise again in man, but that alone will rise again which belonged to the truth of the human nature of the individual, and this reaches the aforesaid perfection in number and quantity by being detached and multiplied.

The second opinion, since it maintains that what is produced from food is needed for the perfection of quantity in the individual and for the multiplication that results from generation, has to admit that something of this product from food shall rise again; not all, however, but only so much as is required for the perfect restoration of human nature in all its individuals. Hence this opinion asserts that all that was in the substance of the seed will rise again in this man who was begotten of this seed, because this belongs chiefly to the truth of human nature in him, while of that which afterwards he derives from nourishment, only so much will rise again in him as is needed for the perfection of his quantity, and not all, because this does not belong to the perfection of human nature, except in so far as nature requires it for the perfection of quantity. Since however this nutrimental humour is subject to ebb and flow the restoration will be effected in this order, that what first belonged to the sub-

stance of a man's body will all be restored, and of that which was added secondly, thirdly, and so on, as much as is required to restore quantity. This is proved by two reasons. First, because that which was added was intended to restore what was wasted at first, and thus it does not belong principally to the truth of human nature to the same extent as that which came first. Secondly, because the addition of extraneous humour to the first radical humour results in the whole mixture not sharing the truth of the specific nature as perfectly as the first did; and the Philosopher instances as an example[2] the mixing of water with wine, which always weakens the strength of the wine, so that in the end the wine becomes watery, so that although the second water is drawn into the species of wine, it does not share the species of wine as perfectly as the first water added to the wine. Even so that which is secondly changed from food into flesh does not so perfectly attain to the species of flesh as that which was changed first, and consequently does not belong in the same degree to the truth of human nature nor to the resurrection. Accordingly it is clear that this opinion maintains that the whole of what belongs to the truth of human nature principally will rise again, but not the whole of what belongs to the truth of human nature secondarily.

The third opinion differs somewhat from the second and in some respects agrees with it. It differs in that it maintains that whatever is under the form of flesh and bone all belongs to the truth of human nature, because this opinion does not distinguish as remaining in man during his whole lifetime any signate matter that belongs essentially and primarily to the truth of human nature, besides something ebbing and flowing, that belongs to the truth of human nature merely on account of the perfection of quantity, and not on account of the primary being of the species, as the second opinion asserted. But it states that all the parts that are not beside the intention of the nature generated belong to the truth of human nature as regards what they have of the species, since thus they remain, but not as regards what they have of matter since thus they are indifferent to ebb and flow; so that we are to understand that the same thing happens in the parts of one man as in the whole population of a city, for each individual is cut off from the population by death, while others take their place; and so the parts of the people flow back and forth materi-

[1] Q. II, A. I.

[2] *Generation and Corruption*, I, 5 (322[a]31).

ally, but remain formally, since these others occupy the very same offices and positions from which the former were withdrawn, so that the commonwealth is said to remain the selfsame. In like manner, while certain parts are on the ebb and others are being restored to the same shape and position, all the parts flow back and forth as to their matter, but remain as to their species; and nevertheless the selfsame man remains.

On the other hand, the third opinion agrees with the second, because it holds that the parts which come secondly do not reach the perfection of the species so perfectly as those which come first, and consequently the third opinion asserts that the same thing rises again in man as the second opinion maintains, but not for quite the same reason. For it holds that the whole of what is produced from the seed will rise again, not because it belongs to the truth of human nature otherwise than that which comes after, but because it shares the truth of human nature more perfectly—which same order the second opinion applied to those things that are produced afterwards from food, in which point also these two opinions agree.

Reply Obj. 1. A natural thing is what it is, not from its matter but from its form; therefore, although that part of matter which at one time was under the form of bovine flesh rises again in man under the form of human flesh, it does not follow that the flesh of an ox rises again, but the flesh of a man; otherwise one might conclude that the clay from which Adam's body was fashioned shall rise again. The second opinion, however, grants this argument.

Reply Obj. 2. That rib did not belong to the perfection of the individual in Adam, but was directed to the multiplication of the species. Hence it will rise again not in Adam but in Eve, just as the seed will rise again, not in the begetter, but in the begotten.

Reply Obj. 3. According to the first opinion it is easy to reply to this argument, because the flesh that is eaten never belonged to the truth of human nature in the eater, but it did belong to the truth of human nature in him whose flesh was eaten, and thus it will rise again in the latter but not in the former. But according to the second and third opinions, each one will rise again in that in which he approached nearest to the perfect participation of the power of the species, and if he approached equally in both, he will rise again in that in which he was first, because in that he first was directed to the

resurrection by union with the rational soul of that man. Hence if there were any surplus in the flesh eaten not belonging to the truth of human nature in the first man, it will be possible for it to rise again in the second. Otherwise what belonged to the resurrection in the first will rise again in him and not in the second. But in the second its place is taken either by something of that which was the product from other food, or if he never partook of any other food than human flesh, the substitution is made by Divine power so far as the perfection of quantity requires, as it does in those who die before the perfect age. Nor does this take away from numerical identity, as neither does the ebb and flow of parts.

Reply Obj. 4. According to the first opinion this argument is easily answered. For that opinion asserts that the seed is not from the surplus food, so that the flesh eaten is not changed into the seed of which the child is begotten. But according to the other two opinions we must reply that it is impossible for the whole of the flesh eaten to be changed into seed, because it is after much separation that the seed is distilled from the food, since seed is the ultimate surplus of food. That part of the eaten flesh which is changed into seed belongs to the truth of human nature in the one born of the seed more than in the one of whose flesh the seed was the product. Hence, according to the rule already laid down (REPLY 3), whatever was changed into the seed will rise again in the person born of the seed, while the remaining matter will rise again in him of whose flesh the seed was the product.

Reply Obj. 5. The embryo is not concerned with the resurrection before it is animated by a rational soul, in which state much has been added to the seminal substance from the substance of food, since the child is nourished in the mother's womb. Consequently on the supposition that a man partook of such food, and that some one were begotten of its surplus, that which was in the seminal substance will indeed rise again in the one begotten of that seed; unless it contain something that would have belonged to the seminal substance in those from whose flesh being eaten the seed was produced, for this would rise again in the first but not in the second. The remainder of the eaten flesh, not being changed into seed, will clearly rise again in the first; the Divine power supplying deficiencies in both. The first opinion is not troubled by this objection, since it does not hold the seed to be from the surplus food, but there are many other reasons against it as may be seen in the Second Book of the Sentences (ii. *Sent.* d. 30).[1]

ARTICLE 5. *Whether Whatever Was Materially in a Man's Members Will All Rise Again?*

We proceed thus to the Fifth Article: It would seem that whatever was materially in a man's members will all rise again.

Objection 1. For the hair, it seems, is less concerned in the resurrection than the other members. Yet whatever was in the hair will all rise again, if not in the hair, at least in other parts of the body, as Augustine says,[2] quoted in the text (iv. *Sent.* d. 44).[3] Much more therefore whatever was materially in the other members will all rise again.

Obj. 2. Further, Just as the parts of the flesh are perfected as to species by the rational soul, so are the parts as to matter. But the human body is directed to the resurrection through being perfected by a rational soul. Therefore not only the parts of species but also the parts of matter will all rise again.

Obj. 3. Further, The body derives its totality from the same cause as it derives its divisibility into parts. But division into parts belongs to a body in respect of matter the disposition of which is quantity in respect of which it is divided. Therefore totality is ascribed to the body in respect of its parts of matter. If then all the parts of matter rise not again, neither will the whole body rise again, which cannot be admitted.

On the contrary, The parts of matter are not permanent in the body but ebb and flow, as stated in the book on *Generation and Corruption.*[4] If, therefore, all the parts of matter rise again, either the body of one who rises again will be very dense, or it will be immoderate in quantity.

Further, whatever belongs to the truth of human nature in one man can all be a part of matter in another man, if the latter were to partake of his flesh. Therefore if all the parts of matter in one man were to rise again it follows that in one man there will rise again that which belongs to the truth of human nature in another, which is absurd.

I answer that, What is in man materially is not directed to the resurrection except in so far as it belongs to the truth of human nature, because it is in this respect that it bears a re-

lation to the human souls. Now all that is in man materially belongs indeed to the truth of human nature in so far as it has something of the species, but not all, if we consider the totality of matter; because all the matter that was in a man from the beginning of his life to the end would surpass the quantity due to his species, as the third opinion states (A. 4), which opinion seems to me more probable than the others. Therefore the whole of what is in man will rise again, if we speak of the totality of the species which is dependent on quantity, shape, position and order of parts, but the whole will not rise again if we speak of the totality of matter.

The second and first opinions, however, do not make this distinction, but distinguish between parts both of which have the species and matter. But these two opinions agree in that they both state that what is produced from the seed will all rise again even if we speak of totality of matter, while they differ in this that the first opinion maintains that nothing will rise again of that which was engendered from food, while the second holds that something, but not all, of it will rise again, as stated above (A. 4).

Reply Obj. 1. Just as all that is in the other parts of the body will rise again, if we speak of the totality of the species, but not if we speak of material totality, so is it with the hair. In the other parts something accrues from nourishment which causes growth, and this is accounted as another part, if we speak of totality of species, since it occupies another place and position in the body, and is under other parts of dimension, and there accrues something which does not cause growth, but serves to make up for waste by nourishing; and this is not accounted as another part of the whole considered in relation to the species, since it does not occupy another place or position in the body than that which was occupied by the part that has passed away, although it may be accounted another part if we consider the totality of matter. The same applies to the hair. Augustine, however, is speaking of the cutting of hair that was a part causing growth of the body; therefore it must rise again, not however as regards the quantity of hair, lest it should be immoderate, but it will rise again in other parts as deemed expedient by Divine providence. Or else he refers to the case when something will be lacking to the other parts, for then it will be possible for this to be supplied from the surplus of hair.

---

[1] Q. II, A. 1; cf. Part I, Q. CXIX, A. 1.
[2] *City of God,* XXII, 19 (PL 41, 780); *Enchir.* LXXXIX (PL 40, 273).   [3] QR II, 1001.   [4] Aristotle, I, 5 (321[b]24).

Reply Obj. 2. According to the third opinion parts of species are the same as parts of matter, for the Philosopher does not make this distinction[1] in order to distinguish different parts, but in order to show that the same parts may be considered both in respect of species, as to what belongs to the form and species in them, and in respect of matter, as to that which is under the form and species. Now it is clear that the matter of the flesh has no relation to the rational soul except in so far as it is under such a form, and consequently by reason of it it is directed to the resurrection. But the first and second opinions which draw a distinction between parts of species and parts of matter say that although the rational soul perfects both parts, it does not perfect parts of matter except by means of the parts of species, and so they are not equally directed to the resurrection.

Reply Obj. 3. In the matter of things subject to generation and corruption it is necessary to presuppose indefinite dimensions before the reception of the substantial form. Consequently division which is made according to these dimensions belongs properly to matter. But complete and definite quantity comes to matter after the substantial form; therefore division that is made in reference to definite quantity regards the species especially when definite position of parts belongs to the essence of the species, as in the human body.

QUESTION LXXXI
OF THE QUALITY OF THOSE WHO RISE AGAIN
(In Four Articles)

WE must now consider the quality of those who rise again. Under this head there are four points of inquiry: (1) Whether all will rise again in the youthful age? (2) Whether they will be of equal stature? (3) Whether all will be of the same sex? (4) Whether they will rise again to the animal life?

ARTICLE 1. *Whether All Will Rise Again of the Same Age?*

We proceed thus to the First Article: It would seem that all will not rise again of the same, namely the youthful age.

Objection 1. Because God will take nothing pertaining to man's perfection from those who rise again, especially from the blessed. Now age pertains to the perfection of man, since old age is the age that demands reverence. Therefore the old will not rise again of a youthful age.

Obj. 2. Further, Age is reckoned according to the length of past time. Now it is impossible for past time not to have passed. Therefore it is impossible for those who were of greater age to be brought back to a youthful age.

Obj. 3. Further, That which belonged most to the truth of human nature in each individual will especially rise again in him. Now the sooner a thing was in man the more would it seem to have belonged to the truth of human nature, because in the end, through the strength of the species being weakened the human body is likened to watery wine according to the Philosopher.[2] Therefore if all are to rise again of the same age, it is more fitting that they should rise again in the age of childhood.

On the contrary, It is written (Eph. 4. 13): *Until we all meet . . . unto a perfect man, unto the measure of the age of the fulness of Christ.* Now Christ rose again of youthful age, which begins about the age of thirty years, as Augustine says.[3] Therefore others also will rise again of a youthful age.

Further, Man will rise again at the most perfect stage of nature. Now human nature is at the most perfect stage in the age of youth. Therefore all will rise again of that age.

I answer that, Man will rise again without any defect of human nature, because as God founded human nature without a defect, even so will He restore it without defect. Now human nature has a twofold defect. First, because it has not yet attained to its ultimate perfection. Secondly, because it has already gone back from its ultimate perfection. The first defect is found in children, the second in the aged, and consequently in each of these human nature will be brought by the resurrection to the state of its ultimate perfection which is in the youthful age, at which the movement of growth terminates, and from which the movement of decrease begins.

Reply Obj. 1. Old age calls for reverence not on account of the state of the body which is at fault, but on account of the soul's wisdom which is taken for granted on account of its being advanced in years. Therefore in the elect there will remain the reverence due to old age on account of the fulness of Divine wisdom which will be in them, but the defect of old age will not be in them.

Reply Obj. 2. We speak of age not as re-

---

[1] *Generation and Corruption*, I, 5 (321ᵇ24).

[2] *Ibid.*, I, 10 (328ᵃ26).

[3] *City of God*, XXII, 15 (PL 41, 777).

gards the number of years, but as regards the state which the human body acquires from years. Hence Adam is said to have been formed in the youthful age on account of the particular condition of body which he had at the first day of his formation. Thus the argument is not to the point.

Reply Obj. 3. The strength of the species is said to be more perfect in a child than in a young man, as regards the ability to transform nourishment in a certain way, even as it is more perfect in the seed than in the mature man. In youth, however, it is more perfect as regards the term of completion. Therefore that which belonged principally to the truth of human nature will be brought to that perfection which it has in the age of youth, and not to that perfection which it has in the age of a child, wherein the humours have not yet reached their ultimate disposition.

ARTICLE 2. *Whether All Will Rise Again of the Same Stature?*

We proceed thus to the Second Article: It would seem that all will rise again of the same stature.

Objection 1. For just as man is measured by dimensive quantity, so is he by the quantity of time. Now the quantity of time will be reduced to the same measure in all, since all will rise again of the same age. Therefore the dimensive quantity will also be reduced to the same measure in all, so that all will rise again of the same stature.

Obj. 2. Further, The Philosopher says[1] that "all things of the same nature have a certain limit and measure of size and growth." Now this limitation can only arise by virtue of the form, with which the quantity as well as all the other accidents ought to agree. Therefore since all men have the same specific form, there should be the same measure of quantity in respect of matter in all, unless an error should occur. But the error of nature will be set right at the resurrection. Therefore all will rise again of the same stature.

Obj. 3. Further, It will be impossible for man in rising again to be of a quantity proportionate to the natural power which first formed his body, for otherwise those who could not be brought to a greater quantity by the power of nature will never rise again of a greater quantity, which is false. Therefore that quantity must be proportionate to the power which will restore the human body by the resurrection,

[1] *Soul*, II, 4 (416ᵃ16).

and to the matter from which it is restored. Now the self-same, namely the Divine, power will restore all bodies, and all the ashes from which the human bodies will be restored are equally disposed to receive the action of that power. Therefore the resurrection of all men will bring them to the same quantity, and so the same conclusion follows.

On the contrary, Natural quantity results from each individual's nature. Now the nature of the individual will not be altered at the resurrection. Therefore neither will its natural quantity. But all are not of the same natural quantity. Therefore all will not rise again of the same stature.

Further, Human nature will not be restored by resurrection to glory or to punishment. But there will not be the same quantity of glory or punishment in all those who rise again. Neither therefore will there be the same quantity of stature.

I answer that, At the resurrection human nature will be restored not only in the selfsame species but also in the selfsame individual, and consequently we must observe in the resurrection what is requisite not only to the specific but also to the individual nature. Now the specific nature has a certain quantity which it neither exceeds nor fails without error, and yet this quantity has certain degrees of latitude and is not to be attached to one fixed measure; and each individual in the human species aims at some degree of quantity befitting his individual nature within the bounds of that latitude, and reaches it at the end of his growth, if there has been no error in the working of nature, resulting in the addition of something to or the subtraction of something from the aforesaid quantity, the measure of which is gauged according to the proportion of heat as expanding, and of humidity as expansive, in point of which all are not of the same power. Therefore all will not rise of the same quantity, but each one will rise again of that quantity which would have been his at the end of his growth if nature had not erred or failed, and the Divine power will subtract or supply what was excessive or lacking in man.

Reply Obj. 1. It has already been explained (A. 1, REPLY 2) that all are said to rise again of the same age, not as though the same length of time were befitting to each one, but because the same state of perfection will be in all, which state is indifferent to a great or small quantity.

Reply Obj. 2. The quantity of a particular

individual corresponds not only to the form of the species, but also to the nature or matter of the individual; therefore the conclusion does not follow.

Reply Obj. 3. The quantity of those who will be raised from the dead is not proportionate to the restoring power, because the latter does not belong to the power of the body,—nor to the ashes, as to the state in which they are before the resurrection,—but to nature which the individual had at first. Nevertheless if the formative power on account of some defect was unable to effect the due quantity that is befitting to the species, the Divine power will supply the defect at the resurrection, as in dwarfs, and in like manner in those who by immoderate size have exceeded the due bounds of nature.

ARTICLE 3. *Whether All Will Rise Again of the Male Sex?*

We proceed thus to the Third Article: It would seem that all will rise again of the male sex.

Objection 1. For it is written (Eph. 4. 13) that we shall all meet *unto a perfect man,* etc. Therefore there will be none but the male sex.

Obj. 2. Further, In the world to come "all pre-eminence will cease," as a gloss observes[1] on I Cor. 15. 24. Now woman is subject to man in the natural order. Therefore women will rise again not in the female but in the male sex.

Obj. 3. Further, That which is produced incidentally and beside the intention of nature will not rise again, since all error will be removed at the resurrection. Now the female sex is produced beside the intention of nature, through a fault in the formative power of the seed, which is unable to bring the matter of the fetus to the male form; therefore the Philosopher says[2] that the female is "a misbegotten male." Therefore the female sex will not rise again.

On the contrary, Augustine says:[3] "Those are wiser, it seems, who doubt not that both sexes will rise again."

Further, At the resurrection God will restore man to what He made him at the creation. Now He made woman from the man's rib (Gen. 2. 22). Therefore He will also restore the female sex at the resurrection.

I answer that, Just as, considering the nature of the individual, a different quantity is due to different men, so also, considering the nature of the individual, a different sex is due to different men. Moreover, this same diversity is becoming to the perfection of the species, the different degrees of which are filled by this very difference of sex and quantity. Therefore just as men will rise again of various stature, so will they rise again of different sex. And though there be difference of sex there will be no shame in seeing one another, since there will be no lust to invite them to shameful deeds which are the cause of shame.

Reply Obj. 1. When it is said that we shall all meet *Christ unto a perfect man,* this refers not to the male sex but to the strength of soul which will be in all, both men and women.

Reply Obj. 2. Woman is subject to man on account of the frailty of nature, as regards both vigour of soul and strength of body. After the resurrection, however, the difference in those points will be not on account of the difference of sex, but by reason of the difference of merits. Hence the conclusion does not follow.

Reply Obj. 3. Although the begetting of a woman is beside the intention of a particular nature, it is in the intention of universal nature, which requires both sexes for the perfection of the human species. Nor will any defect result from sex as stated above (REPLY 2).

ARTICLE 4. *Whether All Will Rise Again to Animal Life?*

We proceed thus to the Fourth Article: It would seem that they will rise again to the animal life, or in other words that they will make use of the acts of the nutritive and generative powers.

Objection 1. For our resurrection will be conformed to Christ's. But Christ is said to have eaten after His resurrection (John 21.; Luke 24). Therefore, after the resurrection men will eat, and in like manner beget.

Obj. 2. Further, The distinction of sexes is directed to generation; and in like manner the instruments which serve the nutritive power are directed to eating. Now man will rise again with all these. Therefore he will exercise the acts of the generative and nutritive powers.

Obj. 3. Further, The whole man will be beatified both in soul and in body. Now beatitude or happiness, according to the Philosopher,[4] consists in a perfect operation. Therefore it must be that all the powers of the soul and all

---

[1] *Glossa* Lombardi (PL 191, 1679); cf. *Glossa ordin.* (VI, 58B); Augustine, QQ. LXXXIII, qu. 69 (PL 40, 76).
[2] *Generation of Animals,* II, 3 (737ª24).
[3] *City of God,* XXII, 17 (PL 41, 778).
[4] *Ethics,* I, 7 (1098ª15); I, 13 (1102ª5); X, 7 (1177ª12).

the members have their respective acts after the resurrection. And so the same conclusion follows as above.

Obj. 4. Further, After the resurrection there will be perfect joy in the blessed. Now such a joy includes all pleasures, since happiness is a state rendered perfect by the accumulation of all goods, and the perfect is that which lacks nothing. Since then there is much pleasure in the act of the generative and nutritive powers it would seem that such acts belonging to animal life will be in the blessed, and much more in others, who will have less spiritual bodies.

On the contrary, It is written (Matt. 22. 30): *In the resurrection they shall neither marry nor be married.*

Further, Generation is directed to supply the defect resulting from death, and to the multiplication of the human race, and eating is directed to make up for waste, and to increase quantity. But in the state of the resurrection the human race will already have the number of individuals preordained by God, since generation will continue up to that point. In like manner each man will rise again in due quantity; neither will death be any more, nor any waste affect the parts of man. Therefore the acts of the generative and nutritive powers would be void of purpose.

I answer that, The resurrection will not be necessary to man on account of his primary perfection, which consists in the integrity of those things that belong to his nature, since man can attain to this in his present state of life by the action of natural causes; but the necessity of the resurrection regards the attainment of his ultimate perfection, which consists in his reaching his ultimate end. Consequently those natural operations which are directed to cause or preserve the primary perfection of human nature will not be in the resurrection; such are the actions of the animal life in man, the action of the elements on one another, and the movement of the heavens; therefore all these will cease at the resurrection. And since to eat, drink, sleep, beget, pertain to the animal life, being directed to the primary perfection of nature, it follows that they will not be in the resurrection.

Reply Obj. 1. When Christ partook of that meal, His eating was an act, not of necessity as though human nature needed food after the resurrection, but of power, so as to prove that He had resumed the true human nature which He had in that state wherein He ate and drank with His disciples. There will be no need

of such proof at the general resurrection, since it will be evident to all. Hence Christ is said to have eaten by dispensation in the sense in which lawyers say that "a dispensation is a relaxation of the general law"[1] because Christ made an exception to that which is common to those who rise again (namely not to partake of food) for the aforesaid motive. Hence the argument does not prove.

Reply Obj. 2. The distinction of sexes and the difference of members will be for the restoration of the perfection of human nature both in the species and in the individual. Hence it does not follow that they are without purpose, although they lack their animal operations.

Reply Obj. 3. These operations do not belong to man as man, as also the Philosopher states,[2] and so the happiness of the human body does not consist in them. But the human body will be glorified by an overflow from the reason whereby man is man, in so far as the body will be subject to reason.

Reply Obj. 4. As the Philosopher says[3] the pleasures of the body are medicinal, because they are applied to man for the removal of weariness; or again, they are unhealthy, in so far as man indulges in those pleasures inordinately, as though they were real pleasures, just as a man whose taste is vitiated delights in things which are not delightful to the healthy. Consequently it does not follow that such pleasures as these belong to the perfection of happiness, as the Jews[4] and Turks[5] maintain, and certain heretics known as the Chiliasts asserted;[6] who, moreover, according to the Philosopher's teaching,[7] would seem to have an unhealthy appetite, since according to him none but spiritual pleasures are pleasures absolutely, and to be sought for their own sake. Therefore these alone are requisite for Happiness.

[1] Cf. Raymond of Pennafort, *Summa,* bk. iii, tit. 29, sect. 2 (346ᵃ); *Glossa ordin. in Decretum,* pt. ii, causa i, Q. 7, can. 5, *Requisitis* (i, 563ᵃ).

[2] *Ethics,* x, 7 (1177ᵇ26).

[3] *Ibid.,* vii, 14 (1154ᵃ26); x, 5 (1175ᵇ16).

[4] Cf. UJE, art. "Future Life" (iv, 484); TJE, art. "Paradise" (ix, 515), where the texts from the Rabbinical Scriptures are cited.

[5] Cf. the Koran, chap. 36 (SL 364); chap. 44 (SL 404).

[6] Or Millenarians; especially Cerinthus; see Caius Romanus, *Disputatio adv. Proclum,* in Eusebius, *Hist. Eccl.* iii, 28 (PG 20, 273; cf. PG 10, 25); Epiphanius, *Adv. Haeres.,* bk. iii, t. ii, haeres. 77, n. 36 (PG 42, 696); Augustine, *City of God,* xx, 7 (PL 41, 667), *De Haeres.,* chap. 8 (PL 42, 27); cf. DTC, art. *Cérinthe* (ii, 2154); art. *Millénarisme* (x, 1761).

[7] *Ethics,* vii, 14 (1154ᵇ20); x, 5 (1176ᵃ10).

QUESTION LXXXII

OF THE CONDITION OF THE BLESSED AFTER THEIR RESURRECTION

(*In Four Articles*)

WE must now consider the conditions under which the blessed rise again, and (1) the impassibility of their bodies; (2) their subtlety (Q. LXXXIII); (3) their agility (Q. LXXXIV); (4) their clarity (Q. LXXXV). Under the first head there are four points of inquiry: (1) Whether at the resurrection the saints will rise again impassible in body? (2) Whether all will be equally impassible? (3) Whether this impassibility renders the glorious bodies insensible? (4) Whether in them all the senses are in act?

ARTICLE 1. *Whether the Bodies of the Saints Will Be Impassible After the Resurrection?*

We proceed thus to the First Article: It seems that the bodies of the saints will not be impassible after the resurrection.

Objection 1. For everything mortal is passible. But man, after the resurrection, will be a mortal rational animal, for such is the definition of man, which will never be dissociated from him. Therefore the body will be passible.

Obj. 2. Further, Whatever is in potency to the form of another thing is passible in relation to something else; for this is what is meant by being passive to another thing.[1] Now the bodies of the saints will be in potency to the form of another thing after the resurrection, since matter, according as it is under one form, does not lose its potency to another form. But the bodies of the saints after the resurrection will have matter in common with the elements, because they will be restored out of the same matter of which they are now composed. Therefore they will be in potency to another form, and thus will be passible.

Obj. 3. Further, According to the Philosopher,[2] contraries have a natural inclination to be active and passive towards one another. Now the bodies of the saints will be composed of contraries after the resurrection, even as now. Therefore they will be passible.

Obj. 4. Further, In the human body the blood and humours will rise again, as stated above (Q. LXXX, A. 3). Now, sickness and such passions arise in the body through the antipathy of the humours. Therefore the bodies of the saints will be passible after the resurrection.

Obj. 5. Further, Actual defect is more inconsistent with perfection than potential defect. But passibility denotes merely potential defect. Since then there will be certain actual defects in the bodies of the blessed, such as the scars of the wounds in the martyrs, even as they were in Christ, it would seem that their perfections will not suffer, if we grant their bodies to be passible.

On the contrary, Everything passible is corruptible, because increase of passion results in loss of substance. Now the bodies of the saints will be incorruptible after the resurrection, according to I Cor. 15. 42, *It is sown in corruption, it shall rise in incorruption.* Therefore they will be impassible.

Further, The stronger is not passive to the weaker. But no body will be stronger than the bodies of the saints, of which it is written (I Cor. 15. 43): *It is sown in weakness, it shall rise in power.* Therefore they will be impassible.

I answer that, We speak of a thing being passive in two ways. First in a broad sense, and thus every reception is called a passion, whether the thing received be fitting to the receiver and perfect it, or contrary to it and corrupt it. The glorious bodies are not said to be impassible by the removal of this kind of passion, since nothing pertaining to perfection is to be removed from them. In another way we use the word passive properly, and thus Damascene defines passion (*De Fide Orthod.* ii, 22)[3] as being "a movement contrary to nature." Hence an immoderate movement of the heart is called its passion, but a moderate movement is called its operation. The reason of this is that whatever is patient is drawn to the bounds of the agent, since the agent assimilates the patient to itself, so that, therefore, the patient as such is drawn beyond its own bounds within which it was confined. Accordingly taking passion in its proper sense there will be no potentiality to passion in the bodies of the saints after resurrection. Therefore they are said to be impassible.

The reason however of this impassibility is assigned differently by different persons. Some ascribe it to the condition of the elements, which will be different then from what it is now. For they say that the elements will remain then, as to substance, yet that they will be deprived of their active and passive qualities. But this does not seem to be true, because the active and passive qualities belong to the perfection of the elements, so that if the elements were

---

[1] Aristotle, *Generation and Corruption*, I, 7 (323ᵇ29).
[2] *Ibid.* (324ᵃ2).
[3] PG 94, 941.

restored without them in the body of the man that rises again, they would be less perfect than now. Moreover since these qualities are the proper accidents of the elements, being caused by their form and matter, it would seem most absurd for the cause to remain and the effect to be removed.

Therefore others say that the qualities will remain, but deprived of their proper activities, the Divine power so doing for the preservation of the human body. This however would seem to be untenable, since the action and passion of the active and passive qualities is necessary for the mixture (of the elements), and according as one or the other preponderates the mixed (bodies) differ in their respective temperaments, and this must apply to the bodies of those who rise again, for they will contain flesh and bones and like parts, all of which demand different temperaments. Moreover, according to this, impassibility could not be one of their gifts, because it would not imply a disposition in the impassible substance, but merely an external preventive to passion, namely the power of God, which might produce the same effect in a human body even in this state of life.

Consequently others say that in the body itself there will be something preventing the passion of a glorified body, namely the nature of a fifth[1] or heavenly body, which they maintain enters into the composition of a human body, to the effect of blending the elements together in harmony so as to be fitting matter for the rational soul; but that in this state of life, on account of the preponderance of the elemental nature, the human body is passible like other elements, whereas in the resurrection the nature of the fifth body will predominate, so that the human body will be made impassible in likeness to the heavenly body. But this cannot stand, because the fifth body does not enter materially into the composition of a human body, as was proved above.[2] Moreover it is absurd to say that a natural power, such as the power of a heavenly body, should endow the human body with a property of glory, such as the impassibility of a glorified body, since the Apostle ascribes to Christ's power the transformation of the human body, because *such as is the heavenly, such also are they that are heavenly* (I Cor. 15. 48), and *He will reform the body of our lowness, made like to the body*

[1] The other four being the elements. This fifth element was known to the peripatetic philosophers as the quintessence, of which they held heavenly bodies to be formed.
[2] St. Thomas, *In Sent.*, dist. XVII, Q. 3, A. 1; cf. Part. I, Q. XCI, A. 1, Reply 2.

of His glory, according to the operation whereby also He is able to subdue all things unto Himself (Phil. 3. 21). And again, a heavenly nature cannot exercise such power over the human body as to take from it its elemental nature which is passible by reason of its essential constituents.

Consequently we must say otherwise that all passion results from the agent overcoming the patient, for otherwise it would not draw it to its own bounds. Now it is impossible for agent to overcome patient except through the weakening of the hold which the form of the patient has over its matter, if we speak of the passion which is against nature, for it is of passion in this sense that we are speaking now; for matter is not subject to one of two contraries, except through the cessation or at least the lessening of the hold which the other contrary has on it. Now the human body and all that it contains will be perfectly subject to the rational soul, even as the soul will be perfectly subject to God. Therefore it will be impossible for the glorified body to be subject to any change contrary to the disposition whereby it is perfected by the soul. And consequently those bodies will be impassible.

Reply Obj. 1. According to Anselm (*Cur Deus Homo*, ii, 11),[3] "mortal is included in the philosophers' definition of man, because they did not believe that the whole man could be ever immortal," for they had no experience of man otherwise than in this state of mortality. Or we may say that since, according to the Philosopher,[4] essential differences are unknown to us, we sometimes employ accidental differences in order to signify essential differences from which the accidental differences result. Hence "mortal" is put in the definition of man, not as though mortality were essential to man, but because that which causes passibility and mortality in the present state of life, namely composition of contraries, is essential to man, but it will not cause it then, on account of the triumph of the soul over the body.

Reply Obj. 2. Potency is twofold, tied (*ligata*) and free; and this is true not only of active but also of passive potency. For the form ties the potency of matter, by determining it to one thing, and it is thus that it overcomes it. And since in corruptible things form does not perfectly overcome matter, it cannot tie it completely so as to prevent it from sometimes receiving a disposition contrary to the

[3] PL 158, 411.
[4] *Metaphysics*, VII, 12 (1038ª13).

form through some passion. But in the saints after the resurrection, the soul will have complete dominion over the body, and it will be altogether impossible for it to lose this dominion, because it will be immutably subject to God, which was not the case in the state of innocence. Consequently those bodies will retain substantially the same potency as they have now to another form; yet that potentiality will remain tied by the triumph of the soul over the body, so that it will never be realized by actual passion.

Reply Obj. 3. The elemental qualities are the instruments of the soul, as stated in the book on the *Soul*,[1] for the heat of fire in an animal's body is directed in the act of nutrition by the soul's power. When, however, the principal agent is perfect, and there is no defect in the instrument, no action proceeds from the instrument except in accordance with the disposition of the principal agent. Consequently in the bodies of the saints after the resurrection, no action or passion will result from the elemental qualities that is contrary to the disposition of the soul which has the preservation of the body in view.

Reply Obj. 4. According to Augustine (*Ep. ad Consent.* ccv, 1)[2] "the Divine power is able to remove whatever qualities He will from this visible and tangible body, other qualities remaining." Hence even as in a certain respect He deprived the flames of the Chaldees' furnace of the power to burn, since the bodies of the children were preserved without hurt, while in another respect that power remained, since those flames consumed the wood, so will He remove passibility from the humours while leaving their nature unchanged. It has been explained in the Article how this is brought about.

Reply Obj. 5. The scars of wounds will not be in the saints, nor were they in Christ, in so far as they imply a defect, but as signs of the most steadfast virtue whereby the saints suffered for the sake of justice and faith, so that this will increase their own and others' joy.[3] Hence Augustine says:[4] "We feel an undescribable love for the blessed martyrs so as to desire to see in that kingdom the scars of the wounds in their bodies, which they bore for Christ's name. Perhaps indeed we shall see them, for this will not make them less comely

but more glorious. A certain beauty will shine in them, a beauty though in the body, yet not of the body but of virtue." Nevertheless those martyrs who have been maimed and deprived of their limbs will not be without those limbs in the resurrection of the dead, for to them it is said (Luke 21. 18): *A hair of your head shall not perish.*

ARTICLE 2. *Whether All Will Be Equally Impassible?*

We proceed thus to the Second Article: It would seem that all will be equally impassible.

Objection 1. For a gloss on I Cor. 15. 42, *It is sown in corruption,* says that all have equal immunity from suffering.[5] Now the gift of impassibility consists in immunity from suffering. Therefore all will be equally impassible.

Obj. 2. Further, Negations are not subject to be more or less. Now impassibility is a negation or privation of passibility. Therefore it cannot be greater in one subject than in another.

Obj. 3. Further, A thing is more white if it have less admixture of black. But there will be no admixture of passibility in any of the saints' bodies. Therefore they will all be equally impassible.

On the contrary, Reward should be proportionate to merit. Now some of the saints were greater in merit than others. Therefore, since impassibility is a reward, it would seem to be greater in some than in others.

Further, Impassibility is divided against the gift of clarity. Now the latter will not be equal in all, according to I Cor. 15. 41. Therefore neither will impassibility be equal in all.

I answer that, Impassibility may be considered in two ways, either in itself, or in respect of its cause. If it be considered in itself, since it denotes a mere negation or privation, it is not subject to be more or less, but will be equal in all the blessed. On the other hand, if we consider it in relation to its cause, thus it will be greater in one person than in another. Now its cause is the dominion of the soul over the body, and this dominion is caused by the soul's unchangeable enjoyment of God. Consequently in one who enjoys God more perfectly, there is a greater cause of impassibility.

Reply Obj. 1. This gloss is speaking of impassibility in itself and not in relation to its cause.

---

[1] Aristotle, II, 4 (415^{b}18).
[2] PL 33, 943.
[3] Cf. Part III, Q. LIV, A. 4, reply 3.
[4] *City of God,* XXII, 19 (PL 41, 782).

[5] *Glossa ordin.* (VI, 59B); *Glossa interl.* (VI, 59r); *Glossa Lombardi* (PL 191, 1687); see Hugh of St. Cher, *In Univ. Test.* (VII, 118va).

Reply Obj. 2. Although negations and privations considered in themselves are not increased nor diminished, yet they are subject to increase and lessening in relation to their causes. Thus a place is said to be more darksome from having more and greater obstacles to light.

Reply Obj. 3. Some things increase not only by receding from their contrary, but also by approach to a term; in this way light increases. Consequently impassibility also is greater in one subject than in another, although there is no possibility remaining in any one.

ARTICLE 3. *Whether Impassibility Excludes Actual Sensation from Glorified Bodies?*

We proceed thus to the Third Article: It would seem that impassibility excludes actual sensation from glorified bodies.

Objection 1. For according to the Philosopher,[1] "sensation is a kind of passion." But the glorified bodies will be impassible. Therefore they will not have actual sensation.

Obj. 2. Further, Natural change precedes spiritual[2] change, just as natural being precedes intentional being. Now glorified bodies, by reason of their impassibility, will not be subject to natural change. Therefore they will not be subject to spiritual change which is requisite for sensation.

Obj. 3. Further, Whenever the sense is put in act, with the new reception there is a new judgment. But in that state there will be no new judgment, because "our thoughts will not then be changeable," as Augustine says (*De Trin.* xv, 16).[3] Therefore there will be no actual sensation.

Obj. 4. Further, When one of the soul's powers is in act, the acts of the other powers are less intense. Now the soul will be supremely intent on the act of the contemplative power in contemplating God. Therefore the soul will have no actual sensation whatever.

On the contrary, It is written (*Apoc.* 1. 7): *Every eye shall see Him.* Therefore there will be actual sensation.

Further, According to the Philosopher,[4] "the animate is distinct from the inanimate by sensation and movement." Now there will be actual movement since they shall run to and fro like sparks among the reeds (Wisd. 3. 7). Therefore there will also be actual sensation.

I answer that, All are agreed that there is

some sensation in the bodies of the blessed; otherwise the bodily life of the saints after the resurrection would be likened to sleep rather than to watchfulness. Now this is not befitting that perfection, because in sleep a sensible body is not in the ultimate act of life, for which reason sleep is described in the *Ethics* as half-life.[5] But there is a difference of opinion as to the mode of sensation.

For some say that the glorified bodies will be impassible, and consequently not susceptible to strange impressions, and much less so than the heavenly bodies, because they will have actual sensations, not by receiving species from sensibles, but by emission of species. But this is impossible, since in the resurrection, the specific nature will remain the same in man and in all his parts. Now the nature of sense is to be a passive power as the Philosopher proves.[6] Therefore if the saints, in the resurrection, were to have sensations by emitting and not by receiving species, sense in them would not be a passive but an active power, and thus it would not be the same specifically with sense as it is now, but would be some other power bestowed on them; for just as matter never becomes form, so a passive power never becomes active.

Consequently others say that the senses will be actualized by receiving species, not indeed from external sensibles, but by an outflow from the higher powers, so that as now the higher powers receive from the lower, so on the contrary the lower powers will then receive from the higher. But this mode of reception does not result in real sensation, because every passive power, according to its specific character, is determined to some special active principle, since a power as such bears relation to that with respect to which it is said to be the power. Therefore since the proper active principle in external sensation is a thing existing outside the soul and not an intention thereof existing in the imagination or reason, if the organ of sense be not moved by external things but by the imagination or other higher powers, there will be no true sensation. Hence we do not say that madmen or other witless persons (in whom there is this kind of outflow of species towards the organs of sense, on account of the powerful influence of the imagination) have real sen-

---

[1] *Soul,* II, 5, 11 (416ᵇ33; 423ᵇ31).
[2] *Animalem,* as though it were derived from *animus*—the mind.
[3] PL 42, 1079.   [4] *Soul,* I, 2 (403ᵇ25).

[5] This is what Aristotle says: "The good and the bad are in sleep least distinguishable; hence men say that for half their lives there is no difference between the happy and the unhappy." (*Ethics,* I, 13–1102ᵇ3).

[6] *Soul,* II, 5, 11 (416ᵇ33; 423ᵇ31).

sations, but that it seems to them that they have sensations.

Consequently we must say with others that sensation in glorified bodies will result from the reception of things outside the soul. It must, however, be observed that the organs of sense are changed by things outside the soul in two ways. First by a natural change, when namely the organ is disposed by the same natural quality as the thing outside the soul which acts on that organ; for instance, when the hand is heated by touching a hot object, or becomes fragrant through contact with a fragrant object. Secondly, by a spiritual change, as when a sensible quality is received in an instrument according to a spiritual mode of being, when, namely, the species or the intention of a quality, and not the quality itself is received; thus the pupil receives the species of whiteness and yet does not itself become white. Accordingly the first reception does not cause sensation, properly speaking, because the senses are receptive of species in matter but without matter; that is to say without the material being which the species had outside the soul.[1] This reception changes the nature of the recipient, because in this way the quality is received according to its material being. Consequently this kind of reception will not be in the glorified bodies, but the second, which of itself causes actual sensation, without changing the nature of the recipient.

Reply Obj. 1. As already explained, by this passion that takes place in actual sensation and is no other than the aforesaid reception of species, the body is not drawn away from natural quality, but is perfected spiritually. And so the impassibility of glorified bodies does not exclude this kind of passion.

Reply Obj. 2. Every subject of passion receives the action of the agent according to its mode. Accordingly if there be a thing that is naturally adapted to be changed by an active principle, with a natural and a spiritual change, the natural change precedes the spiritual change, just as natural precedes intentional being. If however a thing be naturally adapted to be changed only with a spiritual change it does not follow that it is changed naturally. For instance the air is not receptive of colour, according to its natural being, but only according to its spiritual being, and therefore in this way alone is it changed; but, on the contrary, inanimate bodies are changed by sensible qualities only naturally and not spiritually. But in the

glorified bodies there cannot be any natural change, and consequently there will be only spiritual change.

Reply Obj. 3. Just as there will be new reception of species in the organs of sensation, so there will be new judgment in the common sense, but there will be no new judgment on the point in the intellect; such is the case with one who sees what he knew before. The saying of Augustine, that "there our thoughts will not be changeable," refers to the thoughts of the intellectual part; therefore it is not to the point.

Reply Obj. 4. When one of two things is the type of the other, the attention of the soul to the one does not hinder or lessen its attention to the other; thus a physician while considering urine is not less but more able to bear in mind the rules of his art concerning the colours of urine. And since God is apprehended by the saints as the type of all things that will be done or known by them, their attention to perceiving sensibles, or to contemplating or doing anything else will in no way hinder their contemplation of God, nor conversely. Or we may say that the reason why one power is hindered in its act when another power is intensely engaged is because one power does not alone suffice for such an intense operation unless it is assisted by receiving from the principle of life the inflow that the other powers or members should receive. And since in the saints all the powers will be most perfect, one will be able to operate intensely without thereby hindering the operation of another power, even as it was with Christ.

ARTICLE 4. *Whether in the Blessed, After the Resurrection, All the Senses Will Be in Act?*

We proceed thus to the Fourth Article: It would seem that all the senses are not in act there.

Objection 1. For touch is the first of all the senses.[2] But the glorified body will lack the actual sense of touch, since the sense of touch becomes actual by the changing of an animal body by some external body preponderating in some one of the active or passive qualities which touch is capable of discerning, and such a change will then be impossible. Therefore all the senses will not be in act there.

Obj. 2. Further, The sense of taste assists the action of the nutritive power. Now after the resurrection there will be no such action,

[1] Aristotle, *Soul*, II, 12 (424[a]21).

[2] *Ibid.*, II, 2 (413[b]4).

as stated above (Q. LXXXI, A. 4). Therefore taste would be useless there.

Obj. 3. Further, Nothing will be corrupted after the resurrection because the whole creature will be invested with a certain virtue of incorruption. Now the sense of smell cannot have its act without some corruption having taken place, because smell is not perceived without a volatile evaporation consisting in a certain dissolution. Therefore the sense of smell is not there in its act.

Obj. 4. Further, "Hearing assists teaching."[1] But the blessed, after the resurrection, will require no teaching by means of sensible things, since they will be filled with Divine wisdom by the very vision of God. Therefore hearing will not be there.

Obj. 5. Further, Seeing results from the pupil receiving the species of the thing seen. But after the resurrection this will be impossible in the blessed. Therefore there will be no actual seeing there, and yet this is the most noble of the senses. The minor is proved thus:—That which is actually lightsome is not receptive of a visible species; and consequently a mirror placed under the sun's rays does not reflect the image of a body opposite to it. Now the pupil like the whole body will be endowed with clarity. Therefore it will not receive the image of a coloured body.

Obj. 6. Further, According to the science of perspective, whatever is seen is seen at an angle. But this does not apply to the glorified bodies. Therefore they will not have actual sense of sight. The minor is proved thus: Whenever a thing is seen at an angle, the angle must be proportionate to the distance of the thing seen, because what is seen from a greater distance is less seen and at a lesser angle, so that the angle may be so small that nothing is seen of the object. Therefore if the glorified eye sees at an angle, it follows that it sees things within a certain distance, and that consequently it does not see a thing from a greater distance than we see now, and this would seem very absurd. And thus it would seem that the sense of sight will not be actual in glorified bodies.

On the contrary, A power joined to its act is more perfect than one not so joined. Now human nature in the blessed will be in its greatest perfection. Therefore all the senses will be actual there.

Further, The sensitive powers are nearer to the soul than the body is. But the body will be rewarded or punished on account of the merits or demerits of the soul. Therefore all the senses in the blessed will also be rewarded, and in the wicked will be punished, with regard to pleasure and pain or sorrow which consist in the operation of the senses.

I answer that, There are two opinions on this question. For some say that in the glorified bodies there will be all the sensitive powers, but that only two senses will be in act, namely touch and sight. Nor will this be owing to defective senses, but from lack of medium and object. Nor will the senses be useless, because they will conduce to the integrity of human nature and will show forth the wisdom of their Creator. But this it seems is untrue, because the medium in these senses is the same as in the others. For in the sight the medium is the air, and this is also the medium in hearing and smelling.[2] Again, the taste, like the touch, has the medium in contact, since taste is a kind of touch.[3] Smell also which is the object of the sense of smell will be there, since the Church sings that the bodies of the saints will be a most sweet smell. There will also be vocal praise in heaven; hence Augustine says on Ps. 149. 6, *The high praises of God shall be in their mouth,* that hearts and tongues shall not cease to praise God.[4] The same is had on the authority of a gloss[5] on II Esdr. 12. 27, *With singing and with cymbals.* Therefore, according to others we must say that smelling and hearing will be in act there, but taste will not be in act, in the sense of being changed by the taking of food or drink, as appears from what we have said (Q. LXXXI, A. 4) unless perhaps we say that there will be taste in act through the tongue being changed by some neighbouring humour.

Reply Obj. 1. The qualities perceived by the touch are those which constitute the animal body. Therefore the body of an animal has, through its tangible qualities according to the present state of life, a natural aptitude to be changed with a natural and spiritual alteration by the object of touch. For this reason the touch is said to be the most material of the senses, since it has a greater measure of material change connected with it. Yet material change is only accidentally related to the act of sensation which is effected by a spiritual change. Consequently the glorified bodies, which by reason of their impassibility are immune

---

[1] Aristotle, *Sense and the Sensible,* 1 (437ª5).

[2] Aristotle, *Soul,* 11, 7, 9 (419ª32; 421ᵇ8).

[3] *Ibid.,* 11, 9 (421ª19); cf. *Sense and the Sensible,* 4 (441ª3).

[4] *Enarr. in Ps.* (PL 37, 1955).

[5] *Glossa ordin.* (11, 266F); Bede (PL 91, 913).

from natural change, will be subject only to spiritual change by tangible qualities. Thus it was with the body of Adam, which could neither be burnt by fire, nor pierced by sword, although he had the sense of such things.

Reply Obj. 2. Taste, in so far as it is the perception of food, will not be in act; but perhaps it will be possible in so far as it is a judge of flavours in the way mentioned above Reply 1.

Reply Obj. 3. Some have considered smell to be merely a volatile evaporation. But this opinion cannot be true; which is evident from the fact that vultures hasten to a corpse on perceiving the odour from a very great distance, although it would be impossible for an evaporation to travel from the corpse to a place so remote, even though the whole corpse were to be dissolved into vapour. This is confirmed by the fact that sensible objects at an equal distance exercise their influence in all directions, so that smell changes the medium sometimes, and the instrument of sensation with a spiritual change, without any evaporation reaching the organ. That some evaporation should be necessary is due to the fact that smell in bodies is mixed with humidity; therefore it is necessary for dissolution to take place in order for the smell to be perceived. But in the glorified bodies odour will be in its ultimate perfection, being in no way hampered by humidity; therefore it will affect the organ with a spiritual change, like the odour of a volatile evaporation. Such will be the sense of smell in the saints, because it will not be hindered by any humidity, and it will know not only of the excellence of odours, as happens with us now on account of the very great humidity of the brain, but also of the minutest differences of odours.

Reply Obj. 4. In heaven there will be vocal praise (though indeed some think otherwise), and in the blessed it will affect the organ of hearing by a merely spiritual change. Nor will it be for the sake of learning whereby they may acquire knowledge, but for the sake of the perfection of the sense and for the sake of pleasure. How it is possible for the voice to give sound there, we have already stated.[1]

Reply Obj. 5. The intensity of light does not hinder the spiritual reception of the image of colour, so long as the pupil retains its diaphanous nature; thus it is evident that however much the air be filled with light, it can be the medium of sight, and the more it is illumined, the more clearly are objects seen through it,

[1] Thomas, *In Sent.*, dist. II, Q. 2, A. 2, Reply 5.

unless there be a fault through defective sight. The fact that the image of an object placed in opposition to a mirror directly opposite the sun's rays does not appear therein, is not due to the reception being hindered, but to the hindering of reflection, because for an image to appear in a mirror it must be thrown back by an opaque body, for which reason lead is affixed to the glass in a mirror. The sun's ray dispels this opacity so that no image can appear in the mirror. But the clarity of a glorified body does not destroy the diaphanous nature of the pupil, since glory does not destroy nature; and consequently the greatness of clarity in the pupil renders the sight keen rather than defective.

Reply Obj. 6. The more perfect the sense the less does it require to be changed in order to perceive its object. Now the smaller the angle at which the sight is affected by the visible object, the less is the organ altered. Hence it is that a stronger sight can see from a distance more than a weaker sight, because the greater the distance the smaller the angle at which a thing is seen. And since the sight of a glorified body will be most perfect it will be able to see by the very least alteration (of the organ), and consequently at a very much smaller angle than now, and therefore from a much greater distance.

QUESTION LXXXIII
Of the Subtlety of the Bodies of the Blessed

(In Six Articles)

We must now consider the subtlety of the bodies of the blessed. Under this head there are six points of inquiry: (1) Whether subtlety is a property of the glorified body? (2) Whether by reason of this subtlety it can be in the same place with another not glorified body? (3) Whether by a miracle two bodies can be in the same place? (4) Whether a glorified body can be in the same place with another glorified body? (5) Whether a glorified body necessarily requires a place equal to itself? (6) Whether a glorified body is palpable?

Article 1. *Whether Subtlety Is a Property of the Glorified Body?*

We proceed thus to the First Article: It would seem that subtlety is not a property of the glorified body.

Objection 1. For the properties of glory surpass the properties of nature, even as the clarity of glory surpasses the clarity of the sun, which is the greatest in nature. Accordingly if subtlety be a property of the glorified body, it would seem that the glorified body will be more subtle than anything which is subtle in nature, and thus it will be more subtle than the wind and the air, which was condemned by Gregory in the city of Constantinople, as he relates (*Moral.* xiv, 56).[1]

Obj. 2. Further, As heat and cold are simple qualities of bodies, that is, of the elements, so is subtlety. But heat and other qualities of the elements will not be intensified in the glorified bodies any more than they are now; in fact they will be more reduced to the mean. Neither, therefore, will subtlety be in them more than it is now.

Obj. 3. Further, Subtlety is in bodies as a result of scarcity of matter, and therefore bodies that have less matter within equal dimensions are said to be more subtle; as fire in comparison with air, and air as compared with water, and water as compared with earth. But there will be as much matter in the glorified bodies as there is now, nor will their dimensions be greater, as appears from what we said above (Q. LXXX, AA. 4, 5; Q. LXXXI, A. 2). Therefore they will not be more subtle then than now.

On the contrary, It is written (I Cor. 15. 44): *It is sown a corruptible body, it shall rise a spiritual,* that is, a spirit-like, *body.* But the subtlety of a spirit surpasses all bodily subtlety. Therefore the glorified bodies will be most subtle.

Further, The more subtle a body is the more exalted it is. But the glorified bodies will be most exalted. Therefore they will be most subtle.

I answer that, Subtlety takes its name from the power to penetrate. Hence it is said[2] that a subtle thing "fills all the parts and the parts of parts." Now that a body has the power of penetrating may happen through two causes. First, through smallness of quantity, especially in respect of depth and breadth, but not of length, because penetration regards depth, and therefore length is not an obstacle to penetration. Secondly, through paucity of matter, and so rarity is synonymous with subtlety, and since in rare bodies the form is more predominant over the matter, the term subtlety has been

transferred to those bodies which are most perfectly subject to their form, and are most fully perfected by them; thus we speak of subtlety in the sun and moon and like bodies, just as gold and similar things may be called subtle, when they are most perfectly complete in their specific being and power. And since incorporeal things lack quantity and matter, the term subtlety is applied to them, not only by reason of their substance, but also on account of their power. For just as a subtle thing is said to be penetrative, for the reason that it reaches to the inmost part of a thing, so is an intellect said to be subtle because it reaches to the insight of the intrinsic principles and the hidden natural properties of a thing. In like manner a person is said to have subtle sight, because he is able to perceive by sight things of the smallest size; and the same applies to the other senses. Accordingly people have differed by ascribing subtlety to the glorified bodies in different ways.

For certain heretics, as Augustine relates,[3] ascribed to them the subtlety whereby spiritual substances are said to be subtle, and they said that at the resurrection the body will be transformed into a spirit, and that for this reason the Apostle describes as being spiritual the bodies of those who rise again (I Cor. 15. 44). But this cannot be maintained. First, because a body cannot be changed into a spirit, since there is no community of matter between them, and Boëthius proves this (*De duab. Nat.* vi).[4] Secondly, because, if this were possible, and one's body were changed into a spirit, one would not rise again a man, for a man naturally consists of a soul and body. Thirdly, because if this were the Apostle's meaning, just as he speaks of spiritual bodies, so would he speak of natural (*animale*) bodies, as being changed into souls (*animam*): and this is clearly false.

Hence certain heretics said that the body will remain at the resurrection, but that it will be endowed with subtlety by means of rarefaction, so that human bodies in rising again will be like the air or the wind, as Gregory relates (*Moral.* xiv, 56).[5] But this again cannot be maintained, because our Lord had a palpable body after the Resurrection, as appears from the last chapter of Luke, and we must believe that His body was supremely subtle. Moreover the human body will rise again with flesh and bones, as did the body of our Lord, according to Luke 24. 39, *A spirit hath not flesh and*

---

[1] PL 75, 1077.
[2] Aristotle, *Generation and Corruption,* II, 2 (330ᵃ1).

[3] *City of God,* XIII, 22 (PL 41, 395).
[4] PL 64, 1350.   [5] PL 75, 1078.

bones *as you see Me to have,* and Job 19. 26, *In my flesh I shall see God,* my Saviour, and the nature of flesh and bone is incompatible with the aforesaid rarity.

Consequently another kind of subtlety must be assigned to glorified bodies, by saying that they are subtle on account of the most complete perfection of the body. But this completeness is explained by some in relation to the fifth, or heavenly, essence, which will be then predominant in them. This, however, is impossible, since first of all the fifth essence can in no way enter into the composition of a body, as we have shown above.[1] Secondly, because granted that it entered into the composition of the human body, it would be impossible to account for its having a greater predominance over the elemental nature then than now, unless either the amount of the heavenly nature in human bodies were increased (thus human bodies would not be of the same stature, unless perhaps elemental matter in man were decreased, which is inconsistent with the integrity of those who rise again), or unless elemental nature were endowed with the properties of the heavenly nature through the latter's dominion over the body, and in that case a natural power would be the cause of a property of glory, which seems absurd.

Hence others say that the aforesaid completeness by reason of which human bodies are said to be subtle will result from the dominion of the glorified soul (which is the form of the body) over the body, by reason of which dominion the glorified body is said to be spiritual, as being wholly subject to the spirit. The first subjection whereby the body is subject to the soul is to the effect of its participating in its specific being, in so far as it is subject to the soul as matter to form; and secondly it is subject to the soul in respect of the other operations of the soul, in so far as the soul is a principle of movement. Consequently the first reason for spirituality in the body is subtlety, and, after that, agility and the other properties of a glorified body. Hence the Apostle, as the masters expound,[2] in speaking of spirituality indicates subtlety. Hence Gregory says (*Moral.* xiv, 56)[3] that the glorified body "is said to be subtle as a result of a spiritual power."

This suffices for the *Replies to the Objections* which refer to the subtlety of rarefaction.

---

[1] *In Sent.,* d. XVII, Q. III, A. I.
[2] Cf. Albert, *In Sent.,* IV, d. XLIV, A. 23 (BO XXX, 574).
[3] PL 75, 1077.

ARTICLE 2. *Whether By Reason of This Subtlety a Glorified Body Is Able To Be in the Same Place With Another Body Not Glorified?*

We proceed thus to the Second Article: It would seem that by reason of this subtlety a body is able to be in the same place with another body not glorified.

Objection 1. For according to Philip. 3. 21, He *will reform the body of our lowness made like to the body of His glory.* Now the body of Christ was able to be in the same place with another body, as appears from the fact that after His Resurrection He went in to His disciples, the doors being shut (John 20. 19, 26). Therefore also the glorified bodies by reason of their subtlety will be able to be in the same place with other bodies not glorified.

Obj. 2. Further, Glorified bodies will be superior to all other bodies. Yet by reason of their superiority certain bodies, namely the solar rays, are able now to occupy the same place together with other bodies. Much more therefore is this befitting glorified bodies.

Obj. 3. Further, A heavenly body cannot be severed, at least as regards the substance of the spheres; hence it is written (Job 37. 18) that *the heavens . . . are most strong, as if they were of molten brass.* If then the subtlety of a glorified body will not enable it to be in the same place together with another body, it will never be able to ascend to the empyrean,[4] and this is erroneous.

Obj. 4. Further, A body which is unable to be in the same place with another body can be hindered in its movement or even surrounded by others standing in its way. But this cannot happen to glorified bodies. Therefore they will be able to be together in the same place with other bodies.

Obj. 5. Further, As point is to point, so is line to line, surface to surface, and body to body. Now two points can be coincident, as in the case of two lines touching one another, and two lines when two surfaces are in contact with one another, and two surfaces when two bodies touch one another, because contiguous things are "those whose boundaries coincide."[5] Therefore it is not against the nature of a body to be in the same place together with another body. Now whatever excellence is possible to the na-

---

[4] The empyrean was the highest of the concentric spheres or heavens, and was identified by Christian writers with the abode of God. Cf. Part I, Q. LVI, A. 3.
[5] Aristotle, *Physics,* VI, I (231ª22); cf. V, 3 (226ᵇ23).

ture of a body will all be bestowed on the glorified body. Therefore a glorified body, by reason of its subtlety, will be able to be in the same place together with another body.

On the contrary, Boëthius says (*De Trin.* 1):[1] "Difference of accidents makes distinction in number. For three men differ not in genus, nor in species, but in their accidents. If we were to remove absolutely every accident from them, still each one has a different place; and it is quite inconceivable that they should all occupy the same place." Therefore if we suppose two bodies to occupy the same place, there will be but one body numerically.

Further, Glorified bodies have more congruity with place than do angelic spirits. But angelic spirits, according to some, could not be distinguished numerically unless they were in different places; for the same reason they held that they must be in a place, and that they could not have been created before the world. Much more therefore must they say that no two bodies can be in the same place.

I answer that, It cannot be maintained that a glorified body, by reason of its subtlety, is able to be in the same place with another body, unless the obstacle to its being now in the same place with another body be removed by that subtlety. Some say that in the present state this obstacle is its grossness by virtue of which it is able to occupy a place, and that this grossness is removed by the gift of subtlety. But there are two reasons why this cannot be maintained. First because the grossness which the gift of subtlety removes is a kind of defect, for instance a lack of order of matter in not being perfectly subject to its form. For all that pertains to the integrity of the body will rise again in the body, both as regards the matter and as regards the form. And the fact that a body is able to fill a place belongs to it by reason of that which pertains to its integrity, and not on account of any defect of nature. For since fulness is opposed to vacancy, that alone does not fill a place, which being put in a place, nevertheless leaves a place vacant. Now a vacuum is defined by the Philosopher[2] as being "a place not filled by a sensible body." And a body is said to be sensible by reason of its matter, form, and natural accidents, all of which pertain to the integrity of nature. It is also plain that the glorified body will be sensible even to touch, as evidenced by the body of our Lord (Luke 24. 39), nor will it lack matter, or form, or natural

accidents, namely heat, cold, and so forth. Hence it is evident that the glorified body, the gift of subtlety notwithstanding, will fill a place, for it would seem madness to say that the place in which there will be a glorified body will be empty. Secondly their argument does not avail because to hinder the co-existence of a body in the same place is more than to fill a place. For if we suppose dimensions separate from matter, those dimensions do not fill a place. Hence some who held the possibility of a vacuum said that a vacuum is a place in which such dimensions exist apart from a sensible body, and yet those dimensions hinder another body from being together with them in the same place. This is made clear by the Philosopher,[3] where he considers it impossible for a mathematical body, which is nothing but separate dimensions, to be together with another natural sensible body. Consequently, granted that the subtlety of a glorified body hindered it from filling a place, nevertheless it would not follow that for this reason it is able to be in the same place with another body, since the removal of the lesser does not involve the removal of the greater.

Accordingly it seems that the obstacle to our body's being now in the same place with another body can in no way be removed by the gift of subtlety. For nothing can prevent a body from occupying the same place together with another body, except something in it that requires a different place, since nothing is an obstacle to identity save that which is a cause of distinction. Now this distinction of place is not required by any quality of the body, because a body does not demand a place by reason of its quality; and so if we remove from a body the fact of its being hot or cold, heavy or light, it still retains the necessity of the aforesaid distinction, as the Philosopher makes clear,[4] and as is self-evident. In like manner neither can matter cause the necessity of this distinction, because matter does not occupy a place except through its dimensive quantity. Again neither does form occupy a place, unless it have a place through its matter.

It remains therefore that the necessity for two bodies occupying each a distinct place results from the nature of dimensive quantity, to which a place is essentially befitting. For this forms part of its definition, since dimensive quantity is quantity occupying a place. Hence it is that if we remove all else in a thing

[1] PL 64, 1249.
[2] *Physics*, IV, 6, 7 (213ª27; 214ª6).

[3] *Ibid.*, IV, 1, 8 (209ª6; 216ᵇ6; *Metaphysics*, III, 2 (998ª13).   [4] *Physics, loc. cit.*

from it, the necessity of this distinction is found in its dimensive quantity alone. Thus take the example of a separate line, supposing there to be two such lines, or two parts of one line, they must occupy distinct places, for otherwise one line added to another would not make something greater, and this is against common sense (*communes conceptiones*). The same applies to surfaces and mathematical bodies. And since matter demands place, through being the subject of dimension, the above necessity results in placed matter, so that just as it is impossible for there to be two lines, or two parts of a line, unless they occupy distinct places, so is it impossible for there to be two matters, or two parts of matter, without there be distinction of place. And since distinction of matter is the principle of the distinction between individuals, it follows that, as Boëthius says (*De Trin.* 1),[1] "we cannot possibly conceive two bodies occupying one place," so that this distinction of individuals requires this difference of accidents. Now subtlety does not deprive the glorified body of its dimension; therefore it in no way removes from it the above necessity of occupying a distinct place from another body. Therefore the subtlety of a glorified body will not enable it to be in the same place together with another body, but it will be possible for it to be together with another body by the operation of the Divine power, even as the body of Peter had the power whereby the sick were healed at the passing of Peter's shadow (Acts 5. 15) not through any inherent property, but by the power of God for the upbuilding of the faith. Thus will the Divine power make it possible for a glorified body to be in the same place together with another body for the perfection of glory.

Reply Obj. 1. That Christ's body was able to be together with another body in the same place was not due to its subtlety, but resulted from the power of His Godhead after His resurrection, even as in His birth. Hence Gregory says (*Hom.* xxvi *in Ev.*):[2] "The same body went into His disciples the doors being shut, which to human eyes came from the closed womb of the Virgin at His birth." Therefore there is no reason why this should be befitting to glorified bodies on account of their subtlety.

Reply Obj. 2. Light is not a body as we have said above (ii. *Sent.*, Q. XIII, A. 3; Part I, Q. LXVII, A. 2). Hence the objection proceeds on a false supposition.

Reply Obj. 3. The glorified body will pass

through the heavenly spheres without severing them, not by virtue of its subtlety, but by the Divine power, which will assist them in all things at will.

Reply Obj. 4. From the fact that God will come to the aid of the blessed at will in whatever they desire, it follows that they cannot be surrounded or imprisoned.

Reply Obj. 5. As stated in the *Physics*,[3] "place is not befitting a point"; hence if it be said to be in a place, this is only accidental, because the body of which it is a term is in a place. And just as the whole place corresponds to the whole body, so the term of the place corresponds to the term of the body. But it happens that two places have one term, even as two lines terminate in one point. And consequently though two bodies must be in distinct places, yet the same term of two places corresponds to the two terms of the two bodies. It is in this sense that the bounds of contiguous bodies are said to coincide.

ARTICLE 3. *Whether It Is Possible, By a Miracle, for Two Bodies To Be in the Same Place?*

We proceed thus to the Third Article: It would seem that not even by a miracle is it possible for two bodies to be in the same place.

Objection 1. For it is not possible that, by a miracle, two bodies be at once two and one, since this would imply that contradictions are true at the same time. But if we suppose two bodies to be in the same place, it would follow that those two bodies are one. Therefore this cannot be done by a miracle. The minor is proved thus. Suppose two bodies A and B to be in the same place. The dimensions of A will either be the same as the dimensions of the place, or they will differ from them. If they differ, then some of the dimensions will be separate, which is impossible, since the dimensions that are within the bounds of a place are not in a subject unless they are in a placed body. If they are the same, then for the same reason the dimensions of B will be the same as the dimensions of the place. Now things that are the same with one and the same thing are the same with one another. Therefore the dimensions of A and B are the same. But two bodies cannot have identical dimensions just as they cannot have the same whiteness. Therefore A and B are one body and yet they were two. Therefore they are at the same time one and two.

[1] PL 64, 1249.   [2] PL 76, 1197.   [3] Aristotle, IV, 5 (212b24).

Obj. 2. Further, A thing cannot be done miraculously either against the common principles, for instance that the part is not less than the whole, since what is contrary to common principles implies a direct contradiction; or contrary to the conclusions of geometry which are infallible deductions from common principles, —for instance that the three angles of a triangle should not be equal to two right angles. In like manner nothing can be done to a line that is contrary to the definition of a line, because to sever the definition from the defined is to make two contradictories true at the same time. Now it is contrary both to the conclusions of geometry and to the definition of a line for two bodies to be in the same place. Therefore this cannot be done by a miracle.

The minor is proved as follows: It is a conclusion of geometry that two circles touch one another only at a point. Now if two circular bodies were in the same place, the two circles described in them would touch one another as a whole. Again it is contrary to the definition of a line that there be more than one straight line between two points, yet this would be the case were two bodies in the same place, since between two given points in the various surfaces of the place, there would be two straight lines corresponding to the two bodies in that place.

Obj. 3. Further, It would seem impossible that by a miracle a body which is enclosed within another should not be in a place, for then it would have a common and not a proper place, and this is impossible. Yet this would follow if two bodies were in the same place. Therefore this cannot be done by a miracle.

The minor is proved thus. Supposing two bodies to be in the same place, the one being greater than the other as to every dimension, the lesser body will be enclosed in the greater, and the place occupied by the greater body will be its common place; while it will have no proper place, because no given surface of the body will contain it, and this is essential to place. Therefore it will not have a proper place.

Obj. 4. Further, Place corresponds in proportion to the thing placed. Now it can never happen by a miracle that the same body is at the same time in different places, except by some kind of change, as in the Sacrament of the Altar. Therefore it can in no way happen by a miracle that two bodies be together in the same place.

On the contrary, The Blessed Virgin gave birth to her Son by a miracle. Now in this hallowed birth it was necessary for two bodies to be together in the same place, because the body of her child when coming forth did not break through the enclosure of her virginal purity. Therefore it is possible for two bodies to be miraculously together in the same place.

Further, This may again be proved from the fact that our Lord went in to His disciples, the doors being shut (John 20. 19, 26).

I answer that, As shown above (A. 2) the reason why two bodies must be in two places is that distinction in matter requires distinction in place. Therefore we observe that when two bodies merge into one, each loses its distinct being, and one indistinct being accrues to the two combined, as in the case of mixtures. Hence it is impossible for two bodies to remain two and yet be together unless each retain its distinct being which it had before, according as each of them was a being undivided in itself and distinct from others. Now this distinct being depends on the essential principles of a thing as on its proximate causes, but on God as on the first cause. And since the first cause can preserve a thing in being, though the second causes be done away, as appears from the first proposition of *De Causis*,[1] therefore by God's power and by that alone it is possible for an accident to be without substance as in the Sacrament of the Altar. Likewise by the power of God, and by that alone, it is possible for a body to retain its distinct being from that of another body, although its matter be not distinct as to place from the matter of the other body; and thus it is possible by a miracle for two bodies to be together in the same place.

Reply Obj. 1. This argument is sophistical because it is based on a false supposition, or begs the question. For it supposes the existence, between two opposite surfaces of a place, of a dimension proper to the place, with which dimension a dimension of the body put in occupation of the place would have to be identified, because it would then follow that the dimensions of two bodies occupying a place would become one dimension, if each of them were identified with the dimension of the place. But this supposition is false, because if it were true whenever a body acquires a new place, it would follow that a change takes place in the dimensions of the place or of the thing placed, since it is impossible for two things to become newly one unless one of them is changed.

But if, as in the case in truth, no other dimensions belong to a place than those of the thing occupying the place, it is clear that the

[1] Sect. 1 (BA 1633).

argument proves nothing, but begs the question, because according to this nothing else has been said but that the dimensions of a thing placed are the same as the dimensions of the place; excepting that the dimensions of the thing placed are contained within the bounds of the place, and that the distance between the bounds of a place is commensurate with the distance between the bounds of the thing placed, just as the former would be distant by their own dimensions if they had them. Thus that the dimensions of two bodies be the dimensions of one place is nothing else than that two bodies be in the same place, which is the chief question at issue.

Reply Obj. 2. Granted that by a miracle two bodies be together in the same place, nothing follows either against common principles, or against the definition of a line, or against any conclusions of geometry. For, as stated above (A. 2), dimensive quantity differs from all other accidents in that it has a special reason of individuality and distinction, namely on account of the placing of the parts, besides the reason of individuality and distinction which is common to it and all other accidents, arising namely from the matter which is its subject. Thus then one line may be understood as being distinct from another, either because it is in another subject (in which case we are considering a material line), or because it is placed at a distance from another (in which case we are considering a mathematical line, which is understood apart from matter). Accordingly if we remove matter, there can be no distinction between lines save in respect of a different placing, and in like manner neither can there be a distinction of points, nor of surfaces, nor of any dimensions whatever. Consequently geometry cannot suppose one line to be added to another, as being distinct from it unless it is distinct as to place. But supposing by a Divine miracle a distinction of subject without a distinction of place, we can understand a distinction of lines; and these are not distant from one another in place, on account of the distinction of subjects.

Again we can understand a difference of points, and thus different lines described on two bodies that are in the same place are drawn from different points to different points; for the point that we take is not a point fixed in the place, but in the placed body, because a line is not said to be drawn otherwise than from a point which is its term. In like manner the two circles described in two spherical bodies that

occupy the same place are two, not on account of the difference of place, for otherwise they could not touch one another as a whole, but on account of the distinction of subjects, and thus while wholly touching one another they still remain two. Even so a circle described by a placed spherical body touches, as a whole, the other circle described by the locating body.

Reply Obj. 3. God could make a body not to be in a place; and yet supposing this, it would not follow that a certain body is not in a place, because the greater body is the place of the lesser body, by reason of its surface which is described by contact with the terms of the lesser body.

Reply Obj. 4. It is impossible for one body to be miraculously in two places locally (for Christ's body is not locally on the altar), although it is possible by a miracle for two bodies to be in the same place. Because to be in several places at once is incompatible with the individual, by reason of its having being undivided in itself, for it would follow that it is divided as to place. On the other hand, to be in the same place with another body is incompatible with the individual as distinct from anything else. Now the nature of unity is perfected in indivision,[1] while distinction from others is a result of the nature of unity. Therefore that one same body be locally in several places at once implies a contradiction, even as for a man to lack reason, while for two bodies to be in the same place does not imply a contradiction, as explained above. Hence the comparison fails.

ARTICLE 4. *Whether One Glorified Body Can Be in the Same Place Together With Another Glorified Body?*

We proceed thus to the Fourth Article: It would seem that a glorified body can be in the same place together with another glorified body.

Objection 1. Because where there is greater subtlety there is less resistance. If then a glorified body is more subtle than a non-glorified body, it will offer less resistance to a glorified body, and so if a glorified body can be in the same place with a non-glorified body, much more can it with a glorified body.

Obj. 2. Further, Even as a glorified body will be more subtle than a non-glorified body, so will one glorified body be more subtle than another. Therefore if a glorified body can be in the same place with a non-glorified body, a more subtle glorified body can be in the same place with a less subtle glorified body.

[1] Aristotle, *Metaphysics*, v, 6 (1016ᵇ3).

Obj. 3. Further, The body of heaven is subtle, and will then be glorified. Now the glorified body of a saint will be able to be in the same place with the body of heaven, since the saints will be able at will to travel to and from earth. Therefore two glorified bodies will be able to occupy the same place.

On the contrary, The glorified bodies will be spiritual, that is like spirits in a certain respect. Now two spirits cannot be in the same place, although a body and a spirit can be in the same place, as stated above (i. *Sent.* d. 37, Q. III, A. 3; Part I, Q. LII, A. 3). Therefore neither will two glorified bodies be able to be in the same place.

Further, If two bodies occupy the same place, one is penetrated by the other. But to be penetrated is a mark of imperfection which will be altogether absent from the glorified bodies. Therefore it will be impossible for two glorified bodies to be in the same place.

I answer that, The property of a glorified body does not make it able to be in the same place with another glorified body, nor again to be in the same place with a non-glorified body. But it would be possible by the Divine power for two glorified bodies or two non-glorified bodies to be in the same place, even as a glorified body with a non-glorified body. Nevertheless it is not fitting for a glorified body to be in the same place with another glorified body, both because a becoming order will be observed in them, which demands distinction, and because one glorified body will not be in the way of another. Consequently two glorified bodies will never be in the same place.

Reply Obj. 1. This argument supposes that a glorified body is able by reason of its subtlety to be in the same place with another body, and this is not true.

The same answer applies to the *Second Objection.*

Reply Obj. 3. The body of heaven and the other bodies will be said equivocally to be glorified, in so far as they will have a certain share in glory, and not as though it were becoming for them to have the gifts of glorified human bodies.

ARTICLE 5. *Whether By Virtue of Its Subtlety a Glorified Body Will No Longer Need To Be in a Place Equal to Itself?*

We proceed thus to the Fifth Article: It would seem that by virtue of its subtlety a glorified body will no longer need to be in a place equal to itself.

Objection 1. For the glorified bodies will be made like to the body of Christ according to Phil. 3. 21. Now Christ's body is not bound by this necessity of being in a place equal to itself; therefore it is contained whole under the small or great dimensions of a consecrated host. Therefore the same will be true of the glorified bodies.

Obj. 2. Further, The Philosopher proves[1] that two bodies are not in the same place, because it would follow that the greatest body would occupy the smallest place, since its various parts could be in the same part of the place, for it makes no difference whether two bodies or however many be in the same place. Now a glorified body will be in the same place with another body, as is commonly admitted. Therefore it will be possible for it to be in any place however small.

Obj. 3. Further, Even as a body is seen by reason of its colour, so is it measured by reason of its quantity. Now the glorified body will be so subject to the spirit that it will be able at will to be seen, and not seen, especially by a non-glorified eye, as evidenced in the case of Christ. Therefore its quantity will be so subject to the spirit's will that it will be able to be in a little or great place, and to have a little or great quantity at will.

On the contrary, The Philosopher says[2] that whatever is in a place is in a place equal to itself. Now the glorified body will be in a place. Therefore it will occupy a place equal to itself.

Further, The dimensions of a place and of that which is in that place are the same, as shown in the *Physics.*[3] Therefore if the place were larger than that which is in the place the same thing would be greater and smaller than itself, which is absurd.

I answer that, A body is not related to place except through the medium of its proper dimensions, in respect of which a located body is confined through contact with the locating body. Hence it is not possible for a body to occupy a place smaller than its quantity, unless its proper quantity be made in some way less than itself, and this can only be understood in two ways. First, by a variation in quantity in respect of the same matter, so that in fact the matter which at first is subject to a greater quantity is afterwards subject to a lesser. Some have held this to be the case with the glorified bodies, saying that quantity is subject to them

---

[1] *Physics,* IV, 6 (213b6).
[2] *Ibid.,* IV, 4 (210b34).
[3] Aristotle, IV, 8 (216b8).

at will, so that at their will they are able to have a great quantity, and when they will a small quantity. But this is impossible, because no movement affecting that which is intrinsic to a thing is possible without passion to the detriment of its substance. Hence in incorruptible, that is heavenly, bodies, there is only local movement, which is not according to something intrinsic. Thus it is clear that change of quantity in respect of matter would be incompatible with the impassibility and incorruptibility of a glorified body. Moreover, it would follow that a glorified body would be sometimes rarer and sometimes denser, because since it cannot be deprived of any of its matter, sometimes the same matter would be under great dimensions and sometimes under small dimensions, and thus it would be rarefied and densified, which is impossible. Secondly, that the quantity of a glorified body become smaller than itself may be understood by a variation of place, in such a way, that is, that the parts of a glorified body insinuate themselves into one another, so that it is reduced in quantity however small it may become. And some have held this to be the case, saying that by reason of its subtlety a glorified body will be able to be in the same place with a non-glorified body, and that in like manner its parts can be one within the other, so much so that a whole glorified body will be able to pass through the minutest opening in another body, and thus they explain how Christ's body came out of the Virgin's womb; and how it went into His disciples, the doors being shut. But this is impossible, both because the glorified body will not be able, by reason of its subtlety, to be in the same place with another body, and because, even if it were able to be in the same place with another body, this would not be possible if the other were a glorified body, as many say; and again because this would be inconsistent with the right disposition of the human body, which requires the parts to be in a certain fixed place and at a certain fixed distance from one another. Therefore this will never happen, not even by a miracle. Consequently we must say that the glorified body will always be in a place equal to itself.

Reply Obj. 1. Christ's body is not locally in the Sacrament of the Altar, as stated above (iv. *Sent.* d. 10, Q. 1, A. 1, reply 5; Part III, Q. LXXVI, A. 5).

Reply Obj. 2. The Philosopher's argument is that for the same reason one part might permeate another. But this permeation of the parts of a glorified body into one another is impos-

sible, as stated above. Therefore the objection does not prove.

Reply Obj. 3. A body is seen because it acts on the sight; but that it does or does not act on the sight causes no change in the body. Hence it is not unfitting that it can be seen when it will, and not seen when it will. On the other hand, being in a place is not an action proceeding from a body by reason of its quantity, as being seen is by reason of its colour. Consequently the comparison fails.

ARTICLE 6. *Whether the Glorified Body, By Reason of Its Subtlety, Will Be Impalpable?*

We proceed thus to the Sixth Article: It would seem that the glorified body, by reason of its subtlety, is impalpable.

Objection 1. For Gregory says (*Hom.* xxvi *in Ev.*):[1] "What is palpable must be corruptible." But the glorified body is incorruptible. Therefore it is impalpable.

Obj. 2. Further, Whatever is palpable resists one who handles it. But that which can be in the same place with another does not resist it. Since then a glorified body can be in the same place with another body, it will not be palpable.

Obj. 3. Further, Every palpable body is tangible. Now every tangible body has tangible qualities in excess of the qualities of the one touching it. Since then in the glorified bodies the tangible qualities are not in excess but are reduced to a supreme degree of equality, it would seem that they are impalpable.

On the contrary, Our Lord rose again with a glorified body; and yet His body was palpable, as appears from Luke 24. 39: *Handle, and see; for a spirit hath not flesh and bones.* Therefore the glorified bodies also will be palpable.

Further, This is the heresy of Eutychius, Bishop of Constantinople,[2] as Gregory states (*Moral.* xiv, 56),[3] for he said that "in the glory of the resurrection our bodies will be impalpable."

I answer that, Every palpable body is tangible, but not conversely. For every body is tangible that has qualities whereby the sense of touch has a natural aptitude to be affected; and so air, fire, and the like are tangible bodies, but a palpable body, in addition to this, resists the touch; therefore the air which never resists that which passes through it, and is most easily pierced, is tangible indeed but not palpable.

[1] PL 76, 1198.
[2] Cf. Part III, Q. LIV, A. 2.
[3] PL 75, 1078.

Accordingly it is clear that a body is said to be palpable for two reasons, namely on account of its tangible qualities, and on account of its resisting that which touches it, so as to hinder it from piercing it. And since the tangible qualities are hot and cold and so forth, which are not found save in heavy and light bodies, which through being contrary to one another are therefore corruptible, it follows that the heavenly bodies, which by their nature are incorruptible, are sensible to the sight but not tangible, and therefore neither are they palpable. This is what Gregory means when he says (*loc. cit.* obj. 1) that "whatever is palpable must be corruptible." Accordingly the glorified body has by its nature those qualities which have a natural aptitude to affect the touch, and yet since the body is altogether subject to the spirit, it is in its power thereby to affect or not to affect the touch. In like manner it is able by its nature to resist any other passing body, so that the latter cannot be in the same place together with it, although, according to its pleasure, it may happen by the Divine power that it occupy the same place with another body, and thus offer no resistance to a passing body. Therefore according to its nature the glorified body is palpable, but it is possible for it to be impalpable to a non-glorified body by a supernatural power. Hence Gregory says (*loc. cit.*) that "our Lord offered His flesh to be handled, which He had brought in through the closed doors, so as to afford a complete proof that after His resurrection His body was unchanged in nature though changed in glory."

Reply Obj. 1. The incorruptibility of a glorified body does not result from the nature of its component parts; and it is on account of that nature that whatever is palpable is corruptible, as stated above.[1] Hence the argument does not prove.

Reply Obj. 2. Although in a way it is possible for a glorified body to be in the same place with another body, nevertheless the glorified body has it in its power to resist at will any one touching it, and thus it is palpable.

Reply Obj. 3. In the glorified bodies the tangible qualities are not reduced to the real mean that is measured according to equal distance from the extremes, but to the proportionate mean, according as is most becoming to the human complexion in each part. Therefore the touch of those bodies will be most delightful, because a power always delights in a becoming object, and is grieved by excess.

[1] Cf. also Q. LXXXII, A. 1.

QUESTION LXXXIV
OF THE AGILITY OF THE BODIES
OF THE BLESSED
(*In Three Articles*)

WE must now consider the agility of the bodies of the blessed in the resurrection. Under this head there are three points of inquiry: (1) Whether the glorified bodies will be agile? (2) Whether they will move? (3) Whether they will move instantaneously?

ARTICLE 1. *Whether the Glorified Bodies Will Be Agile?*

We proceed thus to the First Article: It would seem that the glorified bodies will not be agile.

Objection 1. For that which is agile by itself needs not to be carried in order to move. But the glorified bodies will, after the resurrection, be taken up by the angels (according to a gloss)[2] in the clouds *to meet Christ, into the air* (I Thess. 4. 16). Therefore the glorified bodies will not be agile.

Obj. 2. Further, No body that moves with labour and pain can be said to be agile. Yet the glorified bodies will move thus, since the principle of their movement, namely the soul, moves them counter to their nature, for otherwise they would always move in the same direction. Therefore they are not agile.

Obj. 3. Further, Of all the animal operations sense surpasses movement in nobility and priority. Yet no property is ascribed to glorified bodies as perfecting them in sensation. Therefore neither should agility be ascribed to them as perfecting them in movement.

Obj. 4. Further, Nature gives different animals instruments of different disposition according to their different powers; hence she does not give instruments of the same disposition to slow as to fleet animals. Now God's works are much more orderly than those of nature. Since then the glorified body's members will have the same disposition, shape and quantity as they now have, it would seem that it will have no agility other than it has now.

On the contrary, It is written (I Cor. 15. 43): *It is sown in weakness, it shall rise in power,* that is, according to a gloss,[3] "movable and living." But mobility can only signify agility in movement. Therefore the glorified bodies will be agile.

[2] *Glossa interl.* (VI, 112r); *Glossa* Lombardi (PL 192, 304).
[3] *Glossa interl.* (VI, 59v); *Glossa* Lombardi (PL 191, 1687).

Further, Slowness of movement would seem especially inconsistent with the nature of a spirit. But the glorified bodies will be most spiritual according to I Cor. 15. 44. Therefore they will be agile.

I answer that, The glorified body will be altogether subject to the glorified soul, so that not only will there be nothing in it to resist the will of the spirit, for it was even so in the case of Adam's body, but also from the glorified soul there will flow into the body a certain perfection, by which it will become adapted to that subjection, and this perfection is called "the gift" of the glorified body. Now the soul is united to body not only as its form, but also as its mover; and in both ways the glorified body has to be most perfectly subject to the glorified soul. Therefore even as by the gift of subtlety the body is wholly subject to the soul as its form, from which it derives its specific being, so by the gift of agility it is subject to the soul as its mover, so that it is prompt and apt to obey the spirit in all the movements and actions of the soul.

Some, however, ascribe the cause of this agility to the fifth, that is the heavenly essence, which will then be predominant in the glorified bodies. But of this we have frequently observed that it does not seem probable (Q. LXXXII, A. 1; Q. LXXXIII, A. 1). Therefore it is better to ascribe it to the soul, from which glory flows to the body.

Reply Obj. 1. Glorified bodies are said to be borne by the angels and also on the clouds, not as though they needed them, but in order to signify the reverence which both angels and all creatures will show them.

Reply Obj. 2. The more the power of the moving soul dominates over the body, the less is the labour of movement, even though it be counter to the body's nature. Hence those in whom the moving power is stronger, and those who through exercise have the body more adapted to obey the moving spirit, labour less in being moved. And since, after the resurrection, the soul will perfectly dominate the body, both on account of the perfection of its own power, and on account of the glorified body's aptitude resulting from the outflow of glory which it receives from the soul, there will be no labour in the saints' movements, and thus it may be said that the bodies of the saints will be agile.

Reply Obj. 3. By the gift of agility the glorified body will be rendered apt not only for local movement but also for sensation, and for the execution of all the other operations of the soul.

Reply Obj. 4. Even as nature gives to fleeter animals instruments of a different disposition in shape and quantity, so God will give to the bodies of the saints a disposition other than that which they have now, not indeed in shape and quantity, but in that property of glory which is called agility.

ARTICLE 2. *Whether the Saints Will Never Use Their Agility for the Purpose of Movement?*

We proceed thus to the Second Article: It would seem that the saints will never use their agility for the purpose of movement.

Objection 1. For, according to the Philosopher,[1] "movement is the act of the imperfect." But there will be no imperfection in glorified bodies. Neither therefore will there be any movement.

Obj. 2. Further, All movement is on account of some need, because whatever is in motion is moved for the sake of obtaining some end. But glorified bodies will have no need, since as Augustine says (*De Spiritu et Anima,* lxiii),[2] "all thou willest will be there, and nothing that thou willest not." Therefore they will not move.

Obj. 3. Further, According to the Philosopher (*De Cælo et Mundo,* ii),[3] that which shares the Divine goodness without movement shares it more excellently than that which shares it with movement. Now the glorified body shares the Divine goodness more excellently than any other body. Since then certain bodies like the heavenly bodies, will remain altogether without movement, it seems that much more will human bodies remain so.

Obj. 4. Further, Augustine says (*De Vera Relig.* xii)[4] that the soul being established in God will in consequence establish its body. Now the soul will be so established in God, that in no way will it move away from Him. Therefore in the body there will be no movement caused by the soul.

Obj. 5. Further, The more noble a body is, the more noble a place is due to it; hence Christ's body which is the most exalted of all has the highest place of all, according to Heb. 7. 26, *Made higher than the heavens,* where a gloss says,[5] "in place and dignity." And again each glorified body will, in like manner, have a place befitting it according to the measure of

[1] *Physics,* III, 2 (201ᵇ31).
[2] Alcher of Clairvaux, *De Spir. et An.,* chap. 64 (PL 40, 828); cf. Augustine, *De Trin.,* XIII, 7 (PL 42, 1020).
[3] *Heavens,* II, 12 (292ᵇ7).   [4] PL 34, 132.
[5] *Glossa interl.* on Heb. 1.3 (VI, 134r); *Glossa* Lombardi on Heb. 1.3 (PL 192, 407).

its dignity. Now a fitting place is one of the conditions pertaining to glory. Since then after the resurrection the glory of the saints will never vary, neither by increase nor by decrease, because they will then have reached the final term of all, it would seem that their bodies will never leave the place assigned to them, and consequently will not be moved.

On the contrary, It is written (Isa. 40. 31): *They shall run and not be weary, they shall walk and not faint;* and (Wisd. 3. 7): *(The just) shall run to and fro like sparks among the reeds.* Therefore there will be some movement in glorified bodies.

I answer that, It is necessary to suppose that the glorified bodies are moved sometimes, since even Christ's body was moved in His ascension, and likewise the bodies of the saints, which will arise from the earth, will ascend to the empyrean. But even after they have climbed the heavens, it is likely that they will sometimes move according as it pleases them, so that by actually putting into practice that which is in their power, they may show forth the excellence of Divine wisdom, and that furthermore their vision may be refreshed by the beauty of the variety of creatures, in which God's wisdom will shine forth with great evidence; for sense can only perceive that which is present, although glorified bodies can perceive from a greater distance than non-glorified bodies. And yet movement will in no way diminish their happiness which consists in seeing God, for He will be everywhere present to them; thus Gregory says of the angels (*Hom.* xxxiv *in Ev.*)[1] that "wherever they are sent their course lies in God."

Reply Obj. 1. Local movement changes nothing that is intrinsic to a thing, but only that which is without, namely place. Hence that which is moved locally is perfect as to those things which are within,[2] although it has an imperfection as to place, because while it is in one place it is in potency with regard to another place, since it cannot be in several places at the same time, for this belongs to God alone. But this defect is not inconsistent with the perfection of glory, as neither is the defect whereby a creature is formed from nothing. Hence such defects will remain in glorified bodies.

Reply Obj. 2. A person is said to need a thing in two ways, namely absolutely and relatively. One needs absolutely that without which one cannot retain one's being or one's perfection, and thus movement in glorified bodies will not

be on account of a need, because their happiness will suffice them for all such things. But we need a thing relatively when without it some end we have in view cannot be obtained by us, or not so well, or not in some particular way. It is thus that movement will be in the blessed on account of need, for they will be unable to show forth their moving power in actual practise unless they are in motion, since nothing prevents a need of this kind being in glorified bodies.

Reply Obj. 3. This argument would prove if the glorified body were unable even without movement to share the Divine goodness much more perfectly than the heavenly bodies, which is untrue. Hence glorified bodies will be moved, not in order to gain a perfect participation in the Divine goodness (since they have this through glory), but in order to show the soul's power. On the other hand, the movement of the heavenly bodies could not show their power except the power they have in moving lower bodies to generation and corruption, which is not becoming to that state. Hence the argument does not prove.

Reply Obj. 4. Local movement takes nothing away from the stability of the soul that is established in God, since it does not affect that which is intrinsic to a thing, as stated above (REPLY 1).

Reply Obj. 5. The fitting place assigned to each glorified body according to the degree of its dignity belongs to the accidental reward. Nor does it follow that this reward is diminished whenever the body is outside its place, because that place pertains to reward not as actually containing the body located there (since nothing flows from it into the glorified body, but rather does it receive splendour from the glorified body), but as being due to merits. Therefore, though out of that place, they will still continue to rejoice in it.

ARTICLE 3. *Whether the Movement of the Saints Will Be Instantaneous?*

We proceed thus to the Third Article: It would seem that the movement of the saints will be instantaneous.

Objection 1. For Augustine says[3] that "wherever the spirit wills there will the body be." Now the movement of the will, according to which the spirit wishes to be anywhere, is instantaneous. Therefore the body's movement will be instantaneous.

Obj. 2. Further, The Philosopher[4] proves

---

[1] PL 76, 1255.   [2] Aristotle, *Physics*, VIII, 7 (261^{a}20).

[3] *City of God*, XXII, 30 (PL 41, 801).

[4] *Physics* IV, 8 (215^{b}19).

that there is no movement through a vacuum, because it would follow that something moves instantaneously, since a vacuum offers no resistance whatever to a thing that is in motion, whereas the plenum offers resistance; and so there would be no proportion between the speed of movement in a vacuum and that of movement in a plenum, since the ratio of movements in point of speed is as the ratio of the resistance offered by the medium. Now the velocities of any two movements that take place in time must be proportional, since any one space of time is proportional to any other. But in like manner no full place can resist a glorified body since this can be in the same place with another body, no matter how this may occur; even as neither can a vacuum resist a body. Therefore if it moves at all, it moves instantaneously.

Obj. 3. Further, The power of a glorified soul surpasses the power of a non-glorified soul, out of all proportion so to speak. Now the nonglorified soul moves the body in time. Therefore the glorified soul moves the body instantaneously.

Obj. 4. Further, Whatever is moved equally soon to what is near and what is distant, is moved instantaneously. Now such is the movement of a glorified body, for however distant the space to which it is moved, the time it takes to be moved is imperceptible; hence Augustine says (QQ. *De Resurrectione, Ep.* CII, Q. 1)[1] that the glorified body "reaches equally soon to any distance, like the sun's ray." Therefore the glorified body is moved instantaneously.

Obj. 5. Further, Whatever is in motion is moved either in time or in an instant. Now after the resurrection the glorified body will not be moved in time, since time will not be then according to Apoc. 10. 6. Therefore this movement will be instantaneous.

On the contrary, In local movement space, movement and time are equally divisible, as is demonstrated in the *Physics*.[2] Now the space traversed by a glorified body in motion is divisible. Therefore both the movement and the time are divisible. But an instant is indivisible. Therefore this movement will not be instantaneous.

Further, A thing cannot be at the same time wholly in one place and partly in another place, since it would follow that the remaining part is in two places at the same time, which is impossible. But whatever is in motion is partly in a term from which and partly in a term to

which, as is proved in the *Physics*,[3] while whatever has been in motion is wholly in the term to which the movement is directed, and it is impossible at the same time for it to be moved and to have been moved. Now that which is moved instantaneously is being moved and has been moved at the same time. Therefore the local movement of a glorified body cannot be instantaneous.

I answer that, Opinion is much divided on this point. For some say that a glorified body passes from one place to another without passing through the interval, just as the will passes from one place to another without passing through the interval, and that consequently it is possible for the movement of a glorified body like that of the will to be instantaneous. But this will not hold, because the glorified body will never attain to the dignity of the spiritual nature, just as it will never cease to be a body. Moreover, when the will is said to move from one place to another, it is not essentially transferred from place to place, because in neither place is it contained essentially, but it is directed to one place after being directed by the intention to another, and in this sense it is said to move from one place to another.

Hence others say that it is a property of the nature of a glorified body, since it is a body, to pass through the interval and consequently to be moved in time, but that by the power of glory, which raises it to a certain infinitude above the power of nature, it is possible for it not to pass through the interval, and consequently to be moved instantaneously. But this is impossible, since it implies a contradiction, which is proved as follows. Suppose a body which we will call Z to be in motion from A to B. It is clear that Z, as long as it is wholly in A is not in motion; and in like manner when it is wholly in B, because then the movement is past. Therefore if it is at any time in motion it must be neither wholly in A nor wholly in B. Therefore while it is in motion, it is either nowhere, or partly in A and partly in B, or wholly in some other intervening place, say C, or partly in A and C and partly in C and B. But it is impossible for it to be nowhere, for then there would be a dimensive quantity without a place, which is impossible. Nor again is it possible for it to be partly in A and partly in B without being in some way in the intervening space; for since B is a place distant from A, it would follow that in the intervening space the part of Z which is in B is not continuous with the part

[1] PL 33, 372.
[2] Aristotle, VI, 4 (235[a]13).
[3] Aristotle, VI, 6 (236[b]19).

which is in A. Therefore it follows that it is either wholly in C, or partly in C, and partly in some other place that intervenes between C and A, say D, and so forth. Therefore it follows that Z does not pass from A to B unless first of all it be in all the intervening places, unless we suppose that it passes from A to B without ever being moved, which implies a contradiction, because the very succession of places is local movement. The same applies to any change whatever having two opposite terms, each of which is something positive, but not to those changes which have only one positive term, the other being a pure privation, since between affirmation and negation or privation there is no fixed distance; and so that which is in the negation may be nearer to or more remote from affirmation, and conversely, by reason of something that causes either of them or disposes thereto, so that while that which is moved is wholly under a negation it is changed into affirmation, and *vice versa;* therefore in such things to be changing precedes to be changed, as is proved in the *Physics*.[1] Nor is there any comparison with the movement of an angel, because being in a place is predicated equivocally of a body and an angel. Hence it is clear that it is altogether impossible for a body to pass from one place to another, unless it pass through every interval.

And therefore others grant this, and yet they maintain that the glorified body is moved instantaneously. But it follows from this that a glorified body is at the same instant in two or more places together, namely in the ultimate term, and in all the intervening places, which is impossible. To this, however, they reply that, although it is the same instant really, it is not the same logically, like a point at which different lines terminate. But this is not enough, because an instant measures the instantaneous, according to its reality and not according to our way of considering it. Therefore an instant through being considered in a different way is not rendered capable of measuring things that are not simultaneous in time, just as a point through being considered in a different way does not make it possible for one point of place to contain things that are locally distant from one another.

Hence others with greater probability hold that a glorified body moves in time, but that this time is so short as to be imperceptible; and that nevertheless one glorified body can pass through the same space in less time than an-

other, because there is no limit to the divisibility of time, no matter how short a space we may take.

Reply Obj. 1. "That which is little lacking is as it were not lacking at all," as it is stated in the *Physics*.[2] Therefore we say: "I do so and so at once," when it is to be done after a short time. It is in this sense that Augustine speaks when he says that "wheresoever the will shall be, there shall the body be at once." Or we may say that in the blessed there will never be a disordered will, so that they never will wish their body to be instantaneously where it cannot be, and consequently whatever instant the will shall choose, at that same instant the body will be in whatever place the will shall determine.

Reply Obj. 2. Some have demurred to this proposition of the Philosopher's, as the Commentator thereon observes.[3] They say that the ratio of one whole movement to another whole movement is not necessarily as the ratio of one resisting medium to another resisting medium, but that the ratio of the intervening mediums gives us the ratio of retardations attending the movements on account of the resistance of the medium. For every movement has a certain fixed speed, either fast or slow, through the mover overcoming the movable, even if there is no resistance on the part of the medium, as is clear in the case of heavenly bodies, which have nothing to hinder their movement; and yet they do not move instantaneously, but in a fixed time proportionate to the power of the mover in comparison with the movable. Consequently it is clear that even if we suppose something to move in a vacuum, it does not follow that it moves instantaneously, but that nothing is added to the time which that movement requires in the aforesaid proportion of the mover to the movable, because the movement is not retarded.

But this reply, as the Commentator observes (*ibid.*), proceeds from an error in the imagination; for it is imagined that the retardation resulting from the resistance of the medium is a part of movement added to the natural movement, the quantity of which is in proportion to the mover in comparison with the movable, as when one line is added to another, for the proportion of one total to the other is not the same as the proportion of the lines to which an addition has been made.[4] And so there

---

[1] Aristotle, VI, 5 (235^{b}6).

[2] Aristotle, II, 5 (197^{a}29).

[3] Averroes, *In Phys.* IV, comm. 71 (IV, 160C); Averroes has reference to Avempace.

[4] The same applies to mathematical quantities: for instance the ratio of $2+1$ to $4+1$ is not as 2 to 4.

would not be the same proportion between one whole sensible movement and another, as between the retardations resulting from the resistance of the medium. This is an error of the imagination, because each part of a movement has as much speed as the whole movement, while not every part of a line has as much of the dimensive quantity as the whole line has. Hence any retardation or acceleration affecting the movement affects each of its parts, which is not the case with lines, and consequently the retardation that comes to a movement is not another part of the movement, whereas in the case of the lines that which is added is a part of the total line.

Consequently, in order to understand the Philosopher's argument, as the Commentator explains (*ibid.*), we must take the whole as being one, that is we must take not only the resistance of the movable to the moving power, but also the resistance of the medium through which the movement takes place, and again the resistance of anything else, so that we take the amount of retardation in the whole movement as being proportionate to the moving power in comparison with the resisting movable, no matter in what way it resist, whether by itself or by reason of something extrinsic. For the movable must always resist the mover somewhat, since mover and moved, agent and patient, as such, are opposed to one another. Now sometimes it is to be observed that the moved resists the mover by itself, either because it has a force inclining it to a contrary movement, as appears in violent movements, or at least because it has a place contrary to the place which is in the intention of the mover; and resistance of this kind even heavenly bodies offer their movers. Sometimes the movable resists the power of the mover by reason only of something else and not by itself. This is seen in the natural movement of heavy and light things, because by their very form they are inclined to such a movement, for the form is an impression of their generator, which is the mover as regards heavy and light bodies. On the part of matter we find no resistance, neither of a force inclining to a contrary movement nor of a contrary place, since place is not due to matter except in so far as the latter, being circumscribed by its dimensions, is perfected by its natural form. Hence there can be no resistance save on the part of the medium, and this resistance is connatural to their movement. Sometimes again the resistance results from both, as may be seen in the movements of animals.

Accordingly when in a movement there is no resistance save on the part of the movable, as in the heavenly bodies, the time of the movement is measured according to the proportion of the mover to the movable, and the Philosopher's argument does not apply to these, since if there be no medium at all their movement is still a movement in time. On the other hand, in those movements where there is resistance on the part of the medium only, the measure of time is taken only according to the obstacle on the part of the medium, so that if the medium be removed there will be no longer an obstacle; and so either it will move instantaneously, or it will move in an equal time through a vacuum and through a plenum, because granted that it moves in time through a vacuum, that time will bear some proportion to the time in which it moves through a plenum.

Now it is possible to imagine another body more subtle in the same proportion than the body which filled the space, and then if this body fill some other equal space it will move in as little time through that plenum as it did previously through a vacuum, since by as much as the subtlety of the medium is increased by so much is the length of time decreased, and the more subtle the medium the less it resists. But in those other movements where resistance is offered by both the movable and the medium, the quantity of time must be proportionate to the power of the mover as compared with the resistance of both movable and medium together. Hence granted that the medium be taken away altogether, or that it cease to hinder, it does not follow that the movement is instantaneous, but that the time is measured according only to the resistance of the movable. Nor will there be any inconsistency if it move in an equal time through a vacuum, and through a space filled with the most subtle body imaginable, since the greater the subtlety we ascribe to the medium the less is it naturally inclined to retard the movement. Therefore it is possible to imagine so great a subtlety as will naturally retard the movement less than does the resistance of the movable, so that the resistance of the medium will add no retardation to the movement.

It is therefore evident that although the medium offer no resistance to the glorified bodies, in so far as it is possible for them to be in the same place with another body, nevertheless their movement will not be instantaneous, because the movable body itself will resist the moving power, from the very fact that it has a determinate place, as we have said in reference to the heavenly bodies.

Reply Obj. 3. Although the power of a glorified soul surpasses immeasurably the power of a non-glorified soul, it does not surpass it infinitely, because both powers are finite; hence it does not follow that it causes instantaneous movement. And even if its power were absolutely infinite, it would not follow that it causes an instantaneous movement, unless the resistance of the movable were overcome altogether. Now although the resistance of the movable to the mover that results from opposition to such a movement by reason of its being inclined to a contrary movement, can be altogether overcome by a mover of infinite power, nevertheless the resistance it offers through contrariety towards the place which the mover intends by the movement cannot be overcome altogether, except by depriving it of its being in such and such a place or position. For just as white resists black by reason of whiteness, and all the more according as whiteness is the more distant from blackness, so a body resists a certain place through having an opposite place, and its resistance is all the greater according as the distance is greater. Now it is impossible to take away from a body its being in some place or position, unless one deprive it of its corporeity, by reason of which it requires a place or position; therefore so long as it retains the nature of a body, it can in no way be moved instantaneously, however greater be the moving power. Now the glorified body will never lose its corporeity, and therefore it will never be possible for it to be moved instantaneously.

Reply Obj. 4. In the words of Augustine, the speed is said to be equal because the excess of one over the other is imperceptible, just as the time taken by the whole movement is imperceptible.

Reply Obj. 5. Although after the resurrection the time which is the measure of the heaven's movement will be no more, there will nevertheless be time resulting from the before and after in any kind of movement.

QUESTION LXXXV

OF THE CLARITY OF THE BODIES
OF THE BLESSED

(*In Three Articles*)

WE must now consider the clarity of the bodies of the blessed at the resurrection. Under this head there are three points of inquiry: (1) Whether there will be clarity in the glorified bodies? (2) Whether this clarity will be visible to the non-glorified eye? (3) Whether a glorified body will of necessity be seen by a non-glorified body?

ARTICLE 1. *Whether Clarity Is Becoming to the Glorified Body?*

We proceed thus to the First Article: It would seem that clarity is unbecoming to the glorified body.

Objection 1. Because according to Avicenna (*Natural.* vi, 3),[1] "every luminous body consists of transparent parts." But the parts of a glorified body will not be transparent, since in some of them, such as flesh and bones, earth is predominant. Therefore glorified bodies are not lightsome.

Obj. 2. Further, Every lightsome body hides one that is behind it; therefore one luminary behind another is eclipsed, and a flame of fire prevents one seeing what is behind it. But the glorified bodies will not hide that which is within them, for as Gregory says on Job 28. 17, *Gold or crystal cannot equal it* (*Moral.* xviii, 48):[2] "There," that is in the heavenly country, "the grossness of the members will not hide one's mind from another's eyes, and the very harmony of the body will be evident to the bodily sight." Therefore those bodies will not be lightsome.

Obj. 3. Further, Light and colour require a contrary disposition in their subject, since "light is the extreme point of visibility in an indeterminate body; colour in a determinate body."[3] But glorified bodies will have colour, for as Augustine says,[4] "the body's beauty is harmony of parts with a certain charm of colour," and it will be impossible for the glorified bodies to lack beauty. Therefore the glorified bodies will not be lightsome.

Obj. 4. Further, If there be clarity in the glorified bodies, it will need to be equal in all the parts of the body, just as all the parts will be equally impassible, subtle and agile. But this is not becoming, since one part has a greater disposition to clarity than another, for instance the eye than the hand, the spirits than the bones, the humours than the flesh or nerves. Therefore it would seem unfitting for those bodies to be lightsome.

On the contrary, It is written (Matt. 13. 43): *The just shall shine as the sun in the kingdom of their Father,* and (Wisd. 3. 7): *The*

---

[1] Chap. 2 (10va).   [2] PL 76, 84.
[3] Aristotle, *Sense and the Sensible,* 3 (439ᵃ26).
[4] *City of God,* XXII, 19 (PL 41, 781).

just shall shine, and shall run to and fro like sparks among the reeds.

Further, It is written (I Cor. 15. 43): *It is sown in dishonour, it shall rise in glory,* which refers to clarity, as evidenced by the previous context where the glory of the rising bodies is compared to the clarity of the stars. Therefore the bodies of the saints will be lightsome.

I answer that, It is necessary to assert that after the resurrection the bodies of the saints will be lightsome, on account of the authority of Scripture which makes this promise. But the cause of this clarity is ascribed by some to the fifth or heavenly essence, which will then predominate in the human body. Since, however, this is absurd, as we have often remarked (Q. LXXXIV, A. I), it is better to say that this clarity will result from the overflow of the soul's glory into the body. For whatever is received into anything is received not according to the mode of the source from which it flows, but according to the mode of the recipient. Therefore clarity which in the soul is spiritual is received into the body as corporeal. And consequently according to the greater clarity of the soul by reason of its greater merit, so too will the body differ in clarity, as the Apostle affirms (I Cor. 15. 41). Thus in the glorified body the glory of the soul will be known, even as through a crystal is known the colour of a body contained in a crystal vessel, as Gregory says[1] on Job. 28. 17, *Gold or crystal cannot equal it.*

Reply Obj. 1. Avicenna is speaking of a body that has clarity through the nature of its component parts. It is not thus but rather by the merit of virtue that the glorified body will have clarity.

Reply Obj. 2. Gregory compares the glorified body to gold on account of clarity, and to crystal on account of its transparency. Therefore it seems we should say that they will be both transparent and lightsome; for that a lightsome body is not transparent is owing to the fact that the clarity of that body results from the density of the lightsome parts, and density is opposed to transparency. Then, however, clarity will result from another cause, as stated above, and the density of the glorified body will not deprive it of transparency, as neither does the density of a crystal deprive crystal.

Some, on the other hand, say that they are compared to crystal not because they are transparent, but on account of this likeness, for just as that which is enclosed in crystal is visible,

[1] *Moral.,* XVIII, 48 (PL 76, 84).

so the glory of the soul enclosed in the glorified body will not be hidden. But the first explanation is better, because it safeguards better the dignity of the glorified body, and is more consistent with the words of Gregory.

Reply Obj. 3. The glory of the body will not destroy nature but will perfect it. Therefore the body will retain the colour due to it by reason of the nature of its component parts, but in addition to this it will have clarity resulting from the soul's glory. Thus we see bodies which have colour by their nature aglow with the resplendence of the sun, or from some other cause extrinsic or intrinsic.

Reply Obj. 4. Even as the clarity of glory will overflow from the soul into the body according to the mode of the body, and is there otherwise than in the soul, so again it will overflow into each part of the soul according to the mode of that part. Hence it is not unreasonable that the different parts should have clarity in different ways, according as they are differently disposed thereto by their nature. Nor is there any comparison with the other gifts of the body, for the various parts of the body are not differently disposed in their regard.

ARTICLE 2. *Whether the Clarity of the Glorified Body Is Visible to the Non-Glorified Eye?*

We proceed thus to the Second Article: It would seem that the clarity of the glorified body is invisible to the non-glorified eye.

Objection 1. For the visible object should be proportionate to the sight. But a non-glorified eye is not proportionate to see the clarity of glory, since this differs generically from the clarity of nature. Therefore the clarity of the glorified body will not be seen by a non-glorified eye.

Obj. 2. Further, The clarity of the glorified body will be greater than the clarity of the sun is now, since the clarity of the sun also will then be greater than it is now, as it is said,[2] and the clarity of the glorified body will be much greater still, for which reason the sun and the entire world will receive greater clarity. Now a non-glorified eye is unable to gaze on the very orb of the sun on account of the greatness of its clarity. Therefore still less will it be able to gaze on the clarity of a glorified body.

Obj. 3. Further, A visible object that is opposite the eyes of the seer must be seen, unless there is some lesion to the eye. But the clarity of a glorified body that is opposite to non-glorified eyes is not necessarily seen by them,

[2] Isaias 30.26; Peter Lombard, *Sent.,* IV, d. 48, chap. 5 (QR II, 1025).

which is evident in the case of the disciples who saw our Lord's body after the resurrection, without witnessing its clarity. Therefore this clarity will be invisible to a non-glorified eye.

On the contrary, A gloss on Philip. 3. 21, *Made like to the body of His glory,* says:[1] "It will be like the clarity which He had in the Transfiguration." Now this clarity was seen by the non-glorified eyes of the disciples. Therefore the clarity of the glorified body will be visible to non-glorified eyes also.

Further, The wicked will be tortured in the judgment by seeing the glory of the just, according to Wisd. 5. 2. But they would not fully see their glory unless they gazed on their clarity. Therefore, etc.

I answer that, Some have asserted that the clarity of the glorified body will not be visible to the non-glorified eye, except by a miracle. But this is impossible, unless this clarity were so named equivocally, because light by its essence has a natural tendency to move the sight, and sight by its essence has a natural tendency to perceive light, even as the true is in relation to the intellect, and the good to the appetite. Therefore if there were a sight altogether incapable of perceiving a light, either this sight is so named equivocally, or else this light is. This cannot be said in the point at issue, because then nothing would be made known to us when we are told that the glorified bodies will be lightsome; in the same way a person who says that a dog [the dog star] is in the heavens conveys no knowledge to one who knows no other dog than the animal. Hence we must say that the clarity of a glorified body is naturally visible to the non-glorified eye.

Reply Obj. 1. The clarity of glory will differ generically from the clarity of nature as to its cause but not as to its species. Hence just as the clarity of nature is, by reason of its species, proportionate to the sight, so too will the clarity of glory be.

Reply Obj. 2. Just as a glorified body is not passible to a passion of nature but only to a passion of the soul, so in virtue of its property of glory it acts only by the action of the soul. Now intense clarity does not disturb the sight, in so far as it acts by the action of the soul, for thus it rather gives delight, but it disturbs it in so far as it acts by the action of nature by heating and destroying the organ of sight, and by scattering the spirits asunder. Hence, though the clarity of a glorified body surpasses

the clarity of the sun, it does not by its nature disturb the sight but soothes it. Therefore this clarity is compared to the jasper-stone (Apoc. 21. 11).

Reply Obj. 3. The clarity of the glorified body results from the merit of the will and therefore will be subject to the will, so as to be seen or not seen according to its command. Therefore it will be in the power of the glorified body to show forth its clarity or to hide it, and this was the opinion of Præpositinus.[2]

ARTICLE 3. *Whether a Glorified Body Will Be Necessarily Seen By a Non-Glorified Body?*

We proceed thus to the Third Article: It would seem that a glorified body will be necessarily seen by a non-glorified body.

Objection 1. For the glorified bodies will be lightsome. Now a lightsome body reveals itself and other things. Therefore the glorified bodies will be seen of necessity.

Obj. 2. Further, Every body which hides other bodies that are behind it is necessarily perceived by the sight, from the very fact that the other things behind it are hidden. Now the glorified body will hide other bodies that are behind it from being seen, because it will be a coloured body. Therefore it will be seen of necessity.

Obj. 3. Further, Just as quantity is something in a body, so is the quality by which a body is seen. Now quantity will not be subject to the will, so that the glorified body be able to be of greater or smaller quantity. Therefore neither will the quality of visibility be subject to the will, so that a body be able not to be seen.

On the contrary, Our body will be glorified in being made like to the body of Christ after the resurrection. Now after the resurrection Christ's body was not necessarily seen; in fact it vanished from the sight of the disciples at Emmaus (Luke 24. 31). Therefore neither will the glorified body be necessarily seen.

Further, There the body will be in complete obedience to the will. Therefore as the soul wills the body will be visible or invisible.

I answer that, A visible object is seen according as it acts on the sight. Now there is no change in a thing through its acting or not acting on an external object. Therefore a glorified body may be seen or not seen without any property pertaining to its perfection being changed. Consequently it will be in the power

---

[1] *Glossa interl.* (VI, 102v); *Glossa* Lombardi (PL 192, 251).

[2] According to William of Auxerre, *Summa Aurea,* PT. IV (297rb); see Albert, *In Sent.,* IV, d. XLIV, A. 28 (BO XXX, 581).

of a glorified soul for its body to be seen or not seen, even as any other action of the body will be in the soul's power; otherwise the glorified body would not be a perfectly obedient instrument of its principal agent.

Reply Obj. 1. This clarity will be obedient to the glorified body so that this will be able to show it or hide it.

Reply Obj. 2. A body's colour does not prevent its being transparent except in so far as it affects the sight, because the sight cannot be affected by two colours at the same time, so as to perceive them both perfectly. But the colour of the glorified body will be completely in the power of the soul, so that it can thereby act or not act on the sight. Hence it will be in its power to hide or not to hide a body that is behind it.

Reply Obj. 3. Quantity is inherent to the glorified body itself, nor would it be possible for the quantity to be altered at the soul's bidding without the glorified body suffering some alteration incompatible with its impassibility. Hence there is no comparison between quantity and visibility, because even this quality whereby it is visible cannot be removed at the soul's bidding, but the action of that quality will be suspended, and thus the body will be hidden at the soul's command.

QUESTION LXXXVI

OF THE CONDITIONS UNDER WHICH
THE BODIES OF THE DAMNED WILL
RISE AGAIN
(*In Three Articles*)

WE must next consider the conditions in which the bodies of the damned will rise again. Under this head there are three points of inquiry: (1) Whether the bodies of the damned will rise again with their deformities? (2) Whether their bodies will be corruptible? (3) Whether they will be impassible?

ARTICLE I. *Whether the Bodies of the Damned Will Rise Again With Their Deformities?*

We proceed thus to the First Article: It would seem that the bodies of the damned will rise again with their deformities.

Objection 1. For that which was appointed as a punishment for sin should not cease unless the sin is forgiven. Now the lack of limbs that results from mutilation, as well as all other bodily deformities, are appointed as punishments for sin. Therefore these deformities will not be taken away from the damned, seeing that they will not have received the forgiveness of their sins.

Obj. 2. Further, Just as the saints will rise again to final happiness, so the wicked will rise again to final unhappiness. Now when the saints rise again nothing will be taken from them that can pertain to their perfection, and therefore nothing pertaining to the defect or unhappiness of the wicked will be taken from them at the resurrection. But such are their deformities. Therefore, etc.

Obj. 3. Further, Just as deformity is a defect of the passible body, so is slowness of movement. Now slowness of movement will not be taken from the bodies of the damned at the resurrection, since their bodies will not be agile. Therefore for the same reason neither will their deformity be taken away.

On the contrary, It is written (I Cor. 15. 52): *The dead shall rise again incorruptible;* where a gloss says:[1] "The dead, that is sinners, or all the dead in general shall rise again incorruptible, that is without the loss of any limbs." Therefore the wicked will rise again without their deformities.

Further, There will be nothing in the damned to lessen the sense of pain. But sickness hinders the sense of pain by weakening the organ of sense, and in like manner the lack of a limb would prevent pain from affecting the whole body. Therefore the damned will rise again without these defects.

I answer that, Deformity in the human body is of two kinds. One arises from the lack of a limb; thus we say that a mutilated person is deformed, because he lacks due proportion of the parts to the whole. Deformities of this kind, without any doubt, will not be in the bodies of the damned, since all bodies of both wicked and good will rise again whole. Another deformity arises from the undue disposition of the parts, by reason of undue quantity, quality, or place,—which deformity is, moreover, incompatible with due proportion of parts to whole. Concerning these deformities and like defects such as fevers and similar ailments which sometimes result in deformity, Augustine remained undecided and doubtful (*Enchir.* xcii)[2] as the Master remarks (iv. *Sent.* d. 44).[3] Among modern masters, however, there are two opinions on this point.

For some say that such deformities and defects will remain in the bodies of the damned, because they consider that those who are damned are sentenced to utmost unhappiness, from which no affliction should be taken away.

[1] *Glossa* Lombardi (PL 191, 1691); cf. *Glossa interl.* (VI, 60r).   [2] PL 40, 274.   [3] QR II, 1002.

But this would seem unreasonable. For in the restoration of the rising body we look to its natural perfection rather than to its previous condition; hence those who die under perfect age will rise again in the stature of youth, as stated above (Q. LXXXI, A. 1). Consequently those who had natural defects in the body, or deformities resulting from them, will be restored without those defects or deformities at the resurrection, unless the demerit of sin prevent; and so if a person rise again with such defects and deformities, this will be for his punishment. Now the mode of punishment is according to the measure of guilt. And a sinner who is about to be damned may be burdened with less grievous sins and yet have deformities and defects which one who is about to be damned has not, while burdened with more grievous sins. Therefore if he who had deformities in this life rise again with them, while the other who had them not in this life, and therefore, as is clear, will rise again without them, though deserving of greater punishment, the mode of the punishment would not correspond to the amount of guilt; in fact it would seem that a man is more punished on account of the pains which he suffered in this world, which is absurd.

Hence others say with more reason, that He Who fashioned nature will wholly restore the body's nature at the resurrection. Therefore whatever defect or deformity was in the body through corruption, or weakness of nature or of natural principles (for instance fever, partial blindness, and so forth) will be entirely done away at the resurrection, whereas those defects in the human body which are the natural result of its natural principles, such as heaviness, passibility, and the like, will be in the bodies of the damned, while they will be removed from the bodies of the elect by the glory of the resurrection.

Reply Obj. 1. Since in every tribunal punishment is inflicted according to the jurisdiction of the tribunal, the punishments which in this temporal life are inflicted for some particular sin are themselves temporal, and do not extend beyond the term of this life. Hence although the damned are not pardoned their sins, it does not follow that there they will undergo the same punishments as they have in this world; but the Divine justice demands that there they shall suffer more severe punishment for eternity.

Reply Obj. 2. There is no parity between the good and the wicked, because a thing can be altogether good, but not altogether evil. Hence the final happiness of the saints requires that they should be altogether exempt from all evil, whereas the final unhappiness of the wicked will not exclude all good, because "if a thing be wholly evil it destroys itself," as the Philosopher says.[1] Hence it is necessary for the good of their nature to underlie the unhappiness of the damned, which good is the work of their perfect Creator, Who will restore that same nature to the perfection of its species.

Reply Obj. 3. Slowness of movement is one of those defects which are the natural result of the principles of the human body; but deformity is not, and consequently the comparison fails.

ARTICLE 2. *Whether the Bodies of the Damned Will Be Incorruptible?*

We proceed thus to the Second Article: It would seem that the bodies of the damned will be corruptible.

Objection 1. For everything composed of contraries must necessarily be corruptible. Now the bodies of the damned will be composed of the contraries of which they are composed even now, for otherwise they would not be the same, neither specifically nor, in consequence, numerically. Therefore they will be corruptible.

Obj. 2. Further, If the bodies of the damned will not be corruptible, this will be due either to nature, or to grace, or to glory. But it will not be by nature, since they will be of the same nature as now; nor will it be by grace or glory, since they will lack these things altogether. Therefore they will be corruptible.

Obj. 3. Further, It would seen inconsistent to withdraw the greatest of punishments from those who are in the highest degree of unhappiness. Now death is the greatest of punishments, as the Philosopher declares.[2] Therefore death should not be withdrawn from the damned, since they are in the highest degree of unhappiness. Therefore their bodies will be corruptible.

On the contrary, It is written (Apoc. 9. 6): *In those days men shall seek death, and shall not find it, and they shall desire to die, and death shall fly from them.*

Further, The damned will be punished with an everlasting punishment both in soul and body (Matt. 25. 46): *These shall go into everlasting punishment.* But this would not be possible if their bodies were corruptible. Therefore their bodies will be incorruptible.

I answer that, Since in every movement there

---

[1] *Ethics,* IV, 5 (1126ᵃ12).   [2] *Ibid.,* III, 6 (1115ᵃ26).

must be a principle of movement, movement or change may be withdrawn from a movable in two ways: first through absence of a principle of movement, secondly through an obstacle to the principle of movement. Now corruption is a kind of change, and consequently a body which is corruptible on account of the nature of its principles may be rendered incorruptible in two ways. First by the total removal of the principle which leads to corruption, and in this way the bodies of the damned will be incorruptible. For since the heaven is the first principle of alteration in virtue of its local movement, and all other secondary agents act in virtue of it and as though moved by it, it follows that at the cessation of the heavenly movement there is no longer any agent that can change the body by altering it from its natural property. Therefore after the resurrection, and the cessation of the heavenly movement, there will be no quality capable of altering the human body from its natural quality. Now corruption, like generation, is the term of alteration. Hence the bodies of the damned will be incorruptible, and this will serve the purpose of Divine justice, since living for ever they will be punished for ever. This is in keeping with the demands of Divine justice, as we shall state further on (A. 3; Q. XCIX, A. 1), even as now the corruptibility of bodies serves the purpose of Divine providence, by which through the corruption of one thing another is generated.

Secondly, this happens through the principle of corruption being hindered, and in this way the body of Adam was incorruptible, because the conflicting qualities that exist in man's body were withheld by the grace of innocence from conducing to the body's dissolution, and much more will they be withheld in the glorified bodies, which will be wholly subject to the spirit. Thus after the general resurrection the two above modes of incorruptibility will be united together in the bodies of the blessed.

Reply Obj. 1. The contraries of which bodies are composed are conducive to corruption as secondary principles. For their first active principle is the heavenly movement. Therefore given the movement of the heaven, it is necessary for a body composed of contraries to be corrupted unless some more powerful cause prevent it, whereas if the heavenly movement be withdrawn, the contraries of which a body is composed do not suffice to cause corruption, even in accordance with nature, as explained above. But the philosophers were ignorant of a cessation in the heavenly movement, and con-

sequently they held that a body composed of contraries is without fail corrupted in accordance with nature.

Reply Obj. 2. This incorruptibility will result from nature, not as though there were some principle of incorruption in the bodies of the damned, but on account of the cessation of the active principle of corruption, as shown above.

Reply Obj. 3. Although death is the greatest of punishments absolutely, yet nothing prevents death conducing, in a certain respect, to a cessation of punishments; and consequently the removal of death may contribute to the increase of punishment. For as the Philosopher says,[1] "Life is pleasant to all, for all desire to be . . . But we must not apply this to a wicked or corrupt life, nor one passed in sorrow." Accordingly just as life is pleasant absolutely, but not the life that is passed in sorrows, so too death, which is the privation of life, is painful absolutely, and the greatest of punishments, since it deprives one of the primary good, namely being, with which other things are withdrawn. But in so far as it deprives one of a wicked life, and of such as is passed in sorrow, it is a remedy for pains, since it puts an end to them; and consequently the withdrawal of death leads to the increase of punishments by making them everlasting. If however we say that death is penal by reason of the bodily pain which the dying feel, without doubt the damned will continue to feel a far greater pain. Therefore they are said to be in everlasting death, according to the Psalm (48. 15): Death shall feed upon them.

ARTICLE 3. Whether the Bodies of the Damned Will Be Impassible?

We proceed thus to the Third Article: It would seem that the bodies of the damned will be impassible.

Objection 1. For, according to the Philosopher,[2] "increase of passion results in loss of substance." Now "if a finite thing be continually lessened, it must at length be done away."[3] Therefore if the bodies of the damned will be passible, and will be always suffering, they will at length be done away and corrupted, and this has been shown to be false (A. 2). Therefore they will be impassible.

Obj. 2. Further, Every agent likens the patient to itself. If then the bodies of the damned are passive to the fire the fire will liken them to

---

[1] Ethics, IX, 9 (1170ᵃ22).
[2] Topics, VI, 6 (145ᵃ3).
[3] Aristotle, Physics, I, 4 (187ᵇ25); cf. III, 6 (206ᵇ7).

itself. Now fire does not consume bodies except in so far as in likening them to itself it disintegrates them. Therefore if the bodies of the damned will be passible they will at length be consumed by the fire, and thus the same conclusion follows as before.

Obj. 3. Further, Those animals, for instance the salamander, which are said to remain living in fire without being destroyed,[1] are not distressed by the fire, because an animal is not distressed by bodily pain unless the body in some way is hurt thereby. If therefore the bodies of the damned can, like these animals, remain in the fire without being corrupted, as Augustine asserts,[2] it would seem that they will suffer no distress there, which would not be the case unless their bodies were impassible. Therefore, etc.

Obj. 4. Further, If the bodies of the damned be passible, the pain resulting from their suffering, it seems, will surpass all present bodily pain, even as the joy of the saints will surpass all present joy. Now in this life it sometimes happens that the soul is severed from the body through excess of pain. Much more therefore if those bodies will be passible, the souls will be separate from the bodies through excess of pain, and thus those bodies will be corrupted, which is false. Therefore those bodies will be impassible.

On the contrary, It is written (I Cor. 15. 52): *And we shall be changed:* and a gloss says:[3] "We,—the good alone,—will be changed with the unchangeableness and impassibility of glory."

Further, Even as the body co-operates with the soul in merit, so does it co-operate in sin. Now on account of the former co-operation not only the soul but also the body will be rewarded after the resurrection. Therefore in like manner the bodies of the damned will be punished, which would not be the case were they impassible. Therefore they will be passible.

I answer that, The principal cause of the bodies of the damned not being consumed by the fire will be the Divine justice by which their bodies will be consigned to everlasting punishment. Now the Divine justice is served also by the natural disposition, whether on the part of the passive body or on the part of the active causes; for since passiveness is a kind of receptiveness, there are two kinds of passion, cor-responding to two ways in which one thing is receptive of another. For a form may be received into a subject materially according to its natural being, just as the air receives heat from fire materially; and corresponding to this manner of reception there is a kind of passion which we call passion of nature. In another way one thing is received into another spiritually by way of an intention, just as the likeness of whiteness is received into the air and in the pupil; this reception is like that whereby the soul receives the likeness of things. Therefore corresponding to this mode of reception is another mode of passion which we call passion of the soul.

Since therefore after the resurrection and the cessation of the heavenly movement it will be impossible for a body to be altered by its natural quality, as stated above (A. 2), it will not be possible for any body to be passive with a passion of nature. Consequently as regards this mode of passion the bodies of the damned will be impassible even as they will be incorruptible. Yet after the heaven has ceased to move, there will still remain the passion which is after the manner of the soul, since the air will both receive light from the sun, and will convey the variety of colours to the sight. Therefore in respect of this mode of passion the bodies of the damned will be passible. But the glorified bodies, although they receive something, and are in a manner patient to sensation, will nevertheless not be passive, since they will receive nothing to distress or hurt them, as will the bodies of the damned, which for this reason are said to be passible.

Reply Obj. 1. The Philosopher is speaking of the passion whereby the patient is changed from its natural disposition. But this kind of passion will not be in the bodies of the damned, as stated above.

Reply Obj. 2. The likeness of the agent is in the patient in two ways. First, in the same way as in the agent, and thus it is in all univocal agents, for instance a thing that is hot makes another thing hot, and fire generates fire. Secondly, otherwise than in the agent, and thus it is in all equivocal agents. In these it happens sometimes that a form which is in the agent spiritually is received into the patient materially; thus the form of the house built by the craftsman is materially in itself, but spiritually in the mind of the craftsman. On the other hand, sometimes it is in the agent materially, but is received into the patient spiritually; thus whiteness is materially on the wall in which it is received, while it is spiritually in the pupil and

---

[1] Cf. Aristotle, *History of Animals*, v, 19 (552^{b}10).

[2] *City of God*, XXI, 2, 4 (PL 41, 710, 712).

[3] *Glossa* Lombardi (PL 191, 1691); cf. *Glossa interl.* (VI, 60r).

in the transferring medium. And so it is in the case at issue, because the species which is in the fire materially is received spiritually into the bodies of the damned; thus it is that the fire will assimilate the bodies of the damned to itself, without, nevertheless, consuming them.

Reply Obj. 3. According to the Philosopher in the treatise on the *Properties of the Elements*,[1] no animal can live in fire. Galen also (*De simp, medic.*)[2] says that there is no body which at length is not consumed by fire, although sometimes certain bodies may remain in fire without hurt, such as ebony. The instance of the salamander is not altogether apposite, since it cannot remain in the fire without being at last

[1] An anonymous Arabian work ascribed to Aristotle, translated by Gerard of Cremona; cf. Grabmann, *Forschungen*, p. 249; Sarton, *Introduction to the History of Science*, vol. I, p. 135; vol. II, p. 340; cf. Albert the Great, *De Causis et Proprietatibus Elementorum*, BK. I, tr. I, chap. 2 (BO IX, 590). Cf. Aristotle, *Generation af Animals*, II, 4 (737ª1); *Soul*, I, 5 (411ª9); *Meteorology*, IV, 4 (382ᵇ6).

[2] Cf. *De Simplicium Medicamentorum ac Facultatibus*, II, 3 (KU XI, 468); I, 11 (KU XI, 399); III, 9 (KU XI, 557); this work is translated into Latin by Gerard of Toledo; cf. Thorndike, *A History of Magic and Experimental Science*, BK. IV, chap. 38 (MM II, 89); see also Galen, *De Elementis ex Hippocrate*, I, 6 (KU I, 471).

consumed, as do the bodies of the damned in hell. Nor does it follow that because the bodies of the damned suffer no corruption from the fire, they therefore are not tormented by the fire, because the sensible object has a natural aptitude to please or displease the senses not only as regards its natural action of stimulating or injuring the organ, but also as regards its spiritual action, since when the sensible object is duly proportioned to the sense, it pleases, while the contrary is the result when it is in excess or defect. Hence subdued colours and harmonious sounds are pleasing, whereas discordant sounds displease the hearing.

Reply Obj. 4. Pain does not sever the soul from the body according as it is confirmed to a power of the soul which feels the pain, but according as the passion of the soul leads to the body being changed from its natural disposition. Thus it is that we see that through anger the body becomes heated, and through fear, chilled; but after the resurrection it will be impossible for the body to be changed from its natural disposition, as stated above (A. 2). Consequently, however great the pain will be, it will not sever the body from the soul.

TREATISE ON THE LAST THINGS

QUESTION LXXXVII

Of the knowledge which, after rising again, men will have at the judgment concerning merits and demerits

(*In Three Articles*)

In the next place we must treat of those things which follow the resurrection. The first of these to be considered will be the knowledge, which after rising again, men will have at the judgment, concerning merits and demerits; the second will be the general judgment itself, as also the time and place at which it will be (Q. LXXX-VIII); thirdly we shall consider who will judge and who will be judged (Q. LXXXIX); fourthly we shall treat of the form wherein the judge will come to judge (Q. XC); and fifthly we shall consider what will be after the judgment, the state of the world and of those who will have risen again (Q. XCI).

Under the first head there are three points of inquiry: (1) Whether at the judgment every man will know all his sins? (2) Whether every one will be able to read all that is on another's conscience? (3) Whether one will be able at one glance to see all merits and demerits?

ARTICLE 1. *Whether After the Resurrection Every One Will Know What Sins He Has Committed?*

We proceed thus to the First Article: It seems that after the resurrection everyone will not be able to know all the sins he has committed.

Objection 1. For whatever we know, either we receive it newly through the senses, or we draw it from the treasure house of the memory. Now after the resurrection men will be unable to perceive their sins by means of sense, because they will be things of the past, while sense perceives only the present; and many sins will have escaped the sinner's memory, and he will be unable to recall them from the treasure house of his memory. Therefore after rising again one will not have knowledge of all the sins one has committed.

Obj. 2. Further, It is stated in the text (iv *Sent.* d. 43)[1] that "there are certain books of the conscience, in which each one's merits are inscribed." Now one cannot read a thing in a book, unless it be marked down in the book, and sin leaves its mark upon the conscience according to a gloss of Origen[2] on Rom. 2. 15, *Their conscience bearing witness*, etc., which mark, it seems, is nothing else than the guilt or stain. Since then in many persons the guilt or stain of many sins is blotted out by grace, it would seem that one cannot read in one's conscience all the sins one has committed, and thus the same conclusion follows as before.

Obj. 3. Further The greater the cause the greater the effect. Now the cause which makes us grieve for the sins which we recall to memory is charity. Since then charity is perfect in the saints after the resurrection, they will grieve exceedingly for their sins if they recall them to memory; yet this is impossible, seeing that according to Apoc. 21. 4, *Sorrow and mourning shall flee away* from them.[3] Therefore they will not recall their own sins to memory.

Obj. 4. Further, At the resurrection the damned will be to the good they once did as the blessed to the sins they once committed. Now it seems that the damned after rising again will have no knowledge of the good they once did, since this would greatly alleviate their pain. Neither therefore will the blessed have any knowledge of the sins they had committed.

On the contrary, Augustine says[4] that "a kind of Divine energy will come to our aid, so that we shall recall all our sins to mind."

Further, As human judgment is to outward testimony, so is the Divine judgment to the testimony of conscience, according to I Kings 16. 7, *Man seeth those things that appear, but the Lord beholdeth the heart.* Now man cannot pass a perfect judgment on a matter unless evidence be taken on all the points that need to be judged. Therefore, since the Divine judgment is most perfect, it is necessary for the conscience to witness to everything that has to be judged. But all works, both good and evil, will have to be judged (II Cor. 5. 10): *We must all be manifested before the judgment seat of*

---

[1] Lombard (QR II, 996).
[2] *Glossa Lombardi* (PL 191, 1346); Origen, *In Rom.* (PG 14, 894).
[3] The quotation is from Isa. 35.10. The text of the Apocalypse has: *Nor mourning, nor crying, nor sorrow shall be any more.* [4] *City of God,* XX, 14 (PL 41, 680).

Christ, that every one may receive the proper things of the body, according as he hath done, whether it be good or evil. Therefore each one's conscience must retain all the works he has done, whether good or evil.

I answer that, According to Rom. 2. 15, 16, *In the day when God shall judge* each one's conscience will bear witness to him, and his thoughts will accuse and defend him. And since in every judicial hearing, the witness, the accuser, and the defendant need to be acquainted with the matter on which judgment has to be pronounced, and since at the general judgment all the works of men will be submitted to judgment, every man then will have to know all his works. Therefore each man's conscience will be as a book containing his deeds on which judgment will be pronounced, even as in the human court of law we make use of records. Of these books it is written in the Apocalypse 20. 12): *The books were opened: and another book was opened, which is the book of life; and the dead were judged by those things which were written in the books* (Vulg.,—*book*) *according to their works.* According to Augustine's exposition,[1] the books which are here said to be opened denote the saints of the New and Old Testaments in whom God's commandments are exemplified." Hence Richard of S. Victor (*De judic. potest.*)[2] says: "Their hearts will be like the code of law." But the book of life, of which the text goes on to speak, signifies each one's conscience, which is said to be one single book, because the one Divine power will cause all to recall their deeds, and this energy, in so far as it reminds a man of his deeds, is called the book of life.[3] Or else we may refer the first books to the conscience, and by the second book we may understand the Judge's sentence as expressed in His providence.

Reply Obj. 1. Although many merits and demerits will have escaped our memory, yet there will be none of them but will remain somewhat in its effect, because those merits which are not deadened will remain in the reward accorded to them, while those that are deadened remain in the guilt of ingratitude, which is increased through the fact that a man sinned after receiving grace. In like manner those demerits which are not blotted out by repentance remain in the debt of punishment due to them, while those which have been blotted out by repentance remain in the remembrance of repentance,

which they will recall together with their other merits. Hence in each man there will be something whereby he will be able to recollect his deeds. Nevertheless, as Augustine says,[4] the Divine energy will especially conduce to this.

Reply Obj. 2. Each one's conscience will bear certain marks of the deeds done by him; and it does not follow that these marks are the guilt alone, as stated above.

Reply Obj. 3. Although charity is now the cause of sorrow for sin, yet the saints in heaven will be so full of joy that they will have no room for sorrow; and so they will not grieve for their sins, but rather will they rejoice in the Divine mercy, whereby their sins are forgiven them. Even so do the angels rejoice now in the Divine justice whereby those whom they guard fall headlong into sin through being abandoned by grace, and whose salvation none the less they eagerly watch over.

Reply Obj. 4. The wicked will know all the good they have done, and this will not diminish their pain; indeed, it will increase it, because the greatest sorrow is to have lost many goods, for which reason Boëthius says (*De Consol.* ii, 4)[5] that "the greatest misfortune is to have been happy."

ARTICLE 2. *Whether Every One Will Be Able To Read All That Is In Another's Conscience?*[2]

We proceed thus to the Second Article: It seems that it will be impossible for every one to read all that is in another's conscience.

Objection 1. For the knowledge of those who rise again will not be clearer than that of the angels, equality with whom is promised us after the resurrection (Matt. 22. 30). Now angels cannot read one another's thoughts in matters dependent on the free-choice, and so they need to speak in order to notify such things to one another. Therefore after rising again we shall be unable to read what is contained in another's conscience.

Obj. 2. Further, Whatever is known is known either in itself, or in its cause, or in its effect. Now the merits or demerits contained in a person's conscience cannot be known by another in themselves, because God alone enters the heart and reads its secrets. Neither will it be possible for them to be known in their cause, since all will not see God Who alone can act on the will, from which merits and demerits proceed. Nor again will it be possible to know them from their effect, since there will be many demerits, which through being wholly blotted

---

[1] *City of God,* xx, 14 (PL 41, 680).   [2] PL 196, 1182.
[3] Cf. Part I, Q. XXIV, A. 1, Reply 1; see Augustine, *City of God,* xx, 14 (PL 41, 680).   [4] *Loc. cit.*   [5] PL 63, 677.

out by repentance will leave no effect remaining. Therefore it will not be possible for every one to know all that is in another's conscience.

Obj. 3. Further, Chrysostom says (*Hom.* xxxi *in Ep. ad Hebr.*),[1] as we have quoted before (iv. *Sent.* d. 17):[2] "If thou remember thy sins now, and frequently confess them before God and beg pardon for them, thou wilt very soon blot them out; but if thou forget them, thou wilt then remember them unwillingly, when they will be made public, and declared before all thy friends and foes, and in the presence of the holy angels." Hence it follows that this publication will be the punishment of man's neglect in omitting to confess his sins. Therefore the sins which a man has confessed will not be made known to others.

Obj. 4. Further, It is a relief to know that one has had many associates in sin, so that one is less ashamed of them. If therefore every one were to know the sin of another, each sinners shame would be much diminished, which is unlikely. Therefore every one will not know the sins of all.

On the contrary, A gloss on I Cor. 4. 5, *will . . . bring to light the hidden things of darkness,* says:[3] "Deeds and thoughts both good and evil will then be revealed and made known to all."

Further, The past sins of all the good will be equally blotted out. Yet we know the sins of some saints, for instance of Magdalen, Peter, and David. Therefore in like manner the sins of the other elect will be known, and much more those of the damned.

I answer that, At the last and general judgment the Divine justice, which now is in many ways hidden, must appear evidently to all. Now the sentence of one who condemns or rewards cannot be just unless it be delivered according to merits and demerits. Therefore just as both judge and jury have to know the merits of a case in order to deliver a just verdict, so is it necessary, in order that the sentence appear to be just, that all who know the sentence should be acquainted with the merits. Hence, since every one will know of his reward or condemnation, so will every one else know of it, and consequently as each one will recall his own merits or demerits, so will he know those of others.

This is the more probable and more common opinion, although the Master (iv. *Sent.* 4, 43)[4] says the contrary, namely that a man's sins

blotted out by repentance will not be made known to others at the judgment. But it would follow from this that neither would his repentance for these sins be perfectly known, which would detract considerably from the glory of the saints and the praise due to God for having so mercifully delivered them.

Reply Obj. 1. All the preceding merits or demerits will come to a certain amount in the glory or unhappiness of each one rising again. Consequently through eternal things being seen all things in their conscience will be visible, especially as the Divine power will conduce to this so that the Judge's sentence may appear just to all.

Reply Obj. 2. It will be possible for a man's merits or demerits to be made known by their effects as stated above (REPLY 1), or by the power of God, although the power of the created intellect is not sufficient for this.

Reply Obj. 3. The manifestation of his sins to the confusion of the sinner is a result of his neglect in omitting to confess them. But that the sins of the saints be revealed cannot be to their confusion or shame, as neither does it bring confusion to Mary Magdalen that her sins are publicly recalled in the Church, because shame is "fear of disgrace," as Damascene says (*De Fide Orthod.* ii, 15),[5] and this will be impossible in the blessed. But this manifestation will bring them great glory on account of the penance they did, even as the confessor hails a man who courageously confesses great crimes. Sins are said to be blotted out because God does not see them for the purpose of punishing them.

Reply Obj. 4. The sinner's confusion will not be diminished, but on the contrary increased, through his seeing the sins of others, for in seeing that others are blameworthy he will all the more acknowledge himself to be blamed. For that confusion be diminished by a cause of this kind is owing to the fact that shame regards the esteem of men, who esteem more lightly that which is customary. But then confusion will regard the esteem of God, which weighs every sin according to the truth, whether it be the sin of one man or of many.

ARTICLE 3. *Whether All Merits and Demerits, One's Own As Well As Those of Others, Will Be Seen By Anyone at a Single Glance?*

We proceed thus to the Third Article: It would seem that not all merits and demerits, one's own as well as those of others, will be seen by anyone at a single glance.

---

[1] PG 63, 217.   [2] QR II, 855; cf. Gratian, *Decretum,* pt. II, causa 33, Q. 3, De Poenit., dist. 1, append. ad Can. 87 (RF I, 1184).   [3] *Glossa interl.* (VI, 38v); *Glossa Lombardi* (PL 191, 1566).   [4] QR II, 998.

[5] PG 94, 932; cf. Aristotle, *Ethics,* IV, 9 (1128^{b}11).

Objection 1. For things considered singly are not seen at one glance. Now the damned will consider their sins singly and will bewail them, and therefore they say (Wisd. 5. 8): *What hath pride profited us?* Therefore they will not see them all at a glance.

Obj. 2. Further, The Philosopher says[1] that "we do not arrive at understanding several things at the same time." Now merits and demerits, both our own and those of others, will not be visible save to the intellect. Therefore it will be impossible for them all to be seen at the same time.

Obj. 3. Further, The intellect of the damned after the resurrection will not be clearer than the intellect of the blessed and of the angels is now, as to the natural knowledge by which they know things by innate species. Now by such knowledge the angels do not see several things at the same time. Therefore neither will the damned be able then to see all their deeds at the same time.

On the contrary, A gloss on Job 8. 22, *They . . . shall be clothed with confusion,* says:[2] "As soon as they shall see the Judge, all their evil deeds will stand before their eyes." Now they will see the Judge suddenly. Therefore in like manner will they see the evil they have done, and for the same reason all others.

Further, Augustine[3] considers it unfitting that at the judgment a material book should be read containing the deeds of each individual written in it, for the reason that it would be impossible to measure the size of such a book, or the time it would take to read. But in like manner it would be impossible to estimate the length of time one would require in order to consider all one's merits and demerits and those of others if one saw these various things one after the other. Therefore we must admit that each one sees them all at the same time.

I answer that, There are two opinions on this question. For some say that one will see all merits and demerits, both one's own and those of others, at the same time in an instant. This is easily credible with regard to the blessed, since they will see all things in the Word, and consequently it is not unreasonable that they should see several things at the same time. But with regard to the damned, a difficulty presents itself, since their intellect is not raised so that they can see God and all else in Him. Therefore others say that the wicked will see all

their sins and those of others generically at the same time, and this suffices for the accusation or absolution necessary for the judgment; but that they will not see them all down to each single one at the same time. But neither does this seem consonant with the words of Augustine,[4] who says that they will count them all with one glance of the mind; and what is known generically is not counted. Hence we may choose a middle way, by holding that they will consider each sin not instantaneously, but in a very short time, the Divine power coming to their aid. This agrees with the saying of Augustine[5] that "they will be discerned with wondrous rapidity." Nor is this impossible, since in a space of time, however short, there is potentially an infinite number of instants. This suffices for the *replies to the objections* on either side of the question.

QUESTION LXXXVIII
OF THE GENERAL JUDGMENT, AS TO THE TIME AND PLACE AT WHICH IT WILL BE
(In Four Articles)

WE must next consider the general judgment, as to the time and place at which it will be. Under this head there are four points of inquiry: (1) Whether there will be a general judgment? (2) Whether as regards the inquiry it will be conducted by word of mouth? (3) Whether it will take place at an unknown time? (4) Whether it will take place in the valley of Josaphat?

ARTICLE 1. *Whether There Will Be a General Judgment?*

We proceed thus to the First Article: It would seem that there will not be a general judgment.

Objection 1. For according to Nahum 1. 9, following the Septuagint version, *God will not judge the same thing a second time.* But God judges now of man's every work, by assigning punishments and rewards to each one after death, and also by rewarding and punishing certain ones in this life for their good or evil deeds. Therefore it would seem that there will be no other judgment.

Obj. 2. Further, In no judicial inquiry is the sentence carried out before judgment is pronounced. But the sentence of the Divine judgment on man regards the acquisition of the kingdom or exclusion from the kingdom (Matt. 25. 34, 41). Therefore since some obtain possession of the kingdom now and some

---

[1] *Topics,* II, 10 (114b34).
[2] *Glossa ordin.* (III, 23F); cf. Gregory the Great, *Moral.,* VIII, 53 (PL 75, 857).   [3] *City of God,* XX, 14 (PL 41, 680).
[4] *Ibid.*   [5] *Ibid.*

are excluded from it for ever, it would seem that there will be no other judgment.

Obj. 3. Further, The reason why certain things are submitted to judgment is that we may come to a decision about them. Now before the end of the world each of the damned is awarded his damnation, and each of the blessed his happiness. Therefore, etc.

On the contrary, It is written (Matt. 12. 41): *The men of Nineve shall rise in judgment with this generation, and shall condemn it.* Therefore there will be a judgment after the resurrection.

Further, It is written (John 5. 29): *They that have done good things shall come forth unto the resurrection of life, but they that have done evil, unto the resurrection of judgment.* Therefore it would seem that after the resurrection there will be a judgment.

I answer that, Just as operation refers to the beginning from which things receive their being, so judgment belongs to the term, in which they are brought to their end. Now we distinguish a twofold operation in God. One is that by which He first gave things their being, by fashioning their nature and by establishing the distinctions which contribute to their perfection; from this work God is stated to have rested (Gen. 2. 2). His other operation is that by which He works in governing creatures, and of this it is written (John 5. 17): *My Father worketh until now; and I work.* Hence we distinguish in Him a twofold judgment, but in the reverse order. One corresponds to the work of governance which cannot be without judgment, and by this judgment each one is judged individually according to his works, not only as adapted to himself, but also as adapted to the government of the universe. Hence one man's reward is delayed for the good of others (Heb. 11. 13, 39, 40), and the punishment of one conduces to the profit of another. Consequently it is necessary that there should be another, and that a general judgment corresponding on the other hand with the first formation of things in being, in order that, namely, just as then all things proceeded immediately from God, so at length the world will receive its ultimate completion, by each one receiving finally his own personal due. Hence at this judgment the Divine justice will be made manifest in all things, whereas now it remains hidden, because at times some persons are dealt with for the profit of others otherwise than their manifest works would seem to require. For this same reason there will then be a general separation of the good from the wicked, because there will be no further motive for the good to profit by the wicked, or the wicked by the good, for the sake of which profit the good are meanwhile mingled with the wicked, so long as this state of life is governed by Divine providence.

Reply Obj. 1. Each man is both an individual person and a part of the whole human race, and so a twofold judgment is due to him. One, the particular judgment, is that to which he will be subjected after death, when he will receive according as he has done in the body, not indeed entirely but only in part, since he will receive not in the body but only in the soul. The other judgment will be passed on him as a part of the human race; thus a man is said to be judged according to human justice even when judgment is pronounced on the community of which he is a part. Hence at the general judgment of the whole human race by the general separation of the good from the wicked, it follows that each one will be judged. And yet God will not judge the same thing a second time, since He will not inflict two punishments for one sin, and the punishment which before the judgment was not inflicted completely will be completed at the last judgment, after which the wicked will be tormented at the same time in body and soul.

Reply Obj. 2. The sentence proper to this general judgment is the general separation of the good from the wicked, which will not precede this judgment. Yet even now, as regards the particular sentence on each individual, the judgment does not at once take full effect, since even the good will receive an increase of reward after the judgment, both from the added glory of the body and from the completion of the number of the saints. The wicked also will receive an increase of torment from the added punishment of the body and from the completion of the number of damned to be punished, because the more numerous those with whom they will burn, the more will they themselves burn.

Reply Obj. 3. The general judgment will regard more directly the generality of men than each individual to be judged, as stated above. Therefore although before that judgment each one will be certain of his condemnation or reward, he will not know of the condemnation or reward of everyone else. Hence the necessity of the general judgment.

ARTICLE 2. *Whether the Judgment Will Take Place by Word of Mouth?*

We proceed thus to the Second Article: It would seem that this judgment, as regards the inquiry and sentence, will take place by word of mouth.

Objection 1. For according to Augustine,[1] "it is uncertain how many days this judgment will last." But it would not be uncertain if the things we are told will take place at the judgment were to be accomplished only in the mind. Therefore this judgment will take place by word of mouth and not only in the mind.

Obj. 2. Further, Gregory says (*Moral.* xxvi, 29)[2] and he is quoted in the text:[3] "Those at least will hear the words of the Judge, who have confessed their faith in Him by words." Now this cannot be understood as referring to the inner word, because thus all will hear the Judge's words, since all the deeds of other men will be known to all both good and wicked. Therefore it seems that this judgment will take place by word of mouth.

Obj. 3. Further, Christ will judge according to His human form, so as to be visible in the body to all. Therefore in like manner it seems that He will speak with the voice of the body, so as to be heard by all.

On the contrary, Augustine says[4] that the book of life which is mentioned Apoc. 20. 12, 15 "is a kind of Divine energy enabling each one to remember all his good or evil works, and to discern them with the gaze of the mind, with wondrous rapidity, his knowledge accusing or defending his conscience, so that all and each will be judged at the same moment." But if each one's merits were discussed by word of mouth, all and each could not be judged at the same moment. Therefore it would seem that this judgment will not take place by word of mouth.

Further, The sentence should correspond proportionately to the testimony. Now the testimony both of accusation and of defence will be mental, according to Rom. 2. 15, 16, *Their conscience bearing witness to them, and their thoughts between themselves accusing or also defending one another in the day when God shall judge the secrets of men.* Therefore, it seems, this sentence and the entire judgment will take place mentally.

I answer that, It is not possible to come to any certain conclusion about the truth of this question. It is, however, the more probable opinion that the whole of this judgment, whether as regards the inquiry, or as regards the accusation of the wicked and the approval of

the good, or again as regards the sentence on both, will take place mentally. For if the deeds of each individual were to be related by word of mouth, this would require an inconceivable length of time. Thus Augustine says[5] that if we suppose the book, from the pages of which all will be judged according to Apoc. 20., to be "a material book, who will be able to conceive its size and length? or the length of time required for the reading of a book that contains the entire life of every individual?" Nor is less time required for telling by word of mouth the deeds of each individual than for reading them if they were written in a material book. Hence, probably we should understand that the details set forth in Matt. 25. will be fulfilled not by word of mouth but mentally.

Reply Obj. 1. The reason why Augustine says that it is uncertain how many days this judgment will last is precisely because it is not certain whether it will take place mentally or by word of mouth. For if it were to take place by word of mouth, a considerable time would be necessary; but if mentally, it is possible for it to be accomplished in an instant.

Reply Obj. 2. Even if the judgment is accomplished solely in the mind, the saying of Gregory stands, since though all will know their own and others' deeds, as a result of the Divine energy which the Gospel describes as speech (Matt. 25. 34-46), nevertheless those who have had the faith which they received through God's words will be judged from those very words, for it is written (Rom. 2. 12): *Whosoever have sinned in the Law shall be judged by the Law.* Hence in a special way something will be said to those who had been believers which will not be said to unbelievers.

Reply Obj. 3. Christ will appear in body, so that the Judge may be recognized in the body by all, and it is possible for this to take place suddenly. But speech which is measured by time would require an immense length of time if the judgment took place by word of mouth.

ARTICLE 3. *Whether the Time of the Future Judgment Is Unknown?*

We proceed thus to the Third Article: It would seem that the time of the future judgment is not unknown.

Objection 1. For just as the holy Fathers looked forward to the first coming, so do we look forward to the second. But the holy Fathers knew the time of the first coming, as proved by the number of weeks mentioned in

---

[1] *City of God*, xx, 1 (PL 41, 569).   [2] PL 76, 379.
[3] Peter Lombard, *Sent.*, iv, d. 47, chap. 3 (QR ii, 1019).
[4] *City of God*, xx, 14 (PL 41, 680).
[5] *Ibid.*

Dan. 9; therefore the Jews are reproached for not knowing the time of Christ's coming (Luke 12. 56): *You hypocrites, you know how to discern the face of the heaven and of the earth, but how is it that you do not discern this time?* Therefore it would seem that the time of the second coming when God will come to judgment should also be determinate to us.

Obj. 2. Further, We arrive by means of signs at the knowledge of the things signified. Now many signs of the coming judgment are declared to us in Scripture (Matt. 24.; Mark 13.; Luke 21.). Therefore we can arrive at the knowledge of that time.

Obj. 3. Further, The Apostle says (I Cor. 10. 11): *It is on us that the ends of the world are come,*[1] and (I John 2. 18): *Little children, it is the last hour,* etc. Since then it is a long time since these things were said, it would seem that now at least we can know that the last judgment is nigh.

Obj. 4. Further, There is no need for the time of the judgment to be hidden, except that each one may be careful to prepare himself for judgment, being in ignorance of the appointed time. Yet the same care would still be necessary even were the time known for certain, because each one is uncertain about the time of his death, of which Augustine says (*Ep. ad Hesych.* cxcix, 1)[2] that "as each one's last day finds him, so will the world's last day find him." Therefore there is no necessity for the time of the judgment to be uncertain.

On the contrary, It is written (Mark 13. 32): *Of that day or hour no man knoweth, neither the angels in heaven, nor the Son, but the Father.* The Son, however, is said not to know in so far as He does not impart the knowledge to us.

Further, It is written (I Thess. 5. 2): *The day of the Lord shall so come as a thief in the night.* Therefore it seems, since the coming of a thief in the night is altogether uncertain, the day of the last judgment is altogether uncertain.

I answer that, God is the cause of things by His knowledge. Now He communicates both these things to His creatures, since He both endows some with the power of action on others, of which they are the cause, and bestows on some the knowledge of things. But in both cases He reserves something to Himself, for He operates certain things wherein no creature co-operates with Him, and again He knows certain things which are unknown to any mere creature. Now this should apply to none more than to those things which are subject to the Divine power alone, and in which no creature co-operates with Him. Such is the end of the world when the day of judgment will come. For the world will come to an end by no created cause, even as it derived its being immediately from God. Therefore the knowledge of the end of the world is fittingly reserved to God. Indeed our Lord seems to assign this very reason when He said (Acts 1. 7): *It is not for you to know the times or moments which the Father hath put in His own power,* as, though He were to say, "which are reserved to His power alone."

Reply Obj. 1. At His first coming Christ came secretly according to Isa. 45. 15, *Verily Thou art a hidden God, the God of Israel, the Saviour.* Hence, that He might be recognized by believers, it was necessary for the time to be fixed beforehand with certainty. On the other hand, at the second coming, He will come openly, according to Ps. 49. 3, *God shall come manifestly.* Consequently there can be no error about the knowledge of His coming. Hence the comparison fails.

Reply Obj. 2. As Augustine says, in his letter to Hesychius concerning the day of judgment (*Ep.* cxcix, 9),[3] "the signs mentioned in the Gospels do not all refer to the second advent which will happen at the end of the world, but some of them belong to the time of the sack of Jerusalem, which is now a thing of the past, while some, in fact many of them, refer to the advent whereby He comes daily to the Church, whom He visits spiritually when He dwells in us by faith and love."

Moreover, the details mentioned in the Gospels and Epistles in connexion with the last coming are not sufficient to enable us to determine the time of the judgment, for the trials that are foretold as announcing the proximity of Christ's coming occurred even at the time of the Early Church, in a degree sometimes more sometimes less marked, so that even the days of the apostles were called the last days (Acts 2. 17) when Peter expounded the saying of Joel 2. 28, *It shall come to pass in the last days,* etc., as referring to that time. Yet it was already a long time since then, and sometimes there were more and sometimes less afflictions in the Church. Consequently it is impossible to decide after how long a time it will take place, nor fix the month, year, century, or thousand

---

[1] *These things ... are written for our correction, upon whom the ends of the world are come.*   [2] PL 33, 905.   [3] PL 33, 914.

years as Augustine says in the same book (*loc. cit.*). And even if we are to believe that at the end these calamities will be more frequent, it is impossible to fix what amount of such calamities will immediately precede the judgment day or the coming of Antichrist, since even at the time of the Early Church persecutions were so bitter, and the corruptions of error were so numerous, that some looked forward to the coming of Antichrist as being near or imminent, as related in Eusebius' *History of the Church* (vi, 7)[1] and in Jerome's book *De Viris Illustribus*.[2]

Reply Obj. 3. The statement, *It is the last hour* and similar expressions that are to be found in Scripture do not enable us to know the exact length of time. For they are not intended to indicate a short length of time, but to signify the last state of the world, which is the last age of all, and it is not stated definitely how long this will last. Thus neither is fixed duration appointed to old age, which is the last age of man, since sometimes it is seen to last as long as or even longer than all the previous ages, as Augustine remarks.[3] Hence also the Apostle (II Thess. 2. 2) disclaims the false meaning which some had given to his words, by believing that the day of the Lord was already at hand.

Reply Obj. 4. Notwithstanding the uncertainty of death, the uncertainty of the judgment conduces to watchfulness in two ways. First, as regards the thing that is not known, since its delay is equal to the length of man's life, so that on either side uncertainty provokes him to greater care. Secondly, for the reason that a man is careful not only of his own person, but also of his family, or of his city or kingdom, or of the whole Church, the length of whose duration is not dependent on the length of man's life. And yet each of these must be so ordered that the day of the Lord finds us not unprepared.

ARTICLE 4. *Whether the Judgment Will Take Place in the Valley of Josaphat?*

We proceed thus to the Fourth Article: It would seem that the judgment will not take place in the valley of Josaphat or in the surrounding locality.

Objection 1. For at least it will be necessary for those to be judged to stand on the ground, and those alone to be raised aloft whose business it will be to judge. But the whole land of promise would not be able to contain the multitude

of those who are to be judged. Therefore it is impossible for the judgment to take place in the neighbourhood of that valley.

Obj. 2. Further, To Christ in His human form judgment is given that He may judge justly, since He was judged unjustly in the court of Pilate, and bore the sentence of an unjust judgment on Golgotha. Therefore these places would be more suitably appointed for the judgment.

Obj. 3. Further, Clouds result from the exhalation of vapours. But then there will be no evaporation or exhalation. Therefore it will be impossible for the just to be taken up in the clouds to met Christ, into the air, and consequently it will be necessary for both good and wicked to be on the earth, so that a much larger place than this valley will be required.

On the contrary, It is written (Joel 3. 2): *I will gather together all nations and will bring them down into the valley of Josaphat, and I will plead with them there.*

Further, It is written (Acts 1. 11): (*This Jesus*) . . . *shall so come as you have seen Him going into heaven.* Now He ascended into heaven from Mount Olivet which overlooks the valley of Josaphat. Therefore He will come to judge in the neighbourhood of that place.

I answer that, We cannot know with any great certainty the manner in which this judgment will take place, nor how men will gather together to the place of judgment; but it may be gathered from Scripture that in all probability He will descend in the neighbourhood of Mount Olivet, even as He ascended from there, so as to show that He who descends is the same as He who ascended.

Reply Obj. 1. A great multitude can be enclosed in a small space. And all that is required is that in the neighbourhood of that locality there be a space, however great, to contain the multitude of those who are to be judged, provided that Christ can be seen from there, since being raised in the air, and shining with exceeding glory, He will be visible from a great distance.

Reply Obj. 2. Although through being sentenced unjustly Christ merited His judiciary power, He will not judge with the appearance of infirmity wherein He was judged unjustly, but under the appearance of glory wherein He ascended to the Father. Hence the place of His ascension is more suitable to the judgment than the place where He was condemned.

Reply Obj. 3. In the opinion of some the name of clouds is here given to certain con-

[1] PG 20, 535.   [2] Chap. 52 (PL 23, 695).
[3] QQ. LXXXIII, Qu. 58 (PL 40, 43).

densations of the light shining from the bodies of the saints, and not to evaporations from earth and water. Or we may say that those clouds will be produced by Divine power in order to show the parallel between His coming to judge and His ascension, so that He Who ascended in a cloud may come to judgment in a cloud.

Again the cloud on account of its refreshing influence indicates the mercy of the Judge.

QUESTION LXXXIX

OF THOSE WHO WILL JUDGE AND OF THOSE WHO WILL BE JUDGED AT THE GENERAL JUDGMENT

(*In Eight Articles*)

WE must next consider who will judge and who will be judged at the general judgment. Under this head there are eight points of inquiry: (1) Whether any men will judge together with Christ? (2) Whether the judicial power corresponds to voluntary poverty? (3) Whether the angels also will judge? (4) Whether the demons will carry out the Judge's sentence on the damned? (5) Whether all men will come up for judgment? (6) Whether any of the good will be judged? (7) Whether any of the wicked will be judged? (8) Whether the angels also will be judged?

ARTICLE 1. *Whether Any Men Will Judge Together With Christ?*

We proceed thus to the First Article: It would seem that no men will judge with Christ.

Objection 1. For it is written (John 5. 22, 23): *The Father . . . hath given all judgment to the Son, that all men may honour the Son.* Therefore, etc.

Obj. 2. Further, Whoever judges has authority over that which he judges. Now those things about which the coming judgment will have to be, such as human merits and demerits, are subject to Divine authority alone. Therefore no one is able to judge of those things.

Obj. 3. Further, This judgment will take place not vocally but mentally. Now the publication of merits and demerits in the hearts of all men (which is like an accusation or approval), or the repayment of punishment and reward (which is like the pronouncement of the sentence) will be the work of God alone. There none but Christ Who is God will judge.

On the contrary, It is written (Matt. 19. 28): *You also shall sit on twelve seats judging the twelve tribes of Israel.* Therefore, etc.

Further, The Lord will enter into judgment with the ancients of His people (Isa. 3. 14). Therefore it would seem that others also will judge together with Christ.

I answer that, "To judge" has several meanings. First it is used causally as it were, when we say it of that which proves that some person ought to be judged. In this sense the expression is used of certain people in comparison, in so far as some are shown to be deserving of judgment through being compared with others; for instance (Matt. 12. 41): *The men of Nineve shall rise in judgment with this generation, and shall condemn it.* To rise in judgment thus is common to the good and the wicked.

Secondly, the expression "to judge" is used equivalently, so to say; for consent to an action is considered equivalent to doing it. Therefore those who will consent with Christ the Judge, by approving His sentence, will be said to judge. In this sense it will belong to all the elect to judge, and so it is written (Wisd. 3. 7, 8): *The just . . . shall judge nations.*

Thirdly, a person is said to judge as an assessor and by likeness, because he is like the judge in that his seat is raised above the others, and thus assessors are said to judge.[1] Some say that the perfect to whom judiciary power is promised (Matt. 19. 28) will judge in this sense, namely that they will be raised to the dignity of assessors, because they will appear above others at the judgment, and go forth *to meet Christ, into the air.* But this apparently does not suffice for the fulfilment of our Lord's promise (*ibid.*): *You shall sit . . . judging,* for He would seem to make judging something additional to sitting.

Hence there is a fourth way of judging, which will belong to perfect men as containing the decrees of Divine justice according to which men will be judged; thus a book containing the law might be said to judge, and so it is written (Apoc. 20. 12):[2] (*Judgment took her seat) and the books were opened.* Richard of S. Victor expounds this judging in this way (*De judic. potest.*),[3] and therefore he says: "Those who persevere in Divine contemplation, who read every day the book of wisdom, transcribe, so to speak, in their hearts whatever they grasp by their clear insight of the truth"; and further on: "What else are the hearts of those who judge, divinely instructed in all truth, but a codex of the law?"

---

[1] An assessor is one who sits by the judge.
[2] Cf. Dan. 7.10.   [3] PL 196, 1182.

Since, however, judging denotes an action exercised on another person, it follows that, properly speaking, he is said to judge who pronounces judgment on another. But this happens in two ways. First, by his own authority, and this belongs to the one who has dominion and power over others, and to whose ruling those who are judged are subject, and therefore it belongs to him to pass judgment on them. In this sense to judge belongs to God alone. Secondly, to judge is to acquaint others of the sentence delivered by another's authority, that is to announce the verdict already given. In this way perfect men will judge, because they will lead others to the knowledge of Divine justice, that these may know what is due to them on account of their merits, so that this very revelation of justice is called judgment. Hence Richard of S. Victor says (*loc. cit.*) that for "the judges to open the books of their decree in the presence of those who are to be judged signifies that they open their hearts to the gaze of all those who are below them, and that they reveal their knowledge in whatever pertains to the judgment."

Reply Obj. 1. This objection considers the judgment of authority which belongs to Christ alone, and the same answer applies to the *Second Objection.*

Reply Obj. 3. There is no reason why some of the saints should not reveal certain things to others, either by way of enlightenment, as the higher angels enlighten the lower, or by way of speech as the lower angels speak to the higher.

ARTICLE 2. *Whether the Judicial Power Corresponds to Voluntary Poverty?*

We proceed thus to the Second Article: It would seem that the judicial power does not correspond to voluntary poverty.

Objection 1. For it was promised to none but the twelve apostles (Matt. 19. 28): *You shall sit on twelve seats, judging*, etc. Since then those who are voluntarily poor are not all apostles, it would seem that the judicial power does not correspond to all.

Obj. 2. Further, To offer sacrifice to God of one's own body is more than to do so of outward things. Now martyrs and also virgins offer sacrifice to God of their own body, while the voluntarily poor offer sacrifice of outward things. Therefore the sublimity of the judicial power is more in keeping with martyrs and virgins than with those who are voluntarily poor.

Obj. 3. Further, It is written (John 5. 45): *There is one that accuseth you, Moses in whom you trust,*—"because you believe not his voice," according to a gloss,[1] and (*ibid.* 12. 48): *The word that I have spoken shall judge him in the last day.* Therefore the fact that a man propounds a law, or exhorts men by word to lead a good life, gives him the right to judge those who scorn his utterances. But this belongs to teachers. Therefore it is more competent to teachers than to those who are poor voluntarily.

Obj. 4. Further, Christ through being judged unjustly merited as man to be judge of all in His human nature, according to John 5. 27, *He hath given Him power to do judgment, because He is the Son of man.* Now those who suffer persecution for justice' sake are judged unjustly. Therefore the judicial power belongs to them rather than to the voluntarily poor.

Obj. 5. Further, A superior is not judged by his inferior. Now many who will have made lawful use of riches will have greater merit than many of the voluntarily poor. Therefore the voluntarily poor will not judge where those are to be judged.

On the contrary, It is written (Job 36. 6): *He saveth not the wicked, and He giveth judgment to the poor.*

Further, A gloss on Matt. 19. 28, *You who have left all things* (Vulg.,—*You who have followed Me.*) says:[2] "Those who left all things and followed God will be the judges; those who made right use of what they had lawfully will be judged," and thus the same conclusion follows as before.

I answer that, The judicial power is due especially to poverty on three counts. First, by reason of fitness, since voluntary poverty belongs to those who despise all the things of the world and cleave to Christ alone. Consequently there is nothing in them to turn away their judgment from justice, so that they are rendered able to be judges as loving the truth of justice above all things. Secondly, by reason of merit, since exaltation corresponds by way of merit to humility. Now of all the things that make man contemptible in this world humility is the chief, and for this reason the excellence of judicial power is promised to the poor, so that he who humbles himself for Christ's sake shall be exalted. Thirdly, because poverty disposes a man to the aforesaid manner of judging. For the reason why one of the saints will be said to

---

[1] *Glossa interl.* (v, 203v); Bede, *In Joann.* (PL 92, 704).
[2] *Glossa ordin.* (v, 60A); Gregory the Great, *Moral.*, x, 31 (PL 75, 950).

judge, as stated above (A. 1), is that he will have the heart instructed in all Divine truth which he will be thus able to make known to others. Now in the advancement to perfection, the first thing that occurs to be renounced is external wealth, because this is the last thing of all to be acquired. And that which is last in the order of generation is the first in the order of destruction; therefore among the beatitudes whereby we advance to perfection, the first place is given to poverty. Thus judicial power corresponds to poverty, in so far as this is the first disposition to the aforesaid perfection. Hence also it is that this same power is not promised to all who are voluntarily poor, but to those who leave all and follow Christ in accordance with the perfection of life.

Reply Obj. 1. According to Augustine,[1] "we must not imagine that because He says that they will sit on twelve seats, only twelve men will judge with Him; otherwise since we read that Matthias was appointed apostle in the place of the traitor Judas, Paul who worked more than the rest will have nowhere to sit as judge." Hence "the number twelve," as he states,[2] "signifies the whole multitude of those who will judge, because the two parts of seven, namely three and four, being multiplied together make twelve." Moreover twelve is a perfect number, being the double of six, which is a perfect number.

Or, speaking literally, He spoke to the twelve apostles in whose person he made this promise to all who follow them.

Reply Obj. 2. Virginity and martyrdom do not dispose man to retain the precepts of Divine justice in his heart in the same degree as poverty does; just as also, on the other hand, outward riches choke the word of God by the cares which they entail (Luke 8. 14). Or we may reply that poverty does not suffice alone to merit judicial power, but is the fundamental part of that perfection to which the judicial power corresponds. Therefore among those things regarding perfection which follow after poverty we may reckon both virginity and martyrdom and all the works of perfection; yet they do not rank as high as poverty, since the beginning of a thing is its chief part.

Reply Obj. 3. He who propounded the law or urged men to good will judge, in the causal sense, because others will be judged in reference to the words he has uttered or propounded. Hence the judicial power does not properly correspond to preaching or teaching. Or we may

reply that, as some say, three things are required for the judicial power: first that one renounce temporal cares, lest the mind be hindered from the contemplation of wisdom; secondly that one possess Divine justice by way of habit both as to knowledge and as to observance; thirdly that one should have taught others this same justice; and this teaching will be the perfection whereby a man merits to have judicial power.

Reply Obj. 4. Christ humbled Himself in that He was judged unjustly, for *He was offered because it was His own will* (Isa. 53. 7); and by His humility He merited His exaltation to judicial power, since all things are made subject to Him (Philip. 2. 8, 9). Hence, judicial power is more due to them who humble themselves of their own will by renouncing temporal goods, on account of which men are honoured by worldlings, than to those who are humbled by others.

Reply Obj. 5. An inferior cannot judge a superior by his own authority, but he can do so by the authority of a superior, as in the case of a judge-delegate. Hence it is not unfitting that it be granted to the poor as an accidental reward to judge others, even those who have higher merit in respect of the essential reward.

ARTICLE 3. *Whether the Angels Will Judge?*

We proceed thus to the Third Article: It would seem that the angels will judge.

Objection 1. For it is written (Matt. 25. 81): *When the Son of man shall come in His majesty, and all the angels with Him.* Now He is speaking of His coming to judgment. Therefore it would seem that also the angels will judge.

Obj. 2. Further, The orders of the angels take their names from the offices which they fulfil. Now one of the angelic orders is that of the Thrones, which would seem to pertain to the judicial power, since a throne is the judicial bench, a royal seat, a professor's chair. Therefore some of the angels will judge.

Obj. 3. Further, Equality with the angels is promised the saints after this life (Matt. 22. 30). If then men will have this power of judging, much more will the angels have it.

On the contrary, It is written (John 5. 27): *He hath given Him power to do judgment, because He is the Son of man.* But the angels have not the human nature in common with Him. Neither therefore do they share with Him in the judicial power.

Further, The same person is not judge and judge's minister. Now in this judgment the an-

---

[1] *City of God*, xx, 5 (PL 41, 663).   [2] *Ibid.*

gels will act as ministers of the Judge and, according to Matt. 13. 41: *The Son of man shall send His angels and they shall gather out of His kingdom all scandals.* Therefore the angels will not judge.

I answer that, The judge's assessors must be conformed to the judge. Now judgment is ascribed to the Son of man because He will appear to all, both good and wicked, in His human nature, although the whole Trinity will judge by authority. Consequently it is necessary also for the Judge's assessors to have the human nature, so as to be visible to all, both good and wicked. Hence it is not fitting for the angels to judge, although in a certain sense we may say that the angels will judge, namely by approving the sentence.

Reply Obj. 1. As a gloss on this passage observes,[1] the angels will come with Christ, not to judge, but "as witnesses of men's deeds, because it was under their guardianship that men did well or ill."

Reply Obj. 2. The name of Thrones is given to angels in reference to the judgment which God is ever pronouncing, by governing all things with supreme justice, of which judgment angels are in a way the executors and promulgators. On the other hand, the judgment of men by the man Christ will require human assessors.

Reply Obj. 3. Equality with angels is promised to men as regards the essential reward. But nothing hinders an accidental reward from being bestowed on men to the exclusion of the angels, as in the case of the virgins' and martyrs' crowns; and the same may be said of the judicial power.

Article 4. *Whether the Demons Will Carry Out the Sentence of the Judge on the Damned?*

We proceed thus to the Fourth Article: It would seem that the demons will not carry out the sentence of the Judge on the damned after the day of judgment.

Objection 1. For, according to the Apostle (I Cor. 15. 24): *He will then bring to nought all principality, and power, and virtue* (Vulg.,— *When He shall have brought to nought,* etc.). Therefore all supremacy will cease then. But the carrying out of the Judge's sentence implies some kind of supremacy. Therefore after the judgment day the demons will not carry out the Judge's sentence.

Obj. 2. Further, The demons sinned more

grievously than men. Therefore it is not just that men should be tortured by demons.

Obj. 3. Further, Just as the demons suggest evil things to men, so good angels suggest good things. Now it will not be the duty of the good angels to reward the good, but this will be done by God, immediately by Himself. Therefore neither will it be the duty of the demons to punish the wicked.

On the contrary, Sinners have subjected themselves to the devil by sinning. Therefore it is just that they should be subjected to him in their punishments, and punished by him as it were.

I answer that, The Master in the text of iv. *Sent.* d. 47[2] mentions two opinions on this question, both of which seem consistent with Divine justice, because it is just for man to be subjected to the devil for having sinned, and yet it is unjust for the demon to be over him. Accordingly the opinion which holds that after the judgment day the demons will not be placed over men to punish them, regards the order of Divine justice on the part of the demons punishing; while the contrary opinion regards the order of Divine justice on the part of the men punished.

Which of these opinions is nearer the truth we cannot know for certain. Yet I think it truer to say that just as, among the saved, order will be observed so that some will be enlightened and perfected by others (because all the orders of the heavenly hierarchies will continue for ever), so, too, will order be observed in punishments, men being punished by demons, lest the Divine order, whereby the angels are placed between the human nature and the Divine, be entirely set aside. Therefore just as the Divine illuminations are conveyed to men by the good angels, so too the demons execute the Divine justice on the wicked. Nor does this in any way diminish the punishment of the demons, since even in torturing others they are themselves tortured, because then the fellowship of the unhappy will not lessen but will increase unhappiness.

Reply Obj. 1. The supremacy which, it is declared, will be brought to nought by Christ in the time to come must be taken in the sense of the supremacy which is in keeping with the state of this world, wherein men are placed over men, angels over men, angels over angels, demons over demons, and demons over men; in every case so as either to lead towards the end or to lead astray from the end. But then, when

---

[1] *Glossa ordin.* (v, 77E); John Chrysostom, *In Matt.,* hom. LXXIX (PG 58, 717).

[2] QR II, 1021.

all things will have attained to that end, there will be no supremacy to lead astray from the end or to lead to it, but only that which maintains in the end, good or evil.

Reply Obj. 2. Although the demerit of the demons does not require that they be placed over men, since they made men subject to them unjustly, yet this is required by the order of their nature in relation to human nature, since "natural goods remain in them unimpaired" as Dionysius says (*Div. Nom.* iv).[1]

Reply Obj. 3. The good angels are not the cause of the principal reward in the elect, because all receive this immediately from God. Nevertheless the angels are the cause of certain accidental rewards in men, in so far as the higher angels enlighten those beneath them, both angels and men, concerning certain hidden things of God, which do not belong to the essence of Happiness. In like manner the damned will receive their principal punishment immediately from God, namely the everlasting banishment from the Divine vision; but there is no reason why the demons should not torture men with other sensible punishments. There is, however, this difference, that merit exalts, whereas sin debases. Therefore since the angelic nature is higher than the human, some on account of the excellence of their merit will be so far exalted as to be raised above the angels both in nature and reward, so that some angels will be enlightened by some men. On the other hand, no human sinners will, on account of a certain degree of virtue, attain to the eminence that attaches to the nature of the demons.

ARTICLE 5. *Whether All Men Will Be Present at the Judgment?*

We proceed thus to the Fifth Article: It would seem that men will not all be present at the judgment.

Objection 1. For it is written (Matt. 19. 28): *You . . . shall sit on twelve seats, judging the twelve tribes of Israel.* But all men do not belong to those twelve tribes. Therefore it would seem that men will not all be present at the judgment.

Obj. 2. Further, The same apparently is to be gathered from Ps. 1. 5, *The wicked shall not rise again in judgment.*

Obj. 3. Further, A man is brought to judgment that his merits may be discussed. But some there are who have acquired no merits, such as children who died before reaching the perfect age. Therefore they need not be

[1] Sect. 23 (PG 3, 725).

present at the judgment. Now there are many such. Therefore it would seem that men will not all be present at the judgment.

On the contrary, It is written (Acts 10. 42) that Christ *was appointed by God to be judge of the living and of the dead.* Now this division comprises all men, no matter how the living be distinct from the dead. Therefore all men will be present at the judgment.

Further, It is written (Apoc. 1. 7): *Behold He cometh with the clouds, and every eye shall see Him.* Now this would not be so unless all were present at the judgment. Therefore, etc.

I answer that, The judicial power was bestowed on Christ as man, in reward for the humility which He showed forth in His passion. Now in His passion He shed His blood for all in point of sufficiency, although through meeting with an obstacle in some, it did not have its effect in all. Therefore it is fitting that all men should assemble at the judgment, to see His exaltation in His human nature, in respect of which *He was appointed by God to be judge of the living and of the dead.* (Acts, 10. 42)

Reply Obj. 1. As Augustine says,[2] "It does not follow from the saying, 'Judging the twelve tribes of Israel,' that the tribe of Levi, which is the thirteenth, is not to be judged, or that they will judge that people alone, and not other nations." The reason why all other nations are denoted by the twelve tribes is because they were called by Christ to take the place of the twelve tribes.

Reply Obj. 2. The words, *The wicked shall not rise in judgment,* if referred to all sinners, mean that they will not arise to judge. But if the wicked denote unbelievers, the sense is that they will not rise to be judged because they are *already judged* (John 3. 18). All, however, will rise again to assemble at the judgment and witness the glory of the Judge.

Reply Obj. 3. Even children who have died before reaching the perfect age will be present at the judgment, not to be judged, but to see the Judge's glory.

ARTICLE 6. *Whether the Good Will Be Judged at the Judgment?*

We proceed thus to the Sixth Article: It would seem that none of the good will be judged at the judgment.

Objection 1. For it is declared (John 3. 18) that *he that believeth in Him is not judged.* Now all the good believed in Him. Therefore they will not be judged.

[2] *City of God,* xx, 5 (PL 41, 663).

Obj. 2. Further, Those who are uncertain of their bliss are not blessed; hence Augustine proves (*Gen. ad Lit.* xi, 17)[1] that the demons were never blessed. But the saints are now blessed. Therefore they are certain of their Happiness. Now what is certain is not submitted to judgment. Therefore the good will not be judged.

Obj. 3. Further, Fear is incompatible with Happiness. But the last judgment, which above all is described as terrible, cannot take place without inspiring fear into those who are to be judged. Hence Gregory observes on Job. 41. 16 *When he shall raise him up, the angels shall fear,* etc. (*Moral.* xxxiv, 7):[2] "Consider how the conscience of the wicked will then be troubled, when even the just are disturbed about their life." Therefore the blessed will not be judged.

On the contrary, It would seem that all the good will be judged, since it is written (II Cor. 5. 10): *We must all be manifested before the judgment seat of Christ, that every one may receive the proper thing of the body, according as he hath done, whether it be good or evil.* Now there is nothing else to be judged. Therefore all, even the good, will be judged.

Further, The "general" includes all. Now this is called the general judgment. Therefore all will be judged.

I answer that, The judgment comprises two things, namely the discussion of merits and the payment of rewards. As regards the payment of rewards, all will be judged, even the good, since the Divine sentence will appoint to each one the reward corresponding to his merit. But there is no discussion of merits save where good and evil merits are mingled together. Now those who build on the foundation of faith, *gold, silver, and precious stones* (I Cor. 3. 12), by devoting themselves wholly to the Divine service, and who have no marked admixture of evil merit, are not subjected to a discussion of their merits. Such are those who have entirely renounced the things of the world and are solicitously thoughtful of the things that are of God; therefore they will be saved but will not be judged. Others, however, build on the foundation of faith, wood, hay, stubble; they, in fact, love worldly things and are as busy about earthly concerns, yet so as to prefer nothing to Christ, but strive to redeem their sins with alms, and these have an admixture of good with evil merits. Hence they are subjected to a discussion of their merits, and consequently in

this account will be judged, and yet they will be saved.

Reply Obj. 1. Since punishment is the effect of justice, while reward is the effect of mercy, it follows that punishment is more especially ascribed antonomastically to judgment which is the act of justice, so that judgment is sometimes used to express condemnation. It is thus that we are to understand the words quoted, as a gloss on the passage remarks.[3]

Reply Obj. 2. The merits of the elect will be discussed, not to remove the uncertainty of their Happiness from the hearts of those who are to be judged, but that it may be made manifest to us that their good merits outweigh their evil merits, and thus God's justice be proved.

Reply Obj. 3. Gregory is speaking of the just who will still be in mortal flesh, and so he had already said: "Those who will still be in the body, although already brave and perfect, yet through being still in the flesh must be troubled with fear in the midst of such a whirlwind of terror." Hence it is clear that this fear refers to the time immediately before the judgment, most terrible indeed to the wicked, but not to the good, who will have no apprehension of evil.

The *arguments in the contrary sense* consider judgment as regards the payment of rewards.

ARTICLE 7. *Whether the Wicked Will Be Judged?*

We proceed thus to the Seventh Article: It would seem that none of the wicked will be judged.

Objection 1. For even as damnation is certain in the case of unbelievers, so is it in the case of those who die in mortal sin. Now it is declared because of the certainty of damnation (John 3. 18): *He that believeth not is already judged.* Therefore in like manner neither will other sinners be judged.

Obj. 2. Further, The voice of the Judge is most terrible to those who are condemned by His judgment. Now according to the text of iv. *Sent.* d. 47[4] and in the words of Gregory (*Moral.* xxvi, 27)[5] "the Judge will not address Himself to unbelievers." If therefore He were to address Himself to the believers about to be condemned, the unbelievers would reap a benefit from their unbelief, which is absurd.

On the contrary, It would seem that all the wicked are to be judged, because all the wicked

[1] PL 34, 438. [2] PL 76, 726.

[3] *Glossa interl.* (v, 196r); *Glossa ordin.* (v, 196A). Cf. Augustine, *In Joann., tract* XII (PL 35, 1490).
[4] QR II, 1019. [5] PL 76, 379.

will be sentenced to punishment according to the degree of their guilt. But this cannot be done without a judicial pronouncement. Therefore all the wicked will be judged.

I answer that, The judgment as regards the sentencing to punishment for sin concerns all the wicked, while the judgment as regards the discussion of merits concerns only believers. Because in unbelievers the foundation of faith is lacking, wtihout which all subsequent works are deprived of the perfection of a right intention, so that in them there is no admixture of good and evil works or merits requiring discussion. But believers in whom the foundation of faith remains have at least a praiseworthy act of faith, which though it is not meritorious without charity, yet is in itself directed to merit, and consequently they will be subjected to the discussion of merits. And so, believers who were at least counted as citizens of the City of God will be judged as citizens, and sentence of death will not be passed on them without a discussion of their merits; but unbelievers will be condemned as foes, who usually among men, are exterminated without their merits being discussed.

Reply Obj. 1. Although it is certain that those who die in mortal sin will be damned, nevertheless since they have an admixture of certain things connected with meriting well, it is necessary for the manifestation of Divine justice, that their merits be subjected to discussion, in order to make it clear that they are justly banished from the city of the saints, of which they appeared outwardly to be citizens.

Reply Obj. 2. Considered under this special aspect the words addressed to the believers about to be condemned will not be terrible, because they will reveal in them certain things pleasing to them, which it will be impossible to find in unbelievers, since *without faith it is impossible to please God* (Heb. 11. 6). But the sentence of condemnation which will be passed on them all will be terrible to all of them.

The *argument in the contrary sense* considered the judgment of retribution.

ARTICLE 8. *Whether at the Coming Judgment the Angels Will Be Judged?*

We proceed thus to the Eighth Article: It would seem that the angels will be judged at the coming judgment.

Objection 1. For it is written (I Cor. 6. 3): *Know you not that we shall judge angels?* But this cannot refer to the state of the present time. Therefore it should refer to the judgment to come.

Obj. 2. Further, It is written concerning Behemoth or Leviathan, whereby the devil is signified (Job 40. 28): *In the sight of all he shall be cast down;* and (Mark 1. 24)[1] the demon cried out to Christ: *Why art Thou come to destroy us before the time?* for, according to a gloss,[2] "the demons seeing our Lord on earth thought they were to be judged immediately." Therefore it would seem that a final judgment is in store for them.

Obj. 3. Further, It is written (II Pet. 2. 4): *God spared not the angels that sinned, but delivered them drawn down by infernal ropes to the lower hell, unto torments, to be reserved unto judgment.* Therefore it seems that the angels will be judged.

On the contrary, It is written (Nahum 1. 9) according to the Septuagint version: *God will not judge the same thing a second time.* But the wicked angels are already judged, and therefore it is written (John 16. 11): *The prince of this world is already judged.* Therefore the angels will not be judged in the time to come.

Further, Goodness and wickedness are more perfect in the angels than in men who are wayfarers. Now some men, good and wicked, will not be judged. Therefore neither will good or wicked angels be judged.

I answer that, The judgment of discussion in no way concerns either the good or the wicked angels, since neither is any evil to be found in the good angels, nor is any good liable to judgment to be found in the wicked angels. But if we speak of the judgment of retribution, we must distinguish a twofold retribution. One corresponds to the angels' personal merits and was made to both from the beginning, when some were raised to happiness, and others plunged into the depths of woe. The other corresponds to the merits, good or evil, procured through the angels, and this retribution will be made in the judgment to come, because the good angels will have an increased joy in the salvation of those whom they have prompted to deeds of merit, while the wicked will have an increase of torment through the manifold downfall of those whom they have incited to evil deeds. Consequently the judgment will not regard the angels directly, neither as judging

---

[1] The reference should be Matt. 8.29: *Art Thou come hither to torment us before the time?* The text of Mark reads: *Art thou come to destroy us?*

[2] *Glossa ordin.* (v, 92A); Bede, *In Mark,* bk. 1 (PL 92, 141).

nor as judged, but only men; but it will regard the angels indirectly somewhat, in so far as they were concerned in men's deeds.

Reply Obj. 1. This saying of the Apostle refers to the judgment of comparison, because certain men will be found to be placed higher than the angels.

Reply Obj. 2. The demons will then be cast down in the sight of all because they will be imprisoned for ever in the dungeon of hell, so that they will no more be free to go out, since this was permitted to them only in so far as they were directed by Divine providence to try the life of man.

The same answer applies to the *Third Objection.*

QUESTION XC
OF THE FORM OF THE JUDGE IN COMING TO THE JUDGMENT
(*In Three Articles*)

WE must now consider the form of the Judge in coming to the judgment. Under this head there are three points of inquiry: (1) Whether Christ will judge under the form of His humanity? (2) Whether He will appear under the form of His glorified humanity? (3) Whether His Godhead can be seen without joy?

ARTICLE 1. *Whether Christ Will Judge Under the Form of His Humanity?*

We proceed thus to the First Article: It would seem that Christ will not judge under the form of His humanity.

Objection 1. For judgment requires authority in the judge. Now Christ has authority over the quick and the dead as God, for thus is He the Lord and Creator of all. Therefore He will judge under the form of His Godhead.

Obj. 2. Further, Invincible power is requisite in a judge; therefore it is written (Eccles. 7. 6): *Seek not to be made a judge, unless thou have strength enough to extirpate iniquities.* Now invincible power belongs to Christ as God. Therefore He will judge under the form of the Godhead.

Obj. 3. Further, It is written (John 5. 22, 23): *The Father . . . hath given all judgment to the Son, that all men may honour the Son, as they honour the Father.* Now equal honour to that of the Father is not due to the Son in respect of his human nature. Therefore He will not judge under His human form.

Obj. 4. Further, It is written (Dan. 7. 9): *I beheld till thrones were placed and the Ancient*

of days sat. Now the thrones signify judicial power, and God is called the Ancient by reason of His eternity, according to Dionysius (*Div. Nom.* x).[1] Therefore it becomes the Son to judge as being eternal; and consequently not as man.

Obj. 5. Further, Augustine says (*Tract.* xix *in Joann.*),[2] and it is quoted in the text,[3] that "the resurrection of the soul is the work of the Word the Son of God, and the resurrection of the body is the work of the Word made the Son of man in the flesh." Now that last judgment regards the soul rather than the body. Therefore it becomes Christ to judge as God rather than as man.

On the contrary, It is written (John 5. 27): *He hath given Him power to do judgment, because He is the Son of man.*

Further, It is written (Job 36. 17): *Thy cause hath been judged as that of the wicked,*—"by Pilate" according to a gloss—therefore, *cause and judgment thou shalt recover,*— "that thou mayest judge justly," according to the gloss.[4] Now Christ was judged by Pilate with regard to His human nature. Therefore He will judge under the human nature.

Further, To Him it belongs to judge who made the law. Now Christ gave us the law of the Gospel while appearing in the human nature. Therefore He will judge under that same nature.

I answer that, Judgment requires a certain authority in the judge. Therefore it is written (Rom. 14. 4): *Who art thou that judgest another man's servant?* Hence it is becoming that Christ should judge in respect of His having authority over men to whom chiefly the last judgment will be directed. Now He is our Lord not only by reason of the Creation, since *the Lord He is God, He made us and not we ourselves* (Ps. 99. 3), but also by reason of the Redemption, which pertains to Him in respect of His human nature. Therefore *to this end Christ died and rose again, that He might be Lord both of the dead and of the living* (Rom. 14. 9). But the goods of the Creation would not suffice us to obtain the reward of eternal life without the addition of the benefit of the Redemption, on account of the obstacle accruing to created nature through the sin of our first parent. Hence, since the last judgment is

---

[1] Sect. 2 (PG 3, 937).
[2] PL 35, 1552.
[3] Peter Lombard, *Sent.,* IV, d. 48, chap. 3 (QR II, 1024).
[4] Cf. Bonaventure, *In Sent.,* IV, d. 48. A. 1, Q. 1, sed contra 2 (QR IV, 984); see Augustine, *Serm. ad Popul.,* serm. CXXVII, 7 (PL 38, 711).

directed to the admission of some to the kingdom, and the exclusion of others from it, it is becoming that Christ should preside at that judgment under the form of His human nature, since it is by favour of that same nature's Redemption that man is admitted to the kingdom. In his sense it is stated (Acts 10. 42) that *He . . . was appointed by God to be Judge of the living and of the dead.* And because by redeeming mankind He restored not only man but all creatures without exception,— since all creatures are bettered through man's restoration, according to Coloss. 1. 20, *Making peace through the blood of His cross, both as to things on earth, and the things that are in heaven,*— it follows that through His Passion Christ merited lordship and judicial power not over man alone, but over all creatures, according to Matt. 28. 18, *All power is given to Me, in heaven and in earth.*

Reply Obj. 1. Christ, in respect of His Divine nature, has authority of lordship over all creatures by right of creation; but in respect of His human nature He has authority of lordship merited through His Passion. The latter is secondary so to speak and acquired, while the former is natural and eternal.

Reply Obj. 2. Although Christ as man has not of Himself invincible power resulting from the natural power of the human species, nevertheless there is also in His human nature an invincible power derived from His Godhead, whereby all things are subjected under His feet (I Cor. 15. 25-28; Heb. 2. 8, 9). Hence He will judge in His human nature indeed, but by the power of His Godhead.

Reply Obj. 3. Christ would not have sufficed for the redemption of mankind had He been a mere man. Therefore from the very fact that He was able as man to redeem mankind, and thereby obtained judicial power, it is evident that He is God, and consequently is to be honoured equally with the Father, not as man but as God.

Reply Obj. 4. In that vision of Daniel the whole order of the judicial power is clearly expressed. This power is in God Himself as its first origin, and more especially in the Father Who is the fount of the entire Godhead; therefore it is stated in the first place that the *Ancient of days sat.* But the judicial power was transmitted from the Father to the Son, not only from eternity in respect of the Divine nature, but also in time in respect of the human nature wherein He merited it. Hence in this vision it is further stated (*verses* 13, 14): *Lo, one like the Son of man came with the clouds of heaven, and He came even to the Ancient of days. . . . And He gave Him power and glory, and a kingdom.*

Reply Obj. 5. Augustine is speaking by a kind of appropriation, so as to trace the effects which Christ wrought in the human nature to causes somewhat similar to them. And since we are made to the image and likeness of God in respect of our soul, and are of the same species as the man Christ in respect of our body, he ascribes to the Godhead the effects wrought by Christ in our souls, and those which He wrought or will work in our bodies he ascribes to His flesh; although His flesh, as being the instrument of His Godhead, has also its effect on our souls as Damascene asserts (*De Fide Orthod.* iii, 15),[1] according to the saying of Heb. 9 14, that His *blood* hath cleansed *our conscience from dead works.* And thus that *the Word was made flesh* is the cause of the resurrection of souls; and therefore also according to His human nature He is fittingly the Judge not only of bodily but also of spiritual goods.   .

ARTICLE 2. *Whether at the Judgment Christ Will Appear in His Glorified Humanity?*

We proceed thus to the Second Article: It would seem that at the judgment Christ will not appear in his glorified humanity.

Objection 1. For a gloss on John 19. 37, *They shall look on him whom they pierced,* says:[2] "Because He will come in the flesh wherein He was crucified." Now He was crucified in the form of weakness. Therefore He will appear in the form of weakness and not in the form of glory.

Obj. 2. Further, It is stated (Matt. 24. 30) that *the sign of the Son of man shall appear in heaven,* namely, "the sign of the cross," as Chrysostom says (*Hom.* lxxvi *in Matt.*),[3] for "Christ when coming to the judgment will show not only the scars of His wounds but even His most shameful death." Therefore it seems that He will not appear in the form of glory.

Obj. 3. Further, Christ will appear at the judgment under that form which can be gazed upon by all. Now Christ will not be visible to all, good and wicked, under the form of His glorified humanity, because the eye that is not glorified does not seem to be proportioned to

---

[1] PG 94, 1049; 1060.
[2] *Glossa interl.* (v, 240r); Augustine, *In Joann.*, **tr. cxx** (PL 35, 1954); cf. Bede, *In Joann.* (PL 92, 916).
[3] PG 58, 698.

see the clarity of a glorified body. Therefore He will not appear under a glorified form.

Obj. 4. Further, That which is promised as a reward to the just is not granted to the unjust. Now it is promised as a reward to the just that they shall see the glory of His humanity (John 10. 9): *He shall go in, and go out, and shall find pastures,* that is refreshment in His Godhead and humanity," according to the commentary of Augustine,[1] and Isa. 33. 17: *His eyes shall see the King in his beauty.* Therefore He will not appear to all in His glorified form.

Obj. 5. Further, Christ will judge in the form in which He was judged; hence a gloss on John 5. 21, *So the Son also giveth life to whom He will,* says:[2] "He will judge justly in the form wherein He was judged unjustly, that He may be visible to the wicked." Now He was judged in the form of weakness. Therefore He will appear in the same form at the judgment.

On the contrary, It is written (Luke 21. 27): *Then they shall see the Son of man coming in a cloud with great power and majesty.* Now majesty and power pertain to glory. Therefore He will appear in the form of glory.

Further, He who judges should be more conspicuous than those who are judged. Now the elect who will be judged by Christ will have a glorified body. Much more therefore will the Judge appear in a glorified form.

Further, As to be judged pertains to weakness, so as to judge pertains to authority and glory. Now at His first coming when Christ came to be judged, He appeared in the form of weakness. Therefore at the second coming, when He will come to judge, He will appear in the form of glory.

I answer that, Christ is called the mediator of God and men (I Tim. 2. 5) because He satisfies for men and intercedes for them to the Father, and confers on men things which belong to the Father, according to John 17. 22, *The glory which Thou hast given Me, I have given to them.* Accordingly then both these things belong to Him in that He communicates with both extremes, for in that He communicates with men, He takes their part with the Father, and in that He communicates with the Father, He bestows the Father's gifts on men. Since then at His first coming He came in order to make satisfaction for us to the Father, He came in the form of our weakness. But since at His second coming He will come in order to execute the Father's

justice on men, He will have to show forth His glory which is in Him by reason of His communication with the Father. And therefore He will appear in the form of glory.

Reply Obj. 1. He will appear in the same flesh, but not under the same form.

Reply Obj. 2. The sign of the cross will appear at the judgment, to denote not a present but a past weakness, so as to show how justly those were condemned who scorned so great mercy, especially those who persecuted Christ unjustly. The scars which will appear in His body will not be due to weakness, but will indicate the exceeding power whereby Christ overcame His enemies by His Passion and infirmity. He will also show forth His most shameful death, not by bringing it sensibly before the eye, as though He suffered it there, but by the things which will appear then, namely the signs of His past Passion, He will recall men to the thought of His past death.

Reply Obj. 3. A glorified body has it in its power to show itself or not to show itself to an eye that is not glorified, as stated above (Q. LXXXV, A. 2, REPLY 3). Hence Christ will be visible to all in His glorified form.

Reply Obj. 4. Even as our friend's glory gives us pleasure, so the glory and power of one we hate is most displeasing to us. Hence as the sight of the glory of Christ's humanity will be a reward to the just, so will it be a torment to Christ's enemies; therefore it is written (Isa. 26. 11): *Let the envious people see and be confounded and let fire* (that is, envy)[3] *devour Thy enemies.*

Reply Obj. 5. Form is taken there for human nature wherein He was judged and likewise will judge; but not for a quality of nature, namely of weakness, which will not be the same in Him when judging as when judged.

ARTICLE 3. *Whether the Godhead Can Be Seen by the Wicked Without Joy?*

We proceed thus to the Third Article: It would seem that the Godhead can be seen by the wicked without joy.

Objection 1. For there can be no doubt that the wicked will know with the greatest cerainty that Christ is God. Therefore they will see His Godhead, and yet they will not rejoice in seeing Christ. Therefore it will be possible to see it without joy.

Obj. 2. Further, The perverse will of the wicked is not more adverse to Christ's humanity than to His Godhead. Now the fact that they

---

[1] Alcher of Clairvaux, *De Spir. et An.,* IX (PL 40, 785).
[2] *Glossa ordin.* (V, 202B); Augustine, *In Joann.,* tr. XXIX (PL 35, 1553).
[3] *Glossa interl.* (IV, 49V).

will see the glory of His humanity will conduce to their punishment, as stated above (A. 2, REPLY 4). Therefore if they were to see His Godhead, there would be much more reason for them to grieve rather than rejoice.

Obj. 3. Further, The course of the affections is not a necessary sequel to that which is in the intellect; hence Augustine says[1] "The intellect precedes, the affections follow slowly or not at all." Now vision regards the intellect, while joy regards the affections. Therefore it will be possible to see the Godhead without joy.

Obj. 4. Further, Whatever is received into a thing is received according to the mode of the receiver and not of the received. But whatever is seen is, in a way, received into the seer. Therefore although the Godhead is in itself supremely enjoyable, nevertheless when seen by those who are plunged in grief, it will give no joy but rather displeasure.

Obj. 5. Further, As sense is to the sensible thing, so is the intellect to the intelligible thing. Now in the senses, "to the unhealthy palate bread is painful, to the healthy palate sweet," as Augustine says,[2] and the same happens with the other senses. Therefore since the damned have the intellect indisposed, it would seem that the vision of the uncreated light will give them pain rather than joy.

On the contrary, It is written (John 17. 3): *This is eternal life: That they may know Thee, the . . . true God.* Therefore it is clear that the essence of Happiness consists in seeing God. Now joy is essential to Happiness. Therefore the Godhead cannot be seen without joy.

Further, The essence of the Godhead is the essence of truth. Now it is delightful to every one to see the truth, and therefore "all naturally desire to know," as stated at the beginning of the *Metaphysics*.[3] Therefore it is impossible to see the Godhead without joy.

Further, If a certain vision is not always delightful, it happens sometimes to be painful. But intellectual vision is never painful since "the pleasure we take in understanding has no grief opposed to it," according to the Philosopher.[4] Since then the Godhead cannot be seen save by the intellect, it seems that the Godhead cannot be seen without joy.

I answer that, In every object of appetite or of pleasure two things may be considered, namely the thing which is desired or which gives pleasure, and the aspect of desirability or pleas-

urableness in that thing. Now according to Boëthius (*De Hebdom.*)[5] "that which is can have something besides what it is, but 'being' itself has no admixture of anything else beside itself." Hence that which is desirable or pleasant can have an admixture of something rendering it undesirable or unpleasant, but the very aspect of pleasurableness has not and cannot have anything mixed with it rendering it unpleasant or undesirable. Now it is possible for things that are pleasurable, by participation of goodness which is the aspect of desirability or pleasurableness, not to give pleasure when they are apprehended, but it is impossible for that which is good by its essence not to give pleasure when it is apprehended. Therefore since God is essentially His own goodness, it is impossible for the Godhead to be seen without joy.

Reply Obj. 1. The wicked will know most clearly that Christ is God, not through seeing His Godhead, but on account of the most manifest signs of His Godhead.

Reply Obj. 2. No one can hate the Godhead considered in itself, as neither can one hate goodness itself. But God is said to be hated by certain persons in respect of some of the effects of the Godhead, in so far as He does or commands something contrary to their will. Therefore the vision of the Godhead can be painful to no one.

Reply Obj. 3. The saying of Augustine applies when the thing apprehended previously by the intellect is good by participation and not essentially, such as all creatures are; therefore there may be something in them by reason of which the affections are not moved. In like manner God is known by wayfarers through His effects, and their intellect does not attain to the very essence of His goodness. Hence it is not necessary that the affections follow the intellect, as they would if the intellect saw God's essence which is His goodness.

Reply Obj. 4. Grief denotes not a disposition but a passion. Now every passion is removed if a stronger contrary cause supervene, and does not remove that cause. Accordingly the grief of the damned would be done away if they saw God in His essence.

Reply Obj. 5. The indisposition of an organ removes the natural proportion of the organ to the object that has a natural aptitude to please, and therefore the pleasure is hindered. But the indisposition which is in the damned does not remove the natural proportion whereby

---

[1] *Enarr.* in *Ps.*, Ps. 118, serm. 8, on verse 20 (PL 37, 1522).   [2] *Confessions*, VII, 20 (PL 32, 744).
[3] Aristotle, I, 1 (980ª21).   [4] *Topics*, I, 13 (106ª38).   [5] PL 64, 1311.

they are directed to the Divine goodness, since its image always remains in them. Hence the comparison fails.

QUESTION XCI
OF THE QUALITY OF THE WORLD AFTER THE JUDGMENT
(*In Five Articles*)

WE must next discuss the quality which the world and those who rise again will have after the judgment. Here a threefold matter offers itself to our consideration: (1) The state and quality of the world. (2) The state of the blessed (Q. XCII). (3) The state of the wicked (Q. XCVII).

Under the first head there are five points of inquiry: (1) Whether there will be a renewal of the world? (2) Whether the movement of the heavenly bodies will cease? (3) Whether the heavenly bodies will be more brilliant? (4) Whether the elements will receive an additional clarity? (5) Whether the animals and plants will remain?

ARTICLE 1. *Whether the World Will Be Renewed?*

We proceed thus to the First Article: It would seem that the world will never be renewed.

Objection 1. For nothing will be but what was at some time as to its species: *What is it that hath been? the same thing that shall be* (Eccl. 1. 9). Now the world never had any disposition other than it has now as to essential parts, both genera and species. Therefore it will never be renewed.

Obj. 2. Further, Renewal is a kind of alteration. But it is impossible for the universe to be changed, because whatever is changed argues some alterant that is not changed, and which nevertheless is a subject of local movement, and it is impossible to place such a thing outside the universe. Therefore it is impossible for the world to be renewed.

Obj. 3. Further, It is stated (Gen. 2. 2) that *God . . . rested on the seventh day from all His work which He had done,* and holy men explain that He rested from forming new creatures.[1] Now when things were first established, the mode imposed upon them was the same as they have now in the natural order. Therefore they will never have any other.

Obj. 4. Further, The disposition which things have now is natural to them. Therefore if they be altered to another disposition, this disposition will be unnatural to them. Now whatever is unnatural and accidental cannot last for ever.[2] Therefore this disposition acquired by being renewed will be taken away from them, and thus there will be a cycle of changes in the world as Empedocles[3] and Origen (*Peri Archon,* ii, 3)[4] maintained, and after this world there will be another, and after that again another.

Obj. 5. Further, Newness of glory is given to the rational creature as a reward. Now where there is no merit, there can be no reward. Since then insensible creatures have merited nothing, it would seem that they will not be renewed.

On the contrary, It is written (Isa. 65. 17): *Behold I create new heavens and a new earth, and the former things shall not be in remembrance;* and (Apoc. 21. 1): *I saw a new heaven and a new earth. For the first heaven and the first earth was gone.*

Further, The dwelling should befit the dweller. But the world was made to be man's dwelling. Therefore it should befit man. Now man will be renewed. Therefore the world will be likewise.

Further, Every beast loveth its like (Ecclus. 13. 19), and so it is evident that likeness is the reason of love. Now man has some likeness to the universe, for which reason he is called "a little world."[5] Hence man loves the whole world naturally and consequently desires its good. Therefore, that man's desire be satisfied the universe must also be made better.

I answer that, We believe all corporeal things to have been made for man's sake, and therefore all things are stated to be subject to him (Ps. 8. 8). Now they serve man in two ways, first, as sustenance to his bodily life, secondly, as helping him to know God, since man sees the invisible things of God by the things that are made (Rom. 1. 20). Accordingly glorified man will in no way need creatures to render him the first of these services, since his body will be altogether incorruptible, the Divine power effecting this through the soul which it will glorify immediately. Again man will not

---

[1] Cf. Augustine, *Gen. ad litt.,* IV, 12 (PL 34, 304); Bede, *In Pentat.,* BK. I, on Gen. 2.2 (PL 91, 202); cf. *Glossa ordin.* on Gen. 2.2 (I, 34C).

[2] Aristotle, *Heavens,* I, 2 (269[b]6); cf. II, 3 (286[a]17).

[3] Cf. Aristotle, *Physics,* VIII, 1 (252[a]19); Empedocles, in Diels, *Die Fragmente,* n. 17 (I, 229); cf. Albert the Great, *In de Cælo,* I, tr. 4, chap. 1 (BO IV, 92); *In Sent.,* IV, d. 43, A. 1, sed contra 2 (BO XXX, 501); cf. Duhem, *Le Système du Monde* (I, 75, 76). See above, Q. LXXVII, A. 1.

[4] PG 11, 128; III, 5 (PG 11, 331).

[5] Cf. Aristotle, *Physics,* VIII, 2 (252[b]26).

need the second service as to intellectual knowledge, since by that knowledge he will see God immediately in His essence. The carnal eye, however, will be unable to attain to this vision of the Essence; therefore that it may be fittingly comforted in the vision of God, it will see the Godhead in Its corporeal effects, wherein manifest proofs of the Divine majesty will appear, especially in Christ's flesh, and secondarily in the bodies of the blessed, and afterwards in all other bodies. Hence those bodies also will need to receive a greater inflow from the Divine goodness than now, not indeed so as to change their species, but so as to add a certain perfection of glory, and such will be the renewal of the world. Therefore at the one same time, the world will be renewed, and man will be glorified.

Reply Obj. 1. Solomon is speaking there of the natural course; this is evident from his adding: *Nothing under the sun is new.* For since the movement of the sun follows a circle, those things which are subject to the sun's power must have some kind of circular movement. This consists in the fact that things which were before return the same in species but different in the individual.[1] But things belonging to the state of glory are not *under the sun.*

Reply Obj. 2. This argument considers natural change which proceeds from a natural agent, which acts from natural necessity. For such an agent cannot produce different dispositions, unless it be itself disposed differently. But things done by God proceed from freedom of will, and therefore it is possible, without any change in God Who wills it, for the universe to have at one time one disposition, and another at another time. Thus this renewal will not be reduced to a cause that is moved, but to an immovable principle, namely God.

Reply Obj. 3. God is stated to have ceased on the seventh day forming new creatures, since nothing was made afterwards that was not previously in some likeness either generically, or specifically, or at least as in a seminal principle, or even as in an obediential potency. I say then that the future renewal of the world preceded in the works of the six days by way of a remote likeness, namely in the glory and grace of the angels. Moreover it preceded in the obediential potency which was then bestowed on the creature to the effect of its receiving this same renewal by the Divine agency.

Reply Obj. 4. This disposition of newness will be neither natural nor contrary to nature,

[1] Aristotle, *Generation and Corruption*, II, 11 (338^{b}16).

but above nature (just as grace and glory are above the nature of the soul), and it will proceed from an everlasting agent which will preserve it for ever.

Reply Obj. 5. Although, properly speaking, insensible bodies will not have merited this glory, yet man merited that this glory should be bestowed on the whole universe, in so far as this conduces to man's increase of glory. Thus a man merits to be clothed in more splendid robes, which splendour the robes in no way merited themselves.

ARTICLE 2. *Whether the Movement of the Heavenly Bodies Will Cease?*

We thus proceed to the Second Article: It seems that when the world is thus renewed the movement of the heavenly bodies will not cease.

Objection 1. For it is written (Gen. 8. 22): *All the days of the earth . . . cold and heat, summer and winter, night and day shall not cease.* Now night and day, summer and winter result from the movement of the sun. Therefore the movement of the sun will never cease.

Obj. 2. Further, It is written (Jerem. 31. 35, 36): *Thus saith the Lord Who giveth the sun for the light of the day, the order of the moon and of the stars for the light of the night: Who stirreth up the sea, and the waves thereof roar . . . . If these ordinances shall fail before Me . . . then also the seed of Israel shall fail, so as not to be a nation before Me for ever.* Now the seed of Israel shall never fail, but will remain for ever. Therefore the laws of day and of the sea waves, which result from the heavenly movement, will remain for ever. Therefore the movement of the heaven will never cease.

Obj. 3. Further, The substance of the heavenly bodies will remain for ever. Now it is useless to admit the existence of a thing unless you admit the purpose for which it was made, and the heavenly bodies were made in order *to divide the day and the night,* and to be *for signs, and for seasons, and for days and for years* (Gen. 1. 14). But they cannot do this except by movement. Therefore their movement will remain for ever, for otherwise those bodies would remain without a purpose.

Obj. 4. Further, In this renewal of the world the whole world will be bettered. Therefore no body will be deprived of what pertains to its perfection. Now movement belongs to the perfection of a heavenly body, because "those bodies participate of the Divine goodness by their movement."[1] Therefore the movement of the heaven will not cease.

Obj. 5. Further, The sun successively gives light to the various parts of the world, by reason of its circular movement. Therefore if the circular movement of the heaven ceases, it follows that in some part of the earth's surface there will be perpetual darkness, which is unbecoming to the above mentioned renewal.

Obj. 6. Further, If the movement were to cease, this could only be because movement causes some imperfection in the heaven, for instance wear and tear, which is impossible, since this movement is natural, and the heavenly bodies are impassible; therefore they are not worn out by movement.[2] Therefore the movement of the heaven will never cease.

Obj. 7. Further, A potency is useless if it is not reduced to act. Now in whatever position the heavenly body is placed it is in potency to another position. Therefore unless this potency is reduced to act, it would remain useless, and would always be imperfect. But it cannot be reduced to act save by local movement. Therefore it will always be in motion.

Obj. 8. Further, If a thing is indifferent in relation to more than one thing, either both are ascribed to it, or neither. Now the sun is indifferent to being in the east or in the west; otherwise its movement would not be uniform throughout, since it would move more rapidly to the place which is more natural to it. Therefore either neither position is ascribed to the sun, or both. But neither both nor neither can be ascribed to it, except successively by movement; for if it stands still, it has to stand in some position. Therefore the solar body will always be in motion, and in like manner all other heavenly bodies.

Obj. 9. Further, The movement of the heaven is the cause of time. Therefore if the movement of the heaven fail, time must fail, and if this were to fail, it would fail in an instant. Now an instant is defined as "the beginning of the future and the end of the past."[3] Consequently there would be time after the last instant of time, which is impossible. Therefore the movement of the heavens will never cease.

Obj. 10. Further, Glory does not remove nature. But the movement of the heaven is natural. Therefore it is not deprived of its movement by glory.

On the contrary, It is stated (Apoc. 10. 6)

that the angel who appeared, *swore by him that liveth for ever and ever . . . that time shall be no longer,* namely after the seventh angel shall have sounded the trumpet, at the sound of which *the dead shall rise again* (I Cor. 15. 52). Now if time is not, there is no movement of the heaven. Therefore the movement of the heaven will cease.

Further: Thy sun shall go down no more, and thy moon shall not decrease (Isa. 60. 20). Now the setting of the sun and the phases of the moon are caused by the movement of the heavens. Therefore the heavenly movement will cease at length.

Further, It is shown in the treatise on *Generation and Corruption*[4] that "the movement of the heaven is for the sake of continual generation in this lower world." But generation will cease when the number of the elect is complete. Therefore the movement of the heaven will cease.

Further, All movement is for some end.[5] But all movement for an end ceases when the end is obtained. Therefore either the movement of the heaven will never obtain its end, and thus it would be useless, or it will cease at length.

Further, Rest is more noble than movement, because things are more likened to God, Who is supremely immovable, by being themselves unmoved. Now the movement of lower bodies terminates naturally in rest. Therefore since the heavenly bodies are far nobler, their movement terminates naturally in rest.

I answer that, There are three opinions touching this question. The first is of the philosophers who assert that the movement of the heaven will last for ever. But this is not in keeping with our faith, which holds that the elect are in a certain number preordained by God, so that the begetting of men will not last for ever, and for the same reason, neither will other things that are directed to the begetting of men, such as the movement of the heaven and the variations of the elements. Others say that the movement of the heaven will cease naturally. But this again is false, since every body that is moved naturally has a place in which it rests naturally, to which it is moved naturally, and from which it is not moved except by violence. Now no such place can be assigned to the heavenly body, since it is not more natural to the sun to move towards a point in the east than to move away from it, and so either its movement would not be al-

---

[1] Aristotle, *Heavens*, II, 12 (292[b]7).

[2] *Ibid.*, II, 1 (284[a]14).

[3] Aristotle, *Physics*, VIII, 1 (251[b]21).

[4] Aristotle, II, 10 (336[a]25).

[5] Aristotle, *Metaphysics*, II, 2 (994[b]15).

together natural, or its movement would not naturally terminate in rest. Hence we must agree with others who say that the movement of the heaven will cease at this renewal of the world, not indeed by any natural cause, but as a result of the will of God. For the body in question, like other bodies, was made to serve man in the two ways above mentioned (A. 1), and hereafter in the state of glory man will no longer need one of these services, that namely in respect of which the heavenly bodies serve man for the sustenance of his bodily life. Now in this way the heavenly bodies serve man by their movement, in so far as by the heavenly movement the human race is multiplied, plants and animals needful for man's use generated, and the temperature of the atmosphere rendered conducive to health. Therefore the movement of the heavenly body will cease as soon as man is glorified.

Reply Obj. 1. These words refer to the earth in its present state, when it is able to be the principle of the generation and corruption of plants. This is evident from its being said there: *All the days of the earth, seed time and harvest,* etc. And it is to be granted absolutely that as long as the earth is fit for seed time and harvest, the movement of the heaven will not cease.

We reply in like manner to *Obj.* 2 that the Lord is speaking there of the duration of the seed of Israel with regard to the present state. This is evident from the words: *Then also the seed of Israel shall fail, so as not to be a nation before Me for ever.* For after this state there will be no succession of days, and therefore the laws also which He had mentioned will cease after this state.

Reply Obj. 3. The end which is there assigned to the heavenly bodies is their proximate end, because it is their proper act. But this act is directed further to another end, namely the service of man, which is shown by the words of Deut. 4. 19: *Lest perhaps lifting up thy eyes to heaven, thou see the sun and the moon and all the stars of heaven, and being deceived by error thou adore and serve them, which the Lord thy God created for the service of all the nations, that are under heaven.* Therefore we should form our judgment of the heavenly bodies from the service of man, rather than from the end assigned to them in Genesis. Moreover the heavenly bodies, as stated above, will serve glorified man in another way; hence it does not follow that they will remain without a purpose.

Reply Obj. 4. Movement does not belong to the perfection of a heavenly body, except in so far as thereby it is the cause of generation and corruption in this lower world, and in that respect also this movement makes the heavenly body participate the Divine goodness by way of a certain likeness of causality. But movement does not belong to the perfection the substance of the heaven, which substance will remain. Therefore it does not follow that when this movement ceases, the substance of the heaven will lose something of its perfection.

Reply Obj. 5. All the elemental bodies will have in themselves a certain clarity of glory. Hence though part of the surface of the earth may not be lit up by the sun, there will by no means be any darkness there.

Reply Obj. 6. A gloss of Ambrose on Rom. 8. 22, *Every creature groaneth,* etc. says[1] that "all the elements labour to fulfil their offices: thus the sun and moon fill the places appointed to them not without work; this is for our sake, and so they will rest when we are taken up to heaven." This work, in my opinion, does not signify that any stress or passion occurs to these bodies from their movement, since this movement is natural to them and in no way violent, as is proved in the book on the *Heavens.*[2] But work here denotes a defect in relation to the term to which a thing tends. Hence since this movement is ordained by Divine providence to the completion of the number of the elect, it follows that as long as the latter is incomplete, this movement has not reached the term to which it was ordered; hence it is said metaphorically to labour, as a man who has not what he intends to have. This defect will be removed from the heaven when the number of the elect is complete. Or it may refer to the desire of the future renewal, which it awaits from the Divine disposal.

Reply Obj. 7. In a heavenly body there is no potency that can be perfected by place, or that is made for this end which is to be in such and such a place. But potency to situation in a place is related to a heavenly body as the craftsman's potency to construct various houses of one kind; for if he construct one of these he is not said to have the potency uselessly, and in like manner in whatever situation a heavenly body be placed, its potency to be in a place will not remain incomplete or without a purpose.

[1] *Glossa ordin.* (VI, 19B); *Glossa* Lombardi (PL 191, 1445); Ambrosiaster, *In Rom.* (PL 17, 131).
[2] Aristotle, I, 2 (269^{b}2); cf. II, 1 (284^{a}14).

Reply Obj. 8. Although a heavenly body, so far as regards its nature, is equally inclined to every situation that it can possibly occupy, nevertheless in comparison with things outside it, it is not equally inclined to every situation, but in respect of one situation it has a more noble disposition in comparison with certain things than in respect of another situation; thus in our regard the sun has a more noble disposition at day-time than at night-time. Hence it is probable, since the entire renewal of the world is directed to man, that the heaven will have in this renewal the most noble situation possible in relation to our dwelling there. Or, according to some, the heaven will rest in that situation in which it was made, for otherwise one of its revolutions would remain incomplete. But this argument seems improbable, for since a revolution of the heaven takes no less than 36,000 years to complete, it would follow that the world must last that length of time, which does not seem probable. Moreover according to this it would be possible to know when the world will come to an end. For we may conclude with probability from astronomers in what position the heavenly bodies were made, by taking into consideration the number of years that have elapsed since the beginning of the world, and in the same way it would be possible to know the exact number of years it would take them to return to a like position; but the time of the world's end is stated to be unknown.

Reply Obj. 9. Time will at length cease, when the heavenly movement ceases. Yet that last "now" will not be the beginning of the future. For the definition quoted applies to the "now" only as continuous with the parts of time, not as terminating the whole of time.

Reply Obj. 10. The movement of the heaven is said to be natural, not as though it were part of nature in the same way as we speak of natural principles, but because it has its principle in the nature of a body, not indeed its active but its receptive principle. Its active principle is a spiritual substance, as the Commentator says on the treatise on the *Heavens*;[1] and consequently it is not unreasonable for this movement to be done away by the renewal of glory, since the nature of the heavenly body will not alter through the cessation of that movement.

We grant the other *objections* which argue *in the contrary sense*, namely the first three, because they conclude in due manner. But since the remaining two seem to conclude that the

[1] Bk. I, comm. 5 (v, 5E).

movement of the heaven will cease naturally, we must reply to them.

To the first, then, we reply that movement ceases when its purpose is attained, provided this is a sequel to, and does not accompany the movement. Now the purpose of the heavenly movement, according to philosophers, accompanies that movement, namely the imitation of the Divine goodness in the causality of that movement with respect to this lower world. Hence it does not follow that this movement ceases naturally.

To the second we reply that although immobility is nobler absolutely than movement, yet movement in a subject which thereby can acquire a perfect participation of the Divine goodness is nobler than rest in a subject which is altogether unable to acquire that perfection by movement. For this reason the earth which is the lowest of the elements is without movement, although God Who is exalted above all things is without movement, by Whom the more noble bodies are moved. Hence also it is that the movements of the higher bodies might be held to be perpetual, so far as their natural power is concerned, and never to terminate in rest, although the movement of lower bodies terminates in rest.

ARTICLE 3. *Whether the Brightness of the Heavenly Bodies Will Be Increased at This Renewal?*

We proceed thus to the Third Article: It would seem that the brightness of the heavenly bodies will not be increased at this renewal.

Objection 1. For this renewal as regards the lower bodies will be caused by the cleansing fire. But the cleansing fire will not reach the heavenly bodies. Therefore the heavenly bodies will not be renewed by receiving an increase of brightness.

Obj. 2. Further, Just as the heavenly bodies are the cause of generation in this lower world by their movement, so are they by their light. But, when generation ceases, movement will cease as stated above (A. 2). Therefore in like manner the light of the heavenly bodies will cease rather than increase.

Obj. 3. Further, If the heavenly bodies will be renewed when man is renewed, it follows that when man deteriorated they deteriorated likewise. But this does not seem probable, since these bodies are unalterable as to their substance. Therefore neither will they be renewed when man is renewed.

Obj. 4. Further, If they deteriorated then, it

follows that their deterioration was on a par with the amelioration which, it is said, will accrue to them at man's renewal. Now it is written (Isa. 30. 26) that *the light of the moon shall be as the light of the sun.* Therefore in the original state before sin the moon shone as much as the sun does now. Therefore whenever the moon was over the earth, it made it to be day as the sun does now, which is proved manifestly to be false from the statement of Gen. 1. 16 that the moon was made *to rule the night.* Therefore when man sinned, the heavenly bodies were not deprived of their light; and so their light will not be increased, so it seems, when man is glorified.

Obj. 5. Further, The brightness of the heavenly bodies, like other creatures, is directed to the use of man. Now, after the resurrection, the brightness of the sun will be of no use to man, for it is written (Isa. 60. 19): *Thou shalt no more have the sun for thy light by day, neither shall the brightness of the moon enlighten thee,* and (Apoc. 21. 23): *The city hath no need of the sun, nor of the moon to shine in it.* Therefore their brightness will not be increased.

Obj. 6. Further, It would not be a wise craftsman who would make very great instruments for the making of a small work. Now man is a very small thing in comparison with the heavenly bodies, which by their huge bulk surpass the size of man almost beyond comparison; in fact the size of the whole earth in comparison with the heaven is as a point compared with a sphere, as astronomers say.[1] Since then God is most wise it would seem that man is not the end of the creation of the heavens, and so it does not seem that the heaven should deteriorate when he sinned, or that it should be bettered when he is glorified.

On the contrary, It is written (Isa. 30. 26): *The light of the moon shall be as the light of the sun, and the light of the sun shall be sevenfold.*

Further, The whole world will be renewed for the better. But the heaven is the more noble part of the corporeal world. Therefore it will be changed for the better. But this cannot be unless it shine out with greater brightness. Therefore its brightness will be bettered and will increase.

Further, Every creature that groaneth and travaileth in pain, awaiteth the revelation of the glory of the children of God (Rom. 8. 21, 22).[2] Now such are the heavenly bodies, as a gloss says[3] on the same passage. Therefore they await the glory of the saints. But they would not await it unless they were to gain something by it. Therefore their brightness will increase thereby, since it is their chief beauty.

I answer that, The renewal of the world is directed to the end that after this renewal has taken place God may become visible to man by signs so manifest as to be perceived as it were by his senses. Now creatures lead to the knowledge of God chiefly by their comeliness and beauty, which show forth the wisdom of their Maker and Governor; therefore it is written (Wisd. 13. 5): *By the greatness of the beauty and of the creature, the Creator of them may be seen, so as to be known thereby.* And the beauty of the heavenly bodies consists chiefly in light; hence it is written (Ecclus. 43. 10): *The glory of the stars is the beauty of heaven, the Lord enlighteneth the world on high.* Hence the heavenly bodies will be bettered, especially as regards their brightness. But to what degree and in what way this betterment will take place is known to Him alone Who will bring it about.

Reply Obj. 1. The cleansing fire will not cause the form of the renewal, but will only dispose to it, by cleansing from the vileness of sin and the impurity resulting from the mingling of bodies, and this is not to be found in the heavenly bodies. Hence although the heavenly bodies are not to be cleansed by fire, they are nevertheless to be Divinely renewed.

Reply Obj. 2. Movement does not denote perfection in the thing moved, considered in itself, since movement is the act of that which is imperfect, although it may pertain to the perfection of the body in so far as the latter is the cause of something. But light belongs to the perfection of a lightsome body, even considered in its substance, and consequently after the heavenly body has ceased to be the cause of generation, its brightness will remain, while its movement will cease.

Reply Obj. 3. A gloss on Isa. 30. 26, *The light of the moon shall be as the light of the sun,* says:[4] "All things made for man's sake deteriorated at his fall, and sun and moon diminished in light." This diminishment is under-

---

[1] Ptolemy, *Syntaxis Mathematica* (*Almagest.*), 1, 6 (HB 1, 20); cf. Averroes, *In De Cælo,* BK. II, comm. 110 (V, 171G); see Duhem, *Le Système du Monde* (1, 477).

[2] *The creature also itself shall be delivered from the servitude of corruption, into the liberty of the children of God. For we know that every creature groaneth and travaileth in pain,* etc.   [3] *Glossa ordin.* (VI, 19B); *Glossa* Lombardi (PL 191, 1445).

[4] *Glossa interl.* (IV, 57v).

stood by some to mean a real lessening of light. Nor does it matter that the heavenly bodies are by nature unalterable, because this alteration was brought about by the Divine power.

Others, however, with greater probability, take this diminishment to mean, not a real lessening of light, but a lessening in reference to man's use; because after sin man did not receive as much benefit from the light of the heavenly bodies as before. In the same sense we read (Gen. 3. 17, 18): *Cursed is the earth in thy work. . . . Thorns and thistles shall it bring forth to thee;* although it would have brought forth thorns and thistles before sin, but not as a punishment to man.

Nor does it follow that, supposing the light of the heavenly bodies not to have been lessened essentially through man sinning, it will not really be increased at man's glorification, because man's sin wrought no change upon the state of the universe, since both before and after sin man had an animal life, which needs the movement and generation of a corporeal creature; but man's glorification will bring a change upon the state of all corporeal creatures, as stated above (A. 1). Hence there is no comparison.

Reply Obj. 4. This lessening, according to the more probable opinion, refers not to the substance but to the effect. Hence it does not follow that the moon while over the earth would have made it to be day, but that man would have derived as much benefit from the light of the moon then as now from the light of the sun. After the resurrection, however, when the light of the moon will be increased in very truth, there will be night nowhere on earth but only in the centre of the earth, where hell will be, because then, as stated, the moon will shine as brightly as the sun does now; the sun seven times as much as now, and the bodies of the blessed seven times more than the sun, although there is no authority or reason to prove this.

Reply Obj. 5. A thing may be useful to man in two ways. First, by reason of necessity, and thus no creature will be useful to man because he will have complete sufficiency from God. This is signified (Apoc. 21. 23) by the words quoted, according to which that *city hath no need of the sun, nor of the moon.* Secondly, on account of a greater perfection, and thus man will make use of other creatures, yet not as necessary to him in order to obtain his end, in which way he makes use of them now.

Reply Obj. 6. This is the argument of Rabbi Moses who endeavours to prove[1] that the world was by no means made for man's use. Therefore he maintains that what we read in the Old Testament about the renewal of the world, as instanced by the quotations from Isaias, is said metaphorically,[2] and that even as the sun is said to be darkened in reference to a person when he encounters a great sorrow so as not to know what to do (which way of speaking is customary to Scripture), so on the other hand the sun is said to shine brighter for a person, and the whole world to be renewed, when he is brought from a state of sorrow to one of very great joy. But this is not in harmony with the authority and commentaries of holy men. Consequently we must answer this argument by saying that although the heavenly bodies far surpass the human body, yet the rational soul surpasses the heavenly bodies far more than these surpass the human body. Hence it is not unreasonable to say that the heavenly bodies were made for man's sake; not, however, as though this were the principal end, since the principal end of all things is God.

ARTICLE 4. *Whether the Elements Will Be Renewed By an Addition of Brightness?*

We proceed thus to the Fourth Article: It would seem that the elements will not be renewed by receiving some kind of brightness.

Objection 1. For just as light is a quality proper to a heavenly body, so are hot and cold, wet and dry, qualities proper to the elements. Therefore as the heaven is renewed by an increase of brightness, so ought the elements to be renewed by an increase of active and passive qualities.

Obj. 2. Further, Rarity and density are qualities of the elements, and the elements will not be deprived of them at this renewal. Now the rarity and density of the elements would seem to be an obstacle to brightness, since a bright body needs to be condensed, for which reason the rarity of the air seems incompatible with brightness, and in like manner the density of the earth which is an obstacle to transparency. Therefore it is impossible for the elements to be renewed by the addition of brightness.

Obj. 3. Further, It is agreed that the damned will be in the earth. Yet they will be in darkness not only internal but also external. Therefore the earth will not be endowed with bright-

---

[1] *Guide,* III, 13 (FR 274).
[2] *Op. cit.,* II, 29 (FR 204, 207).

ness in this renewal, nor for the same reason will the other elements.

Obj. 4. Further, Increase of brightness in the elements implies an increase of heat. If therefore at this renewal the brightness of the elements be greater than it is now, their heat will likewise be greater; and thus it would seem that they will be changed from their natural qualities, which are in them according to a fixed measure, and this is absurd.

Obj. 5. Further, The good of the universe which consists in the order and harmony of the parts is more excellent than the good of any individual creature. But if one creature be bettered, the good of the universe is done away, since there will no longer be the same harmony. Therefore if the elemental bodies, which according to their natural degree in the universe should be devoid of brightness, were to be endowed with brightness, the prefection of the universe would be diminished thereby rather than increased.

On the contrary, It is written (Apoc. 21. 1): *I saw a new heaven and a new earth.* Now the heaven will be renewed by an increase of brightness. Therefore the earth and likewise the other elements will also.

Further, The lower bodies, like the higher, are for man's use. Now the corporeal creature will be rewarded for its services to man, as a gloss of Ambrose seems to say[1] on Rom. 8. 22, *Every creature groaneth.* Therefore the elements will be glorified as well as the heavenly bodies.

Further, Man's body is composed of the elements. Therefore the elemental particles that are in man's body will be glorified by the addition of brightness when man is glorified. Now it is fitting that whole and part should have the same disposition. Therefore it is fitting that the elements themselves should be endowed with brightness.

I answer that, Just as there is a certain order between the heavenly spirits and the earthly, that is, human spirits, so is there an order between heavenly bodies and earthly bodies. Since then the corporeal creature was made for the sake of the spiritual and is ruled thereby, it follows that corporeal things are dealt with similarly to spiritual things. Now in this final consummation of things the lower spirits will receive the properties of the higher spirits, because men will be as the angels in heaven (Matt. 22. 30); and this will be accomplished by conferring the highest degree of perfection on that in which the human spirit agrees with the angelic. Therefore, in like manner, since the lower bodies do not agree with the heavenly bodies except in the nature of light and transparency,[2] it follows that the lower bodies are to be perfected chiefly as regards brightness. Hence all the elements will be clothed with a certain brightness, not equally, however, but according to their mode; for it is said that the earth on its outward surface will be as transparent as glass, water as crystal, the air as heaven, fire as the lights of heaven.

Reply Obj. 1. As stated above (A. 1), the renewal of the world is directed to the effect that man even by his senses may as it were see the Godhead by manifest signs. Now the most spiritual and subtle of our senses is the sight. Consequently all the lower bodies need to be bettered, chiefly as regards the visible qualities the principle of which is light. On the other hand, the elemental qualities regard the touch, which is the most material of the senses, and the excess of their contrariety is more displeasing than pleasant; but excess of light will be pleasant, since it has no contrariety, except on account of a weakness in the organ, such as will not be then.

Reply Obj. 2. The air will be bright, not as casting forth rays, but as an enlightened transparency; while the earth, although it is opaque through lack of light, yet by the Divine power its surface will be clothed with the glory of brightness, without prejudice to its density.

Reply Obj. 3. The earth will not be glorified with brightness in the infernal regions; but instead of this glory, that part of the earth will have the rational spirits of men and demons, who though weak by reason of sin are nevertheless superior to any corporeal quality by the dignity of their nature. Or we may say that, even though the whole earth is glorified, the wicked will nevertheless be in exterior darkness, since even the fire of hell, while shining for them in one respect, will be unable to enlighten them in another.

Reply Obj. 4. This brightness will be in these bodies even as it is in the heavenly bodies, in which it causes no heat, because these bodies will then be unalterable, as the heavenly bodies are now.

Reply Obj. 5. The order of the universe will not be done away by the betterment of the elements, because all the other parts will also be bettered, and so the same harmony will remain.

---

[1] *Glossa ordin.* (VI, 19B); *Glossa* Lombardi (PL 191, 1445); Ambrosiaster *In Rom.* (PL 17, 131).

[2] Aristotle, *Soul,* II, 7 (418ᵃ7).

ARTICLE 5. *Whether the Plants and Animals Will Remain in This Renewal?*

We proceed thus to the Fifth Article: It would seem that the plants and animals will remain in this renewal.

Objection 1. For the elements should be deprived of nothing that belongs to their adornment. Now the elements are said to be adorned by the animals and plants. Therefore they will not be removed in this renewal.

Obj. 2. Further, Just as the elements served man, so also did animals, plants, and mineral bodies. But on account of this service the elements will be glorified.[1] Therefore both animals and plants and mineral bodies will be glorified likewise.

Obj. 3. Further, The universe will remain imperfect if anything belonging to its perfection is removed. Now the species of animals, plants, and mineral bodies belong to the perfection of the universe. Since then we must not say that the world will remain imperfect when it is renewed, it seems that we should assert that the plants and animals will remain.

Obj. 4. Further, Animals and plants have a more noble form than the elements. Now the world, at this final renewal, will be changed for the better. Therefore animals and plants should remain rather than the elements, since they are nobler.

Obj. 5. Further, It is unfitting to assert that the natural appetite will be frustrated. But by their natural appetite animals and plants desire to be for ever, if indeed not as regards the individual, at least as regards the species; and to this end their continual generation is directed.[2] Therefore it is unfitting to say that these species will at length cease to be.

On the contrary, If plants and animals are to remain, either all of them will, or some of them. If all of them, then dumb animals, which had previously died, will have to rise again, just as men will rise again. But this cannot be asserted, for since their form comes to nothing, they cannot resume the same identical form. On the other hand if not all but some of them remain, since there is no more reason for one of them remaining for ever rather than another, it would seem that none of them will. But whatever remains after the world has been renewed will remain for ever, generation and corruption being done away. Therefore plants and animals will altogether cease after the renewal of the world.

Further, According to the Philosopher[3] the species of animals, plants, and the like corruptible things, are not perpetuated except by the continuance of the heavenly movement. Now this will cease then. Therefore it will be impossible for those species to be perpetuated.

Further, If the end cease, those things which are directed to the end should cease. Now animals and plants were made for the upkeep of human life; hence it is written (Gen. 9. 3): *Even as the green herbs have I delivered all flesh to you* (Vulg.,—*have I delivered them all to you*). Therefore when men's animal life ceases, animals and plants should cease. But after this renewal animal life will cease in man. Therefore neither plants nor animals ought to remain.

I answer that, Since the renewal of the world will be for man's sake it follows that it should be conformed to the renewal of man. Now by being renewed man will pass from the state of corruption to incorruptibility and to a state of everlasting rest, and therefore it is written (I Cor. 15. 53): *This corruptible must put on incorruption, and this mortal must put on immortality;* and consequently the world will be renewed in such a way as to throw off all corruption and remain for ever at rest. Therefore it will be impossible for anything to be the subject of that renewal, unless it be a subject of incorruption. Now such are the heavenly bodies, the elements, and man. For the heavenly bodies are by their very nature incorruptible both as to their whole and as to their part, the elements are corruptible as to their parts but incorruptible as a whole, while men are corruptible both in whole and in part, but this is on the part of their matter not on the part of their form, the rational soul namely, which will remain incorrupt after the corruption of man. On the other hand, dumb animals, plants, and minerals, and all mixed bodies, are corruptible both in their whole and in their parts, both on the part of their matter which loses its form, and on the part of their form which does not remain actually; and thus they are in no way subjects of incorruption. Hence they will not remain in this renewal, but those things alone which we have mentioned above.

Reply Obj. 1. These bodies are said to adorn the elements, in so far as the general active and passive forces which are in the elements are applied to specific actions; hence they adorn the elements in their active and passive state. But this state will not remain in the elements.

---

[1] Cf. A. 4, on the contrary, 2.

[2] Aristotle, *Generation and Corruption*, II, 10 (336[b]27).

[3] *Ibid.* (336[a]15).

Therefore there is no need for animals or plants to remain.

Reply Obj. 2. Neither animals nor plants nor any other bodies merited anything by their services to man, since they lack free choice. However, certain bodies are said to be rewarded in so far as man merited that those things should be renewed which are adapted to be renewed. But plants and animals are not adapted to the renewal of incorruption, as stated above. Therefore for this very reason man did not merit that they should be renewed, since no one can merit for another, or even for himself, that which another or himself is incapable of receiving. Hence, granted even that dumb animals merited by serving man, it would not follow that they are to be renewed.

Reply Obj. 3. Just as several kinds of perfection are ascribed to man (for there is the perfection of created nature and the perfection of glorified nature), so also there is a twofold perfection of the universe, one corresponding to this state of changeableness, the other corresponding to the state of a future renewal. Now plants and animals belong to its perfection according to the present state, and not according to the state of this renewal, since they are no capable of it.

Reply Obj. 4. Although animals and plants as to certain other respects are more noble than the elements, the elements are more noble in relation to incorruption, as explained above.

Reply Obj. 5. The natural desire to be for ever that is in animals and plants must be understood in reference to the movement of the heaven, so that they may continue in being as long as the movement of the heaven lasts, for there cannot be an appetite for an effect to last longer than its cause. Therefore if at the cessation of movement in the first movable body, plants and animals cease as to their species, it does not follow that the natural appetite is frustrated.

QUESTION XCII

Of the Vision of the Divine Essence
IN REFERENCE TO THE BLESSED

(*In Three Articles*)

In the next place we must consider matters concerning the blessed after the general judgment. We shall consider: (1) Their vision of the Divine essence in which their Happiness consists chiefly. (2) Their Happiness and their mansions (Q. XCIII). (3) Their relations with the damned (Q. XCIV). (4) Their gifts, which are contained in their Happiness (Q. XCV). (5) The crowns

which perfect and adorn their Happiness (Q. XCVI).

Under the first head there are three points of inquiry: (1) Whether the saints will see God in His essence? (2) Whether they will see Him with the eyes of the body? (3) Whether in seeing God they will see all that God sees?

ARTICLE 1. *Whether the Human Intellect Can Attain to the Vision of God in His Essence?*

We proceed thus to the First Article: It would seem that the human intellect cannot attain to the vision of God in His essence.

Objection 1. For it is written (John 1. 18): *No man hath seen God at any time;* and Chrysostom in his commentary says (*Hom.* xv *in Joann.*)[1] that "not even the heavenly essences, namely the Cherubim and Seraphim, have ever been able to see Him as He is." Now, only equality with the angels is promised to men (Matt. 22. 30): *They . . . shall be as the angels of God in heaven.* Therefore neither will the saints in heaven see God in His essence.

Obj. 2. Further, Dionysius argues thus (*Div. Nom.* i):[2] Knowledge is only of existing things. Now whatever exists is finite, since it is confined to a certain genus, and therefore God, since He is infinite, is above all existing things. Therefore there is no knowledge of Him, and He is above all knowledge.

Obj. 3. Further, Dionysius (*De Myst. Theol.* i)[3] shows that the most perfect way in which our intellect can be united to God is when it is united to Him as to something unknown. Now that which is seen in its essence is not unknown. Therefore it is impossible for our intellect to see God in His essence.

Obj. 4. Further, Dionysius says (*Ep. ad Caium Monach.*)[4] that "the darkness,"—for thus he calls the abundance of light,—"which screens God is impervious to all illuminations, and hidden from all knowledge; and if anyone in seeing God understood what he saw, he saw not God Himself, but one of those things that are His." Therefore no created intellect will be able to see God in His essence.

Obj. 5. Further, According to Dionysius (*Ep. ad Doroth.*)[5] "God is invisible on account of His surpassing glory." Now His glory surpasses the human intellect in heaven even as on the way. Therefore since He is invisible on the way, so will He be in heaven.

---

[1] PG 59, 98.
[2] Sect. 1 (PG 3, 588); cf. chap. IV. sect. 3 (PG 3, 697).
[3] Sect. 1 (PG 3, 997).   [4] *Epist.*, 1 (PG 3, 1065).
[5] *Epist.*, v (PG 3, 1073).

Obj. 6. Further, Since the intelligible is the perfection of the intellect, there must be proportion between intelligible and intellect, as between the visible and the sight. But there is no possible proportion between our intellect and the Divine essence, since an infinite distance separates them. Therefore our intellect will be unable to attain to the vision of the Divine essence.

Obj. 7. Further, God is more distant from our intellect than the created intelligible is from our senses. But the senses can in no way attain to the sight of a spiritual creature. Therefore neither will our intellect be able to attain to the vision of the Divine essence.

Obj. 8. Further, Whenever the intellect understands something actually it needs to be informed with the likeness of the object understood, which likeness is the principle of the intellectual operation terminating in that object, even as heat is the principle of heating. Accordingly if our intellect understands God, this must be by means of some likeness informing the intellect itself. Now this cannot be the very essence of God, since form and things informed must have one being, while the Divine essence differs from our intellect in essence and being. Therefore the form by which our intellect is informed in understanding God must be a likeness impressed by God on our intellect. But this likeness, being something created, cannot lead to the knowledge of God, except as an effect leads to the knowledge of its cause. Therefore it is impossible for our intellect to see God except through His effect. But to see God through His effect is not to see Him in His essence. Therefore our intellect will be unable to see God in His essence.

Obj. 9. Further, The Divine essence is more distant from our intellect than any angel or intelligence. Now according to Avicenna (*Met.* iii, 8),[1] "the existence of an intelligence in our intellect does not imply that its essence is in our intellect," because in that case our knowledge of the intelligence would be a substance and not an accident, "but that its impression is in our intellect." Therefore neither is God in our intellect, so as to be understood by us, except in so far as an impression of Him is in our intellect. But this impression cannot lead to the knowledge of the Divine essence, for since it is infinitely distant from the Divine essence, it degenerates to another species, much more than if the species of a white thing were to degenerate to the species of a black thing. There-

fore, just as a person in whose sight the species of a white thing degenerates to the species of a black thing, on account of an indisposition in the organ, is not said to see a white thing, so neither will our intellect be able to see God in His essence, since it understands God only by means of this impression.

Obj. 10. Further, "In things separate from matter that which understands is the same as that which is understood."[2]

Now God is supremely separate from matter. Since then our intellect, which is created, cannot attain to be an uncreated essence, it is impossible for our intellect to see God in His essence.

Obj. 11. Further, Whatever is seen in its essence is known as to what it is. But our intellect cannot know of God what He is, but only what He is not, as Dionysius (*De Cæl. Hier.* ii)[3] and Damascene (*De Fide Orthod.* i, 4)[4] declare. Therefore our intellect will be unable to see God in His essence.

Obj. 12. Further, Every infinite thing, as such, is unknown. But God is in every way infinite. Therefore He is altogether unknown. Therefore it will be impossible for Him to be seen in His essence by a created intellect.

Obj. 13. Further, Augustine says (*De Videndo Deo: Ep.* cxlvii, 15):[5] "God is by nature invisible." Now that which is in God by nature cannot be otherwise. Therefore it is impossible for Him to be seen in His essence.

Obj. 14 Further, Whatever is in one way and is seen in another way is not seen as it is. Now God is in one way and will be seen in another way by the saints in heaven; for He is according to His own mode, but will be seen by the saints according to their mode. Therefore He will not be seen by the saints as He is, and thus will not be seen in His essence.

Obj. 15. Further, That which is seen through a medium is not seen in its essence. Now God will be seen in heaven through a medium which is the light of glory, according to Ps. 35. 10, *In Thy light we shall see light.* Therefore He will not be seen in His essence.

Obj. 16. Further, In heaven God will be seen face to face, according to I Cor. 13. 12. Now when we see a man face to face, we see him through his likeness. Therefore in heaven God will be seen through His likeness, and consequently not in His essence.

On the contrary, It is written (I Cor. 13. 12): *We see now through a glass in a dark manner,*

---

[1] 82va.

[2] Aristotle, *Soul,* III, 4 (430ᵃ3).   [3] Sect. 3 (PG 3, 140).

[4] PG 94, 800.   [5] PL 33, 613.

but then face to face. Now that which is seen face to face is seen in its essence. Therefore God will be seen in His essence by the saints in heaven.

Further, It is written (I John 3. 2): *When He shall appear we shall be like to Him, because we shall see Him as He is.* Therefore we shall see Him in His essence.

Further, A gloss on I Cor. 15. 24, *When He shall have delivered up the kingdom to God and the Father,* says:[1] "Where," that is, in heaven, "the essence of Father, Son, and Holy Ghost shall be seen, this is given to the clean of heart alone and is the highest happiness." Therefore the blessed will see God in His essence.

Further, It is written (John 14. 21): *He that loveth Me shall be loved of My Father; and I will love him, and will manifest Myself to him.* Now that which is manifested is seen in its essence. Therefore God will be seen in His essence by the saints in heaven.

Further, Gregory commenting (*Moral.* xviii, 54)[2] on the words of Exod. 33. 20, *Man shall not see Me and live,* disapproves of the opinion of those who said that "in this abode of bliss God can be seen in His glory but not in His nature; for His glory differs not from His nature." But His nature is His essence. Therefore He will be seen in His essence.

Further, The desire of the saints cannot be altogether frustrated. Now the common desire of the saints is to see God in His essence, according to Exod. 33. 13, *Show me Thy glory;* Ps. 79. 20, *Show Thy face and we shall be saved;* and John 14. 8, *Show us the Father and it is enough for us.* Therefore the saints will see God in His essence.

I answer that, Even as we hold by faith that the last end of man's life is to see God, so the philosophers maintained that man's ultimate happiness is to understand immaterial substances according to their being. Hence in reference to this question we find that philosophers and theologians encounter the same difficulty and the same difference of opinion. For some philosophers held that our possible intellect can never come to understand separate substances; thus Alfarabi expresses himself at the end of his *Ethics,*[3] although he says the contrary in his book *On the Intelligence,*[4] as the Commentator attests (*De Anima,* iii).[5] In like manner certain theologians held that the hu-

man intellect can never attain to the vision of God in His essence. On either side they were moved by the distance which separates our intellect from the Divine essence and from separate substances. For since the intellect in act is in some way one with the intelligible in act, it would seem difficult to understand how the created intellect is made in any way to be an uncreated essence. Therefore Chrysostom says (*Hom.* xv *in Joann.*),[6] "How can the creature see the uncreated?" Those who hold the possible intellect to be the subject of generation and corruption, as being a power dependent on the body, encounter a still greater difficulty not only as regards the vision of God but also as regards the vision of any separate substances.

But this opinion is altogether untenable. First, because it is in contradiction to the authority of canonical scripture, as Augustine declares (*De Videndo Deo: Ep.* cxlvii, 5).[7] Secondly because, since understanding is an operation most proper to man, it follows that his happiness must be held to consist in that operation when perfected in him. Now since the perfection of an intelligent being as such is the intelligible thing, if in the most perfect operation of his intellect man does not attain to the vision of the Divine essence, but to something else, we shall be forced to conclude that something other than God makes man happy; and since the ultimate perfection of a thing consists in its being united to its principle, it follows that something other than God is the effecting principle of man, which is absurd, according to us, and also according to the philosophers, who maintain that our souls emanate from the separate substances, so that finally we may be able to understand these substances. Consequently, according to us, it must be asserted that our intellect will at length attain to the vision of the Divine essence, and according to the philosophers, that it will attain to the vision of separate substances.

It remains, then, to examine how this may come about. For some, like Alfarabi and Avempace, held that from the very fact that our intellect understands any intelligibles whatever, it attains to the vision of a separate substance. To show this they proceed in two ways. The first is that just as the specific nature is not diversified in various individuals, except as united to various individuating principles, so the form understood is not diversified in me and you, except in so far as it is united to various imaginary forms; and consequently

---

[1] *Glossa ordin.* (vi, 58A); *Glossa* Lombardi (PL 191, 1679).   [2] PL 76, 93.
[3] In Averroes, *In De An.,* iii, comm. 36, dig., pt. i (vi, 2, 175D, 178A).   [4] 68vb; cf. Averroes, *loc. cit.*
[5] *Loc. cit.;* cf. *Epist. De Intellectu* (ix, 157B).   [6] PG 59, 98.   [7] PL 33, 601.

when the intellect separates the form understood from the imaginary forms, there remains a quiddity understood, which is one and the same in the various persons understanding it, and such is the quiddity of a separate substance. Hence, when our intellect attains to the supreme abstraction of any intelligible quiddity, it thereby understands the quiddity of the separate substance that is similar to it.[1]

The second way is that our intellect has a natural aptitude to abstract the quiddity from all intelligible objects having a quiddity. If, then, the quiddity which it abstracts from some particular individual be a quiddity without a quiddity, the intellect by understanding it understands the quiddity of the separate substance which has a like disposition, since separate substances are subsisting quiddities without quiddities; for the quiddity of a simple thing is the simple thing itself, as Avicenna says.[2] On the other hand if the quiddity abstracted from this particular sensible be a quiddity that has a quiddity, it follows that the intellect has a natural aptitude to abstract this quiddity, and consequently since we cannot go on infinitely, we shall come to some quiddity without a quiddity, and this is what we understand by a separate quiddity.[3]

But this way does not seem to be enough. First, because the quiddity of the material substance, which the intellect abstracts, is not of the same character as the quiddity of the separate substances, and consequently from the fact that our intellect abstracts the quiddities of material things and knows them, it does not follow that it knows the quiddity of a separate substance, especially of the Divine essence, which more than any other is of a different character from any created quiddity. Secondly, because granted that it be of the same character, nevertheless the knowledge of a composite thing would not lead to the knowledge of a separate substance, except in the point of the most remote genus, namely substance; and such a knowledge is imperfect unless it reach to the properties of a thing. For to know a man only as an animal is to know him only in a restricted sense and potentially; and much less is it to know only the nature of substance in him. Hence to know God thus, or other separate substances, is not to see the essence of God or the quiddity of a separate substance,

but to know Him in His effect and in a mirror as it were.

For this reason Avicenna in his *Metaphysics*[4] propounds another way of understanding separate substances, namely, that separate substances are understood by us by means of intentions of their quiddities, such intentions being likenesses of their substances, not indeed abstracted from them, since they are immaterial, but impressed by them on our souls. But this way also seems inadequate to the Divine vision which we seek. For it is agreed that "whatever is received into anything is in it after the mode of the recipient," and consequently the likeness of the Divine essence impressed on our intellect will be according to the mode of our intellect, and the mode of our intellect falls short of a perfect reception of the Divine likeness. Now the lack of perfect likeness may occur in as many ways, as unlikeness may occur. For in one way there is a deficient likeness, when the form is participated according to the same specific nature, but not in the same measure of perfection; such is the defective likeness in a subject that has little whiteness in comparison with one that has much. In another way the likeness is yet more defective, when it does not attain to the same specific nature but only to the same generic nature; such is the likeness of an orange-coloured or yellowish object in comparison with a white one. In another way, still more defective is the likeness when it does not attain to the same generic nature, but only to a certain analogy or proportion; such is the likeness of whiteness to man, in that each is a being, and in this way every likeness received into a creature is defective in comparison with the Divine essence. Now in order that the sight know whiteness, it is necessary for it to receive the likeness of whiteness according to its specific nature, although not according to the same manner of being, because the form has a manner of being in the sense other from that which it has in the thing outside the soul; for if the form of yellowness were received into the eye, the eye would not be said to see whiteness. In like manner in order that the intellect understand a quiddity, it is necessary for it to receive its likeness according to the same specific nature, although there may possibly not be the same manner of being on either side; for the form which is in the intellect or sense is not the principle of knowledge according to its manner of being on both sides, but according

---

[1] Reference in Alfarabi not known; for Avempace see Averroes, *In De An.*, III, comm. 36, dig., PT. III (VI, 2; 181, A).

[2] *Meta.*, V, 5 (90ra).

[3] Alfarabi, *De Intellectu* (68vb); cf. Averroes, *loc. cit.*

[4] Tr. III, chap. 8 (82va).

to the aspect which it shares with the thing outside. Hence it is clear that by no likeness received in the created intellect can God be understood, in such a way that His essence is seen immediately. And for this reason those who held the Divine essence to be seen in this way alone said that the essence itself will not be seen, but a certain brightness, as it were a radiance of it. Consequently neither does this way suffice for the Divine vision that we seek.

Therefore we must take the other way, which also certain philosophers held, namely Alexander[1] and Averroes (*De Anima,* iii).[2] For since in every knowledge some form is required by which the object is known or seen, this form by which the intellect is perfected so as to see separate substances is neither a quiddity abstracted by the intellect from composite things, as the first opinion maintained, nor an impression left on our intellect by the separate substance, as the second opinion affirmed, but the separate substance itself united to our intellect as its form, so as to be both that which is understood, and that by which it is understood. And whatever may be the case with other separate substances, we must nevertheless allow this to be our way of seeing God in His essence, because by whatever other form our intellect were informed, it could not be led thereby to the Divine essence. This, however, must not be understood as though the Divine essence were in reality the form of our intellect, or as though from it and our intellect there resulted one being absolutely, as in natural things from the natural form and matter, but the meaning is that the proportion of the Divine essence to our intellect is as the proportion of form to matter. For whenever two things, one of which is the perfection of the other, are received into the same recipient, the proportion of one to the other, namely of the more perfect to the less perfect, is as the proportion of form to matter; thus light and colour are received into a transparent thing, light being to colour as form to matter. When therefore intellectual light is received into the soul, together with the indwelling Divine essence, though they are not received in the same way, the Divine essence will be to the intellect as form to matter. And that this suffices for the intellect to be able to see the Divine essence by the Divine essence itself may be shown as follows.

As from the natural form (by which a thing has being) and matter there results one thing absolutely, so from the form by which the intellect understands, and the intellect itself, there results one thing in understanding. Now in natural things a self-subsistent thing cannot be the form of any matter if that thing has matter as one of its parts, since it is impossible for matter to be the form of a thing. But if this self-subsistent thing be a form only, nothing hinders it from being the form of some matter and becoming that by which the composite itself is,[3] as appears in the case of the soul. Now in the intellect we must take the intellect itself in potency as matter, and the intelligible species as form; so that the intellect actually understanding will be the composite as it were resulting from both. Hence if there is a self-subsistent thing that has nothing in itself besides that which is intelligible, such a thing can by itself be the form by which the intellect understands. Now a thing is intelligible in respect of its actuality and not of its potency.[4] The sign of this is that an intelligible form needs to be abstracted from matter and from all the properties of matter. Therefore, since the Divine essence is pure act, it will be possible for it to be the form by which the intellect understands; and this will be the beatific vision. Hence the Master says (ii. *Sent.* d. 1)[5] that the union of the body with the soul is an illustration of the blessed union of the spirit with God.

Reply Obj. 1. The words quoted can be explained in three ways, according to Augustine (*De Videndo Deo: Ep.* cxlvii, 6).[6] In one way as excluding corporeal vision, whereby no one ever saw or will see God in His essence; secondly, as excluding intellectual vision of God in His essence from those who dwell in this mortal flesh; thirdly, as excluding the vision of comprehension from a created intellect. It is thus that Chrysostom understands the saying, and therefore he adds: "By seeing, the evangelist means a most clear perception, and such a comprehension as the Father has of the Son." This also is the meaning of the evangelist, since he adds: *The only-begotten Son Who is in the bosom of the Father, He hath declared Him;* his intention being to prove the Son to be God from His comprehending God.

Reply Obj. 2. Just as God, by His infinite essence, surpasses all existing things which have

---

[1] Alexander of Aphrodisias, *De An.,* III (SA II, 107). Cf. Averroes, *In De An.,* BK. III, comm. 36, dig., pt. I (VI, 2; 175E, 177A); Albert, *In De An.* III, iii, 6 (BO V, 378).
[2] Comm. 36, dig., PT. V (VI, 185c).

[3] Literally,—and becoming the that-by-which-it-is of the composite itself.
[4] Aristotle, *Metaphysics,* IX, 9 (1051[a]29).
[5] QR I, 311.   [6] PL 33, 603.

a determinate being, so His knowledge, whereby He knows, is above all knowledge. Therefore as our knowledge is to our created essence, so is the Divine knowledge to His infinite essence. Now two things contribute to knowledge, namely, the knower and the thing known. Again, the vision by which we shall see God in His essence is the same by which God sees Himself, as regards that by which He is seen, because as He sees Himself in His essence, so shall we also see Him. But as regards the knower there is the difference that is between the Divine intellect and ours. Now in the order of knowledge the object known follows the form by which we know, since by the form of a stone we see a stone, but the efficacy of knowledge follows the power of the knower; thus he who has stronger sight sees more clearly. Consequently in that vision we shall see the same thing that God sees, namely His essence, but not so effectively.

Reply Obj. 3. Dionysius is speaking there of the knowledge whereby wayfarers know God by a created form, by which our intellect is informed so as to see God. But as Augustine says[1] "God evades every form of our intellect," because whatever form our intellect conceives, that form is out of proportion to the Divine essence. Hence He cannot be fathomed by our intellect, but our most perfect knowledge of Him as wayfarers is to know that He is above all that our intellect can conceive, and thus we are united to Him as to something unknown. In heaven, however, we shall see Him by a form which is His essence, and we shall be united to Him as to something known.

Reply Obj. 4. God is light (John i. 9). Now illumination is the impression of light on an illuminated object. And since the Divine essence is of a different mode from any likeness of it impressed on the intellect, he (Dionysius) says that the "Divine darkness is impervious to all illumination," because, that is, the Divine essence, which he calls darkness on account of its surpassing brightness, remains undemonstrated by the impression of our intellect, and consequently is hidden from all knowledge. Therefore if anyone in seeing God conceives something in his mind, this is not God but one of God's effects.

Reply Obj. 5. Although the glory of God surpasses any form by which our intellect is informed now, it does not surpass the Divine essence, which will be the form of our intellect in heaven. And therefore although it is invisible now, it will be visible then.

Reply Obj. 6. Although there can be no proportion between finite and infinite, since the excess of the infinite over the finite is indeterminate, there can be proportionateness or a likeness to proportion between them, for just as a finite thing is equal to some finite thing, so is an infinite thing equal to an infinite thing. Now in order that a thing be known totally, it is sometimes necessary that there be proportion between knower and known, because the power of the knower needs to be adequate to the knowableness of the thing known, and equality is a kind of proportion. Sometimes, however, the knowableness of the thing surpasses the power of the knower, as when we know God, or conversely when He knows creatures, and then there is no need for proportion between knower and known, but only for proportionateness, so that, namely, as the knower is to the knowable object, so is the knowable object to the fact of its being known; and this proportionateness suffices for the infinite to be known by the finite, or conversely.

We may also reply that proportion according to the strict sense in which it is employed signifies a relationship of quantity to quantity based on a certain fixed excess or equality, but is further transferred to denote any relationship of any one thing to another; and in this sense we say that matter should be proportionate to its form. In this sense nothing hinders our intellect, although finite, being described as proportionate to the vision of the Divine essence; but not to the comprehension of it, on account of its immensity.

Reply Obj. 7. Likeness and distance are twofold. One is according to agreement in nature; and thus God is more distant from the created intellect than the created intelligible is from the sense. The other is according to proportionateness; and thus it is the other way about, for sense is not proportionate to the knowledge of the immaterial, as the intellect is proportionate to the knowledge of anything immaterial whatsoever. It is this likeness and not the former that is required for knowledge, for it is clear that the intellect understanding a stone is not like it in its natural being; thus also the sight apprehends red honey and red gall, though it does not apprehend sweet honey, for the redness of gall is more becoming to honey as visible, than the sweetness of honey to honey.

---

[1] *Serm. ad Pop.*, serm. CXVII.2 (PL 38, 662); the same is found in Alexander of Hales, *Summa Theol.*, pt. I, n. 333 (QR I, 492); Bonaventure, *In Sent.*, BK. I, d. 22, A. I, Q. I (QR I, 390).

Reply Obj. 8. In the vision wherein God will be seen in His essence, the Divine essence itself will be the form, as it were, of the intellect, by which it will understand; nor is it necessary for them to become one in being, but only to become one as regards the act of understanding.

Reply Obj. 9. We do not uphold the saying of Avicenna as regards the point at issue, for in this other philosophers also disagree with him. Unless perhaps we might say that Avicenna refers to the knowledge of separate substances, in so far as they are known by the habits of speculative sciences and the likeness of other things. Hence he makes this statement in order to prove that in us knowledge is not a substance but an accident. Nevertheless, although the Divine essence is more distant as to the property of its nature from our intellect than is the substance of an angel, it surpasses it in the point of intelligibility, since it is pure act without any admixture of potency, which is not the case with other separate substances. Nor will that knowledge by which we shall see God in His essence be in the genus of accident as regards that by which He will be seen, but only as regards the act of the one who understands Him, for this act will not be the very substance either of the person understanding or of the thing understood.

Reply Obj. 10. A substance that is separate from matter understands both itself and other things, and in both cases the authority quoted can be verified. For since the very essence of a separate substance is of itself intelligible and actual, through being separate from matter, it is clear that when a separate substance understands itself, that which understands and that which is undersood are absolutely identical, for it does not understand itself by an intention abstracted from itself, as we understand material objects. And this is apparently the meaning of the Philosopher[1] as indicated by the Commentator.[2]

But when it understands other things, the thing actually understood becomes one with the intellect in act, in so far as the form of the thing understood becomes the form of the intellect, in so far as the intellect is in act; not that it becomes identified with the essence of the intellect, as Avicenna proves (*De Natural.* vi),[3] because the essence of the intellect remains one under two forms whereby it understands two things in succession, in the same way as primary matter remains one under vari-

ous forms. Hence also the Commentator (*De Anima.* iii)[4] compares the possible intellect, in this respect, to primary matter. Thus it by no means follows that our intellect in seeing God becomes the very essence of God, but that the latter is compared to it as its perfection or form.

Reply Obj. 11. These and all like authorities must be understood to refer to the knowledge by which we know God on the way, for the reason given above.

Reply Obj. 12. The infinite is unknown if we take it in the privative sense, as such, because it indicates removal of completion, from which knowledge of a thing is derived. Therefore the infinite amounts to the same as matter subject to privation, as stated in the *Physics*.[5] But if we take the infinite in the negative sense, it indicates the absence of limiting matter, since even a form is in some way limited by its matter. Hence the infinite in this sense is of itself most knowable; and it is in this way that God is infinite.

Reply Obj. 13. Augustine is speaking of bodily vision, by which God will never be seen. This is evident from what precedes: "For no man hath seen God at any time, nor can any man see Him as these things which we call visible are seen; in this way He is by nature invisible even as He is incorruptible." As, however, He is by nature supremely being, so He is in Himself supremely intelligible. But that He is for a time not understood by us is owing to our defect; therefore that He is seen by us after being unseen is owing to a change not in Him but in us.

Reply Obj. 14. In heaven God will be seen by the saints as He is, if this be referred to the mode of the object seen, for the saints will see that God has the mode which He has. But if we refer the mode to the knower, He will not be seen as He is, because the created intellect will not have so great an efficacy in seeing as the Divine essence has to the effect of being seen.

Reply Obj. 15. There is a threefold medium both in bodily and in intellectual vision. The first is the medium *under which* the object is seen, and this is something perfecting the sight so as to see in general, without determining the sight to any particular object. Such is bodily light in relation to bodily vision; and the light of the agent intellect in relation to the possible intellect, in so far as this light is a medium.

[1] *Soul*, III, 4 (430ª3).
[2] *In De An.*, III, comm. 15 (VI, 159F).   [3] 25vb.
[4] Comm. 5 (VI, 138F, 149E, 151D); comm. 36, dig., V (VI, 185C).   [5] Aristotle, III, 7 (207ᵇ35).

The second is the light *by which* the object is seen, and this is the visible form, by which either sight is determined to a special object, for instance by the form of a stone to know a stone. The third is the medium *in which* it is seen, and this is something by gazing on which the sight is led to something else; thus by looking in a mirror it is led to see the things reflected in the mirror, and by looking at an image it is led to the thing represented by the image. In this way, too, the intellect from knowing an effect is led to the cause, or conversely. Accordingly in the heavenly vision there will be no third medium, so that, namely, God be known by the images of other things, as He is known now, for which reason we are said to see now in a glass; nor will there be the second medium, because the essence itself of God will be that whereby our intellect will see God. But there will only be the first medium, which will upraise our intellect so that it will be possible for it to be united to the uncreated substance in the aforesaid manner. Yet this medium will not cause that knowledge to be mediate, because it does not come in between the knower and the thing known, but is that which gives the knower the power to know.

Reply Obj. 16. Corporeal creatures are not said to be seen immediately, except when that which in them is capable of being brought into conjunction with the sight is in conjunction with it. Now they are not capable of being in conjunction with the sight by their essence on account of their materiality; hence they are seen immediately when their image is in conjunction with the sight. But God is able to be united to the intellect by His Essence; therefore He would not be seen immediately unless His essence were united to the intellect; and this vision, which is effected immediately, is called vision of face. Moreover the likeness of the corporeal thing is received into the sight according to the same aspect as it is in the thing, although not according to the same mode of being. Therefore this likeness leads to the thing directly; but no likeness can lead our intellect in this way to God, as shown above. And for this reason the comparison fails.

ARTICLE 2. *Whether After the Resurrection the Saints Will See God With the Eyes of the Body?*

We proceed thus to the Second Article: It would seem that after the resurrection the saints will see God with the eyes of the body.

Objection 1. Because the glorified eye has greater power than one that is not glorified. Now the blessed Job saw God with his eyes (Job 42. 5): *With the hearing of the ear, I have heard Thee, but now my eye seeth Thee.* Much more therefore will the glorified eye be able to see God in His essence.

Obj. 2. Further, It is written (Job 19. 26): *In my flesh I shall see God my Saviour* (Vulg., —*my God*). Therefore in heaven God will be seen with the eyes of the body.

Obj. 3. Further, Augustine, speaking of the sight of the glorified eyes, expresses himself as follows:[1] "A greater power will be in those eyes, not to see more keenly, as certain serpents or eagles are reported to see (for whatever acuteness of vision is possessed by these animals they can see only corporeal things), but to see even incorporeal things." Now any power that is capable of knowing incorporeal things can be upraised to see God. Therefore the glorified eyes will be able to see God.

Obj. 4. Further, The disparity of corporeal to incorporeal things is the same as of incorporeal to corporeal. Now the incorporeal eye can see corporeal things. Therefore the corporeal eye can see the incorporeal. And consequently the same conclusion follows.

Obj. 5. Further, Gregory, commenting on Job 4. 16, *There stood one whose countenance I knew not,* says (*Moral.* v, 34):[2] "Man who had he been willing to obey the command, would have been spiritual in the flesh, became, by sinning, carnal even in mind." Now through becoming carnal in mind, "he thinks only of those things which he draws to his soul by the images of bodies (*ibid.*)." Therefore when he will be spiritual in the flesh (which is promised to the saints after the resurrection), he will be able even in the flesh to see spiritual things. Therefore the same conclusion follows.

Obj. 6. Further, Man can be beatified by God alone. Now he will be beatified not only in soul but also in body. Therefore God will be visible not only to his intellect but also to his flesh.

Obj. 7. Further, Even as God is present to the intellect by His essence, so will He be to the senses, because He will be *all in all* (I Cor. 15. 28). Now He will be seen by the intellect through the union of His essence with the intellect. Therefore He will also be visible to the sense.

[1] *City of God*, XXII, 29 (PL 41, 799).
[2] PL 75, 712.

On the contrary, Ambrose, commenting on Luke I. 11, *There appeared to him an angel,* says:[1] "God is not sought with the eyes of the body, nor surveyed by the sight, nor clasped by the touch." Therefore God will by no means be visible to the bodily sense.

Further, Jerome, commenting on Isa. 6. 1, *I saw the Lord sitting,* says:[2] "The Godhead not only of the Father, but also of the Son and of the Holy Ghost is visible, not to carnal eyes, but only to the eyes of the mind, of which it is said: 'Blessed are the pure in heart.'"

Further, Jerome says again (as quoted by Augustine, *Ep.* cxlvii, 23):[3] "An incorporeal thing is invisible to a corporeal eye." But God is supremely incorporeal. Therefore, etc.

Further, Augustine says (*De Videndo Deo, Ep.* cxlvii, 11):[4] "No man hath seen God as He is at any time, neither in this life, nor in the angelic life, in the same way as these visible things which are seen with the corporeal sight." Now the angelic life is the life of the blessed, wherein they will live after the resurrection. Therefore, etc.

Further, According to Augustine (*De Trin.* xiv, 4),[5] "man is said to be made to God's image in that he is able to see God." But man is in God's image as regards his mind, and not as regards his flesh. Therefore he will see God with his mind and not with his flesh.

I answer that, A thing is perceived by the senses of the body in two ways, directly and indirectly. A thing is perceived directly if it can act directly on the bodily senses. And a thing can act directly either on sense as such or on a particular sense as such. That which acts directly in this second way on a sense is called a proper sensible, for instance colour in relation to the sight, and sound in relation to the hearing. But as sense as such makes use of a bodily organ, nothing can be received therein except corporeally, since whatever is received into a thing is in it after the mode of the recipient. Hence all sensibles act on the sense as such, according to their magnitude, and consequently magnitude and all that follows on it, such as movement, rest, number, and the like, are called common sensibles, and yet are direct objects of sense.

An indirect object of sense is that which does not act on the sense, neither as sense nor as a particular sense, but is joined to those things that act on sense directly; for instance Socrates, the son of Diares, a friend, and the like which are known *per se* by the intellect in the universal, and in the particular are the object of the cogitative power in man, and of the estimative power in other animals. The external sense is said to perceive things of this kind, although *per accidens,* when the apprehensive power (whose province it is to know *per se* this thing known), from that which is sensed *per se,* apprehends them at once and without any doubt or discourse (thus we see that a person is alive from the fact that he speaks). Otherwise the sense is not said to perceive it even accidentally.

I say then that God can in no way be seen with the eyes of the body, or perceived by any of the senses, as that which is seen *per se,* neither here, nor in heaven; for if that which belongs to sense as such be removed from sense, there will be no sense, and in like manner if that which belongs to sight as sight be removed from sight, there will be no sight. Accordingly seeing that sense as sense perceives magnitude, and sight as such a sense perceives colour, it is impossible for the sight to perceive that which is neither colour nor magnitude, unless we call it a sense equivocally. Since then sight and sense will be specifically the same in the glorified body as in a non-glorified body, it will be impossible for it to see the Divine essence as a thing *per se* visible; yet it will see it as is visible *per accidens,* because on the one hand the bodily sight will see so great a glory of God in bodies, especially in the glorified bodies and most of all in the body of Christ, and, on the other hand, the intellect will see God so clearly, that God will be perceived in things seen with the eye of the body, even as life is perceived in speech. For although our intellect will not then see God from seeing His creatures, yet it will see God in His creatures seen corporeally. This manner of seeing God corporeally is indicated by Augustine,[6] as is clear if we take note of his words, for he says: "It is very credible that we shall so see the mundane bodies of the new heaven and the new earth, as to see most clearly God everywhere present, governing all corporeal things, not as we now see the invisible things of God as understood by those that are made, but as when we see men . . . we do not believe but see that they live."

Reply Obj. 1. This saying of Job refers to the spiritual eye, of which the Apostle says (Eph. 1. 18): *The eyes of our* (Vulg.,—*your*) *heart enlightened.*

Reply Obj. 2. The passage quoted does not

[1] PL 15, 1624.   [2] PL 24, 94.   [3] PL 33, 621.
[4] PL 33, 609.   [5] PL 42, 1040.
[6] *City of God,* XXII, 29 (PL 41, 800).

mean that we are to see God with the eyes of the flesh, but that, in the flesh, we shall see God.

Reply Obj. 3. In these words Augustine speaks as one inquiring and conditionally. This appears from what he had said before: "Therefore they will have an altogether different power, if they shall see that incorporeal nature"; and then he goes on to say: "Accordingly a greater power," etc., and afterwards he explains himself.

Reply Obj. 4. All knowledge results from some kind of abstraction from matter. Therefore the more a corporeal form is abstracted from matter, the more is it a principle of knowledge. Hence it is that a form existing in matter is in no way a principle of knowledge, while a form existing in the senses is somewhat a principle of knowledge, in so far as it is separated from matter, and a form existing in the intellect is still better a principle of knowledge. Therefore the spiritual eye, from which the obstacle to knowledge is removed, can see a corporeal object; but it does not follow that the corporeal eye, in which the cognitive power is deficient as participating in matter, is able to know perfectly incorporeal objects of knowledge.

Reply Obj. 5. Although the mind that has become carnal cannot think but of things received from the senses, it thinks of them immaterially. In like manner whatever the sight apprehends, it must always apprehend it corporeally; therefore it cannot know things which cannot be apprehended corporeally.

Reply Obj. 6. Happiness is the perfection of man as man. And since man is man not through his body but through his soul, and the body is essential to man, in so far as it is perfected by the soul, it follows that man's happiness does not chiefly consist other than in an act of the soul, and passes from the soul on to the body by a kind of overflow, as explained above (Q. LXXXV, A. 1). Yet our body will have a certain Happiness from seeing God in sensible creatures, and especially in Christ's body.

Reply Obj. 7. The intellect can perceive spiritual things, whereas the eyes of the body cannot; therefore the intellect will be able to know the Divine essence united to it, but the eyes of the body will not.

ARTICLE 3. *Whether the Saints, Seeing God, See All That God Sees?*

We proceed thus to the *Third Article:* It would seem that the saints, seeing God in His essence, see all that God sees in Himself.

Objection 1. For as Isidore says:[1] "The angels know all things in the Word of God, before they happen." Now the saints will be equal to the angels of God (Matt. 22. 30). Therefore the saints also in seeing God see all things.

Obj. 2. Further, Gregory says (*Dial.* iv, 33):[2] "Since all see God there with equal clearness, what do they not know, who know Him Who knows all things?," and he refers to the blessed who see God in His essence. Therefore those who see God in His essence know all things.

Obj. 3. Further, It is stated in the book on the *Soul*[3] that "when an intellect understands the greatest things, it is all the more able to understand the least things." Now God is the greatest of intelligible things. Therefore the power of the intellect is greatly increased by understanding Him. Therefore the intellect seeing Him understands all things.

Obj. 4. Further, The intellect is not hindered from understanding a thing except by this surpassing it. Now no creature surpasses the intellect that understands God, since, as Gregory says (*Dial.* ii, 35),[4] "to the soul which sees its Creator all Creatures are small." Therefore those who see God in His essence know all things.

Obj. 5. Further, Every passive power that is not reduced to act is imperfect. Now the possible intellect of the human soul is a power that is passive as it were to the knowledge of all things, since "the possible intellect is in which all are in potentiality."[5] If then in that happiness it were not to understand all things, it would remain imperfect, which is absurd.

Obj. 6. Further, Whoever sees a mirror sees the things reflected in the mirror. Now all things are reflected in the Word of God as in a mirror, because He is the type and likeness of all. Therefore the saints who see the Word in its essence see all created things.

Obj. 7. Further, According to Prov. 10. 24, *to the just their desire shall be given.* Now the just desire to know all things, since all men desire naturally to know, and nature is not done away by glory. Therefore God will grant them to know all things.

Obj. 8. Further, Ignorance is one of the penalties of the present life. Now all penalty will be removed from the saints by glory. Therefore all ignorance will be removed, and consequently they will know all things.

Obj. 9. Further, The Happiness of the saints

---

[1] *Sent.*, I, 10 (PL 83, 556).   [2] PL 77, 376.
[3] Aristotle, III, 4 (429[b]3).   [4] PL 66, 200.
[5] Aristotle, *Soul*, III, 5 (430[a]14).

is in their soul before being in their body. Now the bodies of the saints will be reformed in glory to the likeness of Christ's body (Philip. 3. 21). Therefore their souls will be perfected in likeness to the soul of Christ. Now Christ's soul sees all things in the Word. Therefore all the souls of the saints will also see all things in the Word.

Obj. 10. Further, The intellect, like the senses, knows all the things with the likeness of which it is informed. Now the Divine essence shows a thing forth more clearly than any other likeness of it. Therefore since in that blessed vision the Divine essence becomes the form as it were of our intellect, it would seem that the saints seeing God see all.

Obj. 11. Further, The Commentator says (*De Anima,* iii),[1] that "if the agent intellect were the form of the possible intellect, we should understand all things." Now the Divine essence represents all things more clearly than the agent intellect. Therefore the intellect that sees God in His essence knows all things.

Obj. 12. Further, The lower angels are enlightened by the higher about the things they are ignorant of, for the reason that they do not now know all things. Now after the day of judgment, one angel will not enlighten another, for then all superiority will cease, as a gloss observes[2] on I Cor. 15. 24, *When He shall have brought to nought,* etc. Therefore the lower angels will then know all things, and for the same reason all the other saints who will see God in His essence.

On the contrary, Dionysius says (*Cæl. Hier.* vi):[3] "The higher angels cleanse the lower angels from ignorance." Now the lower angels see the Divine essence. Therefore an angel while seeing the Divine essence may be ignorant of certain things. But the soul will not see God more perfectly than an angel. Therefore the souls seeing God will not necessarily see all things.

Further, Christ alone has the spirit not *by measure* (John 3. 34). Now it becomes Christ, as having the spirit without measure, to know all things in the Word; therefore it is stated in the same place (*verse* 35) that the *Father . . . hath given all things into His hand.* Therefore none but Christ is able to know all things in the Word.

Further, The more perfectly a principle is

known, the more of its effects are known thereby. Now some of those who see God in His essence will know God more perfectly than others. Therefore some will know more things than others, and consequently every one will not know all things.

I answer that, God by seeing His essence knows all things whatsoever that are, shall be, or have been; and He is said to know these things by His knowledge of vision, because He knows them as though they were present in likeness to corporeal vision. Moreover by seeing this essence He knows all that He can do, although He never did them, nor ever will, for otherwise He would not know His power perfectly, since a power cannot be known unless its objects be known; and this is called His science or knowledge of simple intelligence.

Now it is impossible for a created intellect, by seeing the Divine essence, to know all that God can do, because the more perfectly a principle is known, the more things are known in it; thus in one principle of demonstration one who is quick of intelligence sees more conclusions than one who is slow of intelligence. Since then the extent of the Divine power is measured according to what it can do, if an intellect were to see in the Divine essence all that God can do, its perfection in understanding would equal in extent the Divine power in producing its effects, and thus it would comprehend the Divine power, which is impossible for any created intellect to do.

Yet there is a created intellect, namely the soul of Christ, which knows in the Word all that God knows by the knowledge of vision. But regarding others who see the Divine essence there are two opinions. For some say that all who see God in His essence see all that God sees by His knowledge of vision. This, however, is contrary to the sayings of holy men,[4] who hold that angels are ignorant of some things; and yet it is clear that according to faith all the angels see God in His essence. Therefore others say that others than Christ, although they see God in His essence, do not see all that God sees because they do not comprehend the Divine essence. For it is not necessary that he who knows a cause should know all its effects, unless he comprehend the cause, and a created intellect is not able to do this. Consequently of those who see God in His essence, each one sees in His essence so much the

---

[1] *Comm.* 36, dig., pt. v (VI, 183D).

[2] *Glossa ordin.* (VI, 58B); *Glossa* Lombardi (PL 191, 1670).

[3] Chap. 10, sect. 3 (PG 3, 273); cf. *De Eccl. Hier.,* VI, PT. III, sect. 6 (PG 3, 537).

[4] Cf. Dionysius, *Eccl. Hier.,* VI, PT. 3, sect. 6 (PG 3, 537); Jerome, *In Ephes.,* BK. II (PL 26, 515); John Chrysostom, *In Ephes.,* hom. VII (PG 62, 49).

more things according as he sees the Divine essence the more clearly, and hence it is that one is able to instruct another concerning these things. Thus the knowledge of the angels and of the souls of the saints can go on increasing until the day of judgment, even as other things pertaining to the accidental reward. But afterwards it will increase no more, because then will be the final state of things, and in that state it is possible that all will know everything that God knows by the knowledge of vision.

Reply Obj. 1. The saying of Isidore, that "the angels know in the Word all things before they happen," cannot refer to those things which God knows only by the knowledge of simple intelligence, because those things will never happen, but it must refer to those things which God knows only by the knowledge of vision. Even of these he does not say that all the angels know them all, but that perhaps some do, and that even those who know do not know all perfectly. For in one and the same thing there are many intelligible aspects to be considered, such as its various properties and relations to other things, and it is possible that while one thing is known in common by two persons, one of them perceives more aspects, and that the one learns these aspects from the other. Hence Dionysius says (*Div. Nom.* iv)[1] that "the lower angels learn from the higher angels the intelligible aspects of things." Therefore it does not follow that even the angels who know all creatures are able to see all that can be understood in them.

Reply Obj. 2. It follows from this saying of Gregory that this blessed vision suffices for the seeing of all things on the part of the Divine essence, which is the medium by which one sees, and by which God sees all things. That all things, however, are not seen is owing to the deficiency of the created intellect which does not comprehend the Divine essence.

Reply Obj. 3. The created intellect sees the Divine essence not according to the mode of that same essence, but according to its own mode which is finite. Hence its efficacy in knowing would need to be infinitely increased by reason of that vision in order for it to know all things.

Reply Obj. 4. Defective knowledge results not only from excess and deficiency of the knowable thing in relation to the intellect, but also from the fact that the aspect of knowableness is not united to the intellect; thus sometimes the sight does not see a stone, through

the likeness of the stone not being united to it. And although the Divine essence which is the type of all things is united to the intellect of one who sees God, it is united to it not as the type of all things, but as the type of some and of so much the more according as one sees the Divine essence more fully.

Reply Obj. 5. When a passive power is perceptible by several perfections in order, if it is perfected with its ultimate perfection it is not said to be imperfect, even though it lack some of the preceding dispositions. Now all knowledge by which the created intellect is perfected is ordered to the knowledge of God as its end. Therefore he who sees God in His essence, even though he know nothing else, would have a perfect intellect; nor is his intellect more perfect through knowing something else besides Him, except in so far as it sees Him more fully. Hence Augustine says:[2] "Unhappy is he who knoweth all these (namely, creatures), and knoweth not Thee; but happy whoso knoweth Thee, though he know not these. And whoso knoweth both Thee and them is not the happier for them, but for Thee only."

Reply Obj. 6. This mirror has a will, and even as He will show Himself to whom He will, so will He show in Himself whatsoever He will. Nor does the comparison with a material mirror hold, for it is not in its power to be seen or not to be seen.

We may also reply that in a material mirror both thing and mirror are seen under their proper form; although the mirror is seen through a form received from the thing itself, whereas the stone is seen through its proper form reflected in some other thing, where the reason for seeing the one is the reason for seeing the other. But in the uncreated mirror a thing is seen through the form of the mirror, just as an effect is seen through the likeness of its cause and conversely. Consequently it does not follow that whoever sees the eternal mirror sees all that is reflected in that mirror, since he who sees the cause does not of necessity see all its effects, unless he comprehend the cause.

Reply Obj. 7. The desire of the saints to know all things will be fulfilled by the mere fact of their seeing God, just as their desire to possess all good things will be fulfilled by their possessing God. For as God suffices the affections in that He has perfect goodness, and by possessing Him we possess all goods as it were, so does the vision of Him suffice the in-

---

[1] Sect. 2 (PG 3, 696).   [2] *Confessions*, v, 7 (PL 32, 708).

tellect: *Lord, show us the Father and it is enough for us* (John 14. 8).

Reply Obj. 8. Ignorance properly so called denotes a privation and thus is it a punishment; for in this way ignorance is nescience of things, the knowledge of which is a duty or a necessity. Now the saints in heaven will not be ignorant of any of these things. Sometimes, however, ignorance is taken in a broad sense of any kind of nescience, and thus the angels and saints in heaven will be ignorant of certain things. Hence Dionysius says (*loc. cit.*) that "the angels will be cleansed from their ignorance (*nescientia*)." In this sense ignorance is not a penalty but a defect. Nor is it necessary for all such defects to be done away by glory, for thus we might say that it was a defect in Pope Linus that he did not attain to the glory of Peter.

Reply Obj. 9. Our body will be conformed to the body of Christ in glory, in likeness but not in equality, for it will be endowed with clarity even as Christ's body, but not equally. In like manner our soul will have glory in likeness to the soul of Christ, but not in equality thereto; thus it will have knowledge even as Christ's soul, but not so great, so as to know all as Christ's soul does.

Reply Obj. 10. Although the Divine essence is the type of all things knowable, it will not be united to each created intellect according as it is the type of all. Hence the objection proves nothing.

Reply Obj. 11. The agent intellect is a form proportionate to the possible intellect; even as the potency of matter is proportionate to the power of the natural agent, so that whatsoever is in the passive power of matter or of the possible intellect is in the active power of the agent intellect or of the natural agent. Consequently if the agent intellect become the form of the possible intellect, the latter must of necessity know all those things to which the power of the agent intellect extends. But the Divine essence is not a form proportionate to our intellect in this sense. Hence the comparison fails.

Reply Obj. 12. Nothing hinders us from saying that after the judgment day, when the glory of men and angels will be consummated once for all, all the blessed will know all that God knows by the knowledge of vision, yet so that not all will see all in the Divine essence. Christ's soul, however, will see clearly all things therein, even as it sees them now, while others will see therein a greater or lesser number of things according to the degree of clearness

with which they will know God, and thus Christ's soul will enlighten all other souls concerning those things which it sees in the Word better than others. Hence it is written (Apoc. 21. 23): *The glory of God shall enlighten the city of Jerusalem* (Vulg.,—*hath enlightened it*), *and the Lamb is the lamp thereof.* In like manner the higher souls will enlighten the lower (not indeed with a new enlightening, so as to increase the knowledge of the lower), but with a kind of continued enlightenment; thus we might understand the sun to enligthen the atmosphere while at a standstill. Therefore it is written (Dan. 12. 3): *They that instruct many to justice* shall shine *as stars for* all eternity. The statement that the superiority of the orders will cease refers to their present ordered ministry in our regard, as is clear from the same gloss.

QUESTION XCIII
OF THE HAPPINESS OF THE SAINTS AND THEIR MANSIONS
(*In Three Articles*)

WE must next consider the happiness of the saints and their mansions. Under this head there are three points of inquiry: (1) Whether the happiness of the saints will increase after the judgment? (2) Whether the degrees of happiness should be called mansions? (3) Whether the various mansions differ according to various degrees of charity?

ARTICLE 1. *Whether the Happiness of the Saints Will Be Greater After the Judgment Than Before?*

We proceed thus to the First Article: It would seem that the happiness of the saints will not be greater after the judgment than before.

Objection 1. For the nearer a thing approaches to the Divine likeness, the more perfectly does it participate happiness. Now the soul is more like God when separated from the body than when united to it. Therefore its happiness is greater before being reunited to the body than after.

Obj. 2. Further, Power is more effective when it is united than when divided. Now the soul is more united when separated from the body than when it is joined to the body. Therefore it has then greater power for operation, and consequently has a more perfect share of happiness, since this consists in an act.

Obj. 3. Further, Happiness consists in an act

of the speculative intellect. Now the intellect, in its act, makes no use of a bodily organ, and consequently by being reunited to the body the soul does not become capable of more perfect understanding. Therefore the soul's happiness is not greater after than before the judgment.

Obj. 4. Further, Nothing can be greater than the infinite, and so the addition of the finite to the infinite does not result in something greater than the infinite by itself. Now the beatified soul before its reunion with the body is rendered happy by rejoicing in the infinite good, namely God; and after the resurrection of the body it will rejoice in nothing else except perhaps the glory of the body, and this is a finite good. Therefore their joy after the resumption of the body will not be greater than before.

On the contrary, A gloss on Apoc. 6. 9, *I saw under the altar the souls of them that were slain,* says:[1] "At present the souls of the saints are under the altar, that is, less exalted than they will be." Therefore their happiness will be greater after the resurrection than after their death.

Further, Just as happiness is bestowed on the good as a reward, so is unhappiness awarded to the wicked. But the unhappiness of the wicked after reunion with their bodies will be greater than before, since they will be punished not only in the soul but also in the body. Therefore the happiness of the saints will be greater after the resurrection of the body than before.

I answer that, It is manifest that the happiness of the saints will increase in extent after the resurrection, because their happiness will then be not only in the soul but also in the body. Moreover, the soul's happiness also will increase in extent, seeing that the soul will rejoice not only in its own good, but also in that of the body. We may also say that the soul's happiness will increase in intensity.[2] For man's body may be considered in two ways: first, as being dependent on the soul for its completion; secondly, as containing something that hampers the soul in its operations, through the soul not perfectly completing the body. As regards the first way of considering the body, its union with the soul adds a certain perfection to the soul, since every part is imperfect, and is completed in its whole; therefore the whole is to the part as form to matter. Consequently the soul is more perfect in its natural being, when it is in

the whole—namely, man who results from the union of soul and body—than when it is a separate part. But as regards the second consideration the union of the body hampers the perfection of the soul, and so it is written (Wisd. 9. 15) that *the corruptible body is a load upon the soul.* If, then, there be removed from the body all those things by which it hampers the soul's action, the soul will be more perfect absolutely while existing in such a body than when separated from it. Now the more perfect a thing is in being, the more perfectly is it able to operate; therefore the operation of the soul united to such a body will be more perfect than the operation of the separated soul. But the glorified body will be a body of this description, being altogether subject to the spirit. Therefore, since happiness consists in an operation, the soul's happiness after its reunion with the body will be more perfect than before. For just as the soul separated from a corruptible body is able to operate more perfectly than when united to it, so after it has been united to a glorified body, its operation will be more perfect than while it was separated. Now every imperfect thing desires its perfection. Hence the separated soul naturally desires reunion with the body, and on account of this desire which proceeds from the soul's imperfection, its operation by which it is borne towards God is less intense. This agrees with the saying of Augustine (*Gen. ad Lit.* xii, 35)[3] that "on account of the body's desire it is held back from tending with all its might to that sovereign good."

Reply Obj. 1. The soul united to a glorified body is more like to God than when separated from it, in so far as when united it has more perfect being. For the more perfect a thing is the more it is like to God; even so the heart, the perfection of whose life consists in movement, is more like to God while in movement than while at rest, although God is never moved.

Reply Obj. 2. A power which by its own nature is capable of being in matter is more effective when it is in matter than when separated from matter, although absolutely speaking a power separate from matter is more powerful.

Reply Obj. 3. Although in the act of understanding the soul does not make use of the body, the perfection of the body will in some way conduce to the perfection of the intellectual operation in so far as through being united

---

[1] *Glossa ordin.* (VI, 250A).
[2] Cf. Part I–II, Q. IV, A. 5, where St. Thomas retracts this statement.
[3] PL 34, 483.

to a glorified body the soul will be more perfect in its nature, and consequently more effective in its operation, and accordingly the good itself of the body will conduce instrumentally, as it were, to the operation wherein happiness consists; thus the Philosopher asserts[1] that external goods conduce instrumentally to the happiness of life.

Reply Obj. 4. Although finite added to infinite does not make a greater thing, it makes more things, since finite and infinite are two things, while infinite taken by itself is one. Now the greater extent of joy regards not a greater thing but more things. Therefore joy is increased in extent, through referring to God and to the body's glory, in comparison with the joy which referred to God. Moreover, the body's glory will conduce to the intensity of the joy that refers to God, in so far as it will conduce to the more perfect operation whereby the soul tends to God, since the more perfect is a becoming operation, the greater the delight, as stated in the *Ethics*.[2]

ARTICLE 2. *Whether the Degrees of Happiness Should Be Called Mansions?*

We proceed thus to the Second Article: It would seem that the degrees of happiness should not be called mansions.

Objection 1. For happiness implies the notion of a reward, whereas mansion denotes nothing pertaining to a reward. Therefore the various degrees of happiness should not be called mansions.

Obj. 2. Further, mansion seems to denote a place. Now the place where the saints will be beatified is not corporeal but spiritual, namely God Who is one. Therefore there is but one mansion, and consequently the various degrees of happiness should not be called mansions.

Obj. 3. Further, As in heaven there will be men of various merits, so are there now in purgatory, and were in the limbo of the fathers. But various mansions are not distinguished in purgatory and limbo. Therefore in like manner neither should they be distinguished in heaven.

On the contrary, It is written (John 14. 2): *In My Father's house there are many mansions,* and Augustine expounds this in reference to the different degrees of rewards (*Tract.* lxvii *in Joann.*).[3]

Further, In every well-ordered city there is a distinction of mansions. Now the heavenly kingdom is compared to a city (Apoc. 21. 2).

Therefore we should distinguish various mansions there according to the various degrees of happiness.

I answer that, Since local movement precedes all other movements, terms of movement, distance and the like are derived from local movement to all other movements according to the Philosopher.[4] Now the end of local movement is a place, and when a thing has arrived at that place it remains there at rest and is maintained in it. Hence in every movement this very rest at the end of the movement is called an establishment (*collocatio*) or mansion. Therefore since the term movement is transferred to the actions of the appetite and will, the attainment of the end of an appetitive movement is called a mansion or establishment, so that the unity of a house corresponds to the unity of happiness, which unity is on the part of the object, and the plurality of mansions corresponds to the differences of happiness on the part of the blessed; even so we observe in natural things that there is one same place above to which all light objects tend, whereas each one reaches it more closely according as it is lighter, so that they have various mansions corresponding to their various lightness.

Reply Obj. 1. Mansion implies the notion of end and consequently of reward which is the end of merit.

Reply Obj. 2. Though there is one spiritual place, there are different degrees of approaching to it, and the various mansions correspond to these.

Reply Obj. 3. Those who were in limbo or are now in purgatory have not yet attained to their end. Therefore various mansions are not distinguished in purgatory or limbo, but only in heaven and hell, wherein is the end of the good and of the wicked.

ARTICLE 3. *Whether the Various Mansions Are Distinguished According to the Various Degrees of Charity?*

We proceed thus to the Third Article: It would seem that the various mansions are not distinguished according to the various degrees of charity.

Objection 1. For it is written (Matt. 25. 15): *He gave to every one according to his proper virtue* (Douay,—*ability*). Now the proper ability of a thing is its natural power. Therefore the gifts also of grace and glory are distributed according to the different degrees of natural power.

---

[1] *Ethics*, I, 8, 9 (1099^{a}33; ^{b}27).
[2] *Ibid.*, X, 4 (1174^{b}19).   [3] PL 35, 1812.

[4] *Physics*, VIII, 9 (265^{b}17).

Obj. 2. Further, It is written (Ps. 61. 12): *Thou wilt render to every man according to his works.* Now that which is rendered is the measure of happiness. Therefore the degrees of happiness are distinguished according to the diversity of works and not according to the diversity of charity.

Obj 3. Further, Reward is due to act and not to habit; hence it is not the strongest who are crowned but those who engage in the conflict,[1] and *he . . . shall not be* (Vulg.,—*is not*) *crowned except he strive lawfully.* Now happiness is a reward. Therefore the various degrees of happiness will be according to the various degrees of works and not according to the various degrees of charity.

On the contrary, The more one will be united to God the happier will one be. Now the measure of charity is the measure of one's union with God. Therefore the diversity of happiness will be according to the difference of charity.

Further, If one thing follows absolutely from another thing absolutely, the increase of the former follows from the increase of the latter. Now to have happiness follows from having charity. Therefore to have greater happiness follows from having greater charity.

I answer that, The distinguishing principle of the mansions or degrees of happiness is twofold, namely proximate and remote. The proximate principle is the difference of disposition which will be in the blessed, from which will result the difference of perfection in them in respect to the beatific operation, while the remote principle is the merit by which they have obtained that happiness. In the first way the mansions are distinguished according to the charity of heaven, which the more perfect it will be in any one, the more will it render him capable of the Divine clarity, on the increase of which will depend the increase in perfection of the Divine vision. In the second way the mansions are distinguished according to the charity of the way. For our actions are meritorious not by the very substance of the action, but only by the habit of virtue with which they are informed. Now every virtue obtains its meritorious efficacy from charity, which has the end itself for its object. Hence the diversity of merit is all traced to the diversity of charity, and thus the charity of the way will distinguish the mansions by way of merit.

Reply Obj. 1. In this passage "virtue" denotes not the natural ability alone, but the natural ability together with the endeavour to obtain grace. Consequently virtue in this sense will be a kind of material disposition to the measure of grace and glory that one will receive. But charity is the formal complement of merit in relation to glory, and therefore the distinction of degrees in glory depends on the degrees of charity rather than on the degrees of the aforesaid virtue.

Reply Obj. 2. Works in themselves do not demand the payment of a reward, except as informed by charity, and therefore the various degrees of glory will be according to the various degrees of charity.

Reply Obj. 3. Although the habit of charity or of any virtue whatever is not a merit to which a reward is due, it is none the less the principle and reason of merit in the act, and consequently according to its diversity is the diversity of rewards. This does not prevent our observing a certain degree of merit in the act considered generically, not indeed in relation to the essential reward which is joy in God, but in relation to some accidental reward, which is joy in some created good.

QUESTION XCIV

OF THE RELATIONS OF THE SAINTS TOWARDS THE DAMNED

(In Three Articles)

WE must next consider the relations of the saints towards the damned. Under this head there are three points of inquiry: (1) Whether the saints see the sufferings of the damned? (2) Whether they pity them? (3) Whether they rejoice in their sufferings?

ARTICLE 1. *Whether the Blessed in Heaven Will See the Sufferings of the Damned?*

We proceed thus to the First Article: It would seem that the blessed in heaven will not see the sufferings of the damned.

Objection 1. For the damned are more cut off from the blessed than wayfarers. But the blessed do not see the deeds of wayfarers; therefore a gloss on Isa. 63. 16, *Abraham hath not known us,* says:[2] "The dead, even the saints, know not what the living, even their own children, are doing." Much less therefore do they see the sufferings of the damned.

Obj. 2. Further, Perfection of vision depends on the perfection of the visible object; hence the Philosopher says[3] that "the most perfect operation of the sense of sight is when the sense is most disposed with reference to the most

---

[1] Aristotle, *Ethics,* I, 8 (1099ᵃ4).   [2] *Glossa interl.* (IV, 102v).   [3] *Ethics,* X, 4 (1174ᵇ14).

beautiful of the objects which fall under the sight." Therefore, on the other hand, any deformity in the visible object redounds to the imperfection of the sight. But there will be no imperfection in the blessed. Therefore they will not see the sufferings of the damned wherein there is extreme deformity.

On the contrary, It is written (Isa. 66. 24): *They shall go out and see the carcasses of the men that have transgressed against Me;* and a gloss says:[1] "The elect will go out by understanding or seeing manifestly, so that they may be urged the more to praise God."

I answer that, Nothing should be denied the blessed that belongs to the perfection of their happiness. Now everything is known the more for being compared with its contrary, because when contraries are placed beside one another they become more conspicuous. Therefore in order that the happiness of the saints may be more delightful to them and that they may render more copious thanks to God for it, they are allowed to see perfectly the sufferings of the damned.

Reply Obj. 1. This gloss speaks of what the departed saints are able to do by nature, for it is not necessary that they should know by natural knowledge all that happens to the living. But the saints in heaven know distinctly all that happens both to wayfarers and to the damned. Hence Gregory says (*Moral.* xii, 21)[2] that Job's words (14. 21), *"Whether his children come to honour or dishonour, he shall not understand,"* "do not apply to the souls of the saints, because since they possess the glory of God within them, we cannot believe that external things are unknown to them."

Reply Obj. 2. Although the beauty of the thing seen conduces to the perfection of vision, there may be deformity of the thing seen without imperfection of vision, because the species of things by which the soul knows contraries are not themselves contrary. Therefore also God Who has most perfect knowledge sees all things, beautiful and deformed.

ARTICLE 2. *Whether the Blessed Pity the Unhappiness of the Damned?*

We proceed thus to the Second Article: It would seem that the blessed pity the unhappiness of the damned.

Objection 1. For pity proceeds from charity, and charity will be most perfect in the blessed. Therefore they will most especially pity the sufferings of the damned.

---

[1] *Glossa ordin.* (IV, 108E); cf. Jerome, *In Isaiam* (PL 24, 702).   [2] PL 75, 999.

Obj. 2. Further, The blessed will never be so far from taking pity as God is. Yet in a sense God compassionates our afflictions, and therefore He is said to be merciful.

On the contrary, Whoever pities another shares somewhat in his unhappiness. But the blessed cannot share in any unhappiness. Therefore they do not pity the afflictions of the damned.

I answer that, Mercy or compassion may be in a person in two ways: first by way of passion, secondly by way of choice. In the blessed there will be no passion in the lower part except as a result of the reason's choice. Hence compassion or mercy will not be in them, except by the choice of reason. Now mercy or compassion comes of the reason's choice when a person wishes another's evil to be dispelled; therefore in those things which, in accordance with reason, we do not wish to be dispelled, we have no such compassion. But so long as sinners are in this world they are in such a state that without prejudice to the Divine justice they can be taken away from a state of unhappiness and sin to a state of happiness. Consequently it is possible to have compassion on them both by the choice of the will,—in which sense God, the angels and the blessed are said to pity them by desiring their salvation,—and by passion, in which way they are pitied by the good men who are in the state of wayfarers. But in the future state it will be impossible for them to be taken away from their unhappiness, and consequently it will not be possible to pity their sufferings according to right reason. Therefore the blessed in glory will have no pity on the damned.

Reply Obj. 1. Charity is the principle of pity when it is possible for us out of charity to wish the cessation of a person's unhappiness. But the saints cannot desire this for the damned, since it would be contrary to Divine justice. Consequently the argument does not prove.

Reply Obj. 2. God is said to be merciful in so far as He succours those whom it is befitting to be released from their afflictions in accordance with the order of wisdom and justice, not as though He pitied the damned, except perhaps in punishing them less than they deserve.

ARTICLE 3. *Whether the Blessed Rejoice in the Punishment of the Wicked?*

We proceed thus to the Third Article: It would seem that the blessed do not rejoice in the punishment of the wicked.

Objection 1. For rejoicing in another's evil

pertains to hatred. But there will be no hatred in the blessed. Therefore they will not rejoice in the unhappiness of the damned.

Obj. 2. Further, The blessed in heaven will be in the highest degree conformed to God. Now God does not rejoice in our afflictions. Therefore neither will the blessed rejoice in the afflictions of the damned.

Obj. 3. Further, That which is blameworthy in a wayfarer has no place whatever in a comprehensor. Now it is most reprehensible in a wayfarer to take pleasure in the pains of others, and most praiseworthy to grieve for them. Therefore the blessed in no way rejoice in the punishment of the damned.

On the contrary, It is written (Ps. 57. 11): *The just shall rejoice when he shall see the revenge.*

Further, It is written (Isa. 56. 24): *They shall satiate* (Douay,—*They shall be a loathsome sight to all flesh*) *the sight of all flesh.* Now satiety denotes refreshment of the mind. Therefore the blessed will rejoice in the punishment of the wicked.

I answer that, A thing may be a matter of rejoicing in two ways. First, in itself, when one rejoices in a thing as such, and thus the saints will not rejoice in the punishment of the wicked. Secondly, accidentally, by reason namely of something joined to it; and in this way the saints will rejoice in the punishment of the wicked, by considering therein the order of Divine justice and their own deliverance, which will fill them with joy. And thus the Divine justice and their own deliverance will be the direct cause of the joy of the blessed, while the punishment of the damned will cause it indirectly.

Reply Obj. 1. To rejoice in another's evil as such belongs to hatred, but not to rejoice in another's evil by reason of something joined to it. Thus a person sometimes rejoices in his own evil as when we rejoice in our own afflictions, as helping us to merit life: *My brethren count it all joy when you shall fall into divers temptations* (Jas. 1. 2).

Reply Obj. 2. Although God rejoices not in punishments as such, He rejoices in them as being ordered by His justice.

Reply Obj. 3. It is not praiseworthy in a wayfarer to rejoice in another's afflictions as such, yet it is praiseworthy if he rejoice in them as having some good joined to them. However it is not the same with a wayfarer as with a comprehensor, because in a wayfarer the passions often forestall the judgment of reason, and

yet sometimes such passions are praiseworthy, as indicating the good disposition of the mind, as in the case of shame, pity and repentance for evil; but in a comprehensor there can be no passion but such as follows the judgment of reason.

QUESTION XCV
OF THE GIFTS OF THE BLESSED
(*In Five Articles*)

WE must now consider the gifts of the blessed under which head there are five points of inquiry: (1) Whether any gifts should be assigned to the blessed? (2) Whether a gift differs from happiness? (3) Whether it is fitting for Christ to have gifts? (4) Whether this is fitting to the angels? (5) Whether three gifts of the soul are rightly assigned?

ARTICLE 1. *Whether Any Gifts Should Be Assigned as Dowry to the Blessed?*

We proceed thus to the First Article: It would seem that no gifts[1] should be assigned to the blessed.

Objection 1. For a dowry (Cod. v, 12, *De jure dot.* 20; Dig. xxiii, 3, *De jure dot.*)[2] is given to the bridegroom for the upkeep of the burdens of marriage. But the saints do not resemble the bridegroom but the bride, as being members of the Church. Therefore they receive no dowry.

Obj. 2. Further, The dowry is given not by the bridegroom's father, but by the father of the bride (Cod. v, 11, *De dot. promiss.* 7; Dig. xxiii, 2, *De rit. nup.*).[3] Now all the beatific gifts are bestowed on the blessed by the father of the bridegroom, that is, Christ: *Every best gift and every perfect gift is from above coming down from the Father of lights* (Jas. 1. 17). Therefore these gifts which are bestowed on the blessed should not be called a dowry.

Obj. 3. Further, In carnal marriage a dowry is given that the burdens of marriage may be the more easily borne. But in spiritual marriage there are no burdens, especially in the state of the Church triumphant. Therefore no dowry should be assigned to that state.

Obj. 4. Further, A dowry is not given save on the occasion of marriage.[4] But a spiritual marriage is contracted with Christ by faith in the state of the Church militant. Therefore if a dowry is befitting the blessed, for the same reason it will be befitting the saints who are

---

[1] The Latin *dos* (gift) signifies a dowry.
[2] KR II, 205b; KR I, 336a. [3] KR II, 204a; KR I, 331b.
[4] Cf. *Dig.*, XXIII, 3, leg. 3 (KR I, 335b).

wayfarers. But it is not befitting the latter, and therefore neither is it befitting the blessed.

Obj. 5. Further, A dowry pertains to external goods, which are styled goods of fortune, whereas the reward of the blessed will consist of internal goods. Therefore they should not be called a dowry.

On the contrary, It is written (Eph. 5. 32): *This is a great sacrament: but I speak in Christ and in the Church.* Hence it follows that the spiritual marriage is signified by the carnal marriage. But in a carnal marriage the dowered bride is brought to the dwelling of the bridegroom. Therefore since the saints are brought to Christ's dwelling when they are beatified, it would seem that they are dowered with certain gifts.

Further, A dowry is appointed to carnal marriage for the ease of marriage. But the spiritual marriage is more blissful than the carnal marriage. Therefore a dowry should be especially assigned to it.

Further, The adornment of the bride is part of the dowry. Now the saints are adorned when they are taken into glory, according to Isa. 61. 10, *He hath clothed me with the garments of salvation . . . as a bride adorned with her jewels.* Therefore the saints in heaven have a dowry.

I answer that, Without doubt the blessed when they are brought into glory are dowered by God with certain gifts for their adornment, and this adornment is called their dowry by the masters. Hence the dower of which we speak now is defined thus: "The dowry is the everlasting adornment of soul and body, adequate to life, lasting for ever in eternal happiness." This description is taken from a likeness to the material dowry whereby the bride is adorned and the husband provided with an adequate support for his wife and children, and yet the dowry remains inalienable from the bride, so that if the marriage union be severed it reverts to her. As to the reason of the name there are various opinions. For some say that the name dowry is taken not from a likeness to the corporeal marriage, but according to the manner of speaking whereby any perfection or adornment of any person whatever is called an endowment; thus a man who is proficient in knowledge is said to be endowed with knowledge, and in this sense Ovid employed the word endowment (*De Arte Amandi,* i, 538):[1] "By whatever endowment thou canst please, strive to please." But this does not seem quite

fitting, for whenever a term is employed to signify a certain thing principally, it is not usually transferred to another save by reason of some likeness. Therefore since by its primary meaning a dowry refers to carnal marriage, it follows that in every other application of the term we must observe some kind of likeness to its principal meaning.

Consequently others say that the likeness consists in the fact that in carnal marriage a dowry is properly a gift bestowed by the bridegroom on the bride for her adornment when she is taken to the bridegroom's dwelling, and that this is shown by the words of Sichem to Jacob and his sons (Gen. 34. 12): *Raise the dowry, and ask gifts,* and from Exod. 22. 16: *If a man seduce a virgin . . . and lie with her, he shall endow her, and have her to wife.* Hence the adornment bestowed by Christ on the saints, when they are brought into the abode of glory, is called a dowry. But this is clearly contrary to what jurists say, to whom it belongs to treat of these matters. For they say[2] that a dowry, properly speaking, is a donation on the part of the wife made to those who are on the part of the husband, in view of the marriage burden which the husband has to bear, while that which the bridegroom gives the bride is called "a donation in view of marriage."[3] In this sense dowry is taken (III Kings 9. 16) where it is stated that *Pharao the king of Egypt, took Gezer . . . and gave it for a dowry to his daughter, Solomon's wife.* Nor do the authorities quoted prove anything to the contrary. For although it is customary for a dowry to be given by the maiden's parents, it happens sometimes that the bridegroom or his father gives the dowry instead of the bride's father. And this happens in two ways: either by reason of his very great love for the bride as in the case of Sichem's father Hemor, who on account of his son's great love for the maiden, wished to give the dowry which he had a right to receive; or as a punishment on the bridegroom, that he should out of his own possessions give a dowry to the virgin seduced by him, whereas he should have received it from the girl's father. In this sense Moses speaks in the passage quoted above. Therefore in the opinion of others we should hold that in carnal marriage a dowry, properly speaking, is that which is given by those on the wife's side to those on the husband's side, for the bearing of the marriage burden, as stated above. Yet the difficulty remains how

[1] DD 176.

[2] Cf. Raymond of Pennafort, *Summa,* bk. iv, tit. xxv, sect. 1 (534ᵃ).   [3] *Ibid.,* sect. 2 (534ᵇ).

this meaning can be adapted to the case in point, since the heavenly adornments are given to the spiritual spouse by the Father of the Bridegroom. This shall be made clear by replying to the objections.

Reply Obj. 1. Although in carnal marriage the dowry is given to the bridegroom for his use, yet the ownership and control belong to the bride, which is evident by the fact that if the marriage be dissolved, the dowry reverts to the bride according to law.[1] Thus also in spiritual marriage, the very adornments bestowed on the spiritual bride, namely the Church in her members, belong indeed to the Bridegroom, in so far as they conduce to His glory and honour, yet to the bride as adorned by them.

Reply Obj. 2. The Father of the Bridegroom, that is of Christ, is the Person of the Father alone, while the Father of the bride is the whole Trinity, since that which is effected in creatures belongs to the whole Trinity. Hence in spiritual marriage these endowments, properly speaking, are given by the Father of the bride rather than by the Father of the Bridegroom. Nevertheless, although this endowment is made by all the Persons, it may be in a manner appropriated to each Person. To the Person of the Father, as endowing, since He possesses authority; and fatherhood in relation to creatures is also appropriated to Him, so that He is Father of both Bridegroom and bride. To the Son it is appropriated in so far as it is made for His sake and through Him; and to the Holy Ghost, in so far as it is made in Him and according to Him, since love is the reason of all giving.

Reply Obj. 3. That which is effected by the dowry belongs to the dowry by its nature, and that is the ease of marriage, while that which the dowry removes, namely the marriage burden which is lightened thereby, belongs to it accidentally; thus it belongs to grace by its nature to make a man just, but accidentally to make an ungodly man just. Accordingly, though there are no burdens in the spiritual marriage, there is the greatest gladness; and that this gladness may be perfected the bride is dowered with gifts, so that by their means she may be happily united with the bridegroom.

Reply Obj. 4. The dowry is usually settled on the bride not when she is espoused, but when she is taken to the bridegroom's dwelling, so as to be in the presence of the bridegroom, since *while we are in the body we are absent from the Lord* (II Cor. 5. 6). Hence the gifts

[1] *Dig.*, XXIV, tit. III, leg. I, 2 (KR I, 356a; 356b).

bestowed on the saints in this life are not called a dowry, but those which are bestowed on them when they are received into glory, where the Bridegroom delights them with His presence.

Reply Obj. 5. In spiritual marriage inward comeliness is required, and therefore it is written (Ps. 44. 14): *All the glory of the king's daughter is within*, etc. But in carnal marriage outward comeliness is necessary. Hence there is no need for a dowry of this kind to be appointed in spiritual marriage as in carnal marriage.

ARTICLE 2. *Whether the Dowry Is the Same As Happiness?*

We proceed thus to the Second Article: It would seem that the dowry is the same as happiness.

Objection 1. For as appears from the definition of dowry (A. 1), the dowry is the everlasting adornment of body and soul in eternal happiness. Now the happiness of the soul is an adornment of the soul. Therefore happiness is a dowry.

Obj. 2. Further, A dowry signifies something whereby the union of bride and bridegroom is rendered delightful (A. 1). Now such is happiness in the spiritual marriage. Therefore happiness is a dowry.

Obj. 3. Further, According to Augustine (*De Trin.* i, 8)[2] vision "is the whole substance of happiness." Now vision is accounted one of the dowries. Therefore happiness is a dowry.

Obj. 4. Further, Enjoyment (*fruitio*) gives happiness. Now enjoyment is a dowry. Therefore a dowry gives happiness and thus happiness is a dowry.

Obj. 5. Further, According to Boëthius (*De Consol.* iii, 2),[3] "happiness is a state made perfect by the aggregate of all good things." Now the state of the blessed is perfected by the dowries. Therefore the dowries are a part of happiness.

On the contrary, The dowries are given without merits, whereas happiness is not given, but is awarded in return for merits. Therefore happiness is not a dowry.

Further, happiness is one only, whereas the dowries are several. Therefore happiness is not a dowry.

Further, happiness is in man according to that which is principal in him,[4] whereas a dowry is also appointed to the body. Therefore dowry and happiness are not the same.

[2] PL 42, 831; cf. *Enarr. in Ps.*, Ps. 90.16 (PL 37, 1169).
[3] PL 63, 724.　　[4] Aristotle, *Ethics*, X, 7 (1177ᵃ12).

I answer that, There are two opinions on this question. For some say that happiness and dowry are the same in reality but differ in aspect, because dowry regards the spiritual marriage between Christ and the soul, whereas happiness does not. But it seems that this cannot be since Happiness consists in an operation, whereas a dowry is not an operation, but a quality or disposition. Therefore according to others it must be stated that happiness and dowry differ even in reality, happiness being the perfect operation itself by which the soul is united to God, while the dowries are habits or dispositions or any other qualities directed to this same perfect operation, so that they are ordered to happiness rather than instead of being in it as its parts.

Reply Obj. 1. Happiness properly speaking, is not an adornment of the soul, but something resulting from the soul's adornment, since it is an operation, while its adornment is a certain comeliness of the blessed themselves.

Reply Obj. 2. Happiness is not directed to the union but is the union itself of the soul with Christ. This union is by an operation, whereas the dowries are gifts disposing to this same union.

Reply Obj. 3. Vision may be taken in two ways. First, actually, that is for the act itself of vision; and thus vision is not a dowry, but happiness itself. Secondly, it may be taken habitually, that is for the habit whereby this act is elicited, namely the clarity of glory, by which the soul is enlightened from above to see God, and thus it is a dowry and the principle of happiness, but not happiness itself. The same answer applies to *Obj.* 4.

Reply Obj. 5. Happiness is the sum of all goods not as though they were essential parts of happiness, but as being in a way ordered to happiness, as stated above.

ARTICLE 3. *Whether It Is Fitting That Christ Should Receive a Dowry?*

We proceed thus to the Third Article: It would seem fitting that Christ should receive a dowry.

Objection 1. For the saints will be conformed to Christ through glory, according to Philip. 3. 21, *Who will reform the body of our lowness made like to the body of His glory.* Therefore Christ also will have a dowry.

Obj. 2. Further, In the spiritual marriage a dowry is given in likeness to a carnal marriage. Now there is a spiritual marriage in Christ which is peculiar to Him, namely of the two natures in one Person, in regard to which the human nature in Him is said to have been espoused by the Word, as a gloss has it[1] on Ps. 18. 6, *He hath set His tabernacle in the sun,* etc., and Apoc. 21. 3, *Behold the tabernacle of God with men.* Therefore it is fitting that Christ should have a dowry.

Obj. 3. Further, Augustine says[2] that Christ, according to the Rule of Tyconius, on account of the unity of the mystic body that exists between the head and its members, calls Himself also the Bride and not only the Bridegroom, as may be gathered from Isa. 61. 10, *As a bridegroom decked with a crown, and as a bride adorned with her jewels.* Since then a dowry is due to the bride, it would seem that Christ ought to receive a dowry.

Obj. 4. Further, A dowry is due to all the members of the Church, since the Church is the spouse. But Christ is a member of the Church according to I Cor. 12. 27, *You are the body of Christ, and members of member,* that is, "of Christ," according to a gloss.[3] Therefore the dowry is due to Christ.

Obj. 5. Further, Christ has perfect vision, fruition, and joy. Now these are the dowries. Therefore, etc.

On the contrary, A distinction of persons is requisite between the bridegroom and the bride. But in Christ there is nothing personally distinct from the Son of God Who is the Bridegroom, as stated in John 3. 29, *He that hath bride is the bridegroom.* Therefore since the dowry is allotted to the bride or for the bride, it would seem unfitting for Christ to have a dowry.

Further, The same person does not both give and receive a dowry. But it is Christ Who gives spiritual dowries. Therefore it is not fitting that Christ should have a dowry.

I answer that, There are two opinions on this point. For some say that there is a threefold union in Christ. One is the union of concord, whereby He is united to God in the bond of love; another is the union of condescension (*dignativa*), whereby the human nature is united to the Divine; the third is the union whereby Christ is united to the Church. They say, then, that as regards the first two unions it is fitting for Christ to have the dowries as such, but as regards the third, it is fitting for Him to have the dowries in the most excellent de-

---

[1] *Glossa ordin.* (III, 110F); *Glossa* Lombardi (PL 191, 208); Augustine, *Enarr. in Ps.* (PL 36, 161).
[2] *Christian Doctrine,* III, 31 (PL 34, 82).   [3] *Glossa* Lombardi (PL 191, 1657); cf. *Glossa interl.* (VI, 53r).

gree, considered as to that in which they consist, but not considered as dowries; because in this union Christ is the bridegroom and the Church the bride, and a dowry is given to the bride as regards property and control, although it is given to the bridegroom as to use. But this does not seem fitting. For in the union of Christ with the Father by the concord of love, even if we consider Him as God, there is not said to be a marriage, since it implies no subjection such as is required in the bride towards the bridegroom. Nor again in the union of the human nature with the Divine, whether we consider the Personal union or that which regards the conformity of will, can there be a dowry, properly speaking, for three reasons. First, because in a marriage where a dowry is given there should be likeness of nature between bridegroom and bride, and this is lacking in the union of the human nature with the Divine; secondly, because there is required a distinction of persons, and the human nature is not personally distinct from the Word; thirdly, because a dowry is given when the bride is first taken to the dwelling of the bridegroom and thus would seem to belong to the bride, who from being not united becomes united; but the human nature, which was assumed into the unity of Person by the Word, never was otherwise than perfectly united. Therefore in the opinion of others we should say that the notion of dowry is either altogether unbecoming to Christ, or not so properly as to the saints, but that the things which we call dowries befit Him in the highest degree.

Reply Obj. 1. This conformity must be understood to refer to the thing which is a dowry and not to the notion of a dowry being in Christ, for it is not requisite that the thing in which we are conformed to Christ should be in the same way in Christ and in us.

Reply Obj. 2. Human nature is not properly said to be a bride in its union with the Word, since the distinction of persons, which is requisite between bridegroom and bride, is not observed therein. That human nature is sometimes described as being espoused in reference to its union with the Word is because it has a certain act of the bride, in that it is united to the Bridegroom inseparably, and in this union is subject to the Word and ruled by the Word, as the bride by the bridegroom.

Reply Obj. 3. If Christ is sometimes spoken of as the Bride, this is not because He is the Bride in very truth, but in so far as He personifies His spouse, namely the Church, who is united to Him spiritually. Hence nothing hinders Him, in this way of speaking, from being said to have the dowries, not that He Himself is dowered, but the Church.

Reply Obj. 4. The term Church is taken in two senses. For sometimes it denotes the body only, which is united to Christ as its Head. In this way alone has the Church the character of spouse, and in this way Christ is not a member of the Church, but is the Head from which all the members receive. In another sense the Church denotes the head and members united together; and thus Christ is said to be a member of the Church, in so far as He fulfils an office distinct from all others, by pouring forth life into the other members, although He is not very properly called a member, since a member implies a certain restriction, whereas in Christ spiritual good is not restricted but is absolutely entire, so that He is the entire good of the Church, nor is He together with others anything greater than He is by Himself. Speaking of the Church in this sense, the Church denotes not only the bride, but the bridegroom and bride, in so far as one thing results from their spiritual union. Consequently although Christ is called a member of the Church in a certain sense, He can by no means be called a member of the bride, and therefore the idea of a dowry is not fitting to Him.

Reply Obj. 5. There is here a fallacy of accident, for these things are not befitting to Christ if we consider them under the aspect of dowry.

ARTICLE 4. *Whether the Angels Receive the Dowries?*

We proceed thus to the Fourth Article: It would seem that the angels receive dowries.

Objection 1. For a gloss on Cant. 6. 8, *One is my dove,* says:[1] "One is the Church among men and angels." But the Church is the bride, and therefore it is fitting for the members of the Church to have the dowries. Therefore the angels have the dowries.

Obj. 2. Further, A gloss on Luke 12. 36, *And you yourselves like to men who wait for their Lord, when he shall return from the wedding,* says:[2] "Our Lord went to the wedding when

---

[1] Cf. among the works of Cassiodorus, *In Cant.* (PL 70, 1091); among the works of Isidore, *In Cant.* (PL 83, 1128); Bede, *In Cant.,* bk. V (PL 91, 1182).

[2] *Glossa ordin.* (v, 158E); Bede, *In Luc.,* bk. IV (PL 92, 495).

after His resurrection the new Man espoused to Himself the angelic host." Therefore the angelic hosts are the spouse of Christ and consequently it is fitting that they should have the dowries.

Obj. 3. Further, The spiritual marriage consists in a spiritual union. Now the spiritual union between the angels and God is no less than between beatified men and God. Since, then, the dowries of which we treat now are assigned by reason of a spiritual marriage, it would seem that they are becoming to the angels.

Obj. 4. Further, A spiritual marriage demands a spiritual bridegroom and a spiritual bride. Now the angels are by nature more conformed than men to Christ as the supreme spirit. Therefore a spiritual marriage is more possible between the angels and Christ than between men and Christ.

Obj. 5. Further, A greater conformity is required between the head and members than between bridegroom and bride. Now the conformity between Christ and the angels suffices for Christ to be called the Head of the angels. Therefore for the same reason it suffices for Him to be called their bridegroom.

On the contrary, Origen at the beginning of the prologue to his commentary on the Canticles,[1] distinguishes four persons, namely "the bridegroom with the bride, the young maidens, and the companions of the bridegroom"; and he says that "the angels are the companions of the bridegroom." Since then the dowry is due only to the bride, it would seem that the dowries are not becoming to the angels.

Further, Christ espoused the Church by His Incarnation and Passion; hence this is foreshadowed in the words (Exod. 4. 25), *A bloody spouse thou art to me.* Now by His Incarnation and Passion Christ was not otherwise united to the angels than before. Therefore the angels do not belong to the Church, if we consider the Church as spouse. Therefore the dowries are not becoming to the angels.

I answer that, Without any doubt, whatever pertains to the endowments of the soul is befitting to the angels as it is to men. But considered under the aspect of dowry they are not as becoming to the angels as to men, because the character of bride is not so properly becoming to the angels as to men. For there is required a conformity of nature between bridegroom and bride, that is that they should be of the same species. Now men are in con-

[1] Trans. of Rufinus (PG 13, 63).

formity with Christ in this way, since He took human nature, and by so doing became conformed to all men in the specific nature of man. On the other hand, He is not conformed to the angels in unity of species, neither as to His Divine nor as to His human nature. Consequently the notion of dowry is not so properly becoming to angels as to men. Since, however, in metaphorical expressions, it is not necessary to have a likeness in every respect, we must not argue that one thing is not to be said of another metaphorically on account of some lack of likeness; and consequently the argument we have adduced does not prove that the dowries are unbecoming absolutely to the angels, but only that they are not so properly befitting to angels as to men, on account of the aforesaid lack of likeness.

Reply Obj. 1. Although the angels are included in the unity of the Church, they are not members of the Church according to conformity of nature, if we consider the Church as bride; and thus it is not properly fitting for them to have the dowries.

Reply Obj. 2. Espousal is taken there in a broad sense, for union without conformity of specific nature, and in this sense nothing prevents our saying that the angels have the dowries taking these in a broad sense.

Reply Obj. 3. In the spiritual marriage although there is no other than a spiritual union, those whose union answers to the idea of a perfect marriage should agree in specific nature. Hence espousal does not properly befit the angels.

Reply Obj. 4. The conformity between the angels and Christ as God is not such as suffices for the notion of a perfect marriage, since so far are they from agreeing in species that there is still an infinite distance between them.

Reply Obj. 5. Not even is Christ properly called the Head of the angels, if we consider the head as requiring conformity of nature with the members. We must observe, however, that although the head and the other members are parts of an individual of one species, if we consider each one by itself, it is not of the same species as another member, for a hand is another specific part from the head. Hence, speaking of the members in themselves, the only conformity required among them is one of proportion, so that one receive from another, and one serve another. Consequently the conformity between God and the angels suffices for the notion of head rather than for that of bridegroom.

ARTICLE 5. *Whether Three Dowries of the Soul Are Suitably Assigned?*

We proceed thus to the Fifth Article: It would seem unfitting to assign to the soul three dowries, namely, vision, love and enjoyment.

Objection 1. For the soul is united to God according to the mind wherein is the image of the Trinity in respect of the memory, understanding, and will. Now love regards the will, and vision the understanding. Therefore there should be something corresponding to the memory, since enjoyment pertains not the memory but the will.

Obj. 2. Further, The beatific dowries are said to correspond to the virtues of the way, which united us to God, and these are faith, hope, and charity, whereby God Himself is the object. Now love corresponds to charity, and vision to faith. Therefore there should be something corresponding to hope, since enjoyment corresponds rather to charity.

Obj. 3. Further, We enjoy God by love and vision only, since "we are said to enjoy those things which we love for their own sake," as Augustine says.[1] Therefore enjoyment should not be put as a distinct dowry from love.

Obj. 4. Further, Comprehension is required for the perfection of happiness: *So run that you may comprehend* (I Cor. 9. 24). Therefore we should put a fourth dowry.

Obj. 5. Further, Anselm says (*De Simil.* xlviii)[2] that the following pertain to the soul's happiness: "wisdom, friendship, concord, power, honour, security, joy," and consequently the above dowries are assigned unsuitably.

Obj. 6. Further, Augustine says[3] that "in that Happiness God will be seen unendingly, loved without wearying, praised untiringly." Therefore praise should be added to the aforesaid dowries.

Obj. 7. Further, Boëthius affirms five things pertaining to happiness (*De Consol.* iii, 10)[4] and these are: Sufficiency, which wealth offers; joy, which pleasure offers; celebrity, which fame offers; security, which power offers; reverence, which dignity offers. Consequently it seems that these should be reckoned as dowries rather than the aforesaid.

I answer that, All agree in affirming three dowries of the soul, in different ways however. For some say that the three dowries of the soul are vision, love, and enjoyment; others say

they are vision, comprehension, and enjoyment; others, vision, delight, and comprehension. However, all these reckonings come to the same, and their number is assigned in the same way. For it has been said (A. 2) that a dowry is something inherent to the soul, and directing it to the operation in which happiness consists. Now two things are required in this operation: its essence, which is vision; and its perfection, which is delight. For happiness must be a perfect operation. Again, a vision is delightful in two ways: first, on the part of the object, by reason of the thing seen being delightful; secondly, on the part of the vision, by reason of the seeing itself being delightful, even as we delight in knowing evil things, although the evil things themselves delight us not. And since this operation wherein ultimate happiness consists must be most perfect, this vision must be delightful in both ways.

Now in order that this vision be delightful on the part of the vision, it needs to be made connatural to the seer by means of a habit; while for it to be delightful on the part of the visible object, two things are necessary, namely that the visible object be suitable, and that it be united to the seer. Accordingly for the vision to be delightful on its own part a habit is required to elicit the vision, and thus we have one dowry, which all call vision. But on the part of the visible object two things are necessary. First, suitableness, which regards the affections,—and in this respect some account love as a dowry, others enjoyment (in so far as enjoyment regards the affective part) since what we love most we consider most suitable. Secondly, union is required on the part of the visible object, and thus some account comprehension, which is nothing else than to have God present and to hold Him within oneself; while others assign enjoyment, not of hope, which is ours while on the way, but of possession,[5] which is in heaven.

Thus the three dowries correspond to the three theological virtues, namely vision to faith, comprehension (or enjoyment in one sense) to hope, and enjoyment (or delight according to another reckoning) to charity. For perfect enjoyment such as will be had in heaven includes delight and comprehension, for which reason some take it for the one, and some for the other.

Others, however, ascribe these three dowries to the three powers of the soul, namely vision to the rational, delight to the concupiscible,

---

[1] *Christian Doctrine*, I, 4 (PL 34, 20).
[2] Eadmer (PL 159, 627).
[3] *City of God*, XXII, 30 (PL 41, 802).   [4] PL 63, 764.
[5] Literally "of the reality"—*non spei. . . . sed rei.*

and enjoyment to the irascible powers, seeing that this enjoyment is acquired by a victory. But this is not said properly, because the irascible and concupiscible powers are not in the intellectual but in the sensitive part, whereas the dowries of the soul are assigned to the mind.

Reply Obj. 1. Memory and understanding have but one act: either because understanding is itself an act of memory, or—if understanding denote a power—because memory does not proceed to act save through the medium of the understanding, since it belongs to the memory to retain knowledge. Consequently there is only one habit, namely knowledge, corresponding to memory and understanding, and therefore only one dowry, namely vision, corresponds to both.

Reply Obj. 2. Enjoyment corresponds to hope, in so far as it includes comprehension which will take the place of hope, since we hope for that which we have not yet; therefore hope chafes somewhat on account of the distance of the beloved, for which reason it will not remain in heaven, but will be succeeded by comprehension.

Reply Obj. 3. Enjoyment as including comprehension is distinct from vision and love, but otherwise than love from vision. For love and vision denote different habits, the one belonging to the intellect, the other to the affective power. But comprehension, or enjoyment as denoting comprehension, does not signify a habit distinct from those two, but the removal of the obstacles which made it impossible for the mind to be united to God by actual vision. This is brought about by the habit of glory freeing the soul from all defects; for instance by making it capable of knowledge without phantasms, of complete control over the body, and so forth, thus removing the obstacles which result in our being pilgrims from the Lord.

Reply Obj. 4 is clear from what has been said.

Reply Obj. 5. Properly speaking, the dowries are the immediate principles of the operation in which perfect happiness consists and by which the soul is united to Christ. The things mentioned by Anselm do not answer to this description, but they are such as in any way accompany or follow happiness, not only in relation to the Bridegroom, to Whom wisdom alone of the things mentioned by him refers, but also in relation to others. They may be either one's equals, to whom friendship refers as regards the union of affections, and concord as regards consent in actions, or one's inferiors, to whom power refers, so far as inferior things are ordered by superior, and honour as regards

that which inferiors offer to their superiors. Or again (they may accompany or follow Happiness) in relation to oneself: to this security refers as regards the removal of evil, and joy as regards the attainment of good.

Reply Obj. 6. Praise, which Augustine mentions as the third of those things which will obtain in heaven, is not a disposition to happiness but rather a sequel to happiness, because from the very fact of the soul's union with God, in which happiness consists, it follows that the soul breaks forth into praise. Hence praise has not the necessary conditions of a dowry.

Reply Obj. 7. The five things aforesaid mentioned by Boëthius are certain conditions of happiness, but not dispositions to happiness or to its act, because happiness by reason of its perfection has of itself alone and undividedly all that men seek in various things, as the Philosopher declares.[1] Accordingly Boëthius shows that these five things obtain in perfect happiness, because they are what men seek in temporal happiness. For they pertain either, as security, to immunity from evil; or to the attainment either of the suitable good, as joy, or of the perfect good, as sufficiency, or to the manifestation of good, as celebrity, in so far as the good of one is made known to others, or as reverence, as indicating that good or the knowledge of it, for reverence is the showing of honour which bears witness to virtue. Hence it is evident that these five should not be called dowries, but conditions of happiness.

QUESTION XCVI
Of the aureoles
(*In Thirteen Articles*)

In the next place we must consider the aureoles. Under this head there are thirteen points of inquiry: (1) Whether the aureoles differ from the essential reward? (2) Whether they differ from the fruit? (3) Whether a fruit is due to the virtue of continence only? (4) Whether three fruits are fittingly assigned to the three parts of continence? (5) Whether an aureole is due to virgins? (6) Whether it is due to martyrs? (7) Whether it is due to doctors? (8) Whether it is due to Christ? (9) Whether to the angels? (10) Whether it is due to the human body? (11) Whether three aureoles are fittingly assigned? (12) Whether the virgin's aureole is the greatest? (13) Whether one has the same aureole in a higher degree than another?

[1] *Ethics*, i, 7 (1097^{b}14); x, 7 (1177^{a}32).

ARTICLE 1. *Whether the Aureole Is the Same As the Essential Reward Which Is Called the Aurea?*

We proceed thus to the First Article: It would seem that the aureole is not distinct from the essential reward which is called the aurea.

Objection 1. For the essential reward is Happiness itself. Now according to Boëthius (*De Consol.* iii, 2),[1] happiness is "a state rendered perfect by the aggregate of all goods." Therefore the essential reward includes every good possessed in heaven, so that the aureole is included in the aurea.

Obj. 2. Further, More and less do not change a species. But those who keep the counsels and commandments receive a greater reward than those who keep the commandments only, nor it seems does their reward differ, except in one reward being greater than another. Since then the aureole denotes the reward due to works of perfection it would seem that it does not signify something distinct from the aurea.

Obj. 3. Further, Reward corresponds to merit. Now charity is the root of all merit. Since then the aurea corresponds to charity, it would seem that there will be no reward in heaven other than the aurea.

Obj. 4. Further, "All the blessed are taken into the angelic orders," as Gregory declares (*Hom.* xxxiv *in Ev.*).[2] Now as regards the angels, "though some of them receive certain gifts in a higher degree, nothing is possessed by any of them exclusively, for all gifts are in all of them, though not equally, because some are endowed more highly than others with gifts which, however, they all possess," as Gregory says (*ibid.*).[3] Therefore as regards the blessed, there will be no reward other than that which is common to all. Therefore the aureole is not a distinct reward from the aurea.

Obj. 5. Further, A higher reward is due to higher merit. If, then, the aurea is due to works which are of obligation, and the aureole to works of counsel, the aureole will be more perfect than the aurea, and consequently should not be expressed by a diminutive [*Aureola*, that is, a little aurea]. Therefore it would seem that the aureole is not a distinct reward from the aurea.

On the contrary, A gloss on Exod. 25. 24, 25, *Thou shalt make . . . another little golden*

crown (*coronam aureolam*), says:[4] "This crown denotes the new hymn which the virgins alone sing in the presence of the Lamb." Therefore apparently the aureole is a crown awarded not to all, but especially to some, whereas the aurea is awarded to all the blessed. Therefore the aureole is distinct from the aurea.

Further, A crown is due to the fight which is followed by victory: *He . . . is not crowned except he strive lawfully* (II Tim. 2. 5). Hence where there is a special kind of conflict, there should be a special crown. Now in certain works there is a special kind of conflict. Therefore they deserve a special kind of crown, which we call an aureole.

Further, The Church militant comes down from the Church triumphant: *I saw the Holy City,* etc. (Apoc. 21. 2). Now in the Church militant special rewards are given to those who perform special deeds, for instance a crown to the conqueror, a prize to the runner. Therefore the same should obtain in the Church triumphant.

I answer that, Man's essential reward, which is his Happiness, consists in the perfect union of the soul with God, in so far as it enjoys God perfectly as seen and loved perfectly. Now this reward is called a crown or aurea metaphorically, both with reference to merit which is gained by a kind of conflict,—since *the life of man upon earth is a warfare* (Job 7. 1),—and with reference to the reward whereby in a way man is made a participator of the Godhead, and consequently endowed with regal power: *Thou hast made us to our God a kingdom,* etc. (Apoc. 5. 10); for a crown is the proper sign of regal power.

In like manner the accidental reward which is added to the essential has the character of a crown. For a crown signifies some kind of perfection, on account of its circular shape, so that for this very reason it is becoming to the perfection of the blessed. Since, however, nothing can be added to the essential but what is less than it, the additional reward is called an aureole. Now something may be added in two ways to this essential reward which we call the aurea. First, in consequence of a condition attaching to the nature of the one rewarded; thus the glory of the body is added to the Happiness of the soul, and so this same glory of the body is sometimes called an *aureole.* Thus a gloss of Bede[5] on Exod. 25. 25, *Thou . . . shalt make another little golden crown,* says that "finally the aureole is added, when it is stated in the

[1] PL 63, 724.
[2] PL 76, 1255; cf. Peter Lombard, *Sent.*, II, d. 9, chap. 6 (QR I, 349).   [3] PL 76, 1252.

[4] *Glossa ordin.* (I, 178B); Bede, *De Tabernaculo,* I, 6 (PL 91, 410).   [5] *Ibid.*

Scriptures that a higher degree of glory is in store for us when our bodies are resumed." But it is not in this sense that we speak of an aureole now. Secondly, in consequence of the nature of the meritorious act. Now this has the character of merit on two counts, from which also it has the character of good. First, namely, from its root which is charity, since it is referred to the last end, and thus there is due to it the essential reward, namely the attainment of the end, and this is the aurea. Secondly, from the very genus of the act which derives a certain praiseworthiness from its due circumstances, from the habit eliciting it and from its proximate end, and thus is due to it a kind of accidental reward which we call an aureole; and it is in this sense that we regard the aureole now. Accordingly it must be said that an aureole denotes something added to the aurea, a kind of joy, that is in the works one has done, in that they have the character of a signal victory, for this joy is distinct from the joy in being united to God, which is called the aurea. Some, however, affirm that the common reward, which is the aurea, receives the name of aureole, according as it is given to virgins, martyrs, or doctors, even as money receives the name of debt through being due to some one, though the money and the debt are altogether the same. And that nevertheless this does not imply that the essential reward is any greater when it is called an aureole, but that it corresponds to a more excellent act, more excellent not in intensity of merit but in the manner of meriting, so that although two persons may have the Divine vision with equal clearness, it is called an aureole in one and not in the other, in so far as it corresponds to higher merit as regards the way of meriting. But this would seem contrary to the meaning of the gloss quoted above. For if aurea and aureole were the same, the aureole would not be described as added to the aurea. Moreover, since reward corresponds to merit, a more excellent reward must correspond to this more excellent way of meriting, and it is this excellence that we call an aureole. Hence it follows that an aureole differs from the aurea.

Reply Obj. 1. Happiness includes all the goods necessary for man's perfect life consisting in his perfect operation. Yet some things can be added not as being necessary for that perfect operation as though it were impossible without them, but as adding to the glory of happiness. Hence they regard the well-being of happiness and a certain fitness of happiness. Even so civic happiness is embellished by nobil-

ity and bodily beauty and so forth, and yet it is possible without them as stated in the *Ethics*;[1] and in this way is the aureole in comparison with the Happiness of heaven.

Reply Obj. 2. He who keeps the counsels and the commandments always merits more than he who keeps the commandments only, if we gather the notion of merit in works from the very genus of those works; but not always if we gauge the merit from its root, charity, since sometimes a man keeps the commandments alone out of greater charity than one who keeps both commandments and counsels. For the most part, however, the contrary happens, because "the proof of love is in the performance of deeds," as Gregory says (*Hom.* xxx *in Ev.*).[2] Therefore it is not the more excellent essential reward that is called an aureole, but that which is added to the essential reward without reference to the essential reward of the possessor of an aureole being greater, or less than, or equal to the essential reward of one who has no aureole.

Reply Obj. 3. Charity is the first principle of merit, but our actions are the instruments, so to speak, by which we merit. Now in order to obtain an effect there is required not only a due disposition in the first mover, but also a right disposition in the instrument. Hence something principal results in the effect with reference to the first mover, and something secondary with reference to the instrument. Therefore in the reward also there is something on the part of charity, namely the aurea, and something on the part of the kind of work, namely the aureole.

Reply Obj. 4. All the angels merited their happiness by the same kind of act, namely by turning to God, and consequently no particular reward is found in anyone which another has not in some way. But men merit happiness by different kinds of acts, and so the comparison fails.

Nevertheless among men what one seems to have specially, all have in common in some way, in so far as each one, by charity, deems another's good his own. Yet this joy whereby one shares another's joy cannot be called an aureole, because it is not given him as a reward for his victory, but regards more the victory of another; but a crown is awarded the victors themselves and not to those who rejoice with them in the victory.

Reply Obj. 5. The merit arising from charity is more excellent than that which arises from the kind of action, just as the end to which

[1] Aristotle, I, 8 (1099ᵃ24).   [2] PL 76, 1220.

charity directs us is more excellent than the things directed to that end, and with which our actions are concerned. Therefore the reward corresponding to merit by reason of charity, however little it may be, is greater than any reward corresponding to an action by reason of its genus. Hence aureole is used as a diminutive in comparison with aurea.

ARTICLE 2. Whether the Aureole Differs from the Fruit?

We proceed thus to the Second Article: It would seem that the aureole does not differ from the fruit.

Objection 1. For different rewards are not due to the same merit. Now the aureole and the hundredfold fruit correspond to the same merit, according to a gloss[1] on Matt. 13. 8, Some a hundredfold. Therefore the aureole is the same as the fruit.

Obj. 2. Further, Augustine says (De Virgin. xlv)[2] that "the hundredfold fruit is due to the martyrs, and also to virgins." Therefore the fruit is a reward common to virgins and martyrs. But the aureole also is due to them. Therefore the aureole is the same as the fruit.

Obj. 3. Further, There are only two rewards in Happiness, namely the essential, and the accidental which is added to the essential. Now that which is added to the essential reward is called an aureole (A. 1), as evidenced by the statement (Exod. 25. 25) that the little crown (aureola) is added to the crown. But the fruit is not the essential reward, for in that case it would be due to all the blessed. Therefore it is the same as the aureole.

On the contrary, Things which are not divided in the same way are not of the same nature. Now fruit and aureole are not divided in the same way, since aureole is divided into the aureole of virgins, of martyrs, and of doctors, whereas fruit is divided into the fruit of the married, of widows, and of virgins. Therefore fruit and aureole are not the same.

Further, If fruit and aureole were the same, the aureole would be due to whomsoever the fruit is due. But this is manifestly untrue, since a fruit is due to widowhood, while an aureole is not. Therefore, etc.

I answer that, Metaphorical expressions can be taken in various ways, according as we find resemblances to the various properties of the thing from which the comparison is taken. Now since fruit, properly speaking, is applied to material things born of the earth, we employ it variously in a spiritual sense, with reference to the various conditions that obtain in material fruits. For the material fruit has sweetness whereby it refreshes so far as it is used by man; again it is the last thing to which the operation of nature attains; moreover it is that to which husbandry looks forward as the result of sowing or any other process.

Accordingly fruit is taken in a spiritual sense sometimes for that which refreshes, as being the last end, and according to this signification we are said to enjoy (frui) God perfectly in heaven, and imperfectly on the way. From this signification we have fruition which is a dowry, but we are not speaking of fruit in this sense now.

Sometimes fruit signifies spiritually that which refreshes only, though it is not the last end; and thus the virtues are called fruits, since "they refresh the mind with genuine sweetness," as Ambrose says.[3] In this sense fruit is taken (Gal. 6. 22): The fruit of the Spirit is charity, joy, etc. Nor again is this the sense in which we speak of fruit now, for we have treated of this already.

We may, however, take spiritual fruit in another sense, in likeness to material fruit, according as material fruit is a profit expected from the labour of husbandry, so that we call fruit that reward which man acquires from his labour in this life, and thus every reward which by our labours we shall acquire for the future life is called a fruit. In this sense fruit is taken (Rom. 6. 22): You have your fruit unto sanctification, and the end life everlasting. Yet neither in this sense do we speak of fruit now, but we are treating of fruit as being the product of seed, for it is in this sense that our Lord speaks of fruit (Matt. 13. 23), where He divides fruit into thirtyfold, sixtyfold, and hundredfold. Now fruit is the product of seed in so far as the seed power is capable of transforming the humours of the soil into its own nature; and the more efficient this power, and the better prepared the soil, the more plentiful fruit will result. Now the spiritual seed which is sown in us is the Word of God; therefore the more a person is transformed into a spiritual nature by withdrawing from carnal things, the greater is the fruit of the Word in him. Accordingly the fruit of the Word of God differs from the aurea and the aureole, in that the aurea consists in the joy

---

[1] Glossa ordin. (v, 45A).
[2] PL 40, 423; cf. Glossa ordin. (v, 45A).

[3] Cf. De Parad., XIII (PL 14, 325); De Spir. Sancto, I, 12 (PL 16, 764); cf. Peter Lombard, In Sent., I, d. 1, chap. 3 (QR I, 19).

one has in God, and the aureole in the joy one has in the perfection of one's works, while the fruit consists in the joy that the worker has in his own disposition as to his degree of spirituality to which he has attained through the seed of God's Word.

Some, however, distinguish between aureole and fruit, by saying that the aureole is due to the fighter, according to II Tim. 2. 5, *He . . . shall not be crowned, except he strive lawfully,* while the fruit is due to the labourer, according to the saying of Wisdom 3. 15, *The fruit of good labours is glorious.* Others again say that the aurea regards conversion to God, while the aureole and the fruit regard things directed to the end; yet so that the fruit regards the will rather, and the aureole the body. Since, however, labour and strife are in the same subject and about the same matter, and since the body's reward depends on the soul's, these explanations of the difference between fruit, aurea and aureole would only imply a logical difference, and this cannot be, since fruit is assigned to some to whom no aureole is assigned.

Reply Obj. 1. There is nothing incongruous if various rewards correspond to the same merit according to the various things contained therein. Therefore to virginity corresponds the aurea in so far as virginity is kept for God's sake at the command of charity; the aureole, in so far as virginity is a work of perfection having the character of a signal victory; and the fruit, in so far as by virginity a person acquires a certain spirituality by withdrawing from carnal things.

Reply Obj. 2. Fruit, according to the proper acceptation as we are speaking of it now, does not denote the reward common to martyrdom and virginity, but that which corresponds to the three degrees of continency. This gloss which states that the hundredfold fruit corresponds to martyrs takes fruit in a broad sense, according as any reward is called a fruit, the hundredfold fruit thus denoting the reward due to any perfect works whatever.

Reply Obj. 3. Although the aureole is an accidental reward added to the essential reward, nevertheless not every accidental reward is an aureole, but only that which is assigned to works of perfection, whereby man is most conformed to Christ in the achievement of a perfect victory (A. 1). Hence it is not unfitting that another accidental reward, which is called the fruit, be due sometimes to the withdrawal from a carnal life.

ARTICLE 3. *Whether a Fruit Is Due to the Virtue of Continence Alone?*

We proceed thus to the Third Article: It would seem that a fruit is not due to the virtue of continence alone.

Objection 1. For a gloss on I Cor. 15. 41, *One is the glory of the sun,* says[1] that "the worth of those who have the hundredfold fruit is compared to the glory of the sun; to the glory of the moon those who have the sixtyfold fruit; and to the stars those who have the thirtyfold fruit." Now this difference of glory, in the meaning of the Apostle, regards any difference whatever of happiness. Therefore the various fruits should correspond to none but the virtue of continence.

Obj. 2. Further, Fruits are so called from fruition. But fruition belongs to the essential reward which corresponds to all the virtues. Therefore, etc.

Obj. 3. Further, Fruit is due to labour: *The fruit of good labours is glorious* (Wis. 3. 15). Now there is greater labour in fortitude than in temperance or continence. Therefore fruit does not correspond to continence alone.

Obj. 4. Further, It is more difficult not to exceed the measure in food which is necessary for life, than in sexual matters without which life can be sustained; and thus the labour of frugality is greater than that of continence. Therefore fruit corresponds to frugality rather than to continence.

Obj. 5. Further, Fruit implies refreshment, and refreshment regards especially the end. Since then the theological virtues have the end for their object, namely God Himself, it would seem that to them especially the fruit should correspond.

On the contrary is the statement of the gloss[2] on Matt. 13. 23, *The one a hundredfold,* which assigns the fruits to virginity, widowhood, and conjugal continence, which are parts of continence.

I answer that, A fruit is a reward due to a person in that he passes from the carnal to the spiritual life. Consequently a fruit corresponds especially to that virtue which more than any other frees man from subjection to the flesh. Now this is the effect of continence, since it is by sexual pleasures that the soul is especially subject to the flesh; so much so that in the carnal act, according to Jerome,[3] not even the

---

[1] *Glossa ordin.* (VI, 59A) ;*Glossa* Lombardi (PL 191, 1686).

[2] *Glossa ordin.* (V, 45A); cf. Augustine, *De Virgin.*, XLV (PL 40, 423).

[3] Cf. Origen, *In Num.*, hom. VI (PG 12, 610); see Jerome, *Epist.*, XXII, *Ad Eustoch.* (PL 22, 409).

spirit of prophecy touches the heart of the prophet, nor "is it possible to understand anything in the midst of that pleasure," as the Philosopher says.[1] Therefore fruit corresponds to continence rather than to another virtue.

Reply Obj. 1. This gloss takes fruit in a broad sense, according as any reward is called a fruit.

Reply Obj. 2. Fruition does not take its name from fruit by reason of any comparison with fruit in the sense in which we speak of it now, as evidenced by what has been said.

Reply Obj. 3. Fruit, as we speak of it now, corresponds to labour not as resulting in fatigue, but as resulting in the production of fruit. Hence a man calls his crops his labour, in so far as he laboured for them, or produced them by his labour. Now the comparison to fruit, as produced from seed, is more adapted to continence than to fortitude, because man is not subjected to the flesh by the passions of fortitude, as he is by the passions with which continence is concerned.

Reply Obj. 4. Although the pleasures of the table are more necessary than the pleasures of sex, they are not so strong; therefore the soul is not so much subjected to the flesh by them.

Reply Obj. 5. Fruit is not taken here in the sense in which enjoyment applies to refreshment in the end, but in another sense as stated above (A. 2). Hence the argument proves nothing.

ARTICLE 4. *Whether Three Fruits Are Fittingly Assigned to the Three Parts of Continence?*

We proceed thus to the Fourth Article: It would seem that three fruits are unfittingly assigned to the three parts of continence.

Objection 1. For twelve fruits of the Spirit are assigned, *charity, joy, peace,* etc. (Gal. 5. 22). Therefore it seems that we should assign only three.

Obj. 2. Further, Fruit denotes a special reward. Now the reward assigned to virgins, widows, and married persons is not a special reward, because all who are to be saved are comprised under one of these three, since no one is saved who lacks continence, and continence is adequately divided by these three. Therefore three fruits are unfittingly assigned to these three.

Obj. 3. Further, Just as widowhood surpasses conjugal continence, so does virginity surpass widowhood. But the excess of sixtyfold over thirtyfold is not as the excess of a hundredfold over sixtyfold; neither in arithmetical proportion, since sixty exceeds thirty by thirty, and a

hundred exceeds sixty by forty; nor in geometrical proportion, since sixty is twice thirty and a hundred surpasses sixty as containing the whole and two-thirds of it. Therefore the fruits are unfittingly adapted to the degrees of continence.

Obj. 4. Further, The statements contained in Holy Writ stand for all time: *Heaven and earth shall pass away, but My words shall not pass away* (Luke 21. 33), whereas human institutions are liable to change every day. Therefore human institutions are not to be taken as a criterion of the statements of Holy Writ, and it would seem in consequence that the explanation of these fruits given by Bede is unfitting. For he says (*Expos. in Luc.* 3. 8)[2] that "the thirtyfold fruit is assigned to married persons, because in the signs drawn on the 'abacus' the number 30 is denoted by the thumb and index finger touching one another at the tips as though kissing one another, so that the number 30 denotes the embraces of married persons. The number 60 is denoted by the contact of the index finger above the middle joint of the thumb, so that the index finger by lying over the thumb and weighing on it, signifies the burden which widows have to bear in this world. When, however, in the course of enumeration we come to the number 100 we pass from the left to the right hand, so that the number 100 denotes virginity, which has a share in the angelic excellence; for the angels are on the right hand, that is, in glory, while we are on the left on account of the imperfection of the present life.

I answer that, By continence, to which the fruit corresponds, man is brought to a kind of spiritual nature, by withdrawing from carnal things. Consequently various fruits are distinguished according to the various manners of the spirituality resulting from continence. Now there is a certain spirituality which is necessary, and one which is superabundant. The spirituality that is necessary consists in the rectitude of the spirit not being disturbed by the pleasures of the flesh, and this obtains when one makes use of carnal pleasures according to the order of right reason. This is the spirituality of married persons. Spirituality is superabundant when a man withdraws himself entirely from those carnal pleasures which stifle the spirit. This may be done in two ways: either in respect of all time past, present, and future, and this is the spirituality of virgins; or in respect of a particular time, and this is the spirituality of widows.

---

[1] *Ethics,* VII, 11 (1152^{b}18).

[2] PL 92, 432; see Jerome, *Adv. Jovin.* (PL 23, 223).

Accordingly to those who keep conjugal continence, the thirtyfold fruit is awarded; to those who keep the continence of widows, the sixtyfold fruit; and to those who keep virginal continence, the hundredfold fruit, and this for the reason given by Bede quoted above, although another motive may be found in the very nature of the numbers. For 30 is the product of 3 multiplied by 10. Now 3 is the number of everything, as stated in the book on the *Heavens*,[1] and contains a certain perfection common to all, namely of beginning, middle, and end. Therefore the number 30 is fittingly assigned to married persons, in whom no other perfection is added to the observance of the Decalogue, signified by the number 10, than the common perfection without which there is no salvation. The number six the multiplication of which by 10 amounts to 60 has perfection from its parts, being the aggregate of all its parts taken together. Therefore it corresponds fittingly to widowhood, in which we find perfect withdrawal from carnal pleasures as to all its circumstances (which are the parts so to speak of a virtuous act), since widowhood uses no carnal pleasures in connexion with any person, place, or any other circumstance, which was not the case with conjugal continence. The number 100 corresponds fittingly to virginity, because the number 10 of which 100 is a multiple is the limit of numbers, and in like manner virginity occupies the limit of spirituality, since no further spirituality can be added to it. The number 100 also being a square number has perfection from its figure, for a square figure is perfect through being equal on all sides, since all its sides are equal. Therefore it is adapted to virginity in which incorruption is found equally as to all times.

Reply Obj. 1. Fruit is not taken there in the sense in which we are taking it now.

Reply Obj. 2. Nothing obliges us to hold that fruit is a reward that is not common to all who will be saved. For not only the essential reward is common to all, but also a certain accidental reward, such as joy in those works without which one cannot be saved. Yet it may be said that the fruits are not becoming to all who will be saved, as is evidently the case with those who repent in the end after leading an incontinent life, for to such no fruit is due but only the essential reward.

Reply Obj. 3. The distinction of the fruits is to be taken according to the species and figures of the numbers rather than according to their quantity. Nevertheless even if we regard the excess in point of quantity, we may find an explanation. For the married man abstains only from one that is not his, the widow from both hers and not hers, so that in the latter case we find the notion of double, just as 60 is the double of 30. Again 100 is 60+40, which latter number is the product of 4×10, and the number 4 is the first solid and square number. Thus the addition of this number is fitting to virginity, which adds perpetual incorruption to the perfection of widowhood.

Reply Obj. 4. Although these numerical signs are a human institution, they are founded somewhat on the nature of things, in so far as the numbers are denoted in gradation, according to the order of the aforesaid joints and contacts.

ARTICLE 5. *Whether an Aureole Is Due on Account of Virginity?*

We proceed thus to the Fifth Article: It would seem that an aureole is not due on account of virginity.

Objection 1. For where there is greater difficulty in the work, a greater reward is due. Now widows have greater difficulty than virgins in abstaining from the works of the flesh. For Jerome says (*Ep. ad Ageruch.*)[2] that the greater difficulty certain persons experience in abstaining from the allurements of pleasure, the greater their reward, and he is speaking in praise of widows. Moreover, the Philosopher says[3] that "young women who have been deflowered desire sexual intercourse the more for the recollection of the pleasure." Therefore the aureole which is the greatest reward is due to widows more than to virgins.

Obj. 2. Further, If an aureole were due to virginity, it would be especially found where there is the most perfect virginity. Now the most perfect virginity is in the Blessed Virgin, and therefore she is called the Virgin of virgins; and yet no aureole is due to her because she experienced no conflict in being continent, for she was not infected with the corruption of the fomes. Therefore an aureole is not due to virginity.

Obj. 3. Further, A special reward is not due to that which has not been at all times praiseworthy. Now it would not have been praiseworthy to observe virginity in the state of innocence, since then was it commanded: *Increase and multiply and fill the earth* (Gen. 1. 28); nor again during the time of the Law,

---

[1] Aristotle, I, 1 (268a9).

[2] *Epist.* (PL 22, 1047).

[3] *History of Animals*, VII, 1 (581b20).

since the barren were accursed. Therefore an aureole is not due to virginity.

Obj. 4. Further, The same reward is not due to virginity observed, and virginity lost. Yet an aureole is sometimes due to lost virginity; for instance if a maiden is violated unwillingly at the order of a tyrant for confessing Christ. Therefore an aureole is not due to virginity.

Obj. 5. Further, A special reward is not due to that which is in us by nature. But virginity is inborn in every man both good and wicked. Therefore an aureole is not due to virginity.

Obj. 6. Further, As widowhood is to the sixtyfold fruit, so is virginity to the hundred-fold fruit, and to the aureole. Now the sixty-fold fruit is not due to every widow, but only, as some say, to one who vows to remain a widow. Therefore it would seem that neither is the aureole due to any kind of virginity, but only to that which is observed by vow.

Obj. 7. Further, Reward is not given to that which is done of necessity, since all merit depends on the will. But some are virgins of necessity, such as those who are naturally cold-blooded, and eunuchs. Therefore an aureole is not always due to virginity.

On the contrary, A gloss on Exod. 25. 25: *Thou shalt also make a little golden crown* (*coronam aureolam*) says.[1] "This crown denotes the new hymn which the virgins sing in the presence of the Lamb, those, namely, who follow the Lamb wherever He goes." Therefore the reward due to virginity is called an aureole.

Further, It is written (Isa. 56. 4): *Thus saith the Lord to the eunuchs;* and the text continues (*verse* 5): *I will give to them . . . a name better than sons and daughters;* and a gloss says:[2] "This refers to their peculiar and transcendent glory." Now the eunuchs *who have made themselves eunuchs for the kingdom of heaven* (Matt. 19. 12) denote virgins. Therefore it would seem that some special reward is due to virginity, and this is called the aureole.

I answer that, Where there is a notable kind of victory, a special crown is due. Therefore since by virginity a person wins a signal victory over the flesh, against which a continuous battle is waged: *The flesh lusteth against the spirit,* etc. (Gal. 5. 17), a special crown called the aureole is due to virginity. This indeed is the common opinion of all; but all are not agreed

as to the kind of virginity to which it is due.

For some say that the aureole is due to the act. So that she who actually remains a virgin will have the aureole provided she be of the number of the saved. But this would seem unreasonable, because in this case those who have the will to marry and nevertheless die before marrying would have the aureole. Hence others hold that the aureole is due to the state and not to the act, so that those virgins alone merit the aureole who by vow have placed themselves in the state of observing perpetual virginity. But this also seems unreasonable, because it is possible to have the same intention of observing virginity without a vow as with a vow. Hence it may be said otherwise that merit is due to every virtuous act commanded by charity. Now virginity comes under the genus of virtue in so far as perpetual incorruption of mind and body is an object of choice, as appears from what has been said above.[3] Consequently the aureole is due to those virgins alone who had the purpose of observing perpetual virginity, whether or no they have confirmed this purpose by vow,—and this I say with reference to the aureole in its proper signification of a reward due to merit,— although this purpose may at some time have been interrupted, integrity of the flesh remaining nevertheless, provided it be found at the end of life, because virginity of the mind may be restored, although virginity of the flesh cannot.

If however, we take the aureole in its broad sense for any joy added to the essential joy of heaven, the aureole will be applicable even to those who are incorrupt in flesh, although they had not the purpose of observing perpetual virginity. For without doubt they will rejoice in the incorruption of their body, even as the innocent will rejoice in having been free from sin, although they had no opportunity of sinning, as in the case of baptized children. But this is not the proper meaning of an aureole, although it is very commonly taken in this sense.

Reply Obj. 1. In some respects virgins experience a greater conflict in remaining continent; and in other respects, widows, other things being equal. For virgins are inflamed by concupiscence, and by the desire of experience, which arises from a certain curiosity as it were, which makes man more willing to see what he has never seen. Sometimes, moreover, this concupiscence is increased by their esteeming the pleasure to be greater that it is in reality, and

---

[1] *Glossa ordin.* (I, 178B); Bede, *De Tabernaculo,* I, 6 (PL 91, 410).

[2] *Glossa interl.* (IV, 93r); Augustine, *De Virgin.,* xxv (PL 40, 409).

[3] *In Sent.,* IV, d. 33, Q. 3, AA. 1, 2.

by their failing to consider the grievances attaching to this pleasure. In these respects widows experience the lesser conflict, yet theirs is the greater conflict by reason of their recollection of the pleasure. Moreover, in different subjects one motive is stronger than another according to the various conditions and dispositions of the subject, because some are more susceptible to one, and others to another. However, whatever we may say of the degree of conflict, this is certain,—that the virgin's victory is more perfect than the widow's, for the most perfect and most brilliant kind of victory is never to have yielded to the foe; and the crown is due, not to the battle but to the victory gained by the battle.

Reply Obj. 2. There are two opinions about this. For some say that the Blessed Virgin has not an aureole in reward of her virginity, if we take aureole in the proper sense as referring to a conflict, but that she has something more than an aureole, on account of her most perfect purpose of observing virginity. Others say that she has an aureole even in its proper signification, and that a most transcendent one, for though she experienced no conflict, she had a certain conflict of the flesh, but owing to the exceeding strength of her virtue, her flesh was so subdued that she did not feel this conflict. This, however, would seem to be said without reason, for since we believe the Blessed Virgin to have been altogether immune from the inclination of the fomes on account of the perfection of her sanctification, it is wicked to suppose that there was in her any conflict with the flesh, since such conflict is only from the inclination of the fomes, nor can temptation from the flesh be without sin, as declared by a gloss[1] on II Cor. 12. 7, *There was given me a sting of my flesh.* Hence we must say that she has an aureole properly speaking, so as to be conformed in this to those other members of the Church in whom virginity is found; and although she had no conflict by reason of the temptation which is of the flesh, she had the temptation which is of the enemy, who feared not even Christ (Matt. 4.).

Reply Obj. 3. The aureole is not due to virginity except as adding some excellence to the other degrees of continence. If Adam had not sinned, virginity would have had no perfection over conjugal continence, since in that case marriage would have been honourable, and the marriage-bed unsullied, for it would not have been dishonoured by lust; hence virginity

would not then have been observed, nor would an aureole have been due to it. But the condition of human nature being changed, virginity has a special beauty of its own, and consequently a special reward is assigned to it.

During the time of the Mosaic law, when the worship of God was to be continued by means of the carnal act, it was not altogether praiseworthy to abstain from carnal intercourse; therefore no special reward would be given for such a purpose unless it came from a Divine inspiration, as is believed to have been the case with Jeremias and Elias, of whose marriage we do not read.[2]

Reply Obj. 4. If a virgin is violated, she does not forfeit the aureole, provided she retain unfailingly the purpose of observing perpetual virginity, and in no way consent to the act. Nor does she forfeit virginity thereby; and this is maintained whether she be violated for the faith, or for any other cause whatever. But if she suffer this for the faith, this will count to her for merit, and will be a kind of martyrdom. Therefore Lucy said: "If thou causest me to be violated against my will, my chastity will receive a double crown";[3] not that she has two aureoles of virginity, but that she will receive a double reward, one for observing virginity, the other for the outrage she has suffered. Even supposing that one thus violated should conceive, she would not for that reason forfeit her virginity; nor would she be equal to Christ's mother, in whom there was integrity of the flesh together with integrity of the mind.

Reply Obj. 5. Virginity is inborn in us as to that which is material in virginity, but the purpose of observing perpetual incorruption, from which virginity derives its merit, is not inborn, but comes from the gift of grace.

Reply Obj. 6. The sixtyfold fruit is due, not to every widow, but only to those who retain the purpose of remaining widows, even though they do not make it the matter of a vow, even as we have said in regard to virginity.

Reply Obj. 7. If cold-blooded persons and eunuchs have the will to observe perpetual incorruption even though they were capable of sexual intercourse, they must be called virgins and merit the aureole, for they make a virtue of necessity. If, on the other hand, they have the will to marry if they could, they do not merit the aureole. Hence Augustine says (*De Sancta Virgin.* xxiv):[4] "For those like eunuchs

---

[1] *Glossa ordin.* (VI, 76E); *Glossa* Lombardi (PL 192, 84); Augustine, *City of God*, XIX, 4 (PL 41, 629).

[2] Cf. Jerome, *Epist.*, XXII (PL 22, 408).
[3] Office of St. Lucy; *lect.*, VI (Dominican **Breviary**, December 13th).   [4] PL 40, 408.

whose bodies are so formed that they are unable to beget, it suffices when they become Christians and keep the commandments of God, that they have a mind to have a wife if they could, in order to rank with the faithful who are married."

ARTICLE 6. *Whether an Aureole Is Due to Martyrs?*

We proceed thus to the Sixth Article: It would seem that an aureole is not due to martyrs.

Objection 1. For an aureole is a reward given for works of supererogation, and therefore Bede commenting on Exod. 25. 25, *Thou shalt also make another . . . crown*, says:[1] "This may be rightly referred to the reward of those who by freely choosing a more perfect life go beyond the general commandments." But to die for confessing the faith is sometimes an obligation, and not a work of supererogation, as appears from the words of Rom. 10. 10, *With the heart, we believe unto justice, but with the mouth confession is made unto salvation.* Therefore an aureole is not always due to martyrdom.

Obj. 2. Further, According to Gregory[2] "the freer the service, the more acceptable it is." Now martyrdom has a minimum of freedom, since it is a punishment inflicted by another person with force. Therefore an aureole is not due to martyrdom, since it is accorded to surpassing merit.

Obj. 3. Further, Martyrdom consists not only in suffering death externally, but also in the interior act of the will; therefore Bernard in a sermon on the Holy Innocents[3] distinguishes three kinds of martyr,—in will and not in death, as John; in both will and death, as Stephen; in death and not in will, as the Innocents. Accordingly if an aureole were due to martyrdom, it would be due to voluntary rather than external martyrdom, since merit proceeds from will. Yet such is not the case. Therefore an aureole is not due to martyrdom.

Obj. 4. Further, Bodily suffering is less than mental, which consists of internal sorrow and afflictions of soul. But internal suffering is also a kind of martyrdom; therefore Jerome says in a sermon on the Assumption:[4] "I should say rightly that the Mother of God was both virgin and martyr, although she ended her days in peace; thus: 'Thine own soul a sword hath

pierced'—namely for her Son's death." Since then no aureole corresponds to interior sorrow, neither should one correspond to outward suffering.

Obj. 5. Further, Penance itself is a kind of martyrdom, and so Gregory says (*Hom.* iii *in Ev.*):[5] "Although persecution has ceased to offer the opportunity, yet the peace we enjoy is not without its martyrdom, since even if we no longer yield the life of the body to the sword, yet do we slay fleshly desires in the soul with the sword of the spirit." But no aureole is due to penance which consists in external works. Neither therefore is an aureole due to every external martyrdom.

Obj. 6. Further, An aureole is not due to an unlawful work. Now it is unlawful to lay hands on oneself, as Augustine declares,[6] and yet the Church celebrates the martyrdom of some who laid hands upon themselves in order to escape the fury of tyrants, as in the case of certain women at Antioch (Eusebius,—*Eccles. Hist.* viii, 12).[7] Therefore an aureole is not always due to martyrdom.

Obj. 7. Further, It happens at times that a person is wounded for the faith, and survives for some time. Now it is clear that such a one is a martyr, and yet it seems an aureole is not due to him, since his conflict did not last until death. Therefore an aureole is not always due to martyrdom.

Obj. 8. Further, Some suffer more from the loss of temporal goods than from the affliction even of their own body, and this is shown by their bearing many afflictions for the sake of gain. Therefore if they are despoiled of their temporal goods for Christ's sake they would seem to be martyrs, and yet an aureole is not apparently due to them. Therefore the same conclusion follows as before.

Obj. 9. Further, A martyr would seem to be no other than one who dies for the faith, and so Isidore says (*Etym.* vii, 11):[8] "They are called martyrs in Greek, witnesses in Latin, because they suffered in order to bear witness to Christ, and strove unto death for the truth." Now there are virtues more excellent than faith, such as justice, charity, and so forth, since these cannot be without grace, and yet no aureole is due to them. Therefore it seems neither is an aureole due to martyrdom.

Obj. 10. Further, Even as the truth of faith

---

[1] *De Tabernaculo*, I, 6 (PL 91, 409).

[2] Cf. Gratian, *Decretum*, Pt. II, causa 23, Q. 6, append. ad can. 4 (RF I, 949); cf. Augustine, *De Adult. Conjung.*, I, 14 (PL 40, 459).

[3] PL 183, 130.　　　[4] *Epist.*, IX (PL 30, 142).

[5] PL 76, 1089.

[6] *City of God*, I, 17, 20, 26 (PL 41, 31; 34; 39).

[7] PG 20, 769; cf. John Chrysostom, *Hom. de SS. Mart. Bernice et Prosdoce* (PG 50, 639); Ambrose, *De Virg.*, III, 7 (PL 16, 241).　　　[8] PL 82, 290.

is from God, so is all other truth, as Ambrose declares,[1] since "every truth by whomsoever uttered is from the Holy Ghost." Therefore if an aureole is due to one who suffers death for the truth of faith, in like manner it is also due to those who suffer death for any other virtue; and yet apparently this is not the case.

Obj. 11. Further, The common good is greater than the good of the individual. Now if a man die in a just war in order to save his country, an aureole is not due to him. Therefore even though he be put to death in order to keep the faith that is in himself, no aureole is due to him; and consequently the same conclusion follows as above.

Obj. 12. Further, All merit proceeds from free choice. Yet the Church celebrates the martyrdom of some who had not the use of free choice. Therefore they did not merit an aureole; and consequently an aureole is not due to all martyrs.

On the contrary, Augustine says (*De Sancta Virgin.* xlvi):[2] "No one, I think, would dare prefer virginity to martyrdom." Now an aureole is due to virginity, and consequently also to martyrdom.

Further, The crown is due to one who has striven. But in martyrdom the strife presents a special difficulty. Therefore a special aureole is due to martyrdom.

I answer that, Just as in the spirit there is a conflict with the internal concupiscences, so is there in man a conflict with the passion that is inflicted from without. Therefore, just as a special crown, which we call an aureole, is due to the most perfect victory by which we triumph over the concupiscences of the flesh, in a word, to virginity, so too an aureole is due to the most perfect victory that is won against external assaults.

Now the most perfect victory over passion caused from without is considered from two points of view. First from the greatness of the passion. Now among all passions inflicted from without, death holds the first place, just as sexual concupiscences are chief among internal passions. Consequently, when a man conquers death and things directed to death, his is a most perfect victory. Secondly, the perfection of victory is considered from the point of view of the motive of conflict, when, namely, a man strives for the most honourable cause, which is Christ Himself.

Both these things are to be found in martyr-

dom, which is death suffered for Christ's sake; for it is not the pain but the cause that makes the martyr. Consequently an aureole is due to martyrdom as well as to virginity.

Reply Obj. 1. To suffer death for Christ's sake is, absolutely speaking, a work of supererogation, since every one is not bound to confess his faith in the face of a persecutor; yet in certain cases it is necessary for salvation, when, that is, a person is seized by a persecutor and interrogated as to his faith which he is then bound to confess. Nor does it follow that he does not merit an aureole. For an aureole is due to a work of supererogation, not as such, but as having a certain perfection. Therefore so long as this perfection remains, even though the supererogation cease, one merits the aureole.

Reply Obj. 2. A reward is due to martyrdom, not in respect to the exterior infliction, but because it is suffered voluntarily, since we merit only through that which is in us. And the more that which one suffers voluntarily is difficult and naturally contrary to the will, the more is the will that suffers it for Christ's sake shown to be firmly established in Christ, and consequently a higher reward is due to him.

Reply Obj. 3. There are certain acts which, in their very selves, contain intense pleasure or difficulty, and in such the act always adds to the character of merit or demerit, since in the performance of the act, the will, on account of the aforesaid intensity, must undergo a change from the state in which it was before. Consequently, other things being equal, one who performs an act of lust sins more than one who merely consents in the act, because in the very act the will is increased. In like manner since in the act of suffering martyrdom there is a very great difficulty, the will to suffer martyrdom does not reach the degree of merit due to actual martyrdom by reason of its difficulty; although indeed it may possibly attain to a higher reward if we consider the root of merit, since the will of one man to suffer martyrdom may possibly proceed from a greater charity than another man's act of martyrdom. Hence one who is willing to be a martyr may by his will merit an essential reward equal to or greater than that which is due to an actual martyr. But the aureole is due to the difficulty inherent to the conflict itself of martyrdom, and so it is not due to those who are martyrs only in will.

Reply Obj. 4. Just as pleasures of touch, which are the matter of temperance, hold the

---

[1] Cf. *In I Cor.,* on 12.3 (PL 17, 258).
[2] PL 40, 424.

chief place among all pleasures both internal and external, so pains of touch surpass all other pains. Consequently an aureole is due to the difficulty of suffering pains of touch, for instance, from blows and so forth, rather than to the difficulty of bearing internal sufferings, by reason of which, however, one is not properly called a martyr, except by a kind of comparison. It is in this sense that Jerome speaks.

Reply Obj. 5. The sufferings of penance are not a martyrdom properly speaking, because they do not consist in things directed to the causing of death, since they are directed merely to the taming of the flesh; and if any one go beyond this measure, such afflictions will be deserving of blame. However such afflictions are spoken of as a martyrdom by a kind of comparison, and they surpass the sufferings of martyrdom in duration but not in intensity.

Reply Obj. 6. According to Augustine[1] it is lawful to no one to lay hands on himself for any reason whatever unless, perhaps it be done by Divine impulse as an example of fortitude that others may despise death. Those to whom the objection refers are believed to have brought death on themselves by Divine stirring, and for this reason the Church celebrates their martyrdom.

Reply Obj. 7. If any one receive a mortal wound for the faith and survive, without doubt he merits the aureole, as appears in the case of blessed Cecilia who survived for three days,[2] and many martyrs who died in prison.[3] But, even if the wound he receives is not mortal, yet is the occasion of his dying, he is believed to merit the aureole (although some say that he does not merit the aureole if he happens to die through his own carelessness or neglect). For this neglect would not have occasioned his death except on the supposition of the wound which he received for the faith, and consequently this wound previously received for the faith is the original occasion of his death, so that he would not seem to lose the aureole for that reason, unless his neglect were such as to involve a mortal sin, which would deprive him of both aurea and aureole. If, however, by some chance or other he were not to die of the mortal wound, or again if the wounds received were not mortal, and he were to die while in prison, he would still merit the aureole. Hence the martyrdom of some saints is celebrated in the Church because they died in prison, having been wounded long before, as in the case of Pope Marcellus.[4]

Accordingly in whatever way suffering for Christ's sake be continued unto death, whether death ensue or not, a man becomes a martyr and merits the aureole. If, however, it be not continued unto death, this is not a reason for calling a person a martyr, as in the case of the blessed Sylvester, whose feast the Church does not solemnize as a martyr's, since he ended his days in peace, although previously he had undergone certain sufferings.

Reply Obj. 8. Even as temperance is not about pleasures of money, honours, and the like, but only about pleasures of touch as being the principal of all, so fortitude is about dangers of death as being the greatest of all.[5] Consequently the aureole is due to such injuries only as are inflicted on a person's own body and are of a nature to cause death. Accordingly whether a person lose his temporal possessions, or his good name, or anything else of the kind, for Christ's sake, he does not for that reason become a martyr, nor merit the aureole. Nor is it possible in an ordered way to love external things more than one's body, and disordered love does not help one to merit an aureole; nor again can sorrow for the loss of corporeal things be equal to the sorrow for the slaying of the body and other like things.

Reply Obj. 9. The sufficient motive for martyrdom is not only confession of the faith, but any other virtue, not civic but infused, that has Christ for its end. For one becomes a witness of Christ by any virtuous act, in so far as the works which Christ perfects in us bear witness to His goodness. Hence some virgins were slain for virginity which they desired to keep, for instance blessed Agnes and others whose martyrdom is celebrated by the Church.[6]

Reply Obj. 10. The truth of faith has Christ for end and object, and therefore its confession if suffering be added to it, merits an aureole, not only on the part of the end but also on the part of the matter. But the confession of any other truth is not a sufficient motive for martyrdom by reason of its matter, but only on the part of the end; for instance if a person were willing to be slain for Christ's sake rather than sin against Him by telling any lie whatever.

Reply Obj. 11. The uncreated good surpasses all created good. Hence any created end,

---

[1] *City of God*, I, 17, 20, 26 (PL 41, 31, 34, 39).

[2] Feast of St. Caecilia, 22 Nov., *lect.* 6, Dominican Breviary.

[3] Baronius, *Annales Eccl.*, ad annum 323 (IV, 57ª).

[4] Cf. *Acta Sanctorum*, die. 16 Jan., 1, 4 (BL II, 376ª).

[5] Aristotle, *Ethics*, III, 6 (1115ª24).

[6] Cf. *Acta Sanctorum*, die 21 Jan. (BL II, 718ª).

whether it be the common or a private good, cannot confer so great a goodness on an act as can the uncreated end, when, that is, an act is done for God's sake. Hence when a person dies for the common good without referring it to Christ, he will not merit the aureole; but if he refer it to Christ he will merit the aureole and he will be a martyr; for instance if he defends his country from the attack of an enemy who designs to corrupt the faith of Christ, and suffers death in that defence.

Reply Obj. 12. Some say that the use of reason was by the Divine power accelerated in the Innocents slain for Christ's sake, even as in John the Baptist while yet in his mother's womb, and in that case they were truly martyrs in both act and will, and have the aureole. Others say, however, that they were martyrs in act only and not in will; and this seems to be the opinion of Bernard, who distinguishes three kinds of martyrs, as stated above (obj. 3). In this case the Innocents, even as they do not fulfil all the conditions of martyrdom, and yet are martyrs in a sense, in that they died for Christ, so too they have the aureole, not in all its perfection, but by a kind of participation, in so far as they rejoice in having been slain in Christ's service; thus it was stated above (A. 5) in reference to baptized children, that they will have a certain joy in their innocence and carnal integrity.

ARTICLE 7. *Whether an Aureole Is Due to Doctors?*

We proceed thus to the Seventh Article: It would seem that an aureole is not due to doctors.

Objection 1. For every reward to be had in the life to come will correspond to some act of virtue. But preaching or teaching is not the act of a virtue. Therefore an aureole is not due to teaching or preaching.

Obj. 2. Further, Teaching and preaching are the result of studying and being taught. Now the things that are rewarded in the future life are not acquired by a man's study, since we merit not by our natural and acquired gifts. Therefore no aureole will be merited in the future life for teaching and preaching.

Obj. 3. Further, Exaltation in the life to come corresponds to humiliation in the present life, because *he that humbleth himself shall be exalted* (Matt. 23. 12). But there is no humiliation in teaching and preaching; in fact they are occasions of pride, for a gloss on Matt. 4. 5, *Then the devil took Him up,* says[1]

[1] *Glossa ordin.* (v, 15F).

that the devil deceives many who are puffed up with the honour of the master's chair. Therefore it would seem that an aureole is not due to preaching and teaching.

On the contrary, A gloss on Eph. 1. 18, 19, *That you may know . . . what is the exceeding greatness,* etc., says:[2] "The holy doctors will have an increase of glory above that which all have in common." Therefore, etc.

Further, A gloss on Cant. 8. 12, *My vineyard is before me,* says:[3] "He describes the peculiar reward which He has prepared for His doctors." Therefore doctors will have a peculiar reward, and we call this an aureole.

I answer that, Just as by virginity and martyrdom a person wins a most perfect victory over the flesh and the world, so is a most perfect victory gained over the devil when a person not only refuses to yield to the devil's assaults, but also drives him out, not from himself alone, but from others also. Now this is done by preaching and teaching, and so an aureole is due to preaching and teaching, even as to virginity and martyrdom. Nor can we admit, as some affirm, that it is due to prelates only, who are able to preach and teach by virtue of their office, but it is due to all whosoever exercise this act lawfully. Nor is it due to prelates, although they have the office of preaching, unless they actually preach, since a crown is due not to the habit, but to the actual strife, according to II Tim. 5, *He . . . shall not be* (Vulg.,—*is not*) *crowned, except he strive lawfully.*

Reply Obj. 1. Preaching and teaching are acts of a virtue, namely mercy, and therefore they are reckoned among the spiritual almsdeeds.

Reply Obj. 2. Although ability to preach and teach is sometimes the outcome of study, the practice of teaching comes from the will, which is informed with charity infused by God; and thus its act can be meritorious.

Reply Obj. 3. Exaltation in this life does not lessen the reward of the other life, except for him who seeks his own glory from that exaltation; moreover he who turns that exaltation to the profit of others acquires thereby a reward for himself. Still, when it is stated that an aureole is due to teaching, this is to be understood of the teaching of things pertaining to salvation, by which teaching the devil is expelled from men's hearts, as by a kind of spir-

[2] *Glossa ordin.* (VI, 90E); *Glossa* Lombardi (PL 192, 177).
[3] *Glossa ordin.* (III, 367F).

itual weapon, of which it is said (II Cor. 10. 4): *The weapons of our warfare are not carnal but spiritual* (Vulg.,—*but mighty to God*).

ARTICLE 8. *Whether an Aureole is Due to Christ?*

We proceed thus to the Eighth Article: It would seem that an aureole is due to Christ.

Objection 1. For an aureole is due to virginity, martyrdom, and teaching. Now these three were pre-eminently in Christ. Therefore an aureole is especially due to Him.

Obj. 2. Further, Whatever is most perfect in human things must be especially ascribed to Christ. Now an aureole is due as the reward of most excellent merits. Therefore it is also due to Christ.

Obj. 3. Further, Cyprian says (*De Habit. Virg.*)[1] that "virginity bears a likeness to God." Therefore the exemplar of virginity is in God. Therefore it would seem that an aureole is due to Christ even as God.

On the contrary, An aureole is described as joy in being conformed to Christ. Now no one is conformed or likened to himself, as the Philosopher says.[2] Therefore an aureole is not due to Christ.

Further, Christ's reward was never increased. Now Christ had no aureole from the moment of His conception, since then He had never fought. Therefore He never had an aureole afterwards.

I answer that, There are two opinions on this point. For some say that Christ has an aureole in its strict sense, seeing that in Him there is both conflict and victory, and consequently a crown in its proper acceptation. But if we consider the question carefully, although the notion of aurea or crown is becoming to Christ, the notion of aureole is not. For from the very fact that aureole is a diminutive term it follows that it denotes something possessed by participation and not in its fulness. Therefore an aureole is becoming to those who participate in the perfect victory by imitating Him in Whom the fulness of perfect victory is realised. And therefore, since in Christ the notion of victory is found chiefly and fully, for by His victory others are made victors,—as shown by the words of John 16. 33, *Have confidence, I have overcome the world,* and Apoc. 5. 5, *Behold the lion of the tribe of Juda . . . hath prevailed,*—it is not fitting for Christ to have an aureole, but to have something from which all aureoles are derived. Hence it is writ-

ten (Apoc. 3. 21): *To him that shall overcome, I will give to sit with Me in My throne, as I also have overcome, and am set down in My Father's throne* (Vulg.,—*With My Father in His throne*). Therefore we must say with others that although there is nothing of the nature of an aureole in Christ, there is nevertheless something more excellent than any aureole.

Reply Obj. 1. Christ was most truly virgin, martyr, and doctor; yet the corresponding accidental reward in Christ is a negligible quantity in comparison with the greatness of His essential reward. Hence He has not an aureole in its proper sense.

Reply Obj. 2. Although the aureole is due to a most perfect work, yet with regard to us, so far as it is a diminutive term, it denotes the participation of a perfection derived from one in whom that perfection is found in its fulness. Accordingly it implies a certain inferiority, and thus it is not found in Christ in Whom is the fulness of every perfection.

Reply Obj. 3. Although in some way virginity has its exemplar in God, that exemplar is not homogeneous. For the incorruption of God, which virginity imitates, is not in God in the same way as in a virgin.

ARTICLE 9. *Whether an Aureole Is Due to the Angels?*

We proceed thus to the Ninth Article: It would seem that an aureole is due to the angels.

Objection 1. For Jerome (*Serm. de Assump.*)[3] speaking of virginity says: "To live without the flesh while living in the flesh is to live as an angel rather than as a man"; and a gloss on I Cor. 7. 26, *For the present necessity,* says[4] that "virginity is the portion of the angels." Since then an aureole corresponds to virginity, it would seem due to the angels.

Obj. 2. Further, Incorruption of the spirit is more excellent than incorruption of the flesh. Now there is incorruption of spirit in the angels, since they never sinned. Therefore an aureole is due to them rather than to men incorrupt in the flesh and who have sinned at some time.

Obj. 3. Further, An aureole is due to teaching. Now angels teach us by cleansing, enlightening, and perfecting us, as Dionysius says (*Hier. Eccles.* vi, 10).[5] Therefore at least the aureole of doctors is due to them.

---

[1] PL 4, 477.   [2] *Metaphysics*, X, 3 (1054^{b}6).

[3] *Epist.*, IX (PL 30, 131).

[4] *Glossa ordin.* (VI, 43E); *Glossa* Lombardi (PL 191, 1596); Augustine, *De Virgin.*, XIII (PL 40, 401).

[5] PG 3, 273.

On the contrary, It is written (II Tim. 2. 5): *He . . . shall not be* (Vulg.,—*is not*) *crowned, except he strive lawfully.* But there is no conflict in the angels. Therefore an aureole is not due to them.

Further, An aureole is not due to an act that is not performed through the body; therefore it is not due to lovers of virginity, martyrdom, or teaching, if they do not practise them outwardly. But angels are incorporeal spirits. Therefore they have no aureole.

I answer that, An aureole is not due to the angels. The reason of this is that an aureole, properly speaking, corresponds to some perfection of surpassing merit. Now those things which make for perfect merit in man are connatural to angels, or belong to their state in general, or to their essential reward. Therefore the angels have not an aureole in the same sense as an aureole is due to men.

Reply Obj. 1. Virginity is said to be an angelic life, in so far as virgins imitate by grace what angels have by nature. For it is not owing to a virtue that angels abstain altogether from pleasures of the flesh, since they are incapable of such pleasures.

Reply Obj. 2. Perpetual incorruption of the spirit in the angels merits their essential reward, because it is necessary for their salvation, since in them recovery is impossible after they have fallen.

Reply Obj. 3. The acts whereby the angels teach us belong to their glory and their common state; therefore they do not thereby merit an aureole.

ARTICLE 10. *Whether an Aureole Is Also Due to the Body?*

We proceed thus to the *Tenth Article:* It would seem that an aureole is also due to the body.

Objection 1. For the essential reward is greater than the accidental. But the dowries which belong to the essential reward are not only in the soul but also in the body. Therefore there is also an aureole which pertains to the accidental reward.

Obj. 2. Further, Punishment in soul and body corresponds to sin committed through the body. Therefore a reward both in soul and in body is due to merit gained through the body. But the aureole is merited through works of the body. Therefore an aureole is also due to the body.

Obj. 3. Further, A certain fulness of virtue will shine forth in the bodies of martyrs, and

will be seen in their bodily scars; therefore Augustine says:[1] "We feel an undescribable love for the blessed martyrs so as to desire to see in that kingdom the scars of the wounds in their bodies, which they bore for Christ's name. Perhaps indeed we shall see them, for this will not make them less comely, but more glorious. A certain beauty will shine in them, a beauty, though in the body, yet not of the body but of virtue." Therefore it would seem that the martyr's aureole is also in his body; and in like manner the aureoles of others.

On the contrary, The souls now in heaven have aureoles, and yet they have no body. Therefore the proper subject of an aureole is the soul and not the body.

Further, All merit is from the soul. Therefore the whole reward should be in the soul.

I answer that, Properly speaking the aureole is in the mind, since it is joy in the works to which an aureole is due. But even as from the joy in the essential reward, which is the aurea, there results a certain comeliness in the body, which is the glory of the body, so from the joy in the aureole there results a certain bodily comeliness, so that the aureole is chiefly in the mind, but by a kind of overflow it shines forth in the body.

This suffices for the *Replies to the Objections.* It must be observed, however, that the beauty of the scars which will appear in the bodies of the martyrs cannot be called an aureole, since some of the martyrs will have an aureole in which such scars will not appear, for instance those who were put to death by drowning, starvation, or the squalor of prison.

ARTICLE 11. *Whether Three Aureoles Are Fittingly Assigned, Those of Virgins, of Martyrs, and of Doctors?*

We proceed thus to the *Eleventh Article:* It would seem that the three aureoles of virgins, martyrs, and doctors are unfittingly assigned.

Objection 1. For the aureole of martyrs corresponds to their virtue of fortitude, the aureole of virgins to the virtue of temperance, and the aureole of doctors to the virtue of prudence. Therefore it seems that there should be a fourth aureole corresponding to the virtue of justice.

Obj. 2. Further, A gloss on Exod. 25. 25: *A polished crown,* etc., says[2] that "a golden (*aurea*) crown is added, when the Gospel promises eternal life to those who keep the com-

---

[1] *City of God,* XXII, 19 (PL 41, 782).
[2] *Glossa ordin.* (I, 178B); Bede, *De Tabernaculo,* I, 6 (PL 91, 409).

mandments: 'If thou wilt enter into life, keep the commandments' (Matt. 19. 17). To this is added the little golden crown (*aureola*) when it is said: 'If thou wilt be perfect, go and sell all that thou hast, and give to the poor'" (*ibid.* 21). Therefore an aureole is due to poverty.

Obj. 3. Further, A man subjects himself wholly to God by the vow of obedience; therefore the greatest perfection consists in the vow of obedience. Therefore it would seem that an aureole is due to obedience.

Obj. 4. Further, There are also many other works of supererogation in which one will rejoice in the life to come. Therefore there are many aureoles besides the above three.

Obj. 5. Further, Just as a man spreads the faith by preaching and teaching, so does he by publishing written works. Therefore a fourth aureole is due to those who do this.

I answer that, An aureole is an exceptional reward corresponding to an exceptional victory; therefore the three aureoles are assigned in accordance with the exceptional victories in the three conflicts which beset every man. For in the conflict with the flesh, he above all wins the victory who abstains altogether from sexual pleasures which are the chief of this kind; and such is a virgin. Therefore an aureole is due to virginity. In the conflict with the world, the chief victory is to suffer the world's persecution even until death. Therefore the second aureole is due to martyrs who win the victory in this battle. In the conflict with the devil, the chief victory is to expel the enemy not only from oneself but also from the hearts of others; this is done by teaching and preaching, and consequently the third aureole is due to doctors and preachers.

Some, however, distinguish the three aureoles in accordance with the three powers of the soul, by saying that the three aureoles correspond to the three chief acts of the soul's three highest powers. For the act of the rational power is to publish the truth of faith even to others, and to this act the aureole of doctors is due; the highest act of the irascible power is to overcome even death for Christ's sake, and to this act the aureole of martyrs is due; and the highest act of the concupiscible power is to abstain altogether from the greatest carnal pleasures, and to this act the aureole of virgins is due.

Others again, distinguish the three aureoles in accordance with those things whereby we are most excellently conformed to Christ. For He was the mediator between the Father and the world. Hence He was a doctor, by manifest-

ing to the world the truth which He had received from the Father; He was a martyr, by suffering the persecution of the world; and He was a virgin, by His personal purity. Therefore doctors, martyrs and virgins are most perfectly conformed to Him, and for this reason an aureole is due to them.

Reply Obj. 1. There is no conflict to be observed in the act of justice as in the acts of the other virtues. Nor is it true that to teach is an act of prudence; in fact rather is it an act of charity or mercy,—in so far as it is by such habits that we are inclined to the practice of such an act,—or again of wisdom, as directing it.

We may also reply, with others, that justice embraces all the virtues, and therefore a special aureole is not due to it.

Reply Obj. 2. Although poverty is a work of perfection, it does not take the highest place in a spiritual conflict, because the love of temporal goods assails a man less than carnal concupiscence or persecution whereby his own body is broken. Hence an aureole is not due to poverty, but judicial power is due to it, by reason of the humiliation consequent upon poverty. The gloss quoted takes aureole in the broad sense for any reward given for excellent merit.

We reply in the same way to the *Third and Fourth Objections.*

Reply Obj. 5. An aureole is due to those who commit the sacred doctrine to writing, but it is not distinct from the aureole of doctors, since the compiling of writing is a way of teaching.

ARTICLE 12. *Whether the Virgin's Aureole Is the Greatest of All?*

We proceed thus to the Twelfth Article: It would seem that the virgin's aureole is the greatest of all.

Objection 1. For it is said of virgins (Apoc. 14. 4) that they *follow the Lamb whithersoever He goeth,* and (*ibid.* 3) that *no other man could say the canticle* which the virgins sang. Therefore virgins have the most excellent aureole.

Obj. 2. Further, Cyprian (*De Habit. Virg.*)[1] says of virgins that they are "the more illustrious portion of Christ's flock." Therefore the greater aureole is due to them.

Obj. 3. Again, it would seem that the martyr's aureole is the greatest. For Haymo, commenting on Apoc. 14. 3, *No man could say the hymn,* says[2] that "virgins do not all take prece-

[1] PL 4, 455.　　　　[2] *In Apoc.* (PL 117, 1106).

dence of married folk; but only those who in addition to the observance of virginity are by the tortures of their passion on a par with married persons who have suffered martyrdom." Therefore martyrdom gives virginity its precedence over other states, and consequently a greater aureole is due to virginity.

Obj. 4. Again, it would seem that the greatest aureole is due to doctors. For the Church militant is modelled after the Church triumphant. Now in the Church militant the greatest honour is due to doctors (I Tim. 5. 17): *Let the priests that rule well be esteemed worthy of double honour, especially they who labour in the word and doctrine.* Therefore a greater aureole is due to them in the Church triumphant.

I answer that, Precedence of one aureole over another may be considered from two standpoints. First, from the point of view of the conflicts, that aureole being considered greater which is due to the more strenuous battle. Looking at it thus the martyr's aureole takes precedence of the others in one way, and the virgin's in another. For the martyr's battle is more strenuous in itself, and more intensely painful, while the conflict with the flesh is fraught with greater danger, since it is more lasting and threatens us at closer quarters. Secondly, from the point of view of the things about which the battle is fought, and thus the doctor's aureole takes precedence of all others, since this conflict is about intelligible goods, while the other conflicts are about sensible passions. Nevertheless, the precedence that is considered in view of the conflict is more essential to the aureole, since the aureole, according to its proper character, regards the victory and the battle, and the difficulty of fighting which is viewed from the standpoint of the battle is of greater importance than that which is considered from our standpoint through the conflict being at closer quarters. Therefore the martyr's aureole is the greatest absolutely of all; for this reason a gloss on Matt. 5. 10, says[1] that "all the other beatitudes are perfected in the eighth, which refers to the martyrs," namely, *Blessed are they that suffer persecution.* For this reason, too, the Church in enumerating the saints together places the martyrs before the doctors and virgins. Yet nothing hinders the other aureoles from being more excellent in some particular way. And this suffices for the *Replies to the Objections.*

[1] *Glossa ordin.* (v, 19A); Augustine, *De Serm. Dom.*, I, 3 (PL 34, 1234).

ARTICLE 13. *Whether One Person Has an Aureole more Excellently Than Another Person?*

We proceed thus to the Thirteenth Article: It would seem that one person has not the aureole either of virginity, or of martyrdom, or of doctrine more perfectly than another person.

Objection 1. For things which have reached their term are not subject to intension or lessening. Now the aureole is due to works which have reached their term of perfection. Therefore an aureole is not subject to intension or lessening.

Obj. 2. Further, Virginity is not subject to being more or less, since it denotes a kind of privation, and privations are not subject to intension or lessening. Therefore neither does the reward of virginity, the virgin's aureole, that is, receive intension or lessening.

On the contrary, The aureole is added to the aurea. But the aurea is more intense in one than in another. Therefore the aureole is also.

I answer that, Since merit is somewhat the cause of reward, rewards must be diversified according as merits are diversified, for the intension or lessening of a thing follows from the intension or lessening of its cause. Now the merit of the aureole may be greater or lesser. Therefore the aureole may also be greater or lesser.

We must observe, however, that the merit of an aureole may be intensified in two ways: first, on the part of its cause, secondly on the part of the work. For there may happen to be two persons, one of whom, out of lesser charity, suffers greater torments of martyrdom, or is more constant in preaching, or again withdraws himself more from carnal pleasures. Accordingly, intension not of the aureole but of the aurea corresponds to the intension of merit derived from its root, while intension of the aureole corresponds to intension of merit derived from the kind of act. Consequently it is possible for one who merits less in martyrdom as to his essential reward to receive a greater aureole for his martyrdom.

Reply Obj. 1. The merits to which an aureole is due do not reach the term of their perfection absolutely, but according to their species, even as fire is specifically the most subtle of bodies. Hence nothing hinders one aureole being more excellent than another, even as one fire is more subtle than another.

Reply Obj. 2. The virginity of one may be greater than the virginity of another by reason of a greater withdrawal from that which is contrary to virginity, so that virginity is stated to be greater in one who avoids more the occasions of corruption. For in this way privations may increase, as when a man is said to be more blind if he is removed further from the possession of sight.

QUESTION XCVII
OF THE PUNISHMENT OF THE DAMNED
(*In Seven Articles*)

IN due sequence we must consider those things that concern the damned after the judgment: (1) The punishment of the damned, and the fire by which their bodies will be tormented; (2) matters relating to their will and intellect (Q. XCVIII); (3) God's justice and mercy in regard to the damned (Q. XCIX).

Under the first head there are seven points of inquiry: (1) Whether in hell the damned are tormented with the sole punishment of fire? (2) Whether the worm by which they are tormented is corporeal? (3) Whether their weeping is corporeal? (4) Whether their darkness is material? (5) Whether the fire whereby they are tormented is corporeal? (6) Whether it is of the same species as our fire? (7) Whether this fire is beneath the earth?

ARTICLE 1. *Whether in Hell the Damned Are Tormented By the Sole Punishment of Fire?*

We proceed thus to the First Article: It would seem that in hell the damned are tormented by the sole punishment of fire.

Objection 1. For in Matt. 25. 41, where their condemnation is declared, mention is made of fire only, in the words: *Depart from Me, you cursed, into everlasting fire.*

Obj. 2. Further, Even as the punishment of purgatory is due to venial sin, so is the punishment of hell due to mortal sin. Now no other punishment but that of fire is stated to be in purgatory, as appears from the words of I Cor. 3. 13: *The fire shall try every man's work, of what sort it is.* Therefore neither in hell will there be a punishment other than of fire.

Obj. 3. Further, Variety of punishment affords a respite, as when one passes from heat to cold. But we can admit no respite in the damned. Therefore there will not be various punishments, but that of fire alone.

On the contrary, It is written (Ps. 10. 7): *Fire and brimstone and storms of winds shall be the portion of their cup.*

Further, It is written (Job. 24. 19): *Let him pass from the snow waters to excessive heat.*

I answer that, According to Basil (*Hom.* i *in Ps.* 28),[1] at the final cleansing of the world there will be a separation of the elements, whatever is pure and noble remaining above for the glory of the blessed, and whatever is ignoble and sordid being cast down for the punishment of the damned, so that just as every creature will be to the blessed a matter of joy, so will all the elements conduce to the torture of the damned, according to Wis. 5. 21, *the whole world will fight with Him against the unwise.* This is also becoming to Divine justice, that whereas they departed from One by sin, and placed their end in material things which are many and various, so should they be tormented in many ways and from many sources.

Reply Obj. 1. It is because fire is most painful, through its abundance of active force, that the name of fire is given to any torment if it be intense.

Reply Obj. 2. The punishment of purgatory is not intended chiefly to torment, but to cleanse; therefore it should be inflicted by fire alone which is above all possessed of cleansing power. But the punishment of the damned is not directed to their cleansing. Consequently the comparison fails.

Reply Obj. 3. The damned will pass from the most intense heat to the most intense cold, without this giving them any respite, because they will suffer from external agencies not by the change of their body from its original natural disposition, and the contrary passion affording a respite by restoring an equable or moderate temperature, as happens now, but by a spiritual action, in the same way as sensible objects act on the senses, being perceived by impressing the organ with their forms according to their spiritual and not their material being.

ARTICLE 2. *Whether the Worm of the Damned Is Corporeal?*

We proceed thus to the Second Article: It would seem that the worm by which the damned are tormented is corporeal.

Objection 1. For flesh cannot be tormented by a spiritual worm. Now the flesh of the damned will be tormented by a worm: *He will give fire and worms into their flesh* (Judith 16. 21), and: *The vengeance on the flesh of the ungodly is fire and worms* (Ecclus. 7. 19). Therefore that worm will be corporeal.

Obj. 2. Further, Augustine says:[2] "Both,

[1] PG 29, 297; cf. *In Hexaëm.,* hom. VI (PG 29, 121).
[2] *City of God,* XXI, 9 (PL 41, 725).

namely fire and worm, will be the punishment of the body." Therefore, etc.

On the contrary, Augustine says:[1] "The unquenchable fire and the restless worm in the punishment of the damned are explained in various ways by different persons. Some refer both to the body, some, both to the soul; others refer the fire, in the literal sense, to the body, the worm to the soul metaphorically, and this seems the more probable."

I answer that, After the day of judgment, no animal or mixed body will remain in the renewed world except only the body of man, because the former are not directed to incorruption, nor after that time will there be generation or corruption. Consequently the worm ascribed to the damned must be understood to be not of a corporeal but of a spiritual nature, and this is the remorse of conscience, which is called a worm because it originates from the corruption of sin, and torments the soul, as a corporeal worm born of corruption torments by gnawing.

Reply Obj. 1. The very souls of the damned are called their flesh because they were subject to the flesh. Or we may reply that the flesh will be tormented by the spiritual worm, according as the afflictions of the soul overflow into the body, both here and hereafter.

Reply Obj. 2. Augustine speaks by way of comparison. For he does not wish to assert absolutely that this worm is material, but that it is better to say that both are to be understood materially than that both should be understood only in a spiritual sense, for then the damned would suffer no bodily pain. This is clear to anyone that examines the context of his words in this passage.

ARTICLE 3. *Whether the Weeping of the Damned Will Be Corporeal?*

We proceed thus to the Third Article: It would seem that the weeping of the damned will be corporeal.

Objection 1. For a gloss on Luke 13. 28, *There will be weeping*, says[2] that "the weeping with which our Lord threatens the wicked is a proof of the resurrection of the body." But this would not be the case if that weeping were merely spiritual. Therefore, etc.

Obj. 2. Further, The pain of the punishment corresponds to the pleasure of the sin, according to Apoc. 18. 7: *As much as she hath glorified herself and lived in delicacies, so much tor-*

---

ment and sorrow give ye to her. Now sinners had internal and external pleasure in their sin. Therefore they will also have external weeping.

On the contrary, Corporeal weeping results from dissolving into tears. Now there cannot be a continual dissolution from the bodies of the damned, since nothing is restored to them by food; for everything finite is consumed if something be continually taken from it. Therefore the weeping of the damned will not be corporeal.

I answer that, Two things are to be observed in corporeal weeping. One is the resolution of tears: and as to this corporeal weeping cannot be in the damned, since after the day of judgment, the movement of the first movable being at an end, there will be neither generation, nor corruption, nor bodily change, and in the resolution of tears that humour needs to be generated which is shed forth in the shape of tears. Therefore in this respect it will be impossible for corporeal weeping to be in the damned. The other thing to be observed in corporeal weeping is a certain agitation and disturbance of the head and eyes, and in this respect weeping will be possible in the damned after the resurrection, for the bodies of the damned will be tormented not only from without, but also from within, according as the body is affected at the instance of the soul's passion towards good or evil. In this sense weeping is a proof of the body's resurrection, and corresponds to the pleasure of sin, experienced by both soul and body.

This suffices for the *Replies to the Objections.*

ARTICLE 4. *Whether the Damned Are in Material Darkness?*

We proceed thus to the Fourth Article: It would seem that the damned are not in material darkness.

Objection 1. For commenting on Job 10. 22, *But everlasting horror dwelleth*, Gregory says (*Moral.* ix, 66):[3] "Although that fire will give no light for comfort, yet, that it may torment the more it does give light for a purpose, for by the light of its flame the wicked will see their followers whom they have drawn thither from the world." Therefore the darkness there is not material.

Obj. 2. Further, The damned see their own punishment, for this increases their punishment. But nothing is seen without light. Therefore there is no material darkness there.

---

[1] *Ibid.*, xx, 22 (PL 41, 694).

[2] *Glossa ordin.* (v, 161F); Jerome, *In Matt.*, 1, on 8.12 (PL 26, 53); Bede, *In Matt.*, 11, on 8.12 (PL 92.41).

[3] PL 75, 915.

Obj. 3. Further, There the damned will have the power of sight after being reunited to their bodies. But this power would be useless to them unless they see something. Therefore, since nothing is seen unless it be in the light, it would seem that they are not in absolute darkness.

On the contrary, It is written (Matt. 22. 13): *Bind his hands and his feet, and cast him into the exterior darkness.* Commenting on these words Gregory says (*Moral.* ix, 65):[1] "If this fire gave any light, he would by no means be described as cast into exterior darkness."

Further, Basil says (*Hom.* i *in Ps.* 28, 7, *The voice of the Lord divideth the flame of fire*)[2] that by God's might the brightness of the fire will be separated from its power of burning, so that its brightness will conduce to the joy of the blessed, and the heat of the flame to the torment of the damned." Therefore the damned will be in material darkness.

Other points relating to the punishment of the damned have been decided above (Q. LXXXVI, A. 3).[3]

I answer that, The disposition of hell will be such as to be adapted to the utmost unhappiness of the damned. Therefore accordingly both light and darkness are there, in so far as they are most conducive to the unhappiness of the damned. Now seeing is in itself pleasant for, as stated in the *Metaphysics,*[4] "the sense of sight is most valued, because thereby many things are known." Yet it happens accidentally that seeing is painful, when we see things that are hurtful to us, or displeasing to our will. Consequently in hell the place must be so disposed for seeing as regards light and darkness that nothing be seen clearly, and that only such things be dimly seen as are able to bring anguish to the heart. Therefore, absolutely speaking, the place is dark. Yet by Divine disposition, there is a certain amount of light, as much as suffices for seeing those things which are capable of tormenting the soul. The natural situation of the place is enough for this, since in the centre of the earth, where hell is said to be, fire cannot be otherwise than thick and cloudy, and reeky as it were.

Some hold that this darkness is caused by the massing together of the bodies of the damned, which will so fill the place of hell with their numbers, that no air will remain, so that there will be no translucid body that can be

the subject of light and darkness, except the eyes of the damned, which will be darkened utterly.

This suffices for the *Replies to the Objections.*

ARTICLE 5. *Whether the Fire of Hell Will Be Corporeal?*

We proceed thus to the Fifth Article: It would seem that the fire of hell whereby the bodies of the damned will be tormented will not be corporeal.

Objection 1. For Damascene says (*De Fide Orthod.* iv, 27):[5] "The devil, and demons, and his man, namely Antichrist, together with the ungodly and sinners, will be cast into everlasting fire, not material fire, such as that which we have, but such as God knoweth." Now everything corporeal is material. Therefore the fire of hell will not be corporeal.

Obj. 2. Further, The souls of the damned when severed from their bodies are cast into hell fire. But Augustine says (*Gen. ad Lit.* xii, 32):[6] "In my opinion the place to which the soul is committed after death is spiritual and not corporeal." Therefore, etc.

Obj. 3. Further, Corporeal fire in the mode of its action does not follow the mode of guilt in the person who is burnt at the stake, but rather does it follow the mode of humid and dry, for in the same corporeal fire we see both good and wicked suffer. But the fire of hell, in its mode of torture or action, follows the mode of guilt in the person punished; therefore Gregory says (*Dial.* iv, 43):[7] "There is indeed but one hell fire, but it does not torture all sinners equally. For each one will suffer as much pain according as his guilt deserves." Therefore this fire will not be corporeal.

On the contrary, He says (*Dial.* iv, 29):[8] "I doubt not that the fire of hell is corporeal, since it is certain that bodies are tortured there."

Further, It is written (Wisd. 5. 21): *The . . . world shall fight . . . against the unwise.* But the whole world would not fight against the unwise if they were punished with a spiritual and not a corporeal punishment. Therefore they will be punished with a corporeal fire.

I answer that, There have been many opinions about the fire of hell. For some philosophers, as Avicenna,[9] not believing in the resurrection, thought that the soul alone would be punished after death. And as they considered it impossible for the soul, being incor-

---

[1] PL 75, 912.
[2] PG 29, 297; cf. *In Hexaëm.*, hom. VI (PG 29, 121).
[3] Cf. also Q. LXX, A. 3; *In Sent.*, IV, d. 44, Q. 3, A. I.
[4] Aristotle, I, I (980ª23).

[5] PG 94, 1225.   [6] PL 34, 480.
[7] PL 77, 401.   [8] PL 77, 368.
[9] *Meta.*, tr. IX, chap. 7 (106vb).

poreal, to be punished with a corporeal fire, they denied that the fire by which the wicked are punished is corporeal, and pretended that all statements as to souls being punished in future after death by any corporeal means are to be taken metaphorically. For just as the joy and happiness of good souls will not be about any corporeal object, but about something spiritual, namely the attainment of their end, so will the torment of the wicked be merely spiritual, in that they will be grieved at being separated from their end, the desire for which is in them by nature. Therefore, just as all descriptions of the soul's delight after death that seem to denote bodily pleasure,—for instance, that they are refreshed, that they smile, and so forth,—must be taken metaphorically, so also are all such descriptions of the soul's suffering as seem to imply bodily punishment,—for instance, that they burn in fire, or suffer from the stench, and so forth. For as spiritual pleasure and pain are unknown to the majority, these things need to be declared under the figure of corporeal pleasures and pains, in order that men may be moved the more to the desire or fear of them.

Since, however, in the punishment of the damned there will be not only pain of loss corresponding to the turning away that was in their sin, but also pain of sense corresponding to the conversion, it follows that it is not enough to hold the above manner of punishment. For this reason Avicenna himself (loc. cit.) added another explanation, by saying that the souls of the wicked are punished after death not by bodies but by likenesses of bodies; just as in a dream it seems to a man that he is suffering various pains on account of such images being in his imagination. Even Augustine seems to hold this kind of punishment (Gen. ad Lit. xii, 32),[1] as is clear from the text.

But this would seem an unreasonable statement. For the imagination is a power that makes use of a bodily organ, so that it is impossible for such visions of the imagination to occur in the soul separated from the body, as in the soul of the dreamer. Therefore Avicenna also (loc. cit.), that he might avoid this difficulty, said that the soul separated from the body uses as an organ some part of the heavenly body, to which the human body needs to be conformed, in order to be perfected by the rational soul, which is like the movers of the heavenly body,—thus following somewhat the opinion of certain philosophers of old, who

maintained that souls return to the stars that are their compeers.

But this is absolutely absurd according to the Philosopher's teaching, since the soul uses a definite bodily organ, even as art uses definite instruments, so that it cannot pass from one body to another, as Pythagoras is stated[2] to have maintained.[3] As to the statement of Augustine we shall say below how it is to be answered (Reply 2).

However, whatever we may say of the fire that torments the separated souls, we must admit that the fire which will torment the bodies of the damned after the resurrection is corporeal, since one cannot fittingly apply a punishment to a body unless that punishment itself be bodily. Therefore Gregory (Dial. iv, 29)[4] proves the fire of hell to be corporeal from the very fact that the wicked will be cast there after the resurrection. Again Augustine, as quoted in the text of iv. Sent. d. 44,[5] clearly admits[6] that the fire by which the bodies are tormented is corporeal. And this is the point at issue for the present. We have said elsewhere (Q. LXX, A. 3) how the souls of the damned are punished by this corporeal fire.

Reply Obj. 1. Damascene does not absolutely deny that this fire is material, but that it is material as our fire, since it differs from ours in some of its properties. We may also reply that since that fire does not change bodies as to their matter, but acts on them for their punishment by a kind of spiritual action, it is for this reason that it is stated not to be material, not as regards its substance, but as to its punitive effect on bodies and, still more, on souls.

Reply Obj. 2. The assertion of Augustine may be taken in this way, that the place whither souls are conveyed after death is described as incorporeal in so far as the soul is there not corporeally, that is as bodies are in a place, but in some other spiritual way, as angels are in a place. Or we may reply that Augustine is expressing an opinion without deciding the point, as he often does in those books.

Reply Obj. 3. That fire will be the instrument of Divine justice inflicting punishment. Now an instrument acts not only by its own power and in its own way, but also by the power of the principal agent, and as directed by it. Therefore although fire is not able, of its own

---

[1] PL 34, 481.

[2] Aristotle, Soul, I, 3 (407ᵇ22).

[3] Cf. Diogenes Laertes, who quotes the verse Zenophon puts in the mouth of Pythagoras; cf. Diels, Doxographi Graeci, pp. 557, 587.

[4] PL 77, 368.   [5] QR II, 1003.

[6] City of God, XXI, 10 (PL 41, 725).

power, to torture certain persons more or less, according to the measure of sin, it is able to do so nevertheless in so far as its action is regulated by the ordering of Divine justice; even so the fire of the furnace is regulated by the forethought of the smith, according as the effect of his art requires.

ARTICLE 6. Whether the Fire of Hell Is of the Same Species As Ours?

We proceed thus to the Sixth Article: It would seem that this fire is not of the same species as the corporeal fire which we see.

Objection 1. For Augustine says,[1] and is quoted in the text,[2] "In my opinion no man knows of what kind is the everlasting fire, unless the Spirit of God has revealed it to anyone." But all or nearly all know the nature of this fire of ours. Therefore that fire is not of the same species as this.

Obj. 2. Further, Gregory commenting on Job 20. 26, A fire that is not kindled shall devour him, says (Moral. xv, 29.)[3] "Bodily fire needs bodily fuel in order to become fire; neither can it be except by being kindled, nor live unless it be renewed. On the other hand the fire of hell, since it is a bodily fire, and burns in a bodily way the wicked cast therein, is neither kindled by human endeavour, nor kept alive with fuel, but once created endures unquenchably; at one and the same time it needs no kindling, and lacks not heat." Therefore it is not of the same nature as the fire that we see.

Obj. 3. Further, The everlasting and the corruptible differ essentially, since they agree not even in genus, according to the Philosopher.[4] But this fire of ours is corruptible, whereas the other is everlasting: Depart from Me, you cursed, into everlasting fire (Matt. 25. 41). Therefore they are not of the same nature.

Obj. 4. Further, It belongs to the nature of this fire of ours to give light. But the fire of hell gives no light; hence the saying of Job 18. 5: Shall not the light of the wicked be extinguished? Therefore . . . . as above.

On the contrary, According to the Philosopher,[5] "every water is of the same species as every other water." Therefore in like manner every fire is of the same species as every other fire.

Further, It is written (Wisd. 11. 17): By what things a man sinneth by the same also he is tormented. Now men sin by the sensible things of this world. Therefore it is just that they should be punished by those same things.

I answer that, As stated in the book on Meteorology,[6] fire has other bodies for its matter, for the reason that of all the elements it has the greatest power of action. Hence fire is found under two conditions: in its own matter, as existing in its own sphere, and in a strange matter, whether of earth, as in burning coal, or of air, as in the flame. Under whatever conditions however fire be found, it is always of the same species, so far as the nature of fire is concerned, but there may be a difference of species as to the bodies which are the matter of fire. Therefore flame and burning coal differ specifically, and likewise burning wood and red-hot iron; nor does it signify, as to this particular point, whether they be kindled by force, as in the case of iron, or by a natural intrinsic principle, as happens with sulphur. Accordingly it is clear that the fire of hell is of the same species as the fire we have, so far as the nature of fire is concerned. But whether that fire subsists in its proper matter, or if it subsists in a strange matter, whatever that matter may be, we know not. And in this way it may differ specifically from the fire we have, considered materially. It has, however, certain properties differing from our fire, for instance that it needs no kindling, nor is kept alive by fuel. But the differences do not argue a difference of species as regards the nature of the fire.

Reply Obj. 1. Augustine is speaking of that fire with regard to its matter, and not with regard to its nature.

Reply Obj. 2. This fire of ours is kept alive with fuel, and is kindled by man, because it is introduced into a foreign matter by art and force. But that other fire needs no fuel to keep it alive, because either it subsists in its own matter, or is in a foreign matter, not by force but by nature from an intrinsic principle. Therefore it is kindled not by man but by God, Who fashioned its nature. This is the meaning of the words of Isaias (30. 33): The breath of the Lord is as a torrent of brimstone kindling it.

Reply Obj. 3. Even as the bodies of the damned will be of the same species as now, although now they are corruptible, whereas then they will be incorruptible, both by the ordering of Divine justice, and on account of the cessation of the heavenly movement, so is

[1] City of God, xx, 16 (PL 41, 682).
[2] Peter Lombard, Sent., iv, d. 44, chap. 6 (QR ii, 1003).
[3] PL 75, 1098.
[4] Metaphysics, x, 10 (1058ᵇ26).
[5] Topics, i, 5 (103ᵃ19).

[6] Aristotle, iv, 1 (379ᵃ16).

it with the fire of hell by which those bodies will be punished.

Reply Obj. 4. To give light does not belong to fire according to any mode of existence, since in its own matter it gives no light; therefore it does not shine in its own sphere according to the philosophers, and in like manner in certain foreign matters it does not shine, as when it is in an opaque earthly substance such as sulphur. The same happens also when its brightness is obscured by thick smoke. Therefore that the fire of hell gives no light is not sufficient proof of its being of a different species.

ARTICLE 7. *Whether the Fire of Hell Is Beneath the Earth?*

We proceed thus to the Seventh Article: It would seem that this fire is not beneath the earth.

Objection 1. For it is said of the damned (Job. 18. 18), *And God shall remove him out of the globe* (Douay,—*world*). Therefore the fire whereby the damned will be punished is not beneath the earth but outside the globe.

Obj. 2. Further, Nothing violent or accidental can be everlasting. But this fire will be in hell for ever. Therefore it will be there not by force but naturally. Now fire cannot be under the earth save by violence. Therefore the fire of hell is not beneath the earth.

Obj. 3. Further, After the day of judgment the bodies of all the damned will be tormented in hell. Now those bodies will fill a place. Consequently, since the multitude of the damned will be very great, for *the number of fools is infinite* (Eccl. 1. 15), the space containing that fire must also be very great. But it would seem unreasonable to say that there is so great a hollow within the earth, since all the parts of the earth naturally tend to the centre. Therefore that fire will not be beneath the earth.

Obj. 4. Further, *By what things a man sinneth, by the same also he is tormented* (Wisd. 11. 17). But the wicked have sinned on the earth. Therefore the fire that punishes them should not be under the earth.

On the contrary, It is written (Isa. 14. 9): *Hell below was in an uproar to meet Thee at Thy coming.* Therefore the fire of hell is beneath us.

Further, Gregory says (*Dial.* iv, 42):[1] "I see not what hinders us from believing that hell is beneath the earth.

Further, A gloss on Jonas 2. 4, *Thou hast cast*

[1] PL 77, 401.

me forth . . . into the heart of the sea, says,[2] "that is, into hell," and in the Gospel (Matt. 12. 40) the words *in the heart of the earth* have the same sense, for as the heart is in the middle of an animal, so is hell supposed to be in the middle of the earth.

I answer that, As Augustine says,[3] and he is quoted in the text,[4] "I am of opinion that no one knows in what part of the world hell is situated, unless the Spirit of God has revealed this to some one." Therefore Gregory (*Dial.* iv, 42)[5] having been questioned on this point answers: "About this matter I dare not give a rash decision. For some have thought hell to be in some part of the earth's surface; others think it to be beneath the earth." He shows the latter opinion to be the more probable for two reasons. First from the very meaning of the word. These are his words: "If we call it the nether regions *(infernus)*, for the reason that it is beneath us *(inferius)*, what earth is in relation to heaven, such should be hell in relation to earth." Secondly, from the words of Apoc. 5. 3: *No man was able, neither in heaven, nor on earth, nor under the earth, to open the book,* where the words "in heaven" refer to the angels, "on earth" to men living in the body, and "under the earth" to souls in hell.

Augustine too (*Gen. ad Lit.* xii, 34)[6] seems to indicate two reasons for the congruity of hell being under the earth. One is that "since the souls of the departed sinned through love of the flesh, they should be treated as the dead flesh is accustomed to be treated, by being buried beneath the earth." The other is that heaviness is to the body what sorrow is to the spirit, and joy (of spirit) is as lightness (of body). Therefore "just as in reference to the body, all the heavier things are beneath the others, if they are placed in order of gravity, so in reference to the spirit, the lower place is occupied by whatever is more sorrowful"; and thus even as the empyrean is a fitting place for the joy of the elect, so the lowest part of the earth is a fitting place for the sorrow of the damned. Nor does it signify that Augustine (*ibid.*) says that "hell is stated or believed to be under the earth," because he withdraws this (*Retract.* ii, 24)[7] where he says: "I think I should have said that hell is beneath the earth, rather than have given the reason why it is stated or believed to be under the earth."

[2] *Glossa interl.* (IV. 375r).
[3] *City of God,* XX, 16 (PL 41, 682).
[4] Lombard, *Sent.,* IV, d. 44, chap. 6 (QR II, 1003).
[5] PL 77, 400.
[6] PL 34, 482.   [7] PL 32, 640.

However, some philosophers have maintained that hell is situated beneath the terrestrial orb, but above the surface of the earth, on that part which is opposite to us. This seems to have been the meaning of Isidore when he asserted that "the sun and the moon will stop in the place wherein they were created, lest the wicked should enjoy this light in the midst of their torments."[1] But this is no argument, if we assert that hell is under the earth. We have already stated how these words may be explained (Q. XCI, A. 2).

Pythagoras held[2] the place of punishment to be in a fiery sphere situated, according to him, in the middle of the whole world, and he called it the prison-house of Jupiter as Aristotle relates.[3] It is, however, more in keeping with Scripture to say that it is beneath the earth.

Reply Obj. 1. The words of Job, *God shall remove him out of the globe,* refer to the surface of the earth, that is from this world. This is how Gregory expounds it (*Moral.* xiv, 22)[4] where he says: "He is removed from the globe when, at the coming of the heavenly judge, he is taken away from this world wherein he now prides himself in his wickedness." Nor does globe here signify the universe, as though the place of punishment were outside the whole universe.

Reply Obj. 2. Fire continues in that place for all eternity by the ordering of Divine justice, although according to its nature an element cannot last for ever outside its own place, especially if things were to remain in this state of generation and corruption. The fire there will be of the very greatest heat, because its heat will be all gathered together from all parts, through being surrounded on all sides by the cold of the earth.

Reply Obj. 3. Hell will never lack sufficient room to admit the bodies of the damned, since hell is accounted one of the three things that *never are satisfied* (Prov. 30. 15, 16). Nor is it unreasonable that God's power should maintain within the bowels of the earth a hollow great enough to contain all the bodies of the damned.

Reply Obj. 4. It does not follow of necessity that *by what things a man sinneth, by the same also he is tormented,* except as regards the principal instruments of sin, because man having

sinned in soul and body will be punished in both. But it does not follow that a man will be punished in the very place where he sinned, because the place due to the damned is other from that due to wayfarers. We may also reply that these words refer to the punishments inflicted on man on the way, according as each sin has its corresponding punishment, since "every disordered love is its own punishment," as Augustine states.[5]

QUESTION XCVIII

Of the Will and Intellect of the Damned

(In Nine Articles)

We must next consider matters pertaining to the will and intellect of the damned. Under this head there are nine points of inquiry: (1) Whether every act of will in the damned is evil? (2) Whether they ever repent of the evil they have done? (3) Whether they would rather not be than be? (4) Whether they would wish others to be damned? (5) Whether the wicked hate God? (6) Whether they can demerit? (7) Whether they can make use of the knowledge acquired in this life? (8) Whether they ever think of God? (9) Whether they see the glory of the blessed?

ARTICLE 1. *Whether Every Act of Will in the Damned Is Evil?*

We proceed thus to the First Article: It would seem that not every act of will in the damned is evil.

Objection 1. For according to Dionysius (*Div. Nom.* iv),[6] "the demons desire the good and the best, namely to be, to live, to understand." Since, then, men who are damned are not worse off than the demons, it would seem that they also can have a good will.

Obj. 2. Further, As Dionysius says (*ibid.*),[7] "evil is altogether involuntary." Therefore if the damned will anything, they will it as something good or apparently good. Now a will that is directly ordered to good is itself good. Therefore the damned can have a good will.

Obj. 3. Further, Some will be damned who, while in this world, acquired certain habits of virtue, for instance heathens who had civic virtues. Now a will elicits praiseworthy acts by reason of virtuous habits. Therefore there may be praiseworthy acts of the will in some of the damned.

---

[1] Cf. *Glossa ordin.*, on Isa. 60.19 (IV, 99A); cf. also Isidore, *De Ord. Creatur.*, v (PL 83, 924); XIII (PL 83, 946); *Etymol.*, XIV, 9 (PL 82, 526).

[2] Diogenes Laertes, *Vitae et Placita Clarorum Philosophorum*, VIII, 1, 31 (DD 211).

[3] *Heavens*, II, 13 (293ᵇ1).   [4] PL 75, 1053.

[5] *Confessions*, I, 19 (PL 32, 670).

[6] Sect. 23 (PG 3, 725).   [7] Sect. 32 (PG 3, 732).

On the contrary, An obstinate will can never be inclined except to evil. Now men who are damned will be obstinate even as the demons. Therefore their will can never be good.

Further, As the will of the damned is in relation to evil, so is the will of the blessed in regard to good. But the blessed never have an evil will. Neither therefore have the damned any good will.

I answer that, A twofold will may be considered in the damned, namely the deliberate will and the natural will. Their natural will is theirs not of themselves but of the Author of nature, Who gave nature this inclination which we call the natural will. Therefore since nature remains in them, it follows that the natural will in them can be good. But their deliberate will is theirs of themselves, according as it is in their power to be inclined by their affections to this or that. This will is in them always evil, and this because they are completely turned away from the last end of a right will, nor can a will be good except it be directed to that same end. Hence even though they will some good, they do not will it well so that one be able to call their will good on that account.

Reply Obj. 1. The words of Dionysius must be understood of the natural will, which is nature's inclination to some particular good. And yet this natural inclination is corrupted by their wickedness, in so far as this good which they desire naturally is desired by them under certain evil circumstances.

Reply Obj. 2. Evil, as evil, does not move the will, but in so far as it is thought to be good. Yet it comes of their wickedness that they esteem that which is evil as though it were good. Hence their will is evil.

Reply Obj. 3. The habits of civic virtue do not remain in the separated soul, because those virtues perfect us only in the civic life which will not remain after this life. Even though they remained, they would never come into action, being enchained, as it were, by the obstinacy of the mind.

ARTICLE 2. *Whether the Damned Repent of the Evil They Have Done?*

We proceed thus to the Second Article: It would seem that the damned never repent of the evil they have done.

Objection 1. For Bernard says on the Canticle[1] that "the damned ever consent to the evil they have done." Therefore they never repent of the sins they have committed.

Obj. 2. Further, To wish one had not sinned is a good will. But the damned will never have a good will. Therefore the damned will never wish they had not sinned, and thus the same conclusion follows as above.

Obj. 3. Further, According to Damascene (*De Fide Orthod.* ii, 4),[2] "death is to man what their fall was to the angels." But the angel's will is irrevocable after his fall, in that he cannot withdraw from the choice whereby he previously sinned. Therefore the damned also cannot repent of the sins committed by them.

Obj. 4. Further, The wickedness of the damned in hell will be greater than that of sinners in the world. Now in this world some sinners repent not of the sins they have committed, either through blindness of mind, as heretics, or through obstinacy, as those *who are glad when they have done evil, and rejoice in most wicked things* (Prov. 2. 14). Therefore, etc.

On the contrary, It is said of the damned (Wisd. 5. 3): *Repenting within themselves* (Vulg.,—*Saying within themselves, repenting*).

Further, The Philosopher says[3] that "the wicked are full of repentance; for afterwards they are sorry for that in which previously they took pleasure." Therefore the damned, being most wicked, repent all the more.

I answer that, A person may repent of sin in two ways: in one way directly, in another way accidentally. He repents of a sin directly who hates sin as such; and he repents accidentally who hates it on account of something connected with it, for instance punishment or something of that kind. Accordingly the wicked will not repent of their sins directly, because consent in the malice of sin will remain in them; but they will repent accidentally, in so far as they will suffer from the punishment inflicted on them for sin.

Reply Obj. 1. The damned will wickedness, but shun punishment, and thus accidentally they repent of wickedness committed.

Reply Obj. 2. To wish one had not sinned on account of the shamefulness of vice is a good will; but this will not be in the wicked.

Reply Obj. 3. It will be possible for the damned to repent of their sins without turning their will away from sin, because in their sins they will shun not what they previously desired, but something else, namely the punishment.

---

[1] Cf. *De Consider.*, v, 12 (PL 182, 802); *De Grat. et Lib. Arb.*, IX (PL 182, 1017); cf. Albert, *In Sent.*, IV, d. 50, A. 3, sed contra 1 (BO XXX, 689).

[2] PG 94, 877.   [3] *Ethics*, IX, 4 (1166[b]24).

Reply Obj. 4. However obstinate men may be in this world, they repent of the sins accidentally if they are punished for them. Thus Augustine says (QQ. LXXXIII, qu. 36):[1] "We see the most savage beasts are deterred from the greatest pleasures by fear of pain."

ARTICLE 3. *Whether the Damned By Right and Deliberate Reason Would Will Not To Be?*

We proceed thus to the Third Article: It would seem impossible for the damned, by right and deliberate reason, to will not to be.

Objection 1. For Augustine says (*De Lib. Arb.* iii, 7):[2] "Consider how great a good it is to be, since both the happy and the unhappy will it; for to be and yet to be unhappy is a greater thing than not to be at all."

Obj. 2. Further. Augustine argues thus (*ibid.* 8):[3] Preference supposes election. But not to be is not a matter of choice since it has not the appearance of good, for it is nothing. Therefore not to be cannot be more desirable to the damned than to be.

Obj. 3. Further, The greater evil is the more to be shunned. Now not to be is the greatest evil, since it removes good altogether, so as to leave nothing. Therefore not to be is more to be shunned than to be unhappy; and thus the same conclusion follows as above.

On the contrary, It is written (Apoc. 9. 6): *In those days men . . . shall desire to die, and death shall fly from them.*

Further, The unhappiness of the damned surpasses all unhappiness of this world. Now in order to escape the unhappiness of this world, it is desirable to some to die, and so it is written (Ecclus. 41. 3, 4): *O death, thy sentence is welcome to the man that is in need, and to him whose strength faileth; who is in a decrepit age, and that is in care about all things, and to the distrustful that loseth wisdom* (Vulg.,— *patience*). Much more, therefore, is "not to be" desirable to the damned according to their deliberate reason.

I answer that, Not to be may be considered in two ways. First, in itself, and thus it can in no way be desirable, since it has no aspect of good, but is pure privation of good. Secondly, it may be considered as a relief from a painful life or from some unhappiness, and thus not to be takes on the aspect of good, since "to lack an evil is a kind of good" as the Philosopher says.[4] In this way it is better for the damned

not to be than to be unhappy. Hence it is said (Matt. 26. 24): *It were better for him, if that man had not been born,* and (Jerem. 20. 14): *Cursed be the day wherein I was born,* where a gloss of Jerome observes:[5] "It is better not to be than to be evilly." In this sense the damned can prefer not to be, according to their deliberate reason.

Reply Obj. 1. The saying of Augustine is to be understood in the sense that not to be is a matter of choice not in itself but accidentally, as putting an end to unhappiness. For when it is stated that to be and to live are desired by all naturally, we are not to take this as referable to an evil and corrupt life, and a life of unhappiness, as the Philosopher says,[6] but absolutely.

Reply Obj. 2. Non being is subject to choice, not in itself, but only accidentally, as stated already (REPLY 1).

Reply Obj. 3. Although not to be is very evil, in so far as it removes being, it is very good, in so far as it removes unhappiness, which is the greatest of evils, and thus it is preferred not to be.

ARTICLE 4. *Whether in Hell the Damned Would Wish Others Were Damned Who Are Not Damned?*

We proceed thus to the Fourth Article: It would seem that in hell the damned would not wish others were damned who are not damned.

Objection 1. For it is said (Luke 16. 27, 28) of the rich man that he prayed for his brethren, lest they should come *into the place of torments.* Therefore in like manner the other damned would not wish, at least, their friends in the flesh to be damned in hell.

Obj. 2. Further, The damned are not deprived of their inordinate affections. Now some of the damned loved inordinately some who are not damned. Therefore they would not desire their evil, that is, that they should be damned.

Obj. 3. Further, the damned do not desire the increase of their punishment. Now if more were damned, their punishment would be greater, even as the joy of the blessed is increased by an increase in their number. Therefore the damned desire not the damnation of those who are saved.

On the contrary, A gloss on Isa. 14. 9, *are*

---

[1] PL 40, 25.   [2] PL 32, 1280.
[3] PL 32, 1281.   [4] *Ethics,* V, 1 (1129^{b}8).

[5] *Glossa ordin.* (IV, 139E); Jerome, *In Jerem.* (PL 24, 838).
[6] *Ethics,* IX, 9 (1170^{a}22).

risen up from their thrones, says:[1] "The wicked are comforted by having many companions in their punishment."

Further, Envy reigns supreme in the damned. Therefore they grieve for the happiness of the blessed, and desire their damnation.

I answer that, Even as in the blessed in heaven there will be most perfect charity, so in the damned there will be the most perfect hate. Therefore as the saints will rejoice in all goods, so will the damned grieve for all goods. Consequently the sight of the happiness of the saints will give them very great pain; hence it is written (Isa. 26. 11): *Let the envious people see and be confounded, and let fire devour Thy enemies.* Therefore they will wish all the good were damned.

Reply Obj. 1. So great will be the envy of the damned that they will envy the glory even of their kindred, since they themselves are supremely unhappy, for this happens even in this life, when envy increases. Nevertheless they will envy their kindred less than others, and their punishment would be greater if all their kindred were damned, and others saved, than if some of their kindred were saved. For this reason the rich man prayed that his brethren might be warded from damnation, for he knew that some are guarded therefrom. Yet he would rather that his brethren were damned as well as all the rest.

Reply Obj. 2. Love that is not based on virtue is easily cut off, especially in evil men, as the Philosopher says.[2] Hence the damned will not preserve their friendship for those whom they loved inordinately. Yet the will of them will remain perverse, because they will continue to love the cause of their inordinate loving.

Reply Obj. 3. Although an increase in the number of the damned results in an increase of each one's punishment, so much the more will their hatred and envy increase that they will prefer to be more tormented with many rather than less tormented alone.

ARTICLE 5. *Whether the Damned Hate God?*

We proceed thus to the Fifth Article: It would seem that the damned do not hate God.

Objection 1. For, according to Dionysius (*Div. Nom.* i),[3] "the beautiful and good that is the cause of all goodness and beauty is be-

loved of all." But this is God. Therefore God cannot be the object of anyone's hate.

Obj. 2. Further, No one can hate goodness itself, as neither can one will badness itself, since "evil is altogether involuntary," as Dionysius asserts (*Div. Nom.* iv).[4] Now God is goodness itself. Therefore no one can hate Him.

On the contrary, It is written (Ps. 73. 23): *The pride of them that hate Thee ascendeth continually.*

I answer that, The appetite is moved by good or evil apprehended. Now God is apprehended in two ways, namely in Himself, as by the blessed, who see Him in His essence; and in His effects, as by us and by the damned. Since, then, He is goodness by His essence, He cannot in Himself be displeasing to any will; therefore whoever sees Him in His essence cannot hate Him. On the other hand, some of His effects are displeasing to the will in so far as they are opposed to any one, and accordingly a person may hate God not in Himself, but by reason of His effects. Therefore the damned, perceiving God in His punishment, which is the effect of His justice, hate Him, even as they hate the punishment inflicted on them.

Reply Obj. 1. The saying of Dionysius refers to the natural appetite; and even this is rendered perverse in the damned, by that which is added to it by their deliberate will, as stated above (A. 1. REPLY 1).

Reply Obj. 2. This argument would prove if the damned saw God in Himself, as being in His essence.

ARTICLE 6. *Whether the Damned Demerit?*

We proceed thus to the Sixth Article: It would seem that the damned demerit.

Objection 1. For the damned have an evil will, as stated in the last Distinction of iv. *Sent.*[5] But they demerited by the evil will that they had here. Therefore if they do not demerit there, their damnation is to their advantage.

Obj. 2. Further, The damned are on the same footing as the demons. Now the demons demerit after their fall, and thus God inflicted a punishment on the serpent, who induced man to sin (Gen. 3. 14, 15). Therefore the damned also demerit.

Obj. 3. Further, An inordinate act that proceeds from a deliberate will is not excused from demerit, even though there be necessity of which one is oneself the cause, for the drunken man deserves a double punishment

---

[1] *Glossa ordin.* (IV, 32E); cf. Jerome, *In Isaiam* (PL 24, 165).
[2] *Ethics,* VIII, 8 (1159b7).   [3] Sect. 10 (PG 3, 708).
[4] Sect. 32 (PG 3, 732).
[5] Dist. 50, chap. 1 (QR II, 1032).

if he commit a crime through being drunk.[1] Now the damned were themselves the cause of their own obstinacy, owing to which they are under a kind of necessity of sinning. Therefore since their act proceeds from their free choice, they are not excused from demerit.

On the contrary, Punishment is divided against fault. Now the perverse will of the damned proceeds from their obstinacy, which is their punishment. Therefore the perverse will of the damned is not a fault by which they may demerit.

Further, After reaching the last term there is no further movement, or advancement in good or evil. Now the damned, especially after the judgment day, will have reached the last term of their damnation, since "then there will cease to be two cities," according to Augustine (*Enchir.* cxi).[2] Therefore after the judgment day the damned will not demerit by their perverse will, for if they did their damnation would be augmented.

I answer that, We must draw a distinction between the damned before the judgment day and after. For all are agreed that after the judgment day there will be neither merit nor demerit. The reason for this is because merit or demerit is directed to the attainment of some further good or evil, and after the day of judgment good and evil will have reached their ultimate consummation, so that there will be no further addition to good or evil. Consequently, good will in the blessed will not be a merit but a reward, and evil will in the damned will be not a demerit but a punishment only. For works of virtue belong especially to the state of happiness, and their contraries to the state of unhappiness.[3]

On the other hand, some say that, before the judgment day, both the good merit and the damned demerit. But this cannot apply to the essential reward or to the principal punishment, since in this respect both have reached the term. Possibly, however, this may apply to the accidental reward, or secondary punishment, which are subject to increase until the day of judgment. Especially may this apply to the demons, or to the good angels, by whose activities some are drawn to salvation, whereby the joy of the blessed angels is increased, and some to damnation, whereby the punishment of the demons is augmented.[4]

Reply Obj. 1. It is in the highest degree unprofitable to have reached the highest degree of evil, the result being that the damned are incapable of demerit. Hence it is clear that they gain no advantage from their sin.

Reply Obj. 2. Men who are damned are not occupied in drawing others to damnation, as the demons are, for which reason the latter demerit as regards their secondary punishment.

Reply Obj. 3. The reason why they are not excused from demerit is not because they are under the necessity of sinning, but because they have reached the highest of evils.

However, the necessity of sinning of which we are ourselves the cause, in so far as it is a necessity, excuses from sin, because every sin needs to be voluntary; but it does not excuse, in so far as it proceeds from a previous act of the will, and consequently the whole demerit of the subsequent sin would seem to belong to the previous sin.

ARTICLE 7. *Whether the Damned Can Make Use of the Knowledge They Had in This World?*

We proceed thus to the Seventh Article: It would seem that the damned are unable to make use of the knowledge they had in this world.

Objection 1. For there is very great pleasure in the consideration of knowledge. But we must not admit that they have any pleasure. Therefore they cannot make use of the knowledge they had previously, by applying their consideration to it.

Obj. 2. Further, The damned suffer greater pains than any pains of this world. Now in this world, when one is in very great pain, it is impossible to consider any intelligible conclusions, through being distracted by the pains that one suffers. Much less therefore can one do so in hell.

Obj. 3. Further, The damned are subject to time. But "length of time is the cause of forgetfulness."[5] Therefore the damned will forget what they knew here.

On the contrary, It is said to the rich man who was damned (Luke 16. 25): *Remember that thou didst receive good things in thy lifetime*, etc. Therefore they will consider about the things they knew here.

Further, The intelligible species remain in the separated soul, as stated above (Q. LXX,

---

[1] *Ethics*, III, 5 (1113^{b}31).   [2] PL 40, 284.
[3] Aristotle, *Ethics*, I, 10 (1100^{b}9).
[4] Cf. Part I, Q. LXII, A. 9, Reply 3; Part II–II, Q. XIII, A. 4, Reply 2.
[5] Aristotle, *Physics*, IV, 13 (222^{b}19).

A. 2, reply 3; Part I, Q. LXXXIX, A. 6). Therefore, if they could not use them these would
remain in them to no purpose.

I answer that, Even as in the saints, on account of the perfection of their glory, there
will be nothing but what is a matter of joy,
so there will be nothing in the damned but what
is a matter and cause of sorrow; nor will anything that can pertain to sorrow be lacking,
so that their unhappiness is consummate. Now
the consideration of certain things known brings
us joy, in some respect, either on the part of the
things known, because we love them, or on
the part of the knowledge, because it is fitting
and perfect. There may also be a reason for
sorrow both on the part of the things known,
because they are of a grievous nature, and on
the part of the knowledge, if we consider its
imperfection; for instance a person may consider his defective knowledge about a certain
thing, which he would desire to know perfectly.
Accordingly, in the damned there will be actual
consideration of the things they knew previously as matters of sorrow, but not as a cause
of pleasure. For they will consider both the
evil they have done, and for which they were
damned, and the delightful goods they have
lost, and on both counts they will suffer torments. Likewise they will be tormented with
the thought that the knowledge they had of
speculative matters was imperfect, and that
they missed its highest degree of perfection
which they might have acquired.

Reply Obj. 1. Although the consideration of
knowledge is delightful in itself, it may accidentally be the cause of sorrow, as explained
above.

Reply Obj. 2. In this world the soul is united
to a corruptible body, and therefore the soul's
consideration is hindered by the suffering of
the body. On the other hand, in the future
life the soul will not be so drawn by the
body, but however much the body may suffer,
the soul will have a most clear view of
those things that can be a cause of anguish
to it.

Reply Obj. 3. Time causes forgetfulness accidentally, in so far as the movement of which
it is the measure is the cause of change. But
after the judgment day there will be no movement of the heavens; therefore neither will it
be possible for forgetfulness to result from
any lapse of time however long. Before the
judgment day, however, the separated soul is
not changed from its disposition by the heavenly movement.

ARTICLE 8. *Whether the Damned Will Ever
Think of God?*

We proceed thus to the Eighth Article: It
would seem that the damned will sometimes
think of God.

Objection 1. For one cannot hate a thing
actually unless one think about it. Now the
damned will hate God, as stated in the text
of the fourth book of the *Sentences* in the last
Distinction.[1] Therefore they will think of God
sometimes.

Obj. 2. Further, The damned will have remorse of conscience. But the conscience suffers
remorse for deeds done against God. Therefore
they will sometimes think of God.

On the contrary, Man's most perfect thoughts
are those which are about God, whereas the
damned will be in a state of the greatest imperfection. Therefore they will not think of God.

I answer that, One may think of God in two
ways. First, in Himself and according to that
which is proper to Him, namely that He is the
fount of all goodness, and thus it is altogether
impossible to think of Him without delight, so
that the damned will by no means think of Him
in this way. Secondly, according to something
accidental as it were to Him in His effects,
such as His punishments, and so forth, and
in this respect the thought of God can bring
sorrow, so that in this way the damned will
think of God.

Reply Obj. 1. The damned do not hate God
except because He punishes and forbids what
is agreeable to their evil will, and consequently
they will think of Him only as punishing and
forbidding. This suffices for the *Reply to the
Second Objection*, since conscience will not
have remorse for sin except as forbidden by
the Divine commandment.

ARTICLE 9. *Whether the Damned See the
Glory of the Blessed?*

We proceed thus to the Ninth Article: It
would seem that the damned do not see the
glory of the blessed.

Objection 1. For they are more distant from
the glory of the blessed than from the happenings of this world. But they do not see what
happens in regard to us; hence Gregory commenting on Job. 14. 21, *Whether his children
come to honour* etc. says (*Moral.* xii, 21):[2]
"Even as those who still live know not in what
place are the souls of the dead, so the dead

[1] Dist. 50, chap. 2 (QR II, 1034).
[2] PL 75, 999.

who have lived in the body know not the things which regard the life of those who are in the flesh." Much less, therefore, can they see the glory of the blessed.

Obj. 2. Further, That which is granted as a great favour to the saints in this life is never granted to the damned. Now it was granted as a great favour to Paul to see the life in which the saints live for ever with God, as the gloss on II Cor. 12. 2 states.[1] Therefore the damned will not see the glory of the saints.

On the contrary, It is stated (Luke 16. 23) that the rich man in the midst of his torments *saw Abraham . . . and Lazarus in his bosom.*

I answer that, The damned, before the judgment day, will see the blessed in glory, in such a way as to know, not what that glory is like, but only that they are in a state of glory that surpasses all thought. This will trouble them, both because they will, through envy, grieve for their happiness, and because they have forfeited that glory. Hence it is written (Wisd. 5. 2) concerning the wicked: *Seeing it* they *shall be troubled with terrible fear.* After the judgment day, however, they will be altogether deprived of seeing the blessed; nor will this lessen their punishment, but will increase it, because they will bear in remembrance the glory of the blessed which they saw at or before the judgment, and this will torment them. Moreover they will be tormented by finding themselves considered unworthy even to see the glory which the saints merit to have.

Reply Obj. 1. The happenings of this life would not, if seen, torment the damned in hell as the sight of the glory of the saints. Therefore the things which happen here are not shown to the damned in the same way as the saints' glory; although also of the things that happen here, those are shown to them which are capable of causing them sorrow.

Reply Obj. 2. Paul looked upon that life wherein the saints live with God, by actual experience of it and by hoping to have it more perfectly in the life to come. Not so the damned, and therefore the comparison fails.

QUESTION XCIX

OF GOD'S MERCY AND JUSTICE TOWARDS THE DAMNED

(In Five Articles)

WE must next consider God's justice and mercy towards the damned, under which head there are five points of inquiry: (1) Whether by

---

[1] *Glossa interl.* (VI, 76r); *Glossa* Lombardi (PL 192, 79).

Divine justice an eternal punishment is inflicted on sinners? (2) Whether by God's mercy all punishment both of men and of demons comes to an end? (3) Whether at least the punishment of men comes to an end? (4) Whether at least the punishment of Christians has an end? (5) Whether there is an end to the punishment of those who have performed works of mercy?

ARTICLE 1. *Whether By Divine Justice an Eternal Punishment Is Inflicted on Sinners?*

We proceed thus to the First Article: It would seem that an eternal punishment is not inflicted on sinners by Divine justice.

Objection 1. For the punishment should not exceed the fault: *According to the measure of the sin shall the measure also of the stripes be* (Deut. 25. 2). Now fault is temporal. Therefore the punishment should not be eternal.

Obj. 2. Further, Of two mortal sins one is greater than the other, and therefore one should receive a greater punishment than the other. But no punishment is greater than eternal punishment, since it is infinite. Therefore eternal punishment is not due to every sin; and if it is not due to one, it is due to none, since they are not infinitely distant from one another.

Obj. 3. Further, A just judge does not punish except in order to correct, and therefore it is stated[2] that "punishments are a kind of medicine." Now, to punish the wicked eternally does not lead to their correction, nor to that of others, since then there will be no one in future who can be corrected thereby. Therefore eternal punishment is not inflicted for sins according to Divine justice.

Obj. 4. Further, No one wishes that which is not desirable for its own sake, except on account of some advantage. Now God does not wish punishment for its own sake, for He delights not in punishment.[3] Since then no advantage can result from the perpetuity of punishment, it would seem that He ought not to inflict such a punishment for sin.

Obj. 5. Further, Nothing accidental lasts for ever.[4] But punishment is one of those things that happen accidentally, since it is contrary to nature. Therefore it cannot be everlasting.

Obj. 6. Further, The justice of God would seem to require that sinners should be brought to nothing, because on account of ingratitude a person deserves to lose all benefits; and among other benefits of God there is being

---

[2] Aristotle, *Ethics*, II, 3 (1104[b]17).
[3] Cf. Wisd. 1.13.
[4] Aristotle, *Heavens*, I, 2 (269[b]6); cf. II, 3 (286[a]17).

itself. Therefore it would seem just that the sinner who has been ungrateful to God should lose his being. But if sinners be brought to nothing, their punishment cannot be everlasting. Therefore it would seem out of keeping with Divine justice that sinners should be punished for ever.

On the contrary, It is written (Matt. 25. 46): *These,* namely the wicked, *shall go into everlasting punishment.*

Further, As reward is to merit, so is punishment to guilt. Now, according to Divine justice, an eternal reward is due to temporal merit: *Every one who seeth the Son and believeth in Him hath* (Vulg.,—*that everyone . . . may have*) *life everlasting.* Therefore according to Divine justice an everlasting punishment is due to temporal guilt.

Further, According to the Philosopher,[1] punishment is meted according to the dignity of the person sinned against, so that a person who strikes one in authority receives a greater punishment than one who strikes anyone else. Now whoever sins mortally sins against God, Whose commandments he breaks, and Whose honour he gives another, by placing his end in some one other than God. But God's majesty is infinite. Therefore whoever sins mortally deserves infinite punishment; and consequently it seems just that for a mortal sin a man should be punished for ever.

I answer that, Since punishment is measured in two ways, namely according to the degree of its severity, and according to its length of time, the measure of punishment corresponds to the measure of fault, as regards the degree of severity, so that the more grievously a person sins the more grievously is he punished: *As much as she hath glorified herself and lived in delicacies, so much torment and sorrow give ye to her* (Apoc. 18. 7). The duration of the punishment does not, however, correspond with the duration of the fault, as Augustine says,[2] for adultery which is committed in a short space of time is not punished with a momentary penalty even according to human laws. But the duration of punishment regards the disposition of the sinner, for sometimes a person who commits an offence in a city is rendered by his very offence worthy of being cut off entirely from the fellowship of the citizens, either by perpetual exile or even by death; sometimes however he is not rendered worthy of being cut off entirely from the fellowship of

the citizens, and therefore in order that he may become a fitting member of the State, his punishment is prolonged or curtailed, according as is expedient for his amendment, so that he may live in the city in a becoming and peaceful manner.

So too, according to Divine justice, sin renders a person worthy to be altogether cut off from the fellowship of God's city, and this is the effect of every sin committed against charity, which is the bond uniting this same city together. Consequently, for mortal sin which is contrary to charity a person is expelled for ever from the fellowship of the saints and condemned to everlasting punishment, because as Augustine says,[3] "as men are cut off from this perishable city by the penalty of the first death, so are they excluded from that imperishable city by the punishment of the second death." That the punishment inflicted by the earthly state is not regarded as everlasting is accidental, either because man does not endure for ever, or because the state itself comes to an end. Therefore if man lived for ever, the punishment of exile or slavery, which is pronounced by human law, would remain in him for ever. On the other hand, as regards those who sin in such a way as not to deserve to be entirely cut off from the fellowship of the saints, such as those who sin venially, their punishment wil be so much the shorter or longer according as they are more or less fit to be cleansed, through sin clinging to them more or less; this is observed in the punishments of this world and of purgatory according to Divine justice.

We find also other reasons given by the saints why some are justly condemned to everlasting punishment for a temporal sin. One is because they sinned against an eternal good by despising eternal life. This is mentioned by Augustine:[4] "He is become worthy of eternal evil, who destroyed in himself a good which could be eternal." Another reason is because man sinned in his own eternity; therefore Gregory says (*Dial.* iv, 44),[5] "it belongs to the great justice of the judge that those should never cease to be punished who in this life never ceased to desire sin." And if it be objected that some who sin mortally propose to amend their life at some time, and that these accordingly would not be deserving of eternal punishment, it must be replied according to some that Gregory speaks of the will that is made manifest by the deed. For he who falls into mortal sin of his

---

[1] *Ethics,* v, 5 (1132ᵇ28).
[2] *City of God,* XXI, 11 (PL 41, 725).
[3] *Ibid.* (PL 41, 726).
[4] *Ibid.,* 12 (PL 41, 727).   [5] PL 77, 404.

own will puts himself in a state from which he cannot be rescued unless God help him; therefore from the very fact that he is willing to sin, he is willing to remain in sin for ever. For man is *a wind that goeth,* namely to sin, *and returneth not* by his own power (Ps. 77. 39).[1] Thus if a man were to throw himself into a pit from which he could not get out without help, one might say that he wished to remain there for ever, whatever else he may have thought himself. Another and a better answer is that from the very fact that he commits a mortal sin, he places his end in a creature; and since the whole of life is directed to its end, it follows that for this very reason he directs the whole of his life to that sin, and is willing to remain in sin for ever if he could do so with impunity. This is what Gregory says on Job 41. 23, *He shall esteem the deep as growing old* (*Moral.* xxxiv, 19):[2] "The wicked only put an end to sinning because their life came to an end; they would indeed have wished to live for ever, that they might continue in sin for ever, for they desire rather to sin than to live."

Still another reason may be given why the punishment of mortal sin is eternal, because thereby one offends God Who is infinite. Therefore since punishment cannot be infinite in intensity, because the creature is incapable of an infinite quality, it must be infinite at least in duration. And again there is a fourth reason for the same, because guilt remains for ever, since it cannot be remitted without grace, and men cannot receive grace after death; nor should punishment cease so long as guilt remains.

Reply Obj. 1. Punishment does not have to be equal to fault as to the amount of duration, as is seen to be the case also with human laws. We may also reply with Gregory[3] that although sin is temporal in act, it is eternal in will.

Reply Obj. 2. The degree of intensity in the punishment corresponds to the degree of gravity in the sin; therefore mortal sins unequal in gravity will receive a punishment unequal in intensity but equal in duration.

Reply Obj. 3. The punishments inflicted on those who are not altogether expelled from the society of their fellow-citizens are intended for their correction, whereas those punishments whereby certain persons are wholly banished from the society of their fellow-citizens are not intended for their correction, although they may be intended for the correction and tranquillity of the others who remain in the state. Accordingly the damnation of the wicked is for the correction of those who are now in the Church; for punishments are intended for correction not only when they are being inflicted, but also when they are decreed.

Reply Obj. 4. The everlasting punishment of the wicked will not be altogether useless. For they are useful for two purposes. First, because thereby the Divine justice is safeguarded which is acceptable to God for its own sake. Hence Gregory says (*Dial.* iv, 44):[4] "Almighty God on account of His loving kindness delights not in the torments of the unhappy, but on account of His justice. He is for ever unappeased by the punishment of the wicked."

Secondly, they are useful, because the elect rejoice therein, when they see God's justice in them, and realize that they have escaped them. Hence it is written (Ps. 57. 12): *The just shall rejoice when he shall see the revenge,* etc., and (Isa. 66. 24): *They,* namely the wicked, *shall be a loathsome sight*[5] *to all flesh,* namely to the saints, as a gloss says.[6] Gregory expresses himself in the same sense:[7] "The wicked are all condemned to eternal punishment, and are punished for their own wickedness. Yet they will burn to some purpose, namely that the just may all both see in God the joys they receive, and perceive in them the torments they have escaped, for which reason they will acknowledge themselves for ever the debtors of Divine grace, the more that they will see how the evils which they overcame by its assistance are punished eternally."

Reply Obj. 5. Although the punishment relates to the soul accidentally, it relates essentially to the soul infected with guilt. And since guilt will remain in the soul for ever, its punishment also will be everlasting.

Reply Obj. 6. Punishment corresponds to fault, properly speaking, in respect of the lack of order in the fault, and not of the dignity in the person offended; for if the latter were the case, a punishment of infinite intensity would correspond to every sin. Accordingly, although a man deserves to lose his being from the fact that he has sinned against God, the author of his being, yet, in view of the lack of order of the act itself, loss of being is not due to him,

---

[1] Cf. *Glossa interl.* (III, 199v); *Glossa* Lombardi (PL 191, 736); Augustine, *Enarr. in Ps.* (PL 36, 998).
[2] PL 76, 738.　　[3] *Ibid.*
[4] PL 77, 404.
[5] *Ad satietatem visionis,* which St. Thomas takes to signify being satiated with joy.
[6] *Glossa interl.* (IV, 108v); Jerome, *In Isaiam* (PL 24, 703).　　[7] *Loc. cit.*

since being is presupposed to merit and demerit, nor is being lost or corrupted by the lack of order of sin; and consequently privation of being cannot be the punishment due to any sin.

ARTICLE 2. *Whether By God's Mercy All Punishment of the Damned, Both Men and Demons, Comes to an End?*

We proceed thus to the Second Article: It would seem that by God's mercy all punishment of the damned, both men and demons, comes to an end.

Objection 1. For it is written (Wisd. 11. 24): *Thou hast mercy upon all, O Lord, because Thou canst do all things.* But among all things the demons also are included, since they are God's creatures. Therefore also their punishment will come to an end.

Obj. 2. Further, *God hath concluded all in sin* (Vulg.,—*unbelief*), *that He may have mercy on all* (Rom. 11. 32). Now God has concluded the demons under sin, that is to say, He permitted them to be concluded. Therefore it would seem that in time He has mercy even on the demons.

Obj. 3. Further, As Anselm says (*Cur Deus Homo,* ii, 4),[1] "it is not just that God should permit the utter loss of a creature which He made for happiness." Therefore, since every rational creature was created for happiness, it would seem unjust for it to be allowed to perish altogether.

On the contrary, It is written (Matt. 25. 41): *Depart from Me, you cursed, into everlasting fire, which is prepared for the devil and his angels.* Therefore they will be punished eternally.

Further, Just as the good angels were made happy through turning to God, so the bad angels were made unhappy through turning away from God. Therefore if the unhappiness of the wicked angels comes at length to an end, the happiness of the good will also come to an end, which cannot be admitted.

I answer that, As Augustine says[2] "Origen erred in maintaining that the demons will at length, through God's mercy, be delivered from their punishment." But this error has been condemned by the Church for two reasons. First because it is clearly contrary to the authority of Holy Writ (Apoc. 20. 9, 10): *The devil who seduced them was cast into the pool of fire and brimstone, where both the beasts and*

the false prophets (Vulg.,—*the beast and false prophet,* etc.) *shall be tormented day and night for ever and ever,* which is the Scriptural expression for eternity. Secondly, because this opinion exaggerated God's mercy in one direction and depreciated it in another. For it would seem equally reasonable for the good angels to remain in eternal happiness and for the wicked angels to be eternally punished. Therefore just as he maintained that the demons and the souls of the damned are to be delivered at length from their sufferings, so he maintained that the angels and the souls of the blessed will at length pass from their happy state to the unhappiness of this life.

Reply Obj. 1. God, for His own part, has mercy on all. Since, however, his mercy is ruled by the order of His wisdom, the result is that it does not reach to certain people who render themselves unworthy of that mercy, as do the demons and the damned who are obstinate in wickedness. And yet we may say that even in them His mercy finds a place, in so far as they are punished less than they wholly deserve but not that they are entirely delivered from punishment.

Reply Obj. 2. In the words quoted the distribution (of the predicate) regards the genera and not the individuals, so that the statement applies to men in the state of wayfarer, because, that is, He had mercy both on Jews and on Gentiles, but not on every Gentile or every Jew.

Reply Obj. 3. Anselm means that it is not just with regard to appropriateness to God's goodness, and is speaking of the creature generically. For it does not become the Divine goodness that a whole genus of creature fail of the end for which it was made; therefore it is unbecoming for all men or all angels to be damned. But there is no reason why some men or some angels should perish for ever, because the intention of the Divine will is fulfilled in the others who are saved.

ARTICLE 3. *Whether God's Mercy Suffers At Least Men To Be Punished Eternally?*

We proceed thus to the Third Article: It would seem that God's mercy does not suffer at least men to be punished eternally.

Objection 1. For it is written (Gen. 6. 3): *My spirit shall not remain in man for ever, because he is flesh,* where "spirit" denotes indignation, as a gloss observes.[3] Therefore, since God's indignation is not distinct from His punishment, man will not be punished eternally.

---

[1] PL 158, 402.

[2] *City of God,* XXI, 17, 23 (PL 41, 731; 735); cf. Origen *Peri Archon,* I, 6 (PG 11, 165; 168).

[3] *Glossa interl.* (I, 50r); Bede, *In Pentat.* (PL 91, 224).

Obj. 2. Further, The charity of the saints in this life makes them pray for their enemies. Now they will have more perfect charity in that life. Therefore they will pray then for their enemies who are damned. But the prayers of the saints cannot be in vain, since they are most acceptable to God. Therefore at the saints' prayers the Divine mercy will in time deliver the damned from their punishment.

Obj. 3. Further, God's foretelling of the punishment of the damned belongs to the prophecy of threats. Now the prophecy of threats is not always fulfilled, as appears from what was said of the destruction of Nineve (Jonas 3.); and yet it was not destroyed as foretold by the prophet, who also was troubled for that very reason (4. 1). Therefore it would seem that much more will the threat of eternal punishment be commuted by God's mercy for a more lenient punishment, when this will be able to give sorrow to none but joy to all.

Obj. 4. Further, The words of Ps. 76. 8 are to the point, where it is said: *Will God then be angry for ever?* (Vulg.,—*Will God then cast off for ever?*) But God's anger is His punishment. Therefore, etc.

Obj. 5. Further, A gloss on Isa. 14. 19, *But thou art cast out*, etc., says:[1] "Even though all souls shall have rest at last, thou never shalt," and it refers to the devil. Therefore it would seem that all human souls shall at length have rest from their pains.

On the contrary, It is written (Matt. 25. 46) of the elect together with the damned: *These shall go into everlasting punishment: but the just, into life everlasting.* But it is inadmissible that the life of the just will ever have an end. Therefore it is inadmissible that the punishment of the damned will ever come to an end.

Further, As Damascene says (*De Fide Orthod.* ii, 4)[2] "death is to men what their fall was to the angels." Now after their fall the angels could not be restored. Therefore neither can man after death. And thus the punishment of the damned will have no end.

I answer that, As Augustine says,[3] some evaded the error of Origen by asserting that the demons are punished everlastingly, while holding that all men, even unbelievers, are at length set free from punishment. But this statement is altogether unreasonable. For just as the demons are obstinate in wickedness and therefore have to be punished for ever, so too are the souls of men who die without charity, since "death is to men what their fall was to the angels," as Damascene says (*loc. cit.*).

Reply Obj. 1. This saying refers to man generically, because God's indignation was at length removed from the human race by the coming of Christ. But those who were unwilling to be included or to remain in this reconciliation effected by Christ, perpetuated the Divine anger in themselves, since no other way of reconciliation is given to us save that which is through Christ.

Reply Obj. 2. As Augustine[4] and Gregory (*Moral.* xxxiv, 19)[5] say, the saints in this life pray for their enemies that they may be converted to God, while it is yet possible for them to be converted. For if we knew that they were foreknown to death, we should no more pray for them than for the demons. And since for those who depart this life without grace there will be no further time for conversion, no prayer will be offered for them, neither by the Church militant, nor by the Church triumphant. For that which we have to pray for them is, as the Apostle says (II Tim. 2. 25, 26), that *God may give them repentance to know the truth, and they may recover themselves from the snares of the devil.*

Reply Obj. 3. A punishment threatened prophetically is only then commuted when there is a change in the merits of the person threatened. Hence: *I will suddenly speak against a nation and against a kingdom, to root out and to pull down and to destroy it. If that nation . . . shall repent of their evil, I also will repent of the evil that I have thought to do to them* (Jer. 18. 7). Therefore, since the merits of the damned cannot be changed, the threatened punishment will always be fulfilled in them. Nevertheless the prophecy of threats is always fulfilled in a certain sense, because as Augustine says:[6] "Nineve has been overthrown, that was evil, and a good Nineve is built up, that was not; for while the walls and the houses remained standing, the city was overthrown in its wicked ways."

Reply Obj. 4. These words of the Psalm refer to the vessels of mercy, which have not made themselves unworthy of mercy, because in this life (which may be called God's anger on account of its unhappiness) He changes vessels of mercy into something better. Hence the Psalm continues (*verse* 11): *This is the*

---

[1] *Glossa interl.* (IV, 33v).
[2] PG 94, 877.
[3] *City of God*, XXI, 17, 18 (PL 41, 731, 732).

[4] *City of God*, XXI, 24 (PL 41, 736).
[5] PL 76, 739. Cf. also *Dial.*, IV, 44 (PL 77, 404).
[6] *Op. cit.*, XXI, 24 (PL 41, 739).

change of the right hand of the most High. We may also reply that they refer to mercy as granting a relaxation but not setting free altogether if it be referred also to the damned. Hence the Psalm does not say: *Will He from His anger shut up His mercies?* but *in His anger,* because the punishment will not be done away entirely; but His mercy will have effect by diminishing the punishment while it continues.

Reply Obj. 5. This gloss is speaking not absolutely but on an impossible supposition in order to throw into relief the greatness of the devil's sin, or of Nabuchodonosor's.

ARTICLE 4. *Whether the Punishment of Christians Is Brought To an End By the Mercy of God?*

We proceed thus to the Fourth Article: It would seem that at least the punishment of Christians is brought to an end by the mercy of God.

Objection 1. *For he that believeth and is baptized shall be saved* (Mark 16. 16). Now this applies to every Christian. Therefore all Christians will at length be saved.

Obj. 2. Further, It is written (John 6. 55): *He that eateth My body and drinketh My blood hath eternal life.* Now this is the meat and drink of which Christians partake in common. Therefore all Christians will be saved at length.

Obj. 3. Further, *If any man's work burn, he shall suffer loss: but he himself shall be saved, yet so as by fire* (I Cor. 3. 15), where it is a question of those who have the foundation of the Christian faith. Therefore all such persons will be saved in the end.

On the contrary, It is written (I Cor. 6. 9): *The unjust shall not possess the kingdom of God.* Now some Christians are unjust. Therefore Christians will not all come to the kingdom of God, and consequently they will be punished for ever.

Further, It is written (II Pet. 2. 21): *It had been better for them not to have known the way of justice, than after they have known it, to turn back from that holy commandment which was delivered to them.* Now those who know not the way of truth will be punished for ever. Therefore Christians who have turned back after knowing it will also be punished for ever.

I answer that, According to Augustine[1] there have been some who predicted a delivery from eternal punishment not for all men, but only

[1] *City of God,* XXI, 19 (PL 41, 733).

for Christians; although they stated the matter in different ways. For some said that whoever received the sacraments of faith would be immune from eternal punishment. But this is contrary to the truth, since some receive the sacraments of faith, and yet have not faith, without which *it is impossible to please God* (Heb. 11. 6). Therefore others said that those alone will be exempt from eternal punishment who have received the sacraments of faith, and professed the Catholic faith. But against this it would seem to be that at one time some people profess the Catholic faith, and afterwards abandon it, and these are deserving not of a lesser but of a greater punishment, since according to II Pet. 2. 21, *it had been better for them not to have known the way of justice than, after they have known it, to turn back.* Moreover it is clear that heresiarchs who renounce the Catholic faith and invent new heresies sin more grievously than those who have conformed to some heresy from the first. And therefore some have maintained that those alone are exempt from eternal punishment who persevere to the end in the Catholic faith, however guilty they may have been of other crimes. But this is clearly contrary to Holy Writ, for it is written (James 2. 20): *Faith without works is dead,* and (Matt. 7. 21) *Not every one that saith to Me, Lord, Lord, shall enter into the kingdom of heaven: but he that doth the will of My Father Who is in heaven;* and in many other passages Holy Scripture threatens sinners with eternal punishment. Consequently those who persevere in the faith unto the end will not all be exempt from eternal punishment, unless in the end they prove to be free from other crimes.

Reply Obj. 1. Our Lord speaks there of formed faith *that worketh by love* (Vulg.,— charity, Gal. 5. 6) in which whosoever dies shall be saved. But to this faith not only is the error of unbelief opposed, but also any mortal sin whatsoever.

Reply Obj. 2. The saying of our Lord refers not to those who partake only sacramentally, and who sometimes by receiving unworthy *eat and drink judgment* to themselves (I Cor. 11. 29), but to those who eat spiritually and are incorporated with Him by charity, which incorporation is the effect of the sacramental eating, in those who approach worthily. Therefore, so far as the power of the sacrament is concerned, it brings us to eternal life, although sin may deprive us of that fruit, even after we have received worthily.

Reply Obj. 3. In this passage of the Apostle the foundation denotes formed faith, upon which whosoever shall build venial sins *shall suffer loss,* because he will be punished for them by God; yet *he himself shall be saved* in the end *by fire,* either of temporal tribulation, or of the punishment of purgatory which will be after death.

ARTICLE 5. *Whether All Those Who Perform Works of Mercy Will Be Punished Eternally?*

We proceed thus to the Fifth Article: It would seem that all who perform works of mercy will not be punished eternally, but only those who neglect those works.

Objection 1. For it is written (James 2. 13): *Judgment without mercy to him that hath not done mercy;* and (Matt. 5. 7): *Blessed are the merciful for they shall obtain mercy.*

Obj. 2. Further, (Matt. 25. 35-46) we find a description of our Lord's discussion with the damned and the elect. But this discussion is only about works of mercy. Therefore eternal punishment will be awarded only to such as have omitted to practise works of mercy; and consequently the same conclusion follows as before.

Obj. 3. Further, It is written (Matt. 6. 12): *Forgive us our debts, as we also forgive our debtors,* and further on (*verse* 14): *For if you will forgive men their offences, your heavenly Father will forgive you also your offences.* Therefore it would seem that the merciful, who forgive others their offences, will themselves obtain the forgiveness of their sins, and consequently will not be punished eternally.

Obj. 4. Further, A gloss of Ambrose on I Tim. 4. 8, *Godliness is profitable to all things,* says:[1] "The sum total of a Christian's rule of life consists in mercy and godliness. Let a man follow this, and though he should suffer from the inconstancy of the flesh, without doubt he will be scourged, but he will not perish, whereas he who can boast of no other exercise but that of the body will suffer everlasting punishment." Therefore those who persevere in works of mercy, though they be shackled with fleshly sins, will not be punished eternally; and thus the same conclusion follows as before.

On the contrary, It is written (I Cor. 6. 9, 10): *Neither fornicators, . . . nor adulterers,* etc., *shall possess the kingdom of God.* Yet many are such who practise works of mercy. Therefore the merciful will not all come to the

eternal kingdom, and consequently some of them will be punished eternally.

Further, It is written (James 2. 10): *Whosoever shall keep the whole law, but offend in one point, is become guilty of all.* Therefore whoever keeps the law as regards the works of mercy and omits other works, is guilty of transgressing the law, and consequently will be punished eternally.

I answer that, As Augustine says in the book quoted above,[2] some have maintained that not all who have professed the Catholic faith will be freed from eternal punishment, but only those who persevere in works of mercy, although they be guilty of other crimes. But this cannot stand, because without charity nothing can be acceptable to God, nor does anything profit unto eternal life in the absence of charity. Now it happens that certain persons persevere in works of mercy without having charity. Therefore nothing profits them to the meriting of eternal life, or to exemption from eternal punishment, as may be gathered from I Cor. 13. 3. Most evident is this in the case of those who lay hands on other people's property, for after seizing on many things, they nevertheless spend something in works of mercy. We must therefore conclude that all whosoever die in mortal sin, neither faith nor works of mercy will free them from eternal punishment, not even after any length of time whatever.

Reply Obj. 1. Those will obtain mercy who show mercy in an ordered manner. But those who while merciful to others are neglectful of themselves do not show mercy in an ordered manner; rather do they strike at themselves by their evil actions. Therefore such persons will not obtain the mercy that sets free altogether, even if they obtain that mercy which rebates somewhat their due punishment.

Reply Obj. 2. The reason why the discussion refers only to the works of mercy is not because eternal punishment will be inflicted on none but those who omit those works, but because eternal punishment will be remitted to those who after sinning have obtained forgiveness by their works of mercy, making unto themselves *friends of the mammon of iniquity* (Luke 16. 9).

Reply Obj. 3. Our Lord said this to those who ask that their debt be forgiven, but not to those who persist in sin. Therefore the repentant alone will obtain by their works of mercy the forgiveness that sets them free altogether.

Reply Obj. 4. The gloss of Ambrose speaks of the inconstancy that consists in venial sin,

---

[1] *Glossa* Lombardi (PL 192, 348); cf. *Glossa ordin.* (VI, 120A); Ambrosiaster (PL 17, 500).

[2] *City of God,* XXI, 22 (PL 41, 735).

from which a man will be freed through the works of mercy after the punishment of purgatory, which he calls a scourging. Or, if he speaks of the inconstancy of mortal sin, the sense is that those who while yet in this life fall into sins of the flesh through frailty are disposed to repentance by works of mercy. Therefore such a one will not perish, that is to say, he will be disposed by those works not to perish, through grace bestowed on him by our Lord, Who is blessed for evermore. Amen.

THE GREAT IDEAS, Volumes 2 and 3